Collectors' Information Bureau's

COLLECTIBLES

MARKET GUIDE & PRICE INDEX

Limited Edition: Plates • Figurines • Cottages • Bells • Graphics • Ornaments • Dolls • Steins

Thirteenth Edition

Your Complete Source for Information on Limited Edition Collectibles

Collectors' Information Bureau
Barrington, Illinois

Distributed by Wallace-Homestead,
a division of Chilton Book Company

Manufactured in the United States of America

Library of Congress Catalog Card Number: 95-71406

ISBN 0-930785-20-7 Collectors' Information Bureau

ISBN 0-87069-745-5 Wallace-Homestead

CREDITS

Book Design and Graphics
Wright Design, Grand Rapids, Michigan

Original Photography (covers and color section)
Camacho & Assoc., Dundee, Illinois

Inquiries to the Collectors' Information Bureau should be mailed to 5065 Shoreline Rd., Suite 200, Barrington, Illinois 60010
Phone (708) 842-2200

FORWARD

Dear Collector,

I am pleased to present you with the latest edition of the COLLECTIBLES MARKET GUIDE & PRICE INDEX. It represents the culmination of a year's efforts that began with in-depth interviews of industry experts, followed by exhaustive research on clubs, artists, and secondary market values. The result is an "encyclopedia of collectibles" that includes over 80 feature articles, profiles of 200 artists and secondary market prices for more than 45,000 limited edition collectibles.

In the 560 pages that follow, you'll learn about insuring your collectibles as well as the fine points of buying and selling on the secondary market. You'll join us as we look back at the history of limited edition collectibles. And you'll look ahead with us as we share the insights of dozens of industry experts, who have helped us take a glimpse at where the future of collectibles is headed. You'll read about how to best care for your treasures so they maintain their beauty and value for years to come. You'll even learn to "talk collectibles" with the help of our extensive "Glossary of Terms," featuring the most commonly used words and phrases in the field of collectibles.

Finally, you'll find the most comprehensive Price Index to limited edition collectibles at your fingertips in the last 200 pages of this book. Our prices are gathered by surveying over 300 secondary market dealers. These dealers report back to us the actual prices paid by collectors in recent purchases of limited edition collectibles that have been retired or closed. We know of no more up-to-date and thorough resource available to collectors that covers the categories of plates, dolls, figurines, cottages, bells, steins, ornaments and graphics. Its extensive use by the insurance industry is a testimony to its value.

We hope you'll enjoy the opportunity that this book —as well as the other Collectors' Information Bureau newsletters, directories and price guides — offers you to enhance your collecting hobby.

On behalf of the 80 companies who participate as members of the Collectors' Information Bureau and our staff of writers and researchers, I invite you to join us on a fascinating trip through the wonderful world of collectibles. We're glad you could join us!

Cordially,

Peggy Veltri

Peggy Veltri
Executive Director

P.S. With a field as vast and dynamic as collectibles, it's difficult to anticipate and answer all your questions in one book. We are anxious to help you find answers, though, and invite you to call us with your questions on collectibles at: (708) 842-2200. We look forward to chatting with you.

ACKNOWLEDGMENTS

The Collectors' Information Bureau wishes to thank the following persons and companies who deserve special recognition for their invaluable contributions to the creation of this book.

CONTRIBUTING WRITERS

Catherine Bloom
Gail Cohen
Kim Fynewever
Jack McCarthy
Kelly Womer

DESIGN AND PRODUCTION

Douglas Frens of AD DESIGN INC., Grand Rapids, MI, for designing and producing the cover artwork.

Kris Wiley and Mike Policka of WRIGHT DESIGN, Grand Rapids, MI, for their work on the design and production of the book.

PHOTOGRAPHY

Mike Camacho and the staff of CAMACHO & ASSOCIATES in West Dundee, IL, for creating the original photography for the cover and the 32-page color section.

PRINTING

Robert Ryder of TOTAL BUSINESS FORMS, Grand Rapids, MI, for the printing of this book.

AND A SPECIAL THANK YOU TO THE STAFF OF THE COLLECTORS' INFORMATION BUREAU...

Joan Barcal
Sue Knappen
Michelle Malwitz
Arlene Utz
Carol Van Elderen
Debbie Wojtysiak
Cindy Zagumny

FOR THEIR TIRELESS EFFORTS TO HELP COLLECTORS HAVE FUN AS THEY LEARN MORE ABOUT THEIR FAVORITE HOBBY...COLLECTING.

To the CIB Panel of Dealers...

Finally, we wish to thank the panel of over 300 limited edition retailers and secondary market experts whose knowledge and dedication have helped make our Price Index possible. We wish we could recognize each of them by name, but they have agreed that to be singled out in this manner might hinder their ability to maintain an unbiased view of the marketplace.

FRONT COVER

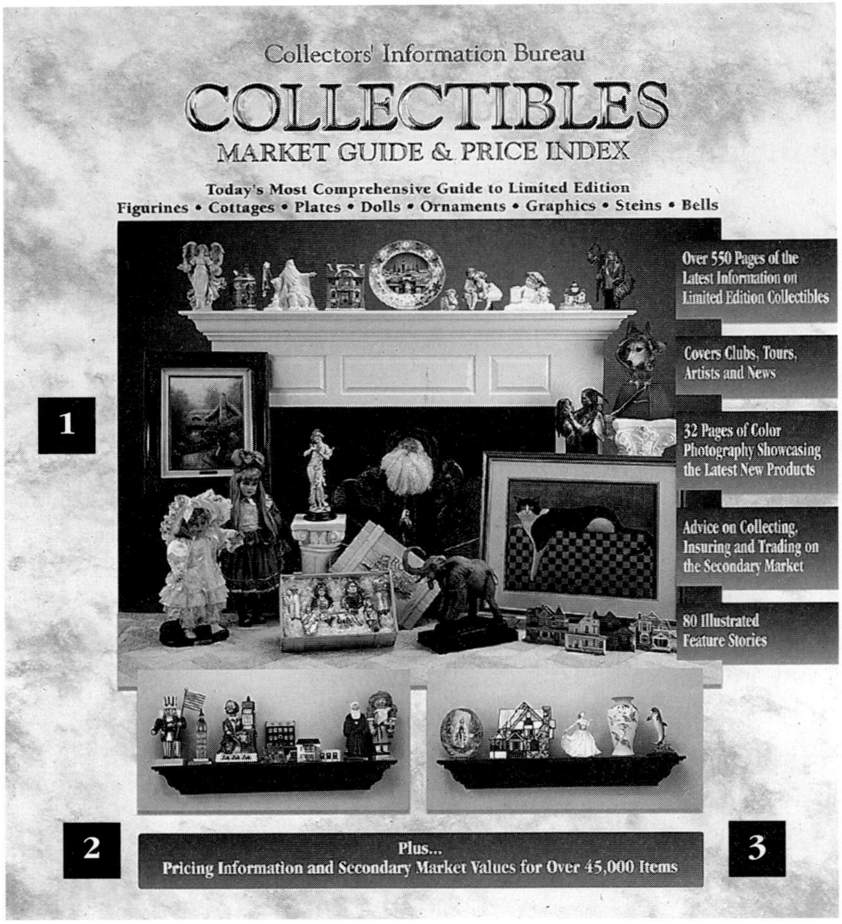

Photo 1:

On the mantel, from left to right: Roman Inc.'s *Seraphim Classics™* "Allysa-Nature's Angel," Anheuser-Busch Inc.'s "The Golden Retriever" Stein, Department 56's *Snowbabies* "Jack Frost- A Touch of Winter's Magic," George Z. Lefton Co.'s "Colonial Village News," Royal Copenhagen/Bing & Grondhal's "1995 Centennial Platter," M.I. Hummel's "Honey Lover," Lladró's "Ten and Growing," Cast Art Industries' "Picture Perfect," Harbour Lights' "Point Fermin," and Lance Corp.'s "The War Bonnet."

In front of the fireplace, from left to right: Lightpost Publishing's "Autumn at Ashley's Cottage," The Wimbledon Collection's "Victoria," Seymour Mann, Inc.'s "Alyssa," Armani's "Melody," Kurt S. Adler, Inc.'s "Roma" Ornament Set, Classic Collectables by Uniquely Yours' "Renaissance Santa," Creart U.S.A.'s "Elephant Tracks," The Greenwich Workshop's "Pavane in Gold," Shelia's Inc.'s "Victorian Springtime II," Legends' "Each, to the Other," and Rick Cain Studios' "Fire and Ice."

Photo 2:

From left to right: Old World Christmas' "Uncle Sam Nutcracker," Fraser International's "Big Ben," WACO Corp.'s *Melody in Motion* "Willie The Conductor," Hawthorne Architectural Register's "McKenna's Cottage," My Friends & Me "My Savannah Friends," R.R. Creations Inc.'s *Amish Collection* "Milk Cans," "Amish House" and "Buggies in a Row," Great American Taylor Collectibles Corp.'s "Timothy Claus-Ireland," and Midwest of Cannon Falls' "Clara" Nutcracker from the *Nutcracker Fantasy Series*.

Photo 3:

From left to right: The Bradford Exchange's "Our Lady of Lourdes," Forma Vitrum's "Brookview Bed & Breakfast," Royal Doulton's "Deborah," The Fenton Art Glass Co.'s "Hummingbird Burmese Vase," and Maruri U.S.A.'s "Dolphin."

BACK COVER

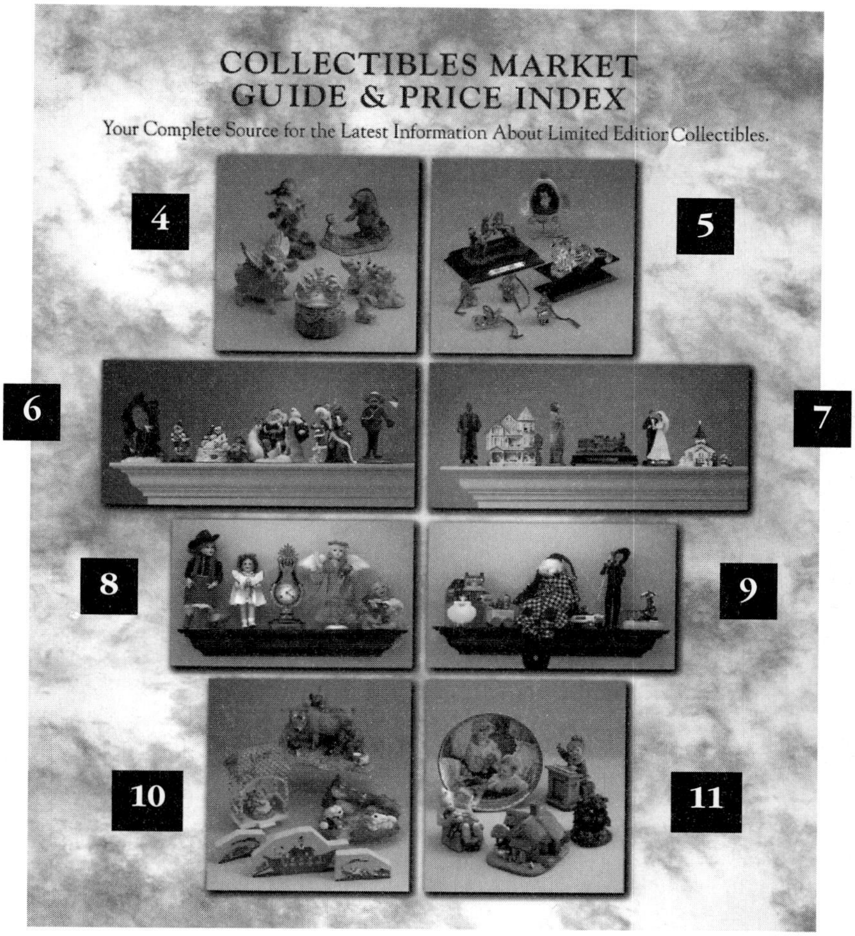

PHOTO 4:

From top to bottom, left to right: Rawcliffe Corp.'s "Angel Fairy of the Summer," Precious Art/Panton's *Krystonia* "Gurney Foot and Shadra," Calabar Creations' *Angelic Pigasus Collection's* "Angelo," Enesco's "It's a Par-Tea," and Flambro's *Pocket Dragons* "Telling Secrets" and "Tumbly."

PHOTO 5:

From top to bottom, left to right: *eggspressions!* "Angel Bunny," The Tudor Mint's "Meeting of the Unicorns," Swarovski's "Inspiration Africa-The Lion," and Hand & Hammer Silversmiths' "Alice in Wonderland" set of four ornaments.

PHOTO 6:

From left to right: June McKenna Collectibles Inc.'s "Peaceful Journey," Christopher Radko's "On Top of the World," Cavanagh Group International's "Always" Polar Bear, Possible Dreams' *Crinkle Claus* "Netherland Santa," United Design Corp.'s "The Story of Christmas," Lenox Collection's Santa, "A Christmas Wish," and Annalee Mobilitee Dolls' "Canadian Mountie."

PHOTO 7:

From left to right: Sarah's Attic's "Martin Luther King, Jr.," Michael's Limited's "Maple Lane," Miss Martha Originals' "Bessie Smith," Ganz' Western and Atlantic Railroad "The General," Today's Creations' *Times to Remember* "With This Ring," and BAND Creations' "Best Friends-River Song."

Photo 8:

From left to right: The Hamilton Collection's "Savannah," The Lawton Doll Company's "Katie and Her Kewpie," The Franklin Mint's "Marie Antoinette" Clock, Georgetown Collection's "Arielle, The Spring Angel," and The Ashton Drake Galleries' "I Wish You Love."

Photo 9:

From left to right: Brandywine Woodcrafts' *Country Lane* "General Store," Margaret Furlong Designs' "Limited Edition Angel -95, Faith Angel," Attic Babies' "Spirit of Christmas-Santy," Hallmark's "Dragnet" car, Byers' Choice Ltd.'s "Lamplighter," and Ron Lee's World of Clowns' "Fillet of Sole."

PHOTO 10:

From top to bottom, left to right: Schmid's "Blossom's Best," Pacific Rim Import Corp.'s *Bunny Toes* "Gazebo" and "Winifred with Blooms," VickiLane's "Sunny Daze," and The Cat's Meow's "Noah's Ark."

PHOTO 11:

From top to bottom, left to right: Reco International's "Moments of Love," ANRI U.S.'s "I Know, I Know," *M.I. Hummel's* "Just Dozing," Lilliput Lane's "Bargate Tea Room," and The Boyds Collections Ltd.'s "Elliott's Tree."

TABLE OF CONTENTS

Background

Features

Reference Section

COLLECTORS' INFORMATION BUREAU MEMBERSHIP ROSTER

Collectors' Information Bureau (CIB) is a not-for-profit business league whose mission is to serve and educate collectors, members and dealers, and to provide them with credible, comprehensive and authoritative information on limited edition collectibles and their current values.

Kurt S. Adler, Inc.
Anheuser-Busch, Inc.
Annalee Mobilitee Dolls, Inc.
ANRI U.S.
G. Armani Society
The Ashton-Drake Galleries
Attic Babies
BAND Creations
The Boyds Collection Ltd.
The Bradford Exchange
Brandywine Woodcrafts, Inc.
Byers' Choice Ltd.
Cain Studios
Calabar Creations
Cast Art Industries, Inc.
Cavanagh Group International
Christopher Radko
Classic Collectables by Uniquely Yours
Creart
Department 56, Inc.
The Walt Disney Company
Duncan Royale
eggspressions! inc.
Enesco Corporation
FJ Designs Inc./The Cat's Meow
The Fenton Art Glass Company
Flambro Imports, Inc.
Forma Vitrum
The Franklin Mint
Fraser International
Margaret Furlong Designs
GANZ
Georgetown Collection
Goebel of North America
Great American Taylor Collectibles Corp.
The Greenwich Workshop
Hallmark Cards, Inc.
The Hamilton Collection*
Hand & Hammer Silversmiths
Harbour Lights
Hawthorne Architectural Register
M.I. Hummel Club*
Ladie and Friends, Inc.
The Lance Corporation
The Lawton Doll Company
Ron Lee's World of Clowns
George Z. Lefton Co.
Legends
Lenox Collections
Lilliput Lane
Lladró
Seymour Mann, Inc.
Maruri U.S.A.
June McKenna Collectibles Inc.
Media Arts Group, Inc.
Michael's Limited
Midwest of Cannon Falls
Miss Martha Originals, Inc.
My Friends and Me
Old World Christmas
Pacific Rim Import Corp.
PenDelfin Studios
Possible Dreams
Precious Art/Panton
R.R. Creations, Inc.
Rawcliffe Corporation
Reco International Corp.*
Roman, Inc.*
Royal Copenhagen/Bing & Grondahl
Royal Doulton
Sarah's Attic
Schmid
Shelia's Collectibles
Swarovski America Limited
Today's Creations, Inc.
The Tudor Mint, Inc.
United Design Corporation
VickiLane, Inc.
WACO Products Corporation
The Wimbledon Collection

*Charter Member

A BRIEF HISTORY OF LIMITED EDITION COLLECTIBLES

An Ever-Expanding Market Embraces Collectible Plates, Steins, Bells, Dolls, Graphics, Figurines, Cottages and Ornaments

Many collectibles "sages" point to the introduction of Bing & Grondahl's 1895 "Behind the Frozen Window" porcelain plate as the beginning of contemporary collecting. Indeed, for the first time this blue-and-white beauty boasted the prime ingredient of what we now call "collectibility": a defined limited edition. Yet hundreds of years before Harald Bing unveiled the premier plate in this century-old series, artists were creating decorative steins, bells and dolls. And many of these pieces were considered so spectacular that their owners preserved them as heirlooms – setting the stage for today's strong primary and secondary markets.

As production techniques evolved and improved, art studios found ways to reproduce original works of art as graphic prints, limited edition figurines and cottages. And the tradition of decorating a stately pine tree at Christmas nurtured collectors' love for ornaments – a fine art medium that now attracts devotees all year 'round.

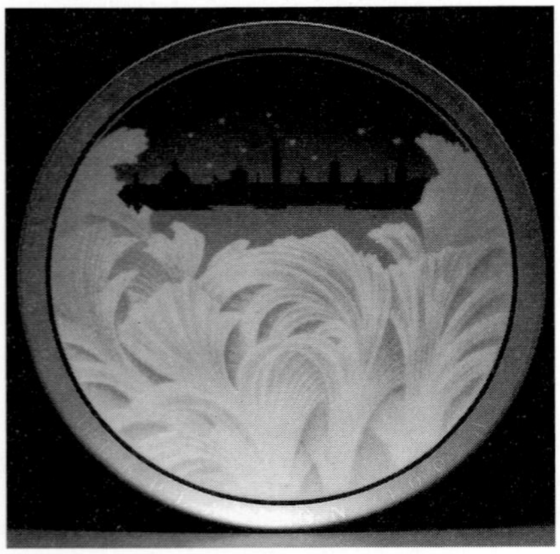

Bing & Grondahl's "Centennial Plate" features the timeless image of "Behind the Frozen Window," the world's very first and most famous Christmas plate.

Plates and Steins Become Works of Art

In many ancient cultures, even primitive peoples considered it essential that their humblest utensils be gracefully designed and elegantly decorated. Thus plates and steins – originally meant simply for eating and drinking – evolved into things of beauty. Indeed, at a certain point, some of these pieces "crossed over" and became objects of art: much too treasured to be subjected to the wear and tear of everyday use.

The Bing & Grondahl Christmas plates themselves have made this transition beautifully. When Harald Bing introduced "Behind the Frozen Window" in 1895, his intention was that the pretty, blue-and-white plate be used for presenting Christmas treats as gifts. There has been a new Bing & Grondahl annual plate every year since – yet only a few Danish "traditionalists" would ever think to serve food today on their treasured "B&Gs" – especially since some of the early pieces command hundreds or even thousands of dollars at auction!

As for steins, these sturdy drinking vessels originally appeared on the European scene hundreds of years ago. Many of them had hinged lids, which could be closed to avoid the pollution of the contents. As steinmakers became more and more innovative with their colorful decorations and bas-relief lid adornments, the practice of collecting steins for display and artistic enjoyment evolved over time.

Some traditional stein collectors enjoy seeking out rare steins from the "glory days" (pre-World War I) of German manufacturers like Villeroy & Boch. Others are just now discovering the pleasures of stein ownership with unique new pieces and handsome reproductions from firms like Anheuser-Busch.

The "Mirror of Truth" stein and plate, the fourth and final issues in the Archive Series, *present turn-of-the-century art from the Anheuser-Busch archives.*

Historic Bells Inspire Today's New Editions

Today many of us treasure delicate little bells of crystal, porcelain or silver, and show them off as collectors' items in our homes. Their tinkling sounds are music to our ears. Yet these elegant "bell collectibles" enjoy a dynamic heritage and an essential place in the history of nations. The first bells of ancient Greece, Rome, Egypt and Asia were used for religious ceremonies, to sound warnings, or to indicate that an area was "all clear" after a military attack. In addition, bells play a part in many of our most delightful memories and historical events: from the old school bell to the wintry sound of sleigh bells to that perennial symbol of freedom, The Liberty Bell.

The transition from large, crude bells of iron or bronze to the lovely pieces we show off in our homes was hastened by the introduction of Royal Bayreuth's "Sunbonnet Babies" at the turn of the century. These are acknowledged as the first-ever limited edition bells, paving the way for contemporary bell series from Goebel, Enesco, and Lladro, among many others.

The Oldest Collectibles of All

There is evidence that dolls may hold the distinction of being the earliest collectible, since their existence has been traced back as far as 2000 B.C. The doll's role as confidante and friend transcends time and culture. When the ruins of Pompeii and Hurculaneum were uncovered in modern times, the perfectly preserved body of a child was found still clutching her doll.

While the 19th century was renowned as the "Golden Age" of dollmaking in Germany and France, many of today's dollmakers are reviving these elegantly dressed dolls of hand-painted bisque and soft kid leather. At the same time, an active secondary market continues for "baby boomer" favorites like Barbie and G.I. Joe.

Bringing back famous dolls of the past, Wendy Lawton designed "Katie and Her Kewpie" from the Classic Playthings Collection. *The very first kewpie doll was made by Rose O'Neill in 1909.*

Treasured by contemporary bell collectors, Lladró's Annual Christmas Bell *series has brought holiday cheer since 1987. This beautifully detailed bell can also be displayed as a Christmas ornament.*

Graphic Prints Bring Fine Art into the Home

At one time, only royalty and the rich could aspire to acquire the works of contemporary art masters. But just as the Industrial Revolution made it possible for "everyday people" to own mass-produced furniture, appliances and clothing, advancements in art techniques and printing now allow most of us to enjoy fine art at home.

Over the last few centuries, a number of reproduction techniques – including lithography, woodcuts, engravings and serigraphy – have opened up this new world of affordable graphics for collectors. Indeed, graphics by artists whose original paintings cost $5,000...$15,000... $30,000 and more now may be acquired for just a few hundred dollars – sometimes even less, depending upon the print's size, medium and edition limit.

Many a collector has entered the contemporary art field with the initial purchase of a plate or small figurine, and then discovered the joy of owning the same artist's graphic prints. By the same token, some graphics collectors later discover that their favorite painters' works also may be enjoyed on porcelain plates or as three-dimensional figurines. Such renowned names as Gregory Perillo, Sandra Kuck, Edna Hibel, Thomas Kinkade, Norman Rockwell, and scores of other artists have had their work reproduced in graphic form as well as on plates, figurines or other collector's media.

From Original Sculptures to Affordable Figurines

While the Renaissance masters once created priceless "one of a kind" sculptures in marble and stone, today's collector revels in the variety of figural art now available in a host of price ranges. Many generations ago, the "lost wax" casting method revolutionized the world of art by allowing one original sculpture to serve as the basis for a mold in which an edition of bronzes could be cast. Then in the 1930s, Royal Worcester of England joined forces with the gifted sculptress, Dorothy Doughty. Together the studio and artist created *Birds of America*, renowned today as the first limited edition

M. I. Hummel *figurines have been capturing the spirit of children for over 60 years since they were first introduced at the Leipzig Fair in 1935. This charming figurine entitled "To Keep You Warm" (HUM 759) will knit her way into your heart! A companion piece, "Nimble Fingers," will be released in 1996.*

The Dickens' Village© *series from Department 56, Inc. was introduced in 1984 with seven original porcelain shops and the "Village Church." New introductions have been added yearly to this popular lighted village which celebrates the bustling and joyous atmosphere of the holidays in Victorian England.*

collection of porcelain sculpture.

Miss Doughty's achievement seems all the more spectacular considering the intricacy of her step-by-step process. She supervised the creation of between 20 and 40 molds to capture every detail of each original sculpture. Even today, admirers marvel at her ability to portray birds and flowers with absolute fidelity to nature.

Miss Doughty's work set the stage for fine art sculpture studios of the late 20th century including Boehm and Cybis in the United States, and Lladro in Spain. Yet these "high end" figurines and sculptures account for only a portion of the market. Many collectors delight in the ownership of smaller, less complex pieces featuring animals, flowers, children, and even cartoon characters. In addition, today's world of figurines encompasses crystal, and cold-casting in various materials, as well as the traditional porcelain and bronze.

Collectors Invest in "Real Estate"

As one frequent traveler said playfully in a recent conversation, "My husband and I purchase real estate just about everywhere we visit!" No, they are not billionaires – rather, they're among the thousands of collectors who have succumbed to "cottage fever" over the past two decades.

From the English images of David Winter and David Tate, to the romantic visions of Thomas Kinkade and the nostalgic Americana of Norman Rockwell, today's collectible cottage market covers a great deal of ground. Also beloved by many are the lighted houses of Department 56 and a range of other lighted homes, shops and lighthouses.

While cottages are still considered part of the "figurine world" because of their three-dimensional quality, recent years have also shown an upswing in collector excitement over the nearly two-dimensional wooden homes of The Cat's Meow, Shelia's Inc., Brandywine Collectibles, R.R. Creations and others.

Ornaments Transcend the Holidays with Year-Round Good Cheer

The concept of decorating a tree at Christmas stretches back to Germany in the early 19th century. In the glassmaking city of Lauscha, beautiful glass ball ornaments were first made. Then in the 1850s, Louis Greiner-Schlotfeger discovered a way to "silver" the balls so that they would shine with a mirror-like glow.

The dime-store mogul Frank Woolworth imported $25.00 worth of the German glass ornaments in 1880, willing to take a risk that American consumers might like them. The pretty decorations were an immediate sell-out, leading to a proliferation of ornaments in wax, paper, tinsel, crystal, porcelain, sterling silver, and many other art media.

While some collectors covet the elegant silver ornaments of Halls, Reed and Barton, Towle, and Shreve, Crump and Lowe, a host of others find themselves "hooked on Hallmark." The famed greeting card maker introduced its first ornaments in the 1970s, and since then has set the pace with thousands of whimsical and attractive offerings.

Indeed, there are ornaments today on most every theme collectors can imagine, and many of them are suitable for display any time of the year. Whether it's a crystal ornament shimmering in front of a sunny window, or a *Precious Moments*® character adding charm to a collector's favorite room – it's clear that ornaments aren't just for Christmas anymore.

For today's collectors, a bit of background on the origins of their favorite art medium can add richness to their enjoyment and understanding. In this brief article, you've learned "the basics" on the history of each collectible category that is covered in this authoritative book. Now read on...

Made from an antique mold, this classic ornament from Old World Christmas is titled "Holly Heart."

TRENDS IN TODAY'S MARKETPLACE

Expert Observers Share Insights with Limited Edition Collectors

The popularity of "Angel of Sharing," and other plates from Sandra Kuck's Precious Angels *series, reflects collectors' renewed interest in faith and hope.*

"Buy only what you like"... "Secondary market potential should be the icing on the cake – not the main reason for selecting an item"... "Show off and enjoy your collectibles – don't store them in a closet or under a bed." Advice like this to collectors is as timeless as a blue-and-white Christmas plate. Yet from year to year and decade to decade there are meaningful changes in the marketplace – and many collectors like to stay abreast of these trends in order to make more informed choices for their personal holdings. That's why Collectors' Information Bureau has gathered a panel of experts to reveal some of the more important new directions in today's world of collecting. These "collectibles gurus" don't always agree, but you'll find their thoughts provocative, authoritative, and intriguing!

Figurines Lead All Other Collectibles in Popularity

Our first question to the experts centered on collectible art media. We wanted to know which media are most sought-after in today's market...and why. The lion's share of our respondents replied with just one word: "Figurines." From the adorable and affordable *Enesco Cherished Teddies™* and Cast Art Industries' *Dreamsicles™*, to the sophistication of Lladró porcelain and Swarovski crystal, the figurine art market offers something for every taste and pocketbook. Yet for all the dominance of figurines as a "medium of choice," some of our experts offered a different viewpoint.

David MacMahan, president of Forma Vitrum, noted the strength of villages. These series of collectible cottages often carry a literary, historical or architectural theme. As MacMahan said, "Villages remain strong because they may be accessorized and changed with each new season for year-round display. Villages are an interactive collectible that allows collectors to design the scene and create the mood. They can build their own unique dreamlands and become a part of the scene."

The growth of Christmas collectibles as a year-round collecting theme was noted by Debra Mosier of Old World Christmas®. "The warmth and excitement surrounding the Christmas holidays are feelings people would like to keep all year long. Christmas ornaments and wooden collectibles provide them with a way to capture that magic," she said.

Collectibles Reflect Societal Change

When asked what general trends in society might affect collectors' choices, our respondents offered a wonderful range of ideas. For example, Marlene Marcus, product development manager at Reco International Corp., commented on the diversity of today's American culture. She observed, "As much as we see trends in society, such as environmentalism, return to basics, marriage and children, we also see a wealth of differences. We have become an 'eclectic' society, and I believe this is very much reflected in the collectibles which are popular today.

"Just as some examples, people seem to appreciate wit and humor, as shown by the success of the 'Santa Paws' plate from The Franklin Mint. Collectibles featuring identifiable names, such as Coca-Cola®, STAR TREK®, and even McDonalds, familiar things that we have known for a long time, bring us comfort in a quickly changing world. Totally different is the interest in faith and the hope that someone really is looking out for us, as demonstrated by the overwhelming popularity of angels, such as the *Precious Angels* collection by Sandra Kuck."

Ms. Marcus continues, "One trend which cannot be denied, is the trend towards spending much more time at home. The availability to do shopping, banking and many other services electronically, the entertainment available through home theater and computer, the ability to work from one's home, is making the home the center of our lives."

Licensed products, such as "Sylvester's Holiday High Jinks" from Possible Dreams, continue to grow in diversity and prominence in today's world of collecting.

One collecting trend that appeals to home decorators focuses on cottages and villages. Collectors are displaying their village scenes all year 'round, often with seasonal accents. Here, an autumn setting enhances the charms of the lighted "Mayor's Mansion" from Forma Vitrum.

David Faas, the consumer services manager for Lladró USA, named three trends that he believes are most reflected in today's collectibles: family values, patriotism, and fantasy/whimsy/nostalgia. He says, "People have become more aware and drawn toward family. Figurines that capture family unity and devotion are strong. Collectibles that capture family occasions such as weddings, communions, new baby, anniversary and parents with children are growing in popularity.

"Love of country appears to be on the upswing. Recently Lladró introduced an astronaut with an American flag called 'The Apollo Landing' to very enthusiastic reviews. A new limited edition figurine called 'Abraham Lincoln' is quite popular with collectors.

"While life becomes increasingly hectic for many collectors, they long for items that can 'take them away' from today's fast-paced lifestyles. Many collectors collect items of fantasy or whimsy to remind them of simple times, enchanting times," Faas concludes.

The vice president of marketing for Goebel of North America, William A. Belmont, Jr., reported succinctly that today's trends are "nature and environment, space limitation, and spiritualism." To illustrate, he noted the popularity of wildlife subjects in homage to nature, the enjoyment of miniatures which take up little space in the home, and the trend of collecting heavenly angels.

Peter Nourjian of Possible Dreams believes, "The biggest trends today seem to be entertainment driven. Naturally, licensed collectibles relating to the movie or personality spotlighted are going to have the biggest appeal. And with baby boomers coming into the collector's fold, quality will become more important to appeal to their more refined tastes."

Finally, Gideon Oberweger, vice president of Seymour Mann, takes a contrarion point of view to the discussion of trends. As he comments, "Trends in society do not affect collectibles as much as people may wish. Subjects dear to the heart which convey an emotion are always more popular than 'trendy' collectibles – this is why subjects such as birds, cats, bears and roses remain the best sellers."

A theme of religious faith and hope shines through in the Roman, Inc. Millenium™ *series of annual Christmas plates and companion ornaments. Both the plate and ornament, shown here, are entitled "Cause of Our Joy."*

Lladró's "Abraham Lincoln" figurine offers a fine example of the patriotic-theme figurines that have attracted collectors in recent years.

Advice on Selecting Artists and Collectibles to Purchase

When asked who the "hottest" artists are today, many respondents cited the artists under contract to their own firms or studios. In addition, names like David Tate, Thomas Kinkade, Sandra Kuck, Sam Butcher, Priscilla Hillman, David Winter, and Christopher Radko came up often.

What's more, Sam Caggiula, manager of corporate communications for The Franklin Mint, had some specific advice on how to get started with a collection. We asked him what he would recommend to a collector with $500 to spend over the next year.

"First, decide what it is that you want to collect," suggests Caggiula. "This task sounds easy enough, but it does require some planning. There are simply too many 'things' that are or become collectibles. You've got to know – or at least have an idea – what type of collectible you want. It could be collector plates, porcelain dolls, die cast replicas, books, Christmas ornaments, or salt-n-pepper shakers, but it's helpful to have a type of collectible in mind before you begin collecting.

"If you can't quite decide, then take your research on the road. Visit museums, antique stores, craft shows, yard sales, and of course, collectible expos. The other alternative is to read a few of the many and varied collectible publications now available to the public."

The Year 2000...and Beyond

To round out our discussion, we asked our experts to look into their crystal balls and predict what collecting will be like circa 2005. Our respondent from Ganz predicts secondary market transactions on the Internet. Several individuals mentioned the continued strength of classic collectibles – items that have been popular for many decades and will continue to attract loyal buyers. Others commented that the market is saturated currently, and that only the "quality" artists, producers and marketers will survive.

Ronald T. Jedlinski, president of Roman, Inc., believes that the turn of the century itself will affect collecting. As he notes, "Millennium will have a big impact on what people will buy and read about. The coming of the end of the Millennium and the attendant uncertainty it generates has given rise to a surge in the return to the spiritual. Collectible producers are responding to this wave with collectibles reflecting images people associate with the Millennium."

To conclude on a more pragmatic note, Peter Nourjian of Possible Dreams believes that the future can be found in "Licensing, licensing, licensing. Big-budgeted Hollywood and TV-generated properties will rule!"

Collectors appreciate the wit and humor displayed in works of collectible art such as The Franklin Mint's "The Santa Paws Plate."

Advice from the Experts: Short Tips for Collectors

Here are a few quick hints from some of today's most knowledgeable collectibles producers and marketers:

To become a smart buyer:

- Obtain every bit of educational material possible about your collection. Go to antique shows – there are always lots of books available on just about any possible collectible. Ask your retailer to obtain as much information from the manufacturer as is available. – Nancy G. Fenton, The Fenton Art Glass Company

- Join the appropriate Collectors Society to be informed, entertained and educated about your favorite collectibles. – David Faas, Lladró USA

- Attend manufacturer-sponsored events and collectible expositions. Work with just one or two retailers exclusively, and choose them for their dedicated, knowledgeable staffs. – Claire Golata, Lilliput Lane

To better display and care for your collectibles:

- Create levels and layers on shelves and cabinets, to make collections more distinctive and easier to appreciate. Almost anything will do as "risers": books, covered boxes, or gift boxes wrapped in fabric or paper. – Linda Masterson, Enesco Corporation

- Invest in a good display case for your collectibles. You will be able to enjoy them while protecting them from dust, smoke, etc. Also, purchase insurance for your collection – better safe than sorry. – Gideon Oberweger, Seymour Mann Inc.

- Those little cordless keyboard vacuums are great for keeping collections dust free – and safe! – Linda Masterson, Enesco Corporation

- Keep an inventory of all items in the collection, including photos. Some insurance companies cover collectibles on homeowner insurance policies. – Debra Mosier, Old World Christmas

- Most boxes fold flat for storage and should be kept to increase the value of a retired piece. – Peter Nourjian, Possible Dreams

THE SECONDARY MARKET

A Basic Guide for Collectors on Buying and Selling Sold-Out Limited Editions

They add sparkle and individuality to our home decor and provide daily enjoyment and inspiration to their owners. They make ideal conversation pieces for visitors, and coveted heirlooms to pass to the next generation. Even without considering their secondary market potential, limited edition collectibles reign among the most delightful of all possessions. In fact, many collectors are so enchanted by the sheer beauty of their holdings that they never even consider the possibility of price appreciation. Yet it is a wise collector who keeps abreast of the secondary market – and knows how to use it to their advantage if the opportunity or need should arise.

In this brief introduction, we'll provide an overview of the "how-tos" of market trading. Then, in our "ask the experts" section, you'll gain insights into some of the nuances of buying and selling collectibles on the aftermarket.

Limited Editions and the Law of Supply and Demand

The price of a limited edition collectible on the secondary market is a function of supply and demand. For example, an item that is in relatively limited supply and is experiencing

– ASK THE EXPERTS –

I'm a collector who is considering trading on the secondary market. What advice do you have for me?

OHI Exchange Division of Opa's Haus, Inc., New Braunfels, Texas; Ken Armke

"If selling, find a store or exchange service to sell for you on a commission basis – that is, unless you feel you have exceptional marketing skills. If buying, decide if you are buying strictly for pleasure or whether you are buying at least partially for 'investment.' If it's for pleasure, simply buy what you can afford and what pleases you. If it's for investment, then a) buy for a short-term return; today's collectibles have not been proven over a long term, and b) buy items you like, because you may 'get stuck' with them!"

Animation Fascination/Classic Endeavors, Joliet, Illinois; Dee Brandt

"Know who you are dealing with! Never mail payments to a post office box or answer a 'blind ad.' If not sure of your contact, use a referral service such as the Collectors' Information Bureau."

Collectible Exchange Inc., New Middletown, Ohio; Connie Eckman

"Manufacturer-sponsored collector clubs are one of the best sources for reliable information about a particular line. You can also ask the manufacturer if they recommend any secondary market services – many do."

Lighthouse Trading Company, Limerick, Pennsylvania; Matt Rothman

"First, understand that a secondary market trade takes time. Be patient and find out if the price you are asking is in line with the market. The more realistic the price, the faster the piece will sell."

Gift Music Book & Collectibles, Chicago Heights, Illinois; Joe Schulte

"Buy the oldest piece in a series that you can afford now, and fill in the middle of the collection later. First in a series almost always goes up faster than the rest."

Swan Seekers Network, Phoenix, Arizona; Maret Webb A.I.A.

"First, realistically assess the condition of your piece. Today's secondary market buyers demand perfection, and flawed merchandise is not tolerated. Scrutinize the item for damage or factory imperfections prior to offering it for sale. Buyers want the correct original packaging, and a realistic selling price may be compromised significantly without the box, certificate, sleeve, etc. A deduction of at least 10% for each missing element is not unreasonable. Pack well and ship fully insured. Require an adult signature for delivery of the parcel. Finally, understand how price guides work. The value printed in a price guide is what it may cost to buy the item. For a prospective buyer, this is good information to know when you go shopping for a collectible on the secondary market, as the price guide can give you a benchmark. A private seller generally will not be able to get 'book' price, but may receive 50% to 70% of the current retail value of an item."

– ASK THE EXPERTS –

What is it about "members-only" pieces from collectors' clubs that makes them such strong secondary market performers?

Collector's Marketplace, Montrose, Pennsylvania, Renée Tyler

"Few people actively bought members-only pieces until recently. The result is that there aren't lots of these pieces around. Additionally, certain manufacturers are limiting these pieces and supplying them on a first-come first-served basis. This approach drives the market wild."

Crystal Reef, Foster City, California; Blaine Garfolo

"There are two things which strongly contribute to the performance of members-only pieces on the secondary market: limited availability and history. Members-only pieces are produced typically for only a single year. Because of this, they are in a sense a limited piece since only club members may purchase them. History plays the second role. A members-only piece can be purchased by the club member only – not by the dealer. When a new collector starts collecting, they can only purchase current members-only pieces. Stores may have back stock on retired pieces, but only previous collectors have the members-only pieces. When one of these members-only pieces becomes available on the secondary market, it is quickly snatched up by a new collector. This members-only piece represents the new collector's link with the history of the collection."

A Work of Art, Valhalla, New York; Joan Lewis

"As more and more people become members of collectors societies, there are more collectors to vie for the previously produced members-only pieces that are no longer available from the manufacturer. Combined with the breakage factor, the number of pieces available is even more limited, tending to put more buying pressure on these pieces."

great demand may appreciate in value. Similarly, if an item is part of a large edition that has not caught the attention and affection of a great number of collectors, it may not see any appreciation in price.

Some novice collectors assume that the lower the edition size, the most likely it is that an item will rise in price later. This may not necessarily be true, since an item must exist in sufficient quantity to "penetrate the market," in order for significant price appreciation to occur. People need to know about the item in order to build word of mouth and demand. Indeed, there have been collector plates limited by firing periods in which tens of thousands of a certain issue were made. Such items may well rise sharply in price if there is more demand than supply available once the edition closes.

Changes in supply and demand occur quite regularly. Over time, the supply of an item may diminish, particularly if the piece is fragile. Likewise, the demand for a particular piece may change as collectors' tastes and interests evolve. For example, a revival of interest in a "popular culture" subject such as a classic TV show or a renowned performer can result in an upturn in price for items inspired by that subject. Likewise, the death of a prominent artist may lead to a temporary surge in the price of his or her works.

As a result of these changes in supply and demand, collectors should realize that prices can and do fluctuate on the secondary market, sometimes quite dramatically. As prices rise, they may reach a level that collectors feel is unreasonable. As a result, demand falls. Once demand begins to fall, sellers may lower their price in order to make the sale. This may continue until collectors again feel that the value for the piece is reasonable and begin buying again. When that happens, demand may outpace supply and the cycle could begin again.

Going It Alone Vs. Using a Broker's Services

While some collectors believe they will save money by attempting to buy or sell on their own, the services of a knowledgeable broker are often well worth the cost of his or her commission. Brokers do the work for you: placing ads, making telephone contacts, ensuring that you are paid or that an item you purchase is delivered safely. In most cases, the seller pays the commission, which may vary from as low as 10% to 30% or more.

When comparing brokers and the prices they advertise, be aware that there are several possible listing methods. Some brokers list the price the buyer will pay, while others list the price the seller will receive. Shipping costs may or may not be included in these prices; if in doubt, ask for clarification.

Make sure you are aware of all surcharges and costs associated with working with a particular broker or buy-sell service. Some may require you to pay a subscription fee, a listing fee, or a surcharge for use of a credit card.

The Collectors' Information Bureau's *Directory to Secondary Market Retailers* features over 150 aftermarket brokers with full-page histories to help collectors learn more about each broker's business practices.

- ASK THE EXPERTS -

What should I look for in buying a new collectible if I am concerned about its future secondary market appreciation?

Gift Music Book & Collectibles, Chicago Heights, Illinois; Joe Schulte

"Strong name; history of appreciation; limited or exclusive availability (the less, the better); first in series; member, show, or mail-order-only promos; signed by a major artist; short production run (one year or less on the market); few discounters or 'gray market' able to sell them; and one that you like in case the market gets soft. Also, if the piece doesn't ship well (breaks easily), and you get one in mint condition, hold onto it for awhile: it'll go up."

Animation Fascination/Classic Endeavors, Joliet, Illinois; Dee Brandt

"Check the track record of the collection over the past six months. A steady climber is better than an overnight sensation. Only invest what you can afford – only buy what you like, and remember collectibles are at the top of the pyramid in high-risk investments."

Collectible Exchange Inc., New Middletown, Ohio; Connie Eckman

"Unless you can afford the risk, it's best not to speculate. If I could predict the secondary market, I wouldn't be working for a living, I would spend my time shopping!"

- ASK THE EXPERTS -

How should I choose a secondary market trading firm to assist me?

Crystal Reef, Foster City, California; Blaine Garfolo

"Look for an exchange that has collectors for employees as they tend to be more sensitive to the needs of collectors."

The Crystal Connection, Peoria, Illinois; Robin Yaw

"Check out their credentials – ask for references. What's the payment method – is there a waiting period before payment is made by the firm to the seller? Get a 'fact sheet' from the firm outlining all their procedures."

A Work of Art, Valhalla, New York; Joan Lewis

"Make sure that the secondary market firm has a strong knowledge of the collectible in which you are interested. I think it is also important to like the people you are dealing with. If they seem a little shifty or high pressure, or if they do not return your calls promptly or do not seem involved with what they're doing, they are probably not for you."

Gift Music Book & Collectibles, Chicago Heights, Illinois; Joe Schulte

"The five most important attributes of secondary market dealer are: 1) Service – we'll call fifty sources to find an item at the best price for our customers. 2) Flexibility – adapt to customer needs. 3) Takes credit cards – this covers everyone's liabilities. 4) Fair prices – not always highest or lowest. 5) Tenacious – we will call six months to a year later if the item a collector wanted shows up."

All that glitters and shines... comes to life in a stunning group of collectible treasures. Top Row (left to right): Swarovski Silver Crystal *South Sea Series* "Dolphin" and *Sparkling Fruit Series* "Large Pineapple." Middle Row: Swarovski Silver Crystal *Endangered Species* "Mother Kangaroo with Baby" and *When We Were Young* "Rocking Horse." Bottom Row: *eggspressions!* "Eternity," Goebel of North America's Steinbach Crystal "American Indian Camp," and *eggspressions!* "Mother's Pride."

The many faces of Santa...and other holiday characters are captured in collectibles that show the serious and silly sides of these universally loved figures. Top Row (left to right): United Design's "Getting Santa Ready," June McKenna Collectibles' "Light of Christmas", Cast Art Industries' "Santa's Kingdom," and Possible Dreams' "Jolly Traveller." Middle Row: Ladie and Friends' "The Little Ones at Christmas," Lladró's "A Christmas Wish," Christopher Radko's "Department Store Santa," Possible Dreams' "Giving Thanks," and ANRI U.S.'s "Checking It Twice." Bottom Row: Lance Corp.'s "Stars & Stripes Santa," Possible Dreams' "A Good Round," Christopher Radko's "Bishop," June McKenna Collectibles' "Peaceful Journey" and Annalee Mobilitee Dolls' " 'Puppies for Christmas' Santa."

Top Row (left to right): Duncan Royale's "Mongolian" Santa, Possible Dreams' "A Frisky Friend," Byers' Choice Ltd.'s "Working Santa," Possible Dreams' "Sounds of Christmas." Middle Row: June McKenna Collectibles' "Christmas Lullaby," Old World Christmas' "Merlin" and "Regal Father Christmas," Kurt S. Adler Inc.'s "Arm Chair Quarterback," Cavanagh Group International's "Santa at the Fireplace." Bottom Row: Byers' Choice Ltd.'s "Couple in Sleigh" and "Salvation Army Girl with 'War Cry'," and WACO Products' "Girl Caroler" and "Boy Caroler."

Time-honored traditions of the holidays...

are captured for generations to come in these sometimes whimsical and always wonderful Christmas collectibles. Top Row (left to right): Reco International's "Dear Santa," Hallmark Keepsake Ornaments' "Murray® Fire Truck," June McKenna Collectibles' "Finishing Touch," Roman Inc.'s *1920's Clothlike* "American Santas Through the Decades," Pacific Rim Import's *Bunny Toes* "Douglas-Frosty Friends," and Schmid's "Belsnickles' 9-inch Teal" Santa. Middle Row: Midwest of Cannon Falls' "Santa on Reindeer" Ornament, Christopher Radko's "Bubbly," Enesco's "T-Bird," Royal Copenhagen/Bing & Grondahl's "Christmas Around the World 1995," ANRI U.S.'s "First Christmas Stocking," and Christopher Radko's "My Favorite Chimp." Bottom Row: Old World Christmas' "Waldkirchen Father Christmas Nutcracker," Classic Collectables by Uniquely Yours' "Scrooge," "Children Carolers," and "Adult Carolers."

Top Row: (left to right) Christopher Radko's "On Top of the World," Old World Christmas' "Sugarplum Fairy Nutcracker," and Christopher Radko's "Little Prince." Bottom Row: Kurt S. Adler Inc.'s *Camelot Series'* "Queen Guenevere Steinbach Nutcracker," Great American Taylor Collectibles *Old World Santas* "Tomba Claus-South Africa," Royal Copenhagen's "Christmas Around the World Ornament" and Great American Taylor Collectibles *Old World Santas* "Lars Claus-Norway." On the Riser: Great American Taylor Collectibles *Old World Santas* "Raymond Claus-Galapagos Islands" and "Stach Claus-Poland."

Warm and wonderful memories... of Christmas' gone by are evoked by a host of holiday collectibles. Top Row: (left to right) Department 56's *Winter Silhouette Christmas Concerto* "Cellist," "Harpist," and "Violinist," *eggspressions!* "Beary Pink Christmas" Band Creations' "River Song" and "Monthly Angels." Middle Row: Department 56's "We'll Plant the Starry Pines" and "Bringing Starry Pines," Cavanagh Group International's "Polar Bear Family," Ganz's *Little Cheesers* "Light of the World," Schmid's "Bah Humbug." Hanging Ornaments: Hand & Hammer Silversmiths' "Fabergé Egg" and "Joy," Hallmark Keepsake Ornaments' "Christmas Cardinal," and Hand & Hammer Silversmiths' "1995 Annual Star." Bottom Row: The Ashton Drake Galleries' "Beneath the Mistletoe," M.I. Hummel Club's "Ride Into Christmas," and United Design's "Into the Wind Victorian."

Top Row (left to right): Hand & Hammer Silversmiths' "The Night Before Christmas" (set of 4), Royal Copenhagen/Bing & Grondahl's "Jubilee Edition - The Capitol" and "Christmas Plate 1995," Pacific Rim Import Corp.'s *Bristol Township* "King's Gate School." Middle Row: George Z. Lefton Co's "Mundt Manor," Old World Christmas' "Santa in Sleigh," Department 56's "Hather Harness" and "Chelsea Market Curiosities Monger & Cart." Bottom Row: Forma Vitrum's "Community Chapel," Midwest of Cannon Falls' "Clara," Lilliput Lane's "Plum Cottage" Ornament, and Department 56's *Christmas in the City* "Heritage Museum of Art" and "Holiday Field Trip."

The mystery, magic and wonder of Angels... and other religious themes are translated into an array of collectibles that inspire, comfort and amuse. Top Row (left to right): Cast Art Industries' *Dreamsicles* "Picture Perfect," *eggspressions!* "Angel of Hope," Margaret Furlong's "2-inch Wreath Angel", "3-inch Flower Garland Angel," "4-inch Flower Garland Angel" and "Faith Angel," Ganz's "Angelic Teachings," and *eggspressions!* "Oh, Holy Night." Middle Row: United Design's "The Gift '95," Roman Inc.'s *1995 Millenium Plate* "Cause of Our Joy" and *Seraphim Classics* "Seraphina-Heaven's Helper," ANRI U.S.'s "Angel of Kindness," Cast Art Industries' *Heavenly Classics* "On Wings of Love." Bottom Row: United Design's "A Little Closer to Heaven," Fenton Art Glass' "Radiant Angel," Georgetown Collection's "Arielle-The Spring Angel," and United Design's "Guardian Angel, Lion and Lamb, Light."

Top Row (left to right): VickiLane's "He Sets My Heart Free," Reco International's "Angel of Laughter," Band Creations' *Best Friends* "Noah's Ark." Middle Row: Roman Inc.'s Americana Collection "Noah & Friends" and Ladie and Friends, Inc.'s "The Little Angel." Bottom Row: Roman Inc.'s *Fontanini* "Heirloom Nativity," ANRI U.S.'s "Mary and Infant" from *The Vatican Library Collection* and Sarah's Attic's "Dignity Angel."

Love and marriage... are celebrated in a collection of serious and sweet collectibles. Top Row (left to right): Ganz's "Holy Mortrimony," Today's Creations' "With This Ring," Band Creations' *Best Wishes* "Anniversary," Today's Creations' "Slice of Life," VickiLane's "Wedding Bunnies," Today's Creations' "First Dance." Middle Row: Today's Creations' "Bride," Forma Vitrum's "Trinity Church," Duncan Royale's *Jubilee Dancers* "Bliss." Bottom Row: Annalee Mobilitee Dolls' "Valentine Girl Bear," Seymour Mann's "Dove Bell," Lladró's "I Love You Truly," Ganz's "Match Made in Heaven," Annalee Mobilitee Doll's "Valentine Boy Bear."

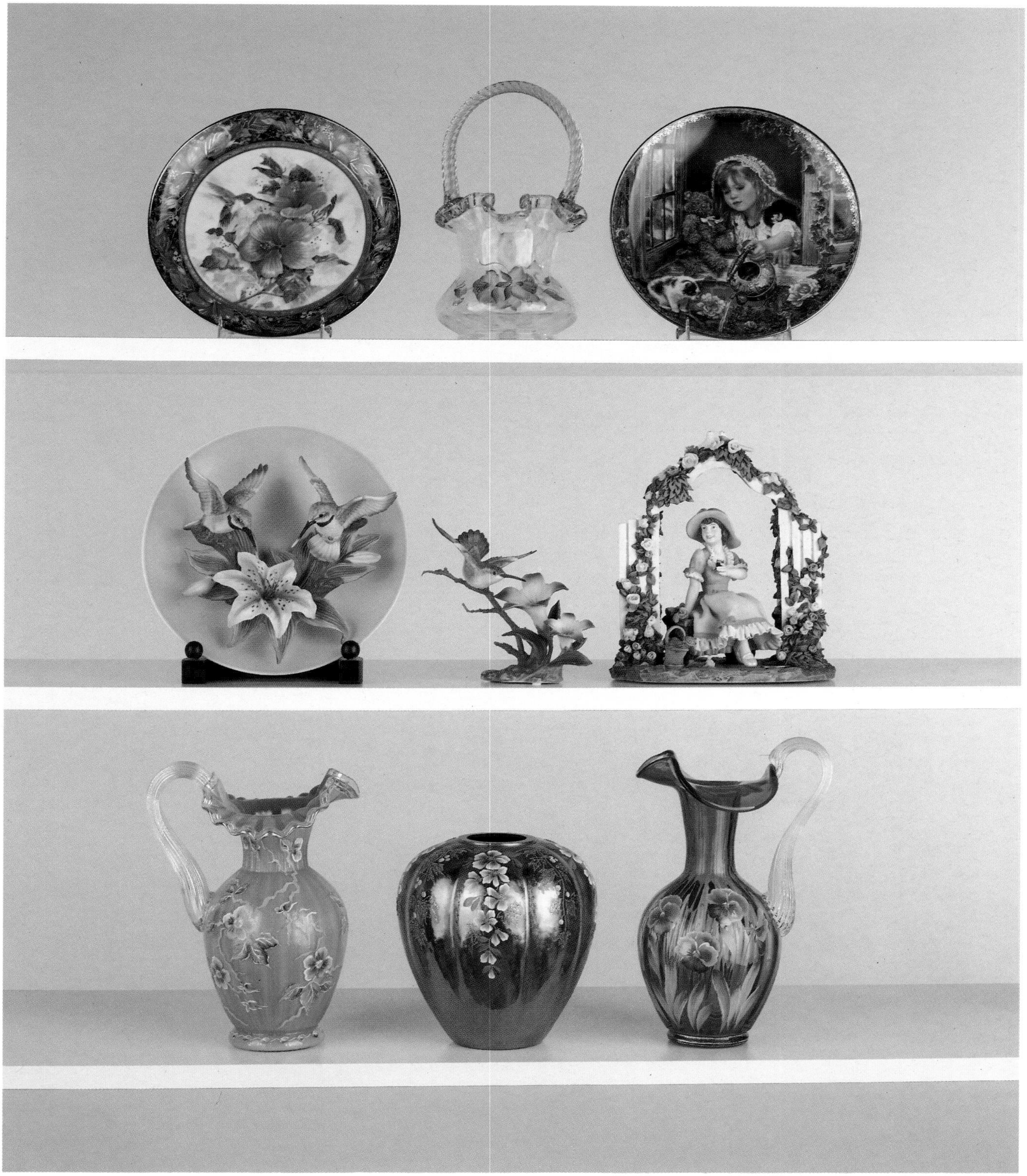

Garden delights... grace collectible plates and vases from some of America's premier collectibles manufacturers. Top Row (left to right): The Franklin Mint's "Imperial Hummingbird Plate," The Fenton Art Glass Company's "Hand-Painted Trellis Basket," Reco International's "Moments of Caring." Middle Row: Seymour Mann's "Hummingbird Duo Plate," Maruri U.S.A.'s "Violet Crowned Hummingbirds with Gentian," and Cavanagh Group International's "The Girl in Rose Arbor." Bottom Row: The Fenton Art Glass Company's "Victorian Art Glass Pitcher," "Favrene Ginger Jar" (base and lid not shown) and "Pansies on Cranberry 10-1/2" Pitcher."

The sweet innocence of childhood... is reflected in a charming assortment of collectibles. Top Row (left to right): M.I. Hummel Club's "Honey Lover" and "Friend or Foe," PenDelfin's "Teddy," Miss Martha Originals' "Issie" and "Honey." Middle Row: Sarah's Attic's "Love & Hugs," M.I. Hummel Club's "Come Back Soon," ANRI U.S.'s "Tender Care," and Enesco's "Sharing the Common Thread of Love." Bottom Row: M.I. Hummel Club's "Strike Up The Band," Miss Martha Originals' "Gina," Calabar Creations' "Little Count" from *The Jazzy Five Collection.*

Mythical creatures and magical fairies... work their spells in a myriad of collectible treasures. Top Row (left to right): Precious Art/Panton's "Moplos," "Escublar," and "Dubious Alliance," and Lance Corporation's "Have & Have Knot." Middle Row: The Tudor Mint's "The Visionary," "The Magical Encounter," and "The Unicorn of Justice," Precious Art/Panton's "Schnoogles," Flambro Imports' *Pocket Dragons* "Watson" and "Elementary My Dear." Bottom Row: The Tudor Mint's "The Great Earth Dragon," Rawcliffe's *Wish Fairies* "Love" and "Fun," "Fall" *Angel Fairy of the Seasons*, and Precious Art/Panton's "One Unhappy Ride."

Figures from literature and history... hold a special fascination for artists and collectors alike. Top row (left to right): Royal Doulton's "Charles Dickens," The Bradford Exchange's "Gettysburg," and Sarah's Attic's "Praise the Lord IV." Bottom Row: Lance Corp.'s "General Robert E. Lee, CSA," Miss Martha Originals' "Bessie Smith," Sarah's Attic's "Buffalo Soldier," and Midwest of Cannon Fall's "Paul Bunyan Nutcracker."

The fun and fascinating world of sports... has long been an inspiration for collectible artists. Top Row (left to right): The Boyds Collections' "Sebastion's Prayer," Flambro's *The Negro Leagues™* Baseball Ornament "Brooklyn Royal Giants," VickiLane's *Golfer Bunny* "Fore You," and Cast Art Industries' *Cuddl'somes'* "Cubby." Middle Row: Miss Martha Originals' "William," The Bradford Exchange's "Joe Montana - King of Comebacks," Flambro's *The Negro Leagues* "Atlanta Black Crackers 1940" and "Homestead Grays 1938." Bottom Row: Ron Lee's World of Clowns' "Practice Swing," Calabar Creations' "Certain Tee" from *The Tee Club Collection* and "Strike So Sweet" from *Yesterday's Friends Collection* and Hallmark Keepsake Ornaments' "Shaquille O'Neal."

Animal antics take center stage...in a fanciful assortment of collectible treasures. Top Row (left to right): Anheuser-Busch Inc.'s "This Bud's For You" Plate, June McKenna Collectibles' "Christmas Down on the Farm," and Possible Dreams' "Clem Jingles." Middle Row: Calabar Creation's *Angelic Pigasus Collection's* "Angelo," Reco International's "You Quack Me Up," VickiLane's "Sunnydaze," Possible Dreams' "Buttercup." Bottom Row: Schmid's "Velveteen Rabbit," Anheuser-Busch Inc.'s "Horseplay," Cast Art Industries *Cuddl'somes* "Dress Up," and Cavanagh Group International's "Boy at the Well."

Top Row (left to right): The Boyds *Bears & Friends™ Bearstone* Collection's "Ms. Bruin & Bailey...The Lesson," "The Nurse," and "Celeste-The Angel Rabbit," Ganz's "Balderdash," and The Boyds Collections Ltd.'s "Bailey the Baker with Sweetie Pie." Middle Row: Enesco's *Cherished Teddies* "Our Hearts Belong to You," PenDelfin's "Jacky," "New Boy," and "Pepper," VickiLane's Blossom "Hopping Forward," and PenDelfin's "Mike." Bottom Row: Pacific Rim Imports' *Bunny Toes* "Charlotte-Best of the Bunch," The Hamilton Collections' "Jack and Jill," The Bradford Exchange's "Time for a Little Something," and Pacific Rim Import's *Bunny Toes* "Maggie-Joy of Giving."

Lifestyles of Native Americans...and the beauty found in nature provide the inspiration behind a great number of modern collectibles. Top Row (left to right): Legends' "Hunter's Quest," Maruri U.S.A.'s "Wild Wings," and Legends' "Rapture." Bottom Row: Legends' "Each, to the Other," Rick Cain Studios' "Winged Victor," and Legends' "Winds of Memory."

Top Row (left to right): Lance Corporation's "Warrior's Rescue," The Bradford Exchange's "Winter's Calm," The Tudor Mint's "Apache - Tonto Warrior." Middle Row: Anheuser-Busch Inc.'s "Golden Retreiver" Stein, The Hamilton Collection's "A Wolf's Pride," and Reco International's "Peace at Last." Bottom Row: Rick Cain Studios' "Family Tree," Anheuser-Busch Inc.'s "The Great Horned Owl" Stein, and Rick Cain Studios' "Arctic Heir."

The strength and beauty found in wildlife... are captured for collectors to enjoy in a stirring array of figurines and steins. Top row (left to right): Rick Cain Studios' "Transcendental White Wolf" and "Fire & Ice," and Creart's "Moose." Bottom Row: Creart's "Grumbler" Cape Buffalo," Legends' "Scent in the Air," and Creart's "Over the Top" Puma.

Images of seas and shores...hold a special place in many collectors' hearts. Top Row (left to right): Harbour Lights' "Point Fermin," "Cape Hatteras," "New Canal" and "Round Island." Middle Row: Creart's "Puffins," Harbour Lights' "Jupiter," Maruri U.S.A.'s "Ocra Mother & Baby." Bottom Row: Forma Vitrum's "Patriot's Point," Michael's Limited's "Peggy's Cove Light," Pacific Rim Imports' *Bristol Waterfront* "Bristol Channel Lighthouse," and George Z. Lefton Co.'s "Cape Hatteras Lighthouse."

Wit and whimsy translate lovingly...into an amusing assortment of figurines. Top Row (left to right): Ron Lee's World of Clowns' "Just Plain Tired," Midwest of Cannon Falls' "Creepy Hollow" Limited Edition Skeleton Cinema, and Ron Lee's World of Clowns' "Fillet of Sole." Bottom Row: Duncan Royale's "History of Clowns-Montebank," Byers' Choice's "Butcher" and "Dog with Sausages," and WACO Products' "Willie the Conductor."

Pop culture is preserved... in a variety of charming collectibles. Top Row (left to right): George Z. Lefton Co.'s "Pepsi Billboard," Hallmark Keepsake Ornament's "Space Shuttle," and George Z. Lefton Co.'s "Patriot's Diner." Middle Row: Schmid's "Pumbaa, Simba and Timon" Music Box, The Franklin Mint's "Sgt. Pepper's Lonely Hearts Club Band" Musical Bell Jar, Hallmark Keepsake Ornament's "Solo in the Spotlight" and Schmid's "Betty Boop as Scarlet." Bottom Row: Royal Doulton's "Captain Hook," The Franklin Mint's "Jukebox Jamboree Musical Sculpture," and Enesco's "Solo in the Spotlight."

Candy colored cottages...and other architectural beauties take us back to a simpler, more elegant time. Top Row (left to right): My Friends & Me "Boss House" and "91 East Bay St.," Michael's Limited's "River Belle Steamer." Middle Row: My Friends & Me "Cathedral of St. John the Baptist-1898," Shelia's "Eclectic Blue," "Edwardian Green," "Brandywine" and "Queen Rose." Bottom Row: Midwest of Cannon Falls' "Cottontail Lane Lighted Rosebud Manor," Michael's Limited's "Victorian Living" and "1905 Maple Lane."

Top Row (left to right): Michael's Limited's "Mountain Homestead," My Friends & Me "Pettingell House," "Owens Thomas House" and "The Herb House." Second Row: Band Creation's "Roseman Bridge," R.R. Creations' "Nathaniel Porter Inn," "Black Horse Inn," and "Herlong Mansion." Third Row: Brandywine Collectibles' "Country Lane General Store," "Hometown X Brick Church," "Hometown X Gift Shop," "Country Lane School" and "Hometown X Doll Shop." Bottom Row: Midwest of Cannon Falls' "Cannon Valley" Lighted Dairy Barn, The Cat's Meow Village "Creamery Bridge," "Becky Thatcher's House," "Sideshow" and "John Coffin House."

Decorating with collectibles...brings greater rewards to this growing hobby. Top Row (left to right): MAGI Entertainment Products' "To Elvis with Love." Middle Row: The Greenwich Workshop's "Into the Wilderness" Book and "Our Ladies of the Front Lawn." Bottom Row: The Greenwich Workshop's "Day Lilies" fine art poster and "Alphabet Soup" Book.

Top Row: (left to right) Lilliput Lane's "Chipping Coombe" and "Fountains Abbey." Bottom Row: Lightpost Publishing's "Luxembourg Gardens" by Thomas Kinkade, Lilliput Lane's "Gertrude's Garden" and "Harvest Mill."

The many faces of woman... Mother and friend, teacher and confidante are among the roles depicted in today's collectibles celebrating womanhood. Top Row (left to right): Lladró's "Spring Splendor," Royal Doulton's "When I was Young" and "Deborah," Lladró's "Ready to Learn." Bottom Row: Giuseppe Armani's "Diana," Royal Doulton's "Hello Daddy," Lladró's "Good Night" and Giuseppe Armani's "Minerva."

Giuseppe Armani's *Via Veneto* "Marina," "Nicole" and "Valentina."

Sugar and spice...and everything nice is reflected in a sweet selection of limited edition collectible dolls and plates. Top Row (left to right): Seymour Mann's "Sugarplum Fairy for McRaes," The Ashton-Drake Galleries' "Now I Lay Me Down to Sleep," and Georgetown Collection's "Caroline." Bottom Row: Attic Babies' "Fertile Myrtle" and The Franklin Mint's "Coca Cola® Heirloom Collector Doll-Megan."

Top Row (left to right): The Hamilton Collection's "Chelsea" and "Love One Another," Enesco's "He Loves Me," Ladie and Friends' "Jillian Bowman." Bottom Row: Seymour Mann's "Carlotta" and The Ashton-Drake Galleries' "Elizabeth."

Amusing and adorable dolls...are created to reflect the childlike simplicity of days gone by. Top Row (left to right): Attic Babies' "Jessabell," Ladie and Friends' "Leona High" and "Regina Bowman." Bottom Row: Attic Babies' "Ruby Begonia," "Petunia Kay Alvertie" and "Old Raggedy Noah."

HOW TO CARE FOR YOUR COLLECTIBLE TREASURES

A Compendium of Do's and Don'ts To Help Keep Your Favorite Limited Editions in Excellent Condition

Figurines, bells, cottages, miniatures and other collectibles may be displayed safely in a handsome hardwood cabinet such as this one from Van Hygan & Smythe. Holding collectibles up to 5-3/4" high, the unit comes with appropriate hardware for hanging or it may also be set on a tabletop.

One of the wonderful qualities of limited edition collectibles is their permanence: most are durable works of art that can be handed down from generation to generation as an enduring legacy of love and distinction. Yet without proper care, these heirloom-quality pieces may lose their original beauty, brightness and appeal. Here are some simple tips that will enable you to keep your most precious treasures in prime condition for decades to come.

Collector Plates

The lion's share of collector plates are made of porcelain or china. These durable materials are highly resistant to chipping and breakage unless they are dropped on a hard surface. Because most plates have their decorations permanently fired on, they keep their bright good looks with a minimum of care. Most fired plates can be wiped with a damp cloth, or even washed gently by hand in a sink of lukewarm water with mild soap.

Porous, unglazed surfaces or hand-painted, unfired plates should never be immersed in water – dusting is the only safe way to freshen them. Also, if your plate has been hand-signed by the artist, it is best not to immerse it in water since the signature may not be adequately sealed.

There are plates made of crystal, wood, stoneware, resin, and many other substances. For care of unusual materials, seek the advice of the plate's manufacturer. If in doubt, treat your plate as you would any other item made of that material.

One final word to the wise: most collector plates are unsuitable for containing food due to the lead content of their decals or paints.

Figurines, Cottages, Bells and Steins

In general, three-dimensional works of art need more care in cleaning and handling than do collector plates. When handling, lift the piece by its base, handle or a sturdy part since delicate parts may snap under pressure. To clean, dust gently with a feather duster or a small shaving brush.

If your piece has been designated safe for washing by its manufacturer, line your double sink with towels and move the faucet out of the way. Fill one sink with a mild soap solution and the other with clear, lukewarm water. Use distilled water if your area has hard water. Dip the figurine carefully in the soapy water, and use a soft brush to clean nooks and crannies. Rinse in the second sink, using a plastic or paper cup to pour water over the piece. For a final rinse, fill a towel-lined sink with vinegar rinse (one-half cup vinegar to a gallon of water). Air dry the figurines, making sure not to place them on wooden surfaces until the unglazed bottoms are completely dry.

Dolls

The delicate porcelain faces, hands and other body parts of fine dolls should be dusted lightly to keep them fresh and pretty. It is best not to "play hairdresser" with a doll's hair – just smooth the hair back in place lightly with your fingers rather than trying to comb out and re-style. As for a doll's clothing, the main enemies of fine fabrics are dust and sunlight – so avoid both in displaying your treasures. If clothing becomes soiled, dry cleaning is the best option unless you are sure the fabric can be washed without damage or shrinking. Many avid collectors invest in handsome, glass and wood display boxes and cases that protect dolls from dirt and too much handling.

Christmas Ornaments

While some collectors now enjoy showing off their ornaments all year, many still pack them away after the holidays. Using the original packing material is wise – but if you no longer have it, you might purchase special ornament storage cases sold by closet/organizational stores and catalogs. For truly unique or heirloom ornaments, you might select an artifact storage box such as those used by museums.

Another option – suggested by a collector of Christopher Radko ornaments – is to use stackable, sealable rubber tray containers lined with bubble wrap. Individual ornaments then can be wrapped loosely in an acid-free paper such as Bounty® microwaveable paper towels. Add a humidity-absorbing packet in each tray and the ornaments are ready for storage.

Graphics

A museum-mounted, framed print behind glass is well protected, yet should still be hung out of direct sunlight and extreme temperatures to prevent fading and moisture build-up. Unframed prints lose beauty and value from overhandling, so invest in binders made especially for their storage within protective acetate sheets. There are also attractive wooden furniture pieces with shallow drawers meant to hold unframed prints in safety.

This broken Lladró figurine has been restored to its original beauty by experienced restorers at Old World Restorations, Inc., utilizing non-destructive methods and reversible materials to achieve restorations invisible to the naked eye.

COLLECTIBLES RESTORATION SERVICES

When a favorite collectible becomes damaged and it is scarce or has special sentimental value, collectors often prefer to have it restored rather than accept an insurance company settlement that requires turning over the broken pieces in exchange for its cash value. A qualified restorer can do wonders in repairing your treasures if damage or breakage occurs. A skillful restoration may recover 50% to 100% of an item's original issue price. The following restoration experts are recommended by the member companies of COLLECTORS' INFORMATION BUREAU. Services are listed in alphabetical order by state.

China & Crystal Clinic
1808 N. Scottsdale
Tempe, AZ 85281
1-800-658-9197

Attic Unlimited
22435 E. La Palma
Yorba Linda, CA 92686
(714) 692-2940

Foster Art Restoration
711 West 17th St., Suite C-12
Costa Mesa, CA 92627
1-800-824-6967

Geppetto's Restoration
31121 Via Colinas, Suite 1003
Westlake Village, CA 91362
(818) 889-0901

Delly Griffin (Harbour Lights and David Winter Cottages)
2626 Paxton Ave.
Palmdale, CA 93551
(805) 266-1328

Just Enterprises
2790 Sherwin Ave. #10
Ventura, CA 93003
(805) 644-5837

Restorations by Linda
1759 Hemlock St.
Fairfield, CA 94533
(707) 422-6497

Venerable Classics
645 Fourth St., Suite 208
Santa Rosa, CA 95404
(707) 575-3626

C.R.C. Workshop
16 Drumlin Hill
Groton, MA 01450
(508) 448-5252

Beth Haley
(Sebastian miniatures only)
16 Chestnut St.
P.O. Box 895
Marblehead, MA 01945
(617) 631-2267

Baer Specialty Shop
259 E. Browning Rd.
Bellmawr, NJ 08031
(609) 931-0696

Witherspoon Studios
17 Locke Court
W. Trenton, NJ 08628
1-800-883-2605

Ceramic Restoration of Westchester, Inc.
81 Water St.
Ossining, NY 10562
(914) 762-1719

China & Glass Repair Studios
282 Main St.
Eastchester, NY 10709
(914) 337-1977

Imperial China
27 and 24 North Park Ave.
Rockville Center, NY 11570
(516) 764-7311

Restoration Unlimited
3009 W. Genesee St.
Syracuse, NY 13219
(315) 488-7123

Old World Restorations
347 Stanley Ave.
Cincinnati, OH 45226
(513) 321-1911

Wiebold Studio, Inc.
413 Terrace Place
Terrace Park, OH 45174
(513) 831-2541

Attic Babies Doll Hospital
(Attic Babies only)
P.O. Box 912
Drumright, OK 74030
(918) 352-4414

Byers' Choice Ltd.
(Byers' Choice figurines only)
4355 County Line Rd.
Chalfont, PA 18914
(215) 822-6700

Lizzie High Doll Hospital
(Lizzie High dolls only)
220 North Main Street
Sellersville, PA 18960
1-800-76-DOLLS

Creart U.S.A.
(Creart sculptures only)
309 E. Ben White Blvd. #103
Austin, TX 78704
(512) 707-2699

June McKenna Collectibles, Inc.
(June McKenna collectibles only)
P.O. Box 1540-205 Haley Road
Ashland, VA 23005
(804) 798-2024

INSURING AND PROTECTING YOUR COLLECTIBLES

Ten Things That Every Collector Needs to Know to Guard Their Treasures from Loss

Not too long ago, a friend and avid plate collector called me, obviously upset, and told me a story that I never would have believed had I heard it from anyone else.

One evening, she and her husband returned to their suburban home to find some of her most valuable collector plates, which she had been proudly displaying on a plate rail in her living room, laying smashed on the floor.

There was no sign of forced entry, and nothing else in the house had been taken or vandalized. The "who" "how" and "why" of the broken plates remained a mystery, until a few heart-broken and worry-filled days later when my friend was first alarmed, then relieved, to see a field mouse, which had somehow made its way inside, scurrying across the now-empty plate rail.

Although the culprit was finally caught, the story does not have a particularly happy ending. Because the plates were not covered at their replacement value by her homeowners' insurance policy, my friend's broken works of art – worth many hundreds of dollars – were insured for only a small fraction of their true price.

While most of us will never have to deal with rogue mice wreaking havoc among our treasures, the lesson to be learned from this story is "when it comes to protecting the things you love, be prepared for anything, because anything can happen – and not just to other people."

If you're like most people, the things you collect are highly personal reflections of your personality and your interests, and it would be difficult for any of us to put a price tag on the treasures we've lovingly acquired through the years. But the fact is, many collections also represent a sizable financial investment – one that may have appreciated considerably in price since they were first purchased.

An effective method of documenting a collection, the use of a video camera allows collectors to visually record their collectibles as well as voice record all pertinent information about individual pieces.

Should the unthinkable happen and your collection is lost through fire, flood, earthquake, storms, theft, or even intruding wildlife, your loss could easily exceed the amount that is specified by your insurance coverage, unless you act now to protect these highly-valued assets.

Ten Important Steps

Here are ten steps that every collector should take right now, to assure that your loss will be minimized should you be faced with a catastrophe.

1. **Keep all receipts.** Even if you purchase a collectible from a friend or a neighbor, make sure you get a receipt for each piece you acquire, and make sure that it clearly identifies the item bought and the price you paid for it.

2. **Jot down crucial information on a piece of paper and staple it to the item's receipt:**

- Item name or description
- Name of manufacturer
- Year of issue
- Artist's name
- Limited edition number
- Series number
- Special markings
- Cost at issue (if different than purchase price)
- Place of purchase
- Date of purchase
- Any other information you deem necessary

3. **Augment this information with a visual record.** All too often, collectors overlook this relatively simple, yet very effective, method of documenting their collections.

You can do this in a variety of ways. The simplest may be to save all brochures or catalogs which feature the items purchased. One drawback to this method is that such materials are not always readily available.

We recommend that you either

photograph or videotape each item in your collection. If you choose to use still photography, be sure to take a shot of it as it is displayed in your home, and then close-up shots capturing any significant markings such as the backstamp, artist signature, and/or limited edition number.

Video-taping is gaining in popularity as the method of choice to document entire collections. Video cameras are typically easy to use, and they give you the opportunity to voice record all pertinent information about the piece while you are taping. As with still photography, videotape each item as it is displayed, using close-ups to record all details which might contribute to the item's worth.

4. **Get very rare or one-of-a-kind pieces appraised.** Unlike collectibles which are issued in open or limited editions, it may be difficult or impossible to substantiate a claim for any unique items in your collection because there are no current market indicators to help determine the item's replacement cost.

Should your collection include a one-of-a-kind or other rare item, you may have to have it appraised in order to establish its worth. In this case, we recommend that you use a qualified appraiser. To find one, start by checking in your local yellow pages, or talk to a museum curator. Your insurance agent may also be able to offer suggestions of qualified individuals. Doing this now will be worth the time and cost if the appraised pieces are lost or destroyed. Note: Give high consideration to members of the American Society of Appraisers. They have passed rigorous certifying tests and are considered to be highly qualified. After you've decided on two or three appraisers, ask for references and check them. Use only appraisers for whom you have received high recommendations.

5. **Keep all these records off site.** You'll want to be sure that all your documentation – receipts, item information, appraisals, and photographs or videotape – is stored safely in a secured location away from your collection so you can easily retrieve it in the event of catastrophe. We recommend you maintain these records in the safety-deposit or lock box where you keep your other vitally important papers.

6. **Read your insurance policy carefully.** This may seem obvious, yet every year, thousands of collectors are surprised after making a claim to find that their treasured belongings are uninsured or underinsured. And by then it is too late to do anything about it.

So take the time right now to review your homeowners' or renters' insurance policy to make sure your collectibles will be adequately covered in the event of a loss. Pay particular attention to whether yours is a cash-value policy or a replacement value policy. Typically, under the terms of a cash-value policy, the insured items are covered for their value at the time the items were purchased. Replacement value policies, on the other hand, usually cover your insured items for the amount it would take to replace them at the time you make a claim. In light of the fact that some collectibles escalate in value over time, you might want to make sure that yours is a "replacement value" policy.

7. **If you have any questions, talk to your insurance agent.** Make sure you ask him or her if special coverage is required to fully insure all your collectibles.

For many collectibles, a floater or rider will be required. This is a policy in which you "schedule" each piece individually for its replacement cost. Many companies have a fine arts or personal articles floater that covers collectibles for the full replacement cost of the item.

If your collection is of extremely high value, your insurer may require you to hold a special lines policy. This is a policy designed to cover unusual or relatively expensive items, and the premiums are typically very high.

Remember that in purchasing insurance coverage, you are always faced with a variety of options. Be certain that you discuss all your special concerns with your agent to make sure you have the coverage you want and need. And don't forget to ask such important questions as:

- Does the floater cover all risks, i.e., flood, fire, theft, etc.?
- Is there a deductible? If so, what is it?
- Does the policy cover breakage? If not, what is the additional cost?
- What constitutes breakage?
- Are the items covered if they are taken off-premises?

Before meeting with the agent, spend an evening or two jotting down any potential losses you think may arise and then ask your agent if the policies you are considering, cover you in each instance. If not, look for another policy.

8. **Update your policy information regularly.** In most cases, if your collection appreciates to a higher value than when it was scheduled, your insurance company is required to reimburse you for only the scheduled value. Because of this, you should be certain to reschedule your collectibles at least once a year, or whenever the collection experiences a drastic change in price. Also, don't forget to add newly acquired additions to your collection.

9. **Should a loss occur, refer to the *Collectibles Market Guide and Price Index* to determine current values.** This highly respected reference source is published by the Collectors' Information Bureau at the beginning of each year. Considered the industry standard, it is recognized by insurers as one of the most reliable and credible sources available. The price index section lists over 45,000 collectibles and their current market prices. An updated price index is available at mid-year in the *Collectibles Price Guide*. Make sure you refer to the most up-to-date price index to determine the most current value of your collectibles.

10. **Exercise extra care in displaying and caring for your collectibles.** By far, the most efficient and most desirable way to keep your collection intact is to keep it out of harm's way in the first place. Make sure your displays are well constructed and offer no threat to the collectibles themselves. Keep figurines away from the edge of shelves and tables, and check to see that wall items are firmly secured to the wall in their frames or hangers.

Take special care when dusting and cleaning all these items, and check the maker's recommendations for the safest, most effective cleaning procedures to follow.

KURT S. ADLER, INC.

The World's Leading Resource for Christmas Accessories and Collectibles

Kurt S. Adler, Inc. presents "Toys for Good Boys and Girls," a Fabriché™ Santa figurine that features a design recreated from the Smithsonian Museum Archives.

Christmas may only come once a year, but at Kurt S. Adler, Inc., it always looks like Christmas. In fact, over the years Kurt S. Adler, Inc. has become almost synonymous with the great holiday of Christmas. Nearly 50 years ago, Kurt S. Adler virtually founded the Christmas decorating industry when he established Kurt S. Adler, Inc./Santa's World. Mr. Adler, a soft-spoken, charming businessman, brought a European flavor and sense of fashion and integrated it with American tastes, bringing a new look to Christmas in the United States. These efforts built the foundation for the company's success today with its current position as the world's leading resource for holiday decorative accessories and as a leader in the collectibles world.

Mr. Adler enjoys reminiscing about his nearly half-century of bringing Yuletide joy to so many people. He traveled the world over in search of unique decorative accessories that would capture the imagination of post-war America. When he wasn't buying and designing new products, Mr. Adler traveled all over the U.S. selling merchandise out of his case of samples. Gifted with the talent for knowing his market and a keen eye for appealing designs and colors, he carried prototypes of his ideas overseas. There, he worked with factories to develop the finest products, using the best materials at the most affordable prices. He quickly learned that the American consumer was quality-conscious and that his products would have to meet stringent standards for his company to succeed in the marketplace.

During its history, the firm has been recognized for many breakthroughs and significant achievements. Ornaments have always been one of the mainstays of the line. Kurt S. Adler, Inc. was the first to design, develop, import and distribute ornaments that were crafted of high-quality materials including better woods, ceramic, stained glass, resin, higher quality plastics, and capiz shell, a byproduct of mother-of-pearl. The firm also introduced the Old World art of wood-turned ornaments to the Orient. In the mid-1950s and well into the 1960s, Kurt S. Adler, Inc. imported the first "quality-made" snowglobes from West Germany. These snowglobes, also called snowdomes, featured Christmas scenes with Santa and other holiday characters. Many of these ornaments and accessories were saved and collected by Americans throughout the years. These consumers have become familiar with the company's products and learned to trust the Kurt S. Adler, Inc. name.

In the early 1970s, utilizing the unique talents of its veteran holiday accessory designer Marjorie Grace Rothenberg, Kurt S. Adler, Inc. introduced cornhusk ornaments. These items include the famous cornhusk mice and angels which depict human characters in fabric and lace costumes. Today, cornhusk mice ornaments are designed for every season and are still highly sought-after by collectors. Marjorie creates collectibles in her country studio at the foothills of the Berkshire Mountains, where she continues to design cornhusk mice ornaments, Fabriché™ figurines and ornaments that depict Santa and Mrs. Claus wearing their trademark gold wedding bands.

During the 1980s, Kurt S. Adler, Inc. introduced The *Louis Nichole Heirloom Collection*, one of the most elegant ornament lines ever produced. This group, which was designed by renowned home furnishings designer Louis Nichole, featured Victorian styled doll ornaments dressed in elaborate fabric and lace costumes with stunning colors. These collectibles reinforced the firm's position in the high fashion end of the Christmas market.

In the 1980s, Kurt S. Adler, Inc. introduced *The Smithsonian Carousel Series*, which features ornaments that represent small replicas of antique carousel animal figures found on merry-go-rounds in the Smithsonian Museum Archives. These museum-quality reproductions feature hand-painted designs and the exact detailing of original, turn-of-the-century carousel animal figures.

Kurt S. Adler, Inc. retains the largest team of first-class, exclusive designers "under one roof" that creates collectible holiday ornaments and accessories in a broad variety of looks and styles. Kurt S. Adler, Inc. is credited for designing the first ornaments and figurines featuring African-American Santas and Santas designed in a variety of unique and whimsical settings.

Charter members of The Steinbach Collectors Club will receive the exclusive opportunity to purchase "King Wenceslaus," an 18" members-only nutcracker. This handsome nutcracker features the good king in his regal attire, hand-painted and hand-turned in the Steinbach Factory.

Steinbach Nutcrackers and Smokers Widely Recognized for Tremendous Demand and Soaring Values

Since it began marketing collectible nutcrackers just a few years ago, Kurt S. Adler, Inc. has enjoyed a tremendous response to the line. Kurt S. Adler, Inc. is sponsoring the Steinbach Collectors Club, which provides free gifts, newsletters and brochures, and offers Charter Members the opportunity to purchase the members-only "King Wenceslaus" Nutcracker.

Kurt S. Adler, Inc. markets and distributes limited edition nutcrackers and smoking figures from the famous Steinbach factory, located in Hohenhameln in the northern region of Germany. For six generations, the Steinbachs have been handcrafting fine nutcrackers and smokers and today are world-renowned for quality and craftsmanship. One of the first limited edition nutcrackers was "Merlin The Magician," which recently sold for over $2,000 on the secondary market after its 1991 release at a retail price of $185.

The *Steinbach Limited Edition Nutcracker Collection* is quite extensive. The *Camelot Series* includes "Queen Guinevere," "Sir Galahad," "Sir Lancelot," "King Arthur" and "Merlin The Magician." The *Tales of Sherwood Forest Series* includes "Friar Tuck" and "Robin Hood," while *The Famous Chieftains* features "Chief Black Hawk," "Chief Red Cloud" and "Chief Sitting Bull." The *Christmas Legends Series* offers the "1930 Santa," "St. Nicholas" and "Father Christmas." The *American Presidents Series* includes "Teddy Roosevelt," "Abraham Lincoln" and "George Washington," while "Benjamin Franklin" is the first issue in *The Great Inventors Series*.

Award-Winning *Polonaise™ Collection*

The tremendous popularity and recognition for *The Polonaise™ Christmas Collection* was evidenced in the spring of 1995 when it received the "Best Glass Ornament Collection" at the Collectors Jubilee in Tulsa, Oklahoma. Molded glass ornaments are handcrafted in Poland in the age-old tradition of European master glassblowers. The ornaments feature hand-workmanship that is very involved, performed by Europe's most highly skilled and well-trained artisans who create forms and fashion shapes by hand-blowing glass. Boxed sets include a limited edition "Wizard of Oz" set, "Ancient Egyptians," "Antique Trains," "Roman Empire," "Holy Family" and more.

Rosemary Volpi's *Timeless Treasures*

Rosemary Volpi is a gifted doll artist who is well-known for her sensitive Christmas figures. She recently created *The Timeless Treasures Collection, which* includes "Neapolitan Angels," that range in size from 7" to 12" and are reproduced from her originals. She also designed the "Woodland Santa" and other holiday figures.

Jocelyn Mostrom's Doll Ornaments

Nationally recognized in the doll world as the woman who raised the American craft of cornhusk doll making into a fine art, Jocelyn Mostrom has contributed to The *KSA Storybook Collection* with humorous renditions and romantic interpretations from classic nursery rhymes and fairytales. She also created *The Small Wonders of the World*, an international collection featuring brother and sister pairs of porcelain dolls dressed in traditional folk costumes crafted of paper twist. Her turn-of-the-century collection includes Victorian styled musicians and snow children. Jocelyn's dolls stand approximately 5" to 6" in height and can be displayed or used as tree ornaments.

Christmas Legends by Paul Bolinger

Paul F. Bolinger, the famed Californian woodcarver, combines both fine art and folkart techniques in his stylized

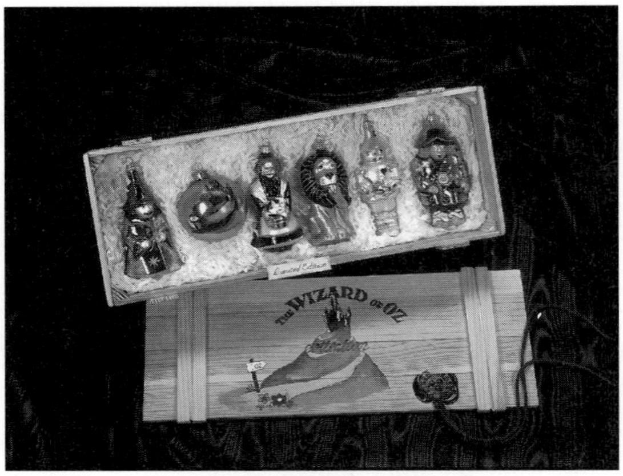

The limited edition "Wizard of Oz" six-piece set is from Kurt S. Adler, Inc.'s award-winning Polonaise™ Collection. *The boxed set features hand-blown glass ornaments depicting Dorothy, The Tin Man, The Scarecrow, The Cowardly Lion, The Wizard and The Wizard of Oz ball ornament.*

"Bountiful" is a unique 18" figurine designed exclusively by famed woodcarver Paul F. Bolinger for the Christmas Legends *series in the KSA Collectibles line from Kurt S. Adler, Inc.*

Christmas Legends series of figurines and ornaments. Cast in wood resin directly from originals and hand-painted by skilled artisans, these gift-giver legends are shown with distinctive looks and personalities. Many are inspired from old German and Celtic lore.

Adorable *Holly Bearies*

Holly Bearies features ornaments and figurines depicting bears that are "Looking for a Home in Your Heart." Each bear is distinguished by its own playful character and personality and is designed by veteran artist and avid teddy bear collector Holly Adler. These resin and wooden bears are offered in a broad variety of themes, from sports and professional settings to traditional Christmas motifs.

Whimsical Fabriché™ Sculptures

Fabriché™ sculptures are guaranteed for unparalleled design, superior quality and skillful workmanship. They feature a mixed media technique based on the Old World art of papier maché combined with modern methods and materials. The *Fabriché™ Collection* features the designs of Marjorie Grace Rothenberg, the KSA Design Team and reproductions of original designs found in the Smithsonian Museum Archives. Fabriché™ figurines and ornaments include exquisite angels and Santa and Mrs. Claus, designed in many whimsical professional, transportation and sports settings.

Whimsical *Hole-In-The-Wall Gang*

The *Hole-In-The-Wall Gang*, designed by Kandy Schlesinger, is a collection of whimsical mice living in their own city, beyond that mouse hole in the wall. These ornaments depict mice scurrying about performing daily routines in a humorous fashion.

Kurt S. Adler, Inc.
1107 Broadway
New York, NY 10010
(212) 924-0900
Fax (212) 807-0575

COLLECTORS' CLUB

The Steinbach Collectors Club
Kurt S. Adler, Inc.
1107 Broadway
New York, NY 10010
(800) 243-9627

Annual Dues: $40.00
Club Year: Anniversary of Sign-Up Date

Benefits:
- Membership Gift: 7" Nutcracker
- Redemption Certificate for Members-Only Nutcracker
- Newsletter
- Club Portfolio
- Membership Card and Certificate
- Special Edition Pin
- Color Brochures

ANHEUSER-BUSCH, INC.

Collectors Express Their Love for the "King of Beers®" and Their Appreciation of a 500-Year-Old Craft with Anheuser-Busch Steins

Beer making is a form of true artistry to a master brewer – and for centuries, handsome beer steins have been created to contain and protect the delicious results of this careful blending of hops, malt and grain. While the earliest steins were mainly functional, the past 100 years have seen the creation of true works of art. German firms like Villeroy & Boch and Gerz offered steins in the 1800s that today can bring hundreds of thousands of dollars on the auction market. And while these collectible steins may be out of financial reach for many of us, since 1975 Anheuser-Busch's remarkable *Collector Series* has captured the glories of 19th-century steins at affordable prices.

All Anheuser-Busch steins are crafted with the same dedication to perfection that makes Budweiser® and the firm's other beers so honored and renowned. Some feature classic themes, while others boast contemporary topics. The steins of character and celebration are ready for actual use, or they can be preserved in "mint condition" as cherished display pieces.

"Budweiser Salutes the Navy" is the name of this handsome stein combining images of air and sea operations as well as an anchor chain sculptured handle and harmonizing chain-motif trim. The Budweiser logo with Navy mascot completes this impressive work of art.

The Leading Brewer Also Sets the Pace in Stein Artistry

Anheuser-Busch has reigned as the world's larg-est brewer for nearly four decades with record annual sales of 88.5 million barrels of beer in 1994. Founded in St. Louis, Missouri, in 1852, the firm forged an association with several renowned stein manufacturers in the mid-1970s to create its own fine steins. Collaborators included the Ceramarte stein factory in Brazil and classic German stein makers including Gerz, Thewalt and Rastal – making it possible for Anheuser-Busch to offer a greater variety of steins with each passing year.

A whimsical baseball mitt stein entitled "Play Ball" features a baseball emblazoned with the red Budweiser bowtie logo.

At first, the concept was to create commemorative pieces and rewards for Anheuser-Busch beer wholesalers. But the steins were so attractive to collectors that Anheuser-Busch was inspired to test the retail sale of steins in 1980. Results were astounding: in the first year alone, 50,000 *Holiday* steins were sold. By 1990, annual sales of the *Holiday* stein had topped the 1,000,000 unit mark!

Anheuser-Busch "Breweriana" Also Intrigues Stein Collectors

Anheuser-Busch steins have proven so attractive to collectors that some aficionados boast ownership of almost every piece introduced since 1975. In addition to steins, many of these enthusiasts also collect what is known as "breweriana" – such stein accouterments as bottles, cans, labels and signs.

While many Anheuser-Busch steins focus on brewery heritage for their subject matter, others showcase holiday celebrations, or non-profit organizations supported by Anheuser-Busch. The firm also commissions local and national artists based upon their specialties to create "theme" steins.

Gerz and Anheuser-Busch Join Forces

Anheuser-Busch works in an exclusive joint venture with S.P. Gerz GMBH and Gerz Inc., the largest manufacturer of handcrafted steins in Germany, and its U.S. subsidiaries. Gerz, founded in 1897, is well known among collectors for its high-quality, handcrafted steins. This landmark association makes Anheuser-Busch – already the world's largest marketer of collectible steins – the exclusive North American distributor and marketing agent of a line of steins designed and produced by Gerz: the *Gerz Meisterwerke Collection.*

The first in the series of limited edition steins, titled "Santa's Mail Bag," captures the warmth and spirit of giving presents during the holiday season. This premier stein was issued in an edition of 5,000 pieces, and is part of *The Saturday Evening Post Christmas Collection*, featuring designs by

Norman Rockwell. The second in the series is entitled "Santa's Helper," and it portrays a beloved Post cover by famed illustrator J. C. Leyendecker. Third in the collection is "All I Want for Christmas," another Leyendecker favorite.

Several other recent introductions have been made possible through the Gerz/Anheuser-Busch alliance. For example, the "Rosie the Riveter" stein honors all the women who answered the wartime call to keep America's factories working in the 1940s. Representing the *Portrait of America* series, it portrays a Norman Rockwell Post cover illustration. A Rockwell "Triple Self-Portrait" stein honors the 100th anniversary of Norman Rockwell's birth. Also by Rockwell and created by Gerz and Anheuser-Busch is "The Dugout" stein, featuring the September 4, 1948 cover illustration from the *Post*; a portrait of the disconsolate Chicago dugout in the midst of a disastrous season.

Showing the range of the Gerz/Anheuser-Busch collaboration are four additional steins. "Mallard" is a special, full-dimensional deep relief ceramic stein portraying a richly colored mallard duck. "Giant Panda" shows a playful giant panda that appears to be reaching out of the stein for a bamboo shoot. The "Winchester 'Model 94' Centennial" stein honors the most famous of all lever-action rifles, and comes topped with a pewter lid-top figurine of the signature Winchester horse and rider. Finally, the "John F. Kennedy" stein – first in the *American Heritage* series – presents a presidential portrait.

From the Hunter's Companion *series, this is "Golden Retriever," a stein paying tribute to this noble breed both with bas-relief artistry and a handsome, ceramic figurine on its pewter-rimmed lid.*

Anheuser-Busch's "A&Eagle Trademark" stein offers historic images from the company's proud tradition as the makers of Budweiser. Company trademarks from the 1890s-1900s, 1910s and 1930s are depicted, with alternating panels of the Bevo Fox.

Birds of Prey Offers Final Issue While Anheuser-Busch Figurines Debut

The "Great Horned Owl" stein – fourth and final edition in Anheuser-Busch's celebrated *Birds of Prey* series – showcases this formidable hunter in all his majesty and grace. The bird's deep-forest habitat, finely feathered body and sharp-eyed face area are beautifully illustrated in detailed ceramic relief – surely a fitting choice to conclude the *Birds of Prey* collection.

Meanwhile, Anheuser-Busch unveils a new series of handsome, hand-painted figurines with two recent issues: "Buddies," and "Horseplay." "Buddies" captures the bright-eyed curiosity of two playful golden retriever puppies in porcelain bisque. The sculpture is inspired by an illustration by nature artist Marlowe Urdahl. The second-edition "Horseplay" depicts three Dalmatian puppies mischievously tugging away at one of the Clydesdales' harnesses. It was inspired by an illustration by Paul Radtke.

Hunter's Companion and *A&Eagle* Steins Win Collectors' Attention

A series of noble canines in the field star in Anheuser-Busch's *Hunter's Companion* collection, which debuted with "The Labrador." Handcrafted by Ceramarte in Brazil, each ceramic relief stein in the series stands 8-1/4" tall and features a pewter lid topped by a unique canine figurine. The second *Hunter's Companion* is "Golden Retriever." Each stein in this limited edition is individually gift boxed and numbered with a Certificate of Authenticity.

The "A&Eagle Trademark Stein" premiered Anheuser-Busch's historical *A&Eagle* series, featuring three early versions of the famous A& Eagle trademark dating from 1872 to 1885. The third stein in the series, introduced in 1995, is called "A&Eagle Trademark III" stein. It features an antique design by artist Don Langeneckert as well as trademarks spanning the 1890s to the 1930s. There will be four steins in all in this collection, each handcrafted by Ceramarte of Brazil, gift-boxed, individually numbered, and accompanied by a Certificate of Authenticity.

A Cordial Invitation to Join the Anheuser-Busch Collectors Club

The Anheuser-Busch Collectors Club made its debut on January 1, 1995, with two unique collectible steins as enticements for charter members. The old-world flavor of the Budweiser Clydesdales and the Anheuser-Busch Brew House Clock Tower is captured exquisitely on two steins, both handcrafted by Ceramarte of Brazil and available to members only.

The "Budweiser Clydesdales at the Bauernhof" stein is part of the Anheuser-Busch Collectors Club membership kit, available at Authorized Collectors Club Dealers. It depicts the regal eight-horse Budweiser Clydesdale hitch pulling an antique beer wagon emerging from the European-inspired Bauernhof Courtyard in St. Louis. Club members may order the "Brew House Clock Tower" stein, introduced in June 1995. It features a stunning design modeled after a century-old six-story building, and is the first Anheuser-Busch stein with a working clock.

The charter membership fee of $35.00 provides new members with many benefits including: the "Clydesdales" stein already mentioned, valued at $60.00; a history and information-filled binder; a one-year subscription to the club's quarterly magazine, *First Draft*; a personalized membership card; and a redemption certificate for the exclusive "Brew House Clock Tower" stein. For information on how to join, collectors may call the club at 1-800-305-2582.

A great deal of the fun of owning Anheuser-Busch steins resides in the enjoyment of showing them off. Secondary market price rises after prompt sell-outs for many steins bode well for continued growth in the Anheuser-Busch stein market. And with expansion ongoing in collector plates, ornaments and figurines, the firm continues to unveil new designs and styles – all aimed at continuing the stein-making quality and tradition established by Anheuser-Busch more than 20 years ago.

Anheuser-Busch, Inc.
Retail Sales Department
2700 South Broadway
St. Louis, MO 63118
(800) 325-1154
Fax (314) 577-9656

COLLECTORS' CLUB

The Anheuser-Busch Collectors Club
2700 South Broadway
St. Louis, MO 63118
(800) 305-2582

Annual Dues: $35.00
Club Year: Anniversary of Sign-Up Date

Benefits:
- Membership Gift: Stein
- Redemption Certificate for Members-Only Stein
- Quarterly Magazine, *First Draft*
- Personalized Membership Card
- Binder Which Includes Information on the History of Anheuser-Busch, Inc. and the Manufacturing of Steins

ANNALEE MOBILITEE DOLLS

Annalee Demonstrates New England Charm at Annual Annalee Doll Society Auction Extravaganza

One of the charming additions to the Annalee Doll line for 1995-96 is the 10" "Red Treetop Angel" (Item No. 7274). Its suggested retail price is $37.50.

A visit to an Annalee Doll Society* Auction Weekend is enough to restore anyone's faith in good old American values. While relaxing in the sunshine with friends, visitors enjoy historical costumes and crazy getups, wonderful food and drink under festive tents, and the drama of skyrocketing auction prices on the rarest and most coveted of Annalee's* collectible dolls, from '50s classics to today's one-of-a-kind "Artist's Proofs."

Annalee Thorndike presides over the event, her ready smile a warm welcome to collectors nationwide who converge on Meredith, New Hampshire. And as always, Annalee's husband Chip – joined by sons Townsend (Town) and Chuck – is present to make sure all their guests are having the time of their lives.

To the uninitiated, this auction can provide a real awakening. One-of-a-kind pieces may sell for hundreds or thousands of dollars, and Annalee designs from the early years attract furious bidding. The all-time record-breaker, a "Halloween Girl" doll from the '50s, brought $6,600 at the 1995 auction. That same day, a 20" Santa Claus from the same period sold for $3,300. Another highlight of the Summer Auction is the unveiling of the Doll Society's exclusive "Folk Hero™" doll and the auction of its Artist's Proof – one of several one-of-a-kind Proof dolls auctioned yearly for charitable purposes.

Prices are only part of the excitement, however. Collectors can choose from a wide range of designs and special products each year, at prices from $5.95 and up. The most recent Annalee catalog and *Collector* magazine features limited-edition pieces based on themes like sports, careers, diverse cultures and more. The rest of the line is drawn largely from seasonal and holiday themes.

Brought to life in the form of flowers, human figures, holiday characters, and animals, the line varies widely. All, however, share the same sense of timeless whimsy and – naturally – the same sunny, crinkly-eyed smile that lights up the face of Annalee Thorndike herself!

Where It All Began

Annalee and Chip Thorndike never suspected that Annalee's whimsical dolls would captivate collectors worldwide. In fact, doll making began as a hobby for a teenage Annalee, who first made them in the 1930s, "just for fun." When friends saw how special her characters could be, they asked Annalee to create designs for them, too.

Eventually, she began selling her pieces through the League of New Hampshire Craftsmen, to merchants for their holiday displays, and to family and friends. When she married Chip in 1941, however, she was content to join him on his chicken farm and start a family. The Harvard-educated Chip wanted nothing more than to enjoy the farmer's simple life. Indeed, it was not until 1953, after the chicken industry moved southward, that the Thorndikes "phased out" the chickens and officially transferred their energies to the establishment of Annalee Mobilitee Dolls*, Incorporated.

Despite outside jobs and hard work on the farm, the Thorndikes had realized that providing for their family would require a change, and they decided to commit themselves to doll making, hoping that the public's love of her happy little characters could support them. The young family pitched in, determined to try. The public became entranced by Annalee's dolls, and soon word spread far beyond New Hampshire. Chuck and Town recall that their childhood years were surrounded by their mother's designs. In the early days of Annalee Mobilitee™ Dolls, the family farmhouse *was* their "Factory in the Woods," and every available space

The "Goin' Fishin' Logo Kid" is the 1995-96 Logo doll for Annalee Doll Society members. This charming doll has a retail value of $50, but it is one of the many benefits of annual membership in the Doll Society, which is just $29.95.

was piled with dolls in various stages of completion. Doll fever seems to have stayed with the Thorndike boys, since today Chuck is CEO and President, and Town is Director of Development for the company.

In the early days, Annalee wondered if she could continue to create new designs, but her innovative spirit has never waned. Now, with Chuck and Town involved in the creative process, it seems that the possibilities remain unlimited. Yet no matter how many dolls they create, the Thorndikes remain devoted to the same careful craftsmanshp that has served them well since the 1950s.

Each doll begins with a conceptual drawing, which is fine-tuned until it meets with Annalee's approval. Then, a manual for each new doll's design is prepared to ensure that every department performs every detail correctly. Annalee passes judgment on the positioning of every doll that leaves the studio – each is equipped with a flexible frame that allows the utmost in "poseability." Chip continues to design accessories – from the wooden skis of the early days to wooden boats for the recently released fishing dolls.

The Thorndike family has chosen to keep the dolls as handcrafted as possible, and make each an individual, with a variety of facial expressions for each "character." To keep the line fresh, the Thorndikes retire dolls and add new dolls or variations yearly. When a doll retires it may eventually join the ranks of the "auction successes" that are so actively pursued by collector/investors.

The Annalee Doll Society: Join The Club

Ever since the Annalee Doll Society was initiated in 1983 to meet the needs of Annalee collectors, it has provided fun and opportunity for these enthusiasts. With a membership in the tens of thousands and growing, the Society offers many benefits. The Membership Kit includes a yearly 7" Logo Kid doll, annual pin and membership card, a special-edition Annalee Felt Pin, and a subscription to *The Collector*, a full-color quarterly magazine devoted to Annalee's dolls and collectors, including a doll listing of valuable dolls available through Annalee's Antique and Collectible Doll Shop. Other benefits include admission to Doll Society events and eligibility to purchase exclusive, signed and numbered dolls available only to Doll Society members.

While the value of the current Logo Kid alone is $50.00, the Kid and all other benefits are available to Doll Society members for only $29.95 annually. For more information or to join the Doll Society, contact any Doll Society Sponsor Store or call 1-800-43-DOLLS.

Reaching Out

The Thorndikes participate enthusiastically in philanthropy today as they have all their lives. They believe in using their success to better society – and not simply by making donations. This family gets involved.

The Thorndikes often use the popularity of their dolls to support a variety of causes. By featuring the logo or theme of the group they wish to benefit on an original Annalee creation, the Thorndikes draw attention to that group's needs. By donating the price paid for the Artist's Proof at auction and setting aside a percentage of the total proceeds from the sales of that item, they are able to address these needs. The dolls are often marketed through the Doll Society, whose members appreciate the value of these extremely limited-run items.

During each annual Annalee Doll Society Auction Weekend, Annalee's auctions several of their Artist Proofs and donates the proceeds to favorite causes including health, education (Annalee's sponsors the Thorndike Scholarship Fund, dedicated to assisting Annalee employees and their families), conservation, homelessness, and the arts. To demonstrate their commitment to the environment, Annalee created the "Two-in-a-Tent" mouse, featuring two mice snuggling in a pup tent. Proceeds from this work of art have benefitted the New Hampshire Land Trust.

During Operation Desert Storm in 1991, the Thorndikes met with the Chairman of the Joint Chiefs of Staff General Colin Powell and White House Chief of Staff John Sununu, presenting General Powell with the first 7" "Desert Storm Mouse." Annalee's donation of 500 of the mice and 1,500 special "Desert Mouse Head" pins were delivered to American troops in the Gulf. In addition, ten percent of the proceeds from the sale of every "Desert Mouse" and "Desert Mouse Head" pin was donated to the American Red Cross. More recently, the "Mississippi Levee Mouse" and "California Mud Slide Mouse" were created to raise funds for flood relief in the wake of the flooding of 1993 and 1995. Ten percent of its proceeds will be donated to flood relief efforts.

Meet The Artist

While the Annual Auction Weekend draws capacity crowds to Meredith, New Hampshire, the Thorndikes are always delighted to welcome visitors. The Annalee Doll Museum and Town

Always energetic, upbeat and smiling, Annalee and Chip Thorndike are a familiar sight to visitors at the Factory in the Woods in Meredith, New Hampshire. Chip often creates charming accessories to enhance the dolls designed by his gifted wife, Annalee.

Thorndike's Antique and Classic Car Collection are within walking distance of one another, and convenient to Lake Winnipesaukee's many attractions. But for those who can't make the trek to New Hampshire, Annalee and the family provide another way to "meet the artist" – they travel throughout the country, not only visiting collectible shows, but dropping in on Doll Society Sponsor Stores as well. A visit to one of these nearly 300 sponsors brings out crowds of Annalee admirers and collectors, eager for the chance to meet Annalee or Chuck, talk with them, and have them sign autograph cards or personal items.

Similarly, the realization that many collectors are unable to get all the way to New Hampshire led Annalee's to move the Fall Auction to Williamsburg, Virginia, in 1994, and to Nashville, Tennessee, in 1995. This allowed Southern and Midwestern collectors a chance to share in the Annalee auction experience.

Always cheery and upbeat herself, Annalee Thorndike proclaims her goal as a simple one: she simply wants to "make people smile." With the happy expressions on her dolls' faces to cheer every admirer, this artist meets her goal with grace and enthusiasm. From "Thorndikes' Eggs and Auto Parts" to the delightful world of Annalee Mobilitee Dolls, the Thorndikes' success story warms the hearts of all who experience the joy of Annalee, her family, and her appealing Annalee dolls.

Annalee Mobilitee Dolls, Inc.
P.O. Box 1137
Reservoir Road
Meredith, NH 03253-1137
(800) 433-6557
Fax (603) 279-6659

COLLECTORS' CLUB/MUSEUM

Annalee Doll Society
P.O. Box 1137
Meredith, NH 03253-1137
1-800-43-DOLLS

Annual Dues: $29.95
Club Year: Anniversary of Sign-Up Date

Benefits:
- Membership Gift: 7" Doll, Membership Pin and Card
- Opportunity to Purchase Members-Only Folk Hero Doll
- Quarterly Magazine, *The Collector*
- Buy/Sell Matching Service
- Members-Only Auctions
- Special Members-Only Event Pieces

Annalee Doll Museum
50 Reservoir Road
Meredith, NH 03253
(603) 279-3333

Hours: Daily from 9 a.m. - 5 p.m. Closed during the winter months.
Admission Fee: None

The Annalee Doll Museum features rare and older Annalee Dolls, as well as a videotaped presentation featuring the history of the company and interviews with Annalee. A Gift Shop is also open to visitors.

ANRI U.S.

Sculptures in Wood Carve Out Old Traditions and New Collectors

From the Vatican Library Collection, *Mary and the Infant Jesus are part of the "Holy Land" nativity authorized by the Biblioteca Apostolica Vaticana. The nativity is accompanied by a signed certificate noting ANRI's collaboration with the Vatican Library for this exclusive collection introduced in 1995.*

In an age of automated machines, assembly lines and computers, there's still a small workshop nestled in the Dolomite Mountains of Northern Italy where time-honored traditions remain untouched by modern technology.

Since 1912, ANRI has been creating beautiful wood sculptures that combine traditional craftsmanship with a continuous search for new expressions. From religious figurines and nativities to those portraying playful children, the limited edition woodcarvings have become family heirlooms. No matter what artist, style or figurine a collector chooses, each woodcarving has very low edition sizes of only 250, 500 or, at the most, 1,000 pieces.

ANRI woodcarvings are among the few collectibles in the world that are truly handcrafted works of art. Each sculpture is carved by skilled artisans from a single block of aged, alpine maple and then delicately painted in oils. No two collectible wood sculptures are alike.

With the continued popularity and appreciation for these sculptures, ANRI of Italy launched a new company in 1995 to distribute its collectibles in the United States. ANRI U.S., based in the Dallas area, helps new collectors turn today's wood sculptures into tomorrow's memories.

The History of ANRI's Woodcarved Nativities

During the 15th century, a unique transformation was taking place in the Groden Valley of Italy, where ANRI makes its home. Grodeners, already known for their fine lace and cloth, were turning their talents to the art of woodcarving. They especially focused on wooden nativity figures that recreated the first Christmas and captured the hearts of Europeans.

Grodeners left a permanent mark on the history of nativities. They were the first to add snow to the Bethlehem scene. This feature, coupled with the intricate detail of their carvings, quickly endeared Groden nativities to churches and collectors throughout Europe. By the 18th century, the Groden Valley became one of the world's primary sources of handcarved nativities. By 1800, two-thirds of the valley's population made their living from woodcarving. Unfortunately, competition led to undercutting on price, and quality began to suffer. So during the late 1800s, Luis Riffeser and later his son, Anton, set out to create woodcarvings that would meet the highest standards of artistry and quality. Anton Riffeser founded The House of ANRI (taken from the first two letters of his first and last name), where he brought together the valley's finest woodcarvers under one roof. Today, four generations of Riffesers later, ANRI is still home to world-famous artists, Groden master woodcarvers and painters. And faithful to the philosophy of its founder, ANRI proudly continues the tradition of nativity woodcarvings begun by their ancestors more than 300 years ago.

Sculptors Carry on the ANRI Tradition of Excellence

Collectors can choose from a wide variety of nativities and sculptures created exclusively for ANRI by a team of artists and designers who bring their

Created by Juan Ferrandiz, "Tender Care" portrays a shepherdess kneeling beside her lamb. As with the artist's other works, the 6-inch figurine captures childhood delight and love.

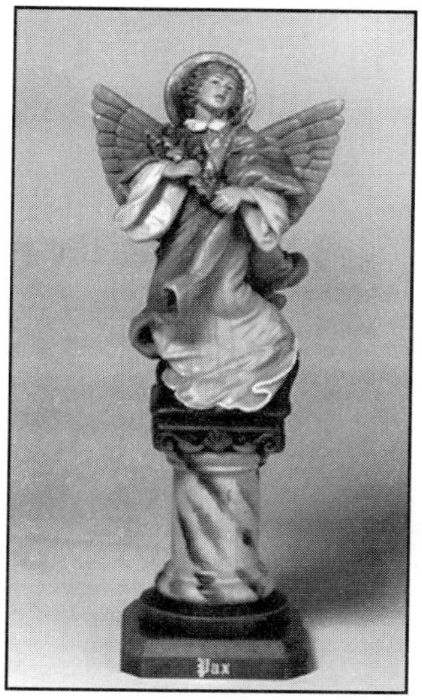

Introduced in 1995, the Heavenly Angels *collection is the first ANRI creation by American artist Charlotte Hallett. In "Angel of Peace," the cherub stands on a pillar and wears a golden halo. The woodcarving is limited to 250 pieces and is available in a painted or natural finish.*

personal styles and talents to each piece. A native of Groden Valley, Ulrich Bernardi has made a life of modelling and designing religious figurines, cherubs and other figures in the spirit of European folklore. Simple attire and innocent expressions characterize his work, which has graced the ANRI studio for more than three decades. He also created the Florentine crèche, which is more ornate and captures the glory of Italy's most fabled city of Renaissance art.

Professor Karl Kuolt, who passed away in 1937, was a student at the Munich School of Art and the Munich Academy. Besides a large number of well-known monuments and memorial chapels throughout Southern Germany, he also created countless smaller works which are now housed in museums and private collections. ANRI's world-famous nativity figurines bear his name and artistry. ANRI has also made additions to the Kuolt crèches with animals and shepherds. New or traditional, each Kuolt piece spreads a message of peace.

Walter Bacher apprenticed to a well-known sculptor at the age of 14. Then he attended two years of art school in Munich and four additional years at the Academy of Art. His works are displayed in churches and museums in Europe and overseas, and one of his most famous creations is an ANRI nativity.

Childhood Innocence Through the Artistry of Juan Ferrandiz and Sarah Kay

For more than 25 years, Spanish artist Juan Ferrandiz has shared his talent with ANRI collectors. Through his artwork, Ferrandiz seeks to create a world of love, unity and compassion. His drawings are translated into three-dimensional collectible woodcarvings, including the Holy Family, traditional nativity characters and animals. The nativity scenes celebrate the innocence of children and animals, both of which bear gentle expressions of happiness.

For more than a decade, Australian artist Sarah Kay has enjoyed worldwide recognition for her interpretations of childhood pastimes. Her association with ANRI began in 1983, when her drawings were first transformed into hand-carved figurines. Her sweet-faced children can be found doing everything from hanging Christmas stockings to heading to the river bank to go fishing. Sarah Kay has also created miniatures and a wonderful Santa Claus figurine series.

Heavenly Angels Descend on ANRI

Created by American artists William and Charlotte Hallett, the *Heavenly Angels* collection was introduced in 1995 as a series of four limited edition pieces. The first in the series, "Angel of Peace" features an angel standing atop a column and wearing a flowing robe. Her face is framed by a halo applied in gold leaf. "Angel of Kindness" portrays a haloed angel with a tiny bird perched on her hand. Each woodcarving is limited to 250 pieces and is available in a painted or natural finish. The Halletts work in their Massachusetts studio, where they have created some privately commissioned pieces for churches throughout the United States.

ANRI Announces *Vatican Library* Collection

Inspired by artwork in the Vatican Library, ANRI proudly introduced another nativity series in 1995. The Biblioteca Apostolica Vaticana authorized ANRI to exclusively reproduce some of its treasures in wood in *The Vatican Library Collection.* The first introduction included a two-piece Holy Family in both the 4-inch and 6-inch sizes. An ox and donkey also joined the set with figurines of kings, shepherds and sheep to be added in upcoming years. The "Holy Land" nativity is accompanied by a signed certificate ensuring outstanding craftsmanship and guaranteeing the collaboration between ANRI and the Vatican Library.

The Making of an ANRI Sculpture Requires Patience and Skill

Each ANRI figurine – whether carved by Bernardi or recreated from the artwork of Ferrandiz – begins with wood from hand-picked Alpine maple trees available only in Austria. The maples are chopped down during the winter, then cut into boards which are left standing for two to three years so the sap will be completely drained. Only unblemished sections of the tree are used.

Frequent inspections of the wood

As an addition to the nativity by Ulrich Bernardi, this shepherd boy and his cat greet the Holy Family. The figurine is available in three sizes – 4, 6 or 8 inches.

Designed by Australian artist Sarah Kay, "I Know, I Know" portrays a school girl anxiously raising her hand to answer a teacher's question. The wood sculpture is available in a 4" edition limited to 500 pieces and a 6" edition limited to 250 pieces.

ensure that flaws in texture, shape, grain or any number of other elements are detected. Control is so tight that only 20 percent of the wood originally cut ever reaches the carver's table.

Once the rough cut is completed by lathe, the sculptor then uses progressively smaller and finer tools to gradually work his way toward the extremely detailed carving. At this stage of the process, any slip destroys the sculpture. When the carving is completed, the piece arrives in the hands of painters, who use special transparent oils to adorn the figurine.

The entire process, from the raw piece of wood to the copyrighted work of art, is continuously monitored for quality control, thus exemplifying the skill handed down from generations.

ANRI U.S. Establishes Increased Presence in America

ANRI Woodcarvings were introduced to American collectors in 1936. But to enhance the company's presence in America, the sales, marketing and distribution of ANRI's collectibles in the United States is now under the management of the new ANRI U.S. "Our network of loyal retailers convinced us that we needed to invest in the future of ANRI's role within the American marketplace," said Ernst Riffeser, the fourth generation of the family who has brought the figurines to collectors for more than a century. "I am fully committed to the U.S. market and the thousands of collectors who appreciate ANRI's creations."

ANRI Introduces Collector's Society

Along with the opening of ANRI U.S. in 1995, the ANRI Collector's Society was launched for collectors to enjoy the handcarved wood sculptures even more. Benefits include full-color newsletters, an authorized ANRI Collector's Society Retailer listing, color catalog featuring all the current pieces, membership certificate, exclusive Society woodcarvings and the opportunity to benefit from the available resources of the ANRI research department to identify older sculptures. Charter Year members also received a wristwatch.

The first exclusive woodcarving offered to members was "On My Own," designed by Sarah Kay. The sculpture portrays a toddler with outstretched arms taking her first important step in life. The annual membership fee is $40. For information, call (800) 763-ANRI or write to the ANRI Collector's Society, P.O. Box 2087, Quincy, MA 02269-2087.

ANRI U.S.
P.O. Box 380760
1126 So. Cedar Ridge, Ste. 111
Duncanville, TX 75138
(800) 730-ANRI
Fax (214) 283-3522

COLLECTORS' CLUB/TOUR

ANRI Collector's Society
P.O. Box 2087
Quincy, MA 02269-2087
(800) 763-ANRI (2674)

Annual Dues: $40.00
Club Year: Society Year–January-December
Collector's Year–Anniversary of Sign-Up Date

Benefits:
- Membership Gift
- Reservation Card to Acquire Members-Only Figurine
- Newsletter Published Three Times Yearly
- Membership Card
- Buy/Sell Matching Service through Newsletter
- Full Color ANRI Catalog
- Authorized Retailer Listing
- In-House Research Department
- In-Store ANRI Master Carver Events
- Travel Opportunities to ANRI Workshop in Italy

ANRI Woodcarvings Tour
Groden Valley
Italy

Hours: By advance reservation through ANRI Collector's Society, P.O. Box 2087, Quincy, MA 02269, (800) 763-ANRI

Admission: Only for Members of ANRI Collector's Society

Club members visiting the ANRI Workshop receive a guided tour of the facility including the painting and carving studios.

G. ARMANI SOCIETY AND ARMANI COLLECTION

Italian Artist Brings About a Renaissance in Hand-Made Sculptures

As one of Italy's most famous sculptors, Giuseppe Armani spends many hours in his home studio, where he creates his original works of art. Armani's renowned and elegant styles reflect the glorious artistic legacy of Tuscany, birthplace of the Renaissance.

Residing and working in the heart of Tuscany, Giuseppe Armani is surrounded by the works of artistic giants. Michelangelo Buonarroti and Leonardo da Vinci, Renaissance legends both, are his inspiration. In his studio, Armani today sculpts to the same ancient rhythms that resounded in the studios of the 15th century Maestros. The legacy of those geniuses inspire Armani to sculpt modern masterpieces.

Even though his work is acclaimed throughout the world, Giuseppe Armani still strives to expand his sculptural horizons. Currently while working on commissions from Disney, Armani is creating a glorious group of religious figurines.

Giuseppe Armani was born in Calci, a quaint little town not far from Pisa. Like children all over the world, young Giuseppe (known as "Beppe" to his many friends) loved to play. But for Beppe, the only game in town he thought worth playing was "drawing pictures." On walls or on any other flat surface, Armani sketched animals, trees and fairy-tale characters. Giuseppe and his family moved to Pisa when he was 14 because Calci lacked inspirational material suitable for an aspiring artist. He mined the artistic treasures of two other renowned Renaissance cities: Siena and Florence. Over the next ten years, Armani taught himself Art and Anatomy. He assidulously immersed himself in the techniques, textures and styles of Michelangelo, da Vinci, Donatello and Pisano. Eventually, he apprenticed himself to a master-sculptor.

Following an Artistic Heritage

Tuscany, the birthplace of the Italian Renaissance, enjoys a recognized cultural tradition in figurative art. Similar to other art forms, sculpture faithfully records the human experience. In Tuscany, the art of sculpture has been handed down from generation to generation since the Etruscans. Michelangelo and da Vinci, who were both capable of sculpting as well as painting, debated throughout their lives about which form of art best and most faithfully represented reality. While Michelangelo asserted that only the multi-sided shapes of sculpture could achieve this purpose, da Vinci argued that only painting, even though created on a flat surface, had the elements of perspective and color, without which, any attempt at representing reality would fail. Particularly in Italy, the art of creating sculpture became an accepted way of expression. People yearned to own and enjoy extraordinary three-dimensional art – in the privacy of their own homes.

Although Armani disciplined himself to study painting and other two-dimensional art, only sculpture resonated in consonance with his uniquely artistic soul. His professional career soon began in Pisa, where he sculpted in the oblique shadows of the Leaning Tower.

Florence Sculture d'Arte Studios Brings Armani's Works to Collectors

In 1975, Armani and Florence Sculture d'Arte began an inspired, exclusive and extraordinarily successful relationship. The factory of Florence Sculture d'Arte is located in the heart of Tuscany where Florence, Siena, Volterra and San Gimignano nestle among lush, rolling hills. The primary ambition of the founders of the Florence factory was to create an environment in which the best Italian sculptors and painters could flourish.

No one living or visiting Tuscany is immune to the pervading artistic atmosphere created by the Renaissance Masters. In this environment, Florence Sculture d'Arte, with its superior sculptors and the natural skills of its fine Tuscan craftsmen, has produced exemplary Armani figurines for more than two decades.

A Work of Art From Start to Finish

At Florence Sculture d'Arte, the sculpture process begins when Armani creates an original piece in clay. Although the artist began his career chiseling in the classic medium of marble, he considers clay a magical material that allows him to massage and manipulate it into incredibly lifelike works of art. About three weeks is required for the artist to sculpt a new figurine. Once the original is completed, it is fired in a kiln at very high temperatures and then smoothed. From this piece, a flexible mold is made using a special technique that allows faithful replication of the original. The mold is then filled with a liquid compound, which hardens in several hours. The figurine is taken out of the mold and hand polished with extreme care. Intricate pieces are cast separately and mounted to form a solid piece. Finally, each sculpture is hand-painted according to the original model conceived by Armani.

"People often ask me how I am able to create new sculptures," Armani once said. "Sculpting comes naturally to me, but the process is not easy to explain. Think about what relaxes you the most. Perhaps you enjoy cooking. When you are chopping vegetables, or measuring ingredients, your mind is clear except for the task at hand. You become totally focused on the food: its texture, and smell — the art of cooking. When you finally present the meal, and it's a success, you get a wonderful feeling inside. And so it is for me with sculpting."

Created exclusively for the 1995 Disneyana convention in Orlando, Florida, "Beauty and the Beast" captures the warmth and magic of the classic fairy tale. In this scene, Belle and the almost human Beast, having found true love, are tenderly holding hands.

Mythology Comes to Life

Two of Giuseppe Armani's newest sculptures are "Diana" and "Minerva." Diana, child of the great god Jupiter, is the goddess of The Hunt. When she was a very little child, Jupiter sat her on his enormous knee and magnanimously asked his precocious girl what gifts she wanted him to give her. She rapidly reeled off a list of things which included a flowing hunting tunic; a bow and arrow like Apollo's (her twin brother); eternal virginity; 60 young nymphs as her companions and all the mountains in the world in which to live and roam.

Minerva, though gentler than Diana, shared many of her traits. She was the goddess of Skilled Art. Minerva invented the flute, trumpet, earthenware pot, ox yoke, chariot and ships. She was the first to teach mathematics and all of the domestic arts such as: cooking, weaving and spinning.

"Diana" — the daughter of Jupiter — always carries her bow and arrow as she roams the mountains protecting children. The sculpture shows the intricate details and expressions beautifully captured by Giuseppe Armani.

Armani has sculpted Diana as a chaste beauty who roams mountain ranges seeking to protect children in danger. It is the wise and gentle side of Minerva that Armani chose to sculpt. The doves that flutter around her show her preference for peace, even though she possesses the terrible power to wage devastating wars.

Since both "Diana" and "Minerva" are classic mythological figures, Armani has sculpted them in the classic style of the Renaissance masters.

Inspiration from Childhood Trips to Rome

When Armani was a very small boy, his parents took him to Rome once a year. For a child from a tiny town outside Pisa, Rome was in a wholly different solar system — big, bustling and filled with noise and excitement. Armani has recently successfully captured the cosmopolitan nature of Via Veneto, a famous tree-lined street in Rome where fashion, fettucini and film meet. Via Veneto is home to some of the world's most fashionable shops, hotels and cafes. Giuseppe Armani's poised, beautiful and thoroughly modern models are dressed for today. Armani has even dared to put one flamboyant figurine called "Marina" in slacks — quite a departure from ancient Greek tunics!

Armani Participates in Disneyana Convention

Giuseppe Armani enjoys meeting with collectors, who admire his work; it was with great pride and happy anticipation that Armani once again decided to accept an invitation to participate in and make a personal appearance at the 1995 Disneyana Convention in Orlando, Florida. Exclusively for the 1995 convention, Armani sculpted a captivating "Beauty and the Beast." It takes the genius of Giuseppe Armani to breathe life into statues. "Beauty and the Beast" depicts the compelling drama of beautiful Belle's search for true love and the Beast's redemption through her love.

G. Armani Society Unites Collectors

The Society was launched for collectors to: learn more about the artist himself, meet fellow collectors, go "behind the scenes" of the studio, find out about new introductions, have the opportunity to acquire exclusive merchandise and participate in members-only activities. Dues are $40.00 for the first year, with renewal memberships at $27.50 per year. Members-only figurines include some of Armani's most inspired works, as unveiled in the quarterly Society publication, "The Review."

Armani is an artist on a double mission: dedicated to his collectors and impelled to bring beauty into their lives. It is for the collector that Armani creates art for today, and it is for the Armani collector that he continues to sculpt wondrous and compelling figurines out of space, air and imagination.

Giuseppe Armani Society
Miller Import Corp.
300 Mac Lane
Keasbey, NJ 08832
(800) 3-ARMANI
Fax: (908) 417-0031

Giuseppe Armani rekindles mythological characters and stories with this introduction named "Minerva," the goddess of Skilled Art. A pair of doves flock around the beautiful woman, showing her gentle side and devotion to peace.

COLLECTORS' CLUB

Giuseppe Armani Society
300 Mac Lane
Keasbey, NJ 08832
(800) 3-ARMANI

Annual Dues: $40.00 - Renewal: $27.50
Club Year: January-December

Benefits:
- Membership Gift: Armani Figurine
- Opportunity to Purchase Members-Only Figurines
- Quarterly Magazine, *The Review*
- Membership Card
- Special "Members Events" Throughout the Year

ASHTON-DRAKE GALLERIES

In Just Ten Years, The Ashton-Drake Galleries Has Become America's Top Doll Company! Everyone Wants to Know: What's Their Secret?

When The Ashton-Drake Galleries opened in 1985, collectors wondered what this new company was all about. At the time, collector plates were "king" and interest in limited edition figurines was growing, but dolls? Too expensive, even non-collectors said. But, producing a quality doll with personality and affordability built-in was the goal of Ashton-Drake, an offshoot of The Bradford Exchange. Challenge in place, they began to work toward what many thought an impossible goal. Who could have imagined so extraordinary an outcome from so simple a beginning as this...

His name was "Jason." Her name was "Heather." They first met at a bustling office in a Chicago suburb ten years ago. He looked dashing in his powder blue clown suit. Her peach dress, bare toes, pillow and white bonnet charmed everyone who saw her.

"What a doll!" collectors said when "Jason," then "Heather," debuted at collector shows across the U.S. Who could argue with rave reviews? Today, "Jason" and "Heather" are the revered "first-borns" of The Ashton-Drake Galleries. They now boast lots of brothers and sisters as Ashton-Drake continues to introduce additional, exclusive editions for doll lovers around the world.

Babe Ruth was never more eloquently immortalized. Award-winning sculptor Titus Tomescu bats a thousand with his realistic, limited edition offering, "The 60th Home Run." A sandy base with solid brass plate bears an impression of The Babe's signature!

How did Ashton-Drake become the recognized leader in the design, manufacture and marketing of high quality collectible dolls in ten short years? The answer is no mystery: Lifelike, beautifully designed dolls at affordable prices. Many say Ashton-Drake literally "reinvented" the collectible doll industry...a statement few can argue.

A Simple Philosophy Behind the Name

Behind the simple philosophy of "lifelike dolls at affordable prices" stands an army of creative minds devoted to picking talented doll artists (some well known...others stars-in-the-making) and embracing new materials, styles and looks. Their efforts show! Ashton-Drake makes dolls that appeal to collectors of every age and interest.

Among the recent ideas explored by Ashton-Drake are personalized babies, dolls scented to excite the senses, mini-dolls, dolls that talk, and moveable, musical dolls. Whether porcelain or vinyl, all Ashton-Drake dolls have a common denominator: each creation is the epitome of personality-filled art, a goal that's at the very heart of Ashton-Drake.

Many founding members of Ashton-Drake have stayed around to shepherd this decade's innovations and its growing family of artists and designers. If you're already an Ashton-Drake fan, you've seen the results of experience and flair. If you're not currently an observer of this dynamic company's efforts, you're in for a treat. Read on to discover why Ashton-Drake Galleries has set a standard for excellence that's become the industry benchmark!

The Start of the Dream Team...

With an eye to the future, the Ashton-Drake start-up team used visionary talent scouts to find doll artists willing to take a chance on the fledgling company. If Ashton-Drake grew, artists were assured their designs would reach collectors across America. The search had hardly begun when Yolanda Bello was discovered. Her work seemed the ideal starting-point for Ashton-Drake. Her dolls were lifelike and endearing. They had the perfect "look" for the new company's launch.

Happily, Bello shared the dream. She longed to expand her audience beyond the local following she already enjoyed. A passionate crusader for peace, love and spirituality, Bello saw her dolls as tiny missionaries and welcomed the chance to spread her philosophy through her art. Working tirelessly through the first days of her association with Ashton-Drake, Yolanda's premier doll, "Jason," was born. This blue-suited, now-pricey premier doll is a near-legend.

Today, Yolanda Bello carefully balances her successes of yesterday with the wishes of contemporary collectors. Fashioning small versions of her best selling dolls (including the landmark "Jason" and "Heather"), miniature *Picture Perfect Babies®*, filled with nostalgia, now greet her adoring public. But Yolanda didn't stop with her miniatures, she also pioneered Ashton-Drake's *Heirloom Ornaments*.

These tiny classics are petite sensations. "Jason," "Heather," "Matthew," "Sarah," "Michael"...indeed, every member of the original *Picture Perfect Babies* gang is now an ornament. These perennial delights make ideal shelf

These babies are legends in their own time! Authentic recreations of first Yolanda Bello designs, award-winning Picture Perfect Babies® miniatures keep Ashton-Drake Galleries at the forefront of doll innovation!

and mantle decorations when they're not enhancing Christmas trees in December. Additional ornaments are "waiting in the wings." Collectors can expect surprises in the year ahead as the Ashton-Drake ornament collection expands.

If you think Ashton-Drake's launch of *Picture Perfect Babies* ornaments completes the list of new Yolanda Bello ideas, think again. Collectors enamored with her award-winning, porcelain "Meagan Rose" doll wrote to say how much they wished their children could own a less fragile version of this precious doll. Voila! A vinyl "Meagan Rose" now delights doll fans of all ages. She looks exactly like her namesake. A quilted blanket and pillow complete every little girl's dream. Bello fans wonder what she'll think of next!

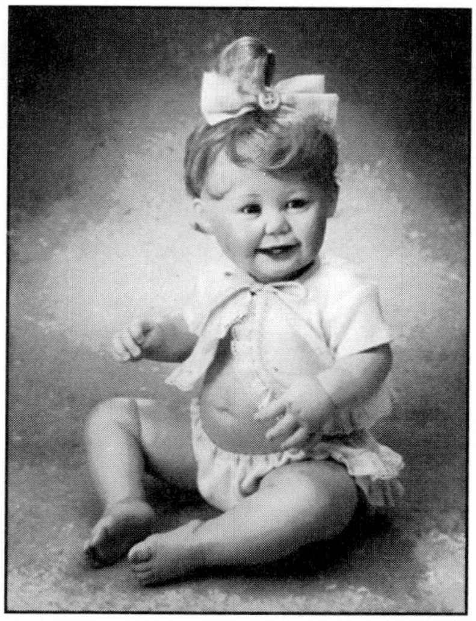

Winner of awards...and hearts..."Cute as a Button" is everything little porcelain girls are made of! Sculptor Titus Tomescu's "first-born" launched Ashton-Drake's popular Barely Yours *collection.*

The Galleries' Award-Winning Artist Family Grows

With Yolanda Bello firmly entrenched as grand matriarch of dolls for The Ashton-Drake Galleries, other artisans were carefully scouted to join the elite family. One star is sculptor Titus Tomescu. Titus looks much too young to be "the dad" of the lifelike babies he designs for Ashton-Drake, but talent sometimes blooms early, and awards for Titus' "Cute as a Button" confirm his genius.

Collectors confess they can't decide what to look at first when they see Tomescu's "Cute as a Button." The T-shirt with embroidered applique? The signature button in baby's realistic hair? Ruffled panties? Many insist her "poseability" makes "Cute as a Button" a winner! Whatever it is, that secret is propelling Titus Tomescu into stardom.

And lest you conclude that his designs appeal only to the maternal side of our collecting senses, take a peek at the lifelike "Babe Ruth" Titus sculpted to commemorate the sports legend! "The 60th Home Run" has such realistic detail, you can almost hear the pop of the bat!

Turning away from the roar of the ball park, we enter a world that's filled with wonder. Lights dim! A curtain opens. From the wings, a tiny ballerina emerges. She's "My Little Ballerina," a rising star in the doll world. Not only is "My Little Ballerina" deliciously poseable, she also comes with her own costume and accessory-filled trunk!

"My Little Ballerina," the brainchild of award-winning sculptor/doll designer Kathy Barry-Hippensteel, is a perfect example of the kind of

The "My Little Ballerina" collection is crafted in a hand-numbered edition ending forever in 1995! She is 16" tall and comes all dressed for her performance. Collectors may acquire additional costumes in a darling, pink trunk filled with surprises.

diversity that continues to fuel Ashton-Drake's mission and the sort of concept that has jump-started in-house design innovations like *Calendar Babies.* This unique concept combines practicality with collector passion for surrounding themselves with dolls year-round.

Collectors subscribing to *Calendar Babies* receive a 25" x 11" master calendar of fine wood with a complete set of date and month tiles. A shadowbox showcases a darling array of "dolls of the month"...each dressed to celebrate a special occasion. There's calendar fun for everyone with this one-of-a-kind collection.

Another perennial Ashton-Drake favorite, Cindy McClure, continues to shine as the distinguished winner of many "Doll of the Year" awards. Her newest originals are recreations of her favorite era: the days of Victoriana. Cindy's flair for dramatic costume design makes her sweet collectible tots a category unto themselves. *Victorian Nursery Heirloom Collection* dolls and the *Cross-Stitch* collection exemplify a sensitive style that's beloved by collectors across the country.

Joyce Wolf's *Nursery Newborns*

A doll collector's dream! Keep track of every year, for years to come, with this perpetual calendar starring tiny dolls dressed to celebrate each month. This mini-collection will be noticed and admired!

double the thrill of doll ownership by combining the look of tiny infants with innovative, real-life twists. Collectors can "adopt" their favorite infant by gender, then dress him or her for a first outing...in the most adorable Christmas outfit anyone could imagine...or in a pristine christening outfit marking this sacred occasion.

Renowned doll creator Wendy Lawton brings her genius to Ashton-Drake with a trail of awards and a national following. A gifted clothing designer, Wendy's dolls win awards for their wonderful faces and the sophisticated clothing they wear; a hallmark of her talent. Thorough research and a passion for historical detail distinguish her work from all others and bring to the Ashton-Drake family of artists and designers a recognized leader.

Inspiring Visions Continue the Legacy

When Julie Good-Krüger first approached Ashton-Drake with her idea for crafting the Holy Family as a limited edition doll collection, she couldn't have picked a better time. Ashton-Drake's strong move into the world of inspirational dolls was already making headlines and her new collection would be the perfect addition. Today, Julie's *Oh, Holy Night* dolls include three adorable wise men, a shepherd boy and a Gloria Angel!

Based on another beloved Christmas story, "The Little Drummer Boy" is moveable and musical. He literally takes collectors back in time to the birth of Baby Jesus as he beats his drum to the accompaniment of the beloved "Little Drummer Boy" tune. Big brown eyes gazing upward, "Little Drummer Boy" looks for divine guidance as he slowly approaches the stable with his gift of song.

Given the early popularity of "Little Drummer Boy," and country-wide excitement of Julie Good-Krüger's *Oh, Holy Night* collection, Ashton-Drake's award-winning artist Titus Tomescu sculpted a highly unusual doll series of scenes depicting the life of Jesus as an adult. Already well-known for his realistic *Barely Yours* collection, debuting with "Cute as a Button," Titus was given the go-ahead to develop this sacred series.

Messages of Hope introduced "Little Children Come to Me" to a ready-made audience of appreciative collectors. Even seasoned Ashton-Drake staffers were impressed and concluded that with such artists as Yolanda Bello, Cindy McClure, Joyce Wolf, Kathy Barry-Hippensteel, Titus Tomescu, Julie Good-Krüger, Wendy Lawton, Dianna Effner and others, the next ten years will be a rocket ride to the stars...a ride doll collectors will be queued up to join!

The Ashton-Drake Galleries
9200 N. Maryland Avenue
Niles, IL 60714
(800) 634-5164
Fax (708) 966-3026

ATTIC BABIES

Rediscovering the Simple Joys of Childhood

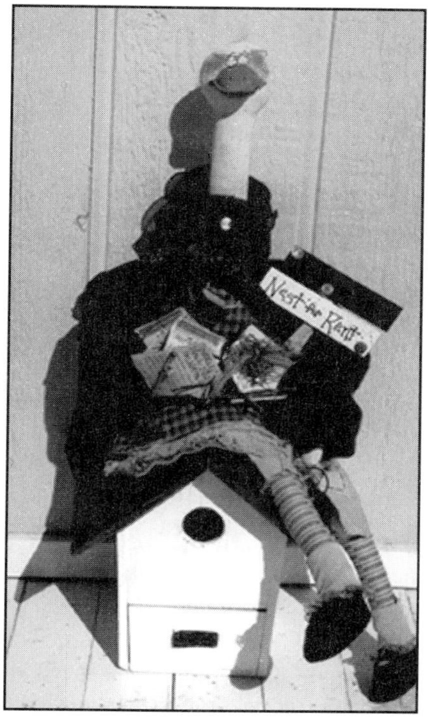

Realtor (and ostrich) "Elmira Truelove" is 28" tall and comes with her own birdhouse.

"Even though growing up can sometimes make us tuck away the very best in all of us – the hopes, the dreams, the sense of possibility – the child is alive and well in all of us. And rediscovering that is one of life's greatest joys."

This, to Attic Babies™ founder and designer Marty Maschino-Walker, is the voice of experience. It has also been her inspiration throughout her life, and especially in the nine years that her company has been in existence – the inspiration that has brought hundreds of whimsical rag dolls and teddy bear creations into our lives – and that has helped her thousands of collectors rediscover the simple joys of childhoods past. This special understanding of Marty's that everyone, someday, returns to their own "attic" is in large part what makes her designs so irresistible.

From Home-Based Business to Award-Winning Company

Attic Babies began as a home-based business in 1987. Marty was pregnant at the time – and she'd found that the rag dolls and teddy bears that she'd been exhibiting at arts and crafts shows were exceptionally popular – not to mention the fact that they were much easier to carry around for the pregnant artist!

Based on her local success, Marty decided in 1987 to invest in exhibiting at the Dallas Gift Market, and sent 16 designs to the show. Interest from the retail trade was exceptional, and orders came in by the droves. Once the show was over, she realized that, while she worked very well under pressure, she just couldn't handle this new level of demand by herself.

So Marty hired some local women who liked the idea of being able to sew at home, watch kids if they needed to, and earn some money while they were at it. True to her instincts, success continued to follow, and to make a long but wonderful story short – what has become Attic Babies today, continued to grow over the next two years – and in the process Marty found her first building to house production. She's now re-located three times, each time to larger facilities. The company now resides in Drumright, Oklahoma – halfway between Tulsa and Oklahoma City. Marty now designs Attic Babies in a 15,000 square foot facility where almost 100 employees bring her designs to life every day. The office and factory are open Monday through Thursday, and factory tours can be arranged Monday through Thursday, from 9:30 a.m. until 2:30 p.m.

Aside from what is to Marty the privilege of having brought hundreds of designs to life, it has been a special thrill in the last nine years to have been: chosen in 1990 as Oklahoma's Small Business Person of the Year; invited to Washington, D.C. to present Mrs. Bush with a special rendition of the First Lady entitled "Grammy Bar;" and invited to the National Governor's Convention in 1993, to present specially designed dolls which commemorated Native Oklahoma to all of the Governors' spouses.

It's been pretty exciting, to say the least. And so, you just have to ask – what does the future hold for Attic Babies? "That's a tough question. One day at a time is just about as much excitement as anyone can stand around here!" quips Marty. Whatever shape it all takes, she is living proof of the adage "do what you love, the money will follow" – so we'd say the future looks very bright indeed.

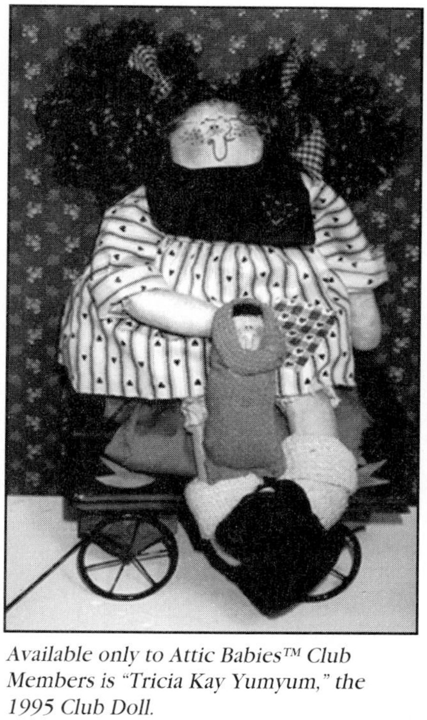

Available only to Attic Babies™ Club Members is "Tricia Kay Yumyum," the 1995 Club Doll.

Distinct Personalities and Original Names Make Attic Babies Unique

If there is such a thing, your average Attic Baby is an extremely cuddly rag doll or teddy bear – and no two are ever exactly alike. But there's much, much more variety in the products – especially the hilarious parodies that come to life from Marty's visions of the "ultimate professional" – whether doctor, lawyer, sports figure, or even her favorite members of the animal kingdom.

One thing is for certain – each design has its own distinctive personality, and a hysterical name to match. Part of the charisma of Attic Babies is wrapped up in those names which Marty develops – names like "Fertile Mertle," "Virtuous Vergie," "Luscious Lulu" and "Fatty Matty" to name a very few. Most of the designs and names alike are influenced by friends and family in Marty's own charmed life – inspired by both childhood and recent memories.

Attic Babies are not developed as collections or series, although there are common threads which are sustained from one design season to the next – Marty designs twice a year – which make for wonderful collections. Each has its own personality, and while they are all limited in production – each "living their lives with great service and loyalty" as Marty would say – many are number-limited in small editions, or are limited by year of production, as are all of Marty's heartwarming Santas.

Almost without exception, though, every Attic Baby can be customized to make it very much a collector's very own one-of-a-kind – from your choice of fabric color, to personalization of accessories, to choice of size and the degree of choice which makes each design a unique character that forms an indelible bond between doll and collector.

An impromptu gathering of Attic Babies includes "Mary Jane Hackensack," a little girl with her wagon full of blocks; "Scruffy Gilhooley," a little boy bear with tricycle who's looking for Poo; "Epple Moneyworth," a felt bunny with wheelbarrow, ready for gardening; and "Albert P. Thigpen," a froggle going a-courtin' with bouquet and trusty fiddle in hand.

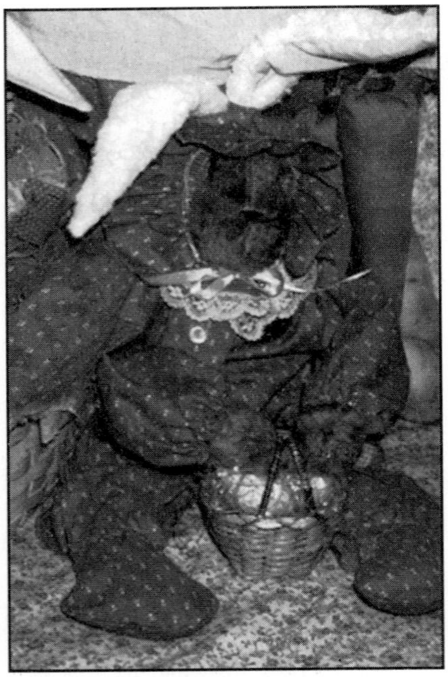

"Ms. Kizzie Tiddle E. Winks" is a bear whose not-so-secret desire is to be a bunny. At 18" tall, she is available in country colors.

Imagination, Experience and Common Sense Go Into Each Attic Babies Design

Attic Babies are the original tea-stained muslin dolls of their kind – and everything in the way that they're made adds charm and whimsy to the delightful concepts which their designer develops.

From Marty's initial prototype, the ingenuity, imagination and experience of her production staff takes over in all the areas which she believes are so critically important to making an Attic Baby a very high-touch collectible. This includes sourcing the right fabric, layering and cutting it just right, developing the accessories, making sure that the facial expressions in production match the prototype, and insuring that Attic Babies are as affordable as they are cute.

"The whole process hasn't really changed significantly in nine years. Just a few more hands out there," says Marty. As with nature, there is a beauty in the simple elegance and common sense that goes into making each and every Attic Baby.

Between design seasons, when Marty can schedule a block of time away from the family she loves very much, she goes on signing tours that take her from coast to coast, with dozens of stops in just a few weeks. It keeps her in touch not only with her retail stores, but more importantly – her thousands of collectors. Says Marty, "They are a constant, heaven-sent source of humility to me. After nine years, their connection to what I do is not only gratifying, it's downright perplexing!"

Collectors Club Continues to Grow

Attic Babies Collectors' Club began in 1992, and membership has almost doubled every year since. Many Club Members have become great friends with Attic Babies staff over the years – and Club Members are constantly calling each other to keep in touch with the latest news. They've even established their own contact network on Prodigy!

One way or another, Club Members get all the information. A quarterly newsletter is both informative and whimsically humorous in a true-to-form way. Members also receive regular mailings with details on signings, appearances at major collectibles shows, and updates on both new designs and retiring dolls. Special offers are often made to Club Members only – everything from T-shirts, buttons, and mugs to an annual Club Doll which is numbered and hand-signed by Marty.

Initial membership is $30.00, and renewals thereafter are $20.00. Marty and all the office staff at Attic Babies believe their Club is truly special. "Our Club Members know our names, and we know theirs. It's really turned into a mutual admiration society. We're truly blessed."

Marty Maschino-Walker is the designer of Attic Babies – the whimsical, tea-stained rag dolls that are a tribute to a rediscovered childhood.

Attic Babies
P.O. Box 912
Drumright, OK 74030
(918) 352-4414
Fax (918) 352-4767

COLLECTORS' CLUB/TOUR

Attic Babies Collectors' Club
P.O. Box 912
Drumright, OK 74030
(918) 352-4414

Annual Dues: $30.00 - Renewal: $20.00
Club Year: Anniversary of Sign-Up Date

Benefits:

- Membership Gift: T-Shirt and Button
- Opportunity to Purchase Members-Only Doll
- Quarterly Newsletter, "News From The Attic"
- Membership Card
- Buy/Sell Matching Service

Attic Babies Factory Tour
Rt. 1 Box 487
Drumright, OK 74030
(918) 352-4414

Hours: Monday through Thursday, 9:30 a.m. - 2:30 p.m.
Admission Fee: None

Visitors can tour the 15,000 square foot Attic Babies Factory and see how the delightful Attic Babies rag dolls "come to life."

BAND CREATIONS

BAND Creations Incorporates Friendship, Romance and History into Collectible Figurines

Since BAND Creations was established in 1988 by Dennis Sowka, it has distributed numerous lines of giftware items by different artists to the collectible world. Sowka's 17 years of experience with inspirational, Christmas and collectible items prior to starting BAND Creations provides him with a knowledge of the artists and pieces that are most admired by collectors.

Currently, BAND Creations exclusively distributes the popular *Best Friends* figurines created by talented artists Jeanette Richards and Sandra Penfield. BAND is also creating excitement in the collectibles field with the introduction of its new collectible lines – *America's Covered Bridges*.

Own A Piece of American History

In 1994, BAND introduced the *America's Covered Bridges* series to its vast and impressive lines of giftware items. The collection of 22 bridges features replicas of historical American bridges built during the mid 1800s and early 1900s at various sites across the U.S., which have been carefully selected and researched prior to creation.

The bridges capture the history and romance of the structures that have linked farmlands with generations of memories. A few of the famous bridges included in the *America's Covered Bridges* series are the well-known tourist attraction, "Narrows Covered Bridge," in Parke County, Indiana; the oldest covered bridge in the West, "Wawona Covered Bridge," within Yosemite National Park; and the "Roseman Covered Bridge" in Madison County, Iowa, the inspiration for the romantic novel. Each of the replicas comes with its own history card detailing such information as the story and date of the bridges construction, the bridges location, world guide number, and a few interesting anecdotes.

BAND Creations unique covered bridges collectibles are handcrafted of poly resin and carefully hand-painted to capture the bridges' individual design and character. The *America's Covered Bridges* feature great attention to detail in everything from the color and texture of the external constructions to the interior truss designs. The bridges come with an attractive wood base and a metal plaque. They range in size from 6" to 10" long and retail for $29.95 to $39.95.

BAND Creations is already selecting and researching additional bridges to be included in the *America's Covered Bridges* series in the future.

Quiet Country Life Is Represented in BAND's New *Best Friends* "RiverSong" Collection

BAND Creations, Jeanette Richards and Sandra Penfield have again combined their creative talents in the artists new *Best Friends* "RiverSong" collection, which reflects the quiet majesty of a small village on the St. Croix River. The quaint village homes and townspeople are the newest addition to Richard's and Penfield's *Best Friends* lines of adorable miniatures. Each of the collectible "RiverSong" buildings is decorated to capture the festive and warm feelings of small-town life. The miniatures also double as candle votives. Richards says, "We based 'RiverSong' on the small river town where we live. It's here that we enjoy the simple pleasures of country living and the various activities of our children."

The new miniature village collection, which is hand-painted and constructed of poly resin, ranges in size from 2" for the citizens to 7" for the houses. They are available for the suggested retail prices of $14.00 to $30.00, or $255.40 for the complete 28-piece set.

Spanning waterways, farmlands and generations of cherished memories, BAND Creations brings unique charm and character to the "Knox Covered Bridge" in Chester County, Pennsylvania, as part of the America's Covered Bridge *series.*

BAND Creations Adds the New "Noah's Ark" to Its Popular Line of *Best Friends* Miniatures

He gathered the animals two by two.
Noah and his wife,
they made quite a crew.

The animals were housed both fore
and aft, while two less popular
rode on the raft.

The rain came down,
forty nights 'til at last appeared land,
the most beautiful of sights.

They all rejoiced as the ark
came to shore. The rainbow,
His promise to flood nevermore.

"RiverSong," the make believe town on the banks of the St. Croix River, becomes a winter playland for BAND Creations' Best Friends *series.*

Jeanette Richards and Sandra Penfield bring their poem to life in their new Noah's Ark creation for BAND Creations. The artists biblical boat figurine is the latest addition to their *Best Friends* line.

Noah's Ark features Noah and his wife sailing happily along in the main ark, surrounded by a variety of their animal friends including monkeys and colorful parrots. In addition, an attached raft is the form of transportation for two adorable skunks.

Richards and Penfield have designed their new 7" tall Noah's Ark out of durable poly resin material and have carefully hand-painted each piece in bright colors. Everything from the straw roof on the ark's cabin, to the bananas on the palm tree and Noah's and his wife's smiling faces, feature the artists attention to detail.

The complete 10-piece set of the *Best Friends* "Noah's Ark" is available now for the suggested retail price of $62.00. In addition, collectors can purchase the decorative ark separately for the suggested retail price of $42.00 and the animals separately for $20.00.

BAND Creations' replica of "The Humpback Covered Bridge," located in Allegheny County, Virginia, captures the history and romance of this unique structure built in 1835. This bridge, with no middle supports, is believed to be the only one of its design in the United States.

Meet the BAND Creations Artists

The creators of BAND Creations *Best Friends* collections, Jeanette Richards and Sandra Penfield have discovered the excitement of creating a world of clay miniatures. Combining their varied talents, creative abilities and formal education, they have succeeded in capturing the simplicity of the American spirit.

Jeanette, from Rocky River, Ohio, studied art in Washington, D.C. and received her B.A. in English and Art from the University of Dayton, Ohio. Growing up in a family of artists, illustration was her first love.

Sandra grew up in Detroit Lakes, Minnesota, and received a B.S. in Art from the University of North Dakota. She taught art and shared her talents through her woodcut prints.

Their mutual interest in art brought Richards and Penfield together in Hudson, Wisconsin, where they became partners in a graphic design business in 1984. Always experimenting with new ideas, they created their first Christmas Angel in October 1990. Using the limitless boundaries of clay, their designs soon evolved to encompass all the facets of friendship and family life. Their collections for BAND Creations include *Best Friends* "O Joyful Night" nativity set, "First Friends Begin at Childhood," "Monthly Angels," "RiverSong," "Winter Wonderland," "Angel Wishes," "A Star is Born," "Noah's Ark" and the popular Angel Pin Cards.

He gathered the animals two by two... Artists Jeanette Richards and Sandra Penfield's "Noah's Ark" is surrounded by a joyful crew!

BAND Creations
28427 N. Ballard
Lake Forest, IL 60045
(800) 535-3242
Fax (708) 816-3695

BING & GRONDAHL

One Hundred Years of Beloved Artistry: Bing & Grondahl, The Company That Pioneered Plate Collecting

The plate that started a tradition! "Behind the Frozen Window" is the first collector plate ever made, limited to 400! Today, F.A. Hallin's design is coveted by collectors and sells for up to $8,000 on the secondary market!

The year was 1895. Denmark prepared for a festive Yuletide season, readying presents to usher in the season of Jesus' birth. As was the custom, generous Danes prepared gifts of candy, cake and fruits to thank members of their household staff for their loyalty and hard work. Treats were elaborately presented on plates made of metal or wood. No one's quite sure when or how this delightful custom began, but it would be hard to say who enjoyed it more: the grateful giver or happy receiver!

As fate would have it, Harald Bing, one of the founders of Bing & Grondahl (producer of fine dinnerware and other renowned pottery) became intrigued by the presentation of holiday plates. He wondered if the custom could be expanded to all Danish society. Determined to test the idea during the 1895 Christmas season, Bing & Grondahl issued an elegant porcelain plate commissioned of artist F. A. Hallin. Called "Behind the Frozen Window," this hand-painted limited edition showcased the Copenhagen skyline as seen through a frosty window pane. Drenched in signature blue and white, the message "Jule Aften" (Christmas Eve) was gently scrolled around the bottom of the plate.

Bing's idea was embraced by the Danish public with enthusiasm and "Behind the Frozen Window" became a legendary work of art. Made in an edition size of just 400, all plates sold out in quick order, despite a 'hefty' price tag of 50¢ per plate! Today, these rare finds continue to be called the most valuable collector plates ever, commanding an average of $8,000.00 on today's secondary market!

A Company Dedicated to Preserving Memories

To appreciate Bing & Grondahl's pioneering collector plate, some background history is helpful. In 1853, 42 years before "Behind the Frozen Window" was made, artist Frederick Grondahl, with brothers Meyer and Jacob Bing, shared a vision: the continuation of an art style pioneered by the legendary Danish sculptor Thorvaldsen. Hoping Thorvaldsen's style would have country-wide appeal, the three men merged their resources, energy and ideas to open a factory dedicated to crafting replicas of the sculptor's work.

Initially, Bing & Grondahl manufactured and sold figurines, but the popularity of these sculptures was so significant, Danish consumers clamored for more variety. Elated, Bing & Grondahl produced elegant dinnerware and coffee services. This remarkable collection rapidly became a benchmark of tabletop fashion across Denmark.

By 1889, the company's distinguished evolution came into the spotlight at the Paris World's Fair. There, a dinner service called *Heron*, by Bing & Grondahl artistic director Pietro Krohn, was unveiled to an adoring public. Visitors from around the world admired *Heron's* bold design and the unique decorating technique used to finish each piece. That same look and finish was selected just six years later, when Harald Bing brought his idea for making a "holiday plate" in the now highly-recognized cobalt glazed finish, to the company. "Behind the Frozen Window" was the result...a history of plate art had begun.

The Idea of "Collecting" Cobalt Plates Spreads Like Wildfire!

Bing & Grondahl's idea for producing limited edition Christmas plates spread beyond the border of Denmark rapidly. Holiday plates fast became a continental passion. Despite unrest and political upheaval, plates continued to be made at Bing & Grondahl's factory through the first World War, the Depression and even during the Nazi occupation. Somehow, materials, desire and resolution kept the tradition alive.

With each Christmas season during these troubled times, a new artistic reflection of the year's events poured from the hands and hearts of the Bing & Grondahl artisans. Fishing boats, quaint homes, gentle animals, Danish landmark buildings, people of all ages and holy symbols graced plates fabricated during the first World War and Depression. Pastoral art featuring horses, churches, a farm and Danish landmarks soothed spirits during World War II, and ushered in the long-awaited peace. Reverently, Bing & Grondahl issued artist Margrethe Hyldal's "Commemoration Cross in Honor of Danish Sailors Who Lost Their Lives During World War II" as its 1946 plate.

It was inevitable that American service men, stationed in Europe, would notice and admire Bing & Grondahl's distinct plates. Soldiers and sailors purchased them to bring home to family and friends, and, of course, Americans with an eye for fine detail and old world charm fell in love! Before long, America joined the now-impressive list of over 70 countries awaiting annual Christmas editions as eagerly as the Danes each year.

How Bing & Grondahl Treasures Are Made

The process of creating a fine Bing & Grondahl collector plate has remained virtually unchanged for 100 years! First, years of drawing, planning and subject evaluation are undertaken by the staff to pick the ideal art. When everyone has agreed on the design, a master sculptor crafts a bas-relief model.

Painstakingly, a plaster of Paris copy is sculpted. This will determine the all-important master mold, so it must be perfection. Finally, a cast bronze image becomes central to the production process, acting as the permanent master. From it, plaster molds are recreated and only 20 plates are made from each before the plaster is destroyed. This is a demanding production method, but one that must be followed to meet stringent quality control standards.

Plates are now ready for firing and decorating in the world-famous "underglaze technique" that has made Bing & Grondahl famous. Colors are applied carefully by artisans receiving special training. Because exact shades of blue don't emerge until the final firing has taken place, craftsmen must know how to adjust the intensity of their colors to attain a perfect finished product.

Bringing to mind Bing & Grondahl's first Christmas plate, "The Towers of Copenhagen" visually escorts collectors through the famous gates of Tivoli Gardens, bordered by frozen swirls and a star of wonder.

Before the final firing, the authentification process must be completed. The date and artist's initials are placed on the backstamp. Finally, the distinguished Bing & Grondahl logo is applied. Each plate is carefully dipped into glaze, then fired. In the kiln, kaolin, quartz and feldspar meld into a hard paste over a 48 hour period. The precise 2700 degree Fahrenheit temperature melts the glaze and creates an everlasting, glass-like surface of shimmering "Copenhagen Cobalt Blue."

If an issue is examined and found undesirable for a reason determined by the quality control team, the plate is destroyed. Since production of all Bing & Grondahl plates are strictly limited by year, this examination process is particularly critical. Of course, all molds are destroyed at the end of a year's production.

An Expanded Library and Distinguished Designers

The very first Christmas plate introduced by Harald Bing debuted just eight years after Orville and Wilber Wright invented the airplane. Since that time, Bing & Grondahl has offered collectors an ever-growing library of delights, such as Mother's Day plates, annual bells, thimbles, Christmas bells and a figurine of the year.

Bing & Grondahl works hard to expand its collection of offerings to include the perfect gifts for newlyweds, anniversary and birthday celebrants and just about every gift-giving occasion Americans can dream up. The idea of a dated collectible to celebrate a special occasion is becoming increasingly more popular. In fact, many collections begin with the birth of a child, marriage or to honor the year of a child's special event, such as a first communion, graduation or confirmation.

Parent company Royal Copenhagen's 88th Christmas annual edition is the splendid "Christmas at the Manor House." Gift boxed, "Christmas at the Manor House" is also issued as an ornament, bell and collectible cup, saucer and 24K, gold-plated spoon!

Regardless of the event it commemorates, every stunning new issue created at the Bing & Grondahl design studios comes from the hands and hearts of a brilliant family of artists. Past masters include Friis, Larsen, Bonfils, Thelander, Hallin, Hyldahl and other greats. More recently, Jorgen Nielsen and Sven Vestergaard have shown their distinct creative spirits on Bing and Grondahl collectible art.

Each of these artists has contributed mightily to the Bing & Grondahl success story and will forever be an honored member of its artistic family. Today, over 350 figurines and hundreds of 'Blue and White' classics form the base of the Bing & Grondahl library. From this eclectic mix, colorful annual eggs, delicate porcelain spring flower plates, annual animal figurines, new Christmas plate series and fabulous ornaments are introduced each year to the delight of an adoring public.

The Celebration That's Lasted One Hundred Years

As a tribute to the tradition that started a century ago, Bing & Grondahl marks this centennial with several

Intertwined spruce twigs, pine cones and glowing candles graciously circle the first-ever Bing & Grondahl "Centennial Platter." Only 7,500 of these 13" masterpieces will be made and sold world-wide.

landmark issues. The first, a series of five limited editions, replicate the most popular motifs from that past 100 years. Each six-inch plate features a hand-applied, 24K gold rim. The first in this exquisite retro plate collection debuted in 1991. Called "Crows Enjoying Christmas," this recreated 1899 plate was snapped up by collectors. In 1995, the series culminated with the re-issuing of a 24K gold-banded "Behind the Frozen Window."

Unveiled in 1995, the magnificent "Centennial Platter" bears the image of the 101st Christmas plate art. Amply sized at 13", collectors can recreate days of Christmas past in Denmark by serving sweets on this commemorative platter before putting it on display. The "Centennial Platter" features a unique, 2-1/2" border lavished with spruce twigs, pine cones and candles. Limited to just 7,500 pieces, this platter marks the only time a Christmas Jubilee Edition has been designed as anything other than a plate!

For Bing & Grondahl, a 100th anniversary celebration could literally be called "icing on the cake." Awards, recognition and spectacular attention has come to the company that pioneered collector plate art.

Before and since becoming part of the Royal Copenhagen group of companies, world-wide recognition has abounded. Royal courts in Denmark, Sweden and the United Kingdom have saluted Bing & Grondahl's considerable contribution to art collecting and major museums count outstanding examples of Bing & Grondahl art among their collections.

But accepting laudits is only part of this legendary company's history. Bing & Grondahl has also presented commemorative gifts to other nations as tributes of friendship. A good example is the Bicentennial Eagle, limited to just 100 figures, crafted in honor of the 200th anniversary of the United States. "Eagle #1" was presented to the White House – the meaningful gift from one friend to another – in much the same way a neighbor might have given a plate of home-baked cookies to a good friend in Denmark one hundred years ago.

Become a part of history and start your own tradition today with a fine collectible treasure from Bing and Grondahl!

Royal Copenhagen/Bing & Grondahl
27 Holland Avenue
White Plains, NY 10603
(914) 428-8222
Fax (914) 428-8251

THE BOYDS COLLECTION, LTD.

Bears...Hares...Tabbies and a Zoo-Full of Offbeat Critters Give Collectors New Reasons to Laugh Out Loud

Collectors with a taste for whimsy, an eye for quality, and a heart for nostalgia have made a great discovery called the Boyds Collection, Ltd. This zoo-full of plush and sculptured animals resides, in perfect harmony, somewhere between the heartstrings and funny bone.

The Boyds Collection isn't your average animal menagerie. It's the wackiest collection of party animals you've ever met! Hunting for their stomping grounds? Look about ten miles west of the hills and battlefields of Gettysburg in McSherrystown, Pennsylvania. Here, Gary Lowenthal and his wife Tina spend their days happily conversing with bears, cats, hares and moose – make that meese.

Given the "beastly nature" of the Lowenthal business, most folks wonder how it got so formal a name as The Boyds Collection, Ltd. Fact is, the Lowenthals ran a thriving antique business in Boyds, Maryland, for years. When they launched their collectibles business, it didn't seem right to tamper with success, so the name stayed.

The Boyds Collection began with a successful library of duck decoys. These jewels, sized from nine inches to three feet, kept Gary busy from dawn to dusk. He painted, antiqued, packaged, sold and shipped his decoy designs, while Tina handled business operations. It was inevitable that their home-based industry would grow "like wild."

By 1982, they moved from their 1880s home to a "newer" building (circa 1890). A thriving industry crafting precious replicas of whimsical, old-fashioned critters was, say the hares, off and running.

Old Fashioned Philosophy...New Fangled Success

When a collector acquires a huggable teddy, tabby, hare or other furry member of the Boyds menagerie, they get more than a plush animal. They also get a big slice of philosophy, detailed inside the hangtag suspended from each Boyds original. It's "stamped" for authenticity by one of the official Boyds bears hired for the job (rumor has it he works for peanuts). Read the inside of the tag and discover a mix of fun, sincerity and facts about how, and why, each critter is made. Collectors learn the Boyds Collection has been around since 1979, that the cast resin *Bearstone Collection™* launched a popular second division, and that their formula for dreaming up new characters keeps things hopping creatively.

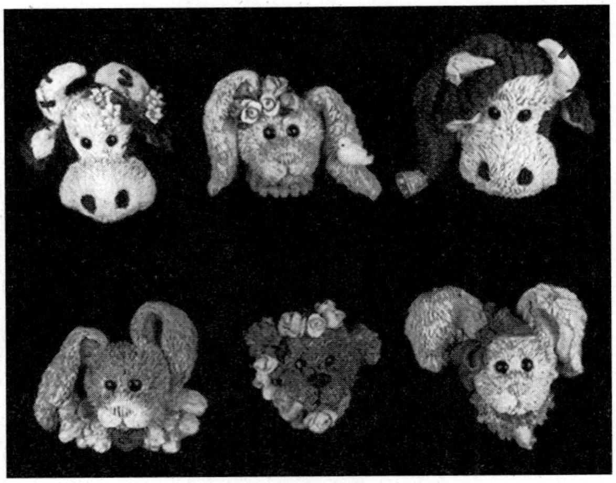

Some say Boyds Collection Bearware *Pins are "crittercal" fashion statements. Get ready to collect 'em all: "Bailey," "M. Harrison," Santa, some Incognito Cows, plus a single Moose looking for love. They're sensational on sweaters and shirts!*

While there's no standard formula for coming up with new designs for plush animals, the process usually begins with Gary Lowenthal's sketches. A stickler for perfection, there are sometimes 20 or 30 refinements made to the original before it starts the production circuit. Depending upon complexity, seamstresses cut patterns by hand or machine, embroiderers make their magic and bears are hand-brushed and inspected three times. It's a long, exacting process, but well worth the wait!

In the case of cast resin collectibles, Gary's conceptual sketch is translated into clay, studied, revised and reworked. When everyone agrees that the look is perfect, it's cast as "White Wear," then handed to a master painter to select a color pallet. Only then is the issue ready to be produced in accordance with the colors and detail of the original.

By-the-way, before a cast resin critter is "born," the official Boyds Pawprint is painted or embossed onto the newcomer. This Symbol of Authenticity promises perfection!

Meet A Few of the Boyds' Boyz (and the Ladies, too)

Describing Boyds Collection animals is like trying to describe your own kids. Each one is precious, unique, irresistible in his or her own way. There are currently more than 350 plush bears, hares, moose and assorted critters in Boyds' growing library of delights. They're showcased, to perfection, in a delightful collector catalog.

Open the cover and you'll first encounter 15 *Board of Directors™*, bean bag bears with funny names like "Binkie," "Dufus" and "Otis." Ten flop-eared hares and ten tabbies, all of plush, pose for the cameras on pages three and four. There's even a litter of five *Mitten Kittens™*, part of *The Archive Series™*, named for British poets "Browning," "Byron," "Tennyson," "Keats" and "Shelly," to be specific. *Mitten Kittens* are fully jointed and fashioned with over 30 separate pieces!

If domestic animals aren't your bag, the Boyds folks have something special for you: wild and woolly farm creatures and exotic animals you're more likely to see in a circus than in the wild. Collectors of the *Farmyard Series™* may choose from cows, pigs and ewes with funny names ranging in size from 7" to a grand 16". Lions, elephants and monkeys in the Circus™ grouping are anything but ferocious-looking!

Boyds has experimented with various materials outside of plush and come up with some winning combinations. *Bean Curlies™*, unique bean bag bears and hares of soft sherpa fleece, and *The Chenille Group™*, "soft and squooshie" critters sewn from what might be the most comforting material on the planet, are particular favorites.

What collection would be complete without an adorable gathering of Christmas animals? As always, Boyds has the holiday covered. *T.J.'s Best Dressed™...Let it Snow™*, boasts Santa bears, moose and mice all dressed up in red robes with holiday trim. The Christmas party continues with *Northern Lights™*, whimsical, fully-jointed bears and moose featuring hand-embroidered detailing. To be sure no Boyds collector's tree goes "undressed," there's even a gathering of small 4-1/2" to 7-1/2" animals, mini-dolls and angels.

Bailey Bear helps Simone after a tumble on "Thin Ice." If you've ever had a good friend help you out (especially when they were right and you were wrong!), this collectible confection is the perfect "Thanks," "I'm glad we're friends" or "Bless you!" gift.

Talk about a harey twist on life! "Myrtle Believe" could be mistaken for a TV antennae since she's getting such great reception from collectors.

There's more...but you'll want to get your paws on a catalog to see every adorable Boyds bean bag delight for yourself. If you can't locate a plush catalog at your local Boyds' dealer, please send $2.50 to the Boyds Collection Ltd., Somethin' Ta Say Dept. C.I.B., Gettysburg, PA 17325-4385.

Vintage and New Bears & Hares Are Today's Big Stars

The folks at Boyds are the proud parents of a collection of resin sculptures called *The Folkstone Collection™*. Part of the *Boyds Bears & Friends Collection™*, The Folkstones are one-of-a-kind original sculptures made of cast resin and designed to melt collector hearts.

Among the *Folkstone* family, collectors will meet up with an unlikely gathering of the "N.Q.G.A.'s" (That's "Not Quite Guardian Angels"), farmer cows, bunnies with ears reaching almost to the clouds and a group of the most outrageous snowmen you'll ever see. Add a moose with a fascination for bells and a few versions of Santa guaranteed to tickle the funny bone, and you've got yourself a mighty popular collection of resin pencil figures.

Then there's the *The Bearstone Collection™*. Don't count on seeing only bears in this series. A select group of bunnies, moose and a cow snuck in and weren't discovered until after the *Bearstone* catalog had gone to press! One glimpse at the cast resin *Bearstone Collection* tends to start a chuckle. Discover sports heroes, holiday dudes (like angels and Santas), some dainty dressers and an entrepreneur or two. Retired members of *The Bearstone Collection* hold lofty positions and are now available only on the secondary market.

Folkstones and *Bearstones* reflect the true benchmarks of collectibility. Based on traditional folk art themes, they're hand-painted, individually numbered, gift boxed, and of course, each comes with a Certificate of Authenticity.

The Dreams and Dreamers Who "Make It All Happen"

Behind the curly chenille...behind the hand-stitched noses and precious poses...an army of creative spirits back the Lowenthal success story. Of particular note, licensed artists lend their names and talents to some of the most remarkable plush and resin personalities collectors have ever seen. To understand how everyone came together, you'll want to acquaint yourself with the leader of all this madness: Gary M. Lowenthal.

Lowenthal likes to refer to himself as the "Head Bean." You'll likely find the nom de plume dotting his publications, chatty newsletters and hang tags. Actually, wherever the spirit moves him, Gary's alter ego, "Head Bean," appears. A child of the raging 60's, Lowenthal survived a New York City upbringing with his offbeat humor intact. Thus, no one was surprised when he earned a masters degree in biology before heading to the Fiji Islands in the South Pacific, courtesy of the Peace Corps. This, quite naturally, led to a great longing for civilization

"Smith Witter II" is Boyds' ultimate yuppie bear. A 17", jointed beanbag bear made of ultra long, curly chenille, he sports paw pads and a bow of material Bearberry's of London would be proud to use.

and all of its hedonistic trappings. Deciding the most logical place to work out these rediscovered sentiments would be the wilds of Bloomingdale's, Gary set off on an exotic, new adventure in retailing.

Following seven years in purchasing, design and merchandising in the Big Apple, Lowenthal did what anyone with a zest for life would do: he bid adieu to Bloomingdale's and started the antique shop of his dreams, described at the beginning of this story. The rest, he might say, is harestory.

Understanding the mind set of shoppers from his rich (if not harey) Bloomingdale's days, Gary Lowenthal recognized early-on that talent keeps a growing company at the forefront of innovation. He enthusiastically sought artisans who might not otherwise have an opportunity to break into the national giftware limelight. Talented Gae Sharp brought her bean bag creations to Boyds, and soon other designers were on board. This happy mix has resulted in new introductions that have made a lot of people (bears, hares and moose) happy.

Inevitably, all this talent and enthusiasm resulted in national recognition and awards for the Boyds Collection. This started Gary thinking about how to better reach his audience. Because Boyds does not sell directly to collectors, a two-faceted plan was devised to reach both shop keepers and collectors. Toward that end, colorful brochures, the enticing catalog mentioned, even a newspaper publication, full of fun reading, are being published. These days, merchants and collectors feel very connected to Boyds via such lively publications.

If you pick up a copy of the *Boyds Bear Retail Inquirer*, prepare for anything! There could be a biography of a new designer, the inside story on a new series of collectible flags, retirement bulletins, updates on Boyds limited editions nominated for awards – even a classified section. Boyds fans from across the country looking for hard-to-find bears and hares hope to locate kindred souls willing to part with a special collectible; but something tells us this doesn't happen often.

In sum, it's a comfort to know that a company like The Boyds Collection exists in 1995. As today's world races quickly along, everyone has too much to do – and too little time to do it in! But at the center of the whirlwind, how delightful it is to know that somewhere, not far from Gettysburg, a family of folks dedicated to bringing a huge helping of yesterday into our world, exists.

They're the kind of people who take time to put a young artist's profile on the inside of their catalog...who make a point of calling their flags "big hummers" so no one mistakes their size...who quote Susan Powter's *Stop the Insanity* in their headlines...and who still believe a good bear is better than all the tranquilizers in the world.

The Boyds Collection Ltd.
Somethin' Ta Say Dept.
Gettysburg, PA 17325-4385

THE BRADFORD EXCHANGE

New Plate Artist Hall of Fame Marks the 100th Anniversary of Plate Collecting

For more than 20 years, The Bradford Exchange has played a unique dual role in the limited edition plate market, serving collectors interested in acquiring both new releases and back-issue plates. Just as significant, the firm displays almost 800 historic issues spanning 100 years at the Bradford Museum of Collector's Plates. Now – in celebration of the centennial of plate collecting – the Exchange has unveiled a special exhibit to be permanently housed at the Museum: the Plate Artist Hall of Fame.

Since its founding in 1973, The Bradford Exchange has become one of the world's most successful marketers of new collector's plates. Over the years, it has introduced many innovative series, continually expanding the boundaries of plate collecting in the process.

The marketing of newly issued, or primary market plates, however, is only one aspect of the services provided by the Exchange. The company also operates an organized, orderly secondary market where collectors can buy and sell back-issue plates. To eliminate the risk of buying and selling plates long-distance, The Bradford Exchange guarantees both ends of the trades it brokers. Only Bradford-recommended plates are eligible for trading on the Exchange.

Celebrating a Century of Collector's Plates

The year 1995 marked the 100th anniversary of limited edition collector's plates: an event commemorated by the Exchange with the introduction of a special Bradford Museum exhibit, "Collector's Plates: The First 100 Years." Located at museum headquarters in Niles, Illinois, the centennial retrospective, which is the first of its kind anywhere in the world, includes "Behind the Frozen Window" – the premier collector's plate issued in 1895 by the famed Danish porcelain house of Bing & Grøndahl.

On permanent exhibit at the Bradford Museum of Collector's Plates is the Plate Artist Hall of Fame, which debuted during the grand opening of the centennial exhibit in May 1995. In recognition of their outstanding contributions to the art of collector's plates, five individuals were named inaugural inductees. Honored artists Thomas Kinkade, Sandra Kuck and Lena Liu attended the grand opening along with Thomas Rockwell, representing his late father, Norman Rockwell. The fifth honoree was Charles Fracé.

Master wildlife artist Charles Fracé is especially known for his portrayals of big cats, such as the jaguar in "Mystic Realm."

Charles Fracé Wins Honors for Wildlife Art

Hall of Fame inductee Charles Fracé strives to find the soul in the animals he paints. "Each animal has an inner spiritual quality that makes it unique," Fracé says. "I try to portray that sense of personality, as well as the beauty of the animal."

Driven by reverence for the subjects he paints and enormous artistic talent, Fracé has attracted a large and devoted following among plate collectors since the 1990 release of his series for The Bradford Exchange entitled *Nature's Lovables*. Enthusiastic response to this and seven subsequent series – including *The World's Most Magnificent Cats, Soaring Majesty* and *Nature's Playmates* – has prompted his Hall of Fame selection.

What makes Fracé's work stand out from the rest? Says one admirer: "The fur is so lifelike you could fluff it." Says another, "When you look at a Fracé, it looks like the animal is going to walk right out of the print."

Since the earliest years of his wildlife art career, Fracé has been an active supporter of conservationist causes. In 1987, he established the Fracé Fund for Wildlife Preservation, which annually awards major grants to conservation organizations large and small, including wildlife parks and zoos. It is Fracé's hope that his art might also serve to prolong the existence of endangered animals by bringing people closer to the awesome – but fragile – beauty of nature. As the artist says, "I think I just try to paint what I feel, and hope that people feel the same thing I do when they view my work."

The "Painter of Light" Earns His Place in the Hall of Fame

A unifying element infuses all of the art of Thomas Kinkade: the luminous glow of light. His mastery of painting light – whether recreated on collector's plates, canvas lithographs or limited edition prints on paper – has earned him the title of the "Painter of Light." A student of the 19th century school of painters known as "Luminists," Kinkade has developed his own variations – what he thinks of as "more of a Romantic Realism, using light."

Kinkade's first collector's plate, issued in 1991, was the award-winning "Chandler's Cottage," part of the

An oval shape and a delicate filigree border add to the charm of "Lamplight Brooke" by Thomas Kinkade.

Garden Cottages of England series. Since then, his artwork has been featured on ten more plate series for The Bradford Exchange – including *Home for the Holidays*, *Home Is Where the Heart Is*, and *Thomas Kinkade's Lamplight Village* – winning additional awards along the way.

Kinkade's work is so captivating that, in just four short years, his plates have become some of the most popular and sought-after on the market. In recognition of his achievements, he has been named as one of the first Hall of Fame artists.

Another Award for the Much-Honored Sandra Kuck

One of the most popular artists in the collectibles field, Sandra Kuck adds Plate Artist Hall of Fame honors to her countless awards for limited edition plates, prints and dolls. Kuck celebrates childhood, family and friends in her warmly nostalgic works – presenting dreamy, yet realistic depictions of women and children that summon tender memories of childhood.

"Me First," Kuck's first plate, was issued in 1979. But it wasn't until the 1983 release of "Sunday Best" that she began to attract a large and devoted following among plate collectors worldwide. Since then, she has produced a succession of widely acclaimed and sought-after plate series, including *Sugar and Spice*, *Precious Angels*, and *Moments at Home*.

"My fantasy is to have lived at the turn of the century, and that's what I paint," Sandra Kuck confides. By her own definition, she is "hard working, disciplined, and compassionate." As she explains, "I try to put a single positive thought into each work I do, a message that reaffirms our culture's shared love of beauty and family."

"Moments of Caring" is a recent example of Sandra Kuck's talent for creating romantic portraits of children that recall Victorian times.

Nature Inspires the Gentle Art of "Hall of Famer" Lena Liu

Lena Liu's delicate, pastel-hued scenes of flowers, birds and butterflies have captivated plate collectors since the debut of her first series for The Bradford Exchange, *On Gossamer Wings*, in 1988. Her distinctive style is the result of her personal experience with both Eastern and Western cultures. An intriguing mix of romance and realism, it brought a new look to nature-themed collector's plates, combining highly detailed subjects with softly colored backgrounds.

Eight subsequent collections showcasing her work have been introduced in the past seven years, including *Floral Greetings from Lena Liu* and *Lena Liu's Hummingbird Treasury*. Along the way, she has earned legions of fans and numerous honors, including "Artist of the Year" in both the U.S. and Canada, and "Plate of the Year" in the U.S. These achievements gain full recognition through her induction into the Plate Artist Hall of Fame.

Raised in Taiwan, Liu was trained from a young age in traditional Oriental painting by Chinese masters. A United States resident since 1972, Liu found new inspiration for her work in the flora and fauna of North America. Even while painting Western subjects, however, she continues to employ many of the tools of conventional Chinese art – much to the delight of collectors.

Lena Liu's delicate, pastel-hued paintings of flowers, birds and butterflies have been recreated on plates such as "Circle of Love."

America's Favorite Artist Is Inducted Posthumously

On the 100th anniversary of his birth in 1994, Norman Rockwell still reigned as both the best-known and best-liked American artist, according to a survey. If Rockwell were alive, according to his son, Thomas, the unassuming illustrator would have been surprised by his continued popularity. "My father certainly didn't realize that there would be this amount of interest in his work years after he had done it. He painted for an immediate use – magazine covers and illustrations – and nobody thought there would be all of these secondary uses."

But there have been scores of such uses in recent decades, with Rockwell's famous magazine covers, advertising art and calendar illustrations inspiring hundreds of collector's plates and other limited editions. Norman Rockwell loved people. He was inspired by them, and it showed. So it's no wonder that people in turn love

Norman Rockwell's lively sense of humor is obvious in "Triple Self-Portrait," part of a series issued to commemorate the centennial of the artist's birth.

Norman Rockwell, earning him the first posthumous induction into the Plate Artist Hall of Fame.

Bradford Museum Invites Collectors' Visits

Almost 800 plates spanning the 100-year history of collector's plates beckon visitors to the Bradford Museum of Collector's Plates in Niles, Illinois. Open from 9 a.m. to 5 p.m. Monday through Friday and 10 a.m. to 4 p.m. Saturday and Sunday, the museum is closed for major holidays. Admission charge is $2.00 for adults, $1.00 for senior citizens, and free for children under 12.

As museum visitors, collectors will have the opportunity to review the rich history of 100 years of plate collecting, and enjoy tributes to the wonderful painters whose creations have earned them a place in the Plate Artist Hall of Fame.

The Bradford Exchange
9333 Milwaukee Avenue
Niles, IL 60714
(800) 323-5577

COLLECTORS' MUSEUM

The Bradford Museum of Collector's Plates
9333 Milwaukee Avenue
Niles, IL 60714
(708) 966-2770

Hours: Monday through Friday, 9 a.m. - 5 p.m.;
Saturday and Sunday, 10 am. - 4 p.m.

Admission Fee: $2.00 for adults; $1.00 for Senior Citizens;
Free for Children under 12 Years of Age.

The Bradford Museum of Collector's Plates houses almost 800 plates, spanning the 100-year history of collector's plates.

BRANDYWINE WOODCRAFTS, INC.

Captures the Heart of America

Collectors of miniature buildings from Brandywine Woodcrafts Inc. can expect a few twists to inspire their imaginations, rekindle their memories...and capture their hearts.

For starters there will be additions to Brandywine's *Country Lane* collection, created in 1995. *Country Lane* combines flat, wooden, detailed print backgrounds with cast resin hand-painted accents on the foregrounds to achieve a three-dimensional effect. At approximately 6.5" x 6.5", *Country Lane* houses are slightly larger than those in other Brandywine collections. They're complemented by Brandywine's line of accessories.

The initial installment of *Country Lane* featured the "Dairy Farm" with barn doors, haystack and pitchfork; the "Farm House," a traditional southern home with shady porch and clothesline laden with quilts for sale; the "Country School," based on a rural Virginia elementary school including its own school bus; the "Berry Farm," with "berry special crafts;" and the "General Store," offering cider, jelly, flour and farm supplies.

Designs for new *Country Lane* houses are kept secret until release time, but collectors can expect them to retain the collection's focus on the nostalgic sights and activities from the old-time farm communities that still dot the American landscape.

Another Brandywine focus is the company's personalization service, which allows collectors to add a unique touch to buildings that hold special meaning for them. Although Brandywine has been offering personalization for several years, some collectors aren't aware of how they can take advantage of it to build value and diversity for their own collections, or to add a special touch to gifts.

The "Hometown School" is one of more than 50 creations in Brandywine's Hometown *collection.*

Any buildings from Brandywine's *Country Lane*, *Hometown* and *Downtown USA* collections can be personalized to reflect family names and interests, historic places and events, and even whimsy. For example, the *Country Lane* "General Store" might be personalized to recall the store down the road from Grandma's Farm. The *Hometown* "Antiques Shop" can be customized to carry the name of a collector's favorite shopping spot. And the *Downtown USA* "Train Station" might bear the name of a station remembered from a childhood hometown.

Personalization is done by hand with brush and acrylic paint. Many dealers personalize Brandywine products in their shops, while others prefer to have it accomplished at the company's manufacturing facility.

1996 promises to be the year that Brandywine collectors in the Midwest and West see the results of their requests for increased product availability, as the company continues to add shops to its roster of dealers. Additionally, the company is building a computerized database of collectors to help determine other means of serving its customers.

"Mercy Drive," from Brandywine's Downtown USA *collection, honors people in the medical professions.*

"We Can Make It Ourselves"

Marlene Dragar Whiting of Yorktown, Virginia, Brandywine's founder, continues to design and handpaint the originals from which all Brandywine products are made. Hers is an eye for detail that's rarely matched in Americana.

"We can make it ourselves," was the motto in the Dragar household in Pittsburgh, Pennsylvania, when Marlene was growing up. Her mother Sophie taught her to sew, knit and crochet, and, assuming that anyone could accomplish intricate handwork, Marlene studied organic chemistry and English in college.

It was only after marrying Air Force pilot Truman C. Whiting Jr. and finding herself coping with frequent moves and separations that Marlene became hooked on tole painting. To afford classes, she designed appliqued infant quilts, seat covers, burp cloths and bibs in Phoenix, Arizona.

When Truman later served in Iran, quilt supplies weren't available in local bazaars, so Marlene designed gingerbread house kits and macramé items handcrafted with local supplies. The Shah was expelled in 1979, and with him the Whitings and their young son and daughter. It was back to Phoenix and a job teaching tole painting, and then to Yorktown, where the humid climate foiled an attempt at oil painting.

To solve this problem, Marlene invested $50.00 in acrylics and brushes and painted wooden cutouts of cows, ducks and hearts. Miniature buildings were soon to follow.

Brandywine's "Halloween House," from the Treasured Times *collection, is one of several miniature houses that celebrates the occasions close to the heart.*

"I've always been fascinated with the little shops, businesses and homes that small towns have in common," Marlene says. "From my childhood I remember how the shops were operated by friends and family. These memories stick with you forever, and they're the ones I incorporate into our buildings."

Handmade, from the Beginning

Brandywine began on a kitchen table. It was 1981 when Marlene took a basketfull of her homemade folk art to a gift shop in historic Hilton Village, Virginia. These were the wooden hearts and such that Truman had cut with a band saw and that she hand-painted.

The owner was busy, so Marlene left the basket on the floor while she browsed. Moments later, the owner ran up. Customers had seen the basket and wanted to buy everything in it.

Soon, Marlene was commissioned to make miniature buildings based on those in Hilton Village. Another order came from Colonial Williamsburg (today Brandywine is their official miniature house builder), and Brandywine Woodcrafts Inc. was off and running.

The company is still based in Yorktown, but it has outgrown the kitchen table – and the house, and the garage, and its first manufacturing facility. In 14 years, Brandywine has gone from two to 20 employees and from one to 22 home-based artisans. Sales have doubled every year since 1992, and in 1994 the company moved into a new 9,400 square foot facility.

Over the years, one thing hasn't changed: the company's family outlook. Truman was appointed president/CEO of Brandywine in 1994, after a 30-year aviation career.

Something for Every Collector

Brandywine Woodcrafts Inc. has two

The "Dairy Farm" and other three-dimensional miniature houses from Brandywine's new Country Lane *collection are quickly becoming collector favorites.*

divisions: Brandywine Collectibles and Brandywine Woodcrafts.

The Brandywine Collectibles Division produces cast resin hand-painted buildings and accessories. Marlene sculpts the original of every cast piece from clay. After the original has been baked, a mold is made from it and cast in virtually indestructible resin. Each is then sanded and painted completely by hand. No silk-screening is involved.

Brandywine Collectibles are historic, generic and whimsical in nature.

Historic collections include *Williamsburg and Yorktown, Virginia; Old Salem, North Carolina; Seymour, Indiana; and Barnesville, Ohio,* as well as *Patriots* and *Custom* renditions. On the back of these buildings, collectors find labels providing historic information.

Generic buildings are in two collections, *Treasured Times* and *Hometown.*

Treasured Times celebrates the happy moments with such buildings as the "Birthday Houses," "New Baby Houses," "Mother's Day Houses," "Happy Valentine's Day House" and the "Halloween House." Each is a collectible, as designs are limited to production of 750 pieces.

Hometown is perhaps the most popular of the cast resin lines. The *Hometown* series includes nostalgic representations of buildings from small towns across our country, from the "General Store" to the "Fire Company" to the "Dress Shop" to the "Brick Church" – more than 50 so far. Brandywine introduces a new *Hometown* series every six months to coincide with major gift show cycles, and retires each *Hometown* series after two years on the market.

In the way of whimsy, Brandywine offers the *North Pole* collection, replete with the "Claus Haus," "Candy Cane Factory," "Sugarplum Bakery," "Elf Club" and a dozen other visions from everyone's favorite northern locale.

Miniature buildings in the *Treasured Times* and *Hometown* collections are individually numbered in sequence and hand-signed by Marlene. All cast pieces are shipped in distinctive tote boxes and come with a postcard that collectors can send, in order to receive a free Certificate of Authenticity and register their purchase.

To accompany these buildings, Brandywine offers some 20 accessories, such as trees, carts, wagons and even a snowman.

Williamsburg and other picturesque locales are represented in Brandywine's various historic collections.

Handpainted Look, Not Price

The Brandywine Woodcrafts Division produces wooden miniature buildings in a group called *Downtown USA*. *Downtown USA* pieces are flat, and each is made by affixing a highly-detailed print of Marlene's original painting to the wood. Before cutting and finishing, each print is covered with a clear "environmentally-friendly mystery substance," which protects it. The result is a hand-painted look without a hand-painted price.

Downtown USA includes more than 70 designs, available in individual pieces or linked together in 16 street scenes, each containing four buildings and a street sign on a single piece of wood. Brandywine will even build a unique street scene using a customer's favorite four buildings and street sign, personalized as requested.

Mercy Drive, one of the newest street scenes, honors those in the medical professions, with the "Optical Shop," "Family Practice," "General Hospital" and "Dentistry." *Second Street*, another recent addition, features the "Police Station," "Car Care Garage" and "Diner."

Downtown USA pieces are rapidly becoming favorites for their attractive pricing, tremendous detail and personalized signs.

Custom Work Recreates History

Brandywine recently completed special designs of The Ryman Auditorium in Nashville, Tennessee; the famous Lynchburg, Tennessee, Hardware & General Store; the Abingdon, Virginia, Barter Theatre; and the Maryland Statehouse, among others. Collectors can call Brandywine to find out how to purchase those special pieces.

Brandywine Woodcrafts
104 Greene Drive
Yorktown, VA 23692-4800
(804) 898-5031
Fax (804) 898-6895

BYERS' CHOICE LTD.

Carolers Share the Christmas Spirit for All Seasons

Collectors are welcome to visit the Byers' Choice Christmas Gallery in Bucks County, Pennsylvania, where visitors can enjoy seeing the first figurines, production process and displays of more than 400 Carolers in beautiful winter settings. At the center's grand opening in 1994, it was a dream come true for (left to right) Jeff Byers, Bob Byers, Sr., Joyce Byers and Bob Byers, Jr.

In Bucks County, Pennsylvania, Joyce and Bob Byers celebrate Christmas all year round. There's lampposts flickering on cobblestone streets, shop windows brimming with toys, and musicians performing on one street corner and a Salvation Army band on the other. There's a postman delivering holiday cards, students walking to their school house, a children's Nativity pageant at a country church, skaters sliding across a frozen mill pond, and Santa's workshop filled ceiling high with toys.

From the beloved Charles Dickens' novel *A Christmas Carol,* there's the Cratchit family in their humble home, while Scrooge wanders throughout the village. Of course, Carolers are singing everywhere you look.

These winter wonderland scenes greet Joyce and Bob as they go to work every day at Byers' Choice Ltd., which they built on the spirit of Christmas. For nearly two decades, the Byers have been creating a joyous choir of limited edition Caroler figurines that rekindle days gone by and the gentle beauty of the holiday season. From a Victorian Mrs. Claus to a man roasting chestnuts, each has its own personality and story to share.

Located in the company's Chalfont, Pennsylvania, production facility is the Byers' Choice Christmas Gallery, which opened in 1994 to display more than 400 figurines in various winter vignettes. Collectors are invited to stop by the gallery, where they learn the history of the Carolers and see firsthand the reason why these singing characters have found a special place in the hearts of collectors around the world.

Charles Dickens and Christmas Inspire First Caroler Figurines

During a trip to London in the 1960s, Joyce and Bob were browsing in an antique shop when they spotted a unique series of porcelain figures that appeared to step right from the pages of a Charles Dickens' tale. The timeless pieces captured the warm, traditional flavor of 19th century England.

When she returned home, Joyce came across a set of papier-maché choir figures that reminded her of the spirit of Christmas. While debating whether or not to purchase these as gifts, she was suddenly struck by a clever idea. She could create caroling figures that combine the feeling of 19th century England *and* Christmas.

An amateur artist with a degree in fashion design, Joyce began working on the project using materials she had at home: plaster, papier-maché, wire, paint and stacks of assorted fabrics. She was already adept at making crafts, which she enjoyed seeing come to life right before her eyes. Dressed in wintertime attire, each figurine opened its rounded mouth to sing favorite Christmas songs – just like carolers who go door to door during the holiday season. Joyce's first figurines reminded her of the classic characters from *A Christmas Carol,* so she simply called them The Carolers.

Byers' Choice Reaches New Markets

Family members adored The Carolers. Christmas shopping for Joyce soon became much easier, as many of the Byers' friends and relatives began asking for the figurines as gifts. A neighbor suggested taking the figurines to craft and antique shows, where they sold out quickly and word spread about Joyce's delightful creations. At one show, a New York display

This traditional grouping of Carolers shows the Victorian beauty and harmony of the Byers' Choice Ltd. line. Led by a matronly conductor, each child and adult figurine looks upward and sings out with joy.

All bundled up for a wintry day, this caroling couple happily sings from their wooden sleigh. They're ready to deliver the holiday spirit and a basket of gifts.

company official told Bob that his firm would be interested in buying figurines if they could be enlarged and altered according to the needs of its customers. Joyce rose to the challenge, thus sealing the fate of Byers' Choice Ltd.

Over the next years, Joyce, Bob and their two sons spent much of each autumn making figurines for friends, craft fairs, a few stores and the display company. As the demand grew, the family became busier in other seasons. After The Carolers began overtaking the Byers' dining room, they converted their garage to a workshop. In 1981, with the addition of full-time helpers, the family hobby was incorporated with Bob and Joyce officially casting their lot with the Carolers.

A Collectible Business That's All in the Family

Today, Byers' Choice Ltd. is still a family business that hires skilled handcrafters and professionally trained artists. In order to keep up with all the orders, the Byers had to make some changes in both the manufacturing process and, to a limited extent, the appearance of the figurines. While today's Carolers are very different from those produced in the early years, almost everyone agrees that the current look captures the Dickensian Christmas spirit even better.

Joyce still sculpts all of the faces and designs most of the clothing for each Caroler. Meanwhile, Bob tends to the financial and administrative side of the business. He also directs the company's extensive charitable giving to a host of local, national and international concerns. In 1987, son Robert took on the job of overseeing the figurine production process. Son Jeffrey joined the family business in 1990 as marketing manager. The company and its 150 employees moved into a larger facility in 1994. With a lot of hard work and imagination, Bob and Joyce have watched their hobby grow into a successful family business dedicated to serving the customer and, through their philanthropy, the community.

A Family Album of Carolers

The family of Caroler figurines gets better each year and many of the older ones have become valuable collectors' items. Within the collection, there are various series and styles for everyone to enjoy. The *Traditional Carolers* portray men and women, boys and girls, and grandmothers and grandfathers dressed in wools, felts and plaids. They hold everything from scrolls and wreaths to muffs and snowballs. Each of the figurines is designed with a matching partner and is produced in an edition of 100 pieces.

The *Victorian Carolers* wear elegant satins, velvets, lace and furs. These are also produced in pairs limited to 100 of each design. *Victorian Mothers* pushing prams or helping their toddlers learn to walk have also been created.

In 1992, Joyce created the first *Salvation Army* figurine to celebrate the season of giving. A new piece is introduced annually with a portion of the proceeds benefitting the work of the agency.

In 1983, Joyce began working on a series of Caroler figurines based on *A Christmas Carol*. "Scrooge" in his nightgown was the first piece and one or two figures were added each year for the next decade. First and second editions were produced. Now the cast of characters – from the "Fezziwigs" to "Marley's Ghost" – is complete. All but a few second edition pieces have been retired. With the close of the *Christmas Carol*, Joyce then began work on *The Nutcracker Suite* series in 1993. The figurines, which began with "Marie," are based on the German tale written by E.T.A. Hoffman that inspired Tchaikovsky to write his magical Christmas ballet.

The *Cries of London* series recreates the 19th century street vendors who often chanted catchy songs to get their customers' attention. Each year, Joyce designs a new figurine in the series, and the previous year's piece is retired.

In addition to a variety of Santas from around the world, Mrs. Claus and other holiday characters, Byers' Choice also offers specialty figurines, including choir directors, postmen, parsons and school children.

These two Carolers celebrate the season of sharing and caring as well as the dedicated work of the Salvation Army and its volunteers. Since 1992, Byers' Choice has introduced an annual Salvation Army *figurine with part of the proceeds benefitting the agency.*

Sitting down at a piano, "Louise" leads children in a chorus of Christmas songs. "Marie," the first in The Nutcracker Suite *series, holds a wooden nutcracker while "Fritz" rides a stick horse. The figurines are inspired by the magical Christmas ballet based on E.T.A. Hoffman's book.*

Gallery Welcomes Collectors to Christmas at Byers' Choice

The Byers' Choice Christmas Gallery displays many Carolers from the past and present. Joyce and Bob always received many requests from collectors to tour the place where The Carolers are made, but the old facility wasn't set up to handle this activity. When the blueprints were drawn for the new Byers' Choice building, a special wing was conceived and dedicated to collectors. This visitors' center features scenes where collectors and Christmas aficionados can view The Carolers strolling among the streets of a London-like city, acting out roles in *A Christmas Carol* and much more.

Visitors can also see Joyce's very first Carolers, retired pieces, a video of the company's history, and an observation deck overlooking the production floor.

A rotating selection of 200 Carolers, as well as other Christmas-related gifts, are sold at the Emporium. As one Caroler fan said: "It is indeed Christmas 365 days a year at Byers' Choice." The gallery is open to the public Monday through Saturday from 10 a.m. to 4 p.m. It is closed holidays and for the month of January. For information and directions, call (215) 822-0150.

"Caroler Chronicle" Keeps Collectors Up To Date

From the beginning, Byers' Choice has received wonderful letters from fans telling how much the Caroler figurines mean to them. An overwhelming number of questions prompted the company to publish the "Caroler Chronicle," a color newsletter published three times a year. The "Caroler Chronicle" highlights stories behind various figurines, upcoming special events or introductions, and a chronological index of characters and the years of production.

Byers' Choice Ltd.
P.O. Box 158
Chalfont, PA 18914
(215) 822-6700
Fax (215) 822-3847

COLLECTORS' MUSEUM

Byers' Choice Christmas Gallery & Emporium
4355 County Line Rd.
Chalfont, PA 18914
(215) 822-0150

Hours: Monday through Saturday, 10 a.m.-4 p.m. Closed Sundays, Holidays and in January.

Admission Fee: None

Visitors to the Byers' Choice Christmas Gallery enjoy a self-guided tour through the museum which displays old and new Caroler® figurines. They can also see a video of the company's history and view the production floor from an observation deck. Selected gifts and caroling figures are sold at the Emporium.

CAIN STUDIOS

Rick Cain's "Multi Imagery" Technique Captivates Collectors Who Are Intrigued by the Natural World

"I work in what I call multi imagery: a wolf might have several other small wolves hidden from immediate view just waiting to be discovered," says Rick Cain, the guiding light behind the Gainesville, Florida-based Cain Studios.

"I am ever changing as a part of the human experience, and so my art follows my changes. Doing wildlife sculpture is one way of communicating with a large audience on common ground," Cain continues.

"Cain Studios was started as a way to get my art to a wider audience by way of cast limited editions. Our company is composed of people from many walks of life who work according to a team philosophy – taking care of their work in a harmonious manner knowing each piece created is the most important piece they touch, to its ultimate purchaser.

"Through these wildlife sculptures, we celebrate the creation of creatures great and small who share the world with us. When I sculpt, I use nature's abstraction, nature's call for us to identify with her. This comes through in wood shapes, stone fragments of a mountain, or other materials as they present themselves to me."

An Artist from Earliest Childhood

At an age when most boys are set on becoming astronauts or firemen or baseball players, Rick Cain had already determined that he would be an artist. Born in an Air Force Base hospital in Tucson, Arizona, Cain found it necessary to adjust to frequent moves and school changes required of his military family. Young Rick found his security and strength in his artistic ability.

"My parents were bent on my being anything other than an artist," Cain recalls. "All I wanted to be was an artist. At the age of eight I announced, 'I will be a famous artist someday.' Wow! It happened!"

The talented youth would surprise (and sometimes frustrate) his teachers and his parents as he relentlessly pursued his goal. At a tender age, he began teaching himself to be an artist. Every day he would practice, mastering the techniques of pencil drawing, for instance – sketching forms, giving them depth and dimension – studying human and animal anatomy, and training in matters of precision and detail until it all flowed naturally for him.

At the age of 20, Rick Cain discovered wood as an art medium. Yet he did not limit himself to creating designs in the wood – he soon moved on to releasing the shapes and images inherent in the wood itself. He was living in Florida now, and the gnarled and weathered tropical hardwoods revealed their personalities in his hands as he brought out wizened old men's faces and graceful human and animal forms.

Within months after starting to sculpt in wood, Cain was showing at his first art exhibit. Since then his work has been in hundreds of juried art shows and exhibitions. He has been honored with numerous awards, including a First Place in the Canadian International Woodcarving Exhibition. What's more, Cain has been selected to participate in the New York International Sculpture Fair and the Walt Disney Festival of the Masters.

Another important recognition for Cain is his membership in the National Museum and Gallery Registration Association. In addition, Cain's original works, as well as his limited edition sculptures, hold places of prestige in private and public collections throughout the world.

A Philosopher-Artist Shares His World View

Rick Cain is a deeply introspective person who examines his own motivations and feelings as thoroughly as he studies the wood he sculpts. He firmly believes that his talent is a gift that he is charged with using to the fullest. He asks himself, "Why do people buy my art? Do they collect wolves or wildlife, and my work happens to fit that category? Sometimes, of course, yes, but most people buy my work because it speaks to them on a creative level. They recognize and respond to the Creative Force behind the work and, guess what? That's not me!

"Oh, yes, I carve each original myself, but I am not creativity. I am a vehicle, a medium. I believe that I am a caretaker of a talent given to me by the grace of God – that universal principle that orders chaos, and created that, too!"

As for his method of work, Cain explains: "I sit and sit, studying wood – its knots, bends, curves, its color, its smell. All these things are a joy to me – a collection of associated peaceful

"Fire and Ice," measuring 17-1/2"H x 8-1/2"W x 10-1/2"D, is one of the most dramatic wolf sculptures Rick Cain has carved.

"Transcendental White Wolf" is one of a pair of sculptures carved in 1995. It's companion piece is entitled "Transcendental Grey Wolf."

feelings that get me to the place in me that becomes Zen meditation."

Rick Cain's Goal Is to Serve the Collector

Cain believes he has gained considerable insight into those who love his work by watching them as they discover his art. "Where is the excitement in finding that new collectible," he asks himself. "Is it in that object you see? No, that feeling, that warmth is inside of you. That thing is just an object. Your viewing it is what makes the collectible beautiful.

"What is collectible? Something you hold dear and near...something precious to your heart? Memories of love, friends, good times and sometimes objects – things we cherish. So, yes, my art is collectible and is sold in all 50 United States, I'm proud to say, and in several international markets."

An Overview of the Creations from Cain Studios

Sleek shore birds, bold eagles, noble Native Americans and elegant fantasy figures combine with many other natural and imaginative subjects to make up the diverse collections of Cain Studios Inc. While most of Rick Cain's works are meant as decorative sculpture, he sometimes adds a functional touch: pieces like "The Hatchling," "Innerview," and "Box Turtle" serve as boxes for small treasures.

Many of Cain's limited edition pieces already have sold out and are available only on the secondary market. But this prolific artist continues to add new works to the collection on a regular basis.

One particularly popular collection has the arctic wolf as its focus. The first piece was the "Arctic Moon." This beautiful white and pastel sculpture sold out in a very short time. Rick Cain has received letters from devoted collectors telling him how the "Arctic Moon" touched them in a special way.

Immediately following the sell out of "Arctic Moon," Rick created "Arctic Son." This piece is a beautiful companion piece to the "Arctic Moon." The demand was so great for another arctic wolf that this piece was introduced as a special Christmas sculpture. "Arctic Son" sold out in a record four days.

In 1994, Rick Cain Studios introduced "Midnight Son," the third piece in the *Arctic Wolf* series. "Midnight Son" was created for members of the Rick Cain Studios' Collectors Guild and was only available during the calendar year of 1994. 1,225 pieces were created in this time-limited edition, and now "Midnight Son" is only available on the secondary market.

During 1995 Rick Cain continued to capture the spirit and elegance of the North American wolf. One piece, "Fire and Ice" has become one of Rick's signature works. "Fire and Ice" is a stunning representation of the wolf in its two major guises-arctic and continental. On the front, a serene wolf stares past the viewer with the calm placid glare of a magnificent animal that is one with its environment. On the reverse, the animal's fur has adapted for the long, snowy winter; and his eyes appear hooded, as he begins to contemplate the long struggle for survival ahead until spring. This is an absolute must for wolf devotees and followers of Rick Cain's career.

Rick Cain also carved a pair of sculptures, "Transcendental White Wolf" and "Transcendental Grey Wolf," that meld the bust of a wolf with the natural flow of a swirling piece of North Carolina hardwood. Again, they are painted to represent the wolf in its two main colorings on the North American continent.

Growing as an artist and a person, Rick continues to expand his knowledge and talent. He intensively studied the wolf's anatomy in 1994 and feels that he is closer to capturing the true essence of this magnificent species.

Another theme Rick Cain has followed over the years is revealing the grace and beauty of the creatures of the seas. In 1995, he released "Mergence," a humpback whale riding on the crest of a wave, offset by the earth. As the whales continue their remarkable return from the edge of extinction, Rick Cain has captured the essence of the species and its precarious balance with the earth.

An Opportunity to Join the Rick Cain Studios Collectors Guild

1995 has been designated "The Year of the Elephant" at Rick Cain Studios. The 1995 exclusive Rick Cain Collectors Guild Membership Sculpture is "Family Tree," 10"H x 10"W x 8"D, a work that will be treasured by collectors throughout their lifetime. A hauntingly beautiful piece; several elephants merge and commingle in one spectrum – never completely in focus, never completely disappearing.

For 1995, the benefits for Guild Membership have increased dramatically. Collectors receive quarterly updates on the status of all pieces in the Rick Cain line, whether actively in production or on the secondary market. In addition, collectors receive frequent updates on new releases, as well as any special information about Rick and the Studio. Also, included is a T-shirt in this year's membership package, along with the variety of notecards, posters and stickers traditionally a part of the Guild Membership. Available immediately, serious collectors of Rick Cain's sculpture, as well as new admirers, can order their kit through a local dealer or call the Studio at 1-800-535-3949 for more information. Membership dues for 1995 are $35.00.

Rick Cain Studios
619 S. Main St.
Gainesville, FL 32601
(800) 535-3949
Fax (904) 377-7038

"Mergence" is an exciting depiction of a humpback whale in balance with the earth. It measures 14"H x 14"W x 5-1/2"D.

COLLECTORS' CLUB

Rick Cain Studios Collectors Guild
619 S. Main St.
Gainesville, FL 32601
(800) 535-3949

Annual Dues: $35.00
Club Year: Anniversary of Sign-Up Date

Benefits:
- Membership Kit: T-Shirt, Notecards, Posters, Stickers and Sculpture Index
- Opportunity to Purchase Members-Only Sculpture
- Quarterly Newsletter
- Free Registration of All Sculptures Purchased

CALABAR CREATIONS

Limited Edition Collectibles Celebrate a Colorful World Between Dreams and Reality

Tony Van and his company Character Collectibles were already well-established in the giftware industry when he met artist Pete Apsit. But it was a meeting that would put a new face – and eventually a new name – on Van's company.

The pair teamed up to introduce Pete's "critters" made out of a material known as hydrostone, which gave the animals a warm, country charm. Three years later, Character Collectibles had tripled the number of items in its line that quickly extended far beyond the company's original country themes. The designs, which ranged from humorous pigs to whimsical cows, established a different direction for Character Collectibles, signaling the time to branch out and expand its horizons. Calabar Creations was born. As its motto says: In the Land of Calabar Colorful Art Life And Beauty Are Raised.

All aboard the "Pigmobile" for a trip filled with fun and adventure. From the Pig Hollow™ *series created by artist Pete Apsit, this 3" figurine takes the whimsical pigs off the farm and into town.*

Creations from the Heart and Hands of Pete Apsit

With a collectibles career spanning 25 years and a host of admiring collectors, Pete Apsit is one of today's most renowned sculptors. His new era of figurines for Calabar Creations dawns with what he and Tony Van call "a tribute to all American children." Each figurine recognizes the fact that children and animals hold a special place in everyone's heart.

From childhood photographs snapped by the father of Art Director Danielle Aphessetche, the Daddy's Girl™ *series captures an innocent picture of youth. "Spring Harvest" features Danielle proudly holding a freshly cut bouquet of flowers.*

Apsit's creations reflect his California attitude – the belief that life is a gift to be enjoyed. Apsit believes that through the eyes of children he can bring home a message that little ones allow us to see life unblemished by stress and complications.

Apsit's children are not "sweet little sophisticated darlings" impeccably dressed and well-mannered. Instead, they belong to a fresh, free "kid society" where innocence prevails, but misbehavior inevitably occurs. It's a place where old clothes sure feel better than Sunday best and where friends, including animals, are the most precious gifts on earth. Apsit's children are unencumbered by class barriers, racial prejudice and adult inhibitions. With Apsit's careful workmanship, the expressions on each figurine tell a story without saying a word. "If it's a cute type of thing with expression in its face and it's telling a story, people will collect it," says Apsit, who finds inspiration from his children and grandchildren. "When children do something really well, they get such a proud look on their faces. That's why expression is the most important part of a piece. If it doesn't have expression, you've missed it."

Working in a studio near his home in Bakersfield, California, Apsit sculpts next to a big window listening to talk radio or classical music. "I work quite fast. I sit down, and within five minutes I have an idea," he says. "I don't know what a piece will look like until I'm done."

New Series Welcome Children and Animals

Apsit's *Little Farmers*, which shows the joy of rural life on a farm, was the first series that established Calabar Creations in the limited edition market. Today, Apsit is constantly designing new series, each with its own fine details, meaning, innocence, humor or memories.

Angelic Pigasus™ features golden winged pigs limited in time not quantity. The first retirement was "Anna" in June 1995. Every six months thereafter, one more cold-cast porcelain pig will be retired to make room in the line for more introductions.

The *Little Professionals™* series shows children trying different occupations on for size. There's "Little Red" struggling with a firehose, "Little Florence" wrapping bandages around her friend, "Little Miss Market" selling lemonade and "Little Angelo" painting with her palette and brush.

Junior Murphy's Law™ is a comical look into the tried-and-true philosophy of, "If something can go wrong, it will." The figurines, which are limited to 5,000 pieces, portray hard-luck kids doing everything from tossing pizza dough on their heads to watching a puppy steal hot dog links.

Days of Innocence™ launched with three figurines that portray the tender moments of childhood. "To Grandma's," "A Letter From Grandma" and "Dear God" are each limited in edition to 5,000. *Kiti Kondo™* is a special home for kittens who happily sit for an afternoon tea.

Introductions Added to Favorite Series

Known as the landmark collection of Calabar Creations, the *Yesterday's Friends™* series continues adding to its wonderful troupe of happy youngsters. In 1995, an all-star team of three boys joined the collection in the figurines titled "Fly High," "Pop Up!" and "Out!" The boys enjoy America's favorite pastime – caring more about having fun than winning or losing the game. The line also includes the friends reading books, playing basketball, dressing up like an Indian chief, washing a pig and gliding along on a soap box scooter.

The ever popular *Angelic Pigasus* series welcomes two new additions, a charming signature piece and "Allegria," with arms spread wide and a heavenly glance. This figurine would make believers of anyone that pigs can fly!

Listen closely and imagine soulful, spirited music melting through the air. The *Jazzy Kids* have arrived to join the *Little Professionals* series. Coaxed from clay by the skilled hands of Pete Apsit, this joyful Dixieland quintet exists to serenade you with all their heart and soul. "Little Count" sets melody, "Little Gypsy" keeps time on the tambourine, "Little Desi" beats the bongos, "Little Ringo" plays his drum, and "Little Louis" blares away on trumpet.

Calabar's newest series is the *Grandpions™*, the grand champions of "have beens" and "wannabes." This humorous collection of dwarfed professionals, sportsmen and hobbyists are sure to unwrinkle many grumpy faces. From the faithful fireman "Old Red" to the doughnut-eating police officer "The Finest," everyone knows someone who looks and acts like a *Grandpion*!

Apsit also created *Daddy's Girl*, which is inspired by old photographs found in the family albums of Calabar Creations Art Director Danielle Aphessetche. As an avid photographer, Danielle's father used his hobby to capture the precious moments of his daughter's childhood. Now Apsit has turned these photographic memories into three-dimensional figurines for all to recall special days gone by. Recent introductions include "Spring Harvest" with Danielle holding a bunch of colorful flowers and "Summer" finding Danielle sitting on a fence post. In "Peek-a-Boo," the little girl looks at the world from upside down.

In keeping with his fascination for swines, Apsit has added more to the fun-loving family of *Pig Hollow*. The pigs are now off the farm and heading on a camping trip in their "Pigmobile." "Pendelton" is pitching the tent, "Pot Belly" is cooking dinner over the fire, "Pepin" is eating watermelon and "Pilar" is scrubbing the clothes on a washboard. The pigs also found a new home in a beautiful castle, which is bustling with activity. "Prude" watches television in the living room, "Pristine Pig" makes sure everything is spotless in the bathroom, "Prof" reads a book to "Plopsy," and "Pig Kahuna" lounges on the sofa.

Listen closely and imagine soulful, spirited music melting through the air ... the Jazzy Kids *have arrived! Coaxed from clay by the skilled hands of Pete Apsit, this joyful Dixieland quintet exists to serenade you with all their heart and soul.*

It's off to grandmother's house for this little girl, who has her overstuffed suitcase, teddy bear and a special gift ready for the trip. "To Grandma's" is a heartwarming introduction to the Days of Innocence™ *series that shows the softer side of childhood.*

Classic Series Still Charm Collectors

Although some lines don't have any new introductions, they are still available for collectors to enjoy and complete their collections. Undoubtedly inspired by Apsit's first bad encounter with the serious game of golf, *Tee Club™* hits the course with a group of grouchy old men showing those true-to-life expressions on the

From the Angelic Pigasus *series created by sculptor Pete Apsit, "Allegria" with arms spread wide and a heavenly glance would make believers of anyone that pigs can fly!*

green. There's golfers like "TEEd-off" who broke his club and "Prac-TEEs" with a pail of golf balls.

As a seasonal greeting, Apsit created *Santa Venture™*, which shows another side of St. Nick. Santa personally tests the toys, makes sure even the smallest animals receive a Christmas gift, takes a rest along his delivery route and hitches up a donkey when his reindeer go on strike. These moments and others open everyone's eyes to Santa's colorful personality and adventures.

Red Moon Children™, created by western artist Richard Myer, centers on memories of when the West was still open, and young Americans of the frontier were blessed with an unclouded view of the world. Each limited edition figurine, which comes with a miniature book, reflects an atmosphere of peace, calm and simplicity.

Personal Attention to Detail

Each Calabar Creations work begins as a clay original designed by the artist. The company's art department then uses this piece as a master for producing a mold. The master is poured from a hard-cast material able to withstand the rigors of many mold formings. Several masters are created because a production mold rapidly loses its ability to reproduce intricate details and variety in texture – both of which are Calabar Creation trademarks.

At this stage, unpainted samples called "whites" are sent to Danielle Aphessetche, the company's art director and colorist. She chooses the colors for the piece and paints the "white" prototype. The artisans in the factory pour and cure the figurines, which are then meticulously cleaned and polished. The painter duplicates the original color scheme. After inspection, each piece receives its brass registration plaque. Finally, the figurine is ready to be gift boxed and shipped to stores for collectors.

A Commitment to Excellence and Beauty

The commitment of Calabar Creations is to offer figurines that will give pleasure both to the eyes and the soul; works of art that will touch a child's curiosity and awaken the sleeping child in all adults. Calabar Creations strives to portray a world between dreamland and reality...a land where children are wise and adults are allowed to dream...a special corner of the world filled with laughter and rainbows. After all, in the land of CALABAR: Colorful Art Life And Beauty Are Raised.

Meet "Old Red" from The Grandpions, *a new collection by Calabar Creations. This faithful fighter of fires is just one of 20 in the lovable collection sculpted by Pete Apsit. This humorous collection of dwarfed professionals, sportsmen and hobbyists are sure to unwrinkle many grumpy faces.*

Calabar Creations
1941 S. Vineyard
Ontario, CA 91761
(909) 930-9978
Fax (909) 930-9928

CAST ART INDUSTRIES, INC.

Bringing Figurines to Collectors from a Variety of Artists

Picture Perfect" is one of the limited edition Dreamsicles. *So far, all of the retired limited editions have increased in value on the secondary market.*

Just over four years ago, California-based Cast Art Industries took the collectible gift market by storm with the introduction of the now-popular *Dreamsicles®* collection. Since that time, the company has produced the works of additional talented artists representing a wide range of styles and subjects. The result is an exciting array of collectible figurines certain to please any collector.

Cast Art Industries was founded in December 1990 by Scott Sherman, Frank Colapinto and Gary Barsellotti, three friends with more than 50 years of combined experience in the gift industry. Sherman was formerly a Florida corporate president, who, despite his youth, had substantial experience in administration and marketing. Colapinto, a long time resident of California, has spent most of his career building a national sales force in the gift industry. Barsellotti, Italian-born and trained, is an expert in the manufacturing of fine quality figurines.

The company began as a manufacturer, securing contracts to produce decorative boxes, figurines, lamps and souvenir items for other companies. Within a few months, Cast Art signed exclusive contracts with independent artists and was producing and selling its own product lines. The success of the designs, and the consistent high quality of the reproductions, quickly caused the collecting world to take notice and made Cast Art one of the fastest-growing companies in the industry.

The *Dreamsicles®* Phenomenon

In March 1991, Cast Art introduced *Dreamsicles®*, a group of 31 adorable cherub and animal figurines designed by artist Kristin Haynes. Kristin's fresh approach to a timeless subject was an instant hit with the gift-buying public, and *Dreamsicles* rapidly became one of the most popular new lines in the world of collectibles.

The collection now numbers over 250 designs and includes animals, holiday pieces, Christmas ornaments, and a birthday collection in addition to a growing variety of cherubs. All are hand-cast and hand-painted, then decorated with dried flowers to assure that no two are ever exactly alike.

Within one year, the *Dreamsicles* line received national recognition as the Best Selling New Category at the Gift Creations Concepts (GCC) industry show in Minneapolis. In addition, *Dreamsicles* has been recognized as the #1 selling general gift line, and Kristin has received numerous industry awards.

In a relatively short time, *Dreamsicles* have gained recognition in the collectibles category with collector pieces. *Giftbeat Newsletter* recently ranked *Dreamsicles* as the country's #2 collectible line, after *Precious Moments* and ahead of *Heritage Village* and *Cherished Teddies*. Each of the limited edition *Dreamsicles* cherubs, consisting of 10,000 pieces signed and numbered by the artist, sold out in a few months and became a valued

"Three Cheers," by Kristin Haynes, celebrates the third year of growth and fun for the Dreamsicles® Collectors Club. The 4-3/8" figurine is free to Club members as the "Symbol of Membership" for 1995.

collectors' piece.

This success is highly unusual, since most items of this type are not recognized as true collectibles until several years after release. Virtually all designs in the line have attained a collectible status, and many of the retired figurines have already shown substantial price increases in the secondary market.

In response to public demand, Cast Art is actively engaged in a licensing program which offers leading manufacturers of a variety of products the use of the *Dreamsicles* designs and logo. These delightful cherubs are appearing on such items as collector plates, candles, garden accessories, rubber stamps, counted cross-stitch patterns, plush toys and a variety of stationery products.

In addition, Cast Art has introduced a *Dreamsicles Gift Collection* which features beautifully decorated porcelain and ceramic items including collectors bells, decorated boxes, coffee mugs, tea sets, picture frames, gift bags and more, all adorned with colorful artwork depicting the popular cherubs.

Cast Arts Cuddl'somes™ *line is a collection of unique teddy bears and other animals that have captured the hearts of bear lovers everywhere.*

Cuddl'somes™ Delight Bear Lovers

When Cast Art recently introduced its *Cuddl'somes™* line, the initial response was far greater than they had anticipated, exceeding even the successful *Dreamsicles*. It was Cast Art's first indication that they might have not one, but two collectible lines destined for success. This collection of 52 teddy bears and other adorable animal figurines is based on several original designs by Kristin Haynes, as interpreted and expanded by the in-house design team of Steve and Gigi Hackett.

Each figurine in the *Cuddl'somes* collection is intricately detailed and hand-painted to perfection. In addition, these adorable figurines are competitively priced, starting at under $10.00.

Cuddl'somes feature fanciful characters including teddy bear pirates, cowboys, firemen and sports figures, as well as delightful cows, pigs and more. This unique collection of precious teddy bears and their adorable animal friends is designed right and priced right, making the collection an instant winner.

In fact, two *Cuddl'somes* figurines were nominated for the sixth annual TOBY® awards in the category of "Figurine Bear-Manufacturer." The popularity of this line has led to Cast Art's introduction of *Cuddl'somes* water globes and Christmas ornaments.

Other Creative Product Lines

As part of its goal to create figurines for every collector, Cast Art uses different artists who develop a variety of designs.

In addition to *Cuddl'somes*, the husband and wife team of Steve and Gigi Hackett have created *Animal Attraction™*, a group of offbeat animal characters. The line includes dancing bears, "flasher" cows, and a variety of hilarious pigs in bikinis, aerobics outfits, "punker" attire and other poses. The tongue-in-cheek, slightly off-color attitudes of the collection represent a substantial departure from Cast Art's other lines, and make *Animal Attraction* popular with youthful collectors.

The success of their collaboration is further evidenced by *Story Time Treasures™*. This grouping depicts a new approach to six timeless children's classics, from *Peter Rabbit to The Frog Prince*. Each sculpture consists of the title character reading the bedtime story to his youngster, and reminds us of the joys of sharing a special moment and a good book with a child.

For those who enjoy the humorous side of life, there are few collections which compare to the whimsical *Cuckoo Corners™*, a mythical place populated by a growing collection of offbeat characters who remind us of people we know and love. Introduced in 1993, these lighthearted designs by the multi-talented Kristen Haynes have rapidly become favorites with collectors everywhere. From screaming babies to silly seniors, they remind us of our own friends and relatives in their best and worst moods. The collection of 59 pieces portrays a wide range of emotions, some subtle, some outrageous, yet all with a keen empathy for the human spirit which sets Kristin apart from other artists.

Wildlife™, a humorous assortment of porcelain animals from the "wild," was introduced by Cast Art in 1994. Designed by Barbara and Bob Sullivan, these whimsical figurines feature a variety of animals, everything from penguins to camels to puppy dogs. Each *Wildlife* figurine is carefully fired at 2350 degrees Fahrenheit, giving the clay a translucent quality, and turning the glaze into glass which creates the distinctive look of china.

Dreamsicles Collectors Club

The Dreamsicles Collectors' Club, formed in 1993, continues to be one of the nation's fastest growing collector organizations. The Club offers members the opportunity to share their appreciation of the charm and beauty of Kristin Haynes' adorable cherubs and animals. They have the chance to purchase Members-Only figurines, many of which have already become highly collectible. Figurines such as "Daydream Believer" and "Makin' A List" are among the unique designs that only Club members have been able to purchase. Other benefits including a free "Symbol of Membership" figurine, a Club binder and printed photo guide to the collection, an embossed personalized membership card, and a subscription to the colorful "Club-House" newsletter. The newsletter allows members to be the first to learn about new product introductions, retirements and much more. Annual membership dues are $27.50.

Cast Art Industries, Inc.
1120 California Ave.
Corona, CA 91719
(800) 932-3020
Fax (909) 270-2852

COLLECTORS' CLUB

Dreamsicles Collectors' Club
1120 California Ave.
Corona, CA 91719
(800) 437-5818

Annual Dues: $27.50 - Renewal: $23.50
Club Year: Anniversary of Sign-Up Date

Benefits:
- Membership Gift: Cherub Figurine
- Opportunity to Purchase Members-Only Cherub Figurine
- Quarterly "ClubHouse Newsletter"
- Three Ring Binder
- Personalized, Embossed Membership Card
- Buy/Sell "Wish List" in Newsletter
- "Guide To The Dreamsicles" Photo Book

CAVANAGH GROUP INTERNATIONAL

It's the Real Thing! The Story Behind Cavanagh Group International's Refreshing Collectible Delights

It's hard to recall a time when Coca-Cola® wasn't our favorite national drink! From coast-to-coast, the "Coke" logo fanned across billboards and magazines from April to September, even before the turn-of-the-century. In 1931, folks at Coca-Cola's corporate headquarters realized they needed to change our nation's seasonal mindset about their drink. After all, Coca-Cola tastes just as good in the winter as it does in the summer. They set out to make their point with a revolutionary ad campaign.

Commissioning highly regarded illustrator Haddon Sundblom to paint Santa Claus, plans were made to introduce America's favorite drink to America's holiday hero. The marriage was a happy success. Sundblom's burly, fun-loving Santa debuted on the pages of *The Saturday Evening Post* magazine in 1931. Just about everyone in America read the *Post*, so the Coca-Cola Santa quickly became America's most recognized St. Nick!

Inspired by a 1917 calendar produced by Coca-Cola, "Calendar Girl Swinging" is part of the Calendar Girls Series *within the* Coca-Cola Heritage Collection. *Only resin crafting and hand-painting can create such delicate ruffles, buds and other realistic touches on this figurine.*

Happily, that still holds true today...thanks to Cavanagh Group International. Established in 1990, Cavanagh has made the Coca-Cola Santa Claus image a flagship of collectible art, carrying the heritage of this heartwarming symbol toward the new millennium with designs collectors from coast-to-coast collect and adore year 'round.

A Heritage of Art Meets a Group of Funny Polar Bears

From the first day it began advertising, the Coca-Cola Bottling Company put its heart and soul into its ads and set records for the numbers of "give-aways" presented to Coke drinkers across America. There were glasses and calendars. Serving trays and wallets. Post cards. Blotters. Cards. Match books. Even sheet music! Some of this art, much from the turn-of-the-century, was selected to be placed on items made for *The Coca-Cola Heritage Collection*.

For Coca-Cola collectors with a passion for "the real thing," Santa Claus figurines, musicals and snowglobes based on Haddon Sundblom's 1951 "Good Boys and Girls" illustration fill the bill. Each hand-painted resin delight is impressively sized and authentically detailed. A classic, bordered collector plate is included in this library. As always, a die-struck medallion attests to each piece's authenticity.

Far removed from classic Sundblom Santa figurines, musicals and snowglobes, are everyone's favorite contemporary television stars: members of the *Coca-Cola Polar Bear Collection*. You've seen these guys and laughed at their antics: each is roly-poly and sugar white! Fans can now have their polar bears in a snowglobe. On a musical base. As a figurine. Or in a whimsical group, posing for a 'family' portrait!

When you're hot, you're hot—even when you're cold! Behold the world-renowned Coca-Cola Polar Bear in signature muffler frolicking on the ice with feisty offspring and a Coke to make the day perfect! The "Polar Bear Family Figurine Musical," from the Always Coca-Cola *series, is made of resin, hand-painted and embellished with a Coca-Cola seal in its base.*

Each is made of hand-painted resin with an official die-struck medallion.

For 1995, the bears appeared as two limited edition ornaments. One is shown on a bottle opener, the other on a snowboard. These two join the 1994 bears who skate, sled, deliver Coke and, of course, sneak an ice cold bottle of their favorite drink from a nearby vending machine. Also new for 1995: four bear ornaments dressed in adorable outfits, wearing ear muffs, stocking hats and formal bow ties. "Cousins" of this happy group unveiled in 1995: enchanting, miniature plush polar bear ornaments.

Coca-Cola Landmark Designs Distinguish the '95 Collection

In addition to the lavishly made collectible art described above, 1995

Coca-Cola introductions gave collectors plenty to cheer about. Four high-quality porcelain buildings are slated for construction in the *Coca-Cola Town Square Collection.* Each rekindles the spirit and memories of days-gone-by, when life was gentle and simple. Merchants welcome these new businesses to *Coca-Cola's Town Square* in '95: "Light House Point Snack Bar," "Grist Mill Restaurant," the "Sweete Shoppe" and the "Bottling Works." Each new building bears a special decal indicating year of release. Now a community of 21 buildings, *Coca-Cola Town Square* has the distinction of having retired nine buildings, three on Christmas, 1994. Many are selling on the secondary market for several times their original price.

Of course, no town would be complete without realistic accessories, so Cavanagh introduces four new pieces to display with *Coca-Cola Town Square.* There's a young couple sitting together on a park bench, rambunctious boys throwing snowballs, a couple of skiers relaxing on the slopes and a horse pulling a lunch wagon filled with all the delights a hungry villager could wish for.

Down the road, stop at the *Coca-Cola North-Pole Bottling Works.* Building on the success of an ornament series of the same theme, Cavanagh debuts ten sculptures for 1995 depicting Santa's elves running a Coca-Cola bottling plant when they're not making or delivering gifts. Three "corner buildings" show both sides of each structure in detail, and seven figures give collectors a peek at the three operations the busy elves run during "the off season." New facades, introduced over the next three years, will complete the series.

Finally, a shimmering new collection of silk on glass Christmas ornaments astonishes collectors of all ages! Called *Santa on Silk,* this elegant series combines European lithographed silk over fine glass balls. Assembled in the United States, these six exquisite holiday ornaments feature the Coca-Cola Santa based on ad designs beginning in 1931. As is Cavanagh's practice, some of the 1995 *Santa on Silk* ornaments will be retired at the end of 1995. These retirements make select Coca-Cola collectibles the rarest limited editions of all!

It's Christmas Every Day For Cavanagh's Coca-Cola Club

The portrait is dignified. The message is clear: "Go ahead and sign up." This invitation, offered by a smiling Coca-Cola Santa toasting with an old-fashioned fountain glass of Coke, is the first thing a shopper sees on a brochure for Cavanagh's Coca-Cola Christmas Collectors Society. The Society is old-fashioned fun. Members are invited to celebrate Christmas twelve months a year as Cavanagh makes sure Club perks are value-packed, educational and festive.

From the moment a new member's application reaches the Cavanagh offices, special treatment is afforded the Coca-Cola art collector. A membership kit speeds its way via the U.S. Mail—no reindeer involved here! Inside, a personalized membership card in signature red with white snowflakes awaits. There's a red-bordered membership certificate, ready for framing, and a quarterly subscription to the Christmas Collector Society's information-packed newsletter. Every three months, this publication arrives filled with announcements of new art, retirements, facts behind the design and manufacture of Coca-Cola collectibles, trends and much, much more.

A unique gift, crafted exclusively for members, is also sent to Society members when they join. This authentic collectible is drawn from the archives of the Coca-Cola Company. For 1995, the membership gift is a delightful Santa ornament circled with a halo of evergreen and perfect for illuminating when hung in front of a Christmas tree light.

Members covet invitations to purchase special limited edition art not offered to non-members. The 1995 Members-Only exclusive is the extraordinary First Edition Collectors Lithograph, "It Will Refresh You Too," inspired by Haddon Sundblom's original illustration. Embossed with the Society seal, this impressive 22" x 28"" lithograph is ready-to-frame and hang. There's more! Browse the Society Members-Only Catalog and you know this is no ordinary collectors club. Members can purchase shirts, tote bags, mugs, a binder and other delights to show the world that their membership in Cavanagh's Coca-Cola Christmas Collectors Society is a joy all year long.

Keys to the Realm of Joy, Tradition and Fun

"We've been given the keys to the Coca-Cola Company archives," says John F. Cavanagh, president of the Cavanagh Group International, "and we're creating a line of high-quality, authentic collectibles. It's a wonderful opportunity for collectors to discover and enjoy a wealth of Coca-Cola art and advertising images by such renowned artists as Haddon Sundblom, N.C. Wyeth and Norman Rockwell." These words sum up the goals and promises of a young company committed to sharing, with millions of Americans, the rich heritage of Coca-Cola art. The

The musical "Santa on the Steps" prepares to deliver gifts and memories! Artist Haddon Sundblom created an original Coca-Cola ad in 1931 that lives on as this extraordinary sculpture. Fashioned of resin and hand-painted in a rainbow of shimmering colors, this impressive figure is part of the Coca-Cola Heritage Collection.

current Cavanagh Collection shows these goals are being met with remarkable vision. This year's variety is breathtaking in size and scope.

The Coca-Cola Heritage Collection, mentioned earlier in this article when we spotlighted the 1995 introductions, includes ornaments, figurines, musicals, polar bears and snowglobes. Within this popular category, *The Coca Cola North Pole Bottling Works* introduces a new collection of corner buildings and accessories sure to charm collectors the moment they discover these magnificently detailed collectible buildings and the helpers who inhabit and visit them.

An astonishing array of other Coca-Cola treats awaits collector pleasure, as well. There are elaborate sculptures of Santa sold as *Major Musical* collectibles. *Miniature Musicals* follow Santa, elves and the Coca-Cola Polar Bear on their Christmas adventures. Crystal-clear *Coca-Cola Santa Snowglobes* shower Santa and the Coke Polar Bear with white flakes as they show up in the most unlikely places. The *Santa Claus Trim-a-Tree* galaxy is a sight to behold, as well. Dozens of ornaments, each inspired by a vintage illustration, swing happily from branches. Collectors may purchase these ornaments individually or as sets. Many have been retired!

Norman Rockwell's signature look distinguished this 1933 portrait of a young boy enjoying a Coke as he patiently awaits a bite on his line! Now a gloriously bordered limited edition collector plate, "Boy Fishing" bears the official seal of Coca-Cola authorized art. This Rockwell delight is also part of the Coca-Cola Heritage Collection.

"From our initial offering of four ornaments in 1990 to our present collection of more than 150 individual pieces, we've been able to respond to the strong desires of collectors who can't get enough Coca-Cola collectible art," John Cavanagh smiles. He sits back and reviews the past five years with an observation that sums up Cavanagh's promise to the fans enriching their lives with Coca-Cola collectibles. "We're committed to continually expanding the breadth and depth of our Coca-Cola treasures. Our collectors can count on us for spectacular, heartwarming art crafted so expertly, these vintage collectibles will become the heirlooms of tomorrow."

Cavanagh Group International
1000 Holcomb Woods Pkwy.
#440-B
Roswell, GA 30078
(800) 895-8100
Fax (404) 643-1172

COLLECTORS' CLUB

Cavanagh's Coca-Cola Christmas Collectors Society
P.O. Box 420157
Atlanta, GA 30342
(800) 653-1221

Annual Dues: $25.00
Club Year: January-December

Benefits:
- Membership Gift: Authentic Collectible Drawn from the Archives of the Coca-Cola Company
- Opportunity to Purchase Members-Only Collectible
- Quarterly Newsletter
- Membership Certificate, Suitable for Framing
- Personalized Membership Card
- Periodic Offers on Special Items Reserved for Society Members

CHRISTOPHER RADKO

Celebrating a Decade of Holiday Memories and Traditions

In 1995, members of the Christopher Radko Starlight Family of Collectors had the opportunity to purchase "Dash Away All." The members-only ornament is part of a wide range of exclusive benefits awaiting collectors who enjoy the fine quality, craftsmanship and nostalgia of the collection.

For Christopher Radko, what appeared to be his family's loss has turned into a colorful and nostalgic gain for collectors around the world. It all began in 1984 when the holiday season was unfolding according to the Radko family tradition. While Christopher was growing up in Scarsdale, New York, the highlight of his family's Christmas was decorating the tree with their astonishing collection of blown-glass ornaments. Three generations of Radkos had collected more than 2,000 of the handcrafted treasures. As a boy, Christopher loved to slide under the fresh pine tree's lowest branches, where he was mesmerized by the reflection of the bubble lights, twinkling stars and shimmering spheres.

But in 1984, as Christopher was performing his annual chore of removing sap and needles from the old tree stand, he decided that a new one was needed. After shopping around, he bought a stand guaranteed to hold up an 18-foot tree – a good 4 feet taller than the Radko's own tree. With the new stand, the old traditions still continued as family members trimmed the tree.

One cold December morning, however, a loud crash suddenly changed the idyllic scene. Despite its guarantee, the stand buckled and the tree fell to the floor, shattering more than half of the fragile decorations.

"I was absolutely heartbroken because those ornaments were our family's direct link to the traditions and memories of four generations of Christmas celebrations," Christopher recalls. "Even though I knew there was no way I could replace the ornaments my great-grandmother and grandmother had handed down, I thought that the least I could do was buy some substitutes so our tree wouldn't look so forlorn."

He searched in the stores near his hometown and shopped the major department stores all over New York City. Sadly, he discovered that most ornaments were being made from plastic and other mysterious materials. The few glass ornaments that he found were poorly crafted, and the painted details were frightful. Needless to say, it was a depressing Christmas for the Radko family.

Reviving a Turn-of-the-Century Technique

The following spring, while Christopher was visiting relatives in Poland, a cousin introduced him to a farmer who once made blown-glass ornaments. He said he might be able to make several new ones. There was only one catch: Christopher had to supply him with detailed drawings of the kinds of ornaments he wanted. Upon seeing the designs, the glassblower said that they were just like the ornaments that his father and grandfather had made before World War II and that although he had never made such complicated pieces, he would be happy to try.

After Christopher returned to the United States with his newly crafted glass ornaments, family members and friends clamored for glorious glass ornaments of their own. At that point, he realized that he had discovered not only a need but his own niche for fulfilling the demand.

Today, a decade later, Christopher engages the services of nearly 800 Polish, German, Czech and Italian glassblowers who masterfully create limited editions of his ornaments. The 1995 line features more than 750 dazzling designs with ideas coming from memories of his family's antique ornaments as well as his other inspirations: architecture, fabrics, films and museum collections. It takes about a week to make each ornament, which is blown, silvered, lacquered, painted and glittered entirely by hand. Designs range from the traditional Santa Claus to a pipe-smoking monkey and rabbits to Persian peacocks.

"My company's success has allowed me to revive Christmas crafts and techniques that were all but lost," Christopher says. "As a Christmas artist with my annual collection of new designs, I am reviving a tradition of designing that had its heyday at the turn of the century. My glassblowers are uncovering old molds and relearning skills that their cottage industry hasn't used in 70 years. Now, even young apprentice glassblowers are being trained in the traditions of their great-grandfathers, ensuring that fine glass ornament making will continue

Created to benefit AIDS-related organizations and raise awareness about the disease, "On Wings of Hope" features an angel with shimmering details and vibrant colors. Each year, Christopher Radko divides the proceeds from the ornament among different agencies that serve those with AIDS.

into the next century. That's something to celebrate!"

Collection Marks Its 10th Anniversary

The collection of glass ornaments also had something to celebrate: its 10th anniversary throughout 1995. In honor of the occasion, Christopher introduced "On Top of the World" as his special Santa Claus for the year.

For collectors to always remember the occasion and enjoy all the ornaments offered to date, Christopher published a 10th anniversary book. The 200-plus-page volume pictures all the ornaments along with articles on the traditions, manufacturing and creative uses of Christopher's ornaments. The book is available in two versions: the 10th anniversary commemorative book limited in edition to 2,500 pieces and bound in leather with a slip case, and the standard version with a hardcover and dust protector.

For the first time, Christopher also introduced the *Boutique Collection* featuring a silk scarf in four color selections, three different tie styles, unisex boxer shorts, a 500-piece jigsaw puzzle, shopping bags and wrapping paper – all of which showcase his renowned ornaments.

New Ornaments Offer Something For Everyone

Because half of the ornaments in the line are retired or changed in some way each year, Christopher's ornaments become highly collectible. For 1995, following the success of "A Partridge in a Pear Tree" and "Two Turtle Doves," another ornament has been added to the *Twelve Days of Christmas* series. Like previous introductions, "Three French Hens" was inspired by the holiday song and is limited to 10,000 pieces with a hand-numbered tag.

For 1995, Snow White has also joined the collection. "And Snowy Makes Eight" is a numbered and pre-packed introduction that includes all seven dwarfs and Snow White straight from the popular children's story. Christopher also introduced two three-year limited series sets. The "Three Wise Men" is limited to 15,000 sets with hand-numbered tags. This is the first part of the company's three-year Nativity set. *The Nutcracker Suite* features the 1995 debuts of "Clara," "Toy Soldier" and "Herr Drosselmeier," each hand-numbered and limited to 15,000 sets.

The 1995 event piece – only available during Christopher Radko presentations nationwide – is "Forever Lucy." Continuing his tradition of raising funds to spread awareness and support the fight against AIDS and pediatric cancer, Christopher has introduced several new ornaments to help others. "On Wings of Hope" will benefit various AIDS-related organizations while "Christmas Puppy Love" will go toward pediatric cancer agencies. Christopher is also proud of the fact that organizations such as World Wildlife Fund, the Smithsonian Institution and the Metropolitan Museum of Art have commissioned limited editions of his ornaments. His ornaments are also bought year-round as gifts for birthdays, anniversaries, housewarming parties and bridal or baby showers.

Starlight Club Welcomes Ornament Collectors

All collectors seem to find something captivating and comforting in the ornaments. Even Vice President Al Gore, Elton John, Katharine Hepburn, Bruce Springsteen, Dolly Parton, Mikhail Barishnikov and Hillary Rodham Clinton are numbered among the devoted Christopher Radko collectors.

Many other fans around the world have joined the Christopher Radko Starlight Family of Collectors. Launched in 1993, this collectors' club offers members exclusive pieces and keeps them up to date on the latest introductions. For 1995, a $50.00 membership included the gift ornament "Purrfect Present," personalized and embossed membership card, an annual

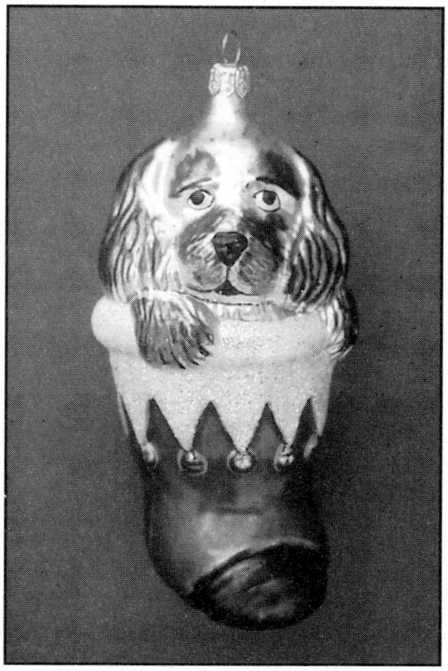

Christopher Radko strongly believes in giving something back to others – and he is an ardent supporter of pediatric cancer agencies. Proceeds from "Christmas Puppy Love," which features a dog in a Christmas stocking, will benefit that cause.

"Three French Hens," the 1995 introduction to the Twelve Days of Christmas *series, follows in the popular tradition of the holiday song. The ornament is limited to 10,000 pieces with a hand-numbered tag.*

ornament button, the 10th anniversary cloisonne collector's pin, 10th anniversary Collector's Catalogue, subscription to the quarterly *Starlight* publication, and a linen bound *Starlight* and Collector's Catalogue storage folio. Members also received a voucher entitling them to purchase the members-only figurine, which for 1995 was titled "Dash Away All."

"I am supported by thousands of loyal collectors who recognize the care and extraordinary quality each ornament represents," Christopher said. And now, thanks to Christopher Radko and the holiday mishap at his family's home more than 10 years ago, any collector can trim a tree with old-fashioned, blown-glass ornaments without going to Europe to find them.

Christopher Radko
P.O. Box 238
Dobbs Ferry, NY 10522
(800) 71-RADKO
Fax: (914) 693-3770

COLLECTORS' CLUB

Starlight Family of Collectors
P.O. Box 238
Dobbs Ferry, NY 10522
(800) 71-RADKO

Annual Dues: $50.00 - Renewal: $45.00
Club Year: January-December

Benefits:
- Membership Gift: Ornament
- Opportunity to Purchase Members-Only Ornament
- Quarterly Magazine, *Starlight*
- *Starlight* Folio
- Personalized Membership Card
- Annual Ornament Button
- Exclusive Christopher Radko Pin
- Tenth Anniversary Catalogue

CLASSIC COLLECTABLES BY UNIQUELY YOURS

Recalling Timeless Treasures from the Past and Expanding for the Future

"Countryside Santa" carries a burlap sack overflowing with toys in this 1995 figurine limited in edition to 300 pieces. With his fur-trimmed coat and walnut base, signed by artist Eileen Tisa, the Santa proudly stands 33" tall.

Classic Collectables by Uniquely Yours experienced a turning point in 1995 through a business venture that has introduced more collectors to the company's nostalgic and handcrafted designs. MeraVic, an international wholesale distributor of decorative accessories and silk flowers, took under its wings the beautiful creations of Uniquely Yours owner/artist Eileen Tisa. MeraVic also represents and displays Eileen's life-like figurines in its catalogs and showrooms across the country.

This wide-spread visibility and recognition are something Eileen never imagined when she sat down one day to help her 8-year-old son Jimmy create a work of art out of clay. Eileen felt compelled to find new creative challenges for Jimmy, who already had a school painting displayed in a "Young Artist of 1978" exhibit in Philadelphia. So together they sculpted the clay only to discover that Jimmy much preferred painting, while Eileen unearthed a talent for creating human likenesses.

Eileen's sculpted faces soon topped bottles and clay-covered wire armatures. She also brushed up on her sewing skills to design clothing for these little people that would become friends to thousands of collectors.

Humble Beginnings from a Classic Christmas Tale

Always inspired by the holiday season and Charles Dickens' beloved classic, *A Christmas Carol*, Eileen chose Bob Cratchit, Tiny Tim, Ebenezer Scrooge, Marley and the story's other memorable characters as subjects for her first creations. From Scrooge's bah-humbug frown to the ghosts' haunting eyes, the figurines seemed to step right out of the pages of the book. Tisa also created a cast of supporting characters: choir boys, children on sleds and carolers. Many of these initial sculptures were wrapped up as special gifts for friends and family.

Tisa also became fascinated with flower design, especially silk bridal arrangements. In 1989, she began selling her silk flowers and other crafts at mall shows and church bazaars, where visitors fell in love with her handmade figurines. As her talent for creating new costumes and concepts blossomed, so did her character's faces, expressions and personality. She soon developed a small-but-growing number of collectors who followed her progress. Classic Collectibles by Uniquely Yours was born in 1989 with Tisa introducing various Santa figurines as well as "The Little Match Girl" from Hans Christian Andersen's tale. That charming work was retired in 1992.

On the Road to Success with New Creations

In 1990, Eileen stood at the crossroads. Her husband of 22 years, Jim, passed away at the age of 44. She had to decide whether to abandon her small but not yet profitable craft business in order to find other employment. Or she could try to find a way to make a living with her artistic talents. Only months before her husband's death, Eileen had registered, on a whim, to share a friend's booth at the Eastern Regional Gift Show in Valley Forge, Pennsylvania. She kept her commitment of attending the show, where her figurines were an overwhelming success. With the help of Tisa's parents, an aunt who could sew, and her son, she filled all the orders requested by the wholesale gift buyers. Her career decision had been made.

Tisa found comfort and encouragement in keeping herself immersed in her work. Prior to the show, she had managed to create two limited edition Santas, "Kris Kringle" and "Father Christmas." Both have since been retired.

Following her success in Valley Forge, Eileen developed more introductions, including "Saint Nicholas" and "Jolly Saint Nick," a pipe-smoking Santa. Both of these pieces remain in the company's line because of their on-going popularity. The mother-and-daughter duo of "Christmas Shoppers" also debuted at that time.

The company also briefly experimented with miniature characters from *A Christmas Carol*, but Eileen thought they were too tedious and time consuming. The "Victorian Band" became part of the regular Dickens' line for about a year before retiring in 1991. "Lighting the Menorah," a vignette honoring Hanukkah, was also produced and retired in 1991.

As sales figures and the number of

This one-of-a-kind "English Santa" delivers the holiday spirit from times gone by. Wearing a maroon, fur-trimmed coat and long white beard, the detailed figurine was introduced in 1993.

collectors grew, the company also branched out from its traditional Santas and fictional characters. "Pilgrims" and "Trick or Treaters" (an adorable witch and devil) were hits. Springtime favorites include "The Girl With the Bunnies," "The Boy With the Easter Basket," "Bride," "Groom," "The Victorian Girl," "Boy With a Hoop," a variety of ladies in Victorian finery, and men in top hats and tails to accompany them. Others included "The Country Woman," "Mother and Daughter," "The African Woman" and "The African Man" – both of which were dressed in colorful costumes.

One-Of-A-Kind Figurines Attract Avid Collectors

Each year, Classic Collectables by Uniquely Yours produces a dozen or so "one-of-a-kind" Santas that are sold at gift shows. Although priced higher than the limited edition pieces, the "one-of-a-kind" Santas are quickly purchased by buyers who know the figurines in turn will be snatched up by avid collectors. Many are bought by art and craft galleries and some have found their way to such places as England, Germany and Ireland.

Eye-catching accessories, historically accurate designs and richly crafted costumes complement the unusual themes in these creations, such as "Backwoods Santa," "Old West Santa," "The Victorian Treetop Angel," "English Countryside Santa" and "Black Santa on a Tricycle" (which is also available in a Caucasian version).

Handcrafted Santas in all Sizes and Places

While the Dickens' line, smaller Santas and "one-of-a-kind" pieces are always in demand, the company reports that the larger Santas are by far the "runaway best sellers." The majestic 33" "Countryside Santa," new for 1995, is dressed in a deep red wool coat generously trimmed with plush fur. Like most of the Santas, he stands on a walnut base and carries lots of tiny gifts ranging from a toy rocking horse to a Christmas tree.

Others include the 33" "Victor-ian Santa," the 25" "Renaissance Santa" and the popular 33" "Olde World Santa." These limited edition, signed and dated Santas have been incorporated into many display windows to draw customers into shops.

Based on the realism she breathes into all her creations, Eileen was commissioned to design several display figures for the holiday store windows of Crouch and Fitzgerald, a New York-based leather goods retailer located on busy Madison Avenue. The project fulfilled her childhood dream of creating commercial displays that attract the undivided attention of rushing passersby. The Crouch and Fitzgerald display featured four, 4' Santas, including a St. Nick in a nightshirt and cap packing his suitcase for a trip to the North Pole. Mr. Claus wears a three-piece suit as he leads a board meeting with his industrious staff of elves. The third Santa sits in a toy-laden truck rather than the traditional sleigh. The fourth features Mrs. Claus in outdoor garb shopping at the store.

Establishing a National Reputation and New Collectors

With more designs and confidence under her belt, Eileen attended larger gift shows, where national not just regional buyers saw the variety of figurines that she had to offer. As the word spread, Classic Collectables by Uniquely Yours began to grow well beyond what Tisa's home could accommodate. What started in the kitchen and a small back bedroom soon took over the entire house and garage. Eileen's parents even kept her figurines and materials in their garage and basement.

In 1993, Eileen leased a workshop and office outside of Philadelphia in nearby Delaware County, Pennsylvania. With additional space and the help of local crafts people, the business quickly expanded with distribution from coast to coast. The company recently leased another 2,250 square feet to keep up with the daily orders. The business boom has also helped the local economy by employing mothers and senior citizens who welcome the extra income and opportunity for part-time work.

Despite her company's tremendous growth, Eileen still hand sculpts the

Limited in edition to 250 pieces, "Jolly St. Nick" was retired in 1995. With a pipe, sack of toys and traditional attire, this Santa reflects the company's attention to detail that makes each figurine a treasured collectible and work of art.

Inspired by the writings of Charles Dickens, artist Eileen Tisa paid her own tribute to A Christmas Carol *by creating a cast of the book's unforgettable characters. The figurines "Marley's Ghost," "Ghost of Christmas Present" and "Ghost of Christmas Past" bring the classic story to life.*

face of each figurine and makes the molds. The designs are then molded in a life-like composition clay and hand-painted. Under the artist's watchful eye, the clothing and construction of each figurine is completed with meticulous attention to detail. All materials and wooden bases are made in the United States, with the exception of a few accessories.

The response from retailers and collectors has been overwhelming. "Adding new accounts has been important to our growth, but nothing makes me happier than hearing from a small shop owner who calls to tell me that she or he 'no sooner got the figurines unpacked – and they were gone,'" says Eileen. Store owners also report that the detail, price and quality of Eileen's creations keep collectors coming back for more!

With the lines now represented by MeraVic, Classic Collectables by Uniquely Yours plans to continue reaching new collectors and creating new designs. "We feel assured the business will continue its rapid progress because of our success at keeping most of our customers even from those early shows," Eileen says.

Classic Collectables By Uniquely Yours
P.O. Box 16861
Philadelphia, PA 19142
(610) 586-6266
Fax (610) 522-2259

CREART

Living Sculptures That Celebrate the Beauty of Wildlife

Since the Stone Age, people have admired and depended on animals. Proof of this reverence is found in murals, artifacts and carvings throughout the world. But not everyone shared this appreciation for nature's creatures as evidenced by their extinction and the environmental destruction over the past hundred years. Today, society is beginning to realize its mistakes which have caused an imbalance in nature. Once again, respect for the environment and wildlife is becoming an important part of daily life, resulting in the protection of many animals and a return to the beauty of nature. This philosophy is embodied in all of Creart's work.

When Creart designs its sculptures, the company pays tribute to wildlife. People take pleasure in bringing a portrayal of wildlife into their home, as a companion in their everyday environment.

Company's Artisans Show Devotion to Nature

Creart is devoted to the understanding and appreciation of nature and will continue to offer only high-quality, realistic sculptures that are genuine representations of the earth's animals. Creart's artists share a true love for animals and believe their work is in harmony with nature. These sincere emotions result in a sculpture that is a masterful achievement in animal art.

This incredible beauty and realism first attracted Creart U.S.A. President Carlos Estevez and his wife, Minerva, to the sculptures. While on vacation in Mexico City, they saw the work in a famous department store. "We were looking for something interesting to buy, when suddenly there they were – these amazing animal sculptures!" explains Estevez.

After some intense research, the pair found the studio where a new process of manufacturing was being used to give these sculptures a consistent high quality. The singular designs, as Estevez and his wife soon discovered, were being crafted by a team of sculptors, each of whom was a master in his own right. The group was led by a man named Emilio Martinez and included Francisco Contreras and Vicente Perez.

As life-time friends, Martinez and Contreras attended Mexico City's National School of Plastic Arts and studied under some of the nation's finest masters. While Martinez went to work for a figurine candleholder company, Contreras worked independently as a sculptor and painter. Perez studied at the same school and had made reproductions of archeological pieces in Mexico's Anthropology Museum of Natural History in Mexico City, home of one of the largest collection of pre-Columbian artifacts. Together, Martinez, Contreras, Perez and Creart's Mexico Director Leon del Rio founded Creart in 1979.

What distinguishes the style of the original Creart artisans? Estevez explains that Martinez especially loves to sculpt soft, round animals. Contreras is an innovator whose models all feature a new approach. Perez handles the very detailed subjects. "Every piece goes through Vincente's hands for the final detailing and approval," notes Estevez, who began importing the sculptures in 1987.

From Collectors' Input to Detailed Sculptures

One of the most interesting facets of Creart is its reliance on the tastes and needs of collectors to dictate which animals it will produce. In fact, Creart's very first step in creating a new piece is asking collectors which subjects they are interested in seeing, how those subjects should be portrayed, what size they should be and how much they

This beautiful creature is magnificently captured in the environment of its daily life in "Ambushing Puma," created by artist Barbara Nelson. Limited to 1,950 pieces, the figurine was among the first pieces that Nelson designed for Creart.

As part of the Nature's Care Collection, *artist Francisco Contreras captures the warm personality and charm of koalas and their babies. Titled "The Land Down Under," the four-piece collection is each limited to 2,500 pieces.*

should cost. The responses from collectors are given considerable attention, after which a subject, together with its posture and environment, is selected. Then, a model sketch is developed for anatomy, proportion and muscle tone.

At this point, Creart's sculptors create an original plastiline statue – from which models are made – and the best of these models is trimmed, detailed and photographed from many different angles. Skilled artisans then construct molds, the most delicate parts of which are reinforced with steel or fiberglass rods that are invisible in the finished piece.

The molds are subsequently filled with the material that Estevez says works best in producing the necessary high-relief detail. This is an exclusive marble compound that offers exceptional reproduction qualities due to its stability, weight, resistance, impermeability, high density and balance. Because this marble/resin compound is less rigid than pure marble, Creart pieces can often be repaired to look like new.

Highly skilled artisans hand-decorate each figurine with as many as 24 different colors to achieve a natural texture that can't be duplicated on glass or porcelain. Then a lusterless, transparent lacquer is applied to make cleaning the figurine easy with just a damp cloth. An exceptionally thorough quality control department checks the finished piece for any flaw. If each sculpture is found acceptable, it is then numbered as part of a limited edition, which when closed, is never reopened for any reason. The sculpture is mounted on an appropriate stand and individually boxed along with a certificate request card which collectors can mail to Creart to obtain a personalized, limited edition certificate.

Always Striving for Excellence and Representational Art at Its Best

Creart U.S.A. President Estevez is an artist himself. His continuing love of art led to his producing rodeo posters and selling his work at the Houston Livestock Show and Rodeo in Texas. His first Creart sculpture, which featured a pair of otters basking on a rock, was produced for collectors in the spring of 1993. The Nature Company of Berkeley, California, was so impressed that the firm became the major purchaser of this sculpture for its more than 100 stores in the United States and Canada.

Syndi Scott, buyer for The Nature Company, calls Creart one of the most successful and profitable lines sold by her firm. "Each piece of Creart is as biologically accurate as it is beautiful because it's representational art at its best, as well as being fine quality, limited edition art," she says. In fact, Scott notes, "This firm perfectly represents our mission statement at The Nature Company: to provide fine quality products devoted to the observation, understanding and appreciation of the natural world."

Distinguished by its quality and detail, Creart is also considered very affordable. "Ever since we began," explains Estevez, "we've dedicated ourselves to the connoisseur collector. Therefore, we can't make any compromises regarding the complexity or quality of our pieces. Collectors understand the value of our sculptures."

Wildlife Artists Add Talents to Collection

In keeping the commitment to producing only the best in wildlife sculpture, Estevez searched for talented, accomplished artists in the United States and found the answers in Barbara Nelson and Jim Robison. Nelson, a sculptor in wood and bronze, obtained a degree in wildlife biology from the University of Massachusetts. In 1989, she first received international recognition by winning the title of

Among the most popular pieces in the Creart line, "Singing to the Moon I" and "Singing to the Moon II" (foreground) were beautifully designed by Vicente Perez to show the lonely howl of wolves. Each is limited in edition to 1,500 pieces and is part of the American Wildlife *series.*

"Second Best in World Lifesize" with "Ringnecked Pheasant." She was the featured sculptor for the 1995 Southwestern Wildlife Exposition.

Her first sculptures for Creart were pumas titled "Ambushing" and "Briefly Rest." The superior quality reflected in all her sculptures is why she is recognized by collectors and fellow artists as among the top in her field.

Robison's love for wildlife is evident through all his work. Robison, an avid outdoorsman, and his wife, Sheri, live in a small rural town, and inspiration for his work comes from watching wildlife on his farm. He has received numerous carving achievements through the years. His sculptures have been exhibited in the Leigh Yawkey Woodson Art Museum and featured on television. Jim was also recognized for his Creart sculpture, "Gyrfalcon," by receiving a 1994 *Collector Editions* magazine "Award of Excellence" nomination.

Creart's Series Capture a Kingdom of Wildlife

Creart has seven series in its line of beautiful wildlife sculptures: *African Wildlife, Wild American Edition, American Wildlife, Horses and Cattle, From Asia and Europe, The Nature's Care Collection* and *Birds of Prey*, plus the *Stylus* line.

Africa is the source of a rich, unparalleled array of wildlife. So it's only fitting that the *African Wildlife* series continues to grow each year. This series includes the giraffe, zebra and many others. The more recent releases in this series are the "Grumbler" Cape Buffalo and "Elephant Tracks."

The *Wild American Edition* features various animal heads, including the "White Blizzard Wolf" and "Cape Buffalo." Both are limited to 1,500 sculptures. The company's popular *American Wildlife* collection is the largest series in the Creart line. This group includes the popular "Singing to the Moon I & II" and "Standing White Tail Deer." Newer releases include the "Over the Top" Puma, "Out of the Den" Puma and "Moose." From Alaska to the Mexican border at the Rio Grande River, a contaminated environment has endangered many of these animals. But with an on-going campaign educating and showing the importance of wildlife, many have begun to understand the importance and need to protect nature.

Creart's *Horses and Cattle* series includes highly detailed horses by artists Martinez and Perez. They are treasured by horse lovers everywhere. Some of the series includes the "Arabian Horse," "Running Horse," "Thoroughbred Horse" and "Quarter Horse."

From Asia and Europe is a smaller series which includes the "Indian Elephant Mother and Baby," "Bengal Tiger" and "Giant Panda." The *Nature's Care Collection* is a series of smaller sculptures which depicts a mother's tender care and love for her young. A popular edition in this collection was the 1995 release "The Land Down Under," a four-piece collection of adorable koalas. Contreras magnificently captured their charm and gentle nature.

The *Birds of Prey* series includes the "Gyrfalcon" and "Vigilant Eagle" by Robison. With the *Stylus* line, Creart responded to customer needs by offering a unique collection of animals that are less detailed but offer collectors the same quality and excellence for which Creart is synonymous. The Creart family proudly teams master sculptors, artisans and technicians, whose ideas of quality are the achievement of the living dimension.

The African Wildlife *series continues growing each year, thanks in part to this realistic addition titled "Elephant Tracks." Designed by artist Vicente Perez, the figurine is limited to 1,500 pieces.*

Creart
209 E. Ben White
Suite 103
Austin, TX 78704
(800) 343-1505
Fax (512) 707-9918

DEPARTMENT 56®, INC.

Just Imagine . . . Snow-Laden Trees, Wreaths at the Windows, and Welcome Mats Out . . . The Tradition Begins

From the Dickens' Village *series comes these quaint pieces entitled "Portobello Road Thatched Cottages."*

"Department 56" may seem a curious name for a firm that designs and manufactures nostalgic, collectible villages. How the name originated is a story that intrigues the firm's many loyal collectors.

Before Department 56, Inc. became an independent corporation, it was part of a large parent company that used a numbering system to identify each of its departments. While Department 21 was administration and Department 54 was the gift warehouse, the name assigned to wholesale gift imports was "Department 56."

Department 56, Inc. originally began by importing fine Italian basketry. However, a new product line introduced in 1977 set the groundwork for the collectible products of today. Little did the company's staff realize that their appealing group of four lighted houses and two churches would pave the way for one of the late-20th century's most popular collectibles.

These miniature buildings were the beginning of *The Original Snow Village®*. Each design was handcrafted of ceramic, and hand-painted to create all the charming details of an "olden day" village. To create the glow from the windows, a switched cord and bulb assembly was included with each individually boxed piece.

Collectors could see the little lighted buildings as holiday decorations under a Christmas tree or on the mantel. Glowing lights gave the impression of cozy homes and neighborhood buildings with happy, bustling townsfolk in a wintry setting. Sales were encouraging, so Department 56, Inc. decided to develop more *Snow Village* pieces to add to their 1978 line.

Word of mouth and consumer interest helped Department 56 realize *The Original Snow Village* collection would continue. Already there were reports of collectors striving to own each new piece as it was introduced.

By 1979, the Department 56, Inc. staff made an important operational decision. In order to keep *The Original Snow Village* at a reasonable size, buildings would have to be retired from production each year to make room for new designs. Being new to the world of collectibles, they did not realize the full impact of this decision. Collectors who had not yet obtained a retired model would attempt to seek out that piece on the secondary market. This phenomenon has led to reports that early *Snow Village* pieces may be valued at considerably more than their original issue price.

Today, as in the past, the Department 56 architects continue to keep the Village alive by bringing collectors new techniques and new materials, all of which result in an exciting array of buildings and charming accessories.

The Heritage Village Collection® From Department 56, Inc.

Love of holiday traditions sparked the original concept of *The Heritage Village Collection*. When decorating our homes, we are often drawn to objects reminiscent of an earlier time. Holiday memories wait, hidden in a bit of wrinkled tissue or a dusty box, until that time each year, when rediscovered, we unpack our treasures and are magically transported to a beloved time and place.

The first *Heritage Village* grouping was *The Dickens' Village® Series* introduced in 1984. Extensive research, charming details and the fine hand-painting of the seven original porcelain shops and "Village Church" established them as favorites among collectors.

Other series followed with the introduction of *The New England Village®, The Alpine Village©, Christmas In The City®, The Little Town of Bethlehem©, The North Pole©*, and in 1994, *The Disney Parks Village Series*. Each of these ongoing collectible series has been researched for authenticity and has the same attention to detail as the original Dickens' Village.

As each of the villages began to grow, limited edition pieces were added, along with trees, street lamps, and accessory groupings to complete the nostalgic charm of each collection. Each lighted piece is stamped in the bottom with its designated series name, title, year of introduction, and Department 56, Inc. logo to assure authenticity.

Each model is packed in its own individual styrofoam storage carton and illustrated sleeve. A special compartment in the boxing of all lighted pieces holds a UL-approved switched cord and bulb. This method not only protects the pieces during shipping, but also provides a convenient way of repacking and storing the collection for many years.

Each grouping within *The Heritage Village Collection* captures the holiday spirit of a bygone era. *Dickens' Village*, for instance, portrays the bustling, hearty and joyous atmosphere of the holidays in Victorian England. *New England Village* brings back memories of "over the river and through the woods," with a journey through the countryside.

The *Alpine Village* recreates the charm of a quaint mountain town, where glistening snow and clear lakes fed by icy streams dot the landscape. *Christmas In The City* evokes memories of busy sidewalks, street corner Santas, friendly traffic cops and bustling crowds amid cheery shops, town-houses and theaters.

In 1987, Department 56, Inc. introduced *The Little Town of Bethlehem*. The unique 12-piece set reproduces the essence of the birthplace of Jesus. This complete village scene continues to inspire and hearten those who celebrate Christmas everywhere.

In 1991, Department 56, Inc. presented *The North Pole Series*. The brightly lit *North Pole* buildings and accompanying accessories depict the wonderful Santa Claus legend with charm and details that bring childhood dreams to life for the young and the young-at-heart.

Santa and his reindeer are charmingly portrayed in these whimsical figurines, "To His Team He Gave a Whistle" and " Sleigh Full of Toys and St. Nicholas Too," from the All Through The House *series.*

In 1994, *The Disney Parks Village Series* became the newest addition to *The Heritage Village Collection*. Replicas of Disney theme park buildings are accompanied by Mickey and Minnie Mouse, along with other coordinated accessories. This new line has caught the eye of Department 56 collectors and Disney fans alike.

"Lift me Higher, I Can't Reach" (left) and "Stringing Fallen Stars" represent the Snowbabies *collection of finely detailed bisque porcelain collectibles with hand-painted faces and hand-applied frosty bisque crystals.*

Celebrate *Snowbabies*® and Other Department 56 Favorites

Another collectible series from Department 56, Inc. is *Snowbabies©*. These adorable, whimsical figurines have bright blue eyes and creamy white snowsuits covered by flakes of new-fallen snow. They sled, make snowballs, ride polar bears and frolic with their friends. Since their introduction, *Snowbabies* have enchanted collectors around the country and have brightened the imagination of all of us who celebrate the gentle play of youthful innocence.

Each of the finely detailed bisque porcelain collectibles, with hand-painted faces and hand-applied frosty bisque snow crystals, is complete in its own gold foil stamped storybook box.

In 1989, a line of pewter miniature *Snowbabies* was introduced, to the great delight of collectors of miniatures. These tiny treasures are made from many of the same designs as their bisque counterparts, and come packaged in little white gift boxes sprinkled with gold stars.

Every year, new *Snowbaby* friends are introduced in these very special collections.

In addition to *Snowbabies* and the Villages, several other series have caught the loyal Department 56 collectors' fancy.

Winter Silhouette™ is a collection of highly detailed white porcelain figurines, many with pewter, silver, gold or red accents. *Winter Silhouette* has an elegant simplicity that brings back Christmas visions of family pleasures in a bygone era.

Introduced in 1991, *Merry Makers®* are chubby little monks dressed in dark green robes. Standing just under four inches tall, each of these delightful friars is handcrafted of porcelain, and hand-painted. They work, play and sing together in happy harmony.

The year 1991 also saw the beginning of another new series, *All Through The House®*. Featuring backdrops and furniture, as well as figurines, these highly detailed pieces

The proper Edwardian Bears, "Nanny Maybold & Baby Arthur," are part of the delightful Upstairs, Downstairs Bears *series.*

offer warm, nostalgic memories inspired by the activities they portray. Made of cold cast porcelain and beautifully hand-painted, this charming collection celebrates family traditions *All Through The House*.

In 1994, a new collectible series was introduced called *The Upstairs, Downstairs Bears™*. Once upon a time...there was a household of proper Edwardian Bears. They resided in a large stately townhouse at Number 49 Theodore Square. Some of the bears lived Upstairs and some of the bears lived Downstairs. From the original designs by Carol Lawson, the well-known English illustrator and author, each of these enchanting, hand-painted resin bears are presented on mahogany bases with porcelain bottom stamps.

Snowbunnies™ are the latest introductions from Department 56, Inc. *Snowbunnies* collectibles are made of creamy bisque porcelain with delicate touches of pink on their ears and on the springtime bows tied around their necks. Their little bunny suits are covered with tiny bisque crystals, and their small cheerful faces are hand-painted with care. *Snowbunnies* are sure to hop into the springtime hearts of collectors everywhere.

Collectors Discover the Wide Range of Department 56, Inc. Creations

In addition to the popular collectibles already mentioned, Department 56, Inc. continues to develop colorful and innovative giftware, as well as ongoing lines for Spring and Easter, Christmas Trim, and many beautiful Christmas ornaments.

Seldom does a firm win the attention and loyalty of collectors as quickly as Department 56, Inc. has done since its first *Original Snow Village* buildings debuted in 1977. As one enthusiast stated, "A company can't make an item collectible. People have to make it collectible, and the people have discovered Department 56."

Department 56, Inc.
P.O. Box 44456
Eden Prairie, MN 55344-1456
(800) 548-8696

COLLECTORS' TOUR

One Village Place Showroom Tour
6436 City West Parkway
Eden Prairie, MN 55344
(800) LIT-TOWN (548-8696)

Reservations required. Call for further information.

Admission Fee: None

Collectors are greeted by staff members and are guided through historical displays of *The Original Snow Village, The Heritage Village Collection* and *Snowbabies*, plus a look at all the current giftware produced by Department 56, Inc.

WALT DISNEY CLASSICS COLLECTION

The Magic of Disney Welcomes the *Enchanted Places* Series

For more than 60 years, generations of moviegoers have grown up with a host of memorable Disney characters that seem a part of life. Everyone can recall the innocence and wonder of Bambi and his woodland friends. There's the artistic brilliance of *Fantasia*, with its Cupids, Centaurettes and Mushroom Dancers filling the screen. Cinderella found her Prince Charming and lived happily ever after. Audiences soared with Peter Pan on his adventures with the villain Captain Hook and the tick-tocking crocodile. And, of course, Mickey Mouse always makes everyone smile.

The *Walt Disney Classics Collection* brings a new dimension to these beloved characters, places and scenes that have warmed the hearts of children and adults. First introduced in 1992, the award-winning collection has its roots in animation with its more than 40 fine sculptures based on animated Disney films. With the Collection, Disney's cast of characters has gone from the big screen and into the homes of collectors around the world.

"Moments are what a film is essentially made of," said Roy E. Disney, vice-chairman of the board for The Walt Disney Company. "The notion that you can recreate some of those as a sculpture is pretty spectacular. The *Walt Disney Classics Collection* does this so well that the lifelikeness and believability of these pieces will catch your imagination and earn your affection like the original screen versions."

Disney Launches *Enchanted Places* Series

While millions have been touched by the warmth and charm of the Disney characters, many have also been intrigued by the imaginary worlds in which they live – worlds that were brought to life through the beautiful background art found only in Disney animation.

For the first time, these unforgettable film settings have been captured in a unique collection of fine animation art sculptures called *Disney's Enchanted Places*. Each hand-painted sculpture is a work of art, replicating the look, mood and style of the original background art used in the film.

"White Rabbit's House," an animation art sculpture from Disney's Enchanted Places, *perfectly duplicates the unique color combinations, asymmetrical lines and flamboyant detail of the famous scene from* Alice in Wonderland. *The suggested retail price is $175.*

The design and use of backgrounds have changed dramatically over the years. They have gone from flat, simple layouts to elaborate scenes of make-believe places such as the zany White Rabbit's House in *Alice In Wonderland*, Gepetto's Toy Shop in *Pinocchio* or the ominous Cave of Wonders in *Aladdin*.

The first three *Enchanted Places* sculptures, released in the summer of 1995, were "The Seven Dwarfs' Cottage" from *Snow White and the Seven Dwarfs*, "White Rabbit's House" from *Alice in Wonderland*, and "Woodcutter's Cottage" from *Sleeping Beauty*. Collectors are invited to register their sculptures to receive an official "property deed" signed by the animated owners.

"It's really quite astonishing that all the wonderment of these beautiful film settings has been recreated on such a small scale with the *Enchanted Places* collection," said John Hench, Disney artist and guiding spirit behind the creation of the series. "The richness of detail in the three-dimensional sculptures could never be replicated in the two dimensions of a picture."

Turning Two-Dimensional Artwork Into Three-Dimensional Works of Art

Walt Disney himself felt the use of backgrounds was key to the storytelling process. He brought a variety of classically trained artists to the studio and challenged them to develop film settings that would enhance the dramatic quality of the film. They sought this inspiration from a variety of resources including countless books, illustrations, architectural designs and locations worldwide.

To fully capture the rich detail found in these style-setting backgrounds, *Enchanted Places* artists study original layout drawings, paintings and the films themselves. They must also understand proper scale and envision unseen angles and viewpoints like the back of the "Seven Dwarfs' Cottage." It's this type of in-depth research and knowledge that enables Disney artists to transform these two-dimensional masterpieces into three-dimensional works of art.

Each *Enchanted Places* sculpture is originally sculpted in clay, then cast in a mixture of alabaster, marble and resin,

The Walt Disney Classics Collection *introduces* Disney's Enchanted Places, *recapturing the charm and magic of original film settings. "Woodcutter's Cottage," from* Sleeping Beauty *features detailed painting techniques that convey textures as varied as weathered wood and damp moss. The suggested retail price is $170.*

which is specially formulated to capture even the most minute detail. Small props such as the Dwarfs' picks, axes and shovels are cast individually in fine pewter then carefully hand-painted to enhance each sculpture, giving it that extra Disney touch.

Painting is one of the most complex and challenging parts of the creative process. Artists must treat each sculpture as a three-dimensional painting, using both oil and water colors and blending and shading to create the illusion of light, shadow and special textures such as weathered wood or old brick.

Because of this unique painting process, no two sculptures are exactly alike, which is why each piece is hand-numbered. They can evoke fond childhood memories and give everyone the chance to revisit some of the most magical places that until now only existed in fairy tales.

Walt Disney *Classics Collection* Recreates Disney Favorites with Perfection

Just as Disney artists painstakingly ensure perfection in the *Enchanted Places* series, each exquisite piece in the entire *Walt Disney Classics Collection* goes through several challenging processes to create a new genre – the animation art sculpture.

"It's a frozen moment in the duration of a Disney film," said Andreas Deja, a Disney animator. "We probably all experience scenes in these films we wish could go on longer, but of course they don't because they're telling a story and they have to move onto the next story point. That's the language of the film. What the *Classics Collection* does is hold it for you. If you have one of those moments in front of you interpreted in three dimensions as a sculpture, it is a whole new experience, and you come to appreciate the beautiful design, color and life of these characters."

Artists begin by going back to the original animation and studying original film references, sketches, painted cels, production drawings and video prints. From these, they select which magical storytelling moments to recreate such as Bambi meeting the little skunk named Flower or Donald Duck admiring Daisy's photograph. Through the use of Disney animators, each piece features specific designs to help convey the character's personality whether it's Goofy's flying ears and off-balance stance from *Symphony Hour* or the dancing pigs from *Three Little Pigs*. The sculptures are then painted using the same color palette as the original film. Captain Hook's vibrant appearance as he lunges for Peter Pan requires 30 colors and multiple kiln firings to make the original film hues.

Finally, animators always stretch to add that extra touch for believability – known at Disney as "plussing." The *Classics Collection* continues that tradition by uniquely combining the porcelain with materials such as blown glass, crystal or platinum to further the Disney "illusion of life."

"We learned as we began developing the *Walt Disney Classics Collection* that Disney really could bring magic to porcelain by applying the same principles we apply to animation, to our theme parks, to all the other things that Disney is known and loved for," said Susanne Lee, vice president of

Created by Disney artists with the utmost attention to detail and authenticity, "Snow White and the Seven Dwarfs" is among the memorable scenes from the Walt Disney Classics Collection.

The second in the American Folk Heroes *series created exclusively for Walt Disney Collectors Society members, "Slue Foot Sue" twirls her lasso as she rides a giant catfish down the river. The scene recreates the moment Pecos Bill first laid eyes on her. The suggested retail price is $695.*

Disney Collectibles.

The backstamp on each sculpture includes Walt Disney's signature logo, the name of the film and a special symbol to denote the year in which the piece was produced. Each piece also comes with a special Certificate of Authenticity signed by Roy E. Disney.

Limited Edition Collectibles Bring Back Memories

Within the Collection are special hand-numbered limited editions, annual editions and anniversary commemoratives that have become sought after by collectors. Among the most popular limited edition sculptures are "He Can Call Me A Flower If He Wants To" from the *Bambi* scene, "A Lovely Dress For Cinderelly" from the *Cinderella* scene, "Who's Afraid of the Big Bad Wolf?" from the *Three Little Pigs* scene and "A Firefly, A Pixie! Amazing!" from the *Peter Pan* scene.

The collection also features many scenes and characters that have never been portrayed in three dimensions, including Clarabelle Cow and Horace Horsecollar from *Symphony Hour* and Mickey and Minnie in the "rubber hose" animation style from the early black-and-white cartoon short *The Delivery Boy*.

Sharing the Magic with the Walt Disney Collectors Society

In 1993, the Walt Disney Collectors Society was launched to further celebrate the beauty of these animated sculptures and support the Collection. It's the first Disney-sponsored membership organization for collectors and Disney enthusiasts.

Members receive many benefits including a membership gift, which in past years has featured sculptures of Jiminy Cricket, the Cheshire Cat and Dumbo. Society members also have the special opportunity to acquire exclusive pieces, including those in the *Holiday Ornament*, *Animator's Choice* and *American Folk Heroes* series.

The third annual *Animator's Choice* sculpture brought back Cruella De Vil, everyone's favorite villainess from *101 Dalmatians*. Past characters in the series have included Donald Duck as "Admiral Duck" in *Sea Scouts*, and Mickey Mouse as "The Brave Little Tailor."

The second in the *American Folk Heroes* series was "Slue Foot Sue," the one true love of Pecos Bill, which was the debut sculpture. In 1995, the Society announced its first offering from the *Holiday Ornament* series. The ornament portrays Dumbo as he splashes in his first bath.

To join the Walt Disney Collectors Society, collectors can visit a Walt Disney Classics Collection dealer or call (800) WD-CLSIX.

The Walt Disney Company
500 South Buena Vista Street
Burbank, CA 91521-6876
(800) WD-CLSIX (678-6528)
Fax (818) 842-6039

COLLECTORS' CLUB

Walt Disney Collectors Society
P.O. Box 11090
Des Moines, IA 50336-1090
(800) 678-6528

Annual Dues: 1 Year – $55.00 for 1 Year; 2 Years – $99.00
Club Year: January-December

Benefits:
- Membership Gift: Disney Sculpture
- Redemption Certificate for Members-Only Figurine and Ornament
- Quarterly Magazine, *Sketches*
- Hard-bound Folio
- Personalized Membership Card
- Cloisonne Membership Pin
- "Newsflashes," Mailed to Members Announcing Special Events or Figurines

DUNCAN ROYALE

Bringing Santa Claus and a World of Fine Collectibles into the Hearts of Collectors

Back in 1983, Duncan Royale re-introduced Santa Claus to the world. But it wasn't simply the familiar jolly St. Nick with a flowing white beard, round belly, rosy cheeks, red coat and a team of reindeer waiting for the Christmas Eve adventure. The company's *History of Santa Claus Collection* retraced the origins, personalities and folklore surrounding this famous symbol of the holidays and good will.

For Duncan Royale, the rest is also history. The popular collection took the collectible market by storm and prepared the way for the company to launch other lines. Today, Duncan Royale offers hundreds of collectible pieces portraying everything from angels to "Little Rascals" characters and jazz musicians to clowns.

Under the leadership of Catherine Duncan, the company promises to continue its growth while still celebrating the many faces of Santa Claus and the holiday season.

In Greece, St. Basil's Day – also known as New Year's Day – is the time for exchanging gifts. Highly honored by the Greeks, "St. Basil" is considered the gift bringer and now appears in the Santa III *collection.*

Santa Series Delivers Magic for Duncan Royale

For more than a decade, Duncan Royale has been manufacturing limited edition cold cast porcelain figurines. It began with the *Santa I Collection*, which included 12 different Santas from around the world. Through extensive research, artists uncovered literature, history and mythology regarding Santa Claus, all of which influenced the present-day notion of St. Nick.

This research appears in a beautiful hard-cover book with the history of each Santa figurine for everyone to read about. The full-color book was so popular that it went to many printings, even after the collection was retired and sold out. The collectors of *Santa I* have enjoyed an average increase as high as any on the secondary market. The Nast Santa has sold for more than $5,000 yet originally retailed for only $90.00.

The Duncan Royale line now boasts *Santa II and III, Christmas Images, The History of Classic Entertainers* (retired with limited availability), *Masks of the Clown* (retired with limited availability), *The Early Americans, Ebony* collection, *Jazz Man, Buckwheat Collection, Jubilee Dancers, Ebony Angel, Greatest Gift ... Love, Family & Friends, Calendar Secrets* (retired with limited availability), and *Woodland Fairies*. Many lines are available in 18", 12" and 6" sizes while others appear on full-size and 3 1/2" mini plates. *Santa I and II* have been produced as Christmas ornaments.

Diverse Lines Join Santa Claus

In 1987, Duncan Royale introduced the *History of Classic Clowns and Entertainers*. This 24-piece collection chronicles the evolution of clowns and entertainers during the past 4,000 years – from Greco-Roman times through the 20th century with Bob Hope. A beautifully illustrated, hard-cover collector's book, *History of Classic Clowns and Entertainers*, puts in writing the memorable stories of these endearing champions of comedy who made everyone laugh.

"Auguste" is known to be a fun-loving, whiteface clown. In the History of Classic Clowns and Entertainers *collection, the comical character shows exactly why he found a target for his pranks and often became a scene stealer.*

One of the most delightful Duncan Royale inventions in the late 1980s was the *Woodland Fairies* series: a group of delightful characters capturing the antics of magical forest folk. Each character bears the name of a favorite tree or flower, including "Cherry," "Mulberry," "Apple," "Sycamore" and "Almond Blossom."

Calendar Secrets depicts the celebrations, traditions and legends of the 12 months of the year. They also illustrate the history of each month of the Roman calendar as the secrets unfold. To complement this magnificent collection, Duncan Royale has introduced a *Calendar Secrets* book, colorfully illustrated and filled with historical information and the lore behind how our calendar was formed and how the months were named. The collection is now retired, but some figurines are still available at stores nationwide.

America is a "new" country at just over 200 years of age. Since today's professionals enjoy learning about their counterparts of the past, Duncan Royale captured the essence of colonial careers in *The Early Americans*. Each individual honored in a limited edition figurine was selected for outstanding skills, as well as the ability to use imagination and humor to pave the way for others. The occupations include fireman, salesman, doctor, storekeeper, secretary and lawyer.

Inspired by the "Little Rascals" character from the famous "Our Gang" comedies, the *Buckwheat Collection* shows the renowned youngsters in a variety of popular poses and activities. Crafted by hand and painted in many bright colors, the figurine scenes show *Buckwheat* making a mess of his painting chore, smiling for the camera, and sitting beside his dog with the trademark bull's-eye marking.

According to Danish folklore, "Julenisse" would always leave gifts on Christmas Eve. From storybooks and traditional tales, this kind-hearted gnome is now remembered in the Santa III *collection.*

Collections Celebrate African-American Culture

The *Ebony* collection was created in tribute to African-American life, accomplishments and culture. This heritage has become one of the strongest building blocks of American society as we know it today. The musical forerunners of Soul, Gospel, Rock n' Roll, Blues and Jazz are deeply imbedded in Black American culture. The *Ebony* collection highlights numerous compelling personalities from these diverse musical "roots." Each figurine is individually numbered with an edition limited to 5,000 pieces. These endearing characters are sure to be treasured by collectors for years to come.

Another African-American collection is *Jubilee Dancers*. The collection spotlights energetic African dancers in colorful, traditional garb. Among the most recent introductions is "Bliss," a wedding couple celebrating the joyous bond of marriage. Limited to 5,000 pieces, "Bliss" is hand-painted and individually numbered. The other five figurines in the grouping are: "Lottie," "Lamar," "Fallana," "Keshia" and "Wilfred."

Family and Friends is the latest addition to the ongoing Ebony collection. Premiering the *Family and Friends* collection are five delightful figurines which depict a family on a picnic. "Millie" and "Agnes" are two friends sharing a lively conversation. In "Daddy," a father holds up a baby, while "Mommy and Me" shows a mother and daughter playing ring-around-the-rosie. A darling baby and his best friend, a large shaggy dog, look into a picnic basket in "Lunchtime." Each figurine in the series, created from an original sculpture by talented artist Shelley Tincher Buonaiuto, is hand-painted, individually numbered and limited to an edition of 5,000 pieces.

From the Jubilee Dancers *collection, "Lottie" shows off her traditional African-American dress and a wide smile. The highly detailed and colorful figurine stands about 12" tall.*

New Production Process Developed For Duncan Royale Figurines

A new process for creating the cold cast porcelain figurines has been invented by Duncan Royale's director of artists, Donna Pemberton. A patent is pending on this vibrant breakthrough. Donna has been experimenting with hundreds of formulas during her tenure with Duncan Royale, and now all new lines will incorporate Donna's molds and formulas.

Each Duncan Royale collection emerges as a result of hours of painstaking research and creative production. After the theme for a collection is developed, artists sketch renderings that exemplify the theme, tradition and history of each personality. When final drawings and colors are selected, the sculptor breathes dimension and "stop-frame action" into each character, adding detail and depth as directed by Catherine Duncan.

Molds are cast from the original clay sculpture, and the porcelain figurines are produced by a cold cast process which captures minute and intricate details. Precision hand-painting strokes each piece with vivid, vibrant color. On some pieces, 40 colors and shades may be used to obtain the desired hues. Each piece receives a limited edition number and its own mini book that tells a brief story about the figure. All Duncan Royale collectibles are security-packed in their own handsome gift boxes.

From the new Family and Friends *collection, "Agnes" and "Millie" share the latest news and gossip during a family picnic. The figurines are created from original sculptures by artist Shelley Tincher Buonaiuto and are limited to an edition of 5,000.*

New Artists Add Creative Touch

Catherine Duncan recently announced the commissioning of several new artists, including Michael and Shelley Tincher Buonaiuto. The artists will each develop their own unique line of products for Duncan Royale for introduction in 1996. Catherine has worked very closely with the in-house artists and commissioned artists throughout Duncan Royale's history. She has helped create the most popular items in Duncan Royale's wide range of collectibles.

Overseeing all in-house and commissioned artists is Donna Pemberton. At the tender age of four, Donna decided to devote her life to art – which has progressed from fingerpainting to ceramics, to painting and sculpting in all mediums. Donna's original work has been commissioned and purchased by such art collectors as John DuPont, Dick Clark and Herb Albert, just to name a few.

The sculptures of Michael and Shelley Buonaiuto use an unusual combination of various clays, porcelain and stoneware in a single work of art. Collectors are drawn to this pair's work not only for the technical achievement but also the highly personal quality that gives each piece a unique life and expression.

Invitation to Join the Duncan Royale Collectors Club

For those interested in learning more about these popular artists and lines, a membership in the Duncan Royale Collectors Club will answer any questions, preview upcoming introductions and provide exclusive opportunities. Members are invited to acquire special members-only pieces and to buy or sell Duncan Royale back issues on the exclusive Royale Exchange.

The "Royal Courier" is an informative and exciting newsletter that gives collectors news about product releases, company history, special offerings and more. Much-anticipated retirements are also announced in the newsletter.

Duncan Royale
1141 S. Acacia Ave.
Fullerton, CA 92631
(714) 879-1360
Fax: (714) 879-4611

COLLECTORS' CLUB

Duncan Royale Collectors Club
1141 S. Acacia Ave.
Fullerton, CA 92631
(714) 879-1360

Annual Dues: $30.00
Club Year: Anniversary of Sign-Up Date

Benefits:
- Membership Gift: Porcelain Bell Ornament
- Opportunity to Purchase Members-Only Figurines
- Quarterly Newsletter, "Royale Courier"
- Elegant Binder
- Membership Card
- Membership Certificate
- Catalog of Duncan Royale Limited Editions
- Free Regisration of Members' Collection

eggspressions!® inc.

At *eggspressions!*, Everything is Sunny Side Up

Like a shell opening to reveal its pearl, "Elegant Choice" is one of many collectible treasures in the "eggsclusive!" catalog. A genuine goose egg rests in an 18K gold-plated stand. Encrusted with Austrian crystals and gold, "Elegant Choice" features a creamy satin lining.

Mention decorated eggs to a passer-by and you're bound to trigger images of Easter bunnies, chocolate and marzipan!

Whisper decorated eggs to a collector and *eggspect* a look of delight. Savvy limited edition collectors know that decorated eggs are "hot" these days, a regal return to the Old World splendor made famous by Peter Carl Fabergé, jeweler to the last Czar of Russia. Fabergé set the standard for glittering masterworks with his *eggsceptional* works of art. Now, contemporary versions of these eggs are back – more wondrous than ever – thanks to an innovative South Dakota company named ***eggspressions!® inc.***, that makes decorated eggshells which *eggspress* the talents of their many artists.

Yes, Virginia, it's a real eggshell!

The exclamation point says it all. ***eggspressions!*** is today's benchmark for collectible eggs. Each "hatchling" is sentimental. Traditional. And ecologically "green." Thanks to their recycling efforts, even the insides are consumed when these *eggstraordinary* collectibles are made.

eggspressions! gives new meaning to the term "decorated egg." Though operating just three short years, they are roaring toward the future with all the ingredients necessary for success and growth: *eggspressive* artists; an *eggspert* staff; and a business philosophy that encourages creativity and *eggscellence*. In sum, ***eggspressions!*** collectible art is something to cluck about!

How the Dream Was Hatched

The Black Hills of South Dakota are the stuff of which western lore is made: Mount Rushmore's presidential faces overlook ghostly echos of cowboy and Indian skirmishes. Just down the road a piece, artist-designer and visionary-free-spirit Connie Drew oversees ***eggspressions!*** Known to wax poetic over the quintessential egg, Connie quickly convinces even the most *eggnorant* listener of their perfection.

"Eggs are wonderful and mystical," Connie *eggsplains*. "I think that God looked down from heaven and pondered 'What should I package LIFE into?' And He came up with the shape of an egg – it's nature's perfect package."

Citing a wealth of symbolism – birth, resurrection and good luck, for starters – Connie merges her feelings with the best genes an egg lover could have: Her grandmother and mother are descended from Czechoslovakian stock. Given her imagination, heritage and fascination with egg decoration, it's understandable that Connie would grow up with her own "CONtribution" to the art. Encouraged by craft magazines and armed with a passion for artistic challenges, Connie began making *eggsotic* eggs as gifts. Like many pioneers, her first efforts were nothing to crow about.

"Thirty years ago, the craft industry hadn't caught up with the 'eggers' yet, so our pieces were pretty primitive," she recalls. Fortunately, practice made perfect. Soon, Connie found herself juxtaposed between old and new world styles. Her inclination? Do 'em all...*eggsperiment* with everything! *Eggspect* the *eggsceptional!* Stealing hinges from old purses and discombobulating pieces of old jewelry to get the findings she needed was typical of Connie's approach. It worked!

As her *eggciting* business took on a life of its own, Connie realized she could no longer handle its rapid *eggspansion* alone. Friend Sandy

Surprise! Musical "Angel Bunny" and her baby wait to be discovered amid flowers and foliage inside this 6-1/2" goose egg. Open the shell, embellished with pearls, flowers and golden trim, and let the tune, "Edelweiss," lull your spirit. Only 250 of "Angel Bunny" eggsist!

Horwitz, with 20 years of jewelry experience under his belt, joined the *Egg Force* and the two opened the doors to ***eggspressions! inc.*** on July 14, 1992. The rest, as Connie might say, is *eggstory*.

Which Came First.... the Chicken or the Emu?

Like Connie's *eggstraordinary* designs, the process of creating a limited edition collectible *eggspression* is fanciful and *eggsacting*. Ideas are formulated in the "brooder," a special room for creative thought, tucked into their 10,000 square foot purple and green "eggplant." Here, supplies, materials, thoughts and energy merge to become new designs. Innovative thought is highly encouraged in the "brooder."

When the conceptual work concludes, "Nesters," Connie's affectionate name for the artists who make the eggs, bring designs to life with a flourish. Using infertile eggs (never from endangered species) supplied by domestic breeders, "Nesters" turn guinea, quail, pigeon, duck, goose, emu, rhea, ostrich and, of course, chicken eggs, into works of art. First, each is emptied of its contents via a tiny hole drilled into the egg. Contents are carefully *eggstracted* with compressed air. Then the eggshell is sterilized and dried. The edible portion of the eggs find their way into the pantries of local charitable organizations.

Babies breath and forget-me-nots surround the cradle as the baby bunny enjoys "Sweet Dreams" inside this cozy, 6" goose egg. Delicate green and white flowers nestle on a yellow, pearl finished outer shell. An open edition, "Sweet Dreams" is sheer enchantment!

Old World Splendor From the "Egg Plant"

At the center of the ***eggspressions!*** universe is a style of egg beloved by Connie Drew, for it's the decorating method she first learned from her mother. Called "Czeggs®," these delicate Czechoslovakian-styled eggs might be called a spiritual anchor at ***eggspressions!*** New Czeggs are eagerly anticipated by collectors each spring!

The drop-pull method for creating Czeggs is intriguing. After the eggs are emptied of their contents and cleaned, warm wax is dropped gently onto the shell, then "pulled" across the surface of the egg. Motifs are rich with Old World symbols. Many tell sacred stories. Once complete, Czeggs are dipped into a heavy lacquer. Drying takes an entire day, but when the process is complete, each egg glows with resilience and is ready to be embellished with genuine Austrian crystals and other touches.

Because Czeggs are entrenched in the Christian symbolism of their origins, contemporary designs are infused with the same inspired messages. Included in the *Easter Collection* are "The Last Supper," "The Crucifixion" and "The Resurrection." But as we stated earlier, Easter eggs are just the beginning of the ***eggspressions!*** story.

New World Delights: The Limited Edition Egg Hatches

"It's been a challenge to take what was basically a cottage industry and turn decorative eggs into collectibles," Sandy Horwitz, ***eggspressions!*** president remarks. But the challenge was met *egg-on* and today, special limited edition eggs from the ***eggspressions!*** "eggplant" are eagerly awaited by collectors around the world.

Christmas dreams linger as cherry red Austrian crystals frame a magnificently trimmed tree with a miniature wooden train circling its base. One of the most popular stars in a galaxy of other Christmas collectibles, "Choo-Choo Christmas" is fashioned of a goose egg trimmed with red ribbon and golden rope. A 9" stand makes this art shine!

Since the new company was organized in 1992, "firsts" have become commonplace. A premier "eggsclusives!" catalog debuted in 1994, containing ***eggspressions!*** first line of limited editions. Innovative gold tags and Certificates of Authenticity were designed to distinguish ***eggspressions!*** collectible art. A corporate mission to limit editions to small numbers delights collectors "in the know." Since an ***eggspressions!*** limited edition collectible egg has never *eggsceeded* a limit of 500, collectors are assured of *eggsclusivity*. Given the several hundred thousand egg collectors estimated in the U.S. alone, ***eggspressions!*** is truly at the forefront of limited edition collectible egg art.

By the way, ***eggspressions!*** boasts not one but four "sold out" eggs. "Passion," "Holiday Memories," "Purrfect Hug" and "Angel of Love" are available only on the secondary market these days – if you can find an owner willing to part with their treasure at any price! It's a good bet you'll find this list *eggspanding* as the popularity of egg collecting flourishes.

When is an Egg Not an Egg? When It's a Musical...a Jewel Box...an Ornament!

Music boxes, created from goose eggs, are astonishing accomplishments! Cleaned egg shells are painted, marked, hinged and cut with *eggsquisite* precision. A musical mechanism is inserted, followed by a special compound designed to add weight to the finished music box. Signature Austrian crystals, surrounded by other high quality trim and decorations, are added to produce elegant keepsakes enhanced by melodies that collectors adore.

In 1995, musicals "Angel Bunny" and "Reflections on Ice" followed in the *eggsteps* of the highly successful "Holiday Memories" musical egg lauded by collectors in 1994. In addition to these musical limited editions, the artistic spirits at ***eggspressions!*** have fashioned "special edition" music boxes for shops across America. As you can imagine, these *eggclusives* are in great demand!

Similar in size and design to music boxes, ***eggspressions!*** keepsake jewel boxes are breathtaking. Their varied styles and delicate embellishments charm and delight. Of particular note, the popular "Elegant Choice" and "Secret Garden" are beloved by collectors.

Finally, holiday ornaments for spring and Christmas display have become an *eggsciting* new avenue for the company. Driven by collector enthusiasm, an ever-*eggspanding* library of ornaments now includes wedding, anniversary, birthday and nature subjects. Given their philosophy of trying lots of new things to offer something for every egg collector, it's going to be mighty *eggsciting* to watch this company spread its wings in years to come!

Time *magazine says 69% of all Americans believe in angels. Collectors beholding "Angel Divine" could drive that figure higher! Suspended in the 5" shell of a hand-carved goose egg, "Angel Divine," limited to an edition of 250, is surrounded by angel hair 'clouds,' blue and green flowers, shimmering Austrian crystals and hand-painted doves.*

The *Eggsuberant* Spirit Behind the Vision

Ask the "Nesters," "Who drives the corporate spirit?" and you'll get a unified answer: Connie Drew. ***eggspressions!*** is her baby; it's seen in the diverse way the company looks, does business, and *eggsperiments* with innovative ideas to offer a splendid variety of collectible egg art to the American public.

"Outside the shell," Connie's personal world is a galaxy of color, wonder and fun. She lives her art, surrounding herself with soul comforts: twinkling stars, butterflies, Scarlett O'Hara dolls "draped in the drapes," bronze sculptures, Broadway music memorabilia, an *eggspanding* collection of opulent Judith Leiber purses (shaped like eggs, of course) and eggs, eggs, eggs. A *spe-shell* "unicorner" in her office contains dozens of the mythical creatures. But none more splendid than Connie, who's easy to spot in a crowd! She paints each fingernail a different color, dresses in purple and carries a Maschino purse fashioned like a goose. And then there's the shoes...! But no matter what she wears, Connie can be found working the kind of hours only a free spirit with a passion for her work could have the stamina to maintain.

"If you have a job you love, you'll never work another day in your life," Connie assures us as she ventures forth on a brand new day ready to discover, generate and *shellabrate* surprises along the way! An *eggspert*? You know it. But her world view *eggstends* far beyond the business built from the dreams of her childhood. Truth is, Connie Drew is an *eggspert* at living life as it was meant to be lived – and that's no yolk!

eggspressions! inc.
1635 Deadwood Avenue
Rapid City, SD 57702
(800) 551-9138
Fax (605) 342-8699

ENESCO CORPORATION

Collectibles for Every Collector

Enesco Corporation, one of the most respected names in the giftware industry, has been regarded as a leader in its field for thirty-six years. Credited with being among the most innovative and trend-setting designers and producers of fine gifts and collectibles, Enesco continues its steady growth and prominence worldwide.

The introduction of the now-famous Enesco *Precious Moments®* Collection catapulted Enesco from being a gift designer to its expanded role as a leading collectibles producer. Today Enesco has an international following of collectors with such award-winning collections as *Cherished Teddies®, Memories of Yesterday®, Small World of Music™, Treasury of Christmas Ornaments®* and many others.

Love, Caring and Sharing with the *Precious Moments* Collection

It was in 1978 that simple drawings of teardrop-eyed children evolved into The Enesco *Precious Moments* Collection. Under the guidance of Enesco President Eugene Freedman, the children with soulful expressions and inspirational titles soon became a phenomenon in the collectibles industry and are now the number one collectible in the country.

Adapted from the work of artist Sam Butcher, the *Precious Moments* Collection of porcelain bisque figurines has touched collectors with messages of love, caring and sharing. Even with his remarkable vision for the Collection, Freedman could not have foreseen the deep attachment collectors have for these teardrop-eyed figurines.

In June of 1995, Enesco launched the Century Circle Retailer program for 35 of its *Precious Moments* retailers. The new program gives consumers the opportunity to purchase exclusive, limited edition porcelain bisque figurines and product from these retailers. Century Circle Retailers are chosen for their commitment to support and maintain the integrity of the Collection. They have also shown extraordinary support to the hundreds of thousands of *Precious Moments* collectors and Club members throughout the country.

For collectors to communicate, exchange information and learn more about the Collection, Enesco sponsored the Precious Moments Collectors' Club in 1981. By the end of the charter year, tens of thousands had joined. Today the Enesco Precious Moments Collectors' Club is the largest club of its kind in the world and has been honored several times as the Collectors' Club of the Year by the National Association of Limited Edition Dealers (NALED), including the 1995 Collectors' Club of the Year. The Enesco Precious Moments Birthday Club was formed in 1985 to introduce children to collectibles and is celebrating its Tenth Anniversary during 1996. Both clubs have more than 500,000 members.

As a first-time introduction, Enesco Corporation is offering two personalized figurines as part of the Precious Moments® *Collection. The figurine of a stork with a baby bear is designed to include baby's name, birth date, weight and height in pink writing for girls and blue writing for boys. The girl with birthday cake figurine can be personalized by having a name imprinted on the cake.*

Memories of Yesterday Collection Develops Strong Following

While the *Precious Moments* Collection has flourished for more than fifteen years, other Enesco collectible lines have gained an enthusiastic collector following. Introduced in 1988, the *Memories of Yesterday* Collection is based on the work of famed British artist Mabel Lucie Attwell (1879-1965), regarded at the foremost illustrator of children in England this century.

The Collection portrays chubby-legged children of the '20s and '30s and is ranked among the country's top ten collectibles. In support of the collection, Enesco established the Memories of Yesterday Collector's Society, which officially began in 1991. In November of 1995, the Memories of Yesterday Collectors' Society celebrated its Fifth Anniversary with a Society Social.

Music, Magic and Motion with the *Small World of Music* Collection

The Enesco Musical Society also began its charter year in 1991 and supports the Enesco *Small World of Music* Collection of deluxe action musicals. More than 12 years ago, Enesco introduced the first of its action musicals by combining creativity, new technology, ambitious engineering and fine craftsmanship.

Subjects for the action musicals range from mice dancing on a grand piano to dalmatians frolicking in a fire truck, to "The Majestic," an old fashioned ferris wheel with flickering lights, motion and its own cassette deck that plays a tape of calliope music. These action musicals have earned numerous international awards and are highly sought-after throughout the world.

The Enesco Cherished Teddies® *Collection celebrates autumn with "Falling for You," a 3-1/2" figurine which features a bear sitting inside a bushel basket of leaves, holding a pin-wheel*

Cherished Teddies Wins Worldwide Recognition

Only introduced in 1992, the *Cherished Teddies* Collection has received international recognition from collectors and the collectibles industry. The adorable teddy bear figurines have found a special place in the hearts of collectors with their warm expressions and universal appeal.

Designed by artist and children's author Priscilla Hillman, each cold cast figurine comes with a Certificate of Adoption and its own name so collectors can "adopt" the teddy bear. Hillman's illustrations have also been recreated in the *Calico Kittens™* Collection, featuring cats and messages of love and friendship, and the *Priscilla's Mouse Tales™* Collection, which is based on well-known nursery rhymes.

On July 29, 1995, the first-ever nationwide *Cherished Teddies* Founder's Day event was held in honor of the Enesco *Cherished Teddies* Collection, the Cherished Teddies Club and the 100th Anniversary of Cherished Teddies Town, which is the imaginary town where the club bears reside.

The Enesco Cherished Teddies Club was formed on January 1, 1995, and currently has over 80,000 mem"bears" and has become one of Enesco's fastest growing clubs.

Enesco *Treasury of Christmas Ornaments* Sponsors Collectors' Club

With Christmas ornaments continuing as one of the fastest growing collectibles, the Enesco *Treasury of Christmas Ornaments* Collection has become a year-round collector favorite. Subjects for the extensive Collection include classic characters such as Mickey Mouse and GARFIELD as well as recognized licenses, including Disney, Parker Brothers, General Mills, McDonald's and Coca-Cola. Intricate detail, creativity and the use of familiar objects such as eyeglasses, teacups and utensils also characterize the Collection.

The popularity of the Collection resulted in the formation of the Treasury of Christmas Ornaments Collectors' Club, which began its Charter Year on July 1, 1993.

Enesco Forms Third Corporate Division — International Collections

In late 1994, Enesco formed the International Collections division as a marketing group to oversee the recent acquisitions of Lilliput Group PLC, Border Fine Arts, Otagiri Co. and Via Vermont. The division has since grown to include Calik's Artistry, Winterthur and the Elisa Collection.

The "Solo In The Spotlight, 1960" musical figurine recently introduced by Enesco Corporation portrays Barbie as a brunette. Limited to 2,500 pieces, this popular porcelain musical is part of the From Barbie™ With Love *collection and plays the tune "Turn Around."*

Collectibles include Lilliput Lane, a collection of miniature cottages, buildings and villages, Border Fine Arts, a collection of high-quality collectible animal sculptures, and the Elisa Collection of limited edition, contemporary ceramic sculptures based on the art work of Spanish sculptor Montserrat Ribes. Via Vermont, a producer of fine art glass giftware, and Calik's Artistry, a collection of hand-blown glass ornaments, are also produced as collectible lines. Otagiri is the producer of fine giftware and home accent products, and the Winterthur Collection is home decorative accessories based on antiques in Francis du Pont's Winterthur home.

The International Collections division adds diversification to Enesco by providing a solid foundation in the home decor and home accents market.

Lucy & Me and Other Enesco Collectibles

The year Sam Butcher's drawings were transformed into the *Precious Moments* Collection, Enesco discovered another artist. Lucy Rigg had been making teddy bears out of baker's clay for almost ten years when Freedman decided to turn her creations into porcelain bisque figurines in 1978. The *Lucy & Me®* Collection features teddy bears dressed up as familiar subjects and objects from flowers to pizza. The charming and whimsical appeal of these teddy bears has kept the collection growing in size and popularity over the past 15 years.

Enesco began a business relationship with Disney in 1989 as a licensee for Mickey & Co. giftware. To further enhance their relationship, Enesco acquired the rights, in 1995, to produce merchandise based on the Disney movie *Pocahontas*, making this new line Enesco's largest Disney collection. Merchandise includes ceramic and resin figurines, musicals, ornaments, banks, photo frames and waterballs based on the main human characters in the story. Enesco also recently acquired the license to produce giftware based on Disney's 34th full-length animated movie, *The Hunchback of Notre Dame*, to be released in June of 1996.

Enesco's *From Barbie™, With Love* Collection features authentically reproduced nostalgic and modern Barbie porcelain plates, musicals and accessory items. The Collection includes many limited edition pieces that capture the doll's glamour, beauty, style and careers over a period of 35 years.

In addition to a talented staff of nearly 60 artists and designers, Enesco also has collectibles from such well-known artists as Karen Hahn (*Laura's Attic™*), Mary Rhyner-Nadig (*Mary's Moo Moos, This Little Piggy, Mary's Hen House*), Ellen Williams (*Sisters and Best Friends*), Walt Disney (*Mickey & Co.*), Lesley Anne Ivory (*Ivory Cats*), Kathy Wise, Ed Van Rosemalen, Warren Kimble, Carol Endres, Bush Prisby, June Somerford (*Melly & Friends*), Peter Fagan (*Pennywhistle Lane/Centimental Bears*) and Klaus Wickl (*Gnomes*).

As collectors discriminately seek new collections for lasting appeal and interest, Enesco always discovers classics and new art to meet the demand. Based on its success with the *Precious Moments* Collection and its other popular collections, Enesco will certainly be a driving force in collectibles in the 1990s and beyond.

Enesco Corporation
225 Windsor Dr.
Itasca, IL 60143
(708) 875-5300
Fax (708) 875-5858

COLLECTORS' CLUBS

Enesco Cherished Teddies Club
P.O. Box 91796
Elk Grove Village, IL 60009-9179
(708) 875-5422

Annual Dues: $17.50
Club Year: January 1-December 31

Benefits:
- Membership Gift: Symbol of Membearship Figurine
- Opportunity to Purchase Two Membears Only Figurines
- Newspaper, *The Town Tattler*
- Key to Cherished Teddies Town Lapel Pin
- Membearship Certificate
- Decorative Easel

Enesco Precious Moments Birthday Club
P.O. Box 689
Itasca, IL 60143-0689
(708) 875-5411

Annual Dues: $20.00 for One Year – $38.00 for Two Years
Club Year: July 1-June 30

Benefits:
- Membership Gift: Symbol of Membership Figurine
- Opportunity to Purchase Members Only Porcelain Bisque Collectibles
- Newsletter, "Good News Parade"
- Personalized, Ready-To-Frame Certificate of Membership
- Personal Happy Birthday Card

Enesco Precious Moments Collectors' Club
P.O. Box 1466
Elk Grove Village, IL 60009-1466
(708) 875-5411

Annual Dues: $27.00
Club Year: January1-December 31

Benefits:
- Membership Gift: Symbol of Membership Figurine
- Opportunity to Purchase Members-Only Figurines
- Newsletter, "The GOODNEWSLETTER"
- Official Binder • Membership Card
- Official Gift Registry • Special Mailings
- Full Color Pocket Guide to The Enesco *Precious Moments* Collection
- Precious Moments Collectors' Club Cookie Cutter
- Invitations to Local and Regional Chapter Conventions

Enesco Treasury of Christmas Ornaments Collectors' Club
P.O. Box 773
Elk Grove Village, IL 60009-0773
(708) 875-5404

Annual Dues: $20.00
Club Year: January 1-December 31

Benefits:
- Membership Gift: Symbol of Membership Ornament
- Opportunity to Purchase Members-Only Ornaments
- Newsletter, "Treasured Times"
- Personalized Membership Card
- Collectors' Guide to the Treasury Collection
- Complimentary Lapel Pin for Renewing Members

Memories of Yesterday Collectors' Society
P.O. Box 245
Elk Grove Village, IL 60009-0245
(708) 875-5799

Annual Dues: $22.50
Club Year: January1-December 31

Benefits:
- Membership Gift: Symbol of Membership Figurine
- Opportunity to Purchase Members-Only Offerings
- Quarterly Newsletter, "Sharing Memories..."
- Personalized Membership Card • Gift Registry
- Set of Exclusvie Stationery
- Exclusive Brooch for Renewing Members

FJ DESIGNS, INC./THE CAT'S MEOW VILLAGE

America's Heritage Handcrafted in Miniature

Faline Fry Jones: creator of The Cat's Meow Village™.

With her bright smile and lively personality, Faline Fry Jones makes a wonderful "art ambassador" for her own delightful *The Cat's Meow Village™*. Created by Ms. Jones, these miniature, handcrafted buildings have delighted collectors for 13 years. What's more, Faline's marvelous accessories – everything from classic "Burma Shave Signs" to a "Rubbermaid Train Car" – add historical significance and warmhearted charm to each *Village* collection.

Faline's designs were in demand from the earliest days of her business – when she developed her concept of architectural reproductions of America's past while working in the basement of her home. Local Ohio gift shops sold the collectibles as fast as she could create them! When she entered the Columbus Gift Mart, the onslaught of orders was remarkable. By the Spring of 1984, 800 dealers were carrying *The Cat's Meow Village™* and Faline had hired 19 employees.

At first, the artist designed only fictitious buildings, but her initial attempts at creating replicas of actual buildings and historical landmarks earned great collector enthusiasm. In 1989, a new facility opened to house Faline's 130-member team of employees. Retirement of the first *Village* collectibles and the formation of the national Cat's Meow Collector's Club during that same period catapulted the *Village* into the national and international arena.

Another landmark event took place on August 9, 1993: the first-ever Cat's Meow Convention in Wooster, Ohio. Nearly 4,000 avid collectors gathered at the Wayne County Fair Grounds to celebrate the 10th anniversary of *The Cat's Meow Village™*. They viewed displays, enjoyed the Village museum, shopped in the company store, and chatted with Faline in her autograph tent, and through an auction helped raise over $9,000 for the Children's Defense Fund.

A Thriving Business Retains the "Family Touch"

As they did from the beginning, Faline Fry Jones' family members play an important part in the creation of her unique collectibles. In addition, more than 300 people are involved in producing Faline's irresistible buildings and accessories. Faline prides herself on providing opportunities for women, including numerous leadership roles, as well as opportunities to complete work at home or on "flex-time."

Even while her company grows and flourishes, Faline remains the driving force behind each design. Her camera is a constant companion when traveling, and she continues to take leads from her faithful collectors. She thrives on researching U.S. history and selects all the items in the regular product line. Casper, the famous *Village* black cat and trademark of an original Cat's Meow, appears on every piece along with Faline's signature.

Each *Village* piece travels through a painstaking, seven-stage production process which includes hand-tracing of pattern, hand-cutting, screen printing, and individual hand-finishing. Products are made from a wood medium, which proves ideal both for cutting and screen printing, and for long-term durability in display.

A Corporate Commitment to Community Service

An annual portion of the profits from the sale of *The Cat's Meow Village™* goes to the National Arbor Day Foundation. In addition, each year Faline selects different series and donates a portion of the first year's sales to other, established charitable organizations such as the American Red Cross, Salvation Army, United Negro College Fund, National Sudden Infant Death Syndrome Foundation, and the Children's Defense Fund.

This commitment to the larger community fits with the company's corporate values, which center on a positive work environment, mutual cooperation and support, friendliness, honesty, efficiency, clarity and partnership.

Historic Buildings Highlight Recent *Village* Introductions

Architectural gems from coast to coast inspired Faline's introductions for 1995. Her *California Mission Series* will retire at the end of the year 2000 and includes the renowned church buildings: "Mission San Luis Rey," "Mission San Buenaventura," "Mission Dolores" and "Mission San Juan Bautista."

The *Mt. Rushmore Presidential Series*, the 1995 Collectors Club Edition, covers four renowned edifices: "Tuckahoe Plantation," "Theodore

Roosevelt Birthplace," "Metamora Courthouse," and "George Washington Birthplace." In addition, the Club Gift House for 1995 is "Eleanor Roosevelt House."

Series XIII of the Village pieces was one Faline was ready to skip for superstitious reasons, until she realized she could simply place two images of Casper on each piece. "You've heard the saying 'two negatives equal a positive,'" she relates, referring to the so-called "bad luck" a black cat like Casper could bring. Included in this series are replicas of eight charming "vintage" buildings from around the nation including "Hospital," "Alvanas & Coe Barbers," "Schneider's Bakery," "YMCA," "Cedar School," "Public Library," "Needleworker" and "Susquehanna Antiques." All of these items are set to retire on December 31, 2000.

Also unveiled during 1995 was an appealing *Annual Edition Collection* – each with a special paw print mark added to the building. These pieces are limited in production to the year of introduction only. They include: "Becky Thatcher House," first of four in the *Mark Twain's Hannibal Series*; "Creamery Bridge," first of four in the *Covered Bridge Series*; "Sideshow," first of four in the *Circus Series*; and John Coffin House, first of four in the *Martha's Vineyard Series*.

Wonderful Victorian homes in the *Daughters of the Painted Ladies Series* were introduced April 1, 1995 to retire at the end of the year 2000. They include: "Barber Cottage," "Hall Cottage," "The Painted Lady" and "The Fan House." From the *Historic Nauvoo Series* – focused on the restored village of Nauvoo, Illinois – come these Village beauties: "Cultural Hall," "J. Browning Gunsmith," "Printing Office," and "Stoddard Home & Tinsmith." Introduced June 1, 1995, these four pieces also will retire on December 31, 2000.

The *Shaker Village Series* offers the "Great Stone Dwelling," "Meetinghouse," "Trustees Office" and "Round Barn," while the *Bed and Breakfast Series* combines "Kinter House Inn," "Southmoreland," "Victorian Mansion" and "Glen Iris." All will be available until retirement at the end of the year 2000.

A *New York Christmas Series* – available only from June 1, 1995 until December 31 of the same year – includes "Clement C. Moore House," "Fulton Market," "St. Marks-In-The Bowery," and "Fraunces Tavern." Also on the Christmas theme are a series of ornaments available during that same limited time period in 1995: "Yaquina Bay Light," "Holly Hill Farmhouse," "Carnegie Library," "Unitarian Church," "St. James General Store," and "North Central School."

New accessory pieces introduced at various points throughout 1995 all are slated to retire on December 31, 2000. They add a great deal of ambiance and charm to a home display of *Village* pieces, and they include everything from trees, railroad cars and mission bells, to fences, signs and ball players.

A "surprise" release in mid-1995, the *New Life Celebration Series*, offers collectors the added attraction of personalization for certain *Village* pieces. In addition, many popular *Village* issues introduced since 1990 are still available from dealers or are only recently retired.

Series XIII of The Cat's Meow Village™ *features two black Caspers (the Cat's Meow trademark cat) on each building. Introduced in 1995, these pieces will retire at the end of the year 2000. They include: (top row, left to right) "Cedar School," "Schneider's Bakery," "Needleworker," "YMCA," and (bottom row, left to right) "Hospital," "Susquehanna Antiques," "Public Library" and "Alvanas & Coe Barbers."*

Collectors Are Warmly Invited to "Join the Club"

The Cat's Meow Collectors Club is one of the fastest growing collectors clubs in the country with more than 35,000 members in the first five years of its existence. Its exclusive Club pieces already have exhibited strong secondary market growth as well. Weekly, Club personnel receive approximately 500 letters and answer about 100 phone calls from members across the country.

New members pay an enrollment fee of $25.00, for which they receive a Free Club Gift House, Free Club Logo Gift, a Membership Card, Club Notebook with color product sheets for the year, a subscription to "The Mews" Club Newsletter, a subscription to the "Village Exchange" with secondary market information, and access to the Custom Search program featuring custom designs. Renewing members pay $22.00 per year for the same benefits. Canadians and individuals outside the U.S. pay $5.00 additional (American dollars only).

Cat's Meow enthusiasts enjoy a standing invitation to visit Club headquarters in Wooster, Ohio, and tour the production facilities for the *Village* collections. Tours take place each weekday Monday through Friday at 10:00 a.m. and 1:00 p.m.

A Future With International Flair

While the *Village* first won popularity in Ohio and Pennsylvania, each year brings more and more geographic diversity to *The Cat's Meow Village™* collector family. Expansion into the West Coast is enhanced by Faline's development of buildings and accessories highlighting the West and Southwest. The firm has entered the international market, which will help boost the firm's dealer roster from the present 2,900 to nearly 4,000.

The *Village* will have new, special, one-year editions while reviving a long-time favorite: Christmas ornaments. More and more buildings featuring American heritage are in the works, and there will be future Conventions to celebrate milestones. Whatever surprises are in store for collectors, however, Faline Fry Jones and her crew promise that the charm and craftsmanship which have established *The Cat's Meow Village* will remain at the center of each new venture.

The birth of Faline's daughter, Grace Elizabeth, in 1993 inspired her to create this Nursery Rhyme *series, including: (top row, left to right) "House That Jack Built," "Cat & The Fiddle," "Crooked House;" and (bottom row, left to right) "Street Lamp," "Old Woman In The Shoe" and "Peter, Peter Pumpkin Eater."*

FJ Designs, Inc.
Makers of Cat's Meow Village
2163 Great Trails Drive
Wooster, OH 44691-3738
(216) 264-1377
Fax (216) 263-0219

COLLECTORS' CLUB/TOUR

Cat's Meow Collectors Club
Box 635
Wooster, OH 44691-0635
(216) 264-1377 Ext. 225

Annual Dues: $25.00 - Renewal: $22.00
Club Year: Anniversary of Sign-Up Date

Benefits:
- Membership Gift: Choice of Club Logo Umbrella or Collectors Club Accessory, "Westtown Water Tower"
- Opportunity to Purchase Members-Only Piece
- Quarterly Newsletter, "Mews"
- Subscription to the "Village Exchange"
- Membership Card
- Club Notebook
- Custom Search Program for Dealer Exclusives

FJ Designs, "The Cat's Meow" Factory Tour
2163 Great Trails Drive
Wooster, OH 44691
(216) 264-1377 Ext. 200

Hours: Monday through Friday, 10 a.m. and 1 p.m.
Closed major holidays.

Admission Fee: None

The tour of the production facilities at FJ Designs takes approximately 30 minutes. Visitors are able to watch skilled artisans produce the handcrafted *Cat's Meow Village™* collections.

FENTON ART GLASS

A Continuing Celebration in Fine Glass

The year: 2005. The event: an extravaganza to mark the 100th anniversary of Fenton Art Glass. Today – with less than 10 years to go before this remarkable milestone – Fenton family members and artists work in a concerted effort to continue their company's rise as one of America's leading creators of collector's items.

Each year Fenton introduces new collectibles in the spirit of the company's long-standing philosophy: the production of unique glass treatments featuring the age-old techniques of handcraftsmanship, conveyed from generation to generation.

A Family of Innovative Glass Artists

The Fenton Art Glass Company was founded in 1905 by Frank L. Fenton and his brother John, in an old glass factory building in Martins Ferry, Ohio. Here, they painted decorations on glass blanks made by other firms. The Fentons had trouble getting the glass they wanted when they wanted it, and soon decided to produce their own. The first glass from the Fenton factory in Williamstown, West Virginia, was made on January 2, 1907.

One of the first colors produced by the new company was called Chocolate Glass, and in late 1907, Fenton introduced iridescent pressed glass. (Fifty years later this glass was called Carnival Glass.) Iridescent glass was still selling in the 1920s, but it was made in delicate pastel colors with very little pattern in a treatment called "stretch glass." High quality Carnival Glass now sells for as much as $600 to $4,500 a piece. Recently, a rare piece sold for $22,500.

A Perfume Bottle Brightens the Depression for Fenton

During the 1930s and 1940s, Fenton Art Glass struggled to survive the Depression and war shortages. Fenton included production of mixing bowls and orange juice reamers to keep people working, but did not hold back on developing beautiful new colors. Jade, Mandarin Red, Mulberry and Peach Blow from this period are eagerly sought by Fenton collectors today.

Fenton recovered after the Depression with the help of a little hobnail perfume bottle designed at the behest of the Allen B. Wrisley Company. The bottle business made Fenton well again and also opened new business for hobnail glass and antique reproductions of Victorian glass.

Frank and Bill Fenton Assume Leadership Roles

Between 1948 and 1949, the top three members of Fenton's original management died, and brothers Frank M. Fenton, age 33, and Bill Fenton, age 25, took over as President and Vice-President of Sales respectively. The next five years were rough ones, but then milk glass began to sell beautifully all over the country. Fenton's hobnail milk glass became the company's bread-and-butter line.

The team of Frank and Bill Fenton led the factory through significant growth for the next 30-plus years. Together they continued to develop new designs based on the flexibility and character of handmade glass.

A Third Generation of Leadership

In February, 1986, the leadership of Fenton Art Glass passed to the third generation when George W. Fenton became President. Bill Fenton is Chairman of the Board and Frank is retired, but both are at work every day as advisors. Today there are 11 family members working in the management of The Fenton Art Glass Company. With 450 employees, the company is now the largest producer of handmade colored glass giftware in the United States.

While a number of hand glass companies have closed their doors over the past 15 years, Fenton has survived and grown by continuing to be flexible, and by offering a constant stream of new products to the market.

An Array of Jewel-Like Fenton Glass Creations

Fenton Art Glass is renowned for creating beautiful and unique colors in glass. These include exotic glass varieties in rich shades such as Cranberry,

This bell, vase and basket – introduced as part of Fenton's 90th Anniversary Collection *for a one-year period – combine a classic coloration called Celeste Blue with hand-painted Coralene Floral. Celeste Blue was first developed in 1921 and has not been offered in the Fenton line since the mid-1920s. The raised "Coralene" texture is achieved with ground-up glass and adds texture and dimension to each piece.*

Mulberry, Opalescent and Burmese. Fenton's iridescent "Carnival" glass enjoys a history extending back to 1907, and fiery Opalescent gleams in transparent colored glass that shades to opaque white. With an appreciation of the past and an eye to the future, Fenton brings back the rare collectible treatments of bygone eras while continually developing new and exciting colors to coordinate with new decorating trends.

At Fenton, each piece of glassware is an individual creation from a skilled hand glassworker. As seasoned collectors know, only an unfeeling machine can produce "glass armies" of unvarying detail. Much of the charm of true Fenton Art Glass comes from its stretched and fluted shapes that can only be created by hand.

Like most experts, the master glassworker makes this craft appear simple. Even so, if you watch the people making Fenton glass, you will see the hundreds of appraising glances that carefully assay each piece as it passes from hand to hand. Many of the looks say proudly, "That's mine, I created it."

Fenton has its own mould shop, which enhances the company's ability to develop and introduce new designs. Patterns and designs are chipped into the cast iron moulds by hand. Many Fenton creations are painted by hand by individual artists who proudly sign each piece.

Special Fenton Offerings Intrigue Collectors

Each year, Fenton Art Glass produces new editions for several popular series which are strictly limited editions. These include the *Family Signature* series, *Historical Collection*, *Connoisseur Collection*, *Collectible Eggs*, and *Christmas*, *Valentines* and *Easter* limited editions.

The *Family Signature* series includes a few select pieces which represent the glass worker's and decorator's finest creations. Classic moulds from the past inspire the *Historical Collection* pieces, all made in unique colors and treatments. The *Connoisseur Collection* features a small grouping of art objects made in exotic glass treatments.

For Christmas, Fenton produces an annual limited edition collection including a plate, bell, fairy light and lamp – all entirely hand-painted. For Valentines, Fenton introduces new items each year in a Cranberry Opalescent Heart pattern, as well as one to three items in the Mary Gregory style of painting. Mouthblown eggs and hand-pressed collectible eggs are showcased in Fenton's Easter offerings.

What's more, Fenton Showcase Dealers now may offer two exclusive Fenton special items each year. In 1995, the Showcase Dealer exclusives were: one additional *Family Signature* series item in Cranberry Opalescent, signed by President George Fenton; and one exclusive Burmese piece from the special *90th Anniversary* collection.

Fenton Collectors Benefit by Knowledge of Glass Markings

The Handler's Mark, Decorator's Signature, and Fenton Logo represent three markings that "savvy" Fenton collectors should know. A "Handler's Mark" – different for each craftsman – is applied to each Fenton basket by the highly skilled person who attaches the handle. The "Decorator's Signature" appears on the bottom of each hand-painted piece, and the "Fenton Logo" is placed on each piece of glass to permanently mark it as authentically Fenton.

Fenton logos vary slightly depending upon when the piece was made and what type of glass it represents. These markings help collectors to authenticate their holdings and evaluate possible purchases on the secondary market.

Clubs and Tours Enhance Fenton Collecting

Fenton invites collectors to join one or both of the national organizations formed in celebration of Fenton Art Glass. The Fenton Art Glass Collectors of America (FAGCA) was chartered in 1977. With 20 local chapters, the organization has over 5,000 current members. The National Fenton Glass Society was formed in 1990 and incorporated in Ohio in 1991.

Regular 45-minute tours of the Fenton Art Glass factory and museum take place Monday through Friday. Collectors are invited to call the Fenton Gift Shop at (304) 375-7772 for specifics on the free tours of the Williamstown, West Virginia facility.

The Fenton Tradition: Born of a Proud Glassmaking History

For three millennia, glass has delighted and served people in their homes, their industries, and their places of worship. The first industry in the American colonies was a hand glass shop started at Jamestown, Virginia, in 1608. In America, glassware reached a new zenith during the last half of the 1800s, as a newly united nation grew to its full destiny.

It is this tradition of the glassmaker's art which is painstakingly recreated in Fenton Art Glass. Now, as they approach their Centennial as a family-owned company, the Fentons take pride in the fact that Fenton glass has itself become a modern American tradition. To every beholder, Fenton handmade glass gives back a little store

Don Fenton's signature appears on this Spruce Green "Hex Vase," which features hand-painted flowers and a butterfly. Pieces like this from the Fenton Family Signature *series are available for a limited time each year.*

of the affection that went into its making. No gift seems quite as intimate in its ability to convey this care and regard. And to those who collect, display and use Fenton Art Glass pieces, this may be the greatest gift of all.

The Fenton Art Glass Company
700 Elizabeth Street
Williamstown, WV 26187
(304) 375-6122
Fax (304) 375-6459

The "Burmese Hummingbird Vase," part of Fenton's 90th Anniversary Special Burmese Offering, is hand-painted with gold accents, and signed by its artist. It is limited to 790 pieces.

COLLECTORS' CLUBS/MUSEUM/TOUR

Fenton Art Glass Collectors of America (FAGCA)
P.O. Box 384
Williamstown, WV 26187
(304) 375-6196

Annual Dues: $15.00 - Associate Membership: $2.00
Club Year: Anniversary of Sign-Up Date

Benefits:
- Opportunity to Purchase Members-Only Glass Piece
- Bi-monthly Newsletter, "The Butterfly Net"
- Buy/Sell Matching Service through Newsletter
- Annual Convention
- Local Club Chapters

National Fenton Glass Society (NFGS)
P.O. Box 4008
Marietta, OH 45750

Annual Dues: $15.00 - Associate Membership: $2.00
Club Year: Anniversary of Sign-Up Date

Benefits:
- Opportunity to Purchase Members-Only Glass Pieces
- Bi-monthly Newsletter, "The Fenton Flyer"
- Buy/Sell Matching Service
- Annual Convention and Auctions
- Local Club Chapters

Fenton Art Glass Company Museum & Tour
420 Caroline Ave.
Williamstown, WV 26187
(304) 375-7772

Hours: Monday through Saturday, 8:30 a.m. - 4:30 p.m.
Closed on major holidays and the first two weeks in July.
Admission Fee: Museum: $1.00 Adults: $.50 Children
Tour: Free

The Fenton Art Glass Museum offers examples of Ohio Valley glass with major emphasis on Fenton glass made from 1905 to 1955. A 30-minute movie on the making of Fenton glass is shown throughout the day.

The 40-minute factory tour allows visitors to watch highly skilled craftsmen create handmade glass from its moulten state to the finished product. A gift shop is also located on the premises.

FLAMBRO IMPORTS, INC.

Emmett Kelly, Jr. Was Just the Beginning...Many Collectibles Now Carry the Line "Exclusively Flambro"

When Louis and Stanley Flamm started Flambro Imports, Inc. in 1965, they had no idea how successful their business would become! Farsightedness, savvy business 'know-how' and creative thinking turned out to be the "right stuff" for Flambro, whose name has become synonymous with the word 'collectible.' Thirty years later, this company, which took off by promoting 'America's Favorite Clown' - Emmett Kelly, Jr., has expanded to include many "Exclusively Flambro" lines, and is growing internationally as well!

Flambro's Remarkable History

Initially, the Flamm brothers sold promotional merchandise used as give-aways and door-busters (loss-leaders to entice new customers into stores). At that time, many ceramic products in the U.S. were made in Japan, and of low quality. Business proved so successful, Flambro, who had been buying from other importers, decided to join the importing business themselves. They continued importing inexpensive promotional items until the 1970s when they began importing better-quality giftware from Taiwan.

During the '70s, many less expensive ceramic factories turned to Taiwan, not Japan, since the labor market could support a low-cost, high-quality product. In those days, many key employees joined other competitors or started their own factories. Instigated via a friendship between Louis Flamm and one of the top porcelain manufacturers, ten leading porcelain producers banded together to form the TTTMA (Taiwan Tao Tsu - Ceramics - Manufacturers Association) in 1978, when industry control was greatly needed. TTTMA's purpose was to cooperate in the purchase of raw materials, share technology and information and stop corporate espionage. Each factory who joined produced a different item. Flambro was named U.S. representative of the group, and in 1980, ten additional factories joined the association.

In 1972, Allan Flamm joined his father, Louis, as a Flambro Sales Executive. In 1975, Allan was promoted to Vice President of Sales, then to Company President when Louis retired in 1982. Stanley Flamm, Allan's uncle, died in 1975. In January of 1995, Louis died, but not before seeing Flambro enter its 30th year of business.

In 1994, Flambro, under Allan's leadership, joined forces with Collectible World Studios of Stoke-On-Trent, England. This collectible firm, run by President Bill Dodd, named Flambro its sole USA distributor for their highly successful collectible lines, *Pocket Dragons* and *Piggin'*. With sales and collector club memberships growing rapidly and internationally, this alliance is proving to be a major success.

Flambro's Philosophy and a Peek at the Future

Flambro's company philosophy is to keep their collectors happy! Today, happy means knowing the collectors' ideals of high quality and reasonable price in a desirable piece of merchandise. As collector demands grow, so do Flambro's efforts to provide excellent product, promotions, sales, service and customer satisfaction. Company growth is rapid with sales up, current lines expanding and new collectibles being introduced. Many new lines are labeled "Exclusively Flambro" - another 'self-promotion' in terms of retailer and consumer recognition.

Flambro's strength has always rested with its limited edition collectibles, especially since signing its first licensing agreement with Emmett Kelly, Jr. in 1980. Today, they carry a full range of collectible merchandise. 1996 will see the addition of *Peanuts* character items and the National Hockey League. Flambro's goal is to carry products to make and keep every collector happy!

Inspired Product Lines Attract Fans of All Ages

The *Emmett Kelly, Jr.* series, begun in 1980, was Flambro's first claim to fame! Its phenomenal success has helped early limited edition pieces soar in value on the secondary market - now worth many times their original retail price. Emmett Kelly, Jr. collectibles have expanded from the first porcelain lines and annual limited edition pieces to include newer resin series: *Real Rags*, fashioned after EKJ's famous tattered suits; *Images of Emmett*, displaying a distinct likeness to EKJ's facial features; and the *Little Emmett* line, created in celebration of EKJ's 70th birthday in 1994.

Little Emmett, a reflection of Emmett's childhood, is an adorable line that brings out the 'kid' in collectors of

"35 Years of Clowning" (left) depicts Emmett in full makeup on a regal elephant standing atop a fine wood base with brass nameplate. On the right, "Emmett Kelly Jr.'s All-Star Circus 20th Anniversary" sculpture is a masterpiece of complexity and color. Both are 1995 limited editions.

all ages. It provides a positive image for children, is of interest to parents and grandparents, and features birthday figurines from ages one to ten, musicals, bookends, vignette figurines and more. New pieces are added annually.

Pocket Dragons, part of Flambro's alliance with Collectible World Studios, is proving to be a highly-successful line. Created by nationally-known artist/sculptor, Real Musgrave, these collectibles originated from his childhood love of dragons and an interest in bringing "magic" to life. *Pocket Dragons* are mischievous and playful, with a keen desire to hide in cozy corners and collectors' pockets. Real's love for his creations is of special interest to collectors. New *Pocket Dragons* are introduced annually.

Piggin', another line Flambro distributes nationally for CWS, is a comical pig line created by English artist David Corbridge. A self-proclaimed pig lover, David designs his collection with English humor. New pieces appear annually.

Flambro Products – Something For Every Collector

From Joan Berg Victor's imagination comes the collectible Christmas villages, *Pleasantville* and *Santaville*, created exclusively for Flambro. Based on the book, *Pleasantville 1893*, this town captures the simplicity of small-town, turn-of-the-century America, inviting the collector to step back in time, meet the make-believe townfolk and enjoy their easy way of life. The village consists of vignettes: Main Street, Orchard Street, Elm Street, River Road and Balcomb's Farm, each adding to *Pleasantville's* charm.

Santaville - The Christmas That Almost Never Was, offers an enchanting look at the North Pole. This unique village, based on a poem written by Stanley Wiklinski with creative concept by Joan, takes the collector inside the working world of Santa, his elfin helpers and their critter assistants. Many pieces are created from a tree, and the buildings offer a cut-out back view of what's going on inside. "Father Christmas' Ice Castle" and the "Baby's Toy Shoppe" are two of *Santaville's* fascinating pieces.

In 1994, Flambro created baseball collectibles, with official licensing by Major League Baseball Properties. *Major League Baseball Santa* ornaments, superbly detailed and painted, are dressed in uniforms of today's favorite teams. *The Cooperstown Collection* recreates fond memories of a bygone baseball era, and includes action-posed Santa figurines and ornaments in uniforms of yesterday's great teams, and musical waterglobes with detailed bases that play "Take Me Out to the Ball Game." Both baseball lines grow on a yearly basis, with the addition of more teams to the lists.

Great African-American baseball players, and the teams that nurtured their dreams, receive Flambro's MVP Award as The Negro Leagues *opened the 1995 season. The series includes: collectible figurines sporting authentic logos of legendary teams, ornaments, coffee mugs, baseball ornaments, magnets, lapel pins and a collector's plate.*

1995 introduced *The Negro Leagues*, a tribute to the professional African-American teams of yesterday. This series, honoring the achievements of great teams and players, includes figurines, Santa ornaments, baseball ornaments, lapel pins, magnets, coffee mugs and a multi-logo collector plate.

Fascinating new resin technology is behind Flambro's whimsical pen line, *The Pen Station*. Created by Systems Technologies of New York, who chose Flambro as its sole sales/marketing partner in this exciting venture, the line presently includes pens and bases with Christmas, cat, zodiac, fruit, vegetable and sports designs. Patents are pending on the process alone, so more is sure to follow.

Meet Flambro's "Star Performers"

Emmett Kelly, Jr.'s earliest memories are of the circus and performing! Born in November 1924, to two circus aerialists, Emmett Kelly, Sr. and wife Eva, Emmett spent his early years traveling with his parents and the circus. As a young man, he joined the Navy. He served during World War II in the Pacific, participating in three invasions, including Okinawa and Iwo Jima.

His life as a clown began in the mid-60s. His dad decided that Emmett, Jr. should carry on the Weary Willie character he had created during the Depression. Emmett altered Weary Willie a little, added a crownless hat, and became Emmett Kelly, Jr! For many years, EKJ has provided a special joy for fans who throng to get his autograph and peek at 'America's Favorite Clown.'

Joan Berg Victor's diversified background has played a part in her creative work with Flambro. Raised in the Midwest, she earned degrees from Newcomb College, the Women's College of Tulane University and Yale University. Over the years, Joan has written and illustrated over two dozen books, many created for children. As her own children grew older, she adapted her books to their interest level. Joan's favorite book is the one on which the *Pleasantville* village is based. Her drawings and paintings can be found in private and museum collections across the country, and she has been featured in *Fortune* magazine and *The Wall Street Journal*.

Real Musgrave has always been an artist. While young, he took private art lessons. Throughout his school years, he came to realize the creative world he could produce might bring him great joy, fame and fortune. Later, he graduated with a BFA in drawing, painting and printmaking from Texas

The 1995 Pocket Dragons. *These precious tricksters are individual delights - displayed as a group, they're sheer magic.*

Tech University where he also studied sociology and anthropology. This unusual combination of science and fine art led Real to see everyday events in a "magical," whimsical way.

Real and his wife Muff developed and marketed limited edition etchings and prints featuring the *Pocket Dragons*, wizards and gargoyles. In 1978, Muff quit her job to become Real's full-time creative partner. Real has won awards and licensed his art for greeting cards, posters, etc. His whimsical style attracted Bill Dodd, President of Collectible World Studios in England. Soon, *The Whimsical World of Pocket Dragons* was launched, with production of the *Pocket Dragon* figurines.

As creator of *Piggin'*, David Corbridge combines interests in wildlife, painting, drawing, illustrating, sculpting – and pigs! Having lived on an English farm for years, he developed a keen understanding of pigs, their personalities and idiosyncratic ways. David fondly states, "To know pigs is to love them." The dominant appeal of *Piggin'* collectibles is David's English sense of humor, displayed not only on each pig's face, but in their names as well.

Important Information About Popular Flambro Collector Clubs

Flambro sponsors several fun-filled collector clubs. The Emmett Kelly, Jr. Collectors' Society is a select group of collectors who share affection and admiration for America's favorite clown. The Little Emmett Collectors' Club – a club with the focus on children, but open to collectors of all ages – is a way to spark childrens' interest in the art of collecting. Parents and grandparents are especially welcome.

Pleasantville 1893 Historical Preservation Society is a must for true collectors of the *Pleasantville 1893 Storybook Village*, and the Pocket Dragons and Friends Collectors Club is a necessity for all lovers of these magical green characters.

Flambro Imports
1530 Ellsworth Industrial Drive
Atlanta, GA 30318
(404) 352-1381
Fax (404) 352-2150

COLLECTORS' CLUBS

EKJ Collectors' Society
P.O. Box 93507, Atlanta, GA 30377-0507
(800) EKJ-CLUB
Annual Dues: $30.00
Renewal: $15.00 for One Year
$50.00 for Four Years
Club Year: January-December
Collectors' Year: Anniversary of Sign-Up Date

Benefits:
- Membership Gift: Collectors' Plaque
- Redemption Coupon for Members-Only Figurine
- Quarterly Newsletter, "EKJournal"
- Binder
- Membership Card
- EKJ Catalog
- Toll Free Collectors' Hotline
- EKJ Lapel Pin
- Free Registration of Figurines
- Annual Collector Registry Listing
- Special Club-Sponsored Events

Little Emmett Collectors' Society
P.O. Box 93507, Atlanta, GA 30377-0507
(800) EKJ-CLUB
Annual Dues: $10.00
Club Year: Anniversary of Sign-Up Date

Benefits:
- Personalized Membership Card
- Quarterly Newsletter, "What's News with Little Emmett"
- Bookmark
- Cut-Out Color Mask
- Collectors' Catalog
- Little Emmett Activity Book
- Little Emmett Puzzle
- Toll Free Collectors' Hotline

Pleasantville 1893 Historical Preservation Society
P.O. Box 93507, Atlanta, GA 30377-0507, (800) 355-CLUB
Annual Dues: $30.00
Renewal: $15.00
Club Year: January-December
Collectors' Year: Anniversary of Sign-Up Date

Benefits:
- Membership Gift: Lighted "Pleasantville Gazette" Building
- Quarterly Newsletter, "The Pleasantville Gazette"
- Membership Card
- Collectors' Catalog
- Lapel Pin
- Toll Free Collectors Hotline
- Bisque Porcelain Christmas Ornament from the Pleasantville Coll.

Pocket Dragons and Friends Collectors Club
P.O. Box 93507, Atlanta, GA 30377-0507
(800) 355-CLUB
Annual Dues: $29.50
Two Year Enrollment: $54.00
Club Year: June 1 - May 30
Collectors' Year: Anniversary of Sign-Up Date

Benefits:
- Membership Gift: Pocket Dragons Figurine
- Redemption Coupon for Members-Only Figurine
- Quarterly Magazine, *Pocket Dragons Gazette*
- Membership Card
- Collectors' Catalog
- Lapel Pin
- Toll Free Collectors Hotline
- Invitations to Special Appearances by Real Musgrave
- Travel Opportunities to Tour Collectible World Studios in England

FORMA VITRUM

Bill Job and Forma Vitrum Give New Meaning to the Words "Beautiful Glass"

Stained glass is an elegant, timeless art form with roots in 19th century America. Brought to prominence by Louis C. Tiffany, his pioneering techniques are world renowned. From Tiffany's glass cutting methods to precise assembly techniques and wrapped-copper soldering processes, Tiffany art has delighted collectors for over one hundred years. Inspired by Tiffany and other glass craftsmen, artist Bill Job carries on their time-honored traditions. Some say he has single-handedly turned stained glass art from a "studio craft" into a contemporary collectible category.

A Tennessee native, Bill's interest in houses began as a child, spurred by his brother's architectural studies. Later, Victorian dwellings in San Francisco and Portland, Oregon, inspired him. Bill studied post and beam construction, hoping to use it to build a dream home of his own some day. His studies helped him do just that: build dream homes – thousands of them. Each is a unique and wonderful construction of stained glass, now available, and affordable for collectors around the world.

The Journey That Dreams Built

When Bill Job realized people shared his love of stained glass but few could afford it, he decided to change that. He turned to mainland China for the skilled hands and patience needed to craft affordable stained glass. Bill's studies in philosophy had already introduced him to Chinese culture, and his family was delighted at the prospect of moving abroad. As soon as he was granted permission by the Chinese government, Bill became one of the first Americans to own a company on the mainland.

By 1989, Bill's stained glass rivaled the quality and grace of Tiffany. He designed, instructed and oversaw the crafting of his ideas using American stained glass. Believing it to be the finest in the world, Bill learned new methods of scoring, cutting and wrapping individual pieces in copper foil tape before soldering sections together. He became adroit at applying the patina required to oxidize a solder (this gives stained glass creations a look of antiquity), then applying silicon oil to seal the solder and stop the oxidation process.

Initially, Tiffany reproduction lamp shades were the company's mainstay, but Bill expanded his offerings to sun catchers, art panels and detailed little houses lit from within by a bulb or candle. The houses were favorites of Bill's family. They convinced him to test them in America. Always ready for new adventures, Bill packed his samples, rented a booth at a trade show and left China for California.

A Fortuitous Meeting with David MacMahan

At the January, 1993 Los Angeles Gift Show, interest in Bill's stained glass was keen, but not overwhelming. During a break, Bill struck up a conversation with gadget and toy promoter David MacMahan. MacMahan, an inventor of gifts that make people laugh and cope with stress, was curious about Job's creations. The moment he saw the houses, David recognized the enormous potential of Bill's designs.

The two quickly realized their business and personal outlooks were compatible, too. By show's end, a partnership was launched with a handshake. Bill would design and create. David would promote and market. The business was born when the two picked the Latin words "forma" (beautiful) and "vitrum," (glass) as the new firm's name. Next, designs were divided into two collections: *The Vitreville Collection*, a series of structures with a "small, home-town feeling," and the *Woodland Village*, a whimsical village of houses named for animals. That accomplished, Bill returned to China with exciting news of the company's formation.

Building a Town: See How It Grows

Bill and David decided the town of *Vitreville* would be built the way small towns grew in America, beginning with homes for residents. Each structure was designed in a traditional style, reflective of people who built houses to last generations. Then, every house was named for the profession of its resident. Next, churches, lighthouses and other buildings were added. Before long, these first issues began to sell briskly! Two *Vitreville* collection

Shingled walls of 373 pieces of glass and pewter invite the world to spend a tranquil weekend at "Brookview Bed and Breakfast." Stone fireplaces, made of fused glass, look just like river rock. Only 1,250 buildings were created for worldwide distribution. This outstanding issue was sold out before the first one reached store shelves!

An Award of Excellence nominee by Collector Editions *magazine, "Thompson's Drug," created from 219 pieces of glass and pewter, features an arched entry awning and hand-numbered brass artist signature plate. Issued for worldwide distribution in limits of just 5,000, "Thompson's Drug" sold out in one year!*

designs reached landmark status a year later. In January 1994, "The Bavarian Chapel" and "Pillars of Faith" were retired after approximately 2,400 of each was produced. By March of 1994, they were completely sold out.

These days, collectors may add "Maplewood Elementary," the "Vitreville Post Office," the "Breadman's Bakery" and the award-nominated "Thompson's Drug" to their collections. *Collector Editions* magazine and the National Association of Limited Edition Dealers selected "Thompson's Drug" as a 1994 award nominee. In addition, "Brookview Bed and Breakfast," Bill's most complex work, has become a highly sought after favorite. Inspired by a house built in Oregon, circa 1892, 1,250 of these limited editions were officially sold out before the first piece shipped.

Finally, every small town in America prides itself on its houses of worship. *Vitreville* collectors may choose from "Country Church," "Community Chapel," "Tiny Town Church," "Trinity Church," and the retired "Bavarian Church" and "Pillars of Faith" to enhance collections.

Forma Vitrum Launches Two Lighthouse Collections

Americans have strong ties to our seacoasts, so Bill's next challenge was designing romantic lighthouses. The Forma Vitrum *Coastal Classics* collection includes six. "Carolina," "Michigan" and "Maine," range in complexity from 41 to 74 pieces of glass. "Sailor's Knoll Lighthouse," "Lookout Point Lighthouse" and "Patriot's Point Lighthouse" round out the current series, each constructed of finely cut sections of American stained glass.

1995 debuted Forma Vitrum's newest innovative replica lighthouse collection: *Coastal Heritage*. This limited edition series was developed under the guidance and sponsorship of the U.S. Lighthouse Society. Only 1,995 of each of the first introductions will be produced to commemorate the year this series was introduced. Every piece comes with a history of the actual lighthouse, and a 50¢ donation will be given to the Society to help with its lighthouse preservation efforts.

Bill Job's *Coastal Heritage* is a true wonder. Using techniques developed after two years of research and experimentation, the result is astonishing. No artist has ever merged so many mediums to create such exacting replicas. American glass is hand-cut and soldered with blown, slumped and fused stained glass and spin cast metals. Many of the towers are blown cylinders of glass to replicate authentic shaping and dimension. Diamond drills cut door and window openings. The incorporation of fiber optics replicates a true beacon shining from each lighthouse!

Debuting the *Coastal Heritage* collection is "Sandy Hook, New Jersey," the oldest lighthouse in the U.S. This 10" tall masterwork is limited to a worldwide edition of 3,759 (1,995 plus 1,764 symbolizing the year the real lighthouse was built). Collectors can expect yearly additions, each crafted using Bill Job's revolutionary new glass techniques!

Extra Special Touches that Make Forma Vitrum Unique

Bill tries to remain impartial about his designs, but pin him down, and he'll confess *Woodland Village* is his personal favorite. Perhaps it's because the buildings are fashioned of curvy glass, more difficult to cut than straight pieces. Maybe it's memories of designing the series with his 12-year-old daughter beside him. Whatever the reason, collectors still 'flock' to *Woodland Village*, with its quaint, animal-named houses: "The Owl House," "The Raccoon House," "The Chipmunk House," "The Rabbit House" and "The Badger House."

Woodland Village is inspired by an imaginary community of tiny people who live peacefully in a forest, free from illness and crime. Their appreciation for nature inspires dwelling names, and according to the *Woodland Village* legend, each house is so beautifully lit, villagers nap by day so they can enjoy the glow coming

Revolutionary design methods make "Sandy Hook, New Jersey," a replica of the oldest lighthouse in the U.S., one-of-a-kind. Limited to a worldwide edition of 3,759 (1,995 plus 1,764 symbolizing the year the real lighthouse was built), fiber optics help create a glowing tribute to innovation and beauty.

from their homes after dark.

Enjoy Your Collection Year-Round

Forma Vitrum collectors prize selecting lifelike accessories to compliment their villages year-round, so realistic accent pieces are a major development focus for the company. Home displays are enhanced by trees, flowers, *Vitreville* residents and 'everyday' touches like signs, benches, fences and lamp posts. Each is perfectly scaled to help collectors personalize their realistic displays.

Authentification is also important to Forma Vitrum. Before each structure is boxed, a number is inscribed by hand and Bill Job's artist signature plate is attached. Additionally, all Forma Vitrum collectibles may be registered with the company by using the form included with each design.

A Future as Bright as the Town Itself

To make sure collectors have everything they want (including the formation of the Forma Vitrum Collectors' Club in the near future and lots of opportunities to meet the artist), Bill communicates regularly with them. A quarterly newsletter, "The Vitreville Voice," broadcasts all the latest product news, and Bill puts as much enthusiasm into his tours as he does his writings. In 1995, his appearances included California, Texas, Minnesota, Wisconsin, Iowa, North Dakota, Arizona, Oklahoma, Indiana and everywhere else he can fit into his schedule.

Whether it's the annual International Collectible Expositions or visits to some of the 2,500 shops selling Forma Vitrum art in Canada, Japan, Australia or the U.S., Bill is one of America's foremost hands-on artists, enjoying standing-room-only at personal appearances. One of the reasons Bill can be here...there...and everywhere...is the faithful hand of Forma Vitrum president David MacMahan and an energetic staff in China and stateside. Bill knows his dream is in able hands when he's out and about. The partnership he and David share is just one good reason the future looks bright.

The remainder of the credit goes to Bill's family. Cheerfully exploring a new country and culture with as much enthusiasm as the man who brought them to China, wife Kitty and daughters Patti and Christy have had the opportunity to do what few families have. They've not only witnessed a dream come true — they also helped make that wish a reality for someone they love and respect.

Knowing his vision and energy has helped make stained glass collectible art affordable for people across America is truly Bill Job's greatest joy.

Forma Vitrum
20414 N. Main Street
Cornelius, NC 28031
(800) 596-9963
Fax (704) 892-5438

THE FRANKLIN MINT

The Franklin Mint: Excellence in Artistic Mastery Delights and Surprises Collectors with an Eye for Perfection and a Heart for Tradition

Historians have a passion for exploring the habits and passions of societies here and abroad. Their languages. Various foods. Mysterious traditions. Exotic clothing. But perhaps the most fascinating subject of all is a culture's rich artistic base. Even today, nothing fascinates social scientists more than the artifacts primitive and advanced societies covet.

Consider the wealth of treasures emerging from the past. Cave drawings. Arrowheads. Bits of carved clay mined from an earth now covered by centuries of time. Whether a shiny crystal plucked from a riverbed or the whittled symbol of luck and fortune, who can resist gathering treasures and keeping them as reminders of special places and unforgettable moments?

Our propensity for gathering and saving helps mark the stepping stones of our growth as distinct societies. Those changes are wonderfully reflected in the evolution of the artifacts we revere: Pre-Columbian carvings. Native folk art. Classic oil paintings. A heritage of decorated eggs commissioned of the famous Peter Carl Fabergé.

In every culture, collectible art has taken its rightful place – been given as gifts and beloved as keepsakes. Styles have emerged and new artisans have brought their own talents to changing and enhancing these treasures. Whether we live in a house, a hut, a tent or a castle, each memento picked for its subject matter, elegance, rarity or memory, ultimately finds a home in our heart.

Sixty years after it debuted, this American icon still symbolizes the wild, defiant spirit of America! Recreated in 1:24 scale, this beauty is hand-assembled, incredibly detailed, painted by hand and loaded with real moving parts! This 1032 V-8 Coupe is authorized by the Ford Motor Company and sells for an astonishing $90.

A legacy for collecting memories established, let us visit a fine art studio flourishing for the past three decades called The Franklin Mint. This haven of innovation and artistry provides incomparable works of historic significance destined to become the prized heirlooms of tomorrow. The award-winning artists of The Franklin Mint use the skills of their hands and the love in their hearts to create treasures of timeless beauty . . . and endless fascination.

As the millennium approaches, these gifted artisans commit themselves to providing the world with the most extraordinary personal luxury items for today...tomorrow...and forever.

Collector Wishes Are Answered, with a Flourish, Each Time New Franklin Mint Art Debuts

The Franklin Mint is a place where dreams begin. Located deep in the heart of the historic Brandywine River Valley, The Franklin Mint is the home of some of the most talented people in the world. Artists in every discipline, designers, sculptors, jewelers, engravers, medallists, doll and model makers, work together in an environment of unlimited creative freedom and endless inspiration.

In their quest for perfection, these individuals create works of art to which few can compare. Extraordinary sculpture in porcelain, pewter, crystal and bronze. The world's finest commemorative coins and stamps. Authentic replicas of historic masterpieces. Award-winning heirloom collector dolls. Books handcrafted in old-world tradition. Collector plates of universal appeal. Furnishings of uncompromising quality and craftsmanship for the home. The ultimate in die-cast automotive classics. Jewelry ablaze with the most precious of gems, gleaming with the richness of gold and silver. Miniature sculptures preserved under a crystal-clear dome. Classic games the whole family can share and enjoy. Acquisitions of taste, beauty and supreme artistry. Personal treasures destined to command attention and admiration.

Prestigious Organizations... Worldwide...Benefit from The Franklin Mint's Galaxy of Renowned Artists

The achievements of great artists, distinguished organizations and master craftspeople are shared with collectors around the world through the resources of The Franklin Mint. Beautiful showpieces include those from The Vatican in Rome, and masterworks from renowned art museums like the Louvre in Paris and the Victoria and Albert in London. Franklin collectors also share in the majesty of time-honored institutions with the House of Fabergé, The House of Coppini, and The Princess Grace Foundation.

In 1995, The Franklin Mint and Royal Doulton signed an agreement providing the Mint the rights to market Royal Doulton and Minton collector plates throughout the world.

Models authorized by Rolls-Royce, Mercedes-Benz, General Motors, Lamborghini and Ferrari grace The Franklin Mint list of offerings, as do works created in collaboration with important environmental causes like the World Wildlife Fund, the Humane Society and Conservation International.

Fabulous fashion classics from

Coca-Cola art...prized by collectors worldwide...created by renowned artist Haddon Sundblom. Santa and his elves sparkle beneath a 5-1/2" crystal dome which is the first of its kind, authorized by the Coca-Cola Company and available for only $37.50.

Franklin emerge in creative coalition with Bill Blass, Adolpho, Givenchy, Bob Mackie, Hanae Mori and Mary McFadden. The Franklin Mint classics of literature include famed works of award-winning authors like Norman Mailer, E.L. Doctrow, Michael Crichton and John Updike. And inspiring masterpieces, from world-renowned artists including Norman Rockwell, Andrew Wyeth, Erte and Peter Max, also intrigue Franklin collectors.

Museums and Governments Rely Upon The Franklin Mint for Commemorative Art to Celebrate Heritage and Pride

Much of The Franklin Mint's finest work involves the creation of commemorative art – for governments, major museums, and prestigious organizations on all seven continents. Commemorative partners include the United Nations, the International Olympic Committee, the Royal Geographic Society and the World Wildlife Fund.

Franklin Mint originals honor those who share the spirit of heritage and pride such as The White House Historical Association, the National Historical Society and the Western Heritage Museum. Franklin also shares in the concerns of distinguished cultural organizations as The Kabuki National Theater, La Scala in Milan and the Royal Shakespeare Theatre.

In search of treasures from the Far East and the Wild West...from the frozen North to the deep South...from the Caribbean to the Gold Coast and from enchanted fairy tale kingdoms to the realms of royalty, The Franklin Mint scans the globe to create works of art to touch the innermost places of the heart.

The Franklin Mint Brings Alive the Forgotten Treasures of Exotic Societies for All Collectors

The Franklin Mint has never forgotten that the traditions of the past inspire the creations of today...and the treasures of tomorrow. Thus, from the ancient civilizations of the Egyptians and Etruscans, come new works to rival those buried for thousands of years.

From the depths of Atlantis to the gods of ancient Greece and Rome come new masterpieces of sculpture to rival those found only in the world's most prestigious museums and private collections. From the dynasties of the Ming to priceless works created for the Czars of Imperial Russia come porcelains of incomparable beauty and splendor.

From the masters of the Renaissance to sparkling reflections of the New Age come treasures that speak of power, and individual achievement. From Asia's mighty warriors to America's legendary heroes come works of history, heritage and pride.

Futuristic magic! Precision cast pieces of sterling silver and 24K gold go "Where no man has gone before," aboard the U.S.S. Enterprise for the ultimate chess challenge. Paramount Pictures' authorization and authentication make this game of the future unmatched at $195.

Gallery Stores Take Collector Delight to New Heights

For those collectors who prefer to see and touch things before they buy, like the Mint's beautiful "Scarlett O'Hara" or "Marilyn Monroe" dolls, The Franklin Mint has expanded its retail locations to more than 50 sites in 1995. Its retail operations allow collectors to view and hold the products they will enjoy for many, many years.

The Franklin Mint Gallery Stores were designed by renowned retail space designer Harvey Bernstein, who created a museum-style environment befitting The Franklin Mint's product line – with marble pedestals, pin-point lighting and an open floor plan.

Franklin Mint's Distinguished Collection Earns Awards... Laudits...and a Reputation for Incomparable Quality

Since its founding, The Franklin Mint has brought pleasure and enjoyment to millions of collectors the world over, with works of art that bring to life memorable characters that have

Doll master Maryse Nicole's first bride doll combines lush romance with splendor. "Vanessa's" bisque porcelain body is fully jointed; sapphire crystal eyes sparkle beneath natural lashes. Gowned and veiled in shimmering white taffeta, iridescent lace, silk blooms, tulle and pearls, "Vanessa" carries ribbon roses and is available for $750.

touched our hearts.

These include the legendary Scarlett O'Hara and the dashing Rhett Butler from the most romantic love story of all time - *Gone With The Wind*, and Dorothy and Toto, the Tin Man, Scarecrow and the Cowardly Lion from the unforgettable *Wizard of Oz*. The Franklin Mint is also proud to offer the world-famous illustrations of Charles Dana Gibson, whose legendary Gibson Girl art set the standard of beauty at the turn-of-the-century.

Franklin also works exclusively with one of America's favorite doll artists, the beloved "Sparkle Queen," Maryse Nicole, and with some of Europe's most famous doll artists, including Sylvia Natterer and Gerda Neubacher.

Collectors enjoy timeless tributes to legends of the silver screen like The Duke, John Wayne, and with portraits that recapture the glamour of the one - the only - Marilyn Monroe. All in all, a collection of works of art with a precious heritage and a never-ending future of beauty.

Following the signing of their agreement, Stuart Lyon, Chief Executive of Royal Doulton and Lynda Resnick, Vice Chairman of The Franklin Mint, view historic pattern styles at Royal Doulton headquarters in Stoke-on-Trent, England and discuss joint, future projects.

Nothing But the Best For Adventurous Collectors

For those driven to new heights of excitement and new levels of achievement, Franklin Mint Precision Models are simply miles ahead. These fine die-cast automotive replicas include classics from the past, like the Rolls-Royce Silver Ghost, the Mercedes Gullwing, the Ford Model-T, the Duesenberg Twenty Grand, and all-American legends like Harley-Davidson, the Petty Nascar, the Cadillac Eldorado and the Chevrolet Bel Air.

Franklin also presents Europe's elite dream machines: the fabulous Ferrari, the Porsche 911 and the Bugatti Royale. Collectors get on the fast track with The Southern Crescent, fly high with Shoo-Shoo Baby and put out fires with the Ahrens-Fox Fire Engine. In addition, there are daring innovations like the Lamborghini Countach, and America's hottest sports car, the Corvette Sting Ray.

Cartoon Legends Find Homes in the Hearts of Americans of Every Age Thanks to The Franklin Mint

The Franklin Mint works together with those at the forefront of the entertainment industry: Paramount Pictures, Twentieth Century Fox and Turner Home Entertainment. Franklin also shares a partnership with great "families" like Warner Brothers and Parker Brothers to bring to life some of the most lovable characters of all time: The Jetsons, The Flintstones, the Road Runner, and Bugs Bunny, just to name a few.

Franklin creates classic games the whole family will share and enjoy such as the Collector's Edition of "The Looney Tunes Chess Set," and with all-time favorites like Scrabble and Monopoly.

Creating magic with the one and only Walt Disney Company, Franklin had paid tribute to Walt Disney's genius with sculpture and dolls of sheer enchantment like Mickey and Minnie Mouse, the beautiful Snow White and the unforgettable Cinderella.

Leading The Franklin Mint Family Into the Future, Stewart and Lynda Rae Resnick's Vision Continues

The Franklin Mint is guided by Lynda and Stewart Resnick, who serve as Vice Chairman and Chairman. As such, they are committed to preserving and honoring the great artistic and historical traditions of the past - and to creating new works of art for today's collector. They are also community and civic leaders, lending their talents, support and expertise to institutions including The National Gallery of Art, The Metropolitan Museum of Art and The Los Angeles County Museum of Art. As the 21st century approaches, Mr. and Mrs. Resnick lead The Franklin Mint into a future destined for glorious achievement in the fine art field.

The Franklin Mint
Franklin Center, PA 19091
(800) 225-5836
Fax (610) 459-6880

COLLECTORS' MUSEUM

The Franklin Mint Museum
U.S. Route 1
Media, PA 19091
(610) 459-6881

Hours: Monday through Saturday, 9:30 a.m.-4:30 p.m.; Sunday, 1 p.m.-4:30 p.m. Closed Major Holidays.

Admission Fee: None

Exhibits at The Franklin Mint Museum include sculpture, dolls, books, die-cast models, stamps and other collectibles. In one wing of the museum, a new exhibit is opened every two months. Special events are scheduled throughout the year, and exclusive Franklin Mint products are available at the Gallery Store, located within the museum.

FRASER INTERNATIONAL, INC.

Presenting Souvenirs of British and American History for Your Home

Do you fancy a country cottage, authentic in every detail? Have you dreamed of life in a British castle, complete with soaring towers and centuries of rich history? Find yourself fascinated by momentous buildings like The Tower of London or The White House? Thanks to Ian MacGregor Fraser of Scotland, now you may indulge these "real estate fantasies" without ever leaving your living room. He recreates all of these renowned sites and more in completely authentic miniature works of art.

When Fraser began creating his cottages, castles and historic landmarks about nine years ago, he had just three helpers. By 1988, he had formed Fraser Creations, was employing 200 people, and Great Britain's Prince Philip had presented him with the Scottish Enterprise Award for the best and most creative new industry in Scotland. Today, close to 300 artisans have a hand in creating Fraser's miniatures, and there are about 150 designs in the line. Most are issued in open editions, although about 100 designs have been retired, 70 of them in December, 1993. Pieces vary in height from about one to ten inches, and in price from $20.00 to $300.

During the late 1980s and early 1990s, some of Fraser's cottages and castles found their way into the United States, primarily via American tourists returning from trips to the United Kingdom. It wasn't until mid-1993 that his work became readily available here, when Fraser International Inc. became the company's exclusive United States distributor.

Enthusiasm in the American Marketplace

Fraser exhibited at both the Long Beach, California, and South Bend, Indiana, collectible expositions, and collectors' response to his work was enthusiastic.

"What we've done in the American market, sales wise, in such a short time is greater than we've achieved elsewhere," says Fraser. "It's really our biggest success. American collectors are by far the most intelligent and well-versed collectors in the world. In addition, their awareness of the secondary market is truly impressive," he adds.

Fraser International's wonderfully detailed sculptures for the American Heritage *collection include two versions of "The White House" (center front and back) as well as models of the "Jefferson Memorial (left) and "Lincoln Memorial" (right). The larger "White House" piece includes the 32 trees planted by American presidents ranging from John Quincy Adams to George Bush.*

The artistic talent behind these popular pieces was born in a cottage in the Scottish lowlands, currently resides in Edinburgh and has a deep love for his homeland. "To me," he says, "Scotland is the most beautiful country in the world. I could never live anywhere else." Although never formally trained in art, he has more than thirty years experience working with various media: painting in oil and watercolor, creating silkscreen prints and copper pictures, and sculpting figurines; he's even created 60-foot murals in fiberglass. He's now settled into designing miniatures, something he likes, as he can do it "sitting down." And his sitting down to miniatures is a bonanza for collectors.

Fraser Creations is family owned and operated. A few of the company's employees assist in the sculpting, but Fraser finishes every piece, has the last word regarding the execution of the sculpture and usually adds a last minute personal touch. His wife Marion is head of quality control. Their daughter Myriam is in charge of the air-brush department. Their son Colin manages the factory and product distribution in all countries except the United States.

Long Hours in the Studio Produce Wonderfully Detailed Originals

Fraser's employees know him as a quiet man who, in his own words, is a "workaholic." When he sculpts, he keeps his attention on his work. Days merge into nights, holidays get swallowed up, and he stays with a piece until it is done perfectly to his own impeccable standards. "When I start something new, I get completely involved with it. It absorbs me," he says. This could be frustrating for his family, as it takes him from three days to two weeks to execute a design, depending on its complexity. Only his steadily increasing travel agenda and his golden retriever, Sultan, can get him away from his studio.

Collectors see another side of him, however. He's a fount of knowledge about the buildings he replicates in miniature, and if you ask him about their history, you'll discover an outgoing man whose soft Scottish brogue and enthusiasm for the architectural heritage of the British Isles is sure to charm you.

The Creative Process for Sculptor Fraser

Before starting a sculpture, Fraser prefers to see the building he will be depicting in miniature, although he also refers to his extensive collection of architectural photographs. After he's sculpted a wax model, a master mold is made. Then comes injection molds, which are used for the working models. The pieces are made of either Crystacle, Alpha K or resin. After the pieces are cast, they go to the fettling department, where rough edges are removed and the pieces are checked for errors.

Once approved, the Crystacle and Alpha K pieces go through a paint dip for the base color (the resin pieces are cast in the color, and so are not dipped). Next, they are painted by hand, with one painter generally staying with a piece until it is finished. Working with a range of sable brushes, the painters spend about two days to complete a small piece; however, they usually work on three or four simultaneously. When the paint is dry, each one is flocked with green felt.

Large trees, bridges and a babbling brook surround "The Red Lion Tavern" in this uplifting work of art from Fraser's Classic Cottage *collection. Creator Ian MacGregor Fraser prides himself on creating a 360° perspective for all of his pieces – meaning that they are equally embellished from every angle of view.*

The Honor of Patronage by the British Royal Family

Fraser's historical accuracy and attention to detail caught the interest of Britain's Royal Family, and shops owned by them in various castles and landmarks carry the full range of historical buildings in the artist's *British Heritage* collection. The Queen's own properties, including "Windsor Castle" and "Balmoral Castle," highlight this collection, along with other world-renowned landmarks of London and surrounding areas. "Buckingham Palace" is a particularly imposing piece, featuring surrounding grounds and environs, as well as the enormous palace itself.

The *British Heritage* collection also presents many of England's most revered religious structures, such as "Westminster Abbey," "St. Paul's Cathedral," and "Canterbury Cathedral." In tribute to William Shakespeare, there are "Anne Hathaway's Cottage" and "Shakespeare's Birthplace."

That collection now is mirrored on our side of the Atlantic, with the recent introduction of Fraser's *American Heritage* collection. The first pieces in the collection depict "The White House," the "Lincoln Memorial," and the "Jefferson Memorial."

Many pieces in the *Heritage* collections are issued in two sizes. The larger works are up to ten inches high and depict a building and its surrounding area; the ten-inch sculpture of "The White House," for example, includes The President's Park, a road, fountain and flowers. The smaller pieces range from about one to three inches in height and focus on the building. The

From Fraser's the British Heritage *collection come two of England's most memorable landmarks, "Big Ben" (left) and "Westminster Abbey."*

large pieces sell for about $150 each, while the small ones are available for about $50.00.

As mentioned earlier, Fraser retired some 70 designs in 1993. He did so to make way for more than eighty new designs that were introduced during 1994, with more to come in the near future. These new works are strong on environment, on each building's setting and the plant and animal life surrounding it.

The *German* collection recreates all the aspects of classic German towns, including two chapels, several elegant homes in various architectural styles, and "Holstein Town Gates," "Alstadter Town Hall," and "Mayor Toppler's Little House."

Fraser plans to continue making frequent visits to United States collectibles expositions, and he enjoys meeting collectors. He has an open-door policy at his factory, located in the town of Penicuik, just four miles from Edinburgh. Collectors may visit his factory, he says, where he'll welcome them and arrange a tour of the facilities.

Portions of this feature are reprinted with permission from an article by Katherine Holden that appeared in Collector Editions *magazine. Collectors' Information Bureau thanks Ms. Holden and* Collector Editions *for their generous cooperation.*

Fraser International
5990 N. Belt East, Unit 606
Humble, TX 77396
(800) 878-5448
Fax (713) 441-7707

From the British Heritage *collection, Fraser presents three historical works of art inspired by renowned sites. They are (clockwise from upper right): "St. Paul's Cathedral," "The White Tower," and "The Tower of London."*

MARGARET FURLONG DESIGNS

America's Favorite Angel Design Receives Her Inspiration from Heaven and Earth

If you have a chance to meet Margaret Furlong, don't turn it down! This dynamo of energy and high-powered talent is sure to enchant you. If *she* doesn't, her work will. Ask Margaret what drives her spirit and she will list God, her family and the beauty of nature. Splendid angels are the gifts she gives, joyfully, to our world of limited edition collectible art.

Furlong's road to so lofty a place as angel designer was filled with twists, turns and a series of equilibrium-jarring moves. On one occasion, a thousand white angels emerged from her kiln a rosy pink (and yes, she had the courage to break them), testing her patience and sense of humor. This is just one memory Margaret Furlong has of the early days when her business grew so fast, it surprised even Furlong. But, Margaret managed to master each challenge, emerging wiser and more committed to her art.

Armed with a Masters Degree in Fine Arts from the University of Nebraska, Margaret taught briefly, then retired from shepherding students to establish her first studio. There, Furlong pioneered "Midwest Snowscapes" in her signature color: white. Today, her work is a hundred light years from her snowscape era. A fortuitous experiment, making angels from seashells left over from a commissioned project, propelled her to fame in the collectible art industry.

Starting a Company with Dreams and Faith

When Margaret Furlong studied the array of "leftover" shells lying about her studio in 1979, she realized these gracefully-shaped wonders looked like natural angels. By sculpting clay faces and delicate embellishments, a personality emerged from each shell. When her initial batch of angels was finished and displayed, Furlong knew this avenue of design was God's plan for her. "I began my business with a commitment to share, in all of my designs, the things I held dear to my heart..." Margaret recalls. "My first angel was also a tribute to my recent personal commitment to Christianity."

Margaret recalls her first year as being "rather slow and laborious." Much time was spent learning production techniques and marketing. With no one to represent her designs, it was up to her to do it, so this one-woman-band managed to juggle every role with grace. Somehow, she even managed to fall in love and plan a wedding. Happily, Jerry Alexander was a supportive soul who encouraged his wife's dream. All he asked was that she move her dream west – to Seattle!

Relocating to the Northwest from Nebraska meant a disruption of major proportions. A new city. New neighbors. New lifestyle! Settling into the basement garage of a condominium in suburban Seattle, Margaret stoically recalls how she "started over." This move proved to be a blessing in disguise. This would be the year Furlong would stretch her wings and fly...just like the angels she creates.

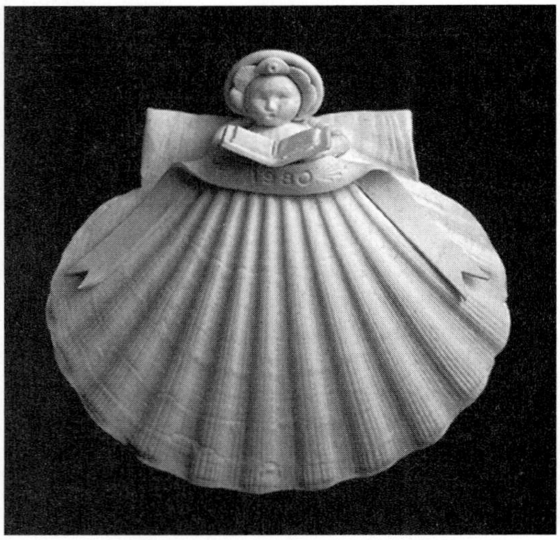

Margaret Furlong's premier limited edition angel celebrates her first venture into collectibles. The first of five angels in the Musical *series, "The Caroler Angel" helped start today's mega-trend in angel collecting!*

Taking Margaret Furlong Designs National

Soon after moving to Seattle, Margaret declared she was ready to go national. She set up a more elaborate marketing plan, recruited sales representatives and printed materials showcasing her designs. The business was flourishing when another geographic jog, just down the road to Salem, Oregon, made Margaret realize Furlong Designs had grown beyond her ability to handle it alone. Husband Jerry Alexander agreed. He gave up his job to become a full-time partner, bringing considerable fiscal and administrative skills to the company.

Since the move to Oregon, it's been non-stop growth for the business, and not just the kind of 'mundane' growth you might imagine.

Margaret Furlong's angels caught the eye of President and Mrs. Ronald Reagan. A selection of Furlong creations was requested to decorate the Reagan's personal tree at the White House in 1981. Each angel hung proudly, surrounded by family heirlooms.

Given this remarkable exposure, it wasn't long before the media took notice. America's top publications featured Margaret's work in their holiday issues. *Victoria, Victorian Homes, Country Home, Traditional Home, Country Living, Gourmet, Redbook, Good Housekeeping* and *Ladies Home Journal* are just a few of the magazines spreading the joy of Furlong angels to

Peek at the face of the infant cradled in this beautiful angel's arms and you'll glimpse Margaret Furlong's sheer joy at having given birth to her daughter Caitlin! "The Messiah Angel," issued in 1994, is the last of the five Joyeux Noel *angels.*

millions of readers.

In 1983, Margaret produced her most distinguished work of art, Caitlin Alexander. The birth of a daughter spurred Margaret's artistic spirit to new heights. Now, she had an angel of her very own to treasure!

First Margaret Furlong Limited Editions Take Flight

Margaret Furlong's *Musical* series, launched in 1980, was her first limited edition series. For five consecutive years, Margaret's definition of the "true meaning of Christmas," was given to the world. The first, "Caroler Angel," depicts an angel holding a hymnal and singing a song of joy. Only 3,000 were made. The following year, "The Lyrist Angel" made her appearance holding a lyre. This angel melted hearts and sold fast. In 1982, "The Lutist Angel," fashioned in the style of the Renaissance masters and limited to 3,000, debuted.

By the time "The Concertinist Angel" was unveiled for the 1983 Christmas season, Margaret Furlong's audience had grown to huge proportions. They eagerly awaited her surprises and were not disappointed when they saw the dainty halo, holly and berry accents and delicate folds of her concertina. When the series concluded, in 1984, fans were reluctant to see it end but agreed the final issue, "The Herald Angel," was a spectacular finale. Crowned with roses and olive branches, "The Herald Angel" proved the perfect conclusion to an outstanding collection.

In 1985, Furlong debuted her next series: *Gifts From God*, also limited to 3,000 of each design. The new series captivated collectors with lavish touches: tiny shells, a cross, primrose, tulips, crocus, the sun and stars and other glorious gifts of nature reflecting the miracle of Jesus' birth, His life on earth and glorious resurrection. The *Gifts From God* collection includes "The Charis Angel" (Charis means grace gift from God), "Hallelujah Angel," "Angel of Light," "The Celestial Angel" and "The Coronation Angel."

Heralding Margaret's Newest Designs and First Retirements

The last decade of the century was reason for celebration. 1990 saw the introduction of the *Joyeux Noel* collection, a five-year series of angels limited to 10,000 of each design. Every figure has a fanciful name. "Celebration Angel," "Thanks-giving Angel," "Joyeux Noel Angel," "Star of Bethlehem Angel" and "Messiah Angel." Each design showcases Margaret's growth and working relationship with God.

"Messiah Angel," the final piece in the *Joyeux Noel* series, is particularly memorable. Sketches of Caitlin, Margaret's daughter, inspired the face of the child on this final figure in the collection. This highly personal design, celebrating both Jesus' birth and the miracle of motherhood, may be the most popular of Margaret's angels to date. Collectors seem to see in it a bit of the divine influence that guides Margaret Furlong's hands.

With the completion of *Joyeux Noel,* a new series, *Flora Angelica*, was prepared for its 1995 unveiling. *Flora Angelica* combines the radiance of angels with the symbolism of flowers. This series is limited to just 10,000 of each annual angel, beginning with the "Faith Angel." A tribute to belief and love, "Faith Angel" holds a delicate bouquet of roses and is crowned with a dainty headdress of roses and leaves. Each angel in this five-year collection will share God's floral delights with the world. Toward this end, Margaret has also introduced new 2", 3" and 4" angels with a botanical theme for 1995.

In the tradition of fine collectible art, retirements are an important part of Margaret Furlong's commitment to give collectors true limited editions. 1995 marks the retirement of both the 3" and 4" "Dove" angels, created in 1984 to celebrate Caitlin's birth. The "Dove" joins the "Star" angel and the "Trumpeter" angel, both of which were retired in 1994.

The Sky's the Limit for Margaret Furlong Designs

Visually wander through one of Margaret Furlong's new catalogs, and

Margaret Furlong's introduction of the new Flora Angelica *series showcases her love of flowers and God's bountiful gifts of nature. "The Faith Angel," introduced in 1995, is limited to just 10,000 angels.*

you'll understand how far her gift for design has blossomed: Discover delicate morning stars, charming hearts, fragile snowflakes, spiraling icicles, elegant tassels and whimsical shell fish – all inspired by enchanting gifts from the sea. Each of Margaret Furlong's unique designs is proudly made in the United States using the exacting techniques and standards she pioneered back in Nebraska.

Today, Margaret Furlong's dreams and creations have come full circle. Each is a reflection of her personal commitment to quality, value and good design. Toward that end, Margaret uses a meticulous production process that moves her creations from prototype to first modeling, from carving to a master mold, all with methodical care. Each step of the crafting and finishing process is overseen by Margaret and her growing staff of artisans and crafters, now numbering more than 85!

With all this excitement, growth and responsibility, it's hard to imagine Margaret has a spare moment, yet she makes herself available to her faithful collectors with tours of her soon-to-be-expanded studios and production facility in Salem, Oregon, and as many personal appearances as she can fit into her schedule.

Margaret Furlong fans may already have heard the rumor that a collector club is in the stars, and you've not finished reading about the other exciting changes planned for Margaret Furlong Designs in the coming years. But you can be sure that the future promises many new challenges and more blessings. With God's help, her family's encouragement and collector support, the sky's the limit...and that's exactly where this popular collectible artist is headed.

Margaret Furlong Designs
210 State Street
Salem, OR 97301
(503) 363-6004
Fax (503) 371-0676

COLLECTORS' TOUR

Margaret Furlong Designs Studio Tour
210 State Street
Salem, OR 97301
(503) 363-6004

Hours: Monday through Friday, 8 a.m.-5 p.m. Please phone for an appointment.

Admission Fee: None

Visitors can tour the production area at Margaret Furlong Designs Studio where skilled craftspeople make each porcelain design by hand.

GANZ

Little Cheesers Leads to Big Success and More Collectibles to Squeak About

Join the Little Cheesers *for a hummin', strummin', foot-tapping day in Cheeserville! From the piano to the banjo, this band of mice plays some down-home tunes in* A Little Country Music *series from the popular collection.*

Ganz began in 1950 as a small, family-owned and operated company that originally produced stuffed teddy bears. The business gave a new start to the Ganz family, who fled to Austria, Germany, and ultimately to Canada after the Nazi army invaded their native Rumania. With $100 of the family's own money and lots of hard work, Ganz (known then as Ganz Bros. Toys Limited) grew steadily and crossed the border into the United States, where the company became recognized for its fine quality plush animals.

But in 1991, company President Howard Ganz made a conscious decision to expand its product line beyond toys to include figurines, mugs, novelties, frames and other gifts. The savvy move welcomed the birth of the *Little Cheesers*, an adorable line of collectible mouse figurines that became an instant hit at its 1991 debut and has since paved a new path of success for Ganz. Today, *Little Cheesers* heads the company's continued growth and prominence in the collectibles industry. Besides the community of old-fashioned mice from Cheeserville, Ganz has introduced collectors to a gallery of collectibles ranging from cows and pigs to teddy bears and angels.

Little Cheesers Opens a New World of Adventures

"A long time ago," starts a page in the book called *The Historical Chronicle of Cheeserville*, "the *Little Cheesers* lived in the Old World. They made their homes in tree stumps, toadstools and burrows. Very cleverly, they used leaves for umbrellas, blossoms for drinking cups and spider webs for fishing nets. Then one day, some of the *Little Cheesers* made a courageous voyage across the Billowing Sea to the New World where they settled and built a new way of life. Instead of living in tree trunks, they learned to make cozy cottages from clapboards and shingles."

Little Cheesers share their new way of life through more than 200 miniature figurines, each bearing a name, story and charming personality that has warmed the hearts of collectors around the world. The *Little Cheesers* population keeps growing around various themes: a picnic, wedding, Christmas celebration, family traditions, springtime and fall holidays.

Although Frowzy Roquefort III spins a fictional tale about the *Little Cheesers* in the fully illustrated book, *The Historical Chronicles of Cheeserville*, the collection's real story began in 1990 when gift industry veteran William R. Dawson traveled to the Far East. There he discovered a special line of mice figurines, which he named *Little Cheesers* and introduced in January 1991. In July of that year, Ganz made special arrangements to purchase *Little Cheesers*.

Christine Thammavongsa, product designer and director of the Ganz Collectibles division, is the on-going creative force behind the collection. Besides sketching each mouse, Christine names the characters and develops all the delightful stories of their lives and pastimes. Since the *Little Cheesers* care about the environment and their neighbors, Christine's designs also capture the tender spirit of family togetherness and love.

Christine recently completed a hardcover *Little Cheesers* storybook called *More Precious Than Gold* that tells a tale of the Woodsworth twins, Little Truffle and Sweet Cicely. These mice

Christine Thammavongsa created Grandma's Attic *to rekindle warm memories of old-fashioned and well-worn teddy bears that seem real to children. Balderdash, Tootoo, Crumples & Creampuff and Bumblebeary (clockwise from the top) are among the bears that play make-believe games in the attic. The figurines stand about two to three inches tall.*

learn the valuable lessons of sharing, caring for Mother Nature, helping each other and understanding that one child is more precious than gold, silver or even diamonds. Christine is the ghost writer for Frowsy Roquefort III, the "author" of the storybook.

Fun is easy to round up in Cowtown, *an udderly cool collectible introduced in 1993. Pictured from left to right are: "Bull Rogers," "Cowlamity Jane," "Buffalo Bull Cody," "Moo West," "Old MooDonald" and "Gloria Bovine & Rudolph Bullentino." They join a herd of other cow figurines that rank among the most popular lines at Ganz.*

Special *Little Cheesers* Retirements and Additions

Each year, Ganz announces the retirement of selected *Little Cheesers* figurines to make way for new introductions. Once a piece is retired, it may be acquired through retailers until their stock is sold out. The first ten pieces were retired in 1991 and sold out within four months. Ganz now announces retirements twice a year in July and December.

In 1993, Ganz also introduced the first limited edition *Little Cheesers* figurines, including Frowzy Roquefort III reading from a book, Blossom Thistledown and Hickory Harvestmouse rowing a boat in "Gently Down the Stream" and the festive "Santa's Sleigh."

Other forest friends have also joined the *Little Cheesers. The Silverwoods* – close relatives of the *Little Cheesers* – make an annual Christmas pilgrimage across the Billowing Sea. They have grey fur to add a new dimension and personality to anyone's collection. In Cloverdale Clearing, just a hop away from Gooseberry Grove on the Cheeserville map, a group of adorable bunnies shares their favorite activities. *Little Hoppers* are the long-eared friends of the *Little Cheesers.*

Life is wonderful in Pigsville, *where the days are long and lazy and the townsfolk are friendly, playful pigs! Designed by Christine Thammavongsa, the humorous figurines include "Bakin' at the Beach," "True Love," "Tipsy," "Wee Little Piggy" and a pig pen of other favorites.*

Collectors' Club Celebrates *Little Cheesers*

To share the joys, adventures and latest news around Cheeserville, Ganz introduced the Little Cheesers Collectors' Club in 1993. Members receive a membership figurine, membership card, club binder, "Cheeserville Gazette" newsletter and redemption certificates for special member's only pieces throughout the year. The colorful newsletter previews upcoming introductions, answers collectors' questions, sponsors contests, offers display tips, announces retirements and tells interesting insider facts about the collection.

Quality Craftsmanship Goes Into Each Collectible

Whether its a figurine for Club members or the latest addition to the picnic scene, Christine's process for creating each *Little Cheesers* piece requires many careful and time-consuming steps. To begin, Christine sketches the characters she has in mind and then presents them to a sculptor in the Far East who brings her work to life in three dimensions. Christine and the sculptor work together to perfect each detail before an original model is produced. A mixture of finely ground porcelain, resin and other ingredients are poured in the molds. *Little Cheesers* figurines are handcrafted in cold cast resin which allows for exceptional detail, durability, texture and color.

The *Little Cheesers* figurines are then hand-painted with water-based paints, producing a striking finish to complement their personalities. The process is repeated in Christine's other creations that reflect the same attention to detail.

A Barn Yard Of Collectible Friends

The *Cowtown* collection, released in 1993, was an original Ganz creation inspired by Christine's childhood memories and visits to her grandparents' farms. The herd of whimsical cow figurines include "Ma & Pa Cattle," "Pocowhantis," "King Cowmooamooa," "Sheriff Bull Masterson," "Cowlamity Jane" and "Buffalo Bull Cody." Wonderful experiences on the farm also influenced Christine's *Pigsville* collection, introduced in 1993. The

"All at once the precious Angels went tumbling down through space and now they are all searching for a perfect little place." This 1995 line of cherubic figurines represents the little angels in everyone's life. A Perfect Little Place *features angels enjoying favorite childhood pastimes.*

carefree pigs enjoy relaxing days from the barn to the beach as they strike humorous poses. The collections also include ornaments, plush, mugs and other accessories. In keeping with the barnyard theme, Christine also created *Cock-A-Doodle Corners* featuring "home-grown" chickens.

More Creations from the Studio of Christine Thammavongsa

Christine's pencils, paintbrushes and imagination have brought to life old-fashioned teddy bears that play make-believe games in *Grandma's Attic*, which premiered in 1995. The story accompanying the collection tells about a 5-year-old girl whose grandmother led her to the corner of the attic, where a well-worn toy chest was hidden under piles of clothes and books. "She gently placed a tiny brass key in the palm of my hand and shared a special secret with me, a secret she had shared with my mother many years before," the story reads. Inside the trunk were vintage teddy bears that the girl's great-grandmother patiently stitched by hand. With names like Dumblekin, Bumblebeary and Balderdash, the anything - but - ordinary bears invite the girl to join in their afternoon games.

Collectors can also discover the charming world of a *Perfect Little Place* as envisioned by Howard Ganz and Christine Thammavongsa. Introduced in 1995, the hand-painted resin figurines feature cherubic and child-like angels that are searching for a wonderful home on earth. Christine has also created *Watching Over You*, a line of classical angel figurines expressing the feelings of motherhood that she has experienced since the birth of her daughter.

Street Scenes and Trains Find a Home With Collectors

Christine also oversees the development of other lines. Introduced in 1995, *Just Around The Corner* is designed for collectors to create their own towns from an authentic selection of shops, restaurants, businesses and apartments that can be joined together to construct endless combinations of winding historic streets. Created by Ganz artist Lisa Sunarth, the first series features an Old Boston flavor with brick buildings, arched doorways and charming storefronts. The buildings in the second series capture the rugged and pioneering spirit of the Old West and life in Tombstone.

Trains Gone By, launched in 1995, features highly detailed resin figurines that recreate famous trains dating back to the mid-1800s. The 10" trains are limited in edition to 5,000, with 1,000 of those pieces also designed to make authentic sound effects. The first five introductions include locomotives from the nation's most recognized railroads: Pennsylvania, Western & Atlantic, Santa Fe, New York Central and Central Pacific. With its continued success in the collectibles industry, Ganz plans to stay right on track by introducing and developing other lines. Of course, Cheeserville will also keep growing with a delightful cast of characters that has collectors around the world following all the adventures and excitement.

Ganz
908 Niagara Falls Blvd.
North Tonawanda, NY 14120-2060
(800) 724-5902
(905) 851-6669

COLLECTORS' CLUB

Little Cheesers Collectors' Club
908 Niagara Falls Blvd.
North Tonawanda, NY 14120-2060
(800) 724-5902

Annual Dues: $27.00 - Renewal: $24.00
Club Year: Anniversary of Sign-Up Date

Benefits:
- Membership Gift: "Welcome to the Club" figurine
- Redemption Certificate for Members-Only Items
- Bi-annual Newsletter, "Cheeserville Gazette"
- Club Binder
- Personalized Membership Card
- Buy/Sell Matching Service through Newsletter
- Item Checklist
- Birthday Cards, Special Mailings, Contests

GEORGETOWN COLLECTION

The Studio That Puts the Doll Artist "In Charge"

Multi-award-winning artist Linda Mason's "Lavender Dreams," standing 15-1/2" tall and retailing for $150, comes complete with her own upholstered chair and miniature book.

The artists who create the dolls that bring such joy to collectors are an amazing group: talented, intuitive and possessed of a truly astonishing understanding of children and their world. Without these gifted virtuosos, the doll realm would be a poorer place indeed.

All of which accounts for why Georgetown Collection, from its studios in Portland, Maine, always insists that the doll artists must have creative control over each doll they design. The result? The finest collectible dolls for today – and tomorrow – in the tradition of the priceless heirloom dolls of yesterday.

Each doll produced by Georgetown, in fact, is an *Artist's Edition*®, the collector's guarantee that the doll is crafted, finished and painted by hand – with every stage subject to the total control and approval of the artist who created that doll. This unusual commitment to excellence is available only to the dolls created for the Georgetown Collection.

Top-Notch Artistic Talents Make Creative Decisions

"We do things differently here," explains Jeff McKinnon, Georgetown's President and founder. "To begin with, we give our artists total artistic control over their dolls. They do what *they* feel is right, so the end product is *their* design rather than some 'composite idea' by an anonymous group." Because artistic control rests in the hands of the artists, notes McKinnon, Georgetown is able to attract such superb talent – and produce dolls that are among the most popular with collectors.

As an example, McKinnon points out Georgetown's current crop of talent, a list that sounds like a "Who's Who" among leading doll artists: Linda Mason, Ann Timmerman, Carol Theroux and Sissel Skille, as well as talented newcomers to the field such as Pamela Phillips, Joyce Reavey, Anne DiMartino, Jutta Kissling, Barbara Prusseit and Marlene Sirko. Further proof of this studio's achievements is provided by the industry press: feature-length articles on the company and/or its artists have appeared in *Contemporary Doll, Dolls* and *Doll Reader* magazines. And then there are the awards: over the past several years, the dolls produced for Georgetown Collection have garnered a total of 17 nominations and six awards!

Extraordinary Quality Control; Responsive Customer Service

As partner and supporter of great doll artists, McKinnon explains, Georgetown also insists that only top quality components be used in the making of its dolls. "Among the tradespeople who produce our porcelain, wigs and the material for our costuming, we have a reputation for accepting only the very best quality. So that's what we get – consistently."

Responsive customer service is another important reason for the firm's continued success. "This," says McKinnon, "comes down to simply working harder. At Georgetown, we treat all our customers as individuals, and we listen to what they tell us. The success of our program is proven by how many of our collectors come back to us again and again." And it's not just the customers who remain faithful to Georgetown: "Since our company first began," notes McKinnon, "we've had very little turnover in our employees, our artists or our suppliers."

A Popular, New Georgetown Newsletter

All this fruitful give-and-take between the company, its artists, employees, suppliers, and its customers, has resulted in the creation of something new and extremely useful for collectors. This is the quarterly newsletter entitled "News from Georgetown" that keeps collectors abreast of the latest information on doll artists, their work, personal appearances and awards, as well as on various Georgetown employees – customer service representatives, for instance – whom customers talk with and might enjoy learning more about.

"We knew there was a need for something like this newsletter," notes McKinnon, "but we never expected such an enormous response. We've

Pamela Phillips' new doll for Georgetown Collection, "Madeleine & Harry" – standing 18" high and retailing for $140 – offers collectors not only an adorable little girl, but a fluffy white puppy, as well.

always considered our employees, artists, suppliers and customers to be a kind of large, extended family, so it's very gratifying to learn that our customers feel this way, too." Collectors interested in receiving an initial copy of "News from Georgetown" can write to Georgetown Collection, P.O. Box 9730, Portland, ME 04104-5030. The initial copy is free, and a further subscription costs only $4.95 – "just to pay for postage and handling," explains McKinnon.

Honors for Georgetown Artists Linda Mason and Pamela Phillips

One of the topics about which the newsletter keeps collectors informed is the latest awards to be handed out to Georgetown artists. And there are always plenty of these! Among the many honors Georgetown artist Linda Mason has won, for instance, is the *Dolls* magazine "Award of Excellence" for an unprecedented three years in a row. Mason, who says she has always loved dolls, as well as the romance of things Victorian, has just created "Lavender Dreams," her first doll in Georgetown's *Victorian Fantasies™* collection.

Pamela Phillips, a relative newcomer to Georgetown, won her *Dolls* magazine "Award of Excellence" in 1994 and has three of her dolls nominated for *Doll Reader's* "Doll of the Year" award in 1995. Portraiture has always been Pamela's first love, and her enormous skill at creating faces as true-to-life as they are beautiful is apparent in her latest work for Georgetown – "Madeleine and Harry." This unique work features a little girl dressed in red, white and blue, together with her adorable dog, a fluffy white West Highland Terrier.

Awards to Ann Timmerman, Joyce Reavey and Marlene Sirko

Popular artist Ann Tim-merman has won an International Doll Exhibition (IDEX) award, as well as receiving two recent nominations from *Doll Reader* for her cherubic angels in Georgetown's *Little Bit of Heaven™* series. Likewise, Marlene Sirko – whose first Georgetown doll "Amanda" sports her own set of ice skates – was previously honored with a *Doll Reader* "Doll of the Year" award.

Another Georgetown artist Joyce Reavey, whose spunky children are becoming a staple of doll collectors, is also the recipient of a *Dolls* magazine "Award of Excellence." All five of the above doll artists – plus European baby doll artist Barbara Prusseit – are discussed in greater detail in the *Artists Profile* section later in this book.

In addition to the six dollmakers just mentioned, the Georgetown Collection also works with several other popular doll artists, whose creations have brought joy and delight to collectors worldwide.

Carol Theroux's *Buffalo Clan* and the *Faraway Friends* of Sissel Skille

Georgetown artist Carol Theroux is considered one of the finest artists now painting Native American subjects, and she has been an honored exhibitor at America's most prestigious invitational Western art shows. Drawing from her own Native American ancestry, Carol has created several beautifully crafted dolls, each of which the artist researches carefully for authenticity and accuracy.

What this means to the collector is that every detail – from necklace to moccasins – has been perfected to the artist's satisfaction. Carol Theroux's dolls for Georgetown now include "Winter Baby" in her traditional blanket-like coat, called a capote, the sister and brother team of "Buffalo Child" and "Buffalo Boy," "Golden Flower" and "Little Fawn's Papoose."

When the very first word a young girl speaks aloud is "doll," is it any wonder she would go on to create dolls of her own? Such is the case with Norwegian artist Sissel Skille, whose *Faraway Friends™* collection for Georgetown includes the enchanting little Norwegian girl "Kristin," "Mariama" from Senegal and "Dara," a delightful kite flyer from Thailand. The dolls in this series celebrate the special friendship shared by young pen pals.

Skating up a storm is Marlene Sirko's "Amanda," a new doll for Georgetown Collection that is brimming with vitality. "Amanda" stands 15-1/2" high and retails for $120.

Soft as moonlight, Ann Timmerman's "Sweetdreams and Moonbeams" for Georgetown Collection is alive with enchantment. With its soft sculpture moon included, the doll is 10" seated and retails for $130.

Sissel, who has always loved children, expresses that love not only in doll making but in teaching in a Norwegian school system, where she can watch her charges progress from tiny tots into young adults. While her original dolls were all one-of-a-kind and very expensive, Sissel is now reaching a much wider audience via her creations for Georgetown.

The *Class Portraits* of Jutta Kissling and Anne DiMartino's *Little Dreamers*

For years Jutta Kissling worked in public relations, helping entrepreneurs bring their creative work to the public eye. As a long-time doll lover, Jutta at last decided to try her hand at doll making. Completely self-taught, she mastered the technique of porcelain doll making and eventually her dolls became known throughout Europe.

Now, Jutta has completed her first creation for Georgetown: "Anna," a lovely European schoolgirl in the *Class Portraits™* collection. This is the first of Jutta's dolls to be made available to American collectors, and quite a prize she is! Complete with schoolbooks and a bouquet of tulips, "Anna" expresses both excitement and uncertainty, as her first class picture is about to be taken.

"Strong feelings are an important part of life," says Anne DiMartino, and this sculptor-turned-doll maker has discovered that dolls are wonderful creations through which to express these feelings. In her Georgetown collection called *Little Dreamers™*, Anne has brought to life two exquisite dolls: "Beautiful Buttercup" and "Julie," both of which demonstrate the beauty that can be found in real-life emotions.

"What I love most about children," notes Anne, "is the freedom they feel to show their emotions. Their faces reflect everything in their hearts – love, sadness, excitement, glee – and it's all there for us to see and to share with them." And those amazing emotions, so difficult to achieve, are exactly what Anne has brought to each of her dolls.

A Continuing Commitment to Excellence

Over the past decade, the Georgetown Collection has built a strong reputation for award-winning doll art, as well as a growing coterie of enthusiastic collectors. In the decade ahead, Georgetown will continue this devotion to excellence. And it will work, as always, with a small cadre of the world's most honored doll artists – whose complete creative control promises collectors an array of dolls that will exceed their very highest expectations.

Georgetown Collection
866 Spring Street
Portland, ME 04104-5030
(800) 626-3330
Fax (207) 775-6457

GOEBEL OF NORTH AMERICA

M.I. Hummel® Artworks Lead a Host of Fine Collectibles and Distinctive Licensed Products

With a wistful wave of his hankie, a young boy bids adieu to a 25-year collection tradition. "Come Back Soon" is the final edition of the beloved M.I. Hummel Annual Plate Series. *A matching figurine is also available.*

It was 125 years ago that Franz Detleff Goebel and his son, William, founded F. & W. Goebel in Coburg, Germany. Since then, five generations of the family have stood at the helm, directing a company whose diversified line now includes handcrafted figurines, porcelain and crystal collectibles, and decorative accessories – all distinctive products prized for high-quality workmanship and design.

Goebel already had earned a fine reputation for product innovation when the firm introduced the famed *M.I. Hummel* figurines in 1935. After World War II, the popularity of the *M.I. Hummel* figurines grew rapidly in the United States, prompting Goebel to establish its first distribution company there in 1968.

Today, the United States represents Goebel's largest single "international" market. Renamed Goebel of North America in 1994, the company currently handles over a dozen distinct lines of gifts and collectible products.

The Latest Creations Inspired by Sister Maria Innocentia Hummel's Art

Franz Goebel, the Goebel founder's great-grandson and fourth-generation owner of the firm, is credited with striking a unique product development arrangement with Sister Maria Innocentia Hummel and the Convent of Siessen. This provided Goebel with the worldwide exclusive rights to transform the artist's drawings into three-dimensional products. The pact remains in force today, as evidenced by a host of appealing new *M.I. Hummel* products introduced recently.

The newcomers to the *M.I. Hummel* collection continue to capture the wide-eyed innocence and tender charm of childhood. Handcrafted and hand-painted by artisans at the Goebel factory in Germany, each new figurine, plate, and bell bears the Goebel backstamp and the signature of the late Sister Maria Innocentia Hummel.

A Wide-Ranging Collection of *M.I. Hummel* Treasures

The year 1995 marked the 60th anniversary of *M.I. Hummel* figurines. In honor of the occasion, W. Goebel Porzellanfabrik of Germany has produced a special edition "Puppy Love Plaque." Offered for one year only, this delightful display plaque features the endearing "Puppy Love" motif, the very first *M.I. Hummel* figurine created in 1935 and retired in 1988.

The new collection is an eclectic one, with something to appeal to every taste. Those who are partial to little girls will say "thank heavens" when they see the nimble knitter, "To Keep You Warm," and "Pixie," a saucy pigtailed imp. Another darling child, "Ooh, My Tooth," is a winsome reminder of one of the more painful passages of youth. This figurine boasts a first-issue and special event backstamp and was available only in the United States and Canada at certain in-store events during 1995.

Boys will be boys, any time, any place. "The Angler" recalls the pride and pleasure every young fisherman feels when he lands his first catch. "Just Dozing" captures the sweet serenity of a wee one at rest. Add a note of merriment to any room with "Strike Up the Band," the tenth release in the *Century Collection* category. This lively quartet of rosy-cheeked music-makers will be produced for only one year and is accompanied by a Certificate of Authenticity.

Ring in the holidays with the annual dated *"Christmas Bell"* and its matching hanging ornament, figurine, and dated plate. Titled "Festival Harmony with Flute," this adorable band of musical cherubs is the third in a series of four annual groupings. The miniature dated plate made a special debut in 1995. It is finished in soft tones of gold and green and features the same coloration and motif as the yule figurine, ornament and bell.

Plate fanciers will welcome "Come Back Soon," the final edition of the

The year 1995 marked the 60th anniversary of M.I. Hummel *figurines. To mark the occasion and celebrate, this special edition "Puppy Love Plaque" made its debut.*

renowned *M.I. Hummel Annual Plate Series* of 25 that began in 1971. The cheerful fellow extending his hand to bid farewell is also available in a matching figurine. Rounding out the new plate issues is the final edition of the *Friends Forever* series. Titled "Surprise," this plate depicts two buddies in a field of flowers who are

The M.I. Hummel *Anniversary Clock, "Goose Girl," was made in Germany and features a ceramic, bas-relief rendering of the famous portrait of girl and geese. The clock itself is flanked by pillars of polished brass and enclosed in a crystal dome. The 12"-high time piece is battery powered for quiet, efficient, virtually maintenance-free operation and comes with a one-year warranty.*

startled by a buzzing bumblebee.

Because Sister Maria Innocentia Hummel produced such a wealth of artwork during her lifetime, there are enough images available to provide wonderful new subjects for many years to come. The Convent of Siessen, where she lived and worked, continues to receive royalties from Goebel to endow charities and benevolent programs throughout the world.

Produced by W. Goebel Porzellanfabrik of Germany, each of these hand-made pieces features the famous incised *M.I. Hummel* signature on the base of the figurine to indicate its authenticity. Production time varies according to the size and complexity of each piece. For example, a six-inch *M. I. Hummel* figurine can require as many as 700 hand operations and can take as long as several weeks to complete. Such pieces are created by highly skilled artisans who have been trained by Goebel, beginning with a three-year apprenticeship program.

Bette Ball and Karen Kennedy Keep Yesterday's Memories Alive

Goebel's gifted doll designers, Bette Ball and Karen Kennedy, have not forgotten their childhood memories. In fact, they cherish the innocence and delight so much that they have made it the basis of their careers — sharing visions of gentle days gone by in a marvelous array of limited edition porcelain dolls, many of which are musical.

Each creation, whether it be from the *Victoria Ashlea Originals*®, *Dolly Dingle*®, *Betty Jane Carter*®, *Carol Anne*®, *Goebel Angels*® or *Charlot Byj*® series, is a masterpiece of fine detailing, craftsmanship and tasteful design. The goal of Ms. Ball and Ms. Kennedy is to capture the imagination and love of discerning collectors today and for many generations to come.

The Success of *Dolly Dingle*

In 1983, Bette Ball and her daughter Ashlea were browsing through an antique shop and happened upon a box of old *Dolly Dingle* cut-outs. Ms. Ball recalls, "As a child, I made an army of paper dolls and supplied them with enormous wardrobes." The cut-out character of *Dolly Dingle* was destined to win her heart. Goebel bought the rights to this early twentieth-century cut-out doll originally owned by Grace Drayton.

By 1985, *Dolly Dingle* had become "America's Sweetheart" in the form of lifelike, three-dimensional dolls created by Bette Ball. That year, Ms. Ball earned the prestigious "Doll of the Year" (DOTY) Award for her creation of a sixteen-inch *Dolly Dingle* musical

Bette Ball designed this wonderful collection of Dolly Dingle *dolls for Goebel. Ms. Ball gained the rights to the original cut-out doll designs of Grace Drayton, and created these three-dimensional "Dollies" in a variety of sizes, themes, and costumes.*

doll. Today, the *Dolly Dingle* line continues to win admirers all over the world. Indeed, you can see Ms. Ball's creations in over 50 museums across the globe. *Dolly Dingle's* family tree grows new members each year. The branches include the Sweeties, the Blossoms, the Twinkles, the Snooks, the Tingles, the Dumplings, the Bumps, and many others.

Goebel Presents Masterpieces in Miniature

Working in harmony with gifted contemporary artists like Peter Yenawine and Douglas Norrgard, Goebel offers a remarkable array of miniature figurines. Yenawine's *Nature's Moments* sculptures in crystal and precious metals feature graceful birds, fish and animals in their favorite habitats — be they mountain summits, coral reefs, arctic islands or backyard baths. Norrgard combines his accomplished artistry with a gift for storytelling, presenting "Once Upon a Winter's Day" — Vignette to recall a childhood memory.

Also in miniature, Goebel offers the tiny novelty clocks of Paul Larsen, created in collaboration with Gordon Converse. What's more, Norman Rockwell's classic *Portraits of America* now are available as handsome miniatures – a series of cameos and vignettes based on some of America's most popular paintings.

A Diverse Array of Artists and Media – All From Goebel

Rockwell's *Portraits of America* not only inspire Goebel Miniatures, but also a wonderful series of regular size plates and figurines. Goebel Crystal – which is 24% full lead crystal made in Germany – offers a dazzling selection of animals, Disney characters, and classic cars.

Goebel's Steinbach designs combine crystal and molten glass to offer marvelously detailed, engraved designs, presented on bold geometric shapes. Goebel Gifts include pieces for Easter and Christmas presentation, as well as precious *Snowbirds* that make a fine gift for any occasion. The *Christmas Treasures* designed by Goebel include colorful, intricately painted angels, Santas, nativity scenes, and other holiday delights.

The Goebel family of products continues to grow with works in porcelain, crystal, and other fine media from talented artists of the past and present. Ranging in appeal from contemporary tastes to traditional Americana, each line is identified by the highly regarded "Goebel" brand, or one of several distinctive licenses. What's more, each is intended to bring lasting pleasure to its purchaser or gift recipient – a five-generation Goebel tradition since 1871.

Goebel of North America
Goebel Plaza
P.O. Box 10, Rte. 31
Pennington, NJ 08534-0010
(609) 737-8700
Fax (609) 737-1545

The "Once Upon a Winter's Day" – Vignette by Douglas Norrgard is one of Goebel's Masterpieces in Miniature. The vignette includes seven hand-painted bronze sculptures, and relates a childhood memory with great visual eloquence.

THE GREAT AMERICAN® TAYLOR COLLECTIBLES CORP.

A World of Collecting from Teddy Bears to Santa Claus

These adorable members of The Taylor Bear Family *were among the first works of art from The Great American Taylor Collectibles Corp. They include grandparents "Glyn" and "Marcie," their daughter "Elizabeth" and her husband "Beauregard," and the grandchildren "Suzy" and "Sidney."*

With their soulful, shoe-button eyes and cuddly good looks, the *Taylor Bears™* of The Great American® Taylor Collectibles Corp. were born to win collectors' hearts. Indeed, these wonderful folk art bear characters established Great American as an important new force in the world of collecting – soon after the North Carolina company's founding in 1980 by its namesake, Jack Taylor.

More than 100 different designs in *The Taylor Bear Family™* have introduced a marvelous clan of bears dressed in bright clothing and ready for fun and adventure. Favorite characters include "Glyn" and "Marcie," their daughter "Elizabeth," her husband "Beauregard" and the grandchildren "Suzy" and "Sidney."

Although they are cold cast before hand-painting, these adorable bears boast a hand-carved look reminiscent of the great, classic folk arts of their Carolina roots. The original *Taylor Bear Family* retired in 1989, but they were succeeded by another marvelous collection, *The Taylor Bear Professionals™*. Most of these doctors, firefighters, teachers, nurses and other "hard-working" bears are still available today. Sadly, their creator, Glyn Snow, died in 1989: a tragedy for all those who love the *Taylor Bears*.

Old World Santas Find New Collectors

While the bears hold a special place in people's hearts, perhaps Great American's most beloved line of all is Lancy Smith's *Old World Santas*, which were introduced in 1988. Each year, five new originals are carved in wood and five from the past are retired. Each year's set "lives" three years before retirement. All are serially numbered, gift boxed and – as is traditional with Great American collectibles – come with rights to full-color personalized Certificates of Ownership. All the collector needs to do is mail the blue request card enclosed with each figurine to acquire this attractive certificate with its gold seal: a personalized document handsome enough for framing.

Each of the *Old World Santas* is completely made in the United States from an oak-like, cold cast material, then hand-painted to perfection by skilled artists in North Carolina's Sandhills. Pieces range in height from 6" to 8" and the issue price for active editions is $29.00 each.

The first 20 *Old World Santas* already have been retired, with secondary market trading well underway for most pieces.

The 1993 collection, which retired at the end of 1995, featured "Franz" of Switzerland, "Otto" of Germany, "Vito" of Italy, "Bjorn" of Sweden and "Ryan" of Canada. The pieces also come with interesting and personal stories, as if they were real people. "Otto," for example lives in Wiesbaden, Germany. His great-grandfather was a Prussian general who loved to have his men march to drums. Every Christmas, "Otto" marches along the Rhine River, beating his drums and distributing toys to the

Among the most popular Great American lines is Lancy Smith's Old World Santas, *which were introduced in 1988. The 1995 introductions include (from left to right): "Lars" of Norway, "Tomba" of South Africa, "Butch" of the United States, "Raymond" of the Galapagos Islands and "Stach" of Poland.*

Collectors can join the Great American Collectors' Guild by simply purchasing one of the company's special Collectors Club pieces, including "Winston" and "Timothy." In addition to enjoying these finely crafted pieces, collectors will receive a free one-year membership and receive three issues of the Club newsletter.

delight of girls and boys.

Retired at the end of 1994 were the Santas first unveiled in 1992. They are: "Jacques" of France, "Mickey" of Ireland, "Terry" of Denmark, "Jose" of Spain and "Stu" from Poland. "Stu" even has his own special story. It seems he's from Warsaw and can't stand clutter or dust. So he carries his straw broom everywhere to keep everything tidy. The pieces, retired in 1994, are already selling on the secondary market for between $36.00 and $50.00.

First introduced in 1994 and available through 1996 are these wonderful Santas: "Ivan" of Russia, "Desmond" of England, "Gord" of Canada, "Wilhelm" of Holland, and "Angus" of Scotland. "Angus" hails from Aberdeen, Scotland, where he and his pet Scotty dog, McNeil, raise Aberdeen Angus cattle on a nearby ranch. "Angus" plays checkers with the Lord Mayor of Aberdeen every Tuesday night, and McNeil entertains them by dancing on his hind legs when he hears the Lord Mayor's bagpipes played on his CD.

Introduced in 1995 are "Lars" of Lillihammer, Norway, who is so glad that the Olympics are over so he can get back to his serious salmon fishing; "Tomba" of South Africa; "Butch" of the United States, who is a fireman when not playing Santa Claus; "Raymond" of the Galapagos Islands; and "Stach" of Poland.

Collectors can also join the Great American Collectors' Guild for free by purchasing one of the company's special Collectors Club pieces. Collectors will receive a free one-year membership and receive three issues of the Club newsletter. The current special Club pieces are "Winston" and "Timothy," who lives on the River Shannon in Limerick with his favorite leprechaun named Shenanigan. "Winston" retires in 1995 and "Timothy" in 1996. "William," the first edition piece, retired in 1994 and has appreciated in value on the secondary market.

Each year, five new pieces join the Jim Clement Santas *collection and the same number of pieces are retired. The figurines that retired in 1995 were (top row from left to right): "Down the Chimney," "The Day After Christmas," "Mr. Egg," "Santa With Hobby Horse" and "Golfer Santa." Retiring in 1996 are (second row from left to right): "Tennis Santa," "Night After Christmas," "Noah," "Bald Santa With Rover," "Big Santa With Toys." The third row contains the 1997 retirees: "Doe A Deer," "Ho! Ho! Ho! Stuck in the Chimney," "Silent Night," "Mountain Dream." "Visions of Sugar Plums" is on the bottom row along with "Kris Jingle," the first edition Collectors' Guild piece that retires in 1996.*

The Ruskins™ *are here to share words of conservative wisdom and wit! Designed by artist Kevin Cagle and Jack Taylor, the line features these little devils that offer their insights on everything from family values to the value of good cigars.*

Jim Clement's Santas Carve a New Niche

Jim Clement's 15 wood carving Santas were introduced in 1994 and have become extremely popular. As a master artisan from Ellijay, Georgia, Jim carves five new pieces each year and five are retired to ensure the line continues to contain only 15 subjects. Jim added "Kris Jingle" in 1995, his first edition Collectors' Club piece which is available both as a figurine and as a handsome lamp with a rich burgundy shade.

His other 1995 lamps, which are all serially numbered, include "Clementine Cat," "Uncle Sam," "Toy Soldier" and "Roosevelt Rooster." The figurines that retired in 1995 were: "Down the Chimney," "The Day After Christmas," "Mr. Egg," "Santa With Hobby Horse" and "Golfer Santa." Retiring in 1996 are: "Tennis Santa," "Night After Christmas," "Noah," "Bald Santa With Rover," "Big Santa With Toys" and "Kris Jingle." The 1997 retirees will be "Doe A Deer," "Ho! Ho! Ho! Stuck in the Chimney," "Silent Night," "Mountain Dream" and "Visions of Sugar Plums." They range in price from $13.75 to $70.00 each.

Ruskins™ Share Words of Wisdom

Another promising artist is Kevin Cagle from the Sandhills of North

Great American's newest collectible line is New York Townhouses *crafted by award-winning architect Richard Banks. These turn-of-the-century designs recreate some of the finest townhouses owned by New York City's elite. Richard has researched and handcrafted in wood the originals of these townhouses on a 1/8" scale.*

Carolina. Kevin and Jack Taylor designed a line of *Ruskin™* figurines – conservative little devils who know the truth and have true courage to speak it ... with a smile. Each *Ruskin* comes with a special story. "Ruskin #1," which retired at the end of 1995, gives wisdom on the family: "Folks, we need to return this country to its traditional family values..."

"Ruskin #2," retiring in December 1996, offers wisdom on our national wealth: "Folks, our national wealth is not a fixed amount of money that can be divided, but is a dynamic that depends for its continuation and growth on liberty and individual initiative, things that as a country we should nurture carefully." "Ruskin #3" talks about hard work and good cigars while "Ruskin #4," wearing a red jacket, promotes speaking the truth. Both will retire at the end of 1997. "Ruskin #5" and "Ruskin #6" are dressed as an angel and a devil, and will retire in 1998. The *Ruskins*, which sell for about $20.00 each, are gift boxed and serially numbered.

New York Townhouses Bring Back Memories

To combine his love of architecture, art and history, Richard Banks has created miniature historical townhouses built for the wealthy movers and shakers of 19th century New York. With more than 25 years of professional experience, Richard has been a university teacher, president of an international architecture and planning firm, head of his own design and real estate development group and construction management consultant to the Mayor of New York City on large-scale projects. Now he's building *New York Townhouses* – on a small scale.

From Fifth Avenue to 82nd Street, Richard has meticulously researched and handcrafted in wood the originals of these elite townhouses on a 1/8" scale.

Great American Taylor Collectible Corp.
Dept. BIC Box 428
Aberdeen, NC 28388
(910) 944-7447
Fax (910) 944-7449

COLLECTORS' CLUB

The Great American Collectors' Guild
P.O. Box 428
Aberdeen, NC 28315
(910) 944-7447

Annual Dues: Free with purchase of Club Piece
Club Year: January-December

Benefits:
- Newsletter Published Three Times Yearly
- Buy/Sell Matching Service
- Tour of Factory Available

THE GREENWICH WORKSHOP

Bringing "Art as Entertainment" into People's Lives Is The Greenwich Workshop's Mission

As the leading North American publisher of art and art-inspired products, including limited edition fine art prints, art books, videos, art furniture and figurines, as well as an innovator in the art entertainment industry, The Greenwich Workshop sees its mission as bringing art into our lives to enhance everyday entertainment and enjoyment. And The Greenwich Workshop believes that there is more than just one way to do it. The art, artists and offerings of the Workshop are as varied as the people who collect them. Be it a limited edition fine art print, a book, an art furnishings frame, porcelain figurine, silk neck tie with a favorite artist's image or an entertaining video, the works of The Greenwich Workshop and their family of artists can take you into the realms of the imagination, preserve a favorite experience in the wilderness, explore new lands, commemorate our history and cultural heritage, or quite simply create a beautiful impression.

"Everyone enjoys art regardless of their level of knowledge and personal taste. Although few of us are fortunate enough to have access to original works of art by outstanding artists," says David Usher, co-founder and chairman of The Greenwich Workshop, "many of us can enjoy them in the form of limited edition fine art prints, posters, books, or a high-quality porcelain figurine in our homes."

Journey into the wilderness to witness one of our planet's most magnificent animals in his natural habitat. "Golden Silhouette" is from Simon Combes' exciting The Great Cats Adventure *series.*

Greenwich's Window on the World Is Opened by Today's Most Accomplished Artists

The Greenwich Workshop is proud to offer wildlife artist Simon Combes' one-of-a-kind collection: *The Great Cats Adventure*. Prints in this series capture and preserve, on canvas and print, and bring to our attention the tenuous status of endangered feline predators as they have never before been seen. Collectors discover in Combes' detailed works a sensitivity and eye for color that makes *The Great Cats Adventure* a popular contemporary series. Look for a picture of "Golden Silhouette" in this article! It gives you a sample of the power and grace of Combes' magnificent animal art.

For fans of Native American art, painter Howard Terpning's sensitive studies are unrivaled. Terpning's reputation for authentic art depicting our indigenous peoples is so remarkable, he's been called "The Storyteller of the Native American People." Current Greenwich Workshop prints by Terpning are in great demand from coast-to-coast.

Few contemporary artists have known the adulation, awards and success of Bev Doolittle. The Greenwich Workshop counts her western spiritual works among its current best sellers. Doolittle has sold more prints than any other artist worldwide; some say her "Prayer for the Wild Things" will remain a benchmark for every artist wishing to infuse their paintings with spiritual reminders of nature's majesty.

Reknowned for his best-selling, groundbreaking book Dinotopia®, *artist James Gurney again ventures into a world of fantasy in his new book* The World Beneath. *"Exhultation" is the dynamic art created to grace the book's cover.*

Fantasy...History...Folk Art and Fairy Tales

Because American collectors have eclectic tastes and enjoy variety, The Greenwich Workshop represents the work of today's most innovative artists. Who hasn't heard of James Gurney, creator of the international best-seller *Dinotopia*? Images of Gurney's land, where dinosaurs and people live in harmony, are available as fine art prints from Greenwich. By the way, if you're a fantasy buff and love lots of bright color and imaginative detail in your prints, James Christensen's work is right up your alley. His charming works (self-described as 'a little left of reality') are eagerly collected by art fans of every age.

Just down the sky a piece from Gurney and Christensen, the adventurous world of aviation history awaits. William S. Phillips' sold out print, "The Giant Begins to Stir," artfully depicts the flight of the Doolittle Raiders when they dominated the skies over 50 years ago during World War II. The historic value of this print doesn't rest with the art alone; collectors will discover counter-signatures of Doolittle and the surviving crew members of the 16-aircraft armada featured in this exciting print.

The Greenwich Workshop recently published two highly notable works which commemorate aviation history: The flights of the Enola Gay ("Dawn, the World Forever Changed," also by Phillips), and Bock's Car (Craig Kodera's "Lonely Flight to Destiny"). Each pays tribute to our bravest men and their daring missions which many believed helped to bring an end to the war in the Pacific.

Countersignatures of ten crewman (including General Paul Tibbets, command pilot of the Enola Gay) appear on these dynamic prints. As an added note, when these legendary heroes were assembled to sign the prints, the idea for a documentary took shape. "The Men Who Brought The Dawn," produced by The Greenwich Workshop, debuted this fall.

From the dangerous skies over the Pacific to the more idyllic places of the heart in America, The Greenwich Workshop also offers a superior variety of popular subjects to suit every taste. Popular folk artist John Simpkins' bold colors and simple lines have captured hearts of every age. Both adults and children flock to Scott Gustafson's fanciful fairy tales and nursery rhymes, done in his opulent painting style. Finally, discover the soft light twinkling from the windows in artist Paul Landry's "Morning Mist," featured in this article.

Windows reflect light everywhere after a drenching rain! Paul Landry's "Morning Mist" exemplifies his masterful ability to make us feel we're standing on this street.

Music to Soothe the Spirit...Art to Warm the Soul

As an innovator in today's art entertainment arena, The Greenwich Workshop is exploring a variety of media to bring art into every facet of our lives. A prime example is "Art in Concert™," an entertainment combining visual and audio elements. Developed exclusively by The Greenwich Workshop, "Art in Concert" brings together legendary musicians, composers, artists and painters.

The premier "Art in Concert" production, which was awarded a Grammy this year, pairs two legends: Grammy award-winning musician/composer Paul Winter and the inspired art of Bev Doolittle. This marriage of sights and sounds meshes Paul Winter's composition "Prayer For the Wild Things" with Bev's best-selling, award-winning artwork of the same title. Viewers are treated to a sensory celebration when they see and hear these glorious works. A second "Art in Concert" matches James Christensen's wonderful "Evening Angels" image with a new composition by the Emmy-award winning composer Kurt Bestor. Stay tuned!

Four years ago, The Greenwich Workshop pioneered a film and video project presenting art as 'a living experience.' This innovative program, called "The Living Canvas," takes viewers into a work of art to examine the people, events, emotions and stories that emerge from the heart and hand of the artist. Among the stories presented in "The Living Canvas" are "Memories of War," a documentary that details the surprise attack at Clark Field on Pearl Harbor in December 1941.

It was the first ever documentary picked for airing on a Pay-Per-View channel. Based on its success, The Greenwich Workshop took "The Living Canvas," hosted by actor Billy Dee Williams, to Public Television, where it aired initially on WNET, New York. Subsequently, over 300 more stations around the country broadcast this program.

Stephen Lyman's "Cathedral Snow" exemplifies the artist's sensitive view of nature. Lyman's prints are best-sellers. His new book, Into the Wilderness, *was released in the fall of 1995.*

Keeping Company with Some of America's Giants

Though The Greenwich Workshop is just 23 years old, it has had a remarkable evolution. Beginning as a publisher of limited edition fine art prints, Greenwich has expanded its scope to include licensing, art furnishings, porcelain figurines and book publishing. Distinguished among its first offerings was the best selling book, *Dinotopia*, which has sold over one million copies. Now, over 16 titles are in print, including *The World Beneath* (James Gurney's newest book, slated for publication in Fall, 1995) and Bev Doolittle's *New Magic*, also a Fall, 1995, release.

Perennial favorite Stephen Lyman's new book, *Into the Wilderness*, combines his "light in the wilderness" painting style and photography with an inspiring text. Lyman shows readers the natural wonders of Yosemite and the American Northwest as they've never before been seen. A classic example of Stephen Lyman's gentle eye for nature's magic can be found in this article!

In addition to publishing, The Greenwich Workshop debuts a new collection of three-dimensional figurines from world-famous artists James Christensen, Scott Gustafson and Will Bullas. Called *The Greenwich Workshop Collection*, each delightful figure in this new library is highly detailed, hand-painted and beautifully colored. Because each artist supervises

James Christensen's imaginative "Mother Goose" and her trusty transportation are about to take collectors on a magical journey into the imagination. This sculpture, a premier Greenwich Workshop Collection *figurine, inaugurates this new venture into three-dimensional art.*

the creation of his work...to be sure each is exactly as he imagined them...collectors are guaranteed something out-of-the-ordinary. Be sure to ask your favorite authorized Greenwich dealer to advise you as soon as The Greenwich Workshop Collection debuts!

Finally, partnerships with some of this nation's most dynamic multi-media companies are also being forged. The Greenwich Workshop has formed alliances with Universal, Columbia Pictures, Turner Publishing, Hallmark Cards, Inc., Bruce McGaw Publishing, Barnes and Noble, Random House, Mattel and Lenox. You can look forward to an exciting array of art, books, music, entertainment, giftware and collectible introductions as the new millennium approaches!

Stretching the Boundries While Remembering the Planet

When Greenwich Workshop was first established in 1972, no one could predict its meteoric success. But a combination of business savvy, foresight and a feel for America's eclectic taste in art and entertainment has given The Greenwich Workshop invaluable insight into the future. Without self-imposed limits, this young company can soar in new directions and find homes for its new introductions all over the world.

At present, the company distributes its limited edition fine art prints and other art-inspired offerings through a network of authorized dealers across the United States, Canada and the United Kingdom. To efficiently serve the Canadian and British markets, Greenwich U.S. oversees The Greenwich Workshop, Ltd. of Scarborough, Ontario, Canada and Greenwich Workshop Europe, located in Upton-upon-Severn, England.

The Greenwich Workshop also operates a select number of retail galleries specializing in original art. Named "Big Horn Galleries," these are located in Fairfield, Connecticut; Cody, Wyoming; Aspen, Colorado and Carmel, California.

Though growing by leaps and bounds in terms of international recognition and the scope of art it develops, The Greenwich Gallery continues to stay focused on its corporate mission. Toward that end, a never-ending search for new talent continues. Once an artist becomes a member of the Greenwich family, he or she is welcomed into a supportive environment of creative freedom. Importantly, artists associated with Greenwich share a concern for our fragile planet and our cultural heritage.

Throughout its existence, The Greenwich Workshop is proud to have made donations valued at more than three million dollars to various not-for-profit organizations related to health, the environment, public service, history and cultural preservation. This legacy will continue for as long as The Greenwich Workshop is privileged

The Greenwich Workshop
One Greenwich Place
Shelton, CT 06484
(800) 243-4246
Fax (203) 925-0262

HALLMARK CARDS, INC.

Hallmark Keepsake Ornaments Revolutionize the Way Americans Decorate for Christmas

Based on the work of popular Dutch artist Marjolein Bastin, the designs in the 1995 Nature's Sketchbook *collection feature highly detailed bas-relief sculpture and delicate hand-painting. "Raising a Family," shown above, was sculpted by Keepsake Ornament artist Joyce Lyle. The collection is part of the Keepsake Ornament Showcase which was first introduced in 1993.*

Imagine holiday celebrations before the introduction of Hallmark Keepsake Ornaments: Americans decorated their Christmas trees with mass-produced glass balls, along with tinsel and garland. Maybe children personalized an ornament with glitter, sequins or lace.

From their first introduction more than 20 years ago, Hallmark Keepsake Ornaments began a delightful tradition of treating American families to a treasure chest of choices for holiday decorating. Today, thanks to technological innovations and the special touch of each Keepsake Ornament studio artist, the designs include light, motion and sound, and an array of specially designed ornaments crafted for thousands of ornament-collecting enthusiasts each year.

How the Magic Began

Clara Johnson Scroggins, a renowned authority on ornament collecting, offers a perspective on the role of Hallmark Keepsake Ornaments in the world of collectibles. "Hallmark was the very first company to date glass ornaments and to apply artistic designs on a printed band," Ms. Scroggins observes. "Hallmark was also the first to put a glass ornament in its own box, making it collectible as well as giftable. No one had ever done that before."

Other "firsts" followed. Hallmark's *Here Comes Santa* series, first introduced in 1979, holds the distinction as the longest-running Keepsake Ornament series. In 1980, "Heavenly Minstrel" and "Checking It Twice" introduced the category of *Special Edition* ornaments. *Artists' Favorites* – a selection of ornaments featuring the signature of the artist – joined the collection in 1987. Year after year, the Keepsake Ornament studio – now made up of over a dozen full-time artists – continues to create touching, whimsical and inspirational designs.

Milestones in Hallmark Keepsake Ornament History

1973 – Hallmark introduces Keepsake Ornaments with a collection of six decorated ball ornaments and 12 yarn figures.

1975 – First handcrafted Keepsake Ornaments debut.

1976 – "Baby's First Christmas" is the industry's first commemorative ornament. By 1989, Hallmark offers commemorative ornaments through child's 5th Christmas, along with an array of other commemoratives for family and friends.

1979 – First edition of the *Here Comes Santa* series, the longest-running Keepsake Ornament series, is introduced.

1980 – The first two *Special Edition* ornaments are introduced: "Heavenly Minstrels" and "Checking It Twice."

1983 – Clara Johnson Scroggins, renowned collector, publishes the first complete guide to Hallmark Keepsake Ornaments. The sixth edition of this book, *Keepsake Ornaments: A Collector's Guide, 1973 - 1993* was published in 1993.

1984 – Lighted Keepsake Ornaments appear, paving the way for the addition of music, motion and even talking Keepsake Magic Ornaments.

1987 – Hallmark organizes the Keepsake Ornament Collector's Club. Today, the Club is more than 200,000 members strong, making it one of the largest collector organizations in the nation.

1987 – Artists' Favorites, a selection of ornaments each featuring the signature of the designer, first appear.

1988 – Hallmark offers the first Keepsake Miniature Ornaments – the industry's first complete line of miniature ornaments.

1991 – Kansas City, Missouri, site of the international headquarters of Hallmark Cards, Inc., hosts the first National Hallmark Keepsake Ornament Collector's Club Convention.

1991 – First Hallmark Keepsake Ornaments for Easter are introduced.

1993 – Hallmark introduces Anniversary Editions, four ornaments commemorating 20 years of Keepsake Ornaments. The first Keepsake Ornament in the *Holiday BARBIE™* series is introduced. The series is based on Mattel's annual special edition Happy Holidays BARBIE® dolls.

1993 – Hallmark introduces the Keepsake Ornament Showcase line, a premiere offering featuring 19 ornaments in four distinctive theme groups: Folk Art Americana, Old-World Silver, Portraits in Bisque and Holiday Enchantment.

1993 – First Personalized Keepsake Ornaments appear with 12 Keepsake Ornaments that may be personalized with name, date or even a phrase. "Messages of Christmas" becomes the first ornament that consumers can

"Santa's Roadster," the 17th design in the Here Comes Santa *series, was sculpted for 1995 by Linda Sickman.* Here Comes Santa, *which began in 1979, is the longest-running Keepsake Ornament Collector's Series.*

record with their own message to be replayed season after season.

1993 – First Keepsake Ornament inspired by a collector appears. "Look for the Wonder" is designed in honor of the Keepsake Ornament Convention's costume contest winner Joanne Pawelek.

1994 – In honor of the 35th anniversary of BARBIE®, a new Hallmark series of nostalgic ornament designs begins with "BARBIE™ - Debut 1959."

1995 – Lighted Keepsake Miniature Ornaments light up the tree. Silent motors for *Keepsake Magic Ornaments* also debut.

1995 – Keepsakes celebrates the 15th anniversary of the *Rocking Horse* series with a special "Anniversary Edition Pewter Rocking Horse."

1995 – For the first time, members of the Keepsakes Ornament Collector's Club appear in photo holder ornaments. Members entered their favorite photos in a contest with several different categories. Winning photos were inserted in the photo holders during the manufacturing process.

Popular Characters and Cultural Change

Hallmark Keepsake Ornaments pioneered many changes through the years, and they continue to change with the times. While family and friends will always select ornaments to commemorate special memories and milestones, choices now include ornaments that salute popular characters, personalities and cultural change. Who would have predicted that BARBIE would find her place on a Christmas tree? Or Superman? Or Shaquille O'Neal? Keepsake Ornaments also celebrate current movies, such as the popular Disney® films *Lion King* and *Pocahontas*. Even Keepsake Miniature Ornaments feature celluloid stars. The charm of "Tiny Toon Adventures," "Pebbles" and "Bamm-Bamm" and others, helps to form a three-dimensional scrapbook of memories and personal interests on today's Christmas trees.

"Even with so many ornaments commemorating events and tales of times past, the way we decorate our Christmas trees reflects our lives today," Scroggins says.

As an example, Keepsake Ornaments traditionally commemorate historic events in innovative ways. "The Eagle Has Landed" captures the drama of the moment when astronaut Neil Armstrong first stepped on the moon more than 25 years ago. The ornament is complete with the actual recorded transmission from the moon, including the famous phrase, "One small step for man, one giant leap for mankind."

Another commemorative collection that found a special spot in collectors' hearts is *The Wizard of Oz* collection. Because of a natural fondness for happy endings, collectors seem to delight that "The Tin Man" received a heart, "The Scarecrow" a brain, and "The Cowardly Lion" received courage. And, of course, "Dorothy and Toto" got to go home.

Current changes in home and workplace environments are reflected in Keepsake Ornaments depicting answering machines, computers and tape recorders. "Santa's Answering Machine" delivers the outgoing message: "Ho, Ho, Ho! I'm out packing my sleigh now, so be sure to leave your Christmas wishes. Wait for the jingle bells!" "People Friendly" brings the concept of personalization to a computer screen, which can highlight messages such as Secretary Friendly or Student Friendly. "Messages of Christmas" took personalization the next step, giving consumers the chance to record their own message to be enjoyed season after season. Shaped as an AM/FM radio and tape recorder, the ornament was introduced in 1993.

STAR TREK® took Christmas trees where no tree had gone before. First introduced in 1991 to commemorate the celebration of STAR TREK'S 25th anniversary, "The Starship Enterprise" quickly became one of the most sought-after designs in Keepsake Ornament history. Other STAR TREK® successes followed in subsequent years, including the addition of "Captain James T. Kirk, STAR TREK®" and "Captain Jean-Luc Picard, STAR TREK®: THE NEXT GENERATION™" in 1995. Each of the captains is featured in an environment aboard his ship.

Investing in Collectibles

The STAR TREK phenomenon is one illustration of the value collectors discover in their Keepsake Ornament collections. Meredith DeGood, a respected authority on the collector's market, observes that an ornament's value may be attributable to its popularity or its scarcity. DeGood says ornaments that bring the highest price on the collector's market aren't necessarily the rarest. She believes ornaments like "Cool Yule," the first design in the *Frosty Friends* series, may be fetching high prices simply because so many people are looking for it, not necessarily because it is rare.

A nostalgic BARBIE™ Keepsake Ornament Collector's Series *began in 1994 with "BARBIE™ – Debut 1959." The 1995 edition features the elegant "Solo in the Spotlight" design.*

The Keepsake Ornament studio artists add their special touch to each Keepsake Ornament design. Pictured are (from left to right): Studio Manager Jack Benson with artists Joyce Lyle, Ed Seale, LaDene Votruba and—at the bottom of the photo—Linda Sickman.

Collector-friendly Guides

The *Keepsake Ornament Collector's Guide*, written by Clara Johnson Scroggins and published in collaboration with Hallmark, was first available in 1983 to assist collectors in keeping track of their collections. The guide has been updated regularly, with a special anniversary edition published in 1993. Another helpful resource for collectors is the *Dream Book*, a catalog published by Hallmark each year, featuring an array of more than 200 brand-new Keepsake Ornaments. Designs are not repeated; each is issued for one year only.

In 1995, Hallmark debuted a new format for the *Dream Book*. In addition to a fresh design, more pages, larger format and decorating ideas, the book features the Keepsake Ornament artists who sculpted or designed each ornament. In response to collectors' requests, the book also contains special thoughts about some of the designs from the artists who created them. When one reads about the artists' perspectives, one learns that Keepsake Ornaments start with the heart, which explains the strong emotional impact of each ornament.

Keepsake Ornament Collector's Club

The emotional attachment collectors feel for their Keepsake Ornaments is one reason the Keepsake Ornament Collector's Club now has more than 200,000 members nationwide. For thousands of Americans, collecting ornaments has become a year-round hobby – a way of preserving treasured memories and extending the magic of Christmas throughout the year.

"Ornament collecting is a fairly recent phenomenon that simply has skyrocketed," says Lynn Wylie, National Keepsake Ornament Collector's Club manager. "People enjoy collecting Keepsake Ornaments because it's rewarding, affordable and fun."

Hallmark Keepsake Ornament Collector's Club Timeline

1987 – For this Charter Year, Hallmark designs the first members-only Keepsake Ornament and publishes the first issue of the *Collector's Courier* newsletter exclusively for Club members.

1988 – First Keepsake Treasury Binder is offered to all members; first limited-edition order opportunity for Club members.

1989 – First time "Keepsake of Membership" ornament is personalized; beginning of Artist's Appearances.

1991 – First national Collector's Club Convention with more than 700 attendees.

1993 – Hallmark celebrates the 20th anniversary of Keepsake Ornaments; two national Collector's Club Conventions are held due to overwhelming demand; *Keepsake Ornaments: A Collector's Guide, 1973-1993* is written by Clara Johnson Scroggins and published in collaboration with Hallmark.

1994 – First Hallmark Keepsake Ornament traveling EXPO is held in eight cities throughout the nation.

Hallmark Cards, Inc.
Hallmark Keepsake Ornament Collector's Club #161, P.O. Box 412734
Kansas City, MO 64141-2734

COLLECTORS' CLUB/VISITOR CENTER

Keepsake Ornament Collector's Club
P.O. Box 419034
Kansas City, MO 64141-6034

Annual Dues: $20.00
Club Year: January-December

Benefits:
- Membership Gift: Three to Four "Keepsake of Membership" Ornaments
- Opportunity to Purchase Exclusive Club Edition Ornaments
- Quarterly Newsletter, "Collector's Courier"
- Personalized Membership Card
- Conventions or Other Special Events
- Local Club Chapters
- Preview of Products
- Early Mailing of *Dream Book*

Hallmark Visitors Center
P.O. Box 419580, Mail Drop 132
Kansas City, MO 64141-6580
(816) 274-5672

Hours: Monday through Friday, 9 a.m. - 5 p.m.; Saturday, 9:30 a.m - 4:30 p.m. Open most holidays.

Admission: None – Free Parking with 3-hour validation.
Reservations required for groups of ten or more.
Located on Hallmark Square in the Crown Center Complex one mile south of downtown Kansas City, Missouri, The Hallmark Visitors Center brings you the sights and sounds of Hallmark, past and present. View a 40-foot historical time line with memorabilia from more than 80 years of Hallmark history, enjoy video exhibits, a film presentation and more.

THE HAMILTON COLLECTION

Renowned Artists and New Initiatives Keep Hamilton a Step Ahead in the World of Limited Edition Collectibles

The year: 1978. The plate: "Clara and Nutcracker." For the first time, The Hamilton Collection introduced a major limited edition collector plate – and the response was extraordinary! Winner of multiple honors and a strong performer on the secondary market, Shell Fisher's ballet-theme "Clara" set the stage for Hamilton's emergence as a leading direct response marketer of collectibles. Since then, the Jacksonville, Florida-based firm has won scores of honors – and set numerous sales records – with its collectible dolls, plates and figurines. What's more, Hamilton continues its innovative ways with planned introductions of miniature cottages, plaques and ornaments.

Over the last year or two, Hamilton's top performers included *Precious Moments®* and *Dreamsicles®* plates, as well as the adorable *Cherished Teddies®* figurine collection. *STAR TREK™* plates – long a favorite of Hamilton collectors – continue their run of popularity, while Victorian and wildlife themes by top artists also intrigue art lovers. What's more, Hamilton continues to forge fruitful associations with some of today's most gifted doll designers, including Connie Walser Derek, Connie Johnston and Virginia Turner.

Heavenly *Dreamsicles* Make Their Plate Debut

Month after month, dealer polls reveal that the charming little *Dreamsicles* cherubs reign as one of today's most popular giftware figurines. Created by artist Kristin Haynes, the *Dreamsicles* began their life in three dimensions. Now – thanks to an exclusive association with The Hamilton Collection – these roly-poly cherubs star in their own plate collection as well – a *Dreamsicles* first.

The premiere plate, "The Flying Lesson," features a central scene of an apprehensive cherub and his two "flying tutors." The little angel is proud of his brand-new wings, but now he has to "take the plunge and give 'em a try!" Each heavenly cherub boasts his own heartwarming personality and expression. One tutor boldly claps his pupil on the back, urging the little hero to "go for it," while the other...soft-eyed and gentle...reads step-by-step directions from the "How to Fly" book. Meanwhile in the background, a brand-new flyer steadies herself for her first "solo spin."

The original *Dreamsicles* progressed from a series of pieces artist Haynes perfected while living in California. Some were crafted of cement in large sizes – as lawn ornaments – while others were smaller and cast in materials better suited for indoor display. The characteristic dried flower "halos" worn by *Dreamsicles* cherubs came about by experimentation. "Dried flowers are so popular, I just popped a little wreath on the cherub's head," Ms. Haynes recalls of a whim she followed one day. "It added so much – such a neat touch!"

Priscilla Hillman Presents *Monthly Friends to Cherish*

Bursting with irresistible charm and personality, the award-winning *Cherished Teddies* collection from Enesco has won the hearts of collectors all over the country. Now, The Hamilton Collection has joined forces with Enesco Corporation to present the *Monthly Friends to Cherish* figurine collection, featuring 12 irresistible teddy bears, one to help collectors celebrate each month of the year.

"Oscar" the October Bear visits neighbors and friends to enjoy lots of tricks and treats. The December bear's festive holiday attire shows her love for Christmas, from the holly on her Santa cap to the candy cane on the present she's holding. Each of the other 10 teddies boasts just such seasonal adornments and touches, and all are expertly crafted and hand-painted.

With *Cherished Teddies* recently voted the best-selling figurine in the nation's heartland according to *Collector's Mart* magazine, it's clear their admirers consider these much more than "bear necessities." In fact, teddy bear lovers everywhere have pronounced the *Monthly Friends to Cherish* a true "honey" of a collection!

An Encounter With...The Borg

Considering the continuing fascination for the original *STAR TREK* plate collection and the many collectible series and special editions that have followed the Starship Enterprise crew, it comes as no surprise that *STAR TREK: The Next Generation™* also has

"The Flying Lesson" by Kristin Haynes premieres The Hamilton Collection's Dreamsicles™ *plate collection.*

"A Wolf's Pride" by David Geenty represents the first issue in a Hamilton sculpture collection titled Wolves of the Wilderness.

inspired a host of popular Hamilton collectibles. Among the most recent is "The Best of Both Worlds," a fine porcelain plate that premiers a series entitled *STAR TREK: The Next Generation™ – The Episodes.*

In this work of art by renowned cinematic painter Keith Birdsong, a cataclysmic, all-consuming spiral of events thrusts the entire crew of the Starship Enterprise into a confrontation with their great adversary, the Borg. This is an alien species whose very existence knows but one command – to assimilate all other life forms. Now the Borg seeks to annihilate humankind, and the crew must stop them.

This stunning drama so astounded the television industry that "The Best of Both Worlds" was honored with four Emmy nominations. Now it premieres a dazzling plate series of montage scenes from the series' most exciting and provocative shows.

Love's Messengers Capture the Glories of Victoriana

Artist and designer John Grossman is considered one of the world's leading authorities on Victorian paper keepsakes. Twenty years ago, this California painter happened into an antique shop, a visit that changed his life forever. Fascinated with the Victorian antique paper mementos, he found them to be an unending source of inspiration and the foundation for a passion that has grown into a distinguished collectibles career.

Over the years, Grossman has acquired a treasury of exquisite paper memorabilia, which he fashions into wonderfully touching collages such as the one which appears on "To My Love" – premiere issue in the *Love's Messengers* plate collection.

Like previous Grossman plate series featuring Victorian children and holiday themes, "To My Love" displays a wonderful, central image: in this case an adorable cupid holding a beautiful floral wreath – the universal symbol of affection. Surrounding this vision of romantic love are all manner of roses, lace, forget-me-nots and trinkets: the perfect expression of Victorian style.

Nature's Beautiful Creatures...Captured in Three Dimension

Two recent series of hand-painted sculptures from The Hamilton Collection pay tribute to beloved creatures of the wild. *Little Friends of the Arctic* premieres with "The Young Prince," while *Wolves of the Wilderness* unveils "A Wolf's Pride."

"The Young Prince" – an adorable polar bear baby – is as cute and playful as he can be. One day he will grow up to be ruler of his snow-bound kingdom. But for now, he seems content to rest on his crystal ice throne, dreaming of his next adventure. Handcrafted of fine porcelain and painted by hand, "The Young Prince" comes complete with a handsome, lead crystal base. Other pieces in the collection will present additional charming baby animals of the polar region.

"A Wolf's Pride" is the creation of British artist David Geenty, who spent much of his childhood on his parents' ranch in Southeast Africa. There his love of nature was nurtured, while his father led photographers and other lovers of nature on safaris through the bush. According to Geenty, *Wolves of the Wilderness* is intended "to draw attention to the importance of preserving America's rich natural history, as represented by its indigenous wolf population."

This first issue focuses on three handsome, curious pups, nestled against their mother for safety and warmth. Meticulously crafted and hand-painted, it lets viewers admire an animal that is highly intelligent and remarkably skilled as a hunter, caring for its young with tenderness and pride.

A Trio of Enchanting Dolls Showcase Three Designers' Gifts

The Hamilton Collection has become a major force in the contemporary doll market over the last decade, with collectors offering kudos for the firm's ability to "team up" with some of the world's most honored doll designers. Foremost among these is Connie Walser Derek, who brings a unique and lovable personality to each of her doll creations.

Take "Chelsea" for example – who is becoming such a big girl and quite a pro at sitting up. In this newly mastered position, she's discovering so many exciting things around her...like her shoelaces which are sure to keep her busy for hours! So marvelously true-to-life as she reaches for her laces, "Chelsea" is crafted of fine, bisque porcelain, painted by hand and inscribed with Connie Walser Derek's signature. In her lavender and rose floral playsuit, "Chelsea" is dressed for a day of fun and discovery!

Next, you're invited to meet "Savannah" by the gifted new artist Connie Johnston. "Savannah" is a sweet little cowgirl from the wide open prairie, and her cornflower blue eyes and sun-kissed charm are sure to steal your heart! All dressed up in her toe-tapping best, "Savannah" proudly shows off her new boots she'll wear to tonight's rodeo. Her Western-style outfit is cheery and wholesome as the

Dressed in her Western best, lovely "Savannah" is the creation of gifted doll designer Connie Johnston.

sky is big and blue. And her pretty hand is accented by a delicate, heart-shaped silver-tone ring.

Don't forget lovely "Amelia," the creation of award-winning doll artist Virginia Turner. All dressed up in a beautiful gown, she presents a timeless portrait of innocence and friendship. "Amelia" wears her hair upswept with a lacy, silk flower-trimmed bow, and her lace-trimmed slip and bloomers coordinate with her matching socks. Pretty shoes with satin ribbon, floral accents and faux pearls complete this sweet child's attire – and she holds an adorable plush teddy named "Cinnamon!"

Never content to rest on their laurels, Hamilton Collection officials constantly draw upon their worldwide resources to develop even more delightful collector plates, figurines and dolls for the future. What's more, with works in innovative new media like miniature cottages, plaques and ornaments under development, the future for Hamilton collectors remains full of bright anticipation.

The Hamilton Collection
4810 Executive Park Court
Jacksonville, FL 32216-6069
(800) 228-2945
Fax (904) 279-1339

HAND & HAMMER SILVERSMITHS

A Renowned Family of Silversmiths Makes Its Mark with Handcrafted Collectibles and a Traditional Craft

Chip deMatteo (left) and Philip Thorp founded Hand & Hammer Silversmiths and today lead a team of talented artisans from the company's studio in Woodbridge, Virginia. Both learned and perfected their trade from Chip's father, Bill deMatteo, Jr.

During the bustling 1920s in New York City, William deMatteo, Sr. began perfecting a craft that would inspire three generations of his family and reach audiences around the world from presidents to royalty. As a 16-year-old Italian immigrant, deMatteo transformed silver into beautiful, shimmering works of art. He became a premier silversmith – sharing the mysteries and secrets of his trade with his son, William (Bill) deMatteo, Jr., who in 1979 founded Hand & Hammer Silversmiths.

Today, the thriving business is guided by Bill's son, Chip deMatteo, and his partner Philip Thorp. They follow in the same time-worn traditions as the elder deMatteo, who set the family on a course to become world renowned for their silver collectible ornaments and jewelry.

The company's creations have graced rooms at the White House. American presidents have commissioned gifts for Queen Elizabeth II, Anwar Sadat, Menacham Begin and Winston Churchill. Leading companies call upon Hand & Hammer Silversmiths to design exclusive gifts for their customers. But whether presented to a dignitary or cherished by collectors nationwide, each piece reflects the deMatteo's legacy and the rich heritage of silversmithing.

A Legacy of Excellence Follows Three Generations

Bill deMatteo, Jr. settled his young family in Colonial Williamsburg, where he became a master silversmith during the 1950s and directed a workshop of more than 100 craftsmen. His designs were recognized beyond the historic streets of Williamsburg. John F. Kennedy selected a pair of solid silver lanterns for the Oval Office. Richard Nixon commissioned a silver globe, and Gerald Ford was presented with a miniature Liberty Bell.

The deMatteos also strongly advocated preserving the integrity and tradition of their craft, which Bill taught to hundreds of apprentices and journeymen. His two most talented pupils were Philip Thorp and Chip deMatteo.

By the time he was 10 years old, Chip started doing chores around the shop and showing a remarkable talent for silversmithing. After college, Chip moved to Washington D.C., where he played the "starving artist" role for several years. During that time, Chip supplemented his income doing silver work for his father and Philip, who was then Bill's foremost journeyman silversmith.

Along with several other silversmiths from Williamsburg, Bill, Phil and Chip moved to Alexandria, Virginia, in the late 1970s to set up their own shop at Hand & Hammer Silversmiths. The unique designs that are the hallmark of Hand & Hammer's work began to shine. As the studio attracted more craftsmen, the small shop in Old Town Alexandria was bursting at the seams. To meet the demands of growth, Hand & Hammer and its centuries-old craft jumped into the 21st century with a spacious, high-tech, custom-designed shop in Woodbridge, Virginia. It is from here that all the beautiful Hand & Hammer pieces are created today.

The Creation of a Hand & Hammer Design

Silversmithing is an art that predates written history. Bright white and lustrous in its natural state, silver is the most reflective material on the earth and the best conductor of heat and electricity. An ancient treatise on metals proclaimed: "He who wished to be acclaimed a master silversmith must be a good universal master in many arts, for the kind of work which comes to his hand are infinite. Those who work in silver must outdistance all other craftsmen in learning and achievement to the same degree that their materials outdistance other metals in nobility."

Each Hand & Hammer design comes from the mastery, heart and hands of Chip deMatteo. From his drawing table, he turns his quick sketches into complete, scaled pictures. From there, they become actual patterns sculpted by hand in either wax or metal. Making the pattern is an exacting process, often taking many weeks to complete.

Attention to detail at this stage is critical to the successful outcome of the prototype, from which molds for the casting process will be made. Hand & Hammer's ornaments are cast using the age-old "lost wax" method in which a casting model is made and then destroyed as part of the difficult, time-

As intricate and timeless as its jeweled counterpart, this "Fabergé Egg" sterling silver ornament captures the intricate beauty and elegance found in all works by Hand & Hammer Silversmiths. The ornament measures 2-3/4".

consuming process. Lost wax casting is much preferred over machine stamping because it yields a piece with greater detail and allows the designer more creativity in terms of overall form, shape or size.

After it is cast, each piece must be "finished" in the Woodbridge shop. This is accomplished through a series of abrasives. The first step is tumbling, a procedure in which pieces are placed with abrasives in a rotating barrel for an entire day. The next steps involve progressive hand-polishing with a succession of finer and finer abrasives until the piece's silver surface resembles a shiny mirror. Hand & Hammer's polishers, Tim, Cherie, Bill and Art, have been with the company for a long time, as it takes many years to develop the skills needed to make the pieces of raw silver come to life.

The shop is supervised by Gene Sutton, who like Phil Thorp and Chip deMatteo, was trained by Bill deMatteo in Williamsburg. The pieces are all held to a rigorous quality check at each stage of finishing, so only the finest works of art leave the shop. Of course, there is still more to be done. Washing, wrapping and packaging takes time and careful effort. Employees Pam, Kathy and Phyllis ensure everything that goes out to stores nationwide is first-rate.

A Tradition of Contemporary Designs and Childhood Favorites

Chip deMatteo is always asked: "Where do you get the ideas for your wonderful designs?" According to him, it's one of the hardest questions to answer. "I've always been creative," he explains. "When I was little, the most fun to me was figuring out how to make something or to find out how something worked. I got into trouble for taking apart the seat of a school bus to see how it was put together.

"But I can have an idea buzzing around in my head for a long time before I figure out how I want it to look as an ornament or piece of jewelry. Sometimes I'll agonize over a design and sometimes it comes out just right on the first try. It's a whole new process each time. That's why it's always interesting," he says with a smile.

While original designs take most of Chip's time, he also enjoys working from old and famous drawings. The *Alice In Wonderland* set of four ornaments was designed using the original John Tenniel drawings for Lewis Carroll's classic story. "Those were fun to do," says Chip.

"Tenniel's drawings are what everyone refers to when they talk about *Alice In Wonderland*, and I think ours turned out very well. By contrast, look at our *Christmas Carol* set of four ornaments. I wanted to illustrate the Charles Dickens book in my own way, and I'm pleased with the result." In 1995, Hand & Hammer introduced a set of four ornaments illustrating Clement Moore's beloved poem *'Twas the Night Before Christmas*.

In recent years, Chip has enjoyed designing sterling silver charms for bracelets. He did a set of charms portraying *Alice in Wonderland*, The *Wizard of Oz* and *Mother Goose*, as well as a full line of Beatrix Potter's delightful creatures in miniature. "The Beatrix Potter pieces are wonderful and working from her original drawings in England was a real thrill for me," Chip says. "People have a wonderful nostalgic response to her little animals." Each year, Hand & Hammer adds another piece to the Peter Rabbit line.

Hand & Hammer Silversmiths also continues existing lines with its "1995 Silver Bells," "1995 Star" and the "Three French Hens" from the *12 Days of Christmas*.

Custom Designs for Companies and Collectors Nationwide

Over the years, Chip has designed more than 500 ornaments with some in collaboration with his father. Many of these also have been sold through finer department and gift stores. In addition, some of Hand & Hammer's most collectible designs are series produced exclusively for the world's most honored institutions, museums and private companies.

Since 1963, Shreve, Crump & Low of Boston has commissioned Hand & Hammer to create exclusive ornaments, including two notable series, *Boston Landmarks* and *Landmarks of America*. Also in Boston, the Museum

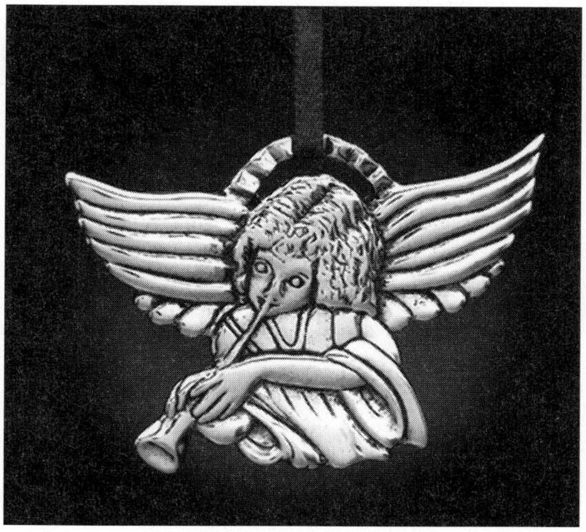

A perfect addition to any Christmas tree, "Heralding Angel" proclaims the holiday season in this sterling silver ornament, which measures 2".

Each year, Hand & Hammer Silversmiths introduces a dated sterling silver star. Limited to the year of issue, "1995 Star" is a six-pointed creation by Chip deMatteo.

of Fine Arts has commissioned Hand & Hammer's ornaments for its Christmas catalog since 1979. The museum's series have included an annual snowflake and pieces based on a Kate Greenaway collection. Other special subjects include an annual angel for the Smithsonian catalog and San Francisco Scenes for Shreve & Co.

Keeping Collectors Up To Date with the Latest Creations

With the tremendous growth of the company and its continuous introduction of new designs, Hand & Hammer collectors often ask for a complete list of collectibles from their favorite studio. This request inspired the 1979 introduction of "Silver Tidings," the newsletter of the Hand & Hammer Collectors' Club. The entire list is updated and published annually, along with occasional newsletters that mention the latest collectibles and where to find them.

Hand & Hammer's Collectors' Club membership is free, and the Club sponsors store and show appearances by Chip deMatteo and Philip Thorp. Collectors may sign up for the Club through participating Collectors' Club retailers or by calling Hand & Hammer at 1-800-SILVERY.

Despite all the new pieces coming out of the Hand & Hammer workshop, Chip says he still has many more ideas in his head – and never grows tired of creating new designs. "I have so much to keep me interested," he says. "I work with people I like and I make beautiful things. That's what keeps me going."

Three generations of silversmiths and a tradition of excellence will also keep Hand & Hammer going for a long, long time.

Hand & Hammer Silversmiths
2610 Morse Lane
Woodbridge, VA 22192
(800) SILVERY
Fax (703) 491-2031

COLLECTORS' CLUB

Hand & Hammer Collectors' Club
2610 Morse Lane
Woodbridge, VA 22192
(800) SILVERY

Annual Dues: None
Club Year: January 1-December 31

Benefits:
- Newsletter, "Silver Tidings"
- Complete List of Hand & Hammer Ornaments, Updated Annually
- Club Sponsored Artist Events

HARBOUR LIGHTS

Collectible Lighthouses of the World

Nothing indicates the prosperity or intelligence of a nation more clearly than the facilities which it affords for the safe approach of the mariner to the shore.

—Report of the Lighthouse Board, 1868

Since the earliest days of man, when fires were lit atop hills to guide fishermen safely into port, mariners have struggled to develop nighttime navigational aids. The oldest known lighthouse, dating back to 300 B.C., was built by the Egyptians on the island of Pharos, at the entrance to the harbor of Alexandria. As time went by, lamps and reflectors replaced fires, and lighthouses became a commonplace sight throughout the European continent, America, and beyond.

Bill Younger's Dream Becomes Reality

Lighthouses have always symbolized strength and hope in the face of adversity. When Bill Younger, the founder of Harbour Lights, was just a small boy, his uncle would often take him fishing on the Chesapeake Bay. At night, as he watched the flickering lights of the distant lighthouses, he was reminded of an earlier time, when the diligence of a light keeper was the only thing to prevent a ship from being dashed to pieces on dangerous shoals.

A natural storyteller, Bill has always had a deep and abiding appreciation of history. Growing up in the nation's capitol gave him ample opportunity to visit museums and historical sites. His love for old buildings, and architecture in general, planted the seeds that would eventually become Harbour Lights. Bill believes that any study of American history would be incomplete without examining the role that lighthouses have played in shaping our destiny.

The idea for Harbour Lights began to form in 1989, when the Postal Service issued a collection of stamps in honor of our nation's lighthouses. Bill felt inspired to create a line of lighthouse sculptures that would accurately depict American architecture. With a solid background in collectible buildings behind him - Younger was the first representative in the United States to market David Winter Cottages - he set about to transform his ideas into a three-dimensional form.

Working closely with his family, Bill's dream became a reality, when in the spring of 1991, Harbour Lights was introduced to the general public. Rather than developing a single artist, he decided to work with a small team of staff sculptors. The reasons are two-fold. For one thing, our coastal lighthouses were built by many different individuals, and are quite unique in their own right. Also, Bill felt that the underlying goal of Harbour Lights was to promote maritime history and architecture, rather than a particular artist. In each re-creation, he wants to achieve a rendering that is so accurate, it is unmistakable for the real thing. At the same time, he has made a sincere effort not to stifle the creativity of the artists.

The original collection consisted of 17 pieces, including two of America's most famous lighthouses, Boston Harbor and Cape Hatteras. Boston Harbor Light has a particularly special meaning to Bill. It was the first lighthouse to be erected in the American colonies in 1713. Destroyed by the British just prior to the signing of the Declaration of Independence, the original tower was not replaced until 1783. The newly erected tower has endured and protected mariners to this day, and has remained a symbol of our nation's nautical tradition. Although automation has made the need for light keepers all but unnecessary, the Coast Guard has determined that Boston Light will be our last manned lighthouse.

"Jupiter Island, FL" is part of Harbour Lights Gulf Coast Series. *It is without a doubt, the most recognized lighthouse on the Florida coast. "Jupiter Island" measures 7" x 5", is limited to 9,500 hand-numbered pieces, and retails for a suggested $77.00.*

A Thriving Family Business

Like many great ideas, Harbour Lights is a family affair. The first 17 pieces were chosen by Bill, his wife Nancy, daughters Kim and Tori Dawn, and Tori's husband, Harry Hine. Since then, the pieces have been chosen through popular request by consumers. The current collection consists of more than 50 pieces from all regions of the country and will soon expand to include lighthouses from Canada and other parts of the world.

Much of the original research was carried out by Bill's daughter, Kim Andrews. Kim currently serves as Managing Director and is responsible for the day-to-day operations of the company, as well as direction of the staff artists. Since retiring from work with John Hine, Ltd., Bill Younger is devoting full time to research and promotion of Harbour Lights. He has personally visited dozens of lighthouses in the United States and other countries, often in quite remote settings. To understand what life may have been like growing up in a real lighthouse setting, Bill has also made an effort to interview children of light keepers.

Harbour Lights collectibles are cast from several durable substances, including hydrostone (a gypsum material) and cold-cast porcelain. Both materials are renown for their strength and hardness. These are made into a pouring mixture and cast, capturing extremely fine detail in every figure. Before a new piece is considered "ready" for production and release, an enormous amount of time is spent on review and inspection.

Earlier editions were generally limited to productions of 5,500 hand-numbered pieces, and then ceremoniously retired. Most of the original 17 are currently sold out and can only be obtained on the secondary market. To accomodate an ever-expanding collector base, future releases may number up to 9,500 pieces. Upon retirement, the original molds are completely destroyed, never to be used again.

Tori Dawn Younger Hine is the origination painter for Harbour Lights. She is well known as the first promotional painting artist in the U. S. for David Winter Cottages. A talented artist who began honing her skills at the tender age of eight, she accepts her responsibilities seriously, sometimes working around the clock to complete an assignment. Capturing beauty and emotion in a miniature sculpture is no easy task. Tori Dawn uses a combination of oil-based paints, as well as acrylic to achieve the desired effect. If you look carefully at each of her lighthouse reproductions, you can feel a part of our history coming through, from the weathered brick and stone towers to the sun worn roofs of the keeper's cottages.

Award-Winning Lighthouses

The United States is blessed with some of the finest shoreline in the world and has a rich maritime history. Since the early 1700s, our forefathers have taken prudent steps to provide lighted navigational aids for our brave mariners. To honor these important sentinels, Harbour Lights has created lighthouse series from the Northeast, Great Lakes, Southeast, Western and Gulf Coast regions.

Each limited edition collectible created by Harbour Lights is carefully hand-painted and hand-numbered. It comes complete with its own history, Certificate of Authenticity, and registration card. Late in 1994, Harbour Lights introduced its first open edition piece, "Cape Hatteras, NC" as part of the *Great Lighthouses of the World* collection. This important series will feature select famous lighthouses from all over the world. While generally smaller than the limited edition series, the open edition collection will be subject to the same exacting standards of quality that have made Harbour Lights so popular among collectors.

The reception to Harbour Lights has been overwhelming. In four short years, they have become the collectors' choice for serious lighthouse afficionados. Wayne Wheeler, President of the U. S. Lighthouse Society, has spoken of Harbour Lights as "quite simply the best quality lighthouse collectible available." In point of fact, it is the only lighthouse line to be honored with national awards. In 1994 "St. Simon's Lighthouse, Georgia" received the prestigious "Award of Excellence," voted by the readers of *Collector Editions* magazine. This year "Cape Neddick (Nubble Light), Maine" was named a finalist for the same award. In 1994, "Cape Hatteras, NC" was presented with a meritorious "Achievement Award" by The National Association of Limited Edition Dealers (NALED). In 1995, NALED named Harbour Lights as one of five finalists for the industry's top honor, "Collectible of the Year."

The first 5,000 pieces of the Great Lakes Stamp Series *were issued in matched, numbered sets and included complimentary First Day Issue Postage Stamps! The series includes "Spectacle Reef, MI," "St. Joseph North Pier Lights, MI," "Split Rock Light, MN," "Marblehead Light, OH" and "30 Mile Point, Somerset, NY."*

Harbour Lights Collector's Society

In April of 1995, Harbour Lights achieved a major milestone, with the introduction of the Harbour Lights Collector's Society. With the founding

Harbour Lights 1995-96 Charter Year Membership Collectible, "Point Fermin, CA," is well known for its exquisite Victorian keeper's quarters. It measures 5.5" x 5.5" amd will retail for a suggested $80.00.

of the society, members will have an opportunity to share with fellow enthusiasts the joys of collecting and expand their knowledge of lighthouses and maritime history. Memberships are renewable on an annual basis and cost just $30.00 per year.

For those fortunate enough to join the Collector's Society during the 1995 - 1996 Charter Period, there are a number of exciting benefits. Privileges include:

- A Charter Membership Certificate, suitable for framing.
- A redemption letter to purchase the Charter Membership piece, "Point Fermin, CA." "Point Fermin" is well known for the exquisite Victorian keeper's quarters that accompany this charming lighthouse.
- All Charter Members will receive a limited edition watercolor print of "Point Fermin, CA." Each museum quality print will be beautifully matted and framed; signed and numbered by artist Mark Sherman.
- A limited edition cloisonné "Point Fermin Lighthouse" pin.
- A Charter Year Membership Card.
- A free subscription to the quarterly newsletter, "The Lighthouse Legacy," accompanied by a handsome binder.

The Future

Harbour Lights will continue to expand its collection in the coming months. Sculptors are currently working on foreign lighthouses, and the *Great Lighthouses of the World* will soon become a reality. In the course of his travel and research, Bill Younger has visited lighthouses in China, England, Russia and Finland.

"Lighthouses are just beginning to touch the imagination of the public," says Younger. "People are coming to appreciate their historical importance." He loves to speak at gatherings of collectors and lighthouse enthusiasts, entertaining audiences with nautical lore. Before finishing a presentation, he encourages everyone present to join a lighthouse preservation group.

The days of lighthouse keepers climbing tower steps to keep an oil lantern burning are long past, but their memory is not forgotten. Lighthouses and the courageous men and women who accepted the call as keepers of the light, will always remain an important part of our heritage. It is to them and their legacy that Harbour Lights dedicates these fine works of art.

Harbour Lights
8130 La Mesa Blvd.
La Mesa, CA 91941
(800) 365-1219
Fax (619) 579-1911

COLLECTORS' CLUB

Harbour Lights Collector's Society
8130 La Mesa Blvd.
La Mesa, CA 91941
(800) 365-1219

Annual Dues: $30.00
Club Year: Anniversary of Sign-Up Date

Benefits:

- Free Annual Membership Gift
- Redemption Coupon for Members-Only Lighthouse
- Membership Certificate Suitable for Framing
- Quarterly Newsletter, "Lighthouse Legacy"
- Specialty Binder
- Membership Card
- Cloisonne Pin

HAWTHORNE ARCHITECTURAL REGISTER

A Host of Handsome Miniature Buildings Inspired by Art Masters Thomas Kinkade, Charles Wysocki, M.I. Hummel, and Norman Rockwell

Anyone who reads the business pages knows that housing starts have been down for some time, and the real estate market is sluggish – especially compared to the "boom years" of the 1980s. But the 1990s are developing a housing sales boom of their own, at least in one segment: miniature buildings and villages based on the works of world-renowned artists.

Leading the way in this housing market upswing is Hawthorne Architectural Register: a top marketer of highly detailed architectural sculptures. Although these pieces range from just three to eight inches tall, they beautifully capture every aspect of emotion, style and detail found in the artist's paintings. Hawthorne's cottages bring the artist's paintings to life.

Hawthorne's "listings" include houses in styles ranging from 18th-century native stone cottages to antebellum mansions to Victorian. However, no matter what style they are, all Hawthorne buildings must meet standards of excellence which the company has established in the following areas: faithful representation of the artist's work and intentions; quality of sculptural detail at scale; authenticity of architectural detail; authenticity of environmental details; and statement of edition and required documentation.

Recent issues from Hawthorne call upon the talent and inspiration of some of the most gifted art masters of the present, including Thomas Kinkade and Charles Wysocki; and the past, including M.I. Hummel and Norman Rockwell. In addition to sculptures of buildings, Hawthorne also draws upon these artists' works to create a wide range of accessories and figurines to increase the fantasy aspects and emotional involvement of the buildings.

"Olde Porterfield Gift Shoppe" represents one issue in Thomas Kinkade's Christmas Memories, *a collection of quaint holiday cottages from the world-renowned Painter of Light™.*

From the series entitled Thomas Kinkade's Enchanted Cottages *comes "McKenna's Cottage" – cozy, warm, and delightfully whimsical.*

The Renowned Painter of Light™ Joins Forces With Hawthorne

For more than a decade, Thomas Kinkade has been creating remarkable landscape paintings and collectible prints. Winner of numerous awards, he travels the world to research and sketch ideas for his work. Honored with the title Painter of Light™, Kinkade delights his admirers with works that seem to glow with a unique radiance.

When Kinkade first visited the English countryside, he fell in love with its cozy cottages, verdant fields and rolling hills. In a magnificent series of vivid oil paintings, Kinkade recreated the charm and beauty of these small country villages of England. And now Hawthorne has captured the emotion of Kinkade's paintings in several remarkable collections of handcrafted cottage sculptures.

Thomas Kinkade's Candlelight Cottages collection of eight pieces begins with "Olde Porterfield Tea Room," the very first recreation of one of Mr. Kinkade's famous canvases for the three-dimensional cottage sculpture medium. Hawthorne's marvelous sculpture allows the artist's legions of admirers to rediscover all the charm and detail of this original art, now brought to life with meticulous sculpting, and careful hand-painting.

Another Hawthorne collection of Kinkade's works begins with "McKenna's Cottage." Entitled *Thomas Kinkade's Enchanted Cottages*, this series welcomes admirers to a world of peace and enchantment. Every detail is beautifully handcrafted, from the straw of the thatched roofs, to the landscaping which provides the perfect setting for each architectural gem.

Share the Joy of Thomas Kinkade's Old-Fashioned Christmas

The Christmas we love to remember was a gentle time of warmth, wonder and love. And now Hawthorne's *Thomas Kinkade's Christmas Memories* collection brings life to a joyous Christmas celebration in a lovely and inviting place. Quaint little curiosity shops like "Olde Porterfield Gift Shoppe" are part of the tiny, tucked-away villages that dot the English countryside. From the signpost that stands at the edge of the walk, to the snow that blankets the roof, trees, and walk, the "Olde Porterfield Gift Shoppe" has been meticulously crafted and hand-painted to Thomas Kinkade's exacting standards – the ideal premiere for this collection of eight holiday landscapes.

Charles Wysocki Welcomes Collectors to *Peppercricket Grove*

Master of Americana Charles Wysocki has created a special place where handsewn quilts, horsedrawn wagons and homemade joy add comfort to a wonderful way of life. He invites collectors to take a leisurely stroll through charming and peaceful *Peppercricket Grove* – and in doing so to discover this much-honored painter's very first sculpture.

"Peppercricket Farms" premieres *Wysocki's Peppercricket Grove* sculptured cottage collection. Inspired by the famous painting of the same name, it captures all the whimsy and wonder of Wysocki's world – now in three dimensions. For the first time ever, Wysocki's admirers can see the back of "Peppercricket Farms" – a unique, new perspective created exclusively for this sculpture with Charles Wysocki's personal involvement. What's more, each sculpture is carefully painted and decorated by hand to capture the beauty and detail of Wysocki's original art.

Popular artist Charles Wysocki recently introduced his first-ever sculpture, "Peppercricket Farms," *through Hawthorne Architectural Register. It marks the premiere of the* Peppercricket Grove *sculptured cottage collection.*

"Angels Duet" is the first-ever lighted ceramic cottage sculpture to depict the beloved art of M.I. Hummel. It is issued exclusively through Hawthorne Porchlight Collections™.

Bring the Charms of *M.I. Hummel's* Bavarian Village to Your Home

Imagine a quaint Bavarian village at Christmastime, full of charm and spirit. Magic is everywhere...the sweet aroma of holiday pastries...carefree sounds of rosy-cheeked children at play...the children so dear and special to M.I. Hummel. This beloved artist's children recall timeless images of innocence and hope. And now, in "Angels Duet" and "Village Bakery," their world is recaptured in lighted sculptures that feature some of M.I. Hummel's own most beloved images. "Angel's Duet" portrays a Bavarian village church featuring the Hummel cherubs known as "Angel's Duet" and "Candle Light." "Village Bakery" showcases a reproduction of M.I. Hummel's classic little baker carrying a mouth-watering goody fresh from the oven.

Introduced by Hawthorne Porchlight Collections™, each issue in the *Bavarian Village* collection combines handcraftsmanship with meticulous hand-painting to reproduce the distinctive tones and hues of an *M.I. Hummel* figurine. The *Hummel* images themselves glow with the light inside their pretty buildings – and they emerge in rich detail through a carefully-controlled, 18-color process involving three separate porcelain firings.

Come Home for a Rockwell Christmas

"Welcome to Stockbridge," reads the sign outside Norman Rockwell's famous Massachusetts home town, and now Rockwell's family invites us all to join them there for *Rockwell's Christmas in Stockbridge.* Based on Rockwell's famous painting "Mainstreet, Stockbridge," Hawthorne Porchlight Collections™ introduced this series as the first lighted village ever authorized by The Norman Rockwell Family Trust – an official Centennial Edition issued in honor of the 100th anniversary of the artist's birth.

Each sculpture beckons with its bright lights, and we are drawn to relive the small-town Christmas that "America's Favorite Illustrator" himself held so dear. From Rockwell's own studio to the town bank, country store, insurance agency and other Main Street fixtures, Stockbridge comes alive as an enchanting village. Each sculpture is hand-painted, and each glows with soft light shining through its windows on all four sides.

Hawthorne Miniatures Add Vitality to Your Sculpture Collection

Hawthorne's Stockbridge or any other Christmas village gains even more life and realism with the addition of the Hawthorne Miniatures — an inspired selection of people, trees, vehicles and accessories that complete the scene of a bustling and happy home town. Sets featuring people include: "The Skating Pond," "Decorating the Tree," "Shopkeeper and Travelers," "Bringing Home the Tree," "Christmas Shopping," "Slipping and Sliding," "Greetings and Games," and "Norman Rockwell and a Trio of Merry Carolers."

To enhance a village even further, there are automobile sets including "Village Vehicles," "Vintage V-8s," and "Roaring Roadsters." More atmosphere can be added with the "Snow-covered Evergreen Tree Set" and the "Old-fashioned Streetlight Set."

With a selection from Hawthorne, collectors enjoy the opportunity to become "real estate moguls" while they rediscover the gentle joys of everyday life through the eyes of some of today's most honored artists. From the English countryside of Thomas Kinkade, to the sleepy Bavarian village of M.I. Hummel to the "small-town U.S.A." of Charles Wysocki and Norman Rockwell, these marvelous, architecturally significant buildings captivate and charm us all.

Charming figurines and accessories from Hawthorne Miniatures make a collector's Christmas village come alive. Available pieces — all created to scale with the village buildings — include vehicles, evergreen trees, streetlights, a skating pond, and townspeople in various groupings.

Now collectors can experience the New England charms of Rockwell's Christmas in Stockbridge *with this collection of enchanting, lighted sculptures depicting the town where "America's Favorite Illustrator" lived and worked. The series is authorized by the artist's family through The Norman Rockwell Family Trust.*

Hawthorne Architectural Register
9210 N. Maryland Avenue
Niles, IL 60714
Customer Service (800) 772-4277
Ordering Number (800) 327-0327

M. I. HUMMEL CLUB®

Loyal Club Members and Collectors Celebrate the Enduring Spirit of Sister M. I. Hummel

"I Brought You a Gift" (HUM 479) is the new member gift provided to each individual who joins the M. I. Hummel Club for the first time. She is retiring as of May 31, 1996. Crafted with care in Germany, this charming figurine carries on the enduring tradition of Sister M. I. Hummel and her art. It has a retail value of $85 U.S. and $105 Canadian, but it is provided to new Club members for free.

She drew and painted them practically from the time she could first hold a pencil: the rosy-cheeked, bright-eyed youngsters who surrounded her during her happy German childhood. Sister Maria Innocentia Hummel delighted in the energy and optimism of little ones – and she captured their charm in hundreds of drawings that brought cheer to all at the Convent of Siessen. As a member of the Sisters of the Third Order of St. Francis, Sister M. I. Hummel came to understand that her finest service to the Lord would be to share her talent for art. But little did she know that this marvelous gift would provide pleasure to collectors all over the world for generations after her death.

The brilliance of this shy German nun might never have been known outside the convent community had it not been for the vision of Franz Goebel. As the fourth-generation family member to head the company bearing his name, Goebel was always on the lookout for promising new artists. In 1879, the Duke of Saxe-Coburg-Gotha first granted permission for the Goebel Company to create kiln-fired porcelain figurines. Originally founded in 1871 to manufacture marbles, slates and slate pencils, Goebel artisans already had spent four decades earning an international reputation for porcelain craftsmanship when Franz Goebel discovered Sister M. I. Hummel in 1934.

While strolling through gift shops in Munich, Goebel happened upon a little store that specialized in religious images. A display of greeting cards captivated him: it was the art of Sister M. I. Hummel! Simple and touching in their innocence, the drawings spoke to Goebel like nothing else he had seen in Munich. It struck him that this would be the perfect basis for a new line of figurines.

Franz Goebel wrote to Sister Hummel, proposing that his artists translate her two-dimensional drawings into three-dimensional figurines. At first, the gentle nun hesitated. But when Goebel arranged a meeting among himself, Sister Hummel, and the Mother Superior of the convent, a historic agreement was reached. Goebel assured the sisters that the figurines would be completely true to the original artwork. He promised that they would be handcrafted to meet the highest quality standards. He gave Sister Hummel and the Convent of Siessen final artistic control. Indeed, he stated that once she approved an original figurine, her signature would be incised on the base of each piece. What's more, beginning then and to this very day, part of the proceeds of each figurine is provided to the convent and then sent to charitable organizations throughout the world.

The first *M. I. Hummel* figurines were unveiled at the 1935 Leipzig Fair, where buyers from all over Europe expressed their excitement at the art's uniqueness and fresh charm. The figurines were a tremendous success, and everyone looked forward to long years of happy productivity from the gifted nun of Siessen.

Alas, the hardships of World War II took their toll on the convent and on Sister M. I. Hummel herself. She fell ill and died in 1946 at the age of 37. Ironically, her fame was spreading quickly across the Atlantic at the time of her death. American GIs were bringing the adorable child-subject figurines home to America as special gifts for family and friends. When they got the news about the popularity of the "Hummels," American gift sellers and department stores flocked to order them and to share them with a wider audience. And since Sister M. I. Hummel had been prolific in her short life, there were still many drawings to serve as inspiration.

How an *M.I. Hummel* Drawing Becomes a Hand-Painted Figurine

Today, collectors all over the world await each new *M. I. Hummel* presentation, brought to life by the gifted artisans of Goebel. The process of creating an *M. I. Hummel* figurine is long and involved, performed by a team of dedicated masters. Each new artist must serve a three-year apprenticeship under the watchful eye of senior Goebel craftspeople before joining the prestigious ranks of the *M. I. Hummel* "team." This long apprenticeship is necessary because of the exacting, ten-step process required to craft each *M. I. Hummel* work of art. The ten steps are: sculpting, model-cutting, moldmaking, casting, assembling, bisque firing, glazing, glaze firing, decorating, and decor firing(s).

To begin, the sculptor creates a clay model using Sister M. I. Hummel's original art as the basis. The Convent of Siessen must approve each model before prototypes are crafted for moldmaking. A single figurine may require as many as 40 individual mold pieces! To make the molds, individual parts are embedded in clay. Then plaster of paris is poured over them to make the master mold. The working model is made of acrylic resin, and then a series of working molds are devised – again using plaster of paris. More than one working mold is required because each mold must be rejected as soon as it loses its exactness of detail.

In casting, liquid porcelain "slip" is poured into the working mold. Excess slip is poured out after about 20 minutes, leaving the shell of the figurine. Next, individual pieces of the figurine are assembled, using more slip to join them. After smoothing to remove seams, the assembled figurines dry at room temperature for about one week. Bisque firing at approximately 2100°F follows, during which each figurine shrinks in size and emerges with a powdery white finish. Glaze firing at 1870°F comes next, after figurines are hand-dipped and sprayed with a tinted liquid glaze. At this stage, the Goebel trademark also is fired onto the base.

Collectors who are celebrating fifteen years of membership in the M. I. Hummel Club are privileged to acquire "Honey Lover" (HUM 312), an exclusive figurine created to mark this special anniversary.

For decorating, thousands of individual colors have been developed in Goebel's own laboratories. The goal is to approximate the varied palette used by Sister M. I. Hummel herself. To produce an edition of figurines, highly skilled painters follow a decorated sample which has been approved by the Convent of Siessen. The initials under the base of each figurine indicate a final decorating check before decor firing commences at approximately 1100°F. As many as three decor firings may be necessary to fuse the colors permanently to each porcelain figurine. All in all, an *M. I. Hummel* figurine requires many weeks to produce, including a total of over 700 detailed hand operations. This painstaking process has been the standard of excellence for Goebel ever since the first *M. I. Hummel* figurines were produced 60 years ago.

Members Enjoy the Many Benefits of the M. I. Hummel Club®

Ever since 1977, collectors of *M. I. Hummel* figurines have relished the friendship, the fun, and the special privileges that come with membership in the M. I. Hummel Club. For the affordable annual fee of $45 (U.S.) and $60 (Canadian), a new member may join the oldest collectors' club of its kind. Renewing members pay a smaller fee: currently $35 (U.S) and $47.50 (Canadian). Each new member receives a special welcome gift, currently a charming *M. I. Hummel* figurine called "I Brought You a Gift." Interested members need to act quickly because she'll be retiring as of May 31, 1996. Renewing members also are sent a yearly token of appreciation, such as the 1994-95 piece, "From Me to You." Each of these figurines carries a retail value of $85 U.S. or $105 Canadian – at least double the membership or renewal fee.

Members of the Club are privileged also to acquire other special *M. I. Hummel* works of art created with their pleasure in mind. There is an annual exclusive figurine, available only to Club members. Most recent of these issues is the adorable "Country Suitor." There is also a Preview Edition called "Strum Along," available only to Club members for two years. This piece bears a special M. I. Hummel Club backstamp, but after the preview period ends, it may become an open edition available to everyone – then bearing the non-exclusive regular Goebel backstamp. What's more, the Club celebrates its long-time members by offering them the opportunity to purchase figurines to mark their personal anniversaries as Club members. Five-year Club members are provided with special redemption certificates for "Flower Girl," while ten-year members may acquire "The Little Pair," and fifteen-year veterans are eligible for "Honey Lover."

As one of the most comprehensive collectors' clubs in the world, the M. I. Hummel Club offers a wide range of services and special opportunities to members. These include Collectors' Market, Research Service, Annual Essay Contests, Travel Opportunities, and Local Chapters. Collectors' Market is a free service to M. I. Hummel Club members who wish to buy and or sell any Goebel collectible. The Club endeavors to match potential buyers with individuals who wish to sell the same item. Then the buyer contacts the potential seller to negotiate a price. Research Service is available to members who wish to authenticate older Goebel pieces they may own. When the Club is sent a clear photograph or drawing of the piece's markings, mold numbers and trademarks, as well as a photograph of the entire piece, such facts as authenticity, identity, age, background and production history can often be provided.

The M. I. Hummel Club sponsors an Annual Essay Contest for members. The recent "Say It With Song" contest asked members to compose original song lyrics which expressed the way they felt about *M. I. Hummel* figurines set to the tune of a well-known song of their choice. Winning entries earned *M. I. Hummel* figurine awards ranging in retail value from $300 to $1,200.

An annual range of Travel Opportunities afford Club members the opportunity to see the world,

The adorable figurine, "Country Suitor" (HUM 760), is the M. I. Hummel Club's Exclusive Edition for 1995-96.

spend time with their fellow *M.I. Hummel* collectors, and tour the legendary W. Goebel Porzellanfabrik. There are tours offering a variety of destinations throughout Europe, and – of course – Sister M. I. Hummel's homeland of Germany.

Members say that one of the most personal pleasures of Club membership is the chance to become active in one of the over 140 Local Club Chapters throughout North America. At no additional cost, Club membership brings each individual a subscription to a Local Chapter newsletter, a Local Chapter patch and membership card sticker, and invitations to Regional Conferences. If there is no Local Chapter in a collector's home area, he or she is invited to start one with the help of the Club's Local Chapter Services division.

In addition to all of these benefits, Club members also receive: a subscription to *Insights*, the Club's colorful and informative quarterly magazine; a Membership Card; and a handsome binder filled with a collector's log, price list and facts about *M. I. Hummel* history and production.

Surely the gentle young Sister M. I. Hummel could never have dreamed that her charming drawings would continue to captivate millions for decades after her death. But today, the delightful and varied *M. I. Hummel* figurines are considered among the world's most cherished collectibles. And members of the M. I. Hummel Club enjoy the best opportunities of all to share in the delights of Sister Hummel's art and the warm friendship of fellow collectors!

M.I. Hummel Club
Goebel Plaza
P.O. Box 11
Pennington, NJ 08534-0011
(800) 666-2582
Fax (609) 737-1545

COLLECTORS' CLUB/MUSEUM

M.I. Hummel Club
Goebel Plaza
P.O. Box 11
Pennington, NJ 08534-0011
(800) 666-CLUB

Annual Dues: $45.00 - Renewal: $35.00
Canada: $60.00 - Renewal: $47.50
Club Year: June 1 to May 31

Benefits:

- Membership Gift: *M.I. Hummel* Figurine. Renewing Members Receive a Yearly Token of Appreciation Figurine.
- Opportunity to Purchase Members-Only Figurine and Preview Editions
- Quarterly Magazine, *Insights*
- Buy/sell Matching Service through Collectors' Market
- Research Service
- Annual Essay Contests
- Travel Opportunities
- Local Club Chapters
- Membership Card
- Binder Includes Collector's Log, Price List and *M.I. Hummel* History and Production Facts

The Hummel Museum
199 Main Plaza
New Braunfels, TX 78130
(210) 625-5636

Hours: Monday through Saturday, 10 am. - 5p.m., Sunday, noon-5p.m.
Admission Fee: $5.00 Adults; $4.50 Seniors; $3.00 Students

The Hummel Museum displays the world's largest collection of Sister Maria Innocentia Hummel's original art. This one-of-a-kind museum offers guided tours, video presentations, historical vignette rooms of Sister Hummel's personal items, extensive display of rare *M.I. Hummel* figurines with over 1,100 on exhibit. The Museum Gift Shop offers a great variety of Hummel collectibles.

LADIE AND FRIENDS, INC.

Celebrating Ten Years of *Lizzie High®* Dolls

Just about a decade ago, the creators of the *Lizzie High®* line of dolls tapped into an idea rooted in the simplicity of childhood memories. It began in a moment of wonder when founder Barbara Wisber picked up a small wooden ball and started rolling it around in her fingers. "I wonder...what can I make with this?" she asked herself.

A simple question evolved into a simple solution. In an inspired moment, she took a paint brush, dabbed two tiny dots on the ball of wood, and invented a well-known trademark in the collectible doll world. It flowered into a cottage industry that has since outgrown the cottage.

Early Lizzie High® *dolls had names borrowed directly from Peter Wisber's family tree. From left to right are: "Flossie High" (Peter's great grandmother); "Lizzie High" (Peter's great-great grandmother); "Johanna Valentine" (Peter's mother) and "Mary Valentine" (Peter's grandmother).*

Lizzie High Dolls Retain Their Original Sense of Simplicity

The evolution of *Lizzie High* through the past decade has seen a series of wooden dolls develop from primitive beginnings to a level of sophistication that still retains that original sense of simplicity. Enlisting the artistic talents and moral support of her husband Peter, Barbara dove into her childhood and came up with ideas for dolls that are tied to universal delights: games to be played, friends to be made, wonderlands to be explored, adventures to be lived, lessons to be learned. She suggests these ideas through short phrases on the tags tied to each doll that hint at whole worlds where children keep their childhood intact, where pets frolic in harmless mischief, and where the good humor of life's little pleasures shine through two well-placed child's eyes on a wooden ball.

Dolls' Names Inspired from Peter Wisber's Family Tree

The first nine dolls created for introduction at the January 1985 giftware shows were very simple indeed. Six little girls wore simple muslin frocks with a variety of shawls and kerchiefs in country plaids, and three young boys in painted overalls sported checkered neckerchiefs. The tales that accompanied these dolls could have been from simpler times a hundred years ago, or from gentler times a childhood ago. These characters care for a pet goose, a prize-winning pig and a baby brother. They jump rope, make wreaths, and love to dress up in their Sunday best. They love picnics, gathering fruit for mom's pies and jams, and gathering eggs to earn money for dance lessons and candy.

The dolls' names are as inspired as their beginnings were humble. Most names spring from Peter's family Bible and history. His family had extensive genealogical studies made and can trace their roots back through a tree blossoming with names filled with history and charm. "Lizzie High" was the first character, and most of the next eight names came naturally from great-great grandmother Lizzie's Good Book: Sabina Valentine, Emma High, Rebecca Bowman, Mary Valentine, Wendel Bowman and Luther Bowman. Since those early beginnings, there have been over 200 characters, each with its own name, a distinct personality, and a message that suggests a story that could go on forever. Most of the original dolls have been retired. Many have been brought back in a new form. Even "Lizzie High" is in her Second Edition as she goes into her second decade. Generally, the newer editions display more detail and animation than the original editions. They appear to embrace a larger world than they previously did. Part of the reason for this is the inclusion of more extensive complementary accessories such as tiny books, animals, wagons, buttons, bows and hats.

The animals in particular add clever moments of humor to each doll's story. Peter sculpts them in clay, then they're cast in a resin that holds not only their shapes, but also their character. Tiny kittens bat at each other, geese strut to some whimsical unheard tune, bunnies flop over their own ears, and they all look as if they absolutely belong with the doll they're with.

Other developments over the last ten years include the creation of "event pieces." Each piece is a miniature version of a full-size character, and each piece is only available for one year at sanctioned *Lizzie High* dealer parties.

The Little Ones Grow in Popularity

Barbara and Peter have found that their line of *The Little Ones*, the smaller-sized dolls, are becoming as popular as the full-sized dolls. *The Little Ones* are not given a particular name, they're universal children expressing a moment each of us might recognize as a childhood memory, rich in detail and evoking an expression of "Oh, yes, I remember when...." Some of these are seasonal – children with a sled and with a snowman, wearing a Halloween mask and carrying a trick-or-treat bag, waving their pinwheels at the Independence Day parade, or gathered 'round a Christmas tree. Barbara and Peter believe that as many people are choosing to live in smaller homes, they'll always have room for *The Little Ones*.

Lizzie High Society News Covered in the "Lizzie High Notebook"

In order to provide *Lizzie High* fans with the literature and information they were requesting, the Wisbers began The Lizzie High Society™ in 1992. Membership includes a subscription to the semi-annual publication called the "Lizzie High Notebook"™. The Notebook is designed as a black and white marble-patterned composition book most of us are familiar with from our school days. It's divided into sections such as "Arithmetic" where news of the dolls that are being added and subtracted from the collection can be found, along with collectors' wishlists for hard-to-find dolls and listings of collectors' dolls that are available for purchase. "Art" might include pictures sent in from collectors who have clever ways of displaying their dolls. "History" recalls tidbits of *Lizzie High* doll history and sometimes family history uncovered in the genealogical research. "Reading" is often a fascinating little story sent in by fans, like the principal from a Central Pennsylvania elementary school who displays her dolls in her office, and her kids love it.

A new feature will be appearing in future Notebooks – "Lizzie's Diary" will translate the brief suggestions of life found on each doll's tag into whole story lines, with dolls interacting with other dolls, and where each stays in character and develops a life beyond what was intended at the original inception of their accompanying tale. Most of the stories will come from suggestions sent in by collectors. Take *Lizzie High's* own tale that reads, "Lizzie High...walks her goose Lily to the pond every day before school...she's always late...." That might evolve into a story of a little girl who dawdles and dawdles, running on her own clock, frustrating teachers, parents and friends, yet experiencing a rich and wonderful world of discovery at her own speed.

Another of the benefits that comes with membership in the Lizzie High Society is a series of pewter ornaments that depict each of the first nine dolls introduced in 1985. This series started in the term that coincided with the Tenth Anniversary of the dolls. The first character cast as a 4" ornament was "Lizzie High." Number two in the series is "Rebecca Bowman." Each character is only available to club members during one term, and these are becoming treasured collectibles in their own right.

"Little Lizzie High," the first Special Event Edition, is available during the Tenth Anniversary year of Lizzie High® *dolls.*

Dolls Develop from Happy Childhood Memories

The evolution of any particular *Lizzie High* doll isn't always a planned event, and it's never the result of an extensive corporate study, research of marketing trends, or the product of some task force assigned to match a doll's form to a desired bottom-line-profit figure. It begins with memory – from Barbara's memory. There is no drawing to work from, nor plan to develop. Just as she did when she turned that ball of wood over in her hands, each new doll comes to her as a result of playing with little bits of stuff. Perhaps Barbara will find a piece of fabric she likes in a store one day. She'll purchase a small sample of it, take it to her studio, and somewhere in its tiny folds she'll find an idea, a starting point. Barbara will see a button here, an accessory there, and she'll play with wood and miniature toys. She ties it all together with a memory from her childhood, or from the happy childhoods of her children, and eventually a rough prototype will appear. Somewhere along the line, she'll ask Peter, "What do you think?" and together they will shape the animals and accessories needed to complete the

"Lizzie High, Second Edition" represents the "new" look in Lizzie High® *dolls.*

picture, although it's more like a sculpture. Barbara and Peter discuss shapes, patterns, colors, and poses, and then names and tag lines, and all the other bits and pieces that form these remarkable dolls. They involve carpenters, painters and detailers, seamstresses, and assemblers to put all the whimsy together, and quality inspectors to ensure each doll meets the standards *Lizzie High* collectors have come to expect.

While the dolls have evolved a great deal from the simple characters of a decade ago, and the popularity of the collection has grown far beyond what Barbara and Peter could have imagined ten years back, it's still their intention to evoke the fondest of life's little pleasures as seen through the eyes of the child within each collector.

Ladie and Friends, Inc.
220 North Main Street
Sellersville, PA 18960
(800) 76-DOLLS
Fax (215) 453-8155

COLLECTORS' CLUB/MUSEUM

The Lizzie High Society
220 North Main Street
Sellersville, PA 18960
(800) 76-DOLLS

Annual Dues: $25 - Renewal: $15.00
Club Year: January-December

Benefits:
- Membership Gift: Pewter Lapel Pin of Lizzie High Logo
- Opportunity to Purchase Members-Only Doll
- Bi-annual Newsletter, "Lizzie High Notebook"
- Complete Color Catalog in Leather-grained Binder
- Membership Card
- 4" Pewter Ornament Depicting One of the First Nine Dolls from 1985
- Buy/Sell Matching Service

Lizzie High Museum
A Country Gift Shoppe
Rt. 313, Dublin Pike
Dublin, PA 18917
(215) 249-9877

Hours: Monday through Saturday, 10 a.m. - 5p.m., Extended Holiday Hours

Admission Fee: None

All retired *Lizzie High* Dolls are on display in the museum, and current dolls are available in the gift shop.

THE LANCE CORPORATION

Fine Metal and Porcelain Sculpture Produced in New England for Over Twenty-five Years

" The Rainmaker" – 1994-95 Chilmark American West *Redemption Special by Michael Boyett.*

The Lance Corporation has begun its second quarter-century in the art metal sculpture field. Grounded in American history and culture, Lance nonetheless prides itself on innovation–both in sculptural subjects and in fine art techniques. Indeed, since 1968, Lance has been recognized as a pacesetter in the field of fine art sculpture.

From its picturesque hometown of Hudson, Massachusetts, Lance offers renowned lines of fine art sculpture–each with its own personaltiy and following. Some pieces are crafted in fine pewter, others are handpainted over pewter, while still others are hand-painted over cast porcelain. Yet all the works of Chilmark, Hudson Pewter and Sebastian Miniatures meet Lance's high standards of quality, historical accuracy and detail in every stage of creation and production.

Don Polland and the Chilmark Polland Collectors Society Enter a New Era

Like the characters of the Old West he depicts in his work, Chilmark artist Don Polland is a true pioneer. While we may never know if he was the first to sculpt scenes of the American West in miniature scale, he certainly has become the most prolific. With well over 100 individual designs to his credit—in bronze, fine pewter and porcelain—Don has earned his place next to Remington, Russell and Fraser, and contemporary artists such as McCarthy and Beeler. Don Polland has invested over 25 years of his life to an art form and a body of work that has integrity and permanence.

The 22-year association between sculptor Don Polland and The Lance Corporation enters a new phase as Polland has "handed over the reins" of the Polland Collectors Society to Ron Larson, president of Lance.

"We are delighted that Don has chosen us to operate the Collectors Society. Don has many loyal collectors, a number of whom have been with him since we first began producing his miniature pewters in 1973. Some have been members of his Society from its inception in 1987; they are old friends of Chilmark, too".

For his part, Polland is extremely happy that the move has been made. "With Chilmark and Lance taking over the management of the Polland Collectors Society, I hope to have the time to do more sculpting."

The Polland Collectors Society was started and has been run by the Polland Studios since 1987. Chilmark now assumes operation of the Collectors Society and will continue to provide the high level of product and service expected by collectors and society members.

Chilmark Awarding Winning Sculpture – *American West, Civil War, Mickey & Co.*

In addition to the work of Don Polland, the Chilmark line has expanded over the years to include the *Civil War* sculptures of Francis J. Barnum, *American West* studies by Michael Boyett, Joe Slockbower and Anne McGrory and Lowell Davis' *Americana* subjects. The most rapidly expanding category over the past few years has been the *Mickey & Co.* designs, which find Mickey and his pals revolutionizing the world of art metal sculpture.

The body of Chilmark sculpture currently available has captured the attention of the collectibles industry, and since 1990, 12 different designs, by six different artists, have been nominated for awards. Eight of these nominees have won awards from prestigious organizations such as *Collector Editions* magazine, the National Association of Limited Edition Dealers and The Walt Disney Company.

"The Children's Nativity Pageant" from Hudson Pewter Villagers Collection

"Christ Kindle, Switzerland" from Hudson's Père Nöel Collection *is a limited edition of 3,500.*

Hudson - Old Favorites and Exciting New Collections

As Mickey Mouse continues to transcend time and age groups, The Lance Corporation offers Fine Pewter *Mickey & Co.* gift items in addition to the limited editions. The World of Mickey (and Minnie!) continues to find favor with collectors of Disneyana and gift-givers alike. The *Mickey and Co.* Birthday and Music Trains, Barnyard Symphony and Carousel, along with keychains and ormanents, offer something for everyone.

Hudson Pewter Villagers - A Nostalgic Winter Wonderland

While there are many village scenes in today's collectibles market, the *Hudson Villagers* collection is unique because the focus is on the people–the heartbeat of any community–rather than a town's buildings. Crisply detailed nostalgic turn-of-the-century characters combine with props and accessories that let collectors create a delightful small town winter wonderland. Each of the pewter pieces is enhanced by bright, hand-painted touches that make the shimmering metal seem all the more beautiful.

Villagers pieces celebrate the joys of hometown Christmas, complete with sliding hill and skating pond at the Town Common, Christmas tree stand, a quaint country church and the children's homemade stable for the annual Christmas pageant. The *Villagers* offer Hudson collectors the opportunity to build a fine art collection in pewter with a combination of open, annual editions and limited edition offerings that provide year-round enjoyment.

A New Twist on Old Favorite

One of the most popular collections in the Hudson line, since its introduction in the early 1980s, continues to be the *Noah's Ark* collection. Over the years, Lance has added more than one hundred different members of the animal family as well as "Noah" and "Mrs. Noah," of course. It is the longest running Hudson Pewter collection to date.

In 1995, Hudson's oldest collection spurred a great idea for the newest and youngest grouping, *Ark Babies*. Young animals adorned with pink and blue bows take the story of Noah's Ark to the younger set. Complete with the beautiful wicker bassinet "ark," the collection has already begun to attract collectors attention – not only the young but the young at heart.

The *Père Nöel* Collection

Hudson's *Père Nöel Collection* is a medley of the many faces of Santa. Every nation and nationality has recognized its own version of Santa Claus – "Père Nöel" in France, "St. Nikkolo" in Austria, "Father Christmas" in England and "Christ Kindle" of Switzerland. Although his garments changed from decade to decade and his name has varied from country to country, the generosity and spirit of old St. Nicholas has survived through legend and fable.

Cindy Smith, *Père Nöel* artist, has been designing and producing handmade, limited edition sculptures for over 12 years. Her first collection for The Lance Corporation was a collection of woodland fairies and folks called Shirelings who dwell in a land known as *cp smithshire*.

The faces and personalities of each and every one of her figures are unique and sculpted directly from the images seen in Cindy's own mind's eye. She carefully researches costuming and has a gift for small details which may be overlooked by others. The color schemes for each limited edition sculpture are developed by Cindy and her palette evokes warm, down-to-earth feelings.

Sebastian Miniatures - Still Young at Heart at Fifty-Eight

America's longest continually produced collectible line, Sebastian Miniatures have been hand cast and hand-painted in New England since 1938. The figures exhibit pure American flavor, depicting themes including historic, nostalgic, and "ordinary people doing ordinary things." The feeling is one of reminiscence and a stirring of memories of days gone by.

In the 1950s, Baston developed a "story-series plan," selling his Sebastian Miniatures as themed groupings. Baston's Sebastian Miniatures were seen as collectible 20 years before the huge collectibles boom of the 1970s.

In 1976, The Lance Corporation took over production and national distribu-

"California or Bust!" from the Chilmark Mickey & Co. *collection is available in a Fine Pewter Edition of 250 and a Bronze Edition of 25.*

tion of Sebastian Miniatures. As the company was inundated with requests for information from people who had old miniatures, it was obvious that Mr. Baston's sales approach had indeed spurred thousands of long time Sebastian collectors. The result was The Sebastian Miniatures Collectors Society. Today after 15-plus years as an organized information center, it is one of the oldest, active collectors clubs in the country.

The Sebastian Miniature Legacy

Baston's son "Woody" worked in the Sebastian Studio throughout his youth and later went on to earn a bachelor's degree in sculpture. Under his father's tutelage, Woody designed his first miniature for the line in 1981. Since his father's death in 1984, Woody has been the sole creative force in the continuation of Sebastian Miniatures.

Lance Corporation
321 Central Street
Hudson, MA 01749
(508) 568-1401
Fax (508) 568-8741

COLLECTORS' CLUBS/MUSEUM

The Chilmark Polland Collectors Society
The Lance Corporation
321 Central St.
Hudson, MA 01749
(508) 568-1401
Annual Dues: $45.00
Club Year: Anniversary of Sign-Up Date

Benefits:
- Membership Gift: Pewter Figurine
- Opportunity to Purchase Members-Only Sculpture
- Bi-annual Newsletter, "Collector's Review"
- Membership Card
- Tours Upon Request

The Chilmark Registry
The Lance Corporation
321 Central St.
Hudson, MA 01749
(508) 568-1401
Annual Dues: Free Upon Registration of a Chilmark Sculpture
Club Year: Up to 5-Year Free Membership

Benefits:
- Two Annual Redemption Certificates for Members-Only Sculptures
- Quarterly Newsletter, "Chilmark Report"
- Tours Upon Request
- Buy/Sell Matching Service
- Annual Price Guide Updates
- Listing of Showcase Dealers
- Color Brochures on New Introductions
- Invitations to Special Events

The Pangaean Society
Official Collectors Club of cp smithshire™
The Lance Corporation
321 Central St., Hudson, MA 01749
(508) 568-1401
Annual Dues: $25.00
Club Year: Anniversary of Sign-Up Date

Benefits:
- Membership Gift: Sculpture
- Opportunity to Purchase Members-Only Sculpture
- Bi-annual Newsletter, "Shirespeak"
- Membership Card
- Enameled "Merlin" Pin
- Buy/Sell Matching Service
- Tours Upon Request
- Invitations to Special Events

Sebastian Miniatures Collectors Society
The Lance Corporation
321 Central St.
Hudson, MA 01749
(508) 568-1401
Annual Dues: $29.50
Club Year: Anniversary of Sign-Up Date

Benefits:
- Membership Gift: Figurine
- Buy/Sell Matching Service
- Membership Card
- Annual Value Register and Updates
- Opportunity to Purchase Members-Only Figurine
- Newsletter, "Sebastian Collectors Society News/Sebastian Exchange"
- Invitations to Special Events Including Stacy's Sebastian Festival and Midwest Fair
- Tours Upon Request

Official Sebastian Miniatures Museum
Stacy's Gifts and Collectibles
Walpole Mall
E. Walpole, MA 02032
(800) STACYS1
Hours: Monday through Saturday, 10 a.m.-9:30 p.m., Sunday, 1 p.m.-6 p.m.

Admission Fee: None

The Official Sebastian Miniatures Museum houses the largest public display of Sebastian Miniatures Figurines spanning "America's oldest continually produced collectible lines" from 1938 to the present.

THE LAWTON DOLL COMPANY

Limited Edition Dolls Tell Timeless Stories for All to Enjoy

Robert Burns immortalized haggis – the favorite Scottish sausage – in his "Address to a Haggis." The writer's birthday is celebrated yearly as the bagpipes play and the haggis is brought steaming to the table. From the Cherished Customs *collection, "Piping the Haggis" is an all-porcelain, 14" doll with an edition of 350 issues.*

Hidden in the pages of classic books and tales, Wendy Lawton finds a world of adventure and beauty waiting to be shared. There's *Anne of Green Gables, Little Women, Oliver Twist* and *Tom Sawyer*. There's memorable stories and poems by Emily Dickinson, Robert Burns, William Wordsworth, Charles Dickens and volumes of other beloved writers. There's childhood favorites of *Alice In Wonderland, Snow White, The Nutcracker* and *Little Red Riding Hood*. And who can forget *The Velveteen Rabbit* or *Peter and the Wolf*?

Books fill Lawton's shelves and mind. She readily admits to being a storyteller, of sorts, but instead of illustrating her discoveries, thoughts and dreams on paper, Lawton adds an extra dimension. Inspired by her literary friends, Lawton brings the timeless stories to life through dolls that can perfectly recite each line without saying a word.

Since the late 1970s, Lawton has created nearly 150 different limited edition dolls reflecting her love of literature, art and music. The hand-crafted porcelain dolls also show her commitment to quality, creativity and design – trademarks that have won accolades and admiration from collectors around the world. "I hope the dolls bring enjoyment and spark the imagination," Lawton says.

The California-based Lawton Doll Company, which was formed in 1983, continues this tradition of excellence with new introductions that send Lawton into the library and studio where she always feels at home.

Childhood Pastimes Inspire Dollmaking Career

Lawton seemed destined to become a dollmaker. She has collected dolls for as long as she can remember, beginning with her first pair of small plastic babies purchased at Woolworth's for five cents each. Lawton and her younger sister spent hours playing with their dolls, taking them in strollers on downtown shopping trips, sewing their clothes and curling their hair. Lawton and her dolls, it seemed, were inseparable. Even her childhood photo album reveals Lawton holding a doll in nearly every picture. When she got her first job at the age of 18, she spent her first paycheck on a doll from Italy.

In college, Lawton studied home economics and art – which turned out to be a perfect combination and preparation for doll making. Although she never took any sculpting classes, she experimented by making dolls from bread dough and plaster. "Dollmaking was a natural outgrowth of my love for dolls," Lawton says.

But it wasn't until 1978 that she set her heart on creating her first porcelain doll. Lawton searched for someone who could show her how to make a portrait doll of her newborn daughter, Rebecca. She found a wonderful teacher, Mrs. Thelma Hanke, who had been making and repairing dolls for nearly 50 years. "She taught me dollmaking from the first clay sculpture all the way through moldmaking to the final china paint," Lawton recalls. "I even learned how to make a hand-wefted wig!"

Lawton then began creating commissioned portrait dolls, which were first sold in 1979 in California. Today, the dolls find homes from coast to coast as Wendy and her husband Keith Lawton and partners Jim and Linda Smith oversee the business and keep up with the demand. Together, they have set the company on a successful course.

New Dolls Add to Popular Series

The Lawton Doll Company is perhaps best known for its porcelain characters inspired by the heroes and heroines of children's storybooks. Introduced in 1983, the first limited edition doll was "Alice In Wonderland." Only 100 pieces were made.

During the New York Toy Fair, the company annually issues an entirely new line of dolls, which consistently sell out each year. The porcelain dolls are limited in production to an average of 350 pieces to ensure quality and the special charm of each creation.

The new dolls are welcome additions to on-going series, including *Early American Portrait, Gentle Pursuits, Once Upon A Rhyme, Grand Tour, Childhood Classics, Cherished Cust-*

oms, Christmas Legends, Memories and Melodies, Folktales and Fairy Stories and *Classic Playthings* .

In 1994, Lawton introduced a new line of posable dolls with fully jointed wooden bodies, inspired by her own collection of antique post-World War I dolls. Each hand-carved wooden doll has 13 joints, a technique that was a year in the making and is becoming a favorite among some collectors. "I love the fact that these dolls are interactive," Lawton says.

The first wooden body dolls in 1994 were "Abigail," "Emily" and "At Aunty's House." In 1995, Lawton introduced 11 new dolls, three of which had wooden bodies: "Eugenia's Literary Salon," "Lucy Gray" and "Carrie and Sophia Grace."

As always, literature is the common thread among all her dolls. "The ideas don't just come out of my head but they come from all over," she says. "I spend a lot of time reading, going into bookstores, and watching the decorating field for colors and trends."

The age-old tale of Rapunzel *is told anew in this intricately handworked version of the fairytale classic. "Rapunzel" is all-porcelain and stands 14" tall. The doll from the* Folktales and Fairy Stories *collection is issued in an edition of 350.*

For "African Safari," the 1995 introduction to the *Grand Tour* series, Lawton read books and biographies by Denys Finch-Hatten, Beryl Markham, Isak Dinesen and others who wrote about and lived in Africa. This adventurous doll carries pieces of their stories and comes with a wardrobe of clothes for all occasions, whether a luncheon party or a trek up Kilamanjaro. From the rattan trunk to the intricately crafted camera and binoculars, this was a once-in-a-lifetime piece for Lawton. "I have never had so much fun researching and designing a doll as I have had with 'African Safari,' " Lawton says.

Dolls Crafted with Pride and Commitment to Quality

Once Lawton has finished the research for a doll, she begins the painstaking process of creating a prototype. She sculpts a new head for each doll edition, giving it a life of its own. (The only dolls with the same mold are two sets of twins.) That first sculpt undergoes three molding stages, with refinements after each step. At the same time, Lawton's initial sketches for costuming give way to fabric selection, pattern drafting and sample garment creation. Meanwhile, wigs are selected and props are designed. These initial stages require anywhere from three weeks to three months – and sometimes longer.

The edition of the dolls is created one by one, following the same process for each piece. The entire doll is crafted in America. The costume is cut and sewn, props, hats and accessories are made, greenware is poured, and the body is soft-fired. Next, the head, arms, legs and torso are fired under high temperatures. Once all six porcelain parts are complete, they are sanded before the cheeks are painted and fired. Painting, shading and highlighting the lips come next before another firing. Then the eyelashes and eyebrows are painted before the final firing.

To put the porcelain doll together, Lawton's artisans carefully string the doll together. The doll's shimmering eyes are set and cleaned, and the wig is added and styled along with the clothing and accessories. Finally each doll is numbered, registered and carefully boxed for shipment.

Bessie proudly displays her cherished doll, the Bye Lo Baby, which was issued in the 1920s as one of the milestone dolls of the century. From the Classic Playthings *collection, "Bessie and her Bye Lo Baby" is all-porcelain and 14" tall. The doll is issued in an edition of 750 pieces.*

Not counting the process involved in making the costume, props and accessories, there are 56 different hand operations required to make one Lawton doll. Because of strict quality control, more than half of all the dolls are rejected at one step or another before they win the right to represent the studio in the marketplace. Each doll requires about 25 hours of individual attention, including firing time and up to ten hours of hand labor for creation and costuming.

"The concept and quality make them different from any other dolls," Lawton says. "Collectors appreciate the little touches and we're very picky." The tiny accessories help the dolls tell their stories. There are handmade leather shoes, a tiny nutcracker, hand-painted Ukrainian eggs, a Swarovski crystal added to a crown, a wooden Windsor nanny rocker and original photos reproduced from an African safari.

The smallest details make a big difference. At one of her many appearances around the country, Lawton recalls a bespectacled young girl who couldn't stop staring at a doll named "Ginger," that also wore eyeglasses. Finally with a burst of excitement, the girl exclaimed: "I just love that doll!" "The collectors, no matter what age they are, identify with something in the dolls," Lawton says. "We love the dolls that we see ourselves in. The collectors love the details."

Lawton Collectors Guild

In 1989, the Lawton Collectors Guild was launched to inform collectors about the latest introductions, artist appearances, stories behind the dolls and even the artist's favorite books! "It gratifies me that there are so many loyal collectors," Lawton says. "Literature, music and arts are the theme of the dolls – and they attract people of like minds. Doll collecting can be a wonderful tool to expand our horizons."

Members have the opportunity each year to acquire the exclusive Guild Doll. For 1995, collectors can custom design their own doll appropriately named "Uniquely Yours." Her face remains the same, but collectors can choose from different hair and eye colors and four different costume ensembles. Besides the Guild Doll, members also receive a membership card, Lawton logo pin, subscription to the quarterly newsletter along with a three-ring binder. For more information, contact Lawton Collectors Guild, P.O. Box 969, Turlock, California 95381.

The Lawton Doll Company
548 North First Street
Turlock, CA 95380
(209) 632-3655
Fax (209) 632-6788

Carrying her perfectly scaled copy of Emily Dickinson, Eugenia embarks on her weekly outing to discuss favorite books and authors. "Eugenia's Literary Salon" is porcelain with a jointed wooden body. The 16" doll from the Gentle Pursuits *collection is limited to an edition of 350 issues.*

COLLECTORS' CLUB/TOUR

Lawton Collectors Guild
P.O. Box 969
Turlock, CA 95381
(209) 632-3655

Annual Dues: $20.00 - Renewal: $10.00
Club Year: January 1-December 31

Benefits:
- Membership Gift: Binder, Cloissone Logo Pin, Membership Card
- Opportunity to Purchase Members-Only Doll
- Quarterly Newsletter
- Buy/Sell Matching Service Through Ads in Newsletter

The Lawton Doll Company Factory Tour
548 North First Street
Turlock, CA 95380
(209) 632-3655

Hours: Call to Schedule Tour
Admission Fee: None

Visitors enjoy a guided tour through the factory, viewing the production of Wendy Lawton dolls.

RON LEE'S WORLD OF CLOWNS

Bringing Collectors Smiles, Magic and Childhood Dreams

As the last vestige of sun slips behind the trees, its final glow filters through the windows to focus on a huge room abundantly decorated with every conceivable clown artifact. Like a spotlight capturing an entertainer, the elongated rays pinpoint an artist intently at work. As the artist concentrates on the mass of clay in one hand and the small tool in the other, a new clown creation soon emerges from the creative mind and talented fingers of Ron Lee.

In a household filled with active sounds of his family, "Hobo Joe" was born. So were "Puppy Love," "Snowdrifter," "Heartbroken Harry" and countless other clown characters. Thriving in a room bursting with his energy as well as that of his wife and four children, Ron diligently follows an arduous daily routine that could easily include sculpting a new figurine, sketching a life-size carousel animal, writing a newsletter for his Collectors Club, making a personal appearance at a collectible shop or helping raise money for charity.

His non-stop energy and outgoing personality are apparent as four, five or even six new ideas could be hatching at the same time. While his highly competent staff often has difficulty keeping up with such a busy schedule, Ron avows it's "the only way to go." If you ask Ron Lee why he chose sculpting instead of other forms of art, he will simply tell you: "I need to be able to touch, to feel, to turn, to lift, to know it has dimension, a sense of reality. Even though the figurines I create are, what would you say, fanciful, if I could hold them in my hands, to me they suddenly become alive. They take on life and seem real, almost like children to be cherished and cared for."

Clowns, Clowns and More Clowns From Ron Lee

Recently establishing himself as the foremost sculptor of classic cartoon character limited edition sculptures, Ron returned to the basics in 1993. That year, he introduced more than 50 new clowns, focusing on the traditional antics of the circus and adventures under the big top. "Although I enjoy creating all these wonderful cartoon characters in three dimensions and in complete scenes, I really felt a need to get back to my 'clowning around' roots," he candidly admitted.

Presented in a broad spectrum of primary and pastel colors, the clowns range in height from 5 to 18 inches. There are clowns with cars, clowns with boats, clowns with trains, clowns with planes, and just clowns being clowns. Lollipop-colored favorites catch everyone's eyes as balloons and umbrellas often fly high above the scene.

As the breathtaking centerpiece of Ron Lee's factory and museum in Henderson, Nevada, this grand Carousel takes visitors on a trip back to their childhood. The $250,000 Carousel spins with lights, music, animals and action.

A Dream of a Lifetime Comes True

As 1994 drew to a close, Ron and his wife, Jill – whose immense job is to ensure all the design and production of the pieces come together – realized a lifelong dream. They moved their complete factory to Henderson, Nevada, located just outside Las Vegas. Not only did they completely move everything, but they created a tourist attraction that draws hundreds of visitors daily. Within the 30,000 sq. ft. facility, guests discover a museum of circus and clown memorabilia, the famed Jitters Gourmet Cafe, Ron's personal archives, the Ron Lee Gallery and the company's very own clown who leads everyone through a self-guided tour of the making of a clown or animation sculpture from start to finish.

To top off this magnificent attraction, children of all ages can ride the full-size, $250,000 Carousel. Within these confines, one can do it all: learn about the history of the clown, view Ron's artistry since his youth, eat lunch, browse or shop at the Gallery, and, of course, go 'round and 'round to the exhilarating music of the glorious Carousel.

Ron Lee makes everyone smile with his fun-loving clowns. In these sculptures, the clown dresses up like a fireman with his trusty Dalmatian, gives flowers to his sweetheart, and takes a snooze on the chair.

New Clown Sculptures and a Life-like Mural Delight Collectors

In the summer of 1995, Ron introduced a special series of limited edition sculptures – all dozen of which were highly detailed, exquisitely painted and featured a variety of clowns in unique scenes. These clowns are in the smaller size category, but each character is so clearly defined that its appearance is magnificent to behold. There's a clown wedding cake as well as a clown bathing, snoozing, painting and sitting in a doghouse, just to name a few.

Ron also created larger-than-life clowns. Covering a 53-foot wall at the Henderson facility, a hand-painted and original mural depicts a parade of clowns. Ron chose a small portion of this mural and created two delightful clown scenes entitled "Leading the Way" and "Want to Ride." Based on the mural, each vignette includes several characters and circus animals. These two new sculpture collections have a very low edition size of only 750. Throughout the year, Ron will be designing other clown scenes from this very astonishing mural. All of Ron Lee's sculptures are individually hand-painted by a staff of talented artists and are limited to low edition sizes.

Sylvester is in for a rough time as he and his sidekick Tweety roam the range in the Looney Tunes collection by Ron Lee. Wearing a cowboy hat, Tweety tries to brand Sylvester with an iron portraying a picture of himself! There are eight different sculptures in the collection.

Ron Lee Heads West With Favorite Looney Tunes Characters

In 1995, Ron also created and designed an extraordinary collection of Looney Tunes sculptures with the popular cartoon characters stirring up trouble along their trail to settle the Old West. There's Tweety branding Sylvester, while Penelope serenades Pepe saloon style. Sheriff Bugs guards the General Store and the Tasmanian Devil is the consummate "Heap Big Chief." These are just four of the eight sculptures in the collection, which features low edition sizes to enhance collectibility. The pieces are also meticulously hand-painted, manufactured in the finest pewter and metal, and 24-K gold plated.

Ron Lee Expands His World to Include Limited Edition Plates

Ron Lee – recognized sculptor of heirloom quality cartoon characters and clown and circus-theme collectibles – recently ventured into another area. He introduced his own series of collector plates focusing on his famous "Hobo Joe" clown character.

"I waited to present this series because I wanted to convey a special feeling in the designs," he said. "Whenever I create art, whether a single sculpture or a scene featuring numerous characters, I strive to evoke emotion that will translate to all the viewers of my work."

These plates have evolved into vividly colored, gold accented trimmed works of art portraying complete scenes featuring the antics of that lovable hero of the downtrodden, "Hobo Joe." Working to deliver the utmost quality in collectible plates, Ron Lee proudly presented a total of five irresistible designs that certainly complement his collectible "Hobo Joe" clown sculptures.

"Holy Cow, Batman! It's Ron Lee!"

Commemorating the hit movie and crime-fighting pair of Gotham City, Ron Lee designed a "Batman and Robin" sculpture that is so lifelike, they all but leap off the top of the building that they're standing on. With the characters in their full and familiar costumes, the sculptures convey the duo's power and personality. Ron's tireless energy is always apparent as his creativity covers all the bases. From the clowns that have captivated young and old alike for centuries to the latest popular characters on television and the big screen, Ron shares his artistry with everyone.

One of Ron Lee's most popular characters, "Hobo Joe," can also be enjoyed in a five-issue plate series. The first in the series is "No Vacancy" produced in the finest quality porcelain, gold banded, and individually numbered and certified.

Ron Lee's World of Clowns
330 Carousel Parkway
Henderson, NV 89014
(702) 434-1700

COLLECTORS' CLUB/TOUR

Ron Lee's Collectors Club
330 Carousel Parkway
Henderson, NV 89014
(702) 434-1700

Annual Dues: $28.50
Club Year: Anniversary of Sign-Up Date

BENEFITS:
- Membership Gift: New Clown Sculpture Each Year
- Quarterly Newsletter
- Annual Convention
- Brochures on New Products
- Members-Only Pieces

Ron Lee's World of Clowns
330 Carousel Parkway
Henderson, NV 89014
(702) 434-1700

Hours: Daily, 9 a.m.-6 p.m.
Admission: Free; $1 for carousel ride.

Visitors enjoy a self-guided tour featuring a start-to-finish demonstration of how a clown sculpture is developed and produced. Curious clown-lovers can view the gallery, archives and circus memorabilia.

GEORGE Z. LEFTON CO.

Villages Capture the Magic of American Traditions

Join us today on a journey back in time to a *Colonial Village* where the pace is slower, neighbors are friendlier, and everyone understands the joy of caring and sharing! This ideal vision of "small town USA" comes alive in Lefton's beloved *Colonial Village Collection* – a group of buildings and wonderful accessories that has been winning a place in the hearts and homes of collectors since 1987.

Now approaching its 10th-anniversary year, the *Colonial Village Collection* has grown from just a few buildings and citizens, to a prospering community of more than 100 buildings and countless neighbors. What's more, each addition has been artfully conceived and crafted with ultimate care. And if the buildings are the heart of the Collection, its accessories and people are surely its soul.

Each building in the Collection is hand-painted and handcrafted of fine ceramic, with vibrant color and detail. Each comes with a Deed of Title that explains the history of the building and symbolizes "ownership" of that particular piece of "real estate."

Among the most impressive recent introductions is the Collection's fifth limited edition building, the "Wycoff Manor." This stately home for senior citizens adds a wonderful new dimension of caring and compassion to the town. The edition is strictly limited to 5,500 pieces.

A Colorful Treat: *The Illustrated Collector's Guide & History*

To complement Lefton's *Colonial Village Collection* – and light the way for the future – company Chairman George Z. Lefton introduced a handsome book: the *Illustrated Collector's Guide & History.* Beautifully rendered in full color, the book includes every building and accessory introduced to date in the Collection – including retired pieces, limited editions, special editions, and suspended pieces. Now in its fifth edition, the book contains a wonderful tale that narrates beautiful photos of detailed *Colonial Village* vignettes.

The inviting lights inside the "Colonial Savings & Loan" (Item #01321) let the folks of the Colonial Village *know that Banker Arthur Pemberton is ready to help them out with loans and financial advice. This hand-painted work of art is typical of the charm and quality of Lefton's* Colonial Village Collection.

The story, "Searching for Rover," introduces a canine hero and then tells of the frightful day when Rover's family awoke to find that their beloved dog had disappeared. The search for Rover takes readers on a trip through the Village, where its buildings, businesses and people come to life. Young Lenny Mullen, Rover's frantic owner, asks everyone he meets to keep a lookout for Rover – and so they do. After many adventures and near-misses, Lenny finally finds his beloved Rover at "Rainy Days Barn" – helping to watch over his new canine family of six adorable puppies and their mother, a dog named Spot.

This eventful tour of *Colonial Village* enables its readers to meet the citizens, explore the architecture, and enjoy a delightful journey through the town that a host of collectors have grown to love. *The Illustrated Collector's Guide & History* book is available from Lefton's Collectors' Service Bureau, attention Guide & History, Post Office Box 09178, Chicago, Illinois 60609-9970.

Collectors' Service Bureau Keeps *Colonial Village* Enthusiasts Informed

While the *Colonial Village Collection* does not have a collectors club, it does have a quarterly newsletter to which thousands of readers subscribe. Subscribers of the "Colonial Village News" get first-hand, "hot-off-the-presses" news about the goings-on in the

The "Colonial Village News," issued quarterly, can be acquired in yearly subscriptions for just $2.00 to cover postage and handling. An Official Deed of Ownership accompanies each Colonial Village Collection *building. In addition, missing deeds may be acquired through Lefton's Collectors' Service Bureau in Chicago.*

Village. They are the first to know of upcoming product retirements, new introductions to the Collection, events locations, and collectible show information.

The "News" is free with just a $2.00 annual fee for shipping and handling of the four yearly issues. Collectors may call Lefton at 1-800-628-8492 to begin subscribing.

That same number serves as the Lefton Consumer Hotline, where collectors may call to locate a stocking retailer near them – a dealer that carries all of Lefton's collectible lines. In addition to newsletter subscriptions, the Hotline handles orders for replacement Deeds of Ownership, provides product brochures and catalogs, offers up-to-date retirement announcement information and new product introductions, and sells the *Guide & History* book.

In 1995, the first formal events program for *Colonial Village* collectors began, centered around an events-only building entitled the "Bayside Inn." This exclusive building is available only through retailers who hosted *Colonial Village* events during 1995.

Lefton's *Historic American Lighthouse Collection*

The majesty and mystery of the sea can belong to collectors – right in their own homes – when they acquire the *Historic American Lighthouses* from Lefton. First introduced in 1992, these fully illuminated beacons of light have been carefully researched for authenticity, then handcrafted and hand-painted to reflect the care and quality that is so much a part of each original structure.

Lighthouses depicted in this collection are located throughout the country, from east to west coast and the lakes in-between. The series has subsets distinguished by their geography, including "Atlantic," "Southern," "Great Lakes," and "Pacific Coast." In the case where an important lighthouse is no longer standing, Lefton has created the mold for its work of art from renderings in historical archives.

In addition to the larger "lights," which range up to 11" in height proportional to the original building, Lefton also offers a charming collection of *Little Lighthouses*. As carefully detailed as the full-size originals, each lighthouse in this collection stands about 6" tall. They are not lighted like the full-size replicas, but still are shining examples of high-quality ceramic collectibles.

"Toledo Harbor" (Item #01331) from Lefton's Historic American Lighthouse Collection *depicts the famous 1904 Great Lakes lighthouse located on a concrete pier in Maumee Bay. Its issue price is $47.00.*

To honor America's great and long history of lighthouses, a portion of the proceeds from each lighthouse is donated to the United States Lighthouse Society, a non-profit organization dedicated to the restoration and preservation of these national treasures.

Each of the over 40 full-size lighthouse replicas now available comes complete with an embossed hangtag detailing its construction, location, and the history of the original, plus a UL-listed cord and bulb with on/off switch. There are over 36 *Little Lighthouses* available, as well.

To receive a colorful catalog that pictures the entire *Historic American Lighthouse Collection*, plus miniatures, musicals and lighthouse ornaments, collectors may call Lefton's Collectors' Service Bureau at the number quoted earlier. The cost of the catalog is $4.00, and it also may be acquired from Lefton's stocking retailers.

Take a Trip Down Memory Lane with Lefton's *Roadside USA Collection*

With six colorful series of nostalgic collectibles, Lefton's *Roadside USA Collection* captures the charm of an earlier American era with its landmark eateries, billboards, transportation modes, and firefighters.

The *Great American Diner* series was first introduced in 1994 with eight styles of classic roadside eating establishments in the premier edition. Fondly known as the "Spectacular Vernaculars," Lefton's *Roadside Delites* continues the Diner series with ten incredible places to stop for "eats": "The Coffee Pot," "Airplane Cafe," "Zep Diner," "The Dog House," "Kone Inn," and five more. Each of these diners – created by award-winning artist/designer David Stravitz, is shaped likes the item it names – wonderfully quirky!

To complement the diners along a collector's personal roadside display, Lefton offers *Billboards of Yesteryear*, a dozen handsome, richly colored signs recreating famous American advertising motifs and billboard foundations from decades past. Products and concepts promoted on the licensed

Lefton's Great American Diners *– from the* Roadside USA Collection *– includes this wonderful old diner known as "The Star Light" (Item #01178) – a uniquely American culinary and architectural statement.*

billboards include: World War II images like "Work for Victory" and "Women at Work;" Smokey the Bear's messages such as "Remember, Only You Can Prevent Forest Fires!" and "Smokey's Friends Don't Play With Matches;" and product promotions for "Kew-Bee Bread," Pepsi-Cola's "More Bounce to the Ounce," and Campbell's Soups' "Eat Soup – And Keep Well." There are also a couple of renowned Ford billboard images – for the Model T and for 1950's "Quiet as a Ford."

Where transportation modes are concerned, Lefton portrays both *Railroad Depots and Trolleys.* The railroad's "Sentimental Journey" includes famous stations from the Atchison, Topeka & Santa Fe line as well as the Erie, B&O, Western Maryland and Wisconsin Central railroads. The "tribute to trolleys and cable cars" features beloved models including the historic San Francisco Cable Cars from "Market Street" and "City Hall 6," Cleveland's "Payne Avenue" railway, and old-fashioned cars from North Chicago, Sioux City, and Baltimore.

Lefton's *Firehouses* – affectionately known as the "Great Halls of Fire," include images of architectural marvels originally built in brick, concrete and steel, stone, wood, and clapboard. They proudly watched over towns in Colorado, New Jersey, New York, New England, Chicago, and Seattle – and they have been lovingly recreated down to the last brick, fire engine and flagpole waving "Old Glory."

From the small-town America of the *Colonial Village Collection* to the legacy of *Historic Lighthouses* and the nostalgia of *Roadside USA*, Lefton recreates a warmhearted world for collectors to explore. And with the services of the firm's Collectors' Service Bureau, each owner of Lefton's "real estate" can maximize their enjoyment in acquisition and display.

George Z. Lefton Co.
3622 S. Morgan St.
Chicago, IL 60609
(800) 628-8492

LEGENDS

Bronze and Pewter Combine With Vermeil of Brass and 24K Gold in Brilliant Mixed Media® Creations

When a team of four brothers launched Legends® in 1986, they were already renowned for their fine art sculptures for giftware-related companies like American Express and Walt Disney Productions. Since then, Legends has dramatically impacted the world of collectibles with works ranging from small-scale issues to full-sized gallery sculptures.

The company's subject matter is remarkably broad as well: encompassing authentic Native American figures, Western and Civil War history, and endangered wildlife. Through the everlasting medium of sculpture, Legends fine art sculpture proudly represents and preserves the inspiring heritage of the Native American Indian, as well as many other significant American heroes, leaders and legends who grace the annals of our nation's history.

Committed to environmental and wildlife conservation, Legends actively supports the work of various non-profit organizations, such as Defenders of Wildlife, the Grounded Eagle Foundation, and the World Wildlife Fund. Additionally, Legends maintains its commitment to the preservation and advancement of today's Native Americans through significant donations that support vital organizations such as the Native American Rights Fund (NARF), Red Cloud Indian School in South Dakota, and the American Indian Dance Theatre.

The Latest Releases from Legends

From the warrior hunters of Michael Boyett's *The Animal Dreamer Collection* to the legendary dancer of Willy Whitten's "Rapture," the artists of Legends capture the drama and dignity of Native American life – and the glories of the wildlife of their western homelands.

Michael Boyett has been specially commissioned to create a stunning five-piece series, *The Animal Dreamer Collection*, exclusively for Legends. Each sculpture reflects the interdependent relationship that existed between the warrior hunter and the wild creatures which roamed the untamed frontier.

"He Hunts With the Eagle Medicine" by Michael Boyett premieres The Animal Dreamer Collection *for Legends. The 10"-high sculpture has been issued in a certified limited edition of 950 pieces.*

The collection's first release, "He Hunts With the Eagle Medicine," presents a warrior using the swiftness and cunning of an eagle to lead him in the hunt. The second introduction, "Buffalo Runner," offers Boyett's presentation of the supreme cunning and courage exhibited by the buffalo hunters of days past.

David Lemon's "Winds of Memory," the second release from the five-piece *Western Memories Premiere Edition*, depicts the legendary Sacajawea in her later years. She remembers wearing the same blanket she wears now, one she had as a young girl with the Lewis and Clark Expedition, sitting on the banks of a river looking down into the face of her newborn son.

"Each, to the Other" offers artist Christopher Pardell's romantic tribute to the transformative power of love and marriage. This poignant piece – second in Pardell's *Culture Covenant Premier Edition* for Legends – features a young Native American couple reflecting upon the powerful change wrought by the tribal ceremony of marriage.

David Lemon's "Winds of Memory" sculpture captures Sacajawea as an older woman, remembering her days as part of the Lewis and Clark Expedition with her infant son as her companion.

With "Scent in the Air," Kitty Cantrell has once again captured the wolf as one of the most majestic examples of wild America. In this specially commissioned sculpture for Legends, the wolf has caught a scent in the air and wrinkles his nose slightly to track its origin. Meanwhile, the wind ruffles his beautiful fur.

"Rapture" by Willy Whitten represents a stunning, specially commissioned sculpture which artfully depicts a moment in the Native American Ghost Dance. At the moment this sculpture portrays, the dancer's costume still stands in its pose, while the dancer has just vanished into the sky.

The Ghost Dancer has just ascended to the sky, leaving his costume still in dance position, in this mystical work of art entitled "Rapture." It is the creation of sculptor Willy Whitten, exclusively for Legends.

A Host of Gifted Sculptors Contribute Their Talents to Legends

Because of their complete dedication to quality and integrity in the creation of fine art sculpture, Legends has attracted some of America's most honored sculptors of Native American and wildlife subjects. The firm's current endeavors include associations with Christopher Pardell, Kitty Cantrell, Willy Whitten, Dan Medina, David Lemon, and Michael Boyett.

Christopher A. Pardell was one of the first artists to join the Legends family. "My work is about more than just excitement and motion and fear," he says. "It's about the bittersweet mixture of joy and sorrow that we all know, we all feel. When they poured the slab for my studio, I carved a motto into the concrete as it hardened. It says, 'Life is a performance artwork, make yours beautiful.'"

Kitty D. Cantrell is known for her striking sculptures of North American wildlife, with wolves, eagles and humpback whales among her favorite subjects. A member of a half-dozen environmental associations, Ms. Cantrell donates a portion of the proceeds from her art to the Nature Conservancy, the World Wildlife Fund and the Grounded Eagle Foundation.

Willy Whitten is a self-taught artist, yet acknowledged as a master craftsman. Fluent in an extensive variety of media and techniques, Whitten finds fascination with the beauty and variety of Native American costume and its wealth of symbolism.

Dan Medina's artistic genius shines through in his award-winning works. Research is essential to his craft, but his true inspiration springs from within. As he says, "To portray emotion and form in metal – that is the essence of art. It all starts in the mind."

David Lemon, a member of the prestigious American Indian and Cowboy Artists Association, is a mesmerizing storyteller as well as an inspired sculptor. "You have to be thick-skinned to be an artist," Lemon says. "Your art is your soul – those are my thoughts and feelings out there on the table for people to comment on or criticize. Or worst of all, ignore."

Michael Boyett's moving style was born of his interest in heroic and historic America, coupled with a strength in realism. Wounded in battle during an enemy ambush, his experience as an infantryman during the years of the Vietnam War burned a deep sensitivity into his nature which carries over into his works of art.

The Mixed Media® Creative Process

Legends has always remained in the forefront of new concepts and innovations in the collectibles and fine art markets – most notably in the conception and creation of Mixed Media®. This significant and valuable contribution to the world of limited edition fine art sculpture combines multiple brilliant media, including Legends Bronze, Fine Pewter, Brass Vermeil, 24K Gold Vermeil, Lucite®, and many other vibrant metals and hot torched-acid patinas. Also used periodically are Black Nickel, Rose Copper Vermeil, Sunrise Gold Copper Vermeil and Flame Copper Vermeil.

When Legends unveiled their first Mixed Media™ work in 1987, collectors immediately recognized the uniqueness of this stunning new concept in fine art sculpture. And while imitators have surfaced over the years, Legends remains the only studio to create each of its works using the authentic colors of the actual metals to create color on the sculpture – never paints or dyes.

The step-by-step crafting process for a Legends sculpture begins when a Legends artist creates an original work. This sculptural original may require many months – sometimes years – of sculpting and re-sculpting soft clay before the original is finalized in the form of plastiline. From these masters, working models are created.

Each piece is sectioned into many tiny component parts to help Legends create the intricate detail found in all of their sculptures. They are then placed into molds for the creation of individual cavities. Hot molten metal is poured into these cavities and is left until it cools down to room temperature.

Each component part is tirelessly hand-cleaned and refitted by foundry artisans with over two decades of experience. Handwork with fine stainless steel tools recovers detail lost in the soldering process. The finished Mixed Media work is oxidized to a deep black patina and then relieved by hand with steel wool and sand to bring back highlights of the original metals. Only then is the piece appointed with the unique characteristics that make Legends

Kitty Cantrell portrays a stunning wolf in this 11-1/2"-high sculpture from Legends, entitled "Scent in the Air."

sculptures the leaders in today's fine art marketplace.

Starlite Collector's Society Boasts Free Membership

Legends supports its collectors through the Starlite Collector's Society (SCS) – formerly Legends Collectors Society – an exclusive, free membership program that collectors receive upon the purchase of any Legends limited edition sculpture. As members, collectors acquire a personalized SCS membership i.d. number which provides access to a wide range of services and opportunities, as well as many other valuable and exclusive benefits.

Among the most coveted of these benefits is the opportunity for collectors to acquire new sculptures before the open market release. Also important is *Starlite*, the quarterly full-color magazine featuring all new releases. In addition, the SCS records sculpture titles, insurance, and secondary market activity for safekeeping as a service to Starlite Collector's Society members, and provides assistance in sculpture appraisal.

It has been only a few short years since Legends developed the masterful innovation of Mixed Media and began creating sculptures using that exquisite media. Since then, this California-based firm has earned a strong – and growing – reputation for integrity, sculptural excellence and innovation. Considering these factors – and the company's commitment to historical accuracy and old-world craftsmanship in fine metal – the "Legends tradition" stands to flourish and grow for generations to come.

Legends
2665D Park Center Drive
Simi Valley, CA 93065
(800) 726-9660
Fax (805) 520-9670

Christopher Pardell's "Each to the Other" represents the second release in the Culture Covenant Premier Edition *from Legends. The sculpture offers a romantic tribute to the transformative power of love and marriage, featuring a young Native American couple.*

COLLECTORS' CLUB

Starlite Collector's Society
2665-D Park Center Drive
Simi Valley, CA 93065
(800) 726-9660

Annual Dues: Free Upon Purchase of a Legends' Sculpture
Club Year: Anniversary of Sign-Up Date

Benefits:
- Quarterly Full-Color Magazine, *Starlite*
- Personalized SCS I.D. Number
- Opportunity to Acquire New Sculptures Before the Open Market Release
- Special Event Pieces Available
- Record Keeping Services
- Appraisal Service

LENOX COLLECTIONS

"The Lenox Difference" Is a 100-Year-Old Tradition of Excellence Carried Forward in Every Work of Art

It began in 1889. A young artist-potter named Walter Scott Lenox founded a company dedicated to the daring proposition that an American firm could create the finest china in the world. He possessed a zeal for *perfection* that he applied to the relentless pursuit of his artistic goals.

In the years that followed, Lenox china became the first American chinaware ever exhibited at the National Museum of Ceramics, in Sevres, France. In 1918, Lenox received the singular honor of being the first American company to create the official state table service for The White House.

Lenox China has been in use at The White House ever since, commissioned by Presidents and First Ladies of four different eras. Works of Lenox may also be found in more than half our Governors' mansions. They are in United States embassies around the world, and they have been specially commissioned for gifts of state.

Today, in every work of art created by Lenox Collections, the traditions begun by Walter Scott Lenox are carried forward.

The Lenox Tradition

On one occasion in the struggling early days of the firm, Walter Scott Lenox took an eminent guest on a tour through the new workshops. They stopped before a kiln and watched as craftsmen removed chinaware representing an investment of $2,000 (quite a large sum in those days). Lenox looked at the pieces with his usual piercing scrutiny and noticed a tiny flaw in every one, possibly visible only to him. Before Lenox could voice his dismay, the enthusiastic visitor cried out, "This is exhilarating. Such excitement!" "Yes," Lenox replied. Without hesitation, he then ordered everything that had just come out of the kiln to be destroyed.

The Lenox Difference

Lenox Collections today creates works in many mediums. In every case, it maintains an unbending position regarding *quality*. The collector will see this difference in the detail of each Lenox hand-painted porcelain sculpture...in the fiery, hand-polished luster of each Lenox crystal bowl, sculpture or vase...and, of course, in the flawless finish of every piece of Lenox china.

This quest for excellence in artistry has earned Lenox the privilege of creating authorized works for famed organizations throughout the world, from the Smithsonian Institution in Washington, D.C. to the famed Palace Museum in Peking's Forbidden City.

Lenox Craftsmanship

From the company's very beginning, Walter Scott Lenox stopped at nothing to locate the most gifted craftsmen both in America and abroad. When he set out to reproduce a special, pearlescent china, nothing would do but to send to Ireland for those potters who knew the craft best. Having served as an apprentice himself, Lenox realized that craftsmanship is what bridges the gulf between dream and reality.

Now, in our own time, Lenox Collections literally searches the world to find the craftsmen most particularly skilled in producing each special work. And these craftsmen are then challenged to surpass themselves – to apply their gifts to a standard of excellence that is *unique* in all the world.

Lenox Beauty...To Endure Forever

On the subject of beauty, Walter Scott Lenox schooled his company to satisfy only one critic – posterity. His goal was to create art that would live forever.

Today, this goal remains unchanged. Every work of art Lenox Collections creates is a message to collectors, and to the world, about the company's firm

"Neuschwanstein" is the remarkable re-creation of a king's fantasy. The castle's four buildings, two courtyards, seven towers and 293 windows are portrayed with breathtaking detail by master miniaturist Ron Spicer. The sculpture is handcrafted in an artist's blend of resin porcelain and painted entirely by hand. Neuschwanstein" is 8" long by 6" high, including base.

commitment to uphold its founder's mission. Lenox works are created today to endure for generations and to be treasured by collectors a hundred years from now.

Lenox and Its Collectors

Throughout its history, Lenox has attracted some of the most exacting customers in the world...from the royal patron who commissioned a service of the most elegant china to set a table for 1,000 guests...to heads of state and dignitaries from countries throughout the world. From United States Presidents Wilson and Roosevelt to Truman and Reagan, each has turned to Lenox, confident of receiving the very best.

Today, Lenox Collections conducts an ongoing search for great talent and has extended its patronage to gifted artists of many different lands. To earn the Lenox hallmark, the highest standards must be met. Every nature subject must be shown completely true to life. Each historical piece must be authentic in every detail, and all works must be infused with the fire of imagination.

The Lenox Pledge of Satisfaction

Lenox Collections takes pride in offering works of uncompromisingly high standards of quality, crafted with care and dedication by skilled artisans. The Lenox goal, in every case, is to meet the highest expectations of artistry and fine workmanship. Therefore, if a collector is ever less than completely satisfied, Lenox will either replace the work or refund the purchase price.

Similarly, if a work is ever broken or damaged, Lenox will strive to satisfy the collector as well. If the edition is still open and a replacement is available, Lenox will send it to the owner at only one-half the current price of the work.

Lenox Collections invites collectors to share in the Lenox heritage of excellence. And the company pledges to make today's collectors as satisfied as the Presidents, First Ladies and royalty who have gone before.

"Golden Splendor" is the first collector plate by the outstanding nature artist Catherine McClung. This award-winning artist portrays beautiful birds in their glorious natural setting. The 8-1/4" plate is crafted of Lenox ivory china to the quality standard that has made Lenox collector plates prized for generations.

The Tradition Continues with Lenox Collector Plates

Lenox entered the collectible plate market in 1902 by introducing bone china dinnerware with special-order decorations. It was William Morley, perhaps the most celebrated artist in the company's early history, who set the standard for superior artistry with these original custom-order plates. Orchids, first requested in 1906, were among Morley's best subjects. A set of 18 portrait plates that were created at this time were auctioned in 1979 for $14,000.

Today, Lenox Collections offers fine art plates by some of today's most highly regarded artists.

Catherine McClung, nationally recognized for her paintings of birds, has been awarded Best of Show at the Chicago Art Exhibition, and featured in the Birds in Art Exhibition at the prestigious Leigh Yawky Woodson Museum. *Nature's Collage* is the artist's first plate collection.

Lynn Bywaters creates Santas robed in regal splendor, adorned in snowy ermine, embroidered in silver and gold. Collectors can acquire *The Magic of Christmas*, a collection of Lynn Bywater's Santas, directly from Lenox Collections.

There are few artists today who enjoy as much critical and collector acclaim as folk artist Warren Kimble. His work is featured in prestigious collections all over the world. Now, collectors can acquire some of Warren Kimble's most sought-after art in his first-ever Lenox plate collection – *The Warren Kimble Barnyard Animals*.

Lenox Supports Conservation Efforts

Because of illegal poaching and shrinking habitats, many of the worlds' magnificent animals face extinction. To raise awareness of their plight, the artists of Lenox work with wildlife organizations such as the Smithsonian Institution's National Zoological Park in Washington, D.C., the National Foundation to Protect America's Eagles™ and the Rainforest Alliance. Together, Lenox Collections and the specialists of these organizations create works of art to serve as constant reminders that our animals, and their natural habitats, must be preserved to prevent their extinction.

Lenox Porcelain and Crystal

The difference that Lenox demands in quality of workmanship, artistry and imagination may be observed in every one of today's classic porcelain and crystal sculptures.

One stunning example of Lenox hand-painted porcelain wildlife sculpture is the "African Elephant Calf." This work has been sculpted under the supervision of specialists at the

Smithsonian Institution's National Zoological Park in Washington, D.C.

With "Prim & Proper," the artists of Lenox have captured feline grace in Lenox Crystal. This elegant pair of crystal cats – one clear, one frosted – can stand alone, or they can nestle together producing an interplay of contours and contrasts.

The grace of the dolphin is portrayed in a work of art in pure white bone china glistening with a touch of gold. Dramatic and elegant, "Dance of the Dolphins" is a true showpiece.

These are but a few of today's best-known Lenox sculptures.

Lenox Looks to the Future

Never a company to rest on its laurels, Lenox Collections actively seeks opportunities to collaborate with prestigious organizations to bring today's collectors fascinating new works of art.

Collectors can watch for exciting creations, authorized by Turner Entertainment, which celebrate the drama and passion of *Gone With the Wind*. And car enthusiasts will be pleased to hear that Lenox Collections, in association with the Chevrolet Motor Division, will be crafting new works to "rev" the engine of the most dedicated collector.

The Tradition Lives On

Walter Scott Lenox died in 1920 at the age of 60, but his dream lives on in the work of today's talented Lenox artists, designers and craftsmen. And in the remarkable works of art that are cherished, treasured and enjoyed by generations of collectors across America and around the world.

Lenox Collections
1170 Wheeler Way
Langhorne, PA 19047
(800) 225-1779
Fax (215) 750-7362

Fluid feline grace is captured in a work of art that combines the clarity of polished crystal with the luster of frosted crystal. A sleek and sophisticated pair, "Prim and Proper" are etched with the Lenox hallmark, symbol of incomparable quality.

LILLIPUT LANE

There's a Place Known as Lilliput Lane...Somewhere Between England...Artist David Tate's Dreams...and Collector Fantasies

"Jones the Butcher" boasts the freshest mutton. And stop at the "The Greengrocers," too. Tots will be angelic after a visit to "The Toy Shop," but if their behavior isn't perfect, a treat from "Penny Sweets" will suffice. Find every enchantment in this delightful mini-series!

Americans who have never visited the United Kingdom tend to think of England in legendary, symbolic terms. Crown jewels. Big Ben. A civilized cup of tea.

Americans who *have* walked the streets of London, Bradford, Bath, Penzance and England's other charming hamlets and cities, know that clocks and kings are but a sampling of a culture steeped in tradition. Some say, "if you wish to know England, you must first understand her architecture." If that's true, you'll want to meet David Tate and hear about his efforts to preserve the rich architectural heritage of the British Isles. As founder of Lilliput Lane, Tate has managed to pack centuries of structural wonders into the burgeoning library of collectible treasures he designs and markets all over the globe.

Today, Tate's mission to preserve British architecture has taken him beyond the English Channel. The architectural styles of continental Europe have become a passion, too. The now-International Lilliput collection includes charming German structures, cozy dwellings from the Netherlands, French country houses – even Americana!

To find out how David Tate accomplished his vision, read on. Sample the gardens. Peek in windows! But be forewarned – once you visit this idyllic world, you might not want to leave Lilliput Lane.

A "Cottage Industry" Becomes a Cottage Phenomenon

Born in 1945 in the Yorkshire district of England, David Tate was the only son of a small, close-knit family. A creative child, he showed a remarkable aptitude for drawing, earning an art scholarship at the age of ten. Just five years later, Tate's artistic education was halted when family obligations required a job to help with expenses. Putting his art ambition on hold, he pursued an eclectic variety of work as a salesman, photographer, British fiberglass industry executive and public relations expert.

Fortuitously, Tate's public relations experience was in the ceramics industry. When he decided to resurrect his life's ambition to be an artist, his knowledge of ceramics would serve him well. Tate and his wife moved to Penrith, in northern England's Lake District. Not far from the Scottish border and his village of birth, he restored an old farm house, creating living quarters and a studio.

All that was left to be done before the work began was to bestow a name on his new venture. Given Tate's love of English literature, he fondly recalled Jonathan Swift's classic *Gulliver's Travels*, picking the name Lilliput Lane. Now his adventure was about to begin.

Tate's Philosophy: Be Fanciful... Be Professional!

Personally supervising the search for new subjects to sculpt, David Tate is a stickler for authenticity and detail – qualities that make his cottages stand out. He has been known to study mountains of books and to rummage through crates of photographs, looking for a single cottage of a particular vernacular styling. For the uninitiated, "vernacular" describes a distinct type of building found only in one area. Thus, both adobe structures in the Southwest and the brownstones of New York City could be called "vernacular." Each is unique to its region and the culture of the area.

Once a vernacular style had been selected for the Lilliput Lane collection, 20th century embellishments, added to the building since its construction, are eliminated as the first model is shaped. This assures collectors the finished piece will be completely representative of its original era. When the model is complete, a silicone mold is made.

Cottages are then fashioned of "amorphite," a material lauded for its fine detailing and undercuts. After

Town and villages are proud of their local tea rooms! The biscuits are hot and fresh and the sweet aroma of tea comforts the soul! Step into one of Lilliput Lane's new tea rooms and you're bound to want to sit awhile and reminisce.

unmolding, sculptures are "fettled" (cleaned) to remove excess material, dipped in sealant and dried.

The fabrication of every limited edition collectible made by Lilliput Lane is predicated upon quality. Tate urges his staff to think professionally at all times. Whether a member of the studio art staff, a customer service representative, or a Lilliput Lane Club staff member, all employees are in accord with the company's founder: "Lilliput Lane's business policy is built on quality. We strive to do everything professionally. Whether it's painting a flower garden or answering collector questions, we'll always put our most professional foot forward!"

At "Langdale Cottage," the wassail bowl greets visitors and the smell of pine boughs strung throughout the little house is the stuff of which Christmas dreams are made!

Lilliput Lane Comes to America - A Club Is Launched

Lilliput Lane's subsidiary, Gift Link, Inc., launched the United States distribution of cottages in 1988. By 1993, the bond between the parent British corporation and American group had become so strong, a unanimous decision to re-name the American company "Lilliput, Incorporated" was reached.

Meanwhile, in England, Lilliput Lane was experiencing its own phenomenon: record growth...far beyond original projections. A decision to put the Lilliput Group plc, the parent company of Lilliput Lane Ltd., on the London Stock Exchange was reached! This move, in November, 1993, was just the first of many advancements. Less than a year later, in October 1994, Lilliput Group plc was acquired by Stanhome, Inc., making Lilliput Lane the newest family member of the prestigious Enesco Corporation.

Corporate changes in place, Lilliput could now put its creative energies into projects and programs beloved by collectors. At the top of the list was the Lilliput Lane Collectors' Club, originally formed in 1986. Now an astonishing 70,000 strong, worldwide Club membership continues to grow at a remarkable rate.

Each year, members eagerly anticipate a Members-Only gift cottage ("Thimble Cottage" is the 1995/96 exclusive); a new color catalog; a subscription to the Club's quarterly magazine, *Gulliver's World*; and a card that allows members to reserve the newest Members-Only Redemption piece. Lilliput proudly presents "Porlock Down" to 1995/96 members, and always looks forward to hearing about the thrill collectors experience upon seeing their Club Special Redemption cottage for the first time.

Awards...Rewards...the New Art That Makes Lilliput Unique

Each year, attempting to write about Lilliput Lane's awards, retirements, new issues and distinguishing achievements becomes harder, for the list grows so rapidly. At present, just over 200 cottages have been retired while 210 structures are now available to collectors! These numbers are precedent-setting.

Of the numerous awards won by David Tate designs, "Convent in the Woods," picked "Best Collectible of Show" at the 1990 South Bend Exposition the same year *Collector Editions* "Award of Excellence" went to "Periwinkle Cottage" are particular favorites. But awards tell only part of the story. The heart of this company's success is found in the diversity that makes new issues "winners" from the moment they debut. Consider the delights collectors may choose this year:

The snow-covered steps at "Rydal Cottage" have been swept clean in anticipation of your visit! Inside, a fire burns merrily as children peek from icy windows to share their Christmas joy.

- *THE VILLAGE SHOP COLLECTION:*

Come visit Midland villages and towns in England and see country shops in miniature! There's "Penny Sweets," "The Greengrocers," "The Toy Shop," "Jones the Butcher," "The China Shop" and "The Bakery." But, don't be surprised if you smell fresh-baked scones when you see this collection in person!

- *THE ENGLISH TEA ROOM COLLECTION*

Every town, and most villages in England, has at least one tea room. It's a mecca for news-sharing, chatting and taking a moment to reflect on the day's events. Lilliput Lane's *English Tea Room Collection* highlights the exquisite differences in tea rooms across Britain. Though "Grandma Batty's Tea Room" and "Bargate Cottage Tea Room," are located at opposite ends of England, both are charming examples of romantic English tea rooms beloved by the people of Britain.

- *HISTORIC CASTLES OF BRITAIN*

Britain would not be Britain without her fabulous castles. Splendid monuments to days-gone-by, British castles have never been more eloquently rendered than in this intricate collection of miniatures. Collectors will be enthralled by tiny details: classic, medieval fortifications and foreboding towers. Traditional moats make these 19th century castles impenetrable to all but the bravest knights!

• *CHRISTMAS AT LILLIPUT LANE*

If Father Christmas chose to copy Santa Claus and climb down rooftops, he'd surely love the chimneys and roofs atop these 12 miniature marvels! Designed with the festive Yuletide season in mind, *Christmas at Lilliput Lane* is a wonderland of snow-covered dwellings. The *Christmas at Lilliput Lane* collection also includes an annual ornament, strictly limited to its year of issue!

The Journey Down Lilliput Lane Continues

Could David Tate have foreseen the heights his company would reach on the fateful day he chose to leave the security of his job to jump-start his business in 1982? Probably not. Artistic visionaries tend to be focused on the intriguing mysteries of creating "something from nothing" rather than wondering about the future.

Who's that waiting in the entryway of "Patterdale Cottage?" This elegant cottage is decorated from top to bottom in anticipation of the gala Christmas homecoming welcoming the entire family!

In the years bridging today and his move to Penrith, much attention has come to David Tate. In 1988, his name was placed on an Honors List compiled by British citizens saluting those who have made outstanding contributions to England's prestige and economy. Soon after, he was invested as an M.B.E. by Queen Elizabeth II. As a Member of the Order of the Royal Empire, many wondered if the dizzying parade of laudits had reached its pinnacle. But David Tate's Lilliput Lane collectibles continued to flourish. The company was twice named one of England's Five Top Companies by the Confederation of British Industry and Tate also accepted the Queen's Award for Export from former Prime Minister Margaret Thatcher. David Tate was also the recipient of the 1995 International Collectible Artist Award.

At age 15, David Tate came to terms with the fact that his dream would have to be put on hold for a while. That's exactly what he did...put it on hold. What's to be learned from the philosophy David Tate adopted at so early an age? Perhaps its that putting a dream on hold tends to makes it doubly sweet when it's realized...at last.

Behold the architectural wonders of bygone days! These castles are historic monuments accurately rendered in exquisite detail. Beloved by noble families...and the sites of exquisite balls...each castle is a tribute to the combined talent of the Lilliput Lane family!

Lilliput Lane
P.O. Box 665
Elk Grove Village, IL 60009-0665
(800) 545-5478
Fax (708) 875-5360

COLLECTORS' CLUB

Lilliput Lane Collectors' Club
P.O. Box 665
Elk Grove Village, IL 60009-0665
(800) -LILLIPUT

Annual Dues: One Year: $40.00 - Two Years: $65.00
Club Year: May 1-April 30
Collector's Year – Anniversary of Sign-Up Date

Benefits:

- Membership Gift
- Card to Reserve Members-Only Redemption piece
- Quarterly Newsletter, "Gulliver's World"
- Binder (Optional Purchase)
- Membership Card
- Special Selections Catalog
- Buy/Sell Matching Service (Referrals Only)
- Travel Opportunities to Tour the Lilliput Lane Studios in Penrith, England
- Painter's Demonstrations & "Paint Your Own" Cottage Events

LLADRÓ

Journey into a World of Beauty and Romance

The year was 1951 when three brothers, Juan, José and Vicente, pooled their talents and finances to start a ceramic-making operation in Almacera, Spain. The kiln built by the brothers on the family patio that year was a meager one capable only of firing ceramics. However, the products that issued forth from that furnace set in motion several decades of growth and development that has made the name Lladró synonymous with quality collectible porcelain.

There are few, if any, historical parallels to the notable success of this company which, from the start, concentrated almost exclusively on its production of ceramic figurines at the expense of the utilitarian wares which normally provide the backbone of a ceramic studio's prosperity. This emphasis reflects the predominantly sculptural sympathies of the brothers. Their ability to parlay their artistic preferences into a vast collection of internationally renown porcelain, however, is due to none other than their artistic talents, business acumen and foresight.

Laying the Cornerstone for Success

Born to the luscious agricultural lands of southern Spain, Juan, José and Vicente are the sons of Juan Lladró Cortina and Rosa Dolz Pastor. Their father was a day laborer who taught his sons to appreciate the land for its qualities as a malleable material, which could be shaped into porcelain. Their mother, as uncomplicated as she was intelligent, imbued her sons with a sensitivity for small things while setting their sights on a successful and financially rewarding future.

The brothers became laborers themselves while very young, toiling in the family fields while pursuing their formal training. On his own time, each brother attended the Escuela de Artes y Oficios de San Carlos where Juan and José focused on painting and Vicente on sculpting. Apprenticeships further enhanced their training and bolstered their confidence, leading them to the construction of their kiln. They began to investigate new procedures for glazing and firing. The diminutive flowers that were their first production pieces attracted unexpected numbers of customers and from these sales blossomed new economic possibilities and plans.

Today, finely detailed and delicate flowers still play an important role in the decoration of Lladró porcelain with their constant and fragile presence.

The year 1953 was a turning point for the Lladró brothers. As masters of making-do, they built a kiln with discarded bricks from the Altos Hornos (High Kilns) at Sagunto. Although still rather rudimentary, this kiln could produce the temperatures necessary to vitrify porcelain. And from the moment they first handled porcelain, they have explored its many possibilities. In 1955, the brothers opened a shop in Valencia and in 1958 laid the foundation for their first factory in the neighboring town of Tavernes Blanques. Their highly specialized endeavors attracted teams of workers with experience in the field of porcelain artistry and manufacturing, laying the cornerstone for Lladró's success.

From the early years, when they modeled their vases in the style of Dresden or Sevres, to the stylizations of flowers, animals and figures of the present, the Lladró brothers have shared their special visions of the world of everyday through the medium of porcelain. Their subjects are diverse, including those already explored in the arts of ancient Greece and Rome, as well as juvenile, religious and literary figurines.

After nearly forty years, Lladró's studies in color, form and posture continue to represent a never-ending fountain of invention, a constant merging of technical expertise and supreme artistry. Lladró truly is "Art in fine porcelain."

"Ten and Growing," the Lladró Society's tenth anniversary figurine, available in 1995 to members only.

Celebrating the Lladró Society's 10th Anniversary

When the famed Spanish porcelain firm first announced plans for an international collectors society in 1985, few could have predicted the worldwide impact. Today, the Lladró Society looks back on a decade of successes in providing inspiration, information and enjoyment to Lladró aficionados around the world.

In 1995 the Society celebrated its tenth anniversary in grand Lladró style with elegant receptions for members attended by members of the Lladró family, exclusive Society figurines for members only, and a deluxe 54-page edition of *Expressions* magazine.

"Ten and Growing," was created for members-only with a tenth anniversary backstamp on its base. The charming figurine recalls a special time and a special moment — first love, first kiss. Like the Society, the two children so enchantingly portrayed are "Ten and Growing."

As a special tribute, charter members of the Lladró Society were honored with a figurine, "Now and Forever." They alone were eligible to redeem this figurine in its introductory year. Each "Now and Forever" redeemed by a charter member featured a personalized backstamp reading "Charter Member, 1985-1995." Thereafter, the figurine will be available to all members who celebrate their personal tenth anniversary with the Lladró Society.

Gala anniversary receptions were held in Chicago, Los Angeles and New York City. Society members were invited to socialize with members of the Lladró family, dine, reminisce and hear plans for their Society's future.

Leading the Society into the Future

In 1995 Rosa María Lladró assumed the new position of Lladró Society President, thereby assuring a close involvement by the Lladró family with Society planning worldwide. Margarita Arriagada became Lladró Society Director for the U.S. replacing the retiring founding Director Hugh Robinson.

In 1995 "Now and Forever" was introduced for Lladró Society Charter Members only. Thereafter it will become available to members as they celebrate their personal tenth anniversary with the Society.

Rosa María Lladró grew up with close ties to the family business. She absorbed the artistic atmosphere of the Lladró Studios which were situated next to her parent's home. As youngsters she and her siblings and cousins played in the studios, drawing, painting and sculpting alongside the artisans who were crafting the world-famous figurines. Besides her playful childhood experiences, Rosa María has impressive academic credentials in law and business. She joins her sister Mari Carmen, and her cousins, Rosa and Juan Vicente, to represent the second generation on the Lladró family council which also includes the three founding brothers.

Margarita Arriagada, Lladró USA Sales Director for the Western United States, has had a lengthy relationship with and admiration for Lladró. Speaking about her new position, Margarita commented, "Lladró represents many things to me, from fine, handcrafted product to an organization built on human values, integrity and quality. In this spirit of pride and joy, I will continue to advance the Society's mission to inform and entertain its members."

Lladró Enhances Membership Benefits

The Lladró Society New Member Package welcomes members to "journey into a world of beauty and romance." The Package overflows with gifts: a high quality Lladró leather key case featuring a small porcelain Lladró logo on the snap, the Society's official porcelain plaque bearing the signatures of the three Lladró brothers, an introductory issue of *Expressions* and a registration form to activate the membership. The New Member Package box serves as a hard-cover binder for *Expressions*, the Society's quarterly magazine.

A special Lladró videotape makes an additional benefit for new members. This fascinating video dramatically highlights the intricate process required to create a beautiful figurine by Lladró. It will be mailed on receipt of each new member's registration form.

"Three Sisters" series of annual Society figurines began with "Basket of Love," in 1994, followed by "Afternoon Promenade," shown above, in 1995.

For New and Renewing Members — A Host of Benefits and Services

High on the list of membership benefits is the opportunity to acquire exclusive figurines which are introduced annually and made available to Society members only. In 1985, the first of these charming figurines, "Little Pals" made its debut at an original price of $95. At recent Lladró auctions "Little Pals" has commanded from $3,000 to $4,000 in intense bidding battles. The second annual figurine to be introduced, "Little Traveler," has garnered $1,500 to $2,000. Indeed, every retiring members-only figurine has attracted strong secondary market trading as new Society members seek to complete their collections with previous years' issues. Yet for most Lladró connoisseurs, the demonstrated investment potential of their beloved figurines plays only a minor part in their enjoyment of collecting.

In 1994 the Society introduced the first figurine in a Lladró first-time members-only series of three. "Three Sisters" were to arrive one annually through 1996. Beginning with "Basket of Love," followed by "Afternoon Promenade," the sisters rapidly won hearts. The Sisters were the latest in the Society's widely admired members-only collection of fine figurines.

All Society members are entitled to VIP services, as well as privileges and benefits not available to the general public. Among them are: a resident archivist to aid in identifying figurines and to report prices from public auctions (not affiliated with Lladró) for retired figurines and sold-out editions. General information includes the care of figurines, the location of Authorized Lladró Dealers, and information on replacement parts or restoration services for damaged pieces. (Lladró offers a unique Lladró Assurance Program that covers all figurines purchased through an Authorized Lladró Dealer in the U.S.).

The "Lladró Antique News" is an informative newsletter that provides an update on activity by Lladró in the sec-

The Lladró Society New Member Package. Each Package includes a porcelain plaque, leather key case, Expressions *magazine and handsome blue binder.*

ondary market. Compiled by an independent consultant, "Lladró Antique News" is published twice a year and mailed to members along with *Expressions*.

Lladró's award-winning publication, *Expressions* features articles and stories of special interest to people who love fine porcelain figurines. Readers are kept informed of special appearances by Juan, José and Vicente Lladró, as well as other members of the Lladró family and Society Director for the U.S., Margarita Arriagada.

The Society sponsors popular events such as signing tours by Lladró family members and trips to Spain that conclude with a tour of the famed Lladró facilities. Members also receive a member card identifying them as an Associate Member of the showcase Lladró Museum in New York City, where the world's largest collection of retired and one-of-a-kind Lladró porcelain is on display.

For more information contact the Lladró Society, One Lladró Drive, Moonachie, NJ 07074, (800)634-9088.

Lladro Society
1 Lladro Drive
Moonachie, NJ 07074
(800) 634-9088
Fax (201) 807-1168

COLLECTORS' CLUB/MUSEUM

Lladro Society
1 Lladro Drive
Moonachie, NJ 07074
(800) 634-9088

Annual Dues: $40.00 - Renewal: $27.50
Club Year: Anniversary of Sign-Up Date

Benefits:
- Membership Gift: Porcelain Plaque and Leather Key Case
- Opportunity to Purchase Members-Only Figurine
- Quarterly Magazine, *Expressions*
- Membership Card
- Binder
- Lladro Video
- Associate Membership to the Lladro Museum in New York City
- Renewal Gift
- Figurine Research Service
- Society-sponsored Trips to Spain
- Members-Only Signing Events

Lladro Museum and Galleries
43 West 57th St.
New York, NY 10019
(212) 838-9341

Hours: Tuesday through Saturday, 10 a.m. - 5:30 p.m.
Admission Fee: None

The Lladro Museum includes the largest collection of retired Lladro porcelains – over 1,000 pieces occupy three floors of the building.

SEYMOUR MANN, INC.

Innovative Design and Accessible Pricing Are the Hallmark of Leading Marketer of Collectible Porcelain Dolls

Currently celebrating its 25th anniversary in the collectibles arena, Seymour Mann, Inc. is using the opportunity to undertake the most significant year of expansion in its history. Introduction of new dolls is at a record high, and the addition of several new artists brings the number of doll designers in the Seymour Mann Gallery to a total of 15. In addition, the company has just increased its New York headquarters space by 33%, opened a new showroom in Los Angeles and completely renovated its showroom in Atlanta.

As the company enters its second quarter-century, it will continue to play a leadership role in the ever-changing doll industry. Many of the recent turns of events in the collectible doll arena are fueled by the discerning collector's growing reluctance to accept "generic" doll heads and inferior costuming. In the tradition the company established when it first opened its doors, Seymour Mann will continue to use doll artists who specialize in unique, distinctive, "human" faces and who pride themselves on using only the most extraordinary fabrics and trim for their costumes.

Founder and President Seymour Mann continues his mandate that every collectible from his company must be above all else a work of art. And with each new award and product honor he receives, this credo is justified by critics and connoisseurs, by professional journals and societies, and by consumer response.

In 1995 alone, the company received eight coveted honors for design of collectible dolls from the three most prestigious award-giving institutions in the collectible field. The Collectors' Society of America named "Sparkle, the Sugar Plum Faerie," by Edna Dali, its third-place winner for Outstanding Doll produced during 1994. *Dolls* magazine named six Seymour Mann creations as nominees for the journal's 1995 Awards of Excellence: "Princess and the Frog" and "Dulcie," both by Carolyn Wang; "Lady Windemere" by Gwen McNeil and "Cara" by Eda Mann. Award of Excellence winners were "Hope" by Eda Mann and "Guinevere" by Pamela Phillips, which also received a DOTY (Doll of the Year) Award from *Doll Reader* magazine. These nominations brought to a total of 15 the number of awards for which Seymour Mann dolls had been nominated in the previous 12-month period.

"Cara," a collectible porcelain doll by Edna Dali for Seymour Mann, Inc., received a 1995 Award of Excellence nomination from Dolls *magazine and is featured on the cover of the company's new catalog.*

Seymour and Eda Mann A Family of Artists

Artist Eda Mann has been a designer for her husband's company since the very beginning – 1965. Eda was born in London and spent her youth studying art under the tutelage of her father and two uncles, all three professional artists. When Eda was 16, the family emigrated to the United States, where her father became a well-known society artist during the 1930s and 1940s. He also created many movie posters for such studios as MGM and Columbia Pictures.

Eda studied art at the National Academy of Design in New York, where she won many awards for her sculpture and paintings. She also worked as a fashion designer, a talent that is still on display in her costume designs for Seymour Mann dolls. Over the years, her works have been acquired by such institutions as the Metropolitan Museum of Art in New York and the National Academy of Design.

Seymour met Eda while he was working as a professional musician and band leader in the '30s. After their courtship and marriage, the Manns combined their talents to form a partnership: Eda designed figurines and other decorative accessories, and Seymour marketed her creations. They carried her design talent and his marketing genius into the tabletop, giftware and collectible fields, and Seymour Mann, Inc. soon grew to be a leader in those arenas.

In the meantime, Eda had begun to create dolls for her daughters – and later her granddaughters – and it occurred to her husband that these delightful creations might also be added to their company's assets. By the late 1970s, Seymour Mann, Inc. began to transform Eda's "hobby" into a treasury of collectibles. Since then the Seymour Mann line of collectible dolls has grown to include many hundreds of dolls, and the company has become renowned worldwide as a leading resource of collectible dolls that are works of art at affordable prices.

The Seymour Mann *Connoisseur Collection* and *Signature Series*

By the 1990s, Seymour Mann, Inc. had evolved into a doll artists' company, whose member artists were becoming as well known as the name Seymour Mann. In addition to Eda Mann herself, the company's *Connoisseur Collection* featured works by such top names as Paulette Aprile, June Amos Grammer, Hanna Hyland, Pat Kolesar, Hal Payne and Michelle Severino.

The *Connoisseur Collection* was solidly established as a premiere resource for collectible dolls in the under-$150 retail price range, and Seymour felt strongly committed to providing top-quality collectible dolls at such moderate prices. At the same time, however, he heard the beginnings of a groundswell demand for something never seen before in this market – artists' dolls at prices so favorable that even novice collectors could begin to acquire them. Thus was born the Seymour Mann *Signature Series*.

It was Seymour's idea that the *Signature Series* would give doll artists an opportunity to reach a wider audience by producing larger editions at lower prices. The series debuted at the 1992 International Toy Fair and was an immediate success. Today, both the *Connoisseur Collection* and the *Signature Series* occupy enviable positions of leadership in the moderate-priced categories of collectible porcelain dolls.

"Lady Windemere" by Gwen McNeill, is one of several collectible porcelain dolls from Seymour Mann, Inc. to be honored by a Dolls magazine 1995 Award of Excellence nomination.

Noted doll designer Paulette Aprile explains the unique niche occupied by Seymour Mann, Inc.: "As an artist, I can produce only a very limited number of dolls, and therefore, my dolls are available to only a few collectors. By working with Seymour Mann, I can offer comparable quality at a much more affordable price to a broader range of collectors. Since Seymour is married to a well-known artist, his company is especially attuned to working with designers and very sensitive to our needs and wishes."

Whimsical ceramic teapots are among the most popular items in the wide range of collectible decorative accessories available from Seymour Mann, Inc.

The Seymour Mann Gallery

Today, Seymour Mann's "stable" of doll artists has evolved into a true "studio"—a creative environment where artists can give expression to the full range of their talents and, at the same time, effectively reach audiences with differing budgets for the acquisition of collectible dolls. Known as the Seymour Mann Gallery, this modern "atelier" includes not only the artists whose works form the *Connoisseur Collection* and the *Signature Series*, but also newer talents like Sandra Bilato, Margie Costa, Edna Dali, Gwen McNeil, Pamela Phillips, Valerie Pike, Lynne Randolph, C.K. Wang and Catherine Wang.

CEO Gideon S. Oberweger is a guiding influence on the artists in the Seymour Mann Gallery and on the direction of the company itself. A founding member of the company's management team, Gideon uses his marketing and sourcing expertise to identify and select overseas manufacturers that can best capture the essence of each artist's distinctive work.

"Each artist brings a new set of challenges," Gideon observes. "We don't want artists' work to compete with one another, so we have to be very selective in granting commissions. In addition, when an artist works in another medium, it doesn't always translate easily into porcelain.

"It's critical to our success," he continues, "to select manufacturers that can provide the best reproductions of each artist's dolls. We closely supervise the manufacture of each doll in order to transform the original into a first-rate collectible work. Some adjustments have to be made to accommodate cost and production objectives, but these decisions are always made with the full participation of the artist and are never made by the manufacturer alone."

Asked to name his favorite doll, Gideon answers: "That's easy–'Hope.' Eda, who is several times a grandmother, was distressed by the effect of world events on children, from Bosnia to Rwanda. So she created a guardian angel holding three children, one Black, one White, one Asian. Eda doesn't see 'Hope' as a political statement—she doesn't believe in politicizing art—but as an emotional plea to save children, who are our hope for the future."

Collectible Giftware and Decorative Accessories

While dolls have made Seymour

Mann a household name, the company continues its commitment to its other lines of collectible porcelains – giftware, tabletop, Christmas items and decorative accessories. In these fields also, the company has staked a reputation for itself on the strength of the design talent it has discovered and employed.

Just this year, the company's limited edition bisque porcelain "Hummingbird Bell," by Mario Bernini, received *Collector Editions* magazine's Award of Excellence. The entire Bernini series includes a bell, music box and three-dimensional plate, each depicting one of six native American birds surrounded by flowers.

In past years, the company has received similar accolades for such products as "Reindeer Stable" by Lorraine Sciola; "Gingerbread Dreams" by Janet Sauerby; "Shoebox Elf" by Mary Alice Byerly; and "Christmas Cat" by Kenji.

Seymour Mann, Inc. also offers a complete line of collectible ceramic teapots in a variety of distinct designs, from Oriental elephants and cats to art deco triangles to fruit and vegetable motifs.

Asked to comment on the future, Gideon Oberweger stresses the company's efforts to hold down prices. "We've begun to see a market backlash against high-priced collectibles from unknown designers. Our challenge is to keep our work – be it a doll, a teapot or a limited edition plate – truly exquisite – and therefore desirable to the collector, but also affordable."

And what drives and inspires his artists and his management team, including himself? "Collectibles are a wonderful, rewarding business. Each day we get letters and pictures from collectors who share the joy our creations have brought into their lives. Who could ask for more?"

Seymour Mann, Inc.
225 Fifth Avenue
Showroom #102
New York, NY 10010
(212) 683-7262
Fax (212) 213-4920

"Sparkle the Sugar Plum Faerie," designed by Edna Dali for Seymour Mann, Inc., was named third-place winner for Outstanding Doll of 1994 by the Collectors' Society of America.

COLLECTORS' CLUB

Seymour Mann, Inc. Doll Club
230 Fifth Avenue, Suite 1500
New York, NY 10001
(212) 683-7262

Annual Dues: $17.50
Club Year: January-December

Benefits:
- Membership Gift: Poster
- Newsletter
- Membership Card
- Buy/Sell Matching Service
- Special Members-Only Dolls

MARURI U.S.A.

Making the Ancient Art of Priceless Porcelain Today's Collectible Sensations

The art of creating exquisite porcelain sculptures requires two things above all else: talented art masters and a total commitment to quality. In the entire world, there are no more than a score of studios achieving true excellence in porcelain. You're probably familiar with some of their names. The European houses of Royal Worcester and Meissen earned their reputations centuries ago. American producers Cybis and Boehm are always counted among the finest in the world. But when it comes to contemporary mastery, few can compare to the dynamic company that took its place among the world's best gift and collectible producers just ten short years ago: Maruri.

Maruri is a Japanese company with roots firmly planted in Seto, Japan. There, highly skilled artisans produce the world's most respected and collected porcelain giftware and collectibles. This legacy began centuries ago and continues today. Maruri's entry into the American market just ten years ago has attracted the attention of collectors, gift shop owners and the media. In sum, Maruri has, in a short amount of time, proven itself a powerful force in today's giftware and limited edition collectibles industries.

A Family Business Flourishes in Central Japan

Long before America discovered the magic of porcelain art, Japan's ceramics industry flourished in the fabled ceramic capital of Seto. Located in central Japan, near the exotic, old-world capital of Nagoya, this region boasted the finest family-oriented workshops in the land. One particularly successful enterprise was started by the Mizuno brothers who carefully selected the name "Maruri" for their design studio. The "ri" means "benefits." "Maru" is a time-honored symbol for a circle symbolizing the never-ending nature of classic, fine art.

With such an appropriate name, how could the company help but flourish? The studio quickly earned a distinguished reputation for excellent bone china, delicate figurines and true-to-nature bird and animal sculptures. When at last the name "Maruri" became established in the United States, a remarkable thing happened. Collectors began to use Maruri as a benchmark of comparison for all other wildlife sculptures on the market.

Standards of Excellence Set Maruri Apart from All Others

Today, Maruri prides itself on upholding the "studied approach" in the creation of its limited edition sculptures. Every flower, eagle, bird and animal takes many days to complete using a multi-step process that has been followed faithfully over the years.

Artisans begin by crafting multiple molds for a single piece. By making individual molds, every detail is captured to perfection. Once the molds are approved, creamy feldspar mixture in the form of liquid slip is carefully poured. This Grand Feu formula is the same one used in ancient times. It continues to be the preferred ceramic material today, prized for its excellent finished look and feel.

Molds are filled to a specific thickness, then allowed to dry very slowly to meet Maruri's stringent specifications. Only when a proper degree of hardness is reached are pieces carefully removed from their molds and placed together. Seam lines and points of juncture are smoothed and refined. Everything is done by hand to ensure a seamless work of art guaranteed to delight collectors everywhere.

Sculptures are next placed in a temperature-controlled drying room, carefully braced between support molds because the hardening process will continue for several days. When sufficiently dry, a sculpture is placed in a kiln and fired for 16 hours. During this critical period, temperatures in the kiln are brought to an ideal degree of heat. Then the kiln is subtly cooled to complete the firing process.

This American bald eagle figurine is from Maruri's American Eagle Gallery*. These soaring eagles are 8-3/4" high and sell for $110. Like all Maruri eagles, this powerful pair is hand-painted and comes with a wood base and Certificate of Authenticity.*

Maruri artisans carefully inspect sculptures as soon as they are removed from their kilns. As many as 35% to 40% may be eliminated as 'less than perfect.' Those passing inspection are sandblasted to a brilliant, strong finish. At last, highly trained artists paint every sculpture by hand in subtle tones chosen by color experts. Finally, the sculpture is ready to be wrapped and shipped to fine shops across the world.

The Maruri Studios Proudly Present "Independent Spirit," and Other Aviary Delights

From time to time, Maruri introduces a complex and distinguished work of art featuring several figures as

Detail so realistic, collectors can hear the cry of these eagles! The newest Maruri Studio Collection *sculpture is "Independent Spirit." Sequentially numbered and stringently limited to 3,500, this fine porcelain and bronze limited edition has a handsome wood base and comes with a Certificate of Authenticity.*

a single work of art. "Independent Spirit" is such a piece. A gathering of sturdy bronze tree branches reach up to support two American bald eagles fiercely battling for dominance of the sky. Their expressive faces are powerful and bold. Wings flare out to reveal astonishing detail. A pallet of realistic colors stroke every inch of this porcelain masterwork.

To create such a complex figure, eagles, wings, tree branches and trunks must all be created independently of one another. Fusing of the individual pieces takes place as it's molded, assembled and painted. It's an arduous process, but well worth the time it takes.

Individually numbered and limited to just 3,500 pieces for world-wide distribution, "Independent Spirit" is a remarkable 14" high on its wood base. A Certificate of Authenticity accompanies this new sculpture, priced at just $395.

Because birds are so popular, Maruri's "Delicate Motion" was designed and produced for collectors of fine aviary art. This sculpture features three violet-crowned hummingbirds circling a bright spray of morning glories. Like "Independent Spirit," "Delicate Motion" is sequentially numbered and limited to 3,500 pieces, world-wide. This remarkable porcelain and bronze figure comes on a wood base and includes a Certificate of Authenticity. Its issue price is $325.

Happily, "Delicate Motion" is but one of Maruri's hummingbird offerings. *The Maruri Hummingbird Collection* also showcases this elusive winged creature. And, for collectors of other types of birds, *Eyes of the Night*, an exotic owl series and a fragile pair of snow-white doves called "Wings of Love" may also be found in Maruri's porcelain aviary.

Savvy collectors are well-aware that Maruri collectible bird sculptures are known for their secondary market performance. Consider, for example, artist W.D. Gaither's "American Bald Eagle I." Introduced by Maruri in 1981 at $165, the figure commanded $600 on the secondary market one year later...$1,750 by 1995! This stunning increase exemplifies Maruri's commitment to producing art rich in detail that also may have great aftermarket potential.

A Polar Expedition Unlike Any You've Seen Before

Few of us will ever have the privilege of seeing polar bears, harp seals, arctic foxes and penguins in their natural environments, so Maruri brings these magnificent animals and birds to you in the *Polar Expedition* collection. Each replica of its real-life cousin is hand-painted in natural colors and so real, you can almost feel the cold!

From the mighty "Polar Bear" to the delightful "Baby Seal," from a formally dressed "Emperor Penguin" to an "Arctic Fox" so real you'll swear you can imagine him scampering behind a bluff, discover a wonderland of gentle faces and soft shapes in the *Polar Expedition* collection. If you haven't yet seen the figures in this series, we invite you to take a peek at "Baby Harp Seals," depicted in this article.

As always, each sculpture in the *Polar Expedition* library comes with Maruri's Certificate of Authenticity. It's your assurance that each member of the *Polar Expedition* family has been made with all the quality and care for which Maruri is known worldwide.

Maruri's exquisite hummingbird family competes with nature for realism! Part of a 16-piece collection that ranges in price from $95 to $150, this mother feeding her babies is an excellent example of Maruri's attention to the smallest detail.

Maruri Travels to Africa to Preserve Magnificent Animals

Maruri artisans transported their talent and vision from the icy Arctic to the plains and savannas of exotic Africa when they announced the debut of *Gentle Giants*, a stunning collection of African elephant sculptures. In this series, five African elephants are fashioned of fine porcelain and detailed so exquisitely, every wrinkle shows!

Gentle Giants collectors may choose from a single, standing baby elephant...a sitting baby elephant...or a playful pair of youngsters!

Everyone's favorite subject, a mother and child, is also included, as well as a beautiful pair of adult elephants. A fine wood base showcases these limited editions, and a Certificate of Authenticity is included.

Fortunately, *Gentle Giants* isn't the only African collection Maruri has developed. A signature collection, designed by noted artist W.D. Gaither and called *African Safari*, shares

These dark-eyed "Baby Harp Seals" are among the delights collectors find in Maruri's Polar Expedition *sculpture collection. Also featured are realistic "Arctic Fox," "Emperor Penguin" and other wonders.*

Gaither's actual experiences in Zululand, South Africa, with collectors. Every sight provided new vistas. The artist sketched and photographed elephants, rhinos, buffalo, lions, leopards, kudus, impalas and other great beasts. Each served as inspiration for his true-to-life *African Safari* animal series.

Maruri Presents Horses from Around the World

Relatively new to the Maruri library is a bold collection of equines entitled *Horses of the World.* From a common prehistoric ancestor, horse breeds have developed independently. Today, each has its own distinct look, behavior and style. Some are strong. Others are fast. Some breeds are known for their endurance; others for their beauty.

Maruri designers recognize certain breeds as standard-bearers, the best of breeds. Each of the following is represented in the *Horses of the World* collection, attractively priced from $145 to $175:

• The dignified "Clydesdale," known for its sweet disposition and strength, has historically been used for farm work and transporting coal from Scottish mines.

• The sleek "Thoroughbred," originating in England, is now most often found streaking across race courses at lightening speed! They are also considered one of the most beautiful breeds on earth.

• The gentle "American Quarter Horse" is beloved by horse fans for its agility, intelligence and good temper. The Quarter Horse is a favorite of those just learning to ride.

• In France, the "Camargue" is known as the 'White Horse of the Sea' despite having a sleek, dark coat at birth! By the time they reach adulthood, Camargues have turned snowy-white.

• The distinct "Paint" was everyone's favorite mount in the Old West. Its broken color patterns provided good camouflage as "cowboys and Indians" chased each other across the Badlands of America.

• Finally, the magnificent "Arabian" is the oldest purebred in the world. Arabians are known for their great stamina, intelligence and gentle love of human companions.

As Maruri broadens and extends its creative wings, its future is limitless. Age-old methods and award-winning sculptors with a boost from the newest porcelain technology promise lasting works of fine art, generation after generation. Today, Maruri continues its time-honored tradition of providing enduring tributes to some of the world's most enchanting creatures.

Maruri U.S.A.
7541 Woodman Place
Van Nuys, CA 91405
(800) 5-MARURI
Fax (818) 780-9871

JUNE MCKENNA® COLLECTIBLES, INC.

Yes, in Virginia There are Many Santa Clauses!

Surrounded by many of her Santa carvings, June McKenna holds her 1993 12" Limited Edition Santa – "Saint Nickolas."

In the year 1897, "Virginia" and "Santa Claus" were forever linked in an editorial response to a young girl's question, "Is there a Santa Claus?" Today the spirit of Santa symbolized in Francis P. Church's famous reply continues through the carvings of an artist from Virginia named June McKenna®. Each Christmas, our childhood beliefs surrounding the mystical figure of Santa are rekindled in all of us. Yet this seasonal ritual can now be enjoyed throughout the year thanks to June McKenna® Collectibles, Inc.

The Santa figurines carved by June McKenna reflect the beauty and joy which captivates the world each year during the Christmas season. Each carving is an expression of this artist whose sense of identity is closely linked with everything related to Christmas. Through her carvings, June McKenna has found a unique way to share with all of her collectors her childhood memories of the holiday season she loves to live each day of the year.

Santa's Workshop

Just north of Richmond, Virginia, lies the historic town of Ashland, home of June McKenna® Collectibles, Inc. This innovative family business began as a home craft and hobby enterprise in the late 1970s. Today, it has become the producer of some of the most popular collectibles in the United States and is best known for its Santas. The success and phenomenal growth of this company is due to the artistic talents and organizational skills of June and Dan McKenna.

June and Dan met and were married in the early 1970s and today have two sons, Scott and Joey. During the first years of their marriage, Dan worked as an electrician while June was a homemaker raising their two sons. During her "spare" moments, June began to develop her artistic interests and talents by creating several types of home crafts which she sold at local craft fairs.

June's career as a sculptress began in an interesting way. One day June's oldest son Scott asked her for some help with his third grade science project. He was studying dinosaurs and was attempting to make a model of a brontosaurus. With Mom's help, some cornstarch and salt, the hard-working pair made a dinosaur to be proud of! Spurred on by the successful completion of the dinosaur, June began experimenting with her newly discovered skills and developed a technique for creating figurines.

By the early 1980s, June had won several awards at craft shows, and her figurines were becoming increasingly popular in her regional area. June and Dan began to wonder if the product they were making was popular enough to support a full-time business rather than a part-time hobby. One day in the spring of 1982, Dan decided to resign from his job as an electrician and devote all his time and energy into helping June make the business a success. And, "the rest of the story" is the successful history of a multimillion dollar business.

Why June McKenna Collectibles?

Many people often wonder what

sets one collectible apart from another. Some collectors admire the beauty and detail that some artists manage to paint or carve in their product. Other collectors are attracted to the variety of products a single artist creates. Whatever reasons collectors have for their initial investment in an artist's product, artists hope that collectors will continue their interest and add to their collection over the years. But with so many outstanding types of collectibles available today, it is often difficult to decide what to collect. In regards to June McKenna Collectibles, there is little doubt why some individuals initially choose to collect these figurines – incredible detail and superior craftsmanship, as well as a variety of product lines. However, one of the reasons why collectors continue to collect June McKenna® Collectibles is – June McKenna!

What a Personality

Anyone who has ever met June McKenna is overwhelmed by her "southern charm." To say that June is a very personable individual is quite an understatement. Yet, the flair she brings to the collectible industry is refreshing and has helped her develop a friendly bond between artist and collectors.

In order to keep her collectors informed about her new carvings, June publishes a semi-annual newsletter entitled "Visions." Each spring and fall, collectors look forward to their newsletter which describes and illustrates June's latest figurines. One of the most eagerly read sections of the newsletter is June's schedule of personal appearances.

June makes herself available to her collectors many times each year through personal appearances at selected retail stores. At these personal appearances, June signs her carvings and autographs. To make these events even more exciting, June introduced a special line of figurines in 1989. These carvings properly called "Personal Appearance Santas," are only available at June's personal appearances.

During the last several years, June has continued to find unique ways to foster the bond she has worked so hard to build between herself and collectors. She recently published the *June McKenna® Collector's Guide*, created the June McKenna Collector's Society, and sponsored the June McKenna® Festival.

June McKenna® Collector's Guide

In order to meet the needs of collectors and retailers, June published the *June McKenna® Collector's Guide* late in 1993. This guide book has been called "collector friendly" by several collectible publications and is designed with the collector in mind. The guide book is over 250 pages and includes 270 color photos of many of June's carvings. The first 2,500 copies were produced in a limited edition, personally signed and numbered by June.

One of the reasons that the guide book has received high marks from the collectible industry is its overall design. The guide book is a leather covered gold-plated spiral notebook. Each chapter is sequentially numbered, allowing future pages to be added, which keeps the guide book up-to-date. June plans to add new pages to the guide every two years.

June McKenna Collector's Society

Due to the growing number of collectors purchasing June McKenna® Collectibles, June began a collector's club in 1994. The immediate response from the public was overwhelming. More than two thousand individuals joined the June McKenna® Collector's Society as charter members.

June's image as "an artist who never misses a detail," is also reflected in her work with the Society. As an annual member of the Society, each collector receives a carved figurine (ornament size) which is a replication of one of June's registered edition Santas. Members also receive the newsletter, "Visions," updated pages for the guide book (every two years), and other special gifts included in the annual membership kit. Lastly, members have the right to purchase "members-only" figurines carved by June each year.

The June McKenna Festival

As if June didn't have enough to do, she decided to sponsor a Festival. The "First Annual June McKenna® Festival" was held on Labor Day weekend 1994. The Festival was such a huge success that June hopes to hold a Festival each year. The purpose of the Festival, according to June, is to bring collectors together for a "gala event." The Festival is just another way for June to stay in touch with her collectors "up close and personal." Highlights of the Festival include a Friday evening dinner followed by a presentation by June, and an auction of rare and difficult-to-find

June McKenna creates a variety of figurines each year. Pictured are the 12" Limited Edition Santa; the Toy Car, an addition to the Train series; Snowmen; Angels and her smaller Santas.

June McKenna figurines on Saturday.

According to many of the collectors who have attended the festivals, the atmosphere surrounding the event reminds them of the Christmas season. This perception of the Festival best describes the place June McKenna holds throughout the collectible industry. Whenever someone asks about Christmas and Santa collectibles, June McKenna's name is usually the first mentioned in the conversation.

What's Next?

It is very hard to believe that June has been able to achieve so much in such a short period of time. As soon as one project is successfully completed, June always seems to come up with another interesting adventure. If we didn't know any better, we'd think that June was Santa in disguise, cleverly planning her next act secretly at her "Santa like" workshop. At least we can be sure of one thing, "yes, (in) Virginia, there is a Santa!"

June McKenna Collectibles, Inc.
P.O. Box 846
Ashland, VA 23005
(804) 798-2024
Fax (804) 798-2618

June is shown doing what she loves to do best – talking to collectors at the June McKenna® Festival.

COLLECTORS' CLUB/TOUR

June McKenna Collector's Club
P.O. Box 1540
Ashland, VA 23005
(804) 798-2024

Annual Dues: $45.00
Club Year: April 1 - March 31

Benefits:
- Membership Gift: Replica of Registered Edition Santa
- Opportunity to Purchase Members-Only Figurine
- Bi-annual Newsletter, "Visions"

June McKenna® Collectibles, Inc. Factory Tour
205 Haley Rd.
Ashland, VA 23005
(804) 798-2024

Admission Fee: None
Hours: Monday through Friday, 9 a.m. - 3 p.m.

The tour shows visitors where June McKenna figurines are finished and prepared for shipment.

MEDIA ARTS GROUP INC.

A Growing Member of the Collectibles Community

There is a "new kid on the block" in the collectibles industry: Media Arts Group Inc. MAGI, as it is more familiarly called, is the corporate umbrella that includes Lightpost Publishing Inc., John Hine Studios and the newest member of the family, MAGI Entertainment Products. Together, these businesses represent fresh, exciting, innovative collectibles for a wide range of today's collectors.

The company was founded in 1990 to publish the limited edition lithographs of award-winning artist Thomas Kinkade. Its growth has been phenomenal, and, in August 1994, Media Arts Group Inc. became a public corporation listed on NASDAQ (ARTS).

Thomas Kinkade – *Painter of Light™*

The consistent growth of Lightpost Publishing can be attributed to the remarkable artwork of Thomas Kinkade. Regarded as one of America's most popular artists, Kinkade's limited edition canvas and paper lithographs have become the standard in the art publishing industry. Using an exclusive process, Lightpost is able to authentically replicate the quality and color of each Thomas Kinkade painting. Renowned as the *Painter of Light™*, Kinkade imparts "light" into each of his works – in the style of the 19th century luminists – and Lightpost has developed a method of capturing that light in its canvas lithographs, making them unique.

Second in the new Hometown Memories *series, "Hometown Chapel," has been introduced by Lightpost Publishing. This enchanting country church first appeared in the background of "Hometown Memories" and now forms the subject of Thomas Kinkade's latest issue.*

Thomas Kinkade has received numerous honors, been profiled in a number of leading publications and made many appearances on national radio and television programs. Kinkade was honored by NALED in 1993, 1994 and 1995 with the prestigious "Lithograph of the Year Award," receiving four of five nominations in the 1995 award. He received the prestigious 1995 NALED "Artist of the Year Award." He received a 1993 and 1994 *Collector Editions* "Award of Excellence" for Lithographs over $100. *US Art Magazine* named Kinkade an "Artist To Watch In 1995" and Kinkade was named "Artist of the Year" at the 1995 Collectors Jubilee.

The Thomas Kinkade Collection is supported by the Thomas Kinkade Collectors' Society, which was organized in 1993. As part of their benefits, members receive an exclusive Membership Lithograph and the opportunity to purchase a limited edition Members Only Lithograph, especially created by the artist. Worldwide membership in 1995 was close to 20,000 members.

The newest introduction by British sculptor David Winter is a portrayal of his family retreat in Ireland. Limited to 4,500 pieces worldwide, "Newton Millhouse" comes with a special David Winter video and scrapbook, which give collectors a very personal glimpse into the private life of this distinguished artist.

John Hine Studios Joins the MAGI Family

In 1993, John Hine Studios became a wholly owned business, bringing its world-famous *David Winter Cottages Collection* into the MAGI family of collectibles. English sculptor David Winter is regarded as one of the foremost creators of miniature architectural structures. His whimsical, nostalgic cottages of British lifestyle have been an award-winning line since it was introduced to U.S. collectors in the early 1980s.

The Collection was named "Collectible of the Year" by NALED in both 1987 and 1988, and David Winter was named "Artist of the Year" in 1991. He has earned numerous other awards over the years. The Studios and Workshops of John Hine Limited are located at Eggars Hill, Hampshire, England, and the Collection continues to be created and produced in the U.K.

The David Winter Cottages Collectors' Guild began in 1986 and has more than 45,000 members world-

Alpine Christmas, the unique new lighted village from Illuminations by John Hine Studios, includes six independent structures, plus a park with pond. The "Clock Tower" has a working clock in it, and using patented technology, this beautifully sculpted architectural structure can be illuminated individually now and added to later.

wide. Member benefits include a variety of items, including an exclusive Membership Cottage. During the membership year, members have the opportunity to purchase at least two Members Only Cottages sculpted exclusively for the Guild. In addition to the International Guild, there are a number of regional and local collector groups that are dedicated to *David Winter Cottages*, including England and Australia.

In addition to David Winter, John Hine Studios is home to several other collectible lines. *Father Time Clocks* and *The Shoemaker's Dream* collections are created by sculptor Jon Herbert, who began his career at the Studios as a mouldmaker for *David Winter Cottages*. His two collectible lines continue to win collector support.

New Lines and Artists Add Breadth and Depth to MAGI

A roster of new lines and artists were added to John Hine Studios in 1995. These include artists Gary Patterson, Ted Slack, Gavin Fifield and Matt Danko.

Illuminations by John Hine Studios is a lighted village collection with self-contained electrical system, for which the company is in the process of obtaining a patent. The highly detailed, miniature architectural structures will portray houses and buildings synonymous with different cities or attractions around the world. Sculpting of the unique line will be undertaken by different artisans, based on expertise and interests.

The first two introductions are *Alpine Christmas*, a snow-covered collection of structures surrounding a miniature skating pond; and *London By Gaslight*, a completely resculpted collection of English buildings portraying Victorian England's most famous city. Utilizing new technology, *Illuminations* provides collectors with a safe, colorful, illuminated display that will enhance enjoyment for the entire family.

Artist Gary Patterson has been called "creator of smiles" because of his ability to take serious situations and artistically make people laugh at themselves. He has used sports as a primary subject for his intricate, richly detailed artwork, which has earned him international acclaim. It is estimated that Gary Patterson's art is owned or recognized by more than 250 million people worldwide.

The *Gary Patterson Collec-tions* initially include a collection of figurines and trophies based on characters in his artwork, as well as a line of limited edition, signed and numbered, framed and matted lithographs of his art. There will also be smaller, unframed, open edition prints.

British sculptor Ted Slack has created a whimsical collection of treehouses called *Woodly Wise*, a mythical land inhabited by elusive keepers of the land called Twiggs. Slack is recognized for his highly detailed, miniature structures, which he has created over the past decade. This newest collection combines a lifelong love of nature with his interest in unusual architectural structures.

Another English sculptor, Gavin Fifield, has been introduced to the United States with a fanciful collection of beautiful lighted fairytale-inspired cottages. The *Gavin Fifield Collection* is his first U.S. collectible. It will debut in 1996.

Artist Matthew Danko has worked in the U.S. collectibles industry for the past 25 years, creating everything from memorable greeting cards to dolls and folk art. His new line is the *Once Upon A Story Collection*, a unique storybook-doll collectible. The collection utilizes mixed-media to create movable *StoryScenes™* that each include a named doll that is the subject of the individual storybook, which comes with every vignette. The dolls are handmade, hand-painted and fully dressed. Each *StoryScene* is comprised of freestanding items that can be moved about, rearranged and placed wherever the collector chooses.

MAGI Entertainment Focuses on Entertainment-Based Licensed Products

The newest subsidiary in Media Arts Group is MAGI Entertainment Products, which recently signed a two-year, multi-film agreement with MCA/Universal Studios to produce and market limited edition art and collectible products based on selected films. A completely new collectible

Artist Gary Patterson depicts the ultimate golf setting in this highly detailed lithograph from Lightpost Publishing entitled "World of Golf."

Limited to 2,950 pieces, "Wendy House" is the first limited edition in the Woodly Wise *collection of intricate treehouse sculptures created by British sculptor Ted Slack.*

movie memorabilia product called *CinemaClips™*, has been introduced by MAGI Entertainment and features a 35mm film clip on an oversized movie ticket with artwork from the film. The first product launched was based on three 1995 Universal films: *Casper*, *Apollo 13* and *Waterworld*. MAGI Entertainment is also marketing limited edition art and three-dimensional products under the banner of Universal Studios Art Editions by MAGI.

In addition to motion picture-related licensed product, MAGI Entertainment Products will create and market collectible memorabilia for sports, music, theatre and familiar personalities. *Recollections* by *Lightpost Classic Clips™*, a nostalgic collection of historic and cultural art and memorabilia, has introduced new licenses and new product concepts for such familiar faces as Elvis, the Cowardly Lion and Rhett Butler. They will be joined later by a star-studded cast for the enjoyment of collectors.

Media Arts Group Inc. is headquartered in San Jose, California, with production and distribution facilities in San Jose, Houston and the United Kingdom. The company also exhibits at major gift and collectible shows and maintains showrooms in major markets.

Media Arts Group
Ten Almaden Blvd. 9th Floor
San Jose, CA 95113
(800) 544-4890
Fax (408) 947-4640

COLLECTORS' CLUBS

Thomas Kinkade Collectors' Society
P.O. Box 90267
San Jose, CA 95109
(800) 366-3733

Annual Dues: $45.00 – 2-Year: $75.00
Club Year: January-December
Collector's Year: Anniversary of Sign-Up Date

Benefits:
- Membership Gift: Pencil Sketch Lithograph
- Opportunity to Purchase Members-Only Canvas and Paper Lithograph
- Special Collector Benefit Certificates for Free Frame with Purchase of Members-Only Canvas Lithograph
- Quarterly Newsletter, "The Beacon"
- Membership Card
- National and Regional Special Events

David Winter Cottages Collectors' Guild
P.O. Box 90038
San Jose, CA 95109-3038
(800) 366-3733

Annual Dues: $40.00 – 2-Year: $75.00
Club Year: Anniversary of Sign-Up Date

Benefits:
- Membership Gift: Membership Cottage
- Opportunity to Purchase Members-Only Cottages
- Quarterly Newsletter, "Cottage Country"
- Membership Card and Certificate
- National and Regional special Events and Tour Signings
- Advance Mailings

MICHAEL'S LIMITED

Brian Baker's Déjà Vu Collection Welcomes Memories Through Architectural Wall Sculptures

Michael's Limited began with a block of clay that has turned into neighborhood blocks that may look like your hometown. There's "Old White Church," "Main Street Cafe," "County Bridge," "Dinard Mansion," "Victorian Tower House" and other houses and buildings inspired by architecture around the world. It's also the world of *Brian Baker's Déjà Vu Collection*, where beautiful sculptures bring back warm memories and let everyone explore familiar places. "We believe when you study one of these works of art, you get the feeling you've been there before," says Michael O'Connell, president of Michael's Limited.

Members of the Brian Baker's Collector's Club had the opportunity to add "Welcome Home" to their collection in 1995. The members-only redemption sculpture features a small, inviting cottage complete with heart cut outs on the shutters to potted plants on the front door step. Brian created the piece based on the Carpenter's Gothic style.

From the Imagination and Creativity of Artisans

Michael O'Connell began his career with Walt Disney Productions working for the company's Imagineering department, which designs and brings to life the famous theme parks. In 1976, Michael left Walt Disney Productions to pursue other interests, including model railroading. As a result, he developed Chooch Enterprises, Inc., a leading manufacturer of model railroad hobby products. By 1980, Chooch Enterprises, Inc. moved to Seattle, where the company continues serving the hobby industry.

For several years, Michael was also interested in creating architectural wall decor. However, it wasn't until 1987 that Brian Baker, an employee of Chooch Enterprises, Inc., made the dream into a reality. It all started with Brian's simple request for a block of clay so that he could make a Christmas present for a friend. Brian's sculpture not only inspired Michael, but is also inspired an idea. Brian had sculpted the first "Hotel Couronne," launching his career and the creation of Michael's Limited. Today *Brian Baker's Déjà Vu Collection* is one of the most exciting collectibles and decorative accessories in the gift industry.

World Travels Inspire Collection

From Europe to Mexico and Thailand to America, Brian Baker's zest for life comes from his fascination for history and the arts. When he isn't busy creating new sculptures, Brian can be found exploring the Pacific Northwest or searching for adventure in a distant land. The culture and architecture of the world inspire him to share his experiences through the collection.

Born in 1962, Brian was raised in Seattle's Puget Sound area. In 1981, he started working for a gift company specializing in framed plaques featuring calligraphy and strips of decorative European braid. In just five years, Brian advanced quickly within the company, acquiring valuable gift industry knowledge and developing his craft.

But Brian embarked on his most ambitious adventure in 1986 when he began a solo trip around the world. He toured throughout Asia and then parts of Europe. In Paris, Brian was enchanted by paintings that captured the character and personality of the charming buildings. This inspired him to delve into the wonderful European heritage. His keen interest quickly spread to a love for the varied styles of American architecture.

Over the years, Brian's travels have taken him to more than 40 countries from the Far East and Middle East to Europe and the South Pacific. And he has stories to tell from each destination. Brian has found beautiful architecture and friendly people throughout the world. He likes Bali for its fascinating culture and Germany for its medieval

Brian Baker first remembers visiting Philadelphia when he was only three years old. When he returned as an adult, he rediscovered a place rich in history with colonial brick rowhouses. He recreated his impressions in "Philadelphia," which he dedicated to two late friends. You'll find a red umbrella by the door, representing the gift given to him by one of those friends.

castles and lush landscapes. He often visits friends in Mexico and explores remnants of the country's ancient civilizations. In Sweden, Brian has nearly 100 distant relatives. He has visited the Scandinavian country three times.

After his travels around the world, Brian returned home to Redmond, Washington, in 1986. At this time, he began working for Michael O'Connell. After he made his first wall hanging sculpture, Michael suggested he create a few more. The finished sculptures were shown at the San Francisco Gift Show. The rest, as they say, is history.

Building a *Déjà Vu Collection* Sculpture

Brian crafts each new building similar to the way each is actually constructed, including additions and remodeling. He lets the building "create itself." Brian's clay sculpting talents represent the first in a series of important and often difficult steps leading to the finished work. The second step involves forming a mold for casting. All of the designs are hand cast in fine bonded stone. Brian then carefully develops a color scheme suitable for the building and its place in the overall collection. His first proof is reproduced to establish a sample for an excellent team of artisans, who carefully completes dozens of designs – each one faithful to Brian's original.

Brian's trademark in the collection is an umbrella. Although not every building has one, there is often an umbrella hidden in the shadows or quietly tucked away in a corner. Some people think the umbrellas represent the well-known rainy days in Seattle, but Brian tells a different story. "On my first building – #1000, the original "Hotel Couronne" – I wanted a hungry French cat sitting by the door," Brian explains. "I could not seem to design a cat that pleased me, so I left the cat's tail as the handle and made the body into an umbrella. This result became a souvenir of the rainy day when I first saw the building in Rouen."

This same detail-oriented creativity goes into every sculpture. At his sculpting table, he takes great care and pride in creating each house. Brian tries to become a resident of the building, imagining the people who would live or work there. This is just his way of bringing history to life and making one feel like Déjà Vu – you've been there before.

An Open Door to Brian Baker's Déjà Vu Collectors' Club

With the tremendous response to the collection, the Brian Baker's Déjà Vu Collectors' Club was founded in 1993. Each year, the club unveils a membership piece and an exclusive building that only members have the opportunity to acquire. For 1995, "Marie's Cottage" was the symbol of membership sculpture, inspired by a small home located on an island in Casco Bay, just north of Portland, Maine. The cottage belongs to the Mead family and is a tribute to Marie Mead, a recently retired and pioneering Michael's Limited sales representative in New Jersey. "Welcome Home," the members-only redemption sculpture for 1995 is based on a house in a restored Toronto neighborhood called Cabbagetown. The small cottage represents the Carpenter's Gothic style.

Limited Editions Make Places More Special

"Amsterdam Canal" is the only limited edition sculpture to be signed and numbered by Brian. The beautiful piece reflects another one of Brian's favorite places. He was impressed by Amsterdam's 6,700 houses and buildings under the care of the National Trust, which makes it the largest historical city in Europe. During the 17th century, the city reached its golden age with canals dug around medieval walls and powerful merchants constructing richly decorated buildings to flaunt their wealth. Today, more than 1,000 bridges cross the city's 160 canals, and the best way of getting around is still by boat. Limited to only 1,000 pieces, "Amsterdam Canal" sold out in 1993.

"Southern Mansion," the first sculp-

Among the most popular pieces in Brian Baker's Déjà Vu Collection, *"Cottage House" was created in two versions: blue and white. This white home was first introduced in 1987 and retired in December 1994. The cozy home represents the bungalow, where Americans settled down after World War II to start a family.*

ture from the collection to be limited to the year of production, was released in February 1995. "Philadelphia," a 1995 numbered limited edition of 1,500 sculptures, was inspired by Brian's collector friends in Louisville, Kentucky. They gave him a red umbrella during the 1993 Christmas season. On the umbrella were many signatures and drawings of Brian's first house and the Old Kentucky Home, which were sketched by the late Kelly Ostrander. That fall, while Brian was in Philadelphia, a close friend named Raleigh Pettaway passed away. So Brian dedicated "Philadelphia" to Kelly and Raleigh. You'll find Kelly's red umbrella at the door.

Adding to the Collection and Retiring All-Time Favorites

For the first time, accessories to the collection were released in 1995. From a weeping willow to a dog house, the 17 sculptures bring a welcome addition to the collection and complement the nostalgic buildings. For 1996, the collection introduced a "Japanese Tea House" and "Japanese Pine" accessory set, "Country Christmas" and "Village Pharmacy."

To make room in the collection for more handcrafted introductions, a sculpture may be retired, thus no longer be produced. "Cottage House," the famous post-World War II bungalow, was among the earliest sculptures created and the first to be retired. "Cottage House" was the small home where America "began again" and settled down after the war. This little house also represents the baby boom, the cozy place where the family rebuilt its faith in America and a hope for a better world. The sculpture was released in two colors: blue (#1531) and white (#1530). In June 1988, the blue version was retired, followed in December 1994 by the best-selling white cottage.

Michael's Limited
P.O. Box 217
Redmond, WA 98052-0217
(800) 835-0181
Fax (206) 861-0608

COLLECTORS' CLUB

Brian Baker's Déjà Vu Collectors' Club
PRDV
P.O. Box 217
Redmond, WA 98052-0217
(800) 835-0181

Annual Dues: $35.00
Club Year: March1 to March 1

Benefits:
- Membership Gift: Symbol of Membership Sculpture
- Opportunity to Purchase Members-Only Redemption Sculpture
- Bi-annual Newsletter, "Brian's Backyard"
- Membership Card
- Artist Appearances

MIDWEST OF CANNON FALLS

Designed in the Heartland, Crafted Around the World

In a scenic river valley in southern Minnesota - just 30 minutes from the Twin Cities, the small town of Cannon Falls has an unmistakable midwestern charm. With its down-to-earth hospitality and naturally inspiring environment, there's no better home for one of the country's leading designers of collectibles and giftware.

Welcome to Midwest of Cannon Falls!

Midwest of Cannon Falls was founded in 1955 by Kenneth W. Althoff as a small, family-owned business specializing in importing European products. Over the years, Midwest has grown to be an industry leader in designing collectibles and giftware. Since 1985, Kathleen Brekken, daughter of Mr. Althoff, has served as President and CEO, guiding the company into its present position of unparalleled success.

Today, Midwest's line features more than 5,000 products including seasonal giftware, exclusive collectibles and distinctive home decor. While the company continues to import fine collectibles from the Erzgebirge region in Germany, the majority of its line is now exclusively designed by Midwest and crafted around the world.

Distinctive Lighted Houses and Figurines

With its talented team of designers, Midwest has created several collections of popular lighted houses and figurines.

Recreate touching stories of America's heartland with the lifelike accessories and porcelain lighted houses of *Cannon Valley™*. From the neighborly "Ace's Garage" and "Church" to the authentic "Four Square Farmhouse" and "Grain Elevator," *Cannon Valley* continues to rekindle memories of small town living. In 1995, this celebration of American tradition has grown to ten porcelain lighted houses including the new "Dairy Barn," limited to 5,000 pieces. Choose from over 50 true-to-life accessories from the "Farm Cat" and "Dog" to "Parking Meters" and "Telephone Poles." Authentically sculpted and hand-painted, every collectible evokes a wonderful feeling of a simpler place and time. Come home to this nostalgic collection, and feel the warm sunshine of the countryside every day of the year.

"Skeleton Cinema," limited to 5,000 pieces, is one of 13 hauntingly memorable houses in the Creepy Hollow *collection. Lighted from within, each eerie estate casts ghostly shadows to fill any room with the holiday spirit.*

Bring Halloween to life with the wickedly amusing characters and lighted porcelain houses of *Creepy Hollow™*. As the leading line of Halloween collectibles, *Creepy Hollow* is the first to provide collectors with both the sights and sounds of the season. Lighted from within, the eerie estates cast ghostly shadows to fill your home with the holiday spirit. In 1995, treat yourself to the "Skeleton Cinema" - the collection's first limited edition lighted house. Or if collectors are superstitious, they can collect all 13 of *Creepy Hollow's* hauntingly memorable houses. From the battery-operated "Pumpkin Street Lamps" to the light-activated blinking eyes and spooky musical sounds of the "Hinged Tomb With Ghoul," *Creepy Hollow* offers over 40 accessories to make decorating for Halloween really a scream!

Invite the charming bunnies and lighted cottages of *Cottontail Lane™* into your home. Follow the lights of "Town Hall," and meet all the residents in this enchanting springtime village. Visit the "Rosebud Manor," where pastel flowers brightly bloom. Down at the local "Boutique," every bunny becomes a spring beauty. In 1995, Midwest has added four porcelain lighted houses including the limited edition "Rosebud Manor." The current collection features 15 porcelain lighted houses and over 50 accessories. You'll even find a cobblestone road and street lights that actually illuminate this adorable city! Each collectible is sculpted in precious detail and delicately hand-painted. With *Cottontail Lane* beautifully displayed in their homes, collectors can celebrate the wonderful feeling of spring anytime.

Enjoy an endless adventure of fun

Absolutely entrancing, Lou Schifferl's images have an heirloom quality that touches the hearts of collectors everywhere. "Bearing Gifts" is just one of the extraordinary pieces featured in Midwest's Folk Art Gallery Collection.

and friendship. *MouseKins™ Tales of Town & Country* shares the heartfelt stories between two tiny mice families. Although distanced by many miles and different lifestyles, they are forever bonded by a very special relationship. The complete collection features over 50 ornaments and figurines that celebrate every season from Valentine's Day and Easter to Halloween and Christmas.

Extraordinary Folk Art

In addition to its collectible lighted houses and figurines, Midwest develops partnerships with exceptional artists creating exclusive collections that feature unique works of art.

Discover the legends and lore of limited edition folk art collectibles from the *Leo R. Smith III Collection*. Every year, Midwest introduces new limited edition folk art collectibles from this nationally-recognized woodcarver. With his remarkable carving and rare insight, Leo R. Smith III brings the legends of the Mississippi River Valley to life. The complete collection features over 35 seasonal ornaments and figurines, as well as year-round images that appear beautifully in the home any day of the year. Hand-cast in resin, each piece is a precise reproduction of Mr. Smith's original woodcarving. Hand-painted and numbered, every collectible includes a legend card and Certificate of Authenticity.

Create conversation with the original designs featured in *Folk Art Gallery Collection™*. The first of its kind in the collectibles industry, this extraordinary collection features an exciting group of American folk artists. Inscribed with the artist's signature, each piece is a faithful reproduction of the original design. From traditional to contemporary, every artist specializes in different mediums. No other collection combines this diversity and originality to benefit both folk art enthusiasts and the artists. In 1995, you'll find a complete selection of over 60 seasonal and year-round ornaments and figurines.

Exquisite German Collectibles

For over 50 years, Midwest has been sharing handcrafted German treasures with collectors. Today, the company's line features over 250 nutcrackers, as well as smokers, pyramids, blown glass ornaments and wood-turned figures.

Experience the "best of the Erzgebirge" nutcrackers with the *Ore Mountain Collection™*. As the largest U.S. importer of these handcrafted treasures, Midwest unveiled this extraordinary collector's series in 1994. Every wooden figure is imported from the nutcracker's 17th century birthplace in the Erzgebirge region of Germany. Each one is crafted with virtually the identical workmanship that made the nutcracker famous over 250 years ago. From traditional images like soldiers and Santas to contemporary figures like cowboys and golfers, Midwest has carefully preserved the tradition of the Erzgebirge in every *Ore Mountain* nutcracker. In addition to over 70 nutcrackers, the *Ore Mountain Collection* features two limited edition series - *Nutcracker Fantasy* and *A Christmas Carol*.

See how the legend of the nutcracker lives on through the exquisite German craftsmanship of *Christian Ulbricht Nutcrackers*. A world-renowned master in the art of German woodcrafting, Christian Ulbricht creates nutcrackers with exceptional warmth and personality. Each one

Authored by Midwest founder Ken Althoff, The Nutcracker Collector's Guide *features everything from the history of Germany's Erzgebirge region and how nutcrackers are made to the basics of starting a collection.*

Only a whisper is heard as Santa glides through the starry night on his snowy-white reindeer. Exclusively from Midwest of Cannon Falls, "Santa on Reindeer" is the second issue in the limited edition ornament series from Leo R. Smith III.

features the highest detail imaginable - a tradition for perfection passed down through the Ulbricht family since 1709. Even today, every Ulbricht nutcracker is created entirely with German parts and labor. In 1995, Midwest remains the largest U.S. distributor of *Christian Ulbricht* with over 40 nutcrackers including 25 exclusive designs and two limited edition series - *Traditional Santas* and *American Folk Heroes*.

Discover the collectible figurines of *Wendt & Kühn*. Truly an art form, wood-turned figures have been created in the Erzgebirge for generations. Of all the family workshops, *Wendt & Kühn* is recognized as one of the finest. Founded in 1915, the company continues to thrive over 80 years later under family ownership by reproducing the founders' original designs. Midwest is the exclusive distributor of this collection in the U.S. and Canada. With their limited availability, these wood-turned figurines are cherished by collectors around the world. In addition to figurines, Midwest's collection of over 80 *Wendt & Kühn* designs includes ornaments, music boxes and candleholders.

Available at specialty gift shops and department stores across the U.S. and Canada, Midwest continues to offer an extensive variety of exclusive collectibles that appeal to the distinctive taste and personality of every individual. Call 1-800-377-3335 to locate your nearest retailer.

Midwest of Cannon Falls
32057 64th Avenue
P.O. Box 20
Cannon Falls, MN 55009-0020
(800) 377-3335
Fax (507) 263-7752

MISS MARTHA ORIGINALS

All God's Children Figurines Capture the Essence of Childhood and Memories of "Way Back When"

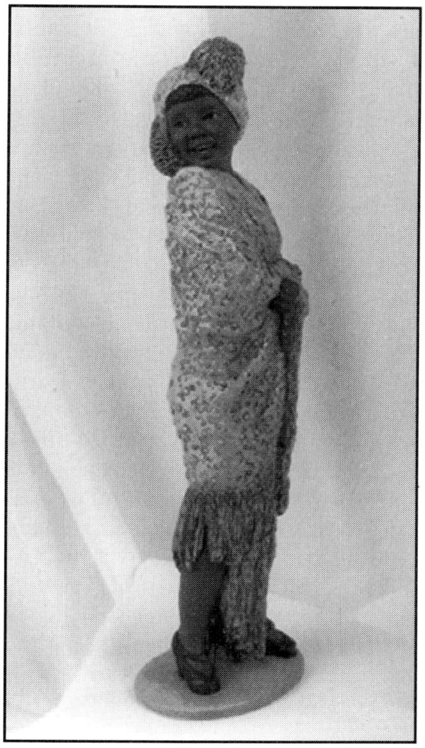

From the Miss Martha Originals Historical Series, *"Bessie Smith" was known to many as the "Empress of the Blues" because of her incredible musical talent. In 1923 her record "Downhearted Blues/Gulf Coast Blues" was the first recording by a black singer to sell over a million copies. She holds an honored place as one of the most important women in the history of American music.*
"Bessie Smith" is 10" high, crafted of a resin and pecan shell flour mixture, and retails for $70.00.

Without a doubt it was the carefree summer days spent on her grandmother's farm that most influenced Martha Holcombe as a child. Those delightful days of long ago still rest warmly in her heart and translate often into the beautiful children that she sculpts today. Summers spent in the Appalachian foothills of Northeast Alabama were filled with days of swimming, fishing, picking cotton and riding the old mule; along with raiding grandmother's watermelon patch.

Ms. Holcombe is a self-taught artist and never stops looking for inspiration for her artwork. Collectors of the *All God's Children* line of figurines keep her supplied with photographs of their loved ones which often inspire Martha Holcombe's art, as well as the names she gives each figurine. Yet, it is God that she credits for her artistic gifts, and it is His love for all His children that is the message of her work.

A native of Alabama, Ms. Holcombe is the mother of three children: Lisa, Keith and Kim. She holds a degree in Mental Health Technology with professional certificates in Counseling, Bible and Christian Education. She is the proud grandmother of Garrett and Alexandria, both of whom are represented by Members-Only club pieces.

How It All Began For Miss Martha

Miss Martha Originals, Inc. began in 1980 with a simple doll pattern design. In order to meet a pledge for a new roof for her church, Gadsden First Church of the Nazarene, she created a soft-sculpture doll that she sold at the church bazaar. Later that initial doll pattern was sold by mail, with proceeds given to the church. It was from the children in her Sunday School class that she was given the name, Miss Martha. It stuck and seemed like just the right name for her company, since it was the needs of the church that gave her the impetus to enter the business world.

The one doll pattern grew to a box of patterns and then enough to fill her garage. Eventually it was necessary to move to a vacant store building, then two store buildings, then in 1985 to a brand-new facility in the Gadsden Industrial Park. The new facility soon became too small, and after continued expansion, it became apparent that a second facility was needed. In 1992 Miss Martha Originals purchased the Coca-Cola plant in Gadsden and moved all administrative offices, the showroom, and the warehouse to that location, giving the original facility increased production capabilities.

It was not the doll patterns that created this sensational growth but the introduction of eight figurines that Miss Martha sculpted and introduced in 1985 that started the company on its dynamic growth spurt. In search of a name for her adorable sculpted children, she simply drew from a favorite Bible verse: "See how much the Father has loved us! His love is so great that we are called God's Children" (1 John 3:1). Thus the name, *All God's Children* was given to the beautiful sculptures by Miss Martha.

At its inception, Miss Martha Originals worked with many United States companies to produce the pecan shell/resin castings from Martha Holcombe's original sculptures. But after the first year the quality did not meet with the artist's high standards, so the decision was made to learn to do the entire process at the plant in Gadsden. The *All God's Children* line is crafted with pride in the U.S.A., at the Gadsden, Alabama, factory.

All God's Children Collectors Celebrate the Precious Memories of Childhood

Each summer for the past five years, collectors have traveled from far and wide to attend the annual All God's Children Family Reunion in Gadsden, Alabama. The 1995 reunion was the biggest yet with over 3,000 collectors coming to meet Miss Martha, and enjoying a day of fellowship, fun, and home-spun love with other collectors and their families.

The reunion is definitely a highlight for collectors from across the land, as they get together for a day of food, friendship, meeting Miss Martha and getting pieces signed, as well as buying and trading at the swap meet. And into all of the above is a jammed-packed day of entertainment and fun.

In 1995 the *All God's Children* line celebrated its tenth anniversary and through the years has won the hearts of its enthusiastic collectors. For some, it is the warm nostalgic vision of times "way back when" that Miss Martha creates in her three-dimensional portraits of African-American children. Yet for others, it is the face of each child which seems to reflect the heart of childhood in all its innocence, tenderness and beauty. In a letter to Miss Martha, Karen Berry of Portland, Oregon, says, "I believe AGC's universal appeal lies in your unique talent for capturing an instant in childhood, and making it last forever."

"William," a 1995 introduction, is every mother's precious child. From the hole in the knee of his pants to the dream he holds in his heart, M. Holcombe's sculpture has again captured the essence of childhood in this delightful, everyday situation. While his clothes are a little rumpled after hours of practice, his face reflects the hope of the future - possibly a home run! "William" is 6" high and retails for $38.00.

Laurie Dudenhoefer of New Brighton, Pennsylvania, says, "I love the manner in which you have captured and honored black children with your God-given talent."

Collector's Club Continues to Delight Collectors

Thousands of other collectors of Miss Martha Originals also have discovered the fun, sharing and touch of family that comes with membership in the *All God's Children* Collector's Club. The annual fee of just $20.00 entitles members to the following benefits: a free figurine, a membership card, free subscription to a quarterly magazine, announcements of special appearances by Martha Holcombe, exclusive invitations to special events such as the annual reunion, opportunity to buy the exclusive "members only" figurine, and a personal checklist to keep accurate records of the collection.

Martha Holcombe keeps a busy schedule dividing her time between sculpting and personal appearances across the country. The Collector's Club magazine keeps collectors notified of upcoming signings, and they are among the first in line to meet the gentle-mannered artist and have their collectibles signed.

Miss Martha Originals and the All God's Children Collector's Club has widespread appeal because there is a little bit of child still left in each of our hearts. These delightfully sculpted children help us to reach back and touch a time when our lives were filled with a sense of awesome wonder.

Richard Gass of Bowen and Associates explained that "The beautiful faces seem to fascinate and capture the viewer's heart immediately." He further added, "that one of the statements I hear most often from collectors and dealers alike is that they truly feel the *All God's Children* collection is one of the most affordable collectible lines in the marketplace." With open edition figurines starting as low as $24.00, these adorable sculptures certainly are a joy to own as well as a good value.

Historical Series Premiered in 1989

While the nostalgic children figurines were being embraced by collectors across the country, Martha began in 1989 to turn her thoughts toward African-American history. She does all of her own research before sculpting each original figurine in the series. This has enriched and challenged her own daily life, as she encounters the determination, vision, and courage that men and women in Black history have unselfishly given as a legacy to the generations that followed.

Her first introduction in 1989 was "Harriet Tubman," who played an influential part in the Underground Railroad, as she bravely faced all odds while securing safety for those yearning for freedom. The "Harriet Tubman" sculpture retired in 1994 but is still a much loved and sought after figurine.

The series includes men and women whose lives have impacted and enriched this nation. The series proudly includes other great historical figures such as "Frederick Douglass," "Ida B. Wells," "Mary Bethune," "George Washington Carver," and the newest introduction "Mary Mahoney" – the first black registered nurse in the United States.

Don Neal, a collector for many years and president of the local New Jersey All God's Children Collector's Club says, "Harriet Tubman was the first piece I purchased." He adds that because "Martha sculpts her own line, you can feel the love she puts into each piece – somehow it just seems to come through. She puts herself into the artwork which gives a truth to it – a genuineness. There is a dignity to the line that is captivating and reflects that she views her art as a ministry."

Miss Martha Originals Created in the U.S.A.

The development of each Miss Martha Original figurine requires an intense period of research, sculpting, and painstaking production. The process begins when Martha Holcombe sculpts the original figurine using soft clay. In the mold room,

"Issie," premiered in the spring of 1995 with five other ragdolls in the latest series by sculptress M. Holcombe named, All God's Children Ragbabies. *Cute and a bit whimsical, each ragbaby in the series has its name and a special message stamped on the bottom of the figurine. "Issie," putting on an old pair of shoes with a hole in the sole, carries the message - 'Bless my sole!' At 2-3/4" high, "Issie" retails for $33.00.*

silicone rubber is then poured over the original sculpture making the first master.

Next, the master prototypes are cast, and the first castings are sent back to Martha for approval. Production molds are then made, and each separate mold is marked with a number which appears on each figurine crafted with that mold. Any one mold can be used only 50 to 75 times before it is destroyed to avoid loss of detail.

Figurines are cast using a special blend of resins and pecan shell flour, washed in a special solution, and then the bottoms of the figurine are sanded. Mold seams are removed and each piece is inspected for quality.

Figurines are painted by skilled craftspeople, with the quality control department inspecting the painting, doing necessary touch-ups and painting of facial features. Antiquing stain is applied next, followed by finishing touches such as hairbows. After a final quality control inspection, figurines are boxed for shipment.

To authenticate each figurine, the signature of M. Holcombe, the name of the piece, copyright line, the phrase "God is Love," and the mold number are etched in. A Certificate of Authenticity is provided with each figurine at the time of purchase. Each collector is invited to establish a personal number for the *All God's Children* pieces through their retailer. As figurines retire, they are then available only on the secondary market.

Additional Collections Sculpted by Miss Martha

In the spring of 1995, Miss Martha introduced a new series called *All God's Children Ragbabies.* With nine pieces in the collection at the present time, these whimsical, ragdoll cuties add still another dimension to the collection sculpted by M. Holcombe. "Issie" has already been singled out by many collectors as a favorite.

Two other collections created by the artist were the *Miss Martha Collection* in which all pieces are now retired; and the *Endearing Memories Series.* Both of these series are more intricate in detail and of a slightly smaller stature, but beautifully capture the tenderness and dignity that is a reflection of Martha Holcombe's goal in creating her art: "I sculpt only with the desire that Jesus Christ will be honored through my work."

Miss Martha Originals, Inc.
P.O. Box 5038
Glencoe, AL 35905
(205) 492-0221
Fax (205) 492-0261

COLLECTORS' CLUB/SHOWROOM

All God's Children Collector's Club
P.O Box 5038
Glencoe, AL 35905
(205) 492-0221

Annual Dues: $20.00
Club Year: June 1-May 31
Collector Year: Anniversary of Sign-Up Date

Benefits:
- Membership Gift: Figurine
- Opportunity to Purchase Members-Only Figurine
- Quarterly Magazine
- Membership Card
- Invitation to Annual "Family Reunion"
- Personal Checklist to Keep Accurate Records of Collection
- Local Club Chapters

Miss Martha Originals, Inc. Showroom
P.O. Box 5038
Glencoe, AL 35905
(205) 492-0221

Hours: Monday through Thursday, 8 a.m.-5 p.m.; Friday, 8 a.m.-Noon
Admission Fee: None

Located at 1119 Chastain Blvd. in Gadsden, Alabama, the showroom displays every figurine sculpted by Martha Holcombe including *All God's Children, Miss Martha Collection, Endearing Memories Collection* and *Ragbabies.*

MY FRIENDS AND ME

Taking a Step Back in Time through Historical Miniature Homes and Buildings

From her studio in the historic village of Hudson, Ohio, Donna Karen Rasbach creates the wonderful historic homes, shops, farms and landmark buildings of My Friends and Me. Hudson was one of the first villages in America to adopt a plan for historic preservation, and it remains among the finest such villages – still architecturally intact – in the country. Originally, Hudson served as inspiration for Donna Karen's miniature, hand-cast buildings. And although the artist's reproductions now encompass a much larger geographic span, they all promote a historic consciousness of the charm and history of a turn-of-the-century village.

As Donna Karen explains, "I want to preserve as much history and architectural detail of the original buildings as possible. What can't be replicated in a sculpture is recaptured in the exclusive historic deed enclosed in the gift box."

The *Main Street Friends*, *Public Square Friends*, *Village Friends* and *Country Friends* collections all are based on real-life buildings and stories of real people. Reflecting typical American architecture, these miniatures include: pioneer homes; classical styles associated with the architecture builders brought to the Western Reserve; Greek and Gothic Revival styles; and Victorian architecture, popular during the heyday of the railroad boom. My Friends and Me will continue to introduce new pieces to these collections – the originals offered by Donna Karen and her firm.

Enthusiastic Collectors Request Reproductions from Sites Across the USA

When collectors discovered the original My Friends and Me collections, Donna Karen began to hear from people across the United States – often with requests for a wider range of subject matter. To fulfill these requests, My Friends and Me has expanded to new collections. *My Chautauqua Friends* collection from New York includes the grand Victorian-style summer hotel, "The Athenaeum," as well as quaint Victorian cottages, and the landmark "Miller Bell Tower," a site where thousands of Americans found their way to Chautauqua by steamship.

Taking a step back in time to experience the grace and charm of the Old South, Donna Karen created the *My Savannah Friends* collection. Collectors are invited to enjoy the "Davenport House," one of America's finest examples of Federal architecture. Also depicted is the "Owens Thomas House," representing English Regency architecture, and "The Herb House," home of the creator of the first experimental garden in America. Collectors cherish these antebellum mansions and the beautiful architecture to be found in Savannah, which is one of the largest Historic Landmark Districts in the nation.

As Donna Karen herself comments, "The garden city, planned in 1733 by General Oglethorpe, sits high on a bluff overlooking the mighty river where cotton was 'white gold' in this busy seaport." She invites collectors to "Stroll the boulevards lined with massive oaks veiled in Spanish moss...to spacious parks and squares embellished by statues and fountains."

The Artist's Childhood Inspires Elegant Buildings

After spending a part of every year of her childhood at her grandparents' home in Charleston, South Carolina, Donna Karen was inspired to do her *Rainbow Row Friends* collection. Originally built as shops on Bay Street in the 1700s, these historic buildings, sporting sherbet-colored paint, now enjoy a new life as a famous tourist attraction.

In honor of her second residence, South Carolina, Donna Karen has recently introduced a new *South Carolina Friends* collection, in response to a request by the State Board of Tourism and Recreation. The reproductions include some of the few historic buildings spared by General Sherman's March to the Sea. Among those represented are the "Governor's Mansion," "Capital," "Lace House,"

The My Country Friends *collection allows "visitors" to (from left to right) stroll down the country lane to "Turner's Mill" for some Perfection flour, to the "Post Office" to visit and pick up the mail, and then on to the "Thompson Bank Barn" to see the farm.*

Donna Karen's My Chautauqua Friends *collection welcomes us to this wonderful "summer place" in New York with its wicker-filled porches, window boxes of flowers, and peaceful, tree-lined streets. Highlights of the Chautauqua "tour" are, from left to right: "Athenaeum Hotel," "Miller Bell Tower," "Brown's Bungalow," "Smith Cottage," "Jane's Cottage," and "Morris Cottage."*

"Boyleston House" and "Longstreet Theatre."

Also in response to requests – particularly from collectibles dealers – My Friends and Me has introduced the *My East Coast Friends* lighthouse collection beginning with the well-known "Tybee Island" and "Harbour Town" Hilton Head lighthouses.

Historically Significant Artwork Presented with Loving Care

Every piece in the My Friends and Me collections is beautifully packaged in its own attractive gift box with tissue paper. Included is an identification label on the building, box, and a label for display. Information offered comprises the name of the building, date of construction, name of the collection, the year introduced, copyright and a symbol for the year of production.

Donna Karen visits and selects each historic building that is reproduced. Her extensive research of the history of the buildings and owners provides the information to transform her models back to their original appearances.

What cannot be replicated in a sculpture is recaptured in the historic deed enclosed in each gift box. A favorite of collectors, each of these hand-rolled parchment scrolls is tied with a tiny gold bow. The deed includes a short history or story complete with American proverb. There are spaces provided for collectors to fill "Grantee" (to) and "Grantor" (from), as well as the date, occasion, year mark and property number.

Collectors and Dealers May Commission Their Own Architecturally Significant "Real Estate"

As a courtesy to the requests of My Friends and Me collectors and dealers, custom service is available with a minimum production of 90 pieces. My Friends and Me dealers can request reproductions exclusive to their stores, as well. To create such pieces, Donna Karen requests a minimum of twelve 35mm color prints of the building, with two copies of each print. She needs a front view "straight on," as well as side views and detail pictures of windows, doors, roof, foundation, etc.

Whether part of a standard collection or a custom creation, each four-to-six-inch My Friends and Me building has a three-dimensional facade so porches stand out, columns are realistic, and doorways are recessed. Each building is hand-cast in cold resin and completely hand-painted with a brush. This touch by a skilled artisan makes each building unique. All buildings have the distinctive My Friends and Me logo stamped on them for easy identification. The number of buildings produced each year is limited due to the intensive hand labor involved.

So beloved are many of Donna

Take a step back in time and experience the grace and charm of the Old South, as portrayed in Donna Karen's My Savannah Friends *collection. In the back row, left to right, are: "Davenport House," "Cathedral of St. John the Baptist," "Andrew Low House," and "The Herb House." In the front row, left to right, are: "Owens Thomas House" and "The Pink House."*

From the My Rainbow Row Friends *collection comes "89 East Bay Street." Built in 1787, this handsome home belonged to John Deas Jr., a descendant of a prominent family of wealthy merchants and planters.*

Karen's buildings that she receives messages of thanks, kudos and awards from around the country. For example, James S. Roberts, Mayor of the City of Medina, Ohio, issued an official Proclamation of Appreciation to Donna Karen for the "Medina City Engine House."

Mayor Roberts' proclamation reads, in part, as follows: "Whereas The 'Engine House' of the City of Medina is a perfect example of Donna Karen's precise attention to detail and a piece that anyone would be proud to own; and, Whereas Donna Karen needs to be commended for the extensive research she has done on each and every piece created – they are by far 'works of art;' and, Now Therefore, I, James S. Roberts, Mayor of the City of Medina, do hereby extend sincere appreciation to Donna Karen Rasbach of the My Friends and Me Collections."

Hudson, Ohio Sparks a Nationwide Enthusiasm

There might never have been a My Friends and Me if it had not been for the "historical inspiration" in Donna Karen's own "stomping grounds" of Hudson, Ohio. To her delight, early research turned up many references to the artist's current hometown, including favorable comparisons to Williamsburg, Virginia, and Charleston, South Carolina. Donna Karen learned that she had "this architectural gem right here in my backyard," and therefore made the Hudson landmarks early "stars" of her collection.

"People come from all over the country to see Hudson," Donna Karen reports proudly, and it is clear that no matter how diverse her collections grow, the Ohio town will remain special in her heart. "People (locally) drive by these buildings every day without giving them a second thought." Now that Hudson's finest architecture appears in the same collection with the "crown jewels" of Chautauqua, Charleston, and other famous historical cities, she hopes that her own city's wonders will be more fully appreciated and treasured.

My Friends and Me
P.O. Box 2274
Hudson, OH 44236
(216) 650-6157
Fax (216) 650-2342

OLD WORLD CHRISTMAS

Creating Tomorrow's Heirlooms Today

1995 marked Old World Christmas' celebration of their 20th anniversary. It was back in 1975 that Tim and Beth Merck, owners of Old World Christmas, decided to branch out from their locally-owned antique business into the fledgling market of collectible-quality tree ornaments. With their creative talent and hard work Old World Christmas has flourished, and millions of homes throughout the country will be trimmed with the Mercks' exclusive decorations this Christmas.

Old World Christmas began more or less by accident. The Mercks owned a retail store in Spokane, Washington, in which they sold antiques they imported directly from Europe. During a buying trip in Europe, they purchased a large assortment of German Christmas decorations, inspired by the heirloom ornaments Beth's grandmother had put on her Christmas trees. This new venture proved to be extremely successful, and before long, Beth and Tim were not only selling to retail customers, but were wholesaling their decorations to local merchants as well. Soon they phased out their antiques business to pursue Christmas in earnest. As Tim Merck says with a chuckle, "Handling ornaments is much easier than moving pianos, armoires and sideboards!" Shortly thereafter, they commissioned a family workshop in Germany and began working directly with the manufacturers.

The Bells, Stars and Stripes and Santas from Old World Christmas' Patriotic Ornament Series *celebrate our nation's freedom and the spirit of Christmas.*

Beth eventually became very involved in developing both color schemes and original designs, and soon the business began to flourish. Since the very beginning, the company has held the philosophy that it is creating tomorrow's heirlooms today. As they use only the finest of raw materials, creating each piece individually to the most exacting of standards, heirloom quality is guaranteed. Old World Christmas will settle for nothing less.

Patriotic Theme Featured in New Series

Beth Merck's most recent additions to the Old World Christmas product lines include a patriotic ornament series, a 10th addition to the series of Santa Lights, first introduced in 1985, and, exclusive to Old World Christmas, the *E.M. Merck Signature Series* of nutcrackers.

Old World Christmas is proud to introduce its patriotic ornament collection commemorating the 50th anniversary of World War II's end and honoring our brave veterans who fought for our freedom and peace. We can reflect and be thankful that today's Christmas celebrations are free from the pain, suffering and blight clouding the Christmases in Europe and the world during the war.

Uncle Sam is the epitome of American patriotism. As reflected in E.M. Merck's most recent addition to Old World Christmas's line of unique and distinctive nutcrackers, this "Uncle Sam" nutcracker is destined to inspire pride and respect in the youngest of hearts during the Christmas season. From his jaunty hat to his patriotic attire, this magnificent nutcracker is destined to be a cherished collector's piece as it inspires collectors to recall the dedication and patriotism of our war heroes, as well as their desire to be home for the Christmas holidays and in the presence of loved ones.

Also, mouth-blown and intricately hand-painted with the care and quality that has become the trademark of Old World Christmas, their bright and colorful glass patriotic ornament theme will enliven and enrich any tree. Made from antique molds, the cheerful ornaments celebrate the freedom and joy the heart of our nation shares with the spirit of Christmas. Bells, Stars and Stripes, Santas and many more ornament patterns shine in tribute to the peace and liberty of Christmas and America. The reds, whites and blues sparkling with Christmas cheer will be proud additions to Christmas trees "from sea to shining sea."

Ten-Year Tradition of *Santa Lights* Continues

Old World Christmas' "Santa in Sleigh" is the tenth anniversary edition in the *Santa Light* series. Since its first Santa Light in 1985, these annual introductions have become collectible additions to holiday celebrations throughout the country. The excitement surrounding these pieces is overwhelming! Each year, before the design for the new Santa Light has been announced, Old World Christmas receives several calls each day requesting information on the forthcoming light.

E.M. Merck fashions each finely crafted glass light after a lovable, familiar Santa figure. The *Santa Lights* come complete with a wood base, U.L. approved cord with switch, and light bulb. Each piece is presented in a glossy red box featuring a full-color picture of the *Santa Light.* A brass "Ten Year Anniversary Edition" commemorative plaque is included with each "Santa in Sleigh" Light and may, at the option of the owner, be applied to the wooden base.

To ensure their continuing importance as collectibles and to make room for new introductions, each design is retired after three years. The earliest designs are now coveted collectibles sought after by Christmas enthusiasts everywhere.

Meet E.M. Merck

A common thread throughout the successes of Old World Christmas lies in the acclaimed talents of its artist, E.M. Merck. Old World Christmas is sure that all avid collectors of their ornaments and collectibles are more than curious about who is the design genius behind the fabulous products that grace their trees, wreaths, garlands and showcases. Well, today you, the reader, are in for a treat as Old World Christmas would like you to meet its talented artist and premier designer, E.M. Merck.

Beth, as she likes to be called, began designing for Old World Christmas ten years ago. It was at this time that she and her husband, Tim Merck, joined forces with the German family workshop, Inge-Glas, to produce mouth-blown glass ornaments for importation into the United States.

"Santa in Sleigh" Light commemorates the Tenth Anniversary of the Santa Light Series *from Old World Christmas.*

Talented artist and premier designer, E.M. Merck, is the creative force behind Old World Christmas' successful line of ornaments and collectibles.

Skilled glassblowers from the tiny village of Neustadt, Germany, use actual antique molds to produce the majority of the ornaments, and Beth creates all of the painting designs. Her attention to detail, exceptional eye for color and intuition about collectibles has helped to create a tremendous demand for Old World Christmas products. Her talents were nurtured by her many years of studying fine arts, art history, and German cultural traditions at Pomona College, Gonzaga University and Eastern Washington University.

In addition to her glass ornament designs, Beth is also the creative genius behind all of the Old World Christmas light covers, *Santa Lights*, and exclusive nutcracker designs. Where does she receive her design inspiration? Beth was quoted in the October 1992 issue of *Collector's Mart* magazine as approaching new projects "with the idea in mind of what a child would think seeing this for the first time. I want the child to have feelings of awe, amazement, warmth." This sentiment is certainly clearly depicted and brought to life in all of Beth's work.

The most recent additions to Beth's extensive design portfolio are exclusive nutcrackers that are produced by a German wood workshop. These unique designs have won the hearts of collectors and dealers alike. E.M. Merck's new designs in 1995 include, among others, the Uncle Sam nutcracker, a Cowboy nutcracker, a Panda, a Pharmacist, an Attorney, and also a Sugar Plum Fairy nutcracker. This "Sugar Plum Fairy" is very special, not only because it is hand-produced with Old World Christmas's trademark standards of quality and attention to detail, but because when one purchases this unique collectible, Old World Christmas donates a portion of the proceeds to the Juvenile Diabetes Foundation. All of Beth's designs possess incredible detail, whimsy and charm, and all in this new series are signed by the artist herself.

Creating Ornaments in the Old World Tradition

The steps involved in creating tomorrow's heirlooms are numerous. Several times each year, Tim and Beth Merck travel to Germany, where they monitor the multitude of steps and tremendous amount of tedious details involved in making each piece. A large number of their ornaments are still blown in cottages nestled in small towns in northern Bavaria, but whether they are produced in the cottages or in the family-owned factory, the process Inge-Glas follows is exactly as it was one hundred years ago.

Each ornament is made from a "blank" which is a small hollow ball of glass with a 6" hollow stem. The glassblower heats the ball of glass over a Bunsen burner until it is red hot. He then sets that portion of the blank into the bottom half of the mold, covers it with the top half and blows on the stem until the molten glass conforms to the shape of the mold. He then removes the ornament from the mold, reheats it a second time and gives it one last puff. This extra step tempers the ornament, preventing stress cracks. Many of these molds were lost for years when German products were out of favor due to wars or changes in decorating styles. Thousands of molds disappeared forever during this time because they were

The 9" "Sugar Plum Fairy" from the E.M. Merck Signature Collection *retails for $55.00. Old World Christmas donates a portion of the sales from this charming nutcracker to the Juvenile Diabetes Foundation.*

converted into cobblestones for streets and building materials for homes.

Silvering the ornament is the next step. A mixture of silver nitrate, ammonia and distilled water is poured into the ornament, followed by a few drops of a combination of saltpeter, sugar and distilled water. The solution is an unappealing brown until the ornament is dipped into a hot water bath where it magically turns into silver. This process gives the ornament its mirror-like interior and greatly enhances its reflectivity. Next it is dipped into an iron chloride solution, rinsed in clear water, and is then placed upside down on a nail and placed in a drying oven. Each one of Old World Christmas's ornaments goes through all of these silvering steps regardless of its final color.

When the ornament is dry, a painter hand-dips it into the appropriate background paint. It is then put back to dry. From there it is taken to an artist's table for painting. Applying each color is a separate step and the ornament is set aside to dry before the next color may be added.

Next, glitter is applied where needed, the stem is broken off, and the trademark star cap is put in place. It is difficult to estimate how much time is involved in making each ornament as each mold is different, but obviously a tremendous amount of labor is required. The steps are numerous, and the quality of the final product is unsurpassed.

Collectors' Club Offers Many Benefits

As these items inspire collectibility, naturally Old World Christmas has begun a Collectors' Club. Formed three years ago, the Club was designed in response to tremendous demand from avid collectors across the country to obtain more information about Old World Christmas and its history, as well as gain access to information on limited edition pieces, exclusively for Club members only. The benefits of the Club are numerous. For a $30.00 annual membership fee, Club members receive a 100-page full-color guide featuring beautiful pictures of all the items currently available in Old World Christmas' line. Club members also receive informative newsletters containing articles on new and retiring products, and stories, perhaps on the making of the wooden nutcrackers or the history behind the trademark star cap.

Another valuable benefit to becoming a Club member is the opportunity to purchase special members-only pieces. Every year Old World Christmas introduces new products, designed by their artist only for members of the Club, and every year they retire the previous years' pieces, thus guaranteeing their collectibility. For 1995 the Collectors' Club featured a glass ornament called the "Large Christmas Carousel" and a special member of the *EM Merck Signature Series* of nutcrackers, the "Konigsee King." Both of these valuable pieces are handcrafted and imported from Germany, and are available to Club members through their favorite Old World Christmas retailer.

And, in addition to all this, members also receive a complimentary gift upon joining or renewing their Club membership. Free to Club members is another exclusive German collectible entitled "A Heavenly Gift." Having a retail value of $32.50, this carefully painted angel reflector ornament adorned with spun glass and a delicate wire wrap is destined to become a treasured family heirloom.

The Club is a fun and informative way to communicate valuable information to Old World Christmas' most avid and dedicated supporters – the private collector. Hopefully with the continued success of the Collectors' Club and with Beth's artistic genius and inspiration, Old World Christmas will continue to spark magic and joy in the hearts of Christmas enthusiasts everywhere, remaining a vital force in the collectibles market for many years to come.

Old World Christmas
P.O. Box 8000
Spokane, WA 99203
(509) 534-9000
Fax (509) 534-9098

COLLECTORS' CLUB

Old World Christmas Collectors' Club
P.O. Box 8000 – Department C
Spokane, WA 99203
(800) 962-7669

Annual Dues: $30.00
Club Year: Anniversary of Sign-Up Date

Benefits:
- Membership Gift: "Angel Reflector"
- Opportunity to Purchase Members-Only Pieces
- Quarterly Newsletter, "Old World Christmas Star"
- Buy/Sell Matching Service through Newsletter
- 100-Page, Full-Color, Collectors' Guide Detailing Complete Current Product Line
- Local Retailer Listings

PACIFIC RIM IMPORT CORP.

Bristol Township and *Waterfront Collections* Set Sail With English Charm

With its winding exterior stairway, the "Bristol Channel Lighthouse" shines its blinking light to passing ships. Introduced in 1995, the third porcelain lighthouse to the Bristol Waterfront *line stands 8-1/2" tall and sells for about $30.00.*

Nestled along the Avon and Fromme Rivers in England, there's a quaint waterfront village that was once known around the world for its bustling trading port. For two centuries, Bristol claimed the country's second most important shipping center. With a harbor in the heart of the city, the Bristol skyline reflected an interesting mix of ship masts and church spires. But during World War II, nearly half of the city was destroyed.

Today, Bristol is experiencing a revival – not only along its old cobblestone streets but through a porcelain village collection by Pacific Rim Import Corporation. Known as the *Bristol Township Collection*, the collectibles have built a new niche for the company and put a new twist on the popularity of cottages. *Bristol Township*, introduced in the spring of 1990 with seven pieces, and followed quickly by six more, was the company's first venture into a line of collectibles. A few years later, the *Bristol Waterfront* line brought back the city's nautical roots. Pacific Rim Import Corp. has since dedicated itself to other collectible lines while turning *Bristol Township* into a very unique village.

The Founding of *Bristol Township*

Bristol Township Collection wasn't initially envisioned or created from its namesake British city. Instead, artist Pat Sebern was asked to draw a half dozen designs of porcelain buildings for Pacific Rim, which wanted to explore new avenues. She came up with a tiny village of charming Victorian buildings, including a manor, cottage and livery stable. When it came time to name the new collection, Sebern proposed "Bristol," which seemed to add an Olde English flavor to the buildings while distinguishing it from other cottages on the market.

But with the name, Sebern became more interested in the story behind Bristol and its harbor. Inspired by this, Sebern submitted drawings in 1991 for a waterfront version of *Bristol Township*. She traveled to Britain, where she studied the Victorian architecture, read about Bristol's past, and experienced firsthand the city's waterfront views. She was particularly intrigued by the harbor areas of western England, where she took photos and made sketches of small but important details. She traveled from London to Bristol where history books chronicled the major damage that the city suffered during World War II. Many wonderful buildings were ultimately replaced by new ones. Fortunately, Sebern spent time in the archives of the city's main library to study line drawings, descriptions and a few photographs of old Bristol buildings and landmarks as they appeared before the war.

Sebern also visited several coastal cities with waterfront architecture. Original stone work remained on many towers and bridges, and every neighborhood seemed to boast a major church. Numerous coaching inns and pubs lined the streets, many with their founding dates etched in stone. Hanging signs made of wood and resembling book illustrations adorned most buildings. These displayed the owner's or business' name with great flair, and gave information about each shop to villagers passing by.

Innovative Yet Traditional Designs Reflect Bristol's Olde World Charm

Returning to Pacific Rim headquarters in Seattle, Sebern began working these ideas into new designs. The *Waterfront* buildings were creatively designed to appear suspended above water. To achieve this effect, Sebern undercut the bottom edge and added boardwalks and pilings. Small hanging signs were developed on wire brackets to fit into small holes in the porcelain buildings. Mounted at the corners or near the doors of these pieces, the signs help recreate the traditional rustic street scenes with most shops and inns bearing two or three. The signs identify the "Customs House" and "Admiralty Shipping." They tell that the "Rusty Knight Inn" provides extra moorage for travelers' boats. To further add to the realistic scenes, a felt ground cover depicting cobblestones and brick roads was developed to properly display the collector villages. The designs are screen printed on felt with various color backgrounds. This creates the look of stony roads, courtyards and narrow lanes often seen in the English

This porcelain light cover ornament portraying the popular "Portshead Lighthouse" was the first in a dated series. The lighthouse, which measures 4-1/2" and retails for about $10.00, captures the quaint waterfront architecture.

countryside and older parts of cities. The product can be cut into individual lanes or be placed down like a blanket with the buildings arranged on top.

Another unusual feature is the light, which is mounted in the bottom of each building. All four sides of the building are illuminated, allowing collectors to set up the scenes from any angle, as the light bulb is hidden from view. The cords can then run down through the felt to create a neighborhood of cobblestone or brick lanes instead of a maze of electrical wiring. The introduction of the *Waterfront* also created a wave of collector demand for a product that resembled water. In response, Pacific Rim packaged Bristol Bay Reflective Film. When used over a smooth cardboard or foam board, the product puts the buildings exactly where they should be: on the waterfront.

Additions Keep *Bristol's* Population and Popularity Growing

Pacific Rim, which was founded about 40 years ago, had its first group of collectibles, *Bristol Township*, produced in Taiwan. While experimenting with different ideas, a few goals remained constant: striving for the highest quality and compatibility with other cottages on the market. Production on all *Bristol Township* pieces was eventually moved to China in 1992. Shortly thereafter, the *Waterfront* pieces were introduced and appeared in stores in time for the 1992 holiday season. At this time, the first lighthouse was also approved for production with its unique two-light design. It features an old stone and timber building with a pier at one end. Its stone tower has a second light that extends up inside and blinks through the cut out windows. In 1994, a second light house, "Portshead Lighthouse," was added. In 1995, a third lighthouse, "Bristol Channel Lighthouse," joined the collection.

In 1993, six pieces were retired, most of which are available now only on the secondary market. The most popular of these was the "Iron Horse Livery," an interesting building that has four hanging signs.

Artist Builds New Cottages Through a Labor of Love

Sebern continues researching new ideas for future introductions to the *Bristol Township Collection*. Sebern, a self-taught artist, began her career as a fashion illustrator and then spent several years involved in Western fine art. When she first joined Pacific Rim Import Corporation in the late 1980s, she did floral design and window display. But a new direction was taken when the opportunity arose to design porcelain houses and establish a collectible group for the company. With each cottage, Sebern carefully researches the architecture and style of the buildings to ensure accuracy.

In 1994, four new buildings were added to the collection. *Bristol Township* (the non-waterfront group) was joined by the "Shotwick Inn and Surgery," a colorful inn where the local doctor also hangs his shingle; and "Surrey Road Church" with its stone arched windows and cross on top. The *Waterfront* line was increased by the "Portshead Lighthouse" with a blinking tower light and no Christmas decor; and the "Tattler Foghorn Inn" combination that includes a newspaper, print shop and inn all rolled into one.

Also introduced were four sets of very small resin figures that inhabit the township: a set of eight caroler musicians, two smaller sets of villagers and an additional group of popular waterfront characters. In 1995, the third lighthouse with its exterior stairway and blinking light was joined by a much requested school. As part of the original *Bristol Township*, "King's Gate School" features four brick chimneys and a coal bin. A porcelain light cover ornament portraying the popular "Portshead Lighthouse" was also introduced in 1995 and is the first in a dated ornament series. The *Bristol Township* and *Waterfront* continue to attract additional admirers with prices ranging from $25.00 to $45.00.

Bunny Toes and *Birthday Bunnies* Celebrate Life's Special Moments

With the popularity of the *Bristol Township Collection*, Pacific Rim introduced a second group of collectibles in

Designed by artist Pat Seburn, "Beth – Back to School" marks that memorable time in September. The adorable bunny walks to school carrying her books, chalkboard and an apple for the teacher.

"Pieter — Higher Education" portrays an adventurous bunny climbing a fence on his way home from school. The Birthday Bunnies *collection by artist Pat Sebern features figurines representing memorable scenes from every month of the year.*

the spring of 1994. *Bunny Toes* debuted with "Tillie and Timothy" in their spring gardens while "Winifred and Wendell" scooped up arms full of tulips. These adorable characters stand about 3" tall and are created in cold cast resin. Delicate watercolor details grace each piece and give the bunnies a heartwarming appeal.

The original *Bunny Toes* group carries a springtime theme and includes a flowered gazebo and garden trellis accessories. A large light-up piece of "Willis and Winifred" is also available. With the summer of 1995, *Birthday Bunnies* came bounding onto the scene. Designed by Sebern, this group of bunnies is leaping into every season as they commemorate birthdays, childhood and all the simple pleasures of growing up. There are 24 figurines as two bunnies represent each month of the year. "Molly" and "Chester" can be found in February while "Anabell" and "Nicholas" romp through July. Wearing the charming country attire of pinafores and overalls, these bunnies portray typical childhood activities. They tell stories of sand castles, snowmen, wishing wells and kites. *Bunny Toes* and *Birthday Bunnies* are affordably priced between $13.00 and $20.00. With its product line of thousands of items, Pacific Rim truly lives up to its motto of a "Company For All Seasons."

Pacific Rim Import Corp.
5930 4th Avenue South
Seattle, WA 98108
(800) 425-5932
Fax (206) 767-9179

PENDELFIN STUDIOS

From Favorite Fairy Tales to Cheerful Rabbits: Timeless Collectibles with A Heart

On the day that Elizabeth the Second was crowned Queen of England, two young English women also set out on a new course by founding their own business. It began as a quiet hobby for Jeannie Todd and Jean Walmsley Heap, who both enjoyed modeling small clay figures as gifts for their friends. Jean designed and modeled their very first piece – a witch flying against the moon with a wide-eyed cat on her shoulder.

Soon their enterprise grew too large for their English garden hut and spilled over into Jeannie's kitchen. They eventually moved their business to a small shop that attracted customers from the surrounding areas. Today, the company, now known as PenDelfin Studios, is reaching collectors around the world with its traditional collectibles designed to capture the heart and imagination.

Little did they know back in 1953 that their at-home venture would become their international claim to fame.

PenDelfin Begins with a Child's Dream

For PenDelfin founder Jean Walmsley Heap, her artistic talent can be traced to childhood illnesses. The times resting and recovering presented idyllic opportunities for Jean to dream and sketch her visions with colored pencils. As soon as she began sketching, her symptoms were forgotten.

By the age of ten, Jean began selling her pictures with a view to buying a wooden hut "to live and paint in." This idea was discouraged, but permission was granted to use the broom cupboard under the stairs which she called "Studio One."

Three years later, Jean was awarded a scholarship to the Burnley School of Art, where she trained under the guidance of distinguished artist Noel H. Leaver. He had great faith in Jean's talents, teaching her clay modeling as well as painting and composition.

Later, Jean began exhibiting child studies and flower paintings regularly in art galleries. During World War II, she was commissioned by the Canadian Red Cross to design large murals for the bare walls of wartime nurseries, as a gift to the children of Britain.

Jean and friend Jeannie Todd then teamed up to start their own company. Since they lived in the shadow of Pendle Hill (the old Witch Hill of "Mist over Pendle") and were creating elfin characters, the partners selected Pendle and Elfin – hence PenDelfin – for their company's name. A broomstick was added to their trademark for good luck.

Jean's strengths were designing and modeling. Jeannie would steer the model-making and casting processes. Friends and relatives helped as unpredictable calamities peppered their first days, such as the time boiling rubber fumes clung to the walls of the Todd house. (The modeling process was moved to her kitchen since the hut had no electricity.) Saucepans burned up with regularity. Each woman sacrificed a treasured pressure cooker for the sake of their craft. They persevered undaunted and determined. In the end, an 8-inch high "Pendle Witch" emerged from their efforts. The artists had proven themselves ready for a real studio!

From a childhood dream to an international company, PenDelfin founder Jean Walmsley Heap enjoys more than four decades of success with her collectibles business. She serves as chairman of PenDelfin.

Doreen Noel Roberts (known as Dorian) arrived at PenDelfin in 1954 to learn about the business. Today, her designs are the heartbeat of the company.

A New, Larger Home For PenDelfin

PenDelfin Studios was established in a shop in the village of Harle Syke. Initially, Jean's character, "Little Thrifty," was slated for casting, but first efforts were a disaster. The stove was destroyed and the finished product looked like anything but "Little Thrifty." They turned their attention back to a familiar subject: the witch.

This sculpture proved to be a charm. Before long, Pendle Hill witches were selling with great vigor at a local inn. Neither Jean nor Jeannie's first wish was to produce figures simply for the money. However, "business is business," they agreed. Witch production at PenDelfin went into full swing.

Various other models followed, but it wasn't until Jean created "Father Rabbit" that orders began to roll in. PenDelfin Studios began opening offices in Canada, the United States and England.

New Artist Volunteers to Join the Company

As the company grew, the pair also found some much-needed artistic help. In 1954, the studio had become a gathering place for local artisans and job seekers – including Doreen Noel Roberts (known as Dorian) who wandered in looking for employment, and by the time she left, an unpaid position was hers. She agreed to work in return for a complete education in the business (and an agreement to allow her pet hen Sylvana to accompany her to work).

After absorbing each step of production, Doreen ultimately became a designer and sculptor of the famous PenDelfin rabbits. She now designs and models full time for PenDelfin and is a member of its Board of Directors, as well as a partner in the PenDelfin Design Unit.

PenDelfin Thrives Through Decades of Change and Growth

New molding methods, state-of-the-art equipment, modern management systems and a growing list of new sculptures pushed PenDelfin into the 1960s. Makeshift work stations helped for awhile. Then the seams again began to burst. Another move was the only answer – this time, to three floors with a private elevator. PenDelfin had arrived!

Larger quarters heralded international distribution. In 1965, PenDelfin officially entered the North American markets. In the midst of this came yet another move to Brennand Mill where more efficient casting systems were designed and personnel expansion marked the next 12 years.

By the time PenDelfin's owners celebrated the 20th anniversary of the move into Jeannie's garden hut, another landmark event had taken place: a permanent home was found. In 1973, PenDelfin bought half a building called Cameron Mill. The founders watched in amazement as 140 employees moved into 32,000 square feet.

The new space was mind-boggling: elegant offices and three elevators moved employees in and out. There was room for a beautiful design studio and space galore for the installation of the company's pride and joy: a special casting machine which quickened production time while still employing handcrafting steps.

In general, the year of the move into Cameron Mill brought a welcome mix of excitement. PenDelfin began to attract attention from the media. A gold-stamped invitation to tea with Queen Elizabeth arrived. Accepting this much-coveted invitation was a culmination of years of hard work – especially for Jeannie, who died a year later.

In 1976, PenDelfin expanded geographically. Jean found a perfect haven for the design unit in Wales. Jean, staff members and assorted animals relocated belongings to an old Welsh farm on the Lleyn Peninsula. For the next 14 years, both Cameron Mill and Wales experienced unparalleled success until a phone call on the night of June 11, 1986, announced the unthinkable: Cameron Mill had gone up in flames during the night. Newspapers described it as "the million pound blaze." To some, the end of PenDelfin seemed inevitable.

"Forty Winks and "Vanilla," designed by Doreen Noel Roberts, are from PenDelfin's adorable Bed Series *and* Picnic Series.

From the Rubble, a Renewed Commitment

As hopeless as the situation might have seemed, a determined PenDelfin family spent little time grieving. One week after the fire, a message arrived in Wales stating: "We are back in production." Jean ignored requests to stay in Wales, arriving at the charred building in hat and boots. She helped move salvageable items to 10,000 square feet of dry flooring at the rear of the building.

Workers brought chairs and tables from home. Meanwhile, negotiations to purchase the other half of the Mill began before the first mop hit the floor. Miraculous as it may seem, holiday decorations were being strung across the refurbished facility by Christmas. Staff members gleefully congratulated each other and happily celebrated the holidays. This incident, more than any other, describes the character of PenDelfin folks.

PenDelfin Family Circle Collectors Club Welcomes New Members

Today, the tradition, dedication and quality continue with new introduc-

"Bellman" is ready to announce all the news! Designed by Jean Walmsley Heap, this confident rabbit is the 1995 membership figurine for the PenDelfin Family Circle Collectors Club. Along with other benefits, members receive the figurine free with their membership.

In 1995, members of the PenDelfin Family Circle Collectors Club had the opportunity to acquire "Georgie and the Dragon," a whimsical figurine designed by Doreen Noel Roberts. The figurine was available exclusively to members.

tions and opportunities for collectors to discover the magic of PenDelfin. The PenDelfin Family Circle Collectors Club completed its third successful year in 1995 and continues to grow with hundreds of new members each month. 1995 club members received a free charismatic little rabbit named "Bellman," specially designed by Jean Walmsley Heap. Members also had the privilege of acquiring "Georgie and the Dragon," the 1995 exclusive Members-Only piece. The friendly rabbit and dragon are sculpted on a base unique to PenDelfin.

Other membership benefits include a subscription to the quarterly "PenDelfin Times" newsletter, a membership card which entitles members to attend special events, and the opportunity to take a tour of the PenDelfin Studio in England. Membership fees are $30.00 in the United States and $40.00 in Canada.

For information on the PenDelfin Family Circle Collectors Club, please write to: Miller Import Corp., 230 Spring Street, N.W., Suite 1238, Atlanta Gift Mart, Atlanta, GA, 30303; or phone (404) 523-3380 or (800) 872-4876.

Collectors simply can't resist the annual event figurine. PenDelfin's 1995 "Event Piece" was available for purchase at special store promotions and artist events through the end of the year.

PenDelfin Continues Looking to the Future

Collectors not familiar with PenDelfin's cheery rabbits, fairy tale characters, mice, elves, pixies, "real estate," wagons, decorative figures and displays may marvel at how this little company grew from a wooden hut in an English garden to an international company. Couple PenDelfin's eclectic history with the endearing collectible art coming from individual hearts and minds, and success is understandable. The PenDelfin product is timeless and the dedicated staff at PenDelfin combines artistic genius, tenacity and loyalty with a commitment to excellence that assures continued and ever-growing success.

PenDelfin Studios
Miller Import Corp.
300 Mc Lane
Keasbey, NJ 08832
(800) 547-2006
Fax (908) 417-0031

COLLECTORS' CLUB

PenDelfin Family Circle
Miller Import Corp.
230 Spring St. N.W., Suite 1238
Atlanta Gift Mart
Atlanta, GA 30303
(404) 523-3380 or (800) 872-4876

Annual Dues: $30.00
Club Year: January-December
Collector Year: Anniversary of Sign-Up Date

Benefits:
- Membership Gift: Figurine
- Opportunity to Purchase Members-Only Figurine
- Quarterly Newsletter, "The PenDelfin Times"
- Membership Card and Certificate
- Buy/Sell Matching Service
- Special Events
- Local Club Chapters

POSSIBLE DREAMS® LTD.

Clothtique® Originals Open Up World of Possibilities

Recreated from a Dec. 4, 1920, Saturday Evening Post *cover portrait, this Clothtique Santa reviews his holiday finances in "Balancing the Budget." The 11" figurine features the popular Clothtique blend of stiffened cloth, resin and porcelain for a unique look.*

It has been said that creativity lies in the eyes of those who look at the same old thing and see something brand new. Leni Miler and Warren Stanley took that philosophy to heart when they founded Possible Dreams Ltd. Teaming up in a small business that focused on designing, modeling and producing porcelain inspirational products, the pair began to look beyond the religious giftware market to find a need for high quality porcelain in the general collectibles area.

In 1983, Possible Dreams launched a line of figurines, including clowns and carousel horses. The response was discouraging: too much competition matched by too little experience. But there was a flicker of encouragement that came in the form of a limited edition Santa dropped into the line at the last minute. Its overwhelming success set a new course for Possible Dreams, and the search began for more items to build the company into a Christmas specialty house.

In 1984, Stanley discovered a wonderful line of stiffened cloth angels and Santas, which would soon become the flagship of the Possible Dreams line. At first, production problems curtailed the success of the Santas, but the angels were an instant hit. Several names were suggested to describe the new product line including Clothtique – which was added to the gift market vocabulary and has since added Possible Dreams as a collectibles leader.

Clothtique Originals Builds a Firm Foundation

For the company that took an unknown process for stiffening cloth and nurtured it into one of the country's leading giftware lines, every day is a holiday. The company's collectibles go beyond the Christmas season. Now after more than a decade, Clothtique Originals from Possible Dreams has grown from a few angels and a handful of Santas to a broad offering of elegant collectibles. Providing inspiration are some of America's most renowned artists: Tom Browning, Judith Ann Griffith, Lynn Bywaters, Jan Brett, Judi Vaillancourt and Thomas Blackshear, to name a few. Pepsi-Cola®, *The Saturday Evening Post* covers by Norman Rockwell and J.C. Leyendecker, Warner Bros.®, and most recently, Garfield® have also joined the Clothtique family.

Creation of a Clothtique Original

Centuries ago, a process much like Clothtique originated in Southern Europe. Yet for most of today's art masters, the concept was completely new. The artists and designers at Possible Dreams perfected the technique. The resulting medium combines charm, beauty and a special, life-like "feel" that is unique to Clothtique Originals by Possible Dreams.

This blend of old-world artistry and modern technology, as well as the mixture of porcelain, resin and cloth makes Clothtique figurines look realistic. The textures of fur, rich fabrics, embroidered tapestry and soft folds of a robe come alive in each piece.

Clothtique Santas and Other Figurines Deliver Originality and Memories

Santas remain the most popular Clothtique figurines, with new introductions that let collectors share the Christmas spirit all year. Sometimes – as in "Homespun Holiday" featuring an African-American Santa – the legendary character is portrayed in his traditional role and red garb to make his delivery for December 25.

Other times, a special friend joins Santa. In "Frisky Friend," Santa has an overzealous puppy. "Special Treat" features Santa holding an adorable baby deer along with his traditional bag of toys. Some Clothtique Santas also feature exquisite European Victorians dressed in luxurious greens, blues and whites with tapestry and fur trim. Their faces reflect an Old World nobility from vibrant eyes to beards rich with a sculptured integrity.

The *American Artists Collection* showcases the talents of artists, who bring their own touch to Santas and the Clothtique process. Among the introductions is "Santa Fe Santa" by Virginia Wiseman, who captures the familiar Southwest feeling of blue jeans, peasant shirts and a string of hot chili peppers. Lisa Nilsson's "Riding High" shows St. Nick in a fur-trimmed Old World outfit, wheeling around on a tricycle with a basket of goodies.

From Warner Bros., Possible Dreams is making show-biz history by dressing

Bugs Bunny in a Clothtique Santa suit. Yosemite Sam, Sylvester and Tweety are also part of the *Looney Tunes Collection*, a classic cast of superstars with a universal appeal to all ages.

But Santas are just part of the year round selection of figures. Londonshire is a fantasy isle complete with clothtique animal citizenry, while the *Lifestyle Collection* features every day professionals dressed in smart Clothtique wardrobes ranging from doctors to firefighters.

The Santa Claus Network

Collectors who find themselves caught up in the magic of the Clothtique Santas may want to join The Santa Claus Network from Possible Dreams. Each member receives many benefits including a free Clothtique Santa, available exclusively to SCN members. Membership offers the opportunity to purchase another exclusive Santa each year, as well as a subscription to a colorful, quarterly newsletter, a complete directory of Clothtique Santas in the *Collectors Guide Book*, and a personal membership card. All this is available for $25.00 annually. (Add $5.00 more for memberships outside the continental United States.) Write to address listed.

More Holiday Magic

Beyond the Clothtique realm are many other holiday gifts and collectibles that capture traditional themes and the season of giving in a whole new light. *Candy Colored Christmas®* borrows coloration from 1950s ribbon-candy to create a dazzling surface on ceramic and porcelain. From stocking holders to ornaments, this line catches the attention of those who want something original and unique. *Crinkle Claus®* is a clan of cold cast characters finished in a wrinkly, puckered texture that proved a big winner in 1995. Borrowing the same idea and procedure, *Crinkle Crackers* are zany officers elaborately dressed in military garb reminiscent of Gilbert & Sullivan. *Santa Go Round™* are roly poly originals, sculpted in cold cast and hand-painted to capture a detailed expression of Christmas fun and delight.

Santa hops aboard a tricycle filled with a basket of gifts in "Riding High" from the American Artists Collection. *Designed by artist Lisa Nilsson, the Clothtique Santa wears a fur-trimmed outfit as he pedals his bike and rings a bell to announce his arrival.*

From the renowned studios of Vaillancourt Folk Art comes another relic of Christmas past. Like all the wonderful Santa designs and antique candy mold creations that Judi Vaillancourt has created for Possible Dreams, *Vaillancourt Cats* combine nostalgia and innovation. Wide-eyed stares full of curiosity and realistic fur coloration make this ceramic collection perfect for feline fanciers.

From the Crinkle Claus *collection, Santa climbs down a snow-covered chimney. The collection gets its distinctive name from the elaborate texture, wrinkly puckers and pleats that give each figurine an animated quality.*

Artist David Wenzel catches Santas in the midst of sledding, skiing, fishing and other outdoor activities. *Santa Antics* is crafted in cold cast for exquisite detailing in the faces and wardrobe. *Baby's First Christmas* celebrates a new addition to the family with a collection of delicate, handcrafted ornaments.

Possible Dreams technicians are always experimenting with new materials to give the products a new — or old — look. Santas and angels in the *Artiva™* collection are crafted from an innovative process that makes Santas and angels appear as though they were discovered in an old dusty attic. Despite its crackled surface and yellowing of age, *Artiva* pieces are lightweight and soft to the touch.

Other Possible Dreams' products include waterdomes, hinged hanging ornaments that open to cherished scenes, and tins to hold gifts the old-fashioned way.

Year-Round Collectibles

Besides the holiday collectibles, Possible Dreams has created lines that extend past the holidays. Mache Mystique®, a technique using hand-pulped Abaca and rice straw paper delicately shaped and bound, hand-dyed and painted, brings the *People of the World*™ collection to life. Researched and authenticated to determine the look that best expresses a cultural identity, the collection portrays American Indians, Africans, Kabuki Actors and Samurai Warriors. *Kidoughs*™ show off adorable little girls in Shirley Temple dresses and curly-locks hair. The figurines are made of a soft resin and painted in pastels. The girls' tiny hands clutch either dolls, bears, teapots or other favorite childhood toys.

In *The Thickets at Sweetbriar*™, never before has such artistry and diligence to detail been applied to a realm of endearing characters. Each personality from the collection seems to have popped out of the dusty pages of a Victorian classic, elegantly dressed in authentic period costumes accentuated by full-color blossoms.

Creativity lies in the eyes of those who look at the same old thing and see something brand new. From outside resources and an in-house creative staff come a steady flow of new ideas to rekindle memories of the past. For at Possible Dreams, illuminating the past in a new light is what keeps the fire lit under its business.

"Parsley Divine" and "Clem Jingles" sing a few carols together in their classic Victorian finery. The figurines are part of The Thickets of Sweetbriar *collection that features a cast of endearing characters.*

Possible Dreams
6 Perry Drive
Foxboro, MA 02035
(508) 543-5412
Fax (508) 543-4255

COLLECTORS' CLUB

Santa Claus Network®
c/o Possible Dreams
6 Perry Drive
Foxboro, MA 02035
(508) 543-6667

Annual Dues: $25.00 ($30.00 Outside Continental U.S.)
Club Year: Anniversary of Sign-Up Date

Benefits:
- Membership Gift: Clothtique Santa
- Opportunity to Purchase Members-Only Santa
- Quarterly Newsletter
- Embossed Membership Card
- Collectors Guide Book – Directory of Clothtique Santas
- Buy/Sell Matching Service Through Newsletter

PRECIOUS ART/PANTON

A World of Collecting from Fantasy to Fun

From the Krystonia *collection, "Barlow" has stumbled across "Okinawathe" and his mate "Tinchachuik." These creatures are as mystified at what to do with "Barlow" as he is afraid of them!*

When Precious Art/Panton first began in 1980, the company's new line of products reflected an ancient tradition. Pictures, music boxes and other accessories captured the distinctive look of Chokin art, a beautiful 13th century Japanese technique that features engraved designs on copper, gold and silver plates. These engravings used by Samurai warriors marked the beginning of a long and creative list of products that would find its way to America.

Since many of the Chokin items were musicals, Precious Art soon found a niche in this area. At one time, 90 percent of its introductions were musicals with other items including beveled and etched glass boxes along with redwood and oak jewelry boxes. The success of the company's musicals led to the creation of the first up-and-down movement carousel. These limited edition pieces brought Precious Art into the collectibles market and paved a path for the company's most popular collection – *Krystonia.*

In 1987, Precious Art opened the door to the *World of Krystonia* – a whimsical place filled with mysterious, magical adventures. This mystical land of expansive deserts, towering mountains and lush valleys boasts an assortment of inhabitants that come to life as hand-painted figurines. But *Krystonia* also has put a new twist on collecting. Corresponding storybooks tell the tale of this make-believe kingdom, with the fourth book published in 1995.

The fascinating books give collectors an opportunity to not only further enjoy their quality figurines but to also follow the storylines of their favorite characters from "Grumblypeg Grunch" to "Kephren." It's an up-close and personal approach that sparks the imagination and has led to great success for Precious Art/Panton.

A Land of New Beginnings That Has No End

Since its inception in 1987 with 19 figurines, *Krystonia* has delighted collectors of all ages with its continuing introductions and stories filled with humorous anecdotes, colorful personalities and struggles of good versus evil. The four *Krystonia* books reveal the magic found throughout the wonderful land, where the search is always on for magical krystals. Whoever controls the krystals rules all of *Krystonia.*

The evil "N'Borg" dreams of the day he will sit at the top. Under his power, *Krystonia* would become a bleak and barren wasteland, a winter with no end. With his henchdragon "N'Grall" and his legion of snords, "N'Borg" won't rest until his conquest of *Krystonia* is complete. From his menacing castle "Krak N'Borg," he waits for the day he will cast the darkest of spells and crush the Council of Wizards. He also has a score to settle with "Klip" for taking away his beautiful "N'Leila."

The Council of Wizards looks out for the best interests of *Krystonia,* wanting the land to be filled with peace and harmony. Working from the Obelisk, the Council has successfully thwarted all of "N'Borg's" conniving plans. Since the day "Azael" first founded the Council, the members have joined to strengthen and improve *Krystonia.* Their diverse spell-casting abilities make them a formidable foe. By whispering their charm words through the krystals, the wizards have cast the most wonderful spells – while showing they're an interesting cast of characters. If you need rest, call on "Turfen" – a change in the weather, there's "Shepf." For utter confusion, look to "Haaph." "Rueggan," the tinkerer, spends his time bringing ancient machines back to life – often with hilarious results.

"Poffles" and "Trumph" jump from the pages of storybooks that tell the magical tales of a land called Krystonia. *These fun-loving characters – along with many collectors worldwide – delight in the adventures found in this make-believe kingdom.*

In this figurine, little "Shadra" is daydreaming about "Escublar the Emperor Dragon," a hero in Krystonia *for saving the land from evil. She's imagining what the emperor looks like – dressed in a purple robe and jewels with a noble expression.*

"Graffyn" may have the toughest job of all the wizards. He negotiates the transportation contracts with the dragon's leader "Grumblypeg Grunch." Nowhere is there a more zany bunch than The Dragon Society of Carin Tor. "Zanzibar" is always looking for adventure even if he has to make it up. "Jumbly" can't stop juggling, and "Stoope the Stupendous" can't wait to show off his latest magic trick. Maybe he will make himself disappear.

The *Krystonia* stories also tell about the trolls, "Maj-Drons" and the dreaded "Hagga-Beast." Remember you are safe in the comfort of the words of "Kephren." Who is "Kephren" you say? He is the teller of tales and translator of scrolls that arrive daily by dragon transport. From these scrolls, he recounts the exciting stories for the *Krystonia* books. Do not be deceived by his comfortable position, for since the arrival of the mysterious Root, his life has been disrupted more than he would care.

Never a Day Without a New Collector

The Krystonia Collectors Club lets everyone enjoy these magical stories and characters even more. The troll "Twingnuk" is the members-only figurine for 1995. His cart, which he uses to mine for krystals in the mountains of Kappah, is a free gift for members. The concept of having a related gift and members-only figurine was started in the club's third year and has been very popular. Members also receive a quarterly newsletter, in which the introduction is narrated by a *Krystonia* character. With 1996 marking the 10th anniversary of *Krystonia*, special surprises are planned. A one-year membership in the club is $25.00. For information, write the Krystonia Collectors Club, 110 E. Ellsworth, Ann Arbor, MI 48108.

The Founding of *Krystonia* and Its Wonderful Tales

Krystonia started in a tiny factory in England, where its creators tapped into the British tradition of excellence and generations of skilled artisans. Although Precious Art's original product lines were produced in the Far East, company officials decided to change locations, knowing the collection needed special care in combining high-quality collectibles with enjoyable stories. *Krystonia* quickly outgrew its original studios and a modern facility was built in Chesterton, England, where all of Precious Art's English products are now produced. Using cold-cast porcelain, the hand-painted figurines and every sculpted detail are carefully monitored throughout the production process. Of course, each character must have its own sparkling krystal adornment for the finishing touch.

While *Krystonia* is made in England, the collection was born from the hearts and minds of David Lee Woodard and Pat Chandok. They spend countless hours making sure that no two characters are the same, while leading a creative team of artists who breath life into every *Krystonia* resident. Without just the right design and color, each figurine may never make it to the production stage. Once it is ready for production, the hardest part follows: deciding on a name. This could take weeks. After all, you must remember that there are no "Bob" the dragons in *Krystonia*.

Storylines for the books come from Dave, Pat and Mark Scott. They collaborate to bring to life all the different characters and adventures. After one book is completed, they start planning the next – which is sure to be filled with pages of fantasy and fun.

New Lines Celebrate the Beauty of Nature

Always looking to develop new products, Precious Art/Panton introduced two lines in 1995. While different in appearance, *Rainforest Children* and *Funny Galore* both reflect an ecological theme. *Rainforest Children* symbolizes the bond among children, wildlife and nature. With their homes being destroyed, the *Rainforest Children* seek help to save the planet with their animal kingdom friends, which are portrayed as endangered and unprotected species. *Rainforest Children* was created to show the inevitability of extinction if no one shows concern for the environment. A portion of the sales of this new line is donated to

Created by Mary Ann Orr, a South African artist, the Funny Galore *collection celebrates the humor, color and beauty of nature. There's* Funny Birds, Funny Frogs *and* Funny Cats *to make everyone laugh. Each figurine is brightly painted for a whimsical look.*

Rainforest Children *shows the special, unspoken bond between children and nature. In this figurine, a child nestles up against a tiger, just one of several endangered or unprotected species that the* Rainforest Children *want to help save. A portion of the sales of this collection is donated to Conservation International.*

Conservation International.

Funny Galore is the creation of Mary Ann Orr, a South African artist. After Mary Ann and her family found themselves caught up in the trappings of a young Yuppie lifestyle, they sold everything and escaped to an idyllic forest on the coast. Returning to the very roots of nature, they decided to make a living in the pottery business. In order to tempt her dormant artistic soul out of hibernation, Mary Ann used clay to reveal her feelings about the relationship between man and nature. She found herself fascinated by "how enormous the controversy of issues such as water pollution, air pollution and over population of man had affected our little creatures."

She may not be an authority on ecological issues, but she realizes many feel powerless and watch helplessly as scientists, biologists and politicians shape the future of the planet. Without wanting to ponder the "doom and disaster" of these issues, she chose instead to highlight the adaptability and pristine beauty of nature, which comes across in her colorful work.

Mary Ann's brightly painted animals are bound to make anyone smile. Her *Funny Birds* result from a mixture of feathered friends. *Funny Cats* find their names from *Puss In Boots* and *Funny Frogs* get their names from the silly noises that they make. This is only the start of Mary Ann's work for Precious Art.

Besides these new collections and *Krystonia*, Precious Art/Panton also features several other lines. The *Safari Kingdom* and *Mischievous Mice* were introduced in 1989. *Safari Kingdom* features African and American animals in their natural habitats and often in mother and baby poses. The *Mischievous Mice* cold cast figurines eat fruit, climb on old books or live humbly and happily in an old can. What's next? The future looks bright not only in the land of *Krystonia* but throughout the company, which will continue growing with more introductions and stories from a far-away magical land.

Precious Art/Panton
110 E. Ellsworth Road
Ann Arbor, MI 48108
(313) 677-3510
Fax (313) 677-3412

COLLECTORS' CLUB

Krystonia Collectors Club
110 E. Ellsworth Road
Ann Arbor, MI 48108
(313) 677-3510

Annual Dues: $25.00
Club Year: February 1-January 31

Benefits:
- Membership Gift: Figurine
- Opportunity to Purchase Members-Only Figurine
- Quarterly Newsletter, "Phargol-Horn"
- Membership Card
- Store Events/Artist Signings

R.R. CREATIONS, INC.

Over One Million 'Windows on the World' Now Open Nationwide

What began as 'an open window of opportunity' became Doreen and Dave Ross' dream! Starting from a modest garage in Pratt, Kansas, R.R. Creations, under the Ross' guidance, has become one of the state's most distinguished small businesses.

Real estate. More than stocks, bonds or money markets, real estate has always been America's favorite investment! Buy a house and treasure it because it's uniquely yours. As a bonus, the longer you live there, the more valuable the property becomes.

R.R. Creations, a dynamic, young Midwest company with a passion for real estate, couldn't agree with this philosophy more. They've made one million buildings...and it's likely they'll make 200,000 more in the year ahead! Amazingly, not one required a plot of land or a building permit, because these distinct structures are finely crafted wood miniatures, styled and manufactured exclusively for the collectibles market.

Dave and Doreen Ross, owners of R.R. Creations, have single-handedly put miniature wood houses on the collectibles map. Each time they place their trademark logo, an open window, on a finished piece, they move one step closer to a shared dream. "The open window symbolizes something we both believe in," explains Doreen. "When God closes a door, He opens a window."

Doreen and husband Dave not only believe this inspired saying, they live it. Recalling the job loss that might have taken them away from the town they loved, both Rosses realized the choice was up to them.

If they stayed, they would need a way to earn a living, so Doreen asked Dave what he thought about making and selling wood miniature buildings, showcasing the distinct architectural styles of the Midwest. After much prayer and considerable research, the couple sprung into action. "We set up a carpentry shop in the family garage," Doreen recalls fondly. "We started without even knowing what a silk screen looked like!"

History Repeats Itself All Over America

When the Rosses begin creating a new design, they carefully select structures for their historic and aesthetic appeal. Their first creation, the "Pratt County Courthouse," established their signature style. Since then, an exciting array of landmark buildings have come from the busy workshops of R.R. Creations. Recent examples are typical of the range and scope of the company's offerings: Susan B. Anthony's residence, Betsy Ross' home and the houses of John F. Kennedy, Mark Twain and Harriet Beecher Stowe.

In addition to creating the homesteads of "the rich and the famous," the Rosses also craft custom-made 'memories to order.' Collectors provide a photograph of a beloved home, school, courthouse or other special place. The Rosses will then make as few as 12 for them at a reasonable $10.00 to $20.00 each. "Whether or not we like the building a customer asks us to recreate is never an issue. We just want to make it as accurately as possible," Doreen Ross assures us. "The people just love them because it's their special memory. Each time we make and paint a building, we try to see it through their eyes."

By the way, houses, schools and other typical requests are occasionally interspersed with a challenge to make something that's never been done before. Dave and Doreen fondly recall some of the more unusual requests coming their way, such as the high school band seeking replicas of their equipment truck as a fund raiser, an order for the creation of football stadiums and an unforgettable request for ten-seated outhouses!

Doreen believes the possibilities for such creations are endless. "There are so many opportunities to do different buildings, many of which no longer exist. Even a small town can afford to have our miniature wood buildings done affordably, capturing forever a beloved memory. We all know people who collect a single subject, like a firehouse because their grandfather or dad

A simple piece of wood and a set of detailed sketches eventually became a brightly colored collection of buildings in an amazing variety of architectural styles. Over one million have been sold...and R.R. Creations is only nine years old!

Collectors look for the benchmark 'open window' on every R.R. Creations building. It's applied by silk screening carefully cut wood to ensure a perfectly detailed and affordable limited edition treasure.

was a fireman. These are the kinds of 'unforgettable memories' we recreate every day," she adds.

The Crafting of a Typical Open Window Treasure

The Rosses love to innovate, but when it comes to the process they use to craft their buildings, there are no experiments or short cuts.

In the beginning, absolute quality was assured because Doreen and Dave performed every step in the production process themselves. They did the research, cut the wood, hand-painted the finished product and marketed it. Happily, growth has forced an expansion. Though Dave and Doreen are still hands-on owners, a skilled staff of Pratt residents now help the company enjoy its meteoric growth.

The division of labor takes advantage of Dave and Doreen's unique talents. Dave and his crew handle the actual production of each piece. Doreen and her staff then guide the cut wood through a computer-based drafting and design system that allows everyone to see exactly how the trim, color and embellishments will appear on the building, even before the silk screen is produced. Color separations are done on site. Screening takes place only after background colors and edges are hand-painted onto the cut forms.

Only when each structure has been dried, sealed, inspected and declared perfect do the Rosses add their signature, certifying it a true R.R. Creation. By the way, early versions of their window logo were burned into the bottom of each piece, but contemporary buildings display a silk-screened logo on the reverse side, adjacent to the historical fact sheet applied to the back of every structure.

From the Heartland to Harrod's to Hollywood!

Not long ago, millions of people shopping at London's famous store, Harrod's, had a chance to see an assortment of R.R. Creations' charming Midwest buildings. This appearance was the happy result of the state of Kansas' search for the best examples of Midwest craftsmanship for an "American Frontier" promotion.

During the preliminary search, the competition seemed formidable! "There were 500 booths set up at the Harrod's market in Wichita," Doreen recalls. "Everyone wanted to show their best wares and many booths showcased more than one line, so you can imagine how many products from Kansas were represented!" Happily, the Rosses learned their buildings were among only six companies selected to make the journey across the Atlantic.

"We were so fortunate to have been picked," Doreen says, recalling the 16 R.R. Creations on display at Harrod's. The experience inspired both Rosses to think about spreading their geographic wings. No sooner were those hopeful thoughts exchanged than the Rosses heard of another trade show in Wichita sponsored by America's Shopping Channel, QVC.

Again competing this time with 250 other companies for the few slots QVC hoped to fill, the Rosses talked with network representatives about their *Amish Collection*. The ten minute chat was less than memorable, and the Rosses went home vowing they'd be on QVC one day. Imagine their shock when a phone call from the network came just two days later requesting an immediate shipment of 1,000 complete sets – that's 5,000 pieces – of the Amish village!

The rest, as they say, is history. Soon, Doreen and her Amish village were being beamed to 50 million homes across the United States plus an additional 17 million homes in England and Mexico.

Special Limited Editions Promise Exclusivity

When the Rosses sat down to begin their long-term planning in 1993, they decided the time had come to give collectors 'true limited edition works of art.' Beginning in 1994, every R.R. Creations structure was numbered, and all series were stringently limited to just 2,500.

The "limited edition decision" proved a popular one. Shops selling their buildings were thrilled. So were collectors, who could now look forward to all-important retirements such as these 1993 series, now no longer in production: the *Historical Collection II, Williamsburg Collection II, In the Country Series II* and *Christmas Memories Series II.* These collections join *Grandpas Farm Collection Series II, On the Square Series II* and *Amish Collection Series II* as prime candidates for strong secondary market activity in the years ahead.

Members of the Open Window Club House delight in all the information they receive about their personal real estate! Historical data is plentiful and members have the unique opportunity to choose their own gift from R.R. Creations comprehensive catalog of delights.

QVC, the popular television shopping network, knew their customers when they selected this example of true Americana, the Amish Collection, *to show to the nation. The Rosses were thrilled to have received an initial order for 5,000 pieces just two days after the series was previewed.*

R.R. Creations Celebrates Its Growing Collectors Club

Countrywide fans of R.R. Creations' miniatures have taken their passion one step further: they've joined the Open Window Club House Collectors Club. Even the name is like a fresh, spring breeze, and benefits for members are plentiful.

New and renewing members receive something out-of-the-ordinary: their choice of a free, hand-signed building from the company's current collection. Unlike collector clubs offering a single gift of the same style to everyone, the Open Window Club House encourages individual choice. The only proviso: the style must be in production.

Each year, a special "Members-Only" piece is created exclusively for Club Members. These are the rarest collectible offerings of all. 1995 members are given a chance to acquire a lovely handcrafted mill in a barnwood stain. Open Window Club Members also look forward to receiving a hard-bound catalog of all available designs that's updated twice yearly.

An official newsletter, "Club House News," is packed with information, published bi-annually and eagerly awaited. Fees are $22.50 initially; members renew each year for $19.50.

In addition to these terrific membership perks, a multi-purchase gratitude rebate program is now in place to reward loyal collectors.

As a service to those seeking to track and evaluate their collections, the Rosses have established a toll-free telephone line. You are invited to call 1-800-779-3610 to get information about any building ever crafted by the Rosses or call 1-800-779-3610 to book a fascinating tour of R.R. Creations, if you happen to be coming through Kansas. Advance notice is required, but the stop is both fun and educational...well worth the trip!

Those who wish information by mail may write to Debi Gaston at R.R. Creations, Inc., P.O. Box 8707, Pratt, Kansas 67124. You can be sure there will be a friendly voice at the end of the phone line or a cheery smile on the face of the person opening your letter. After all, the reason the Rosses started their company was as simple as not wanting to leave the small town they had grown to love with its friendly hearts and talented hands!

R. R. Creations
P.O. Box 8707
Pratt, KS 67124
(800) 779-3610
Fax (316) 672-5850

COLLECTORS' CLUB/TOUR

Open Window Club House Collectors Club
P.O. Box 8707
Dept. Club
Pratt, KS 67124
(800) 779-3610

Annual Dues: $22.50 - Renewal: $19.50
Club Year: Anniversary of Sign-Up Date

Benefits:
- Membership Gift: Choice of Hand-Signed Building from Current Line
- Opportunity to Purchase Members-Only Piece
- Bi-annual Newsletter, "Club House News"
- Hard-Bound Catalog with Binder
- Personaized Membership Card
- Buy/Sell Matching Service

Open Window Video Tour
P.O. Box 8707
Pratt, KS 67124
(800) 779-3610

Hours: Tour is limited to groups only and must be scheduled in advance.
Admission Fee: None

The tour includes a history of R.R. Creations, tour of the showroom, drafting demonstration and a video tour of the manufacturing facilities.

RAWCLIFFE CORPORATION

From Historical Classics to Whimsical Fantasy, Rawcliffe's Diverse Products Delight Collectors of All Ages

Rawcliffe offers collectible items for virtually every wild and domestic animal, sport, pet, hobby, avocation, pastime, personality type, and caricature – from "generic" giftware items for all occasions to highly specific items for each person's "passion." All Rawcliffe designs begin with original artist sculptures. Then they transform each designer's creativity into a finely detailed and meticulously manufactured piece. Whether you treasure pewter's fine patina or favor angels perched on hand-blown iridescent glass bubbles, there's a Rawcliffe collectible to delight collectors of all ages.

Classic Collection (L-R) – B-17 Bomber, World War II Fleet Tugboat, 1956 T-Bird Hardtop, all-American classics that are reproduced in handsome detail.

Rawcliffe's Distinctive *Classic Collection* Immortalizes History

Automobiles, airplanes and ships – classics that shaped American history. Rawcliffe's new *Classic Collection* captures the best state-of-the-art technology that America had to offer over the past 50 years. Each detailed replica is hand-cast and hand-finished of America's finest pewter.

Included with each collectible is a booklet of classic and fascinating facts. One of the favorites from this collection is the B-17 Bomber. Also known as the "Flying Fortress," the B-17 was a high altitude heavy bomber used extensively in WWII. However, toward the end of the battles, several "war weary" models were stripped of their equipment and used as pilotless radio-controlled flying bombs. (Actual size: 4-1/2" L, 6-1/4" wing span.)

Another classic is the World War II Tugboat. Tugs have always played a vital role in transportation and commerce, but they truly proved themselves in action during World War II. Tugs towed two artificial harbors across the Channel during the first hectic weeks of the Allied invasion, foiling Hitler's generals, who thought that only regular ports like Cherbourg or LeHavre would be used for an attack. (Actual size: 5-3/4" L x 2-1/8" W x 3" H.)

The 1956 T-Bird Hardtop maintained a stable and comfortable 90-100 m.p.h. cruising speed, especially over the roughly surfaced roads of Europe. Because most European sports cars could not attain these speeds, a remarkable 32,000 T-Birds were sold in the U.S. and abroad in 1956. (Actual size: 4-1/2" L x 1-3/4" W.)

Other replicas which are currently available in the collection are: World War II Submarine, B-52 Bomber, F4U-1 Corsair, P-51 Mustang, DC-3, Porsche 928, and the VW Beetle. Suggested retail prices for the *Classic Collection* range from $70.00 to $129.

Licensed Products are Collectible Favorites

Rawcliffe is proud to be an authorized licensee for *Looney Tunes™* characters, and for ships and characters from the ever-popular *Star Wars™* and *Star Trek™* series. Serious Trekkies appreciate the limited edition "Deep Space Nine™ Space Station" on its custom marble base ($300) and the "USS Enterprise NCC-1701-D" ($100), along with ships and characters from all the syndicated TV shows and movies. *Star Wars* aficionados can handsomely display three limited edition pieces on their wood bases: Han Solo's "Millennium Falcon" ($95.00), Darth Vader's "TIE Fighter" ($135) and Luke Skywalker's "X-Wing Fighter" ($95.00). Over two dozen *Star Wars* figurines and ships are

Star Trek® *"Deep Space Nine™ Space Station," produced in an edition limited to 4,500 pieces, sits atop a custom marble base.*

reproduced in open editions. A line of keychains and mugs features many of the science fiction logos, insignias, characters and ships in a portable form.

Award-Winning Fantasy Artist Hap Henriksen Sculpts for Rawcliffe

Depicted on keychains, mugs and as figurines, *Looney Tunes®* characters are reproduced in fine pewter from the original sculptures of Hap Henriksen. A founding member of the National Academy of Fantastic Art, Henriksen's award-winning fantasy and science fiction creations have gained him an international reputation. He has captured in great detail all the favorite *Looney Tunes* characters exclusively for Rawcliffe Corp. Featured in the open edition are "Yosemite Sam," "Tasmanian Devil," "Wile E. Coyote," "Road Runner," "Daffy Duck," "Sylvester" and "Porky Pig." Figurines stand between 3" and 4" high and carry a suggested retail of $25.00 to $30.00.

Jessica deStefano's *Bubble Fairies™* Celebrate Friendship and Nature

Original sculptures by artist Jessica deStefano feature delightful hand-painted resin fairies perched atop iridescent glass bubbles. *Bubble Fairies™* encompass open stock and limited edition pieces retailing from $30.00 to $150, including *Wish Fairies™*, *Angel Fairies of the Seasons™*, *The Rainbow Collection™*, *Garden Fairies™*, *The Four Seasons™*, and *Bubble Fairy* ornaments. Twelve captivating *Wish Fairies™* are designed as a gift and greeting card in one. A sprinkle of magic fairy dust bestows the giver's best wishes for "Rainbows," "Fun," "Love," "Dreams," "Happiness," "Good Fortune," "Health," "Good Luck," "Friendship," "Success," "Sunshine" and "Laughter." An additional 12 *Star Wish Fairies™* will be released later in 1995. For every *Wish Fairy* purchased, a donation is made to Amos House in Providence, Rhode Island, to support their programs for needy individuals and families. *Wish Fairies* have a

Looney Tunes® *(L-R) – "Yosemite Sam," "Daffy Duck," "Taz," "Wile E. Coyote" and "Road Runner" are posed as their own outrageous selves.*

Bubble Fairies™ *(L-R) — "Rainbows"* Wish Fairy™, *"Fun"* Wish Fairy™, *Limited Edition "Summer"* Angel Fairy of the Seasons™, *and "Love"* Wish Fairy™ *delight fairy collectors of all ages.*

suggested retail price of $30.00.

The newest additions to the enchanting *Bubble Fairies* line are the four *Angel Fairies of the Seasons™*, depicting the special Angels who lovingly protect nature's animals the whole year through. The "Angel Fairy of Spring" gathers a basket of ducklings, and together they brave the wind and rain. "Angel Fairy of Summer" quenches the thirst of parched throats and very dry roots with welcomed rainwater. "Angel Fairy of Fall" helps two baby squirrels gather the autumn harvest to store for the long winter ahead, and "Angel Fairy of Winter" cradles a bird with a broken wing and carries it safely through the freezing storm. The edition is limited to 4,500 pieces of each figurine, with a suggested retail price of $95.00.

Rawcliffe's new line of delightful *Mischievous Fairies™* are being sculpted by deStefano and will be available later this year.

Rawcliffe Corporation
155 Public Street
Providence, RI 02903
(800) 343-1811
Fax (401) 751-8545

RECO INTERNATIONAL CORP.

Committed Leadership and Award-Winning Artists Keep Reco at the Pinnacle of Collectibles Excellence for Nearly Three Decades

Sandra Kuck's "Moments of Caring" warms our hearts as a sweet little girl – surrounded by real and stuffed animal friends – waters her pretty flowers. The open window and the graceful vines make this a welcoming image, and the child's lovely face and glowing complexion provide each viewer with a sense of happy well-being.

When Heio Reich founded Reco International Corp. in 1967, his goal was to provide American collectors with a panorama of world-class collectibles in a host of fine art media. As a native of Berlin, Germany, Reich enjoyed a great many contacts with European art studios. Thus Reco gained fame by introducing plates from some of Europe's most celebrated makers, including Fuerstenberg, Royale, Dresden, Royal Germania, Crystal, King's and Moser.

Many of the plates Reco imported to the United States have risen substantially in price since their introduction in the late 1960s and early 1970s. But Reich sensed a golden opportunity in 1977, and he steered his business in a whole new direction. Since then, Reco International has reigned as one of the nation's top producers of limited edition plates by renowned American painters like Sandra Kuck, John McClelland and Jody Bergsma.

While some studios specialize in only one area such as child-subject art or wildlife, Reco seeks out artists of excellence in many different subjects and styles. Sandra Kuck's Victorian children and the fantasy visions of Jody Bergsma take center stage in the current Reco line-up. Retired from the active plate market, John McClelland nonetheless remains an all-time collector favorite for his paintings of adorable children. In the past, Dot and Sy Barlowe created vivid portraits of wildlife and nature for Reco, while Clemente Micarelli painted homages to the ballet, religious events and weddings. Subjects as diverse as Edwardian bears and military art also may be found in the Reco archives.

A Pledge to Collectors: Only the Very Best

While Reco's productions represent a panorama of art styles, media and subjects, Heio Reich's company philosophy unites all Reco creations with a shared vision of excellence. Reich's goal for Reco is that the company creates objects to bring enjoyment, a life-long interest and hobby to collectors, meanwhile providing beautiful products for the public. Reco's commitment to produce only the very best art on plates and in other media will continue into the future – just as it has since 1967.

Reich and his artists have never sought personal glory or awards – indeed, they consider their finest accolade the gleam in a happy collector's eyes. Even so, Heio Reich has been the recipient of most every prestigious honor available to a collectibles marketer or producer. These include "Vendor of the Year," "Producer of the Year," the "Lee Benson Memorial Award," the "International Collectible Achievement Award" and the "Silver Chalice Award" for selected plates. Reich has long been an active member and leader in the National Association of Limited Edition Dealers (NALED) and the Plate Makers Guild, and he was a charter member of the Board of Directors of Collectors' Information Bureau.

What's more, John McClelland and Sandra Kuck have been lauded at scores of conventions and collectors' gatherings with "Plate of the Year," "Artist of the Year," and many other honors. Indeed, Ms. Kuck is acknowledged as the most honored collectibles artist of all time – including an unprecedented six consecutive "Artist of the Year" awards from the National Association of Limited Edition Dealers. Heio Reich is particularly proud that Reco International Corp. has exhibited at every South Bend Collectibles Exposition since the famous show's inception over 20 years ago.

"Peace at Last" by Jody Bergsma explores the natural relationship of Native American peoples with the wildlife that grace their glorious lands. A proud eagle forms the backdrop for a full-body portrait of an Indian brave with his horse, celebrating a victory that will bring peace to his people. This work of art is the second issue in Ms. Bergsma's Totems of the West *plate collection.*

The Renowned Plate Maker Offers Works in Other Popular Media

Although Reco's fame stems primarily from works of art in fine porcelain, the firm has marketed and manufactured pieces in many other materials and media over the years. The early King's plates, for example, featured delicate, bas-relief floral motifs, and the Royale Germania plates were crafted of gleaming crystal.

Say the name "Reco" to a contemporary collector, however, and he or she is most likely to think of porcelain plates with art by Kuck, McClelland and Bergsma. Another important concentration for Reco in the porcelain plate realm is what Heio Reich likes to call "Special Occasions" plates. The firm's early European-made series often focused on Christmas, Mother's Day, Father's Day and Easter. Sandra Kuck's Christmas series – showing little ones in holiday scenes – have won many a collector's heart. Ms. Kuck also has created original art to honor Mother's Day, christenings, weddings, and other memorable days.

Reco crafts figurines both in shimmering porcelain and using the cold-cast method: a medium which is growing in popularity because of the intricate detail it can capture. John McClelland's silky white angels helped establish Reco as an important maker of three-dimensional art. Now Jody Bergsma enhances this well-earned reputation with the adorable animals in her *Laughables* line.

Sandra Kuck's precious children seemed destined to come alive as elegant, collectible dolls – and Reco was up to the challenge of creating heirloom-quality bisque beauties. Ms. Kuck's lovely characters are captured in fine porcelain and painted to enhance the delicate blush of a cheek...the grace of a child's tiny fingers and hands. The dolls' costumes faithfully portray Ms. Kuck's love for Victoriana and whimsy – with flowing frocks, charming accessories, and marvelous trimmings in ribbon and lace. What's more, each Sandra Kuck doll tells a story – in fact, the doll *herself* is sharing a story in a recent Kuck introduction, "Reading with Teddy."

Using Proverbs 22:17 – "A cheerful heart is good medicine" – as inspiration, Jody Bergsma created these adorable figurines called Laughables. *They are, clockwise from center top: "Whiskers & Willie," "Sunny," "Daisy & Jeremiah," "Annie, George & Harry," "Millie & Mittens" and "Patches & Pokey." Each comes complete with its own humorous saying for life's ups and downs.*

Ever on the alert for new ways to share the art of favorite painters with collector friends, Reco has diversified its offerings to include music boxes and keepsake boxes, each enhanced by beloved artwork. Some of the boxes are handcrafted of walnut and mahogany, while others are made of shimmering porcelain.

Reco Nurtures An Extended Family of Artists

Reco International remains a family-owned business, and the firm cultivates a warm and friendly atmosphere: both in its internal operations and in its relationships with artists. Each Reco employee takes a personal interest in the products they help create, and in the artists whose work inspires each new edition.

Although John McClelland now is retired from the creation of collector plate art, many of his works are still available on the primary and secondary markets. Later series may be acquired at issue price through many dealers, while earlier McClelland favorites are available only at auctions and through exchanges of various types. Reco International continues to receive scores of letters from McClelland fans and collectors, and it is clear that the personable artist remains a favorite for many.

Sandra Kuck has charmed Reco collectors with her romantic and nostalgic portraits for more than 15 years. Ever since her "Sunday Best" plate was introduced in 1983, Ms. Kuck has reigned as the "sweetheart" of collectors throughout North America and beyond. She enjoys a remarkable gift for intricate detail work, as well as a deep love for "all things Victorian." Combine this with her ability to capture the fresh-faced innocence of little ones, and it is easy to understand why collectors are so devoted to Ms. Kuck and her creations.

Jody Bergsma has a whimsical and joyous heart, which she displays in all her fantasy art. Her unicorns and dragons combine mystery with beauty, and her "Little People" and animals are equally endearing. Ms. Bergsma recently has expanded her repertoire beyond watercolor prints and collectors plates to include the *Laughables* figurines – a lighthearted group of animal portraits that are sure to bring a smile to each

Lucky Teddy! His owner – a beautiful little girl with a lacy Victorian frock, silky slippers, and a flower-trimmed hat – has decided to read him a book called Teddy's Adventures! *For the occasion, this cuddly stuffed bear has donned his own wire-rimmed glasses. This whimsical doll charmer was designed by Sandra Kuck and is entitled "Reading with Teddy."*

recipient. What's more, the artist shows her contemplative side in a plate series entitled *Totems of the West.* To create this dramatic collection, Ms. Bergsma traveled extensively and studied the spiritual forces that Native American tribes consider sacred.

Sandra Kuck Collectors Enjoy the Kuck Newsletter

Reco International Corp. publishes a bi-annual newsletter to keep collectors informed about Sandra Kuck and the wonderful artwork she creates. The newsletter provides an "up-close and personal" glimpse into the world of this lovely, warm lady and her world of "updated Victoriana." It also offers Kuck collectors news about upcoming products and their availability.

To add your name to the mailing list and receive the Sandra Kuck Newsletter at no charge, simply send your name and address to: Sandra Kuck Newsletter, c/o Reco International Corp., P.O. Box 951, Port Washington, New York 11050.

Reco International Corp.
150 Haven Avenue
Port Washington, NY 11050
(516) 767-2400
Fax (516) 767-2409

ROMAN, INC.

Premier Collectible Producer Meets Demand for Angels for All Reasons, All Seasons with Magnificent Works by American, European Artists

"Alyssa–Nature's Angel" is the first in a series of limited edition figurines for Roman, Inc.'s popular Seraphim Classics™ *collection.*

With a 32-year history of successfully responding to collector angel needs, Roman, Inc. finds itself in the unique position of being perfectly equipped with a variety of breathtaking masterpieces for the current upsurge in angel collectibles interest. The company lists more than 400 kinds and 16 collections of angels in a virtual kaleidoscope of sizes, shapes and mediums. They range from porcelain bisque, resin and papier maché to sinamay, acrylic, brass, fabric and glass.

Seraphim Classics™ by Seraphim Studio Rank as Top U.S. Angels

Currently, Roman, Inc. is the nation's leading angel resource with collections featuring celestial messengers that have captured collectors' hearts and minds. Whether you've browsed casually or you are an avid fan of angels, you have heard of or seen the *Seraphim Classics™* angels from Roman, Inc. that are currently ranked as the most popular in the United States. Ethereal beauties with graceful flowing robes and tresses featuring gloriously sculpted wings, they embody the romantic classical style reminiscent of Michelangelo and subsequent fine art of the 1700s and 1800s. The seemingly translucent resin figurines by Roman's Seraphim Studio are being unanimously hailed by collectors as heavenly masterpieces.

Seraphim Studio artists created original art in 1995 for the exquisite first *Seraphim Classics* limited edition figure, "Alyssa - Nature's Angel," who rapidly found her home in prized collections. Spring '95 introductions included a collection of 4" miniature figures, postcards and a full color journal, all featuring the complete set of 12 angels. Collectors eagerly anticipate 1996 when the Seraphim Studio debuts six new figures, four ornaments, a pin and a nativity.

Fontanini Heirloom Nativity Angels by Simonetti Set Standards

"We've always held prominence in this area because of our long-standing relationship with Italy's famous House of Fontanini® and their master sculptor Elio Simonetti," explains owner and Chief Executive Officer Ronald T. Jedlinski. "The Fontanini angels and cherubs are so breathtaking that Simonetti's designs have become a standard many try to emulate. That is why Fontanini instituted worldwide copyrights that Roman, Inc. diligently defends as the exclusive Fontanini source in North America."

Simonetti has created over 200 master sculptures for angels and cherubs during his 40-year career with the Fontanini family. Many collectors hail the magnificent life-sized Heirloom Nativity that is featured in the hit movie *Home Alone* and graces the Pope's private quarters in the Vatican as Simonetti and Fontanini's crowning achievement. These 50" tall masterpieces exhibit the full scope of the gifted Simonetti's sculpting and the Fontanini dedication to their almost 90-year tradition of excellence in artistry and crafting.

Speaking of the most recent character he has created for this famous set, Simonetti has long believed the angel is a very important element in his celebration of the birth of Christ, and had always planned to add it to the life-sized Nativity. It is fortuitous that his inspiration to shape this figure with his gifted hands came at a time when all attention is focused so strongly on angels.

The history of the House of Fontanini is one steeped in tradition and family values. In 1908, the family

One of a host of celestial messengers ranked as the top angel collection in the nation, the Seraphim Classics™ *collection embodies ethereal beauty with unequaled grace and elegance. "Seraphina–Heaven's Keeper" portrays a graceful angel ministering to a babe in her arms.*

The best-seller Millenium™ Series *of limited edition plates and companion ornaments will issue editions annually until the year 2000.*

patriarch, Emanuele Fontanini, launched the company when he began working with the finest sculptors and painters in Tuscany, Italy, to craft figures and decorations of heirloom quality in a one-room workshop. His sons joined him and, in turn, passed their tradition of superior craftsmanship to their sons. Today, the humble workshop has given way to spacious facilities 60 miles from Florence, in Bagni di Lucca, a region steeped in the rich heritage of the glorious Renaissance period.

The creation of the Fontanini figures is truly a family affair from concept to completion. The exquisite sculptures begin in the skilled hands of Simonetti. A meticulous molding process follows under vigilant Fontanini supervision. Finally, each figure is painstakingly painted by hand by artisans utilizing skills passed from generation to generation in their families.

During his four decades with the House of Fontanini, Simonetti has fine-tuned his already superlative artistry with his current work reflecting the maturing of his perceptions and talents. He explores new and unique areas of design in the crafting of a duo of 12" celestial musicians. Divine in detail with golden flowered accents on the front of their flowing gowns, these sophisticated, stylized angels can stand alone or with the 12" *Heirloom Nativity Collection.*

In 1991, the master sculptor pledged to resculpt all the original 5" Nativity figures he created at the outset of his career with Fontanini. As he resculpts the new concepts, the originals are retired. Simonetti resculpted the 5" standing and kneeling angels that were retired the previous year. Since 1991, 11 five-inch Nativity figures have been retired.

Plate, Ornament *Seraphim™ Collection* and *Millenium™ Series* Earn Laurels

FARO Studios of Italy is the font of creativity that brings international limited edition plates of incomparable beauty to aficionados of this medium. Beginning with the *Millenium™ Series* in 1992 and continuing until the year 2000, FARO's designer Ennio Morcaldo has drafted art that sculptor Alfonso Lucchesi fashions into bas relief plates of infinite grace. Themes center around the birth of the Blessed Child focusing on the Madonna and always featuring angels in either central roles as in "The Annunciation" or supportive as in "Peace on Earth." These tremendously popular plates of pristine white oxolyte also have companion ornaments reflecting the grace and flow of the sculpting in miniature. Oxolyte is a blending of polymer resin and powdered alabaster. When polished, the plates and ornaments resemble marble.

"Rosalyn - Rarest of Heaven" – the first limited edition in the *Seraphim Collection* from FARO has proven rare, indeed, by garnering the *Collector Editions* 1995 "Award of Excellence" honor in its category. The 1995 issue in this plate collection featuring angels is "Helena - Heaven's Herald" – a portrayal of an angel with gloriously sculpted wings full spread with a dove perched on her hand. *Seraphim Collection* companion ornaments again mirror Rosalyn and Helena in exquisitely detailed mini-form.

Angela Tripi Creates Museum Gallery Messengers

Sicilian sculptor Angela Tripi has forged a reputation for distinctive renderings of historical and biblical subjects. Her talent for instilling character into her unique sculptures has earned Tripi "Collectible Sculpture of Show" at the California International Collectibles Exposition in 1991. First, Tripi shapes and molds the clay, her preferred medium, into sculptures whose features reflect her years of studying the people of her homeland. Her figures are then costumed in garments of fabric, dramatically draped and fixed to a hard finish using a secret family formula. Tripi then hand paints each character, even the patterns on the cloth. Roman translates her originals into durable resin, faithfully preserving every nuance.

First, Tripi created angels for her religious nativities that have earned acclaim and best sculpture honors in Palermo and Sorrento. Next, Tripi explored heaven's creatures further with limited editions figures and ornaments including "Serenade," "Rhapsody" and "Sonata" figurines and annual ornaments.

Home-Grown Jauquet Contributes Americana Winged Creatures

With exhibits in the Smithsonian Institute and top U.S. galleries and features in magazines, word is spreading on the country charm of Bill Jauquet's woodcarvings. His sculpts in aged white cedar preserve a vanishing, more relaxed way of life in America. His deceptively simple renderings of life in rural America, including Amish, farm and Native American themes, are also giving him a successful entry into the collectibles world.

Jauquet's Midwestern charm surfaces in his *Americana Collection*, which provides a whimsical look into rural America, complete with barnyard animals and folksy characters. The collection expanded into Christmas with the addition of Santa Claus figures, ornaments and a limited edition plate. In 1996, Jauquet will introduce a collection of angels. Jauquet took his imagination to another level when he debuted *Molly's World* in 1995. A loving gift to his baby granddaughter, *Molly's World* is a collection of whimsical animals that mirror the wondrous active imaginations of small children.

Why Angels?

The reasons behind the ongoing popularity of angels are as infinite as the heavens are high. Some collectors cite the sense of hope and protection that angels offer; others value the spirituality angels provide in difficult times. Perhaps the world's most prolific angel collector (and a member of the Fontanini Collectors' Club), Joyce Berg of Beloit, Wisconsin, boasts more than 10,000 angels in her collection. Like the majority of angel collectors, she began collecting long before it became in vogue, when traveling through Florida in 1976. Joyce happened upon an antique store with cherubs in the window. The rest, as they say, is angel history. Her Fontanini figures are among the most cherished in her collection. Joyce's devotion to angels has sparked a group of women in Beloit to create an angel museum, paying tribute to a variety of celestial messengers.

Avid collectors such as these are the reason Roman, Inc. will continue to offer "the most angels this side of heaven," as well as a wide variety of distinctive collectibles.

Roman, Inc.
555 Lawrence Avenue
Roselle, IL 60172-1599
(708) 529-3000
Fax (708) 529-1121

"Rosalyn–Rarest of Heaven" is a Collector Editions *award-winning plate from the FARO Studios* Seraphim Collection.™

COLLECTORS' CLUB/TOUR

Fontanini Collectors' Club^{SM}
555 Lawrence Avenue
Roselle, IL 60172
(800) 729-7662

Annual Dues: $19.50 - Renewal: $17.50
Club Year: Anniversary of Sign-Up Date

Benefits:
- Membership-Gift: Symbol-of-Membership Figure
- Opportunity to Purchase Members-Only Figure
- Quarterly Newsletter, "The Fontanini Collector"
- Binder with Club Logo
- Personalized Membership Card
- Club Pin
- Fontanini Registry Guide
- Research Service
- Advance Notice of Tour Appearances by Fontanini Family Members
- Travel Opportunities
- Contests

House of Fontanini Studio Tour in Italy
c/o The Fontanini Collectors' Club
555 Lawrence Avenue
Roselle, IL 60172
(800) 729-7662

Hours: Advance Reservations through the Fontanini Collectors' Club
Admission Fee: None

For collectors planning a trip to Italy, the House of Fontanini offers tours of their facilities in Bagni di Luca, Italy.

ROYAL DOULTON

Child Figures and a Family of Collectibles Continue a Tradition of Excellence

Generations of collectors have treasured the figurines from the famed British firm of Royal Doulton. Whether historical legends, childhood storybook favorites, 17th century women or images of nature, the three-dimensional works of art open the doors to a world of discovery. It is a world that has attracted many thousands of collectors, most of whom started off with a solitary figurine but were drawn back again and again to the memories and passion found in every piece.

Each character tells its own story through the captivating expressions, fine detail, remarkable design and painstaking craftsmanship that are international hallmarks of Royal Doulton. Many figurines have become heirlooms, passed down for children and future generations to enjoy. Fittingly, children have always held an important place in the collection.

Bringing Back Childhood Memories

Introduced in 1913, the first child figurine ever produced by Royal Doulton was titled "Darling." Inspired by poems by A.A. Milne and Robert Louis Stevenson, the figurine received its name after Queen Mary picked it out during a visit to the Royal Doulton factory and exclaimed, "Isn't he a darling!" She – and many other collectors – immediately fell in love with the small child dressed in a white nightgown. A version of this figurine still exists in the current product line.

Since then, many other childhood subjects have been produced over the years, including such favorites as "This Little Pig," "Bo Peep" and "Dinky Do."

In the past several years, Royal Doulton has focused on creating more figures to evoke a certain nostalgia for childhood days gone by. A range of figures which shows a little girl with a dog in several poses has been a most sought after group from Royal Doulton. These figures include "Sit," "Buddies," "Reward" and "Let's Play."

Still a popular theme with collectors, childhood offers continuing inspiration to Royal Doulton's artists. In keeping with this tradition and the popularity of these childhood subjects, several figurines were introduced in 1994: "Flowers For Mother," "Young Melody," "First Recital," "Mother's Helper," "A Posy for You" and "Special Friend," the first boy figurine in recent years.

Also introduced was "Hello Daddy" which portrays a little girl greeting her father over an old-fashioned, metal telephone. The figurines were designed to celebrate memorable family moments, such as "First Recital" and "Young Melody" to mark musical achievements while "Mother's Helper" and "Hello Daddy" pay tribute to the special relationship between parent and child.

In the spring of 1995, another range of three child figures premiered to the delight of collectors. "Hometime" portrays a little girl carrying her bookbag home from school while her dog trails alongside. "What's the Matter?" features another girl nursing her sick teddy bear back to health. A girl in her red dress carefully holds her lollipop in "Special Treat."

Royal Doulton has also introduced additions to previous series that bring back the joys of youth. "Dinnertime" shows a little girl holding a supper bowl while her grey poodle anxiously awaits his meal. Pets and children are familiar combinations in other subjects. "Home At Last" features a little girl lovingly cradling her cat, and "Faithful Friend" features another girl holding her spaniel. "Storytime" finds a little girl sitting on a bench reading her favorite nursery rhyme – the title of which actually appears in the book.

Royal Doulton is always planning more child figures, including a follow-up ballerina to the existing "Ballet Shoes" and "Little Ballerina," as well as other little boys.

The warm bond between a father and daughter inspired this china figurine titled "Hello Daddy." A little girl calls up her father using an old-fashioned telephone, which adds a special touch to the piece. Modelled by artist Nada Pedley, the figurine was introduced in the fall of 1994.

Bunnykins Continues a Rich Tradition

Children and adults have also enjoyed other series that bring animals to life. *Bunnykins* was created by Royal Doulton in 1934 and has since become the delight of three generations. The lovable characters help celebrate the many happy moments in family life. Whether the rabbits are getting ready for bedtime or playing in the snow, each piece is designed to treasure today and tomorrow as even more new generations discover the adventures of *Bunnykins*. The most recent introductions include "Goodnight," "New Baby," "Girl Skater" and "Boy Skater."

Children always seem to find special friends in pets. In "Dinnertime," "Faithful Friend" and "Home At Last" (from left to right), Royal Doulton shows little girls giving tender loving care to their poodle, spaniel and cat. In "Storytime," another girl reads her favorite nursery rhyme.

Beatrix Potter's Famous Characters

Lifted from the pages of *The Tales of Peter Rabbit*, Royal Doulton has introduced the beloved characters from Beatrix Potter's timeless books. Among the most recent additions, "Mr. McGregor" has the distinction of being the only human figure in the collection. "Peter Ate A Radish" shows the rabbit's antics, that always seem to get him into trouble, and is perhaps the most popular image of the mischievous character. All of the pieces in this popular Beatrix Potter collection are faithful to the gentle nature of the original illustrations.

Royal Doulton Relives History and Romance

The *Royal Doulton Figure Collection* is now more varied and extensive than ever, with hundreds of different subjects. Besides the child figures, Royal Doulton is renowned for its pretty ladies dressed in the most fashionable attire of their day. Characters from literature and legend are portrayed in china and resin. Recent additions include "Sherlock Holmes," "Gulliver" and "Richard the Lionheart."

The first large-scale prestige sculpture in 15 years, "Charge of the Light Brigade" commemorates a glorious defeat in 1854 when 673 gallant British cavalry men faced the mighty mass of Russian guns during the Crimean War. Introduced in 1995, the magnificent work of art is made in bone china and features a soldier holding leather reins and a metal lance, rifle and sword. Because of the intricate detail and complexity of the piece, each figure takes months to make and must be special ordered.

Many famous characters have also been immortalized on the limited edition character and toby jugs: Cyrano de Bergerac, Robin Hood, Confucius, Captain Bligh, Abraham Lincoln, George Washington, Charles Dickens and Alfred Hitchcock, just to name a few. Collectors can also join the Royal Doulton International Collectors Club to acquire exclusive figurines and stay up to date on the latest introductions.

A Historical View of Royal Doulton

As the world's largest manufacturer and distributor in the premium ceramic tableware and giftware market, Royal Doulton has come a long way from its humble beginnings. In 1815, John Doulton invested in a small pottery plant in London that produced practical and decorative stoneware. His son, Sir Henry Doulton, extended the product range to include sanitary ware, drain pipes and other related items, thereby establishing the business at the forefront of the ceramics industry. In 1877, the business acquired an interest in a factory in Stoke-on-Trent and later began producing bone china tableware at that site.

In 1901, H.M. King Edward VII authorized Doulton to use the word "Royal" to describe its products. Production expanded in the 1930s to include figurines and other giftware items. In 1966, Royal Doulton was the first china manufacturer to be awarded The Queen's Award for Technological Advancement. The company's brands now include Royal Crown Derby, Minton, Royal Albert and Royal Doulton.

Attention to Detail and Tradition

Royal Doulton artists who paint the colorful costumes, facial expressions and subtle skin tones of the *Figure Collection* follow in a tradition that dates back to the 19th century. During the 1890s, one of the company's most

Many little girls around the world dream of dancing on stage in a famous ballet. And their dreams all begin in the dance studio, as they lace up their slippers and put on their pink tutus. In this heart-warming figurine titled "Ballet Shoes," a girl takes a step toward her aspirations in the spotlight.

A popular theme for collectors, childhood inspired these three 1995 bone china figures titled (from left to right) "Hometime," "What's the Matter?" and "Special Treat." A girl strides out purposely clutching her school bag as she's followed by her puppy in "Hometime." "What's the Matter?" is a question posed by a concerned girl cradling her teddy bear, who she suspects is ill. "Special Treat" is the reward of a big yellow lollipop for a good girl.

distinguished art directors, Charles Noke, modeled the earliest examples, "Cardinal Wolsey" and "Queen Catherine." By 1909, Noke wanted to revive the genre of Staffordshire figures and the first productions, based on classical and literary themes, caused quite a stir among critics.

More extensive production of the figure series began in 1920 after Doulton received rave reviews at the British Industries Fair. Since then, new additions have constantly been designed and more than 1,000 different figures have been created.

Royal Doulton has its own in-house design team, combining artistic talent and technical expertise. Giftware ranges have also increasingly been designed to incorporate new working practices and decorating techniques, such as spray painting, the use of color clay, and the use of lithographic transfers for fine detail. These changes have resulted in greater consistency in quality, greater productivity, and the reduction of various decorating costs. Of course, a high level of hand work will always be maintained.

Royal Doulton
701 Cottontail Lane
Somerset, NJ 08873
(800) 68-CHINA
Fax (908) 356-9467

COLLECTORS' CLUB/TOURS

Royal Doulton International Collectors Club
701 Cottontail Lane
Somerset, NJ 08873
(800) 582-2102

Annual Dues: $25.00
Club Year: Anniversary of Sign-Up Date

Benefits:
- Opportunity to Purchase Members-Only Figurines
- Quarterly Magazine
- National Newsletter
- Advance Information on Introductions
- Historical Enquiry Service
- Invitations to Michael Doulton Events and Childsworld Artisan Events

Royal Doulton Factory Tours
Nile Street
Burslem Stoke-on-Trent Staffs ST6 2AJ
England
01144 1782 292292

Hours: Monday through Friday, 10:30 a.m. and 2 p.m.

Admission Fee: Nominal charge. For safety reasons the tour is not available for babies or children under ten years of age.

The Royal Doulton Factory Tour takes you behind the scenes at the world's leading fine china company. The tour also includes the Sir Henry Doulton Gallery, displaying examples of Royal Doulton products spanning over 170 years, and a factory gift shop.

Beswick Factory Tours
Gold Street
Longton Stoke-on-Trent ST3 2JP
England
01144 1782 292292
Hours: Monday through Friday, 10:15 a.m. and 2 p.m.
Admission Fee: Nominal charge. For safety reasons the tour is not available for babies or children under ten years of age.

The guided tour of the Beswick Factory allows visitors to see most stages of production of the Royal Doulton Character Jugs, animal models, studies of Beatrix Potter characters and *Bunnykins*. The Beswick Museum is open immediately before tours commence, and the Factory Gift Shop offers a wide selection of items from the John Beswick Studios.

SARAH'S ATTIC, INC.

The Journey to a Dream

"The Tuskegee Airman," a product of World War II was released by Sarah's Attic in June, 1995 (from the Sarah's Attic Historical Collection).

Sarah Johnston Schultz first graced this earth on a cold winter's day in the picturesque little village of Chesaning, Michigan. Sarah still calls this little town home. The influence of a small-town childhood coupled with the various experiences of running a nationwide business have helped Sarah to form her personal philosophy and thus the company philosophy of **Love**, **Respect** and **Dignity**. The purpose for and the effectiveness of each piece is carefully weighed before its debut. If it does not portray the qualities of Love, Respect and Dignity, the project is scuttled. Thus Sarah Schultz and Sarah's Attic, Inc. are as one.

Dreams Begin in Childhood

Sarah Johnston Schultz, daughter of William and Louise Johnston, was born in Chesaning, Michigan on February 23, 1943. She was "forever creative" and "ready for action." Little Sarah was the village's first paper girl. When she was not peddling papers or doing other chores, she was scooting about town on her bike, stopping to chat with friends both old and new.

Sarah and her father loved to fish, and when the time could be spared, the two could be found with fishing poles, wading the waters near the dam of the Shiawassee River. The father-daughter closeness is evident in many of Sarah's creations including "Contentment" which sold out in 1992. This endearing figurine portrays Sarah and her beloved father enjoying their very favorite pastime and captures those profound feelings of Love, Respect and Dignity that they had for each other.

Sarah graduated from Our Lady of Perpetual Help High School, and later married her childhood sweetheart, Jack "Jackboy" Schultz. While Sarah worked at Michigan Bell Telephone Company, Jack attended college and received his degree in pharmacy. After graduation, Jack went to work in his father's pharmacy, which he and Sarah eventually purchased, and Sarah developed a thriving gift department in the store. During these lean years, Sarah had five children: Mark, Tim, Tom, Julie and Mike. Tim and Julie have joined their mother in her business, while Mark and Tom have pursued other careers, but still help out when needed. Mike is currently attending Michigan State University.

The Dream Begins

Sarah's hectic life became even busier when she discovered that the best-selling gift items in the Schultz Country Pharmacy were her own creations. Items such as her stenciled slates, boards, pictures and sweet-faced dolls were in much demand. A sales representative suggested that she market her own creations, and after careful consideration, she decided, "Why not?" Demands on her time were already great, but since she was "itching" for some of her creativity to emerge, she began to create in earnest.

Sarah's business rapidly expanded from the dining room table, to a 5' by 20' room in the back of the very cramped pharmacy. In 1984, no longer able to "fit" everything and everybody into the available space, Sarah and company moved to the "Attic" which consisted of 1,200 square feet of floor space located above the pharmacy.

In 1986, pecan resin figurines replaced stenciled rulers and slates as the company's top sellers. The members of *Sarah's Gang*, "Tillie," "Willie," "Cupcake," "Twinkie," "Katie," "Whimpy" and baby "Rachael," became best sellers. Even though their poses and locales have changed through the years, they remain a mainstay of Sarah's Attic, Inc.

As the business grew, so did the need for more room. After much soul-searching and worry, Sarah purchased and remodeled a 10,000 square-foot grocery store on the Shiawassee River near the dam and close to the spot where she and her father had fished years earlier. It was the right decision, and today the production operations are located in this building. The art room, mail room and business offices remain in the "Attic" above the pharmacy. Despite all of the moves and growth in the company, Love, Respect and Dignity remain as the solid foundation for each collectible produced by Sarah's Attic.

Specializing in Dreams

Each of the collections created by Sarah and Sarah's Attic reflects a personal experience from the past or the present. For example, Sarah became

The Tender Moments-From Our Heart to Yours Collection *was created to promote awareness for special needs people. Sarah's Attic donates a portion of the proceeds from the sale of these figurines to two charities that help special children and adults, The Starlight Foundation and Hear Now.*

seriously ill with rheumatic fever when she was a child. Her father was very concerned and often brought angel figurines to her. To honor that special memory, the *Angels in the Attic Collection* was created.

In the past, it appeared that African-Americans were being ignored in the collectibles industry. Sarah saw the need for tasteful figurines to be created in their honor. Sarah's Attic filled that void by creating realistic black figurines that have become an important part of the company and of the collectibles industry. Sarah recalled the black family she grew up with in Chesaning, and from this enjoyable time in her life, the *Black Heritage Collection* was created.

The *Daisy Petals* series from the *Cherished Memories Collection* depicts Sarah's beloved children in their formative years. Thus "Spike" (Mark), "Sparky" (Tim), "Bomber" (Tom), "Jewel" (Julie) and "Stretch" (Mike) were born. To complete the family, "Sally Booba" (Sarah) and "Jack Boy" (Jack) came into existence. The *Cookie Kids & Friends©* also has memorable ties to the early days of the Schultz family. The growing business of Sarah's Attic allowed Sarah less time with her children. Years later, these "guilty feelings" led to the creation of the *Cookie Kids & Friends Collection.*

During the long illness of her mother Louise, Sarah searched for little pick-me ups to take to her. Sarah looked for mementos that would remind her mother of the pleasant chores and delightful activities that she cherished when she and her late husband, Willie Bill, were younger, healthy and raising their family. This was an impossible task because nothing was available. That difficult time in Sarah's life was the inspiration for the *Labor of Love Collection* which is currently in production. Although "Angel Willie Bill" and "Angel Louise" have departed this earth, they remain an influence on all that is created at Sarah's Attic.

The company continues to appreciate the efforts of the courageous patriots that have made America great. The *Spirit of America* and the *Black Heritage Collections* continue to feature pioneers that practiced a philosophy very similar to that of Sarah's Attic – Love, Respect and Dignity. Each one of these noble patriots has carved their niche in the history of the United States of America.

The *Tender Moments-From Our Heart to Yours Collection*, portraying children in wheelchairs, as well as the "Love and Hugs" figurine showing a child "signing" love and hugs, were created to promote awareness for people with special needs. A portion of the proceeds from the sale of these figurines is contributed to several charities.

The Dream Continues

The company continues to adapt to today's changing society. In 1994, Sarah's Attic was granted permission by the Martin Luther King, Jr. Estate to create figurines portraying Dr. King, his family and his world. This collection has proven very popular, and pieces are continually being added to it. Sarah's Attic has been given permission by Rosa Parks to create a figurine in her honor. This amazing likeness, which was recently released, has also been a great success.

Keeping abreast of today's trends, Sarah's Attic has granted licensing to several companies to produce company-related items including afghans and glitter domes.

The Sarah's Attic Forever Friends Collector's Club is a very important part of the company. The fifth club year began June 1, 1995 and continues through May 31, 1996. The free membership piece is entitled "Friends Forever" and features a lovable little African-American angel girl and a

To honor the memory of Dr. Martin Luther King, Jr., Sarah's Attic introduced the "Martin Luther King, Jr." figurine and sign and the "Coretta Scott King" figurine. These first three pieces in the Martin Luther King, Jr. Collection *are limited in production to December 31, 1996.*
** Licensed by the Estate of Martin Luther King, Jr., 1994*

Those joining the Sarah's Attic Forever Friends Collector's Club in 1995-96 receive the free membership figurine entitled, "Friends Forever."

Caucasian angel boy perched on a crescent moon atop a cloud of friendship. The Members-Only Redemption pieces are titled "Playtime Pals" and "Horsin' Around." In "Playtime Pals" an Afro-American angel boy and girl frolic with their rocking horse and favorite toys. "Horsin' Around" finds an adorable Caucasian angel boy and girl cavorting with their rocking horse and toys. These special pieces, along with additional club benefits and the tender loving care that members receive during the year, make the Sarah's Attic Forever Friends Collector's Club very unique. Both club pieces are additions to the *Labor of Love Collection*. The piece, "Flags in Heaven," offered only at promotional events, is also part of the *Labor of Love Collection*.

Many accolades have come to Sarah and Sarah's Attic, Inc. over the years. Each one has a special place in Sarah's heart. One of the highlights was receiving the 1992 Michigan Wholesale/Retail Entrepreneur of the Year award. This was a magnificent tribute to Sarah and the company that had come so far, overcoming many obstacles, in nine short years. From Chesaning's little paper girl to Michigan's Entrepreneur of the Year is a giant step. Only in America and only with the help of good people and Sarah's philosophy of Love, Respect and Dignity could the dream come true.

Speaking of dreams – Sarah has in her dreams a theme park promoting Love, Respect and Dignity, as well as Sarah's Attic shelters for the homeless. Those who know Sarah realize that her dreams are very likely to come true.

Sarah's Attic, Inc.
126-1/2 West Broad
P.O. Box 448
Chesaning, MI 48616
(800) 4-FRIEND
Fax (517) 845-3477

COLLECTORS' CLUBS

Sarah's Attic Forever Friends Collector's Club
P.O. Box 448
Chesaning, MI 48616
(800) 4-FRIEND

Annual Dues: $32.50
Club Year: June 1-May 31

Benefits:
- Membership Gift: "Forever Friends" Figurine
- Opportunity to Purchase Members-Only Figurines
- Newsletter, "Attic Updates"
- Folder to Hold Newsletters
- Catalogs
- Special Mailings
- Local Club Chapters

SCHMID

Lowell Davis and *Belsnickles* Continue the Schmid Tradition of Bringing Fine Collectibles to American Collectors

Drawing upon his childhood memories of farm and family, artist Lowell Davis has captured American rural life. In "Mother's Day," a cat proudly watches over her kittens. The tender scene reminds Davis that throughout life's changes "there's one thing that has always remained the same and that is having a wonderful mother."

The Stock Market Crash of 1929 signaled the end for many companies across the country as the grips of the Great Depression tightened the belts of Americans and dashed their hopes. For Paul Schmid, that time of desperation became a source of inspiration. The economic downturn closed the door on his successful commodities career but opened another door to a lifelong dream. He always believed that Americans would enjoy owning many works of art created in his homeland of Germany. This was his opportunity to prove it.

These fine gifts and collectibles weren't available in the United States in the early 1930s. But by 1935, Schmid could see his plans falling into place after discovering the charming Goebel figurines by Sister M.I. Hummel as well as ANRI woodcarvings from Italy. The company soon introduced Americans to these works of art, and now the family-run company has grown to become one of the world's leading suppliers of collectibles. Today, Schmid is still introducing collectors to quality products and leading artists who take everyone from down on the farm and back to centuries-old legends of Christmas.

Lowell Davis Serves a Slice of Rural Americana

In 1979, Schmid went to America's Heartland to find a Missouri farmer-turned-artist who would turn everyone's attention to the humor, critters and nostalgia of rural life. Since then, Lowell Davis has become one of the country's foremost artists who restores the days of "way back when." Davis himself once tried to escape the past only to find it held the best that life has to offer. This discovery shapes the artist and his work.

Davis was born into a humble farm family in Red Oak, Missouri, during the Great Depression – just as Schmid was getting off the ground on the East Coast. For him, life was living in the back of a general store (his family lost the farm), wearing clothes his mother sewed from empty feed sacks, milking the family's jersey cow, and listening to the old timers spin yarns as they whittled around a pot-bellied stove.

As soon as he was of age, he "escaped" to the Air Force, but not before becoming adept at whittling and painting. Following his military service, Davis landed a job as an art director for a Dallas advertising agency. But as Davis recalls: "It all came tumbling down. Liberal living is fine for awhile, but someday it all catches up with you. I lost everything, just everything, overnight." Everything but his artistic abilities.

He headed back to Red Oak in search of his roots and found a ghost town. Seeing the storybook simplicity of his childhood in the deteriorating barnboard, Davis knew what he had to do: preserve through art the values of that simpler time for future generations. That's exactly what he has accomplished by designing his limited edition lithographs, figurines, ornaments and collector plates from Schmid. He includes a personal story with each piece, describing his thoughts and country tales.

Davis continues to draw upon the antics of barnyard animals and childhood tales as the subjects and inspiration for his work. In his spare time, he uses his 40-acre farm in Carthage, Missouri, as his canvas, faithfully restoring an entire 1930s town, board by board, as a living monument to rural life in America. Davis, an inductee into the Agriculture Hall of Fame, is still at home on his farm and in his art studio behind the goat yard.

Farm Club Welcomes Collectors

Formed in 1985, the Lowell Davis Farm Club is going strong with an ever-growing membership dedicated to celebrating life's simple pleasures. Farm Club members enjoy many benefits not available to other folks, including a gift especially designed by Davis as a reminder of the joys of country living. New and renewing members also receive a free subscription to the "Lowell Davis Farm Club Gazette," *Lowell Davis Collector's Guide* and a Farm Club cap. During the year, they have the opportunity to purchase a members-only figurine.

Farm Club members always look forward to reading the latest issue of the "Gazette," published three times a year. This full-color newsletter offers information about new figurines, upcoming events, special promotions and all the news from the farm. Each issue also includes an authentic country-style recipe straight out of Davis' own kitchen.

Farm life isn't always filled with tranquility as Lowell Davis shows in "Sticks and Stones," which portrays Hayseed, the old tomcat on the farm. The cat has to put up with birds that enjoy pestering him – probably, as Davis warns, because Hayseed gets to close to their nests.

The *Lowell Davis Collector's Guide*, published once a year, includes full-color photographs of all the figurines in the collection, along with their year of introduction. The Guide also features information on all retired figurines, which collectors find especially helpful when looking for pieces on the secondary market. As for the Lowell Davis Farm Club cap, collectors have been spotted wearing it from the mall to the beach.

From a Nickel to the *Belsnickle*

Schmid also found the talents of another Missourian, who brings antique Santas to life. Inspired by the hand-sculpted, papier-maché figures of Linda Lindquist Baldwin, the *Belsnickle Collection* of figurines and ornaments is crafted of hollowed cold cast porcelain. It's an unusual and fascinating medium that perfectly mimics the look and feel of the original sculptures and is painted entirely by hand in authentic colors, including teal, grey, ecru and blue.

If you grew up without ever hearing about *Belsnickles*, you're probably not alone. But Baldwin is a *Belsnickle* success story. And it all began with a simple nickel – the one Baldwin spent in 1986 at a yard sale to purchase a book about antique Santas. Not only has she become something of a legend among Santa collectors, her *Belsnickles* are on exhibit at the Museum of American Folk Art in New York and on file for a future exhibit at the Smithsonian Institution. They are included in *The Spirit of Christmas*, a hard-cover book published by Leisure Arts and in a *Better Homes and Gardens* book of paper crafts. In addition, Baldwin has been featured on CNN Headline News and NBC Evening News, as well as *Woman's World*, and many other magazine and newspaper articles.

Because of the time required to sculpt and hand-paint each figure (up to 25 hours for some), Baldwin can only complete from 80 to 100 every year – not nearly enough to keep up with the demand. "The response to my *Belsnickles* has been so overwhelming that I finally realized I needed help in making them more widely available," she says. "I chose Schmid because, to me, they have the best reputation in the business. But I really didn't dream they would be able to replicate my work so well. When they showed me the first samples, I could not believe it. I was just stunned, they were so gorgeous."

Like Baldwin's originals, the *Belsnickles Collection* is comprised of three distinct Santa figurines, all based on her own research into the legend of these traditional Christmas figures that date back many hundreds of years. The stern, long-limbed and benevolent *Belsnickle* is from 19th century Germany. The *Belsnickle* counterpart is Father Christmas, also tall and lean, but carrying fruit, nuts and candy for those who have been good. The Roly-Poly is the transitional Santa of early 20th century America – round, red-cheeked and elfish, much like the Santa we all know today.

A U.S. nickel has been imbedded in the bottom of each figurine and some of the Santas even contain rare or newly minted coins. This symbolizes the history behind these unique pieces, which began when Baldwin spent five cents on the antique Santa book. She was mesmerized by the photographs she found inside and disappointed to learn that the price of the antique papier-maché Santas cost up to $6,000. So she set out to make her own, even though she never took an art class in her life.

While Baldwin continues creating her one-of-a-kind originals, she is tremendously excited about her partnership with Schmid. "I grew up on a farm in the Ozarks with no running water or electricity," she says. "Thanks to my *Belsnickles*, I now feel like Cinderella at the ball! I hope I never hear the stroke of midnight!"

Continuing Three Generations of Excellence

The *Belsnickles Collection* follows the company's long-standing commitment to quality and to providing

Enchanting beyond compare, this "Fourth Annual Santa" from the Belsnickle Collection *has all the makings of an instant classic. Beautifully detailed in the collection's signature style, this snoozing Santa was handcrafted and hand-painted from an original sculpture by folk artist Linda Lindquist Baldwin. Limited to 1995 production, the Santa measures 8" with an issue price of $45.00.*

This antique reproduction "Ivory Santa" from the Belsnickle Collection *conveys a sense of gentle goodwill. Standing 12-1/2" tall, this handcrafted and hand-painted collectible was created of resin to mimic the look and feel of Linda Lindquist Baldwin's original sculptures. The figurine has an issue price of $70.00.*

collectibles that will be cherished for many years to come. "From the time my grandfather first started selling giftware to New England shopkeepers in the 1930s, he insisted that Schmid must be known for its quality and service," Paul Schmid III once said.

That philosophy has held for more than 60 years with the company's licensed products and its own figurines, musicals, ornaments and other collectibles. From Disney characters to Lowell Davis' critters and Beatrix Potter to *Belsnickles*, Schmid will continue in the steps of its founder, who turned a dream into reality.

Schmid
55 Pacella Park Dr.
Randolph, MA 02368-1795
(617) 961-3000
Fax: (617) 961-4355

COLLECTORS' CLUB/TOUR

Lowell Davis Farm Club
55 Pacella Park Dr.
Randolph, MA 02368-1795
(617) 961-3000

Annual Dues: $25.00 - Renewel: $20.00
Club Year: Anniversary of Sign-Up Date

Benefits:
- Membership Gift: Lowell Davis Figurine and Official Lowell Davis Farm Cap
- Opportunity to Purchase Members-Only Figurine
- Subscription to the "Lowell Davis Farm Club Gazette"
- Membership Card
- *Lowell Davis Collector's Guide* and Dealer Listing
- Announcements of Special Appearances by Lowell Davis
- Invitation to Farm Events
- Coloring Book with Story Written and Ilustrated by Lowell Davis
- Local Club Chapters

Red Oak II
Rt. 1
Carthage, MO 64836
(417) 358-9018

Hours: Monday through Saturday, 10 a.m.-6 p.m.; Sunday, 10 a.m.-5 p.m. Closed January and February.

Admission Fee: None; $1.00 Admission to the Belle Star Museum

Visit the 1930s town recreated by artist Lowell Davis which includes the Belle Star Museum, Gas Station, Blacksmith Shop, Elmira School, Salem Country Church, Parsonage, General Store/Gift Shop, Feed and Seed Store, Mother-in-Law House, The Bird Song, Sawmill and four Bed and Breakfasts.

SHELIA'S COLLECTIBLES

Tour the Country as History Repeats Itself — in Miniature Buildings

As a young girl growing up in the South in the 1940s and 1950s, Shelia Thompson was raised in true Southern fashion — young women were not expected to further their education beyond high school, let alone aspire to own their own companies! Like most Southern women, Shelia's own grandmother believed that a woman's role as a good mother and good wife was the best that life could offer — a true measure of success. It was in this atmosphere that Shelia Thompson, who always excelled artistically, was never encouraged to pursue her talents, except as they related to being a wife and mother.

So how did Shelia's Collectibles get its start and continue to expand to its present success? How did Shelia Thompson become known as the "woman who makes history every day?" And how is it that Shelia Thompson, both wife and mother, presents seminars to women's groups today about the secret of success as a self-taught artist: "Don't impose limitations! Are credentials important? They may open doors faster, but it is your drive, determination and desire, and being in the right place at the right time, that makes all the difference in the world."

Early Beginnings

During her childhood, Shelia Thompson loved anything related to art. "As a child, you assume that if you can do it, everyone else can too," explains Shelia. "It wasn't until later that I discovered my artistic talent was a gift, a part of me that couldn't be denied. At four or five, I used to carefully remove the family portraits from the wall and trace the outline of my ancestors' faces and try to draw their eyes and lips. I would then take these masterpieces to my grandmother, but never did tell her how I composed my pictures!"

Thompson's artistic endeavors continued in high school. Anytime there was an art project in high school, she headed the committee, whether it was making posters or creating backdrops for the school plays. Years later, Thompson's love of art turned into a hobby, as she cared for her two young daughters and experimented with various materials and media.

"This house oozes Southern," according to Shelia Thompson. She is, of course, referring to "Tara," from the popular Gone With The Wind *series.*

Many collectible companies were started by women who sought innovative ways to add income to meet their families' needs, and Shelia is no exception. This talented artist was looking for a way to raise some extra cash for the holidays in 1978 and decided to make wall-mounted Mallard ducks to sell at the famed Charleston Market. These ducks were a hit, Shelia caught the entrepreneurial bug, and Shelia's Collectibles was launched!

With the Charleston Market at her fingertips, Shelia observed thousands of tourists passing through this historic market looking for something to take home as a remembrance. Shelia's love for old houses, combined with numerous requests from customers asking for historic buildings, made it a natural for her to begin creating miniature wooden replicas of historic houses and public buildings. Shelia began this venture by creating the *Charleston* series, and today, Shelia's Collectibles' series span the nation.

Shelia has always taken great pride in developing concepts that are uniquely and distinctively hers. With this goal in mind, she researched the market and thus created an interpretation with an exciting new look: the layered facade house. "I wanted each miniature replica to look as if you could actually walk into the building," explains Shelia. Instead of creating designs on both sides of the structures, Shelia felt collectors would appreciate learning some of the history of the locales; therefore, the backs of all pieces contain pertinent facts about the residences, the people who built them and other fascinating information. For example, "Ivy Green," Helen Keller's birthplace, featured a message in braille on the back of this Collector Society piece, and members received the written transcription in their Society notebooks.

Today, the Shelia's Collectibles manufacturing facility hums with activity, as each house designed by Shelia begins as a block of wood, which is first sanded. The wood is then cut to design specifications and sprayed with its base color of paint. The house begins to take shape, as artisans print the designated design on each wood form. Roofs are hand-painted, in addition to the beautiful bushes, flowers and trees which grace each structure: a trademark of Shelia's attractive houses. The layers of the houses are then assembled, forming complete pieces. "We're always improving our quality," explains Shelia. "We experiment with raw materials such as wood and paint. We try different color combinations and locate different ways to create sharper details, such as our laser cutting methods."

Backed By History

Shelia's deep appreciation of history is apparent upon examining the company's product line. "What started out as my love of old houses and customers' requests for historic buildings, has evolved into our mission of acting as ambassadors to help people appreciate the history of the United States," relates Shelia. "Our country is so diversified, whether you're studying the South and the effects of the Civil War or the beautiful plantations, or the North, where you can appreciate the significance of our forefathers responsible for signing the Declaration of Independence and what they contributed to history – the buildings they built, the homes in which they lived and the meetings that took place. Of course, we can't forget the western expansion to California, the famous Gold Rush and the architectural styles unique to this region. Now that I have grandchildren, I understand the importance of preserving the past. We hope to encourage people to appreciate their heritage by saving it for their grandchildren and, in turn, their grandchildren."

How does an artist go about selecting her subject matter? For Shelia Thompson, the ideas came naturally. Once she introduced the *Charleston* series and observed collectors' enthusiasm for historic areas, Shelia proceeded to research and select sites around the country to launch other historic series. Although Shelia and her husband and business partner Jim, travel extensively to locate buildings for their historical miniature house series, they rely on recommendations from collectors and retailers, who send postcards, photographs and news clippings to share their recommendations. Most of Shelia's series are ongoing, as she selects historic cities that according to the artist, "include so many wonderful buildings that I could add to them my entire lifetime and never run out of sites!" Some of these ongoing series include *Savannah, Williamsburg, Martha's Vineyard, Key West, West Coast Lighthouses, American Barns, Jazzy New Orleans, Plantations, Amish Village, Atlanta* and *San Francisco.*

A new category for Shelia's collectibles, nine painted metal ornaments debut this stunning collection, which includes the "Drayton House." Located in Charleston, this house is nicknamed the 'Chinese Chippendale' because of the Medieval European and Chinese architectural influences.

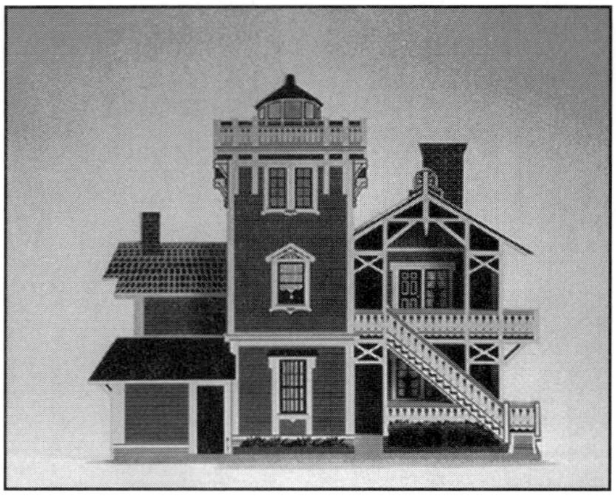

Part of the West Coast Lighthouse *series, "East Brother Light" is one of seven lighthouses located in the San Francisco Bay area. This structure more closely resembles a home than a lighthouse.*

Innovations that Shape Shelia's

Although Shelia creates miniature homes in various architectural styles, she is best known for her lovely Victorian homes, which collectors admire for their intricate gingerbread motifs, expansive entrances, turrets, and lace curtains at the windows. The *Victorian Springtime* series features a Victorian home from every state, complete with springtime flowers in bloom to commemorate this lovely season. On the back of each piece is the history of the house, along with the State bird, tree, flower, motto and nickname. Five homes will be added to this series each year until all 50 states are represented.

One of Shelia's favorite annual introductions is what the company calls the *Artist's Choice* series. Shelia describes this strictly limited edition series as "the freedom to have the ability to explore those things no one is asking for and to offer them as part of my line!" Prior releases have included such innovations as the "Mail-Order Victorians," four striking Victorian homes from George F. Barber's catalog of home plans dating back to the 1800s.

Always interested in experimenting with various techniques, Shelia achieved a glow-in-the-dark look in her *Ghost Houses* series. Collectors beware, because this series includes all real, documented ghost houses, with folklore included on the back of each piece! Stemming from a fascination with ghosts, Shelia also studied the various moon phases and introduced two houses per year featuring a moon phase, which glows in the dark.

Another 'first' for Shelia's Collectibles is their venture into licensing, and the firm began in grand style with the introduction of everyone's favorite, *Gone With The Wind.* "Collectors' enthusiasm for memorabilia and items related to this epic novel and movie were so overwhelming," reminisces Shelia, "that we obtained a license through Turner Entertainment to create favorite landmarks such as 'Tara,' and 'Twelve Oaks.'" The designs were all approved by the licensing firm, and each piece bears the Turner trademark and licensing information.

Just when Shelia thought her miniature replicas couldn't get any smaller, a large firm known for their metalwork ornaments, contacted the artist regarding the creation of painted metal ornaments. Prototypes were created,

From the San Francisco *series comes "Eclectic Blue," aptly named for its shades of blue and somewhat unconventional style, with all of the "swirls and turns," as Shelia describes.*

and much to Shelia's delight, they were historically accurate, right down to the coloration of each original structure. Nine ornaments debuted the collection, carefully selected by Shelia from her existing series. Lighthouses, Victorian homes and a cottage from the *Martha's Vineyard* series were painstakingly created, and each includes a 'romance card' featuring historical facts.

Looking to the Future

Shelia's Collectibles is certainly a company on the move, as the firm is constantly seeking exciting projects to parlay into wonderful collector series. Plans include more licensing opportunities like the *Gone With The Wind* series, in addition to locating ways to use Shelia's images on other materials, as they did with the Christmas ornaments. Collectors can keep current on news about the company through membership in the Collectors Society, with benefits including the chance to obtain exclusive Society pieces, and information about Shelia and her latest introductions and travels. Collectors will be particularly interested in hearing that Shelia's Collectibles has ventured into television, with appearances on "Start to Finish" on the Discovery Channel and "The Contemporary Collectibles Show," the first industry-wide television show for collectors.

Shelia Thompson is a Southern woman, proud of her heritage, who followed her dreams like other artists, to create artwork for collectors' enjoyment. "I strive for quality and a sense of color and design. When I create a piece of artwork, I'm saying something about myself and the way I interpret life. Anytime you buy an artist's work, you're truly buying a piece of that artist who has put his or her heart and soul into the project. But above all, what makes my job so rewarding is the collectors that I meet while traveling and the letters I receive. It's a real honor to recreate historical buildings and to put them on the real estate market, an honor I will enjoy for many years to come!"

Shelia's Collectibles
P.O. Box 31028
Charleston, SC 29417
(800) 227-6564
Fax (803) 556-0040

COLLECTORS' CLUB/TOUR

Shelia's Collectors Society
1856 Belgrade Avenue, Bldg. C
Charleston, SC 29407
(803) 766-0485 or (800) 227-6564

Annual Dues: $25.00 - Renewal: $20.00
Club Year: Anniversary of Sign-Up Date

Benefits:
- Special Society Gift
- Opportunity to Purchase Members-Only House
- Quarterly Newsletter
- Binder
- Personalized Membership Card Issued Annually
- Members-Only Tour of Shelia's Collectibles

Shelia's Collectibles Tour
1856 Belgrade Avenue
Charleston, SC 29407
(803) 766-0485 or (800) 227-6564

Hours: Monday through Friday by Appointment Only
Admission: For Shelia's Collectors Society Members Only

Members of Shelia's Collectors Society are welcome to tour the art studio and manufacturing facility of Shelia's Collectibles.

SWAROVSKI

One Hundred Years of Crystal Perfection

In 1895, together with his family, 33 year old Daniel Swarovski left Georgenthal in northern Bohemia and headed for the tiny village of Wattens in the Austrian Tyrol to set up his own company. Even as an adolescent, this son of a glass cutter had made exploratory attempts to improve the manual cutting of crystal jewelry stones. Not long after, Daniel Swarovski had a vision of making affordable high-quality jewelry stones available throughout the world. Then, during a visit to the International Electricity Exhibition in Vienna, he saw the inventions of Edison, Siemens and Schuckert and decided to develop a machine that would cut crystal jewelry stones with previously unknown perfection and precision. Having done so, he decided to leave his birthplace, which had been a major center for the manufacture of crystal jewelry stones since the 17th century, and settle in Tyrol, which offered him the hydroelectric power he needed for his machines.

By the end of the century, Swarovski's crystal stones were synonymous with perfectly cut crystal jewelry stones in the world's major fashion centers.

In 1911, Swarovski and his three sons, Wilhelm, Friedrich and Alfred, set up a laboratory and found a way of producing their own raw material, pure crystal. In their striving for ever-higher quality and independence, they established principles that are still central to the company success to this day.

Still headquartered in Wattens in the Austrian Tyrol, Swarovski is the world's leading manufacturer of full cut crystal and is still run by the descendants of its founder, Daniel Swarovski, now in the fourth generation.

Today, Swarovski products range from jewelry stones used by the fashion, jewelry, lighting and cosmetic packaging industries to gift items, collectibles, decorative objects and their own fashion accessories and jewelry lines. Other product lines include precision optical instruments, grinding tools and abrasives, and other industrial items.

Swarovski Celebrates 100th Anniversary in 1995

In 1995, Swarovski, celebrated its centennial. The company's success is still very much based on the principle set by its founder generations ago: the constant striving for perfection, a belief in the importance of innovation and a corporate culture in which a sense of responsibility towards the company and its employees are of central importance.

Swarovski Silver Crystal introduced the "Centenary Swan" available only in 1995. Included was a decorative column display, a perfect way to display the exquisitely cut swan. A "maxi" swan was also introduced and is available indefinitely. Both were designed by Swarovski designer, Anton Hirzinger.

The Swarovski Collectors Society organized special events and activities to commemorate this special occasion, including 10-day centenary tours. Following the footsteps of Daniel Swarovski, the tour started in Prague where Swarovski patented his first invention, then went on to Vienna where he visited the First International Electricity Exhibition in 1883. The

Founded in 1895 by Daniel Swarovski, the Swarovski factory is still headquartered in Wattens in the beautiful Austrian Tyrol.

climax of the tour was a visit to the Austrian Tyrol, home to Swarovski since 1895.

The Swarovski Collectors Society renewal gift for 1995 was a miniature swan, the smallest in the series of swans designed for the centenary year. Also available exclusively for members was a crystal-studded swan brooch, and a centenary coin for members visiting Wattens in 1995. Members could stamp their own coins at the ancient mint in the historic town of Hall in the Tyrol or obtain it from the Swarovski Crystal Shop in Wattens.

The highlight of the centenary year was the opening of the "Swarovski Crystal Worlds" in Wattens. Designed by the internationally renowned multi-media artist Andre Heller, it is a half-underground, half-aboveground structure with an internal volume of 600,000 cubic feet. Inside the structure is a series of rooms and halls that highlight the aesthetic qualities of crystal. For instance, one room is actually a dome made of 590 mirrors that gives those inside the feeling of being inside a crystal. Located adjacent to the company's factory in Wattens, Austria, "Swarovski Crystal Worlds" also features the work of important contemporary artists including Salvador Dali and Keith Haring. Also included are a cafeteria, a lounge for SCS members and a retail shop.

Available only in 1995, the "Centenary Swan" was intoduced by Swarovski Silver Crystal to celebrate its 100th Anniversary. A decorative column was included to display this exquisitely cut swan.

Swarovski Silver Crystal

A tiny crystal mouse introduced in 1976 marked the beginning of a new era for Swarovski. The mouse was the first item in the Swarovski Silver Crystal line, which today consists of over 120 gift items and collectibles featuring 20 theme groups, including *Our Woodland Friends*, *South Sea*, and *When We Were Young*. The brilliant, full cut crystal designs of animals, fruits and other decorative objects, are available at more than 13,000 selected retailers worldwide.

Newer introductions in the Silver Crystal line include the "Angel" and "Sir Penguin" by Adi Stocker, and a 4-piece "miniature" train set designed by Gabriele Stamey.

First Swarovski Silver Crystal Limited Edition

For the first time ever, Swarovski Silver Crystal introduced its first limited edition, "The Eagle," early in 1995. Created by Adi Stocker, one of the company's best known designers, it admirably captures the power and grace of a Golden eagle about to launch into flight. Society members were offered this masterpiece on a "first come–first serve" basis, and only 2,900 U.S. Society members were lucky enough to acquire this special edition. Each piece is unique, due to its individual number indelibly lasered into the base of the artwork. It rests on a handcrafted mahogany base bearing the signature of Adi Stocker and the year of introduction.

"The Eagle's" bill and talons are crafted of solid sterling silver and the piece was accompanied by a Certificate of Authenticity signed by Helmut Swarovski and Adi Stocker.

Will Swarovski Silver Crystal introduce other limited editions in the future? We'll just have to wait and see.

Swarovski Collectors Society

The success and popularity of

Swarovski: The Magic of Crystal, *written by jewelry historian Vivienne Becker, documents the history of Swarovski from its foundation in 1895 until today.*

Swarovski Silver Crystal, together with the fact that it has so many devoted followers, led to the foundation of the Swarovski Collectors Society (SCS) in 1987. Today, SCS boasts more than 200,000 members in 25 countries.

Membership benefits include special limited editions created exclusively for SCS members, a bi-annual full color magazine; membership renewal gifts; invitations to special events, exhibitions, and seminars; and organized visits to Wattens, the home of Swarovski. The membership fee is $35 – renewal: $25.

Swarovski: The Magic of Crystal

A lavishly illustrated, 160-page book telling the story of Swarovski has been published in six languages: English, German, Italian, French, Spanish and Dutch. Written by Vivienne Becker, jewelry historian, *Swarovski: The Magic of Crystal* documents the history of the traditional family firm from its foundation in 1895 on to the present day, with the main emphasis on the Swarovski Silver Crystal figurines first launched in 1976. Anyone interested in reading more about Swarovski's history is able to obtain the book at Swarovski Silver Crystal retail outlets and distinguished book stores worldwide.

Swarovski America Limited
2 Slater Road
Cranston, RI 02920
(800) 426-3088
Fax (401) 463-8459

COLLECTORS' CLUB/VISITOR CENTER

Swarovski Collectors Society
2 Slater Road
Cranston, RI 02920
(800) 426-3088

Annual Dues: $35.00 - Renewal: $25.00
Club Year: Anniversary of Sign-Up Date

Benefits:
- Opportunity to Purchase SCS Annual Edition Figurine
- Membership Certificate: 40mm Swarovski Paperweight
- Complimentary Renewal Gift
- Bi-annual Magazine, *Swarovski Collector*
- Bi-annual Newsletter
- Travel Opportunities
- Designer Signature Sessions, Special Events, Exhibitions, Seminars

The Swarovski Crystal Shop & Visitor Center
A-6112 Wattens
Innstrasse 1
Austria
(43-5224-5886)

Hours: May to September – Monday through Saturday, 8 a.m. - 6 p.m., Sunday, 8 a.m. - Noon
October to April – Monday through Friday, 8 a.m. - 6 p.m., Saturday, 8 a.m. - Noon

Admission Fee: None

The Swarovski Crystal Shop & Visitor Center displays all Swarovski crystal brands, as well as unique articles from other leading manufactures. Members of Swarovski Collectors Society are given a special welcome in the lounge. Exhibits highlight engraving, various glass techniques and gem cutting.

TODAY'S CREATIONS INC.

Times to Remember Captures Every Memorable Aspect of the Bridal Experience

A flowing white gown...a bouquet of gorgeous flowers...a towering wedding cake...a romantic first dance with the handsome bridegroom. These are just a few of the memorable aspects that help make a wedding day perfect. And now, thanks to Today's Creations, every bride (or bride-to-be) can experience the emotion and excitement of that wonderful wedding again and again. For this New Jersey-based firm unveiled, in May 1995, a stunning set of contemporary bridal figurines called *Times to Remember*.

In six original works of art, *Times to Remember* portrays the universal feelings of brides, grooms and their happy families. When introduced in order, these elegant figurines tell the story of a wedding day to cherish.

Al Gordon, artist for Today's Creations Inc., is putting the final touches on the illustration of "With This Ring." Mr. Gordon's illustrations became the blueprints for Today's Creations' unique bridal figurines.

First we see the loving mother, helping her daughter put the finishing touches on her gown, make-up and hairstyle. "Mother and Bride" will bring a happy tear to the eye of many women who recall just such an intimate moment – a few last-minute bits of advice from the doting mother...the nervous bride's need for reassurance that she looks her best...the profession of everlasting love between mother and daughter.

Next we observe "Bride with Bouquet," the classic photographic portrait subject. Fresh and graceful as the flowers she holds near her heart, the bride wears an expression of expectation and love as she prepares for this – the most important commitment of her young life.

"With This Ring" portrays the high point of the marriage ceremony, as the bride says "I do" to her adoring husband. The most dramatic moment of the wedding, this moment seals the covenant of marriage before God and before all the assembled family and guests.

Two wonderful figurines introduce us to the reception festivities, and both involve traditional dances. "The First Dance" symbolizes the beginning of the bride and groom's life together as they dance to their special song. Then "Daddy's Little Girl" saves a dance for that first man in her life, as the loving father embraces his daughter and admires the beautiful young woman he and her mother have raised.

The final figurine in this first suite of six is called "Slice of Life." It depicts yet another classic moment from the American wedding scene as the bride and groom slice the first few pieces of wedding cake to feed each other and pose for the camera.

Each of these heart-touching vignettes is captured in an 8"-tall figurine, cold cast to ensure that every marvelous detail is preserved to perfection. Collectors have the choice of a hand-painted version of each figurine, or a pristine, all-white style that appears particularly contemporary in display. For those who enjoy musical figurines, "The First Dance" and "Daddy's Little Girl" both are made available in versions with built-in musical movements.

The *Times to Remember* collection carries a limited edition of 5,000 for each work of art. What's more, an original poem has been composed and included with each figurine – an addition that provides all the more depth and emotional power to this remarkable fine art presentation. All figurines come with a wooden base and brass name plate, and a Certificate of Authenticity is included in every beautifully designed gift box.

The Creative Minds Behind *Times to Remember*

Devotion and determination have been the hallmarks of the creative process for *Times to Remember* and

Today's Creations. The team at Today's Creations includes Marty Miller and Randy Gordon, each of whom brought unique skills and insights to their association.

Marty Miller directed the research model for the *Times to Remember* project, ensuring that every aspect would be completely reflective of the American wedding tradition. Miller's background includes doing research grants for the Federal Government. This professional skill offered the team a unique and insightful way of extracting information and ideas. The question Miller always asked himself and his partner was, "How do we make it better?"

Randy Gordon has a history that is somewhat unique for a "player" in the collectibles industry. His background includes being a player in minor league baseball for the Detroit Tigers. As an athlete, he has always strived for perfection. Indeed as a bowler, he has achieved perfection with five perfect 300 games to his credit! This dedication has carried over to his business career and shows in the excellence of the *Times to Remember* collection.

The initial concept for a bridal series of figurines came from Randy Gordon, who serves as Vice-President of Sales and Marketing for Marty Miller Marketing. The Miller firm is a sales, marketing and design company specializing in the collectibles market. Its namesake, Marty Miller, has 20 years experience in the field, while Gordon brings a decade of experience to the *Times to Remember* creative process.

Using Randy Gordon's concept of a bridal focus, the team conducted extensive research in the bridal market. They learned several facts which indicated that collectors would happily embrace the concept of *Times to Remember.* First and foremost, no manufacturer had ever before sculpted all the significant scenes of a wedding. Most such sculptural works centered only on the bride herself. Second, most bridal figurines were Victorian in style – not representative of the brides of today. Third, the only available contemporary bridal figurines carried very high price tags.

The mission for *Times to Remember* became clear. Today's Creations would develop an entire series of 1990s-style bridal figurines at moderate prices, intended to appeal to the bride and groom of today. The firm's goal would be to achieve a realistic, yet appealing, portrayal of special wedding participants and events.

Artist Al Gordon Brings the Dream to Reality

The illustrator for *Times to Remember*, Al Gordon, has over 30 years of experience in all aspects of the art and collectibles fields. His impressive portfolio includes time spent running his own design group, developing original characters, and working for many major licensing companies. Al Gordon has illustrated Disney and Looney Tunes characters, and he also boasts the unique ability to translate reality into a two-dimensional illustration. These illustrations became the blueprints for the three-dimensional, hand-sculpted figurines you see today.

The inspiration behind Al Gordon's work was Sue, his wife for over 40 years. The love, respect and friendship they shared through the years showed in the passion of Al's designs. She was with him throughout his career and remained by his side through the completion of these first six *Times to Remember* designs. Sadly, Sue lost her battle with lung cancer in May 1994, and did not see the final pieces. Al has dedicated this *Times to Remember* series to the memory of his loving wife.

Production Begins

Bill Berzack, president of Today's Creations, has been importing products to the United States for over 20 years. His knowledge of the production studios in various lands provided the final piece to the creative puzzle. When Bill first showed Al's illustrations to officials at his chosen studio, the

Artist Al Gordon, with over 30 years experience in all aspects of the art and collectibles fields, is shown with a small sampling of the characters he has illustrated. His diversified talent enabled Today's Creations to create the Times to Remember *bridal figurine series.*

"With This Ring," beautifully captures one of the special moments of the wedding ceremony. Limited to 5,000 pieces, the hand-painted figurine recalls the joy and happiness of this blessed occasion.

sculptor's response was, "These are the best illustrations I've ever seen." Everyone was convinced that Today's Creations had something special – an impression that was further reinforced by the outstanding sculptures that emerged. They far exceeded the creative team's expectations!

Times to Remember Sets the Stage for Today's Creations

While the *Times to Remember* figurines are sure to attract brides of all generations, research shows that the current bridal market is booming. In 1991 alone there were almost 2,500,000 marriages in the United States, which generated over $32,000,000,000 in retail sales. With gift and collectible retailers expanding their bridal displays, these marvelous figurines are sure to be showcased in a wide variety of stores. And with almost 70% of all weddings occurring between April and October, the May 1995 introduction of the collection was timed perfectly for both stores and consumers.

Not content to rest on their laurels, the creators of *Times to Remember* already have a second series of collectibles well underway. Titled *Today's Heroes*, these works of art will be sculpted in a 1990s contemporary and realistic style. Each figurine will portray a much-honored profession, with the first piece inspired by the fireman.

Over 200 photos of firemen in action were taken to ensure accuracy in the final portrayal of pose, uniform and equipment. Depicted in completely authentic detail, the fireman and others in the *Today's Heroes* series will be available in 1996.

As Today's Creations carves out its niche in the gift and collectibles field, careful research will remain the firm's hallmark. The creative team's goal is to present contemporary collectibles that break new ground while inspiring and pleasing America's discerning collectors.

Today's Creations, Inc.
167 Main Street
Lodi, NJ 07644
(800) 5-TODAYS
Fax (201) 472-4793

THE TUDOR MINT INC.

A Fantasy World of *Myth and Magic* Portrayed in Shimmering Figurines With Brilliant Crystals

Houston, Texas, marks the new American home of The Tudor Mint Inc. – and a cause for celebration among all those who love the fantasy world of *Myth and Magic.* This new company has been created especially to serve the interests of Myth & Magic Collectors' Club members who reside in the United States. It is also the route through which The Tudor Mint's figurines now enter America for distribution to shops throughout the country.

The principal persons in the company are: President Graham Hughes (United Kingdom); Vice-President and USA Manager Bruce Kollath; Secretary Richard Power (United Kingdom); Treasurer Louis DeCou; and Operations Manager Chuck Smith. American collectors first enjoyed the opportunity to meet club officials and see Tudor Mint collections at the Long Beach and South Bend collectibles shows during 1995.

The British Origins of The Tudor Mint Inc.

Birmingham, at the heart of the English Midlands, once was the home of many jewelers who lived and worked there for generations, producing fine-quality, detailed work. One such craftsman was Walter Archibald Parker Watson.

In 1915, Watson sold his business to A.H. Power and C. Flint, who kept his name when they established their new company – W.A.P. Watson Limited – presumably to retain the reputation he had established over a number of years. Power and Flint originally produced costume jewelry under the trade name of *Exquisite Jewellery.* The business did well and by 1935, products included souvenirs such as ashtrays, sweet dishes, condiment sets, cake stands, letter openers and keepsake spoons.

During World War II, the company's workshops were turned over to essential war production, making small, precise components. In 1945, after the war, W.A.P. Watson resumed its costume jewelry and souvenir business. In 1954, the company moved out of the jewelry quarter to a three-acre site in Solihull, England, where it still remains today. With room to expand, W.A.P. Watson became the second largest manufacturer of costume jewelry in the United Kingdom.

Graham Hughes joined W.A.P. Watson on November 1, 1970 as company secretary – at a time when business was thriving. In the late 1970s, though, the arrival of "cheap products" in costume jewelry brought large declines in the firm's jewelry sales. As a result, new product ideas were being developed by Mr. Hughes. All of these new product ideas were created and tested under the name "Tudor Mint" in order to create a quality base upon which to establish the giftware side of the business.

Graham Hughes went on to become the Managing Director of The Tudor Mint Ltd. Changes were also made within the company structure: The Watson Group Limited was created as the holding company, with W.A.P. Watson Limited being the trading company (hence the "WAPW" nameplate on all Tudor Mint products).

A range of silver and gilt-plated animals, each incorporating a crystal, was developed and named *Crystalflame.* This was a successful line for The Tudor Mint until 1988, when sales had peaked and were beginning to drop. Graham Hughes realized that a new giftware line was needed to take its place. *Myth and Magic* was this collection.

At over 9" in height, "The Power of Crystal" serves as the most intricate and largest study in the Myth and Magic *collection.*

The International Debut of *Myth and Magic*

The Tudor Mint's chief designer was invited to submit drawings for a collection of dragons, wizards, castles and mythical creatures, to be manufactured incorporating crystals. She presented 25 original designs, from which 12 were sculpted and first shown at a trade show in Birmingham. As soon as the collection became available in stores, it was an instant success. The same was true when *Myth and Magic* debuted in the United States in February 1989.

The Myth and Magic Collectors' Club was founded in the United Kingdom in 1990 because the products already had earned an incredible following. By the end of July 1990, 3,000 members had been enrolled. The popularity of the club continued to increase, and the United States division opened May 1, 1991 through Fantasy Creations of New York City. In 1991, a distributorship was opened in Canada: SAMACO Trading Limited. SAMACO then launched a

Genuine crystals sparkle and boast a whole rainbow of colors in "The Earth Dragon" from the Myth and Magic *collection.*

Canadian division of the Collectors' Club in May, 1992.

In early 1994, W.A.P. Watson Limited and Graham Hughes realized that in order to reach full market potential in the United States, it would be necessary for The Tudor Mint to have a physical presence in North America. The central United States location and the availability of experienced management personnel, trained staff, and an expert collectibles sales force gave rise to the decision to locate this fully owned subsidiary in Houston.

The Tudor Mint Inc. became the official and exclusive distributor for all Tudor Mint products and the headquarters for the United States division of the Myth and Magic Collectors' Club on January 1, 1995. This offered a fresh beginning for Tudor Mint products, which now are sold mostly through retail shops instead of through other distributors or directly to the public. The company's main goals include re-establishing its line to increase its collectibility, and increasing visibility in the marketplace.

The Tudor Mint: Product Information

New releases from The Tudor Mint are launched each January and July, with retirements announced each July for December 31 implementation. Annual "One Year Only Studies" are released in January and retire on December 31 of the same year. "Extravaganza Studies" debut at the annual Collector "Extravaganza" hosted by The Tudor Mint Ltd. in England. The Extravaganza is a special show for Tudor Mint collectors only, with about 800 - 1,000 attendees annually. All Tudor Mint artists are in attendance, and collectors also enjoy entertainment and contests. The "Extravaganza Studies" are available only on the day of this event. "Exhibition Only Studies" are sculpted for the purpose of small exhibitions or events, and again are available for purchase only on the day of the event.

Myth and Magic remains the showpiece of The Tudor Mint Ltd. product line which consists of wizards, dragons, unicorns, pegasus, and other fantasy figurines. From 1" miniature studies with one crystal, to 9" extra large studies with more than five crystals, this varied line serves as the focus of the collectors' club. In addition to figurines of various sizes and prices, there are *Myth and Magic* jewelry, memorabilia and miscellaneous items like key rings, trinket boxes and letter openers, a chess set, and "club studies" released specifically for club members.

The *Arthurian Legend* Collection was a direct result of the widespread interest in *Myth and Magic*. All figurines are based on reading done by Chief Designer Sharon Riley, from sources such as Mallory's *Le Morte d' Arthur*, and John Boorman's film *Excalibur*.

The *J.R. Tolkien Collection* was created in response to requests by collectors, and all figurines are based on the stories of Tolkien including *The Hobbit* and *Lord of the Rings*.

Dark Secrets, launched in January, 1994, is kept separate from *Myth and Magic* because the subject matter consists of skulls, skeletons and demons. Introduced in 1993 as an "experiment," "The Keeper of the Skulls," sold 25,000 pieces in the first year alone. As a direct result, the *Dark Secrets* collection and its three chambers, for Skulls, Demons and Skeletons, were born.

Launched in 1995 in the United States the *Native American Collection* features 12 subjects depicting the life of certain tribes in the 1800s. Tribes featured include Apache, Comanche, Arapaho, Sioux and others. Each of the 12 figurines is available in silver or bronze finish.

Fine Designs and Careful Craftsmanship Bring Tudor Mint Products to Life

Tudor Mint products are not made of pewter, but rather their manufacturing process allows for figurines with more definition than pewter can achieve. The pieces, called "antique, silver plate figurines," have varied tones of gray rather than appearing to be all of one color, and they are highly detailed in their sculpture. What's

"The Unicorn" was one of the first Myth and Magic *studies ever introduced. Its simple elegance illustrates the beauty and grace of a unicorn.*

"Reflections," introduced in July 1995, is a unique study. If you look closely, you can see the dragon's reflection in the crystal!

more, these pieces are truly collectibles rather than giftware: each has its own individual name and the number of images is limited to provide the proper drama and distinctiveness for each.

Most figurines from The Tudor Mint have one designer and one model maker. Each designer and model maker works on various models within each collection. The very first designer (now Chief Designer) is Sharon Riley, and the first model maker (now Chief Model Maker) is Roger Gibbons. Other designers for The Tudor Mint include Jessica Watson and Helen Coventry, while other model makers include Mark Locker, Anthony Slocombe and Steve Darnley.

The manufacturing process is a unique one that includes many steps: from drawing to design to model sculpting, master mould making, production, antiquing, burnishing, and the addition of crystals. Finally, each new study must survive The Drop Test! It is boxed and shrink wrapped, then dropped from shoulder height eight times – onto each face and corner. Only when it has successfully passed this final test is it ready for shipment.

Club Members Enjoy Special Benefits

The Myth and Magic Collectors' Club is the only United States club of its kind for collectors of fantasy figurines. With about 20,000 members worldwide, the club focuses attention on *Myth and Magic* products – all of which feature genuine, beautifully cut crystals and an exceptional value. For a $37.50 annual fee, members receive a free yearly presentation piece, a club membership card, a catalog of the current collection and updates, two issues of the popular "Methtintdour Times" newsletter, special purchase opportunities, and opportunities to win valuable prizes.

Collectors may correspond with The Myth and Magic Collectors' Club at The Tudor Mint Inc., P.O. Box 431729, Houston, Texas 77243-1729. The phone number is (713) 462-0076.

The Tudor Mint
P.O. Box 431729
Houston, TX 77243-1729
(713) 462-0076
Fax (713) 462-0170

COLLECTORS' CLUB

Myth and Magic Collectors' Club
c/o The Tudor Mint
P.O. Box 431729
Houston, TX 77243-1729
(713) 462-0076

Annual Dues: $37.50
Club Year: July 1 - June 30

Benefits:
- Membership Gift: Figurine
- Renewal Gift
- Redemption Cards for Members-Only Figurines
- Bi-annual Newsletter, "Methtintdour Times"
- Membership Card
- Invitation to Attend "Extravaganza," held in England
- Current Catalog, Plus Updates

UNITED DESIGN

Capturing Nature's Beauty and Life's Simple Pleasures With Creativity and Hands-On Craftsmanship

Gary and Jeanie Clinton, founders of United Design, have worked hand-in-hand to build their Oklahoma-based company that also includes a gift shop. Figurines from the White Christmas *collection are among the thousands on display and for sale.*

When Gary and Jeanie Clinton first started their pottery business, they worked side by side in a tiny chicken coop. Today, they have a zoo of creations that has turned their backyard hobby into a thriving multi-national company. United Design currently offers 16 product catalogs with more than 3,000 different items that capture nature's beauty, diversity and mystery. As noted in its mission statement, the Oklahoma-based company is "inspired by the joy and wonder of the world around us."

People ask, "Did you ever think you'd get to this point,'" says Jeanie. "But consciously, we did dream that it would happen." The Clintons launched their business in 1973, building it around a love of animals and an uncanny talent that would eventually turn the animal kingdom into a host of highly successful product lines. "We had been art students at the University of Oklahoma," explains Jeanie. "I'd been making pottery and started selling it on weekends at craft fairs. Then I started making it full time. That sort of just grew."

Gary received his master of fine arts degree in 1975. "But I was enjoying making things more than I thought I'd enjoy teaching," Gary says. The next couple of years found Gary and Jeanie making pottery in their back yard studio and setting up booths at craft shows. They made $300 at their first fair to put a down payment on two pottery kilns. With the growing demand for their handmade items, the Clintons hired their first employee in 1976. "We began getting more and more business, so we hired another person," recalls Gary. With this extra helping hand, Gary and Jeanie created more products – and more customers – that fit in with their goals for the business. Things haven't stopped since.

Over 700 employees in its Noble, Purcell and Wekoka, Oklahoma, locations now produce the detailed figurines ranging from teddy bears and Dalmatians to Santa Claus and angels. A sister facility in Norwich, Ontario, produces some of the product lines for distribution in Canada, and a European sales and distribution company is headquartered in Nottingham, England.

Like their employees, the Clintons work as a team, dividing their business responsibilities according to their personal strengths. Jeanie is in manufacturing and operations while Gary is in charge of the various stages of product development. "If I had been on my own, I'd still just have my little studio," Gary confides. "Jeanie is good at working on day-to-day projects. She's very pragmatic and practical. She's the heartbeat of our operation. I'm more of a dreamer, and the combination works really well." Their dreams, ideas and hard work go into all the new and continuing lines that have made United Design a resounding success.

Winging Their Way To United Design . . . *Teddy Angels*

Divinely down-to-earth characters have descended on United Design. The *Teddy Angels* collection, which features lovable teddy bears with wings, was inspired by antique and contemporary teddies. Created by sculptor Penni Jo Jonas, each *Teddy Angels* character has something very special to share through uplifting sentiments and messages that address everyday situations. There's "Cowboy Murray" dressed in boots to say "Have a doo-da day." "Old Bear" carries his well-traveled suitcase to proclaim: "Always remember your way home." Each figurine also comes with a *Teddy Angels* story booklet describing the collection's origin and mission.

Santa Claus and Angels Continue To Delight Collectors

No legend is more filled with wonder and magic than Santa Claus. Introduced in 1986, *The Legend of Santa Claus* collection has become a beloved limited edition collectible and year-round tradition for many families. The hand-cast, hand-painted figurines designed by the company's creative artisans make the collection a tremendous hit with Santa collectors worldwide.

The *Angels Collection* sends messengers and messages of good tidings. The limited edition collectibles have spurred a tremendous response since debuting in 1991. One very special figurine in the collection is titled "The Gift." Designed exclusively to support the work of The Starlight Foundation, the highly detailed figurine symbolizes the dreams and wishes that can come true for chronically and terminally ill children. A new figurine is designed each year to benefit this worthy cause.

A Menagerie of Stone Critters

Dalmatians, turtles, frogs, owls, eagles, otters, bears, bunnies, pigs and cows! What more could a collector ask for? United Design's *Stone Critters The Animal Collection* offers those and more than 400 creatures that have become America's most popular collectible animal figurine. Every phase of a *Stone Critters* creation – from the heartwarming poses and expressions to the sculptured detail, to the hand-painting and finishing – achieves a natural look. Realistic eyes are also added, which seem to magically bring the *Stone Critters* to life. Whether a collector is just beginning or looking for a special piece to add to a collection, the *Stone Critters* line is a great place to start and end.

"Sweetie" is among the heavenly characters in the Teddy Angels *collection. Each piece is inscribed with its own special sentiment and sculpted by Penni Jo Jonas.*

Eggstra! Eggstra! Bunnies Are A Hopping Success

The normally quiet Cottontail Valley just north of United Design is abuzz with a flurry of furry activity. Creating the commotion are designs hopping down the bunny trail in the *Easter Bunny Family Collection*. The collection started in 1988 when sculptor Donna Kennicutt created the first seven designs. Since then, this popular collectible has continued to multiply to the delight of many Easter Bunny enthusiasts. In 1993, *Easter Bunny Family Miniatures*, a co-creation of Penni Jo Jonas and Dianna Newburn, were added to the collection. Kennicutt designed the adorable *Easter Bunny Family Babies* in 1994. Though not limited in edition, the collection has several designs that are retired each year and replaced by new creations. The seven original designs were retired in 1991.

Communicating With Collectors

Collectors of the *Easter Bunny Family* and the limited edition Santas and Angels have the opportunity to receive the annual "The Legend of Santa Claus," "Angels Collection" and "Eggspress" newsletters. These publications inform collectors about new releases and retirements, provide a checklist of available pieces, and often give a sneak peek at upcoming introductions that sculptors are working on. Collectors are also invited to visit and tour United Design's Oklahoma facility, where they can get a fascinating and first-hand glimpse at the manufacturing process. A showroom also displays thousands of the company's figurines.

A Masterful Attention To Detail

Most United Design products are made in the heart of America: Noble, Oklahoma. Each design begins as a simple idea in someone's imagination – the Clintons, a sculptor or even collectors who submit concepts. United Design's team of talented sculptors include Ken Memoli, Larry Miller, Dianna Newburn, Donna Kennicutt, Suzan Bradford, Penni Jo Jonas, Midge Ramsey and Terri Russell.

Created to benefit The Starlight Foundation, this 1994 figurine titled "The Gift" was limited to 5,000 pieces and sculpted by Dianna Newburn. From its Angels Collection, *United Design creates an annual piece for the non-profit organization.*

The figurine production starts in the studio of one of United Design's gifted artists. Using their hands and a variety of tools, the sculptors capture the idea in a three-dimensional clay design.

Once the clay sculpture is complete, a master mold is made by applying latex or silicone over the original, layer by layer. The first hard cast model from the mold is called a "master." The master is returned to the sculptor to be reworked for exact detail. Production molds are then created. Two raw materials are used for casting the majority of United Design's products: a bonded porcelain and Hydrostone, which is mined in Oklahoma. Each material allows for great surface detail.

Casting is actually done by hand by mixing the material, which is poured into molds. When set, the mold is removed – like taking off a glove from your hand – and what results is a near-perfect replica of the original sculpture. From the pouring room, each item makes its way to what is called a "fettling" area. Here, precision drills are used to remove any extra or unwanted material which may be on the cast piece. This clean-up operation prepares each piece for the hand-painting process.

The painting is done using both regular brushes and airbrush techniques depending on the desired effect. Because of the hand-painting process, it can truly be said that no two pieces are exactly alike. Every item is an original! Supplementing the artisans at United Design is a "cottage industry" – or a group of home painters. These independent workers check out the pieces to paint and return them when finished. The cottage industry phenomenon has been an exciting part of the growth at United Design.

Near the end of the production cycle, United Design adds those trademark eyes, either glass or plastic depending on which gives the most life-like appearance. A final inspection is done before the item is carefully packed and ready to find a new home.

Dedication To Quality Guides United Design

Though the days of the backyard chicken coop are long gone, Gary and Jeanie are still active in the daily activities of the company. This husband-and-wife team strives to retain the down-home values, family atmosphere and team cooperation that has guided the company for more than 20 years. Devotion to creativity, quality and hands-on craftsmanship have distinguished United Design from the rest.

United Design Corporation
P.O. Box 1200
Noble, OK 73068
(800) 527-4883
Fax (405) 360-4442

Two enthusiastic collectors of the Easter Bunny Family *suggested the adorable idea for this 1995 addition titled "Easter Cookies." Artist Donna Kennicutt created the collection in 1988.*

COLLECTORS' TOUR

United Design Gift Shop & Factory Tour
1600 N. Main
Noble, OK 73068
(800) 527-4883

Hours: Tours – Monday through Friday at 10 a.m. and 1 p.m.
Gift Shop – Monday through Friday, 8 a.m. - 6 p.m.; Saturdays in November and December, 10 a.m. - 4 p.m. (Open First Saturday of the Month During the Rest of the Year, 10 a.m. - 4 p.m.).

Admission Fee: None

The tour of the United Design factory, which lasts about 25 minutes, shows visitors how figurines are made, beginning with a clay sculpture, through molding, casting, hand-painting and finishing.

VICKILANE, INC.

A World of Collectibles to Share Life's Joy, Memories and Beauty

Imagine for a moment that you have captured a dream, a moment of your pleasant memories or sweet imaginary thoughts – and that you can magically hold them in your hand. It's a make-believe wish that becomes reality with VickiLane, Inc. Through each whimsical and charming creation by VickiLane, you'll find yourself recalling happy days gone by, fond remembrances and warm emotions.

The world of VickiLane is filled with innocence and soft expressions, as seen in creations that capture something inside the eye and heart of the beholder. It's a realm of imagination, innocent delight and subtle expressions. Each precious, handcrafted design also reveals a part of artist Vicki Anderson, who shares her own feelings and messages about living life to the fullest. As VickiLane continues to grow, so does the special memories found throughout the collection and in the mind of its creator.

Vicki Anderson's Artistic Beginnings

For Vicki, art has always been as much a part of life as breathing. She grew up in a family brimming with creativity. Her parents, Jack and Viletta West, met while attending Denver Art School and actively pursued their interest in art throughout their lives. Vicki's mother also founded the renowned Viletta China Company. Before Vicki entered kindergarten, her father started teaching her how to draw. On Sunday mornings in church, she would sketch pictures of the preacher and other members in the congregation.

By the time she reached high school, Vicki had already discovered that she was blessed with marketable – and remarkable – artistic talent. It was also in high school that she first met Ron Anderson. After they attended community college together in Roseburg, Oregon, the pair got married, thus forming a partnership that has grown both personally and professionally. The Andersons' artistic collaboration began with a plan to fulfill their dreams of higher education. But they needed a way to pay their tuition at the University of Oregon, where Vicki was an art major and Ron studied computer science and math. In the early 1970s, mushroom sculptures were the rage. So they pooled their talents to design and market a line of sculptured mushrooms, whimsical turtles, children and calligraphy prints – works of art that were soon among the most coveted Saturday Market "finds."

Ministry Grows Into Family Business

Back then, the Andersons believed that their little business would only be a temporary part of their lives, a financial boost to fund their college education. They sold the business in 1977 after Ron completed his ministerial studies at Portland Bible College, and they were called to pastor a church in a small town.

In 1983, the couple launched VickiLane Inc. from a corner of their garage to help support themselves. In the midst of their ministry in 1985, Ron and Vicki began to realize that their study, experience and faith had prepared them for a new area of service. Vicki's creations with their uplifting messages could become a ministry. Even though VickiLane has become their full-time occupation, they still devote countless hours as lay ministers in their local church and as supporters of its missions.

With a sense of destiny in their hearts, Ron and Vicki set out to make a mark in the gift and collectible business. Their mission: "Create an experience of beauty and delight that will uplift every heart. Make a positive impact through the products we design, the ideas we stimulate and the jobs we create." These and other similar phrases have been part of the simple philosophy underlying every step of their journey.

From the time she reached high school, Vicki Anderson had already discovered her remarkable artistic talents. Today Vicki is the creative force and inspiration behind VickiLane. Through her imagination and enthusiasm, she designs and sculpts each masterpiece in her make-believe collection.

"This is my inspiration as I work in sculpture and water color: to communicate the truly important experiences of life, to capture the beauty of creation, to capture a moment of pure joy and to express a childlike faith," says Vicki.

Celebrating Life's Little Pleasures

Continuing the experience that began in the 1970s, Vicki's work is still in demand and in touch with the times. Most of her current designs are devoted to figurines featuring bunnies, mice, cats, pigs, teddy bears, lambs, dogs and sea life. Each animal is a charming character with a story that offers a slice of life and encouragement. Ron says his wife has a "sixth sense" for knowing what collectors want in a figurine or painting.

To keep up on the latest trends and techniques, Vicki is constantly developing her skills. It's a way of life. She carefully observes current design styles, finds out the desires and needs of people, and analyzes the best works of contemporary artists. Then she lets her creativity freely wander. "It's not an analytical or scientific thing," she says of her mental process. "But rather a felt thing – stemming from a desire to express my true self." Vicki has a deep appreciation for the best art from every era of history and is aware that it subtly influences her own work, helping her meld current trends with long-standing traditions.

Items she created years ago are still popular, yet each new piece seems to elevate the artist's "personal best." "Collectors are always curious to know what Vicki will come up with next," explains her husband. "I, too, am full of a sense of anticipation as to how her creative talents will unfold. I believe we have only seen a thumb sketch of the high quality work she will create in the years to come."

Vicki Anderson recalls the childhood fun of playing "cowboys and Indians" in "I Gotcha" and "Sneaking Up On You." Benjamin and April dress up for an afternoon adventure in the handcrafted figurines, which sell for about $25.00 each.

"Summer Daze" catches two day-dreaming bunnies, Benjamin and Rachael, resting next to a babbling brook. With its inviting forest setting of rocks, trees, bushes and flowers, the figurine brings back childhood memories and makes you wish you were there! The figurine is limited to 500 pieces, each signed by the artist and individually numbered.

Meet VickiLane's Friends

In 1986, Vicki began sculpting the line of *Sweet Thumpins* bunnies as cute little gifts. "But people started collecting them," she says. Now there's an entire community of bunnies, including April, Blossom, Cinnamon, Spice, Benjamin and all their friends and family. They're always enjoying favorite childhood activities, walking down the aisle in a wedding or simply relaxing on a warm summer day.

Each figurine also comes with a story, like the one for the 1995 introductions of "I Gotcha" and "Sneaking Up On You." Take, for example, Benjamin, an adventurous bunny that happened upon a dusty toy box hidden away in the attic. To his surprise, the chest had a cowboy and Indian outfit that he quickly took to his friend April's house. April put on the feathered headdress and Benjamin wore the cowboy hat and chaps before they headed out to play in the woods. "That night at the supper table, the two tired bunnies couldn't stop talking about their costumes and adventures in the woods. It had been a special day, and one they would long remember." These memories and others are part of the warmth and popularity of the collection.

Besides these bunnies and the *Lil' Blessings* collection of miniature bunny angels, there's a host of other fun-loving characters. *Blessings From Above* is Vicki's first series of angelic children, which have a wide-eyed excitement. She also created *Cowlectibles*, a line of cow figurines. "I'm constantly building on each of the lines," Vicki says.

In 1993, the company also began retiring specific pieces to make more room in the collection for Vicki's other creative ideas. Some of the pieces are also limited in edition.

Join the VickiLane Collectors' Club

Collectors all over the country had been asking when VickiLane would start a collectors' club. So in 1993 Vicki launched the club with the first membership figurine appropriately called "The Secret's Out."

With their membership, collectors receive a special figurine, a newsletter three times a year, club button, membership card and a Certificate of

Blossom joyfully plays hopscotch, smiling and concentrating on hitting each square. Whenever the adorable bunny tries to do something perfectly, her floppy ears turn up just a bit. "Hopping Forward" is the 1995 membership figurine of the VickiLane Collectors' Club.

Authenticity. The annual cost of membership is $28.00. Each newsletter shares the stories behind each character, along with a collector profile and information about retirements, upcoming artist visits and introductions. The VickiLane Collectors' Club newsletter also publishes profiles on members across the country. For information on joining, contact VickiLane Collectibles, 3233 NE Cadet Ave., Portland, Oregon, 97220; or call (800) 456-4259. The Andersons also enjoy hearing from collectors whether through letters or in person at shows or store appearances.

A Warm Welcome to the World of VickiLane

Ron and Vicki Anderson invite collectors to take a walk down VickiLane with them ... and to meet all the delightful personalities created from the artist's thoughts and imagination. As friends of VickiLane, collectors have the opportunity to read about each design, listen to the heart of the designer and begin to appreciate the depth of feeling in each wonderful creation. The tales found with these collectible figurines offer a marvelous world of adventure as they open the pathway to VickiLane: a magical land filled with beauty.

With destiny in their hearts and a positive philosophy, the Andersons have set out to make an impact on the gift and collectibles industry. Vicki feels fortunate to be able to put her talents to work in this outstanding way. And with her family surrounding her, she loves every minute and looks forward to bringing more designs to life.

VickiLane
3233 NE Cadet Ave.
Portland, OR 97220
(800) 678-4254
Fax (503) 251-5916

COLLECTORS' CLUB

VickiLane Collectors' Club
3233 NE Cadet Ave.
Portland, OR 97220
(800) 456-4259

Annual Dues: $28.00
Club Year: Anniversary of Sign-Up Date

Benefits:
- Membership Gift: Figurine
- Newsletter Published Three Times Yearly
- Membership Card
- Club Button

WACO PRODUCTS CORPORATION

Melody In Motion Moves Toward More Success and Magic

With music, motion and magic, WACO Products Corporation has found a winning combination that hits all the right notes. For the past 10 years, WACO has brought together fine art and advanced technology to create a line of delightful *Melody In Motion* figurines, which have found a home with collectors all over the world.

These creations are prized for their fine porcelain sculptures, beautiful studio-recorded music and complex, life-like movements. From a lovable hobo named "Willie" to classic holiday scenes featuring Santa Claus, *Melody In Motion* musicals truly bring magic to life. Each has a special story that's waiting to be told.

Time, Technology, Quality and Excellence Make Musical Masterpieces

Before the musicals entertain collectors, each piece undergoes a lengthy production process.

The *Melody In Motion* porcelain figurines are molded from sculptures created by the award-winning Japanese master sculptor Seiji Nakane. Handcrafted in Seto – the porcelain capital of Japan – each figurine is faithfully reproduced by highly skilled artisans to match Nakane's original sculptures.

Fore! Willie tries his hand at golfing in "The Longest Drive" – an ironic title since the ball simply falls off the tee. The musical plays "Blue Skies" as Willie moves from side to side.

Crafted from pure clay found only in Seto, the figurines are then fired to a bisque finish before trained artisans put on the final touch by hand-painting each detail. The figurines are fired for a second time and thoroughly inspected to ensure that every piece meets the exact specifications of the original artwork.

State-of-the-art technology and solid state sound reproduction inside every *Melody In Motion* figurine create an electro-mechanical device that activates the music and graceful movements. This makes every *Melody In Motion* figurine unique. A high-quality precision motor drives a gear train that activates a maze of cams and levers to set in motion the realistic movements in each figurine. Each part of the mechanical device is custom made for that style figurine, with each mechanism designed and engineered to achieve a specific movement. This advanced technology is truly exceptional, and is comparable to that found in high-quality appliances and camcorders.

Adding music to complete the story of each figurine is achieved by selecting the appropriate tune and musical instrument. The selected song is then recorded in a sound studio by professional musicians. The music's high quality is evident in everything from the Tchaikovsky theme played by a professional concert cellist to the carousel music recorded from working carousel band organs from around the world.

Combining the art of porcelain with precision technology, each figurine is presented as a tableau that tells a story to spark a collector's imagination. *Melody In Motion* figurines, which can only be produced in limited quantities due to their complex design and painstaking craftsmanship, are exceptional both in beauty and technology.

It's Willie's lucky day! The hobo that has become one of the most popular Melody In Motion *characters collects his winnings in "Jackpot Willie." The musical plays "We're In The Money" as Willie moves his head back and forth.*

A Musical Legacy and History of "Automata"

Although the *Melody in Motion* figurines are unique in today's collectible market, the concept of moving figures and mankind's fascination with "automata" can be traced to centuries-old traditions. As early as the 3rd century B.C., during the Han dynasty in China, a mechanical orchestra was handcrafted for the Emperor. In those days, these entertaining devices were powered by water movement or air pressure. By the mid-15th century, wind-up spring mechanisms were introduced and they became a portable power source for automata. By the end of the 1700s, very intricate automatons in human form were created by master artisans – who were only able to produce a few pieces in their lifetime. All were made for wealthy persons and only a handful of those works survive. Today, they can only be found in museums or private collections. *Melody In Motion* follows in this rich legacy with figurines that delight collectors of all ages.

Melody In Motion: The Willie Collection

The character of "Willie" is at the heart of *Melody in Motion* – and warms the hearts of collectors. The hobo brings back special memories and timeless stories about friendship, happiness and life with new introductions each year that chronicle his adventures. To celebrate *Melody In Motion's* 10th anniversary, Willie brings together his feathered friends and conducts an imaginary orchestra to play "When You're Smiling." As he sways, the chirping doves turn the already happy moment into a celebration. "Jackpot Willie" drops a quarter in the slot to come out a winner! As his head moves back and forth in amazement of his luck, the red light flashes to announce Willie's success. He whistles "We're In The Money" as he scrambles to fit all his

In "Chattanooga Choo Choo," Willie whistles the song of the same name while he waits for the train. He's ready to climb aboard as his head moves up and down to look at the track.

winnings into his overworked hat. In "Chattanooga Choo Choo," Willie finds himself on the move again, this time waiting to hitch a ride on his favorite box car. With his bags ready to toss on board, he looks up and down the tracks as he whistles "Chattanooga Choo Choo." In "The Longest Drive," Willie thinks he hit the golf ball far down the fairway. But the ball simply fell off the tee, where it sits as Willie moves his head to the tune "Blue Skies." "Willie The Yodeler" rolls out a barrel of fun and a few oom-pahs! The musical plays "German Folksong/Yodeling."

Melody In Motion: The Carousel Collection

The "Grand Carousel" is the show piece of the *Melody In Motion* line. Standing 22-1/2" tall and weighing 25 pounds, it is a wonder of animation and music. The pre-production process took Seiji Nakane more than a year, and the completion of the first Carousel was a two-year project. This combination of "beauty" (porcelain) and "beast" (motors, gears and audio system) has emerged as one of the masterworks in the contemporary collectibles field. It is as magnificent in appearance as it is in technological achievement. With flashing lights, two levels of moving animals, intricate details and brilliant colors, the carousel is a childhood fantasy crowded with golden lions, purple elephants and legendary griffins. The carousel comes with two audio tapes of authentic band music. The audio tape player, which is built into the base, also plays standard cassette tapes.

The *Melody In Motion* collection also boasts three additional carousels of various sizes and features. The "Blue Danube Carousel" features colorful horses moving gracefully up and down their shiny gold poles to the popular tune "Blue Danube Waltz." "Victoria Park Carousel" is sculpted in exquisite detail and delicately painted in soft pastels. This grand carousel plays the glorious melody "Under the Double Eagle." The "King of Clowns Carousel" displays two exquisitely sculpted reliefs crowned with a scallop-shaped edge.

As much of a tradition as holiday gatherings, WACO introduces a Santa Claus figurine each year. For 1995, Santa relaxes in his chair to read a stack of children's letters while an old-time radio plays "Deck The Halls."

The artisan's touch can be seen from the extravagant flourishes and energetic clowns to the lively and nostalgic organ music.

Melody In Motion: The Clock Collection

"Willie" and other characters star in the *Melody In Motion* clocks that keep everyone on time. The collection features eight hand-made and hand-painted porcelain figurines complete with beautiful, built-in clocks. Of course, each piece also has music and movement. There's "Low Pressure Job," "Day's End," "Willie The Golfer," "The Artist," "Wall St. Willie" and "Clockpost Willie" – all portraying the collection's signature character.

In addition, "Grandfather Clock" shows a distinguished gentleman in his rocking chair as he smokes his pipe and rocks back and forth to the rhythmic tune of "The Syncopated Clock." Finally, "Golden Mountain Clock" portrays three gnomes pushing ore cars through a tunnel, while two others work their pick axes into the gold mine walls to the tune "Viennese Musical Clock."

Melody In Motion: The Santa Collection and Retired Pieces

Each year since 1986, WACO has introduced an annual Santa. And each year, these appealing "St. Nick" sculptures have sold out and retired. For 1995, the official *Melody In Motion* Santa relaxes in his favorite chair to read letters from children throughout the world. His favorite song "Deck The Halls" plays on an old-time radio while Santa's head turns to and fro as he swings his foot.

In addition, there are more than 30 limited edition *Melody In Motion* figurines that have been retired or will soon receive that honor. The success and popularity of the line is evident in the strong interest of collectors for these older additions.

Classic Scenes Come To Life with *Melody In Motion*

Even the 1930s "Coca-Cola" calendars created by Norman Rockwell become more nostalgic when put with music and motion. The Coca-Cola® brand musical figurine based on the artist's drawing "Gone Fishin'" takes a look back to simpler days, country life and the lazy summer days of youth. It was a time when nothing could be better than a trip down to the fishing hole on a hot summer's day. The musical plays the tune "Thank God I'm A Country Boy."

This Coca-Cola brand musical figurine is based on Norman Rockwell's painting "Gone Fishin'" when a country boy spends a lazy summer day at the fishing hole.

Share In The Magic with the Melody In Motion Collectors Society

To support the collection of fine musicals, WACO invites collectors to experience the magic first hand by joining the Melody In Motion Collectors Society. Dues are $27.50 for the first year or $50.00 for a two-year membership. Collectors also have the opportunity to purchase gift memberships for family and friends.

As members, collectors receive the exclusive figurine titled "Best Friends" which is a special gift from sculptor Seiji Nakane. If "Best Friends" were available in stores, it would sell for $45.00 or more. Members also receive a personal Membership Card, complimentary annual subscription to the "Melody Notes" newsletter, the latest *Melody In Motion* catalog and a $10.00 member coupon which can be applied to the purchase of any figurine except the Members' Only issue.

Members will also receive a Personal Redemption Certificate entitling them to purchase the Society's limited edition figurine created exclusively for members. "Willie The Collector," a 9-3/4" work of art, has assembled his own miniature collection. His head moves as he whistles "When The Saints Go Marching In." The same tune is heard in the background as if it were played by the miniature "Willie The Trumpeter" that he holds.

To celebrate Melody In Motion's *10th anniversary, Willie leads a choir of his feathered friends to the tune "When You're Smiling." Titled "Willie The Conductor," the clown sways with the music.*

WACO Products Corp.
I-80 & New Maple Avenue
P.O. Box 898
Pine Brook NJ 07058-0898
(201) 882-1820
Fax (201) 882-3661

COLLECTORS' CLUB

Melody In Motion Collectors Club
WACO Products Corporation
I-80 & New Maple Avenue
P.O. Box 898
Pine Brook, NJ 07058-0898
(201) 882-1820

Annual Dues: $27.50
Club Year: Anniversary of Sign-Up Date

Benefits:
- Membership Gift: Porcelain Bisque Figurine
- Redemption Certificate for Members-Only Figurine
- Bi-annual Newsletter, "Melody Notes"
- Membership Card & Certificate
- Two Members "Savings" Coupons
- Melody In Motion Catalog
- Personal Purchasing Record
- Retired Edition Summary
- List of Collectors' Centers

THE WIMBLEDON COLLECTION

Porcelain Dolls That Are "Distinctive By Design"

Gustave Wolff fostered his artistic skills through years of formal schooling, while daughter Gretchen seemed to absorb talent through osmosis across the kitchen table. Whether their creations reflect the unusual of "Cryin' Over Spilt Milk" and "Bad Hair Day," or perhaps the more elaborate "American Beauty" and "Victoria," the artistic design team is committed to the distinctive, as well as the affordable, collectible product. With these aspects serving as their foundation, the Wolff's have forged one of the hottest partnerships in today's doll industry.

Educated at Northland College and the University of Wisconsin-Madison, Gustave, known as Fritz, apprenticed under renowned ceramicist Robert Eckels. He remained in Madison for teaching purposes a few years after the completion of his master's degree. He soon became accidently interested in the sculpting process of fine porcelain, when a graduate student requested his assistance with a sculpting assignment. One means of assistance led to the beginning of a fledging doll business in the early '70s. At that time, many of Fritz's creations modeled a "basic" appearance in both sculpt and artistic design. It wasn't until his oldest daughter entered the picture in the mid-'80s, that the clay molds began to reflect a much different appearance.

Gretchen started voicing her amazingly profound design opinions while still in junior high. Her work became reality when Gustave began noticing his daughter's keen eye for true-to-life expression and perfected dress. Surprisingly, though, Gretchen has not experienced the artistic education and training that has helped shape Gustave's doll making career. Genes, many, many family table discussions and a highly adept photographic memory seem to best explain the younger Wolff's talents.

Dolls for Every Type of Collector

When Fritz first started in the doll business, he found that the public was looking for inexpensive porcelain dolls. He started The Wimbledon Collection line with dolls that retailed for $20.00 to $50.00 each. As doll collecting became more popular and more manufacturers got into the collectible doll business, the consumers' tastes began to change. True doll collectors wanted more detailing of facial features, real eyelashes, and in general, a more sophisticated look than the old "white" porcelain, inexpensive dolls of a few years back. As the dolls improved, prices skyrocketed. Consumers were now willing to spend hundreds of dollars for a well-made heirloom-quality porcelain doll.

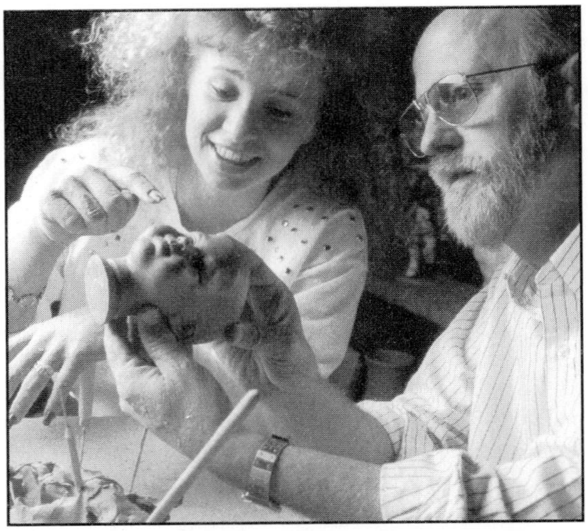

Fritz and Gretchen Wolff examine a clay doll head that Fritz has just finished sculpting.

Fritz and Gretchen decided that within this new market they could really put their talents to work. In 1992, they came up with their designer series line called *The Gustave F. Wolff & Gretchen M. Wolff Designer Series Dolls.*

Each piece in this set is available signed and numbered from the artist in a limited edition size of 600. Each of the 600 collectible pieces is complete with a gorgeous mahogany base, brass name plaque, artist hand-signed signature and signed/numbered Certificate of Authenticity. These hand-signed dolls retail anywhere from $115 to $350 each. They range in size from 18" to 22" tall.

The designer line is also produced in an open edition which has the artist's signature engraved into the porcelain on the back of the doll's neck. These dolls do not come with a signed and numbered certificate or a mahogany base. They do come with a regular Wimbledon Collection Certificate of Authenticity. The open edition designer dolls retail for between $100 to $300 each.

Although Fritz and Gretchen now have their own *Designer Series* of porcelain dolls, they have not forgotten the consumer who may still want to purchase an inexpensive "generic" porcelain doll for a special friend or as a start-up to a doll collection. Many other releases from the Wolff team are not limited in their edition size nor personally autographed by the respective artist. These dolls retail from $40.00 to $100 each and range in size from 12" to 20". All clothing for these dolls is designed by either Fritz or Gretchen.

"Hands On" Business

The Wimbledon Collection is definitely a "hands on" business. Gretchen and Fritz do all their own sculpting with water based clay. No other artists are involved in their doll-making process. Speaking of Gretchen, Fritz says, "She's been fooling with clay her whole life, and she was very much interested in the art end of the business since she was a little girl. Now she's not only an accomplished sculptor in her own right, but also an expert in material and cloth. So, when I'm designing a dress, I'll depend on her for ideas for fabric and so forth."

Along with doing their own sculpting, both Fritz and Gretchen attend all the major trade shows throughout the year. While at the trade shows, they pick up ideas for new designs from their customers. Customers will come into their booth with suggestions on themes, names and what they think would sell best in their various locations. Fritz and Gretchen keep all of these ideas in mind when designing their new pieces.

The majority of the time, the final look of the doll is not known until the very end. Both artists start with a head and create a face. "I then design the clothing to go with that particular face. After I get that done, I find a name that fits," explains Fritz.

Gretchen uses mostly images in her mind when sculpting a new doll. Neither artist uses a real model. "I think that I subconsciously take pictures in my mind of faces or expressions that I've seen from people at the mall or on the street. These images seem to stay with me and come out in the clay when I sculpt," Gretchen says. The majority of the Wolff's designs depict character not beauty. Fritz has said many times over "that not everyone looks like Miss America," and this is the type of real life expressions and facial features that both father and daughter try to portray in their sculpting.

"Keightley," Gretchen Wolff's 1993 Christmas doll, was a finalist at The Canadian Collectible of the Year Awards 1993.

"Susie," sculpted by Fritz Wolff, has been one of the best-selling designer dolls offered by The Wimbledon Collection. "Susie" was one of the first designs available in 1992, and the signed edition was sold out before she ever entered Wimbledon's distribution center.

1993 *Platinum Edition*

The *Designer Series*, introduced in 1992, was so well received, that in 1993, Fritz and Gretchen decided to show their appreciation of everyone's support of their artistic endeavors. They each designed one special doll that would be strictly limited to 600 pieces each. Each doll would be hand-signed and numbered and come with a large mahogany base which featured an engraved silver-plated plaque. Once the 600 pieces were made, the molds were broken, never to be used again. The dolls were available to dealers on an allotment basis. Both dolls retailed for around $200 each.

Fritz designed the impish looking "Connor." "Connor" was 20" tall and dressed in a white cotton lace dress accented by a pink satin ribbon and floral scarf around her neck. Her clothing was completed with lacy white bobby socks and white shoes. "Connor's" smiling face was accented by a winking eye and human hair eyelashes. A straw hat decorated with hand-made silk flowers sat atop her blonde curly locks. "Connor" held an ice cream cone in her hand.

"Melanie" (20" tall) was Gretchen's *Platinum Edition* creation. She sported a blue floral print jumper with a white blouse underneath. The jumper was trimmed in white lace, and "Melanie" wore a 14K gold plated brooch on her blouse. "Melanie's" outfit included white stockings and white shoes. Her smiling face was accented by sparkling brown eyes which featured human hair eyelashes and brown curly hair. In her hair, "Melanie" wore a headband made entirely of hand-made silk flowers.

1995 Releases

Latest releases from The Wimbledon Collection continue to depict the distinct character and fine design which have made the company's unique father-daughter design team a constant in today's fine, collectible doll market. "Mommy, my shoe and sock came off" is yet another expressive creation from artist Gustave F. Wolff and the fine line of Wimbledon porcelain dolls. Also referred to as "Daphne," the 20" tall doll was released in the Spring of 1995. She is designed with an incredibly soft facial expression, a mauve dress accented by Swedish imported lace and again, "Daphne" depicts – in the finest bone porcelain available – an all too common theme of many playful young

"Melanie," Gretchen Wolff's 1993 Platinum Edition *doll, was strictly limited to 600 pieces before the mold was broken.*

girls. Perhaps most appealing is "Daphne's" striking big blue eyes framed by human hair eyelashes. Gustave proclaims their size and clarity to be the best ever produced in a Wimbledon creation. "Daphne" is available from The Wimbledon Collection in a signed and numbered edition of 600 pieces.

Also from the father-daughter design team's studio comes "Anissa," a Wimbledon collector's long-anticipated, signed and numbered bride doll, also released in the spring of 1995. Limited to 600, "Anissa's" full-length, snow-white gown and cascading veil add authenticity to to her exquisite design. Collectors have appreciated her dark brown eyes and curly dark hair, which seem to lift "Anissa" to life over the purity of her gown. At 20" tall, she is innocently beautiful and a definite collectible creation from the Wolff family designers!

Fall 1995 Releases

"Nettie" is off to school with a very determined look upon her face. The teacher has asked all of the students to pick their favorite bird and give an oral report to the class about that bird. "Nettie's" favorite bird is the goose, and she is determined to get an A+ on her report. She is carrying a hand-woven basket filled with genuine goose down for all the children to see and feel. "Nettie" has on her favorite blue floral print dress with white overlay, blue shoes and white bobby socks. Momma even let her wear her favorite gold brooch with pearl insert. At 20" tall, "Nettie" is the first African-American doll to appear in the *Gustave and Gretchen Wolff Designer Series.* She features medium brown skin, sparkling brown eyes and dark brown curly hair. One of Gustave's best sculptures in 25 years, "Nettie" is available in a signed and numbered edition of 600 pieces.

"Andrew" just loves it when Mommy reads him stories about old time explorers and sailors. He gets dressed in his favorite red striped sailor suit with matching hat, pulls on his tube socks and blue tennis shoes, grabs his miniature wooden ship, and he's ready to "Cast Off!" and find the nearest water puddle to dream about discovering strange new exotic lands. "Andrew's" cheerful smiling face is complimented by sparkling blue eyes featuring human hair eyelashes and blonde hair. Designed by Gustave F. Wolff, he is a must for every doll lover's collection. "Andrew" is also available in a signed and numbered edition of 600 pieces.

The Wimbledon Collection
P.O. Box 21948
Lexington, KY 40522
(606) 277-8531
Fax (606) 277-9231

MEET THE ARTISTS

Biographies of Some of Today's Most Popular and Talented Artists in the Field of Limited Edition Collectibles

Some of the best-known artists in today's world of limited edition collectibles are showcased in the following articles. This listing provides an introduction to many of these talented men and women whose works bring pleasure to collectors world-wide.

HOLLY ADLER

Collectors, friends and neighbors await the works of Holly Adler with delight and anticipation. Her sun-drenched studio in Andover, Minnesota, is a menagerie of sketches, wood carvings, prototypes, books, paint brushes and fabrics – reminders of a dedicated, hard-working artist.

As a designer for Kurt S. Adler, Inc. for the past decade, Holly has developed new major themes featuring Christmas ornaments and decorative accessories and designs for Christmas products for leading licensors. Holly designs Christmas accessories and collectibles in wood, resins and fabrics.

Having accumulated more than 300 teddy bears, some of which she designed herself, Holly decided to introduce her very special bears to the world. In 1995, Holly created the *Holly Bearies Collection*, which features collectible ornaments and figurines depicting teddy bears – each with its own playful character and personality – that are "Looking for a Home in Your Heart."

Holly believes that the hand-made decorations and collectibles she creates today are destined to become the treasured keepsakes and heirlooms of tomorrow.

MARTYN ALCOCK

Martyn Alcock became a modeller for Royal Doulton at the John Beswick studio in 1986. He began work on several figure subjects for *Bunnykins*, including "Policeman" and "Schoolboy" (1988). Since then, he has modelled numerous additions to the *Bunnykins*, culminating in 1994's *Sixtieth Anniversary Bunnykins* .

Martyn has contributed several studies of Beatrix Potter characters to the *Royal Albert* figure collection, including "Peter and the Red Handkerchief" and "Christmas Stocking." He also recreated several of the most popular Beatrix Potter subjects in a large size.

Like all the modellers in the Beswick studio, Martyn has been encouraged to show his versatility, and more recently has turned his hand to character jugs. His first character jug, "Captain Hook," was selected to be Royal Doulton's *Character Jug of the Year* for 1994. He also modelled the charming miniature "Snowman" character jug.

Away from the studio, Martyn spends time with his family and still finds time to play goalkeeper for Royal Doulton's Nile Street soccer team.

As Martyn says, "To know that people enjoy and appreciate my work is the most rewarding part of my job."

VICKI ANDERSON

In the world of VickiLane where make-believe and reality thrive side by side, each work of art transmits the feelings, thoughts and blessings of Vicki Elaine Anderson to every collector with love.

Growing up in a household brimming with creativity, Vicki took art lessons from her mother and created successful designs for her parents' business, Viletta China.

In 1970, Vicki married Ron Anderson. Vicki, an art major, and Ron, a computer science and math major, pooled their talents to design and market a line of sculptured mushrooms, whimsical turtles, children and calligraphy prints. The business provided the income to finish their studies both at the University of Oregon and Portland Bible College. After selling their first company, they spent a number of years pastoring a church while Vicki continued her art work, including teaching classes at a community college.

In 1985, Ron and Vicki decided to launch VickiLane, a gift and collectible company. Their philosophy is to "make a positive impact through the life we lead, the products we design, the ideas we stimulate, and the jobs we create."

PATRICIA ANDREWS

In recent years, Keepsake Ornament artist Patricia Andrews has become known for her Keepsake Ornament sculptures depicting BARBIE®. The first of these designs was the first edition in the *Holiday BARBIE™* Collector's Series which

debuted in 1993. In addition to the *Holiday BARBIE™* series, the first of a new, nostalgic BARBIE™ series was introduced in 1994 with "BARBIE™ - Debut 1959." Patricia also portrayed the rare, brunette version of the first BARBIE® doll in a members-only, 1995 Keepsake Ornament Collector's Club Edition ornament.

Other favorites by Patricia include the 1995 Keepsake Ornaments "A Celebration of Angels," "Heaven's Gift," "Baby's First Christmas," and the delightful "New Home" and "Christmas Patrol" designs.

Patricia began her career at Hallmark 19 years ago. She was an engraving instructor before joining the Keepsake Ornament staff eight years ago. She is married to Dill Rhodus, who also designs Keepsake Ornaments.

DANIELLE A. APHESSETCHE

As art director at Calabar Creations, Danielle's warm spirit and optimistic outlook is mirrored on each new design and collection. Danielle's cheerful book-lined studio is a testament to the thoughtful and creative research she puts into each design. She is valued for the coloration, names and stories of all Calabar figurines.

A native of France, Danielle earned a diploma for ceramic art and sculpture and another for drawing and design from the State School of Applied Art and her teaching credentials from the Ecole Normale D'Instituteurs. Later she earned her master of art degree in design from the University of Bordeaux and a second master of arts from California State University at Fullerton.

She traveled extensively in Europe and won several of the highest awards from the French School of Beaux Art. Danielle taught art before her marriage but later immigrated to the United States. She enjoys working in her beautiful and bountiful garden and spending time with her husband and three grown children.

PETE APSIT

Born in Los Angeles, Pete Apsit majored in art at the University of Southern California. He enjoys working from his Bakersfield studio where he can be near his wife and children.

One Christmas, Pete was short of money and chose to sculpt a whale for his brother. Impressed with the statue's rugged artistry, his brother convinced Pete to quit his job and form the Apsit Brothers of California Co., which manufactured and sold statuary. In 1977, Pete separated from his brother and created California Originals, a company offering free-lance designs.

For Calabar Creations, Pete created the limited edition series *Little Farmers*, *Yesterday's Friends* and *Daddy's Girl* in tribute to America's children.

A jovial, life-loving person, Pete has created many collections that fit his bubbly personality, such as *SantaVenture*, *Tee Club*, and *The Grandpions*. His humorous Santas reveal the "other side" of Santa Claus. His golfers' facial expressions depict with humor and empathy the strong emotions hidden in the seemingly peaceful game of golf. *The Grandpions* are collections of dwarfed professionals, sportsmen and hobbyists that are sure to unwrinkle many grumpy faces.

GIUSEPPE ARMANI

Born in Calci, a quaint little town not far from Pisa, Italy, Giuseppe Armani found it lacking in inspirational material suitable for a young and avid artist. As an adolescent, he felt impelled to seek his future elsewhere. He set out to mine the artistic treasures of the great triumvirate of quintessential renaissance cities – Pisa, Siena and Florence – and he struck gold!

Beginning his professional career in Pisa, Armani worked in the workshop of a gallery located directly opposite The Leaning Tower. In 1975, Florence Sculture d'Arte and Armani began an inspired, exclusive and extraordinarily successful relationship. Armani and Florence Sculture d' Arte are currently forming a workshop in the tradition of the renowned Renaissance workshops, enabling the world's most talented sculptors to work with and learn from the master sculptor himself, Giuseppe Armani.

Armani's mythic, almost mystical, ability to put character and "soul" into his sculptures continues to amaze, astound and intrigue us. The geniuses of the Renaissance have inspired Armani to sculpt modern masterpieces. Giuseppe Armani Creates Art For Today!

MABEL LUCIE ATTWELL

British artist Mabel Lucie Attwell sold her first drawing before she was 16 to a London publisher. From there, Attwell worked as an artist to pay for art school.

Attwell married illustrator Harold Earnshaw. They had two sons and a daughter, Peggy, who became the "Attwell child," the toddler with large eyes, a winsome expression and often a large bow in her hair.

Attwell's earliest published illustrations for gift books, children's books and fairy tales appeared in 1905. Her distinctive treatment of children as cherubic, chubby-legged and winsome was established early in her career. Throughout her career, her art was always in demand – even by the Royal Family. As a toddler, Prince Charles was presented with a set of nursery china bearing Attwell's illustrations, and Princess Margaret chose Attwell's artwork for personal Christmas cards.

After Attwell's death in 1964, Enesco licensed the rights to translate her artwork into porcelain bisque figurines for the *Enesco Memories of Yesterday®* collection, which premiered in 1988.

BRIAN BAKER

Brian Baker's fascination for history, art and architecture has taken him to over 40 countries, from Europe to Mexico. Brian's discoveries have inspired him to share those experiences with others through the creation of the *Déjà Vu Collection* from Michael's Limited.

Brian believes each building creates itself, but really it's the charming way he sculpts and his attention to detail. He hand-casts the designs in fine bonded stone and carefully develops a color scheme for each building.

Brian's trademark is an umbrella. Watch for one hidden in the shadows or tucked away in a corner of many of his sculptures. Brian explains, "On my first building, I wanted a hungry French cat sitting by the door. I couldn't seem to design a cat that pleased me, so I left the cat's tail as the handle and made the body into an umbrella."

The *Déjà Vu Collection* is Brian Baker's way of bringing history to life and making you feel like you've been there before.

LINDA LINDQUIST BALDWIN

Christmas collectors just love the *Belsnickles* – antique reproduction Santas of hollowed cold cast porcelain – created to mimic the look and feel of Missouri artist Linda Lindquist Baldwin's original papier-maché sculptures.

Their creation started with a single nickel – the amount Linda spent on a book about antique Santas. Now, every Schmid *Belsnickle* features a U.S. nickel embedded at the base, with limited editions containing a newly minted nickel for the introduction year. Select limited edition pieces feature a rare coin to enhance collectibility.

Linda's *Belsnickles* are on exhibit at the Museum of American Folk Art in New York and on file for a future exhibit at the Smithsonian. They are included in *The Spirit of Christmas* and in a *Better Homes and Gardens* book of paper crafts. Linda has been featured by "CNN Headline News," "NBC Evening News" and in magazine and newspaper articles across the country.

The *Belsnickle Collection* is comprised of three historically distinct Santa figures – long-limbed, stern Belsnickle from 19th century Germany, the Roly Poly Santa of early 20th century America, and the tall, benevolent Father Christmas. Whatever form they take, Schmid's *Belsnickles* are unforgettable.

BETTE BALL

As director of doll design for Goebel of North America, Bette Ball is the award-winning designer of the highly acclaimed *Betty*

Jane Carter®, *Goebel Angel Dolls®* and *Victoria Ashlea Originals®* porcelain dolls. She is known and appreciated by doll collectors for her uncompromising quality of design.

Bette double majored in Fine Arts and Costume Design in art school. Her paintings hang in many private collections around the world, and she enjoys an international reputation for her design in fine china and giftware.

She is a recipient of the prestigious DOTY award and NALED "Doll of the Year" awards. Bette's dolls have been honored by acceptance in more than 50 museums worldwide.

Bette has endeared herself to countless admirers through personal and television appearances, where she lends her vibrant personality to discussions on designing and collecting dolls.

DOT AND SY BARLOWE

Collaborating as fellow artists at New York's Museum of Natural History in the 1940s, Dot and Sy Barlowe have been illustrating since then – together and separately – and earning national recognition for their historic and naturalist art.

The Barlowes have illustrated nature books such as *Seashores*, *Trees of America* and *Amphibians of North America* for some of the largest publishing houses in America.

In addition, the Barlowes have contributed illustrations to Audubon Society guides and to *The Audubon Society Encyclopedia of North American Birds*. They also teach nature illustration and botany at the Parsons School of Design in New York. Their works have been honored with numerous awards and exhibitions at the Society of Illustrators in New York and Expo '67 in Montreal.

Reco International Corp. has presented an eight-plate *Vanishing Animal Kingdoms* collection by Sy and a *Gardens of Beauty* plate collection by Dot, as well as a series of animal figurines by both artists. Other recent introductions include *Town & Country Dogs* and *Our Cherished Seas* plate series.

FRANCIS J. BARNUM

Born and raised in Ohio's Cuyahoga River Valley, Francis J. Barnum joined the Chilmark Gallery in the midst of a 35 year career as a designer, modelmaker and sculptor. Barnum has now made a name for himself as a historian and prominent artist in the realm of Civil War sculpture.

Barnum has designed the *Civil War* collection commemorating America's most remembered war through depictions of well-known leaders, as well as anonymous heroes, in fine pewter,

MetalART™ and bronze. Painstaking research and attention to the smallest details are obvious in Barnum's work. In addition to bringing a sense of high drama to his scenes, he captures the very emotions of his characters.

Numbering over 75 pieces in 1995, the Barnum *Civil War* collection takes us from Gettysburg to Shiloh to Antietam and runs the gamut of emotions from victory to defeat.

KATHY BARRY-HIPPENSTEEL

Kathy Barry-Hippensteel, a sculptor of child and baby dolls, has received widespread acclaim for their lifelike quality and has been bestowed with many awards.

"Chen" was nominated for a *Dolls* magazine 1989 "Award of Excellence" and received the National Association of Limited Edition Dealers' 1990 "Achievement Award." In 1992, "Patricia, My First Tooth" doll, from the *Happiness Is...* collection, was nominated for *Dolls'* "Award of Excellence" and *Doll Reader's* "Doll of the Year" award. In 1993, "Tickles" – the first issue in the *Joys of Summer* collection and one of her most sought-after dolls – was nominated for the same two awards.

In 1994, the International Doll Exposition (IDEX) recognized Kathy, giving her international acclaim. She displays art in France and the U.S., while both her "Tickles" and "Elizabeth's Homecoming" dolls have received prestigious "Canadian Collectibles of the Year Award" from *Collectibles Canada*.

Kathy hopes "to bring a smile to people's faces. If I can make something that hugs somebody's heart and makes them smile, then I've done what I set out to do."

PRESCOTT "WOODY" BASTON, JR.

In 1938, Prescott Baston was asked by a friend to sculpt a pair of figures for her to sell at her restaurant. From this modest beginning came *Sebastian Miniatures*. Over a 46 year period, Baston sculpted more than 1,200 designs and variations, many of which are highly collectible today.

Baston's son, Prescott Jr. or "Woody," worked in the Sebastian Studio throughout his youth and later earned a bachelor's degree in sculpture from Boston University. Under his father's tutelage, Woody designed his first miniature, "First Kite," in 1981. Since Baston, Sr.'s death in 1984, Woody has been the sole creative force behind *Sebastian Miniatures*, America's oldest continually produced collectible line.

Woody has sculpted over 300 miniatures including figures in both cold cast porcelain and pewter, as well as Christmas ornaments. Currently offered series include *Santa's World*, *Sunday Afternoon in the Park*, *The Sebastian Firefighter Collection* and *Lighthouses*.

YOLANDA BELLO

In 1995, doll artist Yolanda Bello celebrated her tenth anniversary at Ashton-Drake Galleries.

As a child in Venezuela, Bello "restyled" her dolls into new and exciting characters. At age 14, Bello moved to Chicago, Illinois, where she worked as a figurine sculptor and pursued doll design and sculpture in her spare time. In 1981, Bello created a pair of porcelain Spanish girl dolls, which turned doll making into a full-time profession.

Since then, Bello has earned more than 60 awards, including a "Doll of the Year®" award in 1985 for one of her studio dolls, and in 1993, for her Ashton-Drake doll, "Meagan Rose."

Bello's designs range from dolls portraying characters in the opera *Carmen*, to her most sought-after limited edition dolls, such as *Yolanda's Picture-Perfect Babies®*, her first dolls for Ashton-Drake. They sold out years ago but are available again, in the brand-new forms of porcelain mini-dolls and ornaments.

Bello is still best-known for her Ashton-Drake dolls, including *Yolanda's Lullaby Babies®*, *Yolanda's Heaven-Scent* collection, and *Yolanda's Rainbow of Love* collection, featuring babies of many ethnic origins.

JODY BERGSMA

Attending a small college in Vancouver, Canada, Jody Bergsma was influenced by the Canadian impressionists called the "Group of Seven." In 1978, she travelled to Europe and painted in southern France, Venice and Florence, ending her studies in Athens and the Greek Islands. Returning home, Bergsma withdrew from her engineering studies and became a serious, full-time artist.

Along with many one-woman shows of her abstract watercolors, Jody has released over 300 different "Little People" prints through the Jody Bergsma Gallery. She teamed up with Reco International to produce her first plate series, *Guardians of the Kingdom*. Since then, they have produced a Mother's Day series, two Christmas Series, *The Castles and Dreams* series and her newest, *Magic Companions*. Her recent trip to the Queen Charlotte Islands inspired many new prints based on the rich heritage and customs of the natives and a plate series entitled *Totems of the West*.

Inspired by the proverb, "A Cheerful Heart Is Good Medicine," Jody designed the *Laughables*, a line of figurines, bringing a joyful chuckle to all who receive them.

ULRICH BERNARDI

Born in the Groden Valley of Northern Italy's Dolomite Mountains, Ulrich Bernardi dreamed of becoming a woodcarver. There, woodcarving has been passed from generation to

generation for more than 300 years.

Bernardi's grandfather, an altar builder, and grandmother, an ornamental wood sculptress, inspired him and shared their knowledge and skills with him. During World War II, Bernardi, a deeply religious man, applied those skills by carving madonnas and crucifixes which he gave as symbols of hope to soldiers heading to the battlefields.

Bernardi earned a master of art degree at the Academy of Art in St. Ulrich and served a four-year apprenticeship with a master woodcarver. At age 30, his sculpture of a madonna earned him the rank of master woodcarver.

Working with the House of ANRI for more than 35 years, Bernardi's religious woodcarvings, including the Florentine Nativity presented to Pope John Paul II, and his woodcarvings of Australian artist Sarah Kay have earned him a worldwide reputation for finely detailed, inspirational art.

KEITH BIRDSONG

Keith Birdsong may not be a space traveler, but as a former parachutist, he knows the breathtaking excitement of hurtling through space – and that's an experience he's drawn upon to create some of the most thrilling *STAR TREK*® illustrations ever seen.

Avid "trekkies" know him as the gifted illustrator of every issue of Pocket Books' fantastically successful *STAR TREK* paperback series for the past four years. Now, collectors can enjoy the talents of this self-taught artist from Oklahoma through his stellar plate painting of the "U.S.S. Enterprise™ NCC-1701" as the premier issue in a new collection for The Hamilton Collection entitled *STAR TREK: The Voyagers*. This collection is dedicated to the most famous spaceships seen in the *STAR TREK* series.

PAUL BOLINGER

Debuting for Kurt S. Adler, Inc. in 1994, Paul Bolinger specializes in distinctive stylized Old World Santas. Ever since receiving a chisel from a friend for Christmas, he has taught himself the art of woodcarving from relief carving to carving in the round. He creates holiday legends from his "Three Bears Cottage" studio in the Santa Cruz Mountains in California.

Selected as one of the top 200 American craftsmen by *Early American Life* magazine, Paul combines both fine art and folk art techniques to hand-carve each of his Santas.

His *Christmas Legends* collection, designed exclusively for KSA Collectibles from Kurt S. Adler, Inc., includes hand-painted Santas cast in wood resin directly from his originals. New collectibles feature Corn Cob Pipe and North Pole sign ornaments, candle holders and novelty ornaments. "Bountiful," an elegant, large Santa, is featured in the *Christmas Legends* series, along with "Cookie Claus" and "No Hair Day Santa." Each of Paul's characters, whether they're inspired from old German and Celtic lore or are just whimsical creations, are based on an original humorous tale that he created.

MICHAEL BOYETT

Michael Boyett is recognized as one of the most important sculptors of the American West. His works are exhibited in Western galleries and museums throughout the United States, including exhibitions at the inauguration of President Carter, The George Phippen Memorial Art Show, Texas Rangers Hall of Fame, and the Texas Art Classic.

Born in Boise, Idaho, Boyett's childhood passion for drawing and carving propelled him into a career in fine arts. After serving in the Vietnam War, he received bachelor's and master's degrees in Fine Arts from Stephen F. Austin State University.

Boyett worked exclusively in bronze until 1979, when The Lance Corporation began casting his miniature scale sculptures in pewter. His works for Chilmark include the *Legacy of Courage* Indian series, *Flat Out for Red River Station* and *He Who Taunts the Enemy*.

His work for Legends® represents the interdependent relationship that existed between the Native American warrior hunter and wild creatures. Creating each detailed sculpture with a sense of movement, Michael hopes that "each of my pieces will give viewers the impression that they have actually witnessed the event portrayed."

SUZAN BRADFORD

Suzan Bradford's background, education and own natural talent have combined to provide us with the inspired figurine sculptor Suzan is today. Her freelance and commissioned artworks are in private collections across the country.

Suzan defines herself as primarily a self-taught artist. Always adventuresome, Suzan explores the mediums of drawing, oil painting, watercolor, bronzes and lithographs as she does sculpture.

Suzan, who joined United Design in 1985, has been instrumental in making *The Legend of Santa Claus™* one of the most sought-after Santa collections available. She is also responsible for creating the first design in the *Angels Collection* and the *Fancy Frames™* offering.

In Suzan's free time, she has turned her talents to renovating her pre-statehood Norman, Oklahoma, home.

RICK BROWN

With a combined passion for drawing, painting and football, Omaha native Rick Brown knew he could be happy with only one career – as a sports artist.

After college at the University of Nebraska-Omaha, Rick moved to California where he studied at the Art Center College of Design in Pasadena, and at Long Beach State. Afterwards, he landed a position with a major California studio working with noted illustrators.

In 1984, Rick began freelancing with an impressive client list that includes Disney, Universal Studios, Milton Bradley, Pro-Line and Pro-Set trading cards, and NFL Properties.

His skill and success in combining acrylics, airbrush and brush painting brought him to the attention of The Bradford Exchange, which recently released the first series of collector's plates to feature his vibrant art, *The Great Super Bowl Quarterbacks*.

TOM BROWNING

Tom Browning found that art was an important part of his childhood, and what he wanted to do with his life. Today, he is one of America's leading artists. His work is displayed at galleries throughout the West and Northwest including Settlers West in Tucson and Wadles Gallery in Santa Fe. He is a member of the Northwest Rendezvous Group (NWR) in Helena, Montana.

In addition to painting full time, Browning and his wife Joyce own and operate Arbor Green Publishers, where they publish and distribute the popular *Santa's Time Off™* greeting cards and prints.

Tom Browning's work is also featured in the *American Artist Collection®* and the *Santa's Time Off™* porcelain collection from Possible Dreams.

Browning describes himself as a quiet, sensitive person who produces "a picture that is simple and straightforward."

MICHAEL AND SHELLEY TINCHER BUONAIUTO

The sculptures of Michael and Shelley Buonaiuto use an unusual combination of various clays, porcelain and stoneware in a single work. Collectors are drawn to their work not only for the technical achievement but also for the highly personal quality that gives each piece a unique life and expression.

At the University of Massachusetts, Shelley studied painting and etching, and Michael studied architecture and sculpture. Unable to find a direction in art, Shelley studied flute and music theory at The New England Conservatory in Boston. Later in New York, Shelley studied and taught sacred dance, and began working in pottery to capture the tranquility of ancient Asian Buddhas and DaVinci's madonnas. Her work is also influenced by her love for music and dance.

Feeling a need for change and fresh inspiration, Michael and Shelley sold their house and moved to Santa Fe via South America.

Michael began working in pottery in 1975. Although his figures are fairly realistic, he is influenced by the art objects and ceremonies of primitive cultures. He finds inspiration by watching the earth and clouds out of an airplane window, from dream imagery or even by walking through a fish market.

In their spare time, Michael improves his Haitian drumming and Shelley is pursuing a degree in art therapy, as well as beginning a new series of art pieces to be cast in bronze.They are under commission from Duncan Royale.

FRANCES BURTON

Frances Elaine Montgomery Burton has always loved art. After completing the Famous Artist Course, she began her training as a Fenton decorator in 1973. For the next ten years, she balanced work with raising her children. Later returning to Fenton full-time, she quickly progressed from decorator to trainer, designer, head designer and finally department supervisor.

In her spare time, Frances likes walking, sewing and growing the beautiful flowers she later brings to life on glass. Her delicate floral Vining Garden design enhanced the beauty of Fenton's Transparent Seamist Green Glass.

Romance novels and old movies also capture her interest. She is content when curled by the fire with a good book, her three cats, and Nikki, the dog. Frances and Lanny, her husband of 25 years, love to escape to Vermillion on Lake Erie where they fish, share the quiet beauty and their dream of residing there someday.

SAM BUTCHER

Sam Butcher began his artistic career creating the teardrop-eyed children with inspirational messages for use on greeting cards and posters. In 1978, Enesco President and CEO, Eugene Freedman, transformed Butcher's two-dimensional art into the popular three-dimensional *Precious Moments®* Collection.

Butcher creates all artwork for the Collection and coordinates with Enesco and the Precious Moments Design Studio in Japan to create dozens of new subjects each year, all inspired by personal events and collector requests. Butcher also creates contemporary art, depicting men, women and children.

Butcher's faith and art led to the construction of the Precious

Moments Chapel in Carthage, Missouri, which houses a myriad of artwork, stained glass windows and a painted ceiling, all featuring *Precious Moments* children.

Butcher has been honored with a multitude of awards within the collectibles industry including the 1988 "Special Recognition Award," 1992 "Artist and Collectible of the Year," and 1994 "Figurine and Ornament of the Year," all by the National Association of Limited Edition Dealers.

The father of seven children and grandfather of 13, Butcher divides his time between his home on the Chapel grounds, his residence near Chicago and the overseas studio.

JOYCE F. BYERS

Joyce Fritz Byers' artistic curiosity at age 12 had expanded from sewing doll costumes to include sculpture and oil painting. She earned a degree in Home Economics at Drexel University and after graduation, took a position designing children's clothing.

By the late 1960s, Joyce had married Bob Byers and lived with their two sons in Bucks County, Pennsylvania.

Joyce began making caroling Christmas figures, first for herself, and then as gifts for her family and friends. For about ten years, Joyce perfected the construction methods and refined her sculpting skills.

In the late 1970s, the demand for the Carolers® became so great that with Bob's assistance, they turned a hobby into a business.

Joyce sculpts each original face in clay and designs the costumes. She teaches artisans the skills necessary for quantity production of the hand-made Byers' Choice figurines. This handwork imparts each figurine with the delightful personality sought by nearly 150,000 collectors.

The incredible success of Byers' Choice figurines has enabled Bob and Joyce to share the joy of giving in Christmas' true spirit. Each year, they give a substantial amount of their company's profits to charities.

RICK CAIN

Since an early age, Rick Cain has pursued a career as an artist. Born into a military family in 1953, Rick found security and strength in his art during adjustments to numerous moves around the country. Every day he taught himself the techniques that have remained constant in all his work – attention to detail, depth and dimension in both human and animal form.

Beginning wood working at age 20, Rick progressed rapidly past merely creating designs in the wood to "releasing" the shapes and images inherent in the wood. By this time, Rick had settled in Florida, and the indigenous tropical hardwoods lent themselves beautifully to the wizened old men's faces and graceful forms that he created.

Within months of his first showing at an art exhibit, his professional career flourished with participation in hundreds of juried art shows and exhibitions. He has been recognized with numerous awards.

In 1988, Rick made the decision to offer his work in limited editions. Rick's original works and limited edition sculptures are in private and public collections throughout the world.

KITTY D. CANTRELL

Award-winning artist and environmentalist Kitty Cantrell is known for her striking sculptures of North American wildlife. Intricately designed and detailed, her Mixed Media® sculptures capture expressions of animals that have never known human touch such as wolves, eagles and humpback whales. Through her sculptures, people can better understand the earth's wild creatures. "If my sculptures can make people think about wildlife and appreciate the importance of wildlife, then maybe they will feel compelled to help protect it."

After researching an animal, Cantrell produces a rough sculpture out of soft clay to check for composition and form. She then forms a master sculpture – authentic to scale and anatomically accurate – and coats it with silicone rubber and plaster casting. When the mold is ready, she sends it to the Legends® foundry where a resin cast is made. Pewter is used as a base for the sculptures which are covered with various metals – bronze, copper and 24K gold. Using actual hot-torched acid patinas, not paints or dyes, the metals are beautifully colored to bring the sculptures to life.

For her work including bronzes and pastels, Cantrell has received several awards. She resides in Southern California with her husband, sculptor Erik Fredsti, and their many animals.

PAT CHANDOK AND DAVID LEE WOODARD

The art of collaboration is alive and well at Precious Art's *World of Krystonia* with Pat Chandok and David Woodard heading a creative team. They have worked together to produce some of the gift industry's most innovative products – from carousel ponies to fantasy figurines and music boxes.

A native of Bombay, India, Pat Chandok brings a sphere of Asian influence. After finishing her schooling, she married and moved to the U.S., where her love of business and fine art directed her into the giftware industry.

In 1975, Dave, already a friend, joined Pat, bringing with him an impressive array of marketing, merchandising and sales skills. In 1980, the pair began importing and distributing their own giftware, which became so successful that they closed their retail shops.

Pat and Dave's early success in oriental designs led into musical items, including the market's first up-and-down carousel. In 1987, they premiered the award-winning *World of Krystonia*, a whimsical make-believe kingdom. With three books on the market and a fourth in the making, collectors can read about their favorite characters. Creating new figurines for their stories is one of Pat and Dave's most rewarding tasks. Whatever the results, the collector is always the first in the minds and hearts of this creative pair.

JAMES C. CHRISTENSEN

James Christensen fills his art with wonderful people, places and things as real as your adult dreams and as beloved as your childhood memories. He has created a unique kinetic kingdom, "a land a little left of reality," where human emotions are often manifested as fish or fowl, utilizing the viewer's own imagination.

His art-inspired offerings from The Greenwich Workshop include porcelain figurines; Art Furnishings; unique Bookcase Puzzles; *Evening Angels*, an Art in Concert™ art and music collaboration with composer Kurt Bestor; and, from The Greenwich Workshop Press, *A Journey of Imagination*.

After studying painting at the University of California and Brigham Young University, Christensen has had one-man shows in the West and the Northeast. His work is prized in America and Europe, and has been included in the *New York Society of Illustrators Annual* and Japan's *Outstanding American Illustrators* book.

Christensen is now a professor of art at Brigham Young University. He has been part of The Greenwich Workshop family of artists since 1985.

JOYCE CLEVELAND

Animals, nature and children are the focus of Joyce Cleveland's artwork. By the time she graduated from Syracuse University, top greeting card companies were already interested in her creations. She immediately began designing party goods and three-dimensional items. Often traveling to Japan, Taiwan and Hong Kong on design trips, she later went back and lived in Taiwan to get a better understanding of factory capabilities.

In 1973, Joyce formed her own company, J. Cleveland Design Inc. Her work ranged from creating textile designs to children's products and packaging, yet she found time to illustrate three children's books.

Joyce enjoys doing a wide variety of designs, from humorous to cute, to realistic wildlife. "I like to make people smile, laugh and have fun with life as well as appreciate the beauty of nature."

Joyce Cleveland is currently designing for Possible Dreams.

LAURA COBABE

To be a great doll designer, two qualities are particularly important – exceptional artistic ability and a deep, abiding love of children. This unique combination can be found in Laura Cobabe, who creates wonderfully animated collector dolls.

The very first doll Laura entered in competition, "Dustin," won a blue ribbon. Today, her dolls continue to win awards, including the coveted "Rolf Ericson Award for Outstanding Doll Sculpture" for "Amber," and back-to-back "Doll of the Year" awards for "Brianna" in 1992 and "Tamika" in 1993. And her adorable trick-or-treater doll, "Lil' Punkin," was nominated for a 1994 DOTY award. Her most recent creation is "Nica" for The Hamilton Collection.

Laura spends so much of her time making her dolls look authentic – from their decorative costumes to their realistic child features – that she only makes five dolls a year. A percentage of the money these dolls draw is donated to the Adam Walsh Children's Fund to give children a chance for a better future.

FRANCISCO "PACO" CONTRERAS

Born on January 8, 1945 in Puebla, Mexico, Francisco "Paco" Contreras studied at the National School of Plastics Arts, San Carlos, of the National University Autonomy of Mexico. After graduating in Graphic Design, Paco joined his artist friends to form Creaciones and Reproduciones Artisticas (Creart) in Mexico City.

Meanwhile, he studied drawing with Maestro Jose Luis Cuevas and artistic anatomy with Maestro Emilio Castaneda. In 1987, Paco left the company to dedicate his time to ceramics, working with Maestro Soledad Hernandez.

Returning to Creart in 1992 with new ideas and spirit, Paco created seven of the nine sculptures in Creart's 1993 *Nature's Care Collection*. His creative talent was behind Creart's "Wild American" Bison, "Cape Buffalo," "Moose" and the 1995 *The Land Down Under* – a four-piece limited edition collection of koalas.

His attention to detail produces high-quality realistic sculptures. He states, "When I begin a sculpture, I begin an adventure, seeking to find the most that can be accomplished in my work. It brings me great joy when I achieve this goal that I long to begin again to feel this jubilation."

DAVID CORBRIDGE

A uniquely talented person, David Corbridge combines passionate interests in conservation, wildlife, drawing, painting, illustrating, sculpting, education...and pigs! Living on an English farm in a remote part of County Durham where there is abundant wildlife, Corbridge has developed a keen understanding of pigs by closely watching their personalities and idiosyncratic ways. As he fondly says, "To know pigs is to love them!"

Corbridge is a much sought-after lecturer and exhibiting artist

who spends his time studying wildlife and expressing his feelings through writing, sculpture, painting and drawing. He enjoys sharing his love of nature with others, especially collectors who have fallen in love with the *Piggin'* line. His English sense of humor is a dominant reason for the appeal of this collectible series produced by Collectible World Studios in England and exclusively distributed in the U.S. by Flambro Imports.

HELEN COVENTRY

Helen Coventry joined W.A.P. Watson Ltd. in 1991 (parent company to The Tudor Mint), and has worked on designs for jewelry, display stands and packaging, including the new *Myth and Magic* box design for 1995.

Helen's first *Myth and Magic* figurine was "The Rising of the Phoenix" and since then she has designed "The Wizard of the Skies" and most of the "Demon" studies from the *Dark Secrets* line. Many of the exciting 1995 introductions have been designed by Helen.

Despite being involved in creating original artwork these days, Helen actually specialized in photography for her degree in design at North Staffordshire Polytechnic.

KEN CROW

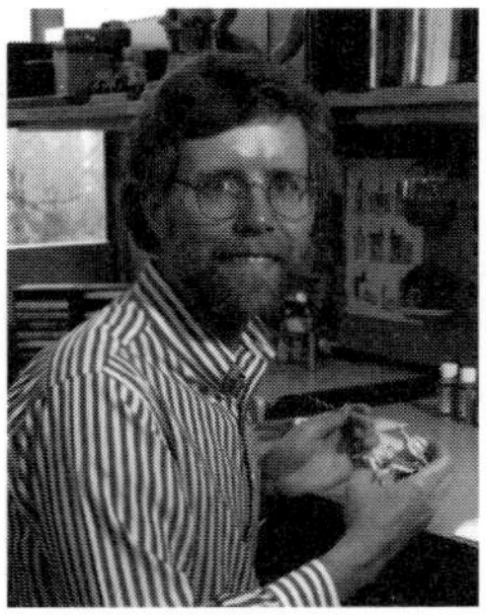

When Ken Crow sculpted Keepsake Ornaments based on Disney's 1994 animated feature film, *The Lion King*, it was truly a dream come true. A native of Long Beach, California, Ken grew up near Disneyland. "It was always a dream of mine to do something for Disney," the artist explains. "...In my opinion, nobody pushes art as far as Disney does." The Keepsake Ornaments inspired by *The Lion King* include "Simba and Nala," "Mufasa and Simba," and the comical "Timon and Pumbaa," and the Keepsake Magic Ornament "Mufasa, Sarabi and Simba."

Ken followed up this first dream come true with yet another, sculpting characters from Disney's animated feature film *Pocahontas* for the 1995 *Pocahontas Collection* of Keepsake Ornaments.

Ken's sculptures are imaginative and playful, often including movement. Recent examples of his sense of fun can be found in the 1995 "In Time With Christmas," "Santa's Serenade" and the Keepsake Miniature Ornament Collector's Series, *Santa's Little Big Top*.

EDNA DALI

A graduate of Ben-Gurion University in Israel, Edna Dali immigrated to Nottingham, England, in 1977, where she studied painting and sculpting. She and her family later moved to the United States. She continued her art studies in Massachusetts, where she first became interested in doll sculpture. This interest has won her a "Public's Favorite Award" at IDEX and two "Awards of Excellence" from *Dolls* magazine.

Edna creates a few one-of-a-kind dolls, much prized by high-end collectors, as well as limited edition dolls that are more accessible to the amateur collector. She makes her home in Ra'Anna, Israel, with her husband Avi and their three children, Tamir, Assaf and Ma'ayan. Her recent creations for the Seymour Mann Gallery include "Patricia," "Stacy" and "Cara," nominee for *Dolls* magazine's 1995 "Award of Excellence."

STEVE DARNLEY

Born in 1962, Steve Darnley worked for W.A.P. Watson Ltd. (parent of The Tudor Mint) for three years in casting and mold making, then left for nearly five years before returning as a model maker in 1991. Although always interested in model making, he has never had any formal training and joined the company on the merits of his self-taught skills gained using tools handmade by his father. As a new model maker, he tended to work initially on souvenirs but now is much more involved with *Myth and Magic*. His first study was "Banishing the Dragon." He also sculpted "The Armoured Dragon" (a favorite of his), "The Hatchlings" and a number of *Dark Secrets'* studies. He prides himself on trying to make the back side of his studies as interesting as the front side, this part not being covered by the original design drawings which allows for greater creativity.

LOWELL DAVIS

Painter and sculptor Lowell Davis appreciates the nostalgic search by Americans for the "good ol' days." Under his grandfather's guidance, Lowell began drawing animals and learned to whittle from the old-timers who sat around the family store.

Leaving this peaceful setting, Lowell became the art director for a major ad agency in Dallas. Later, he returned to Missouri's Ozark Mountains and found a 1930s farmhouse and a simpler way of life. Schmid recognized Davis' talent and began to produce his complete line of figurines, limited edition plates and other collectibles. Over the years, Davis scoured the countryside for buildings and farm implements to make his Fox Fire Farm an authentic 1930s working farm and to recreate the town of his youth. He bought several Red Oak homes and businesses, moved them 23 miles to his farm, and restored them to their original grandeur, which he now calls Red Oak II.

Collectors from all over the world have come to visit Davis' farm. They return home with the knowledge that their collectibles, carefully crafted by Lowell Davis, are truly an authentic slice of Americana.

RAY DAY

Since 1973, Ray Day has painted America's rural landscape in watercolor and published limited edition originals. From 1986, Ray's watercolors have been published on limited edition porcelain plates. Ray's watercolors bring enjoyment to collectors who find pleasure in the nostalgic and historic. He finds inspiration all over America...from coast to coast... from noted landmarks to hidden treasures.

At the invitation of Lilliput Lane, Ray has created the *American Landmarks* collection. He sculpts each building based on actual locations in wax, then sends it to the Lilliput Lane Studios in Penrith, England, where molding, casting and painting takes place.

Ray has spent 33 years teaching high school art and theater. In addition, he and his wife Eileen continue to publish his watercolors from their southern Indiana home.

Ray serves on the Rural Landmarks Council of the Historic Landmarks Foundation in Indiana. He encourages collectors to join protective societies in order "to be informed of preservation needs and efforts throughout the country."

CHIP DEMATTEO

Growing up in a restored home in Colonial Williamsburg, Chip deMatteo watched his father, William, set off for his silversmith's shop. As a child, he enjoyed spending time in his father's shop, and by age ten, he was actually doing small jobs.

Eventually, Chip studied art in college and then spent a few years as a "starving artist" in Washington, D.C. Meanwhile, he supplemented his income with silver work for his father.

In the late 1970s, Chip, his father and a partner Philip Thorp formed Hand & Hammer Silversmiths in Alexandria, Virginia. Since 1981, Chip has been the sole designer for Hand & Hammer, creating more than 400 ornament designs.

Using the "lost-wax" technique, Chip has designed a number of highly sought-after series. Especially popular are the *Bell*, *Star*, and *Twelve Days of Christmas* series, in addition to the *Beatrix Potter*, *Night Before Christmas* and *Alice in Wonderland* collections.

JESSICA DESTEFANO

Over the past 20 years, Jessica deStefano has created collectibles for The Franklin Mint, The Danbury Mint and Rawcliffe Corporation. After apprenticing under several members of the National Sculpture Society, she specialized in creating limited edition chess sets, including a Watergate Chess Set which now resides in Washington, D. C.

Since 1988, deStefano has been sculpting the *Bubble Fairies™* collection for Rawcliffe Corporation. Dedicated to her father's memory, deStefano explains: "When I was small, although he was not well, my Dad would occasionally push me on the swing and sing his favorite song – 'I'm forever blowing bubbles, pretty bubbles in the air...they fly so high, nearly touch the sky...'" *Bubble Fairies™* are mixed media collectibles, blending a resin figurine with a hand-blown irridescent glass bubble and nylon wings. The result is a light and airy sculpture that captures the essence of these delightful creatures.

Says deStefano, "When people ask me where *Bubble Fairies™* come from, I answer 'somewhere over the rainbow.' I believe that there is a beautiful dreamer in every child and that child never dies. That's why even adults love fairies so much."

BEV DOOLITTLE

Bev Doolittle has set the world's record for the number of commissioned limited edition prints sold, and the book *The Art of Bev Doolittle* has more than 350,000 copies in print.

Following the announcement of a "hiatus for creative exploration," the anticipation was great for her 1995 fine art print "Two More Indian Horses," and her book *New Magic*, which is offered in a Collector's Edition with a new signed and numbered limited edition print.

After graduating from the Art Center College of Design in Los Angeles, Bev became involved in advertising art and television commercial production with her husband, Jay. However, she had a strong desire to create her own art and be close to nature.

Now with both goals accomplished, Bev's talents in the medium of transparent watercolor have won her a worldwide following. Often referred to as a 'camouflage' artist, Bev thinks of herself as a 'concept painter' who uses camouflage to get her story across. "For me, camouflage is a means to an end, not an end in itself. My meaning and message are never hidden."

CONNIE DREW

"I wasn't born, I was hatched," says South Dakota native Connie Drew with a wink. Her long love affair with decorated eggs started very early when her mother and grandmother taught her the art of drop-pull egg decorating, a Czechoslovakian tradition she calls CZEGGS.

Throughout the years, Connie's hobby *eggspanded* to a full-time business. Her turn toward *eggsquisite* collectibles happened over 25 years ago when she saw her first decorated ostrich egg. Connie *eggsclaims*, "It was the biggest egg I had ever seen." So she bought it and has been *collEGGting* and designing ever since.

Today, Connie's art form uses modern techniques and equipment to create designs that would rival Fabergé, the famous

Russian Jeweler to the czar. And yes, they are all made out of real eggshells. The future is bright and *eggciting* for *eggspressions!* because the world's oldest form of gift giving has become today's hottest collectible.

CARLOS ESTEVEZ

Creart U.S.A. President and contributing artist, Carlos Estevez, showed a natural talent for painting and drawing at a young age.

Born in Colombia, South America, he attended the Seminary and Navy School. In 1969, he moved to New York City to continue his education, receiving a bachelor's degree in technical science and civil engineering.

For 12 years, Carlos worked for a civil engineering firm in Houston. During this time, he won many awards from the El Campa Art League.

In 1987, Carlos joined Creart, working in marketing. He produced his first sculpture, "Sea Otters," for Creart in 1992, and created "Puffins," "Catamountain," and "Out of the Den" Puma. Carlos is also the creative artist behind the 1995 series titled *African Water Hole*. This series depicts African animals gathering at the precious water hole. The first sculpture was "Cheetahs" – a beautiful representation of these animals in their graceful refinement.

"Even though we, as artists, are imitators of God's creation," says Carlos, "I find delight in what can be accomplished. In my work I can make tangible the beauty of our wildlife."

DECLAN FEARON

A standard of Irish folklore for centuries, the Blarney Stone is believed to bestow the gifts of good luck and eloquence upon all who kiss it. People have traveled long distances for this opportunity.

Thanks to Declan Fearon, a journey to your local collectible store is all that's necessary to share in the enchantment through *Declan's Finnians: Guardians of the Blarney Stone*. These colorful, handcrafted characters with tales on Story Cards bear a stone chip from the same quarry that was the source for the historic Blarney Castle. Fearon and his wife, Camilla, collaborated on the Finnians' concept and design.

Fearon personally brought a bit of Ireland to the Fightin' Irish in 1994 by presenting a piece of quarry stone to University of Notre Dame's Head Football Coach, Lou Holtz.

A successful businessman for over 30 years, Fearon is a native of the capital of Ireland and studied at the University of Dublin.

PAT FORD

Pat Ford is influenced by all the roles that have fulfilled her unique life – that of mother, wife, and consummate artist. Her development as a naturalist artist came out of her own experi-

ence. "I married an outdoorsman. Instead of going to the opera or ballet, we went camping, raised horses and cattle...the boys were interested in wildlife and we took care of injured animals and birds."

Of her art she says, "I'm doing what I do best and what I enjoy most." Ford not only brings her tremendous talent into each painting, but also does textbook and field research on each animal she paints. Her dedication to factual detail takes her art one step beyond photorealism.

Each painting takes about three weeks. Sometimes she will paint 18 hours a day, seven days a week. The rest of her time is spent in wildlife refuges, or dedicating time and her artwork to raise funds for Ducks Unlimited®. Anheuser-Busch features her art on limited edition steins and collectibles.

CHARLES FRACÉ

Although especially known for his paintings of big cats, Charles Fracé is captivated by all wildlife subjects, ranging from wolves and grizzly bears to mountain goats and harp seals. "Every time I sit down to paint, I get excited about the painting, the animal and the exploration ahead," says Fracé.

Believing that nothing substitutes for seeing animals firsthand, Fracé has traveled the globe to conduct field studies and to observe animals at zoos and private breeding compounds throughout the U.S.

Featured in more than 300 one-man shows throughout the U.S. and Canada, Fracé has been honored by a number of museums, including the Smithsonian's National Museum of Natural History, the Leigh Yawkey Woodson Art Museum and the Denver Museum of Natural History. Most recently, he was one of the first five artists inducted into The Bradford Exchange Plate Artist Hall of Fame.

Fracé's paintings have been reproduced on eight plate series available from The Bradford Exchange, including *The World's Most Magnificent Cats* and *Kingdom of Great Cats: The Gold Signature Collection*.

TOBIN FRALEY

Renowned carousel restorer and author Tobin Fraley, whose fascination with carousels goes back to his childhood experiences at his grandfather's amusement park, has been involved with carousel restoration for more than three decades. Recently Fraley signed on with George Zoltan Lefton Company to design an exclusive collection of colorful, hand-painted carousel figures.

Under his own publishing

company, Zephyr Press, he has published more than 100 wall calendars and a coffee table book, *The Carousel Animal*, which traces the rich history of the carousel from its beginnings to the early 20th century. As a gift designer for Hallmark Galleries and Willitts Designs, Fraley has created original carousel collections and ornaments.

Of his association with Lefton and the new carousel collection, Fraley comments: "I believe carousels are an artistic category that will never die. The carousel is something that everyone has experienced – it has universal appeal."

MARGARET FURLONG

Margaret Furlong Alexander combines her "commitment to personal and spiritual values" with her artistic gifts in producing the beautiful white porcelain angels, stars and other designs for her company, Margaret Furlong Designs.

Margaret's love affair with white began when she started sculpting abstract snowscapes in Nebraska in the '70s. Her first angel ornament appeared in 1979, after she combined several shell forms, a molded face, a textured coil and a tapered trumpet into a "shell angel" from unshaded and unglazed porcelain.

Since then she has married, moved to Seattle and then to Salem, Oregon, where her business is thriving and she and her husband Jerry are raising their daughter Caitlin.

Margaret divides her time between her family, home studio and the Carriage House Studio. Her staff of more than 90 produces over 120 different designs, which are sold throughout the country.

Margaret views each new design as a gift from God that she can share with all her collectors. And her genuineness, wisdom and joy are worth sharing, both as visions of pure white angels and as an example for others.

W.D. GAITHER

W.D. "Bill" Gaither is a multi-faceted artist with thousands of paintings and prints on display in galleries and private collections all over America.

As a sculptor and painter, Gaither's special gift stems from his immersion in the world of wildlife with his involvement in several environmental and wildlife conservation organizations. His workshops hold books on a myriad of subjects, mounted specimens, dozens of sketches and partially completed sculptures.

Gaither creates works which are active, fluid and alive – never static or frozen. His wildlife studies reflect a living moment in the animal's life in the wild – feeding, running, attacking, playing, leaping, soaring or charging.

Gaither's first sculpture in association with the Maruri Studio premiered in 1982. Since then, wildlife art connoisseurs eagerly await each Maruri introduction – many of which sell out immediately and begin rising in value.

ROGER GIBBONS

Born in 1954, Roger Gibbons started his career as a precious stones salesman in Birmingham's Jewelry Quarter before gaining an apprenticeship in W.A.P. Watson Ltd.'s Model Making Department (parent of The Tudor Mint). Part of his training involved a three-year jewelry course at Mid-Warwickshire College of Higher Education under Rex Billingham. Since then, he has worked on fashion jewelry, souvenirs, giftware, Crystalflame and Victorian scenes that launched The Tudor Mint name. Roger modeled the first *Myth and Magic* figurines from Sharon Riley's designs and has worked on a great number since. However, as Chief Model Maker, he also has administrative duties to consider and doesn't sculpt quite as much as he has done in the past. In 1994, he celebrated 20 years with the company.

NATE GIORGIO

Even before his 1991 debut as a limited edition plate artist, Nate Giorgio had already made a name for himself in the arts. He has created commissioned artwork of several famous celebrities, including Michael Jackson, Quincy Jones, Madonna, Prince and Johnny Cash.

Giorgio's world-tour program cover and 1989 calendar for Michael Jackson was enthusiastically received, leading him to create not only many movie posters and entertainment companies' logos but also numerous pieces for collectors throughout the United States and England.

Working in mixed media, including oils, pastels and watercolors, Giorgio explores and celebrates the spirit of the entertainer. "It's not photographic or realistic. I try to really capture their personalities," says Giorgio.

His four plate series available from The Bradford Exchange – *The Beatles Collection*, *Elvis Presley Hit Parade*, *Superstars of Country Music* and *Remembering the King* – have also captured some of music's legendary entertainers.

JULIE GOOD-KRÜGER

For Julie Good-Krüger, life as a doll artist includes living and working in Amish country's Strasburg, Pennsylvania where she, her husband and daughter live in a stone grist mill. The influence of the Amish inspired her to create the *Amish Blessings* doll collection for The Ashton-Drake Galleries.

In high school, Julie enjoyed reading doll magazines and creating small sculptures on plaques. Her interest in dolls waned in college until the late 1970s when she began experimenting with doll making to earn extra money for graduate school.

Perfecting her craft for three years, Julie finally introduced her first original child dolls to the public. Since then, her dolls have won numerous awards, including 1988 and 1989 "Doll of the Year" award nominations, and in 1995, a "Doll of the Year" award nomination for "I Wish You Love."

Since *Amish Blessings*, Julie has created three other collections for Ashton-Drake: the *Oh Holy Night* nativity collection, the *Baby Talk* collection, and the *All I Wish for You* collection of baby angels, of which the DOTY® award nominee doll, "I Wish You Love," is the first issue.

AL GORDON

After majoring in fine arts at Columbia University, Al Gordon became one of the early illustrators for Marvel Comics and also worked for Walt Disney Studios. His abilities as a graphic artist led to opportunities with NBC and ABC networks. Now, Al serves as art director for Marty Miller Marketing (the design team for Today's Creations).

As head of his own design studio, A.G. Graphics, his award winning package designs and illustrations have been utilized by most major toy manufacturers. Specializing in licensed characters from Mickey Mouse to Power Rangers, he has designed product and created showroom displays for numerous companies for the International Toy Fair in New York City.

The love, respect and friendship Al shared with his wife, Sue, for over 40 years showed in his designs for the *Times to Remember Collection* from Today's Creations. Sadly, Sue lost her battle with lung cancer in 1994 and did not see the final pieces. Al has dedicated this *Times to Remember* series to the memory of his loving wife.

JAMES GRIFFIN

Born in Ontario, Canada, James Griffin came to the U.S. with his family at age five. Earning a bachelor's degree from Pratt Institute, he has exhibited at numerous locations from New York and the Midwest to South America.

His illustrations have appeared in publications, ranging from *Good Housekeeping* to *The Wall Street Journal*. Listed in *Who's Who in American Art*, he has also illustrated for such publishing and media giants as Harcourt Brace Jovanovich, Random House, Doubleday, NBC and Warner Communications.

He cites the great illustrators of the past – including Norman Rockwell and N.C. Wyeth – as important influences on his artwork, along with Japanese prints, Mughal miniatures and Gustav Klimt.

A seasoned world traveler who draws on other cultures for inspiration, Griffin has toured France, Italy, Japan, Mexico, Turkey, Morocco, India and Nepal. He has lived in England, Peru and Brazil. He currently resides in New York's Hudson Valley with his wife Tabita and their cat Pushkin.

Griffin's work has appeared in three plate series available from The Bradford Exchange – *Casablanca*, *World War II: A Remembrance*, and *Battles of the American Civil War*.

JUDITH ANN GRIFFITH

Growing up in rural Pennsylvania, it was natural for Judith Ann Griffith to start drawing pictures of birds and animals at an early age. Later she attended an art college in Philadelphia and, after graduation, worked for a large greeting card company. There, her artistic style naturally continued to grow.

Today, Judith lives in the Ozark Mountains of Arkansas, a wooded setting she discovered while on a vacation. She finds inspiration surrounded by vast natural areas. "I've spent most of my life in the woods of Pennsylvania and Arkansas. When I'm not painting, I hike or garden, and have learned much from nature, especially from the great sentient forests."

Judith's artwork celebrates a deep reverence for life, and for the beauty and peace which truly exist on earth. She hopes that her art is an inspiration for others to work in love and harmony for the well-being of life on this planet.

Judith Ann Griffith has designed figurines for the *American Artist Collection*® from Possible Dreams.

JOHN GROSSMAN

"I feel a tremendous responsibility to conserve and preserve these old images," artist John Grossman says of his 200,000-piece collection of Victorian paper keepsakes. "But as an artist, I also love taking an old design and transforming it into something new."

After attending the Minneapolis School of Art, Grossman honed his skills at the Cours de la Civilization Francais at the Sorbonne in Paris.

With his gift for art and his natural appreciation for "all things Victorian," Grossman has been able to assemble and share his remarkable collection of antique Victorian keepsakes and mementos in the form of appealing collages. These Victorian keepsake collages are now available to collectors in the form of a limited edition plate series entitled *Romantic Victorian Keepsakes* under the commission of The Hamilton Collection.

In celebration of a festive Victorian Christmas, Grossman created another plate series of porcelain collages entitled *Victorian Christmas Memories*, beginning with "A Visit From St. Nicholas."

JAMES GURNEY

James Gurney's ability to recreate moments of history with scientific accuracy and to imagine fantastic realms in a wealth of detail has resulted in the creation of *Dinotopia*®, a place where

humans and dinosaurs live in peaceful interdependence. Selling more than a million copies, *Dinotopia* (1992) has won numerous awards. The next *Dinotopia* adventure, *The World Beneath* (1995), features more than 160 full color illustrations.

To develop this new land, Gurney consulted experts at several museums, including The Smithsonian. Wanting to make things "as believable as possible," Gurney has done extensive work with historic realism. While pursuing anthropology at the University of California at Berkeley, he assisted at the Lowie Museum of Anthropology. He continued at the Pasadena Art Center College of Design and then traveled across America armed with sketchbook and tape recorder for two years.

Gurney's paintings have been exhibited by the New York Society of Illustrators, the Cleveland Museum of Natural History and the National Geographic Society.

SCOTT GUSTAFSON

Scott Gustafson's interpretations of classic fairy tales and stories show his love for stories. "My work creates an opportunity to revisit and reacquaint people with stories and make them accessible, so you might feel like you're visiting old friends."

Gustafson was first introduced to The Greenwich Workshop in 1992, and in less than a year, he became one of the most popular artists in the realm of limited edition prints, which include *Touched by Magic* (depicting Cinderella), *Goldilocks and the Three Bears*, *Little Red Riding Hood*, *The Frog Prince*, *Snow White and the Seven Dwarfs*, *Humpty Dumpty*, *Pat-a-Cake*, *The Alice in Wonderland Suite*, and *Jack and the Beanstalk*.

His classic, opulent style has appeared in such magazines as *The Saturday Evening Post* and *Playboy*. Gustafson has illustrated anew such classics as *The Night Before Christmas*, *The Nutcracker* and *Peter Pan* and created new stories with *Alphabet Soup* and *The Animal Orchestra*.

Scott's artwork has been interpreted in three dimensional works included in the recently introduced figurine collectibles line called *The Greenwich Workshop Collection*.

STEVE AND GIGI HACKETT

Steve and Gigi Hackett are a talented husband and wife team whose figurines have been produced by Cast Art Industries since 1993.

Steve apprenticed with the Disney organizations and left to undertake freelance commissions, including one-of-a-kind sculptures for the rich and famous. Together with his wife Gigi, a unique team approach and wry sense of humor have made vital contributions to several delightful collectible series.

Animal Attractions™ is an assortment of humorous portrayals of favorite pigs and dancing bears. *Story Time Treasures™* are representations of beloved children's stories, from *The Three Pigs* to *The Frog Prince*, each depicting a parent animal reading to his youngster. The Hacketts and artist Kristin Haynes have also developed *Cuddl'somes™*, a line of teddy bears and other animal figurines.

These wonderful collectible figurines, like all Cast Art products, are painstakingly hand-cast and hand-painted, and are sold in fine gift and collectibles stores.

HANS HENRIK HANSEN

Born in 1952, Hans Henrik Hansen graduated from the Academy of Applied Art in Copenhagen with an emphasis on graphic design.

For 12 years, he was the principal decorator at the retail store for the Royal Copenhagen Porcelain Manufactory, where his window decorations were the rage of fashionable Copenhagen.

Since 1987, Hansen has been devoted almost exclusively to creating designs and illustrations for the porcelain manufactory. His first Christmas series, *Jingle Bells*, was very successful.

With the introduction of the *Santa Claus* collection in 1989, Hansen became the first artist since 1895 to create a colorful Christmas plate for Bing & Grondahl.

For the first time since 1908, Royal Copenhagen issued a series of six annual Christmas plates and coordinating ornaments titled *Christmas in Denmark*. The original art for this epoch-making series was created by Hans Henrik Hansen.

KRISTIN HAYNES

Raised in Utah, Kristin Haynes is the product of an extremely artistic family. She majored in fine arts at the University of Utah and then moved with husband Scott to California in 1978 to pursue their careers – his in music, hers in sculpture. Kristin began creating a group of cherubs, animals, and other storybook characters which became popular with fans throughout southern California. Demand grew so great that Kristin began searching for a partner to help make reproductions in commercial quantities.

After showing her samples to Cast Art Industries, a gift manufacturing company, they agreed that the line must maintain its unique characteristics – manufactured from natural gypsum materials, handcrafted, and offered at an affordable price. The line, named *Dreamsicles®*, became one of the fastest growing in collectibles history.

Kristin's *Dreamsicles* now include more than 250 cherubs and animals, and she continues to create new designs from her farmhouse studio. In addition, *Cuckoo Corners™*, a collection of humorous characters, and several *Cuddl'somes™* teddy bears continue to be collectors' favorites.

JEAN WALMSLEY HEAP

By age ten, Jean Walmsley Heap began selling her drawings with a dream of buying a wooden hut "to live and paint in." She gained permission to use the broom cupboard under the stairs instead and called it "Studio One."

Three years later, Jean trained under Noel H. Leaver, A.R.C.A. at the Burnley School of Art. Later she began exhibiting child studies and flower paintings regularly in art galleries. During WWII, the Canadian Red Cross commissioned her to design large wall murals for wartime nurseries, as a gift to the children of Britain.

In 1953, Jean and her friend Jeannie Todd began the hobby that would give them international fame. In a tiny garden hut, Jean designed and modeled their very first piece – a witch, flying against the moon, with a wide-eyed cat on her shoulder – in honor of Pendle Hill, known as the Hill of Witches. Various other models followed, but orders did not roll in until Jean modeled "Father Rabbit." The "hobby" grew into what is now PenDelfin Studios with Jean as chairman and with offices in Canada, the U.S. and England.

HAP HENRIKSEN

For over 20 years, Hap Henriksen has delighted collectors throughout the world with his *Fantastic Art* collectibles, most recently sculpting for United Design, Lilliput Lane and Land of Legend. Now the award-winning Henriksen is putting his incredible talents to use in designing an entire line of fine pewter figurines of all the favorite *Looney Tunes™* characters. Under Rawcliffe Corporation's license with Warner Bros., such cartoon personalities as Road Runner, Daffy Duck, Wile E. Coyote, Tazmanian Devil, Porky Pig, Tweety Bird and Sylvester come to life being their own outrageous selves.

A master of detail, Henriksen's intricate and precise artistry has drawn accolades from the National Academy of Fantastic Art, the Delaware Art Museum, the Royal Toy & Model Museum of London, and the National Museum of Science Fiction & Fantasy in Houston, Texas. In 1989 and 1990, he was a popular featured speaker at the International Collectibles Exhibition in South Bend, Indiana.

Henriksen maintains studios in both Kansas and Texas, but his work is appreciated worldwide. Rawcliffe is proud to have him on board, capturing the essence of *Looney Tunes™*, a unique slice of Americana.

JON HERBERT

Jon Herbert, a talented British sculptor, has been known to American collectors for years but made his first United States collector appearance in 1995 for John Hine Studios.

Herbert's works first came to the United States in 1988 with the *The Shoemaker's Dream*, a collection of cottages sculpted in the shape of a variety of shoes and boots. A special "Military Boot" was crafted by Herbert in 1995 exclusively for military personnel, to commemorate the 50th anniversary of the end of World War II.

Herbert also sculpted and designed *The Father Time Clocks* collection, which premiered in 1991 and a collection of miniature clock sculptures in 1995.

Herbert began his career with John Hine Studios as a mouldmaker, making the intricate moulds for David Winter Cottages. His work begins with drawings, which cover a wide gamut of fantasy subjects, and from there, he proceeds to sculpt his original creations. Since joining John Hine Limited in 1987, his talents and his collections have attracted collectors around the world.

PEGGY HERRICK

Already a talented designer, Peggy Herrick discovered woodcarving over ten years ago. Through the carving of smiling animals, Peggy realized that she had found an artistic home.

Peggy's husband, a life-long woodworker, introduced her to an air-powered die grinder. With this tool, Peggy could further express her creativity and keep up with the demand for her unique and extraordinary pieces. After applying her whimsically hand-painted final touches, Peggy introduces another member to her enchanting animal kingdom – creating a smile on the original piece, as well as on the faces of everyone who sees it.

Midwest of Cannon Falls is pleased to present an exclusively-designed collection of precise reproductions of folk art pieces by Peggy Herrick. Her original ornaments and figures are certain to generate smiles on the faces of collectors and folk art enthusiasts alike.

PRISCILLA HILLMAN

Childhood memories of sketching at the kitchen table with her twin sister, Greta, influenced Priscilla Hillman's charming illustrations and uplifting children's books that have touched the hearts of collectors worldwide.

After writing and illustrating the children's books *Tumpy Rumple* and *Squeaky Nibble*, Western Publishing saw her work and asked her to illustrate several of its books. From there, she illustrated and wrote nine *Merry Mouse* books for Doubleday. In 1995, Enesco Corporation transformed her drawings of *Merry Mouse* into a giftware collection of figurines, titled *Mouse Tales*.

After recovering from a serious back problem in the late 1980s, Priscilla sent sketches of teddy bears to Enesco President and CEO, Eugene Freedman, who transformed them into the *Cherished Teddies® Collection* in 1992. Since its debut, the Collection has been honored with several awards, including "Collectible of the Year" and "Figurine of the Year" by NALED. Priscilla was recognized in 1994 as the "Artist of the Year."

Priscilla also designed the *Enesco Calico Kittens™ Collection*, based on messages of friendship and love for Enesco in 1994, and recently created a new bunny giftware line titled *My Blushing Bunnies*.

TORI DAWN YOUNGER HINE

As a child, Tori Dawn Hine exhibited natural artistic talent. At eight years old, she was submitting drawings to national publications, and at nine, she undertook formal training in the use of oils, acrylics and pastels.

In 1985, Tori Dawn's father, Bill Younger, introduced David Winter Cottages in the United States. The following year, his gifted daughter traveled to England to study cottage painting and became the first American painting artist for John Hine Studios.

During one of her visits to England, Tori Dawn met Harry Hine, whom she married in 1990. They currently live in San Diego where Tori Dawn keeps busy with her two boys and an active painting schedule.

When her father and sister Kim, founded Harbour Lights in 1991, Tori Dawn extended her cottage painting skills to lighthouse miniatures. As origination painter for Harbour Lights, she has earned accolades from collectors for her ability to capture romance and drama in each new release.

GERNOT HIRSCH

From a family of porcelain painters, Gernot Hirsch, production manager and a master painter, began his career with W. Goebel Porzellanfabrik (producer of *M.I. Hummel* figurines) in 1957.

After completing the three-year apprenticeship program and passing the porcelain painting exam given by the Chamber of Commerce and Industry in Coburg, Gernot developed his professional skills in various painting departments at Goebel. In 1962 he was promoted to Painting Supervisor.

Continuing to train and participate in special courses, Gernot became a Master of Industrial Arts in 1973. For many years, he served as Project Leader of special tasks in the Time and Motion Studies Department.

In 1986, Gernot was awarded, and maintains today, the position of head of Goebel's plant in Teuschnitz, where he supervises all aspects of operations including training the many new and talented painters. In addition, Gernot has participated in promotions in Japan, Australia, Germany and other European countries.

Married and living in Roedental, Gernot enjoys chess, choir singing, hiking and painting with water colors in his spare time.

ANTON HIRZINGER

Anton Hirzinger has lived in Kramsach, Tyrol, home of the famous Technical School for Glass Craft and Design, since he was born in 1955. "Even as a child, I was fascinated by glass production and knew at a very early age that when I grew up I wanted to make it my career," says Anton, who studied at his "hometown school." He initially worked as a hollow glass craftsman at a small company.

Now, Anton has been working for Swarovski for more than eight years. He initially started work in the Swarovski Crystal Shop in Wattens, providing countless visitors from all over the world a closer insight to glass and crystal craftmanship. Transferring to the Design Center in 1991, Anton created the Swarovski Silver Crystal "Pelican" and "Owlet." His greatest achievement so far is the "Centenary Swan" design, a commemorative edition for the company's 100th anniversary in 1995.

In his spare time, Anton and his family walk through Tyrol's beautiful countryside and ski in winter.

MARTHA HOLCOMBE

Martha Holcombe creates children whose expressions and situations reflect the tenderness, innocence and love of childhood. For Martha, each year is marked by the children "born" in that year, such as "Booker T." in 1985 and "Betsy and Bean" in 1988. In 1995 she introduced a new series called *All God's Children Ragbabies* that are adorable, whimsical and tickle the heart with their charming situations and sayings.

Known to many as Miss Martha, she creates from her heart and deep personal faith. Martha's childhood memories of growing up in the Appalachian foothills of northeast Alabama have inspired her sculptured art and have made her one of America's foremost artisans.

Her handcrafted cold-cast figures depict African-American children in delightful situations. Each piece, sculpted by Martha, is made entirely in the USA at Miss Martha Originals, located in Gadsden, Alabama.

Martha is pleased and humbled that her "children" have been so lovingly embraced by collectors across the country. For her, the high point of sculpting is the loving response and encouragement that collectors share with her.

FRANCES HOOK

The collectibles, art and publishing business communities saluted the inimitable artistry and spirit of the late Frances Hook by establishing a foundation in her name to foster young artists' studies. Since its inception following Hook's death in 1983, the Frances Hook Scholarship Fund currently awards over $55,000 in awards and scholarships to art students from first grade to college undergraduates.

A scholarship to the Pennsylvania Museum of Art led to the development of Hook's style in pastel and her unique manner of capturing the spirit and vitality of children. Her talent is evident in her renderings of famous 1960s Northern Tissue children.

Having illustrated children's books, Hook joined her husband Richard to successfully illustrate *The Living Bible* by Tyndale House Publishers.

Through her association with Roman, Inc., Hook's illustrations are reproduced in the form of limited edition figurines, plates and prints.

Much of Frances Hook's work can be seen today in the Frances Hook Museum and Gallery located in the Old School of Mishicot, Wisconsin.

SISTER MARIA INNOCENTIA HUMMEL

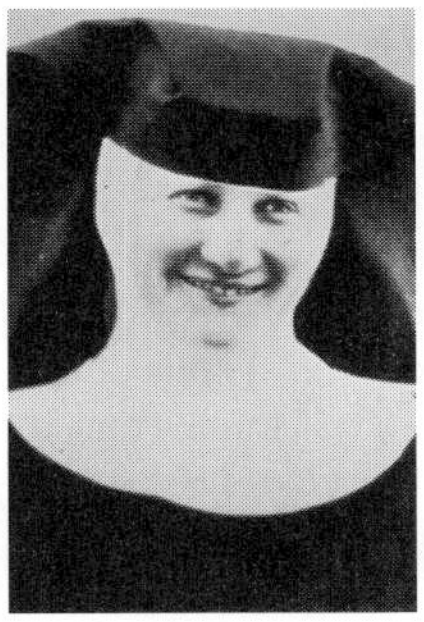

Sister Maria Innocentia Hummel created hundreds of colorful and charming sketches, drawings and paintings of children. Her work is the basis for scores of appealing, hand-painted fine earthenware figurines, as well as limited edition plates and bells, created and offered exclusively by W. Goebel Porzellanfabrik of Germany.

Born Berta Hummel in Bavaria in 1909, she had inclinations toward art from an early age. She graduated from the Munich Academy of Applied Art, meanwhile devoting much of her energy toward her religion.

After graduation, Berta entered a convent, taking the name Sister Maria Innocentia. Because the convent of Siessen, a teaching order, was quite poor, she sold some of her artwork in the form of postcards to raise money. In 1934, Franz Goebel, the fourth-generation head of the porcelain-producing firm, discovered her art.

The first *M.I. Hummel figurines* debuted at the Leipzig Fair in 1935, and since then have been popular with collectors around the world. Sadly, Sister M.I. Hummel died in 1946 at the age of 37, not yet aware of her full triumph as an artist.

CLIFF JACKSON

Cliff Jackson started his career as an artist while a youngster in Georgia, filling sketchbooks with the faces and places in his small hometown.

Later, winning a scholarship to the School of Visual Arts in New York City, Jackson honed his talents for illustration and design, graduating with a degree in fine arts and an appreciation for the dual roles of artist and educator. Jackson has taught drawing to schoolchildren and practices his art as an independent illustrator, designer and sculptor for corporate and private clients across America. His combined works include book jackets, magazine illustrations and sculptures.

Five three-dimensional plate series for The Bradford Exchange have featured his work: *Egypt: Splendors of an Ancient World*, *Field Pup Follies*, *Immortals of the Diamond*, *A Visit from St. Nick*, *Native Legends: Chiefs of Destiny* and *Winnie the Pooh and Friends*.

"I want the image to look alive and soft," Jackson says, "which is hard to do on clay. I try to make the plates as high relief as possible, bringing more depth."

BILL JAUQUET

Bill Jauquet's wood carvings chronicle a lifestyle little changed from American history's early years. Whimsical portraits spring from Jauquet's appreciation of the humor inherent in working with unpredictable livestock and weather. His impishness also surfaces in a holiday theme that embraces two styles of Santas – solemnly slender and playfully plump.

The *Bill Jauquet Americana Collection*, exclusive to Roman, Inc., features resin reproductions faithfully capturing the hand-wrought look, natural charm and power of each Jauquet original wood sculpture. The Wisconsin artist's carvings are worked directly from his mind's vision. Using aged cedar, Bill first roughs out the log with power tools. Then he planes and rasps the wood to achieve the desired form. After sanding and sealing, he applies stain or paint to achieve an antiqued look.

Jauquet's 1979 sculpture of a swan for his wife's antiques/folk art shop started him on the pursuit of art full-time. Now Jauquet's work appears in fine galleries nationwide and has been acquired by the Smithsonian Institute, corporations and celebrities.

BILL JOB

Raised in the Tennessee mountains, Bill Job learned to appreciate the local craftsmen's skills. First working with wood and then glass, Bill began reproducing the famous Tiffany lamp shades. Pursuing his interest in traveling, Bill eventually settled with his family on mainland China's east coast in 1987. Combining his love of the natives with western management practices, he built a large studio to create glass treasures. Bill immediately gained recognition for his beautiful Tiffany style lamps, and as a pioneer in business, he became one of the first Americans granted permission for sole proprietorship of his own company in China.

Bill's latest collection for Forma Vitrum, *Coastal Heritage*, is a

series of limited edition lighthouse replicas which are sponsored by the U.S. Lighthouse Society. The original Bill Job stained glass collectible villages – *Vitreville, Woodland Village* and *Coastal Classics* – are handcrafted from the highest quality American stained glass. When completed, each piece is truly an individual work of art with its own color and cut variations, but all reflect the style, detail and quality of his design.

PENNI JO JONAS

Penni Jo Jonas made her first figurines in her kitchen and sold them at craft shows. The miniature teddy bear she made for her daughter's doll house was the inspiration for a series of similar bears. Using colored clays, a food processor, and a toaster oven, Penni Jo created miniature teddy bears that propelled her into the national spotlight among collectible figurine artists.

Penni Jo still uses the toaster oven, along with many other innovative tools, to create just the right detail needed in her sculptures.

Having joined United Design in 1989, Penni Jo designs and sculpts several other collectible figurine editions, including *Itty Bitty Critters™* and the small and miniature angels in the *Angels Collection*.

These days, Penni Jo is keeping busy creating some exciting new works, including a brand new collection of teddy bear angels called *Teddy Angels™*.

FALINE FRY JONES

Faline Fry Jones developed her concept of architectural reproductions of America's past in the basement of her home in 1982. She patterned her designs after actual buildings and historic landmarks no longer in existence, naming them *The Cat's Meow Village™*.

By 1989, a new facility was built for the 130 member-team of employees, and the firm's name was changed to FJ Designs. Today, FJ Designs is a highly successful multi-million dollar international collectibles company.

Faline has won several awards for her business and artistic efforts, including the Small Business of the Year and Entrepreneur of the Year from the Wooster Area Chamber of Commerce in 1989 and Business of the Year from the North Central Business Journal in 1994.

In addition to FJ Designs and motherhood, Faline is active in several local and national organizations and serves on the board of directors at Junior Achievement and the Wooster Area Chamber of Commerce.

RU KATO

Wearing many hats at a time, Ru Kato's talents, as a producer, ex-musician, creative officer and President of WACO Products, served him well on orchestrating the *Melody In Motion (MIM)* development team including Seiji Nakane, Chief Sculptor.

In 1972, WACO Japan introduced "Whistling Hobo," a painted resin figurine equipped with a mechanical whistling device, but his whistling was not entertaining. Going back to the drawing board, MIM's research and development team introduced the first porcelain figurines with motion and music – "Willie The Trumpeter," "Willie The Hobo" and "Willie The Whistler" in 1985.

Although Ru calls America his home, he frequently travels to Japan to work with those involved in *Melody In Motion's* production.

A quiet man, Ru Kato prefers a background role when it comes to the promotion of MIM. As *Melody In Motion* celebrates its 10th Anniversary, Ru is pleased that so many enjoy what took so many years to create. He still lives by the same motto that he had in 1972..."Never Give Up."

GARRI KATZ

As a child in the Soviet Union, Garri Katz drew and painted to calm his fears during World War II. After the war, Katz studied at the Odessa Institute of Fine Arts, before launching his career as a painter and illustrator.

In 1973, having immigrated to Israel, Katz painted religious and historic subjects and his celebrations of everyday life in Israel, which he displayed in many one-man shows in Israel. Then in 1984, Katz began a series of shows in the U.S. sponsored by patrons who discovered his genius on trips to Israel. Today, art connoisseurs from all over purchase Katz' paintings and watercolors for as high as $12,000 each. His works are on display in Israel, Belgium, Germany, Canada and the U.S. Katz resides in Florida.

Katz's first limited edition collector plate series, *Great Stories from the Bible* – eight plates which portray a memorable moment from a beloved Bible story – represents a commission from Reco International Corp.

EMMETT KELLY, JR.

Emmett Kelly, Jr.'s earliest childhood memories are of the circus and performing. Born in November 1924 to Emmett and Eva Kelly, Sr., circus performers, Emmett spent his early years traveling with his parents. During his school years, he lived with relatives and later joined the Navy. Emmett served during World War II in the Pacific and participated in three invasions, including Okinawa and Iwo Jima.

In the mid-60's, Emmett's life as a clown began. Although alienated from his father for many years, they put aside their differences when both agreed that Emmett would continue the Weary Willie character that his father created during the Depression. Emmett changed the Weary Willie image somewhat, putting on a crownless hat and billing himself as Emmett Kelly, Jr.

Throughout his many years of clowning, "America's Favorite Clown" has given a special joy to clown lovers everywhere.

BUD KEMPER

Although Bud Kemper's childhood interest was in music, his high school music teacher persuaded him to submit his paintings to the local college. Bud was awarded a scholarship to Washington University, where he obtained a Bachelor of Fine Arts in Illustration. After serving in the military, he received a Master of Fine Arts in Painting from the University of Kansas. Bud is a member of the New York Society of Illustrators and the American Society of Portrait Artists.

Bud has consistently received presitigious awards in his field, including seven Society of Illustration Awards, Communication Art Annuals, and numerous awards from local and regional shows.

Bud's style of painting has been developed from raw talent, formal education and 37 years of practice and teaching painting.

Bud, a master painter, can paint any subject in a unique way. "I do portraits because I like people and enjoy working with them. I also like to paint wildlife and landscapes. I guess I don't like to paint just one thing all the time."

Bud's artwork is also featured on Anheuser-Busch steins.

KAREN KENNEDY

A love affair with fashion design and dolls began at an early age for Goebel's talented doll designer Karen Kennedy. In the artisitc atmosphere of Goebel's atelier, she is free to combine both loves by creating exclusive costumes for *Victoria Ashlea Originals®*, *Carol Anna®* and *Charlot Byj®* doll lines.

Three of Karen's designs were accepted into museums: Victorian Doll Museum in North Chili, New York, Hobby City Doll and Toy Museum in Anaheim, California, and Mary Stolz Doll and Toy Museum in East Stroudsburg, Pennsylvania.

Karen loves to meet with collectors personally to share her knowledge and thoughts on collecting and has appeared on television many times to promote her appearances.

Karen is a quickly rising young star for Goebel of North America.

DONNA KENNICUTT

Primarily self taught, Donna Kennicutt says she loved art during her high school years but never pursued it as a career until her children were grown. Even then, her painting and sculpting began as a hobby. Her talent, however, won her wide recognition as she was soon voted one of the state's outstanding women artists.

Donna's subjects for her cast bronze pieces were primarily animals, which gave her an ideal background for creating the originals for the animal figurines produced by United Design. They are now in private collections across the United States and in several foreign countries.

One of the most popular collectible editions Donna has created and sculpted since coming to United Design is the *Easter Bunny Family™* collection. She is also responsible for *Children's Garden of Critters™* and many of the *Stone Critters™* and *Animal Magnetism®* designs.

THOMAS KINKADE

Thomas Kinkade is renowned for infusing light into his canvas lithographs, which are published by Lightpost Publishing in San Jose, California. A modern day impressionist, Kinkade has received numerous national awards, including the 1994 "Lithograph of the Year Award" from the National Association of Limited Edition Dealers and the 1995 *Collector Editions* "Award of Excellence." He was honored as a charter inductee into The Bradford International Hall of Fame for plate artists.

Though his family did not have wealth, Kinkade often says they were "rich in the greatest form of wealth – a nurturing and affirming love."

Kinkade studied art at the University of California at Berkeley and at the Art Center College of Design in Pasadena.

While writing *The Artist's Guide to Sketching* with James Gurney, Kinkade painted some 600 scenic backgrounds for the animated motion picture, *Fire and Ice* in a two-year period.

A devout Christian and family-oriented individual, Thomas Kinkade draws on personal experience for much of his artistic inspiration. Many of his scenes of peace, tranquility and nostalgia are based on family travels and memories.

PAT KOLESAR

As an avid doll collector, Pat Kolesar complained that all dolls look the same, and in 1979, she decided to take matters into her own hands. Today, she is well known for dolls whose faces reveal the varied and unpredictable moods of children. Her realistic dolls show on the outside what people feel on the inside.

Pat has won more than 40 blue ribbons at regional and national UFDC conventions. She has also received eight "Dolls of Excellence" nominations from *Dolls* magazine, including one

each for "Enoc the Eskimo Boy," "Baby Cakes" and "Baby Cake Crumbs," all for the Seymour Mann Gallery. In addition, she has designed several of Seymour Mann's most popular dolls, including "Clair Mann," "Enid," "Sparkle," "Kissing Kyle," "Kissing Kelly" and "Kissing Casey."

A former student of artist Nat Ramer, Pat is an accomplished painter and sculptor. Among her commissions are a portrait doll of former Treasury Secretary William Simon. Several of her dolls are on display in museums across the country.

SANDRA KUCK

Sandra Kuck, a talented artist, echoes her strong sense of family and appreciation for beauty in all of her works.

While attending UCLA and The Art Student's League in New York, Sandra realized her love for painting children. Her husband, John, encouraged her to pursue her dream. But Sandra did not begin to devote much time to her work until their two children were in school.

In 1979, Heio Reich, President of Reco International Corp., discovered her paintings of children in a Long Island gallery. Sandra's career skyrocketed with the creation of the plate "Sunday Best" in 1983. Since then, NALED honored her with many awards, including an unprecedented six-time honor as "Artist of the Year."

Constantly working, Sandra's recent works include the *Moments at Home* plate series, a new Mother's Day collection debuting with "Home Is Where the Heart Is," the *Victorian Christmas* series introduced with "Dear Santa," and "God's Gift," a portrait of a mother and infant, released as a Christening Plate. She also released the third doll in the *Childhood Doll Collection*, "Reading With Teddy," along with a collection of *Angel Ornaments*.

PAUL LANDRY

Paul Landry's prints portray halcyon days of the sea and shore in bright, airy and lush colors which are worth treasuring.

A native of Nova Scotia and the grandson of two sea captains, Landry naturally took to the sea for amusement and occupation. Developing his artistic talent, he brought his sketchbook along while pulling up nets and traps with local fishermen.

At 17, Landry became an apprentice photo-engraver. He then attended the Nova Scotia College of Art and the Art Students League in New York City. He traveled from Canada to the Midwest, plying his photo-engraving trade and pursuing his interest in commercial art.

Finally he settled in Connecticut, where he taught at Westport's Famous Artists School, wrote the popular textbook *On Drawing and Painting*, and continued to paint seaside villages and American towns.

Landry's paintings attract a growing audience, thanks to their beauty and romantic, stirring nostalgia. In 1984, The Greenwich Workshop published the first of its many Paul Landry fine art prints.

PAUL LARSEN

Native Californian Paul Larsen came to Goebel Miniatures with his own wealth of experience, having completed over 700 wax and clay masters for the manufacture of buckles, coins, plaques and statuary work. But, as a protege of the renowned Bob Olszewski, he became a master of miniatures himself. "I love detail," Larsen says, "And that's what miniatures are about."

Larsen's virtuosity and expertise are evident in everything from classic period pieces to cartoon characters and miniature clocks. His new collection of *Classic Timepieces* made its public debut in 1995 at the International Collectible Exposition in Long Beach. The *M.I. Hummel* "Honey Lover" pendant is Paul's work, and his "Mickey's Self-Portrait" was a sell-out at last year's Disneyana convention.

WENDY LAWTON

Wendy Lawton has loved dolls for as long as she can remember. "I learned much of what I know as an adult, from my play as a child," she says. "People often forget that toys are the tools of childhood. Since dolls represent humans, interactive play with dolls, actually helps to develop the ability to relate to others effectively." Mrs. Lawton's other great interest in her early years was literature and art. "My sister and I loved to 'tell stories on paper'. I've never lost that desire to illustrate stories in a unique way, so it was a natural outgrowth that I now tell stories illustrated by dolls."

Mrs. Lawton's designs have garnered an impressive array of honors over the last ten years. With more than 40 industry awards to her credit, including six "Dolls of the Year" awards and two "Dolls of Excellence" awards, Mrs. Lawton continues to create dolls that are both collectible and critically acclaimed. But more importantly, Wendy's dolls are cherished by collectors the world over.

DAVID LEMON

David Lemon, a member of the American Indian and Cowboy Artists Association (A.I.C.A.), traces his artistic yearnings as far back as kindergarten, when he impressed the girls by drawing their portraits.

Through his father's and grandparents' stories, David

developed an interest in the Old West. His parents encouraged him in his art, despite calls from his fifth grade teacher that he spent his time drawing cowboys and Indians.

In his senior year of high school, David signed up for a ceramics class where his teacher suggested he sculpt using terra-cotta clay. His efforts earned him three scholarships. After serving 12 years in the U.S. Navy, David finally went beyond sculpture as a hobby when he won first place in the Utah State Fair of 1977.

"You have to be thick-skinned to be an artist," Lemon said. "Your art is your soul." The bountiful accolades Lemon has received for his work through the years are sufficient to dispel his fears of being ignored. Currently a resident of Montana, David creates sculptures for Legends® that speak of the people who toiled and sacrificed to build a new nation.

ANTHONY LEON

Illustrator Anthony Leon knew early on that painting was going to be more than a hobby.

After 12 years and hundreds of illustrations for dozens of major corporations, Leon, who relies on a hand-held brush and the added versatility of an airbrush, is now one of the artists commissioned by Anheuser-Busch, Inc.

Leon was influenced by N.C. Wyeth's use of atmosphere in his mood-setting scenes of knights and castles which illustrate *Treasure Island* and *Robin Hood*. Leon's depiction of the World Famous Clydesdales in the exceptional Charter Member Issue Stein for the Anheuser-Busch Collectors Club is an outstanding example of his own use of this technique. Leon beautifully depicted the majestic eight-horse hitch pulling an antique beer wagon from the European-inspired Bauernhof Courtyard at Grant's Farm on this handcrafted stein in genuine ceramic relief.

Two oval vignettes – one showcasing the elaborate harnessware and festive braided mane, and the second illustrating the Dalamatian trained to protect the horses and guard the wagon – frame the central image of the stein.

LENA LIU

Born in Tokyo during her father's tour of duty for the Chinese Nationalist government, Lena Liu later moved with her family to Taipei, Taiwan, where her talent was recognized early.

She took Oriental art lessons under Professors Sun Chia-Chin and Huang Chun-Pi. Moving to the United States, she graduated from the School of Architecture and Design in New York/Buffalo in 1974 and U.C.L.A's graduate school. Working for an architectural firm until 1977, she then began painting full time.

Her distinctive style has made her a hit since the 1988 debut of her first collector's plate series. An intriguing mix of romance and realism, the series combines detailed subjects with softly colored backgrounds.

Eight subsequent collections showcase her work over the past seven years, including *Floral Greetings from Lena Liu* and *Lena Liu's Hummingbird Treasury*. Along the way, she earned numerous honors, including "Artist of the Year" in both the U.S. and Canada, "Plate of the Year" in the U.S., and recently was one of the first artists inducted into The Bradford Exchange Plate Artist Hall of Fame.

MARK LOCKER

Model making has always interested Mark Locker ever since his grandfather taught him to carve wood as a boy. As one of W.A.P. Watson's (parent of The Tudor Mint) two solderers nine years ago (now there are twelve), he pestered Roger Gibbons to teach him the craft's finer skills. Eventually, Roger said, "Come and find out for yourself" – and Mark was thrown in at the deep end as a full-time model maker.

Just prior to the beginning of the *Myth and Magic* line, Mark worked on the Victorian scenes before becoming "Mister Fantasy and Legend" to Roger's "Mister Myth and Magic." But Fantasy and Legend did not work out, and Mark has since sculpted a number of *Myth and Magic* studies, as well as turning his hand to other requirements. His favorite study is "The Tortured Skull" (*Dark Secrets*), as he worked hard to get the anatomy just right. He also admires Anthony Slocombe's work on "The Dragon of Darkness."

G.M. LOWENTHAL

Raised on Manhattan Island, G.M. Lowenthal, Chief Designer and President of The Boyds Collection Ltd., received a B.S. and M.S. in Biology from Alfred University. Then, as a "Child of the Sixties," he left for the Fiji Islands and the Peace Corps.

Later, G.M. returned to New York City and began purchasing, designing and merchandising at Bloomingdales. Taking a bold step, G.M. moved to rural Boyds, Maryland, to start The Boyds Collection Ltd., an out-of-the-way antique shop. In a restored 1800's farmhouse, G.M. built his business, designing the miniature ceramic "Gnome Homes" and hand-carved wood duck decoys.

Moving his business and growing family to Gettysburg, Pennsylvania, in 1987, G.M. teamed up with Gae Sharp and began designing a line of award-winning collectible plush animals called *Boyds Bears*. In 1992, G.M. introduced the *Boyds Bears and Friends Collection™*. In 1993, the *Folkstones*, whimsical folk art figurines, were introduced, and in August of 1995, the new line of *Yesterday's Child...the Dollstone Collection™* was unveiled, adding to the growing line of Boyds Collectibles.

STEPHEN LYMAN

Stephen Lyman is an explorer who paints elusive moments in nature.

Lyman enrolled at Pasadena's Art Center School of Design to learn more about the commercial art field and then began a commercial illustration career in Los Angeles. Later he returned to Idaho to explore and develop his own painting style.

Lyman has been sharing the wonder of the natural world with collectors since 1983 when his first limited edition print was published by The Greenwich Workshop. He has been a frequent participant in the prestigious international "Birds in Art" show at the Leigh Yawkey Woodson Art Museum and was invited to be "Artist of the Year" at the 1991 Pacific Rim Wildlife Art Show.

The latest image from Lyman's "firelight" works is titled "Midnight Fire," and his most recent limited edition fine art print is "Cathedral Snow." Recently released, Lyman's book *Into the Wilderness* features his wilderness and wildlife artwork and photography. A limited edition fine art print, "Evening Star" will accompany the Collector's Edition of the book.

EMILIO MARTINEZ

Born in June of 1947 in Mexico City, Emilio Martinez attended the National School of Plastic Arts, majoring in commercial drafting and publicity art for television, with specialization in displays. He was tutored in paint technique by Maestro Rafael Rodriguez and studied composition and enamel in copper under Maestro Ayaco Tsuru.

Emilio's heart, however, was in creation and design, so he started working for a company designing pottery and candles. Striving for independence and development of his own style, Emilio continued his studies in painting and sculpture.

He helped found Creart and is in charge of the art department.

Emilio's love for nature and wildlife, combined with his talent, result in the creation of his excellent wildlife sculptures. His originality, realism and detail are evident in his "Cape Buffalo," "Standing Whitetail Deer" and the *Stylus Equestrian Collection*.

In the peaceful surroundings of his studio, Emilio faces each day by saying, "Today I am working on my masterpiece."

MARTY MASCHINO-WALKER

Marty Maschino-Walker is president, founder and designer of *Attic Babies™*, a rag doll manufacturing company in Drumright, Oklahoma. A talent for design and a love for dolls found Marty exhibiting her creations at local craft shows for many years and led to her first home-based business in 1986. But her success in 1987 at the Dallas Gift Market and continued success has forced her to move the business three times to larger facilities, where she now employs approximately 100 people.

Along the way, special honors have come her way. In 1990, she was chosen as Oklahoma's Small Business Person of the Year, and also presented Mrs. Bush with "Grammy Bar," a special characterization of the First Lady. In 1993, she designed special dolls commemorating Native Oklahoma for each Governor's spouse attending the National Governors' Convention. And in 1995, collectors from across the country awarded Attic Babies the "Best Dolls Under $100" at the 2nd Annual Collectors' Jubilee.

Marty's whimsical babies shine with her own carefree and charismatic charm. While many of Marty's designs are signed and numbered limited editions, none of her Babies retires until "it has lived its life with great service."

LINDA MASON

Few doll artists have been more often honored than Linda Mason, who has been on the high road ever since creating her first doll. In an unprecedented achievement, Mason won the *Dolls* magazine "Award of Excellence" three years in a row – in 1991, for "Bridget Quinn;" in 1992, for "Many Stars;" and in 1993, for "Tulu" – all from Georgetown's *American Diary Doll™* series. Not surprisingly, her doll "Lian Ying," newest in this series, has been nominated for a 1995 "Award of Excellence."

All told, this popular artist is a six-time winner of that award, as well as a winner of *Doll Reader's* prestigious "Doll of the Year" award. And Mason's entire *American Diary Doll™* series was nominated for the *Doll Reader* special award for "Concept of the Year."

Never one to allow success to alter her work habits, Mason continues to work carefully and slowly, sculpting only a few new designs each year, with "Lavender Dreams" from Georgetown's *Victorian Fantasies™* collection as her latest.

JOHN McCLELLAND

Some years back, John McClelland created a life-sized portrait of his daughter Susan. The portrait was used for an ad in a trade magazine, and Miles Kimball, the mail order company, spotted it and asked McClelland to do a Christmas cover for their catalog. That was the beginning of an association which continues today.

In the mid-1970s, Reco International arranged for the artist to create limited edition plates. McClelland today is one of the field's most celebrated artists with numerous "Plate of the Year" and "Artist of the Year" awards. He also has designed several figurine series and a number of limited edition lithographs.

McClelland is a portraitist and has taught both intermediate and advanced classes in portrait painting. Scores of his illustrations have appeared in *The Saturday Evening Post*, *Redbook*, *American* and *Readers Digest*, and he has written two "how to" books for artists.

Among his works for Reco are *The Treasured Songs of Childhood*, *The Wonder of Christmas* and *A Children's Garden* plate series, as well as *The Children's Circus Doll Collection*, based upon the popular Reco plate series.

CINDY M. MCCLURE

Cindy McClure is one of a few artists in the world to win the prestigious "Doll of the Year" award (DOTY) from the International Doll Academy in 1986 and 1987. Most recently, she won the *Dolls* "Award of Excellence" for her original wax-over-porcelain issue named *Cross-Stitch* – an exclusive porcelain edition by The Ashton-Drake Galleries. Her Ashton-Drake doll "Victorian Lullaby" has been nominated for the 1995 *Dolls* "Award of Excellence." In all, Cindy has captured more than 20 awards.

Today, Cindy's dolls are eagerly sought by collectors because her originals and some of her Ashton-Drake issues have appreciated considerably on the secondary market.

Most collectors, however, are attracted to her dolls for her ability to capture the sensitive and appealing portraits of children. And her flair for costume design has resulted in the creation of two new Ashton-Drake collections – *Victorian Nursery Heirloom* and *Cross-Stitch* – portraying McClure's love for the Victorian era.

ANNE TRANSUE MCGRORY

Anne McGrory has always been interested in wildlife and nature. She received her bachelor's degree with an emphasis in wildlife art illustration from the Rhode Island School of Design in 1981. After graduation, she did illustrations for the Massachusetts Audubon Society and for the next three years designed jewelry for a manufacturer in Belmont, Massachusetts. From this experience, Anne developed an interest in three-dimensional art.

McGrory began sculpting for The Lance Corporation in 1985, where she helped in several product innovations, including three-dimensional art based on the paintings of Frederic Remington and the concept of "hidden image" sculpture.

Her collections in Chilmark Pewter and MetalART™ include *The OffCanvas™ Collection*, *The Seekers* and *Kindred Spirits*. Two of McGrory's Chilmark sculptures, "Buffalo Vision" and "Brother Wolf" have been honored in being nominated for *Collector Editions* "Award of Excellence."

JUNE MCKENNA

A self-taught sculptor, June McKenna is an acclaimed carver of detailed Santa figurines. Although June carves other types of

figurines, her name has become synonymous with Santa throughout the collectibles industry, and she is referred to by some as the "Santa Lady."

Everyone wonders how June continues to create such imaginative carvings each year. June would tell you that Christmas has played an important role in her life, and she lives each day as if it was Christmas. With so many happy memories about the Christmas season, June incorporates a cast of Christmas characters such as elves, reindeer, carolers, snowmen, angels and even Mrs. Santa into her carvings along with Santa.

June's mind is unlimited in regards to how she envisions Santa and his helpers. Therefore, it is quite probable that June will be carving unique and wonderful Santa figurines for years to come.

GWEN MCNEILL

In a career only ten years old, Gwen McNeill has become one of the leading doll artists in Australia. She began by making reproduction porcelain dolls but felt limited by the painting and finishing techniques. After perfecting her own methods, she began to design and sell her own dolls. In addition to creating dolls, she now teaches painting and sculpture in Australia and serves as an expert judge in doll competitions around the world.

Gwen first came to the New York Toy Fair in 1993. Since then she has become a leading doll artist among U.S. collectors. While Gwen's specialty is modern dolls, she is equally at home working with period costumes.

Her fanciful "Lady Windemere" for Seymour Mann received a 1995 nomination for an "Award of Excellence" from *Dolls* magazine. Another McNeill favorite for Seymour Mann is "Chelsea."

DAN MEDINA

A self-taught illustrator, painter and sculptor, Dan Medina's award-winning artistic genius has proven that he possesses genuine God-given talents.

Early on in his career, Dan realized that he would only be able "to see as far as my eyes would allow me to." This realization led Dan to sculpting – a world balanced in logic, spirit, and creativity, and influenced by Renaissance artists Michelangelo and Leonardo daVinci.

Before creating, Dan researches his subject to ensure its authenticity and sense of motion. "To portray emotion and form in metal – that is the essence of art," says Medina. "It all starts in the mind." He begins to sculpt only when he is satisfied with the two-dimensional image.

Through his work, Dan sees the world with his heart, using his hands and eyes as the conduits to express the human experience. "The kinetics and emotions of the human body, along with the pure beauty of nature, flourish through art."

As Legends' Art Director, Dan expresses that working within

the organization has allowed him to find a balance between science and art.

KEN MEMOLI

Ken Memoli was surrounded from an early age by the cultural riches of New England, which included artists such as Calder, Rockwell and D.C. French. With an inspired interest in nature and the arts, Ken studied sculpture at the University of Hartford Art School, melding his experience into a line of outdoor animal statuary.

Ken's talent in sculpting animals brought him to the attention of United Design, where he now works sculpting many of the company's large life-like *Animal Classics™* figurines and animal statuary for the *Stone Garden™* line.

As well as the intricately detailed wildlife and domestic animals Ken creates, he also sculpts figurines for the company's limited edition series *The Legend of Santa Claus™*. The *Angels Collection* features many of Ken's inspired designs, too.

In addition to his sculpture, which he works on daily in his studio, Ken enjoys photography and playing the guitar.

E.M. MERCK

E.M. Merck's success as a bright and popular artist is well represented by her ever-growing series of ornament designs and her *Signature Collection* of nutcrackers for Old World Christmas. Merck's attention to detail, eye for color and intuition about collectibles has furthered the demand for Old World Christmas' heirloom quality mouth-blown ornaments, which are produced by skilled glassblowers in Germany.

E.M. Merck studied fine arts, art history and German cultural traditions at Pomona College, Gonzaga University and Eastern Washington University. Her ornament and nutcracker designs have been nominated for *Collector Editions* "Award of Excellence," and her talents have been showcased in newspaper articles and on radio talk shows. However, her true gratification and feeling of Christmas comes from watching children enjoy the treasures she creates and carrying on Old World Christmas' tradition of bringing affordable, high-quality collectibles to consumers.

RICHARD MEYER

Richard Meyer has an insatiable desire to create three-dimensional art. He finds reality and art a challenge.

Sculpting for over 20 years, his formal training began at Brigham Young University and moved on to the Art Student League and the Sculpture Center. He works from his California home and is a member of the American Indian and Cowboy Artists. He is inspired by themes from the Great West, and his well known bronze sculptures grace the collections of such

notables as Roy Rogers and Gene Autry.

Meyer's latest creations for Calabar Creations take us on a journey to the Western Frontier where the modern cowboy works and plays in contemporary settings and dignified Native Americans in traditional attire inspire reverence. He hopes collectors will enjoy sharing this journey and see each piece as an artistic reality.

CLEMENTE MICARELLI

Clemente Micarelli studied art at both the Pratt Institute and The Art Students League in New York and the Rhode Island School of Design.

His paintings have been exhibited in numerous shows and have won many awards. Represented nationally by Portraits, Inc. and C.C. Price Gallery in New York, Micarelli has painted the portraits of prominent personalities throughout the United States and Europe.

The artist has done fashion illustrations for many leading department stores and has taught at the Rhode Island School of Design, the Art Institute of Boston and the Scituate Arts Association and South Shore Art Center.

For Reco International, Micarelli has created *The Nutcracker Ballet* plate series, a *Wedding Series* of plates and bells and *The Glory of Christ Collection*, a plate series depicting revered events in the life of Jesus Christ.

LARRY MILLER

Larry Miller's love for the work he does is evident in the charming humor and rich detail he sculpts into his designs.

Larry graduated from the University of Oklahoma with a Bachelor of Fine Arts in Design, yet he credits an art professor at the former Oklahoma College of Liberal Arts in Chickasha as the person who inspired his career in art and design.

After working in graphic arts, Larry came to United Design in 1981 because of the opportunity to work in three dimensional art. Larry had always loved the feel and texture of sculpture, so working independently, he developed his technique by sculpting western bronzes.

Larry is credited with creating several of *The Legend of Santa Claus™* limited edition figurines, many of the *Animal Classics™* – a series of large, exceptionally life-like animals – and many designs in the *Stone Garden™* line.

MARY MONTEIRO

Unlike many artists, Mary Monteiro wasn't drawn to art as a child. Her first introduction came when she entered a university program. After only two years of study, it became evident that the

program wasn't moving fast enough for her. For the next four years, she immersed herself in private studies with artist Eugene Tonoff where she focused on portraiture and oil painting. She then built a successful commercial and fine arts career. Despite this success, she still longed "to get in touch with the spiritual part of myself."

After five years of studying and experiencing Eastern Religion, Mary re-entered the field of commercial art, this time to search for a style that was uniquely her own. She thought that, "it was time to paint and draw what was inside of me."

Inside she found kittens, toys, teddy bears and Christmas wreaths which soon became greeting cards. She also found angels and children which were transformed into fine porcelain figurines from Possible Dreams. Today, these designs provide her with "a way to share my feelings and thoughts with others."

JOCELYN MOSTROM

Jocelyn Mostrom first came to national recognition as the woman who raised the American craft of cornhusk doll making into a fine art. She utilized a primitive folk art to design wonderful porcelain dolls, which took up to 60 hours to make.

Aiming to give each doll a sense of timelessness and universal appeal, she captures the lifestyles of favorite historical periods and transforms them into exquisite doll designs. Known for creating dolls with unique personalities, she depicts them with open-mouths, outstretched arms and bodies-in-motion.

Recently Jocelyn created 5" dolls that also double as Christmas ornaments for the *KSA Storybook Collection*, which include "Bo Peep," "Alice in Wonderland," "Red Riding Hood," "Boy Blue" and "Cinderella." In addition, she has created the *When I Grow Up* series of children playing dress-up as a doctor, nurse, firefighter, teacher and golfer. Jocelyn also expanded her current collections, portraying Kwanza, an American cowboy and cowgirl, children from Ireland and Mexico for *Small Wonders of the World*, and also musicians and snow children for the *Royal Heritage Collection*.

REAL MUSGRAVE

(Sampsel/Preston Photographic Design)

Real Musgrave is an artist who follows a whimsical muse. The *Pocket Dragons*, wizards and other creatures that Real sculpts spring to life from the complex and wonderful world he has created in drawings and paintings for over 20 years. Those finely detailed drawings bespeak the heritage of beautifully illustrated children's books from the turn of the century, but to everything he adds a vision of gentleness and humor which is uniquely his own.

Together Real and his wife Muff developed and marketed a line of limited edition etchings and prints featuring the *Pocket Dragons*, wizards, gargoyles and friends. In 1978, Muff quit her job to become Real's full-time creative partner.

Real's work has won awards and been exhibited in shows at major museums, art institutes and galleries. Today, Real is recognized as one of the foremost fantasy artists in the world. The *Pocket Dragons* appear on greeting cards, posters, and other products, as well as the delightful sculptures produced by Collectible World Studios in England and exclusively distributed in the U.S. by Flambro Imports, Inc.

ALLYSON NAGEL

The name of Allyson Nagel's company, A.N. Original, reflects her passion for perfection, resulting in authentic art with fascinating personality. In her South Dakota studio, she creates whimsical egg characters, stars with personality and unique dolls entirely by hand, using no molds. Her labor-intensive art form requires hand sculpting distinctive faces full of character, firing to a bisque in her kiln and meticulous hand-painting.

Reflecting on her success garnering recognition and coveted "Judge's Choice" awards, Nagel says, "I started out in portraiture. My turn to crafting dolls began when the noted doll maker Faith Wick viewed my work and asked me if I would make faces for dolls."

Nagel turned her attention to designing porcelain eggs with personalities...even dressing them! This new idea turned into a successful, intriguing new egg collection, *Sunny Side Up™*, for Roman, Inc.

For her encore, Nagel's *Home Gnomes™* dolls, *Starlight Starbright* and *Soul Sisters* collections are charming America.

SEIJI NAKANE

Born in Tajimi, Gifu prefecture of Japan in 1938, Seiji Nakane, award-winning master sculptor, graduated from Tajii Art and Industrial School and studied art in Asia and Europe. Fascinated by the porcelain-making industry in Seto, he began working in clay at age 18, which he continued in addition to painting in oil and watercolor.

Captivated by Seiji's figurines, which seem almost alive with personality, WACO Products Corporation used a selection of his figurines as prototypes for the first *Melody In Motion* introductions.

Billed as "the only porcelain, moving, animated sound musical collectible," the *Melody In Motion* figurines have set collectors' hearts singing.

Merging art and technology, each meticulously hand-painted and assembled figurine is fitted with gears, cams, motor, amplifier and speaker. Taking four weeks to create, the lifelike figurines move and sing. Established in 1992, the *Melody In Motion* Collectors Society teaches collectors about this fascinating process and the artist who inspired it all.

BARBARA NELSON

Born and raised in Massachusetts, Barbara Nelson obtained a degree in Wildlife Biology from the University of Massachusetts in 1978. She now maintains her studio and resides on a small horse farm in Minneapolis, Minnesota.

Nelson held positions with the U.S. Forest Service, U.S. Fish and Wildlife Service, and Iowa Department of Natural Resources (DNR) before becoming a full-time sculptor in the early 1980s. She also served five years as a commissioner for the Iowa DNR.

In 1989, she won the title of Second in World Lifesize with a "Ringnecked Pheasant," and in 1991, won Third in World with "Ruffed Grouse." Recognized as one of the top wood and bronze sculptors, Barbara was the Featured Sculptor for the 1995 Southeastern Wildlife Exposition and has been selected to create the Masterpiece Carving for the 1995 Easton Waterfowl Festival.

Her sculptures for Creart – "Ambushing" Puma, "Briefly Rest" Pumas, "Red-tailed Hawk" and "Mourning Dove" – reflect a superior quality. Her desire is "to create art that the discriminating collector cannot forget – work that has impact and value."

DIANNA NEWBURN

Dianna Newburn has always enjoyed doing creative works, and when her children were small, she taught decorative painting. Dianna would take some of her own works to craft fairs, but her real talent and love of sculpture was discovered as she experimented with making miniature clay dolls. Dianna says, "Part of the reason I love doing this so much is because I have three sons and no daughters. Now I have my dolls to dress up."

In 1990, Dianna's work had become so popular, she was exhausted from trying to keep up with the demand. That was when she joined the staff of United Design, where she continues to create dolls and figurines for many different collections.

Currently, Dianna is sculpting figurines for the *Angels Collection*. She has created several designs for the limited edition series and the small angels. Dianna is also kept busy working on *Angel Babies™* and *Itty Bitty Critters™*.

MARYSE NICOLE

Born in the French wine country, Maryse Nicole's father, a guitarist, and mother, a ballroom dancer, introduced her to show business. As a child, Maryse travelled all over Europe, Venezuela, Chicago and finally to California, and became fluent in French, English, Spanish and Italian.

Wherever she is, Maryse is always looking for joyful and artistic

ways to express her own unique personality and style. Originally a professional singer, Maryse created dolls as a hobby. She carried her trademark, a dazzling, beaded costume that sparkled on stage, to TV when she began selling her dolls through television, and collector's nicknamed her the "Sparkle Queen."

Today, singing is a hobby to her doll designing. As Executive Director of The Franklin Mint Heirloom Dolls in Los Angeles, Maryse personally sculpts each original porcelain doll, oversees the intricate hand-painting and carefully selects each fabric, trim and accessory for her dolls.

"When I am with collectors, it's like seeing an old friend," says Maryse. "Their friendship and love for my dolls makes it all worthwhile."

JORGEN NIELSEN

Jorgen Nielsen joined the artists and manufacturers at Royal Copenhagen Porcelain Manufactory in 1959. Since then he has ambitiously pursued various types of artistry at Royal Copenhagen and abroad.

Although he was originally trained as an onglaze painter, Nielsen began working in 1965 as a painter of unique underglaze vases. After a two-year study tour to Japan, he returned to onglaze painting for a few years.

From 1976 to 1986, Nielsen worked under the tutelage of ceramist Nils Thorsson, using the media of faience, porcelain and stoneware.

Currently, Jorgen Nielsen works on a freelance basis for Royal Copenhagen and manages his own painting studio.

DOUGLAS NORRGARD

Douglas Norrgard is more than an accomplished artist – he is a skilled storyteller. His newly introduced Goebel Miniatures "Once Upon a Winter's Day" relates a childhood memory with such visual eloquence that no words are needed.

Trained as a painter both here and abroad, Douglas didn't realize until later in his career that sculpture was his true calling. On a trip to Japan in 1985, he watched a sculptor turn a lifeless lump of clay into a figurine that seemed to come alive in his hands. The classically trained painter became a self-taught sculptor.

"What I strive for," Douglas explains, "is the feeling beyond the form. I want people to be able to relate to my work with their hearts as well as their eyes."

Collector reponse to his first commission for Goebel Miniatures indicates he has achieved that goal.

DON PALMITER

Don Palmiter's Keepsake Ornament designs just keep on rolling! He is the sculptor for such popular designs as the *Classic American Cars* series, the Keepsake Ornament *Kiddie Car Classics* series, and the *All-American Truck* series. Don has also sculpted many designs for *Kiddie Car Classics* – a collection of die-cast, scale-model replicas of authentic pedal cars from Hallmark. As a car enthusiast, Don has had a lifelong affection for classic automobiles. He has owned a 1962 Corvair, 1963 Rolls Royce Silver Cloud and a 1968 Corvette.

Another popular series, *Nostalgic Houses and Shops*, also features several of Don's designs, including the 1995 "Town Church."

A Hallmark employee for over 28 years, Don joined the company after high school and spent several years as an engraver. During his first three years in the Keepsake Ornament studio, Don worked on collectibles, including the *Hometown America* and *Mary and Friends* collections.

CHRISTOPHER PARDELL

Christopher Pardell, one of Legends® first artists, began sculpting at age four. After pursuing a university art education, he left after two years frustrated with the "narrow viewpoints."

At 21, Christopher apprenticed as a moldmaker for a commercial statuary company owned and operated by Italian immigrants trained in the Old World style. He rapidly learned the skills to excel as an artist and a sculptor.

Never sketching his designs on paper, Christopher composes all of his work in three dimensional maquette, which explains the beauty of line and sense of action that is his trademark.

Christopher is drawn to the aesthetic of the human figure and strives to capture the tragedy and nobility of the human endeavor. For him, the history of Native Americans, defiantly holding to their traditions and beliefs in the face of opposition, exemplifies the human condition. In sculpting, Christopher strives to shape his feelings for humanity, so that we can see how much of ourselves exist in each other.

In his wish to pass on his realizations, Christopher formed an apprenticeship program that gives young artists Old World training.

GARY PATTERSON

Artist/humorist Gary Patterson made his first venture into gifts and collectibles with Media Arts Group Inc. in 1995, with a series of three-dimensional figurines, limited edition and open lithographs of his famous illustrations.

Widely known by an estimated 250 million people as the "creator of smiles" for his highly detailed, richly insightful – yet witty and humorous – portraits of life through sports scenes, Gary Patterson has earned many accolades over the years, including induction into the Basketball Hall of Fame, Sports Artist of the Year and Art Director for an Academy Award-winning film. However, Gary has not limited his talent to sports. Among his most famous paintings are his unique, whimsical and appealing cats and a charming little mouse he calls "Boo."

He is often described as having "put a mirror in front of all of us and has shown that in smiling through our tears, the unbearable can become bearable and even laughable." His world-famous works are exhibited in the Los Angeles County Museum of Art and have been enjoyed on television and in newspapers and magazines over the past 25 years.

DONNA PEMBERTON

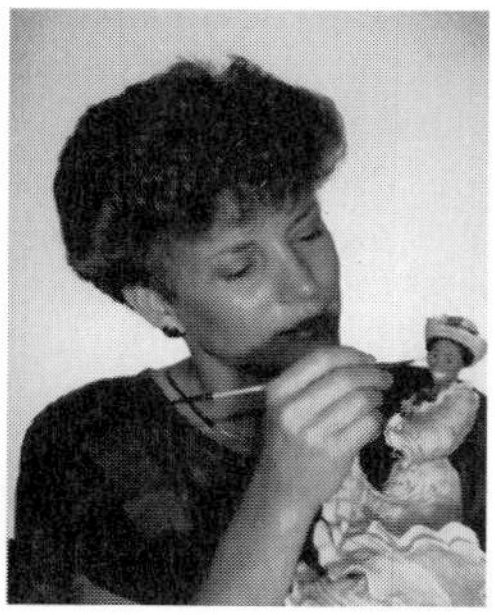

Donna Pemberton, the vibrant Director of Artists for Duncan Royale, showed a remarkable talent for drawing at the early age of four. Her art progressed from finger painting to ceramics, sculpting, and graphic arts. Donna received her formal training at U.C.L.B., where she was one of the few students elected for the coveted ceramic program. Since graduating at the top of her class, Donna works with some of the world's best known and highly qualified artists in various disciplines.

Donna's original work, which she creates in her own studio in Orange County, California, has been commissioned and purchased by such well-known art collectors as John Dupont, Dick Clark and Herb Albert, to name a few.

At Duncan Royale, Donna's wide range of responsibilities include assisting with the development of new products and color schemes, working with staff and commissioned artists, supervising the development of catalogs and brochures, assisting with figurine repair and communicating with collectors.

VICENTE PEREZ

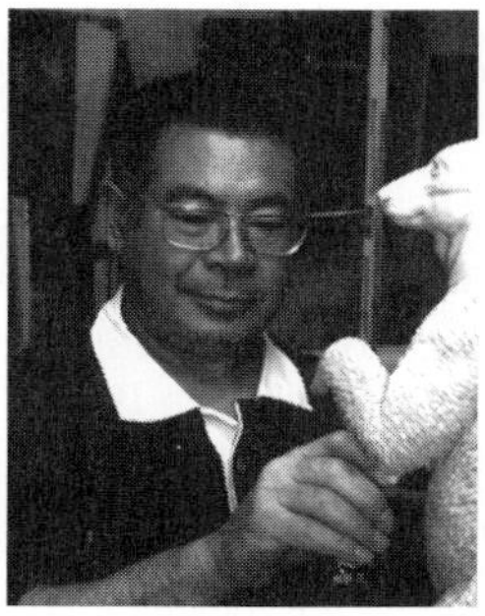

Vicente Perez is not satisfied just to produce a beautiful sculpture; he attempts to "give life" to his pieces. In his opinion, "realism is the beauty of our work."

Born in Veracruz, Mexico, Vicente studied at the National School of Plastic Arts. He began studying with the maestros, Humberto Pedraza and Francisco Zuniga. Later, Vicente taught clay and plastics modeling for 15 years at The Technical School of Mexico. For several years, he made replicas of pre-hispanic sculptures at the National Institute of Anthropology and History, giving him experience in molding, casting and sculpting.

Vicente co-founded, with Emilio Martinez, Creart, a leading manufacturer of wildlife sculptures, where he expressed his ideas in over 60 original models, including "The Sound of Warning" Elephant, "Over the Top" Puma, "Wild American Series" Puma and "Singing to the Moon I & II." Not only a Creart sculptor, Vicente finishes the master plastiline sculptures and makes the primary and production molds.

Nature and conservation are Vicente's passion. "I feel that somehow, my work is cooperating with nature."

PAMELA PHILLIPS

A creative painter and portrait artist since childhood, Pamela Phillips recently began designing dolls. As she explains, "I saw a face so compelling it could only be expressed in sculpture. After much trial, but mostly error, I made my first doll."

Although a newcomer to the doll field, Phillips' work has already been graced with major nominations and awards. In 1994, she received three nominations for *Dolls* magazine's "Award of Excellence," one of which, the 26-inch "Anna," won. Now, two of her dolls have been nominated for *Doll Reader's* "Doll of the Year" award for 1995: "Mary Elizabeth and her Jumeau," first in the *Yesterday's Dream™* collection from the Georgetown Collection and "Caroline" for Georgetown's elegant *Sweethearts of Summer™* collection.

Pamela created some of her first dolls for the Seymour Mann Gallery; these dolls – "Alyssa" and "Nizhoni" – both received a 1993 *Dolls* magazine nomination for "Awards of Excellence" as well as being nominated for a DOTY. In addition, her doll for Seymour Mann, "Guinevere," received both an "Award of Excellence" nomination and a DOTY nomination from *Doll Reader* magazine.

VALERIE PIKE

A resident of Australia's Gold Coast, Valerie Pike's first artistic efforts were in oil portraits. Later she turned to hand-painted clothing and soft sculpture, which she regards as a natural progression toward doll sculpting. The people she sees around her inspire her lifelike creations, which have won many enthusiasts in the South Pacific.

Valerie sculpts her dolls from a water-based clay, from which she makes a mold for the porcelain head, shoulder plate, hands and feet. She designs her own body patterns and often makes her own wigs from mohair.

Until recently Valerie's dolls were produced only in limited editions of ten to twenty-five. By joining the Seymour Mann Studios, she now makes her works available in editions of 5,000 each. Her first Seymour Mann doll will be introduced at Toy Fair in 1996.

DON POLLAND

Don Polland describes himself as a "self-taught experimenter." He cannot remember a time when he was not making figures, even as a boy. In 1966, he began a new hobby – sculpting miniatures of the American West.

In 1973, a series of miniature sculptures of Bicentennial events by Robert Sullivan caught Polland's eye. They were cast in pewter, not bronze, for Royal Worcester by The Lance Corporation. "The thing that interested me," remembers Polland, "was how quickly you could read the detail in the pieces – the eyes, the folds of the clothing, the buttons on the shirt."

Polland asked Lance if they would cast his miniatures, and they introduced three *American West* pewter sculptures in 1974. Today, over 20 years later, Polland and Chilmark have created an innovative and immense body of art owned and appreciated by more than 50,000 people around the world.

BARBARA PRUSSEIT

Those tiny hands...that little cooing voice...the fresh-as-a-snowflake smell.... That's right: It's baby time at Georgetown Collection, and the creator of all this delight is a new artist – Barbara Prusseit. Barbara hails from the German region of Bavaria, and, until recently, only Europeans knew and loved her baby dolls. Now, she's creating them for Georgetown, and the first arrival is "Good as Gold," the premier issue in the *Gifts from Heaven™* collection.

This tiny treasure, a mere 13 inches, sleeps in a pose that's sheer perfection, with a secret smile that says "Somebody loves me" and hands and toes so lifelike they might start wiggling at any moment. Barbara explains that her husband, a physician, has helped her learn the art of anatomy. Everything else – from the pose to the clothes – is the design of this talented artist.

CHRISTOPHER RADKO

When Christopher Radko began designing his collection of fine glass Christmas ornaments ten years ago, there were only 50 styles in the collection. Today, there are over 750 fabulous designs – a crowning achievement of a decade of Christopher's personal design, development and plain hard work.

Growing up with diverse traditions handed down from relatives in Poland, Austria and France, Christopher remembers that, "Christmas was like being at the United Nations. We had carols, food and ornaments from all over Europe."

In an effort to replace his family's lost ornament collection – caused by their Christmas tree falling over – Christopher started designing and creating ornaments "with the quality of the old days."

His desire to create exquisitely blown and intricately decorated ornaments leads Christopher to select only expert craftsmen in Italy, the Czech Republic, Germany and Poland. He visits the cottage factories and retrains glass blowers and decorators in the art perfected by their own great-grandparents. Through his designs, Christopher has put both quality and magic back into Christmas.

LYNNE RANDOLPH

An avid sketch artist and painter since childhood, Lynne Randolph turned to calligraphy after the birth of her second child. From there she progressed to sculpting, a phase she describes as "a classic plaster-all-over-the-kitchen-floor story." While on vacation in 1990, she visited a doll shop in Maine, where she admired some porcelain baby dolls. "I was instantly fascinated," she remembers, "and I said to my husband 'I have to learn to do this.'" Soon afterwards she created her first original doll, "Rachel Beth," using her own daughter as a model.

Her many awards include a DOTY nomination from *Doll Reader*. Her favorite dolls for the Seymour Mann Gallery include "Tiffany," "Meredith" and "Ginnie." Speaking of her dolls, she says, "They are a gentle reminder that children are ours to protect, nurture and love."

JOYCE REAVEY

What artist could create both the charm and innocence of "Clarissa Comes Calling" (Georgetown's *Pictures of Innocence™* series) and the delightfully mud-splattered "Mr. Mischief" (first in the *Boys Will Be Boys™* collection)? It should come as no surprise that Joyce Reavey, the mother of three, portrays the cheer and challenge of parenting with love and a good-natured sense of humor. "My inspiration," she laughs, "comes from seeing my own kids tromping into the house every day, bringing mud and wildlife adventures to share."

Reavey has an eye for the opulence of Victoriana, too, as witnessed by "Catherine," the new doll in the *Age of Romance™* collection. Every detail of this ravishing beauty's wedding gown – from its rich fabric and lace to the floral headpiece – bespeaks Victorian style. Reavey is yet another Georgetown Collection artist who has been honored with a *Dolls* magazine "Award of Excellence" nomination.

MARTHA REYNOLDS

Vibrant – a wonderful word that describes both Martha Reynolds and her art.

A Fenton designer for over four years, Martha constantly experiments with new materials and styles, creating designs that range from simple and contemporary to the ornate and richly embellished look of Victorian glass.

Martha has frequently been honored with design awards since graduating cum laude from Shepherd College. Her "Best of

Show" awards cover a variety of media including sculpture, watercolor and woodcuts. In 1993, the Society for Glass and Ceramic Decorators honored her with their prestigious Vandenoever Award.

Few artists choose to paint on glass because it is difficult to adjust to the different background colors, shapes and the non-absorbent slick surfaces. Martha welcomes these challenges and her ringing laughter lifts everyone's spirits when deadlines are short.

Look for more of Martha's glass painting in the *90th Anniversary* and *Connoisseur* collections from Fenton Art Glass.

MARY RHYNER-NADIG

As a teenager, Mary Rhyner-Nadig considered being a veterinarian but planned to enjoy art as a hobby. But when she showed a sketch to a friend's father, he told her she could make a living with art.

Mary, who has been with the Enesco Corporation since 1990 and is a Senior Product Designer, studied at the American Academy of Art in Chicago. Enesco has honored Mary with the "Division Designer of the Year" and "Associate of the Month" awards, and the "Stanhome Achievement Award" from Stanhome, Enesco's parent company.

Mary designs her figurines in watercolors and colored pencils, and she gets her inspiration from antique stores, flea markets and other shops, as well as from magazines and catalogs. Mary's most recent Enesco lines, *This Little Piggy* and *Santa's Special Deerlivery™*, together with *Mary's Moo Moos*, *Cute As A Button™*, *Cream & Cocoa* and *Partners in Crime™* have become the talk of the industry.

Mary says, "When I walk into a store and I see the product I worked on, I'm in disbelief. I'll ask myself, 'Did I really do that?'"

JEANETTE RICHARDS AND SANDRA PENFIELD

The artists of the *Best Friends* collection, Jeanette Richards and Sandra Penfield, have discovered the excitement of creating a world of clay miniatures that capture the true essence of friendship.

Jeanette, from Rocky River, Ohio, studied art in Washington, D.C. and received a B.A. in English and Art from the University of Dayton, Ohio. Growing up in a family of artists, her first love was illustration.

Sandra, from Detroit Lakes, Minnesota, received a B.S. in Art from the University of North Dakota. She taught art and shared it through her woodcut prints.

The pair's mutual interest in art brought them together in

Hudson, Wisconsin, where they became partners in a graphic design business in 1984.

In 1990, Jeanette and Sandra created the first figure in the *Best Friends* series for BAND Creations, recreating their experiences along the St. Croix River. These designs soon evolved to include all the facets of friendship and family life. The line includes *Monthly Angels, Angel Wishes, Noah's Ark, First Friends Begin at Childhood, Winter Wonderland, O Joyful Night* and the *Town of RiverSong*.

LUCY RIGG

Lucy Rigg began making baker's clay teddy bear figurines in 1969 while awaiting the birth of her daughter, Noelle. She decorated the nursery with her first teddy bears, but friends and family were so enchanted with the original creations that Lucy began making them for others.

Teddy bear collectors bought her hand-painted clay dough bears, known as "Rigglets," at street fairs. To keep up with the growing demand, she imposed a quota on herself to make 100 teddy bears per day.

As her teddy bears became more popular, Lucy formed her own company. In the late 1970s, Enesco Corporation President Eugene Freedman approached Lucy and proposed turning her hand-made teddy bears into a line of porcelain bisque figurines and accessories. Since Enesco introduced the *Lucy & Me®* Collection in 1978, it has enjoyed steady support from collectors and teddy bear lovers.

Lucy continues to operate Lucy & Company, designing diaries, baby announcements, calendars and her "teddy bear" version of popular children's books.

SHARON RILEY

Sharon Riley joined W.A.P. Watson Ltd. (parent of The Tudor Mint) as a designer in 1983 and apart from an 'O' level in Art, is an entirely self-taught artist. In the past decade, she has worked on all aspects of the company's products and was responsible for the first 12 *Myth and Magic* designs launched in 1989. As Chief Designer for The Tudor Mint, she has generated more ideas for studies than any other designer. Her favorite models are "The Dragon of the Underworld" and "Dactrius." She likes the effect of dragons coiling themselves around objects. Sharon's son, Daniel, was born around the same time she designed the Collectors' Club study "Playmates" – hence the little cherub on the piece.

SUSAN RIOS

At age 13, Susan Rios' artistic talent became apparent in her pen and ink explorations which led to a summer scholarship at Cal State Northridge. Her artistic ventures, however, led her to

abandon her college classes to explore the worlds of graphic design and flower arrangement.

After her daughter's birth, Susan decided to evolve her artwork from avocation to vocation. Since then, she has balanced her busy schedule of painter and homemaker.

A self-taught painter, Susan derived her influences from Matisse and Monet. Whether they depict lush gardens, floral sanctuaries or intimate corners furnished in wicker chairs and overstuffed love seats, her acrylic paintings offer a feeling of coziness, peacefulness and a sense of familiarity.

Relying on her inborn gifts of tenacity and discipline to struggle through a painting's beginning stages, Susan relishes the distinct moment when she can step back and begin to feel the "harmony and wholeness" of her artwork. Her works are published by Lightpost.

DOREEN NOEL ROBERTS

Doreen Noel Roberts, poet and painter, was born in Burnley, Lancashire, England, and comes from a long line of artists. She spent two years at college in business training, which was followed by a short instructive spell as an accounting clerk.

In 1954, Doreen joined PenDelfin Studios Ltd., via the Burnley Artists' Society, where her natural talents were developed by Jean Walmsley Heap, chairman of PenDelfin. After absorbing each step of production over the years, Doreen ultimately became a designer and sculptor of the famous PenDelfin rabbits. She now designs and models full-time for PenDelfin and is a member of its board of directors, as well as a partner in the PenDelfin Design Unit.

JIM ROBISON

Born in Pekin, Illinois, Jim Robison, a self-taught artist, began carving duck decoys at age 12 and later decorative wildfowl wood sculptures.

Jim and his wife Sheri live in Hopedale, Illinois, on a fifty-acre farm where they enjoy watching wildlife and Jim finds inspiration for his work.

Jim's interest in birds has led him into the art of falconry and raptor conservation. As director of the Raptor Resource Project, he hopes to reintroduce the peregrine falcon.

A world-class contender in wildfowl carving, Jim's sculptures have been selected on three occasions to be exhibited in the Leigh Yawkey Woodson Art Museum's "Birds In Art" exhibit and also in the Illinois State Museum. His work has been featured in *People* magazine and in a film for NBC's Junior Hall of Fame

Show. Jim has also been honored by the National Ducks Unlimited Corporation for his generous woodcarving donations.

Jim became a part of Creart's limited edition family when he was commissioned to create the *Birds of Prey* collection, which includes "Gyrfalcon" and "Vigilant Eagle." His next release is an Urban Release Peregrine Falcon.

NORMAN ROCKWELL

The most popular American artist and illustrator of the 20th century, Norman Rockwell, sold his first cover illustration to *The Saturday Evening Post* in 1916. By 1920, he was the *Post's* top illustrator. His trademark style, a realistic technique highlighted by a warm and whimsical sense of humor, is best summed up by him: "I paint life as I would like it to be."

Through the years, Rockwell created classic illustrations for *Life*, *McCall's* and *Boy's Life*, and for many advertisers. Among his best works, "The Four Freedoms" raised more than $130 million in war bonds during World War II, and the *American Family* series, portrayed in more than 70 sketches for the Massachusetts Mutual Life Insurance Company, is on display in The Norman Rockwell Museum.

In the 1970s, Rockwell's illustrations became some of the most sought-after subjects for limited edition collectibles. The Norman Rockwell Gallery offers only those collectibles bearing The Norman Rockwell Family Trust's official authorization seal. Also, Hawthorne Architectural Register distributes three-dimensional cottage sculptures based on his original artwork.

Rockwell continued as an artist and illustrator in his Stockbridge, Massachusetts, studio until his death in 1978.

ANITA MARRA ROGERS

Not long ago, Anita Marra Rogers took her Keepsake Ornament sculpting a long, long way – into space. Her 1995 Keepsake Ornament designs, "Captain Jean-Luc Picard" from STAR TREK®: THE NEXT GENERATION™ and "Captain James T. Kirk" of STAR TREK®, showcase her talent for sculpting realistic likenesses of popular characters.

Anita is also known for her popular *Puppy Love* collector's series designs as well as the popular Keepsake Ornaments "Lulu and Family," "Jolly Dolphin," and "Holiday Teatime." For 1995, Anita sculpted an ornate design for the first ornament in the new *Christmas Visitors* series, "St. Nicholas."

Anita knew she'd found her artistic calling from the first time she visited the Keepsake Ornament studio. After teaching herself to sculpt and submitting a portfolio, Anita was hired as a part-time artist. The Kansas City, Missouri, native went on to become a full-time artist in 1987.

CINDY MARSCHNER ROLFE

Noted artist Cindy Marschner Rolfe has taken the doll collecting world by storm with her innovative creations and their adorable, lifelike expressions.

"I make my dolls as lifelike and appealing as possible so that, hopefully, they will remind collectors of their own children and grandchildren," Cindy says.

She credits her father for recognizing and developing her talent. When she was young, she watched for hours while he sketched and carved wood products. That initial interest in art prompted her many years later to teach herself to sculpt. The resulting clay babies were so much admired by neighbors and family members that Cindy developed her talent further, finally agreeing to sell her dolls to the public.

"Shannon," a doll created for The Hamilton Collection, was inspired by Cindy's young daughter, who loves to pose for pictures and served as a wonderful model for the irresistible doll.

BRONWEN ROSS

Creator of *The Thickets At Sweetbriar*™, internationally renowned artist Bronwen Ross has always been captivated by the beauty of flora and fauna. A self-taught artist with no formal training, Bronwen began drawing at an early age, often creating stories as she went along.

Bronwen has a precise eye for detail and a colorful imagination. When working on new artwork, she never does a preliminary sketch. Instead, she visualizes what she'll paint, seeing the artwork on blank paper before she even picks up a brush.

Bronwen's creations for Possible Dreams entwine the detailed intricacies of nature with the romantic renderings of a bygone era. *The Thickets At Sweetbriar* collection includes charming cats, bunnies and mice dressed in Victorian costume and accented with beautiful flowers, feathers and butterflies.

Living in rural Missouri, Bronwen is inspired by the nature around her. She enjoys pressing flowers and using her garden florals as models. Her work has been reproduced on greeting cards, stationery and limited edition prints and has been shown in *Good Housekeeping* magazine.

DOREEN M. ROSS

Doreen Ross is always on the lookout for new and interesting buildings or ways to make a process better at the company she and her husband, David started – R.R. Creations.

As a very craft-oriented person, Doreen is always renewing or redecorating something at home or at the office. Working hard has paid off, as R.R. Creations recently emerged into the foreign market by producing buildings from Denmark, and several of R.R.'s collectibles have been highlighted at Harrod's of London. Doreen hopes to double the number of shops that carry the

Open Window collection in the next year.

For a person who thinks of herself as the "Queen of QVC," Doreen fulfilled her dream in 1995 by having a collection of three buildings and two accessories represented on the QVC shopping network.

A few on her office staff have made the statement that she is one to "jump into the fire" with new ideas and challenges. But her philosophy is that "anything is possible with the Lord." She enjoys a challenge, even friendly competition, because the pressure has a profound effect on creativity.

MARJORIE GRACE ROTHENBERG

Marjorie Grace Rothenberg, also known affectionately as MGR, received her first commissions to illustrate children's books and magazine and advertising art while in high school.

In 1970, MGR became art director at Kurt S. Adler, Inc. For 20 years, she frequently travelled abroad to work with talented artisans. Along with Mr. Kurt S. Adler, MGR is one of the early pioneers of the Christmas trade. Under their guidance, she taught a Far East cottage craft industry the fine art of Christmas design.

Now a grandmother, MGR works mostly in her studio in the Berkshires' foothills. "It is here," says Marjorie, "that I draw constant inspiration..." and create "little people." Starting with a detailed drawing, Marjorie then oversees the sculpting, painting, sewing and trimming of each figure to her standards.

Designing exclusively for Kurt S. Adler, Inc., MGR is well-known for the cornhusk mice ornaments, depicting human characters and created for Christmas and Easter holidays. Recently, she designed many new Fabriché™ figurines and ornaments in fine fabric maché, featuring Santa, Mrs. Claus, elves and other holiday characters. Look for MGR's signature trademark, a gold wedding band, on all her Fabriché Santas and Mrs. Claus.

SUSAN RYAN

Susan Ryan's dream of going to art school was delayed by marriage and five children. In 1990 when the last child graduated from high school, Ryan graduated from Madison Area Technical College with a degree in commercial art.

Although Ryan has painted outdoor scenes, flowers, people and animals, the majority of her commissioned work is animals.

She has painted a long list of field trial labrador and golden retrievers. The most famous, "Lottie of Candlewood Kennels," is the only three-time National Field Champion in history

Ryan's experience in painting hunting dog breeds led to a referral to Anheuser-Busch. She has designed and painted the Setters, Golden Retrievers and Beagle Steins in the *Hunters Companion* collectibles series.

Susan Ryan continues to work out of her home studio located in Madison, Wisconsin, painting subjects for future prints and commission portraits.

BARBI SARGENT

Barbi Sargent is known as "one of the most reproduced artists in the world" because of her thousands of greeting card designs exchanged around the world since 1966. Today her renderings weave into the tapestry of American gifts and collectibles, surfacing as popular greeting cards, collections, dolls, books and prints.

Drawing since age two, Sargent later earned a scholarship to the Cooper School of Commercial Art. She began creating greeting cards at age 18 leading to the creation of characters like "Gretchen" and "Poppyseed" which achieved her national fame.

Years later, an inspirational meeting with renowned artist Edna Hibel encouraged Sargent to form Barbie Sargent and Company, Inc. in 1989 to produce greeting cards, fine art prints and licensed designs.

Sargent's volunteer work with youngsters at the Cleveland Clinic Foundation inspired her *Tender Expressions™* character, "Sunshine," for Roman, Inc. Sargent donates all royalities from two pledge figurines to the Tender Expressions Endowment Fund for vital programs at The Cleveland Clinic Foundation Children's Hospital. Roman contributes a matching donation.

LOU AND PAM SCHIFFERL

Growing up in a family that nurtured creativity, Lou Schifferl spent hours watching his father's skillful woodcrafting. And then in turn, Lou inspired his daughter Pam.

A treasured woodcrafting tradition passed down through three generations continues through the father-daughter artistic team of Lou and Pam Schifferl. Combining their shared love for woodcarving and their distinctive styles, they create folk art that excites the imagination. The Schifferls' images of Christmas have a remarkably nostalgic appearance – an heirloom quality that touches the heart.

Midwest of Cannon Falls proudly offers exclusive reproductions of the Schifferls' imaginative folk art pieces. Folk art lovers and collectors alike will want to include these delightful ornaments and figures among their holiday treasures.

KANDY SCHLESINGER

"It's impossible to grow up and live in the Blue Ridge Mountains and not be touched by the mystical beauty and folklore," says folk artist Kandy Schlesinger. "These mountains reflect a spirit, strength and simplicity that has been an inspiration for much of my work and is inherent to all that I am."

Kandy employs many mediums to give life to her incredible array of Santas, wizards, animals, witches and other whimsical creatures in her art. She is equally comfortable working with clay, wood, fabric or paint.

Kandy is a whirlwind of energy and emits a tremendous sense of excitement in each project she does for Kurt S. Adler, Inc. Her inspiration can be sparked by a scrap of material, the flash of a mental image or piece of oddly shaped wood. Each work reflects the best of American country art. She has designed the *Kandy's Folkart* and *Hole-in-the-Wall Gang* collections, both exclusively available from Kurt S. Adler, Inc.

SARAH SCHULTZ

While working in her husband's pharmacy managing the gift department in 1983, Sarah Schultz observed that the best selling products were her original creations – stenciled slates, boards, pictures and dolls.

Many of Sarah's creations come from her memories. For example, when Sarah developed rheumatic fever as a child, her father began an angel collection for her. Through prayers, her father's faith and the angels, she recovered. Later, in dedication to her father who passed away, and to everyone who has lost a loved one, Sarah created the collection, *Angels in the Attic*.

While delivering the daily paper as a child to an African-American family living nearby, Sarah developed a loving friendship with them which inspired her to create the *Black Heritage Collection*.

As a firm believer in love, respect and dignity, Sarah paints a heart on each piece to symbolize these words. The signature heart also guarantees the product's unmatched quality and originality. This guarantee assures collectors that much love and pride were put into creating, painting and shipping the product.

ED SEALE

As the creator of such well-loved Keepsake Ornament favorites as *Tender Touches*, *Fabulous Decade* and *Heart of Christmas*, Ed Seale has become widely known by collectors.

In 1994, Ed's Keepsake Ornament depicting "The Eagle Has Landed," was a hit with collectors. The ornament featured a depiction of the first lunar landing – including a recording of the actual transmission from the moon.

Since 1991, Ed has delighted Keepsake Miniature Ornament fans with sets featuring tiny mice engaged in various activities. "Tiny Treasures," a charming group of mice primping for their holiday debut, was offered in 1995.

Ed has always loved crafting beautiful objects with his hands. Born in Toronto, Canada, he grew up in southern Ontario. As a young man, he worked as a carpenter and a boat builder. His interest eventually turned to art, and in 1968 he joined Hallmark. He has been creating Keepsake Ornaments since 1980.

PAT SEBERN

Beginning her art career in fashion illustration, Pat Sebern moved into the fine arts in the early 1970s.

Living in Colorado, her greatest interest was in western art. Activities with horses and frontier re-enactments provided good research material, and she exhibited her art widely for several years.

In 1988, a job change took her to Washington State where she joined Pacific Rim Import Corp. She began designing a new porcelain collectible village entitled *Bristol Township*. To develop Bristol's seaport concept, Pat traveled to England and studied several Victorian seaside locations.

Eventually, *Bristol* became the market's first waterfront style porcelain village. She has continued to develop accessory and display products for the collection.

Recently, Pat has been involved in the development of a second line of collectibles for Pacific Rim. *Bunny Toes*, a series of small resin bunnies, is leaping off her drawing tablet with *Birthday Bunnies* being the newest variation. She doesn't have much time to paint anymore but feels very blessed to have such a creative job.

MARK SHERMAN

Studying at New York's Art Student's League and in California with Rex Brandt and Joseph Mugnaini, Mark Sherman's paintings have appeared in juried exhibitions and are included in many private and corporate collections. His creations in pastels, oil and watercolors reveal his wide range of interests and talents.

Currently a professor in San Diego, Mark instructs a studio art class for the humanities program. Travels with his family in North America and Europe have inspired many of his transparent watercolors. A long time admirer of our nations' lighthouses, Mark naturally chose "Old Point Loma," only a few miles from his home, as the subject of his first lighthouse watercolor.

Beginning with the 1995 *Harbour Lights Calendar*, Mark has been commissioned to offer 12 original lighthouse watercolors for the annual publication. He also created a beautiful watercolor rendering of "Point Fermin Lighthouse, CA" to launch the Harbour Lights Collectors Society. Signed and numbered museum-quality prints of "Point Fermin" will be framed and given as gifts to Charter Society Members.

LINDA SICKMAN

Artist Linda Sickman has created some of the most popular Keepsake Ornaments, including designs for the *Rocking Horse*

series. The *Rocking Horse* series celebrated its 15th year with Linda's 1995 Anniversary Edition "Pewter Rocking Horse." Linda also created the *Tin Locomotive* series, *Yuletide Central* series, and the *Folk Art American* collection of Keepsake Showcase Ornaments. She has contributed several designs to the long-running *Here Comes Santa* series and, in 1995, sculpted "Precious Creations," a unique Keepsake Miniature Ornament depicting endangered animals from the sea, earth and sky.

A native of Clinton, Missouri, Linda often evokes memories of her hometown at Christmas in her work. After 31 years with Hallmark, she remains as creative as ever. "I keep fresh by constantly trying something different – a new medium, such as working with wax, clay, wood or plastic, or new ways to make each new design more interesting..." she says.

ELIO SIMONETTI

Creating the life-sized Fontanini® Heirloom Nativity sculptures is a crowning achievement of Elio Simonetti's distinguished artistic career with the renowned House of Fontanini. Receiving the Fontanini family gift of a 50" nativity, Pope John Paul II said of Simonetti's breathtaking masterpiece, "I hope God grants him a long life to continue his fantastic sculpting."

Countless people worldwide share this appreciation for Simonetti's talent and the fine Fontanini craftsmanship when viewing life-sized nativities in American movies like *Home Alone*, famous European cathedrals and parades.

Working with the Fontaninis for 40 years, Master Sculptor Simonetti pledged to resculpt all his early 5" subjects bringing to them the maturing of his perception and skills.

Born in Lucca in 1942, Simonetti attended the Liceo for art for a few years but abandoned his studies for full-time work to help support his large family.

Recently, Simonetti has turned his magical touch to exploration of one of his favorite themes – angels.

MARLENE SIRKO

Vitality is the key to Marlene Sirko's creations. When this doll artist was young, her relatives and friends noticed that Marlene had a gift for painting. Today, the artist still recalls the thrill when, at age 16, she received her first oil paints set. Her studies at the Pennsylvania Academy of the Fine Arts led her to sculpting, which in turn led her to the creation of dolls – one of which won a *Doll Reader* magazine "Doll of the Year" award.

Marlene loves to portray the incredible natural talent of children – often using her own two as inspiration. "Every child is gifted in some way," she says, "whether it's in painting, playing a musical instrument or throwing a baseball." Her creations for Georgetown Collection include a doll based on one of her childhood dreams – skating. Named "Amanda," this 15-1/2" beauty is poseable, so collectors can display her in their favorite skating poses!

GERHARD SKROBEK

Gerhard Skrobek, a master sculptor of the Goebel company, was born in Silesia, the northernmost part of Germany, subsequently moving with his family to Berlin. There, surrounded by museum art treasures and encouraged by his artist mother, Skrobek became immersed in the artistic tradition. From early childhood, he was fascinated with sculpture and its many artistic forms. He studied at the Reimann-schule in Berlin, a renowned private academy of arts, and continued his studies in Coburg. Through a professor, he was introduced to porcelain sculpture at W. Goebel Porzellanfabrik.

Skrobek joined Goebel in 1951, becoming one of its leading sculptors and eventually the predominant interpreter of Sister Maria Innocentia Hummel's drawings into three-dimensional form.

According to his interpretation, Skrobek is able to capture the life and vitality of two-dimensional art through the use of a textured surface in the sculpting process. Skrobek is articulate and personable, and a delight to meet and talk with about *M.I. Hummel* figurines.

TED SLACK

British sculptor, Ted Slack finds that combining his love of nature with a long-time fascination for the unusual has resulted in his ability to create the unique. In his newest achievement, *Woodly Wise* for John Hine Studios, Ted Slack demonstrates his artistic talent and his penchant for incorporating whimsy, architecture and natural beauty in these remarkably miniature treehouses.

As a budding artist, Slack found old churches, windmills, buildings and boats along river banks as interesting drawing subjects. But his main interest was in the dilapidation and decay of castle ruins, old buildings and quaint cottages.

At 16, he was accepted at an art school in Cambridge and later completed his diploma in Art and Design at Sunderland.

Returning to England, Slack took a position with a master craftsman working on the renovation of buildings and discovered he enjoyed sculpting in miniature. This led to his joining Lilliput Lane Ltd., where he devoted himself full-time to the sculpting of miniature architectural structures and cottages.

In his home studio, Slack now combines his many years of sculpting, traveling, research and architecture to create his treehouses. His three sons contribute, each in his own way, to the creation of *Woodly Wise*.

JOSEPH SLOCKBOWER

Indians have always held a special fascination for Joseph Slockbower, who studied drawing and sculpting at California State University, Long Beach in the late 1970s. He started researching the Indian culture, customs, beliefs and costuming, striving to capture physical features, as well as the right expression and the true spirit of each subject. Joe believes that, "Just as every detail on the person or subject is critical to the finished piece, so is the soul or spiritual aspect of the subject."

Joe joined forces with The Lance Corporation in 1991. His striking collections for the Chilmark Pewter line include *The Great Chiefs*, *Guardians of the Plains* and *Legends of the Wild West: The Lawman*. His "Chief Joseph," MetalART™ bust from *The Great Chiefs* collection was awarded the 1992 *Collector Editions* "Award of Excellence."

ANTHONY SLOCOMBE

Like Roger Gibbons, Anthony Slocombe studied under Rex Billingham at Mid-Warwickshire College for Further Education. After an initial three-year stint with W.A.P. Watson (parent of The Tudor Mint), he left but returned four years later. During his time away, Anthony worked for Citadel Miniatures, sculpting fantasy figurines, which helped him when he later found himself immersed in creating *Myth and Magic*. His first model was "Le Morte D'Arthur." Anthony likes to give his pieces a hard edge, especially the dragons, and "The Dragon of Darkness" is a favorite of his. His son (age 8) has been immortalized on more than one study: his initials (JOS) can be seen on "The Well of Aspirations" and the name "Jack" appears on "The Chamber of the Skulls."

Anthony was born in Hall Green, Birmingham, in 1962 and after moving all around Britain, now finds himself back in Hall Green.

CINDY SMITH

Born and raised in Irwin, Pennsylvania, Cindy Smith has been designing and producing handmade, limited edition clay sculptures for nearly 12 years. Her works have been eagerly sought by collectors, some of whom have waited up to a year for a single piece.

Her choice of subject matter – traditional and whimsical Santas, woodland fairies and folk art – all come from a special place in her heart.

The faces and personalities of every figure are unique and sculpted directly from the images in Cindy's mind. She carefully researches costuming and has a gift for small details which may be overlooked by others. The color schemes for each sculpture are developed by Cindy and her palette evokes warm, down-to-earth feelings. Her *cp smithshire™* and *Pére Nöel* collections for The Lance Corporation embody all of the varied talents of this skilled American artist.

LEO R. SMITH III

Woodcarver Leo R. Smith III believes "the artist is a reflection of the environment." His choice of inspirational atmosphere is the picturesque town of Fountain City, Wisconsin. This Mississippi River town and its surrounding woodlands are a rich source of legends and folklore captured in Leo's folk art pieces.

Largely self-taught, Leo creates his original carvings in the studio adjacent to his home. After sculpting a clay model of his design, Leo begins handcarving the wood sculpture – a process that often requires months. Leo and his wife Marilyn then develop a color scheme and bring the character to life through hand-painting.

Midwest of Cannon Falls offers an exclusive collection of resin reproductions of Smith's carvings. Richly detailed and individually numbered for authenticity, these limited edition figures and ornaments bring the legends of the Mississippi River Valley to collectors and folk art lovers alike.

IRENE SPENCER

Irene Spencer, a pillar of the collectibles world and one of America's most beloved artists, became the first female to design a limited edition plate in 1972. Today, Spencer ranks as one of the industry's most popular artists. She has received many honors, including "Litho and Plate of the Year," "Silver Chalice Award," "Artist of the Year" and the NALED "Award of Devotion."

The talented artist credits her adherence to her life's philosophy for much of her success: "My intention in creating is to express, with my best technical ability, a depth of feeling that defies verbal description." Her moving portrayals of that loving and endearing bond between mother and child attest to Spencer's superb artistry.

Powerful emotions are aroused by Spencer's many collectibles, including plates, sculptures and ornaments based on her celebrated themes of love, as well as her penchant for cats' mischievous antics.

GABRIELE STAMEY

Born in the small Tyrolean town, Worgl, Gabriele Stamey began her professional career designing aesthetic, hand-blown stemware after studying at the Technical School of Glassmaking and Design of Kramsach/Tyrol.

In 1986, Gabriele accepted a full-time design position with

Swarovski Silver Crystal. Her professional skills and lively imagination were immediately evident in her first designs comprising a whimsical "Miniature-Cockerel," a "Miniature-Hen" and three "Miniature-Chicks" in fine cut crystal.

Inspired by her two sons, she created the new theme group, "When We Were Young," which brings back childhood memories. One design in this series, "Silver Crystal Express" – a cut crystal train complete with "Locomotive," "Tender" and three "Wagons" – is dedicated to man's fascination with flight and travel. Another piece, the "Santa Maria," is the flagship which Gabriele designed especially for the "Columbus Quincentennial."

To balance her demanding job, Gabriele relaxes with her family and her hobbies, such as hiking, swimming, art and music.

MICHAEL STAMEY

Born in Munich, West Germany, in 1951, Michael Stamey now lives and works in the Austrian Tyrol, where he studied at the College of Glassmaking and Design.

In 1977, he began designing for Swarovski Silver Crystal. Among his designs are the "Rose," and most figurines in the "South Sea" theme, including "Dolphin" and "Maritime Trio." An avid snorkeler, Stamey loves to watch the light change underwater and witness the abundant sea life when vacationing on the Mediterranean.

Stamey also created the Annual Edition pieces, "Lead Me" - The Dolphins, "Save Me" - The Seals, and "Care For Me" - The Whales for the Swarovski Collectors Society series, *Mother and Child*, and the "Kudu" in the *Inspiration Africa* series.

The most important thing in his life and his artistic work is nature. "If you just look at something beautiful or complex long enough, parallels to Nature become obvious," says Stamey.

SCOTT STEARMAN

Born in 1953, Scott Stearman was raised the son of a minister and spent most of his childhood in the Midwest. Beginning to sculpt in the early 1980s, his fascination with three-dimensional art had become a full time career by 1985. He built his studio and log home in the Colorado Rockies above Colorado Springs where he lives with his wife Hermine.

Scott has accepted commissions from corporations, organizations and individuals. While many of his sculptures are in private collections, his life-size and larger works have been placed in public locations.

As a sculptor, he has pursued the classical tradition of realism. "It seems to me that the best way to communicate ideas is to use language that is understood by everyone. My desire is that when someone looks at the work I have created over my lifetime, they will see a sincere body of work that reflects the dignity of the human spirit, the glory of God in creation, and the wonder of life."

HERR CHRISTIAN & KARLA STEINBACH

Herr Christian and Karla Steinbach are the current President and Vice President of the Steinbach Factory, the world-famous producer of nutcrackers and smoking figures in Germany. Together they oversee product development and manufacturing of limited edition collectibles for Kurt S. Adler, Inc.

Christian, especially known for his own "Old World Charm," captivates collectors with insights and lore, signs nutcrackers and smokers, and has been known to perform impromptu repair work.

Born November 1957 in the town of Schneeberg in the Erzgebirge Mountains in Germany, Karla is destined to become the sixth generation to head the company when Herr Christian retires.

Founded in 1832, the Steinbach company continues to manufacture nutcrackers, smoking figures, ornaments and music boxes in the Old World tradition. Each piece is handcrafted and hand-painted from the finest northern European wood and represents the best examples of the medieval art of wood turning.

ADI STOCKER

Born in St. Johann in Tyrol, Austria, Adi Stocker studied at the College of Glassmaking and Design. After graduating in 1977, he worked in a glass studio in New Hampshire for four years. Then he traveled around the world for a year, visiting Japan, China, Thailand, Nepal and India. Upon his return, he began working for Swarovski.

In 1992, Adi and his wife moved into their newly built home in St. Ulrich am Pillersee. From his atelier there he creates his newest figures but maintains contact with his colleagues in Wattens. Since his son's birth in 1993, he enjoys the contentment of family life.

His Swarovski Silver Crystal designs include the limited edition "Eagle" and "Polar Bear." His creation, the "Lion," rounded off the *Inspiration Africa* trilogy for the Swarvoski Collectors Society as the 1995 Annual Edition. Designer objects such as jewelry boxes and pen holders designed for Swarovski Selection in 1992, testify to Adi's highly diversified talent. He also developed various miniatures in the *Swarovski Crystal Memories* line.

DAVID STRAVITZ

David Stravitz owns one of America's most important collections of New York architectural photographs and has donated a portion to the Library of Congress. His fascination for architecture and the design and beauty of diners of the 20's, 30's

and 40's led him to create the *Roadside USA Collection* for George Z. Lefton Co. in order to preserve a piece of Americana.

As Stravitz explains, "This [project] was for the pure enjoyment of recreating some of America's best! I brought back to life the color and designs of diners often left unattended for years and in ruin...recreating each feature to perfection!" Since then, he has created five additional series as part of *Roadside USA – Billboards of Yesteryear, Firehouses, Cable and Trolley Cars, Railroad Depots*, and *Roadside Delites*.

David has been awarded over 100 patents, copyrights and trademarks. He has designed, developed and manufactured products for numerous clients including *Readers Digest, Business Week*, RCA, CBS, Danbury Mint, Lenox, Time-Life and others.

ROBERT TANENBAUM

Renowned as a gifted entertainment-theme artist, Robert Tanenbaum has been commissioned to create numerous portraits of America's most famous personalities, as well as movie posters for many top films.

Tanenbaum established himself as a superbly talented portrait artist in 1977 when his portrait of Howard Hughes for Hughes Aircraft astounded them with its realism, though only a few photographs existed of the eccentric genius at age 33. Word of the artist's remarkable abilities spread quickly, and other coveted Hollywood commissions soon followed.

Although Tanenbaum had little formal artistic training prior to college, he won the All-College Self-Portrait contest in his freshman year at Washington University in St. Louis. Since then, the artist has earned a number of honors, which include becoming one of 22 artists nationwide certified by the American Portrait Society.

Tanenbaum entered a new phase of his prolific career with his series of collector plate portraits for The Hamilton Collection, entitled *The Best of Baseball*, beginning with "The Legendary Mickey Mantle," and the new plate series, entitled the *Drivers of Victory Lane*, beginning with "Bill Elliott."

DAVID TATE

David Tate formed Lilliput Lane in 1982 with family and friends, which has become the United Kingdom's leading producer of miniature cottages. Their friendliness and open style of management has brought David and the company many accolades, such as the Queen investing David as a Member of the Order of the British Empire (M.B.E.).

David had no formal art training but has successfully painted in oils and watercolors and worked with some great sculptors. With Robert Glen, a Kenyan sculptor, he helped create the "Los Colinas Mustangs" near Fort Worth in Dallas.

Having acquired specialist skills in the fiberglass industry, David created unique and complex models of England's architectural history. Many of Lilliput Lane's systems still in use today were his inventions. He now spends most of his time with his creative team at Penrith, England, as the technical and art director. When not in his studio, he takes photographs of original medieval cottages either as inspiration for new Lilliput models or to include in his evocative and inspiring audio-visual shows, which he presents around the world with his wife Sandra.

RANDY TATE

Inspired by the whimsy of everyday life, Randy D. Tate of Sycamore, Illinois, creates a refreshing variety of light-hearted woodcarvings.

Each with its own colorful personality, his folk art pieces vary from spirited birdhouses and lively gameboards to festive holiday ornaments. With every new design, Randy combines his precise hand-carving techniques with a witty perspective to distinguish his specialities from other folk artists.

Midwest of Cannon Falls is pleased to offer folk art enthusiasts and avid collectors exclusive reproductions of Randy Tate's imaginative carvings. This folk art will fill the home with holiday cheer and inspire the spirit of giving throughout the year.

CHRISTINE THAMMAVONGSA

Born in rural Ontario, Christine Thammavongsa has always kept close to nature and simple country ways. By age 12, Christine was determined to pursue art as a career despite her teacher's advice to follow her interests in literature and natural sciences. However, Christine has combined her interests in writing and nature with her Ganz creations, most notably as author and illustrator of *More Precious Than Gold*.

As both product designer and director of Ganz Collectibles, Christine's attention to detail and creativity have put their mark on several successful lines. Howard Ganz, company President, selected her to design the *Little Cheesers®* line in mid-1991. The 1993 *Cowtown®* collection was inspired by memories of visits to her grandparents' farms. Farm experiences also influence her sketches for the *Pigsville®* collection.

For 1995, Christine created old-fashioned teddy bears who play make-believe in *Grandma's Attic™* and cherubic angels who search for a *Perfect Little Place™* on earth. *Watching Over You™*, which initially consists of three classical angels, expresses the motherly feelings Christine experienced over the birth of her daughter Tanisha in 1993.

SHELIA THOMPSON

As a young girl growing up in the South, Shelia Thompson showed an aptitude for art by removing the family portraits off the wall to study and then hone her talents. In high school, Shelia headed up numerous committees, creating posters and play backdrops.

Shelia's Collectibles was founded in 1978 when this self-taught artist discovered a creative way to increase her family's income by making wooden replicas of historic houses to sell at the Charleston City Market.

Shelia's work can be best recognized by the layered facade interpretation she gives each building, with colorful foliage and a fascinating history on the back. She is most well known for, but not limited to, her creations of Victorian-style houses.

Shelia is highly creative and imaginative, as shown by her designs, including the *Ghost House* series which glows in the dark; her first licensed series, *Gone With The Wind*; and a new category: painted metal ornaments. Shelia was the recipient of the 1995 Collectors' Jubilee award for the "Best Unlighted House."

ANNALEE THORNDIKE

Annalee Davis Thorndike was destined for doll-making fame almost in spite of herself. Coming from an artistic family, Annalee loved to watch her mother sew, and they made doll clothes together. "I never played 'house' with dolls," says Annalee, "I just made clothes."

After graduating from high school, in order to "cough up some money to help at home," Annalee began making dolls, selling them through the League of New Hampshire Craftsmen.

In 1941, Annalee married Charles "Chip" Thorndike, son of a distinguished Boston surgeon. Chip, a free-spirited individual, preferred poultry farming. When the poultry business in New Hampshire went south, their farm became the "Factory in the Woods" for Annalee's doll hobby turned business. By the 1960s, an entire work force was involved in meeting the demand for Annalee dolls. With a work force of 400, Annalee's has become a leader in the Christmas and gift industry.

CHUCK THORNDIKE

Chuck Thorndike inherited the family's artistic talents and serves as CEO and President of Annalee Dolls.

Born March 17, 1945, Chuck attended Meredith schools, Paul Smith College, the University of New Hampshire, and is a Vietnam veteran. Chuck, also an inventor, designed and patented a device for lifting logs and stones, and has made many improvements to doll-making tools and its assembly process. His wife Karen established the Annalee Gift Shop, which opened over 20 years ago in Meredith. They have two sons and a daughter.

Chuck's hobbies have centered around seasonal sports activities found in New Hampshire's lakes and mountains, which inspire ideas for dolls.

Chuck recalls growing up in a household where, at one time, Rhode Island Red hens roamed the premises of the Thorndike poultry farm, and where Annalee Dolls covered the tables and beds, and a squadron of doll makers worked around the dining room table. "My brother and I both agree it was an enchanted childhood," he says.

ANN TIMMERMAN

When she began creating dolls as a child in Alabama, Ann Timmerman used any material available, from clay to corn husks. Now, as one of Georgetown Collection's premier doll artists, she works with the best materials available to produce the company's famous *Artist's Editions®*. Timmerman is known for her ability to portray the essence of each particular character in the face of the doll she creates.

Awards and honors are starting to pile at her feet. At the 1993 International Doll Exhibition (IDEX), "Sweet Strawberry" from the *Portraits of Perfection™* series was voted an IDEX award in the category of porcelain dolls available for under $500. In her popular *Portraits of Perfection™* series, new dolls include "Apple Dumpling" and "Blackberry Blossom." Her most recent dolls for Georgetown – "Noelle the Christmas Angel" and "Arielle the Spring Angel," from the *Little Bit of Heaven™* collection, were both honored with 1995 award nominations from *Doll Reader* magazine.

EILEEN TISA

Eileen Tisa liked to make a point of joining her only child Jimmy in his activities. Little did she know that when they sat down to work with some clay, she would discover something new about herself – a talent and joy in sculpting human likenesses.

Although Eileen's sculpted faces were primitive at first, they soon were topping bottles and then clay-covered wire armatures. She also developed her sewing skills to design clothing for her little people. Inspired by the Christmas season, Eileen chose characters from Charles Dickens' classic, *A Christmas Carol*, as subjects for her first creations.

In 1990, Eileen's husband of 22 years, Jim, passed away. She contemplated abandoning her small and not yet very profitable craft business to find other employment, but decided to first share a booth with a friend at the Eastern Regional Gift Show at Valley Forge, Pennsylvania. The show proved an overwhelming success for Classic Collectables by Uniquely Yours. Since then, the company has produced a variety of figurines and gained nationwide recognition.

TITUS TOMESCU

A renowned artist and sculptor even before he created his first fine-porcelain doll, "Cute as a Button," Titus Tomescu is today one of the leading names in the doll collecting world. His dolls have been praised for the lifelike realism and intricate detailing that captures each doll's distinctive personality.

Among his most recent achievements are the "Babe Ruth" doll, and the "I Am the Good Shepherd" doll, an original issue in the *Messages of Hope* collection and recipient of a prestigious nomination for *Doll Reader* magazine's 1995 "Doll of the Year" award. Tomescu is the creator of the now-legendary *Snow-Babies™* dolls. The first issue, "Beneath the Mistletoe," received a prized nomination for 1995 *Dolls* magazine's "Award of Excellence." Tomescu's "Cute as a Button" doll continues to be one of the most sought-after all-porcelain dolls, receiving both 1994 "Doll Award of Excellence" and "Doll of the Year" awards.

ANGELA TRIPI

Determination and a lifelong dream have brought Italy's Angela Tripi to her current status as a world-class artist. This gifted sculptor has come far since the days she abandoned formal art study to help with family finances.

Born in 1941, Tripi showed early signs of talent – first painting; then sculpting in terra cotta. She fired her initial primitive figures in a makeshift oven. For 15 years, Tripi worked in an office by day and devoted all her spare time to shaping clay into figures reflecting the Sicilian peasants she knows so well.

Before her discovery by Roman, Inc. President Ron Jedlinski, Tripi achieved recognition with exhibitions in Italy, France and Japan. Her nativities in Palermo's Villa Niscemi and Sorrento have earned best sculpture honors.

Today, Tripi creates masterpieces in her Palermo workshop for *The Museum Collection of Angela Tripi*, a distinctive gallery of limited edition sculptures for Roman, Inc., which earned her the 1991 "Collectible of Show," sculpting category, at the Long Beach Collectible Show.

VIRGINIA EHRLICH TURNER

Virginia Ehrlich Turner remembers her mother, father and other family members gently trying to dissuade her from becoming an artist when she grew up – no one believed she had enough "imagination" to accomplish this lifelong dream.

But today after much success, Virginia says that it is probably this "non-imaginative" approach to her craft that has made her little "characters" so popular with collectors. She describes her dolls as "characters" because she doesn't care for the "pretty baby-type" dolls but rather real children with real personalities. Virginia's rare ability to capture children's expressions has become the unmistakable trademark of Turner Dolls, which she began in 1982 when a retired ceramics teacher gave her his kiln. At that time, Turner Dolls was one of just three companies in the U.S. producing entirely handcrafted dolls.

In 1991, Virginia's doll "Hannah" was chosen for an "Award of Excellence" by *Dolls* magazine. And "Michelle" was the first doll she created for The Hamilton Collection.

CHRISTIAN ULBRICHT

The legend of the nutcracker lives on through the finely handcrafted and lovingly detailed works of Christian Ulbricht. His delightful nutcrackers and smoking men are the culmination of a woodcrafting tradition born deep in Germany's Erzgebirge region.

The Ulbricht family began woodcrafting in 1705. Today, the tradition continues with Christian Ulbricht's company, *Messrs. Holzhunst Christian Ulbricht*, located in the Bavarian town of Lauingen. Together with his wife Inge, daughter Ines and son Gunther, Ulbricht has built a successful business creating original designs renowned for their attention to detail and unique sense of whimsy. The Ulbrichts pride themselves on developing only products that are made with 100% German materials and labor.

For more than 20 years, Midwest of Cannon Falls has been bringing the art of Christian Ulbricht to America. To both collectors and admirers, his works are German treasures destined to delight generations to come.

JUDI VAILLANCOURT

Judi Vaillancourt has an uncanny ability to adapt old designs and blend them into contemporary works. The creative force behind Vaillancourt Folk Art, she has been an artistic talent since her youth. Over the years, she has designed and created various pieces of colonial furniture; developed a line of antique-style clocks; painted various scenes and portraits; and designed and constructed custom fireplace mantels. Judi became interested in antiques as a teenager.

In 1984, Judi began experimenting with antique chocolate molds by filling them with chalkware, a plaster-like substance, and hand-painting each piece. By chance, she was invited to display one of her pieces at a local folk art show where she received orders for 30 more. A hobby soon became a business, and Vaillancourt Folk Art was born.

Today, Judi Vaillancourt is best known for her ability to bring an historical perspective, along with a personal warmth, to all her creations, including her Clothtique® Santas for Possible Dreams.

SVEN VESTERGAARD

Sven Vestergaard became an apprentice at the Royal Copenhagen Porcelain Manufactory at the age of 16. Four years later, he was given the highest award – the Silver Medal – and remained at the factory as an overglaze painter until 1959.

He then worked as a designer at Denmark's oldest newspaper, *Berlinske Tidenade*, as well as at various advertising agencies. In 1965, he returned to the factory as a draftsman and became the head of Royal Copenhagen's drawing office in 1976.

Vestergaard has become well known and respected throughout the world for his designs for Royal Copenhagen's *Christmas*, *Olympic*, *Hans Christian Andersen*, *National Parks of America* and *Mother's Day* plates and *Children's Day* series.

Vestergaard lives 30 miles south of Copenhagen on an estate originally owned by nobility, where he creates the many themes for Royal Copenhagen plates and his oil paintings of peaceful Danish landscapes, animals and nature.

JOAN BERG VICTOR

Joan Berg Victor, renowned artist, designer and author, has created *Pleasantville 1893* exclusively for Flambro Imports.

Born and raised in the Midwest, Victor earned her undergraduate degree with honors from Newcomb College, the Women's College of Tulane University, where she not only received academic honors, but was elected Miss Tulane. At Yale University, Victor was awarded a Master of Fine Arts degree with honors.

A highly regarded draftsman, her drawings and paintings can be found in private and museum collections. Her subjects have appeared in *Fortune* magazine, *The New York Times* and *The Wall Street Journal*.

Through the years, Victor has written and illustrated over two dozen books for both young children and adults. Her favorite book, of course, is *Pleasantville 1893*.

Her newest venture is a wonderful collectible Christmas village entitled *Santaville – The Christmas That Almost Never Was*. Based on an endearing poem, conceived and illustrated by Victor and written by Stanley Wiklinski, *Santaville* was created exclusively for Flambro Imports. The village invites the collector to get a first-hand peek at the working world of Santa and all his helpers.

JESSICA WATSON

Jessica Watson studied at Birmingham University and gained a first class BA degree in Fine Arts. She originally joined The Tudor Mint in 1987 and among other things, worked on designs for bookmarks and Crystalflame. During the next two years, she took time off to obtain a Post Graduate Certificate of Education.

When Jessica returned in 1990, *Myth and Magic* was already in full swing, and she recalls enjoying the challenge of working on a project requiring such a great deal of imagination. In college, she specialized in painting and drawing, and her color work can be seen in the illustrations for Allan Frost's *The Stracyl of Unity*. Among Jessica's favorite studies are "The Dark Dragon" and "The Dragon of Darkness." She also admires in particular some of Sharon Riley's larger designs, such as "The VII Seekers of Knowledge" and "The Dragon Master."

WENDT & KÜHN

More than 80 years have passed since Grete Wendt and her friend Grete Kühn first created their little hand-turned wood figurines in the German village of Grünhainichen.

Among the best-loved Wendt & Kühn figures are the delightful little angel musicians with the trademarked eleven dots on green wings – a statement of authenticity for collectors. Uniquely-crafted Santas and charming village children add to this wonderful collection. Each piece is beautifully hand-painted and hand-finished by craftsmen who honor the design and workmanship originated by Wendt & Kühn in 1915. Today, under the leadership of Grete's nephew, Hans Wendt, the tradition of quality and craftsmanship continues in the Erzgebirge region of Germany.

In the *Wendt & Kühn Collection*, the designs available to collectors are reproductions of the originals created over 80 years ago. Midwest of Cannon Falls is proud to be the exclusive U.S. distributor of these treasured collectibles.

MARLENE WHITING

Marlene Whiting of Yorktown, Virginia, is well-known among collectors of miniature buildings for her ability to capture the spirit and charm that define Americana.

The founder of Brandywine Woodcrafts Inc. grew up in Pittsburgh in the late 1940s and 1950s, fascinated by the color and diversity of the small shops, businesses and homes of the city's neighborhoods. It's these memories, along with her love of architecture, literature and gardening, that she's incorporated into her nostalgic, historic and whimsical collections since Brandywine's beginning in 1981.

Though Brandywine has grown from a kitchen-table pastime to a full-fledged manufacturing operation, Marlene has insisted that the company never lose sight of its family orientation. Indeed, she still designs, sculpts and handpaints the original of every Brandywine creation. Her husband Tru serves as the company's president, while her mother, son and daughter participate in manufacturing and promotional activities.

WILLY WHITTEN

Skilled in a variety of media and techniques, Willy Whitten is a self-taught artist who is now a master craftsman. His interest in art began at a young age, but an exhibition he viewed at the Museum of Art in Los Angeles in his late twenties made him realize he wanted to sculpt for a living.

Gifted with natural talent and unique vision, Willy acquired extensive modeling and design experience in the field of cinematic special effects. In the last decade, he has been a creative artist on more than two dozen films, including *Ghostbusters* and *The Terminator*. His sets and animatronic characters can be found in theme parks such as Universal Tours and Disneyland.

Willy's greatest artistic love, and his most renowned, is sculpting miniatures. To all his work Willy brings an expressiveness and realism, demonstrating the ability to capture the sense of a person's character and inner identity. He realized his dream of seeing that work "come alive in the brilliant dimension of metal," when he began working with Legends®.

Originally from Indiana, Willy now resides in southern California with his wife Linda.

KLAUS WICKL

A native of Salzburg, Austria, sculptor-designer Klaus Wickl loves nature and rural life and says he immigrated to America in 1984 because he was attracted by "America's free pioneer spirit, its love of the land and its survival."

Fascinated by Rien Poortvliet's illustrations of Gnomes, Wickl made three-dimensional sculptures and traveled to The Netherlands to meet with the artist. After several trips for advice and approvals, Klaus Wickl Studios introduced the first Gnomes figurines in 1988.

Wickl says he designed and sculpted the Gnomes to "share the message of living in a more perfect society in harmony with both nature and each other." The sculptor sees the Gnomes as a means of stimulating environmental and ecological awareness. Wickl created a storyland where each of the Gnomes has a purpose and a place in his natural setting.

In joining with Enesco in this venture, Wickl hopes to broaden the influence of the Gnomes and to spread their message to new and appreciative audiences worldwide.

PRESTON WILLINGHAM

In the past 14 years, Preston Willingham has completed nine commissions of public sculpture on permanent display, two war memorials for public parks and 12 private commissions for offices and homes in marble, bronze, glass and aluminum. One of the public sculptures has been named a historic monument by the Governor and Cabinet of the State of Florida. Another resides in a library of a former President of the United States.

Of his pieces, nothing has been more emotionally moving than "From a Child's Heart" – the first of a new series which features porcelain figurines with *inspirational messages* from the hearts of children – since this represents the relationship and emotions Preston shares with his son Noah. These exquisite sculptures are distributed by WACO Products.

DAVID WINTER

Gifted British sculptor David Winter has gained worldwide acclaim for his unique miniature cottages, with their remarkable detail and whimsical touches – including the illusive Mouse. Winter tries to convey the feeling of life in the past, by recreating the buildings in which people lived and worked in days gone by.

Born in Catterick, Yorkshire, David, the son of an army colonel and famed sculptor Faith Winter, created his own clay sculptures as his mother worked. In 1979, John Hine approached Faith to work on a dimensional heraldic plaque project, and she recommended her son.

Following the failure of the plaque venture, David sculpted his first miniature cottage, "Mill House." The sculpture was taken to a local gift shop, where it sold the same afternoon. Soon, David Winter Cottages were available in several shops and soon spread worldwide. From a single painter, an entire "cottage industry" was born.

David won the coveted "Collectible of the Year Award" from NALED in 1987 and 1988 and "Artist of the Year" in 1991, among other awards over the years.

BARBARA AND PETER WISBER

Barbara and Peter Wisber have been bringing *The Family* and *Friends of Lizzie High®* as a collaborative effort and labor of love to delighted collectors since 1985.

When Barbara decided to add dolls to their already popular folk art line, she took her ideas to Peter who turned her sketch into a doll cut out of pine and standing on two egg-shaped feet. Each doll was given an old-fashioned name borrowed from Peter's family tree and an accompanying "tale" to enhance their charm.

Married in 1971, they first lived on a large working farm and later moved to a farmhouse in Bucks County when they started a family. Happy childhood memories and the joys of raising their two children shine forth in additions to the *Lizzie High* collection. Peter's talents also extend to sculpting an array of adorable little animals added to many *Lizzie High* characters.

Barbara and Peter have parlayed the joys of their partnership into a successful line of lovingly crafted dolls that bring joy to the hearts and homes of an ever-growing number of collectors.

GUSTAVE AND GRETCHEN WOLFF

Educated at Northland College and the University of Wisconsin-Madison, Gustave Wolff became interested in porcelain sculpting by accident, when a graduate student requested his assistance with a sculpting assignment. From there, he began a fledgling doll business in the early 1970s. His creations had a "basic" appearance in both sculpture and artistic design.

Then in the mid-'80s, with young Gretchen's keen eye for true-to-life expression and perfection in costuming, his clay molds began to reflect a much different appearance. With no formal education, Gretchen's talent seems best explained by genes, many family discussions, and a highly photographic memory.

The Wolff's latest releases for The Wimbledon Collection – "Victoria...blowing bubbles," "Paige...bad hair day," "Daphne...Mommy, my shoe and sock came off!" and "Princess Nakoma" – continue to depict their distinct character and fine design. Whether their creations reflect the unusual or the more elaborate, this artistic team is committed to distinctive and affordable collectibles.

CHARLES WYSOCKI

Charles Wysocki, a Detroit native who now lives in Joshua Tree and Lake Arrowhead, California, is a painter who is a lot like his art. Looking into Wysocki's laughing eyes sparks the same feelings as one of his paintings – charming.

His homey, vividly-colored scenes of New England set in the 1700s and 1800s reveal intricate details and whimsical touches that provide insights into the lives of early Americans. Sold as limited edition prints through The Greenwich Workshop, Wysocki's paintings have steadily gained popularity since 1979.

Today his limited edition prints are carried by more than 1,000 galleries, and his collector's plates have taken the market by storm. Now he brings his unique vision to the sculpture medium for the first time with the *Peppercricket Grove* cottage collection from Hawthorne Architectural Register.

MANUELLA YATES

Many children have read the wonderful tales written by Beatrix Potter and therefore have become familiar with the adventures of characters such as Jemima Puddleduck, Peter Rabbit and Tom Kitten. After 16 years Manuella Yates, a ceramic artisan at the Royal Doulton Design Studios in the United Kingdom, has mastered the expertise required in handpainting the various subjects of Beatrix Potter, *Bunnykins* and *Brambly Hedge*.

She has worked in other areas of ceramic manufacturing for over 25 years. Among her favorite figures to paint are "Lady Mouse" and "Peter Rabbit." Some of Yates work includes "Bedtime Bunnykins," "Be Prepared," "Benjamin Bunny Wakes Up" and the ever popular "Peter Rabbit" figurines. With her considerable expertise, Yates produces intricately hand-painted pieces.

Yates enjoys talking about her work, the techniques and the folk legends surrounding the Royal Doulton family of figurines. Her knowledge of Royal Doulton products and their history fascinate many, and the signing of her name to a figurine selection is a very special and rare opportunity for long-time collectors and first-time purchasers alike.

BILL YOUNGER

If Bill Younger could have his way, all lighthouses would be open to the public. As a child, he would often observe lighthouses during fishing expeditions on the Chesapeake Bay. Those memories and his love for history, old buildings and architecture, provided fertile ground for the dream that has become Harbour Lights.

As founder and conceptual artist, Bill feels that Harbour Lights' purpose is to promote history and maritime tradition. In each lighthouse miniature, he hopes to achieve a rendering that is not only aesthetically pleasing, but also as accurate as the real thing.

To research new lighthouse editions, Bill often travels to deserted locations far off the beaten path. On some of these trips, he has had to walk for several hours, sometimes through water. "When I finally arrive at the lighthouse, I forget all of the difficulties. I'm immediately taken into the past and reminded of the families that worked and played there."

MARTIN ZENDRON

Born in the medieval town of Hall in Tyrol, Austria, Martin Zendron now lives and works only a few miles away in Wattens, the home of Swarovski.

In his late teens, Martin attended the College of Glassmaking and Design of Kramsach/Tyrol, where he studied glass design with a special course in cutting and engraving. After graduation, he worked for a well-known Tyrolean retailer specializing in glass objects. There his work came to Swarovski's attention, where he became a designer in 1988.

His first creations for Swarovski were the "Harp" and the "Lute," followed by the "Grand Piano," which all reveal a rare artistic talent and craftsmanship. He also created the first piece in the *Inspiration Africa* series, the "Elephant," for the Swarovski Collectors Society.

Although Martin spends much of his spare time in the mountains, his real passion is deep-sea diving. For him, it is a wonderful way of relaxing from the precision and concentration required for his work with Swarovski.

BOOKS, MAGAZINES AND NEWSLETTERS

The following publications are designed to keep you current on the latest news about limited edition collectibles. In addition, many manufacturers and collector clubs publish newsletters that will help you enjoy your hobby to the fullest. See the club listing on page 336 for information about club publications.

— BOOKS —

A COLLECTORS GUIDE TO MYTH AND MAGIC
by John Hughes and Chris Wotton. Collectables Publishing Limited.

AMERICAN TEDDY BEAR ENCYCLOPEDIA
by Linda Mullins. Hobby House Press.

THE CHILMARK COLLECTION
by Glenn S. Johnson and James E. Secky. Commonwealth Press, Worcester, Massachusetts.

CHRISTMAS THROUGH THE DECADES
by Robert Brenner. Schiffer Publishing.

DECK THE HALLS
by Robert Merck. Abbeville Press.

DIRECTORY TO LIMITED EDITION COLLECTIBLE STORES
by Diane Carnevale Jones. Collectors' Information Bureau, Barrington, Illinois.

DIRECTORY TO SECONDARY MARKET RETAILERS
by Collectors' Information Bureau.

FENTON GLASS, THE FIRST TWENTY-FIVE YEARS (1905-1930)
by William Heacock. Richardson Printing.

FENTON GLASS, THE SECOND TWENTY-FIVE YEARS (1931-1955)
by William Heacock. Richardson Printing.

FENTON GLASS, THE THIRD TWENTY-FIVE YEARS (1956-1980)
by William Heacock. Richardson Printing.

LLADRÓ – THE MAGIC WORLD OF PORCELAIN
by Several. Salvat.

MORE PRECIOUS THAN GOLD (A CHEESERVILLE TALE)
by Christine Thammavongsa. GANZ.

NUMBER ONE PRICE GUIDE TO M.I. HUMMEL FIGURINES, PLATES, MINIATURES AND MORE
by Robert Miller. Portfolio Press.

THE OFFICIAL LLADRÓ COLLECTION IDENTIFICATION CATALOG AND PRICE GUIDE
by Glenn S. Johnson. Lladró Collectors Society.

THE OFFICIAL MSA IDENTIFICATION AND PRICE GUIDE TO THE CHILMARK COLLECTION
by Glenn S. Johnson and Ann Hagenstein. Grafacon, Hudson, Massachusetts.

THE SEBASTIAN MINIATURE COLLECTION
by Glenn S. Johnson. Commonwealth Press, Worcester, Massachusetts.

THE STRACYL OF UNITY
by Allan Frost. AJF Desk Top Publishing.

SWAROVSKI: THE MAGIC OF CRYSTAL
by Vivienne Becker. Abrams, New York.

VALUE REGISTER HANDBOOK FOR SEBASTIAN MINIATURES
by Paul J. Sebastian. The Sebastian Exchange, Lancaster, Pennsylvania.

— MAGAZINES/NEWSLETTERS —

AMERICAN ARTIST
1515 Broadway
New York, NY 10036
(212)536-5178

ANTIQUES & COLLECTING
1006 S. Michigan Avenue
Chicago, IL 60605
(312)939-4767

THE ANTIQUE TRADER
P.O. Box 1050
Dubuque, IA 52004
(800)334-7165

CIB REPORT & SHOWCASE
5065 Shoreline Road, Suite 200
Barrington, IL 60010
(708)842-2200

COLLECTOR EDITIONS
170 Fifth Avenue
New York, NY 10010
(800)347-6969

COLLECTOR'S MART
700 E. State Street
Iola, WI 54990
(715)445-2214

COLLECTORS NEWS
P.O. Box 156
Grundy City, IA 50638
(319)824-6981

CONTEMPORARY DOLL COLLECTOR
30595 8 Mile
Livonia, MI 48152-1798
(810)477-6650

DOLLS MAGAZINE
170 Fifth Avenue, 12th Floor
New York, NY 10010
(800)347-6969

THE DOLL READER
6405 Flank Drive
Harrisburg, PA 17112
(717)657-9555

DOLL WORLD
P.O. Box 420077
Palm Coast, FL 32142-9895

FIGURINES & COLLECTIBLES
6405 Flank Drive
Harrisburg, PA 17112
(717)657-9555

KOVELS ON ANTIQUES & COLLECTIBLES
P.O. Box 420347
Palm Coast, FL 32142-0347
(800)829-9158

KOVELS SPORTS COLLECTIBLES
P.O. Box 420026
Palm Coast, FL 32142-0026
(800)829-9158

MINIATURE COLLECTOR
30595 8 Mile
Livonia, MI 48152-1798
(810) 477-6650

SOUTHWEST ART
P.O. Box 460535
Houston, TX 77056
(713)850-0990

TEDDY BEAR AND FRIENDS
6405 Flank Drive
Harrisburg, PA 17112
(717)657-9555

TEDDY BEAR REVIEW
170 Fifth Avenue, 12th Floor
New York, NY 10010
(800)347-6969

U.S. ART COLLECTIBLES
220 S. 6th Street, Suite 500
Minneapolis, MN 55402
(612)339-7571

WILDLIFE ART NEWS
4725 Highway 7
St. Louis Park, MN 55416
(612)927-9056

NATIONAL COLLECTORS' CLUBS

	Annual Dues/Renewals	Club Year	Membership Gift	Members-Only Piece	Club Publication	Binder	Membership Card	Buy-Sell Matching Service	Local Chapters	Tours/Special Events	Other Benefits
All God's Children Collector's Club* **Miss Martha Originals** P.O. Box 5038, Glencoe, AL 35905 (205) 492-0221	$ 20.	June 1- May 31	●	●	4/yr.		●		●	●	Personal Checklist
The Anheuser-Busch Collectors Club* 2700 South Broadway, St. Louis, MO 63118 (800) 305-2582	35.	Anniv. of Sign-Up Date	●	●	4/yr.	●	●				
Annalee Doll Society* P.O. Box 1137, Meredith, NH 03253-1137 (800) 43-DOLLS	29.95	Anniv. of Sign-Up Date	●	●	4/yr.		●	●		●	Membership Pin Members-Only Event Pieces
ANRI Collector's Society* P.O. Box 2087, Quincy, MA 02269-2087 (800) 763-ANRI (2674)	40.	Jan.- Dec.	●	●	3/yr.		●	●		●	ANRI Catalog Research Dept. Authorized Retailer Listing
G. Armani Society* 300 Mac Lane, Keasbey, NJ 08832 (800) 3-ARMANI	40./27.50	Jan.- Dec.	●	●	4/yr.		●			●	
Attic Babies Collectors' Club* P.O. Box 912, Drumright, OK 74030 (918) 352-4414	30./20.	Anniv. of Sign-Up Date	●	●	4/yr.		●	●		●	
Brian Baker's Déjà Vu Collectors' Club* **Michael's Ltd.** PRDV, P.O. Box 217, Redmond, WA 98052-0217 (800) 835-0181	35.	Mar. 1- Mar. 1	●	●	2/yr.		●			●	
The Belleek Collectors International Society 9893 Georgetown Pike, Suite 525 Great Falls, VA 22066 (800)-BELLEEK	35.	Anniv. of Sign-Up Date	●	●	3/yr.		●		●	●	Membership Certificate
Boehm Porcelain Society 25 Fairfacts Street, Trenton, NJ 08638 (800) 257-9410	15.	Jan.- Dec.		●	1/yr.			●		●	Catalogs
Michael Boyett Collectors Registry P.O. Box 632012, Nacogdoches, TX 75963 (409) 560-4477	None	Jan.- Dec.			2/yr.					●	
Rick Cain Studios Collectors Guild* 619 S. Main Street, Gainesville, FL 32601 (800) 535-3949	35.	Anniv. of Sign-Up Date	●	●	4/yr.						Free Registration of All Sculptures
Caithness Collectors' Club - Caithness Glass Inc. 141 Lanza Ave., Bldg. 12, Garfield, NJ 07026 (201) 340-3330	35.	Anniv. of Sign-Up Date	●	●	●	●	●			●	
Cat's Meow Collectors Club* Box 635, Wooster, OH 44691-0635 (216) 264-1377 Ext. 225	25./22.	Anniv. of Sign-Up Date	●	●	4/yr.		●				Club Notebook Custom Search Program
Cavanagh's Coca-Cola Christmas Collectors Society* P.O. Box 420157, Atlanta, GA 30342 (800) 653-1221	25.	Jan.- Dec.	●	●	4/yr.		●				Membership Certificate Special Items Offer
The Chilmark Polland Collectors Society* **The Lance Corporation** 321 Central Street, Hudson, MA 01749 (508) 568-1401	45.	Anniv. of Sign-Up Date	●	●	2/yr.		●			●	
The Chilmark Registry* - The Lance Corporation 321 Central Street, Hudson, MA 01749 (508) 568-1401	None	Up to 5 yrs. Free		●	4/yr.			●		●	Free Upon Registration of Chilmark Sculpture. Price Guide Updates
Lowell Davis Farm Club* - Schmid 55 Pacella Park Drive, Randolph, MA 02368-1795 (617) 961-3000	25./20.	Anniv. of Sign-Up Date	●	●	●		●		●	●	Collector's Guide, Cap, Coloring Book
Walt Disney Collectors Society* P.O. Box 11090, Des Moines, IA 50336-1090 (800) 678-6528	55.-1yr. 99.-2 yrs.	Jan.- Dec.	●	●	4/yr.	●	●			●	Cloissone Pin, "Newsflashes"
Dreamsicles Collectors' Club* - Cast Art 1120 California Avenue, Corona, CA 91719 (800) 437-5818	27.50/ 23.50	Anniv. of Sign-Up Date	●	●	4/yr.	●	●	●			Photo Book

* For more information, see company feature articles (pp. 53 - 292).

NATIONAL COLLECTORS' CLUBS

Club	Annual Dues/Renewals	Club Year	Membership Gift	Members-Only Piece	Club Publication	Binder	Membership Card	Buy-Sell Matching Service	Local Chapters	Tours/Special Events	Other Benefits
Duncan Royale Collectors Club* 1141 S. Acacia Ave., Fullerton, CA 92631 (714) 879-1360	$ 30.	Anniv. of Sign-Up Date	●	●	4/yr.	●	●				Certificate, Catalog, Free Figurine Registration
EKJ Collectors' Society* - Flambro Imports P.O. Box 93507, Atlanta, GA 30377-0507 (800) EKJ-CLUB	30./15.	Jan.-Dec.	●	●	4/yr.	●	●			●	EKJ Pin and Catalog Free Figurine Registration Collector Registry Listing
Enchantica Collectors Club P.O. Box 200, Waterville, OH 43566 (419) 878-0034	27.50	Jan.-Dec.	●	●	2/yr.		●			●	
Enesco Cherished Teddies Club* P.O. Box 91796, Elk Grove Village, IL 60009-9179 (708) 875-5422	17.50	Jan. 1-Dec. 31	●	●	●						Lapel Pin, Easel, Certificate
Enesco Precious Moments Birthday Club* P.O. Box 689, Itasca, IL 60143-0689 (708) 875-5411	20.-1yr. 38.-2yrs.	July 1-June 30	●	●	●						Certificate, Happy Birthday Card
Enesco Precious Moments Collectors' Club* P.O. Box 1466, Elk Grove Village, IL 60009-1466 (708) 875-5411	27.	Jan. 1-Dec. 31	●	●	●	●	●			●	Gift Registry, Pocket Guide, Cookie Cutter Special Mailings
Enesco Treasury of Christmas Ornaments Collectors' Club* P.O. Box 773, Elk Grove Village, IL 60009-0773 (708) 875-5404	20.	Jan. 1-Dec. 31	●	●	●		●				Lapel Pin, Collectors' Guide
Fenton Art Glass Collectors of America (FAGCA)* P.O. Box 384, Williamstown, WV 26187 (304) 375-6196	15.	Anniv. of Sign-Up Date		●	6/yr.			●	●	●	
National Fenton Glass Society (NFGS)* P.O. Box 4008, Marietta, OH 45750	15.	Anniv. of Sign-Up		●	6/yr.			●	●	●	
Fontanini Collectors' Club* - Roman, Inc. 555 Lawrence Avenue, Roselle, IL 60172 (800) 729-7662	19.50/ 17.50	Anniv. of Sign-Up Date	●	●	4/yr.	●	●			●	Registry Guide, Pin, Research Service, Contests
The Great American Collectors' Club* P.O. Box 428, Aberdeen, NC 28315 (910) 944-7447	None	Jan.-Dec.		●	3/yr.			●		●	Membership Free with Purchase of Club Piece
Jan Hagara Collectors' Club 40114 Industrial Park, Georgetown, TX 78626 (512) 863-9499	44./39.	July 1-June 30	●	●	4/yr.	●	●	●	●	●	Cloisonne Pin, Contest, Drawings, Savings on Products
Hallmark Keepsake Ornament Collector's Club* P.O. Box 419034, Kansas City, MO 64141-6034	20.	Jan.-Dec.	●	●	4/yr.		●	●	●	●	Early Mailing of *Dreambook*
Hand & Hammer Collectors' Club* 2610 Morse Lane, Woodbridge, VA 22192 (800) SILVERY	None	Jan. 1-Dec. 31			●					●	Updated List of Ornaments
Harbour Lights Collectors Society* 8130 La Mesa Blvd., La Mesa, CA 91941 (800) 365-1219	30.	Anniv. of Sign-Up Date	●	●	4/yr.	●	●		●	●	Cloissone Pin
Edna Hibel Society P.O. Box 9721, Coral Springs, FL 33075 (407) 848-9663	20.-1yr. 35.-2yrs.	Anniv. of Sign-Up Date	●	●	4/yr.		●		●	●	Previews of Hibel Artworks
Mark Hopkins Bronze Guild 21 Shorter Industrial Blvd., Rome, GA 30165-1838 (800) 678-6564	None				2/yr.			●			
M.I. Hummel Club* Goebel Plaza, P.O. Box 11 Pennington, NJ 08534-0011 (800) 666-CLUB	45./35.	June 1-May 31	●	●	4/yr.	●	●	●	●	●	Research Service Essay Contests
Iris Arc Collectors Society 114 East Haley Street, Santa Barbara, CA 93101 (805) 963-3661	25.	Anniv. of Sign-Up Date	●	●	2 yr.		●	●		●	

* For more information, see company feature articles (pp. 53 - 292).

NATIONAL COLLECTORS' CLUBS

Club	Annual Dues/Renewals	Club Year	Membership Gift	Members-Only Piece	Club Publication	Binder	Membership Card	Buy-Sell Matching Service	Local Chapters	Tours/Special Events	Other Benefits
Thomas Kinkade Collectors' Society* **Media Arts Group Inc.** P.O. Box 90267, San Jose, CA 95109 (800) 366-3733	$45.-1yr. 75.-2yrs.	Jan.- Dec.	●	●	4/yr.		●			●	Free Frame with Purchase of Members-Only Canvas Lithograph
Krystonia Collectors Club* **Precious Art** 110 E. Ellsworth, Ann Arbor, MI 48108 (313) 677-3510	25.	Feb. 1- Jan. 31	●	●	4/yr.		●			●	
Lawton Collectors Guild* P.O. Box 969, Turlock, CA 95381 (209) 632-3655	20./10.	Jan. 1- Dec. 31	●	●	4/yr.	●	●	●		●	
Lilliput Lane Collectors' Club* P.O. Box 665, Elk Grove Village, IL 60009-0665 (800)-LILLIPUT	40.-1yr. 65.-2yrs.	May 1- Apr. 30	●	●	4/yr.	●	●	●		●	Catalog
Little Cheesers Collectors' Club* - GANZ 908 Niagara Falls Blvd., North Tonawanda, NY 141201-2060 (800) 724-5902	27./24.	Anniv. of Sign-Up Date	●	●	2/yr.	●	●	●			Item Checklist, Contests, Birthday Cards, Special Mailings
Little Emmett Collectors' Society* **Flambro Imports** P.O. Box 93507, Atlanta, GA 30377-0507 (800) EKJ-CLUB	10.	Anniv. of Sign-Up Date			4/yr.		●				Bookmark, Mask, Activity Book, Puzzle, Catalog
The Lizzie High Society* - Ladie and Friends 220 North Main Street, Sellersville, PA 18960 (800) 76-DOLLS	25./15.	Jan.- Dec.	●	●	2/yr.	●	●	●		●	Pewter Ornament
Lladró Society* 1 Lladró Drive, Moonachie, NJ 07074 (800) 634-9088	40./27.50	Anniv. of Sign-Up Date	●	●	4/yr.	●	●			●	Video, Research Service Assoc. Membership to Lladró Museum
Seymour Mann, Inc. Doll Club* 230 Fifth Avenue, Suite 1500, New York, NY 10001 (212) 683-7262	17.50	Jan.- Dec.	●	●	●		●	●			
June McKenna Collector's Club* P.O. Box 1540, Ashland, VA 23005 (804) 798-2024	45.	Apr. 1- Mar. 31	●	●	2/yr.					●	
Melody In Motion Collectors Club* **WACO Products Corporation** I-80 & New Maple Avenue, P.O. Box 898 Pine Brook, NJ 07058-0898 (201) 882-1820	27.50	Anniv. of Sign-Up Date	●	●	2/yr.		●				Catalog, "Savings" Coupons, Personal Purchasing Record, Retired Edition Summary List of Collectors' Centers
Memories of Yesterday Collectors' Society* **Enesco Corporation** P.O. Box 245, Elk Grove Village, IL 60009-0245 (708) 875-5799	22.50	Jan. 1- Dec. 31	●	●	4/yr.		●				Gift Registry, Brooch, Stationery
Myth and Magic Collectors' Club* - The Tudor Mint P.O. Box 431729, Houston, TX 77243-1729 (713) 462-0076	37.50	July 1- June 30	●	●	2/yr.		●			●	Catalog and Updates
Old World Christmas Collectors' Club* P.O. Box 8000 — Department C, Spokane, WA 99203 (800) 962-7669	30.	Anniv. of Sign-Up Date	●	●	4/yr.			●			Collectors' Guide Local Retailer Listings
Open Window ClubHouse Collectors Club* **R.R. Creations** P.O. Box 8707, Dept. Club, Pratt, KS 67124 (800) 779-3610	22.50/ 19.50	Anniv. of Sign-Up Date	●	●	2/yr.	●	●	●		●	
The Pangaean Society* **Official Collectors Club of cp smithshire** **The Lance Corporation** 321 Central Street, Hudson, MA 01749 (508) 568-1401	25.	Anniv. of Sign-Up Date	●	●	2/yr.		●	●		●	Pin
PenDelfin Family Circle* - Miller Import Corp. 230 Spring Street N.W., Atlanta Gift Mart, Suite 1238 Atlanta, GA 30303 (404) 523-3380 or (800) 872-4876	30.	Jan.- Dec.	●	●	4/yr.		●	●	●	●	Membership Certificate

* For more information, see company feature articles (pp. 53 - 292).

NATIONAL COLLECTORS' CLUBS

Club	Annual Dues/Renewals	Club Year	Membership Gift	Members-Only Piece	Club Publication	Binder	Membership Card	Buy-Sell Matching Service	Local Chapters	Tours/Special Events	Other Benefits
Pennibears Collectors Club 1413 N.E. Lincoln Avenue, Moore, OK 73160 (405) 799-0006	$5.	Anniv. of Sign-Up Date		●	4/yr.		●				
Pleasantville 1893 Historical Preservation Society* Flambro Imports P.O. Box 93507, Atlanta, GA 30377-0507 (800) 355-CLUB	30./15.	Jan.-Dec.	●		4/yr.		●				Pin, Catalog, Christmas Ornament
Pocket Dragons and Friends Collectors Club* Flambro Imports P.O. Box 93507, Atlanta, GA 30377-0507 (800) 355-CLUB	29.50-1yr. 54.-2yrs.	June 1-May 30	●	●	4/yr.		●			●	Pin, Catalog
Red Mill Collectors Society One Hunters Ridge, Summersville, WV 26651 (304) 872-5237	15.	Mar. 31 and Sept. 30			4/yr.		●	●			
Royal Doulton International Collectors Club* 701 Cottontail Lane, Somerset, NJ 08873 (800) 582-2102	25.	Anniv. of Sign-Up Date		●	4/yr.					●	Historical Enquiry Services Advance Mailings
Sandicast Collectors Guild P.O. Box 910079, San Diego, CA 92191 (800) 722-3316	25.	Anniv. of Sign-Up Date	●		2/yr.			●		●	
Sarah's Attic Forever Friends Collector's Club* P.O. Box 448, Chesaning, MI 48616 (800) 4-FRIEND	32.50	June 1-May 31	●	●	●	●			●		Catalogs, Special Mailings
Santa Claus Network* - Possible Dreams 6 Perry Drive, Foxboro, MA 02035 (508) 543-6667	25.	Anniv. of Sign-Up Date	●	●	4/yr.		●	●			Collectors Guide Book
Sebastian Miniatures Collectors Society* The Lance Corporation 321 Central Street, Hudson, MA 01749 (508) 568-1401	29.50	Anniv. of Sign-Up Date	●	●	●		●	●		●	Annual Value Register and Updates
The Shade Tree Cowboy Collectors Society 6210 NW 124th Place, Gainesville, FL 32653 (800) 327-6923	None				4/yr.						Free Registration of Cowboy Figurines Advance Mailings
Shelia's Collectors Society* 1856 Belgrade Avenue, Bldg. C Charleston, SC 29407 (803) 766-0485 or (800) 227-6564	25./20.	Anniv. of Sign-Up Date	●	●	4/yr.	●	●			●	
Starlight Family of Collectors* Christopher Radko P.O. Box 238, Dobbs Ferry, NY 10522 (800) 71-RADKO	50./45.	Jan.-Dec.	●	●	4/yr.	●	●				Button, Pin, Catalog
Starlite Collector's Society* - Legends 2665-D Park Center Drive, Simi Valley, CA 93065 (800) 726-9660	None				4/yr.						Record-Keeping Services Appraisal Service, Advance Notice of New Sculptures
The Steinbach Collectors Club* - Kurt S. Adler, Inc. 1107 Broadway, New York, NY 10010 (800) 243-9627	40.		●	●	●		●				Portfolio, Pin, Brochures
Swarovski Collectors Society* 2 Slater Road, Cranston, RI 02920 (800) 426-3088	35./25.	Anniv. of Sign-Up Date	●	●	2/yr.					●	
Bill Vernon Collectors Society 6210 NW 124th Place, Gainesville, FL 32653 (800) 327-6923	None				●						Free Registration of Figurines Advance Mailings
VickiLane Collectors' Club* 3233 NE Cadet Avenue, Portand, OR 97220 (800) 456-4259	28.	Anniv. of Sign-Up Date	●		3/yr.		●				Club Button
David Winter Cottages Collectors' Guild* Media Arts Group, Inc. P.O. Box 90038, San Jose, CA 95109-3038 (800) 366-3733	40.-1yr. 75.-2yrs.	Anniv. of Sign-Up Date	●	●	4/yr.		●			●	Advance Mailings Membership Certificate

* For more information, see company feature articles (pp. 53 - 292).

DIRECTORY OF COLLECTIBLES MANUFACTURERS

"Who's Who" in Limited Edition Collectibles

This directory provides some basic information about many companies actively involved in today's field of limited edition collectibles. In addition to the company's name, address, phone and fax numbers, the category of collectibles that each company specializes in is also included. Collectors can find this listing helpful when inquiring about a firm's products and services.

Kurt S. Adler, Inc.
1107 Broadway
New York, NY 10010
(212) 924-0900
Fax: (212) 807-0575
Specialty: See article on page 53

Amaranth Productions
P.O. Box 3505
Huntington Beach, CA
92605-3505
(714) 841-9972
Fax: (714) 847-1090
Specialty: Dolls

Amazze Gifts
1030 Sunnyside Road
Vermilion, OH 44089
(800) 543-6759
Fax: (216) 967-519
Specialty: Stained glass cottages and landmark lighthouses

American Artists
66 Poppasquash Road
Bristol, RI 02809
(401) 254-1191
Fax: (401) 254-8881
Specialty: Equestrian lithos and plates

American Artist Portfolio, Inc.
9625 Tetley Drive
Somerset, VA 22972
(703) 672-0400
Fax: (703) 672-0286
Specialty: Graphics

American Greetings Corp.
One American Road
Cleveland, OH 44144
(216) 252-7300
Fax: (216) 252-6751
Specialty: Christmas ornaments and plates

Anheuser Busch, Inc.
2700 South Broadway
St. Louis, MO 63118
(800) 325-1154
Fax: (314) 577-9656
Specialty: See article on page 56

Anna-Perenna Inc.
35 River Street
New Rochelle, NY 10801
(914) 633-3777
Fax: (914) 633-8727
Specialty: Figurines, ornaments and plates

Annalee Mobilitee Dolls, Inc.
P.O. Box 1137
Meredith, NH 03253-1137
(800) 433-6557
Fax: (603) 279-6659
Specialty: See article on page 59

ANRI U.S.
P.O. Box 380760
1126 So. Cedar Ridge, Ste. 111
Duncanville, TX 75138
(800) 730-ANRI
Fax: (214) 283-3522
Specialty: See article on page 62

G. Armani Society/
Miller Import Corp.
300 Mac Lane
Keasbey, NJ 08832
(800) 3-ARMANI
Fax: (908) 417-0031
Specialty: See article on page 65

Artists of the World
2915 N. 67th Place
Scottsdale, AZ 85251
(602) 946-6361
Fax (602) 941-8918
Specialty: DeGrazia plates and figurines

The Ashton-Drake Galleries
9200 N. Maryland Avenue
Niles, IL 60714
(800) 634-5164
Fax: (708) 966-3026
Specialty: See article on page 68

Attic Babies
P.O. Box 912
Drumright, OK 74030
(918) 352-4414
Fax: (918) 352-4767
Specialty: See article on page 71

Autom
5226 S. 31st Place
Phoenix, AZ 85040
(602) 243-5200
Specialty: Figurines and ornaments

The B & J Company
P.O. Box 67
Georgetown, TX 78626
(512) 863-8318
Fax: (512) 863-0833
Specialty: Dolls, figurines, miniatures and plates

BAND Creations
28427 N. Ballard
Lake Forest, IL 60045
(800) 535-3242
Fax: (708) 816-3695
Specialty: See article on page 74

Marty Bell Fine Art
9314 Eton Avenue
Chatsworth, CA 91311
(800) 637-4537
Fax: (818) 709-7668
Specialty: Graphics

Belleek Collector International Society
9893 Georgetown Pike
Great Falls, VA 22066
(800) - BELLEEK
Fax: (703) 847-6201
Specialty: Belleek china and plates

Jody Bergsma Galleries
1344 King Street
Bellingham, WA 98226
(800) BERGSMA
Fax: (206) 647-2758
Specialty: Graphics and plates

Boehm Porcelain Studio
25 Fairfacts Street
Trenton, NJ 08638
(800) 257-9410
Fax: (609) 392-1437
Specialty: Dolls, figurines and plates

The Boyds Collection Ltd.
Somethin' Ta Say Dept.
Gettysburg, PA 17325-4385
Specialty: See article on page 80

Michael Boyett Studio
P.O. Box 632012
Nacogdoches, TX 75963
(409) 560-4477
Specialty: Figurines and graphics

The Bradford Exchange
9333 Milwaukee Avenue
Niles, IL 60714
(800) 323-5577
Specialty: See article on page 83

Bradley Doll
1400 N. Spring Street
Los Angeles, CA 90012
(213) 221-4162
Fax: (213) 221-8272
Specialty: Dolls

Brandywine Collectibles
104 Greene Dr.
Yorktown, VA 23692
(804) 898-5031
Fax: (804) 898-6895
Specialty: See article on page 86

Briant & Sons
5250 SW Tomahawk
Redmond, OR 97756
(503) 923-1473
Fax: (503) 923-7403
Specialty: Plate hangers and accessories

Buccellati Silver Ltd.
P.O. Box 360
East Longmeadow, MA 01028
(413) 525-4800
Fax: (413) 525-8877
Specialty: Ornaments

Byers' Choice Ltd.
P.O. Box 158
Chalfont, PA 18914
(215) 822-6700
Fax: (215) 822-3847
Specialty: See article on page 89

Rick Cain Studios
619 S. Main Street
Gainesville, FL 32601
(800) 535-3949
Fax: (904) 377-7038
Specialty: See article on page 92

Cairn Studio
P.O. Box 489
Davidson, NC 28036
(704) 892-3581
Specialty: Figurines

Caithness Glass Inc.
141 Lanza Avenue, Bldg. 12
Garfield, NJ 07026
(201) 340-3330
Fax: (201) 340-9415
Specialty: Glass paperweights

Calabar Creations
1941 S. Vineyard Avenue
Ontario, CA 91761
(909) 930-9978
Fax: (909) 930-9928
Specialty: See article on page 95

Cameo Guild Studios
5217 Verdugo Way, Suite D
Camarillo, CA 93012
(805) 388-1223
Specialty: California missions, miniatures and plates

L.M. Cape Craftsmen, Inc.
415 Peanut Road
Elizabethtown, NC 28337
(800) 262-5447
Fax: (949) 862-4611
Specialty: Figurines

Cardew Design
c/o Portmeirion USA
91 Great Hill Road
P.O. Box 5
Naugatuck, CT 06770
(203) 729-8255
Specialty: Teapots

Cast Art Industries, Inc.
1120 California Avenue
Corona, CA 91719
(800) 932-3020
Fax: (909) 270-2852
Specialty: See article on page 98

Cavanagh Group International
1000 Holcomb Woods Pkwy.
#440-B
Roswell, GA 30078
(800) 895-8100
Fax: (404) 643-1172
Specialty: See article on page 101

Cazenovia Abroad
67 Albany Street
Cazenovia, NY 13035
(315) 655-3433
Fax: (315) 655-4249
Specialty: Sterling silver figurines and ornaments

Chimera Studios
3708 E. Hubbard
Mineral Wells, TX 76067
(800) 843-4647
Specialty: Figurines

Christopher Radko
P.O. Box 238
Dobbs Ferry, NY 10522
(800) 71-RADKO
Fax: (914) 693-3770
Specialty: See article on page 104

Classic Collectables by
Uniquely Yours
P.O. Box 16861
Philadelphia, PA 19142
(610) 586-6266
Fax: (610) 522-2259
Specialty: See article on page 107

Clay Art
239 Utah Avenue
So. San Francisco, CA 94080
(415) 244-4970
Fax: (415) 244-4979
Specialty: Masks

Sandy Clough Studio
25 Trail Road
Marietta, GA 30064-1535
(404) 428-9406
Specialty: Limited edition prints

The Constance Collection
Rt.1, Box 538
Midland, VA 22728
(703) 788-4500
Fax: (703) 788-4100
Specialty: Figurines

M. Cornell Importers, Inc.
1462-18th St. N.W.
St. Paul, MN 55112
(612) 633-8690
Fax: (612) 636-3568
Specialty: Steins and teapots

Country Artists USA
9515 Gerwig Lane, Ste. 112
Columbia, MD 21046
(410) 290-8990
Fax: (410) 290-5480
Specialty: Figurines

Creart
209 E. Ben White, Suite 103
Austin, TX 78704
(800) 343-1505
Fax: (512) 707-9918
Specialty: See article on page 110

Cross Gallery, Inc.
180 N. Center
(Mail: P.O. Box 4181)
Jackson Hole, WY 83001
(307) 733-2200
Fax: (307) 733-1414
Specialty: Graphics, ornaments and plates

Crystal World
3 Borinski Road, Suite B
Lincoln Park, NJ 07035
(201) 633-0707
Specialty: Crystal figurines

Cybis
65 Norman Avenue
Trenton, NJ 08618
(609) 392-6074
Specialty: Figurines and ornaments

Daddy's Long Legs
c/o KVK INC.
300 Bank Street
Southlake, TX 76092
(817) 488-4644
Specialty: Dolls

Andrew D. Darvas Inc.
2165 Dwight Way
Berkeley, CA 94704
(510) 843-7838
Fax: (510) 843-1815
Specialty: Bossoms characters and wall masks

Department 56, Inc.
P.O. Box 44456
Eden Prairie, MN 55344-1456
(800) 548-8696
Specialty: See article on page 113

The Walt Disney Company
500 South Buena Vista Street
Burbank, CA 91521-6876
(800) WD-CLSIX
Specialty: See article on page 116

Donjo Studios Inc.
31149 Via Colinas Suite 609
Westlake Village, CA 91362
(818) 865-2390
Fax: (818) 865-0996
Specialty: Crystal figurines and miniatures

Dram Tree/C.U.I.
1502 N. 23rd Street
Wilmington, NC 28405
(910) 251-1110
Specialty: Steins

Duncan Royale
1141 S. Acacia Avenue
Fullerton, CA 92631
(714) 879-1360
Fax: (714) 879-4611
Specialty: See article on page 119

Ebeling & Reuss Co.
P.O. Box 1289
Allentown, PA 18105-1289
(610) 366-8304
Fax: (610) 366-8307
Specialty: Figurines and teacups

Egg Fantasy
4040 Schiff Drive
Las Vegas, NV 89103
(702) 368-7747
Specialty: Egg creations

eggspressions! inc.
1635 Deadwood Avenue
Rapid City, SD 57702
(800) 551-9138
Fax: (605) 342-8699
Specialty: See article on page 122

Eklund's Ltd.
1701 W. St. Germain
St. Cloud, MN 56301
(612) 252-1318
Specialty: Plates; horse and wildlife

Enesco Corporation
225 Windsor Drive
Itasca, IL 60143
(708) 875-5300
Specialty: See article on page 125

Federica Doll Company
4501 W. Highland Road
Milford, MI 48380
(810) 887-9575
Fax: (810) 887-9575
Specialty: Dolls

The Fenton Art Glass Company
700 Elizabeth Street
Williamstown, WV 26187
(304) 375-6122
Fax: (304) 375-6459
Specialty: See article on page 131

Figaro Import Corporation
325 South Flores Street
San Antonio, TX 78204-1178
(210) 225-1167
Specialty: Figurines

Figi Graphics
3636 Gateway Center
San Diego, CA 92102
(619) 262-8811
Fax: (619) 264-7781
Specialty: Figurines

FJ Designs, Inc.
Makers of Cat's Meow Village
2163 Great Trails Drive
Wooster, OH 44691-3738
(216) 264-1377
Fax: (216) 263-0219
Specialty: See article on page 128

Flambro Imports
1530 Ellsworth Industrial Dr.
Atlanta, GA 30318
(404) 352-1381
Fax: (404) 352-2150
Specialty: See article on page 134

Forma Vitrum
20414 N. Main Street
Cornelius, NC 28031
(800) 596-9963
Fax: (704) 892-5438
Specialty: See article on page 137

The Franklin Mint
Franklin Center, PA 19091
(800) 225-5836
Fax: (610) 459-6880
Specialty: See article on page 140

Fraser International
5990 N. Belt East, Unit 606
Humble, TX 77396
(800) 878-5448
Fax: (713) 441-7707
Specialty: See article on page 143

Margaret Furlong Designs
210 State Street
Salem, OR 97301
(503) 363-6004
Fax: (503) 371-0676
Specialty: See article on page 146

Ganz
908 Niagara Falls Blvd.
North Tonawanda, NY 14120-2060
(800) 724-5902
Fax: (905) 851-6669
Specialty: See article on page 149

Michael Garman Productions, Inc.
2418 W. Colorado Avenue
Colorado Springs, CO 80904
(800) 874-7144
Fax: (719) 471-3659
Specialty: Figurines

Gartlan USA
One Greentree Centre, Ste. 201
Marlton, NJ 08053
(609) 988-5466
Fax: (609) 596-8359
Specialty: Figurines and plates

Georgetown Collection
P.O. Box 9730
Portland, ME 04104
(800) 626-3330
Fax: (207) 775-6457
Specialty: See article on page 152

Goebel of North America
Goebel Plaza
P.O. Box 10, Rte. 31
Pennington, NJ 08534-0010
(609) 737-8700
Fax: (609) 737-1545
Specialty: See article on page 155

Good-Krüger Dolls
1842 William Penn Way, Ste.A
Lancaster, PA 17601
(717) 399-3602
Specialty: Dolls

Great American Doll Co.
438 E. Katella Avenue #226
Orange, CA 92667
(800) VIP-DOLL
Specialty: Dolls

Great American Taylor Collectilbles Corp.
Dept. BIC, P.O. Box 428
Aberdeen, NC 28315
(910) 944-7447
Fax: (910) 944-7449
Specialty: See article on page 158

The Greenwich Workshop
One Greenwich Place
Shelton, CT 06484
(800) 243-4246
Fax: (203) 925-0262
Specialty: See article on page 161

Dave Grossman Creations
1608 N. Warson Road
St. Louis, MO 63132
(800) 325-1655
Fax: (314) 423-7620
Specialty: Figurines and plates

Gund Inc.
1 Runyons Lane, P.O. Box H
Edison, NJ 08818
(908) 248-1500
Specialty: Bears; stuffed toys

H & G Studios Inc.
5660 Corporate Way
West Palm Beach, FL 33407
(407) 615-9900
Fax: (407) 615-8400
Specialty: Decorative and music boxes, graphics and plates

Hadley House
11001 Hampshire Avenue S.
Bloomington, MN 55438
(800) 927-0880
Fax: (612) 943-8098
Specialty: Cottages, graphics, ornaments, plates, steins

Jan Hagara Collectables, Inc.
40114 Industrial Park Circle
Georgetown, TX 78626
(512) 863-3072
Fax: (512) 869-2093
Specialty: Dolls, miniature figurines and plates

Hallmark Cards, Inc.
Keepsake Ornament Collectors Club #161
P.O. Box 412734
Kansas City, MO 64141-2734
Specialty: See article on page 164

The Hamilton Collection
4810 Executive Park Court
Jacksonville, FL 32216-6069
(800) 228-2945
Specialty: See article on page 167

Hand & Hammer Silversmiths
2610 Morse Lane
Woodbridge, VA 22192
(800) SILVERY
Fax: (703) 491-2031
Specialty: See article on page 170

Harbour Lights
8130 La Mesa Blvd.
La Mesa, CA 91941
(619) 579-1820
Fax: (619) 579-1911
Specialty: See article on page 173

Harmony Kingdom
225 Fifth Avenue, Suite 623
New York, NY 10010
(800) 318-3815
Fax: (212) 684-3686
Specialty: Figurines/ collectible box

Hawthorne Architectural Register
9210 N. Maryland Avenue
Niles, IL 60714
(800) 772-4277 customer service
(800) 327-0327 ordering
Specialty: See article on page 176

Heirloom Editions Ltd.
25100-B So. Normandie Ave.
Harbor City, CA 90710
(310) 539-5587
Fax: (310) 539-8891
Specialty: Bells, Staffordshire dogs & teapots, and thimbles

Heirloom Ltd.
4330 Margaret Circle
Mound, MN 55364
(612) 474-2402
Specialty: Dolls and lithos

The Heritage Collections, Ltd.
6647 Kerns Road
Falls Church, VA 22042-4231
(703) 533-7800
Fax: (703) 533-7801
Specialty: Music boxes, ornaments, paperweights

Edna Hibel Studio
P.O. Box 9967
Riviera Beach, FL 33419
(407) 848-9633
Fax: (407) 848-9640
Specialty: Bells, crystal, dolls, figurines, graphics (original lithographs and serigraphs, limited edition reproductions), ornaments and plates

Mark Hopkins Sculptures
21 Shorter Industrial Blvd.
Rome, GA 30165-1838
(800) 678-6564
Fax: (706) 235-2814
Specialty: Sculptures

M.I. Hummel Club
Division of Goebel Art GmbH,
Goebel Plaza
P.O. Box 11
Pennington, NJ 08534-0011
(800) 666-2582
Fax: (609) 737-1545
Specialty: See article on page 179

Incolay Studios Inc.
445 N. Fox Street
San Fernando, CA 91340
(818) 365-2521
Specialty: Plates

Iris Arc Crystal
114 East Haley Street
Santa Barbara, CA 93101
(805) 963-3661
Fax: (805) 965-2458
Specialty: Crystal and figurines

Janco Studio
P.O. Box 30012
Lincoln, NE 68503
(800) 490-1430
Fax: (402) 435-1430
Specialty: Figurines, miniatures and ornaments

Kaiser Porcelain (US)
2045 Niagara Falls Blvd.
Niagara Falls, NY 14304
(800) 287-0077
Fax: (716) 297-2749
Specialty: Figurines and plates

Mark Klaus LTD
P.O. Box 470758
Broadview Heights, OH 44147-0758
(216) 582-5003
Specialty: Figurines

Ladie and Friends, Inc.
220 North Main Street
Sellersville, PA 18960
(800) 76DOLLS
Fax: (215) 453-8155
Specialty: See article on page 182

Lalique
400 Veterans Blvd.
Carlstadt, NJ 07072
(800) CRISTAL
Specialty: Crystal and plates

The Lance Corporation
321 Central Street
Hudson, MA 01749
(508) 568-1401
Fax: (508) 568-8741
Specialty: See article on page 185

The Lawton Doll Company
548 North First
Turlock, CA 95380
(209) 632-3655
Fax: (209) 632-6788
Specialty: See article on page 188

Ron Lee's World of Clowns
330 Carousel Pkwy.
Henderson, NV 89014
(800) 829-3928
Fax: (702) 434-4310
Specialty: See article on page 191

George Z. Lefton Co.
3622 S. Morgan St.
Chicago, IL 60609
(800) 628-8492
Specialty: See article on page 194

Legacy Works
4020 Will Rogers Parkway, Suite 700
Oklahoma City, OK 73108
(800) 460-3661
Fax: (405) 948-1784
Specialty: Figurines

Legends
2665D Park Center Drive
Simi Valley, CA 93065
(800) 726-9660
Fax: (805) 520-9670
Specialty: See article on page 197

Lemax, Inc.
25 Pequot Way
Canton, MA 02021
(617) 821-4555
Fax: (617) 821-4455
Specialty: Christmas village collectibles and accessories

Lenox Collections
1170 Wheeler Way
Langhorne, PA 19047
(800) 225-1779
Fax: (215) 750-7362
Specialty: See article on page 200

Lilliput Lane
P.O. Box 665
Elk Grove Village, IL 60009-0665
(800) 545-5478
Specialty: See article on page 203

Lladro Society
1 Lladro Drive
Moonachie, NJ 07074
(800) 634-9088
Fax: (201) 807-1168
Specialty: See article on page 206

Lynette Decor Products
1559 W. Embassy Street
Anaheim, CA 92802
(800) 223-8623
Fax: (714) 956-0653
Specialty: Collectible displays and accessories

Magus Fine Arts & Collectibles, Inc.
9437 Kilimanjaro Rd.
Columbia, MD 21045
(301) 596-6156
Specialty: Dolls

Seymour Mann, Inc.
225 Fifth Avenue
Showroom #102
New York, NY 10010
(212) 683-7262
Fax: (212) 213-4920
Specialty: See article on page 209

M C K Gifts Inc.
P.O. Box 621848
Littleton, CO 80162-1814
(303) 789-9394
Specialty: Figurines

Marty Sculpture, Inc.
P.O. Box 15067
Wilmington, NC 28408
(800) 654-0478
Specialty: Figurines

Maruri, U.S.A.
7541 Woodman Place
Van Nuys, CA 91405
(800) 5-MARURI
Fax: (818) 780-9871
Specialty: See article on page 212

June McKenna Collectibles, Inc.
P.O. Box 846
Ashland, VA 23005
(804) 798-2024
Fax: (804) 798-2618
Specialty: See article on page 215

Media Arts Group
Ten Almaden Blvd. 9th floor
San Jose, CA 95113
(800) 544-4890
Fax: (408) 947-4640
Specialty: See article on page 218

Michael's Limited
P.O. Box 217
Redmond, WA 98052-0217
(800) 835-0181
Fax: (206) 861-0608
Specialty: See article on page 221

Midwest of Cannon Falls
32057 64th Avenue
P.O. Box 20
Cannon Falls, MN 55009-0020
(800) 377-3335
Fax: (507) 263-7752
Specialty: See article on page 224

Miss Martha Originals, Inc.
P.O. Box 5038
Glencoe, AL 35905
(205) 492-0221
Fax: (205) 492-0261
Specialty: See article on page 227

The Moss Portfolio
1 Poplar Grove Lane
Mathews, VA 23109
(804) 725-7378
Specialty: Graphics

Munro Enterprises, Inc.
P.O. Box 200
Waterville, OH 43566
(419) 878-0034
Fax: (419) 878-2535
Specialty: Bronzes, figurines and graphics

My Friends and Me
P.O. Box 2274
Hudson, OH 44236
(216) 650-6157
Fax: (216) 650-2342
Specialty: See article on page 230

Napoleon
P.O. Box 860
Oakes, PA 19456
(610) 666-1650
Fax: (610) 666-1379
Specialty: Capidimonte figurines

New Masters Publishing Co., Inc.
2301 14th Street, Ste. 105
Gulfport, MS 39501
(601) 863-5145
Fax: (601) 863-5145
Specialty: Bronzes and graphics

No. American Bear Co.
401 North Wabash, Suite 500
Chicago, IL 60611
(312) 329-0020
Fax: (312) 329-1417
Specialty: Teddy Bears

Oldenburg Originals
W5061 Pheasant Valley Road
Waldo, WI 53093
(414) 528-7127
Fax: (414) 528-7127
Specialty: Limited edition and porcelain original dolls

Old World Christmas
P.O. Box 8000
Spokane, WA 99203
(509) 534-9000
Fax: (509) 534-9098
Specialty: See article on page 233

Olszewski Studios
355 N. Lantana, Suite 500
Camarillo, CA 93010
(805) 374-9990
Fax: (805) 484-4993
Specialty: Miniature figurines

Opa's Haus, Inc.
1600 River Road
New Braunfels, TX 78132
(210) 629-1191
Fax: (210) 629-0153
Specialty: Steins

Orrefors of Sweden
140 Bradford Drive
Berlin, NJ 08009
(609) 768-5400
Fax: (609) 768-9726
Specialty: Figurines and ornaments

Pacific Rim Import Corp.
5390 4th Avenue South
Seattle, WA 98108
(800) 425-5932
Fax: (206) 767-9179
Specialty: See article on page 236

Past Impressions
P.O. Box 188
Belvedere, CA 94920
(415) 358-9075
Fax: (415) 358-8676
Specialty: Graphics

PenDelfin Studios
c/o Miller Import Corp.
300 Mac Lane
Keasbey, NJ 08832
(800) 547-2006
Fax: (908) 417-0031
Specialty: See article on page 239

Penni Jo's Originals Ltd.
1413 N.E. Lincoln Ave.
Moore, OK 73160
(405) 799-0006
Specialty: Pennibears, miniature figurines and plates

Pickard Inc.
782 Pickard Ave.
Antioch, IL 60002
(708) 395-3800
Specialty: Plates

Polland Studios
P.O. Box 1146
Prescott, AZ 86301-1146
(520) 778-1900
Fax: (520) 778-4034
Specialty: Pewter figurines

Porsgrunds Porselaensfabrik
A/S – P.O. Box 100
N-3907 Porsgrunn/Norway
+4735550040
Fax: +4735559110
Specialty: Christmas plates

Porterfield's
5020 Yaple Avenue
Santa Barbara, CA 93111
(805) 964-1824
Fax: (805) 964-1862
Specialty: Plates

Possible Dreams
6 Perry Drive
Foxboro, MA 02035
(508) 543-6667
Fax: (508) 543-4255
Specialty: See article on page 242

Precious Art/Panton
110 E. Ellsworth Road
Ann Arbor, MI 48108
(313) 677-3510
Fax: (313) 677-3412
Specialty: See article on page 245

R.R. Creations
P.O. Box 8707
Pratt, KS 67124
(800) 779-3610
Fax: (316) 672-5850
Specialty: See article on page 248

Rawcliffe Corporation
155 Public Street
Providence, RI 02903
(800) 343-1811
Fax: (401) 751-8545
Specialty: See article on page 251

Reco International
150 Haven Avenue
Port Washington, NY 11050
(516) 767-2400
Fax: (516) 767-2409
Specialty: See article on page 254

Red Mill Mfg., Inc.
1023 Arbuckle Road
Summersville, WV 26651
(304) 872-5231
Fax: (304) 872-5234
Specialty: Character and wildlife figurines

Harold Rigsby Graphics
4108 Scottsville Rd.
Glasgow, KY 42141
(800) 892-4984
Specialty: Graphics

Roman, Inc.
555 Lawrence Avenue
Roselle, IL 60172-1599
(708) 529-3000
Fax: (708) 529-1121
Specialty: See article on page 257

Royal Copenhagen/
Bing & Grondahl
27 Holland Avenue
White Plains, NY 10603
(914) 428-8222
Fax: (914) 428-8251
Specialty: See artictle on page 77

Royal Doulton
701 Cottontail Lane
Somerset, NJ 08873
(800) 68-CHINA
Fax: (908) 356-9467
Specialty: See article on page 260

Royal Worcester
Severn Street
Worcester, England
(01905) 23221
Fax: (01905) 23601
Specialty: Figurines, ornaments and plates

Helen Sabatte Designs, Inc.
6041 Acacia Avenue
Oakland, CA 94618
(510) 653-4616
Fax: (510) 547-5806
Specialty: Figurines

Saint-Alexis Santons
P.O. Box 307
Searsport, ME 04974
(800) 829-0243
Fax: (207) 548-0244
Specialty: Figurines and villages

Salvino, Inc.
1379 Pico Street, Ste. 103
Corona, CA 91719
(909) 273-7850
Fax: (909) 279-3409
Specialty: Sports figurines

Sandicast, Inc.
8480 Miralani Drive
San Diego, CA 92126
(800) 722-3316
Fax: (619) 695-061
Specialty: Cast stone animal figurines

Sarah's Attic
126-1/2 West Broad
P.O. Box 448
Chesaning, MI 48616
(800) 4-FRIEND
Fax: (517) 845-3477
Specialty: See article on page 263

Schmid
55 Pacella Park Drive
Randolph, MA 02368-1795
(617) 961-3000
Fax: (617) 961-4355
Specialty: See article on page 266

Sculpture Workshop Designs
510 School Rd. P.O. Box 420
Blue Bell, PA 19422
(215) 643-7447
Fax: (215) 643-7447
Specialty: Sterling silver ornaments

Second Nature Design
110 S. Southgate Bldg. C-4, #2
Chandler, AZ 85226
(602) 961-3963
Specialty: Figurines

Shade Tree Creations
6210 NW 124th Place
Gainesville, FL 32653
(904) 462-1830
Fax: (904) 462-1799
Specialty: Figurines

Shelia's Inc.
P.O. Box 31028
Charleston, SC 29417
(800) 227-6564
Fax: (803) 556-0040
Specialty: See article on page 269

Shenandoah Designs International
P.O. Box 911
Rural Retreat, VA 24368
(800) 338-7644
Specialty: Figurines

Silver Deer Ltd.
963 Transport Way
Petaluma, CA 94954
(800) 729-3337
Fax: (303) 449-0653
Specialty: Figurines

Spencer Collin Lighthouses
2 Government Street
Kittery, ME 03904
(207) 439-6016
Fax: (204) 439-5787
Specialty: Lighthouses

Steiff USA
200 Fifth Avenue Ste. 1205
New York, NY 10010
(212) 675-2727
Fax: 212 779-2594
Specialty: Plush bears

Studio Collection
69 Thomas Lane
Falmouth, MA 02540
(800) 314-7748
Fax: (508) 548-8829
Specialty: Figurines and ornaments

Swarovski America Limited
2 Slater Road
Cranston, RI 02920
(800) 426-3088
Fax: (401) 463-8459
Specialty: See article on page 272

Sylvestri Sales
225 Fifth Avenue, Room 120
New York, NY 10010
(212) 684-1870
Fax: (212) 684-3207
Specialty: Figurines and ornaments

Talsco of Florida
5427 Crafts Street
New Port Richey, FL 34652
(813) 847-6370
Fax: (813) 847-6786
Specialty: Collectible accessories, glass displays and plate frames

Jack Terry Fine Art Publishing
25251 Freedom Trail
Kerrville, TX 78028
(210) 367-4242
Fax: (210) 367-4243
Specialty: Limited edition prints and sculptures

Texas Stamps
P.O. Box 42388
Houston, TX 77242-2388
(800) 779-4100
Fax: (713) 266-7706
Specialty: Stamps-individual and collections

Angela Trotta Thomas
1107 E. Longwood Drive
Clarks Summit, PA 18411
(717) 586-0774
Fax: (717) 586-0774
Specialty: Nostalgic water color painting

Timeless Creations
333 Continental Blvd.
El Segundo, CA 90245-5012
(310) 524-2000
Specialty: Dolls

Today's Creations, Inc.
167 Main Street
Lodi, NJ 07644
(800) 5-TODAYS
Fax: (201) 472-4793
Specialty: See article on page 275

Towle Silversmiths
144 Addison Street
Boston, MA 02128
(617) 568-1300
Fax: (617) 568-9185
Specialty: Bells and ornaments

The Tudor Mint
P.O. Box 431729
Houston, TX 77243-1729
(713) 462-0076
Fax: (713) 462-0170
Specialty: See article on page 278

Glynda Turley Prints, Inc.
P.O. Box 112
Heber Springs, AR 72543
(800) 633-7931
Fax: (501) 362-5020
Specialty: Prints

United Design
P.O. Box 1200
Noble, OK 73068
(800) 527-4883
Fax: (405) 360-4442
Specialty: See article on page 281

Vaillancourt Folk Art
145 Armsby Road
Sutton, MA 01590
(508) 865-9183
Fax: (508) 865-4140
Specialty: Figurines

Bill Vernon Studios
6210 NW 124th Place
Gainesville, FL 32653
(904) 462-1830
Fax: (904) 462-1799
Specialty: Figurines

VF Fine Arts
11191 Westheimer #202
Houston, TX 77042
(713) 461-1944
Specialty: Graphics

VickiLane
3233 NE Cadet Avenue
Portland, OR 97220
(800) 678-4254
Fax: (503) 251-5916
Specialty: See article on page 284

Viking Import House
690 NE 13th Street
Ft. Lauderdale, FL 33304
(800) 327-2297
Specialty: Bells, dolls, figurines, ornaments, plates and steins

Viletta China Company
10130 Mula Road
Stafford, TX 77477
(713) 564-2400
Fax: (713) 564-3882
Specialty: Plates

WACO Products Corp.
I-80 & New Maple Avenue
P.O. Box 898
Pine Brook, NJ 07058-0898
(201) 882-1820
Fax: (201) 882-3661
Specialty: See article on page 287

The Susan Wakeen Doll Company
425 Bantam Road
P.O. Box 1321
Litchfield, CT 06759
(203) 567-0007
Fax: (203) 567-4636
Specialty: Dolls

Wallace Silversmiths
175 McClellan Highway
E. Boston, MA 02128-9114
(617) 561-2200
Fax: (617) 568-9185
Specialty: Bells and ornaments

Waterford Crystal
1330 Campus Parkway
Wall, NJ 07719
(908) 938-5800
Specialty: Crystal

Wedgwood
1330 Campus Parkway
Wall, NJ 07719
(908) 938-5800
Specialty: Ornaments and plates

Wild Wings
South Highway 61
Lake City, MN 55041
(800) 445-4833
Specialty: Plates and prints

Willitts Designs
1129 Industrial Avenue
Petaluma, CA 94952
(800) 358-9184
Fax: (707) 769-0304
Specialty: Figurines, graphics, ornaments and plates

W.T. Wilson Limited Editions
185 York Avenue
Pawtucket, RI 02860
(800) 722-0485
Specialty: Bells and figurines

The Wimbledon Collection
P.O. Box 21948
Lexington, KY 40522
(606) 277-8531
Fax: (606)277-9231
Specialty: See article on page 290

Windstone Editions
13012 Saticoy Street #3
North Hollywood, CA 91605
(800) 982-4464
Fax: (818) 982-4674
Specialty: Castles, dinosaur, fantasy and gargoyle figurines

Winston Roland Ltd.
1909 Oxford Street E.
Unit 17
London, Ont. CAN N5V 2Z7
(519) 659-6601
Fax: (519) 659-2923
Specialty: Graphics and plates

R. John Wright Dolls
15 West Main Street
Cambridge, NY 12816
(518) 677-8566
Specialty: Bears and dolls

Donald Zolan Studio
29 Cambridge Drive
Hershey, PA 17033
(717) 534-2446
Specialty: Bells and plates

Johannes Zook Originals
P.O. Box 256
Midland, MI 48640
(517) 835-9388
Specialty: Dolls

NALED

National Association of Limited Edition Dealers

Formed in 1976, NALED is a national group of retail and wholesale merchants who are in the specialized market of selling limited edition collectibles. The National Headquarters for NALED is located at 5235 Monticello Street, Dallas, Texas 75206, (800) HI-NALED.

ALABAMA
COLLECTIBLE COTTAGE, Gardendale, AL, 205-631-2413
COLLECTIBLE COTTAGE, Birmingham, AL, 205-988-8551
MARGO COLLECTIBLES, Cullman, AL, 205-734-1452
OLD COUNTRY STORE, Gadsen, AL, 205-492-7659
OLDE POST OFFICE, Trussville, AL, 205-655-7292
TOMORROW'S TREASURES, Birmingham, AL, 205-838-1887
TRADITIONS GIFT SHOP, Albertville AL, 205-891-2903

ARIZONA
ANNIE'S HALLMARK, Tucson, AZ, 602-790-7430
ARTISAN COLLECTORS GALLERY, THE, Mesa, AZ, 602-833-0495
BONA'S CHRISTMAS ETC, Tucson, AZ, 602-885-3755
FOX'S GIFTS & COLLECTABLES, Scottsdale, AZ, 602-947-0560
LAWTON'S GIFTS & COLLECTIBLES, Chandler, AZ, 602-899-7977
MARYLYN'S COLLECTIBLES, Tucson, AZ, 602-293-4603
MILLIE'S HALLMARK, Phoenix AZ, 602-893-3777
RUTH'S HALLMARK SHOP, Cottonwood, AZ, 602-634-8050

CALIFORNIA
ALLOVIO GALLERY, THE, Roseville, CA, 916-782-5330
BLEVINS PLATES 'N THINGS, Vallejo, CA, 707-642-7505
BUNNY HUTCH, THE, Fair Oaks, CA, 916-967-7044
CAMEO GIFTS & COLLECTIBLES, Temecula, CA, 909-676-1635
CAPRICE, Northridge, CA, 818-363-0796
CARDTOWNE HALLMARK, Garden Grove, CA, 714-537-5240
CAROL'S GIFT SHOP *, Artesia, CA, 310-924-6335
COLLECTIBLE CORNER, Placentia, CA, 714-528-3079
COLLECTIBLES UNLIMITED, Woodland Hills, CA, 818-703-6173
COLLECTOR'S WORLD, Montrose, CA, 818-248-9451
CRYSTAL AERIE, Fremont, CA, 510-791-0298
DANA DRUG STORE, Burbank, CA, 818-562-1177
DODIE'S FINE GIFTS & COLLECTIBLES, Woodland, CA, 916-668-1909
DOLLS GIFTS & MORE, Danville, CA, 510-831-8981
DOLLS GIFTS & MORE, San Ramon, CA, 510-830-9546
EASTERN ART, Victorville, CA, 619-241-0166
EASTLAND HALLMARK & STATIONERS, Ojai, CA, 805-646-8963
ENCORE CARDS & GIFTS, Cypress, CA, 714-761-1266
EVA MARIE DRY GROCER, Redondo Beach, CA, 310-375-8422
FRAME GALLERY, THE, Chula Vista, CA, 619-422-1700
FRAN'S HALLMARK, Red Bluff, CA, 916-527-6789
FRIENDS COLLECTIBLES, Canyon Country, CA, 805-298-2232
GALLERIA GIFTS, Reedley, CA, 209-638-4060
GALLERY DECOR, Arcadia, CA, 818-445-7679
GIFT GALLERY NORTHRIDGE PHARMACY, Northridge, CA, 818-349-7000
HEIRLOOMS OF TOMORROW, Fullerton, CA, 714-525-1522
HIDDEN COTTAGE, THE, Simi Valley, CA, 805-584-2252
KENNEDY'S COLLECTIBLES & GIFTS, Sacramento, CA, 916-973-8754
LENA'S GIFT GALLERY *, San Mateo, CA, 415-342-1304
LESLIE'S HALLMARK SHOP, Ventura, CA, 805-644-2331
LOUISE MARIE'S FINE GIFTS, Livermore, CA, 510-449-5757
MARGIE'S GIFTS & COLLECTIBLES, Torrance, CA, 310-378-2526
MARY ANN'S CARDS, GIFTS & COL, Yorba Linda, CA, 714-777-0999
MC CURRY'S HALLMARK, Citrus Heights, CA, 916-969-9452
MC CURRY'S HALLMARK, Sacramento, CA, 916-925-6485
MC CURRY'S HALLMARK, Sacramento, CA, 916-567-9952
MUSICAL MOMENTS & COLLECTIBLES, Shingle Spgs, CA, 916-677-2221
NORTHERN LIGHTS, San Rafael, CA, 415-457-2884
NYBORG CASTLE, Martinez, CA, 510-930-0200
P M COLLECTABLES, Cupertino, CA, 408-725-8858
PARDINI'S GIFTS & COLLECTIBLES, Stockton, CA, 209-957-2414
RUG RAT COLLECTABLES, Monterey, CA, 408-657-1055
RUMMEL'S VILLAGE GUILD, Montebello, CA, 213-722-2691
RYSTAD'S LIMITED EDITIONS, San Jose, CA, 408-279-1960
SUGARBUSH GIFT GALLERY, San Marcos, CA, 619-599-9945
SUTTER STREET EMPORIUM, Folsom, CA, 916-985-4647
TOMORROW'S TREASURES, Riverside, CA, 909-354-5731
VICTORIA'S COTTAGE, Newhall, CA, 805-287-9387
VILLAGE PEDDLER, La Habra, CA, 310-694-6111
WEE HOUSE FINE GIFTS & COLLECTIBLES, Irvine, CA, 714-552-3228
WILSON GALLERIES, Fresno, CA, 209-224-2223
WONDERLAND COLLECTIBLES, Fresno, CA, 209-435-1002

COLORADO
GIFT HOUSE, THE, Lakewood, CO, 303-922-7279
GRECO COLLECTIBLES, Aurora CO, 303-755-6048
KATHIE'S IMPORT CHALET, Englewood, CO, 303-761-1740
KENT COLLECTION, THE, Englewood, CO, 303-761-0059
KING'S GALLERY OF COLLECTABLES, Colorado Springs, CO, 719-636-2228
NOEL - THE CHRISTMAS SHOP, Vail, CO, 303-476-6544
PLATES ETC, Arvada, CO, 303-420-0752
QUALITY GIFTS & COLLECTIBLES, Colorado Springs, CO, 719-599-0051
SWISS MISS SHOP, Cascade, CO, 719-684-9679
TOBACCO LEAF, Lakewood, CO, 303-274-8720

CONNECTICUT
COLLECTIBLES, Hawleyville, CT, 203-790-1011
MAURICE NASSER *, New London, CT, 203-443-6523
NEW ENGLAND HOUSE OF COLLECTIBLES, Meriden, CT, 203-634-7509
PERIWINKLE, Vernon, CT, 203-872-2904
REVAY'S GARDENS & GIFT SHOP, East Windsor, CT, 203-623-9068
TAYLOR'D TOUCH, THE, Marlborough, CT, 203-295-9377
UTOPIA COLLECTABLES & FINE GIFTS, Oxford, CT, 203-888-0233
WINDSOR SHOPPE, North Haven, CT, 203-239-4644

DELAWARE
GIFT DESIGN GALLERIES, Dover, DE, 302-734-3002
HOBBY HOUSE OF GIFTS, Townsend, DE, 302-378-1408
PEREGOY'S GIFTS, Wilmington, DE, 302-999-1155
TULL BROTHERS, Seaford, DE, 302-629-3071
WASHINGTON SQUARE LIMITED, Newark, DE, 302-453-1776

FLORIDA
CARDS N' GIFTS GALORE, Daytona Beach, FL, 904-255-6624
CAROL'S HALLMARK SHOP, Tampa, FL, 813-960-8807
CHRISTMAS COLLECTION, Altamonte Springs, FL, 407-862-5383
CHRISTMAS PALACE, THE, Hialea Gardens, FL, 305-558-5352
CHRISTMAS SHOPPE, THE, Tallahassee, FL, 904-422-8990
CHRISTMAS SHOPPE, Miami, FL, 305-255-5414
CLASSIC CARGO, Destin, FL, 904-837-8171
CORNER GIFTS, Pembroke Pines, FL, 305-432-3739
ENTERTAINER, THE, Jacksonville, FL, 904-725-1166
GALLERY OF ANTIQUES & COLLECTIBLES, Jacksonville, FL, 904-783-6787
GIFT GALLERY, THE, Palm Harbor, FL, 813-786-1984
GIFTS UNLIMITED, Miami, FL, 305-253-0146
HEIRLOOM COLLECTIBLES, Clearwater FL, (813)797-8007
HEIRLOOMS OF TOMORROW, North Miami, FL, 305-899-0920
HUNT'S COLLECTIBLES, Satellite Beach, FL, 407-777-1313
JOHNSTONS HALLMARK, Tampa, FL, 813-968-2625
METHODIST FOUNDATION GIFT SHOPS, Jacksonville, FL, 904-798-8210
PAPER MOON, West Palm Beach, FL, 407-684-2668
PARK AVENUE GALLERY, Winter Park, FL, 407-644-1545
SUN ROSE GIFTS, Indian Harbor Beach, FL, 407-773-0550
VILLAGE PLATE COLLECTOR *, Cocoa, FL, 407-636-6914

GEORGIA
BECKY'S SMALL WONDERS, Helen, GA, 706-878-3108
CHAMBERHOUSE, Canton, GA, 404-479-9115
COTTAGE GARDEN, Macon, GA, 912-743-9897
CREATIVE GIFTS, Augusta, GA, 706-796-8794
GALLERY II, Atlanta, GA, 404-458-5858
GLASS ETC, Atlanta, GA, 404-493-7936
HEART OF COUNTRY, Fayetteville, GA, 404-460-0337
IMPRESSIONS, Brunswick, GA, 912-265-1624
MTN CHRISTMAS-MTN MEMORIES, Dahlonega, GA, 706-864-9115
PAM'S HALLMARK SHOP, Fayetteville, GA, 404-461-3041

PLUM TREE, Tucker, GA, 404-491-9433
SACKS ROUTE 1, Warm Springs, GA, 706-655-9093
SWAN GALLERIES, Stone Mountain, GA, 404-498-1324
WESSON'S, Helen, GA, 706-878-3544
WHIMSEY MANOR, Warner Robins, GA, 912-328-2500

HAWAII

OUR HOUSE COLLECTIBLE GIFT GALLERY, Honolulu, HI, 808-593-1999

IDAHO

CINNAMON TREE GIFT & COL. GALLERY, Pocatello, ID, 208-232-6371

ILLINOIS

BITS OF GOLD JEWELRY & GIFTS, Nashville, IL, 618-327-4261
C A JENSEN, LaSalle, IL, 815-223-0377
CHRYSLER BOUTIQUE, Effingham, IL, 217-342-4864
CLASS ACT, LAKE ZURICH, IL, 708-540-7700
COLLECTOR'S PARADISE, Monmouth, IL, 309-734-3690
CONTINENTAL GIFTS, Wheaton, IL, 708-653-3055
COUNTRY OAK COLLECTABLES, Schaumburg, IL, 708-529-0290
CROWN CARD & GIFT SHOP, Chicago, IL, 312-282-6771
DORIS COLLECTIBLES, St Peter, IL, 618-349-8780
EUROPEAN IMPORTS & GIFTS, Niles, IL, 708-967-5253
FINE & FANCY, Aurora, IL, 708-898-1130
GATZ COLLECTABLES, Wheeling, IL, 708-541-4033
GIFTIQUE OF LONG GROVE, Long Grove, IL, 708-634-9171
GLORY B!, Carthage, IL, 217-357-2599
GRIMM'S HALLMARK - WEST, St Charles, IL, 708-513-7008
GUZZARDO'S HALLMARK, Kewanee, IL, 309-852-5621
HALL JEWELERS & GIFTS LTD, Moweaqua, IL, 217-768-4990
HAWK HOLLOW, Galena, IL, 815-777-3616
HUMMEL KORNER & GIFTS, Wheeling, IL, 708-215-2908
JBJ THE COLLECTORS SHOP, Champaign, IL, 217-352-9610
KIEFER'S GALLERIES LTD, LaGrange, IL, 708-354-1888
KIEFER'S GALLERY OF C HILL, Plainfield, IL, 815-436-5444
KRIS KRINGLE HAUS, Geneva, IL, 708-208-0400
LYNN'S & COMPANY, Arlington Heights, IL, 708-870-1188
MAY HALLMARK SHOP, Woodridge, IL, 708-985-1008
MC HUGH'S GIFTS & COLLECTIBLES, Rock Island, IL, 309-788-9525
PAINTED PLATE LTD EDITION, O'Fallon IL, 618-624-6987
PEGGY'S HALLMARK SHOP, Bloomington, IL, 309-663-1977
PEGGY'S HALLMARK SHOP, Normal, IL, 309-452-5831
POTPOURRI CARD & GIFT, Bolingbrook, IL, 708-759-8222
POTPOURRI CARD & GIFT, Westchester, IL, 708-562-1440
RANDALL DRUG & GIFTS, Aurora, IL, 708-907-8700
ROYALE IMPORTS, Lisle, IL, 708-357-7002
RUTH'S HALLMARK, Bloomingdale, IL, 708-894-7890
SANDY'S DOLLS & COLLECTABLES INC, Palos Heights, IL, 708-423-0070
SOMETHING SO SPECIAL, Rockford, IL, 815-226-1331
STONE'S HALLMARK SHOPS, Rockford, IL, 815-399-4481
STRAWBERRY HOUSE, Libertyville, IL, 708-816-6129
STROHL'S LIMITED EDITIONS, Shelbyville, IL, 217-774-5222
TICK TOCK GIFT SHOP, Aurora, IL, 708-851-7767
TRICIA'S TREASURES, Fairview Hgts, IL, 618-624-6334
WHYDE'S HAUS, Canton, IL, 309-647-8823

INDIANA

ANGEL LIGHT, Mishawaka, IN, 219-256-9403
ART & CRAFT GALLERY, Corydon, IN, 812-738-4147
BEA'S HALLMARK, Indianapolis, IN, 317-888-8408
CARD & GIFT GALLERY, Indianapolis, IN, 317-783-1555
CAROL'S CRAFTS, Nashville, IN, 812-988-6388
CURIO SHOPPE, Greensburg, IN, 812-663-6914
DEARLY YOURS, Noblesville, IN, 317-773-3098
GIFT BOX, THE, Logansport, IN, 219-753-8442
HILBISH DRUG, La Porte, IN, 219-362-2247
JORGENSENS, Fort Wayne, IN, 219-432-5519
LANDMARK GIFTS & ANTIQUES, Kokomo, IN, 317-456-3488
LOUISE'S HALLMARK, St John, IN, 219-365-3837
NANA'S, Butler, IN, 219-868-5634
ROSE MARIE'S, Evansville, IN, 812-423-7557
ROSIE'S CARD & GIFT SHOP, Newburgh, IN, 812-853-3059
SMUCKER DRUGS, Middlebury, IN, 219-825-2485
TEMPTATIONS GIFTS, Valparaiso, IN, 219-462-1000
TOMORROW'S TREASURES, Muncie, IN, 317-284-6355
WALTER'S COLLECTIBLES, Princeton, IN, 812-386-3992
WATSON'S *, New Carlisle, IN, 219-654-8600

IOWA

COLLECTION CONNECTION, Des Moines, IA, 515-276-7766
DAVE & JANELLE'S, Mason City, IA, 515-423-6377
DAVIS COLLECTIBLES, Waterloo, IA, 319-232-0050
HAWK HOLLOW, Bellevue, IA, 319-872-5467
JAKOBSON DRUG & HALLMARK SHOP, Osage, IA, 515-732-5452
VAN DEN BERG'S, Pella, IA, 515-628-2533

KANSAS

CAROL'S DECOR, Salina, KS, 913-823-1739 Ext 186

KENTUCKY

ANN'S HALLMARK, Lexington, KY, 606-266-9101
ANN'S HALLMARK, Florence, KY, 606-342-7595
BETSY'S HALLMARK, Benton, KY, 502-527-1848
KAREN'S GIFTS, Louisville, KY, 502-425-3310
STORY BOOK KIDS, Florence, KY, 606-525-7743

LOUISANA

AD LIB GIFTS, Metairie, LA, 504-835-8755
GALILEAN, THE, Leesville, LA, 318-239-6248
LA TIENDA, Lafayette, LA, 318-984-5920
PARTRIDGE CHRISTMAS SHOPS, Covington, LA, 504-892-4477
PLATES AND THINGS, Baton Rouge, LA, 504-753-2885
PLUM TREE, Lake Charles, LA, 318-439-9526
PONTALBA COLLECTIBLES, New Orleans, LA, 504-524-8068
SANTA'S QUARTERS, New Orleans, LA, 504-581-5820

MAINE

CHRISTMAS SHOPPE, THE, East Holden, ME, 207-989-4887
GIMBEL & SONS COUNTRY STORE, Boothbay Harbor, ME, 207-633-5088
HERITAGE GIFTS, Oakland, ME, 207-465-3910

MARYLAND

BODZER'S COLLECTIBLES, Baltimore, MD, 410-931-9222
CALICO MOUSE, Glen Burnie, MD, 410-760-2757
CALICO MOUSE, Annapolis, MD, 410-266-7204
CALICO MOUSE, Annapolis, MD, 301-261-2441
CHERRY TREE CARDS & GIFTS, Laurel, MD, 301-498-8528
EDWARDS STORES, Ocean City, MD, 410-289-7000
ELLEN'S HALLMARK, Bel Air, MD, 410-838-0284
HANDS OF TIME CLOCKS & COLLECTIBLES, Savage, MD, 301-206-3281
KEEPSAKES & COLLECTIBLES, Owings Mill, MD, 410-356-3578
MUSIC BOX, THE, Baltimore, MD, 410-727-0444
PENN DEN, Bowie, MD, 301-262-2430
PRECIOUS GIFTS, Ellicott City, MD, 410-461-6813
TIARA GIFTS, Wheaton, MD, 301-949-0210
TOMORROW'S TREASURES, Bel Air, MD, 410-893-7965
WANG'S GIFTS & COLLECTIBLE, Bel Air, MD, 410-838-2626
WANG'S GIFTS & COLLECTIBLES, White Marsh, MD, 410-931-7388

MASSACHUSETTS

GIFT GALLERY, Webster, MA, 508-943-4402
HONEYCOMB GIFT SHOPPE, Wakefield, MA, 617-245-2448
KAY'S HALLMARK, Tewksbury, MA, 508-851-7790
LEONARD GALLERY, Springfield, MA, 413-733-9492
MERRY CHRISTMAS SHOPPE, Whitman, MA, 617-447-6677
PAPER STORE, THE, Bedford, MA, 617-275-3232
PAPER STORE, THE, Maynard, MA, 508-897-3338
SAVAS LIMITED, Hanson, MA, 617-294-0177
SHROPSHIRE CURIOSITY SHOP II, Shrewsbury, MA, 508-799-7200
SHROPSHIRE CURIOSITY SHOP II, Shrewsbury, MA, 508-842-5001
SHROPSHIRE CURIOSITY SHOP I, Shrewsbury, MA, 508-842-4202
STACY'S GIFTS & COLLECTIBLES, East Walpole, MA, 508-668-4212
WARD'S, Burlington, MA, 617-229-0068
WARD'S, Medford, MA, 617-395-4099
WAYSIDE COUNTRY STORE, Marlboro, MA, 508-481-3458

MICHIGAN

1/2 OFF CARD SHOP, Bay City, MI, 517-686-9820
1/2 OFF CARD SHOPS, Southfield, MI, 810-851-4358
1/2 OFF CARD SHOP, Taylor, MI, 313-374-2450
AFTER EFFECTS, Clinton Twp, MI, 810-791-2265
CARAVAN GIFTS & COLLECTIBLES, Fenton, MI, 810-629-4212
CINDY'S HALLMARK, Sturgis, MI, 616-651-1424
DEE'S HALLMARK, Clinton Twp, MI, 810-792-5510
DOLL LEE GIFTS & COLLECTIBLES, Roseville, MI, 810-771-4438
ELLE STEVENS JEWELERS, Ironwood, MI, 906-932-5679
ELSIE'S HALLMARK SHOP, Petoskey, MI, 616-347-5270
EMILY'S GIFTS, DOLLS, COLLECTIBLES, St Clair Shores, MI, 810-777-5250
FRITZ GIFTS & COLLECTIBLES, Monroe, MI, 313-241-6760
GEORGIA'S GIFT GALLERY, Plymouth, MI, 313-453-7733
HARPOLD'S, South Haven, MI, 616-637-3522
HOUSE OF CARDS & GIFTS, Sturgis, MI, 616-651-6011
HOUSE OF CARDS & COLLECTIBLES, Macomb, MI, 313-247-2000
JACQUELYNS GIFTS, Warren, MI, 810-296-9211
KEEPSAKE GIFTS, Kimball, MI, 810-985-5855
KNIBLOE GIFT CORNER, Jackson, MI, 517-782-6846
LAKEVIEW CARD & GIFT SHOP, Battle Creek, MI, 616-962-0650
MILLER'S UNIQUE GIFTS, Tecumseh, MI, 517-423-3848
MOMBER PHARMACY & GIFTS, Sparta, MI, 616-887-7323
PEWTER CLASSICS, Grand Rapids, MI, 616-942-8822
PINOCCHIO'S INC, Frankenmuth, MI, 517-652-2751
PLATE LADY, Livonia, MI, 313-261-5220
ROBINETTE'S GIFT BARN, Grand Rapids, MI, 616-361-7180
SCHULTZ GIFT GALLERY, Pinconning, MI, 517-879-3110
SPECIAL THINGS, Sterling Heights, MI, 810-739-4030
TOUCH OF COUNTRY, Howell, MI, 517-546-5995
TROY STAMP & COIN EXCHANGE, Troy, MI, 810-528-1181
VEENA'S CARDS & COLLECTIBLES, Farmington Hills, MI, 810-489-4060

MINNESOTA
ANDERSEN HALLMARK, Albert Lea, MN, 507-373-0996
BJORNSON IMPORTS, Mound, MN, 612-474-3957
COLLECTIBLES SHOWCASE, Bloomington, MN, 612-854-1553
GUSTAF'S, Lindstrom, MN, 612-257-6688
HELGA'S HALLMARK, Cambridge, MN, 612-689-5000
HUNT HALLMARK CARD & GIFT, Rochester, MN, 507-289-5152
HUNT SILVER LAKE DRUG & GIFT, Rochester, MN, 507-289-0749
MARY D'S DOLLS & BEARS & SUCH, Minneapolis, MN, 612-424-4375
ODYSSEY, Rochester, MN, 507-288-6629
ODYSSEY, Mankato, MN, 507-388-2006
ODYSSEY GIFTS, Mankato, MN, 507-388-2004
SEEFELDT'S GALLERY, Roseville, MN, 612-631-1397

MISSOURI
DICKENS GIFT SHOPPE, Branson, MO, 417-334-2992
ELLY'S, Kimmswick, MO, 314-467-5019
EMILY'S HALLMARK, Chesterfield, MO, 314-391-8755
FIRST CAPITOL TRADING POST, St Charles, MO, 314-946-2883
HELEN'S GIFTS & ACCESSORIES, Rolla, MO, 314-341-2300
K C COLLECTIBLES & GIFTS, Kansas City, MO, 816-741-2448
OAK LEAF GIFTS, Osage Beach, MO, 314-348-0190
TOBACCO LANE, Cape Girardeau, MO, 314-651-3414
TRA-ART LTD, Jefferson City, MO, 314-635-8278
UNIQUE GIFT SHOPPE, Springfield, MO, 417-887-5476

MONTANA
TRADITIONS, Missoula, MT, 406-543-3177

NEBRASKA
L & L GIFTS, Fremont, NE, 402-727-7275
MANGELSEN'S, Omaha, NE, 402-339-3922
MARIANNE K FESTERSEN *, Omaha, NE, 402-393-4454
SHARRON SHOP, Omaha, NE, 402-393-8311
WOOD 'N DOLL, North Platte, NE, 308-534-3618

NEW HAMPSHIRE
STRAW CELLAR, THE, Wolfeboro, NH, 603-569-1516

NEW JERSEY
CHINA ROYALE INC, Englewood, NJ, 201-568-1005
CHRISTMAS CAROL, Flemington, NJ, 908-782-0700
CLASSIC COLLECTIONS, Livingston, NJ, 201-992-8605
COLLECTORS CELLAR, Pine Beach, NJ, 908-341-4107
COLLECTORS EMPORIUM, Secaucus, NJ, 201-863-2977
CRAFT EMPORIUM, Waldwick, NJ, 201-670-0022
EMJAY SHOP, Stone Harbor, NJ, 609-368-1227
EXTRA SPECIAL TOUCH INC, Pompton Lakes, NJ, 201-835-5441
GIFT CARAVAN, North Arlington, NJ, 201-997-1055
GIFT GALLERY, Paramus, NJ, 201-845-0940
GIFT GALLERY, Edison, NJ, 908-494-3939
GIFT WORLD, Maple Shade, NJ, 609-321-1500
J C'S HALLMARK, Old Bridge, NJ, 908-826-8208
JIANA INC, Union, NJ, 201-492-1728
KATIE'S KACHE, Red Bank, NJ, 908-576-1777
LA MAISON CAPRI, Atlantic City, NJ, 609-345-4305
LITTLE TREASURES, Rutherford, NJ, 201-460-9353
MEYER HOUSE GIFT SHOP, Newfoundland, NJ, 201-697-7122
MOLK BROTHERS, Elmwood Park, NJ, 201-796-8377
NOTES-A-PLENTY GIFT SHOPPE, Flemington, NJ, 908-782-0700
OAKWOOD CARD & GIFT SHOP, Edison, NJ, 908-549-9494
OLD WAGON GIFTS, Colts Neck, NJ, 908-780-6656
SOMEONE SPECIAL, Cherry Hill, NJ, 609-424-1914
SOMEONE SPECIAL, W Berlin, NJ, 609-768-7171
TOM'S GARDEN WORLD, McKee City, NJ, 609-641-4522
WESTON'S LIMITED EDITIONS, Eatontown, NJ, 908-935-0301
ZASLOW'S FINE COLLECTIBLES *, Matawan, NJ, 908-583-1499
ZASLOW'S FINE COLLECTIBLES, Middletown, NJ, 908-957-9560

NEW MEXICO
COVERED WAGON GIFTS & COLLECTIBLES, Rudioso, NM, 505-257-4591
LORRIE'S COLLECTIBLES, Albuquerque, NM, 505-292-0020

NEW YORK
ANDREW'S COLLECTIBLES, Buffalo, NY, 716-823-4131
ANN'S HALLMARK CARDS & GIFTS, Newburgh, NY, 914-564-5585
ANN'S HALLMARK SHOPPE, Newburgh, NY, 914-562-3149
CANAL TOWN COUNTRY STORE, Rochester, NY, 716-424-4120
CANAL TOWN COUNTRY STORE, Rochester, NY, 716-225-5070
CANAL TOWN COUNTRY STORE, Irondequoit, NY, 716-338-3670
CERAMICA GIFT GALLERY, New York, NY, 212-354-9216
CLASSIC GIFT GALLERY, Centereach, NY, 516-467-4813
CLIFTON PARK COUNTRY STORE, Clifton Park, NY, 518-371-0585
CLOCK MAN GALLERY, Poughkeepsie, NY, 914-473-9055
COLLECTIBLES, Poughkeepsie, NY, 914-298-0226
COLLECTIBLY YOURS, Spring Valley, NY, 914-425-9244
CORNER COLLECTIONS, Hunter, NY, 518-263-4141
COUNTRY GALLERY, Fishkill, NY, 914-897-2008
COW HARBOR FINE GIFTS & COLLECTIBLES, Northport, NY, 516-261-7907
CROWN SHOPPE, Rockville Centre, NY, 516-536-2712
CRYSTAL CAVE, THE, Woodhaven, NY, 718-441-0144
DAYDREAMS, Latham, NY, 518-783-7513
ELLIE'S LTD ED & COLLECTIBLES, Selden, NY, 516-698-3467
ELLIE'S LTD ED & COLLECTIBLES, Miller Place, NY, 516-698-3467
FLOWERS & MORE, Clarence, NY, 716-759-2988
FOREVER CHRISTMAS, Hyde Park, NY, 914-229-2969
GRANDMA'S COUNTRY CORNERS, Albany, NY, 518-459-1209
ISLAND TREASURES, Staten Island, NY, 718-698-1234
LIL' SUSIES KEEPSAKES & COLLECTIBLES, Shirley, NY, 516-281-9481
LIMITED COLLECTOR, Corning, NY, 607-936-6195
LIMITED EDITION, THE *, Merrick, NY, 516-623-4400
LYN GIFT SHOP, Lynbrook, NY, 516-593-6500
MARESA'S CANDELIGHT GIFT SHOPPE, Port Jefferson, NY, 516-331-6245
PAUL'S ECONOMY PHARMACY, Staten Island, NY, 718-442-2924
PLATE COTTAGE, St James, NY, 516-862-7171
PRECIOUS GIFT GALLERY, Levittown, NY, 516-579-3562
PREMIO, Massapequa, NY, 516-795-3050
SIX SIXTEEN GIFT SHOPS, Bellmore, NY, 516-221-5829
VILLAGE GIFT SHOP, Tonawanda, NY, 716-695-6589

NEVADA
CARLAN'S FINE GIFTS, Las Vegas, NV, 702-734-6003
JAN'S HALLMARK, Reno, NV, 702-825-2205
OOH'S AND AH'S, Las Vegas, NV, 702-870-2078

NORTH CAROLINA
AUNT EDYE'S COLLECTIBLES, Charlotte, NC, 704-545-2658
BUSH STATIONERS & GIFTS, Charlotte, NC, 704-333-4438
GIFT ATTIC, Raleigh, NC, 919-781-1822
GIFT ATTIC, Raleigh, NC, 919-781-1822
MC NAMARA'S *, Highlands, NC, 704-526-5551
OLDE WORLD CHRISTMAS SHOPPE, Asheville, NC, 704-274-4819
PLEASURES & TREASURES, Greensboro, NC, 910-855-1301
PLEASURES & TREASURES, High Point, NC, 910-855-1301
TINDER BOX, Charlotte, NC, 704-366-5164
TINDER BOX, Charlotte, NC, 704-568-8798
TINDER BOX, Pineville, NC, 704-542-6115
TINDER BOX OF WINSTON-SALEM, Winston-Salem, NC, 919-765-9511

NORTH DAKOTA
BJORNSON IMPORTS, Grand Forks, ND, 701-775-2618
FRAMEMAKER, Grand Forks, ND, 701-775-9675
JUNIQUE'S, Bismarck, ND, 701-258-3542

OHIO
ALADDIN LAMP, Lima, OH, 419-224-5612
ARTIST'S TOUCH, THE, New Bremen, OH, 419-629-3815
BELLFAIR COUNTRY STORES, Dayton, OH, 513-426-3921
BETTY'S HALLMARK, Twinsburg, OH, 216-425-1661
CABBAGES & KINGS, Grand Rapids, OH, 419-832-2709
CELLAR CACHE, Put-in-Bay, OH, 419-285-2738
CHRISTMAS TREASURE CHEST, Ashland, OH, 419-289-2831
COLLECTION CONNECTION, Piqua, OH, 513-778-9909
COLLECTOR'S GALLERY, Marion, OH, 614-387-0602
COLLECTOR'S OUTLET, Mentor On The Lake, OH, 216-257-1141
COMSTOCK'S COLLECTIBLES, Medina, OH, 216-725-4656
CURIO CABINET, Worthington, OH, 614-885-1986
EASTERN ART, Parma, OH, 216-888-6277
EMPORIUM, THE, Bucyrus, OH, 419-562-1943
EXCALIBUR GIFTS, Sandusky, OH, 419-626-3539
GIFT GARDEN, No Olmsted, OH, 216-777-0116
GINGERBREAD HOUSE GIFTS & COL, West Milton, OH, 513-698-3477
HIDDEN TREASURES, Huron, OH, 419-433-2585
HOUSE OF TRADITION, Perrysburg, OH, 419-874-1151
KATHRYN'S GALLERY OF GIFTS, Solon, OH, 216-498-0234
LAKE CABLE GIFTS & COLLECTIBLES, Canton, OH, 216-494-4173
LAKESHORE LTD, Huron, OH, 419-433-6168
LITTLE RED GIFT HOUSE, Birmingham, OH, 216-965-5420
LITTLE SHOP ON THE PORTAGE, Woodville, OH, 419-849-3742
LOLA & DALE GIFTS & COLLECTIBLES, Parma Heights, OH, 216-885-0444
MUSIK BOX HAUS, Vermilion, OH, 216-967-4744
NORTH HILL GIFT SHOP, Akron, OH, 216-535-4811
OLDE TYME CLOCKS, Cincinnati, OH, 513-741-9188
PORCELLANA LTD, Hamilton, OH, 513-868-1511
ROCHELLE'S FINE GIFTS, Toledo, OH, 419-472-7673
SAXONY IMPORTS, Cincinnati, OH, 513-621-7800
SCHUMM PHARMACY HALLMARK & GIFTS, Rockford, OH, 419-363-3630

SETTLER'S COLLECTIONS, Middlefield, OH, 216-632-1009
STORY BOOK KIDS, Cincinnati, OH, 513-769-5437
STRAWBERRY PATCH, Brunswick, OH, 216-225-7796
STRUBLES OF SHELBY, Shelby, OH, 419-342-2136
STUHLDREHER FLORAL CO, Mansfield, OH, 419-524-5911
TOWNE CENTRE SHOPPE, Streetsboro, OH, 216-626-3106
UP-TOWNE FLOWER & GIFT SHOPPE, Worthington, OH, 614-889-1001

OKLAHOMA

COLONIAL FLORISTS, Stillwater, OK, 405-372-9166
CURIOSITY SHOP, THE, Ada, OK, 405-332-5355
DODY'S HALLMARK, Lawton, OK, 405-353-8379
EARL'S JEWELERS, Cushing, OK, 918-225-1685
EMPORIUM - THE GIFT SHOPPE, THE, Ponca City, OK, 405-762-5345
NORTH POLE CITY, Oklahoma City, OK, 405-685-6635
PERFECT TOUCH, Tulsa, OK, 918-496-8118
SHIRLEY'S GIFTS, Ardmore, OK, 405-223-2116
SUZANNE'S COLLECTORS GALLERY *, Miami, OK, 918-542-3808
W D GIFTS, Okmulgee, OK, 918-756-2229

OREGON

CROWN SHOWCASE, Portland, OR, 503-280-0669
DAS HAUS-AM-BERG, Salem, OR, 503-363-0669
KESSEL'S COLLECTIBLES & GIFT SHOPPEE, Salem, OR, 503-362-5342
MANCKE'S COLLECTIBLES, Salem, OR, 503-371-3157
PRESENT PEDDLER, Beaverton, OR, 503-641-6364
TICKLED PINK, Portland, OR, 503-297-4102
TREASURE CHEST GIFT SHOP, Gresham, OR, 503-667-2999

PENNSYLVANIA

BOB'S CARDS & GIFTS, Southampton. PA, 215-364-2872
COLLECTOR'S CHOICE, Pittsburgh, PA, 412-366-4477
COLLECTOR'S MARKETPLACE, Montrose, PA, 717-278-4094
DEN, THE, Lahaska, PA, 215-794-8493
DIGBY'S SIDE DOOR, Mc Murray PA, 412-941-3750
DUTCH INDOOR VILLGE, Lancaster, PA, 717-299-2348
EMPORIUM COLLECTIBLES GALLERY, Erie, PA, 814-833-2895
EUROPEAN TREASURES, Pittsburgh, PA, 412-421-8660
GIFT DESIGN GALLERIES, Wilkes-Barre, PA, 717-822-6704
GIFT DESIGN GALLERIES, Whitehall, PA, 610-266-1266
GILLESPIE JEWELER COLLECTORS GALLERY *, Northampton, PA, 215-261-0882
GOLDCRAFTERS, Springfield, PA, 610-544-9521
JAMIE'S COLLECTABLES, Reading, PA, 610-373-4270
KRINGLE'S CHRISTMAS BARN & COTTAGE, Scotrun, PA, 717-629-3122
LAUCHNOR'S GIFTS & COLLECTABLES, Trexlertown, PA, 610-398-3008
LIMITED EDITIONS, Forty Fort, PA, 717-288-0940
LIMITED PLATES & COLLECTIBLES, Collegeville, PA, 610-489-7799
MARIE'S GIFT SHOP, Tafton, PA, 717-226-3345
MOLE HOLE OF PEDDLERS VILLAGE, THE, Lahaska, PA, 215-794-7572
NEWTOWN SQUARE GLASS & CHINA, Newtown Square, PA, 610-353-7726
PICCADILLY CENTRE, Duncansville, PA, 814-695-8383
SAVILLE'S LIMITED EDITIONS, Pittsburgh, PA, 412-366-5458
SHAKER TREE STUDIO, Hermitage, PA, 412-347-4141
SOMEONE SPECIAL, Bensalem, PA, 215-245-0919
SPECIAL ATTRACTIONS, Sayre, PA, 717-888-9433
THINGS COLLECTIBLE, Feasterville, PA, 215-355-4733
TODAY'S TREASURES, Pittsburgh, PA, 412-341-5233
WISHING WELL, Reading, PA, 610-921-2566
YEAGLE'S, Lahaska, PA, 215-794-7756

RHODE ISLAND

GOLDEN GOOSE, Smithfield, RI, 401-949-9940

SOUTH CAROLINA

ABRAMS DOLLS & COLLECTIBLES, Conway, SC, 803-248-9198
CHRISTMAS CELEBRATION, Greenville, SC, 803-242-1804
CHRISTMAS CELEBRATION, Mauldin, SC, 803-277-7373
CHRISTY'S CHRISTMAS, Cayce, SC, 803-794-5152
CURIOSITY SHOPPE, THE, Darlington, SC, 803-665-8686
DUANE'S HALLMARK CARD & GIFT SHOP, Columbia, SC, 803-772-2624
TINDER BOX, Myrtle Beach, SC, 803-272-2336
TINDER BOX, Myrtle Beach, SC, 803-626-2654

SOUTH DAKOTA

AKERS GIFTS & COLLECTIBLES, Sioux Falls, SD, 605-339-1325
GIFT GALLERY, Brookings, SD, 605-692-9405

TENNESSEE

CALICO BUTTERFLY, Memphis, TN, 901-362-8121
COX'S HALLMARK SHOP, Maryville, TN, 615-982-0421
GIFTS UNIQUE, Lenoir City, TN, 615-986-1211
HOUR GLASS II, Chattanooga, TN, 615-877-2328
ORANGE BLOSSOM, Martin, TN, 901-587-5091
PAPILLON INC, Chatanooga, TN, 615-499-2997
PATTY'S HALLMARK, Murfreesboro, TN, 615-890-8310
STAGE CROSSING GIFTS & COLLECTIBLES, Bartlett, TN, 901-372-4438

TEXAS

BETTY'S COLLECTABLES LTD *, Harlingen, TX, 210-423-8234
CHRISTMAS TREASURES, Baytown, TX, 713-421-1581
COLLECTIBLE HEIRLOOMS, Friendswood, TX, 713-486-5023
ELOISE'S COLLECTIBLES, Katy, TX, 713-578-6655
ELOISE'S COLLECTIBLES, Houston, TX, 713-783-3611
ELOISE'S GIFTS & ANTIQUES, Rockwall, TX, 214-771-6371
GALAXY HALLMARK SHOP, Houston, TX, 713-335-1211
GIFTS CARTOONS COLLECTIBLES, Hurst, TX, 817-590-0324
HOLIDAY HOUSE, Huntsville, TX, 409-295-7338
KEEPSAKES & KOLLECTIBLES, Spring, TX, 713-353-9233
LACEY'S HALLMARK, Pasadena, TX, 713-998-7171
LOUJON'S GIFTS, Sugar Land, TX, 713-980-1245
MR C COLLECTIBLE CENTER, Carrollton, TX, 214-242-5100
OPA'S HAUS, New Braunfels, TX, 210-629-1191
SHEPHERD'S SHOPPE, THE, San Antonio, TX, 210-342-4811
SUNSHINE HOUSE GALLERY, Plano, TX, 214-424-5015
TIMES & CHIMES, Friendswood, TX, 713-488-1574

UTAH

RIVERTON DRUG & GIFT, Riverton, UT, 801-254-7407

VIRGINIA

CREEKSIDE COLLECTIBLES & GIFTS, Winchester, VA, 703-662-0270
GAZEBO GIFTS, Newport News, VA, 804-591-8387
PLATE SHOPPE, THE, Alexandria, VA, 703-360-1708

WASHINGTON

CHALET, THE, Tacoma, WA, 206-564-0326
GOLD SHOPPE'S COLLECTORS GALLERY, Tacoma, WA, 206-473-4653
LORETTA'S GIFTS & COLLECTIBLES, Poulsbo, WA, 360-779-7171
NATALIA'S COLLECTIBLES, Woodinville, WA, 206-481-4575
SERENDIPITY GIFTS & COLLECTIBLES, Puyallup, WA, 206-770-1990
STEFAN'S EUROPEAN GIFTS, Yakima, WA, 509-457-5503
TANNENBAUM SHOPPE, Leavenworth, WA, 509-548-7014

WEST VIRGINIA

ARACOMA DRUG GIFT GALLERY, Logan, WV, 304-752-3812
FENTON GIFT SHOP, Williamstown, WV, 304-375-7772

WISCONSIN

A COUNTRY MOUSE, Milwaukee, WI, 414-281-4210
BEAUCHENE'S LTD ED, Thiensville, WI, 414-242-0170
CENTURY COIN SERVICE, Green Bay, WI, 414-494-2719
COLLECTIBLES ETC INC, Port Washington, WI, 414-355-4545
GREEN TREE GIFTS & COLLECTIBLES, Manitowoc, WI, 414-684-4300
JAN'S HALLMARK & GIFT GALLERY, Delavan, WI, 414-728-8447
JANE'S COUNTRY COLLECTIBLES, Random Lake, WI, 414-994-4747
KRISTMAS KRINGLE SHOPPE, Fond Du Lac, WI, 414-922-3900
P J'S COLLECTIBLES, Green Bay, WI, 414-437-3443
P J'S HALLMARK SHOP, Marinette, WI, 715-735-3940
SPIRIT OF CHRISTMAS, Mayville, WI, 414-387-4648
TIVOLI IMPORTS, Milwaukee, WI, 414-774-7590

INTERNATIONAL MEMBERS

AUSTRALIA

LIBERTY LANE, Sydney, NSW Aust, 011-61-2-261-3595

CANADA

BAKEROSA COLLECTIBLES & BOOKS, London, Ont CAN, 519-472-0827
CHORNYJS'-HADKE, Sault Ste Marie, Ont CAN, 705-253-0315
DURAND'S LTD ED, Calgary, Alberta CAN, 403-277-0008
OVER THE RAINBOW COLLECTABLES, Islington, Ont CAN, 416-622-6835
PLATEFINDERS, Edmonton, Alberta CAN, 403-435-3603
TOMORROW'S TREASURES, Bobcaygeon, Ont CAN, 705-738-2147

ENGLAND

CASTLE CHINA GROUP, Warwick, ENG, 44-1926-419102

CONVENTIONS AND SPECIAL EVENTS

A Look at the Exciting World of Collectibles

National Collector Conventions

The International Collectible Exposition is the world's premier showcase for the limited edition collectible industry. The show attracts collectors from around the country and features collectibles manufacturers from around the world.

Attending a national manufacturer-sponsored collectibles convention offers collectors the opportunity to enhance their collecting hobby. Several hundred attractive booths display exciting new products, and well-known artists are on hand to meet collectors and sign autographs. Collectors can attend informative seminars, participate in Swap 'n Sells and enjoy other fun-filled events.

The International Collectible Exposition holds two shows yearly. In spring of 1996 the Expo will be held at the Meadowlands Exposition Center in Secaucus, New Jersey. The show is open to retailers only on April 11-12, and to the public on April 13-14, 1996.

The summer International Collectible Exposition, traditionally held in South Bend, Indiana, will take place at the Rosemont Convention Center in Rosemont, Illinois. The show will be open to retailers only on June 27-28 and to the public on June 29-30, 1996. For more information, please contact McRand International, Ltd., Expositions, One Westminster Place, Lake Forest, IL 60045, (708) 295-4444.

The 3rd Annual Collectors' Jubilee, a "celebration of collection" is scheduled for April 26-28, 1996 at Expo Square in Tulsa, Oklahoma. The three-day event features manufacturers, artists, retailers and publications from around the country and the world. The show's 500-plus booths showcase collectibles from teddy bears to dolls, antiques to contemporary figurines, and toys to fine art.

One of the most exciting events at the International Collectible Exposition is the "Opening Ceremony Artist Parade." The Parade delights collectors and features renowned collectible artists from around the world.

Indicative of the compassion that is a trademark of the collectibles' industry, the 1995 Collectors' Jubilee included The Oklahoma City Disaster Relief Booth which raised almost $10,000 for "Feed The Children." The proceeds were earmarked for the parents of children killed in the explosion of the Alfred P. Murrah Federal Building.

Lorrie and Ray Kiefer were honored for their many years of service to the National Association of Limited Edition Dealers (NALED) at the Achievement Awards Banquet in July 1995. NALED President Kevin Samara (center) presented the Kiefers with a special "Thank You" gift.

For show information, contact The Collectors' Jubilee, 622 East Main St., Suite 107, Jenks, OK 74037, (918) 298-8881.

The Collectors' Jubilee hosts "The Collectors' Choice Awards" ceremony honoring the best collectibles in over 21 different categories. Accepting the awards for "Best Lighted House" and "Best Decorative Accessory" were Forma Vitrum's stained glass artist Bill Job and Pia Colon, Vice-President of the company.

Special Events

The unparalleled artistry and inimitable spirit of the late Frances Hook inspired the formation of The Frances Hook Scholarship Fund which fosters the studies of young U.S. artists.

The generosity and caring of many members of the collectibles industry is expressed through a variety of special events supported by collectibles companies. Whether it's helping children's causes, young artists or the fine arts, the heart of the collectibles industry is beating strong with concern that translates into commitment.

The Frances Hook Scholarship Fund

The Frances Hook Scholarship Fund is the collectibles art and publishing business communities' highest tribute to the superlative artistry and inimitable spirit of the late Frances Hook. Inspired by Hook's love for children, this foundation was established in her name to foster the studies of young U.S. artists.

Limited edition collectibles' companies who generously support the Frances Hook Scholarship Fund include: Roman, Inc., Enesco Corporation, Media Arts Group, Gifts & Decorative Accessories, Flambro, Cast Art Industries, Department 56, Lefton, Goebel, and The Bradford Exchange. These companies have joined hands in a consortium of support by issuing a three-year Challenge Pledge of $100,000 to the Frances Hook Scholarship Fund to raise matching dollars in support of young artists everywhere.

The not-for-profit organization accepts contributions for this program which are tax deductible to the fullest extent of the law. To learn how you can support the efforts of the Frances Hook Scholarship Fund write to P.O. Box 597346, Chicago, IL 60659 or call (708) 673-ARTS.

Hundreds of young patients in the Shriner's Nationwide Hospital Network receive Christmas gifts annually from Roman, Inc. Shriner's patient Andres Diaz of Aurora, Illinois, enjoys a talk with Ronald T. Jedlinski, Roman CEO and owner, and his wife Diane, who annually donate thousands of toys to bed-bound children in 20 Shriner's hospitals across the country.

The Greenwich Workshop and The National Arbor Day Foundation have joined forces in 1995 to publicize the artistic efforts of elementary students who participated in the annual Arbor Day National Poster Contest. This year's winning poster, titled "Trees are terrific...and forests are too!," was created by Justin Grimm. The Greenwich Workshop will publish 5,000 full-color posters of Justin's original artwork for display in 5th grade classrooms across the country. Justin is pictured with renowned and best-selling wilderness artist Bev Doolittle.

James P. Gallagher, (center) Director of The Bradford Exchange Board of Governors, offers his congratulations to the first artists to be inducted in The Bradford Exchange Plate Artist Hall of Fame. Pictured are (left to right, holding crystal plaques) inductees Thomas Kinkade, Sandra Kuck and Lena Liu, and Thomas Rockwell, who accepted the honor on behalf of his father, the late Norman Rockwell. The fifth inductee, Charles Fracé, was unable to attend the May 1995 ceremonies.

GLOSSARY

You can better appreciate your hobby by acquainting yourself with terms commonly used by collectors and dealers to describe limited edition collectibles. This list is not all-inclusive, but it will provide a good starting point for approaching the collectibles field.

Acid-free. A description of paper and materials treated to remove the acids that cause deterioration.

Alabaster. A fine-textured gypsum which is usually white and translucent. Some collectors' plates are made of a material called ivory alabaster which is not translucent, but has the look and patina of old ivory.

Allotment. The number within a limited edition which a manufacturer allows to a given dealer, direct marketer or collector.

Annual. The term is used to describe a plate or other limited edition which is issued yearly. Many annual plates commemorate holidays or anniversaries, and they are commonly named by that special date, i.e. the Annual Bing & Grondahl Christmas plate.

Artist/gallery/publishers' proofs. Originally, the first few prints in an edition of lithographs were used to test colors and then given to the artist. They were not numbered but were signed. Artist's proofs are not considered part of the edition. Gallery and publishers' proofs are used as a means of increasing the number of prints in an edition.

Baby doll. A doll with the proportions of a baby; with a short-limbed body and lips parted to take a nipple.

Back issue. An issue in a series other than the issue that is currently being produced. It can be either open or closed and may or may not be available.

Backstamp. The information on the back of a plate or other limited edition which documents it as part of a limited edition. This information may be hand-painted onto the plate, or it may be incised, or applied as a transfer (decal). Information which typically appears on the backstamp includes the name of the series, name of the item, year of issue, some information about the subject, the artist's name and/or signature, the edition limit, the item's number within that edition, initials of the firing master or production supervisor, etc.

Band. Also known as a rim, as in "24K gold banded, or rimmed." A popular finishing technique is to band plates and bells with gold, platinum or silver which is then adhered to the plate through the firing process. Details from the primary artwork may also be adapted to form a decorative rim.

Bas-relief. A technique in which the collectible has a raised design. This design may be achieved by pouring liquid material into a mold before firing, or by applying a three-dimensional design element to the flat surface of a plate, figurine or other "blank" piece.

Bavaria. A section of Germany that is one of the world's richest sources of kaolin clay, an essential component of fine porcelain. The region is home to a number of renowned porcelain factories.

Bisque or biscuit. A fired ware which has neither a glaze nor enamel applied to it. Bisque may be white or colored. The name comes from its biscuit-like, matte texture.

Body. The basic form of a plate, figurine, bell or other collectible, or its component materials.

Bone ash. Fire is used to reduce animal bones to calcium phosphate, a powder which is an ingredient of bone china or porcelain.

Bone china/bone porcelain. Bone porcelain is similar to hard porcelain in its ingredients, except that bone ash is the main component of the mix and is the primary contributor to the vitrification and translucency. Bone clay allows for extreme thinness and translucency without sacrificing strength or durability.

Bottomstamp. The same as a backstamp, but usually refers to documentation material found on the bottom of a figurine or the inside of a bell.

Bye-lo-baby. Grace Storey Putman copyrighted this life-sized baby doll (three days old) in 1922. This style of baby doll is a favorite among limited edition collectors.

Cameo. Relief decoration with a flat surface around it similar to the look of a jeweler's cameo. A technique used by Wedgwood, Incolay, Avondale and others.

Cancelled plate. A plate that was planned as part of a series, but never produced because of technical problems or lack of interest in early issues.

Canvas transfer process. A lithograph is treated with a latex emulsion. The paper is removed and the image on the latex emulsion is placed on a cotton duck canvas. It is then topcoated, retouched and highlighted by hand before being hand-numbered.

Capodimonte. Originally a fine porcelain poduced at a "castle on the mountain" overlooking Naples, the term currently describes a highly ornate style rather than an actual product. Frequently features flowers, fruits and courtly or native figures.

Cast. The process of creating a copy of an original model by pouring liquid clay or slip into a mold.

Ceramic. The generic term for a piece which is made of some form of clay and finished by firing at high temperatures.

Certificate/Certificate of Authenticity. A document which accompanies a limited edition item to establish its place within the edition. Certificates may include information such as the series name, item title, artist's name and/or signature, brief description of the item and its subject, signatures of sponsoring and marketing organizations' representatives, and other documentation material along with the item's individual number or a statement of the edition limit.

Character dolls. These dolls are often created to resemble actors or celebrities. Character dolls also include fairytale images, folk heroes and cartoon characters.

Chasing. A sculpting process in which tiny hammers and punches are used to create decorative details on ornaments.

China. Originally "china" referred to all wares which came from China. Now the term means products which are fired at a high temperature. China usually consists of varying percentages of kaolin clay, feldspar and quartz. Also see "porcelain".

Cinnabar. A red mineral found in volcanic regions, and an ingredient in mercury. It is used to create collectors' items.

Cire perdue. See lost wax.

Clay. A general term for materials used to make ceramic items. Pliable when moist, clay becomes hard and strong when fired. It may be composed of any number of earthen materials.

Cloissone. An enameling process in which thin metal strips are soldered on the base of a piece to create a pattern. Then, various enamels are poured in to provide the color.

Closed edition. A limited edition that is no longer being issued because it has reached the designated limit, or no longer has market appeal.

Closed end edition. A series with a pre-determined, and usually pre-announced, number of issues.

Cobalt blue. Also known as Copenhagen blue, this rich color was an early favorite because it was the only color that could withstand high firing temperatures needed for glazing. Cobalt oxide is a black powder when applied, but fires to a deep blue.

Cold cast. A relatively new process which combines polyester resins and a variety of materials (metal powders, ground porcelain, wood shavings and other natural materials). The combination is forced into a mold or die under high pressure and a forging process occurs. Allows for exceptional detailing which can be easily hand-painted.

Collector plate. A limited edition plate which is created to be collected for its decorative appearance.

Commemorative. An item created to mark a special date, holiday or event.

Dealer. An individual or store where collectors can purchase collectibles at retail prices.

Decal. Also known as a transfer, this is a lithographic or silkscreen rendering of a piece of artwork, which is applied to ceramic or other materials and then fired on to fuse it to the surface.

Delftware. Heavy earthenware coated with an opaque white glaze that contains tin oxide. First developed in Delft, Holland in the 16th century.

Drafting. Process for shaping metal into hollowware.

Earthenware. A non-vitrified ceramic made of ball clay, kaolin and pegmatite. Remains porous until glazed and fired at a low temperature.

Edition. A term referring to the number of items created with the same name and decorations.

Embossing. A process of producing an image in relief by using dies or punches on a surface.

Engraving. An intaglio process in which an image is cut into the surface. Term also used to describe a print made by an engraving process.

Etched design. Decoration produced by cutting into a surface with acid. An acid-resisant paint or wax is applied and the design is inscribed through this coating. When immersed in acid, the acid etches the surface to form the design.

Faience. Named after an Italian town, Faenza, faience is similar to Delftware and Majolica because it is earthenware coated with a glaze that contains tin oxide.

Feldspar. When decomposed, this mineral becomes kaolin, which is the essential ingredient in china and porcelain. Left in its undercomposed form, feldspar adds hardness to a ware.

Fire. To heat, and thus harden, a ceramic ware in a kiln.

Firing period. A time period—usually 10-to-75 days, which serves to limit an edition, usually of plates. The number of items is limited to the capacity of the manufacturer over that 10-to-75 days.

First issue. The premiere item in a series, whether closed-ended or open-ended.

French bronze. Also known as "spelter," this is zinc refined to 99.97% purity. It has been used as an alternative to bronze for casting for more than a century.

Glaze. The liquid material which is applied to a ware for various purposes. Cosmetically, it provides shine and decorative value. It also makes the item more durable. Decorations may be applied before or after glaze is applied.

Graphic. A print produced by one of the "original" print processes such as etching, engraving, woodblocks, lithographs and serigraphs. This term is frequently used interchangeably with "print".

Greenware. Undecorated ceramic before it is fired.

Hallmark. The mark or logo of the manufacturer of an item.

Hard paste porcelain. The hardest porcelain made, this material uses feldspar to enchance vitrification and translucency, and is fired at about 2642 degrees Fahrenheit.

Hydro-stone. The hardest form of gypsum cement from which many limited edition collectibles are produced. A registered trademark of the United States Gypsum Co.

Incised. Writing or design which is etched or inscribed into a piece to provide a backstamp or decorative design.

Incolay stone. A man-made material combining minerals including carnelian and crystal quartz. Used by Incolay Studios to make cameo-style collectibles.

Inlay. To fill an etched or incised design with another material such as enamel, metal or jewels.

In stock. A term used to refer to an item of a given edition still available from the producers' inventory.

Issue. As a verb, to introduce. As a noun, the term means an item within a series.

Issue Price. The price established by the manufacturer or principal marketer when a collectible is introduced.

Jasper ware. Josiah Wedgwood's unglazed stoneware material, first introduced in the 1770s. Although jasper is white in its original form, it can be stained a medium blue called "Wedgwood Blue," or a darker blue, black, green, lilac, yellow, brown and gray. Colored Wedgwood "bodies" are often decorated with white bas-relief, or vice/versa.

Kaolin. The essential ingredient in china and porcelain, this special clay is found in several spots throughout the world. Many famous porcelain factories are located near these deposits.

Lead crystal. Lead oxide is added to glass to give it weight, brilliance and a clear ring. Lead crystal has a lead oxide content of 24%, while "full" lead crystal contains more than 30%.

Limited edition. An item produced only in a certain quantity or only during a certain time period. Collectible editions are limited by: specific numbers, years, specific time periods or firing periods.

Limoges. A town in France with rich deposits of kaolin clay and other essential ingredients for making china and porcelain. Home of a number of famed porcelain manufacturers.

Lost wax. An ancient method used by sculptors to create a detailed wax "positive" which is then used to form a ceramic "negative" shell. This shell becomes the original mold used in the creation of finely carved three-dimensional pieces.

Majolica. Similar to Delftware and Faience, this glazed earthenware was first produced on the Spanish island, Majorca.

Market. The organized buy-sell medium for collectibles.

Marks or markings. The logo or insignia which certifies that an item was made by a particular firm.

Miniatures. Collectibles, including figurines, plates, graphics, dolls, ornaments and bells, which are very small originals or smaller versions of larger pieces. Usually finely detailed, many figurine miniatures are created using the lost wax process.

Mint condition. The term originated in coin collecting. In limited edition collectibles, it means that an item is still in its original, like-new condition, with all accompanying documents.

Mold. The form that supplies the shape of a plate, bell, figurine or other items.

Open-ended series. A collection of plates or other limited editions which appear at intervals, usually annually, with no limit as to the number of years it will be produced. For example, the Bing & Grondahl Christmas series has been produced annually since 1895, with no end in sight.

Overglaze. A decoration which is applied to an item after its original glazing and firing.

Paste. The raw material of porcelain before shaping and firing. See "slip."

Pewter. An alloy containing at least 85% tin.

Polyester resin. A bonding compound mixed with powdered, ground or chipped materials (pulverized porcelain, wood, shells and other materials) to form cold-cast products. Cold-cast porcelain is made by mixing resin with porcelain dust; cold-cast bronze is made by blending resin with ground bronze.

Porcelain. Made of kaolin, quartz and feldspar, porcelain is fired at up to 1450 degrees centigrade. Porcelain is noted for its translucency and its true ring. Also called "china".

Pottery. Ceramic ware, more specifically that which is earthenware or non-vitrified. Also a term for manufacturing plants where such objects are made and fired.

Primary market. The first buy-sell market used by manufacturers to reach collectors. Sold at issue price, collectibles are offered to the public through retailers, direct mail and home shopping networks.

Print. A photomechanical reproduction process such as offset, lithography, collotypes and letterpress.

Printed remarque. A hand drawn image by the artist that is photomechanically reproduced in the margin of a print.

Queen's ware. Cream-colored earthenware developed by Josiah Wedgwood; now used as a generic term for similar materials.

Quote. The average selling price of a collectible at any given time. It may be the issue price, or above or below.

Release price. The price for which each print in the edition is sold until the edition is sold out and a secondary market is established.

Relief. A raised design in various levels above a background.

Remarque. A hand-drawn original image by the artist, either in pencil, pen and ink, watercolor or oil that is sketched in the margin of a limited edition print.

Resin. See polyester resin.

Sculpted crystal. A general term for products made by assembling faceted Austrian crystal prisms with a 32 % lead content

Second. An item which is not first quality and should not be included in the limited edition. Normally, such items are destroyed or at least marked on the backstamp or bottomstamp to indicate they are not first quality.

Secondary market. Once the original edition has been sold out, the buying and selling among collectors, through dealers or exchanges, takes place on the "secondary" market.

Secondary market price. The price a customer is willing to sell or buy an item for once it is no longer available on the primary market. These prices will vary from one part of the country to another, depending on the supply and demand for the collectible.

Serigraphy. A direct printing process used by artists to design, make and print their own stencils. A serigraph differs from other prints in that its images are created with paint films instead of printing inks.

Signed and numbered. Each print is signed and consecutively numbered by the artist, in pencil, either in the image area or in the margin. Edition size is limited.

Signed in the plate. The only signature on the artwork is reproduced from the artist's original signature. Not necessarily limited in edition size.

Signed only. Usually refers to a print that is signed without consecutive numbers. May not be limited in edition size.

Silver crystal. Faceted Austrian crystal prisms with a 32% lead content used to produce sculpted crystal. The name is registered by Swarovski.

Silverplate. A process of manufacturing ornaments in which pure silver is electroplated onto a base metal, usually brass or pewter.

Slip. A creamy material used to fill the molds in making greenware. Formulas for slip are closely guarded secrets.

Soft paste. A mixture of clay and ground glass first used in Europe to produce china. The vitrification point of soft paste is too low to produce the hardness required for true porcelain.

Sold out. The classification given to an edition which has been 100% sold out by the producer.

Spin casting. A process of casting multiple ornaments from rubber molds; commonly used for low-temperature metals such as pewter.

Sterling silver. An alloy of 92-1/2% pure silver and 7-1/2% copper.

Stoneware. A vitrified ceramic material, usually a silicate clay that is very hard, heavy and impervious to liquids and most stains.

Terra cotta. A reddish earthenware or a general term for any fired clay.

Tin glaze. The glaze on Delftware, Faience or Majolica. This material results in a heavy white and opaque surface after firing.

Transfer. See decal.

Translucency. Allowing light to shine through a nontransparent object. A positive quality of fine china or porcelain.

Triptych. A three-panel art piece, often of religious significance.

Underglaze. A decoration which is applied before the final glazing and firing of an item. Most often, such decorations are painted by hand.

Vinyl. A relatively new synthetic material developed with the special properties of color, durability and skin-like texture which is molded into collectible dolls.

Vitrification. The process by which ceramic artwork becomes vitrified or totally nonporous at high temperatures.

Collectors' Information Bureau

PRICE INDEX 1996

Limited Edition

Plates • Figurines • Cottages • Bells • Graphics • Christmas Ornaments • Dolls • Steins

This index includes thousands of the most widely traded limited editions in today's collectibles market. It is based on surveys and interviews with several hundred of the most experienced and informed limited edition dealers in the United States, as well as many independent market advisors.

HOW TO USE THIS INDEX

Listings are set up using the following format:

Enesco Corporation ❶

Precious Moments Figurines ❷ **— S. Butcher** ❸

❹	❺	❻	❼	❽	❾
1979	Praise the Lord Anyhow-E1374B	Retrd.	1982	8.00	65-155

❶ Enesco Corporation = Company Name

❷ Precious Moments Figurines = Series Name

❸ S. Butcher = Artist's Name. The word "Various" may also be indicated, meaning that several artists have created pieces within the series. The artist name then appears after the title of the collectible. In some cases, the artist's name will be indicated after the series name "with exceptions noted." If company staff artists have created the piece, no artist name is listed.

❹ 1979 = Year of Issue

❺ Praise the Lord Anyhow-E1374B = Title of the collectible. Many titles also include the model number for further identification purposes.

❻ Retrd. = Edition Limit. In this case, the collectible is no longer available. The edition limit category generally refers to the number of items created with the same name and decoration. Edition limits may indicate a specific number (i.e. 10,000) or the number of firing days for plates (i.e. 100-day, the capacity of the manufacturer to produce collectibles during a given firing period). Refer to "Open," "Suspd.," "Annual," and "Yr. Iss." under "Terms and Abbreviations" below.

❼ 1982 = Year of Retirement. May also indicate the year the manufacturer ceased production of the collectible. If N/A appears in this column, it indicates the information is not available at this time, but research is continuing.
Note: In the plate section, the year of retirement may not be indicated because many plates are limited to firing days and not years.

❽ 8.00 = Original Issue Price in U.S. Dollars

❾ 65-155 = Current Quote Price reflected may show a price or price range. Quotes are based on interviews with retailers across the country, who provide their actual sales transactions. Quotes have been rounded up to the nearest dollar. Quote may also reflect a price increase for pieces that are not retired or closed.

A Special Note to Beatrix Potter, Boyds Bears, Cherished Teddies, Disney Classics, Goebel Miniatures, M.I. Hummel and Precious Moments Collectors: *These collectibles are engraved with a special annual mark. This emblem changes with each production year. The secondary market value for each piece varies because of these distinctive yearly markings. Our pricing reflects an average for all years.*

A Special Note to Hallmark Keepsake Ornament Collectors: *All quotes in this section are for ornaments in mint condition in their original box.*

A Special Note to Department 56 Collectors: *Year of Introduction indicates the year in which the piece was designed, sculpted and copyrighted. It is possible these pieces may not be available to the collectors until the following calendar year.*

TERMS AND ABBREVIATIONS

Annual = Issued once a year.
A/P = Artist Proof.
Closed = An item or series no longer in production.
G/P = Gallery Proof.
N/A = Not available at this time.
Open = Not limited by number or time, available until manufacturer stops production, "retires" or "closes" the item or series.
Retrd. = Retired.
S/N = Signed and Numbered.
S/O = Sold Out.
Set = Refers to two or more items issued together for a single price.
Suspd. = Suspended (not currently being produced: may be produced in the future).
Unkn. = Unknown.
Yr. Iss. = Year of issue (limited to a calendar year).
28-day, 10-day, etc. = Limited to this number of production (or firing) days, usually not consecutive.

BELLS

ANRI

Juan Ferrandiz Musical Christmas Bells - J. Ferrandiz

YEAR ISSUE		EDITION LIMIT	YEAR RETD.	ISSUE PRICE	QUOTE U.S.$
1976	Christmas	Yr.Iss.	1976	25.00	80
1977	Christmas	Yr.Iss.	1977	25.00	80
1978	Christmas	Yr.Iss.	1978	35.00	75
1979	Christmas	Yr.Iss.	1979	48.00	60
1980	Little Drummer Boy	Yr.Iss.	1980	60.00	63
1981	The Good Shepherd Boy	Yr.Iss.	1981	63.00	63
1982	Spreading the Word	Yr.Iss.	1982	63.00	63
1983	Companions	Yr.Iss.	1983	63.00	63
1984	With Love	Yr.Iss.	1984	55.00	55

Wooden Christmas Bells - J. Ferrandiz

YEAR ISSUE		EDITION LIMIT	YEAR RETD.	ISSUE PRICE	QUOTE U.S.$
1976	Christmas	Yr.Iss.	1976	6.00	50
1977	Christmas	Yr.Iss.	1977	7.00	40
1978	Christmas	Yr.Iss.	1978	10.00	40
1979	Christmas	Yr.Iss.	1979	13.00	25-30
1980	The Christmas King	Yr.Iss.	1980	18.00	19
1981	Lighting The Way	Yr.Iss.	1981	19.00	19
1982	Caring	Yr.Iss.	1982	19.00	19
1983	Behold	Yr.Iss.	1983	19.00	19
1985	Nature's Dream	Yr.Iss.	1985	19.00	19

Artists of the World

DeGrazia Bells - T. DeGrazia

YEAR ISSUE		EDITION LIMIT	YEAR RETD.	ISSUE PRICE	QUOTE U.S.$
1980	Festival of Lights	5,000	N/A	40.00	85
1980	Los Ninos	7,500	N/A	40.00	125
1980	Los Ninos (signed)	500	N/A	80.00	200

Belleek

Belleek Bells - Belleek

YEAR ISSUE		EDITION LIMIT	YEAR RETD.	ISSUE PRICE	QUOTE U.S.$
1988	Bell, 1st Ed.	Yr.Iss.		38.00	38
1989	Tower, 2nd Ed.	Yr.Iss.		35.00	35
1990	Leprechaun, 3rd Ed.	Yr.Iss.		30.00	30
1991	Church, 4th Ed.	Yr.Iss.		32.00	32
1992	Cottage, 5th Ed.	Yr.Iss.		30.00	30
1993	Pub, 6th Ed.	Yr.Iss.		30.00	30
1994	Castle, 7th Ed.	Yr.Iss.		30.00	30

Twelve Days of Christmas - Belleek

YEAR ISSUE		EDITION LIMIT	YEAR RETD.	ISSUE PRICE	QUOTE U.S.$
1991	A Partridge in a Pear Tree	Yr.Iss.		30.00	30
1992	Two Turtle Doves	Yr.Iss.		30.00	30
1993	Three French Hens	Yr.Iss.		30.00	30
1994	Four Calling Birds	Yr.Iss.		30.00	30
1995	Five Golden Rings	Yr.Iss.		30.00	30

Dave Grossman Designs

Norman Rockwell Collection - Rockwell-Inspired

YEAR ISSUE		EDITION LIMIT	YEAR RETD.	ISSUE PRICE	QUOTE U.S.$
1975	Faces of Christmas NRB-75	Retrd.	N/A	12.50	35
1976	Drum for Tommy NRB-76	Retrd.	N/A	12.00	30
1976	Ben Franklin (Bicentennial)	Retrd.	N/A	12.50	25
1980	Leapfrog NRB-80	Retrd.	N/A	50.00	60

Enesco Corporation

Cherished Teddies - P. Hillman

YEAR ISSUE		EDITION LIMIT	YEAR RETD.	ISSUE PRICE	QUOTE U.S.$
1992	906530-Angel Bell	Suspd.		20.00	50-75

Memories of Yesterday Bell - M. Attwell

YEAR ISSUE		EDITION LIMIT	YEAR RETD.	ISSUE PRICE	QUOTE U.S.$
1990	Here Comes the Bride-God Bless Her-523100	Suspd.		25.00	25
1994	Time For Bed-525243	Open		25.00	25

Precious Moments Annual Bells - S. Butcher

YEAR ISSUE		EDITION LIMIT	YEAR RETD.	ISSUE PRICE	QUOTE U.S.$
1981	Let the Heavens Rejoice-E-5622-	Retrd.	1981	15.00	235-250
1982	I'll Play My Drum for Him-E-2358	Retrd.	1982	17.00	75-80
1983	Surrounded With Joy-E-0522	Retrd.	1983	18.00	70-75
1984	Wishing You a Merry Christmas-E-5393	Retrd.	1984	19.00	45
1985	God Sent His Love-15873	Retrd.	1985	19.00	45-50
1986	Wishing You a Cozy Christmas-102318	Retrd.	1986	20.00	50
1987	Love is the Best Gift of All-109835	Retrd.	1987	22.50	38-45
1988	Time To Wish You a Merry Christmas-115304	Retrd.	1988	25.00	40-45
1989	Oh Holy Night-522821	Retrd.	1989	25.00	35-40
1990	Once Upon A Holy Night-523828	Retrd.	1990	25.00	40
1991	May Your Christmas Be Merry-524182	Retrd.	1991	25.00	40
1992	But The Greatest Of These Is Love-527726	Retrd.	1992	25.00	42-50
1993	Wishing You The Sweetest Christmas-530174	Retrd.	1993	25.00	42-50
1994	Your're As Pretty as a Christmas Tree-604216	Yr.Iss.	1994	27.50	37

Precious Moments Various Bells - S. Butcher

YEAR ISSUE		EDITION LIMIT	YEAR RETD.	ISSUE PRICE	QUOTE U.S.$
1981	Jesus Loves Me (B)-E-5208	Suspd.		15.00	50
1981	Jesus Loves Me (G)-E-5209	Suspd.		15.00	55-60
1981	Prayer Changes Things-E-5210	Suspd.		15.00	55-60
1981	God Understands-E-5211	Retrd.	N/A	15.00	35-50
1981	We Have Seen His Star-E-5620	Suspd.		15.00	50-60
1981	Jesus Is Born-E-5623	Suspd.		15.00	50-65
1982	The Lord Bless You and Keep You-E-7175	Suspd.		17.00	35-55
1982	The Lord Bless You and Keep You-E-7176	Suspd.		17.00	55-65
1982	The Lord Bless You and Keep You-E-7179	Suspd.		22.50	55-85
1982	Mother Sew Dear-E-7181	Suspd.		17.00	40-50
1982	The Purr-fect Grandma-E-7183	Suspd.		17.00	45-60

Fenton Art Glass Company

American Classic Series - M. Dickinson

YEAR ISSUE		EDITION LIMIT	YEAR RETD.	ISSUE PRICE	QUOTE U.S.$
1986	Jupiter Train, 6 1/2" on Opal Satin	5,000	1986	50.00	50
1986	Studebaker-Garford Car, 6 1/2" on Opal Satin	5,000	1986	50.00	50

Artist Series - Various

YEAR ISSUE		EDITION LIMIT	YEAR RETD.	ISSUE PRICE	QUOTE U.S.$
1982	After The Snow - D. Johnson	15,000	1982	14.50	15
1983	Winter Chapel - D. Johnson	15,000	1984	15.00	15
1985	Flying Geese - D. Johnson	15,000	1985	15.00	15
1986	The Hummingbird - D. Johnson	15,000	1986	15.00	15
1987	Out in the Country - L. Everson	15,000	1987	15.00	15
1988	Serenity - F. Burton	5,000	1988	16.50	17
1989	Househunting - D. Barbour	5,000	1989	16.50	17

Childhood Treasurers Series - Various

YEAR ISSUE		EDITION LIMIT	YEAR RETD.	ISSUE PRICE	QUOTE U.S.$
1983	Teddy Bear, 4 1/2" - D. Johnson	15,000	1983	15.00	15
1984	Hobby Horse, 4 1/2" - L. Everson	15,000	1984	15.00	15
1985	Clown, 4 1/2" - L. Everson	15,000	1985	17.50	18
1986	Playful Kitten, 4 1/2" - L. Everson	15,000	1986	15.00	15
1987	Frisky Pup, 4 1/2" - D. Barbour	15,000	1987	15.00	15
1988	Castles in the Air, 4 1/2" - D. Barbour	5,000	1988	16.50	17
1989	A Child's Cuddly Friend, 4 1/2" - D. Johnson	5,000	1989	16.50	17

Christmas - Various

YEAR ISSUE		EDITION LIMIT	YEAR RETD.	ISSUE PRICE	QUOTE U.S.$
1978	Christmas Morn - M. Dickinson	Yr.Iss.	1978	25.00	25
1979	Nature's Christmas - K. Cunningham	Yr.Iss.	1979	30.00	30
1980	Going Home - D. Johnson	Yr.Iss.	1980	32.50	33
1981	All Is Calm - D. Johnson	Yr.Iss.	1981	35.00	35
1982	Country Christmas - R. Spindler	Yr.Iss.	1982	35.00	35
1983	Anticipation - D. Johnson	7,500	1983	35.00	35
1984	Expectation - D. Johnson	7,500	1984	37.50	38
1985	Heart's Desire - D. Johnson	7,500	1986	37.50	38
1987	Sharing The Spirit - L. Everson	Yr.Iss.	1987	37.50	38
1987	Cardinal in the Churchyard - D. Johnson	4,500	1987	29.50	30
1988	A Chickadee Ballet - D. Johnson	4,500	1988	29.50	30
1989	Downy Pecker - Chisled Song - D. Johnson	4,500	1989	29.50	30
1990	A Blue Bird in Snowfall - D. Johnson	4,500	1990	29.50	30
1990	Sleigh Ride - F. Burton	3,500	1990	39.00	39
1991	Christmas Eve - F. Burton	3,500	1991	35.00	35
1992	Family Tradition - F. Burton	3,500	1992	39.00	39
1993	Family Holiday - F. Burton	3,500	1993	39.50	40
1994	Silent Night - F. Burton	2,500	1994	45.00	45
1995	Our Home Is Blessed - F. Burton	2,500		45.00	45

Christmas Limited Edition - M. Reynolds, unless otherwise noted

YEAR ISSUE		EDITION LIMIT	YEAR RETD.	ISSUE PRICE	QUOTE U.S.$
1992	Winter on Twilight Blue, 6 1/2"	2,500	1992	29.50	30
1993	Manager Scene on Ruby, 6 1/2"	2,500	1993	39.50	40
1993	Reindeer on Blue, 6 1/2"	2,500	1993	30.00	30
1993	Floral on Green-Musical, 6 1/2"	2,500	1993	39.50	40
1994	Magnolia on Gold, 6 1/2"	1,000	1994	35.00	35
1994	Angel on Ivory, 6 1/2"	1,000	1994	39.50	40
1994	Partridge on Ruby-Musical 6 1/2"	1,000	1994	48.50	49
1995	Bow & Holly on Ivory, 6 1/2"	900		39.50	40
1995	Chickadee on Gold, 6 1/2"	900		39.50	40
1995	Iced Poinsettia on Ruby, 5 1/2"	900		45.00	45
1995	Angel, Heavenly Bell, 5 3/4" - R. Spindler	1,900		35.00	35

Connoisseur Bell - Various

YEAR ISSUE		EDITION LIMIT	YEAR RETD.	ISSUE PRICE	QUOTE U.S.$
1983	Bell, Burmese Hndpt.- L. Everson	2,000	1983	50.00	95
1983	Craftsman Bell, White Satin Carnival - Fenton	3,500	1983	25.00	50
1984	Bell, Famous Women's Ruby Satin Irid. - Fenton	3,500	1984	25.00	50
1985	Bell, 6 1/2" Burmese, Hndpt. L. Everson	2,500	1985	55.00	95
1986	Bell, Burmese-Shells, Hndpt. D. Barbour	2,500	1986	60.00	100
1988	Bell, 7" Wisteria, Hndpt. L. Everson	4,000	1988	45.00	85
1989	Bell, 7" Handpainted Rosalene Satin - L. Everson	3,500	1989	50.00	75
1991	Bell, 7" Roses on Rosalene, Hndpt. - M. Reynolds	2,000	1991	50.00	60

Designer Series - Various

YEAR ISSUE		EDITION LIMIT	YEAR RETD.	ISSUE PRICE	QUOTE U.S.$
1983	Lighthouse Point, 6" M. Dickinson	1,000	1983	55.00	55
1983	Down Home, 6" - G. Finn	1,000	1983	55.00	55
1984	Smoke 'N Cinders, 6" M. Dickinson	1,250	1984	55.00	55
1984	Majestic Flight, 6" B. Cumberledge	1,250	1984	55.00	55
1985	In Season, 6" - M. Dickinson	1,250	1985	55.00	55
1985	Nature's Grace, 6" B. Cumberland	1,250	1985	55.00	55
1985	Statue of Liberty, 6" - S. Bryan	1,250	1985	55.00	55
1986	Statue of Liberty, 6" - S. Bryan	1,250	1986	55.00	55

Mary Gregory - M. Reynolds

YEAR ISSUE		EDITION LIMIT	YEAR RETD.	ISSUE PRICE	QUOTE U.S.$
1993	Bell, 6" Ruby	Closed	1993	49.00	49
1994	Bell, 6" Ruby - Loves Me, Loves Me Not	Closed	1994	49.00	49
1995	Bell, 6 1/2"	Closed	1995	49.00	49

Mother's Day Series - Various

YEAR ISSUE		EDITION LIMIT	YEAR RETD.	ISSUE PRICE	QUOTE U.S.$
1980	New Born - L. Everson	Closed	1980	25.00	25
1981	Gentle Fawn - L. Everson	Closed	1981	27.50	28
1982	Nature's Awakening - L. Everson	Closed	1982	28.50	29
1983	Where's Mom - L. Everson	Closed	1983	28.50	29
1984	Precious Panda - L. Everson	Closed	1984	28.50	29
1985	Mother's Little Lamb - L. Everson	Closed	1985	35.00	35
1990	White Swan - L. Everson	Closed	1990	35.00	35
1990	White Swan (Musical) L. Everson	Closed	1990	45.00	45
1991	Mother's Watchful Eye M. Reynolds	Closed	1991	35.00	35
1992	Let's Play With Mom M. Reynolds	Closed	1992	37.50	38
1993	Mother Deer - M. Reynolds	Closed	1993	39.50	40
1994	Loving Puppy - M. Reynolds	Closed	1994	39.50	40

Valentine's Day Series - M. Reynolds

YEAR ISSUE		EDITION LIMIT	YEAR RETD.	ISSUE PRICE	QUOTE U.S.$
1992	Bell, 6" Vining Hearts Hndpt. Opal Irid.	Closed	1992	35.00	35

Goebel/M.I. Hummel

M.I. Hummel Collectibles Annual Bells - M. I. Hummel

YEAR ISSUE		EDITION LIMIT	YEAR RETD.	ISSUE PRICE	QUOTE U.S.$
1978	Let's Sing 700	Closed	N/A	50.00	50
1979	Farewell 701	Closed	N/A	70.00	70
1980	Thoughtful 702	Closed	N/A	85.00	85
1981	In Tune 703	Closed	N/A	85.00	85
1982	She Loves Me, She Loves Me Not 704	Closed	N/A	90.00	90
1983	Knit One 705	Closed	N/A	90.00	90
1984	Mountaineer 706	Closed	N/A	90.00	90
1985	Sweet Song 707	Closed	N/A	90.00	90
1986	Sing Along 708	Closed	N/A	100.00	100
1987	With Loving Greetings 709	Closed	N/A	110.00	110
1988	Busy Student 710	Closed	N/A	120.00	120
1989	Latest News 711	Closed	N/A	135.00	135
1990	What's New? 712	Closed	N/A	140.00	140
1991	Favorite Pet 713	Closed	N/A	150.00	150
1992	Whistler's Duet 714	Closed	N/A	160.00	160

Gorham

Currier & Ives - Mini Bells - Currier & Ives

YEAR ISSUE		EDITION LIMIT	YEAR RETD.	ISSUE PRICE	QUOTE U.S.$
1976	Christmas Sleigh Ride	Annual		9.95	35
1977	American Homestead	Annual		9.95	25
1978	Yule Logs	Annual		12.95	20
1979	Sleigh Ride	Annual		14.95	20
1980	Christmas in the Country	Annual		14.95	20
1981	Christmas Tree	Annual		14.95	18
1982	Christmas Visitation	Annual		16.50	18
1983	Winter Wonderland	Annual		16.50	18
1984	Hitching Up	Annual		16.50	18
1985	Skaters Holiday	Annual		17.50	18
1986	Central Park in Winter	Annual		17.50	18
1987	Early Winter	Annual		19.00	19

Mini Bells - N. Rockwell

YEAR ISSUE		EDITION LIMIT	YEAR RETD.	ISSUE PRICE	QUOTE U.S.$
1981	Tiny Tim	Annual		19.75	20
1982	Planning Christmas Visit	Annual		20.00	20

Various - N. Rockwell

YEAR ISSUE		EDITION LIMIT	YEAR RETD.	ISSUE PRICE	QUOTE U.S.$
1975	Sweet Song So Young	Annual		19.50	50
1975	Santa's Helpers	Annual		19.50	30
1975	Tavern Sign Painter	Annual		19.50	30
1976	Flowers in Tender Bloom	Annual		19.50	40
1976	Snow Sculpture	Annual		19.50	45
1977	Fondly Do We Remember	Annual		19.50	55
1977	Chilling Chore (Christmas)	Annual		19.50	35
1978	Gaily Sharing Vintage Times	Annual		22.50	23
1978	Gay Blades (Christmas)	Annual		22.50	23
1979	Beguiling Buttercup	Annual		24.50	27
1979	A Boy Meets His Dog (Christmas)	Annual		24.50	30
1980	Flying High	Annual		27.50	28
1980	Chilly Reception (Christmas)	Annual		27.50	28
1981	Sweet Serenade	Annual		27.50	28
1981	Ski Skills (Christmas)	Annual		27.50	28
1982	Young Mans Fancy	Annual		29.50	30
1982	Coal Season's Coming	Annual		29.50	30
1983	Christmas Medley	Annual		29.50	30
1983	The Milkmaid	Annual		29.50	30
1984	Tiny Tim	Annual		29.50	30
1984	Young Love	Annual		29.50	30
1984	Marriage License	Annual		32.50	33
1984	Yarn Spinner	5,000		32.50	33
1985	Yuletide Reflections	5,000		32.50	33
1986	Home For The Holidays	5,000		32.50	33
1986	On Top of the World	5,000		32.50	33
1987	Merry Christmas Grandma	5,000		32.50	33
1987	The Artist	5,000		32.50	33
1988	The Homecoming	15,000		37.50	38

Hallmark Galleries

Enchanted Garden - E. Richardson

YEAR	ISSUE	EDITION LIMIT	YEAR RETD.	ISSUE PRICE	QUOTE U.S. $
1992	Fairy Bunny (porcelain) 3500QHG3012	9,500	1994	35.00	35

Kirk Stieff

Bell - Kirk Stieff

YEAR	ISSUE	EDITION LIMIT	YEAR RETD.	ISSUE PRICE	QUOTE U.S. $
1992	Santa's Workshop	3,000		40.00	40
1993	Santa's Reindeer	Closed	N/A	30.00	30

Musical Bells - Kirk Stieff

YEAR	ISSUE	EDITION LIMIT	YEAR RETD.	ISSUE PRICE	QUOTE U.S. $
1977	Annual Bell 1977	Closed	N/A	17.95	75-120
1978	Annual Bell 1978	Closed	N/A	17.95	80
1979	Annual Bell 1979	Closed	N/A	17.95	50
1980	Annual Bell 1980	Closed	N/A	19.95	50
1981	Annual Bell 1981	Closed	N/A	19.95	75
1982	Annual Bell 1982	Closed	N/A	19.95	60-120
1983	Annual Bell 1983	Closed	N/A	19.95	50-60
1984	Annual Bell 1984	Closed	N/A	19.95	40
1985	Annual Bell 1985	Closed	N/A	19.95	50
1986	Annual Bell 1986	Closed	N/A	19.95	55
1987	Annual Bell 1987	Closed	N/A	19.95	45
1988	Annual Bell 1988	Closed	N/A	22.50	35-45
1989	Annual Bell 1989	Closed	N/A	25.00	25
1990	Annual Bell 1990	Closed	N/A	27.00	27
1991	Annual Bell 1991	Closed	N/A	28.00	35
1992	Annual Bell 1992	Closed	N/A	30.00	30
1993	Annual Bell 1993	Closed	N/A	30.00	30
1994	Annual Bell 1994	Open	N/A	30.00	35

Lance Corporation

Hudson Pewter Bicentennial Bells - P.W. Baston

YEAR	ISSUE	EDITION LIMIT	YEAR RETD.	ISSUE PRICE	QUOTE U.S. $
1974	Benjamin Franklin	Closed	1977	Unkn.	70-80
1974	George Washington	Closed	1977	Unkn.	30-40
1974	James Madison	Closed	1977	Unkn.	30-40
1974	John Adams	Closed	1977	Unkn.	100-125
1974	Thomas Jefferson	Closed	1977	Unkn.	40-50

Lenox China

Songs of Christmas - Unknown

YEAR	ISSUE	EDITION LIMIT	YEAR RETD.	ISSUE PRICE	QUOTE U.S. $
1991	We Wish You a Merry Christmas	Yr.Iss.	1992	49.00	49
1992	Deck the Halls	Yr.Iss.	1993	53.00	53
1993	Jingle Bells	Yr.Iss.	1994	57.00	57
1994	Silver Bells	Yr.Iss.	1995	62.00	62

Lenox Collections

Bird Bells - Unknown

YEAR	ISSUE	EDITION LIMIT	YEAR RETD.	ISSUE PRICE	QUOTE U.S. $
1991	Bluebird	Open		57.00	57
1991	Chickadee	Open		57.00	57
1991	Hummingbird	Open		57.00	57
1992	Robin Bell	Open		57.00	57

Carousel Bell - Unknown

YEAR	ISSUE	EDITION LIMIT	YEAR RETD.	ISSUE PRICE	QUOTE U.S. $
1992	Carousel Horse	Open		45.00	45

Crystal Christmas Bell - Lenox

YEAR	ISSUE	EDITION LIMIT	YEAR RETD.	ISSUE PRICE	QUOTE U.S. $
1981	Partridge in a Pear Tree	15,000	1981	55.00	55
1982	Holy Family Bell	15,000	1982	55.00	55
1983	Three Wise Men	15,000	1983	55.00	55
1984	Dove Bell	15,000	1984	57.00	57
1985	Santa Claus Bell	15,000	1985	57.00	57
1986	Dashing Through the Snow Bell	15,000	1986	64.00	64
1987	Heralding Angel Bell	15,000	1987	76.00	76
1991	Celestial Harpist	15,000	1991	75.00	75

Lenox Crystal

Annual Bell Series - Lenox

YEAR	ISSUE	EDITION LIMIT	YEAR RETD.	ISSUE PRICE	QUOTE U.S. $
1987	Partridge Bell	Yr.Iss.	1990	45.00	45
1988	Angel Bell	Open	1991	45.00	45
1989	St. Nicholas Bell	Open	1991	45.00	45
1990	Christmas Tree Bell	Open	1993	49.00	49
1991	Teddy Bear Bell	Yr.Iss.	1992	49.00	49
1992	Snowman Bell	Yr.Iss.	1993	49.00	49
1993	Nutcracker Bell	Yr.Iss.	1994	49.00	49
1994	Candle Bell	Yr.Iss.	1995	49.00	49

Lladro

Lladro Bell - Lladro

YEAR	ISSUE	EDITION LIMIT	YEAR RETD.	ISSUE PRICE	QUOTE U.S. $
XX	Crystal Wedding Bell L4500	Closed	N/A	N/A	195

Lladro Christmas Bell - Lladro

YEAR	ISSUE	EDITION LIMIT	YEAR RETD.	ISSUE PRICE	QUOTE U.S. $
1987	Christmas Bell - L5458M	Annual	1987	29.50	50-75
1988	Christmas Bell - L5525M	Annual	1988	32.50	30-50
1989	Christmas Bell - L5616M	Annual	1989	32.50	105-120
1990	Christmas Bell - L5641M	Annual	1990	34.50	55-65
1991	Christmas Bell - L5803M	Annual	1991	37.50	40
1992	Christmas Bell - L5913M	Annual	1992	37.50	45
1993	Christmas Bell - L6010M	Annual	1993	37.50	40-70
1994	Christmas Bell - L6139M	Annual	1994	39.50	40
1995	Christmas Bell - L6206M	Annual		39.50	40

Lladro Limited Edition Bell - Lladro

YEAR	ISSUE	EDITION LIMIT	YEAR RETD.	ISSUE PRICE	QUOTE U.S. $
1994	Eternal Love 7542M	Annual		95.00	95

Old World Christmas

Porcelain Christmas - E.M. Merck

YEAR	ISSUE	EDITION LIMIT	YEAR RETD.	ISSUE PRICE	QUOTE U.S. $
1988	1st Edition Santa Bell	Retrd.	1988	10.00	10
1989	2nd Edition Santa Bell	Retrd.	1989	10.00	10

Reed & Barton

Noel Musical Bells - Reed & Barton

YEAR	ISSUE	EDITION LIMIT	YEAR RETD.	ISSUE PRICE	QUOTE U.S. $
1980	Bell 1980	Closed	1980	20.00	50
1981	Bell 1981	Closed	1981	22.50	45
1982	Bell 1982	Closed	1982	22.50	40
1983	Bell 1983	Closed	1983	22.50	55
1984	Bell 1984	Closed	1984	22.50	55
1985	Bell 1985	Closed	1985	25.00	40
1986	Bell 1986	Closed	1986	25.00	55
1987	Bell 1987	Closed	1987	25.00	55
1988	Bell 1988	Closed	1988	25.00	28-40
1989	Bell 1989	Closed	1989	25.00	40
1990	Bell 1990	Closed	1990	27.50	30
1991	Bell 1991	Closed	1991	30.00	30
1992	Bell 1992	Closed	1992	30.00	40
1993	Bell 1993	Yr.Iss.	1993	30.00	30
1994	Bell 1994	Yr.Iss.	1994	30.00	30
1995	Bell 1995	Yr.Iss.		30.00	30

Yuletide Bell - Reed & Barton

YEAR	ISSUE	EDITION LIMIT	YEAR RETD.	ISSUE PRICE	QUOTE U.S. $
1981	Yuletide Holiday	Closed	1981	14.00	14
1982	Little Shepherd	Closed	1982	14.00	14
1983	Perfect Angel	Closed	1983	15.00	15
1984	Drummer Boy	Closed	1984	15.00	15
1985	Caroler	Closed	1985	16.50	17
1986	Night Before Christmas	Closed	1986	16.50	17
1987	Jolly St. Nick	Closed	1987	16.50	17
1988	Christmas Morning	Closed	1988	16.50	17
1989	The Bell Ringer	Closed	1989	16.50	17
1990	The Wreath Bearer	Closed	1990	18.50	19
1991	A Special Gift	Closed	1991	22.50	23
1992	My Special Friend	Closed	1992	22.50	23
1993	My Christmas Present	Yr.Iss.	1993	22.50	23
1994	Holiday Wishes	Yr.Iss.	1994	22.50	23
1995	Yuletide Bell	Yr.Iss.		22.50	23

River Shore

Norman Rockwell Single Issues - N. Rockwell

YEAR	ISSUE	EDITION LIMIT	YEAR RETD.	ISSUE PRICE	QUOTE U.S. $
1981	Grandpa's Guardian	7,000		45.00	45
1981	Looking Out to Sea	7,000		45.00	95
1981	Spring Flowers	347		175.00	175

Rockwell Children Series I - N. Rockwell

YEAR	ISSUE	EDITION LIMIT	YEAR RETD.	ISSUE PRICE	QUOTE U.S. $
1977	First Day of School	7,500		30.00	75
1977	Flowers for Mother	7,500		30.00	60
1977	Football Hero	7,500		30.00	75
1977	School Play	7,500		30.00	75

Rockwell Children Series II - N. Rockwell

YEAR	ISSUE	EDITION LIMIT	YEAR RETD.	ISSUE PRICE	QUOTE U.S. $
1978	Dressing Up	15,000		35.00	50
1978	Five Cents A Glass	15,000		35.00	40
1978	Future All American	15,000		35.00	52
1978	Garden Girl	15,000		35.00	40

Roman, Inc.

Annual Fontanini Christmas Crystal Bell - E. Simonetti

YEAR	ISSUE	EDITION LIMIT	YEAR RETD.	ISSUE PRICE	QUOTE U.S. $
1991	Bell 1991	Closed	1991	30.00	30
1992	Bell 1992	Closed	1992	30.00	30
1993	Bell 1993	Closed	1993	30.00	30

Annual Nativity Bell - I. Spencer

YEAR	ISSUE	EDITION LIMIT	YEAR RETD.	ISSUE PRICE	QUOTE U.S. $
1990	Nativity	Closed	N/A	15.00	15
1991	Flight Into Egypt	Closed	N/A	15.00	15
1992	Gloria in Excelsis Deo	Closed	N/A	15.00	15
1993	Three Kings of Orient	Closed	N/A	15.00	15

F. Hook Bells - F. Hook

YEAR	ISSUE	EDITION LIMIT	YEAR RETD.	ISSUE PRICE	QUOTE U.S. $
1985	Beach Buddies	15,000		25.00	28
1986	Sounds of the Sea	15,000		25.00	28
1987	Bear Hug	15,000		25.00	28

The Masterpiece Collection - Various

YEAR	ISSUE	EDITION LIMIT	YEAR RETD.	ISSUE PRICE	QUOTE U.S. $
1979	Adoration - F. Lippe	Open		20.00	20
1980	Madonna with Grapes - P. Mignard	Open		25.00	25
1981	The Holy Family - G. Notti	Open		25.00	25
1982	Madonna of the Streets - R. Ferruzzi	Open		25.00	25

Schmid

Berta Hummel Christmas Bells - B. Hummel

YEAR	ISSUE	EDITION LIMIT	YEAR RETD.	ISSUE PRICE	QUOTE U.S. $
1972	Angel with Flute	Yr.Iss.	1972	20.00	75
1973	Nativity	Yr.Iss.	1973	15.00	80
1974	The Guardian Angel	Yr.Iss.	1974	17.50	45
1975	The Christmas Child	Yr.Iss.	1975	22.50	45
1976	Sacred Journey	Yr.Iss.	1976	22.50	25
1977	Herald Angel	Yr.Iss.	1977	22.50	50
1978	Heavenly Trio	Yr.Iss.	1978	27.50	40
1979	Starlight Angel	Yr.Iss.	1979	38.00	45
1980	Parade into Toyland	Yr.Iss.	1980	45.00	55
1981	A Time to Remember	Yr.Iss.	1981	45.00	55
1982	Angelic Procession	Yr.Iss.	1982	45.00	50
1983	Angelic Messenger	Yr.Iss.	1983	45.00	55
1984	A Gift from Heaven	Yr.Iss.	1984	45.00	75
1985	Heavenly Light	Yr.Iss.	1985	45.00	75
1986	Tell the Heavens	Yr.Iss.	1986	45.00	45
1987	Angelic Gifts	Yr.Iss.	1987	47.50	48
1988	Cheerful Cherubs	Yr.Iss.	1988	52.50	55
1989	Angelic Musician	Yr.Iss.	1989	53.00	55
1990	Angel's Light	Yr.Iss.	1990	53.00	53
1991	Message From Above	5,000	1991	58.00	58
1992	Sweet Blessings	5,000	1992	65.00	65
1993	Silent Wonder	5,000	1993	58.00	58

Berta Hummel Mother's Day Bells - B. Hummel

YEAR	ISSUE	EDITION LIMIT	YEAR RETD.	ISSUE PRICE	QUOTE U.S. $
1976	Devotion for Mothers	Yr.Iss.	1976	22.50	55
1977	Moonlight Return	Yr.Iss.	1977	22.50	45
1978	Afternoon Stroll	Yr.Iss.	1978	27.50	45
1979	Cherub's Gift	Yr.Iss.	1979	38.00	45
1980	Mother's Little Helper	Yr.Iss.	1980	45.00	45
1981	Playtime	Yr.Iss.	1981	45.00	45
1982	The Flower Basket	Yr.Iss.	1982	45.00	45
1983	Spring Bouquet	Yr.Iss.	1983	45.00	45
1984	A Joy to Share	Yr.Iss.	1984	45.00	45

Disney Annuals - Disney Studios

YEAR	ISSUE	EDITION LIMIT	YEAR RETD.	ISSUE PRICE	QUOTE U.S. $
1985	Snow Biz	10,000	1985	16.50	17
1986	Tree for Two	10,000	1986	16.50	17
1987	Merry Mouse Medley	10,000	1987	17.50	18
1988	Warm Winter Ride	10,000	1988	19.50	20
1989	Merry Mickey Claus	10,000	1989	23.00	23
1990	Holly Jolly Christmas	10,000	1990	26.50	27
1991	Mickey & Minnie's Rockin' Christmas	10,000	1991	26.50	27

RFD Bell - L. Davis

YEAR	ISSUE	EDITION LIMIT	YEAR RETD.	ISSUE PRICE	QUOTE U.S. $
1979	Blossom	Closed	N/A	65.00	300-400
1979	Kate	Closed	N/A	65.00	300-400
1979	Willy	Closed	N/A	65.00	400
1979	Caruso	Closed	N/A	65.00	300
1979	Wilbur	Closed	N/A	65.00	300-350
1979	Old Blue Lead	Closed	N/A	65.00	275-300
1980	Cow Bell "Blossom"	Closed	N/A	65.00	65
1980	Mule Bell "Kate"	Closed	N/A	65.00	65
1980	Goat Bell "Willy"	Closed	N/A	65.00	65
1980	Rooster Bell "Caruso"	Closed	N/A	65.00	65
1980	Pig Bell "Wilbur"	Closed	N/A	65.00	65
1980	Dog Bell "Old Blue and Lead"	Closed	N/A	65.00	65

Seymour Mann, Inc.

Connoisseur Collection - M. Bernini

YEAR	ISSUE	EDITION LIMIT	YEAR RETD.	ISSUE PRICE	QUOTE U.S. $
1995	Bluebird CLT-15	Open		15.00	15
1995	Canary CLT-12	Open		15.00	15
1995	Cardinal CLT-9	Open		15.00	15
1995	Dove CLT-3	Open		15.00	15
1995	Hummingbird CLT-6	Open		15.00	15
1995	Pink Rose CLT-72	Open		15.00	15
1995	Robin CLT-18	Open		15.00	15
1995	Swan CLT-52	Open		15.00	15

CHRISTMAS ORNAMENTS

All God's Children

Angel Dumpling - M. Holcombe

YEAR	ISSUE	EDITION LIMIT	YEAR RETD.	ISSUE PRICE	QUOTE U.S. $
1993	Eric-1570	Retrd.	1994	22.50	30-45
1994	Erica-1578	Retrd.	1995	22.50	23

Christmas Ornaments - M. Holcombe

YEAR	ISSUE	EDITION LIMIT	YEAR RETD.	ISSUE PRICE	QUOTE U.S. $
1987	Cameo Ornaments,set /12 D1912	Retrd.	1988	144.00	1325-2040
1987	Doll Ornaments set/ 24 - D1924	Retrd.	1988	336.00	2000-3200
1993	Santa with Scooty-1571	Retrd.	1994	22.50	30-60

Anheuser-Busch, Inc.

A & Eagle Collector Ornament Series - A.-Busch, Inc.

YEAR	ISSUE	EDITION LIMIT	YEAR RETD.	ISSUE PRICE	QUOTE U.S. $
1991	Budweiser Girl-Circa 1890's N3178	Open		15.00	15
1992	1893 Columbian Exposition N3649	Open		15.00	15
1993	Greatest Triumph N4089	Open		15.00	15

Christmas Ornaments - Various

YEAR	ISSUE	EDITION LIMIT	YEAR RETD.	ISSUE PRICE	QUOTE U.S. $
1992	Clydesdales Mini Plate Ornaments N3650 - S. Sampson	Open		23.00	23
1993	Budweiser Six-Pack Mini Plate Ornaments N4220 - M. Urdahl	Retrd.	1994	10.00	10

Annalee Mobilitee Dolls, Inc.

Christmas Ornaments - A. Thorndike

YEAR	ISSUE	EDITION LIMIT	YEAR RETD.	ISSUE PRICE	QUOTE U.S. $
1985	Clown Head	5,701	N/A	6.95	175
1987	3" Elf	1,950	1989	12.95	325
1992	3" Skier	8,332	N/A	14.45	175

CHRISTMAS ORNAMENTS

ANRI

Disney Four Star Collection - Disney Studios

YEAR ISSUE		EDITION LIMIT	YEAR RETD.	ISSUE PRICE	QUOTE U.S.$
1989	Maestro Mickey	Yr.Iss.	1989	25.00	25
1990	Minnie Mouse	Yr.Iss.	1990	25.00	25

Ferrandiz Message Collection - J. Ferrandiz

YEAR ISSUE		EDITION LIMIT	YEAR RETD.	ISSUE PRICE	QUOTE U.S.$
1989	Let the Heavens Ring	1,000	1992	215.00	215
1990	Hear The Angels Sing	1,000	1992	225.00	225

Ferrandiz Woodcarvings - J. Ferrandiz

YEAR ISSUE		EDITION LIMIT	YEAR RETD.	ISSUE PRICE	QUOTE U.S.$
1988	Heavenly Drummer	1,000	1992	175.00	225
1989	Heavenly Strings	1,000	1992	190.00	190

Sarah Kay's First Christmas - S. Kay

YEAR ISSUE		EDITION LIMIT	YEAR RETD.	ISSUE PRICE	QUOTE U.S.$
1994	Sarah Kay's First Christmas	500		140.00	140
1995	First Xmas Stocking 57502	500		99.00	99

Armani

Christmas - G. Armani

YEAR ISSUE		EDITION LIMIT	YEAR RETD.	ISSUE PRICE	QUOTE U.S.$
1991	Christmas Ornament 799A	Retrd.	1991	11.50	45
1992	Christmas Ornament 788F	Retrd.	1992	23.50	24
1993	Christmas Ornament 892P	Retrd.	1993	25.00	25
1994	Christmas Ornament 801P	Retrd.	1994	25.00	35
1995	Christmas Ornament 640P	Yr.Iss.		30.00	30

Artaffects

Annual Bell Ornaments - G. Perillo

YEAR ISSUE		EDITION LIMIT	YEAR RETD.	ISSUE PRICE	QUOTE U.S.$
1985	Home Sweet Wigwam	Yr.Iss.		14.00	25
1986	Peek-A-Boo	Yr.Iss.		15.00	25
1987	Annual Bell Ornament	Yr.Iss.		15.00	25
1988	Annual Bell Ornament	Yr.Iss.		17.50	25
1989	Annual Bell Ornament	Yr.Iss.		17.50	25
1990	Annual Bell Ornament	Yr.Iss.		17.50	25
1991	Annual Bell Ornament	Yr.Iss.		19.50	25

Annual Christmas Ornaments - G. Perillo

YEAR ISSUE		EDITION LIMIT	YEAR RETD.	ISSUE PRICE	QUOTE U.S.$
1985	Papoose Ornament	Unkn.		14.00	30
1986	Christmas Cactus	Unkn.		15.00	50
1987	Annual Ornament	Unkn.		15.00	35
1988	Annual Ornament	Yr.Iss.		18.00	25
1989	Annual Ornament	Yr.Iss.		18.00	25
1990	Annual Ornament	Yr.Iss.		19.50	25
1991	Annual Ornament	Yr.Iss.		19.50	25

Artists of the World

De Grazia Annual Ornaments - T. De Grazia

YEAR ISSUE		EDITION LIMIT	YEAR RETD.	ISSUE PRICE	QUOTE U.S.$
1986	Pima. Indian Drummer Boy	Yr.Iss.	1986	28.00	400-500
1987	White Dove	Yr.Iss.	1987	30.00	85-120
1988	Flower Girl	Yr.Iss.	1988	33.00	75-110
1989	Flower Boy	Yr.Iss.	1989	35.00	75-100
1990	Pink Papoose	Yr.Iss.	1990	35.00	65-120
1990	Merry Little Indian	10,000	1990	88.00	95-125
1991	Christmas Prayer (Red)	Yr.Iss.	1991	50.00	75-95
1992	Bearing Gift	Yr.Iss.	1992	55.00	65-75
1993	Lighting the Way	Yr.Iss.	1993	58.00	65-75
1994	Warm Wishes	Yr.Iss.	1994	65.00	65-75
1995	Little Prayer (White)	Yr.Iss.	1995	49.50	50-65
1995	Heavenly Flowers	Yr.Iss.		65.00	65
1995	My Beautiful Rocking Horse	1,995		125.00	125

Attic Babies

Christmas Decorations- M. Maschino

YEAR ISSUE		EDITION LIMIT	YEAR RETD.	ISSUE PRICE	QUOTE U.S.$
1993	Raggedy Santa Wreath	Retrd.	1994	101.95	102
1992	Stocking	Retrd.	1994	55.95	56

Wooden Ornaments - M. Maschino

YEAR ISSUE		EDITION LIMIT	YEAR RETD.	ISSUE PRICE	QUOTE U.S.$
1993	Angel	Retrd.	1994	21.95	22
1993	Snowman	Retrd.	1994	17.95	18
1993	Stocking	Retrd.	1994	25.95	26

Band Creations, Inc.

Best Friends - Richards/Penfield

YEAR ISSUE		EDITION LIMIT	YEAR RETD.	ISSUE PRICE	QUOTE U.S.$
1994	4 Assorted Angel Ornaments	Open		5.00	5
1995	Double Angels	Open		8.00	8

Best Friends-A Star is Born - Richards/Penfield

YEAR ISSUE		EDITION LIMIT	YEAR RETD.	ISSUE PRICE	QUOTE U.S.$
1995	Baseball Boy	Open		6.00	6
1995	Baseball Girl	Open		6.00	6
1995	Basketball Boy	Open		6.00	6
1995	Basketball Girl	Open		6.00	6
1995	Cheerleader Girl	Open		6.00	6
1995	Football Boy	Open		6.00	6
1995	Golfer Boy	Open		6.00	6
1995	Golfer Girl	Open		6.00	6
1995	Hockey Boy	Open		6.00	6
1995	Soccer Boy	Open		6.00	6
1995	Soccer Girl	Open		6.00	6
1995	Swimmer Boy	Open		6.00	6
1995	Swimmer Girl	Open		6.00	6

Bing & Grondahl

Christmas - Various

YEAR ISSUE		EDITION LIMIT	YEAR RETD.	ISSUE PRICE	QUOTE U.S.$
1985	Christmas Eve at the Farmhouse - E. Jensen	Closed	1985	19.50	20
1986	Silent Night, Holy Night E. Jensen	Closed	1986	19.50	30
1987	The Snowman's Christmas Eve E. Jensen	Closed	1987	22.50	23
1988	In the King's Garden - E. Jensen	Closed	1988	25.00	25
1989	Christmas Anchorage E. Jensen	Closed	1989	27.00	27
1990	Changing of the Guards E. Jensen	Closed	1990	32.50	35
1991	Copenhagen Stock Exchange E. Jensen	Closed	1991	34.50	35
1992	Christmas at the Rectory J. Steensen	Closed	1992	36.50	37
1993	Father Christmas in Copenhagen - J. Nielsen	Closed	1993	36.50	37
1994	A Day at the Deer Park J. Nielsen	Closed	1994	36.50	37
1995	The Towers of Copenhagen J. Nielsen	Closed	1995	37.50	38
1996	Winter at the Old Mill - J. Nielsen	Yr.Iss.		37.50	38

Christmas In America - J. Woodson

YEAR ISSUE		EDITION LIMIT	YEAR RETD.	ISSUE PRICE	QUOTE U.S.$
1986	Christmas Eve in Williamsburg	Closed	1986	12.50	40-90
1987	Christmas Eve at the White House	Closed	1987	15.00	25-60
1988	Christmas Eve at Rockefeller Center	Closed	1988	18.50	19
1989	Christmas in New England	Closed	1989	20.00	20
1990	Christmas Eve at the Capitol	Closed	1990	20.00	35
1991	Independence Hall	Closed	1991	23.50	24
1992	Christmas in San Francisco	Closed	1992	25.00	35
1993	Coming Home For Christmas	Closed	1993	25.00	30
1994	Christmas Eve in Alaska	Closed	1994	25.00	45
1995	Christmas Eve in Mississippi	Closed	1995	25.00	25

Santa Around the World - H. Hansen

YEAR ISSUE		EDITION LIMIT	YEAR RETD.	ISSUE PRICE	QUOTE U.S.$
1995	Santa in Greenland	Yr.Iss.	1995	25.00	25

Santa Claus

YEAR ISSUE		EDITION LIMIT	YEAR RETD.	ISSUE PRICE	QUOTE U.S.$
1989	Santa's Workshop	Yr.Iss.	1989	20.00	60
1990	Santa's Sleigh	Yr.Iss.	1990	20.00	48
1991	The Journey	Yr.Iss.	1991	24.00	45
1992	Santa's Arrival	Yr.Iss.	1992	25.00	36
1993	Santa's Gifts	Yr.Iss.	1993	25.00	36
1994	Christmas Stories	Yr.Iss.	1994	25.00	25

Boyds Collection Ltd.

The Bearstone Collection ™ - G. M. Lowenthal

YEAR ISSUE		EDITION LIMIT	YEAR RETD.	ISSUE PRICE	QUOTE U.S.$
1994	'Charity'-Angel Bear with Star 2502	Open		9.45	10-15
1994	'Faith'-Angel Bear w/Trumpet 2500	Open		9.45	10-15
1994	'Hope'-Angel Bear w/Wreath 2501	Open		9.45	10-15
1995	'Edmund'...Believe 2505	Open		9.45	10-15
1995	'Elliot with Tree' 2507	Open		9.45	10-15
1995	'Manheim' the Moose with Wreath 2506	Open		9.45	10-15

The Folkstone Collection ™ - G.M. Lowenthal

YEAR ISSUE		EDITION LIMIT	YEAR RETD.	ISSUE PRICE	QUOTE U.S.$
1995	Father Christmas 2553	Open		9.45	10
1995	Jean Claude & Jacque...the Skiers 2561	Open		9.45	10
1995	Jingles the Snowman with Wreath 2562	Open		9.45	10
1995	Nicholai with Tree 2550	Open		9.45	10
1995	Nicholas the Giftgiver 2551	Open		9.45	10
1995	Olaf...Let it Snow 2560	Open		9.45	10
1995	Sliknick in the Chimney 2552	Open		9.45	10

Brandywine Collectibles

Custom Collection - M. Whiting

YEAR ISSUE		EDITION LIMIT	YEAR RETD.	ISSUE PRICE	QUOTE U.S.$
1989	Lorain Lighthouse	Closed	1992	9.00	9
1994	Smithfield Clerk's Office	Open		9.00	9
1991	Smithfield VA. Courthouse	Closed	1992	9.00	9

Williamsburg Ornaments - M. Whiting

YEAR ISSUE		EDITION LIMIT	YEAR RETD.	ISSUE PRICE	QUOTE U.S.$
1988	Apothocary	Closed	1991	9.00	9
1988	Bootmaker	Closed	1991	9.00	9
1989	Cole Shop	Closed	1991	9.00	9
1988	Finnie Quarter	Closed	1991	9.00	9
1989	Gunsmith	Closed	1991	9.00	9
1994	Gunsmith	360	1994	9.50	10
1989	Music Teacher	Closed	1991	9.00	9
1988	Nicolson Shop	Closed	1991	9.00	9
1988	Tarpley's Store	Closed	1991	9.00	9
1988	Wigmaker	Closed	1991	9.00	9
1989	Windmill	Closed	1991	9.00	9

Calabar Creations

Angelic Pigasus - P. Apsit

YEAR ISSUE		EDITION LIMIT	YEAR RETD.	ISSUE PRICE	QUOTE U.S.$
1995	Adagio AP75361	Open		5.00	5
1995	Alba AP75351	Open		5.00	5
1995	Ambrose AP75372	Open		5.00	5
1995	Andante AP75381	Open		5.00	5
1995	Angelica AP75312	Open		5.00	5
1995	Anna AP75321	Open		5.00	5
1995	Aria AP75341	Open		5.00	5

Cast Art Industries

Dreamsicles Ornaments - K. Haynes

YEAR ISSUE		EDITION LIMIT	YEAR RETD.	ISSUE PRICE	QUOTE U.S.$
1992	Bear-DX274	Retrd.	1994	6.00	6
1992	Bunny-DX270	Retrd.	1994	6.00	6
1992	Cherub On Cloud-DX263	Retrd.	1994	6.00	6
1992	Cherub With Moon-DX260	Retrd.	1994	6.00	6
1992	Cherub With Star-DX262	Retrd.	1994	6.00	6
1992	Lamb-DX275	Retrd.	1994	6.00	6
1992	Piggy-DX271	Retrd.	1994	6.00	6
1992	Praying Cherub-DX261	Retrd.	1994	6.00	6
1992	Raccoon-DX272	Retrd.	1994	6.00	6
1992	Squirrel-DX273	Retrd.	1994	6.00	6

The Cat's Meow

1985 Christmas Ornaments - F. Jones

YEAR ISSUE		EDITION LIMIT	YEAR RETD.	ISSUE PRICE	QUOTE U.S.$
1985	Bancroft House	Retrd.	1986	4.00	40
1985	Chapel	Retrd.	1986	4.00	N/A
1985	Grayling House	Retrd.	1986	4.00	40
1985	Morton House	Retrd.	1986	4.00	N/A
1985	Rutledge House	Retrd.	1986	4.00	75
1985	School	Retrd.	1986	4.00	N/A

1987 Christmas Ornaments - F. Jones

YEAR ISSUE		EDITION LIMIT	YEAR RETD.	ISSUE PRICE	QUOTE U.S.$
1987	Blacksmith Shop	Retrd.	1988	5.00	60
1987	District #17 School	Retrd.	1988	5.00	60
1987	Globe Corner Bookstore	Retrd.	1988	5.00	60
1987	Kennedy Birthplace	Retrd.	1988	5.00	26-75
1987	Set/4	Retrd.	1988	20.00	175-200

1995 Christmas Ornaments - F. Jones

YEAR ISSUE		EDITION LIMIT	YEAR RETD.	ISSUE PRICE	QUOTE U.S.$
1995	Carnegie Library	12/95		8.75	9
1995	Holly Hill Farmhouse	12/95		8.75	9
1995	North Central School	12/95		8.75	9
1995	St. James General Store	12/95		8.75	9
1995	Unitarian Church	12/95		8.75	9
1995	Yaquina Bay Light	12/95		8.75	9

1996 Christmas Ornaments - F. Jones

YEAR ISSUE		EDITION LIMIT	YEAR RETD.	ISSUE PRICE	QUOTE U.S.$
1996	Christ Church	12/96		9.00	9
1996	Deerfield Post Office	12/96		9.00	9
1996	Gimbel & Sons Country Store	12/96		9.00	9
1996	Hook Windmill	12/96		9.00	9
1996	Maple Manor	12/96		9.00	9
1996	Parsonage	12/96		9.00	9

Cavanagh Group Intl.

Coca-Cola Christmas Collectors Society Members' Only - Sundblom

YEAR ISSUE		EDITION LIMIT	YEAR RETD.	ISSUE PRICE	QUOTE U.S.$
1993	Ho Ho Ho	Closed	1993	Gift	N/A
1994	Fishing Bear	Closed	1994	Gift	N/A
1995	Hospitality	12/95		Gift	N/A

Coca-Cola Brand Heritage Collection - Sundblom

YEAR ISSUE		EDITION LIMIT	YEAR RETD.	ISSUE PRICE	QUOTE U.S.$
1995	Christmas Is Love	Open		10.00	10
1995	Santa at the Mantle	Open		10.00	10
1995	Ssshhh!	Open		10.00	10

Coca-Cola Brand Historical Building - CGI

YEAR ISSUE		EDITION LIMIT	YEAR RETD.	ISSUE PRICE	QUOTE U.S.$
1991	1930's Service Station	Closed	1994	9.99	10-13
1991	Early Coca-Cola Bottling Company	Closed	1994	9.99	10-13
1991	Jacob's Pharmacy	Closed	1994	9.99	10-13
1991	The Pemberton House	Closed	1994	9.99	10-13

Coca-Cola Brand North Pole Bottling Works - CGI

YEAR ISSUE		EDITION LIMIT	YEAR RETD.	ISSUE PRICE	QUOTE U.S.$
1995	Barrel of Bears	Open		8.99	9
1993	Blast Off	Open		8.99	9
1993	Delivery for Santa	Open		8.99	9
1993	Fill 'er Up	Closed	1994	8.99	9
1995	Fountain Glass Follies	Open		8.99	9
1993	Ice Sculpting	Open		8.99	9
1993	Long Winter's Nap	Open		8.99	9
1993	North Pole Express	Closed	1994	8.99	9
1995	North Pole Flying School	Open		8.99	9
1994	Power Drive	Open		8.99	9
1994	Santa's Refreshment	Open		8.99	9
1994	Seltzer Surprise	Open		8.99	9
1993	Thirsting for Adventure	Closed	1994	8.99	9
1994	Tops Off Refreshment	Open		8.99	9
1993	Tops on Refreshment	Open		8.99	9

Coca-Cola Brand Polar Bear - CGI

YEAR ISSUE		EDITION LIMIT	YEAR RETD.	ISSUE PRICE	QUOTE U.S.$
1994	Downhill Sledder	Open		8.99	9
1994	North Pole Delivery	Open		8.99	9
1995	Polar Bear in Bottle Opener	Open		8.99	9
1994	Skating Coca-Cola Polar Bear	Open		8.99	9
1995	Snowboardin' Bear	Open		8.99	9
1994	Vending Machine Mischief	Open		8.99	9

Coca-Cola Brand Trim A Tree Collection - Sundblom

YEAR ISSUE		EDITION LIMIT	YEAR RETD.	ISSUE PRICE	QUOTE U.S.$
1994	Busy Man's Pause	Open		9.99	10
1991	Christmas Is Love	Closed	1992	9.99	13
1993	Decorating the Tree	Closed	1994	9.99	13
1993	Extra Bright Refreshment	Closed	1994	9.99	13

YEAR ISSUE		EDITION LIMIT	YEAR RETD.	ISSUE PRICE	QUOTE U.S.$
1994	For Sparkling Holidays	Open		9.99	10
1990	Happy Holidays	Closed	1992	9.99	20
1992	Happy Holidays	Closed	1993	9.99	10
1995	It Will Refresh You Too	Open		9.99	10
1990	Merry Christmas and a Happy New Year	Closed	1991	9.99	22-45
1995	Please Pause Here	Open		9.99	10
1990	Santa on Stool	Closed	1993	9.99	13
1990	Season's Greetings	Closed	1991	9.99	13
1992	Sshhh!	Closed	1992	9.99	15
1994	Things Go Better with Coke	Open		9.99	10
1991	A Time to Share	Closed	1993	9.99	13
1993	Travel Refreshed	Open		9.99	10

Cazenovia Abroad

Carousel - Various

YEAR ISSUE		EDITION LIMIT	YEAR RETD.	ISSUE PRICE	QUOTE U.S.$
1991	Flag Horse-A301CFH - Herschell-Spillman	2,649		75.00	75
1991	Fishing Cat-A302CFH - Cernigliaro	2,649		75.00	75
1991	Flirting Rabbit-A303CFH - Cernigliaro	2,649		75.00	75
1992	Sneaky Tiger-A304LST - C. Looff	2,649		82.50	83
1992	Spillman Polar Bear-A305HPB - Herschell-Spillman	2,649		82.50	83
1992	Rose Horse-A306PRH - C.W. Parker	2,649		82.50	83
1994	Flying Mane Jumping-A307LFM - Illions	2,649		82.50	83
1994	Pig-A308DP - Cernigliaro	2,649		82.50	83
1994	Zebra-A309DZ - Cernigliaro	2,649		82.50	83
1995	PTC Lion-A310PL - Philadelphia Toboggan Co.	2,649		82.50	83
1995	Hershall Frog-A311HSF - Hershall	2,649		82.50	83
1995	S&G Armor Horse-A312SGAH - Stein & Goldstein	2,649		82.50	83

Christmas Ornaments - Unknown

YEAR ISSUE		EDITION LIMIT	YEAR RETD.	ISSUE PRICE	QUOTE U.S.$
1968	Teddy Bear-P101TB	Unkn.		9.00	60
1968	Elephant-P102E	Unkn.		9.00	60
1968	Duck-P103D	Unkn.		9.00	60
1968	Bunny-P104B	Unkn.		9.00	60
1968	Cat-P105C	Unkn.		9.00	60
1968	Rooster-P106R	Unkn.		10.00	60
1968	Standing Angel-P107SA	Unkn.		9.00	70
1968	Tiptoe Angel-P108TTA	Unkn.		10.00	60
1969	Fawn-P109F	Unkn.		12.00	65
1970	Snow Man-P110SM	Unkn.		12.00	60
1970	Peace-P111P	Unkn.		12.00	60
1970	Porky-P112PK	Unkn.		15.00	60
1971	Kneeling Angel-P113KA	Unkn.		15.00	80
1972	Rocking Horse-P114RH	Unkn.		15.00	80
1973	Treetop Angel-P115TOP	Unkn.		10.00	65
1974	Owl-P116O	Unkn.		15.00	60
1975	Star-P117ST	Unkn.		15.00	60
1976	Hatching Chick-P118CH	Unkn.		15.00	60
1977	Raggedy Ann-P119RA	Unkn.		18.00	65
1978	Shell-P120SH	Unkn.		20.00	65
1979	Toy Soldier-P121TS	Unkn.		20.00	60
1980	Burro-P122BU	Unkn.		20.00	60
1981	Clown-P123CL	Unkn.		25.00	60
1982	Rebecca-P124RE	Unkn.		25.00	60
1983	Raggedy Andy-P125AND	Unkn.		28.00	65
1983	Mouse-P126MO	Unkn.		28.00	70
1984	Cherub-P127CB	Unkn.		30.00	70
1985	Shaggy Dog-P132SD	Unkn.		45.00	60
1986	Peter Rabbit-P133PR	Unkn.		50.00	60
1986	Big Sister-P134BS	Unkn.		60.00	70
1986	Little Brother-P135LB	Unkn.		55.00	70
1987	Lamb-P136LA	Unkn.		60.00	70
1987	Sea Horse-P137SE	Unkn.		35.00	50
1988	Partridge-P138PA	Unkn.		70.00	80
1988	Squirrel-P139SQ	Unkn.		70.00	80
1984	Reindeer & Sleigh-H100	Unkn.		1250.00	1500
1989	Swan-P140SW	Open		45.00	60
1990	Moravian Star-P141PS	Open		65.00	60
1991	Hedgehog-P142HH	Open		65.00	70
1991	Bunny Rabbit-P143BR	Open		65.00	70
1991	Angel-P144A	Open		63.00	70
1992	Humpty Dumpty-P145HD	Open		70.00	70
1994	Father Christmas-P146FC	Open		70.00	70
1995	9 1/2" Treetopper P2921	Open		250.00	250
1995	Globe, Joy of the World ME002	Open		70.00	70

Twelve Days of Christmas - J. Kall

YEAR ISSUE		EDITION LIMIT	YEAR RETD.	ISSUE PRICE	QUOTE U.S.$
1994	Partridge in a Pear Tree A401PP	Open		85.00	85
1994	Two Turtle Doves A402TT	Open		85.00	85
1994	Three French Hens A403TF	Open		85.00	85
1994	Four Calling Birds A404FC	Open		85.00	85
1994	Five Golden Rings A405FG	Open		85.00	85

Christopher Radko

Christopher Radko Family of Collectors - C. Radko

YEAR ISSUE		EDITION LIMIT	YEAR RETD.	ISSUE PRICE	QUOTE U.S.$
1993	Angels We Have Heard on High SP1	Retrd.	1993	50.00	425-600
1994	Starbuck Santa SP3	Retrd.	1994	75.00	75
1995	Dash Away All SP7	Yr.Iss.		34.00	34
1995	Purrfect Present SP8	Yr.Iss.		Gift	N/A

10 Year Anniversary - C. Radko

YEAR ISSUE		EDITION LIMIT	YEAR RETD.	ISSUE PRICE	QUOTE U.S.$
1995	On Top of the World SP6	Yr.Iss.		32.00	32

1987 Holiday Collection - C. Radko

YEAR ISSUE		EDITION LIMIT	YEAR RETD.	ISSUE PRICE	QUOTE U.S.$
1987	Baby Balloon 8832	Retrd.	N/A	7.95	95
1987	Birdhouse 8873	Retrd.	1987	10.00	100
1987	Buds in Bloom (pink) 8824	Retrd.	N/A	16.00	125
1987	Circle of Santas 8811	Retrd.	N/A	16.95	100
1987	Double Royal Drop 8856	Retrd.	1991	25.00	70
1987	Grecian Column 8842	Retrd.	1990	9.95	95
1987	Hot Air Balloon 885	Retrd.	N/A	15.00	100
1987	Lilac Sparkle 1814	Retrd.	N/A	15.00	125
1987	Mushroom in Winter 8862	Retrd.	1993	12.00	85
1987	Ripples on Oval 8844	Retrd.	1987	6.00	85
1987	Royal Diadem 8860	Retrd.	1987	25.00	135
1987	Royal Porcelain 8812	Retrd.	N/A	16.95	100
1987	Satin Scepter 8847	Retrd.	1987	8.95	100
1987	Simply Cartiere 8817	Retrd.	N/A	16.95	125
1987	Striped Balloon 8877	Retrd.	N/A	16.95	60
1987	Twin Finial 8857	Retrd.	N/A	23.50	100

1988 Holiday Collection - C. Radko

YEAR ISSUE		EDITION LIMIT	YEAR RETD.	ISSUE PRICE	QUOTE U.S.$
1988	Alpine Flowers 22	Retrd.	N/A	16.00	30
1988	Celestial 4	Retrd.	N/A	15.00	35
1988	Christmas Fanfare 50	Retrd.	1988	15.00	125
1988	Crown Jewels 74	Retrd.	1993	15.00	30
1988	Double Royal Star 56	Retrd.	1991	23.00	60
1988	Faberge Oval 3	Retrd.	N/A	15.00	30
1988	Gilded Leaves 13	Retrd.	N/A	16.00	125
1988	Mushroom Winter 62	Retrd.	1993	10.00	30
1988	Royal Porcelain 12	Retrd.	1991	16.00	35
1988	Stained Glass 16	Retrd.	1990	16.00	125
1988	Zebra - Tiger 886	Retrd.	N/A	15.00	60

1989 Holiday Collection - C. Radko

YEAR ISSUE		EDITION LIMIT	YEAR RETD.	ISSUE PRICE	QUOTE U.S.$
1989	Alpine Flowers 9-43	Retrd.	N/A	17.00	30
1989	Baroque Angel 9-11	Retrd.	1989	17.00	95
1989	Charlie Chaplin (blue hat) 9-55	Retrd.	1990	8.50	45-75
1989	Double Top 9-71	Retrd.	1989	7.00	40
1989	Elf on Ball (matte) 9-62	Retrd.	1990	9.50	45
1989	Fisher Frog 9-65	Retrd.	1991	7.00	40
1989	Grecian Urn 9-69	Retrd.	1989	9.00	35
1989	Hurricane Lamp 9-67	Retrd.	1989	7.00	45
1989	Joey Clown (light pink) 9-58	Retrd.	1992	9.00	60
1989	Kim Ono 9-57	Retrd.	1990	6.50	45
1989	King Arthur (Lt. Blue) 9-103	Retrd.	1991	12.00	45
1989	Lilac Sparkle 9-7	Retrd.	1989	17.00	30
1989	Lucky Fish 9-73	Retrd.	1989	6.50	30
1989	Parachute 9-68	Retrd.	1989	6.50	20
1989	Royal Rooster 9-18	Retrd.	1993	17.00	20
1989	Seahorse 9-54	Retrd.	1992	10.00	60
1989	Serpent 9-72	Retrd.	N/A	7.00	18
1989	Shy Kitten 9-66	Retrd.	N/A	7.00	45
1989	Shy Rabbit 9-61	Retrd.	N/A	7.00	50
1989	Small Reflector 9-76	Retrd.	N/A	7.50	32
1989	Smiling Sun 9-59	Retrd.	N/A	7.00	45
1989	Walrus 9-63	Retrd.	1990	8.00	95
1989	Zebra 9-10	Retrd.	1991	17.50	95

1990 Holiday Collection - C. Radko

YEAR ISSUE		EDITION LIMIT	YEAR RETD.	ISSUE PRICE	QUOTE U.S.$
1990	Angel on Harp 46	Retrd.	1990	9.00	40
1990	Ballooning Santa 85	Retrd.	1991	20.00	60
1990	Bathing Baby 70	Retrd.	N/A	11.00	37
1990	Calla Lilly 38	Retrd.	N/A	7.00	20-50
1990	Carmen Miranda 18	Retrd.	1991	19.00	95
1990	Christmas Cardinals 16	Retrd.	1992	18.00	50-60
1990	Conch Shell 65	Retrd.	1991	9.00	25
1990	Crowned Prince 56	Retrd.	1990	14.00	45
1990	Dublin Pipe 40	Retrd.	1990	14.00	50
1990	Eagle Medallion 67	Retrd.	1990	9.00	85
1990	Early Winter 24	Retrd.	1990	10.00	40
1990	Emerald City 92	Retrd.	1990	7.50	45
1990	Fat Lady 35	Retrd.	N/A	7.00	20
1990	Father Christmas 76	Retrd.	N/A	7.00	15
1990	Frog Under Balloon 58	Retrd.	1991	14.00	45
1990	Goggle Eyes 44	Retrd.	1990	9.00	45
1990	Golden Puppy 53	Retrd.	1990	8.00	95
1990	Happy Gnome 77	Retrd.	1991	8.00	40
1990	Holly Ball 4	Retrd.	N/A	19.00	60
1990	Joey Clown (red striped) 55	Retrd.	N/A	14.00	35
1990	Kim Ono 79	Retrd.	1990	6.00	55
1990	King Arthur (Red) 72	Retrd.	N/A	16.00	95
1990	Lullaby 47	Retrd.	1990	9.00	35
1990	Maracca 94	Retrd.	1990	9.00	75
1990	Mother Goose (blue bonnet/pink shawl) 52	Retrd.	N/A	10.00	45
1990	Nativity 36	Retrd.	1990	6.00	25
1990	Peacock (on snowball) 74	Retrd.	N/A	18.00	50
1990	Pierre Le Berry	Retrd.	N/A	10.00	45
1990	Polish Folk Dance 13	Retrd.	N/A	19.00	125
1990	Proud Peacock 74	Retrd.	N/A	18.00	50
1990	Roly Poly Santa (Red bottom) 69	Retrd.	N/A	13.00	60
1990	Rose Lamp 96	Retrd.	1990	14.00	75
1990	Santa on Ball 80	Retrd.	1991	16.00	45
1990	Silent Movie (black hat) 75	Retrd.	1990	8.50	45
1990	Small Nautilus Shell 78	Retrd.	N/A	7.00	22
1990	Smiling Kite 63	Retrd.	1990	14.00	45
1990	Snowball Tree 71	Retrd.	1990	17.00	45-95
1990	Snowman on Ball 45	Retrd.	1990	14.00	75
1990	Spin Top 90	Retrd.	N/A	11.00	35
1990	Sunburst Fish (green/yellow) 68	Retrd.	N/A	13.00	28
1990	Tuxedo Penquin 57	Retrd.	1990	8.00	N/A
1990	Walrus 59	Retrd.	1990	8.50	45
1990	Yarn Fight 23	Retrd.	N/A	17.00	100

1991 Holiday Collection - C. Radko

YEAR ISSUE		EDITION LIMIT	YEAR RETD.	ISSUE PRICE	QUOTE U.S.$
1991	All Weather Santa 137	Retrd.	1992	32.00	70
1991	Altar Boy 18	Retrd.	1992	16.00	31
1991	Anchor America 65	Retrd.	1992	21.50	38
1991	Apache 42	Retrd.	N/A	8.50	40
1991	Aspen 76	Retrd.	1992	20.50	60
1991	Aztec 141	Retrd.	1991	21.50	60
1991	Aztec Bird 41	Retrd.	1992	20.00	85
1991	Ballooning Santa 110	Retrd.	1991	23.00	60
1991	Barnum Clown 56	Retrd.	1991	15.00	85
1991	Blue Rainbow 136	Retrd.	1992	21.50	40
1991	Bowery Kid 50	Retrd.	1991	14.50	70
1991	By the Nile 124	Retrd.	1992	21.50	50
1991	Chance Encounter 104	Retrd.	1992	13.50	35
1991	Chimney Santa 12	Retrd.	N/A	14.50	35
1991	Clown Drum 33	Retrd.	1991	14.00	40
1991	Comet 62	Retrd.	1991	9.00	35
1991	Cosette 16	Retrd.	1991	16.00	40-55
1991	Dapper Shoe 89	Retrd.	1991	10.00	85
1991	Dawn & Dust 34	Retrd.	N/A	14.00	24-35
1991	Deco Floral 133	Retrd.	1991	22.00	60
1991	DecoSparkle 134	Retrd.	1992	21.00	95
1991	Dutch Boy 27	Retrd.	1991	11.00	30-45
1991	Dutch Girl 28	Retrd.	1991	11.00	30-45
1991	Edwardian Lace 82	Retrd.	1991	21.50	60
1991	Einstein Kite 98	Retrd.	N/A	20.00	75
1991	Elf Reflector 135	Retrd.	1992	23.00	50
1991	Fanfare 126	Retrd.	1992	21.50	98
1991	Fisher Frog 44	Retrd.	1991	11.00	45
1991	Florentine 83	Retrd.	N/A	22.00	40
1991	Flower Child 90	Retrd.	1991	13.00	40
1991	Frog Under Balloon 53	Retrd.	N/A	16.00	45
1991	Fruit in Balloon 40	Retrd.	N/A	22.00	150
1991	Fu Manchu 11	Retrd.	N/A	15.00	68
1991	Galaxy 120	Retrd.	1991	21.50	75
1991	Grapefruit Tree 113	Retrd.	N/A	23.00	150-200
1991	Harvest 3	Retrd.	N/A	13.50	25
1991	Hatching Duck 35	Retrd.	1991	14.00	50
1991	Hearts & Flowers Finial 158	Retrd.	1993	53.00	95
1991	Her Majesty 39	Retrd.	1991	21.00	45
1991	Her Purse 88	Retrd.	N/A	10.00	55
1991	Holly Ball 156	Retrd.	N/A	22.00	60
1991	Irish Laddie 10	Retrd.	1991	12.00	60
1991	Jemima's Child 111	Retrd.	1991	16.00	35-45
1991	King Arthur (Blue) 95	Retrd.	N/A	18.50	N/A
1991	Lion's Head 31	Retrd.	N/A	16.00	35
1991	Madonna & Child 103	Retrd.	N/A	15.00	25-45
1991	Melon Slice 99	Retrd.	N/A	18.00	31
1991	Mother Goose 57	Retrd.	N/A	11.00	35
1991	Olympiad 125	Retrd.	1992	22.00	40
1991	Peruvian 74	Retrd.	1991	21.50	60
1991	Pierre Le Berry 2	Retrd.	1993	14.00	45
1991	Pipe Smoking Monkey 54	Retrd.	1991	11.00	32-45
1991	Polish Folk Art 116	Retrd.	N/A	20.50	45
1991	Prince on Ball (pink/blue/green) 51	Retrd.	1991	15.00	45
1991	Prince Umbrella 21	Retrd.	1991	15.00	70
1991	Proud Peacock 37	Retrd.	N/A	23.00	37
1991	Rainbow Bird 92	Retrd.	1991	16.00	45
1991	Raspberry & Lime 96	Retrd.	1991	12.00	50
1991	Red Star 129	Retrd.	1992	21.50	40
1991	Sally Ann 43	Retrd.	1991	8.00	35
1991	Santa Bootie 55	Retrd.	1993	10.00	35
1991	Shirley 15	Retrd.	1991	16.00	50-75
1991	Shy Elf 1	Retrd.	1991	10.00	40-70
1991	Sitting Bull 107	Retrd.	1992	16.00	73
1991	Sleepy Time Santa 52	Retrd.	N/A	15.00	95
1991	Star Quilt 139	Retrd.	1991	21.50	40
1991	Sunburst Fish 108	Retrd.	N/A	15.00	28
1991	Sunshine 67	Retrd.	N/A	22.00	40
1991	Tabby 46	Retrd.	1991	8.00	30-50
1991	Tiffany 68	Retrd.	1991	22.00	50
1991	Tiger 5	Retrd.	N/A	15.00	35
1991	Trigger 114	Retrd.	1991	15.00	100
1991	Trumpet Man 100	Retrd.	1992	21.00	35
1991	Tulip Fairy 63	Retrd.	1992	16.00	65
1991	Vienna 1901 127	Retrd.	1992	21.50	N/A
1991	Villandry 87	Retrd.	1991	21.00	144
1991	Woodland Santa 38	Retrd.	N/A	14.00	55
1991	Zebra (glittered) 79	Retrd.	1991	22.00	60

1992 Holiday Collection - C. Radko

YEAR ISSUE		EDITION LIMIT	YEAR RETD.	ISSUE PRICE	QUOTE U.S.$
1992	Alpine Flowers 162	Retrd.	1992	28.00	36
1992	Aspen 120	Retrd.	1992	26.00	50
1992	Barbie's Mom 69	Retrd.	1992	18.00	45
1992	Butterfly Bouquet 119	Retrd.	1992	26.50	33
1992	By the Nile 139	Retrd.	1992	27.00	33-40
1992	Cabaret (see-through) 159	Retrd.	1993	28.00	60
1992	Candy Trumpet man (red) 98	Retrd.	1992	27.00	75
1992	Celestial 129	Retrd.	N/A	26.00	40
1992	Cheerful Sun 50	Retrd.	N/A	18.00	25
1992	Chevron 160	Retrd.	1992	28.00	35
1992	Choir Boy 114	Retrd.	1992	24.00	30
1992	Christmas Cardinals 123	Retrd.	1992	26.00	60
1992	Christmas Rose 143	Retrd.	1992	25.50	60
1992	Circus lady 54	Retrd.	1992	12.00	15
1992	Clown Snake 62	Retrd.	N/A	22.00	27
1992	Cowboy Santa 94	Retrd.	N/A	24.00	N/A

YEAR ISSUE		EDITION LIMIT	YEAR RETD.	ISSUE PRICE	QUOTE U.S.$
1992	Delft Design 124	Retrd.	1992	26.50	35
1992	Diva 73	Retrd.	1992	17.00	20-50
1992	Dolly Madison 115	Retrd.	1992	17.00	21
1992	Downhill Racer 76	Retrd.	1992	34.00	42
1992	Elephant on Parade 141	Retrd.	1992	26.00	75
1992	Elephant Reflector 181	Retrd.	N/A	17.00	25
1992	Elf Reflectors 136	Retrd.	1992	28.00	36
1992	Faberge 148	Retrd.	N/A	26.50	55
1992	Faith, Hope & Love 183	Retrd.	1992	12.00	N/A
1992	Floral Cascade Tier Drop 175	Retrd.	1992	32.00	41-45
1992	Florentine 131	Retrd.	N/A	27.00	40
1992	Folk Art Set 95	Retrd.	1992	10.00	13
1992	Forest Friends 103	Retrd.	1992	14.00	18
1992	Fruit in Balloon 83	Retrd.	N/A	28.00	150-250
1992	Gabriel's Trumpets 188	Retrd.	N/A	20.00	25
1992	Harlequin Tier Drop 74	Retrd.	1992	36.00	65
1992	Harold Lloyd Reflector 218	Retrd.	1992	70.00	100
1992	Her Slipper 56	Retrd.	1992	17.00	22
1992	Holly Finial 200	Retrd.	N/A	70.00	83
1992	Ice Pear 241	Retrd.	N/A	20.00	45
1992	Ice Poppies 127	Retrd.	1992	26.00	60
1992	Jumbo 99	Retrd.	N/A	31.00	36
1992	King of Prussia 149	Retrd.	1992	27.00	33-35
1992	Kitty Rattle 166	Retrd.	1993	18.00	95
1992	Little League 53	Retrd.	1992	20.00	25-35
1992	Merry Christmas Maiden 137	Retrd.	1992	26.00	N/A
1992	Mother Goose 37	Retrd.	N/A	15.00	25
1992	Neopolitan Angels 152	Retrd.	1992	27.00	55
1992	Norweigian Princess 170	Retrd.	1992	15.00	22
1992	Pierre Winterberry 64	Retrd.	1993	17.00	45
1992	Pink Lace Ball (See Through) 158	Retrd.	1992	28.00	60
1992	Primary Colors 108	Retrd.	1992	30.00	43
1992	Quilted Hearts (Old Salem Museum) 194	Retrd.	N/A	27.50	60
1992	Rainbow Parasol 90	Retrd.	1992	30.00	30
1992	Royal Scepter 77	Retrd.	1992	36.00	98
1992	Russian Imperial 112	Retrd.	1992	25.00	80
1992	Russian Star 130	Retrd.	1992	26.00	32-40
1992	Santa in Winter White 106	Retrd.	N/A	28.00	100
1992	Seahorse (pink) 92	Retrd.	1992	20.00	86
1992	Serpents of Paradise 97	Retrd.	N/A	13.00	30
1992	Siberian Sleighride (pink) 154	Retrd.	N/A	27.00	65
1992	Sitting Bull 93	Retrd.	1992	26.00	75
1992	Sleepytime Santa (pink) 81	Retrd.	N/A	18.00	50
1992	Sloopy Snowman 328	Retrd.	N/A	19.90	56
1992	Sputniks 134	Retrd.	1992	25.50	32
1992	St. Nickcicle 107	Retrd.	N/A	26.00	33
1992	Star of Wonder 177	Retrd.	1992	27.00	35
1992	Stardust Joey 110	Retrd.	1992	16.00	45
1992	Talking Pipe (black stem) 104	Retrd.	N/A	26.00	48
1992	Thunderbolt 178	Retrd.	1993	60.00	75
1992	Tiffany Bright 161	Retrd.	1992	28.00	N/A
1992	To Grandma's House 239	Retrd.	N/A	20.00	N/A
1992	Topiary 117	Retrd.	N/A	30.00	150-275
1992	Tropical Fish 109	Retrd.	N/A	17.00	60
1992	Tulip Fairy 57	Retrd.	1992	18.00	45
1992	Tuxedo Santa 88	Retrd.	1993	22.00	95
1992	Two Sided Santa Reflector 102	Retrd.	1992	28.00	50
1992	Victorian Santa & Angel Balloon 122	Retrd.	1992	68.00	150
1992	Vienna 1901 128	Retrd.	1992	27.00	40
1992	Virgin Mary 46	Retrd.	1992	20.00	29
1992	Wacko's Brother, Doofus 55	Retrd.	N/A	20.00	65
1992	Water Lilies 133	Retrd.	1992	26.00	50
1992	Winter Wonderland 156	Retrd.	1992	26.00	33
1992	Woodland Santa 111	Retrd.	N/A	20.00	55
1992	Ziegfeld Follies 126	Retrd.	1992	27.00	56

1993 Holiday Collection - C. Radko

1993	Aladdin's Lamp 237	Retrd.	N/A	20.00	27
1993	Alpine Village 420	Retrd.	1993	23.80	35
1993	Angel of Peace 132	Retrd.	1993	17.00	24
1993	Apache 357	Retrd.	1993	13.90	40
1993	Auld Lang Syne 246	Retrd.	N/A	15.00	40
1993	Bell House Boy 291	Retrd.	1993	21.00	28
1993	Beyond the Stars 108	Retrd.	1993	18.50	20
1993	Bishop of Myra 327	Retrd.	1993	19.90	50
1993	Blue Top 114	Retrd.	1993	16.00	16
1993	Calla Lilly 314	Retrd.	N/A	12.90	23
1993	Center Ring (Exclusive) 192	Retrd.	1993	30.80	38
1993	Centurian 224	Retrd.	1993	25.50	31
1993	Chimney Sweep Bell 294	Retrd.	1993	26.00	28
1993	Christmas Express 394 (Garland)	Retrd.	N/A	58.00	200
1993	Christmas Stars 342	Retrd.	N/A	14.00	21
1993	Cinderella's Bluebirds 145	Retrd.	1993	25.90	26
1993	Circle of Santas Finial 413	Retrd.	N/A	69.00	163
1993	Circus Seal 249	Retrd.	1993	28.00	60
1993	Class Clown 332	Retrd.	N/A	21.00	60
1993	Confucius 363	Retrd.	1993	19.00	28
1993	Copenhagen 166	Retrd.	1993	26.80	55
1993	Crowned Passion 299	Retrd.	1993	23.00	50
1993	Crystal Rainbow 308	Retrd.	N/A	29.90	60
1993	Deco Snowfall 147	Retrd.	1993	26.80	33
1993	Deer Drop 304	Retrd.	N/A	34.00	100
1993	Downhill Racer 195	Retrd.	1993	30.00	36
1993	Emerald Wizard 279	Retrd.	N/A	18.00	45
1993	Emperor's Pet 253	Retrd.	1993	22.00	29
1993	Enchanted Gardens 341	Retrd.	1993	5.50	13
1993	English Kitchen 234	Retrd.	1993	26.00	28
1993	Evening Star Santa 409	Retrd.	1993	59.00	85
1993	Forest Friends 250	Retrd.	1993	28.00	35
1993	French Rose 152	Retrd.	1993	26.60	27-33
1993	Geisha Girls 261	Retrd.	1993	11.90	12-19
1993	Gold Fish 158	Retrd.	1993	25.80	26
1993	Grandpa Bear 260	Retrd.	1993	12.80	13-20
1993	Grecian Urn 231	Retrd.	1993	23.00	23
1993	Gypsy Girl 371	Retrd.	1993	16.00	35
1993	Holiday Spice 422	Retrd.	1993	24.00	24
1993	Honey Bear 352	Retrd.	1993	13.90	40
1993	Ice Star Santa 405	Retrd.	1993	38.00	125-300
1993	Jack Frost (blue) 333	Retrd.	N/A	23.00	30
1993	Joey B. Clown 135	Retrd.	N/A	26.00	60
1993	Just Like Grandma Lg. 200	Retrd.	N/A	7.20	15
1993	Just Like Grandmas Sm. 200	Retrd.	N/A	7.20	20
1993	Kitty Rattle 374	Retrd.	1993	17.80	25
1993	Light in the Windows 229	Retrd.	1994	24.50	30
1993	Little Doggie 180	Retrd.	1993	7.00	15
1993	Little Eskimo 355	Retrd.	N/A	13.90	21
1993	Majestic Reflector 312	Retrd.	1993	70.00	70
1993	Midas Touch 162	Retrd.	N/A	27.80	50-70
1993	Monkey Man 97	Retrd.	1993	16.00	35
1993	Monterey 290	Retrd.	1993	15.00	40
1993	Mr. & Mrs. Claus 121	Retrd.	1993	17.90	18
1993	Mushroom Elf 267	Retrd.	N/A	17.90	25
1993	Nellie (Italian ornament) 225	Retrd.	1993	27.50	85
1993	North Woods 317	Retrd.	1993	26.80	60-75
1993	One Small Leap 222	Retrd.	N/A	26.00	50
1993	Pagoda 258	Retrd.	1993	8.00	15
1993	Pennsylvania Dutch 146	Retrd.	1993	26.80	33
1993	Polar Bears 112A	Retrd.	1993	15.50	15
1993	Pompadour 344	Retrd.	1993	8.80	11
1993	Purse 389	Retrd.	1993	15.60	16
1993	Quartet 392	Retrd.	1993	3.60	11
1993	Rainbow Reflector 154	Retrd.	1993	26.60	35
1993	Rainbow Shark 277	Retrd.	N/A	18.00	40
1993	Rainy Day Friend 206	Retrd.	N/A	22.00	40
1993	Rose Pointe Finial 323	Retrd.	1993	34.00	34
1993	Sail by Starlight 339	Retrd.	1993	11.80	14-19
1993	Santa Tree 320	Retrd.	N/A	66.00	200
1993	Saraband 140	Retrd.	1993	27.80	35
1993	Serenade Pink 157	Retrd.	1993	26.80	55
1993	Shy Rabbit 280	Retrd.	N/A	14.00	48
1993	The Skating Bettinas 242	Retrd.	N/A	29.00	60
1993	Sloopy Snowman 328	Retrd.	1993	19.90	55
1993	Smitty 378	Retrd.	N/A	17.90	25
1993	Snow Dance 247	Retrd.	N/A	29.00	75
1993	Snowday Santa 98	Retrd.	1993	20.00	27
1993	Spider & the Fly 393	Retrd.	1993	6.40	14
1993	St. Nick's Pipe 330	Retrd.	N/A	4.40	25
1993	Star Children 208	Retrd.	1993	18.00	50
1993	Starlight Santa 348	Retrd.	N/A	11.90	19
1993	Stocking Stuffers 236	Retrd.	1993	16.00	23
1993	Sweetheart 202	Retrd.	1993	16.00	18
1993	Talking Pipe 373	Retrd.	N/A	26.00	48
1993	Texas Star 338	Retrd.	1993	7.50	8
1993	Tuxedo Santa 117	Retrd.	1993	21.90	29
1993	Tweeter 94	Retrd.	1993	3.20	6
1993	U-Boat 353	Retrd.	1993	15.50	23
1993	V.I.P. 230	Retrd.	1993	23.00	75
1993	Waddles 95	Retrd.	1993	3.80	11
1993	Winterbirds 164	Retrd.	1993	26.80	27

1994 Holiday Collection - C. Radko

1994	Leader of the Band 94-915D (wh pants) - signed	Retrd.	1994	25.00	360
1994	Leader of the Band 94-915D (wh pants) - unsigned	Retrd.	1994	25.00	85
1994	Mr. Smedley Drysdale 37	Retrd.	N/A	44.00	115
1994	Shivers 262	Retrd.	N/A	25.00	69
1994	Xenon 304	Retrd.	N/A	38.00	75

Aids Awareness - C. Radko

1993	A Shy Rabbit's Heart 462	Retrd.	1993	15.00	75-300
1994	Frosty Cares SP5	Retrd.	1994	25.00	40-75
1995	On Wings of Hope SP10	Yr.Iss.		30.00	30

Event Only - C. Radko

1993	Littlest Snowman 347S	Retrd.	1993	15.00	32-50
1994	Roly Poly 94125E	Retrd.	1994	22.00	65
1995	Forever Lucy 91075E	Yr.Iss.		32.00	32

Limited Edition Ornaments - C. Radko

1995	And Snowy Makes Eight 169 (set of 8)	15,000		125.00	125

Nativity Series - C. Radko

1995	Three Wise Men WM (set of 3)	15,000		90.00	90

Nutcracker Series - C. Radko

1995	Nutcracker Suite 1 NC1 (set of 3)	15,000		90.00	90

Pediatrics Cancer Research - C. Radko

1994	A Gifted Santa 70	Retrd.	1994	25.00	50-100
1995	Christmas Puppy Love SP11	Yr.Iss.		30.00	30

South Bend Special - C. Radko

1995	Polar Express (lilac) 950-76-SB	Retrd.	1995	24.95	75

Twelve Days of Christmas - C. Radko

1993	Partridge in a Pear Tree SP2	5,000	1993	35.00	650-1000
1994	Two Turtle Doves SP4	10,000	1994	28.00	100-250
1995	Three French Hens SP9	10,000		34.00	34

Cybis

Christmas Collection - Cybis

1983	1983 Holiday Bell	Yr.Iss.		145.00	1000
1984	1984 Holiday Ball	Yr.Iss.		145.00	700
1985	1985 Holiday Angel	Yr.Iss.		75.00	500
1986	1986 Holiday Cherub Ornament	Yr.Iss.		75.00	500
1987	1987 Heavenly Angels	Yr.Iss.		95.00	400
1988	1988 Holiday Ornament	Yr.Iss.		95.00	375

Dave Grossman Creations

Gone With the Wind Ornaments - Various

1987	Ashley - D. Geenty	Closed	N/A	15.00	45
1994	Gold Plated GWO-00 - Unknown	Open		13.00	13
1994	Limited Edition GWO-94 - Unknown	Yr.Iss.		25.00	25
1989	Mammy - D. Geenty	Closed	N/A	20.00	20
1991	Prissy - Unknown	Closed	N/A	20.00	20
1993	Rhett (White Suit) GWO-93 - Unknown	Closed	N/A	20.00	20
1987	Rhett - D. Geenty	Closed	N/A	15.00	45
1988	Rhett and Scarlett - D. Geenty	Closed	N/A	20.00	40
1992	Scarlett (Green Dress) - Unknown	Closed	N/A	20.00	20
1990	Scarlett (Red Dress) - D. Geenty	Closed	N/A	20.00	20
1987	Scarlett - D. Geenty	Closed	N/A	15.00	45
1994	Scarlett GWO-94 - Unknown	Yr.Iss.		20.00	20
1987	Tara - D. Geenty	Closed	N/A	15.00	45

Rockwell Collection-Annual Rockwell Ball - Rockwell-Inspired

1975	Santa with Feather Quill NRO-01	Retrd.	N/A	3.50	25
1976	Santa at Globe NRO-02	Retrd.	N/A	4.00	25
1977	Grandpa on Rocking Horse NRO-03	Retrd.	N/A	4.00	12
1978	Santa with Map NRO-04	Retrd.	N/A	4.50	12
1979	Santa at Desk with Mail Bag NRO-05	Retrd.	N/A	5.00	12
1980	Santa Asleep with Toys NRO-06	Retrd.	N/A	5.00	10
1981	Santa with Boy on Finger NRO-07	Retrd.	N/A	5.00	10
1982	Santa Face on Winter Scene NRO-08	Retrd.	N/A	5.00	10
1983	Coachman with Whip NRO-9	Retrd.	N/A	5.00	10
1984	Christmas Bounty Man NRO-10	Retrd.	N/A	5.00	10
1985	Old English Trio NRO-11	Retrd.	N/A	5.00	10
1986	Tiny Tim on Shoulder NRO-12	Retrd.	N/A	5.00	10
1987	Skating Lesson NRO-13	Retrd.	N/A	5.00	10
1988	Big Moment NRO-14	Retrd.	N/A	5.50	6
1989	Discovery NRO-15	Retrd.	N/A	6.00	6
1990	Bringing Home The Tree NRO-16	Retrd.	N/A	6.00	6
1991	Downhill Daring NRO-17	Retrd.	N/A	6.00	6
1992	On The Ice NRO-18	Retrd.	N/A	6.00	6
1993	Granps NRO-19	Retrd.	N/A	6.00	6
1994	Triple Self Portrait-Commemorative NRO-20	Yr.Iss.		6.00	6

Rockwell Collection-Annual Rockwell Figurine Ornaments - Rockwell-Inspired

1978	Caroler NRX-03	Retrd.	N/A	15.00	45
1979	Drum for Tommy NRX-24	Retrd.	N/A	20.00	30
1980	Santa's Good Boys NRX-37	Retrd.	N/A	20.00	30
1981	Letters to Santa NRX-39	Retrd.	N/A	20.00	30
1982	Cornettist NRX-32	Retrd.	N/A	20.00	30
1983	Fiddler NRX-83	Retrd.	N/A	20.00	30
1984	Christmas Bounty NRX-84	Retrd.	N/A	20.00	30
1985	Jolly Coachman NRX-85	Retrd.	N/A	20.00	30
1986	Grandpa on Rocking Horse NRX-86	Retrd.	N/A	20.00	30
1987	Skating Lesson NRX-87	Retrd.	N/A	20.00	30
1988	Big Moment NRX-88	Retrd.	N/A	20.00	25
1989	Discovery NRX-89	Retrd.	N/A	20.00	20
1990	Bringing Home The Tree NRX-90	Retrd.	N/A	20.00	20
1991	Downhill Daring B NRX-91	Retrd.	N/A	20.00	20
1992	On The Ice	Retrd.	N/A	20.00	20
1993	Granps NRX-93	Retrd.	N/A	24.00	24
1993	Marriage License First Christmas Together NRX-m1	Retrd.	N/A	30.00	30
1994	Merry Christmas NRX-94	Yr.Iss.		24.00	24

Department 56

Bisque Light-Up, Clip-on Ornaments - Department 56

1986	Angelic Lite-up 8260-0	Open		4.00	4
1987	Anniversary Love Birds, (pair) w/brass ribbon 8353-4	Closed	1988	4.00	4
1986	Dessert, 6 asst. 7100-5	Closed	1987	5.00	5
1985	Humpty Dumpty 3525-4	Closed	1986	4.50	5
1990	Owl w/clip 8344-5	Closed	1994	5.00	14
1986	Plum Pudding 7101-3	Closed	1987	4.50	5
1989	Pond-Frog w/clip 8347-0	Closed	1991	5.00	5
1989	Pond-Snail w/clip 8347-0	Closed	1991	5.00	40-55
1988	Rabbit w/clip 8350-0	Open		4.00	17
1987	Shells, set/4 8349-6	Closed	1991	14.00	14
1986	Shooting Star 7106-4	Closed	1987	5.50	6
1990	Snowbaby Penquin, w/clip 7940-5	Closed	1992	5.00	5
1990	Snowbaby Polar Bear, w/clip 7941-3	Closed	1992	5.00	5
1985	Snowbirds, (pair) w/clip 8357-7	Open		5.00	5
1985	Snowbirds, set/6 8367-4	Closed	1988	15.00	15
1985	Snowbirds, set/8 8358-5	Closed	1988	20.00	20

YEAR ISSUE		EDITION LIMIT	YEAR RETD.	ISSUE PRICE	QUOTE U.S.$
1985	Snowmen, 3 asst. 8360-7	Closed	1988	10.50	11
1986	Teddy Bear w/clip 8262-7	Closed	1991	5.00	5
1986	Truffles Sampler, set/4 7102-1	Closed	1987	17.50	18
1986	Winged Snowbird 8261-9	Closed	1988	2.50	3
1989	Woodland-Field Mouse w/clip 8348-8	Closed	1991	5.00	45-55
1989	Woodland-Squirrel w/clip 8348-8	Closed	1991	5.00	48-58

CCP Ornaments-Flat -Department 56

YEAR ISSUE		EDITION LIMIT	YEAR RETD.	ISSUE PRICE	QUOTE U.S.$
1986	Christmas Carol Houses, set/3 (6504-8)	Closed	1989	13.00	45-70
1986	•The Cottage of Bob Cratchit & Tiny Tim	Closed	1989	4.35	N/A
1986	•Fezziwig's Warehouse	Closed	1989	4.35	N/A
1986	•Scrooge and Marley Countinghouse	Closed	1989	4.35	N/A
1986	New England Village, set/7 (6536-6)	Closed	1989	25.00	300
1986	•Apothecary Shop	Closed	1989	3.50	40
1986	•Brick Town Hall	Closed	1989	3.50	50
1986	•General Store	Closed	1989	3.50	55
1986	•Livery Stable & Boot Shop	Closed	1989	3.50	40-50
1986	•Nathaniel Bingham Fabrics	Closed	1989	3.50	20-55
1986	•Red Schoolhouse	Closed	1989	3.50	40-70
1986	•Steeple Church	Closed	1989	3.50	150-225

Christmas Carol Character Ornaments-Flat -Department 56

YEAR ISSUE		EDITION LIMIT	YEAR RETD.	ISSUE PRICE	QUOTE U.S.$
1986	Christmas Carol Characters, set of 3 (6505-6)	Closed	1987	13.00	40-60
1986	•Bob Cratchit & Tiny Tim	Closed	1987	4.35	35-75
1986	•Poulterer	Closed	1987	4.35	30
1986	•Scrooge	Closed	1987	4.35	35-75

Miscellaneous Ornaments - Department 56

YEAR ISSUE		EDITION LIMIT	YEAR RETD.	ISSUE PRICE	QUOTE U.S.$
1988	Balsam Bell Brass Dickens' Candlestick, 6244-8	Closed	1989	3.00	15
1986	Cherub on Brass Ribbon, 8248-1	Closed	1988	8.00	66
1988	Christmas Carol- Bob & Mrs. Cratchit, 5914-5	Closed	1989	18.00	36-45
1988	Christmas Carol- Scrooge's Head, 5912-9	Closed	1989	13.00	30-35
1988	Christmas Carol- Tiny Tim's Head, 5913-7	Closed	1989	10.00	25-35
1984	Dickens 2-sided Tin Ornaments, set of 6, 6522-6	Closed	1985	12.00	440
1984	•Abel Beesley Butcher	Closed	1985	2.00	45
1984	•Bean and Son Smithy Shop	Closed	1985	2.00	45
1984	•Crowntree Inn	Closed	1985	2.00	45
1984	•Golden Swan Baker	Closed	1985	2.00	45
1984	•Green Grocer	Closed	1985	2.00	45
1984	•Jones & Co. Brush & Basket Shop	Closed	1985	2.00	45
1994	Dickens Village Dedlock Arms Ornament, 9872-8, (porcelain, gift boxed)	Closed	1994	12.50	15-25
1983	Snow Village Wood Ornaments, set of 6, 5099-7	Closed	1984	30.00	N/A
1983	•Carriage House	Closed	1984	5.00	50
1983	•Centennial House	Closed	1984	5.00	100
1983	•Countryside Church	Closed	1984	5.00	125
1983	•Gabled House	Closed	1984	5.00	75
1983	•Pioneer Church	Closed	1984	5.00	75-125
1983	•Swiss Chalet	Closed	1984	5.00	75
1986	Teddy Bear on Brass Ribbon, 8263-5	Closed	1988	7.00	70

Snowbabies Ornaments - Department 56

YEAR ISSUE		EDITION LIMIT	YEAR RETD.	ISSUE PRICE	QUOTE U.S.$
1994	Be My Baby 6866-7	Open		15.00	25
1986	Crawling, Lite-Up, Clip-On, 7953-7	Closed	1992	7.00	30
1994	First Star Jinglebaby, 6858-6	Open		10.00	11
1994	Gathering Stars in the Sky, 6855-1	Open		12.50	13
1994	Juggling Stars in the Sky 6867-5	Open		15.00	15
1994	Just For You Jinglebaby 6869-1	Open		11.00	11
1994	Little Drummer Jinglebaby, 6859-4	Open		10.00	11
1987	Mini, Winged Pair, Lite-Up, Clip-On, 7976-6	Open		9.00	12
1987	Moon Beams, 7951-0	Open		7.50	9
1991	My First Star, 6811-0	Open		7.00	8
1989	Noel, 7988-0	Open		7.50	8
1995	Overnight Delivery, 759-5 (Event Piece)	Open		10.00	10
1990	Penguin, Lite-Up, Clip-On, 7940-5	Closed	1992	5.00	15-20
1990	Polar Bear, Lite-Up, Clip-On, 7941-3	Closed	1992	5.00	17
1990	Rock-A-Bye Baby, 7939-1	Open		7.00	8
1986	Sitting, Lite-Up, Clip-On, 7952-9	Closed	1990	7.00	30-50
1992	Snowbabies Icicle With Star, 6825-0	Open		16.00	16
1987	Snowbaby Adrift Lite-Up, Clip-On, 7969-3	Closed	1990	8.50	100-150
1986	Snowbaby on Brass Ribbon, 7961-8	Closed	1989	8.00	145-180
1993	Sprinkling Stars in the Sky, 6848-9	Open		12.50	13
1989	Star Bright, 7990-1	Open		7.50	8
1992	Starry, Starry Night, 6830-6	Open		12.50	13
1994	Stars in My Stocking Jinglebaby 6868-3	Open		11.00	11
1989	Surprise, 7989-8	Closed	1994	12.00	15-30
1991	Swinging On a Star, 6810-1	Open		9.50	10
1988	Twinkle Little Star, 7980-4	Closed	1990	7.00	80-120
1993	Wee...This is Fun!, 6847-0	Open		13.50	14
1986	Winged, Lite-Up, Clip-On, 7954-5	Closed	1990	7.00	35-45

Village Light-Up Ornaments - Department 56

YEAR ISSUE		EDITION LIMIT	YEAR RETD.	ISSUE PRICE	QUOTE U.S.$
1987	Christmas Carol Cottages, set of 3 (6513-7)	Closed	1989	17.00	50-65
1987	•The Cottage of Bob Cratchit & Tiny Tim	Closed	1989	6.00	20-28
1987	•Fezziwig's Warehouse	Closed	1989	6.00	25-30
1987	•Scrooge & Marley Countinghouse	Closed	1989	6.00	15-25
1987	Dickens' Village, set of 14 (6521-8, 6520-0)	Closed	1989	84.00	400
1987	Dickens' Village, set of 6 (6520-0)	Closed	1989	36.00	85-175
1987	•Barley Bree Farmhouse	Closed	1989	6.00	20-40
1987	•Blythe Pond Mill House	Closed	1989	6.00	40
1987	•Brick Abbey	Closed	1989	6.00	90
1987	•Chesterton Manor House	Closed	1989	6.00	45
1987	•Kenilworth Castle	Closed	1989	6.00	60
1987	•The Old Curiosity Shop	Closed	1989	6.00	45
1985	Dickens' Village, set of 8 (6521-8)	Closed	1989	48.00	200
1985	•Abel Beesley Butcher	Closed	1989	6.00	25
1985	•Bean and Son Smithy Shop	Closed	1989	6.00	20-35
1985	•Candle Shop	Closed	1989	6.00	25-35
1985	•Crowntree Inn	Closed	1989	6.00	65
1985	•Dickens' Village Church	Closed	1989	6.00	40-50
1985	•Golden Swan Baker	Closed	1989	6.00	20-30
1985	•Green Grocer	Closed	1989	6.00	20-30
1985	•Jones & Co. Brush & Basket Shop	Closed	1989	6.00	30-40
1987	New England Village, set of 13 (6533-1, 6534-0)	Closed	1989	78.00	700-750
1987	New England Village, set of 6 (6534-0)	Closed	1989	36.00	200-275
1987	•Craggy Cove Lighthouse	Closed	1989	6.00	125-140
1987	•Jacob Adams Barn	Closed	1989	6.00	60
1987	•Jacob Adams Farmhouse	Closed	1989	6.00	60
1987	•Smythe Woolen Mill	Closed	1989	6.00	135-145
1987	•Timber Knoll Log Cabin	Closed	1989	6.00	115-125
1987	•Weston Train Station	Closed	1989	6.00	35-65
1986	New England Village, set of 7 (6533-1)	Closed	1989	42.00	325
1986	•Apothecary Shop	Closed	1989	6.00	20
1986	•Brick Town Hall	Closed	1989	6.00	40
1986	•General Store	Closed	1989	6.00	38
1986	•Livery Stable & Boot Shop	Closed	1989	6.00	30
1986	•Nathaniel Bingham Fabrics	Closed	1989	6.00	38
1986	•Red Schoolhouse	Closed	1989	6.00	70-80
1986	•Steeple Church	Closed	1989	6.00	135

Duncan Royale

History Of Santa Claus - Duncan Royale

YEAR ISSUE		EDITION LIMIT	YEAR RETD.	ISSUE PRICE	QUOTE U.S.$
1992	Santa I (set of 12)	Open		144.00	144
1992	Santa II (set of 12)	Open		144.00	144

Enesco Corporation

Cherished Teddies - P. Hillman

YEAR ISSUE		EDITION LIMIT	YEAR RETD.	ISSUE PRICE	QUOTE U.S.$
1995	Cupid Bear Flying - 103608	Suspd.		13.00	13
1995	Girl Flying Cupid - 103616	Suspd.		13.00	13
1995	Teddy with Ice Skates dated 95 141232	Open		12.50	13
1995	Baby Angel on Cloud - 141240	Open		13.50	14
1995	Boy/Girl with Banner - 141259	Open		13.50	14
1994	Bundled Up For The Holidays -617229	Open		15.00	15
1994	Beary Christmas Dated 1994 -617253	Yr.Iss.		15.00	18-30
1995	Mrs Claus Xmas dated 95 625426	Open		12.50	13
1995	Elf Bear W/Doll - 625434	Open		12.50	13
1995	Elf Bear W/Stuffed Reindeer 625442	Open		12.50	13
1995	Teddies Santa Bear - 651370	Open		12.50	13
1995	Elf Bears/Candy Cane - 651389	Open		12.50	13
1993	Girl w/Muff (Alice) dated 1993 912832	Yr.Iss.		13.50	25-40
1994	Drummer Boy Dated 1994 912891	Yr.Iss.		10.00	20
1993	3 Asst. Angel - 912980	Open		12.50	13
1993	Baby Girl dated 1993 - 913006	Yr.Iss.		12.50	25-32
1993	Baby Boy dated 1993 - 913014	Yr.Iss.		12.50	25-32
1993	Jointed Teddy Bear -914894	Suspd.		12.50	23
1992	Bear In Stocking, dated 1992-950653	Yr.Iss.		16.00	25-50
1992	Angel - 950777	Suspd.		12.50	24-40
1992	Beth On Rocking Reindeer 950793	Suspd.		20.00	30-45
1992	3 Asst. Christmas Sister Bears 951226	Suspd.		12.50	13

Enesco Treasury of Christmas Ornaments - Various

YEAR ISSUE		EDITION LIMIT	YEAR RETD.	ISSUE PRICE	QUOTE U.S.$
1983	Wide Open Throttle-E-0242	3-Yr.	1985	12.00	35
1983	Baby's First Christmas-E-0271	Yr.Iss.	1983	6.00	N/A
1983	Grandchild's First Christmas-E-0272	Yr.Iss.	1983	5.00	N/A
1983	Baby's First Christmas-E-0273	3-Yr.	1985	9.00	N/A
1983	Toy Drum Teddy-E-0274	4-Yr.	1986	9.00	N/A
1983	Watching At The Window-E-0275	3-Yr.	1985	13.00	N/A
1983	To A Special Teacher-E-0276	7-Yr.	1989	5.00	15
1983	Toy Shop-E-0277	7-Yr.	1989	8.00	50
1983	Carousel Horse-E-0278	7-Yr.	1989	9.00	20
1981	Look Out Below-E-6135	2-Yr.	1982	6.00	N/A
1982	Flyin' Santa Christmas Special 1982-E-6136	Yr.Iss.	1982	9.00	75
1981	Flyin' Santa Christmas Special 1981-E-6136	Yr.Iss.	1981	9.00	N/A
1981	Sawin' Elf Helper-E-6138	2-Yr.	1982	6.00	40
1981	Snow Shoe-In Santa-E-6139	2-Yr.	1982	6.00	35
1981	Baby's First Christmas 1981-E-6145	Yr.Iss.	1981	6.00	N/A
1981	Our Hero-E-6146	2-Yr.	1982	4.00	N/A
1981	Whoops-E-6147	2-Yr.	1982	3.50	N/A
1981	Whoops, It's 1981-E-6148	Yr.Iss.	1981	7.50	75
1981	Not A Creature Was Stirring-E-6149	2-Yr.	1982	4.00	25
1984	Joy To The World-E-6209	2-Yr.	1985	9.00	35
1984	Letter To Santa-E-6210	2-Yr.	1985	5.00	30
1984	Lucy & Me Photo Frames-E-6211	3-Yr.	1986	5.00	N/A
1984	Lucy & Me Photo Frames-E-6211	3-Yr.	1986	5.00	N/A
1984	Lucy & Me Photo Frames-E-6211	3-Yr.	1986	5.00	N/A
1984	Lucy & Me Photo Frames-E-6211	3-Yr.	1986	5.00	N/A
1984	Lucy & Me Photo Frames-E-6211	3-Yr.	1986	5.00	N/A
1984	Lucy & Me Photo Frames-E-6211	3-Yr.	1986	5.00	N/A
1984	Lucy & Me Photo Frames-E-6211	3-Yr.	1986	5.00	N/A
1984	Baby's First Christmas 1984-E-6212 - Gilmore	Yr.Iss.	1984	10.00	30
1984	Merry Christmas Mother-E-6213	3-Yr.	1986	10.00	30
1984	Baby's First Christmas 1984-E-6215	Yr.Iss.	1984	6.00	N/A
1984	Ferris Wheel Mice-E-6216	2-Yr.	1985	9.00	30
1984	Cuckoo Clock-E-6217	2-Yr.	1985	8.00	40
1984	Muppet Babies Baby's First Christmas-E6222 - J. Henson	Yr.Iss.	1984	10.00	45
1984	Muppet Babies Baby's First Christmas-E6223 -J. Henson	Yr.Iss.	1984	10.00	45
1984	Garfield Hark! The Herald Angel-E-6224 - J. Davis	2-Yr.	1985	7.50	35
1984	Fun in Santa's Sleigh-E-6225 J. Davis	2-Yr.	1985	12.00	35
1984	Deer! Odie-E-6226 -J. Davis	2-Yr.	1985	6.00	30
1984	Garfield The Snow Cat-E-6227 J. Davis	2-Yr.	1985	12.00	35
1984	Peek-A-Bear Baby's First Christmas-E-6228	3-Yr.	1986	10.00	N/A
1984	Peek-A-Bear Baby's First Christmas-E-6229	3-Yr.	1986	9.00	N/A
1984	Owl Be Home For Christmas-E-6230	2-Yr.	1985	10.00	23
1984	Santa's Trolley-E-6231	3-Yr.	1986	11.00	50
1984	Holiday Penguin-E-6240	3-Yr.	1986	1.50	15-20
1984	Little Drummer-E-6241	5-Yr.	1988	2.00	N/A
1984	Happy Holidays-E-6248	2-Yr.	1985	2.00	N/A
1984	Christmas Nest-E-6249	2-Yr.	1985	3.00	25
1984	Bunny's Christmas Stocking-E-6251	Yr.Iss.	1984	2.00	15
1984	Santa On Ice-E-6252	3-Yr.	1986	2.50	25
1984	Treasured Memories The New Sled-E-6256	2-Yr.	1985	7.00	N/A
1984	Up On The House Top-E-6280	6-Yr.	1989	9.00	N/A
1984	Penguins On Ice-E-6280	2-Yr.	1985	7.50	N/A
1984	Grandchild's First Christmas 1984-E-6286	Yr.Iss.	1984	5.00	N/A
1984	Grandchild's First Christmas1984-E-6286	Yr.Iss.	1984	5.00	N/A
1984	Godchild's First Christmas-E-6287	3-Yr.	1986	7.00	N/A
1984	Santa In The Box-E-6292	2-Yr.	1985	6.00	N/A
1984	Carousel Horse-E-6913	2-Yr.	1985	1.50	N/A
1983	Arctic Charmer-E-6945	2-Yr.	1984	7.00	N/A
1982	Victorian Sleigh-E-6946	4-Yr.	1985	9.00	15
1983	Wing-A-Ding Angel-E-6948	3-Yr.	1985	7.00	50
1982	A Saviour Is Born This Day-E-6949	8-Yr.	1989	4.00	18
1982	Crescent Santa-E-6950 - Gilmore	4-Yr.	1985	10.00	50
1982	Baby's First Christmas 1982-E-6952	Yr.Iss.	1982	10.00	N/A
1982	Polar Bear Fun Whoops, It's 1982-E-6953	Yr.Iss.	1982	10.00	75
1982	Holiday Skier-E-6954 - J. Davis	5-Yr.	1986	7.00	N/A
1982	Toy Soldier 1982-E-6957	Yr.Iss.	1982	6.50	N/A
1982	Merry Christmas Grandma-E-6975	3-Yr.	1984	5.00	N/A
1982	Carousel Horses-E-6958	3-Yr.	1984	8.00	20-40
1982	Dear Santa-E-6959 - Gilmore	8-Yr.	1989	10.00	25
1982	Penguin Power-E-6977	2-Yr.	1983	6.00	15
1982	Bunny Winter Playground 1982-E-6978	Yr.Iss.	1982	10.00	N/A
1982	Baby's First Christmas 1982-E-6979	Yr.Iss.	1982	10.00	N/A
1982	Carousel Horses-E-6980	4-Yr.	1986	8.00	N/A
1982	Grandchild's First Christmas 1982-E-6983	Yr.Iss.	1982	5.00	73
1982	Merry Christmas Teacher-E-6984	4-Yr.	1985	7.00	N/A
1983	Garfield Cuts The Ice-E-8771 J. Davis	3-Yr.	1985	6.00	45
1984	A Stocking Full For 1984-E-8773 - J. Davis	Yr.Iss.	1984	6.00	N/A
1983	Stocking Full For 1983-E-8773 J. Davis	Yr.Iss.	1983	6.00	N/A
1985	Santa Claus Balloon-55794	Yr.Iss.	1985	8.50	20
1985	Carousel Reindeer-55808	4-Yr.	1988	12.00	33
1985	Angel In Flight-55816	4-Yr.	1988	8.00	23
1985	Christmas Penguin-55824	4-Yr.	1988	7.50	43
1985	Merry Christmas Godchild-55832 - Gilmore	5-Yr.	1989	8.00	N/A
1985	Baby's First Christmas-55840	2-Yr.	1986	15.00	N/A
1985	Old Fashioned Rocking Horse-55859	2-Yr.	1986	10.00	15
1985	Child's Second Christmas-55867	5-Yr.	1989	11.00	N/A
1985	Fishing For Stars-55875	5-Yr.	1989	9.00	25
1985	Baby Blocks-55883	2-Yr.	1986	12.00	N/A
1985	Christmas Toy Chest-55891	5-Yr.	1989	10.00	N/A
1985	Grandchild's First Ornament-55921	5-Yr.	1989	7.00	30

CHRISTMAS ORNAMENTS

YEAR ISSUE		EDITION LIMIT	YEAR RETD.	ISSUE PRICE	QUOTE U.S.$
1985	Joy Photo Frame-55956	Yr.Iss.	1985	6.00	N/A
1985	We Three Kings-55964	Yr.Iss.	1985	4.50	20
1985	The Night Before Christmas-55972	2-Yr.	1986	5.00	N/A
1985	Baby's First Christmas 1985-55980	Yr.Iss.	1985	6.00	N/A
1985	Baby Rattle Photo Frame-56006	2-Yr.	1986	5.00	N/A
1985	Baby's First Christmas 1985-56014 - Gilmore	Yr.Iss.	1985	10.00	N/A
1985	Christmas Plane Ride-56049 - L. Rigg	6-Yr.	1990	10.00	N/A
1985	Scottie Celebrating Christmas-56065	5-Yr.	1989	7.50	25
1985	North Pole Native-56073	2-Yr.	1986	9.00	N/A
1985	Skating Walrus-56081	2-Yr.	1986	9.00	20
1985	Ski Time-56111 - J. Davis	Yr.Iss.	1985	13.00	N/A
1985	North Pole Express-56138 - J. Davis	Yr.Iss.	1985	12.00	N/A
1985	Merry Christmas Mother-56146 - J. Davis	Yr.Iss.	1985	8.50	N/A
1985	Hoppy Christmas-56154 - J. Davis	Yr.Iss.	1985	8.50	N/A
1985	Merry Christmas Teacher-56170 - J. Davis	Yr.Iss.	1985	6.00	N/A
1985	Garfield-In-The-Box-56189 - J. Davis	Yr.Iss.	1985	6.50	25
1985	Merry Christmas Grandma-56197	Yr.Iss.	1985	7.00	N/A
1985	Christmas Lights-56200	2-Yr.	1986	8.00	N/A
1985	Victorian Doll House-56251	Yr.Iss.	1985	13.00	40
1985	Tobaoggan Ride-56286	4-Yr.	1988	6.00	15
1985	Look Out Below-56375	Yr.Iss.	1985	8.50	40
1985	Flying Santa Christmas Special-56383	2-Yr.	1986	10.00	N/A
1985	Sawin Elf Helper-56391	Yr.Iss.	1985	8.00	N/A
1985	Snow Shoe-In Santa-56405	Yr.Iss.	1985	8.00	50
1985	Our Hero-56413	Yr.Iss.	1985	5.50	N/A
1985	Not A Creaturxe Was Stirring-56421	2-Yr.	1986	4.00	N/A
1985	Merry Christmas Teacher-56448	Yr.Iss.	1985	9.00	N/A
1985	A Stocking Full For 1985-56464 - J. Davis	Yr.Iss.	1985	6.00	25
1985	St. Nicholas Circa 1910-56659	5-Yr.	1989	6.00	15
1985	Christmas Tree Photo Frame-56871	4-Yr.	1988	10.00	N/A
1990	Deck The Halls-566063	3-Yr.	1992	12.50	N/A
1988	Making A Point-489212 - G.G. Santiago	3-Yr.	1990	10.00	N/A
1988	Mouse Upon A Pipe-489220 - G.G. Santiago	2-Yr.	1989	10.00	12
1988	North Pole Deadline-489387	3-Yr.	1990	13.50	25
1988	Christmas Pin-Up-489409	2-Yr.	1989	11.00	30
1988	Airmail For Teacher-489425 - Gilmore	3-Yr.	1990	13.50	N/A
1986	1st Christmas Together 1986-551171	Yr.Iss.	1986	9.00	15-35
1986	Elf Stringing Popcorn-551198	4-Yr.	1989	10.00	20-30
1986	Christmas Scottie-551201	4-Yr.	1989	7.00	15-30
1986	Santa and Child-551236	4-Yr.	1989	13.50	25-50
1986	The Christmas Angel-551244	4-Yr.	1989	22.50	75
1986	Carousel Unicorn-551252 - Gilmore	4-Yr.	1989	12.00	38
1986	Have a Heavenly Holiday-551260	4-Yr.	1989	9.00	N/A
1986	Siamese Kitten-551279	4-Yr.	1989	9.00	36
1986	Old Fashioned Doll House-551287	4-Yr.	1989	15.00	N/A
1986	Holiday Fisherman-551309	3-Yr.	1988	8.00	40
1986	Antique Toy-551317	3-Yr.	1988	9.00	N/A
1986	Time For Christmas-551325 - Gilmore	4-Yr.	1989	13.00	N/A
1986	Christmas Calendar-551333	2-Yr.	1987	7.00	N/A
1986	Merry Christmas-551341 - Gilmore	3-Yr.	1988	8.00	98
1986	The Santa Claus Shoppe Circa 1905-551562 - J. Grossman	4-Yr.	1989	8.00	15
1986	Baby Bear Sleigh-551651 - Gilmore	3-Yr.	1988	9.00	30
1986	Baby's First Christmas 1986-551678 - Gilmore	Yr.Iss.	1986	10.00	20
1986	First Christmas Together-551708	3-Yr.	1988	6.00	10
1986	Baby's First Christmas-551716	3-Yr.	1988	5.50	10
1986	Baby's First Christmas 1986-551724	Yr.Iss.	1986	6.50	30
1986	Peek-A-Bear Grandchild's First Christmas-	Yr.Iss.	1986	6.00	23
1986	Peek-A-Bear Present-552089	4-Yr.	1989	2.50	N/A
1986	Peek-A-Bear Present-552089	4-Yr.	1989	2.50	N/A
1986	Peek-A-Bear Present-552089	4-Yr.	1989	2.50	N/A
1986	Peek-A-Bear Present-552089	4-Yr.	1989	2.50	N/A
1986	Merry Christmas 1986-552186 - L. Rigg	Yr.Iss.	1986	8.00	N/A
1986	Merry Christmas 1986-552534 - L. Rigg	Yr.Iss.	1986	8.00	N/A
1986	Lucy & Me Christmas Tree-552542 - L. Rigg	3-Yr.	1988	7.00	25
1986	Santa's Helpers-552607	3-Yr.	1988	2.50	N/A
1986	My Special Friend-552615	3-Yr.	1988	6.00	N/A
1986	Christmas Wishes From Panda-552623	3-Yr.	1988	6.00	N/A
1986	Lucy & Me Ski Time-552658 - L. Rigg	2-Yr.	1987	6.50	30
1986	Merry Christmas Teacher-552666	3-Yr.	1988	6.50	N/A
1986	Country Cousins Merry Christmas, Mom	3-Yr.	1988	7.00	23
1986	Country Cousins Merry Christmas, Dad	3-Yr.	1988	7.00	23
1986	Country Cousins Merry Christmas, Mom-552712	4-Yr.	1989	7.00	23
1986	Country Cousins Merry Christmas, Dad-552712	4-Yr.	1989	7.00	25
1986	Grandmother's Little Angel-552747	4-Yr.	1989	8.00	N/A
1987	Puppy's 1st Christmas-552909	2-Yr.	1988	4.00	N/A
1987	Kitty's 1st Christmas-552917	2-Yr.	1988	4.00	25
1987	Merry Christmas Puppy-552925	2-Yr.	1988	3.50	N/A
1987	Merry Christmas Kitty-552933	2-Yr.	1988	3.50	N/A
1986	I Love My Grandparents-553263	Yr.Iss.	1986	6.00	N/A
1986	Merry Christmas Mom & Dad-553271	Yr.Iss.	1986	6.00	N/A
1986	S. Claus Hollycopter-553344	4-Yr.	1989	13.50	35
1986	From Our House To Your House-553360	3-Yr.	1988	15.00	40
1986	Christmas Rattle-553379	3-Yr.	1988	8.00	35
1986	Bah, Humbug!-553387	4-Yr.	1989	9.00	N/A
1986	God Bless Us Everyone-553395	4-Yr.	1989	10.00	15
1987	Carousel Mobile-553409	3-Yr.	1989	15.00	50
1986	Holiday Train-553417	4-Yr.	1989	10.00	N/A
1986	Lighten Up!-553603 - J. Davis	5-Yr.	1990	10.00	N/A
1986	Gift Wrap Odie-553611 - J. Davis	Yr.Iss.	1986	7.00	20
1986	Merry Christmas-553646	4-Yr.	1989	8.00	N/A
1987	M.V.B. (Most Valuable Bear)-554219	2-Yr.	1988	3.00	N/A
1987	M.V.B. (Most Valuable Bear)-554219	2-Yr.	1988	3.00	N/A
1987	M.V.B. (Most Valuable Bear)-554219	2-Yr.	1988	3.00	N/A
1987	M.V.B. (Most Valuable Bear)-554219	2-Yr.	1988	3.00	N/A
1988	1st Christmas Together-554537 - Gilmore	3-Yr.	1990	15.00	N/A
1988	An Eye On Christmas-554545 - Gilmore	3-Yr.	1990	22.50	60
1988	A Mouse Check-554553 - Gilmore	3-Yr.	1990	13.50	45
1988	Merry Christmas Engine-554561	2-Yr.	1989	22.50	35
1989	Sardine Express-554588 - Gilmore	2-Yr.	1990	17.50	30
1988	1st Christmas Together 1988-554596	Yr.Iss.	1988	10.00	N/A
1988	Forever Friends-554626 - Gilmore	2-Yr.	1989	12.00	27
1988	Santa's Survey-554642	2-Yr.	1989	35.00	75-100
1989	Old Town's Church-554871 - Gilmore	2-Yr.	1990	17.50	20
1988	A Chipmunk Holiday-554898 - Gilmore	3-Yr.	1990	11.00	25
1988	Christmas Is Coming-554901	3-Yr.	1990	12.00	12
1988	Baby's First Christmas 1988-554928	Yr.Iss.	1988	7.50	N/A
1988	Baby's First Christmas 1988-554936 - Gilmore	Yr.Iss.	1988	10.00	25
1988	The Christmas Train-554944	3-Yr.	1990	15.00	N/A
1988	Li'l Drummer Bear-554952 - Gilmore	3-Yr.	1990	12.00	12
1987	Baby's First Christmas-555061	3-Yr.	1989	12.00	N/A
1987	Baby's First Christmas-555088	3-Yr.	1989	7.50	N/A
1987	Baby's First Christmas-555118	3-Yr.	1989	6.00	N/A
1987	Sugar Plum Bearies-555193	2-Yr.	1988	4.50	N/A
1987	Garfield Merry Kissmas-555215 - J. Davis	3-Yr.	1989	8.50	30
1987	Sleigh Away-555401	3-Yr.	1989	12.00	N/A
1987	Merry Christmas 1987-555428 - L. Rigg	Yr.Iss.	1987	8.00	N/A
1987	Merry Christmas 1987-555436 - L. Rigg	Yr.Iss.	1987	8.00	N/A
1987	Lucy & Me Storybook Bear-555444 - L. Rigg	3-Yr.	1989	6.50	N/A
1987	Time For Christmas-555452 - L. Rigg	3-Yr.	1989	12.00	20
1987	Lucy & Me Angel On A Cloud-555487 - L. Rigg	3-Yr.	1989	8.00	35
1987	Teddy's Stocking-555940 - Gilmore	3-Yr.	1989	10.00	N/A
1987	Kitty's Jack-In-The-Box-555959	3-Yr.	1989	11.00	30
1987	Merry Christmas Teacher-555967	3-Yr.	1989	7.50	N/A
1987	Mouse In A Mitten-555975	3-Yr.	1989	7.50	N/A
1987	Boy On A Rocking Horse-555983	3-Yr.	1989	12.00	18
1987	Peek-A-Bear Letter To Santa-555991	2-Yr.	1988	8.00	30
1987	Garfield Sugar Plum Fairy-556009 - J. Davis	3-Yr.	1989	8.50	20
1987	Garfield The Nutcracker-556017 - J. Davis	4-Yr.	1990	8.50	35
1987	Home Sweet Home-556033 - Gilmore	3-Yr.	1989	15.00	40
1987	Baby's First Christmas-556041	4-Yr.	1990	10.00	20
1987	Little Sailor Elf-556068	3-Yr.	1989	10.00	28
1987	Carousel Goose-556076	3-Yr.	1989	17.00	40
1987	Night Caps-556084	2-Yr.	1988	5.50	N/A
1987	Night Caps-556084	2-Yr.	1988	5.50	N/A
1987	Night Caps-556084	2-Yr.	1988	5.50	N/A
1987	Night Caps-556084	2-Yr.	1988	5.50	N/A
1987	Rocking Horse Past Joys-556157	3-Yr.	1989	10.00	20
1987	Partridge In A Pear Tree-556173 - Gilmore	3-Yr.	1989	9.00	35
1987	Carousel Lion-556025 - Gilmore	3-Yr.	1989	12.00	25
1987	Skating Santa 1987-556211	Yr.Iss.	1987	13.50	75
1987	Baby's First Christmas 1987-556238 - Gilmore	Yr.Iss.	1987	10.00	25
1987	Baby's First Christmas 1987-556254	Yr.Iss.	1987	7.00	25
1987	Teddy's Suspenders-556262	4-Yr.	1990	8.50	22
1987	Baby's First Christmas 1987-556297	Yr.Iss.	1987	2.00	N/A
1987	Baby's First Christmas 1987-556297	Yr.Iss.	1987	2.00	N/A
1987	Beary Christmas Family-556300	2-Yr.	1988	2.00	N/A
1987	Beary Christmas Family-556300	2-Yr.	1988	2.00	N/A
1987	Beary Christmas Family-556300	2-Yr.	1988	2.00	N/A
1987	Beary Christmas Family-556300	2-Yr.	1988	2.00	N/A
1987	Beary Christmas Family-556300	2-Yr.	1988	2.00	N/A
1987	Beary Christmas Family-556300	2-Yr.	1988	2.00	N/A
1987	Merry ChristmasTeacher-556319	2-Yr.	1988	2.00	N/A
1987	Merry ChristmasTeacher-556319	2-Yr.	1988	2.00	N/A
1987	Merry ChristmasTeacher-556319	2-Yr.	1988	2.00	N/A
1987	Merry ChristmasTeacher-556319	2-Yr.	1988	2.00	N/A
1987	1st ChristmasTogether 1987-556335	Yr.Iss.	1987	9.00	18
1987	Country Cousins Katie Goes Ice Skating-	3-Yr.	1989	8.00	30
1987	Country Cousins Scooter Snowman-556386	3-Yr.	1989	8.00	30
1987	Santa's List-556394	3-Yr.	1989	7.00	23
1987	Kitty's Bed-556408	3-Yr.	1989	12.00	30
1987	Grandchild's First Christmas-556416	3-Yr.	1989	10.00	N/A
1987	Two Turtledoves-556432 - Gilmore	3-Yr.	1989	9.00	30
1987	Three French Hens-556440 - Gilmore	3-Yr.	1989	9.00	30
1988	Four Calling Birds-556459 - Gilmore	3-Yr.	1990	11.00	30
1987	Teddy Takes A Spin-556467	4-Yr.	1990	13.00	35
1987	Tiny Toy Thimble Mobile-556475	2-Yr.	1988	12.00	35
1987	Bucket O'Love-556491	2-Yr.	1988	2.50	N/A
1987	Bucket O'Love-556491	2-Yr.	1988	2.50	N/A
1987	Puppy Love-556505	3-Yr.	1989	6.00	N/A
1987	Peek-A-Bear My Special Friend-556513	4-Yr.	1990	6.00	30
1987	Our First Christmas Together-556548	3-Yr.	1989	13.00	20
1987	Three Little Bears-556556	3-Yr.	1989	7.50	15
1987	Lucy & Me Mailbox Bear-556564 - L. Rigg	4-Yr.	1990	3.00	N/A
1987	Twinkle Bear-556572 - Gilmore	3-Yr.	1989	8.00	N/A
1987	I'm Dreaming Of A Bright Christmas-556602	2-Yr.	1988	2.50	N/A
1987	I'm Dreaming Of A Bright Christmas-556602	2-Yr.	1988	2.50	N/A
1987	Christmas Train-557196	3-Yr.	1989	10.00	N/A
1988	Dairy Christmas-557501 - M. Cook	2-Yr.	1989	10.00	30
1988	Merry Christmas 1988-557595 - L. Rigg	Yr.Iss.	1988	10.00	N/A
1988	Merry Christmas 1988-557609 - L. Rigg	Yr.Iss.	1988	10.00	N/A
1988	Toy Chest Keepsake-558206 - L. Rigg	3-Yr.	1990	12.50	30
1988	Teddy Bear Greetings-558214 - L. Rigg	3-Yr.	1990	8.00	30
1988	Jester Bear-558222 - L. Rigg	2-Yr.	1989	8.00	N/A
1988	Night-Watch Cat-558362 - J. Davis	3-Yr.	1990	13.00	35
1988	Christmas Thim-bell-558389	Yr.Iss.	1988	4.00	30
1988	Christmas Thim-bell-558389	Yr.Iss.	1988	4.00	N/A
1988	Christmas Thim-bell-558389	Yr.Iss.	1988	4.00	N/A
1988	Christmas Thim-bell-558389	Yr.Iss.	1988	4.00	N/A
1988	Baby's First Christmas-558397 - D. Parker	3-Yr.	1990	16.00	30
1988	Christmas Tradition-558400 - Gilmore	2-Yr.	1989	10.00	25
1988	Stocking Story-558419 - G.G. Santiago	3-Yr.	1990	10.00	23
1988	Winter Tale-558427 - G.G. Santiago	2-Yr.	1989	6.00	N/A
1988	Party Mouse-558435 - G.G. Santiago	3-Yr.	1990	12.00	30
1988	Christmas Watch-558443 - G.G. Santiago	2-Yr.	1989	11.00	32
1988	Christmas Vacation-558451 - G.G. Santiago	3-Yr.	1990	8.00	23
1988	Sweet Cherub-558478 - G.G. Santiago	3-Yr.	1990	7.00	8
1988	Time Out-558486 - G.G. Santiago	2-Yr.	1989	11.00	N/A
1988	The Ice Fairy-558516 - G.G. Santiago	3-Yr.	1990	23.00	45-55
1988	Santa Turtle-558559	2-Yr.	1989	10.00	35
1988	The Teddy Bear Ball-558567	3-Yr.	1990	10.00	25
1988	Turtle Greetings-558583	2-Yr.	1989	8.50	25
1988	Happy Howladays-558605	Yr.Iss.	1988	7.00	15
1988	Special Delivery-558699 - J. Davis	3-Yr.	1990	9.00	30
1988	Deer Garfield-558702 - J. Davis	3-Yr.	1990	12.00	30
1988	Garfield Bags O' Fun-558761 - J. Davis	Yr.Iss.	1988	3.30	N/A
1988	Gramophone Keepsake-558818	2-Yr.	1989	13.00	20
1988	North Pole Lineman-558834 - Gilmore	2-Yr.	1989	10.00	50
1988	Five Golden Rings-559121 - Gilmore	3-Yr.	1990	11.00	25
1988	Six Geese A-Laying-559148 - Gilmore	3-Yr.	1990	11.00	25
1988	Pretty Baby-559156 - R. Morehead	3-Yr.	1990	12.50	25
1988	Old Fashioned Angel-559164 - R. Morehead	3-Yr.	1990	12.50	20
1988	Two For Tea-559776 - Gilmore	3-Yr.	1990	20.00	35-40
1988	Merry Christmas Grandpa-560065	3-Yr.	1990	8.00	N/A
1990	Reeling In The Holidays-560405 - M. Cook	2-Yr.	1991	8.00	15
1991	Walkin' With My Baby-561029 - M. Cook	2-Yr.	1992	10.00	N/A
1989	Scrub-A-Dub Chipmunk-561037 - M. Cook	2-Yr.	1990	8.00	20
1989	Christmas Cook-Out-561045 - M. Cook	2-Yr.	1990	9.00	20
1989	Sparkles-561843 - S. Zimnicki	3-Yr.	1991	17.50	25-28
1989	Bunkie-561835 - S. Zimnicki	3-Yr.	1991	22.50	30
1989	Popper-561878 - S. Zimnicki	3-Yr.	1991	12.00	25

CHRISTMAS ORNAMENTS

YEAR ISSUE		EDITION LIMIT	YEAR RETD.	ISSUE PRICE	QUOTE U.S.$
1989	Seven Swans A-Swimming-562742 - Gilmore	3-Yr.	1991	12.00	23
1989	Eight Maids A-Milking-562750 - Gilmore	3-Yr.	1991	12.00	23
1989	Nine Dancers Dancing-562769 - Gilmore	3-Yr.	1991	15.00	23
1989	Baby's First Christmas 1989-562807	Yr.Iss.	1989	8.00	20
1989	Baby's First Christmas 1989-562815 - Gilmore	Yr.Iss.	1989	10.00	N/A
1989	First Christmas Together 1989-562823	Yr.Iss.	1989	11.00	N/A
1989	Travelin' Trike-562882 - Gilmore	3-Yr.	1991	15.00	15
1989	Victorian Sleigh Ride-562890	3-Yr.	1991	22.50	23
1991	Santa Delivers Love-562904 - Gilmore	2-Yr.	1992	17.50	18
1989	Chestnut Roastin'-562912 - Gilmore	2-Yr.	1990	13.00	13
1990	Th-Ink-In' Of You-562920 - Gilmore	2-Yr.	1991	20.00	30
1989	Ye Olde Puppet Show-562939	2-Yr.	1990	17.50	34
1989	Static In The Attic-562947	2-Yr.	1990	13.00	25
1989	Mistle-Toast 1989-562963 - Gilmore	Yr.Iss.	1989	15.00	25
1989	Merry Christmas Pops-562971 - Gilmore	3-Yr.	1991	12.00	12
1990	North Pole Or Bust-562998 - Gilmore	2-Yr.	1991	25.00	25
1989	By The Light Of The Moon-563005 - Gilmore	3-Yr.	1991	12.00	24
1989	Stickin' To It-563013 - Gilmore	2-Yr.	1990	10.00	12
1989	Christmas Cookin'-563048 - Gilmore	3-Yr.	1991	22.50	25
1989	All Set For Santa-563080 -Gilmore	3-Yr.	1991	17.50	25
1990	Santa's Sweets-563196 - Gilmore	2-Yr.	1991	20.00	20
1990	Purr-Fect Pals-563218	2-Yr.	1991	8.00	8
1989	The Pause That Refreshes-563226	3-Yr.	1991	15.00	35
1989	Ho-Ho Holiday Scrooge-563234 - J. Davis	3-Yr.	1991	13.50	30
1989	God Bless Us Everyone-563242 - J. Davis	3-Yr.	1991	13.50	30
1989	Scrooge With The Spirit-563250 - J. Davis	3-Yr.	1991	13.50	30
1989	A Chains Of Pace For Odie-563269 - J. Davis	3-Yr.	1991	12.00	25
1990	Jingle Bell Rock 1990-563390 - G. Armgardt	Yr.Iss.	1990	13.50	30
1989	Joy Ridin'-563463 - J. Davis	2-Yr.	1990	15.00	30
1989	Just What I Wanted-563668 - M. Peters	3-Yr.	1991	13.50	14
1990	Pucker Up!-563676 - M. Peters	3-Yr.	1992	11.00	11
1989	What's The Bright Idea-563684 - M. Peters	3-Yr.	1991	13.50	14
1990	Fleas Navidad-563978 - M. Peters	3-Yr.	1992	13.50	25
1990	Tweet Greetings-564044 - J. Davis	2-Yr.	1991	15.00	30
1990	Trouble On 3 Wheels-564052 - J. Davis	3-Yr.	1992	20.00	35
1989	Mine, All Mine!-564079 - J. Davis	Yr.Iss.	1989	15.00	40
1989	Star of Stars-564389 - J. Jonik	3-Yr.	1991	9.00	15
1990	Hang Onto Your Hat-564397 - J. Jonik	3-Yr.	1992	8.00	15
1990	Fireplace Frolic-564435 - N. Teiber	2-Yr.	1991	25.00	32
1989	Hoe! Hoe! Hoe!-564761	Yr.Iss.	1989	20.00	35
1991	Double Scoop Snowmouse-564796 - M. Cook	3-Yr.	1993	13.50	14
1990	Christmas Is Magic-564826 - M. Cook	2-Yr.	1991	10.00	10
1990	Lighting Up Christmas-564834 - M. Cook	2-Yr.	1991	10.00	10
1989	Feliz Navidad! 1989-564842 - M. Cook	Yr.Iss.	1989	11.00	40
1989	Spreading Christmas Joy-564850 - M. Cook	3-Yr.	1991	10.00	10
1989	Yuletide Tree House-564915 - J. Jonik	3-Yr.	1991	20.00	20
1990	Brewnig Warm Wishes-564974	2-Yr.	1991	10.00	10
1990	Yippie-I-Yuletide-564982 - Hahn	3-Yr.	1992	15.00	15
1990	Coffee Break-564990 - Hahn	3-Yr.	1992	15.00	15
1990	You're Sew Special-565008 - Hahn	Yr.Iss.	1990	20.00	35
1989	Full House Mouse-565016 - Hahn	2-Yr.	1990	13.50	25
1989	I Feel Pretty-565024 - Hahn	3-Yr.	1991	20.00	30
1990	Warmest Wishes-565032 - Hahn	3-Yr.	1992	15.00	15
1990	Baby's Christmas Feast-565040 - Hahn	3-Yr.	1992	13.50	14
1990	Bumper Car Santa-565083 - G.G. Santiago	Yr.Iss.	1990	20.00	40
1989	Special Delivery(Proof Ed.)-565091 - G.G. Santiago	Yr.Iss.	1989	12.00	15
1990	Ho! Ho! Yo-Yo!(Proof Ed.)-565105 - G.G. Santiago	Yr.Iss.	1990	12.00	15
1989	Weightin' For Santa-565148 - G.G. Santiago	3-Yr.	1991	7.50	8
1989	Holly Fairy-565199 - C.M. Baker	Yr.Iss.	1989	15.00	45
1990	The Christmas Tree Fairy-565202 - C.M. Baker	Yr.Iss.	1990	15.00	40
1989	Christmas 1989-565210 - L. Rigg	Yr.Iss.	1989	12.00	38
1989	Top Of The Class-565237 - L. Rigg	3-Yr.	1991	11.00	11
1989	Deck The Hogs-565490 - M. Cook	2-Yr.	1990	12.00	14
1989	Pinata Ridin'-565504 - M. Cook	2-Yr.	1990	11.00	N/A
1989	Hangin' In There 1989-565598 - K. Wise	Yr.Iss.	1989	10.00	20
1990	Meow-y Christmas 1990-565601 - K. Wise	Yr.Iss.	1990	10.00	25
1990	Seaman's Greetings-566047	2-Yr.	1991	11.00	24
1990	Hang In There-566055	3-Yr.	1992	13.50	14
1991	Pedal Pushin' Santa-566071	Yr.Iss.	1991	20.00	30
1990	Merry Christmas Teacher-566098	2-Yr.	1991	11.00	11
1990	Festive Flight-566101	2-Yr.	1991	11.00	11
1990	Santa's Suitcase-566160	3-Yr.	1992	25.00	25
1989	The Purr-Fect Fit!-566462	3-Yr.	1991	15.00	35
1990	Tumbles 1990-566519 - S. Zimnicki	Yr.Iss.	1990	16.00	25
1990	Twiddles-566551 - S. Zimnicki	3-Yr.	1992	15.00	30
1991	Snuffy-566578 - S. Zimnicki	3-Yr.	1993	17.50	18
1990	All Aboard-567671 - Gilmore	2-Yr.	1991	17.50	18
1989	Gone With The Wind-567698	Yr.Iss.	1989	13.50	30
1989	Dorothy-567760	Yr.Iss.	1989	12.00	35
1989	The Tin Man-567779	Yr.Iss.	1989	12.00	25
1989	The Cowardly Lion-567787	Yr.Iss.	1989	12.00	25
1989	The Scarecrow-567795	Yr.Iss.	1989	12.00	25
1990	Happy Holiday Readings-568104	2-Yr.	1991	8.00	8
1989	Christmas 1989-568325 - L. Rigg	Yr.Iss.	1989	12.00	N/A
1991	Holiday Ahoy-568368	2-Yr.	1992	12.50	13
1991	Christmas Countdown-568376	3-Yr.	1993	20.00	20
1989	Clara-568406	Yr.Iss.	1989	12.50	20
1990	The Nutcracker-568414	Yr.Iss.	1990	12.50	30
1991	Clara's Prince-568422	Yr.Iss.	1991	12.50	18
1989	Santa's Little Reindear-568430	2-Yr.	1990	15.00	25
1991	Tuba Totin' Teddy-568449	3-Yr.	1993	15.00	15
1990	A Calling Home At Christmas-568457	2-Yr.	1991	15.00	15
1991	Love Is The Secret Ingredient-568562 - L. Rigg	2-Yr.	1992	15.00	15
1990	A Spoonful of Love-568570 - L. Rigg	2-Yr.	1991	10.00	10
1990	Christmas Swingtime 1990-568597 - L. Rigg	Yr.Iss.	1990	13.00	N/A
1990	Christmas Swingtime 1990-568600 - L. Rigg	Yr.Iss.	1990	13.00	N/A
1990	Bearing Holiday Wishes-568619 - L. Rigg	3-Yr.	1992	22.50	23
1990	Smitch-570184 - S. Zimnicki	3-Yr.	1992	22.50	23
1991	Twinkle & Sprinkle-570206 - S. Zimnicki	3-Yr.	1993	22.50	23
1990	Blinkie-570214 - S. Zimnicki	3-Yr.	1992	15.00	15
1990	Have A Coke And A SmileÔ-571512	3-Yr.	1992	15.00	25
1990	Fleece Navidad-571903 - M. Cook	2-Yr.	1991	13.50	25
1990	Have a Navaho-Ho-Ho 1990-571970 - M. Cook	Yr.Iss.	1990	15.00	35
1990	Cheers 1990-572411 - T. Wilson	Yr.Iss.	1990	13.50	22
1990	A Night Before Christmas-572438 - T. Wilson	2-Yr.	1991	17.50	18
1990	Merry Kissmas-572446 - T. Wilson	2-Yr.	1991	10.00	30
1991	Here Comes Santa Paws-572535 - J. Davis	3-Yr.	1993	20.00	20
1990	Frosty Garfield 1990-572551 - J. Davis	Yr.Iss.	1990	13.50	35
1990	Pop Goes The Odie-572578 - J. Davis	2-Yr.	1991	15.00	30
1991	Sweet Beams-572586 - J. Davis	2-Yr.	1992	13.50	14
1990	An Apple A Day-572594 - J. Davis	2-Yr.	1991	12.00	12
1990	Dear Santa-572608 - J. Davis	3-Yr.	1992	17.00	17
1991	Have A Ball This Christmas-572616 - J. Davis	Yr.Iss.	1991	15.00	15
1990	Oh Shoosh!-572624 - J. Davis	3-Yr.	1992	17.00	17
1990	Little Red Riding Cat-572632 - J. Davis	Yr.Iss.	1990	13.50	33
1991	All Decked Out-572659 - J. Davis	2-Yr.	1992	13.50	14
1990	Over The Rooftops-572721 - J. Davis	2-Yr.	1991	17.50	28-35
1990	Garfield NFL Los Angeles Rams-572764 - J. Davis	2-Yr.	1991	12.50	13
1990	Garfield NFLCincinnati Bengals-573,000 - J. Davis	2-Yr.	1991	12.50	13
1990	Garfield NFLCleveland Browns-573019 - J. Davis	2-Yr.	1991	12.50	13
1990	Garfield NFL Houston Oiliers-573027 - J. Davis	2-Yr.	1991	12.50	13
1990	Garfield NFL Pittsburg Steelers-573035 - J. Davis	2-Yr.	1991	12.50	13
1990	Garfield NFL Denver Broncos-573043 - J. Davis	2-Yr.	1991	12.50	13
1990	Garfield NFLKansas City Chiefs-573051 - J. Davis	2-Yr.	1991	12.50	13
1990	Garfield NFL Los Angeles Raiders-573078 - J. Davis	2-Yr.	1991	12.50	13
1990	Garfield NFL San Diego Chargers-573086 - J. Davis	2-Yr.	1991	12.50	13
1990	Garfield NFL Seattle Seahawks-573094 - J. Davis	2-Yr.	1991	12.50	13
1990	Garfield NFL Buffalo Bills-573108 - J. Davis	2-Yr.	1991	12.50	13
1990	Garfield NFL Indianapolis Colts-573116 - J. Davis	2-Yr.	1991	12.50	13
1990	Garfield NFL Miami Dolphins-573124 - J. Davis	2-Yr.	1991	12.50	13
1990	Garfield NFL New England Patriots-573132 - J. Davis	2-Yr.	1991	12.50	13
1990	Garfield NFL New York Jets-573140 - J. Davis	2-Yr.	1991	12.50	13
1990	Garfield NFL Atlanta Falcons-573159 - J. Davis	2-Yr.	1991	12.50	13
1990	Garfield NFL New Orleans Saints-573167 - J. Davis	2-Yr.	1991	12.50	13
1990	Garfield NFL San Francisco 49ers-573175 - J. Davis	2-Yr.	1991	12.50	13
1990	Garfield NFL Dallas Cowboys-573183 - J. Davis	2-Yr.	1991	12.50	13
1990	Garfield NFL New York Giants-573191 - J. Davis	2-Yr.	1991	12.50	13
1990	Garfield NFL Philadelphia Eagles-573205 - J. Davis	2-Yr.	1991	12.50	13
1990	Garfield NFL Phoenix Cardinals-573213 - J. Davis	2-Yr.	1991	12.50	13
1990	Garfield NFL Washington Redskins-573221 - J. Davis	2-Yr.	1991	12.50	13
1990	Garfield NFL Chicago Bears-573248 - J. Davis	2-Yr.	1991	12.50	13
1990	Garfield NFL Detroit Lions-573256 - J. Davis	2-Yr.	1991	12.50	13
1990	Garfield NFL Green Bay Packers-573264 - J. Davis	2-Yr.	1991	12.50	13
1990	Garfield NFLMinnesota Vikings-573272 - J. Davis	2-Yr.	1991	12.50	13
1990	Garfield NFL Tampa Bay Buccaneers-573280 - J. Davis	2-Yr.	1991	12.50	13
1991	Tea For Two-573299 - Hahn	3-Yr.	1993	30.00	50
1991	Hot Stuff Santa-573523	Yr.Iss.	1991	25.00	30
1990	Merry Moustronauts-573558 - M. Cook	3-Yr.	1992	20.00	40
1991	Santa Wings It-573612 - J. Jonik	3-Yr.	1993	13.00	13
1990	All Eye Want For Christmas-573647 - Gilmore	3-Yr.	1992	27.50	32
1990	Stuck On You-573655 - Gilmore	2-Yr.	1991	12.50	13
1990	Professor Michael Bear, The One Bear Band-573663 - Gilmore	3-Yr.	1992	22.50	28
1990	A Caroling Wee Go-573671 - Gilmore	3-Yr.	1992	12.00	12
1990	Merry Mailman-573698 - Gilmore	2-Yr.	1991	15.00	30
1990	Deck The Halls-573701 - Gilmore	3-Yr.	1992	22.50	30
1990	You're Wheel Special-573728 - Gilmore	3-Yr.	1992	15.00	15
1991	Come Let Us Adore Him-573736 - Gilmore	2-Yr.	1992	9.00	9
1991	Moon Beam Dreams-573760 - Gilmore	3-Yr.	1993	12.00	12
1991	A Song For Santa-573779 - Gilmore	3-Yr.	1993	25.00	25
1990	Warmest Wishes-573825 - Gilmore	Yr.Iss.	1990	17.50	25
1991	Kurious Kitty-573868 - Gilmore	3-Yr.	1993	17.50	18
1990	Old Mother Mouse-573922 - Gilmore	2-Yr.	1991	17.50	20-32
1990	Railroad Repairs-573930 - Gilmore	2-Yr.	1991	12.50	25
1990	Ten Lords A-Leaping-573949 - Gilmore	3-Yr.	1992	15.00	25
1990	Eleven Drummers Drumming-573957 - Gilmore	3-Yr.	1992	15.00	25
1990	Twelve Pipers Piping-573965 - Gilmore	3-Yr.	1992	15.00	25
1990	Baby's First Christmas 1990-573973 - Gilmore	Yr.Iss.	1990	10.00	N/A
1990	Baby's First Christmas 1990-573981 - Gilmore	Yr.Iss.	1990	12.00	N/A
1991	Peter, Peter Pumpkin Eater-574015 - Gilmore	2-Yr.	1992	20.00	30
1990	Little Jack Horner-574058 - Gilmore	2-Yr.	1991	17.50	35
1991	Mary, Mary Quite Contrary-574066 - Gilmore	2-Yr.	1992	22.50	33
1991	Through The Years-574252 - Gilmore	Yr.Iss.	1991	17.50	18
1991	Holiday Wing Ding-574333	3-Yr.	1993	22.50	23
1991	North Pole Here I Come-574597	3-Yr.	1993	10.00	10
1991	Christmas Caboose-574856 - Gilmore	2-Yr.	1992	25.00	30
1990	Bubble Trouble-575038 - Hahn	3-Yr.	1992	20.00	35
1991	Merry Mother-To-Be-575046 - Hahn	3-Yr.	1993	13.50	14
1990	A Holiday 'Scent' Sation-575054 - Hahn	3-Yr.	1992	15.00	30
1990	Catch Of The Day-575070 - Hahn	3-Yr.	1992	25.00	25
1990	Don't Open 'Til Christmas-575089 - Hahn	3-Yr.	1992	17.50	18
1990	I Can't Weight 'Til Christmas-575119 - Hahn	3-Yr.	1992	16.50	30
1991	Deck The Halls-575127 - Hahn	2-Yr.	1992	15.00	25
1990	Mouse House-575186	3-Yr.	1992	16.00	16
1991	Dream A Little Dream-575593	2-Yr.	1992	17.50	18
1991	Christmas Two-gether-575615 - L. Rigg	3-Yr.	1993	22.50	23
1991	Christmas Trimmings-575631	2-Yr.	1992	17.00	17
1991	Gumball Wizard-575658 - Gilmore	2-Yr.	1992	13.00	13
1991	Crystal Ball Christmas-575666 - Gilmore	2-Yr.	1992	22.50	23
1990	Old King Cole-575682 - Gilmore	2-Yr.	1991	20.00	29
1991	Tom, Tom The Piper's Son-575690 - Gilmore	2-Yr.	1992	15.00	33
1991	Tire-d Little Bear-575852 - L. Rigg	Yr.Iss.	1991	12.50	13
1990	Baby Bear Christmas 1990-575860 - L. Rigg	Yr.Iss.	1990	12.00	28
1991	Crank Up The Carols-575887 - L. Rigg	2-Yr.	1992	17.50	18
1990	Beary Christmas 1990-576158 - L. Rigg	Yr.Iss.	1990	12.00	12
1991	Christmas Swingtime 1991-576166 - L. Rigg	Yr.Iss.	1991	13.00	13
1991	Christmas Swingtime 1991-576174 - L. Rigg	Yr.Iss.	1991	13.00	13
1991	Christmas Cutie-576182	3-Yr.	1993	13.50	14
1991	Meow Mates-576220	3-Yr.	1993	12.00	12
1991	Frosty The Snowmant-576425	3-Yr.	1993	15.00	15
1991	Ris-ski Business-576719 - T. Wilson	2-Yr.	1992	10.00	10
1991	Pinocchio-577391 - J. Davis	3-Yr.	1993	15.00	15

CHRISTMAS ORNAMENTS

YEAR ISSUE		EDITION LIMIT	YEAR RETD.	ISSUE PRICE	QUOTE U.S.$
1990	Yuletide Ride 1990-577502 - Gilmore	Yr.Iss.	1990	13.50	50
1990	Tons of Toys-577510	Yr.Iss.	1990	13.00	30
1990	McHappy Holidays-577529	2-Yr.	1991	17.50	25
1990	Heading For Happy Holidays-577537	3-Yr.	1992	17.50	18
1990	'Twas The Night Before Christmas-577545	3-Yr.	1992	17.50	18
1990	Over One Million Holiday Wishes!-577553	Yr.Iss.	1990	17.50	30
1990	You Malt My Heart-577596	2-Yr.	1991	25.00	25
1991	All I Want For Christmas-577618	2-Yr.	1992	20.00	20
1991	Things Go Better With Coke™-580597	3-Yr.	1993	17.00	17
1991	Christmas To Go-580600 - M. Cook	Yr.Iss.	1991	22.50	23
1991	Have A Mariachi Christmas-580619 - M. Cook	2-Yr.	1992	13.50	14
1991	Christmas Is In The Air-581453	Yr.Iss.	1991	15.00	15
1991	Holiday Treats-581542	Yr.Iss.	1991	17.50	18
1991	Christmas Is My Goal-581550	2-Yr.	1992	17.50	18
1991	A Quarter Pounder With Cheerr-581569	3-Yr.	1993	20.00	20
1991	From The Same Mold-581798 - Gilmore	3-Yr.	1993	17.00	17
1991	The Glow Of Christmas-581801	2-Yr.	1992	20.00	20
1991	All Caught Up In Christmas-583537	2-Yr.	1992	10.00	10
1991	Lights..Camera..Kissmas!-583626 - Gilmore	Yr.Iss.	1991	15.00	35
1991	Sweet Steed-583634 - Gilmore	3-Yr.	1993	15.00	15
1991	Dreamin' Of A White Christmas-583669 - Gilmore	2-Yr.	1992	15.00	15
1991	Merry Millimeters-583677 - Gilmore	3-Yr.	1993	17.00	17
1991	Here's The Scoop-583693	2-Yr.	1992	13.50	20
1991	Happy Meal® On Wheels-583715	3-Yr.	1993	22.50	23
1991	Christmas Kayak-583723	2-Yr.	1992	13.50	14
1991	Marilyn Monroe-583774	Yr.Iss.	1991	20.00	20
1991	A Christmas Carol-583928 - Gilmore	3-Yr.	1993	22.50	23
1991	Checking It Twice-583936	2-Yr.	1992	25.00	25
1991	Merry Christmas Go-Round-585203 - J. Davis	3-Yr.	1993	20.00	20
1991	Holiday Hideout-585270 - J. Davis	2-Yr.	1992	15.00	15
1991	Our Most Precious Gift-585726	Yr.Iss.	1991	17.50	18
1991	Christmas Cheer-585769	2-Yr.	1992	13.50	14
1991	Fired Up For Christmas-586587 - Gilmore	2-Yr.	1992	32.50	33
1991	One Foggy Christmas Eve-586625 - Gilmore	3-Yr.	1993	30.00	30
1991	For A Purr-fect Mom-586641 - Gilmore	Yr.Iss.	1991	12.00	12
1991	For A Special Dad-586668 - Gilmore	Yr.Iss.	1991	17.50	18
1991	With Love-586676 - Gilmore	Yr.Iss.	1991	13.00	13
1991	For A Purr-fect Aunt-586692 - Gilmore	Yr.Iss.	1991	12.00	12
1991	For A Dog-Gone Great Uncle-586706 - Gilmore	Yr.Iss.	1991	12.00	12
1991	Peddling Fun-586714 - Gilmore	Yr.Iss.	1991	16.00	16
1991	Special Keepsakes-586722 - Gilmore	Yr.Iss.	1991	13.50	14
1991	Hats Off To Christmas-586757 - Hahn	Yr.Iss.	1991	22.50	23
1991	Baby's First Christmas 1991-586935	Yr.Iss.	1991	12.50	13
1991	Jugglin' The Holidays-587028	2-Yr.	1992	13.00	13
1991	Santa's Steed-587044	Yr.Iss.	1991	15.00	15
1991	A Decade of Treasures-587052 - Gilmore	Yr.Iss.	1991	37.50	75
1991	Mr. Mailmouse-587109 - Gilmore	2-Yr.	1992	17.00	17
1991	Starry Eyed Santa-587176	2-Yr.	1992	15.00	15
1991	Lighting The Way-588776	2-Yr.	1992	20.00	20
1991	Rudolph-588784	2-Yr.	1992	17.50	18
1989	Tea For Two-693758 - N. Teiber	2-Yr.	1990	12.50	30
1990	Holiday Tea Toast-694770 - N. Teiber	2-Yr.	1991	13.50	14
1991	It's Tea-lightful-694789	2-Yr.	1992	13.50	14
1989	Tea Time-694797 - N. Teiber	2-Yr.	1990	12.50	30
1989	Bottom's Up 1989-830003	Yr.Iss.	1989	11.00	32
1990	Sweetest Greetings 1990-830011 - Gilmore	Yr.Iss.	1990	10.00	27
1990	First Class Christmas-830038 - Gilmore	3-Yr.	1992	10.00	10
1989	Caught In The Act-830046 - Gilmore	3-Yr.	1991	12.50	13
1989	Readin' & Ridin'-830054 - Gilmore	3-Yr.	1991	13.50	34
1991	Beary Merry Mailman-830151 - L. Rigg	3-Yr.	1993	13.50	14
1990	Here's Looking at You!-830259 - Gilmore	2-Yr.	1991	17.50	18
1991	Stamper-830267 - S. Zimnicki	Yr.Iss.	1991	13.50	14
1991	Santa's Key Man-830461 - Gilmore	2-Yr.	1992	11.00	11
1991	Tie-dings Of Joy-830488 - Gilmore	Yr.Iss.	1991	12.00	12
1990	Have a Cool Yule-830496 - Gilmore	3-Yr.	1992	12.00	27
1990	Slots of Luck-830518 - Hahn	2-Yr.	1991	13.50	45-60
1991	Straight To Santa-830534 - J. Davis	2-Yr.	1992	13.50	14
1991	Letters To Santa-830925 - Gilmore	2-Yr.	1992	15.00	15
1991	Sneaking Santa's Snack-830933 - Gilmore	3-Yr.	1993	13.00	13
1991	Aiming For The Holidays-830941 - Gilmore	2-Yr.	1992	12.00	12
1991	Ode To Joy-830968 - Gilmore	3-Yr.	1993	10.00	10
1991	Fittin' Mittens-830976 - Gilmore	3-Yr.	1993	12.00	12
1991	The Finishing Touch-831530 - Gilmore	Yr.Iss.	1991	10.00	10
1991	A Real Classic-831603 - Gilmore	Yr.Iss.	1991	10.00	10
1991	Christmas Fills The Air-831921 - Gilmore	3-Yr.	1993	12.00	12
1991	Deck The Halls-860573 - M. Peters	3-Yr.	1993	12.00	12
1991	Bathing Beauty-860581 - Hahn	3-Yr.	1993	13.50	35
1992	Sparky & Buffer-561851 - S. Zimnicki	3-Yr.	1994	25.00	25
1992	Moonlight Swing-568627 - L. Rigg	3-Yr.	1994	15.00	15
1992	Carver-570192 - S. Zimnicki	Yr.Iss.	1992	17.50	18
1992	A Rockin' GARFIELD Christmas-572527 - J. Davis	2-Yr.	1993	17.50	18
1992	The Nutcracker-574023 - Gilmore	3-Yr.	1994	25.00	25
1992	Humpty Dumpty-574244 - Gilmore	2-Yr.	1993	25.00	25
1992	Music Mice-Tro!-575143	2-Yr.	1993	12.00	12
1992	On Target Two-Gether-575623	Yr.Iss.	1992	17.00	17
1992	Rock-A-Bye Baby-575704 - Gilmore	2-Yr.	1993	13.50	14
1992	Queen of Hearts-575712 - Gilmore	2-Yr.	1992	17.50	18
1992	Tasty Tidings-575836 - L. Rigg	Yr.Iss.	1992	13.50	14
1992	Bearly Sleepy-578029 - Gilmore	Yr.Iss.	1992	17.50	18
1992	Spreading Sweet Joy-580465	Yr.Iss.	1992	13.50	14
1992	Ring My Bell-580740 - J. Davis	Yr.Iss.	1992	13.50	14
1992	4 x 4 Holiday Fun-580783 - J. Davis	2-Yr.	1993	20.00	20
1992	The Holidays Are A Hit-581577	2-Yr.	1993	17.50	18
1992	Tip Top Tidings-581828	2-Yr.	1993	13.00	13
1992	Christmas Lifts The Spirits-582018	2-Yr.	1993	25.00	25
1992	A Pound Of Good Cheers-582034	2-Yr.	1993	17.50	18
1992	Sweet as Cane Be-583642 - Gilmore	3-Yr.	1994	15.00	15
1992	Sundae Ride-583707	2-Yr.	1993	20.00	20
1992	The Cold, Crisp Taste Of Coke-583766	3-Yr.	1994	17.00	17
1992	Sew Christmasy-583820	3-Yr.	1994	25.00	25
1992	Catch A Falling Star-583944 - Gilmore	2-Yr.	1993	15.00	15
1992	Swingin' Christmas-584096	2-Yr.	1993	15.00	15
1992	Mc Ho, Ho, Ho-585181	3-Yr.	1994	22.50	23
1992	Holiday On Ice-585254 - J. Davis	3-Yr.	1994	17.50	18
1992	Fast Track Cat-585289 - J. Davis	3-Yr.	1994	17.50	18
1992	Holiday Cat Napping-585319 - J. Davis	2-Yr.	1993	20.00	20
1992	The Finishing Touches-585610 - T. Wilson	2-Yr.	1993	17.50	18
1992	Jolly Ol' Gent-585645 - J. Jonik	3-Yr.	1994	13.50	14
1992	A Child's Christmas-586358	3-Yr.	1994	25.00	25
1992	Festive Fiddlers-586501	Yr.Iss.	1992	20.00	25
1992	La Luminaria-586579 - M. Cook	2-Yr.	1993	13.50	14
1992	Cozy Chrismas Carriage-586730 - Gilmore	2-Yr.	1993	22.50	23
1992	Small Fry's First Christmas-586749	2-Yr.	1993	17.00	17
1992	Friendships Preserved-586765 - Hahn	Yr.Iss.	1992	22.50	23
1992	Window Wish List-586854 - Gilmore	2-Yr.	1993	30.00	30
1992	Through The Years-586862 - Gilmore	Yr.Iss.	1992	17.50	18
1992	Baby's First Christmas 1992-586943	Yr.Iss.	1992	12.50	13
1992	Firehouse Friends-586951 - Gilmore	Yr.Iss.	1992	22.50	23
1992	Bubble Buddy-586978 - Gilmore	2-Yr	1993	13.50	14
1992	The Warmth Of The Season-586994	2-Yr.	1993	20.00	20
1992	It's A Go For Christmas-587095 - Gilmore	2-Yr.	1993	15.00	15
1992	Post-Mouster General-587117 - Gilmore	2-Yr.	1993	20.00	20
1992	To A Deer Baby-587168	Yr.Iss.	1992	18.50	19
1992	Moon Watch-587184	2-Yr.	1993	20.00	20
1992	Guten Cheers-587192	Yr.Iss.	1992	22.50	23
1992	Put On A Happy Face-588237	2-Yr.	1993	15.00	15
1992	Beginning To Look A Lot Like Christmas-588253	2-Yr.	1993	15.00	15
1992	A Christmas Toast-588261	2-Yr.	1993	20.00	20
1992	Merry Mistle-Toad-588288	2-Yr.	1993	15.00	15
1992	Tic-Tac-Mistle-Toe-588296	3-Yr.	1994	23.00	23
1992	Heaven Sent-588423 - J. Penchoff	2-Yr.	1993	12.50	13
1992	Holiday Happenings-588555 - Gilmore	3-Yr.	1994	30.00	30
1992	Seed-son's Greetings-588571 - Gilmore	3-Yr.	1994	27.00	27
1992	Santa's Midnight Snack-588598 - Gilmore	2-Yr.	1993	20.00	20
1992	Trunk Of Treasures-588636	Yr.Iss.	1992	30.00	30
1992	Festive Newsflash-588792	2-Yr.	1993	17.50	18
1992	A-B-C-Son's Greetings-588806	2-Yr.	1993	16.50	17
1992	Hoppy Holidays-588814	Yr.Iss.	1992	13.50	14
1992	Fireside Friends-588830	2-Yr.	1993	20.00	20
1992	Christmas Eve-mergency-588849	2-Yr.	1993	27.00	27
1992	A Sure Sign Of Christmas-588857	2-Yr.	1993	22.50	23
1992	Holidays Give Me A Lift-588865	2-Yr.	1993	30.00	30
1992	Yule Tide Together-588903	2-Yr.	1993	20.00	20
1992	Have A Soup-er Christmas-588911	2-Yr.	1993	17.50	18
1992	Christmas Cure-Alls-588938	2-Yr.	1993	20.00	20
1992	Dial 'S' For Santa-589373	2-Yr.	1993	25.00	25
1992	Joy To The Whirled-589551 - Hahn	2-Yr.	1993	20.00	20
1992	Merry Make-Over-589586 - Hahn	3-Yr.	1994	20.00	20
1992	Campin' Companions-590282 - Hahn	3-Yr.	1994	20.00	20
1992	Fur-Ever Friends-590797 - Gilmore	2-Yr.	1993	13.50	14
1992	Tee-rific Holidays-590827	3-Yr.	1994	25.00	25
1992	Spinning Christmas Dreams-590908 - Hahn	3-Yr.	1994	22.50	23
1992	Christmas Trimmin'-590932	3-Yr.	1994	17.00	17
1992	Wrappin' Up Warm Wishes-593141	Yr.Iss.	1992	17.50	18
1992	Christmas Biz-593168	2-Yr.	1993	22.50	23
1992	Holiday Take-Out-593508	Yr.Iss.	1992	17.50	18
1992	A Christmas Yarn-593516 - Gilmore	Yr.Iss.	1992	20.00	20
1992	Treasure The Earth-593826 - Hahn	2-Yr.	1993	25.00	25
1992	Toyful' Rudolph-593982	2-Yr.	1993	22.50	23
1992	Take A Chance On The Holidays-594075	3-Yr.	1994	20.00	20
1992	Lights.Camera.Christmas! -594369	3-Yr.	1994	20.00	20
1992	Spirited Stallion-594407	Yr.Iss.	1992	15.00	15
1992	A Watchful Eye-595713	Yr.Iss.	1992	15.00	15
1992	Good Catch-595721	Yr.Iss.	1992	12.50	13
1992	Squirrelin' It Away-595748 - Hahn	Yr.Iss.	1992	12.00	12
1992	Checkin' His List-595756	Yr.Iss.	1992	12.50	13
1992	Christmas Cat Nappin'	Yr.Iss.	1992	12.00	12
1992	Bless Our Home-595772	Yr.Iss.	1992	12.00	12
1992	Salute the Season-595780 - Hahn	Yr.Iss.	1992	12.00	12
1992	Fired Up For Christmas-595799	Yr.Iss.	1992	12.00	12
1992	Speedin' Mr. Snowman-595802 - M. Rhyner	Yr.Iss.	1992	12.00	12
1992	Merry Christmas Mother Earth-595810 - Hahn	Yr.Iss.	1992	11.00	11
1992	Wear The Season With A Smile-595829	Yr.Iss.	1992	10.00	10
1992	Jesus Loves Me-595837 - Hahn	Yr.Iss.	1992	10.00	10
1992	Merry Kisses-831166	2-Yr.	1993	17.50	18
1992	Christmas Is In The Air-831174	2-Yr.	1993	25.00	25
1992	To The Point-831182	2-Yr.	1993	13.50	14
1992	Poppin' Hoppin' Holidays-831263 - Gilmore	Yr.Iss.	1992	25.00	25
1992	Tankful Tidings-831271 - Gilmore	2-Yr.	1993	30.00	30
1992	Ginger-Bred Greetings-831581 - Gilmore	Yr.Iss.	1992	12.00	12
1992	A Gold Star For Teacher-831948 - Gilmore	3-Yr.	1994	15.00	15
1992	A Tall Order-832758 - Gilmore	3-Yr.	1994	12.00	12
1992	Candlelight Serenade-832766 - Gilmore	2-Yr.	1993	12.00	12
1992	Holiday Glow Puppet Show-832774 - Gilmore	3-Yr.	1994	15.00	15
1992	Christopher Columouse-832782 - Gilmore	Yr.Iss.	1992	12.00	12
1992	Cartin' Home Holiday Treats-832790	2-Yr.	1993	13.50	14
1992	Making Tracks To Santa-832804 - Gilmore	2-Yr.	1993	15.00	15
1992	Special Delivery-832812	2-Yr.	1993	12.00	12
1992	A Mug Full Of Love-832928 - Gilmore	Yr.Iss.	1992	13.50	14
1992	Have A Cool Christmas-832944 - Gilmore	Yr.Iss.	1992	13.50	14
1992	Knitten' Kittens-832952 - Gilmore	Yr.Iss.	1992	17.50	18
1992	Holiday Honors-833029 - Gilmore	Yr.Iss.	1992	15.00	15
1992	Christmas Nite Cap-834424 - Gilmore	3-Yr.	1994	13.50	14
1992	North Pole Peppermint Patrol-840157 - Gilmore	2-Yr.	1993	25.00	25
1992	A Boot-iful Christmas-840165 - Gilmore	Yr.Iss.	1992	20.00	20
1992	Watching For Santa-840432	2-Yr.	1993	25.00	25
1992	Special Delivery-840440	Yr.Iss.	1992	22.50	23
1993	I'm Dreaming of a White-Out Christmas-566144	2-Yr.	1994	22.50	23
1993	Born To Shop-572942	Yr.Iss.	1993	26.50	35
1993	Toy To The World-575763	2-Yr.	1994	25.00	25
1993	Bearly Balanced-580724	Yr.Iss.	1993	15.00	15
1993	Joyeux Noel-582026	2-Yr.	1994	24.50	25
1993	Holiday Mew-Sic-582107	2-Yr.	1994	20.00	20
1993	Santa's Magic Ride-582115	2-Yr.	1994	24.00	24
1993	Warm And Hearty Wishes-582344	Yr.Iss.	1993	17.50	18
1993	Cool Yule-582352	Yr.Iss.	1993	12.00	12
1993	Have A Holly Jell-O Christmas-582387	Yr.Iss.	1993	45.00	45
1993	Festive Firemen-582565 - Gilmore	2-Yr.	1994	17.00	17
1993	Light Up Your Holidays With Coke-583758	Yr.Iss.	1993	27.50	28
1993	Pool Hall-idays-584851	2-Yr.	1994	19.90	20
1993	Bah Humbug-585394 - Davis	Yr.Iss.	1993	15.00	15
1993	Chimer-585777 - Zimnicki	Yr.Iss.	1993	25.00	25
1993	Sweet Whiskered Wishes-585807	Yr.Iss.	1993	17.00	17
1993	Grade "A" Wishes From Garfield -585823 - Davis	2-Yr.	1994	20.00	20
1993	Tree For Two-586781 - Gilmore	2-Yr.	1994	17.50	18
1993	A Bright Idea-586803 - Gilmore	2-Yr.	1994	22.50	23
1993	Baby's First Christmas 1993-585823 - Gilmore	Yr.Iss.	1993	17.50	18
1993	My Special Christmas-586900 - Gilmore	Yr.Iss.	1993	17.50	18
1993	Baby's First Christmas Dinner-587001	Yr.Iss.	1993	12.00	12
1993	A Pause For Claus-588318	2-Yr.	1994	22.50	23

CHRISTMAS ORNAMENTS

YEAR ISSUE		EDITION LIMIT	YEAR RETD.	ISSUE PRICE	QUOTE U.S.$
1993	Not A Creature Was Stirring...-588663 - Gilmore	2-Yr.	1994	27.50	28
1993	Terrific Toys-588644	Yr.Iss.	1993	20.00	20
1993	Christmas Dancer-588652	Yr.Iss.	1993	15.00	15
1993	Countin' On A Merry Christmas-588954	2-Yr.	1994	22.50	23
1993	To My Gem-589004	Yr.Iss.	1993	27.50	28
1993	Christmas Mall Call-589012	2-Yr.	1994	20.00	20
1993	Spreading Joy-589047	2-Yr.	1994	27.50	28
1993	Pitter-Patter Post Office-589055	2-Yr.	1994	20.00	20
1993	Happy Haul-idays-589098	2-Yr.	1994	30.00	30
1993	Hot Off ThePress-589292	2-Yr.	1994	27.50	28
1993	Designed With You In Mind-589306	2-Yr.	1994	16.00	16
1993	Seeing Is Believing-589381 - Gilmore	2-Yr.	1994	20.00	20
1993	Roundin' Up Christmas Together-590800	Yr.Iss.	1993	25.00	25
1993	Toasty Tidings-590940	2-Yr.	1994	20.00	20
1993	Focusing On Christmas-590983 - Gilmore	2-Yr.	1994	27.50	28
1993	Dunk The Halls-591009	2-Yr.	1994	18.50	19
1993	Mice Capades-591386 - Hahn	2-Yr.	1994	26.50	27
1993	25 Points For Christmas-591750	Yr.Iss.	1993	25.00	25
1993	Carving Christmas Wishes-592625 - Gilmore	2-Yr.	1994	25.00	25
1993	Celebrating With A Splash-592692	Yr.Iss.	1993	17.00	17
1993	Slimmin' Santa-592722	Yr.Iss.	1993	18.50	24
1993	Plane Ol' Holiday Fun-592773	Yr.Iss.	1993	27.50	28
1993	Smooth Move, Mom-593176	Yr.Iss.	1993	20.00	20
1993	Tool Time, Yule Time-593192	Yr.Iss.	1993	18.50	19
1993	Speedy-593370 - Zimnicki	2-Yr.	1994	25.00	25
1993	On Your Mark, Set, Is That To Go?-593524	Yr.Iss.	1993	13.50	14
1993	Do Not Open 'Til Christmas-593737 - Hahn	2-Yr.	1994	15.00	15
1993	Greetings In Stereo-593745 - Hahn	Yr.Iss.	1993	19.50	20
1993	Tangled Up For Christmas-593974	2-Yr.	1994	14.50	15
1993	Sweet Season's Eatings-594202	Yr.Iss.	1993	22.50	23
1993	Have A Darn Good Christmas-594229 - Gilmore	2-Yr.	1994	21.00	21
1993	The Sweetest Ride-594253 - Gilmore	2-Yr.	1994	18.50	19
1993	Lights...Camera...Christmas -594369	Yr.Iss.	1993	20.00	20
1993	Have A Cheery Christmas, Sister-594687	Yr.Iss.	1993	13.50	14
1993	Say Cheese-594962 - Gilmore	2-Yr.	1994	13.50	14
1993	Christmas Kicks-594989	Yr.Iss.	1993	17.50	18
1993	Time For Santa-594997 - Gilmore	2-Yr.	1994	17.50	18
1993	Holiday Orders-595004	Yr.Iss.	1993	20.00	20
1993	T'Was The Night Before Christmas-595012	Yr.Iss.	1993	22.50	23
1993	Sugar Chef Shoppe-595055 - Gilmore	2-Yr.	1994	23.50	24
1993	Merry Mc-Choo-Choo-595063	Yr.Iss.	1993	30.00	30
1993	Basketful Of Friendship-595098	Yr.Iss.	1993	20.00	20
1993	Rockin' With Santa-595195	2-Yr.	1994	13.50	14
1993	Christmas-To-Go-595217	Yr.Iss.	1993	25.50	26
1993	Sleddin' Mr. Snowman-595275	2-Yr.	1994	13.00	13
1993	A Kick Out Of Christmas-595373	2-Yr.	1994	10.00	10
1993	Friends Through Thick And Thin-595381	2-Yr.	1994	10.00	10
1993	See-Saw Sweethearts-595403	2-Yr.	1994	10.00	10
1993	Special Delivery For Santa-595411	2-Yr.	1994	10.00	10
1993	Top Marks For Teacher-595438	2-Yr.	1994	10.00	10
1993	Home Tweet Home-595446	2-Yr.	1994	10.00	10
1993	Clownin' Around-595454	2-Yr.	1994	10.00	10
1993	Heart Filled Dreams-595462	2-Yr.	1994	10.00	10
1993	Merry Christmas Baby-595470	2-Yr.	1994	10.00	10
1993	Your A Hit With Me, Brother-595535 - Hahn	Yr.Iss.	1993	10.00	10
1993	For A Sharp Uncle-595543	Yr.Iss.	1993	10.00	10
1993	Paint Your Holidays Bright-595551 - Hahn	2-Yr.	1994	10.00	10
1993	You Got To Treasure The Holidays, Man'-596051	Yr.Iss.	1993	22.50	23
1993	Ariel's Under-The-Sea Tree-596078	Yr.Iss.	1993	20.00	20
1993	Here Comes Santa Claws-596086	Yr.Iss.	1993	22.50	35
1993	You're Tea-Lighting, Mom!-596094	Yr.Iss.	1993	17.50	18
1993	Hearts A Glow-596108	Yr.Iss.	1993	18.50	35
1993	Love's Sweet Dance-596116	Yr.Iss.	1993	25.00	25
1993	Holiday Wishes-596124	Yr.Iss.	1993	15.00	15
1993	Hangin Out For The Holidays-596132	Yr.Iss.	1993	15.00	35
1993	Magic Carpet Ride-596140	Yr.Iss.	1993	20.00	20
1993	Holiday Treasures-596159	Yr.Iss.	1993	18.50	35
1993	Happily Ever After-596167	Yr.Iss.	1993	22.50	23
1993	The Fairest Of Them All-596175	Yr.Iss.	1993	18.50	19
1993	December 25...Dear Diary-596809 - Hahn	2-Yr.	1994	10.00	10
1993	Wheel Merry Wishes-596930 - Hahn	2-Yr.	1994	15.00	15
1993	Good Grounds For Christmas-596957 - Hahn	Yr.Iss.	1993	24.50	25
1993	Ducking The Season's Rush-597597	Yr.Iss.	1993	17.50	18
1993	Here Comes Rudolph®-597686	2-Yr.	1994	17.50	18
1993	It's Beginning To Look A Lot Like Christmas-597694	Yr.Iss.	1993	22.50	23
1993	Christmas In The Making-597716	Yr.Iss.	1993	20.00	20

YEAR ISSUE		EDITION LIMIT	YEAR RETD.	ISSUE PRICE	QUOTE U.S.$
1993	Mickey's Holiday Treasure-597759	Yr.Iss.	1993	12.00	12
1993	Dream Wheels-597856	Yr.Iss.	1993	29.50	50-75
1993	All You Add Is Love-598429	Yr.Iss.	1993	18.50	19
1993	Goofy About Skiing-598631	Yr.Iss.	1993	22.50	23
1993	A Toast Ladled With Love-830828 - Hahn	2-Yr.	1994	15.00	15
1993	Christmas Is In The Air-831174	2-Yr.	1994	25.00	35
1993	Delivered to The Nick In Time-831808 - Gilmore	2-Yr.	1994	13.50	14
1993	Sneaking A Peek-831840 - Gilmore	2-Yr.	1994	10.00	10
1993	Jewel Box Ballet-831859 - Hahn	2-Yr.	1994	20.00	20
1993	A Mistle-Tow-831867 - Gilmore	2-Yr.	1994	15.00	15
1993	Grandma's Liddle Griddle-832936 - Gilmore	Yr.Iss.	1993	10.00	10
1993	To A Grade "A" Teacher-833037 - Gilmore	2-Yr.	1994	10.00	10
1993	Have A Cool Christmas-834467 - Gilmore	2-Yr.	1994	10.00	10
1993	For A Star Aunt-834556 - Gilmore	Yr.Iss.	1993	12.00	12
1993	Watching For Santa-840432	2-Yr.	1994	25.00	30
1994	Sending You A Season's Greetings - 550140 - Butcher	Yr.Iss.	1994	25.00	25
1994	Goofy Delivery - 550639	Yr.Iss.	1994	22.50	23
1994	Happy Howl-idays - 550647	Yr.Iss.	1994	22.50	23
1994	Christmas Crusin' - 550655	Yr.Iss.	1994	22.50	23
1994	Holiday Honeys - 550663	Yr.Iss.	1994	20.00	20
1994	May Your Holiday Be Brightened With Love - 550698 - Butcher	Yr.Iss.	1994	15.00	15
1994	May All Your Wishes Come True - 550701 - Butcher	Yr.Iss.	1994	20.00	20
1994	Baby's First Christmas - 550728 - Butcher	Yr.Iss.	1994	20.00	20
1994	Baby's First Christmas- 550736 - Butcher	Yr.Iss.	1994	20.00	20
1994	Our First Christmas Together - 550744 - Butcher	Yr.Iss.	1994	25.00	25
1994	Drumming Up A Season Of Joy- 550752 - Butcher	Yr.Iss.	1994	18.50	19
1994	Friendships Warm The Holidays - 550760 - Butcher	Yr.Iss.	1994	20.00	20
1994	Dropping In For The Holidays - 550779 - Butcher	Yr.Iss.	1994	20.00	20
1994	Ringing Up Holiday Wishes - 550787 - Butcher	Yr.Iss.	1994	18.50	19
1994	A Child Is Born - 550795 - Butcher	Yr.Iss.		25.00	25
1994	Tis The Season To Go Shopping - 550817 - Butcher	Yr.Iss.	1994	22.50	23
1994	The Way To A Mouse's Heart - 550922	Yr.Iss.	1994	15.00	15
1994	Teed-Off Donald - 550930	Yr.Iss.	1994	15.00	15
1994	Holiday Show-Stopper - 550949	Yr.Iss.		15.00	15
1994	Answering Christmas Wishes - 551023	Yr.Iss.	1994	17.50	18
1994	Pure Christmas Pleasure - 551066	Yr.Iss.		20.00	20
1994	Good Tidings, Tidings, Tidings, Tidings - 551333	Yr.Iss.		20.00	20
1994	From Our House To Yours - 551384 - Gilmore	Yr.Iss.	1994	25.00	25
1994	Sugar 'N' Spice For Someone Nice - 551406 - Gilmore	Yr.Iss.	1994	30.00	30
1994	Picture Perfect Christmas - 551465	Yr.Iss.	1994	15.00	15
1994	Toodles - 551503 - Zimnicki	Yr.Iss.	1994	25.00	25
1994	A Bough For Belle! - 551554	Yr.Iss.		18.50	19
1994	Ariel's Christmas Surprise! - 551570	Yr.Iss.	1994	20.00	20
1994	Merry Little Two-Step - 551589	Yr.Iss.		12.50	13
1994	Sweets For My Sweetie - 551600	Yr.Iss.	1994	15.00	15
1994	Friends Are The Spice of Life - 551619 - Hahn	Yr.Iss.		20.00	20
1994	Cool Cruise - 551635	19,640		20.00	20
1994	A Christmas Tail - 551759	Yr.Iss.		20.00	20
1994	Merry Mischief- 551767	Yr.Iss.	1994	15.00	15
1994	L'il Stocking Stuffer - 551791	Yr.Iss.	1994	17.50	18
1994	Once Upon A Time - 551805	Yr.Iss.	1994	15.00	15
1994	Wishing Upon A Star - 551813	Yr.Iss.	1994	18.50	19
1994	A Real Boy For Christmas - 551821	Yr.Iss.		15.00	15
1994	Minnie's Holiday Treasure - 552216	Yr.Iss.	1994	12.00	12
1994	Sweet Holidays - 552259 - Butcher	Yr.Iss.	1994	11.00	11
1994	Special Delivery - 561657	Yr.Iss.	1994	20.00	20
1994	Merry Miss Merry - 564508 - Hahn	Yr.Iss.	1994	12.00	12
1994	Santa Delivers - 564567	Yr.Iss.	1994	12.00	12
1994	Buttons 'N' Bow Boutique - 578363 - Gilmore	Yr.Iss.		22.50	23
1994	A Sign of Peace - 581992	Yr.Iss.	1994	18.50	19
1994	Wishing You Well At Christmas - 582050	Yr.Iss.	1994	25.00	25
1994	Ahoy Joy! - 582085	Yr.Iss.	1994	20.00	20
1994	Santa...Phone Home - 582166	Yr.Iss.	1994	25.00	25
1994	Christmas Swishes - 582379	Yr.Iss.	1994	17.50	18
1994	The Latest Scoop From Santa - 582395 - Gilmore	Yr.Iss.	1994	18.50	19
1994	Chiminy Cheer - 582409 - Gilmore	Yr.Iss.	1994	22.50	23
1994	Cozy Candlelight Dinner - 582417 - Gilmore	Yr.Iss.	1994	25.00	25
1994	Fine Feathered Festivities - 582425 - Gilmore	Yr.Iss.	1994	22.50	23
1994	Joy From Head To Hose - 582433 - Gilmore	Yr.Iss.	1994	15.00	15
1994	Yuletide Yummies - 584835 - Gilmore	Yr.Iss.	1994	20.00	20

YEAR ISSUE		EDITION LIMIT	YEAR RETD.	ISSUE PRICE	QUOTE U.S.$
1994	Merry Christmas Tool You, Dad - 584886	Yr.Iss.	1994	22.50	23
1994	Exercising Good Taste - 584967	Yr.Iss.	1994	17.50	18
1994	Holiday Chew-Chew - 584983 - Gilmore	Yr.Iss.	1994	22.50	23
1994	Mine, Mine, Mine - 585815 - Davis	Yr.Iss.	1994	20.00	20
1994	To The Sweetest Baby - 588725 - Gilmore	Yr.Iss.	1994	18.50	19
1994	Rockin' Ranger - 588970	Yr.Iss.	1994	25.00	25
1994	Peace On Earthworm - 588989	Yr.Iss.	1994	20.00	20
1994	Good Things Crop Up At Christmas - 589071	Yr.Iss.	1994	25.00	25
1994	Christmas Crossroads - 589128	Yr.Iss.	1994	20.00	20
1994	Have A Ball At Christmas - 590673	Yr.Iss.	1994	15.00	15
1994	Have A Totem-ly Terrific Christmas - 590819	Yr.Iss.	1994	30.00	30
1994	Cocoa 'N' Kisses For Santa- 591939	Yr.Iss.		22.50	23
1994	On The Road With Coke™ - 592528	Yr.Iss.		25.00	25
1994	What's Shakin' For Christmas - 592668	Yr.Iss.	1994	18.50	19
1994	"A" For Santa - 592676	Yr.Iss.	1994	17.50	18
1994	Christmas Fly-By - 592714	Yr.Iss.	1994	15.00	15
1994	Santa...You're The Pops! - 593761	Yr.Iss.	1994	22.50	23
1994	Purdy Packages, Pardner! - 593834	Yr.Iss.	1994	20.00	20
1994	Handle With Care - 593842	Yr.Iss.	1994	20.00	20
1994	To Coin A Phrase, Merry Christmas - 593877	Yr.Iss.	1994	20.00	20
1994	Featured Presentation - 593885	Yr.Iss.	1994	20.00	20
1994	Christmas Fishes From Santa Paws - 593893	Yr.Iss.	1994	18.50	19
1994	Melted My Heart - 594237 - Gilmore	Yr.Iss.	1994	15.00	15
1994	Finishing First - 594342 - Gilmore	Yr.Iss.	1994	20.00	20
1994	Yule Fuel - 594385	Yr.Iss.	1994	20.00	20
1994	Toy Tinker Topper - 595047 - Gilmore	Yr.Iss.	1994	20.00	20
1994	Santa Claus Is Comin' - 595209	Yr.Iss.	1994	20.00	20
1994	Seasoned With Love - 595268	Yr.Iss.	1994	22.50	23
1994	Sweet Dreams - 595489	Yr.Iss.	1994	12.50	13
1994	Peace On Earth - 595497	Yr.Iss.	1994	12.50	13
1994	Christmas Two-gether - 595500	Yr.Iss.	1994	12.50	13
1994	Santa's L'il Helper - 595519	Yr.Iss.	1994	12.50	13
1994	Expecting Joy - 595527 - Hahn	Yr.Iss.	1994	12.50	13
1994	Sweet Greetings - 595578	Yr.Iss.	1994	12.50	13
1994	Ring In The Holidays - 595586 - Hahn	Yr.Iss.	1994	12.50	13
1994	Grandmas Are Sew Special - 595594	Yr.Iss.	1994	12.50	13
1994	Holiday Catch - 595608 - Hahn	Yr.Iss.	1994	12.50	13
1994	Bubblin' with Joy - 595616	Yr.Iss.	1994	12.50	13
1994	Good Friends Are Forever - 595950 - Gilmore	Yr.Iss.	1994	13.50	14
1994	Christmas Tee Time - 596256	Yr.Iss.		25.00	25
1994	Have a Merry Dairy Christmas - 596264	Yr.Iss.	1994	22.50	23
1994	Happy Holi-date - 596272 - Hahn	Yr.Iss.		22.50	23
1994	O' Come All Ye Faithful - 596280 - Hahn	Yr.Iss.	1994	15.00	15
1994	One Small Step... - 596299 - Hahn	19,690		30.00	30
1994	To My Favorite V.I.P. - 596698	Yr.Iss.	1994	20.00	20
1994	Building Memories - 596876 - Hahn	Yr.Iss.	1994	25.00	25
1994	Open For Business - 596906 - Hahn	Yr.Iss.	1994	17.50	18
1994	Twas The Nite Before Christmas - 597643 - Gilmore	Yr.Iss.	1994	18.50	19
1994	I Can Bear-ly Wait For A Coke™ - 597724	Yr.Iss.		18.50	19
1994	Gallant Greeting- 598313	Yr.Iss.	1994	20.00	20
1994	Merry Menage - 598321	Yr.Iss.	1994	20.00	20
1994	Bundle Of Joy - 598992	Yr.Iss.	1994	10.00	10
1994	Bundle Of Joy - 599018	Yr.Iss.	1994	10.00	10
1994	Have A Dino-mite Christmas - 599026 - Hahn	Yr.Iss.	1994	18.50	19
1994	Good Fortune To You - 599034	Yr.Iss.	1994	25.00	25
1994	Building a Sew-man - 599042	Yr.Iss.	1994	18.50	19
1994	Merry Memo-ries - 599050	Yr.Iss.	1994	22.50	23
1994	Ski-son's Greetings - 599069	Yr.Iss.	1994	20.00	20
1994	Holiday Freezer Teaser - 599085 - Gilmore	Yr.Iss.	1994	25.00	25
1994	Almost Time For Santa - 599093 - Gilmore	Yr.Iss.	1994	25.00	25
1994	Santa's Secret Test Drive - 599107 - Gilmore	Yr.Iss.	1994	20.00	20
1994	You're A Wheel Cool Brother - 599115 - Gilmore	Yr.Iss.	1994	22.50	23
1994	Hand-Tossed Tidings - 599166	Yr.Iss.	1994	17.50	18
1994	Tasty Take Off - 599174	Yr.Iss.	1994	20.00	20
1994	Formula For Love - 599530 - Olsen	Yr.Iss.	1994	10.00	10
1994	Santa's Ginger-bred Doe - 599697 - Gilmore	Yr.Iss.	1994	15.00	15
1994	Nutcracker Sweetheart - 599700	Yr.Iss.	1994	15.00	15
1994	Merry Reindeer Ride - 599719	Yr.Iss.	1994	20.00	20
1994	Santa's Sing-A-Long - 599727 - Gilmore	Yr.Iss.	1994	20.00	20
1994	A Holiday Opportunity - 599735	Yr.Iss.		20.00	20
1994	Holiday Stars - 599743	Yr.Iss.	1994	20.00	20
1994	The Latest Mews From Home - 653977	Yr.Iss.	1994	16.00	16
1994	You're A Winner Son! - 834564 - Gilmore	Yr.Iss.	1994	18.50	19

CHRISTMAS ORNAMENTS

YEAR ISSUE		EDITION LIMIT	YEAR RETD.	ISSUE PRICE	QUOTE U.S.$
1994	Especially For You - 834580 - Gilmore	Yr.Iss.	1994	27.50	28
1995	How...Do I Love Thee - 104949	Yr.Iss.		22.50	23
1995	Swishing You Sweet Greetings - 105201	Yr.Iss.		20.00	20
1995	Planely Delicious - 109665	Yr.Iss.		20.00	20
1995	Home For The Howl-i-days - 111732	Yr.Iss.		20.00	20
1995	Time For Refreshment - 111872	Yr.Iss.		20.00	20
1995	Holiday Bike Hike 111937	Yr.Iss.		20.00	20
1995	Ho, Ho, Hole in One! - 111953	Yr.Iss.		20.00	20
1995	No Time To Spare at Christmas - 111961	Yr.Iss.		20.00	20
1995	Hustling Up Some Cheer - 112038	Yr.Iss.		20.00	20
1995	Scoring Big at Christmas - 112046	Yr.Iss.		20.00	20
1995	Serving Up the Best 112054	Yr.Iss.		17.50	18
1995	Sea-sons Greetings, Teacher 112070 - Gilmore	Yr.Iss.		17.50	18
1995	Siesta Santa - 112089 - Gilmore	Yr.Iss.		25.00	25
1995	We've Shared Sew Much - 112097 - Gilmore	Yr.Iss.		25.00	25
1995	Toys To Treasure - 112119	Yr.Iss.		20.00	20
1995	To Santa, Post Haste - 112151- Gilmore	Yr.Iss.		15.00	15
1995	Yule Logon For Christmas Cheer - 122513	Yr.Iss.		20.00	20
1995	Pretty Up For The Holidays - 125830 - Butcher	Yr.Iss.		20.00	20
1995	You Bring The Love to Christmas - 125849 - Butcher	Yr.Iss.		15.00	15
1995	Happy Birthday Jesus 125857 - Butcher	Yr.Iss.		15.00	15
1995	Let's Snuggle Together For Christmas - 125865 - Butcher	Yr.Iss.		15.00	15
1995	I'm In A Spin Over You - 125873 - Butcher	Yr.Iss.		15.00	15
1995	Our First Christmas Together - 125881 - Butcher	Yr.Iss.		22.50	23
1995	Twinkle, Twinkle Christmas Star - 125903 - Butcher	Yr.Iss.		17.50	18
1995	Bringing Holiday Wishes To You - 125911 - Butcher	Yr.Iss.		22.50	23
1995	You Pull The Strings To My Heart - 125938 - Butcher	Yr.Iss.		20.00	20
1995	Baby's First Christmas - 125946 - Butcher	Yr.Iss.		15.00	15
1995	Baby's First Christmas - 125954 - Butcher	Yr.Iss.		15.00	15
1995	Friends Are The Greatest Treasure - 125962 - Butcher	20,000		25.00	25
1995	4-Alarm Christmas - 128767 - Gilmore	Yr.Iss.		17.50	18
1995	Truckin' - 128813	Yr.Iss.		25.00	25
1995	T-Bird - 128821	19,550		20.00	20
1995	57 HVN - 128848	Yr.Iss.		20.00	20
1995	Corvette - 128856	Yr.Iss.		20.00	20
1995	Mom's Taxi - 128872	Yr.Iss.		25.00	25
1995	Choc Full of Wishes - 128945	Yr.Iss.		20.00	20
1995	Have a Coke and a Smile™ - 128953	Yr.Iss.		22.50	23
1995	Trunk Full of Treasures - 128961	20,000		25.00	25
1995	Make Mine a Coke - 128988	Yr.Iss.		25.00	25
1995	Dashing Through the Snow - 128996	Yr.Iss.		20.00	20
1995	Happy Yuleglide - 129003	Yr.Iss.		17.50	18
1995	Santa's Speedway - 129011	Yr.Iss.		20.00	20
1995	You're My Cup of Tea - 129038	Yr.Iss.		20.00	20
1995	Crackin' a Smile - 129046	Yr.Iss.		17.50	18
1995	Rx:Mas Greetings - 129054	Yr.Iss.		17.50	18
1995	Merry McMeal - 129070	Yr.Iss.		17.50	18
1995	Above the Crowd - 129089	Yr.Iss.		20.00	20
1995	Mickey at the Helm - 132063	Yr.Iss.		17.50	18
1995	Caddy - 132705	Yr.Iss.		20.00	20
1995	Jackpot Joy! - 132896 - Hahn	Yr.Iss.		17.50	18
1995	Get in the Spirit...Recycle - 132918 - Hahn	Yr.Iss.		17.50	18
1995	Miss Merry's Secret - 132934 - Hahn	Yr.Iss.		20.00	20
1995	...Good Will Toward Men - 132942 - Hahn	19,450		25.00	25
1995	Friendships Bloom Through All Seasons - 132950 - Hahn	Yr.Iss.		22.50	23
1995	Merry Monopoly - 132969	Yr.Iss.		22.50	23
1995	The Night B 4 Christmas - 134848 - Hahn	Yr.Iss.		20.00	20
1995	Bubblin' With Joy - 136581	Yr.Iss.		15.00	15
1995	Minnie's Merry Christmas - 136611	Yr.Iss.		20.00	20
1995	Makin' Tracks With Mickey - 136662	Yr.Iss.		20.00	20
1995	Mickey's Airmail - 136670	Yr.Iss.		20.00	20
1995	Holiday Bound - 136689	Yr.Iss.		20.00	20
1995	Goofed-Up - 136697	Yr.Iss.		20.00	20
1995	On The Ball At Christmas - 136700	Yr.Iss.		15.00	15
1995	Sweet on You - 136719	Yr.Iss.		22.50	23
1995	Nutty About Christmas - 137030	Yr.Iss.		22.50	23
1995	Tinkertoy Joy - 137049	Yr.Iss.		20.00	20
1995	Starring Roll At Christmas - 137057	Yr.Iss.		17.50	18
1995	A Thimble of the Season - 137243 - Gilmore	Yr.Iss.		22.50	23
1995	A Little Something Extra...Extra - 137251	10,000		25.00	25
1995	The Maze Of Our Lives - 139599 - Hahn	Yr.Iss.		17.50	18
1995	A Sip For Good Measure - 139610	Yr.Iss.		17.50	18
1995	Christmas Fishes, Dad - 139629 - Hahn	Yr.Iss.		17.50	18
1995	Christmas Is In The Bag - 139645	Yr.Iss.		17.50	18
1995	Gotta Have a Clue - 139653	Yr.Iss.		20.00	20
1995	Fun In Hand - 139661	Yr.Iss.		17.50	18
1995	Christmas Cuddle - 139688	Yr.Iss.		20.00	20
1995	Dreamin Of the One I Love - 139696	Yr.Iss.		25.00	25
1995	Sneaking a Peek - 139718	Yr.Iss.		22.50	23
1995	Christmas Eve Mischief - 139726	Yr.Iss.		17.50	18
1995	All Tucked In - 139734	Yr.Iss.		15.00	15
1995	Merry Christmas To Me - 139742	Yr.Iss.		20.00	20
1995	Looking Our Holiday Best - 139750	Yr.Iss.		25.00	25
1995	Christmas Vacation - 142158	Yr.Iss.		20.00	20
1995	Just Fore Christmas - 142174	Yr.Iss.		15.00	15
1995	Christmas Belle - 142182	Yr.Iss.		20.00	20
1995	Tail Waggin' Wishes - 142190	Yr.Iss.		17.50	18
1995	Holiday Ride - 142204	Yr.Iss.		17.50	18
1995	A Carousel For Ariel - 142212	Yr.Iss.		17.50	18
1995	On The Move At Christmas - 142220 - Hahn	Yr.Iss.		17.50	18
1995	T-Bird - 146838	Yr.Iss.		20.00	20
1995	Sweet Harmony - 586773 - Gilmore	Yr.Iss.		17.50	18
1995	Yule Tide Prancer - 588660	Yr.Iss.		15.00	15
1995	Baby's Sweet Feast - 588733 - Gilmore	Yr.Iss.		17.50	18
1995	A Well, Balanced Meal For Santa - 592633	Yr.Iss.		17.50	18
1995	Salute - 593133	Yr.Iss.		22.50	23
1995	Filled To The Brim - 595039 - Gilmore	Yr.Iss.		25.00	25

Enesco Treasury of Christmas Ornaments Collectors' Club- Various

YEAR ISSUE		EDITION LIMIT	YEAR RETD.	ISSUE PRICE	QUOTE U.S.$
1993	The Treasury Card (Club) - T0001 - Gilmore	Yr.Iss.	1993	20.00	20
1993	Together We Can Shoot For The Stars (Club) - TR931 - Hahn	Yr.Iss.	1993	17.50	18
1993	Can't Weights For The Holidays (Club) - TR932	Yr.Iss.	1993	18.50	19
1994	Seedlings Greetings (Club) - TR933 - Hahn	Yr.Iss.	1994	22.50	23
1994	Spry Fry (Club) - TR934	Yr.Iss.	1994	15.00	15
1995	You're the Perfect Fit - T0002 - Hahn	Yr.Iss.	1995	Gift	N/A
1995	You're the Perfect Fit - T0102 (Charter Members) - Hahn	Yr.Iss.	1995	Gift	N/A
1995	Things Go Better With Coke™- TR951	Yr.Iss.	1995	15.00	15
1995	Buttoning Up Our Holiday Best- TR952 - Gilmore	Yr.Iss.	1995	22.50	23
1995	Holiday High-Light- TR953 - Gilmore	Yr.Iss.	1995	15.00	15
1995	First Class Christmas- TR954 - Gilmore	Yr.Iss.	1995	22.50	23

Memories of Yesterday - M. Attwell

YEAR ISSUE		EDITION LIMIT	YEAR RETD.	ISSUE PRICE	QUOTE U.S.$
1988	Baby's First Christmas 1988-520373	Yr.Iss.		13.50	25
1988	Special Delivery! 1988-520381	Yr.Iss.		13.50	25-38
1989	Baby's First Christmas-522465	Open		15.00	15-20
1989	Christmas Together-522562	Open		15.00	15-25
1989	A Surprise for Santa-522473 (1989)	Yr.Iss.		13.50	20-30
1990	Time For Bed-524638	Yr.Iss.		15.00	15-30
1990	New Moon-524646	Suspd.		15.00	15-25
1990	Moonstruck-524794	Retrd.	1992	15.00	15-25
1991	Just Watchin' Over You-525421	Retrd.	1994	17.50	18
1991	Lucky Me-525448	Retrd.	1993	16.00	20
1991	Lucky You-525847	Retrd.	1993	16.00	20
1991	Star Fishin'-525820	Open		16.00	16
1991	S'no Use Lookin' Back Now!-527181(dated)	Yr.Iss.		17.50	28
1992	Merry Christmas, Little Boo-Boo-528803	Open		37.50	38
1992	I'll Fly Along To See You Soon-525804 (1992 Dated Bisque)	Yr.Iss.		16.00	18
1992	Mommy, I Teared It-527041(Five Year Anniversary Limited Edition)	Yr.Iss.		15.00	20
1992	Star Light. Star Bright-528838	Open		16.00	16
1992	Swinging Together-580481(1992 Dated Artplas)	Yr.Iss.		17.50	22
1992	Sailin' With My Friends-587575 (Artplas)	Open		25.00	25
1993	Wish I Could Fly To You-525790 (dated)	Yr.Iss.		16.00	16
1993	May All Your Finest Dreams Come True-528811	Open		16.00	16
1993	Bringing Good Wishes Your Way-592846 (Artplas)	Open		25.00	25
1994	Give Yourself a Hug From Me!-529109 ('94 Dated)	Yr. Iss.		17.50	18
1994	Just Dreaming of You-524786	Open		16.00	16
1994	Bout Time I Came Along to See You-592854 (Artplas)	Open		17.50	18
1995	Happy Landings (Dated 1995) 522619	Yr.Iss.		16.00	16
1995	Now I Lay Me Down to Sleep 527009	Open		15.00	15
1995	I Pray the Lord My Soul to Keep 527017	Open		15.00	15

Memories of Yesterday Event Item Only - Enesco

YEAR ISSUE		EDITION LIMIT	YEAR RETD.	ISSUE PRICE	QUOTE U.S.$
1993	How 'Bout A Little Kiss?-527068	Yr.Iss.		16.50	50

Memories of Yesterday Society Member's Only - M. Attwell

YEAR ISSUE		EDITION LIMIT	YEAR RETD.	ISSUE PRICE	QUOTE U.S.$
1992	With Luck And A Friend, I's In Heaven-MY922	Yr.Iss.		16.00	20
1993	I'm Bringing Good Luck-Wherever You Are	Yr.Iss.		16.00	22

Miss Martha's Collection - M. Holcombe

YEAR ISSUE		EDITION LIMIT	YEAR RETD.	ISSUE PRICE	QUOTE U.S.$
1993	Caroline - Always Someone Watching Over Me - 350532	Closed	1994	25.00	50
1993	Arianna - Heavenly Sounds H/O - 350567	Closed	1994	25.00	50
1992	Baby in Basket - 369454	Closed	1994	25.00	31
1992	Baby In Swing - 421480	Retrd.	1993	25.00	50
1992	Girl Holding Stocking - 421499	Closed	1994	25.00	30-50
1992	Girl/Bell In Hand - 421502	Retrd.	1993	25.00	50

Precious Moments - S. Butcher

YEAR ISSUE		EDITION LIMIT	YEAR RETD.	ISSUE PRICE	QUOTE U.S.$
1983	Surround Us With Joy-E-0513	Yr.Iss.		9.00	50-60
1983	Mother Sew Dear-E-0514	Open		9.00	17-32
1983	To A Special Dad-E-0515	Suspd.		9.00	30-54
1983	The Purr-fect Grandma-E-0516	Open		9.00	17-32
1983	The Perfect Grandpa-E-0517	Suspd.		9.00	30-39
1983	Blessed Are The Pure In Heart -E-0518	Yr.Iss.		9.00	45
1983	O Come All Ye Faithful-E-0531	Suspd.		10.00	55
1983	Let Heaven And Nature Sing-E-0532	Retrd.	1986	9.00	24-35
1983	Tell Me The Story Of Jesus-E-0533	Suspd.		9.00	36-57
1983	To Thee With Love-E-0534	Retrd.	1989	9.00	25-55
1983	Love Is Patient-E-0535	Suspd.		9.00	46-52
1983	Love Is Patient-E-0536	Suspd.		9.00	60
1983	Jesus Is The Light That Shines-E-0537	Suspd.		9.00	60-70
1982	Joy To The World-E-2343	Suspd.		9.00	40-66
1982	I'll Play My Drum For Him-E-2359	Yr.Iss.		9.00	100
1982	Baby's First Christmas-E-2362	Suspd.		9.00	33-70
1982	The First Noel-E-2367	Suspd.		9.00	66
1982	The First Noel-E-2368	Retrd.	1984	9.00	36-68
1982	Dropping In For Christmas-E-2369	Retrd.	1986	9.00	36-55
1982	Unicorn-E-2371	Retrd.	1988	10.00	40-60
1982	Baby's First Christmas-E-2372	Suspd.		9.00	35-45
1982	Dropping Over For Christmas-E-2376	Retrd.	1985	9.00	29-60
1982	Mouse With Cheese-E-2381	Suspd.		9.00	98-115
1982	Our First Christmas Together-E-2385	Suspd.		10.00	26-55
1982	Camel, Donkey & Cow (3 pc. set)-E2386	Suspd.		25.00	55-90
1984	Wishing You A Merry Christmas-E-5387	Yr.Iss.		10.00	35
1984	Joy To The World-E-5388	Retrd.	1987	10.00	30-50
1984	Peace On Earth-E-5389	Suspd.		10.00	30-45
1984	May God Bless You With A Perfect Holiday Season-E-5390	Suspd.		10.00	20-30
1984	Love Is Kind-E-5391	Suspd.		10.00	24-35
1984	Blessed Are The Pure In Heart-E-5392	Yr.Iss.		10.00	40
1981	But Love Goes On Forever-E-5627	Suspd.		6.00	78-115
1981	But Love Goes On Forever-E-5628	Suspd.		6.00	80-125
1981	Let The Heavens Rejoice-E-5629	Yr.Iss.		6.00	200
1981	Unto Us A Child Is Born-E-5630	Suspd.		6.00	40-70
1981	Baby's First Christmas-E-5631	Suspd.		6.00	45-60
1981	Baby's First Christmas-E-5632	Suspd.		6.00	45-85
1981	Come Let Us Adore Him (4pc. set)-E-5633	Suspd.		22.00	115-150
1981	Wee Three Kings (3pc. set)-E-5634	Suspd.		19.00	100-129
1981	We Have Seen His Star-E-6120	Retrd.	1984	6.00	40-60
1985	Have A Heavenly Christmas-12416	Open		12.00	19-30
1995	He Covers The Earth With His Beauty - 142689	Yr.Iss.		30.00	30
1995	He Covers The Earth With His Beauty - 142662	Yr.Iss.		17.00	17
1995	Our First Christmas Together - 142700	Yr.Iss.		18.50	19
1995	Baby's First Christmas - 142719	Yr.Iss.		17.50	18
1995	Baby's First Christmas - 142727	Yr.Iss.		17.50	18
1985	God Sent His Love-15768	Yr.Iss.		10.00	35
1985	May Your Christmas Be Happy-15822	Suspd.		10.00	30-48
1985	Happiness Is The Lord-15830	Suspd.		10.00	20-37
1985	May Your Christmas Be Delightful-15849	Suspd.		10.00	15-35
1985	Honk If You Love Jesus-15857	Suspd.		10.00	23-35
1985	Baby's First Christmas-15903	Yr.Iss.		10.00	42
1985	Baby's First Christmas-15911	Yr.Iss.		10.00	30-45
1986	Shepherd of Love-102288	Suspd.		10.00	35
1986	Wishing You A Cozy Christmas-102326	Yr.Iss.		10.00	40
1986	Our First Christmas Together-102350	Yr.Iss.		10.00	15-39
1986	Trust And Obey-102377	Open		10.00	17-30
1986	Love Rescued Me-102385	Open		10.00	17-23
1986	Angel Of Mercy-102407	Open		10.00	17-30
1986	It's A Perfect Boy-102415	Suspd.		10.00	30
1986	Lord Keep Me On My Toes-102423	Retrd.	1990	10.00	30-50
1986	Serve With A Smile-102431	Suspd.		10.00	20-30
1986	Serve With A Smile-102458	Suspd.		10.00	30
1986	Reindeer-102466	Yr.Iss.		11.00	145-200
1986	Rocking Horse-102474	Suspd.		10.00	25
1986	Baby's First Christmas-102504	Yr.Iss.		10.00	25

YEAR ISSUE		EDITION LIMIT	YEAR RETD.	ISSUE PRICE	QUOTE U.S.$
1986	Baby's First Christmas-102512	Yr.Iss.		10.00	25
1987	Bear The Good News Of Christmas-104515	Yr.Iss.		12.50	20
1987	Baby's First Christmas-109401	Yr.Iss.		12.00	40
1987	Baby's First Christmas-109428	Yr.Iss.		12.00	40
1987	Love Is The Best Gift Of All-109770	Yr.Iss.		11.00	35
1987	I'm A Possibility-111120	Suspd.		11.00	12-25
1987	You Have Touched So Many Hearts-112356	Open		11.00	17-30
1987	Waddle I Do Without You-112364	Open		11.00	17-30
1987	I'm Sending You A White Christmas-112372	Suspd.		11.00	20-25
1987	He Cleansed My Soul-112380	Open		12.00	17-25
1987	Our First Christmas Together-112399	Yr.Iss.		11.00	25-35
1988	To My Forever Friend-113956	Open		16.00	19-35
1988	Smile Along The Way-113964	Suspd.		15.00	30
1988	God Sent You Just In Time-113972	Suspd.		13.50	30
1988	Rejoice O Earth-113980	Retrd.	1991	13.50	28-38
1988	Cheers To The Leader-113999	Suspd.		13.50	28-35
1988	My Love Will Never Let You Go-114006	Suspd.		13.50	32
1988	Baby's First Christmas-115282	Yr.Iss.		15.00	17-25
1988	Time To Wish You A Merry Christmas-115320	Yr.Iss.		13.00	42
1995	Joy From Head To Mistletoe 150126	Yr.Iss.		8.50	9
1995	You're "A" Number One In My Book, Teacher - 150142	Yr.Iss.		8.50	9
1995	Joy To The World - 150320	Yr.Iss.		10.00	10
1988	Our First Christmas Together-520233	Yr.Iss.		13.00	21
1988	Baby's First Christmas-520241	Yr.Iss.		15.00	22
1988	You Are My Gift Come True-520276	Yr.Iss.		12.50	20
1988	Hang On For The Holly Days-520292	Yr.Iss.		13.00	15-25
1991	Sno-Bunny Falls For You Like I Do-520438	Yr.Iss.		15.00	15
1989	Christmas is Ruff Without You-520462	Yr.Iss.		13.00	13-30
1990	Wishing You A Purr-fect Holiday-520497	Yr.Iss.		15.00	20-35
1993	Slow Down & Enjoy The Holidays-520489	Yr.Iss.		16.00	16
1989	May All Your Christmases Be White-521302 (dated)	Suspd.		15.00	25-35
1990	Glide Through the Holidays-521566	Retrd.	1992	13.50	25-40
1990	Dashing Through the Snow-521574	Suspd.		15.00	15-25
1989	Our First Christmas Together-521558	Yr.Iss.		17.50	30
1990	Don't Let the Holidays Get You Down-521590	Retrd.	1994	15.00	29-45
1989	Oh Holy Night-522848	Yr.Iss.		13.50	14-30
1989	Make A Joyful Noise-522910	Open		15.00	17
1989	Love One Another-522929	Open		17.50	19-25
1990	Friends Never Drift Apart-522937	Open		17.50	19-27
1989	I Believe In The Old Rugged Cross-522953	Suspd.		15.00	30
1989	Peace On Earth-523062	Yr.Iss.		25.00	60-70
1989	Baby's First Christmas-523194	Yr.Iss.		15.00	25
1989	Baby's First Christmas-523208	Yr.Iss.		15.00	30
1990	Baby's First Christmas-523798	Yr.Iss.		15.00	20
1990	Baby's First Christmas-523771	Yr.Iss.		15.00	20
1990	Once Upon A Holy Night-523852	Yr.Iss.		15.00	25
1990	Bundles of Joy-525057	Yr.Iss.		15.00	25-35
1990	Our First Christmas Together-525324	Yr.Iss.		17.50	18-25
1990	May Your Christmas Be A Happy Home-523704	Yr.Iss.		27.50	35
1992	Good Friends Are For Always-524131	Open		15.00	17
1991	Our First Christmas Together-522945	Yr.Iss.		17.50	18-25
1991	Happy Trails Is Trusting Jesus-523224	Suspd.		15.00	16-30
1991	May Your Christmas Be Merry (on Base)-526940	Yr.Iss.		30.00	35
1991	Baby's First Christmas (Girl)-527092	Yr.Iss.		15.00	25
1991	Baby's First Christmas (Boy)-527084	Yr.Iss.		15.00	25
1991	May Your Christmas Be Merry-524174	Yr.Iss.		15.00	25
1991	The Good Lord Always Delivers-527165	Suspd.		15.00	25
1992	Baby's First Christmas-527475	Yr.Iss.		15.00	17
1992	Baby's First Christmas-527483	Yr.Iss.		15.00	17
1992	But The Greatest of These Is Love-527696	Yr.Iss.		15.00	20-30
1992	Our First Christmas-528870	Yr.Iss.		17.50	18-25
1992	But The Greatest of These Is Love-527734 (on Base)	Yr.Iss.		30.00	35
1992	Lord, Keep Me On My Toes-525332	Open		15.00	17-18
1993	Share in The Warmth of Christmas-527211	Open		15.00	17
1992	I'm Nuts About You-520411	Yr.Iss.		15.00	15-25
1993	Wishing You the Sweetest Christmas-530190	Yr.Iss.		30.00	30-45
1993	Wishing You the Sweetest Christmas-530212	Yr.Iss.		15.00	15-28
1993	Our First Christmas Together-530506	Yr.Iss.		17.50	18
1993	It's So Uplifting to Have a Friend Like You-528846	Open		16.00	17
1993	Baby's First Christmas-530859	Yr.Iss.		15.00	15
1993	Baby's First Christmas-530867	Yr.Iss.		15.00	15
1993	Sugartown Chapel Ornament-530484	Yr.Iss.		17.50	18
1994	Sam's House - 530468	Yr.Iss.		17.50	18
1994	Our 1st Christmas Together 529206	Yr.Iss.		18.50	19-27
1994	Baby's 1st Christmas - 530263	Yr.Iss.		16.00	16
1994	Baby's 1st Christmas - 530255	Yr.Iss.		16.00	16
1994	Bringing You A Merry Christmas - 528226	Open		16.00	16
1994	Onward Christmas Soldiers - 527327	Open		16.00	16
1994	Sending You A White Christmas - 528218	Open		16.00	16
1994	You're As Pretty As A Christmas Tree - 530387	Yr.Iss.		30.00	30
1994	You're As Pretty As A Christmas Tree - 530395	Yr.Iss.		16.00	16
1994	You Are Always In My Heart 530972	Yr.Iss.		16.00	16-28
1995	Hippo Holidays - 520403	Yr.Iss.		17.00	17

Precious Moments Club 15th Anniversary Commemorative Edition - S. Butcher

1993	15 Years Tweet Music Together -530840	Yr.Iss.		15.00	18-50

Precious Moments DSR Open House Weekend Ornaments - S. Butcher

1992	The Magic Starts With You-529648	Yr.Iss.		16.00	30
1993	An Event For All Seasons-529974	Yr.Iss.		15.00	20
1994	Take A Bow Cuz You're My Christmas Star - 520470	Yr.Iss.	1994	16.00	22
1995	Merry Chrismoose-150134	Yr.Iss.		17.00	17

Precious Moments Easter Seal Commemorative Ornaments - S. Butcher

1994	It's No Secret What God Can Do-244570	Yr.Iss.		6.50	7
1995	Take Time To Smell The Flowers - 128899	Yr.Iss.		7.50	8
1996	You Can Always Count on Me - 152579	Yr.Iss.		6.50	7

Precious Moments Special Edition Members' Only - S. Butcher

1993	Loving, Caring And Sharing Along The Way-PM040 (Club Appreciation)	Yr.Iss.		12.50	15
1994	You Are The End of My Rainbow-PM041	Yr.Iss.		15.00	15

Precious Moments Sugartown - S. Butcher

1995	Dr. Sugar's Office - 530441	Yr.Iss.		8.75	9
1995	Dr. Sugar's Office Display PMB053	Open		8.75	9

Flambro Imports

Emmett Kelly Jr. Christmas Ornaments - Undis.

1989	1989 65th Birthday	Yr.Iss.	1989	24.00	85-135
1990	1990 30 Years Of Clowning	Yr.Iss.	1990	30.00	125-160
1991	1991 EKJ With Stocking & Toys	Yr.Iss.	1991	30.00	30
1992	1992 Home For Christmas	Yr.Iss.	1992	24.00	65
1993	1993 Christmas Mail	Yr.Iss.	1993	25.00	65
1994	1994 '70 Birthday Commemorative	Yr.Iss.	1994	24.00	40-55
1995	1995 20th Anniversary All Star Circus	Yr.Iss.	1995	25.00	25

Little Emmett Ornaments - M. Wu

1995	Little Emmett Christmas Wrap	Open		11.50	12
1995	Little Emmett Deck the Neck	Open		11.50	12

Ganz

Cowtown/The Christmas Collection - C. Thammavongsa

1995	Bells on Cowtail Ring	Open		11.50	12
1994	Bronco Bully	Open		13.00	13
1995	Buckets of Joy	Open		12.00	12
1994	Calf-in-the Box	Open		12.50	13
1994	Christmoos Eve	Open		12.00	12
1995	Dairy Christmas	Open		11.50	12
1994	Downhill Dare Debull	Open		12.00	12
1994	Hallemooah	Open		12.00	12
1995	Holy Cow	Open		12.00	12
1994	Jingle Bull	Open		15.50	16
1994	Li'l Red Gliding Hoof	Open		12.00	12
1994	Little Drummer Calf	Open		12.00	12
1995	Moo, Moo, Moo	Open		11.50	12

Little Cheesers/The Christmas Collection - C. Thammavongsa, unless otherwise noted

1992	Abner Appleton Ornament - GDA/Thammavongsa	Open		15.00	15
1994	All I Want For Christmas	Closed	1994	13.50	14
1994	Angel	Open		8.00	8
1995	Annual Angel 1995	Open		10.50	11
1993	Baby's First X'mas Ornament	Retrd.	1995	12.50	13
1994	Candy Cane Caper	Open		9.00	9
1994	Cheeser Snowman	Closed	1994	5.00	5
1994	Chelsea's Stocking Bell	Open		15.50	16
1994	Cousin Woody Playing Flute	Closed	1994	10.00	10
1993	Dashing Through the Snow Ornament	Open		11.00	11
1994	Grandpa Blowing Horn	Closed	1994	10.00	10
1994	Hickory Playing Cello	Closed	1994	10.00	10
1992	Jenny Butterfield Ornament GDA/Thammavongsa	Open		17.00	17
1992	Jeremy With Teddy Bear Ornament - GDA/Thammavongsa	Open		13.00	13
1995	Light of the World Bell	Open		16.00	16
1993	Little Stocking Stuffer Ornament	Open		10.50	11
1992	Little Truffle Ornament GDA/Thammavongsa	Open		9.50	10
1995	Mama Claus' Special Recipe	Open		11.50	12
1993	Medley Meadowmouse X'mas Bell Ornament	Open		17.00	17
1994	Medley Playing Drum	Closed	1994	5.50	6
1992	Myrtle Meadowmouse Ornament - GDA/Thammavongsa	Open		15.00	15
1995	Noel	Open		10.50	11
1993	Our First Christmas Together Ornament	Open		18.50	19
1994	Peace on Earth	Open		8.00	8
1992	Santa Cheeser Ornament GDA/Thammavongsa	Open		14.00	14
1993	Santa's Little Helper Ornament	Open		11.00	11
1994	Santa's Workshop	Open		10.00	10
1993	Skating Into Your Heart Ornament	Open		10.00	10
1995	Skiing Santa	Open		10.00	10
1994	Sleigh Ride	Closed	1994	9.00	9
1995	Snow Cheeser II	Open		6.50	7
1994	Swinging Into the Season	Open		11.00	11
1994	Violet With Snowball	Closed	1994	5.50	6

Little Cheesers/The Silverwoods - C. Thammavongsa

1995	Angel Above	Open		8.50	9
1994	Christmas Surprise	Open		8.50	9
1994	Comfort and Joy	Open		6.00	6
1994	Deck the Halls	Open		9.50	10
1994	Giddy Up!	Open		8.50	9
1995	Harps of Gold	Open		8.50	9
1994	Hickory Dickory Dock	Open		9.50	10
1995	Joyful Sounds	Open		8.50	9
1994	Mrs. Claus	Open		9.00	9
1995	Over The Hills	Open		8.50	9
1994	Santa Silverwood	Open		9.00	9
1994	Xmas Express	Open		8.50	9

Perfect Little Place/Christmas Collection - C.Thammavongsa

1995	Angel of Light	Open		12.00	12

Pigsville/The Christmas Collection - C. Thammavongsa

1994	Caroler	Open		10.00	10
1994	Christmas Treats	Open		9.00	9
1994	Drummer Pig	Open		10.00	10
1995	Fa-La-La-La-La	Open		9.50	10
1995	Heaven Sent	Open		10.50	11
1994	Joy to the World	Open		10.00	10
1994	Lovestruck	Open		10.50	11
1994	Santa Pig	Open		11.00	11
1994	Wheeeeee! Piggy	Open		9.00	9

The Precious Steeples Collection - Ganz/L. Sunarth

1995	Florence Cathedral	Open		11.00	11
1995	Notre-Dame Cathedral	Open		11.00	11
1995	St. Patrick's Cathedral	Open		11.00	11
1995	St. Paul's Cathedral	Open		11.00	11
1995	St. Peter's Basilica	Open		11.00	11
1995	Westminster Abbey	Open		11.00	11

Goebel of North America

Angel Bell 3" - Goebel

1994	Angel w/Clarinet - Red	Closed	1994	17.50	18
1995	Angel w/Harp - Blue	Yr.Iss.		17.50	18

Angel Bells - 3 Asst. Colors - Goebel

1976	Angel Bell w/Clarinet (3 colors)	Closed	N/A	8.00	8
1976	Angel Bell w/Clarinet (white bisque)	Closed	N/A	6.00	6
1977	Angel Bell w/Mandolin (3 colors)	Closed	N/A	8.50	9
1977	Angel Bell w/Mandolin (white bisque)	Closed	N/A	6.50	7
1978	Angel Bell w/Harp (3 colors)	Closed	N/A	9.00	9
1978	Angel Bell w/Harp (white bisque)	Closed	N/A	7.00	7
1979	Angel Bell w/Accordian (3 colors)	Closed	N/A	9.50	10
1979	Angel Bell w/Accordian (white bisque)	Closed	N/A	7.50	8
1980	Angel Bell w/Saxaphone (3 colors)	Closed	N/A	10.00	10
1980	Angel Bell w/Saxaphone (white bisque)	Closed	N/A	8.00	8
1981	Angel Bell w/Music (3 colors)	Closed	N/A	11.00	11
1981	Angel Bell w/Music (white bisque)	Closed	N/A	9.00	9
1982	Angel Bell w/French Horn (3 colors)	Closed	N/A	11.75	12
1982	Angel Bell w/French Horn (white bisque)	Closed	N/A	9.75	10
1983	Angel Bell w/Flute (3 colors)	Closed	N/A	12.50	13

YEAR ISSUE		EDITION LIMIT	YEAR RETD.	ISSUE PRICE	QUOTE U.S.$
1983	Angel Bell w/Flute (white bisque)	Closed	N/A	10.50	11
1984	Angel Bell w/Drum (3 colors)	Closed	N/A	14.00	14
1984	Angel Bell w/Drum (white bisque)	Closed	N/A	12.00	12
1985	Angel Bell w/Trumpet (3 colors)	Closed	N/A	14.00	14
1985	Angel Bell w/Trumpet (white bisque)	Closed	N/A	12.00	12
1986	Angel Bell w/Bells (3 colors)	Closed	N/A	15.00	15
1986	Angel Bell w/Bells (white bisque)	Closed	N/A	12.50	13
1987	Angel Bell w/Conductor (3 colors)	Closed	N/A	16.50	17
1987	Angel Bell w/Conductor (white bisque)	Closed	N/A	13.50	14
1988	Angel Bell w/Candle (3 colors)	Closed	N/A	17.50	18
1988	Angel Bell w/Candle (wh. bisque)	Closed	N/A	15.00	15
1989	Angel Bell w/Star (3 colors)	Closed	N/A	20.00	20
1989	Angel Bell w/Star (white bisque)	Closed	N/A	17.50	18
1990	Angel Bell w/Lantern (3 colors)	Closed	N/A	22.50	23
1990	Angel Bell w/Lantern (white bisque)	Closed	N/A	20.00	20
1991	Angel Bell w/Teddy (3 colors)	Closed	N/A	25.00	25
1991	Angel Bell w/Teddy (wh. bisque)	Closed	N/A	22.50	23
1992	Angel Bell w/Doll (3 colors)	Closed	N/A	27.50	28
1992	Angel Bell w/Doll (white bisque)	Closed	N/A	25.00	25
1993	Angel Bell w/Rocking Horse (3 colors)	Closed	N/A	30.00	30
1993	Angel Bell w/Rocking Horse (white bisque)	Closed	N/A	27.50	28
1994	Angel Bell w/Clown (3 colors)	Open		34.50	35
1994	Angel Bell w/Clown (white bisque)	Open		29.50	30
1995	Angel Bell w/Train (3 colors)	Open		37.00	37
1995	Angel Bell w/Train (white bisque)	Open		30.50	31

Charlot Byj Annual Ornaments - Charlot Byj

1986	Santa Lucia Angel	Closed	N/A	18.00	25
1987	Christmas Pageant	Closed	N/A	20.00	20
1988	Angel with Sheet Music	Closed	N/A	22.00	22
1990	Girl In Sleigh	Closed	N/A	30.00	30
1991	Baby On Moon	Closed	N/A	35.00	35

Charlot Byj Baby Ornaments - Charlot Byj

1986	Baby Ornament	Closed	N/A	18.00	18
1987	Baby Snow	Closed	N/A	20.00	20
1988	Baby's 1st Stocking	Closed	N/A	27.50	28

Co-Boy Annual Ornaments - G. Skrobek

1986	Coboy with Wreath	Closed	N/A	18.00	25
1987	Coboy with Candy Cane	Closed	N/A	25.00	25
1988	Coboy with Tree	Closed	N/A	30.00	30

Goebel/M.I. Hummel

M.I. Hummel Annual Figurine Ornaments - M.I. Hummel

1988	Flying High 452	Closed	N/A	75.00	125
1989	Love From Above 481	Closed	N/A	75.00	100
1990	Peace on Earth 484	Closed	N/A	80.00	85-100
1991	Angelic Guide 571	Closed	N/A	95.00	95-125
1992	Light Up The Night 622	Closed	N/A	100.00	95-125
1993	Herald on High 623	Closed	N/A	155.00	180

M.I. Hummel Collectibles Christmas Bell Ornaments - M.I. Hummel

1989	Ride Into Christmas 775	Closed	N/A	35.00	70
1990	Letter to Santa Claus 776	Closed	N/A	37.50	50
1991	Hear Ye, Hear Ye 777	Closed	N/A	40.00	40
1992	Harmony in Four Parts 778	Closed	N/A	50.00	50
1993	Celestial Musician 779	Closed	N/A	50.00	50
1994	Festival Harmony w/Mandolin 780	Closed	N/A	50.00	50
1995	Festival Harmony w/Flute 781	Yr. Iss.		55.00	50

M.I. Hummel Collectibles Miniature Ornaments - M.I. Hummel

1993	Celestial Musician 646	Open		90.00	110
1994	Festival Harmony w/Mandolin 647	Open		95.00	110
1995	Festival Harmony w/Flute 648	Yr. Iss.		100.00	110

Gorham

Annual Crystal Ornaments - Gorham

1985	Crystal Ornament	Closed	1985	22.00	22
1986	Crystal Ornament	Closed	1986	25.00	25
1987	Crystal Ornament	Closed	1987	25.00	25
1988	Crystal Ornament	Closed	1988	28.00	28
1989	Crystal Ornament	Closed	1989	28.00	28
1990	Crystal Ornament	Closed	1990	30.00	30
1991	Crystal Ornament	Closed	1991	35.00	35
1992	Crystal Ornament	Closed	1992	32.50	33
1993	Crystal Ornament	Closed	1993	32.50	33

Annual Snowflake Ornaments - Gorham

1970	Sterling Snowflake	Closed	1970	10.00	300-600
1971	Sterling Snowflake	Closed	1971	10.00	75-125
1972	Sterling Snowflake	Closed	1972	10.00	75-125
1973	Sterling Snowflake	Closed	1973	11.00	75-130
1974	Sterling Snowflake	Closed	1974	18.00	70-110
1975	Sterling Snowflake	Closed	1975	18.00	35-85
1976	Sterling Snowflake	Closed	1976	20.00	45-90
1977	Sterling Snowflake	Closed	1977	23.00	35-75
1978	Sterling Snowflake	Closed	1978	23.00	50-75
1979	Sterling Snowflake	Closed	1979	33.00	50-90
1980	Silverplated Snowflake	Closed	1980	15.00	100-200
1981	Sterling Snowflake	Closed	1981	50.00	125-300
1982	Sterling Snowflake	Closed	1982	38.00	55-90
1983	Sterling Snowflake	Closed	1983	45.00	100
1984	Sterling Snowflake	Closed	1984	45.00	55-90
1985	Sterling Snowflake	Closed	1985	45.00	55-130
1986	Sterling Snowflake	Closed	1986	45.00	55-90
1987	Sterling Snowflake	Closed	1987	50.00	55-70
1988	Sterling Snowflake	Closed	1988	50.00	60
1989	Sterling Snowflake	Closed	1989	50.00	60
1990	Sterling Snowflake	Closed	1990	50.00	60
1991	Sterling Snowflake	Closed	1991	55.00	60
1992	Sterling Snowflake	Closed	1992	50.00	60
1993	Sterling Snowflake	Closed	1993	50.00	50

Archive Collectible - Gorham

1988	Victorian Heart	Closed	1988	50.00	75
1989	Victorian Wreath	Closed	1989	50.00	65
1990	Elizabethan Cupid	Closed	1990	60.00	60
1991	Baroque Angels	Closed	1991	55.00	70
1992	Madonna and Child	Closed	1992	50.00	50
1993	Angel With Mandolin	Closed	1993	50.00	50

Baby's First Christmas Crystal - Gorham

1991	Baby's First Rocking Horse	Closed	1994	35.00	35

Hadley House

Annual Christmas Series - T. Redlin

1994	Almost Home	Yr.Iss.		19.95	20
1995	Sharing the Evening	Yr.Iss.		19.95	20

Hallmark Galleries

Enchanted Garden - E. Richardson

1992	Neighborhood Dreamer 1500QHG3014	19,500	1994	15.00	15

Hallmark Keepsake Ornaments

1973 Hallmark Keepsake Collection - Keepsake

1973	Betsey Clark 250XHD100-2	Yr.Iss.	1973	2.50	60-85
1973	Betsey Clark-(1st Ed.) 250XHD 110-2	Yr.Iss.	1973	2.50	125
1973	Christmas Is Love 250XHD106-2	Yr.Iss.	1973	2.50	80
1973	Elves 250XHD103-5	Yr.Iss.	1973	2.50	80
1973	Manger Scene 250XHD102-2	Yr.Iss.	1973	2.50	75
1973	Santa with Elves 250XHD101-5	Yr.Iss.	1973	2.50	85

1973 Keepsake Yarn Ornaments - Keepsake

1973	Angel 125XHD78-5	Yr.Iss.	1973	1.25	23
1973	Blue Girl 125XHD85-2	Yr.Iss.	1973	1.25	23
1973	Boy Caroler 125XHD83-2	Yr.Iss.	1973	1.25	30
1973	Choir Boy 125XHD80-5	Yr.Iss.	1973	1.25	28
1973	Elf 125XHD79-2	Yr.Iss.	1973	1.25	25
1973	Green Girl 125XHD84-5	Yr.Iss.	1973	1.25	25
1973	Little Girl 125XHD82-5	Yr.Iss.	1973	1.25	20
1973	Mr. Santa 125XHD74-5	Yr.Iss.	1973	1.25	25
1973	Mr. Snowman 125XHD76-5	Yr.Iss.	1973	1.25	25
1973	Mrs. Santa 125XHD75-2	Yr.Iss.	1973	1.25	23
1973	Mrs. Snowman 125XHD77-2	Yr.Iss.	1973	1.25	23
1973	Soldier 100XHD81-2	Yr.Iss.	1973	1.00	22

1974 Hallmark Keepsake Collection - Keepsake

1974	Angel 250QX110-1	Yr.Iss.	1974	2.50	75
1974	Betsey Clark-(2nd Ed.) 250QX 108-1	Yr.Iss.	1974	2.50	47-85
1974	Buttons & Bo (Set of 2) 350QX113-1	Yr.Iss.	1974	3.50	50
1974	Charmers 250QX109-1	Yr.Iss.	1974	2.50	23-45
1974	Currier & Ives (Set of 2) 350QX112-1	Yr.Iss.	1974	3.50	42-55
1974	Little Miracles (Set of 4) 450QX115-1	Yr.Iss.	1974	4.50	55
1974	Norman Rockwell 250QX106-1	Yr.Iss.	1974	2.50	45-95
1974	Norman Rockwell 250QX111-1	Yr.Iss.	1974	2.50	85
1974	Raggedy Ann and Andy(4/set) 450QX114-1	Yr.Iss.	1974	4.50	75
1974	Snowgoose 250QX107-1	Yr.Iss.	1974	2.50	75

1974 Keepsake Yarn Ornaments - Keepsake

1974	Angel 150QX103-1	Yr.Iss.	1974	1.50	28
1974	Elf 150QX101-1	Yr.Iss.	1974	1.50	23
1974	Mrs. Santa 150QX100-1	Yr.Iss.	1974	1.50	23
1974	Santa 150QX105-1	Yr.Iss.	1974	1.50	25
1974	Snowman 150QX104-1	Yr.Iss.	1974	1.50	23
1974	Soldier 150QX102-1	Yr.Iss.	1974	1.50	23

1975 Handcrafted Ornaments: Adorable - Keepsake

1975	Betsey Clark 250QX157-1	Yr.Iss.	1975	2.50	225
1975	Drummer Boy 250QX161-1	Yr.Iss.	1975	2.50	295
1975	Mrs. Santa 250QX156-1	Yr.Iss.	1975	2.50	275
1975	Raggedy Andy 250QX160-1	Yr.Iss.	1975	2.50	375
1975	Raggedy Ann 250QX159-1	Yr.Iss.	1975	2.50	295
1975	Santa 250QX155-1	Yr.Iss.	1975	2.50	250

1975 Handcrafted Ornaments: Nostalgia - Keepsake

1975	Drummer Boy 350QX130-1	Yr.Iss.	1975	3.50	115-175
1975	Joy 350QX132-1	Yr.Iss.	1975	3.50	125-175
1975	Locomotive (dated) 350QX127-1	Yr.Iss.	1975	3.50	110-175
1975	Peace on Earth (dated) 350QX131-1	Yr.Iss.	1975	3.50	95-165
1975	Rocking Horse 350QX128-1	Yr.Iss.	1975	3.50	112-125
1975	Santa & Sleigh 350QX129-1	Yr.Iss.	1975	3.50	125

1975 Keepsake Property Ornaments - Keepsake

1975	Betsey Clark (Set of 2) 350QX167-1	Yr.Iss.	1975	3.50	25-45
1975	Betsey Clark (Set of 4) 450QX168-1	Yr.Iss.	1975	4.50	50
1975	Betsey Clark 250QX163-1	Yr.Iss.	1975	2.50	40
1975	Betsey Clark-(3rd Ed.) 300QX133-1	Yr.Iss.	1975	3.00	30-75
1975	Buttons & Bo (Set of 4) 500QX139-1	Yr.Iss.	1975	5.00	50
1975	Charmers 300QX135-1	Yr.Iss.	1975	3.00	30-45
1975	Currier & Ives (Set of 2) 250QX164-1	Yr.Iss.	1975	2.50	40
1975	Currier & Ives (Set of 2) 400QX137-1	Yr.Iss.	1975	4.00	40
1975	Little Miracles (Set of 4) 500QX140-1	Yr.Iss.	1975	5.00	40
1975	Marty Links 300QX136-1	Yr.Iss.	1975	3.00	50
1975	Norman Rockwell 250QX166-1	Yr.Iss.	1975	2.50	37-55
1975	Norman Rockwell 300QX134-1	Yr.Iss.	1975	3.00	37
1975	Raggedy Ann 250QX165-1	Yr.Iss.	1975	2.50	50
1975	Raggedy Ann and Andy(2/set) 400QX138-1	Yr.Iss.	1975	4.00	65

1975 Keepsake Yarn Ornaments - Keepsake

1975	Drummer Boy 175QX123-1	Yr.Iss.	1975	1.75	25
1975	Little Girl 175QX126-1	Yr.Iss.	1975	1.75	20
1975	Mrs. Santa 175QX125-1	Yr.Iss.	1975	1.75	22
1975	Raggedy Andy 175QX122-1	Yr.Iss.	1975	1.75	40
1975	Raggedy Ann 175QX121-1	Yr.Iss.	1975	1.75	35
1975	Santa 175QX124-1	Yr.Iss.	1975	1.75	22

1976 Bicentennial Commemoratives - Keepsake

1976	Bicentennial '76 Commemorative 250QX211-1	Yr.Iss.	1976	2.50	60
1976	Bicentennial Charmers 300QX198-1	Yr.Iss.	1976	3.00	60
1976	Colonial Children (Set of 2) 4 400QX208-1	Yr.Iss.	1976	4.00	40-65

1976 Decorative Ball Ornaments - Keepsake

1976	Cardinals 225QX205-1	Yr.Iss.	1976	2.30	50
1976	Chickadees 225QX204-1	Yr.Iss.	1976	2.30	50

1976 First Commemorative Ornament - Keepsake

1976	Baby's First Christmas 250QX211-1	Yr.Iss.	1976	2.50	150

1976 Handcrafted Ornaments: Nostalgia - Keepsake

1976	Drummer Boy 400QX130-1	Yr.Iss.	1976	3.50	160
1976	Locomotive 400QX222-1	Yr.Iss.	1976	3.50	165
1976	Peace on Earth 400QX223-1	Yr.Iss.	1976	3.50	95-175
1976	Rocking Horse 400QX128-1	Yr.Iss.	1976	3.50	165

1976 Handcrafted Ornaments: Tree Treats - Keepsake

1976	Angel 300QX176-1	Yr.Iss.	1976	3.00	150-195
1976	Reindeer 300QX 178-1	Yr.Iss.	1976	3.00	115
1976	Santa 300QX177-1	Yr.Iss.	1976	3.00	200
1976	Shepherd 300QX175-1	Yr.Iss.	1976	3.00	100

1976 Handcrafted Ornaments: Twirl-Abouts - Keepsake

1976	Angel 450QX171-1	Yr.Iss.	1976	4.50	130-165
1976	Partridge 450QX174-1	Yr.Iss.	1976	4.50	195
1976	Santa 450QX172-1	Yr.Iss.	1976	4.50	100-125
1976	Soldier 450QX173-1	Yr.Iss.	1976	4.50	95

1976 Handcrafted Ornaments: Yesteryears - Keepsake

1976	Drummer Boy 500QX184-1	Yr.Iss.	1976	5.00	125-150
1976	Partridge 500QX183-1	Yr.Iss.	1976	5.00	115
1976	Santa 500QX182-1	Yr.Iss.	1976	5.00	165
1976	Train 500QX181-1	Yr.Iss.	1976	5.00	135-160

1976 Property Ornaments - Keepsake

1976	Betsey Clark (Set of 3) 450QX218-1	Yr.Iss.	1976	4.50	50
1976	Betsey Clark 250QX210-1	Yr.Iss.	1976	2.50	38-42
1976	Betsey Clark-(4th Ed.) 300QX 195-1	Yr.Iss.	1976	3.00	75-100
1976	Charmers (Set of 2) 350QX215-1	Yr.Iss.	1976	3.50	35-55
1976	Currier & Ives 250QX209-1	Yr.Iss.	1976	2.50	40
1976	Currier & Ives 300QX197-1	Yr.Iss.	1976	3.00	50
1976	Happy the Snowman (Set of 2) 350QX216-1	Yr.Iss.	1976	3.50	55
1976	Marty Links (Set of 2) 400QX207-1	Yr.Iss.	1976	4.00	45
1976	Norman Rockwell 300QX196-1	Yr.Iss.	1976	3.00	80
1976	Raggedy Ann 250QX212-1	Yr.Iss.	1976	2.50	65
1976	Rudolph and Santa 250QX213-1	Yr.Iss.	1976	2.50	75

1976 Yarn Ornaments - Keepsake

1976	Caroler 175QX126-1	Yr.Iss.	1976	1.75	28
1976	Drummer Boy 175QX123-1	Yr.Iss.	1976	1.75	23
1976	Mrs. Santa 175QX125-1	Yr.Iss.	1976	1.75	22
1976	Raggedy Andy 175QX122-1	Yr.Iss.	1976	1.75	40
1976	Raggedy Ann 175QX121-1	Yr.Iss.	1976	1.75	35
1976	Santa 175QX124-1	Yr.Iss.	1976	1.75	24

1977 Christmas Expressions Collection - Keepsake

1977	Bell 350QX154-2	Yr.Iss.	1977	3.50	40
1977	Mandolin 350QX157-5	Yr.Iss.	1977	3.50	65
1977	Ornaments 350QX155-5	Yr.Iss.	1977	3.50	65
1977	Wreath 350QX156-2	Yr.Iss.	1977	3.50	65

1977 Cloth Doll Ornaments - Keepsake

1977	Angel 175QX220-2	Yr.Iss.	1977	1.75	50

YEAR ISSUE		EDITION LIMIT	YEAR RETD.	ISSUE PRICE	QUOTE U.S.$
1977	Santa 175QX221-5	Yr.Iss.	1977	1.75	60-80

1977 Colors of Christmas - Keepsake

1977	Bell 350QX200-2	Yr.Iss.	1977	3.50	35-43
1977	Candle 350QX203-5	Yr.Iss.	1977	3.50	55
1977	Joy 350QX201-5	Yr.Iss.	1977	3.50	45
1977	Wreath 350QX202-2	Yr.Iss.	1977	3.50	30-55

1977 Commemoratives - Keepsake

1977	Baby's First Christmas 350QX131-5	Yr.Iss.	1977	3.50	60-75
1977	First Christmas Together 350QX132-2	Yr.Iss.	1977	3.50	40-65
1977	For Your New Home 350QX263-5	Yr.Iss.	1977	3.50	120
1977	Granddaughter 350QX208-2	Yr.Iss.	1977	3.50	150
1977	Grandmother 350QX260-2	Yr.Iss.	1977	3.50	150
1977	Grandson 350QX209-5	Yr.Iss.	1977	3.50	150
1977	Love 350QX262-2	Yr.Iss.	1977	3.50	95
1977	Mother 350QX261-5	Yr.Iss.	1977	3.50	75

1977 Decorative Ball Ornaments - Keepsake

1977	Christmas Mouse 250QX134-2	Yr.Iss.	1977	3.50	65
1977	Rabbit 250QX139-5	Yr.Iss.	1977	2.50	95
1977	Squirrel 250QX138-2	Yr.Iss.	1977	2.50	115
1977	Stained Glass 250QX152-2	Yr.Iss.	1977	3.50	40-70

1977 Holiday Highlights - Keepsake

1977	Drummer Boy 350QX312-2	Yr.Iss.	1977	3.50	40-65
1977	Joy 350QX310-2	Yr.Iss.	1977	3.50	45
1977	Peace on Earth 350QX311-5	Yr.Iss.	1977	3.50	65
1977	Star 350QX313-5	Yr.Iss.	1977	3.50	50

1977 Metal Ornaments - Keepsake

1977	Snowflake Collection (Set/4) 500QX 210-2	Yr.Iss.	1977	5.00	95

1977 Nostalgia Collection - Keepsake

1977	Angel 500QX182-2	Yr.Iss.	1977	5.00	90-125
1977	Antique Car 500QX180-2	Yr.Iss.	1977	5.00	50-65
1977	Nativity 500QX181-5	Yr.Iss.	1977	5.00	135
1977	Toys 500QX183-5	Yr.Iss.	1977	5.00	155

1977 Peanuts Collection - Keepsake

1977	Peanuts (Set of 2) 400QX163-5	Yr.Iss.	1977	4.00	75
1977	Peanuts 250QX162-2	Yr.Iss.	1977	2.50	55
1977	Peanuts 350QX135-5	Yr.Iss.	1977	3.50	60

1977 Property Ornaments - Keepsake

1977	Betsey Clark -(5th Ed.) 350QX264-2	Yr.Iss.	1977	3.50	480
1977	Charmers 350QX153-5	Yr.Iss.	1977	3.50	50
1977	Currier & Ives 350QX130-2	Yr.Iss.	1977	3.50	55
1977	Disney (Set/2) 400QX137-5	Yr.Iss.	1977	4.00	75
1977	Disney 350QX133-5	Yr.Iss.	1977	3.50	45
1977	Grandma Moses 350QX150-2	Yr.Iss.	1977	3.50	100-175
1977	Norman Rockwell 350QX151-5	Yr.Iss.	1977	3.50	70

1977 The Beauty of America Collection - Keepsake

1977	Desert 250QX159-5	Yr.Iss.	1977	2.50	25
1977	Mountains 250QX158-2	Yr.Iss.	1977	2.50	15
1977	Seashore 250QX160-2	Yr.Iss.	1977	2.50	50
1977	Wharf 250QX161-5	Yr.Iss.	1977	2.50	30-50

1977 Twirl-About Collection - Keepsake

1977	Bellringer 600QX192-2	Yr.Iss.	1977	6.00	45-55
1977	Della Robia Wreath 450QX193-5	Yr.Iss.	1977	4.50	90-115
1977	Snowman 450QX190-2	Yr.Iss.	1977	4.50	55-75
1977	Weather House 600QX191-5	Yr.Iss.	1977	6.00	85-95

1977 Yesteryears Collection - Keepsake

1977	Angel 600QX172-2	Yr.Iss.	1977	6.00	85
1977	House 600QX170-2	Yr.Iss.	1977	6.00	100-125
1977	Jack-in-the-Box 600QX171-5	Yr.Iss.	1977	6.00	100-120
1977	Reindeer 600QX173-5	Yr.Iss.	1977	6.00	105-140

1978 Colors of Christmas - Keepsake

1978	Angel 350QX354-3	Yr.Iss.	1978	3.50	40
1978	Candle 350QX357-6	Yr.Iss.	1978	3.50	85
1978	Locomotive 350QX356-3	Yr.Iss.	1978	3.50	45
1978	Merry Christmas 350QX355-6	Yr.Iss.	1978	3.50	50

1978 Commemoratives - Keepsake

1978	25th Christmas Together 350QX269-3	Yr.Iss.	1978	3.50	35
1978	Baby's First Christmas 350QX200-3	Yr.Iss.	1978	3.50	80
1978	First Christmas Together 350QX218-3	Yr.Iss.	1978	3.50	45
1978	For Your New Home 350QX217-6	Yr.Iss.	1978	3.50	75
1978	Granddaughter 350QX216-3	Yr.Iss.	1978	3.50	55
1978	Grandmother 350QX267-6	Yr.Iss.	1978	3.50	50
1978	Grandson 350QX215-6	Yr.Iss.	1978	3.50	45
1978	Love 350QX268-3	Yr.Iss.	1978	3.50	55
1978	Mother 350QX266-3	Yr.Iss.	1978	3.50	40

1978 Decorative Ball Ornaments - Keepsake

1978	Drummer Boy 350QX252-3	Yr.Iss.	1978	3.50	55
1978	Hallmark's Antique Card Collection Design 350QX220-3	Yr.Iss.	1978	3.50	40
1978	Joy 350QX254-3	Yr.Iss.	1978	3.50	45
1978	Merry Christmas (Santa) 350QX202-3	Yr.Iss.	1978	3.50	45-55
1978	Nativity 350QX253-6	Yr.Iss.	1978	3.50	150
1978	The Quail 350QX251-6	Yr.Iss.	1978	3.50	45
1978	Yesterday's Toys 350QX250-3	Yr.Iss.	1978	3.50	55

1978 Handcrafted Ornaments - Keepsake

1978	Angel 400QX139-6	Yr.Iss.	1981	4.50	85-95
1978	Angels 800QX150-3	Yr.Iss.	1978	8.00	345
1978	Animal Home 600QX149-6	Yr.Iss.	1978	6.00	125-175
1978	Calico Mouse 450QX137-6	Yr.Iss.	1978	4.50	145
1978	Carrousel Series-(1st Ed.) 600QX146-3	Yr.Iss.	1978	6.00	400
1978	Dough Angel 400QX139-6	Yr.Iss.	1981	5.50	90
1978	Dove 450QX190-3	Yr.Iss.	1978	4.50	125
1978	Holly and Poinsettia Ball 600QX147-6	Yr.Iss.	1978	6.00	85
1978	Joy 450QX138-3	Yr.Iss.	1978	4.50	70-85
1978	Panorama Ball 600QX145-6	Yr.Iss.	1978	6.00	135
1978	Red Cardinal 450QX144-3	Yr.Iss.	1978	4.50	150-175
1978	Rocking Horse 600QX148-3	Yr.Iss.	1978	6.00	85
1978	Schneeberg Bell 800QX152-3	Yr.Iss.	1978	8.00	190
1978	Skating Raccoon 600QX142-3	Yr.Iss.	1978	6.00	85-95

1978 Holiday Chimes - Keepsake

1978	Reindeer Chimes 450QX320-3	Yr.Iss.	1980	4.50	60

1978 Holiday Highlights - Keepsake

1978	Dove 350QX310-3	Yr.Iss.	1978	3.50	125
1978	Nativity 350QX309-6	Yr.Iss.	1978	3.50	80
1978	Santa 350QX307-6	Yr.Iss.	1978	3.50	75
1978	Snowflake 350QX308-3	Yr.Iss.	1978	3.50	65

1978 Little Trimmers - Keepsake

1978	Drummer Boy 250QX136-3	Yr.Iss.	1978	2.50	55-75
1978	Praying Angel 250QX134-3	Yr.Iss.	1978	2.50	90
1978	Santa 250QX135-6	Yr.Iss.	1978	2.50	65
1978	Set of 4 - 250QX355-6	Yr.Iss.	1978	10.00	400-425
1978	Thimble Series (Mouse)-First Ed. 250QX133-6	Yr.Iss.	1978	2.50	250-300

1978 Peanuts Collection - Keepsake

1978	Peanuts 250QX203-6	Yr.Iss.	1978	2.50	50
1978	Peanuts 250QX204-3	Yr.Iss.	1978	2.50	60
1978	Peanuts 350QX205-6	Yr.Iss.	1978	3.50	50
1978	Peanuts 350QX206-3	Yr.Iss.	1978	3.50	50

1978 Property Ornaments - Keepsake

1978	Betsey Clark-(6th Ed.) 350QX 201-6	Yr.Iss.	1978	3.50	60
1978	Disney 350QX207-6	Yr.Iss.	1978	3.50	75
1978	Joan Walsh Anglund 350QX221-6	Yr.Iss.	1978	3.50	65
1978	Spencer Sparrow 350QX219-6	Yr.Iss.	1978	3.50	50

1978 Yarn Collection - Keepsake

1978	Green Boy 200QX123-1	Yr.Iss.	1979	2.00	25
1978	Green Girl 200QX126-1	Yr.Iss.	1979	2.00	20
1978	Mr. Claus 200QX340-3	Yr.Iss.	1979	2.00	23
1978	Mrs. Claus 200QX125-1	Yr.Iss.	1979	2.00	22

1979 Collectible Series - Keepsake

1979	Bellringer-(1st Ed.) 10QX147-9	Yr.Iss.	1979	10.00	400
1979	Carousel-(2nd Ed.) 650QX146-7	Yr.Iss.	1979	6.50	165-185
1979	Here Comes Santa-(1st Ed.) 900QX155-9	Yr.Iss.	1979	9.00	600
1979	Snoopy and Friends 800QX141-9	Yr.Iss.	1979	8.00	125
1979	Thimble-(2nd Ed.) 300QX131-9	Yr.Iss.	1980	3.00	145-175

1979 Colors of Christmas - Keepsake

1979	Holiday Wreath 350QX353-9	Yr.Iss.	1979	3.50	35-45
1979	Partridge in a Pear Tree 350QX351-9	Yr.Iss.	1979	3.50	35-45
1979	Star Over Bethlehem 350QX352-7	Yr.Iss.	1979	3.50	75
1979	Words of Christmas 350QX350-7	Yr.Iss.	1979	3.50	85

1979 Commemoratives - Keepsake

1979	Baby's First Christmas 350QX208-7	Yr.Iss.	1979	3.50	22-30
1979	Baby's First Christmas 800QX154-7	Yr.Iss.	1979	8.00	175
1979	Friendship 350QX203-9	Yr.Iss.	1979	3.50	18
1979	Granddaughter 350QX211-9	Yr.Iss.	1979	3.50	23-35
1979	Grandmother 350QX252-7	Yr.Iss.	1979	3.50	10
1979	Grandson 350QX210-7	Yr.Iss.	1979	3.50	20-35
1979	Love 350QX258-7	Yr.Iss.	1979	3.50	17-30
1979	Mother 350QX251-9	Yr.Iss.	1979	3.50	10-23
1979	New Home 350QX212-7	Yr.Iss.	1979	3.50	45
1979	Our First Christmas Together 350QX209-9	Yr.Iss.	1979	3.50	45
1979	Our Twenty-Fifth Anniversary350QX 250-7	Yr.Iss.	1979	3.50	20-28
1979	Teacher 350QX213-9	Yr.Iss.	1979	3.50	15

1979 Decorative Ball Ornaments - Keepsake

1979	Behold the Star 350QX255-9	Yr.Iss.	1979	3.50	40
1979	Black Angel 350QX207-9	Yr.Iss.	1979	3.50	25
1979	Christmas Chickadees 350QX204-7	Yr.Iss.	1979	3.50	30
1979	Christmas Collage 350QX257-9	Yr.Iss.	1979	3.50	16-28
1979	Christmas Traditions 350QX253-9	Yr.Iss.	1979	3.50	35
1979	The Light of Christmas 350QX256-7	Yr.Iss.	1979	3.50	18-28
1979	Night Before Christmas 350QX214-7	Yr.Iss.	1979	3.50	40

1979 Handcrafted Ornaments - Keepsake

1979	Christmas Eve Surprise 650QX157-9	Yr.Iss.	1979	6.50	65
1979	Christmas Heart 650QX140-7	Yr.Iss.	1979	6.50	104-115
1979	Christmas is for Children 500QX135-9	Yr.Iss.	1980	5.00	80-95
1979	A Christmas Treat 500QX134-7	Yr.Iss.	1980	5.00	85
1979	The Downhill Run 650QX145-9	Yr.Iss.	1979	6.50	135-175
1979	The Drummer Boy 800QX143-9	Yr.Iss.	1979	8.00	125
1979	Holiday Scrimshaw 400QX152-7	Yr.Iss.	1979	4.00	205-225
1979	Outdoor Fun 800QX150-7	Yr.Iss.	1979	8.00	135-150
1979	Raccoon 650QX142-3	Yr.Iss.	1979	6.50	85
1979	Ready for Christmas 650QX133-9	Yr.Iss.	1979	6.50	95-150
1979	Santa's Here 500QX138-7	Yr.Iss.	1979	5.00	55-75
1979	The Skating Snowman 500QX139-9	Yr.Iss.	1980	5.00	65-80

1979 Holiday Chimes - Keepsake

1979	Reindeer Chimes 450QX320-3	Yr.Iss.	1980	4.50	75
1979	Star Chimes 450QX137-9	Yr.Iss.	1979	4.50	75

1979 Holiday Highlights - Keepsake

1979	Christmas Angel 350QX300-7	Yr.Iss.	1979	3.50	95
1979	Christmas Cheer 350QX303-9	Yr.Iss.	1979	3.50	95
1979	Christmas Tree 350QX302-7	Yr.Iss.	1979	3.50	75
1979	Love 350QX304-7	Yr.Iss.	1979	3.50	88
1979	Snowflake 350QX301-9	Yr.Iss.	1979	3.50	40

1979 Little Trimmer Collection - Keepsake

1979	Angel Delight 300QX130-7	Yr.Iss.	1979	3.00	60
1979	A Matchless Christmas 400QX132-7	Yr.Iss.	1979	4.00	65-75
1979	Santa 300QX135-6	Yr.Iss.	1979	3.00	55
1979	Thimble Series-Mouse 300QX133-6	Yr.Iss.	1979	3.00	150-225

1979 Property Ornaments - Keepsake

1979	Betsey Clark-Seventh Edition 350QX 201-9	Yr.Iss.	1979	3.50	40
1979	Joan Walsh Anglund 350QX205-9	Yr.Iss.	1979	3.50	25-35
1979	Mary Hamilton 350QX254-7	Yr.Iss.	1979	3.50	15-25
1979	Peanuts (Time to Trim) 350QX202-7	Yr.Iss.	1979	3.50	40
1979	Spencer Sparrow 350QX200-7	Yr.Iss.	1979	3.50	30-35
1979	Winnie-the-Pooh 350QX206-7	Yr.Iss.	1979	3.50	35

1979 Sewn Trimmers - Keepsake

1979	Angel Music 200QX343-9	Yr.Iss.	1980	2.00	20
1979	Merry Santa 200QX342-7	Yr.Iss.	1980	2.00	20
1979	The Rocking Horse 200QX340-7	Yr.Iss.	1980	2.00	23
1979	Stuffed Full Stocking 200QX341-9	Yr.Iss.	1980	2.00	20

1979 Yarn Collection - Keepsake

1979	Green Boy 200QX123-1	Yr.Iss.	1979	2.00	20
1979	Green Girl 200QX126-1	Yr.Iss.	1979	2.00	18
1979	Mr. Claus 200QX340-3	Yr.Iss.	1979	2.00	20
1979	Mrs. Claus 200QX125-1	Yr.Iss.	1979	2.00	20

1980 Collectible Series - Keepsake

1980	The Bellringers-(2nd Ed.)15QX157-4	Yr.Iss.	1980	15.00	60-85
1980	Carrousel-(3rd Ed.) 750QX141-4	Yr.Iss.	1980	7.50	140-165
1980	Frosty Friends-(1st Ed.)650QX 137-4	Yr.Iss.	1980	6.50	600
1980	Here Comes Santa-(2nd Ed.)12QX 143-4	Yr.Iss.	1980	12.00	110-180
1980	Norman Rockwell-(1st Ed.) 650QX306-1	Yr.Iss.	1980	6.50	250
1980	Snoopy & Friends-(2nd Ed.) 900QX154-1	Yr.Iss.	1980	9.00	100-125
1980	Thimble-(3rd Ed.) 400QX132-1	Yr.Iss.	1980	4.00	175

1980 Colors of Christmas - Keepsake

1980	Joy 400QX350-1	Yr.Iss.	1980	4.00	23

1980 Commemoratives - Keepsake

1980	25th Christmas Together 400QX206-1	Yr.Iss.	1980	4.00	20
1980	Baby's First Christmas 12QX156-1	Yr.Iss.	1980	12.00	50
1980	Baby's First Christmas 400QX200-1	Yr.Iss.	1980	4.00	30
1980	Beauty of Friendship 400QX303-4	Yr.Iss.	1980	4.00	60
1980	Black Baby's First Christmas 400QX 229-4	Yr.Iss.	1980	4.00	30
1980	Christmas at Home 400QX210-1	Yr.Iss.	1980	4.00	35
1980	Christmas Love 400QX207-4	Yr.Iss.	1980	4.00	40
1980	Dad 400QX214-1	Yr.Iss.	1980	4.00	9-18
1980	Daughter 400QX212-1	Yr.Iss.	1980	4.00	40
1980	First Christmas Together 400QX205-4	Yr.Iss.	1980	4.00	40
1980	First Christmas Together 400QX305-4	Yr.Iss.	1980	4.00	30-55
1980	Friendship 400QX208-1	Yr.Iss.	1980	4.00	10-20
1980	Granddaughter 400QX202-1	Yr.Iss.	1980	4.00	35
1980	Grandfather 400QX231-4	Yr.Iss.	1980	4.00	10-20
1980	Grandmother 400QX204-1	Yr.Iss.	1980	4.00	20
1980	Grandparents 400QX213-4	Yr.Iss.	1980	4.00	40

YEAR ISSUE		EDITION LIMIT	YEAR RETD.	ISSUE PRICE	QUOTE U.S.$
1980	Grandson 400QX201-4	Yr.Iss.	1980	4.00	20-35
1980	Love 400QX302-1	Yr.Iss.	1980	4.00	65
1980	Mother 400QX203-4	Yr.Iss.	1980	4.00	11-23
1980	Mother 400QX304-1	Yr.Iss.	1980	4.00	35
1980	Mother and Dad 400QX230-1	Yr.Iss.	1980	4.00	11-23
1980	Son 400QX211-4	Yr.Iss.	1980	4.00	25-35
1980	Teacher 400QX209-4	Yr.Iss.	1980	4.00	10-20

1980 Decorative Ball Ornaments - Keepsake

1980	Christmas Cardinals 400QX224-1	Yr.Iss.	1980	4.00	35
1980	Christmas Choir 400QX228-1	Yr.Iss.	1980	4.00	85
1980	Christmas Time 400QX226-1	Yr.Iss.	1980	4.00	30
1980	Happy Christmas 400QX222-1	Yr.Iss.	1980	4.00	30
1980	Jolly Santa 400QX227-4	Yr.Iss.	1980	4.00	30
1980	Nativity 400QX225-4	Yr.Iss.	1980	4.00	125
1980	Santa's Workshop 400QX223-4	Yr.Iss.	1980	4.00	20-30

1980 Frosted Images - Keepsake

1980	Dove 400QX308-1	Yr.Iss.	1980	4.00	25-40
1980	Drummer Boy 400QX309-4	Yr.Iss.	1980	4.00	25
1980	Santa 400QX310-1	Yr.Iss.	1980	4.00	20

1980 Handcrafted Ornaments - Keepsake

1980	The Animals' Christmas 800QX150-1	Yr.Iss.	1980	8.00	40-65
1980	Caroling Bear 750QX140-1	Yr.Iss.	1980	7.50	140-150
1980	Christmas is for Children 550QX135-9	Yr.Iss.	1980	5.50	95
1980	A Christmas Treat 550QX134-7	Yr.Iss.	1980	5.50	75
1980	A Christmas Vigil 900QX144-1	Yr.Iss.	1980	9.00	185
1980	Drummer Boy 550QX147-4	Yr.Iss.	1980	5.50	55-95
1980	Elfin Antics 900QX142-1	Yr.Iss.	1980	9.00	225
1980	A Heavenly Nap 650QX139-4	Yr.Iss.	1981	6.50	20-45
1980	Heavenly Sounds 750QX152-1	Yr.Iss.	1980	7.50	70-95
1980	Santa 1980 550QX146-1	Yr.Iss.	1980	5.50	90
1980	Santa's Flight 550QX138-1	Yr.Iss.	1980	5.50	95-115
1980	Skating Snowman 550QX139-9	Yr.Iss.	1980	5.50	80
1980	The Snowflake Swing 400QX133-4	Yr.Iss.	1980	4.00	45
1980	A Spot of Christmas Cheer 800QX153-4	Yr.Iss.	1980	8.00	145

1980 Holiday Chimes - Keepsake

1980	Reindeer Chimes 550QX320-3	Yr.Iss.	1980	5.50	25
1980	Santa Mobile 550QX136-1	Yr.Iss.	1981	5.50	25-50
1980	Snowflake Chimes 550QX165-4	Yr.Iss.	1981	5.50	35

1980 Holiday Highlights - Keepsake

1980	Three Wise Men 400QX300-1	Yr.Iss.	1980	4.00	30
1980	Wreath 400QX301-4	Yr.Iss.	1980	4.00	85

1980 Little Trimmers - Keepsake

1980	Christmas Owl 400QX131-4	Yr.Iss.	1982	4.00	45
1980	Christmas Teddy 250QX135-4	Yr.Iss.	1980	2.50	80-135
1980	Clothespin Soldier 350QX134-1	Yr.Iss.	1980	3.50	40
1980	Merry Redbird 350QX160-1	Yr.Iss.	1980	3.50	50-65
1980	Swingin' on a Star 400QX130-1	Yr.Iss.	1980	4.00	65-85
1980	Thimble Series-A Christmas Salute 400QX131-9	Yr.Iss.	1980	4.00	175

1980 Old-Fashioned Christmas Collection - Keepsake

1988	In a Nutshell 550QX469-7	Yr.Iss.	1988	5.50	24-33

1980 Property Ornaments - Keepsake

1980	Betsey Clark 650QX307-4	Yr.Iss.	1980	6.50	60
1980	Betsey Clark's Christmas 750QX194-4	Yr.Iss.	1980	7.50	35
1980	Betsey Clark-Eighth Edition 400QX 215-4	Yr.Iss.	1980	4.00	28
1980	Disney 400QX218-1	Yr.Iss.	1980	4.00	30
1980	Joan Walsh Anglund 400QX217-4	Yr.Iss.	1980	4.00	13-25
1980	Marty Links 400QX221-4	Yr.Iss.	1980	4.00	11-23
1980	Mary Hamilton 400QX219-4	Yr.Iss.	1980	4.00	20
1980	Muppets 400QX220-1	Yr.Iss.	1980	4.00	40
1980	Peanuts 400QX216-1	Yr.Iss.	1980	4.00	30

1980 Sewn Trimmers - Keepsake

1980	Angel Music 200QX343-9	Yr.Iss.	1980	2.00	20
1980	Merry Santa 200QX342-7	Yr.Iss.	1980	2.00	20
1980	The Rocking Horse 200QX340-7	Yr.Iss.	1980	2.00	22
1980	Stuffed Full Stocking 200QX341-9	Yr.Iss.	1980	2.00	25

1980 Special Editions - Keepsake

1980	Checking it Twice 20QX158-4	Yr.Iss.	1981	20.00	175-195
1980	Heavenly Minstrel 15QX156-7	Yr.Iss.	1980	15.00	345

1980 Yarn Ornaments - Keepsake

1980	Angel 300QX162-1	Yr.Iss.	1981	3.00	10
1980	Santa 300QX161-4	Yr.Iss.	1981	3.00	9
1980	Snowman 300QX163-4	Yr.Iss.	1981	3.00	9
1980	Soldier 300QX164-1	Yr.Iss.	1981	3.00	9

1981 Collectible Series - Keepsake

1981	Bellringer - 3rd Edition 1500QX441-5	Yr.Iss.	1981	15.00	70-95
1981	Carrousel - 4th Edition 900QX427-5	Yr.Iss.	1981	9.00	70-95
1981	Frosty Friends - 2nd Edition 800QX433-5	Yr.Iss.	1981	8.00	300-425
1981	Here Comes Santa - 3rd Ed.1300QX438-2	Yr.Iss.	1981	13.00	295

YEAR ISSUE		EDITION LIMIT	YEAR RETD.	ISSUE PRICE	QUOTE U.S.$
1981	Norman Rockwell - 2nd Edition 850QX 511-5	Yr.Iss.	1981	8.50	30-45
1981	Rocking Horse - 1st Ed. 900QX 422-2	Yr.Iss.	1981	9.00	495-650
1981	Snoopy and Friends - 3rd Ed. 1200QX436-2	Yr.Iss.	1981	12.00	95
1981	Thimble - 4th Edition 450QX413-5	Yr.Iss.	1981	4.50	150

1981 Commemoratives - Keepsake

1981	25th Christmas Together 450QX707-5	Yr.Iss.	1981	4.50	15-23
1981	25th Christmas Together 550QX504-2	Yr.Iss.	1981	5.50	22
1981	50th Christmas 450QX708-2	Yr.Iss.	1981	4.50	10-20
1981	Baby's First Christmas 1300QX440-2	Yr.Iss.	1981	13.00	40-50
1981	Baby's First Christmas 550QX516-2	Yr.Iss.	1981	5.50	30
1981	Baby's First Christmas 850QX513-5	Yr.Iss.	1981	8.50	11-20
1981	Baby's First Christmas-Black 450QX602-2	Yr.Iss.	1981	4.50	25
1981	Baby's First Christmas-Boy 450QX 601-5	Yr.Iss.	1981	4.50	25-30
1981	Baby's First Christmas-Girl 450QX 600-2	Yr.Iss.	1981	4.50	25-30
1981	Daughter 450QX607-5	Yr.Iss.	1981	4.50	30-40
1981	Father 450QX609-5	Yr.Iss.	1981	4.50	10-20
1981	First Christmas Together 450QX706-2	Yr.Iss.	1981	4.50	25-30
1981	First Christmas Together 550QX505-5	Yr.Iss.	1981	5.50	25
1981	Friendship 450QX704-2	Yr.Iss.	1981	4.50	30
1981	Friendship 550QX503-5	Yr.Iss.	1981	5.50	20-30
1981	The Gift of Love 450QX705-5	Yr.Iss.	1981	4.50	15-25
1981	Godchild 450QX603-5	Yr.Iss.	1981	4.50	10-20
1981	Granddaughter 450QX605-5	Yr.Iss.	1981	4.50	15-30
1981	Grandfather 450QX701-5	Yr.Iss.	1981	4.50	20
1981	Grandmother 450QX702-2	Yr.Iss.	1981	4.50	10-20
1981	Grandparents 450QX703-5	Yr.Iss.	1981	4.50	15-20
1981	Grandson 450QX604-2	Yr.Iss.	1981	4.50	15-30
1981	Home 450QX709-5	Yr.Iss.	1981	4.50	20
1981	Love 550QX502-2	Yr.Iss.	1981	5.50	48
1981	Mother 450QX608-2	Yr.Iss.	1981	4.50	10-18
1981	Mother and Dad 450QX700-2	Yr.Iss.	1981	4.50	17
1981	Son 450QX606-2	Yr.Iss.	1981	4.50	30
1981	Teacher 450QX800-2	Yr.Iss.	1981	4.50	12

1981 Crown Classics - Keepsake

1981	Angel 450QX507-5	Yr.Iss.	1981	4.50	15-25
1981	Tree Photoholder 550QX515-5	Yr.Iss.	1981	5.50	20-30
1981	Unicorn 850QX516-5	Yr.Iss.	1981	8.50	15-25

1981 Decorative Ball Ornaments - Keepsake

1981	Christmas 1981 450QX809-5	Yr.Iss.	1981	4.50	15-25
1981	Christmas in the Forest 450QX813-5	Yr.Iss.	1981	4.50	145
1981	Christmas Magic 450QX810-2	Yr.Iss.	1981	4.50	15-25
1981	Let Us Adore Him 450QX811-5	Yr.Iss.	1981	4.50	40-65
1981	Merry Christmas 450QX814-2	Yr.Iss.	1981	4.50	15-22
1981	Santa's Coming 450QX812-2	Yr.Iss.	1981	4.50	15-25
1981	Santa's Surprise 450QX815-5	Yr.Iss.	1981	4.50	25
1981	Traditional (Black Santa) 450QX801-5	Yr.Iss.	1981	4.50	50-95

1981 Fabric Ornaments - Keepsake

1981	Calico Kitty 300QX403-5	Yr.Iss.	1981	3.00	20
1981	Cardinal Cutie 300QX400-2	Yr.Iss.	1981	3.00	10-22
1981	Gingham Dog 300QX402-2	Yr.Iss.	1981	3.00	11-20
1981	Peppermint Mouse 300QX401-5	Yr.Iss.	1981	3.00	35

1981 Frosted Images - Keepsake

1981	Angel 400QX509-5	Yr.Iss.	1981	4.00	33
1981	Mouse 400QX508-2	Yr.Iss.	1981	4.00	25
1981	Snowman 400QX510-2	Yr.Iss.	1981	4.00	25

1981 Hand Crafted Ornaments - Keepsake

1981	Candyville Express 750QX418-2	Yr.Iss.	1981	7.50	90
1981	Checking It Twice 2250QX158-4	Yr.Iss.	1981	23.00	195
1981	Christmas Dreams 1200QX437-5	Yr.Iss.	1981	12.00	200-225
1981	Christmas Fantasy 1300QX155-4	Yr.Iss.	1982	13.00	68-85
1981	Dough Angel 550QX139-6	Yr.Iss.	1981	5.50	80
1981	Drummer Boy 250QX148-1	Yr.Iss.	1981	2.50	45
1981	The Friendly Fiddler 800QX434-2	Yr.Iss.	1981	8.00	75
1981	A Heavenly Nap 650QX139-4	Yr.Iss.	1981	6.50	50
1981	Ice Fairy 650QX431-5	Yr.Iss.	1981	6.50	85-95
1981	The Ice Sculptor 800QX432-2	Yr.Iss.	1982	8.00	90-100
1981	Love and Joy 900QX425-2	Yr.Iss.	1981	9.00	75-95
1981	Mr. & Mrs. Claus 1200QX448-5	Yr.Iss.	1981	12.00	115-125
1981	Sailing Santa 1300QX439-5	Yr.Iss.	1981	13.00	200-290
1981	Space Santa 650QX430-2	Yr.Iss.	1981	6.50	75-110
1981	St. Nicholas 550QX446-2	Yr.Iss.	1981	5.50	40-50
1981	Star Swing 550QX421-5	Yr.Iss.	1981	5.50	60
1981	Topsy-Turvy Tunes 750QX429-5	Yr.Iss.	1981	7.50	66-80
1981	A Well-Stocked Stocking 900QX154-7	Yr.Iss.	1981	9.00	85

1981 Holiday Chimes - Keepsake

1981	Santa Mobile 550QX136-1	Yr.Iss.	1981	5.50	40
1981	Snowflake Chimes 550QX165-4	Yr.Iss.	1981	5.50	25
1981	Snowman Chimes 550QX445-5	Yr.Iss.	1981	5.50	25-30

1981 Holiday Highlights - Keepsake

1981	Christmas Star 550QX501-5	Yr.Iss.	1981	5.50	15-30

YEAR ISSUE		EDITION LIMIT	YEAR RETD.	ISSUE PRICE	QUOTE U.S.$
1981	Shepherd Scene 550QX500-2	Yr.Iss.	1981	5.50	27

1981 Little Trimmers - Keepsake

1981	Clothespin Drummer Boy 450QX408-2	Yr.Iss.	1981	4.50	30-45
1981	Jolly Snowman 350QX407-5	Yr.Iss.	1981	3.50	40-60
1981	Perky Penguin 350QX409-5	Yr.Iss.	1982	3.50	45-60
1981	Puppy Love 350QX406-2	Yr.Iss.	1981	3.50	30-40
1981	The Stocking Mouse 450QX412-2	Yr.Iss.	1981	4.50	90-115

1981 Plush Animals - Keepsake

1981	Christmas Teddy 500QX404-2	Yr.Iss.	1981	5.50	22
1981	Raccoon Tunes 550QX405-5	Yr.Iss.	1981	5.50	15-23

1981 Property Ornaments - Keepsake

1981	Betsey Clark 900QX423-5	Yr.Iss.	1981	9.00	60-75
1981	Betsey Clark Cameo 850QX512-2	Yr.Iss.	1981	8.50	20-30
1981	Betsey Clark-9th Ed450QX 802-2	Yr.Iss.	1981	4.50	23-33
1981	Disney 450QX805-5	Yr.Iss.	1981	4.50	15-30
1981	The Divine Miss Piggy 1200QX425-5	Yr.Iss.	1982	12.00	80-95
1981	Joan Walsh Anglund 450QX804-2	Yr.Iss.	1981	4.50	10-23
1981	Kermit the Frog 900QX424-2	Yr.Iss.	1981	9.00	80-95
1981	Marty Links 450QX808-2	Yr.Iss.	1981	4.50	10-20
1981	Mary Hamilton 450QX806-2	Yr.Iss.	1981	4.50	10-20
1981	Muppets 450QX807-5	Yr.Iss.	1981	4.50	20-35
1981	Peanuts 450QX803-5	Yr.Iss.	1981	4.50	15-35

1982 Brass Ornaments - Keepsake

1982	Brass Bell 1200QX460-6	Yr.Iss.	1982	12.00	20
1982	Santa and Reindeer 900QX467-6	Yr.Iss.	1982	9.00	40-50
1982	Santa's Sleigh 900QX478-6	Yr.Iss.	1982	9.00	20-35

1982 Collectible Series - Keepsake

1982	The Bellringer-4th Ed. 1500QX455-6	Yr.Iss.	1982	15.00	80-95
1982	Carrousel Series-5th Ed. 1000QX478-3	Yr.Iss.	1982	10.00	90-100
1982	Clothespin Soldier-1st Ed. 500QX458-3	Yr.Iss.	1982	5.00	110-125
1982	Frosty Friends-3rd Ed. 800QX452-3	Yr.Iss.	1982	8.00	125-275
1982	Here Comes Santa-4th Ed. 1500QX464-3	Yr.Iss.	1982	15.00	125-135
1982	Holiday Wildlife-1st Ed. 700QX313-3	Yr.Iss.	1982	7.00	340-375
1982	Rocking Horse-2nd Ed. 1000QX 502-3	Yr.Iss.	1982	10.00	375-425
1982	Snoopy and Friends-4th Ed. 1000QX478-3	Yr.Iss.	1982	13.00	75-85
1982	Thimble-5th Ed. 500QX451-3	Yr.Iss.	1982	5.00	75
1982	Tin Locomotive-1st Ed. 1300QX460-3	Yr.Iss.	1982	13.00	500-600

1982 Colors of Christmas - Keepsake

1982	Nativity 450QX308-3	Yr.Iss.	1982	4.50	40-50
1982	Santa's Flight 450QX308-6	Yr.Iss.	1982	4.50	38-45

1982 Commemoratives - Keepsake

1982	25th Christmas Together 450QX211-6	Yr.Iss.	1982	4.50	10-20
1982	50th Christmas Together 450QX212-3	Yr.Iss.	1982	4.50	10-20
1982	Baby's First Christmas (Boy)450QX 216-3	Yr.Iss.	1982	4.50	20-25
1982	Baby's First Christmas (Girl)450QX 207-3	Yr.Iss.	1982	4.50	20-25
1982	Baby's First Christmas 1300QX455-3	Yr.Iss.	1982	13.00	50
1982	Baby's First Christmas 550QX302-3	Yr.Iss.	1982	5.50	25-40
1982	Baby's First Christmas-Photoholder 650QX312-6	Yr.Iss.	1982	6.50	22
1982	Christmas Memories 650QX311-6	Yr.Iss.	1982	6.50	20
1982	Daughter 450QX204-6	Yr.Iss.	1982	4.50	35
1982	Father 450QX205-6	Yr.Iss.	1982	4.50	20
1982	First Christmas Together 450QX211-3	Yr.Iss.	1982	4.50	35
1982	First Christmas Together 550QX302-6	Yr.Iss.	1982	5.50	20-25
1982	First Christmas Together 850QX306-6	Yr.Iss.	1982	8.50	20-35
1982	FirstChristmas Together-Locket 1500QX456-3	Yr.Iss.	1982	15.00	25-40
1982	Friendship 450QX208-6	Yr.Iss.	1982	4.50	17
1982	Friendship 550QX304-6	Yr.Iss.	1982	5.50	15-25
1982	Godchild 450QX222-6	Yr.Iss.	1982	4.50	15-20
1982	Granddaughter 450QX224-3	Yr.Iss.	1982	4.50	15-30
1982	Grandfather 450QX207-6	Yr.Iss.	1982	4.50	18
1982	Grandmother 450QX200-3	Yr.Iss.	1982	4.50	15
1982	Grandparents 450QX214-6	Yr.Iss.	1982	4.50	17
1982	Grandson 450QX224-6	Yr.Iss.	1982	4.50	18-30
1982	Love 450QX209-6	Yr.Iss.	1982	4.50	10-20
1982	Love 550QX304-3	Yr.Iss.	1982	5.50	30
1982	Moments of Love 450QX209-3	Yr.Iss.	1982	4.50	10-18
1982	Mother 450QX205-3	Yr.Iss.	1982	4.50	10-20
1982	Mother and Dad 450QX222-3	Yr.Iss.	1982	4.50	10-20
1982	New Home 450QX212-6	Yr.Iss.	1982	4.50	10-20
1982	Sister 450QX208-3	Yr.Iss.	1982	4.50	15-30
1982	Son 450QX204-3	Yr.Iss.	1982	4.50	12-30
1982	Teacher 450QX214-3	Yr.Iss.	1982	4.50	12
1982	Teacher 650QX312-3	Yr.Iss.	1982	6.50	18
1982	Teacher-Apple 550QX301-6	Yr.Iss.	1982	5.50	13

CHRISTMAS ORNAMENTS

1982 Decorative Ball Ornaments - Keepsake

YEAR ISSUE		EDITION LIMIT	YEAR RETD.	ISSUE PRICE	QUOTE U.S.$
1982	Christmas Angel 450QX220-6	Yr.Iss.	1982	4.50	25
1982	Currier & Ives 450QX201-3	Yr.Iss.	1982	4.50	12-23
1982	Santa 450QX221-6	Yr.Iss.	1982	4.50	15-20
1982	Season for Caring 450QX221-3	Yr.Iss.	1982	4.50	23

1982 Designer Keepsakes - Keepsake

1982	Merry Christmas 450QX225-6	Yr.Iss.	1982	4.50	10-20
1982	Old Fashioned Christmas 450QX227-6	Yr.Iss.	1982	4.50	40
1982	Old World Angels 450QX226-3	Yr.Iss.	1982	4.50	22
1982	Patterns of Christmas 450QX226-6	Yr.Iss.	1982	4.50	15-22
1982	Stained Glass 450QX228-3	Yr.Iss.	1982	4.50	15-22
1982	Twelve Days of Christmas 450QX203-6	Yr.Iss.	1982	4.50	30

1982 Handcrafted Ornaments - Keepsake

1982	Baroque Angel 1500QX456-6	Yr.Iss.	1982	15.00	175
1982	Christmas Fantasy 1300QX155-4	Yr.Iss.	1982	13.00	59
1982	Cloisonne Angel 1200QX145-4	Yr.Iss.	1982	12.00	95
1982	Cowboy Snowman 800QX480-6	Yr.Iss.	1982	8.00	50
1982	Cycling Santa 2000QX435-5	Yr.Iss.	1983	20.00	120-150
1982	Elfin Artist 900QX457-3	Yr.Iss.	1982	9.00	42-50
1982	Embroidered Tree - 650QX494-6	Yr.Iss.	1982	6.50	40
1982	Ice Sculptor 800QX432-2	Yr.Iss.	1982	8.00	75
1982	Jogging Santa 800QX457-6	Yr.Iss.	1982	8.00	35-50
1982	Jolly Christmas Tree 650QX465-3	Yr.Iss.	1982	6.50	80
1982	Peeking Elf 650QX419-5	Yr.Iss.	1982	6.50	25-40
1982	Pinecone Home 800QX461-3	Yr.Iss.	1982	8.00	125-175
1982	Raccoon Surprises 900QX479-3	Yr.Iss.	1982	9.00	125
1982	Santa Bell 1500QX148-7	Yr.Iss.	1982	15.00	45-60
1982	Santa's Workshop 1000QX450-3	Yr.Iss.	1983	10.00	75-85
1982	The Spirit of Christmas 1000QX452-6	Yr.Iss.	1982	10.00	105-125
1982	Three Kings 850QX307-3	Yr.Iss.	1982	8.50	17-25
1982	Tin Soldier 650QX483-6	Yr.Iss.	1982	6.50	30-45

1982 Holiday Chimes - Keepsake

1982	Bell Chimes 550QX494-3	Yr.Iss.	1982	5.50	30
1982	Tree Chimes 550QX484-6	Yr.Iss.	1982	5.50	50

1982 Holiday Highlights - Keepsake

1982	Angel 550QX309-6	Yr.Iss.	1982	5.50	20-35
1982	Christmas Magic 550QX311-3	Yr.Iss.	1982	5.50	22-29
1982	Christmas Sleigh 550QX309-3	Yr.Iss.	1982	5.50	75

1982 Ice Sculptures - Keepsake

1982	Arctic Penguin 400QX300-3	Yr.Iss.	1982	4.00	10-20
1982	Snowy Seal 400QX300-6	Yr.Iss.	1982	4.00	12-19

1982 Little Trimmers - Keepsake

1982	Christmas Kitten 400QX454-3	Yr.Iss.	1983	4.00	38
1982	Christmas Owl 450QX131-4	Yr.Iss.	1982	4.50	35
1982	Cookie Mouse 450QX454-6	Yr.Iss.	1982	4.50	48-60
1982	Dove Love 450QX462-3	Yr.Iss.	1982	4.50	40-55
1982	Jingling Teddy 400QX477-6	Yr.Iss.	1982	4.00	25-40
1982	Merry Moose 550QX415-5	Yr.Iss.	1982	5.50	45-60
1982	Musical Angel 550QX459-6	Yr.Iss.	1982	5.50	115-125
1982	Perky Penguin 400QX409-5	Yr.Iss.	1982	4.00	35

1982 Property Ornaments - Keepsake

1982	Betsey Clark 850QX305-6	Yr.Iss.	1982	8.50	25
1982	Betsey Clark-10th ed. 450QX215-6	Yr.Iss.	1982	4.50	22-33
1982	Disney 450QX217-3	Yr.Iss.	1982	4.50	20-35
1982	The Divine Miss Piggy 1200QX425-5	Yr.Iss.	1982	12.00	125
1982	Joan Walsh Anglund 450QX219-3	Yr.Iss.	1982	4.50	8-20
1982	Kermit the Frog 1100QX495-6	Yr.Iss.	1982	11.00	70-95
1982	Mary Hamilton 450QX217-6	Yr.Iss.	1982	4.50	10-20
1982	Miss Piggy and Kermit 450QX218-3	Yr.Iss.	1982	4.50	35
1982	Muppets Party 450QX218-6	Yr.Iss.	1982	4.50	35
1982	Norman Rockwell 450QX202-3	Yr.Iss.	1982	4.50	25
1982	Norman Rockwell-3rd ed.850QX305-3	Yr.Iss.	1982	8.50	10-25
1982	Peanuts 450QX200-6	Yr.Iss.	1982	4.50	15-30

1983 Collectible Series - Keepsake

1983	The Bellringer-5th Ed. 1500QX 403-9	Yr.Iss.	1983	15.00	90-130
1983	Carrousel-6th Ed. 1100QX401-9	Yr.Iss.	1983	11.00	50
1983	Clothespin Soldier-2nd Ed. 500QX402-9	Yr.Iss.	1983	5.00	34-50
1983	Frosty Friends-4th Ed. 800QX400-7	Yr.Iss.	1983	8.00	275-300
1983	Here Comes Santa-5th Ed. 1300QX 403-7	Yr.Iss.	1983	13.00	250-295
1983	Holiday Wildlife-2nd Ed. 700QX 309-9	Yr.Iss.	1983	7.00	60-75
1983	Porcelain Bear-1st Ed. 700QX428-9	Yr.Iss.	1983	7.00	85-95
1983	Rocking Horse-3rd Ed. 1000QX417-7	Yr.Iss.	1983	10.00	250-295
1983	Snoopy and Friends -5th Ed.1300QX416-9	Yr.Iss.	1983	13.00	85
1983	Thimble - 6th Ed. 500QX401-7	Yr.Iss.	1983	5.00	35-45
1983	Tin Locomotive - 2nd Ed. 1300QX404-9	Yr.Iss.	1983	13.00	295

1983 Commemoratives - Keepsake

1983	25th Christmas Together 450QX224-7	Yr.Iss.	1983	4.50	20
1983	Baby's First Christmas 1400QX402-7	Yr.Iss.	1983	14.00	30-40
1983	Baby's First Christmas 450QX200-7	Yr.Iss.	1983	4.50	23-30
1983	Baby's First Christmas 450QX200-9	Yr.Iss.	1983	4.50	25
1983	Baby's First Christmas 700QX302-9	Yr.Iss.	1983	7.00	23
1983	Baby's First Christmas 750QX301-9	Yr.Iss.	1983	7.50	15
1983	Baby's Second Christmas 450QX226-7	Yr.Iss.	1983	4.50	30
1983	Child's Third Christmas 450QX226-9	Yr.Iss.	1983	4.50	25
1983	Daughter 450QX203-7	Yr.Iss.	1983	4.50	25-43
1983	First Christmas Together 450QX208-9	Yr.Iss.	1983	4.50	30
1983	First Christmas Together 600QX306-9	Yr.Iss.	1983	6.00	15-23
1983	First Christmas Together 600QX310-7	Yr.Iss.	1983	6.00	15-38
1983	First Christmas Together 750QX301-7	Yr.Iss.	1983	7.50	15-25
1983	First Christmas Together-Brass Locket 1500QX 432-9	Yr.Iss.	1983	15.00	30-40
1983	Friendship 450QX207-7	Yr.Iss.	1983	4.50	20
1983	Friendship 600QX305-9	Yr.Iss.	1983	6.00	10-20
1983	Godchild 450QX201-7	Yr.Iss.	1983	4.50	16
1983	Grandchild's First Christmas 400QX430-9	Yr.Iss.	1983	14.00	20-35
1983	Grandchild's First Christmas 600QX 312-9	Yr.Iss.	1983	6.00	10-22
1983	Granddaughter 450QX202-7	Yr.Iss.	1983	4.50	30
1983	Grandmother 450QX205-7	Yr.Iss.	1983	4.50	17
1983	Grandparents 650QX429-9	Yr.Iss.	1983	6.50	10-22
1983	Grandson 450QX201-9	Yr.Iss.	1983	4.50	15-30
1983	Love 1300QX422-7	Yr.Iss.	1983	13.00	20-40
1983	Love 450QX207-9	Yr.Iss.	1983	4.50	43
1983	Love 600QX305-7	Yr.Iss.	1983	6.00	9-20
1983	Love 600QX310-9	Yr.Iss.	1983	6.00	40
1983	Love Is a Song 450QX223-9	Yr.Iss.	1983	4.50	30
1983	Mom and Dad 650QX429-7	Yr.Iss.	1983	6.50	14-25
1983	Mother 600QX306-7	Yr.Iss.	1983	6.00	20-25
1983	New Home 450QX210-7	Yr.Iss.	1983	4.50	15-30
1983	Sister 450QX206-9	Yr.Iss.	1983	4.50	23
1983	Son 450QX202-9	Yr.Iss.	1983	4.50	25-35
1983	Teacher 450QX224-9	Yr.Iss.	1983	4.50	15
1983	Teacher 600QX304-9	Yr.Iss.	1983	6.00	15
1983	Tenth Christmas Together 650QX430-7	Yr.Iss.	1983	6.50	15-25

1983 Crown Classics - Keepsake

1983	Enameled Christmas Wreath 900QX 311-9	Yr.Iss.	1983	9.00	10-15
1983	Memories to Treasure 700QX303-7	Yr.Iss.	1983	7.00	25
1983	Mother and Child 750QX302-7	Yr.Iss.	1983	7.50	20-40

1983 Decorative Ball Ornaments - Keepsake

1983	1983 450QX220-9	Yr.Iss.	1983	4.50	27
1983	Angels 500QX219-7	Yr.Iss.	1983	5.00	24
1983	The Annunciation 450QX216-7	Yr.Iss.	1983	4.50	30
1983	Christmas Joy 450QX216-9	Yr.Iss.	1983	4.50	15-30
1983	Christmas Wonderland 450QX221-9	Yr.Iss.	1983	4.50	95
1983	Currier & Ives 450QX215-9	Yr.Iss.	1983	4.50	8-19
1983	Here Comes Santa 450QX217-7	Yr.Iss.	1983	4.50	37
1983	An Old Fashioned Christmas 450QX2217-9	Yr.Iss.	1983	4.50	25
1983	Oriental Butterflies 450QX218-7	Yr.Iss.	1983	4.50	30
1983	Season's Greeting 450QX219-9	Yr.Iss.	1983	4.50	10-22
1983	The Wise Men 450QX220-7	Yr.Iss.	1983	4.50	30-40

1983 Handcrafted Ornaments - Keepsake

1983	Angel Messenger 650QX408-7	Yr.Iss.	1983	6.50	85-95
1983	Baroque Angels 1300QX422-9	Yr.Iss.	1983	13.00	130
1983	Bell Wreath 650QX420-9	Yr.Iss.	1983	6.50	35
1983	Brass Santa 900QX423-9	Yr.Iss.	1983	9.00	23
1983	Caroling Owl 450QX411-7	Yr.Iss.	1983	4.50	32-40
1983	Christmas Kitten 400QX454-3	Yr.Iss.	1983	4.00	35
1983	Christmas Koala 400QX419-9	Yr.Iss.	1983	4.00	20-32
1983	Cycling Santa 2000QX435-5	Yr.Iss.	1983	20.00	195
1983	Embroidered Heart 650QX421-7	Yr.Iss.	1983	6.50	25
1983	Embroidered Stocking 650QX479-6	Yr.Iss.	1983	6.50	10-22
1983	Hitchhiking Santa 800QX424-7	Yr.Iss.	1983	8.00	40
1983	Holiday Puppy 350QX412-7	Yr.Iss.	1983	3.50	15-30
1983	Jack Frost 900QX407-9	Yr.Iss.	1983	9.00	60
1983	Jolly Santa 350QX425-9	Yr.Iss.	1983	3.50	20-35
1983	Madonna and Child 1200QX428-7	Yr.Iss.	1983	12.00	26-45
1983	Mailbox Kitten 650QX415-7	Yr.Iss.	1983	6.50	40-60
1983	Mountain Climbing Santa 650QX407-7	Yr.Iss.	1984	6.50	25-40
1983	Mouse in Bell 1000QX419-7	Yr.Iss.	1983	10.00	65
1983	Mouse on Cheese 650QX413-7	Yr.Iss.	1983	6.50	30-50
1983	Old-Fashioned Santa 1100QX409-9	Yr.Iss.	1983	11.00	55-65
1983	Peppermint Penguin 650QX408-9	Yr.Iss.	1983	6.50	30-50
1983	Porcelain Doll, Diana 900QX423-7	Yr.Iss.	1983	9.00	16-33
1983	Rainbow Angel 550QX416-7	Yr.Iss.	1983	5.50	112-125
1983	Santa's Many Faces 600QX311-6	Yr.Iss.	1983	6.00	30
1983	Santa's on His Way 1000QX426-9	Yr.Iss.	1983	10.00	35
1983	Santa's Workshop 1000QX450-3	Yr.Iss.	1983	10.00	60
1983	Scrimshaw Reindeer 800QX424-9	Yr.Iss.	1983	8.00	20-35
1983	Skating Rabbit 800QX409-7	Yr.Iss.	1983	8.00	55
1983	Ski Lift Santa 800QX418-7	Yr.Iss.	1983	8.00	50-75
1983	Skiing Fox 800QX420-7	Yr.Iss.	1983	8.00	30-38
1983	Sneaker Mouse 450QX400-9	Yr.Iss.	1983	4.50	30-40
1983	Tin Rocking Horse 650QX414-9	Yr.Iss.	1983	6.50	50
1983	Unicorn 1000QX426-7	Yr.Iss.	1983	10.00	40-65

1983 Holiday Highlights - Keepsake

1983	Christmas Stocking 600Qx303-9	Yr.Iss.	1983	6.00	20-40
1983	Star of Peace 600QX304-7	Yr.Iss.	1983	6.00	20
1983	Time for Sharing 600QX307-7	Yr.Iss.	1983	6.00	40

1983 Holiday Sculptures - Keepsake

1983	Heart 400QX307-9	Yr.Iss.	1983	4.00	50
1983	Santa 400QX308-7	Yr.Iss.	1983	4.00	20-35

1983 Property Ornaments - Keepsake

1983	Betsey Clark 650QX404-7	Yr.Iss.	1983	6.50	35
1983	Betsey Clark 900QX440-1	Yr.Iss.	1983	9.00	32
1983	Betsey Clark-11th Edition 450QX211-9	Yr.Iss.	1983	4.50	30
1983	Disney 450QX212-9	Yr.Iss.	1983	4.50	50
1983	Kermit the Frog 1100QX495-6	Yr.Iss.	1983	11.00	35
1983	Mary Hamilton 450QX213-7	Yr.Iss.	1983	4.50	40
1983	Miss Piggy 1300QX405-7	Yr.Iss.	1983	13.00	225
1983	The Muppets 450QX214-7	Yr.Iss.	1983	4.50	40-50
1983	Norman Rockwell 450QX215-7	Yr.Iss.	1983	4.50	50
1983	Norman Rockwell-4th Ed. 750QX 300-7	Yr.Iss.	1983	7.50	35
1983	Peanuts 450QX212-7	Yr.Iss.	1983	4.50	15-30
1983	Shirt Tales 450QX214-9	Yr.Iss.	1983	4.50	25

1984 Collectible Series - Keepsake

1984	Art Masterpiece- 1st Ed. 650QX349-4	Yr.Iss.	1984	6.50	13-19
1984	The Bellringer - 6th & Final Ed. 1500QX438-4	Yr.Iss.	1984	15.00	38
1984	Betsey Clark - 12th Ed. 500QX249-4	Yr.Iss.	1984	5.00	25-35
1984	Clothespin Soldier -3rd Ed. 500QX447-1	Yr.Iss.	1984	5.00	29
1984	Frosty Friends -5th Ed. 800QX437-1	Yr.Iss.	1984	8.00	65-85
1984	Here Comes Santa -6th Ed. 1300QX438-4	Yr.Iss.	1984	13.00	75-90
1984	Holiday Wildlife - 3rd Ed. 725QX 347-4	Yr.Iss.	1984	7.25	20-30
1984	Norman Rockwell - 5th Ed. 750QX341-1	Yr.Iss.	1984	7.50	24-35
1984	Nostalgic Houses and Shops-1st Ed. 1300QX 448-1	Yr.Iss.	1984	13.00	195-225
1984	Porcelain Bear- 2nd Ed. 700QX454-1	Yr.Iss.	1984	7.00	25-35
1984	Rocking Horse - 4th Ed. 1000QX435-4	Yr.Iss.	1984	10.00	70-80
1984	Thimble - 7th Ed. 500QX430-4	Yr.Iss.	1984	5.00	40-60
1984	Tin Locomotive- 3rd Ed. 1400QX440-4	Yr.Iss.	1984	14.00	75-90
1984	The Twelve Days of Christmas-1st Ed. 600QX 3484	Yr.Iss.	1984	6.00	275-425
1984	Wood Childhood Ornaments- 1st Ed. 650QX 439-4	Yr.Iss.	1984	6.50	40-50

1984 Commemoratives - Keepsake

1984	Baby's First Christmas 1400QX438-1	Yr.Iss.	1984	14.00	35-40
1984	Baby's First Christmas 1600QX904-1	Yr.Iss.	1984	16.00	50-55
1984	Baby's First Christmas 600QX340-1	Yr.Iss.	1984	6.00	25-40
1984	Baby's First Christmas 700QX300-1	Yr.Iss.	1984	7.00	20-25
1984	Baby's First Christmas-Boy 450QX240-4	Yr.Iss.	1984	4.50	27
1984	Baby's First Christmas-Girl 450QX340-1	Yr.Iss.	1984	4.50	20-40
1984	Baby's Second Christmas 450QX241-1	Yr.Iss.	1984	4.50	25-40
1984	Baby-sitter 450QX253-1	Yr.Iss.	1984	4.50	13
1984	Child's Third Christmas 450QX261-1	Yr.Iss.	1984	4.50	20
1984	Daughter 450QX244-4	Yr.Iss.	1984	4.50	25-35
1984	Father 600QX257-1	Yr.Iss.	1984	6.00	20
1984	First Christmas Together 1500QX436-4	Yr.Iss.	1984	15.00	20-40
1984	First Christmas Together 1600QX904-4	Yr.Iss.	1984	16.00	40
1984	First Christmas Together 450QX245-1	Yr.Iss.	1984	4.50	15-25
1984	First Christmas Together 600QX342-1	Yr.Iss.	1984	6.00	10-22
1984	First Christmas Together 750QX340-4	Yr.Iss.	1984	7.50	15-25
1984	Friendship 450QX248-1	Yr.Iss.	1984	4.50	18
1984	From Our Home to Yours 450QX248-4	Yr.Iss.	1984	4.50	50
1984	The Fun of Friendship 600QX343-1	Yr.Iss.	1984	6.00	20-35
1984	A Gift of Friendship 450QX260-4	Yr.Iss.	1984	4.50	25
1984	Godchild 450QX242-1	Yr.Iss.	1984	4.50	20
1984	Grandchild's First Christmas110QX460-1	Yr.Iss.	1984	11.00	15-30

CHRISTMAS ORNAMENTS

YEAR ISSUE		EDITION LIMIT	YEAR RETD.	ISSUE PRICE	QUOTE U.S.$
1984	Grandchild's First Christmas450QX257-4	Yr.Iss.	1984	4.50	15
1984	Granddaughter 450QX243-1	Yr.Iss.	1984	4.50	30
1984	Grandmother 450QX244-1	Yr.Iss.	1984	4.50	15
1984	Grandparents 450QX256-1	Yr.Iss.	1984	4.50	18
1984	Grandson 450QX242-4	Yr.Iss.	1984	4.50	20-30
1984	Gratitude 600QX344-4	Yr.Iss.	1984	6.00	12
1984	Heartful of Love 1000QX443-4	Yr.Iss.	1984	10.00	45
1984	Love 450QX255-4	Yr.Iss.	1984	4.50	15-25
1984	Love...the Spirit of Christmas450QX247-4	Yr.Iss.	1984	4.50	20-42
1984	The Miracle of Love 600QX342-4	Yr.Iss.	1984	6.00	25-35
1984	Mother 600QX343-4	Yr.Iss.	1984	6.00	18
1984	Mother and Dad 650QX258-1	Yr.Iss.	1984	6.50	15-25
1984	New Home 450QX245-4	Yr.Iss.	1984	4.50	95
1984	Sister 650QX259-4	Yr.Iss.	1984	6.50	20-32
1984	Son 450QX243-4	Yr.Iss.	1984	4.50	15-30
1984	Teacher 450QX249-1	Yr.Iss.	1984	4.50	15
1984	Ten Years Together 650QX258-4	Yr.Iss.	1984	6.50	15-25
1984	Twenty-Five Years Together650QX259-1	Yr.Iss.	1984	6.50	20

1984 Holiday Humor - Keepsake

YEAR ISSUE		EDITION LIMIT	YEAR RETD.	ISSUE PRICE	QUOTE U.S.$
1984	Bell Ringer Squirrel 1000QX443-1	Yr.Iss.	1984	10.00	20-40
1984	Christmas Owl 600QX444-1	Yr.Iss.	1984	6.00	20-32
1984	A Christmas Prayer 450QX246-1	Yr.Iss.	1984	4.50	10-23
1984	Flights of Fantasy 450QX256-4	Yr.Iss.	1984	4.50	20
1984	Fortune Cookie Elf 450QX452-4	Yr.Iss.	1984	4.50	35-40
1984	Frisbee Puppy 500QX444-4	Yr.Iss.	1984	5.00	40-50
1984	Marathon Santa 800QX456-4	Yr.Iss.	1984	8.00	40
1984	Mountain Climbing Santa 650QX407-7	Yr.Iss.	1984	6.50	35
1984	Musical Angel 550QX434-4	Yr.Iss.	1984	5.50	70
1984	Napping Mouse 550QX435-1	Yr.Iss.	1984	5.50	40-50
1984	Peppermint 1984 450Q452-1	Yr.Iss.	1984	4.50	25-50
1984	Polar Bear Drummer 450QX430-1	Yr.Iss.	1984	4.50	30
1984	Raccoon's Christmas 900QX447-7	Yr.Iss.	1984	9.00	35-55
1984	Reindeer Racetrack 450QX254-4	Yr.Iss.	1984	4.50	10-23
1984	Roller Skating Rabbit 500QX457-1	Yr.Iss.	1985	5.00	20-35
1984	Santa Mouse 450QX433-4	Yr.Iss.	1984	4.50	50
1984	Santa Star 550QX450-4	Yr.Iss.	1984	5.50	33-40
1984	Snowmobile Santa 650QX431-4	Yr.Iss.	1984	6.50	35-40
1984	Snowshoe Penguin 650QX453-1	Yr.Iss.	1984	6.50	55
1984	Snowy Seal 400QX450-1	Yr.Iss.	1985	4.00	25
1984	Three Kittens in a Mitten 800QX431-1	Yr.Iss.	1985	8.00	40-50

1984 Keepsake Magic Ornaments - Keepsake

YEAR ISSUE		EDITION LIMIT	YEAR RETD.	ISSUE PRICE	QUOTE U.S.$
1984	All Are Precious 800QLX704-1	Yr.Iss.	1985	8.00	15-25
1984	Brass Carrousel 900QLX707-1	Yr.Iss.	1984	9.00	95
1984	Christmas in the Forest 800QLX703-4	Yr.Iss.	1984	8.00	14-20
1984	City Lights 1000QLX701-4	Yr.Iss.	1984	10.00	50
1984	Nativity 1200 QLX700-1	Yr.Iss.	1985	12.00	20-30
1984	Santa's Arrival 1300QLX702-4	Yr.Iss.	1984	13.00	50-65
1984	Santa's Workshop 1300QLX700-4	Yr.Iss.	1985	13.00	45-62
1984	Stained Glass 800QLX703-1	Yr.Iss.	1984	8.00	19
1984	Sugarplum Cottage 1100QLX701-1	Yr.Iss.	1986	11.00	40-45
1984	Village Church 1500QLX702-1	Yr.Iss.	1985	15.00	35-50

1984 Limited Edition - Keepsake

YEAR ISSUE		EDITION LIMIT	YEAR RETD.	ISSUE PRICE	QUOTE U.S.$
1984	Classical Angel 2750QX459-1	Yr.Iss.	1984	28.00	105

1984 Property Ornaments - Keepsake

YEAR ISSUE		EDITION LIMIT	YEAR RETD.	ISSUE PRICE	QUOTE U.S.$
1984	Betsey Clark Angel 900QX462-4	Yr.Iss.	1984	9.00	20-35
1984	Currier & Ives 450QX250-1	Yr.Iss.	1984	4.50	35
1984	Disney 450QX250-4	Yr.Iss.	1984	4.50	25-38
1984	Katybeth 900QX463-1	Yr.Iss.	1984	9.00	20-33
1984	Kit 550QX453-4	Yr.Iss.	1984	5.50	28
1984	Muffin 550QX442-1	Yr.Iss.	1984	5.50	25-33
1984	The Muppets 450QX251-4	Yr.Iss.	1984	4.50	20-35
1984	Norman Rockwell 450QX251-4	Yr.Iss.	1984	4.50	25
1984	Peanuts 450QX252-1	Yr.Iss.	1984	4.50	20-33
1984	Shirt Tales 450QX252-4	Yr.Iss.	1984	4.50	20
1984	Snoopy and Woodstock 750QX439-1	Yr.Iss.	1984	7.50	90

1984 Traditional Ornaments - Keepsake

YEAR ISSUE		EDITION LIMIT	YEAR RETD.	ISSUE PRICE	QUOTE U.S.$
1984	Alpine Elf 600QX452-1	Yr.Iss.	1984	6.00	32-40
1984	Amanda 900QX432-1	Yr.Iss.	1984	9.00	20-30
1984	Chickadee 600QX451-4	Yr.Iss.	1984	6.00	33-40
1984	Christmas Memories Photoholder 650QX300-4	Yr.Iss.	1984	6.50	25
1984	Cuckoo Clock 1000QX455-1	Yr.Iss.	1984	10.00	47
1984	Gift of Music 1500QX451-1	Yr.Iss.	1984	15.00	65-95
1984	Holiday Friendship 1300QX445-1	Yr.Iss.	1984	13.00	30
1984	Holiday Jester 1100QX437-4	Yr.Iss.	1984	11.00	20-35
1984	Holiday Starburst 500QX253-4	Yr.Iss.	1984	5.00	20
1984	Madonna and Child 600QX344-1	Yr.Iss.	1984	6.00	40
1984	Needlepoint Wreath 650QX459-4	Yr.Iss.	1984	6.50	12
1984	Nostalgic Sled 600QX442-4	Yr.Iss.	1984	6.00	15-30
1984	Old Fashioned Rocking Horse 750QX346-4	Yr.Iss.	1984	7.50	10-20
1984	Peace on Earth 750QX341-4	Yr.Iss.	1984	7.50	30
1984	Santa 750QX458-4	Yr.Iss.	1984	7.50	15
1984	Santa Sulky Driver 900QX436-1	Yr.Iss.	1984	9.00	20-35
1984	A Savior is Born 450X254-1	Yr.Iss.	1984	4.50	33
1984	Twelve Days of Christmas1500QX 415-9	Yr.Iss.	1984	15.00	95
1984	Uncle Sam 600QX449-1	Yr.Iss.	1984	6.00	50
1984	White Christmas 1600QX905-1	Yr.Iss.	1984	16.00	70-95

1985 Collectible Series - Keepsake

YEAR ISSUE		EDITION LIMIT	YEAR RETD.	ISSUE PRICE	QUOTE U.S.$
1985	Art Masterpiece-2nd Ed.675QX377-2	Yr.Iss.	1985	6.75	15
1985	Betsey Clark-13th & final Ed.500QX263-2	Yr.Iss.	1985	5.00	25-35
1985	Clothespin Soldier-4th Ed.550QX471-5	Yr.Iss.	1985	5.50	20-30
1985	Frosty Friends-6th Ed.850QX482-2	Yr.Iss.	1985	8.50	63
1985	Here Comes Santa-7th Ed.1400QX496-5	Yr.Iss.	1985	14.00	60
1985	Holiday Wildlife-4th Ed.750QX376-5	Yr.Iss.	1985	7.50	20-30
1985	Miniature Creche-1st Ed.875QX482-5	Yr.Iss.	1985	8.75	30-40
1985	Norman Rockwell-6th Ed.750QX374-5	Yr.Iss.	1985	7.50	22-33
1985	Nostalgic Houses and Shops-(2nd Ed.)-1375QX497-5	Yr.Iss.	1985	13.75	80-110
1985	Porcelain Bear-3rd Ed.750QX479-2	Yr.Iss.	1985	7.50	38-60
1985	Rocking Horse-5th Ed.1075QX493-2	Yr.Iss.	1985	10.75	55-65
1985	Thimble-8th Ed.550QX472-5	Yr.Iss.	1985	5.50	24-35
1985	Tin Locomotive-4th Ed.1475QX497-2	Yr.Iss.	1985	14.75	54-80
1985	Twelve Days of Christmas-2nd Ed. 650QX371-2	Yr.Iss.	1985	6.50	70-75
1985	Windows of the World-1st Ed.975QX490-2	Yr.Iss.	1985	9.75	98-105
1985	Wood Childhood Ornaments-2nd Ed. 700QX472-2	Yr.Iss.	1985	7.00	45-50

1985 Commemoratives - Keepsake

YEAR ISSUE		EDITION LIMIT	YEAR RETD.	ISSUE PRICE	QUOTE U.S.$
1985	Baby Locket 1600QX401-2	Yr.Iss.	1985	16.00	35-38
1985	Baby's First Christmas 1500QX499-2	Yr.Iss.	1985	15.00	50-55
1985	Baby's First Christmas 1600QX499-5	Yr.Iss.	1985	16.00	45-55
1985	Baby's First Christmas 500QX260-2	Yr.Iss.	1985	5.00	25
1985	Baby's First Christmas 575QX370-2	Yr.Iss.	1985	5.75	21
1985	Baby's First Christmas 700QX478-2	Yr.Iss.	1985	7.00	18
1985	Baby's Second Christmas 600QX478-5	Yr.Iss.	1985	6.00	35
1985	Baby-sitter 475QX264-2	Yr.Iss.	1985	4.75	9
1985	Child's Third Christmas 600QX475-5	Yr.Iss.	1985	6.00	40-50
1985	Daughter 550QX503-2	Yr.Iss.	1985	5.50	15-25
1985	Father 650QX376-2	Yr.Iss.	1985	6.50	10
1985	First Christmas Together 1300QX493-5	Yr.Iss.	1985	13.00	25-40
1985	First Christmas Together 1675QX400-5	Yr.Iss.	1985	16.75	30
1985	First Christmas Together 475QX261-2	Yr.Iss.	1985	4.75	24
1985	First Christmas Together 675QX370-5	Yr.Iss.	1985	6.75	20
1985	First Christmas Together 800QX507-2	Yr.Iss.	1985	8.00	15
1985	Friendship 675QX378-5	Yr.Iss.	1985	6.75	17
1985	Friendship 775QX506-2	Yr.Iss.	1985	7.75	10
1985	From Our House to Yours 775QX520-2	Yr.Iss.	1985	7.75	10
1985	Godchild 675QX380-2	Yr.Iss.	1985	6.75	15
1985	Good Friends 475QX265-2	Yr.Iss.	1985	4.75	15-30
1985	Grandchild's First Christmas 1100QX495-5	Yr.Iss.	1985	11.00	15-24
1985	Grandchild's First Christmas 500QX260-5	Yr.Iss.	1985	5.00	15
1985	Granddaughter 475QX263-5	Yr.Iss.	1985	4.75	20-30
1985	Grandmother 475QX262-5	Yr.Iss.	1985	4.75	14
1985	Grandparents 700QX380-5	Yr.Iss.	1985	7.00	10
1985	Grandson 475QX262-2	Yr.Iss.	1985	4.75	30
1985	Heart Full of Love 675QX378-2	Yr.Iss.	1985	6.75	10-20
1985	Holiday Heart 800QX498-2	Yr.Iss.	1985	8.00	20-30
1985	Love at Christmas 575QX371-5	Yr.Iss.	1985	5.75	40
1985	Mother 675QX372-2	Yr.Iss.	1985	6.75	10-15
1985	Mother and Dad 775QX509-2	Yr.Iss.	1985	7.75	12-23
1985	New Home 475QX269-5	Yr.Iss.	1985	4.75	30
1985	Niece 575QX520-5	Yr.Iss.	1985	5.75	11
1985	Sister 725QX506-5	Yr.Iss.	1985	7.25	15-25
1985	Son 550QX502-5	Yr.Iss.	1985	5.50	35-45
1985	Special Friends 575QX372-5	Yr.Iss.	1985	5.75	10
1985	Teacher 600QX505-2	Yr.Iss.	1985	6.00	10-20
1985	Twenty-Five Years Together800QX500-5	Yr.Iss.	1985	8.00	20
1985	With Appreciation 675QX375-2	Yr.Iss.	1985	6.75	10

1985 Country Christmas Collection - Keepsake

YEAR ISSUE		EDITION LIMIT	YEAR RETD.	ISSUE PRICE	QUOTE U.S.$
1985	Country Goose 775QX518-5	Yr.Iss.	1985	7.75	10-16
1985	Old-Fashioned Doll 1450QX519-5	Yr.Iss.	1985	15.00	40
1985	Rocking Horse Memories 1000QX518-2	Yr.Iss.	1985	10.00	10-15
1985	Sheep at Christmas 825QX517-5	Yr.Iss.	1985	8.25	30
1985	Whirligig Santa 1250QX519-2	Yr.Iss.	1985	13.00	13-27

1985 Heirloom Christmas Collection - Keepsake

YEAR ISSUE		EDITION LIMIT	YEAR RETD.	ISSUE PRICE	QUOTE U.S.$
1985	Charming Angel 975QX512-5	Yr.Iss.	1985	9.75	15-25
1985	Keepsake Basket 1500QX514-5	Yr.Iss.	1985	15.00	15-20
1985	Lacy Heart 875QX511-2	Yr.Iss.	1985	8.75	20-30
1985	Snowflake 650QX510-5	Yr.Iss.	1985	6.50	10-23
1985	Victorian Lady 950QX513-2	Yr.Iss.	1985	9.50	25

1985 Holiday Humor - Keepsake

YEAR ISSUE		EDITION LIMIT	YEAR RETD.	ISSUE PRICE	QUOTE U.S.$
1985	Baker Elf 575QX491-2	Yr.Iss.	1985	5.75	20-30
1985	Beary Smooth Ride 650QX480-5	Yr.Iss.	1986	6.50	15-25
1985	Bottlecap Fun Bunnies 775QX481-5	Yr.Iss.	1985	7.75	30-35
1985	Candy Apple Mouse 750QX470-5	Yr.Iss.	1985	6.50	45-65
1985	Children in the Shoe 950QX490-5	Yr.Iss.	1985	9.50	30-50
1985	Dapper Penguin 500QX477-2	Yr.Iss.	1985	5.00	30
1985	Do Not Disturb Bear 775QX481-2	Yr.Iss.	1986	7.75	16-33
1985	Doggy in a Stocking 550QX474-2	Yr.Iss.	1985	5.50	25-40
1985	Engineering Mouse 550QX473-5	Yr.Iss.	1985	5.50	18-25
1985	Ice-Skating Owl 500QX476-5	Yr.Iss.	1985	5.00	15-25
1985	Kitty Mischief 500QX474-5	Yr.Iss.	1986	5.00	15-25
1985	Lamb in Legwarmers 700QX480-2	Yr.Iss.	1985	7.00	15-25
1985	Merry Mouse 450QX403-2	Yr.Iss.	1986	4.50	20-30
1985	Mouse Wagon 575QX476-2	Yr.Iss.	1985	5.75	48-60
1985	Nativity Scene 475QX264-5	Yr.Iss.	1985	4.75	30
1985	Night Before Christmas 1300QX449-4	Yr.Iss.	1985	13.00	30-45
1985	Roller Skating Rabbit 500QX457-1	Yr.Iss.	1985	5.00	19
1985	Santa's Ski Trip 1200QX496-2	Yr.Iss.	1985	12.00	40-60
1985	Skateboard Raccoon 650QX473-2	Yr.Iss.	1986	6.50	25-42
1985	Snow-Pitching Snowman 450QX470-2	Yr.Iss.	1986	4.50	25
1985	Snowy Seal 400QX450-1	Yr.Iss.	1985	4.00	16
1985	Soccer Beaver 650QX477-5	Yr.Iss.	1986	6.50	15-25
1985	Stardust Angel 575QX475-2	Yr.Iss.	1985	5.75	30-36
1985	Sun and Fun Santa 775QX492-5	Yr.Iss.	1985	7.75	40
1985	Swinging Angel Bell 1100QX492-5	Yr.Iss.	1985	11.00	40
1985	Three Kittens in a Mitten 800QX431-1	Yr.Iss.	1985	8.00	35
1985	Trumpet Panda 450QX471-2	Yr.Iss.	1985	4.50	15-25

1985 Keepsake Magic Ornaments - Keepsake

YEAR ISSUE		EDITION LIMIT	YEAR RETD.	ISSUE PRICE	QUOTE U.S.$
1985	All Are Precious 800QLX704-1	Yr.Iss.	1985	8.00	12-25
1985	Baby's First Christmas 1650QLX700-5	Yr.Iss.	1985	17.00	30-40
1985	Chris Mouse-1st edition1250QLX703-2	Yr.Iss.	1985	13.00	72-88
1985	Christmas Eve Visit 1200QLX710-5	Yr.Iss.	1985	12.00	33
1985	Katybeth 1075QLX710-2	Yr.Iss.	1985	10.75	30-43
1985	Little Red Schoolhouse 1575QLX711-2	Yr.Iss.	1985	15.75	70-95
1985	Love Wreath 850QLX702-5	Yr.Iss.	1985	8.50	19-30
1985	Mr. and Mrs. Santa 1450QLX705-2	Yr.Iss.	1986	15.00	73-90
1985	Nativity 1200 QLX700-1	Yr.Iss.	1985	12.00	18-28
1985	Santa's Workshop 1300QLX700-4	Yr.Iss.	1985	13.00	58
1985	Season of Beauty 800QLX712-2	Yr.Iss.	1985	8.00	20-30
1985	Sugarplum Cottage 1100QLX701-1	Yr.Iss.	1985	11.00	45
1985	Swiss Cheese Lane 1300QLX706-5	Yr.Iss.	1985	13.00	34-50
1985	Village Church 1500QLX702-1	Yr.Iss.	1985	15.00	35-50

1985 Limited Edition - Keepsake

YEAR ISSUE		EDITION LIMIT	YEAR RETD.	ISSUE PRICE	QUOTE U.S.$
1985	Heavenly Trumpeter 2750QX405-2	Yr.Iss.	1985	28.00	70-100

1985 Property Ornaments - Keepsake

YEAR ISSUE		EDITION LIMIT	YEAR RETD.	ISSUE PRICE	QUOTE U.S.$
1985	Betsey Clark 850QX508-5	Yr.Iss.	1985	8.50	30
1985	A Disney Christmas 475QX271-2	Yr.Iss.	1985	4.75	30
1985	Fraggle Rock Holiday 475QX265-5	Yr.Iss.	1985	4.75	23
1985	Hugga Bunch 500QX271-5	Yr.Iss.	1985	5.00	30
1985	Kit the Shepherd 575QX484-5	Yr.Iss.	1985	5.75	24
1985	Merry Shirt Tales 475QX267-2	Yr.Iss.	1985	4.75	20
1985	Muffin the Angel 575QX483-5	Yr.Iss.	1985	5.75	24
1985	Norman Rockwell 475QX266-2	Yr.Iss.	1985	4.75	30
1985	Peanuts 475QX266-5	Yr.Iss.	1985	4.75	30
1985	Rainbow Brite and Friends 475QX 268-2	Yr.Iss.	1985	4.75	25
1985	Snoopy and Woodstock 750QX491-5	Yr.Iss.	1985	7.50	42-75

1985 Traditional Ornaments - Keepsake

YEAR ISSUE		EDITION LIMIT	YEAR RETD.	ISSUE PRICE	QUOTE U.S.$
1985	Candle Cameo 675QX374-2	Yr.Iss.	1985	6.75	15
1985	Christmas Treats 550QX507-5	Yr.Iss.	1985	5.50	18
1985	Nostalgic Sled 600QX442-4	Yr.Iss.	1985	6.00	20
1985	Old-Fashioned Wreath 750QX373-5	Yr.Iss.	1985	7.50	22
1985	Peaceful Kingdom 575QX373-2	Yr.Iss.	1985	5.75	30
1985	Porcelain Bird 650QX479-5	Yr.Iss.	1985	6.50	30
1985	Santa Pipe 950QX494-2	Yr.Iss.	1985	9.50	25
1985	Sewn Photoholder 700QX379-5	Yr.Iss.	1985	7.00	35
1985	The Spirit of Santa Claus -Special Ed. 2250QX 498-5	Yr.Iss.	1985	23.00	75-95

1986 Christmas Medley Collection - Keepsake

YEAR ISSUE		EDITION LIMIT	YEAR RETD.	ISSUE PRICE	QUOTE U.S.$
1986	Christmas Guitar 700QX512-6	Yr.Iss.	1986	7.00	20-25
1986	Favorite Tin Drum 850QX514-3	Yr.Iss.	1986	8.50	30
1986	Festive Treble Clef 875QX513-3	Yr.Iss.	1986	8.75	10-28
1986	Holiday Horn 800QX514-6	Yr.Iss.	1986	8.00	20-33
1986	Joyful Carolers 975QX513-6	Yr.Iss.	1986	9.75	35-40

1986 Collectible Series - Keepsake

YEAR ISSUE		EDITION LIMIT	YEAR RETD.	ISSUE PRICE	QUOTE U.S.$
1986	Art Masterpiece-3rd & Final Ed. 675QX350-6	Yr.Iss.	1986	6.75	20-33

CHRISTMAS ORNAMENTS

YEAR ISSUE		EDITION LIMIT	YEAR RETD.	ISSUE PRICE	QUOTE U.S.$
1986	Betsey Clark: Home for Christmas-1st Ed. 500QX277-6	Yr.Iss.	1986	5.00	30-35
1986	Clothespin Soldier-5th Ed. 550QX406-3	Yr.Iss.	1986	5.50	20-30
1986	Frosty Friends-7th Ed. 850QX405-3	Yr.Iss.	1986	8.50	50-70
1986	Here Comes Santa-8th Ed. 1400QX404-3	Yr.Iss.	1986	14.00	45-65
1986	Holiday Wildlife-5th Ed. 750QX321-6	Yr.Iss.	1986	7.50	20-30
1986	Miniature Creche-2nd Ed. 900QX407-6	Yr.Iss.	1986	9.00	55
1986	Mr. and Mrs. Claus-1st Ed. 1300QX402-6	Yr.Iss.	1986	13.00	100-125
1986	Norman Rockwell-7th Ed. 775QX321-3	Yr.Iss.	1986	7.75	20-30
1986	Nostalgic Houses and Shops-3rd Ed. 1375QX403-3	Yr.Iss.	1986	13.75	255
1986	Porcelain Bear-4th Ed. 775QX405-6	Yr.Iss.	1986	7.75	28-45
1986	Reindeer Champs-1st Ed. 750QX422-3	Yr.Iss.	1986	7.50	130-150
1986	Rocking Horse-6th Ed. 1075QX401-6	Yr.Iss.	1986	10.75	55-65
1986	Thimble-9th Ed. 575QX406-6	Yr.Iss.	1986	5.75	20-30
1986	Tin Locomotive-5th Ed. 1475QX403-6	Yr.Iss.	1986	14.75	50-75
1986	Twelve Days of Christmas-3rd Ed. 650QX378-6	Yr.Iss.	1986	6.50	40-50
1986	Windows of the World-2nd Ed. 1000QX408-3	Yr.Iss.	1986	10.00	60-95
1986	Wood Childhood Ornaments-3rd Ed. 750QX407-3	Yr.Iss.	1986	7.50	20-50

1986 Commemoratives - Keepsake

YEAR ISSUE		EDITION LIMIT	YEAR RETD.	ISSUE PRICE	QUOTE U.S.$
1986	Baby Locket 1600QX412-3	Yr.Iss.	1986	16.00	19-27
1986	Baby's First Christmas 550QX271-3	Yr.Iss.	1986	5.50	25
1986	Baby's First Christmas 600QX380-3	Yr.Iss.	1986	6.00	15-25
1986	Baby's First Christmas 900QX412-6	Yr.Iss.	1986	9.00	32-38
1986	Baby's First Christmas Photoholder 800QX379-2	Yr.Iss.	1986	8.00	17
1986	Baby's Second Christmas 650QX413-3	Yr.Iss.	1986	6.50	22-30
1986	Baby-Sitter 475QX275-6	Yr.Iss.	1986	4.75	10
1986	Child's Third Christmas 650QX413-6	Yr.Iss.	1986	6.50	20-27
1986	Daughter 575QX430-6	Yr.Iss.	1986	5.75	35-50
1986	Father 650QX431-3	Yr.Iss.	1986	6.50	12
1986	Fifty Years Together 1000QX400-6	Yr.Iss.	1986	10.00	20
1986	First Christmas Together 1200QX409-6	Yr.Iss.	1986	12.00	30-35
1986	First Christmas Together 1600QX400-3	Yr.Iss.	1986	16.00	28
1986	First Christmas Together 475QX270-3	Yr.Iss.	1986	4.75	10-20
1986	First Christmas Together 7000QX379-3	Yr.Iss.	1986	7.00	10-20
1986	Friends Are Fun 475QX272-3	Yr.Iss.	1986	4.75	40
1986	Friendship Greeting 800QX427-3	Yr.Iss.	1986	8.00	15
1986	Friendship's Gift 600QX381-6	Yr.Iss.	1986	6.00	15
1986	From Our Home to Yours 600QX383-3	Yr.Iss.	1986	6.00	15
1986	Godchild 475QX271-6	Yr.Iss.	1986	4.75	15
1986	Grandchild's First Christmas 1000QX411-6	Yr.Iss.	1986	10.00	14
1986	Granddaughter 475QX273-6	Yr.Iss.	1986	4.75	25
1986	Grandmother 475QX274-3	Yr.Iss.	1986	4.75	12
1986	Grandparents 750QX432-3	Yr.Iss.	1986	7.50	10-23
1986	Grandson 475QX273-3	Yr.Iss.	1986	4.75	12-24
1986	Gratitude 600QX432-6	Yr.Iss.	1986	6.00	10
1986	Husband 800QX383-6	Yr.Iss.	1986	8.00	15
1986	Joy of Friends 675QX382-3	Yr.Iss.	1986	6.75	18
1986	Loving Memories 900QX409-3	Yr.Iss.	1986	9.00	35
1986	Mother 700QX382-6	Yr.Iss.	1986	7.00	12-21
1986	Mother and Dad 750QX431-6	Yr.Iss.	1986	7.50	10-20
1986	Nephew 675QX381-3	Yr.Iss.	1986	6.25	7-12
1986	New Home 475QX274-6	Yr.Iss.	1986	4.75	65
1986	Niece 600QX426-6	Yr.Iss.	1986	6.00	10
1986	Season of the Heart 4750QX270-6	Yr.Iss.	1986	4.75	10-18
1986	Sister 675QX380-6	Yr.Iss.	1986	6.75	15
1986	Son 575QX430-3	Yr.Iss.	1986	5.75	30-35
1986	Sweetheart 1100QX408-6	Yr.Iss.	1986	11.00	50-70
1986	Teacher 475QX275-3	Yr.Iss.	1986	4.75	9
1986	Ten Years Together 750QX401-3	Yr.Iss.	1986	7.50	25
1986	Timeless Love 600QX379-6	Yr.Iss.	1986	6.00	30
1986	Twenty-Five Years Together800QX410-3	Yr.Iss.	1986	8.00	25

1986 Country Treasures Collection - Keepsake

YEAR ISSUE		EDITION LIMIT	YEAR RETD.	ISSUE PRICE	QUOTE U.S.$
1986	Country Sleigh 1000QX511-3	Yr.Iss.	1986	10.00	29
1986	Little Drummers 1250QX511-6	Yr.Iss.	1986	12.50	20-35
1986	Nutcracker Santa 1000QX512-3	Yr.Iss.	1986	10.00	30-50
1986	Remembering Christmas 865QX510-6	Yr.Iss.	1986	8.75	30
1986	Welcome, Christmas 825QX510-3	Yr.Iss.	1986	8.25	20-35

1986 Holiday Humor - Keepsake

YEAR ISSUE		EDITION LIMIT	YEAR RETD.	ISSUE PRICE	QUOTE U.S.$
1986	Acorn Inn 850QX424-3	Yr.Iss.	1986	8.50	25-30
1986	Beary Smooth Ride 650QX480-5	Yr.Iss.	1986	6.50	20
1986	Chatty Penguin 575QX417-6	Yr.Iss.	1986	5.75	15-22
1986	Cookies for Santa 450QX414-6	Yr.Iss.	1986	4.50	17-30
1986	Do Not Disturb Bear 775QX481-2	Yr.Iss.	1986	7.75	15-25
1986	Happy Christmas to Owl 600QX418-3	Yr.Iss.	1986	6.00	14-25
1986	Heavenly Dreamer 575QX417-3	Yr.Iss.	1986	5.75	21-35
1986	Jolly Hiker 500QX483-2	Yr.Iss.	1987	5.00	17-30
1986	Kitty Mischief 500QX474-5	Yr.Iss.	1986	5.00	25
1986	Li'l Jingler 675QX419-3	Yr.Iss.	1987	6.75	22-40
1986	Merry Koala 500QX415-3	Yr.Iss.	1987	5.00	23
1986	Merry Mouse 450QX403-2	Yr.Iss.	1986	4.50	22
1986	Mouse in the Moon 550QX416-6	Yr.Iss.	1987	5.50	28-45
1986	Open Me First 725QX422-6	Yr.Iss.	1986	7.25	31
1986	Playful Possum 1100QX425-3	Yr.Iss.	1986	11.00	30-35
1986	Popcorn Mouse 675QX421-3	Yr.Iss.	1986	6.75	40-55
1986	Puppy's Best Friend 650QX420-3	Yr.Iss.	1986	6.50	25-30
1986	Rah Rah Rabbit 700QX421-6	Yr.Iss.	1986	7.00	40
1986	Santa's Hot Tub 1200QX426-3	Yr.Iss.	1986	12.00	55-60
1986	Skateboard Raccoon 650QX473-2	Yr.Iss.	1986	6.50	40
1986	Ski Tripper 675QX420-6	Yr.Iss.	1986	6.75	12-22
1986	Snow Buddies 800QX423-6	Yr.Iss.	1986	8.00	38
1986	Snow-Pitching Snowman 450QX470-2	Yr.Iss.	1986	4.50	23
1986	Soccer Beaver 650QX477-5	Yr.Iss.	1986	6.50	25
1986	Special Delivery 500QX415-6	Yr.Iss.	1986	5.00	17-30
1986	Tipping the Scales 675QX418-6	Yr.Iss.	1986	6.75	15-30
1986	Touchdown Santa 800QX423-3	Yr.Iss.	1986	8.00	42
1986	Treetop Trio 975QX424-6	Yr.Iss.	1987	11.00	32
1986	Walnut Shell Rider 600QX419-6	Yr.Iss.	1987	6.00	15-26
1986	Wynken, Blynken and Nod 975QX424-6	Yr.Iss.	1986	9.75	42

1986 Lighted Ornament Collection - Keepsake

YEAR ISSUE		EDITION LIMIT	YEAR RETD.	ISSUE PRICE	QUOTE U.S.$
1986	Baby's First Christmas1950QLX710-3	Yr.Iss.	1986	19.50	45
1986	Chris Mouse-2nd Edition1300QLX705-6	Yr.Iss.	1986	13.00	75
1986	Christmas Classics-1st Edition 1750QLX704-3	Yr.Iss.	1986	17.50	85
1986	Christmas Sleigh Ride 2450QLX701-2	Yr.Iss.	1986	24.50	120-145
1986	First Christmas Together2200QLX707-3	Yr.Iss.	1986	14.00	43
1986	General Store 1575QLX705-3	Yr.Iss.	1986	15.75	43-60
1986	Gentle Blessings 1500QLX708-3	Yr.Iss.	1986	15.00	110-175
1986	Keep on Glowin' 1000QLX707-6	Yr.Iss.	1987	10.00	37-50
1986	Merry Christmas Bell 850QLX709-3	Yr.Iss.	1986	8.50	15-25
1986	Mr. and Mrs. Santa 1450QLX705-2	Yr.Iss.	1986	14.50	65-95
1986	Santa and Sparky-1st Edition 2200QLX703-3	Yr.Iss.	1986	22.00	95
1986	Santa's On His Way 1500QLX711-5	Yr.Iss.	1986	15.00	63-75
1986	Santa's Snack 100QLX706-6	Yr.Iss.	1986	10.00	40-58
1986	Sharing Friendship 850QLX706-3	Yr.Iss.	1986	8.50	17
1986	Sugarplum Cottage 1100QLX701-1	Yr.Iss.	1986	11.00	45
1986	Village Express 2450QLX707-2	Yr.Iss.	1987	24.50	87-120

1986 Limited Edition - Keepsake

YEAR ISSUE		EDITION LIMIT	YEAR RETD.	ISSUE PRICE	QUOTE U.S.$
1986	Magical Unicorn 2750QX429-3	Yr.Iss.	1986	27.50	85-100

1986 Property Ornaments - Keepsake

YEAR ISSUE		EDITION LIMIT	YEAR RETD.	ISSUE PRICE	QUOTE U.S.$
1986	Heathcliff 750QX436-3	Yr.Iss.	1986	7.50	20-33
1986	Katybeth 700QX435-3	Yr.Iss.	1986	7.00	25
1986	Norman Rockwell 475QX276-3	Yr.Iss.	1986	4.75	26
1986	Paddington Bear 600QX435-6	Yr.Iss.	1986	6.00	25-40
1986	Peanuts 475QX276-6	Yr.Iss.	1986	4.75	30
1986	Shirt Tales Parade 475QX277-3	Yr.Iss.	1986	4.75	18
1986	Snoopy and Woodstock 800QX434-6	Yr.Iss.	1986	8.00	45-50
1986	The Statue of Liberty 600QX384-3	Yr.Iss.	1986	6.00	10-25

1986 Special Edition - Keepsake

YEAR ISSUE		EDITION LIMIT	YEAR RETD.	ISSUE PRICE	QUOTE U.S.$
1986	Jolly St. Nick 2250QX429-6	Yr.Iss.	1986	22.50	50-75

1986 Traditional Ornaments - Keepsake

YEAR ISSUE		EDITION LIMIT	YEAR RETD.	ISSUE PRICE	QUOTE U.S.$
1986	Bluebird 725QX428-3	Yr.Iss.	1986	7.25	40-50
1986	Christmas Beauty 600QX322-3	Yr.Iss.	1986	6.00	10
1986	Glowing Christmas Tree 700QX428-6	Yr.Iss.	1986	7.00	15
1986	Heirloom Snowflake 675QX515-3	Yr.Iss.	1986	6.75	10-22
1986	Holiday Jingle Bell 1600QX404-6	Yr.Iss.	1986	16.00	30-54
1986	The Magi 475QX272-6	Yr.Iss.	1986	4.75	20
1986	Mary Emmerling: American Country Collection 795QX275-2	Yr.Iss.	1986	7.95	25
1986	Memories to Cherish 750QX427-6	Yr.Iss.	1986	7.50	25
1986	Star Brighteners 600QX322-6	Yr.Iss.	1986	6.00	17

1987 Artists' Favorites - Keepsake

YEAR ISSUE		EDITION LIMIT	YEAR RETD.	ISSUE PRICE	QUOTE U.S.$
1987	Beary Special 475QX455-7	Yr.Iss.	1987	4.75	20-30
1987	December Showers 550QX448-7	Yr.Iss.	1987	5.50	25-38
1987	Three Men in a Tub 800QX454-7	Yr.Iss.	1987	8.00	20-30
1987	Wee Chimney Sweep 625QX451-9	Yr.Iss.	1987	6.25	15-30

1987 Christmas Pizzazz Collection - Keepsake

YEAR ISSUE		EDITION LIMIT	YEAR RETD.	ISSUE PRICE	QUOTE U.S.$
1987	Christmas Fun Puzzle 800QX467-9	Yr.Iss.	1987	8.00	16-30
1987	Doc Holiday 800QX467-7	Yr.Iss.	1987	8.00	43
1987	Happy Holidata 650QX471-7	Yr.Iss.	1988	6.50	15-30
1987	Holiday Hourglass 800QX470-7	Yr.Iss.	1987	8.00	25
1987	Jolly Follies 850QX466-9	Yr.Iss.	1987	8.50	40
1987	Mistletoad 700QX468-7	Yr.Iss.	1988	7.00	30
1987	St. Louie Nick 775QX453-9	Yr.Iss.	1988	7.75	20-32

1987 Collectible Series - Keepsake

YEAR ISSUE		EDITION LIMIT	YEAR RETD.	ISSUE PRICE	QUOTE U.S.$
1987	Betsey Clark: Home for Christmas-2nd Ed. 500QX272-7	Yr.Iss.	1987	5.00	15-25
1987	Clothespin Soldier-6th & Final Ed. 550QX480-7	Yr.Iss.	1987	5.50	20-30
1987	Collector's Plate-1st Ed. 800QX481-7	Yr.Iss.	1987	8.00	65-75
1987	Frosty Friends -8th Ed. 850QX440-9	Yr.Iss.	1987	8.50	55-60
1987	Here Comes Santa-9th Ed. 1400QX484-7	Yr.Iss.	1987	14.00	45-70
1987	Holiday Heirloom-1st Ed./ limited ed. 2500QX485-7	Yr.Iss.	1987	25.00	50
1987	Holiday Wildlife -6th Ed. 750QX371-7	Yr.Iss.	1987	7.50	15-25
1987	Miniature Creche -3rd Ed. 900QX481-9	Yr.Iss.	1987	9.00	24-38
1987	Mr. and Mrs. Claus-2nd Ed. 132QX483-7	Yr.Iss.	1987	13.25	55-75
1987	Norman Rockwell-8th Ed.775QX370-7	Yr.Iss.	1987	7.75	15-25
1987	Nostalgic Houses and Shops-4th Ed. 483QX483-9	Yr.Iss.	1987	14.00	65-75
1987	Porcelain Bear-5th Ed. 775QX442-7	Yr.Iss.	1987	7.75	25-40
1987	Reindeer Champs-2nd Ed. 750QX480-9	Yr.Iss.	1987	7.50	45-55
1987	Rocking Horse-7th Ed.1075QX482-9	Yr.Iss.	1987	10.75	40-60
1987	Thimble-10th Ed. 575QX441-9	Yr.Iss.	1987	5.75	25-30
1987	Tin Locomotive-6th Ed. 1475QX484-9	Yr.Iss.	1987	14.75	65
1987	Twelve Days of Christmas-4th Ed. 650QX370-9	Yr.Iss.	1987	6.50	35-40
1987	Windows of the World-3rd Ed. 1000QX482-7	Yr.Iss.	1987	10.00	25-40
1987	Wood Childhood Ornaments-4th Ed. 750QX441-7	Yr.Iss.	1987	7.50	17-27

1987 Commemoratives - Keepsake

YEAR ISSUE		EDITION LIMIT	YEAR RETD.	ISSUE PRICE	QUOTE U.S.$
1987	Baby Locket 1500QX461-7	Yr.Iss.	1987	15.00	15-30
1987	Baby's First Christmas 600QX372-9	Yr.Iss.	1987	6.00	20-25
1987	Baby's First Christmas 975QX411-3	Yr.Iss.	1987	9.75	30-35
1987	Baby's First Christmas Photoholder 750QX4661-9	Yr.Iss.	1987	7.50	30
1987	Baby's First Christmas-Baby Boy475QX274-9	Yr.Iss.	1987	4.75	20-27
1987	Baby's First Christmas-Baby Girl 475QX274-7	Yr.Iss.	1987	4.75	22
1987	Baby's Second Christmas 575QX460-7	Yr.Iss.	1987	5.75	32
1987	Babysitter 475QX279-7	Yr.Iss.	1987	4.75	10-20
1987	Child's Third Christmas 575QX459-9	Yr.Iss.	1987	5.75	30
1987	Dad 600QX462-9	Yr.Iss.	1987	6.00	20-40
1987	Daughter 575QX463-7	Yr.Iss.	1987	5.75	26-35
1987	Fifty Years Together 800QX443-7	Yr.Iss.	1987	8.00	25
1987	First Christmas Together 1500QX446-9	Yr.Iss.	1987	15.00	30
1987	First Christmas Together 475QX272-9	Yr.Iss.	1987	4.75	10-22
1987	First Christmas Together 650QX371-9	Yr.Iss.	1987	6.50	10-20
1987	First Christmas Together 800QX445-9	Yr.Iss.	1987	8.00	38
1987	First Christmas Together 950QX446-7	Yr.Iss.	1987	9.50	30-40
1987	From Our Home to Yours 475QX279-9	Yr.Iss.	1987	4.75	50
1987	Godchild 475QX276-7	Yr.Iss.	1987	4.75	20
1987	Grandchild's First Christmas900QX460-9	Yr.Iss.	1987	9.00	24
1987	Granddaughter 600QX374-7	Yr.Iss.	1987	6.00	15-25
1987	Grandmother 475QX277-9	Yr.Iss.	1987	4.75	15
1987	Grandparents 475QX277-7	Yr.Iss.	1987	4.75	18
1987	Grandson 475QX276-9	Yr.Iss.	1987	4.75	20-27
1987	Heart in Blossom 600QX372-7	Yr.Iss.	1987	6.00	25
1987	Holiday Greetings 600QX375-7	Yr.Iss.	1987	6.00	13
1987	Husband 700QX373-9	Yr.Iss.	1987	7.00	12
1987	Love is Everywhere 475QX278-7	Yr.Iss.	1987	4.75	25
1987	Mother 650QX373-7	Yr.Iss.	1987	6.50	12-20
1987	Mother and Dad 700QX462-7	Yr.Iss.	1987	7.00	22
1987	New Home 600QX376-7	Yr.Iss.	1987	6.00	30
1987	Niece 475QX275-9	Yr.Iss.	1987	4.75	13
1987	Sister 600QX474-7	Yr.Iss.	1987	6.00	15
1987	Son 575QX463-9	Yr.Iss.	1987	5.75	45
1987	Sweetheart 1100QX447-9	Yr.Iss.	1987	11.00	20-30
1987	Teacher 575QX466-7	Yr.Iss.	1987	5.75	21
1987	Ten Years Together 700QX444-7	Yr.Iss.	1987	7.00	25
1987	Time for Friends 475QX280-7	Yr.Iss.	1987	4.75	22
1987	Twenty-Five Years Together750QX443-9	Yr.Iss.	1987	7.50	15-30
1987	Warmth of Friendship 600QX375-9	Yr.Iss.	1987	6.00	12
1987	Word of Love 800QX447-7	Yr.Iss.	1987	8.00	10-30

1987 Holiday Humor - Keepsake

YEAR ISSUE		EDITION LIMIT	YEAR RETD.	ISSUE PRICE	QUOTE U.S.$
1987	Bright Christmas Dreams 725QX440-7	Yr.Iss.	1987	7.25	75-85
1987	Chocolate Chipmunk 600QX456-7	Yr.Iss.	1987	6.00	45-55
1987	Christmas Cuddle 575QX453-7	Yr.Iss.	1987	5.75	25-35
1987	Dr. Seuss: The Grinch's Christmas 475QX278-3	Yr.Iss.	1987	4.75	45-60

CHRISTMAS ORNAMENTS

YEAR ISSUE		EDITION LIMIT	YEAR RETD.	ISSUE PRICE	QUOTE U.S.$
1987	Fudge Forever 500QX449-7	Yr.Iss.	1987	5.00	25-40
1987	Happy Santa 475QX456-9	Yr.Iss.	1987	4.75	29
1987	Hot Dogger 650QX471-9	Yr.Iss.	1987	6.50	25-30
1987	Icy Treat 450QX450-9	Yr.Iss.	1987	4.50	20-30
1987	Jack Frosting 700QX449-9	Yr.Iss.	1987	7.00	30-50
1987	Jammie Pies 475QX283-9	Yr.Iss.	1987	4.75	18
1987	Jogging Through the Snow725QX457-7	Yr.Iss.	1987	7.25	22-40
1987	Jolly Hiker 500QX483-2	Yr.Iss.	1987	5.00	18
1987	Joy Ride 1150QX440-7	Yr.Iss.	1987	11.50	42-50
1987	Let It Snow 650QX458-9	Yr.Iss.	1987	6.50	15-24
1987	Li'l Jingler 675QX419-3	Yr.Iss.	1987	6.75	22-36
1987	Merry Koala 500QX415-3	Yr.Iss.	1987	5.00	17
1987	Mouse in the Moon 550QX416-6	Yr.Iss.	1987	5.50	21
1987	Nature's Decorations 475QX273-9	Yr.Iss.	1987	4.75	35
1987	Night Before Christmas 650QX451-7	Yr.Iss.	1988	6.50	19-33
1987	Owliday Wish 650QX455-9	Yr.Iss.	1988	6.50	14-25
1987	Paddington Bear 550QX472-7	Yr.Iss.	1987	5.50	25-35
1987	Peanuts 475QX281-9	Yr.Iss.	1987	4.75	33
1987	Pretty Kitten 1100QX448-9	Yr.Iss.	1987	11.00	35
1987	Raccoon Biker 700QX458-7	Yr.Iss.	1987	7.00	15-30
1987	Reindoggy 575QX452-7	Yr.Iss.	1988	5.75	35-45
1987	Santa at the Bat 775QX457-9	Yr.Iss.	1987	7.75	20-30
1987	Seasoned Greetings 625QX454-9	Yr.Iss.	1987	6.25	15-30
1987	Sleepy Santa 625QX450-7	Yr.Iss.	1987	6.25	35-40
1987	Snoopy and Woodstock 725QX472-9	Yr.Iss.	1987	7.25	40-50
1987	Spots 'n Stripes 550QX452-9	Yr.Iss.	1987	5.50	15-25
1987	Treetop Dreams 675QX459-7	Yr.Iss.	1988	6.75	15-30
1987	Treetop Trio 1100QX425-6	Yr.Iss.	1987	11.00	25
1987	Walnut Shell Rider 600QX419-6	Yr.Iss.	1987	6.00	18

1987 Keepsake Collector's Club - Keepsake

YEAR ISSUE		EDITION LIMIT	YEAR RETD.	ISSUE PRICE	QUOTE U.S.$
1987	Carrousel Reindeer QXC580-7	Yr.Iss.	1987	Unkn.	55-65
1987	Wreath of Memories QXC580-9	Yr.Iss.	1988	Unkn.	48-55

1987 Keepsake Magic Ornaments - Keepsake

YEAR ISSUE		EDITION LIMIT	YEAR RETD.	ISSUE PRICE	QUOTE U.S.$
1987	Angelic Messengers 1875QLX711-3	Yr.Iss.	1987	18.75	53-60
1987	Baby's First Christmas 1350QLX704-9	Yr.Iss.	1987	13.50	32-55
1987	Bright Noel 700QLX705-9	Yr.Iss.	1987	7.00	18-33
1987	Chris Mouse-3rd Edition1100QLX705-7	Yr.Iss.	1987	11.00	60
1987	Christmas Classics-2nd Ed.1600ZLX702-9	Yr.Iss.	1987	16.00	50-75
1987	Christmas Morning 2450QLX701-3	Yr.Iss.	1988	24.50	33-50
1987	First Christmas Together 1150QLX708-7	Yr.Iss.	1987	11.50	45-50
1987	Good Cheer Blimp 1600QLX704-6	Yr.Iss.	1987	16.00	52-59
1987	Keeping Cozy 1175QLX704-7	Yr.Iss.	1987	11.75	30-35
1987	Lacy Brass Snowflake 1150QLX709-7	Yr.Iss.	1987	11.50	16-30
1987	Loving Holiday 2200QLX701-6	Yr.Iss.	1987	22.00	38-55
1987	Memories are Forever Photoholder 850QLX706-7	Yr.Iss.	1987	8.50	33
1987	Meowy Christmas 1000QLX708-9	Yr.Iss.	1987	10.00	40-63
1987	Santa and Sparky-2nd Edition1950QLX701-9	Yr.Iss.	1987	19.50	65-75
1987	Season for Friendship 850QLX706-9	Yr.Iss.	1987	8.50	11-20
1987	Train Station 1275QLX703-9	Yr.Iss.	1987	12.75	41-50

1987 Lighted Ornament Collection - Keepsake

YEAR ISSUE		EDITION LIMIT	YEAR RETD.	ISSUE PRICE	QUOTE U.S.$
1987	Keep on Glowin' 1000QLX707-6	Yr.Iss.	1987	10.00	37-50
1987	Village Express 2450QLX707-2	Yr.Iss.	1987	24.50	87-120

1987 Limited Edition - Keepsake

YEAR ISSUE		EDITION LIMIT	YEAR RETD.	ISSUE PRICE	QUOTE U.S.$
1987	Christmas is Gentle 1750QX444-9	Yr.Iss.	1987	17.50	35-75
1987	Christmas Time Mime 2750QX442-9	Yr.Iss.	1987	27.50	46-65

1987 Old-Fashioned Christmas Collection - Keepsake

YEAR ISSUE		EDITION LIMIT	YEAR RETD.	ISSUE PRICE	QUOTE U.S.$
1987	Country Wreath 575QX470-9	Yr.Iss.	1987	5.75	30
1987	Folk Art Santa 525QX474-9	Yr.Iss.	1987	5.25	20-33
1987	In a Nutshell 550QX469-7	Yr.Iss.	1988	5.50	15-30
1987	Little Whittler 600QX469-9	Yr.Iss.	1987	6.00	25-33
1987	Nostalgic Rocker 650QX468-9	Yr.Iss.	1987	6.50	26-33

1987 Special Edition - Keepsake

YEAR ISSUE		EDITION LIMIT	YEAR RETD.	ISSUE PRICE	QUOTE U.S.$
1987	Favorite Santa 2250QX445-7	Yr.Iss.	1987	22.50	32-45

1987 Traditional Ornaments - Keepsake

YEAR ISSUE		EDITION LIMIT	YEAR RETD.	ISSUE PRICE	QUOTE U.S.$
1987	Christmas Keys 575QX473-9	Yr.Iss.	1987	5.75	20-33
1987	Currier & Ives: American Farm Scene 475QX282-9	Yr.Iss.	1987	4.75	20-30
1987	Goldfinch 700QX464-9	Yr.Iss.	1987	7.00	50-85
1987	Heavenly Harmony 1500QX465-9	Yr.Iss.	1987	15.00	25-35
1987	I Remember Santa 475QX278-9	Yr.Iss.	1987	4.75	33
1987	Joyous Angels 775QX465-7	Yr.Iss.	1987	7.75	27
1987	Norman Rockwell: Christmas Scenes 475QX282-7	Yr.Iss.	1987	4.75	27
1987	Promise of Peace 650QX374-9	Yr.Iss.	1987	6.50	17-25
1987	Special Memories Photoholder 675QX464-7	Yr.Iss.	1987	6.75	15-27

1988 Artist Favorites - Keepsake

YEAR ISSUE		EDITION LIMIT	YEAR RETD.	ISSUE PRICE	QUOTE U.S.$
1988	Baby Redbird 500QX410-1	Yr.Iss.	1988	5.00	15-20
1988	Cymbals of Christmas 550QX411-1	Yr.Iss.	1988	5.50	25-30
1988	Little Jack Horner 800QX408-1	Yr.Iss.	1988	8.00	15-28
1988	Merry-Mint Unicorn 850QX423-4	Yr.Iss.	1988	8.50	20
1988	Midnight Snack 600QX410-4	Yr.Iss.	1988	6.00	15-23
1988	Very Strawbeary 475QX409-1	Yr.Iss.	1988	4.75	13-22

1988 Christmas Pizzazz Collection - Keepsake

YEAR ISSUE		EDITION LIMIT	YEAR RETD.	ISSUE PRICE	QUOTE U.S.$
1988	Happy Holidata 650QX471-7	Yr.Iss.	1988	6.50	15-30
1988	Mistletoad 700QX468-7	Yr.Iss.	1988	7.00	20-30
1988	St. Louie Nick 775QX453-9	Yr.Iss.	1988	7.75	15-22

1988 Collectible Series - Keepsake

YEAR ISSUE		EDITION LIMIT	YEAR RETD.	ISSUE PRICE	QUOTE U.S.$
1988	Betsey Clark: Home for Christmas-(3rd Ed.) 500QX271-4	Yr.Iss.	1988	5.00	25
1988	Collector's Plate-(2nd Ed.)800QX406-1	Yr.Iss.	1988	8.00	45-50
1988	Five Golden Rings-(5th Ed.)650QX371-4	Yr.Iss.	1988	6.50	30
1988	Frosty Friends-(9th Ed.)875QX403-1	Yr.Iss.	1988	8.75	55-65
1988	Here Comes Santa-(10th Ed.)1400QX400-1	Yr.Iss.	1988	14.00	40-48
1988	Holiday Heirloom-(2nd Ed.) 2500QX406-4	Yr.Iss.	1988	25.00	24
1988	Holiday Wildlife-(7th Ed.)775QX371-1	Yr.Iss.	1988	7.75	14-24
1988	Mary's Angels-(1st Ed.)500QX407-4	Yr.Iss.	1988	5.00	43-65
1988	Miniature Creche-(4th Ed.)850QX403-4	Yr.Iss.	1988	8.50	21-34
1988	Mr. and Mrs. Claus-(3rd Ed.)1300QX401-1	Yr.Iss.	1988	13.00	55
1988	Norman Rockwell-(9th Ed.)775QX370-4	Yr.Iss.	1988	7.75	14-23
1988	Nostalgic Houses and Shops-(5th Ed.) 1450QX401-4	Yr.Iss.	1988	14.50	45-60
1988	Porcelain Bear-(6th Ed.)800QX404-4	Yr.Iss.	1988	8.00	25-40
1988	Reindeer Champs-(3rd Ed.)750QX405-1	Yr.Iss.	1988	7.50	30-37
1988	Rocking Horse-(8th Ed.)1075QX402-4	Yr.Iss.	1988	10.75	40-55
1988	Thimble-(11th Ed.)575QX405-4	Yr.Iss.	1988	5.75	15-25
1988	Tin Locomotive-(7th Ed.)1475QX400-4	Yr.Iss.	1988	14.75	53-60
1988	Windows of the World-(4th Ed.) 1000QX402-1	Yr.Iss.	1988	10.00	25-35
1988	Wood Childhood-(5th Ed.)750QX404-1	Yr.Iss.	1988	7.50	25

1988 Commemoratives - Keepsake

YEAR ISSUE		EDITION LIMIT	YEAR RETD.	ISSUE PRICE	QUOTE U.S.$
1988	Baby's First Christmas (Boy)475QX272-1	Yr.Iss.	1988	4.75	21
1988	Baby's First Christmas (Girl)475QX272-4	Yr.Iss.	1988	4.75	21
1988	Baby's First Christmas 600QX372-1	Yr.Iss.	1988	6.00	20
1988	Baby's First Christmas 750QX470-4	Yr.Iss.	1988	7.50	28
1988	Baby's First Christmas 975QX470-1	Yr.Iss.	1988	9.75	40
1988	Baby's Second Christmas 600QX471-1	Yr.Iss.	1988	6.00	33
1988	Babysitter 475QX279-1	Yr.Iss.	1988	4.75	10
1988	Child's Third Christmas 600QX471-4	Yr.Iss.	1988	6.00	25-30
1988	Dad 700QX414-1	Yr.Iss.	1988	7.00	25
1988	Daughter 575QX415-1	Yr.Iss.	1988	5.75	50-55
1988	Fifty Years Together 675QX374-1	Yr.Iss.	1988	6.75	10-20
1988	First Christmas Together 475QX274-1	Yr.Iss.	1988	4.75	23
1988	First Christmas Together 675QX373-1	Yr.Iss.	1988	6.75	20-30
1988	First Christmas Together 900QX489-4	Yr.Iss.	1988	9.00	25-35
1988	Five Years Together 475QX274-4	Yr.Iss.	1988	4.75	12-22
1988	From Our Home to Yours 475QX279-4	Yr.Iss.	1988	4.75	17
1988	Godchild 475QX278-4	Yr.Iss.	1988	4.75	10-20
1988	Granddaughter 475QX277-4	Yr.Iss.	1988	4.75	10-25
1988	Grandmother 475QX276-4	Yr.Iss.	1988	4.75	20
1988	Grandparents 475QX277-1	Yr.Iss.	1988	4.75	15-20
1988	Grandson 475QX278-1	Yr.Iss.	1988	4.75	15-25
1988	Gratitude 600QX375-4	Yr.Iss.	1988	6.00	12
1988	Love Fills the Heart 600QX374-4	Yr.Iss.	1988	6.00	25
1988	Love Grows 475QX275-4	Yr.Iss.	1988	4.75	32
1988	Mother 650QX375-1	Yr.Iss.	1988	6.50	20
1988	Mother and Dad 800QX414-4	Yr.Iss.	1988	8.00	20
1988	New Home 600QX376-1	Yr.Iss.	1988	6.00	25
1988	Sister 800QX499-4	Yr.Iss.	1988	8.00	33
1988	Son 575QX415-4	Yr.Iss.	1988	5.75	40-55
1988	Spirit of Christmas 475QX276-1	Yr.Iss.	1988	4.75	21
1988	Sweetheart 975QX490-1	Yr.Iss.	1988	9.75	11-22
1988	Teacher 625QX417-1	Yr.Iss.	1988	6.25	20
1988	Ten Years Together 475QX275-1	Yr.Iss.	1988	4.75	10-20
1988	Twenty-Five Years Together 675QX373-4	Yr.Iss.	1988	6.75	10-19
1988	Year to Remember 700QX416-4	Yr.Iss.	1988	7.00	25

1988 Hallmark Handcrafted Ornaments - Keepsake

YEAR ISSUE		EDITION LIMIT	YEAR RETD.	ISSUE PRICE	QUOTE U.S.$
1988	Americana Drum 775QX488-1	Yr.Iss.	1988	7.75	40-45
1988	Arctic Tenor 400QX472-1	Yr.Iss.	1988	4.00	10-20
1988	Christmas Cardinal 475QX494-1	Yr.Iss.	1988	4.75	10-20
1988	Christmas Cuckoo 800QX480-1	Yr.Iss.	1988	8.00	30
1988	Christmas Memories 650QX372-4	Yr.Iss.	1988	6.50	25
1988	Christmas Scenes 475QX273-1	Yr.Iss.	1988	4.75	18
1988	Cool Juggler 650QX487-4	Yr.Iss.	1988	6.50	20
1988	Feliz Navidad 675QX416-1	Yr.Iss.	1988	6.75	25-33
1988	Filled with Fudge 475QX419-1	Yr.Iss.	1988	4.75	32
1988	Glowing Wreath 600QX492-1	Yr.Iss.	1988	6.00	15
1988	Go For The Gold 800QX417-4	Yr.Iss.	1988	8.00	20-30
1988	Goin' Cross-Country 850QX476-4	Yr.Iss.	1988	8.50	24
1988	Gone Fishing 500QX479-4	Yr.Iss.	1989	5.00	16
1988	Hoe-Hoe-Hoel 500QX422-1	Yr.Iss.	1988	5.00	11-20
1988	Holiday Hero 500QX423-1	Yr.Iss.	1988	5.00	20
1988	Jingle Bell Clown 1500QX477-4	Yr.Iss.	1988	15.00	20-35
1988	Jolly Walrus 450QX473-1	Yr.Iss.	1988	4.50	18-25
1988	Kiss from Santa 450QX482-1	Yr.Iss.	1989	4.50	23
1988	Kiss the Claus 500QX486-1	Yr.Iss.	1988	5.00	10-18
1988	Kringle Moon 550QX495-1	Yr.Iss.	1988	5.00	35
1988	Kringle Portrait 750QX496-1	Yr.Iss.	1988	7.50	25-35
1988	Kringle Tree 650QX495-4	Yr.Iss.	1988	6.50	39
1988	Love Santa 500QX486-4	Yr.Iss.	1988	5.00	20
1988	Loving Bear 475QX493-4	Yr.Iss.	1988	4.75	15-20
1988	Nick the Kick 500QX422-4	Yr.Iss.	1988	5.00	23
1988	Noah's Ark 850QX490-4	Yr.Iss.	1988	8.50	20
1988	Old-Fashioned Church 400QX498-1	Yr.Iss.	1988	4.00	23
1988	Old-Fashioned School House 400QX497-1	Yr.Iss.	1988	4.00	23
1988	Oreo 400QX481-4	Yr.Iss.	1989	4.00	11-20
1988	Par for Santa 500QX479-1	Yr.Iss.	1988	5.00	20
1988	Party Line 875QX476-1	Yr.Iss.	1989	8.75	22-30
1988	Peanuts 475QX280-1	Yr.Iss.	1988	4.75	45
1988	Peek-a-boo Kittens 750QX487-1	Yr.Iss.	1989	7.50	21
1988	Polar Bowler 500QX478-4	Yr.Iss.	1989	5.00	10-20
1988	Purrfect Snuggle 625QX474-4	Yr.Iss.	1988	6.25	15-30
1988	Sailing! Sailing! 850QX491-1	Yr.Iss.	1988	8.50	25
1988	Santa Flamingo 475QX483-4	Yr.Iss.	1988	4.75	16-33
1988	Shiny Sleigh 575QX492-4	Yr.Iss.	1988	5.75	20
1988	Slipper Spaniel 450QX472-4	Yr.Iss.	1988	4.50	10-20
1988	Snoopy and Woodstock 600QX474-1	Yr.Iss.	1988	6.00	35-40
1988	Soft Landing 700QX475-1	Yr.Iss.	1988	7.00	15-25
1988	Sparkling Tree 600QX483-1	Yr.Iss.	1988	6.00	19
1988	Squeaky Clean 675QX475-4	Yr.Iss.	1988	6.75	15-25
1988	Starry Angel 475494-4	Yr.Iss.	1988	4.75	20
1988	Sweet Star 500QX418-4	Yr.Iss.	1988	5.00	20-33
1988	Teeny Taster 475QX418-1	Yr.Iss.	1989	4.75	25-30
1988	The Town Crier 550QX473-4	Yr.Iss.	1988	5.50	15-25
1988	Travels with Santa 1000QX477-1	Yr.Iss.	1988	10.00	26-40
1988	Uncle Sam Nutcracker 700QX488-4	Yr.Iss.	1988	7.00	21-40
1988	Winter Fun 850QX478-1	Yr.Iss.	1988	8.50	17-27

1988 Hallmark Keepsake Ornament Collector's Club - Keepsake

YEAR ISSUE		EDITION LIMIT	YEAR RETD.	ISSUE PRICE	QUOTE U.S.$
1988	Angelic Minstrel 2750QXC408-4	Yr.Iss.	1988	27.50	39-59
1988	Christmas is Sharing 1750QXC407-1	Yr.Iss.	1988	17.50	31-49
1988	Hold on Tight QXC570-4	Yr.Iss.	1988	Unkn.	75
1988	Holiday Heirloom-(2nd Ed.) 2500QXC406-4	Yr.Iss.	1988	25.00	23-37
1988	Our Clubhouse QXC580-4	Yr.Iss.	1988	Unkn.	33-50
1988	Sleighful of Dreams 800QC580-1	Yr.Iss.	1988	8.00	48-75

1988 Holiday Humor - Keepsake

YEAR ISSUE		EDITION LIMIT	YEAR RETD.	ISSUE PRICE	QUOTE U.S.$
1988	Night Before Christmas 650QX451-7	Yr.Iss.	1988	6.50	18-33
1988	Owliday Wish 650QX455-9	Yr.Iss.	1988	6.50	14-25
1988	Reindoggy 575QX452-7	Yr.Iss.	1988	5.75	20-25
1988	Treetop Dreams 675QX459-7	Yr.Iss.	1988	6.75	15-25

1988 Keepsake Magic Ornaments - Keepsake

YEAR ISSUE		EDITION LIMIT	YEAR RETD.	ISSUE PRICE	QUOTE U.S.$
1988	Baby's First Christmas 2400QLX718-4	Yr.Iss.	1988	24.00	43-60
1988	Bearly Reaching 950QLX715-1	Yr.Iss.	1988	9.50	40
1988	Chris Mouse-(4th Ed.)875QLX715-4	Yr.Iss.	1988	8.75	60
1988	Christmas Classics-(3rd Ed.) 1500QLX716-1	Yr.Iss.	1988	15.00	30
1988	Christmas is Magic 1200QLX717-1	Yr.Iss.	1988	12.00	35-55
1988	Christmas Morning 2450QLX701-3	Yr.Iss.	1988	24.50	33-50
1988	Circling the Globe 1050QLX712-4	Yr.Iss.	1988	10.50	45
1988	Country Express 2450QLX721-1	Yr.Iss.	1988	24.50	67-75
1988	Festive Feeder 1150QLX720-4	Yr.Iss.	1988	11.50	40-50
1988	First Christmas Together 1200QLX702-7	Yr.Iss.	1988	12.00	35-40
1988	Heavenly Glow 1175QLX711-4	Yr.Iss.	1988	11.75	19-29
1988	Kitty Capers 1300QLX716-4	Yr.Iss.	1988	13.00	45
1988	Kringle's Toy Shop 2450QLX701-7	Yr.Iss.	1988	25.00	35-60
1988	Last-Minute Hug 1950QLX718-1	Yr.Iss.	1988	19.50	45
1988	Moonlit Nap 875QLX713-4	Yr.Iss.	1988	8.75	20-30
1988	Parade of the Toys 2200QLX719-4	Yr.Iss.	1988	22.00	53
1988	Radiant Tree 1175QLX712-1	Yr.Iss.	1988	11.75	24
1988	Santa and Sparky-(3rd Ed.)1950QLX719-1	Yr.Iss.	1988	19.50	43
1988	Skater's Waltz 1950QLX720-1	Yr.Iss.	1988	19.50	36-62
1988	Song of Christmas 850QLX711-1	Yr.Iss.	1988	8.50	15-30
1988	Tree of Friendship 850QLX710-4	Yr.Iss.	1988	8.50	23

1988 Keepsake Miniature Ornaments - Keepsake

YEAR ISSUE		EDITION LIMIT	YEAR RETD.	ISSUE PRICE	QUOTE U.S.$
1988	Baby's First Christmas	Yr.Iss.	1988	6.00	12
1988	Brass Angel	Yr.Iss.	1988	1.50	20
1988	Brass Star	Yr.Iss.	1988	1.50	20
1988	Brass Tree	Yr.Iss.	1988	1.50	20
1988	Candy Cane Elf	Yr.Iss.	1988	3.00	20
1988	Country Wreath	Yr.Iss.	1988	4.00	11

YEAR ISSUE		EDITION LIMIT	YEAR RETD.	ISSUE PRICE	QUOTE U.S.$
1988	Family Home-(1st Ed.)	Yr.Iss.	1988	8.50	45
1988	First Christmas Together	Yr.Iss.	1988	4.00	11
1988	Folk Art Lamb	Yr.Iss.	1988	2.50	14-23
1988	Folk Art Reindeer	Yr.Iss.	1988	2.50	13-20
1988	Friends Share Joy	Yr.Iss.	1988	2.00	15
1988	Gentle Angel	Yr.Iss.	1988	2.00	15
1988	Happy Santa	Yr.Iss.	1988	4.50	19
1988	Holy Family	Yr.Iss.	1988	8.50	13
1988	Jolly St. Nick	Yr.Iss.	1988	8.00	25-35
1988	Joyous Heart	Yr.Iss.	1988	3.50	15-30
1988	Kittens in Toyland-(1st Ed.)	Yr.Iss.	1988	5.00	15-30
1988	Little Drummer Boy	Yr.Iss.	1988	4.50	19-26
1988	Love is Forever	Yr.Iss.	1988	2.00	15
1988	Mother	Yr.Iss.	1988	3.00	12
1988	Penguin Pal-(1st Ed.)	Yr.Iss.	1988	3.75	27
1988	Rocking Horse-(1st Ed.)	Yr.Iss.	1988	4.50	20-42
1988	Skater's Waltz	Yr.Iss.	1988	7.00	14-22
1988	Sneaker Mouse	Yr.Iss.	1988	4.00	14-20
1988	Snuggly Skater	Yr.Iss.	1988	4.50	27
1988	Sweet Dreams	Yr.Iss.	1988	7.00	14-22
1988	Three Little Kitties	Yr.Iss.	1988	6.00	13-19

1988 Old Fashioned Christmas Collection - Keepsake

1988	In A Nutshell 550QX469-7	Yr.Iss.	1988	5.50	24-33

1988 Special Edition - Keepsake

1988	The Wonderful Santacycle 2250QX411-4	Yr.Iss.	1988	22.50	34-45

1989 Artists' Favorites - Keepsake

1989	Baby Partridge 675QX452-5	Yr.Iss.	1989	6.75	10-15
1989	Bear-i-Tone 475QX454-2	Yr.Iss.	1989	4.75	10-20
1989	Carousel Zebra 925QX451-5	Yr.Iss.	1989	9.25	15-20
1989	Cherry Jubilee 500QX453-2	Yr.Iss.	1989	5.00	15-25
1989	Mail Call 875QX452-2	Yr.Iss.	1989	8.75	15-20
1989	Merry-Go-Round Unicorn 1075QX447-2	Yr.Iss.	1989	10.75	22
1989	Playful Angel 675QX453-5	Yr.Iss.	1989	6.75	15-25

1989 Collectible Series - Keepsake

1989	Betsey Clark: Home for Christmas-(4th Ed.) 500QX230-2	Yr.Iss.	1989	5.00	25-36
1989	Christmas Kitty (1st Ed.) 1475QX544-5	Yr.Iss.	1989	14.75	20-32
1989	Collector's Plate-(3rd Ed.) 825QX461-2	Yr.Iss.	1989	8.25	32-40
1989	Crayola Crayon (1st Ed.) 875QX435-2	Yr.Iss.	1989	8.75	42-55
1989	Frosty Friends-(10th Ed. 925QX457-2	Yr.Iss.	1989	9.25	32-50
1989	The Gift Bringers (1st Ed.) 500QX279-5	Yr.Iss.	1989	5.00	21
1989	Hark! It's Herald (1st Ed.) 675QX455-5	Yr.Iss.	1989	6.75	24-30
1989	Here Comes Santa (11th Ed.)1475QX458-5	Yr.Iss.	1989	14.75	44-50
1989	Mary's Angels-(2nd Ed.) 575QX454-5	Yr.Iss.	1989	5.75	45-65
1989	Miniature Creche (5th Ed. 925QX459-2	Yr.Iss.	1989	9.25	15-25
1989	Mr. and Mrs. Claus-(4th Ed.) 1325QX 457-5	Yr.Iss.	1989	13.25	30-50
1989	Nostalgic Houses and Shops-(6th Ed.) 1425QX458-2	Yr.Iss.	1989	14.25	45-60
1989	Porcelain Bear (7th Ed.) 875QX461-5	Yr.Iss.	1989	8.75	20-33
1989	Reindeer Champs-(4th Ed.) 775QX456-2	Yr.Iss.	1989	7.75	16-26
1989	Rocking Horse (9th Ed.) 1075QX462-2	Yr.Iss.	1989	10.75	31-43
1989	Thimble (12th Ed.) 575QX455-2	Yr.Iss.	1989	5.75	18-25
1989	Tin Locomotive (8th Ed.) 1475QX460-2	Yr.Iss.	1989	14.75	52-60
1989	Twelve Days of Christmas (6th Ed.) 675QX381-2	Yr.Iss.	1989	6.75	20-25
1989	Windows of the World (5th Ed.) 1075QX462-5	Yr.Iss.	1989	10.75	20-30
1989	Winter Surprise (1st Ed.) 1075QX427-2	Yr.Iss.	1989	10.75	25-32
1989	Wood Childhood Ornaments-(6th Ed.) 775QX459-5	Yr.Iss.	1989	7.75	15-25

1989 Commemoratives - Keepsake

1989	Baby's Fifth Christmas 675QX543-5	Yr.Iss.	1989	6.75	18-25
1989	Baby's First Christmas 675QX381-5	Yr.Iss.	1989	6.75	20
1989	Baby's First Christmas 725QX449-2	Yr.Iss.	1989	7.25	75-85
1989	Baby's First Christmas Photoholder 625QX468-2	Yr.Iss.	1989	6.25	50
1989	Baby's First Christmas-Baby Boy 475QX272-5	Yr.Iss.	1989	4.75	18
1989	Baby's First Christmas-Baby Girl 475QX272-2	Yr.Iss.	1989	4.75	20
1989	Baby's Fourth Christmas 675QX543-2	Yr.Iss.	1989	6.75	18-25
1989	Baby's Second Christmas 675QX449-5	Yr.Iss.	1989	6.75	30-45
1989	Baby's Third Christmas 675QX469-5	Yr.Iss.	1989	6.75	23-30
1989	Brother 625QX445-2	Yr.Iss.	1989	6.25	15-20
1989	Dad 725QX442-5	Yr.Iss.	1989	7.25	15-25
1989	Daughter 625QX443-2	Yr.Iss.	1989	6.25	20-25
1989	Festive Year 775QX384-2	Yr.Iss.	1989	7.75	10-20
1989	Fifty Years Together Photoholder 875QX486-2	Yr.Iss.	1989	8.75	12-20
1989	First Christmas Together 475QX273-2	Yr.Iss.	1989	4.75	25
1989	First Christmas Together 675QX383-2	Yr.Iss.	1989	6.75	15-25
1989	First Christmas Together 675QX485-2	Yr.Iss.	1989	9.75	15-25
1989	Five Years Together 475QX273-5	Yr.Iss.	1989	4.75	22
1989	FortyYears Together Photoholder 875QX545-2	Yr.Iss.	1989	8.75	17
1989	Friendship Time 975QX413-2	Yr.Iss.	1989	9.75	30
1989	From Our Home to Yours 625QX384-5	Yr.Iss.	1989	6.25	15
1989	Godchild 625QX311-2	Yr.Iss.	1989	6.25	15
1989	Granddaughter 475QX278	Yr.Iss.	1989	4.75	23
1989	Granddaughter's First Christmas 675QX382-2	Yr.Iss.	1989	6.75	10-23
1989	Grandmother 475QX277-5	Yr.Iss.	1989	4.75	18
1989	Grandparents 475QX277-2	Yr.Iss.	1989	4.75	18
1989	Grandson 475QX278-5	Yr.Iss.	1989	4.75	15-23
1989	Grandson's First Christmas 675QX382-5	Yr.Iss.	1989	6.75	10-18
1989	Gratitude 675QX385-2	Yr.Iss.	1989	6.75	14
1989	Language of Love 625QX383-5	Yr.Iss.	1989	6.25	22
1989	Mom and Dad 975QX442-5	Yr.Iss.	1989	9.75	24
1989	Mother 975QX440-5	Yr.Iss.	1989	9.75	25-30
1989	New Home 475QX275-5	Yr.Iss.	1989	4.75	25
1989	Sister 475QX279-2	Yr.Iss.	1989	4.75	10-20
1989	Son 625QX444-5	Yr.Iss.	1989	6.25	24
1989	Sweetheart 975QX486-5	Yr.Iss.	1989	9.75	35
1989	Teacher 575QX412-5	Yr.Iss.	1989	5.75	15-25
1989	Ten Years Together 475QX274-2	Yr.Iss.	1989	4.75	30
1989	Twenty-five Years Together Photoholder 875QX485-5	Yr.Iss.	1989	8.75	17
1989	World of Love 475QX274-5	Yr.Iss.	1989	4.75	30-35

1989 Hallmark Handcrafted Ornaments - Keepsake

1989	Peek-a-boo Kittens 750QX487-1	Yr.Iss.	1989	7.50	21

1989 Hallmark Keepsake Ornament Collector's Club - Keepsake

1989	Christmas is Peaceful 1850QXC451-2	Yr.Iss.	1989	18.50	30-45
1989	Collect a Dream 900QXC428-5	Yr.Iss.	1989	9.00	43-65
1989	Holiday Heirloom-(3rd Ed.)2500QXC460-5	Yr.Iss.	1989	25.00	29-39
1989	Noelle 1975QXC448-3	Yr.Iss.	1989	19.75	50-60
1989	Sitting Purrty QXC581-2	Yr.Iss.	1989	Unkn.	25-45
1989	Visit from Santa QXC580-2	Yr.Iss.	1989	Unkn.	38-55

1989 Holiday Traditions - Keepsake

1989	Camera Claus 575QX546-5	Yr.Iss.	1989	5.75	12-23
1989	A Charlie Brown Christmas 475QX276-5	Yr.Iss.	1989	4.75	30-40
1989	Cranberry Bunny 575QX426-2	Yr.Iss.	1989	5.75	17
1989	Deer Disguise 575QX426-5	Yr.Iss.	1989	5.75	17-25
1989	Feliz Navidad 675QX439-2	Yr.Iss.	1989	6.75	18-30
1989	The First Christmas 775QX547-5	Yr.Iss.	1989	7.75	14-16
1989	Gentle Fawn 775QX548-5	Yr.Iss.	1989	7.75	13-20
1989	George Washington Bicentennial 625QX386-2	Yr.Iss.	1989	6.75	10-20
1989	Gone Fishing 500QX479-4	Yr.Iss.	1989	5.75	17
1989	Gym Dandy 575QX418-5	Yr.Iss.	1989	5.75	10-18
1989	Hang in There 525QX430-5	Yr.Iss.	1989	5.25	33
1989	Here's the Pitch 575QX545-5	Yr.Iss.	1989	5.75	12-20
1989	Hoppy Holidays 775QX469-2	Yr.Iss.	1989	7.75	13-24
1989	Joyful Trio 975QX437-2	Yr.Iss.	1989	9.75	17
1989	A Kiss™ From Santa 450QX482-1	Yr.Iss.	1989	4.50	20
1989	Kristy Claus 575QX424-5	Yr.Iss.	1989	5.75	10-15
1989	Norman Rockwell 475QX276-2	Yr.Iss.	1989	4.75	20-25
1989	North Pole Jogger 575QX546-2	Yr.Iss.	1989	5.75	12-23
1989	Old-World Gnome 775QX434-5	Yr.Iss.	1989	7.75	15-30
1989	On the Links 575QX419-2	Yr.Iss.	1989	5.75	16-23
1989	Oreo® Chocolate Sandwich Cookies 400QX481-4	Yr.Iss.	1989	4.00	15
1989	Owliday Greetings 400QX436-5	Yr.Iss.	1989	4.00	13-20
1989	Paddington Bear 575QX429-2	Yr.Iss.	1989	5.75	15-20
1989	Party Line 875QX476-1	Yr.Iss.	1989	8.75	27
1989	Peek-a-Boo Kitties 750QX487-1	Yr.Iss.	1989	7.50	16-22
1989	Polar Bowler 500QX478-4	Yr.Iss.	1989	5.75	17
1989	Sea Santa 575QX415-2	Yr.Iss.	1989	5.75	13-25
1989	Snoopy and Woodstock 675QX433-2	Yr.Iss.	1989	6.75	20-30
1989	Snowplow Santa 575QX420-5	Yr.Iss.	1989	5.75	12-22
1989	Special Delivery 525QX432-5	Yr.Iss.	1989	5.25	15-25
1989	Spencer Sparrow, Esq. 675QX431-2	Yr.Iss.	1990	6.75	16-23
1989	Stocking Kitten 675QX456-5	Yr.Iss.	1990	6.75	17
1989	Sweet Memories Photoholder 675QX438-5	Yr.Iss.	1989	6.75	25
1989	Teeny Taster 475QX418-1	Yr.Iss.	1989	4.75	17

1989 Keepsake Magic Collection - Keepsake

1989	Angel Melody 950QLX720-2	Yr.Iss.	1989	9.50	25
1989	The Animals Speak 1350QLX723-2	Yr.Iss.	1989	13.50	78-125
1989	Baby's First Christmas 3000QLX727-2	Yr.Iss.	1989	30.00	47-65
1989	Backstage Bear 1350QLX721-5	Yr.Iss.	1989	13.50	29
1989	Busy Beaver 1750QLX724-5	Yr.Iss.	1989	17.50	35-50
1989	Chris Mouse-(5th Ed.) 950QLX722-5	Yr.Iss.	1989	9.50	51-60
1989	Christmas Classics-(4th Ed.) 1350QLX724-2	Yr.Iss.	1989	13.50	27-43
1989	First Christmas Together1750QLX734-2	Yr.Iss.	1989	17.50	33-45
1989	Forest Frolics-(1st Ed.)2450QLX728-2	Yr.Iss.	1989	24.50	83
1989	Holiday Bell 1750QLX722-2	Yr.Iss.	1989	17.50	29-35
1989	Joyous Carolers 3000QLX729-5	Yr.Iss.	1989	30.00	47-70
1989	Kringle's Toy Shop 2450QLX701-7	Yr.Iss.	1989	24.50	40-60
1989	Loving Spoonful 1950QLX726-2	Yr.Iss.	1989	19.50	32-38
1989	Metro Express 2800QLX727-5	Yr.Iss.	1989	28.00	72-80
1989	Moonlit Nap 875QLX713-4	Yr.Iss.	1989	8.75	23
1989	Rudolph the Red-Nosed Reindeer 1950QLX725-2	Yr.Iss.	1989	19.50	50-70
1989	Spirit of St. Nick 2450QLX728-5	Yr.Iss.	1989	24.50	60-75
1989	Tiny Tinker 1950QLX717-4	Yr.Iss.	1989	19.50	60-65
1989	Unicorn Fantasy 950QLX723-5	Yr.Iss.	1989	9.50	17

1989 Keepsake Miniature Ornaments - Keepsake

1989	Acorn Squirrel 450QXM568-2	Yr.Iss.	1989	4.50	9
1989	Baby's First Christmas 600QXM573-2	Yr.Iss.	1989	6.00	11-20
1989	Brass Partridge 300QXM572-5	Yr.Iss.	1989	3.00	10
1989	Brass Snowflake 450QXM570-2	Yr.Iss.	1989	4.50	13
1989	Bunny Hug 300QXM577-5	Yr.Iss.	1989	3.00	7-11
1989	Country Wreath 450QXM573-1	Yr.Iss.	1989	4.50	12
1989	Cozy Skater 450QXM573-5	Yr.Iss.	1989	4.50	11
1989	First Christmas Together 850QXM564-2	Yr.Iss.	1989	8.50	12
1989	Folk Art Bunny 450QXM569-2	Yr.Iss.	1989	4.50	10
1989	Happy Bluebird 450QXM566-2	Yr.Iss.	1989	4.50	13
1989	Holiday Deer 300QXM577-2	Yr.Iss.	1989	3.00	12
1989	Holy Family 850QXM561-1	Yr.Iss.	1989	8.50	15
1989	Kittens in Toyland-(2nd Ed.) 450QXM561-2	Yr.Iss.	1989	4.50	15-20
1989	Kitty Cart 300QXM572-2	Yr.Iss.	1989	3.00	7
1989	The Kringles-(1st Ed.)600QXM562-2	Yr.Iss.	1989	6.00	26-33
1989	Little Soldier 450QXM567-5	Yr.Iss.	1989	4.50	15-24
1989	Little Star Bringer 600QXM562-2	Yr.Iss.	1989	6.00	18
1989	Load of Cheer 600QXM574-5	Yr.Iss.	1989	6.00	12-20
1989	Lovebirds 600QXM563-5	Yr.Iss.	1989	6.00	9-15
1989	Merry Seal 600QXM575-5	Yr.Iss.	1989	6.00	11-15
1989	Mother 600QXM564-5	Yr.Iss.	1989	6.00	10-15
1989	Noel R.R.-(1st Ed.) 850QXM576-2	Yr.Iss.	1989	8.50	33-43
1989	Old English Village-(2nd Ed.) 850QXM561-5	Yr.Iss.	1989	8.50	20-38
1989	Old-World Santa 300QXM569-5	Yr.Iss.	1989	3.00	8
1989	Penguin Pal-(2nd Ed.)450QXM560-2	Yr.Iss.	1989	4.50	14-20
1989	Pinecone Basket 450QXM573-4	Yr.Iss.	1989	4.50	8
1989	Puppy Cart 300QXM571-5	Yr.Iss.	1989	3.00	10-22
1989	Rejoice 300QXM578-2	Yr.Iss.	1989	3.00	10
1989	Rocking Horse-(2nd Ed.) 450QXM560-5	Yr.Iss.	1989	4.50	23
1989	Roly-Poly Pig 300QXM571-2	Yr.Iss.	1989	3.00	14
1989	Roly-Poly Ram 300QXM570-5	Yr.Iss.	1989	3.00	13
1989	Santa's Magic Ride 850QXM563-2	Yr.Iss.	1989	8.50	13-20
1989	Santa's Roadster 600QXM566-5	Yr.Iss.	1989	6.00	15-20
1989	Scrimshaw Reindeer 450QXM568-5	Yr.Iss.	1989	4.50	8
1989	Sharing a Ride 850QXM576-5	Yr.Iss.	1989	8.50	10-15
1989	Slow Motion 600QXM575-2	Yr.Iss.	1989	6.00	11-17
1989	Special Friend 450QXM565-2	Yr.Iss.	1989	4.50	11-14
1989	Starlit Mouse 450QXM565-5	Yr.Iss.	1989	4.50	15
1989	Stocking Pal 450QXM567-2	Yr.Iss.	1989	4.50	10
1989	Strollin' Snowman 450QXM574-2	Yr.Iss.	1989	4.50	12-18
1989	Three Little Kitties 600QXM569-4	Yr.Iss.	1989	6.00	19

1989 New Attractions - Keepsake

1989	Balancing Elf 675QX489-5	Yr.Iss.	1989	6.75	23
1989	Cactus Cowboy 675QX411-2	Yr.Iss.	1989	6.75	33-44
1989	Claus Construction 775QX488-5	Yr.Iss.	1990	7.75	25-35
1989	Cool Swing 625QX487-5	Yr.Iss.	1989	6.25	33
1989	Country Cat 625QX467-2	Yr.Iss.	1989	6.25	16
1989	Festive Angel 675QX463-5	Yr.Iss.	1989	6.75	20
1989	Goin' South 425QX410-5	Yr.Iss.	1989	4.25	25
1989	Graceful Swan 675QX464-2	Yr.Iss.	1989	6.75	20
1989	Horse Weathervane 575QX463-2	Yr.Iss.	1989	5.75	15
1989	Let's Play 725QX488-2	Yr.Iss.	1989	7.25	27
1989	Nostalgic Lamb 675QX466-5	Yr.Iss.	1989	6.75	15
1989	Nutshell Dreams 575QX465-5	Yr.Iss.	1989	5.75	14-23
1989	Nutshell Holiday 575QX465-2	Yr.Iss.	1990	5.75	17-27
1989	Nutshell Workshop 575QX487-2	Yr.Iss.	1989	5.75	15-22
1989	Peppermint Clown 2475QX450-5	Yr.Iss.	1989	24.75	25-50
1989	Rodney Reindeer 675QX407-2	Yr.Iss.	1989	6.75	15
1989	Rooster Weathervane 575QX467-5	Yr.Iss.	1989	5.75	15
1989	Sparkling Snowflake 775QX547-2	Yr.Iss.	1989	7.75	25
1989	TV Break 625QX409-2	Yr.Iss.	1989	6.25	20
1989	Wiggly Snowman 675QX489-2	Yr.Iss.	1989	6.75	25

1989 Special Edition - Keepsake

1989	The Ornament Express 2200QX580-5	Yr.Iss.	1989	22.00	40-45

1990 Artists' Favorites - Keepsake

1990	Angel Kitty 875QX4746	Yr.Iss.	1990	8.75	20-25
1990	Donder's Diner 1375QX4823	Yr.Iss.	1990	13.75	20
1990	Gentle Dreamers 875QX4756	Yr.Iss.	1990	8.75	18-28
1990	Happy Woodcutter 975QX4763	Yr.Iss.	1990	9.75	23
1990	Mouseboat 775QX4753	Yr.Iss.	1990	7.75	13-18
1990	Welcome, Santa 1175QX4773	Yr.Iss.	1990	11.75	25

CHRISTMAS ORNAMENTS

1990 Collectible Series - Keepsake

YEAR ISSUE		EDITION LIMIT	YEAR RETD.	ISSUE PRICE	QUOTE U.S.$
1990	Betsey Clark: Home for Christmas-(5th Ed.) 500QX2033	Yr.Iss.	1990	5.00	20-25
1990	Christmas Kitty-(2nd Ed.) 1475QX4506	Yr.Iss.	1990	14.75	25-33
1990	Cinnamon Bear-(8th Ed.) 875QX4426	Yr.Iss.	1990	8.75	20-32
1990	Cookies for Santa-(4th Ed.) 875QX4436	Yr.Iss.	1990	8.75	35
1990	CRAYOLA Crayon-Bright Moving Colors-(2nd Ed.) 875QX4586	Yr.Iss.	1990	8.75	40-45
1990	Fabulous Decade-(1st Ed.) 775QX4466	Yr.Iss.	1990	7.75	30-45
1990	Festive Surrey-(12th Ed.) 1475QX4923	Yr.Iss.	1990	14.75	29-43
1990	Frosty Friends-(11th Ed.) 975QX4396	Yr.Iss.	1990	9.75	26
1990	The Gift Bringers-St. Lucia -(2nd Ed.) 500QX2803	Yr.Iss.	1990	5.00	20
1990	Greatest Story-(1st Ed.) 1275QX4656	Yr.Iss.	1990	12.75	31
1990	Hark! It's Herald-(2nd Ed.) 675QX4463	Yr.Iss.	1990	6.75	20-27
1990	Heart of Christmas-(1st Ed.) 1375QX4726	Yr.Iss.	1990	13.75	50-80
1990	Holiday Home-(7th Ed.) 1475QX4696	Yr.Iss.	1990	14.75	50-60
1990	Irish-(6th Ed.) 1075QX4636	Yr.Iss.	1990	10.75	20-32
1990	Mary's Angels-Rosebud-(3rd Ed.) 575QX4423	Yr.Iss.	1990	5.75	40-45
1990	Merry Olde Santa-(1st Ed.) 1475QX4736	Yr.Iss.	1990	14.75	65-75
1990	Popcorn Party-(5th Ed.) 1375QX4393	Yr.Iss.	1990	13.75	40-50
1990	Reindeer Champs-Comet -(5th Ed.) 775QX4433	Yr.Iss.	1990	7.75	19-29
1990	Rocking Horse-(10th Ed.) 1075QX4646	Yr.Iss.	1990	10.75	50-58
1990	Seven Swans A-Swimming -(7th Ed.) 675QX3033	Yr.Iss.	1990	6.75	19-29
1990	Winter Surprise-(2nd Ed.) 1075QX4443	Yr.Iss.	1990	10.75	20-30

1990 Commemoratives - Keepsake

YEAR ISSUE		EDITION LIMIT	YEAR RETD.	ISSUE PRICE	QUOTE U.S.$
1990	Across The Miles 675QX3173	Yr.Iss.	1990	6.75	15
1990	Baby's First Christmas 675QX3036	Yr.Iss.	1990	6.75	15-22
1990	Baby's First Christmas 775QX4856	Yr.Iss.	1990	7.75	35
1990	Baby's First Christmas 975QX4853	Yr.Iss.	1990	9.75	23-30
1990	Baby's First Christmas-Baby Boy 475QX2063	Yr.Iss.	1990	4.75	15-23
1990	Baby's First Christmas-Baby Girl 475QX2066	Yr.Iss.	1990	4.75	12-22
1990	Baby's First Christmas-Photo Holder 775QX4843	Yr.Iss.	1990	7.75	23-30
1990	Baby's Second Christmas 675QX4683	Yr.Iss.	1990	6.75	30-35
1990	Brother 575QX4493	Yr.Iss.	1990	5.75	15
1990	Child Care Giver 675QX3166	Yr.Iss.	1990	6.75	13
1990	Child's Fifth Christmas 675QX4876	Yr.Iss.	1990	6.75	20
1990	Child's Fourth Christmas 675QX4873	Yr.Iss.	1990	6.75	20-25
1990	Child's Third Christmas 675QX4866	Yr.Iss.	1990	6.75	23-30
1990	Copy of Cheer 775QX4486	Yr.Iss.	1990	7.75	19
1990	Dad 675QX4533	Yr.Iss.	1990	6.75	17-25
1990	Dad-to-Be 575QX4913	Yr.Iss.	1990	5.75	21
1990	Daughter 575QX4496	Yr.Iss.	1990	5.75	15-30
1990	Fifty Years Together 975QX4906	Yr.Iss.	1990	9.75	19
1990	Five Years Together 475QX2103	Yr.Iss.	1990	4.75	19
1990	Forty Years Together 975QX4903	Yr.Iss.	1990	9.75	20
1990	Friendship Kitten 675QX4142	Yr.Iss.	1990	6.75	20-25
1990	From Our Home to Yours 475QX2166	Yr.Iss.	1990	4.75	20
1990	Godchild 675QX3167	Yr.Iss.	1990	6.75	17
1990	Granddaughter 475QX2286	Yr.Iss.	1990	4.75	15-23
1990	Granddaughter's First Christmas 675QX3106	Yr.Iss.	1990	6.75	15-23
1990	Grandmother 475QX2236	Yr.Iss.	1990	4.75	17
1990	Grandparents 475QX2253	Yr.Iss.	1990	4.75	17
1990	Grandson 475QX2293	Yr.Iss.	1990	4.75	15-20
1990	Grandson's First Christmas 675QX3063	Yr.Iss.	1990	6.75	15-23
1990	Jesus Loves Me 675QX3156	Yr.Iss.	1990	6.75	15
1990	Mom and Dad 875QX4593	Yr.Iss.	1990	8.75	16-25
1990	Mom-to-Be 575QX4916	Yr.Iss.	1990	5.75	25-33
1990	Mother 875QX4536	Yr.Iss.	1990	8.75	30
1990	New Home 675QX4343	Yr.Iss.	1990	6.75	26
1990	Our First Christmas Together 475QX2136	Yr.Iss.	1990	4.75	20
1990	Our First Christmas Together 675QX3146	Yr.Iss.	1990	6.75	21
1990	Our First Christmas Together 975QX4883	Yr.Iss.	1990	9.75	20-35
1990	Our First Christmas Together-Photo Holder Ornament 775QX4886	Yr.Iss.	1990	7.75	20
1990	Peaceful Kingdom 475QX2106	Yr.Iss.	1990	4.75	20
1990	Sister 475QX2273	Yr.Iss.	1990	4.75	19
1990	Son 575QX4516	Yr.Iss.	1990	5.75	15-30
1990	Sweetheart 1175QX4893	Yr.Iss.	1990	11.75	25
1990	Teacher 775QX4483	Yr.Iss.	1990	7.75	16
1990	Ten Years Together 475QX2153	Yr.Iss.	1990	4.75	19
1990	Time for Love 475QX2133	Yr.Iss.	1990	4.75	10-22
1990	Twenty-Five Years Together 975QX4896	Yr.Iss.	1990	9.75	19

1990 Holiday Traditions - Keepsake

YEAR ISSUE		EDITION LIMIT	YEAR RETD.	ISSUE PRICE	QUOTE U.S.$
1990	Spencer Sparrow, Esq. 675QX431-2	Yr.Iss.	1990	6.75	15
1990	Stocking Kitten 675QX456-5	Yr.Iss.	1990	6.75	11-15

1990 Keepsake Collector's Club - Keepsake

YEAR ISSUE		EDITION LIMIT	YEAR RETD.	ISSUE PRICE	QUOTE U.S.$
1990	Armful of Joy 800QXC445-3	Yr.Iss.	1990	8.00	40-45
1990	Club Hollow QXC445-6	Yr.Iss.	1990	Unkn.	35-40
1990	Crown Prince QXC560-3	Yr.Iss.	1990	Unkn.	39

1990 Keepsake Magic Ornaments - Keepsake

YEAR ISSUE		EDITION LIMIT	YEAR RETD.	ISSUE PRICE	QUOTE U.S.$
1990	Baby's First Christmas 2800QLX7246	Yr.Iss.	1990	28.00	48-60
1990	Beary Short Nap 1000QLX7326	Yr.Iss.	1990	10.00	20-30
1990	Blessings of Love 1400QLX7363	Yr.Iss.	1990	14.00	45-50
1990	Children's Express 2800QLX7243	Yr.Iss.	1990	28.00	65-75
1990	Chris Mouse Wreath 1000QLX7296	Yr.Iss.	1990	10.00	28-45
1990	Christmas Memories 2500QLX7276	Yr.Iss.	1990	25.00	47
1990	Deer Crossing 1800QLX7213	Yr.Iss.	1990	18.00	41-50
1990	Elf of the Year 1000QLX7356	Yr.Iss.	1990	10.00	16-25
1990	Elfin Whittler 2000QLX7265	Yr.Iss.	1990	20.00	37-55
1990	Forest Frolics 2500QLX7236	Yr.Iss.	1990	25.00	55-75
1990	Holiday Flash 1800QLX7333	Yr.Iss.	1990	18.00	25-39
1990	Hop 'N Pop Popper 2000QLX7353	Yr.Iss.	1990	20.00	75-95
1990	Letter to Santa 1400QLX7226	Yr.Iss.	1990	14.00	28-35
1990	The Littlest Angel 1400QLX7303	Yr.Iss.	1990	14.00	27-45
1990	Mrs. Santa's Kitchen 2500QLX7263	Yr.Iss.	1990	25.00	50-80
1990	Our First Christmas Together 1800QLX7255	Yr.Iss.	1990	18.00	26-46
1990	Partridges in a Pear 1400QLX7212	Yr.Iss.	1990	14.00	35
1990	Santa's Ho-Ho-Hoedown 2500QLX7256	Yr.Iss.	1990	25.00	75-90
1990	Song and Dance 2000QLX7253	Yr.Iss.	1990	20.00	60-95
1990	Starlight Angel 1400QLX7306	Yr.Iss.	1990	14.00	27-37
1990	Starship Christmas 1800QLX7336	Yr.Iss.	1990	18.00	35-55

1990 Keepsake Miniature Ornaments - Keepsake

YEAR ISSUE		EDITION LIMIT	YEAR RETD.	ISSUE PRICE	QUOTE U.S.$
1990	Acorn Wreath 600QXM5686	Yr.Iss.	1990	6.00	10
1990	Air Santa 450QXM5656	Yr.Iss.	1990	4.50	10
1990	Baby's First Christmas 850QXM5703	Yr.Iss.	1990	8.50	12-17
1990	Basket Buddy 600QXM5696	Yr.Iss.	1990	6.00	10
1990	Bear Hug 600QXM5633	Yr.Iss.	1990	6.00	12
1990	Brass Bouquet 600QMX5776	Yr.Iss.	1990	6.00	6
1990	Brass Horn 300QXM5793	Yr.Iss.	1990	3.00	8
1990	Brass Peace 300QXM5796	Yr.Iss.	1990	3.00	8
1990	Brass Santa 300QXM5786	Yr.Iss.	1990	3.00	7
1990	Brass Year 300QXM5833	Yr.Iss.	1990	3.00	8
1990	Busy Carver 450QXM5673	Yr.Iss.	1990	4.50	9
1990	Christmas Dove 450QXM5636	Yr.Iss.	1990	4.50	12
1990	Cloisonne Poinsettia 1050QMX5533	Yr.Iss.	1990	10.75	22-35
1990	Coal Car 850QXM5756	Yr.Iss.	1990	8.50	18-25
1990	Country Heart 450QXM5693	Yr.Iss.	1990	4.50	9
1990	First Christmas Together 600QXM5536	Yr.Iss.	1990	6.00	12
1990	Going Sledding 450QXM5683	Yr.Iss.	1990	4.50	13
1990	Grandchild's First Christmas 600QXM5723	Yr.Iss.	1990	6.00	11
1990	Holiday Cardinal 300QXM5526	Yr.Iss.	1990	3.00	10
1990	Kittens in Toyland 450QXM5736	Yr.Iss.	1990	4.50	18
1990	The Kringles 600QXM5753	Yr.Iss.	1990	6.00	20-28
1990	Lion and Lamb 450QXM5676	Yr.Iss.	1990	4.50	8
1990	Loving Hearts 300QXM5523	Yr.Iss.	1990	3.00	8
1990	Madonna and Child 600QXM5643	Yr.Iss.	1990	6.00	10
1990	Mother 450QXM5716	Yr.Iss.	1990	4.50	11-17
1990	Nativity 450QXM5706	Yr.Iss.	1990	4.50	11-17
1990	Nature's Angels 450QMX5733	Yr.Iss.	1990	4.50	15-25
1990	Panda's Surprise 450QXM5616	Yr.Iss.	1990	4.50	12
1990	Penguin Pal 450QXM5746	Yr.Iss.	1990	4.50	14-20
1990	Perfect Fit 450QXM5516	Yr.Iss.	1990	4.50	10
1990	Puppy Love 600QXM5666	Yr.Iss.	1990	6.00	13
1990	Rocking Horse 450QXM5743	Yr.Iss.	1990	4.50	17-25
1990	Ruby Reindeer 600QXM5816	Yr.Iss.	1990	6.00	11
1990	Santa's Journey 850QXM5826	Yr.Iss.	1990	8.50	18
1990	Santa's Streetcar 850QQXM5766	Yr.Iss.	1990	8.50	15
1990	School 850QXM5763	Yr.Iss.	1990	8.50	16-25
1990	Snow Angel 600QXM5773	Yr.Iss.	1990	6.00	13
1990	Special Friends 600QXM5726	Yr.Iss.	1990	6.00	12
1990	Stamp Collector 450QXM5623	Yr.Iss.	1990	4.50	9
1990	Stringing Along 850QXM5606	Yr.Iss.	1990	8.50	16
1990	Sweet Slumber 450QXM5663	Yr.Iss.	1990	4.50	10
1990	Teacher 450QXM5653	Yr.Iss.	1990	4.50	8
1990	Thimble Bells 600QXM5543	Yr.Iss.	1990	6.00	20-28
1990	Type of Joy 450QXM5646	Yr.Iss.	1990	4.50	8
1990	Warm Memories 450QXM5713	Yr.Iss.	1990	4.50	10
1990	Wee Nutcracker 850QXM5843	Yr.Iss.	1990	8.50	14

1990 Limited Edition - Keepsake

YEAR ISSUE		EDITION LIMIT	YEAR RETD.	ISSUE PRICE	QUOTE U.S.$
1990	Christmas Limited1975 QXC476-6	38700	1990	19.75	75-125
1990	Dove of Peace 2475QXC447-6	25400	1990	24.75	75
1990	Sugar Plum Fairy 2775QXC447-3	25400	1990	27.75	60

1990 New Attractions - Keepsake

YEAR ISSUE		EDITION LIMIT	YEAR RETD.	ISSUE PRICE	QUOTE U.S.$
1990	Baby Unicorn 975QX5486	Yr.Iss.	1990	9.75	15-23
1990	Bearback Rider 975QX5483	Yr.Iss.	1990	9.75	25
1990	Beary Good Deal 675QX4733	Yr.Iss.	1990	6.75	13
1990	Billboard Bunny 775QX5196	Yr.Iss.	1990	7.75	18
1990	Born to Dance 775QX5043	Yr.Iss.	1990	7.75	15-25
1990	Chiming In 975QX4366	Yr.Iss.	1990	9.75	23
1990	Christmas Croc 775QX4373	Yr.Iss.	1990	7.75	13-25
1990	Christmas Partridge 775QX5246	Yr.Iss.	1990	7.75	13-23
1990	Claus Construction 775QX4885	Yr.Iss.	1990	7.75	15-20
1990	Country Angel 675QX5046	Yr.Iss.	1990	6.75	195
1990	Coyote Carols 875QX4993	Yr.Iss.	1990	8.75	17-25
1990	Cozy Goose 575QX4966	Yr.Iss.	1990	5.75	14
1990	Feliz Navidad 675QX5173	Yr.Iss.	1990	6.75	20-30
1990	Garfield 475QX2303	Yr.Iss.	1990	4.75	10-20
1990	Gingerbread Elf 575QX5033	Yr.Iss.	1990	5.75	20-25
1990	Goose Cart 775QX5236	Yr.Iss.	1990	7.75	14
1990	Hang in There 675QX4713	Yr.Iss.	1990	6.75	15-23
1990	Happy Voices 675QX4645	Yr.Iss.	1990	6.75	14
1990	Holiday Cardinals 775QX5243	Yr.Iss.	1990	7.75	14-23
1990	Home for the Owlidays 675QX5183	Yr.Iss.	1990	6.75	13
1990	Hot Dogger 775QX4976	Yr.Iss.	1990	7.75	14-20
1990	Jolly Dolphin 675QX4683	Yr.Iss.	1990	6.75	20-30
1990	Joy is in the Air 775QX5503	Yr.Iss.	1990	7.75	20-25
1990	King Klaus 775QX4106	Yr.Iss.	1990	7.75	13-20
1990	Kitty's Best Pal 675QX4716	Yr.Iss.	1990	6.75	15-23
1990	Little Drummer Boy 775QX5233	Yr.Iss.	1990	7.75	19
1990	Long Winter's Nap 675QX4703	Yr.Iss.	1990	6.75	22
1990	Lovable Dears 875QX5476	Yr.Iss.	1990	8.75	18
1990	Meow Mart 775QX4446	Yr.Iss.	1990	7.75	21
1990	Mooy Christmas 675QX4933	Yr.Iss.	1990	6.75	25
1990	Norman Rockwell Art 475QX2296	Yr.Iss.	1990	4.75	20
1990	Nutshell Chat 675QX5193	Yr.Iss.	1990	6.75	14-28
1990	Nutshell Holiday 575QX465-2	Yr.Iss.	1990	5.75	17-28
1990	Peanuts 475QX2233	Yr.Iss.	1990	4.75	12-28
1990	Pepperoni Mouse 675QX4973	Yr.Iss.	1990	6.75	15-20
1990	Perfect Catch 775QX4693	Yr.Iss.	1990	7.75	11-18
1990	Polar Jogger 575QX4666	Yr.Iss.	1990	5.75	17
1990	Polar Pair 575QX4626	Yr.Iss.	1990	5.75	25
1990	Polar Sport 775QX5156	Yr.Iss.	1990	7.75	20
1990	Polar TV 775QX5166	Yr.Iss.	1990	7.75	18
1990	Polar V.I.P. 575QX4663	Yr.Iss.	1990	5.75	16
1990	Polar Video 575QX4633	Yr.Iss.	1990	5.75	16
1990	Poolside Walrus 775QX4986	Yr.Iss.	1990	7.75	20
1990	S. Claus Taxi 1175QX4686	Yr.Iss.	1990	11.75	25-30
1990	Santa Schnoz 675QX4983	Yr.Iss.	1990	6.75	30
1990	SNOOPY and WOODSTOCK 675QX4723	Yr.Iss.	1990	6.75	20-30
1990	Spoon Rider 975QX5496	Yr.Iss.	1990	9.75	19
1990	Stitches of Joy 775QX5186	Yr.Iss.	1990	7.75	28
1990	Stocking Kitten 675QX456-5	Yr.Iss.	1990	6.75	7
1990	Stocking Pals 1075QX5493	Yr.Iss.	1990	10.75	20-25
1990	Three Little Piggies 775QX4996	Yr.Iss.	1990	7.75	14-24
1990	Two Peas in a Pod 475QX4926	Yr.Iss.	1990	4.75	30

1990 Special Edition - Keepsake

YEAR ISSUE		EDITION LIMIT	YEAR RETD.	ISSUE PRICE	QUOTE U.S.$
1990	Dickens Caroler Bell-Mr. Ashbourne 2175QX5056	Yr.Iss.	1990	21.75	40-53

1991 Artists' Favorites - Keepsake

YEAR ISSUE		EDITION LIMIT	YEAR RETD.	ISSUE PRICE	QUOTE U.S.$
1991	Fiddlin' Around 775QX4387	Yr.Iss.	1991	7.75	18
1991	Hooked on Santa 775QX4109	Yr.Iss.	1991	7.75	22
1991	Noah's Ark 1375QX4867	Yr.Iss.	1991	13.75	38-50
1991	Polar Circus Wagon 1375QX4399	Yr.Iss.	1991	13.75	25-30
1991	Santa Sailor 975QX4389	Yr.Iss.	1991	9.75	18-25
1991	Tramp and Laddie 775QX4397	Yr.Iss.	1991	7.75	18-39

1991 Club Limited Editions - Keepsake

YEAR ISSUE		EDITION LIMIT	YEAR RETD.	ISSUE PRICE	QUOTE U.S.$
1991	Galloping Into Christmas 1975QXC4779	28,400	1991	19.75	55
1991	Secrets for Santa 2375QXC4797	28,700	1991	23.75	48

1991 Collectible Series - Keepsake

YEAR ISSUE		EDITION LIMIT	YEAR RETD.	ISSUE PRICE	QUOTE U.S.$
1991	1957 Corvette-(1st Ed.)1275QX4319	Yr.Iss.	1991	12.75	150-195
1991	Betsey Clark: Home for Christmas (6th Ed.) 500QX2109	Yr.Iss.	1991	5.00	19-29
1991	Checking His List (6th Ed.) 1375QX4339	Yr.Iss.	1991	13.75	38
1991	Christmas Kitty-(3rd Ed.) 1475QX4377	Yr.Iss.	1991	14.75	25-33
1991	CRAYOLA CRAYON-Bright Vibrant Carols-(3rd Ed.) 975QX4219	Yr.Iss.	1991	9.75	25-40
1991	Eight Maids A-Milking-(8th Ed.) 675QX3089	Yr.Iss.	1991	6.75	20-30
1991	Fabulous Decade-(2nd Ed.) 775QX4119	Yr.Iss.	1991	7.75	20-40
1991	Fire Station-(8th Ed.) 1475QX4139	Yr.Iss.	1991	14.75	60
1991	Frosty Friends-(12th Ed.) 975QX4327	Yr.Iss.	1991	9.75	40
1991	The Gift Bringers-Christkind (3rd Ed.) 500QX2117	Yr.Iss.	1991	5.00	24
1991	Greatest Story-(2nd Ed.) 1275QX4129	Yr.Iss.	1991	12.75	25-30
1991	Hark! It's Herald (3rd Ed.) 675QX4379	Yr.Iss.	1991	6.75	20-30
1991	Heart of Christmas-(2nd Ed.) 1375QX4357	Yr.Iss.	1991	13.75	38
1991	Heavenly Angels-(1st Ed.) 775QX4367	Yr.Iss.	1991	7.75	15-37
1991	Let It Snow! (5th Ed.) 875QX4369	Yr.Iss.	1991	8.75	28
1991	Mary's Angels-Iris (4th Ed.) 675QX4279	Yr.Iss.	1991	6.75	30-40

YEAR ISSUE		EDITION LIMIT	YEAR RETD.	ISSUE PRICE	QUOTE U.S.$
1991	Merry Olde Santa-(2nd Ed.) 1475QX4359	Yr.Iss.	1991	14.75	65-80
1991	Peace on Earth-Italy (1st Ed.) 1175QX5129	Yr.Iss.	1991	11.75	26-35
1991	Puppy Love-(1st Ed.) 775QX5379	Yr.Iss.	1991	7.75	40-48
1991	Reindeer Champ-Cupid (6th Ed.) 775QX4347	Yr.Iss.	1991	7.75	20-30
1991	Rocking Horse-(11th Ed.) 1075QX4147	Yr.Iss.	1991	10.75	30-35
1991	Santa's Antique Car-(13th Ed.) 1475QX4349	Yr.Iss.	1991	14.75	18-47
1991	Winter Surprise-(3rd Ed.) 1075QX4277	Yr.Iss.	1991	10.75	20-35

1991 Commemoratives - Keepsake

1991	Across the Miles 675QX3157	Yr.Iss.	1991	6.75	14
1991	Baby's First Christmas 1775QX5107	Yr.Iss.	1991	17.75	43
1991	Baby's First Christmas 775QX4889	Yr.Iss.	1991	7.75	23-35
1991	Baby's First Christmas-Baby Boy475QX2217	Yr.Iss.	1991	4.75	15-20
1991	Baby's First Christmas-Baby Girl475QX2227	Yr.Iss.	1991	4.75	15-20
1991	Baby's First Christmas-Photo Holder 775QX4869	Yr.Iss.	1991	7.75	25-30
1991	Baby's Second Christmas 675QX4897	Yr.Iss.	1991	6.75	22-30
1991	The Big Cheese 675QX5327	Yr.Iss.	1991	6.75	18
1991	Brother 675QX5479	Yr.Iss.	1991	6.75	18
1991	A Child's Christmas 975QX4887	Yr.Iss.	1991	9.75	17
1991	Child's Fifth Christmas 675QX4909	Yr.Iss.	1991	6.75	20
1991	Child's Fourth Christmas 675QX4907	Yr.Iss.	1991	6.75	20
1991	Child's Third Christmas 675QX4899	Yr.Iss.	1991	6.75	26
1991	Dad 775QX5127	Yr.Iss.	1991	7.75	19
1991	Dad-to-Be 575QX4879	Yr.Iss.	1991	5.75	15
1991	Daughter 575QX5477	Yr.Iss.	1991	5.75	18-40
1991	Extra-Special Friends 475QX2279	Yr.Iss.	1991	4.75	15
1991	Fifty Years Together 875QX4947	Yr.Iss.	1991	8.75	20
1991	Five Years Together 775QX4927	Yr.Iss.	1991	7.75	19
1991	Forty Years Together 775QX4939	Yr.Iss.	1991	7.75	19
1991	Friends Are Fun 975QX5289	Yr.Iss.	1991	9.75	22
1991	From Our Home to Yours 475QX2287	Yr.Iss.	1991	4.75	14-22
1991	Gift of Joy 875QX5319	Yr.Iss.	1991	8.75	18-25
1991	Godchild 675QX5489	Yr.Iss.	1991	6.75	18
1991	Granddaughter 475QX2299	Yr.Iss.	1991	4.75	21
1991	Granddaughter's First Christmas 675QX5119	Yr.Iss.	1991	6.75	18-25
1991	Grandmother 475QX2307	Yr.Iss.	1991	4.75	15-20
1991	Grandparents 475QX2309	Yr.Iss.	1991	4.75	15
1991	Grandson 475QX2297	Yr.Iss.	1991	4.75	15-22
1991	Grandson's First Christmas 675QX5117	Yr.Iss.	1991	6.75	12-24
1991	Jesus Loves Me 775QX3147	Yr.Iss.	1991	7.75	16
1991	Mom and Dad 975QX5467	Yr.Iss.	1991	9.75	25
1991	Mom-to-Be 575QX4877	Yr.Iss.	1991	5.75	20-25
1991	Mother 975QX5457	Yr.Iss.	1991	9.75	25-35
1991	New Home 675QX5449	Yr.Iss.	1991	6.75	26
1991	Our First Christmas Together 475QX2229	Yr.Iss.	1991	4.75	20
1991	Our First Christmas Together 675QX3139	Yr.Iss.	1991	6.75	23
1991	Our First Christmas Together 875QX4919	Yr.Iss.	1991	8.75	27-35
1991	Our First Christmas Together-Photo Holder 875QX4917	Yr.Iss.	1991	8.75	25-30
1991	Sister 675QX5487	Yr.Iss.	1991	6.75	18
1991	Son 575QX5469	Yr.Iss.	1991	5.75	15-30
1991	Sweetheart 975QX4957	Yr.Iss.	1991	9.75	18-25
1991	Teacher 475QX2289	Yr.Iss.	1991	4.75	12
1991	Ten Years Together 775QX4929	Yr.Iss.	1991	7.75	18
1991	Terrific Teacher 675QX5309	Yr.Iss.	1991	6.75	16
1991	Twenty -Five Years Together 875QX4937	Yr.Iss.	1991	8.75	18
1991	Under the Mistletoe 875QX4949	Yr.Iss.	1991	8.75	19

1991 Keepsake Collector's Club - Keepsake

1991	Beary Artistic 1000QXC7259	Yr.Iss.	1991	10.00	32-40
1991	Hidden Treasure/Li'l Keeper 1500QXC4769	Yr.Iss.	1991	15.00	38

1991 Keepsake Magic Ornaments - Keepsake

1991	Angel of Light 3000QLT7239	Yr.Iss.	1991	30.00	60
1991	Arctic Dome 2500QLX7117	Yr.Iss.	1991	25.00	45-55
1991	Baby's First Christmas 3000QLX7247	Yr.Iss.	1991	30.00	55-90
1991	Bringing Home the Tree-2800QLX7249	Yr.Iss.	1991	28.00	51-65
1991	Chris Mouse Mail 1000QLX7207	Yr.Iss.	1991	10.00	25-40
1991	Elfin Engineer 1000QLX7209	Yr.Iss.	1991	10.00	23
1991	Father Christmas 1400QLX7147	Yr.Iss.	1991	14.00	28-40
1991	Festive Brass Church 1400QLX7179	Yr.Iss.	1991	14.00	21-33
1991	Forest Frolics 2500QLX7219	Yr.Iss.	1991	25.00	68
1991	Friendship Tree 1000QLX7169	Yr.Iss.	1991	10.00	24
1991	Holiday Glow 1400QLX7177	Yr.Iss.	1991	14.00	30
1991	It's A Wonderful Life 2000QLX7237	Yr.Iss.	1991	20.00	40-75
1991	Jingle Bears 2500QLX7323	Yr.Iss.	1991	25.00	45-58
1991	Kringles's Bumper Cars-2500QLX7119	Yr.Iss.	1991	25.00	46-55
1991	Mole Family Home 2000QLX7149	Yr.Iss.	1991	20.00	35-50
1991	Our First Christmas Together-2500QXL7137	Yr.Iss.	1991	25.00	45-60
1991	PEANUTS 1800QLX7229	Yr.Iss.	1991	18.00	65
1991	Salvation Army Band 3000QLX7273	Yr.Iss.	1991	30.00	55-80
1991	Santa Special 4000QLX7167	Yr.Iss.	1992	40.00	55-80
1991	Santa's Hot Line 1800QLX7159	Yr.Iss.	1991	18.00	32-42
1991	Ski Trip 2800QLX7266	Yr.Iss.	1991	28.00	50-60
1991	Sparkling Angel 1800QLX7157	Yr.Iss.	1991	18.00	27-37
1991	Starship Enterprise 2000QLX7199	Yr.Iss.	1991	20.00	300-500
1991	Toyland Tower 2000QLX7129	Yr.Iss.	1991	20.00	37-45

1991 Keepsake Miniature Ornaments - Keepsake

1991	All Aboard 450QXM5869	Yr.Iss.	1991	4.50	17
1991	Baby's First Christmas 600QXM5799	Yr.Iss.	1991	6.00	10-21
1991	Brass Church 300QXM5979	Yr.Iss.	1991	3.00	9
1991	Brass Soldier 300QXM5987	Yr.Iss.	1991	3.00	9
1991	Bright Boxers 450QXM5877	Yr.Iss.	1991	4.50	10-17
1991	Busy Bear 450QXM5939	Yr.Iss.	1991	4.50	12
1991	Cardinal Cameo 600QXM5957	Yr.Iss.	1991	6.00	17
1991	Caring Shepherd 600QXM5949	Yr.Iss.	1991	6.00	17
1991	Cool 'n' Sweet 450QXM5867	Yr.Iss.	1991	4.50	20
1991	Country Sleigh 450QXM5999	Yr.Iss.	1991	4.50	14
1991	Courier Turtle 450QXM5857	Yr.Iss.	1991	4.50	14
1991	Fancy Wreath 450QXM5917	Yr.Iss.	1991	4.50	14
1991	Feliz Navidad 600QXM5887	Yr.Iss.	1991	6.00	15
1991	Fly By 450QXM5859	Yr.Iss.	1991	4.50	17
1991	Friendly Fawn 600QXM5947	Yr.Iss.	1991	6.00	17
1991	Grandchild's First Christmas 450QXM5697	Yr.Iss.	1991	4.50	14
1991	Heavenly Minstrel 975QXM5687	Yr.Iss.	1991	9.75	21-30
1991	Holiday Snowflake 300QXM5997	Yr.Iss.	1991	3.00	12
1991	Inn-(4th Ed.) 850QXM5627	Yr.Iss.	1991	8.50	20-30
1991	Key to Love 450QXM5689	Yr.Iss.	1991	4.50	16
1991	Kittens in Toyland-(4th Ed.) 450QXM5639	Yr.Iss.	1991	4.50	14-20
1991	Kitty in a Mitty 450QXM5879	Yr.Iss.	1991	4.50	13
1991	The Kringles-(3rd Ed.) 6000QXM5647	Yr.Iss.	1991	6.00	20-25
1991	Li'l Popper 450QXM5897	Yr.Iss.	1991	4.50	16
1991	Love Is Born 600QXM5959	Yr.Iss.	1991	6.00	18
1991	Lulu & Family 600QXM5677	Yr.Iss.	1991	6.00	14-20
1991	Mom 600QXM5699	Yr.Iss.	1991	6.00	17
1991	N. Pole Buddy 450QXM5927	Yr.Iss.	1991	4.50	18
1991	Nature's Angels-(2nd Ed.) 450QXM5657	Yr.Iss.	1991	4.50	21
1991	Noel 300QXM5989	Yr.Iss.	1991	3.00	12
1991	Our First Christmas Together 600QXM5819	Yr.Iss.	1991	6.00	17
1991	Passenger Car-(3rd Ed.) 850QXM5649	Yr.Iss.	1991	8.50	22-27
1991	Penquin Pal-(4th Ed.) 450QXM5629	Yr.Iss.	1991	4.50	17
1991	Ring-A-Ding Elf 850QXM5669	Yr.Iss.	1991	8.50	18
1991	Rocking Horse-(4th Ed.) 450QXM5637	Yr.Iss.	1991	4.50	21
1991	Seaside Otter 450QXM5909	Yr.Iss.	1991	4.50	13
1991	Silvery Santa 975QXM5679	Yr.Iss.	1991	9.75	23
1991	Special Friends 850QXM5797	Yr.Iss.	1991	8.50	18
1991	Thimble Bells-(2nd Ed.) 600QXM5659	Yr.Iss.	1991	6.00	15-25
1991	Tiny Tea Party Set of 6 2900QXM5827	Yr.Iss.	1991	29.00	142-150
1991	Top Hatter 600QXM5889	Yr.Iss.	1991	6.00	17
1991	Treeland Trio 850QXM5899	Yr.Iss.	1991	8.50	17
1991	Upbeat Bear 600QXM5907	Yr.Iss.	1991	6.00	16
1991	Vision of Santa 450QXM5937	Yr.Iss.	1991	4.50	14
1991	Wee Toymaker 850QXM5967	Yr.Iss.	1991	8.50	15
1991	Woodland Babies 600QXM5667	Yr.Iss.	1991	6.00	15-25

1991 New Attractions - Keepsake

1991	All-Star 675QX5329	Yr.Iss.	1991	6.75	21
1991	Basket Bell Players 775QX5377	Yr.Iss.	1991	7.75	21
1991	Bob Cratchit 1375QX4997	Yr.Iss.	1991	13.75	22-33
1991	Chilly Chap 675QX5339	Yr.Iss.	1991	6.75	18
1991	Christmas Welcome 975QX5299	Yr.Iss.	1991	9.75	23
1991	Christopher Robin 975QX5579	Yr.Iss.	1991	9.75	35-40
1991	Cuddly Lamb 675QX5199	Yr.Iss.	1991	6.75	20
1991	Dinoclaus 775QX5277	Yr.Iss.	1991	7.75	23
1991	Ebenezer Scrooge 1375QX4989	Yr.Iss.	1991	13.75	27-43
1991	Evergreen Inn 875QX5389	Yr.Iss.	1991	8.75	16
1991	Fanfare Bear 875QX5337	Yr.Iss.	1991	8.75	19
1991	Feliz Navidad 675QX5279	Yr.Iss.	1991	6.75	13-25
1991	Folk Art Reindeer 875QX5359	Yr.Iss.	1991	8.75	18
1991	GARFIELD 775QX5177	Yr.Iss.	1991	7.75	20-28
1991	Glee Club Bears 87566QX4969	Yr.Iss.	1991	8.75	18
1991	Holiday Cafe 875QX5399	Yr.Iss.	1991	8.75	15
1991	Jolly Wolly Santa 775QX5419	Yr.Iss.	1991	7.75	15-26
1991	Jolly Wolly Snowman 775QX5427	Yr.Iss.	1991	7.75	15-23
1991	Jolly Wolly Soldier 775QX5429`	Yr.Iss.	1991	7.75	15-23
1991	Joyous Memories-Photoholder 675QX5369	Yr.Iss.	1991	6.75	16-25
1991	Kanga and Roo 975QX5617	Yr.Iss.	1991	9.75	50
1991	Look Out Below 875QX4959	Yr.Iss.	1991	8.75	20
1991	Loving Stitches 875QX4987	Yr.Iss.	1991	8.75	30
1991	Mary Engelbreit 475QX2237	Yr.Iss.	1991	4.75	28
1991	Merry Carolers 2975QX4799	Yr.Iss.	1991	29.75	95
1991	Mrs. Cratchit 1375QX4999	Yr.Iss.	1991	13.75	31
1991	Night Before Christmas 975QX5307	Yr.Iss.	1991	9.75	23
1991	Norman Rockwell Art 500QX2259	Yr.Iss.	1991	5.00	22
1991	Notes of Cheer 575QX5357	Yr.Iss.	1991	5.75	14
1991	Nutshell Nativity 675QX5176	Yr.Iss.	1991	6.75	22
1991	Nutty Squirrel 575QX4833	Yr.Iss.	1991	5.75	14
1991	Old-Fashioned Sled 875QX4317	Yr.Iss.	1991	8.75	18
1991	On a Roll 675QX5347	Yr.Iss.	1991	6.75	20
1991	Partridge in a Pear Tree 975QX5297	Yr.Iss.	1991	9.75	19
1991	PEANUTS® 500QX2257	Yr.Iss.	1991	5.00	16-23
1991	Piglet and Eeyore 975QX5577	Yr.Iss.	1991	9.75	48
1991	Plum Delightful 875QX4977	Yr.Iss.	1991	8.75	19
1991	Polar Classic 675QX5287	Yr.Iss.	1991	6.75	18
1991	Rabbit 975QX5607	Yr.Iss.	1991	9.75	25-30
1991	Santa's Studio 875QX5397	Yr.Iss.	1991	8.75	16
1991	Ski Lift Bunny 675QX5447	Yr.Iss.	1991	6.75	18
1991	SNOOPY and WOODSTOCK 675QX5197	Yr.Iss.	1991	6.75	28-35
1991	Snow Twins 875QX4979	Yr.Iss.	1991	8.75	20
1991	Snowy Owl 775QX5269	Yr.Iss.	1991	7.75	19
1991	Sweet Talk 875QX5367	Yr.Iss.	1991	8.75	23
1991	Tigger 975QX5609	Yr.Iss.	1991	9.75	110
1991	Tiny Tim 1075QX5037	Yr.Iss.	1991	10.75	24-40
1991	Up 'N'Down Journey 975QX5047	Yr.Iss.	1991	9.75	27
1991	Winnie-the Pooh 975QX5569	Yr.Iss.	1991	9.75	55-60
1991	Yule Logger 875QX4967	Yr.Iss.	1991	8.75	17-27

1991 Special Edition - Keepsake

1991	Dickens Caroler Bell-Mrs. Beaumont-2175QX5039	Yr.Iss.	1991	21.75	45-50

1992 Artists' Favorites - Keepsake

1992	Elfin Marionette1175QX5931	Yr.Iss.	1992	11.75	23
1992	Mother Goose 1375QX4984	Yr.Iss.	1992	13.75	30
1992	Polar Post 875QX4914	Yr.Iss.	1992	8.75	19
1992	Stocked With Joy 775QX5934	Yr.Iss.	1992	7.75	22
1992	Turtle Dreams 875QX4991	Yr.Iss.	1992	8.75	28
1992	Uncle Art's Ice Cream 875QX5001	Yr.Iss.	1992	8.75	23

1992 Collectible Series - Keepsake

1992	1966 Mustang-(2nd Ed.) 1275QX4284	Yr.Iss.	1992	12.75	40-55
1992	Betsey's Country Christmas-(1st Ed.) 500QX2104	Yr.Iss.	1992	5.00	20-35
1992	CRAYOLA CRAYON-Bright Colors (4th Ed.) 975QX4264	Yr.Iss.	1992	9.75	25-35
1992	Fabulous Decade-(3rd Ed.) 775QX4244	Yr.Iss.	1992	7.75	35-45
1992	Five-and-Ten-Cent Store (9th Ed.) 1475QX4254	Yr.Iss.	1992	14.75	27-43
1992	Frosty Friends (13th Ed.) 975QX4291	Yr.Iss.	1992	9.75	22-30
1992	The Gift Bringers-Kolyada (4th Ed.) 500QX2124	Yr.Iss.	1992	5.00	15-23
1992	Gift Exchange (7th Ed.) 1475QX4294	Yr.Iss.	1992	14.75	30-40
1992	Greatest Story (3rd Ed.) 1275QX4251	Yr.Iss.	1992	12.75	24
1992	Hark! It's Herald (4th Ed.) 775QX4464	Yr.Iss.	1992	7.75	18-25
1992	Heart of Christmas (3rd Ed.) 1375QX4411	Yr.Iss.	1992	13.75	30
1992	Heavenly Angels (2nd Ed.) 775QX4454	Yr.Iss.	1992	7.75	19-30
1992	Kringle Tours (14th Ed.) 1475QX4341	Yr.Iss.	1992	14.75	27-40
1992	Mary's Angels-Lily (5th Ed.) 675QX4274	Yr.Iss.	1992	6.75	45-50
1992	Merry Olde Santa (3rd Ed.) 1475QX4414	Yr.Iss.	1992	14.75	35-50
1992	Nine Ladies Dancing (9th Ed.) 675QX3031	Yr.Iss.	1992	6.75	20
1992	Owliver (1st Ed.) 775QX4544	Yr.Iss.	1992	7.75	15-20
1992	Peace On Earth-Spain (2nd Ed.) 1175QX5174	Yr.Iss.	1992	11.75	21-28
1992	Puppy Love (2nd Ed.) 775QX4484	Yr.Iss.	1992	7.75	35-42
1992	Reindeer Champs-Donder (7th Ed.) 875QX5284	Yr.Iss.	1992	8.75	26-33
1992	Rocking Horse (12th Ed.) 1075QX4261	Yr.Iss.	1992	10.75	25-40
1992	Sweet Holiday Harmony (6th Ed.) 875QX4461	Yr.Iss.	1992	8.75	19-29
1992	Tobin Fraley Carousel (1st Ed.) 2800QX4891	Yr.Iss.	1992	28.00	14-23
1992	Winter Surprise (4th Ed.) 1175QX4271	Yr.Iss.	1992	11.75	27-33

1992 Collectors' Club - Keepsake

1992	Chipmunk Parcel Service 675QXC5194	Yr.Iss.	1992	6.75	21
1992	Rodney Takes Flight 975QXC5081	Yr.Iss.	1992	9.75	22
1992	Santa's Club List 1500QXC7291	Yr.Iss.	1992	15.00	35-40

1992 Commemoratives - Keepsake

1992	Across the Miles 675QX3044	Yr.Iss.	1992	6.75	14
1992	Anniversary Year 975QX4851	Yr.Iss.	1992	9.75	18-25
1992	Baby's First Christmas 775QX4641	Yr.Iss.	1992	7.75	21
1992	Baby's First Christmas 775QX4644	Yr.Iss.	1992	7.75	18-35
1992	Baby's First Christmas-Baby Boy 475QX2191	Yr.Iss.	1992	4.75	14
1992	Baby's First Christmas-Baby Girl 475QX2204	Yr.Iss.	1992	4.75	15-20
1992	Baby's First Christmas1875QX4581	Yr.Iss.	1992	18.75	35-40

YEAR ISSUE		EDITION LIMIT	YEAR RETD.	ISSUE PRICE	QUOTE U.S.$
1992	Baby's Second Christmas 675QX4651	Yr.Iss.	1992	6.75	20-40
1992	Brother 675QX4684	Yr.Iss.	1992	6.75	14
1992	A Child's Christmas 975QX4574	Yr.Iss.	1992	9.75	19
1992	Child's Fifth Christmas 675QX4664	Yr.Iss.	1992	6.75	15
1992	Child's Fourth Christmas 675QX4661	Yr.Iss.	1992	6.75	15-25
1992	Child's Third Christmas 675QX4654	Yr.Iss.	1992	6.75	15-25
1992	Dad 775QX4674	Yr.Iss.	1992	7.75	18
1992	Dad-to-Be 675QX4611	Yr.Iss.	1992	6.75	17
1992	Daughter 675QX5031	Yr.Iss.	1992	6.75	22-30
1992	For My Grandma 775QX5184	Yr.Iss.	1992	7.75	14
1992	For The One I Love 975QX4884	Yr.Iss.	1992	9.75	20
1992	Friendly Greetings 775QX5041	Yr.Iss.	1992	7.75	16
1992	Friendship Line 975QX5034	Yr.Iss.	1992	9.75	20-30
1992	From Our Home To Yours 475QX2131	Yr.Iss.	1992	4.75	15
1992	Godchild 675QX5941	Yr.Iss.	1992	6.75	19
1992	Grandaughter 675QX5604	Yr.Iss.	1992	6.75	17
1992	Grandaughter's First Christmas 675QX4634	Yr.Iss.	1992	6.75	18
1992	Grandmother 475QX2011	Yr.Iss.	1992	4.75	17
1992	Grandparents 475QX2004	Yr.Iss.	1992	4.75	17
1992	Grandson 675QX5611	Yr.Iss.	1992	6.75	17
1992	Grandson's First Christmas 675QX4621	Yr.Iss.	1992	6.75	20
1992	Holiday Memo 775QX5044	Yr.Iss.	1992	7.75	15
1992	Love To Skate 875QX4841	Yr.Iss.	1992	8.75	18
1992	Mom 775QX5164	Yr.Iss.	1992	7.75	18
1992	Mom and Dad 975QX4671	Yr.Iss.	1992	9.75	35
1992	Mom-to-Be 675QX4614	Yr.Iss.	1992	6.75	17-25
1992	New Home 875QX5191	Yr.Iss.	1992	8.75	18-25
1992	Our First Christmas Together 875QX4694	Yr.Iss.	1992	8.75	20-25
1992	Our First Christmas Together 675QX3011	Yr.Iss.	1992	6.75	19
1992	Our First Christmas Together 975QX5061	Yr.Iss.	1992	9.75	20-35
1992	Secret Pal 775QX5424	Yr.Iss.	1992	7.75	15
1992	Sister 675QX4681	Yr.Iss.	1992	6.75	16
1992	Son 675QX5024	Yr.Iss.	1992	6.75	20-30
1992	Special Cat 775QX5414	Yr.Iss.	1992	7.75	17
1992	Special Dog 775QX5421	Yr.Iss.	1992	7.75	30
1992	Teacher 475QX2264	Yr.Iss.	1992	4.75	17
1992	V. P. of Important Stuff 675QX5051	Yr.Iss.	1992	6.75	14
1992	World-Class Teacher 775QX5054	Yr.Iss.	1992	7.75	20

1992 Easter Ornaments - Keepsake

1992	Easter Parade (1st Ed.) 675QEO8301	Yr.Iss.	1992	6.75	25-30
1992	Egg in Sports (1st Ed.) 675QEO9341	Yr.Iss.	1992	6.75	25-35

1992 Limited Edition Ornaments - Keepsake

1992	Christmas Treasures 2200QXC5464	15,500	1992	22.00	22
1992	Victorian Skater (w/ base) 2500QXC4067	14,700	1992	25.00	35

1992 Magic Ornaments - Keepsake

1992	Angel Of Light 3000QLT7239	Yr.Iss.	1992	30.00	30
1992	Baby's First Christmas 2200QLX7281	Yr.Iss.	1992	22.00	88-95
1992	Chris Mouse Tales (8th Ed.) 1200QLX7074	Yr.Iss.	1992	12.00	25-30
1992	Christmas Parade 3000QLX7271	Yr.Iss.	1992	30.00	54-60
1992	Continental Express 3200QLX7264	Yr.Iss.	1992	32.00	60-70
1992	The Dancing Nutcracker 3000QLX7261	Yr.Iss.	1992	30.00	40-60
1992	Enchanted Clock 3000QLX7274	Yr.Iss.	1992	30.00	53-60
1992	Feathered Friends 1400QLX7091	Yr.Iss.	1992	14.00	29
1992	Forest Frolics-(4th Ed.) 2800QLX7254	Yr.Iss.	1992	28.00	52-60
1992	Good Sledding Ahead 2800QLX7244	Yr.Iss.	1992	28.00	55
1992	Lighting the Way 1800QLX7231	Yr.Iss.	1992	18.00	39
1992	Look! It's Santa 1400QLX7094	Yr.Iss.	1992	14.00	30-40
1992	Nut Sweet Nut 1000QLX7081	Yr.Iss.	1992	10.00	22
1992	Out First Christmas Together 2000QLX7221	Yr.Iss.	1992	20.00	40-45
1992	PEANUTS® (2nd Ed.) 1800QLX7214	Yr.Iss.	1992	18.00	45-55
1992	Santa Special 4000QLX7167	Yr.Iss.	1992	40.00	80
1992	Santa Sub 1800QLX7321	Yr.Iss.	1992	18.00	34-40
1992	Santa's Answering Machine 2200QLX7241	Yr.Iss.	1992	22.00	43
1992	Under Construction 1800QLX7324	Yr.Iss.	1992	18.00	35-42
1992	Watch Owls 1200QLX7084	Yr.Iss.	1992	12.00	24-30
1992	Yuletide Rider 2800QLX7314	Yr.Iss.	1992	28.00	52-60

1992 Miniature Ornaments - Keepsake

1992	A+ Teacher 375QXM5511	Yr.Iss.	1992	3.75	8
1992	Angelic Harpist 450QXM5524	Yr.Iss.	1992	4.50	13
1992	Baby's First Christmas 450QXM5494	Yr.Iss.	1992	4.50	18
1992	The Bearymores(1st Ed.) 575QXM5544	Yr.Iss.	1992	5.75	15-20
1992	Black-Capped Chickadee 300QXM5484	Yr.Iss.	1992	3.00	13
1992	Box Car (4th Ed.) Noel R.R. 700QXM5441	Yr.Iss.	1992	7.00	13-23
1992	Bright Stringers 375QXM5841	Yr.Iss.	1992	3.75	14
1992	Buck-A-Roo 450QXM5814	Yr.Iss.	1992	4.50	14
1992	Christmas Bonus 300QXM5811	Yr.Iss.	1992	3.00	8
1992	Christmas Copter 575QXM5844	Yr.Iss.	1992	5.75	15
1992	Church (5th Ed.) Old English V. 700QXM5384	Yr.Iss.	1992	7.00	20-30
1992	Coca-Cola Santa 575QXM5884	Yr.Iss.	1992	5.75	16
1992	Cool Uncle Sam 300QXM5561	Yr.Iss.	1992	3.00	14
1992	Cozy Kayak 375QXM5551	Yr.Iss.	1992	3.75	12
1992	Fast Finish 375QXM5301	Yr.Iss.	1992	3.75	12
1992	Feeding Time 575QXM5481	Yr.Iss.	1992	5.75	16
1992	Friendly Tin Soldier 450QXM5874	Yr.Iss.	1992	4.50	10-18
1992	Friends Are Tops 450QXM5521	Yr.Iss.	1992	4.50	10
1992	Gerbil Inc. 375QXM5924	Yr.Iss.	1992	3.75	11
1992	Going Places 375QXM5871	Yr.Iss.	1992	3.75	10
1992	Grandchild's First Christmas 575QXM5501	Yr.Iss.	1992	5.75	13
1992	Grandma 450QXM5514	Yr.Iss.	1992	4.50	15
1992	Harmony Trio-Set of Three 1175QXM5471	Yr.Iss.	1992	11.75	20
1992	Hickory, Dickory, Dock 375QXM5861	Yr.Iss.	1992	3.75	13
1992	Holiday Holly 975QXM5364	Yr.Iss.	1992	9.75	20
1992	Holiday Splash 575QXM5834	Yr.Iss.	1992	5.75	12
1992	Hoop It Up 450QXM5831	Yr.Iss.	1992	4.50	11
1992	Inside Story 725QXM5881	Yr.Iss.	1992	7.25	15-20
1992	Kittens in Toyland (5th Ed.) 450QXM5391	Yr.Iss.	1992	4.50	15
1992	The Kringles-(4th Ed.) 600QXM5381	Yr.Iss.	1992	6.00	16-23
1992	Little Town of Bethlehem 300QXM5864	Yr.Iss.	1992	3.00	18
1992	Minted For Santa 375QXM5854	Yr.Iss.	1992	3.75	14
1992	Mom 450QXM5504	Yr.Iss.	1992	4.50	14
1992	Nature's Angels (3rd Ed.) 450QXM5451	Yr.Iss.	1992	4.50	15-20
1992	The Night Before Christmas 1375QXM5541	Yr.Iss.	1992	13.75	27-35
1992	Perfect Balance 300QXM5571	Yr.Iss.	1992	3.00	13
1992	Polar Polka 450QXM5534	Yr.Iss.	1992	4.50	14
1992	Puppet Show 300QXM5574	Yr.Iss.	1992	3.00	12
1992	Rocking Horse (5th Ed.) 450QXM5454	Yr.Iss.	1992	4.50	14-20
1992	Sew Sew Tiny (set/6) 2900QXM5794	Yr.Iss.	1992	29.00	55
1992	Ski For Two 450QXM5821	Yr.Iss.	1992	4.50	14
1992	Snowshoe Bunny 375QXM5564	Yr.Iss.	1992	3.75	12
1992	Snug Kitty 375QXM5554	Yr.Iss.	1992	3.75	13
1992	Spunky Monkey 300QXM5921	Yr.Iss.	1992	3.00	13
1992	Thimble Bells (3rd Ed.) 600QXM5461	Yr.Iss.	1992	6.00	15-20
1992	Visions Of Acorns 450QXM5851	Yr.Iss.	1992	4.50	15
1992	Wee Three Kings 575QXM5531	Yr.Iss.	1992	5.75	18
1992	Woodland Babies (2nd Ed.) 600QXM5444	Yr.Iss.	1992	6.00	14

1992 New Attractions - Keepsake

1992	Bear Bell Champ 775QX5071	Yr.Iss.	1992	7.75	16
1992	Caboose 975QX5321	Yr.Iss.	1992	9.75	20
1992	Cheerful Santa 975QX5154	Yr.Iss.	1992	9.75	35
1992	Coal Car 975QX5401	Yr.Iss.	1992	9.75	19
1992	Cool Fliers 1075QX5474	Yr.Iss.	1992	10.75	20-25
1992	Deck the Hogs 875QX5204	Yr.Iss.	1992	8.75	15-23
1992	Down-Under Holiday 775QX5144	Yr.Iss.	1992	7.75	18
1992	Egg Nog Nest 775QX5121	Yr.Iss.	1992	7.75	16
1992	Eric the Baker 875QX5244	Yr.Iss.	1992	8.75	18
1992	Feliz Navidad 675QX5181	Yr.Iss.	1992	6.75	18
1992	Franz the Artist 875QX5261	Yr.Iss.	1992	8.75	18
1992	Freida the Animals' Friend 875QX5264	Yr.Iss.	1992	8.75	16-25
1992	Fun on a Big Scale 1075QX5134	Yr.Iss.	1992	10.75	22
1992	GARFIELD 775QX5374	Yr.Iss.	1992	7.75	18
1992	Genius at Work 1075QX5371	Yr.Iss.	1992	10.75	20
1992	Golf's a Ball 675QX5984	Yr.Iss.	1992	6.75	28
1992	Gone Wishin' 875QX5171	Yr.Iss.	1992	8.75	19
1992	Green Thumb Santa 775QX5101	Yr.Iss.	1992	7.75	17
1992	Hello-Ho-Ho 975QX5141	Yr.Iss.	1992	9.75	16-23
1992	Holiday Teatime 1475QX5431	Yr.Iss.	1992	14.75	28
1992	Holiday Wishes 775QX5131	Yr.Iss.	1992	7.75	17
1992	Honest George 775QX5064	Yr.Iss.	1992	7.75	18
1992	Jesus Loves Me 775QX3024	Yr.Iss.	1992	7.75	15
1992	Locomotive 975QX5311	Yr.Iss.	1992	9.75	43-60
1992	Loving Shepherd 775QX5151	Yr.Iss.	1992	7.75	15
1992	Ludwig the Musician 875QX5281	Yr.Iss.	1992	8.75	15-20
1992	Mary Engelbreit Santa Jolly Wolly 775QX5224	Yr.Iss.	1992	7.75	8
1992	Max the Tailor 875QX5251	Yr.Iss.	1992	8.75	20
1992	Memories to Cherish 1075QX5161	Yr.Iss.	1992	10.75	20
1992	Merry "Swiss" Mouse 775QX5114	Yr.Iss.	1992	7.75	15
1992	Norman Rockwell Art 500QX2224	Yr.Iss.	1992	5.00	19
1992	North Pole Fire Fighter 975QX5104	Yr.Iss.	1992	9.75	21
1992	Otto the Carpenter 875QX5254	Yr.Iss.	1992	8.75	21
1992	Owl 975QX5614	Yr.Iss.	1992	9.75	20
1992	Partridge In a Pear Tree 875QX5234	Yr.Iss.	1992	8.75	19
1992	PEANUTS® 500QX2244	Yr.Iss.	1992	5.00	15-23
1992	Please Pause Here 1475QX5291	Yr.Iss.	1992	14.75	31-45
1992	Rapid Delivery 875QX5094	Yr.Iss.	1992	8.75	21
1992	Santa's Hook Shot 1275QX5434	Yr.Iss.	1992	12.75	29
1992	Santa's Roundup 875QX5084	Yr.Iss.	1992	8.75	20-25
1992	A Santa-Full! 975QX5991	Yr.Iss.	1992	9.75	30-40
1992	Silver Star 2800QX5324	Yr.Iss.	1992	28.00	54-60
1992	Skiing 'Round 875QX5214	Yr.Iss.	1992	8.75	18
1992	SNOOPY® and WOODSTOCK 875QX5954	Yr.Iss.	1992	8.75	19-29
1992	Spirit of Christmas Stress 875QX5231	Yr.Iss.	1992	8.75	15-23
1992	Stock Car 975QX5314	Yr.Iss.	1992	9.75	19
1992	Tasty Christmas 975QX5994	Yr.Iss.	1992	9.75	19-25
1992	Toboggan Tail 775QX5459	Yr.Iss.	1992	7.75	16
1992	Tread Bear 875QX5091	Yr.Iss.	1992	8.75	23

1992 Special Edition - Keepsake

1992	Dickens Caroler Bell-Lord Chadwick (3rd Ed.) 2175QX4554	Yr.Iss.	1992	21.75	38-50

1992 Special Issues - Keepsake

1992	Elvis 1475QX562-4	Yr.Iss.	1992	14.75	15-35
1992	Santa Maria 1275QX5074	Yr.Iss.	1992	12.75	20-30
1992	Shuttlecraft Galileo 2400QLX733-1	Yr.Iss.	1992	24.00	35-60

1993 Anniversary Edition - Keepsake

1993	Frosty Friends 2000QX5682	Yr.Iss.	1993	20.00	20-50
1993	Glowing Pewter Wreath 1875QX5302	Yr.Iss.	1993	18.75	38
1993	Shopping With Santa 2400QX5675	Yr.Iss.	1993	24.00	25-50
1993	Tannenbaum's Dept. Store 2600QX5612	Yr.Iss.	1993	26.00	54-60

1993 Artists' Favorites - Keepsake

1993	Bird Watcher 975QX5252	Yr.Iss.	1993	9.75	15-20
1993	Howling Good Time 975QX5255	Yr.Iss.	1993	9.75	18
1993	On Her Toes 875QX5265	Yr.Iss.	1993	8.75	18
1993	Peek-a-Boo Tree 1075QX5245	Yr.Iss.	1993	10.75	20-30
1993	Wake-Up Call 875QX5262	Yr.Iss.	1993	8.75	18

1993 Collectible Series - Keepsake

1993	1956 Ford Thunderbird (3rd Ed.) 1275QX5275	Yr.Iss.	1993	12.75	25-35
1993	Barbie 1475QX5725	Yr.Iss.	1993	14.75	115-125
1993	Betsey's Country Christmas (2nd Ed.) 500QX2062	Yr.Iss.	1993	5.00	20
1993	Cozy Home (10th Ed.) 1475QX4175	Yr.Iss.	1993	14.75	32-40
1993	CRAYOLA CRAYON-Bright Shining Castle (5th Ed.) 1075QX4422	Yr.Iss.	1993	11.00	22-35
1993	Fabulous Decade (4th Ed.) 775QX4475	Yr.Iss.	1993	7.75	14-20
1993	A Fitting Moment (8th Ed.) 1475QX4202	Yr.Iss.	1993	14.75	20-40
1993	Frosty Friends (14th Ed.) 975QX4142	Yr.Iss.	1993	9.75	22-35
1993	The Gift Bringers-The Magi (5th Ed.) 500QX2065	Yr.Iss.	1993	5.00	10-18
1993	Happy Haul-idays (15th Ed.) 1475QX4102	Yr.Iss.	1993	14.75	26-33
1993	Heart Of Christmas-(4th Ed.) 1475QX4482	Yr.Iss.	1993	14.75	20-30
1993	Heavenly Angels (3rd Ed.) 775QX4945	Yr.Iss.	1993	7.75	18
1993	Humpty-Dumpty (1st Ed.) 1375QX5282	Yr.Iss.	1993	13.75	28-34
1993	Mary's Angels-Ivy (6th Ed.) 675QX4282	Yr.Iss.	1993	6.75	15-30
1993	Merry Olde Santa-(4th Ed.) 1475QX4842	Yr.Iss.	1993	14.75	27-40
1993	Owliver (2nd Ed.) 775QX5425	Yr.Iss.	1993	7.75	17
1993	Peace On Earth-Poland (3rd Ed.) 1175QX5242	Yr.Iss.	1993	11.75	21-45
1993	Peanuts (1st Ed.) 975QX5315	Yr.Iss.	1993	9.75	35-55
1993	Puppy Love (3rd Ed.) 775QX5045	Yr.Iss.	1993	7.75	25
1993	Reindeer Champs-Blitzen (8th Ed.) 875QX4331	Yr.Iss.	1993	8.75	21
1993	Rocking Horse (13th Ed.) 1075QX4162	Yr.Iss.	1993	10.75	27-35
1993	Ten Lords A-Leaping (10th Ed.) 675QX3012	Yr.Iss.	1993	6.75	17
1993	Tobin Fraley Carousel (2nd Ed.) 2800QX5502	Yr.Iss.	1993	28.00	40-55
1993	U.S. Christmas Stamps (1st Ed.) 1075QX5292	Yr.Iss.	1993	10.75	25-40

1993 Commemoratives - Keepsake

1993	Across the Miles 875QX5912	Yr.Iss.	1993	8.75	18
1993	Anniversary Year 975QX5972	Yr.Iss.	1993	9.75	18
1993	Apple for Teacher 775QX5902	Yr.Iss.	1993	7.75	16
1993	Baby's First Christmas 1075QX5515	Yr.Iss.	1993	10.75	21
1993	Baby's First Christmas 1875QX5512	Yr.Iss.	1993	18.75	40
1993	Baby's First Christmas 775QX5522	Yr.Iss.	1993	7.75	21
1993	Baby's First Christmas 775QX5525	Yr.Iss.	1993	7.75	20-30
1993	Baby's First Christmas-Baby Boy 475QX2105	Yr.Iss.	1993	4.75	13
1993	Baby's First Christmas-Baby Girl 475QX2092	Yr.Iss.	1993	4.75	11
1993	Baby's Second Christmas 675QX5992	Yr.Iss.	1993	6.75	20-25
1993	Brother 675QX5542	Yr.Iss.	1993	6.75	14
1993	A Child's Christmas 975QX5882	Yr.Iss.	1993	9.75	22
1993	Child's Fifth Christmas 675QX5222	Yr.Iss.	1993	6.75	16
1993	Child's Fourth Christmas 675QX5215	Yr.Iss.	1993	6.75	13-25
1993	Child's Third Christmas 675QX5995	Yr.Iss.	1993	6.75	15-25
1993	Coach 675QX5935	Yr.Iss.	1993	6.75	15
1993	Dad 775QX5855	Yr.Iss.	1993	7.75	16

YEAR ISSUE	EDITION LIMIT	YEAR RETD.	ISSUE PRICE	QUOTE U.S.$
1993 Dad-to-Be 675QX5532	Yr.Iss.	1993	6.75	15-25
1993 Daughter 675QX5872	Yr.Iss.	1993	6.75	13-20
1993 Godchild 875QX5875	Yr.Iss.	1993	8.75	15-20
1993 Grandchild's First Christmas 675QX5552	Yr.Iss.	1993	6.75	15
1993 Granddaughter 675QX5635	Yr.Iss.	1993	6.75	15
1993 Grandmother 675QX5665	Yr.Iss.	1993	6.75	15
1993 Grandparents 475QX2085	Yr.Iss.	1993	4.75	14
1993 Grandson 675QX5632	Yr.Iss.	1993	6.75	15
1993 Mom 775QX5852	Yr.Iss.	1993	7.75	14-20
1993 Mom and Dad 975QX5845	Yr.Iss.	1993	9.75	14-25
1993 Mom-to-Be 675QX5535	Yr.Iss.	1993	6.75	14
1993 Nephew 675QX5735	Yr.Iss.	1993	6.75	14
1993 New Home 775QX5905	Yr.Iss.	1993	7.75	40-50
1993 Niece 675QX5732	Yr.Iss.	1993	6.75	14
1993 Our Christmas Together 1075QX5942	Yr.Iss.	1993	10.75	22
1993 Our Family 775QX5892	Yr.Iss.	1993	7.75	17
1993 Our First Christmas Together 1875QX5955	Yr.Iss.	1993	18.75	37
1993 Our First Christmas Together 675QX3015	Yr.Iss.	1993	6.75	15
1993 Our First Christmas Together 875QX5952	Yr.Iss.	1993	8.75	18-25
1993 Our First Christmas Together 975QX5642	Yr.Iss.	1993	9.75	15-30
1993 People Friendly 875QX5932	Yr.Iss.	1993	8.75	17
1993 Sister 675QX5545	Yr.Iss.	1993	6.75	16-23
1993 Sister to Sister 975QX5885	Yr.Iss.	1993	9.75	40-50
1993 Son 675QX5865	Yr.Iss.	1993	6.75	12-25
1993 Special Cat 775QX5235	Yr.Iss.	1993	7.75	15
1993 Special Dog 775QX5962	Yr.Iss.	1993	7.75	15
1993 Star Teacher 575QX5645	Yr.Iss.	1993	5.75	14
1993 Strange and Wonderful Love 875QX5965	Yr.Iss.	1993	8.75	17
1993 To My Grandma 775QX5555	Yr.Iss.	1993	7.75	17
1993 Top Banana 775QX5925	Yr.Iss.	1993	7.75	19
1993 Warm and Special Friends 1075QX5895	Yr.Iss.	1993	10.75	25

1993 Easter Ornaments - Keepsake

YEAR ISSUE	EDITION LIMIT	YEAR RETD.	ISSUE PRICE	QUOTE U.S.$
1993 Easter Parade (2nd Ed.) 675QEO8325	Yr.Iss.	1993	6.75	18
1993 Egg in Sports (2nd Ed.) 675QEO8332	Yr.Iss.	1993	6.75	18
1993 Springtime Bonnets (1st Ed. 775QEO8322	Yr.Iss.	1993	7.75	25

1993 Keepsake Collector's Club - Keepsake

YEAR ISSUE	EDITION LIMIT	YEAR RETD.	ISSUE PRICE	QUOTE U.S.$
1993 It's In The Mail 1000QXC5272	Yr.Iss.	1993	10.00	21
1993 Trimmed With Memories 1200QXC5432	Yr.Iss.	1993	12.00	38

1993 Keepsake Magic Ornaments - Keepsake

YEAR ISSUE	EDITION LIMIT	YEAR RETD.	ISSUE PRICE	QUOTE U.S.$
1993 Baby's First Christmas 2200QLX7365	Yr.Iss.	1993	22.00	40-45
1993 Bells Are Ringing 2800QLX7402	Yr.Iss.	1993	28.00	40-60
1993 Chris Mouse Flight (9th Ed.) 1200QLX7152	Yr.Iss.	1993	12.00	28
1993 Dog's Best Friend 1200QLX7172	Yr.Iss.	1993	12.00	22-35
1993 Dollhouse Dreams 2200QLX7372	Yr.Iss.	1993	22.00	38-50
1993 Forest Frolics (5th Ed.) 2500QLX7165	Yr.Iss.	1993	25.00	48-53
1993 Home On The Range 3200QLX7395	Yr.Iss.	1993	32.00	63-70
1993 The Lamplighter 1800QLX7192	Yr.Iss.	1993	18.00	34-40
1993 Last-Minute Shopping 2800QLX7385	Yr.Iss.	1993	28.00	41-60
1993 North Pole Merrython 2500QLX7392	Yr.Iss.	1993	25.00	45-50
1993 Our First Christmas Together 2000QLX7355	Yr.Iss.	1993	20.00	39-45
1993 PEANUTS® (3rd Ed.) 1800QLX7155	Yr.Iss.	1993	18.00	34-43
1993 Radio News Flash 2200QLX7362	Yr.Iss.	1993	22.00	40-45
1993 Raiding The Fridge1600QLX7185	Yr.Iss.	1993	16.00	35-40
1993 Road Runner and Wile E. Coyote 3000QLX7415	Yr.Iss.	1993	30.00	68-75
1993 Santa's Snow-Getter 1800QLX7352	Yr.Iss.	1993	18.00	39
1993 Santa's Workshop 2800QLX7375	Yr.Iss.	1993	28.00	54-60
1993 Song Of The Chimes 2500QLX7405	Yr.Iss.	1993	25.00	50-55
1993 Winnie The Pooh 2400QLX7422	Yr.Iss.	1993	24.00	50

1993 Limited Edition Ornaments - Keepsake

YEAR ISSUE	EDITION LIMIT	YEAR RETD.	ISSUE PRICE	QUOTE U.S.$
1993 Gentle Tidings 2500QXC5442	17,500	1993	25.00	50
1993 Sharing Christmas 2000QXC5435	16,500	1993	20.00	45

1993 Miniature Ornaments - Keepsake

YEAR ISSUE	EDITION LIMIT	YEAR RETD.	ISSUE PRICE	QUOTE U.S.$
1993 'Round The Mountain 725QXM4025	Yr.Iss.	1993	7.25	17
1993 Baby's First Christmas 575QXM5145	Yr.Iss.	1993	5.75	10-15
1993 The Bearymores (2nd Ed.). 575QXM5125	Yr.Iss.	1993	5.75	17
1993 Cheese Please 375QXM4072	Yr.Iss.	1993	3.75	7
1993 Christmas Castle 575QXM4085	Yr.Iss.	1993	5.75	13
1993 Cloisonne Snowflake 975QXM4012	Yr.Iss.	1993	9.75	18
1993 Country Fiddling 375QXM4062	Yr.Iss.	1993	3.75	9
1993 Crystal Angel 975QXM4015	Yr.Iss.	1993	9.75	53-75
1993 Ears To Pals 375QXM4075	Yr.Iss.	1993	3.75	8
1993 Flatbed Car (5th Ed.) 700QXM5105	Yr.Iss.	1993	7.00	13-20
1993 Grandma 450QXM5162	Yr.Iss.	1993	4.50	12
1993 I Dream Of Santa 375QXM4055	Yr.Iss.	1993	3.75	11
1993 Into The Woods 375QXM4045	Yr.Iss.	1993	3.75	8
1993 The Kringles (5th Ed.) 575QXM5135	Yr.Iss.	1993	5.75	14
1993 Learning To Skate 300QXM4122	Yr.Iss.	1993	3.00	8
1993 Lighting A Path 300QXM4115	Yr.Iss.	1993	3.00	8
1993 March Of The Teddy Bears (1st Ed.) 500QX2403	Yr.Iss.	1993	4.50	13-25
1993 Merry Mascot 375QXM4042	Yr.Iss.	1993	3.75	9
1993 Mom 450QXM5155	Yr.Iss.	1993	4.50	12
1993 Monkey Melody 575QXM4092	Yr.Iss.	1993	5.75	13
1993 Nature's Angels-(4th Ed.) 450QXM5122	Yr.Iss.	1993	4.50	10-15
1993 The Night Before Christmas (2nd Ed.) 4505QXM5115	Yr.Iss.	1993	4.50	16
1993 North Pole Fire Truck 475QXM4105	Yr.Iss.	1993	4.75	10
1993 On The Road (1st Ed.) 575QXM4002	Yr.Iss.	1993	5.75	12-25
1993 Pear-Shaped Tones 375QXM4052	Yr.Iss.	1993	3.75	7
1993 Pull Out A Plum 575QXM4095	Yr.Iss.	1993	5.75	12
1993 Refreshing Flight 575QXM4112	Yr.Iss.	1993	5.75	14
1993 Rocking Horse (6th Ed.) 450QXM5112	Yr.Iss.	1993	4.50	13
1993 Secret Pals 375QXM5172	Yr.Iss.	1993	3.75	10
1993 Snuggle Birds 575QXM5182	Yr.Iss.	1993	5.75	14
1993 Special Friends 450QXM5165	Yr.Iss.	1993	4.50	9
1993 Thimble Bells (4th Ed.) 575QXM5142	Yr.Iss.	1993	5.75	14
1993 Tiny Green Thumbs, Set/6, 2900QXM4032	Yr.Iss.	1993	29.00	36-50
1993 Toy Shop 6th Ed.) 700QXM5132	Yr.Iss.	1993	7.00	18
1993 Visions Of Sugarplums 725QXM4022	Yr.Iss.	1993	7.25	15
1993 Woodland Babies (3rd Ed.) 575QXM5102	Yr.Iss.	1993	5.75	14

1993 New Attractions - Keepsake

YEAR ISSUE	EDITION LIMIT	YEAR RETD.	ISSUE PRICE	QUOTE U.S.$
1993 Beary Gifted 775QX5762	Yr.Iss.	1993	7.75	18
1993 Big on Gardening 975QX5842	Yr.Iss.	1993	9.75	18
1993 Big Roller 875QX5352	Yr.Iss.	1993	8.75	17
1993 Bowling For ZZZ's 775QX5565	Yr.Iss.	1993	7.75	18
1993 Bugs Bunny 875QX5412	Yr.Iss.	1993	8.75	24
1993 Caring Nurse 675QX5785	Yr.Iss.	1993	6.75	19
1993 Christmas Break 775QX5825	Yr.Iss.	1993	7.75	18
1993 Clever Cookie 775QX5662	Yr.Iss.	1993	7.75	16-23
1993 Curly 'n' Kingly 1075QX5285	Yr.Iss.	1993	10.75	21
1993 Dunkin' Roo 775QX5575	Yr.Iss.	1993	7.75	15
1993 Eeyore 975QX5712	Yr.Iss.	1993	9.75	16-25
1993 Elmer Fudd 875QX5495	Yr.Iss.	1993	8.75	18-25
1993 Faithful Fire Fighter 775QX5782	Yr.Iss.	1993	7.75	19
1993 Feliz Navidad 875QX5365	Yr.Iss.	1993	9.75	18
1993 Fills the Bill 875QX5572	Yr.Iss.	1993	8.75	17
1993 Great Connections 1075QX5402	Yr.Iss.	1993	10.75	20-25
1993 He Is Born 975QX5362	Yr.Iss.	1993	9.75	35-40
1993 High Top-Purr 875QX5332	Yr.Iss.	1993	8.75	20-25
1993 Home For Christmas 775QX5562	Yr.Iss.	1993	7.75	15
1993 Icicle Bicycle 975QX5835	Yr.Iss.	1993	9.75	18
1993 Kanga and Roo 975QX5672	Yr.Iss.	1993	9.75	23
1993 Little Drummer Boy 875QX5372	Yr.Iss.	1993	8.75	20
1993 Look For Wonder 1275QX5685	Yr.Iss.	1993	12.75	26
1993 Lou Rankin Polar Bear 975QX5745	Yr.Iss.	1993	9.75	21-28
1993 Makin' Music 975QX5325	Yr.Iss.	1993	9.75	18
1993 Making Waves 975QX5775	Yr.Iss.	1993	9.75	23
1993 Mary Engelbreit 500QX2075	Yr.Iss.	1993	5.00	14
1993 Maxine 875QX5385	Yr.Iss.	1993	8.75	14-23
1993 One-Elf Marching Band 1275QX5342	Yr.Iss.	1993	12.75	26
1993 Owl 975QX5695	Yr.Iss.	1993	9.75	19
1993 PEANUTS® 500QX2072	Yr.Iss.	1993	5.00	17
1993 Peep Inside 1375QX5322	Yr.Iss.	1993	13.75	18-28
1993 Perfect Match 875QX5772	Yr.Iss.	1993	8.75	19
1993 The Pink Panther 1275QX5755	Yr.Iss.	1993	12.75	20-27
1993 Playful Pals 1475QX5742	Yr.Iss.	1993	14.75	27-35
1993 Popping Good Times 1475QX5392	Yr.Iss.	1993	14.75	28
1993 Porky Pig 875QX5652	Yr.Iss.	1993	8.75	19-25
1993 Putt-Putt Penguin 975QX5795	Yr.Iss.	1993	9.75	19
1993 Quick As A Fox 875QX5792	Yr.Iss.	1993	8.75	12-18
1993 Rabbit 975QX5702	Yr.Iss.	1993	9.75	19
1993 Ready For Fun 775QX5124	Yr.Iss.	1993	7.75	17
1993 Room For One More 875QX5382	Yr.Iss.	1993	8.75	45-50
1993 Silvery Noel 1275QX5305	Yr.Iss.	1993	12.75	20-30
1993 Smile! It's Christmas 975QX5335	Yr.Iss.	1993	9.75	18
1993 Snow Bear Angel 775QX5355	Yr.Iss.	1993	7.75	16
1993 Snowbird 775QX5765	Yr.Iss.	1993	7.75	16
1993 Snowy Hideaway 975QX5312	Yr.Iss.	1993	9.75	15-20
1993 Star Of Wonder 675QX5982	Yr.Iss.	1993	6.75	33
1993 Superman 1275QX5752	Yr.Iss.	1993	12.75	35-50
1993 The Swat Team 1275QX5395	Yr.Iss.	1993	12.75	28
1993 Sylvester and Tweety 975QX5405	Yr.Iss.	1993	9.75	30-35
1993 That's Entertainment 875QX5345	Yr.Iss.	1993	8.75	18
1993 Tigger and Piglet 975QX5705	Yr.Iss.	1993	9.75	40-50
1993 Tin Airplane 775QX5622	Yr.Iss.	1993	7.75	25-30
1993 Tin Blimp 775QX5625	Yr.Iss.	1993	7.75	15-20
1993 Tin Hot Air Balloon 775QX5615	Yr.Iss.	1993	7.75	15-20
1993 Water Bed Snooze 975QX5375	Yr.Iss.	1993	9.75	21
1993 Winnie the Pooh 975QX5715	Yr.Iss.	1993	9.75	28-40

1993 Showcase Folk Art Americana - Keepsake

YEAR ISSUE	EDITION LIMIT	YEAR RETD.	ISSUE PRICE	QUOTE U.S.$
1993 Angel in Flight 1575QK1052	Yr.Iss.	1993	15.75	40
1993 Polar Bear Adventure 1500QK1055	Yr.Iss.	1993	15.00	55
1993 Riding in the Woods 1575QK1065	Yr.Iss.	1993	15.75	55
1993 Riding the Wind 1575QK1045	Yr.Iss.	1993	15.75	42
1993 Santa Claus 1675QK1072	Yr.Iss.	1993	16.75	225

1993 Showcase Holiday Enchantment - Keepsake

YEAR ISSUE	EDITION LIMIT	YEAR RETD.	ISSUE PRICE	QUOTE U.S.$
1993 Angelic Messengers 1375QK1032	Yr.Iss.	1993	13.75	40
1993 Bringing Home the Tree 1375QK1042	Yr.Iss.	1993	13.75	35
1993 Journey to the Forest 1375QK1012	Yr.Iss.	1993	13.75	32
1993 The Magi 1375QK1025	Yr.Iss.	1993	13.75	37
1993 Visions of Sugarplums 1375QK1005	Yr.Iss.	1993	13.75	35

1993 Showcase Old-World Silver - Keepsake

YEAR ISSUE	EDITION LIMIT	YEAR RETD.	ISSUE PRICE	QUOTE U.S.$
1993 Silver Dove of Peace 2475QK1075	Yr.Iss.	1993	24.75	15-35
1993 Silver Santa 2475QK1092	Yr.Iss.	1993	24.75	25-55
1993 Silver Sleigh 2475QK1082	Yr.Iss.	1993	24.75	35
1993 Silver Stars and Holly 2475QK1085	Yr.Iss.	1993	24.75	55

1993 Showcase Portraits in Bisque - Keepsake

YEAR ISSUE	EDITION LIMIT	YEAR RETD.	ISSUE PRICE	QUOTE U.S.$
1993 Christmas Feast 1575QK1152	Yr.Iss.	1993	15.75	33
1993 Joy of Sharing1575QK1142	Yr.Iss.	1993	15.75	32
1993 Mistletoe Kiss1575QK1145	Yr.Iss.	1993	15.75	32
1993 Norman Rockwell-Filling the Stockings 1575QK1155	Yr.Iss.	1993	15.75	36
1993 Norman Rockwell-Jolly Postman 1575QK1142	Yr.Iss.	1993	15.75	36

1993 Special Editions - Keepsake

YEAR ISSUE	EDITION LIMIT	YEAR RETD.	ISSUE PRICE	QUOTE U.S.$
1993 Dickens Caroler Bell-Lady Daphne-(4th Ed.) 2175QX5505	Yr.Iss.	1993	21.75	50
1993 Julianne and Teddy 2175QX5295	Yr.Iss.	1993	21.75	40-50

1993 Special Issues - Keepsake

YEAR ISSUE	EDITION LIMIT	YEAR RETD.	ISSUE PRICE	QUOTE U.S.$
1993 Holiday Barbie™ -(1st Ed.) 1475QX572-5	Yr.Iss.	1993	14.75	78-150
1993 Messages of Christmas 3500QLX747-6	Yr.Iss.	1993	35.00	40
1993 Star Trek® The Next Generation 2400QLX741-2	Yr.Iss.	1993	24.00	50-65

1994 Artists' Favorites - Keepsake

YEAR ISSUE	EDITION LIMIT	YEAR RETD.	ISSUE PRICE	QUOTE U.S.$
1994 Cock-a-Doodle Christmas 895QX5396	Yr.Iss.	1994	8.95	14-30
1994 Happy Birthday Jesus 1295QX5423	Yr.Iss.	1994	12.95	19-29
1994 Keep on Mowin' 895QX5413	Yr.Iss.	1994	8.95	15-20
1994 Kitty's Catamaran 1095QX5416	Yr.Iss.	1994	10.95	18
1994 Making It Bright 895QX5403	Yr.Iss.	1994	8.95	14-20

1994 Collectible Series - Keepsake

YEAR ISSUE	EDITION LIMIT	YEAR RETD.	ISSUE PRICE	QUOTE U.S.$
1994 1957 Chevy-(4th Ed.) 1295QX5422	Yr.Iss.	1994	12.95	25-30
1994 Baseball Heroes-Babe Ruth (1st Ed.) 1295QX5323	Yr.Iss.	1994	12.95	35-55
1994 Betsey's Country Christmas (3rd Ed.) 500QX2403	Yr.Iss.	1994	5.00	14
1994 Cat Naps (1st Ed.) 795QX5313	Yr.Iss.	1994	7.95	20-35
1994 CRAYOLA CRAYON-Bright Playful Colors-(6th Ed.) 1095QX5273	Yr.Iss.	1994	10.95	23
1994 Fabulous Decade-(5th Ed.) 795QX5263	Yr.Iss.	1994	7.95	12-25
1994 Frosty Friends (15th Ed.) 995QX5293	Yr.Iss.	1994	9.95	20-25
1994 Handwarming Present (9th Ed.) 1495QX5283	Yr.Iss.	1994	14.95	11-30
1994 Heart of Christmas-(5th Ed.) 1495QX5266	Yr.Iss.	1994	14.95	28
1994 Hey Diddle Diddle-(2nd Ed.) 1395QX5213	Yr.Iss.	1994	13.95	35-40
1994 Kiddie Car Classics-(1st Ed.) 1395QX5426	Yr.Iss.	1994	13.95	35-65
1994 Makin' Tractor Tracks (16th Ed.) 1495QX5296	Yr.Iss.	1994	14.95	50
1994 Mary's Angels-Jasmine (7th Ed.) 695QX5276	Yr.Iss.	1994	6.95	12-25
1994 Merry Olde Santa-(5th Ed.) 1495QX5256	Yr.Iss.	1994	14.95	25-35
1994 Neighborhood Drugstore-(11th Ed.)1495QX5286	Yr.Iss.	1994	14.95	28-33
1994 Owliver-(3rd Ed.) 795QX5226	Yr.Iss.	1994	7.95	19
1994 PEANUTS®-Lucy-(2nd Ed.) 995QX5203	Yr.Iss.	1994	9.95	18-30
1994 Pipers Piping-(11th Ed.) 695QX3183	Yr.Iss.	1994	6.95	17
1994 Puppy Love-(4th Ed.) 795QX5253	Yr.Iss.	1994	7.95	18
1994 Rocking Horse-(14th Ed.) 1095QX5016	Yr.Iss.	1994	10.95	22
1994 Tobin Fraley Carousel-(3rd Ed.) 2800QX5223	Yr.Iss.	1994	28.00	45-60
1994 Xmas Stamp-(2nd Ed.) 1095QX5206	Yr.Iss.	1994	10.95	20-25
1994 Yuletide Central-(1st Ed.) 1895QX5316	Yr.Iss.	1994	18.95	40-50

1994 Commemoratives - Keepsake

YEAR ISSUE	EDITION LIMIT	YEAR RETD.	ISSUE PRICE	QUOTE U.S.$
1994 Across the Miles 895QX5656	Yr.Iss.	1994	8.95	18
1994 Anniversary Year 1095QX5683	Yr.Iss.	1994	10.95	22

YEAR ISSUE		EDITION LIMIT	YEAR RETD.	ISSUE PRICE	QUOTE U.S.$
1994	Baby's First Christmas 1295QX5743	Yr.Iss.	1994	12.95	27
1994	Baby's First Christmas 1895QX5633	Yr.Iss.	1994	18.95	30-40
1994	Baby's First Christmas 795QX5713	Yr.Iss.	1994	7.95	20
1994	Baby's First Christmas Photo 795QX5636	Yr.Iss.	1994	7.95	15-23
1994	Baby's First Christmas-Baby Boy 500QX2436	Yr.Iss.	1994	5.00	14-25
1994	Baby's First Christmas-Baby Girl 500QX2433	Yr.Iss.	1994	5.00	10-15
1994	Baby's Second Christmas 795QX5716	Yr.Iss.	1994	7.95	20
1994	Brother 695QX5516	Yr.Iss.	1994	6.95	17
1994	Child's Fifth Christmas 695QX5733	Yr.Iss.	1994	6.95	14
1994	Child's Fourth Christmas 695QX5726	Yr.Iss.	1994	6.95	15
1994	Child's Third Christmas 695QX5723	Yr.Iss.	1994	6.95	15
1994	Dad 795QX5463	Yr.Iss.	1994	7.95	17
1994	Dad-To-Be 795QX5473	Yr.Iss.	1994	7.95	17
1994	Daughter 695QX5623	Yr.Iss.	1994	6.95	15
1994	Friendly Push 895QX5686	Yr.Iss.	1994	8.95	20
1994	Godchild 895QX4453	Yr.Iss.	1994	8.95	15-22
1994	Godparents 500QX2423	Yr.Iss.	1994	5.00	17
1994	Grandchild's First Christmas 795QX5676	Yr.Iss.	1994	7.95	18
1994	Granddaughter 695QX5523	Yr.Iss.	1994	6.95	16
1994	Grandma Photo 695QX5613	Yr.Iss.	1994	6.95	7
1994	Grandmother 795QX5673	Yr.Iss.	1994	7.95	15-20
1994	Grandpa 795QX5616	Yr.Iss.	1994	7.95	17
1994	Grandparents 500QX2426	Yr.Iss.	1994	5.00	15
1994	Grandson 695QX5526	Yr.Iss.	1994	6.95	17
1994	Mom 795QX5466	Yr.Iss.	1994	7.95	17
1994	Mom and Dad 995QX5666	Yr.Iss.	1994	9.95	22
1994	Mom-To-Be 795QX5506	Yr.Iss.	1994	7.95	16
1994	Nephew 795QX5546	Yr.Iss.	1994	7.95	17
1994	New Home 895QX5663	Yr.Iss.	1994	8.95	15-20
1994	Niece 795QX5543	Yr.Iss.	1994	7.95	17
1994	Our Family 795QX5576	Yr.Iss.	1994	7.95	17
1994	Our First Christmas Together 1895QX5706	Yr.Iss.	1994	18.95	40
1994	Our First Christmas Together 695QX3186	Yr.Iss.	1994	6.95	15
1994	Our First Christmas Together 995QX4816	Yr.Iss.	1994	9.95	20
1994	Our First Christmas Together 995QX5643	Yr.Iss.	1994	9.95	20-30
1994	Our First Christmas Together Photo 895QX5653	Yr.Iss.	1994	8.95	20
1994	Secret Santa 795QX5736	Yr.Iss.	1994	7.95	18
1994	Sister 695QX5513	Yr.Iss.	1994	6.95	17
1994	Sister to Sister 995QX5533	Yr.Iss.	1994	9.95	21
1994	Son 695QX5626	Yr.Iss.	1994	6.95	10-15
1994	Special Cat 795QX5606	Yr.Iss.	1994	7.95	17
1994	Special Dog 795QX5603	Yr.Iss.	1994	7.95	17
1994	Thick 'N' Thin 1095QX5693	Yr.Iss.	1994	10.95	23
1994	Tou Can Love 895QX5646	Yr.Iss.	1994	8.95	20

1994 Easter Ornaments - Keepsake

YEAR ISSUE		EDITION LIMIT	YEAR RETD.	ISSUE PRICE	QUOTE U.S.$
1994	Baby's First Easter 675QEO8153	Yr.Iss.	1994	6.75	18
1994	Carrot Trimmers 500QEO8226	Yr.Iss.	1994	5.00	5
1994	CRAYOLA CRAYON-Colorful Spring 775QEO8166	Yr.Iss.	1994	7.75	26
1994	Daughter 575QEO8156	Yr.Iss.	1994	5.75	14
1994	Divine Duet 675QEO8183	Yr.Iss.	1994	6.75	15
1994	Easter Art Show 775QEO8193	Yr.Iss.	1994	7.75	16
1994	Egg Car-(1st Ed.) 775QEO8093	Yr.Iss.	1994	7.75	28
1994	Golf-(3rd Ed.) 675QEO8133	Yr.Iss.	1994	6.75	18
1994	Horn-(3rd Ed.) 675QEO8136	Yr.Iss.	1994	6.75	18
1994	Joyful Lamb 575QEO8206	Yr.Iss.	1994	5.75	14
1994	PEANUTS® 775QEO8176	Yr.Iss.	1994	7.75	25-47
1994	Peeping Out 675QEO8203	Yr.Iss.	1994	6.75	14
1994	Riding a Breeze 575QEO8213	Yr.Iss.	1994	5.75	14
1994	Son 575QEO8163	Yr.Iss.	1994	5.75	14
1994	Springtime Bonnets-(2nd Ed.) 775QEO8096	Yr.Iss.	1994	7.75	20-25
1994	Sunny Bunny Garden, set/3 1500QEO8146	Yr.Iss.	1994	15.00	28
1994	Sweet as Sugar 875QEO8086	Yr.Iss.	1994	8.75	18
1994	Sweet Easter Wishes Tender Touches 875QEO8196	Yr.Iss.	1994	8.75	23
1994	Treetop Cottage 975QEO8186	Yr.Iss.	1994	9.75	18
1994	Yummy Recipe 775QEO8143	Yr.Iss.	1994	7.75	19

1994 Keepsake Collector's Club - Keepsake

YEAR ISSUE		EDITION LIMIT	YEAR RETD.	ISSUE PRICE	QUOTE U.S.$
1994	First Hello 500QXC4846	Yr.Iss.	1994	5.00	15
1994	Happy Collecting 300QXC4803	Yr.Iss.	1994	3.00	17
1994	Holiday Pursuit 1175QXC4823	Yr.Iss.	1994	11.75	12
1994	Mrs. Claus' Cupboard 5500QXC4843	Yr.Iss.	1994	55.00	55
1994	On Cloud Nine 1200QXC4853	Yr.Iss.	1994	12.00	25
1994	Sweet Bouquet 850QXC4806	Yr.Iss.	1994	8.50	9
1994	Tilling Time 500QXC8256	Yr.Iss.	1994	5.00	20

1994 Keepsake Magic Ornaments - Keepsake

YEAR ISSUE		EDITION LIMIT	YEAR RETD.	ISSUE PRICE	QUOTE U.S.$
1994	Away in a Manager 1600QLX7383	Yr.Iss.	1994	16.00	38
1994	Baby's First Christmas 2000QLX7466	Yr.Iss.	1994	20.00	35-42
1994	Candy Cane Lookout 1800QLX7376	Yr.Iss.	1994	18.00	35-53
1994	Chris Mouse Jelly-Tenth Ed. 1200QLX7393	Yr.Iss.	1994	12.00	16-30
1994	Conversations With Santa 2800QLX7426	Yr.Iss.	1994	28.00	35-55
1994	Country Showtime 2200QLX7416	Yr.Iss.	1994	22.00	45
1994	The Eagle Has Landed 2400QLX7486	Yr.Iss.	1994	24.00	30-60
1994	Feliz Navidad 2800QLX7433	Yr.Iss.	1994	28.00	50-56
1994	Forest Frolics-6th Ed. 2800QLX7436	Yr.Iss.	1994	28.00	53-60
1994	Gingerbread Fantasy-Special Edition 4400QLX7382	Yr.Iss.	1994	44.00	97
1994	Kringle Trolley 2000QLX7413	Yr.Iss.	1994	20.00	40-50
1994	Maxine 2000QLX7503	Yr.Iss.	1994	20.00	38-43
1994	PEANUTS®-(4th Ed.) 2000QLX7406	Yr.Iss.	1994	20.00	35-43
1994	Peekaboo Pup 2000QLX7423	Yr.Iss.	1994	20.00	42
1994	Rock Candy Miner 2000QLX7403	Yr.Iss.	1994	20.00	35-40
1994	Santa's Sing-Along 2400QLX7473	Yr.Iss.	1994	24.00	55
1994	Tobin Fraley-(1st Ed.) 3200QLX7496	Yr.Iss.	1994	32.00	67-75
1994	Very Merry Minutes 2400QLX7443	Yr.Iss.	1994	24.00	43-48
1994	White Christmas 2800QLX7463	Yr.Iss.	1994	28.00	45-60
1994	Winnie the Pooh Parade 3200QLX7493	Yr.Iss.	1994	32.00	65

1994 Limited Editions - Keepsake

YEAR ISSUE		EDITION LIMIT	YEAR RETD.	ISSUE PRICE	QUOTE U.S.$
1994	Jolly Holly Santa 2200QXC4833	N/A	1994	22.00	22
1994	Majestic Deer 2500QXC4836	N/A	1994	25.00	25

1994 Miniature Ornaments - Keepsake

YEAR ISSUE		EDITION LIMIT	YEAR RETD.	ISSUE PRICE	QUOTE U.S.$
1994	Babs Bunny 575QXM4116	Yr.Iss.	1994	5.75	12
1994	Baby's First Christmas 575QXM4003	Yr.Iss.	1994	5.75	13
1994	Baking Tiny Treats, set/6 2900QXM4033	Yr.Iss.	1994	29.00	38-58
1994	Beary Perfect Tree 475QXM4076	Yr.Iss.	1994	4.75	9
1994	The Bearymores-(3rd Ed.) 575QXM5133	Yr.Iss.	1994	5.75	15
1994	Buster Bunny 575QXM5163	Yr.Iss.	1994	5.75	12
1994	Centuries of Santa-(1st Ed.) 600QXM5153	Yr.Iss.	1994	6.00	15-25
1994	Corny Elf 450QXM4063	Yr.Iss.	1994	4.50	10
1994	Cute as a Button 375QXM4103	Yr.Iss.	1994	3.75	10
1994	Dazzling Reindeer-Pr. Ed. 975QXM4026	Yr.Iss.	1994	9.75	19
1994	Dizzy Devil 575QXM4133	Yr.Iss.	1994	5.75	13
1994	Friends Need Hugs 450QXM4016	Yr.Iss.	1994	4.50	12
1994	Graceful Carousel 75QXM4056	Yr.Iss.	1994	7.75	17
1994	Hamton 575QXM4126	Yr.Iss.	1994	5.75	12
1994	Hat Shop (7th Ed.) 700QXM5143	Yr.Iss.	1994	7.00	10-18
1994	Have a Cookie 575QXM5166	Yr.Iss.	1994	5.75	15
1994	Hearts A-Sail 575QXM4006	Yr.Iss.	1994	5.75	11
1994	Jolly Visitor 575QXM4053	Yr.Iss.	1994	5.75	15
1994	Jolly Wolly Snowman 375QXM4093	Yr.Iss.	1994	3.75	11
1994	Journey to Bethlehem 575QXM4036	Yr.Iss.	1994	5.75	12
1994	Just My Size 375QXM4086	Yr.Iss.	1994	3.75	9
1994	Love Was Born 450QXM4043	Yr.Iss.	1994	4.50	12
1994	March of the Teddy Bears-(2nd Ed.) 450QXM5106	Yr.Iss.	1994	4.50	10-15
1994	Melodic Cherub 375QXM4066	Yr.Iss.	1994	3.75	10
1994	A Merry Flight 575QXM4073	Yr.Iss.	1994	5.75	12
1994	Mom 450QXM4013	Yr.Iss.	1994	4.50	10
1994	Nature's Angels-(5th Ed.) 450QXM5126	Yr.Iss.	1994	4.50	12
1994	Night Before Christmas-(3rd Ed.) 450QXM5123	Yr.Iss.	1994	4.50	13
1994	Noah's Ark (special edition) 2450QXM4106	Yr.Iss.	1994	24.50	45-50
1994	Nutcracker Guild-(1st Ed.) 575QXM5146	Yr.Iss.	1994	5.75	15-20
1994	On the Road-(2nd Ed.) 575QXM5103	Yr.Iss.	1994	5.75	13
1994	Plucky Duck 575QXM4123	Yr.Iss.	1994	5.75	12
1994	Pour Some More 575QXM5156	Yr.Iss.	1994	5.75	12
1994	Rocking Horse-(7th Ed.) 450QXM5116	Yr.Iss.	1994	4.50	11
1994	Scooting Along 675QXM5173	Yr.Iss.	1994	6.75	14
1994	Stock Car-(6th Ed.) 700QXM5113	Yr.Iss.	1994	7.00	17
1994	Sweet Dreams 300QXM4096	Yr.Iss.	1994	3.00	10-20
1994	Tea With Teddy 725QXM4046	Yr.Iss.	1994	7.25	16

1994 New Attractions - Keepsake

YEAR ISSUE		EDITION LIMIT	YEAR RETD.	ISSUE PRICE	QUOTE U.S.$
1994	All Pumped Up 895QX5923	Yr.Iss.	1994	8.95	18
1994	Angel Hare 895QX5896	Yr.Iss.	1994	8.95	19
1994	Batman 1295QX5853	Yr.Iss.	1994	12.95	27-35
1994	Beatles Gift Set 4800QX5373	Yr.Iss.	1994	48.00	95-110
1994	BEATRIX POTTER The Tale of Peter Rabbit 500QX2443	Yr.Iss.	1994	5.00	15
1994	Big Shot 795QX5873	Yr.Iss.	1994	7.95	17
1994	Busy Batter 795QX5876	Yr.Iss.	1994	7.95	17
1994	Candy Caper 895QX5776	Yr.Iss.	1994	8.95	19
1994	Caring Doctor 895QX5823	Yr.Iss.	1994	8.95	19
1994	Champion Teacher 695QX5836	Yr.Iss.	1994	6.95	16
1994	Cheers to You! 1095QX5796	Yr.Iss.	1994	10.95	24
1994	Cheery Cyclists 1295QX5786	Yr.Iss.	1994	12.95	29
1994	Child Care Giver 795QX5906	Yr.Iss.	1994	7.95	16
1994	Coach 795QX5933	Yr.Iss.	1994	7.95	17
1994	Colors of Joy 795QX5893	Yr.Iss.	1994	7.95	17
1994	Cowardly Lion 995QX5446	Yr.Iss.	1994	9.95	25-50
1994	Daffy Duck 895QX5415	Yr.Iss.	1994	8.95	20
1994	Daisy Days 995QX5986	Yr.Iss.	1994	9.95	10
1994	Deer Santa Mouse (2) 1495QX5806	Yr.Iss.	1994	14.95	29
1994	Dorothy and Toto 1095QX5433	Yr.Iss.	1994	10.95	45-55
1994	Extra-Special Delivery 795QX5833	Yr.Iss.	1994	7.95	17
1994	Feelin' Groovy 795QX5953	Yr.Iss.	1994	7.95	21
1994	A Feline of Christmas 895QX5816	Yr.Iss.	1994	8.95	25
1994	Feliz Navidad 895QX5793	Yr.Iss.	1994	8.95	15-20
1994	Follow the Sun 895QX5846	Yr.Iss.	1994	8.95	18
1994	Fred and Barney 1495QX5003	Yr.Iss.	1994	14.95	27-35
1994	Friendship Sundae 1095QX4766	Yr.Iss.	1994	10.95	20-25
1994	GARFIELD 1295QX5753	Yr.Iss.	1994	12.95	27
1994	Gentle Nurse 695QX5973	Yr.Iss.	1994	6.95	15-20
1994	Harvest Joy 995QX5993	Yr.Iss.	1994	9.95	10
1994	Hearts in Harmony 1095QX4406	Yr.Iss.	1994	10.95	21
1994	Helpful Shepherd 895QX5536	Yr.Iss.	1994	8.95	20
1994	Holiday Patrol 895QX5826	Yr.Iss.	1994	8.95	19
1994	Ice Show 795QX5946	Yr.Iss.	1994	7.95	17
1994	In the Pink 995QX5763	Yr.Iss.	1994	9.95	21
1994	It's a Strike 895QX5856	Yr.Iss.	1994	8.95	18
1994	Jingle Bell Band 1095QX5783	Yr.Iss.	1994	10.95	24-30
1994	Joyous Song 895QX4473	Yr.Iss.	1994	8.95	17
1994	Jump-along Jackalope 895QX5756	Yr.Iss.	1994	8.95	18
1994	Kickin' Roo 795QX5916	Yr.Iss.	1994	7.95	17
1994	Kringle's Kayak 795QX5886	Yr.Iss.	1994	7.95	18
1994	LEGO®'S 1095QX5453	Yr.Iss.	1994	10.95	22-30
1994	Lou Rankin Seal 995QX5456	Yr.Iss.	1994	9.95	20
1994	Magic Carpet Ride 795QX5883	Yr.Iss.	1994	7.95	20-25
1994	Mary Engelbreit 500QX2416	Yr.Iss.	1994	5.00	15
1994	Merry Fishmas 895QX5913	Yr.Iss.	1994	8.95	18
1994	Mistletoe Surprise (2)1295QX5996	Yr.Iss.	1994	12.95	26
1994	Norman Rockwell 500QX2413	Yr.Iss.	1994	5.00	15
1994	Open-and-Shut Holiday 995QX5696	Yr.Iss.	1994	9.95	21
1994	Out of This World Teacher 795QX5766	Yr.Iss.	1994	7.95	19
1994	Practice Makes Perfect 795QX5863	Yr.Iss.	1994	7.95	17
1994	Red Hot Holiday 795QX5843	Yr.Iss.	1994	7.95	17
1994	Reindeer Pro 795QX5926	Yr.Iss.	1994	7.95	17
1994	Relaxing Moment 1495QX5356	Yr.Iss.	1994	14.95	30
1994	Road Runner and Wile E. Coyote 1295QX5602	Yr.Iss.	1994	12.95	20-27
1994	Scarecrow 995QX5436	Yr.Iss.	1994	9.95	25-55
1994	A Sharp Flat 1095QX5773	Yr.Iss.	1994	10.95	23
1994	Speedy Gonzales 895QX5343	Yr.Iss.	1994	8.95	15-20
1994	Stamp of Approval 795QX5703	Yr.Iss.	1994	7.95	17
1994	Sweet Greeting (2) 1095QX5803	Yr.Iss.	1994	10.95	21
1994	Tasmanian Devil 895QX5605	Yr.Iss.	1994	8.95	40-60
1994	Thrill a Minute 895QX5866	Yr.Iss.	1994	8.95	18
1994	Time of Peace 795QX5813	Yr.Iss.	1994	7.95	16
1994	Tin Man 995QX5443	Yr.Iss.	1994	9.95	25-50
1994	Tulip Time 995QX5983	Yr.Iss.	1994	9.95	10
1994	Winnie the Pooh/Tigger 1295QX5746	Yr.Iss.	1994	12.95	29
1994	Yosemite Sam 895QX5346	Yr.Iss.	1994	8.95	20
1994	Yuletide Cheer 995QX5976	Yr.Iss.	1994	9.95	10

1994 Personalized Ornaments - Keepsake

YEAR ISSUE		EDITION LIMIT	YEAR RETD.	ISSUE PRICE	QUOTE U.S.$
1994	Baby Block 1495QP6035	Yr.Iss.	1994	14.95	15
1994	Computer Cat 'N' Mouse 1295QP6046	Yr.Iss.	1994	12.95	13
1994	Cookie Time 1295QP6073	Yr.Iss.	1994	12.95	13
1994	Etch-A-Sketch 1295QP6006	Yr.Iss.	1994	12.95	13
1994	Festive Album 1295QP6025	Yr.Iss.	1994	12.95	13
1994	From the Heart 1495QP6036	Yr.Iss.	1994	14.95	15
1994	Goin' Fishin' 1495QP6023	Yr.Iss.	1994	14.95	15
1994	Goin' Golfin' 1295QP6012	Yr.Iss.	1994	12.95	13
1994	Holiday Hello 2495QXR6116	Yr.Iss.	1994	24.95	25
1994	Mailbox Delivery 1495QP6015	Yr.Iss.	1994	14.95	15
1994	Novel Idea 1295QP6066	Yr.Iss.	1994	12.95	13
1994	On the Billboard 1295QP6022	Yr.Iss.	1994	12.95	13
1994	Playing Ball 1295QP6032	Yr.Iss.	1994	12.95	13
1994	Reindeer Rooters 1295QP6056	Yr.Iss.	1994	12.95	13
1994	Santa Says 1495QP6005	Yr.Iss.	1994	14.95	15

1994 Premiere Event - Keepsake

YEAR ISSUE		EDITION LIMIT	YEAR RETD.	ISSUE PRICE	QUOTE U.S.$
1994	Eager for Christmas 1500QX5336	Yr.Iss.	1994	15.00	15

1994 Showcase Christmas Lights - Keepsake

YEAR ISSUE		EDITION LIMIT	YEAR RETD.	ISSUE PRICE	QUOTE U.S.$
1994	Home for the Holidays 1575QK1123	Yr.Iss.	1994	15.75	16
1994	Moonbeams 1575QK1116	Yr.Iss.	1994	15.75	16
1994	Mother and Child 1575QK1126	Yr.Iss.	1994	15.75	16
1994	Peaceful Village 1575QK1106	Yr.Iss.	1994	15.75	16

1994 Showcase Folk Art Americana Collection - Keepsake

YEAR ISSUE		EDITION LIMIT	YEAR RETD.	ISSUE PRICE	QUOTE U.S.$
1994	Catching 40 Winks 1675QK1183	Yr.Iss.	1994	16.75	32
1994	Going to Town 1575QK1166	Yr.Iss.	1994	15.75	35
1994	Racing Through the Snow 1575QK1173	Yr.Iss.	1994	15.75	50
1994	Rarin' to Go 1575QK1193	Yr.Iss.	1994	15.75	35
1994	Roundup Time 1675QK1176	Yr.Iss.	1994	16.75	35

1994 Showcase Holiday Favorites - Keepsake

YEAR ISSUE		EDITION LIMIT	YEAR RETD.	ISSUE PRICE	QUOTE U.S.$
1994	Dapper Snowman 1375QK1053	Yr.Iss.	1994	13.75	14
1994	Graceful Fawn 1175QK1033	Yr.Iss.	1994	11.75	12
1994	Jolly Santa 1375QK1046	Yr.Iss.	1994	13.75	14
1994	Joyful Lamb 1175QK1036	Yr.Iss.	1994	11.75	12
1994	Peaceful Dove 1175QK1043	Yr.Iss.	1994	11.75	12

1994 Showcase Old World Silver Collection - Keepsake

YEAR ISSUE		EDITION LIMIT	YEAR RETD.	ISSUE PRICE	QUOTE U.S.$
1994	Silver Bells 2475QK1026	Yr.Iss.	1994	24.75	25

YEAR	ISSUE	EDITION LIMIT	YEAR RETD.	ISSUE PRICE	QUOTE U.S.$
1994	Silver Bows 2475QK1023	Yr.Iss.	1994	24.75	25
1994	Silver Poinsettias 2475QK1006	Yr.Iss.	1994	24.75	25
1994	Silver Snowflakes 2475QK1016	Yr.Iss.	1994	24.75	25

1994 Special Edition - Keepsake

YEAR	ISSUE	EDITION LIMIT	YEAR RETD.	ISSUE PRICE	QUOTE U.S.$
1994	Lucinda and Teddy 2175QX4813	Yr.Iss.	1994	21.75	41

1994 Special Issues - Keepsake

YEAR	ISSUE	EDITION LIMIT	YEAR RETD.	ISSUE PRICE	QUOTE U.S.$
1994	Barney 2400QLX7506	Yr.Iss.	1994	24.00	50
1994	Barney 995QX5966	Yr.Iss.	1994	9.95	21
1994	Holiday Barbie™ -(2nd Ed.) 1495QX5216	Yr.Iss.	1994	14.95	35-50
1994	Klingon Bird of Prey™ 2400QLX7386	Yr.Iss.	1994	24.00	45
1994	Mufasa/Simba-Lion King 1495QX5406	Yr.Iss.	1994	14.95	30-35
1994	Nostalgic-Barbie™ -(1st Ed.) 1495QX5006	Yr.Iss.	1994	14.95	35
1994	Simba/Nala-Lion King (2) 1295QX5303	Yr.Iss.	1994	12.95	30-35
1994	Simba/Sarabi/Mufasa the Lion King 2000QLX7513	Yr.Iss.	1994	20.00	50-100
1994	Simba/Sarabi/Mufasa the Lion King 3200QLX7513	Yr.Iss.	1994	32.00	50-100
1994	Timon/Pumbaa-Lion King 895QX5366	Yr.Iss.	1994	8.95	30-35

1995 Anniversary Edition - Keepsake

YEAR	ISSUE	EDITION LIMIT	YEAR RETD.	ISSUE PRICE	QUOTE U.S.$
1995	Pewter Rocking Horse 2000QX6167	Yr.Iss.		20.00	20

1995 Artists' Favorite - Keepsake

YEAR	ISSUE	EDITION LIMIT	YEAR RETD.	ISSUE PRICE	QUOTE U.S.$
1995	Barrel-Back Rider 995QX5189	Yr.Iss.		9.95	10
1995	Our Little Blessings 1295QX5209	Yr.Iss.		12.95	13

1995 Collectible Series - Keepsake

YEAR	ISSUE	EDITION LIMIT	YEAR RETD.	ISSUE PRICE	QUOTE U.S.$
1995	1956 Ford Truck -(1st Ed.) 1395QX5527	Yr.Iss.		13.95	14
1995	1969 Chevrolet Camaro -(5th Ed.) 1295QX5239	Yr.Iss.		12.95	13
1995	Bright 'n' Sunny Tepee (7th Ed.) 1095QX5247	Yr.Iss.		10.95	11
1995	Camellia - Mary's Angels (8th Ed.) 695QX5149	Yr.Iss.		6.95	7
1995	Cat Naps -(2nd Ed.) 795QX5097	Yr.Iss.		7.95	8
1995	A Celebration of Angels -(1st Ed.) 1295QX5077	Yr.Iss.		12.95	13
1995	Christmas Eve Kiss (10th Ed.) 1495QX5157	Yr.Iss.		14.95	15
1995	Fabulous Decade (6th Ed.) 795QX5147	Yr.Iss.		7.95	8
1995	Frosty Friends (16th Ed.) 1095QX5169	Yr.Iss.		10.95	11
1995	Jack and Jill -(3rd Ed.) 1395QX5099	Yr.Iss.		13.95	14
1995	Lou Gehrig -(2nd Ed.) 1295QX5029	Yr.Iss.		12.95	13
1995	Merry Olde Santa (6th Ed.) 1495QX5139	Yr.Iss.		14.95	15
1995	Murray® Fire Truck -(2nd Ed.) 1395QX5027	Yr.Iss.		13.95	14
1995	The PEANUTS® Gang -(3rd Ed.) 995QX5059	Yr.Iss.		9.95	10
1995	Puppy Love -(5th Ed.) 795QX5137	Yr.Iss.		7.95	8
1995	Rocking Horse -(15th Ed.) 1095QX5167	Yr.Iss.		10.95	11
1995	Santa's Roadster -(17th Ed.) 1495QX5179	Yr.Iss.		14.95	15
1995	St. Nicholas -(1st Ed.) 1495QX5087	Yr.Iss.		14.95	15
1995	Tobin Fraley Carousel (4th Ed.) 2800QX5069	Yr.Iss.		28.00	28
1995	Town Church -(12th Ed.) 1495QX5159	Yr.Iss.		14.95	15
1995	Twelve Drummers Drumming (12th Ed.) 695QX3009	Yr.Iss.		6.95	7
1995	U.S. Christmas Stamps (3rd Ed.) 1095QX5067	Yr.Iss.		10.95	11
1995	Yuletide Central-(2nd Ed.) 1895QX5079	Yr.Iss.		18.95	19

1995 Commemoratives - Keepsake

YEAR	ISSUE	EDITION LIMIT	YEAR RETD.	ISSUE PRICE	QUOTE U.S.$
1995	Across the Miles 895QX5847	Yr.Iss.		8.95	9
1995	Air Express 795QX5977	Yr.Iss.		7.95	8
1995	Anniversary Year 895QX5819	Yr.Iss.		8.95	9
1995	Baby's First Christmas 1895QX5547	Yr.Iss.		18.95	19
1995	Baby's First Christmas 795QX5549	Yr.Iss.		7.95	8
1995	Baby's First Christmas 795QX5559	Yr.Iss.		7.95	8
1995	Baby's First Christmas 995QX5557	Yr.Iss.		9.95	10
1995	Baby's First Christmas-Baby Boy 500QX2319	Yr.Iss.		5.00	5
1995	Baby's First Christmas-Baby Girl 500QX2317	Yr.Iss.		5.00	5
1995	Baby's Second Christmas 795QX5567	Yr.Iss.		7.95	8
1995	Brother 695QX5679	Yr.Iss.		6.95	7
1995	Child's Fifth Christmas 695QX5637	Yr.Iss.		6.95	7
1995	Child's Fourth Christmas 695QX5629	Yr.Iss.		6.95	7
1995	Child's Third Christmas 795QX5627	Yr.Iss.		7.95	8
1995	Christmas Fever 795QX5967	Yr.Iss.		7.95	8
1995	Christmas Patrol 795QX5959	Yr.Iss.		7.95	8
1995	Dad 795QX5649	Yr.Iss.		7.95	8
1995	Dad-to-Be 795QX5667	Yr.Iss.		7.95	8
1995	Daughter 695QX5677	Yr.Iss.		6.95	7
1995	For My Grandma 695QX5729	Yr.Iss.		6.95	7
1995	Friendly Boost 895QX5827	Yr.Iss.		8.95	9
1995	Godchild 795QX5707	Yr.Iss.		7.95	8
1995	Godparent 500QX2417	Yr.Iss.		5.00	5
1995	Grandchild's First Christmas 795QX5777	Yr.Iss.		7.95	8
1995	Granddaughter 695QX5779	Yr.Iss.		6.95	7
1995	Grandmother 795QX5767	Yr.Iss.		7.95	8
1995	Grandpa 895QX5769	Yr.Iss.		8.95	9
1995	Grandparents 500QX2419	Yr.Iss.		5.00	5
1995	Grandson 695QX5787	Yr.Iss.		6.95	7
1995	Important Memo 895QX5947	Yr.Iss.		8.95	9
1995	In a Heartbeat 895QX5817	Yr.Iss.		8.95	9
1995	Mom 795QX5647	Yr.Iss.		7.95	8
1995	Mom and Dad 995QX5657	Yr.Iss.		9.95	10
1995	Mom-to-Be 795QX5659	Yr.Iss.		7.95	8
1995	New Home 895QX5839	Yr.Iss.		8.95	9
1995	North Pole 911 1095QX5957	Yr.Iss.		10.95	11
1995	Number One Teacher 795QX5949	Yr.Iss.		7.95	8
1995	Our Christmas Together 995QX5809	Yr.Iss.		9.95	10
1995	Our Family 795QX5709	Yr.Iss.		7.95	8
1995	Our First Christmas Together 1695QX5797	Yr.Iss.		16.95	17
1995	Our First Christmas Together 695QX3177	Yr.Iss.		6.95	7
1995	Our First Christmas Together 895QX5799	Yr.Iss.		8.95	9
1995	Our First Christmas Together 895QX5807	Yr.Iss.		8.95	9
1995	Packed With Memories 795QX5639	Yr.Iss.		7.95	8
1995	Sister 695QX5687	Yr.Iss.		6.95	7
1995	Sister to Sister 895QX5689	Yr.Iss.		8.95	9
1995	Son 695QX5669	Yr.Iss.		6.95	7
1995	Special Cat 795QX5717	Yr.Iss.		7.95	8
1995	Special Dog 795QX5719	Yr.Iss.		7.95	8
1995	Two for Tea 995QX5829	Yr.Iss.		9.95	10

1995 Easter Ornaments - Keepsake

YEAR	ISSUE	EDITION LIMIT	YEAR RETD.	ISSUE PRICE	QUOTE U.S.$
1995	3 Flowerpot Friends 1495QEO8229	Yr.Iss.		14.95	24
1995	Baby's First Easter 795QEO8237	Yr.Iss.		7.95	17
1995	Bugs Bunny (Looney Tunes) 895QEO8279	Yr.Iss.		8.95	18
1995	Bunny w/Crayons (Crayola) 795QEO8249	Yr.Iss.		7.95	18
1995	Bunny w/Seed Packets (Tender Touches) 895QEO8259	Yr.Iss.		8.95	19
1995	Bunny w/Water Bucket 695QEO8253	Yr.Iss.		6.95	14
1995	Collector's Plate -(2nd Ed.) 795QEO8217	Yr.Iss.		7.95	8
1995	Daughter Duck 595QEO8239	Yr.Iss.		5.95	12
1995	Easter Beagle (Peanuts) 795QEO8257	Yr.Iss.		7.95	23
1995	Easter Egg Cottages -(1st Ed.) 895QEO8207	Yr.Iss.		8.95	25
1995	Garden Club -(1st Ed.) 795QEO8209	Yr.Iss.		7.95	19
1995	Ham n Eggs 795QEO8277	Yr.Iss.		7.95	16
1995	Here Comes Easter -(2nd Ed.) 795QEO8217	Yr.Iss.		7.95	17
1995	Lily (Religious) 695QEO8267	Yr.Iss.		6.95	10
1995	Miniature Train 495QEO8269	Yr.Iss.		4.95	12
1995	Son Duck 595QEO8247	Yr.Iss.		5.95	12
1995	Springtime Barbie - (1st Ed.) 1295QEO8069	Yr.Iss.		12.95	32
1995	Springtime Bonnets -(3rd Ed.) 795QEO8227	Yr.Iss.		7.95	17

1995 Keepsake Collector's Club - Keepsake

YEAR	ISSUE	EDITION LIMIT	YEAR RETD.	ISSUE PRICE	QUOTE U.S.$
1995	1958 Ford Edsel Citation Convertible 1295QXC4167	Yr.Iss.		12.95	13
1995	Brunette Debut - 1959 1495QXC5397	Yr.Iss.		14.95	15
1995	Christmas Eve Bake-Off 5500QXC4049	Yr.Iss.		55.00	55
1995	Cinderella's Stepsisters 375QXC4159	Yr.Iss.		3.75	4
1995	Collecting Memories 1200QXC4117	Yr.Iss.		12.00	12
1995	Cool Santa 575QXC4457	Yr.Iss.		5.75	6
1995	Cozy Christmas 850QXC4119	Yr.Iss.		8.50	9
1995	Fishing for Fun 1095QXC5207	Yr.Iss.		10.95	11
1995	A Gift From Rodney 500QXC4129	Yr.Iss.		5.00	5
1995	Home From the Woods 1595QXC1059	Yr.Iss.		15.95	16
1995	May Flower 495QXC8246	Yr.Iss.		4.95	5

1995 Keepsake Magic Ornaments - Keepsake

YEAR	ISSUE	EDITION LIMIT	YEAR RETD.	ISSUE PRICE	QUOTE U.S.$
1995	Baby's First Christmas 2200QLX7317	Yr.Iss.		22.00	22
1995	Chris Mouse Tree (11th Ed.) 1250QLX7307	Yr.Iss.		12.50	13
1995	Coming to See Santa 3200QLX7369	Yr.Iss.		32.00	32
1995	Forest Frolics (7th Ed.) 2800QLX7299	Yr.Iss.		28.00	28
1995	Fred and Dino 2800QLX7289	Yr.Iss.		28.00	28
1995	Friends Share Fun 1650QLX7349	Yr.Iss.		16.50	17
1995	Goody Gumballs! 1250QLX7367	Yr.Iss.		12.50	13
1995	Headin' Home 2200QLX7327	Yr.Iss.		22.00	22
1995	Holiday Swim 1850QLX7319	Yr.Iss.		18.50	19
1995	Jukebox Party 2450QLX7339	Yr.Iss.		24.50	25
1995	Jumping for Joy 2800QLX7347	Yr.Iss.		28.00	28
1995	My First HOT WHEELS™ 2800QLX7279	Yr.Iss.		28.00	28
1995	PEANUTS® - (5th Ed.) 2450QLX7277	Yr.Iss.		24.50	25
1995	Santa's Diner 2450QLX7337	Yr.Iss.		24.50	25
1995	Space Shuttle 2450QLX7396	Yr.Iss.		24.50	25
1995	Superman™ 2800QLX7309	Yr.Iss.		28.00	28
1995	Tobin Fraley Holiday Carousel (2nd Ed.) 3200QLX7269	Yr.Iss.		32.00	32
1995	Victorian Toy Box -Special Ed. 4200QLX7357	Yr.Iss.		42.00	42
1995	Wee Little Christmas 2200QLX7329	Yr.Iss.		22.00	22
1995	Winnie the Pooh Too Much Hunny 2450QLX7297	Yr.Iss.		24.50	25

1995 Miniature Ornaments - Keepsake

YEAR	ISSUE	EDITION LIMIT	YEAR RETD.	ISSUE PRICE	QUOTE U.S.$
1995	Alice in Wonderland- (1st Ed.) 675QXM4777	Yr.Iss.		6.75	7
1995	Baby's First Christmas 475QXM4027	Yr.Iss.		4.75	5
1995	Calamity Coyote 675QXM4467	Yr.Iss.		6.75	7
1995	Centuries of Santa- (2nd Ed.) 575QXM4789	Yr.Iss.		5.75	6
1995	Christmas Bells- (1st Ed.) 475QXM4007	Yr.Iss.		4.75	5
1995	Christmas Wishes 375QXM4087	Yr.Iss.		3.75	4
1995	Cloisonne Partridge 975QXM4017	Yr.Iss.		9.75	10
1995	Downhill Double 475QXM4837	Yr.Iss.		4.75	5
1995	Friendship Duet 475QXM4019	Yr.Iss.		4.75	5
1995	Furrball 575QXM4459	Yr.Iss.		5.75	6
1995	Grandpa's Gift 575QXM4829	Yr.Iss.		5.75	6
1995	Heavenly Praises 575QXM4037	Yr.Iss.		5.75	6
1995	Joyful Santa 475QXM4089	Yr.Iss.		4.75	5
1995	Little Beeper 575QXM4469	Yr.Iss.		5.75	6
1995	March of the Teddy Bears -(3rd Ed.) 475QXM4799	Yr.Iss.		4.75	5
1995	Merry Walruses 575QXM4057	Yr.Iss.		5.75	6
1995	Milk Tank Car -(7th Ed.) 675QXM4817	Yr.Iss.		6.75	7
1995	Miniature Clothespin Soldier -(1st Ed.) 375QXM4097	Yr.Iss.		3.75	4
1995	A Moustershire Christmas 2450QXM4839	Yr.Iss.		24.50	25
1995	Murray® "Champion" -(1st Ed.) 575QXM4079	Yr.Iss.		5.75	6
1995	Nature's Angels -(6th Ed.) 475QXM4809	Yr.Iss.		4.75	5
1995	The Night Before Christmas- (4th Ed.) 475QXM4807	Yr.Iss.		4.75	5
1995	Nutcracker Guild -(2nd Ed.) 575QXM4787	Yr.Iss.		5.75	6
1995	On the Road -(3rd Ed.) 575QXM4797	Yr.Iss.		5.75	6
1995	Pebbles and Bamm-Bamm 975QXM4757	Yr.Iss.		9.75	10
1995	Playful Penguins 575QXM4059	Yr.Iss.		5.75	6
1995	Precious Creations 975QXM4077	Yr.Iss.		9.75	10
1995	Rocking Horse -(8th Ed.) 475QXM4827	Yr.Iss.		4.75	5
1995	Santa's Little Big Top- (1st Ed.) 675QXM4779	Yr.Iss.		6.75	7
1995	Santa's Visit 775QXM4047	Yr.Iss.		7.75	8
1995	Starlit Nativity 775QXM4039	Yr.Iss.		7.75	8
1995	Sugarplum Dreams 475QXM4099	Yr.Iss.		4.75	5
1995	Tiny Treasures (set of 6) 2900QXM4009	Yr.Iss.		29.00	29
1995	Tudor House- (8th Ed.) 675QXM4819	Yr.Iss.		6.75	7
1995	Tunnel of Love 475QXM4029	Yr.Iss.		4.75	5

1995 New Attractions - Keepsake

YEAR	ISSUE	EDITION LIMIT	YEAR RETD.	ISSUE PRICE	QUOTE U.S.$
1995	Acorn 500 1095QX5929	Yr.Iss.		10.95	11
1995	Batmobile 1495QX5739	Yr.Iss.		14.95	15
1995	Betty and Wilma 1495QX5417	Yr.Iss.		14.95	15
1995	Bingo Bear 795QX5919	Yr.Iss.		7.95	8
1995	Bobbin' Along 895QX5879	Yr.Iss.		8.95	9
1995	Bugs Bunny 895QX5019	Yr.Iss.		8.95	9
1995	Catch the Spirit 795QX5899	Yr.Iss.		7.95	8
1995	Christmas Morning 1095QX5997	Yr.Iss.		10.95	11
1995	Colorful World 1095QX5519	Yr.Iss.		10.95	11
1995	Cows of Bali 895QX5999	Yr.Iss.		8.95	9
1995	Delivering Kisses 1095QX4107	Yr.Iss.		10.95	11
1995	Dream On 1095QX6007	Yr.Iss.		10.95	11
1995	Dudley the Dragon 1095QX6209	Yr.Iss.		10.95	11
1995	Faithful Fan 895QX5897	Yr.Iss.		8.95	9
1995	Feliz Navidad 795QX5869	Yr.Iss.		7.95	8
1995	Forever Friends Bear 895QX5258	Yr.Iss.		8.95	9
1995	GARFIELD 1095QX5007	Yr.Iss.		10.95	11
1995	Glinda, Witch of the North 1395QX5749	Yr.Iss.		13.95	14
1995	Gopher Fun 995QX5887	Yr.Iss.		9.95	10
1995	Happy Wrappers 1095QX6037	Yr.Iss.		10.95	11
1995	Heaven's Gift 2000QX6057	Yr.Iss.		20.00	20
1995	Hockey Pup 995QX5917	Yr.Iss.		9.95	10
1995	In Time With Christmas 1295QX6049	Yr.Iss.		12.95	13
1995	Joy to the World 895QX5867	Yr.Iss.		8.95	9
1995	LEGO® Fireplace With Santa 1095QX4769	Yr.Iss.		10.95	11
1995	Lou Rankin Bear 995QX4069	Yr.Iss.		9.95	10
1995	The Magic School Bus™ 1095QX5849	Yr.Iss.		10.95	11
1995	Mary Engelbreit 500QX2409	Yr.Iss.		5.00	5

YEAR ISSUE		EDITION LIMIT	YEAR RETD.	ISSUE PRICE	QUOTE U.S.$
1995	Merry RV 1295QX6027	Yr.Iss.		12.95	13
1995	Muletide Greetings 795QX6009	Yr.Iss.		7.95	8
1995	The Olympic Spirit 795QX3169	Yr.Iss.		7.95	8
1995	On the Ice 795QX6047	Yr.Iss.		7.95	8
1995	Perfect Balance 795QX5927	Yr.Iss.		7.95	8
1995	PEZ® Santa 795QX5267	Yr.Iss.		7.95	8
1995	Polar Coaster 895QX6117	Yr.Iss.		8.95	9
1995	Popeye® 1095QX5257	Yr.Iss.		10.95	11
1995	Refreshing Gift 1495QX4067	Yr.Iss.		14.95	15
1995	Rejoice! 1095QX5987	Yr.Iss.		10.95	11
1995	Roller Whiz 795QX5937	Yr.Iss.		7.95	8
1995	Santa in Paris 895QX5877	Yr.Iss.		8.95	9
1995	Santa's Serenade 895QX6017	Yr.Iss.		8.95	9
1995	Santa's Visitors 500QX2407	Yr.Iss.		5.00	5
1995	Simba, Pumbaa and Timon 1295QX6159	Yr.Iss.		12.95	13
1995	Ski Hound 895QX5909	Yr.Iss.		8.95	9
1995	Surfin' Santa 995QX6019	Yr.Iss.		9.95	10
1995	Sylvester and Tweety 1395QX5017	Yr.Iss.		13.95	14
1995	Takin' a Hike 795QX6029	Yr.Iss.		7.95	8
1995	Tennis, Anyone? 795QX5907	Yr.Iss.		7.95	8
1995	Thomas the Tank Engine-No. 1 995QX5857	Yr.Iss.		9.95	10
1995	Three Wishes 795QX5979	Yr.Iss.		7.95	8
1995	Vera the Mouse 895QX5537	Yr.Iss.		8.95	9
1995	Waiting Up for Santa 895QX6106	Yr.Iss.		8.95	9
1995	Water Sports 1495QX6039	Yr.Iss.		14.95	15
1995	Wheel of Fortune® 1295QX6187	Yr.Iss.		12.95	13
1995	Winnie the Pooh and Tigger 1295QX5009	Yr.Iss.		12.95	13
1995	The Winning Play 795QX5889	Yr.Iss.		7.95	8

1995 Personalized Ornaments - Keepsake

1995	Baby Bear 1295QP6157	Yr.Iss.		12.95	13
1995	The Champ 1295QP6127	Yr.Iss.		12.95	13
1995	Computer Cat 'n' Mouse 1295QP6046	Yr.Iss.		12.95	13
1995	Cookie Time 1295QP6073	Yr.Iss.		12.95	13
1995	Etch-A-Sketch® 1295QP6006	Yr.Iss.		12.95	13
1995	From the Heart 1495QP6036	Yr.Iss.		14.95	15
1995	Key Note 1295QP6149	Yr.Iss.		12.95	13
1995	Mailbox Delivery 1495QP6015	Yr.Iss.		12.95	13
1995	Novel Idea 1295QP6066	Yr.Iss.		12.95	13
1995	On the Billboard 1295QP6022	Yr.Iss.		12.95	13
1995	Playing Ball 1295QP6032	Yr.Iss.		12.95	13
1995	Reindeer Rooters 1295QP6056	Yr.Iss.		14.95	15

1995 Premiere Event - Keepsake

1995	Wish List 1500QX5859	Yr.Iss.		15.00	15

1995 Showcase All Is Bright Collection - Keepsake

1995	Angel of Light 1195QK1159	Yr.Iss.		11.95	12
1995	Gentle Lullaby 1195QK1157	Yr.Iss.		11.95	12

1995 Showcase Angel Bells Collection - Keepsake

1995	Carole 1295QK1147	Yr.Iss.		12.95	13
1995	Joy 1295QK1137	Yr.Iss.		12.95	13
1995	Noelle 1295QK1139	Yr.Iss.		12.95	13

1995 Showcase Folk Art Americana Collection - Keepsake

1995	Fetching the Firewood 1595QK1057	Yr.Iss.		15.95	16
1995	Fishing Party 1595QK1039	Yr.Iss.		15.95	16
1995	Guiding Santa 1895QK1037	Yr.Iss.		18.95	19
1995	Learning to Skate 1495QK1047	Yr.Iss.		14.95	15

1995 Showcase Holiday Enchantment Collection - Keepsake

1995	Away in a Manger 1395QK1097	Yr.Iss.		13.95	14
1995	Following the Star 1395QK1099	Yr.Iss.		13.95	14

1995 Showcase Invitation to Tea Collection - Keepsake

1995	Cozy Cottage Teapot 1595QK1127	Yr.Iss.		15.95	16
1995	European Castle Teapot 1595QK1129	Yr.Iss.		15.95	16
1995	Victorian Home Teapot 1595QK1119	Yr.Iss.		15.95	16

1995 Showcase Nature's Sketchbook Collection - Keepsake

1995	Backyard Orchard 1895QK1069	Yr.Iss.		18.95	19
1995	Christmas Cardinal 1895QK1077	Yr.Iss.		18.95	19
1995	Raising a Family 1895QK1067	Yr.Iss.		18.95	19
1995	Violets and Butterflies 1695QK1079	Yr.Iss.		16.95	17

1995 Showcase Symbols of Christmas Collection - Keepsake

1995	Jolly Santa 1595QK1087	Yr.Iss.		15.95	16
1995	Sweet Song 1595QK1089	Yr.Iss.		15.95	16

1995 Showcase Turn-of-the-Century Parade - Keepsake

1995	The Fireman 1695QK1027	Yr.Iss.		16.95	17

1995 Special Edition - Keepsake

1995	Beverly and Teddy 2175QX5259	Yr.Iss.		21.75	22

1995 Special Issues - Keepsake

YEAR ISSUE		EDITION LIMIT	YEAR RETD.	ISSUE PRICE	QUOTE U.S.$
1995	Captain Jean-Luc Picard 1395QXI5737	Yr.Iss.		13.95	14
1995	Captain James T. Kirk 1395QXI5539	Yr.Iss.		13.95	14
1995	Captain John Smith and Meeko 1295QXI6169	Yr.Iss.		12.95	13
1995	Football Legends -(1st Ed.) 1495QXI5759	Yr.Iss.		14.95	15
1995	Holiday Barbie™ -(3rd Ed.) 1495QXI5057	Yr.Iss.		14.95	15
1995	Hoop Stars -(1st Ed.) 1495QXI5517	Yr.Iss.		14.95	15
1995	Percy, Flit and Meeko 995QXI6179	Yr.Iss.		9.95	10
1995	Pocahontas 1295QXI6177	Yr.Iss.		12.95	13
1995	Pocahontas and Captain John Smith 1495QXI6197	Yr.Iss.		14.95	15
1995	Romulan Warbird™ 2400QXI7267	Yr.Iss.		24.00	24
1995	The Ships of Star Trek® 1995QXI4109	Yr.Iss.		19.95	20
1995	Solo in the Spotlight Barbie™-(2nd Ed.)1495QXI5049	Yr.Iss.		14.95	15
1995	Springtime Barbie -(1st Ed.) QEO8069	Yr.Iss.		12.95	13

1995 Special Offer - Keepsake

1995	Charlie Brown 395QRP4207	Yr.Iss.		3.95	4
1995	Linus 395QRP4217	Yr.Iss.		3.95	4
1995	Lucy 395QRP4209	Yr.Iss.		3.95	4
1995	SNOOPY 395QRP4219	Yr.Iss.		3.95	4
1995	Snow Scene 395QRP4227	Yr.Iss.		3.95	4

Hamilton Collection

Christmas Angels - S. Kuck

1994	Angel of Charity	Open		19.50	20
1995	Angel of Joy	Open		19.50	20
1995	Angel of Grace	Open		19.50	20
1995	Angel of Faith	Open		19.50	20

Derek Darlings - N/A

1995	Jessica, Sara, Chelsea (set)	Open		29.85	30

Hand & Hammer

Annual Ornaments - De Matteo

1987	Silver Bells 737	2,700	1987	38.00	66
1988	Silver Bells 792	3,150	1988	39.50	60
1989	Silver Bells 843	3,150	1989	39.50	63
1990	Silver Bells 865	3,615	1990	39.00	50
1990	Silver Bells Rev. 964	4,490	1990	39.00	40
1991	Silver Bells 1080	4,100	1991	39.50	40
1992	Silver Bells 1148	4,100	1992	39.50	40
1993	Silver Bells 1311	Retrd.	1993	39.50	40
1994	Silver Bells 1463	Retrd.	1994	39.50	40
1995	Silver Bells 1597	Yr.Iss.		39.50	40

Hand & Hammer Ornaments - De Matteo

1985	Abigail 613	Suspd.		32.00	50
1991	Alice 1119	Open		39.00	39
1991	Alice in Wonderland 1159	Open		140.00	140
1992	America At Peace 1245	2,000		85.00	100
1992	Andrea 1163	Retrd.	1994	36.00	40
1992	Angel 1213	2,000		39.00	50
1993	Angel 1342	Suspd.		38.00	38
1993	Angel 1993 1405	Suspd.		45.00	50
1985	Angel 607	225	1989	36.00	50
1985	Angel 612	217	1989	32.00	75
1988	Angel 797 (sp)	Unkn.		13.00	13
1988	Angel 818	Suspd.		32.00	45
1993	Angel Bell 1312	Retrd.	1994	38.00	40
1992	Angel with Double Horn 1212	2,000		39.00	50
1991	Angel with Horn 1026	Open		32.00	40
1987	Angel with Lyre 750	Retrd.	1991	32.00	44
1994	Angel with Star 1480	Open		38.00	40
1990	Angel with Star 871	Suspd.		38.00	38
1990	Angel with Violin 1024	Suspd.		39.00	60
1990	Angels 1039	Retrd.	1992	36.00	47
1991	Appley Dapply 1091	Open		39.50	40
1986	Archangel 684	Retrd.	1990	29.00	60
1987	Art Deco Angel 765	Retrd.	1992	38.00	56
1985	Art Deco Deer 620	Suspd.		34.00	55
1985	Audubon Bluebird 615	Suspd.		48.00	125
1985	Audubon Swallow 614	Suspd.		48.00	125
1995	Augusta Golf 1653	Open		39.00	39
1988	Bank 812	400	1989	40.00	100
1989	Barnesville Buggy 1989 950 (sp)	Unkn.		13.00	13
1993	Beantown 1344	Suspd.		38.00	50
1986	Bear Claus 692 (sp)	Unkn.		13.00	13
1990	Beardsley Angel 1040	Retrd.	1991	34.00	70
1984	Beardsley Angel 398	Open		28.00	48
1994	Beatrix Potter Noel 1438	Open		39.50	40
1986	Bicycle 669 (sp)	Unkn.		13.00	30
1984	Bird & Cherub 588 (sp)	Unkn.		13.00	30
1995	Bird Swirl 1502	Open		39.00	39
1990	Blake Angel 961	Suspd.		36.00	40
1992	Bob & Tiny Tim 1242	Open		36.00	40
1990	The Boston Light 1032	Suspd.		39.50	50
1988	Boston State House 819	Open		34.00	40
1987	Buffalo 777	Suspd.		36.00	48
1988	Buggy 817 (sp)	Unkn.		13.00	13
1989	Bugle Bear 935 (sp)	Unkn.		12.00	12
1984	Bunny 582 (sp)	Unkn.		13.00	30
1985	Butterfly 646	Suspd.		39.00	56
1988	Cable Car 848	Suspd.		38.00	75
1993	Cable Car to the Stars 1363	Suspd.		39.00	50
1983	Calligraphic Deer 511	Suspd.		25.00	38
1985	Camel 655 (sp)	Unkn.		13.00	30
1994	Canterbury Star 1441	Suspd.		35.00	35
1994	Cardinal & Holly 1445	Open		38.00	40
1990	Cardinals 870	Retrd.	1994	39.00	40
1990	Carousel Horse 866	1,915	1992	38.00	40
1991	Carousel Horse 1025	Retrd.	1993	38.00	40
1993	Carousel Horse 1993 1321	Retrd.	1993	38.00	40
1989	Carousel Horse 811	2,150	1990	34.00	43
1985	Carousel Pony 618 (sp)	Unkn.		13.00	13
1990	Carriage 960 (sp)	Unkn.		13.00	13
1982	Carved Heart 425	Suspd.		29.00	70
1995	Cat & Fiddle 1658	Open		39.00	39
1987	Cat 754	Suspd.		37.00	37
1990	Cat on Pillow 915 (sp)	Unkn.		13.00	13
1993	Celebrate America 1352	Retrd.	1994	38.00	38
1993	Cheer Mouse 1359	Retrd.	1994	39.00	39
1983	Cherub 528	295	1987	29.00	56
1985	Cherub 642	815	1989	37.00	60
1992	Chocolate Pot 1208	Retrd.	1994	49.50	75
1990	Christmas Seal 931	Unkn.		25.00	25
1986	Christmas Tree 708 (sp)	Unkn.		13.00	13
1988	Christmas Tree 798 (sp)	Unkn.		13.00	13
1990	Church 921	Retrd.	1994	37.00	40
1993	Clara with Nutcracker 1316	Suspd.		38.00	50
1987	Clipper Ship 756	Suspd.		35.00	55
1990	Clown w/Dog 958 (sp)	Unkn.		13.00	13
1990	Cockatoo 969 (sp)	Unkn.		13.00	13
1990	Colonial Capitol 965	Suspd.		39.00	75
1991	Columbus 1140	1,500	1993	39.00	50
1990	Conestoga Wagon 1027	Suspd.		38.00	45
1988	Conn. State House 833	Open		38.00	38
1988	Coronado 864	Suspd.		38.00	75
1990	Covered Bridge 920	Retrd.	1994	37.00	40
1995	Cow & Moon 1660	Open		39.00	39
1991	Cow Jumped Over The Moon 1055	Suspd.		38.00	38
1992	Cowardly Lion 1287	Retrd.	1993	36.00	50
1985	Crane 606	Suspd.		38.00	65
1993	Creche 1351	Open		38.00	40
1984	Crescent Angel 559	Suspd.		30.00	60
1995	Cross 1622	Open		39.00	40
1990	Currier & Ives Set -Victorian Village 923	2,000	1994	140.00	160
1995	Degas Dancer 1650	Open		39.00	39
1992	Della Robbia Ornament 1219	Retrd.	1994	39.00	44
1992	Dorothy 1284	Retrd.	1993	36.00	50
1983	Dove 522 (sp)	Unkn.		13.00	13
1987	Dove 747 (sp)	Unkn.		13.00	13
1988	Dove 786	112	1991	36.00	60
1988	Drummer Bear 773 (sp)	Unkn.		13.00	13
1990	Ducklings 1114	Suspd.		38.00	50
1985	Eagle 652	375	1989	30.00	125
1983	Egyptian Cat 521 (sp)	Unkn.		13.00	13
1988	Eiffel Tower 861	225	1989	38.00	100
1990	Elk 1023 (sp)	Unkn.		13.00	13
1990	Ember 1124	120		N/A	350
1994	Emperor 1439	Retrd.	1995	38.00	50
1994	Esplanade 1523	Open		39.00	39
1995	Esplanade 1667	Open		39.00	39
1995	Faberge Egg 1618	Open		39.00	40
1996	Faberge Egg 1725	Yr.Iss.		39.50	40
1992	Fairy-Tale Angel 1222	Open		36.00	36
1985	Family 659	915	1989	32.00	53
1993	Faneuil Hall 1399	Suspd.		39.00	50
1993	Faneuil Hall 1412	Open		39.50	40
1990	Farmhouse 919	Retrd.	1994	37.00	40
1995	Father Christmas 1715	Open		39.00	39
1990	Father Christmas 970	Open		36.00	40
1990	Ferrel's Angel 1990 1084 (sp)	Unkn.		15.00	15
1991	Fir Tree 1145	Retrd.	1995	39.00	50
1983	Fire Angel 473	315	1985	25.00	53
1990	First Baptist Angel 997	200	1992	35.00	75
1987	First Christmas 771 (sp)	Unkn.		13.00	13
1989	First Christmas 842 (sp)	Unkn.		13.00	13
1990	First Christmas Bear 940	Suspd.		35.00	40
1982	Fleur de Lys Angel 343	320	1985	28.00	75
1990	Flopsy Bunnies 995	Suspd.		39.50	40
1990	Florida State Capitol 1044	2,000		39.50	40
1984	Freer Star 553 (sp)	Unkn.		13.00	30
1995	French Quarter Heart 647	Open		37.00	38
1981	Gabriel 320	Suspd.		25.00	60
1981	Gabriel with Liberty Cap 301	275	1986	25.00	60
1985	George Washington 629	Suspd.		35.00	50
1990	Georgia State Capitol 1042	2,000		39.50	40
1994	Golden Gate Bridge 1429	Suspd.		39.50	50
1990	Goose & Wreath 868	Retrd.	1993	37.00	40
1989	Goose 857	650	1993	37.00	55
1990	Governor's Palace 966	Suspd.		39.00	75
1985	Grasshopper 634	Suspd.		32.00	50
1985	Guardian Angel 616	Suspd.		35.00	48
1993	Gurgling Cod 1397	Open		50.00	50
1991	Gus 1195	200		N/A	150
1986	Hallelujah 686	Suspd.		38.00	56
1985	Halley's Comet 621	432	1990	35.00	75
1995	Hart 1501	Open		38.00	38
1990	Heart Angel 959	Suspd.		39.00	39
1992	Heart of Christmas 1301	500		39.00	60
1994	Heart of Christmas 1440	500		39.00	50
1994	Heart of Christmas 1537	500		39.00	39-50
1995	Heart of Christmas 1682	Yr.Iss.		39.00	39
1985	Herald Angel 641	Retrd.	1989	36.00	60

YEAR ISSUE		EDITION LIMIT	YEAR RETD.	ISSUE PRICE	QUOTE U.S.$
1994	Heralding Angel 1481	Open		39.00	40
1994	Holly 1472	Open		38.00	40
1985	Hosanna 635	715	1988	32.00	64
1995	Hummingbird 1631	Open		39.00	40
1987	Hunting Horn 738	Suspd.		37.00	40
1991	I Love Santa 998	Open		36.00	40
1984	Ibex 584	400	1988	29.00	75
1980	Icicle 009	490	1985	25.00	60
1989	Independence Hall 908	Suspd.		38.00	45
1983	Indian 494	190	1985	29.00	58
1988	Jack in the Box 789	Retrd.	1991	39.50	60
1989	Jack in the Box Bear 936 (sp)	Unkn.		12.00	12
1983	Japanese Snowflake 534	350	1989	29.00	60
1994	Jefferson Hotel 1594	Open		39.00	39
1990	Jemima Puddleduck 1020	Unkn.		30.00	30
1992	Jemima Puddleduck 1992 1167	Retrd.	1992	39.50	40
1990	Jeremy Fisher 992	Open		39.50	40
1990	Joy 1047	Retrd.	1992	39.00	55
1992	Joy 1164	Open		39.50	40
1990	Joy 867	1,140	1993	36.00	40
1995	Kate Greenaway Joy 1651	Open		39.00	39
1995	Kate Greenaway Noel 1515	Open		39.00	39
1995	Kermit Joy 1596	Open		36.00	40
1990	Koala San Diego Zoo 1095	Suspd.		36.00	40
1986	Kringle Bear 723 (sp)	Unkn.		13.00	30
1995	L&T Santa 1700	Yr.Iss.		39.00	39
1989	L&T Ugly Duckling 917	Retrd.	1995	38.00	75
1985	Lafarge Angel 658	Suspd.		32.00	45
1986	Lafarge Angel 710	Suspd.		31.00	45
1990	Landing Duck 1021 (sp)	Unkn.		13.00	13
1991	Large Jemima Puddleduck 1083	Open		49.50	50
1991	Large Peter Rabbit 1116	Open		49.50	50
1991	Large Tailor of Gloucester 1117	Open		49.50	50
1990	Liberty Bell 1028	Suspd.		38.00	45
1985	Liberty Bell 611	Suspd.		32.00	50
1993	Lion and Lamb 1322	Open		38.00	40
1989	Locket Bear 844	Unkn.		25.00	25
1990	Locomotive 1100	Suspd.		39.00	50
1994	Loudoun County C.H. 1611	Open		39.00	39
1994	Lyre 1505	Open		39.00	39
1991	Mad Tea Party 1120	Open		39.00	39
1982	Madonna & Child 388	175	1985	28.00	75
1985	Madonna 666	227	1990	35.00	75
1988	Madonna 787	600	1992	35.00	60
1988	Madonna 809	Suspd.		39.00	50
1988	Madonna 815	Suspd.		39.00	75
1988	Magi 788	Suspd.		39.50	50
1994	Mandoline 1506	Open		39.00	39
1984	Manger 601	Retrd.	1988	29.00	48
1994	Marengo 1482	Open		39.00	39
1992	Marley's Ghost 1243	Open		36.00	40
1994	Marmion Angels 1443	Suspd.		50.00	75
1994	Mass State House 1540	Open		39.00	39
1985	Mermaid 622	Retrd.	1995	35.00	75
1990	Merry Christmas Locket 948	Unkn.		25.00	25
1989	MFA Angel with Tree 906	Suspd.		36.00	55
1989	MFA Durer Snowflake 907	Suspd.		36.00	44
1989	MFA LaFarge Angel set 937	Suspd.		98.00	110
1989	MFA Noel 905	Suspd.		36.00	44
1992	MFA Snowflake 1246	Retrd.	1993	39.00	44
1991	MFA Snowflake 1991 1143	Retrd.	1991	36.00	44
1985	Militiaman 608	Suspd.		25.00	38
1990	Mill 922	Retrd.	1994	37.00	40
1987	Minuteman 776	Suspd.		35.00	100
1985	Model A Ford 604 (sp)	Unkn.		13.00	30
1990	Mole & Rat Wind in Will 944	Suspd.		36.00	36
1991	Mommy & Baby Kangaroo 1078	Retrd.	1993	36.00	36
1991	Mommy & Baby Koala Bear 1077	Retrd.	1993	36.00	36
1991	Mommy & Baby Panda Bear 1079	Retrd.	1993	36.00	40
1991	Mommy & Baby Seal 1075	Retrd.	1993	36.00	36
1991	Mommy & Baby Wolves 1076	Retrd.	1993	36.00	36
1990	Montpelier 1113	Suspd.		36.00	75
1984	Moravian Star 595	Suspd.		38.00	100
1986	Mother Goose 719	Open		34.00	40
1993	Mouse King 1398	Suspd.		38.00	50
1990	Mouse with Candy Cane 916 (sp)	Unkn.		13.00	13
1992	Mrs. Cratchit 1244	Open		36.00	40
1992	Mrs. Rabbit 1181	Open		39.50	40
1991	Mrs. Rabbit 1991 1086	Retrd.	1991	39.50	40
1993	Mrs. Rabbit 1993 1325	Retrd.	1993	39.50	40
1990	Mrs. Rabbit 991	Open		39.50	40
1984	Mt. Vernon Weathervane 602	Suspd.		32.00	50
1990	N. Carolina State Capitol 1043	2,000		39.50	40
1987	Naptime 732	Retrd.	1991	32.00	48
1991	Nativity 1118	Open		38.00	40
1986	Nativity 679	Retrd.	1991	36.00	55
1988	Nativity 821	Suspd.		32.00	75
1995	Night Before Christmas 1600	Open		160.00	160
1988	Night Before Xmas Col. 841	10,000		160.00	275
1986	Nightingale 716	Retrd.	1995	35.00	75
1984	Nine Hearts 572	275	1985	34.00	66
1992	Noah's Ark 1166	Open		36.00	40
1994	Noel 1477	Open		38.00	40
1987	Noel 731	Suspd.		38.00	40
1991	Nutcracker 1151	Open		49.50	50
1991	Nutcracker 1183	Open		38.00	38
1989	Nutcracker 1989 872	1,790	1990	38.00	75
1985	Nutcracker 609	510	1989	30.00	55
1986	Nutcracker 681	1,356	1988	37.00	61
1991	Nutrcracker Suite 1184	Suspd.		38.00	100
1990	Old Fashioned Santa 971	Suspd.		36.00	40
1987	Old Ironsides 767	Suspd.		35.00	45
1988	Old King Cole 824	Retrd.	1990	34.00	43
1985	Old North Church 661	Open		35.00	39
1991	Olivers Rocking Horse 1085	Retrd.	1993	37.00	40
1994	Palace of Fine Arts 1522	Open		39.50	40
1992	Parrot 1233	Open		37.00	37
1993	Partridge & Pear 1328	Open		38.00	40
1990	Patriotic Santa 972	Suspd.		36.00	40
1991	Paul Revere 1158	Open		39.00	39
1994	Paul Revere Lantern 1541	Open		39.00	39
1993	Peace 1327	Suspd.		36.00	36
1995	Peace on Earth 1503	Open		36.00	36
1994	Peachtree Swan 1612	Open		39.00	39
1985	Peacock 603	470	1989	34.00	65
1990	Pegasus 1037	Retrd.	1991	35.00	40
1987	Pegasus 745 (sp)	Unkn.		13.00	13
1995	Peter Rabbit & B Bunny 1492	Open		39.50	40
1993	Peter Rabbit 100th 1383	Retrd.	1993	39.50	45
1990	Peter Rabbit 1990 1018	4,315	1990	39.50	40
1994	Peter Rabbit 1994 1444	Retrd.	1994	39.50	40
1995	Peter Rabbit 1995 1598	Yr.Iss.		39.50	40
1996	Peter Rabbit 1996 1699	Yr.Iss.		39.50	40
1990	Peter Rabbit 993	Open		39.50	40
1990	Peter Rabbit Locket Ornament 1019	Unkn.		30.00	30
1991	Peter Rabbit with Book 1093	Open		39.50	40
1990	Peter's First Christmas 994	Suspd.		39.50	40
1986	Phaeton 683 (sp)	Unkn.		13.00	13
1985	Piazza 653	Suspd.		32.00	55
1991	Pig Robinson 1090	Open		39.50	40
1984	Pineapple 558	Suspd.		30.00	53
1995	Plate & Spoon 1659	Open		39.00	39
1983	Pollock Angel 502	Suspd.		35.00	75
1995	Pooh & Christopher Robin 1668	Open		39.00	39
1995	Pooh Hunny Pot 1663	Open		39.50	40
1995	Pooh with Balloon 1664	Open		39.50	40
1986	Prancer 698	Open		38.00	40
1984	Praying Angel 576	Suspd.		29.00	45
1991	Precious Planet 1142	2,000		120.00	200
1990	Presidential Homes 990	Suspd.		350.00	400
1989	Presidential Seal 858	Suspd.		39.00	150
1992	Princess & The Pea 1247	Retrd.	1995	39.00	50
1993	Public Garden 1370	Suspd.		38.00	50
1995	Public Garden Angel 1701	Open		39.00	39
1993	Puss In Boots 1396	Suspd.		40.00	44
1994	Quatrefoil 1542	Open		50.00	50
1991	Queen of Hearts 1122	Open		39.00	39
1994	R.E. Lee Monument 1446	Open		39.00	39
1988	Rabbit 816 (sp)	Unkn.		13.00	13
1985	Reindeer 656 (sp)	Unkn.		13.00	30
1987	Reindeer 752	Retrd.	1991	38.00	45
1992	Revere Teapot 1207	Retrd.	1994	49.50	75
1987	Ride a Cock Horse 757	Retrd.	1991	34.00	43
1984	Rocking Horse 581 (sp)	Unkn.		13.00	13
1984	Rosette 571	220	1988	32.00	65
1992	Round Teapot 1206	Retrd.	1994	49.50	55
1981	Roundel 109	220	1985	25.00	60
1990	S. Carolina State Capitol 1045	2,000		39.50	40
1986	Salem Lamb 712	Retrd.	1989	32.00	75
1985	Samantha 648	Suspd.		35.00	46
1991	San Francisco Heart 1196	Open		39.00	39
1995	San Francisco House 1685	Open		39.00	39
1990	San Francisco Row House 1071	Suspd.		39.50	50
1990	Santa & Reindeer 929	395	1991	39.00	50
1989	Santa 1989 856	1,715	1989	35.00	60
1990	Santa 1990 869	2,250	1990	38.00	42
1991	Santa 1991 1056	3,750	1992	38.00	40
1987	Santa 741 (sp)	Unkn.		13.00	13
1987	Santa and Sleigh 751	Retrd.	1989	32.00	100
1990	Santa in Balloon 973	Open		36.00	40
1990	Santa in the Moon 941	Suspd.		38.00	40
1990	Santa on Reindeer 974	Suspd.		36.00	100
1986	Santa Skates 715	Suspd.		36.00	45
1987	Santa Star 739	Retrd.	1991	32.00	48
1990	Santa UpTo Date 975	Suspd.		36.00	40
1988	Santa with Scroll 814	250	1991	34.00	44
1983	Sargent Angel 523	690	1987	29.00	56
1992	Scarecrow 1286	Retrd.	1993	36.00	50
1995	Schwarzschild Carillon 1738	Open		39.00	39
1992	Scrooge 1241	Open		36.00	40
1985	Shepherd 617	1,770	1990	35.00	60
1994	Shepherdstown House 1630	Open		39.00	39
1995	SI Angel 1691	Open		39.00	39
1995	SI Teddy Bear 1687	Open		39.00	39
1988	Skaters 790	Retrd.	1991	39.50	50
1994	Skaters in the Park 1617	Open		39.00	40
1995	Skating in the Park 1705	Open		39.00	39
1988	Sleigh 834	Open		34.00	40
1994	Smithsonian Angel 1534	Retrd.	1994	39.00	39
1987	Snow Queen 746	Retrd.	1995	35.00	75
1995	Snowflake 1574	Open		38.00	38
1990	Snowflake 1990 1033	1,415	1990	36.00	45
1993	Snowflake 1993 1394	Retrd.	1993	40.00	44
1994	Snowflake 1994 1486	Retrd.	1994	39.00	39
1995	Snowflake 1995 1652	Yr.Iss.		39.00	40
1986	Snowflake 713	Retrd.	1990	36.00	55
1994	Snowman 1572	Retrd.	1995	39.00	50
1987	Snowman 753	825	1991	38.00	56
1992	St. John Angel 1236	10,000		39.00	50
1992	St. John Lion 1235	10,000		39.00	50
1985	St. Nicholas 670 (sp)	Unkn.		13.00	30
1995	Star 1591	Open		40.00	40
1994	Star 1994 1462	Retrd.	1994	39.50	40
1988	Star 806	311	1990	50.00	200
1988	Star 854	275	1990	32.00	75
1988	Star of the East 785	Retrd.	1992	35.00	48
1990	Steadfast Tin Soldier 1050	Retrd.	1995	36.00	75
1987	Stocking 772 (sp)	Unkn.		13.00	13
1988	Stocking 774 (sp)	Unkn.		13.00	13
1988	Stocking 827 (sp)	Unkn.		13.00	13
1989	Stocking Bear 835 (sp)	Unkn.		13.00	13
1989	Stocking Bear 955 (sp)	Unkn.		12.00	12
1989	Stocking with Toys 956 (sp)	Unkn.		12.00	12
1982	Straw Star 448	590	1986	25.00	50
1983	Sunburst 543	Unkn.		13.00	50
1989	Swan Boat 904	Suspd.		38.00	50
1987	Sweetheart Star 740	Retrd.	1991	39.50	58
1991	Tailor of Gloucester 1087	Open		39.50	40
1985	Teddy 637	Suspd.		37.00	47
1986	Teddy 707	Unkn.		13.00	30
1986	Teddy Bear 685	Retrd.	1991	38.00	58
1990	Teddy Bear Locket 949	Unkn.		25.00	25
1990	Teddy Bear with Heart 957 (sp)	Unkn.		13.00	13
1995	Three Angels 1683	Open		39.50	40
1995	Three French Hens 1621	Open		39.00	40
1988	Thumbelina 803	Retrd.	1995	35.00	75
1992	Tin Man 1285	Retrd.	1993	36.00	50
1990	Toad Wind in Willows 945	Suspd.		38.00	38
1994	Trumpet 1504	Open		39.00	39
1994	Two Turtle Doves 1478	Open		38.00	40
1992	Unicorn 1165	Retrd.	1994	36.00	36
1985	Unicorn 660	Retrd.	1990	37.00	55
1988	US Capitol 820	Open		38.00	40
1984	USHS 1984 Angel 574	Suspd.		35.00	75
1989	USHS Angel 1989 901	Suspd.		38.00	75
1990	USHS Angel 1990 1061	Suspd.		39.00	39
1991	USHS Angel 1991 1139	Suspd.		38.00	50
1995	USHS Angel 1995 1703	Yr.Iss.		39.00	39
1986	USHS Angel 703	Suspd.		35.00	75
1985	USHS Bluebird 631	Suspd.		29.00	38
1994	USHS Dove 1521	Open		39.00	39
1987	USHS Gloria Angel 748	Suspd.		39.00	75
1985	USHS Madonna 630	Suspd.		35.00	75
1985	USHS Swallow 632	Suspd.		29.00	38
1989	Victorian Heart 954 (sp)	Unkn.		13.00	13
1986	Victorian Santa 724	250	1988	32.00	45
1993	Violin 1340	Retrd.	1993	38.00	90
1991	The Voyages Of Columbus 1141	1,500	1993	39.00	50
1991	Waiting For Santa 1123	Retrd.	1993	38.00	38
1994	Weld Boathouse 1447	Open		39.00	39
1991	White Rabbit 1121	Open		39.00	39
1990	White Tail Deer 1022 (sp)	Unkn.		13.00	13
1984	Wild Swan 592	Retrd.	1995	35.00	75
1993	Window 1360	Retrd.	1994	38.00	38
1986	Winged Dove 680	Retrd.	1993	35.00	54
1983	Wise Man 549	Retrd.	1988	29.00	56
1984	Wreath 575 (sp)	Unkn.		13.00	30
1986	Wreath 714	Suspd.		36.00	38
1992	Xmas Tree & Heart 1162	Retrd.	1994	36.00	36
1993	Xmas Tree 1395	Suspd.		40.00	44
1993	Zig Zag Tree 1343	Suspd.		39.00	39

Hawthorne Architectural Register

Rockwell's Main Street (Illuminated) - Rockwell Inspired

1994	Antique Shop and Town Offices	Open		29.90	30
1994	Barn and Library	Open		29.90	30
1994	Red Lion Inn & Rockwell Residence	Open		29.90	30
1994	Studio and Country Store	Open		29.90	30

John Hine N.A. Ltd.

David Winter Ornaments - Various

1991	Christmas Carol - D. Winter	Closed	1991	15.00	15
1991	Christmas in Scotland & Hogmanay - D. Winter	Closed	1991	15.00	15
1991	Mr. Fezziwig's Emporium - D. Winter	Closed	1991	15.00	15
1991	Ebenezer Scrooge's Counting House - D. Winter	Closed	1991	15.00	15
1991	Set - D. Winter	Closed	1991	60.00	50-66
1992	Fairytale Castle - D. Winter	Closed	1992	15.00	15
1992	Fred's Home - D. Winter	Closed	1992	15.00	15
1992	Suffolk House - D. Winter	Closed	1992	15.00	15
1992	Tudor Manor - D. Winter	Closed	1992	15.00	15
1992	Set - D. Winter	Closed	1992	60.00	30-60
1993	The Grange - J. Hine Studios	Closed	1993	15.00	15
1993	Scrooge's School - J. Hine Studios	Closed	1993	15.00	15
1993	Tomfool's Cottage - J. Hine Studios	Closed	1993	15.00	15
1993	Will-O The Wisp - J. Hine Studios	Closed	1993	15.00	15
1993	Set - J. Hine Studios	Closed	1993	60.00	40-60
1994	Old Joe's Beetling Shop - J. Hine Studios	Closed	1994	17.50	18
1994	Scrooge's Family Home - J. Hine Studios	Closed	1994	17.50	18
1994	What Cottage - J. Hine Studios	Closed	1994	17.50	18

June McKenna Collectibles, Inc.

Flatback Ornaments - J. McKenna

1988	1776 Santa	Closed	1991	17.00	45

YEAR ISSUE		EDITION LIMIT	YEAR RETD.	ISSUE PRICE	QUOTE U.S.$
1986	Amish Boy, blue	Closed	1989	13.00	65-275
1986	Amish Boy, pink	Closed	1986	13.00	100-225
1986	Amish Girl, blue	Closed	1989	13.00	275-360
1986	Amish Girl, pink	Closed	1986	13.00	325
1985	Amish Man	Closed	1989	13.00	110-200
1985	Amish Woman	Closed	1989	13.00	100-200
1993	Angel of Peace, white or pink	Closed	1994	30.00	30
1984	Angel with Horn	Closed	1988	14.00	100
1995	Angel with Teddy	Open		30.00	30
1982	Angel With Toys	Closed	1988	14.00	110-160
1995	Angel with Wreath	Open		30.00	30
1994	Angel, Guiding Light ,green, pink & white	Open		30.00	30
1983	Baby Bear in Vest, 5 colors	Closed	1988	11.00	83
1982	Baby Bear, Teeshirt	Closed	1984	11.00	85
1985	Baby Pig	Closed	1988	11.00	100
1983	Baby, blue trim	Closed	1988	11.00	110
1983	Baby, pink trim	Closed	1988	11.00	60-75
1991	Boy Angel, white	Closed	1992	20.00	85-120
1982	Candy Cane	Closed	1984	10.00	375
1993	Christmas Treat	Open		30.00	30
1982	Colonial Man, 3 colors	Closed	1984	12.00	175
1982	Colonial Woman, 3 colors	Closed	1984	12.00	95
1984	Country Boy, 2 colors	Closed	1988	12.00	65
1984	Country Girl, 2 colors	Closed	1988	12.00	60
1995	Country Santa	Open		30.00	30
1993	Elf Bernie	Closed	1994	30.00	30
1990	Elf Jeffrey	Closed	1992	17.00	40
1991	Elf Joey	Closed	1993	20.00	20
1992	Elf Scotty	Closed	1993	25.00	30
1995	Elf-Danny	Open		30.00	30
1994	Elf-Ricky	Open		30.00	30
1994	Elf-Tammy	Open		30.00	30
1988	Elizabeth, sill sitter	Closed	1989	20.00	100-200
1983	Father Bear in Suit, 3 colors	Closed	1988	12.00	70-85
1985	Father Pig	Closed	1988	12.00	50
1993	Final Notes	Closed	1994	30.00	30
1991	Girl Angel, white	Closed	1993	20.00	90-130
1983	Gloria Angel	Closed	1984	14.00	550
1989	Glorious Angel	Closed	1992	17.00	17
1983	Grandma, 4 colors	Closed	1988	12.00	110
1983	Grandpa, 4 colors	Closed	1988	12.00	80
1988	Guardian Angel	Closed	1991	16.00	40
1990	Harvest Santa	Closed	1992	17.00	40
1990	Ho Ho Ho	Closed	1992	17.00	40
1982	Kate Greenaway Boy, 3 colors	Closed	1983	12.00	155
1982	Kate Greenaway Girl, 3 colors	Closed	1983	12.00	125
1982	Mama Bear, Blue Cape	Closed	1984	12.00	75
1983	Mother Bear in Dress, 3 colors	Closed	1988	12.00	73
1985	Mother Pig	Closed	1988	12.00	70
1984	Mr. Claus	Closed	1988	14.00	100
1984	Mrs. Claus	Closed	1988	14.00	100
1994	Mrs. Klaus	Open		30.00	30
1992	Northpole News	Closed	1993	25.00	30
1994	Nutcracker	Open		30.00	30
1993	Old Lamplighter	Closed	1994	30.00	30
1984	Old World Santa, 3 colors	Closed	1989	14.00	75
1984	Old World Santa, gold	Closed	1986	14.00	200
1982	Papa Bear, Red Cape	Closed	1984	12.00	85
1992	Praying Angel	Closed	1993	25.00	30
1985	Primitive Santa	Closed	1989	17.00	128
1983	Raggedy Andy, 2 colors	Closed	1983	12.00	250
1983	Raggedy Ann, 2 colors	Closed	1983	12.00	325
1994	Ringing in Christmas	Open		30.00	30
1995	Santa and His Lil' Helper	Open		40.00	40
1995	Santa Nutcracker	Open		30.00	30
1986	Santa with Bag	Closed	1989	16.00	45
1991	Santa with Banner	Closed	1992	20.00	20
1992	Santa with Basket	Closed	1993	25.00	30
1986	Santa with Bear	Closed	1991	14.00	40
1986	Santa with Bells, blue	Closed	1989	14.00	125
1986	Santa with Bells, green	Closed	1987	14.00	400-425
1988	Santa with Book, blue & red	Closed	1988	17.00	275
1991	Santa with Lights, black or white	Closed	1992	20.00	45
1994	Santa with Pipe	Open		30.00	30
1992	Santa with Sack	Closed	1993	25.00	30
1994	Santa with Skis	Open		30.00	30
1989	Santa with Staff	Closed	1991	17.00	40
1982	Santa with Toys	Closed	1988	14.00	110
1988	Santa with Toys	Closed	1991	17.00	150
1989	Santa with Tree	Closed	1991	17.00	40
1988	Santa with Wreath	Closed	1991	17.00	40
1995	Santa-Teacher	Open		30.00	30
1994	Snow Showers	Open		30.00	30
1983	St. Nick with Lantern (wooden)	Closed	1988	14.00	130
1995	Who's This Frosty?	Open		30.00	30
1989	Winking Santa	Closed	1991	17.00	40

Santa Head Ornament - J. McKenna

YEAR ISSUE		EDITION LIMIT	YEAR RETD.	ISSUE PRICE	QUOTE U.S.$
1995	Moon Shape Santa	Open		17.00	17
1994	Primative	Open		16.00	16
1994	Quick as a Wink	Open		16.00	16
1995	Santa with Holly	Open		17.00	17
1995	Santa with Pipe	Open		17.00	17
1994	Whispering	Open		16.00	16

Kirk Stieff

Colonial Williamsburg - D. Bacorn

YEAR ISSUE		EDITION LIMIT	YEAR RETD.	ISSUE PRICE	QUOTE U.S.$
1992	Court House	Open		10.00	10
1989	Doll ornament, silverplate	Closed		22.00	22
1993	Governors Palace	Open		10.00	10
1988	Lamb, silverplate	Closed		20.00	22
1992	Prentis Store	Open		10.00	10
1987	Rocking Horse, silverplate	Closed		20.00	30
1987	Tin Drum, silverplate	Closed		20.00	30
1983	Tree Top Star, silverplate	Closed		29.50	30
1988	Unicorn, silverplate	Closed		22.00	22
1992	Wythe House	Open		10.00	10

Kirk Stieff Ornaments - Various

YEAR ISSUE		EDITION LIMIT	YEAR RETD.	ISSUE PRICE	QUOTE U.S.$
1994	Angel with Star - J. Ferraioli	Open		8.00	8
1993	Baby's Christmas - D. Bacorn	Open		12.00	12
1993	Bell with Ribbon - D. Bacorn	Open		12.00	12
1992	Cat and Ornament - D. Bacorn	Closed		10.00	10
1993	Cat with Ribbon - D. Bacorn	Open		12.00	12
1983	Charleston Locomotive - D. Bacorn	Closed		18.00	20
1993	First Christmas Together - D. Bacorn	Closed		10.00	10
1993	French Horn - D. Bacorn	Closed		12.00	12
1992	Guardian Angel - J. Ferraioli	Closed		13.00	13
1986	Icicle, sterling silver - D. Bacorn	Closed		35.00	65
1994	Kitten with Tassel - J. Ferraioli	Open		12.00	12
1993	Mouse and Ornament - D. Bacorn	Closed		10.00	10
1992	Repoussé Angel - J. Ferraioli	Open		13.00	13
1992	Repoussé Wreath - J. Ferraioli	Open		13.00	13
1994	Santa with Tassel - J. Ferraioli	Open		12.00	12
1989	Smithsonian Carousel Horse - Kirk Stieff	Closed		50.00	50
1989	Smithsonian Carousel Seahorse - Kirk Stieff	Closed		50.00	50
1994	Teddy Bear - D. Bacorn	Open		8.00	8
1990	Toy Ship - Kirk Stieff	Closed		23.00	23
1984	Unicorn - D. Bacorn	Closed		18.00	20
1994	Unicorn - D. Bacorn	Open		8.00	8
1994	Victorian Skaters - D. Bacorn	Open		8.00	8
1994	Williamsburg Wreath - D. Bacorn	Open		15.00	15
1993	Wreath with Ribbon - D. Bacorn	Open		12.00	12

Kurt S. Adler, Inc.

Children's Hour - J. Mostrom

YEAR ISSUE		EDITION LIMIT	YEAR RETD.	ISSUE PRICE	QUOTE U.S.$
1995	Alice in Wonderland J5751	Open		22.50	23
1995	Bow Peep J5753	Open		27.00	27
1995	Cinderella J5752	Open		28.00	28
1995	Little Boy Blue J5755	Open		18.00	18
1995	Miss Muffet J5753	Open		27.00	27
1995	Mother Goose J5754	Open		27.00	27
1995	Red Riding Hood J5751	Open		22.50	23

Christmas in Chelsea Collection - J. Mostrom

YEAR ISSUE		EDITION LIMIT	YEAR RETD.	ISSUE PRICE	QUOTE U.S.$
1994	Alice, Marguerite W2973	Open		28.00	28
1992	Allison Sitting in Chair W2812	Retrd.	1994	25.50	26
1992	Allison W2729	Retrd.	1993	21.00	21
1992	Amanda W2709	Retrd.	1994	21.00	21
1992	Amy W2729	Retrd.	1993	21.00	21
1992	Christina W2812	Retrd.	1994	25.50	26
1992	Christopher W2709	Retrd.	1994	21.00	21
1992	Delphinium W2728	Open		20.00	20
1995	Edmond With Violin W3078	Open		32.00	32
1994	Guardian Angel With Baby W2974	Open		31.00	31
1992	Holly Hock W2728	Open		20.00	20
1992	Holly W2709	Retrd.	1994	21.00	21
1995	Jose With Violin W3078	Open		32.00	32
1995	Pauline With Violin W3078	Open		32.00	32
1992	Peony W2728	Open		20.00	20
1992	Rose W2728	Open		20.00	20

Cornhusk Mice Ornament Series - M. Rothenberg

YEAR ISSUE		EDITION LIMIT	YEAR RETD.	ISSUE PRICE	QUOTE U.S.$
1994	3" Father Christmas W2976	Open		18.00	18
1994	9" Father Christmas W2982	Open		25.00	25
1995	Angel Mice W3088	Open		10.00	10
1995	Baby's First Mouse W3087	Open		10.00	10
1993	Ballerina Cornhusk Mice W2700	Retrd.	1994	13.50	14
1994	Clara, Prince W2948	Open		16.00	16
1994	Cowboy W2951	Open		18.00	18
1994	Drosselmeir Fairy, Mouse King W2949	Open		16.00	16
1994	Little Pocahontas, Indian Brave W2950	Open		18.00	18
1995	Miss Tammie Mouse W3086	Open		17.00	17
1995	Mr. Jamie Mouse W3086	Open		17.00	17
1995	Mrs. Molly Mouse W3086	Open		17.00	17
1993	Nutcracker Suite Fantasy Cornhusk Mice W2885	Retrd.	1994	15.50	16

Fabriché™ Ornament Series - KS. Adler, unless otherwise noted

YEAR ISSUE		EDITION LIMIT	YEAR RETD.	ISSUE PRICE	QUOTE U.S.$
1994	All Star Santa W1665	Open		27.00	27
1992	An Apron Full of Love W1594 - M. Rothenberg	Open		27.00	27
1995	Captain Claus W1711	Open		25.00	25
1994	Checking His List W1634	Open		23.50	24
1992	Christmas in the Air W1593	Open		35.50	36
1994	Cookies For Santa W1639	Open		28.00	28
1994	Firefighting Friends W1668	Open		28.00	28
1992	Hello Little One! W1561	Open		22.00	22
1994	Holiday Flight W1637 - Smithsonian	Open		40.00	40
1993	Homeward Bound W1596	Open		27.00	27
1992	Hugs And Kisses W1560	Open		22.00	22
1993	Master Toymaker W1595	Open		27.00	27
1992	Merry Chrismouse W1565	Retrd.	1994	10.00	10
1992	Not a Creature Was Stirring W1563	Open		22.00	22
1993	Par For the Claus W1625	Open		27.00	27
1993	Santa With List W1510	Open		20.00	20
1994	Santa's Fishtales W1666	Open		29.00	29
1995	Strike Up The Band W1710	Open		25.00	25

International Christmas - J. Mostrom

YEAR ISSUE		EDITION LIMIT	YEAR RETD.	ISSUE PRICE	QUOTE U.S.$
1994	Cathy, Johnny W2945	Open		24.00	24
1994	Eskimo-Atom, Ukpik W2967	Open		28.00	28
1994	Germany-Katerina, Hans W2969	Open		27.00	27
1994	Native American-White Dove, Little Wolf W2970	Retrd.	1994	28.00	28
1994	Poland-Marissa, Hedwig W2965	Open		27.00	27
1994	Scotland-Bonnie, Douglas W2966	Open		27.00	27
1994	Spain-Maria, Miguel W2968	Open		27.00	27

Little Dickens - J. Mostrom

YEAR ISSUE		EDITION LIMIT	YEAR RETD.	ISSUE PRICE	QUOTE U.S.$
1994	Little Bob Crachit W2961	Open		30.00	30
1994	Little Marley's Ghost W2964	Open		33.50	34
1994	Little Mrs. Crachit W2962	Open		27.00	27
1994	Little Scrooge in Bathrobe W2959	Open		30.00	30
1994	Little Scrooge in Overcoat W2960	Open		30.00	30
1994	Little Tiny Tim W2963	Open		22.50	23

Polonaise™ by Komozja - KSA/Komozja, unless otherwise noted

YEAR ISSUE		EDITION LIMIT	YEAR RETD.	ISSUE PRICE	QUOTE U.S.$
1995	Alarm Clock GP452	Open		25.00	25
1994	Angel Head GP372	Open		18.00	18
1994	Angel w/Bell GP396	Open		20.20	21
1994	Beer Glass GP366	Open		18.00	18
1995	Blessed Mother GP413	Open		22.50	23
1994	Cardinal GP420	Open		18.00	18
1995	Cat in Boot GP478 - Rothenberg	Open		28.00	28
1994	Cat w/Ball GP390	Open		23.00	23
1995	Cat w/Bow GP446	Open		22.50	23
1995	Ceasar GP422	Open		25.00	25
1995	Christ Child GP414	Open		20.00	20
1995	Christmas Tree GP461	Open		22.50	23
1995	Clara GP408	Open		20.00	20
1995	Clown Head 4.5" GP460	Open		25.00	25
1995	Cowboy Head GP462	Open		30.00	30
1995	Creche GP458 - Stefan	Open		28.00	28
1995	Crocodile GP468	Open		28.00	28
1994	Dinosaurs GP397	Open		22.50	23
1995	Dove on Ball GP472 - Stefan	Open		30.00	30
1995	Eagle GP453	Open		28.00	28
1994	Egyptian (12 pc boxed set) GP500	Open		200.00	200
1995	Egyptian set 4 pc. boxed GP500/4	Open		110.00	110
1995	Elephant GP	Open		28.00	28
1995	Fish 4 pc. boxed GP506	Open		110.00	110
1994	Glass Acorn GP342	Open		11.00	11
1994	Glass Angel GP309	Open		18.00	18
1994	Glass Apple GP339	Open		11.00	11
1994	Glass Church GP369	Open		18.00	18
1994	Glass Clown 4" GP301	Open		13.50	14
1994	Glass Clown 6" GP303	Open		22.50	23
1994	Glass Clown 6.5" GP302	Open		22.50	23
1994	Glass Dice GP363	Open		18.00	18
1994	Glass Doll GP377	Open		13.50	14
1994	Glass Gnome GP347	Open		18.00	18
1994	Glass Knight GP304	Open		18.00	18
1994	Glass Owl GP328	Open		20.00	20
1994	Glass Top GP359	Open		9.00	9
1994	Glass Turkey GP326	Open		20.00	20
1994	Golden Cherub Head GP372	Retrd.	1994	18.00	69
1994	Golden Rocking Horse GP355	Retrd.	1994	22.50	23
1995	Goose w/Wreath GP475 - Stefan	Open		30.00	30
1994	Guardman GP407	Open		15.50	16
1995	Herr Drosselmeir GP465 - Rothenberg	Open		30.00	30
1995	Holy Family 3 pc. GP504	Open		84.00	84
1994	Holy Family GP371	Open		28.00	28
1995	Humpty Dumpty GP477 - Stefan	Open		30.00	30
1995	Icicle Santa GP474 - Stefan	Open		25.00	25
1995	Indian GP463	Open		30.00	30
1994	Locomotive GP353	Open		22.50	23
1995	Locomotive GP447	Open		28.00	28
1994	Madonna w/Child GP370	Open		22.50	23
1994	Merlin GP373	Open		20.00	20
1994	Moose King GP406	Open		20.00	20
1994	Nefertiti GP349	Open		25.00	25
1994	Night & Day GP307	Open		22.50	23
1995	Noah's Ark GP469	Open		28.00	28
1994	Nutcracker GP404	Open		20.00	20
1995	Nutcracker Suite 4 pc. boxed GP507	Open		110.00	110
1994	Old Fashion Car GP380	Open		13.50	14
1994	Parrott GP332	Open		15.50	16
1995	Partridge GP467 - Stefan	Open		33.50	34
1994	Peacock 5" GP324	Open		18.00	18
1994	Peacock 7.5" GP323	Open		28.00	28
1995	Peter Pan 4 pc. boxed set GP503	Open		124.00	124
1995	Peter Pan GP419	Open		22.50	23
1994	Pierrot Clown GP405	Open		18.00	18
1995	Polonaise Afro-American Santa GP389/1	Open		25.00	25
1995	Polonaise Cardinal GP473 - Stefan	Open		30.00	30
1995	Polonaise House GP455	Open		25.00	25

YEAR ISSUE		EDITION LIMIT	YEAR RETD.	ISSUE PRICE	QUOTE U.S.$
1995	Polonaise Santa GP389	Open		25.00	25
1994	Puppy GP333	Open		15.50	16
1994	Pyramid GP352	Open		22.50	23
1994	Rocking Horse 4" GP355	Open		22.50	23
1994	Rocking Horse 5" GP356	Open		22.50	23
1995	Roman 7 pc. boxed set GP402	Open		164.00	164
1995	Roman Centurian GP427	Open		22.50	23
1995	Roman set 4 pc. boxed GP402/4	Open		110.00	110
1995	Sailing Ship GP415	Open		30.00	30
1994	Saint Nick GP316	Open		28.00	28
1994	Santa Boot GP375	Open		20.00	20
1994	Santa GP317	Open		22.50	23
1995	Santa GP442	Open		25.00	25
1994	Santa Head 4" GP315	Open		13.50	14
1994	Santa Head 4.5" GP374	Open		18.00	18
1995	Santa Moon GP454 - Stefan	Open		28.00	28
1995	Santa on Goose on Sled GP479	Open		30.00	30
1995	Shark GP417	Open		18.00	18
1994	Snowman w/Parcel GP313	Open		22.50	23
1994	Snowman w/Specs GP312	Open		20.00	20
1994	Sparrow GP 329	Open		15.50	16
1994	Sphinx GP350	Open		22.50	23
1995	St. Joseph GP412	Open		22.50	23
1995	Star Santa GP470 - Stefan	Open		25.00	25
1994	Swan GP325	Open		20.00	20
1994	Teddy Bear GP338	Open		15.50	16
1995	Telephone GP448	Open		25.00	25
1994	Train Coaches GP354	Open		15.50	16
1994	Train Set (boxed) GP501	Open		90.00	90
1995	Treasure Chest GP416	Open		20.00	20
1994	Tropical Fish GP409	Open		22.50	23
1995	Turtle Doves GP471 - Stefan	Open		25.00	25
1994	Tutenkhamen GP348	Open		25.00	25
1995	Wizard of Oz 4 pc. boxed GP505	5,000		124.00	124
1995	Wizard of Oz 6 pc. boxed GP508	5,000	1995	170.00	170
1995	Wizard of Oz Dorothy GP434	Open		25.00	25
1995	Wizard of Oz Lion GP433	Open		22.50	23
1995	Wizard of Oz Scarecrow GP435	Open		25.00	25
1995	Wizard of Oz Tinman GP436	Open		25.00	25
1994	Zodiac Sun GP381	Open		22.50	23

Royal Heritage Collection - J. Mostrom

1993	Anastasia W2922	Retrd.	1994	28.00	28
1995	Benjamin J5756	Open		24.50	25
1995	Blythe J5756	Open		24.50	25
1993	Caroline W2924	Retrd.	1995	25.50	26
1993	Charles W2924	Retrd.	1995	25.50	26
1993	Elizabeth W2924	Retrd.	1995	25.50	26
1994	Ice Fairy, Winter Fairy W2972	Open		25.50	26
1993	Joella W2979	Retrd.	1993	27.00	27
1993	Kelly W2979	Retrd.	1993	27.00	27
1993	Nicholas W2923	Open		25.50	26
1993	Patina W2923	Open		25.50	26
1993	Sasha W2923	Open		25.50	26
1994	Snow Princess W2971	Open		28.00	28

Smithsonian Museum Carousel - KSA/Smithsonian

1987	Antique Bunny S3027/2	Retrd.	1992	14.50	15
1992	Antique Camel S3027/12	Open		15.00	15
1989	Antique Cat S3027/6	Retrd.	1995	14.50	15
1992	Antique Elephant S3027/11	Open		14.50	15
1995	Antique Frog S32027/18	Open		15.50	16
1988	Antique Giraffe S3027/4	Retrd.	1993	14.50	15
1987	Antique Goat S3027/1	Retrd.	1992	14.50	15
1991	Antique Horse S3027/10	Open		14.50	15
1993	Antique Horse S3027/14	Open		15.00	15
1988	Antique Horse S3027/3	Retrd.	1993	14.50	15
1989	Antique Lion S3027/5	Retrd.	1994	14.50	15
1994	Antique Pig S3027/16	Open		15.50	16
1994	Antique Reindeer S3027/15	Open		15.50	16
1991	Antique Rooster S3027/9	Retrd.	1994	14.50	15
1990	Antique Seahorse S3027/8	Open		14.50	15
1993	Antique Tiger S3027/13	Open		15.00	15
1990	Antique Zebra S3027/7	Open		14.50	15
1995	Armored Horse S3027/17	Open		15.50	16

Smithsonian Museum Fabriché™ - KSA/Smithsonian

1992	Holiday Drive W1580	Retrd.	1995	38.00	38
1992	Santa On a Bicycle W1547	Open		31.00	31

Steinbach Ornament Series - KS. Adler

1992	The King's Guards ES300	Open		27.00	27

Lance Corporation

Sebastian Christmas Ornaments - P.W. Baston Jr., unless otherwise noted

1943	Madonna of the Chair - P.W. Baston	25	1943	2.00	150-200
1981	Santa Claus - P.W. Baston	5,000	1981	28.50	30
1982	Madonna of the Chair (Reissue of '43) - P.W. Baston	2,165	1982	15.00	30-45
1985	Home for the Holidays	Closed	1993	10.00	13
1986	Holiday Sleigh Ride	Closed	1993	10.00	13
1987	Santa	Closed	1993	10.00	13
1988	Decorating the Tree	Closed	1993	12.50	13
1989	Final Preparations for Christmas	Closed	1993	13.90	14
1990	Stuffing the Stockings	Closed	1993	14.00	14
1990	Christmas Rose-Red on White (Blossom Shop)	Closed	N/A	22.00	25-35
1991	Merry Christmas	Closed	1993	14.50	15
1992	Final Check	Closed	1993	14.50	15
1993	Ethnic Santa	Closed	1993	12.50	13
1993	Caroling With Santa	Closed	1993	15.00	15
1994	Victorian Christmas Skaters	Closed	1994	17.00	17
1995	Midnight Snacks	Annual	1995	17.00	17

Lenox China

Annual Ornaments - Lenox

1982	1982 Ball	Yr.Iss.	1983	30.00	50-90
1983	1983 Teardrop Shape	Yr.Iss.	1984	35.00	75
1984	1984 Starburst	Yr.Iss.	1985	38.00	65
1985	1985 Bell	Yr.Iss.	1986	37.50	60
1986	1986 The Three Magi	Yr.Iss.	1987	38.50	50
1987	1987 Dickens Village	Yr.Iss.	1988	39.00	45
1988	1988 Ball	Yr.Iss.	1989	39.00	45
1989	1989 Faberge Egg	Yr.Iss.	1990	39.00	39
1990	1990 Bell	Yr.Iss.	1991	42.00	42
1991	1991 Ornament	Yr.Iss.	1992	39.00	39
1992	1992 Ball	Yr.Iss.	1993	42.00	42
1993	1993 Lantern	Yr.Iss.	1994	45.00	45
1994	1994 Star	Yr.Iss.	1995	39.00	39

Days of Christmas - Lenox

1987	Partridge	Retrd.	1992	20.00	20
1988	Two Turtle Doves	Retrd.	1992	20.00	20
1989	Three French Hens	Retrd.	1992	22.50	23
1990	Four Calling Birds	Retrd.	1992	25.00	25
1991	Five Golden Rings	Retrd.	1992	25.00	25
1992	Six Geese a-Laying	Retrd.	1993	25.00	25
1993	Seven Swans	Retrd.	1994	26.00	26
1994	Eight Maids Milking	Retrd.	1995	26.00	26

Holiday Homecoming - Lenox

1988	Hearth	Closed	1990	22.50	23
1989	Door	Closed	1991	22.50	23
1990	Hutch	Closed	1992	25.00	25
1991	Window	Closed	1992	25.00	25
1992	Stove	Closed	1993	25.00	25
1993	Clock	Closed	1994	26.00	26
1994	Lamp	Closed	1995	26.00	26

Yuletide - Lenox

1985	Christmas Tree	Open		16.00	16
1985	Rocking Horse	Closed	1987	16.00	16
1985	Teddy Bear	Closed	1990	18.00	18
1985	Christmas Bells	Closed	1987	16.00	16
1987	Reindeer	Closed	1989	17.00	17
1987	Snow Blossom Snowflake	Closed	1988	17.00	17
1988	Santa with Sleigh	Closed	1989	17.00	17
1989	Santa	Closed	1991	18.00	18
1989	Angel with Horn	Closed	1993	18.00	18
1990	Dove	Open		19.50	20
1991	Snowman	Closed	1995	19.50	20
1992	Goose	Closed	1994	19.50	20
1993	Cardinal	Open		19.50	20
1994	Cat	Open		19.50	20

Lenox Collections

The Christmas Carousel - Lenox

1989	Cat	Open		19.50	20
1989	Elephant	Open		19.50	20
1989	Goat	Open		19.50	20
1989	Hare	Open		19.50	20
1989	Lion	Open		19.50	20
1989	Palomino	Open		19.50	20
1989	Pinto	Open		19.50	20
1989	Polar Bear	Open		19.50	20
1989	Reindeer	Open		19.50	20
1989	Sea Horse	Open		19.50	20
1989	Swan	Open		19.50	20
1989	Tiger	Open		19.50	20
1989	Unicorn	Open		19.50	20
1989	White Horse	Open		19.50	20
1989	Zebra	Open		19.50	20
1989	Black Horse	Open		19.50	20
1990	Camel	Open		19.50	20
1990	Frog	Open		19.50	20
1990	Giraffe	Open		19.50	20
1990	Medieval Horse	Open		19.50	20
1990	Panda	Open		19.50	20
1990	Pig	Open		19.50	20
1990	Rooster	Open		19.50	20
1990	St. Bernard	Open		19.50	20
1990	Set of 24	Open		468.00	468

Lilliput Lane Ltd.

Christmas Ornaments - Lilliput Lane

1992	Mistletoe Cottage	Closed	1992	27.50	35-45
1993	Robin Cottage	Closed	1993	35.00	40
1994	Ivy House	Closed	1994	35.00	40
1995	Plum Cottage	Yr.Iss.		40.00	40

Lladro

Angels - Lladro

1994	Joyful Offering L6125G	Yr.Iss.		245.00	245
1995	Angel of the Stars L6132G	Yr.Iss.		195.00	195

Annual Ornaments - Lladro

1988	Christmas Ball-L1603M	Yr.Iss.	1988	60.00	60-80
1989	Christmas Ball-L5656M	Yr.Iss.	1989	65.00	65-95
1990	Christmas Ball-L5730M	Yr Iss.	1990	70.00	70-90
1991	Christmas Ball-L5829M	Yr.Iss.	1991	52.00	68
1992	Christmas Ball-L5914M	Yr.Iss.	1992	52.00	55
1993	Christmas Ball-L6009M	Yr.Iss.	1993	54.00	54-60
1994	Christmas Ball-L6105M	Yr.Iss.	1994	55.00	55
1995	Christmas Ball-L6207M	Yr.Iss.		55.00	55

Cherub Ornaments - Lladro

1995	Suprised Cherub L6253G	Open		120.00	120
1995	Playing Cherub L6254G	Open		120.00	120
1995	Thinking Cherub L6255G	Open		120.00	120

Dove Ornaments - Lladro

1995	Landing Dove L6266G	Open		49.00	49
1995	Flying Dove L6267G	Open		49.00	49

Miniature Ornaments - Lladro

1988	Miniature Angels-L1604G, Set/3	Yr.Iss.	1988	75.00	130-200
1989	Holy Family-L5657G, Set/3	Yr.Iss.	1990	79.50	100-115
1990	Three Kings-L5729G, Set/3	Yr Iss.	1991	87.50	100-118
1991	Holy Shepherds-L5809G	Yr.Iss.	1991	97.50	125
1993	Nativity Trio-L6095G	Yr.Iss.	1993	115.00	125

Ornaments - Lladro

1992	Snowman-L5841G	Yr.Iss.	1994	50.00	52
1992	Santa-L5842G	Yr.Iss.	1994	55.00	57
1992	Baby's First-1992-L5922G	Yr.Iss.	1992	55.00	55
1992	Our First-1992-L5923G	Yr.Iss.	1992	50.00	50
1992	Elf Ornament-L5938G	Yr.Iss.	1994	50.00	50
1992	Mrs. Claus-L5939G	Yr.Iss.	1994	55.00	57
1992	Christmas Morning-L5940G	Yr.Iss.	1992	97.50	100
1993	Nativity Lamb-L5969G	Yr.Iss.	1994	85.00	85
1993	Baby's First 1993-L6037G	Yr.Iss.	1993	57.00	57
1993	Our First-L6038G	Yr.Iss.	1993	52.00	52

Toy Ornaments - Lladro

1995	Christmas Tree L6261G	Open		75.00	75
1995	Rocking Horse L6262G	Open		69.00	69
1995	Doll L6263G	Open		69.00	69
1995	Train L6264G	Open		69.00	69

Tree Topper Ornaments - Lladro

1990	Angel Tree Topper-L5719G-Blue	Yr.Iss.	1990	115.00	120-200
1991	Angel Tree Topper-L5831G-Pink	Yr.Iss.	1991	115.00	120-200
1992	Angel Tree Topper-L5875G-Green	Yr.Iss.	1992	120.00	120
1993	Angel Tree Topper-L5962G-Lavender	Yr.Iss.	1993	125.00	125

Margaret Furlong Designs

Annual Ornaments - M. Furlong

1980	1980 3" Trumpeter Angel	Closed	1994	12.00	12
1980	1980 4" Trumpeter Angel	Closed	1994	21.00	21
1982	1982 3" Star Angel	Closed	1994	12.00	12
1982	1982 4" Star Angel	Closed	1994	21.00	21
1984	1984 3" Dove Angel	Closed	1995	12.00	12
1984	1984 4" Dove Angel	Closed	1995	21.00	21

Flora Angelica - M. Furlong

1995	Faith Angel	10,000	1995	45.00	45

Gifts from God - M. Furlong

1985	1985 The Charis Angel	3,000	1985	45.00	300
1986	1986 The Hallelujah Angel	3,000	1986	45.00	600-750
1987	1987 The Angel of Light	3,000	1987	45.00	200-250
1988	1988 The Celestial Angel	3,000	1988	45.00	200-250
1989	1989 Coronation Angel	3,000	1989	45.00	175-250

Joyeux Noel - M. Furlong

1990	1990 Celebration Angel	10,000	1994	45.00	100-125
1991	1991 Thanksgiving Angel	10,000	1994	45.00	100-125
1992	1992 Joyeux Noel Angel	10,000	1994	45.00	100-125
1993	1993 Star of Bethlehem Angel	10,000	1994	45.00	100-125
1994	1994 Messiah Angel	10,000	1994	45.00	100-250

Musical Series - M. Furlong

1980	1980 The Caroler	3,000	1980	50.00	100-200
1981	1981 The Lyrist	3,000	1981	45.00	100-200
1982	1982 The Lutist	3,000	1982	45.00	100-200
1983	1983 The Concertinist	3,000	1983	45.00	100-200
1984	1984 The Herald Angel	3,000	1984	45.00	100-200

Midwest of Cannon Falls

Folk Art Gallery Collection - Various

1995	Animal Jester, 2 asst. 13498-6 - P. Herrick	Open		20.00	20
1995	Ballerina Bunny Pull Toy 13500-6 - P. Herrick	Open		23.00	23
1995	Frog and Turtle, 2 asst. 13781-9 - P. Herrick	Open		20.00	20
1995	Jingle Claus Icicle 13491-7 - R. Jones	Open		11.00	11
1995	Jointed Dutch Santa 13494-8 - R. Jones	Open		27.00	27

YEAR ISSUE		EDITION LIMIT	YEAR RETD.	ISSUE PRICE	QUOTE U.S.$
1995	Maypole Dancer, 3 asst. 13616-4 - P. Herrick	Open		15.00	15
1995	Once in a Blue Moon 13497-9 - P. Herrick	Open		15.00	15
1995	Playtime, 2 asst. 13499-3 - P. Herrick	Open		17.00	18
1995	Uncle Sam 13493-1 - R. Jones	Open		22.50	23

Heritage Santa Collection Ornaments - Midwest

YEAR ISSUE		EDITION LIMIT	YEAR RETD.	ISSUE PRICE	QUOTE U.S.$
1991	Father Christmas Dimensional 02945-9	Retrd.	1994	11.50	12
1991	Herr Kristmas Dimensional 02942-8	Retrd.	1993	11.50	12
1990	Herr Kristmas Fabric Mache 05216	Retrd.	1992	18.00	18
1991	MacNicholas Dimensional 02930-5	Retrd.	1994	11.50	12
1990	MacNicholas Fabric Mache 05224	Retrd.	1992	18.00	18
1991	Papa Frost Dimensional 02944-2	Retrd.	1992	11.50	12
1990	Papa Frost Fabric Mache 05232	Retrd.	1992	18.00	18
1992	Pere Noel Dimensional 06773-4	Retrd.	1994	11.50	12
1993	Santa España Dimensional 07376-6	Retrd.	1994	11.50	12
1991	Santa Niccolo Dimensional 02946-6	Retrd.	1993	11.50	12
1992	Santa Nykolai Dimensional 06774-1	Retrd.	1994	11.50	12
1993	Santa O'Nicholas Dimensional 07377-3	Retrd.	1994	11.50	12
1991	Scanda Klaus Dimensional 02941-1	Retrd.	1993	11.50	12
1990	Scanda Klaus Fabric Mache 05208	Retrd.	1992	18.00	18

Leo R. Smith III Collection - L.R. Smith

YEAR ISSUE		EDITION LIMIT	YEAR RETD.	ISSUE PRICE	QUOTE U.S.$
1995	"Angel of Love" 16123-4	3,500		32.00	32
1995	"Angel of Peace" 16199-9	3,500		32.00	32
1995	"Angel of Your Dreams" 16130-2	3,500		32.00	32
1994	Flying Woodsman Santa 11921-1	2,500	1994	35.00	100
1995	Partridge Angel 13994-3	3,500		30.00	30
1995	Santa on Reindeer 13780-2	3,500	1995	35.00	35

Wendt und Kuhn Ornaments - Wendt/Kuhn

YEAR ISSUE		EDITION LIMIT	YEAR RETD.	ISSUE PRICE	QUOTE U.S.$
1978	Angel Clip-on Ornament 00729-7	Open		20.00	24
1991	Angel in Ring Ornament 01208-6	Open		12.00	15
1994	Angel on Moon, Star, 12 asst. 12945-6	Open		20.00	22
1989	Trumpeting Angel Ornament, 2 asst. 09402-0	S/O	N/A	14.00	17

Old World Christmas

Collector Club - E.M. Merck, unless otherwise noted

YEAR ISSUE		EDITION LIMIT	YEAR RETD.	ISSUE PRICE	QUOTE U.S.$
1993	Mr. & Mrs. Claus set 1490	Retrd.	1993	Gift	75-150
1993	Glass Christmas Maidens, set of 4, 1491	Retrd.	1993	35.00	60
1993	Dresdener Drummer Nutcracker 7258	Retrd.	1993	110.00	150-175
1994	Santa in Moon 1492	Retrd.	1994	Gift	N/A
1994	Large Santa in Chimney 1493	Retrd.	1994	42.50	65
1995	Large Christmas Carousel 1587 - Inge-Glas	Yr.Iss.		79.50	80
1995	The Konigsee Nutcracker 7284	Yr.Iss.		125.00	125
1995	Cherub on Reflector 1545 - Inge-Glas	Open		Gift	N/A

Angel & Female - E.M. Merck, unless otherwise noted

YEAR ISSUE		EDITION LIMIT	YEAR RETD.	ISSUE PRICE	QUOTE U.S.$
1993	Angel Above Celestial Ball 1060	Open		41.00	41
1990	Angel Holding Star 1023	Open		7.80	8
1991	Angel of Peace 1033	Open		9.25	10
1990	Angel on Disc 1028	Retrd.	1993	11.70	13
1992	Angel on Form 1044	12/95		9.70	10
1995	Angel with Wings 2306	Open		8.95	9
1990	Antique Style Doll Head 1026	Open		8.45	9
1988	Baby in Bunting 1015	Retrd.	1990	7.70	10
1991	Baby Jesus 1036	Open		9.25	10
1993	Ballerina 1061	Open		14.50	15
1991	Baroque Angel 1031	Open		12.95	13
1991	Blue Praying Angel w/ Wings 1035	Open		8.25	9
1985	Caroling Girl 101062	Retrd.	1990	6.65	14
1991	Cherub 1034	Open		8.80	9
1994	Christmas Cutie 1069	Open		6.50	7
1993	Christmas Girl 1054	Open		6.55	7
1993	Chubby Mushroom Girl 1057	Open		8.00	8
1986	Clip-on Angel with Wings 1004	Open		10.00	11
1995	Clip-on Golden Angel 1075	Open		9.95	10
1985	Doll Head 123209	Retrd.	1989	6.40	9
1994	Double-Sided Egg Baby 1070	Open		7.25	8
1995	Fairytale Princess 1072	Open		10.95	11
1993	Frau Schneemann 1059	Open		16.90	17
1992	Garden Girl 1040	Open		8.25	9
1985	Girl in Blue Dress 1042227	Open		7.00	7
1987	Girl in Grapes 1010	Retrd.	1989	8.45	15
1990	Girl in Polka Dot Dress 1030	Open		12.60	13
1993	Girl on Bell 1055	Open		8.75	9
1987	Girl on Snowball with Teddy 1007	Retrd.	1995	9.25	10
1988	Girl Under Tree 1014	12/95		7.80	8
1990	Girl with Black Cat 1024	Open		9.25	10
1985	Girl with Flowers 101069	Retrd.	1993	7.50	12
1992	Girl with White Kitty 1045	Open		9.25	10
1985	Gold Girl with Tree 1010306	Retrd.	1995	6.25	9
1995	Grandma 2308	Open		11.95	12
1992	Guardian Angel 1043	12/95		8.25	9
1994	Heavenly Angel 1068	Open		11.00	11
1995	Heavenly Splendor 1074 - Inge-Glas	Open		32.50	33
1994	Heidi 1071	Open		9.50	10
1994	Heidi and Peter 1064	Open		11.90	12
1990	Heralding Angel 1029	Open		7.80	8
1992	Honey Child 1042	12/95		7.45	8
1989	Irish Lassie 1021	Open		8.35	9
1995	Large Angel Head 2301	Open		9.95	10
1988	Large Blue Angel 1012	Retrd.	1994	13.40	14
1987	Large Burgundy Angel with Wings 1005	Open		13.00	13
1988	Large Doll Head 1013	Retrd.	1995	11.60	12
1985	Light Blue Angel with Wings 101052	Retrd.	1994	9.25	10
1986	Little Red Riding Hood 1001	Retrd.	1993	9.90	16
1991	Little Tyrolean Girl 1037	Open		7.00	7
1988	Little Witch 1020	Open		8.35	9
1993	Madonna & Child on Form 1056	Open		9.80	10
1992	Madonna 1038	Open		7.55	8
1988	Madonna with Child 1016	Open		12.75	13
1994	Mary 1066	Open		8.25	9
1994	Mermaid 1062	Open		38.90	39
1990	Miniature Mrs. Claus 1027	Open		4.95	5
1988	Miss Liberty 1011	Open		10.35	11
1986	Mrs. Santa Claus 1003	Retrd.	1989	8.90	19
1987	Mushroom Girl 1006	Retrd.	1994	9.25	10
1988	Nativity 1017	Open		10.50	11
1994	Nuremberg Angel 1065	Open		8.25	9
1994	Oma 1067	Open		11.45	12
1987	Pastel Angel with Horn (A) 1008	Open		7.00	7
1988	Pilgrim Girl 1019	Open		9.25	10
1986	Pink Angel with Wings 1002	Retrd.	1988	8.90	14
1991	Praying Angel with Wings 1032	Open		8.55	9
1990	Praying Girl 1025	Retrd.	1993	7.80	11
1993	Purple Angel with Star 1058	Open		8.70	9
1985	Red Girl with Tree 1010309	Retrd.	1995	8.25	9
1993	Red Riding Hood 1053	Open		7.55	8
1992	Shy Girl 1039	Open		9.90	10
1993	Small Blue Angel 1046	Open		6.65	7
1990	Small Girl Head 1022	Open		7.00	7
1985	Small Girl with Tree 101029	12/95		5.85	6
1992	Thumbelina 1041	Open		10.25	11
1993	Triplets in Bed 1051	Open		6.65	7
1988	Victorian Angel 1018	Open		8.35	9
1985	Victorian Girl 101035	Retrd.	1989	5.30	14
1994	Water Baby 1063	Open		8.25	9

Animals - E.M. Merck, unless otherwise noted

YEAR ISSUE		EDITION LIMIT	YEAR RETD.	ISSUE PRICE	QUOTE U.S.$
1990	Assorted Tropical Fish 1229	Open		6.75	7
1990	Baby Bear with Milk Bottle 1235	Open		4.95	5
1993	Bear Above Reflector 1279	Retrd.	1995	33.75	34
1986	Bear in Crib 1203	Retrd.	1994	9.00	9
1995	Bessie 1104 - Inge-Glas	Open		28.50	29
1995	Big Bad Wolf 1103 - Inge-Glas	Open		28.50	29
1984	Black Cat 121016	Open		9.00	9
1993	Brilliant Butterfly 1267	Open		10.70	11
1993	Brilliant Butterfly on Form 1271	Open		7.25	8
1995	Buddy in Basket 1296	Open		23.50	24
1993	Buster 1266	Open		8.35	9
1985	Butterfly on Form 1237447	Open		7.80	8
1989	Calico Kitten 1217	Open		9.90	10
1989	Cat and the Fiddle 1221	Retrd.	1994	7.80	8
1986	Cat in Bag 1204	Open		9.00	9
1993	Cat in House 1260	Open		7.65	8
1985	Cat in Show 121103	Retrd.	1994	7.80	8
1991	Christmas Butterfly 1247	Retrd.	1994	7.00	7
1991	Christmas Carp 1248	Open		7.00	7
1986	Cinnamon Bear 1209	Open		5.20	6
1984	Circus Dog 121021	Retrd.	1994	9.00	9
1993	Circus Dog On Ball 1278	Open		13.20	14
1993	Circus Elephant on Ball 1277	Open		12.00	12
1995	Clip-on Bunny 1297	Open		4.50	5
1994	Cow Jumping Over the Moon 1284	Open		27.75	28
1991	Crocodile 1243	Open		7.35	8
1992	Dog with Trumpet 1253	Open		9.25	10
1989	Fat Fish 1223	Open		5.85	6
1985	Frog 121068	Open		5.85	6
1992	Frog on Lily Pad 1252	Open		6.65	7
1994	Frog Prince 1288	Open		8.10	9
1993	Frog with Banjo on Ball 1274	Open		18.50	19
1991	Goldfish 1249	Open		7.00	7
1994	Grasshopper 1289	Open		10.00	10
1985	Grey Elephant 123420	Open		7.00	7
1993	Grizzly Bear 1265	Open		8.35	9
1986	Honey Bear (A) 1208	Open		5.20	6
1986	Hungry Rabbit 1201	Open		8.55	9
1988	Jumbo Elephant 1213	12/95		9.25	10
1989	King Charles Spaniel 1222	Open		9.90	10
1984	Kitten 121004	Retrd.	1995	7.00	7
1991	Kitten in Slipper 1240	Open		9.25	10
1989	Lady Bug 1215	Open		7.65	8
1994	Large Christmas Bear 1287	Open		44.40	45
1994	Large Christmas Mouse 1286	Open		44.40	45
1989	Large Fish 1214	Retrd.	1993	6.70	12
1993	Large Frog 1262	Open		7.90	8
1992	Large Lady Bug 1254	Open		9.25	10
1994	Large Lion 1285	Open		19.85	20
1991	Large Puppy with Basket 1241	Retrd.	1993	13.25	19
1995	Large Santa Bear 1102 - Inge-Glas	Open		25.00	25
1985	Large Teddy Bear 121089	Retrd.	1988	13.00	18
1993	Large Teddy Bear 1261	Open		15.65	16
1985	Large Three-Sided Head 121088	Retrd.	1994	12.95	16
1995	Large Tropical Fish 1294 - Inge-Glas	Open		32.50	33
1995	Large Turtle 1105 - Inge-Glas	Open		32.50	33
1992	Lion 1251	Open		6.45	7
1991	Lobster 1245	Open		7.35	8
1988	Lucky Pig 1212	Open		8.80	9
1990	Mama Bear 1236	Open		9.90	10
1985	Matte Gold Bear with Heart 1234356	Open		7.00	7
1993	Miniature Frog 1259	Open		3.50	4
1986	Monkey 1205	Retrd.	1994	5.85	9
1993	Monkey with Apple 1258	Open		8.80	9
1987	Mouse 1211	Open		9.90	10
1993	My Darling 1276	Open		6.30	7
1991	Panda Bear 1242	Open		9.25	10
1990	Papa Bear 1237	Open		10.35	11
1993	Pastel Butterfly 1268	12/95		8.45	9
1990	Pastel Fish 1234	Open		6.65	7
1985	Pink Pig 121042	Open		7.80	8
1990	Pink Poodle 1227	Retrd.	1994	8.80	9
1986	Playing Cat 1202	Retrd.	1994	8.80	9
1993	Polar Bear on Icicle 1275	Open		18.50	19
1995	Prize Catch 1299	Open		7.50	8
1992	Proud Pug 1250	Open		9.25	10
1984	Puppy 121010	Retrd.	1994	7.00	7
1989	Rabbit in Tree 1219	Open		8.35	9
1991	Rabbit on Heart 1244	Open		8.00	8
1985	Rainbow Trout 121070	Open		6.75	7
1990	Red Butterfly on Form 1231	Retrd.	1994	8.55	9
1992	Salmon with Tail 1255	Open		9.25	10
1995	Santa Bear 1106 - Inge-Glas	Open		6.50	7
1994	Sea Horse 1282	Open		14.50	15
1993	Sea Serpent 1273	Open		14.65	15
1994	Seal on Ball 1283	Open		24.50	25
1990	Sitting Black Cat 1228	Open		7.00	7
1986	Sitting Dog with Pipe 1206	Retrd.	1995	7.80	11
1991	Sitting Puppy 1246	Retrd.	1994	6.75	7
1985	Small Bunny 121090	Retrd.	1994	5.20	6
1989	Small Goldfish 1224	Open		2.25	3
1990	Small Squirrel 1225	Open		5.75	6
1986	Smiling Dog 1207	Retrd.	1994	7.80	8
1985	Snail 121041	Retrd.	1993	6.70	15
1994	Spark Plug 1292	Open		14.00	14
1993	Specked Trout 1272	Open		7.00	7
1993	Sugar Bear 1257	Open		8.25	9
1994	Ted 1290	Open		7.65	8
1989	Teddy Bear with Bow 1218	Retrd.	1990	6.65	16
1990	Teddy Bear with Bow 1226	Open		5.75	6
1984	Three-Sided: Owl, Dog, Cat 121009	Retrd.	1994	8.55	9
1995	Toby 1298	Open		8.50	9
1994	Tony 1293	Open		17.65	18
1990	Two Kittens in Basket 1230	Open		8.10	9
1993	Velveteen Rabbit 1256	Open		5.75	6
1993	Very Large Christmas Bear 1281	Open		72.50	73
1993	Very Large Christmas Mouse 1280	Open		72.50	73
1990	Weather Frog 1233	Open		8.80	9
1990	West Highland Terrrier 1232	Retrd.	1993	7.45	15
1989	White Kitty 1220	Retrd.	1990	7.45	8
1994	Woodland Squirrel 1291	12/95		21.00	21

Assortment Ornaments - E.M. Merck

YEAR ISSUE		EDITION LIMIT	YEAR RETD.	ISSUE PRICE	QUOTE U.S.$
1985	6 pc Display set, Santa 141039	Open		32.50	33
1992	Assorted Floral Miniatures 1406	Open		55.00	55
1990	Assorted Miniature Figurals 1405	Open		60.00	60
1990	Assorted Shiny Miniature Forms 1404	Open		37.50	38
1986	Replica of Antique Mold 1411	Open		40.00	40
1989	Set of 12 Assorted Small Forms 1403	Open		42.50	43
1989	Twelve Assorted Miniature Forms 1402	Open		37.00	37

Bead Garlands - E.M. Merck

YEAR ISSUE		EDITION LIMIT	YEAR RETD.	ISSUE PRICE	QUOTE U.S.$
1993	Angel Garland 1306	Retrd.	1993	55.00	65-100
1995	Candy & Clowns Garland 1315	Open		69.50	70
1993	Celestial Garland 1303	Retrd.	1993	55.00	60-75
1994	Christmas Train 1310	Open		45.00	45
1993	Clown & Drum Garland 1301	Retrd.	1993	55.00	60
1994	Floral Garland 1312	Open		65.00	65
1993	Frog and Fish Garland 1305	Yr.Iss.		55.00	80-110
1995	Frosty's Snowball Garland 1314	Open		69.50	70
1993	Fruit Garland 1302	Retrd.	1993	55.00	58
1994	North Pole Garland 1313	Open		65.00	65
1995	Old World Rose Garland 1316	Open		69.50	70
1993	Pickle Garland 1304	Retrd.	1993	55.00	100
1993	Santa Garland 1308	Yr.Iss.		55.00	80-110
1994	Stars and Stripes Garland 1309	Open		55.00	55
1993	Teddy Bear & Heart Garland 1307	Retrd.	1993	55.00	100
1994	Woodland Christmas Garland 1311	Open		65.00	65

Butterflies - E.M. Merck

YEAR ISSUE		EDITION LIMIT	YEAR RETD.	ISSUE PRICE	QUOTE U.S.$
1987	Butterfly, Blue with Blue 1905	Retrd.	1991	20.95	28
1987	Butterfly, Gold with Gold 1906	Retrd.	1991	20.95	28
1987	Butterfly, Orange with Orange 1904	Retrd.	1991	20.95	28
1987	Butterfly, Red with Cream 1903	Retrd.	1991	20.95	28
1987	Butterfly, White with Blue 1902	Retrd.	1991	20.95	28
1987	Butterfly, White with Red 1901	Retrd.	1991	20.95	28

Celestial Figures - E.M. Merck

YEAR ISSUE		EDITION LIMIT	YEAR RETD.	ISSUE PRICE	QUOTE U.S.$
1994	Assorted Shiny Stars 2212	Open		4.85	5

YEAR ISSUE		EDITION LIMIT	YEAR RETD.	ISSUE PRICE	QUOTE U.S.$
1987	Blue Man in the Moon 2203	Open		8.45	9
1992	Blue Moon 2206	Open		7.00	7
1993	Brilliant Star on Form 2210	Open		8.70	9
1993	Comet on Form 2209	Open		7.65	8
1992	Confetti Star 2208	Open		8.00	8
1995	Golden Sun 2214	Open		5.95	6
1993	High Noon 2211	Open		5.65	6
1985	Large Gold Star with Glitter 2237139	Retrd.	1993	7.00	7
1985	Man in the Moon 221062	Open		7.00	7
1994	Midnight Moon 2213	Open		8.25	9
1992	Old Sol 2207	Open		7.55	8
1991	Shining Star (A) 2205	Open		7.00	7
1990	Shining Sun 2204	Open		7.00	7
1986	Shooting Star on Ball 2201	Retrd.	1993	6.65	11
1985	Sun/Moon 221027	Retrd.	1993	7.00	7

Churches & Houses - E.M. Merck

YEAR ISSUE		EDITION LIMIT	YEAR RETD.	ISSUE PRICE	QUOTE U.S.$
1993	Barn 2033	Open		9.80	10
1985	Bavarian House 201059	Retrd.	1994	8.00	12
1993	Bunny House 2032	Open		8.45	9
1993	Castle Tower 2029	Open		9.45	10
1990	Christmas Chalet 2014	12/95		8.00	8
1991	Christmas Shop 2020	Open		9.45	10
1993	Church on Bell 2030	Open		11.00	11
1990	Church on Disc 2018	Open		12.50	13
1988	Church/Tree on Form 2008	Open		8.35	9
1991	Country Cottage 2025	Open		8.80	9
1990	Fairy Tale House 2016	Open		9.25	10
1991	Farm Cottage 2022	Open		8.55	9
1986	Farm House 2003	Open		8.45	9
1990	Garden House with Gnome 2011	Retrd.	1993	7.80	12
1986	Gingerbread House (A) 2001	Retrd.	1989	6.55	16
1988	Gingerbread House 2009	Open		9.00	9
1986	House with Blue Roof 2005	Open		7.65	8
1986	House with Peacock 2004	Retrd.	1987	7.45	11
1988	Large Cathedral 2007	Open		9.80	10
1995	Large Gingerbread House 2037	Open		16.95	17
1991	Large Lighthouse/Mill 2023	Open		11.00	11
1993	Large Windmill 2034	Open		13.20	14
1990	Lighthouse 2013	Open		7.90	8
1990	Matte Cream Church 2017	Open		8.00	8
1985	Matte Cream Church 206790-2	Retrd.	1993	6.45	9
1988	Matte White Church 203010	Open		7.80	8
1985	Mill 201094	Retrd.	1990	9.45	21
1992	Mill House 2026	Open		8.35	9
1990	Miniature House 2012	Open		4.95	5
1991	Mission with Sea Gull 2024	Open		9.45	10
1991	Old Town Scene 2021	Open		9.25	10
1985	Rathaus 201051	Retrd.	1989	7.00	14
1992	Rose Cottage 2028	Open		7.00	7
1988	Santa's House 2010	Open		8.00	8
1990	Small Cathedral 2015	Open		8.00	8
1985	Square House 201040	Retrd.	1995	7.80	8
1991	Thatched Cottage 2019	12/95		7.35	8
1993	Turkish Tea House 2031	Open		6.75	7
1994	Victorian Windmill 2035	Open		12.25	13
1992	Watch Tower 2027	Open		9.25	10
1986	Windmill on Form 2006	Retrd.	1988	7.45	19

Clip-On Birds - E.M. Merck

YEAR ISSUE		EDITION LIMIT	YEAR RETD.	ISSUE PRICE	QUOTE U.S.$
1991	Advent Bird 1837	Open		8.00	8
1991	Alpine Bird 1839	Open		7.35	8
1995	American Songbird 1861	Open		6.50	7
1994	Assorted Miniature Songbird 1859	Open		4.00	4
1990	Barn Owl 1829	Open		9.00	9
1995	Baronial Peacock 1872	Open		13.95	14
1991	Bavarian Finch 1835	Open		9.25	10
1986	Bird in Nest 1801	12/95		10.35	11
1985	Bird of Paradise 181101	Retrd.	1994	7.80	9
1985	Blue Bird 181078	12/95		6.65	7
1992	Blue Bird with Topnotch 1845	Open		9.45	10
1991	Brilliant Snowbird 1836	Open		12.95	13
1992	Brilliant Songbird 1841	Open		7.35	8
1991	Canary 1834	Retrd.	1994	7.35	9
1990	Cardinal 1822	Open		9.90	10
1993	Carnival Canary 1852	Open		9.45	10
1990	Christmas Bird 1824	Open		7.00	7
1992	Christmas Finch 1843	Open		7.65	8
1995	Christmas Parrot 1865	Open		9.50	10
1986	Clip-On Rooster 1802	Retrd.	1989	8.00	30
1991	Cockatiel 1838	Open		9.25	10
1985	Cockatoo 181077	Open		8.55	9
1995	Cranberry Peacock 1870	Open		13.95	14
1985	Fancy Peacock 181073	Retrd.	1993	13.50	16
1985	Fancy Pink Peacock 181096	Retrd.	1995	13.95	14
1985	Fantasy Bird with Tinsel Tail 181075	Open		8.00	8
1987	Fat Burgundy Bird 1813	12/95		7.80	8
1985	Fat Songbird 181074	Open		7.80	8
1991	Festive Bird 1832	12/95		7.00	7
1993	Festive Sparrow 1853	Open		6.00	6
1992	Forest Finch 1840	Open		8.00	8
1995	Forest Finch 1871	Open		7.50	8
1986	Gold Bird with Tinsel Tail 1803	Retrd.	1994	7.45	8
1985	Gold Peacock, Tinsel Tail 1872016	Retrd.	1995	8.25	9
1995	Golden Songbird 1864	Open		3.95	4
1995	Golden Swan 1866	Open		9.95	10
1987	Goldfinch 1808	Open		8.55	9
1995	Harvest Bird 1868	Open		7.50	8
1993	Holiday Finch 1849	Open		10.60	11
1993	King Fisher 1850	Open		10.00	10
1984	Large Cockatoo 181025	Retrd.	1994	13.95	14
1985	Large Goldfinch 181085	Retrd.	1994	9.25	10
1992	Large Nightingale 1842	Open		8.00	8
1990	Large Pastel Bird 1827	Open		10.70	11
1985	Large Peacock 187206	Open		10.35	11
1991	Large Peacock with Crown 1830	Retrd.	1994	13.95	14
1990	Large Robin 1821	Open		10.35	11
1992	Large Woodpecker 1846	Open		11.15	12
1987	Lilac Bird 1811	12/95		8.70	9
1993	Love Birds 1856	Open		10.25	11
1995	Magical Frost Bird 1863	Open		12.50	13
1994	Magnificent Peacock 1860	Open		17.75	18
1985	Magnificent Songbird 181086	Retrd.	1994	13.95	14
1985	Medium Peacock w/ Tinsel Tail 187215	12/95		9.00	9
1992	Merry Songbird 1848	Open		7.90	8
1990	Miniature Parrot 1828	12/95		8.45	9
1990	Miniature Peacock 1825	Retrd.	1994	8.35	9
1995	Miniture Love Bird 1862	Open		3.95	4
1985	Nightingale 181083	Open		5.55	6
1985	Nuthatch 181076	12/95		7.00	7
1995	Old World Songbird 1869	Open		8.50	9
1986	Parrot 1804	Open		8.35	9
1987	Partridge 1814	Retrd.	1994	8.80	9
1992	Pastel Canary 1847	Open		7.65	8
1985	Pink Bird w/ Blue Wings 181082	Retrd.	1994	5.55	6
1989	Rainbow Parrot 1820	Open		12.60	13
1987	Red Bird with Medallion 1806	Open		7.80	8
1987	Red Breasted Songbird 1812	12/95		9.25	10
1987	Red Snowbird 1810	Retrd.	1993	8.70	18
1994	Regal Peacock 1857	Open		17.75	18
1987	Robin 1819	Retrd.	1993	8.80	13
1991	Rooster 1831	Open		10.50	11
1987	Royal Songbird 1815	Open		12.75	13
1987	Shiny Gold Bird 1807	12/95		5.55	6
1985	Shiny Red Songbird 181081	Open		5.75	6
1991	Silly Bird 1833	Retrd.	1994	6.75	7
1992	Small Gull 1844	Open		4.95	5
1987	Small Purple Bird 1809	Open		7.00	7
1990	Small Red-Headed Songbird 1823	Retrd.	1995	7.00	7
1987	Snow Owl 1816	Retrd.	1994	9.90	12
1985	Snowbird 181080	Retrd.	1993	8.00	11
1985	Songbird with Topnotch 181099	Open		10.35	11
1990	Tropical Parrot 1826	Retrd.	1994	10.35	11
1993	Tropical Songbird 1854	Open		7.55	8
1995	Turtle Dove 1867	Open		5.95	6
1987	White Cockatoo 1805	Open		7.80	8
1993	Woodland Finch 1851	Open		7.55	8
1994	Woodland Peacock 1858	Open		12.00	12
1993	Woodland Songbird 1855	Open		7.55	8

Clowns & Male Figures - E.M. Merck, unless otherwise noted

YEAR ISSUE		EDITION LIMIT	YEAR RETD.	ISSUE PRICE	QUOTE U.S.$
1984	'Shorty Clown' 241011	Retrd.	1988	5.65	12
1984	'Stop' Keystone Cop 241019	Retrd.	1989	6.65	21
1986	500,000 Clown 2403	Open		10.80	11
1986	Aviator 2402	Retrd.	1994	7.80	8
1986	Baby 2405	Retrd.	1989	6.75	14
1993	Bacchus 2458	Open		6.65	7
1992	Baker 2449	Open		8.35	9
1992	Bavarian 2450	Open		9.25	10
1987	Bavarian with Hat 2428	Open		12.60	13
1990	Black Boy 2439	Retrd.	1995	9.00	9
1995	Blessings 2491	Open		10.95	11
1993	Boxer 2454	Open		7.20	8
1986	Boy Head with Stocking Cap 2411	Retrd.	1993	5.30	8
1985	Boy in Yellow Sweater 241032	Retrd.	1988	7.00	14
1985	Boy on Toy Car 241031	Open		8.45	9
1995	The Champ 2307	Open		7.50	8
1995	Charlie Chaplin 2487 - Inge-Glas	Open		25.00	25
1994	Child in Manger 2472	Open		7.75	8
1995	Child on Snowball 2304	Open		8.95	9
1993	Chimney Sweep 2455	Open		7.55	8
1992	Circus Clown 2452	Open		7.90	8
1986	Clip-on Boy Head 2416	Retrd.	1989	6.45	9
1993	Clown Above Ball 2470	Retrd.	1994	42.00	42
1986	Clown Head in Drum 2412	Open		10.25	11
1986	Clown Head w/ Burgundy Hat 2418	Retrd.	1994	7.00	7
1987	Clown in Red Stocking 2423	Open		8.00	8
1984	Clown in Stocking 241006	Retrd.	1988	6.65	12
1990	Clown on Ball 2444	Open		8.25	9
1984	Clown Playing Bass Fiddle 241005	Open		7.80	8
1986	Clown with Accordion 2409	12/95		10.35	11
1986	Clown with Banjo 2407	Retrd.	1995	7.00	7
1986	Clown with Drum 2408	Retrd.	1995	10.35	11
1986	Clown with Saxophone 2410	Open		10.35	11
1990	Devil Head 2438	Open		8.80	9
1995	Devil with Horns 2485 - Inge-Glas	Open		10.95	11
1985	Dutch Boy 243321	Retrd.	1993	7.55	14
1990	Dwarf 2441	Open		7.00	7
1989	Dwarf with Shovel 2433	Open		7.00	7
1990	English Bobby 2442	Retrd.	1994	8.80	9
1986	Farm Boy 2414	Retrd.	1989	4.95	14
1985	Fat Boy with Sweater & Cap 2442265	Retrd.	1994	5.85	6
1985	Fat Standing Clown 246852	Open		6.55	7
1989	Frosty 2434	Open		7.00	7
1992	Garden Gnome 2448	Open		10.50	11
1988	Gnome in Tree 2431	Open		7.80	8
1986	Gnome Under Mushroom 2417	Retrd.	1993	7.00	10
1988	Harpo 2432	Retrd.	1991	6.20	21
1994	Hot Shot 2473	Open		11.00	11
1993	Humpty Dumpty 2465	Open		8.55	9
1984	Indian Chief with Peace Pipe 241008	Open		7.45	8
1986	Indian in Canoe 2401	Open		10.95	11
1994	Jack Horner 2471	Open		6.50	7
1986	Jester 2419	12/95		7.45	8
1995	Jester on Spiral 2493 - Inge-Glas	Open		32.50	33
1993	Jesus 2460	Open		7.65	8
1994	Jesus on Form 2475	Open		17.65	18
1994	John Bull 2481	Open		9.35	10
1990	Jolly Accordion Player 2443	Open		8.25	9
1987	Jolly Clown Head 2429	Retrd.	1994	12.95	13
1987	Jolly Snowman 2420	Open		8.00	8
1994	Joseph 2477	Open		8.25	9
1984	Keystone Cop 241003	Retrd.	1994	9.90	10
1987	King 2421	Open		10.60	11
1994	King Ludwig 2482	Open		12.75	13
1984	Large Roly-Poly Clown 241024	Open		10.95	11
1993	Large Sad Clown 2466	Open		13.40	14
1989	Leprechaun 2435	Retrd.	1994	7.65	8
1994	Marley 2483	Open		7.75	8
1994	Merlin 2476	Open		17.65	18
1990	Merry Wanderer 2446	Open		12.30	13
1993	Miniature Clown 2464	Open		6.00	6
1993	Monk 2467	Retrd.	1994	7.90	8
1987	Mr. Big Nose 2426	Retrd.	1993	8.00	14
1995	Mr. Sci-Fi 2492 - Inge-Glas	Open		29.50	30
1988	Mushroom Gnome 2430	Retrd.	1989	6.20	10
1994	My Buddy 2474	Open		7.75	8
1995	Pilot with Legs 2484 - Inge-Glas	Open		22.50	23
1993	Pinocchio 2459	Open		9.90	10
1992	Pirate 2451	Open		7.45	8
1986	Pixie with Accordion 2406	Retrd.	1989	4.95	11
1987	Punch 2424	Open		8.70	9
1995	Punch with Legs 2489 - Inge-Glas	Open		22.95	23
1994	Razzle-Dazzle 2479	Open		17.65	18
1994	Roly-Poly 2478	Open		24.00	24
1984	Roly-Poly Keystone Cop 241015	Retrd.	1988	9.90	21
1995	Rosen Cavalier 2490 - Inge-Glas	Open		28.95	29
1993	Sailor 2457	Open		7.55	8
1995	Sailor Boy 2488 - Inge-Glas	Open		7.95	8
1986	Sailor Head 2404	Retrd.	1990	7.45	25
1993	Santa's Helper 2456	Open		6.00	6
1986	School Boy 2415	Retrd.	1989	4.95	10
1984	Scotsman 241017	Retrd.	1988	6.20	18
1990	Scout 2440	Open		9.25	10
1987	Scrooge 2427	Retrd.	1995	8.55	9
1994	Show Time 2480	Open		18.90	19
1989	Small Clown Head 2436	Retrd.	1993	6.65	7
1985	Small Fat Boy 241028	Open		5.55	6
1993	Small Jester 2463	Open		7.35	8
1993	Small Snowman 2462	Open		6.00	6
1992	Snowman in Chimney 2447	Open		10.50	11
1993	Snowman on Icicle 2469	Open		15.45	16
1990	Snowman on Reflector 2445	Retrd.	1993	10.35	14
1989	Snowman with Broom 2437	Open		6.45	7
1993	Turquoise Clown 2461	Open		6.45	7
1986	Uncle Sam 2413	Open		10.80	11
1985	Waiter in Tuxedo 241047	Retrd.	1989	7.00	19
1993	Winking Leprechaun 2453	Open		6.55	7

Collector's Editions - E.M. Merck, unless otherwise noted

YEAR ISSUE		EDITION LIMIT	YEAR RETD.	ISSUE PRICE	QUOTE U.S.$
1995	Admiral Perry 1581 - Inge-Glas	Open		25.00	25
1992	Angel on Balloon 1527	Open		22.50	23
1992	Angel on Swan with Tinsel Wire 1526	Open		21.50	22
1992	Angel with Tinsel Wire 1522	Retrd.	1993	55.00	75
1993	Angel with Wings 1556	Retrd.	1993	12.50	50
1995	Antique Style Airplane 1549 - Inge-Glas	Open		27.50	28
1995	Antique Style Zeppelin 1546	Open		19.95	20
1994	Assorted Pumpkin People 1580	Open		19.75	20
1992	Brilliant Peacock with Wings 1552	Open		23.00	23
1992	Cherub Above Ball 1528	Open		23.65	24
1995	Christmas Eve 1596	Open		12.50	13
1993	Christmas Heart 1593	Retrd.	1993	10.00	16
1995	Christmas Time 1543 - Inge-Glas	Open		39.50	40
1995	Christmas Tree above Star Reflector 1513	2,400		53.00	53
1992	Dresden Santa with Tinsel Wire 1525	Open		21.50	22
1992	Father Christmas on Balloon 1529	Open		22.50	23
1992	Flying Peacock with Wings 1550	12/95		22.50	23
1992	Flying Songbird with Wings 1551	12/95		21.75	22
1993	Guardian Angel with Wire 1562	Open		20.00	20
1993	Hansel and Gretal 1511	2,400		45.00	50
1993	Heavenly Angel 1563	Open		20.00	20
1995	Ho-Ho-Ho 1597 - Inge-Glas	Open		32.50	33
1995	Lg. Christmas Carousel 1585	Open		79.50	80
1990	Night Before Christmas Ball 1501	500	1993	72.50	85-100
1992	Nightingale with Wings 1553	Open		21.00	21
1992	Nutcracker Ornament 1510	Retrd.	1993	33.75	85-150
1995	Parachuting Santa 1547	Open		59.50	60

CHRISTMAS ORNAMENTS

YEAR ISSUE		EDITION LIMIT	YEAR RETD.	ISSUE PRICE	QUOTE U.S.$
1995	Sailing Santa 1598 - Inge-Glas	Open		39.50	40
1993	Santa with Hot Air Balloon 1570	Open		38.85	39
1992	Santa with Tinsel Wire 1521	Retrd.	1993	55.00	65
1992	Santa's Departure 1503	500	1994	72.50	73
1991	Santa's Visit 1502	500	1994	72.50	80
1993	Scrap Victorian Angel on Balloon 1566	Open		50.00	50
1993	Scrap Victorian Santa on Balloon 1565	Open		50.00	50
1992	Snowman with Tinsel Wire 1523	Retrd.	1993	32.50	40
1995	Special Event Santa 1560	5,000		15.00	15
1992	Very Large Ball with Icicle Drop 1532	Open		59.50	60
1992	Very Large Ball with Reflectors 1531	Open		59.50	60
1992	Very Large Drop with Reflectors 1533	Open		59.50	60
1987	Very Large Icicle 1534	Open		59.50	60
1992	Very Large Mushroom with Flower 1530	Open		59.50	60
1995	Very large Wizard w/ Owl 1586	Open		95.00	95
1995	Victorian Child in Manger 1544 - Inge-Glas	Open		27.50	28
1995	Victorian Parosol 1548	Open		25.00	25
1993	Victorian Santa on Heart 1564	Open		12.95	13

Easter - E.M. Merck

YEAR ISSUE		EDITION LIMIT	YEAR RETD.	ISSUE PRICE	QUOTE U.S.$
1988	Gentleman Chick 9311	Retrd.	1993	22.50	23
1988	Gentleman Rabbit 9301	Retrd.	1993	25.00	25
1988	Lady Chick 9312	Retrd.	1993	22.50	23

Easter Light Covers - E.M. Merck

YEAR ISSUE		EDITION LIMIT	YEAR RETD.	ISSUE PRICE	QUOTE U.S.$
1988	Assorted Easter Egg 9331-1	Retrd.	1993	3.95	7
1988	Assorted Pastel Egg 9335-1	Retrd.	1994	2.95	3
1988	Bunny 9333-4	Retrd.	1994	4.20	5
1988	Bunny in Basket 9333-6	Retrd.	1994	4.20	5
1988	Chick 9333-3	Retrd.	1994	4.20	5
1988	Chick in Egg 9333-5	Retrd.	1994	4.20	5
1988	Hen in Basket 9333-1	Retrd.	1994	4.20	5
1988	Rabbit in Egg 9333-2	Retrd.	1994	4.20	5

Fruits & Vegetables - E.M. Merck, unless otherwise noted

YEAR ISSUE		EDITION LIMIT	YEAR RETD.	ISSUE PRICE	QUOTE U.S.$
1994	Apple Slice 2884	Open		9.45	10
1993	Apple Tree 2874	Open		8.90	9
1995	Apple Tree 2888	Open		9.95	10
1990	Apples on Form 2837	Open		9.00	9
1990	Apricot 2831	Open		6.55	7
1993	Asparagus 2876	Open		10.60	11
1984	Banana 281020	Open		8.00	8
1989	Berry 2822	Open		2.70	3
1992	Candied Apple 2860	Open		8.70	9
1986	Carrot with Leaf 2802	Open		7.35	8
1990	Cherries on Form 2825	Retrd.	1993	9.00	10
1993	Chestnut 2869	Open		6.00	6
1989	Cucumber 2820	Retrd.	1989	6.65	12
1991	Double Mushroom 2850	Open		6.65	7
1990	Fancy Strawberry 2845	Open		5.55	6
1994	French Carrot 2886	Open		4.45	5
1990	Fruit Basket 2838	Open		7.80	8
1992	Fruit Basket on Form 2859	Open		9.25	10
1995	Fruit Centerpiece 2893	Open		8.50	9
1990	Fruits on Form 2842	Open		10.35	11
1993	Garlic 2878	Open		7.00	7
1990	Gold Grapes 2840	Open		6.75	7
1988	Gold Walnut 2817	Open		2.00	2
1985	Grapes on Form 281038	Retrd.	1987	7.00	10
1994	Grapes with Butterfly 2887	Open		9.50	10
1986	Grapes with Green Glitter 2807	Open		4.75	5
1987	Green Pepper 2812	Open		8.00	8
1989	Gurken 2823	Open		2.70	3
1991	Harvest Grapes 2854	Open		9.25	10
1995	Indian Corn 2892	Open		10.95	11
1986	Large Acorn 2803	Open		6.65	7
1985	Large Basket of Grapes 281053	12/95		10.35	11
1993	Large Candied Apple 2882	Open		12.95	13
1995	Large Concord Grapes 2889	Open		10.95	11
1993	Large Cornucopia 2877	Open		25.00	25
1995	Large Frosted Grapes 2895 - Inge-Glas	Open		27.50	28
1989	Large Frosted Strawberry 2821	Open		6.00	6
1991	Large Fruit Basket 2849	Open		12.50	13
1990	Large Golden Apple 2829	Open		8.55	9
1984	Large Matte Corn 281033	Open		9.25	10
1985	Large Pear with Leaf 281072	Open		7.35	8
1991	Large Purple Grapes with Leaves 2852	Open		6.75	7
1991	Large Raspberry 2855	Open		7.90	8
1990	Large Red Apple 2828	Open		8.55	9
1985	Large Strawberry 2841432	Retrd.	1993	4.20	7
1990	Large Strawberry w/ Flower 2841	Retrd.	1993	10.50	16
1985	Large Strawberry w/ Glitter 287282	Open		6.45	7
1993	Large Sugar Pear 2881	Open		12.95	13
1992	Large Tomato 2858	Open		7.45	8
1986	Large Walnut 2804	Open		3.60	4
1990	Lime 2839	Open		3.50	4
1988	Miniature Grapes 2816	Open		3.00	3
1993	Miniature Mushrooms 2880	Open		4.00	4
1985	Mr. Apple 281071	Retrd.	1988	6.20	17
1984	Mr. Pear 281023	Retrd.	1993	6.75	7
1993	Mushroom Face 2873	Open		5.85	6
1994	New Potato 2883	Open		5.80	6
1987	Onion 2810	Retrd.	1989	8.25	60
1992	Orange 2857	Open		7.00	7
1994	Orange Slice 2885	Open		9.45	10
1993	Pea Pod 2875	Open		9.60	10
1990	Peach 2846	Open		7.65	8
1993	Pear Face 2871	Open		8.35	9
1986	Pear with Face 2805	Retrd.	1995	7.00	7
1986	Pear with Leaf 2809	Open		5.55	6
1984	Pickle 281018	Open		7.00	7
1987	Plum With Leaf 2813	Open		7.35	8
1987	Potato 2811	Open		8.45	9
1986	Pumpkin Head 2801	Open		7.35	8
1985	Purple Grapes 283765	Open		5.75	6
1990	Raspberry 2835	Retrd.	1993	6.20	7
1990	Red Onion 2896	Open		8.95	9
1991	Red Pepper 2853	Open		9.45	10
1989	Shiny Corn 2818	Open		5.50	6
1992	Shiny Red Apple 2856	Open		6.55	7
1987	Small Apple With Leaf 2814	Open		5.75	6
1989	Small Matte Corn 2819	Open		4.50	5
1986	Small Pear with Leaf 2808	Open		4.75	5
1995	Small Plum 2891	Open		4.50	5
1985	Small Purple Grapes 2841047	Open		4.00	4
1995	Small Rasberry 2890	Open		3.75	4
1988	Small Tomato 2815	Open		4.00	4
1991	Strawberries/Flower/ Form 2851	Retrd.	1994	8.55	9
1986	Strawberry 2806	Open		4.75	5
1990	Strawberry Cluster 2836	12/95		5.20	6
1992	Sugar Grapes 2865	Open		7.45	8
1993	Sugar Harvest Grapes 2866	Open		9.70	10
1992	Sugar Lemon 2862	Open		7.45	8
1992	Sugar Pear 2863	Open		7.00	7
1992	Sugar Plum 2861	Open		7.55	8
1993	Sugar Raspberry 2867	Open		8.55	9
1992	Sugar Strawberry 2864	Open		7.65	8
1990	Sweet Pickle 2833	Open		4.50	5
1993	Translucent Grapes with 18KT Gold 2879	Open		7.25	8
1991	Very Large Apple 2848	Retrd.	1993	10.60	12
1991	Very Large Pear 2847	Retrd.	1993	10.60	12
1985	Very Large Strawberry 281050	Open		9.25	10
1990	Watermelon Slice 2844	Open		11.00	11
1990	White Grapes 2834	Open		6.75	7

Halloween Light Covers - E.M. Merck

YEAR ISSUE		EDITION LIMIT	YEAR RETD.	ISSUE PRICE	QUOTE U.S.$
1989	Dancing Scarecrow 9241-3	Retrd.	1994	7.65	8
1987	Devil 9223-5	Retrd.	1993	3.95	6
1987	Ghost w/Pumpkin 9221-2	Retrd.	1994	3.95	6
1987	Haunted House 9223-1	Retrd.	1994	3.95	6
1987	Jack O'Lantern 9221-1	Retrd.	1993	3.95	6
1989	Man in the Moon 9241-5	Retrd.	1993	7.65	17
1989	Pumpkin Face 9241-6	Retrd.	1994	7.65	8
1987	Pumpkin w/Top Hat 9223-6	Retrd.	1994	3.95	6
1987	Sad Pumpkin 9221-5	Retrd.	1993	3.95	6
1987	Scarecrow 9221-3	Retrd.	1993	3.95	6
1987	Six Halloween Light Covers 9221	Retrd.	1994	25.00	32
1987	Six Halloween Light Covers 9223	Retrd.	1993	25.90	32
1987	Skull 9221-6	Retrd.	1994	3.95	6
1987	Smiling Cat 9223-2	Retrd.	1993	3.95	6
1987	Smiling Ghost 9223-4	Retrd.	1994	3.95	6
1989	Spider 9241-1	Retrd.	1994	7.65	8
1987	Standing Witch 9223-3	Retrd.	1994	3.95	6
1987	Witch Head 9221-4	Retrd.	1993	3.95	6
1989	Witch Head 9241-2	Retrd.	1994	7.65	8
1989	Wizard 9241-4	Retrd.	1993	7.65	19

Hanging Birds - E.M. Merck

YEAR ISSUE		EDITION LIMIT	YEAR RETD.	ISSUE PRICE	QUOTE U.S.$
1988	Bird House 1611	Open		10.35	11
1994	Bird in Nest 1634	Open		19.90	20
1992	Birdie 1620	Open		8.80	9
1985	Blue Bird with Wings 161100	Retrd.	1991	7.65	8
1992	Brilliant Hanging Snowbird 1625	Open		9.80	10
1993	Cardinal on Form 1627	Open		7.55	8
1985	Cardinal with Wings 161098	Retrd.	1994	10.95	11
1984	Chick in Egg 161013	Open		8.25	9
1991	Chick on Form 1619	Retrd.	1993	8.00	9
1984	Cock Robin 161012	Retrd.	1995	7.00	7
1990	Duck 1613	12/95		6.20	7
1992	Exotic Bird 1623	Open		10.35	11
1985	Fancy Peacock 161066	Open		9.25	10
1987	Fat Rooster 1610	Retrd.	1995	10.35	11
1992	Gentleman Chick 1621	Open		7.65	8
1995	Golden Pheasant 1635	Open		11.95	12
1993	Hanging Parrot 1631	Open		9.60	10
1993	Hanging Pastel Bird 1630	Open		10.50	11
1992	Large German Songbird 1624	Open		11.25	12
1986	Large Owl with Stein 1604	Retrd.	1989	10.00	32
1991	Large Parrot on Ball 1617	Retrd.	1995	11.00	11
1992	Messenger Bird 1626	Open		6.75	7
1986	Owl on Form 1601	Open		11.00	11
1986	Parrot in Cage 1606	Open		7.45	8
1993	Parrot on Reflector 1632	Open		12.25	13
1993	Rooster at Hen House 1629	12/95		10.25	11
1986	Rooster on Form 1603	Retrd.	1989	6.65	9
1994	Royal Swan 1633	Open		27.75	28
1986	Small Owl 1607	Open		5.75	6
1992	Snowy Owl 1622	Open		6.00	6
1990	Songbird on Form 1614	Retrd.	1994	8.80	9
1991	Songbird on Heart (A) 1618	Retrd.	1993	8.25	11
1986	Songbirds on Ball 1602	Retrd.	1994	9.25	10
1986	Standing Owl 1608	Open		8.90	9
1993	Stork with Baby 1628	Open		9.60	10
1986	Swan on Form 1605	Open		8.35	9
1988	Swans on Lake 1612	12/95		7.80	8
1985	Turkey 161058	Retrd.	1989	8.00	11
1990	Turkey 1615	Open		9.00	9
1990	Wise Owl 1616	Open		8.35	9

Hearts - E.M. Merck

YEAR ISSUE		EDITION LIMIT	YEAR RETD.	ISSUE PRICE	QUOTE U.S.$
1987	Burgundy Heart with Glitter 3004	12/95		6.75	7
1989	Double Heart 3008	Open		3.00	3
1993	Frost Red Translucent Heart 3012	Open		6.45	7
1992	Heart with Flowers 3010	Retrd.	1993	9.50	12
1987	Heart with Ribbon 3003	Open		8.45	9
1995	Holly Heart 3014	Open		9.50	10
1985	Large Matte Red Heart 306925	Retrd.	1995	5.30	6
1988	Large Red Glitter Heart 3006	Open		8.45	9
1993	Merry Christmas Heart 3013	Open		7.20	8
1985	Pink Heart with Glitter 306767	Open		6.75	7
1992	Scrap Angel on Heart (A) 3011	Open		8.35	9
1986	Small Gold Heart with Star 3001	Retrd.	1993	2.85	6
1986	Small Red Heart with Star 3002	Open		2.95	3
1989	Smooth Heart 3009	Open		2.25	3
1989	Strawberry Heart 3007	Open		3.00	3
1988	Valentine 3005	12/95		5.75	6

Household Items - E.M. Merck

YEAR ISSUE		EDITION LIMIT	YEAR RETD.	ISSUE PRICE	QUOTE U.S.$
1988	Baby's Shoe 3205	Open		7.35	8
1993	Beer Stein 3214	Open		10.95	11
1986	Black Stocking 3203	Retrd.	1993	9.45	32
1995	Cheers 3222	Open		6.95	7
1993	Christmas Shoe 3212	Open		8.25	9
1985	Clip-On Candle 321063	Open		12.95	13
1986	Cuckoo Clock 3202	Open		9.25	10
1993	Elegant Chocolate Pot 3216	Open		12.85	13
1985	Fancy Coffee Pot 321092	Open		13.95	14
1993	Fancy Purse 3215	Open		6.00	6
1993	Fancy Teapot 3213	Open		8.75	9
1992	Flapper Purse 3211	Open		9.25	10
1985	Lady's Fan 321093	Open		6.65	7
1985	Large Purse 321095	Open		7.00	7
1991	Money Bag 3206	Retrd.	1994	7.00	7
1985	Pastel Umbrella (A) 321091	Retrd.	1993	11.00	13
1991	Pipe (A) 3207	Open		9.00	9
1985	Pocket Watch 326729	Open		5.85	6
1986	Red Stocking 3201	Retrd.	1987	9.00	18
1995	Ruby Slipper 3223	Open		6.95	7
1991	Small Cuckoo Clock 3209	Open		7.00	7
1991	Small Wine Barrel 3210	Retrd.	1993	6.30	7
1985	Very Large Pink Umbrella 321103	Retrd.	1986	29.50	46
1985	Wall Clock 321060	Retrd.	1995	11.00	11
1988	Wine Barrel 3204	Retrd.	1990	7.00	12

Icicles - E.M. Merck

YEAR ISSUE		EDITION LIMIT	YEAR RETD.	ISSUE PRICE	QUOTE U.S.$
1988	Long Champagne Icicle 3401	Retrd.	1988	7.25	12
1985	Long Silver Icicle 3450380	Open		7.00	7

Light Covers - E.M. Merck

YEAR ISSUE		EDITION LIMIT	YEAR RETD.	ISSUE PRICE	QUOTE U.S.$
1984	3 Men in a Tub 529007-1	Retrd.	1986	1.60	8
1986	Angel on Bell 529023-5	Retrd.	1991	3.95	8
1995	Angel with Star 5288	Open		3.95	4
1985	Apple 529011-5	Retrd.	1989	3.00	8
1986	Assorted Alphabet Blocks 529043-1	Retrd.	1991	4.50	8
1984	Assorted Animals, set/ 6 529003	Retrd.	1987	10.35	48
1986	Assorted Bells, set of 6 529023	Retrd.	1993	22.50	48
1988	Assorted Birds 529057-1	Retrd.	1990	3.95	8
1986	Assorted Easter Eggs 529031-1	Retrd.	1993	3.00	8
1988	Assorted Fast Food 529055-1	Retrd.	1991	3.95	8
1984	Assorted Figurals, set/ 6 529005	Retrd.	1987	10.35	48
1989	Assorted Fir Cone 529209-1	Retrd.	1991	2.85	7
1993	Assorted Frosty Bell 5275	Retrd.	1993	5.65	7
1985	Assorted Fruit, set of 6 529011	Retrd.	1989	20.00	48
1985	Assorted Heads, set of 6 529009	Retrd.	1988	10.35	48
1986	Assorted Peach Roses 529045-4	Retrd.	1990	3.95	7
1986	Assorted Pink Roses 529045-3	Open		3.95	7
1986	Assorted Red Roses 529045-1	Open		3.95	7
1986	Assorted Roses, set of 6 529045	Retrd.	1991	22.50	48
1985	Assorted Santas, set of 6 529015	Retrd.	1992	20.00	48
1989	Assorted Sea Shells 529301-4	Retrd.	1992	3.50	9
1991	Assorted Snowmen 529305-1	Retrd.	1993	5.55	8
1995	Assorted Snowmen 5301	Open		5.00	5
1995	Assorted Snowmen 5301	Open		3.95	4
1991	Assorted Spun Glass Globe 529213-1	Open		3.50	7
1995	Assorted Tropical Fish 5280	Open		3.95	4
1986	Assorted Yellow Roses 529045-2	Retrd.	1990	3.95	8
1985	Automobile 529019-3	Retrd.	1988	2.70	9
1985	Balloon 529019-2	Retrd.	1988	2.70	9
1984	Bear 519003-3	Retrd.	1987	2.50	9
1986	Blue Father Christmas 529047-3	Retrd.	1992	3.95	10
1986	Bunny 529033-4	Retrd.	1993	3.60	8
1995	Bunny 5293	Open		3.95	4
1986	Bunny in Basket 529033-6	Retrd.	1993	3.60	7
1995	Butterfly on Form 5284	Open		3.95	4
1985	Cable Car 529019-5	Retrd.	1988	2.70	9
1984	Carousel 529005-3	Retrd.	1987	2.70	9
1986	Chick 529033-3	Retrd.	1993	3.60	7
1986	Chick in Egg 529033-5	Retrd.	1993	3.60	8
1988	Christmas Carol 529053	Retrd.	1991	25.00	48
1988	Christmas Tree 529051-4	Retrd.	1992	3.95	7
1984	Church on Ball 529005-6	Retrd.	1987	2.50	10
1995	Circus Clown 5286	Open		3.95	4
1985	Clara-The Doll 529017-1	Retrd.	1989	2.70	8
1985	Clear Icicle 529205-1	Open		3.50	7

CHRISTMAS ORNAMENTS

YEAR ISSUE		EDITION LIMIT	YEAR RETD.	ISSUE PRICE	QUOTE U.S.$
1995	Clear Icicle 5298	Open		3.95	4
1985	Clear Icicles, set of 6 529205	Retrd.	1989	20.00	48
1984	Clown 529001-5	Retrd.	1986	1.60	11
1988	Clown 529051-6	Retrd.	1991	3.95	8
1985	Clown Head 529009-1	Retrd.	1988	1.60	9
1995	Clown on Ball 5297	Open		3.95	4
1995	Cone with Face 5291	Open		3.95	4
1988	Cornucopia 529049-1	Retrd.	1992	3.95	8
1988	Doll 529051-2	Retrd.	1993	3.95	8
1993	Doll Head 5202	Retrd.	1993	5.65	9
1985	Doll Head 529009-4	Retrd.	1988	1.60	7
1988	Drum 529051-1	Retrd.	1992	3.95	7
1988	Ear of Corn 529049-6	Retrd.	1992	3.95	10
1984	Elephant 529003-4	Retrd.	1987	1.60	8
1985	Father Christmas 529009-5	Retrd.	1990	3.00	48
1986	Father Christmas Set 529047	Retrd.	1992	25.00	39
1984	Flower Basket 529005-1	Retrd.	1987	1.60	12
1989	Frog 529303-6	Retrd.	1993	6.45	8
1995	Frog 5296	Open		3.95	4
1993	Frosty Acorn 5276	Retrd.	1994	5.65	8
1993	Frosty Cone 5271	Retrd.	1994	5.65	8
1993	Frosty Icicle 5272	Retrd.	1993	5.65	8
1993	Frosty Red Rose 5277	Retrd.	1993	5.65	8
1993	Frosty Snowman 5270	Retrd.	1993	5.65	8
1993	Frosty Tree 5273	Retrd.	1993	5.65	9
1984	Gnome 529001-1	Retrd.	1986	1.60	7
1985	Grapes 529011-3	Retrd.	1989	3.00	7
1995	Grapes with Leaves 5282	Open		3.95	4
1986	Green Father Christmas 529047-2	Retrd.	1992	3.95	8
1984	Hedgehog 529003-5	Retrd.	1987	1.60	10
1986	Hen in Basket 529033-1	Retrd.	1993	3.60	7
1995	Horse Head 5290	Open		3.95	4
1984	House 529005-2	Retrd.	1987	1.60	10
1995	Humpty Dumpty 5281	Open		3.95	4
1988	Indian 529049-5	Retrd.	1992	3.95	8
1985	King 529013-3	Retrd.	1988	2.70	9
1989	Kitten 529303-3	Retrd.	1993	6.45	8
1984	Lil' Boy Blue 529007-5	Retrd.	1986	1.60	10
1985	Lil' Rascal Head 529009-6	Retrd.	1988	1.60	10
1985	Locomotive 529019-4	Retrd.	1988	2.70	9
1985	Marie-The Girl 529017-3	Retrd.	1989	2.70	9
1985	Mouse King 529017-5	Retrd.	1989	2.70	9
1984	Mrs. Claus 529001-4	Retrd.	1986	1.60	10
1985	Nutcracker 529017-4	Retrd.	1989	2.70	9
1995	Nutcracker King 5294	Open		3.95	4
1986	Nutcracker on Bell 529023-6	Retrd.	1993	3.95	7
1985	Nutcracker Suite Figures, set of 6 529017	Retrd.	1989	19.00	48
1985	Orange 529011-6	Retrd.	1989	3.00	6
1984	Owl 529003-2	Retrd.	1987	1.60	9
1989	Panda 529303-1	Retrd.	1994	6.45	7
1985	Pastel Icicles 529207	Retrd.	1989	N/A	N/A
1984	Peacock 519003-6	Retrd.	1987	2.70	9
1993	Peacock 5203	Retrd.	1993	5.65	8
1985	Pear 529011-1	Retrd.	1989	3.00	9
1988	Pilgrim Boy 529049-3	Retrd.	1992	3.95	8
1988	Pilgrim Girl 529049-4	Retrd.	1992	3.95	8
1985	Pineapple 529011-4	Retrd.	1989	3.00	8
1985	Pink Heart 529201-3	Retrd.	1989	2.85	8
1989	Puppy 529303-4	Retrd.	1994	6.45	8
1986	Purple Father Christmas 529047-6	Retrd.	1992	3.95	9
1984	Queen of Heart 529007-3	Retrd.	1986	2.70	10
1986	Rabbit in Egg 529033-2	Retrd.	1993	3.60	7
1986	Red Father Christmas 529047-1	Retrd.	1992	3.95	9
1986	Red Father Christmas 529047-4	Retrd.	1992	3.95	9
1985	Red Heart 529201-1	Retrd.	1990	2.85	9
1985	Red Riding Hood 529009-2	Retrd.	1988	1.60	9
1986	Rocking Horse on Bell 529023-4	Retrd.	1990	3.95	7
1985	Roly-Poly Santa 529015-6	Retrd.	1989	3.00	9
1995	Round Santa Head 5295	Open		3.95	4
1984	Santa Head 529005-4	Retrd.	1987	2.70	10
1985	Santa Head 529009-3	Retrd.	1988	3.00	9
1995	Santa in Chimney 5292	Open		3.95	4
1986	Santa on Bell 529023-3	Retrd.	1990	3.95	9
1984	Santa on Heart 529005-5	Retrd.	1987	3.00	9
1985	Santa with Tree 529015-3	Retrd.	1992	3.00	9
1985	School Bus 529019-6	Retrd.	1991	2.70	9
1985	Six Red & White Hearts 529201	Retrd.	1989	15.00	15
1992	Six Snowmen 529305	Retrd.	1993	29.00	48
1984	Snowman 519001-2	Retrd.	1986	2.50	8
1995	Snowman 5289	Open		3.95	4
1995	Snowy House 5287	Open		3.95	4
1985	Soldier with Drum 529013-1	Retrd.	1988	2.70	9
1985	Soldier with Gun 529013-2	Retrd.	1988	2.70	9
1985	Soldiers, set of 6 529013	Retrd.	1988	17.95	48
1989	Squirrel 529303-2	Retrd.	1994	6.45	7
1984	Standing Santa 529001-3	Retrd.	1987	3.00	9
1988	Stocking 529051-3	Retrd.	1992	3.95	7
1985	Strawberry 529011-2	Retrd.	1989	3.00	7
1993	Sugar Fruit Basket 5256	Retrd.	1994	5.65	6
1993	Sugar Plum 5253	Retrd.	1993	5.65	6
1985	Sugar Plum Fairy 529017-6	Retrd.	1989	2.70	9
1993	Sugar Strawberry 5251	Retrd.	1993	5.65	6
1989	Swan 529303-5	Retrd.	1994	6.45	8
1986	Teddy Bear 529023-2	Retrd.	1990	3.95	9
1988	Teddy Bear 529051-5	Retrd.	1992	3.95	7
1995	Teddy Bear w/Vest 5283	Open		3.95	4
1986	Teddy Bear with Ball 529041-5	Retrd.	1994	3.95	4
1986	Teddy Bear with Candy Cane 529041-1	Retrd.	1992	3.95	7
1986	Teddy Bear with Nightshirt 529041-4	Retrd.	1994	3.95	4
1986	Teddy Bear with Red Heart 529041-2	Retrd.	1992	3.95	7
1986	Teddy Bear with Tree 529041-3	Retrd.	1992	3.95	7
1986	Teddy Bear with Vest 529041-6	Open	1992	3.95	4
1986	Teddy Bears, set of 6 529041	Retrd.	1991	25.00	48
1988	Thanksgiving, set of 6 529049	Retrd.	1992	25.00	48
1988	Toy, set of 6 529051	Retrd.	1992	25.00	48
1985	Transportation Set 529019	Retrd.	1988	17.90	48
1986	Tree on Bell 529023-1	Retrd.	1991	3.95	7
1985	Tug Boat 529019-1	Retrd.	1988	2.70	9
1988	Turkey 529049-2	Retrd.	1992	3.95	7
1986	White Father Christmas 529047-5	Retrd.	1992	3.95	9
1985	White Heart 529201-2	Retrd.	1989	2.85	7
1995	Wise Owl 5285	Open		3.95	4

Miscellaneous Forms - E.M. Merck, unless otherwise noted

YEAR ISSUE		EDITION LIMIT	YEAR RETD.	ISSUE PRICE	QUOTE U.S.$
1995	Assorted Apricot Tulips 3676	Open		6.95	7
1990	Assorted Christmas Flowers 3626	Retrd.	1994	8.00	8
1990	Assorted Christmas Stars 3620	12/95		7.00	7
1993	Assorted Fantasy Form with Wire 3650	Retrd.	1994	20.00	20
1992	Assorted Northern Stars 3640	Retrd.	1995	6.20	7
1990	Assorted Pastel Fantasy Forms 3627	Open		6.25	7
1995	Assorted Red Tulips 3673	Open		6.95	7
1992	Assorted Spirals 3636	Retrd.	1995	8.25	9
1992	Basket of Roses 3638	Open		11.00	11
1992	Christmas Ball with Roses 3634	Open		9.45	10
1995	Christmas Cactus 3679	Open		32.50	33
1989	Christmas Lantern 3611	Open		7.80	8
1992	Christmas Shamrock 3632	Open		9.25	10
1990	Clip-On Pink Rose 3628	Open		9.25	10
1988	Clip-On Tulip (A) 3605	Retrd.	1995	8.70	9
1993	Crown 3642	Open		8.90	9
1989	Edelweiss 3614	Open		3.00	3
1990	Edelweiss on Form 3618	Retrd.	1995	8.25	9
1992	Fantasy Christmas Form 3635	Open		9.00	9
1995	Firecracker 3663	Open		6.95	7
1995	Flag on Ball 3661	Open		8.50	9
1986	Flower Basket 3601	Open		10.25	11
1989	Flower Bouquet in Basket 3610	Open		9.45	10
1989	Flower with Butterfly 3609	Retrd.	1993	9.75	12
1992	Garden Flowers 3639	Open		9.00	9
1995	Golden Conical Shell 3675	Open		6.95	7
1995	Golden Sea Shell 3674	Open		6.95	7
1995	Harvest Basket 3670	Open		11.50	12
1985	Ice Cream Cone 3637164	Retrd.	1988	14.50	21
1988	Ice Cream Cone with Glitter 3604	Open		13.40	14
1990	Large Conical Shell 3629	Retrd.	1993	8.70	10
1993	Large Conical Shell 3646	Open		7.35	8
1995	Large Peace Rose 3677	Open		9.95	10
1992	Large Ribbed Ball with Roses 3633	Open		7.00	7
1990	Large Sea Shell 3625	Open		8.35	9
1990	Large Snowflake 3622	12/95		13.00	13
1995	Lucky Penny 3664 - Inge-Glas	Open		11.95	12
1993	Lucky Shamrock 3643	Retrd.	1993	7.80	19
1993	Merry Christmas Ball 3645	Open		7.45	8
1989	Morning Glories 3608	Retrd.	1995	8.90	9
1989	Mr. Sunflower 3612	Open		7.80	8
1995	Olympic Torch 3678	Open		32.50	33
1992	Pansy 3637	Open		7.35	8
1995	Patriotic Ball 3666	Open		11.50	12
1995	Patriotic Star 3665	Open		6.95	7
1985	Pink Rose with Glitter 366828	Open		4.95	5
1990	Pink Sea Shell 3623	Open		7.00	7
1990	Poinsettia Blossom 3630	Open		11.60	12
1992	Poinsettia on Form 3631	Open		7.35	8
1990	Poinsettias 3619	Open		9.90	10
1989	Red Rose on Form 3607	Retrd.	1995	5.85	6
1989	Ribbed Ball with Roses 3615	Open		3.00	3
1989	Rose 3616	Open		2.40	3
1990	Shamrock on Form 3621	Open		5.55	6
1989	Shiny Red Clip-On Tulip 3617	Retrd.	1990	7.45	8
1988	Skull 3606	Open		7.35	8
1992	Snowflake on Form 3641	Open		6.75	7
1987	Stars on Form (A) 3602	Open		12.95	13
1995	Street Lamp 3672	Open		11.95	12
1990	Sunburst 3624	Retrd.	1993	8.00	8
1994	Victorian Floral Drop 3659	12/95		22.00	22
1989	Victorian Keepsake 3613	Open		9.25	10

Musical Instruments - E.M. Merck

YEAR ISSUE		EDITION LIMIT	YEAR RETD.	ISSUE PRICE	QUOTE U.S.$
1990	Accordion 3814	Open		8.35	9
1990	Assorted Snow Bells 3816	Open		6.65	7
1989	Bell with Flowers 3805	Open		5.85	6
1986	Cello 3801	Retrd.	1995	6.65	7
1989	Christmas Bells on From 3806	Open		8.35	9
1988	Clip-On Drum 383534	Retrd.	1994	8.00	8
1987	Guitar 3802	Retrd.	1995	6.65	7
1990	Large Banjo 3812	Open		8.35	9
1988	Large Bell with Acorns 3804	Retrd.	1994	9.00	9
1993	Large Bell with Holly 3819	Open		50.00	50
1990	Large Cello 3811	Open		8.35	9
1990	Large Christmas Bell 3808	Retrd.	1995	10.35	11
1988	Large Drum 3803	Open		10.35	11
1990	Large Mandolin 3813	Open		8.35	9
1995	Liberty Bell 3821	Open		5.50	6
1990	Lyre 3809	Retrd.	1995	8.35	9
1995	Patriotic Bell 3823	Open		10.95	11
1990	Small Fancy Drum 3815	Open		7.80	8
1990	Toy Drum 3817	Open		9.25	10
1990	Zither 3810	Open		8.35	9

Porcelain Christmas - E.M. Merck

YEAR ISSUE		EDITION LIMIT	YEAR RETD.	ISSUE PRICE	QUOTE U.S.$
1989	Angel 9435	Retrd.	1994	6.65	7
1988	Bear on Skates 9495	Retrd.	1988	10.00	16
1988	Bunnies on Skies 9494	Retrd.	1988	10.00	16
1987	Father Christmas (A) 9404	Retrd.	1988	11.00	11
1987	Father Christmas w/Cape 9405	Retrd.	1988	11.00	11
1987	Father Christmas w/Toys 9406	Retrd.	1988	11.00	11
1989	Hummingbird 9433	Retrd.	1994	6.65	7
1987	Lighted Angel Tree Top 9420	Retrd.	1992	29.50	30
1989	Nutcracker 9436	Retrd.	1994	6.65	7
1988	Penguin w/Gifts 9496	Retrd.	1988	10.00	14
1989	Rocking Horse 9431	Retrd.	1994	6.65	7
1987	Roly-Poly Santa 9441	Retrd.	1988	6.75	9
1989	Santa 9432	Retrd.	1994	6.65	7
1987	Santa Head 9410	Retrd.	1988	6.55	7
1989	Teddy Bear 9434	Retrd.	1994	6.65	7

Reflectors - E.M. Merck, unless otherwise noted

YEAR ISSUE		EDITION LIMIT	YEAR RETD.	ISSUE PRICE	QUOTE U.S.$
1990	Assorted 6 cm Reflectors 4207	12/95		7.00	7
1990	Assorted Reflectors with Diamonds 4206	Retrd.	1995	9.95	12
1992	Flower in Reflector 4212	Open		9.25	10
1986	Horseshoe Reflector 4203	Retrd.	1989	7.80	12
1987	Large Drop with Indents (A) 4204	Retrd.	1994	12.85	15
1992	Mushrooms in Reflector (A) 4213	Open		9.90	10
1995	Patriotic Reflector 4218 - Inge-Glas	Open		8.95	9
1991	Peacock in Reflector 4208	Open		9.25	10
1991	Pears in Reflector 4209	Open		9.25	10
1986	Pink Reflector 4202	12/95		9.50	10
1992	Poinsettia in Reflector 4211	Open		9.00	9
1994	Reflector on Icicle 4217	Open		27.75	28
1993	Reflector with Tinsel Wire 4215	Open		20.00	20
1992	Scrap Santa in Reflector 4214	Retrd.	1993	8.80	16
1992	Shining Sun Reflector 4210	Open		9.00	9
1994	Small Fantasy Form 4216	Open		22.00	22
1986	Star Pattern Reflector (A) 4201	Retrd.	1994	9.25	11
1990	Strawberry in Reflector 4205	Open		9.25	10

Santas - E.M. Merck, unless otherwise noted

YEAR ISSUE		EDITION LIMIT	YEAR RETD.	ISSUE PRICE	QUOTE U.S.$
1995	All American Santa 4087 - Inge-Glas	Open		89.50	90
1991	Alpine Santa 4047	Open		7.00	7
1992	Belznickel 4055	Open		12.50	13
1985	Blue Father Christmas 4010498	12/95		8.00	8
1993	Blue St. Nick 4067	Open		10.00	10
1990	Blue Victorian St. Nick 4028	Retrd.	1993	9.95	14
1987	Burgundy Father Christmas 4013	Open		7.80	8
1987	Burgundy Santa Claus 4014	Retrd.	1994	13.95	14
1990	Clip-On Victorian St. Nick 4030	Open		11.00	11
1994	Double-Sided Santa Head 4075	Open		8.00	8
1989	Father Christmas 4024	Open		4.25	5
1986	Father Christmas Head 4006	Open		7.80	8
1985	Father Christmas Head 403223	Retrd.	1994	7.80	8
1990	Father Christmas on Form 4046	Open		11.00	11
1985	Father Christmas w/ Basket 403224	Retrd.	1994	7.80	8
1994	Father Christmas w/Chenile 4080	Open		10.80	11
1990	Father Christmas with Toys 4036	Open		13.95	14
1985	Father Christmas w/Tree 401039	Retrd.	1995	8.00	8
1990	Festive Santa Head 4039	12/95		11.00	11
1992	Frontier Santa with Tree 4051	Open		11.00	11
1993	Frosty Santa 4061	Open		10.25	11
1985	Gold Father Christmas 401045	Open		7.45	8
1992	Gold Weihnachtsmann 4052	Open		9.80	10
1986	Green Clip-On Santa 4007	Retrd.	1995	7.80	8
1985	Jolly Father Christmas 401043	12/95		7.00	7
1995	Jolly Santa Head 2302	Open		7.50	8
1987	Jolly Santa Head 4016	Open		8.80	9
1993	Lg. Father Christmas Head 4066	12/95		22.50	23
1995	Large Santa Head 2305	Open		13.95	14
1984	Large Santa In Basket 401001	12/95		12.95	13
1985	Large Santa with Tree 401055	Open		12.60	13
1990	Large Weihnachtsmann 4042	Open		10.25	11
1990	Light Blue St. Nicholas 4029	Retrd.	1994	6.45	7
1987	Matte Red Roly-Poly Santa 4012	Retrd.	1995	7.90	8
1985	Matte Santa Head 401087	Open		8.00	8
1990	Miniature Santa 4032	Open		4.95	5
1990	Old Bavarian Santa 4044	Open		12.50	13
1984	Old Father Christmas Head 401007	Retrd.	1994	7.00	7
1990	Old St. Nick with Toys 4041	Open		13.95	14
1992	Old Swiss Santa 4053	Open		12.50	13
1995	Old World Clip-on Santa 4085	Open		9.95	10
1993	Old World Santa 4068	Open		11.00	11
1994	Old World Santa Head 4074	Open		6.50	7
1989	Old-Fashioned Santa (A) 4019	Retrd.	1995	5.75	6
1990	Old-Fashioned St. Nicholas 4040	Open		11.00	11
1994	Old-Fashioned St. Nick 4077	Open		9.25	10
1985	Parachuting Santa 401056	Open		8.00	8
1995	Patriotic Santa 4086	Open		12.50	13
1986	Pink Clip-On Santa 4011	Retrd.	1994	8.35	9
1985	Pink Father Christmas 4010499	12/95		8.00	8
1993	Purple Belznickel 4060	Open		12.50	13
1993	Purple Father Christmas 4063	Open		8.35	9
1995	Regal Father Christmas 4081	Open		15.95	16

CHRISTMAS ORNAMENTS

YEAR ISSUE		EDITION LIMIT	YEAR RETD.	ISSUE PRICE	QUOTE U.S.$
1992	Roaring 20s Santa 4050	Open		10.00	10
1984	Roly-Poly Santa 401002	Retrd.	1994	7.90	8
1990	Round Jolly Santa Head 4035	Open		11.00	11
1992	Round Santa Head 4054	Open		9.00	9
1995	Salsburger Santa 4084	Open		13.50	14
1989	Santa 4025	Open		4.50	5
1987	Santa Above Ball 4018	Open		13.95	14
1993	Santa Above Bell 4072	Open		36.00	36
1993	Santa Above Reflector 4069	Open		40.00	40
1985	Santa and Tree on Form 401026	12/95		9.25	10
1995	Santa Face on Cone 4083	Open		7.50	8
1989	Santa Hiding in Tree 4023	Open		11.00	11
1987	Santa in Airplane 4017	Open		13.95	14
1986	Santa In Chimney 4005	Retrd.	1995	8.70	9
1993	Santa in Chimney 4059	Open		12.50	13
1985	Santa in Chimney 406912	Retrd.	1989	11.00	17
1991	Santa in Mushroom 4048	Open		8.70	9
1993	Santa in Sleigh 4057	Open		14.65	15
1985	Santa in Tree 401054	Retrd.	1995	7.45	8
1993	Santa in Walnut 4058	Open		7.00	7
1986	Santa On Carriage 4003	Retrd.	1988	10.00	24
1986	Santa On Cone 4002	Retrd.	1993	7.90	14
1986	Santa Under Tree 4001	Open		10.35	11
1995	Santa with Chenille Legs 4088 - Inge-Glas	Open		22.50	23
1986	Santa with Glued-On Tree 4009	12/95		9.00	9
1993	Santa with Staff 4070	Open		10.95	11
1994	Santa's Shop 4079	Open		13.25	14
1995	Shimmering Santa 4082 - Inge-Glas	Open		7.95	8
1986	Small Blue Santa 4010	12/95		5.40	6
1984	Small Old-Fashioned Santa 401022	Retrd.	1994	6.65	7
1985	Small Santa in Basket 401105	12/95		9.25	10
1992	Small Santa on Form 4049	Open		8.00	8
1985	Small Santa with Pack 401065	12/95		5.40	6
1990	Small Victorian Santa Head 4027	Open		7.35	8
1993	Snowy Purple Santa 4056	Open		7.35	8
1990	Snowy Santa 4033	Open		10.95	11
1989	St. Nicholas 4020	Retrd.	1995	10.00	10
1986	St. Nicholas Head 4008	12/95		6.65	7
1985	St. Nicholas on Horse 401064	Open		13.95	14
1995	Standing Santa 2303	Open		13.95	14
1985	Standing Santa 401057	Open		11.00	11
1990	Very Large Belznickel 4037	Open		22.50	23
1993	Very Large Roly-Poly Santa 4071	Open		50.00	50
1987	Very Large Santa Head 4015	Open		13.95	14
1990	Very Large St. Nick Head 4038	Open		22.50	23
1994	Very Merry Santa 4076	Open		7.35	8
1990	Victorian Father Christmas 4045	Open		10.00	10
1994	Victorian Father Christmas 4078	Open		7.35	8
1989	Victorian Santa 4021	Open		8.45	9
1989	Victorian Santa Head 4022	Open		8.35	9
1990	Victorian Scrap Santa 4043	Retrd.	1993	9.70	12
1990	Weihnachtsmann 4034	12/95		9.00	9
1990	Weihnachtsmann with Tree 4031	Open		10.50	11
1990	White Clip-On Santa 4026	Retrd.	1995	7.35	8
1993	Woodland Santa 4062	Open		9.35	10

Toys - E.M. Merck

1993	Cornucopia of Toys 4411	Open		9.50	10
1985	Doll Buggy with Doll 4437138	Retrd.	1994	7.00	7
1986	Dumb-Dumb 4403	Retrd.	1988	6.45	21
1995	King of the Nutcrackers 4415	Open		65.00	65
1990	Large Doll Buggy with Doll 4409	Open		11.50	12
1990	Large Fancy Carousel 4407	Open		12.75	13
1986	Large Nutcracker 4401	Open		13.50	14
1990	Lucky Dice 4406	Open		7.00	7
1988	Nutcracker Guard 4405	Retrd.	1995	8.50	9
1990	Rocking Horse/Tree on Form 4408	Open		12.95	13
1985	Small Carousel 446836	Open		7.00	7
1986	Small Nutcracker 4402	Open		10.00	10
1986	Soccer Ball 4404	Open		7.00	7
1993	Stocking with Toys 4410	Open		13.50	14

Transportation - E.M. Merck, unless otherwise noted

1988	Cable Car 4602	Retrd.	1989	8.45	21
1985	Cable Car 461067	Retrd.	1988	14.95	21
1992	Commemorative Airship 4607	Open		9.25	10
1990	Fancy Steam Locomotive 4606	Open		10.35	11
1990	Fire Truck 4603	Open		8.25	9
1995	Full Sail 4614 - Inge-Glas	Open		27.50	28
1993	Gold Car 4610	Open		9.80	10
1993	Gray Zeppelin 4613	Open		6.75	7
1990	Large Zeppelin 4605	12/95		8.25	9
1985	Locomotive 461069	Retrd.	1993	7.00	16
1992	Locomotive/Tree on Form 4608	Open		12.95	13
1993	Ocean Liner 4611	Open		9.45	10
1985	Old-Fashioned Car 463747	Retrd.	1989	6.25	17
1990	Old-Time Limousine 4604	Open		9.00	9
1992	Race Car 4609	12/95		7.00	7
1986	Rolls Royce 4601	Retrd.	1989	7.90	19
1993	Small Locomotive 4612	Open		9.80	10
1985	Zeppelin 467265	Open		7.00	7

Tree Tops - E.M. Merck, unless otherwise noted

1987	Angel in Indent Tree Top 5009	Retrd.	1995	27.00	27
1987	Angel w/Crown 5007	Retrd.	1993	50.00	65
1986	Blue Angel 5004	Open		47.50	48
1986	Blue Santa 5002	Retrd.	1995	37.50	38
1986	Burgundy Angel 5003	Open		47.50	48
1985	Fancy Gold Spire w/Bells 506266	Retrd.	1993	32.00	40
1985	Fancy Red Spire w/Bells 506269	Retrd.	1993	32.00	40
1992	Fancy Spiral Tree Top 5016	Open		47.50	48
1987	Heart Reflector 5011	Open		25.00	25
1992	Large Spire w/Reflectors 5014	Open		69.50	70
1992	Large Tree Top w/Cherubs 5012	Open		57.50	58
1992	Large Tree Top w/Roses 5015	Open		47.50	48
1992	Miniature Reflector 5013	Open		15.00	15
1995	North Pole Santa Tree Top 5019	Open		45.00	45
1995	Patriotic Tree Top 5020 - Inge-Glas	Open		20.95	21
1986	Red Santa 5001	Open		37.50	38
1985	Santa Head Tree Top 506345	Open		19.35	20
1987	Santa in Indent 5008	Retrd.	1995	25.00	25
1987	Star Reflector 5010	Open		25.00	25
1995	Teddy Bear Tree Top 5021	Open		45.00	45
1986	Two Angels 5005	Open		47.50	48
1993	Very Large Reflector 5017	Open		65.00	65

Trees & Cones - E.M. Merck, unless otherwise noted

1989	Assorted Pearl Cones 4804	Open		3.85	4
1990	Assorted Pine Cones with Leaves 4809	Open		6.75	7
1990	Assorted Shiny Cones 4807	Open		6.55	7
1985	Fir Cone With Glitter 481046	Open		6.45	7
1990	Fir Tree 4813	Open		7.00	7
1985	Green Tree with Glitter 481044	Open		4.50	5
1990	Large Christmas Tree 4815	Open		8.00	8
1995	Large Frosted Jewel Cone 4820 - Inge-Glas	Open		11.50	12
1988	Large Mauve & Champagne Cone 4802	Retrd.	1993	11.85	12
1994	Matte Gold Cone with Snow 486866	Open		4.85	5
1985	Medium Gold Cone w/Glitter 486712-5	Open		3.85	4
1990	Multi-Colored Cone 4810	Open		7.00	7
1990	Multi-Colored Tree 4812	Retrd.	1994	5.55	6
1990	Pine Cone Man 4811	Open		8.25	9
1989	Pine Cone Santa 4805	Open		4.75	5
1988	Smal Fir Cone (A) 4803	Open		4.50	5
1990	Small Christmas Tree 4814	Open		4.95	5
1990	Small Pine Cones with Leaves (A) 4806	Open		5.25	6
1986	Small Red & Gold Cones (A) 4801	Open		3.75	4
1993	Sugar Cone 4817	Open		7.55	8
1992	Tree With Eagle 4816	Open		7.00	7
1985	Very Large Red & Gold Cones 483612	Open		7.00	7

Orrefors

Christmas Ornaments - E. Lagerbulke

1995	Christmas Tree	Yr.Iss.		45.00	45

Christmas Ornaments - O. Alberius

1984	Dove	Yr.Iss.		30.00	45
1985	Angel	Yr.Iss.		30.00	40
1986	Reindeer	Yr.Iss.		30.00	40
1987	Snowman	Yr.Iss.		30.00	40
1988	Sleigh	Yr.Iss.		30.00	40
1989	Christmas Tree "1989"	Yr.Iss.		35.00	40
1990	Holly Leaves And Berries	Yr.Iss.		35.00	40
1991	Stocking	Yr.Iss.		40.00	40
1992	Star	Yr.Iss.		35.00	40
1993	Bell	Yr.Iss.		35.00	40
1993	Baby's1st Christmas	Yr.Iss.		40.00	40
1994	Rocking Horse	Yr.Iss.		40.00	40

Pacific Rim Import Corp.

Bristol Waterfront - P. Sebern

1995	Portshead Lighthouse	Open		10.00	10

Rawcliffe Corporation

Bubble Fairy™ Ornaments - J. deStefano

1993	Blessing Hanging Baby Bubble Fairy	Open		40.00	40
1992	Holly Hanging Baby Bubble Fairy	Open		40.00	40
1993	Joy Hanging Baby Bubble Fairy	Open		40.00	40
1993	Sweetness Hanging Baby Bubble Fairy	Open		40.00	40
1993	Wonder Hanging Baby Bubble Fairy	Open		40.00	40

Reed & Barton

12 Days of Christmas Sterling and Lead Crystal - Reed & Barton

1988	Partridge in a Pear Tree	Yr.Iss.		25.00	40
1989	Two Turtle Doves	Yr.Iss.		25.00	40
1990	Three French Hens	Yr.Iss.		27.50	40
1991	Four Colly birds	Yr.Iss.		27.50	40
1992	Five Golden Rings	Yr.Iss.		27.50	28
1993	Six Geese A Laying	Yr.Iss.		27.50	28
1994	Seven Swans A 'Swimming	Yr.Iss.		27.50	28
1994	Eight Maids A Milking	Yr.Iss.		27.50	28

Carousel Horse - Reed & Barton

1988	Silverplate-1988	Closed	1988	13.50	14
1988	Gold-covered-1988	Closed	1988	15.00	15
1989	Silverplate-1989	Closed	1989	13.50	14
1989	Gold-covered-1989	Closed	1989	15.00	15
1990	Silverplate-1990	Closed	1990	13.50	14
1990	Gold-covered-1990	Closed	1990	15.00	15
1991	Silverplate-1991	Closed	1991	13.50	14
1991	Gold-covered-1991	Closed	1991	15.00	15
1992	Silverplate-1992	Closed	1992	13.50	14
1992	Gold-covered-1992	Closed	1992	15.00	15
1993	Silverplate-1993	Closed	1993	13.50	14
1993	Gold-covered-1993	Closed	1993	15.00	15
1994	Silverplate-1994	Yr.Iss.	1994	13.50	14
1994	Gold-covered-1994	Yr.Iss.	1994	15.00	15
1995	Silverplate-1995	Yr.Iss.		13.50	14
1995	Gold-covered-1995	Yr.Iss.		15.00	15

Christmas Cross - Reed & Barton

1971	Sterling Silver-1971	Closed	1971	10.00	150-300
1971	24Kt. Gold over Sterling-V1971	Closed	1971	17.50	300
1972	Sterling Silver-1972	Closed	1972	10.00	70-150
1972	24Kt. Gold over Sterling-V1972	Closed	1972	17.50	65-105
1973	Sterling Silver-1973	Closed	1973	10.00	60-75
1973	24Kt. Gold over Sterling-V1973	Closed	1973	17.50	55-65
1974	Sterling Silver-1974	Closed	1974	12.95	45-90
1974	24Kt. Gold over Sterling-V1974	Closed	1974	20.00	50-60
1975	Sterling Silver-1975	Closed	1975	12.95	35-90
1975	24Kt. Gold over Sterling-V1975	Closed	1975	20.00	45-50
1976	Sterling Silver-1976	Closed	1976	13.95	45-60
1976	24Kt. Gold over Sterling-V1976	Closed	1976	19.95	45-50
1977	Sterling Silver-1977	Closed	1977	15.00	35-60
1977	24Kt. Gold over Sterling-V1977	Closed	1977	18.50	45-50
1978	Sterling Silver-1978	Closed	1978	16.00	45-90
1978	24Kt. Gold over Sterling-V1978	Closed	1978	20.00	45-55
1979	Sterling Silver-1979	Closed	1979	20.00	45-75
1979	24Kt. Gold over Sterling-V1979	Closed	1979	24.00	32-57
1980	Sterling Silver-1980	Closed	1980	35.00	100-200
1980	24Kt. Gold over Sterling-V1980	Closed	1980	40.00	45-50
1981	Sterling Silver-1981	Closed	1981	35.00	85-100
1981	24Kt. Gold over Sterling-V1981	Closed	1981	40.00	45
1982	Sterling Silver-1982	Closed	1982	35.00	45-100
1982	24Kt. Gold over Sterling-V1982	Closed	1982	40.00	45
1983	Sterling Silver-1983	Closed	1983	35.00	60-100
1983	24Kt. Gold over Sterling-V1983	Closed	1983	40.00	40-45
1984	Sterling Silver-1984	Closed	1984	35.00	45-63
1984	24Kt. Gold over Sterling-V1984	Closed	1984	45.00	45
1985	Sterling Silver-1985	Closed	1985	35.00	45-63
1985	24Kt. Gold over Sterling-V1985	Closed	1985	40.00	40
1986	Sterling Silver-1986	Closed	1986	38.50	45-63
1986	24Kt. Gold over Sterling-V1986	Closed	1986	40.00	40
1987	Sterling Silver-1987	Closed	1987	35.00	45-60
1987	24Kt. Gold over Sterling-V1987	Closed	1987	40.00	40
1988	Sterling Silver-1988	Closed	1988	35.00	40-110
1988	24Kt. Gold over Sterling-V1988	Closed	1988	40.00	40
1989	Sterling Silver-1989	Closed	1989	35.00	40-65
1989	24Kt. Gold over Sterling-V1989	Closed	1989	40.00	40
1990	Sterling Silver-1990	Closed	1990	40.00	45-60
1990	24Kt. Gold over Sterling-1990	Closed	1990	45.00	45
1991	Sterling Silver-1991	Closed	1991	40.00	40-60
1991	24Kt. Gold over Sterling-1991	Closed	1991	45.00	45
1992	Sterling Silver-1992	Closed	1992	40.00	40-60
1992	24Kt. Gold over Sterling-1992	Closed	1992	45.00	45
1993	Sterling Silver-1993	Closed	1993	40.00	45
1993	24Kt. Gold over Sterling-1993	Closed	1993	45.00	45
1994	Sterling Silver-1994	Closed	1994	40.00	40
1994	24Kt. Gold over Sterling-1994	Closed	1994	45.00	45
1995	Sterling Silver-1995	Yr.Iss.		40.00	40
1995	24Kt. Gold over Sterling-1995	Yr.Iss.		45.00	45

Holly Ball - Reed & Barton

1976	1976 Silver plated	Closed	1976	14.00	50
1977	1977 Silver plated	Closed	1977	15.00	50
1978	1978 Silver plated	Closed	1978	15.00	50
1979	1979 Silver plated	Closed	1979	15.00	35

Holly Bell - Reed & Barton

1980	1980 Bell	Closed	1980	22.50	40
1980	Bell, gold plate, V1980	Closed	1980	25.00	45
1981	1981 Bell	Closed	1981	22.50	45
1981	Bell, gold plate, V1981	Closed	1981	27.50	35
1982	1982 Bell	Closed	1982	22.50	50
1982	Bell, gold plate, V1982	Closed	1982	27.50	50
1983	1983 Bell	Closed	1983	23.50	55
1983	Bell, gold plate, V1983	Closed	1983	30.00	50
1984	1984 Bell	Closed	1984	25.00	50
1984	Bell, gold plate, V1984	Closed	1984	28.50	50
1985	1985 Bell	Closed	1985	25.00	50
1985	Bell, gold plate, V1985	Closed	1985	28.50	50
1986	1986 Bell	Closed	1986	25.00	50
1986	Bell, gold plate, V1986	Closed	1986	28.50	50
1987	1987 Bell	Closed	1987	27.50	50
1987	Bell, gold plate, V1987	Closed	1987	30.00	50
1988	1988 Bell	Closed	1988	27.50	55
1988	Bell, gold plate, V1988	Closed	1988	30.00	30
1989	1989 Bell	Closed	1989	27.50	40
1989	Bell, gold plate, V1989	Closed	1989	30.00	30
1990	Bell, gold plate, V1990	Closed	1990	30.00	30
1990	1990 Bell	Closed	1990	27.50	45
1991	Bell, gold plate, V1991	Closed	1991	30.00	30
1991	1991 Bell	Closed	1991	27.50	40
1992	Bell, gold plate, V1992	Closed	1992	30.00	30
1992	Bell, silver plate, 1992	Closed	1992	27.50	45
1993	Bell, gold plate, V1993	Closed	1993	27.50	28
1993	Bell, silver plate, 1993	Closed	1993	30.00	40
1994	Bell, gold plate, 1994	Closed	1994	30.00	30

YEAR ISSUE		EDITION LIMIT	YEAR RETD.	ISSUE PRICE	QUOTE U.S.$
1994	Bell, silver plate, 1994	Closed	1994	27.50	28
1995	Bell, gold plate, 1995	Closed		30.00	30
1995	Bell, silver plate, 1995	Closed		27.50	28

Roman, Inc.

Catnippers - I. Spencer

YEAR ISSUE		EDITION LIMIT	YEAR RETD.	ISSUE PRICE	QUOTE U.S.$
1989	Bow Brummel	Open		15.00	15
1991	Christmas Knight	Open		15.00	15
1988	Christmas Mourning	Open		15.00	15
1991	Faux Paw	Open		15.00	15
1990	Felix Navidad	Open		15.00	15
1989	Happy Holidaze	Open		15.00	15
1991	Holly Days Are Happy Days	Open		15.00	15
1991	Meowy Christmas	Open		15.00	15
1991	Pawtridge in a Purr Tree	Open		15.00	15
1988	Puss in Berries	Open		15.00	15
1988	Ring A Ding-Ding	Open		15.00	15
1989	Sandy Claws	Open		15.00	15
1991	Snow Biz	Open		15.00	15
1990	Sock It to Me Santa	Open		15.00	15
1990	Stuck on Christmas	Open		15.00	15

The Discovery of America - I. Spencer

YEAR ISSUE		EDITION LIMIT	YEAR RETD.	ISSUE PRICE	QUOTE U.S.$
1991	Kitstopher Kolumbus	1,992		15.00	15
1991	Queen Kitsabella	1,992		15.00	15

Fontanini Annual Christmas Ornaments - E. Simonetti

YEAR ISSUE		EDITION LIMIT	YEAR RETD.	ISSUE PRICE	QUOTE U.S.$
1991	1991 Annual (Girl)	Yr.Iss.	1991	8.50	9
1991	1991 Annual (Boy)	Yr.Iss.	1991	8.50	9
1992	1992 Annual (Girl)	Yr.Iss.	1992	8.50	9
1992	1992 Annual (Boy)	Yr.Iss.	1992	8.50	9
1993	1993 Annual (Girl)	Yr.Iss.	1993	8.50	9
1993	1993 Annual (Boy)	Yr.Iss.	1993	8.50	9

Fontanini Limited Edition Ornaments - E. Simonetti

YEAR ISSUE		EDITION LIMIT	YEAR RETD.	ISSUE PRICE	QUOTE U.S.$
1995	The Annunciation	20,000		20.00	20

Millenium Ornament - M. Lucchesi

YEAR ISSUE		EDITION LIMIT	YEAR RETD.	ISSUE PRICE	QUOTE U.S.$
1992	Silent Night	20,000	1992	20.00	20
1993	The Annunciation	20,000	1993	20.00	20
1994	Peace On Earth	20,000	1994	20.00	20
1995	Cause of Our Joy	20,000		20.00	20

Museum Collection of Angela Tripi - A. Tripi

YEAR ISSUE		EDITION LIMIT	YEAR RETD.	ISSUE PRICE	QUOTE U.S.$
1994	1994 Annual Angel Ornament	2,500	1994	49.50	50
1995	1995 Annual Angel Ornament	2,500		49.50	50

Sepaphim Collection by Faro - Faro

YEAR ISSUE		EDITION LIMIT	YEAR RETD.	ISSUE PRICE	QUOTE U.S.$
1994	Rarest of Heaven	20,000		25.00	25
1995	Heaven's Herald	20,000		25.00	25

Vernon Wilson Signature Series - V. Wilson

YEAR ISSUE		EDITION LIMIT	YEAR RETD.	ISSUE PRICE	QUOTE U.S.$
1995	We Three Kings	Open		34.00	34

Royal Doulton

Bunnykins - Unknown

YEAR ISSUE		EDITION LIMIT	YEAR RETD.	ISSUE PRICE	QUOTE U.S.$
1992	Caroling	N/A		19.00	19
1991	Santa Bunny	N/A		19.00	19

Christmas Ornaments - Unknown

YEAR ISSUE		EDITION LIMIT	YEAR RETD.	ISSUE PRICE	QUOTE U.S.$
1993	Together for Christmas	Yr.Iss.		20.00	20
1994	Home For Christmas	Yr.Iss.		20.00	20

Schmid

Disney Annual - Disney Studios

YEAR ISSUE		EDITION LIMIT	YEAR RETD.	ISSUE PRICE	QUOTE U.S.$
1985	Snow Biz	Yr.Iss.	1985	8.50	20
1986	Tree for Two	Yr.Iss.	1986	8.50	15
1987	Merry Mouse Medley	Yr.Iss.	1987	8.50	10
1988	Warm Winter Ride	Yr.Iss.	1988	11.00	45
1989	Merry Mickey Claus	Yr.Iss.	1989	11.00	11
1990	Holly Jolly Christmas	Yr.Iss.	1990	14.00	30
1991	Mickey & Minnie's Rockin' Christmas	Yr.Iss.	1991	14.00	14

Lowell Davis Country Christmas - L. Davis

YEAR ISSUE		EDITION LIMIT	YEAR RETD.	ISSUE PRICE	QUOTE U.S.$
1983	Mailbox	Yr.Iss.	1983	17.50	45-75
1984	Cat in Boot	Yr.Iss.	1984	17.50	60-65
1985	Pig in Trough	Yr.Iss.	1985	17.50	50-75
1986	Church	Yr.Iss.	1986	17.50	35-55
1987	Blossom	Yr.Iss.	1987	19.50	36
1988	Wisteria	Yr.Iss.	1988	19.50	25
1989	Wren	Yr.Iss.	1989	19.50	30-48
1990	Wintering Deer	Yr.Iss.	1990	19.50	30
1991	Church at Red Oak II	Yr.Iss.	1991	25.00	25
1992	Born On A Starry Night	Yr.Iss.	1992	25.00	25
1993	Waiting for Mr. Lowell	Yr.Iss.	1993	20.00	20
1994	Visions of Sugarplums	Yr.Iss.	1994	25.00	25
1995	Bah Humbug	Yr.Iss.	N/A	25.00	25

Seymour Mann, Inc.

Christmas Collection - Various

YEAR ISSUE		EDITION LIMIT	YEAR RETD.	ISSUE PRICE	QUOTE U.S.$
1985	Angel Wall XMAS-523 - J. White	Closed	1988	12.00	12
1989	Christmas Cat in Teacup XMAS-660 - J. White	Closed	1992	13.50	14
1990	Cupid CPD-5 - J. White	Closed	1993	13.50	14
1990	Cupid CPD-6 - J. White	Closed	1993	13.50	14
1986	Cupid Head XMAS-53 - J. White	Closed	1988	25.00	25
1990	Doll Tree Topper OM-124 - J. White	Closed	1993	85.00	85
1991	Elf w/ Reindeer CJ-422 - Jaimy	Closed	1993	9.00	9
1991	Elves w/ Mail CJ-464 - J. White	Closed	1993	30.00	30
1991	Flat Red Santa CJ-115R - Jaimy	Closed	1993	2.88	3
1991	Flat Santa CJ-115 - Jaimy	Closed	1993	7.50	8
1991	Floral Plaque XMAS-911 - J. White	Closed	1993	10.00	10
1991	Flower Basket XMAS-912 - J. White	Closed	1993	10.00	10
1990	Hat w/ Streamers OM-116 - J. White	Closed	1993	20.00	20
1990	Heartlace OM-119 - J. White	Closed	1993	12.00	12
1990	Lace Ball OM-120 - J. White	Closed	1993	10.00	10
1994	Santa w/ Candle CBU-300 - J. White	Open		40.00	40
1994	Santa w/ Child CBU-305 - J. White	Open		40.00	40
1994	Santa w/ Children CBU-304 - J. White	Open		40.00	40
1994	Santa w/ Lamb CBU-301 - J. White	Open		40.00	40
1994	Santa w/ Lantern CBU-303 - J. White	Open		40.00	40
1994	Santa w/ List CBU-307 - J. White	Open		40.00	40
1994	Santa w/ Sled CBU-306 - J. White	Open		40.00	40
1994	Santa w/ Stick CBU-302 - J. White	Open		40.00	40
1986	Santa XMAS-384 - J. White	Closed	1989	7.50	8
1991	Santas, set of 6 CJ-12 - Jaimy	Closed	1993	60.00	60
1990	Tassel OM-118 - J. White	Closed	1993	7.50	8

Christmas Lite-Up Houses - L. Sciola

YEAR ISSUE		EDITION LIMIT	YEAR RETD.	ISSUE PRICE	QUOTE U.S.$
1994	Lite-up Church XMR-21	Open		30.00	30
1994	Lite-up Country House	Open		30.00	30
1994	Lite-up Library XMR-24	Open		30.00	30
1994	Lite-up Mansion XMR-23	Open		30.00	30
1994	Lite-up Restaurant XMR-20	Open		30.00	30
1994	Set/10 Lite-up Houses XMR-10	Open		95.00	95
1994	Set/10 Lite-up Houses XMR-11	Open		95.00	95

Gingerbread Christmas - J. Sauerbrey

YEAR ISSUE		EDITION LIMIT	YEAR RETD.	ISSUE PRICE	QUOTE U.S.$
1991	Gingerbread Angel CJ-411	Closed	1992	7.50	8
1991	Gingerbread House CJ-416	Closed	1992	7.50	8
1991	Gingerbread Man CJ-415	Closed	1992	7.50	8
1991	Gingerbread Mouse/Boot CJ-409	Closed	1992	7.50	8
1991	Gingerbread Mrs. Claus CJ-414	Closed	1992	7.50	8
1991	Gingerbread Reindeer CJ-410	Closed	1992	7.50	8
1991	Gingerbread Santa CJ-408	Closed	1992	7.50	8
1991	Gingerbread Sleigh CJ-406	Closed	1992	7.50	8
1991	Gingerbread Snowman CJ-412	Closed	1992	7.50	8
1991	Gingerbread Tree CJ-407	Closed	1992	7.50	8

Victorian Christmas Collection - Jaimy

YEAR ISSUE		EDITION LIMIT	YEAR RETD.	ISSUE PRICE	QUOTE U.S.$
1991	Couple Against Wind CJ-420	Closed	1993	15.00	15

Shelia's Collectibles

Historical Ornament Collection - S. Thompson

YEAR ISSUE		EDITION LIMIT	YEAR RETD.	ISSUE PRICE	QUOTE U.S.$
1995	Blue Cottage (1st edition) OR001	2-Yr.		15.00	15
1995	Cape Hatteras Light (1st edition) OR007	2-Yr.		15.00	15
1995	Chestnut House (1st edition) OR002	2-Yr.		15.00	15
1995	Drayton House (1st edition) OR003	2-Yr.		15.00	15
1995	East Brother Lighthouse (1st edition) OR008	2-Yr.		15.00	15
1995	Eclectic Blue (1st edition) OR004	2-Yr.		15.00	15
1995	Goeller House (1st edition) OR005	2-Yr.		15.00	15
1995	Point Fermin Light (1st edition) OR009	2-Yr.		15.00	15
1995	Stockton Row (1st edition) OR006	2-Yr.		15.00	15

Swarovski America Ltd.

Holiday Ornaments - Swarovski

YEAR ISSUE		EDITION LIMIT	YEAR RETD.	ISSUE PRICE	QUOTE U.S.$
1981	1981 Snowflake 7563NR35	Yr.Iss.		30.00	300
1987	1987 Holiday Etching-Candle	Yr.Iss.		20.00	100-240
1988	1988 Holiday Etching-Wreath	Yr.Iss.		25.00	50-75
1989	1989 Holiday Etching-Dove	Yr.Iss.		35.00	145-200
1990	1990 Holiday Etching-Merry Christmas	Yr.Iss.		25.00	125-150
1991	1991 Holiday Ornament-Star	Yr.Iss.		35.00	70-90
1992	1992 Holiday Ornament-Star	Yr.Iss.		37.50	50-100
1993	1993 Holiday Ornament-Star	Yr.Iss.		37.50	40-75
1994	1994 Holiday Ornament-Star	Yr.Iss.		37.50	50-95
1995	1995 Holiday Ornament-Star	Yr.Iss.		40.00	40-95

Towle Silversmiths

Christmas Angel Medallions - Towle

YEAR ISSUE		EDITION LIMIT	YEAR RETD.	ISSUE PRICE	QUOTE U.S.$
1991	1991 Angel	Closed	1991	45.00	45-63
1992	1992 Angel	Closed	1992	45.00	45-60
1993	1993 Angel	Closed	1993	45.00	45
1994	1994 Angel	Closed	1994	50.00	50
1995	1995 Angel	Closed	1995	50.00	50

Remembrance Collection - Towle

YEAR ISSUE		EDITION LIMIT	YEAR RETD.	ISSUE PRICE	QUOTE U.S.$
1990	1990 - Old Master Snowflake	Closed	1990	40.00	62
1991	1991 - Old Master Snowflake	Closed	1991	40.00	62
1992	1992 - Old Master Snowflake	Closed	1992	40.00	62
1993	1993 - Old Master Snowflake	Closed	1993	40.00	45
1994	1994 - Old Master Snowflake	Closed	1994	50.00	50
1995	1995 - Old Master Snowflake	Closed	1995	50.00	50

Songs of Christmas Medallions - Towle

YEAR ISSUE		EDITION LIMIT	YEAR RETD.	ISSUE PRICE	QUOTE U.S.$
1978	Silent Night Medallion	Closed	1978	35.00	40-70
1979	Deck The Halls	Closed	1979	35.00	55-80
1980	Jingle Bells	Closed	1980	53.00	60-80
1981	Hark the Hearld Angels Sing	Closed	1981	53.00	150
1982	O Christmas Tree	Closed	1982	35.00	50-80
1983	Silver Bells	Closed	1983	40.00	60-80
1984	Let It Snow	Closed	1984	30.00	55-80
1985	Chestnuts Roasting on Open Fire	Closed	1985	35.00	55-80
1986	It Came Upon a Midnight Clear	Closed	1986	35.00	45-80
1987	White Christmas	Closed	1987	35.00	45-80

Sterling Cross - Towle

YEAR ISSUE		EDITION LIMIT	YEAR RETD.	ISSUE PRICE	QUOTE U.S.$
1994	Sterling Cross	Closed	1994	50.00	50
1995	Christmas Cross	Closed	1995	50.00	50

Sterling Floral Medallions - Towle

YEAR ISSUE		EDITION LIMIT	YEAR RETD.	ISSUE PRICE	QUOTE U.S.$
1983	Christmas Rose	Closed	1983	40.00	50
1984	Hawthorn/Glastonbury Thorn	Closed	1984	40.00	50
1985	Poinsettia	Closed	1985	35.00	55-70
1986	Laurel Bay	Closed	1986	35.00	55-80
1987	Mistletoe	Closed	1987	35.00	55-95
1988	Holly	Closed	1988	40.00	55-70
1989	Ivy	Closed	1989	35.00	55
1990	Christmas Cactus	Closed	1990	40.00	50
1991	Chrysanthemum	Closed	1991	40.00	50
1992	Star of Bethlehem	Closed	1992	40.00	45

Sterling Nativity Medallions - Towle

YEAR ISSUE		EDITION LIMIT	YEAR RETD.	ISSUE PRICE	QUOTE U.S.$
1988	The Angel Appeared	Closed	1988	40.00	80-135
1989	The Journey	Closed	1989	40.00	60-75
1990	No Room at the Inn	Closed	1990	40.00	45-75
1991	Tidings of Joy	Closed	1991	40.00	45-70
1992	Star of Bethlehem	Closed	1992	40.00	45-70
1993	Mother and Child	Closed	1993	40.00	45
1994	Three Wisemen	Closed	1994	40.00	40
1995	Newborn King	Closed	1995	40.00	40

Sterling Twelve Days of Christmas Medallions - Towle

YEAR ISSUE		EDITION LIMIT	YEAR RETD.	ISSUE PRICE	QUOTE U.S.$
1971	Partridge in A Pear Tree	Closed	1971	20.00	500
1972	Two Turtle Doves	Closed	1972	20.00	100-200
1973	Three French Hens	Closed	1973	20.00	100-125
1974	Four Calling Birds	Closed	1974	30.00	100-200
1975	Five Golden Rings	Closed	1975	30.00	75-150
1975	Five Golden Rings (vermeil)	Closed	1975	30.00	200-300
1976	Six Geese-a-Laying	Closed	1976	30.00	90-150
1977	Seven Swans-a-Swimming	Closed	1977	35.00	50-100
1977	Seven Swans-a-Swimming (turquoise)	Closed	1977	35.00	200-300
1978	Eight Maids-a-Milking	Closed	1978	37.00	80-100
1979	Nine Ladies Dancing	Closed	1979	37.00	50-100
1980	Ten Lords-a-Leaping	Closed	1980	76.00	65-100
1981	Eleven Pipers Piping	Closed	1981	50.00	65-100
1982	Twelve Drummers Drumming	Closed	1982	35.00	65-100

Twelve Days of Christmas - Towle

YEAR ISSUE		EDITION LIMIT	YEAR RETD.	ISSUE PRICE	QUOTE U.S.$
1991	Partridge in A Pear Tree In A Wreath	Closed	1991	50.00	50
1992	Two Turtle Doves In A Wreath	Closed	1992	50.00	50
1993	Three French Hens In A Wreath	Closed	1993	50.00	50
1994	Four Calling Birds In A Wreath	Closed	1995	50.00	50

United Design Corp.

Angels Collection-Tree Ornaments™ - P.J. Jonas, unless otherwise noted

YEAR ISSUE		EDITION LIMIT	YEAR RETD.	ISSUE PRICE	QUOTE U.S.$
1992	Angel and Tambourine IBO-422 S. Bradford	Open		20.00	20
1992	Angel and Tambourine, ivory IBO-425 - S. Bradford	Open		20.00	20
1993	Angel Baby w/ Bunny IBO-426 - D. Newburn	Open		23.00	24
1991	Angel Waif, ivory IBO-411	Open		15.00	20
1993	Angel Waif, plum IBO-437	Open		20.00	20
1995	Autumn's Bounty IBO-460	Open		32.00	32
1995	Autumn's Bounty, light IBO-454	Open		32.00	32
1995	Birds of a Feather IBO-457	Open		27.00	27
1990	Crystal Angel IBO-401	Retrd.	1993	20.00	20
1993	Crystal Angel, emerald IBO-446	Open		20.00	20
1990	Crystal Angel, ivory IBO-405	Open		20.00	20
1991	Fra Angelico Drummer, blue IBO-414 - S. Bradford	Open		20.00	20
1991	Fra Angelico Drummer, ivory IBO-420 - S. Bradford	Open		20.00	20
1991	Girl Cupid w/Rose, ivory IBO-413 - S. Bradford	Open		15.00	20
1995	Heavenly Blossoms IBO-458	Open		27.00	27
1993	Heavenly Harmony IBO-428	Open		25.00	30
1993	Heavenly Harmony, crimson IBO-433	Open		22.00	30
1993	Little Angel IBO-430 - D. Newburn	Open		18.00	20
1993	Little Angel, crimson IBO-445 - D. Newburn	Open		18.00	20

YEAR ISSUE		EDITION LIMIT	YEAR RETD.	ISSUE PRICE	QUOTE U.S.$
1992	Mary and Dove IBO-424 S. Bradford	Open		20.00	20
1994	Music and Grace IBO-448	Open		24.00	24
1994	Music and Grace, crimson IBO-449	Open		24.00	24
1994	Musical Flight IBO-450	Open		28.00	28
1994	Musical Flight, crimson IBO-451	Open		28.00	28
1991	Peace Descending, ivory IBO-412	Open		20.00	20
1993	Peace Descending, crimson IBO-436	Open		20.00	20
1993	Renaissance Angel IBO-429	Open		24.00	24
1993	Renaissance Angel, crimson IBO-431	Open		24.00	24
1990	Rose of Sharon IBO-402	Retrd.	1993	20.00	20
1993	Rose of Sharon, crimson IBO-439	Open		20.00	20
1990	Rose of Sharon, ivory IBO-406	Open		20.00	20
1993	Rosetti Angel, crimson IBO-434	Open		20.00	24
1991	Rosetti Angel, ivory IBO-410	Open		20.00	24
1995	Special Wishes IBO-456 - D. Newburn	Open		27.00	27
1995	Spring's Rebirth IBO-452	Open		32.00	32
1992	St. Francis and Critters IBO-423 S. Bradford	Open		20.00	20
1994	Star Flight IBO-447	Open		20.00	20
1990	Star Glory IBO-403	Retrd.	1993	15.00	15
1993	Star Glory, crimson IBO-438	Open		20.00	20
1990	Star Glory, ivory IBO-407	Open		15.00	20
1993	Stars & Lace IBO-427	Open		18.00	20
1993	Stars & Lace, Emerald IBO-432	Open		18.00	20
1995	Summer's Glory IBO-453	Open		32.00	32
1995	Tender Time IBO-459	Open		27.00	27
1990	Victorian Angel IBO-404	Retrd.	1993	15.00	15
1990	Victorian Angel, ivory IBO-408	Open		15.00	20
1993	Victorian Angel, plum IBO-435	Open		18.00	20
1993	Victorian Cupid, crimson IBO-440	Open		15.00	20
1991	Victorian Cupid, ivory IBO-409	Open		15.00	20
1995	Winter's Light IBO-455	Open		32.00	32

VickiLane

Sweet Thumpins - V. Anderson

1994	Secrets Out	Yr.Iss.		15.00	15

Wallace Silversmiths

24K Goldplate Sculptures - Wallace

1988	Angel	Closed	1988	15.99	16
1988	Candy Cane	Closed	1988	15.99	16
1993	Carousel	Closed	1993	10.00	16
1988	Christmas Tree	Closed	1988	15.99	16
1993	Dove	Closed	1993	10.00	10
1988	Dove	Closed	1988	15.99	16
1994	Mother & Child	Closed	1994	16.00	16
1988	Nativity Scene	Closed	1988	15.99	16
1994	Peace Dove	Closed	1994	16.00	16
1993	Ringing Bells	Closed	1993	10.00	10
1988	Snowflake	Closed	1988	15.99	16
1993	Stocking	Closed	1993	10.00	10
1993	Tree	Closed	1993	10.00	10
1993	Wreath	Closed	1993	10.00	10

Annual Pewter Bells - Wallace

1992	Angel	Closed	1992	25.00	30
1993	Santa Holding List	Closed	1993	25.00	25
1994	Large Santa Bell	Closed	1994	25.00	25
1995	Santa Bell	Yr.Iss.		25.00	25

Annual Silverplated Sleigh Bells - Wallace

1971	1st Edition Sleigh Bell	Closed	1971	12.95	1000
1972	2nd Edition Sleigh Bell	Closed	1972	12.95	400-500
1973	3rd Edition Sleigh Bell	Closed	1973	12.95	400-500
1974	4th Edition Sleigh Bell	Closed	1974	13.95	100-200
1975	5th Edition Sleigh Bell	Closed	1975	13.95	100-250
1976	6th Edition Sleigh Bell	Closed	1976	13.95	100-250
1977	7th Edition Sleigh Bell	Closed	1977	14.95	50-100
1978	8th Edition Sleigh Bell	Closed	1978	14.95	40-85
1979	9th Edition Sleigh Bell	Closed	1979	15.95	100-150
1980	10th Edition Sleigh Bell	Closed	1980	18.95	30-50
1981	11th Edition Sleigh Bell	Closed	1981	18.95	80
1982	12th Edition Sleigh Bell	Closed	1982	19.95	80-100
1983	13th Edition Sleigh Bell	Closed	1983	19.95	75-100
1984	14th Edition Sleigh Bell	Closed	1984	21.95	80
1985	15th Edition Sleigh Bell	Closed	1985	21.95	75-100
1986	16th Edition Sleigh Bell	Closed	1986	21.95	35
1987	17th Edition Sleigh Bell	Closed	1987	21.99	30
1988	18th Edition Sleigh Bell	Closed	1988	21.99	30
1989	19th Edition Sleigh Bell	Closed	1989	24.99	25
1990	20th Edition Sleigh Bell	Closed	1990	25.00	25
1990	Special Edition Sleigh Bell, gold	Closed	1990	35.00	70
1991	21st Edition Sleigh Bell	Closed	1991	25.00	25
1992	22nd Edition Sleigh Bell	Closed	1992	25.00	35
1993	23rd Edition Sleigh Bell	Closed	1993	25.00	25
1994	24th Edition Sleigh Bell	Closed	1994	25.00	25
1994	Sleigh Bell, gold	Closed	1994	35.00	35
1995	25th Edition Sleigh Bell	Closed	1995	30.00	30
1995	Sleigh Bell, gold	Closed	1995	35.00	35

Candy Canes - Wallace

1981	Peppermint	Closed	1981	8.95	100-225
1982	Wintergreen	Closed	1982	9.95	30-60
1983	Cinnamon	Closed	1983	10.95	30-50
1984	Clove	Closed	1984	10.95	30-50
1985	Dove Motif	Closed	1985	11.95	30-50
1986	Bell Motif	Closed	1986	11.95	30-80
1987	Teddy Bear Motif	Closed	1987	12.95	30-50
1988	Christmas Rose	Closed	1988	13.99	30-45
1989	Christmas Candle	Closed	1989	14.99	35
1990	Reindeer	Closed	1990	16.00	20
1991	Christmas Goose	Closed	1991	16.00	20
1992	Angel	Closed	1992	16.00	20
1993	Snowmen	Closed	1993	16.00	16
1994	Canes	Closed	1994	17.00	17
1995	Santa	Closed	1995	18.00	18

Cathedral Ornaments - Wallace

1988	1988-1st Edition	Closed	1988	24.99	30-60
1989	1989-2nd Edition	Closed	1989	24.99	25-55
1990	1990-3rd Edition	Closed	1990	25.00	25-50

Grand Baroque Bells - Wallace

1995	Grand Baroque Bell	Yr.Iss.		25.00	25

Grande Baroque 12 Day Series - Wallace

1988	Partridge	Closed	1988	39.99	60-100
1989	Two Turtle Doves	Closed	1989	39.99	60-150
1990	Three French Hens	Closed	1990	40.00	50-100
1991	Four Colly Birds	Closed	1991	40.00	60-125
1992	Five Golden Rings	Closed	1992	40.00	40-60
1993	Six Geese-a-Laying	Closed	1993	40.00	40
1994	Seven Swans-a-Swimming	Open	1994	40.00	40
1995	Eight Maids-a-Milking	Open		40.00	40

Pewter Ornaments - Wallace

1989	Angel with Candles	Closed	1989	9.99	10
XX	Candy Cane	Closed	N/A	9.99	10
1989	Cherub with Horn	Closed	1989	9.99	10
1993	Christmas Tree	Closed	1993	10.00	10
XX	Dove	Closed	N/A	9.99	10
XX	Gingerbread House	Closed	N/A	9.99	10
XX	Rocking Horse	Closed	N/A	9.99	10
1989	Santa	Closed	1989	9.99	10
1994	Santa	Closed	1994	10.00	10
1994	Snowman	Closed	1994	10.00	10
1993	Stocking	Closed	1993	10.00	10
1994	Teddy Bear	Closed	1994	10.00	10
XX	Teddy Bear	Closed	N/A	9.99	10
1989	Teddy Bear	Closed	1989	9.99	10
1994	Toy Soldier	Closed	1994	10.00	10
XX	Toy Soldier	Closed	N/A	9.99	10
1994	Train	Closed	1994	10.00	10
1989	Wreath	Closed	1989	9.99	10
1993	Wreath	Closed	1993	10.00	10

Walt Disney

Classics Collection-Holiday Series - Disney Studios

1995	Presents For My Pals 41087	12/95		50.00	50

Waterford Wedgwood USA

Waterford Crystal Christmas Ornaments - Waterford

1978	1978 Ornament	Annual		25.00	105
1979	1979 Ornament	Annual		28.00	80
1980	1980 Ornament	Annual		28.00	60
1981	1981 Ornament	Annual		28.00	45
1982	1982 Ornament	Annual		28.00	50
1983	1983 Ornament	Annual		28.00	50
1984	1984 Ornament	Annual		28.00	50
1985	1985 Ornament	Annual		28.00	80
1986	1986 Ornament	Annual		28.00	50
1987	1987 Ornament	Annual		29.00	40
1988	1988 Ornament	Annual		30.00	40
1989	1989 Ornament	Annual		32.00	40

DOLLS

Annalee Mobilitee Dolls, Inc.

Doll Society-Animals - A. Thorndike

1985	10" Penguin and Chick	3,000	N/A	29.95	225
1986	10" Unicorn	3,000	N/A	36.95	350
1987	7" Kangaroo	3,000	N/A	37.45	450
1988	5" Owl	3,000	N/A	37.45	300
1989	7" Polar Bear	3,000	N/A	37.50	300
1990	10" Thorndike Chicken	3,000	N/A	37.50	275

Doll Society-Folk Heroes - A. Thorndike

1984	10" Johnny Appleseed	1,500	N/A	80.00	1000
1984	10" Robin Hood	1,500	N/A	90.00	850
1985	10" Annie Oakley	1,500	N/A	95.00	700
1986	10" Mark Twain	2,500	N/A	117.50	500
1987	10" Ben Franklin	2,500	N/A	119.50	525
1988	10" Sherlock Holmes	2,500	N/A	119.50	500
1989	10" Abraham Lincoln	2,500	N/A	119.50	500
1990	10" Betsy Ross	2,500	N/A	119.50	450
1991	10" Christopher Columbus	1,132	N/A	119.50	300
1992	10" Uncle Sam	1,034	N/A	87.50	N/A
1993	10" Pony Express Rider	Yr.Iss.	N/A	97.50	N/A
1994	10" Bean Nose Santa	Yr.Iss.	1994	119.50	N/A
1995	10" Pocahontas	Yr.Iss.		87.50	88

Doll Society-Logo Kids - A. Thorndike

1985	Christmas Logo w/Cookie	3,562	1986	N/A	675
1986	Sweetheart Logo	6,271	1987	N/A	275
1987	Naughty Logo	1,100	1988	N/A	425
1988	Raincoat Logo	13,646	1989	N/A	200
1989	Christmas Morning Logo	16,641	1990	N/A	150
1990	Clown	20,049	1991	N/A	150
1991	Reading Logo	26,516	1992	N/A	125
1992	Back to School Logo	17,524	1993	N/A	90
1993	Ice Cream Logo	Yr.Iss.	1994	N/A	N/A
1994	Dress Up Santa Logo	Yr.Iss	1995	N/A	N/A
1995	Goin' Fishin' Logo	Yr.Iss		29.95	30

Assorted Dolls - A. Thorndike

1987	3" Baby Witch	3,645	1987	13.95	275
1987	3" Bride and Groom	1,053	1987	38.95	375
1983	3" PJ Kid (designer series)	2,360	1983	10.95	200
1971	3" Reindeer Head	N/A	1976	1.00	200
1991	3" Water Baby in Pond Lily	3,720	1991	14.95	175
1984	5" E.P. Boy Bunny	2,583	1984	11.95	200
1984	5" E.P. Girl Bunny	2,790	1984	11.95	200
1983	5" Easter Parade Girl Bunny w/ Music Box	1,167	1983	29.95	400
1963	5" Elf (Lilac)	N/A	1963	2.50	325
1959	5" Man (Special Order)	N/A	1959	N/A	1525
1960	5" Wee Skis	N/A	N/A	3.95	325
1978	7" Airplane Pilot Mouse	2,308	1981	6.95	425
1964	7" Angel in a Blanket	N/A	1964	2.45	325
1984	7" Angel on Star	772	1984	32.95	475
1983	7" Angel w/ Musical Instrument on Music Box	N/A	1983	29.95	425
1960	7" Angel w/ Paper Wings	N/A	1966	N/A	400
1970	7" Artist Mouse	298	1974	3.95	400
1950	7" Baby Angel	N/A	1950	2.45	1650
1960	7" Baby Angel (yellow feather hair)	N/A	1962	N/A	350
1962	7" Baby Angel on Cloud	N/A	1963	2.45	500-700
1980	7" Baby in Bassinet	12,215	1983	13.95	275
1968	7" Baby in Christmas Bag	N/A	1968	2.95	350
1968	7" Baby in Santa's Hat	N/A	1969	2.95	500
1971	7" Baby w/ Bottle	N/A	1971	N/A	300
1979	7" Ballerina	4,700	1979	7.45	275
1967	7" Ballerina Mouse	N/A	1968	3.95	450
1980	7" Ballooning Santa	N/A	1983	49.95	350
1970	7" Bartender Mouse	289	1973	3.95	400
1987	7" BBQ Mouse	1,798	1987	17.95	300
1974	7" Black Santa w/ Oversized Bag	1,638	1975	5.45	550
1977	7" Boating Mouse	1,186	1977	5.95	175
1964	7" Boudoir Puff Baby Angel	N/A	1965	3.95	400
1984	7" Boy w/ Firecracker	1,893	1984	19.95	400
1966	7" Bride & Groom Mice	N/A	1966	3.95	600
1970	7" Bunny (yellow)	3,215	1973	3.95	375
1987	7" Bunny in 10" Carrot Balloon	624	1987	49.95	375
1974	7" Camper in Tent Mouse	468	1974	5.45	325
1968	7" Caroller Boy Mouse w/ Music	N/A	1969	4.45	400
1974	7" Carpenter Mouse	2,687	1978	5.45	275
1978	7" Carpenter Mouse	1,494	1978	6.95	350
1970	7" Christmas Baby on Hat Box	1,894	1971	2.95	350
1965	7" Christmas Dumb Bunny	N/A	1965	3.95	775
1975	7" Christmas Mouse in Santa Mitten	3,959	1976	5.45	375
1977	7" Christmas Mouse in Santa's Mitten	15,916	1979	7.95	175
1975	7" Colonial Boy Mouse	12,739	1976	5.45	350
1975	7" Colonial Girl Mouse	9,338	1976	5.45	350
1965	7" Colored Mouse (Peek)	N/A	1965	3.95	550
1982	7" Cowboy Mouse	3,776	1983	12.95	300
1982	7" Cowgirl Mouse	3,116	1983	12.95	300
1984	7" Cupid in Hanging Heart	2,445	1985	32.95	375
1984	7" Dentist Mouse	2,362	1985	14.95	400
1992	7" Disney Kid	300	1992	59.95	400
1985	7" Dress-Up Boy	1,174	1985	18.95	225
1985	7" Dress-Up Girl	1,536	1985	18.95	225
1993	7" Eric & Shane Boating in Hawaii	100	1993	105.00	750
1979	7" Fishing Mouse	N/A	1979	7.95	275
1972	7" Football Mouse	744	1974	3.95	300
1991	7" Fun in the Sun Kid	300	1991	80.00	300
1962	7" Furcapped Baby	N/A	1962	2.45	400
1967	7" Garden Club Baby	N/A	1969	2.95	575
1979	7" Gardener Mouse	1,939	1980	7.95	325
1974	7" Gardener Mouse	485	1980	5.45	400
1992	7" Gnome w/ Mushroom	1,691	1992	35.95	350
1967	7" Gnome w/ Pajama Suit	N/A	1970	2.95	375
1965	7" Gnome w/ Vest	N/A	1965	2.45	675
1965	7" Hangover Mouse	N/A	1987	3.95	375
1987	7" Hangover Mouse	1,548	1987	13.95	175
1977	7" Hobo Mouse	1,004	1977	5.95	275
1980	7" Hockey Mouse	2,477	1981	9.95	300
1985	7" Hockey Player Kid	1,578	1985	18.95	400
1974	7" Hunter Mouse w/ Bird	690	1975	5.45	325
1981	7" I'm Late Bunny	100	1981	N/A	475
1985	7" Kid w/ Kite	1,084	1985	17.95	300
1965	7" Lawyer Mouse	N/A	1965	3.95	350
1965	7" M/M Indoor Santa	N/A	1966	5.95	500
1970	7" M/M Santa on Ski Bob	N/A	1970	5.95	600
1983	7" M/M Santa w/ Basket	5,105	1983	25.95	300
1959	7" Man (special order)	N/A	1959	N/A	1200
1993	7" Mississippi Levee Mouse	341	1993	N/A	400
1982	7" Mouse w/ Strawberry	10,267	1985	12.95	175
1970	7" Mr. Holly Mouse	1,726	1970	3.95	225
1977	7" Mr. Santa Mouse	7,197	1979	6.00	300
1967	7" Mrs. Holly Mouse	N/A	1976	3.95	350

YEAR ISSUE		EDITION LIMIT	YEAR RETD.	ISSUE PRICE	QUOTE U.S.$
1967	7" Mrs. Santa w/ Fur-Trimmed Cape	N/A	1973	2.95	450
1971	7" Naughty Angel	12,359	1971	10.95	275
1976	7" Needlework Mouse	3,566	1978	6.95	400
1968	7" Patches Pam	N/A	1968	2.95	850
1979	7" Quilting Mouse	213	1979	N/A	375
1991	7" Santa in Tub w/ Rubber Duckie	5,373	1991	33.95	200
1971	7" Santa Mailman	8,296	1974	5.50	375
1972	7" Santa on Ski-Bob w/ Oversized Bag	7,590	1974	7.95	400
1978	7" Santa w/ 10" Reindeer Trimming Christmas Tree	1,621	1978	18.45	425
1963	7" Santa w/ Fur Trimmed Suit	N/A	1967	2.95	400
1969	7" Santa w/ Oversized Bag	N/A	1970	3.95	350
1971	7" Santa w/ Skis and Poles	N/A	1978	5.45	300
1989	7" Science Center Mouse	500	1989	75.00	525
1972	7" Secretary Mouse	727	1974	3.95	500
1970	7" Sherriff Mouse	11	1970	3.95	650
1991	7" Sherriff Mouse #92	1,191	1992	49.50	700
1965	7" Singing Mouse	N/A	1965	3.95	450
1979	7" Skateboard Mouse	1,821	1979	7.95	275
1976	7" Ski Mouse	10,375	1981	6.95	225
1974	7" Sloppy Painter Mouse	349	1974	5.45	550
1971	7" Swimmer Mouse w/ Inner Tube	267	1971	3.95	325
1967	7" Tuckered Mr. & Mrs. Santa Water Bottle	N/A	1969	5.95	400
1973	7" Vacationer Girl Mouse	1,017	1974	4.45	325
1986	7" Witch Mouse w/ Pumpkin Balloon	868	1987	59.95	300
1982	7" Wood Chopper Mouse	1,910	1982	11.95	375
1992	7" Workshop Mouse	6,618	1992	21.95	350
1971	7" Yachtsman Mouse w/ Binnacle	249	1974	3.95	400
1966	7" Yum Yum Bunny	N/A	1966	3.95	700
1968	8" Elephant (Tubby)	N/A	1969	4.95	450
1980	8" Girl BBQ Pig	3,854	1981	9.95	175
1975	8" Lamb	234	1975	8.95	450
1977	8" Rooster	1,642	1977	5.95	350
1959	10" 4th of July Doll	N/A	1959	N/A	1525
1991	10" Aviator Frog w/ Flag	2,110	1991	19.95	425
1957	10" Baby Angel	N/A	1958	8.95	525
1963	10" Ballerina	N/A	1963	5.95	1350
1980	10" Balloon w/ Two 10" Frogs	837	1980	49.95	850
1968	10" Bather (Skinny Minnie w/ Towel)	N/A	1968	5.95	950
1966	10" Bathersome Chick w/ Flippers	N/A	1966	5.95	650
1959	10" Bathing Girl	N/A	1959	7.95	850
1957	10" Bathing Girl	N/A	1957	N/A	1300
1989	10" BBQ Pig	2,471	1989	27.95	325
1964	10" Black (Monk)	N/A	1965	2.95	375
1994	10" Boston Bruins Hockey Player (Signed by team)	2	1994	N/A	500
1966	10" Boy & Girl on Tandem Bike	N/A	1966	20.95	1350
1956	10" Boy Building Boat	N/A	1969	N/A	1550
1950	10" Boy Building Boat	N/A		9.95	1200
1976	10" Boy in Tire Swing	358	1976	6.95	350
1965	10" Boy on Bike	N/A	1965	N/A	600
1980	10" Boy on Raft	1,087	1981	28.95	325
1969	10" Bride & Groom Set	N/A	1969	11.95	800
1967	10" Brown Nun	N/A	1967	2.95	375
1950	10" Calypso Dancer	N/A	1950	N/A	1350
1967	10" Carnaby Street Boy	N/A	1967	3.95	400
1987	10" Carrot Balloon w / 7" Bunny in Basket	624	1987	49.95	500
1970	10" Casualty Ski Elf w/ Crutch & Leg in Cast	2,818	1972	4.50	600
1967	10" Choir Boy (set/3)	N/A	1967	2.95	725
1950	10" Christmas Girl	N/A	1957	N/A	2350
1987	10" Clown	2,699	1987	17.95	425
1971	10" Clown (black & white)	N/A	1971	2.00	300
1969	10" Clown (bright stripes)	N/A	1971	3.95	350
1969	10" Clown (pink w/green polka dots)	N/A	1969	3.95	525
1971	10" Clown w/ Mushroom	45	1971	7.95	850
1975	10" Colonial Drummer Boy	1,846	1976	5.95	375
1989	10" Country Boy Pig	2,566	1989	25.95	175
1989	10" Country Girl Pig	2,367	1989	25.95	175
1982	10" Cyrano de Bergerac	35	1982	N/A	2300
1972	10" Democratic Donkey	861	1972	3.95	450
1960	10" Elf	N/A	1966	N/A	400
1963	10" Elf	N/A	1963	N/A	350
1950	10" Elf	N/A	N/A	N/A	900
1954	10" Elf w/ Cap	N/A	1954	N/A	1150
1978	10" Elf w/ Planter	1,978	1978	6.95	275
1967	10" Elf w/ Skis and Poles	48	1971	2.95	425-900
1959	10" Fisherman & Girl in Boat	N/A	1959	N/A	2550
1963	10" Friar	N/A	1963	2.95	500
1959	10" Girl and Boy on Tandem Bike	N/A	1959	20.95	2200
1965	10" Girl on Bike	N/A	1965	N/A	600
1966	10" Go-Go Boy	N/A	1966	3.95	350
1967	10" Golfer Boy	N/A	1968	5.95	925
1965	10" Golfer Boy Doll	N/A	1965	9.95	700
1966	10" Golfer-Girl Putter	N/A	1968	5.95	925
1957	10" Halloween Girl	N/A	1959	9.95	3200
1965	10" Hiking Doll	N/A	1965	9.95	750
1987	10" Huck Finn (#62)	800	1988	102.95	700
1991	10" Husky w/ 5" Puppy in Dog Sled	2,860	1991	54.95	350
1960	10" Impski	N/A	1966	3.95	500
1960	10" Impski (red)	N/A	1966	3.95	325
1960	10" Impski (white)	N/A	1966	3.95	350
1982	10" Jack Frost Elf w/ 10" Snowflake	N/A	1982	13.50	150
1981	10" Jack Frost Elf w/ 5" Snowflake	5,950	1981	31.95	325
1974	10" Leprechaun w/ Sack	8,834	1974	5.45	350
1959	10" Man (special Order)	N/A	1959	N/A	1400
1964	10" Monk (red robe)	N/A	1965	2.95	800
1965	10" Monk w/ Christmas Tree Planting	N/A	1967	2.95	450
1967	10" Monk w/ Jug	N/A	1969	2.95	375
1970	10" Monk w/ Skis and Poles	1,386	1972	3.95	350
1970	10" Mushroom w/ 7" Santa	1,535	1971	7.95	250
1967	10" Nun (green)	N/A	1967	42.95	700
1994	10" Piper Bear	200	1994	130.00	650
1974	10" Polly Frog Spring Cleaning	580	1974	5.50	325
1965	10" Reindeer	N/A	1965	4.95	425
1975	10" Reindeer w/ 7" Santa	2,429	1976	10.50	400
1964	10" Robin Hood Elf	N/A	1965	2.50	500
1988	10" Scrooge Head	N/A	1988	N/A	325
1984	10" Shriner (special order)	1,000	1984	N/A	875
1987	10" Sitting Frog w/Instrument	2,162	1987	19.95	525
1987	10" Ski Elf	N/A	1987	19.95	350
1971	10" Ski Elf	1,262	1971	3.95	275
1956	10" Skier Girl w/ Broken Leg in Cast	N/A	1957	14.95	1550
1990	10" Spirit of '76	1,080	1990	175.00	550
1965	10" Spring Elf	N/A	1965	2.50	375
1954	10" Spring Girl	N/A	1954	N/A	2350
1957	10" Square Dancer (Girl)	N/A	1959	9.95	900
1950	10" Square Dancers (Boy and Girl)	N/A	1959	9.95	2100
1956	10" Square Dancers (set/8)	N/A	1956	59.95	5200
1987	10" State Trooper (#642)	511	1988	134.00	500
1991	10" Summer Santa #1663	1,926	1991	59.95	425
1967	10" Surfer Boy	N/A	1968	5.95	525
1967	10" Surfer Girl	N/A	1968	5.95	625
1989	10" Three Bunnies w/ Maypole	647	1989	190.00	600
1976	10" Uncle Sam	1,095	1976	5.95	500
1957	10" Valentine Doll	N/A	1957	9.95	1800
1991	10" Victory Ski Doll	1,192	1991	49.50	350
1959	10" Wood Sprite	N/A	1967	N/A	750
1966	10" Workshop Elf	N/A	1966	N/A	425
1976	12" Angel	13,338	1979	10.95	350
1960	12" Baby in Green	N/A	1960	N/A	550
1992	12" Bat	2,107	1992	31.95	225
1965	12" Christmas Bonnet Lady Mouse	N/A	1965	9.95	400
1990	12" Easter Parade Duck w/ Watering Can	2,891	1990	49.95	300
1968	12" Gnome w/ Gay Apron	N/A	1968	5.95	900
1968	12" Laura May Cat	N/A	1971	7.95	900
1981	12" Monkey Boy w/ Banana	N/A	1971	23.95	225
1970	12" Mr. Santa Mouse w/ Toybag	N/A	1971	10.95	525
1967	12" Mrs. Santa w/ Muff	N/A	1969	9.95	550
1968	12" Myrtle Turtle	N/A	1969	6.95	2600
1969	12" Myrtle Turtle	N/A	1969	6.95	800
1969	12" Nightshirt Boy Mouse	N/A	1976	9.95	550
1957	12" Santa	N/A	1957	N/A	925
1954	12" Santa (Bean Nose)	N/A	1957	19.95	1000
1990	12" Santa Duck	506	1991	49.95	300
1967	12" Sneaky Peaky Boy Cat	N/A	1967	6.95	375
1967	12" Yum-Yum Bunny	N/A	1968	9.95	850
1980	14" Dragon w/ Bush Boy	2,130	1982	32.95	300
1955	14" Fireman	N/A	1955	N/A	4750
1990	15" Christmas Dragon	448	1990	49.95	400
1970	16" Christmas Wreath w/ Santa Head	1,662	1974	9.95	375
1972	16" Democratic Donkey	219	1972	12.95	1600
1972	16" Elephant (Republican)	230	1972	12.95	800
1984	18" Aerobic Girl	622	1984	35.95	375
1988	18" Americana Couple #82	7,258	1988	169.95	700
1990	18" Angel w/ Instrument	398	1990	51.95	325
1978	18" Artist Bunny w/ Brush & Palette	2,023	1979	14.00	300
1985	18" Ballerina Bear	918	1985	39.95	275
1980	18" Ballerina Bunny	7,069	1982	27.95	425
1979	18" Ballerina Bunny	2,315	1982	15.95	450
1985	18" Bear w/ Honey Pot & Bee	2,032	1986	41.50	600
1974	18" Bell Hop (special order)	3	1974	N/A	1000
1977	18" Boy Bunny w/Carrot	1,159	1977	13.50	250
1979	18" Boy Frog	3,524	1981	22.95	175
1981	18" Butterfly w/ 10" Elf	2,507	1982	27.95	500
1972	18" Candy Kid Boy	4,350	1973	11.95	775
1972	18" Candy Kid Girl	4,350	1973	11.95	775
1975	18" Caroller Boy	1,024	1975	12.00	400
1973	18" Christmas Panda	437	1973	10.50	600
1975	18" Clown	166	1975	N/A	450
1983	18" Country Girl Bunny w/ Basket	2,905	1983	29.95	400
1984	18" E.P. Girl Bunny	2,952	1984	35.95	350
1976	18" Elephant "Vote '76"	806	1976	8.50	500
1984	18" Fawn w/ Wreath	2,080	1984	32.95	375
1979	18" Girl Frog	3,677	1981	22.95	175
1979	18" Gnome	15,851	1980	19.95	200
1975	18" Horse	221	1976	16.95	375
1968	18" Mrs. Santa w/ Boudoir Cap & Apron	N/A	1968	7.45	250
1968	18" Mrs. Santa w/ Hot Water Bottle	N/A	1968	7.45	525
1990	18" Naughty Kid	1,454	1991	69.95	525
1978	18" Pilgrim Boy	1,213	1978	14.95	275
1964	18" PJ Kid	N/A	1964	6.95	500
1980	18" Santa Frog w/ Toybag	2,126	1980	24.95	450
1971	18" Santa Fur Kid	1,191	1972	7.45	250
1964	18" Santa Kid	N/A	1965	6.95	450
1990	18" Santa Playing w/ Electric Train	168	1990	119.00	350
1987	18" Special Mrs. Santa (special order)	341	1987	N/A	400
1976	18" Uncle Sam	345	1976	16.95	500
1987	18" Workshop Santa (special order)	1,001	1987	N/A	450
1975	18" Yankee Doodle Dandy w/ 18" Horse	437	1976	28.95	900
1981	22" Christmas Giraffe w/ 10" Elf	1,377	1982	36.95	500
1974	22" Christmas Stocking	8,536	1974	4.95	150
1974	22" Leprchaun	199	1974	11.45	650
1970	22" Monkey (chartreuse)	70	1970	10.95	725
1990	22" Spring Elf (yellow)	1,636	1990	34.95	325
1981	22" Sun Mobile	3,003	1985	36.95	475
1954	26" Elf	N/A	1956	9.95	550
1963	26" Friar	N/A	1963	14.95	2500
1979	29" Artist Bunny w/ Brush & Palette	179	1979	42.95	350
1974	29" Bell Hop (special order)	3	1974	29.00	1200
1978	29" Caroller Mouse	658	1978	49.95	775
1976	29" Clown (blue w/ white polka dots)	466	1976	29.95	925
1981	29" Dragon w/ 12 Bush Boy	151	1982	69.95	700
1960	29" Fur Trim Santa	N/A	1979	N/A	1000
1971	29" M/M Tuckered w/ 2 18" Kids	811	1972	51.95	800
1974	29" Motorized See-Saw Bunny Set	43	1975	250.00	1600
1977	29" Mr. Santa Mouse w/ Sack	704	1977	49.95	800
1968	29" Mrs. Indoor Santa	N/A	1968	16.95	475
1977	29" Mrs. Santa Mouse w/ Muff	571	1977	49.95	800
1972	29" Mrs. Snow Woman w/ Cardholder Skirt	331	1972	19.95	700
1990	30" Clown	530	1990	99.95	350
1984	30" Santa in Chair w/ 2 18" Kids	940	1984	169.95	1200
1984	30" Snowgirl w/ Muff	685	1984	79.50	1000
1959	33" Boy & Girl on Tandem Bike	N/A	1959	N/A	4500
1960	36" PJ Kid	N/A	1960	N/A	1200
1980	42" Clown	224	1980	74.95	700
1977	42" Scarecrow	365	1978	61.95	2050
1986	48" Velour Santa	410	1988	269.95	750
1963	Baby Angel Head w/ Santa Hat	N/A	1963	1.00	350
1963	Bath Puff (yellow)	N/A	1965	1.95	325
1968	Bunny Head Pin On	N/A	1968	1.00	400
1950	Cellist	N/A	N/A	N/A	5250
1976	Colonial Boy Head Pin On	N/A	1976	1.50	275
1976	Colonial Girl Head Pin On	N/A	1976	1.50	275
1972	Donkey Head Pin On	1,371	1972	1.00	300
1972	Elephant Head Pin On	1,384	1972	1.00	325
1960	Head Pin	N/A	N/A	N/A	200
1968	Hippy Head (Boy)	N/A	1969	1.00	350
1968	Hippy Head (Girl)	N/A	1969	1.00	350
1960	Man Head Pin-on	N/A	N/A	N/A	800
1970	Monkey Head Pin-on (boy)	153	1973	1.00	275
1970	Monkey Head Pin-on (girl)	153	1973	1.00	275
1971	Monkey Head Pin-on (hot pink)	N/A	1971	1.00	450
1960	Mouse Head Pin-On	N/A	1976	1.00	250
1971	Snowman Head Pin-on	4,040	1972	1.00	200
1971	Snowman Kid	1,374	1971	3.95	450
1985	Tree Skirt	1,332	1985	24.95	350
1989	Two Bunnies on Flexible Flyer Sled	4,104	1990	52.95	325

ANRI

Disney Dolls - Disney Studios

1990	Daisy Duck, 14"	2,500	1991	895.00	895
1990	Donald Duck, 14"	2,500	1991	895.00	895
1989	Mickey Mouse, 14"	2,500	1991	850.00	895
1989	Minnie Mouse, 14"	2,500	1991	850.00	895
1989	Pinocchio, 14"	2,500	1991	850.00	895

Ferrandiz Dolls - J. Ferrandiz

1991	Carmen, 14"	1,000	1992	730.00	730
1991	Fernando, 14"	1,000	1992	730.00	730
1989	Gabriel, 14"	1,000	1991	550.00	575
1991	Juanita, 7"	1,500	1992	300.00	300
1990	Margarite, 14"	1,000	1992	575.00	730
1989	Maria, 14"	1,000	1991	550.00	575
1991	Miguel, 7"	1,500	1992	300.00	300
1990	Philipe, 14"	1,000	1992	575.00	680

Sarah Kay Dolls - S. Kay

1991	Annie, 7"	1,500	1993	300.00	300
1989	Bride to Love And To Cherish	750	1992	750.00	790
1989	Charlotte (Blue)	1,000	1991	550.00	575
1990	Christina, 14"	1,000	1993	575.00	730
1989	Eleanor (Floral)	1,000	1991	550.00	575
1989	Elizabeth (Patchwork)	1,000	1991	550.00	575
1988	Emily, 14"	Closed	1989	500.00	500
1990	Faith, 14"	1,000	1993	575.00	685
1989	Groom With This Ring Doll	750	1992	550.00	730
1989	Helen (Brown)	1,000	1991	550.00	575
1989	Henry	1,000	1991	550.00	575
1991	Janine, 14"	1,000	1993	750.00	750
1988	Jennifer, 14"	Closed	1989	500.00	500
1991	Jessica, 7"	1,500	1993	300.00	300
1991	Julie, 7"	1,500	1993	300.00	300
1988	Katherine, 14"	Closed	1989	500.00	500
1988	Martha, 14"	Closed	1989	500.00	500
1989	Mary (Red)	1,000	1991	550.00	575
1991	Michelle, 7"	1,500	1993	300.00	300

YEAR ISSUE		EDITION LIMIT	YEAR RETD.	ISSUE PRICE	QUOTE U.S.$
1991	Patricia, 14"	1,000	1993	730.00	730
1991	Peggy, 7"	1,500	1993	300.00	300
1990	Polly, 14"	1,000	1993	575.00	680
1988	Rachael, 14"	Closed	1989	500.00	500
1988	Rebecca, 14"	Closed	1989	500.00	500
1988	Sarah, 14"	Closed	1989	500.00	500
1990	Sophie, 14"	1,000	1993	575.00	660
1991	Susan, 7"	1,500	1993	300.00	300
1988	Victoria, 14"	Closed	1989	500.00	500

Ashton-Drake Galleries

All I Wish For You - Good-Kruger

YEAR ISSUE		EDITION LIMIT	YEAR RETD.	ISSUE PRICE	QUOTE U.S.$
1994	I Wish You Love	12/95		79.95	80

America the Beautiful - Y. Bello

YEAR ISSUE		EDITION LIMIT	YEAR RETD.	ISSUE PRICE	QUOTE U.S.$
1995	Billy	12/96		49.95	50
1995	Bobby	12/96		49.95	50

The American Dream - J. Kovacik

YEAR ISSUE		EDITION LIMIT	YEAR RETD.	ISSUE PRICE	QUOTE U.S.$
1994	Patience	12/95		79.95	80
1994	Hope	12/95		79.95	80

Amish Blessings - J. Good-Kruger

YEAR ISSUE		EDITION LIMIT	YEAR RETD.	ISSUE PRICE	QUOTE U.S.$
1990	Rebeccah	Closed	1993	68.00	100-175
1991	Rachel	Closed	1993	69.00	125-195
1991	Adam	Closed	1993	75.00	175-200
1992	Ruth	Closed	1993	75.00	100-150
1992	Eli	Closed	1993	79.95	100-150
1993	Sarah	Closed	1994	79.95	100-150

Amish Inspirations - J. Ibarolle

YEAR ISSUE		EDITION LIMIT	YEAR RETD.	ISSUE PRICE	QUOTE U.S.$
1994	Ethan	12/95		69.95	70
1994	Mary	12/95		69.95	70
1995	Seth	12/96		74.95	75
1995	Anna	12/96		74.95	75

As Cute As Can Be - D. Effner

YEAR ISSUE		EDITION LIMIT	YEAR RETD.	ISSUE PRICE	QUOTE U.S.$
1993	Sugar Plum	Closed	1994	49.95	60-100
1994	Puppy Love	12/95		49.95	50
1994	Angel Face	12/95		49.95	50

Baby Book Treasures - K. Barry-Hippensteel

YEAR ISSUE		EDITION LIMIT	YEAR RETD.	ISSUE PRICE	QUOTE U.S.$
1990	Elizabeth's Homecoming	Closed	1993	58.00	58-80
1991	Catherine's Christening	Closed	1994	58.00	58-65
1991	Christopher's First Smile	Closed	1992	63.00	63-100

Baby Talk - Good-Kruger

YEAR ISSUE		EDITION LIMIT	YEAR RETD.	ISSUE PRICE	QUOTE U.S.$
1994	All Gone	Closed	1995	49.95	60-95
1994	Bye-Bye	12/95		49.95	50
1994	Night, Night	12/95		49.95	50

Barely Yours - T. Tomescu

YEAR ISSUE		EDITION LIMIT	YEAR RETD.	ISSUE PRICE	QUOTE U.S.$
1994	Cute as a Button	Closed	1994	69.95	70
1994	Snug as a Bug in a Rug	12/95		75.00	75
1995	Clean as a Whistle	12/96		75.00	75
1995	Pretty as a Picture	12/96		75.00	75
1995	Good as Gold	12/96		75.00	75

Beautiful Dreamers - G. Rademann

YEAR ISSUE		EDITION LIMIT	YEAR RETD.	ISSUE PRICE	QUOTE U.S.$
1992	Katrina	Closed	1993	89.00	115-125
1992	Nicolette	Closed	1994	89.95	90-150
1993	Brigitte	Closed	1994	94.00	100-150
1993	Isabella	Closed	1994	94.00	100-125
1993	Gabrielle	Closed	1994	94.00	100-125

Born To Be Famous - K. Barry-Hippensteel

YEAR ISSUE		EDITION LIMIT	YEAR RETD.	ISSUE PRICE	QUOTE U.S.$
1989	Little Sherlock	Closed	1991	87.00	70-125
1990	Little Florence Nightingale	Closed	1991	87.00	87-100
1991	Little Davey Crockett	Closed	1994	92.00	92-125
1992	Little Christopher Columbus	Closed	1993	95.00	95-150

Calendar Babies - Ashton-Drake

YEAR ISSUE		EDITION LIMIT	YEAR RETD.	ISSUE PRICE	QUOTE U.S.$
1995	New Year	Open		24.95	25
1995	Cupid	Open		24.95	25
1995	Leprechaun	Open		24.95	25
1995	April Showers	Open		24.95	25
1995	May Flowers	Open		24.95	25
1995	June Bride	Open		24.95	25
1995	Uncle Sam	Open		24.95	25
1995	Sun & Fun	Open		24.95	25
1995	Back to School	Open		24.95	25
1995	Happy Haunting	Open		24.95	25
1995	Thanksgiving Turkey	Open		24.95	25
1995	Jolly Santa	Open		24.95	25

Caught In The Act - M. Tretter

YEAR ISSUE		EDITION LIMIT	YEAR RETD.	ISSUE PRICE	QUOTE U.S.$
1992	Stevie, Catch Me If You Can	Closed	1994	49.95	125-160
1993	Kelly, Don't I Look Pretty?	Closed	1994	49.95	99
1994	Mikey (Look It Floats)	Closed	1994	55.00	55-75
1994	Nickie (Cookie Jar)	12/95		59.95	60
1994	Becky (Kleenex Box)	12/95		59.95	60
1994	Sandy	12/95		59.95	60

Children of Christmas - M. Sirko

YEAR ISSUE		EDITION LIMIT	YEAR RETD.	ISSUE PRICE	QUOTE U.S.$
1994	The Little Drummer Boy	12/95		79.95	80
1994	The Littlest Angel	12/95		79.95	80

Children of Mother Goose - Y. Bello

YEAR ISSUE		EDITION LIMIT	YEAR RETD.	ISSUE PRICE	QUOTE U.S.$
1987	Little Bo Peep	Closed	1988	58.00	125-200
1987	Mary Had a Little Lamb	Closed	1989	58.00	125-200
1988	Little Jack Horner	Closed	1989	63.00	115-150
1989	Miss Muffet	Closed	1991	63.00	63-75

Children Of The Sun - M. Severino

YEAR ISSUE		EDITION LIMIT	YEAR RETD.	ISSUE PRICE	QUOTE U.S.$
1993	Little Flower	Closed	1994	69.95	70
1993	Desert Star	12/95		69.95	70

A Children's Circus - J. McClelland

YEAR ISSUE		EDITION LIMIT	YEAR RETD.	ISSUE PRICE	QUOTE U.S.$
1990	Tommy The Clown	Closed	1993	78.00	78
1991	Katie The Tightrope Walker	Closed	1993	78.00	78
1991	Johnnie The Strongman	Closed	1994	83.00	83
1992	Maggie The Animal Trainer	Closed	1994	83.00	83

Christmas Memories - Y. Bello

YEAR ISSUE		EDITION LIMIT	YEAR RETD.	ISSUE PRICE	QUOTE U.S.$
1994	Christopher	12/95		59.95	60
1994	Joshua	12/95		59.95	60
1994	Stephanie	12/95		59.95	60

Cindy's Playhouse Pals - C. McClure

YEAR ISSUE		EDITION LIMIT	YEAR RETD.	ISSUE PRICE	QUOTE U.S.$
1989	Meagan	Closed	1990	87.00	87-100
1989	Shelly	Closed	1993	87.00	87
1990	Ryan	Closed	1993	89.00	89
1991	Samantha	Closed	1993	89.00	89

Classic Brides of The Century - E. Williams

YEAR ISSUE		EDITION LIMIT	YEAR RETD.	ISSUE PRICE	QUOTE U.S.$
1990	Flora, The 1900s Bride	Closed	1993	145.00	145-150
1991	Jennifer, The 1980s Bride	Closed	1992	149.00	150
1993	Kathleen, The 1930s Bride	Closed	1993	149.95	150

Days of the Week - K. Barry-Hippensteel

YEAR ISSUE		EDITION LIMIT	YEAR RETD.	ISSUE PRICE	QUOTE U.S.$
1994	Monday	12/95		49.95	50
1995	Tuesday	12/96		49.95	50
1995	Wednesday	12/96		49.95	50
1995	Thursday	12/96		49.95	50
1995	Friday	12/96		49.95	50
1995	Saturday	12/96		49.95	50
1995	Sunday	12/96		49.95	50

Dianna Effner's Mother Goose - D. Effner

YEAR ISSUE		EDITION LIMIT	YEAR RETD.	ISSUE PRICE	QUOTE U.S.$
1990	Mary, Mary, Quite Contrary	Closed	1992	78.00	200-250
1991	The Little Girl With The Curl (Horrid)	Closed	1992	79.00	150-225
1991	The Little Girl With The Curl (Good)	Closed	1993	79.00	100-175
1992	Little Boy Blue	Closed	1993	85.00	85-115
1993	Snips & Snails	Closed	1994	85.00	125-200
1993	Sugar & Spice	Closed	1994	89.95	125-150
1993	Curly Locks	12/95		89.95	90

Down The Garden Path - P. Coffer

YEAR ISSUE		EDITION LIMIT	YEAR RETD.	ISSUE PRICE	QUOTE U.S.$
1991	Rosemary	Closed	1994	79.00	79
1991	Angelica	Closed	1994	85.00	85
1993	Amanda by the Shore	Closed	1994	89.95	90

Elvis: Lifetime Of A Legend - L. Di Leo

YEAR ISSUE		EDITION LIMIT	YEAR RETD.	ISSUE PRICE	QUOTE U.S.$
1992	'68 Comeback Special	Closed	1994	99.95	100
1994	King of Las Vegas	Closed	1994	99.95	100

European Fairytales - G. Rademann

YEAR ISSUE		EDITION LIMIT	YEAR RETD.	ISSUE PRICE	QUOTE U.S.$
1994	Little Red Riding Hood	12/95		79.95	80
1995	Snow White	12/96		79.95	80

Family Ties - M. Tretter

YEAR ISSUE		EDITION LIMIT	YEAR RETD.	ISSUE PRICE	QUOTE U.S.$
1994	Welcome Home Baby Brother	12/95		79.95	80
1995	Kiss and Make it Better	12/96		89.95	90
1995	Happily Ever Better	12/96		89.95	90

Father's Touch - L. Di Leo

YEAR ISSUE		EDITION LIMIT	YEAR RETD.	ISSUE PRICE	QUOTE U.S.$
1993	2 A.M. Feeding	Closed	1994	99.95	100

From The Heart - T. Menzenbach

YEAR ISSUE		EDITION LIMIT	YEAR RETD.	ISSUE PRICE	QUOTE U.S.$
1992	Carolin	Closed	1994	79.95	95-125
1992	Erik	Closed	1994	79.95	98

From This Day Forward - P. Tumminio

YEAR ISSUE		EDITION LIMIT	YEAR RETD.	ISSUE PRICE	QUOTE U.S.$
1994	Elizabeth	12/95		89.95	90
1995	Betty	12/96		89.95	90
1995	Beth	12/96		89.95	90
1995	Lisa	12/96		89.95	90

Garden of Inspirations - B. Hanson

YEAR ISSUE		EDITION LIMIT	YEAR RETD.	ISSUE PRICE	QUOTE U.S.$
1994	Gathering Violets	12/95		69.95	70
1994	Daisy Chain	12/95		69.95	70
1995	Heart's Bouquet	12/96		74.95	75
1995	Garden Prayer	12/96		74.95	75

Gene - M. Odom

YEAR ISSUE		EDITION LIMIT	YEAR RETD.	ISSUE PRICE	QUOTE U.S.$
1995	Premiere	12/96		69.95	70
1995	Red Venus	12/96		69.95	70
1995	Monaco	12/96		69.95	70

Growing Young Minds - K. Barry-Hippensteel

YEAR ISSUE		EDITION LIMIT	YEAR RETD.	ISSUE PRICE	QUOTE U.S.$
1991	Alex	Closed	1992	79.00	80-120

Happiness Is... - K. Barry-Hippensteel

YEAR ISSUE		EDITION LIMIT	YEAR RETD.	ISSUE PRICE	QUOTE U.S.$
1991	Patricia (My First Tooth)	Closed	1993	69.00	100-145
1992	Crystal (Feeding Myself)	Closed	1994	69.95	95-125
1993	Brittany (Blowing Kisses)	Closed	1993	69.95	95-125
1993	Joy (My First Christmas)	Closed		69.95	70-100
1994	Candy Cane (Holly)	Closed	1993	69.95	70-120
1994	Patrick (My First Playmate)	Closed	1994	69.95	85-125

Happy Thoughts - K. Barry-Hippensteel

YEAR ISSUE		EDITION LIMIT	YEAR RETD.	ISSUE PRICE	QUOTE U.S.$
1994	Laughter is the Best Medicine	12/95		59.95	60

Heavenly Inspirations - C. McClure

YEAR ISSUE		EDITION LIMIT	YEAR RETD.	ISSUE PRICE	QUOTE U.S.$
1992	Every Cloud Has a Silver Lining	Closed	1994	59.95	95-125
1993	Wish Upon A Star	Closed	1994	59.95	95-125
1994	Sweet Dreams	Closed	1994	65.00	65-100
1994	Luck at the End of Rainbow	Closed	1994	65.00	65-100
1994	Sunshine	Closed	1994	69.95	70-110
1994	Pennies From Heaven	12/95		69.95	70

Heritage of American Quilting - J. Lundy

YEAR ISSUE		EDITION LIMIT	YEAR RETD.	ISSUE PRICE	QUOTE U.S.$
1994	Eleanor	12/95		79.95	80
1995	Abigail	12/96		79.95	80
1995	Louisa	12/96		84.95	85
1995	Ruth Anne	12/96		84.95	85

Heroines from the Fairy Tale Forests - D. Effner

YEAR ISSUE		EDITION LIMIT	YEAR RETD.	ISSUE PRICE	QUOTE U.S.$
1988	Little Red Riding Hood	Closed	1990	68.00	200-300
1989	Goldilocks	Closed	1991	68.00	80-150
1990	Snow White	Closed	1992	73.00	150-200
1991	Rapunzel	Closed	1993	79.00	150-200
1992	Cinderella	Closed	1993	79.00	150-200
1993	Cinderella (Ballgown)	Closed	1994	79.95	150-200

How Little Was I? - K. Barry-Hippensteel

YEAR ISSUE		EDITION LIMIT	YEAR RETD.	ISSUE PRICE	QUOTE U.S.$
1995	Brittany	12/96		59.95	60
1995	Claire	12/96		59.95	60

I Want Mommy - K. Barry-Hippensteel

YEAR ISSUE		EDITION LIMIT	YEAR RETD.	ISSUE PRICE	QUOTE U.S.$
1993	Timmy (Mommy I'm Sleepy)	Closed	1994	59.95	175-195
1993	Tommy (Mommy I'm Sorry)	Closed	1994	59.95	125
1994	Up Mommy (Tammy)	Closed	1994	65.00	90-125

I'm Just Little - K. Barry-Hippensteel

YEAR ISSUE		EDITION LIMIT	YEAR RETD.	ISSUE PRICE	QUOTE U.S.$
1995	I'm a Little Angel	12/96		49.95	50
1995	I'm a Little Devil	12/96		49.95	50

International Festival of Toys and Tots - K. Barry-Hippensteel

YEAR ISSUE		EDITION LIMIT	YEAR RETD.	ISSUE PRICE	QUOTE U.S.$
1989	Chen, a Little Boy of China	Closed	1990	78.00	78-125
1989	Natasha	Closed	1992	78.00	78-100
1990	Molly	Closed	1993	83.00	83
1991	Hans	Closed	1993	88.00	88-100
1992	Miki, Eskimo	Closed	1994	88.00	88

Joys of Summer - K. Barry-Hippensteel

YEAR ISSUE		EDITION LIMIT	YEAR RETD.	ISSUE PRICE	QUOTE U.S.$
1993	Tickles	Closed	1994	49.95	70-125
1993	Little Squirt	Closed	1994	49.95	50-100
1994	Yummy	Closed	1994	55.00	55-100
1994	Havin' A Ball	Closed	1994	55.00	55-100
1994	Lil' Scoop	Closed	1994	55.00	55-100

Just Like Me - B. Bambina

YEAR ISSUE		EDITION LIMIT	YEAR RETD.	ISSUE PRICE	QUOTE U.S.$
1995	Amber	12/96		59.95	60
1995	Tiffany	12/96		59.95	60
1995	Carmen	12/96		59.95	60

The King & I - P. Ryan Brooks

YEAR ISSUE		EDITION LIMIT	YEAR RETD.	ISSUE PRICE	QUOTE U.S.$
1991	Shall We Dance?	Closed	1992	175.00	275-395

Lasting Traditions - W. Hanson

YEAR ISSUE		EDITION LIMIT	YEAR RETD.	ISSUE PRICE	QUOTE U.S.$
1993	Something Old	Closed	1993	69.95	70
1994	Finishing Touch	Closed	1994	69.95	70
1994	Mother's Pearls	Closed	1994	85.00	85
1994	Her Traditional Garter	12/95		85.00	85

Lawton's Nursery Rhymes - W. Lawton

YEAR ISSUE		EDITION LIMIT	YEAR RETD.	ISSUE PRICE	QUOTE U.S.$
1994	Little Bo Peep	12/95		79.95	80
1994	Little Miss Muffet	12/95		79.95	80
1994	Mary, Mary	12/95		85.00	85
1994	Mary/Lamb	12/95		85.00	85

The Legends of Baseball - Various

YEAR ISSUE		EDITION LIMIT	YEAR RETD.	ISSUE PRICE	QUOTE U.S.$
1994	Babe Ruth - T. Tomescu	12/95		79.95	80
1994	Lou Gehrig - T. Tomescu	12/95		79.95	80
1995	Ty Cobb - E. Shelton	12/96		79.95	80

Let's Play Mother Goose - K. Barry-Hippensteel

YEAR ISSUE		EDITION LIMIT	YEAR RETD.	ISSUE PRICE	QUOTE U.S.$
1994	Cow Jumped Over the Moon	12/95		69.95	70
1994	Hickory, Dickory, Dock	12/95		69.95	70

Little Bits - G. Rademan

YEAR ISSUE		EDITION LIMIT	YEAR RETD.	ISSUE PRICE	QUOTE U.S.$
1993	Lil Bit of Sunshine	Closed	1993	39.95	40
1993	Lil Bit of Love	Closed	1994	39.95	40
1994	Lil Bit of Tenderness	Closed	1994	39.95	40
1994	Lil Bit of Innocence	Closed	1994	39.95	40

Little Handfuls - M. Severino

YEAR ISSUE		EDITION LIMIT	YEAR RETD.	ISSUE PRICE	QUOTE U.S.$
1993	Ricky	Closed	1994	39.95	40
1993	Abby	12/95		39.95	40
1993	Josie	12/95		39.95	40

Little House On The Prairie - J. Ibarolle

YEAR ISSUE		EDITION LIMIT	YEAR RETD.	ISSUE PRICE	QUOTE U.S.$
1992	Laura	Closed	1993	79.95	90-125
1993	Mary Ingalls	Closed	1993	79.95	200-350
1993	Nellie Olson	Closed	1994	85.00	95-125
1993	Almanzo	Closed	1994	85.00	95-145
1994	Carrie	Closed	1994	85.00	85-100
1994	Ma Ingalls	12/95		85.00	85
1994	Pa Ingalls	12/95		85.00	85

DOLLS

YEAR	ISSUE	EDITION LIMIT	YEAR RETD.	ISSUE PRICE	QUOTE U.S.$
1995	Baby Grace	12/96		85.00	85

Little Women - W. Lawton

YEAR	ISSUE	EDITION LIMIT	YEAR RETD.	ISSUE PRICE	QUOTE U.S.$
1994	Jo	12/95		59.95	60
1994	Meg	12/95		59.95	60
1994	Beth	12/96		59.95	60
1994	Amy	12/96		59.95	60
1995	Marmie	12/96		59.95	60

The Littlest Clowns - M. Tretter

YEAR	ISSUE	EDITION LIMIT	YEAR RETD.	ISSUE PRICE	QUOTE U.S.$
1991	Sparkles	Closed	1992	63.00	63-100
1991	Bubbles	Closed	1992	65.00	65
1991	Smooch	Closed	1992	69.00	69
1992	Daisy	Closed	1993	69.95	70

Look At Me - L. Di Leo

YEAR	ISSUE	EDITION LIMIT	YEAR RETD.	ISSUE PRICE	QUOTE U.S.$
1993	Rose Marie	Closed	1994	49.95	50
1994	Ann Marie	Closed	1994	49.95	50
1994	Lisa Marie	12/95		55.00	55

Lots Of Love - T. Menzenbach

YEAR	ISSUE	EDITION LIMIT	YEAR RETD.	ISSUE PRICE	QUOTE U.S.$
1993	Hannah Needs A Hug	Closed	1994	49.95	50-100
1993	Kaitlyn	Closed	1994	49.95	60-100
1994	Nicole	12/95		49.95	50

Mainstreet Saturday Morning - M. Tretter

YEAR	ISSUE	EDITION LIMIT	YEAR RETD.	ISSUE PRICE	QUOTE U.S.$
1994	Kenny	12/95		69.95	70
1995	Betty	12/96		69.95	70
1995	Donny	12/96		69.95	70

Memories of Yesterday - M. Attwell

YEAR	ISSUE	EDITION LIMIT	YEAR RETD.	ISSUE PRICE	QUOTE U.S.$
1994	A Friend in Need	12/95		59.95	60
1994	Tomorrow is Another Day	12/95		59.95	60
1995	Beauty is in the Eye of the Beholder	12/96		59.95	60

Messages of Hope - T. Tomescu

YEAR	ISSUE	EDITION LIMIT	YEAR RETD.	ISSUE PRICE	QUOTE U.S.$
1994	Let the Little Children Come to Me	12/95		129.95	130
1995	Good Shepherd	12/96		129.95	130
1995	I Stand at the Door	12/96		129.95	130

Moments To Remember - Y. Bello

YEAR	ISSUE	EDITION LIMIT	YEAR RETD.	ISSUE PRICE	QUOTE U.S.$
1991	Justin	Closed	1994	75.00	75-100
1992	Jill	Closed	1993	75.00	95-125
1993	Brandon (Ring Bearer)	Closed	1994	79.95	80-100
1993	Suzanne (Flower Girl)	Closed	1994	79.95	80-100

My Closest Friend - J. Goodyear

YEAR	ISSUE	EDITION LIMIT	YEAR RETD.	ISSUE PRICE	QUOTE U.S.$
1991	Boo Bear 'N Me	Closed	1992	78.00	150-225
1991	Me and My Blankie	Closed	1993	79.00	95-100
1992	My Secret Pal (Robbie)	Closed	1993	85.00	85
1992	My Beary Best Friend	Closed	1993	79.95	80

My Fair Lady - P. Ryan Brooks

YEAR	ISSUE	EDITION LIMIT	YEAR RETD.	ISSUE PRICE	QUOTE U.S.$
1991	Eliza at Ascot	Closed	1992	125.00	200-350

My Heart Belongs To Daddy - J. Singer

YEAR	ISSUE	EDITION LIMIT	YEAR RETD.	ISSUE PRICE	QUOTE U.S.$
1992	Peanut	Closed	1994	49.95	100-125
1992	Pumpkin	Closed	1994	49.95	90
1994	Princess	Closed	1994	59.95	60

My Little Ballerina - K. Barry-Hippensteel

YEAR	ISSUE	EDITION LIMIT	YEAR RETD.	ISSUE PRICE	QUOTE U.S.$
1994	My Little Ballerina	12/95		59.95	60

Nursery Newborns - J. Wolf

YEAR	ISSUE	EDITION LIMIT	YEAR RETD.	ISSUE PRICE	QUOTE U.S.$
1994	It's A Boy	12/95		79.95	80
1994	It's A Girl	12/95		79.95	80

Oh Holy Night - Good-Krueger

YEAR	ISSUE	EDITION LIMIT	YEAR RETD.	ISSUE PRICE	QUOTE U.S.$
1994	The Holy Family (Jesus, Mary, Joseph)	12/95		129.95	130
1995	The Kneeling King	12/95		59.95	60
1995	The Purple King	12/95		59.95	60
1995	The Blue King	12/95		59.95	60
1995	Shepherd with Pipes	12/95		59.95	60
1995	Shepherd with Lamb	12/95		59.95	60
1995	Angel	12/95		59.95	60

Parade of American Fashion - Stevens/Siegel

YEAR	ISSUE	EDITION LIMIT	YEAR RETD.	ISSUE PRICE	QUOTE U.S.$
1987	The Glamour of the Gibson Girl	Closed	1989	77.00	125-200
1988	The Southern Belle	Closed	1989	77.00	125
1990	Victorian Lady	Closed	1993	82.00	82
1991	Romantic Lady	Closed	1993	85.00	85

Petting Zoo - Y. Bello

YEAR	ISSUE	EDITION LIMIT	YEAR RETD.	ISSUE PRICE	QUOTE U.S.$
1995	Andy	12/96		59.95	60
1995	Kendra	12/96		59.95	60
1995	Cory	12/96		59.95	60
1995	Maddie	12/96		59.95	60

Polly's Tea Party - S. Krey

YEAR	ISSUE	EDITION LIMIT	YEAR RETD.	ISSUE PRICE	QUOTE U.S.$
1990	Polly	Closed	1992	78.00	125
1991	Lizzie	Closed	1992	79.00	79
1992	Annie	Closed	1993	83.00	83-100

Precious Memories of Motherhood - S. Kuck

YEAR	ISSUE	EDITION LIMIT	YEAR RETD.	ISSUE PRICE	QUOTE U.S.$
1989	Loving Steps	Closed	1991	125.00	125
1990	Lullaby	Closed	1993	125.00	125
1991	Expectant Moments	Closed	1993	149.00	195-250
1992	Bedtime	Closed	1993	150.00	150

Pretty in Pastels - J. Goodyear

YEAR	ISSUE	EDITION LIMIT	YEAR RETD.	ISSUE PRICE	QUOTE U.S.$
1994	Precious in Pink	12/95		79.95	80

Rainbow of Love - Y. Bello

YEAR	ISSUE	EDITION LIMIT	YEAR RETD.	ISSUE PRICE	QUOTE U.S.$
1994	Blue Sky	12/95		59.95	60
1994	Yellow Sunshine	12/95		59.95	60
1994	Green Earth	12/95		59.95	60
1994	Pink Flower	12/96		59.95	60
1994	Purple Mountain	12/96		59.95	60
1994	Orange Sunset	12/96		59.95	60

Rockwell Christmas - Rockwell-Inspired

YEAR	ISSUE	EDITION LIMIT	YEAR RETD.	ISSUE PRICE	QUOTE U.S.$
1990	Scotty Plays Santa	Closed	1991	48.00	48
1991	Scotty Gets His Tree	Closed	1992	59.00	59
1993	Merry Christmas Grandma	Closed	1993	59.95	60

Romantic Flower Maidens - M. Roderick

YEAR	ISSUE	EDITION LIMIT	YEAR RETD.	ISSUE PRICE	QUOTE U.S.$
1988	Rose, Who is Love	Closed	1990	87.00	87-125
1989	Daisy	Closed	1993	87.00	87
1990	Violet	Closed	1993	92.00	92
1990	Lily	Closed	1991	92.00	92-125

Season of Dreams - G. Rademann

YEAR	ISSUE	EDITION LIMIT	YEAR RETD.	ISSUE PRICE	QUOTE U.S.$
1994	Autumn Breeze	12/95		79.95	80

Secret Garden - J. Kovacik

YEAR	ISSUE	EDITION LIMIT	YEAR RETD.	ISSUE PRICE	QUOTE U.S.$
1994	Mary	12/95		69.95	70
1995	Colin	12/96		69.95	70
1995	Martha	12/96		69.95	70
1995	Dickon	12/96		69.95	70

A Sense of Discovery - K. Barry-Hippensteel

YEAR	ISSUE	EDITION LIMIT	YEAR RETD.	ISSUE PRICE	QUOTE U.S.$
1993	Sweetie (Sense of Discovery)	Closed	1994	59.95	60-75

Siblings Through Time - C. McClure

YEAR	ISSUE	EDITION LIMIT	YEAR RETD.	ISSUE PRICE	QUOTE U.S.$
1995	Alexandra	12/96		69.95	70
1995	Gracie	12/96		59.95	60

Snow Babies - T. Tomescu

YEAR	ISSUE	EDITION LIMIT	YEAR RETD.	ISSUE PRICE	QUOTE U.S.$
1995	Beneath the Mistletoe	12/95		69.95	70
1995	Follow the Leader	12/96		75.00	75
1995	Snow Baby Express	12/96		75.00	75

Someone to Watch Over Me - K. Barry-Hippensteel

YEAR	ISSUE	EDITION LIMIT	YEAR RETD.	ISSUE PRICE	QUOTE U.S.$
1994	Sweet Dreams	12/95		69.95	70
1995	Night-Night Angel	12/95		24.95	25
1995	Lullaby Angel	12/95		24.95	25
1995	Sleepyhead Angel	12/96		24.95	25
1995	Stardust Angel	12/96		24.95	25
1995	Tuck-Me-In Angel	12/96		24.95	25

Sooo Big - M. Tretter

YEAR	ISSUE	EDITION LIMIT	YEAR RETD.	ISSUE PRICE	QUOTE U.S.$
1993	Jimmy	Closed	1994	59.95	60
1994	Kimmy	12/95		59.95	60

Special Edition Tour 1993 - Y. Bello

YEAR	ISSUE	EDITION LIMIT	YEAR RETD.	ISSUE PRICE	QUOTE U.S.$
1993	Miguel	Closed	1993	69.95	70
1993	Rosa	Closed	1993	69.95	70

Stepping Out - Akers/Girardi

YEAR	ISSUE	EDITION LIMIT	YEAR RETD.	ISSUE PRICE	QUOTE U.S.$
1991	Millie	Closed	1992	99.00	125

Tender Moments - L. Tierney

YEAR	ISSUE	EDITION LIMIT	YEAR RETD.	ISSUE PRICE	QUOTE U.S.$
1995	Tender Love	12/96		49.95	50
1995	Tender Heart	12/96		49.95	50
1995	Tender Care	12/96		49.95	50

Together Forever - S. Krey

YEAR	ISSUE	EDITION LIMIT	YEAR RETD.	ISSUE PRICE	QUOTE U.S.$
1994	Kirsten	12/95		59.95	60
1994	Courtney	12/95		59.95	60
1994	Kim	12/95		59.95	60

Treasured Togetherness - M. Tretter

YEAR	ISSUE	EDITION LIMIT	YEAR RETD.	ISSUE PRICE	QUOTE U.S.$
1994	Tender Touch	12/95		99.95	100
1994	Touch of Love	12/95		99.95	100

Tumbling Tots - K. Barry Hippensteel

YEAR	ISSUE	EDITION LIMIT	YEAR RETD.	ISSUE PRICE	QUOTE U.S.$
1993	Roly Poly Polly	Closed	1994	69.95	70
1994	Handstand Harry	12/95		69.95	70

Two Much To Handle - K. Barry-Hippensteel

YEAR	ISSUE	EDITION LIMIT	YEAR RETD.	ISSUE PRICE	QUOTE U.S.$
1993	Julie (Flowers For Mommy)	Closed	1994	59.95	60-90
1993	Kevin (Clean Hands)	Closed	1995	59.95	70-130

Victorian Dreamers - K. Barry-Hippensteel

YEAR	ISSUE	EDITION LIMIT	YEAR RETD.	ISSUE PRICE	QUOTE U.S.$
1995	Rock-A-Bye/Good Night	12/96		49.95	50
1995	Victorian Storytime	12/96		49.95	50

Victorian Lace - C. Layton

YEAR	ISSUE	EDITION LIMIT	YEAR RETD.	ISSUE PRICE	QUOTE U.S.$
1993	Alicia	Closed	1994	79.95	125-175
1994	Colleen	12/95		79.95	80-85
1994	Olivia	12/95		79.95	80

Victorian Nursery Heirloom - C. McClure

YEAR	ISSUE	EDITION LIMIT	YEAR RETD.	ISSUE PRICE	QUOTE U.S.$
1994	Victorian Lullaby	12/95		129.95	130
1995	Victorian Highchair	12/96		129.95	130
1995	Victorian Playtime	12/96		139.95	140
1995	Victorian Bunny Buggy	12/96		139.95	140

What Little Girls Are Made Of - D. Effner

YEAR	ISSUE	EDITION LIMIT	YEAR RETD.	ISSUE PRICE	QUOTE U.S.$
1994	Peaches and Cream	12/95		69.95	70

Winter Wonderland - K. Barry-Hippensteel

YEAR	ISSUE	EDITION LIMIT	YEAR RETD.	ISSUE PRICE	QUOTE U.S.$
1994	Annie	12/95		59.95	60
1994	Bobby	12/95		59.95	60

Winterfest - S. Sherwood

YEAR	ISSUE	EDITION LIMIT	YEAR RETD.	ISSUE PRICE	QUOTE U.S.$
1991	Brian	Closed	1992	89.00	125
1992	Michelle	Closed	1993	89.95	125
1993	Bradley	Closed	1993	89.95	90-100

The Wonderful Wizard of Oz - M. Tretter

YEAR	ISSUE	EDITION LIMIT	YEAR RETD.	ISSUE PRICE	QUOTE U.S.$
1994	Dorothy	12/95		79.95	80
1994	Scarecrow	12/95		79.95	80
1994	Tin Man	12/95		79.95	80
1994	The Cowardly Lion	12/96		79.95	80

Year Book Memories - Akers/Girardi

YEAR	ISSUE	EDITION LIMIT	YEAR RETD.	ISSUE PRICE	QUOTE U.S.$
1991	Peggy Sue	Closed	1992	87.00	95
1993	Going Steady (Patty Jo)	Closed	1994	89.95	90
1993	Prom Queen (Betty Jean)	Closed	1993	92.00	92

Yesterday's Dreams - M. Oldenburg

YEAR	ISSUE	EDITION LIMIT	YEAR RETD.	ISSUE PRICE	QUOTE U.S.$
1990	Andy	Closed	1993	68.00	68
1991	Janey	Closed	1993	69.00	69

Yolanda's Heaven Scent Babies - Y. Bello

YEAR	ISSUE	EDITION LIMIT	YEAR RETD.	ISSUE PRICE	QUOTE U.S.$
1993	Meagan Rose	Closed	1994	49.95	75-100
1993	Daisy Anne	Closed	1994	49.95	50-100
1993	Morning Glory	12/95		49.95	50
1993	Sweet Carnation	12/95		54.95	55
1993	Lily	12/95		54.95	55
1993	Cherry Blossom	12/95		54.95	55

Yolanda's Lullaby Babies - Y. Bello

YEAR	ISSUE	EDITION LIMIT	YEAR RETD.	ISSUE PRICE	QUOTE U.S.$
1991	Christy (Rock-a-Bye)	Closed	1993	69.00	95-105
1992	Joey (Twinkle, Twinkle)	Closed	1994	69.00	90-100
1993	Amy (Brahms Lullaby)	Closed	1994	75.00	75
1993	Eddie (Teddy Bear Lullaby)	Closed	1994	75.00	75-95
1993	Jacob (Silent Night)	Closed	1994	75.00	75
1994	Bonnie (You Are My Sunshine)	Closed	1994	80.00	80-100

Yolanda's Picture - Perfect Babies - Y. Bello

YEAR	ISSUE	EDITION LIMIT	YEAR RETD.	ISSUE PRICE	QUOTE U.S.$
1985	Jason	Closed	1988	48.00	650-700
1986	Heather	Closed	1988	48.00	225-350
1987	Jennifer	Closed	1989	58.00	225-325
1987	Matthew	Closed	1990	58.00	195-225
1987	Sarah	Closed	1990	58.00	95-175
1988	Amanda	Closed	1990	63.00	125-160
1989	Jessica	Closed	1993	63.00	75-125
1990	Michael	Closed	1992	63.00	125-160
1990	Lisa	Closed	1992	63.00	110-125
1991	Emily	Closed	1992	63.00	100-150
1991	Danielle	Closed	1993	69.00	95-150

Yolanda's Playtime Babies - Y. Bello

YEAR	ISSUE	EDITION LIMIT	YEAR RETD.	ISSUE PRICE	QUOTE U.S.$
1993	Todd	Closed	1994	59.95	60-90
1993	Lindsey	Closed	1994	59.95	65-95
1993	Shawna	Closed	1994	59.95	60-70

Yolanda's Precious Playmates - Y. Bello

YEAR	ISSUE	EDITION LIMIT	YEAR RETD.	ISSUE PRICE	QUOTE U.S.$
1992	David	Closed	1994	69.95	125
1993	Paul	Closed	1994	69.95	125
1994	Johnny	Closed	1994	69.95	70

Young Love - J.W. Smith

YEAR	ISSUE	EDITION LIMIT	YEAR RETD.	ISSUE PRICE	QUOTE U.S.$
1993	First Kiss	Closed	1993	118.00	118
1993	Buttercups	Closed	1994	Set	Set

Attic Babies

Attic Babies' Collector Club - M. Maschino

YEAR	ISSUE	EDITION LIMIT	YEAR RETD.	ISSUE PRICE	QUOTE U.S.$
1992	Burtie Buzbee, SNL	Retrd.	1992	40.00	40
1993	Izzie B. Ruebottom, SNL	277	1993	35.00	35
1994	Sunflower Flossie, SNL	Retrd.	1994	42.00	42
1995	Trisca Kay Yum-Yum, SNL	12/95		40.00	40

Baggie Collection - M. Maschino

YEAR	ISSUE	EDITION LIMIT	YEAR RETD.	ISSUE PRICE	QUOTE U.S.$
1991	Americana Baggie Bear	Retrd.	1994	19.95	22
1991	Americana Baggie Girl	Retrd.	1994	19.95	22
1991	Americana Baggie Rabbit	Retrd.	1994	19.95	22
1991	Americana Baggie Santa	Retrd.	1994	19.95	22
1991	Christmas Baggie Bear	Retrd.	1994	19.95	22
1991	Christmas Baggie Girl	Retrd.	1994	19.95	22
1991	Christmas Baggie Rabbit	Retrd.	1994	19.95	22
1991	Christmas Baggie Santa	Retrd.	1994	19.95	22
1991	Country Baggie Bear	Retrd.	1994	19.95	22
1991	Country Baggie Girl	Retrd.	1994	19.95	22
1991	Country Baggie Rabbit	Retrd.	1994	19.95	22

Mother's Day Angels - M. Maschino

YEAR	ISSUE	EDITION LIMIT	YEAR RETD.	ISSUE PRICE	QUOTE U.S.$
1994	Nattie Fae Tucker, SNL	757	1994	64.95	65

Retired Dolls - M. Maschino

YEAR	ISSUE	EDITION LIMIT	YEAR RETD.	ISSUE PRICE	QUOTE U.S.$
1992	Americana Raggedy Santa 1st edition , SNL	Retrd.	1992	85.95	150
1992	Americana Raggedy Santa 2nd edition , SNL	Retrd.	1992	89.95	90
1989	Annie Fannie	Retrd.	1992	43.95	70-110

DOLLS

YEAR ISSUE		EDITION LIMIT	YEAR RETD.	ISSUE PRICE	QUOTE U.S.$
1987	Bessie Jo	Retrd.	1989	31.95	98
1987	Beth Sue	Retrd.	1991	27.95	75
1988	Bunnifer	Retrd.	1990	39.95	82
1988	Buttons	Retrd.	1991	27.95	28
1992	Candy Applebee	Retrd.	1994	15.95	18
1992	Christopher Columbus SNL	Retrd.	1992	79.95	80
1989	Cotton Pickin' Ninny	Retrd.	1992	47.95	100
1987	Country Clyde	Retrd.	1988	27.95	28
1992	Daddy's Lil Punkin Patty, SNL	Retrd.	1993	79.95	80
1987	Dirty Harry	Retrd.	1991	27.95	55-100
1994	Dollie Boots	Retrd.	1994	79.95	80
1990	Duckie Dinkle	Retrd.	1991	95.95	96
1988	Fester Chester	Retrd.	1994	39.95	50
1990	Frannie Farkle	Retrd.	1991	129.95	130
1990	Frizzy Lizzy	Retrd.	1992	95.95	250
1988	Hannah Lou	Retrd.	1994	39.95	50
1990	Happy Huck	Retrd.	1992	47.95	102
1993	Happy Pappy Claus SNL	805	1994	73.95	74
1987	Harold	Retrd.	1990	27.95	80
1989	Heavenly Heather	Retrd.	1992	59.95	100
1988	Heffy Cheffy	Retrd.	1994	75.95	125
1993	Itty Bitty Santa	Retrd.	1993	5.95	6
1990	Ivan Ivie	Retrd.	1991	129.95	230
1987	Jacob	Retrd.	1988	27.95	100
1993	Jammy Mammy Claus SNL	653	1994	67.95	68
1987	Jenny Lou	Retrd.	1992	35.95	36
1989	Jolly Jim	Retrd.	1992	31.95	32
1990	Jumpin Pumkin Jill	Retrd.	1994	55.95	56
1990	Lampsie Divie Ivie	Retrd.	1991	129.95	230
1988	Lazy Daisy	Retrd.	1992	39.95	60
1988	Lazy Liza Jane	Retrd.	1991	47.95	48
1988	Little Dove	Retrd.	1988	39.95	40
1994	Lollie Ann	Retrd.	1994	39.95	40
1987	Maggie Mae	Retrd.	1991	25.95	28
1991	Maizie Mae	Retrd.	1994	51.95	52
1991	Mandi Mae	Retrd.	1994	51.95	52
1991	Memsie Mae	Retrd.	1994	51.95	52
1994	Merry Ole Farley Fagan Dooberry, SNL	Retrd.	1994	131.95	132
1993	Millie Wilset	2,000	1994	39.95	40
1987	Miss Pitty Pat	Retrd.	1988	27.95	100
1988	Molly Bea	Retrd.	1990	39.95	45-80
1988	Moosey Matilda	Retrd.	1990	39.95	150-300
1993	Mr. Kno Mo Sno, SNL	1,800	1994	51.95	52
1991	Mr. Raggedy Claus, SNL	Retrd.	1992	69.95	120
1991	Mrs. Raggedy Claus, SNL	Retrd.	1992	69.95	120
1989	Ms. Waddles	Retrd.	1990	47.95	48
1987	Muslin Bunny	Retrd.	1993	7.95	8
1987	Muslin Teddy	Retrd.	1993	7.95	8
1988	Naughty Nellie	Retrd.	1990	31.95	85
1993	Old St. Knickerbocker, SNL	Retrd.	1993	79.95	80
1992	Old St. Nick, SNL	Retrd.	1993	95.95	130
1989	Old Tyme Santy	Retrd.	1989	79.95	80
1990	Phylbert Farkle	Retrd.	1991	129.95	225
1991	Pippy Pat	Retrd.	1994	47.95	52
1988	Prissy Missy	Retrd.	1990	31.95	32
1987	Rachel	Retrd.	1988	29.95	85
1987	Raggedy Kitty	Retrd.	1988	29.95	30
1990	Raggedy Ole Chris Cringle 1st edition	Retrd.	1990	189.95	262
1990	Raggedy Ole Chris Cringle 2nd edition	Retrd.	1991	189.95	190
1988	Raggedy Sam	Retrd.	1991	55.95	115
1987	Raggedy Santy 1st edition	Retrd.	1988	75.95	200
1990	Raggedy Santy 2nd edition	Retrd.	1991	89.95	90
1989	Rammy Sammy	Retrd.	1990	43.95	44
1987	Rose Ann	Retrd.	1991	39.95	40
1988	Rotten Wilber	Retrd.	1990	35.95	140
1988	Rufus	Retrd.	1992	35.95	70-80
1990	Salie Ollie Otis	Retrd.	1991	129.95	130
1987	Sally Francis	Retrd.	1993	35.95	62
1987	Sara	Retrd.	1992	39.95	86
1992	Scary Larry Scarecrow, SNL	Retrd.	1994	79.95	80
1988	Silly Willie	Retrd.	1990	39.95	76
1989	Skitty Kitty	Retrd.	1991	43.95	140
1988	Spring Santy	Retrd.	1989	47.95	48
1988	Sweet William	Retrd.	1989	35.95	152
1992	Teeny Weenie Christmas Angel	Retrd.	1994	9.95	12
1992	Teeny Weenie Country Angel	Retrd.	1994	9.95	12
1987	Toddy Sue	Retrd.	1990	27.95	87
1988	Wacky Jackie	Retrd.	1990	39.95	40
1991	Winkie Binkie	Retrd.	1993	53.95	54
1992	Witchy Wanda, SNL	Retrd.	1994	79.95	80
1989	Wood Doll, black-large	Retrd.	1991	36.00	36
1989	Wood Doll, white-large	Retrd.	1991	36.00	36
1989	Wood Doll-medium	Retrd.	1991	31.95	32
1989	Wood Doll-small	Retrd.	1991	23.95	24
1990	Yankee Doodle Debbie	Retrd.	1993	95.95	150
1990	Zitty Zelda, SNL	Retrd.	1993	89.95	176

Tour Babies - M. Maschino

YEAR ISSUE		EDITION LIMIT	YEAR RETD.	ISSUE PRICE	QUOTE U.S.$
1993	Tour Baby 1993	Retrd.	1993	19.95	22
1994	Tour Baby 1994	Retrd.	1994	24.95	25

Valentine Collection - M. Maschino

YEAR ISSUE		EDITION LIMIT	YEAR RETD.	ISSUE PRICE	QUOTE U.S.$
1993	Valentine Bear-Girl	Retrd.	1993	39.95	40
1993	Valentine Bear-Boy	Retrd.	1993	39.95	40
1994	Herwin Heaps-O Hugs	613	1994	39.95	40
1994	Lottie Lots-A Hugs	825	1994	39.95	40
1995	Ruthie Claire	Retrd.	1995	39.95	40

The Collectables Inc.

Collector's Club Doll - P. Parkins

YEAR ISSUE		EDITION LIMIT	YEAR RETD.	ISSUE PRICE	QUOTE U.S.$
1991	Mandy	Closed	1991	360.00	360
1992	Kallie	Closed	1992	410.00	410
1993	Mommy and Me	Closed	1993	810.00	810
1994	Krystal	Closed	1994	380.00	380
1995	Taylor	Yr.Iss.		380.00	380

Angel Series - P. Parkins

YEAR ISSUE		EDITION LIMIT	YEAR RETD.	ISSUE PRICE	QUOTE U.S.$
1992	Angel on My Shoulder	Closed	1993	530.00	530
1994	Guarding the Way	500	1995	950.00	950
1993	My Guardian Angel	500	1993	590.00	590

Butterfly Babies - P. Parkins

YEAR ISSUE		EDITION LIMIT	YEAR RETD.	ISSUE PRICE	QUOTE U.S.$
1989	Belinda	S/O	1990	270.00	375
1992	Laticia	Closed	1993	320.00	320
1990	Willow	Closed	1991	240.00	375

Cherished Memories - P. Parkins, unless otherwise noted

YEAR ISSUE		EDITION LIMIT	YEAR RETD.	ISSUE PRICE	QUOTE U.S.$
1986	Amy and Andrew	S/O	1986	220.00	325
1988	Brittany	Closed	1988	240.00	300
1990	Cassandra	Closed	1990	500.00	550
1989	Generations	Closed	1989	480.00	500
1988	Heather	Closed	1988	280.00	300-350
1988	Jennifer	Closed	1988	380.00	500-600
1988	Leigh Ann & Leland	Closed	1988	250.00	250-300
1988	Tea Time - D. Effner	S/O	1986	380.00	450
1990	Twinkles	Closed	1991	170.00	275

The Collectibles Inc. Dolls - P. Parkins, unless otherwise noted

YEAR ISSUE		EDITION LIMIT	YEAR RETD.	ISSUE PRICE	QUOTE U.S.$
1991	Adrianna	Closed	1992	1350.00	1350
1994	Afternoon Delight	500		410.00	410
1995	Alexus	150		770.00	770
1993	Amber	500	1994	330.00	330
1994	Amber Hispanic	500	1994	340.00	340
1992	Angel on My Shoulder (Lillianne w/CeCe)	500	1993	530.00	530
1990	Bassinet Baby	2,000	1990	130.00	375-425
1991	Bethany	Closed	1992	450.00	450
1995	Brianna	150		590.00	590
1995	Christine	350		390.00	390
1990	Danielle	1,000	1990	400.00	475
1994	Earth Angel	500		195.00	195
1993	Haley	500	1994	330.00	330
1990	In Your Easter Bonnet	1,000	1990	350.00	350
1992	Karlie	500	1992	380.00	380
1991	Kelsie	500	1991	320.00	320
1991	Lauren	S/O	1991	490.00	490
1993	Little Dumpling (Black)	500	1994	190.00	190
1993	Little Dumpling (White)	500	1994	190.00	190
1990	Lizbeth Ann - D. Effner	1,000	1990	420.00	420
1994	Madison	250		350.00	350
1994	Madison Sailor	250		370.00	370
1993	Maggie	500	1994	330.00	330
1992	Marissa	300	1992	350.00	350
1992	Marty	250	1992	190.00	190
1992	Matia	250	1992	190.00	190
1989	Michelle	250	1990	270.00	400-450
1992	Missy	Open		59.00	59
1992	Molly	450	1993	350.00	350
1994	Morgan	250	1995	390.00	390
1994	Morgan in Red	250		390.00	390
1995	A Mother's Love	450		770.00	770
1995	My Little Angel Boy	set		set	set
1995	My Little Angel Girl	450		450.00	450
1991	Natasha	Closed	1992	510.00	510
1992	Shelley	300	1992	450.00	450
1987	Storytime By Sarah Jane	S/O	1990	330.00	475-525
1994	Sugar Plum Fairy	500		250.00	250
1987	Tasha	S/O	1987	290.00	1400
1986	Tatiana	S/O	1986	270.00	1000
1989	Welcome Home - D. Effner	1,000	1990	330.00	475-675
1991	Yvette	300	1992	580.00	580

Enchanted Children - P. Parkins

YEAR ISSUE		EDITION LIMIT	YEAR RETD.	ISSUE PRICE	QUOTE U.S.$
1990	Kara	Closed	1991	550.00	550
1990	Katlin	Closed	1991	550.00	550
1990	Kristin	S/O	1991	550.00	650
1990	Tiffy	S/O	1991	370.00	500

Fairy - P. Parkins

YEAR ISSUE		EDITION LIMIT	YEAR RETD.	ISSUE PRICE	QUOTE U.S.$
1988	Tabatha	1,500	1989	370.00	400-450

Mother's Little Treasures - D. Effner

YEAR ISSUE		EDITION LIMIT	YEAR RETD.	ISSUE PRICE	QUOTE U.S.$
1985	1st Edition	S/O	1985	380.00	1000
1990	2nd Edition	S/O	1990	440.00	475-595

Storybook Series - P. Parkins

YEAR ISSUE		EDITION LIMIT	YEAR RETD.	ISSUE PRICE	QUOTE U.S.$
1995	Jack	300		170.00	170
1995	Jill	300		170.00	170
1995	Little Bo Peep	300		220.00	220
1995	Little Boy Blue	300		170.00	170
1995	Little Red Riding Hood	300		210.00	210
1995	Twinkle, Twinkle Little Star	300		170.00	170

Yesterday's Child - D. Effner, unless otherwise noted

YEAR ISSUE		EDITION LIMIT	YEAR RETD.	ISSUE PRICE	QUOTE U.S.$
1986	Ashley - P. Parkins	Closed	1987	220.00	275
1983	Chad And Charity	Closed	1984	190.00	190
1982	Cleo	Closed	1983	180.00	250
1982	Columbine	Closed	1983	180.00	250
1982	Jason And Jessica	Closed	1983	150.00	300
1984	Kevin And Karissa	Closed	1985	190.00	250-300
1983	Noel	Closed	1984	190.00	240
1984	Rebecca	Closed	1985	250.00	250-300
1986	Todd And Tiffany	Closed	1987	220.00	250

Department 56

Heritage Village Doll Collection - Department 56

YEAR ISSUE		EDITION LIMIT	YEAR RETD.	ISSUE PRICE	QUOTE U.S.$
1987	Christmas Carol Dolls 1000-6 4/set (Tiny Tim, Bob Crachet, Mrs. Crachet, Scrooge)	250	1988	1500.00	1500
1987	Christmas Carol Dolls 5907-2 4/set (Tiny Tim, Bob Crachet, Mrs. Crachet, Scrooge)	Closed	1993	250.00	265-300
1988	Christmas Carol Dolls 1001-4 4/set (Tiny Tim, Bob Crachet, Mrs. Crachet, Scrooge)	350	1989	1600.00	1600
1988	Mr. & Mrs. Fezziwig 5594-8 2/set	Open		172.00	172

Snowbabies Dolls - Department 56

YEAR ISSUE		EDITION LIMIT	YEAR RETD.	ISSUE PRICE	QUOTE U.S.$
1988	Allison & Duncan-Set of 2, 7730-5	Closed	1989	200.00	750-795

Dolls by Jerri

Dolls by Jerri - J. McCloud

YEAR ISSUE		EDITION LIMIT	YEAR RETD.	ISSUE PRICE	QUOTE U.S.$
1986	Alfalfa	1,000		350.00	350
1986	Allison	1,000		350.00	450
1986	Amber	1,000		350.00	850
1986	Annabelle	300		600.00	585
1986	Ashley	1,000		350.00	500
1986	Audrey	300		550.00	550
1982	Baby David	538		290.00	2000
XX	Boy	1,000		350.00	425
1985	Bride	1,000		350.00	400
1986	Bridgette	300		500.00	500
1985	Candy	1,000		340.00	2000
1986	Cane	1,000		350.00	1200
1986	Charlotte	1,000		330.00	450
1984	Clara	1,000		320.00	1200-1500
1986	Clown-David 3 Yrs. Old	1,000		340.00	450
1986	Danielle	1,000		350.00	500
1986	David-2 Years Old	1,000		330.00	550
1986	David-Magician	1,000		350.00	450
XX	Denise	1,000		380.00	550
1986	Elizabeth	1,000		340.00	350
1984	Emily	1,000		330.00	2500
1986	The Fool	1,000		350.00	350
XX	Gina	1,000		350.00	475
XX	Goldilocks	1,000		370.00	600-750
1989	Goose Girl, Guild	Closed		300.00	700
1986	Helenjean	1,000		350.00	500-650
1988	Holly	1,000		370.00	825
1986	Jacqueline	300		500.00	500
XX	Jamie	800		380.00	450
1986	Joy	1,000		350.00	350
XX	Laura	1,000		350.00	500
1989	Laura Lee	1,000		370.00	575
XX	Little Bo Peep	1,000		340.00	450
XX	Little Miss Muffet	1,000		340.00	450
1986	Lucianna	300		500.00	500
1986	Mary Beth	1,000		350.00	350
XX	Megan	750		420.00	550
XX	Meredith	750		430.00	600
1985	Miss Nanny	1,000		160.00	275
1986	Nobody	1,000		350.00	550-650
1986	Princess and the Unicorn	1,000		370.00	400
1986	Samantha	1,000		350.00	550
1985	Scotty	1,000		340.00	1800
1986	Somebody	1,000		350.00	550-750
1986	Tammy	1,000		350.00	900
1985	Uncle Joe	1,000		160.00	250-300
XX	Uncle Remus	500		290.00	450
1986	Yvonne	300		500.00	500

Dynasty Doll

Annual - Various

YEAR ISSUE		EDITION LIMIT	YEAR RETD.	ISSUE PRICE	QUOTE U.S.$
1989	Amber - Unknown	Yr.Iss.		90.00	90
1990	Marcella - Unknown	Yr.Iss.		90.00	90
1991	Butterfly Princess - Unknown	Yr.Iss.		110.00	110
1993	Annual Bride - H. Tertsakian	Yr.Iss.		190.00	190
1993	Ariel - Unknown	Yr.Iss.		120.00	120
1994	Annual Bride - H. Tertsakian	Yr.Iss.		200.00	200
1994	Janie '94 - Unknown	Yr.Iss.		120.00	120
1995	Victoria Jane - H. Tertsakian	Yr.Iss.		160.00	160
1995	Annual Bride - B. Lee	Yr.Iss.		210.00	210

Christmas - Unknown

YEAR ISSUE		EDITION LIMIT	YEAR RETD.	ISSUE PRICE	QUOTE U.S.$
1987	Merrie	Retrd.	N/A	60.00	60
1988	Noel	Retrd.	N/A	80.00	80
1990	Faith	Retrd.	N/A	110.00	110
1991	Joy	Retrd.	N/A	125.00	125
1993	Genevieve	Retrd.	N/A	164.00	164
1994	Gloria '94	5,000	1994	170.00	170
1995	Sparkle	3,500		150.00	150

Dynasty Collection - Various

YEAR ISSUE		EDITION LIMIT	YEAR RETD.	ISSUE PRICE	QUOTE U.S.$
1993	Amanda - Unknown	3,000	1994	195.00	195

YEAR ISSUE		EDITION LIMIT	YEAR RETD.	ISSUE PRICE	QUOTE U.S.$
1994	Amelia - G. Hoyt	1,500	1995	170.00	170
1994	Amy - Unknown	1,500		175.00	175
1993	Angela - Unknown	1,500		195.00	195
1993	Antoinette - H. Tertsakian	5,000	1995	190.00	190
1993	Carley - G. Hoyt	Retrd.	1995	120.00	120
1993	Catherine - H. Tertsakian	5,000	1995	190.00	190
1994	Christina - Unknown	3,500		200.00	200
1994	Gabrielle - S. Kelsey	1,500		180.00	180
1993	Heather - G. Tepper	Retrd.	N/A	160.00	160
1993	Julie - K. Henderson	Retrd.	N/A	175.00	175
1993	Juliet - G. Tepper	Retrd.	N/A	160.00	160
1993	Kadyrose - M. Cohen	Retrd.	1995	145.00	145
1993	Katy - M. Cohen	Retrd.	N/A	135.00	135
1994	Kelsey - S. Kelsey	1,500	1995	225.00	225
1991	Lana - Unknown	Open		85.00	85
1994	Laurelyn - Unknown	2,000	1995	180.00	180
1993	Megan - Unknown	3,500	1994	150.00	150
1993	Nicole - Unknown	Retrd.	N/A	135.00	135
1993	Patricia - Unknown	Open		160.00	160
1994	Rebecca - Unknown	1,500		175.00	175
1993	Shannon - Unknown	1,500		195.00	195
1993	Tami - M. Cohen	7,500	1995	190.00	190
1993	Tory - M. Cohen	7,500	1995	190.00	190

Elke's Originals, Ltd.

Elke Hutchens - E. Hutchens

YEAR ISSUE		EDITION LIMIT	YEAR RETD.	ISSUE PRICE	QUOTE U.S.$
1991	Alicia	250		595.00	700-995
1989	Annabelle	250		575.00	1300-1600
1990	Aubra	250		575.00	850-995
1990	Aurora	250		595.00	850-995
1991	Bellinda	400		595.00	800-895
1992	Bethany	400		595.00	700-895
1991	Braelyn	400		595.00	1300-1700
1991	Brianna	400		595.00	895
1992	Cecilia	435		635.00	750-895
1992	Charles	435		635.00	450-800
1992	Cherie	435		635.00	900
1992	Clarissa	435		635.00	800-895
1993	Daphne	435		675.00	500-800
1993	Deidre	435		675.00	500-800
1993	Desirée	435		675.00	550-800
1990	Kricket	500		575.00	400
1992	Laurakaye	435		550.00	550
1990	Little Liebchen	250		475.00	1000
1990	Victoria	500		645.00	645

Enesco Corporation

Precious Moments Dolls - S. Butcher

YEAR ISSUE		EDITION LIMIT	YEAR RETD.	ISSUE PRICE	QUOTE U.S.$
1981	Mikey, 18"- E-6214B	Suspd.		150.00	175
1981	Debbie, 18"- E-6214G	Suspd.		150.00	240
1982	Cubby, 18"- E-7267B	5,000		200.00	350-450
1982	Tammy, 18"- E-7267G	5,000		300.00	500-600
1983	Katie Lynne, 16"- E-0539	Suspd.		165.00	185
1984	Mother Sew Dear, 18"- E-2850	Retrd.	1985	350.00	300
1984	Kristy, 12"- E-2851	Suspd.		150.00	150
1984	Timmy, 12"- E-5397	Open		125.00	85
1985	Aaron, 12"- 12424	Suspd.		135.00	135
1985	Bethany, 12"- 12432	Suspd.		135.00	135
1985	P.D., 7"- 12475	Suspd.		50.00	80
1985	Trish, 7" - 12483	Suspd.		50.00	100
1986	Bong Bong, 13" - 100455	12,000		150.00	250
1986	Candy, 13" - 100463	12,000		150.00	285
1986	Connie, 12" - 102253	7,500		160.00	240
1987	Angie, The Angel of Mercy - 12491	12,500		160.00	275
1990	The Voice of Spring - 408786	2-Yr.		150.00	150
1990	Summer's Joy - 408794	2-Yr.		150.00	150
1990	Autumn's Praise - 408808	2-Yr.		150.00	150
1990	Winter's Song - 408816	2-Yr.		150.00	170
1991	You Have Touched So Many Hearts- 427527	2-Yr.		90.00	90
1991	May You Have An Old Fashioned Christmas - 417785	2-Yr.		150.00	175
1991	The Eyes Of The Lord Are Upon You (Boy Action Muscial) - 429570	Suspd.		65.00	65
1991	The Eyes Of The Lord Are Upon You (Girl Action Musical) - 429589	Suspd.		65.00	65

Precious Moments-Jack-In-The-Boxes - S. Butcher

YEAR ISSUE		EDITION LIMIT	YEAR RETD.	ISSUE PRICE	QUOTE U.S.$
1991	You Have Touched So Many Hearts-422282	2-Yr.		175.00	175
1991	May You Have An Old Fashioned Christmas-417777	2-Yr.		200.00	200

Precious Moments-Jack-In-The-Boxes-4 Seasons - S. Butcher

YEAR ISSUE		EDITION LIMIT	YEAR RETD.	ISSUE PRICE	QUOTE U.S.$
1990	Voice of Spring-408735	2-Yr.		200.00	200
1990	Summer's Joy-408743	2-Yr.		200.00	200
1990	Autumn's Praise-408751	2-Yr.		200.00	200
1990	Winter's Song-408778	2-Yr.		200.00	200

Ganz

Cowtown - C. Thammavongsa

YEAR ISSUE		EDITION LIMIT	YEAR RETD.	ISSUE PRICE	QUOTE U.S.$
1994	Buffalo Bull Cody	Open		20.00	20
1994	Old MooDonald	Open		20.00	20
1994	Santa Cows	Open		25.00	25

Little Cheesers/Cheeserville Picnic Collection - G.D.A. Group

YEAR ISSUE		EDITION LIMIT	YEAR RETD.	ISSUE PRICE	QUOTE U.S.$
1992	Sweet Cicely Musical Doll In Basket	Open		85.00	85

Georgetown Collection, Inc.

Age of Romance - J. Reavey

YEAR ISSUE		EDITION LIMIT	YEAR RETD.	ISSUE PRICE	QUOTE U.S.$
1994	Catherine	100-day		150.00	150

American Diary Dolls - L. Mason

YEAR ISSUE		EDITION LIMIT	YEAR RETD.	ISSUE PRICE	QUOTE U.S.$
1991	Bridget Quinn	100-day		129.25	130
1991	Christina Merovina	100-day		129.25	130
1990	Jennie Cooper	100-day		129.25	130-155
1994	Lian Ying	100-day		130.00	130
1991	Many Stars	100-day		129.25	130
1992	Rachel Williams	100-day		129.25	130
1993	Sarah Turner	100-day		130.00	130
1992	Tulu	100-day		129.25	130

Baby Kisses - T. DeHetre

YEAR ISSUE		EDITION LIMIT	YEAR RETD.	ISSUE PRICE	QUOTE U.S.$
1992	Michelle	100-day		118.60	119

Beautiful Dreamers - A. DiMartino

YEAR ISSUE		EDITION LIMIT	YEAR RETD.	ISSUE PRICE	QUOTE U.S.$
1994	Beautiful Buttercup	100-day		130.00	130
1995	Julie	100-day		130.00	130

Blessed Are The Children - J. Reavey

YEAR ISSUE		EDITION LIMIT	YEAR RETD.	ISSUE PRICE	QUOTE U.S.$
1994	Faith	100-day		83.00	83

Boys Will Be Boys - J. Reavey

YEAR ISSUE		EDITION LIMIT	YEAR RETD.	ISSUE PRICE	QUOTE U.S.$
1994	Mr. Mischief	100-day		96.00	96

Children of the Great Spirit - C. Theroux

YEAR ISSUE		EDITION LIMIT	YEAR RETD.	ISSUE PRICE	QUOTE U.S.$
1993	Buffalo Child	100-day		140.00	140
1994	Golden Flower	100-day		130.00	130
1994	Little Fawn	100-day		114.00	114
1993	Winter Baby	100-day		160.00	160

Class Portraits - J. Kissling

YEAR ISSUE		EDITION LIMIT	YEAR RETD.	ISSUE PRICE	QUOTE U.S.$
1995	Anna	100-day		140.00	140

Dreams Come True - M. Sirko

YEAR ISSUE		EDITION LIMIT	YEAR RETD.	ISSUE PRICE	QUOTE U.S.$
1995	Amanda	100-day		120.00	120

Faerie Princess - B. Deval

YEAR ISSUE		EDITION LIMIT	YEAR RETD.	ISSUE PRICE	QUOTE U.S.$
1989	Faerie Princess	Closed	N/A	248.00	248

Fanciful Dreamers - A. Timmerman

YEAR ISSUE		EDITION LIMIT	YEAR RETD.	ISSUE PRICE	QUOTE U.S.$
1995	Sweetdreams & Moonbeams	100-day		130.00	130

Faraway Friends - S. Skille

YEAR ISSUE		EDITION LIMIT	YEAR RETD.	ISSUE PRICE	QUOTE U.S.$
1994	Dara	100-day		140.00	140
1993	Kristin	100-day		140.00	140
1994	Mariama	100-day		140.00	140

Favorite Friends - K. Murawska

YEAR ISSUE		EDITION LIMIT	YEAR RETD.	ISSUE PRICE	QUOTE U.S.$
1995	Christina	100-day		130.00	130

Georgetown Collection - Various

YEAR ISSUE		EDITION LIMIT	YEAR RETD.	ISSUE PRICE	QUOTE U.S.$
1995	Buffalo Boy - C. Theroux	100-day		130.00	130
1993	Quick Fox - L. Mason	100-day		138.95	139
1994	Silver Moon - L. Mason	100-day		140.00	140

Gifts From Heaven - B. Prusseit

YEAR ISSUE		EDITION LIMIT	YEAR RETD.	ISSUE PRICE	QUOTE U.S.$
1994	Good as Gold	100-day		88.00	88
1995	Sweet Pea	100-day		88.00	88

Hearts in Song - J. Galperin

YEAR ISSUE		EDITION LIMIT	YEAR RETD.	ISSUE PRICE	QUOTE U.S.$
1994	Angelique	100-day		150.00	150
1992	Grace	100-day		149.60	150
1993	Michael	100-day		150.00	150

Heavenly Messages - M. Sirko

YEAR ISSUE		EDITION LIMIT	YEAR RETD.	ISSUE PRICE	QUOTE U.S.$
1995	Gabrielle	100-day		104.00	104

Kindergarten Kids - V. Walker

YEAR ISSUE		EDITION LIMIT	YEAR RETD.	ISSUE PRICE	QUOTE U.S.$
1992	Nikki	100-day		129.60	130

Let's Play - T. DeHetre

YEAR ISSUE		EDITION LIMIT	YEAR RETD.	ISSUE PRICE	QUOTE U.S.$
1992	Eentsy Weentsy Willie	100-day		118.60	119
1992	Peek-A-Boo Beckie	100-day		118.60	119

Linda's Little Ladies - L. Mason

YEAR ISSUE		EDITION LIMIT	YEAR RETD.	ISSUE PRICE	QUOTE U.S.$
1993	Shannon's Holiday	100-day		169.95	170

Little Bit of Heaven - A. Timmerman

YEAR ISSUE		EDITION LIMIT	YEAR RETD.	ISSUE PRICE	QUOTE U.S.$
1994	Arielle	100-day		130.00	130
1995	Cupid	100-day		135.00	135
1995	Noelle	100-day		130.00	130

Little Bloomers - J. Reavey

YEAR ISSUE		EDITION LIMIT	YEAR RETD.	ISSUE PRICE	QUOTE U.S.$
1995	Darling Daisy	100-day		104.00	104

Little Loves - B. Deval

YEAR ISSUE		EDITION LIMIT	YEAR RETD.	ISSUE PRICE	QUOTE U.S.$
1988	Emma	Closed	N/A	139.20	140
1989	Katie	Closed	N/A	139.20	140
1990	Laura	Closed	N/A	139.20	140
1989	Megan	Closed	N/A	138.00	160

Messengers of the Great Spirit - Various

YEAR ISSUE		EDITION LIMIT	YEAR RETD.	ISSUE PRICE	QUOTE U.S.$
1994	Noatak - L. Mason	100-day		150.00	150
1994	Prayer for the Buffalo - C. Theroux	100-day		120.00	120

Miss Ashley - P. Thompson

YEAR ISSUE		EDITION LIMIT	YEAR RETD.	ISSUE PRICE	QUOTE U.S.$
1989	Miss Ashley	Closed	N/A	228.00	228

Nursery Babies - T. DeHetre

YEAR ISSUE		EDITION LIMIT	YEAR RETD.	ISSUE PRICE	QUOTE U.S.$
1990	Baby Bunting	Closed	N/A	118.20	150
1991	Diddle, Diddle	Closed	N/A	118.20	119
1991	Little Girl	100-day		118.20	119
1990	Patty Cake	Closed	N/A	118.20	119
1991	Rock-A-Bye Baby	100-day		118.20	119
1991	This Little Piggy	100-day		118.20	119

Pictures of Innocence - J. Reavey

YEAR ISSUE		EDITION LIMIT	YEAR RETD.	ISSUE PRICE	QUOTE U.S.$
1994	Clarissa	100-day		137.50	138

Portraits of Perfection - A. Timmerman

YEAR ISSUE		EDITION LIMIT	YEAR RETD.	ISSUE PRICE	QUOTE U.S.$
1993	Apple Dumpling	100-day		149.60	150
1994	Blackberry Blossom	100-day		149.60	150
1993	Peaches & Cream	100-day		149.60	150
1993	Sweet Strawberry	100-day		149.60	150

Prayers From The Heart - S. Skille

YEAR ISSUE		EDITION LIMIT	YEAR RETD.	ISSUE PRICE	QUOTE U.S.$
1995	Hope	100-day		115.00	115

Russian Fairy Tales Dolls - B. Deval

YEAR ISSUE		EDITION LIMIT	YEAR RETD.	ISSUE PRICE	QUOTE U.S.$
1993	Vasilisa	100-day		190.00	190

Small Wonders - B. Deval

YEAR ISSUE		EDITION LIMIT	YEAR RETD.	ISSUE PRICE	QUOTE U.S.$
1991	Abbey	100-day		97.60	98
1990	Corey	100-day		97.60	98
1992	Sarah	100-day		97.60	98

Songs of Innocence - J. Reavey

YEAR ISSUE		EDITION LIMIT	YEAR RETD.	ISSUE PRICE	QUOTE U.S.$
1995	Kelsey	100-day		104.00	104

Sugar & Spice - L. Mason

YEAR ISSUE		EDITION LIMIT	YEAR RETD.	ISSUE PRICE	QUOTE U.S.$
1992	Little Sunshine	100-day		141.10	142
1991	Little Sweetheart	100-day		118.25	119
1991	Red Hot Pepper	100-day		118.25	119

Sweethearts of Summer - P. Phillips

YEAR ISSUE		EDITION LIMIT	YEAR RETD.	ISSUE PRICE	QUOTE U.S.$
1994	Caroline	100-day		140.00	140
1995	Jessica	100-day		140.00	140
1995	Madeleine & Harry	100-day		140.00	140

Tansie - P. Coffer

YEAR ISSUE		EDITION LIMIT	YEAR RETD.	ISSUE PRICE	QUOTE U.S.$
1988	Tansie	Closed	N/A	81.00	81

Victorian Fantasies - L. Mason

YEAR ISSUE		EDITION LIMIT	YEAR RETD.	ISSUE PRICE	QUOTE U.S.$
1995	Amber Afternoon	100-day		150.00	150
1995	Lavender Dreams	100-day		150.00	150

Victorian Innocence - L. Mason

YEAR ISSUE		EDITION LIMIT	YEAR RETD.	ISSUE PRICE	QUOTE U.S.$
1994	Annabelle	100-day		130.00	130

Victorian Splendor - J. Reavey

YEAR ISSUE		EDITION LIMIT	YEAR RETD.	ISSUE PRICE	QUOTE U.S.$
1994	Emily	100-day		130.00	130

Yesterday's Dreams - P. Phillips

YEAR ISSUE		EDITION LIMIT	YEAR RETD.	ISSUE PRICE	QUOTE U.S.$
1994	Mary Elizabeth	100-day		130.00	130

Goebel of North America

Dolly Dingle - B. Ball

YEAR ISSUE		EDITION LIMIT	YEAR RETD.	ISSUE PRICE	QUOTE U.S.$
1995	Melvis Bumps	1,000		99.00	99

Goebel Dolls - B. Ball

YEAR ISSUE		EDITION LIMIT	YEAR RETD.	ISSUE PRICE	QUOTE U.S.$
1995	Brother Murphy	2,000		125.00	125

United States Historical Society - B. Ball

YEAR ISSUE		EDITION LIMIT	YEAR RETD.	ISSUE PRICE	QUOTE U.S.$
1995	Mary	1,500		195.00	195

Victoria Ashlea® Birthstone Dolls - K. Kennedy

YEAR ISSUE		EDITION LIMIT	YEAR RETD.	ISSUE PRICE	QUOTE U.S.$
1995	January-Garnet-912471	2,500		29.50	30
1995	February-Amethyst-912472	2,500		29.50	30
1995	March-Aquamarine-912473	2,500		29.50	30
1995	April-Diamond-912474	2,500		29.50	30
1995	May-Emerald-912475	2,500		29.50	30
1995	June -Lt. Amethyst-912476	2,500		29.50	30
1995	July-Ruby-912477	2,500		29.50	30
1995	August-Peridot-912478	2,500		29.50	30
1995	September-Sapphire-912479	2,500		29.50	30
1995	October-Rosestone-912480	2,500		29.50	30
1995	November-Topaz-912481	2,500		29.50	30
1995	December-Zircon-912482	2,500		29.50	30

Victoria Ashlea® Originals - B. Ball, unless otherwise noted

YEAR ISSUE		EDITION LIMIT	YEAR RETD.	ISSUE PRICE	QUOTE U.S.$
1985	Adele-901172	Closed	1989	145.00	275
1989	Alexa-912214	Closed	1991	195.00	195
1989	Alexandria-912273	Closed	1991	275.00	275
1987	Alice-901212	Closed	1991	95.00	135
1990	Alice-912296 - K. Kennedy	Closed	1992	65.00	65
1992	Alicia-912388	500	1994	135.00	135
1992	Allison-912358	Closed	1993	160.00	165

YEAR ISSUE		EDITION LIMIT	YEAR RETD.	ISSUE PRICE	QUOTE U.S.$
1987	Amanda Pouty-901209	Closed	1991	150.00	215
1988	Amanda-912246	Closed	1991	180.00	180
1993	Amanda-912409	2,000		40.00	40
1984	Amelia-933006	Closed	1988	100.00	100
1990	Amie-912313 - K. Kennedy	Closed	1991	150.00	150
1990	Amy-901262	Closed	1993	110.00	110
1990	Angela-912324 - K. Kennedy	Closed	1994	130.00	135
1988	Angelica-912204	Closed	1991	150.00	150
1992	Angelica-912339	1,000		145.00	145
1990	Annabelle-912278	Closed	1992	200.00	200
1988	Anne-912213	Closed	1991	130.00	150
1990	Annette-912333 - K. Kennedy	Closed	1993	85.00	85
1988	April-901239	Closed	1992	225.00	225
1989	Ashlea-901250	Closed	1992	550.00	550
1988	Ashley-901235	Closed	1991	110.00	110
1992	Ashley-911004	Closed	1994	99.00	105
1986	Ashley-912147	Closed	1989	125.00	125
1986	Baby Brook Beige Dress-912103	Closed	1989	60.00	60
1986	Baby Courtney-912124	Closed	1990	120.00	120
1988	Baby Daryl-912200	Closed	1991	85.00	85
1987	Baby Doll-912184	Closed	1990	75.00	75
1988	Baby Jennifer-912210	Closed	1992	75.00	75
1988	Baby Katie-912222	Closed	1993	70.00	70
1986	Baby Lauren Pink-912086	Closed	1991	120.00	120
1987	Baby Lindsay-912190	Closed	1990	80.00	80
1984	Barbara-901108	Closed	1987	57.00	110
1990	Baryshnicat-912298 K. Kennedy	Closed	1991	25.00	25
1988	Bernice-901245	Closed	1991	90.00	90
1993	Beth-912430 - K. Kennedy	2,000		45.00	45
1992	Betsy-912390	500	1994	150.00	150
1990	Bettina-912310	Closed	1993	100.00	105
1988	Betty Doll-912220	Closed	1993	90.00	90
1987	Bonnie Pouty-901207	Closed	1992	100.00	100
1988	Brandon-901234	Closed	1992	90.00	90
1990	Brandy-912304 - K. Kennedy	Closed	1992	150.00	150
1987	Bride Allison-901218	Closed	1993	180.00	180
1988	Brittany-912207	Closed	1990	130.00	145
1992	Brittany-912365 - K. Kennedy	Closed	1993	140.00	145
1987	Caitlin-901228	Closed	1991	260.00	260
1988	Campbell Kid-Boy-758701	Closed	1988	13.80	14
1988	Campbell Kid-Girl-758700	Closed	1988	13.80	14
1989	Candace-912288 - K. Kennedy	Closed	1992	70.00	70
1992	Carol-912387 - K. Kennedy	1,000		140.00	140
1987	Caroline-912191	Closed	1990	80.00	80
1990	Carolyn-901261 - K. Kennedy	Closed	1993	200.00	200
1992	Cassandra-912355 - K. Kennedy	1,000		165.00	165
1988	Cat Maude-901247	Closed	1993	85.00	85
1986	Cat/Kitty Cheerful Gr Dr-901179	Closed	1990	60.00	60
1987	Catanova-901227	Closed	1991	75.00	75
1988	Catherine-901242	Closed	1992	240.00	240
XX	Charity-912244	Closed	1990	70.00	70
1982	Charleen-912094	Closed	1986	65.00	65
1985	Chauncey-912085	Closed	1988	75.00	110
1988	Christina-901229	Closed	1991	350.00	400
1987	Christine-912168	Closed	1989	75.00	75
1992	Cindy-912384	1,000	1994	185.00	190
1985	Claire-901158	Closed	1988	115.00	160
1984	Claude-901032	Closed	1987	110.00	225
1984	Claudette-901033	Closed	1987	110.00	225
1989	Claudia-901257 - K. Kennedy	Closed	1993	225.00	225
1987	Clementine-901226	Closed	1991	75.00	75
1986	Clown Calypso-912104	Closed	1990	70.00	70
1985	Clown Casey-912078	Closed	1988	40.00	40
1986	Clown Cat Cadwalader-912132	Closed	1988	55.00	55
1987	Clown Champagne-912180	Closed	1989	95.00	95
1986	Clown Christabel-912095	Closed	1988	100.00	150
1985	Clown Christie-912084	Closed	1988	60.00	90
1986	Clown Clarabella-912096	Closed	1989	80.00	80
1986	Clown Clarissa-912123	Closed	1990	75.00	110
1988	Clown Cotton Candy-912199	Closed	1990	67.00	67
1986	Clown Cyd-912093	Closed	1988	70.00	70
1985	Clown Jody-912079	Closed	1988	100.00	150
1982	Clown Jolly-912181	Closed	1991	70.00	70
1986	Clown Kitten-Cleo-912133	Closed	1989	50.00	50
1986	Clown Lollipop-912127	Closed	1989	125.00	225
1984	Clown-901136	Closed	1988	90.00	120
1988	Crystal-912226	Closed	1992	75.00	75
1983	Deborah-901107	Closed	1987	220.00	400
1990	Debra-912319 - K. Kennedy	Closed	1992	120.00	120
1992	Denise-912362 - K. Kennedy	1,000	1994	145.00	175-225
1989	Diana Bride-912277	Closed	1992	180.00	180
1984	Diana-901119	Closed	1987	55.00	135
1988	Diana-912218	Closed	1992	270.00	270
1987	Dominique-901219	Closed	1991	170.00	225
1987	Doreen-912198	Closed	1990	75.00	75
1985	Dorothy-901157	Closed	1988	130.00	275
1992	Dottie-912393 - K. Kennedy	1,000		160.00	160
1988	Elizabeth-901214	Closed	1991	90.00	90
1988	Ellen-901246	Closed	1991	100.00	100
1990	Emily-912303	Closed	1992	150.00	150
1988	Erin-901241	Closed	1991	170.00	170
1990	Fluffer-912293	Closed	1994	135.00	150-225
1985	Garnet-901183	Closed	1988	160.00	295
1990	Gigi-912306 - K. Kennedy	Closed	1994	150.00	150
1986	Gina-901176	Closed	1989	300.00	300
1989	Ginny-912287 - K. Kennedy	Closed	1993	140.00	140
1986	Girl Frog Freda-912105	Closed	1989	20.00	20
1988	Goldilocks-912234 - K. Kennedy	Closed	1992	65.00	65
1986	Googley German Astrid-912109	Closed	1989	60.00	60
1988	Heather-912247	Closed	1990	135.00	150
1990	Heather-912322	Closed	1992	150.00	150
1990	Heidi-901266	2,000		150.00	150
1990	Helene-901249 - K. Kennedy	Closed	1991	160.00	160
1990	Helga-912337	Closed	1994	325.00	325
1984	Henri-901035	Closed	1986	100.00	200
1984	Henrietta-901036	Closed	1986	100.00	200
1992	Hilary-912353	Closed	1993	130.00	135
1992	Holly Belle-912380	500	1994	125.00	125
1982	Holly-901233	Closed	1985	160.00	200
1989	Holly-901254	Closed	1992	180.00	180
1989	Hope Baby w/ Pillow-912292	Closed	1992	110.00	110
1992	Iris-912389 - K. Kennedy	500		165.00	165
1987	Jacqueline-912192	Closed	1990	80.00	80
1990	Jacqueline-912329 - K. Kennedy	Closed	1993	136.00	150-225
1984	Jamie-912061	Closed	1987	65.00	100
1984	Jeannie-901062	Closed	1987	200.00	550
1988	Jennifer-901248	Closed	1991	150.00	150
1988	Jennifer-912221	Closed	1990	80.00	80
1992	Jenny-912374 - K. Kennedy	Closed	1993	150.00	150
1988	Jesse-912231	Closed	1994	110.00	115
1987	Jessica-912195	Closed	1990	120.00	135
1993	Jessica-912410	2,000	1994	40.00	40
1990	Jillian-912323	Closed	1993	150.00	150
1989	Jimmy Baby w/ Pillow-912291 K. Kennedy	Closed	1992	165.00	165
1989	Jingles-912271	Closed	1991	60.00	60
1990	Joanne-912307 - K. Kennedy	Closed	1991	165.00	165
1987	Joy-912155	Closed	1989	50.00	50
1989	Joy-912289 - K. Kennedy	Closed	1992	110.00	110
1987	Julia-912174	Closed	1989	80.00	80
1990	Julia-912334 - K. Kennedy	Closed	1993	85.00	85
1993	Julie-912435 - K. Kennedy	2,000		45.00	45
1990	Justine-901256	Closed	1992	200.00	200
1988	Karen-912205	Closed	1991	200.00	250
1993	Katie-912412	2,000		40.00	40
1993	Kaylee-912433 - K. Kennedy	2,000	1994	45.00	45
1992	Kelli-912361	1,000		160.00	165
1990	Kelly-912331	Closed	1991	95.00	95
1990	Kimberly-912341	1,000		140.00	145
1987	Kittle Cat-912167	Closed	1989	55.00	55
1987	Kitty Cuddles-901201	Closed	1990	65.00	65
1992	Kris-912345 - K. Kennedy	Closed	1992	160.00	160
1989	Kristin-912285 - K. Kennedy	Closed	1994	90.00	95
1984	Laura-901106	Closed	1987	300.00	575
1988	Laura-912225	Closed	1991	135.00	135
1988	Lauren-912212	Closed	1991	110.00	110
1992	Lauren-912363 - K. Kennedy	1,000		190.00	195
1993	Lauren-912413	2,000		40.00	40
1993	Leslie-912432 - K. Kennedy	2,000	1994	45.00	45
1989	Licorice-912290	Closed	1991	75.00	75
1987	Lillian-901199	Closed	1990	85.00	100
1989	Lindsey-901263	Closed	1991	100.00	100
1989	Lisa-912275	Closed	1991	160.00	160
1989	Loni-912276	Closed	1993	125.00	150-185
1985	Lynn-912144	Closed	1988	90.00	135
1992	Margaret-912354 - K. Kennedy	1,000	1994	150.00	150
1989	Margot-912269	Closed	1991	110.00	110
1989	Maria-912265	Closed	1990	90.00	90
1982	Marie-901231	Closed	1985	95.00	95
1989	Marissa-901252 - K. Kennedy	Closed	1993	225.00	225
1988	Maritta Spanish-912224	Closed	1990	140.00	140
1992	Marjorie-912357	Closed	1993	135.00	135
1990	Marshmallow-912294 K. Kenndy	Closed	1992	75.00	75
1985	Mary-912126	Closed	1988	60.00	90
1990	Matthew-901251	Closed	1993	100.00	100
1989	Megan-901260	Closed	1993	120.00	120
1987	Megan-912148	Closed	1989	70.00	70
1989	Melanie-912284 - K. Kennedy	Closed	1992	135.00	135
1990	Melinda-912309 - K. Kennedy	Closed	1991	70.00	70
1988	Melissa-901230	Closed	1991	110.00	110
1988	Melissa-912208	Closed	1990	125.00	125
1989	Merry-912249	Closed	1990	200.00	200
1987	Michelle-901222	Closed	1991	90.00	90
1985	Michelle-912066	Closed	1989	100.00	225
1992	Michelle-912381 - K. Kennedy	Closed	1992	175.00	175
1985	Millie-912135	Closed	1988	70.00	125
1989	Missy-912283	Closed	1993	110.00	115
1988	Molly-912211 - K. Kennedy	Closed	1992	75.00	75
1990	Monica-912336 - K. Kennedy	Closed	1993	100.00	105
1990	Monique-912335 - K. Kennedy	Closed	1993	85.00	85
1988	Morgan-912239 - K. Kennedy	Closed	1992	75.00	75
1990	Mrs. Katz-912301	Closed	1993	140.00	145
1993	Nadine-912431 - K. Kennedy	2,000		45.00	45
1989	Nancy-912266	Closed	1990	110.00	110
1987	Nicole-901225	Closed	1991	575.00	575
1993	Nicole-912411	2,000		40.00	40
1987	Noel-912170	Closed	1989	125.00	125
1992	Noelle-912360 - K. Kennedy	1,000	1994	165.00	170
1990	Pamela-912302	Closed	1991	95.00	95
1986	Patty Artic Flower Print-901185	Closed	1990	140.00	140
1990	Paula-912316	Closed	1992	100.00	100
1988	Paulette-901244	Closed	1991	90.00	90
1990	Penny-912325 - K. Kennedy	Closed	1993	130.00	150-225
1986	Pepper Rust Dr/Appr-901184	Closed	1990	125.00	200
1985	Phyllis-912067	Closed	1989	60.00	60
1989	Pinky Clown-912268 K. Kennedy	Closed	1993	70.00	75
1988	Polly-912206	Closed	1990	100.00	125
1990	Priscilla-912300	Closed	1993	185.00	190
1990	Rebecca-901258	Closed	1992	250.00	250
1988	Renae-912245	Closed	1990	120.00	120
1990	Robin-912321	Closed	1993	160.00	165
1985	Rosalind-912087	Closed	1988	145.00	225
1985	Roxanne-901174	Closed	1988	155.00	275
1984	Sabina-901155	Closed	1988	75.00	N/A
1990	Samantha-912314	Closed	1993	185.00	190
1988	Sandy-901240 - K. Kennedy	Closed	1993	115.00	115
1989	Sara-912279	Closed	1991	175.00	175
1988	Sarah w/Pillow-912219	Closed	1991	105.00	105
1987	Sarah-901220	Closed	1992	350.00	350
1993	Sarah-912408	2,000		40.00	40
1993	Shannon-912434 - K. Kennedy	2,000		45.00	45
1990	Sheena-912338	Closed	1992	115.00	115
1984	Sheila-912060	Closed	1988	75.00	135
1990	Sheri-912305 - K. Kennedy	Closed	1992	115.00	115
1992	Sherise-912383 - K. Kennedy	Closed	1992	145.00	145
1989	Sigrid-912282	Closed	1992	145.00	145
1988	Snow White-912235 K. Kennedy	Closed	1992	65.00	65
1987	Sophia-912173	Closed	1989	40.00	40
1988	Stephanie-912238	Closed	1992	200.00	200
1990	Stephanie-912312	Closed	1993	150.00	150
1984	Stephanie-933012	Closed	1988	115.00	115
1988	Susan-901243	Closed	1991	100.00	100
1990	Susie-912328	Closed	1993	115.00	120
1987	Suzanne-901200	Closed	1990	85.00	100
1989	Suzanne-912286	Closed	1992	120.00	120
1989	Suzy-912295	Closed	1991	110.00	110
1992	Tamika-912382	500	1994	185.00	185
1989	Tammy-912264	Closed	1990	110.00	110
1987	Tasha-901221	Closed	1990	115.00	130
1990	Tasha-912299 - K. Kennedy	Closed	1992	25.00	25
1989	Terry-912281	Closed	1994	125.00	130
1987	Tiffany Pouty-901211	Closed	1991	120.00	160
1990	Tiffany-912326 - K. Kennedy	Closed	1992	180.00	180
1984	Tobie-912023	Closed	1987	30.00	30
1992	Toni-912367 - K. Kennedy	Closed	1993	120.00	120
1990	Tracie-912315	Closed	1993	125.00	125
1992	Trudie-912391	500		135.00	135
1982	Trudy-901232	Closed	1985	100.00	100
1992	Tulip-912385 - K. Kennedy	500	1994	145.00	145
1989	Valerie-901255	Closed	1994	175.00	175
1989	Vanessa-912272	Closed	1991	110.00	110
1984	Victoria-901068	Closed	1987	200.00	1500
1992	Wendy-912330 - K. Kennedy	1,000		125.00	130
1988	Whitney Blk-912232	Closed	1994	62.50	65

Victoria Ashlea® Originals-Tiny Tot Clowns - K. Kennedy

1994	Danielle-912461	2,000		45.00	45
1994	Lindsey-912463	2,000		45.00	45
1994	Lisa-912458	2,000		45.00	45
1994	Marie-912462	2,000		45.00	45
1994	Megan-912460	2,000		45.00	45
1994	Stacy-912459	2,000		45.00	45

Victoria Ashlea® Originals-Tiny Tot School Girls - K. Kennedy

1994	Andrea- 912456	2,000		47.50	48
1994	Christine- 912450	2,000		47.50	48
1994	Monique- 912455	2,000		47.50	48
1994	Patricia- 912453	2,000		47.50	48
1994	Shawna- 912449	2,000		47.50	48
1994	Susan- 912457	2,000		47.50	48

Goebel/M.I. Hummel

M. I. Hummel Collectible Dolls - M. I. Hummel

1964	Chimney Sweep 1908	Closed	N/A	55.00	110
1964	For Father 1917	Closed	N/A	55.00	90
1964	Goose Girl 1914	Closed	N/A	55.00	80
1964	Gretel 1901	Closed	N/A	55.00	125
1964	Hansel 1902	Closed	N/A	55.00	110
1964	Little Knitter 1905	Closed	N/A	55.00	75
1964	Lost Stocking 1926	Closed	N/A	55.00	75
1964	Merry Wanderer 1906	Closed	N/A	55.00	90
1964	Merry Wanderer 1925	Closed	N/A	55.00	110
1964	On Secret Path 1928	Closed	N/A	55.00	80
1964	Rosa-Blue Baby 1904/B	Closed	N/A	45.00	85
1964	Rosa-Pink Baby 1904/P	Closed	N/A	45.00	75
1964	School Boy 1910	Closed	N/A	55.00	80
1964	School Girl 1909	Closed	N/A	55.00	75
1964	Visiting and Invalid 1927	Closed	N/A	55.00	75

M. I. Hummel Porcelain Dolls - M. I. Hummel

1984	Birthday Serenade/Boy	Closed	N/A	225.00	250-300
1984	Birthday Serenade/Girl	Closed	N/A	225.00	250-300
1985	Carnival	Closed	N/A	225.00	250-300
1985	Easter Greetings	Closed	N/A	225.00	250-300
1985	Lost Sheep	Closed	N/A	225.00	250-300
1984	On Holiday	Closed	N/A	225.00	250-300
1984	Postman	Closed	N/A	225.00	250-300
1985	Signs of Spring	Closed	N/A	225.00	250-300

Good-Krüger

Limited Edition - J. Good-Krüger

1990	Alice	Retrd.	1991	250.00	250
1992	Anne	Retrd.	1992	240.00	500
1990	Annie-Rose	Retrd.	1990	219.00	425
1990	Christmas Cookie	Retrd.	1993	199.00	225
1990	Cozy	Retrd.	1992	179.00	275-375
1990	Daydream	Retrd.	1990	199.00	350
1992	Jeepers Creepers (Porcelain)	Retrd.	1992	725.00	800
1991	Johnny-Lynn	Retrd.	1991	240.00	500

YEAR ISSUE		EDITION LIMIT	YEAR RETD.	ISSUE PRICE	QUOTE U.S.$
1991	Moppett	Retrd.	1991	179.00	275
1990	Sue-Lynn	Retrd.	1990	240.00	300
1991	Teachers Pet	Retrd.	1991	199.00	250
1991	Victorian Christmas	Retrd.	1992	219.00	275

Gorham

Beverly Port Designer Collection - B. Port

YEAR ISSUE		EDITION LIMIT	YEAR RETD.	ISSUE PRICE	QUOTE U.S.$
1988	The Amazing Calliope Merriweather 17"	Closed	1990	275.00	1000-1300
1988	Baery Mab 9-1/2"	Closed	1990	110.00	300
1987	Christopher Paul Bearkin 10"	Closed	1990	95.00	275-350
1988	Hollybeary Kringle 15"	Closed	1990	350.00	450
1987	Kristobear Kringle 17"	Closed	1990	200.00	450
1988	Miss Emily 18"	Closed	1990	350.00	1000
1987	Molly Melinda Bearkin 10"	Closed	1990	95.00	200-250
1987	Silver Bell 17"	Closed	1990	175.00	300-700
1988	T.R. 28-1/2"	Closed	1990	400.00	600-650
1987	Tedward Jonathan Bearkin 10"	Closed	1990	95.00	225-400
1987	Tedwina Kimelina Bearkin 10"	Closed	1990	95.00	225-350
1988	Theodore B. Bear 14"	Closed	1990	175.00	550

Bonnet Babies - M. Sirko

YEAR ISSUE		EDITION LIMIT	YEAR RETD.	ISSUE PRICE	QUOTE U.S.$
1993	Chelsea's Bonnet	Closed	1994	95.00	95

Bonnets & Bows - B. Gerardi

YEAR ISSUE		EDITION LIMIT	YEAR RETD.	ISSUE PRICE	QUOTE U.S.$
1988	Belinda	Closed	1990	195.00	450
1988	Annemarie	Closed	1990	195.00	450
1988	Allessandra	Closed	1990	195.00	350
1988	Lisette	Closed	1990	285.00	495
1988	Bettina	Closed	1994	285.00	495
1988	Ellie	Closed	1994	285.00	495
1988	Alicia	Closed	1994	385.00	700
1988	Bethany	Closed	1994	385.00	1350
1988	Jesse	Closed	1994	525.00	675
1988	Francie	Closed	1994	625.00	800

Bride Dolls - D. Valenza

YEAR ISSUE		EDITION LIMIT	YEAR RETD.	ISSUE PRICE	QUOTE U.S.$
1993	Susannah's Wedding Day	9,500	1994	295.00	295

Carousel Dolls - C. Shafer

YEAR ISSUE		EDITION LIMIT	YEAR RETD.	ISSUE PRICE	QUOTE U.S.$
1993	Ribbons And Roses	Closed	1994	119.00	119

Celebrations Of Childhood - L. Di Leo

YEAR ISSUE		EDITION LIMIT	YEAR RETD.	ISSUE PRICE	QUOTE U.S.$
1992	Happy Birthday Amy	Closed	1994	160.00	225

Childhood Memories - D. Valenza

YEAR ISSUE		EDITION LIMIT	YEAR RETD.	ISSUE PRICE	QUOTE U.S.$
1991	Amanda	Closed	1994	98.00	98
1991	Jennifer	Closed	1994	98.00	98
1991	Jessica Anne's Playtime	Closed	1994	98.00	98
1991	Kimberly	Closed	1994	98.00	98

Children Of Christmas - S. Stone Aiken

YEAR ISSUE		EDITION LIMIT	YEAR RETD.	ISSUE PRICE	QUOTE U.S.$
1989	Clara, 16"	Closed	1994	325.00	650
1990	Natalie, 16"	1,500	1994	350.00	500
1991	Emily	1,500	1994	375.00	400
1992	Virginia	1,500	1994	375.00	400

Christmas Traditions - S. Stone Aiken

YEAR ISSUE		EDITION LIMIT	YEAR RETD.	ISSUE PRICE	QUOTE U.S.$
1993	Trimming the Tree	2,500	1994	295.00	295
1993	Chrissy	Closed	1994	150.00	150

Daydreamer Dolls - S. Stone Aiken

YEAR ISSUE		EDITION LIMIT	YEAR RETD.	ISSUE PRICE	QUOTE U.S.$
1992	Heather's Daydream	Closed	1994	119.00	119

Days Of The Week - R./L. Schrubbe

YEAR ISSUE		EDITION LIMIT	YEAR RETD.	ISSUE PRICE	QUOTE U.S.$
1992	Monday's Child	Closed	1994	98.00	98
1992	Tuesday's Child	Closed	1994	98.00	98
1992	Wednesday's Child	Closed	1994	98.00	98
1992	Thurday's Child	Closed	1994	98.00	98
1992	Friday's Child	Closed	1994	98.00	98
1992	Saturday's Child	Closed	1994	98.00	98
1992	Sunday's Child	Closed	1994	98.00	98

Dollie And Me - J. Pilallis

YEAR ISSUE		EDITION LIMIT	YEAR RETD.	ISSUE PRICE	QUOTE U.S.$
1991	Dollie's First Steps	Closed	1994	160.00	225

Dolls of the Month - Gorham

YEAR ISSUE		EDITION LIMIT	YEAR RETD.	ISSUE PRICE	QUOTE U.S.$
1991	Miss January	Closed	1994	79.00	79
1991	Miss February	Closed	1994	79.00	79
1991	Miss March	Closed	1994	79.00	79
1991	Miss April	Closed	1994	79.00	79
1991	Miss May	Closed	1994	79.00	79
1991	Miss June	Closed	1994	79.00	79
1991	Miss July	Closed	1994	79.00	79
1991	Miss August	Closed	1994	79.00	79
1991	Miss September	Closed	1994	79.00	79
1991	Miss October	Closed	1994	79.00	79
1991	Miss November	Closed	1994	79.00	79
1991	Miss December	Closed	1994	79.00	79

The Friendship Dolls - Various

YEAR ISSUE		EDITION LIMIT	YEAR RETD.	ISSUE PRICE	QUOTE U.S.$
1991	Angela-The Italian Traveler S. Nappo	Closed	1994	98.00	98
1991	Kinuko-The Japanese Traveler - S. Ueki	Closed	1994	98.00	98
1991	Meagan-The Irish Traveler L. O'Connor	Closed	1994	98.00	98
1991	Peggy-The American Traveler P. Seaman	Closed	1994	98.00	98

Gift of Dreams - Young/Gerardi

YEAR ISSUE		EDITION LIMIT	YEAR RETD.	ISSUE PRICE	QUOTE U.S.$
1991	Christina (Christmas)	Closed	1994	695.00	695
1991	Elizabeth	Closed	1994	495.00	495
1991	Katherine	Closed	1994	495.00	495
1991	Melissa	Closed	1994	495.00	495
1991	Samantha	Closed	1994	495.00	495

Gifts of the Garden - S. Stone Aiken

YEAR ISSUE		EDITION LIMIT	YEAR RETD.	ISSUE PRICE	QUOTE U.S.$
1991	Alisa	Closed	1994	125.00	250
1991	Deborah	Closed	1994	125.00	250
1991	Holly (Christmas)	Closed	1994	150.00	250
1991	Irene	Closed	1994	125.00	250
1991	Joelle (Christmas)	Closed	1994	150.00	250
1991	Lauren	Closed	1994	125.00	250
1991	Maria	Closed	1994	125.00	250
1991	Priscilla	Closed	1994	125.00	250
1991	Valerie	Closed	1994	125.00	250

Gorham Baby Doll Collection - Aiken/Matthews

YEAR ISSUE		EDITION LIMIT	YEAR RETD.	ISSUE PRICE	QUOTE U.S.$
1987	Christening Day	Closed	1990	245.00	350
1987	Leslie	Closed	1990	245.00	350
1987	Matthew	Closed	1990	245.00	350

Gorham Dolls - S. Stone Aiken, unless otherwise noted

YEAR ISSUE		EDITION LIMIT	YEAR RETD.	ISSUE PRICE	QUOTE U.S.$
1985	Alexander, 19"	Closed	1990	275.00	400
1981	Alexandria, 18"	Closed	1990	250.00	500
1986	Alissa	Closed	1990	245.00	300
1985	Amelia, 19"	Closed	1990	275.00	325
1982	Baby in Apricot Dress, 16"	Closed	1990	175.00	375
1982	Baby in Blue Dress, 12"	Closed	1990	150.00	300
1982	Baby in White Dress, 18" - Gorham	Closed	1990	250.00	350
1982	Benjamin, 18"	Closed	1990	200.00	600
1981	Cecile, 16"	Closed	1990	200.00	800
1981	Christina, 16"	Closed	1990	200.00	425
1981	Christopher, 19"	Closed	1990	250.00	500
1982	Corrine, 21"	Closed	1990	250.00	500
1981	Danielle, 14"	Closed	1990	150.00	300
1981	Elena, 14"	Closed	1990	150.00	650
1982	Ellice, 18"	Closed	1990	200.00	400
1986	Emily, 14"	Closed	1990	175.00	395
1986	Fleur, 19"	Closed	1990	300.00	450
1985	Gabrielle, 19"	Closed	1990	225.00	350
1983	Jennifer, 19" Bridal Doll	Closed	1990	325.00	750
1982	Jeremy, 23"	Closed	1990	300.00	700
1986	Jessica	Closed	1990	195.00	275
1981	Jillian, 16"	Closed	1990	200.00	400
1986	Julia, 16"	Closed	1990	225.00	350
1987	Juliet	Closed	1990	325.00	400
1982	Kristin, 23"	Closed	1990	300.00	575
1986	Lauren, 14"	Closed	1990	175.00	350
1985	Linda, 19"	Closed	1990	275.00	600
1982	M. Anton, 12" - Unknown	Closed	1990	125.00	175
1982	Melanie, 23"	Closed	1990	300.00	600
1981	Melinda, 14"	Closed	1990	150.00	300
1986	Meredith	Closed	1990	295.00	350
1982	Mlle. Jeanette, 12"	Closed	1990	125.00	175
1982	Mlle. Lucille, 12"	Closed	1990	125.00	375
1982	Mlle. Marsella, 12" - Unknown	Closed	1990	125.00	275
1982	Mlle. Monique, 12"	Closed	1990	125.00	275
1982	Mlle. Yvonne, 12" - Unknown	Closed	1990	125.00	375
1985	Nanette, 19"	Closed	1990	275.00	325
1985	Odette, 19"	Closed	1990	250.00	450
1981	Rosemond, 18"	Closed	1990	250.00	750
1981	Stephanie, 18"	Closed	1990	250.00	2000

Gorham Holly Hobbie Childhood Memories - Holly Hobbie

YEAR ISSUE		EDITION LIMIT	YEAR RETD.	ISSUE PRICE	QUOTE U.S.$
1985	Mother's Helper	Closed	1990	45.00	175
1985	Best Friends	Closed	1994	45.00	175
1985	First Day of School	Closed	1994	45.00	175
1985	Christmas Wishes	Closed	1994	45.00	175

Gorham Holly Hobbie For All Seasons - Holly Hobbie

YEAR ISSUE		EDITION LIMIT	YEAR RETD.	ISSUE PRICE	QUOTE U.S.$
1984	Summer Holly 12"	Closed	1994	42.50	195
1984	Fall Holly 12"	Closed	1994	42.50	195
1984	Winter Holly 12"	Closed	1994	42.50	195
1984	Spring Holly 12"	Closed	1994	42.50	195
1984	Set of 4	Closed	1994	170.00	750

Holly Hobbie - Holly Hobbie

YEAR ISSUE		EDITION LIMIT	YEAR RETD.	ISSUE PRICE	QUOTE U.S.$
1983	Blue Girl, 14"	Closed	1994	80.00	245
1983	Blue Girl, 18"	Closed	1994	115.00	295
1983	Christmas Morning, 14"	Closed	1994	80.00	245
1983	Heather, 14"	Closed	1994	80.00	275
1983	Little Amy, 14"	Closed	1994	80.00	245
1983	Robbie, 14"	Closed	1994	80.00	275
1983	Sunday Best, 18"	Closed	1994	115.00	295
1983	Sweet Valentine, 16"	Closed	1994	100.00	295
1983	Yesterday's Memories, 18"	Closed	1994	125.00	375

Imaginary People - R. Tonner

YEAR ISSUE		EDITION LIMIT	YEAR RETD.	ISSUE PRICE	QUOTE U.S.$
1993	Melinda, The Tooth Fairy	2,900	1994	95.00	95

International Babies - R. Tonner

YEAR ISSUE		EDITION LIMIT	YEAR RETD.	ISSUE PRICE	QUOTE U.S.$
1993	Natalia's Matrioshka	Closed	1994	95.00	95

Joyful Years - B. Gerardi

YEAR ISSUE		EDITION LIMIT	YEAR RETD.	ISSUE PRICE	QUOTE U.S.$
1989	Katrina	Closed	1994	295.00	375
1989	William	Closed	1994	295.00	375

Kezi Doll For All Seasons - Kezi

YEAR ISSUE		EDITION LIMIT	YEAR RETD.	ISSUE PRICE	QUOTE U.S.$
1985	Ariel 16"	Closed	1994	135.00	500
1985	Aubrey 16"	Closed	1994	135.00	500
1985	Amber 16"	Closed	1994	135.00	500
1985	Adrienne 16"	Closed	1994	135.00	500
1985	Set of 4	Closed	1994	540.00	1900

Kezi Golden Gifts - Kezi

YEAR ISSUE		EDITION LIMIT	YEAR RETD.	ISSUE PRICE	QUOTE U.S.$
1984	Charity 16"	Closed	1990	85.00	175
1984	Faith 18"	Closed	1990	95.00	195
1984	Felicity 18"	Closed	1990	95.00	195
1984	Grace 16"	Closed	1990	85.00	175
1984	Hope 16"	Closed	1990	85.00	175
1984	Merrie 16"	Closed	1990	85.00	175
1984	Patience 18"	Closed	1990	95.00	195
1984	Prudence 18"	Closed	1990	85.00	195

Legendary Heroines - S. Stone Aiken

YEAR ISSUE		EDITION LIMIT	YEAR RETD.	ISSUE PRICE	QUOTE U.S.$
1991	Guinevere	1,500	1994	245.00	245
1991	Jane Eyre	1,500	1994	245.00	245
1991	Juliet	1,500	1994	245.00	245
1991	Lara	1,500	1994	245.00	245

Les Belles Bebes Collection - S. Stone Aiken

YEAR ISSUE		EDITION LIMIT	YEAR RETD.	ISSUE PRICE	QUOTE U.S.$
1993	Camille	1,500	1994	375.00	395
1991	Cherie	Closed	1994	375.00	475
1991	Desiree	1,500	1994	375.00	395

Limited Edition Dolls - S. Stone Aiken

YEAR ISSUE		EDITION LIMIT	YEAR RETD.	ISSUE PRICE	QUOTE U.S.$
1982	Allison, 19"	Closed	1990	300.00	4500
1983	Ashley, 19"	Closed	1990	350.00	1000
1984	Nicole, 19"	Closed	1990	350.00	875
1984	Holly (Christmas), 19"	Closed	1990	300.00	850
1985	Lydia, 19"	Closed	1990	550.00	1800
1985	Joy (Christmas), 19"	Closed	1990	350.00	695
1986	Noel (Christmas), 19"	Closed	1990	400.00	750
1987	Jacqueline, 19"	Closed	1994	500.00	700
1987	Merrie (Christmas), 19"	Closed	1994	500.00	750
1988	Andrew, 19"	Closed	1994	475.00	750
1988	Christa (Christmas), 19"	Closed	1994	550.00	1500
1990	Amey (10th Anniversary Edition)	Closed	1994	650.00	1100

Limited Edition Sister Set - S. Stone Aiken

YEAR ISSUE		EDITION LIMIT	YEAR RETD.	ISSUE PRICE	QUOTE U.S.$
1988	Kathleen	Closed	1994	550.00	750
1988	Katelin	Set	1994	Set	Set

Little Women - S. Stone Aiken

YEAR ISSUE		EDITION LIMIT	YEAR RETD.	ISSUE PRICE	QUOTE U.S.$
1983	Amy, 16"	Closed	1994	225.00	500
1983	Beth, 16"	Closed	1994	225.00	500
1983	Jo, 19"	Closed	1994	275.00	575
1983	Meg, 19"	Closed	1994	275.00	650

Littlest Angel Dolls - L. Di Leo

YEAR ISSUE		EDITION LIMIT	YEAR RETD.	ISSUE PRICE	QUOTE U.S.$
1992	Merriel	Closed	1994	49.50	50

Nature's Bounty - R. Tonner

YEAR ISSUE		EDITION LIMIT	YEAR RETD.	ISSUE PRICE	QUOTE U.S.$
1993	Jamie's Fruitful Harvest	Closed	1994	95.00	95

Pillow Baby Dolls - L. Gordon

YEAR ISSUE		EDITION LIMIT	YEAR RETD.	ISSUE PRICE	QUOTE U.S.$
1993	On the Move	Closed	1994	39.00	39
1993	Sitting Pretty	Closed	1994	39.00	39
1993	Tickling Toes	Closed	1994	39.00	39

Portrait Perfect Victorian Dolls - R. Tonner

YEAR ISSUE		EDITION LIMIT	YEAR RETD.	ISSUE PRICE	QUOTE U.S.$
1993	Pretty in Peach	2,900	1994	119.00	119

Precious as Pearls - S. Stone Aiken

YEAR ISSUE		EDITION LIMIT	YEAR RETD.	ISSUE PRICE	QUOTE U.S.$
1986	Colette	Closed	1994	400.00	1500
1987	Charlotte	Closed	1994	425.00	750
1988	Chloe	Closed	1994	525.00	850
1989	Cassandra	Closed	1994	525.00	1250
XX	Set	Closed	1994	1875.00	4000

Puppy Love Dolls - R./ L. Schrubbe

YEAR ISSUE		EDITION LIMIT	YEAR RETD.	ISSUE PRICE	QUOTE U.S.$
1992	Katie And Kyle	Closed	1994	119.00	119

Small Wonders - B. Gerardi

YEAR ISSUE		EDITION LIMIT	YEAR RETD.	ISSUE PRICE	QUOTE U.S.$
1988	Madeline	Closed	1990	365.00	365
1988	Marguerite	Closed	1990	425.00	425
1988	Patina	Closed	1990	265.00	265

Southern Belles - S. Stone Aiken

YEAR ISSUE		EDITION LIMIT	YEAR RETD.	ISSUE PRICE	QUOTE U.S.$
1985	Amanda, 19"	Closed	1990	300.00	1400
1986	Veronica, 19"	Closed	1990	325.00	750
1987	Rachel, 19"	Closed	1990	375.00	800
1988	Cassie, 19"	Closed	1990	500.00	875

Special Moments - E. Worrell

YEAR ISSUE		EDITION LIMIT	YEAR RETD.	ISSUE PRICE	QUOTE U.S.$
1991	Baby's First Christmas	Closed	1994	135.00	235
1992	Baby's First Steps	Closed	1994	135.00	135

Sporting Kids - R. Schrubbe

YEAR ISSUE		EDITION LIMIT	YEAR RETD.	ISSUE PRICE	QUOTE U.S.$
1993	Up At Bat	Closed	1994	49.50	80

Tender Hearts - M. Murphy

YEAR ISSUE		EDITION LIMIT	YEAR RETD.	ISSUE PRICE	QUOTE U.S.$
1993	Saying Grace	Closed	1994	119.00	119

Times To Treasure - L. Di Leo

YEAR ISSUE		EDITION LIMIT	YEAR RETD.	ISSUE PRICE	QUOTE U.S.$
1991	Bedtime	Closed	1994	195.00	250
1993	Playtime	Closed	1994	195.00	250

YEAR ISSUE		EDITION LIMIT	YEAR RETD.	ISSUE PRICE	QUOTE U.S.$
1990	Storytime	Closed	1994	195.00	250

Valentine Ladies - P. Valentine

YEAR ISSUE		EDITION LIMIT	YEAR RETD.	ISSUE PRICE	QUOTE U.S.$
1987	Anabella	Closed	1994	145.00	395
1987	Elizabeth	Closed	1994	145.00	450
1988	Felicia	Closed	1994	225.00	325
1987	Jane	Closed	1994	145.00	350
1988	Judith Anne	Closed	1994	195.00	325
1989	Julianna	Closed	1994	225.00	275
1987	Lee Ann	Closed	1994	145.00	325
1988	Maria Theresa	Closed	1994	225.00	350
1987	Marianna	Closed	1994	160.00	400
1987	Patrice	Closed	1994	145.00	325
1988	Priscilla	Closed	1994	195.00	325
1987	Rebecca	Closed	1994	145.00	325
1987	Rosanne	Closed	1994	145.00	325
1989	Rose	Closed	1994	225.00	275
1987	Sylvia	Closed	1994	160.00	350

Victorian Cameo Collection - B. Gerardi

YEAR ISSUE		EDITION LIMIT	YEAR RETD.	ISSUE PRICE	QUOTE U.S.$
1990	Victoria	1,500	1994	375.00	425
1991	Alexandra	Closed	1994	375.00	425

Victorian Children - S. Stone Aiken

YEAR ISSUE		EDITION LIMIT	YEAR RETD.	ISSUE PRICE	QUOTE U.S.$
1992	Sara's Tea Time	1,000	1994	495.00	750
1993	Catching Butterflies	1,000	1994	495.00	495

The Victorian Collection - E. Woodhouse

YEAR ISSUE		EDITION LIMIT	YEAR RETD.	ISSUE PRICE	QUOTE U.S.$
1992	Victoria's Jubilee	Yr.Iss.	1994	295.00	295

Victorian Flower Girls - J. Pillalis

YEAR ISSUE		EDITION LIMIT	YEAR RETD.	ISSUE PRICE	QUOTE U.S.$
1993	Rose	Closed	1994	95.00	95

H & G Studios

Brenda Burke Dolls - B. Burke

YEAR ISSUE		EDITION LIMIT	YEAR RETD.	ISSUE PRICE	QUOTE U.S.$
1989	Adelaine	25		1795.00	3600
1989	Alexandra	125		995.00	2000
1989	Alicia	125		895.00	1800
1989	Amanda	25		1995.00	6000
1989	Angelica	50		1495.00	3000
1989	Arabelle	500		695.00	1400
1989	Beatrice	85		2395.00	2395
1990	Belinda	12		3695.00	3695
1989	Bethany	45		2995.00	2995
1989	Brittany	75		2695.00	2695
1991	Charlotte	20		2395.00	2395
1991	Clarissa	15		3595.00	3595
1992	Dorothea	500		395.00	395
1993	Giovanna	1		7800.00	7800
1993	Melissa	1		7750.00	7750
1991	Sleigh Ride	20		3695.00	3695
1991	Tender Love	25		3295.00	3295

Hallmark

Special Edition Hallmark Barbie Dolls

YEAR ISSUE		EDITION LIMIT	YEAR RETD.	ISSUE PRICE	QUOTE U.S.$
1994	Victorian Elegance Barbie	Yr.Iss.	1994	40.00	110-150
1995	Holiday Memories Barbie	Yr.Iss.	1995	45.00	45

Hallmark Galleries

Mary Engelbreit's Friendship Garden - M. Engelbreit

YEAR ISSUE		EDITION LIMIT	YEAR RETD.	ISSUE PRICE	QUOTE U.S.$
1993	Porcelain Doll-Josephine 6000QHG5003	12,500	1995	60.00	60
1993	Porcelain Doll-Louisa 6500QHG5002	12,500	1995	65.00	65
1993	Porcelain Doll-Margaret 6000QHG5001	12,500	1995	60.00	60

Victorian Memories - J. Greene

YEAR ISSUE		EDITION LIMIT	YEAR RETD.	ISSUE PRICE	QUOTE U.S.$
1992	Abigail 1QHG1019	4,500	1995	125.00	125
1992	Abner 1QHG1018	4,500	1995	110.00	110
1992	Alice 1QHG1020	4,500	1995	125.00	125
1993	Baby Doll Beatrice 2000QHG1029	9,500	1994	20.00	20
1992	Bear-plush bear 3500QHG1011	9,500	1995	35.00	35
1992	Bunny B-plush rabbit 3500QHG1012	9,500	1995	35.00	35
1992	Daisy -plush bear 8500QHG1009	2,500	1995	85.00	85
1992	Emma/miniature doll 2500QHG1016	9,500	1995	25.00	25
1993	Hannah 1QHG1030	2,500	1995	130.00	130
1992	Katherine 1QHG1017	1,200	1995	150.00	150
1994	Mini Jointed Bear Jesse 1200QHG1037	9,500	1995	12.00	12
1992	Olivia 1QHG1021	4,500	1995	125.00	125
1992	Seth-plush bear 4000QHG1007	9,500	1995	40.00	40
1992	Teddy -plush bear 4500QHG1008	9,500	1995	45.00	45

Hamilton Collection

Abbie Williams Doll Collection - A. Williams

YEAR ISSUE		EDITION LIMIT	YEAR RETD.	ISSUE PRICE	QUOTE U.S.$
1992	Molly	Closed	N/A	155.00	200

Annual Connossieur Doll - N/A

YEAR ISSUE		EDITION LIMIT	YEAR RETD.	ISSUE PRICE	QUOTE U.S.$
1992	Lara	7,450		295.00	295

The Antique Doll Collection - Unknown

YEAR ISSUE		EDITION LIMIT	YEAR RETD.	ISSUE PRICE	QUOTE U.S.$
1989	Nicole	Closed	N/A	195.00	300
1990	Colette	Open		195.00	195
1991	Lisette	Open		195.00	225
1991	Katrina	Open		195.00	195

Baby Portrait Dolls - B. Parker

YEAR ISSUE		EDITION LIMIT	YEAR RETD.	ISSUE PRICE	QUOTE U.S.$
1991	Melissa	Closed	1993	135.00	150-185
1992	Jenna	Closed	N/A	135.00	195
1992	Bethany	Open		135.00	135
1993	Mindy	Open		135.00	135

Belles of the Countryside - C. Heath Orange

YEAR ISSUE		EDITION LIMIT	YEAR RETD.	ISSUE PRICE	QUOTE U.S.$
1992	Erin	Open		135.00	135
1992	Rose	Open		135.00	135
1993	Lorna	Open		135.00	135
1994	Gwyn	Open		135.00	135

The Bessie Pease Gutmann Doll Collection - B.P. Gutmann

YEAR ISSUE		EDITION LIMIT	YEAR RETD.	ISSUE PRICE	QUOTE U.S.$
1989	Love is Blind	Closed	N/A	135.00	220
1989	He Won't Bite	Closed	N/A	135.00	135
1991	Virginia	Open		135.00	135
1991	First Dancing Lesson	Open		195.00	195
1991	Good Morning	Open		195.00	195
1991	Love At First Sight	Open		195.00	195

Best Buddies - C.M. Rolfe

YEAR ISSUE		EDITION LIMIT	YEAR RETD.	ISSUE PRICE	QUOTE U.S.$
1994	Jodie	Open		69.00	69
1994	Brandy	Open		69.00	69
1995	Joey	Open		69.00	69

Boehm Christening - Boehm Studio

YEAR ISSUE		EDITION LIMIT	YEAR RETD.	ISSUE PRICE	QUOTE U.S.$
1994	Elena's First Portrait	Open		155.00	155

Boehm Dolls - N/A

YEAR ISSUE		EDITION LIMIT	YEAR RETD.	ISSUE PRICE	QUOTE U.S.$
1994	Elena	Open		155.00	155

Bridal Elegance - Boehm

YEAR ISSUE		EDITION LIMIT	YEAR RETD.	ISSUE PRICE	QUOTE U.S.$
1994	Camille	Open		195.00	195

Bride Dolls - Unknown

YEAR ISSUE		EDITION LIMIT	YEAR RETD.	ISSUE PRICE	QUOTE U.S.$
1991	Portrait of Innocence	Open		195.00	195
1992	Portrait of Loveliness	Open		195.00	195

Brooks Wooden Dolls - P. Ryan Brooks

YEAR ISSUE		EDITION LIMIT	YEAR RETD.	ISSUE PRICE	QUOTE U.S.$
1993	Waiting For Santa	15,000	1994	135.00	200-225
1993	Are You the Easter Bunny?	15,000		135.00	135
1994	Be My Valentine	Open		135.00	135

Catherine Mather Dolls - C. Mather

YEAR ISSUE		EDITION LIMIT	YEAR RETD.	ISSUE PRICE	QUOTE U.S.$
1993	Justine	15,000		155.00	155

Central Park Skaters - Unknown

YEAR ISSUE		EDITION LIMIT	YEAR RETD.	ISSUE PRICE	QUOTE U.S.$
1991	Central Park Skaters	Open		245.00	245

A Child's Menagerie - B. Van Boxel

YEAR ISSUE		EDITION LIMIT	YEAR RETD.	ISSUE PRICE	QUOTE U.S.$
1993	Becky	Open		69.00	69
1993	Carrie	Open		69.00	69
1994	Mandy	Open		69.00	69
1994	Terry	Open		69.00	69

Children To Cherish - N/A

YEAR ISSUE		EDITION LIMIT	YEAR RETD.	ISSUE PRICE	QUOTE U.S.$
1991	A Gift of Innocence	Yr.Iss.		135.00	135
1991	A Gift of Beauty	Open		135.00	135

Cindy Marschner Rolfe Dolls - C. M. Rolfe

YEAR ISSUE		EDITION LIMIT	YEAR RETD.	ISSUE PRICE	QUOTE U.S.$
1993	Shannon	Open		95.00	95
1993	Julie	Open		95.00	95
1993	Kayla	Open		95.00	95
1994	Janey	Open		95.00	95

Cindy Marschner Rolfe Twins - C. M. Rolfe

YEAR ISSUE		EDITION LIMIT	YEAR RETD.	ISSUE PRICE	QUOTE U.S.$
1995	Shelby & Sydney	Open		190.00	190

Cobabe Indians - L. Cobabe

YEAR ISSUE		EDITION LIMIT	YEAR RETD.	ISSUE PRICE	QUOTE U.S.$
1994	Snowbird	Open		135.00	135

Connie Walser Derek Baby Dolls - C.W. Derek

YEAR ISSUE		EDITION LIMIT	YEAR RETD.	ISSUE PRICE	QUOTE U.S.$
1990	Jessica	Closed	1993	155.00	275-395
1991	Sara	Closed	N/A	155.00	180
1991	Andrew	Open		155.00	155
1991	Amanda	Open		155.00	155
1992	Samantha	Open		155.00	155

Connie Walser Derek Baby Dolls II - C. W. Derek

YEAR ISSUE		EDITION LIMIT	YEAR RETD.	ISSUE PRICE	QUOTE U.S.$
1992	Stephanie	Open		95.00	95
1992	Beth	Open		95.00	95

Connie Walser Derek Baby Dolls III - C. W. Derek

YEAR ISSUE		EDITION LIMIT	YEAR RETD.	ISSUE PRICE	QUOTE U.S.$
1994	Chelsea	Open		79.00	79

Connie Walser Derek Dolls - C. W. Derek

YEAR ISSUE		EDITION LIMIT	YEAR RETD.	ISSUE PRICE	QUOTE U.S.$
1992	Baby Jessica	Open		75.00	75
1993	Baby Sara	Open		75.00	75

Connie Walser Derek Toddlers - C. W. Derek

YEAR ISSUE		EDITION LIMIT	YEAR RETD.	ISSUE PRICE	QUOTE U.S.$
1994	Jessie	Open		79.00	79
1994	Casey	Open		79.00	79

Daddy's Little Girls - M. Snyder

YEAR ISSUE		EDITION LIMIT	YEAR RETD.	ISSUE PRICE	QUOTE U.S.$
1992	Lindsay	Open		95.00	95
1993	Cassie	Open		95.00	95
1993	Dana	Open		95.00	95

Dolls by Autumn Berwick - A. Berwick

YEAR ISSUE		EDITION LIMIT	YEAR RETD.	ISSUE PRICE	QUOTE U.S.$
1993	Laura	Open		135.00	135

Dolls By Kay McKee - K. McKee

YEAR ISSUE		EDITION LIMIT	YEAR RETD.	ISSUE PRICE	QUOTE U.S.$
1992	Shy Violet	Closed	1993	135.00	225-236
1992	Robin	Open		135.00	135
1993	Katie Did It!	Open		135.00	135
1993	Ryan	Open		135.00	135

Dolls of America's Colonial Heritage - A. Elekfy

YEAR ISSUE		EDITION LIMIT	YEAR RETD.	ISSUE PRICE	QUOTE U.S.$
1986	Katrina	Open		55.00	55
1986	Nicole	Open		55.00	55
1987	Maria	Open		55.00	55
1987	Priscilla	Open		55.00	55
1987	Colleen	Open		55.00	55
1988	Gretchen	Open		55.00	55

Elaine Campbell Dolls - E. Campbell

YEAR ISSUE		EDITION LIMIT	YEAR RETD.	ISSUE PRICE	QUOTE U.S.$
1994	Emma	Open		95.00	95
1995	Abby	Open		95.00	95

First Recital - N/A

YEAR ISSUE		EDITION LIMIT	YEAR RETD.	ISSUE PRICE	QUOTE U.S.$
1993	Hillary	Open		135.00	135
1994	Olivia	Open		135.00	135

Grobben Ethnic Babies - J. Grobben

YEAR ISSUE		EDITION LIMIT	YEAR RETD.	ISSUE PRICE	QUOTE U.S.$
1994	Jasmine	Open		135.00	135

Grothedde Dolls - N. Grothedde

YEAR ISSUE		EDITION LIMIT	YEAR RETD.	ISSUE PRICE	QUOTE U.S.$
1993	Cindy	Open		69.00	69

Hargrave Dolls - M. Hargrave

YEAR ISSUE		EDITION LIMIT	YEAR RETD.	ISSUE PRICE	QUOTE U.S.$
1994	Angela	Open		79.00	79

Helen Carr Dolls - H. Carr

YEAR ISSUE		EDITION LIMIT	YEAR RETD.	ISSUE PRICE	QUOTE U.S.$
1994	Claudia	Open		135.00	135

Helen Kish II Dolls - H. Kish

YEAR ISSUE		EDITION LIMIT	YEAR RETD.	ISSUE PRICE	QUOTE U.S.$
1992	Vanessa	Open		135.00	135
1994	Jordan	Open		95.00	95

Holiday Carollers - U. Lepp

YEAR ISSUE		EDITION LIMIT	YEAR RETD.	ISSUE PRICE	QUOTE U.S.$
1992	Joy	Open		155.00	155
1993	Noel	Open		155.00	155

Huckleberry Hill Kids - B. Parker

YEAR ISSUE		EDITION LIMIT	YEAR RETD.	ISSUE PRICE	QUOTE U.S.$
1994	Gabrielle	Open		95.00	95
1994	Alexandra	Open		95.00	95

I Love Lucy (Porcelain) - Unknown

YEAR ISSUE		EDITION LIMIT	YEAR RETD.	ISSUE PRICE	QUOTE U.S.$
1990	Lucy	Closed	N/A	95.00	240-300
1991	Ricky	Closed	N/A	95.00	350
1992	Queen of the Gypsies	Closed	N/A	95.00	245
1992	Vitameatavegamin	Closed	N/A	95.00	200-300

I Love Lucy (Vinyl) - Unknown

YEAR ISSUE		EDITION LIMIT	YEAR RETD.	ISSUE PRICE	QUOTE U.S.$
1988	Ethel	Closed	N/A	40.00	100
1988	Fred	Closed	N/A	40.00	100
1990	Lucy	Closed	N/A	40.00	100
1991	Ricky	Closed	N/A	40.00	150
1992	Queen of the Gypsies	Open		40.00	40
1992	Vitameatavegamin	Open		40.00	40

I'm So Proud Doll Collection - L. Cobabe

YEAR ISSUE		EDITION LIMIT	YEAR RETD.	ISSUE PRICE	QUOTE U.S.$
1992	Christina	Open		95.00	95
1993	Jill	Open		95.00	95
1994	Tammy	Open		95.00	95
1994	Shelly	Open		95.00	95

Inga Manders - I. Manders

YEAR ISSUE		EDITION LIMIT	YEAR RETD.	ISSUE PRICE	QUOTE U.S.$
1995	Miss Priss	Open		79.00	79

International Children - C. Woodie

YEAR ISSUE		EDITION LIMIT	YEAR RETD.	ISSUE PRICE	QUOTE U.S.$
1991	Miko	Closed	N/A	49.50	80
1991	Anastasia	Open		49.50	50
1991	Angelina	Open		49.50	50
1992	Lian	Open		49.50	50
1992	Monique	Open		49.50	50
1992	Lisa	Open		49.50	50

Jane Zidjunas Party Dolls - J. Zidjunas

YEAR ISSUE		EDITION LIMIT	YEAR RETD.	ISSUE PRICE	QUOTE U.S.$
1991	Kelly	Open		135.00	135
1992	Katie	Open		135.00	135
1993	Meredith	Open		135.00	135

Jane Zidjunas Toddler Dolls - J. Zidjunas

YEAR ISSUE		EDITION LIMIT	YEAR RETD.	ISSUE PRICE	QUOTE U.S.$
1991	Jennifer	Open		135.00	135
1991	Megan	Open		135.00	160
1992	Kimberly	Open		135.00	135
1992	Amy	Open		135.00	135

Jeanne Wilson Dolls - J. Wilson

YEAR ISSUE		EDITION LIMIT	YEAR RETD.	ISSUE PRICE	QUOTE U.S.$
1994	Priscilla	Open		155.00	155

Johnston Cowgirls - C. Johnston

YEAR ISSUE		EDITION LIMIT	YEAR RETD.	ISSUE PRICE	QUOTE U.S.$
1994	Savannah	Open		79.00	79
1994	Skyler	Open		79.00	79

Join The Parade - N/A

YEAR ISSUE		EDITION LIMIT	YEAR RETD.	ISSUE PRICE	QUOTE U.S.$
1992	Betsy	Open		49.50	50
1994	Peggy	Open		55.00	55

YEAR ISSUE		EDITION LIMIT	YEAR RETD.	ISSUE PRICE	QUOTE U.S.$
1994	Sandy	Open		55.00	55

Joke Grobben Dolls - J. Grobben

YEAR ISSUE		EDITION LIMIT	YEAR RETD.	ISSUE PRICE	QUOTE U.S.$
1992	Heather	Open		69.00	69
1993	Kathleen	Open		69.00	69
1993	Brianna	Open		69.00	69
1994	Bridget	Open		69.00	69

Just Like Mom - H. Kish

YEAR ISSUE		EDITION LIMIT	YEAR RETD.	ISSUE PRICE	QUOTE U.S.$
1991	Ashley	Closed	1993	135.00	250
1992	Elizabeth	Open		135.00	135
1992	Hannah	Open		135.00	135
1993	Margaret	Open		135.00	135

Kay McKee Klowns - K. McKee

YEAR ISSUE		EDITION LIMIT	YEAR RETD.	ISSUE PRICE	QUOTE U.S.$
1993	The Dreamer	15,000		155.00	155

Kuck Fairy - S. Kuck

YEAR ISSUE		EDITION LIMIT	YEAR RETD.	ISSUE PRICE	QUOTE U.S.$
1994	Tooth Fairy	Open		135.00	135

Laura Cobabe Dolls - L. Cobabe

YEAR ISSUE		EDITION LIMIT	YEAR RETD.	ISSUE PRICE	QUOTE U.S.$
1992	Amber	Open		195.00	195
1992	Brooke	Open		195.00	195

Laura Cobabe Dolls II - L. Cobabe

YEAR ISSUE		EDITION LIMIT	YEAR RETD.	ISSUE PRICE	QUOTE U.S.$
1993	Kristen	Open		75.00	75

Laura Cobabe Tall Dolls - L. Cobabe

YEAR ISSUE		EDITION LIMIT	YEAR RETD.	ISSUE PRICE	QUOTE U.S.$
1994	Cassandra	Open		195.00	195
1994	Taylor	Open		195.00	195

Laura Cobabe's Costume Kids - L. Cobabe

YEAR ISSUE		EDITION LIMIT	YEAR RETD.	ISSUE PRICE	QUOTE U.S.$
1994	Lil' Punkin	Open		79.00	79
1994	Little Ladybug	Open		79.00	79
1995	Miss Dinomite	Open		79.00	79

Little Rascals™ - S./J. Hoffman

YEAR ISSUE		EDITION LIMIT	YEAR RETD.	ISSUE PRICE	QUOTE U.S.$
1992	Spanky	Open		75.00	75
1993	Alfalfa	Open		75.00	75
1994	Darla	Open		75.00	75
1994	Buckwheat	Open		75.00	75
1994	Stymie	Open		75.00	75

Littlest Members of the Wedding - J. Esteban

YEAR ISSUE		EDITION LIMIT	YEAR RETD.	ISSUE PRICE	QUOTE U.S.$
1993	Matthew & Melanie	Open		195.00	195

Maud Humphrey Bogart Dolls - Unknown

YEAR ISSUE		EDITION LIMIT	YEAR RETD.	ISSUE PRICE	QUOTE U.S.$
1992	Playing Bridesmaid	Closed	N/A	195.00	225

Maud Humphrey Bogart Doll Collection - M.H. Bogart

YEAR ISSUE		EDITION LIMIT	YEAR RETD.	ISSUE PRICE	QUOTE U.S.$
1989	Playing Bride	Closed	N/A	135.00	225
1990	First Party	Closed	N/A	135.00	150
1990	The First Lesson	Closed	N/A	135.00	149
1991	Seamstress	Closed	N/A	135.00	149
1991	Little Captive	Open		135.00	135
1992	Kitty's Bath	Open		135.00	135

Mavis Snyder Dolls - M. Snyder

YEAR ISSUE		EDITION LIMIT	YEAR RETD.	ISSUE PRICE	QUOTE U.S.$
1994	Tara	Open		95.00	95

Parker-Levi Toddlers - B. Parker

YEAR ISSUE		EDITION LIMIT	YEAR RETD.	ISSUE PRICE	QUOTE U.S.$
1992	Courtney	Open		135.00	135
1992	Melody	Open		135.00	135

Parkins Connisseur - S. Kuck

YEAR ISSUE		EDITION LIMIT	YEAR RETD.	ISSUE PRICE	QUOTE U.S.$
1993	Faith	Open		135.00	135

Parkins Portraits - P. Parkins

YEAR ISSUE		EDITION LIMIT	YEAR RETD.	ISSUE PRICE	QUOTE U.S.$
1993	Lauren	Open		79.00	79
1993	Kelsey	Open		79.00	79
1994	Morgan	Open		79.00	79
1994	Cassidy	Open		79.00	79

Parkins Treasures - P. Parkins

YEAR ISSUE		EDITION LIMIT	YEAR RETD.	ISSUE PRICE	QUOTE U.S.$
1992	Tiffany	Closed	1994	55.00	80
1992	Dorothy	Closed	N/A	55.00	55
1993	Charlotte	Open		55.00	55
1993	Cynthia	Open		55.00	55

Phyllis Parkins Dolls - P. Parkins

YEAR ISSUE		EDITION LIMIT	YEAR RETD.	ISSUE PRICE	QUOTE U.S.$
1992	Swan Princess	9,850		195.00	220-250

Picnic In The Park - J. Esteban

YEAR ISSUE		EDITION LIMIT	YEAR RETD.	ISSUE PRICE	QUOTE U.S.$
1991	Rebecca	Open		155.00	155
1992	Emily	Open		155.00	155
1992	Victoria	Open		155.00	155
1993	Benjamin	Open		155.00	155

Precious Moments - S. Butcher

YEAR ISSUE		EDITION LIMIT	YEAR RETD.	ISSUE PRICE	QUOTE U.S.$
1994	Tell Me the Story of Jesus	Open		79.00	79

Proud Indian Nation - N/A

YEAR ISSUE		EDITION LIMIT	YEAR RETD.	ISSUE PRICE	QUOTE U.S.$
1992	Navajo Little One	Closed	1993	95.00	200
1993	Dressed Up For The Pow Wow	Open		95.00	95
1993	Autumn Treat	Open		95.00	95
1994	Out with Mama's Flock	Open		95.00	95

The Royal Beauty Dolls - Unknown

YEAR ISSUE		EDITION LIMIT	YEAR RETD.	ISSUE PRICE	QUOTE U.S.$
1991	Chen Mai	Open		195.00	195

Russian Czarra Dolls - Unknown

YEAR ISSUE		EDITION LIMIT	YEAR RETD.	ISSUE PRICE	QUOTE U.S.$
1991	Alexandra	Closed	N/A	295.00	350

Sandra Kuck Dolls - S. Kuck

YEAR ISSUE		EDITION LIMIT	YEAR RETD.	ISSUE PRICE	QUOTE U.S.$
1993	A Kiss Goodnight	Open		79.00	79
1994	Teaching Teddy	Open		79.00	79

Santa's Little Helpers - C.W. Derek

YEAR ISSUE		EDITION LIMIT	YEAR RETD.	ISSUE PRICE	QUOTE U.S.$
1992	Nicholas	Open		155.00	155
1993	Hope	Open		155.00	155

Schmidt Dolls - J. Schmidt

YEAR ISSUE		EDITION LIMIT	YEAR RETD.	ISSUE PRICE	QUOTE U.S.$
1994	Kaitlyn	Open		79.00	79

Schrubbe Santa Dolls - R. Schrubbe

YEAR ISSUE		EDITION LIMIT	YEAR RETD.	ISSUE PRICE	QUOTE U.S.$
1994	Jolly Old St. Nick	Open		135.00	135

Simon Indians - S. Simon

YEAR ISSUE		EDITION LIMIT	YEAR RETD.	ISSUE PRICE	QUOTE U.S.$
1994	Meadowlark	Open		95.00	95

Songs of the Seasons Hakata Doll Collection - T. Murakami

YEAR ISSUE		EDITION LIMIT	YEAR RETD.	ISSUE PRICE	QUOTE U.S.$
1985	Winter Song Maiden	9,800		75.00	75
1985	Spring Song Maiden	9,800		75.00	75
1985	Summer Song Maiden	9,800		75.00	75
1985	Autumn Song Maiden	9,800		75.00	75

Star Trek Doll Collection - E. Daub

YEAR ISSUE		EDITION LIMIT	YEAR RETD.	ISSUE PRICE	QUOTE U.S.$
1988	Mr. Spock	Closed	N/A	75.00	150
1988	Captain Kirk	Closed	N/A	75.00	120
1989	Dr. Mc Coy	Closed	N/A	75.00	120
1989	Scotty	Closed	N/A	75.00	120
1990	Sulu	Closed	N/A	75.00	120
1990	Chekov	Closed	N/A	75.00	120
1991	Uhura	Closed	N/A	75.00	120

Storybook Dolls - L. Di Leo

YEAR ISSUE		EDITION LIMIT	YEAR RETD.	ISSUE PRICE	QUOTE U.S.$
1991	Alice in Wonderland	Open		75.00	75

Through The Eyes of Virginia Turner - V. Turner

YEAR ISSUE		EDITION LIMIT	YEAR RETD.	ISSUE PRICE	QUOTE U.S.$
1992	Michelle	Closed	1993	95.00	95
1992	Danielle	Open		95.00	95
1993	Wendy	Open		95.00	95
1994	Dawn	Open		95.00	95

Toddler Days Doll Collection - D. Schurig

YEAR ISSUE		EDITION LIMIT	YEAR RETD.	ISSUE PRICE	QUOTE U.S.$
1992	Erica	Open		95.00	95
1993	Darlene	Open		95.00	95
1994	Karen	Open		95.00	95
1995	Penny	Open		95.00	95

Treasured Toddlers - V. Turner

YEAR ISSUE		EDITION LIMIT	YEAR RETD.	ISSUE PRICE	QUOTE U.S.$
1992	Whitney	Open		95.00	95
1993	Natalie	Open		95.00	95

Vickie Walker 1st's - V. Walker

YEAR ISSUE		EDITION LIMIT	YEAR RETD.	ISSUE PRICE	QUOTE U.S.$
1995	Leah	Open		79.00	79

Victorian Treasures - C.W. Derek

YEAR ISSUE		EDITION LIMIT	YEAR RETD.	ISSUE PRICE	QUOTE U.S.$
1992	Katherine	Open		155.00	155
1993	Madeline	Open		155.00	155

Wooden Dolls - N/A

YEAR ISSUE		EDITION LIMIT	YEAR RETD.	ISSUE PRICE	QUOTE U.S.$
1991	Gretchen	9,850		225.00	280
1991	Heidi	9,850		225.00	200-250

Wright Indian Dolls - D. Wright

YEAR ISSUE		EDITION LIMIT	YEAR RETD.	ISSUE PRICE	QUOTE U.S.$
1994	Sacajawea	Open		135.00	135

Year Round Fun - D. Schurig

YEAR ISSUE		EDITION LIMIT	YEAR RETD.	ISSUE PRICE	QUOTE U.S.$
1992	Allison	Open		95.00	95
1993	Christy	Open		95.00	95
1993	Paula	Open		95.00	95
1994	Kaylie	Open		95.00	95

Zolan Dolls - D. Zolan

YEAR ISSUE		EDITION LIMIT	YEAR RETD.	ISSUE PRICE	QUOTE U.S.$
1991	A Christmas Prayer	Closed	1993	95.00	200-225
1992	Winter Angel	Open		95.00	95
1992	Rainy Day Pals	Open		95.00	95
1992	Quiet Time	Open		95.00	95
1993	For You	Open		95.00	95
1993	The Thinker	Open		95.00	95

Zolan Double Dolls - D. Zolan

YEAR ISSUE		EDITION LIMIT	YEAR RETD.	ISSUE PRICE	QUOTE U.S.$
1993	First Kiss	Open		135.00	135
1994	New Shoes	Open		155.00	155

Jan McLean Originals

Flowers of the Heart Collection - J. McLean

YEAR ISSUE		EDITION LIMIT	YEAR RETD.	ISSUE PRICE	QUOTE U.S.$
1991	Marigold	100		2400.00	2800-3200
1990	Pansy	100		2200.00	2800-3000
1990	Poppy	100		2200.00	2600-2800
1991	Primrose	100		2500.00	2800

Jan McLean Originals - J. McLean

YEAR ISSUE		EDITION LIMIT	YEAR RETD.	ISSUE PRICE	QUOTE U.S.$
1991	Lucrezia	15		6000.00	6000
1990	Phoebe I	25		2700.00	3200

Kurt S. Adler, Inc.

Royal Heritage Collection - J. Mostrom

YEAR ISSUE		EDITION LIMIT	YEAR RETD.	ISSUE PRICE	QUOTE U.S.$
1993	Anastasia J5746	3,000		125.00	125
1993	Good King Wenceslas W2928	2,000		130.00	130
1993	Medieval King of Christmas W2981	2,000	1994	390.00	390
1994	Nicholas on Skates J5750	3,000		120.00	120
1994	Sasha on Skates J5749	3,000		130.00	130

Small Wonders - J. Mostrom

YEAR ISSUE		EDITION LIMIT	YEAR RETD.	ISSUE PRICE	QUOTE U.S.$
1995	America-Hollie Blue W3162	Open		30.00	30
1995	America-Texas Tyler W3162	Open		30.00	30
1995	Ireland-Cathleen W3082	Open		28.00	28
1995	Ireland-Michael W3082	Open		28.00	28
1995	Kwanza-Mufaro W3161	Open		28.00	28
1995	Kwanza-Shani W3161	Open		28.00	28

When I Grow Up - J. Mostrom

YEAR ISSUE		EDITION LIMIT	YEAR RETD.	ISSUE PRICE	QUOTE U.S.$
1995	Dr. Brown W3079	Open		27.00	27
1995	Freddy the Fireman W3163	Open		28.00	28
1995	Melissa the Teacher W3081	Open		28.00	28
1995	Nurse Nancy W3079	Open		27.00	27
1995	Scott the Golfer W3080	Open		28.00	28

Ladie and Friends

Lizzie High Society™ Members-Only Dolls - B.K. Wisber

YEAR ISSUE		EDITION LIMIT	YEAR RETD.	ISSUE PRICE	QUOTE U.S.$
1993	Audrey High-1301	Closed	1992	59.00	300
1993	Becky High-1330	Closed	1994	96.00	275
1994	Chloe Valentine-1351	12/95		79.00	79

The Christmas Concert - B.K. Wisber

YEAR ISSUE		EDITION LIMIT	YEAR RETD.	ISSUE PRICE	QUOTE U.S.$
1990	Claire Valentine-1262	Open		56.00	58
1993	James Valentine-1310	Open		60.00	61
1992	Judith High-1292	Open		70.00	72
1993	Stephanie Bowman-1309	Open		74.00	75

The Christmas Pageant™ - B.K. Wisber

YEAR ISSUE		EDITION LIMIT	YEAR RETD.	ISSUE PRICE	QUOTE U.S.$
1985	"Earth" Angel-1122	Closed	1989	30.00	100
1985	"Noel" Angel (1st Ed.)-1126	Closed	1989	30.00	100
1989	"Noel" Angel (2nd Ed.)-1126	Open		48.00	51
1985	"On" Angel-1121	Closed	1989	30.00	100
1985	"Peace" Angel (1st Ed.)-1120	Closed	1989	30.00	100
1989	"Peace" Angel (2nd Ed.)-1120	Open		48.00	51
1985	Christmas Wooly Lamb-1133	Closed	1991	11.00	35
1985	Joseph and Donkey-1119	Open		30.00	38
1985	Mary and Baby Jesus-1118	Open		30.00	38
1986	Shepherd-1193	Open		32.00	38
1985	Wiseman #1-1123	Open		30.00	38
1985	Wiseman #2-1124	Open		30.00	38
1985	Wiseman #3-1125	Open		30.00	38
1985	Wooden Creche-1132	Open		28.00	32

The Family and Friends of Lizzie High®- B.K. Wisber

YEAR ISSUE		EDITION LIMIT	YEAR RETD.	ISSUE PRICE	QUOTE U.S.$
1987	Abigail Bowman-1199	Closed	1994	40.00	90
1987	Addie High-1202	Open		37.00	42
1990	Albert Valentine-1260	Closed	1995	42.00	45
1986	Alice Valentine (1st Ed.)-1148	Closed	1987	32.00	100
1995	Alice Valentine (2nd Ed.)-1148	Open		56.00	56
1988	Allison Bowman-1229	Open		56.00	60
1985	Amanda High (1st Ed.)-1111	Closed	1988	30.00	100
1990	Amanda High (2nd Ed.)-1111	Closed	1995	54.00	58
1989	Amelia High-1248	Open		45.00	49
1987	Amy Bowman-1201	Closed	1994	37.00	82
1986	Andrew Brown-1157	Closed	1988	45.00	125
1991	Annabelle Bowman-1267	Open		68.00	70
1986	Annie Bowman (1st Ed.)-1150	Closed	1989	32.00	100
1993	Annie Bowman (2nd Ed.)-1150	Open		68.00	69
1993	Ashley Bowman-1304	Open		48.00	49
1992	Barbara Helen-1274	Open		58.00	60
1985	Benjamin Bowman (Santa)-1134	Open		34.00	41
1985	Benjamin Bowman-1129	Closed	1987	30.00	100
1988	Bess High-1241	Open		45.00	49
1988	Betsy Valentine-1245	Open		42.00	45
1994	Bonnie Valentine-1323	Open		35.00	36
1987	Bridget Bowman-1222	Closed	1994	40.00	96
1992	Carol Anne Bowman-1282	Closed	1994	70.00	142
1986	Carrie High (1st Ed.)-1190	Closed	1989	45.00	100
1989	Carrie High (2nd Ed.)-1190	Open		46.00	49
1986	Cassie Yocum (1st Ed.)-1179	Closed	1988	36.00	100
1993	Cassie Yocum (2nd Ed.)-1179	Open		80.00	81
1987	Cat on Chair-1217	Closed	1991	16.00	35
1987	Charles Bowman (1st Ed.)-1221	Closed	1990	34.00	100
1992	Charles Bowman (2nd Ed.)-1221	Closed	1995	46.00	48
1985	Christian Bowman-1110	Closed	1987	30.00	100
1994	Christine Bowman-1332	Open		62.00	63
1993	Christmas Tree w/Cats-1293A	Open		42.00	43
1986	Christopher High-1182	Closed	1992	34.00	72
1985	Cora High-1115	Closed	1987	30.00	100
1991	Cynthia High-1127A	Closed	1995	60.00	62
1988	Daphne Bowman-1235	Closed	1994	38.00	40
1986	David Yocum-1195	Closed	1995	33.00	37
1986	Delia Valentine-1153	Closed	1988	32.00	100
1991	The Department Store Santa-1270	Open		76.00	78
1986	Dora Valentine (1st Ed.)-1152	Closed	1989	30.00	100
1992	Dora Valentine (2nd Ed.)-1152	Open		48.00	50
1986	Edward Bowman (1st Ed.)-1158	Closed	1988	45.00	125
1994	Edward Bowman (2nd Ed.)-1158	Open		76.00	77
1992	Edwin Bowman-1281	Closed	1994	70.00	71

DOLLS

YEAR ISSUE		EDITION LIMIT	YEAR RETD.	ISSUE PRICE	QUOTE U.S.$
1995	Edwina High-1343	Open		56.00	57
1985	Elizabeth Sweetland (1st Ed.)-1109	Closed	1987	30.00	100
1991	Elizabeth Sweetland (2nd Ed.)-1109	Open		56.00	58
1994	Elsie Bowman-1325	Open		64.00	65
1986	Emily Bowman (1st Ed.)-1185	Closed	1990	34.00	100
1990	Emily Bowman (2nd Ed.)-1185	Open		48.00	50
1985	Emma High-1103	Closed	1988	30.00	100
1989	Emmy Lou Valentine-1251	Open		45.00	48
1985	Esther Dunn (1st Ed.)-1127	Closed	1987	45.00	N/A
1991	Esther Dunn (SecondEdition)-1127	Open		60.00	62
1988	Eunice High-1240	Closed	1994	56.00	58
1985	Flossie High (1st Ed.)-1128	Closed	1988	45.00	100-125
1989	Flossie High (2nd Ed.)-1128	Open		54.00	57
1987	The Flower Girl-1204	Closed	1995	17.00	24
1993	Francis Bowman-1305	Open		48.00	49
1994	Gilbert High-1335	Open		65.00	66
1986	Grace Valentine (1st Ed.)-1146	Closed	1989	32.00	100
1991	Grace Valentine (2nd Ed.)-1146	Open		48.00	50
1987	Gretchen High-1216	Closed	1994	40.00	44
1994	Gwendolyn High-1342	Open		56.00	57
1985	Hannah Brown-1131	Closed	1988	45.00	125
1988	Hattie Bowman-1239	Open		40.00	45
1985	Ida Valentine-1116	Closed	1988	30.00	80
1987	Imogene Bowman-1206	Closed	1994	37.00	40
1988	Jacob High-1230	Closed	1994	44.00	46
1994	Jamie Bowman-1324	Open		35.00	36
1988	Janie Valentine-1231	Open		37.00	42
1989	Jason High (alone)-1254A	Open		20.00	24
1989	Jason High (with Mother)-1254	Open		58.00	61
1986	Jenny Valentine-1181	Closed	1989	34.00	110
1986	Jeremy Bowman-1192	Closed	1991	36.00	80
1989	Jessica High (alone)-1253A	Open		20.00	24
1989	Jessica High (with Mother)-1253	Open		58.00	61
1995	Jillian Bowman ((2nd Ed.))-1180	Open		90.00	90
1986	Jillian Bowman (1st Ed.)-1180	Closed	1990	34.00	110
1992	Joanie Valentine-1295	Open		48.00	50
1989	Johann Bowman-1250	Open		40.00	43
1987	Johanna Valentine-1198	Closed	1988	37.00	100
1992	Joseph Valentine-1283	Closed	1995	62.00	64
1994	Josie Valentine-1322	Open		76.00	77
1986	Juliet Valentine (1st Ed.)-1147	Closed	1988	32.00	100
1990	Juliet Valentine (2nd Ed.)-1147	Open		48.00	51
1993	Justine Valentine-1302	Open		84.00	85
1986	Karl Valentine (1st Ed.)-1161	Closed	1988	30.00	100
1994	Karl Valentine (2nd Ed.)-1161	Open		54.00	55
1987	Katie and Barney-1219	Open		38.00	42
1986	Katie Bowman-1178	Closed	1994	36.00	82
1985	Katrina Valentine-1135	Closed	1989	30.00	100
1988	Kinch Bowman-1237	Open		47.00	50
1987	Laura Valentine-1223	Closed	1994	36.00	80
1995	Leona High-1355	Open		68.00	68
1986	Little Ghosts-1197	Open		15.00	18
1987	Little Witch-1225	Open		17.00	23
1985	Lizzie Highr-1100	Open		30.00	38
1985	Louella Valentine-1112	Closed	1991	30.00	100
1989	Lucy Bowman-1255	Open		45.00	48
1985	Luther Bowman (1st Ed.)-1108	Closed	1987	30.00	100
1993	Luther Bowman (2nd Ed.)-1108	Open		60.00	61
1995	Lydia Bowman-1347	Open		54.00	54
1986	Madaleine Valentine (1st Ed.)-1187	Closed	1989	34.00	90
1989	Madaleine Valentine (2nd Ed.)-1187	Open		37.00	40
1986	Maggie High-1160	Closed	1988	30.00	100
1987	Margaret Bowman-1213	Open		35.00	42
1986	Marie Valentine (1st Ed.)-1184	Closed	1990	47.00	125
1992	Marie Valentine (2nd Ed.)-1184	Open		68.00	70
1986	Marisa Valentine (alone)-1194A	Open		33.00	39
1986	Marisa Valentine (w/ Brother Petey)-1194	Open		45.00	50
1994	Marisa Valentine-1333	Open		58.00	59
1986	Marland Valentine-1183	Closed	1990	33.00	100
1990	Marlene Valentine-1259	Closed	1995	48.00	51
1986	Martha High-1151	Closed	1989	32.00	100
1985	Martin Bowman-1117	Closed	1992	30.00	43-85
1988	Mary Ellen Valentine-1236	Open		40.00	44
1985	Mary Valentine-1105	Closed	1988	30.00	88-100
1986	Matthew Yocum-1186	Closed	1988	33.00	100
1995	Mattie Dunn-1344	Open		56.00	57
1988	Megan Valentine-1227	Closed	1994	44.00	94
1987	Melanie Bowman (1st Ed.)-1220	Closed	1990	36.00	125
1992	Melanie Bowman (2nd Ed.)-1220	Closed	1995	46.00	48
1991	Michael Bowman-1268	Open		52.00	54
1994	Minnie Valentine-1336	Open		64.00	65
1989	Miriam High-1256	Open		46.00	49
1986	Molly Yocum (1st Ed.)-1189	Closed	1989	34.00	80-100
1989	Molly Yocum (2nd Ed.)-1189	Open		39.00	42
1993	Mommy-1312	Open		48.00	49
1989	Mrs. Claus-1258	Open		42.00	45
1990	Nancy Bowman-1261	Open		48.00	51
1987	Naomi Valentine-1200	Closed	1993	40.00	88
1992	Natalie Valentine-1284	Closed	1995	62.00	64
1995	Nathan Bowman-1354	Open		70.00	70
1985	Nettie Brown (1st Ed.)-1102	Closed	1987	30.00	100
1988	Nettie Brown (2nd Ed.)-1102	Closed	1995	36.00	39
1985	Nettie Brown (Christmas)-1114	Closed	1987	30.00	100
1987	Olivia High-1205	Open		37.00	42
1987	Patsy Bowman-1214	Closed	1995	50.00	53
1988	Pauline Bowman-1228	Open		44.00	49
1993	Pearl Bowman-1303	Open		56.00	57
1989	Peggy Bowman-1252	Closed	1995	58.00	70
1987	Penelope High-1208	Closed	1991	40.00	100
1993	Penny Valentine-1308	Open		60.00	61
1985	Peter Valentine (1st Ed.)-1113	Closed	1991	30.00	72
1995	Peter Valentine (2nd Ed.)-1113	Open		55.00	55
1988	Phoebe High-1246	Closed	1992	48.00	90
1987	Priscilla High-1226	Closed	1995	56.00	62
1986	Rachel Bowman (1st Ed.)-1188	Closed	1989	34.00	100
1989	Rachel Bowman (2nd Ed.)-1188	Open		34.00	38
1987	Ramona Brown-1215	Closed	1989	40.00	50
1985	Rebecca Bowman (1st Ed.)-1104	Closed	1988	30.00	100
1989	Rebecca Bowman (2nd Ed.)-1104	Open		56.00	60
1987	Rebecca's Mother-1207	Closed	1995	37.00	54
1995	Regina Bowman-1353	Open		70.00	70
1995	Robert Bowman-1348	Open		64.00	64
1985	Russell Dunn-1107	Closed	1987	30.00	100
1988	Ruth Anne Bowman-1232	Closed	1994	44.00	46
1985	Sabina Valentine (1st Ed.)-1101	Closed	1987	30.00	100
1988	Sabina Valentine (2nd Ed.)-1101	Open		40.00	43
1986	Sadie Valentine-1163	Open		45.00	49
1986	Sally Bowman-1155	Closed	1991	32.00	110
1988	Samantha Bowman-1238	Open		47.00	50
1989	Santa (with Tub)-1257	Open		58.00	62
1987	Santa Claus (sitting)-1224	Closed	1991	50.00	61
1993	Santa Claus-1311	Open		48.00	49
1991	Santa's Helper-1271	Open		52.00	54
1986	Sara Valentine-1154	Closed	1994	32.00	38-76
1994	Shirley Bowman-1334	Open		63.00	64
1986	Sophie Valentine-1164	Closed	1991	45.00	125
1995	St. Nicholas-1356	Open		98.00	98
1986	Susanna Bowman-1149	Closed	1988	45.00	125
1986	Thomas Bowman-1159	Closed	1987	30.00	100
1986	Tillie Brown-1156	Closed	1988	32.00	100
1992	Timothy Bowman-1294	Open		56.00	58
1991	Trudy Valentine-1269	Open		64.00	66
1989	Vanessa High-1247	Open		45.00	49
1989	Victoria Bowman-1249	Open		40.00	43
1987	The Wedding (Bride)-1203	Closed	1995	37.00	41
1987	The Wedding (Groom)-1203A	Closed	1995	34.00	37
1985	Wendel Bowman (1st Ed.)-1106	Closed	1987	30.00	100
1992	Wendel Bowman (2nd Ed.)-1106	Open		60.00	62
1992	Wendy Bowman-1293	Open		78.00	80
1986	William Valentine-1191	Closed	1992	36.00	72
1986	Willie Bowman-1162	Closed	1992	30.00	72

The Grummels of Log Hollow™ - B.K. Wisber

YEAR ISSUE		EDITION LIMIT	YEAR RETD.	ISSUE PRICE	QUOTE U.S.$
1986	Aunt Gertie Grummel™ -1171	Closed	1988	34.00	70-110
1986	Aunt Hilda Grummel™ -1174	Closed	1988	34.00	70-110
1986	Aunt Polly Grummel™ -1169	Closed	1988	34.00	70-110
1986	Cousin Lottie Grummel™ -1170	Closed	1988	36.00	70-110
1986	Cousin Miranda Grummel™ 1165	Closed	1988	47.00	70-110
1986	Grandma Grummel™ -1173	Closed	1988	45.00	70-110
1986	Grandpa Grummel™ -1176	Closed	1988	36.00	180
1986	The Little Ones-Grummels™ (boy/girl)-1196	Closed	1988	15.00	40
1986	Ma Grummel™ -1167	Closed	1988	36.00	70-110
1986	Pa Grummel™ -1172	Closed	1988	34.00	70-110
1986	Sister Nora Grummel™-1177	Closed	1988	34.00	70-110
1986	Teddy Bear Bed-1168	Closed	1988	15.00	70-100
1986	Uncle Hollis Grummel™-1166	Closed	1988	34.00	70-110
1986	Washline-1175	Closed	1988	15.00	70-100

The Little Ones at Christmas-Nativity™ - B.K. Wisber

YEAR ISSUE		EDITION LIMIT	YEAR RETD.	ISSUE PRICE	QUOTE U.S.$
1995	Donkey-1362	Open		17.00	17
1995	Little Angel-1359	Open		36.00	36
1995	Little Joseph-1358	Open		31.00	31
1995	Little Mary w/Baby in Manger-1357	Open		33.00	33
1995	Little Ones' Creche-1361	Open		24.00	24
1995	Little Shepherd w/Lamb-1360	Open		45.00	45

The Little Ones at Christmas™ - B.K. Wisber

YEAR ISSUE		EDITION LIMIT	YEAR RETD.	ISSUE PRICE	QUOTE U.S.$
1990	Girl (black) w/Basket of Greens-1263	Open		22.00	26
1990	Girl (white) w/Cookie-1264	Open		22.00	26
1990	Girl (white) w/Gift-1266	Open		22.00	26
1990	Girl (white) w/Tree Garland-1265	Open		22.00	26
1991	Boy (black) w/Santa Photo-1273A	Open		24.00	28
1991	Boy (white) w/Santa Photo-1273	Open		24.00	28
1991	Girl (black) w/Santa Photo-1272A	Open		24.00	28
1991	Girl (white) w/Santa Photo-1272	Open		24.00	28
1993	Boy Peeking (Alone)-1314	Open		22.00	23
1993	Boy Peeking w/Tree-1313	Open		60.00	61
1993	Girl w/Baking Table-1317	Open		38.00	39
1994	Girl w/Greens on Table-1337	Open		46.00	47
1993	Girl w/Note for Santa-1318	Open		36.00	37
1993	Girl Peeking (Alone)-1316	Open		22.00	23
1993	Girl Peeking w/Tree-1315	Open		60.00	61
1995	Little Santa-1364	Open		50.00	50

The Little Ones™ - B.K. Wisber

YEAR ISSUE		EDITION LIMIT	YEAR RETD.	ISSUE PRICE	QUOTE U.S.$
1985	Boy (black) (1st Ed.)-1130	Closed	1989	15.00	45-65
1985	Boy (white) (1st Ed.)-1130	Closed	1989	15.00	45-65
1985	Girl (black) (1st Ed.)-1130	Closed	1989	15.00	45-65
1985	Girl (white) (1st Ed.)-1130	Closed	1989	15.00	45-65
1989	Boy (black) (2nd Ed.)-1130I	Closed	1994	20.00	23
1989	Boy (white) (2nd Ed.)-1130H	Closed	1994	20.00	23
1989	Girl (black)-country color (2nd Edition)-1130G	Closed	1994	20.00	23
1989	Girl (black)-pastels (2nd Edition)-1130E	Closed	1994	20.00	23
1989	Girl (white)-country color (2nd Edition)-1130F	Closed	1994	20.00	23
1989	Girl (white)-pastels (2nd Edition)-1130H	Closed	1994	20.00	23
1992	Boy w/Sled-1289	Open		30.00	32
1992	Clown-1290	Open		32.00	34
1992	Girl Reading-1286	Open		36.00	38
1992	Girl w/Apples-1277	Open		26.00	28
1992	Girl w/Beach Bucket-1275	Open		26.00	28
1992	Girl w/Birthday Gift-1279	Open		26.00	28
1992	Girl w/Christmas Lights-1287	Open		34.00	36
1992	Girl w/Easter Eggs-1276	Open		26.00	28
1992	Girl w/Kitten and Milk-1280	Open		32.00	34
1992	Girl w/Kitten and Yarn-1278	Open		34.00	36
1992	Girl w/Snowman-1288	Open		36.00	38
1992	Girl w/Valentine-1291	Open		30.00	32
1993	4th of July Boy-1307	Open		28.00	29
1993	Ballerina-1321	Open		40.00	41
1995	Basketweaver-1363	Open		48.00	48
1993	Boy w/Easter Flowers-1306	Open		30.00	31
1993	Bunny-1297	Open		36.00	37
1993	Girl Picnicking w/ Teddy Bear-1320	Open		34.00	35
1993	Girl w/Easter Flowers-1296	Open		34.00	35
1993	Girl w/Mop-1300	Open		36.00	37
1993	Girl w/Spinning Wheel-1299	Open		36.00	37
1993	Girl w/Violin-1319	Open		28.00	29
1994	Girl w/Puppy in Tub-1339	Open		43.00	44
1993	4th of July Girl-1298	Open		30.00	31
1994	Boy Dyeing Eggs-1327	Open		30.00	31
1994	Boy w/Pumpkin-1341	Open		29.00	30
1994	Girl Dyeing Eggs-1326	Open		30.00	31
1994	Girl w/Laundry Basket-1338	Open		38.00	39
1994	Girl w/Wagon-1340	Open		42.00	43
1994	Nurse-1328	Open		40.00	41
1994	Teacher-1329	Open		38.00	39

The Pawtuckets of Sweet Briar Lane™ - B.K. Wisber

YEAR ISSUE		EDITION LIMIT	YEAR RETD.	ISSUE PRICE	QUOTE U.S.$
1994	Aunt Lillian Pawtucket™ (2nd Ed.)-1141	Open		58.00	59
1986	Aunt Lillian Pawtucket™ (1st Ed.)-1141	Closed	1989	32.00	110
1987	Aunt Mabel Pawtucket™ -212	Closed	1989	45.00	130
1986	Aunt Minnie Pawtucket™ (1st Ed.)-1136	Closed	1989	45.00	110
1994	Aunt Minnie Pawtucket™ (2nd Edition)-1136	Open		72.00	73
1986	Brother Noah Pawtucket™ -1140	Closed	1989	32.00	110
1987	Bunny Bed-1218	Closed	1989	16.00	110
1987	Cousin Alberta Pawtucket™ 1210	Closed	1989	36.00	110
1986	Cousin Clara Pawtucket™ (1st Ed.)-1144	Closed	1989	32.00	110
1987	Cousin Isabel Pawtucket™ -1209	Closed	1989	36.00	110
1988	Cousin Jed Pawtucket™ -1234	Closed	1990	34.00	110
1988	Cousin Winnie Pawtucket™ 1233	Closed	1990	49.00	110
1994	Flossie Pawtucket™ -1136A	Open		33.00	34
1986	Grammy Pawtucket™ (1st Ed.)-1137	Closed	1989	32.00	110
1994	Grammy Pawtucket™ (2nd Edition)-1137	Open		68.00	69
1995	The Little One Bunnies (1995)-female w/ laundry basket-1211A	Open		33.00	34
1986	The Little One Bunnies-boy (1st Ed.)-1145	Closed	1989	15.00	20
1994	The Little One Bunnies-boy (2nd Ed.)-1145A	Open		33.00	34
1986	The Little One Bunnies-girl (1st Ed.)-1145	Closed	1989	15.00	50
1994	The Little One Bunnies-girl (2nd Ed.)-1145	Open		33.00	34
1986	Mama Pawtucket™ (1st Ed.)-1142	Closed	1989	34.00	110
1994	Mama Pawtucket™ (2nd Ed.)-1142	Open		86.00	87
1986	Pappy Pawtucket™ (1st Ed.)-1143	Closed	1989	32.00	110
1995	Pappy Pawtucket™ (2nd Ed.)-1143	Open		56.00	56
1994	Pawtucket™ Bunny Hutch-1141A	Open		38.00	39
1995	Pawtucket™ Wash Line-1211B	Open		20.00	20
1987	Sister Clemmie Pawtucket™ (1st Ed.)-1211	Closed	1989	34.00	110
1995	Sister Clemmie Pawtucket™ (2nd Ed.)-1211	Open		60.00	60
1986	Sister Flora Pawtucket™ -1139	Closed	1989	32.00	110
1986	Uncle Harley Pawtucket™ (1st Ed.)-1138	Closed	1989	32.00	110
1994	Uncle Harley Pawtucket™ (2nd Ed.)-1138	Open		74.00	75

Special Editions - B.K. Wisber

YEAR ISSUE		EDITION LIMIT	YEAR RETD.	ISSUE PRICE	QUOTE U.S.$
1992	Kathryn Bowman (Limited Edition)-1285	3,000	1992	140.00	500
1994	Prudence Valentine-1331	4,000	1994	180.00	180
1995	Little Lizzie High®-Anniversary Special Event Edition	Yr.Iss.		40.00	40
1995	Lizzie High®-10th Anniversary Signature Edition-1100A	Yr.Iss.		90.00	90

The Thanksgiving Play - B.K. Wisber

YEAR ISSUE		EDITION LIMIT	YEAR RETD.	ISSUE PRICE	QUOTE U.S.$
1988	Indian Squaw-1244	Open		36.00	39
1988	Pilgrim Boy-1242	Open		40.00	43
1988	Pilgrim Girl-1243	Open		48.00	51

Lawtons

Guild Dolls - W. Lawton

Year Issue		Edition Limit	Year Retd.	Issue Price	Quote U.S.$
1989	Baa Baa Black Sheep	1,003	1989	395.00	650
1990	Lavender Blue	781	1990	395.00	400
1991	To Market, To Market	683	1991	495.00	495
1992	Little Boy Blue	510	1992	395.00	395
1993	Lawton Logo Doll	575	1993	350.00	500
1994	Wee Handful	540	1994	250.00	250
1995	Uniquely Yours	12/95		395.00	395

Cherished Customs - W. Lawton

Year Issue		Edition Limit	Year Retd.	Issue Price	Quote U.S.$
1990	The Blessing/Mexico	500	1990	395.00	1000
1992	Carnival/Brazil	750	1992	425.00	425
1992	Cradleboard/Navajo	750	1993	425.00	425
1991	Frolic/Amish	500	1991	395.00	395
1990	Girl's Day/Japan	500	1990	395.00	395
1990	High Tea/Great Britain	500	1990	395.00	450-550
1994	Kwanzaa/Africa	500	1994	425.00	425
1990	Midsommar/Sweden	500	1990	395.00	395
1993	Nalauqataq-Eskimo	500	1993	395.00	395
1991	Ndeko/Zaire	500	1991	395.00	550
1992	Pascha/Ukraine	750	1992	495.00	495
1995	Piping the Haggis	350		495.00	495
1993	Topeng Klana-Java	250	1993	495.00	495

Childhood Classics II® - W. Lawton

Year Issue		Edition Limit	Year Retd.	Issue Price	Quote U.S.$
1994	Girl of the Limberlost	500	1994	425.00	425
1995	Little Lord Fauntleroy	350		450.00	450
1992	Marigold Garden	750	1992	450.00	450
1992	Oliver Twist	750	1992	450.00	450
1992	Peter And The Wolf	750	1992	495.00	495
1993	Tom Sawyer	500	1993	395.00	395
1993	The Velveteen Rabbit	750	1993	395.00	395

Childhood Classics® - W. Lawton

Year Issue		Edition Limit	Year Retd.	Issue Price	Quote U.S.$
1983	Alice In Wonderland	100	1983	225.00	2000
1986	Anne Of Green Gables	250	1986	325.00	1600-2400
1991	The Bobbsey Twins: Flossie	350	1991	364.50	500
1991	The Bobbsey Twins: Freddie	350	1991	364.50	500
1985	Hans Brinker	250	1985	325.00	1800
1984	Heidi	250	1984	325.00	650
1991	Hiawatha	500	1991	395.00	500
1989	Honey Bunch	250	1989	350.00	550
1987	Just David	250	1987	325.00	700
1986	Laura Ingalls	250	1986	325.00	500
1991	Little Black Sambo	500	1991	395.00	650
1988	Little Eva	250	1988	350.00	500-1000
1989	Little Princess	250	1989	395.00	600
1990	Mary Frances	350	1990	350.00	350
1987	Mary Lennox	250	1987	325.00	500
1987	Polly Pepper	250	1987	325.00	450
1986	Pollyanna	250	1986	325.00	1600
1990	Poor Little Match Girl	350	1990	350.00	500
1988	Rebecca	250	1988	350.00	450
1988	Topsy	250	1988	350.00	750

The Children's Hour - W. Lawton

Year Issue		Edition Limit	Year Retd.	Issue Price	Quote U.S.$
1991	Edith With Golden Hair	500	1991	395.00	475
1991	Grave Alice	500	1991	395.00	475
1991	Laughing Allegra	500	1991	395.00	475

Christmas Dolls - W. Lawton

Year Issue		Edition Limit	Year Retd.	Issue Price	Quote U.S.$
1988	Christmas Joy	500	1988	325.00	750-1200
1989	Noel	500	1989	325.00	375
1990	Christmas Angel	500	1990	325.00	325
1991	Yuletide Carole	500	1991	395.00	395

Christmas Legends™ - W. Lawton

Year Issue		Edition Limit	Year Retd.	Issue Price	Quote U.S.$
1992	The Legend Of The Poinsettia	750	1992	395.00	395
1993	The Little Drummer Boy	500	1993	595.00	595
1994	Santa Lucia	350	1994	425.00	425
1995	The Nutcracker	500		595.00	595

Classic Playthings™ - W. Lawton

Year Issue		Edition Limit	Year Retd.	Issue Price	Quote U.S.$
1995	Bessie and Her Bye Lo Baby	750		595.00	595
1994	Katie and Her Kewpie	750	1994	595.00	595
1993	Patricia and Her Patsy®	750	1993	595.00	595

Early American Portrait - W. Lawton

Year Issue		Edition Limit	Year Retd.	Issue Price	Quote U.S.$
1994	Abigail and Jane Augusta	250	1994	995.00	995
1995	Carrie and Sophia Grace	350		1250.00	1250

Folktales And Fairy Stories® - W. Lawton

Year Issue		Edition Limit	Year Retd.	Issue Price	Quote U.S.$
1993	Goldilocks And Baby Bear	350	1993	595.00	495
1992	The Little Emperor's Nightingale	750	1992	425.00	495
1994	Little Gretel	500	1994	395.00	395
1992	Little Red Riding Hood	750	1992	450.00	450
1995	Rapunzel	350		450.00	450
1993	Snow White	500	1993	395.00	395
1992	Swan Princess	750	1992	495.00	495
1992	William Tell, The Younger	750	1992	395.00	395

Gentle Pursuits - W. Lawton

Year Issue		Edition Limit	Year Retd.	Issue Price	Quote U.S.$
1994	Emily and Her Diary	350	1994	795.00	795
1995	Eugenia's Literary Salon	350		795.00	795

Grand Tour™ - W. Lawton

Year Issue		Edition Limit	Year Retd.	Issue Price	Quote U.S.$
1995	African Safari	350		995.00	995
1994	Springtime in Paris	250	1994	895.00	895

Memories And Melodies™ - W. Lawton

Year Issue		Edition Limit	Year Retd.	Issue Price	Quote U.S.$
1993	Apple Blossom Time	500	1993	295.00	295
1995	Easter Parade	250		295.00	295
1993	In The Good Ol' Summertime	500	1993	295.00	295
1994	Let Me Call You Sweetheart	250	1994	295.00	295
1993	Lyda Rose	500	1993	295.00	295
1993	Scarlet Ribbons	500	1993	295.00	295

Newcomer Collection - W. Lawton

Year Issue		Edition Limit	Year Retd.	Issue Price	Quote U.S.$
1987	Ellin Elizabeth, Eyes Closed	49	1987	335.00	750-1000
1987	Ellin Elizabeth, Eyes Open	19	1987	335.00	900-1200

Once Upon A Rhyme - W. Lawton

Year Issue		Edition Limit	Year Retd.	Issue Price	Quote U.S.$
1994	At Aunty's House	350	1994	795.00	750
1995	Lucy Gray	350		795.00	795

Playthings Past - W. Lawton

Year Issue		Edition Limit	Year Retd.	Issue Price	Quote U.S.$
1989	Edward And Dobbin	500	1989	395.00	495-600
1989	Elizabeth And Baby	500	1989	395.00	495-650
1989	Victoria And Teddy	500	1989	395.00	395

Seasons - W. Lawton

Year Issue		Edition Limit	Year Retd.	Issue Price	Quote U.S.$
1988	Amber Autumn	500	1988	325.00	300
1990	Crystal Winter	500	1990	325.00	325
1991	Spring Blossom	500	1991	350.00	350
1989	Summer Rose	500	1989	325.00	375-475

Small Wonders - W. Lawton

Year Issue		Edition Limit	Year Retd.	Issue Price	Quote U.S.$
1993	Jafry	500	1993	149.95	150
1993	Jamilla	500	1993	149.95	150
1993	Meghan	500	1993	149.95	150
1993	Michael	500	1993	149.95	150

Special Edition - W. Lawton

Year Issue		Edition Limit	Year Retd.	Issue Price	Quote U.S.$
1993	Flora McFlimsey	250	1993	895.00	1000
1988	Marcella And Raggedy Ann	2,500	1988	395.00	700-750
1994	Mary Chilton	350	1994	395.00	395

Special Occasion - W. Lawton

Year Issue		Edition Limit	Year Retd.	Issue Price	Quote U.S.$
1990	First Birthday	500	1990	295.00	350
1989	First Day Of School	500	1989	325.00	525
1988	Nanthy	500	1988	325.00	525

Sugar 'n' Spice - W. Lawton

Year Issue		Edition Limit	Year Retd.	Issue Price	Quote U.S.$
1987	Ginger	454	1987	275.00	395-550
1986	Jason	27	1986	250.00	800-1700
1986	Jessica	30	1986	250.00	800-1700
1986	Kersten	103	1986	250.00	550-800
1986	Kimberly	87	1986	250.00	550-800
1987	Marie	208	1987	275.00	450

Timeless Balladsr - W. Lawton

Year Issue		Edition Limit	Year Retd.	Issue Price	Quote U.S.$
1987	Annabel Lee	250	1987	550.00	600-695
1987	Highland Mary	250	1987	550.00	600-875
1988	She Walks In Beauty	250	1988	550.00	600-800
1987	Young Charlotte	250	1987	550.00	850-900

Treasured Tales - W. Lawton

Year Issue		Edition Limit	Year Retd.	Issue Price	Quote U.S.$
1994	The Dreamer	500	1994	395.00	395

Wee Bits - W. Lawton

Year Issue		Edition Limit	Year Retd.	Issue Price	Quote U.S.$
1989	Wee Bit O'Bliss	250	1989	295.00	350
1988	Wee Bit O'Heaven	250	1988	295.00	350
1988	Wee Bit O'Sunshine	250	1988	295.00	350
1988	Wee Bit O'Woe	250	1988	295.00	350
1989	Wee Bit O'Wonder	250	1989	295.00	350

Lenox Collections

Bolshoi Nutcracker Dolls - Unknown

Year Issue		Edition Limit	Year Retd.	Issue Price	Quote U.S.$
1991	Clara	Open		195.00	195

Children of the World - Unknown

Year Issue		Edition Limit	Year Retd.	Issue Price	Quote U.S.$
1991	Amma-The African Girl	Open		119.00	119
1992	Gretchen, German Doll	Open		119.00	119
1989	Hannah, The Little Dutch Maiden	Open		119.00	119
1990	Heather, Little Highlander	Open		119.00	119
1991	Sakura-The Japanese Girl	Open		119.00	119

Children With Toys Dolls - Unknown

Year Issue		Edition Limit	Year Retd.	Issue Price	Quote U.S.$
1991	Tea For Teddy	Open		136.00	136

China Dolls - Cloth Bodies - J. Grammer

Year Issue		Edition Limit	Year Retd.	Issue Price	Quote U.S.$
1985	Amy, 14"	Closed	1990	250.00	N/A
1985	Annabelle, 14"	Closed	1990	250.00	N/A
1985	Elizabeth, 14"	Closed	1990	250.00	N/A
1985	Jennifer, 14"	Closed	1990	250.00	N/A
1985	Miranda, 14"	Closed	1990	250.00	N/A
1985	Sarah, 14"	Closed	1990	250.00	N/A

Country Decor Dolls - Unknown

Year Issue		Edition Limit	Year Retd.	Issue Price	Quote U.S.$
1991	Molly	Open	1994	150.00	150

Ellis Island Dolls - P. Thompson

Year Issue		Edition Limit	Year Retd.	Issue Price	Quote U.S.$
1992	Angelina	Closed	1994	150.00	150
1992	Anna	Closed	1994	152.00	152
1992	Catherine	Closed	1994	152.00	152
1991	Megan	Closed	1994	150.00	150
1991	Stefan	Closed	1994	150.00	150

First Collector Doll - Unknown

Year Issue		Edition Limit	Year Retd.	Issue Price	Quote U.S.$
1992	Lauren	Open		152.00	152

Inspirational Doll - Unknown

Year Issue		Edition Limit	Year Retd.	Issue Price	Quote U.S.$
1992	Blessed Are The Peacemakers	Open		119.00	119

International Baby Doll - Unknown

Year Issue		Edition Limit	Year Retd.	Issue Price	Quote U.S.$
1992	Natalia, Russian Baby	Open		119.00	119

Lenox China Dolls - J. Grammer

Year Issue		Edition Limit	Year Retd.	Issue Price	Quote U.S.$
1984	Abigail, 20"	Closed	1990	425.00	N/A
1984	Amanda, 16"	Closed	1990	385.00	N/A
1984	Jessica, 20"	Closed	1990	450.00	N/A
1984	Maggie, 16"	Closed	1990	375.00	N/A
1984	Maryanne, 20"	Closed	1990	425.00	N/A
1984	Melissa, 16"	Closed	1990	450.00	N/A
1984	Rebecca, 16"	Closed	1990	375.00	N/A
1984	Samantha, 16"	Closed	1990	500.00	N/A

Lenox Victorian Dolls - Unknown

Year Issue		Edition Limit	Year Retd.	Issue Price	Quote U.S.$
1990	Christmas Doll, Elizabeth	Open		195.00	195
1992	Lady at Gala	Open		295.00	295
1989	The Victorian Bride	Open		295.00	295
1991	Victorian Christening Doll	Open		295.00	295

Little Women - Unknown

Year Issue		Edition Limit	Year Retd.	Issue Price	Quote U.S.$
1992	Amy, The Inspiring Artist	Open		152.00	152

Musical Baby Dolls - Unknown

Year Issue		Edition Limit	Year Retd.	Issue Price	Quote U.S.$
1991	Patrick's Lullabye	Open		95.00	95

Nutcracker Dolls - Unknown

Year Issue		Edition Limit	Year Retd.	Issue Price	Quote U.S.$
1993	Nutcracker	Open		195.00	195
1992	Sugarplum	Open		195.00	195

Prima Ballerina Collection - Unknown

Year Issue		Edition Limit	Year Retd.	Issue Price	Quote U.S.$
1992	Odette, Queen of the Swans	Closed	1992	195.00	195

Sibling Dolls - A. Lester

Year Issue		Edition Limit	Year Retd.	Issue Price	Quote U.S.$
1991	Skating Lesson	Open		195.00	195

Mattel

35th Anniversary Dolls by Mattel - Mattel

Year Issue		Edition Limit	Year Retd.	Issue Price	Quote U.S.$
1994	Blonde	Retrd.	1994	39.99	30-50
1994	Brunette	Retrd.	1994	39.99	55-95
1994	Gift Pack	Retrd.	1994	79.97	135-200

Annual Holiday (white) Barbie Dolls - Mattel

Year Issue		Edition Limit	Year Retd.	Issue Price	Quote U.S.$
1988	Holiday Barbie	Retrd.	1990	24.95	500-800
1989	Holiday Barbie	Retrd.	1991	N/A	175-275
1990	Holiday Barbie	Retrd.	1991	N/A	150-225
1991	Holiday Barbie	Retrd.	1993	N/A	200
1992	Holiday Barbie	Retrd.	1992	N/A	125-175
1993	Holiday Barbie	Retrd.	1993	N/A	115-150
1994	Holiday Barbie	Retrd.	1994	44.95	150-200
1995	Holiday Barbie	Open		44.95	45

Bob Mackie Barbie Dolls - B. Mackie

Year Issue		Edition Limit	Year Retd.	Issue Price	Quote U.S.$
1992	Empress Bride Barbie 4247	Retrd.	1992	232.00	750-950
1990	Gold Barbie 5405	Retrd.	1990	120.00	700-900
1993	Masquerade	Retrd.	1993	175.00	400-475
1992	Neptune Fantasy Barbie 4248	Retrd.	1993	160.00	750-950
1991	Platinum Barbie 2703	Retrd.	1991	153.00	650-950
1994	Queen of Hearts	Retrd.	1994	175.00	185-250
1991	Starlight Splendor Barbie 2704	Retrd.	1991	135.00	700-900

Classique Collection - Various

Year Issue		Edition Limit	Year Retd.	Issue Price	Quote U.S.$
1992	Benefit Ball - C. Spencer	Retrd.	1994	59.95	150-190
1993	City Style - J. Goldblatt	Retrd.	1994	59.95	70-125
1993	Opening Night - J. Goldblatt	Retrd.	1994	59.95	75-125

Golden Jubilee - C. Spencer

Year Issue		Edition Limit	Year Retd.	Issue Price	Quote U.S.$
1994	Golden Jubliee	Retrd.	1994	299.00	800-1200

Great Eras - Mattel

Year Issue		Edition Limit	Year Retd.	Issue Price	Quote U.S.$
1993	Flapper	Retrd.	1995	54.00	125-175
1993	Gibson Girl	Retrd.	1995	54.00	95-125

Nostalgic Porcelain Barbie Dolls - Mattel

Year Issue		Edition Limit	Year Retd.	Issue Price	Quote U.S.$
1990	Solo in the Spotlight 7613	Retrd.	1990	198.00	250-350
1990	Sophisticated Lady 5313	Retrd.	1990	198.00	200-275
1989	Wedding Day Barbie 2641	Retrd.	1989	198.00	550-695

The Winter Princess Collection - Mattel

Year Issue		Edition Limit	Year Retd.	Issue Price	Quote U.S.$
1994	Evergreen Princess	Retrd.	1994	59.95	145-175
1994	Evergreen Princess (Red Head)	Retrd.	1994	59.95	495-595
1995	Peppermint Princess	Retrd.	1995	59.95	60
1993	Winter Princess	Retrd.	1993	59.95	500-600

Middleton Doll Company

Christmas Angel Collection - L. Middleton

Year Issue		Edition Limit	Year Retd.	Issue Price	Quote U.S.$
1987	Christmas Angel 1987	4,174	1987	130.00	400-500
1988	Christmas Angel 1988	8,969	1988	130.00	200-250
1989	Christmas Angel 1989	7,500	1991	150.00	190
1990	Christmas Angel 1990	5,000	1991	150.00	190
1991	Christmas Angel 1991	5,000	1992	180.00	200
1992	Christmas Angel 1992	5,000	1995	190.00	190

YEAR ISSUE		EDITION LIMIT	YEAR RETD.	ISSUE PRICE	QUOTE U.S.$
1993	Christmas Angel 1993-Girl	3,144	1995	190.00	190
1993	Christmas Angel 1993 (set)	1,000	1993	390.00	500
1994	Christmas Angel 1994	5,000		190.00	190
1995	Christmas Angel 1995 (white or black)	3,000		190.00	190

First Moments Series - L. Middleton

1984	First Moments (Sleeping)	40,861	1990	69.00	200
1992	First Moments Awake in Blue	1,230	1994	170.00	170
1992	First Moments Awake in Pink	856	1994	170.00	170
1986	First Moments Blue Eyes	14,494	1990	120.00	150
1987	First Moments Boy	6,075	1989	130.00	160
1986	First Moments Brown Eyes	5,324	1989	120.00	150
1987	First Moments Christening (Asleep)	9,377	1992	160.00	250
1987	First Moments Christening (Awake)	16,384	1992	160.00	180
1993	First Moments Heirloom	1,372	1995	190.00	190
1991	First Moments Sweetness	6,323	1995	180.00	180
1994	Sweetness-Newborn	Retrd.	1995	190.00	190

Limited Edition Vinyl - L. Middleton

1993	Amanda Springtime	612	1994	180.00	180
1989	Angel Fancy	5,310	1992	120.00	150
1990	Angel Locks	8,140	1992	140.00	150
1991	Baby Grace	4,862	1991	190.00	250
1994	Beloved-Happy Birthday (Blue)	1,000		220.00	220
1994	Beloved-Happy Birthday (Pink)	1,000		220.00	220
1994	The Bride	1,000	1995	250.00	250
1991	Bubba Batboy	3,925	1994	190.00	190
1992	Cottontop Cherish	3,525	1994	180.00	180
1991	Dear One-Sunday Best	1,371	1994	140.00	140
1991	Devan Delightful	4,520	1994	170.00	170
1990	First Moments-Twin Boy	2,971	1991	180.00	180
1990	First Moments-Twin Girl	2,544	1991	180.00	180
1990	Forever Cherish	5,000	1991	170.00	200
1992	Gracie Mae (Blond Hair)	3,660	1995	250.00	250
1992	Gracie Mae (Brown Hair)	2,551	1994	250.00	250
1993	Gracie Mae (Red Velvet)	100	1993	250.00	250
1994	Joey-Newborn	1,000	1995	180.00	180
1991	Johanna	1,388	1994	190.00	200
1994	Johanna-Newborn	2,000		180.00	180
1985	Little Angel-King-2 (Hand Painted)	Retrd.	1985	40.00	200
1981	Little Angel-Kingdom (Hand Painted)	Retrd.	1981	40.00	300
1991	Missy- Buttercup	4,748	1994	160.00	180
1992	Molly Rose	2,981	1994	196.00	196
1991	My Lee Candy Cane	2,240	1994	170.00	170
1995	Polly Esther "Sock Hop"	1,000	1995	119.00	119
1992	Serenity Berries & Bows	458	1993	250.00	250
1992	Sincerity Petals & Plums	414	1993	250.00	250
1991	Sincerity-Apples n' Spice	1,608	1993	250.00	250
1991	Sincerity-Apricots n' Cream	1,789	1993	250.00	250

Porcelain Collector Series - L. Middleton

1992	Beloved & Bé Bé	362	1994	590.00	590
1993	Cherish - Lilac & Lace	141	1994	500.00	500
1992	Sencerity II - Country Fair	253	1994	500.00	500

Porcelain Limited Edition Series - L. Middleton

1990	Baby Grace	500	1990	500.00	500
1994	Blossom	86	1995	500.00	500
1994	Bride	200	1994	1390.00	1390
1988	Cherish -1st Edition	750	1988	350.00	500
1989	Devan	543	1991	500.00	500
1991	Johanna	381	1992	500.00	500
1991	Molly Rose	500	1991	500.00	500
1989	My Lee	655	1991	500.00	500
1988	Sincerity -1st Edition -Nettie/Simplicity	750	1988	330.00	350-600
1994	Tenderness-Petite Pierrot	250	1994	500.00	500

Vinyl Collectors Series - L. Middleton

1987	Amanda - 1st Edition	3,778	1989	140.00	160
1985	Angel Face	20,200	1989	90.00	150
1994	Angel Kisses Boy	Open		98.00	98
1994	Angel Kisses Girl	Open		98.00	98
1992	Beth	1,414	1994	160.00	160
1986	Bubba Chubbs	5,550	1988	100.00	150-200
1988	Bubba Chubbs Railroader	7,925	1994	140.00	170
1988	Cherish	14,790	1992	160.00	250
1994	Country Boy	Open		118.00	118
1994	Country Boy (Dark Flesh)	Open		118.00	118
1994	Country Girl	Open		118.00	118
1994	Country Girl (Dark Flesh)	Open		118.00	118
1986	Dear One - 1st Edition	4,935	1988	90.00	250
1989	Devan	8,336	1991	170.00	170
1993	Echo	Open		180.00	180
1986	Little Angel - 3rd Edition	15,158	1992	90.00	110
1992	Little Angel Boy	Open		130.00	130
1992	Little Angel Girl	Open		130.00	130
1987	Missy	11,855	1991	100.00	120
1989	My Lee	3,794	1991	170.00	170
1992	Polly Esther	2,137	1994	160.00	160
1988	Sincerity - Limited 1st Ed. - Nettie/Simplicity	3,711	1989	160.00	200-250
1989	Sincerity-Schoolgirl	6,622	1992	180.00	200
1994	Town Boy	Open		118.00	118
1994	Town Boy (Dark Flesh)	Open		118.00	118
1994	Town Girl	Open		118.00	118
1994	Town Girl (Dark Flesh)	Open		118.00	118

Midwest of Cannon Falls

Folk Art Gallery Collection - S. Hale

1994	Bewitching Belinda 11425-4	Retrd.	1994	40.00	40
1994	Gardening Girl 11426-1	Retrd.	1994	45.00	45
1994	Heartfelt Angel 11422-3	Retrd.	1994	37.00	37
1994	Heartfelt Angel 11423-0	Retrd.	1994	20.00	20
1994	Santa Gone Fishing 12029-3	Retrd.	1994	130.00	130
1994	Santa of Christmas Past 12057-6	Retrd.	1994	130.00	130
1994	Sitting Santa 11424-7	Retrd.	1994	30.00	30

Original Appalachian Artworks

Collectors Club Editions - X. Roberts

1987	Baby Otis	Closed	1987	250.00	500
1989	Anna Ruby	Closed	1989	250.00	350-500
1990	Lee Ann	Closed	1990	250.00	400-500
1991	Richard Russell	Closed	1991	250.00	350-500
1992	Baby Dodd	Closed	1992	250.00	300-500
1993	Patti w/ Cabbage Bud Boutonnier	Closed	1993	280.00	280
1994	Mother Cabbage	Closed	1995	150.00	150

Cabbage Patch Kids - X. Roberts

1982	Amy	Closed	1982	125.00	500-700
1983	Andre/Madeira	Closed	1982	250.00	1200
1982	Billie	Closed	1982	125.00	450-700
1982	Bobbie	Closed	1982	125.00	450-700
1984	Daddy's Darlins' Kitten	Closed	1984	300.00	400-500
1984	Daddy's Darlins' Princess	Closed	1984	300.00	400-500
1984	Daddy's Darlins' Pun'kin	Closed	1983	300.00	400-500
1984	Daddy's Darlins' Tootsie	Closed	1984	300.00	400-500
1984	Daddy's Darlins', set of 4	Closed	1984	1600.00	1000-2000
1982	Dorothy	Closed	1982	125.00	700
1982	Gilda	Closed	1982	125.00	700-2500
1994	Little People 27" (Boy)	Closed	1994	325.00	500-650
1993	Little People 27" (Girl)	Closed	1993	325.00	750
1982	Marilyn	Closed	1982	125.00	700-800
1994	Mountain Laurel 'Kids™	Closed	1994	210.00	210
1994	Mountain Laurel Baby Sidney & Baby Lanier	100		390.00	390
1994	Mountain Laurel Easter	200		210.00	210
1994	Mountain Laurel Mysterious Barry	Closed	1994	225.00	225
1994	Mountain Laurel Norma Jean	Closed	1994	225.00	225
1994	Mountain Laurel-St. Patrick Boys	100		210.00	210
1994	Mountain Laurel-St. Patrick Girls	200		210.00	210
1995	Mt. Yonah	Closed	1995	210.00	210
1995	Mt. Yonah Easter	Closed	1995	215.00	215
1995	Mt. Yonah Valentine	Closed	1995	200.00	200
1982	Otis	Closed	1982	125.00	700
1982	Rebecca	Closed	1982	125.00	700
1982	Sybil	Closed	1982	125.00	450-700
1989	Tiger's Eye-Mother's Day	Closed	1989	150.00	150-300
1988	Tiger's Eye-Valentine's Day	Closed	1984	150.00	150-300
1982	Tyler	Closed	1982	125.00	2000-3000
1993	Unicoi Edition	Closed	1993	210.00	210

Cabbage Patch Kids Circus Parade - X. Roberts

1987	Big Top Clown-Baby Cakes	2,000	1987	180.00	300-450
1989	Happy Hobo-Bashful Billy	1,000	1989	180.00	350
1991	Mitzi	1,000	1991	220.00	250-350

Cabbage Patch Kids International - X. Roberts

1983	American Indian/Pair	Closed	1983	300.00	1200
1984	Bavarian/Pair	Closed	1984	300.00	450-800
1983	Hispanic/Pair	Closed	1983	300.00	400
1983	Irish/Pair	Closed	1985	320.00	320
1983	Oriental/Pair	Closed	1983	300.00	1000

Christmas Collection - X. Roberts

1979	X Christmas/Pair	Closed	1979	300.00	5500
1980	Christmas-Nicholas/Noel	Closed	1980	400.00	2600
1982	Christmas-Baby Rudy/Christy Nicole	Closed	1982	400.00	1600
1983	Christmas-Holly/Berry	Closed	1983	400.00	800
1984	Christmas-Carole/Chris	Closed	1984	400.00	600
1985	Christmas-Baby Sandy/Claude	Closed	1985	400.00	400
1986	Christmas-Hilliary/Nigel	Closed	1986	400.00	400
1987	Christmas-Katrina/Misha	Closed	1987	500.00	500
1988	Christmas-Kelly/Kane	Closed	1988	500.00	500
1989	Christmas-Joy	Closed	1989	250.00	600
1990	Christmas-Krystina	Closed	1990	250.00	250
1991	Christmas-Nick	Closed	1991	275.00	275
1992	Christmas-Christy Claus	Closed	1992	285.00	285
1993	Christmas-Rudolph	Closed	1993	275.00	275
1994	Christmas-Natalie	Closed	1994	275.00	275

Convention Baby - X. Roberts

1989	Ashley	Closed	1989	150.00	500
1990	Bradley	Closed	1990	175.00	350-500
1991	Caroline	Closed	1991	200.00	300
1992	Duke	Closed	1992	225.00	300-400
1993	Ellen	Closed	1993	225.00	225
1994	Justin	Closed	1994	238.50	300-500
1995	Fifi	Closed	1995	250.00	250

Happily Ever After - X. Roberts

1993	Bride	Closed	1993	230.00	275
1993	Groom	Closed	1993	230.00	275

Little People - X. Roberts

1978	"A" Blue	Closed	1978	125.00	5000-6000
1978	"B" Red	Closed	1978	100.00	3000-4200
1978	"C" Burgundy	Closed	1978	100.00	1500-1800
1979	"D" Purple	Closed	1979	100.00	800-1000
1979	"E" Bronze	Closed	1979	125.00	700
1982	"PE" New 'Ears Preemie	Closed	1982	140.00	300
1981	"PR II" Preemie	Closed	1981	130.00	250
1980	"SP" Preemie	Closed	1980	100.00	500-750
1982	"U" Unsigned	Closed	1982	125.00	300-400
1980	"U" Unsigned	Closed	1981	125.00	300-400
1980	Celebrity	Closed	1980	200.00	350-650
1980	Grand Edition	Closed	1986	1000.00	1000
1978	Helen Blue	Closed	1978	150.00	6000-7000
1981	New 'Ears	Closed	1981	125.00	125
1981	Standing Edition	Closed	1986	300.00	350-400

Princeton Gallery

Best Friend Dolls - Unknown

1991	Sharing Secrets	Open		78.00	78

Childhood Songs Dolls - Unknown

1991	It's Raining, It's Pouring	Open		78.00	78

Dress Up Dolls - Unknown

1991	Grandma's Attic	Open		95.00	95

Fabrique Santa - Unknown

1991	Christmas Dream	Open		76.00	76

Imaginary People - Unknown

1992	Melinda, Tooth Fairy	Open		95.00	95

Little Ladies of Victorian England - Unknown

1991	Abigail	Open		59.00	59
1993	Beverly	Open		58.50	59
1992	Caroline	Open		58.50	59
1992	Heather	Open		58.50	59
1991	Valerie	Open		58.50	59
1990	Victoria Anne	Open		59.00	59

Rock-N-Roll Dolls - Various

1992	Chantilly Lace - M. Sirko	Open		95.00	95
1991	Cindy at the Hop - M. Sirko	Open		95.00	95
1993	Yellow Dot Bikini - Unknown	Open		95.00	95

Santa Doll - Unknown

1991	Checking His List	Open		119.00	119

Terrible Twos - M. Sirko

1991	One Man Band	Open		95.00	95

Reco International

Childhood Doll Collection - S. Kuck

1994	A Kiss Goodnight	Open		79.00	79
1995	Reading With Teddy	Open		79.00	79
1994	Teaching Teddy His Prayers	Open		79.00	79
1996	Teddy's Picnic	Open		79.00	79

Children's Circus Doll Collection - J. McClelland

1991	Johnny The Strongman	Yr.Iss.		83.00	83
1991	Katie The Tightrope Walker	Yr.Iss.		78.00	78
1992	Maggie The Animal Trainer	Yr.Iss.		83.00	83
1991	Tommy The Clown	Yr.Iss.		78.00	78

Precious Memories of Motherhood - S. Kuck

1993	Bedtime	Retrd.	1994	149.00	149
1992	Expectant Moments	Retrd.	1993	149.00	149
1990	Loving Steps	Retrd.	1992	125.00	150-195
1991	Lullaby	Yr.Iss.		125.00	125

Roman, Inc.

Abbie Williams Collection - E. Williams

1991	Molly	5,000		155.00	155

A Christmas Dream - E. Williams

1990	Carole	5,000		125.00	125
1990	Chelsea	5,000		125.00	125

Classic Brides of the Century - E. Williams

1991	Flora-The 1900's Bride	Yr.Iss.		145.00	145
1992	Jennifer-The 1980's Bride	Yr.Iss.		149.00	149
1993	Kathleen-The 1930's Bride	Yr.Iss.		149.00	149

Ellen Williams Doll - E. Williams

1989	Noelle	5,000		125.00	125
1989	Rebecca 999	7,500		195.00	195

Tyrolean Treasures: Wood Body, Moveable Joint - Unknown

1990	Andrew	2,000		575.00	575
1990	Ann	2,000		650.00	650
1990	David	2,000		650.00	650
1990	Ellan	2,000		575.00	575
1990	Erika	2,000		575.00	575
1990	Karin	2,000		650.00	650
1990	Lisa	2,000		650.00	650
1990	Marisa	2,000		575.00	575
1990	Matthew	2,000		575.00	575

YEAR ISSUE		EDITION LIMIT	YEAR RETD.	ISSUE PRICE	QUOTE U.S. $
1990	Melissa	2,000		650.00	650
1990	Monica	2,000		650.00	650
1990	Nadia	2,000		650.00	650
1990	Sarah	2,000		575.00	575
1990	Susie	2,000		650.00	650
1990	Tina	2,000		650.00	650
1990	Verena	2,000		650.00	650

Sarah's Attic, Inc.

Heirlooms from the Attic - Sarah's Attic

YEAR ISSUE		EDITION LIMIT	YEAR RETD.	ISSUE PRICE	QUOTE U.S. $
1991	Adora 1823	500	1991	90.00	200
1991	All Cloth Muffin Black Doll 1820	Closed	1991	90.00	200
1991	All Cloth Puffin Black Doll 1821	Closed	1991	90.00	200
1992	Angelle Guardian Angel 3569	2,000	1993	170.00	170
1995	Baby Doll 4341	150	1995	300.00	300
1989	Becky Doll 1461	150	1991	120.00	120
1989	Beverly Jane-Black Dress 1496	500	1992	160.00	160
1989	Beverly Jane-Green Dress 1693	500	1992	160.00	160
1989	Beverly Jane-Red Dress 1694	500	1992	160.00	160
1989	Beverly Jane-Sunday's Best 1666	500	1992	160.00	160
1989	Bobby Doll 1462	150	1991	120.00	120
1988	Country Girl Doll 1190	Closed	1988	26.00	26
1986	Cupcake Doll 0039B	Closed	1986	32.00	32
1992	Edie-Country 1834	500	1993	170.00	170
1992	Edie-Playtime 1835	500	1993	170.00	170
1992	Edie-Victorian 1833	500	1993	170.00	170
1992	Emily-Country 1830	500	1993	250.00	250
1992	Emily-Victorian 1829	500	1993	250.00	250
1992	Emma-Country 1837	500	1993	160.00	160
1992	Emma-Playtime 1838	500	1993	160.00	160
1992	Emma-Victorian 1836	500	1993	160.00	160
1991	Enos 1822	500	1991	90.00	200
1989	Freedom-Americana Clown 1472	500	1992	120.00	120
1993	Granny Quilting Lady Doll 3576	Closed	1993	130.00	130
1989	Harmony-Victorian Clown 1464	500	1992	120.00	120
1992	Harpster w/Banjo 3591	Closed	1992	250.00	250
1990	Hickory-Americana 1771	Closed	1993	150.00	150-175
1990	Hickory-Beachtime 1769	2,000	1993	140.00	150-175
1991	Hickory-Christmas 1810	2,000	1993	150.00	150-175
1990	Hickory-Playtime 1768	2,000	1993	140.00	175
1990	Hickory-School Days 1766	2,000	1993	140.00	175
1991	Hickory-Springtime 1814	2,000	1993	150.00	195
1990	Hickory-Sunday's Best 1770	2,000	1993	150.00	195
1990	Hickory-Sweet Dreams 1767	2,000	1993	140.00	175
1992	Hilary-Country 1832	500	1993	200.00	200
1992	Hilary-Victorian 1831	500	1993	200.00	200
1986	Holly Black Angel 0410	Retrd.	1986	34.00	200
1993	Jack Boy Doll 3893	500		130.00	130
1986	Katie Doll 0039F	Closed	1986	32.00	32
1992	Kiah Guardian Angel 3570	2,000	1993	170.00	170
1995	Labor of Love Black Doll 4338	150		300.00	300
1995	Labor of Love White Doll 4339	150		300.00	300
1993	Lilla Quilting Lady Doll 3581	Closed	1993	130.00	130
1988	Lily-Black Doll 2221	Closed	1988	90.00	90
1986	Maggie Cloth Doll 0012	Closed	1989	70.00	120
1986	Maggie Cloth Doll 0039 D	Closed	1986	32.00	32
1986	Matt Cloth Doll 0011	Closed	1989	70.00	120
1986	Matt Cloth Doll 0039 C	Closed	1986	32.00	32
1989	Megan Doll 1752	100	1990	70.00	70
1988	Michael Doll 4015	Closed	1988	44.00	44
1993	Millie Quilting Lady Doll 3586	Closed	1993	130.00	130
1987	Molly Doll 2053	Closed	1988	44.00	44
1988	Mrs. Claus Doll 6284	500	1989	120.00	120
1989	Noel-Christmas Clown 1469	500	1992	120.00	120
1995	Olivia Doll 4340	150		300.00	300
1992	Peace on Earth Santa 3564	200	1992	175.00	350
1986	Priscilla Doll 0030	Closed	1989	140.00	300
1993	Sally Booba Doll 3890	500		130.00	130
1988	Santa Claus Doll 6337	500	1989	120.00	120
1990	Sassafras-Americana 1685	2,000	1993	150.00	175
1990	Sassafras-Beachtime 1683	2,000	1993	140.00	175
1991	Sassafras-Christmas 1809	2,000	1993	150.00	150-175
1990	Sassafras-Playtime 1682	2,000	1993	140.00	175
1989	Sassafras-School Days 1680	2,000	1993	140.00	175
1991	Sassafras-Springtime 1813	2,000	1993	150.00	195
1990	Sassafras-Sunday's Best 1684	2,000	1993	150.00	175
1990	Sassafras-Sweet Dreams 1681	2,000	1993	140.00	195
1989	Scott Doll 1753	100	1990	70.00	70
1988	Smiley Clown Doll 3050	Closed	1988	126.00	126
1986	Spike Doll 0039G	Closed	1986	32.00	32
1989	Spirit of America Santa 1476	500	1993	150.00	200
1994	Star Black Angel 4107	500		120.00	120
1987	Sunshine Doll 3003	Closed	1988	118.00	118
1986	Tillie Doll 0039J	Closed	1986	32.00	32
1995	Tillie Doll 4337	150	1995	300.00	300
1987	Tillie Rag Doll 0344	Closed	1987	32.00	32
1994	Tillie-Clown 9601	1,000		120.00	120
1986	Twinkie Doll 0039A	Closed	1986	32.00	32
1994	Twinkle-White Angel 4108	500		120.00	120
1989	Victor Doll 1468	Closed	1990	120.00	120
1989	Victoria Doll 1467	500	1990	120.00	120
1986	Whimpy Doll 0039E	Closed	1986	32.00	32
1992	Whoopie 3597	Closed	1992	200.00	200
1986	Willie Doll 0039I	Closed	1986	32.00	32
1995	Willie Doll 433	150		300.00	300
1987	Willie Rag Doll 0343	Closed	1987	32.00	32
1994	Willie-Clown Doll 9601	1,000		120.00	120
1992	Wooster 3602	Closed	1992	160.00	160

Seymour Mann, Inc.

Connossieur Doll Collection - E. Mann

YEAR ISSUE		EDITION LIMIT	YEAR RETD.	ISSUE PRICE	QUOTE U.S. $
1991	Abby 16" Pink Dress-C3145	Closed	1993	100.00	100
1995	Abby C-3229	2,500		30.00	30
1994	Abby YK-4533	3,500		135.00	135
1991	Abigail-EP-3	Closed	1993	100.00	100
1991	Abigail-WB-72WM	Closed	1993	75.00	75
1994	Adak PS-412	2,500		150.00	150
1993	Adrienne C-3162	Closed	1994	135.00	135
1995	Aggie PS-435	2,500		80.00	80
1991	Alexis 24" Beige Lace-EP32	Closed	1993	220.00	220
1994	Alice GU-32	2,500		150.00	150
1994	Alice IND-508	2,500	1995	115.00	115
1992	Alice-JNC-4013	Open	1993	90.00	90
1995	Alicia C-3235	2,500		65.00	65
1991	Alicia-YK-4215	Closed	1993	90.00	90
1995	Allison CD-18183	2,500		35.00	35
1995	Allison TR-92	2,500		125.00	125
1994	Ally FH-556	2,500	1995	115.00	115
1994	Alyssa C-3201	2,500	1995	110.00	110
1994	Alyssa PP-1	2,500		275.00	275
1991	Amanda Toast-OM-182	Closed	1993	260.00	260
1995	Amanda TR-96	2,500		135.00	135
1989	Amber-DOM-281A	Closed	1993	85.00	85
1991	Amelia-TR-47	Closed	1993	105.00	105
1991	Amy C-3147	Closed	1993	135.00	135
1995	Amy GU-300A	2,500	1995	30.00	30
1994	Amy OC-43M	2,500		115.00	115
1992	Amy OM-06	2,500	1993	150.00	150
1990	Anabelle C-3080	Closed	1992	85.00	85
1990	Angel DOM-335	Closed	1992	105.00	105
1995	Angel FH-291DP	2,500		70.00	70
1994	Angel LL-956	2,500		90.00	90
1994	Angel SP-460	2,500		140.00	140
1990	Angela C-3084	Closed	1992	105.00	105
1990	Angela C-3084M	Closed	1992	115.00	115
1995	Angela Doll 556	2,500		35.00	35
1995	Angela FH-511	2,500		85.00	85
1995	Angela OM-87	2,500		150.00	150
1995	Angelica FH-291B	2,500		70.00	70
1994	Angelica FH-291E	2,500		85.00	85
1995	Angelica FH-511B	2,500		85.00	85
1995	Angelina FH-291S	2,500		70.00	70
1994	Angelina FH-291S	2,500		85.00	85
1995	Angeline FH-291WG	2,500		75.00	75
1994	Angeline FH-291WG	2,500		85.00	85
1995	Angeline OM-84	2,500		100.00	100
1995	Angelique	2,500		150.00	150
1995	Angelita FH-291G	2,500		70.00	70
1994	Angelita FH-291G	2,500		85.00	85
1994	Angelo OC-57	2,500		135.00	135
1990	Anita FH-277G	Closed	1992	65.00	65
1991	Ann TR-52	Closed	1993	135.00	135
1995	Anna Doll 550	2,500		60.00	60
1995	Annette FH-635	2,500		110.00	110
1991	Annette-TR-59	Closed	1993	130.00	130
1991	Annie YK-4214	Closed	1993	145.00	145
1991	Antoinette FH-452	Closed	1993	100.00	100
1993	Antonia OM-227	2,500	1993	350.00	350
1994	Antonia OM-42	2,500		150.00	150
1995	April CD-2212B	2,500		50.00	50
1991	Arabella-C-3163	Closed	1993	135.00	135
1991	Ariel 34" Blue/White-EP-33	Closed	1993	175.00	175
1995	Ariel OM-81	2,500		185.00	185
1994	Arilene LL-940	2,500	1994	90.00	90
1993	Arlene SP-421	Closed	1993	100.00	100
1988	Ashley C-278	Closed	1990	80.00	80
1989	Ashley C-278	Closed	1993	80.00	80
1990	Ashley FH-325	Closed	1993	75.00	75
1995	Ashley OC-76	2,500		40.00	40
1995	Ashley PS-433	2,500		110.00	110
1994	Atanak PS-414	2,500	1994	150.00	150
1991	Audrey FH-455	2,500	1993	125.00	125
1990	Audrey YK-4089	Closed	1992	125.00	125
1987	Audrina YK-200	Closed	1986	85.00	140
1991	Aurora Gold 22"-OM-181	2,500	1993	260.00	260
1991	Azure AM-15	2,500	1993	175.00	175
1994	Baby Belle C-3193	2,500	1994	150.00	150
1991	Baby Beth-DOLL-406P	2,500	1993	27.50	28
1995	Baby Betsy Doll 336	2,500		75.00	75
1990	Baby Betty YK-4087	Closed	1991	125.00	125
1990	Baby Bonnie SP-341	Closed	1991	55.00	55
1991	Baby Bonnie SP-341	Closed	1993	55.00	55
1991	Baby Bonnie w/Walker Music-DOLL-409	2,500	1993	40.00	40
1990	Baby Brent EP-15	Closed	1991	85.00	85
1991	Baby Brent EP-15	Closed	1993	85.00	85
1991	Baby Carrie DOLL-402P	2,500	1993	27.50	28
1990	Baby Ecru WB-17	Closed	1991	65.00	65
1991	Baby Ecru WB-17	Closed	1993	65.00	65
1991	Baby Ellie Ecru Musical DOLL-402E	2,500	1993	27.50	28
1991	Baby Gloria Black Baby PS-289	Closed	1993	75.00	75
1991	Baby John PS-498	Closed	1993	85.00	85
1989	Baby John PS-49B	Closed	1991	85.00	85
1990	Baby Kate WB-19	Closed	1991	85.00	85
1991	Baby Linda-DOLL-406E	2,500	1993	27.50	28
1990	Baby Nelly-PS-163	Closed	1991	95.00	95
1994	Baby Scarlet C-3194	2,500	1994	115.00	115
1991	Baby Sue-DOLL-402B	2,500	1993	27.50	28
1990	Baby Sue-DOLL-402B	Closed	1992	27.50	28
1990	Baby Sunshine-C-3055	Closed	1992	90.00	90
1995	Barbara PS-439	2,500		65.00	65
1995	Beige Angel FH-291E	2,500		70.00	70
1991	Belinda-C-3164	Closed	1993	150.00	150
1991	Bernetta-EP-40	Closed	1993	115.00	115
1995	Beth OC-74	2,500		40.00	40
1992	Beth-OM-05	Closed	1993	135.00	135
1990	Beth-YK-4099A/B	Closed	1992	125.00	125
1995	Betsy C-3224	2,500		45.00	45
1995	Betsy OM-89B	2,500		125.00	125
1995	Betsy RDK-230	2,500		35.00	35
1991	Betsy-AM-6	Closed	1993	105.00	105
1992	Bette-OM-01	2,500	1993	115.00	115
1990	Bettina-TR-4	Closed	1991	125.00	125
1991	Bettina-YK-4144	Closed	1993	105.00	105
1995	Betty LL-996	2,500		115.00	115
1989	Betty-PS27G	Closed	1993	65.00	125
1990	Beverly-DOLL-335	Closed	1992	110.00	110
1995	Bianca CD-1450C	2,500		35.00	35
1990	Billie-YK-4056V	Closed	1992	65.00	65
1993	Blaine C-3167	Closed	1993	100.00	100
1991	Blaine-TR-61	Closed	1993	115.00	115
1994	Blair YK-4532	3,500	1994	150.00	150
1991	Blythe-CH-15V	Closed	1993	135.00	135
1991	Bo-Peep w/Lamb-C-3128	Closed	1993	105.00	105
1994	Bobbi NM-30	2,500	1994	135.00	135
1994	Brandy YK-4537	3,500	1995	165.00	165
1995	Brenda Doll 551	2,500		60.00	60
1989	Brett-PS27B	Closed	1992	65.00	125
1995	Brianna GU-300B	2,500		30.00	30
1991	Bridget-SP-379	2,500	1993	105.00	105
1995	Brie C-3230	2,500		30.00	30
1995	Brie CD-16310C	2,500		30.00	30
1995	Brie OM-89W	2,500		125.00	125
1995	Britt OC-77	2,500		40.00	40
1995	Brittany Doll 558	2,500		35.00	35
1989	Brittany-TK-4	Closed	1990	150.00	150
1988	Brittany-TK-5	Closed	1990	120.00	120
1994	Bronwyn IND-517	2,500	1994	140.00	140
1991	Brooke-FH-461	2,500	1993	115.00	115
1995	Bryna Doll 555	2,500		35.00	35
1991	Bryna-AM-100B	2,500	1993	70.00	70
1995	Bunny TR-97	2,500		85.00	85
1995	Burgundy Angel FH-291D	2,500		75.00	75
1994	Cactus Flower Indian LL-944	2,500	1994	105.00	105
1990	Caillin-DOLL-11PH	Closed	1992	60.00	60
1995	Caitlin LL-997	2,500		115.00	115
1990	Caitlin-YK-4051V	Closed	1992	90.00	90
1994	Callie TR-76	2,500	1994	140.00	140
1994	Calypso LL-942	2,500	1994	150.00	150
1991	Camellia-FH-457	2,500	1993	100.00	100
1986	Camelot Fairy-C-84	Closed	1988	75.00	225
1993	Camille OM-230	2,500	1994	250.00	250
1995	Candice TR-94	2,500	1995	135.00	135
1995	Carmel TR-93	2,500		125.00	125
1994	Carmen PS-408	2,500	1994	150.00	150
1990	Carole-YK-4085W	Closed	1992	125.00	125
1991	Caroline-LL-838	2,500	1993	110.00	110
1991	Caroline-LL-905	2,500	1993	110.00	110
1995	Carolotta OM-80	2,500		175.00	175
1995	Carrie C-3231	2,500		30.00	30
1994	Casey C-3197	2,500		140.00	140
1995	Catherine RDK-231	2,500		30.00	30
1994	Cathy GU-41	2,500	1994	140.00	140
1995	Cecily Doll 552	2,500		60.00	60
1995	Celene FH-618	2,500		120.00	120
1995	Celestine LL-982	2,500		100.00	100
1990	Charlene-YK-4112	Closed	1992	90.00	90
1992	Charlotte-FH-484	2,500	1993	115.00	115
1995	Chelsea Doll 560	2,500		35.00	35
1992	Chelsea-IND-397	Open	1993	85.00	85
1995	Cherry FH-616	2,500	1994	100.00	100
1991	Cheryl-TR-49	2,500	1993	120.00	120
1991	Chin Chin-YK-4211	Closed	1993	85.00	85
1990	Chin Fa-C-3061	Closed	1992	95.00	95
1990	Chinook-WB-24	Closed	1992	85.00	85
1994	Chris FH-561	2,500	1994	85.00	85
1994	Chrissie FH-562	2,500	1994	85.00	85
1990	Chrissie-WB-2	Closed	1992	75.00	75
1991	Christina-PS-261	Closed	1993	115.00	115
1985	Christmas Cheer-125	Closed	1988	40.00	100
1995	Christmas Kitten IND-530	2,500		100.00	100
1991	Cindy Lou-FH-464	2,500	1993	85.00	85
1994	Cindy OC-58	2,500	1994	140.00	140
1993	Cinnamon JNC-4014	Closed	1993	90.00	90
1988	Cissie-DOM263	Closed	1990	65.00	135
1991	Cissy-EP-56	2,500	1993	95.00	95
1995	Clancy GU-54	2,500	1995	80.00	80
1994	Clara IND-518	2,500	1994	140.00	140
1994	Clara IND-524	2,500	1994	150.00	150
1993	Clare FH-497	2,500	1993	100.00	100
1991	Clare-DOLL-465	Open	1993	100.00	100
1994	Claudette TR-81	2,500	1995	150.00	150
1991	Claudine-C-3146	Closed	1993	95.00	95
1993	Clothilde FH-469	2,500	1993	125.00	125
1995	Cody FH-629	2,500	1995	120.00	120
1991	Colette-WB-7	Closed	1993	65.00	65
1991	Colleen-YK-4163	Closed	1993	120.00	120
1991	Cookie-GU-6	2,500	1993	110.00	110
1994	Copper YK-4546C	3,500		150.00	150
1994	Cora FH-565	2,500		140.00	140

DOLLS

YEAR ISSUE		EDITION LIMIT	YEAR RETD.	ISSUE PRICE	QUOTE U.S.$
1992	Cordelia-OM-009	2,500	1993	250.00	250
1992	Cordelia-OM-09	2,500	1993	250.00	250
1994	Cory FH-564	2,500	1994	115.00	115
1991	Courtney-LL-859	2,500	1993	150.00	150
1991	Creole-AM-17	2,500	1993	160.00	160
1989	Crying Courtney-PS-75	Closed	1992	115.00	115
1988	Crying Courtney-PS75	Closed	1990	115.00	115
1991	Crystal-YK-4237	3,500	1993	125.00	125
1995	Cynthia GU-300C	2,500		30.00	30
1988	Cynthia-DOM-211	3,500	1990	85.00	85
1987	Cynthia-DOM-211	Closed	1986	85.00	85
1990	Daisy-EP-6	Closed	1992	90.00	90
1994	Dallas PS-403	2,500	1994	150.00	150
1995	Danielle MER-808	2,500		65.00	65
1995	Danielle PS-432	2,500		100.00	100
1991	Danielle-AM-5	Closed	1993	125.00	125
1990	Daphne Ecru-C-3025	Closed	1992	85.00	85
1989	Daphne Ecru/Mint Green-C3025	Closed	1990	85.00	85
1995	Darcy FH-636	2,500		80.00	80
1995	Darcy LL-986	2,500		110.00	110
1991	Darcy-EP-47	Closed	1993	110.00	110
1991	Darcy-FH-451	2,500	1993	105.00	105
1991	Daria-C-3122	Closed	1993	110.00	110
1995	Darla LL-988	2,500		100.00	100
1991	Darlene-DOLL-444	2,500	1993	75.00	75
1994	Daryl LL-947	2,500	1994	150.00	150
1991	Dawn-C-3135	Closed	1993	130.00	130
1987	Dawn-C185	Closed	1986	75.00	175
1992	Debbie-JNC-4006	Open	1993	90.00	90
1994	Dee LL-948	2,500	1994	110.00	110
1992	Deidre-FH-473	2,500	1993	115.00	115
1992	Deidre-YK-4083	Closed	1993	95.00	95
1994	Delilah C-3195	2,500	1994	150.00	150
1995	Denise LL-994	2,500		105.00	105
1991	Denise-LL-852	2,500	1993	105.00	105
1991	Dephine-SP-308	Closed	1993	135.00	135
1991	Desiree-LL-898	2,500	1993	120.00	120
1995	Diana RDK-221A	2,500		35.00	35
1995	Diane PS-444	2,500		110.00	110
1990	Diane-FH-275	Closed	1992	90.00	90
1990	Dianna-TK-31	Closed	1992	175.00	175
1995	Dinah OC-79	2,500		40.00	40
1988	Doll Oliver-FH392	Closed	1990	100.00	100
1990	Domino-C-3050	Closed	1992	145.00	200
1992	Dona-FH-494	2,500	1993	100.00	100
1993	Donna DOLL-447	2,500	1993	85.00	85
1995	Donna GU-300D	2,500		30.00	30
1990	Dorothy-TR-10	Closed	1992	135.00	150
1990	Dorri-DOLL-16PH	Closed	1992	85.00	85
1991	Duanane-SP-366	Closed	1993	85.00	85
1995	Dulcie FH-622	2,500		110.00	110
1991	Dulcie-YK-4131V	Closed	1993	100.00	100
1991	Dwayne-C-3123	Closed	1993	120.00	120
1991	Edie -YK-4177	Closed	1993	115.00	115
1990	Eileen-FH-367	Closed	1992	100.00	100
1995	Elaine CD-02210	2,500		50.00	50
1995	Eleanor C16669	2,500		35.00	35
1991	Elisabeth and Lisa-C-3095	2,500	1993	195.00	195
1989	Elisabeth-OM-32	Closed	1990	120.00	120
1991	Elise -PS-259	Closed	1993	105.00	105
1995	Elizabeth Doll 553	2,500		35.00	35
1991	Elizabeth-AM-32	2,500	1993	105.00	105
1989	Elizabeth-C-246P	Closed	1990	150.00	200
1993	Ellen YK-4223	3,500	1994	150.00	150
1995	Ellie FH-621	2,500		125.00	125
1989	Emily-PS-48	Closed	1990	110.00	110
1988	Emily-YK-243V	Closed	1990	70.00	70
1995	Emma Doll 559	2,500		35.00	35
1995	Emma GU-300E	2,500		30.00	30
1991	Emmaline Beige/Lilac-OM-197	Closed	1993	300.00	300
1991	Emmaline-OM-191	2,500	1993	300.00	300
1991	Emmy-C-3099	Closed	1993	125.00	125
1995	Erin RDK-223	2,500		30.00	30
1991	Erin-DOLL-4PH	Closed	1993	60.00	60
1992	Eugenie-OM-225	2,500	1993	300.00	300
1991	Evalina-C-3124	Closed	1993	135.00	135
1994	Faith IND-522	2,500	1994	135.00	135
1994	Faith OC-60	2,500	1994	115.00	115
1995	Fawn C-3228	2,500		55.00	55
1995	Felicia GU-300F	2,500		30.00	30
1990	Felicia-TR-9	Closed	1992	115.00	115
1991	Fifi-AM-100F	Closed	1993	70.00	70
1995	Fleur C16415	2,500		30.00	30
1991	Fleurette-PS-286	2,500	1993	75.00	75
1994	Flora FH-583	2,500	1994	115.00	115
1991	Flora-TR-46	Closed	1993	125.00	125
1994	Florette IND-519	2,500	1994	140.00	140
1988	Frances-C-233	Closed	1990	80.00	125
1989	Frances-C233	Closed	1990	80.00	125
1991	Francesca-AM-14	2,500	1993	175.00	175
1990	Francesca-C-3021	Closed	1992	100.00	175
1994	Gardiner PS-405	2,500		150.00	150
1993	Gena OM-229	Closed	1994	250.00	250
1994	Georgia IND-510	2,500	1995	220.00	220
1995	Georgia IND-528	2,500		125.00	125
1994	Georgia SP-456	2,500		115.00	115
1991	Georgia-YK-4131	Closed	1993	100.00	100
1991	Georgia-YK-4143	Closed	1993	150.00	150
1990	Gerri Beige-YK4094	Closed	1992	95.00	140
1991	Gigi-C-3107	Closed	1993	135.00	135
1991	Ginger-LL-907	Closed	1993	115.00	115
1995	Ginnie FH-619	2,500		110.00	110
1990	Ginny-YK-4119	Closed	1995	100.00	100
1988	Giselle on Goose-FH176	Closed	1990	105.00	225
1992	Giselle-OM-02	Closed	1993	90.00	90
1991	Gloria-AM-100G	2,500	1993	70.00	70
1991	Gloria-YK-4166	Closed	1993	105.00	105
1995	Gold Angel FH-511G	2,500		85.00	85
1995	Green Angel FH-511C	2,500		85.00	85
1995	Gretchen FH-620	2,500	1995	120.00	120
1991	Gretchen-DOLL-446	Open	1993	45.00	45
1991	Gretel-DOLL-434	Closed	1993	60.00	60
1995	Guardian Angel TR-98	2,500		85.00	85
1995	Guardian Angel OM-91	2,500		150.00	150
1991	Hansel and Gretel-DOLL-448V	Closed	1993	60.00	60
1989	Happy Birthday-C3012	Closed	1990	80.00	125
1993	Happy FH-479	2,500	1994	105.00	105
1995	Happy RDK-238	2,500		25.00	25
1994	Hatty/Matty IND-514	2,500		165.00	165
1995	Heather LL-991	2,500		115.00	115
1995	Heather PS-436	2,500		115.00	115
1994	Heather YK-4531	3,500		165.00	165
1993	Hedy FH-449	Closed	1994	95.00	95
1989	Heidi-260	Closed	1990	50.00	95
1991	Helene-AM-29	2,500	1993	150.00	150
1995	Holly CD-16526	2,500		30.00	30
1991	Holly-CH-6	Closed	1993	100.00	100
1991	Honey Bunny-WB-9	Closed	1993	70.00	70
1994	Honey LL-945	2,500		150.00	150
1991	Honey-FH-401	Closed	1993	100.00	100
1991	Hope-FH-434	2,500	1993	90.00	90
1990	Hope-YK-4118	Closed	1992	90.00	90
1995	Hyacinth C-3227	2,500		130.00	130
1994	Hyacinth LL-941	2,500	1995	90.00	90
1990	Hyacinth-DOLL-15PH	Closed	1992	85.00	85
1990	Indian Doll-FH-295	Closed	1992	60.00	60
1994	Indian IND-520	2,500		115.00	115
1991	Indira-AM-4	2,500	1993	125.00	125
1995	Irene GU-56	2,500		85.00	85
1995	Irina RDK-237	2,500		35.00	35
1993	Iris FH-483	2,500	1994	95.00	95
1991	Iris-TR-58	Closed	1993	120.00	120
1995	Ivana RDK-233	2,500		35.00	35
1994	Ivy C-3203	2,500		85.00	85
1991	Ivy-PS-307	Closed	1993	75.00	75
1994	Jacqueline C-3202	2,500		150.00	150
1995	Jamaica LL-989	2,500		75.00	75
1993	Jan Dress-Up OM-12	2,500	1994	135.00	135
1994	Jan FH-584R	2,500		115.00	115
1992	Jan-OM-012	9,200	1993	135.00	135
1991	Jane-PS-243L	Closed	1993	115.00	115
1992	Janet-FH-496	2,500	1993	120.00	120
1990	Janette-DOLL-385	Closed	1992	85.00	85
1991	Janice-OM-194	2,500	1993	300.00	300
1994	Janis FH-584B	2,500		115.00	115
1989	Jaqueline-DOLL-254M	Closed	1990	85.00	85
1995	Jennifer PS-446	2,500		145.00	145
1995	Jenny CD-16673B	2,500		35.00	35
1994	Jenny OC-36M	2,500		115.00	115
1995	Jerri PS-434	2,500		100.00	100
1995	Jessica RDK-225	2,500		30.00	30
1988	Jessica-DOM-267	Closed	1990	90.00	90
1991	Jessica-FH-423	2,500	1993	95.00	95
1992	Jet-FH-478	2,500	1993	115.00	115
1995	Jewel TR-100	2,500		110.00	110
1994	Jillian C-3196	2,500		150.00	150
1993	Jillian SP-428	Closed	1994	165.00	165
1990	Jillian-DOLL-41PH	Closed	1992	90.00	90
1994	Jo YK-4539	3,500	1995	150.00	150
1988	Joanne Cry Baby-PS-50	Closed	1990	100.00	100
1989	Joanne Cry Baby-PS-50	2,500	1991	100.00	100
1990	Joanne-TR-12	Closed	1992	175.00	175
1992	Jodie-FH-495	2,500	1993	115.00	115
1995	Joella CD-16779	2,500		35.00	35
1988	Jolie-C231	Closed	1990	65.00	150
1994	Jordan SP-455	2,500		150.00	150
1995	Joy CD-1450A	2,500		35.00	35
1995	Joy TR-99	2,500		85.00	135
1991	Joy-EP-23V	Closed	1993	130.00	130
1991	Joyce-AM-100J	2,500	1993	35.00	35
1995	Julia C-3234	2,500		100.00	100
1995	Julia RDK-222	2,500		35.00	35
1991	Julia-C-3102	Closed	1993	135.00	135
1988	Julie-C245A	Closed	1990	65.00	160
1990	Julie-WB-35	Closed	1992	70.00	70
1988	Juliette Bride Musical-C246LTM	Closed	1990	150.00	200
1993	Juliette OM-8	2,500	1994	175.00	175
1992	Juliette-OM-08	2,500	1993	175.00	175
1991	Juliette-OM-192	2,500	1993	300.00	300
1995	June CD-2212	2,500		50.00	50
1991	Karen-EP-24	Closed	1993	115.00	115
1990	Karen-PS-198	Closed	1992	150.00	150
1991	Karmela-EP-57	2,500	1993	120.00	120
1995	Karyn RDK-224	2,500		35.00	35
1994	Kate OC-55	2,500		150.00	150
1990	Kate-C-3060	Closed	1992	95.00	95
1990	Kathy w/Bear-TE1	Closed	1992	70.00	70
1994	Katie IND-511	2,500		110.00	110
1989	Kayoko-PS-24	Closed	1991	75.00	175
1994	Kelly YK-4536	3,500		150.00	150
1991	Kelly-AM-8	Closed	1993	125.00	125
1995	Kelsey Doll 561	2,500		35.00	35
1993	Kendra FH-481	2,500	1994	115.00	115
1991	Kerry-FH-396	Closed	1993	100.00	100
1994	Kevin MS-25	2,500		150.00	150
1994	Kevin YK-4543	3,500		140.00	140
1990	Kiku-EP-4	Closed	1992	100.00	100
1991	Kim-AM-100K	2,500	1993	70.00	70
1995	Kimmie CD-15816	2,500		30.00	30
1991	Kinesha-SP-402	2,500	1993	110.00	110
1988	Kirsten-PS-40G	Closed	1990	70.00	70
1989	Kirsten-PS-40G	Closed	1991	70.00	70
1993	Kit SP-426	Closed	1994	55.00	55
1994	Kit YK-4547	3,500		115.00	115
1994	Kitten IND-512	2,500		110.00	110
1995	Kitty IND-527	2,500		40.00	40
1991	Kristi-FH-402	Closed	1993	100.00	100
1991	Kyla-YK-4137	Closed	1993	95.00	95
1994	Lady Caroline LL-938	2,500		120.00	120
1994	Lady Caroline LL-939	2,500		120.00	120
1994	Laughing Waters PS-410	2,500		150.00	150
1990	Laura-DOLL-25PH	Closed	1992	55.00	55
1992	Laura-OM-010	2,500	1993	250.00	250
1991	Laura-WB-110P	Closed	1993	85.00	85
1994	Lauren SP-458	2,500		125.00	125
1990	Lauren-SP-300	Closed	1992	85.00	85
1992	Laurie-JNC-4004	Open	1993	90.00	90
1990	Lavender Blue-YK-4024	Closed	1992	95.00	135
1991	Leigh-DOLL-457	2,500	1993	95.00	95
1991	Leila-AM-2	Closed	1993	125.00	125
1995	Lenore FH-617	2,500		120.00	120
1995	Lenore RDK-229	2,500		50.00	50
1991	Lenore-LL-911	2,500	1993	105.00	105
1991	Lenore-YK-4218	3,500	1995	135.00	135
1995	Leslie LL-983	2,500		105.00	105
1995	Leslie MER-809	2,500		65.00	65
1991	Libby-EP-18	Closed	1993	85.00	85
1990	Lien Wha-YK-4092	Closed	1992	100.00	100
1995	Lila GU-55	2,500		55.00	55
1991	Lila-AM-10	2,500	1993	125.00	125
1991	Lila-FH-404	2,500	1993	100.00	100
1995	Lili CD-16888	2,500		30.00	30
1995	Lily FH-630	2,500		120.00	120
1995	Lily in pink stripe IND-533	2,500	1995	85.00	85
1993	Linda SP-435	Closed	1994	95.00	95
1987	Linda-C190	Closed	1986	60.00	120
1995	Lindsay PS-442	2,500		175.00	175
1994	Lindsay SP-462	2,500		150.00	150
1991	Lindsey-C-3127	Closed	1993	135.00	135
1991	Linetta-C-3166	Closed	1993	135.00	135
1990	Ling-Ling-DOLL	Closed	1992	50.00	50
1989	Ling-Ling-PS-87G	Closed	1991	90.00	90
1988	Lionel-FH206B	Closed	1990	50.00	120
1990	Lisa Beige Accordion Pleat-YK4093	Closed	1992	125.00	125
1991	Lisa-AM-100L	2,500	1993	70.00	70
1990	Lisa-FH-379	Closed	1992	100.00	100
1995	Lisette LL-993	2,500		105.00	105
1995	Little Bobby RDK-235	2,500		25.00	25
1991	Little Boy Blue-C-3159	Closed	1993	100.00	100
1995	Little Lisa OM-86	2,500		125.00	125
1995	Little Lori RDK-228	2,500		20.00	20
1995	Little Lou RDK-227	2,500		20.00	20
1995	Little Mary RDK-234	2,500		25.00	25
1995	Little Patty PS-429	2,500		50.00	50
1994	Little Red Riding Hood FH-557	2,500		140.00	140
1989	Liz -YK-269	Closed	1991	70.00	100
1991	Liz-C-3150	2,500	1993	100.00	100
1990	Liza-C-3053	Closed	1992	100.00	100
1991	Liza-YK-4226	3,500	1993	35.00	35
1991	Lola-SP-363	2,500	1993	90.00	90
1990	Lola-SP-79	Closed	1992	105.00	105
1991	Loni-FH-448	2,500	1993	100.00	100
1994	Loretta SP-457	2,500		140.00	140
1990	Loretta-FH-321	Closed	1992	90.00	90
1991	Lori-EP-52	2,500	1993	95.00	95
1990	Lori-WB-72BM	Closed	1992	75.00	75
1991	Louise-LL-908	2,500	1993	105.00	105
1995	Lucie MER-607	2,500		65.00	65
1989	Lucinda -DOM-293	Closed	1990	90.00	90
1994	Lucinda PS-406	2,500		150.00	150
1988	Lucinda-DOM-293	Closed	1990	90.00	90
1991	Lucy-LL-853	Closed	1993	80.00	80
1992	Lydia-OM-226	2,500	1993	250.00	250
1993	Lynn FH-498	2,500	1994	120.00	120
1995	Lynn LL-995	2,500		105.00	105
1990	Madame De Pompadour-C-3088	Closed	1992	250.00	250
1991	Madeleine-C-3106	Closed	1993	95.00	95
1995	Mae PS-431	2,500		70.00	70
1995	Maggie IND-532	2,500		80.00	80
1992	Maggie-FH-505	Closed	1993	125.00	125
1990	Maggie-PS-151P	Closed	1992	90.00	90
1990	Maggie-WB-51	Closed	1992	105.00	105
1994	Magnolia FH-558	2,500		150.00	150
1989	Mai-Ling-PS-79	2,500	1991	100.00	100
1994	Maiden PS-409	2,500	1995	150.00	150
1994	Mandy YK-4548	3,500		115.00	115
1989	Marcey-YK-4005	3,500	1995	90.00	90
1991	Marcy-TR-55	Closed	1993	135.00	135
1987	Marcy-YK122	Closed	1986	55.00	100
1994	Margaret C-3204	2,500		150.00	150
1989	Margaret-245	Closed	1991	100.00	150
1994	Maria GU-35	2,500		115.00	115
1990	Maria-YK-4116	Closed	1992	85.00	85
1993	Mariah LL-909	Closed	1993	135.00	135
1991	Mariel 18" Ivory-C-3119	Closed	1993	125.00	125
1995	Marielle PS-443	2,500		175.00	175
1995	Marla PS-437	2,500		125.00	125
1995	Martina RDK-232	2,500		35.00	35

YEAR ISSUE		EDITION LIMIT	YEAR RETD.	ISSUE PRICE	QUOTE U.S.$
1995	Mary Ann FH-633	2,500		110.00	110
1994	Mary Ann TR-79	2,500		125.00	125
1995	Mary Elizabeth OC-51	2,500		50.00	50
1994	Mary Jo FH-552	2,500		150.00	150
1994	Mary Lou FH-565	2,500		135.00	135
1994	Mary OC-56	2,500		135.00	135
1991	Maude-AM-100M	2,500	1993	70.00	70
1989	Maureen-PS-84	Closed	1990	90.00	90
1995	Maxine C-3225	2,500		125.00	125
1995	Mc Kenzie LL-987	2,500		100.00	100
1994	Megan C-3192	2,500		150.00	150
1995	Megan RDK-220	2,500		30.00	30
1989	Meimei-PS22	Closed	1990	75.00	225
1990	Melanie-YK-4115	Closed	1992	80.00	80
1991	Melissa-AM-9	Closed	1993	120.00	120
1991	Melissa-CH-3	Closed	1993	110.00	110
1990	Melissa-DOLL-390	Closed	1992	75.00	75
1989	Melissa-LL-794	Closed	1990	95.00	95
1991	Melissa-LL-901	Closed	1993	135.00	135
1992	Melissa-OM-03	2,500	1993	135.00	135
1995	Meredith MER-806	2,500		65.00	65
1991	Meredith-FH-391-P	Closed	1993	95.00	95
1995	Merri MER-810	2,500		65.00	65
1990	Merry Widow 20"-C-3040M	Closed	1992	140.00	140
1990	Merry Widow-C-3040	Closed	1992	145.00	145
1991	Meryl-FH-463	2,500	1993	95.00	95
1991	Michael w/School Books-FH-439B	2,500	1993	95.00	95
1988	Michelle & Marcel-YK176	Closed	1990	70.00	150
1991	Michelle Lilac/Green-EP36	Closed	1993	95.00	95
1991	Michelle w/School Books-FH-439G	Closed	1993	95.00	95
1995	Mindi PS-441	2,500	1995	125.00	125
1995	Mindy LL-990	2,500		75.00	75
1995	Miranda C16456B	2,500		30.00	30
1995	Miranda TR-91	2,500		135.00	135
1991	Miranda-DOLL-9PH	Closed	1993	75.00	75
1984	Miss Debutante Debi	Closed	1987	75.00	180
1994	Miss Elizabeth SP-459	2,500		150.00	150
1989	Miss Kim-PS-25	Closed	1990	75.00	175
1994	Missy FH-567	2,500		140.00	140
1991	Missy-DOLL-464	Closed	1993	70.00	70
1991	Missy-PS-258	Closed	1993	90.00	90
1991	Mon Yun w/Parasol-TR33	2,500	1993	115.00	115
1995	Monica TR-95	2,500		135.00	135
1994	Morning Dew Indian PS-404	2,500		150.00	150
1994	Musical Doll OC-45M	2,500		140.00	140
1991	Nancy -WB-73	2,500	1993	65.00	65
1991	Nancy 21" Pink w/Rabbit-EP-31	Closed	1993	165.00	165
1995	Nancy FH-615	2,500		100.00	100
1992	Nancy-JNC-4001	Open	1993	90.00	90
1990	Nanook-WB-23	Closed	1992	75.00	75
1994	Natalie PP-2	2,500		275.00	275
1995	Natasha TR-90	2,500		125.00	125
1990	Natasha-PS-102	Closed	1992	100.00	100
1991	Nellie-EP-1B	Closed	1993	75.00	75
1991	Nicole-AM-12	Closed	1993	135.00	135
1994	Nikki PS-401	2,500	1995	150.00	150
1994	Nikki SP-461	2,500		150.00	150
1993	Nina YK-4232	3,500	1993	135.00	135
1987	Nirmala-YK-210	Closed	1995	50.00	50
1994	Noel MS-27	2,500		150.00	150
1994	Noelle C-3199	2,500		195.00	195
1994	Noelle MS-28	2,500		150.00	150
1991	Noelle-PS-239V	Closed	1993	95.00	95
1995	Norma C-3226	2,500		135.00	135
1990	Odessa-FH-362	Closed	1992	65.00	65
1994	Odetta IND-521	2,500	1995	140.00	140
1993	Oona TR-57	Closed	1993	135.00	135
1994	Oriana IND-515	2,500		140.00	140
1995	Our First Skates RDK-226/BG	2,500		50.00	50
1994	Paige GU-33	2,500		150.00	150
1995	Paige IND-529	2,500		80.00	80
1994	Pamela LL-949	2,500		115.00	115
1995	Pan Pan GU-52	2,500		60.00	60
1994	Panama OM-43	2,500		195.00	195
1989	Patricia/Patrick-215GBB	Closed	1990	105.00	135
1991	Patti-DOLL-440	2,500	1993	65.00	65
1995	Patty C-3220	2,500		60.00	60
1994	Patty GU-34	2,500		115.00	115
1991	Patty-YK-4221	3,500	1993	125.00	125
1989	Paula-PS-56	Closed	1990	75.00	75
1995	Paulette PS-430	2,500		80.00	80
1989	Pauline Bonaparte-OM68	Closed	1990	120.00	120
1995	Pauline PS-440	2,500		65.00	65
1988	Pauline-YK-230	Closed	1990	90.00	90
1994	Payson YK-4541	3,500		135.00	135
1994	Payton PS-407	2,500	1995	150.00	150
1995	Peaches IND-531	2,500		80.00	80
1994	Pearl IND-523	2,500		275.00	275
1995	Pegeen C-3205	2,500		150.00	150
1994	Peggy TR-75	2,500		185.00	185
1991	Pepper-PS-277	Closed	1993	130.00	130
1994	Petula C-3191	2,500		140.00	140
1991	Pia-PS-246L	Closed	1993	115.00	115
1990	Ping-Ling-DOLL-363RV	Closed	1992	50.00	50
1990	Polly-DOLL-22PH	Closed	1992	90.00	90
1990	Princess Fair Skies-FH-268B	Closed	1992	75.00	75
1994	Princess Foxfire PS-411	2,500		150.00	150
1994	Princess Moonrise YK-4542	3,500		140.00	140
1990	Princess Red Feather-PS-189	Closed	1992	90.00	90
1994	Princess Snow Flower PS-402	2,500	1995	150.00	150
1991	Princess Summer Winds-FH-427	2,500	1993	120.00	120
1994	Priscilla YK-4538	3,500		135.00	135
1990	Priscilla-WB-50	Closed	1992	105.00	105
1991	Prissy White/Blue-C-3140	Closed	1993	100.00	100
1995	Rainie LL-984	2,500		125.00	125
1989	Ramona-PS-31B	Closed	1992	80.00	80
1991	Rapunzel-C-3157	2,500	1993	150.00	150
1987	Rapunzel-C158	Closed	1986	95.00	165
1994	Rebecca C-3177	2,500		135.00	135
1993	Rebecca C-3177	2,500	1993	135.00	135
1989	Rebecca-PS-34V	Closed	1992	45.00	45
1991	Red Wing-AM-30	2,500	1993	165.00	165
1994	Regina OM-41	2,500		150.00	150
1994	Rita FH-553	2,500		115.00	115
1994	Robby NM-29	2,500		135.00	135
1995	Robin C-3236	2,500		60.00	60
1991	Robin-AM-22	Closed	1993	120.00	120
1991	Rosalind-C-3090	Closed	1992	150.00	150
1989	Rosie-290M	Closed	1992	55.00	85
1995	Rusty CD-1450B	2,500		35.00	35
1988	Sabrina -C-208	Closed	1990	65.00	95
1987	Sabrina-C208	Closed	1986	65.00	95
1990	Sabrina-C3050	Closed	1992	105.00	105
1987	Sailorette-DOM217	Closed	1986	70.00	150
1992	Sally-FH-492	2,500	1993	105.00	105
1990	Sally-WB-20	Closed	1992	95.00	95
1991	Samantha-GU-3	Closed	1992	100.00	100
1995	San San GU-53	2,500		60.00	60
1991	Sandra-DOLL-6-PHE	2,500	1992	65.00	65
1992	Sapphires-OM-223	2,500	1993	250.00	250
1992	Sara Ann-FH-474	2,500	1993	115.00	115
1995	Sarah C-3214	2,500		110.00	110
1994	Saretta SP-423	2,500		100.00	100
1993	Saretta SP-423	2,500	1993	100.00	100
1995	Sasha GU-57	2,500		75.00	75
1991	Scarlett-FH-399	2,500	1992	100.00	100
1991	Scarlett-FH-436	2,500	1992	135.00	135
1992	Scarlett-FH-471	2,500	1993	120.00	120
1994	Shaka TR-45	2,500		100.00	100
1993	Shaka TR-45	2,500	1993	100.00	100
1991	Shaka-SP-401	2,500	1992	110.00	110
1991	Sharon 21" Blue-EP-34	Closed	1992	120.00	120
1995	Sharon C-3237	2,500		95.00	95
1991	Shau Chen-GU-2	2,500	1992	85.00	85
1991	Shelley-CH-1	2,500	1992	110.00	110
1995	Shimmering Caroline LL-992	2,500		115.00	115
1990	Shirley-WB-37	Closed	1992	65.00	65
1988	Sister Agnes 14"-C250	Closed	1990	75.00	75
1988	Sister Ignatius Notre Dame-FH184	Closed	1990	75.00	75
1989	Sister Mary-C-249	Closed	1992	75.00	125
1990	Sister Mary-WB-15	Closed	1992	70.00	70
1994	Sister Suzie IND-509	2,500	1995	95.00	95
1988	Sister Teresa-FH187	Closed	1990	80.00	80
1995	Sleeping Beauty OM-88	2,500		115.00	115
1992	Sonja-FH-486	2,500	1994	125.00	125
1995	Sophia PS-445	2,500		125.00	125
1990	Sophie-OM-1	Closed	1992	65.00	65
1991	Sophie-TR-53	2,500	1992	135.00	135
1995	Southern Belle Bride FH-637	2,500		160.00	160
1994	Southern Belle FH-570	2,500		140.00	140
1994	Sparkle OM-40	2,500		150.00	150
1995	Stacy FH-634	2,500		110.00	110
1995	Stacy OC-75	2,500		40.00	40
1991	Stacy-DOLL-6PH	Closed	1992	65.00	65
1990	Stacy-TR-5	Closed	1992	105.00	105
1991	Stephanie Pink & White-OM-196	Closed	1992	300.00	300
1991	Stephanie-AM-11	Closed	1992	105.00	105
1991	Stephanie-FH-467	Closed	1992	95.00	95
1994	Stephie OC-41M	2,500		115.00	115
1990	Sue Chuen-C-3061G	Closed	1992	95.00	95
1994	Sue Kwei TR-73	2,500		110.00	110
1992	Sue-JNC-4003	Closed	1994	90.00	90
1994	Sugar Plum Fairy OM-39	2,500		150.00	150
1991	Summer-AM-33	Closed	1992	200.00	200
1990	Sunny-FH-331	Closed	1992	70.00	70
1989	Sunny-PS-59V	Closed	1992	71.00	71
1989	Susan-DOLL-364MC	Closed	1992	75.00	75
1995	Suzanna Doll 554	2,500		35.00	35
1994	Suzanne LL-943	2,500		105.00	105
1994	Suzie GU-38	2,500		135.00	135
1995	Suzie OC-80	2,500		50.00	50
1993	Suzie SP-422	2,500	1993	164.00	164
1994	Suzie SP-422	2,500		164.00	164
1989	Suzie-PS-32	Closed	1992	80.00	80
1995	Sweet Pea LL-981	2,500		90.00	90
1991	Sybil 20" Beige-C-3131	Closed	1992	135.00	135
1991	Sybil Pink-DOLL-12PHMC	2,500	1992	75.00	75
1995	Sylvie CD-16634B	2,500		35.00	35
1995	Tabitha C-3233	2,500		50.00	50
1994	Taffey TR-80	2,500		150.00	150
1994	Tallulah OM-44	2,500		275.00	275
1991	Tamara-OM-187	Closed	1992	135.00	135
1990	Tania-DOLL-376P	Closed	1992	65.00	65
1989	Tatiana Pink Ballerina-OM-60	Closed	1991	120.00	175
1994	Teresa C-3198	2,500	1995	110.00	110
1995	Terri OM-78	2,500		150.00	150
1989	Terri-PS-104	Closed	1991	85.00	85
1991	Terri-TR-62	Closed	1992	75.00	75
1991	Tessa-AM-19	Closed	1992	135.00	135
1994	Tiffany OC-44M	2,500		140.00	140
1992	Tiffany-OM-014	2,500	1994	150.00	150
1995	Tina OM-79	2,500		150.00	150
1991	Tina-AM-16	Closed	1992	130.00	130
1990	Tina-DOLL-371	Closed	1992	85.00	85
1990	Tina-WB-32	Closed	1992	65.00	65
1994	Tippy LL-946	2,500	1995	110.00	110
1995	Tobey C-3232	2,500		50.00	50
1994	Todd YK-4540	3,500		45.00	45
1990	Tommy-C-3064	Closed	1992	75.00	75
1994	Topaz TR-74	2,500	1995	195.00	195
1988	Tracy-C-3006	Closed	1990	95.00	150
1992	Trina-OM-011	Closed	1994	165.00	165
1994	Trixie TR-77	2,500		110.00	110
1991	Vanessa-AM-34	Closed	1992	90.00	90
1991	Vicki-C-3101	Closed	1992	200.00	200
1991	Violet-EP-41	Closed	1992	135.00	135
1991	Violet-OM-186	2,500	1992	270.00	270
1992	Violette-FH-503	2,500	1994	120.00	120
1994	Virginia TR-78	2,500		195.00	195
1991	Virginia-SP-359	Closed	1992	120.00	120
1987	Vivian-C-201P	Closed	1986	80.00	80
1988	Vivian-C201P	Closed	1990	80.00	80
1991	Wah-Ching Watching Oriental Toddler YK-4175	Closed	1992	110.00	110
1995	Wei Lin GU-44	2,500		70.00	70
1994	Wendy MS-26	2,500		150.00	150
1985	Wendy-C120	Closed	1987	45.00	150
1989	Wendy-PS-51	Closed	1991	105.00	105
1990	Wendy-TE-3	Closed	1992	75.00	75
1990	Wilma-PS-174	Closed	1992	75.00	75
1995	Windy in Rose Print FH-626	2,500	1995	200.00	200
1995	Winnie LL-985	2,500		75.00	75
1995	Winter Wonderland RDK-301	2,500		35.00	35
1995	Woodland Sprite OM-90	2,500		100.00	100
1995	Yelena RDK-236	2,500		35.00	35
1990	Yen Yen-YK-4091	Closed	1992	95.00	95
1992	Yvette-OM-015	2,500	1994	150.00	150

Signature Doll Series - Various

YEAR ISSUE		EDITION LIMIT	YEAR RETD.	ISSUE PRICE	QUOTE U.S.$
1992	Abigail-MS-11 - M. Severino	5,000	1994	125.00	125
1995	Adak PPA-21 - P. Phillips	5,000		110.00	110
1992	Adora-MS-14 - M. Severino	5,000	1994	185.00	185
1995	Alain PPA-19 - P. Phillips	2,500		100.00	100
1992	Alexandria-PAC-19 - P. Aprile	5,000	1995	300.00	300
1991	Alice-MS-7 - M. Severino	5,000		120.00	120
1995	Amanda KSFA-1 - K. Fitzpatrick	5,000		175.00	175
1991	Amber-MS-1 - M. Severino	Closed	1994	95.00	95
1995	Amelia PAC-28 - P. Aprile	5,000		130.00	130
1995	Amy Rose HKHF-200 - H.K. Hyland	5,000		125.00	125
1992	Baby Cakes Crumbs PK-CRUMBS - P. Kolesar	5,000		17.50	18
1992	Baby Cakes Crumbs/Black PK-CRUMBS/B - P. Kolesar	5,000		17.50	18
1991	Becky-MS-2 - M. Severino	5,000	1994	95.00	95
1991	Bianca-PK-101 - P. Kolesar	Closed	1994	120.00	120
1993	Bonnett Baby MS-17W - M. Severino	5,000		175.00	175
1995	Brad HKH-15 - H.K. Hyland	5,000		85.00	85
1992	Bride & Flower Girl-PAC-6 P. Aprile	5,000		600.00	600
1991	Bridgette-PK-104 - P. Kolesar	Closed	1994	120.00	120
1995	Brie PPA-26 - P. Aprile	5,000		180.00	180
1995	Cara DALI-1 - E. Dali	5,000		400.00	400
1995	Casey PPA-23 - P. Phillips	5,000		85.00	85
1992	Cassandra-PAC-8 - P. Aprile	Closed	N/A	450.00	450
1992	Cassie Flower Girl-PAC-9 P. Aprile	Closed	N/A	175.00	175
1992	Celine-PAC-11 - P. Aprile	5,000	1995	165.00	165
1991	Clair-Ann-PK-252 - P. Kolesar	5,000		100.00	100
1992	Clarissa-PAC-3 - P. Aprile	5,000		165.00	165
1992	Cody-MS-19 - M. Severino	Closed	1993	120.00	120
1992	Creole Black-HP-202 - H. Payne	Closed	1993	250.00	250
1992	Cynthia-PAC-10 - P. Aprile	Closed	1993	165.00	165
1991	Daddy's Little Darling-MS-8 M. Severino	5,000		165.00	165
1992	Darla-HP-204 - H. Payne	5,000		250.00	250
1991	Dozy Elf w/ Featherbed MAB-100 - M.A. Byerly	Closed	1991	110.00	110
1991	Duby Elf w/ Featherbed MAB-103 - M.A. Byerly	Closed	1991	110.00	110
1991	Dudley Elf w/ Featherbed MAB-101 - M.A. Byerly	Closed	1991	110.00	110
1991	Duffy Elf w/ Featherbed MAB-102 - M.A. Byerly	Closed	1991	110.00	110
1992	Dulcie-HP-200 - H. Payne	Closed	1993	250.00	250
1992	Dustin-HP-201 - H. Payne	5,000	1993	250.00	250
1995	Eleanore GMNA-100 - G. McNeil	5,000		225.00	225
1991	Enoc-PK-100 - P. Kolesar	5,000		100.00	100
1992	Eugenie Bride-PAC-1 - P. Aprile	5,000		165.00	165
1992	Evening Star-PAC-5 - P. Aprile	Closed	1993	500.00	500
1995	Ginny LR-2 - L. Randolph	5,000		360.00	360
1993	Grace HKH-2 - H. Kahl-Hyland	5,000		250.00	250
1995	Happy JFC-100 - K. Fitzpatrick	5,000		120.00	120
1993	Helene HKH-1 - H. Kahl-Hyland	5,000		250.00	250
1995	Holly GMN-202 - G. McNeil	5,000		150.00	150
1995	Iman PPA-24 - P. Aprile	5,000		110.00	110
1992	Kate-MS-15 - M. Severino	Closed	1993	190.00	190
1995	Latisha PPA-25 - P. Phillips	5,000		110.00	110
1995	Laurel HKH-17R - H.K. Hyland	5,000		110.00	110
1995	Lauren HKH-202 - H.K. Hyland	5,000		150.00	150
1995	Lena PPA-20 - P. Phillips	5,000		120.00	120
1995	Lenore LRC-100 - L. Randolph	5,000		140.00	140
1992	Little Match Girl-HP-205 H. Payne	Closed	1994	150.00	150

YEAR ISSUE		EDITION LIMIT	YEAR RETD.	ISSUE PRICE	QUOTE U.S.$
1992	Little Turtle Indian-PK-110 P. Kolesar	Closed	1993	150.00	150
1995	Lucy HKH-14 - H.K. Hyland	5,000		105.00	105
1992	Megan-MS-12 - M. Severino	5,000	1995	125.00	125
1992	Melanie-PAC-14 - P. Aprile	Closed	1993	300.00	300
1995	Meredith LR-3 - L. Randolph	5,000		375.00	375
1991	Mikey-MS-3 - M. Severino	5,000	1994	95.00	95
1991	Mommy's Rays of Sunshine MS-9 - M. Severino	5,000		165.00	165
1992	Nadia-PAC-18 - P. Aprile	Closed	1993	175.00	175
1995	Natasha HKH-17P - H.K. Hyland	5,000		110.00	110
1995	Nikki HKHF-20 - H.K. Hyland	5,000		125.00	125
1992	Olivia-PAC-12 - P. Aprile	Closed	1993	300.00	300
1995	Patricia DALI-3 - E. Dali	5,000		280.00	280
1991	Paulette-PAC-2 - P. Aprile	5,000		250.00	250
1991	Paulette-PAC-4 - P. Aprile	5,000		250.00	250
1992	Pavlova-PAC-17 - P. Aprile	5,000	1994	145.00	145
1992	Polly-HP-206 - H. Payne	5,000		120.00	120
1991	Precious Baby-SB-100 S. Bilotto	5,000		250.00	250
1991	Precious Pary Time-SB-102 S. Bilotto	5,000		250.00	250
1991	Precious Spring Time-SB-104 - S. Bilotto	Closed	N/A	250.00	250
1992	Raven Eskimo-PK-106 P. Kolesar	Closed	1993	130.00	130
1992	Rebecca Beige Bonnet-MS-17B M. Severino	5,000	1995	175.00	175
1993	Reilly HKH-3 - H. Kahl-Hyland	5,000		260.00	260
1992	Ruby-MS-18 - M. Severino	5,000		135.00	135
1992	Sally-MS-25 - M. Severino	5,000	1993	110.00	110
1995	Shao Ling PPA-22 - P. Phillips	5,000		110.00	110
1991	Shun Lee-PK-102 - P. Kolesar	Closed	N/A	120.00	120
1994	Sis JAG-110 - J. Grammer	5,000	1994	110.00	110
1992	Spanky-HP-25 - H. Payne	5,000	1994	250.00	250
1991	Sparkle-PK-250 - P. Kolesar	5,000		100.00	100
1995	Stacy DALI-2 - E. Dali	5,000		360.00	360
1992	Stacy-MS-24 - M. Severino	Closed	1993	110.00	110
1991	Stephie-MS-6 - M. Severino	Closed	1994	125.00	125
1991	Su Lin-MS-5 - M. Severino	5,000	1994	105.00	105
1991	Susan Marie-PK-103 - P. Kolesar	Closed	1991	120.00	120
1995	Suzie HKH-16 - H.K. Hyland	5,000		100.00	100
1991	Sweet Pea-PK-251 - P. Kolesar	Closed		100.00	100
1995	Tammy LR-4 - L. Randolph	5,000		325.00	325
1994	Tex JAG-114 - J. Grammer	5,000		110.00	110
1995	Tiffany LR-1 - L. Randolph	5,000		370.00	370
1994	Tracy JAG-111 - J. Grammer	5,000		150.00	150
1994	Trevor JAG-112 - J. Grammer	5,000		115.00	115
1992	Vanessa-PAC-15 - P. Aprile	Closed	1993	300.00	300
1992	Victoria w/Blanket-MS-10 M. Severino	Closed	1993	110.00	110
1992	Violetta-PAC-16 - P. Aprile	5,000	1994	165.00	165
1991	Yawning Kate-MS-4 M. Severino	Closed	1994	105.00	105

Susan Wakeen Doll Co. Inc.

The Littlest Ballet Company - S. Wakeen

1985	Cynthia	375		198.00	350
1987	Elizabeth	250		425.00	1000
1985	Jeanne	375		198.00	800
1985	Jennifer	250		750.00	750
1987	Marie Ann	50		1000.00	1000
1985	Patty	375		198.00	400-500

Timeless Creations

Barefoot Children - A. Himstedt

1987	Bastian	Closed	1989	329.00	650-700
1987	Beckus	Closed	1989	329.00	1100-1200
1987	Ellen	Closed	1989	329.00	750-825
1987	Fatou	Closed	1989	329.00	1000-1200
1987	Fatou (Cornroll)	Closed	1989	329.00	1200-1500
1987	Kathe	Closed	1989	329.00	750-825
1987	Lisa	Closed	1989	329.00	600-825
1987	Paula	Closed	1989	329.00	725-750

Blessed Are The Children - A. Himstedt

1988	Friederike	Closed	1990	499.00	1400
1988	Kasimir	Closed	1990	499.00	1600-1850
1988	Makimura	Closed	1990	499.00	1200-1500
1988	Malin	Closed	1990	499.00	1400-1500
1988	Michiko	Closed	1990	499.00	1050-1200

Faces of Friendship - A. Himstedt

1991	Liliane (Netherlands)	2-Yr.	1993	598.00	650-695
1991	Neblina (Switzerland)	2-Yr.	1993	596.00	550-650
1991	Shireem (Bali)	2-Yr.	1993	598.00	500-625

Fiene And The Barefoot Babies - A. Himstedt

1990	Annchen-German Baby Girl	2-Yr.	1992	498.00	600-700
1990	Fiene-Belgian Girl	2-Yr.	1992	598.00	750-800
1990	Mo-American Baby Boy	2-Yr.	1992	498.00	500-650
1990	Taki-Japanese Baby Girl	2-Yr.	1992	498.00	650-900

Heartland Series - A. Himstedt

1988	Timi	Closed	1990	329.00	500-600
1988	Toni	Closed	1990	329.00	500-550

Images of Childhood - A. Himstedt

1993	Kima (Greenland)	2-Yr.	1995	599.00	599
1993	Lona (California)	2-Yr.	1995	599.00	599
1993	Tara (Germany)	2-Yr.	1995	599.00	599

Reflection of Youth - A. Himstedt

1989	Adrienne (France)	Closed	1991	558.00	750-800
1989	Ayoka (Africa)	Closed	1991	558.00	950-1200
1989	Janka (Hungry)	Closed	1991	558.00	650-800
1989	Kai (German)	Closed	1991	558.00	650-800

Summer Dreams - A. Himstedt

1992	Enzo	2-Yr.	1994	599.00	500-650
1992	Jule	2-Yr.	1994	599.00	600-650
1992	Pemba	2-Yr.	1994	599.00	600-650
1992	Sanga	2-Yr.	1994	599.00	500-650

The Wimbledon Collection

D.I. Special - G.&G. Wolff

1995	Ashley A-3027	1,620		100.00	100
1995	Athena A-3034	1,620		100.00	100
1995	Carmella A-3032	1,620		100.00	100
1995	Gabriel A-3033	2,620		100.00	100
1995	Halley A-3026	1,620		100.00	100
1995	Jennifer A-3030	1,620		100.00	100
1995	Josie A-3035	3,120		100.00	100
1995	Laura A-3031	2,620		100.00	100
1995	Nikki A-3028	1,620		100.00	100
1995	Nona A-3024	3,120		100.00	100
1995	Spencer A-3029	2,620		100.00	100
1995	Stephanie A-3025	1,620		100.00	100

Hobby Horse Set - G.&G. Wolff

1991	Cheryl A-083	360	1991	90.00	90
1991	Dixie A-081	360	1991	90.00	90
1991	Donna A-082	360	1991	90.00	90
1991	Linda A-084	360	1991	90.00	90
1991	Patty A-079	360	1991	90.00	90
1991	Polly A-080	360	1991	90.00	90

Platinum Edition, Signed Only - Various

1993	Conner A-2002 - G.F. Wolff	600	1993	200.00	200
1993	Melanie A-2001 - Gr. M. Wolff	600	1993	200.00	200

Pocket Dolls - Various

1994	Abbi A-5006 - Gr. M. Wolff	600		80.00	80
1994	Amelia A-5007 - Gr. M. Wolff	600		80.00	80
1994	Desi A-5004 - Gr. M. Wolff	600		80.00	80
1994	Karmen A-5003 - G.F. Wolff	600		80.00	80
1994	Kendell A-5000 - G.F. Wolff	600		80.00	80
1994	Krystal A-5002 - G.F. Wolff	600		80.00	80
1994	Madison A-5005 - Gr. M. Wolff	600		80.00	80
1994	Mikal A-5001 - G.F. Wolff	600		80.00	80

Teddy Bear Series - G.&G. Wolff

1994	Callie A-3018	360	1995	70.00	70
1994	Lindy A-3016	360	1995	70.00	70
1994	Parrie A-3019	360	1995	70.00	70
1994	Piper A-3017	360	1995	70.00	70
1994	Randi A-3014	360	1995	70.00	70
1994	Riley A-3015	360	1995	70.00	70

The Wimbledon Collection - Various

1992	Abigail (signed) A-104-S G.F. Wolff	600	1994	200.00	200
1992	Abigail A-104 - G.F. Wolff	Retrd.	1994	170.00	170
1992	Alexandra (signed) A-118-S - G.F. Wolff	600	1994	254.00	254
1992	Alexandra A-118 - G.F. Wolff	Retrd.	1994	224.00	224
1990	Alexis A-048 - Gr. M. Wolff	1,200	1991	200.00	200
1989	Alicia A-4089 - G.&G. Wolff	1,000	1991	65.00	65
1993	Alliston A-3002 - G.&G. Wolff	360	1994	120.00	120
1989	Alyson A-047 - G.&G. Wolff	1,000	1991	80.00	80
1990	Amanda A-051 - Gr. M. Wolff	1,000	1991	200.00	200
1989	Amber A-5014 - G.&G. Wolff	1,000	1991	77.00	77
1992	American Beauty (signed) A-111-S - G.F. Wolff	600	1992	255.00	255
1992	American Beauty A-111 G.F. Wolff	Retrd.	1994	224.00	224
1989	Amy A-4070 - G.&G. Wolff	1,000	1990	45.00	45
1989	Anastasia A-011 - G.&G. Wolff	1,000	1993	150.00	150
1989	Andrea A-4092 - G.&G. Wolff	1,000	1990	65.00	65
1995	Andrew A-143 - G.F. Wolff	Open		170.00	170
1995	Andrew (signed) A-143-S G.F. Wolff	600		200.00	200
1989	Angela A-5016 - G.&G. Wolff	1,000	1990	115.00	115
1995	Anissa A-140 - G.F. Wolff	Open		100.00	100
1995	Anissa (signed) A-140-S G.F. Wolff	600		130.00	130
1989	Annessa A-019 - G.&G. Wolff	1,000	1992	85.00	85
1994	April A-098 - G.&G. Wolff	360	1994	80.00	80
1989	Ashley A-4039 - G.&G. Wolff	1,000	1990	48.00	48
1994	Austin (signed) A-132-S Gr. M. Wolff	600		200.00	200
1994	Austin A-132 - Gr. M. Wolff	Open		170.00	170
1991	Autumn A-065 - G.&G. Wolff	1,000	1993	140.00	140
1989	Becky A-4057 - G.&G. Wolff	1,000	1990	48.00	48
1989	Belinda A-029 - G.&G. Wolff	1,000	1992	55.00	55
1992	Berkeley (signed) A-112-S G.F. Wolff	600	1994	360.00	360
1992	Berkeley A-112 - G.F. Wolff	Retrd.	1994	330.00	330
1989	Bethany A-5013 - G.&G. Wolff	1,000	1991	75.00	75
1994	Blackhawk (signed) A-136-S G.F. Wolff	600		254.00	254
1994	Blackhawk A-136 - G.F. Wolff	Open		224.00	224
1989	Bo Peep A-003 - G.&G. Wolff	1,000	1991	95.00	95
1989	Bobbie A-4083 - G.&G. Wolff	1,000	1991	40.00	40
1989	Bonnie A-031 - G.&G. Wolff	1,000	1992	50.00	50
1993	Bradley A-3003 - G.&G. Wolff	Open		134.00	134
1991	Brandi A-078 - G.&G. Wolff	1,000	1994	130.00	130
1989	Brenda A-027 - G.&G. Wolff	1,000	1991	55.00	55
1994	Brianna A-3012 - G.&G. Wolff	360	1994	120.00	120
1989	Brittany A-5011 - G.&G. Wolff	1,000	1991	70.00	70
1994	Brooke (signed) A-139-S G.F. Wolff	600		230.00	230
1994	Brooke A-139 - G.F. Wolff	Open		200.00	200
1989	Brooke A-5002 - G.&G. Wolff	1,000	1990	46.00	46
1989	Caitlin A-4088 - G.&G. Wolff	1,000	1991	75.00	75
1989	Camille A-038 - G.&G. Wolff	1,000	1992	100.00	100
1991	Candi A-090 - G.&G. Wolff	1,000	1992	90.00	90
1994	Candice A-3023 - G.&G. Wolff	360		150.00	150
1989	Carla A-5023 - G.&G. Wolff	1,000	1990	89.00	89
1989	Carole A-015 - G.&G. Wolff	1,000	1991	21.00	21
1989	Caroline A-002 - G.&G. Wolff	1,000	1992	90.00	90
1993	Cassidy (signed) A-122-S Gr. M. Wolff	600		254.00	254
1993	Cassidy A-122 - Gr. M. Wolff	Open		224.00	224
1989	Cassie A-016 - G.&G. Wolff	1,000	1992	130.00	130
1989	Cecilia A-006 - G.&G. Wolff	1,000	1991	70.00	70
1989	Charlotte A-039 - G.&G. Wolff	1,000	1993	100.00	100
1992	Chelsey (signed) A-110-S G.F. Wolff	600	1993	255.00	255
1992	Chelsey A-110 - G.F. Wolff	Retrd.	1994	224.00	224
1991	Christa A-091 - G.&G. Wolff	1,000	1992	230.00	230
1989	Christina A-4086 - G.&G. Wolff	1,000	1991	65.00	65
1989	Christmas Doll A-046 G.&G. Wolff	1,000	1990	N/A	N/A
1994	Christmas Past & Present (signed) A-134-S - G.F. Wolff	600		254.00	254
1994	Christmas Past & Present A-134 G.F. Wolff	Open		224.00	224
1989	Christopher A-4087 G.&G. Wolff	1,000	1990	65.00	65
1989	Cindy A-4085 - G.&G. Wolff	1,000	1990	43.00	43
1995	Cody A-3036 - G. & G. Wolff	Open		150.00	150
1989	Colleen (blue) A-4030-B G.&G. Wolff	1,000	1991	40.00	40
1989	Colleen (pink) A-4030-P G.&G. Wolff	1,000	1991	40.00	40
1989	Corey A-004 - G.&G. Wolff	1,000	1991	72.00	72
1991	Cricket A-066 - G.&G. Wolff	1,000	1992	100.00	100
1992	Crissie (signed) A-102-S Gr. M. Wolff	600	1993	170.00	170
1992	Crissie A-102 - Gr. M. Wolff	Retrd.	1994	140.00	140
1989	Dana A-035 - G.&G. Wolff	1,000	1991	98.00	98
1995	Daphne A-141 - G.F. Wolff	Open		140.00	140
1995	Daphne (signed) A-141-S G.F. Wolff	600		170.00	170
1989	Dee A-5007 - G.&G. Wolff	1,000	1991	60.00	60
1991	Denise A-087 - G.&G. Wolff	1,000	1992	90.00	90
1994	Devon A-3020 - G.&G. Wolff	360	1994	120.00	120
1989	Diane A-045 - G.&G. Wolff	1,000	1992	75.00	75
1992	Don't Cry Over Spilt Milk (signed) A-101-S - G.F. Wolff	600	1992	190.00	190
1992	Don't Cry Over Spilt Milk A-101 - G.F. Wolff	Open		160.00	160
1991	Elise A-077 - G.&G. Wolff	1,000	1993	100.00	100
1989	Elizabeth A-5015 - G.&G. Wolff	1,000	1991	80.00	80
1991	Emma A-073 - G.&G. Wolff	1,000	1992	100.00	100
1992	Erika (signed) A-105-S Gr. M. Wolff	600	1993	200.00	200
1992	Erika A-105 - Gr. M. Wolff	Retrd.	1994	170.00	170
1989	Erika A-4090 - G.&G. Wolff	1,000	1990	65.00	65
1989	Erin A-4033 - G.&G. Wolff	1,000	1991	40.00	40
1989	Faith A-014 - G.&G. Wolff	1,000	1991	50.00	50
1992	Flora (signed) A-120-S G.F. Wolff	600		280.00	280
1992	Flora A-120 - G.F. Wolff	Open		250.00	250
1991	Fran A-064 - G.&G. Wolff	1,000	1992	150.00	150
1990	Franz A-053 - G. F. Wolff	1,000	1992	200.00	200
1990	Grandma's Attic A-052 Gr. M. Wolff	1,000	1991	170.00	170
1989	Gretchen A-4032 - G.&G. Wolff	1,000	1991	37.00	37
1991	Hannah A-076 - G.&G. Wolff	1,000	1992	150.00	150
1989	Heather A-5003 - G.&G. Wolff	1,000	1990	53.00	53
1989	Heidi A-010 - G.&G. Wolff	1,000	1991	80.00	80
1989	Hillary A-5021 - G.&G. Wolff	1,000	1991	90.00	90
1993	Hollis (signed) A-126-S Gr. M. Wolff	600		170.00	170
1993	Hollis A-126 - Gr. M. Wolff	Open		140.00	140
1989	Holly A-4080 - G.&G. Wolff	1,000	1990	36.00	36
1994	Hunter A-3011 - G.&G. Wolff	360	1994	100.00	100
1994	I Just Found Great-Grandma's Babies (signed) A-135-S G.F. Wolff	600		200.00	200
1994	I Just Found Great-Grandma's Babies A-135 - G.F. Wolff	Open		170.00	170
1989	Jackie A-022 - G.&G. Wolff	1,000	1991	80.00	80
1989	Jamie (lavender) A-4088-L - G.&G. Wolff	1,000	1991	38.00	38
1989	Jamie (pink) A-4088-P G.&G. Wolff	1,000	1990	37.00	37
1993	Jamison (signed) A-129-S G.F. Wolff	600		170.00	170
1993	Jamison A-129 - G.F. Wolff	Open		140.00	140
1991	Jeanine A-070 - G.&G. Wolff	1,000	1993	110.00	110
1989	Jennifer A-4058 - G.&G. Wolff	1,000	1991	40.00	40
1991	Jill A-056 - G.&G. Wolff	1,000	1991	90.00	90
1994	Jill A-094 - G.&G. Wolff	360	1994	70.00	70
1989	Jill A-4031 - G.&G. Wolff	1,000	1991	38.00	38
1989	Joanne A-4037 - G.&G. Wolff	1,000	1990	43.00	43
1989	Jodi A-4055 - G.&G. Wolff	1,000	1990	27.00	27
1992	Johnny (signed) A-117-S G.F. Wolff	600	1994	254.00	254
1992	Johnny A-117 - G.F. Wolff	Open		224.00	224

DOLLS/FIGURINES/COTTAGES

YEAR ISSUE		EDITION LIMIT	YEAR RETD.	ISSUE PRICE	QUOTE U.S.$
1993	Jordan A-3006 - G.&G. Wolff	Open		160.00	160
1994	Joy A-092 - G.&G. Wolff	600		80.00	80
1989	Julie A-4081 - G.&G. Wolff	1,000	1990	35.00	35
1993	Kariss (signed) A-125-S Gr. M. Wolff	600	1994	329.00	329
1993	Kariss A-125 - Gr. M. Wolff	Retrd.	1994	300.00	300
1989	Kate A-5001 - G.&G. Wolff	1,000	1990	46.00	46
1989	Kathy A-036 - G.&G. Wolff	1,000	1993	95.00	95
1989	Katrina A-017 - G.&G. Wolff	1,000	1992	77.00	77
1992	Kayla (signed) A-107-S Gr. M. Wolff	600	1993	200.00	200
1992	Kayla A-107 - Gr. M. Wolff	Retrd.	1994	170.00	170
1993	Keightley (signed) A-123-S Gr. M. Wolff	600	1993	254.00	254
1993	Keightley A-123 - Gr. M. Wolff	Retrd.	1993	224.00	224
1989	Kelly A-5018 - G.&G. Wolff	1,000	1990	56.00	56
1993	Kessler (signed) A-127-S G.F. Wolff	600		180.00	180
1993	Kessler A-127 - G.F. Wolff	Open		150.00	150
1989	Kimberly A-5006 - G.&G. Wolff	1,000	1991	64.00	64
1993	Krista (signed) A-124-S G.F. Wolff	600	1994	276.00	276
1993	Krista A-124 - G.F. Wolff	Open		246.00	246
1989	Kristin (blue) A-4040-B G.&G. Wolff	1,000	1990	45.00	45
1989	Kristin (pink) A-4040-P G.&G. Wolff	1,000	1990	45.00	45
1989	Kristy A-001 - G.&G. Wolff	1,000	1992	90.00	90
1989	Kyle A-018 - G.&G. Wolff	1,000	1992	77.00	77
1992	Lacey (signed) A-113-S Gr. M. Wolff	600		330.00	330
1992	Lacey A-113 - Gr. M. Wolff	Open		300.00	300
1994	Larkin (signed) A-130-S G.F. Wolff	600	1994	254.00	254
1990	Laurel A-049 - Gr. M. Wolff	1,200	1991	200.00	200
1994	Lauren A-3022 - G.&G. Wolff	360		150.00	150
1989	Laurie A-030 - G.&G. Wolff	1,000	1992	55.00	55
1992	Leigh Ann (signed) A-108-S - Gr. M. Wolff	600	1995	255.00	255
1992	Leigh Ann A-108 - Gr. M. Wolff	Open	1995	224.00	224
1989	Leslie A-007 - G.&G. Wolff	1,000	1991	80.00	80
1989	Libby A-008 - G.&G. Wolff	1,000	1991	70.00	70
1989	Lindsey A-4093 - G.&G. Wolff	1,000	1991	65.00	65
1994	Lloyd A-3013 - G.&G. Wolff	360	1994	120.00	120
1994	Logan A-3010 - G.&G. Wolff	360		100.00	100
1989	Loving Care A-009 - G.&G. Wolff	1,000	1991	150.00	150
1989	Lucy A-5017 - G.&G. Wolff	1,000	1991	70.00	70
1989	Lydia A-043 - Gr. M. Wolff	3,000	1992	120.00	120
1993	Macy A-3005 - G.&G. Wolff	Open		144.00	144
1991	Maggie A-071 - G.&G. Wolff	1,000	1993	100.00	100
1989	Mandy A-4082 - G.&G. Wolff	1,000	1991	40.00	40
1989	Marcy A-021 - G.&G. Wolff	1,000	1991	150.00	150
1989	Marla A-5012 - G.&G. Wolff	1,000	1991	75.00	75
1991	Martina A-069 - G.&G. Wolff	1,000	1992	130.00	130
1989	Mary A-020 - G.&G. Wolff	1,000	1991	85.00	85
1989	Mattie A-026 - G.&G. Wolff	1,000	1992	50.00	50
1992	McKenzie (signed) A-106-S - G.F. Wolff	600	1992	220.00	220
1992	McKenzie A-106 - G.F. Wolff	Retrd.	1994	190.00	190
1989	Megan A-032 - G.&G. Wolff	1,000	1992	100.00	100
1989	Melissa A-042 - G.&G. Wolff	1,000	1992	150.00	150
1989	Michelle A-037 - G.&G. Wolff	1,000	1992	90.00	90
1994	Miller A-3009 - G.&G. Wolff	360		110.00	110
1989	Mindy A-5005 - G.&G. Wolff	1,000	1991	60.00	60
1994	Mirria A-093 - G.&G. Wolff	360		70.00	70
1989	Missy A-5010 - G.&G. Wolff	1,000	1990	70.00	70
1992	Morgan (signed) A-10S Gr. M. Wolff	600	1992	200.00	200
1992	Morgan A-100 - Gr. M. Wolff	Retrd.	1993	170.00	170
1989	Nancy A-4084 - G.&G. Wolff	1,000	1991	45.00	45
1989	Natalie A-023 - G.&G. Wolff	1,000	1991	95.00	95
1989	Natasha A-005 - G.&G. Wolff	1,000	1991	60.00	60
1995	Nettie A-142 - G.F. Wolff	Open		170.00	170
1995	Nettie (signed) A-142-S G.F. Wolff	600		200.00	200
1993	Noel A-096 - G.&G. Wolff	600	1993	80.00	80
1994	Paige (signed) A-133-S G.F. Wolff	600	1995	254.00	254
1994	Paige A-133 - G.F. Wolff	Open		224.00	224
1993	Palmer A-3007 - G.&G. Wolff	360	1994	150.00	150
1993	Parker A-3001 - G.&G. Wolff	700	1994	120.00	120
1989	Paula A-4068 - G.&G. Wolff	1,000	1990	35.00	35
1991	Penny A-063 - G.&G. Wolff	1,000	1992	150.00	150
1992	Peyton (signed) A-115-S G.F. Wolff	600	1994	255.00	255
1992	Peyton A-115 - G.F. Wolff	Retrd.	1994	224.00	224
1994	Princess Nakoma (signed) A-135-S - G.F. Wolff	600		200.00	200
1994	Princess Nakoma A-135 G.F. Wolff	Open		170.00	170
1991	Rachel A-085 - G.&G. Wolff	1,000	1992	90.00	90
1993	Ramsey A-3004 - G.&G. Wolff	Open		134.00	134
1989	Rebecca (blue) A-4051-B - G.&G. Wolff	1,000	1991	37.00	37
1989	Rebecca (pink) A-4051-P - G.&G. Wolff	1,000	1991	37.00	37
1989	Robin A5004 - G.&G. Wolff	1,000	1991	60.00	60
1989	Rose A-033 - G.&G. Wolff	1,000	1991	45.00	45
1991	Roxanne A-088 - G.&G. Wolff	1,000	1992	90.00	90
1994	Royce Ann A-3021 - G.&G. Wolff	360		150.00	150
1989	Ryan A-034 - G.&G. Wolff	1,000	1991	45.00	45
1989	Sabrina A-4015 - G.&G. Wolff	1,000	1990	75.00	75
1991	Samantha A-062 - G.&G. Wolff	1,000	1992	150.00	150
1989	Samuel A-4014 - G.&G. Wolff	1,000	1991	75.00	75
1989	Sandy A-4056 - G.&G. Wolff	1,000	1991	42.00	42
1991	Sarah A-075 - G.&G. Wolff	1,000	1992	200.00	200
1990	Savannah A-050 - G.F. Wolff	1,200	1991	200.00	200
1992	Shelby (signed) A-109-S Gr. M. Wolff	600		255.00	255
1992	Shelby A-109 - Gr. M. Wolff	Open		224.00	224
1990	Shelly A-054 - G.&G. Wolff	1,000	1991	90.00	90
1991	Snow Queen A-074 G.&G. Wolff	1,000	1992	250.00	250
1989	Sondra A-4054 - G.&G. Wolff	1,000	1990	54.00	54
1989	Sophia A-044 - G.&G. Wolff	1,000	1991	80.00	80
1990	Stacey A-055 - G.&G. Wolff	1,000	1990	80.00	80
1989	Stephanie A-028 - G.&G. Wolff	1,000	1991	55.00	55
1989	Susan A-4052 - G.&G. Wolff	1,000	1991	25.00	25
1992	Susie (signed) A-103-S G.F. Wolff	600	1992	200.00	200
1992	Susie A-103 - G.F. Wolff	Open		170.00	170
1989	Suzanne A-012 - G.&G. Wolff	1,000	1993	100.00	100
1992	Sydney (signed) A-114-S Gr. M. Wolff	600	1994	255.00	255
1992	Sydney A-114 - Gr. M. Wolff	Retrd.	1994	224.00	224
1992	Sylvia (signed) A-119-S Gr. M. Wolff	600	1993	254.00	254
1992	Sylvia A-119 - Gr. M. Wolff	Retrd.	1994	224.00	224
1989	Tamara A-025 - Gr. M. Wolff	1,000	1991	200.00	200
1989	Tara A-041 - G.&G. Wolff	1,000	1991	105.00	105
1992	Tatum (signed) A-116-S G.F. Wolff	600		254.00	254
1992	Tatum A-116 - G.F. Wolff	Open		224.00	224
1991	Taylor A-094 - G.&G. Wolff	1,000	1992	150.00	150
1989	Terri A-013 - G.&G. Wolff	1,000	1991	80.00	80
1989	Tessa A-5020 - G.&G. Wolff	1,000	1991	90.00	90
1989	Tiffany A-040 - G.&G. Wolff	1,000	1991	150.00	150
1994	Tina A-097 - G.&G. Wolff	360	1994	70.00	70
1991	Tonya A-089 - G.&G. Wolff	1,000	1992	90.00	90
1989	Tracy A-024 - G.&G. Wolff	1,000	1992	70.00	70
1991	Tricia A-086 - G.&G. Wolff	1,000	1992	90.00	90
1989	Tricia A-5022 - G.&G. Wolff	1,000	1990	89.00	89
1994	Tyler (signed) A-131-S Gr. M. Wolff	600		254.00	254
1994	Tyler A-131 - Gr. M. Wolff	Open		224.00	224
1994	Victoria (signed) A-138-S G.F. Wolff	600		200.00	200
1991	Victoria A-061 - G.&G. Wolff	1,000	1992	200.00	200
1994	Victoria A-138 - G.F. Wolff	Open		170.00	170
1991	Wendy A-068 - G.&G. Wolff	1,000	1992	130.00	130
1994	Wesley A-3008 - G.&G. Wolff	360		90.00	90
1989	Whitney A-5009 - G.&G. Wolff	1,000	1990	60.00	60

FIGURINES/COTTAGES

All God's Children

Collectors' Club - M. Holcombe

YEAR ISSUE		EDITION LIMIT	YEAR RETD.	ISSUE PRICE	QUOTE U.S.$
1989	Molly -1524	Retrd.	1990	38.00	300-600
1990	Joey -1539	Retrd.	1991	32.00	275-425
1991	Mandy -1540	Retrd.	1992	36.00	180-260
1992	Olivia -1562	Retrd.	1993	36.00	140-200
1993	Garrett -1567	Retrd.	1994	36.00	150-175
1993	Peek-a-Boo	Retrd.	1994	Gift	35-60
1994	Alexandria -1575	Retrd.	1995	36.00	50-85
1994	Lindy	Retrd.	1995	Gift	20-40
1995	Zamika -1581	5/96		36.00	36
1995	Zizi	5/96		Gift	N/A

All God's Children - M. Holcombe

YEAR ISSUE		EDITION LIMIT	YEAR RETD.	ISSUE PRICE	QUOTE U.S.$
1985	Abe -1357	Retrd.	1988	25.00	1000-1425
1989	Adam - 1526	Open		36.00	37
1987	Amy - 1405W	Open		22.00	27
1987	Angel - 1401W	Retrd.	1995	20.00	27-54
1986	Annie Mae 6" -1311	Retrd.	1989	19.00	85-160
1986	Annie Mae 8 1/2" -1310	Retrd.	1989	27.00	200-240
1987	Aunt Sarah - blue -1440	Retrd.	1989	45.00	185-265
1987	Aunt Sarah - red-1440	Retrd.	1989	45.00	250-385
1992	Barney - 1557	Retrd.	1995	32.00	40-75
1988	Bean (Clear Water)-1521	Retrd.	1992	36.00	225-300
1992	Bean (Painted Water)-1521	Retrd.	1993	36.00	125
1987	Becky - 1402W	Retrd.	1995	22.00	32-54
1987	Becky with Patch - 1402W	Retrd.	N/A	19.00	180-225
1987	Ben - 1504	Retrd.	1988	22.00	300-415
1991	Bessie & Corkie - 1547	Open		70.00	70
1992	Beth - 1558	Retrd.	1995	32.00	55-75
1988	Betsy (Clear Water)- 1513	Retrd.	1992	36.00	225-310
1992	Betsy (Painted Water)- 1513	Retrd.	1993	36.00	125
1989	Beverly (sm.)- 1525	Retrd.	1990	50.00	450-590
1991	Billy (lg. stars raised)- 1545	Retrd.	1993	36.00	100-140
1991	Billy (stars imprinted)- 1545	Retrd.	1993	36.00	125-150
1987	Blossom - blue - 1500	Retrd.	1989	60.00	200-380
1987	Blossom - red - 1500	Retrd.	1989	60.00	625-780
1989	Bo - 1530	Retrd.	1994	22.00	50-75
1987	Bonnie & Buttons - 150	Retrd.	1992	24.00	90-140
1985	Booker T - 1320	Retrd.	1988	19.00	1100-1400
1987	Boone - 1510	Retrd.	1989	16.00	100-150
1989	Bootsie - 1529	Retrd.	1994	22.00	50-75
1992	Caitlin - 1554	Retrd.	1994	36.00	65-95
1985	Callie 2 1/4" - 1362	Retrd.	1988	12.00	200-270
1985	Callie 4 1/2" - 1361	Retrd.	1988	19.00	400-490
1988	Calvin - 777	Retrd.	1988	200.00	1500-2000
1987	Cassie - 1503	Retrd.	1989	22.00	100-175
1994	Chantel 1573	Open		39.00	39
1987	Charity - 1408	Retrd.	1994	28.00	60-90
1994	Cheri 1574	Open		38.00	38
1989	David - 1528	Open		28.00	30
1991	Dori (green dress) - 1544	Retrd.	N/A	30.00	275-375
1991	Dori (peach dress) - 1544	Open		28.00	30
1987	Eli - 1403W	Open		26.00	28
1985	Emma - 1322	Retrd.	1994	27.00	1550-1950
1992	Faith - 1555	Retrd.	1993	32.00	70-95
1995	Gina - 1579	Open		38.00	38
1987	Ginnie - 1508	Retrd.	1988	22.00	350-420
1986	Grandma - 1323	Retrd.	1987	30.00	3000-3650
1988	Hannah - 1515	Open		36.00	37
1988	Hope - 1519	Open		36.00	37
1987	Jacob - 1407W	Open		26.00	28
1989	Jeremy - 1523	800	1993	195.00	650-890
1989	Jerome - 1532	Open		30.00	32
1989	Jessica - 1522	800	1993	195.00	650-890
1989	Jessica and Jeremy -1522-1523	Retrd.	1993	390.00	1300-1780
1987	Jessie (no base) -1501W	Retrd.	1989	19.00	300-425
1989	Jessie - 1501	Open		30.00	32
1988	John -1514	Retrd.	1990	30.00	150-225
1989	Joseph - 1537	Open		30.00	30
1991	Joy - 1548	Open		30.00	30
1994	Justin - 1576	Open		37.00	37
1989	Kacie - 1533	Open		38.00	38
1988	Kezia - 1518	Open		36.00	37
1986	Lil' Emmie 3 1/2"-1345	Retrd.	1989	14.00	75-140
1986	Lil' Emmie 4 1/2" -1344	Retrd.	1989	18.00	100-170
1988	Lisa-1512	Retrd.	1991	36.00	150-220
1989	Mary - 1536	Open		30.00	30
1988	Maya - 1520	Retrd.	1993	36.00	90-125
1987	Meg (beige dress) -1505	Retrd.	1988	21.00	900-1125
1988	Meg (blue dress, long hair) -1505	Retrd.	1988	21.00	325-425
1988	Meg (blue dress, short hair) 1505	Retrd.	1988	21.00	700-900
1992	Melissa - 1556	Retrd.	1995	32.00	50-65
1992	Merci - 1559	Open		36.00	37
1986	Michael & Kim - 1517	Open		36.00	38
1988	Moe & Pokey - 1552	Retrd.	1993	16.00	50-65
1987	Moses - 1506	Retrd.	1992	30.00	90-140
1993	Nathaniel-11569	Open		36.00	36
1991	Nellie - 1546	Retrd.	1993	36.00	115-135
1994	Niambi- 1577	Open		34.00	34
1987	Paddy Paw & Lucy - 1553	Suspd.		24.00	60-100
1987	Paddy Paw & Luke - 1551	Suspd.		24.00	60-100
1988	Peanut -1509	Retrd.	1990	16.00	100-155
1989	Preshus - 1538	Open		24.00	24
1987	Primas Jones (w/base) -1377	Retrd.	1988	40.00	675-800
1987	Primas Jones -1377	Retrd.	1988	40.00	650-800
1986	Prissy (Bear) - 1558	Open		18.00	25
1986	Prissy (Moon Pie) - 1557	Open		20.00	32
1986	Prissy with Basket -1346	Retrd.	1989	16.00	100-155
1986	Prissy with Yarn Hair (6 strands) 1343	Retrd.	1989	19.00	200-265
1986	Prissy with Yarn Hair (9 strands) 1343	Retrd.	1989	19.00	375-525
1987	Pud - 1550	Retrd.	1988	11.00	1100-1300
1987	Rachel - 1404W	Open		20.00	28
1992	Rakiya - 1561	Open		36.00	36
1988	Sally -1507	Retrd.	1989	19.00	110-170
1991	Samantha - 1542	Retrd.	1994	38.00	75-100
1991	Samuel - 1541	Retrd.	1994	32.00	50-85
1989	Sasha - 1531	Open		30.00	32
1986	Selina Jane (6 strands) -1338	Retrd.	1989	21.95	200-265
1986	Selina Jane (9 strands) -1338	Retrd.	1989	21.95	400-600
1993	Simon & Andrew - 1565	Open		45.00	45
1986	St. Nicholas-B -1316	Retrd.	1990	30.00	120-145
1986	St. Nicholas-W -1315	Retrd.	1990	30.00	90-140
1992	Stephen (Nativity Shepherd) - 1563	Open		36.00	36
1988	Sunshine - 1535	Open		38.00	38
1993	Sylvia - 1564	Open		36.00	37
1988	Tansi & Tedi (green socks, collar, cuffs)-1516	Retrd.	N/A	30.00	190-295
1988	Tansy & Tedi - 1516	Open		N/A	37
1989	Tara - 1527	Open		36.00	37
1989	Tess - 1534	Open		30.00	32
1990	Thaliyah- 778	Retrd.	1990	200.00	1500-1825
1991	Thomas - 1549	Open		30.00	30
1987	Tiffany - 1511	Open		32.00	32
1994	Tish 1572	Open		38.00	38
1986	Toby 3 1/2"- 1332	Retrd.	1989	13.00	90-140
1986	Toby 4 1/2"- 1331	Retrd.	1989	16.00	115-170
1985	Tom- 1353	Retrd.	1988	16.00	250-415
1986	Uncle Bud 6"- 1304	Retrd.	1991	19.00	100-155
1986	Uncle Bud 8 1/2"- 1303	Retrd.	1991	27.00	275-350
1992	Valerie - 1560	Open		36.00	37
1995	William - 1580	Open		38.00	38
1987	Willie - 1406W	Open		22.00	28
1993	Zack - 1566	Open		34.00	34

All God's Children Ragbabies - M. Holcombe

YEAR ISSUE		EDITION LIMIT	YEAR RETD.	ISSUE PRICE	QUOTE U.S.$
1995	Honey - 4005	Open		33.00	33
1995	Issie - 4004	Open		33.00	33
1995	Ivy - 4008	Open		33.00	33
1995	Josie - 4003	Open		33.00	33
1995	Mitzi - 4000	Open		33.00	33
1995	Muffin - 4001	Open		33.00	33
1995	Puddin - 4006	Open		33.00	33
1995	Punkin - 4007	Open		33.00	33
1995	Sweetie - 4002	Open		33.00	33

Angelic Messengers - M. Holcombe

YEAR ISSUE		EDITION LIMIT	YEAR RETD.	ISSUE PRICE	QUOTE U.S.$
1994	Cieara 2500	Open		38.00	38
1994	Mariah 2501	Open		38.00	38
1995	Sabrina - 2502	Open		38.00	38

Christmas - M. Holcombe

YEAR ISSUE		EDITION LIMIT	YEAR RETD.	ISSUE PRICE	QUOTE U.S.$
1987	1987 Father Christmas-W -1750	Retrd.	N/A	145.00	500-700
1987	1987 Father Christmas-B -1751	Retrd.	N/A	145.00	500-700
1988	1988 Father Christmas-W -1757	Retrd.	N/A	195.00	425-585
1988	1988 Father Christmas-B -1758	Retrd.	N/A	195.00	425-585
1988	Santa Claus-W -1767	Retrd.	N/A	185.00	450-615
1988	Santa Claus-B -1768	Retrd.	N/A	185.00	450-615
1989	1989 Father Christmas-W -1769	Retrd.	N/A	195.00	500-670
1989	1989 Father Christmas-B -1770	Retrd.	N/A	195.00	500-670
1990	1990-91 Father Christmas W -1771	Retrd.	N/A	195.00	450-620
1990	1990-91 Father Christmas B -1772	Retrd.	N/A	195.00	450-620
1991	1991-92 Father Christmas W -1773	Retrd.	N/A	195.00	300-450
1991	1991-92 Father Christmas B -1774	Retrd.	N/A	195.00	300-450
1992	Father Christmas Bust-W -1775	Retrd.	N/A	145.00	250-335
1992	Father Christmas Bust-B -1776	Retrd.	N/A	145.00	250-335

Event Piece - M. Holcombe

YEAR ISSUE		EDITION LIMIT	YEAR RETD.	ISSUE PRICE	QUOTE U.S.$
1994	Uriel 2000	Yr.Iss.	1994	45.00	60-100
1995	Jane 2001 (10 year Anniversary)	Yr.Iss.		45.00	45

Historical Series - M. Holcombe

YEAR ISSUE		EDITION LIMIT	YEAR RETD.	ISSUE PRICE	QUOTE U.S.$
1994	Augustus Walley (Buffalo Soldier) - 1908	Retrd.	1995	95.00	150-200
1994	Bessie Smith- 1909	Open		70.00	70
1992	Dr. Daniel Williams - 1903	Retrd.	1995	70.00	70
1992	Frances Harper - 1905	Open		70.00	70
1991	Frederick Douglass - 1902	Open		70.00	70
1992	George Washington Carver 1907	Open		70.00	70
1989	Harriet Tubman - 1900	Retrd.	1994	65.00	125-200
1992	Ida B. Wells - 1906	Open		70.00	70
1992	Mary Bethune (misspelled) 1904	Retrd.	1992	70.00	150-235
1992	Mary Bethune - 1904	Open		70.00	70
1995	Mary Mahoney - 1911	Open		65.00	65
1995	Richard Allen - 1910	Open		70.00	70
1990	Sojourner Truth - 1901	Open		65.00	65

International Series - M. Holcombe

YEAR ISSUE		EDITION LIMIT	YEAR RETD.	ISSUE PRICE	QUOTE U.S.$
1987	Juan - 1807	Retrd.	1993	26.00	100-140
1987	Kameko - 1802	Open.		26.00	28
1987	Karl - 1808	Open.		26.00	28
1987	Katrina - 1803	Retrd.	1993	26.00	100-140
1987	Kelli - 1805	Open		30.00	30
1987	Little Chief - 1804	Open		32.00	32
1993	Minnie - 1568	Open		36.00	100-140
1987	Pike - 1806	Open		30.00	32
1987	Tat - 1801	Open		30.00	32

Little Missionary Series - M. Holcombe

YEAR ISSUE		EDITION LIMIT	YEAR RETD.	ISSUE PRICE	QUOTE U.S.$
1994	Nakia 3500	Retrd.	1995	40.00	80

Sugar And Spice - M. Holcombe

YEAR ISSUE		EDITION LIMIT	YEAR RETD.	ISSUE PRICE	QUOTE U.S.$
1987	Blessed are the Peacemakers (Eli) -1403	Retrd.	1988	22.00	350-525
1987	Friend Show Love (Becky) -1402	Retrd.	1988	22.00	350-525
1987	Friendship Warms the Heart (Jacob) -1407	Retrd.	1988	22.00	350-525
1987	God is Love (Angel) -1401	Retrd.	1988	22.00	350-525
1987	Jesus Loves Me (Amy) -1405	Retrd.	1989	22.00	350-525
1987	Old Friends are Best (Rachel) 1404	Retrd.	1988	22.00	350-525
1987	Sharing with Friends (Willie) 1406	Retrd.	1988	22.00	350-525

American Artists

Fred Stone Figurines - F. Stone

YEAR ISSUE		EDITION LIMIT	YEAR RETD.	ISSUE PRICE	QUOTE U.S.$
1986	Arab Mare & Foal	2,500		150.00	225
1985	The Black Stallion, bronze	1,500		150.00	175
1985	The Black Stallion, porcelain	2,500		125.00	260
1987	Rearing Black Stallion (Bronze)	1,250		175.00	195
1987	Rearing Black Stallion (Porcelain)	3,500		150.00	175
1986	Tranquility	2,500		175.00	275

Anheuser-Busch, Inc.

Anheuser-Busch Collectible Figurines - Various

YEAR ISSUE		EDITION LIMIT	YEAR RETD.	ISSUE PRICE	QUOTE U.S.$
1994	Buddies N4575 - M. Urdahl	7,500		65.00	65
1995	Horseplay F1 - P. Radtke	7,500		65.00	65

ANRI

Club ANRI - Various

YEAR ISSUE		EDITION LIMIT	YEAR RETD.	ISSUE PRICE	QUOTE U.S.$
1983	Welcome, 4" - J. Ferrandiz	Yr.Iss.	1984	110.00	395
1984	My Friend, 4" - J. Ferrandiz	Yr.Iss.	1985	110.00	400
1984	Apple of My Eye, 4 1/2" - S. Kay	Yr.Iss.	1985	135.00	385
1985	Harvest Time, 4" - J. Ferrandiz	Yr.Iss.	1986	125.00	175-385
1985	Dad's Helper, 4 1/2" - S. Kay	Yr.Iss.	1986	135.00	150-375
1986	Harvest's Helper, 4" - J. Ferrandiz	Yr.Iss.	1987	135.00	175-335
1986	Romantic Notions, 4" - S. Kay	Yr.Iss.	1987	135.00	175-310
1986	Celebration March, 5" J. Ferrandiz	Yr.Iss.	1987	165.00	225-295
1987	Will You Be Mine, 4"- J. Ferrandiz	Yr.Iss.	1988	135.00	175-310
1987	Make A Wish, 4" - S. Kay	Yr.Iss.	1988	165.00	215-325
1987	A Young Man's Fancy, 4" S. Kay	Yr.Iss.	1988	135.00	165-265
1988	Forever Yours, 4" - J. Ferrandiz	Yr.Iss.	1989	170.00	250
1988	I've Got a Secret, 4" - S. Kay	Yr.Iss.	1989	170.00	205
1988	Maestro Mickey, 4 1/2" - Disney Studio	Yr.Iss.	1989	170.00	175
1989	Diva Minnie, 4 1/2" - Disney Studio	Yr.Iss.	1990	190.00	190
1989	I'll Never Tell, 4" - S. Kay	Yr.Iss.	1990	190.00	190
1989	Twenty Years of Love, 4" J. Ferrandiz	Yr.Iss.	1990	190.00	190
1990	You Are My Sunshine, 4" J. Ferrandiz	Yr.Iss.	1991	220.00	220
1990	A Little Bashful, 4" - S. Kay	Yr.Iss.	1991	220.00	220
1990	Dapper Donald, 4" - Disney Studio	Yr.Iss.	1991	199.00	199
1991	With All My Heart, 4" J. Ferrandiz	Yr.Iss.	1992	250.00	250
1991	Kiss Me, 4" - S. Kay	Yr.Iss.	1992	250.00	250
1991	Daisy Duck, 4 1/2" - Disney Studio	Yr.Iss.	1992	250.00	250

ANRI Club - Various

YEAR ISSUE		EDITION LIMIT	YEAR RETD.	ISSUE PRICE	QUOTE U.S.$
1992	You Are My All, 4" - J. Ferrandiz	Yr.Iss.	1993	260.00	260
1992	My Present For You, 4" - S. Kay	Yr.Iss.	1993	270.00	270
1992	Gift of Love - S. Kay	Yr.Iss.	1993	Gift	N/A
1993	Truly Yours, 4" - J. Ferrandiz	Yr.Iss.	1994	290.00	290
1993	Sweet Thoughts, 4" - S. Kay	Yr.Iss.	1994	300.00	300
1993	Just For You - S. Kay	Yr.Iss.	1994	Gift	N/A
1994	Sweet 'N Shy, 4" - J. Ferrandiz	Yr.Iss.	1994	250.00	250
1994	Snuggle Up, 4" - S. Kay	Yr.Iss.	1994	300.00	300
1994	Dapper 'N Dear, 4" - J. Ferrandiz	Yr.Iss.	1994	250.00	250

ANRI Collectors' Society - S. Kay

YEAR ISSUE		EDITION LIMIT	YEAR RETD.	ISSUE PRICE	QUOTE U.S.$
1995	On My Own, 4"	Yr.Iss.		175.00	175

Bernardi Reflections - U. Bernardi

YEAR ISSUE		EDITION LIMIT	YEAR RETD.	ISSUE PRICE	QUOTE U.S.$
1994	Master Carver, 4"	500		350.00	350
1994	Master Carver, 6"	250		600.00	600
1995	Planning the Tour, 4"	500		450.00	450
1995	Planning the Tour, 6"	250		300.00	300

Christmas Firsts - S. Kay

YEAR ISSUE		EDITION LIMIT	YEAR RETD.	ISSUE PRICE	QUOTE U.S.$
1994	Sarah Kay's First Christmas, 4"	500		350.00	350
1994	Sarah Kay's First Christmas, 6"	250		600.00	600
1995	First Xmas Stocking, 4" 57553	500		250.00	250
1995	First Xmas Stocking, 6" 57554	250		395.00	395

Disney Studios Mickey Mouse Thru The Ages - Disney Studios

YEAR ISSUE		EDITION LIMIT	YEAR RETD.	ISSUE PRICE	QUOTE U.S.$
1991	The Mad Dog, 4"	1,000	1991	500.00	375-500
1990	Steam Boat Willie, 4"	1,000	1990	295.00	500

Disney Woodcarving - Disney Studio

YEAR ISSUE		EDITION LIMIT	YEAR RETD.	ISSUE PRICE	QUOTE U.S.$
1991	Bell Boy Donald, 4" 656029	Closed	1991	250.00	250
1991	Bell Boy Donald, 6" 656110	500	1991	400.00	400
1990	Chef Goofy, 2 1/2" 656222	Closed	1991	125.00	125-150
1990	Chef Goofy, 5" 656227	Closed	1991	265.00	265
1989	Daisy, 4" 656021	Closed	1991	190.00	200
1990	Donald & Daisy, 6" 656108	500	1991	700.00	700
1988	Donald Duck, 1 3/4" 656209	Closed	1990	80.00	100
1988	Donald Duck, 2" 656204	Closed	1990	85.00	100-125
1987	Donald Duck, 4" 656004	Closed	1989	150.00	200-250
1988	Donald Duck, 4" 656014	Closed	1990	180.00	200-250
1988	Donald Duck, 6" 656102	500	1988	350.00	500
1989	Donald, 4" 656020	Closed	1991	190.00	200-250
1988	Goofy, 1 3/4" 656210	Closed	1990	80.00	125
1988	Goofy, 2" 656205	Closed	1990	85.00	125
1987	Goofy, 4" 656005	Closed	1989	150.00	200-250
1988	Goofy, 4" 656015	Closed	1990	180.00	200-250
1989	Goofy, 4" 656022	Closed	1991	190.00	200-250
1988	Goofy, 6" 656103	500	1988	380.00	525
1988	Goofy, 6" 656105	500	1991	350.00	400-500
1989	Mickey & Minnie Set, 6" 656106	500	1991	700.00	850
1989	Mickey & Minnie, 20" matched set	50	1991	7000.00	7000
1987	Mickey & Minnie, 6" 656101	500	1987	625.00	1000
1988	Mickey Mouse, 1 3/4" 656206	Closed	1990	80.00	200
1988	Mickey Mouse, 2" 656201	Closed	1990	85.00	100
1990	Mickey Mouse, 2" 656220	Closed	1991	100.00	200
1987	Mickey Mouse, 4" 656001	Closed	1989	150.00	200-250
1988	Mickey Mouse, 4" 656011	Closed	1990	180.00	200-250
1990	Mickey Mouse, 4" 656025	Closed	1991	199.00	200-250
1991	Mickey Skating, 2" 656224	Closed	1991	120.00	125
1991	Mickey Skating, 4" 656030	Closed	1991	250.00	350
1988	Mickey Sorcerer's Apprentice, 2" 656211	Closed	1991	80.00	200-300
1988	Mickey Sorcerer's Apprentice, 4" 656016	Closed	1991	180.00	199
1988	Mickey Sorcerer's Apprentice, 6" 656109	500	1991	350.00	500
1989	Mickey, 10" 656800	250	1991	700.00	1000
1989	Mickey, 20" 656850	50	1991	3500.00	3500
1989	Mickey, 4" 656018	Closed	1991	190.00	300
1988	Mini Donald, 1 3/4" 656204	Closed	1991	85.00	100-125
1989	Mini Donald, 2" 656215	Closed	1991	85.00	100-125
1988	Mini Goofy, 1 3/4" 656205	Closed	1991	85.00	100-125
1989	Mini Goofy, 2" 656217	Closed	1991	85.00	100-125
1988	Mini Mickey, 1 3/4" 656201	Closed	1991	85.00	100-125
1989	Mini Mickey, 2" 656213	Closed	1991	85.00	100-125
1988	Mini Minnie, 1 3/4" 656202	Closed	1991	85.00	100-125
1989	Mini Minnie, 2" 656214	Closed	1991	85.00	100-125
1989	Mini Pluto, 2" 656218	Closed	1991	85.00	100-125
1989	Minnie Daisy, 2" 656216	Closed	1991	85.00	100-125
1988	Minnie Mouse, 2" 656202	Closed	1990	85.00	100-125
1990	Minnie Mouse, 2" 656221	Closed	1991	100.00	100-125
1987	Minnie Mouse, 4" 656002	Closed	1989	150.00	250
1990	Minnie Mouse, 4" 656026	Closed	1991	199.00	200
1988	Minnie Pinocchio, 1 3/4" 656203	Closed	1991	85.00	200-300
1991	Minnie Skating, 2" 656225	Closed	1991	120.00	125
1991	Minnie Skating, 4" 656031	Closed	1991	250.00	350
1989	Minnie, 10" 656801	250	1991	700.00	800
1989	Minnie, 20" 656851	50	1991	3500.00	3500
1989	Minnie, 4" 656019	Closed	1991	190.00	200
1988	Pinocchio, 1 3/4" 656208	Closed	1990	80.00	200-300
1989	Pinocchio, 10" 656802	250	1991	700.00	1000
1988	Pinocchio, 2" 656203	Closed	1990	85.00	85
1989	Pinocchio, 2" 656219	Closed	1991	85.00	100
1989	Pinocchio, 20" 656851	50	1991	3500.00	3500
1987	Pinocchio, 4" 656003 (apple)	Closed	1989	150.00	200-250
1988	Pinocchio, 4" 656013	Closed	1990	180.00	199
1989	Pinocchio, 4" 656024	Closed	1991	190.00	199
1989	Pinocchio, 6" 656107	500	1991	350.00	350
1988	Pluto, 1 3/4" 656207	Closed	1990	80.00	100-125
1988	Pluto, 4" 656012	Closed	1990	180.00	200
1989	Pluto, 4" 656023	Closed	1991	190.00	200
1988	Pluto, 6" 656104	500	1991	350.00	350
1990	Sorcerer's Apprentice w/ crystal, 2" 656223	Closed	1991	125.00	300
1990	Sorcerer's Apprentice w/ crystal, 4" 656028	Closed	1991	265.00	350
1990	Sorcerer's Apprentice w/ crystal, 6" 656109	1,000	1991	475.00	500-600
1990	Sorcerer's Apprentice w/ crystal, 8" 656803	350	1991	790.00	800-900
1990	Sorcerer's Apprentice w/ crystal,16" 656853	100	1991	3500.00	3500

Ferrandiz Boy and Girl - J. Ferrandiz

YEAR ISSUE		EDITION LIMIT	YEAR RETD.	ISSUE PRICE	QUOTE U.S.$
1983	Admiration, 6"	2,250	1983	220.00	295
1990	Alpine Friend, 3"	1,500	1990	225.00	365
1990	Alpine Friend, 6"	1,500	1990	450.00	610
1990	Alpine Music, 3"	1,500	1990	225.00	225
1990	Alpine Music, 6"	1,500	1990	450.00	580
1989	Baker Boy, 3"	1,500	1989	170.00	170
1989	Baker Boy, 6"	1,500	1989	340.00	340
1978	Basket of Joy, 6"	1,500	1978	140.00	350-450
1983	Bewildered, 6"	2,250	1983	196.00	295
1991	Catalonian Boy, 3"	1,500	1993	227.50	228
1991	Catalonian Boy, 6"	1,500	1993	500.00	500
1991	Catalonian Girl, 3"	1,500	1993	227.50	228
1991	Catalonian Girl, 6"	1,500	1993	500.00	500
1976	Cowboy, 6"	1,500	1976	75.00	500-600
1987	Dear Sweetheart, 3"	2,250	1989	130.00	130
1987	Dear Sweetheart, 6"	2,250	1989	250.00	250
1988	Extra, Extra!, 3"	1,500	1988	145.00	145
1988	Extra, Extra!, 6"	1,500	1988	320.00	320
1979	First Blossom, 6"	2,250	1979	135.00	345-375
1987	For My Sweetheart, 3"	2,250	1989	130.00	130
1987	For My Sweetheart, 6"	2,250	1989	250.00	250
1984	Friendly Faces, 3"	2,250	1984	93.00	110
1984	Friendly Faces, 6"	2,250	1984	210.00	225-295
1980	Friends, 6"	2,250	1980	200.00	300-350
1986	Golden Sheaves, 3"	2,250	1986	125.00	125
1986	Golden Sheaves, 6"	2,250	1986	245.00	245
1982	Guiding Light, 6"	2,250	1982	225.00	275-350
1979	Happy Strummer, 6"	2,250	1979	160.00	395
1976	Harvest Girl, 6"	1,500	1976	75.00	400-800
1977	Leading the Way, 6"	1,500	1977	100.00	300-375
1992	May I, Too?, 3"	1,000	1993	230.00	230
1992	May I, Too?, 6"	1,000	1993	440.00	440
1980	Melody for Two, 6"	2,250	1980	200.00	350
1981	Merry Melody, 6"	2,250	1981	210.00	300-350
1989	Pastry Girl, 3"	1,500	1989	170.00	170
1989	Pastry Girl, 6"	1,500	1989	340.00	340
1978	Peace Pipe, 6"	1,500	1978	140.00	325-450
1985	Peaceful Friends, 3"	2,250	1985	120.00	120
1985	Peaceful Friends, 6"	2,250	1985	250.00	295
1986	Season's Bounty, 3"	2,250	1986	125.00	125
1986	Season's Bounty, 6"	2,250	1986	245.00	245
1988	Sunny Skies, 3"	1,500	1988	145.00	145
1988	Sunny Skies, 6"	1,500	1988	320.00	320
1985	Tender Love, 3"	2,250	1985	100.00	125
1985	Tender Love, 6"	2,250	1985	225.00	250
1981	Tiny Sounds, 6"	2,250	1981	210.00	300-350
1982	To Market, 6"	1,500	1982	220.00	295
1977	Tracker, 6"	1,500	1977	100.00	400
1984	Wanderer's Return, 3"	2,250	1984	93.00	135
1984	Wanderer's Return, 6"	2,250	1984	196.00	250
1992	Waste Not, Want Not, 3"	1,000	1993	190.00	200
1992	Waste Not, Want Not, 6"	1,000	1993	430.00	430

Ferrandiz Matching Number Woodcarvings - J. Ferrandiz

YEAR ISSUE		EDITION LIMIT	YEAR RETD.	ISSUE PRICE	QUOTE U.S.$
1990	Alpine Music / Friend, 3"	Closed	1992	450.00	450
1990	Alpine Music / Friend, 6"	Closed	1992	900.00	900
1989	Baker / Pastry, 3"	Closed	1992	340.00	340
1989	Baker / Pastry, 6"	Closed	1992	680.00	680
1991	Catalonian Boy/Girl, 3"	Closed	1992	455.00	455
1991	Catalonian Boy/Girl, 6"	Closed	1992	1000.00	1000
1988	Dear Sweetheart, 3"/For My Sweetheart, 3"	Closed	1989	285.00	495
1988	Dear Sweetheart, 6"/For My Sweetheart, 6"	Closed	1989	525.00	900
1988	Extra, Extra!, 3"/Sunny Skies, 3"	Closed	1992	315.00	315
1988	Extra, Extra!, 6"/Sunny Skies, 6"	Closed	1988	665.00	665
1988	Picnic for Two, 3"/Bon Appetit, 3"	Closed	1991	390.00	390
1988	Picnic for Two, 6"/Bon Appetit, 6"	Closed	1992	845.00	845

Ferrandiz Message Collection - J. Ferrandiz

YEAR ISSUE		EDITION LIMIT	YEAR RETD.	ISSUE PRICE	QUOTE U.S.$
1990	Christmas Carillon, 4 1/2"	2,500	1992	299.00	299
1990	Count Your Blessings, 4 1/2"	5,000	1992	300.00	300

YEAR ISSUE		EDITION LIMIT	YEAR RETD.	ISSUE PRICE	QUOTE U.S.$
1990	God's Creation, 4 1/2"	5,000	1992	300.00	300
1989	God's Miracle, 4 1/2"	5,000	1991	300.00	300
1989	God's Precious Gift, 4 1/2"	5,000	1991	300.00	300
1989	He Guides Us, 4 1/2"	5,000	1991	300.00	300
1989	He is the Light, 4 1/2"	5,000	1991	300.00	300
1989	He is the Light, 9"	5,000	1991	600.00	600
1989	Heaven Sent, 4 1/2"	5,000	1991	300.00	300
1989	Light From Within, 4 1/2"	5,000	1991	300.00	300
1989	Love Knows No Bounds, 4 1/2"	5,000	1991	300.00	300
1989	Love So Powerful, 4 1/2"	5,000	1991	300.00	300

Ferrandiz Mini Nativity Set - J. Ferrandiz

YEAR ISSUE		EDITION LIMIT	YEAR RETD.	ISSUE PRICE	QUOTE U.S.$
1985	Baby Camel, 1 1/2"	Closed	1993	45.00	53
1985	Camel Guide, 1 1/2"	Closed	1993	45.00	53
1985	Camel, 1 1/2"	Closed	1993	45.00	53
1988	Devotion, 1 1/2"	Closed	1993	53.00	53
1985	Harmony, 1 1/2"	Closed	1993	45.00	53
1984	Infant, 1 1/2"	Closed	1993	Set	Set
1988	Jolly Gift, 1 1/2"	Closed	1992	53.00	53
1984	Joseph, 1 1/2"	Closed	1993	Set	Set
1984	Leading the Way, 1 1/2"	Closed	1993	Set	Set
1988	Long Journey, 1 1/2"	Closed	1993	53.00	53
1984	Mary, 1 1/2"	Closed	1993	300.00	540
1986	Mini Angel, 1 1/2"	Closed	1993	45.00	53
1986	Mini Balthasar, 1 1/2"	Closed	1993	45.00	53
1986	Mini Caspar, 1 1/2"	Closed	1993	45.00	53
1986	Mini Free Ride, plus Mini Lamb, 1 1/2"	Closed	1993	45.00	53
1986	Mini Melchoir, 1 1/2"	Closed	1993	45.00	53
1986	Mini Star Struck, 1 1/2"	Closed	1993	45.00	53
1986	Mini The Hiker, 1 1/2"	Closed	1993	45.00	53
1986	Mini The Stray, 1 1/2"	Closed	1993	45.00	53
1986	Mini Weary Traveller, 1 1/2"	Closed	1993	45.00	53
1984	Ox Donkey, 1 1/2"	Closed	1993	Set	Set
1985	Rest, 1 1/2"	Closed	1993	45.00	53
1985	Reverence, 1 1/2"	Closed	1993	45.00	53
1984	Sheep Kneeling, 1 1/2"	Closed	1993	Set	Set
1984	Sheep Standing, 1 1/2"	Closed	1993	Set	Set
1985	Small Talk, 1 1/2"	Closed	1993	45.00	53
1988	Sweet Dreams, 1 1/2"	Closed	1993	53.00	53
1988	Sweet Inspiration, 1 1/2"	Closed	1992	53.00	53
1985	Thanksgiving, 1 1/2"	Closed	1993	45.00	53

Ferrandiz Shepherds of the Year - J. Ferrandiz

YEAR ISSUE		EDITION LIMIT	YEAR RETD.	ISSUE PRICE	QUOTE U.S.$
1982	Companions, 6"	2,250	1982	220.00	275-300
1984	Devotion, 3"	2,250	1984	82.50	125
1984	Devotion, 6"	2,250	1984	180.00	200-250
1979	Drummer Boy, 3"	Yr.Iss.	1979	80.00	250
1979	Drummer Boy, 6"	Yr.Iss.	1979	220.00	400-425
1980	Freedom Bound, 3"	Yr.Iss.	1980	90.00	225
1980	Freedom Bound, 6"	Yr.Iss.	1980	225.00	400
1977	Friendship, 3"	Yr.Iss.	1977	53.50	330
1977	Friendship, 6"	Yr.Iss.	1977	110.00	500-675
1983	Good Samaritan, 6"	2,250	1983	220.00	300-320
1981	Jolly Piper, 6"	2,250	1981	225.00	375
1978	Spreading the Word, 3"	Yr.Iss.	1978	115.00	250-275
1978	Spreading the Word, 6"	Yr.Iss.	1978	270.50	500

Ferrandiz Woodcarvings - J. Ferrandiz

YEAR ISSUE		EDITION LIMIT	YEAR RETD.	ISSUE PRICE	QUOTE U.S.$
1988	Abracadabra, 3"	1,500	1991	145.00	165
1988	Abracadabra, 6"	1,500	1991	315.00	345
1987	Among Friends, 3"	3,000	1990	125.00	151
1987	Among Friends, 6"	3,000	1990	245.00	291
1969	Angel Sugar Heart, 6"	Closed	1973	25.00	2500
1974	Artist, 3"	Closed	1981	30.00	195
1970	Artist, 6"	Closed	1981	25.00	350
1982	Bagpipe, 3"	Closed	1983	80.00	95
1982	Bagpipe, 6"	Closed	1983	175.00	190
1978	Basket of Joy, 3"	Closed	1984	65.00	120
1984	Bird's Eye View, 3"	Closed	1989	88.00	129
1984	Bird's Eye View, 6"	Closed	1989	216.00	700
1987	Black Forest Boy, 3"	3,000	1990	125.00	151
1987	Black Forest Boy, 6"	3,000	1990	250.00	301
1987	Black Forest Girl, 3"	3,000	1990	125.00	151
1987	Black Forest Girl, 6"	3,000	1990	250.00	300-350
1977	The Blessing, 3"	Closed	1982	45.00	150
1977	The Blessing, 6"	Closed	1982	125.00	250
1988	Bon Appetit, 3"	500	1991	175.00	195
1988	Bon Appetit, 6"	500	1991	395.00	440
1974	The Bouquet, 3"	Closed	1981	35.00	175
1974	The Bouquet, 6"	Closed	1981	75.00	325
1982	Bundle of Joy, 3"	Closed	1990	100.00	300
1982	Bundle of Joy, 6"	Closed	1990	225.00	323
1985	Butterfly Boy, 3"	Closed	1990	95.00	140
1985	Butterfly Boy, 6"	Closed	1990	220.00	322
1976	Catch a Falling Star, 3"	Closed	1983	35.00	150
1976	Catch a Falling Star, 6"	Closed	1983	75.00	250
1982	The Champion, 3"	Closed	1985	98.00	110
1982	The Champion, 6"	Closed	1985	225.00	250
1975	Cherub, 2"	Open		32.00	90
1975	Cherub, 4"	Open		32.00	275
1993	Christmas Time, 5"	750		360.00	380
1982	Circus Serenade, 3"	Closed	1988	100.00	160
1982	Circus Serenade, 6"	Closed	1988	220.00	220
1982	Clarinet, 3"	Closed	1983	80.00	100
1982	Clarinet, 6"	Closed	1983	175.00	200
1982	Companions, 3"	Closed	1984	95.00	115
1975	Courting, 3"	Closed	1982	70.00	235
1975	Courting, 6"	Closed	1982	150.00	450
1984	Cowboy, 10"	Closed	1989	370.00	500
1983	Cowboy, 20"	250	1989	2100.00	2100
1976	Cowboy, 3"	Closed	1989	35.00	140-160
1994	Donkey Driver, 3"	Open		160.00	160
1994	Donkey Driver, 6"	Open		360.00	360
1994	Donkey, 3"	Open		200.00	200
1994	Donkey, 6"	Open		450.00	450
1980	Drummer Boy, 3"	Closed	1988	130.00	200
1980	Drummer Boy, 6"	Closed	1988	300.00	400
1970	Duet, 3"	Closed	1991	36.00	165
1970	Duet, 6"	Closed	1991	Unkn.	355
1986	Edelweiss, 10"	Open		500.00	1000
1986	Edelweiss, 20"	250		3300.00	5420
1983	Edelweiss, 3"	Open		95.00	190
1983	Edelweiss, 6"	Open		220.00	450
1982	Encore, 3"	Closed	1984	100.00	115
1982	Encore, 6"	Closed	1984	225.00	235
1979	First Blossom, 3"	Closed	1985	70.00	110
1974	Flight Into Egypt, 3"	Closed	1986	35.00	125
1974	Flight Into Egypt, 6"	Closed	1986	70.00	500
1976	Flower Girl, 3"	Closed	1988	40.00	40
1976	Flower Girl, 6"	Closed	1988	90.00	310
1982	Flute, 3"	Closed	1983	80.00	95
1982	Flute, 6"	Closed	1983	175.00	190
1976	Gardener, 3"	Closed	1984	32.00	195
1976	Gardener, 6"	Closed	1985	65.00	275-350
1975	The Gift, 3"	Closed	1982	40.00	195
1975	The Gift, 6"	Closed	1982	70.00	295
1973	Girl in the Egg, 3"	Closed	1988	30.00	127
1973	Girl in the Egg, 6"	Closed	1988	60.00	272
1973	Girl with Dove, 3"	Closed	1984	30.00	110
1973	Girl with Dove, 6"	Closed	1984	50.00	175-200
1976	Girl with Rooster, 3"	Closed	1982	32.50	175
1976	Girl with Rooster, 6"	Closed	1982	60.00	275
1986	God's Little Helper, 2"	3,500	1991	170.00	255
1986	God's Little Helper, 4"	2,000	1991	425.00	550
1975	Going Home, 3"	Closed	1988	40.00	110
1975	Going Home, 6"	Closed	1988	70.00	240
1986	Golden Blossom, 10"	Open		500.00	1000
1986	Golden Blossom, 20"	250		3300.00	5420
1983	Golden Blossom, 3"	Open		95.00	190
1986	Golden Blossom, 40"	50		8300.00	12950
1983	Golden Blossom, 6"	Open		220.00	450
1982	The Good Life, 3"	Closed	1984	100.00	200
1982	The Good Life, 6"	Closed	1984	225.00	295
1969	The Good Sheperd, 3"	Closed	1988	12.50	121
1971	The Good Shepherd, 10"	Closed	1988	90.00	90
1969	The Good Shepherd, 6"	Closed	1988	25.00	237
1974	Greetings, 3"	Closed	1976	30.00	300
1974	Greetings, 6"	Closed	1976	55.00	475
1982	Guiding Light, 3"	Closed	1984	100.00	115-140
1982	Guitar, 3"	Closed	1983	80.00	95
1982	Guitar, 6"	Closed	1983	175.00	190
1979	Happy Strummer, 3"	Closed	1986	75.00	110
1973	Happy Wanderer, 10"	Closed	1985	120.00	500
1974	Happy Wanderer, 3"	Closed	1986	40.00	105
1974	Happy Wanderer, 6"	Closed	1986	70.00	200
1982	Harmonica, 3"	Closed	1983	80.00	95
1982	Harmonica, 3"	Closed	1983	80.00	95
1982	Harmonica, 6"	Closed	1983	175.00	190
1978	Harvest Girl, 3"	Closed	1986	75.00	110-140
1979	He's My Brother, 3"	Closed	1984	70.00	130
1979	He's My Brother, 6"	Closed	1984	155.00	240
1987	Heavenly Concert, 2"	3,000	1991	200.00	200
1987	Heavenly Concert, 4"	2,000	1991	450.00	550
1969	Heavenly Gardener, 6"	Closed	1973	25.00	2000
1969	Heavenly Quintet, 6"	Closed	1973	25.00	2000
1974	Helping Hands, 3"	Closed	1976	30.00	350
1974	Helping Hands, 6"	Closed	1976	55.00	700
1984	High Hopes, 3"	Closed	1986	81.00	81-100
1984	High Hopes, 6"	Closed	1986	170.00	255
1979	High Riding, 3"	Closed	1984	145.00	200
1979	High Riding, 6"	Closed	1984	340.00	475
1982	Hitchhiker, 3"	Closed	1986	98.00	85-110
1982	Hitchhiker, 6"	Closed	1986	125.00	230
1993	Holiday Greetings, 3"	1,000	1993	200.00	200
1993	Holiday Greetings, 6"	1,000	1993	450.00	450
1975	Holy Family, 3"	Closed	1988	75.00	250
1975	Holy Family, 6"	Closed	1988	200.00	670
1977	Hurdy Gurdy, 3"	Closed	1988	53.00	150
1977	Hurdy Gurdy, 6"	Closed	1988	112.00	390
1975	Inspector, 3"	Closed	1981	40.00	250
1975	Inspector, 6"	Closed	1981	80.00	395
1981	Jolly Piper, 3"	Closed	1984	100.00	120
1977	Journey, 3"	Closed	1983	67.50	175
1977	Journey, 6"	Closed	1983	120.00	400
1977	Leading the Way, 3"	Closed	1984	62.50	120
1976	The Letter, 3"	Closed	1988	40.00	40
1976	The Letter, 6"	Closed	1988	90.00	600
1982	Lighting the Way, 3"	Closed	1984	105.00	150
1982	Lighting the Way, 6"	Closed	1984	225.00	295
1974	Little Mother, 3"	Closed	1981	136.00	290
1974	Little Mother, 6"	Closed	1981	85.00	285
1993	Lots of Gifts, 3"	1,000	1993	200.00	200
1993	Lots of Gifts, 6"	1,000	1993	450.00	450
1975	Love Gift, 3"	Closed	1982	40.00	175
1975	Love Gift, 6"	Closed	1982	70.00	295
1969	Love Letter, 3"	Closed	1982	12.50	150
1969	Love Letter, 6"	Closed	1982	25.00	250
1983	Love Message, 3"	Closed	1990	105.00	151
1983	Love Message, 6"	Closed	1990	240.00	366
1969	Love's Messenger, 6"	Closed	1973	25.00	2000
1992	Madonna With Child, 3"	1,000	1994	190.00	190
1992	Madonna With Child, 6"	1,000	1994	370.00	370
1981	Merry Melody, 3"	Closed	1984	90.00	115
1989	Mexican Boy, 3"	1,500	1993	170.00	175
1989	Mexican Boy, 6"	1,500	1993	340.00	350
1989	Mexican Girl, 3"	1,500	1993	170.00	175
1989	Mexican Girl, 6"	1,500	1993	340.00	350
1975	Mother and Child, 3"	Closed	1983	45.00	150
1975	Mother and Child, 6"	Closed	1983	90.00	295
1981	Musical Basket, 3"	Closed	1984	90.00	115
1981	Musical Basket, 6"	Closed	1984	200.00	225
1986	A Musical Ride, 4"	Closed	1990	165.00	237
1986	A Musical Ride, 8"	Closed	1990	395.00	559
1973	Nature Girl, 3"	Closed	1988	30.00	30
1973	Nature Girl, 6"	Closed	1988	60.00	272
1987	Nature's Wonder, 3"	3,000	1990	125.00	151
1987	Nature's Wonder, 6"	3,000	1990	245.00	291
1974	New Friends, 3"	Closed	1976	30.00	275
1974	New Friends, 6"	Closed	1976	55.00	550
1977	Night Night, 3"	Closed	1983	45.00	120
1977	Night Night, 6"	Closed	1983	67.50	250-315
1992	Pascal Lamb, 3"	1,000	1993	210.00	210
1992	Pascal Lamb, 6"	1,000	1993	460.00	460
1988	Peace Maker, 3"	1,500	1991	180.00	200
1988	Peace Maker, 6"	1,500	1991	360.00	395
1983	Peace Pipe, 10"	Closed	1986	460.00	495
1984	Peace Pipe, 20"	Closed	1986	2200.00	3500
1979	Peace Pipe, 3"	Closed	1986	85.00	120
1988	Picnic for Two, 3"	500	1991	190.00	210
1988	Picnic for Two, 6"	500	1991	425.00	465
1982	Play It Again, 3"	Closed	1984	100.00	120
1982	Play It Again, 6"	Closed	1984	250.00	255
1977	Poor Boy, 3"	Closed	1986	50.00	110
1977	Poor Boy, 6"	Closed	1986	125.00	215
1977	Proud Mother, 3"	Closed	1988	52.50	150
1977	Proud Mother, 6"	Closed	1988	130.00	350
1971	The Quintet, 10"	Closed	1990	100.00	675
1971	The Quintet, 20"	Closed	1990	Unkn.	3000
1969	The Quintet, 3"	Closed	1990	12.50	140
1969	The Quintet, 6"	Closed	1990	25.00	340
1977	Riding Thru the Rain, 10"	Open		400.00	1150
1977	Riding Thru the Rain, 5"	Open		145.00	450
1974	Romeo, 3"	Closed	1981	50.00	250
1974	Romeo, 6"	Closed	1981	85.00	395
1993	Santa and Teddy, 5"	750		360.00	380
1994	Santa Resting on Bag, 5"	750		400.00	400
1987	Serenity, 3"	3,000	1989	125.00	151
1987	Serenity, 6"	3,000	1989	245.00	291
1976	Sharing, 3"	Closed	1983	32.50	130
1976	Sharing, 6"	Closed	1983	32.50	225-275
1984	Shipmates, 3"	Closed	1989	81.00	119
1984	Shipmates, 6"	Closed	1989	170.00	248
1978	Spreading the Word, 3"	Closed	1989	115.00	194
1978	Spreading the Word, 6"	Closed	1989	270.00	495
1980	Spring Arrivals, 10"	Open		435.00	770
1980	Spring Arrivals, 20"	250		2000.00	3360
1973	Spring Arrivals, 3"	Open		30.00	160
1973	Spring Arrivals, 6"	Open		50.00	350
1978	Spring Dance, 12"	Closed	1984	950.00	1750
1978	Spring Dance, 24"	Closed	1984	4750.00	6200
1974	Spring Outing, 3"	Closed	1976	30.00	625
1974	Spring Outing, 6"	Closed	1976	55.00	900
1982	Star Bright, 3"	Closed	1984	110.00	125
1982	Star Bright, 6"	Closed	1984	250.00	295
1981	Stepping Out, 3"	Closed	1984	95.00	110-145
1981	Stepping Out, 6"	Closed	1984	220.00	275
1979	Stitch in Time, 3"	Closed	1984	75.00	125
1979	Stitch in Time, 6"	Closed	1984	150.00	235
1969	Sugar Heart, 3"	Closed	1973	12.50	450
1969	Sugar Heart, 6"	Closed	1973	25.00	525
1975	Summertime, 3"	Closed	1989	35.00	35
1975	Summertime, 6"	Closed	1989	70.00	258
1982	Surprise, 3"	Closed	1988	100.00	150
1982	Surprise, 6"	Closed	1988	225.00	325
1973	Sweeper, 3"	Closed	1981	35.00	130
1973	Sweeper, 6"	Closed	1981	75.00	425
1981	Sweet Arrival Blue, 3"	Closed	1985	105.00	110
1981	Sweet Arrival Blue, 6"	Closed	1985	225.00	255
1981	Sweet Arrival Pink, 3"	Closed	1985	105.00	110
1981	Sweet Arrival Pink, 6"	Closed	1985	225.00	225
1981	Sweet Dreams, 3"	Closed	1990	100.00	140
1982	Sweet Dreams, 6"	Closed	1990	225.00	330
1982	Sweet Melody, 3"	Closed	1985	80.00	90
1982	Sweet Melody, 6"	Closed	1985	198.00	210
1989	Swiss Boy, 3"	Closed	1993	180.00	180
1986	Swiss Boy, 3"	Closed	1993	122.00	162
1986	Swiss Boy, 6"	Closed	1993	245.00	324
1989	Swiss Boy, 6"	Closed	1993	380.00	380
1986	Swiss Girl, 3"	Closed	1993	122.00	122
1989	Swiss Girl, 3"	Closed	1993	200.00	200
1986	Swiss Girl, 6"	Closed	1993	245.00	304
1989	Swiss Girl, 6"	Closed	1993	470.00	470
1971	Talking to Animals, 20"	Closed	1989	Unkn.	3000
1971	Talking to the Animals, 10"	Closed	1989	90.00	600
1969	Talking to the Animals, 3"	Closed	1989	12.50	125
1969	Talking to the Animals, 6"	Closed	1989	45.00	45
1995	Tender Care, 3" 55700/52	Open		125.00	125
1974	Tender Moments, 3"	Closed	1976	30.00	375
1974	Tender Moments, 6"	Closed	1976	55.00	575
1981	Tiny Sounds, 3"	Closed	1984	90.00	105
1982	To Market, 3"	Closed	1984	95.00	115
1977	Tracker, 3"	Closed	1984	70.00	120-200
1980	Trumpeter, 10"	Closed	1986	500.00	500

YEAR ISSUE		EDITION LIMIT	YEAR RETD.	ISSUE PRICE	QUOTE U.S.$
1984	Trumpeter, 20"	Closed	1986	2350.00	3050
1973	Trumpeter, 3"	Closed	1986	69.00	115
1973	Trumpeter, 6"	Closed	1986	120.00	240
1980	Umpapa, 4"	Closed	1984	125.00	140
1982	Violin, 3"	Closed	1983	80.00	95
1982	Violin, 6"	Closed	1983	175.00	195
1976	Wanderlust, 3"	Closed	1983	32.50	125
1975	Wanderlust, 6"	Closed	1983	70.00	450
1988	Winter Memories, 3"	1,500	1991	180.00	195
1988	Winter Memories, 6"	1,500	1991	398.00	440

Limited Edition Couples - J. Ferrandiz

1985	First Kiss, 8"	750	1985	590.00	950
1987	Heart to Heart, 8"	750	1991	590.00	850
1988	A Loving Hand, 8"	750	1991	795.00	850
1986	My Heart Is Yours, 8"	750	1991	590.00	850
1985	Springtime Stroll, 8"	750	1990	590.00	950
1986	A Tender Touch, 8"	750	1990	590.00	850

Sarah Kay Figurines - S. Kay

1985	'Tis the Season, 4"	4,000	1993	95.00	250
1985	'Tis the Season, 6"	Closed	1985	210.00	425
1985	Afternoon Tea, 11"	750	1993	650.00	770
1985	Afternoon Tea, 20"	100	1993	3100.00	3500
1985	Afternoon Tea, 4"	4,000	1990	95.00	185
1985	Afternoon Tea, 6"	4,000	1990	195.00	325-365
1987	All Aboard, 1 1/2"	7,500	1990	50.00	90
1987	All Aboard, 4"	4,000	1990	130.00	185
1987	All Aboard, 6"	2,000	1990	265.00	355
1987	All Mine, 1 1/2"	7,500	1988	49.50	95
1987	All Mine, 4"	4,000	1988	130.00	225
1987	All Mine, 6"	4,000	1988	245.00	465
1986	Always By My Side, 1 1/2"	7,500	1988	45.00	95
1986	Always By My Side, 4"	4,000	1988	95.00	195
1986	Always By My Side, 6"	4,000	1988	195.00	375
1990	Batter Up, 1 1/2"	3,750	1991	90.00	95
1990	Batter Up, 4"	2,000		220.00	265
1990	Batter Up, 6"	2,000		440.00	505
1983	Bedtime, 1 1/2"	7,500	1984	45.00	110
1983	Bedtime, 4"	Closed	1987	95.00	230
1983	Bedtime, 6"	4,000	1987	195.00	435
1994	Bubbles & Bows, 4"	1,000		300.00	300
1994	Bubbles & Bows, 6"	1,000		600.00	600
1986	Bunny Hug, 1 1/2"	7,500	1989	45.00	85
1986	Bunny Hug, 4"	4,000	1989	95.00	172
1986	Bunny Hug, 6"	2,000	1989	210.00	395
1989	Cherish, 1 1/2"	Closed	1991	80.00	95
1989	Cherish, 4"	2,000	1994	199.00	290
1989	Cherish, 6"	2,000	1994	398.00	560
1993	Christmas Basket, 4"	1,000		310.00	290
1993	Christmas Basket, 6"	1,000		600.00	580
1994	Christmas Wonder, 4"	1,000		370.00	370
1994	Christmas Wonder, 6"	1,000		700.00	700
1994	Clowning Around, 4"	1,000		300.00	300
1994	Clowning Around, 6"	1,000		550.00	550
1987	Cuddles, 1 1/2"	7,500	1988	49.50	95
1987	Cuddles, 4"	4,000	1988	130.00	225
1987	Cuddles, 6"	4,000	1988	245.00	465
1984	Daydreaming, 1 1/2"	7,500	1984	45.00	125
1984	Daydreaming, 4"	4,000	1988	95.00	235
1984	Daydreaming, 6"	4,000	1988	195.00	445
1991	Dress Up, 1 1/2"	3,750	1991	110.00	110
1991	Dress Up, 4"	2,000	1993	270.00	270
1991	Dress Up, 6"	2,000	1993	550.00	550
1983	Feeding the Chickens, 1 1/2"	7,500	1984	45.00	110
1983	Feeding the Chickens, 4"	Closed	1987	95.00	250
1983	Feeding the Chickens, 6"	4,000	1987	195.00	450
1991	Figure Eight, 1 1/2"	3,750	1991	110.00	110
1991	Figure Eight, 4"	2,000		270.00	365
1991	Figure Eight, 6"	2,000		550.00	660
1984	Finding Our Way, 1 1/2"	7,500	1984	45.00	135
1984	Finding Our Way, 4"	4,000	1988	95.00	245
1984	Finding Our Way, 6"	2,000	1984	210.00	495
1986	Finishing Touch, 1 1/2"	7,500	1989	45.00	85
1986	Finishing Touch, 4"	4,000	1989	95.00	172
1986	Finishing Touch, 6"	4,000	1989	195.00	312
1989	First School Day, 1 1/2"	Closed	1991	85.00	95
1989	First School Day, 4"	2,000	1993	290.00	350
1989	First School Day, 6"	2,000	1993	550.00	650
1989	Fisherboy, 1 1/2"	Closed	1991	85.00	95
1989	Fisherboy, 4"	2,000	1994	220.00	240
1989	Fisherboy, 6"	1,000	1994	440.00	475
1984	Flowers for You, 1 1/2"	7,500	1984	45.00	125
1984	Flowers for You, 4"	4,000	1988	95.00	250
1984	Flowers for You, 6"	4,000	1988	195.00	450
1991	Fore!!, 1 1/2"	3,750	1991	110.00	115
1991	Fore!!, 4"	2,000		270.00	325
1991	Fore!!, 6"	2,000		550.00	580
1992	Free Skating, 4"	1,000		310.00	325
1992	Free Skating, 6"	1,000		590.00	620
1983	From the Garden, 1 1/2"	7,500	1984	45.00	110
1983	From the Garden, 4"	Closed	1987	95.00	235
1983	From the Garden, 6"	4,000	1987	195.00	450
1989	Garden Party, 1 1/2"	Closed	1991	85.00	95
1989	Garden Party, 4"	2,000	1993	220.00	240
1989	Garden Party, 6"	2,000	1993	440.00	475
1985	Giddyap!, 4"	4,000	1990	95.00	250
1985	Giddyap!, 6"	4,000	1990	195.00	325
1988	Ginger Snap, 1 1/2"	Closed	1990	70.00	90
1988	Ginger Snap, 4"	2,000	1990	150.00	185
1988	Ginger Snap, 6"	1,000	1990	300.00	355
1986	Good As New, 1 1/2"	7,500	1991	45.00	90
1986	Good As New, 4"	4,000	1994	95.00	290
1986	Good As New, 6"	4,000	1994	195.00	500
1983	Helping Mother, 1 1/2"	7,500	1983	45.00	110
1983	Helping Mother, 4"	Closed	1983	95.00	300
1983	Helping Mother, 6"	2,000	1983	210.00	495
1988	Hidden Treasures, 1 1/2"	Closed	1990	70.00	90
1988	Hidden Treasures, 4"	2,000	1990	150.00	185
1988	Hidden Treasures, 6"	1,000	1990	300.00	355
1990	Holiday Cheer, 1 1/2"	3,750	1991	90.00	95
1990	Holiday Cheer, 4"	2,000		225.00	305
1990	Holiday Cheer, 6"	1,000		450.00	610
1989	House Call, 1 1/2"	Closed	1991	85.00	95
1989	House Call, 4"	2,000	1991	190.00	195
1989	House Call, 6"	2,000	1991	390.00	390
1995	I Know, I Know, 4" 57701	500		250.00	250
1995	I Know, I Know, 6" 57702	250		395.00	395
1993	Innocence, 4"	1,000		345.00	315
1993	Innocence, 6"	1,000		630.00	630
1994	Jolly Pair, 4"	1,000		350.00	350
1994	Jolly Pair, 6"	1,000		650.00	650
1993	Joy to the World, 4"	1,000		310.00	290
1993	Joy to the World, 6"	1,000		600.00	580
1987	Let's Play, 1 1/2"	7,500	1990	49.50	90
1987	Let's Play, 4"	4,000	1990	130.00	185
1987	Let's Play, 6"	2,000	1990	265.00	355
1994	Little Chimney Sweep, 4"	1,000		300.00	300
1994	Little Chimney Sweep, 6"	1,000		600.00	600
1987	Little Nanny, 1 1/2"	7,500	1990	49.50	90
1987	Little Nanny, 4"	4,000	1990	150.00	200
1987	Little Nanny, 6"	4,000	1990	295.00	400
1987	A Loving Spoonful, 1 1/2"	7,500	1991	49.50	90
1987	A Loving Spoonful, 4"	4,000	1994	150.00	290
1987	A Loving Spoonful, 6"	4,000	1994	295.00	550
1992	Merry Christmas, 1 1/2"	3,750	1994	110.00	115
1992	Merry Christmas, 4"	1,000	1994	350.00	350
1992	Merry Christmas, 6"	1,000	1994	580.00	580
1995	Mom's Joy, 5" 57902	250		297.00	297
1983	Morning Chores, 1 1/2"	7,500	1983	45.00	110
1983	Morning Chores, 4"	Closed	1983	95.00	300
1983	Morning Chores, 6"	2,000	1983	210.00	550
1993	Mr. Santa, 4"	750		375.00	390
1993	Mr. Santa, 6"	750		695.00	730
1993	Mrs. Santa, 4"	750		375.00	390
1993	Mrs. Santa, 6"	750		695.00	730
1993	My Favorite Doll, 4"	1,000		315.00	315
1993	My Favorite Doll, 6"	1,000		630.00	630
1988	My Little Brother, 1 1/2"	Closed	1991	70.00	90
1988	My Little Brother, 4"	2,000	1991	195.00	225
1988	My Little Brother, 6"	2,000	1991	375.00	450
1988	New Home, 1 1/2"	Closed	1991	70.00	90
1988	New Home, 4"	2,000	1991	185.00	240
1988	New Home, 6"	2,000	1991	365.00	500
1985	Nightie Night, 4"	4,000	1990	95.00	185
1985	Nightie Night, 6"	4,000	1990	195.00	325
1984	Off to School, 1 1/2"	7,500	1984	45.00	125
1984	Off to School, 11"	750		590.00	880
1984	Off to School, 20"	100		2900.00	4200
1984	Off to School, 4"	4,000		95.00	240
1984	Off to School, 6"	4,000		195.00	450
1986	Our Puppy, 1 1/2"	7,500	1990	45.00	90
1986	Our Puppy, 4"	4,000	1990	95.00	185
1986	Our Puppy, 6"	2,000	1990	210.00	355
1988	Penny for Your Thoughts, 1 1/2"	Closed	1991	70.00	90
1988	Penny for Your Thoughts, 4"	2,000		185.00	215
1988	Penny for Your Thoughts, 6"	2,000		365.00	455
1983	Playtime, 1 1/2"	7,500	1984	45.00	110
1983	Playtime, 4"	Closed	1987	95.00	250
1983	Playtime, 6"	4,000	1987	195.00	495
1988	Purrfect Day, 4"	2,000	1991	184.00	215
1988	Purrfect Day, 1 1/2"	Closed	1991	70.00	90
1988	Purrfect Day, 6"	2,000	1991	265.00	455
1992	Raindrops, 1 1/2"	3,750	1994	110.00	110
1992	Raindrops, 4"	1,000	1994	350.00	350
1992	Raindrops, 6"	1,000	1994	640.00	640
1991	Season's Joy, 1 1/2"	3,750	1991	110.00	115
1991	Season's Joy, 4"	2,000		270.00	305
1991	Season's Joy, 6"	1,000		550.00	620
1990	Seasons Greetings, 1 1/2"	3,750	1991	90.00	95
1990	Seasons Greetings, 4"	2,000		225.00	305
1990	Seasons Greetings, 6"	1,000		450.00	610
1990	Shootin' Hoops, 4"	2,000	1993	220.00	225
1990	Shootin' Hoops, 6"	2,000	1993	440.00	450
1990	Shootin' Hoops,1 1/2"	3,750	1991	90.00	95
1985	A Special Day, 4"	4,000	1990	95.00	195
1985	A Special Day, 6"	4,000	1990	195.00	325
1984	Special Delivery, 1 1/2"	7,500	1984	45.00	125
1984	Special Delivery, 4"	4,000	1989	95.00	187
1984	Special Delivery, 6"	4,000	1989	195.00	312-350
1990	Spring Fever, 1 1/2"	3,750	1991	90.00	95
1990	Spring Fever, 4"	2,000		225.00	305
1990	Spring Fever, 6"	2,000		450.00	610
1983	Sweeping, 1 1/2"	7,500	1984	45.00	110
1983	Sweeping, 4"	Closed	1987	95.00	230
1983	Sweeping, 6"	4,000	1987	195.00	435
1986	Sweet Treat, 1 1/2"	7,500	1989	45.00	85
1986	Sweet Treat, 4"	4,000	1989	95.00	172
1986	Sweet Treat, 6"	4,000	1989	195.00	312
1984	Tag Along, 4"	4,000	1988	95.00	225
1984	Tag Along, 6"	4,000	1988	195.00	290
1984	Tag Along,1 1/2"	7,500	1984	45.00	130
1989	Take Me Along, 1 1/2"	Closed	1991	85.00	95
1989	Take Me Along, 4"	2,000		220.00	285
1989	Take Me Along, 6"	1,000		440.00	525
1990	Tender Loving Care, 1 1/2"	3,750	1991	90.00	95
1990	Tender Loving Care, 4"	2,000	1993	220.00	240
1990	Tender Loving Care, 6"	2,000	1993	440.00	475
1986	To Love And To Cherish, 1 1/2"	7,500	1989	45.00	85
1986	To Love and To Cherish, 11"	1,000	1989	Unkn.	667
1986	To Love and To Cherish, 20"	200	1989	Unkn.	3600
1986	To Love And To Cherish, 4"	4,000	1989	95.00	172
1986	To Love And To Cherish, 6"	4,000	1989	195.00	312
1991	Touch Down, 1 1/2"	3,750	1994	110.00	110
1991	Touch Down, 4"	2,000	1994	270.00	270
1991	Touch Down, 6"	2,000	1994	550.00	550
1992	Tulips For Mother, 4"	1,000		310.00	325
1992	Tulips For Mother, 6"	1,000		590.00	620
1983	Waiting for Mother, 1 1/2"	7,500	1984	45.00	110
1983	Waiting for Mother, 11"	750	1987	495.00	795
1983	Waiting for Mother, 4"	Closed	1987	95.00	230
1983	Waiting for Mother, 6"	4,000	1987	195.00	445
1984	Wake Up Kiss, 1 1/2"	7,500	1984	45.00	550
1984	Wake Up Kiss, 4"	4,000	1993	95.00	195
1983	Wake Up Kiss, 6"	2,000	1984	210.00	550
1984	Watchful Eye, 4"	4,000	1988	95.00	235
1984	Watchful Eye, 6"	4,000	1988	195.00	445
1984	Watchful Eye,1 1/2"	7,500	1984	45.00	125
1992	Winter Cheer, 4"	2,000	1993	300.00	300
1992	Winter Cheer, 6"	1,000	1993	580.00	580
1991	Winter Surprise, 1 1/2"	3,750	1994	110.00	110
1991	Winter Surprise, 4"	2,000	1994	270.00	270
1991	Winter Surprise, 6"	1,000	1994	550.00	550
1986	With This Ring, 1 1/2"	7,500	1989	45.00	85
1986	With This Ring, 11"	1,000	1989	Unkn.	668
1986	With This Ring, 20"	200	1989	Unkn.	3600
1986	With This Ring, 4"	4,000	1989	95.00	172
1986	With This Ring, 6"	4,000	1989	195.00	312
1989	Yearly Check-Up, 1 1/2"	Closed	1991	85.00	95
1989	Yearly Check-Up, 4"	2,000	1991	190.00	195
1989	Yearly Check-Up, 6"	2,000	1991	390.00	390
1985	Yuletide Cheer, 4"	4,000	1993	95.00	250
1985	Yuletide Cheer, 6"	Closed	1985	210.00	435

Sarah Kay Mini Santas - S. Kay

1991	Jolly Santa, 1 1/2"	2,500	1993	110.00	110
1991	Jolly St. Nick, 1 1/2"	2,500	1993	110.00	110
1991	Kris Kringle, 1 1/2"	2,500	1993	110.00	110
1991	Sarah Kay Santa, 1 1/2"	2,500	1993	110.00	110

Sarah Kay Santas - S. Kay

1995	Checking It Twice, 4" 57709	500		250.00	250
1995	Checking It Twice, 6" 57710	250		395.00	395
1992	Father Christmas, 4"	750	1994	350.00	350
1992	Father Christmas, 6"	750	1994	590.00	590
1991	A Friend To All, 4"	750	1994	300.00	300
1991	A Friend To All, 6"	750	1994	590.00	590
1989	Jolly Santa, 12"	150	1990	1300.00	1300
1988	Jolly Santa, 4"	750	1989	235.00	300-350
1988	Jolly Santa, 6"	750	1989	480.00	600
1988	Jolly St. Nick, 4"	750	1989	199.00	300-550
1988	Jolly St. Nick, 6"	750	1989	398.00	850
1990	Kris Kringle Santa, 4"	750	1990	275.00	350
1990	Kris Kringle Santa, 6"	750	1990	550.00	550
1989	Santa, 4"	750	1990	235.00	350
1989	Santa, 6"	750	1990	480.00	480

Armani

G. Armani Society Members Only Figurine - G. Armani

1990	Awakening 591C	Closed	1990	137.50	900-1175
1991	Ruffles 745E	Closed	1991	139.00	275-400
1992	Ascent 866C	Closed	1992	195.00	275-375
1993	Venus 881C	Closed	1993	225.00	325-400
1993	Lady Rose (Bonus) 197C	Closed	1993	125.00	175-225
1993	Julie (Bonus) 293P	Closed	1993	90.00	125
1993	Juliette (Bonus) 294P	Closed	1994	90.00	175
1994	Flora 212C	Closed	1994	225.00	265
1994	Aquarius (Bonus) 248C	Closed	1994	125.00	125-155
1994	Harlequin (Bonus) 490C	Closed	1994	300.00	350
1995	Melody 656C	Yr.Iss.		250.00	250-350

G. Armani Society Members Only Event - G. Armani

1990	My Fine Feathered Friends (Bonus)122S	Closed	1991	175.00	360
1991	Peace & Harmony (Bonus) 824C	Closed	1992	300.00	325-360
1992	Springtime 961C	Closed	1992	250.00	350-500
1992	Boy with Dog (Bonus) 407S	Closed	1992	200.00	200
1993	Loving Arms 880E	Closed	1993	250.00	300
1994	Daisy 202E	Closed	1994	250.00	300
1995	Iris 628E	Yr. Iss.		250.00	250

Can-Can Dancers - G. Armani

1989	Two Can-Can Dancers 516C	Closed	1994	820.00	975

Clown Series - G. Armani

1991	Bust of Clown 725E	5,000		500.00	500
1995	Charlie 644C	Open		175.00	175
1994	The Happy Fiddler 478C	Open		360.00	360
1995	Jerry 643C	Open		200.00	200
1994	Sound the Trumpet 476C	Open		300.00	300

Country Series - G. Armani

1994	Back From the Fields 473F	Open		360.00	360
1993	Boy With Accordion 177C	Open		170.00	170
1993	Boy With Accordion 177F	Open		75.00	75
1993	Boy With Flute 890C	Open		175.00	175

YEAR ISSUE		EDITION LIMIT	YEAR RETD.	ISSUE PRICE	QUOTE U.S.$
1993	Boy With Flute 890F	Open		90.00	90
1994	Country Girl with Grapes 215C	Open		230.00	230
1994	Country Girl with Grapes 215F	Open		120.00	120
1994	Fresh Fruits 471F	Open		250.00	250
1993	Girl Tending Flowers 466C	Open		210.00	210
1993	Girl With Chicks 889C	Open		155.00	155
1993	Girl With Chicks 889F	Open		75.00	75
1993	Girl With Sheep 178C	Open		150.00	150
1993	Girl With Sheep 178F	Open		65.00	65
1993	Girl With Wheelbarrow /Flowers 468C	Open		240.00	240
1994	Laundry Girl 214C	Open		230.00	230
1994	Laundry Girl 214F	Open		120.00	120

Florentine Garden - G. Armani

1995	Wisteria 626C	Open		350.00	350
1995	Wisteria 626F	Open		275.00	275

Four Seasons - G. Armani

1990	Lady on Seashore (Summer) 540C	Open		440.00	440
1990	Lady With Bicycle (Spring) 539C	Open		550.00	550
1992	Lady With Fruit (Summer) 182B	Open		135.00	135
1992	Lady With Fruit (Summer) 182C	Open		275.00	275
1992	Lady With Grapes (Fall) 183C	Open		275.00	275
1992	Lady With Grapes (Fall)182B	Open		135.00	135
1990	Lady With Ice Skates (Winter) 542C	Open		400.00	400
1992	Lady With Roses (Spring)181B	Open		135.00	135
1992	Lady With Roses (Spring)181C	Open		275.00	275
1990	Lady With Umbrella (Fall) 541C	Open		475.00	475
1992	Lady With Vegetables (Winter)183B	Open		135.00	135
1992	Lady With Vegetables (Winter)183C	Open		275.00	275

Galleria Collection: Distinguished Dealers - G. Armani

1994	The Falconer 224S	3,000		1000.00	1000
1994	Leda & The Swan 1012T	1,500		500.00	500-625
1993	The Sea Wave 1006T	1,500	1994	500.00	500-625
1993	Spring Herald 1009T	1,500	1994	500.00	500
1993	Spring Water 1007T	1,500	1994	500.00	500-625
1993	Zephyr 1010T	1,500	1994	500.00	500-625

Garden Series - G. Armani

1994	Lady At Well 222C	Open		275.00	275
1994	Lady At Well 222F	Open		150.00	150
1991	Lady with Cornucopie 870C	10,000		600.00	600
1991	Lady with Harp 874C	10,000		500.00	500
1991	Lady with Peacock 871C	10,000		585.00	585
1991	Lady with Violin 872C	10,000		560.00	560

Golden Age - G. Armani

1995	Claire 654C	Open		250.00	250
1995	Claire 654F	Open		100.00	100
1995	Dear Friends 532F	Open		100.00	100
1995	Florence 535C	Open		250.00	250
1995	Florence 535F	Open		155.00	155
1995	Gloria 655C	Open		250.00	250
1995	Gloria 655F	Open		100.00	100
1995	Love and Peace 538C	Open		125.00	125
1995	Stormy Weather 533C	Open		260.00	260
1995	Stormy Weather 533F	Open		135.00	135
1995	Sunday Drive 531C	Open		275.00	275
1995	Sunday Drive 531F	Open		140.00	140
1995	Sunshine Dream 529C	Open		165.00	165
1995	Sunshine Dream 529F	Open		90.00	90
1995	Sweet Dreams 536C	Open		225.00	225
1995	Sweet Dreams 536F	Open		135.00	135

Gulliver's World - G. Armani

1994	The Barrel 659T	1,000		225.00	225
1994	Cowboy 657T	1,000		125.00	125
1994	Getting Clean 661T	1,000		130.00	130
1994	Ray of Moon 658T	1,000		100.00	100
1994	Seranade 660T	1,000		200.00	200

Gypsy Series - G. Armani

1994	Esmeralda-Gypsy Girl 198C	Open		400.00	400
1994	Esmeralda-Gypsy Girl 198F	Open		215.00	215

Little Treasures - G. Armani

1994	Bathtime 357T	Open		50.00	50
1994	Clean Sweep 373T	Open		50.00	50
1994	Girl at the Telephone 364T	Open		50.00	50
1994	Girl with Ice Cream 365T	Open		50.00	50
1994	Little Fisher Boy 362T	Open		37.00	37
1994	Playing the Piano 376T	Open		50.00	50
1994	Sweet Dreams 360T	Open		35.00	35
1994	A Woman's Work 363T	Open		50.00	50

Moonlight Masquerade - G. Armani

1990	Harlequin Lady 740C	Retrd.	1994	450.00	450
1990	Lady Clown with Cane 742C	Retrd.	1994	390.00	390
1990	Lady Clown with Doll 743C	Retrd.	1994	410.00	410
1990	Lady Pierrot 741C	Retrd.	1994	390.00	475
1990	Queen of Hearts 744C	Retrd.	1994	450.00	450

Motherhood - G. Armani

1994	Black Maternity 502C	5,000		500.00	500
1994	Black Maternity 502F	Open		335.00	335
1993	Garden Maternity 188C	Open		210.00	210
1993	Garden Maternity 188F	Open		115.00	115
1994	Kneeling Maternity 216C	Open		275.00	275
1994	Kneeling Maternity 216F	Open		135.00	135
1993	Maternity Embracing 190C	Open		250.00	250
1993	Maternity Embracing 190F	Open		160.00	160
1994	Mother & Child 470F	Open		150.00	150
1992	Mother With Child (Mother's Day) 185B	Open		235.00	235
1992	Mother With Child (Mother's Day) 185C	Open		400.00	400
1994	Mother's Hand 479F	Open		215.00	215
1993	Mother/Child 792C	Open		385.00	385
1993	Mother/Child 792F	Open		250.00	250
1995	Perfect Love 652C	5,000		1200.00	1200
1995	Perfect Love 652F	Open		800.00	800

My Fair Ladies ™ - G. Armani

1995	At Ease 634C	5,000		650.00	650
1995	At Ease 634F	Open		400.00	400
1995	Awaiting 631C	Open		170.00	170
1995	Awaiting 631F	Open		90.00	90
1993	Elegance 195C	5,000		525.00	525
1993	Elegance 195F	Open		300.00	300
1993	Fascination 192C	5,000		500.00	500
1993	Fascination 192F	Open		250.00	250
1987	Flamenco Dancer 389C	5,000		400.00	500
1995	Isadora 633C	3,000		920.00	920
1995	Isadora 633F	Open		500.00	500
1994	Lady w/Umbrella 196C	5,000		335.00	335
1994	Lady w/Umbrella 196F	Open		200.00	200
1987	Lady w/ Book 384C	5,000		300.00	450
1987	Lady w/ Compact 386C	Retrd.	1993	300.00	700-900
1987	Lady w/ Fan 387C	5,000		300.00	400
1987	Lady w/ Great Dane 429C	5,000		365.00	475
1987	Lady w/ Muff 388C	5,000		250.00	450
1989	Lady w/Parrot 616C	5,000		400.00	500
1987	Lady w/ Peacock 385C	Retrd.	1992	380.00	2200-3200
1993	Mahogany 194C	5,000	1995	500.00	500-575
1993	Mahogany 194F	Open		360.00	360
1993	Morning Rose 193C	5,000		450.00	450
1993	Morning Rose 193F	Open		225.00	225
1987	Mother & Child 405C	5,000		410.00	550
1995	Promenade 630C	Open		185.00	185
1995	Promenade 630F	Open		90.00	90
1995	Starry Night 632C	Open		185.00	185
1995	Starry Night 632F	Open		90.00	90

Pearls Of The Orient - G. Armani

1989	Chu Chu San 612C	Retrd.	1994	500.00	550
1989	Lotus Blossom 613C	Retrd.	1994	450.00	475
1989	Madame Butterfly 610C	Retrd.	1994	450.00	500
1989	Turnadot 611C	Retrd.	1994	475.00	500

Premiere Ballerina - G. Armani

1988	Ballerina 508C	Retrd.	1994	430.00	530
1988	Ballerina 517C	Retrd.	1994	325.00	375
1988	Ballerina Group in Flight 518C	Retrd.	1994	810.00	950
1988	Ballerina in Flight 503C	Retrd.	1994	420.00	500
1988	Ballerina with Drape 504C	Retrd.	1994	450.00	575
1990	Fly Dancer 585F	Retrd.	1993	190.00	210
1988	Two Ballerinas 515C	Retrd.	1994	620.00	775

Religious - G. Armani

1994	Baby Jesus 1020C	1,000		175.00	175
1987	Choir Boys 900	5,000		350.00	620
1990	Crucifix Plaque 711C	15,000		265.00	265
1987	Crucifix 1158C	10,000	1990	155.00	600-1000
1993	Crucifix 786C	7,500		250.00	250
1991	Crucifix 790C	15,000		180.00	180
1994	Donkey 1027C	1,000		185.00	185
1994	Joseph 1021C	1,000		500.00	500
1994	La Pieta 802C	5,000		950.00	950
1994	La Pieta 802F	Open		550.00	550
1992	Madonna With Child 787B	Open		260.00	260
1992	Madonna With Child 787C	Open		425.00	425
1992	Madonna With Child 787F	Open		265.00	265
1994	Magi King Gold 1023C	1,000		600.00	600
1994	Magi King Incense 1024C	1,000		600.00	600
1994	Magi King Myrrh 1025C	1,000		450.00	450
1994	Mary 1022C	1,000		365.00	365
1994	Moses 812C	Open		220.00	220
1994	Moses 812F	Open		115.00	115
1994	Ox 1026C	1,000		300.00	300
1994	Renaissance Crucifix 1017T	5,000		250.00	250

Renaissance - G. Armani

1992	Abundance 870C	5,000		600.00	600
1994	Ambrosia 482C	5,000		435.00	435
1994	Angelica 484C	5,000		575.00	575
1992	Aurora-Girl With Doves 884B	Open		220.00	220
1992	Aurora-Girl With Doves 884C	7,500		370.00	370
1991	Bust of Eve 590T	Closed	1991	250.00	700-1200
1992	Dawn 874C	5,000		500.00	500
1993	Freedom-Man And Horse 906C	3,000		850.00	850
1992	Liberty-Girl On Horse 903B	Open		450.00	450
1992	Liberty-Girl On Horse 903C	5,000		750.00	750
1992	Lilac & Roses-Girl w/Flowers 882B	Open		220.00	220
1992	Lilac & Roses-Girl w/Flowers 882C	7,500		410.00	410
1992	Twilight 872C	5,000		560.00	560
1992	Vanity 871C	5,000		585.00	585
1993	Wind Song-Girl With Sail 904C	5,000		520.00	520

Romantic - G. Armani

1994	The Embrace 480C	3,000		1450.00	1450
1993	Girl w/Dog At Fence 886C	Open		350.00	350
1993	Girl w/Dog At Fence 886F	Open		175.00	175
1993	Girl With Ducks 887C	Open		320.00	320
1993	Girl With Ducks 887F	Open		160.00	160
1992	Lady with Doves 858E	Retrd.	1993	250.00	450
1993	Lovers 191C	3,000		450.00	450
1993	Lovers 879C	3,000		570.00	570
1993	Lovers 879F	Open		325.00	325
1993	Lovers On A Swing 942C	Open		410.00	410
1993	Lovers On A Swing 942F	Open		265.00	265
1993	Lovers With Roses 888C	Open		300.00	300
1993	Lovers With Roses 888F	Open		155.00	155
1993	Lovers With Wheelbarrow 891C	Open		370.00	370
1993	Lovers With Wheelbarrow 891F	Open		190.00	190

Romantic Motherhood - G. Armani

1993	Maternity On Swing 941C	Open		360.00	360
1993	Maternity On Swing 941F	Open		220.00	220

Siena Collection - G. Armani

1993	Back From The Fields 1002T	1,000	1995	400.00	425
1994	Country Boy 1014T	2,500		135.00	135
1993	Encountering 1003T	1,000	1995	350.00	370
1993	Fresh Fruit 1001T	2,500	1995	155.00	295
1993	Happy Fiddler 1005T	1,000		225.00	225
1993	Mother's Hand 1008T	2,500		250.00	250
1993	Soft Kiss 1000T	2,500	1995	155.00	155
1993	Sound The Trumpet 1004T	1,000	1995	225.00	250

Special Issues - G. Armani

1991	Discovery of America Plaque 867C	Closed	1994	400.00	400
1993	Mother's Day Plaque 899C	Closed	1993	100.00	100
1995	Mother's Day Plaque-Love/Peace 538C	Yr.Iss.		125.00	125
1994	Mother's Day Plaque-The Swing 254C	Closed	1994	120.00	120

Special Times - G. Armani

1982	Card Players (Cheaters) 3280	Open		400.00	1200
1991	Couple in Car 862C	5,000		1000.00	1000
1991	Doctor in Car 848C	2,000		800.00	800
1994	The Encounter 472F	Open		315.00	315
1994	The Fairy Tale 219C	Open		335.00	335
1994	The Fairy Tale 219F	Open		175.00	175
1982	Girl with Chicks 5122E	Suspd.		95.00	165
1982	Girl with Sheep Dog 5117E	Retrd.	1992	100.00	210
1994	Grandpa's Nap 251C	Open		225.00	225
1994	Lady Doctor 249C	Open		200.00	200
1994	Lady Doctor 249F	Open		105.00	105
1994	Lady Graduate-Lawyer 253C	Open		225.00	225
1994	Lady Graduate-Lawyer 253F	Open		120.00	120
1991	Lady with Car 861C	3,000	1995	900.00	900
1994	Old Acquaintance 252C	Open		275.00	275
1982	Shy Kiss 5138E	Retrd.	1992	125.00	285
1982	Sledding 5111E	Retrd.	1992	115.00	250
1982	Soccer Boy 5109	Open		75.00	180
1994	Story Time 250C	Open		275.00	275

Special Walt Disney Production - G. Armani

1992	Cinderella	Retrd.	1992	500.00	3500-4300
1993	Dopey	Retrd.	1993	125.00	190-250
1993	Snow White 199C	Retrd.	1993	750.00	1000-1300
1994	Ariel (Little Mermaid) 505C	1,500	1994	750.00	1200-1300
1995	Beauty and the Beast	2,000	1995	975.00	975

Sports - G. Armani

1992	Lady Equestrian 910C	Open		315.00	315
1992	Lady Equestrian 910F	Open		155.00	155
1992	Lady Golfer 911C	Open		325.00	325
1992	Lady Golfer 911F	Open		170.00	170
1992	Lady Skater 913C	Open		300.00	300
1992	Lady Skater 913F	Open		170.00	170
1992	Lady Tennis 912C	Open		275.00	275
1992	Lady Tennis 912F	Open		175.00	175

Terra Cotta - G. Armani

1994	Ambrosia 1013T	Open		275.00	275
1994	Angelica 1016T	Open		450.00	450
1994	Country Boy w/ Mushrooms 1014T	2,500		135.00	135
1994	The Embrace 1011T	Open		930.00	930
1994	La Pieta 1015T	Open		550.00	550

Wedding - G. Armani

1994	Black Bride 500C	Open		170.00	170
1994	Black Bride 500F	Open		115.00	115
1994	Black Wedding Waltz 501C	3,000		750.00	750
1994	Black Wedding Waltz 501F	Open		450.00	450
1988	Bride & Groom Wedding 475P	Open		270.00	285
1994	Bride With Column & Vase 488C	Open		260.00	260
1994	Bride With Column & Vase 488F	Open		200.00	200
1992	Bride With Doves 885C	Open		280.00	280
1992	Bride With Doves 885F	Open		220.00	220
1994	Bride With Flower Vase 489C	Open		135.00	135
1994	Bride With Flower Vase 489F	Open		90.00	90
1993	Carriage Wedding 902F	Open		500.00	500
1993	Carriage Wedding902C	2,500		1000.00	1000

YEAR ISSUE		EDITION LIMIT	YEAR RETD.	ISSUE PRICE	QUOTE U.S.$
1993	Garden Wedding 189C	Open		225.00	225
1993	Garden Wedding 189F	Open		120.00	120
1989	Just Married 827C	5,000		950.00	1000
1987	Wedding Couple 407C	Open		525.00	550
1982	Wedding Couple 5132	Open		110.00	190
1991	Wedding Couple At Threshold 813C	7,500		400.00	400
1993	Wedding Couple At Wall 201C	Open		225.00	225
1993	Wedding Couple At Wall 201F	Open		115.00	115
1993	Wedding Couple Forever 791F	Open		250.00	250
1991	Wedding Couple Kissing 815C	7,500		500.00	500
1991	Wedding Couple w/ Bicycle 814C	7,500		600.00	600
1993	Wedding Flowers To Mary 187C	Open		225.00	225
1993	Wedding Flowers To Mary 187F	Open		115.00	115
1994	Wedding Waltz 493C	3,000		750.00	750
1994	Wedding Waltz 493F	Open		450.00	450

Wildlife - G. Armani

1988	Bird Of Paradise 454S	5,000		475.00	500
1990	Bird of Paradise 718S	5,000		550.00	575
1993	Doves With Vase 204S	3,000		375.00	375
1983	Eagle Bird of Prey 3213	Open		210.00	425
1991	Flamingo 713S	5,000		420.00	420
1991	Flying Duck 839S	5,000		470.00	470
1993	Galloping Horse 905S	7,500		465.00	465
1991	Great Argus Pheasant 717S	3,000		600.00	600
1993	Horse Head 205S	Open		140.00	140
1991	Large Owl 842S	5,000		520.00	520
1993	Parrot With Vase 736S	3,000		460.00	460
1988	Peacock 455S	5,000		600.00	675
1988	Peacock 458S	5,000		630.00	700
1993	Peacock With Vase 735S	3,000		375.00	375
1993	Rearing Horse 909S	7,500		515.00	515
1983	Royal Eagle with Babies 3553	Open		215.00	400
1993	Show Horse 907S	7,500		550.00	550
1982	Snow Bird 5548	Open		100.00	180
1990	Soaring Eagle 970S	5,000		620.00	700
1991	Swan 714S	5,000		550.00	550
1990	Three Doves 996S	5,000		670.00	750

Yesteryears - G. Armani

1993	Country Doctor In Car 848C	2,000		800.00	800
1994	Summertime-Lady on Swing 485C	5,000		650.00	650
1994	Summertime-Lady on Swing 485F	Open		450.00	450

Armstrong's

Armstrong's/Ron Lee - R. Skelton

1984	Captain Freddie	7,500		85.00	375-475
1984	Freddie the Torchbearer	7,500		110.00	450-475

Happy Art - W. Lantz

1982	Woody's Triple Self-Portrait	5,000		95.00	325

Pro Autographed Ceramic Baseball Card Plaque - Unknown

1985	Brett, Garvey, Jackson, Rose, Seaver, auto, 3-1/4X5	1,000		150.00	250

The Red Skelton Collection - R. Skelton

1981	Clem Kadiddlehopper	7,500		75.00	150
1981	Freddie in the Bathtub	7,500		80.00	150
1981	Freddie on the Green	7,500		80.00	85
1981	Freddie the Freeloader	7,500		70.00	150
1981	Jr., The Mean Widdle Kid	7,500		75.00	150
1981	San Fernando Red	7,500		75.00	200
1981	Sheriff Deadeye	7,500		75.00	150

The Red Skelton Porcelain Plaque - R. Skelton

1991	All American	1,500		495.00	1200
1994	Another Day	1,994		675.00	575
1992	Independance Day?	1,500		525.00	1000
1993	Red & Freddie Both Turned 80	1,993		595.00	600

Artaffects

Members Only Limited Edition Redemption Offerings - G. Perillo

1983	Apache Brave (Bust)	Closed		50.00	150
1986	Painted Pony	Closed		125.00	175
1991	Chief Crazy Horse	Closed		195.00	195

Limited Edition Free Gifts to Members - G. Perillo

1986	Dolls	Closed		Gift	35
1991	Sunbeam	Closed		Gift	35
1992	Little Shadow	Closed		Gift	35

The Chieftains - G. Perillo

1983	Crazy Horse	5,000		65.00	200
1983	Geronimo	5,000		65.00	135
1983	Joseph	5,000		65.00	250
1983	Red Cloud	5,000		65.00	275
1983	Sitting Bull	5,000		65.00	500

Pride of America's Indians - G. Perillo

1988	Brave and Free	10-day		50.00	150
1989	Dark Eyed Friends	10-day		45.00	75
1989	Kindred Spirits	10-day		45.00	50
1989	Loyal Alliance	10-day		45.00	75
1989	Noble Companions	10-day		45.00	50
1989	Peaceful Comrades	10-day		45.00	50
1989	Small & Wise	10-day		45.00	50
1989	Winter Scouts	10-day		45.00	50

Special Issue - G. Perillo

1984	Apache Boy Bust	Closed	N/A	40.00	75
1984	Apache Girl Bust	Closed	N/A	40.00	75
1985	Lovers	Closed	N/A	70.00	125
1984	Papoose	325		500.00	500
1982	The Peaceable Kingdom	950		750.00	750

The Storybook Collection - G. Perillo

1981	Cinderella	10,000		65.00	95
1982	Goldilocks & 3 Bears	10,000		80.00	110
1982	Hansel and Gretel	10,000		80.00	110
1980	Little Red Ridinghood	10,000		65.00	95

The Tribal Ponies - G. Perillo

1984	Arapaho	1,500		65.00	175-200
1984	Comanche	1,500		65.00	175-200
1984	Crow	1,500		65.00	175-200

The War Pony - G. Perillo

1983	Apache War Pony	495		150.00	175-200
1983	Nez Perce War Pony	495		150.00	175-200
1983	Sioux War Pony	495		150.00	175-200

Artists of the World

DeGrazia Annual Christmas Collection - T. DeGrazia

1992	Feliz Navidad	1,992		195.00	225
1993	Fiesta Angels	1,993		295.00	295
1994	Littlest Angel	1,994		165.00	165
1995	Bethlehem Bound	1,995		195.00	195

DeGrazia Figurine - T. DeGrazia

1990	Alone	S/O	N/A	395.00	595
1995	Apache Mother	3,500		165.00	195
1994	Bearing Gifts	Open		145.00	145
1988	Beautiful Burden	Closed	1990	175.00	200-250
1990	Biggest Drum	Closed	1992	110.00	135
1986	The Blue Boy	Susp.		70.00	125
1992	Coming Home	3,500		165.00	175
1990	Crucifixion	S/O	1995	295.00	295
1990	Desert Harvest	S/O	N/A	135.00	145
1986	Festival Lights	Susp.		75.00	110-150
1994	Fiesta Flowers	3,500		197.50	198
1995	Floral Harvest	Open		175.00	185
1984	Flower Boy	Closed	1992	65.00	185-250
1988	Flower Boy Plaque	Closed	1990	80.00	85
1984	Flower Girl	Susp.		65.00	200-250
1984	Flower Girl Plaque	Closed	1985	45.00	85
1993	Flowers For Mother	Open		145.00	145
1995	Little Farm Boy	Open		145.00	165
1995	Little Helper	3,500		165.00	185
1995	Little Hopi Girl	Open		97.50	110
1985	Little Madonna	Closed	1993	80.00	200-250
1993	Little Medicine Man	Open		175.00	185
1988	Los Ninos	S/O	N/A	595.00	1200
1989	Los Ninos (Artist's Edition)	S/O	N/A	695.00	1600-2000
1987	Love Me	Closed	1992	95.00	175-250
1988	Merrily, Merrily, Merrily	Closed	1991	95.00	220
1986	Merry Little Indian	S/O	N/A	175.00	275
1993	Mother Silently Prays	3,500		345.00	345
1989	My Beautiful Rocking Horse	Open		225.00	275
1995	My Blue Balloon	Open		110.00	115
1989	My First Arrow	Closed	1992	95.00	185-250
1984	My First Horse	Closed	1990	65.00	185-250
1990	Navajo Boy	Closed	1992	110.00	145
1992	Navajo Madonna	Closed	1993	135.00	200
1991	Navajo Mother	3,500		295.00	325
1994	Pedro	Open		145.00	145
1985	Pima Drummer Boy	Closed	1991	65.00	165-200
1994	Rio Grande Dancer	Open		97.50	98
1993	Saddle Up	5,000		195.00	215
1994	Saguaro Dance	2,500		495.00	495
1992	Sun Showers	5,000		195.00	225
1984	Sunflower Boy	Closed	1985	65.00	200-300
1990	Sunflower Girl	Closed	1993	95.00	220
1993	Water Wagon	Open		295.00	295
1995	Wedding Party	Open		175.00	175
1995	Wedding Party Children	Open		75.00	75
1987	Wee Three	Closed	1990	180.00	200
1984	White Dove	Closed	1992	45.00	110-145
1984	Wondering	Closed	1987	85.00	220-275

DeGrazia Nativity Collection - T. DeGrazia

1993	Balthasar	Open		135.00	135
1988	Christmas Prayer Angel (red)	Closed	1991	70.00	200-295
1990	El Burrito	Closed	N/A	60.00	90
1993	El Toro	Open		95.00	98
1993	Gaspar	Open		135.00	135
1985	Jesus	Open		55.00	65
1985	Joseph	Open		100.00	110
1990	Little Prayer Angel (white)	Closed	1992	85.00	300-395
1985	Mary	Open		90.00	100
1993	Melchoir	Open		135.00	135
1985	Nativity Set-3 pc. (Mary, Joseph, Jesus)	Open		275.00	275
1995	Pima Indian Drummer Boy	Open		135.00	135
1991	Shepherd's Boy	Open		95.00	135
1989	Two Little Lambs	Closed	1992	70.00	220

DeGrazia Pendants - R. Olszewski

1987	Festival of Lights 562-P	Suspd.		90.00	275
1985	Flower Girl Pendant 561-P	Suspd.		125.00	200

DeGrazia Platinum Figurine - T. DeGrazia

1995	Little Navajo Music Man	950		165.00	175

DeGrazia Village Collection - T. DeGrazia

1993	Let's Compromise	Open		65.00	65
1992	The Listener	Closed	1992	48.00	48-75
1993	Peace Pipe	Open		65.00	65
1992	Telling Tales	Closed	1992	48.00	48-75
1993	Three Feathers	Open		65.00	65

DeGrazia: Goebel Miniatures - R. Olszewski

1988	Adobe Display 948D	Suspd.		45.00	75-100
1990	Adobe Hacienda (large) Display 958-D	Suspd.		85.00	125-175
1989	Beautiful Burden 554-P	Suspd.		110.00	150-200
1990	Chapel Display 971-D	Suspd.		95.00	125
1986	Festival of Lights 507-P	Suspd.		85.00	150-300
1985	Flower Boy 502-P	Suspd.		85.00	125-200
1985	Flower Girl 501-P	Suspd.		85.00	125-200
1986	Little Madonna 552-P	Suspd.		93.00	175-225
1989	Merry Little Indian 508-P (new style)	Suspd.		110.00	150-200
1987	Merry Little Indian 508-P (old style)	Closed		95.00	300
1991	My Beautiful Rocking Horse 555-P	Suspd.		110.00	165-200
1985	My First Horse 503-P	Suspd.		85.00	145-165
1986	Pima Drummer Boy 506-P	Suspd.		85.00	200-300
1985	Sunflower Boy 551- P	Suspd.		93.00	125-165
1985	White Dove 504-P	Suspd.		80.00	125-150
1985	Wondering 505-P	Suspd.		93.00	125-175

Band Creations, Inc.

America's Covered Bridges - Band Creations

1995	Billie Creek, Parke County, IN	Open		29.95	30
1995	Bridge at the Green, Bennington County, VT	Open		29.95	30
1995	Bunker Hill, Catawba County, NC	Open		29.95	30
1995	Burfordville, Cape Giradeai County, MO	Open		39.95	40
1995	Cedar Creek, Ozaukee County, WI	Open		29.95	30
1995	Chiselville, Bennington County, VT	Open		29.95	30
1995	Elder's Mill, Oconee County, GA	Open		29.95	30
1995	Elizabethton, Carter County, TN	Open		29.95	30
1995	Fallasburg, Kent County, MI	Open		29.95	30
1995	Gilliland, Etowah County, AL	Open		29.95	30
1995	Humpback, Allegheny County, VA	Open		29.95	30
1995	Knox, Chester County, PA	Open		29.95	30
1995	Narrows, Parke County, IN	Open		29.95	30
1995	Old Blenheim, Schoharie County, NY	Open		39.95	40
1995	Philippi, Barbour County, WV	Open		39.95	40
1995	Roberts, Preble County, OH	Open		29.95	30
1995	Robyville, Penobscot County, ME	Open		29.95	30
1995	Roseman, Madison County, IA	Open		29.95	30
1995	Shimenak, Linn County, OR	Open		29.95	30
1995	Thompson Mill, Shelly County, IL	Open		29.95	30
1995	Wawona, Mariposa County, CA	Open		29.95	30
1995	Zumbrota, Goodhue County, MN	Open		29.95	30

Best Friends Angel Pins - Richards/Penfield

1995	Daughter	Open		5.00	5
1995	Friend	Open		5.00	5
1995	Grandmother	Open		5.00	5
1995	Mother	Open		5.00	5
1995	Nurse	Open		5.00	5
1995	Sister	Open		5.00	5
1995	Teacher	Open		5.00	5
1995	Teammate	Open		5.00	5

Best Friends-Angel Wishes - Richards/Penfield

1994	Anniversary	Open		12.00	12
1994	Best Wishes	Open		12.00	12
1994	Bride and Groom	Open		12.00	12
1994	Congratulations	Open		12.00	12
1994	Create A Wish	Open		12.00	12
1994	Get Well	Open		12.00	12
1994	Good Luck	Open		12.00	12
1994	Happy Birthday	Open		12.00	12
1994	Inspirational	Open		12.00	12
1994	New Baby	Open		12.00	12

Best Friends-Angels Of The Month - Richards/Penfield

1993	January	Open		10.00	10
1993	February	Open		10.00	10
1993	March	Open		10.00	10
1993	April	Open		10.00	10
1993	May	Open		10.00	10
1993	June	Open		10.00	10
1993	July	Open		10.00	10
1993	August	Open		10.00	10
1993	September	Open		10.00	10
1993	October	Open		10.00	10

YEAR ISSUE		EDITION LIMIT	YEAR RETD.	ISSUE PRICE	QUOTE U.S.$
1993	November	Open		10.00	10
1993	December	Open		10.00	10

Best Friends-First Friends Begin At Childhood - Richards/Penfield

YEAR ISSUE		EDITION LIMIT	YEAR RETD.	ISSUE PRICE	QUOTE U.S.$
1993	Castles In The Sand (4 pc set)	Open		16.00	16
1993	Checking It Twice (2 pc set)	Open		15.00	15
1993	Dad's Best Pal	Open		15.00	15
1993	Feathered Friends	Open		13.00	13
1993	Fishing Friends	Open		18.00	18
1993	Grandma's Favorite	Open		15.00	15
1993	My "Beary" Best Friend	Open		12.00	12
1993	My Best Friend (2 pc set)	Open		24.00	24
1993	Oh So Pretty	Open		14.00	14
1993	Purr-Fit Friends	Open		12.00	12
1993	Quiet Time	Open		15.00	15
1993	Rainbow Of Friends	Open		24.00	24
1993	Santa's First Visit	Open		15.00	15
1993	Santa's Surprise	Open		14.00	14
1993	Sharing Is Caring	Open		12.00	12
1993	A Wagon Full Of Fun (2 pc set)	Open		15.00	15

Best Friends-Noah's Ark - Richards/Penfield

YEAR ISSUE		EDITION LIMIT	YEAR RETD.	ISSUE PRICE	QUOTE U.S.$
1995	Animals (set of 10)	Open		20.00	20
1995	Noah's Ark & Raft	Open		42.00	42

Best Friends-O Joyful Night Nativity - Richards/Penfield

YEAR ISSUE		EDITION LIMIT	YEAR RETD.	ISSUE PRICE	QUOTE U.S.$
1994	3 Kings (set/3)	Open		24.00	24
1994	Angel on Stable (wall)	Open		16.00	16
1994	Camel and Donkey (set/2)	Open		8.00	8
1995	Camel Standing	Open		6.00	6
1994	Holy Family (Joseph, Mary & Jesus)	Open		16.00	16
1994	Shepard Boy	Open		8.00	8
1995	Shepherd with Sheep (set/7)	Open		8.00	8

Best Friends-RiverSong - Richards/Penfield

YEAR ISSUE		EDITION LIMIT	YEAR RETD.	ISSUE PRICE	QUOTE U.S.$
1994	3 Assorted Carolers	Open		22.00	22
1995	Brick House	Open		19.95	20
1993	Carolers Set UF14 set/5 (3 carolers, 1 lamp post, 1 dog)	Open		30.00	30
1995	Church	Open		19.95	20
1995	Double Angels	Open		8.00	8
1995	Gingerbread House	Open		19.95	20
1995	Skaters Sitting (set/2)	Open		12.00	12
1995	Skaters Standing (set/2)	Open		12.00	12
1995	Snowball Fight (set/3)	Open		15.00	15
1995	Snowmen (set/3)	Open		12.95	13
1995	Stucco House	Open		19.95	20
1995	Wood House	Open		19.95	20

Best Friends-Winter Wonderland - Richards/Penfield

YEAR ISSUE		EDITION LIMIT	YEAR RETD.	ISSUE PRICE	QUOTE U.S.$
1994	3 Assorted White Trees & 3 presents	Open		18.00	18
1994	Accessories; rabbits, teddies, presents (set/3)	Open		4.00	4
1994	Mr. Santa	Open		9.00	9
1994	Mrs. Santa	Open		9.00	9
1994	Reindeer (1 standing, 1 sitting) (set/2)	Open		10.00	10

Bing & Grondahl

Centennial Anniversary Commemoratives - F.A. Hallin

YEAR ISSUE		EDITION LIMIT	YEAR RETD.	ISSUE PRICE	QUOTE U.S.$
1995	Centennial Vase: Behind the Frozen Window	1,250	1995	295.00	295

Boehm Studios

Animal Sculptures - Boehm

YEAR ISSUE		EDITION LIMIT	YEAR RETD.	ISSUE PRICE	QUOTE U.S.$
1969	Adios 400-05	130		1500.00	1900
1977	African Elephant 5006	50		9500.00	14630
1976	American Mustangs 5005	75		3700.00	5665
1981	Appaloosa Horse 40193	75		975.00	1070
1980	Arabian Oryx, pair 50015	60		3800.00	4135
1983	Arabian Stallion (Prancing) 55007	200		1500.00	1565
1983	Arabian Stallion (Rearing) 55006	200		1500.00	1565
1980	Asian Lion 50017	100		1500.00	1645
1979	Bengel Tiger 500-13	12		25000.00	26540
1978	Black Rhinoceros 500-11	50		9500.00	9920
1971	Bobcats 4001	200		1600.00	1990
1982	Buffalo 50022	100		1625.00	1625
1978	Camel & Calf 5009	50		3500.00	3700
1980	Cheetah 50016	100		2700.00	3000
1985	Elephant (white bisque) 200-44B	200		495.00	575
1979	Fallow Deer 500-12	30		7500.00	7500
1971	Foxes 4003	200		1800.00	2360
1975	Giant Panda 5003	100		3800.00	6890
1978	Gorilla 5008	50		3800.00	4550
1982	Greater Kudu 50023	75		7500.00	7500
1952	Hunter 203	250		600.00	1400
1979	Hunter Chase 55001	20		4000.00	4085
1981	Jaguar 50020	100		2900.00	3310
1973	Nyala Antelope 5001	100		4700.00	6560
1976	Otter 5004	75		1100.00	1505
1981	Polar Bear with Cubs 40188	65		1800.00	1875
1957	Polo Player 206	100		850.00	4610
1982	Polo Player on Pinto 55005	50		3500.00	3500
1975	Puma 5002	50		5700.00	6560
1971	Raccoons 4002	200		1600.00	2105
1972	Red Squirrels 4004	100		2600.00	2770
1978	Snow Leopard 5007	75		3500.00	4670
1978	Thoroughbred with Jockey 400-85	25		2600.00	2785
1984	White-tailed Buck 50026	200		1375.00	1660
1979	Young & Free Fawns 50014	160		1875.00	2055

Bird Sculptures - Boehm

YEAR ISSUE		EDITION LIMIT	YEAR RETD.	ISSUE PRICE	QUOTE U.S.$
1980	American Avocet 40134	300		1400.00	1655
1981	American Bald Eagle 40185	655		1200.00	1330
1982	American Eagle (Commemorative) 40215	250		950.00	1150
1982	American Eagle (Symbol of Freedom) 40200	35		16500.00	18560
1957	American Eagle, large 428A	31		225.00	11200
1957	American Eagle, small 428B	76		225.00	9200
1980	American Redstart 40138	225		850.00	1090
1958	American Redstarts 447	500		350.00	2010
1980	American Wild Turkey (life-size) 40115	25		15000.00	16940
1980	American Wild Turkey 40154	75		1800.00	2020
1983	Anna's Hummingbird 10048	300		1100.00	1940
1980	Arctic Tern 40135	350		1400.00	2060
1979	Avocet 100-27	175		1200.00	1345
1972	Barn Owl 1005	350		3600.00	5400
1972	Black Grouse 1006	175		2800.00	3100
1982	Black-eared Bushtit (female) 10038	100		975.00	1045
1982	Black-eared Bushtit (male) 10039	100		975.00	1045
1969	Black-headed Grosbeak 400-03	675		1250.00	1535
1956	Black-tailed Bantams, pair 423	57		350.00	4800
1976	Black-throated Blue Warbler 400-60	200		900.00	1165
1958	Black-throated Blue Warbler 441	500		400.00	1780
1973	Blackbirds, pair 100-13	75		5400.00	6470
1984	Blackburnian Warbler 40253	125		925.00	965
1967	Blue Grosbeak 489	750		1050.00	1530
1982	Blue Jay (with Morning Glories) 40218	300		975.00	1190
1981	Blue Jay (with Wild Raspberries) 40190	350		1950.00	2405
1962	Blue Jays, pair 466	250		2000.00	12300
1973	Blue Tits 1008	300		3000.00	3250
1982	Blue-throated Hummingbird 10040	300		1100.00	1440
1953	Bob White Quail, pair 407	750		400.00	2500
1964	Bobolink 475	500		550.00	1520
1981	Boreal Owl 40172	200		1750.00	1875
1972	Brown Pelican 400-22	100		10500.00	14400
1980	Brown Pelican 40161	90		2800.00	2860
1973	Brown Thrasher 400-26	260		1850.00	1930
1972	Cactus Wren 400-17	225		3000.00	3410
1957	California Quail, pair 433	500		400.00	2730
1979	Calliope Hummingbird 40104	200		900.00	1115
1987	Calliope Hummingbird 40319	500		575.00	595
1978	Canada Geese, pair 400-71	100		4200.00	4200
1977	Cape May Warbler 400-45	400		825.00	990
1977	Cardinals 400-53	200		3500.00	4095
1955	Cardinals, pair 415	500		550.00	3650
1957	Carolina Wrens 422	100		750.00	5400
1983	Catbird 40246	111		1250.00	1250
1965	Catbird 483	500		900.00	2080
1980	Cedar Waxwing 40117	325		950.00	1040
1956	Cedar Waxwings, pair 418	100		600.00	7835
1957	Cerulean Warblers 424	100		800.00	4935
1974	Chaffinch 100-20	125		2000.00	2525
1976	Chickadees 400-61	400		1450.00	1550
1968	Common Tern 497	500		1400.00	6040
1985	Condor 10057	2		75000.00	87710
1979	Costa's Hummingbird 40103	200		1050.00	1200
1967	Crested Flycatcher 488	500		1650.00	3005
1974	Crested Tit 100-18	400		1150.00	1310
1980	Crimson Topaz Hummingbird 40113	310		1400.00	1640
1983	Dove of Peace 40236	709		750.00	1480
1983	Doves with Cherry Blossoms, pair 10049	150		7500.00	10600
1979	Downy Woodpecker 40116	300		950.00	1000
1957	Downy Woodpeckers 427	500		450.00	1760
1976	Eagle of Freedom I 400-50	15		35000.00	51375
1976	Eagle of Freedom II 400-70	200		7200.00	7370
1977	Eastern Bluebird 400-51	300		2300.00	2625
1959	Eastern Bluebirds, pair 451	100		1800.00	12210
1975	Eastern Kingbird 400-42	100		3500.00	4275
1983	Egret (National Audubon Society) 40221	1,029		1200.00	1580
1975	European Goldfinch 100-22	250		1150.00	1400
1973	Everglades Kites 400-24	50		5800.00	7340
1987	Flamingo w/ Young (National Audubon Society) 40316	225		1500.00	1525
1977	Fledgling Brown Thrashers 400-72A	400		500.00	680
1967	Fledgling Canada Warbler 491	750		550.00	2205
1965	Fledgling Great Horned Owl 479	750		350.00	1590
1971	Flicker 400-16	250		2400.00	2770
1983	Forster's Tern (Cresting) 40224	300		1850.00	2080
1983	Forster's Tern (on the Wing) 40223	300		1850.00	2080
1986	Gannet 40287	30		4300.00	4300
1972	Goldcrest 1004	500		650.00	1210
1983	Golden Eagle 10046	25		32000.00	36085
1954	Golden Pheasant, bisque 414B	7		200.00	11375
1954	Golden Pheasant, decorated 414A	7		350.00	19235
1956	Golden-crowned Kinglets 419	500		400.00	2320
1983	Goldfinch 40245	136		1200.00	1200
1961	Goldfinches 457	500		400.00	1830
1982	Great White Egret 40214	50		11500.00	15055
1982	Green Jays, pair 40198	65		3900.00	3900
1966	Green Jays, pair 486	400		1850.00	4120
1973	Green Woodpeckers 100-15	50		4200.00	4890
1979	Grey Wagtail 100-26	150		1050.00	1385
1974	Hooded Warbler 400-30	100		2400.00	3020
1973	Horned Larks 400-25	200		3800.00	4435
1964	Ivory-billed Woodpeckers 474	4		N/A	N/A
1968	Kestrels, pair 492	460		2300.00	3160
1982	Killdeer 40213	125		1075.00	1090
1964	Killdeer, pair 473	300		1750.00	5160
1976	Kingfishers 100-24	200		1900.00	2205
1980	Kirtland's Warble 40169	130		750.00	890
1973	Lapwing 100-14	100		2600.00	3000
1974	Lark Sparrow 400-35	150		2100.00	2340
1973	Lazuli Buntings 400-23	250		1800.00	2455
1981	Least Sandpipers 40136	350		2100.00	2540
1979	Least Tern 40102	350		1275.00	3045
1962	Lesser Prairie Chickens, pair 464	300		1200.00	2390
1971	Little Owl 1002	350		700.00	1390
1973	Long Tail Tits 100-11	200		2600.00	3000
1984	Long-eared Owl 10052	12		6000.00	6260
1984	Magnolia Warbler 40258	246		1100.00	1100
1952	Mallards, pair 406	500		650.00	1745
1957	Meadowlark 435	750		350.00	3180
1963	Mearn's Quail, pair 467	350		950.00	3635
1968	Mergansers, pair 496	440		2200.00	2985
1981	Mockingbird's Nest with Bluebonnet 10033	55		1300.00	1365
1978	Mockingbirds 400-52	350		2200.00	3045
1961	Mockingbirds, pair 459	500		650.00	3970
1963	Mountain Bluebirds 470	300		1900.00	5480
1981	Mourning Dove 40189	300		2200.00	2325
1958	Mourning Doves 443	500		550.00	1490
1971	Mute Swans, life-size, pair 400-14A	3		N/A	N/A
1982	Mute Swans, pair 40219	115		5800.00	6350
1971	Mute Swans, small size, pair 400-14B	400		4000.00	7820
1974	Myrtle Warblers 400-28	210		1850.00	2105
1958	Nonpareil Buntings 446	750		250.00	1165
1981	Northern Oriole 40194	100		1750.00	1900
1967	Northern Water Thrush 490	500		800.00	1420
1971	Nuthatch 1001	350		650.00	1130
1970	Orchard Orioles 400-11	550		1750.00	2305
1981	Osprey 10031	25		17000.00	21070
1981	Osprey 10037	100		4350.00	4710
1970	Oven-bird 400-04	450		1400.00	1790
1985	Parula Warblers 40270	100		2450.00	2465
1965	Parula Warblers 484	400		1500.00	3370
1975	Pekin Robins 400-37	100		7000.00	9680
1984	Pelican 40259	93		1200.00	1235
1973	Peregrine Falcon 100-12	350		4400.00	5470
1981	Peregrine Falcon with Young 40171	105		1850.00	2020
1980	Pheasant 40133	100		2100.00	2175
1984	Pileated Woodpeckers 40250	50		2900.00	2925
1979	Prince Rudolph's Blue Bird of Paradise 40101	10		35000.00	37200
1962	Ptarmigans, pair 463	350		800.00	3465
1974	Purple Martins 400-32	50		6700.00	9150
1979	Racquet-tail Hummingbird 40105	310		1500.00	1965
1985	Racquet-tailed Hummingbird 10053	350		2100.00	2500
1975	Red-billed Blue Magpie 400-44	100		4600.00	6230
1979	Red-breasted Nuthatch 40118	200		800.00	925
1957	Red-winged Blackbirds, pair 426	100		700.00	5590
1954	Ringed-necked Pheasants, pair 409	500		650.00	1810
1976	Rivoli's Hummingbird 100-23	350		950.00	1535
1982	Roadrunner 40199	150		2100.00	2325
1968	Roadrunner 493	500		2600.00	3680
1964	Robin (Daffodils) 472	500		600.00	5650
1977	Robin (Nest) 400-65	350		1650.00	2080
1981	Robin's Nest with Wild Rose 10030	90		1300.00	1380
1981	Rose-breasted Grosbeak 10032	165		1850.00	1880
1983	Royal Terns 10047	75		4300.00	4845
1974	Ruby-throated Hummingbird 100-21	200		1900.00	2825
1977	Ruffed Grouse, pair 400-65	100		4400.00	4485
1960	Ruffed Grouse, pair 456	250		950.00	5080
1966	Rufous Hummingbirds 487	500		850.00	2360
1986	Sandhill Crane 40286 (National Audubon Society)	205		1650.00	1665
1977	Scarlet Tanager 400-41	4		1800.00	4275
1985	Scarlet Tanager 40267	125		2100.00	2125
1977	Scissor-tailed Flycatcher 400-48	100		3200.00	3650
1979	Scops Owl 40114	300		975.00	1415
1973	Screech Owl 100-10	500		850.00	1495
1980	Screech Owl 40132	350		2100.00	3125
1978	Siskens 100-25	250		2100.00	2405
1970	Slate-colored Junco 400-12	500		1600.00	2240
1972	Snow Buntings 400-21	350		2400.00	2700
1985	Soaring Eagle (bisque) 40276B	304		950.00	960
1985	Soaring Eagle (gilded) 40276G	35		5000.00	5290
1956	Song Sparrows, pair 421	50		2000.00	38450
1974	Song Thrushes 100-16	100		2800.00	3590
1974	Stonechats 100-17	150		2200.00	2560
1961	Sugarbirds 460	100		2500.00	14910
1974	Swallows 100-19	125		3400.00	4320
1983	Towhee 40244	75		975.00	1045
1963	Towhee 471	500		350.00	2430

YEAR ISSUE		EDITION LIMIT	YEAR RETD.	ISSUE PRICE	QUOTE U.S.$
1972	Tree Creepers 1007	200		3200.00	3200
1985	Trumpeter Swan 40266 (National Audubon Society)	500		1500.00	1625
1965	Tufted Titmice 482	500		600.00	2040
1965	Varied Buntings 481	300		2200.00	4935
1974	Varied Thrush 400-29	300		2500.00	3115
1969	Verdins 400-02	575		1150.00	1565
1969	Western Bluebirds 400-01	300		5500.00	7020
1971	Western Meadowlark 400-15	350		1425.00	1735
1984	Whooping Crane 40254 (National Audubon Society)	647		1800.00	2025
1971	Winter Robin 1003	225		1150.00	1420
1981	Wood Ducks 40192	90		3400.00	3560
1951	Wood Thrush 400	2		375.00	N/A
1966	Wood Thrushes, pair 485	400		4200.00	8285
1954	Woodcock 413	500		300.00	2060
1982	Wren 10036	50		1700.00	1950
1980	Yellow Warbler 40137	200		950.00	1070
1972	Yellow-bellied Sapsucker 400-18	250		2700.00	3200
1974	Yellow-billed Cuckoo 400-31	150		2800.00	3055
1974	Yellow-headed Blackbird 400-34	75		3200.00	3600
1982	Yellow-shafted Flicker 40220	175		1450.00	1500
1973	Yellowhammers 1009	350		3300.00	4180
1975	Young & Spirited 1976 400-49	1,121		950.00	1610
1969	Young American Eagle 498B	850		700.00	1520
1973	Young American Eagle, Inaugural 498A	100		1500.00	2125

Figurines - Boehm

1986	Amanda with Parasol 10269	27		750.00	750
1986	Aria 67003	100		875.00	875
1986	Aurora 67001	100		875.00	875
1977	Beverly Sills 7006	100		950.00	1010
1986	Celeste 67002	100		875.00	875
1986	Devina 67000	100		875.00	875
1977	Jerome Hines 7007	12		825.00	1000
1986	Jo, Skating 10267	26		750.00	750
1986	Mattina 67004	100		875.00	875
1986	Meg with Basket 10268	26		625.00	625

Floral Sculptures - Boehm

1980	Begonia (pink) 30041	500		1250.00	1470
1980	Bluebonnets 30050	160		650.00	775
1979	Cactus Dahlia 300-33	300		800.00	970
1980	Caprice Iris (pink) 30049	235		650.00	725
1986	Cherries Jubilee Camellia 10388	250		625.00	625
1983	Chrysanthemum 30105	75		1250.00	1464
1985	Chrysanthemum Petal Camellia 30125	500		575.00	600
1972	Chrysanthemums 3005	350		1100.00	2030
1971	Daisies 3002	350		600.00	1045
1981	Daisy (white) 30056	75		975.00	995
1974	Debutante Camellia 3008	500		625.00	865
1973	Dogwood 3003	250		625.00	1035
1981	Dogwood 30045	510		875.00	955
1978	Double Clematis Centerpiece 300-27	150		1500.00	1780
1974	Double Peony 3007	275		575.00	995
1982	Double Peony 30078	110		1525.00	1640
1978	Edward Boehm Camellia 300-23	500		850.00	960
1975	Emmett Barnes Camellia 300-11	425		550.00	770
1985	Emmett Barnes Camellia 30120	275		625.00	630
1983	Empress Camellia (white) 30109	350		1025.00	1050
1974	Gentians 3009	350		425.00	730
1986	Globe of Light Peony 10372	125		475.00	505
1979	Grand Floral Centerpiece 300-35	15		7500.00	8755
1978	Helen Boehm Camellia 300-25	500		600.00	1110
1978	Helen Boehm Daylily 300-20	175		975.00	1140
1978	Helen Boehm Iris 300-19	175		975.00	1190
1979	Honeysuckle 300-34	200		900.00	1055
1986	Icarian Peony Centerpiece 30119	33		2800.00	2865
1981	Julia Hamiter Camellia 30061	300		675.00	745
1985	Kama Pua Hibiscus (orange) 30128	122		1600.00	1615
1984	Lady's Slipper Orchid 30112	76		575.00	575
1982	Magnolia Centerpiece 30101	15		6800.00	6985
1975	Magnolia Grandiflora 300-12	750		650.00	1525
1980	Magnolia Grandiflora 300-47	350		1650.00	1935
1982	Marigolds 30072	150		1275.00	1275
1984	Mary Heatley Begonia 30111	200		1100.00	1125
1980	Miss Indiana Iris (blue) 30049	235		650.00	710
1981	Nancy Reagan Camellia 30076	600		650.00	830
1980	Orchid (pink) 30036	175		725.00	780
1980	Orchid (yellow) 30037	130		725.00	780
1976	Orchid Cactus 300-15	100		650.00	1030
1984	Orchid Centerpiece (assorted) 30016	150		2600.00	2650
1984	Orchid Centerpiece (pink) 30115	350		2100.00	2490
1984	Orchid, Cymbidium 30114	160		575.00	625
1984	Orchid, Odontoglossum 30113	100		575.00	610
1980	Parrot Tulips 30042	300		850.00	1000
1985	Peonies (white) 30118	100		1650.00	1650
1978	Pink Lotus 300-21	175		975.00	1055
1981	Poinsettia 30055	200		1100.00	1230
1982	Pontiff Iris 30097	200		3000.00	3830
1981	Poppies 30058	325		1150.00	1265
1976	Queen of the Night Cactus 300-14	125		650.00	895
1985	Rhododendron (pink, yellow) 30122	125		1850.00	1895
1981	Rhododendron 30064	275		825.00	825
1978	Rhododendron Centerpiece 300-30	350		1150.00	1900
1981	Rose (yellow in shell) 30059	300		1100.00	1160
1986	Rose Centerpiece (yellow) 10370	25		5500.00	5625
1981	Rose Grace de Monaco 30071	350		1650.00	1940
1980	Rose, Alec's Red 30039	500		1050.00	1390
1981	Rose, Annenberg 30051	200		1450.00	1495
1978	Rose, Blue Moon 300-28	500		650.00	915
1985	Rose, Duet 30130	200		1525.00	1550
1980	Rose, Elizabeth of Glamis 30046	500		1650.00	1970
1981	Rose, Grandpa Dickson 30069	225		1200.00	1430
1985	Rose, Helen Boehm 30121	360		1475.00	1480
1982	Rose, Jehan Sadat 30080	200		875.00	1030
1981	Rose, Just Joey 30052	240		1050.00	1050
1981	Rose, Lady Helen 30070	325		1350.00	1520
1982	Rose, Mountbatten 30094	50		1525.00	1665
1981	Rose, Nancy Reagan 35027	1,200		800.00	920
1978	Rose, Pascali 300-24	500		950.00	1520
1982	Rose, Pascali 30093	250		1500.00	1710
1980	Rose, Peach 30038	350		1800.00	2070
1981	Rose, Prince Charles & Lady Diana Centerpiece 30065/6	100		4800.00	6330
1981	Rose, Prince Charles & Lady Diana Floral 30068	600		750.00	850
1982	Rose, Princess Margaret 30095	350		950.00	1170
1982	Rose, Queen Elizabeth 30091	350		1450.00	1790
1982	Rose, Royal Blessing 30099	500		1350.00	1715
1976	Rose, Supreme Peace 300-16	250		850.00	1745
1976	Rose, Supreme Yellow 300-17	250		850.00	1735
1978	Rose, Tropicana 300-22	500		475.00	1075
1981	Rose, Tropicana in Conch Shell 30060	150		1100.00	1100
1983	Rose, Yankee Doodle 30108	450		650.00	700
1982	Royal Bouquet 30092	125		1500.00	1690
1982	Scabious with Japonica 30090	50		1550.00	1575
1985	Seminole Hibiscus (pink) 30129	100		1800.00	1815
1978	Spanish Iris 300-29	500		600.00	760
1983	Spring Centerpiece 30110	100		1125.00	1200
1982	Stewart's Supreme Camellia 30084	350		675.00	710
1973	Streptocalyx Poeppigii 3006	50		3400.00	4485
1971	Swan Centerpiece 3001	135		1950.00	2930
1976	Swan Lake Camellia 300-13	750		825.00	1790
1971	Sweet Viburnum 3004	35		650.00	1395
1982	Tiger Lilies (orange) 30077	350		1225.00	1270
1980	Tree Peony 30043	325		1400.00	1485
1982	Tulips 30089	180		1050.00	1090
1974	Waterlily 300-10	350		400.00	725
1978	Watsonii Magnolia 300-31	250		575.00	680

Boyds Collection Ltd.

The Bearstone Collection ™ - G.M. Lowenthal

1994	Agatha & Shelly-'Scardy Cat' 2246	Open		16.25	17-70
1995	Amelia's Enterprise 'Carrot Juice' 2258	Open		16.25	17-45
1995	Angelica...'the Guardian' 2266	Open		17.95	18-50
1995	Angelica...the Guardian Angel Water Globe 2702	Open		37.50	38
1993	Arthur...with Red Scarf 2003-03	Retrd.	1994	10.50	45-100
1994	Bailey & Emily...'Forever Friends'	Open		34.00	34-90
1994	Bailey & Wixie 'To Have and To Hold' 2017	Open		15.75	16-100
1994	Bailey at the Beach 2020-09	12/95		15.75	16-95
1993	Bailey Bear with Suitcase (old version) 2000	Retrd.	1993	14.20	100-200
1993	Bailey Bear with Suitcase (revised version) 2000	Open		14.20	15-75
1994	Bailey's Birthday 2014	Open		15.95	16-90
1995	Bailey...'The Baker with Sweetie Pie' 2254	Open		12.50	13-60
1995	Bailey...'the Cheerleader' 2268	Open		15.95	16-35
1995	Bailey...'The Honeybear' 2260	Open		15.75	16-50
1993	Bailey...in the Orchard 2006	Open		14.20	15-110
1995	Baldwin...as the Child 2403	Open		14.95	15
1994	Bessie the Santa Cow 2239	Open		15.75	16-80
1993	Byron & Chedda w/Catmint 2010	Retrd.	1994	14.20	40-75
1994	Celeste...'The Angel Rabbit' 2230	Open		16.25	17-100
1994	Charlotte & Bebe...'The Gardeners' 2229	12/95		15.75	16-85
1993	Christian by the Sea 2012	Open		14.20	15-80
1995	Clara...'The Nurse' 2231	Open		16.25	17-175
1994	Clarence Angel Bear (rust) 2029-11	12/95		12.60	13-75
1995	Cookie Catberg...'Knittin' Kitten' 2250	Open		18.75	19-45
1994	Cookie the Santa Cat 2237	12/95		15.25	16-85
1995	Daphne and Eloise...'Women's Work' 2251	Open		18.00	18-45
1993	Daphne Hare & Maisey Ewe 2011	12/95		14.20	15-90
1994	Daphne...The Reader Hare 2226	Open		14.20	15-95
1994	Edmond & Bailey...'Gathering Holly' 2240	Open		24.25	25-90
1994	Elgin the Elf Bear 2236	Open		14.20	15-80
1994	Elliot & Snowbeary 2242	Open		15.25	16-75
1994	Elliot & The Tree 2241	Open		16.25	17-115
1995	Elliot & the Tree Water Globe 2704	Open		35.00	35
1995	Emma...'the Witchy Bear' 2269	Open		16.75	17
1993	Father Chrisbear and Son 2008	Retrd.	1993	15.00	200-250
1994	Grenville & Beatrice...'Best Friends' 2016	Open		26.25	27-150
1995	Grenville & Knute...Football Buddies 2255	Open		19.95	20-45
1993	Grenville & Neville...'The Sign' (prototype) 2099	Retrd.	1993	15.75	50-125
1993	Grenville & Neville...'The Sign' 2099	Open		15.75	16-60
1994	Grenville the Santabear 2030	Open		14.20	15-300
1994	Grenville the Santabear Musical Waterball 2700	Open		35.75	36-75
1994	Grenville...'The Graduate' 2233	Open		16.25	17-70
1995	Grenville...'The Storyteller' 2265	12/95		50.00	50
1993	Grenville...with Green Scarf 2003-04	Retrd.	1994	10.50	185-250
1993	Grenville...with Red Scarf 2003-08	12/95		10.50	11-125
1994	Homer on the Plate 2225	Open		15.75	16-80
1995	Hop-a-Long...'The Deputy' 2247	Open		14.00	14-45
1994	Juliette Angel Bear (ivory) 2029-10	12/95		12.60	13-75
1994	Justina & M. Harrison...'Sweetie Pie' 2015	Open		26.25	27-80
1994	Knute & The Gridiron 2245	Open		16.25	17-60
1994	Kringle & Bailey with List 2235	Open		14.20	15-60
1995	Lefty...'On the Mound' 2253	Open		15.00	15-60
1994	Manheim the 'Eco-Moose' 2243	Open		15.25	16-60
1994	Maynard the Santa Moose 2238	Open		15.25	16-65
1995	Miss Bruin & Bailey 'The Lesson' 2259	Open		18.45	19-55
1993	Moriarty-'The Bear in the Cat Suit' 2005	12/95		13.75	14-85
1995	Neville...as Joseph 2401	Open		14.95	15
1993	Neville...The 'Bedtime Bear' 2002	Open		14.20	15-85
1995	Otis...'Taxtime' 2262	Open		18.75	19-45
1995	Otis...'The Fisherman' 2249-06	Open		15.75	16-45
1994	Sebastian's Prayer 2227	Open		16.25	17-65
1994	Sherlock & Watson-In Disguise 2019	Open		15.75	16-75
1995	Simone & Bailey...'Helping Hands' 2267	Open		25.95	26
1993	Simone De Bearvoire and Her Mom 2001	Open		14.20	15-100
1995	The Stage...the School Pagent 2425	Open		34.95	35
1994	Ted & Teddy 2223	Open		15.75	16-65
1995	Theresa...as Mary 2402	Open		14.95	15
1995	Union Jack...'Love Letters' 2263	Open		18.95	19-40
1993	Victoria...'The Lady' 2004	Open		18.40	19-80
1994	Wilson at the Beach 2020-06	Open		15.75	16-75
1994	Wilson the "Perfesser" 2222	Open		16.25	17-75
1993	Wilson with Love Sonnets 2007	Open		12.60	13-300
1995	Wilson...'the Wonderful Wizard of Wuz' 2261	Open		15.95	16-35

The Folkstone Collection ™ - G.M. Lowenthal

1995	Abigail...Peaceable Kingdom 2829	Open		18.95	19
1994	Angel of Freedom 2820	Open		16.75	17
1994	Angel of Love 2821	Open		16.75	17
1994	Angel of Peace 2822	Open		16.75	17
1994	Beatrice-Birthday Angel 2825	Open		20.00	20
1995	Beatrice...the Giftgiver 2836	Open		17.95	18
1995	Boowinkle Vonhindenmoose...2831	Open		17.95	18
1994	Chilly & Son with Dove 2811	Open		17.75	18-25
1994	Elmer-Cow on Haystacks 2851	Open		19.00	19
1995	Ernest Hemmingmoose...the Hunter 2835	Open		17.95	18
1995	Esmeralda...the Wonderful Witch 2860	Open		17.95	18
1994	Florence-Kitchen Angel 2824	Open		20.00	20
1995	Icabod Mooselman...the Pilgrim 2833	Open		17.95	18
1994	Ida & Bessie-The Gardeners 2852	Open		19.00	19
1995	Jean Claude & Jacques...the Skiers 2815	Open		16.95	17
1994	Jill-Language of Love 2842	Open		19.00	19
1994	Jingle Moose 2830	Open		17.75	18
1994	Jingles & Son withWreath 2812	Open		17.75	18
1994	Lizzie Shopping Angel 2827	Open		20.00	20
1994	Minerva-Baseball Angel 2826	Open		20.00	20
1994	Myrtle-Believe 2840	Open		20.00	20
1995	Na-Nick of the North 2804	Open		17.95	18
1994	Nicholai with Tree 2800	Open		17.75	18-25
1994	Nicholas with Book 2802	Open		17.75	18
1994	Nick on Ice (1st ed. GCC) 3001	3,600	1995	49.95	50
1994	Nick on Ice 3001	Open		32.95	33
1994	Nikki with Candle 2801	Open		17.75	18-25
1995	Northbound Wille 2814	Open		16.95	17
1994	Oceana-Ocean Angel 2823	Open		16.75	17
1994	Peter-The Whopper 2841	Open		19.00	19
1995	Prudence Mooselmaid...the Pilgrim 2834	Open		17.95	18
1994	Rufus-Hoedown 2850	Open		19.00	19
1994	Santa's Challenge (1st ed. GCC) 3002	3,600	1995	49.95	50
1994	Santa's Challenge 3002	Open		32.95	33
1994	Santa's Flight Plan (1st ed. GCC) 3000	3,600	1995	49.95	50
1994	Santa's Flight Plan 3000	Open		32.95	33
1995	Seraphina with Jacob & Rachael...the Choir Angels 2828	Open		19.95	20
1995	Siegfried and Egon...the Sign 2899	Open		18.95	19
1995	Sliknick the Chimney Sweep 2803	Open		17.95	18
1994	Windy with Book 2810	*Open		17.75	18-25

Brandywine Collectibles

Accessories - M. Whiting

1992	Apple Tree/Tire Swing	Open		10.00	10
1991	Baggage Cart	Open		10.50	11
1990	Bandstand	Closed	1992	10.50	11

YEAR	ISSUE	EDITION LIMIT	YEAR RETD.	ISSUE PRICE	QUOTE U.S.$
1994	Elm Tree with Benches	Open		16.00	16
1988	Flag	Open		10.00	10
1990	Flower Cart	Open		13.00	13
1990	Gate & Arbor	Closed	1992	9.00	9
1990	Gooseneck Lamp	Open		7.50	8
1989	Horse & Carriage	Open		13.00	13
1994	Lamp with Barber Pole	Open		10.50	11
1988	Lampost, Wall & Fence	Open		11.00	11
1989	Mailbox, Tree & Fence	Open		10.00	10
1989	Pumpkin Wagon	Open		11.50	12
1991	Street Sign	Open		8.00	8
1987	Summer Tree with Fence	Open		7.00	7
1991	Town Clock	Open		7.50	8
1992	Tree with Birdhouse	Open		10.00	10
1989	Victorian Gas Light	Open		6.50	7
1990	Wishing Well	Open		10.00	10

Barnsville Collection - M. Whiting

YEAR	ISSUE	EDITION LIMIT	YEAR RETD.	ISSUE PRICE	QUOTE U.S.$
1991	B & O Station	Open		28.00	28
1992	Barnesville Church	Open		44.00	44
1991	Bradfield House	Open		32.00	32
1990	Candace Bruce House	Open		30.00	30
1990	Gay 90's Mansion	Open		32.00	32
1992	Plumtree Bed & Breakfast	Open		44.00	44
1990	Thompson House	Open		32.00	32
1990	Treat-Smith House	Open		32.00	32
1991	Whiteley House	Open		32.00	32

Country Lane - M. Whiting

YEAR	ISSUE	EDITION LIMIT	YEAR RETD.	ISSUE PRICE	QUOTE U.S.$
1995	Berry Farm	Open		30.00	30
1995	Country School	Open		30.00	30
1995	Dairy Farm	Open		30.00	30
1995	Farm House	Open		30.00	30
1995	The General Store	Open		30.00	30

Country Lane II - M. Whiting

YEAR	ISSUE	EDITION LIMIT	YEAR RETD.	ISSUE PRICE	QUOTE U.S.$
1995	Antiques & Crafts	Open		30.00	30
1995	Basketmaker	Open		30.00	30
1995	Country Church	Open		30.00	30
1995	Fishing Lodge	Open		30.00	30
1995	Herb Farm	Open		30.00	30
1995	Olde Mill	Open		30.00	30
1995	Spinners & Weavers	Open		30.00	30

Custom Collection - M. Whiting

YEAR	ISSUE	EDITION LIMIT	YEAR RETD.	ISSUE PRICE	QUOTE U.S.$
1988	Burgess Museum	Open		15.50	16
1992	Cumberland County Courthouse	Open		15.00	15
1990	Doylestown Public School	Open		32.00	32
1991	Jamestown Tower	Closed	1991	9.00	9
1990	Jared Coffin House	Open		32.00	32
1989	Lorain Lighthouse	Closed	1992	11.00	11
1992	Loudon County Courthouse	Open		15.00	15
1988	Princetown Monument	Closed	1989	9.70	10
1991	Smithfield VA. Courthouse	Closed	1992	12.00	12
1989	Yankee Candle Co.	Open		13.50	14

Hilton Village - M. Whiting

YEAR	ISSUE	EDITION LIMIT	YEAR RETD.	ISSUE PRICE	QUOTE U.S.$
1987	Dutch House	Closed	1991	8.50	9
1987	English House	Closed	1991	8.50	9
1987	Georgian House	Closed	1991	8.50	9
1987	Gwen's House	Closed	1991	8.50	9
1987	Hilton Firehouse	Closed	1991	8.50	9

Hometown I - M. Whiting

YEAR	ISSUE	EDITION LIMIT	YEAR RETD.	ISSUE PRICE	QUOTE U.S.$
1990	Barber Shop	Closed	1992	14.00	14
1990	General Store	Closed	1992	14.00	14
1990	School	Closed	1992	14.00	14
1990	Toy Store	Closed	1992	14.00	14

Hometown II - M. Whiting

YEAR	ISSUE	EDITION LIMIT	YEAR RETD.	ISSUE PRICE	QUOTE U.S.$
1991	Church	Closed	1993	14.00	14
1991	Dentist	Closed	1993	14.00	14
1991	Ice Cream Shop	Closed	1993	14.00	14
1991	Stitch-N-Sew	Closed	1993	14.00	14

Hometown III - M. Whiting

YEAR	ISSUE	EDITION LIMIT	YEAR RETD.	ISSUE PRICE	QUOTE U.S.$
1991	Basket Shop	Closed	1993	15.50	16
1991	Dairy	Closed	1993	15.50	16
1991	Firehouse	Closed	1993	15.50	16
1991	Library	Closed	1993	15.50	16

Hometown IV - M. Whiting

YEAR	ISSUE	EDITION LIMIT	YEAR RETD.	ISSUE PRICE	QUOTE U.S.$
1992	Bakery	Closed	1994	21.00	21
1992	Country Inn	Closed	1994	21.50	22
1992	Courtnhouse	Closed	1994	21.50	22
1992	Gas Station	Closed	1994	21.00	21

Hometown V - M. Whiting

YEAR	ISSUE	EDITION LIMIT	YEAR RETD.	ISSUE PRICE	QUOTE U.S.$
1992	Antiques Shop	Closed	1995	22.00	22
1992	Gift Shop	Closed	1995	22.00	22
1992	Pharmacy	Closed	1995	22.00	22
1992	Sporting Goods	Closed	1995	22.00	22
1992	Tea Room	Closed	1995	22.00	22

Hometown VI - M. Whiting

YEAR	ISSUE	EDITION LIMIT	YEAR RETD.	ISSUE PRICE	QUOTE U.S.$
1993	Church	Closed	1995	24.00	24
1993	Diner	Closed	1995	24.00	24
1993	General Store	Closed	1995	24.00	24
1993	School	Closed	1995	24.00	24
1993	Train Station	Closed	1995	24.00	24

Hometown VII - M. Whiting

YEAR	ISSUE	EDITION LIMIT	YEAR RETD.	ISSUE PRICE	QUOTE U.S.$
1993	Candy Shop	Open		24.00	24
1993	Dress Shop	Open		24.00	24
1993	Flower Shop	Open		24.00	24
1993	Pet Shop	Open		24.00	24
1993	Post Office	Open		24.00	24
1993	Quilt Shop	Open		24.00	24

Hometown VIII - M. Whiting

YEAR	ISSUE	EDITION LIMIT	YEAR RETD.	ISSUE PRICE	QUOTE U.S.$
1994	Barber Shop	Open		28.00	28
1994	Country Store	Open		28.00	28
1994	Fire Company	Open		28.00	28
1994	Professional Building	Open		28.00	28
1994	Sewing Shop	Open		26.00	26

Hometown IX - M. Whiting

YEAR	ISSUE	EDITION LIMIT	YEAR RETD.	ISSUE PRICE	QUOTE U.S.$
1994	Bed & Breakfast	Open		29.00	29
1994	Cafe/Deli	Open		29.00	29
1994	Hometown Bank	Open		29.00	29
1994	Hometown Gazette	Open		29.00	29
1994	Teddys & Toys	Open		29.00	29

Hometown X - M. Whiting

YEAR	ISSUE	EDITION LIMIT	YEAR RETD.	ISSUE PRICE	QUOTE U.S.$
1995	Brick Church	Open		29.00	29
1995	The Doll Shoppe	Open		29.00	29
1995	General Hospital	Open		29.00	29
1995	The Gift Box	Open		29.00	29
1995	Police Station	Open		29.00	29

Hometown XI - M. Whiting

YEAR	ISSUE	EDITION LIMIT	YEAR RETD.	ISSUE PRICE	QUOTE U.S.$
1995	Antiques	Open		29.00	29
1995	Church II	Open		29.00	29
1995	Grocer	Open		29.00	29
1995	Pharmacy	Open		29.00	29
1995	School II	Open		29.00	29

North Pole Collection - M. Whiting, unless otherwise noted

YEAR	ISSUE	EDITION LIMIT	YEAR RETD.	ISSUE PRICE	QUOTE U.S.$
1992	3 Winter Trees - D. Whiting	Open		10.50	11
1993	Candy Cane Factory	Open		24.00	24
1991	Claus House	Open		24.00	24
1993	Elf Club	Open		24.00	24
1992	Elves Workshop	Open		24.00	24
1991	Gingerbread House	Open		24.00	24
1994	Post Office	Open		25.00	25
1991	Reindeer Barn	Open		24.00	24
1992	Snowflake Lodge	Open		24.00	24
1992	Snowman with St. Sign	Open		11.50	12
1995	Stocking Shop	Open		25.00	25
1992	Sugarplum Bakery	Open		24.00	24
1993	Teddybear Factory	Open		24.00	24
1993	Town Christmas Tree	Open		20.00	20
1994	Town Hall	Open		25.00	25

Old Salem Collection - M. Whiting

YEAR	ISSUE	EDITION LIMIT	YEAR RETD.	ISSUE PRICE	QUOTE U.S.$
1987	Boys School	Open		18.50	19
1987	First House	Open		12.80	13
1987	Home Moravian Church	Open		18.50	19
1987	Miksch Tobacco Shop	Closed	1993	12.00	12
1987	Salem Tavern	Open		20.50	21
1987	Schultz Shoemaker	Open		10.50	11
1987	Vogler House	Open		20.50	21
1987	Winkler Bakery	Open		20.50	21

Patriots Collection - M. Whiting

YEAR	ISSUE	EDITION LIMIT	YEAR RETD.	ISSUE PRICE	QUOTE U.S.$
1992	Betsy Ross House	Open		17.50	18
1992	Washingtons Headquarters	Open		24.00	24

Seymour Collection - M. Whiting

YEAR	ISSUE	EDITION LIMIT	YEAR RETD.	ISSUE PRICE	QUOTE U.S.$
1991	Anderson House	Open		20.00	20
1991	Blish Home	Open		20.00	20
1992	Majestic Theater	Open		22.00	22
1991	Seymour Church	Open		19.00	19
1991	Seymour Library	Open		20.00	20

Treasured Times - M. Whiting

YEAR	ISSUE	EDITION LIMIT	YEAR RETD.	ISSUE PRICE	QUOTE U.S.$
1994	Birthday House	750		32.00	32
1994	Halloween House	750		32.00	32
1994	Mother's Day House	750		32.00	32
1994	New Baby Boy House	750		32.00	32
1994	New Baby Girl House	750		32.00	32
1994	Valentine House	750		32.00	32

Victorian Collection - M. Whiting

YEAR	ISSUE	EDITION LIMIT	YEAR RETD.	ISSUE PRICE	QUOTE U.S.$
1989	Broadway House	Closed	1994	22.00	22
1989	Elm House	Closed	1994	25.00	25
1989	Fairplay Church	Closed	1994	19.50	20
1989	Hearts Ease Cottage	Closed	1994	15.30	16
1989	Old Star Hook & Ladder	Closed	1994	23.00	23
1989	Peachtree House	Closed	1994	22.50	23
1989	Seabreeze Cottage	Closed	1994	15.30	16
1989	Serenity Cottage	Closed	1994	15.30	16
1989	Skippack School	Closed	1994	22.50	23

Williamsburg Collection -M. Whiting

YEAR	ISSUE	EDITION LIMIT	YEAR RETD.	ISSUE PRICE	QUOTE U.S.$
1993	Campbell's Tavern	Open		28.00	28
1988	Colonial Capitol	Open		43.50	44
1988	Court House of 1770	Open		26.50	27
1988	Governor's Palace	Open		37.50	38
1993	Kings Arms Tavern	Open		25.00	25
1988	The Magazine	Open		23.50	24
1988	Wythe House	Open		25.00	25

Yorktown Collection - M. Whiting

YEAR	ISSUE	EDITION LIMIT	YEAR RETD.	ISSUE PRICE	QUOTE U.S.$
1987	Custom House	Open		17.50	18
1993	Digges House	Open		22.00	22
1987	Grace Church	Open		19.00	19
1987	Medical Shop	Open		13.00	13
1987	Moore House	Open		22.00	22
1987	Nelson House	Open		22.00	22
1987	Pate House	Open		19.00	19
1987	Swan Tavern	Open		22.00	22

Byers' Choice Ltd.

Accessories - J. Byers

YEAR	ISSUE	EDITION LIMIT	YEAR RETD.	ISSUE PRICE	QUOTE U.S.$
1995	Cat in Hat	Open		10.00	10
1995	Dog with Sausages	Open		18.00	18

Carolers - J. Byers

YEAR	ISSUE	EDITION LIMIT	YEAR RETD.	ISSUE PRICE	QUOTE U.S.$
1988	Children with Skates	Open		40.00	49
1988	Singing Cats	Open		13.50	16
1986	Singing Dogs	Open		13.00	16
1976	Traditional Adult (1976-80)	Closed	1980	N/A	300-500
1981	Traditional Adult (1981-current)	Open		45.00	45-300
XX	Traditional Adult (undated)	Closed	N/A	N/A	400-700
1978	Traditional Colonial Lady (w/ hands)	Closed	1978	N/A	1500
1986	Traditional Grandparents	Open		35.00	45
1982	Victorian Adult (1st Version)	Closed	1982	32.00	300-400
1982	Victorian Adult (2nd Version/dressed alike)	Closed	1983	46.00	300-400
1983	Victorian Adult (assorted) (2nd Version)	Open		35.00	48
1982	Victorian Child (1st Version w/floppy hats)	Closed	1982	32.00	300-375
1983	Victorian Child (2nd Version/sailor suit)	Closed	1983	33.00	300-400
1983	Victorian Child (assorted)	Open		33.00	48
1988	Victorian Grand Parent	Open		40.00	48

Children of The World - J. Byers

YEAR	ISSUE	EDITION LIMIT	YEAR RETD.	ISSUE PRICE	QUOTE U.S.$
1993	Bavarian Boy	Closed	1993	50.00	175-275
1992	Dutch Boy	Closed	1992	50.00	175-300
1992	Dutch Girl	Closed	1992	50.00	175-300
1994	Irish Girl	Closed	1994	50.00	125-225

Cries Of London - J. Byers

YEAR	ISSUE	EDITION LIMIT	YEAR RETD.	ISSUE PRICE	QUOTE U.S.$
1991	Apple Lady (red stockings)	Closed	1991	80.00	850-1100
1991	Apple Lady (red/wh stockings)	Closed	1991	80.00	900-1200
1992	Baker	Closed	1992	62.00	125-200
1993	Chestnut Roaster	Closed	1993	64.00	173-325
1995	Dollmaker	Closed	1995	64.00	64
1994	Flower Vendor	Closed	1994	64.00	150-200
1995	Girl Holding Doll	Closed	1995	48.00	48

Dickens Series - J. Byers

YEAR	ISSUE	EDITION LIMIT	YEAR RETD.	ISSUE PRICE	QUOTE U.S.$
1990	Bob Cratchit & Tiny Tim (1st Edition)	Closed	1990	84.00	200-250
1991	Bob Cratchit & Tiny Tim (2nd Edition)	Open		86.00	89
1991	Happy Scrooge (1st Edition)	Closed	1991	50.00	200-275
1992	Happy Scrooge (2nd Edition)	Closed	1992	50.00	225
1986	Marley's Ghost (1st Edition)	Closed	1986	40.00	300-450
1987	Marley's Ghost (2nd Edition)	Closed	1992	42.00	200-325
1985	Mr. Fezziwig (1st Edition)	Closed	1985	43.00	450-750
1986	Mr. Fezziwig (2nd Edition)	Closed	1990	43.00	350-600
1984	Mrs. Cratchit (1st Edition)	Closed	1984	38.00	600-1000
1985	Mrs. Cratchit (2nd Edition)	Open		39.00	49
1985	Mrs. Fezziwig (1st Edition)	Closed	1985	43.00	600-750
1986	Mrs. Fezziwig (2nd Edition)	Closed	1990	43.00	350-600
1983	Scrooge (1st Edition)	Closed	1983	36.00	1200-1500
1984	Scrooge (2nd Edition)	Open		38.00	49
1989	Spirit of Christmas Future (1st Edition)	Closed	1989	46.00	220-350
1990	Spirit of Christmas Future (2nd Edition)	Closed	1991	48.00	250-375
1987	Spirit of Christmas Past (1st Edition)	Closed	1987	42.00	300-400
1988	Spirit of Christmas Past (2nd Edition)	Closed	1991	46.00	275-350
1988	Spirit of Christmas Present (1st Edition)	Closed	1988	44.00	300-400
1989	Spirit of Christmas Present (2nd Edition)	Closed	1991	48.00	230-350

Display Figures - J. Byers

YEAR	ISSUE	EDITION LIMIT	YEAR RETD.	ISSUE PRICE	QUOTE U.S.$
1986	Display Adults	Closed	1987	170.00	500
1983	Display Carolers	Closed	1983	200.00	500
1985	Display Children (Boy & Girl)	Closed	1987	140.00	1200-1400
1982	Display Drummer Boy-1st	Closed	1983	96.00	800-1200
1985	Display Drummer Boy-2nd	Closed	1986	160.00	400-600
1981	Display Lady	Closed	1981	N/A	2000
1981	Display Man	Closed	1981	N/A	2000
1985	Display Old World Santa	Closed	1985	260.00	500
1982	Display Santa	Closed	1983	96.00	600
1990	Display Santa-bayberry	Closed	1990	250.00	400-475
1990	Display Santa-red	Closed	1990	250.00	400-475
1984	Display Working Santa	Closed	1985	260.00	500
1987	Mechanical Boy with Drum	Closed	1987	N/A	500-600
1987	Mechanical Girl with Bell	Closed	1987	N/A	500-600

Musicians - J. Byers

YEAR	ISSUE	EDITION LIMIT	YEAR RETD.	ISSUE PRICE	QUOTE U.S.$
1991	Boy with Mandolin	Closed	1991	48.00	175-300

YEAR ISSUE		EDITION LIMIT	YEAR RETD.	ISSUE PRICE	QUOTE U.S.$
1985	Horn Player	Closed	1985	38.00	700-800
1985	Horn Player, chubby face	Closed	1985	37.00	900-1200
1991	Musician with Accordian	Closed	1991	48.00	200-275
1989	Musician with Clarinet	Closed	1989	44.00	400-600
1992	Musician with French Horn	Closed	1992	52.00	100-225
1990	Musician with Mandolin	Closed	1990	46.00	200-275
1986	Victorian Girl with Violin	Closed	1986	39.00	300-400
1983	Violin Player Man (1st Version)	Closed	1983	38.00	1500
1984	Violin Player Man (2nd Version)	Closed	1984	38.00	1500

Nativity - J. Byers

1989	Angel Gabriel	Closed	1991	37.00	150-200
1987	Angel-Great Star (Blonde)	Closed	1991	40.00	220-290
1987	Angel-Great Star (Brunette)	Closed	1991	40.00	250
1987	Angel-Great Star (Red Head)	Closed	1991	40.00	175-275
1987	Black Angel	Closed	1987	36.00	225-285
1990	Holy Family with stable	Closed	1991	119.00	225-375
1989	King Balthasar	Closed	1991	40.00	100-150
1989	King Gaspar	Closed	1991	40.00	100-150
1989	King Melchior	Closed	1991	40.00	100-150
1988	Shepherds	Closed	1991	37.00	100-150

The Nutcracker - J. Byers

1994	Fritz (1st Edition)	Closed	1994	56.00	125-150
1995	Fritz (2nd Edition)	Open		57.00	57
1995	Louise Playing Piano (1st Edition)	Closed	1995	82.00	82
1993	Marie (1st Edition)	Closed	1993	52.00	150-200
1994	Marie (2nd Edition)	Open		53.00	54

Salvation Army Band - J. Byers

1995	Girl with War Cry	Open		55.00	55
1993	Man with Cornet	Open		54.00	56
1992	Woman with Kettle	Open		64.00	67
1992	Woman with Kettle (1st yr. issue)	Closed	1992	64.00	175
1993	Woman with Tambourine	Closed	1995	58.00	59

Santas - J. Byers

1991	Father Christmas	Closed	1992	48.00	135-185
1988	Knecht Ruprecht (Black Peter)	Closed	1989	38.00	150-200
1984	Mrs. Claus	Closed	1991	38.00	200-350
1992	Mrs. Claus (2nd Version)	Closed	1993	50.00	135-150
1986	Mrs. Claus on Rocker	Closed	1986	73.00	600-650
1995	Mrs. Claus' Needlework	Closed	1995	70.00	70
1994	Old Befana	Open		53.00	54
1978	Old World Santa	Closed	1986	33.00	375
1989	Russian Santa	Closed	1989	85.00	400-600
1988	Saint Nicholas	Closed	1992	44.00	150-225
1982	Santa in a Sleigh (1st Version)	Closed	1983	46.00	800
1984	Santa in Sleigh (2nd Version)	Closed	1985	70.00	600-800
1993	Skating Santa	Closed	1993	60.00	125
1987	Velvet Mrs. Claus	Open		44.00	53
1987	Velvet Mrs. Claus (1st yr. issue)	Closed	1987	44.00	115
1978	Velvet Santa	Closed	1993	Unkn.	300
1994	Velvet Santa with Stocking (2nd Version)	Open		47.00	51
1986	Victorian Santa	Closed	1989	39.00	250-300
1990	Weihnachtsmann (German Santa)	Closed	1990	56.00	150-225
1983	Working Santa (1st Version)	Closed	1991	38.00	175
1992	Working Santa (1st yr. issue)	Closed	1992	52.00	115
1992	Working Santa (2nd Version)	Open		52.00	55

Skaters - J. Byers

1991	Adult Skaters	Closed	1994	50.00	50-100
1991	Adult Skaters (1991 version)	Closed	1991	50.00	115-130
1993	Boy Skater on Log	Closed	1993	55.00	100-150
1992	Children Skaters	Open		50.00	52
1992	Children Skaters (1992 version)	Closed	1992	50.00	130
1993	Grandparent Skaters	Closed	1993	50.00	60
1993	Grandparent Skaters (1993 version)	Closed	1993	50.00	145
1995	Man Holding Skates	Open		52.00	52
1995	Woman Holding Skates	Open		52.00	52

Special Characters - J. Byers

1979	Adult Male "Icabod"	Closed	1979	32.00	2400-2600
1988	Angel Tree Top	100	1988	Unkn.	275-375
1994	Baby in Basket	Closed	1994	7.50	10
1989	Black Boy w/skates	Closed	N/A	N/A	400-450
1989	Black Drummer Boy	Closed	N/A	N/A	500-600
1989	Black Girl w/skates	Closed	N/A	N/A	400-450
1983	Boy on Rocking Horse	300	1983	85.00	2500-2900
1987	Boy on Sled	Closed	1987	50.00	275-400
1991	Boy with Apple	Closed	1991	41.00	125-275
1994	Boy with Goose	Closed	1995	49.50	50
1995	Boy with Skis	Open		49.50	50
1991	Boy with Tree	Closed	1994	49.00	150
1995	Butcher	Closed	1995	54.00	54
1987	Caroler with Lamp	Closed	1987	40.00	175-200
1984	Chimney Sweep-Adult	Closed	1984	36.00	1200-1500
1991	Chimney Sweep-Child	Closed	1994	50.00	100-150
1982	Choir Children, boy and girl set	Closed	1986	32.00	400-600
1993	Choir Director,lady/music stand	Closed	1995	56.00	58
1982	Conductor	Closed	1992	32.00	120-150
1994	Constable	Open		53.00	54
1995	Couple in Sleigh	Closed	1995	110.00	110
1982	Drummer Boy	Closed	1992	34.00	150-175
1982	Easter Boy	Closed	1983	32.00	450-550
1982	Easter Girl	Closed	1983	32.00	450-550
1991	Girl with Apple	Closed	1991	41.00	150-250
1991	Girl with Apple/coin purse	Closed	1991	41.00	350-500
1989	Girl with Hoop	Closed	1990	44.00	145-160
1995	Girl with Skis	Open		49.50	50
1982	Icabod	Closed	1982	32.00	1150
1993	Lamplighter	Open		48.00	50
1993	Lamplighter (1st yr. issue)	Closed	1993	48.00	85-100
1982	Leprechauns	Closed	1982	34.00	1200-2000
1988	Mother Holding Baby	Closed	1993	40.00	100-250
1987	Mother's Day	225	1987	125.00	265-400
1988	Mother's Day (Daughter)	Closed	1988	125.00	450
1988	Mother's Day (Son)	Closed	1988	125.00	450-575
1989	Mother's Day (with Carriage)	3,000	1989	75.00	375-450
1994	Nanny	Open		66.00	67
1989	Newsboy with Bike	Closed	1992	78.00	175-250
1985	Pajama Children (painted flannel)	Closed	1989	35.00	250-375
1985	Pajama Children (red flannel)	Closed	1989	35.00	200-280
1990	Parson	Closed	1993	44.00	100-200
1990	Postman	Closed	1993	45.00	150-200
1994	Sandwich Board Man (red board)	Closed	1994	52.00	100-150
1994	Sandwich Board Man (white board)	Open		52.00	53
1993	School Kids	Closed	1994	48.00	75-125
1992	Schoolteacher	Closed	1994	48.00	100-150
1995	Shopper-Man	Open		56.00	56
1995	Shopper-Woman	Open		56.00	56
1981	Thanksgiving Lady (Clay Hands)	Closed	1981	Unkn.	2000
1981	Thanksgiving Man (Clay Hands)	Closed	1981	Unkn.	2000
1994	Treetop Angel	Open		50.00	50
1982	Valentine Boy	Closed	1983	32.00	450-550
1982	Valentine Girl	Closed	1983	32.00	450-550
1990	Victorian Girl On Rocking Horse (blonde)	Closed	1991	70.00	185-275
1990	Victorian Girl On Rocking Horse (brunette)	Closed	1991	70.00	185-275
1992	Victorian Mother with Toddler (Fall/Win-green)	Closed	1993	60.00	150-225
1993	Victorian Mother with Toddler (Spr/Sum-blue)	Closed	1993	61.00	150-225
1992	Victorian Mother with Toddler (Spr/Sum-white)	Closed	1993	60.00	150-225

Store Exclusives-Christmas Loft - J. Byers

1991	Russian Santa	40	1991	100.00	850

Store Exclusives-Country Christmas - J. Byers

1988	Toymaker	600	1988	59.00	800-975

Store Exclusives-Long's Jewelers - J. Byers

1981	Leprechaun (with bucket)	Closed	N/A	N/A	2500

Store Exclusives-Port-O-Call - J. Byers

1986	Cherub Angel-blue	Closed	1987	N/A	275-400
1986	Cherub Angel-cream	Closed	1987	N/A	400
1986	Cherub Angel-pink	Closed	1987	N/A	275-400
1987	Cherub Angel-rose	Closed	1987	N/A	275-400

Store Exclusives-Snow Goose - J. Byers

1988	Man with Goose	600	1988	60.00	300

Store Exclusives-Stacy's Gifts & Collectibles - J. Byers

1987	Santa in Rocking Chair with Boy	100	1987	130.00	1000-1500
1987	Santa in Rocking Chair with Girl	100	1987	130.00	1000-1500

Store Exclusives-Talbots - J. Byers

1994	Man w/Log Carrier	Closed	N/A	N/A	130-150
1990	Victorian Family of Four	Closed	N/A	N/A	375-450

Store Exclusives-Wayside Country Store Exclusives - J. Byers

1988	Colonial Lady s/n	600	1988	49.00	500-600
1986	Colonial Lamplighter s/n	600	1986	46.00	800-1000
1987	Colonial Watchman s/n	600	1987	49.00	600-750
1995	Sunday School Boy	300	1995	52.00	200
1995	Sunday School Girl	300	1995	52.00	200

Store Exclusives-Wooden Soldier - J. Byers

XX	Victorian Lamp Lighter	Closed	N/A	N/A	175-200

Store Exclusives-Woodstock Inn - J. Byers

1987	Skier Boy	200	1987	40.00	250-350
1987	Skier Girl	200	1987	40.00	250-350
1991	Sugarin Kids (Woodstock)	Closed	1991	41.00	300
1988	Woodstock Lady	Closed	1988	41.00	350
1988	Woodstock Man	Closed	1988	41.00	350

Toddlers - J. Byers

1993	Gingerbread Boy	Closed	1994	18.50	40
1993	Package	Closed	1993	18.50	35
1992	Shovel	Closed	1993	17.00	35
1994	Skis	Open		19.00	20
1994	Sled (black toddler)	Closed	1994	19.00	19
1992	Sled (white toddler)	Closed	1993	17.00	20
1995	Sled (white toddler-2nd version)	Open		19.00	20
1991	Sled with Dog/toddler	Closed	1991	30.00	100-175
1992	Snowball	Closed	1994	17.00	35
1994	Snowflake	Closed	1994	18.00	18
1993	Teddy Bear	Closed	1993	18.50	40
1995	Toddler with Wagon	Open		19.50	20
1994	Tree	Open		18.00	20
1995	Victorian Boy Toddler	Open		19.50	20
1995	Victorian Girl Toddler	Open		19.50	20

Calabar Creations

Angelic Pigasus - P. Apsit

1995	Adagio AP75364	Open		18.00	18
1994	Alba AP75353	Open		12.00	12
1995	Allegria AP75395	Open		24.00	24
1995	Ambrose AP75374	Open		22.00	22
1995	Andante AP75384	Open		18.00	18
1994	Angelica AP75315	Open		24.00	24
1995	Angelo AP75335	Open		5.00	5
1994	Angelo AP75335	Open		24.00	24
1994	Anna AP75324	Retrd.	1995	22.00	22
1994	Aria AP75343	Open		12.00	12
1995	Signature Piece AP75405	Open		24.00	24

Daddy's Girl - P. Apsit

1994	All Aboard! DA74804	5,000		20.00	20
1994	Discovery DA74816	5,000		28.00	28
1994	Moil DA74834	5,000		20.00	20
1994	Peek-A-Boo DA74843	5,000		20.00	20
1994	Spring Harvest DA74856	5,000		28.00	28
1995	Summer DA74866	5,000		34.00	34
1994	Teddy Talks DA74826	5,000		40.00	40

Days of Innocence - P. Apsit

1995	Dear God DI74975	5,000		28.00	28
1995	A Letter From Grandma DI74966	5,000		40.00	40
1995	To Grandma's DI74956	5,000		28.00	28

Grandpions - P. Apsit

1995	Alex the Great OM77144	Open		13.00	13
1995	Alley King OM77313	Open		13.00	13
1995	Blue Baron OM77294	Open		13.00	13
1995	Chained OM77234	Open		13.00	13
1995	Doc OM77184	Open		13.00	13
1995	The Finest OM77174	Open		13.00	13
1995	Harleyson OM77164	Open		15.00	15
1995	Ice Proof OM77133	Open		13.00	13
1995	Lady Hope OM77304	Open		13.00	13
1995	Marathon Man OM77224	Open		13.00	13
1995	Martiny OM77264	Open		13.00	13
1995	Mazuma OM77244	Open		13.00	13
1995	Oh Gee! OM77203	Open		13.00	13
1995	Old Red OM77154	Open		13.00	13
1995	Peleman OM77274	Open		13.00	13
1995	Ratchet OM77254	Open		13.00	13
1995	Rocky Road OM77283	Open		13.00	13
1995	See The Birdy OM77193	Open		13.00	13
1995	Struck OM77214	Open		13.00	13
1995	Weed Child OM77323	Open		13.00	13

Junior Murphy's Law - P. Apsit

1995	Extra Topping JM75216	5,000		40.00	40
1995	Fast Food JM75196	5,000		46.00	46
1995	Lucky Me! JM75176	5,000		40.00	40
1995	Milk Fan JM75205	5,000		44.00	44
1995	Robin Tell JM75226	5,000		40.00	40

Little Farmers - P. Apsit

1994	Apple Delivery LF73127	5,000		54.00	54
1993	Between Chores LF73105	5,000		40.00	40
1993	Caring Friend LF73066	5,000		57.00	57
1993	Going Home LF73027	5,000		64.00	64
1993	It's Not For You LF73038	5,000		64.00	64
1994	LF Signature Piece LF73147	Open		40.00	40
1993	Little Lumber Joe LF73077	5,000		64.00	64
1994	Lunch Express LF73117	5,000		76.00	76
1993	Oops! LF73058	5,000		64.00	64
1993	Piggy Ride LF73097	5,000		45.00	45
1993	Playful Kittens LF73016	5,000		64.00	64
1993	Surprise! LF73046	5,000		60.00	60
1993	True Love LF73087	5,000		45.00	45
1994	Vita-Veggie Vendor LF73137	5,000		62.00	62

Little Professionals - P. Apsit

1994	Little Angelo LP75057	5,000		38.00	38
1995	Little Count LP75084	5,000		36.00	36
1995	Little Desi LP75135	5,000		18.00	18
1994	Little Florence LP75065	5,000		44.00	44
1995	Little Gypsy LP75115	5,000		18.00	18
1995	Little Louis LP75106	5,000		18.00	18
1994	Little Miss Market LP75046	5,000		40.00	40
1995	Little Red LP75075	5,000		38.00	38
1995	Little Ringo LP75094	5,000		18.00	18

Pig Hollow - P. Apsit

1994	The After Picture PH75544	Open		12.00	12
1995	Armchair/buttons PH75752	Open		7.00	7
1994	Barn Fun PH75474	Open		15.00	15
1995	Bathroom Vanity PH75703	Open		6.00	6
1995	Double Bed PH75722	Open		9.00	9
1995	Dresser/2-drawer PH75714	Open		8.00	8
1994	Going South PH75533	Open		11.00	11
1994	Just Cute PH75442	Open		9.00	9
1995	Kitchen Counter PH75684	Open		19.00	19
1995	Large Armchair PH75742	Open		8.00	8
1994	Mary Pig PH75524	Open		11.00	11
1994	Move Please PH75462	Open		11.00	11
1994	Nap Time PH75492	Open		11.00	11
1994	Old McPig PH75513	Open		11.00	11
1995	Par PH75674	Open		15.00	15
1995	Pauline PH75873	Open		9.00	9

YEAR ISSUE		EDITION LIMIT	YEAR RETD.	ISSUE PRICE	QUOTE U.S.$
1995	Pelota PH75612	Open		8.00	8
1995	Pendleton PH75822	Open		10.00	10
1995	Pepin PH75842	Open		9.00	9
1995	Pieball PH75633	Open		9.00	9
1995	Pig Kahuna PH75602	Open		9.00	9
1995	Pigmobile PH75853	Open		34.00	34
1995	Pilar PH75832	Open		9.00	9
1994	Pillow Talk PH75453	Open		12.00	12
1995	Plopsy PH75642	Open		8.00	8
1995	Pluckster PH75812	Open		9.00	9
1995	Poirot PH75622	Open		8.00	8
1995	Poof PH75592	Open		8.00	8
1995	Pot Belly PH75883	Open		12.00	12
1995	Pristine Pig PH75573	Open		10.00	10
1995	Prof PH75583	Open		9.00	9
1995	Proof PH75862	Open		12.00	12
1995	Prude Jr. PH75652	Open		8.00	8
1995	Prude PH75663	Open		9.00	9
1994	Reddie PH75554	Open		12.00	12
1995	Sidetable/1 book PH75773	Open		8.00	8
1995	Sidetable/2 doors PH75782	Open		6.00	6
1994	Signature Piece PH75565	Open		19.00	19
1995	Sofa PH75762	Open		14.00	14
1995	Stove/Oven PH75693	Open		7.00	7
1994	Sweet Corn PH75503	Open		9.00	9
1994	Time For School PH75484	Open		15.00	15
1995	TV Console PH75793	Open		7.00	7
1995	Twin Bed PH75732	Open		9.00	9

Santaventure - P. Apsit

YEAR ISSUE		EDITION LIMIT	YEAR RETD.	ISSUE PRICE	QUOTE U.S.$
1994	Almost Done SV73836	5,000		50.00	50
1993	Cart O' Plenty SV73737	5,000		66.00	66
1993	Hooray For Santa SV73757	5,000		59.00	59
1994	In His Dream SV73816	5,000		78.00	78
1994	The Last Mile SV73806	5,000		54.00	54
1993	Nuts For You SV73787	5,000		59.00	59
1993	Pilgrim Santa SV73748	5,000		59.00	59
1993	A Pinch of Advice SV73768	5,000		68.00	68
1994	Reindeer's Strike SV73827	5,000		54.00	54
1993	Santa Tested SV73778	5,000		68.00	68
1993	Santa's Sack Attack SV73796	5,000		60.00	60
1994	Signature Piece SV73577	5,000		60.00	60
1994	Viola! SV73847	5,000		50.00	50

Tee Club - P. Apsit

YEAR ISSUE		EDITION LIMIT	YEAR RETD.	ISSUE PRICE	QUOTE U.S.$
1993	Certain-Tee TC73898	5,000		100.00	100
1993	Naugh-Tee TC73908	5,000		56.00	56
1993	Old Tee-Mer TC73887	5,000		78.00	78
1993	Prac-Tees TC73858	5,000		66.00	66
1993	Putt-Teeing TC73868	5,000		66.00	66
1993	Teed-Off TC73877	5,000		60.00	60

Yesterday's Friends - P. Apsit

YEAR ISSUE		EDITION LIMIT	YEAR RETD.	ISSUE PRICE	QUOTE U.S.$
1993	Bayou Boys RW74456	3,500		80.00	80
1993	Bluester RW74446	7,500		44.00	44
1993	Buddies RW74466	7,500		50.00	50
1994	Caddie Chris RW74527	7,500		34.00	34
1994	Cornered RW74707	7,500		54.00	54
1993	Dinner For Two RW74496	7,500		38.00	38
1994	Equipment Manager RW74596	7,500		34.00	34
1994	Excess RW74726	7,500		50.00	50
1993	Freewheeling RW74436	7,500		48.00	48
1994	Funny Frog RW74745	7,500		44.00	44
1994	Goose Loose RW74635	7,500		40.00	40
1995	High Fly RW74795	7,500		28.00	28
1993	Hop-a-Long Pete RW74539	3,500		80.00	80
1993	Interference RW74506	7,500		42.00	42
1993	Jazzy Bubble RW74486	7,500		37.00	37
1993	Me Big Chief RW74548	7,500		56.00	56
1993	Mike's Magic RW74475	7,500		37.00	37
1995	Out! RW74766	7,500		34.00	34
1994	Parade RW74716	7,500		60.00	60
1995	Pop Up! RW74755	7,500		34.00	34
1994	Read All About It RW74616	7,500		70.00	70
1994	Read-A-Thon RW74694	7,500		40.00	40
1994	Scrub-a-Swine RW74606	7,500		48.00	48
1994	Signature Piece RW74737	Open		54.00	54
1993	Strike So Sweet RW74517	7,500		42.00	42
1994	Tuba Notes RW74688	7,500		54.00	54
1993	Tug-a-Leg RW74557	7,500		56.00	56
1994	What A Smile RW74626	7,500		40.00	40

Cast Art Industries

Dreamsicles Collectors Club - K. Haynes

YEAR ISSUE		EDITION LIMIT	YEAR RETD.	ISSUE PRICE	QUOTE U.S.$
1993	A Star is Born-CD001	Retrd.	1993	Gift	50-100
1994	Daydream Believer-CD100	Retrd.	1994	29.95	60
1994	Join The Fun-CD002	Retrd.	1994	Gift	30
1994	Makin' A List-CD101	Retrd.	1994	47.95	60
1995	Three Cheers-CD003	Yr.Iss.		Gift	N/A
1995	Town Crier-CD102	12/95		24.95	25

Animal Attractions - S.&G. Hackett

YEAR ISSUE		EDITION LIMIT	YEAR RETD.	ISSUE PRICE	QUOTE U.S.$
1993	Cat Dancing-AA026	Suspd.		21.00	21
1993	Feeding Time-AA016	Suspd.		10.00	10
1993	Udderly Ridiculous-AA002	Suspd.		28.00	28
1993	Undelivered Mail-AA015	Suspd.		15.00	15

Cuckoo Corners - K. Haynes

YEAR ISSUE		EDITION LIMIT	YEAR RETD.	ISSUE PRICE	QUOTE U.S.$
1993	Beth Friend-CC063	Suspd.		22.00	22
1993	Dolly House-CC061	Suspd.		22.00	22
1993	Faith Flower Power-CC062	Suspd.		27.00	27
1993	Heidi Hoedown-CC064	Suspd.		27.00	27

Dreamsicles - K. Haynes

YEAR ISSUE		EDITION LIMIT	YEAR RETD.	ISSUE PRICE	QUOTE U.S.$
1995	The 1995 International Collectible Exposition Commemorative Figurine	Retrd.	1995	34.95	100-200
1992	Baby Love-DC147	12/95		7.00	7
1991	Best Pals-DC103	Retrd.	1994	15.00	30
1994	Birthday Party-DC171	Suspd.		13.50	14
1992	Bluebird On My Shoulder-DC115	12/95		19.00	19
1994	Boxful of Stars-DC224	Suspd.		16.00	16
1992	Bundle of Joy-DC142	12/95		7.00	7
1992	Bunny Wall Plaque-5018	Suspd.		22.00	22
1992	Bunny Wall Plaque-5019	Suspd.		22.00	22
1993	By the Silvery Moon-Limited Edition DC253	Retrd.	1994	100.00	295
1992	Caroler - Center Scroll-DC216	12/95		19.00	19
1992	Caroler - Left Scroll-DC218	12/95		19.00	19
1992	Caroler - Right Scroll-DC217	12/95		19.00	19
1991	Cherub and Child-DC100	12/95		15.00	15
1992	Cherub For All Seasons-DC114	12/95		23.00	23
1991	Cherub Wall Plaque-5130	Suspd.		15.00	15
1991	Cherub Wall Plaque-5131	Suspd.		15.00	15
1992	Cherub-Limited Edition DC112	Retrd.	1993	50.00	50
1992	Cherub-Limited Edtion DC111	Retrd.	1992	50.00	50-75
1992	A Child's Prayer-DC145	12/95		7.00	7
1994	Cuddle Blanket-DC153	12/95		6.50	7
1992	Cupid's Bow-DC202	Suspd.		27.00	27
1992	Dance Ballerina Dance-DC140	12/95		37.00	37
1992	Dream A Little Dream-DC144	12/95		7.00	7
1994	Eager to Please-DC154	12/95		6.50	7
1992	Flying Lesson-Limited Edition-DC251	Retrd.	1993	80.00	370
1991	Forever Friends-DC102	Retrd.	1994	15.00	30
1991	Forever Yours-DC110	12/95		44.00	44
1994	Happy Birthday w/hat-DC133	Suspd.		13.50	14
1994	Here's Looking at You-DC172	12/95		25.00	25
1994	I Can Read-DC151	12/95		6.50	7
1991	King Heart "I Love You" Box-5850	Suspd.		37.50	38
1991	King Oval Cow Box-5860	Suspd.		55.00	55
1993	Lg. Candle Holder Boy-DC138	Suspd.		20.00	22
1993	Lg. Candle Holder Girl-DC139	Suspd.		20.00	22
1992	Little Darlin'-DC146	12/95		7.00	7
1993	Little Dickens-DC127	12/95		24.00	24
1992	Littlest Angel-DC143	12/95		7.00	7
1993	Long Fellow-DC126	12/95		24.00	24
1991	Medium Heart Cherub Box-5751	Suspd.		14.00	14
1991	Musician w/Cymbals-5154	Suspd.		22.00	22
1991	Musician w/Drums-5152	Suspd.		22.00	22
1991	Musician w/Flute-5153	Suspd.		22.00	22
1991	Musician w/Trumpet-5151	Suspd.		22.00	22
1992	My Funny Valentine-DC201	Suspd.		17.00	28
1995	Nursery Rhyme-DC229	Suspd.		42.00	42
1991	Octagonal Ballerina Box-5700	Suspd.		9.00	9
1995	Picture Perfect-Limited Edtion DC255	10,000		100.00	100
1991	Queen Octagonal Cherub Box-5804	Suspd.		26.00	26
1991	Queen Rectangle Cat Box-5800	Suspd.		28.75	29
1991	Queen Round Bears Box-5801	Suspd.		28.75	29
1994	The Recital-Limited Editon DC254	Retrd.	1994	135.00	175
1994	Side By Side-DC169	12/95		31.50	32
1992	Sleigh Ride-DC122	Suspd.		15.50	16
1991	Small Cherub with Hanging Ribbon-5104	Suspd.		10.00	10
1991	Small Heart "I Love You" Box-5701	Suspd.		9.00	9
1991	Small Rectangle "Dicky Duck" Box-5703	Suspd.		9.00	9
1991	Small Square Dinosaur Box-5702	Suspd.		9.00	9
1994	Sock Hop-DC222	Suspd.		16.00	16
1991	Speed Racer Box-5750	Suspd.		14.00	14
1994	Sucking My Thumb-DC156	12/95		6.50	7
1994	Surprise Gift-DC152	12/95		6.50	7
1993	Sweet Dreams-DC125	12/95		29.00	29
1994	Sweet Gingerbread-DC223	Suspd.		16.00	16
1993	Teeter Tots-Limited Edition-DC252	Retrd.	1993	100.00	175-295
1991	Train Box-5803	Suspd.		28.75	29
1994	Up All Night-DC155	12/95		6.50	7
1991	You're Special Box-5802	Suspd.		28.75	29

Dreamsicles Animals - K. Haynes

YEAR ISSUE		EDITION LIMIT	YEAR RETD.	ISSUE PRICE	QUOTE U.S.$
1991	Armadillo-5176	Suspd.		14.00	14
1992	Beach Baby-DA615	Suspd.		26.00	26
1992	Blowfish-DA608	Suspd.		10.00	10
1991	Buddy Bear-DA451	Suspd.		7.50	8
1992	Bunny Bookends-DA122	Suspd.		44.00	44
1991	Bunny Hop-DA105	12/95		19.50	20
1992	Cat Nap-DA551	Suspd.		10.00	10
1992	The Cat's Meow-DA552	Suspd.		10.00	10
1992	Crabby-DA607	Suspd.		8.00	8
1992	Cute As A Button-DA553	Suspd.		10.00	10
1991	Dairy Delight-DA381	12/95		28.00	28
1991	Dimples (girl)-DA100	12/95		6.00	6
1992	Dino-DA480	Suspd.		14.00	14
1992	Dodo-DA482	Suspd.		9.00	9
1992	Double fish-DA611	Suspd.		8.00	8
1992	Fat Cat-DA555	Suspd.		26.00	26
1991	Gathering Flowers-DA320	12/95		18.00	18
1992	Helga-DA112	12/95		8.00	8
1991	Hippity Hop- DA106	Suspd.		31.00	31
1991	Honey Bun (boy)-DA101	12/95		6.00	6
1992	Hound Dog-DA568	Suspd.		11.00	11
1991	King Rabbit-DA124	Suspd.		66.00	66
1991	Kitchen Pig-DA345	Suspd.		31.50	32
1991	Lambie Pie-DA328	Suspd.		9.00	9
1992	Largemouth-DA609	Suspd.		8.00	8
1992	Lazy Bones-DA605	Suspd.		14.00	14
1993	Li'l Chick-DA385	Suspd.		7.00	7
1993	Li'l Duck-DA388	Suspd.		7.00	7
1991	Mama Bear-DA452	Suspd.		9.00	9
1992	Man's Best Friend-DA560	Suspd.		11.00	11
1991	Mother Mouse-DA477	Suspd.		10.00	10
1991	Mouse on Skis-DA475	Suspd.		17.00	17
1991	Mr. Bunny- DA107	Suspd.		27.00	27
1991	Mrs. Bunny- DA108	Suspd.		27.00	27
1991	Mutton Chops-DA326	Suspd.		7.50	8
1992	Needlenose-DA610	Suspd.		8.00	8
1992	Octopus' Garden-DA606	Suspd.		10.00	10
1991	P.J. Mouse-DA476	Suspd.		10.00	10
1993	Pal Joey-DA104	12/95		13.50	14
1992	Papa Pelican-DA602	Suspd.		22.00	22
1993	Party Bunny-DA116	Suspd.		19.00	19
1991	Pigmalion-DA340	12/95		6.00	6
1991	Pigtails-DA341	12/95		6.00	6
1992	Pretty Kitty-DA554	Suspd.		15.00	15
1992	Pumpkin Harvest-DA322	Suspd.		19.00	19
1992	Puppy Love-DA562	Suspd.		12.00	12
1992	Red Rover-DA566	Suspd.		17.00	17
1992	Rhino-DA481	Suspd.		14.00	14
1991	Ricky Raccoon-5170	Suspd.		27.00	27
1992	Sarge-DA111	12/95		8.00	8
1992	Scooter-DA567	Suspd.		11.00	11
1992	Slow Poke-DA630	Suspd.		13.00	13
1991	Soap Box Bunny-DA221	12/95		15.00	15
1991	Socrates the Sheep-5029	Suspd.		18.00	18
1992	Splash-DA616	Suspd.		26.00	26
1992	St. Peter Rabbit-DA243	Suspd.		29.00	29
1992	Teddy Bear-DA456	Suspd.		14.00	14
1991	Tiny Bunny-DA102	12/95		7.50	8
1992	Winter's Comin'-DA471	Suspd.		10.00	15
1991	Wooly Bully-DA327	Suspd.		9.00	9

Dreamsicles Calendar Collection - K. Haynes

YEAR ISSUE		EDITION LIMIT	YEAR RETD.	ISSUE PRICE	QUOTE U.S.$
1994	Winter Wonderland (January)-DC180	12/95		24.00	24
1994	Special Delivery (February)-DC181	12/95		24.00	24
1994	Ride Like The Wind (March)-DC182	12/95		24.00	24
1994	Springtime Frolic (April)-DC183	12/95		24.00	24
1994	Love In Bloom (May)-DC184	12/95		24.00	24
1994	Among Friends (June)-DC185	12/95		24.00	24
1994	Pool Pals (July)-DC186	12/95		24.00	24
1994	Nature's Bounty (August)-DC187	12/95		24.00	24
1994	School Days (September)-DC188	12/95		24.00	24
1994	Autumn Leaves (October)-DC189	12/95		24.00	24
1994	Now Give Thanks (November)-DC190	12/95		24.00	24
1994	Holiday Magic (December)-DC191	12/95		24.00	24

Dreamsicles Christmas - K. Haynes

YEAR ISSUE		EDITION LIMIT	YEAR RETD.	ISSUE PRICE	QUOTE U.S.$
1992	Baby Love-DX147	12/95		7.00	7
1992	Bluebird On My Shoulder-DX115	12/95		19.00	19
1992	Bundle of Joy-DX142	12/95		7.00	7
1992	Caroler - Center Scroll-DX216	12/95		19.00	19
1992	Caroler - Left Scroll-DX218	12/95		19.00	19
1992	Caroler - Right Scroll-DX217	12/95		19.00	19
1991	Cherub and Child-DX100	12/95		14.00	14
1992	A Child's Prayer-DX145	12/95		7.00	7
1992	Dream A Little Dream-DX144	12/95		7.00	7
1993	The Finishing Touches-DX248	Retrd.	1994	85.00	115-170
1991	Forever Yours-DX110	12/95		44.00	44
1994	Here's Looking at You-DX172	12/95		25.00	25
1994	Holiday on Ice-DX249	Retrd.	1995	85.00	100
1992	Little Darlin'-DX146	12/95		7.00	7
1993	Little Dickens-DX127	12/95		24.00	24
1992	Littlest Angel-DX143	12/95		7.00	7
1993	Long Fellow-DX126	12/95		24.00	24
1991	Santa Bunny-DX203	Retrd.	1994	32.00	32
1992	Santa In Dreamsicle Land-DX247	Retrd.	1993	85.00	225-350
1994	Side By Side-DX169	12/95		31.50	32
1993	Sweet Dreams-DX125	12/95		29.00	29

Dreamsicles Day Event- K. Haynes

YEAR ISSUE		EDITION LIMIT	YEAR RETD.	ISSUE PRICE	QUOTE U.S.$
1995	1995 Dreamsicles Event Figurine-DC075	12/95		20.00	20

The Cat's Meow

Collector Club Gift - Houses - F. Jones

YEAR ISSUE		EDITION LIMIT	YEAR RETD.	ISSUE PRICE	QUOTE U.S.$
1989	1989 Betsy Ross House	Retrd.	1989	Gift	200
1990	1990 Amelia Earhart	Retrd.	1990	Gift	100
1991	1991 Limberlost Cabin	Retrd.	1991	Gift	50
1992	1992 Abigail Adams Birthplace	Retrd.	1992	Gift	N/A
1993	1993 Pearl S. Buck House	Retrd.	1993	Gift	50
1993	Set of '89-'93	Retrd.	1993	Gift	450
1994	1994 Lillian Gish	Retrd.	1994	Gift	N/A
1995	1995 Eleanor Roosevelt	12/95		Gift	N/A

YEAR ISSUE		EDITION LIMIT	YEAR RETD.	ISSUE PRICE	QUOTE U.S.$
1996	1996 Mother's Day Church	12/96		Gift	N/A

Collector Club - Famous Authors - F. Jones

YEAR ISSUE		EDITION LIMIT	YEAR RETD.	ISSUE PRICE	QUOTE U.S.$
1989	Harriet Beecher Stowe	Retrd.	1989	8.75	N/A
1989	Orchard House	Retrd.	1989	8.75	N/A
1989	Longfellow House	Retrd.	1989	8.75	N/A
1989	Herman Melville's Arrowhead	Retrd.	1989	8.75	800
1989	Set	Retrd.	1989	35.00	750-850

Collector Club - Great Inventors - F. Jones

YEAR ISSUE		EDITION LIMIT	YEAR RETD.	ISSUE PRICE	QUOTE U.S.$
1990	Thomas Edison	Retrd.	1990	9.25	N/A
1990	Ford Motor Co.	Retrd.	1990	9.25	N/A
1990	Seth Thomas Clock Co.	Retrd.	1990	9.25	75
1990	Wright Cycle Co.	Retrd.	1990	9.25	N/A
1990	Set	Retrd.	1990	37.00	400-500

Collector Club - American Songwriters - F. Jones

YEAR ISSUE		EDITION LIMIT	YEAR RETD.	ISSUE PRICE	QUOTE U.S.$
1991	Benjamin R. Hanby House	Retrd.	1991	9.25	N/A
1991	Anna Warner House	Retrd.	1991	9.25	N/A
1991	Stephen Foster Home	Retrd.	1991	9.25	22
1991	Oscar Hammerstein House	Retrd.	1991	9.25	22
1991	Set	Retrd.	1991	37.00	150-300

Collector Club - Signers of the Declaration - F. Jones

YEAR ISSUE		EDITION LIMIT	YEAR RETD.	ISSUE PRICE	QUOTE U.S.$
1992	Josiah Bartlett Home	Retrd.	1992	9.75	N/A
1992	George Clymer Home	Retrd.	1992	9.75	N/A
1992	Stephen Hopkins Home	Retrd.	1992	9.75	N/A
1992	John Witherspoon Home	Retrd.	1992	9.75	N/A
1992	Set	Retrd.	1992	39.00	250

Collector Club -19th Century Master Builders - F. Jones

YEAR ISSUE		EDITION LIMIT	YEAR RETD.	ISSUE PRICE	QUOTE U.S.$
1993	Henry Hobson Richardson	Retrd.	1993	10.25	N/A
1993	Samuel Sloan	Retrd.	1993	10.25	N/A
1993	Alexander Jackson Davis	Retrd.	1993	10.25	N/A
1993	Andrew Jackson Downing	Retrd.	1993	10.25	N/A
1993	Set	Retrd.	1993	41.00	100

Collector Club - Williamsburg Merchants - F. Jones

YEAR ISSUE		EDITION LIMIT	YEAR RETD.	ISSUE PRICE	QUOTE U.S.$
1994	East Carlton Wigmaker	Retrd.	1994	11.15	12
1994	J. Geddy Silversmith	Retrd.	1994	11.15	12
1994	Craig Jeweler	Retrd.	1994	11.15	12
1994	M. Hunter Millinery	Retrd.	1994	11.15	12
1994	Set	Retrd.	1994	44.60	75-95

Collector Club - Mt. Rushmore Presidential Series - F. Jones

YEAR ISSUE		EDITION LIMIT	YEAR RETD.	ISSUE PRICE	QUOTE U.S.$
1995	George Washington Birthplace	12/95		12.00	12
1995	Metamora Courthouse	12/95		12.00	12
1995	Theodore Roosevelt Birthplace	12/95		12.00	12
1995	Tuckahoe Plantation	12/95		12.00	12
1995	Set	12/95		48.00	48

Collector Club - American Holiday Series - F. Jones

YEAR ISSUE		EDITION LIMIT	YEAR RETD.	ISSUE PRICE	QUOTE U.S.$
1996	...And to all a Goodnight	12/96		11.00	11
1996	Boo to You	12/96		11.00	11
1996	Easter's On Its Way	12/96		11.00	11
1996	Let Freedom Ring	12/96		11.00	11

Accessories - F. Jones

YEAR ISSUE		EDITION LIMIT	YEAR RETD.	ISSUE PRICE	QUOTE U.S.$
1990	1909 Franklin Limousine	5-Yr.		4.00	5
1990	1913 Peerless Touring Car	5-Yr.		4.00	5
1990	1914 Fire Pumper	5-Yr.		4.00	5
1983	5" Hedge	Retrd.	1988	3.00	30-50
1983	5" Iron Fence	Retrd.	1988	3.00	30-50
1987	5" Picket Fence	Retrd.	1992	3.00	15
1990	5" Wrought Iron Fence	5-Yr.		3.00	5
1983	8" Hedge	Retrd.	1988	3.25	40
1983	8" Iron Fence	Retrd.	1988	3.25	50
1983	8" Picket Fence	Retrd.	1988	3.25	40-50
1989	Ada Belle	Retrd.	1994	4.00	7
1990	Amish Buggy	5-Yr.		4.00	5
1991	Amish Garden	5-Yr.		4.00	5
1994	Amish Milk Wagon	5-Yr.		4.50	5
1994	Amish Produce Wagon	5-Yr.		4.50	5
1994	Apple Tree	5-Yr.		4.50	5
1987	Band Stand	Retrd.	1992	6.50	13
1991	Barnyard	5-Yr.		4.00	5
1995	Beech & Cherry Tree Row	5-Yr.		4.50	5
1995	Bennington Flag	5-Yr.		4.50	5
1994	Berries & Sheep	5-Yr.		4.50	5
1990	Blue Spruce	5-Yr.		4.00	5
1994	Booker T. Washington Monument	5-Yr.		4.50	5
1996	Bow Bridge	5-Yr.		5.00	5
1995	Burma-Shave Signs	5-Yr.		4.50	5
1990	Bus Stop	5-Yr.		4.00	5
1987	Butch & T.J.	Retrd.	1992	4.00	6-15
1986	Cable Car	Retrd.	1991	4.00	9-18
1993	Cannonball Express	5-Yr.		4.00	5
1986	Carolers	Retrd.	1991	4.00	9-18
1994	Cat & The Fiddle S/2	5-Yr.		4.50	5
1995	Central Park Skaters	5-Yr.		4.50	5
1995	Charles & Lady	5-Yr.		4.50	5
1987	Charlie & Co.	Retrd.	1992	4.00	9-15
1985	Cherry Tree	Retrd.	1990	4.00	30-50
1991	Chessie Hopper Car	5-Yr.		4.00	5
1986	Chickens	Retrd.	1991	3.25	10-18
1993	Chippewa Lake Billboard	5-Yr.		4.00	5
1990	Christmas Tree Lot	5-Yr.		4.00	5
1989	Clothesline	Retrd.	1994	4.00	8
1988	Colonial Bread Wagon	Retrd.	1993	4.00	10
1991	Concert in the Park	5-Yr.		4.00	5
1994	Cornstalks & Turkeys	5-Yr.		4.50	5
1986	Cows	Retrd.	1991	4.00	12-18
1994	Daily Business (wlbg. people)	5-Yr.		4.50	5
1986	Dairy Wagon	Retrd.	1991	4.00	12-18
1995	Dancing Cat & Clipper Ship	5-Yr.		9.00	9
1994	Deer	5-Yr.		4.50	5
1992	Delivery Truck	5-Yr.		4.00	5
1995	Directional Sign	5-Yr.		5.00	5
1986	Ducks	Retrd.	1991	3.25	10-18
1990	Eugene	5-Yr.		4.00	5
1985	Fall Tree	Retrd.	1990	4.00	27-40
1995	Father Serra & Indians	5-Yr.		4.50	5
1987	FJ Express	Retrd.	1992	4.00	15
1986	FJ Real Estate Sign	Retrd.	1991	3.00	18-24
1988	Flower Pots	Retrd.	1993	4.00	6-11
1992	Forsythia Bush	5-Yr.		4.00	5
1993	Garden House	5-Yr.		3.25	5
1994	Garden Wall	5-Yr.		4.50	5
1988	Gas Light	Retrd.	1993	4.00	10
1990	Gerstenslager Buggy	5-Yr.		4.00	7
1993	Getting Directions	5-Yr.		4.00	5
1994	Good Humor Man	5-Yr.		4.50	5
1994	Gracie (in carriage)	5-Yr.		4.50	5
1993	Grape Arbor	5-Yr.		4.00	5
1989	Harry's Hotdogs	Retrd.	1994	4.00	7
1986	Horse & Carriage	Retrd.	1991	4.00	9-15
1987	Horse & Sleigh	Retrd.	1992	4.00	9-15
1996	Hot Air Balloon	5-Yr.		5.00	5
1995	Humpty Dumpty	5-Yr.		9.00	9
1986	Ice Wagon	Retrd.	1991	4.00	9-18
1983	Iron Gate	Retrd.	1988	3.00	50-65
1991	Jack The Postman	5-Yr.		3.25	5
1994	Jacob, Atlee & Noah	5-Yr.		4.50	5
1993	Jennie & George's Wedding	5-Yr.		4.00	5
1993	Johnny Appleseed Statue	5-Yr.		4.00	5
1994	Kearsarge Fire Pumper	5-Yr.		4.50	5
1995	Knickerbockers Ball Team	5-Yr.		4.50	5
1994	Lemonade Stand	5-Yr.		4.50	5
1986	Liberty St. Sign	Retrd.	1991	3.25	9-19
1994	Light Ship	5-Yr.		4.50	5
1983	Lilac Bushes	Retrd.	1988	3.00	200-400
1995	Lion Circus Wagon	5-Yr.		4.50	5
1993	Little Marine	5-Yr.		4.00	5
1990	Little Red Caboose	5-Yr.		4.00	5
1996	Little Red Riding Hood	5-Yr.		5.00	5
1994	Lunch Wagon	5-Yr.		4.50	5
1995	Magnolia Tree	5-Yr.		4.50	5
1988	Mail Wagon	Retrd.	1993	4.00	6-11
1988	Main St. Sign	Retrd.	1993	3.25	7-11
1991	Marble Game	5-Yr.		4.00	5
1986	Market St. Sign	Retrd.	1991	3.25	7-18
1993	Market Wagon	5-Yr.		4.00	5
1991	Martin House	5-Yr.		3.25	5
1994	Moving Truck	5-Yr.		4.50	5
1994	Moving Truck	5-Yr.		4.50	5
1992	Mr. Softee Truck	5-Yr.		4.00	5
1995	Mt. Rushmore	5-Yr.		9.00	9
1987	Nanny	Retrd.	1992	4.00	7-15
1994	Nativity	5-Yr.		15.00	17
1994	Nativity Visitors Trio Set	5-Yr.		19.00	19
1995	Noah's Ark Trio Set	5-Yr.		21.00	21
1996	Noah's Sons Trio Set	5-Yr.		5.00	5
1992	Nutcracker Billboard	5-Yr.		4.00	5
1991	On Vacation	5-Yr.		4.00	5
1996	Owl & PussyCat Went to Sea	5-Yr.		5.00	5
1995	Palm Trees	5-Yr.		9.00	9
1989	Passenger Train Car	Retrd.	1994	4.00	8
1996	Peachtree Street Sign	5-Yr.		5.00	5
1985	Pine Tree	Retrd.	1990	4.00	26-40
1992	Police Car	5-Yr.		4.00	5
1988	Pony Express Rider	Retrd.	1993	4.00	10
1991	Popcorn Wagon	5-Yr.		4.00	5
1985	Poplar Tree	Retrd.	1990	4.00	22-40
1989	Pumpkin Wagon	Retrd.	1994	3.25	7
1989	Quaker Oats Train Car	Retrd.	1994	4.00	7
1987	Railroad Sign	Retrd.	1992	3.00	10-20
1990	Red Maple Tree	5-Yr.		4.00	5
1995	Rose Arbor	5-Yr.		4.50	5
1989	Rose Trellis	Retrd.	1994	3.25	7
1995	Rubbermaid Train Car	5-Yr.		4.50	5
1989	Rudy & Aldine	Retrd.	1994	4.00	7
1993	Rustic Fence	5-Yr.		4.00	5
1994	Salvation Army Band	5-Yr.		4.50	5
1995	San Juan Capistrano Bells	5-Yr.		9.00	9
1990	Santa & Reindeer	5-Yr.		4.00	5
1991	Scarey Harry (Scarecrow)	5-Yr.		4.00	5
1991	School Bus	5-Yr.		4.00	5
1992	School Crossing	5-Yr.		4.00	5
1996	Seagulls	5-Yr.		5.00	5
1992	Silo	5-Yr.		4.00	5
1991	Ski Party	5-Yr.		4.00	5
1988	Skipjack	Retrd.	1993	6.50	10-15
1996	Smucker Train Car	5-Yr.		5.00	5
1989	Snowmen	Retrd.	1994	4.00	7
1996	Soccer Game	5-Yr.		5.00	5
1992	Springhouse	5-Yr.		3.25	5
1994	Stock Train Car	5-Yr.		4.50	5
1988	Street Clock	Retrd.	1993	4.00	7-11
1994	Street Lamp	5-Yr.		4.50	5
1985	Summer Tree	Retrd.	1990	4.00	30-40
1989	Tad & Toni	Retrd.	1994	4.00	7
1996	Tea For Two	5-Yr.		5.00	5
1988	Telephone Booth	Retrd.	1993	4.00	8-18
1986	Touring Car	Retrd.	1991	4.00	9-15
1996	Treehouse	5-Yr.		5.00	5
1994	Trick or Treat	5-Yr.		4.50	5
1990	Tulip Tree	5-Yr.		4.00	5
1988	U.S. Flag	Retrd.	1993	4.00	7-15
1994	U.S. Flag	5-Yr.		4.50	5
1995	Ulric the Undertaker	5-Yr.		4.50	5
1991	USMC War Memorial	5-Yr.		6.50	7
1990	Veterinary Wagon	5-Yr.		4.00	5
1990	Victorian Outhouse	5-Yr.		4.00	5
1991	Village Entrance Sigh	5-Yr.		6.50	7
1995	Vineyard Fence	5-Yr.		4.50	5
1995	Watermelon Wagon	5-Yr.		4.50	5
1990	Watkins Wagon	5-Yr.		4.00	5
1994	Weeping Willow Tree	5-Yr.		4.50	5
1986	Wells, Fargo Wagon	Retrd.	1991	4.00	12-18
1994	Wharf	5-Yr.		4.50	5
1987	Windmill	Retrd.	1992	3.25	10-15
1995	Winter Tree	5-Yr.		4.50	5
1986	Wishing Well	Retrd.	1991	3.25	15-23
1987	Wooden Gate (two-sided)	Retrd.	1992	3.00	10-25
1985	Xmas Pine Tree	Retrd.	1990	4.00	30-50
1985	Xmas Pine Tree w/Red Bows	Retrd.	1990	3.00	175-220
1990	Xmas Spruce	5-Yr.		4.00	5
1994	Yule Tree S/2	5-Yr.		4.50	5

American Barns - F. Jones

YEAR ISSUE		EDITION LIMIT	YEAR RETD.	ISSUE PRICE	QUOTE U.S.$
1992	Bank Barn	5-Yr.		8.50	10
1992	Crib Barn	5-Yr.		8.50	10
1992	Ohio Barn	5-Yr.		8.50	10
1992	Vermont Barn	5-Yr.		8.50	10

Bed & Breakfast Series - F. Jones

YEAR ISSUE		EDITION LIMIT	YEAR RETD.	ISSUE PRICE	QUOTE U.S.$
1995	Glen Iris	5-Yr.		10.00	10
1995	Kinter House Inn	5-Yr.		10.00	10
1995	Southmoreland	5-Yr.		10.00	10
1995	Victorian Mansion	5-Yr.		10.00	10

California Mission Series - F. Jones

YEAR ISSUE		EDITION LIMIT	YEAR RETD.	ISSUE PRICE	QUOTE U.S.$
1995	Mission Dolores	5-Yr.		10.00	10
1995	Mission San Buenaventura	5-Yr.		10.00	10
1995	Mission San Juan Bautista	5-Yr.		10.00	10
1995	Mission San Luis Rey	5-Yr.		10.00	10

Chippewa Amusement Park - F. Jones

YEAR ISSUE		EDITION LIMIT	YEAR RETD.	ISSUE PRICE	QUOTE U.S.$
1993	Ballroom	5-Yr.		9.00	10
1993	Bath House	5-Yr.		9.00	10
1993	Midway	5-Yr.		9.00	10
1993	Pavilion	5-Yr.		9.00	10

Christmas '83-Williamsburg - F. Jones

YEAR ISSUE		EDITION LIMIT	YEAR RETD.	ISSUE PRICE	QUOTE U.S.$
1983	Christmas Church	Retrd.	1983	6.00	N/A
1983	Federal House	Retrd.	1983	6.00	N/A
1983	Garrison House	Retrd.	1983	6.00	N/A
1983	Georgian House	Retrd.	1983	6.00	450
1983	Set	Retrd.	1983	24.00	N/A

Christmas '84-Nantucket - F. Jones

YEAR ISSUE		EDITION LIMIT	YEAR RETD.	ISSUE PRICE	QUOTE U.S.$
1984	Christmas Shop	Retrd.	1984	6.50	N/A
1984	Powell House	Retrd.	1984	6.50	350
1984	Shaw House	Retrd.	1984	6.50	350
1984	Wintrop House	Retrd.	1984	6.50	N/A
1984	Set	Retrd.	1984	26.00	1500

Christmas '85-Ohio Western Reserve - F. Jones

YEAR ISSUE		EDITION LIMIT	YEAR RETD.	ISSUE PRICE	QUOTE U.S.$
1985	Bellevue House	Retrd.	1985	7.00	175
1985	Gates Mills Church	Retrd.	1985	7.00	175
1985	Olmstead House	Retrd.	1985	7.00	175
1985	Western Reserve Academy	Retrd.	1985	7.00	175
1985	Set	Retrd.	1985	27.00	750-900

Christmas '86-Savannah - F. Jones

YEAR ISSUE		EDITION LIMIT	YEAR RETD.	ISSUE PRICE	QUOTE U.S.$
1986	J.J. Dale Row House	Retrd.	1986	7.25	150
1986	Lafayette Square House	Retrd.	1986	7.25	140-150
1986	Liberty Inn	Retrd.	1986	7.25	200
1986	Simon Mirault Cottage	Retrd.	1986	7.25	200
1986	Set	Retrd.	1986	29.00	750

Christmas '87-Maine - F. Jones

YEAR ISSUE		EDITION LIMIT	YEAR RETD.	ISSUE PRICE	QUOTE U.S.$
1987	Cappy's Chowder House	Retrd.	1987	7.75	250
1987	Captain's House	Retrd.	1987	7.75	250
1987	Damariscotta Church	Retrd.	1987	7.75	250
1987	Portland Head Lighthouse	Retrd.	1987	7.75	250
1987	Set	Retrd.	1987	31.00	800-1000

Christmas '88-Philadelphia - F. Jones

YEAR ISSUE		EDITION LIMIT	YEAR RETD.	ISSUE PRICE	QUOTE U.S.$
1988	Elfreth's Alley	Retrd.	1988	7.75	150-200
1988	Graff House	Retrd.	1988	7.75	150-200
1988	The Head House	Retrd.	1988	7.75	150-200
1988	Hill-Physick-Keith House	Retrd.	1988	7.75	150-200
1988	Set	Retrd.	1988	31.00	450-700

Christmas '89-In New England - F. Jones

YEAR ISSUE		EDITION LIMIT	YEAR RETD.	ISSUE PRICE	QUOTE U.S.$
1989	Hunter House	Retrd.	1989	8.00	80-125
1989	The Old South Meeting House	Retrd.	1989	8.00	80-125
1989	Sheldon's Tavern	Retrd.	1989	8.00	125
1989	The Vermont Country Store	Retrd.	1989	8.00	80-125
1989	Set	Retrd.	1989	32.00	250-400

Christmas '90-Colonial Virginia - F. Jones

YEAR ISSUE		EDITION LIMIT	YEAR RETD.	ISSUE PRICE	QUOTE U.S.$
1990	Dulany House	Retrd.	1990	8.00	50-100
1990	Rising Sun Tavern	Retrd.	1990	8.00	70-100

YEAR ISSUE		EDITION LIMIT	YEAR RETD.	ISSUE PRICE	QUOTE U.S.$
1990	Shirley Plantation	Retrd.	1990	8.00	40-100
1990	St. John's Church	Retrd.	1990	8.00	100
1990	St. John's Church (blue)	Retrd.	1990	8.00	150-200
1990	Set	Retrd.	1990	32.00	300-600

Christmas '91-Rocky Mountain - F. Jones

1991	First Presbyterian Church	Retrd.	1991	8.20	50-75
1991	Tabor House	Retrd.	1991	8.20	50-75
1991	Western Hotel	Retrd.	1991	8.20	25-75
1991	Wheller-Stallard House	Retrd.	1991	8.20	25-75
1991	Set	Retrd.	1991	32.80	125-200

Christmas '92-Hometown - F. Jones

1992	August Imgard House	Retrd.	1992	8.50	25-30
1992	Howey House	Retrd.	1992	8.50	19-30
1992	Overholt House	Retrd.	1992	8.50	19-30
1992	Wayne Co. Courthouse	Retrd.	1992	8.50	19-30
1992	Set	Retrd.	1992	34.00	80-100

Christmas '93-St. Charles - F. Jones

1993	Lewis & Clark Center	Retrd.	1993	9.00	13-20
1993	Newbill-McElhiney House	Retrd.	1993	9.00	13-20
1993	St. Peter's Catholic Church	Retrd.	1993	9.00	13-20
1993	Stone Row	Retrd.	1993	9.00	13-20
1993	Set	Retrd.	1993	36.00	65-75

Christmas '94-New Orleans Series - F. Jones

1994	Beauregard-Keyes House	Retrd.	1994	10.00	14
1994	Gallier House	Retrd.	1994	10.00	14
1994	Hermann-Grima House	Retrd.	1994	10.00	14
1994	St. Patrick's Church	Retrd.	1994	10.00	14
1994	Set	Retrd.	1994	40.00	50

Christmas '95-New York Series - F. Jones

1995	Clement C. Moore House	12/95		10.00	10
1995	Fraunces Taver	12/95		10.00	10
1995	Fulton Market	12/95		10.00	10
1995	St. Marks-In-the-Bowery	12/95		10.00	10

Christmas '96-Atlanta Series - F. Jones

1996	Callanwolde	12/96		11.00	11
1996	First Baptist Church	12/96		11.00	11
1996	Fox Theatre	12/96		11.00	11
1996	Margaret Mitchell House	12/96		11.00	11

Circus Series - F. Jones

1996	Ferris Wheel	12/96		10.00	10
1995	Sideshow	12/95		10.00	10

Covered Bridge Series - F. Jones

1995	Creamery Bridge	12/95		10.00	10
1996	Kennedy Bridge	12/96		10.00	10

Daughters of the Painted Lady Series - F. Jones

1995	Barber Cottage	5-Yr.		10.00	10
1995	The Fan House	5-Yr.		10.00	10
1995	Hall Cottage	5-Yr.		10.00	10
1995	The Painted Lady	5-Yr.		10.00	10

Duke of Gloucester Series - F. Jones

1994	Cole Shop	5-Yr.		10.00	10
1994	Nicolson Store	5-Yr.		10.00	10
1994	Pasteur & Galt Apothecary	5-Yr.		10.00	10
1994	Prentis Shop	5-Yr.		10.00	10

Elm Street Series - F. Jones

1994	Blumenthal's	5-Yr.		10.00	10
1994	Clyde's Shoe Repair	5-Yr.		10.00	10
1994	First Congregational Church	5-Yr.		10.00	10
1994	Jim's Hunting & Fishing	5-Yr.		10.00	10

Fairy Tale Series - F. Jones

1996	Gingerbread House	5-Yr.		10.00	10
1996	Grandmother's House	5-Yr.		10.00	10
1996	Seven Dwarf's House	5-Yr.		10.00	10
1996	Three Bear's House	5-Yr.		10.00	10

Fall - F. Jones

1986	Golden Lamb Buttery	Retrd.	1991	8.00	30-45
1986	Grimm's Farmhouse	Retrd.	1991	8.00	45
1986	Mail Pouch Barn	Retrd.	1991	8.00	45-75
1986	Vollant Mills	Retrd.	1991	8.00	35-45
1986	Set	Retrd.	1991	32.00	135-180

Firehouse Series - F. Jones

1994	David Crockett No. 1	5-Yr.		10.00	10
1994	Denver No. 1	5-Yr.		10.00	10
1994	Toledo No. 18	5-Yr.		10.00	10
1994	Vigilant 1891	5-Yr.		10.00	10

Galveston Series - F. Jones

1996	Ashton Villa	5-Yr.		10.00	10
1996	Lemuel Burr House	5-Yr.		10.00	10
1996	Sacred Heart Church	5-Yr.		10.00	10
1996	Trueheart - Adriance Building	5-Yr.		10.00	10

General Store Series - F. Jones

1993	Calef's Country Store	5-Yr.		10.00	10
1993	Davoll's General Store	5-Yr.		10.00	10
1993	Peltier's Market	5-Yr.		10.00	10
1993	S. Woodstock Country Store	5-Yr.		10.00	10

Great Americans Series - F. Jones

1996	Daniel Boone Home	12/96		10.00	10

Green Gables Series - F. Jones

1996	Green Gables House	12/96		10.00	10

Greenwich Village Series - F. Jones

1996	Hudson Gormet	5-Yr.		10.00	10
1996	Mc Nulty's Tea & Coffee	5-Yr.		10.00	10
1996	Three Lives Books	5-Yr.		10.00	10
1996	Vesuvio Bakery	5-Yr.		10.00	10

Hagerstown - F. Jones

1988	J Hager House	Retrd.	1993	8.00	13-40
1988	Miller House	Retrd.	1993	8.00	13-40
1988	Woman's Club	Retrd.	1993	8.00	13-40
1988	The Yule Cupboard	Retrd.	1993	8.00	13-40
1988	Set	Retrd.	1993	32.00	60-140

Historic Nauvoo Series - F. Jones

1995	Cultural Hall	5-Yr.		10.00	10
1995	J. Browning Gunsmith	5-Yr.		10.00	10
1995	Printing Office	5-Yr.		10.00	10
1995	Stoddard Home & Tinsmith	5-Yr.		10.00	10

Liberty St. - F. Jones

1988	County Courthouse	Retrd.	1993	8.00	13-35
1988	Graf Printing Co.	Retrd.	1993	8.00	13-35
1988	Wilton Railway Depot	Retrd.	1993	8.00	13-35
1988	Z. Jones Basketmaker	Retrd.	1993	8.00	13-35

Lighthouse - F. Jones

1990	Admiralty Head	5-Yr.		8.00	10
1990	Cape Hatteras Lighthouse	5-Yr.		8.00	10
1990	Sandy Hook Lighthouse	5-Yr.		8.00	10
1990	Split Rock Lighthouse	5-Yr.		8.00	10

Limited Edition Promotional Items - F. Jones

1993	Convention Museum	Retrd.	1993	12.95	13
1993	F.J. Factory	Open		12.95	13
1994	F.J. Factory/5 Yr. Banner	Retrd.	1994	10.00	15
1993	F.J. Factory/Gold Cat Edition	Retrd.	1993	12.95	490
1994	F.J. Factory/Home Banner	Retrd.	1994	10.00	10
1990	Frycrest Farm Homestead	Retrd.	1991	10.00	125
1992	Glen Pine	Retrd.	1993	10.00	20-35
1993	Nativity Cat on the Fence	Retrd.	1993	19.95	20

Main St. - F. Jones

1987	Franklin Library	Retrd.	1992	8.00	20-40
1987	Garden Theatre	Retrd.	1992	8.00	20-45
1987	Historical Museum	Retrd.	1992	8.00	20-40
1987	Telegraph/Post Office	Retrd.	1992	8.00	20-45
1987	Set	Retrd.	1992	32.00	70-150

Mark Twain's Hannibal Series - F. Jones

1995	Becky Thatcher House	12/95		10.00	10
1996	Hickory Stick	12/96		10.00	10

Market St. - F. Jones

1989	Schumacher Mills	Retrd.	1993	8.00	13-23
1989	Seville Hardware Store	Retrd.	1993	8.00	13-23
1989	West India Goods Store	Retrd.	1993	8.00	13-23
1989	Yankee Candle Company	Retrd.	1993	8.00	13-23

Martha's Vineyard Series - F. Jones

1995	John Coffin House	12/95		10.00	10
1996	West Chop Lighthouse	12/96		10.00	10

Miscellaneous - F. Jones

1985	Pencil Holder	Retrd.	1988	3.95	210
1985	Recipe Holder	Retrd.	1988	3.95	250
1986	School Desk-blue	Retrd.	1988	12.00	N/A
1986	School Desk-red	Retrd.	1988	12.00	175

Nantucket - F. Jones

1987	Jared Coffin House	Retrd.	1992	8.00	20-33
1987	Maria Mitchell House	Retrd.	1992	8.00	20-33
1987	Nantucket Atheneum	Retrd.	1992	8.00	20-33
1987	Unitarian Church	Retrd.	1992	8.00	20-33
1987	Set	Retrd.	1992	32.00	70-100

Nautical - F. Jones

1987	H & E Ships Chandlery	Retrd.	1992	8.00	20-40
1987	Lorain Lighthouse	Retrd.	1992	8.00	20-40
1987	Monhegan Boat Landing	Retrd.	1992	8.00	20-40
1987	Yacht Club	Retrd.	1992	8.00	20-40
1987	Set	Retrd.	1992	32.00	70-140

Neighborhood Event Series - F. Jones

1995	Peter Seitz Tavern & Stagecoach	12/95		12.95	13
1995	Birely Place	12/95		12.95	13
1996	Sea-Chimes	12/96		12.95	13
1996	Bailey-Gombert House	12/96		12.95	13

Nursery Rhyme Series - F. Jones

1994	Crooked House	5-Yr.		10.00	10
1994	House That Jack Built	5-Yr.		10.00	10
1994	Old Woman in the Shoe	5-Yr.		10.00	10
1994	Peter, Peter Pumpkin Eater	5-Yr.		10.00	10

Ohio Amish - F. Jones

1991	Ada Mae's Quilt Barn	5-Yr.		8.00	10
1991	Brown School	5-Yr.		8.00	10
1991	Eli's Harness Shop	5-Yr.		8.00	10
1991	Jonas Troyer Home	5-Yr.		8.00	10

Painted Ladies - F. Jones

1988	Andrews Hotel	Retrd.	1993	8.00	14-23
1988	Lady Amanda	Retrd.	1993	8.00	14-23
1988	Lady Elizabeth	Retrd.	1993	8.00	14-23
1988	Lady Iris	Retrd.	1993	8.00	14-23
1988	Set	Retrd.	1993	32.00	60-80

Roscoe Village - F. Jones

1986	Canal Company	Retrd.	1991	8.00	35-45
1986	Jackson Twp. Hall	Retrd.	1991	8.00	35-45
1986	Old Warehouse Rest.	Retrd.	1991	8.00	35-45
1986	Roscoe General Store	Retrd.	1991	8.00	35-45
1986	Set	Retrd.	1991	32.00	115-150

Series I - F. Jones

1983	Antique Shop	Retrd.	1988	8.00	100-125
1983	Apothecary	Retrd.	1988	8.00	100-125
1983	Barbershop	Retrd.	1988	8.00	80-125
1983	Book Store	Retrd.	1988	8.00	50-125
1983	Cherry Tree Inn	Retrd.	1988	8.00	N/A
1983	Federal House	Retrd.	1988	8.00	60-125
1983	Florist Shop	Retrd.	1988	8.00	60-125
1983	Garrison House	Retrd.	1988	8.00	50-125
1983	Red Whale Inn	Retrd.	1988	8.00	N/A
1983	School	Retrd.	1988	8.00	80-125
1983	Sweetshop	Retrd.	1988	8.00	125
1983	Toy Shoppe	Retrd.	1988	8.00	125
1983	Victorian House	Retrd.	1988	8.00	50-125
1983	Wayside Inn	Retrd.	1988	8.00	N/A
1983	Set of 12 w/1 Inn	Retrd.	1988	96.00	1000-2000
1983	Set of 14 w/ 3 Inns	Retrd.	1988	112.00	2000-3000

Series II - F. Jones

1984	Attorney/Bank	Retrd.	1989	8.00	75-95
1984	Brocke House	Retrd.	1989	8.00	50-95
1984	Church	Retrd.	1989	8.00	50-95
1984	Eaton House	Retrd.	1989	8.00	50-95
1984	Grandinere House	Retrd.	1989	8.00	50-95
1984	Millinery/Quilt	Retrd.	1989	8.00	50-100
1984	Music Shop	Retrd.	1989	8.00	50-95
1984	S&T Clothiers	Retrd.	1989	8.00	60-95
1984	Tobacconist/Shoemaker	Retrd.	1989	8.00	75-95
1984	Town Hall	Retrd.	1989	8.00	150
1984	Set	Retrd.	1989	96.00	525-750

Series III - F. Jones

1985	Allen-Coe House	Retrd.	1990	8.00	40-50
1985	Connecticut Ave. FireHouse	Retrd.	1990	8.00	40-50
1985	Dry Goods Store	Retrd.	1990	8.00	40-50
1985	Edinburgh Times	Retrd.	1990	8.00	40-50
1985	Fine Jewelers	Retrd.	1990	8.00	40-50
1985	Hobart-Harley House	Retrd.	1990	8.00	40-50
1985	Kalorama Guest House	Retrd.	1990	8.00	40-50
1985	Main St. Carriage Shop	Retrd.	1990	8.00	40-50
1985	Opera House	Retrd.	1990	8.00	40-50
1985	Ristorante	Retrd.	1990	8.00	40-50
1985	Set	Retrd.	1990	80.00	350-600

Series IV - F. Jones

1986	Bennington-Hull House	Retrd.	1991	8.00	25-40
1986	Chagrin Falls Popcorn Shop	Retrd.	1991	8.00	25-40
1986	Chepachet Union Church	Retrd.	1991	8.00	25-40
1986	John Belville House	Retrd.	1991	8.00	25-40
1986	Jones Bros. Tea Co.	Retrd.	1991	8.00	25-40
1986	The Little House Giftables	Retrd.	1991	8.00	25-40
1986	O'Malley's Livery Stable	Retrd.	1991	8.00	25-40
1986	Vandenberg House	Retrd.	1991	8.00	25-40
1986	Village Clock Shop	Retrd.	1991	8.00	25-40
1986	Westbrook House	Retrd.	1991	8.00	25-40
1986	Set	Retrd.	1991	80.00	325-450

Series V - F. Jones

1987	Amish Oak/Dixie Shoe	Retrd.	1992	8.00	18-32
1987	Architect/Tailor	Retrd.	1992	8.00	18-32
1987	Congruity Tavern	Retrd.	1992	8.00	18-32
1987	Creole House	Retrd.	1992	8.00	18-32
1987	Dentist/Physician	Retrd.	1992	8.00	18-32
1987	M. Washington House	Retrd.	1992	8.00	18-32
1987	Markethouse	Retrd.	1992	8.00	18-32
1987	Murray Hotel	Retrd.	1992	8.00	18-32
1987	Police Department	Retrd.	1992	8.00	18-32
1987	Southport Bank	Retrd.	1992	8.00	18-32
1987	Set	Retrd.	1992	80.00	200-300

Series VI - F. Jones

1988	Burton Lancaster House	Retrd.	1993	8.00	14-23
1988	City Hospital	Retrd.	1993	8.00	20-45
1988	First Baptist Church	Retrd.	1993	8.00	14-23
1988	Fish/Meat Market	Retrd.	1993	8.00	14-23
1988	Lincoln School	Retrd.	1993	8.00	14-23
1988	New Masters Gallery	Retrd.	1993	8.00	14-23
1988	Ohliger House	Retrd.	1993	8.00	14-23
1988	Pruyn House	Retrd.	1993	8.00	14-23

YEAR ISSUE		EDITION LIMIT	YEAR RETD.	ISSUE PRICE	QUOTE U.S.$
1988	Stiffenbody Funeral Home	Retrd.	1993	8.00	20-45
1988	Williams & Sons	Retrd.	1993	8.00	14-23
1988	Set	Retrd.	1993	80.00	130-200

Series VII - F. Jones

1989	Black Cat Antiques	Retrd.	1994	8.00	15
1989	Hairdressing Parlor	Retrd.	1994	8.00	15
1989	Handcrafted Toys	Retrd.	1994	8.00	15
1989	Justice of the Peace	Retrd.	1994	8.00	15
1989	Octagonal School	Retrd.	1994	8.00	15
1989	Old Franklin Book Shop	Retrd.	1994	8.00	15
1989	Thorpe House Bed & Breakfast	Retrd.	1994	8.00	15
1989	Village Tinsmith	Retrd.	1994	8.00	15
1989	Williams Apothecary	Retrd.	1994	8.00	15
1989	Winkler Bakery	Retrd.	1994	8.00	15

Series VIII - F. Jones

1990	F.J. Realty Company	5-Yr.		8.00	10
1990	Globe Corner Bookstore	5-Yr.		8.00	10
1990	Haberdashers	5-Yr.		8.00	10
1990	Medina Fire Department	5-Yr.		8.00	10
1990	Nell's Stems & Stitches	5-Yr.		8.00	10
1990	Noah's Ark Veterinary	5-Yr.		8.00	10
1990	Piccadilli Pipe & Tobacco	5-Yr.		8.00	10
1990	Puritan House	5-Yr.		8.00	10
1990	Victoria's Parlour	5-Yr.		8.00	10
1990	Walldorff Furniture	5-Yr.		8.00	10

Series IX - F. Jones

1991	All Saints Chapel	5-Yr.		8.00	10
1991	American Red Cross	5-Yr.		8.00	10
1991	Central City Opera House	5-Yr.		8.00	10
1991	City Hall	5-Yr.		8.00	10
1991	CPA/Law Office	5-Yr.		8.00	10
1991	Gov. Snyder Mansion	5-Yr.		8.00	10
1991	Jeweler/Optometrist	5-Yr.		8.00	10
1991	Osbahr's Upholstery	5-Yr.		8.00	10
1991	Spanky's Hardware Co.	5-Yr.		8.00	10
1991	The Treble Clef	5-Yr.		8.00	10

Series X - F. Jones

1992	City News	5-Yr.		8.50	10
1992	Fudge Kitchen	5-Yr.		8.50	10
1992	Grand Haven	5-Yr.		8.50	10
1992	Henyan's Athletic Shop	5-Yr.		8.50	10
1992	Leppert's 5 &10	5-Yr.		8.50	10
1992	Madeline's Dress Shop	5-Yr.		8.50	10
1992	Owl And The Pussycat	5-Yr.		8.50	10
1992	Pickles Pub	5-Yr.		8.50	10
1992	Pure Gas Station	5-Yr.		8.50	10
1993	Shrimplin & Jones Produce	5-Yr.		9.00	10
1992	United Church of Acworth	5-Yr.		8.50	10

Series XI - F. Jones

1993	Barbershop/Gallery	5-Yr.		9.00	10
1993	Haddonfield Bank	5-Yr.		9.00	10
1993	Immanuel Church	5-Yr.		9.00	10
1993	Johann Singer Boots & Shoes	5-Yr.		9.00	10
1993	Pet Shop/Gift Shop	5-Yr.		9.00	10
1993	Police-Troop C	5-Yr.		9.00	10
1993	Stone's Restaurant	5-Yr.		9.00	10
1993	U.S. Armed Forces	5-Yr.		9.00	10
1993	U.S. Post Office	5-Yr.		9.00	10

Series XII - F. Jones

1994	Arnold-Lynch Funeral Home	5-Yr.		10.00	10
1994	Bedford County Courthouse	5-Yr.		10.00	10
1994	Boyd's Drug Strore	5-Yr.		10.00	10
1994	Christmas Tree Hill Gifts	5-Yr.		10.00	10
1994	Foorman-Morrison House	5-Yr.		10.00	10
1994	Haddon Hts. Train Depot	5-Yr.		10.00	10
1994	Historical Society	5-Yr.		10.00	10
1994	Masonic Temple	5-Yr.		10.00	10
1994	Ritz Theater	5-Yr.		10.00	10
1994	Spread Eagle Tavern	5-Yr.		10.00	10

Series XIII - F. Jones

1995	Alvanas & Coe Barbers	5-Yr.		10.00	10
1995	Cedar School	5-Yr.		10.00	10
1995	Hospital	5-Yr.		10.00	10
1995	Needleworker	5-Yr.		10.00	10
1995	Public Library	5-Yr.		10.00	10
1995	Schneider's Bakery	5-Yr.		10.00	10
1995	Susquehanna Antiques	5-Yr.		10.00	10
1995	YMCA	5-Yr.		10.00	10

Series XIV - F. Jones

1996	3 Guys Pizzeria	5-Yr.		10.00	10
1996	Dr. Goodbody III	5-Yr.		10.00	10
1996	Mc Auley School	5-Yr.		10.00	10
1996	Rosie's Fish & Chips	5-Yr.		10.00	10
1996	Stabler Apothecary	5-Yr.		10.00	10
1996	Wayside Inn Grist Mill	5-Yr.		10.00	10
1996	Willa Cather Home	5-Yr.		10.00	10
1996	Winter Clove Inn	5-Yr.		10.00	10

Shaker Village Series - F. Jones

1995	Great Stone Dwelling	5-Yr.		10.00	10
1995	Meetinghouse	5-Yr.		10.00	10
1995	Round Barn	5-Yr.		10.00	10
1995	Trustees Office	5-Yr.		10.00	10

Southern Belles Series - F. Jones

1996	Auburn	12/96		10.00	10

Special Item - F. Jones

1995	Smokey Bear	Retrd.		8.95	10
1994	Smokey Bear w/ 50th stamp	Retrd.	1994	8.95	10

Tradesman - F. Jones

1988	Buckeye Candy & Tobacco	Retrd.	1993	8.00	14-23
1988	C.O. Wheel Company	Retrd.	1993	8.00	14-23
1988	Hermannhof Winery	Retrd.	1993	8.00	14-23
1988	Jenney Grist Mill	Retrd.	1993	8.00	15-50

Washington - F. Jones

1991	National Archives	5-Yr.		8.00	10
1991	U.S. Capitol	5-Yr.		8.00	10
1991	U.S. Supreme Court	5-Yr.		8.00	10
1991	White House	5-Yr.		8.00	10

Waterfront Series - F. Jones

1994	Arnold Transit Company	5-Yr.		10.00	10
1994	Lowell's Boat Shop	5-Yr.		10.00	10
1994	Sand Island Lighthouse	5-Yr.		10.00	10
1994	Seaside Market	5-Yr.		10.00	10

West Coast Lighthouse Series - F. Jones

1994	East Brother Lighthouse	5-Yr.		10.00	10
1994	Heceta Head Light	5-Yr.		10.00	10
1994	Mukilteo Light	5-Yr.		10.00	10
1994	Point Pinos Light	5-Yr.		10.00	10

Wild West - F. Jones

1989	Drink 'em up Saloon	Retrd.	1993	8.00	14-23
1989	F.C. Zimmermann's Gun Shop	Retrd.	1993	8.00	14-23
1989	Marshal's Office	Retrd.	1993	8.00	15-40
1989	Wells, Fargo & Co.	Retrd.	1993	8.00	14-23

Williamsburg Series - F. Jones

1993	Bruton Parish	5-Yr.		10.00	10
1993	Governor's Palace	5-Yr.		10.00	10
1993	Grissell Hay Lodging House	5-Yr.		10.00	10
1993	Raleigh Tavern	5-Yr.		10.00	10

Wine Country Series - F. Jones

1996	Charles Krug Winery	12/96		10.00	10

Cavanagh Group Intl.

Coca-Cola Brand Heritage Collection - Various

1995	Always - CGI	Open		30.00	30
1995	Always-Musical - CGI	Open		50.00	50
1995	Boy at Well - N. Rockwell	10,000		60.00	60
1995	Boy Fishing - N. Rockwell	10,000		60.00	60
1994	Calendar Girl 1916-Music Box - CGI	Open		60.00	60
1994	Eight Polar Bears on Wood-Musical - CGI	10,000		150.00	150
1995	Elaine - CGI	10,000		100.00	100
1995	Girl on Swing - CGI	10,000		80.00	80
1994	Hilda Clark 1901-Music Box - CGI	Open		60.00	60
1994	Hilda Clark 1903-Music Box - CGI	Open		60.00	60
1995	The Homecoming - S. Stearman	7,500	1995	125.00	125
1995	Hospitality - Sundblom	5,000		35.00	35
1994	Santa at His Desk - Sundblom	5,000		80.00	80
1994	Santa at His Desk-Musical - Sundblom	5,000		100.00	100
1994	Santa at His Desk-Snowglobe - Sundblom	Open		45.00	45
1994	Santa at the Fireplace - Sundblom	5,000		80.00	80
1994	Santa at the Fireplace-Musical - Sundblom	5,000		100.00	100
1994	Santa at the Lamppost-Snowglobe - Sundblom	Open		50.00	50
1994	Single Polar Bear on Ice-Snowglobe - CGI	Open		40.00	40
1995	They Remember Me-Musical - Sundblom	5,000		50.00	50
1994	Two Polar Bears on Ice - CGI	Open		25.00	25
1994	Two Polar Bears on Ice-Musical -CGI	Open		45.00	45

Coca-Cola Brand Musical - Various

1993	Dear Santa, Please Pause Here - Sundblom	Open		50.00	50
1994	Santa's Soda Shop - CGI	Open		50.00	50

Coca-Cola Brand North Pole Bottling Works - CGI

1995	Filling Operations	Open		45.00	45
1995	The Kitchen Corner	Open		55.00	55
1995	Making the Secret Syrup	Open		30.00	30
1995	Pipe Maintenance	Open		20.00	20
1995	Quality Control	Open		25.00	25
1995	Restocking the Vending Machine	Open		30.00	30
1995	Santa at His Desk	Open		30.00	30
1995	Santa's Office	Open		50.00	50
1995	Taking a Break	Open		20.00	20
1995	The Vault	Open		25.00	25

Coca-Cola Brand Santa Animations - Sundblom

1991	Ssshh! (1st Ed.)	Closed	1992	99.99	135-285
1992	Santa's Pause for Refreshment (2nd Ed.)	Closed	1993	99.99	135-235
1993	Trimming the Tree (3rd Ed.)	Closed	1994	99.99	135-235
1995	Santa at the Lamppost (4th Ed.)	Open		110.00	110

Coca-Cola Brand Town Square Collection - CGI

1992	Candler's Drugs	Closed	1993	39.99	40-60
1993	City Hall	Closed	1994	39.99	40-60
1995	Coca-Cola Bottling Works	Open		39.99	40
1992	Dee's Boarding House	Closed	1993	39.99	200-400
1992	Dick's Luncheonette	Closed	1993	39.99	40-60
1994	Flying "A" Service Station	Open		39.99	40
1992	Gilbert's Grocery	Closed	1993	39.99	40-60
1995	Grist Mill	Open		39.99	40
1992	Howard Oil	Closed	1993	39.99	100-135
1993	Jacob's Pharmacy	5,000	1993	25.00	200-400
1995	Jenny's Sweet Shoppe	Open		39.99	40
1995	Lighthouse Point Snack Bar	Open		39.99	40
1994	McMahon's General Store	Open		39.99	40
1993	Mooney's Antique Barn	Closed	1994	39.99	40-60
1994	Plaza Drugs	Open		39.99	40
1993	Route 93 Covered Bridge	Open		19.99	20
1994	Station #14 Firehouse	Open		39.99	40
1994	Strand Theatre	Open		39.99	40
1993	T. Taylor's Emporium	Closed	1994	39.99	40-60
1993	The Tick Tock Diner	Open		39.99	40
1994	Town Gazebo	Open		19.99	20
1992	Train Depot	Closed	1993	39.99	175-235

Coca-Cola Brand Town Square Collection Accessories - CGI

1992	"Coca-Cola" Ad Car	Closed	1993	9.00	25
1992	"Coca-Cola" Delivery Truck	Closed	1993	15.00	25
1992	"Gil" the Grocer	Closed	1993	8.00	10
1992	After Skating	Closed	1993	8.00	10
1992	Bringing It Home	Closed	1993	8.00	13
1992	Delivery Man	Closed	1993	8.00	35
1992	Horse-Drawn Wagon	Closed	1993	12.00	25
1992	Thirsty the Snowman	Closed	1993	9.00	14

Classic Collectables by Uniquely Yours

Additional Santas - E. Tisa

1991	Mrs. Claus	Open		36.00	68
1993	Olde English Santa	Open		66.00	94
1993	Russian Santa	Open		72.00	102
1989	Santa at Work	Open		68.00	139
1990	St. Nicholas	Open		76.00	139

Dicken's-A Christmas Carol (Miniatures) - E. Tisa

1987	Belle	Closed	1989	40.00	40
1987	Christmas Past	Closed	1989	40.00	40
1987	Christmas Present	Closed	1989	40.00	40
1987	Christmas Yet to Be	Closed	1989	32.00	32
1987	Father Christmas	Closed	1989	40.00	40
1987	Marley's Ghost	Closed	1989	40.00	40
1987	Mr. Fezzziwig	Closed	1989	40.00	40
1987	Mrs. Cratchit	Closed	1989	42.00	42
1987	Mrs. Fezziwig	Closed	1989	40.00	40
1987	Scrooge	Closed	1989	40.00	40
1987	Tiny Tim & Bob	Closed	1989	60.00	60

Dicken's-A Christmas Carol - E. Tisa

1989	Adult Carolers	Open		78.00	125
1988	Bob Cratchit and Tiny Tim	Open		68.00	122
1988	Boy on Sled	Open		32.00	63
1989	Children Carolers	Open		68.00	119
1989	Christmas Present (vingette w/feast)	Closed	1990	90.00	90
1988	Ghost of Christmas Past	Open		36.00	68
1988	Ghost of Christmas Present	Open		68.00	122
1988	Ghost of Christmas Yet To Be	Open		48.00	102
1988	Girl in a Sleigh	Open		36.00	74
1990	Lighting the Menorrah	Closed	1990	96.00	96
1988	Marley's Ghost	Open		36.00	77
1988	Match Girl w/ Lamppost	Closed	1992	68.00	68
1988	Mr. & Mrs. Fezziwig	Open		78.00	125
1988	Mrs. Crachit	Open		36.00	68
1988	Scrooge	Open		36.00	68
1989	Scrooge & Marley	Closed	1991	78.00	78
1989	Senior Carolers	Open		78.00	125
1986	Single Boy Caroler	Closed	1989	N/A	N/A
1986	Single Girl Caroler	Closed	1989	N/A	N/A
1986	Single Man Caroler	Closed	1989	N/A	N/A
1986	Single Woman Caroler	Closed	1989	N/A	N/A
1989	Victorian Band	Closed	1989	144.00	144

Easter - E. Tisa

1989	Boy w/Easter Basket	Closed	1991	36.00	36
1989	Girl w/Bunnies	Closed	1991	36.00	36

Halloween - E. Tisa

1989	Ghoul	Closed	1991	38.00	38
1989	Trick or Treat-Devil	Closed	1991	36.00	36
1989	Trick or Treat-Witch	Closed	1991	32.00	32

Limited Edition Santas - E. Tisa

1994	Black Santa on Tricycle	600		160.00	228
1995	Countryside Santa	300		396.00	396
1991	European Santa w/Little Girl	1,000		118.00	205
1989	Father Christmas	Closed	1992	138.00	190
1989	Father Christmas-sm.	Closed	1992	48.00	56

YEAR ISSUE		EDITION LIMIT	YEAR RETD.	ISSUE PRICE	QUOTE U.S.$
1990	Jolly St. Nick	250		104.00	184
1989	Kris Kringle	Closed	1992	178.00	230
1989	Olde World Santa	Closed	1992	48.00	56
1993	Olde World Santa	300		270.00	383
1993	Pere Noel	500		350.00	496
1993	Renaissance Santa	450		210.00	326
1994	Santa on Tricycle	600		160.00	228
1993	Traditional Santa in Sleigh	400		160.00	241
1991	Victorian Santa	1,500		196.00	326

Miscellaneous - E. Tisa

1989	African Man	Closed	1990	40.00	40
1989	African Woman	Closed	1990	36.00	36
1988	Bride	Closed	1991	40.00	40
1989	Christmas Child	Closed	1991	22.00	22
1989	Christmas Shopper	Closed	1992	26.00	26
1988	Groom	Closed	1991	40.00	40
1989	Mother & Daughter	Closed	1990	68.00	68

Thanksgiving - E. Tisa

1988	Pilgrim-Man	Closed	1990	40.00	40
1988	Pilgrim-Woman	Closed	1990	38.00	38

Valentine's Day - E. Tisa

1990	Valentine-Boy	Closed	1990	36.00	36
1990	Valentine-Girl	Closed	1990	36.00	36

Victorian - E. Tisa

1989	Victorian Boy w/Hoop	Closed	1991	36.00	36
1989	Victorian Girl	Closed	1991	36.00	36
1989	Victorian Man	Closed	1991	40.00	40
1989	Victorian Treetop Angel	Open		80.00	114
1989	Victorian Woman	Closed	1991	36.00	36

Creart

African Wildlife - Various

1987	African Elephant With Leaf-22 - Martinez	2,500		230.00	298
1987	African Elephant-10 - Perez	2,500	1993	410.00	575
1987	African Lion-61 - Martinez	2,500		260.00	338
1991	Breaking Away Gazelles-256 - Quesada	1,500		650.00	698
1993	Cape Buffalo-412 - Contreras	1,500		418.00	418
1995	Cheetahs-644 - Estevez	950		178.00	178
1987	Cob Antelope-46 - Perez	2,500		310.00	398
1995	Elephant Tracks-472 - Perez	1,500		350.00	350
1987	Giraffe-43 - Perez	2,500		250.00	338
1994	Grumbler Cape Buffalo-451 - Martinez	1,500		498.00	498
1990	Hippopotamus-55 - Quesada	2,500		420.00	438
1995	Lion-448 - Contreras	1,500		298.00	298
1994	Numa Lion's Head-433 - Contreras	2,500		418.00	418
1986	Running Elephant-73 - Perez	2,500		260.00	338
1992	Small African Elephant-271 - Perez	2,500	1993	320.00	320
1991	Sound of Warning Elephant-268 - Perez	2,500		500.00	518
1990	Symbol of Power Lion-40 - Quesada	2,500		450.00	478
1993	Travieso-358 - Perez	1,500		198.00	218
1987	White Rhinoceros-136 - Perez	2,500		330.00	438
1987	Zebra-67 - Perez	2,500		305.00	398

American Wildlife - Various

1994	Ambushing Puma-508 - Nelson	1,950		150.00	150
1986	American Bison-121 - Perez	Susp.		400.00	490
1986	Bald Eagle-70 - Martinez	Susp.		730.00	900
1994	Briefly Rest Pumas-526 - Nelson	1,950		250.00	250
1993	Buenos Dias Jack Rabbit-229 - Martinez	1,500		218.00	218
1992	California Grizzly-238 - Perez	2,500		270.00	278
1995	Canvasback Duck-902 - Nelson	2,500		95.00	95
1994	Catamountain-505 - Estevez	2,500		118.00	118
1990	The Challenge, Rams-82 - Gonzalez	1,500		698.00	738
1990	Dolphin, Back-148 - Perez	2,500		210.00	250
1990	Dolphin, Front-142 - Perez	2,500		210.00	250
1990	Dolphin, Middle-145 - Perez	2,500		210.00	250
1988	Flamingo Flapping-175 - Perez	2,500		230.00	298
1988	Flamingo Head Down-172 - Perez	2,500		230.00	298
1988	Flamingo Upright-169 - Perez	2,500		230.00	298
1994	Freedom Eagle-430 - Martinez	1,500		500.00	500
1990	Gray Wolf-88 - Quesada	2,500		365.00	378
1987	Grizzley Bear-31 - Perez	2,500		210.00	278
1993	Howling Coyote-217 - Martinez	1,500		199.00	218
1989	Jaguar-79 - Gonzalez	500		700.00	750
1988	Mammoth-112 - Martinez	2,500		450.00	578
1991	Mischievous Raccoon-262 - Quesada	2,500		370.00	318
1995	Moose-478 - Contreras	1,500		298.00	298
1995	Mourning Dove-535 - Nelson	1,500		130.00	130
1994	Out of the Den Puma-523 - Estevez	1,500		130.00	130
1990	Over the Clouds Falcon-85 - Martinez	2,500		520.00	538
1994	Over the Top Puma-445 - Perez	1,500		398.00	398
1989	Penguins-R76 - Del Valle	Closed	1992	175.00	175
1995	Pheasant-903 - Nelson	2,500		95.00	95
1985	Pigeons-64 - Perez	Closed	1991	265.00	265
1991	Playmates Sparrows-265 - Martinez	2,500		500.00	518
1986	Polar Bear-58 - Martinez	2,500		200.00	258
1994	Puffins-511 - Estevez	1,500		258.00	258
1987	Puma-130 - Perez	2,500	1994	370.00	470
1995	Ram-295 - Martinez	950		240.00	240
1993	The Red Fox-220 - Contreras	1,500		199.00	218
1994	Red Tail Hawk-520 - Nelson	1,950		130.00	130
1989	Rooster-R40 - Martinez	Closed	1990	290.00	290
1991	Royal Eagle With Snake-259 - Martinez	2,500		700.00	738
1987	Royal Eagle-49 - Martinez	Closed	1992	545.00	598
1993	Scent of Honey Bear-223 - Perez	1,500		398.00	398
1994	Singing to the Moon I Wolf-439 - Perez	1,500		398.00	398
1994	Singing to the Moon II Wolf-442 - Perez	1,500		358.00	358
1992	Soaring Royal Eagle-52 - Martinez	2,500		580.00	598
1992	Standing Whitetail Deer-109 - Martinez	2,500		364.00	378
1991	White Hunter Polar Bear-250 - Gonzalez	2,500		380.00	398
1990	White Tail Deer-151 - Martinez	2,500		380.00	478
1990	White Tail Doe-154 - Martinez	2,500		330.00	418
1990	White Tail Fawn-157 - Martinez	2,500		220.00	290

Birds of Prey - Robison

1994	Gyrfalcon-502	450		1300.00	1300
1994	Vigilant Eagle-517	650		780.00	780

From Asia & Europe - Various

1988	Bengal Tiger-115 - Perez	Suspd.		440.00	520
1986	Deer-4 - Martinez	Closed	1992	560.00	600
1987	Drover of Camels-124 - Martinez	2,500		650.00	718
1990	Giant Panda-244 - Martinez	2,500		280.00	298
1986	Indian Elephant Baby-16 - Perez	Suspd.		200.00	200
1985	Indian Elephant Mother-25 - Perez	Suspd.		485.00	490
1985	Marco Polo Sheep-37 - Martinez	2,500		270.00	318
1987	Royal Owl-133 - Perez	Closed	1992	340.00	370
1995	Striking Power-292 - Perez	950		338.00	338
1985	Tiger-R55 - Martinez	Closed	1990	200.00	200

Horses And Cattle - Various

1989	Apaloosa Horse-100 - Martinez	2,500		260.00	278
1995	Arabian at Folly-475 - Martinez	2,500		298.00	298
1985	Arabian Horse-34 - Martinez	2,500		230.00	298
1989	Arabian Horse-91 - Perez	2,500		260.00	278
1989	Brahma Bull-13 - Gonzalez	2,500		420.00	498
1985	Bull-28 - Martinez	Susp.		285.00	285
1988	Horse Head-139 - Martinez	2,500		440.00	498
1987	Horse In Passage-127 - Martinez	2,500		500.00	558
1989	Lippizzan Horse-94 - Perez	2,500		260.00	278
1992	Pegasus-106 - Perez	2,500		420.00	438
1989	Quarter Horse II-103 - Perez	2,500		260.00	278
1989	Quarter Horse Recoil-1 - Gonzalez	Closed	1993	310.00	310
1993	Rosie Bella-421 - Martinez	950		758.00	758
1985	Running Horse-7 - Martinez	2,500		360.00	458
1995	Running Wind-241 - Martinez	2,500		178.00	178
1989	Thoroughbred Horse-97 - Perez	2,500		260.00	278

Nature's Care Collection - Various

1993	Doe and Fawns-355 - Contreras	2,500		99.00	138
1993	Eagle and Eaglets-352 - Contreras	2,500		120.00	130
1993	Gorilla and Baby-394 - Contreras	2,500		99.00	110
1993	Grizzly and Cubs-340 - Perez	2,500		99.00	118
1993	Jack Rabbit and Young-343 - Martinez	2,500		99.95	120
1993	Lioness and Cubs-346 - Contreras	2,500		99.00	118
1993	Otters-325 - Estevez	2,500		99.95	120
1993	Penguin and Chicks-76 - Perez	2,500		99.00	132
1993	Wolf and Pups-349 - Contreras	2,500		99.00	150

Pets - Various

1989	Boxer-187 - Martinez	Suspd.		135.00	135
1989	Cocker Spaniel American-184 - Martinez	Suspd.		100.00	100
1991	German Shepherd Dog-253 - Martinez	2,500		360.00	388
1989	Great Dane, Brown-193 - Martinez	Suspd.		140.00	140
1989	Great Dane, Harlequi-196 - Martinez	Suspd.		140.00	140
1987	Labrador Retriever-19 - Martinez	2,500		300.00	378
1989	Labrador, Black-214 - Martinez	Suspd.		130.00	130
1989	Labrador, Golden-211 - Martinez	Suspd.		130.00	130
1989	Pointer, Black-202 - Perez	Suspd.		132.00	132
1989	Pointer, Brown-190 - Perez	Suspd.		132.00	132
1989	Poodle-205 - Perez	Suspd.		120.00	120
1989	Saint Bernard-208 - Perez	Suspd.		130.00	130
1989	Schnauzer Miniature-190 - Perez	Suspd.		110.00	110

Stylus - Various

1992	Bronco Busting-319 - Martinez	Open		100.00	100
1992	Horse Head-310 - Martinez	2,500		150.00	150
1992	Imperial Eagle-301 - Martinez	Open		100.00	100
1995	Koala Family-367 - Contreras	2,500		79.50	80
1992	Mare-313 - Martinez	Open		100.00	100
1995	Mother's Love-376 - Contreras	2,500		72.00	72
1992	Mustang-304 - Martinez	Open		100.00	100
1995	Nap Time-370 - Contreras	2,500		67.50	68
1995	Racoon Fishing-481 - Diaz	2,500		72.00	72
1992	Recoil-307 - Martinez	Open		100.00	100
1995	Spring Arrival-379 - Contreras	2,500		98.00	98
1995	Summer Afternoon-382 - Contreras	2,500		98.00	98
1995	Tender Care-373 - Contreras	2,500		72.00	72

Wild America Edition - Various

1993	American Symbol-328 - Contreras	1,500		246.00	258
1992	Puma Head-334 - Perez	900		320.00	338
1992	Twelve Pointer Deer-337 - Perez	900		472.00	490
1993	White Blizzard-331 - Perez	1,500		275.00	278
1993	Wild America Bison-409 - Contreras	1,500		338.00	338

Cybis

Animal Kingdom - Cybis

1971	American Bullfrog	Closed	N/A	250.00	600
1975	American White Buffalo	250		1250.00	4000
1971	Appaloosa Colt	Closed	N/A	150.00	300
1980	Arctic White Fox	100		4500.00	4700
1984	Australian Greater Sulpher Crested Cockatoo	25		9850.00	9850
1985	Baxter and Doyle	400		450.00	450
1985	Beagles, Branigan and Clancy	Open		375.00	625
1968	Bear	Closed	N/A	85.00	400
1981	Beavers, Egbert and Brewster	400		285.00	335
1968	Buffalo	Closed	N/A	115.00	185
XX	Bull	100		150.00	4500
1977	Bunny Pat-a-Cake	Closed	N/A	90.00	150
1976	Bunny, Muffet	Closed	N/A	85.00	150
1985	Bunny, Snowflake	Open		65.00	75
1984	Chantilly, Kitten	Open		175.00	210
1976	Chipmunk w/Bloodroot	225		625.00	675
1969	Colts, Darby and Joan	Closed	N/A	295.00	475
1982	Dall Sheep	50		Unkn.	4250
1986	Dapple Grey Foal	Open		195.00	250
1970	Deer Mouse in Clover	Closed	N/A	65.00	160
1978	Dormouse, Maximillian	Closed	N/A	250.00	285
1978	Dormouse, Maxine	Closed	N/A	195.00	225
1968	Elephant	100		600.00	5000
1985	Elephant, Willoughby	Open		195.00	245
1961	Horse	100		150.00	2000
1986	Huey, the Harmonious Hare	Open		175.00	275
1967	Kitten, Blue Ribbon	Closed	N/A	95.00	500
1975	Kitten, Tabitha	Closed	N/A	90.00	150
1975	Kitten, Topaz	Closed	N/A	90.00	150
1986	Mick, The Melodious Mutt	Open		175.00	275
1985	Monday, Rhinoceros	Open		85.00	150
1971	Nashua	100		2000.00	3000
1978	Pinky Bunny/Carrot	200		200.00	265
1972	Pinto Colt	Closed	N/A	175.00	250
1976	Prairie Dog	Closed	N/A	245.00	345
1965	Raccoon, Raffles	Closed	N/A	110.00	365
1968	Snail, Sir Escargot	Closed	N/A	50.00	300
1980	Squirrel, Highrise	400		475.00	525
1965	Squirrel, Mr. Fluffy Tail	Closed	N/A	90.00	350
1968	Stallion	350		475.00	850
1966	Thoroughbred	350		425.00	1500
1986	White Tailed Deer	50		9500.00	11500

Biblical - Cybis

1984	Christ Child with Lamb	Open		Unkn.	290
1960	Exodus	50		350.00	2600
1960	Flight Into Egypt	50		175.00	2500
1956	Holy Child of Prague	10		1500.00	N/A
XX	Holywater Font "Holy Ghost"	Closed	N/A	15.00	145
1960	Madonna Lace & Rose	Open		15.00	295
1957	Madonna, House of Gold	8		125.00	4000
1963	Moses, The Great Lawgiver	750		250.00	5500
1984	Nativity, Angel, Color	Open		395.00	575
1984	Nativity, Camel, Color	Open		625.00	825
1985	Nativity, Cow, Color	Open		175.00	195
1985	Nativity, Cow, White	Open		125.00	225
1985	Nativity, Donkey, Color	Open		195.00	225
1985	Nativity, Donkey, White	Open		130.00	150
1984	Nativity, Joseph	Open		Unkn.	325
1985	Nativity, Lamb, Color	Open		150.00	195
1985	Nativity, Lamb, White	Open		115.00	125
1984	Nativity, Mary	Open		Unkn.	325
1984	Nativity, Shepherd, Color	Open		395.00	475
1976	Noah	500		975.00	2800
1960	The Prophet	50		250.00	3500
1964	St. Peter	500		Unkn.	1250

Birds & Flowers - Cybis

1985	American Bald Eagle	300		2900.00	3595
1972	American Crested Iris	400		975.00	1150
1976	American White Turkey	75		1450.00	1600
1976	American Wild Turkey	75		1950.00	2200
1977	Apple Blossoms	400		350.00	550
1972	Autumn Dogwood w/Chickadees	350		1100.00	1200
XX	Birds & Flowers	250		500.00	4500
1960	Blue Headed Virio Building Nest	Closed	N/A	60.00	1100
1960	Blue Headed Virio with Lilac	275		1200.00	2200
1961	Blue-Grey Gnatcatchers, pair	200		400.00	2500
XX	Butterfly w/Dogwood	200		Unkn.	350
1968	Calla Lily	500		750.00	1750
1965	Christmas Rose	500		250.00	750
1977	Clematis	Closed	N/A	210.00	315
1969	Clematis with House Wren	350		1300.00	1400
1976	Colonial Basket	100		2750.00	5500

YEAR ISSUE		EDITION LIMIT	YEAR RETD.	ISSUE PRICE	QUOTE U.S.$
1976	Constancy Flower Basket	Closed	N/A	345.00	400
1964	Dahlia, Yellow	350		450.00	1800
1976	Devotion Flower Basket	Closed	N/A	345.00	400
1962	Duckling "Baby Brother"	Closed	N/A	35.00	140
1977	Duckling "Buttercup & Daffodil"	Closed	N/A	165.00	295
1970	Dutch Crocus	350		550.00	750
1976	Felicity Flower Basket	Closed	N/A	325.00	345
1961	Golden Clarion Lily	100		250.00	4500
1974	Golden Winged Warbler	200		1075.00	1150
1975	Great Horned Owl, Color	50		3250.00	7500
1975	Great Horned Owl, White	150		1950.00	4500
1964	Great White Heron	350		850.00	3750
1977	Hermit Thrush	150		1450.00	1450
1959	Hummingbird	Closed	N/A	95.00	950
1963	Iris	250		500.00	4500
1978	Kinglets on Pyracantha	175		900.00	1100
1977	Krestrel	175		1875.00	1925
1971	Little Blue Heron	500		425.00	1500
1963	Magnolia	Closed	N/A	350.00	450-1500
1976	Majesty Flower Basket	Closed	N/A	345.00	400
1970	Mushroom with Butterfly	Closed	N/A	225.00	450
1968	Narcissus	500		350.00	550
1978	Nestling Bluebirds	Closed	N/A	235.00	250
1972	Pansies, China Maid	1,000		275.00	350
1975	Pansies, Chinolina Lady	750		295.00	400
1960	Pheasant	150		750.00	5000
XX	Sandpipers	400		700.00	1500
1985	Screech Owl & Siblings	100		3250.00	3925
XX	Skylarks	350		330.00	1800
1962	Sparrow on a Log	Closed	N/A	35.00	450
1982	Spring Bouquet	200		750.00	750
1957	Turtle Doves	500		350.00	5000
1968	Wood Duck	500		325.00	800
1980	Yellow Condesa Rose	Closed	N/A	Unkn.	255
1980	Yellow Rose	Closed	N/A	80.00	450

Carousel-Circus - Cybis

YEAR ISSUE		EDITION LIMIT	YEAR RETD.	ISSUE PRICE	QUOTE U.S.$
1975	Barnaby Bear	Closed	N/A	165.00	325
1981	Bear, "Bernhard"	325		1125.00	1150
1975	Bicentennial Horse Ticonderoga	350		925.00	4000
1975	Bosun Monkey	Closed	N/A	195.00	425
1981	Bull, Plutus	325		1125.00	2050
1973	Carousel Goat	325		875.00	1750
1973	Carousel Horse	325		925.00	7500
1985	Carousel Unicorn	325		1275.00	2750
1979	Circus Rider "Equestrienne Extraordinaire"	150		2275.00	3500
1977	Dandy Dancing Dog	Closed	N/A	145.00	295
1981	Frollo	1,000		750.00	825
1976	Funny Face Child Head/Holly	Closed	N/A	325.00	750
1982	Giraffe	750		Unkn.	1750
1985	Jumbles and Friend	750		675.00	725
1974	Lion	325		1025.00	1350
1976	Performing Pony "Poppy"	1,000		325.00	1200
1984	Phineas, Circus Elephant	Open		325.00	425
1986	Pierre, the Performing Poodle	Open		225.00	275
1981	Pony	750		975.00	975
1976	Sebastian Seal	Closed	N/A	195.00	200
1974	Tiger	325		925.00	1500
1985	Valentine	Open		335.00	375

Children of the World - Cybis

YEAR ISSUE		EDITION LIMIT	YEAR RETD.	ISSUE PRICE	QUOTE U.S.$
1972	Eskimo Child Head	Closed	N/A	165.00	400
1975	Indian Boy Head	Closed	N/A	425.00	900
1975	Indian Girl Head	Closed	N/A	325.00	900
1978	Jason	Closed	N/A	285.00	375
1978	Jennifer	Closed	N/A	325.00	375
1977	Jeremy	Closed	N/A	315.00	475
1979	Jessica	Closed	N/A	325.00	475

Children to Cherish - Cybis

YEAR ISSUE		EDITION LIMIT	YEAR RETD.	ISSUE PRICE	QUOTE U.S.$
1978	Alice (Seated)	Closed	N/A	350.00	550
1964	Alice in Wonderland	Closed	N/A	50.00	850
1978	Allegra	Closed	N/A	310.00	350
1968	Baby Bust	239		375.00	1000
1963	Ballerina on Cue	Closed	N/A	150.00	700
1960	Ballerina Red Shoes	Closed	N/A	75.00	1200
1968	Ballerina, Little Princess	Closed	N/A	125.00	750
1985	Ballerina, Recital	Open		275.00	275
1985	Ballerina, Swanilda	Open		450.00	725
1985	Beth	Open		235.00	275
1977	Boys Playing Marbles	Closed	N/A	285.00	425
1984	The Choirboy	Open		325.00	345
1985	Clara	Open		395.00	395
1986	Clarissa	Open		165.00	195
1978	Edith	Closed	N/A	310.00	325
1976	Elizabeth Ann	Closed	N/A	195.00	275
1986	Encore Figure Skater	750		625.00	675
1985	Felicia	Open		425.00	525
1985	Figure Eight	750		625.00	750
XX	First Bouquet	250		150.00	300
1966	First Flight	Closed	N/A	50.00	475
1981	Fleurette	1,000		725.00	1075
1973	Goldilocks	Closed	N/A	145.00	525
1974	Gretel	Closed	N/A	260.00	425
1974	Hansel	Closed	N/A	270.00	550
1962	Heide, Color	Closed	N/A	165.00	550
1962	Heide, White	Closed	N/A	165.00	550
1984	Jack in the Beanstalk	750		575.00	575
1985	Jody	Open		235.00	275
1986	Kitri	Open		450.00	550
1978	Lisa and Lynette	Closed	N/A	395.00	475
1978	Little Boy Blue	Closed	N/A	425.00	500
1984	Little Champ	Open		325.00	375
1980	Little Miss Muffet	Closed	N/A	335.00	365
1973	Little Red Riding Hood	Closed	N/A	110.00	475
1986	Lullaby, Blue	Open		125.00	160
1986	Lullaby, Ivory	Open		125.00	160
1986	Lullaby, Pink	Open		125.00	160
1985	Marguerite	Open		425.00	525
1974	Mary, Mary	500		475.00	750
1976	Melissa	Closed	N/A	285.00	425
1984	Michael	Open		235.00	350
1967	Pandora Blue	Closed	N/A	265.00	325
1958	Peter Pan	Closed	N/A	80.00	1000
1971	Polyanna	Closed	N/A	195.00	550
1975	Rapunzel, Apricot	1,500		475.00	1200
1978	Rapunzel, Lilac	1,000		675.00	1000
1972	Rapunzel, Pink	1,000		425.00	1100
1964	Rebecca	Closed	N/A	110.00	360
1985	Recital	Open		275.00	275
1982	Robin	1,000		475.00	850
1982	Sleeping Beauty	750		695.00	1475
1963	Springtime	Closed	N/A	45.00	775
1957	Thumbelina	Closed	N/A	45.00	525
1959	Tinkerbell	Closed	N/A	95.00	1500
1985	Vanessa	Open		425.00	525
1975	Wendy with Flowers	Unkn.		250.00	450
1975	Yankee Doodle Dandy	Closed	N/A	275.00	325

Commemoratives - Cybis

YEAR ISSUE		EDITION LIMIT	YEAR RETD.	ISSUE PRICE	QUOTE U.S.$
1984	1984 Cybis Holiday	Open		145.00	145
1986	1986 Commemorative Egg	Open		365.00	365
1969	Apollo II Moon Mission	111		1500.00	2500
1981	Arion, Dolphin Rider	1,000		575.00	1150
1980	The Bride	100		6500.00	10500
1972	Chess Set	10		30000.00	60000
1967	Columbia	200		1000.00	2500
1967	Conductor's Hands	250		250.00	1500
1971	Cree Indian	100		2500.00	5500
1984	Cree Indian "Magic Boy"	200		4250.00	4995
1975	George Washington Bust	Closed	N/A	275.00	350
1985	Holiday Ornament	Open		75.00	75
1981	Kateri Takakwitha	100		2875.00	2975
1985	Liberty	100		1875.00	4000
1986	Little Miss Liberty	Open		295.00	350
1977	Oceania	200		1250.00	975-1550
1981	Phoenix	100		950.00	950

Everyone's Fun Time (Limnettes) - Cybis

YEAR ISSUE		EDITION LIMIT	YEAR RETD.	ISSUE PRICE	QUOTE U.S.$
1972	Country Fair	500		125.00	200
1972	The Pond	500		125.00	200
1972	The Seashore	500		125.00	200
1972	Windy Day	500		125.00	200

Fantasia - Cybis

YEAR ISSUE		EDITION LIMIT	YEAR RETD.	ISSUE PRICE	QUOTE U.S.$
1974	Cybele	500		675.00	800
1981	Desiree, White Deer	400		575.00	595
1985	Dore'	1,000		575.00	1075
1984	Flight and Fancy	1,000		975.00	1175
1980	Pegasus	500		1450.00	750
1980	Pegaus, Free Spirit	1,000		675.00	775
1981	Prince Brocade Unicorn	500		2200.00	2600
1978	Satin Horse Head	500		1100.00	2800
1977	Sea King's Steed "Oceania"	200		1250.00	1450
1978	Sharmaine Sea Nymph	250		1450.00	1650
1982	Theron	350		675.00	850
1969	Unicorn	500		1250.00	3750
1977	Unicorns, Gambol and Frolic	1,000		425.00	2300

Land of Chemeric - Cybis

YEAR ISSUE		EDITION LIMIT	YEAR RETD.	ISSUE PRICE	QUOTE U.S.$
1977	Marigold	Closed	N/A	185.00	550
1981	Melody	1,000		725.00	800
1985	Oberon	750		825.00	825
1979	Pip, Elfin Player	1,000		450.00	665
1977	Queen Titania	750		725.00	2500
1977	Tiffin	Closed	N/A	175.00	550

North American Indian - Cybis

YEAR ISSUE		EDITION LIMIT	YEAR RETD.	ISSUE PRICE	QUOTE U.S.$
1974	Apache, "Chato"	350		1950.00	3300
1969	Blackfeet "Beaverhead Medicine Man"	500		2000.00	2775
1982	Choctaw "Tasculusa"	200		2475.00	4050
1977	Crow Dancer	200		3875.00	8500
1969	Dakota "Minnehaha Laughing Water"	500		1500.00	2500
1973	Eskimo Mother	200		1875.00	2650
1979	Great Spirit "Wankan Tanka"	200		3500.00	4150
1973	Iriquois "At the Council Fire"	500		4250.00	4975
1969	Onondaga "Haiwatha"	500		1500.00	2450
1971	Shoshone "Sacajawea"	500		2250.00	2775
1985	Yaqui "Deer Dancer"	200		2095.00	2850

Portraits in Porcelain - Cybis

YEAR ISSUE		EDITION LIMIT	YEAR RETD.	ISSUE PRICE	QUOTE U.S.$
1976	Abigail Adams	600		875.00	1300
1973	Ballet-Prince Florimond	200		975.00	1100
1984	Bathsheba	500		1975.00	3250
1965	Beatrice	700		225.00	1800
1979	Berengaria	500		1450.00	2-4700
1986	Carmen	500		1675.00	1975
1982	Desdemona	500		1850.00	4000
1971	Eleanor of Aquitaine	750		875.00	4250
1967	Folk Singer	283		300.00	850
1978	Good Queen Anne	350		975.00	1500
1967	Guinevere	800		250.00	2400
1968	Hamlet	500		350.00	2000
1981	Jane Eyre	500		975.00	1500
1965	Juliet	800		175.00	4000
1985	King Arthur	350		2350.00	3450
1985	King David	350		1475.00	2175
1972	Kwan Yin	350		1250.00	2000
1982	Lady Godiva	200		1875.00	3250
1975	Lady Macbeth	750		850.00	1350
1979	Nefertiti	500		2100.00	3000
1969	Ophelia	800		750.00	4500
1985	Pagliacci	Open		325.00	325
1982	Persephone	200		3250.00	5250
1973	Portia	750		825.00	3750
1976	Priscilla	500		825.00	1500
1974	Queen Esther	750		925.00	1800
1985	Romeo and Juliet	500		2200.00	3400
1968	Scarlett	500		450.00	32-3500
1985	Tristan and Isolde	200		2200.00	2200

Sport Scenes - Cybis

YEAR ISSUE		EDITION LIMIT	YEAR RETD.	ISSUE PRICE	QUOTE U.S.$
1980	Jogger, Female	Closed	N/A	345.00	425
1980	Jogger, Male	Closed	N/A	395.00	475

Theatre of Porcelain - Cybis

YEAR ISSUE		EDITION LIMIT	YEAR RETD.	ISSUE PRICE	QUOTE U.S.$
1981	Columbine	250		2250.00	2250
1978	Court Jester	250		1450.00	1750
1980	Harlequin	250		1575.00	1875
1981	Puck	250		2300.00	2450

When Bells are Ringing (Limnettes) - Cybis

YEAR ISSUE		EDITION LIMIT	YEAR RETD.	ISSUE PRICE	QUOTE U.S.$
1972	Easter Egg Hunt	500		125.00	200
1972	Independence Celebration	500		125.00	200
1972	Merry Christmas	500		125.00	200
1972	Sabbath Morning	500		125.00	200

The Wonderful Seasons (Limnettes) - Cybis

YEAR ISSUE		EDITION LIMIT	YEAR RETD.	ISSUE PRICE	QUOTE U.S.$
1972	Autumn	500		125.00	200
1972	Spring	500		125.00	200
1972	Summer	500		125.00	200
1972	Winter	500		125.00	200

Dave Grossman Creations

6" Gone With The Wind Series - Unknown

YEAR ISSUE		EDITION LIMIT	YEAR RETD.	ISSUE PRICE	QUOTE U.S.$
1994	Ashley GWW-102	Open		40.00	40
1994	Rhett GW-104	Open		40.00	40
1994	Scarlett GWW-101	Open		40.00	40

Gone With The Wind Series - Unknown

YEAR ISSUE		EDITION LIMIT	YEAR RETD.	ISSUE PRICE	QUOTE U.S.$
1993	Belle Waiting GWW-10	Open		70.00	70
1994	Gerald O'Hara GWW-15	Open		70.00	70
1988	Mammy GWW-6	Retrd.		70.00	70
1991	Prissy GWW-8	Open		50.00	50
1993	Rhett & Bonnie GWW-11	Open		80.00	80
1993	Rhett in White Suit GWW-12	Open		70.00	70
1994	Scarlett in Bar B Que Dress GWW-14	Open		70.00	70
1992	Scarlett in Green Dress GWW-9	Open		70.00	70
1987	Tara GWW-5	Retrd.	N/A	70.00	70

Norman Rockwell America Collection - Rockwell-Inspired

YEAR ISSUE		EDITION LIMIT	YEAR RETD.	ISSUE PRICE	QUOTE U.S.$
1993	After The Prom NRP-916	7,500		75.00	75
1989	Bottom of the Sixth NRC-607	Retrd.	N/A	140.00	140
1989	Doctor and Doll NRP-600	Retrd.	N/A	90.00	60
1989	First Day Home NRC-606	Retrd.	N/A	80.00	60
1989	First Haircut NRC-604	Retrd.	N/A	75.00	75
1989	First Visit NRC-605	Retrd.	N/A	110.00	110
1993	Gone Fishing NRP-915	7,500		65.00	65
1989	Locomotive NRC-603	Retrd.	N/A	110.00	110
1993	Missed NRP-914	7,500		110.00	110
1989	Runaway NRC-610	Retrd.	N/A	140.00	140
1989	Weigh-In NRC-611	Retrd.	N/A	120.00	120

Norman Rockwell America Collection-Lg. Ltd. Edition - Rockwell-Inspired

YEAR ISSUE		EDITION LIMIT	YEAR RETD.	ISSUE PRICE	QUOTE U.S.$
1989	Bottom of the Sixth NRP-307	Retrd.	N/A	190.00	190
1989	Doctor and Doll NRP-300	Retrd.	N/A	150.00	150
1989	Runaway NRP-310	Retrd.	N/A	190.00	190
1989	Weigh-In NRP-311	Retrd.	N/A	160.00	175

Norman Rockwell America Collection-Miniatures - Rockwell-Inspired

YEAR ISSUE		EDITION LIMIT	YEAR RETD.	ISSUE PRICE	QUOTE U.S.$
1989	First Day Home MRC-906	Retrd.	N/A	45.00	45
1989	First Haircut MRC-904	Retrd.	N/A	45.00	45

Saturday Evening Post - Rockwell-Inspired

YEAR ISSUE		EDITION LIMIT	YEAR RETD.	ISSUE PRICE	QUOTE U.S.$
1992	After the Prom NRP-916	Open		75.00	75
1994	Almost Grown Up NRC-609	Open		75.00	75
1993	Baby's First Step NRC-604	Open		100.00	100
1993	Bed Time NRC-606	Open		100.00	100
1990	Bedside Manner NRP-904	Open		65.00	65
1990	Big Moment NRP-906	Retrd.	N/A	100.00	135
1990	Bottom of the Sixth NRP-908	Open		165.00	165
1993	Bride & Groom NRC-605	Open		100.00	100
1991	Catching The Big One NRP-909	Open		75.00	75
1992	Choosin Up NRP-912	Retrd.	N/A	110.00	140-150
1990	Daydreamer NRP-902	Open		55.00	55
1990	Doctor and Doll NRP-907	Retrd.	N/A	110.00	150
1994	For A Good Boy NRC-608	Open		100.00	100
1992	Gone Fishing NRP-915	Open		65.00	65
1991	Gramps NRP-910	Open		85.00	85

YEAR ISSUE		EDITION LIMIT	YEAR RETD.	ISSUE PRICE	QUOTE U.S.$
1994	Little Mother NRC-607	Open		75.00	75
1992	Locomotive NRC-603	Open		110.00	110
1992	Missed NRP-914	Open		110.00	110
1990	No Swimming NRP-901	Retrd.	N/A	50.00	50
1991	The Pharmacist NRP-911	Open		70.00	70
1990	Prom Dress NRP-903	Retrd.	N/A	60.00	60
1990	Runaway NRP-905	Open		130.00	130
1994	A Visit with Rockwell (100th Aniversary)-NRP-100	1,994		100.00	100

Saturday Evening Post-Miniatures - Rockwell-Inspired

1991	A Boy Meets His Dog BMR-01	Retrd.	N/A	35.00	35
1991	Downhill Daring BMR-02	Retrd.	N/A	40.00	40
1991	Flowers in Tender Bloom BMR-03	Retrd.	N/A	32.00	32
1991	Fondly Do We Remember BMR-04	Retrd.	N/A	30.00	30
1991	In His Spirit BMR-05	Retrd.	N/A	30.00	30
1991	Pride of Parenthood BMR-06	Retrd.	N/A	35.00	35
1991	Sweet Serenade BMR-07	Retrd.	N/A	32.00	32
1991	Sweet Song So Young BMR-08	Retrd.	N/A	30.00	30

Dave Grossman Designs

Norman Rockwell Collection - Rockwell-Inspired

1982	American Mother NRG-42	Retrd.	N/A	100.00	125
1978	At the Doctor NR-29	Retrd.	N/A	108.00	150-275
1979	Back From Camp NR-33	Retrd.	N/A	96.00	120
1973	Back To School NR-02	Retrd.	N/A	20.00	40-45
1975	Barbershop Quartet NR-23	Retrd.	N/A	100.00	1400
1974	Baseball NR-16	Retrd.	N/A	45.00	160
1975	Big Moment NR-21	Retrd.	N/A	60.00	125
1973	Caroller NR-03	Retrd.	N/A	22.50	75
1975	Circus NR-22	Retrd.	N/A	55.00	145
1983	Country Critic NR-43	Retrd.	N/A	75.00	125
1982	Croquet NR-41	Retrd.	N/A	100.00	135
1973	Daydreamer NR-04	Retrd.	N/A	22.50	60
1975	Discovery NR-20	Retrd.	N/A	55.00	175
1973	Doctor & Doll NR-12	Retrd.	N/A	65.00	150-285
1979	Dreams of Long Ago NR-31	Retrd.	N/A	100.00	125
1976	Drum For Tommy NRC-24	Retrd.	N/A	40.00	95
1980	Exasperated Nanny NR-35	Retrd.	N/A	96.00	100
1978	First Day of School NR-27	Retrd.	N/A	100.00	150
1974	Friends In Need NR-13	Retrd.	N/A	45.00	100
1983	Graduate NR-44	Retrd.	N/A	30.00	50
1979	Grandpa's Ballerina NR-32	Retrd.	N/A	100.00	110
1980	Hankerchief NR-36	Retrd.	N/A	110.00	100-110
1973	Lazybones NR-08	Retrd.	N/A	30.00	250
1973	Leapfrog NR-09	Retrd.	N/A	50.00	600-700
1973	Love Letter NR-06	Retrd.	N/A	25.00	60
1973	Lovers NR-07	Retrd.	N/A	45.00	70
1978	Magic Potion NR-28	Retrd.	N/A	84.00	235
1973	Marble Players NR-11	Retrd.	N/A	60.00	400-450
1973	No Swimming NR-05	Retrd.	N/A	25.00	65-145
1977	Pals NR-25	Retrd.	N/A	60.00	120
1986	Red Cross NR-47	Retrd.	N/A	67.00	100
1973	Redhead NR-01	Retrd.	N/A	20.00	210
1980	Santa's Good Boys NR-37	Retrd.	N/A	90.00	100
1973	Schoolmaster NR-10	Retrd.	N/A	55.00	375
1984	Scotty's Home Plate NR-46	Retrd.	N/A	30.00	60
1983	Scotty's Surprise NRS-20	Retrd.	N/A	25.00	50-60
1974	See America First NR-17	Retrd.	N/A	50.00	125
1981	Spirit of Education NR-38	Retrd.	N/A	96.00	110
1974	Springtime '33 NR-14	Retrd.	N/A	30.00	65
1977	Springtime '35 NR-19	Retrd.	N/A	50.00	65
1974	Summertime '33 NR-15	Retrd.	N/A	45.00	50-60
1974	Take Your Medicine NR-18	Retrd.	N/A	50.00	100
1979	Teacher's Pet NRA-30	Retrd.	N/A	35.00	50
1980	The Toss NR-34	Retrd.	N/A	110.00	150-225
1982	A Visit With Rockwell NR-40	Retrd.	N/A	120.00	100-120
1988	Wedding March NR-49	Retrd.	N/A	110.00	150
1978	Young Doctor NRD-26	Retrd.	N/A	100.00	120
1987	Young Love NR-48	Retrd.	N/A	70.00	120

Norman Rockwell Collection-American Rockwell Series - Rockwell-Inspired

1981	Breaking Home Ties NRV-300	Retrd.	N/A	2000.00	2300
1982	Lincoln NRV-301	Retrd.	N/A	300.00	375
1982	Thanksgiving NRV-302	Retrd.	N/A	2500.00	2650

Norman Rockwell Collection-Boy Scout Series - Rockwell-Inspired

1981	Can't Wait BSA-01	Retrd.	N/A	30.00	50
1981	Good Friends BSA-04	Retrd.	N/A	58.00	65
1981	Good Turn BSA-05	Retrd.	N/A	65.00	100
1982	Guiding Hand BSA-07	Retrd.	N/A	58.00	60
1981	Physically Strong BSA-03	Retrd.	N/A	56.00	60
1981	Scout Is Helpful BSA-02	Retrd.	N/A	38.00	45
1981	Scout Memories BSA-06	Retrd.	N/A	65.00	70
1983	Tomorrow's Leader BSA-08	Retrd.	N/A	45.00	55

Norman Rockwell Collection-Country Gentlemen Series - Rockwell-Inspired

1982	Bringing Home the Tree CG-02	Retrd.	N/A	60.00	75
1982	The Catch CG-04	Retrd.	N/A	50.00	60
1982	On the Ice CG-05	Retrd.	N/A	50.00	60
1982	Pals CG-03	Retrd.	N/A	36.00	45
1982	Thin Ice CG-06	Retrd.	N/A	50.00	60
1982	Turkey Dinner CG-01	Retrd.	N/A	85.00	90

Norman Rockwell Collection-Huck Finn Series - Rockwell-Inspired

1980	Listening HF-02	Retrd.	N/A	110.00	120
1980	No Kings HF-03	Retrd.	N/A	110.00	110
1979	The Secret HF-01	Retrd.	N/A	110.00	130
1980	Snake Escapes HF-04	Retrd.	N/A	110.00	120

Norman Rockwell Collection-Large Limited Editions - Rockwell-Inspired

1975	Baseball NR-102	Retrd.	N/A	125.00	450
1982	Circus NR-106	Retrd.	N/A	500.00	500
1974	Doctor and Doll NR-100	Retrd.	N/A	300.00	1400
1981	Dreams of Long Ago NR-105	Retrd.	N/A	500.00	750
1979	Leapfrog NR-104	Retrd.	N/A	440.00	750
1984	Marble Players NR-107	Retrd.	N/A	500.00	750
1975	No Swimming NR-101	Retrd.	N/A	150.00	550-600
1974	See America First NR-103	Retrd.	N/A	100.00	500-550

Norman Rockwell Collection-Lladro Series - Rockwell-Inspired

1982	Court Jester RL-405	Retrd.	N/A	600.00	15-1600
1982	Daydreamer RL-404	Retrd.	N/A	450.00	1200
1982	Lladro Love Letter RL-400	Retrd.	N/A	650.00	700-800
1982	Practice Makes Perfect RL-402	Retrd.	N/A	725.00	700-800
1982	Springtime RL-406	Retrd.	N/A	450.00	11-1300
1982	Summer Stock RL-401	Retrd.	N/A	750.00	700-800
1982	Young Love RL-403	Retrd.	N/A	450.00	700-800

Norman Rockwell Collection-Miniatures - Rockwell-Inspired

1984	At the Doctor's NR-229	Retrd.	N/A	35.00	35
1979	Back To School NR-202	Retrd.	N/A	18.00	25
1982	Barbershop Quartet NR-223	Retrd.	N/A	40.00	50
1980	Baseball NR-216	Retrd.	N/A	40.00	50
1982	Big Moment NR-221	Retrd.	N/A	36.00	40
1979	Caroller NR-203	Retrd.	N/A	20.00	25
1982	Circus NR-222	Retrd.	N/A	35.00	40
1979	Daydreamer NR-204	Retrd.	N/A	20.00	30
1982	Discovery NR-220	Retrd.	N/A	35.00	45
1979	Doctor and Doll NR-212	Retrd.	N/A	40.00	40
1984	Dreams of Long Ago NR-231	Retrd.	N/A	30.00	30
1982	Drum For Tommy NRC-224	Retrd.	N/A	25.00	30
1984	First Day of School NR-227	Retrd.	N/A	35.00	35
1980	Friends In Need NR-213	Retrd.	N/A	30.00	40
1979	Lazybones NR-208	Retrd.	N/A	22.00	50
1979	Leapfrog NR-209	Retrd.	N/A	32.00	32
1979	Love Letter NR-206	Retrd.	N/A	26.00	50
1979	Lovers NR-207	Retrd.	N/A	28.00	30
1984	Magic Potion NR-228	Retrd.	N/A	30.00	40
1979	Marble Players NR-211	Retrd.	N/A	36.00	38
1979	No Swimming NR-205	Retrd.	N/A	22.00	30
1984	Pals NR-225	Retrd.	N/A	25.00	25
1979	Redhead NR-201	Retrd.	N/A	18.00	50
1983	Santa On the Train NR-245	Retrd.	N/A	35.00	55
1979	Schoolmaster NR-210	Retrd.	N/A	34.00	45
1980	See America First NR-217	Retrd.	N/A	28.00	50
1980	Springtime '33 NR-214	Retrd.	N/A	24.00	80
1982	Springtime '35 NR-219	Retrd.	N/A	24.00	30
1980	Summertime '33 NR-215	Retrd.	N/A	22.00	25
1980	Take Your Medicine NR-218	Retrd.	N/A	36.00	40
1984	Young Doctor NRD-226	Retrd.	N/A	30.00	50

Norman Rockwell Collection-Pewter Figurines - Rockwell-Inspired

1980	Back to School FP-02	Retrd.	N/A	25.00	25
1980	Barbershop Quartet FP-23	Retrd.	N/A	25.00	25
1980	Big Moment FP-21	Retrd.	N/A	25.00	25
1980	Caroller FP-03	Retrd.	N/A	25.00	25
1980	Circus FP-22	Retrd.	N/A	25.00	25
1980	Doctor and Doll FP-12	Retrd.	N/A	25.00	25
1980	Figurine Display Rack FDR-01	Retrd.	N/A	60.00	60
1980	Grandpa's Ballerina FP-32	Retrd.	N/A	25.00	25
1980	Lovers FP-07	Retrd.	N/A	25.00	25
1980	Magic Potion FP-28	Retrd.	N/A	25.00	25
1980	No Swimming FP-05	Retrd.	N/A	25.00	25
1980	See America First FP-17	Retrd.	N/A	25.00	25
1980	Take Your Medicine FP-18	Retrd.	N/A	25.00	25

Norman Rockwell Collection-Rockwell Club Series - Rockwell-Inspired

1982	Diary RCC-02	Retrd.	N/A	35.00	50
1984	Gone Fishing RCC-04	Retrd.	N/A	30.00	55
1983	Runaway Pants RCC-03	Retrd.	N/A	65.00	75
1981	Young Artist RCC-01	Retrd.	N/A	96.00	105

Norman Rockwell Collection-Select Collection, Ltd. - Rockwell-Inspired

1982	Boy & Mother With Puppies SC-1001	Retrd.	N/A	27.50	28
1982	Father With Child SC-1005	Retrd.	N/A	22.00	22
1982	Football Player SC-1004	Retrd.	N/A	22.00	22
1982	Girl Bathing Dog SC-1006	Retrd.	N/A	26.50	27
1982	Girl With Dolls In Crib SC-1002	Retrd.	N/A	26.50	27
1982	Helping Hand SC-1007	Retrd.	N/A	32.00	32
1982	Lemonade Stand SC-1008	Retrd.	N/A	32.00	32
1982	Save Me SC-1010	Retrd.	N/A	35.00	35
1982	Shaving Lesson SC-1009	Retrd.	N/A	30.00	30
1982	Young Couple SC-1003	Retrd.	N/A	27.50	28

Norman Rockwell Collection-Tom Sawyer Miniatures - Rockwell-Inspired

1983	First Smoke TSM-02	Retrd.	N/A	40.00	45
1983	Lost In Cave TSM-05	Retrd.	N/A	40.00	50
1983	Take Your Medicine TSM-04	Retrd.	N/A	40.00	45
1983	Whitewashing the Fence TSM-01	Retrd.	N/A	40.00	50

Norman Rockwell Collection-Tom Sawyer Series - Rockwell-Inspired

1976	First Smoke TS-02	Retrd.	N/A	60.00	235
1978	Lost In Cave TS-04	Retrd.	N/A	70.00	175
1977	Take Your Medicine TS-03	Retrd.	N/A	63.00	235
1975	Whitewashing the Fence TS-01	Retrd.	N/A	60.00	235

Department 56

Alpine Village Series - Department 56

1987	Alpine Church 6541-2	Closed	1991	32.00	150-195
1992	Alpine Shops 5618-9,2/set (Metterniche Wurst, Kukuck Uhren)	Open		75.00	75
1986	Alpine Village 6540-4, 5/set (Bessor Bierkeller, Gasthof Eisl, Apotheke, E. Staubr Backer, Milch-Kase)	Open		150.00	195
1990	Bahnhof 5615-4	Closed	1993	42.00	60-90
1994	Bakery & Chocolate Shop 5614-6	Open		37.50	38
1988	Grist Mill 5953-6	Open		42.00	45
1987	Josef Engel Farmhouse 5952-8	Closed	1989	33.00	900-1050
1993	Sport Laden, 5612-0	Open		50.00	50
1991	St. Nikolaus Kirche 5617-0	Open		37.50	38

Christmas In the City Series - Department 56

1989	5607 Park Avenue Townhouse 5977-3	Closed	1992	48.00	70-90
1989	5609 Park Avenue Townhouse 5978-1	Closed	1992	48.00	70-90
1991	All Saints Corner Church 5542-5	Open		96.00	110
1991	Arts Academy 5543-3	Closed	1993	45.00	65-95
1994	Brokerage House, 5881-5	Open		48.00	48
1987	The Cathedral 5962-5	Closed	1990	60.00	300-350
1992	Cathedral Church of St. Mark 5549-2	3,024	1993	120.00	1600-2300
1988	Chocolate Shoppe 5968-4	Closed	1991	40.00	100-130
1987	Christmas In The City 6512-9, Set /3	Closed	1990	112.00	425-500
1987	•Bakery 6512-9	Closed	1990	37.50	90-125
1987	•Tower Restaurant 6512-9	Closed	1990	37.50	185-225
1987	•Toy Shop and Pet Store 6512-9	Closed	1990	37.50	185-225
1988	City Hall (small) 5969-2	Closed	1991	65.00	145-170
1988	City Hall (standard) 5969-2	Closed	1991	65.00	140-200
1991	The Doctor's Office 5544-1	Closed	1994	60.00	75-95
1989	Dorothy's Dress Shop 5974-9	12,500	1991	70.00	345-400
1994	First Metropolitan Bank 5882-3	Open		60.00	60
1988	Hank's Market 5970-6	Closed	1992	40.00	65-100
1994	Heritage Museum of Art 5883-1	Open		96.00	96
1991	Hollydale's Department Store 5534-4	Open		75.00	85
1995	Ivy Terrace Apartments 5887-4	Open		60.00	60
1991	Little Italy Ristorante 5538-7	Open		50.00	52
1987	Palace Theatre 5963-3	Closed	1989	45.00	875-1000
1990	Red Brick Fire Station 5536-0	Open		55.00	55
1989	Ritz Hotel 5973-0	Closed	1994	55.00	65-95
1987	Sutton Place Brownstones 5961-7	Closed	1989	80.00	800-1000
1992	Uptown Shoppes 5531-0, Set /3 (Haberdashery, City Clockworks, Music Emporium)	Open		150.00	150
1988	Variety Store 5972-2	Closed	1990	45.00	135-185
1993	West Village Shops 5880-7, set of 2 (Potters' Tea Seller, Spring St. Coffee House)	Open		90.00	90
1990	Wong's In Chinatown 5537-9	Closed	1994	55.00	65-85

Dickens' Village Series - Department 56

1991	Ashbury Inn 5555-7	Open		55.00	60
1987	Barley Bree 5900-5, Set of 2 (Farmhouse, Barn)	Closed	1989	60.00	375-425
1990	Bishops Oast House 5567-0	Closed	1992	45.00	60-100
1986	Blythe Pond Mill House 6508-0	Closed	1990	37.00	245-300
1986	By The Pond Mill House 6508-0	Closed	1990	37.00	115-165
1994	Boarding & Lodging School, 5810-6	Open		48.00	48
1993	Boarding and Lodging School, 5809-2 (Christmas Carol Commemorative Piece)	Yr.Iss.	1993	48.00	150-240
1987	Brick Abbey 6549-8	Closed	1989	33.00	335-435
1988	C. Fletcher Public House 5904-8	12,500	1989	35.00	550-650
1986	Chadbury Station and Train 6528-5	Closed	1989	65.00	375-425
1987	Chesterton Manor House 6568-4	7,500	1988	45.00	1600-1875
1986	Christmas Carol Cottages 6500-5, Set /3 (Fezziwig's Warehouse, Scrooge and Marley Counting House, The Cottage of Bob Cratchit & Tiny Tim)	Open		75.00	90
1988	Cobblestone Shops 5924-2, Set of 3	Closed	1990	95.00	350-375
1988	•Booter and Cobbler 5924-2	Closed	1990	32.00	110-135
1988	•T. Wells Fruit & Spice Shop 5924-2	Closed	1990	32.00	88-120
1988	•The Wool Shop 5924-2	Closed	1990	32.00	170-210
1989	Cobles Police Station 5583-2	Closed	1991	37.50	110-150

YEAR ISSUE		EDITION LIMIT	YEAR RETD.	ISSUE PRICE	QUOTE U.S.$
1988	Counting House & Silas Thimbleton Barrister 5902-1	Closed	1990	32.00	80-120
1992	Crown & Cricket Inn (Charles Dickens' Signature Series), 5750-9	Yr.Iss.	1992	100.00	165-200
1989	David Copperfield 5550-6, Set of 3	Closed	1992	125.00	165-225
1989	•Betsy Trotwood's Cottage 5550-6	Closed	1992	42.50	50-80
1989	•Peggotty's Seaside Cottage 5550-6 (green boat)	Closed	1992	42.50	50-70
1989	• Mr. Wickfield Solicitor 5550-6	Closed	1992	42.50	85-110
1989	David Copperfield 5550-6, Set of 3 with tan boat	Closed	1992	125.00	235-300
1989	Peggotty's Seaside Cottage 5550-6 (tan boat)	Closed	1992	42.50	120-200
1994	Dedlock Arms, 5752-5 (Charles Dickens' Signature Series)	Yr.Iss.	1994	100.00	130-165
1985	Dickens' Cottages 6518-8 Set /3	Closed	1988	75.00	900-1100
1985	•Stone Cottage 6518-8	Closed	1988	25.00	425-450
1985	•Thatched Cottage 6518-8	Closed	1988	25.00	175-210
1985	•Tudor Cottage 6518-8	Closed	1988	25.00	400-450
1986	Dickens' Lane Shops 6507-2, Set of 3	Closed	1989	80.00	550-675
1986	•Cottage Toy Shop 6507-2	Closed	1989	27.00	210-265
1986	•Thomas Kersey Coffee House 6507-2	Closed	1989	27.00	150-200
1986	•Tuttle's Pub 6507-2	Closed	1989	27.00	225-300
1984	Dickens' Village Church (cream) 6516-1	Closed	1989	35.00	240-440
1985	Dickens' Village Church (dark) 6516-1	Closed	1989	35.00	150-175
1985	Dickens' Village Church (green) 6516-1	Closed	1989	35.00	345-450
1985	Dickens' Village Church (tan) 6516-1	Closed	1989	35.00	150-180
1985	Dickens' Village Mill 6519-6	2,500	1986	35.00	4000-5000
1995	Dudden Cross Church 5834-3	Open		45.00	45
1991	Fagin's Hide-A-Way 5552-2	Open		68.00	72
1989	The Flat of Ebenezer Scrooge 5587-5	Open		37.50	38
1994	Giggelswick Mutton & Ham, 5822-0	Open		48.00	48
1993	Great Denton Mill, 5812-2	Open		50.00	50
1989	Green Gate Cottage 5586-7	22,500	1990	65.00	250-300
1994	Hather Harness 5823-8	Open		48.00	48
1992	Hembleton Pewterer, 5800-9	Open		72.00	72
1988	Ivy Glen Church 5927-7	Closed	1991	35.00	70-110
1987	Kenilworth Castle 5916-1	Closed	1988	70.00	500-750
1992	King's Road Post Office, 5801-7	Open		45.00	45
1993	Kingford's Brewhouse, 5811-4	Open		45.00	45
1990	Kings Road 5568-9, Set of 2 (Tutbury Printer, C.H. Watt Physician)	Open		72.00	80
1989	Knottinghill Church 5582-4	Open		50.00	55
1995	The Maltings 5833-5	Open		50.00	50
1988	Merchant Shops 5926-9, set/5	Closed	1993	150.00	210-250
1988	•Geo. Weeton Watchmaker 5926-9	Closed	1993	30.00	45-70
1988	•The Mermaid Fish Shoppe 5926-9	Closed	1993	30.00	60-80
1988	•Poulterer 5926-9	Closed	1993	30.00	55-75
1988	•Walpole Tailors 5926-9	Closed	1993	30.00	45-70
1988	•White Horse Bakery 5926-9	Closed	1993	30.00	55-75
1991	Nephew Fred's Flat 5557-3	Closed	1994	35.00	60-75
1988	Nicholas Nickleby 5925-0, Set/ 2	Closed	1991	72.00	145-200
1988	•Nicholas Nickleby Cottage 5925-0	Closed	1991	36.00	70-95
1988	•Wackford Squeers Boarding School 5925-0	Closed	1991	36.00	85-100
1988	Nickolas Nickleby Cottage 5925-0-misspelled	Closed	1991	36.00	95-145
1988	Nickolas Nickleby set of 2, 5925-0-misspelled	Closed	1991	36.00	200-225
1986	Norman Church 6502-1	3,500	1987	40.00	2700-3500
1987	The Old Curiosity Shop 5905-6	Open		32.00	42
1992	Old Michaelchurch, 5562-0	Open		42.00	48
1991	Oliver Twist 5553-0 Set of 2	Closed	1993	75.00	120-150
1991	•Brownlow House 5553-0	Closed	1993	38.00	60-85
1991	•Maylie Cottage 5553-0	Closed	1993	38.00	50-70
1984	The Original Shops of Dickens' Village, 6515-3, Set of 7	Closed	1988	175.00	1200-1400
1984	•Abel Beesley Butcher 6515-3	Closed	1988	25.00	110-150
1984	•Bean And Son Smithy Shop 6515-3	Closed	1988	25.00	180-200
1984	•Candle Shop 6515-3	Closed	1988	25.00	180-225
1984	•Crowntree Inn 6515-3	Closed	1988	25.00	250-385
1984	•Golden Swan Baker 6515-3	Closed	1988	25.00	155-185
1984	•Green Grocer 6515-3	Closed	1988	25.00	165-275
1984	•Jones & Co. Brush & Basket Shop 6515-3	Closed	1988	25.00	280-360
1993	The Pied Bull Inn (Charles Dickens' Signature Series), 5751-7	Closed	1993	100.00	140-200
1994	Portobello Road Thatched Cottages 5824-6, set of 3 (Mr. & Mrs. Pickle, Cobb Cottage, Browning Cottage)	Open		120.00	120
1993	Pump Lane Shoppes,5808-4 set of 3 (Bumpstead Nye Cloaks & Canes, Lomas Ltd. Molasses, W.M. Wheat Cakes & Puddings)	Open		112.00	112
1989	Ruth Marion Scotch Woolens 5585-9	17,500	1990	65.00	350-425
1995	Sir John Falstaff Inn 5753-3(Charles Dickens' Signature Series)	Yr.Iss.		100.00	110-135
1995	Start A Tradition Set, 5832-7 set/13 (The Town Square Shops-Faversham Lamps & Oil, Morston Steak and Kidney Pie, The Town Square Carolers Accessory, set/3, 6 Sisal Trees, Bag of Real Plastic Snow, Cobblestone Road)	Open		85.00	85
1989	Theatre Royal 5584-0	Closed	1992	45.00	65-100
1989	Victoria Station 5574-3	Open		100.00	112
1994	Whittlesbourne Church, 5821-1	Open		85.00	85

Disney Parks Village Series - Department 56

YEAR ISSUE		EDITION LIMIT	YEAR RETD.	ISSUE PRICE	QUOTE U.S.$
1994	Disney Parks Family (Accessory), set of 3 5354-6	Open		32.50	33
1994	Fire Station 5352-0 Disneyland, CA	Open		45.00	45
1994	Mickey and Minnie (Accessory), set /2 5353-8	Open		22.50	23
1994	Mickey's Christmas Shop, set /2 5350-3 Disney World, FL	Open		144.00	144
1994	Olde World Antiques Gate (Accessory) 5355-4	Open		15.00	15
1994	Olde World Antiques, set/2 5351-1 Disney World, FL	Open		90.00	90

Easter Collectibles - Department 56

YEAR ISSUE		EDITION LIMIT	YEAR RETD.	ISSUE PRICE	QUOTE U.S.$
1995	Bisque Chick, Large 2464-3	Open		8.50	9
1995	Bisque Chick, Small, 2465-1	Open		6.50	7
1993	Bisque Duckling, set	Closed	1993	15.00	35
1993	Bisque Duckling, Large 3.5" 7282-6	Closed	1993	8.50	18
1993	Bisque Duckling, Small 2.75" 7281-8	Closed	1993	6.50	15
1994	Bisque Fledgling in Nest, Large 2.75" 2400-7	Closed	1994	6.00	12
1994	Bisque Fledgling in Nest, Small 2.5" 2401-5	Closed	1994	5.00	10
1991	Bisque Lamb, set	Closed	1991	12.50	50-75
1991	Bisque Lamb, Large 4" 7392-0	Closed	1991	7.50	40-50
1991	Bisque Lamb, Small 2.5" 7393-8	Closed	1991	5.00	20-30
1992	Bisque Rabbit, set	Closed	1992	14.00	40-50
1992	Bisque Rabbit, Large 5" 7498-5	Closed	1992	8.00	20-25
1992	Bisque Rabbit, Small 4" 7499-3	Closed	1992	6.00	15-20

Event Piece - Heritage Village Collection Accessory - Department 56

YEAR ISSUE		EDITION LIMIT	YEAR RETD.	ISSUE PRICE	QUOTE U.S.$
1992	Gate House 5530-1	Closed	1992	22.50	50-75

Little Town of Bethlehem Series - Department 56

YEAR ISSUE		EDITION LIMIT	YEAR RETD.	ISSUE PRICE	QUOTE U.S.$
1987	Little Town of Bethlehem 5975-7, Set of 12	Open		150.00	150

New England Village Series - Department 56

YEAR ISSUE		EDITION LIMIT	YEAR RETD.	ISSUE PRICE	QUOTE U.S.$
1993	A. Bieler Farm 5648-0, set/2 (Pennsylvania Dutch Farmhouse, Pennsylvania Dutch Barn)	Open		92.00	95
1988	Ada's Bed and Boarding House (lemon yellow) 5940-4	Closed	1991	36.00	300-350
1988	Ada's Bed and Boarding House (pale yellow) 5940-4	Closed	1991	36.00	125-150
1994	Arlington Falls Church, 5651-0	Open		40.00	42
1989	Berkshire House (medium blue) 5942-0	Closed	1991	40.00	150
1989	Berkshire House (teal) 5942-0	Closed	1991	40.00	95-120
1993	Blue Star Ice Co., 5647-2	Open		45.00	48
1992	Bluebird Seed and Bulb, 5642-1	Open		48.00	48
1995	Brewster Bay Cottage, 5657-0 set/2 (Jeremiah Brewster House, Thomas T. Julian House)	Open		90.00	90
1994	Cape Keag Cannery 5652-9	Open		48.00	48
1990	Captain's Cottage 5947-1	Open		40.00	44
1988	Cherry Lane Shops 5939-0, set/3	Closed	1990	80.00	275-330
1988	•Anne Shaw Toys 5939-0	Closed	1990	27.00	150-175
1988	•Ben's Barbershop 5939-0	Closed	1990	27.00	80-100
1988	•Otis Hayes Butcher Shop 5939-0	Closed	1990	27.00	65-90
1987	Craggy Cove Lighthouse 5930-7	Closed	1994	35.00	65-80
1986	Jacob Adams Farmhouse and Barn 6538-2	Closed	1989	65.00	500-600
1989	Jannes Mullet Amish Barn 5944-7	Closed	1992	48.00	90-110
1989	Jannes Mullet Amish Farm House 5943-9	Closed	1992	32.00	95-120
1991	McGrebe-Cutters & Sleighs 5640-5	Open		45.00	48
1986	New England Village 6530-7, Set/7	Closed	1989	170.00	1150-1250
1986	•Apothecary Shop 6530-7	Closed	1989	25.00	100-120
1986	•Brick Town Hall 6530-7	Closed	1989	25.00	195-230
1986	•General Store 6530-7	Closed	1989	25.00	325-370
1986	•Livery Stable & Boot Shop 6530-7	Closed	1989	25.00	135-155
1986	•Nathaniel Bingham Fabrics 6530-7	Closed	1989	25.00	155
1986	•Red Schoolhouse 6530-7	Closed	1989	25.00	260-300
1986	•Steeple Church (Original) 6530-7	Closed	1989	25.00	125-160
1988	Old North Church 5932-3	Open		40.00	45
1994	Pigeonhead Lighthouse 5653-7	Open		50.00	50
1990	Shingle Creek House 5946-3	Closed	1994	37.50	50-65
1990	Sleepy Hollow 5954-4, Set of 3	Closed	1993	96.00	155-200
1990	•Ichabod Crane's Cottage 5954-4	Closed	1993	32.00	45-70
1990	•Sleepy Hollow School 5954-4	Closed	1993	32.00	75-90
1990	•Van Tassel Manor 5954-4	Closed	1993	32.00	50-75
1990	Sleepy Hollow Church 5955-2	Closed	1993	36.00	50-70
1987	Smythe Woolen Mill 6543-9	7,500	1988	42.00	1050-1200
1986	Steeple Church (Second Version) 6539-0	Closed	1990	30.00	95-110
1992	Stoney Brook Town Hall 5644-8	Open		42.00	42
1987	Timber Knoll Log Cabin 6544-7	Closed	1990	28.00	145-165
1987	Weston Train Station 5931-5	Closed	1989	42.00	250-285
1992	Yankee Jud Bell Casting 5643-0	Open		44.00	44

North Pole Series - Department 56

YEAR ISSUE		EDITION LIMIT	YEAR RETD.	ISSUE PRICE	QUOTE U.S.$
1994	Beard Barber Shop 5634-0	Open		27.50	28
1992	Elfie's Sleds & Skates 5625-1	Open		48.00	48
1994	Elfin Snow Cone Works 5633-2	Open		40.00	40
1993	Express Depot 5627-8	Open		48.00	48
1991	Neenee's Dolls & Toys 5620-0	Open		37.50	36
1990	North Pole 5601-4 Set of 2 (Reindeer Barn, Elf Bunkhouse)	Open		70.00	80
1993	North Pole Chapel 5626-0	Open		45.00	45
1994	North Pole Dolls & Santa's Bear Works 5635-9, set of 3 (North Pole Dolls, Santa's Bear Works, Entrance)	Open		96.00	96
1992	North Pole Post Office 5623-5	Open		45.00	50
1991	North Pole Shops, Set of 2 5621-9 (Orly's Bell & Harness Supply, Rimpy's Bakery)	Open		75.00	75
1992	Obbie's Books & Letrinka's Candy 5624-3	Open		70.00	70
1993	Santa's Lookout Tower 5629-4	Open		45.00	48
1993	Santa's Woodworks 5628-6	Open		42.00	45
1990	Santa's Workshop 5600-6	Closed	1993	72.00	350-400
1991	Tassy's Mittens & Hassel's Woolies 5622-7	Open		50.00	50
1995	Tin Soldier Shop 5638-3	Open		42.00	42

The Original Snow Village Collection - Department 56

YEAR ISSUE		EDITION LIMIT	YEAR RETD.	ISSUE PRICE	QUOTE U.S.$
1986	2101 Maple 5043-1	Closed	1986	32.00	300-375
1990	56 Flavors Ice Cream Parlor 5151-9	Closed	1992	42.00	80-125
1979	Adobe House 5066-6	Closed	1980	18.00	2100-3000
1992	Airport 5439-9	Open		60.00	60
1992	Al's TV Shop 5423-2	Open		40.00	40
1986	All Saints Church 5070-9	Open		38.00	45
1986	Apothecary 5076-8	Closed	1990	34.00	90-115
1981	Bakery 5077-6	Closed	1983	30.00	220-350
1986	Bakery 5077-6	Closed	1991	35.00	65-110
1982	Bank 5024-5	Closed	1983	32.00	500-700
1981	Barn 5074-1	Closed	1984	32.00	400-500
1984	Bayport 5015-6	Closed	1986	30.00	225-240
1986	Beacon Hill House 5065-2	Closed	1988	31.00	135-185
1979	Brownstone 5056-7	Closed	1981	36.00	350-600
1978	Cape Cod 5013-8	Closed	1980	20.00	375-400
1994	Carmel Cottage 5466-6	Open		48.00	48
1982	Carriage House 5021-0	Closed	1984	28.00	335-375
1986	Carriage House 5071-7	Closed	1988	29.00	90-130
1987	Cathedral Church 5019-9	Closed	1990	50.00	100-130
1980	Cathedral Church 5067-4	Closed	1981	36.00	2200-3000
1982	Centennial House 5020-2	Closed	1984	32.00	330-450
1983	Chateau 5084-9	Closed	1984	35.00	375-525
1995	Christmas Cove Lighthouse 5483-6	Open		60.00	60
1991	The Christmas Shop 5097-0	Open		37.50	38
1985	Church of the Open Door 5048-2	Closed	1988	34.00	110-160
1988	Cobblestone Antique Shop 5123-3	Closed	1992	36.00	60-80
1994	Coca-Colar Brand Bottling Plant 5469-0	Open		65.00	65
1995	Coca-Colar Brand Corner Drugstore 5484-4	Open		55.00	55
1989	Colonial Church 5119-5	Closed	1992	60.00	60-100
1980	Colonial Farm House 5070-9	Closed	1982	30.00	275-375
1984	Congregational Church 5034-2	Closed	1985	28.00	650
1988	Corner Cafe 5124-1	Closed	1991	37.00	65-100
1981	Corner Store 5076-8	Closed	1983	30.00	230-300
1976	Country Church 5004-7	Closed	1979	18.00	330-375
1979	Countryside Church 5051-8 Meadowland Series	Closed	1980	25.00	800
1979	Countryside Church 5058-3	Closed	1984	27.50	250-325
1989	Courthouse 5144-6	Closed	1993	65.00	125-180
1992	Craftsman Cottage (American Architecture Series), 5437-2	Open		55.00	55
1987	Cumberland House 5024-5	Open		42.00	45
1993	Dairy Barn, 5446-1	Open		55.00	55
1984	Delta House 5012-1	Closed	1986	32.00	300-500
1985	Depot and Train w/2 Train Cars 5051-2	Closed	1988	65.00	100-165
1993	Dinah's Drive-In, 5447-0	Open		45.00	45
1989	Doctor's House 5143-8	Closed	1992	56.00	85-135
1991	Double Bungalow, 5407-0	Closed	1994	45.00	50-75
1985	Duplex 5050-4	Closed	1987	35.00	135-180
1981	English Church 5078-4	Closed	1982	30.00	350
1981	English Cottage 5073-3	Closed	1982	25.00	285-325
1983	English Tudor 5033-4	Closed	1985	30.00	245-350
1987	Farm House 5089-0	Closed	1992	40.00	60-95
1994	Federal House (American Architecture Series), 5465-8	Open		50.00	50
1991	Finklea's Finery: Costume Shop 5405-4	Closed	1993	45.00	55-75
1983	Fire Station 5032-6	Closed	1984	32.00	600-800
1987	Fire Station No. 2 5091-1	Closed	1989	40.00	175-275
1994	Fisherman's Nook Cabins, 5461-5 set/2, (Fisherman's Nook Bass Cabin, Fisherman's Nook Trout Cabin)	Open		50.00	50
1994	Fisherman's Nook Resort, 5460-7	Open		75.00	75
1982	Flower Shop 5082-2	Closed	1983	25.00	415-500
1976	Gabled Cottage 5002-1	Closed	1979	20.00	335-375
1982	Gabled House 5081-4	Closed	1983	30.00	365-425

YEAR ISSUE		EDITION LIMIT	YEAR RETD.	ISSUE PRICE	QUOTE U.S.$
1984	Galena House 5009-1	Closed	1985	32.00	330-400
1978	General Store (tan) 5012-0	Closed	1980	25.00	670
1978	General Store (white) 5012-0	Closed	1980	25.00	500
1979	Giant Trees 5065-8	Closed	1982	20.00	300-400
1983	Gingerbread HouseBank (Non-lighted) 5025-3	Closed	1984	24.00	300-375
1994	Glenhaven House 5468-2	Open		45.00	45
1992	Good Shepherd Chapel & Church School, 5424-0, set/2	Open		72.00	72
1983	Gothic Church 5028-8	Closed	1986	36.00	240-275
1991	Gothic Farmhouse (American Architecture Series), 5404-6	Open		48.00	48
1983	Governor's Mansion 5003-2	Closed	1985	32.00	200-350
1992	Grandma's Cottage 5420-8	Open		42.00	45
1983	Grocery 5001-6	Closed	1985	35.00	275-400
1992	Hartford House 5426-7	Open		55.00	55
1984	Haversham House 5008-3	Closed	1987	37.00	230-350
1986	Highland Park House 5063-6	Closed	1988	35.00	130-165
1988	Home Sweet Home/House & Windmill 5126-8	Closed	1991	60.00	90-135
1978	Homestead 5011-2	Closed	1984	30.00	225-275
1991	Honeymooner Motel 5401-1	Closed	1993	42.00	60-115
1993	Hunting Lodge, 5445-3	Open		50.00	50
1976	The Inn 5003-9	Closed	1979	20.00	450
1989	J. Young's Granary 5149-7	Closed	1992	45.00	70-90
1991	Jack's Corner Barber Shop 5406-2	Closed	1994	42.00	55-85
1987	Jefferson School 5082-2	Closed	1991	36.00	125-200
1989	Jingle Belle Houseboat 5114-4	Closed	1991	42.00	100-120
1988	Kenwood House 5054-7	Closed	1990	50.00	120-150
1979	Knob Hill (gold) 5055-9	Closed	1981	30.00	370
1979	Knob Hill 5055-9	Closed	1981	30.00	275-400
1981	Large Single Tree 5080-6	Closed	1989	17.00	30-60
1987	Lighthouse 5030-0	Closed	1988	36.00	550-700
1986	Lincoln Park Duplex 5060-1	Closed	1988	33.00	105-140
1979	Log Cabin 5057-5	Closed	1981	22.00	440-500
1984	Main Street House 5005-9	Closed	1986	27.00	235-275
1990	Mainstreet Hardware Store 5153-5	Closed	1993	42.00	60-75
1977	Mansion 5008-8	Closed	1979	30.00	450-650
1988	Maple Ridge Inn 5121-7	Closed	1990	55.00	65-125
1994	Marvel's Beauty Salon 5470-4	Open		37.50	38
1986	Mickey's Diner 5078-4	Closed	1987	22.00	350-600
1979	Mission Church 5062-5	Closed	1980	30.00	1085-1250
1979	Mobile Home 5063-3	Closed	1980	18.00	1800-2500
1990	Morningside House 5152-7	Closed	1992	45.00	45-80
1993	Mount Olivet Church, 5442-9	Open		65.00	65
1976	Mountain Lodge 5001-3	Closed	1979	20.00	300-400
1978	Nantucket 5014-6	Closed	1986	25.00	250-275
1993	Nantucket Renovation 5441-0	Closed	1993	55.00	70-100
1984	New School House 5037-7	Closed	1986	35.00	225-325
1982	New Stone Church 5083-0	Closed	1984	32.00	385
1989	North Creek Cottage 5120-9	Closed	1992	45.00	55-85
1991	Oak Grove Tudor 5400-3	Closed	1994	42.00	55-75
1994	The Original Snow Village Starter Set, 5462-3 (Shady Oak Church, Sunday School Serenade Accessory, 3 assorted Sisal Trees, 1.5 oz. bag of real plastic snow)	Open		50.00	50
1986	Pacific Heights House 5066-0	Closed	1988	33.00	95-120
1988	Palos Verdes 5141-1	Closed	1990	37.50	60-90
1989	Paramount Theater 5142-0	Closed	1993	42.00	85-105
1984	Parish Church 5039-3	Closed	1986	32.00	330-400
1983	Parsonage 5029-6	Closed	1985	35.00	300-400
1995	Peppermint Porch Day Care 5485-2	Open		45.00	45
1989	Pinewood Log Cabin 5150-0	Open		37.50	38
1982	Pioneer Church 5022-9	Closed	1984	30.00	300-375
1985	Plantation House 5047-4	Closed	1987	37.00	110-130
1992	Post Office 5422-4	Open		35.00	38
1990	Prairie House (American Architecture Series), 5156-0	Closed	1993	42.00	55-80
1992	Print Shop & Village News 5425-9	Closed	1994	37.50	60-80
1990	Queen Anne Victorian (American Architecture Series), 5157-8	Open		48.00	50
1986	Ramsey Hill House 5067-9	Closed	1989	36.00	85-140
1987	Red Barn 5081-4	Closed	1992	38.00	75-100
1988	Redeemer Church 5127-6	Closed	1992	42.00	50-90
1985	Ridgewood 5052-0	Closed	1987	35.00	145-200
1984	River Road House 5010-5	Closed	1987	36.00	200-260
1986	Saint James Church 5068-7	Closed	1988	37.00	165-190
1979	School House 5060-9	Closed	1982	30.00	375-400
1988	Service Station 5128-4	Closed	1991	37.50	200-300
1988	Single Car Garage 5125-0	Closed	1990	22.00	45-60
1994	Skate & Ski Shop 5467-4	Open		50.00	50
1982	Skating Pond 5017-2	Closed	1984	25.00	375
1978	Skating Rink, Duck Pond (Set) 5015-3	Closed	1979	16.00	1400
1976	Small Chalet 5006-2	Closed	1979	15.00	400-465
1978	Small Double Trees w/ blue birds 5016-1	Closed	1989	13.50	165
1978	Small Double Trees w/ red birds 5016-1	Closed	1989	13.50	50
1987	Snow Village Factory 5013-0	Closed	1989	45.00	115-145
1987	Snow Village Resort Lodge 5092-0	Closed	1989	55.00	125-145
1993	Snowy Hills Hospital, 5448-8	Open		48.00	48
1986	Sonoma House 5062-8	Closed	1988	33.00	110-150
1991	Southern Colonial (American Architecture Series), 5403-8	Closed	1994	48.00	60-85
1990	Spanish Mission Church 5155-1	Closed	1992	42.00	55-90
1987	Springfield House 5027-0	Closed	1990	40.00	65-100
1985	Spruce Place 5049-0	Closed	1987	33.00	225-325
1987	St. Anthony Hotel & Post Office 5006-7	Closed	1989	40.00	95-130
1992	St. Luke's Church 5421-6	Closed	1994	45.00	60-90
1976	Steepled Church 5005-4	Closed	1979	25.00	475-600
1977	Stone Church (10") 5009-6	Closed	1979	35.00	660-800
1979	Stone Church (8") 5059-1	Closed	1980	32.00	1000
1980	Stone Mill House 5068-2	Closed	1982	30.00	475-600
1988	Stonehurst House 5140-3	Closed	1994	37.50	50-70
1984	Stratford House 5007-5	Closed	1986	28.00	190-245
1982	Street Car 5019-9	Closed	1984	16.00	400
1985	Stucco Bungalow 5045-8	Closed	1986	30.00	335-470
1984	Summit House 5036-9	Closed	1985	28.00	330-425
1982	Swiss Chalet 5023-7	Closed	1984	28.00	400-475
1979	Thatched Cottage 5050-0 Meadowland Series	Closed	1980	30.00	800
1980	Town Church 5071-7	Closed	1982	33.00	425
1983	Town Hall 5000-8	Closed	1984	32.00	375
1986	Toy Shop 5073-3	Closed	1990	36.00	85-100
1980	Train Station w/ 3 Train Cars 5085-6	Closed	1985	100.00	375-425
1984	Trinity Church 5035-0	Closed	1986	32.00	265-300
1979	Tudor House 5061-7	Closed	1981	25.00	310-350
1983	Turn of the Century 5004-0	Closed	1986	36.00	220-352
1986	Twin Peaks 5042-3	Closed	1986	32.00	300-500
1979	Victorian 5054-2	Closed	1982	30.00	340
1983	Victorian Cottage 5002-4	Closed	1984	35.00	325-375
1977	Victorian House 5007-0	Closed	1979	30.00	470
1983	Village Church 5026-1	Closed	1984	30.00	435
1991	Village Greenhouse 5402-0	Open		35.00	36
1988	Village Market 5044-0	Closed	1991	39.00	70-95
1993	Village Public Library, 5443-7	Open		55.00	55
1990	Village Realty 5154-3	Closed	1993	42.00	65
1992	Village Station 5438-0	Open		65.00	65
1988	Village Station and Train 5122-5	Closed	1992	65.00	85-125
1992	Village Vet and Pet Shop 5427-5	Open		32.00	32
1989	Village Warming House 5145-4	Closed	1992	42.00	60-80
1986	Waverly Place 5041-5	Closed	1986	35.00	265-350
1994	Wedding Chapel 5464-0	Open		55.00	55
1985	Williamsburg House 5046-6	Closed	1988	37.00	130-165
1993	Woodbury House, 5444-5	Open		45.00	45
1983	Wooden Church 5031-8	Closed	1985	30.00	330-450
1981	Wooden Clapboard 5072-5	Closed	1984	32.00	220-300

The Original Snow Village Collection Accessories Retired - Department 56

YEAR ISSUE		EDITION LIMIT	YEAR RETD.	ISSUE PRICE	QUOTE U.S.$
1987	3 Nuns With Songbooks 5102-0	Closed	1988	6.00	130
1988	Apple Girl/Newspaper Boy 5129-2, set/2	Closed	1990	11.00	18-30
1979	Aspen Trees 5052-6, Meadowland Series	Closed	1980	16.00	475
1989	Bringing Home The Tree 5169-1	Closed	1992	15.00	22-30
1989	Calling All Cars 5174-8, set/2	Closed	1991	15.00	30-50
1979	Carolers 5064-1	Closed	1986	12.00	90-130
1987	Caroling Family 5105-5, set/3	Closed	1990	20.00	25-40
1980	Ceramic Car 5069-0	Closed	1986	5.00	50-60
1981	Ceramic Sleigh 5079-2	Closed	1986	5.00	58
1987	Children In Band 5104-7	Closed	1989	15.00	25-40
1989	Choir Kids 5147-0	Closed	1992	15.00	26
1991	Christmas Cadillac 5413-5	Closed	1994	9.00	10-20
1987	Christmas Children 5107-1, set/4	Closed	1990	20.00	30-35
1991	Cold Weather Sports 5410-0, set/4	Closed	1994	27.50	35
1991	Come Join The Parade 5411-9	Closed	1992	13.00	20-30
1991	Country Harvest, 5415-1	Closed	1993	13.00	20-35
1988	Doghouse/Cat In Garbage Can,set/2 5131-4	Closed	1992	15.00	25-35
1990	Down the Chimney He Goes, 5158-6	Closed	1993	6.50	10-20
1985	Family Mom/Kids, Goose/Girl 5057-1	Closed	1988	11.00	25-45
1987	For Sale Sign 5108-0	Closed	1989	3.50	5-10
1990	Fresh Frozen Fish 5163-2, set/2	Closed	1993	20.00	30-40
1986	Girl/Snowman, Boy 5095-4	Closed	1987	11.00	55-70
1988	Hayride 5117-9	Closed	1990	30.00	50-70
1990	Here We Come A Caroling, set/3 5161-6	Closed	1992	18.00	20-35
1990	Home Delivery, set /2 5162-4	Closed	1992	16.00	25-45
1986	Kids Around The Tree (large) 5094-6	Closed	1990	15.00	75-90
1986	Kids Around The Tree (small) 5094-6	Closed	1990	15.00	33-55
1990	Kids Decorating the Village Sign, 5134-9	Closed	1993	13.00	16-25
1989	Kids Tree House 5168-3	Closed	1991	25.00	35-55
1988	Man On Ladder Hanging Garland 5116-0	Closed	1992	7.50	17
1984	Monks-A-Caroling (brown) 5040-7	Closed	1988	6.00	45
1983	Monks-A-Caroling (butterscotch) 6459-9	Closed	1984	6.00	60-75
1992	Nanny and the Preschoolers 5430-5, set/2	Closed	1994	27.50	32
1987	Park Bench (green) 5109-8	Closed	1993	3.00	6
1987	Praying Monks 5103-9	Closed	1988	6.00	33-50
1985	Santa/Mailbox 5059-8	Closed	1988	11.00	50-60
1988	School Bus, Snow Plow 5137-3, set/2	Closed	1991	16.00	40-55
1988	School Children 5118-7, set/3	Closed	1990	15.00	25-35
1984	Scottie With Tree 5038-5	Closed	1985	3.00	170
1979	Sheep, 9 White, 3 Black 5053-4 Meadowland Series	Closed	1980	12.00	400
1986	Shopping Girls w/Packages (large) 5096-2	Closed	1988	11.00	40-55
1986	Shopping Girls w/Packages (small) 5096-2	Closed	1988	11.00	30-60
1985	Singing Nuns 5053-9	Closed	1987	6.00	120
1988	Sisal Tree Lot 8183-3	Closed	1991	45.00	80-100
1989	Skate Faster Mom 5170-5	Closed	1991	13.00	22-45
1990	Sleighride 5160-8	Closed	1992	30.00	40-70
1990	Sno-Jet Snowmobile, 5159-4	Closed	1993	15.00	17-30
1987	Snow Kids 5113-6, set/4	Closed	1990	20.00	45-60
1985	Snow Kids Sled, Skis 5056-3	Closed	1987	11.00	45-60
1991	Snowball Fort 5414-3, set/3	Closed	1993	28.00	35-50
1982	Snowman With Broom 5018-0	Closed	1990	3.00	10-20
1989	Statue of Mark Twain 5173-0	Closed	1991	15.00	35-45
1990	SV Special Delivery, 5197-7, set/2	Closed	1992	16.00	38-48
1989	Through the Woods, 5172-1, set/2	Closed	1991	18.00	25-45
1989	US Mailbox 5179-9	Closed	1990	3.50	15-30
1989	US Special Delivery 5148-9, set/2	Closed	1990	16.00	35-50
1989	Village Birds 5180-2, set/6	Closed	1994	3.50	20-35
1991	Village Greetings 5418-6, set/3	Closed	1994	5.00	10
1991	Village Marching Band 5412-7, set/3	Closed	1992	30.00	45-50
1988	Water Tower 5133-0	Closed	1991	20.00	55-75
1989	Water Tower-John Deer 568-0	Closed	1991	20.00	655-900
1992	We're Going to a Christmas Pageant 5435-6	Closed	1994	15.00	18
1991	Winter Fountain, 5409-7	Closed	1993	25.00	40-55
1988	Woodsman and Boy 5130-6, set/2	Closed	1991	13.00	25-35
1988	Woody Station Wagon 5136-5	Closed	1990	6.50	25-50
1991	Wreaths For Sale 5408-9, set/4	Closed	1994	27.50	30-50

Retired Heritage Village Collection Accessories - Department 56

YEAR ISSUE		EDITION LIMIT	YEAR RETD.	ISSUE PRICE	QUOTE U.S.$
1991	All Around the Town, set/2 5545-0	Closed	1993	18.00	25-35
1987	Alpine Village Sign 6571-4	Closed	1993	6.00	12-20
1986	Alpine Villagers, set/3 6542-0	Closed	1992	13.00	30-45
1990	Amish Buggy 5949-8	Closed	1992	22.00	45-55
1990	Amish Family, set/3 5948-0	Closed	1992	20.00	25-45
1990	Amish Family, set/3 5948-0 w/Moustache	Closed	1992	20.00	40-55
1987	Blacksmith, set/3 5934-0	Closed	1990	20.00	60-75
1990	Busy Sidewalks, set/4 5535-2	Closed	1992	28.00	37-50
1984	Carolers, set/3 w/ Lamppost (bl) 6526-9	Closed	1990	10.00	25-45
1984	Carolers, set/3 w/ Lamppost (wh) 6526-9	Closed	1990	10.00	95-135
1990	Carolers on the Doorstep, set/4 5570-0	Closed	1993	25.00	35-45
1988	Childe Pond and Skaters, set/4 5903-0	Closed	1991	30.00	75-90
1986	Christmas Carol Figures, set/3 6501-3	Closed	1990	12.50	60-85
1987	Christmas in the City Sign, 5960-9	Closed	1993	6.00	13-20
1992	Churchyard Gate and Fence, set/3 5563-8	Closed	1992	15.00	40-50
1988	City Bus & Milk Truck, set/2 5983-8	Closed	1991	15.00	20-40
1988	City Newsstand, set/4 5971-4	Closed	1991	25.00	45-60
1987	City People, set/5 5965-0	Closed	1990	27.50	45-55
1987	City Workers, set/4 5967-6	Closed	1988	15.00	35-45
1991	Come into the Inn, 5560-3	Closed	1994	22.00	35
1989	Constables, set/3 5579-4	Closed	1991	17.50	50-65
1986	Covered Wooden Bridge 6531-5	Closed	1990	10.00	37
1989	David Copperfield Characters, set/5 5551-4	Closed	1992	32.50	35-50
1987	Dickens' Village Sign 6569-2	Closed	1993	6.00	10-20
1987	Dover Coach 6590-0	Closed	1990	18.00	65-85
1987	Dover Coach w/o Mustache 6590-0	Closed	1990	18.00	85-115
1989	Farm Animals, set/4 5945-5	Closed	1991	15.00	30-45
1987	Farm People And Animals, set/5 5901-3	Closed	1989	24.00	75-95
1988	Fezziwig and Friends, set/3 5928-5	Closed	1990	12.50	45-60
1989	Heritage Village Sign, 9953-8	Closed	1989	10.00	15-25
1992	Letters for Santa, set/3 5604-9	Closed	1994	30.00	45-55
1986	Lighted Tree With Children & Ladder 6510-2	Closed	1989	35.00	325-350
1987	Maple Sugaring Shed, set/3 6589-7	Closed	1989	19.00	200-250
1991	Market Day, set/3 5641-3	Closed	1993	35.00	40-50
1987	New England Village Sign 6570-6	Closed	1993	6.00	10-18
1986	New England Winter Set, set/5 6532-3	Closed	1990	18.00	40-50
1988	Nicholas Nickleby Characters, set/4 5929-3	Closed	1991	20.00	28-45
1991	Oliver Twist Characters, set/3 5554-9	Closed	1993	35.00	35-55
1988	One Horse Open Sleigh 5982-0	Closed	1993	20.00	30-40
1989	Organ Grinder, set/3 5957-9	Closed	1991	21.00	30-45
1987	Ox Sled (blue pants) 5951-0	Closed	1989	20.00	125-150
1987	Ox Sled (tan pants) 5951-0	Closed	1989	20.00	200-255
1989	Popcorn Vendor, set/3 5958-7	Closed	1992	22.00	25-40
1986	Porcelain Trees, set/2 6537-4	Closed	1992	14.00	30-35
1994	Postern, 9871-0, (Dickens' Village Ten Year Accessory Anniversary Piece)	Closed	1994	17.50	25-35
1988	Red Covered Bridge, 5987-0	Closed	1994	17.00	20-35
1989	River Street Ice House Cart 5959-5	Closed	1991	20.00	40-55
1989	Royal Coach 5578-6	Closed	1992	55.00	65-80
1988	Salvation Army Band, set/6 5985-4	Closed	1991	24.00	55-75
1990	Santa's Little Helpers, set/3 5610-3	Closed	1993	28.00	45-55
1987	Shopkeepers, set/4 5966-8	Closed	1988	15.00	30-45

YEAR ISSUE		EDITION LIMIT	YEAR RETD.	ISSUE PRICE	QUOTE U.S.$
1987	Silo And Hay Shed 5950-1	Closed	1989	18.00	150-185
1987	Skating Pond 6545-5	Closed	1990	24.00	70-85
1990	Sleepy Hollow Characters, set/3 5956-0	Closed	1992	27.50	35-45
1986	Sleighride 6511-0	Closed	1990	19.50	45-65
1988	Snow Children, 5938-2	Closed	1994	17.00	25-35
1987	Stone Bridge 6546-3	Closed	1990	12.00	75-85
1990	Tis the Season, 5539-5	Closed	1994	12.95	23
1990	Trimming the North Pole 5608-1	Closed	1993	10.00	20-28
1989	U.S. Mail Box and Fire Hydrant, 5517-4	Closed	1990	5.00	15-25
1989	Village Blvd., Set of 14 5516-6	Closed	1993	25.00	40-55
1993	Village Express Van (black), 9951-1	Closed	1993	25.00	115-150
1993	Village Express Van (gold), 9977-5 (promotional)	Closed	1993	N/A	1100-1300
1994	Village Express Van-Bachman's, 729-3	Closed	1994	22.50	75
1994	Village Express Van-Bronner's, 737-4	Closed	1994	22.50	55-75
1995	Village Express Van-Canadian 2163-7	Closed	1995	N/A	100-150
1994	Village Express Van-Christmas Dove, 730-7	Closed	1994	25.00	60-75
1994	Village Express Van-European Imports, 739-0	Closed	1994	22.50	45-75
1994	Village Express Van-Fortunoff's, 735-8	Closed	1994	22.50	125-150
1994	Village Express Van-The Incredible Christmas (Pigeon Forge), 732-3	Closed	1994	24.98	60-75
1994	Village Express Van-Limited Edition, 733-1	Closed	1994	25.00	60-80
1994	Village Express Van-The Lemon Tree, 721-8	Closed	1994	30.00	45-75
1994	Village Express Van-Lock, Stock & Barrel, 731-5	Closed	1994	22.50	100-130
1994	Village Express Van-North Pole City, 736-6	Closed	1994	25.00	60-75
1995	Village Express Van-Park West 0755-2	Closed	1995	N/A	350
1994	Village Express Van-Robert's Christmas Wonderland, 734-0	Closed	1994	22.50	50-75
1994	Village Express Van-Stat's, 741-2	Closed	1994	22.50	50-80
1994	Village Express Van-William Glen, 738-2	Closed	1994	22.50	50-75
1994	Village Express Van-Windsor Shoppe, 740-4	Closed	1994	25.00	50-75
1987	Village Express Train (electric, black),5997-8	Closed	1988	89.95	275-375
1988	Village Harvest People, set/4 5941-2	Closed	1991	27.50	40-55
1989	Village Sign with Snowman, 5572-7	Closed	1994	10.00	10-20
1992	Village Street Peddlers, set/2 5804-1	Closed	1994	16.00	20-30
1985	Village Train Brighton, set/3 6527-7	Closed	1986	12.00	400-550
1988	Village Train Trestle 5981-1	Closed	1990	17.00	55-75
1987	Village Well And Holy Cross, set/2 6547-1	Closed	1989	13.00	120-160
1989	Violet Vendor/Carolers/Chestnut Vendor set/3 5580-8	Closed	1992	23.00	30-50
1988	Woodcutter And Son, set/2 5986-2	Closed	1990	10.00	35-45

Snowbabies - Department 56

YEAR ISSUE		EDITION LIMIT	YEAR RETD.	ISSUE PRICE	QUOTE U.S.$
1989	All Fall Down, set of 4 7984-7	Closed	1991	36.00	50-85
1990	All Tired Out, waterglobe 7937-5	Closed	1992	55.00	75-100
1988	Are All These Mine? 7977-4	Open		10.00	13
1995	Are You On My List? 6875-6	Open		25.00	25
1986	Best Friends 7958-8	Closed	1989	12.00	115-160
1994	Bringing Starry Pines 6862-4	Open		35.00	35
1992	Can I Help, Too? 6806-3	18,500	1992	48.00	80-140
1993	Can I Open it Now? 6838-1 (Event Piece)	Closed	1993	15.00	35-50
1993	Can I Open it Now?, mini music box 7648-1	Closed	1994	20.00	42-50
1986	Catch a Falling Star, waterglobe 7967-7	Closed	1987	18.00	550-600
1986	Climbing on Snowball, Bisque Votive w/Candle 7965-0	Closed	1989	15.00	95-120
1987	Climbing On Tree, set/2 7971-5	Closed	1989	25.00	650-850
1993	Crossing Starry Skies 6834-9	Open		35.00	35
1991	Dancing To a Tune, set/3 6808-0	Open		30.00	30
1987	Don't Fall Off 7968-5	Closed	1990	12.50	75-100
1987	Down The Hill We Go 7960-0	Open		20.00	23
1989	Finding Fallen Stars 7985-5	6,000	1989	32.50	165-185
1991	Fishing For Dreams 6809-8	Closed	1994	28.00	35-40
1992	Fishing For Dreams, waterglobe 6832-2	Closed	1994	32.50	40-55
1986	Forest Accessory "Frosty Forest", set/2 7963-4	Open		15.00	20
1988	Frosty Frolic 7981-2	4,800	1989	35.00	775-900
1989	Frosty Fun 7983-9	Closed	1991	27.50	45-70
1993	Frosty Fun, mini music box 7650-3	Closed	1994	20.00	40-50
1986	Give Me A Push 7955-3	Closed	1990	12.00	55-70
1986	Hanging Pair 7966-9	Closed	1989	15.00	120-160
1992	Help Me, I'm Stuck 6817-9	Closed	1994	32.50	40-50
1989	Helpful Friends 7982-0	Closed	1993	30.00	40-65
1986	Hold On Tight 7956-1	Open		12.00	14
1995	I Found The Biggest Star of All! 6874-8	Open		16.00	16
1993	I Found Your Mittens, set/2, 6836-5	Open		30.00	30
1991	I Made This Just For You 6802-0	Open		15.00	15
1992	I Need A Hug 6813-6	Open		20.00	20
1995	I See You!, set/2 6878-0	Open		27.50	28
1991	I'll Put Up The Tree 6800-4	Open		24.00	25
1993	I'll Teach You A Trick 6835-7	Open		24.00	24
1993	I'm Making an Ice Sculpture 6842-0	Open		30.00	30
1986	I'm Making Snowballs 7962-6	Closed	1992	12.00	25-50
1994	I'm Right Behind You!, 6852-7	Open		60.00	60
1989	Icy Igloo 7987-1	Open		37.50	38
1991	Is That For Me 6803-9, set/2	Closed	1993	32.50	40-55
1994	Jack Frost...A Touch of Winter's Magic, 6854-3	Open		90.00	95
1992	Join The Parade 6824-1	Closed	1994	37.50	45-50
1992	Just One Little Candle 6823-3	Open		15.00	15
1989	Let It Snow, waterglobe 7992-8	Closed	1993	25.00	35-45
1993	Let's All Chime In! 6845-4, set/2	Open		37.50	38
1994	Let's Go Skating 6860-8	Open		16.50	17
1992	Let's Go Skiing 6815-2	Closed	1994	15.00	15-20
1994	Lift Me Higher, I Can't Reach 6863-2	Open		75.00	75
1992	Look What I Can Do! 6819-5	Open		16.50	17
1993	Look What I Found 6833-0	Open		45.00	45
1994	Look What I Found, waterglobe 6872-1	Open		32.50	33
1993	Now I Lay Me Down to Sleep 6839-0	Open		13.50	14
1992	Over the Milky Way 6828-4	Open		32.00	32
1991	Peek-A-Boo, waterglobe 7938-3	Closed	1993	50.00	65-80
1989	Penguin Parade 7986-3	Closed	1992	25.00	40-70
1993	Penguin Parade, mini music box 7645-5	Closed	1994	20.00	40-50
1994	Pennies From Heaven 6864-0	Open		17.50	18
1994	Planting Starry Pines, waterglobe 6870-5	Open		32.50	33
1991	Play Me a Tune, waterglobe 7936-7	Closed	1993	50.00	60-85
1993	Play Me a Tune, mini music box 7651-1	Closed	1994	20.00	40-50
1990	Playing Games Is Fun 7947-2	Closed	1993	30.00	45-55
1988	Polar Express 7978-2	Closed	1992	22.00	55-85
1990	Read Me a Story 7945-6	Open		25.00	25
1992	Read Me a Story, waterglobe 6831-4	Open		32.50	33
1993	Reading a Story, mini music box 7649-0	Closed	1994	20.00	42-50
1995	Ring The Bells...It's Christmas! 6876-4	Open		40.00	40
1992	Shall I Play For You? 6820-9	Open		16.50	17
1995	Snowbabies Animated Skating Pond, set/14 7668-6	Open		60.00	60
1993	Snowbabies Picture Frame, Baby's First Smile 6846-2	Open		30.00	30
1987	Snowbabies Riding Sleds, waterglobe 7975-8	Closed	1988	40.00	600
1986	Snowbaby Holding Picture Frame, set/2 7970-7	Closed	1987	15.00	550-695
1986	Snowbaby Nite-Lite 7959-6	Closed	1989	15.00	300-400
1991	Snowbaby Polar Sign 6804-7	Open		20.00	20
1986	Snowbaby Standing, waterglobe 7964-2	Closed	1987	7.50	450-500
1987	Snowbaby with Wings, waterglobe 7973-1	Closed	1988	20.00	500
1993	So Much Work To Do 6837-3	Open		18.00	18
1993	Somewhere in Dreamland 6840-3	Open		85.00	85
1990	A Special Delivery 7948-0	Closed	1994	15.00	20-29
1992	Starry Pines 6829-2, set/2	Open		17.50	18
1992	Stars-In-A-Row, Tic-Tac-Toe 6822-5	Open		32.50	33
1994	Stringing Fallen Stars 6861-6	Open		25.00	25
1994	There's Another One!, 6853-5	Open		24.00	24
1991	This Is Where We Live 6805-5	Closed	1994	60.00	66-85
1992	This Willl Cheer You Up 6816-0	Closed	1994	30.00	45-65
1988	Tiny Trio, set of 3 7979-0	Closed	1990	20.00	125-160
1987	Tumbling In the Snow, set/5 7957-0	Closed	1993	35.00	65-90
1990	Twinkle Little Stars 7942-1, set/2	Closed	1993	37.50	45-75
1992	Wait For Me 6812-8	Closed	1994	48.00	60
1991	Waiting For Christmas 6807-1	Closed	1993	27.50	35-45
1993	We Make a Great Pair 6843-8	Open		30.00	30
1990	We Will Make it Shine 7946-4	Closed	1992	45.00	55-90
1994	We'll Plant the Starry Pines, set/2 6865-9	Open		37.50	38
1995	What Shall We Do Today? 6877-2	Open		32.50	33
1987	When You Wish Upon a Star, music box 7972-3	Closed	1993	30.00	47
1993	Where Did He Go? 6841-1	Open		35.00	35
1994	Where Did You Come From?, 6856-0	Open		40.00	40
1990	Who Are You? 7949-9	12,500	1991	32.50	110-145
1991	Why Don't You Talk To Me 6801-2	Open		24.00	24
1993	Will it Snow Today? 6844-6	Open		45.00	45
1992	Winken, Blinken, and Nod 6814-4	Open		60.00	65
1987	Winter Surprise 7974-0	Closed	1992	15.00	35-50
1990	Wishing on a Star 7943-0	Closed	1994	22.00	30-42
1992	You Can't Find Me! 6818-7	Open		45.00	45
1992	You Didn't Forget Me 6821-7	Open		32.50	33

Snowbabies Pewter Miniatures - Department 56

YEAR ISSUE		EDITION LIMIT	YEAR RETD.	ISSUE PRICE	QUOTE U.S.$
1989	All Fall Down, set of 4, 7617-1	Closed	1993	25.00	33-60
1989	Are All These Mine? 7605-8	Closed	1992	7.00	12-20
1989	Best Friends. 7604-0	Closed	1994	10.00	20
1991	Dancing to a Tune, set/3, 7630-9	Closed	1993	18.00	22-30
1989	Don't Fall Off!, 7603-1	Closed	1994	7.00	15
1989	Finding Fallen Stars, set/2, 7618-0	Closed	1992	12.50	30-40
1989	Frosty Frolic, set of 4, 7613-9	Closed	1993	24.00	30-40
1989	Give Me a Push!, 7601-5	Closed	1994	7.00	14
1989	Helpful Friends, set of 4 7608-2	Closed	1992	13.50	22-35
1991	I Made This Just for You!, 7628-7	Closed	1994	7.00	15
1989	Icy Igloo, w/tree, set of 2 7610-4	Closed	1992	7.50	17-24
1991	Is That For Me?, set of 2, 7631-7	Closed	1993	12.50	15-25
1989	Penguin Parade, set of 4, 7616-3	Closed	1993	12.50	20-30
1990	Playing Games is Fun!, set/2, 7623-6	Closed	1993	13.50	19-30
1989	Polar Express, set of 2, 7609-0	Closed	1992	13.50	25-37
1990	A Special Delivery 7624-4	Closed	1993	7.00	13
1989	Tiny Trio, set of 3, 7615-5	Closed	1993	18.00	25-35
1989	Tumbling in the Snow!, set of 5, 7614-7	Closed	1992	30.00	65-80
1990	Twinkle Little Stars, set of 2, 7621-0	Closed	1993	15.00	23-35
1991	Waiting for Christmas, 7629-5	Closed	1993	13.00	20-30
1989	Winter Surprise!, 7607-4	Closed	1994	13.50	15-30

Village CCP Miniatures - Department 56

YEAR ISSUE		EDITION LIMIT	YEAR RETD.	ISSUE PRICE	QUOTE U.S.$
1987	Christmas Carol Cottages, set/3 6561-7	Closed	1989	30.00	75-90
1987	•The Cottage of Bob Cratchit & Tiny Tim 6561-7	Closed	1989	10.00	30-45
1987	•Fezziwig's Warehouse 6561-7	Closed	1989	10.00	20-30
1987	•Scrooge/ Marley Countinghouse 6561-7	Closed	1989	10.00	30
1987	Dickens' Chadbury Station & Train 6592-7	Closed	1989	27.50	50-80
1987	Dickens' Cottages, set/3 6559-5	Closed	1989	30.00	210
1987	•Stone Cottage 6559-5	Closed	1989	10.00	115-130
1987	•Thatched Cottage 6559-5	Closed	1989	10.00	100
1987	•Tudor Cottage 6559-5	Closed	1989	10.00	115-135
1988	Dickens' Kenilworth Castle 6565-0	Closed	1989	30.00	80-90
1987	Dickens' Lane Shops, set/3 6591-9	Closed	1989	30.00	110-135
1987	•Cottage Toy Shop 6591-9	Closed	1989	10.00	30-60
1987	•Thomas Kersey Coffee House 6591-9	Closed	1989	10.00	50-60
1987	•Tuttle's Pub 6591-9	Closed	1989	10.00	25-50
1987	Dickens' Village Assorted, set/3 6560-9	Closed	1989	48.00	N/A
1987	•Blythe Pond Mill House 6560-9	Closed	1989	16.00	40-45
1987	•Dickens Village Church 6560-9	Closed	1989	16.00	40-85
1987	•Norman Church 6560-9	Closed	1989	16.00	75-110
1987	Dickens' Village Assorted, set/4 6562-5	Closed	1989	60.00	N/A
1987	•Barley Bree Farmhouse 6562-5	Closed	1989	15.00	35-45
1987	•Brick Abbey 6562-5	Closed	1989	15.00	90-125
1987	•Chesterton Manor House 6562-5	Closed	1989	15.00	85-120
1987	•The Old Curiosity Shop 6562-5	Closed	1989	15.00	60-110
1987	Dickens' Village Original, set/7 6558-7	Closed	1989	72.00	240-260
1987	•Abel Beesley Butcher 6558-7	Closed	1989	12.00	30-45
1987	•Bean and Son Smithy Shop 6558-7	Closed	1989	12.00	25-50
1987	•Candle Shop 6558-7	Closed	1989	12.00	25-50
1987	•Crowntree Inn 6558-7	Closed	1989	12.00	25-70
1987	•Golden Swan Baker 6558-7	Closed	1989	12.00	25-45
1987	•Green Grocer 6558-7	Closed	1989	12.00	42
1987	•Jones & Co Brush & Basket Shop 6558-7	Closed	1989	12.00	60
1987	Little Town of Bethlehem, set of 12 5976-5	Closed	1989	85.00	180-220
1988	New England Village Assorted, set/6 5937-4	Closed	1989	85.00	260
1988	•Craggy Cove Lighthouse 5937-4	Closed	1989	14.50	180
1988	•Jacob Adams Barn 5937-4	Closed	1989	14.50	70-80
1988	•Jacob Adams Farmhouse 5937-4	Closed	1989	14.50	60
1988	•Maple Sugaring Shed 5937-4	Closed	1989	14.50	48-60
1988	•Smythe Wollen Mill 5937-4	Closed	1989	14.50	90-110
1988	•Timber Knoll Log Cabin 5937-4	Closed	1989	14.50	30-55
1988	New England Village Original, set/7 5935-8	Closed	1989	72.00	325-475
1988	•Apothecary Shop 5935-8	Closed	1989	10.50	20-50
1988	•Brick Town Hall 5935-8	Closed	1989	10.50	55-70
1988	•General Store 5935-8	Closed	1989	10.50	55-100
1988	•Livery Stable & Boot Shop 5935-8	Closed	1989	10.50	30-60
1988	•Nathaniel Bingham Fabrics 5935-8	Closed	1989	10.50	45
1988	•Red Schoolhouse 5935-8	Closed	1989	10.50	70-90
1988	•Village Steeple Church 5935-8	Closed	1989	10.50	275-325
1986	Victorian Miniatures, set/2 6564-1	Closed	1987	45.00	300
1986	•Church 6564-1	Closed	1987	22.50	N/A
1986	•Estate 6564-1	Closed	1987	22.50	N/A
1986	Victorian Miniatures, set/5 6563-3	Closed	1987	65.00	N/A
1986	Williamsburg Snowhouse Series, set/6	Closed	1987	60.00	500-575
1986	•Williamsburg Church, White 6566-8	Closed	1987	10.00	40
1986	•Williamsburg House Brown Brick 6566-8	Closed	1987	10.00	40
1986	•Williamsburg House, Blue 6566-8	Closed	1987	10.00	60
1986	•Williamsburg House, Brown Clapboard	Closed	1987	10.00	40
1986	•Williamsburg House, Red 6566-8	Closed	1987	10.00	60
1986	•Williamsburg House, White 6566-8	Closed	1987	10.00	75

Disneyana

Disneyana Conventions - Various

YEAR ISSUE		EDITION LIMIT	YEAR RETD.	ISSUE PRICE	QUOTE U.S.$
1992	1947 Mickey Mouse Plush J20967 - Gund	1,000	1992	50.00	100-150
1992	Big Thunder Mountain A26648 - R. Lee	250	1992	1650.00	2000-3000

Year Issue		Edition Limit	Year Retd.	Issue Price	Quote U.S.$
1992	Carousel Horse 022482 - PJ's	250	1992	125.00	265
1992	Carousel Horse Poster (Lithograph)-A26318 R. Souders	2,000	1992	25.00	50
1992	Cinderella 022076 - Armani	500	1992	500.00	3500-4300
1992	Cinderella Castle 022077 - John Hine Studio	500	1992	250.00	1100
1992	Cruella DeVil Doll-porcelain 22554 - J. Wols	25	1992	600.00	3000-3500
1992	Disneyana Logo Charger B. White	25	1992	600.00	3000
1992	Nifty-Nineties Mickey & Minnie 022503 - House of Laurenz	250	1992	650.00	650
1992	Pinocchio - R. Wright	250	1992	750.00	200
1992	Serigraph Diptych Collage (set of 2)-22073 - M. Graves	1,000	1992	900.00	N/A
1992	Steamboat Willie-Resin M. Delle	500	1992	125.00	900-1200
1992	Tinker Bell 022075 - Lladro	1,500	1992	350.00	2200-2700
1992	Two Merry Wanderers 022074 - Goebel	1,500	1992	250.00	800-1200
1992	Walt's Convertible (Cel) - Disney Art Ed.	500	1992	950.00	2300
1993	1947 Minnie Mouse Plush - Gund	1,000	1993	50.00	120
1993	Alice in Wonderland - Malvern	10	1993	8000.00	N/A
1993	Annette Doll - Alexander Doll	1,000	1993	400.00	450
1993	The Band Concert "Maestro Mickey" - Disney Art Ed.	275	1993	2950.00	N/A
1993	The Band Concert-Bronze B. Toma	25	1993	650.00	3000-5000
1993	Bandleader-Resin - M. Delle	1,500	1993	125.00	225-288
1993	Barbershop Quartet (Lithograph) C. Boyer	1,000	1993	350.00	600
1993	Disneyland Bandstand Poster R. Souders	2,000	1993	25.00	25
1993	Dopey - Armani	Retrd.	1993	125.00	190-250
1993	Family Dinner Figurine - C. Boyer	1,000	1993	600.00	1000-1100
1993	Jumper from King Arthur Carousel - PJ's	250	1993	125.00	650
1993	Mickey & Pluto Charger - White/Rhodes	25	1993	850.00	3000
1993	Mickey Mouse, the Bandleader - Arribas Brothers	25	1993	700.00	3000-5000
1993	Mickey's Dreams - R. Lee	250	1993	400.00	600-900
1993	Peter Pan - Lladro	2,000	1993	400.00	1000-1500
1993	Sleeping Beauty Castle - John Hine Studio	500	1993	250.00	450-800
1993	Snow White - Armani	2,000	1993	750.00	1000-1300
1993	Two Little Drummers - Goebel	1,500	1993	325.00	500-650
1993	Walt's Train Celebration - Disney Art Ed.	950	1993	950.00	1800
1994	Ariel - Armani	1,500	1994	750.00	1200-1300
1994	Cinderella/Godmother - Lladro	2,500	1994	875.00	850-1250
1994	Cinderella's Slipper - Waterford	1,200	1994	250.00	450-650
1994	Euro Disney Castle - John Hine Studio	750	1994	250.00	350-450
1994	Jessica & Roger Charger White/Rhodes	25	1994	2000.00	3000-4000
1994	Mickey Triple Self Portrait Goebel Miniatures	500	1994	295.00	800-1000
1994	Minnie Be Patient - Goebel	1,500	1994	395.00	425-480
1994	MM/MN w/House Kinetic - F. Prescott	10	1994	4000.00	N/A
1994	MM/MN/Goofy Limo (Stepin' Out) - Ron Lee	500	1994	500.00	600
1994	Scrooge in Money Bin/Bronze - Carl Barks	100	1994	1800.00	2600-3500
1994	Sleeping Beauty - Malvern	10	1994	5500.00	N/A
1994	Sorcerer Mickey-Bronze - B. Toma	100	1994	1000.00	2000-2500
1994	Sorcerer Mickey-Crystal Arribas Brothers	50	1994	1700.00	2200-3000
1994	Sorcerer Mickey-Resin - M. Delle	2,000	1994	125.00	175-250
1994	Studio Poster - R. Souders	1,000	1994	25.00	N/A
1995	Ah, Venice - M. Pierson	100		2600.00	2600
1995	Ariel's Dolphin Ride - Wyland	250		2500.00	2500
1995	Barbershop Quartet - Goebel Miniatures	750	1995	300.00	400-700
1995	Beauty and the Beast - Armani	2,000	1995	975.00	975
1995	Brave Little Tailor Charger - White/Rhodes	15	1995	2000.00	4500
1995	Celebration-Resin - M. Delle	1,500	1995	125.00	175-250
1995	Donald Duck Mini-Charger White/Rhodes	1,000	1995	75.00	150-275
1995	Ear Force One - R. Lee	500		600.00	600
1995	Engine No. One - R. Lee	500		650.00	650
1995	Fire Station 105 - Lilliput Lane	501	1995	195.00	300-500
1995	For Father - Goebel	1,500		450.00	450
1995	Grandpa's Boys - Goebel	1,500		340.00	340
1995	Mad Minnie Charger White/Rhodes	10	1995	2000.00	4000
1995	Memories - B. Toma	200	1995	1200.00	1300-1650
1995	Neat & Pretty Mickey-Crystal - Arribas	50	1995	1700.00	2500
1995	Neat & Pretty Mickey-Resin M. Delle	2,000	1995	135.00	305
1995	"Night of Stars" Poster R. Souders	1,000		25.00	25
1995	Plane Crazy - Arribas	50	1995	1750.00	3200
1995	The Prince's Kiss - P Gordon	25	1995	250.00	600
1995	"Proud Pocahontas" Lithogragh - D. Struzan	500	1995	195.00	195
1995	Sheriff of Bullet Valley - Barks/Vought	200	1995	1800.00	2300
1995	Showtime - B. Toma	200		1400.00	1400
1995	Simba - Bolae	200		1500.00	1500
1995	Sleeping Beauty Castle Mirror - Gordon	250		1200.00	1200
1995	Sleeping Beauty Dance - Lladro	1,000	1995	1280.00	1500-2500
1995	Sleeping Beauty's Tiara - Waterford	1,500		250.00	250
1995	Snow White's Apple - Waterford	1,500		225.00	300-500
1995	"Snow White & Friends" Brooch/Pendant	25		1500.00	1500
1995	Thru the Mirror - Barks/Vought	200		2600.00	2600
1995	"Uncle Scrooge" Tile - Barks/Vought	50	1995	900.00	2000

Duncan Royale

Collector Club - Duncan Royale

Year Issue		Edition Limit	Year Retd.	Issue Price	Quote U.S.$
1991	Today's Nast	Retrd.	1993	80.00	125
1994	Winter Santa	Retrd.	1994	125.00	125
1995	Santa's Gift	Yr. Iss.		100.00	100

1990 & 1991 Special Event Piece - Duncan Royale

Year Issue		Edition Limit	Year Retd.	Issue Price	Quote U.S.$
XX	Nast & Music	Retrd.	1993	79.95	95

Ebony Collection - Duncan Royale

Year Issue		Edition Limit	Year Retd.	Issue Price	Quote U.S.$
1990	Banjo Man	5,000		80.00	80
1993	Ebony Angel	5,000		170.00	170
1991	Female Gospel Singer	5,000		90.00	90
1990	The Fiddler	5,000		90.00	90
1990	Harmonica Man	5,000		80.00	80
1991	Jug Man	5,000		90.00	90
1992	Jug Tooter	5,000		90.00	90
1992	A Little Magic	5,000		80.00	80
1991	Male Gospel Singer	5,000		90.00	90
1991	Preacher	5,000		90.00	90
1991	Spoons	5,000		90.00	90

Ebony Collection-Buckwheat - Duncan Royale

Year Issue		Edition Limit	Year Retd.	Issue Price	Quote U.S.$
1992	O'Tay	5,000		70.00	90
1992	Painter	5,000		80.00	90
1992	Petee & Friend	5,000		90.00	90
1992	Smile For The Camera	5,000		80.00	90

Ebony Collection-Friends & Family - Duncan Royale

Year Issue		Edition Limit	Year Retd.	Issue Price	Quote U.S.$
1994	Agnes	5,000		100.00	120
1994	Daddy	5,000		120.00	125
1994	Lunchtime	5,000		100.00	100
1994	Millie	5,000		100.00	100
1994	Mommie & Me	5,000		125.00	125

Ebony Collection-Jazzman - Duncan Royale

Year Issue		Edition Limit	Year Retd.	Issue Price	Quote U.S.$
1992	Bass	5,000		90.00	110
1992	Bongo	5,000		90.00	100
1992	Piano	5,000		130.00	140
1992	Sax	5,000		90.00	100
1992	Trumpet	5,000		90.00	100

Ebony Collection-Jubilee Dancers - Duncan Royale

Year Issue		Edition Limit	Year Retd.	Issue Price	Quote U.S.$
1993	Bliss	5,000		200.00	200
1993	Fallana	5,000		100.00	100
1993	Keshia	5,000		100.00	100
1993	Lamar	5,000		100.00	100
1993	Lottie	5,000		125.00	125
1993	Wilfred	5,000		100.00	100

Ebony Collection-Special Releases - Duncan Royale

Year Issue		Edition Limit	Year Retd.	Issue Price	Quote U.S.$
1991	Signature Piece	Open		50.00	50

History of Classic Entertainers - P. Apsit

Year Issue		Edition Limit	Year Retd.	Issue Price	Quote U.S.$
1987	American	Retrd.	1995	160.00	350
1987	Auguste	Retrd.	1995	220.00	350
1987	Greco-Roman	Retrd.	1995	180.00	350
1987	Grotesque	Retrd.	1995	230.00	350
1987	Harlequin	Retrd.	1995	250.00	350
1987	Jester	Retrd.	1995	410.00	700-800
1987	Pantalone	Retrd.	1995	270.00	300
1987	Pierrot	Retrd.	1995	180.00	225
1987	Pulcinella	Retrd.	1995	220.00	350
1987	Russian	Retrd.	1995	190.00	350
1987	Slapstick	Retrd.	1995	250.00	300
1987	Uncle Sam	Retrd.	1995	160.00	350

History of Classic Entertainers II - P. Apsit

Year Issue		Edition Limit	Year Retd.	Issue Price	Quote U.S.$
1988	Bob Hope	Retrd.	1995	250.00	250-295
1988	Feste	Retrd.	1995	250.00	250
1988	Goliard	Retrd.	1995	200.00	300
1988	Mime	Retrd.	1995	200.00	300
1988	Mountebank	Retrd.	1995	270.00	300
1988	Pedrolino	Retrd.	1995	200.00	300
1988	Tartaglia	Retrd.	1995	200.00	250
1988	Thomassi	Retrd.	1995	200.00	300
1988	Touchstone	Retrd.	1995	200.00	300
1988	Tramp	Retrd.	1995	200.00	300
1988	White Face	Retrd.	1995	250.00	300
1988	Zanni	Retrd.	1995	200.00	300

History of Classic Entertainers-Special Releases - P. Apsit

Year Issue		Edition Limit	Year Retd.	Issue Price	Quote U.S.$
1990	Bob Hope-18"	Retrd.	1995	1500.00	1700
1990	Bob Hope-6" porcelain	6,000/yr.		130.00	130
1990	Mime-18"	Retrd.	1995	1500.00	1500
1988	Signature Piece	Retrd.	1995	50.00	50

History of Santa Claus (18") - P. Apsit

Year Issue		Edition Limit	Year Retd.	Issue Price	Quote U.S.$
1989	Kris Kringle-18"	1,000		1500.00	1500
1989	Medieval-18"	1,000		1500.00	1500
1989	Nast-18"	1,000		1500.00	1500
1989	Russian-18"	1,000		1500.00	1500
1989	Soda Pop-18"	1,000		1500.00	1500
1989	St. Nicholas-18"	1,000		1500.00	1500

History of Santa Claus I (6") - P. Apsit

Year Issue		Edition Limit	Year Retd.	Issue Price	Quote U.S.$
1988	Black Peter-6" porcelain	6,000/yr.		40.00	80
1988	Civil War-6" porcelain	6,000/yr.		40.00	80
1988	Dedt Moroz -6" porcelain	6,000/yr.		40.00	80
1988	Kris Kringle-6" porcelain	6,000/yr.		40.00	80
1988	Medieval-6" porcelain	6,000/yr.		40.00	80
1988	Nast-6" porcelain	6,000/yr.		40.00	80
1988	Pioneer-6" porcelain	6,000/yr.		40.00	80
1988	Russian-6" porcelain	6,000/yr.		40.00	80
1988	Soda Pop-6" porcelain	6,000/yr.		40.00	80
1988	St. Nicholas-6" porcelain	6,000/yr.		40.00	80
1988	Victorian-6" porcelain	6,000/yr.		40.00	80
1988	Wassail-6" porcelain	6,000/yr.		40.00	80

History of Santa Claus I -Wood - P. Apsit

Year Issue		Edition Limit	Year Retd.	Issue Price	Quote U.S.$
1987	Black Peter-8" wood	500	1993	450.00	450
1987	Civil War-8" wood	500	1993	450.00	450
1987	Dedt Moroz-8" wood	500	1993	450.00	450
1987	Kris Kringle-8" wood	500	1993	450.00	450
1987	Medieval-8" wood	500	1993	450.00	1200
1987	Nast-8" wood	500	1993	450.00	1500
1987	Pioneer-8" wood	500	1993	450.00	450
1987	Russian-8" wood	500	1993	450.00	450
1987	Soda Pop-8" wood	500	1993	450.00	850
1987	St. Nicholas-8" wood	500	1993	450.00	700
1987	Victorian-8" wood	500	1993	450.00	450
1987	Wassail-8" wood	500	1993	450.00	450

History of Santa Claus II (6") - P. Apsit

Year Issue		Edition Limit	Year Retd.	Issue Price	Quote U.S.$
1988	Alsace Angel-6" porcelain	6,000/yr		80.00	90
1988	Babouska-6" porcelain	6,000/yr		70.00	80
1988	Bavarian-6" porcelain	6,000/yr		90.00	100
1988	Befana-6" porcelain	6,000/yr		70.00	80
1988	Frau Holda-6" porcelain	6,000/yr		50.00	80
1988	Lord of Misrule-6" porcelain	6,000/yr		60.00	80
1988	Magi-6" porcelain	6,000/yr		130.00	150
1988	Mongolian/Asian-6" porcelain	6,000/yr		80.00	90
1988	Odin-6" porcelain	6,000/yr		80.00	90
1988	Pixie-6" porcelain	6,000/yr		50.00	80
1988	Sir Christmas-6" porcelain	6,000/yr		60.00	80
1988	St. Lucia-6" porcelain	6,000/yr		70.00	80

History of Santa Claus III - Duncan Royale

Year Issue		Edition Limit	Year Retd.	Issue Price	Quote U.S.$
1990	Druid	10,000		250.00	250
1991	Grandfather Frost & Snow Maiden	10,000		400.00	400
1991	Hoteisho	10,000		200.00	200
1991	Judah Maccabee	10,000		300.00	300
1990	Julenisse	10,000		200.00	200
1991	King Wenceslas	10,000		300.00	300
1991	Knickerbocker	10,000		300.00	300
1991	Samichlaus	10,000		350.00	350
1991	Saturnalia King	10,000		200.00	200
1990	St. Basil	10,000		300.00	300
1990	Star Man	10,000		300.00	300
1990	Ukko	10,000		250.00	250

History of Santa Claus I - P. Apsit

Year Issue		Edition Limit	Year Retd.	Issue Price	Quote U.S.$
1983	Black Peter	Retrd.	1991	145.00	300-350
1983	Civil War	10,000		145.00	300
1983	Dedt Moroz	Retrd.	1989	145.00	600
1983	Kris Kringle	Retrd.	1988	165.00	1250-1400
1983	Medieval	Retrd.	1988	220.00	1200-1400
1983	Nast	Retrd.	1987	90.00	2200-2500
1983	Pioneer	Retrd.	1989	145.00	250-350
1983	Russian	Retrd.	1989	145.00	550-700
1983	Soda Pop	Retrd.	1988	145.00	1400-1500
1983	St. Nicholas	Retrd.	1989	175.00	800-1250
1983	Victorian	Retrd.	1990	120.00	350-550
1983	Wassail	Retrd.	1991	90.00	300-350

History of Santa Claus II - P. Apsit

Year Issue		Edition Limit	Year Retd.	Issue Price	Quote U.S.$
1986	Alsace Angel	10,000		250.00	300
1986	Babouska	10,000		170.00	200
1986	Bavarian	10,000		250.00	300
1986	Befana	10,000		200.00	250
1986	Frau Holda	10,000		160.00	180
1986	Lord of Misrule	10,000		160.00	200
1986	The Magi	10,000		350.00	400
1986	Mongolian/Asian	10,000		240.00	300
1986	Odin	10,000		200.00	250
1986	The Pixie	10,000		140.00	175
1986	Sir Christmas	10,000		150.00	175
1986	St. Lucia	10,000		180.00	225

History Of Santa Claus-Special Releases - Duncan Royale

Year Issue		Edition Limit	Year Retd.	Issue Price	Quote U.S.$
1992	Nast & Sleigh	5,000		500.00	500
1991	Signature Piece	Open		50.00	50

Painted Pewter Miniatures-Santa 1st Series - Duncan Royale

Year Issue		Edition Limit	Year Retd.	Issue Price	Quote U.S.$
1986	Black Peter	500		30.00	30
1986	Civil War	500		30.00	30
1986	Dedt Moroz	500		30.00	30
1986	Kris Kringle	500		30.00	30
1986	Medieval	500		30.00	30
1986	Nast	500		30.00	30

YEAR ISSUE		EDITION LIMIT	YEAR RETD.	ISSUE PRICE	QUOTE U.S.$
1986	Pioneer	500		30.00	30
1986	Russian	500		30.00	30
1986	Soda Pop	500		30.00	30
1986	St. Nicholas	500		30.00	30
1986	Victorian	500		30.00	30
1986	Wassail	500		30.00	30
1986	Set of 12	500		360.00	360-495

Painted Pewter Miniatures-Santa 2nd Series - Duncan Royale

1988	Alsace Angel	500		30.00	30
1988	Babouska	500		30.00	30
1988	Bavarian	500		30.00	30
1988	Befana	500		30.00	30
1988	Frau Holda	500		30.00	30
1988	Lord of Misrule	500		30.00	30
1988	Magi	500		30.00	30
1988	Mongolian	500		30.00	30
1988	Odin	500		30.00	30
1988	Pixie	500		30.00	30
1988	Sir Christmas	500		30.00	30
1988	St. Lucia	500		30.00	30
1988	Set of 12	500		360.00	360-495

Woodland Fairies - Duncan Royale

1988	Almond Blossom	Retrd.	1993	70.00	70
1988	Apple	Retrd.	1994	70.00	70
1988	Calla Lily	Retrd.	1994	70.00	70
1988	Cherry	10,000		70.00	70
1988	Chestnut	10,000		70.00	70
1988	Christmas Tree	Retrd.	1993	70.00	70
1988	Elm	10,000		70.00	70
1988	Guilder Rose	Retrd.	1994	70.00	70
1988	Lime Tree	Retrd.	1993	70.00	70
1988	Mulberry	10,000		70.00	70
1988	Pear Blossom	Retrd.	1993	70.00	70
1988	Pine Tree	10,000		70.00	70
1988	Poplar	10,000		70.00	70
1988	Sycamore	Retrd.	1993	70.00	70

eggspressions! inc.

Childrens Collection - eggspressions

1994	Jessica	125		240.00	240
1994	Purr-fect Hug	250	1994	150.00	150
1994	Skip A Long	250		118.00	120
1994	Teddy Bear Sing Along	250		114.00	115

Christmas Collection - eggspressions

1994	Angel of Hope	250		130.00	130
1994	Angel of Love	250	1995	110.00	110
1994	Beary Blue Christmas	250		98.00	100
1994	Beary Pink Christmas	250		98.00	100
1994	Caroling Mice	250		120.00	120
1994	Christmas Joy	250		104.00	105
1994	O' Holy Night	250		160.00	160
1994	Santas Little Elves	250		130.00	130
1994	Santas Little Sweetheart	100		98.00	100

Curio Collection - eggspressions

1995	Cabbage Patch	250		105.00	105
1992	Winter Colt (Stand)	Open		104.00	105
1992	Winter Song	Open		99.00	115

Easter Collection - eggspressions

1994	Chicks & Bunnies	Open		88.00	88
1994	Grandmas Goodies	Open		99.00	99
1994	Pre-School Play	Open		108.00	108
1994	Sweet Dreams	Open		99.00	100

Hanging Christmas - eggspressions

1992	Bill & Coo	Open		53.00	55
1992	Candyland	Open		94.00	100
1992	Cardinals	Open		58.00	70
1992	Choo Choo Christmas	Open		124.00	130
1992	Christmas Curiosity	Open		104.00	110
1992	Drummer Bear	Open		97.00	100
1992	Santa's Workshop	125		150.00	150
1992	Tiny Treasures	Open		100.00	110
1992	Winter Wonderland	Open		98.00	105

Hanging Collectibles - eggspressions

1995	Andrea	250		80.00	80
1995	Angel Divine	250		120.00	120
1992	Blue Birds of Happiness	Open		79.00	79
1995	Coo	250		115.00	115
1995	Dawn	250		190.00	190
1995	Father Christmas	250		135.00	135
1992	Golden Crystal	Open		145.00	145
1995	Harvest Fairy	Open		95.00	95
1995	Heavenly	250		120.00	120
1992	Isadora	Open		110.00	130
1995	Jamie	250		80.00	80
1992	Kewpie Doll	Open		99.00	110
1995	Left Behind	250		100.00	100
1992	Love Duet	Open		125.00	140
1992	Love in Flight	Open		95.00	100
1992	McGregor's Garden	Open		98.00	105
1995	Peek N Out	250		55.00	55
1992	Romantique	Open		66.00	75
1995	Santa's Here	250		130.00	130

YEAR ISSUE		EDITION LIMIT	YEAR RETD.	ISSUE PRICE	QUOTE U.S.$
1995	Shining Star	250		72.00	72
1995	Tara	250		80.00	80
1995	Winter Bunny	250		90.00	90
1992	Winter Colt	Open		104.00	105
1995	Woodland Bunnies	250		120.00	120

Jeweled Baskets - eggspressions

1994	Absolutely Amethyst	Open		98.00	100
1994	Pastel & Pearls	Open		112.00	112
1994	Pristine Pearls	Open		118.00	118
1994	Rose Marie	Open		98.00	98

Keepsake Collection - eggspressions

1994	Eternity	250		170.00	170
1994	Golden Harmony	250		160.00	160
1994	Passion	25	1995	500.00	500

Music Boxes - eggspressions

1995	Angel Bunny	250		220.00	220
1994	Holiday Memories	250		190.00	190
1994	Making Spirits Bright	25		300.00	300

Musical Collectibles - eggspressions

1995	First Love	250		190.00	190
1995	Reflections on Ice	250		230.00	230
1995	Royalty	250		170.00	170

Musical Treasure Chests - eggspressions

1992	Lara	Open		115.00	115
1992	Maria	Open		115.00	115

Natures Collection - eggspressions

1994	Love Birds	250		118.00	120
1994	Mother's Pride	250		120.00	120
1994	Spring Melody	250		130.00	130

Romance Collection - eggspressions

1994	Lavender Love	250		130.00	130
1994	Serenade	250		120.00	120
1994	Serenity	250		114.00	115
1994	Wedding in White	250		160.00	160

Southwesten Collection - eggspressions

1992	Storyteller	Retrd.	1995	112.00	130

Treasure Chests - eggspressions

1995	Amber's Treasure	250		120.00	120
1995	Dynasty	25		700.00	700
1992	Ebony	Open		105.00	105
1992	Elegant Choice	Open		167.00	167
1992	Pearl	Open		98.00	98
1995	Princess	250		100.00	100
1992	Secret Garden	Open		158.00	158
1995	Sophia	250		110.00	110
1995	Summertime Fantasy	25		450.00	450
1992	Velvet Princess	Open		170.00	170
1992	Yellow Rose	Open		105.00	105

Whimsical - eggspressions

1992	Colours	Open		45.00	55
1992	Kris Kringle	Open		38.00	45
1992	Marcella	Open		38.00	45
1992	Miss Ellie	Open		38.00	45
1992	Peter	Open		38.00	45
1992	Petunia	Open		38.00	45

Wilderness Collection - eggspressions

1992	Togetherness	Open		95.00	100

Enchantica

Enchantica Collectors Club - Various

1991	Snappa on Mushroom-2101 A. Bill	Retrd.	1991	Gift	10-150
1991	Rattajack with Snail-2102 - A. Bill	Retrd.	1991	60.00	85
1992	Jonquil-2103 - A. Hull	Retrd.	1992	Gift	75
1992	Ice Demon-2104 - K. Fallon	Retrd.	1992	85.00	150
1992	Sea Dragon-2106 - A. Bill	Retrd.	1993	99.00	200-250
1993	White Dragon-2107 - A. Bill	Retrd.	1993	Gift	200
1993	Jonquil's Flight-2108 - A. Bill	Retrd.	1993	140.00	300-375
1994	Verratus-2111 - A. Bill	Retrd.	1994	Gift	60
1994	Mimmer-Spring Fairy-2112 A. Bill	Retrd.	1994	100.00	115
1994	Gorgoyle Cameo piece-2113 - K. Fallon	Retrd.	1994	Gift	10
1995	Destroyer-2116 - A. Hull	Yr.Iss.		100.00	100
1995	Cloudbreaker-2115 - J. Oliver	Yr.Iss.		Gift	N/A

Retired Enchantica Collection - A. Bill, unless otherwise noted

1990	Arangast - Summer Dragon-2026 - K. Fallon	Retrd.	1992	165.00	275
1991	Bledderag, Goblin Twin-2048 - K. Fallon	Retrd.	1993	115.00	140
1988	Blick Scoops Crystals-2015	Retrd.	1991	47.00	70
1992	Breen - Carrier Dragon-2053 K. Fallon	Retrd.	1993	156.00	175
1990	Cellandia-Summer Fairy-2029 - K. Fallon	Retrd.	1992	115.00	170
1989	Chuckwalla-2021	Retrd.	1994	43.00	60
1992	Desert Dragon-2064	Retrd.	1994	175.00	175
1994	Escape (5th Anniversary)-2110	Retrd.	1994	250.00	320
1988	Fantazar- Spring Wizard-2016	Retrd.	1991	132.50	400

YEAR ISSUE		EDITION LIMIT	YEAR RETD.	ISSUE PRICE	QUOTE U.S.$
1991	Flight to Danger-2044 - K. Fallon	Retrd.	1991	3000.00	6500
1990	Fossfex - Autumn Fairy-2030 - K. Fallon	Retrd.	1992	115.00	150-175
1991	Furza - Carrier Dragon-2050 K. Fallon	Retrd.	1993	137.50	165
1988	Gorgoyle - Spring Dragon-2017	Retrd.	1991	132.50	395
1991	Grawlfang '91 Winter Dragon-2046	Retrd.	1994	295.00	325
1989	Grawlfang - Winter Dragon-2019	Retrd.	1991	132.50	450
1988	Hepna Pushes Truck-2014	Retrd.	1994	47.00	65
1988	Hest Checks Crystals-2013	Retrd.	1994	47.00	65
1989	Hobba, Hellbenders Twin Son-2023	Retrd.	1992	69.00	105
1993	Ice Dragon-2109	Retrd.	1994	95.00	95
1988	Jonquil- Dragons Footprint-2004	Retrd.	1991	55.00	90
1992	Manu Manu-Peeper-2105	Retrd.	1993	40.00	60
1991	Ogrod-Ice Troll-2032	Retrd.	1994	235.00	245
1991	Okra, Goblin Princess-2031 K. Fallon	Retrd.	1994	105.00	115
1989	Old Yargle-2020	Retrd.	1994	55.00	75
1992	Olm & Sylphen, Mer-King & Queen-2059	Retrd.	1994	350.00	400
1990	Orolan-Summer Wizard-2025	Retrd.	1992	165.00	300
1991	Quillion-Autumn Witch-2045	Retrd.	1994	205.00	220
1988	Rattajack - Circles-2003	Retrd.	1993	40.00	70
1988	Rattajack - My Ball-2001	Retrd.	1993	40.00	70
1988	Rattajack - Please-2000	Retrd.	1993	40.00	65
1988	Rattajack - Terragon Dreams-2002	Retrd.	1993	40.00	60
1991	Rattajack-Up & Under-2038	Retrd.	1994	65.00	70
1991	Samphire-Carrier Dragon-2049	Retrd.	1994	137.50	150
1988	Snappa Climbs High-2008	Retrd.	1993	25.00	65
1988	Snappa Finds a Collar-2009	Retrd.	1992	25.00	60
1988	Snappa Dozes Off-2011	Retrd.	1993	25.00	60
1988	Snappa Hatches Out-2006	Retrd.	1991	25.00	60
1991	Snappa Nods Off-2043 - A. Hull	Retrd.	1994	30.00	40
1988	Snappa Plays Ball-2010	Retrd.	1993	25.00	60
1991	Snappa Posing-2042 - A. Hull	Retrd.	1994	30.00	40
1991	Snappa Tumbles-2047 - A. Hull	Retrd.	1994	30.00	40
1988	Snappa's First Feast-2007	Retrd.	1993	25.00	60
1991	Snappa-Snowdrift-2041 - A. Hull	Retrd.	1994	30.00	40
1991	Snarlgard - Autumn Dragon-2034 - K. Fallon	Retrd.	1992	337.00	350
1992	Sorren & Gart-2054 - K. Fallon	Retrd.	1994	220.00	300
1992	Spring Wizard and Yim-2060	Retrd.	1993	410.00	425
1990	The Swamp Demon-2028 K. Fallon	Retrd.	1992	69.00	95
1988	Tarbet with Sack-2012	Retrd.	1991	47.00	60
1992	Thrace-Gladiator-2061 K. Fallon	Retrd.	1993	280.00	350
1992	The Throne Citadel-2063 J. Woodward	Retrd.	1994	2000.00	2000
1990	Tuatara-Evil Witch-2027	Retrd.	1994	174.00	185
1989	Vrorst - The Ice Sorcerer-2018	Retrd.	1991	155.00	600
1991	Waxifrade - Autumn Wizard-2033 - K. Fallon	Retrd.	1992	265.00	400

Enesco Corporation

Cherished Teddies Club - P. Hillman

1995	Cub E. Bear CT001	Yr.Iss.		Gift	N/A
1995	Mayor Wilson T.Beary CT951	Yr.Iss.		20.00	20
1995	Hilary Hugabear CT952	Yr.Iss.		17.50	18

Cherished Teddies - P. Hillman

1993	Baby Blocks Displayer- CRT004	Open		40.00	40
1994	Nursery Rhyme Books - CRT013	Open		40.00	40
1995	Boy Bear Cupid - 103551	Suspd.		17.50	28
1995	Girl Bear Cupid - 103586	Suspd.		15.00	30
1995	Cupid Boy/Girl Double - 103594	Suspd.		25.00	45
1995	Boy Bear Flying Cupid - 103608	Open		13.00	25
1995	Girl Bear Flying Cupid - 103616	Open		13.00	25
1995	Bear Cupid Girl 2AT - 103640	Suspd.		15.00	15
1995	Cupid Baby on Pillow 2 Asst - 103659	Suspd.		13.50	14
1995	Margaret "A Cup Full of Love" - 103667	Open		20.00	20
1995	Hope "Our Love Is Ever-Blooming" - 103764	Open		20.00	20
1995	Gail "Catching the First Blooms of Friendship" - 103772	Open		20.00	20
1995	Lisa "My Best Is Always You" - 103780	Open		20.00	20
1995	Donald "Friends Are Egg-ceptional Blessings" - 103799	Open		20.00	20
1995	Bunny "Just In Time For Spring" - 103802	Open		13.50	14
1995	Jennifer "Gathering The Blooms of Friendship" - 103810	Open		22.50	23
1995	Melissa "Every Bunny Needs A Friend" - 103829	Open		20.00	20
1995	Christian "My Prayer Is For You" - 103837	Open		18.50	19
1995	Christine "My Prayer Is For You" - 103845	Open		18.50	19
1995	Kevin "Good Luck To You" - 103896	Open		12.50	13
1995	Peter "You're Some Bunny Special - 104973	Open		17.50	18
1995	Sculpted Irish Plaque - 110981	Open		13.50	14
1995	The Best Is Yet To Come - 127949	Open		12.50	13
1995	The Best Is Yet To Come - 127957	Open		12.50	13
1995	Kiss The Hurt And Make It Well - 127965	Open		15.00	15

FIGURINES/COTTAGES

YEAR ISSUE		EDITION LIMIT	YEAR RETD.	ISSUE PRICE	QUOTE U.S.$
1995	Tucker & Travis "We're in This Together" - 127973	Open		25.00	25
1995	Allison & Alexandria "Two Friends Mean Twice The Love" - 127981	Open		25.00	25
1995	Seth & Sarabeth "We're Beary Good Pals" - 128015	Open		25.00	25
1995	Millie, Christy, Dorothy "A. Love Me Tender, B. Take Me To Your Heart, C. Love Me True" - 128023	Open		12.50	13
1995	Priscilla & Greta "Our Hearts Belong to You" - 128031	19,950		50.00	75-120
1995	Girl Bear on Ottoman Musical - 128058	Open		55.00	55
1995	Earl "Warm Hearted Friends" - 131873	Open		17.50	18
1995	Madeline "A Cup Full of Friendship" - 135593	Open		20.00	20
1995	Marilyn "A Cup Full of Cheer" - 135682	Open		20.00	20
1995	Maureen "Lucky Friend" - 135690	Open		12.50	13
1995	Nickolas "You're At The Top Of My List" - 141100	Yr.Iss.		20.00	23-40
1995	Holly "A Cup of Homemade Love" - 141119	Open		18.50	19
1995	Ginger "Painting Your Holidays With Love" - 141127	Open		22.50	23
1995	Meri "Handsewn Holidays" - 141135	Open		20.00	20
1995	Yule "Building a Sturdy Friendship" - 141143	Open		22.50	23
1995	Amanda "Here's Some Cheer to Last The Year" - 141186	Yr.Iss.		17.50	35
1995	Kristen "Hugs of Love And Friendship" - 141194	Open		20.00	20
1995	Celeste "An Angel To Watch Over You" - 141267	Open		20.00	20
1995	Pat "Falling For You" - 141313	Open		22.50	23
1995	Carrie "The Future 'Beareth' All Things" - 141321	Open		18.50	19
1995	Bea "Bee My Friend" - 141348	Open		15.00	15
1995	Santa's Workshop Nightlight - 141925	Open		75.00	75
1995	Beary Scary Halloween House - 152382	Open		20.00	20
1994	Tiny Ted-Bear "God Bless Us Every One" - 614777	Open		10.00	10
1994	Jacob Bearly "You Will Be Haunted By Three Spirits" - 614785	Open		17.50	18
1994	Gloria "Ghost of Christmas Past, " Garland "Ghost Of Christmas Present", Gabriel "Ghost of Christmas Yet To Come" - 614807	Open		55.00	55
1994	Thanksgiving Quilt -617075	Open		12.00	12
1994	Jedediah "Giving Thanks For Friends" - 617091	Open		17.50	18
1994	Patience "Happiness Is Homemade" - 617105	Open		17.50	18
1994	Phoebe "A Little Friendship Is A Big Blessing" - 617113	Open		13.50	14
1994	Wylie "I'm Called Little Friend" - 617121	Open		15.00	15
1994	Stacie "You Lift My Spirit" - 617148	Open		18.50	19
1994	Taylor "Sail The Seas With Me" - 617156	Open		15.00	15
1994	Willie "Bears Of A Feather Stay Together" -617164	Open		15.00	15
1994	Winona "Fair Feather Friends" - 617172	Open		15.00	15
1994	Breanna "Pumpkin Patch Pals" - 617180	Open		15.00	15
1994	Ingrid "Bundled Up With Warm Wishes" Dated 1994 - 617237	Yr.Iss.		20.00	25-50
1994	Nils "Near And Dear For Christmas" - 617245	Open		22.50	23
1994	Ebearneezer Scrooge "Bah Humbug!" - 617296	Open		17.50	18
1994	Mrs. Cratchit "A Beary Christmas And Happy New Year!" - 617318	Open		18.50	19
1994	Bear Cratchit "And A Very Merry Christmas To You Mr. Scrooge" - 617326	Open		17.50	18
1994	Counting House - 622788	Open		75.00	75
1994	Eric "Bear Tidings Of Joy" - 622796	Open		22.50	23
1994	Sonja "Holiday Cuddles" - 622818	Open		20.00	20
1994	Jack & Jill "Our Friendship Will Never Tumble" - 624772	Open		30.00	30
1994	Little Jack Horner "I'm Plum Happy You're My Friend'" - 624780	Open		20.00	20
1994	Little Miss Muffet "I'm Never Afraid With You At My Side" - 624799	Open		20.00	20
1994	Little Bo Peep "Looking For A Friend Like You" - 624802	Open		22.50	23
1994	Tom, Tom The Piper's Son "Wherever You Go I'll Follow" - 624810	Open		20.00	20
1994	Older Son "Child Of Pride" - 624829	Open		10.00	10
1994	Young Son "Child of Hope" - 624837	Open		9.00	9
1994	Older Daughter "Child Of Love" - 624845	Open		10.00	10
1994	Young Daughter "Child Of Kindness" - 624853	Open		9.00	9
1994	Mother "A Mother's Love Bears All Things" - 624861	Open		20.00	20
1994	Father "A Father Is The Bearer Of Strength" - 624888	Open		13.50	14
1994	Billy "Everyone Needs A Cuddle", Betsey "First Step To Love" Bobbie "A Little Friendship To Share" - 624896	Open		12.50	13
1994	Boy/Girl in Laundry Basket (Musical) - 624926	Open		60.00	60
1994	Bear as Bunny Jointed (Musical) - 625302	Open		60.00	60
1994	Betty "Bubblin' Over With Love" - 626066	Open		18.50	19
1994	Mary, Mary Quite Contrary "Friendship Blooms With Loving Care" - 626074	Open		22.50	23
1994	Bear w/ Goose (Musical) -627445	Open		45.00	45
1994	Bear w/Toy Chest (Musical) - 627453	Open		60.00	60
1994	Bear w/Horse (Musical) - 628565	Open		150.00	150
1994	Bear w/Rocking Reindeer (Musical) - 629618	Open		165.00	165
1994	Wyatt "I'm Called Little Runnig Bear" - 629707	Open		15.00	15
1994	Cow "That's What Friends Are For" - 651095	Open		22.50	23
1994	Cratchit's House - 651362	Open		75.00	75
1994	Boy/Girl in Sled (Musical) - 651435	Open		100.00	100
1994	Baby Boy Jointed (Musical) - 699314	Open		60.00	60
1994	Baby Girl Jointed (Musical) - 699322	Open		60.00	60
1994	Bride/Groom (Musical) - 699349	Open		50.00	50
1995	Cupid Boy Sitting 2 Asst - 869074	Suspd.		13.50	14
1995	Cupid Boy/Girl Double 2 Asst - 869082	Suspd.		18.50	19
1993	Abigail "Inside We're All The Same" - 900362	Suspd.		16.00	30-45
1993	Jointed Bear Christmas (Musical) - 903337	Suspd.		60.00	60
1993	Alice "Cozy Warm Wishes Coming Your Way" (9") - 903620	Suspd.		100.00	100-150
1993	"Friends Like You Are Precious And Few" - 904309	Open		30.00	30
1993	Theadore, Samantha & Tyler "Friendship Weathers All Storms" (musical) - 904546	Suspd.		170.00	170
1993	Daisy "Friendship Blossoms With Love" - 910651	Suspd.		15.00	175-300
1993	Charity "I Found A Friend In Ewe" - 910678	Suspd.		20.00	60-85
1993	Henrietta "A Basketful of Wings" - 910686	Suspd.		22.50	50-75
1993	Chelsea "Good Friends Are A Blessing" -910694	Retrd.	1995	15.00	175-200
1993	Heidi & David "Special Friends" - 910708	Suspd.		25.00	35-45
1993	Priscilla "Love Surrounds Our Friendship" - 910724	Open		15.00	15
1993	Amy "Hearts Quilted With Love" - 910732	Open		13.50	14
1993	Timothy "A Friend Is Forever" - 910740	Suspd.		15.00	25-35
1993	Molly "Friendship Softens A Bumpy Ride" - 910759	Suspd.		30.00	40-55
1993	Marie "Friendship Is A Special Treat" - 910767	Open		20.00	20
1993	Michael & Michelle "Friendship Is A Cozy Feeling" - 910775	Suspd.		30.00	35-55
1993	"Chalking Up Six Wishes" Age 6 - 911283	Open		16.50	17
1993	"Color Me Five" Age 5 - 911291	Open		15.00	15
1993	"Unfolding Happy Wishes Four You" Age 4 - 911305	Open		15.00	15
1993	"Three Cheers For You" Age 3 - 911313	Open		15.00	15
1993	"Two Sweet Two Bear" Age 2 - 911321	Open		13.50	14
1993	"Beary Special One" Age 1 - 911348	Open		13.50	14
1993	"Cradled With Love" Baby - 911356	Open		16.50	17
1993	Tracie & Nicole "Side By Side With Friends" - 911372	Open		35.00	35
1993	Robbie & Rachel "Love Bears All Things" - 911402	Open		27.50	28
1993	Patrick "Thank You For A Friend That's True" - 911410	Open		18.50	19
1993	Patrice "Thank You For The Sky So Blue" - 911429	Open		18.50	19
1993	Thomas "Chuggin' Along", Jonathon "Sail With Me", Harrison "We're Going Places" - 911739	Open		15.00	15
1993	Freda & Tina "Our Friendship Is A Perfect Blend" - 911747	Open		35.00	35
1993	Miles "I'm Thankful For A Friend Like You" - 912751	Open		17.00	17
1993	Gretel "We Make Magic, Me And You" - 912778	Open		18.50	19
1993	Gary "True Friendships Are Scarce" - 912786	Open		18.50	19
1993	Connie "You're A Sweet Treat" - 912794	Open		15.00	15
1993	Prudence "A Friend To Be Thankful For" - 912808	Open		17.00	17
1993	Buckey & Brenda "How I Love Being Friends With You" - 912816	Suspd.		15.00	35-45
1993	Mary "A Special Friend Warms The Season" - 912840	Open		25.00	25
1993	Nativity (Musical) - 912859	Suspd.		60.00	80
1993	"Friendship Pulls Us Through" & "Ewe Make Being Friends Special" - 912867	Open		13.50	14
1993	Alice "Cozy Warm Wishes Coming Your Way" Dated 1993 - 912875	Yr.Iss.		17.50	40-65
1993	Theadore, Samantha & Tyler "Friendship Weathers All Storms (9")" - 912883	Suspd.		160.00	160
1994	Ronnie "I'll Play My Drum For You" - 912905	Open		13.50	14
1993	Carolyn "Wishing You All Good Things" - 912921	Open		22.50	23
1993	Hans "Friends In Toyland" - 912956	Suspd.		20.00	23-45
1993	Bear Playing w/Train (Musical) - 912964	Open		40.00	40
1993	Boy Praying (Musical) - 914304	Open		37.50	38
1993	Girl Praying (Musical) - 914312	Open		37.50	38
1993	Baby in Cradle (Musical) - 914320	Open		60.00	60
1993	Jack January Monthly - 914754 (Also available through Hamilton Collection)	Open		15.00	15
1993	Phoebe February Monthly - 914762 (Also available through Hamilton Collection)	Open		15.00	15
1993	Mark March Monthly - 914770 (Also available through Hamilton Collection)	Open		15.00	15
1993	Alan April Monthly - 914789 (Also available through Hamilton Collection)	Open		15.00	15
1993	May May Monthly - 914797 (Also available through Hamilton Collection)	Open		15.00	15
1993	June June Monthly - 914800 (Also available through Hamilton Collection)	Open		15.00	15
1993	Julie July Monthly - 914819 (Also available through Hamilton Collection)	Open		15.00	15
1993	Arthur August Monthly - 914827 (Also available through Hamilton Collection)	Open		15.00	15
1993	Seth September Monthly - 914835 (Also available through Hamilton Collection)	Open		15.00	15
1993	Oscar October Monthly - 914843 (Also available through Hamilton Collection)	Open		15.00	15
1993	Nichole November Monthly - 914851 (Also available through Hamilton Collection)	Open		15.00	15
1993	Denise December Monthly - 914878 (Also available through Hamilton Collection)	Open		15.00	15
1994	Elizabeth & Ashley "My Beary Best Friend" - 916277	Suspd.		25.00	50
1994	Victoria "From My Heart To Yours" - 916293	Suspd.		16.50	50-100
1994	Kelly "You're My One And Only" -916307	Suspd.		15.00	40-60
1994	Nancy "Your Friendship Makes My Heart Sing" - 916315	Suspd.		15.00	40-65
1994	Bear Holding Harp (Musical) - 916323	Open		45.00	45
1994	Becky "Springtime Happiness" - 916331	Suspd.		20.00	30-50
1994	Courtney "Springtime Is A Blessing From Above" - 916390	Suspd.		15.00	40-75
1994	Bessie "Some Bunny Loves You" - 916404	Suspd.		15.00	50-75
1994	Faith "There's No Bunny Like You" - 916412	Suspd.		20.00	45-65
1994	Henry "Celebrating Spring With You" - 916420	Suspd.		20.00	40-50
1994	Sean "Luck Found Me A Friend In You" - 916439	Open		12.50	13
1994	Kathleen "Luck Found Me A Friend In You" - 916447	Open		12.50	13
1994	Oliver & Olivia "Will You Be Mine?" - 916641	Suspd.		25.00	40-50
1992	Camille "I'd Be Lost Without You" - 950424	Open		20.00	20
1992	Sara "Lov Ya" Jacki Hugs & Kisses", Karen "Best Buddy" - 950432	Open		10.00	10
1992	Katie "A Friend Always Knows When You Need A Hug" - 950440	Open		20.00	20
1992	Anna "Hooray For You" - 950459	Open		22.50	23
1992	Jasmine " You Have Touched My Heart" - 950475	Suspd.		22.50	45-75
1992	Christopher "Old Friends Are The Best Friends" 950483	Open		50.00	50
1992	Zachary "Yesterday's Memories Are Today's Treasures" - 950491	Open		30.00	30
1992	Theadore, Samantha & Tyler "Friends Come In All Sizes" - 950505	Open		20.00	20
1992	Nathaniel & Nellie "It's Twice As Nice With You" - 950513	Open		30.00	30
1992	Jeremy "Friends Like You Are Precious And Few" - 950521	Retrd.	1995	15.00	30-50
1992	Benji "Life Is Sweet, Enjoy" - 950548	Retrd.	1995	13.50	30-50
1992	Joshua "Love Repairs All" - 950556	Open		20.00	20
1992	Blossom & Beth "Friends Are Never Far Apart" - 950564	Open		50.00	50

YEAR ISSUE		EDITION LIMIT	YEAR RETD.	ISSUE PRICE	QUOTE U.S.$
1992	Blossom & Beth "Friends Are Never Far Apart" w/butterfly - 950564	Open		50.00	125
1992	Mandy "I Love You Just The Way You Are" - 950572	Retrd.	1995	15.00	30-75
1992	Beth "Bear Hugs" - 950637	Retrd.	1995	17.50	30-60
1992	Couple in Basket/Umbrella (Musical) - 950645	Open		60.00	60
1992	Douglas "Let's Be Friends" - 950661	Retrd.	1995	20.00	30-60
1992	Maria, Baby & Josh "A Baby Is God's Gift of Love" "Everyone Needs a Daddy"- 950688	Open		35.00	35
1992	Richard "My Gift Is Loving", Edward "My Gift Is Caring", Wilbur"My Gift Is Sharing" - 950718	Open		55.00	55
1992	Sammy "Little Lambs Are In My Care" - 950726	Open		17.50	18
1992	Jacob "Wishing For Love" - 950734	Open		22.50	23
1992	Charlie "The Spirit of Friendshiip Warms The Heart" - 950742	Open		22.50	23
1992	Theadore, Samantha & Tyler "Friendship Weathers All Storms" - 950769	Open		20.00	20
1992	Beth "Happy Holidays, Deer Friend" - 950807	Suspd.		22.50	45
1992	Bear on Rocking Reindeer (Musical) - 950815	Suspd.		60.00	60-80
1992	Signage Plaque - 951005	Open		15.00	15
1992	Steven "A Season Filled With Sweetness" - 951129	Open		20.00	20
1992	Angie "I Brought The Star" - 951137	Open		15.00	15
1992	Theadore, Samantha & Tyler (9") "Friends Come In All Sizes" - 951196	Open		130.00	130
1992	Creche & Quilt - 951218	Open		50.00	50

Cherished Teddies Special Limited Edition - P. Hillman

YEAR ISSUE		EDITION LIMIT	YEAR RETD.	ISSUE PRICE	QUOTE U.S.$
1993	Teddy & Roosevelt "The Book of Teddies 1903-1993" - 624918	Yr.Iss.		20.00	100-175
1993	Holding On To Someone Special-Collector Appreciation Fig.-916285	Yr.Iss.		20.00	150-200
1994	Priscilla Ann "There's No One Like Hue" Collectible Exposition Exclusive available only at Secaucus and South Bend in 1994 and at Long Beach in 1995	Yr.Iss.		24.00	100-175

Maud Humphrey Bogart - Collectors' Club Members Only - M. Humphrey

YEAR ISSUE		EDITION LIMIT	YEAR RETD.	ISSUE PRICE	QUOTE U.S.$
1991	Friends For Life MH911	Closed	N/A	60.00	65
1992	Nature's Little Helper MH921	Closed	N/A	65.00	60-65
1993	Sitting Pretty MH931	Yr.Iss.		60.00	60

Maud Humphrey Bogart - Symbol Of Membership Figurines - M. Humphrey

YEAR ISSUE		EDITION LIMIT	YEAR RETD.	ISSUE PRICE	QUOTE U.S.$
1991	A Flower For You H5596	Closed	N/A	Unkn.	30
1992	Sunday Best M0002	Closed	N/A	Unkn.	30-53
1993	Playful Companions M0003	Yr.Iss.		Unkn.	Unkn.

Maud Humphrey Bogart - M. Humphrey

YEAR ISSUE		EDITION LIMIT	YEAR RETD.	ISSUE PRICE	QUOTE U.S.$
1988	Tea And Gossip H1301	Retrd.	N/A	65.00	45-65
1988	Cleaning House H1303	Retrd.	N/A	60.00	55
1988	Susanna H 1305	Retrd.	N/A	60.00	90-100
1988	Little Chickadees H1306	Retrd.	N/A	65.00	60-65
1988	The Magic Kitten H1308	Retrd.	N/A	66.00	50
1988	Seamstress H1309	Retrd.	N/A	66.00	75-100
1988	A Pleasure To Meet You H1310	Retrd.	N/A	65.00	65-120
1988	My First Dance H1311	Retrd.	N/A	60.00	100-125
1988	Sarah H1312	Retrd.	N/A	60.00	175-275
1988	Sealed With A Kiss H1316	Retrd.	N/A	45.00	60
1988	Special Friends H1317	Retrd.	N/A	66.00	50
1988	School Days H1318	Retrd.	N/A	42.50	55
1988	Gift Of Love H1319	Retrd.	N/A	65.00	40
1988	My 1st Birthday H1320	Retrd.	N/A	47.00	47
1989	Winter Fun H1354	Retrd.	N/A	46.00	50
1992	Stars and Stripes Forever 910201	Retrd.	N/A	75.00	96
1993	Playing Mama 5th Anniv. Figurine 915963	Retrd.	N/A	80.00	80
1993	Playing Mama Event Figurine 915963R	Retrd.	N/A	80.00	80

Maud Humphrey Bogart Victorian Village - M. Humphrey

YEAR ISSUE		EDITION LIMIT	YEAR RETD.	ISSUE PRICE	QUOTE U.S.$
1994	Chirstmas Scene - 655457	Open		50.00	50

Memories of Yesterday - Society Figurines - M. Attwell

YEAR ISSUE		EDITION LIMIT	YEAR RETD.	ISSUE PRICE	QUOTE U.S.$
1991	Welcome To Your New Home-MY911	Yr.Iss.		30.00	45
1991	I Love My Friends-MY921	Yr.Iss.		32.50	35
1993	Now I'm The Fairest Of Them All-MY931	Yr.Iss.		35.00	35
1993	A Little Love Song for You-MY941	Yr.Iss.		35.00	35
1994	Wot's All This Talk About Love-MY942	Yr.Iss.		27.50	28
1995	Sharing the Common Thread of Love- MY951	Yr.Iss.		100.00	100
1995	A Song For You From One That's True - MY952	Yr.Iss.		37.50	38

Memories of Yesterday - Exclusive Membership Figurine - M. Attwell

YEAR ISSUE		EDITION LIMIT	YEAR RETD.	ISSUE PRICE	QUOTE U.S.$
1991	We Belong Together-S0001	Yr.Iss.		Gift	35
1992	Waiting For The Sunshine-S0002	Yr.Iss.		Gift	35
1993	I'm The Girl For You-S0003	Yr.Iss.		Gift	40
1994	Blowing a Kiss to a Dear I Miss-S0004	Yr.Iss.		Gift	N/A
1995	Time to Celebrate-S0005	Yr.Iss.		Gift	N/A

Memories of Yesterday - Exclusive Charter Membership Figurine - M. Attwell

YEAR ISSUE		EDITION LIMIT	YEAR RETD.	ISSUE PRICE	QUOTE U.S.$
1992	Waiting For The Sunshine-S0102	Yr.Iss.		Gift	N/A
1993	I'm The Girl For You-S0103	Yr.Iss.		Gift	N/A
1994	Blowing a Kiss to a Dear I Miss-S0104	Yr.Iss.		Gift	N/A
1995	Time to Celebrate-S0105	Yr.Iss.		Gift	N/A

Memories of Yesterday - M. Attwell

YEAR ISSUE		EDITION LIMIT	YEAR RETD.	ISSUE PRICE	QUOTE U.S.$
1990	Collection Sign-513156	Closed	1993	7.00	7
1989	Blow Wind, Blow-520012	Open		40.00	40
1990	Hold It! You're Just Swell-520020	Suspd.		50.00	50
1990	Kiss The Place And Make It Well-520039	Suspd.		50.00	50
1989	Let's Be Nice Like We Was Before-520047	Suspd.		50.00	50
1989	I'se Spoken For-520071	Retrd.	1991	30.00	30-50
1990	Where's Muvver?-520101	Retrd.	1994	30.00	30
1990	Here Comes The Bride And Groom God Bless 'Em!-520136 (musical)	Suspd.		80.00	80
1989	Daddy, I Can Never Fill Your Shoes-520187	Open		30.00	30
1989	This One's For You, Dear-520195	Suspd.		50.00	50
1989	Should I . . . ?-520209	Suspd.		50.00	50
1990	Luck At Last! He Loves Me-520217	Retrd.	1992	35.00	36-58
1989	Here Comes The Bride-God Bless Her! -9"-520527	2-Yr.	1990	95.00	95-100
1989	We's Happy! How's Yourself?-520616	Retrd.	1991	70.00	85-150
1989	Here Comes The Bride & Groom (musical) God Bless 'Em-520896	Open		50.00	50
1989	The Long and Short of It-522384	Retrd.	1994	32.50	33
1989	As Good As His Mother Ever Made-522392	Open		32.50	32-40
1989	Must Feed Them Over Christmas-522406	Open		38.50	39
1989	Knitting You A Warm & Cozy Winter-522414	Open		37.50	38
1989	Joy To You At Christmas-522449	Open		45.00	45
1989	For Fido And Me-522457	Open		70.00	70
1990	I'm Not As Backwards As I Looks-523240	Open		32.50	33
1990	I Pray The Lord My Soul To Keep-523259	Open		25.00	25
1990	He Hasn't Forgotten Me-523267	Suspd.		30.00	30
1990	Time For Bed 9"-523275	2-Yr.	1991	95.00	125
1990	Got To Get Home For The Holidays-524751(musical)	Retrd.	1994	100.00	100
1990	Hush-A-Bye Baby-524778	Open		80.00	80
1990	Let Me Be Your Guardian Angel-524670	Open		32.50	33
1990	A Dash of Something With Something For the Pot-524727	Open		55.00	55
1990	A Lapful Of Luck-524689	Open		15.00	15
1990	Not A Creature Was Stirrin'-524697	Suspd.		45.00	45
1990	I'se Been Painting-524700	Suspd.		37.50	38
1990	The Greatest Treasure The World Can Hold-524808	Open		50.00	50
1990	Hoping To See You Soon-524824	Suspd.		30.00	30
1991	He Loves Me -9" -525022	2-Yr.	1992	100.00	100
1991	Give It Your Best Shot-525561	Open		35.00	35
1991	Wishful Thinking-522597	Open		45.00	45
1991	Them Dishes Nearly Done-524611	Open		50.00	50
1991	Just Thinking 'bout You-523461 (musical)	Suspd.		70.00	70
1991	Who Ever Told Mother To Order Twins?-520063	Open		33.50	34
1991	Tying The Knot-522678	Open		60.00	60
1991	Pull Yourselves Together Girls, Waists Are In-522783	Open		30.00	30
1991	I Must Be Somebody's Darling-524832	Retrd.	1993	30.00	30
1991	We All Loves A Cuddle-524832	Retrd.	1992	30.00	35
1991	Sitting Pretty-522708	Retrd.	1993	40.00	50
1991	Why Don't You Sing Along?-522600	Retrd.	1995	55.00	55
1991	Wherever I Am, I'm Dreaming of You-	Suspd.		40.00	40
1991	Opening Presents Is Much Fun!-524735	Suspd.		37.50	38
1991	I'm As Comfy As Can Be-525480	Suspd.		50.00	50
1991	Friendship Has No Boundaries (Special Understamp)-525545	Yr.Iss.	1991	30.00	30-50
1991	Could You Love Me For Myself Alone?-525618	Retrd.	1994	30.00	30
1991	Good Morning, Little Boo-Boo-525766	Open		40.00	40
1991	S'no Use Lookin' Back Now!-527203	Open		75.00	75
1992	I Pray the Lord My Soul To Keep (musical)-525596	Suspd.		65.00	65
1992	Time For Bed-527076	Open		30.00	30
1992	Now Be A Good Dog Fido-524581	Open		45.00	45
1992	A Kiss From Fido-523119	Suspd.		35.00	35
1992	I'se Such A Good Little Girl Sometimes-522759	Suspd.		30.00	30
1992	Send All Life's Little Worries Skipping-527505	Open		30.00	30
1992	A Whole Bunch of Love For You-522732	Open		40.00	40
1992	Hurry Up For the Last Train to Fairyland-525863	Suspd.		40.00	40
1992	I'se So Happy You Called-526401	Retrd.	1993	100.00	100
1992	I'm Hopin' You're Missing Me Too-525499	Suspd.		55.00	55
1992	You'll Always Be My Hero-524743	Open		50.00	50
1992	Things Are Rather Upside Down-522775	Suspd.		30.00	30
1992	The Future-God Bless 'Em!-524719	Open		37.50	38
1992	Making Something Special For You-525472	Open		45.00	45
1992	Home's A Grand Place To Get Back To Musical-525553	Retrd.	1995	100.00	100
1992	Five Years Of Memories-525669 (Five Year Anniversary Figurine)	Yr.Iss.	1992	50.00	65
1992	Good Night and God Bless You In Every Way!-525634	Suspd.		50.00	50
1992	Collection Sign-527300	Open		30.00	30
1992	Merry Christmas, Little Boo-Boo-528803	Open		37.50	38
1992	Five Years Of Memories Celebrating Our Five Years1992-525669A	500		N/A	N/A
1993	You Do Make Me Happy-520098	Open		27.50	28
1993	Will You Be Mine?-522694	Open		30.00	30
1993	Here's A Little Song From Me To You Musical-522716	Open		70.00	70
1993	Bringing Good Luck To You-522791	Open		30.00	30
1993	With A Heart That's True, I'll Wait For You-524816	Open		50.00	50
1993	Now I Lay Me Down To Sleep-525413 (musical)	Suspd.		65.00	65
1993	The Jolly Ole Sun Will Shine Again-525502	Retrd.	1994	55.00	55
1993	May Your Flowers Be Even Better Than The Pictures On The Packets-525685	Open		37.50	38
1993	You Won't Catch Me Being A Golf Widow-525715	Open		30.00	30
1993	Having A Wash And Brush Up-527424	Open		35.00	35
1993	A Bit Tied Up Just Now-But Cheerio-527467	Open		45.00	45
1993	Hullo! Did You Come By Underground?-527653	Yr.Iss.	1993	40.00	40
1993	Hullo! Did You Come By Underground? Commemorative Issue: 1913-1993 -527653A	500		N/A	N/A
1993	Look Out-Something Good Is Coming Your Way!-528781	Suspd.		37.50	38
1993	Strikes Me, I'm Your Match-529656	Open		27.50	28
1993	Wot's All This Talk About Love?-529737	Retrd.	1994	100.00	100
1993	Do You Know The Way To Fairyland?-530379	Open		50.00	50
1994	Too Shy For Words-525758	Open		50.00	50
1994	Pleasant Dreams and Sweet Repose-(musical)-526592	Open		80.00	80
1994	Bless 'Em!-523127	Open		35.00	35
1994	Bless 'Em!-523232	Open		35.00	35
1994	Don't Wait For Wishes to Come True-Go Get Them!-527645	Open		37.50	38
1994	Making the Right Connection-529907	Yr.Iss.	1994	30.00	30
1994	The Nativity Pageant-602949	Open		90.00	90
1994	Taking After Mother-525731	Open		40.00	40
1994	Bobbed-526991	Retrd.	1995	32.50	33
1994	Having a Good Ole Laugh-527432	Open		50.00	50
1994	Do Be Friends With Me-529117	Open		40.00	40
1994	Good Morning From One Cheery Soul To Another-529141	Open		30.00	30
1994	May Your Birthday Be Bright And Happy-529575	Open		35.00	35
1994	Thank God For Fido-529753	2-Yr.		100.00	100
1994	Still Going Strong-530344	Open		27.50	28
1994	Comforting Thoughts-531367	Open		32.50	33
1994	With A Heart That's True, I'll Wait For You 524816	Open		50.00	50
1995	Love Begins With Friendship - 602914	Open		50.00	50
1995	A Helping Hand For You - 101192	Open		40.00	40
1995	Wherever You Go, I'll Keep In Touch - 602760	Open		30.00	30
1995	Good Friends Are Great Gifts - 525723	Open		50.00	50
1995	Let's Sail Away Together - 525707	Open		32.50	33
1995	A Friend Like You Is Hard To Find - 101176	Open		45.00	45
1995	You Brighten My Day With A Smile - 522627	Open		30.00	30
1995	Love To You Always - 602752	Open		30.00	30
1995	May You Have A Big Smile For A Long While - 602965	Open		30.00	30
1995	Love To You Today - 602973	Open		30.00	30
1995	Bedtime Tales-set 153400	2,000		60.00	60
1995	Won't You Skate With Me? 134864	5,000		35.00	35
1995	Dear Old Dear, Wish You Were Here 134872	5,000		37.50	38
1995	Boo-Boo's Band Set/5 137758	Open		25.00	25
1995	You're My Sunshine On A Rainy Day 137626	Open		37.50	38
1995	I Comfort Fido And Fido Comforts Me 522813	5,000		50.00	50

YEAR ISSUE		EDITION LIMIT	YEAR RETD.	ISSUE PRICE	QUOTE U.S.$
1995	Join Me For A Little Song 524654	5,000		37.50	38
1996	You Warm My Heart 603007	7,500		35.00	35
1996	We're In Trouble Now! 162299	7,500		37.50	38
1996	Put Your Best Foot Forward 526983	5,000		50.00	50
1996	How Good of God To Make Us All 164135	5,000		50.00	50
1996	We'd Do Anything For You, Dear 530905	5,000		50.00	50
1996	Whenever I Get A Moment-I Think of You 525626	7,500		37.50	38

Memories of Yesterday A Loving Wish For You - M. Attwell

YEAR ISSUE		EDITION LIMIT	YEAR RETD.	ISSUE PRICE	QUOTE U.S.$
1995	Happiness Is Our Wedding Wish - 135178	Open		25.00	25
1995	A Blessed Day For You - 135186	Open		25.00	25
1995	Wishing You A Bright Future - 135194	Open		25.00	25
1995	An Anniversary Is Love - 135208	Open		25.00	25
1995	A Birthday Wish For You - 135216	Open		25.00	25
1995	Bless You, Little One - 135224	Open		25.00	25

Memories of Yesterday Charter 1988 - M. Attwell

YEAR ISSUE		EDITION LIMIT	YEAR RETD.	ISSUE PRICE	QUOTE U.S.$
1988	Mommy, I Teared It-114480	Open		25.00	40-143
1988	Now I Lay Me Down To Sleep-114499	Open		20.00	25-65
1988	We's Happy! How's Yourself?-114502	Open		40.00	45-60
1988	Hang On To Your Luck!-114510	Open		25.00	27-70
1988	How Do You Spell S-O-R-R-Y?-114529	Retrd.	1990	25.00	50-95
1988	What Will I Grow Up To Be?-114537	Suspd.		40.00	45
1988	Can I Keep Her Mommy?-114545	Retrd.	1995	25.00	27-70
1988	Hush!-114553	Retrd.	1990	45.00	75-125
1988	It Hurts When Fido Hurts-114561	Retrd.	1992	30.00	32-75
1988	Anyway, Fido Loves Me-114588	Suspd.		30.00	32-75
1988	If You Can't Be Good, Be Careful-114596	Retrd.	1993	50.00	55-90
1988	Mommy, I Teared It, 9"-115924	Retrd.	1990	85.00	140-195
1988	Welcome Santa-114960	Open		45.00	50-100
1988	Special Delivery-114979	Retrd.	1991	30.00	32-70
1988	How 'bout A Little Kiss?-114987	Retrd.	1995	25.00	27-85
1988	Waiting For Santa-114995	Open		40.00	40-50
1988	Dear Santa. . .-115002	Suspd.		50.00	50
1988	I Hope Santa Is Home . . . 115010	Open		30.00	33-45
1988	It's The Thought That Counts-115029	Suspd.		25.00	29-75
1988	Is It Really Santa?-115347	Open		50.00	55-60
1988	He Knows IF You've Been Bad Or Good-115355	Open		40.00	45-75
1988	Now He Can Be Your Friend, Too!-115363	Open		45.00	50-70
1988	We Wish You A Merry Christmas-115371 (musical)	Suspd.		70.00	70
1988	Good Morning Mr. Snowman-115401	Retrd.	1992	75.00	80-170

Memories of Yesterday Event Item Only - M. Attwell

YEAR ISSUE		EDITION LIMIT	YEAR RETD.	ISSUE PRICE	QUOTE U.S.$
1994	I'll Always Be Your Truly Friend-525693	Yr.Iss.		30.00	30
1995	Wrapped In Love And Happiness 602930	Yr.Iss.		35.00	35

Memories of Yesterday Exclusive Heritage Dealer Figurine - M. Attwell

YEAR ISSUE		EDITION LIMIT	YEAR RETD.	ISSUE PRICE	QUOTE U.S.$
1991	A Friendly Chat and a Cup of Tea-525510	Yr.Iss.		50.00	100
1993	I'm Always Looking Out For You-527440	Yr.Iss.		55.00	55
1994	Loving Each Other Is The Nicest Thing We've Got- 522430	Yr.Iss.		60.00	60
1995	A Little Help From Fairyland 529133	1,995		55.00	55
1995	Friendship Is Meant To Be Shared - 602922	Yr.Iss.		50.00	50

Memories of Yesterday Holiday Snapshots - M. Attwell

YEAR ISSUE		EDITION LIMIT	YEAR RETD.	ISSUE PRICE	QUOTE U.S.$
1995	I'll Help You Mommy 144673	Open		25.00	25
1995	Isn't She Pretty? 144681	Open		25.00	25
1995	I Didn't Mean To Do It 144703	Open		25.00	25
1995	Can I Open Just One? 144711	Open		25.00	25

Memories of Yesterday Memories Of A Special Day - M. Attwell

YEAR ISSUE		EDITION LIMIT	YEAR RETD.	ISSUE PRICE	QUOTE U.S.$
1994	Monday's Child...-531421	Open		35.00	35
1994	Tuesday's Child...-531448	Open		35.00	35
1994	Wednesday's Child...-531405	Open		35.00	35
1994	Thursday's Child...-531413	Open		35.00	35
1994	Friday's Child...-531391	Open		35.00	35
1994	Saturday's Child...-531383	Open		35.00	35
1994	Sunday's Child...-531480	Open		35.00	35
1994	Collector's Commemorative Edition Set of 7, Hand-numbered-528056	1,994		250.00	250

Memories of Yesterday Nativity - M. Attwell

YEAR ISSUE		EDITION LIMIT	YEAR RETD.	ISSUE PRICE	QUOTE U.S.$
1994	Nativity Set of 4 602949	Open		90.00	90
1995	Innkeeper 602892	Open		27.50	28

Memories of Yesterday Once Upon A Fairy Tale™... - M. Attwell

YEAR ISSUE		EDITION LIMIT	YEAR RETD.	ISSUE PRICE	QUOTE U.S.$
1992	Mother Goose-526428	18,000		50.00	50
1992	Mary Had A Little Lamb-526479	18,000		45.00	45
1992	Simple Simon-526452	18,000		35.00	35
1993	Mary, Mary Quite Contrary-526436	18,000		45.00	45
1993	Little Miss Muffett-526444	18,000		50.00	50
1994	Tweedle Dum & Tweedle Dee-526460	10,000		50.00	50

Memories of Yesterday Special Edition - M. Attwell

YEAR ISSUE		EDITION LIMIT	YEAR RETD.	ISSUE PRICE	QUOTE U.S.$
1989	As Good As His Mother Ever Made-522392	9,600		32.50	114-150
1988	Mommy, I Teared It-523488	10,000		25.00	175-325
1990	A Lapful of Luck -525014	5,000		30.00	114-180
1990	Set of Three	N/A		87.50	735

Memories of Yesterday When I Grow Up - M. Attwell

YEAR ISSUE		EDITION LIMIT	YEAR RETD.	ISSUE PRICE	QUOTE U.S.$
1995	When I Grow Up, I Want To Be A Doctor - 102997	Open		25.00	25
1995	When I Grow Up, I Want To Be A Mother - 103195	Open		25.00	25
1995	When I Grow Up, I Want To Be A Ballerina-103209	Open		25.00	25
1995	When I Grow Up, I Want To Be A Teacher - 103357	Open		25.00	25
1995	When I Grow Up, I Want To Be A Fireman - 103462	Open		25.00	25
1995	When I Grow Up, I Want To Be A Nurse - 103535	Open		25.00	25

Miss Martha's Collection - M. Holcombe

YEAR ISSUE		EDITION LIMIT	YEAR RETD.	ISSUE PRICE	QUOTE U.S.$
1993	Erin - Don't Worry Santa Won't Forget Us - 307246	Retrd.	1994	55.00	110
1993	Amber - Mr. Snowman! (waterglobe) - 310476	Closed	1994	50.00	100
1993	Kekisha - Heavenly Peace Musical - 310484	Closed	1994	60.00	120
1993	Whitney - Let's Have Another Party - 321559	Closed	1994	45.00	45-90
1993	Megan - My Birthday Cake! - 321567	Closed	1994	60.00	60-100
1993	Doug - I'm Not Showin' Off - 321575	Closed	1994	40.00	80
1993	Francie - Such A Precious Gift! - 321583	Closed	1994	50.00	100
1993	Alicia - A Blessing From God - 321591	Closed	1994	40.00	160
1993	Anita - It's For You, Mama! - 321605	Closed	1994	45.00	60-90
1994	Jeffrey - Bein' A Fireman Sure Is Hot & Thirsty Work - 350206	Closed	1994	40.00	80
1993	Jess - I Can Fly - 350516	Retrd.	1994	45.00	90
1993	Ruth - Littlest Angel Figurine - 350524	Closed	1994	40.00	80
1993	Stephen - I'll Be The Best Shepherd In The World! - 350540	Closed	1994	40.00	80
1993	Jonathon - Maybe I Can Be Like Santa - 350559	Closed	1994	45.00	90
1994	Charlotte - You Can Be Whatever You Dream - 353191	Closed	1994	40.00	40-80
1992	Lillie - Christmas Dinner! - 369373	Retrd.	1993	55.00	110
1992	Eddie - What A Nice Surprise! - 369381	Retrd.	1994	50.00	100
1992	Kekisha - Heavenly Peace - 421456	Closed	1994	40.00	80
1992	Angela - I Have Wings - 421464	Closed	1994	45.00	160
1992	Amber - Mr. Snowman - 421472	Retrd.	1993	60.00	100
1992	Mar/Jsh/Christopher - Hush Baby! It's Your B-day! Musical - 431362	Closed	1994	80.00	160
1992	Carrie - God Bless America - 440035	Closed	1994	45.00	90
1993	Hallie - Sing Praises To The Lord - 443166	Retrd.	1993	60.00	75-120
1991	Jana - Plant With Love - 443174	Closed	1994	40.00	55-80
1991	Hallie - Sing Praises To The Lord - 443182	Closed	1994	37.50	50-75
1992	Belle/Maize - Not Now, Muffin - 443204	Retrd.	1993	50.00	100
1991	Sammy/Leisha - Sister's First Day Of School - 443190	Retrd.	1993	55.00	60-110
1991	Nate - Hope You Hear My Prayer, Lord - 443212	Closed	1994	17.50	30-75
1991	Sadie - They Can't Find Us Here - 443220	Retrd.	1993	45.00	80-90
1992	Patsy - Clean Clothes For Dolly - 443239	Retrd.	1993	50.00	100
1991	Dawn - Pretty Please, Mama - 443247	Closed	1994	40.00	50-80
1991	Tonya - Hush, Puppy Dear - 443255	Closed	1994	50.00	60-100
1991	Jenny/Jeremiah - Birthday Biscuits, With Love... - 443263	Retrd.	1993	60.00	75-120
1991	Suzi - Mama, Watch Me! - 443271	Retrd.	1993	35.00	45-70
1992	Mattie - Sweet Child - 443298	Retrd.	1993	30.00	30-60
1992	Sara Lou - Here, Lammie - 443301	Retrd.	1993	50.00	100
1992	Angel Tree Topper - 446521	Closed	1994	80.00	160
1992	Mar/Jsh/Christopher - Hush, Baby! It's Your B-day Figurine - 448354	Closed	1994	55.00	110

Precious Moments Collectors Club Welcome Gift - S. Butcher

YEAR ISSUE		EDITION LIMIT	YEAR RETD.	ISSUE PRICE	QUOTE U.S.$
1982	But Love Goes On Forever-Plaque-E-0202	Yr.Iss.		Unkn.	65-100
1983	Let Us Call the Club to Order-E-0303	Yr.Iss.		Unkn.	50-60
1984	Join in on the Blessings-E-0404	Yr.Iss.		Unkn.	45-55
1985	Seek and Ye Shall Find-E-0005	Yr.Iss.		Unkn.	30-55
1986	Birds of a Feather Collect Together-E-0006	Yr.Iss.		Unkn.	40
1987	Sharing Is Universal-E-0007	Yr.Iss.		Unkn.	35
1988	A Growing Love-E-0008	Yr.Iss.		Unkn.	35
1989	Always Room For One More-C-0009	Yr.Iss.		Unkn.	35-45
1990	My Happiness-C-0010	Yr.Iss.		Unkn.	25-50
1991	Sharing the Good News Together-C-0011	Yr.Iss.		Unkn.	35-55
1992	The Club That's Out Of This World-C-0012	Yr.Iss.		Unkn.	30-45
1993	Loving, Caring, and Sharing Along the Way-C-0013	Yr.Iss.		Unkn.	45
1994	You Are the End of My Rainbow-C-0014	Yr.Iss.		Unkn.	50
1995	You're The Sweetest Cookie In The Batch-C-0015	Yr.Iss.		Unkn.	Unkn.

Precious Moments Inscribed Charter Member Renewal Gift - S. Butcher

YEAR ISSUE		EDITION LIMIT	YEAR RETD.	ISSUE PRICE	QUOTE U.S.$
1981	But Love Goes on Forever-E-0001	Yr.Iss.		Unkn.	130-175
1982	But Love Goes on Forever-Plaque-E-0102	Yr.Iss.		Unkn.	55-100
1983	Let Us Call the Club to Order-E-0103	Yr.Iss.		25.00	55
1984	Join in on the Blessings-E-0104	Yr.Iss.		25.00	50
1985	Seek and Ye Shall Find-E-0105	Yr.Iss.		25.00	45-55
1986	Birds of a Feather Collect Together-E-0106	Yr.Iss.		25.00	30-50
1987	Sharing Is Universal -E-0107	Yr.Iss.		25.00	30-50
1988	A Growing Love-E-0108	Yr.Iss.		25.00	30-50
1989	Always Room For One More-C-0109	Yr.Iss.		35.00	40-50
1990	My Happiness-C-0110	Yr.Iss.		Unkn.	35
1991	Sharing The Good News Together-C-0111	Yr.Iss.		Unkn.	25-45
1992	The Club That's Out Of This World-C-0112	Yr.Iss.		Unkn.	30-45
1993	Loving, Caring, and Sharing Along the Way-C-0113	Yr.Iss.		Unkn.	35-50
1994	You Are the End of My Rainbow-C-0114	Yr.Iss.		Unkn.	35
1995	You're The Sweetest Cookie In The Batch-C-0115	Yr.Iss.		Unkn.	Unkn.

Precious Moments Special Edition Members' Only - S. Butcher

YEAR ISSUE		EDITION LIMIT	YEAR RETD.	ISSUE PRICE	QUOTE U.S.$
1981	Hello, Lord, It's Me Again-PM-811	Yr.Iss.		25.00	375-450
1982	Smile, God Loves You-PM-821	Yr.Iss.		25.00	150-255
1983	Put on a Happy Face-PM-822	Yr.Iss.		25.00	165-200
1983	Dawn's Early Light-PM-831	Yr.Iss.		27.50	65-95
1984	God's Ray of Mercy-PM-841	Yr.Iss.		25.00	40-70
1984	Trust in the Lord to the Finish-PM-842	Yr.Iss.		25.00	45-70
1985	The Lord is My Shepherd-PM-851	Yr.Iss.		25.00	65-90
1985	I Love to Tell the Story-PM-852	Yr.Iss.		27.50	50-75
1986	Grandma's Prayer-PM-861	Yr.Iss.		25.00	70-100
1986	I'm Following Jesus-PM-862	Yr.Iss.		25.00	65-90
1987	Feed My Sheep-PM-871	Yr.Iss.		25.00	35-70
1987	In His Time-PM-872	Yr.Iss.		25.00	60-75
1987	Loving You Dear Valentine-PM-873	Yr.Iss.		25.00	35-55
1987	Loving You Dear Valentine-PM-874	Yr.Iss.		25.00	35-50
1988	God Bless You for Touching My Life-PM-881	Yr.Iss.		27.50	40-85
1988	You Just Can't Chuck A Good Friendship-PM-882	Yr.Iss.		27.50	39-50
1989	You Will Always Be My Choice-PM-891	Yr.Iss.		27.50	30-55
1989	Mow Power To Ya-PM-892	Yr.Iss.		27.50	30-55
1990	Ten Years And Still Going Strong-PM-901	Yr.Iss.		30.00	40-55
1990	You Are A Blessing To Me-PM-902	Yr.Iss.		30.00	40-60
1991	One Step At A Time-PM-911	Yr.Iss.		33.00	45-60
1991	Lord, Keep Me In TeePee Top Shape-PM-912	Yr.Iss.		33.00	40-50
1992	Only Love Can Make A Home-PM-921	Yr.Iss.		30.00	40-60
1992	Sowing The Seeds of Love-PM-922	Yr.Iss.		30.00	35-45
1993	His Little Treasure-PM-931	Yr.Iss.		30.00	40
1993	Loving PM-932	Yr.Iss.		30.00	35-60
1994	Caring PM-941	Yr.Iss.		35.00	45
1994	Sharing PM-942	Yr.Iss.		35.00	35
1995	You're One In A Million To Me PM-951	Yr.Iss.		35.00	35
1995	Take Time To Pray PM-952	Yr.Iss.		35.00	35

Precious Moments Club 5th Anniversary Commemorative Edition - S. Butcher

YEAR ISSUE		EDITION LIMIT	YEAR RETD.	ISSUE PRICE	QUOTE U.S.$
1985	God Bless Our Years Together-12440	Yr.Iss.		175.00	300-350

Precious Moments Club 10th Anniversary Commemorative Edition - S. Butcher

YEAR ISSUE		EDITION LIMIT	YEAR RETD.	ISSUE PRICE	QUOTE U.S.$
1988	The Good Lord has Blessed Us Tenfold-114022	Yr.Iss.		90.00	175-250

Precious Moments Club 15th Anniversary Commemorative Edition - S. Butcher

YEAR ISSUE		EDITION LIMIT	YEAR RETD.	ISSUE PRICE	QUOTE U.S.$
1993	15 Happy Years Together: What A Tweet-530786	Yr.Iss.		100.00	115
1993	A Perfect Display of 15 Happy Years - 127817	Yr.Iss.		100.00	115

YEAR ISSUE		EDITION LIMIT	YEAR RETD.	ISSUE PRICE	QUOTE U.S.$
Precious Moments - S. Butcher					
1983	Sharing Our Season Together E-0501	Suspd.		50.00	110-150
1983	Jesus is the Light that Shines E-0502	Suspd.		23.00	50-60
1983	Blessings from My House to Yours-E-0503	Suspd.		27.00	75-110
1983	Christmastime Is for Sharing E-0504	Retrd.	1990	37.00	55-85
1983	Surrounded with Joy-E-0506	Retrd.	1989	21.00	50-85
1983	God Sent His Son-E-0507	Suspd.		32.50	65-90
1983	Prepare Ye the Way of the Lord-E-0508	Suspd.		75.00	100-130
1983	Bringing God's Blessing to You-E-0509	Suspd.		35.00	70-100
1983	Tubby's First Christmas-E-0511	Suspd.		12.00	32-43
1983	It's a Perfect Boy-E-0512	Suspd.		18.50	45-65
1983	Onward Christian Soldiers-E-0523	Open		24.00	35-59
1983	You Can't Run Away from God-E-0525	Retrd.	1989	28.50	80-110
1983	He Upholdeth Those Who Fall-E-0526	Suspd.		35.00	65-95
1987	His Eye Is On The Sparrow-E-0530	Retrd.	1987	28.50	100-125
1979	Jesus Loves Me-E-1372B	Open		7.00	28-125
1979	Jesus Loves Me-E-1372G	Open		7.00	28-130
1979	Smile, God Loves You-E-1373B	Retrd.	1984	7.00	55-135
1979	Jesus is the Light-E-1373G	Retrd.	1988	7.00	50-125
1979	Praise the Lord Anyhow-E-1374B	Retrd.	1982	8.00	65-155
1979	Make a Joyful Noise-E-1374G	Open		8.00	28-125
1979	Love Lifted Me-E-1375A	Retrd.	1993	11.00	45-125
1979	Prayer Changes Things-E-1375B	Suspd.		11.00	135-215
1979	Love One Another-E-1376	Open		10.00	40-120
1979	He Leadeth Me-E-1377A	Suspd.		9.00	76-120
1979	He Careth For You-E-1377B	Suspd.		9.00	90-105
1979	God Loveth a Cheerful Giver-E-1378	Retrd.	1981	11.00	750-850
1979	Love is Kind-E-1379A	Suspd.		8.00	80-150
1979	God Understands-E-1379B	Suspd.		8.00	85-130
1979	O, How I Love Jesus-E-1380B	Retrd.	1984	8.00	85-175
1979	His Burden Is Light-E-1380G	Retrd.	1984	8.00	80-175
1979	Jesus is the Answer-E-1381	Suspd.		11.50	95-140
1979	We Have Seen His Star-E-2010	Suspd.		8.00	66-144
1979	Come Let Us Adore Him-E-2011	Retrd.	1981	10.00	175-250
1979	Jesus is Born-E-2012	Suspd.		12.00	90-110
1979	Unto Us a Child is Born-E-2013	Suspd.		12.00	88-105
1982	May Your Christmas Be Cozy-E-2345	Suspd.		23.00	70-140
1982	May Your Christmas Be Warm-E-2348	Suspd.		30.00	100-140
1982	Tell Me the Story of Jesus-E-2349	Suspd.		30.00	95-112
1982	Dropping in for Christmas-E-2350	Suspd.		18.00	65-115
1987	Holy Smokes-E-2351	Retrd.	1987	27.00	80-135
1982	O Come All Ye Faithful-E-2353	Retrd.	1986	27.50	70-100
1982	I'll Play My Drum for Him-E-2356	Suspd.		30.00	55-77
1982	I'll Play My Drum for Him-E-2360	Open		16.00	30-40
1982	Christmas Joy from Head to Toe-E-2361	Suspd.		25.00	55-80
1982	Camel Figurine-E-2363	Open		20.00	33-50
1982	Goat Figurine-E-2364	Suspd.		10.00	45-75
1982	The First Noel-E-2365	Suspd.		16.00	55-75
1982	The First Noel-E-2366	Suspd.		16.00	60-70
1982	Bundles of Joy-E-2374	Retrd.	1993	27.50	70-100
1982	Dropping Over for Christmas-E-2375	Retrd.	1991	30.00	70-115
1982	Our First Christmas Together-E-2377	Suspd.		35.00	75-150
1982	3 Mini Nativity Houses & Palm Tree-E-2387	Open		45.00	75-110
1982	Come Let Us Adore Him-E-2395 (11pc. set)	Open		80.00	130-175
1980	Come Let Us Adore Him-E2800 (9 pc. set)	Open		70.00	125-175
1980	Jesus is Born-E-2801	Suspd.		37.00	100-240
1980	Christmas is a Time to Share-E-2802	Suspd.		20.00	60-90
1980	Crown Him Lord of All-E-2803	Suspd.		20.00	60-95
1980	Peace on Earth-E-2804	Suspd.		20.00	118-135
1980	Wishing You a Season Filled w/ Joy-E-2805	Retrd.	1985	20.00	80-100
1984	You Have Touched So Many Hearts-E-2821	Open		25.00	38-52
1984	This is Your Day to Shine-E-2822	Retrd.	1988	37.50	81-100
1984	To God Be the Glory-E-2823	Suspd.		40.00	75-85
1984	To a Very Special Mom-E-2824	Open		27.50	38-57
1984	To a Very Special Sister-E-2825	Open		37.50	55-65
1984	May Your Birthday Be a Blessing-E-2826	Suspd.		37.50	75-120
1984	I Get a Kick Out of You-E-2827	Suspd.		50.00	150-200
1984	Precious Memories-E-2828	Open		45.00	45-70
1984	I'm Sending You a White Christmas-E-2829	Open		37.50	55-60
1984	God Bless the Bride-E-2832	Open		35.00	50-60
1986	Sharing Our Joy Together-E-2834	Suspd.		30.00	52-60
1984	Baby Figurines (set of 6)-E-2852	Open		12.00	105-168
1980	Blessed Are the Pure in Heart-E-3104	Suspd.		9.00	25-45
1980	He Watches Over Us All-E-3105	Suspd.		11.00	52-95
1980	Mother Sew Dear-E-3106	Open		13.00	28-80
1980	Blessed are the Peacemakers-E-3107	Retrd.	1985	13.00	65-125
1980	The Hand that Rocks the Future-E-3108	Suspd.		13.00	60-95
1980	The Purr-fect Grandma-E-3109	Open		13.00	28-75
1980	Loving is Sharing-E-3110B	Retrd.	1993	13.00	55-100
1980	Loving is Sharing-E-3110G	Open		13.00	30-100
1980	Be Not Weary In Well Doing-E-3111	Retrd.	1985	14.00	85-145
1980	God's Speed-E-3112	Retrd.	1983	14.00	65-100
1980	Thou Art Mine-E-3113	Open		16.00	40-65
1980	The Lord Bless You and Keep You-E-3114	Open		16.00	45-65
1980	But Love Goes on Forever-E-3115	Open		16.50	38-77
1980	Thee I Love-E-3116	Retrd.	1983	16.50	55-150
1980	Walking By Faith-E-3117	Open		35.00	70-125
1980	Eggs Over Easy-E-3118	Retrd.	1983	12.00	75-125
1980	It's What's Inside that Counts-E-3119	Suspd.		13.00	90-130
1980	To Thee With Love-E-3120	Suspd.		13.00	60-150
1981	The Lord Bless You and Keep You-E-4720	Suspd.		14.00	35-55
1981	The Lord Bless You and Keep You-E-4721	Open		14.00	33-80
1981	Love Cannot Break a True Friendship E-4722	Suspd.		22.50	90-210
1981	Peace Amid the Storm-E-4723	Suspd.		22.50	70-130
1981	Rejoicing with You-E-4724	Open		25.00	45-99
1981	Peace on Earth-E-4725	Suspd.		25.00	60-90
1981	Bear Ye One Another's Burdens-E-5200	Suspd.		20.00	60-105
1981	Love Lifted Me-E-5201	Suspd.		25.00	75-110
1981	Thank You for Coming to My Ade-E-5202	Suspd.		22.50	120-210
1981	Let Not the Sun Go Down Upon Your Wrath-E-5203	Suspd.		22.50	130-175
1981	To A Special Dad-E-5212	Open		20.00	35-79
1981	God is Love-E-5213	Suspd.		17.00	55-104
1981	Prayer Changes Things-E-5214	Suspd.		35.00	100-165
1984	May Your Christmas Be Blessed-E-5376	Suspd.		37.50	67-75
1987	Love is Kind-E-5377	Retrd.	1987	27.50	70-90
1984	Joy to the World-E-5378	Suspd.		18.00	37-50
1984	Isn't He Precious?-E-5379	Open		20.00	30-48
1984	A Monarch is Born-E-5380	Suspd.		33.00	60-75
1984	His Name is Jesus-E-5381	Suspd.		45.00	95-120
1984	For God So Loved the World-E-5382	Suspd.		70.00	115-130
1984	Wishing You a Merry Christmas-E-5383	Yr.Iss.		17.00	45
1984	I'll Play My Drum for Him-E-5384	Open		10.00	16-30
1984	Oh Worship the Lord (B)-E-5385	Suspd.		10.00	50-60
1984	Oh Worship the Lord (G)-E-5386	Suspd.		10.00	55-70
1981	Come Let Us Adore Him-E-5619	Suspd.		10.00	30-45
1981	Donkey Figurine-E-5621	Open		6.00	15-30
1981	They Followed the Star-E-5624	Open		130.00	200-270
1981	Wee Three Kings-E-5635	Open		40.00	75-125
1981	Rejoice O Earth-E-5636	Open		15.00	30-70
1981	The Heavenly Light-E-5637	Open		15.00	30-60
1981	Cow with Bell Figurine-E-5638	Open		16.00	30-50
1981	Isn't He Wonderful (B)-E-5639	Suspd.		12.00	50-75
1981	Isn't He Wonderful (G)-E-5640	Suspd.		12.00	65-80
1981	They Followed the Star-E-5641	Suspd.		75.00	175-230
1981	Nativity Wall (2 pc. set)-E-5644	Open		60.00	120-145
1984	God Sends the Gift of His Love-E-6613	Suspd.		22.50	70-150
1982	God is Love, Dear Valentine-E-7153	Suspd.		16.00	22-40
1982	God is Love, Dear Valentine-E-7154	Suspd.		16.00	22-40
1982	Thanking Him for You-E-7155	Suspd.		16.00	60
1982	I Believe in Miracles-E-7156	Suspd.		17.00	85-115
1987	I Believe In Miracles-E-7156R	Retrd.	1992	22.50	65-85
1982	There is Joy in Serving Jesus-E-7157	Retrd.	1986	17.00	50-65
1982	Love Beareth All Things-E-7158	Open		25.00	38-70
1982	Lord Give Me Patience-E-7159	Suspd.		25.00	45-75
1982	The Perfect Grandpa-E-7160	Suspd.		25.00	60-75
1982	His Sheep Am I-E-7161	Suspd.		25.00	55-85
1982	Love is Sharing-E-7162	Suspd.		25.00	150-190
1982	God is Watching Over You-E-7163	Suspd.		27.50	90-120
1982	Bless This House-E-7164	Suspd.		45.00	180-240
1982	Let the Whole World Know-E-7165	Suspd.		45.00	75-120
1983	If God Be for Us, Who Can Be Against Us-E-9239	Suspd.		27.50	55-70
1983	Love is Patient-E-9251	Suspd.		35.00	65-95
1983	Forgiving is Forgetting-E-9252	Suspd.		37.50	75-100
1983	The End is in Sight-E-9253	Suspd.		25.00	75-100
1983	Praise the Lord Anyhow-E-9254	Retrd.	1994	35.00	55
1983	Bless You Two-E-9255	Open		21.00	40-50
1983	We are God's Workmanship-E-9258	Open		19.00	33-50
1983	We're In It Together-E-9259	Suspd.		24.00	50-70
1983	God's Promises are Sure-E-9260	Suspd.		30.00	55-75
1983	Seek Ye the Lord-E-9261	Suspd.		21.00	37-50
1983	Seek Ye the Lord-E-9262	Suspd.		21.00	50
1983	How Can Two Walk Together Except They Agree-E-9263	Suspd.		35.00	125-160
1963	Press On-E-9265	Open		40.00	55-100
1973	Animal Collection, Teddy Bear-E-9267A	Suspd.		6.50	21-30
1983	Animal Collection, Dog W/ Slippers-E-9267B	Suspd.		6.50	18-25
1983	Animal Collection, Bunny W/ Carrot-E-9267C	Suspd.		6.50	18-31
1983	Animal Collection, Kitty With Bow-E-9267D	Suspd.		6.50	18-22
1983	Animal Collection, Lamb With Bird-E-9267E	Suspd.		6.50	19-25
1983	Animal Collection, Pig W/ Patches-E-9267F	Suspd.		6.50	18-25
1983	Nobody's Perfect-E-9268	Retrd.	1990	21.00	50-75
1987	Let Love Reign-E-9273	Retrd.	1987	27.50	55-85
1983	Taste and See that the Lord is Good-E-9274	Retrd.	1986	22.50	45-80
1983	Jesus Loves Me-E-9278	Open		9.00	17-34
1983	Jesus Loves Me-E-9279	Open		9.00	17-32
1983	To Some Bunny Special-E-9282A	Suspd.		8.00	18-35
1983	You're Worth Your Weight In Gold-E-9282B	Suspd.		8.00	30
1983	Especially For Ewe-E-9282C	Suspd.		8.00	20-37
1983	Peace on Earth-E-9287	Suspd.		37.50	85-125
1983	Sending You a Rainbow-E-9288	Suspd.		22.50	55-95
1983	Trust in the Lord-E-9289	Suspd.		21.00	62-75
1985	Love Covers All-12009	Suspd.		27.50	48-65
1985	Part of Me Wants to be Good-12149	Suspd.		19.00	55-65
1987	This Is The Day Which The Lord Has Made-12157	Suspd.		20.00	52-75
1985	Get into the Habit of Prayer-12203	Suspd.		19.00	35-45
1985	Miniature Clown-12238A	Open		13.50	19-32
1985	Miniature Clown-12238B	Open		13.50	19-32
1985	Miniature Clown-12238C	Open		13.50	19-32
1985	Miniature Clown-12238D	Open		13.50	19-32
1985	It is Better to Give than to Receive-12297	Suspd.		19.00	120-175
1985	Love Never Fails-12300	Open		25.00	35-57
1985	God Bless Our Home-12319	Open		40.00	55-65
1986	You Can Fly-12335	Suspd.		25.00	55-80
1985	Jesus is Coming Soon-12343	Suspd.		22.50	40-70
1985	Halo, and Merry Christmas-12351	Suspd.		40.00	160-180
1985	May Your Christmas Be Delightful-15482	Suspd.		25.00	35-52
1985	Honk if You Love Jesus-15490	Open		13.00	20-35
1985	Baby's First Christmas-15539	Yr.Iss.		13.00	42-45
1985	Baby's First Christmas-15547	Yr.Iss.		13.00	45
1985	God Sent His Love-15881	Yr.Iss.		17.00	30-78
1986	To My Favorite Paw-100021	Suspd.		22.50	50-65
1987	To My Deer Friend-100048	Open		33.00	50-92
1986	Sending My Love-100056	Suspd.		22.50	40-65
1986	O Worship the Lord-100064	Open		24.00	38-49
1986	To My Forever Friend-100072	Open		33.00	44-80
1987	He's The Healer Of Broken Hearts-100080	Open		33.00	50-59
1987	Make Me A Blessing-100102	Retrd.	1990	35.00	75-100
1986	Lord I'm Coming Home-100110	Open		22.50	33-55
1986	Lord, Keep Me On My Toes-100129	Retrd.	1988	22.50	75-100
1986	The Joy of the Lord is My Strength-100137	Open		35.00	50-89
1986	God Bless the Day We Found You-100145	Suspd.		37.50	85-125
1995	God Bless the Day We Found You(Girl)-100145R	Open		60.00	60
1986	God Bless the Day We Found You-100153	Suspd.		37.50	45-85
1995	God Bless the Day We Found You(Boy)-100153R	Open		60.00	60
1986	Serving the Lord-100161	Suspd.		19.00	65-75
1986	I'm a Possibility-100188	Retrd.	1993	21.00	55-70
1987	The Spirit Is Willing But The Flesh Is Weak-100196	Retrd.	1991	19.00	65-80
1987	The Lord Giveth & the Lord Taketh Away-100226	Retrd.	1995	33.50	40-55
1986	Friends Never Drift Apart-100250	Open		35.00	55-75
1986	Help, Lord, I'm In a Spot-100269	Retrd.	1989	18.50	55-65
1986	He Cleansed My Soul-100277	Open		24.00	38-60
1986	Serving the Lord-100293	Suspd.		19.00	30-55
1987	Scent From Above-100528	Retrd.	1991	19.00	60-80
1986	Brotherly Love-100544	Suspd.		37.00	65-95
1987	No Tears Past The Gate-101826	Open		40.00	70-85
1987	Smile Along The Way-101842	Retrd.	1991	30.00	150
1987	Lord, Help Us Keep Our Act Together-101850	Retrd.	1992	35.00	105-125
1986	O Worship the Lord-102229	Open		24.00	38-42
1986	Shepherd of Love-102261	Open		10.00	16-24
1986	Three Mini Animals-102296	Suspd.		13.50	19-30
1986	Wishing You a Cozy Christmas-102342	Yr.Iss.		17.00	39-45
1986	Love Rescued Me-102393	Open		21.00	38-40
1986	Angel of Mercy-102482	Open		19.00	19-40
1986	Sharing our Christmas Together-102490	Suspd.		35.00	65-70
1987	We Are All Precious In His Sight-102903	Yr.Iss.		30.00	65-125
1986	God Bless America-102938	Yr.Iss.		30.00	65-70
1986	It's the Birthday of a King-102962	Suspd.		18.50	35-50
1987	I Would Be Sunk Without You-102970	Open		15.00	20-30
1987	My Love Will Never Let You Go-103497	Open		25.00	38-45
1986	I Believe in the Old Rugged Cross-103632	Open		25.00	35-47
1986	Come Let Us Adore Him-104000 (9 pc. set w/cassette)	Open		95.00	130
1987	With this Ring I...-104019	Open		40.00	65-65
1987	Love Is The Glue That Mends-104027	Suspd.		33.50	50-70
1987	Cheers To The Leader-104035	Open		22.50	30-39
1987	Happy Days Are Here Again-104396	Suspd.		25.00	57-70
1987	A Tub Full of Love-104817	Open		22.50	30-42
1987	Sitting Pretty-104825	Suspd.		22.50	43-60
1987	Have I Got News For You-105635	Suspd.		22.50	30-60
1988	Something's Missing When You're Not Around -105643	Suspd.		32.50	40-75
1987	To Tell The Tooth You're Special-105813	Suspd.		38.50	110-140

YEAR ISSUE		EDITION LIMIT	YEAR RETD.	ISSUE PRICE	QUOTE U.S.$
1988	Hallelujah Country-105821	Open		35.00	45-65
1987	We're Pulling For You-106151	Suspd.		40.00	60-75
1987	God Bless You Graduate-106194	Open		20.00	33-35
1987	Congratulations Princess-106208	Open		20.00	33-35
1987	Lord Help Me Make the Grade-106216	Suspd.		25.00	49-65
1988	Heaven Bless Your Togetherness-106755	Open		65.00	80-87
1988	Precious Memories-106763	Open		37.50	50-55
1988	Puppy Love Is From Above-106798	Retrd.	1995	45.00	55
1988	Happy Birthday Poppy-106836	Suspd.		27.50	39-49
1988	Sew In Love-106844	Open		45.00	55-80
1987	They Followed The Star-108243	Open		75.00	120
1987	The Greatest Gift Is A Friend-109231	Open		30.00	38-55
1988	Believe the Impossible-109487	Suspd.		35.00	50-110
1988	Happiness Divine-109584	Retrd.	1992	25.00	55-85
1987	Wishing You A Yummy Christmas-109754	Suspd.		35.00	50-70
1987	We Gather Together To Ask The Lord's Blessing-109762	Open		130.00	150-169
1988	Meowie Christmas-109800	Open		30.00	40-50
1987	Oh What Fun It Is To Ride-109819	Open		85.00	110-135
1988	Wishing You A Happy Easter-109886	Open		23.00	33-34
1988	Wishing You A Basket Full Of Blessings-109924	Open		23.00	33
1988	Sending You My Love-109967	Open		35.00	45-60
1988	Mommy, I Love You-109975	Open		22.50	30-34
1987	Love Is The Best Gift of All-110930	Yr.Iss.		22.50	45-39
1988	Faith Takes The Plunge-111155	Open		27.50	40-50
1988	Tis the Season-111163	Open		27.50	35-45
1987	O Come Let Us Adore Him (4 pc. 9" Nativity)-111333	Suspd.		200.00	225-275
1988	Mommy, I Love You-112143	Open		22.50	30-36
1987	A Tub Full of Love-112313	Open		22.50	30-36
1988	This Too Shall Pass-114014	Open		23.00	28-37
1988	Some Bunny's Sleeping-115274	Open		15.00	25-35
1988	Our First Christmas Together-115290	Suspd.		50.00	60-80
1988	Time to Wish You a Merry Christmas-115339	Yr.Iss.		24.00	35-50
1995	Love Blooms Eternal-127019	Yr.Iss.		35.00	35
1995	Dreams Really Do Come True-128309	Open		37.50	38
1995	Another Year More Grey Hares-128686	Open		17.50	18
1995	I Give You My Love Forever True-129100	Open		70.00	70
1995	He Hath Made Everything Beautiful in His Time-129151	Open		50.00	50
1995	Happy Hula Days-128694	Yr.Iss.		15.00	15
1995	He Covers the Earth With His Beauty-142654	Yr.Iss.		30.00	30
1995	Come Let Us Adore Him-142735 (large nativity)	Open		50.00	50
1995	Come Let Us Adore Him-142743 (small nativity)	Open		35.00	35
1995	Making A Trail to Bethlehem-142751	Open		30.00	30
1995	I'll Give Him My Heart-150088	Yr.Iss.		20.00	20
1995	Soot Yourself To A Merry Christmas-150096	Yr.Iss.		17.50	18
1995	Making Spirits Bright-150118	Yr.Iss.		18.75	19
1988	Rejoice O Earth-520268	Open		13.00	17-27
1988	Jesus the Savior Is Born-520357	Suspd.		25.00	33-55
1992	The Lord Turned My Life Around-520535	Open		35.00	35
1991	In The Spotlight Of His Grace-520543	Open		35.00	35
1990	Lord, Turn My Life Around-520551	Open		35.00	35-52
1992	You Deserve An Ovation-520578	Open		35.00	35
1989	My Heart Is Exposed With Love-520624	Open		45.00	55-60
1989	A Friend Is Someone Who Cares-520632	Retrd.	1995	30.00	35-55
1989	I'm So Glad You Fluttered Into My Life-520640	Retrd.	1991	40.00	255-350
1995	Wishing You A Happy Bear Hug-520659	Open		27.50	28
1989	Eggspecially For You-520667	Open		45.00	50-60
1989	Your Love Is So Uplifting-520675	Open		60.00	65-79
1989	Sending You Showers Of Blessings-520683	Retrd.	1992	32.50	52-70
1989	Just A LineTo Wish You A Happy Day-520721	Open		65.00	70-79
1989	Friendship Hits The Spot-520748	Open		55.00	60-68
1989	Jesus Is The Only Way-520756	Suspd.		40.00	57-70
1989	Puppy Love-520764	Open		12.50	17-25
1989	Many Moons In Same Canoe, Blessum You-520772	Retrd.	1990	50.00	215-275
1989	Wishing You Roads Of Happiness-520780	Open		60.00	75
1989	Someday My Love-520799	Retrd.	1992	40.00	85-95
1989	My Days Are Blue Without You-520802	Suspd.		65.00	80-135
1989	We Need A Good Friend Through The Ruff Times-520810	Suspd.		35.00	50-60
1989	You Are My Number One-520829	Open		25.00	33-42
1989	The Lord Is Your Light To Happiness-520837	Open		50.00	65
1989	Wishing You A Perfect Choice-520845	Open		55.00	60-67
1989	I Belong To The Lord-520853	Suspd.		25.00	35-50
1990	Heaven Bless You-520934	Open		35.00	30-150
1993	There Is No Greater Treasure Than To Have A Friend Like You -521000	Open		30.00	30
1989	Hello World-521175	Open		15.00	17
1990	That's What Friends Are For-521183	Open		45.00	45-49
1990	Hope You're Up And OnThe Trail Again-521205	Suspd.		35.00	35-45
1993	The Fruit of the Spirit is Love-521213	Yr.Iss.		30.00	30
1991	Take Heed When You Stand-521272	Suspd.		55.00	55-70
1990	Happy Trip-521280	Suspd.		35.00	35-70
1991	Hug One Another-521299	Open		45.00	55
1990	Yield Not To Temptation-521310	Suspd.		27.50	30-50
1990	Faith Is A Victory-521396	Retrd.	1993	25.00	115-185
1990	I'll Never Stop Loving You-521418	Open		37.50	38-53
1991	To A Very Special Mom & Dad-521434	Suspd.		35.00	35-45
1990	Lord, Help Me Stick To My Job-521450	Open		30.00	30-48
1989	Tell It To Jesus-521477	Open		35.00	38-58
1991	There's A Light At The End Of The Tunnel-521485	Open		55.00	55
1991	A Special Delivery-521493	Open		30.00	30
1991	Thumb-body Loves You-521698	Open		55.00	50-65
1990	Sweep All Your Worries Away-521779	Open		40.00	40-130
1990	Good Friends Are Forever-521817	Open		50.00	55-62
1990	Love Is From Above-521841	Open		45.00	45-59
1989	The Greatest of These Is Love-521868	Suspd.		27.50	40-50
1990	Easter's On Its Way-521892	Open		60.00	65-75
1994	Hoppy Easter Friend-521906	Open		40.00	40-43
1991	Perfect Harmony-521914	Open		55.00	55
1993	Safe In The Arms Of Jesus-521922	Open		30.00	30
1989	Wishing You A Cozy Season-521949	Suspd.		42.50	45-62
1990	High Hopes-521957	Suspd.		30.00	35-50
1991	To A Special Mum-521965	Open		30.00	30-33
1993	To The Apple Of God's Eye-522015	Yr.Iss.		32.50	33
1979	May Your Life Be Blessed With Touchdowns-522023	Open		45.00	50-62
1989	Thank You Lord For Everything-522031	Suspd.		55.00	65-85
1994	Now I Lay Me Down To Sleep-522058	Open		30.00	33
1991	May Your World Be Trimmed With Joy-522082	Open		55.00	55-62
1990	There Shall Be Showers Of Blessings-522090	Open		60.00	70
1992	It's No Yolk When I Say I Love You-522104	Suspd.		60.00	60-75
1989	Don't Let the Holidays Get You Down-522112	Retrd.	1993	42.50	80-110
1989	Wishing You A Very Successful Season-522120	Open		60.00	65-70
1989	Bon Voyage!-522201	Open		75.00	80-105
1989	He Is The Star Of The Morning-522252	Suspd.		55.00	60-75
1989	To Be With You Is Uplifting-522260	Retrd.	1994	20.00	22-46
1991	A Reflection Of His Love-522279	Open		50.00	50
1990	Thinking Of You Is What I Really Like To Do-522287	Open		30.00	30-42
1989	Merry Christmas Deer-522317	Open		50.00	55-70
1995	Just A Line To Say You're Special-522864	Open		50.00	50
1989	Isn't He Precious-522988	Suspd.		15.00	25-35
1990	Some Bunny's Sleeping-522996	Suspd.		12.00	12-28
1989	Jesus Is The Sweetest Name I Know-523097	Suspd.		22.50	25-36
1991	Joy On Arrival-523178	Open		50.00	50-60
1990	The Good Lord Always Delivers-523453	Open		27.50	28-35
1990	This Day Has Been Made In Heaven-523496	Open		30.00	33-45
1990	God Is Love Dear Valentine-523518	Open		27.50	28-45
1991	I Will Cherish The Old Rugged Cross-523534	Yr.Iss.		27.50	28-40
1992	You Are The Type I Love-523542	Open		40.00	40
1993	The Lord Will Provide-523593	Yr.Iss.		40.00	40-55
1991	Good News Is So Uplifting-523615	Open		60.00	65
1992	I'm So Glad That God Has Blessed Me With A Friend Like You -523623	Retrd.	1995	50.00	50
1994	I Will Always Be Thinking Of You-523631	Open		45.00	45
1990	Time Heals-523739	Open		37.50	38
1990	Blessings From Above-523747	Retrd.	1994	45.00	50-75
1994	Just Poppin' In To Say Halo - 523755	Open		45.00	45
1991	I Can't Spell Success Without You-523763	Suspd.		40.00	40-60
1990	Once Upon A Holy Night-523836	Yr.Iss.		25.00	45
1992	My Warmest Thoughts Are You-524085	Open		55.00	60
1991	Good Friends Are For Always-524123	Open		27.50	33
1994	Lord Teach Us to Pray-524158	Yr.Iss.		35.00	35
1991	May Your Christmas Be Merry-524166	Yr.Iss.		27.50	33
1995	Walk In The Sonshine-524212	Open		35.00	35
1991	He Loves Me-524263	Yr.Iss.		35.00	35-65
1992	Friendship Grows When You Plant A Seed-524271	Retrd.	1994	40.00	90-100
1993	May Your Every Wish Come True-524298	Open		50.00	50-60
1991	May Your Birthday Be A Blessing-524301	Open		30.00	33-48
1992	What The World Needs Now-524352	Open		50.00	50
1991	May Only Good Things Come Your Way-524425	Open		30.00	38
1993	Sealed With A Kiss-524441	Open		50.00	55
1993	A Special Chime For Jesus-524468	Yr.Iss.		32.50	33
1994	God Cared Enough To Send His Best-524476	Open		50.00	50
1990	Happy Birthday Dear Jesus-524875	Suspd.		13.50	14-27
1992	It's So Uplifting To Have A Friend Like You-524905	Open		40.00	45
1990	We're Going To Miss You-524913	Open		50.00	50-65
1991	Angels We Have Heard On High-524921	Open		60.00	60
1992	Tubby's First Christmas-525278	Open		10.00	10
1991	It's A Perfect Boy-525286	Open		16.50	17
1993	May Your Future Be Blessed-525316	Open		35.00	38
1992	Ring Those Christmas Bells-525898	Open		95.00	100
1992	Going Home-525979	Open		60.00	60-70
1992	I Would Be Lost Without You-526142	Open		27.50	28
1994	Friends 'Til The Very End-526150	Open		40.00	40
1992	You Are My Happiness-526185	Yr.Iss.		37.50	45-75
1994	You Suit Me to a Tee-526193	Open		35.00	35
1994	Sharing Sweet Moments Together-526487	Open		45.00	45
1991	How Could I Ever Forget You-526924	Open		15.00	17
1991	We Have Come From Afar-526959	Suspd.		17.50	18
1993	Bless-Um You-527335	Open		35.00	35
1992	You Are My Favorite Star-527378	Open		55.00	55
1992	Bring The Little Ones To Jesus-527556	Open		90.00	90-110
1992	God Bless The U.S.A.-527564	Yr.Iss.		32.50	40-50
1993	Tied Up For The Holidays-527580	Yr.Iss.		40.00	40
1993	Bringing You A Merry Christmas-527599	Yr.Iss.		45.00	45
1992	Wishing You A Ho Ho Ho-527629	Open		40.00	40
1992	But The Greatest of These Is Love-527688	Yr.Iss.		27.50	35
1992	Wishing You A Comfy Christmas-527750	Open		30.00	30
1993	I Only Have Arms For You-527769	Open		15.00	16
1992	This Land Is Our Land-527777	Yr.Iss.		35.00	44
1994	Nativity Cart-528072	Open		16.00	16
1994	Have I Got News For You-528137	Open		16.00	17
1994	To a Very Special Sister-528633	Open		60.00	60
1993	America You're Beautiful-528862	Yr.Iss.		35.00	35
1993	Ring Out The Good News-529966	Yr.Iss.		27.50	30
1993	Wishing You the Sweetest Christmas-530166	Yr.Iss.		27.50	31
1994	You're As Pretty As A Christmas Tree-530425	Yr.Iss.		27.50	28
1994	Serenity Prayer Girl-530697	Open		35.00	35
1994	Serenity Prayer Boy-530700	Open		35.00	35
1995	We Have Come From Afar-530913	Open		12.00	12
1995	I Only Have Ice For You-530956	Open		27.50	28
1995	What The World Needs Is Love-531065	Open		45.00	45
1994	Money Isn't The Only Green Thing Worth Saving-531073	Open		50.00	50
1995	Vaya Con Dios (To Go With God)-531146	Open		32.50	33-55
1995	Bless Your Sole-531162	Open		25.00	25
1994	The Lord is Counting on You-531707	Open		32.50	33
1994	Dropping In For The Holidays-531952	Open		40.00	40
1995	Hallelujah For The Cross-532002	Open		35.00	35
1995	Sending You Oceans Of Love-532010	Open		35.00	35
1995	I Can't Bear To Let You Go-532037	Open		50.00	50
1995	Lord Help Me To Stay On Course-532096	Open		35.00	35
1994	The Lord Bless You and Keep You-532118	Open		40.00	45
1994	The Lord Bless You and Keep You-532126	Open		30.00	33
1994	The Lord Bless You and Keep You-532134	Open		30.00	33
1994	Luke 2:10-11-532916	Open		35.00	35
1994	Nothing Can Dampen The Spirit of Caring-603864	Open		35.00	35
1995	A Poppy For You-604208	Open		35.00	35

Precious Moments Anniversary Figurines - S. Butcher

YEAR ISSUE		EDITION LIMIT	YEAR RETD.	ISSUE PRICE	QUOTE U.S.$
1984	God Blessed Our Years Together With So Much Love And Happiness-E-2853	Open		35.00	50-60

YEAR ISSUE		EDITION LIMIT	YEAR RETD.	ISSUE PRICE	QUOTE U.S.$
1984	God Blessed Our Year Together With So Much Love And Happiness (1st)-E-2854	Open		35.00	50-60
1984	God Blessed Our Years Together With So Much Love And Happiness (5th)-E-2855	Open		35.00	50-55
1984	God Blessed Our Years Together With So Much Love And Happiness (10th)-E-2856	Open		35.00	50-55
1984	God Blessed Our Years Together With So Much Love And Happiness (25th)-E-2857	Open		35.00	50-65
1984	God Blessed Our Years Together With So Much Love And Happiness (40th)-E-2859	Open		35.00	50-65
1984	God Blessed Our Years Together With So Much Love And Happiness (50th)-E-2860	Open		35.00	50-65
1994	I Still Do-530999	Open		30.00	30
1994	I Still Do-531006	Open		30.00	30

Precious Moments Baby's First - S. Butcher

YEAR ISSUE		EDITION LIMIT	YEAR RETD.	ISSUE PRICE	QUOTE U.S.$
1984	Baby's First Step-E-2840	Suspd.		35.00	70-95
1984	Baby's First Picture-E-2841	Retrd.	1986	45.00	150-225
1985	Baby's First Haircut-12211	Suspd.		32.50	150-200
1986	Baby's First Trip-16012	Suspd.		32.50	210-300
1989	Baby's First Pet-520705	Suspd.		45.00	50-95
1990	Baby's First Meal-524077	Open		35.00	35-45
1990	Baby's First Word-527238	Open		24.00	24-28
1993	Baby's First Birthday-524069	Open		25.00	25

Precious Moments Birthday Club Inscribed Charter Membership Renewal Gift - S. Butcher

YEAR ISSUE		EDITION LIMIT	YEAR RETD.	ISSUE PRICE	QUOTE U.S.$
1987	A Smile's the Cymbal of Joy-B-0102	Yr.Iss.		Unkn.	55-85
1988	The Sweetest Club Around-B-0103	Yr.Iss.		Unkn.	50-75
1989	Have A Beary Special Birthday-B-0104	Yr.Iss.		Unkn.	35-65
1990	Our Club Is A Tough Act To Follow-B-0105	Yr.Iss.		Unkn.	35-50
1991	Jest To Let You Know You're Tops-B-0106	Yr.Iss.		Unkn.	35-45
1992	All Aboard For Birthday Club Fun-B-0107	Yr.Iss.		Unkn.	30-50
1994	Happines is Belonging-B-0108	Yr.Iss.		Unkn.	35
1994	Can't Get Enough of Our Club-B-0109	Yr.Iss.		Unkn.	30
1995	Hoppy Birthday-B-0110	Yr.Iss.		Unkn.	Unkn.

Precious Moments Birthday Club Figurines - S. Butcher

YEAR ISSUE		EDITION LIMIT	YEAR RETD.	ISSUE PRICE	QUOTE U.S.$
1986	Fishing For Friends-BC-861	Yr.Iss.		10.00	145-165
1987	Hi Sugar-BC-871	Yr.Iss.		11.00	100-110
1988	Somebunny Cares-BC-881	Yr.Iss.		13.50	50-75
1989	Can't Bee Hive Myself Without You-BC-891	Yr.Iss.		13.50	50-70
1990	Collecting Makes Good Scents-BC-901	Yr.Iss.		15.00	40-60
1990	I'm Nuts Over My Collection-BC-902	Yr.Iss.		15.00	40
1991	Love Pacifies-BC-911	Yr.Iss.		15.00	35-45
1991	True Blue Friends-BC-912	Yr.Iss.		15.00	29-40
1992	Every Man's House Is His Castle-BC-921	Yr.Iss.		16.50	40-50
1993	I Got You Under My Skin-BC-922	Yr.Iss.		16.00	40
1994	Put a Little Punch In Your Birthday-BC-931	Yr.Iss.		15.00	30
1994	Owl Always Be Your Friend-BC-932	Yr.Iss.		16.00	30
1994	God Bless Our Home-BC-941	Yr.Iss.		16.00	30
1995	Yer A Pel-I-Can Count On-BC-942	Yr.Iss.		16.00	20

Precious Moments Birthday Club Welcome Gift - S. Butcher

YEAR ISSUE		EDITION LIMIT	YEAR RETD.	ISSUE PRICE	QUOTE U.S.$
1986	Our Club Can't Be Beat-B-0001	Yr.Iss.		Unkn.	85
1987	A Smile's The Cymbal of Joy-B-0002	Yr.Iss.		Unkn.	50-65
1988	The Sweetest Club Around-B-0003	Yr.Iss.		Unkn.	45
1989	Have A Beary Special Birthday-B-0004	Yr.Iss.		Unkn.	30-45
1990	Our Club Is A Tough Act To Follow-B-0005	Yr.Iss.		Unkn.	35
1991	Jest To Let You Know You're Tops-B-0006	Yr.Iss.		Unkn.	25-35
1992	All Aboard For Birthday Club Fun-B-0007	Yr.Iss.		Unkn.	30
1994	Happiness Is Belonging-B-0008	Yr.Iss.		Unkn.	20
1994	Can't Get Enough of Our Club-B-0009	Yr.Iss.		Unkn.	Unkn.
1995	Hoppy Birthday-B-0010	Yr.Iss.		Unkn.	Unkn.

Precious Moments Birthday Series - S. Butcher

YEAR ISSUE		EDITION LIMIT	YEAR RETD.	ISSUE PRICE	QUOTE U.S.$
1988	Friends To The End-104418	Suspd.		15.00	35
1987	Showers Of Blessings-105945	Retrd.	1993	16.00	60-75
1988	Brighten Someone's Day-105953	Suspd.		12.50	30-35
1990	To My Favorite Fan-521043	Suspd.		16.00	30-55
1989	Hello World!-521175	Open		13.50	15-30
1993	Hope You're Over The Hump-521671	Open		16.00	16
1990	Not A Creature Was Stirring-524484	Suspd.		17.00	30-40
1991	Can't Be Without You-524492	Open		16.00	17-29
1991	How Can I Ever Forget You-526924	Open		15.00	15
1992	Let's Be Friends-527270	Open		15.00	15-20
1992	Happy Birdie-527343	Open		8.00	17
1993	Happy Birthday Jesus-530492	Open		20.00	20
1994	Oinky Birthday-524506	Open		13.50	14

YEAR ISSUE		EDITION LIMIT	YEAR RETD.	ISSUE PRICE	QUOTE U.S.$
1995	Wishing You A Happy Bear Hug-520659	Open		27.50	28

Precious Moments Birthday Train Figurines - S. Butcher

YEAR ISSUE		EDITION LIMIT	YEAR RETD.	ISSUE PRICE	QUOTE U.S.$
1988	Isn't Eight Just Great-109460	Open		18.50	23
1988	Wishing You Grr-eatness-109479	Open		18.50	23-38
1986	May Your Birthday Be Warm-15938	Open		10.00	16-35
1986	Happy Birthday Little Lamb-15946	Open		10.00	15-39
1986	Heaven Bless Your Special Day-15954	Open		11.00	18-23
1986	God Bless You On Your Birthday-15962	Open		11.00	18-37
1986	May Your Birthday Be Gigantic -15970	Open		12.50	20-38
1986	This Day Is Something To Roar About-15989	Open		13.50	23-40
1986	Keep Looking Up-15997	Open		13.50	23-35
1986	Bless The Days Of Our Youth-16004	Open		15.00	23-38
1992	May Your Birthday Be Mammoth-521825	Open		25.00	25-40
1992	Being Nine Is Just Divine-521833	Open		25.00	25-40

Precious Moments Bless Those Who Serve Their Country - S. Butcher

YEAR ISSUE		EDITION LIMIT	YEAR RETD.	ISSUE PRICE	QUOTE U.S.$
1991	Bless Those Who Serve Their Country (Navy) 526568	Suspd.		32.50	75-125
1991	Bless Those Who Serve Their Country (Army) 526576	Suspd.		32.50	45-55
1991	Bless Those Who Serve Their Country (Air Force) 526584	Suspd.		32.50	45
1991	Bless Those Who Serve Their Country (Girl Soldier) 527289	Suspd.		32.50	45
1991	Bless Those Who Serve Their Country (Soldier) 527297	Suspd.		32.50	40-65
1991	Bless Those Who Serve Their Country (Marine) 527521	Suspd.		32.50	45
1995	You Will Always Be Our Hero 136271	Yr.Iss.		40.00	40

Precious Moments Bridal Party - S. Butcher

YEAR ISSUE		EDITION LIMIT	YEAR RETD.	ISSUE PRICE	QUOTE U.S.$
1984	Bridesmaid-E-2831	Open		13.50	22-30
1985	Ringbearer-E-2833	Open		11.00	17-30
1985	Flower Girl-E-2835	Open		11.00	17-25
1984	Groomsman-E-2836	Open		13.50	22-30
1986	Groom-E-2837	Open		13.50	20-40
1985	Junior Bridesmaid-E-2845	Open		12.50	20-30
1987	Bride-E-2846	Open		18.00	25-30
1987	God Bless Our Family (Parents of the Groom)-100498	Open		35.00	50-55
1987	God Bless Our Family (Parents of the Bride)-100501	Open		35.00	50-60
1987	Wedding Arch-102369	Suspd.		22.50	40-55

Precious Moments Calendar Girl - S. Butcher

YEAR ISSUE		EDITION LIMIT	YEAR RETD.	ISSUE PRICE	QUOTE U.S.$
1988	January-109983	Open		37.50	40-67
1988	February-109991	Open		27.50	38-67
1988	March-110019	Open		27.50	38-50
1988	April-110027	Open		30.00	38-100
1988	May -110035	Open		25.00	30-225
1988	June-110043	Open		40.00	50-112
1988	July-110051	Open		35.00	45-58
1988	August-110078	Open		40.00	45-58
1988	September-110086	Open		27.50	38-40
1988	October-110094	Open		35.00	45-59
1988	November-110108	Open		32.50	38-50
1988	December-110116	Open		27.50	35-75

Precious Moments Clown - S. Butcher

YEAR ISSUE		EDITION LIMIT	YEAR RETD.	ISSUE PRICE	QUOTE U.S.$
XX	I Get a Bang Out of You-12262	Open		30.00	45-55
1986	Lord Keep Me On the Ball-12270	Open		30.00	45-55
1985	Waddle I Do Without You-12459	Retrd.	1989	30.00	75-110
1986	The Lord Will Carry You Through-12467	Retrd.	1988	30.00	78-110

Precious Moments Commemorative 500th Columbus Anniversary - S. Butcher

YEAR ISSUE		EDITION LIMIT	YEAR RETD.	ISSUE PRICE	QUOTE U.S.$
1992	This Land Is Our Land-527386	Yr.Iss.		350.00	400-450

Precious Moments Commemorative Easter Seal - S. Butcher

YEAR ISSUE		EDITION LIMIT	YEAR RETD.	ISSUE PRICE	QUOTE U.S.$
1988	Jesus Loves Me-9" Fig.-104531	1,000		N/A	1800-2000
1987	He Walks With Me-107999	Yr.Iss.		25.00	35-75
1988	Blessed Are They That Overcome-115479	Yr.Iss.		27.50	40-75
1989	Make A Joyful Noise-9" Fig.-520322	1,500		N/A	900-950
1989	His Love Will Shine On You-522376	Yr.Iss.		30.00	50-65
1990	You Have Touched So Many Hearts-9" fig.-523283	2,000		N/A	675-775
1991	We Are God's Workmanship-9" fig.-523879	2,000		N/A	650-725
1990	Always In His Care-524522	Yr.Iss.		30.00	40-55
1992	You Are Such A Purr-fect Friend 9" fig.-526010	2,000		N/A	600-700
1991	Sharing A Gift Of Love-527114	Yr.Iss.		30.00	35-65
1992	A Universal Love-527173	Yr.Iss.		32.50	75
1993	Gather Your Dreams-9" fig.-529680	2,000		N/A	N/A
1993	You're My Number One Friend-530026	Yr.Iss.		30.00	40
1994	It's No Secret What God Can Do-531111	Yr.Iss.		30.00	45

YEAR ISSUE		EDITION LIMIT	YEAR RETD.	ISSUE PRICE	QUOTE U.S.$
1994	You Are The Rose of His Creation-9" fig.-531243	2,000		N/A	N/A
1995	Take Time To Smell the Flowers-524387	Yr.Iss.		30.00	30
1995	He's Got The Whole World In His Hands-9" fig.-526886	Yr.Iss.		N/A	N/A
1996	He Loves Me 9" fig. - 152277	2,000		N/A	N/A
1996	You Can Always Count on Me - 526827	Yr.Iss.		30.00	30

Precious Moments Events Figurines - S. Butcher

YEAR ISSUE		EDITION LIMIT	YEAR RETD.	ISSUE PRICE	QUOTE U.S.$
1988	You Are My Main Event-115231	Yr.Iss.		30.00	45-55
1989	Sharing Begins In The Heart-520861	Yr.Iss.		25.00	60-75
1990	I'm A Precious Moments Fan-523526	Yr.Iss.		25.00	40-50
1990	Good Friends Are Forever-525049	Yr.Iss.		25.00	N/A
1991	You Can Always Bring A Friend-527122	Yr.Iss.		27.50	45-55
1992	An Event Worth Wading For-527319	Yr.Iss.		32.50	30-45
1993	An Event For All Seasons-530158	Yr.Iss.		30.00	50
1994	Memories Are Made of This-529982	Yr.Iss.		30.00	40
1995	Follow Your Heart-528080	Yr.Iss.		30.00	30

Precious Moments Family Christmas Scene - S. Butcher

YEAR ISSUE		EDITION LIMIT	YEAR RETD.	ISSUE PRICE	QUOTE U.S.$
1985	May You Have the Sweetest Christmas-15776	Suspd.		17.00	40-50
1985	The Story of God's Love-15784	Suspd.		22.50	60-75
1985	Tell Me a Story-15792	Suspd.		10.00	25-40
1985	God Gave His Best-15806	Suspd.		13.00	30-45
1985	Silent Night-15814	Suspd.		37.50	75-120
1986	Sharing Our Christmas Together-102490	Suspd.		40.00	70-80
1989	Have A Beary Merry Christmas-522856	Suspd.		15.00	30-40
1990	Christmas Fireplace-524883	Suspd.		37.50	60-85

Precious Moments Growing In Grace - S. Butcher

YEAR ISSUE		EDITION LIMIT	YEAR RETD.	ISSUE PRICE	QUOTE U.S.$
1995	Infant Angel With Newspaper-136204	Open		22.50	23
1995	Age 1 Baby With Cake-136190	Open		25.00	25
1995	Age 2 Girl With Blocks-136212	Open		25.00	25
1995	Age 3 Girl With Flowers-136220	Open		25.00	25
1995	Age 4 Girl With Doll-136239	Open		27.50	28
1995	Age 5 Girl With Lunch Box-136247	Open		27.50	28
1995	Age 6 Girl On Bicycle-136255	Open		30.00	30
1995	Age 16 Sweet Sixteen Girl Holding Sixteen Roses-136263	Open		45.00	45

Precious Moments Musical Figurines - S. Butcher

YEAR ISSUE		EDITION LIMIT	YEAR RETD.	ISSUE PRICE	QUOTE U.S.$
1983	Sharing Our Season Together-E-0519	Retrd.	1986	70.00	117-145
1983	Wee Three Kings-E-0520	Suspd.		60.00	105-130
1983	Let Heaven And Nature Sing-E-2346	Suspd.		55.00	115-130
1982	O Come All Ye Faithful-E-2352	Suspd.		50.00	140-200
1982	I'll Play My Drum For Him-E-2355	Suspd.		45.00	175-225
1979	Christmas Is A Time To Share-E-2806	Retrd.	1984	35.00	140-170
1979	Crown Him Lord Of All-E-2807	Suspd.		35.00	93-110
1979	Unto Us A Child Is Born-E-2808	Suspd.		35.00	95-125
1980	Jesus Is Born-E-2809	Suspd.		35.00	105-135
1980	Come Let Us Adore Him-E-2810	Suspd.		45.00	108-125
1980	Peace On Earth-E-4726	Suspd.		45.00	122-132
1980	The Hand That Rocks The Future-E-5204	Open		30.00	55-85
1980	My Guardian Angel-E-5205	Suspd.		22.50	70-100
1981	My Guardian Angel-E-5206	Suspd.		22.50	80-95
1984	Wishing You A Merry Christmas-E-5394	Suspd.		55.00	80-120
1980	Silent Knight-E-5642	Suspd.		45.00	225-300
1981	Rejoice O Earth-E-5645	Retrd.	1988	35.00	80-125
1981	The Lord Bless You And Keep You-E-7180	Open		55.00	80-100
1981	Mother Sew Dear-E-7182	Open		35.00	55-95
1981	The Purr-fect Grandma-E-7184	Suspd.		35.00	70-100
1981	Love Is Sharing-E-7185	Retrd.	1985	40.00	152-189
1981	Let the Whole World Know-E-7186	Suspd.		60.00	125-190
1985	Lord Keep My Life In Tune (G) (2/set)-12165	Suspd.		50.00	120-140
1984	We Saw A Star-12408	Suspd.		50.00	65-100
1987	Lord Keep My Life In Tune (B) (2/set)-12580	Suspd.		50.00	200-300
1993	God Sent You Just In Time-15504	Retrd.	1989	60.00	90-110
1993	Silent Night-15814	Open		55.00	55-89
1985	Heaven Bless You-100285	Suspd.		45.00	70-78
1986	Our 1st Christmas Together-101702	Retrd.	1992	50.00	97-125
1993	Let's Keep In Touch-102520	Open		85.00	85-115
1993	Peace On Earth-109746	Suspd.		120.00	130
1987	I'm Sending You A White Christmas-112402	Retrd.	1993	55.00	110-135
1987	You Have Touched So Many Hearts-112577	Open		50.00	50-60
1991	Lord Keep My Life In Balance-520691	Suspd.		60.00	68-80
1993	The Light Of The World Is Jesus-521507	Open		65.00	65-87
1992	Do Not Open Till Christmas-522244	Suspd.		75.00	75-90

YEAR ISSUE		EDITION LIMIT	YEAR RETD.	ISSUE PRICE	QUOTE U.S.$
1992	This Day Has Been Made In Heaven-523682	Open		60.00	60
1993	Wishing You Were Here-526916	Open		100.00	100

Precious Moments Rejoice in the Lord - S. Butcher

YEAR ISSUE		EDITION LIMIT	YEAR RETD.	ISSUE PRICE	QUOTE U.S.$
1987	Lord Keep My Life In Tune - 12165	Suspd.		37.50	85-110
1985	There's a Song in My Heart-12173	Suspd.		11.00	30-48
1985	Happiness is the Lord-12378	Suspd.		15.00	30-40
1985	Lord Give Me a Song-12386	Suspd.		15.00	35-45
1985	He is My Song-12394	Suspd.		17.50	35-45

Precious Moments Sammy's Circus - S. Butcher

YEAR ISSUE		EDITION LIMIT	YEAR RETD.	ISSUE PRICE	QUOTE U.S.$
1994	Markie-528099	Open		18.50	19
1994	Dusty-529176	Open		22.50	23
1994	Katie-529184	Open		17.00	17
1994	Tippy-529192	Open		12.00	12
1994	Collin-529214	Open		20.00	20
1994	Sammy-529222	Yr.Iss.		20.00	45
1994	Circus Ten-528196 (Nite-Lite)	Open		90.00	90
1994	Jordan-529168	Open		20.00	20

Precious Moments Spring Catalog - S. Butcher

YEAR ISSUE		EDITION LIMIT	YEAR RETD.	ISSUE PRICE	QUOTE U.S.$
1993	Happiness Is At Our Fingertips-529931	Yr.Iss.	1993	35.00	45-85
1994	So Glad I Picked You As A Friend-524379	Yr.Iss.	1994	40.00	40
1995	Sending My Love Your Way-528609	Yr.Iss.		40.00	40

Precious Moments Sugartown - S. Butcher

YEAR ISSUE		EDITION LIMIT	YEAR RETD.	ISSUE PRICE	QUOTE U.S.$
1992	Chapel-529621	Retrd.	1994	85.00	75-175
1992	Christmas Tree-528684	Retrd.	1994	15.00	30
1992	Grandfather-529516	Retrd.	1994	15.00	15-30
1992	Nativity-529508	Retrd.	1994	20.00	20-40
1992	Philip-529494	Retrd.	1994	17.00	20-35
1992	Aunt Ruth & Aunt Dorothy-529486	Retrd.	1994	20.00	35
1992	Sam Butcher-529567 (1st sign)	Yr.Iss.		22.50	95-175
1993	7 pc. Sam's House Collector's Set-531774	Open		189.00	189
1993	Sam's House Night Light-529605	Open		80.00	85
1993	Fence-529796	Open		10.00	10
1993	Sammy-528668	Open		17.00	17
1993	Katy Lynne-529524	Open		20.00	20
1993	Sam Butcher-529842 (2nd sign)	Yr.Iss.		22.50	45-60
1993	Dusty-529435	Open		17.00	17
1993	Sam's Car-529443	Open		22.50	23
1993	Sugar Town Chapel-530484	Yr.Iss.		17.50	18
1994	Dr. Sam Sugar-530850	Open		17.00	17
1994	Doctor's Office Night Light-529869	Open		80.00	85
1994	Sam's House-530468	Yr.Iss.		17.50	18
1994	Jan-529826	Open		17.00	17
1994	Sugar & Her Dog House-533165	Open		20.00	20
1994	Stork With Baby Sam-529788	Yr.Iss.		22.50	23
1994	Free Christmas Puppies - 528064	Open		18.50	19
1994	7 pc. Doctor's Office Collectors Set-529281	Yr.Iss.		189.00	189
1994	Leon & Evelyn Mae-529818	Open		20.00	20
1994	Village Town Hall Clock-532908	Open		80.00	85
1995	Sam the Conductor -150169	Yr.Iss.		20.00	20
1995	Train Station Night Light -150150	Open		50.00	50
1995	Railroad Crossing Sign -150177	Open		12.00	12
1995	Tammy and Debbie -531812	Open		22.50	23
1995	Donny -531871	Open		22.50	23
1995	Luggage Cart With Kitten And Tag -150185	Open		13.00	13
1995	6 pc. Train Station Collector Set-750193	Yr.Iss.		190.00	190
1995	Dr. Sugar's Office-530441	Yr.Iss.		17.50	18

Precious Moments Sugartown Enhancements - S. Butcher

YEAR ISSUE		EDITION LIMIT	YEAR RETD.	ISSUE PRICE	QUOTE U.S.$
1994	Lamp Post - 529559	Open		8.00	8
1994	Mailbox - 531847	Open		5.00	5
1994	Single Tree - 533173	Open		10.00	10
1994	Cobble Stone Bridge - 533203	Open		17.00	17
1994	Straight Sidewalk - 533157	Open		10.00	10
1994	Double Tree - 533181	Open		10.00	10
1994	Curved Sidewalk - 533149	Open		10.00	10
1995	Street Sign - 532185	Open		5.00	5
1995	Dog And Kitten On Park Bench - 529540	Open		13.00	13
1995	Bus Stop - 150207	Open		8.50	9
1995	Bird Bath - 150223	Open		8.50	9
1995	Fire Hydrant - 150215	Open		5.00	5
1995	Sugartown Enhancement Pack, set/5-152269	Open		45.00	45

Precious Moments The Four Seasons - S. Butcher

YEAR ISSUE		EDITION LIMIT	YEAR RETD.	ISSUE PRICE	QUOTE U.S.$
1985	The Voice of Spring-12068	Yr.Iss.		30.00	150-250
1985	Summer's Joy-12076	Yr.Iss.		30.00	100
1986	Autumn's Praise-12084	Yr.Iss.		30.00	60-75
1986	Winter's Song-12092	Yr.Iss.		30.00	100-140
1986	Set	Yr.Iss.		120.00	550

Precious Moments Two By Two - S. Butcher

YEAR ISSUE		EDITION LIMIT	YEAR RETD.	ISSUE PRICE	QUOTE U.S.$
1993	Noah, Noah's Wife, & Noah's Ark (lighted)-530042	Open		125.00	125-195
1993	Sheep (mini double fig.) -530077	Open		10.00	10
1993	Pigs (mini double fig.) -530085	Open		12.00	12
1993	Giraffes (mini double fig.) -530115	Open		16.00	16
1993	Bunnies (mini double fig.) -530123	Open		9.00	9
1993	Elephants (mini double fig.) -530131	Open		18.00	18
1993	Eight Piece Collector's Set -530948	Open		190.00	190
1994	Llamas-531375	Open		15.00	15
1995	Congratulations You Earned Your Stripes-127809	Open		15.00	15

Fenton Art Glass Company

Collectors Club - Fenton

YEAR ISSUE		EDITION LIMIT	YEAR RETD.	ISSUE PRICE	QUOTE U.S.$
1978	Cranberry Opalescent Baskets w/variety of spot moulds	Yr.Iss.	1978	20.00	75-125
1979	Vasa Murrhina Vases (Variety of colors)	Yr.Iss.	1979	25.00	50-95
1980	Velva Rose Bubble Optic "Melon" Vases	Yr.Iss.	1980	30.00	50-95
1981	Amethyst w/White Hanging Hearts Vases	Yr.Iss.	1981	37.50	125-150
1982	Overlay Baskets in pastel shades (Swirl Optic)	Yr.Iss.	1982	40.00	60-95
1983	Cranberry Opalescent 1 pc. Fairy Lights	Yr.Iss.	1983	40.00	125-295
1984	Blue Burmese w/peloton Treatment Vases	Yr.Iss.	1984	25.00	65-125
1985	Overlay Vases in Dusty Rose w/Mica Flecks	Yr.Iss.	1985	25.00	85
1986	Ruby Iridized Art Glass Vase	Yr.Iss.	1986	30.00	50-150
1987	Dusty Rose Overlay/Peach Blow Interior w/dark blue Crest Vase	Yr.Iss.	1987	38.00	65-95
1988	Teal Green and Milk marble Basket	Yr.Iss.	1988	30.00	55-95
1989	Mulberry Opalescent Basket w/Coin Dot Optic	Yr.Iss.	1989	37.50	75-195
1990	Sea Mist Green Opalescent Fern Optic Basket	Yr.Iss.	1990	40.00	45-75
1991	Rosalene Leaf Basket and Peacock & Dahlia Basket	Yr.Iss.	1991	65.00	90
1992	Blue Bubble Optic Vases	Yr.Iss.	1992	35.00	45-75
1993	Cranberry Opalescent "Jonquil" Basket	Yr.Iss.	1993	35.00	65-95
1994	Cranberry Opalescent Jacqueline Pitcher	Yr.Iss.	1994	55.00	65-125
1994	Rosalene Tulip Vase-1994 Convention Pc.	Yr.Iss.	1994	45.00	95
1995	Fairy Light-Blue Burmese-1995 Convention Pc.	Yr.Iss.	1995	45.00	100-200

1983 Connoisseur Collection - Fenton

YEAR ISSUE		EDITION LIMIT	YEAR RETD.	ISSUE PRICE	QUOTE U.S.$
1983	Basket, 9" Vasa Murrhina	1,000	1983	75.00	110-125
1983	Craftsman Stein, White Satin Carnival	1,500	1983	35.00	50
1983	Cruet/Stopper Vasa Murrhina	1,000	1983	75.00	150-250
1983	Epergne Set, 5 pc. Burmese	500	1983	200.00	450-795
1983	Vase, 4 1/2" Sculptured Rose Quartz	2,000	1983	32.50	50-95
1983	Vase, 7" Sculptured Rose Quartz	1,500	1983	50.00	75-125
1983	Vase, 9" Sculptured Rose Quartz	850	1983	75.00	150-225

1984 Connoisseur Collection - Fenton, unless otherwise noted

YEAR ISSUE		EDITION LIMIT	YEAR RETD.	ISSUE PRICE	QUOTE U.S.$
1984	Basket, 10" Plated Amberina Velvet	1,250	1984	85.00	150-200
1984	Candy Box w/cover, 3 pc. Blue Burmese	1,250	1984	75.00	150-225
1984	Cane, 18" Plated Amberina Velvet	Yr.Iss.	1984	35.00	125
1984	Top Hat, 8" Plated Amberina Velvet	1,500	1984	65.00	135-195
1984	Vase, 9" Rose Velvet Hndpt. Floral - L. Everson	750	1984	75.00	100-175
1984	Vase, 9" Rose Velvet-Mother/Child	750	1984	125.00	150-225
1984	Vase, Swan, 8" Gold Azure	1,500	1984	65.00	150-195

1985 Connoisseur Collection - Fenton, unless otherwise noted

YEAR ISSUE		EDITION LIMIT	YEAR RETD.	ISSUE PRICE	QUOTE U.S.$
1985	Basket, 8 1/2" Buremese, Hndpt. L. Everson	1,250	1985	95.00	175-200
1985	Epergne Set, 4 pc. Diamond Lace Green Opal.	1,000	1985	95.00	125-195
1985	Lamp, 22" Burmese-Butterfly, Hndpt. - L. Everson	350	1985	300.00	575-650
1985	Punch Set, 14 pc. Green Opalescent	500	1985	250.00	375
1985	Vase, 12" Gabrielle Scul. French Opal.	800	1985	150.00	185
1985	Vase, 7 1/2" Burmese-Shell D. Barbour	950	1985	135.00	275-350
1985	Vase, 7 1/2" Chrysanthemums/ Circlet, Hndpt. - L. Everson	1,000	1985	125.00	135-195

1986 Connoisseur Collection - Fenton, unless otherwise noted

YEAR ISSUE		EDITION LIMIT	YEAR RETD.	ISSUE PRICE	QUOTE U.S.$
1986	Basket, Top hat Wild Rose/Teal Overlay	1,500	1986	49.00	60-95
1986	Boudoir Lamp, Cranberry Pearl	750	1986	145.00	200-295
1986	Cruet/Stopper, Cranberry Pearl	1,000	1986	75.00	225
1986	Handled Urn, 13" Cranberry Satin	1,000	1986	185.00	300-325
1986	Handled Vase, 7" French Royale	1,000	1986	100.00	150-195
1986	Lamp, 20" Burmese Shells Hndpt. - D. Barbour	500	1986	350.00	600-650
1986	Vanity Set, 4 pc. Blue Ridge	1,000	1986	125.00	195-295
1986	Vase 10 1/2" Danielle Sandcarved - R. Delaney	1,000	1986	95.00	100-150
1986	Vase, 10 1/2" Misty Morn, Hndpt. - L. Everson	1,000	1986	95.00	100-150

1987 Connoisseur Collection - Various

YEAR ISSUE		EDITION LIMIT	YEAR RETD.	ISSUE PRICE	QUOTE U.S.$
1987	Pitcher, 8" Enameled Azure Hndpt.- L. Everson	950	1987	85.00	100-125
1987	Vase, 7 1/4" Blossom/Bows on Cranberry Hndpt.- D. Barbour	950	1987	95.00	95-150

1988 Connoisseur Collection - Fenton, unless otherwise noted

YEAR ISSUE		EDITION LIMIT	YEAR RETD.	ISSUE PRICE	QUOTE U.S.$
1988	Basket, Irid. Teal Cased Vasa Murrhina	2,500	1988	65.00	125-150
1988	Candy, Wave Crest, CranberryHndpt. - L. Everson	2,000	1988	95.00	125-195
1988	Pitcher, Cased Cranberry/ Opal Teal Ring	3,500	1988	60.00	100-125
1988	Vase, 6" Cased Cranberry/Opal Teal/Irid.	3,500	1988	50.00	85-125

1989 Connoisseur Collection - Fenton, unless otherwise noted

YEAR ISSUE		EDITION LIMIT	YEAR RETD.	ISSUE PRICE	QUOTE U.S.$
1989	Basket, 7" Cranberry w/Crystal Ring Hndpt.- L. Everson	2,500	1989	85.00	100-150
1989	Candy Box, w/cover, Cranberry, Hndpt. - L. Everson	2,500	1989	85.00	100-195
1989	Epergne Set 5 pc., Rosalene	2,000	1989	250.00	350-495
1989	Lamp, 21" Rosalene Satin Hndpt. - L. Everson	1,000	1989	250.00	300-395
1989	Pitcher, Diamond Optic, Rosalene	2,500	1989	55.00	85
1989	Vase, Basketweave, Rosalene	2,500	1989	45.00	60-95
1989	Vase, Pinch, 8" Vasa Murrhina	2,000	1989	65.00	100

1990-85th Anniversary Collection - Various

YEAR ISSUE		EDITION LIMIT	YEAR RETD.	ISSUE PRICE	QUOTE U.S.$
1990	Basket, 5 1/2" Trees on Burmese, Hndpt. - Piper/F. Burton	Closed	1990	57.50	100
1990	Basket, 7" Raspberry on Burmese, Hndpt. - L. Everson	Closed	1990	75.00	100-150
1990	Cruet/Stopper Petite Floral on Burmese, Hndpt. - L. Everson	Closed	1990	85.00	125
1990	Epergne Set, 2 pc. Pt. Floral on Burmese, Hndpt. - L. Everson	Closed	1990	125.00	185
1990	Lamp, 20" Rose Burmese, Hndpt. - Piper/D. Barbour	Closed	1990	250.00	325-395
1990	Lamp, 21" Raspberry on Burmese, Hndpt. - L. Everson	Closed	1990	295.00	395
1990	Vase, 6 1/2" Rose Burmese, Hndpt. - Piper/D. Barbour	Closed	1990	45.00	75
1990	Vase, 9" Trees on Burmese, Hndpt. - Piper/F. Burton	Closed	1990	75.00	125-200
1990	Vase, Fan 6" Rose Burmese, Hndpt. - Piper/D. Barbour	Closed	1990	49.50	85
1990	Water Set, 7 pc. Raspberry on Burmese, Hndpt. - L. Everson	Closed	1990	275.00	400-450

1991 Connoisseur Collection - Various

YEAR ISSUE		EDITION LIMIT	YEAR RETD.	ISSUE PRICE	QUOTE U.S.$
1991	Basket, Floral on Rosalene, Hndpt. - M. Reynolds	1,500	1991	64.00	75
1991	Candy Box, 3 pc. Favrene - Fenton	1,000	1991	90.00	150-195
1991	Fish, Paperweight, Rosalene - Fenton	2,000	1991	30.00	35
1991	Lamp, 20" Roses on Burmese, Hndpt. - Piper/F. Burton	500	1991	275.00	420
1991	Vase, 7 1/2" Raspberry on Burmese, Hndpt. - L. Everson	1,500	1991	65.00	95
1991	Vase, Floral on Favrene, Hndpt. M. Reynolds	850	1991	125.00	295-395
1991	Vase, Fruit on Favrene, Hndpt. - F. Burton	850	1991	125.00	295-395

1992 Connoisseur Collection - Various

YEAR ISSUE		EDITION LIMIT	YEAR RETD.	ISSUE PRICE	QUOTE U.S.$
1992	Covered Box, Poppy/Daisy, Hndpt. - F. Burton	1,250	1992	95.00	125
1992	Pitcher, 4 1/2" Berries on Burmese, Hndpt. - M. Reynolds	1,500	1992	65.00	95-125
1992	Pitcher, 9" Empire on Cranberry, Hndpt. - M. Reynolds	950	1992	110.00	150-195
1992	Vase, 6 1/2" Raspberry on Burmese, Hndpt. - L. Everson	1,500	1992	45.00	80
1992	Vase, 8" Seascape, Hndpt. F. Burton	750	1992	150.00	150
1992	Vase, Twining Floral Rosalene Satin, Hndpt. - M. Reynolds	950	1992	110.00	150

1993 Connoisseur Collection - Various

YEAR ISSUE		EDITION LIMIT	YEAR RETD.	ISSUE PRICE	QUOTE U.S.$
1993	Amphora w/Stand, Favrene, Hndpt. - M. Reynolds	850	1993	285.00	325-395
1993	Bowl, Ruby Stretch w/Gold Scrolls, Hndpt. - M. Reynolds	1,250	1993	95.00	125
1993	Lamp, Spring Woods Reverse Hndpt. - F. Burton	500	1993	595.00	595
1993	Owl Figurine, 6" Favrene - Fenton	1,500	1993	95.00	125
1993	Perfume/Stopper, Rose Trellis Rosalene, Hndpt. - F. Burton	1,250	1993	95.00	110
1993	Vase, 9" Gold Leaves Sand-carved on Plum Irid., M. Reynolds	950	1993	175.00	225
1993	Vase, Victorian Roses Persian Blue Opal., Hndpt. - M. Reynolds	950	1993	125.00	125

1993 Family Signature Collection - Various

YEAR ISSUE		EDITION LIMIT	YEAR RETD.	ISSUE PRICE	QUOTE U.S.$
1993	Basket, 8 1/2" Lilacs - Bill Fenton	Closed	1993	65.00	75
1993	Vase, 9" Alpine Thistle/Ruby Carnival - Frank M. Fenton	Closed	1993	105.00	125
1993	Vase, 9" Cottage Scene - Shelley Fenton	Closed	1993	90.00	100

YEAR ISSUE		EDITION LIMIT	YEAR RETD.	ISSUE PRICE	QUOTE U.S.$
1993	Vase, 10" Vintage on Plum - Don Fenton	Closed	1993	80.00	90
1993	Vase, 11" Cranberry Dec. - George Fenton	Closed	1993	110.00	110

1994 Connoisseur Collection - Various

1994	Bowl, 14" Cranberry Cameo Sandcarved - Reynolds/Delaney	500	1994	390.00	390
1994	Clock, 4 1/2" Favrene, Hndpt. - F. Burton	850	1994	150.00	150
1994	Lamp, Hummingbird Reverse, Hndpt. - F. Burton	300	1994	590.00	750
1994	Pitcher, 10" Lattice on Burmese, Hndpt. - F. Burton	750	1994	165.00	225-250
1994	Vase, 7" Favrene, Hndpt. M. Reynolds	850	1994	185.00	200
1994	Vase, 8" Plum Opalescent, Hndpt. - M. Reynolds	750	1994	165.00	175
1994	Vase, 11" Gold Amberina, Hndpt. - M. Reynolds	750	1994	175.00	175

1994 Family Signature Collection - Various

1994	Basket, 7 1/2" Lilacs - Shelley Fenton	Closed	1994	65.00	65
1994	Basket, 8" Stiegel Green - Bill Fenton	Closed	1994	60.00	75
1994	Basket, 8 1/2" Ruby Carnival - Tom Fenton	Closed	1994	60.00	80
1994	Basket, 11" Autumn Gold Opal - Frank Fenton	Closed	1994	70.00	75
1994	Candy w/cover, 9 1/2" Autumn Leaves - Don Fenton	Closed	1994	60.00	60
1994	Pitcher, 6 1/2" Cranberry - Frank M. Fenton	Closed	1994	85.00	100-125
1994	Vase, 9 1/2" Pansies on Cranberry - Bill Fenton	Closed	1994	95.00	110-150
1994	Vase, 10" Fuchsia - George Fenton	Closed	1994	95.00	125

1995 Connoisseur Collection - M. Reynolds, unless otherwise noted

1995	Amphora w/stand, 10 1/4" Royal Purple, Hndpt.	890		195.00	195
1995	Ginger Jar, 3 Pc. 8 1/2" Favrene, Hndpt.	790		275.00	275
1995	Lamp, 21" Butterfly/Floral Reverse, Hndpt. - F. Burton	300		595.00	595
1995	Pitcher, 9 1/2" Victorian Art Glass, Hndpt.	490		250.00	250
1995	Vase, 7" Aurora Wild Rose, Hndpt.	890		125.00	125

1995 Family Signature Collection - Various

1995	Basket, 8 1/2" Trellis - Lynn Fenton	Closed	1995	85.00	85
1995	Basket, 9 1/2" Coralene Floral - Frank M./Bill Fenton	Closed	1995	75.00	75
1995	Candy w/cover, 9" Red Carnival Mike Fenton	Closed	1995	65.00	65
1995	Pitcher, 9 1/2" Thistle - Don Fenton	Closed	1995	125.00	125
1995	Vase, 7" Gold Pansies on Cranberry - George Fenton	Closed	1995	75.00	75
1995	Vase, 9" Summer Garden on Spruce - Don Fenton	Closed	1995	85.00	85
1995	Vase, 9 1/2" Golden Flax on Cobalt - Shelley Fenton	Closed	1995	95.00	95

American Classic Series - M. Dickinson

1986	Jupiter Train on Opal Satin, Lamp, 23"	1,000	1986	295.00	295-350
1986	Studebaker-Garford Car on Opal Satin, Lamp, 16"	1,000	1986	235.00	275

Christmas - Various

1978	Christmas Morn, Lamp, 16" M. Dickinson	Yr.Iss.	1978	125.00	150
1978	Christmas Morn, Fairy Light M. Dickinson	Yr.Iss.	1978	25.00	35
1979	Nature's Christmas, Lamp, 16" - K. Cunningham	Yr.Iss.	1979	150.00	150
1979	Nature's Christmas, Fairy Light K. Cunningham	Yr.Iss.	1979	30.00	30
1980	Going Home, Lamp, 16" D. Johnson	Yr.Iss.	1980	165.00	165
1980	Going Home, Fairy Light D. Johnson	Yr.Iss.	1980	32.50	33
1981	All Is Calm, Lamp, 16" D. Johnson	Yr.Iss.	1981	175.00	175
1981	All Is Calm, Lamp, 20" - D. Johnson	Yr.Iss.	1981	225.00	225
1981	All Is Calm, Fairy Light D. Johnson	Yr.Iss.	1981	35.00	35
1982	Country Christmas, Lamp, 16" - R. Spindler	Yr.Iss.	1982	175.00	175
1982	Country Christmas, Lamp, 21" - R. Spindler	Yr.Iss.	1982	225.00	225
1982	Country Christmas, Fairy Light - R. Spindler	Yr.Iss.	1982	35.00	35
1983	Anticipation, Fairy Light D. Johnson	7,500	1983	35.00	35
1984	Expectation, Lamp, 10 1/2" D. Johnson	7,500	1984	75.00	75
1984	Expectation, Fairy Light D. Johnson	7,500	1984	37.50	38
1985	Heart's Desire, Fairy Light D. Johnson	7,500	1986	37.50	38
1987	Sharing The Spirit, Fairy Light - L. Everson	Yr.Iss.	1987	37.50	38
1987	Cardinal in the Churchyard, Lamp, 18 1/2" - D. Johnson	500	1987	250.00	278
1987	Cardinal in the Churchyard, Fairy Light - D. Johnson	4,500	1987	29.50	45
1988	A Chickadee Ballet, Lamp, 21" D. Johnson	500	1988	274.00	275
1988	A Chickadee Ballet, Fairy Light - D. Johnson	4,500	1988	29.50	30
1989	Downy Pecker, Lamp, 16" Chisled Song - D. Johnson	500	1989	250.00	250
1989	Downy Pecker, Fairy Light Chisled Song - D. Johnson	4,500	1989	29.50	30
1990	A Blue Bird in Snowfall, Lamp, 21" - D. Johnson	500	1990	250.00	250
1990	A Blue Bird in Snowfall, Fairy Light - D. Johnson	4,500	1990	29.50	35
1990	Sleigh Ride, Lamp, 16" F. Burton	1,000	1990	250.00	250
1990	Sleigh Ride, Fairy Light F. Burton	3,500	1990	39.00	39
1991	Christmas Eve, Lamp, 16" F. Burton	1,000	1991	250.00	250
1991	Christmas Eve, Fairy Light F. Burton	3,500	1991	39.00	39
1992	Family Tradition, Lamp, 20" F. Burton	1,000	1992	250.00	250
1992	Family Tradition, Fairy Light F. Burton	3,500	1992	39.00	39
1993	Family Holiday, Lamp, 16" F. Burton	1,000	1993	265.00	265
1993	Family Holiday, Fairy Light F. Burton	3,500	1993	39.00	39
1994	Silent Night, Lamp, 16" F. Burton	500	1994	275.00	300
1994	Silent Night, Fairy Light F. Burton	1,500	1994	45.00	50
1994	Egg on Stand - F. Burton	1,500	1994	45.00	45
1995	Our Home Is Blessed, Lamp, 21" F. Burton	500		275.00	275
1995	Our Home Is Blessed, Egg F. Burton	1,500		45.00	45

Christmas Limited Edition - M. Reynolds

1992	Egg, 3 1/2" Manager Scene on Ruby	2,500	1992	30.00	30
1992	Egg, 3 1/2" Poinsettia on Crystal Irid.	2,500	1992	30.00	30
1993	Egg, 3 1/2" Angel on Green	2,500	1993	35.00	35
1993	Egg, 3 1/2" Woods on White	2,500	1993	35.00	35
1994	Egg, 3 1/2" Magnolia on Gold	1,500	1994	35.00	35
1994	Egg, 3 1/2" Partridge on Ruby	1,500	1994	35.00	35
1995	Egg, 3 1/2" Bow & Holly on Ivory	900		35.00	35
1995	Egg, 3 1/2" Chickadee on Gold	900		35.00	35
1995	Egg, 3 1/2" Iced Poinsettia on Ruby	900		39.50	40
1995	Angel, Radiant-Musical Base	900		85.00	85
1995	Pitcher, Golden Holiday Pine Cones	900		79.00	79

Collectible Eggs - M. Reynolds, unless otherwise noted

1991	Egg, Gold Design/Salem Blue Irid.	1,500	1991	29.50	30
1991	Egg, Partridge/Seamist Green Irid.	1,500	1991	29.50	30
1991	Egg, Poinsettias/Special Milk Glass	1,500	1991	29.50	30
1991	Egg, Shell/Favrene	1,500	1991	35.00	45
1991	Egg, Skater/Ruby	1,500	1991	29.50	30
1991	Egg, Snow Scene/Sp. Milk	1,500	1991	29.50	30
1991	Egg, White Scene/Black	1,500	1991	29.50	30
1992	Egg, Butterflies/Black	2,500	1992	30.00	30
1992	Egg, Croquet/Clear Carnival	2,500	1992	30.00	30
1992	Egg, Floral & Bronze/Special Milk Glass	2,500	1992	30.00	30
1992	Egg, Iris/Seamist Green	2,500	1992	30.00	30
1992	Egg, Pink Floral/Dusty Rose	2,500	1992	30.00	30
1992	Egg, Unicorn/Twilight Blue	2,500	1992	30.00	30
1993	Egg, Cottage/White Opal	2,500	1993	30.00	30
1993	Egg, Fuchsia Floral/White	2,500	1993	30.00	30
1993	Egg, Paisley/Dusty Rose	2,500	1993	30.00	30
1993	Egg, Sandcarved/Black	1,500	1993	35.00	35
1993	Egg, Scrolling Floral/Green K. Plauche	2,500	1993	30.00	30
1993	Egg, Sea Gulls/Ocean Blue	2,500	1993	30.00	30
1993	Egg, w/gold on Plum K. Plauche	2,500	1993	35.00	35
1993	Egg, w/gold on Ruby	2,500	1993	30.00	30
1994	Egg, Cascading Floral/Pink S. Jackson	2,500	1994	32.50	33
1994	Egg, Metallic Floral/Plum K. Plauche	2,500	1994	32.50	33
1994	Egg, Enameled Flowers/Blue F. Burton	2,500	1994	37.50	38
1994	Egg, Scrolls/Gold	2,500	1994	32.50	33
1994	Egg, Spring Landscape/Opal - S. Jackson	2,500	1994	32.50	33
1994	Egg, Tulips/Sea Mist S. Jackson	2,500	1994	32.50	33
1994	Egg, Violets/Milk Pearl S. Jackson	2,500	1994	32.50	33
1995	Egg, Floral/Blue	2,500		32.50	33
1995	Egg, Floral/Gold	2,500		32.50	33
1995	Egg, Floral/Green	2,500		32.50	33
1995	Egg, Floral/White	2,500		32.50	33
1995	Egg, Hummingbird/Dusty Rose	2,500		35.00	35
1995	Egg, Scene/White	2,500		32.50	33
1995	Egg, Scrolls/Black	2,500		32.50	33

Designer Series - Various

1983	Lighthouse Point, Lamp, 23 1/2", M. Dickinson	150	1983	350.00	400
1983	Lighthouse Point, Lamp, 25 1/2", M. Dickinson	150	1983	350.00	400
1983	Down Home, Lamp, 21" - G. Finn	300	1983	300.00	325
1984	Smoke 'N Cinders, Lamp, 16" M. Dickinson	250	1984	195.00	225
1984	Smoke 'N Cinders, Lamp, 23" M. Dickinson	250	1984	350.00	350
1984	Majestic Flight, Lamp, 16" B. Cumberledge	250	1984	195.00	195
1984	Majestic Flight, Lamp, 23 1/2" B. Cumberledge	250	1984	350.00	350
1985	In Season, Lamp, 16" M. Dickinson	250	1985	225.00	250
1985	In Season, Lamp, 23" M. Dickinson	250	1985	295.00	295
1985	Nature's Grace, Lamp, 16" B. Cumberland	250	1985	225.00	225
1985	Nature's Grace, Lamp, 23" B. Cumberland	295	1985	295	225

Easter Series - M. Reynolds

1995	Fairy Light	Closed	1995	49.00	49

Mary Gregory - M. Reynolds

1994	Basket, 7 1/2" Oval	Closed	1994	59.00	59
1995	Basket, 7 1/2" Oval	Closed	1995	65.00	65
1995	Egg on stand, 4" - Butterfly Delight	Closed	1995	37.50	38

Mouthblown Eggs - Various

1991	Egg, 3 1/2" Mother of Pearl - M. Reynolds	Closed	1991	49.00	49
1991	Egg, 4 1/2" Mother of Pearl - M. Reynolds	Closed	1991	59.00	59
1992	Egg, 5" Petal Pink Iridized - F. Burton	Closed	1992	65.00	65
1992	Egg, 5" Seamist Green Iridized - F. Burton	Closed	1992	65.00	65
1993	Egg, 5" Ocean Blue - M. Reynolds	Closed	1993	69.00	69
1993	Egg, 5" Plum - M. Reynolds	Closed	1993	69.00	69
1994	Egg, 5" Blue - F. Burton	Closed	1994	75.00	75
1994	Egg, 5" Rose - M. Reynolds	Closed	1994	75.00	75
1995	Egg, 5" Gold - M. Reynolds	Closed	1995	75.00	75
1995	Egg, 5" Spruce - M. Reynolds	Closed	1995	75.00	75

Valentine's Day Series - Fenton, unless otherwise noted

1992	Basket, 6" Cranberry Opal/Heart Optic	Closed	1992	50.00	60
1992	Vase, 4" Cranberry Opal/Heart Optic	Closed	1992	35.00	40
1992	Perfume, w/oval stopper Cranberry Opal/Heart Optic	Closed	1992	60.00	95
1993	Basket, 7" Caprice Cranberry Opal/Heart Optic	Closed	1993	59.00	59
1993	Trinket Box, 5" Cranberry Opal/Heart Optic	Closed	1993	79.00	79
1993	Vase, 5 1/2" Melon Cranberry Opal/Heart Optic	Closed	1993	45.00	45
1993	Southern Girl, 8", Hndpt. Opal Satin - M. Reynolds	Closed	1993	49.00	49
1993	Southern Girl, 8", Rose Pearl Irid.	Closed	1993	45.00	45
1994	Basket, 7" Cranberry Opal/Heart Optic	Closed	1994	65.00	65
1994	Vase, 5 1/2" Ribbed Cranberry Opal/Heart Optic	Closed	1994	47.50	48
1994	Perfume, w/ stopper, 5" Cranberry Opal/Heart Optic	Closed	1994	75.00	75
1995	Basket, 8" Melon Cranberry Opal/Heart Optic	Closed	1995	69.00	69
1995	Pitcher, 5 1/2" Melon Cranberry Opal/Heart Optic	Closed	1995	69.00	69
1995	Perfume, w/ heart stopper, Kristen's Floral Hndpt. - M. Reynolds	2,500	1995	49.00	49
1995	Doll, 7", Kristen's Floral Hndpt. Ivory Satin - M. Reynolds	2,500	1995	49.00	49

Fitz And Floyd, Inc.

Holiday Hamlet ®-Accessories - V. Balcou

1993	Blizzard Express Train	Open		95.00	95
1993	Carols in the Snow	Open		30.00	30
1993	Christmas Tree, large	Open		45.00	45
1993	Christmas Tree, small	Open		30.00	30
1994	Hand Car	Open		35.00	35
1993	Silent Night Singers	Open		30.00	30
1993	Village Sign	Open		40.00	40
1993	Village Square Clock	Open		50.00	50

Holiday Hamlet ®-Figurines - V. Balcou

1993	Baby Squirrel	Open		15.00	15
1993	Bell Choir Bunny	Open		15.00	15
1993	Bell Choir Fox	Open		10.00	10
1994	Blessed Mother/Joseph Players	Open		25.00	25
1993	Christmas Carolers	Open		20.00	20
1993	Christmas Carolers, waterglobe	Open		45.00	45
1993	Christmas Treats	Open		15.00	15
1993	The Conductor	Open		10.00	10
1993	Delivering Gifts	Open		20.00	20
1993	Dollmaker	Open		15.00	15
1993	Dollmaker's Apprentice	Open		15.00	15
1993	Dr. B. Well	Open		15.00	15
1993	Dr. Quack & Patient	Open		15.00	15
1993	Gathering Apples	Open		15.00	15
1993	Gathering Pine Boughs	Open		10.00	10
1994	Holiday Hamlet, waterglobe	Open		75.00	75
1994	Little Angels	Open		30.00	30
1993	Mr. Grizzly	Open		20.00	20
1994	Mr. Winterberry, Pie Vendor	2,500	1995	25.00	25

YEAR ISSUE		EDITION LIMIT	YEAR RETD.	ISSUE PRICE	QUOTE U.S.$
1993	Mrs. Grizzly	Open		20.00	20
1993	Nanny Rabbit & Bunnies	Open		20.00	20
1993	Old Royal Elf	Open		20.00	20
1993	The Parson	Open		10.00	10
1993	Pastry Vendor	Open		10.00	10
1994	Poor Shepherds	Open		15.00	15
1994	The Porter	Open		25.00	25
1994	Proud Mother/Father	Open		20.00	20
1993	Santa Claus	Open		25.00	25
1993	Skaters	Open		20.00	20
1993	Squirrel Family	Open		15.00	15
1994	Three Wisemen	Open		20.00	20
1993	Tying the Christmas Garland	Open		20.00	20
1993	Waving Elf	Open		10.00	10
1993	Welcome Banner	Open		20.00	20
1993	Welcoming Elf	Open		10.00	10

Holiday Hamlet ®-Lighted Houses - V. Balcou

YEAR ISSUE		EDITION LIMIT	YEAR RETD.	ISSUE PRICE	QUOTE U.S.$
1994	Christmas Pageant Stage	Open		75.00	75
1993	Doctor's Office	Open		75.00	75
1993	Dollmaker's Cottage	Open		125.00	125
1993	Holiday Hamlet Chapel	Open		75.00	150
1993	Holiday Manor	Open		75.00	75
1994	Mr. Winterberry's Pie Shop	2,500	1995	100.00	350
1993	Railroad Station	Closed	N/A	125.00	350
1994	Snowman Supply Hut	Open		65.00	65
1993	Stocking Stuffer's Workshop	Open		45.00	45
1993	Tavern in the Woods	Closed	1995	125.00	350
1993	Toymaker's Workshop	Open		45.00	45
1994	Whistlestop Junction Train Stop	Open		65.00	65
1994	World's Best Snowman	Open		55.00	55

Flambro Imports

Emmett Kelly Jr. Members Only Figurine - Undis.

YEAR ISSUE		EDITION LIMIT	YEAR RETD.	ISSUE PRICE	QUOTE U.S.$
1990	Merry-Go-Round	Closed	1990	125.00	400-500
1991	10 Years Of Collecting	Closed	1991	100.00	180
1992	All Aboard	Closed	1992	75.00	175
1993	Ringmaster	Closed	1993	125.00	125
1994	Birthday Mail	Closed	1994	100.00	175
1995	Salute To Our Vets	Closed	1995	75.00	75

EKJ Professionals - Undis.

YEAR ISSUE		EDITION LIMIT	YEAR RETD.	ISSUE PRICE	QUOTE U.S.$
1987	Accountant	Retrd.	1994	50.00	100
1991	Barber	Retrd.	1995	50.00	100
1988	Bowler	Retrd.	1994	50.00	100
1991	Carpenter	Open		50.00	50
1991	The Chef	Retrd.	1994	50.00	50
1995	Coach	Open		55.00	55
1990	Computer Whiz	Open		50.00	50
1987	Dentist	Retrd.	1995	50.00	100
1995	Doctor	Open		55.00	55
1987	Doctor	Retrd.	1995	50.00	100
1987	Engineer	Retrd.	1995	50.00	100
1987	Executive	Open		50.00	50
1995	Fireman	Open		55.00	55
1988	Fireman	Retrd.	1994	50.00	100
1990	Fisherman	Open		50.00	50
1995	Golfer	Open		55.00	55
1988	Golfer	Open		50.00	50
1990	Hunter	Open		50.00	50
1995	Lawyer	Open		55.00	55
1987	Lawyer	Retrd.	1995	50.00	100
1988	Mailman	Retrd.	1995	50.00	100
1993	On Maneuvers	Open		50.00	50
1991	Painter	Open		50.00	50
1991	Pharmacist	Open		50.00	50
1990	Photographer	Open		50.00	50
1993	Pilot	Open		50.00	50
1991	Plumber	Retrd.	1994	50.00	100
1995	Policeman	Open		55.00	55
1988	Policeman	Retrd.	1994	50.00	75-100
1990	The Putt	Open		50.00	50
1993	Realtor	Open		50.00	50
1988	Skier	Retrd.	1995	50.00	100
1987	Stockbrocker	Open		50.00	50
1987	Teacher	Retrd.	1995	50.00	100
1993	Veterinarian	Open		50.00	50

Emmett Kelly Jr. - Undis., unless otherwise noted

YEAR ISSUE		EDITION LIMIT	YEAR RETD.	ISSUE PRICE	QUOTE U.S.$
1995	20th Anniversary of All Star Circus	5,000	1995	240.00	250
1995	35 Years of Clowning	5,000	1995	240.00	250
1989	65th Birthday Commemorative	1,989	1989	275.00	1000-2700
1993	After The Parade	7,500		190.00	190
1988	Amen	12,000	1991	120.00	300-400
1991	Artist At Work	7,500		295.00	295
1992	Autumn - D. Rust	Open		60.00	60
1983	The Balancing Act	10,000	1985	75.00	775-1000
1983	Balloons For Sale	10,000	1985	75.00	600-700
1990	Balloons for Sale II	7,500		250.00	250-300
1986	Bedtime	12,000	1991	98.00	325
1984	Big Business	9,500	1987	110.00	900
1990	Convention-Bound	7,500		225.00	230
1986	Cotton Candy	12,000	1987	98.00	375
1988	Dining Out	12,000	1991	120.00	375
1984	Eating Cabbage	12,000	1986	75.00	475
1985	Emmett's Fan	12,000	1986	80.00	475
1986	The Entertainers	12,000	1991	120.00	150-200
1986	Fair Game	2,500	1987	450.00	1650
1991	Finishing Touch	7,500		245.00	245
1991	Follow The Leader	7,500		200.00	200
1994	Forest Friends	7,500		190.00	190
1983	Hole In The Sole	10,000	1986	75.00	300-700
1989	Hurdy-Gurdy Man	9,500	1991	150.00	175-250
1985	In The Spotlight	12,000	1989	103.00	400
1993	Kittens For Sale	7,500		190.00	190
1994	Let Him Eat Cake	3,500	1995	300.00	500-600
1994	The Lion Tamer	7,500		190.00	190
1981	Looking Out To See	12,000	1982	75.00	2200-2500
1986	Making New Friends	9,500	1988	140.00	350
1989	Making Up	7,500	1995	200.00	350
1985	Man's Best Friend	9,500	1989	98.00	550
1990	Misfortune?	3,500	1989	200.00	450
1987	My Favorite Things	9,500	1988	109.00	350-700
1989	No Loitering	7,500	1994	200.00	300
1985	No Strings Attached	9,500	1991	98.00	220-375
1992	No Use Crying	7,500		200.00	200
1987	On The Road Again	9,500	1991	109.00	400
1988	Over a Barrel	9,500	1991	130.00	375
1992	Peanut Butter?	7,500		200.00	200
1984	Piano Player	9,500	1988	160.00	550-650
1992	Ready-Set-Go	7,500		200.00	200
1987	Saturday Night	7,500	1988	153.00	450-625
1983	Spirit of Christmas I	3,500	1984	125.00	2000-3200
1984	Spirit of ChristmasII	3,500	1985	270.00	320-700
1985	Spirit of Christmas III	3,500	1989	220.00	240-700
1986	Spirit of Christmas IV	3,500	1989	150.00	300-400
1987	Spirit of Christmas V	2,400	1989	170.00	300-550
1988	Spirit of Christmas VI	2,400	1989	194.00	400-600
1990	Spirit of Christmas VII	3,500	1990	275.00	425
1991	Spirit of Christmas VIII	3,500	1992	250.00	350
1993	Spirit of Christmas IX	3,500		200.00	200
1993	Spirit of Christmas X	3,500		200.00	200
1994	Spirit of Christmas XI	3,500	1995	200.00	225-250
1995	Spirit of Christmas XII	3,500		200.00	200
1992	Spring - D. Rust	Open		60.00	60
1992	Summer - D. Rust	Open		60.00	60
1981	Sweeping Up	12,000	1982	75.00	1000-1800
1982	The Thinker	15,000	1986	60.00	1100
1987	Toothache	12,000	1995	98.00	195
1990	Watch the Birdie	9,500		200.00	225
1982	Wet Paint	15,000	1983	80.00	800
1988	Wheeler Dealer	7,500	1990	160.00	250
1982	Why Me?	15,000	1984	65.00	425-600
1992	Winter - D. Rust	Open		60.00	60
1983	Wishful Thinking	10,000	1985	65.00	500-700
1993	World Traveler	7,500		190.00	190

Emmett Kelly Jr. A Day At The Fair - Undis.

YEAR ISSUE		EDITION LIMIT	YEAR RETD.	ISSUE PRICE	QUOTE U.S.$
1990	75 Please	Retrd.	1994	65.00	85-125
1991	Coin Toss	Retrd.	1994	65.00	85-125
1990	Look At You	Retrd.	1994	65.00	85-125
1991	Popcorn!	Retrd.	1994	65.00	85-125
1990	Ride The Wild Mouse	Retrd.	1994	65.00	85-125
1990	Step Right Up	Retrd.	1994	65.00	85-125
1992	Stilt Man	Retrd.	1994	65.00	85-125
1990	The Stilt Man	Retrd.	1994	65.00	85-125
1990	Thanks Emmett	Retrd.	1994	65.00	85-125
1990	Three For A Dime	Retrd.	1994	65.00	85-125
1991	The Trouble With Hot Dogs	Retrd.	1994	65.00	85-125
1990	You Can Do It, Emmett	Retrd.	1994	65.00	85-125
1990	You Go First, Emmett	Retrd.	1994	65.00	85-125

Emmett Kelly Jr. Appearance Figurine - Undis.

YEAR ISSUE		EDITION LIMIT	YEAR RETD.	ISSUE PRICE	QUOTE U.S.$
1992	Now Appearing	Open		100.00	100
1993	The Vigilante	Open		75.00	75

Emmett Kelly Jr. Miniatures - Undis.

YEAR ISSUE		EDITION LIMIT	YEAR RETD.	ISSUE PRICE	QUOTE U.S.$
1994	65th Birthday	Retrd.	1994	70.00	75-95
1986	Balancing Act	Retrd.	1992	25.00	125
1986	Balloons for Sale	Retrd.	1993	25.00	105
1995	Bedtime	Open		35.00	35
1988	Big Business	Retrd.	1995	35.00	70
1989	Cotton Candy	Retrd.	1991	30.00	75
1995	Dining Out	Open		35.00	35
1987	Eating Cabbage	Retrd.	1990	30.00	100
1987	Emmett's Fan	Retrd.	1994	30.00	85
1995	The Entertainers	Open		45.00	45
1994	Fair Game	Open		75.00	75
1986	Hole in the Sole	Retrd.	1989	25.00	75-125
1995	Hurdy Gurdy Man	Open		40.00	40
1991	In The Spotlight	Numbrd		35.00	85-125
1986	Looking Out To See	Retrd.	1987	25.00	60-175
1992	Making New Friends	Numbrd		40.00	40
1989	Man's Best Friend?	Retrd.	1994	35.00	65
1990	My Favorite Things	Retrd.	1995	45.00	90
1995	No Loitering	Open		50.00	50
1991	No Strings Attached	Numbrd		35.00	35
1992	On the Road Again	Numbrd		35.00	35
1994	Over a Barrel	Open		30.00	30
1992	Piano Player	Numbrd		50.00	50
1990	Saturday Night	Retrd.	1995	50.00	50
1988	Spirit of Christmas I	Retrd.	1990	40.00	130
1992	Spirit of Christmas II	Retrd.	1995	50.00	50
1990	Spirit Of Christmas III	Retrd.	1993	50.00	90
1993	Spirit of Christmas IV	Numbrd		40.00	40
1994	Spirit of Christmas V	Open		50.00	50
1986	Sweeping Up	Retrd.	1987	25.00	125-175
1986	The Thinker	Retrd.	1991	25.00	135
1986	Wet Paint	Retrd.	1993	25.00	125
1986	Why Me?	Retrd.	1989	25.00	110
1986	Wishful Thinking	Retrd.	1988	25.00	90

Emmett Kelly Jr. Real Rags Collection - Undis.

YEAR ISSUE		EDITION LIMIT	YEAR RETD.	ISSUE PRICE	QUOTE U.S.$
1995	Balloons For Sale 2	Open		120.00	120
1993	Big Business II	Open		140.00	140
1993	Checking His List	Closed	N/A	100.00	115
1994	Eating Cabbage 2	3,000		100.00	100
1994	A Good Likeness	3,000		120.00	120
1995	I've Got Rhythm	Open		140.00	140
1993	Looking Out To See II	Open		100.00	100
1995	No Strings Attached 2	Open		120.00	120
1994	On in Two	3,000		100.00	100
1994	Rudolph Has A Red Nose, Too	3,000		135.00	135
1993	Sweeping Up II	Open		100.00	100
1993	Thinker II	Open		120.00	120
1995	Watch Out Below	Open		120.00	120

Little Emmetts - M. Wu

YEAR ISSUE		EDITION LIMIT	YEAR RETD.	ISSUE PRICE	QUOTE U.S.$
1994	Birthday Haul	Open		30.00	30
1995	Dance Lessons	Open		50.00	50
1994	Little Artist Picture Frame	Open		22.00	22
1994	Little Emmett Fishing	Open		35.00	35
1995	Little Emmett Noel, Noel	Open		40.00	40
1994	Little Emmett Shadow Show	Open		40.00	40
1995	Little Emmett Someday	Open		50.00	50
1994	Little Emmett w/Blackboard	Open		30.00	30
1994	Little Emmett, Counting Lession (Musical)	Open		30.00	30
1994	Little Emmett, Country Road (Musical)	Open		35.00	35
1994	Little Emmett, Raindrops (Musical)	Open		35.00	35
1994	Little Emmett, You've Got a Friend (Musical)	Open		33.00	33
1995	Looking Back Musical Waterglobe	Open		75.00	75
1995	Looking Forward Musical Waterglobe	Open		75.00	75
1994	Playful Bookends	Open		40.00	40
1994	EKJ, Age 1	Open		9.00	9
1994	EKJ, Age2	Open		9.50	10
1994	EKJ, Age 3	Open		12.00	12
1994	EKJ, Age 4	Open		12.00	12
1994	EKJ, Age 5	Open		15.00	15
1994	EKJ, Age 6	Open		15.00	15
1994	EKJ, Age 7	Open		17.00	17
1994	EKJ, Age 8	Open		21.00	21
1994	EKJ, Age 9	Open		22.00	22
1994	EKJ, Age 10	Open		25.00	25

Pleasantville 1893 - J. Berg Victor

YEAR ISSUE		EDITION LIMIT	YEAR RETD.	ISSUE PRICE	QUOTE U.S.$
1990	1st Church Of Pleasantville	Retrd.	1994	35.00	35
1992	Apothecary/Ice Cream Shop	Open		36.00	36
1992	Ashbey House	Open		40.00	40
1993	Balcomb's Barn	Open		40.00	40
1993	Balcomb's Farm (out buildings)	Open		40.00	40
1993	Balcomb's Farmhouse	Open		40.00	40
1990	The Band Stand	Retrd.	1992	12.00	15
1992	Bank/Real Estate Office	Retrd.	1995	36.00	36
1993	Blacksmith Shop	Open		40.00	40
1991	Court House	Open		36.00	36
1992	Covered Bridge	Retrd.	1995	36.00	36
1990	Department Store	Retrd.	1993	25.00	29
1991	Fire House	Open		40.00	40
1994	Gazebo/Bandstand	Open		25.00	25
1990	The Gerber House	Retrd.	1993	30.00	30
1992	Library	Open		32.00	32
1993	Livery Stable and Residence	Open		40.00	40
1990	Mason's Hotel and Saloon	Open		35.00	35
1991	Methodist Church	Open		40.00	40
1992	Miss Fountains Boarding House	Open		48.00	48
1990	Pleasantville Library	Open		32.00	32
1992	Post Office	Retrd.	1995	40.00	40
1992	Railroad Station	Open		40.00	40
1990	Reverend Littlefield's House	Open		34.00	34
1994	Sacred Heart Catholic Church	Open		40.00	40
1994	Sacred Heart Rectory	Open		40.00	40
1991	School Houe	Open		36.00	36
1990	Sweet Shoppe & Bakery	Open		40.00	40
1990	Toy Store	Retrd.	1992	30.00	45
1992	Tubbs, Jr. House	Open		40.00	40

Pleasantville 1893 Members Only - J. Berg Victor

YEAR ISSUE		EDITION LIMIT	YEAR RETD.	ISSUE PRICE	QUOTE U.S.$
1992	Pleasantville Gazette Building	Open		30.00	30

Pocket Dragon Collector Club - R. Musgrave

YEAR ISSUE		EDITION LIMIT	YEAR RETD.	ISSUE PRICE	QUOTE U.S.$
1991	Collecting Butterflies	Retrd.	1992	Gift	105
1992	The Key to My Heart	Retrd.	1993	Gift	95-120
1993	Want A Bite?	Retrd.	1994	Gift	55-65
1993	Bitsy	Retrd.	1994	Gift	N/A
1994	Friendship Pin	Open		Gift	N/A
1994	Blue Ribbon Dragon	Retrd.	1995	Gift	75
1995	Making Time For You	5/96		Gift	N/A

Pocket Dragon Members Only Pieces - R. Musgrave

YEAR ISSUE		EDITION LIMIT	YEAR RETD.	ISSUE PRICE	QUOTE U.S.$
1991	A Spot of Tea Won't You Join Us (set)	Retrd.	1992	75.00	265
1991	Wizard's House Print	Retrd.	1993	39.95	65-100
1992	Book Nook	Retrd.	1993	140.00	200
1993	Pen Pals	Retrd.	1994	90.00	135-150
1994	The Best Seat in the House	Retrd.	1995	75.00	150
1995	Party Time	5/96		75.00	75

Pocket Dragon Appearance Figurines - R. Musgrave

YEAR ISSUE		EDITION LIMIT	YEAR RETD.	ISSUE PRICE	QUOTE U.S.$
1993	A Big Hug	Retrd.	1994	35.00	50
1994	Packed and Ready	Retrd.	1995	47.00	47
1994	Attention to Detail	Open		24.00	24

Pocket Dragon Christmas Editions - R. Musgrave

YEAR ISSUE		EDITION LIMIT	YEAR RETD.	ISSUE PRICE	QUOTE U.S.$
1992	A Pocket-Sized Tree	Retrd.	1992	18.95	95
1993	Christmas Angel	Retrd.	1993	45.00	65-90
1991	I've Been Very Good	Retrd.	1991	37.50	60-90
1989	Putting Me on the Tree	Retrd.	1994	52.50	85
1994	Dear Santa	Retrd.	1995	50.00	55-65
1995	Chasing Snowflakes	12/95		35.00	35

Pocket Dragons - R. Musgrave

YEAR ISSUE		EDITION LIMIT	YEAR RETD.	ISSUE PRICE	QUOTE U.S.$
1990	The Apprentice	Retrd.	1994	22.50	45
1989	Attack	Retrd.	1992	45.00	65-90
1989	Baby Brother	Retrd.	1992	19.50	55
1993	Bath Time	Open		90.00	90
1993	The Book End	Open		90.00	90
1994	A Book My Size	Open		30.00	30
1992	Bubbles	Open		55.00	55
1995	But I am Too Little!	Open		14.50	15
1994	Butterfly Kissess	Open		29.50	30
1994	Candy Cane	Open		55.00	55
1995	Classical Dragon	Open		80.00	80
1994	Coffee Please	Open		24.00	24
1994	Dance Partner	Open		23.00	23
1992	A Different Drummer	Retrd.	1994	32.50	45-75
1989	Do I Have To?	Open		45.00	45
1991	Dragons in the Attic	Open		120.00	120
1989	Drowsy Dragon	Open		27.50	28
1995	Elementary My Dear	Open		35.00	35
1989	Flowers For You	Retrd.	1992	42.50	65-95
1991	Friends	Open		55.00	55
1993	Fuzzy Ears	Open		16.50	17
1989	The Gallant Defender	Retrd.	1992	36.50	80-95
1989	Gargoyle Hoping For Raspberry Teacakes	Retrd.	1990	139.50	485
1994	Gargoyles Just Wanna Have Fun	Open		30.00	30
1989	A Good Egg	Retrd.	1991	36.50	150-165
1995	Hedgehog's Joke	Open		27.00	27
1993	I Ate the Whole Thing	Open		32.50	33
1991	I Didn't Mean To	Open		32.50	33
1991	I'm A Kitty	Retrd.	1993	37.50	55
1994	In Trouble Again	Open		35.00	35
1995	It's a Present	Open		21.00	21
1994	It's Dark Out There	Open		45.00	45
1994	It's Magic	Open		31.00	31
1991	A Joyful Noise	Open		16.50	17
1992	The Juggler	Open		32.50	33
1993	Let's Make Cookies	Open		90.00	90
1992	The Library Cat	Retrd.	1994	38.50	55-85
1993	Little Bit (lapel pin)	Open		16.50	17
1993	Little Jewel (brooch)	Retrd.	1994	19.50	30
1994	A Little Security	Open		20.00	20
1989	Look at Me	Retrd.	1990	42.50	185
1992	Mitten Toes	Open		16.50	17
1994	My Big Cookie	Open		35.00	35
1992	Nap Time	Open		15.00	15
1989	New Bunny Shoes	Retrd.	1992	28.50	75
1989	No Ugly Monsters Allowed	Retrd.	1992	47.50	80
1993	Oh Goody!	Open		16.50	17
1990	One-Size-Fits-All	Retrd.	1993	16.50	35
1992	Oops!	Open		16.50	17
1989	Opera Gargoyle	Retrd.	1991	85.00	195
1992	Percy	Retrd.	1994	70.00	85-125
1991	Pick Me Up	Open		16.50	17
1989	Pink 'n' Pretty	Retrd.	1992	23.90	55
1994	Playing Dress Up	Open		30.00	30
1991	Playing Footsie	Retrd.	1994	16.50	25-30
1989	Pocket Dragon Countersign	Retrd.	1991	50.00	195
1989	The Pocket Minstrel	Retrd.	1991	36.50	125-150
1992	Pocket Posey	Open		16.50	17
1993	Pocket Rider (brooch)	Open		19.50	20
1991	Practice Makes Perfect	Retrd.	1993	32.50	55
1991	Putt Putt	Retrd.	1993	37.50	55-100
1994	Raiding the Cookie Jar	3,500		200.00	200
1993	Reading the Good Parts	Open		70.00	70
1991	Scales of Injustice	Open		45.00	45
1989	Scribbles	Retrd.	1994	32.50	45
1989	Sea Dragon	Retrd.	1991	45.00	125-165
1995	Sees All, Knows All	Open		35.00	35
1989	Sir Nigel Smythebe-Smoke	Retrd.	1993	120.00	145-225
1991	Sleepy Head	Open		37.50	38
1994	Snuggles	Open		35.00	35
1989	Stalking the Cookie Jar	Open		27.50	28
1989	Storytime at Wizard's House	Retrd.	1993	375.00	450-495
1990	Tag-A-Long	Retrd.	1993	15.00	35-40
1989	Teddy Magic	Retrd.	1991	85.00	125-145
1995	Telling Secrets	Open		48.00	48
1991	Thimble Foot	Retrd.	1994	38.50	50-85
1991	Tickle	Open		27.50	28
1989	Toady Goldtrayler	Retrd.	1993	55.00	90-110
1993	Treasure	Open		90.00	90
1995	Tumbly	Open		21.00	21
1991	Twinkle Toes	Open		16.50	17
1992	Under the Bed	2,500		450.00	475
1989	Walkies	Retrd.	1992	65.00	135-165
1995	Watson	Open		22.50	23
1993	We're Very Brave	Open		37.50	38
1989	What Cookie?	Open		38.50	39
1989	Wizardry for Fun and Profit	Retrd.	1992	375.00	500
1993	You Can't Make Me	Open		15.00	15
1989	Your Paint is Stirred	Retrd.	1991	42.50	115
1992	Zoom Zoom	Open		37.50	38

Forma Vitrum

Coastal Classics - B. Job

YEAR ISSUE		EDITION LIMIT	YEAR RETD.	ISSUE PRICE	QUOTE U.S.$
1995	Bayside Beacon Lighthouse 21013	Open		65.00	65
1993	Carolina Lighthouse 21003	Open		65.00	65
1994	Lookout Point Lighthouse 21012	Open		60.00	60
1993	Maine Lighthouse 21002	Open		50.00	50
1993	Michigan Lighthouse 21001	Open		50.00	50
1994	Patriot's Point 29010	Open		70.00	70
1994	Sailor's Knoll Lighthouse 21011	Open		65.00	65

Coastal Heritage - B. Job

YEAR ISSUE		EDITION LIMIT	YEAR RETD.	ISSUE PRICE	QUOTE U.S.$
1995	Cape Neddick (ME) 25002	1,995	1995	140.00	140
1995	Marble Head (OH) 25201	1,995	1995	75.00	75
1995	North Head (WA) 25302	1,995	1995	100.00	100
1995	Old Point Loma (CA) 25301	1,995	1995	100.00	100
1995	Portland Head (ME) 25003	1,995	1995	140.00	140
1995	Sandy Hook (NJ) 25001	3,759	1995	140.00	140
1995	St. Simons (GA) 25101	1,995	1995	120.00	120

Special Production - B. Job

YEAR ISSUE		EDITION LIMIT	YEAR RETD.	ISSUE PRICE	QUOTE U.S.$
1993	The Bavarian Church 11503	Retrd.	1994	90.00	125
1994	Gingerbread House 19111	1,020	1994	100.00	100
1995	Miller's Mill (Musical) 11304	Open		115.00	115
1993	Pillars of Faith Church 11504	Retrd.	1994	90.00	125

Vitreville™ - B. Job

YEAR ISSUE		EDITION LIMIT	YEAR RETD.	ISSUE PRICE	QUOTE U.S.$
1994	"Trinity Church" 11511	7,000		130.00	130
1994	"Vitreville" Post Office 11402	Open		90.00	90
1993	Breadman's Bakery 11301	Open		70.00	70
1994	Brookview Bed & Breakfast 11303	1,250	1994	295.00	350
1993	Candlemaker's Delight 11801	Open		60.00	60
1993	Candymaker's Cottage 11102	Open		65.00	65
1994	Community Church 19510	Open		95.00	95
1993	Country Church 11502	12,500	1994	100.00	100
1993	Doctor's Domain 11201	Open		70.00	70
1995	Fire Station 11403	Open		100.00	100
1995	Major's Manor 11205	Open		85.00	85
1994	Maplewood Elementary School 11401	Open		100.00	100
1993	Painter's Place 11202	Open		70.00	70
1993	Pastor's Place 11101	Open		65.00	65
1993	Roofer's Roost 11203	Retrd.	1994	70.00	70
1993	Tailor's Townhouse 11204	Retrd.	1994	70.00	70
1994	Thompson's Drug 11302	5,000	1994	140.00	200
1993	Tiny Town Church 11501	Open		95.00	95

Woodland Village™ - B. Job

YEAR ISSUE		EDITION LIMIT	YEAR RETD.	ISSUE PRICE	QUOTE U.S.$
1993	Badger House 31003	Open		80.00	80
1993	Chipmunk House 31005	Open		80.00	80
1993	Owl House 31004	Open		80.00	80
1993	Rabbit House 31001	Open		90.00	90
1993	Racoon House 31002	Open		80.00	80

Franklin Mint

Joys of Childhood - N. Rockwell

YEAR ISSUE		EDITION LIMIT	YEAR RETD.	ISSUE PRICE	QUOTE U.S.$
1976	Coasting Along	3,700		120.00	175
1976	Dressing Up	3,700		120.00	175
1976	The Fishing Hole	3,700		120.00	175
1976	Hopscotch	3,700		120.00	175
1976	The Marble Champ	3,700		120.00	175
1976	The Nurse	3,700		120.00	175
1976	Ride 'Em Cowboy	3,700		120.00	175
1976	The Stilt Walker	3,700		120.00	175
1976	Time Out	3,700		120.00	175
1976	Trick or Treat	3,700		120.00	175

Fraser International

Collectors' Society - I. Fraser

YEAR ISSUE		EDITION LIMIT	YEAR RETD.	ISSUE PRICE	QUOTE U.S.$
1993	Peace Haven	Retrd.	1993	39.95	40
1993	Granny Smith's Cottage	Retrd.	1994	25.00	25
1993	St. Stephen's Church	Retrd.	1994	59.50	60
1994	Granny Mac Gregor's Cottage	7/95		29.95	30
1994	Summer Retreat	Yr.Iss.		34.75	35

The British Heritage Collection - I. Fraser

YEAR ISSUE		EDITION LIMIT	YEAR RETD.	ISSUE PRICE	QUOTE U.S.$
1988	Anne Hathaway's Cottage 32 mold #1	Retrd.	N/A	53.00	53
1994	Anne Hathaway's Cottage 32 mold #2	Open		53.00	65
1991	Balmoral Castle 128	Open		115.00	135
1992	Big Ben 154	Open		57.50	70
1991	Buckingham Palace 132	Open		159.50	185
1991	Caernarfon Castle 125	Open		85.00	100
1992	Canterbury Cathedral 153	Open		149.50	175
1991	Cardiff Castle Keep 152	Open		49.50	60
1992	The Cenotaph 172	Open		35.00	40
1989	Cliffords Tower 109	Open		31.50	40
1988	Craigievar Castle 94	Open		59.50	75
1990	Culzean Castle 124	Open		115.00	135
1988	Dove Cottage 99	Open		45.00	55
1987	Edinburgh Castle 43	Open		85.00	99
1987	Eilean Donan Castle 93	Open		85.00	99
1987	The Giant's Causway 75	Open		19.50	25
1987	Holyrood Palace 42	Open		85.00	99
1987	John Knox House 28	Open		39.50	50
1991	Kings College Chapel 133	Open		115.00	135
1991	Leeds Castle 126	Open		85.00	100
1989	Micklegate Bar 111	Open		39.50	50
1991	Nelson's Column 156	Open		39.50	50
1987	Old Leonach Cottage 178	Open		35.00	40
1987	Robert Burn's Cottage 02	Open		23.50	30
1992	The Round Tower 158	Open		59.50	75
1987	Royal & Ancient Clubhouse 44	Open		85.00	99
1992	The Royal Albert Hall 174	Open		59.50	75
1987	The Scott Monument 76	Open		49.50	60
1988	Shakespeare's Birthplace 33 mold #1	Retrd.	N/A	53.00	53
1994	Shakespeare's Birthplace 33 mold #2	Open		53.00	70
1991	St. Margaret's Church 157	Open		59.50	75
1992	St. Pauls Cathedral 134	Open		149.50	175
1990	Stirling Castle 127	Open		115.00	135
1988	The Tower of London 78	Open		99.50	125
1991	Warwick Castle 131	Open		99.50	125
1992	Westminster Abbey 135	Open		149.50	175
1992	The White Tower 151	Open		59.50	75
1989	Windsor Castle 120	Open		99.50	125
1989	York Minster 103	Open		99.50	125

The British Heritage Miniature Collection - I. Fraser

YEAR ISSUE		EDITION LIMIT	YEAR RETD.	ISSUE PRICE	QUOTE U.S.$
1992	Balmoral Castle 165	Open		42.00	50
1995	Beaulieu 214	Open		79.50	80
1995	Blair Castle 217	Open		59.50	60
1992	Braemar Castle 184	Open		48.00	60
1995	Buccleuch Street Tennament 200	Open		59.50	60
1992	Buckingham Palace 169	Open		48.00	60
1992	Castle Fraser 183	Open		48.00	60
1992	Cawdor Castle 186	Open		54.00	70
1993	Claypotts 194	Open		48.00	55
1992	Crathes Castle 187	Open		42.00	50
1992	Drum Castle 180	Open		45.00	55
1995	Duart Castle 215	Open		59.50	60
1995	Dunvegan Castle 218	Open		59.50	60
1992	Durham Cathedral 176	Open		59.50	70
1992	Edinburgh Castle 159	Open		39.00	50
1992	Ely Cathedral 175	Open		51.00	60
1995	Falkland Palace 208	Open		59.50	60
1992	Fyvie Castle 182	Open		48.00	60
1993	Glamis Castle 193	Open		57.50	70
1995	Harlech Castle 219	Open		59.50	60
1992	Holyrood Palace 168	Open		42.00	50
1995	Inverary Castle 220	Open		59.50	60
1995	Iona Abbey 221	Open		59.50	60
1995	Leed's Town Hall 206	Open		69.50	70
1992	Leeds Castle 170	Open		42.00	50
1992	Norwich Cathedral 177	Open		48.00	60
1995	Provand's Lordship 199	Open		55.00	55
1995	Provost Skeng's House 195	Open		69.50	70
1995	The Roman Baths 202	Open		49.50	50
1995	Salsbury Cathedral 207	Open		59.50	60
1995	Scone Palace 216	Open		59.50	60
1992	St. Pauls Cathedral 163	Open		45.00	55
1992	Stirling Castle 161	Open		45.00	55
1993	Stonehenge 189	Open		39.50	45
1992	The Tower of London 166	Open		42.00	50
1992	Urquhart Castle 185	Open		48.00	60
1992	Warwick Castle 167	Open		42.00	50
1992	Westminister Abbey 162	Open		45.00	55
1992	Windsor Castle 164	Open		42.00	50
1995	Woburn Abbey 209	Open		59.50	60
1992	York Minster 160	Open		48.00	60

Classic Cottage Collection - I. Fraser

YEAR ISSUE		EDITION LIMIT	YEAR RETD.	ISSUE PRICE	QUOTE U.S.$
1994	Benmore Croft C24	Open		49.50	50
1994	Birch Cottage C18	Open		39.50	40
1995	Bluebell Cottage C64	Open		22.50	23
1995	The Book Store C57	Open		119.50	120
1994	Buttermere Tearooms C05	Open		29.50	30
1994	Carbis View C54	Open		22.50	23
1995	The Cat & Fiddle Inn C61	Open		75.00	75
1994	Cheddar View C14	Open		34.50	35
1994	Clover Cottage C03	Open		29.50	30
1994	Coniston House C36	Open		59.50	60
1994	Coombe Cottage C55	Open		49.50	50
1994	Crail Cottage C21	Open		49.50	50
1994	Crathie Church C39	Open		75.00	75
1994	Cullin Croft C25	Open		49.50	50
1994	Daisy Cottage C51	Open		22.50	23
1994	Dale Farm C43	Open		99.00	99
1994	Duck Cottage C20	Open		39.50	40
1994	Ennerdale Farm C07	Open		34.50	35
1994	Follyfoot Farm C29	Open		55.00	55
1994	Foxglove Cottage C19	Open		39.50	40
1995	The Fruit Seller C56	Open		69.50	70
1994	Fyne View C02	Open		22.50	23
1994	Gamekeepers Lodge C37	Open		75.00	75
1994	Glengarry Homestead C45	Open		135.00	135
1994	Grannie's Hieland Hame C15	Open		39.50	40
1995	Granny O' Reilly's C66	Open		39.95	40
1995	Hawkhurst Mill C65	Open		375.00	375
1994	Heatherlea Cottage C13	Open		34.50	35
1994	Honey Cottage C50	Open		39.50	40
1994	Honeymoon Hideaway C16	Open		39.50	40
1994	Horseshoe Inn C34	Open		59.50	60
1994	Inverbeg Gatehouse C23	Open		49.50	50
1994	Ivy Cottage C12	Open		34.50	35

YEAR ISSUE		EDITION LIMIT	YEAR RETD.	ISSUE PRICE	QUOTE U.S.$
1994	Kilrea Cottage C31	Open		55.00	55
1994	The Kings Arms C27	Open		49.50	50
1994	Langdale Farm C26	Open		49.50	50
1994	Laurel Bank C38	Open		75.00	75
1994	Lavender Lane C40	Open		75.00	75
1995	The Lifeboat Station C60	Open		59.50	60
1994	Lomond View C35	Open		59.50	60
1994	Merchant's Manor C53	Open		39.50	40
1994	Northborough Manor C46	Open		175.00	175
1994	The Old Anchor Inn C22	Open		49.50	50
1994	The Old Curiosity Shop C08	Open		34.50	35
1995	The Old Rectory C62	Open		55.00	55
1994	Perriwinkle Cottage C01	Open		22.50	23
1994	Polperro Cottage C28	Open		55.00	55
1994	Puffin Lighthouse C30	Open		55.00	55
1994	Ranworth View C10	Open		34.50	35
1994	The Red Lion Tavern C48	Open		375.00	375
1994	Rock Cliff C06	Open		29.50	30
1994	The Rose & Crown C17	Open		39.50	40
1995	Rose Cottage C63	Open		22.50	23
1994	Rosebank C11	Open		34.50	35
1994	Saxmund Smithy C04	Open		29.50	30
1994	Smugglers Hideaway C32	Open		55.00	55
1994	St. Andrews Kirk C47	Open		49.50	50
1995	St. David's Church C59	Open		59.50	60
1994	St. Mary's Chapel C09	Open		34.50	35
1994	Strathmore Loged C44	Open		99.00	99
1994	Swallow Mill C52	Open		39.50	40
1995	The Tall Ships Tavern C58	Open		85.00	85
1994	The Village Post Office C49	Open		55.00	55
1994	Whitesand Lighthouse C33	Open		59.50	60
1994	Windrush Lane C41	Open		75.00	75
1994	The Wine Merchant C42	Open		75.00	75
Countryside in Miniature Collection - I. Fraser					
1988	Acorn Cottage 15	Retrd.	1993	34.00	25
1988	The Barge's Base 58	Retrd.	1993	270.00	270
1991	Belle Cottage 106	Retrd.	1993	17.00	17
1988	Black Isle Cottage 121	Retrd.	1993	32.00	32
1988	The Blacksmith 09	Retrd.	1993	28.00	28
1988	Bluebell Cottage 04	Retrd.	1991	27.00	27
1988	Boatman's House 91	Retrd.	1993	39.00	39
1988	Bridge House 67	Retrd.	1993	27.00	27
1990	Bull & Bush 100	Retrd.	1993	54.00	54
1991	But 'N' Ben 104	Retrd.	1993	17.00	17
1988	Camelot 23 (beige)	Retrd.	1990	44.75	45
1988	Camelot 23 (gray)	Retrd.	1990	44.75	45
1988	Camelot 23 (white)	Retrd.	1990	44.75	45
1990	Castle of Monte Crisco 101	Retrd.	1993	149.75	150
1988	The Chandlery 31 mold #1	Retrd.	1989	54.00	54
1989	The Chandlery 31 mold #2	Retrd.	1993	54.00	54
1988	Chester House 84	Retrd.	1993	75.00	75
1988	Cornish Cottage 35	Retrd.	1990	57.00	57
1988	Cornish-Tin-Mine 18	Retrd.	1990	35.75	36
1988	Cotswold Cottage 20	Retrd.	1990	39.00	39
1988	Cove Cottage 82	Retrd.	1993	32.00	32
1988	Creel Cottage 83	Retrd.	1993	37.00	37
1988	Crooked House 171	Retrd.	1993	37.00	37
1988	Devon Cottage 64	Retrd.	1993	34.00	34
1988	Drover Cottage 85	Retrd.	1991	22.50	23
1988	Fern Cottage 70	Retrd.	1993	21.00	21
1989	Fisherman's Cottage 30	Retrd.	1993	49.50	50
1988	Fisherman's Wharf 66	Retrd.	1991	89.75	90
1991	Fishers Wynd 110	Retrd.	1993	32.00	32
1991	Follyfoot 112	Retrd.	1993	37.00	37
1988	The Forge 47 mold #1	Retrd.	1988	115.00	115
1988	The Forge 47 mold #2	Retrd.	1993	115.00	115
1988	The Forge on Plinth 48	Retrd.	1993	135.00	135
1991	Grannie's Heiland Home 108	Retrd.	1993	21.00	21
1988	Green Gables 19	Retrd.	1990	39.00	39
1988	Greystone Manor 92	Retrd.	1993	54.00	54
1988	Harbor Base 57	Retrd.	1993	140.00	140
1988	Hawthorn Cottage 01	Retrd.	1993	21.00	21
1990	Heather Lea 97	Retrd.	1993	21.00	21
1988	Highbury House 59	Retrd.	1990	101.75	102
1988	Highland Croft 12 mold #1	Retrd.	1990	32.00	32
1990	Highland Croft mold #2	Retrd.	1990	32.00	32
1988	Highland House 81	Retrd.	1993	63.50	64
1988	Hillview Base 56	Retrd.	1993	137.80	138
1988	The Homestead 34	Retrd.	1993	57.00	57
1988	Honeymoon Cottage 87	Retrd.	1993	25.00	25
1991	Horseshoe Inn 115	Retrd.	1993	39.00	39
1988	Irish Cottage 03	Retrd.	1993	25.00	25
1988	Ivy Mews 60	Retrd.	1993	45.00	45
1991	Kent Oast House 123	Retrd.	1993	37.00	37
1988	Kent Oast House 41	Retrd.	1990	75.00	75
1990	Killarney Cottage 96	Retrd.	1993	63.50	64
1988	Lake View 11	Retrd.	1992	28.00	28
1988	Lavender Lane 24	Retrd.	1993	42.00	42
1991	Lifeboat House 118	Retrd.	1993	54.00	54
1988	Lighthouse 17	Retrd.	1993	32.00	32
1988	Lilac Cottage 13	Retrd.	1990	34.00	34
1990	Linden Lea 98	Retrd.	1993	32.00	32
1991	Meadowsweet Farm 116	Retrd.	1993	39.00	39
1988	Merchant's Court 95	Retrd.	1993	291.00	291
1988	The Mill 06	Retrd.	1993	25.00	25
1988	The Millers 49	Retrd.	1991	129.00	129
1988	The Millers on Plinth 50	Retrd.	1991	159.00	159
1988	Milton Manor 36	Retrd.	1991	57.00	57
1988	Morningside 80	Retrd.	1993	300.00	300
1988	Myrtle Cottage 08	Retrd.	1993	28.00	28
1988	Oak Tree Inn 39	Retrd.	1993	69.50	70
1988	Old Antique Shop 61	Retrd.	1993	42.00	42
1988	Old Brig Inn 79	Retrd.	1993	63.50	64
1988	Old Leonach Cottage 90	Retrd.	1990	41.75	42
1988	Old Market 21	Retrd.	1993	39.00	39
1991	The Parsonage 119	Retrd.	1993	63.50	64
1991	Pebble Cottage 105	Retrd.	1993	17.00	17
1988	Ploughman's Cottage 72	Retrd.	1993	99.50	100
1988	Ploughman's Cottage/ Plinth 74	Retrd.	1993	119.50	200
1988	Preston Mill 27	Retrd.	1990	45.00	45
1988	Primrose Cottage 68	Retrd.	1991	33.00	33
1988	Riverside 25	Retrd.	1993	42.00	42
1988	Robert Burns Cottage 26	Retrd.	1990	45.00	45
1991	Rock Cliff 107	Retrd.	1993	17.00	17
1988	Rose Cottage 14	Retrd.	1991	35.75	36
1988	Rowan Cottage 69	Retrd.	1993	21.00	21
1989	Sea View 29	Retrd.	1993	49.50	50
1988	Sheep Farm 16	Retrd.	1993	34.00	34
1988	Shepherd's Cottage 71	Retrd.	1993	99.50	100
1988	Shepherd's Cottage on Plinth 73	Retrd.	1993	119.50	120
1988	Smugglers Cove 05	Retrd.	1993	25.00	25
1988	Snow Church 37	Retrd.	1990	59.75	60
1988	Somerset Cottage 88	Retrd.	1992	32.75	33
1988	Springbank 65	Retrd.	1990	41.75	42
1988	St. Andrews Church 10 mold #1	Retrd.	1990	32.00	32
1990	St. Andrews Church mold #2	Retrd.	1990	32.00	32
1991	St. David's Church 117	Retrd.	1993	42.00	42
1990	St. Georges Church 102	Retrd.	1993	32.00	32
1988	Staging Post 55	Retrd.	1992	389.75	390
1988	Summerside 62	Retrd.	1991	45.00	45
1988	Swan Inn 22	Retrd.	1993	39.00	39
1988	Sweet Hope 07	Retrd.	1993	32.00	32
1988	The Thatchers 51 mold #1	Retrd.	1988	124.00	124
1988	The Thatchers 51 mold #2	Retrd.	1993	124.00	300
1988	The Thatchers on Plinth 52	Retrd.	1993	149.50	150
1991	Tintagel Post Office 122	Retrd.	1993	42.00	42
1988	Tudor Court 53 mold #1	Retrd.	1988	129.00	129
1988	Tudor Court 53 mold #2	Retrd.	1990	129.00	129
1988	Tudor Court on Plinth 54 mold #1	Retrd.	1988	149.50	150
1988	Tudor Court on Plinth 54 mold #2	Retrd.	1990	149.50	250
1988	Tweedale Cottage 89	Retrd.	1991	38.75	39
1991	Village Post Office 114	Retrd.	1993	37.00	37
1988	The Wedding 45 mold #1	Retrd.	1990	115.00	115
1990	The Wedding 45 mold #2	Retrd.	1993	115.00	115
1988	The Wedding on Plinth 46 mold #1	Retrd.	1990	135.00	135
1990	The Wedding on Plinth 46 mold #2	Retrd.	1993	135.00	350
1988	Woodcutters Cottage 63	Retrd.	1991	45.00	45
1988	Yeoman's Cottage 86	Retrd.	1993	25.00	25
German Collection - I. Fraser					
1992	Altstadter Town Hall 140	Open		79.50	90
1992	Holstein Town Gates 141	Open		119.50	130
1992	Mayor Toppler's Little House 143	Open		39.50	45
1990	Schless Neuschwanstein 113	Open		145.00	165
1992	Schloss Badinghagen 142	Open		79.50	90
1992	Schloss Heidelberg 136	Open		155.00	175
1992	Schloss Heidelburg (with snow) 188	Open		165.00	185
1991	Schloss Linderhof 129	Open		155.00	175
1992	St. Coloman Chapel 138	Open		39.50	45
1992	St. Wilhelm Chapel 139	Open		39.50	45
The Miniature Collection - I. Fraser					
1995	Balmoral Castle M105	Open		19.90	20
1995	Edinburgh Castle M101	Open		19.90	20
1995	Stirling Castle M102	Open		19.90	20
1995	The Tower of London M106	Open		19.90	20
1995	Warwick Castle M104	Open		19.90	20
1995	Windsor Castle M103	Open		19.90	20
Washington D.C. Collection - I. Fraser					
1994	Jefferson Memorial A03	Open		49.50	50
1994	Lincoln Memorial A02	Open		49.50	50
1994	White House A01	Open		49.50	50
1994	White House on Base A06	Open		225.00	225
Ganz					
Blazing Spirits Collection - Ganz					
1995	Freedom's Foal	Open		75.00	75
1995	Racing The Wind	Open		55.00	55
1995	Wild Stallion	Open		55.00	55
Carnival Classico Collection - Ganz					
1995	Columbina	Open		52.00	52
1995	Harlequin	Open		52.00	52
1995	Jester	Open		52.00	52
1995	Pierrot	Open		52.00	52
1995	Spaventa	Open		52.00	52
1995	Tartaglia	Open		52.00	52
Cock-A-Doodle Corners Collection - C.Thammavongsa					
1995	Cock-a-Doodle Corners Sign	Open		16.00	16
1995	Coffee Clutch	Open		24.00	24
1995	Country Courting	Open		20.00	20
1995	Follow the Leader	Open		24.00	24
1995	Fresh-Baked	Open		16.50	17
1995	Great Eggspectations	Open		15.00	15
1995	Hen Packed	Open		17.00	17
1995	Home Remedy	Open		21.00	21
1995	Master Craftsman	Open		18.00	18
1995	New Arrival	Open		10.00	10
1995	Organically Grown	Open		22.00	22
1995	Poultry Patrol	Open		16.50	17
Cowtown Collection - C.Thammavongsa					
1994	Amoolia Steerheart	Open		25.00	25
1995	Bedtime Dairy Tales	Open		19.00	19
1993	Buffalo Bull Cody	Open		15.00	15
1996	Bull Cassidy & The Sundance Calf	Open		20.00	20
1993	Bull Masterson	Open		15.00	15
1993	Bull Rogers	Open		17.00	17
1993	Bull Ruth	Retrd.	1994	13.00	13
1995	Buster Cowtown	Open		15.00	15
1993	Buttermilk & Buttercup	Open		16.00	16
1995	A Calf's Best Friend	Open		12.00	12
1993	Cowlamity Jane	Open		15.00	15
1994	Cowsey Jones & The Cannonbull Express	Open		26.50	27
1993	Daisy Moo	Open		11.00	11
1995	Dracowla	Open		15.00	15
1995	Francowstein	Open		12.50	13
1994	Geronimoo	Open		17.00	17
1993	Gloria Bovine & Rudolph Bullentino	Open		20.00	20
1995	Grandma Mooses	Open		15.00	15
1994	Heiferella	Open		16.50	17
1995	Hicowatha & Moonehaha	Open		18.50	19
1995	Holy Mootrimoony	Open		20.00	20
1995	Jack-Cow-Lantern	Open		11.00	11
1993	Jethro Bovine	Retrd.	1994	15.00	15
1994	King Cowmooamooa	Open		16.50	17
1993	Lil' Orphan Angus	Open		11.00	11
1996	Lone-Wrangler	Open		15.00	15
1994	Ma & Pa Cattle	Open		23.50	24
1993	Moo West	Open		15.00	15
1995	Moother's Li'l Rascow	Open		20.00	20
1993	Old MooDonald	Open		13.50	14
1994	Pocowhantis	Open		16.50	17
1995	Scarecow	Open		11.50	12
1994	Set of Three Cacti	Open		17.00	17
1995	Steershot Annie	Open		16.50	17
1995	Supercow	Open		15.00	15
1994	Tchaicowsky	Open		19.00	19
1996	Tender Loving Cow	Open		12.50	13
1994	Texas Lonesteer	10,000		50.00	50
1995	Will Bull Hickock	Open		17.00	17
1995	Yellowsteer National Park	Open		20.00	20
Cowtown/Christmas Collection - C.Thammavongsa					
1994	Billy the Calf	Open		14.00	14
1994	Christmas Cactus	Open		13.50	14
1995	Ellie-Moo's Angel	Open		11.00	11
1995	Here Comes Santa Cow	Open		17.50	18
1995	John Steere	Open		11.00	11
1995	Milk & Cookies	Open		14.50	15
1995	Moo Claus	Open		17.00	17
1995	Polar Bull	Open		17.50	18
1994	Saint Nicowlas	Open		16.00	16
1994	Santa Cows	Open		18.00	18
1994	Santa's Little Heifer	Open		12.50	13
1995	Twinkle Twinkle Little Steer	Open		12.00	12
Cowtown/Fall, Halloween Collection - C.Thammavongsa					
1995	Dracowla	Open		15.00	15
1995	Francowstein	Open		12.50	13
1995	Jack-Cow-Lantern	Open		11.00	11
1995	Scarecow	Open		11.50	12
Cowtown/Valentine Collection - C.Thammavongsa					
1994	I Love Moo	Open		15.00	15
1994	Robin Hoof & Maid Mooian	Open		23.00	23
1994	Romecow & Mooliet	Open		22.00	22
1994	Wanted: A Sweetheart	Open		16.00	16
Grandma's Attic Collection - C.Thammavongsa					
1995	Balderdash	Open		25.00	25
1995	Bumblebeary	Open		10.00	10
1995	Coco & Jiffy	Open		11.00	11
1995	Crumples & Creampuff	Open		13.50	14
1995	Dilly-Dally	Open		13.50	14
1995	Dumblekin	Open		19.00	19
1995	Jelly-Belly	Open		12.00	12
1995	Molly-Coddle	Open		16.00	16
1995	Prince Fuddle-Duddle & Princess Dazzle	Open		17.00	17
1995	Sprinkles	Open		15.00	15
1995	Tootoo	Open		10.00	10
Grandma's Attic/Easter, Springtime Collection - C.Thammavongsa					
1995	Hucklebeary	Open		14.50	15
1995	Lambie-Pie	Open		14.50	15
1995	Slugger	Open		13.00	13
Grandma's Attic/Valentine Collection - C.Thammavongsa					
1995	Abracadabra	Open		14.00	14

YEAR ISSUE		EDITION LIMIT	YEAR RETD.	ISSUE PRICE	QUOTE U.S.$
1995	Cuddles	Open		12.00	12
1995	Skippy and Marmalade	Open		23.00	23
1995	Tickles and Giggles	Open		20.00	20

Just Around the Corner/Boston Collection - Ganz/L. Sunarth

YEAR ISSUE		EDITION LIMIT	YEAR RETD.	ISSUE PRICE	QUOTE U.S.$
1995	Beaux Arts Facade	Open		23.00	23
1995	Clarendon Hall	Open		17.50	18
1995	Display Sign	Open		13.50	14
1995	Fairfield Place	Open		17.50	18
1995	Haydon Press	Open		17.50	18
1995	Jacob Wirth's Co.	Open		19.50	20
1995	Macullar Parker & Co.	Open		15.00	15
1995	Malborough Bank	Open		17.50	18
1995	Melrose Cottage	Open		19.50	20
1995	New England Cutlery & Hardware Shop	Open		17.50	18
1995	State Building	Open		15.00	15
1995	Winthrop & Assoc.	Open		17.50	18
1995	Wm. G. Bell & Co.	Open		22.00	22

Just Around the Corner/Tombstone Collection - Ganz/L. Sunarth

YEAR ISSUE		EDITION LIMIT	YEAR RETD.	ISSUE PRICE	QUOTE U.S.$
1995	Barbershop	Open		15.50	16
1995	Chapel	Open		15.00	15
1995	Clockmaker	Open		14.00	14
1995	The Daily Chronicle	Open		16.00	16
1995	Display Sign	Open		13.50	14
1995	Dry Goods Store	Open		16.00	16
1995	General Store	Open		15.00	15
1995	Mine Co.	Open		15.50	16
1995	Miner's Union Hall	Open		14.00	14
1995	Mint Theater	Open		17.50	18
1995	Saloon	Open		17.50	18
1995	Town Bank	Open		18.00	18
1995	Town Hall	Open		16.00	16

The Lacewing Fairies Collection - Ganz/B. Lemaire

YEAR ISSUE		EDITION LIMIT	YEAR RETD.	ISSUE PRICE	QUOTE U.S.$
1995	Lacewing Fairies Sign	Open		10.00	10
1995	Liana & Her Spellbounde Prince	Open		37.00	37
1995	Liana - Spirit of the Woodes	Open		30.00	30
1995	Liana - The Butterflye Maiden	Open		26.50	27
1995	Salina - Enchantress of the Sea	Open		35.00	35
1995	Salina - Midsummer Night's Dreame	Open		36.00	36
1995	Salina - the Faerie Queene	Open		37.00	37

Little Cheesers/Collectors' Club Pieces - C.Thammavongsa

YEAR ISSUE		EDITION LIMIT	YEAR RETD.	ISSUE PRICE	QUOTE U.S.$
1993	Charter Member	Closed	1994	27.00	27
1994	Fireweed Fox	Closed	1995	15.00	15
1995	Welcome to the Club	Open		27.00	27
1995	The Invention	Open		15.00	15

Little Cheesers/Cheeserville Fall - C.Thammavongsa

YEAR ISSUE		EDITION LIMIT	YEAR RETD.	ISSUE PRICE	QUOTE U.S.$
1995	Bewitched	Open		8.50	9
1995	Candy Bandit	Open		8.50	9
1995	Cornucopia	Open		10.00	10
1995	Peace Offering	Open		8.50	9
1995	Pilgrims	Open		15.50	16
1995	Pumpkin Patch	Open		8.00	8

Little Cheesers/Cheeserville Picnic Collection - Various

YEAR ISSUE		EDITION LIMIT	YEAR RETD.	ISSUE PRICE	QUOTE U.S.$
1991	Auntie Marigold Eating Cookie	Open		13.00	13
1991	Baby Cicely	Retrd.	1995	8.00	8
1991	Baby Truffle	Open		8.00	8
1991	Blossom & Hickory In Love	Open		19.00	19
1995	Cheeserville Tales - C.Thammavongsa	Open		7.50	8
1993	Chuckles The Clown - C.Thammavongsa	Open		16.00	16
1993	Clownin' Around - C.Thammavongsa	Open		10.50	11
1991	Cousin Woody With Bread and Fruit	Open		14.00	14
1991	Fellow With Picnic Hamper	Retrd.	1991	13.00	13
1991	Fellow With Plate Of Cookies	Retrd.	1991	13.00	13
1994	Fiddle-Dee-Dee - C.Thammavongsa	Open		13.00	13
1993	For Someone Special - C.Thammavongsa	Open		13.50	14
1991	Grandmama Thistledown Holding Bread	Open		14.00	14
1991	Grandpapa Thistledown Carrying Basket	Open		13.00	13
1991	Harley Harvestmouse Waving	Open		13.00	13
1991	Harriet Harvestmouse	Retrd.	1993	13.00	13
1995	Hush-A-Bye Baby - C.Thammavongsa	Open		14.00	14
1991	Jenny Butterfield Kneeling	Open		13.00	13
1991	Jeremy Butterfield	Open		13.00	13
1995	Joyful Beginnings - C.Thammavongsa	Open		15.00	15
1991	Lady With Grapes	Retrd.	1991	14.00	14
1993	Little Cheesers Display Plaque - C.Thammavongsa	Open		25.00	25
1991	Little Truffle Eating Grapes	Open		8.00	8
1991	Little Truffle Smelling Flowers	Retrd.	1995	16.50	17
1991	Mama Fixing Sweet Cicely's Hair -	Retrd.	1993	16.50	17
1991	Mama With Rolling Pin	Open		13.00	13
1991	Mama Woodsworth With Crate	Retrd.	1992	14.00	14
1991	Marigold Thistledown Picking Up Jar	Open		14.00	14
1991	Medley Meadowmouse With Bouquet	Open		13.00	13
1994	Melody Maker - C.Thammavongsa	Retrd.	1995	17.00	17
1994	Ooom-Pah-Pah - C.Thammavongsa	Open		13.00	13
1991	Papa Woodsworth	Open		13.00	13
1991	Picnic Buddies	Open		19.00	19
1995	Picnic with Papa - C.Thammavongsa	Open		14.00	14
1995	Playtime - C.Thammavongsa	Open		14.00	14
1995	Read Me A Story - C.Thammavongsa	Open		15.00	15
1993	The Storyteller - C.Thammavongsa	10,000		25.00	25
1994	Strummin' Away - C.Thammavongsa	Open		13.00	13
1993	Sunday Drive - C.Thammavongsa	Open		40.00	40
1993	Sweet Dreams - C.Thammavongsa	Open		27.50	28
1994	Swingin' Sax - C.Thammavongsa	Open		13.00	13
1991	Violet With Peaches	Open		13.00	13
1994	Washboard Blues - C.Thammavongsa	Open		13.00	13
1994	What a Hoot! - C.Thammavongsa	Open		13.00	13
1993	Willy's Toe-Tappin' Tunes - C.Thammavongsa	Open		15.00	15
1993	Words Of Wisdom - C.Thammavongsa	Open		14.00	14

Little Cheesers/Cheeserville Picnic Collection Accessories - G.D.A. Group

YEAR ISSUE		EDITION LIMIT	YEAR RETD.	ISSUE PRICE	QUOTE U.S.$
1994	Mayflower Meadow Base	Open		50.00	50

Little Cheesers/Cheeserville Picnic Mini-Food Acc. - G.D.A. Group

YEAR ISSUE		EDITION LIMIT	YEAR RETD.	ISSUE PRICE	QUOTE U.S.$
1991	Basket Of Apples	Open		2.25	3
1991	Basket Of Peaches	Open		2.00	2
1991	Blueberry Cake	Retrd.	1994	2.50	3
1991	Bread Basket	Open		2.50	3
1991	Candy	Open		2.00	2
1991	Cherry Mousse	Open		2.00	2
1991	Cherry Pie	Retrd.	1991	2.00	2
1991	Chocolate Cake	Open		2.50	3
1991	Chocolate Cheesecake	Open		2.00	2
1991	Doughnut Basket	Open		2.50	3
1991	Egg Tart	Open		1.00	1
1991	Food Basket With Blue Cloth	Retrd.	1994	6.50	7
1991	Food Basket With Green Cloth	Open		7.50	8
1991	Food Basket With Pink Cloth	Retrd.	1994	6.00	6
1991	Food Basket With Purple Cloth	Open		6.00	6
1991	Food Trolley	Retrd.	1991	12.00	12
1991	Hazelnut Roll	Retrd.	1991	2.00	2
1991	Honey Jar	Retrd.	1991	2.00	2
1991	Hot Dog	Open		2.25	3
1991	Ice Cream Cup	Open		2.00	2
1991	Lemon Cake	Retrd.	1991	2.00	2
1991	Napkin In Can	Retrd.	1991	2.00	2
1991	Set Of Four Bottles	Retrd.	1991	10.00	10
1991	Strawberry Cake	Open		2.00	2
1991	Sundae	Open		2.00	2
1991	Wine Glass	Retrd.	1995	1.25	2

Little Cheesers/Cheeserville Picnic Musicals - G.D.A. Group

YEAR ISSUE		EDITION LIMIT	YEAR RETD.	ISSUE PRICE	QUOTE U.S.$
1994	The Bandstand Base	Open		48.50	49
1991	Blossom & Hickory Musical Jewelry Box	Retrd.	1992	65.00	65
1991	Mama & Sweet Cicely Waterglobe	Retrd.	1992	55.00	55
1991	Medley Meadowmouse Waterglobe	Retrd.	1995	47.00	47
1993	Musical "Secret Treasures" Trinket Box	Open		36.00	36
1991	Musical Basket Trinket Box	Open		30.00	30
1991	Musical Floral Trinket Box	Open		32.00	32
1991	Musical Medley Meadowmouse Cookie Jar	Retrd.	1992	75.00	75
1991	Musical Picnic Base	Open		60.00	60
1991	Musical Sunflower Base	Retrd.	1993	65.00	65
1991	Musical Violet Woodsworth Cookie Jar	Retrd.	1992	75.00	75
1992	Sweet Cicely Musical Doll Basket	Open		85.00	85
1993	Wishing Well Musical	Open		50.00	50

Little Cheesers/Christmas Collection - Various

YEAR ISSUE		EDITION LIMIT	YEAR RETD.	ISSUE PRICE	QUOTE U.S.$
1991	Abner Appleton Ringing Bell	Retrd.	1993	14.00	14
1993	All I Want For Christmas - C.Thammavongsa	Open		18.00	18
1994	Angel - C.Thammavongsa	Open		8.00	8
1991	Auntie Blossom With Ornaments	Open		14.00	14
1994	Baby Jesus - C.Thammavongsa	Open		6.50	7
1991	Cheeser Snowman	Retrd.	1994	7.50	8
1993	Christmas Greetings - C.Thammavongsa	Open		16.50	17
1991	Cousin Woody Playing Flute	Open		14.00	14
1994	First Wiseman - C.Thammavongsa	Open		11.00	11
1991	Frowzy Roquefort III Skating	Retrd.	1993	14.00	14
1991	Grandmama & Little Truffle	Retrd.	1993	19.00	19
1991	Grandpapa & Sweet Cicely	Open		19.00	19
1991	Grandpapa Blowing Horn	Retrd.	1994	14.00	14
1991	Great Aunt Rose With Tray	Open		14.00	14
1991	Harley & Harriet Dancing	Retrd.	1993	19.00	19
1991	Hickory Playing Cello	Retrd.	1994	14.00	14
1991	Jenny On Sleigh	Open		16.00	16
1991	Jeremy With Teddy Bear	Open		12.00	12
1994	Joseph - C.Thammavongsa	Open		10.00	10
1995	Joy to the World - C.Thammavongsa	Open		8.00	8
1991	Little Truffle With Stocking	Open		8.00	8
1991	Mama Pouring Tea	Retrd.	1993	14.00	14
1991	Marigold&Oscar Stealing A Christmas Kiss	Open		19.00	19
1994	Mary - C.Thammavongsa	Open		10.00	10
1991	Medley Playing Drum	Open		8.00	8
1991	Myrtle Meadowmouse With Book	Retrd.	1993	14.00	14
1991	Santa Cheeser	Open		13.00	13
1994	Santa's Sleigh - C.Thammavongsa	10,000		22.00	22
1994	Second Wiseman - C.Thammavongsa	Open		11.00	11
1994	Shepherd - C.Thammavongsa	Open		8.50	9
1993	Sleigh Ride - C.Thammavongsa	Retrd.	1995	11.00	11
1995	Tending The Flocks - C.Thammavongsa	Open		9.00	9
1994	Third Wiseman - C.Thammavongsa	Open		10.50	11
1991	Violet With Snowball	Retrd.	1994	8.00	8

Little Cheesers/Christmas Collection Acc. - Various

YEAR ISSUE		EDITION LIMIT	YEAR RETD.	ISSUE PRICE	QUOTE U.S.$
1993	Candleholder-Santa Cheeser - C.Thammavongsa	Open		19.00	19
1993	Candy Cane - C.Thammavongsa	Open		2.00	2
1994	Christmas Collection Base - C.Thammavongsa	Open		50.00	50
1993	Christmas Gift - C.Thammavongsa	Open		3.00	3
1993	Christmas Stocking - C.Thammavongsa	Open		3.00	3
1991	Christmas Tree	Open		9.00	9
1994	Creche Base - C.Thammavongsa	Open		28.50	29
1993	Gingerbread House - C.Thammavongsa	Open		3.00	3
1993	Ice Pond Base - C.Thammavongsa	Open		5.50	6
1991	Lamp Post	Open		8.50	9
1995	Little Cheeser Tree Topper - C.Thammavongsa	Open		34.00	34
1991	Outdoor Scene Base	Retrd.	1993	35.00	35
1991	Parlor Scene Base	Open		37.50	38
1993	Toy Soldier - C.Thammavongsa	Open		3.00	3
1993	Toy Train - C.Thammavongsa	Open		3.00	3

Little Cheesers/Christmas Collection Musicals - Various

YEAR ISSUE		EDITION LIMIT	YEAR RETD.	ISSUE PRICE	QUOTE U.S.$
1992	Jenny Butterfield Christmas Waterglobe GDA/Thammavongsa	Retrd.	1992	55.00	55
1992	Little Truffle Christmas Waterglobe	Retrd.	1995	45.00	45
1992	Musical Santa Cheeser Roly-Poly	Suspd.		55.00	55
1993	Rotating Round Wood Base "I'll be Home for X'mas" - C.Thammavongs	Open		30.00	30
1993	Round Wood Base "We Wish You a Merry X'mas" - C.Thammavongs	Open		25.00	25

Little Cheesers/Circus Party Collection - C.Thammavongsa

YEAR ISSUE		EDITION LIMIT	YEAR RETD.	ISSUE PRICE	QUOTE U.S.$
1995	Balancing Act	Open		8.00	8
1995	Beep-Beep	Open		13.50	14
1995	Cheeserville Choo-Choo	Open		21.00	21
1995	Easy As Cake	Open		15.00	15
1995	Look Ma-No Hands	Open		18.00	18
1995	Woops!	Open		10.50	11

Little Cheesers/Little Hoppers Collection - C.Thammavongsa

YEAR ISSUE		EDITION LIMIT	YEAR RETD.	ISSUE PRICE	QUOTE U.S.$
1994	Bubble Bath	Open		7.50	8
1994	Let's Play Ball	Open		7.00	7
1994	Somebunny Loves You	Open		7.50	8
1994	Sweet Nothings	Open		15.00	15
1994	Tender Loving Care	Open		10.00	10
1994	Tricycle Built for Two	Open		16.00	16

Little Cheesers/Springtime In Cheeserville Accessories - C.Thammavongsa

YEAR ISSUE		EDITION LIMIT	YEAR RETD.	ISSUE PRICE	QUOTE U.S.$
1992	April Showers Bring May Flowers	Open		7.50	8
1992	Decorated With Love	Open		7.50	8
1992	For Somebunny Special	Open		7.50	8

Little Cheesers/Springtime In Cheeserville Musicals - GDA/Thammavongsa

YEAR ISSUE		EDITION LIMIT	YEAR RETD.	ISSUE PRICE	QUOTE U.S.$
1992	Tulips & Ribbons Musical Trinket Box	Closed	1994	28.00	28

Little Cheesers/Springtime In Cheeserville Collection - C.Thammavongsa

YEAR ISSUE		EDITION LIMIT	YEAR RETD.	ISSUE PRICE	QUOTE U.S.$
1993	Ballerina Sweetheart	Open		10.00	10
1992	A Basket Full Of Joy	Open		16.00	16
1994	Birthday Party	Retrd.	1995	22.00	22
1993	Blossom Has A Little lamb	Open		16.50	17
1993	First Kiss	Open		24.00	24
1993	For My Sweatheart	Open		22.00	22
1993	Friends Forever	Open		22.00	22
1995	Fuzzy Friends	Open		9.00	9
1993	Gently Down The Stream	10,000		27.00	27
1994	Get Well	Open		22.00	22
1993	Gift From Heaven	Open		10.00	10

YEAR ISSUE		EDITION LIMIT	YEAR RETD.	ISSUE PRICE	QUOTE U.S.$
1994	Hip Hip Hooray	Open		22.00	22
1992	Hippity-Hop. It's Eastertime!	Open		16.00	16
1993	Hugs & Kisses	Open		11.00	11
1993	I Love You	Open		22.00	22
1995	Little Miracles	Open		8.00	8
1993	Playing Cupid	Open		10.00	10
1992	Springtime Delights	Open		12.00	12
1993	Sugar & Spice	Open		24.00	24
1993	Sunday Stroll	Open		22.00	22
1992	A Wheelbarrow Of Sunshine	Open		17.00	17

Little Cheesers/Valentine Collection - C.Thammavongsa

1993	Ballerina Sweetheart	Open		10.00	10
1995	Be My Angel	Open		10.50	11
1993	First Kiss	Open		24.00	24
1993	For My Sweetheart	Open		22.00	22
1993	Friends Forever	Open		22.00	22
1993	Gently Down the Stream	10,000		27.00	27
1993	Hugs & Kisses	Open		11.00	11
1993	I Love You	Open		22.00	22
1995	My L'il Sweetheart	Open		9.00	9
1993	Playing Cupid	Open		10.00	10
1993	Sugar & Spice	Open		24.00	24
1993	Sunday Stroll	Open		22.00	22

Little Cheesers/Wedding Collection - Various

1993	The Big Day - C. Thammavongsa	Open		20.00	20
1992	Blossom Thistledown (bride) GDA/Thammavongsa	Open		16.00	16
1992	Cousin Woody & Little Truffle GDA/Thammavongsa	Open		20.00	20
1992	Frowzy Roquefort III With Gramophone GDA/Thammavongsa	Open		20.00	20
1992	Grandmama & Grandpapa Thistledown GDA/Thammavongsa	Retrd.	1994	20.00	20
1992	Great Aunt Rose Beside Table GDA/Thammavongsa	Open		20.00	20
1992	Harley & Harriet Harvestmouse GDA/Thammavongsa	Open		20.00	20
1992	Hickory Harvestmouse (groom) GDA/Thammavongsa	Open		16.00	16
1992	Jenny Butterfield/Sweet Cicely (bridesmaids) GDA/Thammavongsa	Retrd.	1995	20.00	20
1992	Little Truffle (ringbearer) GDA/Thammavongsa	Open		10.00	10
1992	Mama & Papa Woodsworth Dancing - GDA/Thammavongsa	Open		20.00	20
1992	Marigold Thistledown & Oscar Bobbins - GDA/Thammavongsa	Open		20.00	20
1992	Myrtle Meadowmouse With Medley - GDA/Thammavongsa	Retrd.	1992	20.00	20
1992	Pastor Smallwood GDA/Thammavongsa	Open		16.00	16
1992	Wedding Procession GDA/Thammavongsa	Open		40.00	40

Little Cheesers/Wedding Collection Accesories - C. Thammavongsa

1993	Banquet Table	Open		14.00	14
1993	Gazebo Base	Open		42.00	42

Little Cheesers/Wedding Collection Mini-Food Acc. - Various

1992	Bible Trinket Box GDA/Thammavongsa	Open		16.50	17
1992	Big Chocolate Cake	Retrd.	1994	4.50	5
1992	Bride Candleholder GDA/Thammavongsa	Open		20.00	20
1992	Cake Trinket Box GDA/Thammavongsa	Open		14.00	14
1992	Candles	Open		3.00	3
1992	Cherry Jello	Open		3.00	3
1992	Chocolate Pastry	Retrd.	1992	2.00	2
1992	Chocolate Pudding	Open		2.50	3
1992	Flour Bag	Retrd.	1992	2.00	2
1992	Flower Vase	Retrd.	1994	3.00	3
1992	Fruit Salad	Open		3.00	3
1993	Gooseberry Champagne C. Thammavongsa	Open		3.00	3
1992	Grass Base GDA/Thammavongsa	Suspd.		3.50	4
1992	Groom Candleholder GDA/Thammavongsa	Open		20.00	20
1992	Honey Pot	Open		2.00	2
1992	Ring Cake	Open		3.00	3
1992	Salt Can	Retrd.	1992	2.00	2
1992	Souffle	Retrd.	1992	2.50	3
1992	Soup Pot	Open		3.00	3
1992	Tea Pot Set	Retrd.	1994	3.00	3
1992	Teddy Mouse	Retrd.	1994	2.00	2
1993	Wedding Cake C. Thammavongsa	Open		4.50	5

Little Cheesers/Wedding Collection Musicals - Various

1993	Blossom & Hickory Musical C. Thammavongsa	Retrd.	1994	50.00	50
1992	Musical Blossom & Hickory Wedding Waterglobe GDA/Thammavongsa	Open		55.00	55
1992	Musical Wedding Base GDA/Thammavongsa	Open		32.00	32
1992	Musical Wooden Base For Wedding Processional	Open		25.00	25
1993	White Musical Wood Base For Gazebo Base "Evergreen" C. Thammavongsa	Open		25.00	25

Perfect Little Place Collection - C.Thammavongsa

1995	All Star Angel	Open		14.00	14
1995	Angel Face	Open		15.00	15
1995	Angel's Food	Open		15.00	15
1995	Divine Intervention	Open		15.00	15
1995	Heaven & Nature	Open		14.00	14
1995	Heavenly Grace	Open		14.00	14
1995	Match Made in Heaven	Open		18.00	18
1995	Paradise	Open		13.00	13
1995	Perfect Little Place	Open		16.00	16
1995	Pray the Lord My Soul to Keep	Open		13.00	13
1995	Ride Like The Wind	Open		15.00	15
1995	Sweet Sleep, Angel Mild	Open		13.50	14

Perfect Little Place/Christmas Collection - C.Thammavongsa

1995	Bearer of Blessings	Open		17.00	17
1995	A Child is Born	Open		21.00	21

Perfect Little Place/Valentine Collection - C.Thammavongsa

1995	Be My Angel	Open		16.00	16
1995	Sweet Innocence	Open		16.00	16
1995	Whispers of Love	Open		21.00	21

Pigsville Accessories - C.Thammavongsa

1995	Bale of Straw	Open		10.00	10
1994	Barn	Open		35.00	35
1995	Outhouse	Open		10.00	10
1994	Silo	Open		15.00	15

Pigsville Collection - C.Thammavongsa, unless otherwise noted

1993	Bakin' at the Beach	Open		11.00	11
1994	Bedtime	Open		9.50	10
1994	Birthday Surprise	Open		9.50	10
1993	Ice Cream Anyone? - G.D.A. Group	Retrd.	1994	9.00	9
1995	Juke Box	Open		12.00	12
1993	Me & My Ice Cream - G.D.A. Group	Retrd.	1994	17.00	17
1996	Melon Patch	Open		11.00	11
1993	Mother Love - G.D.A. Group	Open		13.00	13
1995	Mr. Fix It	Open		14.00	14
1993	Nap Time - G.D.A. Group	Retrd.	1995	11.00	11
1994	Ole Fishing Hole	Open		16.00	16
1995	Open Roads	Open		14.00	14
1993	P.O.P Display Sign	Open		8.00	8
1995	Paradise	Open		10.00	10
1993	Pig at the Beach - G.D.A. Group	Open		9.00	9
1996	Pig Pen Blues	Open		11.00	11
1996	Pig Tails	Open		10.00	10
1995	Piggy Back	Open		10.50	11
1994	Play Ball	Open		11.50	12
1994	Pretty Piglet	Open		8.00	8
1993	Prima Ballerina	Retrd.	1994	11.00	11
1994	Sandcastle	Open		12.00	12
1995	Scrub-A-Dub-Dub	Open		13.50	14
1995	Seeds of Love	Open		14.50	15
1994	Snacktime	Open		11.50	12
1993	Soap Suds - G.D.A. Group	Open		12.00	12
1994	Special Treat	Open		11.50	12
1993	Squeaky Clean - G.D.A. Group	Retrd.	1995	11.00	11
1994	Storytime	Open		13.00	13
1993	Tipsy - G.D.A. Group	Open		9.00	9
1995	Touchdown	Open		11.00	11
1993	True Love	Open		12.00	12
1994	Wedded Bliss	Open		16.00	16
1993	Wee Little Piggy	Open		8.00	8
1996	Yard Work	Open		13.00	13

Pigsville/Christmas Collection - C.Thammavongsa

1994	Christmas Trimmings	10,000		24.00	24
1995	Dear Santa	Open		10.00	10
1994	Joy to the World	Open		10.00	10
1994	Let It Snow	Open		12.00	12
1994	Mistletoe Magic	Open		14.00	14
1995	Mrs. Claus	Open		11.00	11
1995	Oh Christmas Tree	Open		10.50	11
1994	Santa Pig	Open		11.00	11
1995	Tucked into Bed	Open		12.00	12
1994	Yuletide Carols	Open		19.00	19

Pigsville/Fall, Halloween Collection - C.Thammavongsa

1995	Apple Bobbing	Open		10.00	10
1995	Giving Thanks	Open		10.00	10
1995	Pumpkin Pig	Open		11.00	11
1995	Scarecrow	Open		11.00	11

Pigsville/Valentine Collection - C.Thammavongsa

1995	Barn Dance	Open		14.50	15
1994	Champagne & Roses	Open		14.00	14
1995	The Hayloft	Open		11.00	11
1994	I Love You	Open		9.50	10
1994	I'm All Yours	Open		11.50	12
1995	Lover's Lane	Open		17.00	17
1994	Lovestruck	Open		10.00	10
1995	Popping The Question	Open		10.00	10
1995	Secret Admirer	Open		11.00	11
1995	Serenade	Open		10.50	11
1994	Sweetheart Pig	Open		8.00	8
1994	Together Forever	Open		15.00	15

The Precious Steeples Collection - Ganz/L. Sunarth

1995	Display Sign	Open		15.00	15
1995	Florence Cathedral	Open		40.00	40
1995	Notre Dame Cathedral	Open		40.00	40
1995	St. Patrick's Cathedral	Open		40.00	40
1995	St. Paul's Cathedral	Open		40.00	40
1995	St. Peter's Basilica	Open		40.00	40
1995	Westminster Abbey	Open		40.00	40

Trains Gone By Collection - Ganz

1995	C.P. Huntington train	3,000		70.00	70
1995	C.P. Huntington train with sound	2,000		85.00	85
1995	Display Sign	Open		24.00	24
1995	The General train	4,000		70.00	70
1995	The General train with sound	1,000		85.00	85
1995	New York Central train	3,000		70.00	70
1995	New York Central train with sound	2,000		85.00	85
1995	Pennsylvania train	4,000		70.00	70
1995	Pennsylvania train with sound	1,000		85.00	85
1995	Santa Fe train	4,000		70.00	70
1995	Santa Fe train with sound	1,000		85.00	85

Watching Over You Collection - C.Thammavongsa

1995	Angelic Teachings	Open		42.00	42
1995	New Borne Babe	Open		40.00	40
1995	Sweet Dreams Little One	Open		38.00	38

Woodland Santas Collection - C.Thammavongsa

1995	Forest Friends	Open		45.00	45
1995	Lake of the Woods	Open		45.00	45
1995	Santa's Sanctuary	Open		41.00	41

Gartlan USA

Members Only Figurine

1990	Wayne Gretzky-Home Uniform L. Heyda	Closed	1991	75.00	225-450
1991	Joe Montana-Road Uniform F. Barnum	Closed	1992	75.00	150-250
1991	Kareem Abdul-Jabbar - L. Heyda	Closed	1993	75.00	175-250
1992	Mike Schmidt - J. Slockbower	Closed	1993	79.00	150-200
1993	Hank Aaron - J. Slockbower	Closed	1994	79.00	100-125
1994	Shaquille O'Neal - L. Cella	Closed	1995	39.95	75-100

Club Gift

1989	Pete Rose, Plate (8 1/2") B. Forbes	Closed	1990	Gift	125-150
1990	Al Barlick, Plate (8 1/2") M. Taylor	Closed	1991	Gift	110
1991	Joe Montana (8 1/2") - M. Taylor	Closed	1992	Gift	125-175
1992	Ken Griffey Jr., Plate (8 1/2") - M. Taylor	Closed	1993	30.00	70-90
1993	Gordie Howe, Plate (8 1/2") M. Taylor	Closed	1994	30.00	50-90
1994	Shaquille O'Neal, Plate (8 1/2") M. Taylor	Closed	1995	30.00	65-100

Kareem Abdul-Jabbar Sky-Hook Collection - L. Heyda

1989	Kareem Abdul-Jabbar "The Captain"-signed	1,989	1990	175.00	300-550
1989	Kareem Abdul-Jabbar, A/P	100	1990	200.00	550-700
1989	Kareem Abdul-Jabbar, Commemorative	33	1990	275.00	4200-4700

Magic Johnson Gold Rim Collection - Roger

1988	Magic Johnson -"Magic in Motion"	1,737	1989	125.00	500-1000
1988	Magic Johnson A/P-"Magic in Motion", signed	250	1989	175.00	2500
1988	Magic Johnson Commemorative	32	1989	275.00	7000-9000

Mike Schmidt "500th" Home Run Edition - Various

1987	Figurine-signed - Roger	1,987	1988	150.00	825-950
1987	Figurine-signed, A/P - Roger	20	1988	275.00	1400-1700
1987	Plaque-"Only Perfect", A/P Paluso	20	1988	200.00	550
1987	Plaque-"Only Perfect", signed Paluso	500	1988	150.00	225-400

Plaques - Various

1986	George Brett-"Royalty in Motion", signed - J. Martin	2,000	1987	75.00	275
1985	Pete Rose-"Desire to Win", signed - T. Sizemore	4,192	1986	75.00	325
1986	Reggie Jackson A/P-The Roundtripper, signed - J. Martin	44	1987	175.00	400-475
1986	Reggie Jackson-"The Roundtripper" signed - J. Martin	500	1987	150.00	350-400
1987	Roger Staubach, signed C. Soileau	1,979	1988	85.00	250-325

Signed Figurines - Various

1991	Al Barlick - V. Bova	1,989		125.00	125
1993	Bob Cousy - L. Heyda	950		150.00	150
1991	Bobby Hull - The Golden Jet L. Heyda	1,983		150.00	150
1992	Bobby Hull, A/P - L. Heyda	300	1994	350.00	400-600

YEAR ISSUE		EDITION LIMIT	YEAR RETD.	ISSUE PRICE	QUOTE U.S.$
1991	Brett Hull - The Golden Brett L. Heyda	1,986		150.00	150
1992	Brett Hull, A/P - L. Heyda	300	1994	350.00	400-600
1989	Carl Yastrzemski-"Yaz", A/P L. Heyda	250	1990	150.00	500-800
1989	Carl Yastrzemski-"Yaz" L. Heyda	1,989	1990	150.00	400-575
1992	Carlton Fisk - J. Slockbower	1,972		150.00	150
1992	Carlton Fisk, A/P - J. Slockbower	300	1993	350.00	400-700
1990	Darryl Strawberry - L. Heyda	2,500		100.00	100
1994	Eddie Matthews - R. Sun	1,978		195.00	150-195
1994	Frank Thomas - D. Carroll	1,500	1995	225.00	250-450
1990	George Brett - F. Barnum	2,250		225.00	250
1992	Gordie Howe - L. Heyda	2,358	1994	150.00	250-350
1990	Gordie Howe, signed A/P L. Heyda	250	1994	395.00	395
1992	Hank Aaron - F. Barnum	1,982	1994	150.00	225-375
1992	Hank Aaron Commemorative w/displ. case - F. Barnum	755	1994	275.00	275-400
1992	Hank Aaron, A/P - F. Barnum	300	1994	325.00	350
1991	Hull Matched Figurines L. Heyda	950	1993	500.00	500
1992	Isiah Thomas - J. Slockbower	1,990	1994	225.00	225
1989	Joe DiMaggio - L. Heyda	2,214	1990	275.00	1500
1990	Joe DiMaggio- Pinstripe Yankee Clipper - L. Heyda	325	1990	695.00	2000-2800
1991	Joe Montana - F. Barnum	2,250	1991	325.00	400-675
1991	Joe Montana, A/P - F. Barnum	250	1991	500.00	700-1100
1989	John Wooden-Coaching Classics - L. Heyda	1,975		175.00	175
1989	John Wooden-Coaching Classics, A/P - L. Heyda	250		350.00	350
1989	Johnny Bench - L. Heyda	1,989	1990	150.00	225-500
1989	Johnny Bench, A/P - L. Heyda	250	1990	150.00	500-725
1994	Ken Griffey Jr., signed A/P J. Slockbower	300		395.00	395
1991	Ken Griffey, Jr - J. Slockbower	1,989		200.00	225
1993	Kristi Yamaguchi - K. Ling Sun	950		125.00	125
1990	Luis Aparicio - J. Slockbower	1,984		125.00	125
1991	Monte Irvin - V. Bova	1,973		100.00	100
1985	Pete Rose-"For the Record", signed - H. Reed	4,192	1987	125.00	1100-1500
1992	Ralph Kiner - J. Slockbower	1,975		100.00	100
1991	Rod Carew - Hitting Splendor J. Slockbower	1,991		225.00	225
1994	Sam Snead - L. Cella	950		100.00	100
1994	Shaquille O'Neal - R. Sun	500	1995	225.00	275
1992	Stan Musial - J. Slockbower	1,969		200.00	225
1992	Stan Musial, A/P - J. Slockbower	300		300.00	300
1989	Steve Carlton - L. Heyda	3,290	1992	175.00	225-325
1989	Steve Carlton, A/P - L. Heyda	300	1992	350.00	400-500
1989	Ted Williams - L. Heyda	2,654	1990	295.00	400-800
1989	Ted Williams, A/P - L. Heyda	250	1990	650.00	700-1000
1992	Tom Seaver - J. Slockbower	1,992		125.00	125
1994	Troy Aikman - V. Davila	500	1995	225.00	250-450
1991	Warren Spahn - J. Slockbower	1,973	1993	125.00	150-275
1989	Wayne Gretzky - L. Heyda	1,851	1989	225.00	600-1000
1989	Wayne Gretzky, A/P - L. Heyda	300	1989	695.00	1800-2300
1990	Whitey Ford - S. Barnum	2,360		125.00	125
1990	Whitey Ford, A/P - S. Barnum	250		350.00	350
1989	Yogi Berra - F. Barnum	2,150	1994	225.00	225
1989	Yogi Berra, A/P - F. Barnum	250	1994	350.00	350

Genesis

Aquatics Collection - K. Cantrell

YEAR ISSUE		EDITION LIMIT	YEAR RETD.	ISSUE PRICE	QUOTE U.S.$
1994	Ancient Mariner (Sea Turtles)	950		950.00	990
1994	Bringing Up Baby (Humpback Whales)	950		950.00	990
1994	Old Men of the Sea (Sea Otters)	950		990.00	990
1994	Sea Wolves (Killer Whales)	950		950.00	990
1994	Splish Splash (Dolphins)	950		950.00	990

Arctic Collection - K. Cantrell

YEAR ISSUE		EDITION LIMIT	YEAR RETD.	ISSUE PRICE	QUOTE U.S.$
1995	Arctic Hares	2,500		98.00	98
1995	Arctic Owl	2,500		98.00	98
1995	Arctic Wolves	2,500		98.00	98
1995	Harp Seal	2,500		98.00	98
1995	Polar Bear	2,500		98.00	98

Birds of Prey - K. Cantrell

YEAR ISSUE		EDITION LIMIT	YEAR RETD.	ISSUE PRICE	QUOTE U.S.$
1994	Bald Eagle	1,250		350.00	350
1994	Great Horned Owl	1,250		350.00	350

Neptune's Children - K. Cantrell

YEAR ISSUE		EDITION LIMIT	YEAR RETD.	ISSUE PRICE	QUOTE U.S.$
1995	Neptune's Children	1,250		290.00	290
1995	Tranquil Waters	1,250		290.00	290

Ocean Realm - K. Cantrell

YEAR ISSUE		EDITION LIMIT	YEAR RETD.	ISSUE PRICE	QUOTE U.S.$
1994	Dophins (Dolphins in Lucite)	1,250		240.00	250
1994	Humpback Whales	1,250		240.00	250
1994	Manta Ray	1,250		240.00	250
1994	Marlins	1,250		240.00	250
1994	Otters	1,250		240.00	250

River Dwellers - K. Cantrell

YEAR ISSUE		EDITION LIMIT	YEAR RETD.	ISSUE PRICE	QUOTE U.S.$
1994	Construction Crew (Beavers)	950		990.00	990
1994	Ice Follies	950		890.00	950
1994	Salmon Supper	950		990.00	990

Special Commission - K. Cantrell

YEAR ISSUE		EDITION LIMIT	YEAR RETD.	ISSUE PRICE	QUOTE U.S.$
1994	Fragile Planet	950		350.00	350
1995	Heavenly Waters	950		N/A	N/A

Geo. Zoltan Lefton Company

Colonial Village - Lefton

YEAR ISSUE		EDITION LIMIT	YEAR RETD.	ISSUE PRICE	QUOTE U.S.$
1993	Antiques & Curiosities 00723	Open		50.00	50
1990	The Ardmore House 07338	Closed	1995	45.00	90
1993	Baldwin's Fine Jewelry 00722	Open		50.00	50
1991	Belle-Union Saloon 07482	Closed	1994	45.00	85-100
1989	Bijou Theatre 06897	Closed	1990	40.00	300
1994	Black Sheep Tavern 01003	Open		50.00	50
1993	Blacksmith 00720	Open		47.00	47
1992	Brenner's Apothecary 07961	Open		45.00	50
1994	Brown's Book Shop 01001	Open		50.00	50
1993	Burnside 00717	Open		50.00	50
1989	Capper's Millinery 06904	Suspd.		40.00	90-115
1988	City Hall 06340	Suspd.		40.00	75-300
1989	Cobb's Bootery 06903	Suspd.		40.00	140
1990	Coffee & Tea Shoppe 07342	Open		45.00	47
1989	Cole's Barn 06750	Closed	1994	40.00	95
1995	Colonial Savings and Loan 01321	Open		50.00	50
1995	Colonial Village News 01002	Open		50.00	50
1990	Country Post Office 07341	Closed	1994	45.00	65-150
1992	County Courthouse 00233	Open		45.00	50
1991	Daisy's Flower Shop 07478	Open		45.00	47
1993	Dentist's Office 00724	Open		50.00	50
1993	Doctor's Office 00721	Open		50.00	50
1992	Elegant Lady Dress Shop 00232	Open		45.00	50
1988	Engine Co. No. 5 Firehouse 06342	Open		40.00	50
1988	Faith Church 06333	Closed	1991	40.00	200-300
1990	Fellowship Church 07334	Open		45.00	47
1990	The First Church 07333	Open		45.00	47
1988	First Post Office 06343	Open		40.00	50
1988	Friendship Chapel 06334	Closed	1994	40.00	100-150
1993	Green's Grocery 00725	Open		50.00	50
1988	Greystone House 06339	Closed	1995	40.00	47
1989	Gull's Nest Lighthouse 06747	Open		40.00	47
1990	Hampshire House 07336	Open		45.00	50
1990	Hillside Church 11991	Closed	1991	60.00	400-700
1995	Historical Society Museum 01328	Open		50.00	50
1988	House of Blue Gables 06337	Closed	1995	40.00	65
1988	Johnson's Antiques 06346	Closed	1993	40.00	140
1993	Joseph House 00718	Open		50.00	50
1993	Kirby House-CVRA Exclusive 00716	Closed	1994	50.00	75-100
1992	Lakehurst House 11992	Closed	1992	55.00	200-400
1992	Main St. Church 00230	Open		45.00	50
1989	The Major's Manor 06902	Open		40.00	47
1989	Maple St. Church 06748	Closed	1993	40.00	75-250
1993	Mark Hall 00719	Open		50.00	50
1989	Miller Bros. Silversmiths 06905	Suspd.		40.00	90
1994	Mt. Zion Church 11994	Closed	1994	70.00	150-200
1990	Mulberry Station 07344	Open		50.00	65
1995	Mundt Manor 01008	Open		50.00	50
1988	New Hope Church (Musical) 06470	Closed	N/A	40.00	75-88
1990	The Nob Hill 07337	Closed	1995	45.00	75
1992	Northpoint School 07960	Open		45.00	50
1994	Notfel Cabin 01320	Open		50.00	50
1995	O'Doul's Ice House 01324	Open		50.00	50
1988	Old Time Station 06335	Open		40.00	50
1986	Original Set of 6	Unkn.		210.00	N/A
1986	-Charity Chapel 05895	Closed	1989	35.00	250-325
1986	-King's Cottage 05890	Open		35.00	50
1986	-McCauley House 05892	Closed	1988	35.00	240
1986	-Nelson House 05891	Closed	1989	35.00	300-470
1986	-Old Stone Church 05825	Open		35.00	47
1986	-The Welcome Home 05824	Open		35.00	47
1986	Original Set of 6	Unkn.		210.00	N/A
1986	-Church of the Golden Rule 05820	Open		35.00	50
1986	-General Store 05823	Closed	1988	35.00	400-500
1986	-Lil Red School House 05821	Open		35.00	50
1986	-Penny House 05893	Closed	1988	35.00	300-480
1986	-Ritter House 05894	Closed	1989	35.00	300-400
1986	-Train Station 05822	Closed	1989	35.00	300-350
1995	Patriot Bridge 01325	Open		50.00	50
1990	Pierpont-Smithe's Curios 07343	Closed	1993	45.00	100-150
1995	Queensgate 01329	Open		50.00	50
1989	Quincy's Clock Shop 06899	Open		40.00	47
1995	Rainy Days Barn 01323	Open		50.00	50
1994	Real Estate Office -CVRA Exclusive 01006	Open		50.00	50
1988	The Ritz Hotel 06341	Suspd.		40.00	100-200
1994	Rosamond 00988	Open		50.00	50
1990	Ryman Auditorium-Special Edition 08010	Open		50.00	55
1992	San Sebastian Mission 00231	Closed	1995	45.00	50
1991	Sanderson's Mill 07927	Open		45.00	47
1990	Ship's Chandler's Shop 07339	Suspd.		45.00	47
1994	Smith and Jones Drug Store 01007	Open		50.00	50
1991	Smith's Smithy 07476	Closed	1991	45.00	150-200
1994	Springfield 00989	Open		50.00	50
1993	St. James Cathedral 11993	Closed	1993	75.00	200-275
1993	St. Peter's Church w/Speaker 00715	Open		60.00	60
1988	The State Bank 06345	Open		40.00	50
1992	Stearn's Stable 00228	Open		45.00	50
1988	The Stone House 06338	Open		40.00	47
1991	Sweet Shop 07481	Open		45.00	47
1989	Sweetheart's Bridge 06751	Open		40.00	47
1991	The Toy Maker's Shop 07477	Open		45.00	47
1988	Trader Tom's Gen'l Store 06336	Open		40.00	47
1990	The Victoria House 07335	Closed	1993	45.00	75
1989	Victorian Apothecary 06900	Closed	1991	40.00	150
1991	Victorian Gazebo 07925	Open		45.00	45
1989	The Village Bakery 06898	Open		40.00	47
1989	Village Barber Shop 06901	Open		40.00	47
1986	Village Express 05826	Closed	N/A	27.00	145
1992	Village Green Gazebo 00227	Open		22.00	22
1990	Village Hardware 07340	Open		45.00	50
1994	Village Hospital 01004	Open		50.00	50
1992	The Village Inn 07962	Open		45.00	50
1989	Village Library 06752	Open		40.00	47
1988	Village Police Station 06344	Open		40.00	50
1989	Village School 06749	Closed	1991	40.00	100
1991	Watt's Candle Shop 07479	Closed	1994	45.00	70-100
1994	White's Butcher Shop 01005	Open		50.00	50
1991	Wig Shop 07480	Suspd.		45.00	75
1992	Windmilll 00229	Open		45.00	47
1995	Wycoff Manor 11995	5,500		75.00	75
1995	Zachary Peters Cabinet Maker 01322	Open		50.00	50

Colonial Village Special Event - Lefton

YEAR ISSUE		EDITION LIMIT	YEAR RETD.	ISSUE PRICE	QUOTE U.S.$
1995	Bayside Inn 01326	Yr.Iss.		50.00	50

Historic American Lighthouse Collection - Lefton

YEAR ISSUE		EDITION LIMIT	YEAR RETD.	ISSUE PRICE	QUOTE U.S.$
1995	1716 Boston Lighthouse 08607	7,500	1995	50.00	50
1994	Admirality Head, WA 01126	Open		40.00	40
1992	Assateaque, VA 00137	Open		40.00	40
1995	Barneget, NJ 01333	Open		40.00	40
1993	Big Sable Point, MI 00885	Open		40.00	40
1994	Bodie Island, NC 01118	Open		40.00	40
1993	Boston Harbor, MA 00881	Open		40.00	40
1994	Cana Island, WI 01117	Open		40.00	40
1993	Cape Cod, MA 00882	Open		40.00	40
1994	Cape Florida, FL 01125	Open		40.00	40
1992	Cape Hatteras, NC 00133	Open		40.00	40
1992	Cape Henry, VA 00135	Open		40.00	40
1992	Cape Lookout, NC 00134	Open		40.00	40
1994	Cape May, NJ 01013	Closed	1995	40.00	40
1994	Chicago Harbor, IL 01010	Open		40.00	40
1995	Fire Island, NY 01334	Open		40.00	40
1994	Ft. Gratiot, MI 01123	Open		40.00	40
1993	Gray's Harbor, WA 00880	Open		40.00	40
1994	Heceta Head, OR 01122	Open		40.00	40
1995	Jupiter Inlet, FL 01336	Open		40.00	40
1993	Marblehead, OH 00879	Open		40.00	40
1993	Montawk, NY 00884	Open		40.00	40
1994	New London Ledge, CT 01119	Open		40.00	40
1994	Ocracoke, NC 01124	Open		40.00	40
1994	Old Point Loma, CA 01011	Open		40.00	40
1995	Pigeon Point, CA 01289	Open		40.00	40
1995	Point Betsie, MI 01335	Open		47.00	47
1995	Point Cabrillo, CA 01330	Open		47.00	47
1993	Point Wilson, WA 00883	Open		40.00	40
1995	Ponce De Leon, FL 01332	Open		40.00	40
1994	Portland Head, ME 01121	Open		40.00	40
1992	Sandy Hook, NJ 00132	Open		40.00	40
1994	Split Rock, MN 01009	Open		40.00	40
1994	St. Augustine, FL 01015	Open		40.00	40
1994	St. Simons, GA 01012	Open		40.00	40
1995	Toledo Harbor, OH 01331	Open		47.00	47
1994	Tybee Island, GA 01014	Open		40.00	40
1992	West Quoddy Head, ME 00136	Open		40.00	40
1993	White Shoal, MI 00878	Open		40.00	40
1994	Yerba Buena, CA 01120	Open		40.00	40

Goebel of North America

Betsey Clark Figurines - G. Bochmann

YEAR ISSUE		EDITION LIMIT	YEAR RETD.	ISSUE PRICE	QUOTE U.S.$
1972	Bless You	Closed	N/A	18.00	275
1972	Friends	Closed	N/A	21.00	400
1972	Little Miracle	Closed	N/A	25.00	350
1972	So Much Beauty	Closed	N/A	25.00	350

Co-Boy - G. Skrobek

YEAR ISSUE		EDITION LIMIT	YEAR RETD.	ISSUE PRICE	QUOTE U.S.$
1981	Al the Trumpet Player	Closed	N/A	45.00	50-75
1987	Bank-Pete the Pirate	Closed	N/A	80.00	125-150
1987	Bank-Utz the Money Bags	Closed	N/A	80.00	100-125
1981	Ben the Blacksmith	Closed	N/A	45.00	50-75
XX	Bert the Soccer Star	Closed	N/A	Unkn.	50-75
1971	Bit the Bachelor	Closed	N/A	16.00	50-75
1972	Bob the Bookworm	Closed	N/A	20.00	50-75
1984	Brad the Clockmaker	Closed	N/A	75.00	125-150
1972	Brum the Lawyer	Closed	N/A	20.00	50-75
XX	Candy the Baker's Delight	Closed	N/A	Unkn.	50-75
1980	Carl the Chef	Closed	N/A	49.00	50-75
1984	Chris the Shoemaker	Closed	N/A	45.00	50-75
1987	Chuck on His Pig	Closed	N/A	75.00	75
1984	Chuck the Chimney Sweep	Closed	N/A	45.00	50-75
1987	Clock-Cony the Watchman	Closed	N/A	125.00	125-150
1987	Clock-Sepp and the Beer Keg	Closed	N/A	125.00	125-150
1972	Co-Boy Plaque	Closed	N/A	20.00	50-125
XX	Conny the Night Watchman	Closed	N/A	Unkn.	125-150
1980	Doc the Doctor	Closed	N/A	49.00	50-100
XX	Ed the Wine Cellar Steward	Closed	N/A	Unkn.	50-75
1984	Felix the Baker	Closed	N/A	45.00	50-75
1971	Fips the Foxy Fisherman	Closed	N/A	16.00	50-75
1971	Fritz the Happy Boozer	Closed	N/A	16.00	50-75
1981	George the Gourmand	Closed	N/A	45.00	50-75
1980	Gerd the Diver	Closed	N/A	49.00	125-175
1978	Gil the Goalie	Closed	N/A	34.00	50-85
1981	Greg the Gourmet	Closed	N/A	45.00	50-95

YEAR ISSUE		EDITION LIMIT	YEAR RETD.	ISSUE PRICE	QUOTE U.S.$
1981	Greta the Happy Housewife	Closed	N/A	45.00	50-75
1980	Herb the Horseman	Closed	N/A	49.00	50-100
1984	Herman the Butcher	Closed	N/A	45.00	50-75
1984	Homer the Driver	Closed	N/A	45.00	50-75
XX	Jack the Village Pharmacist	Closed	N/A	Unkn.	50-75
XX	Jim the Bowler	Closed	N/A	Unkn.	50-75
XX	John the Hawkeye Hunter	Closed	N/A	Unkn.	50-75
1972	Kuni the Big Dipper	Closed	N/A	20.00	50-75
XX	Mark-Safety First	Closed	N/A	Unkn.	120
1984	Marthe the Nurse	Closed	N/A	45.00	50-75
XX	Max the Boxing Champ	Closed	N/A	Unkn.	135
1971	Mike the Jam Maker	Closed	N/A	16.00	50-75
1980	Monty the Mountain Climber	Closed	N/A	49.00	50-75
1981	Nick the Nightclub Singer	Closed	N/A	45.00	50-75
1981	Niels the Strummer	Closed	N/A	45.00	50-75
1978	Pat the Pitcher	Closed	N/A	34.00	50-75
1984	Paul the Dentist	Closed	N/A	45.00	50-75
1981	Peter the Accordionist	Closed	N/A	45.00	50-75
XX	Petrl the Village Angler	Closed	N/A	Unkn.	50-75
1971	Plum the Pastry Chef	Closed	N/A	16.00	50-75
1972	Porz the Mushroom Muncher	Closed	N/A	20.00	50-75
1984	Rick the Fireman	Closed	N/A	45.00	50-75
1971	Robby the Vegetarian	Closed	N/A	16.00	85
1984	Rudy the World Traveler	Closed	N/A	45.00	50-75
1971	Sam the Gourmet	Closed	N/A	16.00	50-75
1972	Sepp the Beer Buddy	Closed	N/A	20.00	50-75
1984	Sid the Vintner	Closed	N/A	45.00	50-75
1980	Ted the Tennis Player	Closed	N/A	49.00	50-85
1971	Tom the Honey Lover	Closed	N/A	16.00	70
1978	Tommy Touchdown	Closed	N/A	34.00	50-75
XX	Toni the Skier	Closed	N/A	Unkn.	50-75
1972	Utz the Banker	Closed	N/A	20.00	50-75
1981	Walter the Jogger	Closed	N/A	45.00	50-75
1971	Wim the Court Supplier	Closed	N/A	16.00	50-75

Co-Boys-Culinary - Welling/Skrobek

1994	Mike the Jam Maker 301050	Open		30.00	30
1994	Plum the Sweets Maker 301052	Open		30.00	30
1994	Robby the Vegetarian 301054	Open		30.00	30
1994	Sepp the Drunkard 301051	Open		30.00	30
1994	Tom the Sweet Tooth 301053	Open		30.00	30

Co-Boys-Professionals - Welling/Skrobek

1994	Brum the Lawyer 301060	Open		30.00	30
1994	Conny the Nightwatchman 301062	Open		30.00	30
1994	Doc the Doctor 301064	Open		30.00	30
1994	John the Hunter 301063	Open		30.00	30
1994	Utz the Banker 301061	Open		30.00	30

Co-Boys-Sports - Welling/Skrobek

1994	Bert the Soccer Player 301059	Open		30.00	30
1994	Jim the Bowler 301057	Open		30.00	30
1994	Petri the Fisherman 301055	Open		30.00	30
1994	Ted the Tennis Player 301058	Open		30.00	30
1994	Toni the Skier 301056	Open		30.00	30

Goebel Figurines - N. Rockwell

1963	Advertising Plaque 212	Closed	N/A	Unkn.	N/A
1963	Boyhood Dreams (Adventurers between Adventures) 202	Closed	N/A	12.00	350-400
1963	Buttercup Test (Beguiling Buttercup) 209	Closed	N/A	10.00	350-400
1963	First Love (A Scholarly Pace) 210	Closed	N/A	30.00	350-400
1963	His First Smoke 204	Closed	N/A	9.00	350-400
1963	Home Cure 206	Closed	N/A	16.00	350-400
1963	Little Veterinarian (Mysterious Malady) 201	Closed	N/A	15.00	350-400
1963	Mother's Helper (Pride of Parenthood) 203	Closed	N/A	15.00	350-400
1963	My New Pal (A Boy Meets His Dog) 205	Closed	N/A	12.00	350-400
1963	Patient Anglers (Fisherman's Paradise) 211	Closed	N/A	18.00	350-400
1963	She Loves Me (Day Dreamer) 208	Closed	N/A	8.00	350-400
1963	Timely Assistance (Love Aid) 207	Closed	N/A	16.00	350-400

Miniatures-Americana Series - R. Olszewski

1982	American Bald Eagle 661-B	Closed	1989	45.00	250-355
1986	Americana Display 951-D	Open	1995	80.00	105
1989	Blacksmith 667-P	Closed	1989	55.00	135-200
1986	Carrousel Ride 665-B	Closed	1995	45.00	100-150
1985	Central Park Sunday 664-B	Closed	1995	45.00	70
1984	Eyes on the Horizon 663-B	Closed	1995	45.00	175-300
1981	The Plainsman 660-B	Closed	1989	45.00	175-295
1983	She Sounds the Deep 662-B	Closed	1995	45.00	70
1987	To The Bandstand 666-B	Closed	1995	45.00	70

Miniatures-Children's Series - R. Olszewski

1983	Backyard Frolic 633-P	Closed	1995	65.00	100
1980	Blumenkinder-Courting 630-P	Closed	1989	55.00	175-395
1990	Building Blocks Castle (large) 968-D	Closed	1995	75.00	100
1987	Carrousel Days (plain base) 637-P	Closed	1989	85.00	750-815
1987	Carrousel Days 637-P	Closed	1989	85.00	150-270
1988	Children's Display (small)	Closed	1995	45.00	60
1989	Clowning Around 636-P (new style)	Closed	1995	85.00	105
1986	Clowning Around 636-P (old style)	Closed	N/A	85.00	195-220
1984	Grandpa 634-P	Closed	1995	75.00	100-115
1988	Little Ballerina 638-P	Closed	1995	85.00	100-115
1982	Out and About 632-P	Closed	1989	85.00	385-445
1985	Snow Holiday 635-P	Closed	1995	75.00	100
1981	Summer Days 631-P	Closed	1989	65.00	315-370

Miniatures-Classic Clocks - Larsen

1995	Alexis	2,500		200.00	200
1995	Blinking Admiral	2,500		200.00	200
1995	Play	2,500		250.00	250

Miniatures-Disney-Cinderella - Disney

1991	Anastasia 172-P	Suspd.		85.00	95-115
1991	Cinderella 176-P	Suspd.		85.00	85-175
1991	Cinderella's Coach Display 978-D	Suspd.		95.00	110-150
1991	Cinderella's Dream Castle 976-D	Suspd.		95.00	110-135
1991	Drizella 174-P	Suspd.		85.00	95-115
1991	Fairy Godmother 180-P	Suspd.		85.00	95-125
1991	Footman 181-P	Suspd.		85.00	100
1991	Gus 177-P	Suspd.		80.00	85-110
1991	Jaq 173-P	Suspd.		80.00	85-110
1991	Lucifer 175-P	Suspd.		80.00	85-135
1991	Prince Charming 179-P	Suspd.		85.00	95-175
1991	Stepmother 178-P	Suspd.		85.00	95-115

Miniatures-Disney-Peter Pan - Disney

1994	Captain Hook 188-P	Suspd.		160.00	160-200
1992	John 186-P	Suspd.		90.00	110-150
1994	Lost Boy-Fox 191-P	Suspd.		130.00	130
1994	Lost Boy-Rabbit 192-P	Suspd.		130.00	130
1992	Michael 187-P	Suspd.		90.00	110
1992	Nana 189-P	Suspd.		95.00	110
1994	Neverland Display 997-D	Suspd.		150.00	150-175
1992	Peter Pan 184-P	Suspd.		90.00	115-200
1992	Peter Pan's London 986-D	Suspd.		125.00	135
1994	Smee 190-P	Suspd.		140.00	140-165
1992	Wendy 185-P	Suspd.		90.00	110-150

Miniatures-Disney-Pinocchio - Disney

1991	Blue Fairy 693-P	Suspd.		95.00	110-140
1990	Geppetto's Toy Shop Display 965-D	Suspd.		95.00	115-150
1990	Geppetto/Figaro 682-P	Suspd.		90.00	105-125
1990	Gideon 683-P	Suspd.		75.00	95-115
1990	J. Worthington Foulfellow 684-P	Suspd.		95.00	105-135
1990	Jiminy Cricket 685-P	Suspd.		75.00	95-150
1991	Little Street Lamp Display 964-D	Suspd.		65.00	75-125
1992	Monstro The Whale 985-D	Suspd.		120.00	150-250
1990	Pinocchio 686-P	Suspd.		75.00	95-190
1991	Stromboli 694-P	Suspd.		95.00	110-150
1991	Stromboli's Street Wagon 979-D	Suspd.		105.00	120-150

Miniatures-Disney-Snow White - Disney

1987	Bashful 165-P	Suspd.		60.00	95-110
1991	Castle Courtyard Display 981-D	Suspd.		105.00	115-225
1987	Cozy Cottage Display 941-D	Suspd.		35.00	200-325
1987	Doc 162-P	Suspd.		60.00	95-110
1987	Dopey 167-P	Suspd.		60.00	125-200
1987	Grumpy 166-P	Suspd.		60.00	95-110
1987	Happy 164-P	Suspd.		60.00	95-110
1988	House In The Woods Display 944-D	Suspd.		60.00	110-135
1992	Path In The Woods 996-D	Suspd.		140.00	140-195
1987	Sleepy 163-P	Suspd.		60.00	95-110
1987	Sneezy 161-P	Suspd.		60.00	95-110
1987	Snow White 168-P	Suspd.		60.00	125-200
1990	Snow White's Prince 170-P	Suspd.		80.00	120-135
1992	Snow White's Queen 182-P	Suspd.		100.00	115-165
1992	Snow White's Witch 183-P	Suspd.		100.00	115-165
1990	The Wishing Well Display 969-D	Suspd.		65.00	80-150

Miniatures-Disneyana Convention - R. Olszewski

1994	Mickey Self Portrait	500		295.00	750-950

Miniatures-Historical Series - R. Olszewski

1985	Capodimonte 600-P (new style)	Suspd.		90.00	145-195
1980	Capodimonte 600-P (old style)	Closed	1987	90.00	425-565
1983	The Cherry Pickers 602-P	Suspd.		85.00	250-295
1990	English Country Garden 970-D	Open		85.00	110
1989	Farmer w/Doves 607-P	Open		85.00	115
1985	Floral Bouquet Pompadour 604-P	Open		85.00	120
1990	Gentleman Fox Hunt 616-P	Suspd.		145.00	170-190
1988	Historical Display 943-D	Open		45.00	65
1981	Masquerade-St. Petersburg 601-P	Closed	1989	65.00	195-250
1987	Meissen Parrot 605-P	Open		85.00	115
1988	Minton Rooster 606-P	7,500		85.00	115
1984	Moor With Spanish Horse 603-P	Open		85.00	115
1992	Poultry Seller 608-G	1,500		200.00	245

Miniatures-Jack & The Beanstalk - R. Olszewski

1994	Beanseller 742-P	5,000		200.00	210
1994	Jack & The Beanstalk Display 999-D	5,000		225.00	260
1994	Jack and the Cow 743-P	5,000		180.00	195
1994	Jack's Mom 741-P	5,000		145.00	180

Miniatures-Mickey Mouse - Disney

1990	Fantasia Living Brooms 972-D	Suspd.		85.00	185-250
1990	The Sorcerer's Apprentice 171-P	Suspd.		80.00	175-200
1990	Set	Suspd.		165.00	450

Miniatures-Nativity Collection - R. Olszewski

1992	3 Kings Display 987-D	Open		85.00	105
1992	Balthazar 405-P	Open		135.00	200
1994	Camel & Tender 819292	Open		380.00	395
1992	Caspar 406-P	Open		135.00	200
1994	Final Nativity Display 991-D	Open		260.00	275
1994	Guardian Angel 407-P	Open		200.00	225
1991	Holy Family Display 982-D	Open		85.00	95
1991	Joseph 401-P	Open		95.00	130
1991	Joyful Cherubs 403-P	Open		130.00	185
1992	Melchoir 404-P	Open		135.00	200
1991	Mother/Child 440-P	Open		120.00	155
1994	Sheep & Shepherd 819290	Open		230.00	240
1991	The Stable Donkey 402-P	Open		95.00	130

Miniatures-Nature's Moments - Yenawine

1995	Bathing Beauties	Open		95.00	95
1995	Fish Paradise	Open		110.00	110
1995	Gathering Goodies	Open		95.00	95
1995	Hide and Seek	Open		110.00	110
1995	Penguins Plunge	Open		95.00	95
1995	Polar Playground	Open		110.00	110
1995	Preparing for Flight	Open		80.00	80
1995	Robyn Refresher	Open		95.00	95
1995	Summer Surprise	Open		95.00	95
1995	Touch and Go	Open		95.00	95

Miniatures-Night Before Christmas (1st Edition) - R. Olszewski

1990	Eight Tiny Reindeer 691-P	5,000		110.00	135
1990	Mama & Papa 692-P	5,000		110.00	140
1990	St. Nicholas 690-P	5,000		95.00	125
1990	Sugar Plum Boy 687-P	5,000		70.00	100
1990	Sugar Plum Girl 689-P	5,000		70.00	100
1991	Up To The Housetop 966-D	5,000		95.00	115
1990	Yule Tree 688-P	5,000		90.00	110

Miniatures-Oriental Series - R. Olszewski

1986	The Blind Men and the Elephant 643-P	Suspd.		70.00	125-200
1990	Chinese Temple Lion 646-P	Open		90.00	115
1987	Chinese Water Dragon 644-P	Suspd.		70.00	135-175
1990	Empress' Garden Display 967-D	Open		95.00	135
1982	The Geisha 641-P	Suspd.		65.00	195-225
1984	Kuan Yin 640-W (new style)	Suspd.		45.00	155-175
1980	Kuan Yin 640-W (old style)	Closed	1992	40.00	215-295
1987	Oriental Display (small) 945-D	Open		45.00	70
1985	Tang Horse 642-P	Open		65.00	100
1989	Tiger Hunt 645-P	Open		85.00	105

Miniatures-Pendants - R. Olszewski

1986	Camper Bialosky 151-P	Closed	1988	95.00	255-300
1991	Chrysanthemum Pendant 222-P	Open		135.00	155
1991	Daffodil Pendant 221-P	Open		135.00	155
1990	Hummingbird 697-P	Open		125.00	155
1988	Mickey Mouse 169-P	5,000	1989	92.00	225-295
1991	Poinsettia Pendant 223-P	Open		135.00	155
1991	Rose Pendant 220-P	Open		135.00	155

Miniatures-Portrait of America/Saturday Evening Post (Pewter) - N. Rockwell

1989	Bottom Drawer 366-P	7,500	1995	85.00	85
1988	Bottom of the Sixth 365-P	Suspd.		85.00	85-150
1988	Check-Up 363-P	Suspd.		85.00	75-110
1988	The Doctor and the Doll 361-P	Suspd.		85.00	115-150
1991	Home Coming Vignette-Soldier/Mother 990-D	2,000	1995	190.00	200-300
1988	Marbles Champion 362-P	Closed	1995	85.00	75-110
1988	No Swimming 360-P	Closed	1995	85.00	75-110
1988	Rockwell Display-952-D	Closed	1995	80.00	100
1988	Triple Self-Portrait 364-P	Suspd.		85.00	145-225

Miniatures-Special Release-Alice in Wonderland - R. Olszewski

1982	Alice In the Garden 670-P	Closed	1982	60.00	645-720
1984	The Cheshire Cat 672-P	Closed	1984	75.00	450-525
1983	Down the Rabbit Hole 671-P	Closed	1983	75.00	395-470

Miniatures-Special Release-Wizard of Oz - R. Olszewski

1986	The Cowardly Lion 675-P	Closed	1987	85.00	200-325
1992	Dorothy/Glinda 695-P	Closed	1995	135.00	155
1992	Good-Bye to Oz Display 980-D	Open		110.00	160
1988	The Munchkins 677-P	Closed	1995	85.00	100
1987	Oz Display 942-D	Closed	1994	45.00	545-590
XX	Oz Display Set	Closed	1994	410.00	1400-1700
1984	Scarecrow 673-P	Closed	1985	75.00	300-495
1985	Tinman 674-P	Closed	1986	80.00	200-275
1987	The Wicked Witch 676-P	Closed	1995	85.00	105

Miniatures-Special Releases - R. Olszewski

1994	Dresden Timepiece 450-P	750		1250.00	1300
1991	Portrait Of The Artist (convention) 658-P	Closed	1991	195.00	350-565
1991	Portrait Of The Artist (promotion) 658-P	Open		195.00	210
1992	Summer Days Collector Plaque 659-P	Open		130.00	130-160

Miniatures-The American Frontier Collection - Various

1987	American Frontier Museum Display 947-D - R. Olszewski	Suspd.		80.00	115

YEAR ISSUE		EDITION LIMIT	YEAR RETD.	ISSUE PRICE	QUOTE U.S.$
1987	The Bronco Buster 350-B - Remington	Suspd.		80.00	165-190
1987	Eight Count 310-B - Pounder	Suspd.		75.00	95
1987	The End of the Trail 340-B - Frazier	Suspd.		80.00	95-150
1987	The First Ride 330-B - Rogers	Suspd.		85.00	105
1987	Grizzly's Last Stand 320-B - Jonas	Suspd.		65.00	85
1987	Indian Scout and Buffalo 300-B - Bonheur	Suspd.		95.00	95-150

Miniatures-Three Little Pigs - R. Olszewski

YEAR ISSUE		EDITION LIMIT	YEAR RETD.	ISSUE PRICE	QUOTE U.S.$
1991	The Hungry Wolf 681-P	7,500		80.00	110
1991	Little Bricks Pig 680-P	7,500		75.00	110
1989	Little Sticks Pig 678-P	7,500		75.00	110
1990	Little Straw Pig 679-P	7,500		75.00	110
1991	Three Little Pigs House 956-D	7,500		50.00	130

Miniatures-Wildlife Series - R. Olszewski

YEAR ISSUE		EDITION LIMIT	YEAR RETD.	ISSUE PRICE	QUOTE U.S.$
1985	American Goldfinch 625-P	Open		65.00	100
1986	Autumn Blue Jay 626-P	Suspd.		65.00	135-210
1992	Autumn Blue Jay 626-P (Archive release)	Open		125.00	140
1980	Chipping Sparrow 620-P	Open		55.00	90
1987	Country Display (small) 940-D	Open		45.00	70
1990	Country Landscape (large) 957-D	Open		85.00	115
1989	Hooded Oriole 629-P	Open		80.00	105
1990	Hummingbird 696-P	Closed	N/A	85.00	150-200
1987	Mallard Duck 627-P	Open		75.00	110
1981	Owl-Daylight Encounter 621-P	Closed	N/A	65.00	375-410
1983	Red-Winged Blackbird 623-P	Closed	N/A	65.00	150-250
1988	Spring Robin 628-P	Closed	N/A	75.00	150-185
1982	Western Bluebird 622-P	Closed	N/A	65.00	125-180
1984	Winter Cardinal 624-P	Closed	N/A	65.00	225-290

Miniatures-Winter Lights - Norrgard

YEAR ISSUE		EDITION LIMIT	YEAR RETD.	ISSUE PRICE	QUOTE U.S.$
1995	Once Upon a Winter Day	Open		275.00	275

Miniatures-Women's Series - R. Olszewski

YEAR ISSUE		EDITION LIMIT	YEAR RETD.	ISSUE PRICE	QUOTE U.S.$
1980	Dresden Dancer 610-P	Closed	1989	55.00	200-525
1985	The Hunt With Hounds (new style) 611-P	Closed	N/A	75.00	190-225
1981	The Hunt With Hounds (old style) 611-P	Closed	1984	75.00	375-425
1986	I Do 615-P	Closed	N/A	85.00	200-275
1983	On The Avenue 613-P	Closed	1995	65.00	110-125
1982	Precious Years 612-P	Closed	N/A	65.00	195-280
1984	Roses 614-P	Closed	1995	65.00	110-125
1989	Women's Display (small) 950-D	Closed	1995	40.00	65

Goebel/M.I. Hummel

M.I. Hummel Collectors Club Exclusives - M. I. Hummel, unless otherwise noted

YEAR ISSUE		EDITION LIMIT	YEAR RETD.	ISSUE PRICE	QUOTE U.S.$
1977	Valentine Gift 387	Closed	N/A	45.00	400-750
1978	Smiling Through Plaque 690	Closed	N/A	50.00	100-250
1979	Bust of Sister-M.I.Hummel HU-3 - G. Skrobek	Closed	N/A	75.00	200-350
1980	Valentine Joy 399	Closed	N/A	95.00	250-350
1981	Daisies Don't Tell 380	Closed	N/A	80.00	200-350
1982	It's Cold 421	Closed	N/A	80.00	185-350
1983	What Now? 422	Closed	N/A	90.00	200-350
1983	Valentine Gift Mini Pendant 248-P - R. Olszewski	Closed	N/A	85.00	200-400
1984	Coffee Break 409	Closed	N/A	90.00	150-300
1985	Smiling Through 408/0	Closed	N/A	125.00	250-300
1986	Birthday Candle 440	Closed	N/A	95.00	150-350
1986	What Now? Mini Pendant 249-P - R. Olszewski	Closed	N/A	125.00	175-300
1987	Morning Concert 447	Closed	N/A	98.00	140-275
1987	Little Cocopah Indian Girl - T. DeGrazia	Closed	N/A	140.00	200-300
1988	The Surprise 431	Closed	N/A	125.00	150-325
1989	Mickey and Minnie - H. Fischer	Closed	N/A	275.00	300-500
1989	Hello World 429	Closed	N/A	130.00	150-300
1990	I Wonder 486	Closed	N/A	140.00	140-250
1991	Gift From A Friend 485	Closed	N/A	160.00	160-250
1991	Miniature Morning Concert w/ Display 269-P - R. Olszewski	Closed	N/A	175.00	175-250
1992	My Wish Is Small 463/0	Closed	N/A	170.00	170-250
1992	Cheeky Fellow 554	Closed	N/A	120.00	120-130
1993	I Didn't Do It 626	Closed	1995	175.00	175-200
1993	Sweet As Can Be 541	Closed	1995	125.00	125
1994	Little Visitor 563/0	5/96		180.00	200
1994	Little Troubadour 558	5/96		130.00	130
1994	At Grandpa's 621	10,000		1300.00	1300
1994	Miniature Honey Lover Pendant 247-P	5/96		165.00	165
1995	Country Suitor 760	5/97		195.00	195
1995	Strum Along 557	5/97		135.00	135
1995	A Story From Grandma 620	10,000		1300.00	1300

Special Edition Anniversary Figurine For 5/10/15 Year Membership - M.I. Hummel

YEAR ISSUE		EDITION LIMIT	YEAR RETD.	ISSUE PRICE	QUOTE U.S.$
1990	Flower Girl 548 (5 year)	Open		105.00	135
1990	The Little Pair 449 (10 year)	Closed	N/A	170.00	210
1991	Honey Lover 312 (15 year)	Open		190.00	220

M.I. Hummel Collectibles Century Collection - M.I. Hummel

YEAR ISSUE		EDITION LIMIT	YEAR RETD.	ISSUE PRICE	QUOTE U.S.$
1986	Chapel Time 442	Closed	N/A	500.00	1200-1500
1987	Pleasant Journey 406	Closed	N/A	500.00	1500-2650
1988	Call to Worship 441	Closed	N/A	600.00	800-1100
1989	Harmony in Four Parts 471	Closed	N/A	850.00	1200-2000
1990	Let's Tell the World 487	Closed	N/A	875.00	700-1500
1991	We Wish You The Best 600	Closed	N/A	1300.00	1300-1800
1992	On Our Way 472	Closed	N/A	950.00	950-1200
1993	Welcome Spring 635	Closed	N/A	1085.00	1100-1450
1994	Rock-A-Bye 574	Closed	N/A	1150.00	1200
1995	Strike Up the Band 668	Yr. Iss.		1200.00	1200

M.I. Hummel Collectibles Christmas Angels - M.I. Hummel

YEAR ISSUE		EDITION LIMIT	YEAR RETD.	ISSUE PRICE	QUOTE U.S.$
1993	Angel in Cloud 585	Open		25.00	33
1993	Angel with Lute 580	Open		25.00	33
1993	Angel with Trumpet 586	Open		25.00	33
1993	Celestial Musician 578	Open		25.00	33
1993	Festival Harmony with Flute 577	Open		25.00	33
1993	Festival Harmony with Mandolin 576	Open		25.00	33
1993	Gentle Song 582	Open		25.00	33
1993	Heavenly Angel 575	Open		25.00	33
1993	Prayer of Thanks 581	Open		25.00	33
1993	Song of Praise 579	Open		25.00	33

M.I. Hummel Collectibles Figurines - M.I. Hummel

YEAR ISSUE		EDITION LIMIT	YEAR RETD.	ISSUE PRICE	QUOTE U.S.$
1988	The Accompanist 453	Open		Unkn.	110
XX	Adoration 23/I	Open		Unkn.	380
XX	Adoration 23/III	Open		Unkn.	590
XX	Adventure Bound 347	Open		Unkn.	3960
XX	Angel Duet 261	Open		Unkn.	240
XX	Angel Serenade 214/D/I	Open		Unkn.	100
XX	Angel Serenade with Lamb 83	Open		Unkn.	240
XX	Angel with Accordion 238/B	Open		Unkn.	55
XX	Angel with Lute 238/A	Open		Unkn.	55
XX	Angel With Trumpet 238/C	Open		Unkn.	55
XX	Angelic Song 144	Open		Unkn.	160
1995	The Angler 566	Open		Unkn.	350
1989	An Apple A Day 403	Open		Unkn.	300
XX	Apple Tree Boy 142/3/0	Open		Unkn.	155
XX	Apple Tree Boy 142/I	Open		Unkn.	300
XX	Apple Tree Boy 142/V	Open		Unkn.	1320
XX	Apple Tree Girl 141/3/0	Open		Unkn.	155
XX	Apple Tree Girl 141/I	Open		Unkn.	300
XX	Apple Tree Girl 141/V	Open		Unkn.	1320
1991	Art Critic 318	Open		Unkn.	315
XX	Artist, The 304	Open		Unkn.	270
XX	Auf Wiedersehen 153/0	Open		Unkn.	270
XX	Auf Wiedersehen 153/I	Open		Unkn.	325
XX	Autumn Harvest 355	Open		Unkn.	220
XX	Baker 128	Open		Unkn.	215
XX	Baking Day 330	Open		Unkn.	300
XX	Band Leader 129	Open		Unkn.	220
XX	Band Leader 129/4/0	Open		Unkn.	110
XX	Barnyard Hero 195/2/0	Open		Unkn.	180
XX	Barnyard Hero 195/I	Open		Unkn.	330
XX	Bashful 377	Open		Unkn.	215
1990	Bath Time 412	Open		Unkn.	410
XX	Be Patient 197/2/0	Open		Unkn.	215
XX	Be Patient 197/I	Open		Unkn.	325
XX	Begging His Share 9	Open		Unkn.	275
XX	Big Housecleaning 363	Open		Unkn.	315
XX	Bird Duet 169	Open		Unkn.	155
XX	Bird Watcher 300	Open		Unkn.	240
1989	Birthday Cake 338	Open		Unkn.	155
1994	Birthday Present 341/3/0	Open		140.00	155
XX	Birthday Serenade 218/0	Open		Unkn.	325
XX	Birthday Serenade 218/2/0	Open		Unkn.	190
XX	Blessed Event 333	Open		Unkn.	350
XX	Bookworm 3/I	Open		Unkn.	325
XX	Bookworm 8	Open		Unkn.	240
XX	Boots 143/0	Open		Unkn.	220
XX	Boots 143/I	Open		Unkn.	360
XX	Botanist, The 351	Open		Unkn.	220
XX	Boy with Accordion 390	Open		Unkn.	95
XX	Boy with Horse 239/C	Open		Unkn.	60
XX	Boy with Toothache 217	Open		Unkn.	230
XX	Brother 95	Open		Unkn.	220
1988	A Budding Maestro 477	Open		Unkn.	110
XX	Builder, The 305	Open		Unkn.	270
XX	Busy Student 367	Open		Unkn.	175
XX	Call to Glory 739/I	Open		250.00	275
XX	Carnival 328	Open		Unkn.	240
XX	Celestial Musician 188/0	Open		Unkn.	240
1993	Celestial Musician 188/4/0	Open		Unkn.	100
XX	Chick Girl 57/0	Open		Unkn.	180
XX	Chick Girl 57/2/0	Open		Unkn.	160
XX	Chick Girl 57/I	Open		Unkn.	300
XX	Chicken-Licken 385	Open		Unkn.	310
XX	Chicken-Licken 385/4/0	Open		Unkn.	110
XX	Chimney Sweep 12/2/0	Open		Unkn.	130
XX	Chimney Sweep 12/I	Open		Unkn.	240
1989	Christmas Angel 301	Open		Unkn.	275
XX	Christmas Song 343	Open		Unkn.	240
XX	Cinderella 337	Open		Unkn.	315
XX	Close Harmony 336	Open		Unkn.	315
1995	Come Back Soon 545	Open		Unkn.	150
XX	Confidentially 314	Open		Unkn.	315
XX	Congratulations 17	Open		Unkn.	220
XX	Coquettes 179	Open		Unkn.	315
1990	Crossroads (Commemorative) 331	10,000		360.00	450-1000
XX	Crossroads (Original) 331	Open		Unkn.	440
XX	Culprits 56/A	Open		Unkn.	320
1989	Daddy's Girls 371	Open		Unkn.	250
XX	Doctor 127	Open		Unkn.	170
XX	Doll Bath 319	Open		Unkn.	315
XX	Doll Mother 67	Open		Unkn.	230
XX	Easter Greetings 378	Open		Unkn.	220
XX	Easter Time 384	Open		Unkn.	275
1992	Evening Prayer 495	Open		Unkn.	115
XX	Eventide 99	Open		Unkn.	360
XX	A Fair Measure 345	Open		Unkn.	315
XX	Farm Boy 66	Open		Unkn.	250
XX	Favorite Pet 361	Open		Unkn.	315
XX	Feathered Friends 344	Open		Unkn.	300
XX	Feeding Time 199/0	Open		Unkn.	215
XX	Feeding Time 199/I	Open		Unkn.	300
1995	Festival Harmony 693	Open		Unkn.	125
1994	Festival Harmony w/Mandolin 172/4/0	Open		95.00	105
XX	Festival Harmony, with Flute 173/0	Open		Unkn.	340
XX	Festival Harmony, with Mandolin 172/0	Open		Unkn.	340
XX	Flower Vendor 381	Open		Unkn.	270
XX	Follow the Leader 369	Open		Unkn.	1320
XX	For Father 87	Open		Unkn.	230
XX	For Mother 257	Open		Unkn.	220
XX	For Mother 257/2/0	Open		Unkn.	130
XX	Forest Shrine 183	Open		Unkn.	585
1993	A Free Flight 569	Open		Unkn.	215
1991	Friend Or Foe 434	Open		Unkn.	240
XX	Friends 136/I	Open		Unkn.	220
XX	Friends 136/V	Open		Unkn.	1320
1993	Friends Together 662/0	Open		260.00	300
1993	Friends Together 662/I	25,000		475.00	550
XX	Gay Adventure 356	Open		Unkn.	210
1995	Gentle Fellowship (Commemorative) 628	25,000		550.00	550
XX	A Gentle Glow 439	Open		Unkn.	220
XX	Girl with Doll 239/B	Open		Unkn.	60
XX	Girl with Nosegay 239/A	Open		Unkn.	60
XX	Girl with Sheet Music 389	Open		Unkn.	95
XX	Girl with Trumpet 391	Open		Unkn.	95
XX	Going Home 383	Open		Unkn.	340
XX	Going to Grandma's 52/0	Open		Unkn.	290
XX	Good Friends 182	Open		Unkn.	215
XX	Good Hunting 307	Open		Unkn.	270
XX	Good Night 214/C/I	Open		Unkn.	100
XX	Good Shepherd 42	Open		Unkn.	275
XX	Goose Girl 47/0	Open		Unkn.	250
XX	Goose Girl 47/3/0	Open		Unkn.	180
XX	Grandma's Girl 561	Open		Unkn.	160
XX	Grandpa's Boy 562	Open		Unkn.	160
1991	The Guardian 455	Open		Unkn.	180
XX	Guiding Angel 357	Open		Unkn.	95
XX	Happiness 86	Open		Unkn.	145
XX	Happy Birthday 176/0	Open		Unkn.	230
XX	Happy Birthday 176/I	Open		Unkn.	325
XX	Happy Days 150/0	Open		Unkn.	330
XX	Happy Days 150/2/0	Open		Unkn.	190
XX	Happy Days 150/I	Open		Unkn.	500
XX	Happy Pastime 69	Open		Unkn.	175
XX	Happy Traveller 109/0	Open		Unkn.	155
XX	Hear Ye! Hear Ye! 15/0	Open		Unkn.	220
XX	Hear Ye! Hear Ye! 15/2/0	Open		Unkn.	160
XX	Hear Ye! Hear Ye! 15/I	Open		Unkn.	275
XX	Heavenly Angel 21/0	Open		Unkn.	130
XX	Heavenly Angel 21/0/1/2	Open		Unkn.	240
XX	Heavenly Angel 21/I	Open		Unkn.	275
XX	Heavenly Lullaby 262	Open		Unkn.	200
XX	Heavenly Protection 88/I	Open		Unkn.	470
XX	Hello 124/0	Open		Unkn.	240
XX	Home from Market 198/2/0	Open		Unkn.	160
XX	Home from Market 198/I	Open		Unkn.	230
XX	Homeward Bound 334	Open		Unkn.	360
1990	Horse Trainer 423	Open		Unkn.	240
1989	Hosanna 480	Open		Unkn.	110
1989	I'll Protect Him 483	Open		Unkn.	95
1994	I'm Carefree 633	Open		365.00	410
1989	I'm Here 478	Open		Unkn.	110
1989	In D Major 430	Open		Unkn.	220
XX	In The Meadow 459	Open		Unkn.	220
XX	In Tune 414	Open		Unkn.	310
XX	Is It Raining? 420	Open		Unkn.	280
XX	Joyful 53	Open		Unkn.	130
XX	Joyous News 27/III	Open		Unkn.	240
1995	Just Dozing 451	Open		Unkn.	240
XX	Just Fishing 373	Open		Unkn.	250
XX	Just Resting 112/3/0	Open		Unkn.	160
XX	Just Resting 112/I	Open		Unkn.	310
XX	Kindergartner 467	Open		Unkn.	220
XX	Kiss Me 311	Open		Unkn.	315
XX	Knit One, Purl One 432	Open		Unkn.	125
XX	Knitting Lesson 256	Open		Unkn.	550
1991	Land in Sight 530	30,000		1600.00	1600
XX	Latest News 184	Open		Unkn.	320
XX	Let's Sing 110/0	Open		Unkn.	135
XX	Let's Sing 110/I	Open		Unkn.	180
XX	Letter to Santa Claus 340	Open		Unkn.	360
1993	Little Architect 410/I	Open		Unkn.	330
XX	Little Bookkeeper 306	Open		Unkn.	315
XX	Little Cellist 89/I	Open		Unkn.	230
XX	Little Drummer 240	Open		Unkn.	160
XX	Little Fiddler 2/0	Open		Unkn.	240
XX	Little Fiddler 2/4/0	Open		Unkn.	110
XX	Little Fiddler 4	Open		Unkn.	220
XX	Little Gabriel 32	Open		Unkn.	155
XX	Little Gardener 74	Open		Unkn.	130

FIGURINES/COTTAGES

YEAR ISSUE		EDITION LIMIT	YEAR RETD.	ISSUE PRICE	QUOTE U.S.$
XX	Little Goat Herder 200/0	Open		Unkn.	215
XX	Little Goat Herder 200/I	Open		Unkn.	260
XX	Little Guardian 145	Open		Unkn.	160
XX	Little Helper 73	Open		Unkn.	130
XX	Little Hiker 16/2/0	Open		Unkn.	130
XX	Little Hiker 16/I	Open		Unkn.	240
XX	Little Nurse 376	Open		Unkn.	270
XX	Little Pharmacist 322/E	Open		Unkn.	265
XX	Little Scholar 80	Open		Unkn.	230
XX	Little Shopper 96	Open		Unkn.	150
1988	Little Sweeper 171/0	Open		Unkn.	150
XX	Little Sweeper 171/4/0	Open		Unkn.	110
XX	Little Tailor 308	Open		Unkn.	270
XX	Little Thrifty 118	Open		Unkn.	160
XX	Little Tooter 214/H	Open		Unkn.	110
XX	Little Tooter 214/H	Open		Unkn.	135
XX	Lost Stocking 374	Open		Unkn.	155
1995	Lucky Boy (Special Event) 335	25,000		190.00	190
XX	Mail is Here 226	Open		Unkn.	585
1989	Make A Wish 475	Open		Unkn.	220
XX	March Winds 43	Open		Unkn.	170
XX	Max and Moritz 123	Open		Unkn.	240
XX	Meditation 13/0	Open		Unkn.	240
XX	Meditation 13/2/0	Open		Unkn.	155
XX	Merry Wanderer 11/0	Open		Unkn.	215
XX	Merry Wanderer 11/2/0	Open		Unkn.	150
XX	Merry Wanderer 7/0	Open		Unkn.	300
XX	Mischief Maker 342	Open		Unkn.	300
1994	Morning Stroll 375/3/0	Open		170.00	195
XX	Mother's Darling 175	Open		Unkn.	230
XX	Mother's Helper 133	Open		Unkn.	215
XX	Mountaineer 315	Open		Unkn.	230
1991	A Nap 534	Open		Unkn.	130
XX	Not For You 317	Open		Unkn.	265
XX	On Holiday 350	Open		Unkn.	190
XX	On Secret Path 386	Open		Unkn.	270
1989	One For You, One For Me 482	Open		Unkn.	110
1993	One Plus One 556	Open		Unkn.	145
1995	Ooh My Tooth 533 (Special Event)	Open		Unkn.	120
XX	Out of Danger 56/B	Open		Unkn.	320
1993	Parade Of Lights 616	Open		Unkn.	275
XX	The Photographer 178	Open		Unkn.	315
1995	Pixie 768	Open		Unkn.	115
XX	Playmates 58/0	Open		Unkn.	180
XX	Playmates 58/2/0	Open		Unkn.	160
XX	Playmates 58/I	Open		Unkn.	300
1994	The Poet 397/I	Open		220.00	250
XX	Postman 119	Open		Unkn.	220
1989	Postman 119/2/0	Open		Unkn.	155
XX	Prayer Before Battle 20	Open		Unkn.	180
1992	The Professor 320	Open		Unkn.	220
1995	Puppy Love Display Plaque 767	Open		Unkn.	265
XX	Retreat to Safety 201/2/0	Open		Unkn.	175
XX	Retreat to Safety 201/I	Open		Unkn.	330
XX	Ride into Christmas 396/2/0	Open		Unkn.	260
XX	Ride into Christmas 396/I	Open		Unkn.	470
XX	Ring Around the Rosie 348	Open		Unkn.	2860
XX	The Run-A-Way 327	Open		Unkn.	275
1992	Scamp 553	Open		Unkn.	120
XX	School Boy 82/0	Open		Unkn.	215
XX	School Boy 82/2/0	Open		Unkn.	155
XX	School Boy 82/II	Open		Unkn.	500
XX	School Boys 170/I	Open		Unkn.	1320
XX	School Girl 81/0	Open		Unkn.	215
XX	School Girl 81/2/0	Open		Unkn.	155
XX	School Girls 177/I	Open		Unkn.	1320
XX	Sensitive Hunter 6/0	Open		Unkn.	215
XX	Sensitive Hunter 6/2/0	Open		Unkn.	160
XX	Sensitive Hunter 6/I	Open		Unkn.	275
XX	Serenade 85/0	Open		Unkn.	145
XX	Serenade 85/4/0	Open		Unkn.	110
XX	Serenade 85/II	Open		Unkn.	500
XX	She Loves Me, She Loves Me Not 174	Open		Unkn.	210
XX	Shepherd's Boy 64	Open		Unkn.	250
XX	Shining Light 358	Open		Unkn.	95
XX	Sing Along 433	Open		Unkn.	300
XX	Sing With Me 405	Open		Unkn.	340
XX	Singing Lesson 63	Open		Unkn.	135
XX	Sister 98/0	Open		Unkn.	220
XX	Sister 98/2/0	Open		Unkn.	150
XX	Skier 59	Open		Unkn.	220
1990	Sleep Tight 424	Open		Unkn.	240
XX	Smart Little Sister 346	Open		Unkn.	275
XX	Soldier Boy 332	Open		Unkn.	230
XX	Soloist 135	Open		Unkn.	145
XX	Soloist 135/4/0	Open		Unkn.	110
1988	Song of Praise 454	Open		Unkn.	110
1988	Sound the Trumpet 457	Open		Unkn.	110
1988	Sounds of the Mandolin 438	Open		Unkn.	130
XX	Spring Dance 353/0	Open		Unkn.	340
XX	St. George 55	Open		Unkn.	350
XX	Star Gazer 132	Open		Unkn.	225
XX	Stitch in Time 255/4/0	Open		Unkn.	105
XX	Stitch in Time 255/I	Open		Unkn.	315
XX	Stormy Weather 71/2/0	Open		Unkn.	330
XX	Stormy Weather 71/I	Open		Unkn.	495
1992	Storybook Time 458	Open		Unkn.	420
XX	Street Singer 131	Open		Unkn.	210
XX	Surprise 94/3/0	Open		Unkn.	165
XX	Surprise 94/I	Open		Unkn.	315
XX	Sweet Greetings 352	Open		Unkn.	220
XX	Sweet Music 186	Open		Unkn.	220
XX	Telling Her Secret 196/0	Open		Unkn.	325
XX	Thoughtful 415	Open		Unkn.	240
XX	Timid Little Sister 394	Open		Unkn.	470
1995	To Keep You Warm w/ Wooden Chair 759	Open		Unkn.	215
XX	To Market 49/0	Open		Unkn.	315
XX	To Market 49/3/0	Open		Unkn.	175
XX	Trumpet Boy 97	Open		Unkn.	145
1989	Tuba Player 437	Open		Unkn.	290
XX	Tuneful Angel 359	Open		Unkn.	95
XX	Umbrella Boy 152/A/0	Open		Unkn.	630
XX	Umbrella Boy 152/A/II	Open		Unkn.	1600
XX	Umbrella Girl 152/B/0	Open		Unkn.	630
XX	Umbrella Girl 152/B/II	Open		Unkn.	1600
XX	Village Boy 51/0	Open		Unkn.	275
XX	Village Boy 51/2/0	Open		Unkn.	155
XX	Village Boy 51/3/0	Open		Unkn.	130
XX	Visiting an Invalid 382	Open		Unkn.	220
XX	Volunteers 50/0	Open		Unkn.	325
XX	Volunteers 50/2/0	Open		Unkn.	240
XX	Waiter 154/0	Open		Unkn.	230
XX	Waiter 154/I	Open		Unkn.	315
1989	Wash Day 321/4/0	Open		Unkn.	110
XX	Wash Day 321/I	Open		Unkn.	315
XX	Watchful Angel 194	Open		Unkn.	340
XX	Wayside Devotion 28/II	Open		Unkn.	450
XX	Wayside Devotion 28/III	Open		Unkn.	600
XX	Wayside Harmony 111/3/0	Open		Unkn.	160
XX	Wayside Harmony 111/I	Open		Unkn.	300
1993	We Come In Peace (Commemorative) 754	Open		385.00	385
XX	We Congratulate 214/E/II	Open		Unkn.	175
XX	We Congratulate 220	Open		Unkn.	165
XX	Weary Wanderer 204	Open		Unkn.	275
1990	What's New? 418	Open		Unkn.	300
XX	Which Hand? 258	Open		Unkn.	215
1992	Whistler's Duet 413	Open		Unkn.	310
XX	Whitsuntide 163	Open		Unkn.	330
1988	A Winter Song 476	Open		Unkn.	120
XX	With Loving Greetings 309	Open		Unkn.	210
XX	Worship 84/0	Open		Unkn.	175

M.I. Hummel Collectibles Figurines Retired - M.I. Hummel

YEAR ISSUE		EDITION LIMIT	YEAR RETD.	ISSUE PRICE	QUOTE U.S.$
1947	Accordion Boy 185	Closed	1994	Unkn.	200-700
1939	Duet 130	Open	1995	Unkn.	280-2500
1937	Farewell 65 TMK1-5	Closed	1993	Unkn.	240-800
1937	Globe Trotter 79 TMK1-7	Closed	1991	Unkn.	200-700
1937	Lost Sheep 68/0 TMK1-7	Closed	1992	Unkn.	170-300
1955	Lost Sheep 68/2/0 TMK2-7	Closed	1992	7.50	125-300
1935	Puppy Love I TMK1-6	Closed	1988	125.00	275-900
1948	Signs Of Spring 203/2/0 TMK2-6	Closed	1990	120.00	200-1000
1948	Signs Of Spring 203/I TMK2-6	Closed	1990	155.00	250-900
1935	Strolling Along 5 TMK1-6	Closed	1989	115.00	250-900

M.I. Hummel Collectibles Madonna Figurines - M.I. Hummel

YEAR ISSUE		EDITION LIMIT	YEAR RETD.	ISSUE PRICE	QUOTE U.S.$
XX	Flower Madonna, color 10/I/II	Open		Unkn.	470
XX	Madonna with Halo, color 45/I/6	Open		Unkn.	135

M.I. Hummel Collectibles Nativity Components - M. I. Hummel, unless otherwise noted

YEAR ISSUE		EDITION LIMIT	YEAR RETD.	ISSUE PRICE	QUOTE U.S.$
XX	Ox 214/K/I	Open		Unkn.	75
XX	12-Pc. Set Figs. only, Color, 214/A/M/I, B/I, A/K/I, F/I G/I J/I K/I, L/I, M/I, N/I, O/I, 366/I	Open		Unkn.	1680
XX	Angel Serenade 214/D/I	Open		Unkn.	100
XX	Camel Kneeling - Goebel	Open		Unkn.	275
XX	Camel Lying - Goebel	Open		Unkn.	275
XX	Camel Standing - Goebel	Open		Unkn.	275
XX	Donkey 214/J/0	Open		Unkn.	55
XX	Donkey 214/J/I	Open		Unkn.	75
XX	Flying Angel/color 366/I	Open		Unkn.	135
XX	Good Night 214/C/I	Open		Unkn.	110
XX	Holy Family 3 Pcs., Color 214/A/M/I, B/I, A/K/I	Open		Unkn.	440
XX	Holy Family,3 Pcs., Color 214/A/M/0, B/0, A/K/0	Open		Unkn.	330
XX	Infant Jesus 214/A/K/0	Open		Unkn.	45
XX	Infant Jesus 214/A/K/I	Open		Unkn.	70
XX	King, Kneeling 214/M/I	Open		Unkn.	195
XX	King, Kneeling 214M/0	Open		Unkn.	155
XX	King, Kneeling w/ Box 214/N/0	Open		Unkn.	150
XX	King, Kneeling w/Box 214/N/I	Open		Unkn.	175
XX	King, Moorish 214/L/0	Open		Unkn.	165
XX	King, Moorish 214/L/I	Open		Unkn.	200
XX	Lamb 214/O/0	Open		Unkn.	22
XX	Lamb 214/O/I	Open		Unkn.	22
XX	Little Tooter 214/H/0	Open		Unkn.	110
XX	Little Tooter 214/H/I	Open		Unkn.	135
XX	Madonna 214/A/M/0	Open		Unkn.	145
XX	Madonna 214/A/M/I	Open		Unkn.	195
XX	Ox 214/K/0	Open		Unkn.	55
XX	Shepherd Boy 214/G/I	Open		Unkn.	145
XX	Shepherd Kneeling 214/G/0	Open		Unkn.	130
XX	Shepherd Standing 214/F/0	Open		Unkn.	165
XX	Shepherd with Sheep-1 piece 214/F/I	Open		Unkn.	195
XX	Small Camel Kneeling - Goebel	Open		Unkn.	220
XX	Small Camel Lying - Goebel	Open		Unkn.	220
XX	Small Camel Standing - Goebel	Open		Unkn.	220
XX	St. Joseph 214/B/0	Open		Unkn.	145
XX	St. Joseph color 214/B/I	Open		Unkn.	195
XX	Stable only fits12 or 16-pc. HUM214/II Set	Open		Unkn.	110
XX	Stable only, fits 16-piece HUM260 Set	Open		Unkn.	440
XX	Stable only, fits 3-pc. HUM214 Set	Open		Unkn.	50
XX	We Congratulate 214/E/I	Open		Unkn.	175

M.I. Hummel Disneyana Figurines - M.I. Hummel

YEAR ISSUE		EDITION LIMIT	YEAR RETD.	ISSUE PRICE	QUOTE U.S.$
1995	For Father	1,500		450.00	450
1995	Grandpa's Boys	1,500		340.00	340
1994	Minnie Be Patient	1,500	1994	395.00	425-480
1993	Two Little Drummers	1,500	1993	325.00	450-650
1992	Two Merry Wanderers 022074	1,500	1992	250.00	800-1200

M.I. Hummel First Edition Miniatures - M.I. Hummel

YEAR ISSUE		EDITION LIMIT	YEAR RETD.	ISSUE PRICE	QUOTE U.S.$
1991	Accordion Boy -37225	Suspd.		105.00	105-135
1989	Apple Tree Boy -37219	Suspd.		115.00	130-200
1990	Baker -37222	Suspd.		100.00	125-150
1992	Bavarian Church (Display) -37370	Closed	N/A	60.00	60-70
1988	Bavarian Cottage (Display) -37355	Closed	N/A	60.00	75-90
1990	Bavarian Marketsquare Bridge(Display) -37358	Closed	N/A	110.00	110-125
1988	Bavarian Village (Display) -37356	Closed	N/A	100.00	105
1991	Busy Student -37226	Suspd.		105.00	105-135
1990	Cinderella -37223	Suspd.		115.00	120-190
1991	Countryside School (Display) -37365	Closed	N/A	100.00	100-110
1989	Doll Bath -37214	Suspd.		95.00	110-175
1995	Festival Harmony 173/4/0	Open		100.00	100
1992	Goose Girl -37238	Suspd.		130.00	180-225
1989	Little Fiddler -37211	Suspd.		90.00	115-135
1989	Little Sweeper -37212	Suspd.		90.00	115-175
1993	The Mail is Here Clock Tower 826504	Open		495.00	575
1990	Marketsquare Flower Stand (Display) -37360	Closed	N/A	35.00	50-80
1990	Marketsquare Hotel (Display)-37359	Closed	N/A	70.00	90-125
1989	Merry Wanderer -37213	Suspd.		95.00	115-135
1991	Merry Wanderer Dealer Plaque -37229	Closed	N/A	130.00	135
1989	Postman -37217	Suspd.		95.00	135-180
1991	Roadside Shrine (Display)-37366	Closed	N/A	60.00	60
1992	School Boy -37236	Suspd.		120.00	150-180
1991	Serenade -37228	Suspd.		105.00	105-135
1992	Snow-Covered Mountain (Display)-37371	Closed	N/A	100.00	100
1989	Stormy Weather -37215	Suspd.		115.00	130-180
1992	Trees (Display)-37369	Closed	N/A	40.00	40-50
1989	Visiting an Invalid -37218	Suspd.		105.00	130-160
1990	Waiter -37221	Suspd.		100.00	125-140
1992	Wayside Harmony -37237	Suspd.		140.00	165-180
1991	We Congratulate -37227	Suspd.		130.00	130

M.I. Hummel Tree Toppers - M.I. Hummel

YEAR ISSUE		EDITION LIMIT	YEAR RETD.	ISSUE PRICE	QUOTE U.S.$
1994	Heavenly Angel 755	Open		450.00	495

M.I. Hummel Vingettes w/Solitary Domes - M.I. Hummel

YEAR ISSUE		EDITION LIMIT	YEAR RETD.	ISSUE PRICE	QUOTE U.S.$
1992	Bakery Day w/Baker & Waiter 37726	3,000		225.00	225
1992	The Flower Market w/Cinderella 37729	3,000		135.00	135
1992	Winterfest w/Ride Into Christmas 37728	5,000		195.00	195

M.I. Hummel's Temp. Out of Production (including trademarks) - M.I. Hummel

YEAR ISSUE		EDITION LIMIT	YEAR RETD.	ISSUE PRICE	QUOTE U.S.$
XX	16-Pc. Set Figs. only, Color, 214/A/M/I, B/I, A/K/I, C/I, D/I, E/I, F/I, G/I, H/I, J/I, K/I, L/I, M/I, N/I, O/I, 366/I	Suspd.		Unkn.	1990
XX	17-Pc. Set Large Color 16 Figs.& Wooden Stable 260 A-R	Suspd.		Unkn.	4540
XX	Angel Serenade 260/E	Suspd.		Unkn.	345-445
XX	Apple Tree Boy 142/X	Suspd.		Unkn.	17000
XX	Apple Tree Girl 141/X	Suspd.		Unkn.	17000
XX	Blessed Child 78/I/83	Suspd.		Unkn.	45
XX	Blessed Child 78/II/83	Suspd.		Unkn.	50
XX	Blessed Child 78/III/83	Suspd.		Unkn.	60
XX	Bookworm 3/II	Suspd.		Unkn.	675-1350
XX	Bookworm 3/III	Suspd.		Unkn.	1000-2500
XX	Celestial Musician 188/I	Suspd.		Unkn.	395-525
XX	Christ Child 18	Suspd.		Unkn.	130-325
XX	Donkey 260/L	Suspd.		Unkn.	140
XX	Festival Harmony, with Flute 173/II	Suspd.		Unkn.	400-1000
XX	Festival Harmony, with Mandolin 172/II	Suspd.		Unkn.	400-1000
XX	Flower Madonna, color 10/III/II	Suspd.		Unkn.	600-750
XX	Flower Madonna, white 10/I/W	Suspd.		Unkn.	165-420
XX	Flower Madonna, white 10/III/W	Suspd.		Unkn.	470-750
XX	Going to Grandma's 52/I	Suspd.		Unkn.	350-1200
XX	Good Night 260/D	Suspd.		Unkn.	145
XX	Goose Girl 47/II	Suspd.		Unkn.	400-1000
XX	Happy Traveler 109/II	Suspd.		Unkn.	350-1200
XX	Hear Ye! Hear Ye! 15/II	Suspd.		Unkn.	375-1500
XX	Heavenly Angel 21/II	Suspd.		Unkn.	415-1025
XX	Heavenly Protection 88/II	Suspd.		Unkn.	600-1000
XX	Hello 124/I	Suspd.		Unkn.	175-385
XX	Holy Child 70	Suspd.		Unkn.	160-400

YEAR ISSUE		EDITION LIMIT	YEAR RETD.	ISSUE PRICE	QUOTE U.S.$
XX	Hummel Display Plaque 187	Suspd.		Unkn.	150-650
XX	Infant Jesus 260/C	Suspd.		Unkn.	120
1985	Jubilee 416 TMK6	Suspd.		200.00	250-375
XX	King, Kneeling 260/P	Suspd.		Unkn.	480
XX	King, Moorish 260/N	Suspd.		Unkn.	430-500
XX	King, Standing 260/O	Suspd.		Unkn.	500
XX	Little Band 392	Suspd.		Unkn.	250-350
XX	Little Cellist 89/II	Suspd.		Unkn.	500-675
XX	Little Fiddler 2/I	Suspd.		Unkn.	260-650
XX	Little Fiddler 2/II	Suspd.		Unkn.	1100-3000
XX	Little Fiddler 2/III	Suspd.		Unkn.	1200-4000
XX	Little Tooter 260/K	Suspd.		Unkn.	170-195
XX	Lullaby 24/III	Suspd.		Unkn.	450-1800
XX	Madonna 260/A	Suspd.		Unkn.	590
XX	Madonna Holding Child, color 151/II	Suspd.		Unkn.	115
XX	Madonna Holding Child, white 151/W	Suspd.		Unkn.	320
XX	Madonna Praying, color 46/III/6	Suspd.		Unkn.	140-400
XX	Madonna Praying, white 46/0/W	Suspd.		Unkn.	40-195
XX	Madonna Praying, white 46/I/W	Suspd.		Unkn.	70-175
XX	Madonna w/o Halo, color 46/I/6	Suspd.		Unkn.	115-300
XX	Madonna w/o Halo, white 46/I/W	Suspd.		Unkn.	70-175
XX	Madonna w/o Halo, white 45/I/W	Suspd.		Unkn.	70-175
XX	Meditation 13/V	Suspd.		Unkn.	1200-5000
XX	Meditation, color 13/II	Suspd.		Unkn.	400-4500
XX	Merry Wanderer 7/II	Suspd.		Unkn.	850-2200
XX	Merry Wanderer 7/III	Suspd.		Unkn.	925-1300
XX	Merry Wanderer 7/X	Suspd.		Unkn.	12000-20000
XX	Merry Wanderer Stepbase 7/I	Suspd.		Unkn.	320-1200
XX	Ox 260/M	Suspd.		Unkn.	150
XX	School Boys 170/III	Suspd.		Unkn.	1500-2200
XX	School Girls 177/III	Suspd.		Unkn.	1500-2200
XX	Sensitive Hunter 6/II	Suspd.		Unkn.	400-1000
XX	Sheep (Lying) 260/R	Suspd.		Unkn.	100
XX	Sheep (Standing) w/ Lamb 260/H	Suspd.		Unkn.	110
XX	Shepherd Boy, Kneeling 260/J	Suspd.		Unkn.	300
XX	Shepherd, Standing 260/G	Suspd.		Unkn.	525
XX	Spring Cheer 72	Suspd.		Unkn.	165-500
XX	Spring Dance 353/I	Suspd.		Unkn.	500-750
XX	St. Joseph 260/B	Suspd.		Unkn.	520
1984	Supreme Protection 364 TMK6	Suspd.		150.00	350
XX	Telling Her Secret 196/I	Suspd.		Unkn.	430-800
XX	To Market 49/I	Suspd.		Unkn.	420-1100
XX	Village Boy 51/I	Suspd.		Unkn.	250-650
XX	Volunteers 50/I	Suspd.		Unkn.	430-1400
XX	We Congratulate 260/F	Suspd.		Unkn.	400
XX	Worship 84/V	Suspd.		Unkn.	800-2800

Gorham

(Four Seasons) A Boy And His Dog - N. Rockwell

YEAR ISSUE		EDITION LIMIT	YEAR RETD.	ISSUE PRICE	QUOTE U.S.$
1972	A Boy Meets His Dog	2,500	1980	200.00	1300-1575
1972	Adventurers Between Adventures	2,500	1980	Set	Set
1972	The Mysterious Malady	2,500	1980	Set	Set
1972	Pride of Parenthood	2,500	1980	Set	Set

(Four Seasons) A Helping Hand - N. Rockwell

YEAR ISSUE		EDITION LIMIT	YEAR RETD.	ISSUE PRICE	QUOTE U.S.$
1980	Year End Court	2,500	1980	650.00	650-700
1980	Closed For Business	2,500	1980	Set	Set
1980	Swatter's Right	2,500	1980	Set	Set
1980	Coal Seasons Coming	2,500	1980	Set	Set

(Four Seasons) Dad's Boy - N. Rockwell

YEAR ISSUE		EDITION LIMIT	YEAR RETD.	ISSUE PRICE	QUOTE U.S.$
1981	Ski Skills	2,500	1990	750.00	750-800
1981	In His Spirit	2,500	1990	Set	Set
1981	Trout Dinner	2,500	1990	Set	Set
1981	Careful Aim	2,500	1990	Set	Set

(Four Seasons) Four Ages of Love - N. Rockwell

YEAR ISSUE		EDITION LIMIT	YEAR RETD.	ISSUE PRICE	QUOTE U.S.$
1974	Gaily Sharing Vintage Times	2,500	1980	300.00	600-1250
1974	Sweet Song So Young	2,500	1980	Set	Set
1974	Flowers In Tender Bloom	2,500	1980	Set	Set
1974	Fondly Do We Remember	2,500	1980	Set	Set

(Four Seasons) Going On Sixteen - N. Rockwell

YEAR ISSUE		EDITION LIMIT	YEAR RETD.	ISSUE PRICE	QUOTE U.S.$
1978	Chilling Chore	2,500	1980	400.00	650-675
1978	Sweet Serenade	2,500	1980	Set	Set
1978	Shear Agony	2,500	1980	Set	Set
1978	Pilgrimage	2,500	1980	Set	Set

(Four Seasons) Grand Pals - N. Rockwell

YEAR ISSUE		EDITION LIMIT	YEAR RETD.	ISSUE PRICE	QUOTE U.S.$
1977	Snow Sculpturing	2,500	1980	350.00	650-675
1977	Soaring Spirits	2,500	1980	Set	Set
1977	Fish Finders	2,500	1980	Set	Set
1977	Ghostly Gourds	2,500	1980	Set	Set

(Four Seasons) Grandpa and Me - N. Rockwell

YEAR ISSUE		EDITION LIMIT	YEAR RETD.	ISSUE PRICE	QUOTE U.S.$
1975	Gay Blades	2,500	1980	300.00	800-1000
1975	Day Dreamers	2,500	1980	Set	Set
1975	Goin' Fishing	2,500	1980	Set	Set
1975	Pensive Pals	2,500	1980	Set	Set

(Four Seasons) Life With Father - N. Rockwell

YEAR ISSUE		EDITION LIMIT	YEAR RETD.	ISSUE PRICE	QUOTE U.S.$
1983	Big Decision	2,500	1990	250.00	250
1983	Blasting Out	2,500	1990	Set	Set
1983	Cheering The Champs	2,500	1990	Set	Set
1983	A Tough One	2,500	1990	Set	Set

(Four Seasons) Me and My Pal - N. Rockwell

YEAR ISSUE		EDITION LIMIT	YEAR RETD.	ISSUE PRICE	QUOTE U.S.$
1976	A Licking Good Bath	2,500	1980	300.00	900-1250
1976	Young Man's Fancy	2,500	1980	Set	Set
1976	Fisherman's Paradise	2,500	1980	Set	Set
1976	Disastrous Daring	2,500	1980	Set	Set

(Four Seasons) Old Buddies - N. Rockwell

YEAR ISSUE		EDITION LIMIT	YEAR RETD.	ISSUE PRICE	QUOTE U.S.$
1984	Shared Success	2,500	1990	250.00	250
1984	Hasty Retreat	2,500	1990	Set	Set
1984	Final Speech	2,500	1990	Set	Set
1984	Endless Debate	2,500	1990	Set	Set

(Four Seasons) Old Timers - N. Rockwell

YEAR ISSUE		EDITION LIMIT	YEAR RETD.	ISSUE PRICE	QUOTE U.S.$
1982	Canine Solo	2,500	1990	250.00	250
1982	Sweet Surprise	2,500	1990	Set	Set
1982	Lazy Days	2,500	1990	Set	Set
1982	Fancy Footwork	2,500	1990	Set	Set

(Four Seasons) Tender Years - N. Rockwell

YEAR ISSUE		EDITION LIMIT	YEAR RETD.	ISSUE PRICE	QUOTE U.S.$
1979	New Year Look	2,500	1979	500.00	550-650
1979	Spring Tonic	2,500	1979	Set	Set
1979	Cool Aid	2,500	1979	Set	Set
1979	Chilly Reception	2,500	1979	Set	Set

(Four Seasons) Traveling Salesman - N. Rockwell

YEAR ISSUE		EDITION LIMIT	YEAR RETD.	ISSUE PRICE	QUOTE U.S.$
1985	Horse Trader	2,500	1985	275.00	250-275
1985	Expert Salesman	2,500	1985	Set	Set
1985	Traveling Salesman	2,500	1985	Set	Set
1985	Country Pedlar	2,500	1985	Set	Set

(Four Seasons) Young Love - N. Rockwell

YEAR ISSUE		EDITION LIMIT	YEAR RETD.	ISSUE PRICE	QUOTE U.S.$
1973	Downhill Daring	2,500	1973	250.00	1100
1973	Beguiling Buttercup	2,500	1973	Set	Set
1973	Flying High	2,500	1973	Set	Set
1973	A Scholarly Pace	2,500	1973	Set	Set

Miniature Christmas Figurines - Various

YEAR ISSUE		EDITION LIMIT	YEAR RETD.	ISSUE PRICE	QUOTE U.S.$
1979	Tiny Tim - N. Rockwell	Yr.Iss.	1979	15.00	20
1980	Santa Plans His Trip - N. Rockwell	Yr.Iss.	1980	15.00	15
1981	Yuletide Reckoning - N. Rockwell	Yr.Iss.	1981	20.00	20
1982	Checking Good Deeds - N. Rockwell	Yr.Iss.	1982	20.00	20
1983	Santa's Friend - N. Rockwell	Yr.Iss.	1983	20.00	20
1984	Downhill Daring - N. Rockwell	Yr.Iss.	1984	20.00	20
1985	Christmas Santa - T. Nast	Yr.Iss.	1985	20.00	20
1986	Christmas Santa - T. Nast	Yr.Iss.	1986	25.00	25
1987	Annual Thomas Nast Santa - T. Nast	Yr.Iss.	1987	25.00	25

Miniatures - N. Rockwell

YEAR ISSUE		EDITION LIMIT	YEAR RETD.	ISSUE PRICE	QUOTE U.S.$
1982	The Annual Visit	Closed	1990	50.00	75
1981	At the Vets	Closed	1990	27.50	40
1987	Babysitter	15,000	1990	75.00	75
1981	Beguiling Buttercup	Closed	1990	45.00	45
1985	Best Friends	Closed	1990	27.50	28
1987	Between The Acts	15,000	1990	60.00	60
1981	Boy Meets His Dog	Closed	1990	37.50	38
1984	Careful Aims	Closed	1990	55.00	55
1987	Cinderella	15,000	1990	70.00	75
1981	Downhill Daring	Closed	1990	45.00	75
1985	Engineer	Closed	1990	55.00	55
1981	Flowers in Tender Bloom	Closed	1990	60.00	60
1986	Football Season	Closed	1990	60.00	60
1981	Gay Blades	Closed	1990	45.00	75
1984	Ghostly Gourds	Closed	1990	60.00	60
1984	Goin Fishing	Closed	1990	60.00	60
1986	The Graduate	Closed	1990	30.00	40
1984	In His Spirit	Closed	1990	60.00	60
1986	Lemonade Stand	Closed	1990	60.00	60
1986	Little Angel	Closed	1990	50.00	60
1985	Little Red Truck	Closed	1990	25.00	25
1982	Marriage License	Closed	1990	60.00	75
1987	The Milkmaid	15,000	1990	80.00	85
1986	Morning Walk	Closed	1990	60.00	60
1985	Muscle Bound	Closed	1990	30.00	30
1985	New Arrival	Closed	1990	32.50	35
1986	The Old Sign Painter	Closed	1990	70.00	80
1984	Pride of Parenthood	Closed	1990	50.00	50
1987	The Prom Dress	15,000	1990	75.00	75
1982	The Runaway	Closed	1990	50.00	50
1984	Shear Agony	Closed	1990	60.00	60
1986	Shoulder Ride	Closed	1990	50.00	65
1981	Snow Sculpture	Closed	1990	45.00	70
1985	Spring Checkup	Closed	1990	60.00	60
1987	Springtime	15,000	1990	65.00	75
1987	Starstruck	15,000	1990	75.00	80
1981	Sweet Serenade	Closed	1990	45.00	45
1981	Sweet Song So Young	Closed	1990	55.00	55
1985	To Love & Cherish	Closed	1990	32.50	35
1982	Triple Self Portrait	Closed	1990	60.00	90-175
1983	Trout Dinner	15,000	1990	60.00	60
1982	Vintage Times	Closed	1990	50.00	50
1986	Welcome Mat	Closed	1990	70.00	75
1984	Years End Court	Closed	1990	60.00	60
1981	Young Man's Fancy	Closed	1990	55.00	55

Parasol Lady - Unknown

YEAR ISSUE		EDITION LIMIT	YEAR RETD.	ISSUE PRICE	QUOTE U.S.$
1991	On the Boardwalk	Open		95.00	95
1994	Sunday Promenade	Open		95.00	95
1994	At The Fair	Open		95.00	95

Rockwell - N. Rockwell

YEAR ISSUE		EDITION LIMIT	YEAR RETD.	ISSUE PRICE	QUOTE U.S.$
1983	Antique Dealer	7,500	1990	130.00	200
1982	April Fool's (At The Curiosity Shop)	Closed	1990	55.00	100-110
1974	At The Vets	Closed	1990	25.00	65
1974	Batter Up	Closed	1990	40.00	90-235
1975	Boy And His Dog	Closed	1990	38.00	95
1974	Captain	Closed	1990	45.00	95
1984	Card Tricks	7,500	1990	110.00	180
1981	Christmas Dancers	7,500	1990	130.00	195
1988	Confrontation	15,000	1990	75.00	75
1988	Cramming	15,000	1990	80.00	80
1981	Day in the Life Boy II	Closed	1990	75.00	100
1982	A Day in the Life Boy III	Closed	1990	85.00	95
1982	A Day in the Life Girl III	Closed	1990	85.00	150
1988	The Diary	15,000	1990	80.00	80
1988	Dolores & Eddie	15,000	1990	75.00	80
1986	Drum For Tommy	Annual	1986	90.00	N/A
1983	Facts of Life	7,500	1990	110.00	180
1974	Fishing	Closed	1990	50.00	100-125
1988	Gary Cooper in Hollywood	15,000	1990	90.00	90
1976	God Rest Ye Merry Gentlemen	Closed	1990	50.00	1000-1500
1988	Home for the Holidays	7,500	1990	100.00	100
1976	Independence	Closed	1990	40.00	150
1980	Jolly Coachman	7,500	1990	75.00	145
1982	Marriage License	5,000	1990	110.00	400-600
1976	Marriage License	Closed	1990	50.00	175
1982	Merrie Christmas	7,500	1990	75.00	150
1974	Missing Tooth	Closed	1990	30.00	90
1975	No Swimming	Closed	1990	35.00	95-200
1976	The Occultist	Closed	1990	50.00	125-180
1975	Old Mill Pond	Closed	1990	45.00	95
1985	The Old Sign Painter	7,500	1990	130.00	210
1985	Puppet Maker	7,500	1990	130.00	130-200
1987	Santa Planning His Annual Visit	7,500	1990	95.00	95
1984	Santa's Friend	7,500	1990	75.00	160
1976	Saying Grace	Closed	1990	75.00	120
1982	Saying Grace	5,000	1990	110.00	500-600
1984	Serenade	7,500	1990	95.00	165
1974	Skating	Closed	1990	37.50	85
1976	Tackled (Ad Stand)	Closed	1990	35.00	100
1982	Tackled (Rockwell Name Signed)	Closed	1990	45.00	100
1974	Tiny Tim	Closed	1990	30.00	100
1982	Triple Self Portrait	5,000	1990	300.00	400-600
1974	Weighing In	Closed	1990	40.00	125
1981	Wet Sport	Closed	1990	85.00	100

Great American Taylor Collectibles

Great American Collectors' Club - Various

YEAR ISSUE		EDITION LIMIT	YEAR RETD.	ISSUE PRICE	QUOTE U.S.$
1993	William Claus-USA 700s - L. Smith	Retrd.	1994	35.00	70
1994	Winston-England 716 - L. Smith	12/95		35.00	35
1995	Timothy Claus-Ireland 717 - L. Smith	12/96		35.00	35
1995	Kris Jingle 817 - J. Clement	12/96		70.00	70

Jim Clement Collection - J. Clement

YEAR ISSUE		EDITION LIMIT	YEAR RETD.	ISSUE PRICE	QUOTE U.S.$
1994	Bearded Shorty Santa 812	Retrd.	1994	13.50	14
1994	Big Santa w/Toys 813	12/96		70.00	70
1994	Day After Christmas 809	12/95		16.50	17
1995	Doe a Deer 818	12/97		29.00	29
1994	Down the Chimny Santa 814	12/95		28.00	28
1994	Golfer Santa 806	12/95		28.00	28
1995	Ho! Ho! Ho! 819	12/97		11.50	12
1995	Mountain Dream 821	12/97		27.00	27
1994	Mr. Egg Santa 802	12/95		19.50	20
1994	Mrs. Clement's Santa 808	Retrd.	1994	17.00	17
1994	Night After Christmas 810	12/96		16.50	17
1994	Noah Santa 805	12/96		28.00	28
1994	Patriotic Santa 807	Retrd.	1994	20.00	20
1994	Santa High Hat 815	Retrd.	1994	30.00	30
1994	Santa w/Rover 811	12/96		20.00	20
1994	Santa w/Tree 804	Retrd.	1994	15.00	15
1995	Silent Night 820	12/97		29.00	29
1994	Sm. Hobby Horse Santa 803	12/95		28.00	28
1994	Tennis Santa 816	12/96		28.00	28
1995	Visions of Sugar Plums 822	12/97		23.00	23

Lamp Collection - J. Clement

YEAR ISSUE		EDITION LIMIT	YEAR RETD.	ISSUE PRICE	QUOTE U.S.$
1995	Clementine Cat 55LNKS	12/97		70.00	70
1995	Toy Soldier 57LSS	12/97		80.00	80
1995	Uncle Sam 56LRS	12/97		80.00	80

Old World Santas - L. Smith

YEAR ISSUE		EDITION LIMIT	YEAR RETD.	ISSUE PRICE	QUOTE U.S.$
1988	Jangle Claus-Ireland 335s	Retrd.	1990	20.00	135-150
1988	Hans Von Claus-Germany 337s	Retrd.	1990	20.00	135-150
1988	Ching Chang Claus-China 338s	Retrd.	1990	20.00	135-150
1988	Kris Kringle Claus-Switzerland 339s	Retrd.	1990	20.00	135-150
1988	Jingle Claus-England 336s	Retrd.	1990	20.00	135-150
1989	Rudy Claus-Austria 410s	Retrd.	1991	20.00	125
1989	Noel Claus-Belguim 412s	Retrd.	1991	20.00	125
1989	Pierre Claus-France 414s	Retrd.	1991	20.00	125
1989	Nicholai Claus-Russia 413s	Retrd.	1991	20.00	125
1989	Yule Claus-Germany 411s	Retrd.	1991	20.00	125
1990	Matts Claus-Sweden 430s	Retrd.	1992	20.00	75
1990	Vander Claus-Holland 433s	Retrd.	1992	20.00	75
1990	Sven Claus-Norway 432s	Retrd.	1992	20.00	75
1990	Cedric Claus-England 434s	Retrd.	1992	20.00	75
1990	Mario Claus-Italy 431s	Retrd.	1992	20.00	75
1991	Mitch Claus-England 437s	Retrd.	1993	25.00	50

YEAR ISSUE		EDITION LIMIT	YEAR RETD.	ISSUE PRICE	QUOTE U.S.$
1991	Samuel Claus-USA 436s	Retrd.	1993	25.00	50
1991	Duncan Claus-Scotland 439s	Retrd.	1993	25.00	50
1991	Benjamin Claus-Israel 438s	Retrd.	1993	25.00	50
1991	Boris Claus-Russia 435s	Retrd.	1993	25.00	50
1992	Mickey Claus-Ireland 701s	Retrd.	1994	25.00	40-50
1992	Jacques Claus-France 702s	Retrd.	1994	25.00	40-50
1992	Terry Claus-Denmark 703s	Retrd.	1994	25.00	50
1992	José Claus-Spain 704s	Retrd.	1994	25.00	36-50
1992	Stu Claus-Poland 705s	Retrd.	1994	25.00	36-50
1993	Otto Claus-Germany 707s	12/95		27.50	29
1993	Franz Claus-Switzerland 706s	12/95		27.50	29
1993	Bjorn Claus-Sweden 709s	12/95		27.50	29
1993	Ryan Claus-Canada 710s	12/95		27.50	29
1993	Vito Claus-Italy 708s	12/95		27.50	29
1994	Angus Claus-Scotland 713s	12/96		29.00	29
1994	Ivan Claus-Russia 712s	12/96		29.00	29
1994	Desmond Claus-England 715s	12/96		29.00	29
1994	Gord Claus-Canada 714s	12/96		29.00	29
1995	Tomba Claus-South Africa 718s	12/97		29.00	29
1995	Butch Claus-United States 719s	12/97		29.00	29
1995	Lars Claus-Norway 720s	12/97		29.00	29
1995	Stach Claus-Poland 721s	12/97		29.00	29
1995	Raymond Claus-Galapagos Islands 722s	12/97		29.00	29

Hallmark

1994 A North Pole Christmas Merry Miniatures - Hallmark

YEAR ISSUE		EDITION LIMIT	YEAR RETD.	ISSUE PRICE	QUOTE U.S.$
1994	Baby Whale with Hat 350QFM8222	Retrd.	1994	3.50	4
1994	Mrs. Claus 375QFM8286	Retrd.	1994	3.75	4
1994	North Pole Sign 675QFM8333	Retrd.	1994	6.75	7
1994	Penguin Throwing Snowball 275QFM8313	Retrd.	1994	2.75	3
1994	Polar Bear on Skates 375QFM8293	Retrd.	1995	3.75	4
1994	Polar Snuggle Bears 325QFM8323	Retrd.	1995	3.25	4
1994	Seal with Earmuffs 250QFM8272	Retrd.	1994	2.50	3
1994	Sled Dog with Candy Cane 325QFM8306	Retrd.	1994	3.25	4
1994	Snowman 275QFM8316	Retrd.	1994	2.75	3
1994	Tree 275QFM8326	Retrd.	1994	2.75	3
1994	Walrus in Hat with Gifts 300QFM8232	Retrd.	1994	3.00	3
1994	White Arctic Fox on Skates 375QFM8303	Retrd.	1994	3.75	4

1994 At The Beach Merry Miniatures - Hallmark

YEAR ISSUE		EDITION LIMIT	YEAR RETD.	ISSUE PRICE	QUOTE U.S.$
1994	Bear with Surfboard 350QSM8015	Retrd.	1994	3.50	4
1994	Chipmunk on Inflated Horse 350QSM8002	Retrd.	1994	3.50	4
1994	Dock 675QSM8076	Retrd.	1994	6.75	7
1994	Hedgehog Eating Hot Dog 300QSM8026	Retrd.	1994	3.00	3
1994	Hippo in Inner Tube 300QSM8032	Retrd.	1994	3.00	3
1994	Mouse with Sunglasses 250QSM8035	Retrd.	1994	2.50	3
1994	Pail of Seashells 275QSM8052	Retrd.	1994	2.75	3
1994	Rabbit with Ice Cream Cone 275QSM8066	Retrd.	1995	2.75	3
1994	Raccoon with Scuba Gear 375QSM8063	Retrd.	1994	3.75	4

1994 Easter Egg Hunt Miniatures - Hallmark

YEAR ISSUE		EDITION LIMIT	YEAR RETD.	ISSUE PRICE	QUOTE U.S.$
1994	Birds in Nest 375QSM8116	Retrd.	1994	3.75	4
1994	Bunny with Cracked Egg 300QSM8125	Retrd.	1994	3.00	3
1994	Chick in Wagon 375QSM8123	Retrd.	1994	3.75	4
1994	Duck with Egg on Spoon 300QSM8135	Retrd.	1994	3.00	3
1994	Easter Basket 250QSM8145	Retrd.	1995	2.50	3
1994	Egg Wishing Well 675QSM8033	Retrd.	1994	6.75	7
1994	Lamb in Flower Patch 325QSM8132	Retrd.	1995	3.25	4
1994	Mouse with Flower 275QSM8243	Retrd.	1995	2.75	3
1994	Rabbit with Croquet 375QSM8113	Retrd.	1994	3.75	4
1994	Rabbit with Egg-Shaped Watering Can 325QSM8083	Retrd.	1994	3.25	4

1994 Haunted House Party Merry Miniatures - Hallmark

YEAR ISSUE		EDITION LIMIT	YEAR RETD.	ISSUE PRICE	QUOTE U.S.$
1994	Bear Dressed as Bat 300QFM8285	Retrd.	1995	3.00	3
1994	Bunny Alien 375QFM8266	Retrd.	1994	3.75	4
1994	Bunny Super Hero 300QFM8422	Retrd.	1994	3.00	3
1994	Cute Black Kitten 325QFM8273	Retrd.	1994	3.25	4
1994	Fence with Lantern 675QFM8283	Retrd.	1994	6.75	7
1994	Ghost on Tombstone 250QFM8282	Retrd.	1994	2.50	3
1994	Mouse Dressed as Witch 300QFM8292	Retrd.	1994	3.00	3
1994	Pumpkin with Hat 275QFM8276	Retrd.	1994	2.75	3
1994	Squirrel Dressed as Clown 375QFM8263	Retrd.	1994	3.75	4

1994 Heartland Merry Miniatures - Hallmark

YEAR ISSUE		EDITION LIMIT	YEAR RETD.	ISSUE PRICE	QUOTE U.S.$
1994	Bear Mail Man 375QSM8006	Retrd.	1994	3.75	4
1994	Beaver With Card 375QSM8013	Retrd.	1995	3.75	4
1994	Chipmunk With Kite 375QSM8003	Retrd.	1994	3.75	4
1994	Dog With Balloon Heart 250QSM8092	Retrd.	1994	2.50	3
1994	Mailbox 675QSM8023	Retrd.	1994	6.75	7
1994	Owl in Stump 275QSM8085	Retrd.	1994	2.75	3
1994	Rabbit With Heart Cutouts 325QSM8016	Retrd.	1995	3.25	4
1994	Raccoon With Cutout Heart 350QSM8062	Retrd.	1995	3.50	4
1994	Tree Stump and Paint Can 300QSM8075	Retrd.	1994	3.00	3

1994 Patriotic Merry Miniatures - Hallmark

YEAR ISSUE		EDITION LIMIT	YEAR RETD.	ISSUE PRICE	QUOTE U.S.$
1994	Bear with Flag 375QSM8043	Retrd.	1994	3.75	4
1994	Document 275QSM8053	Retrd.	1994	2.75	3
1994	Eagle with Hat 375QSM8036	Retrd.	1994	3.75	4
1994	Flag 675QSM8056	Retrd.	1994	6.75	7
1994	Goat Uncle Sam 300QSM8472	Retrd.	1994	3.00	3
1994	Hedgehog with Fife 350QSM8492	Retrd.	1994	3.50	4
1994	Lamb Betsy Ross with Flag 350QSM8482	Retrd.	1994	3.50	4
1994	Mouse Statue of Liberty 300QSM8475	Retrd.	1994	3.00	3

1994 Thanksgiving Feast Merry Miniatures - Hallmark

YEAR ISSUE		EDITION LIMIT	YEAR RETD.	ISSUE PRICE	QUOTE U.S.$
1994	Basket of Apples 275QFM8356	Retrd.	1995	2.75	3
1994	Beaver with Apple 375QFM8336	Retrd.	1995	3.75	4
1994	Corn Stalk 675QFM8363	Retrd.	1994	6.75	7
1994	Cute Indian Bunny 275QFM8353	Retrd.	1994	2.75	3
1994	Indian Bear with Honey 350QFM8162	Retrd.	1994	3.50	4
1994	Indian Chickadee with Corn 325QFM8346	Retrd.	1994	3.25	4
1994	Indian Squirrel with Pie 300QFM8182	Retrd.	1995	3.00	3
1994	Pilgrim Girl Bunny 375QFM8343	Retrd.	1994	3.75	4
1994	Pilgrim Mouse Praying 300QFM8175	Retrd.	1994	3.00	3

1995 Christmas Merry Miniatures - Hallmark

YEAR ISSUE		EDITION LIMIT	YEAR RETD.	ISSUE PRICE	QUOTE U.S.$
1995	Cameron on Sled 375QFM8199	Open		3.75	4
1995	Caroling Bear 325QFM8307	Open		3.25	4
1995	Caroling Bunny 325QFM8309	Open		3.25	4
1995	Caroling Mouse 300QFM8317	Open		3.00	3
1995	Christmas Tree 675QFM8197	Open		6.75	7
1995	Hamster With Cookie 325QFM8319	Open		3.25	4
1995	Lion and Lamb 400QFM8287	Open		4.00	4
1995	Nutcracker 375QFM8297	Open		3.75	4
1995	Polar Bear on Skates 375QFM8293	Open		3.75	4
1995	Polar Snuggle Bears 325QFM8323	Open		3.25	4
1995	Santa 375QFM8299	Open		3.75	4
1995	Toymaker Beaver 375QFM8289	Open		3.75	4

1995 Easter Merry Miniatures - Hallmark

YEAR ISSUE		EDITION LIMIT	YEAR RETD.	ISSUE PRICE	QUOTE U.S.$
1995	Beauregard 300QSM8047	Open		3.00	3
1995	Cameron Dressed as Bunny 375QSM8029	Open		3.75	4
1995	Cottage Prop 675QSM8027	Open		6.75	7
1995	Duck with Egg on Spoon 300QSM8135	Open		3.00	3
1995	Easter Basket 250QSM8145	Open		2.50	3
1995	Mouse With Flower 275QSM8243	Open		2.75	3
1995	Prince Charming 400QSM8049	Open		4.00	4
1995	Selby 300QSM8039	Open		3.00	3
1995	Stylish Rabbit 375QSM8037	Open		3.75	4

1995 Halloween Merry Miniatures - Hallmark

YEAR ISSUE		EDITION LIMIT	YEAR RETD.	ISSUE PRICE	QUOTE U.S.$
1995	Bear Dressed as Bat 300QFM8285	Open		3.00	3
1995	Cameron in Pumpkin Costume 375QFM8147	Open		3.75	4
1995	Cute Witch 300QFM8157	Open		3.00	3
1995	Friendly Monster 300QFM8159	Open		3.00	3
1995	Haunted House 675QFM8139	Open		6.75	7
1995	Mouse as Witch 300QFM8292	Open		3.00	3
1995	Rhino Mummy 375QFM8149	Open		3.75	4
1995	Stepmother 400QFM8099	Open		4.00	4

1995 St. Patrick's Merry Miniatures - Hallmark

YEAR ISSUE		EDITION LIMIT	YEAR RETD.	ISSUE PRICE	QUOTE U.S.$
1995	Leprechaun 350QSM8119	Open		3.50	4

1995 Summer Merry Miniatures - Hallmark

YEAR ISSUE		EDITION LIMIT	YEAR RETD.	ISSUE PRICE	QUOTE U.S.$
1995	Bear in Clown Costume 375QSM8057	Open		3.75	4
1995	Bride and Groom Bears 375QSM8067	Open		3.75	4
1995	Cameron With Camera 375QSM8077	Open		3.75	4
1995	Fairy Godmother 400QSM8089	Open		4.00	4
1995	Ground Hog 300QSM8079	Open		3.00	3
1995	Rabbit With Ice Cream Cone 275QSM8066	Open		2.75	3
1995	Raccoon and Flower 300QSM8087	Open		3.00	3

1995 Thanksgiving Merry Miniatures - Hallmark

YEAR ISSUE		EDITION LIMIT	YEAR RETD.	ISSUE PRICE	QUOTE U.S.$
1995	Basket of Apples 275QFM8356	Open		2.75	3
1995	Beaver With Apple 375QFM8336	Open		3.75	4
1995	Cameron in Pilgrim Costume 375QFM8169	Open		3.75	4
1995	Chipmunk With Corn 375QFM8179	Open		3.75	4
1995	Indian Squirrel With Pie 300QFM8182	Open		3.00	3
1995	Mouse With Cranberries 300QFM8189	Open		3.00	3
1995	Mouse With Pumpkin 300QFM8187	Open		3.00	3
1995	Pilgrim Turkey 375QFM8177	Open		3.75	4
1995	Pumpkin Carriage 500QFM8127	Open		5.00	5
1995	Thanksgiving Feast 475QFM8167	Open		4.75	5

1995 Valentine Merry Miniatures - Hallmark

YEAR ISSUE		EDITION LIMIT	YEAR RETD.	ISSUE PRICE	QUOTE U.S.$
1995	Bashful Boy With Heart 300QSM8107	Open		3.00	3
1995	Bashful Girl With Heart 300QSM8109	Open		3.00	3
1995	Beaver With Card 375QSM8013	Open		3.75	4
1995	Cameron With Heart 375QSM8009	Open		3.75	4
1995	Christmas Tree 675QFM8197	Open		6.75	7
1995	Cinderella 400QSM8117	Open		4.00	4
1995	Koala Bear With Heart 375QSM8019	Open		3.75	4
1995	Rabbit With Heart Cutouts 325QSM8016	Open		3.25	4
1995	Raccoon With Cutout Heart 350QSM8016	Open		3.50	4
1995	St. Bernard Dog375 QSM8017	Open		3.75	4
1995	Tree With Carved Heart Prop 675QSM8007	Open		6.75	7

Hallmark Galleries

Birds of North America - G.&G. Dooly

YEAR ISSUE		EDITION LIMIT	YEAR RETD.	ISSUE PRICE	QUOTE U.S.$
1992	American Goldfinch 5500QHG9887	2,500	1994	85.00	85
1992	American Robins 2QHG9878	2,500	1994	175.00	175
1992	Cardinal 7500QHG9897	2,500	1994	110.00	110
1992	Cedar Waxwing 8000QHG9889	2,500	1994	120.00	120
1992	Dark-eyed Junco 5500QHG9899	2,500	1994	85.00	85
1992	House Wren 5500QHG9801	2,500	1994	85.00	85
1992	Ovenbird 6500QHG9837	2,500	1994	95.00	95
1992	Red-breasted Nuthatch 5500QHG9802	2,500	1994	95.00	95

Days to Remember-The Art of Norman Rockwell - D. Unruh

YEAR ISSUE		EDITION LIMIT	YEAR RETD.	ISSUE PRICE	QUOTE U.S.$
1993	A Child's Prayer 7500QHG9722	7,500	1995	75.00	75
1992	The Fiddler 9500QHG9708	4,500	1995	95.00	95
1992	The Fiddler-Musical Jewelry Box 4800QHG9711	9,500	1994	48.00	48
1992	Little Spooner-Musical Jewelry Box 4800QHG9712	9,500	1994	48.00	48
1992	Little Spooners 7000QHG9705	4,500	1995	70.00	70
1992	Low and Outside 9500QHG9714	4,500	1995	95.00	95
1992	Marbles Champion 7500QHG9704	4,500	1995	75.00	75
1994	No Swimming 7000QHG9725	4,500	1995	70.00	70
1992	Santa and His Helpers 9500QHG9702	7,500	1995	95.00	95
1992	Saying Grace 1QHG9719	1,500	1995	375.00	375
1993	Secrets 7000QHG9721	7,500	1995	70.00	70
1992	Sleeping Children 1QHG9703	7,500	1995	105.00	105
1992	Springtime 1927 9500QHG9706	4,500	1995	95.00	95
1992	Springtime, 1927-Musical Jewelry Box 4800QHG9713	9,500	1994	48.00	48
1992	The Truth About Santa 8500QHG9720	7,500	1995	85.00	85

Eileen's Richardson's Enchanted Garden - E. Richardson

YEAR ISSUE		EDITION LIMIT	YEAR RETD.	ISSUE PRICE	QUOTE U.S.$
1992	Baby Bunny Hop (bowl) 8500QHG3004	9,500	1994	85.00	85
1992	Bunny Abundance (vase) 7500QHG3005	9,500	1994	75.00	75
1992	Enchanted Garden (vase) 1QHG3006	1,200	1994	115.00	115
1992	Everybunny Can Fly (vase) 7000QHG3007	9,500	1994	70.00	70
1992	Let Them Eat Carrots (pitcher) 7000QHG3013	9,500	1994	70.00	70
1992	Milk Bath (vase) 8000QHG3009	9,500	1994	80.00	80
1993	Peaceable Kingdom Lidded Box 3800QHG3017	9,500	1994	38.00	38
1992	Promenade (bowl) 6500QHG3002	9,500	1994	65.00	65

Innocent Wonders - T. Blackshear

YEAR ISSUE		EDITION LIMIT	YEAR RETD.	ISSUE PRICE	QUOTE U.S.$
1992	Bobo Bipps 1QHG4005	2,500	1995	150.00	150
1992	Dinky Toot 1QHG4004	4,500	1995	125.00	125
1992	Pinkie Poo 1QHG4002	2,500	1995	135.00	135
1992	Pippy Lou 1QHG4006	4,500	1995	150.00	150
1992	Pockets 1QHG4018	4,500	1995	125.00	125
1992	Rectangular Music Box 6000QHG4009	9,500	1995	60.00	60
1992	Square Music Box 4500QHG4008	9,500	1995	45.00	45
1993	Twinky Wink 1QHG4021	4,500	1995	115.00	115
1992	Waggletag 1QHG4001	4,500	1995	125.00	125
1992	Waterdome-Dinky Toot 3500QHG4020	9,500	1994	35.00	35
1992	Wood Base 2000QHG4011	Retrd.	1995	20.00	20
1992	Zip Doodle 1QHG4010	4,500	1995	125.00	125

Kiddie Car Classics - E. Weirick

YEAR ISSUE		EDITION LIMIT	YEAR RETD.	ISSUE PRICE	QUOTE U.S.$
1994	1936 Steelcraft Lincoln Zephyr by Murray 5000QHG9015	19,500		50.00	50
1995	1937 Steelcraft Auburn Luxury Edition QHG9021	24,500		65.00	65

FIGURINES/COTTAGES

YEAR ISSUE		EDITION LIMIT	YEAR RETD.	ISSUE PRICE	QUOTE U.S.$
1995	1937 Steelcraft Chrysler Airflow by Murray (R) L.E. QHG9024	24,500		65.00	65
1992	1940 Murray Airplane 5000QHG9003	14,500	1993	50.00	125-240
1992	1941 Steelcraft Spitfire Airplane 5000QHG9009	19,500		50.00	50
1995	1948 Murray Pontiac QHG9026	Open		50.00	50
1995	1950 Murray Torpedo QHG9020	Open		50.00	50
1992	1953 Murray Dump Truck 4800QHG9012	14,500	1993	48.00	80-115
1992	1955 Murray Champion 4500QHG9008	14,500	1993	45.00	150-185
1992	1955 Murray Dump Truck 4800QHG9011	19,500		48.00	48
1993	1955 Murray Fire Chief 4500QHG9006	19,500		45.00	45
1992	1955 Murray Fire Truck 5000QHG9001	14,500	1993	50.00	150-195
1992	1955 Murray Fire Truck 5000QHG9010	19,500		50.00	50
1993	1955 Murray Ranch Wagon 4800QHG9007	24,500		48.00	48
1992	1955 Murray Red Champion 4500QHG9002	19,500		45.00	45
1995	1955 Murray Royal Deluxe QHG9025	29,500		55.00	55
1992	1955 Murray Tractor and Trailer 5500QHG9004	14,500	1993	55.00	120-175
1994	1956 Garton Dragnet Police Car 5000QHG9016	24,500		50.00	50
1994	1956 Garton Kidillac (Special Edition) 5500QHX9094	Retrd.	1994	50.00	50
1994	1956 GARTON Mark V QHG9022	24,500		45.00	45
1994	1958 Murray Atomic Missile QHG9018	24,500		55.00	55
1995	1959 GARTON Deluxe Kidillac QHG9017	Open		55.00	55
1995	1961 GARTON Casey Jones Locomotive QHG9019	Open		55.00	55
1994	1961 Murray Circus Car 4800QHG9014	24,500		48.00	48
1994	1961 Murray Speedway Pace Car 4500QHG9013	24,500		45.00	45
1995	1962 Murray Super Deluxe Fire Truck QHG9095	Open		55.00	55
1995	1964 GARTON Tin Lizzie QHG9023	Open		50.00	50
1993	1968 Murray Boat Jolly Roger 5000QHG9005	19,500		50.00	50

Little Creations - L. Rankin

YEAR ISSUE		EDITION LIMIT	YEAR RETD.	ISSUE PRICE	QUOTE U.S.$
1993	Basset Hound-Happy Hound 1000QEC1294	Retrd.	1995	10.00	10
1993	Beagle Daydreamin 8500QEC1275	Retrd.	1995	8.50	9
1993	Bear Honey 1200QEC1243	Retrd.	1995	12.00	12
1993	Bulldog-Bone Tired 8500QEC1273	Retrd.	1995	8.50	9
1994	Cat Lookin' for Trouble 1000QEC1227	Retrd.	1995	10.00	10
1993	Frog Ribbett 1000QEC1285	Retrd.	1995	10.00	10
1994	Orangutan Peace & Quiet 1200QEC1228	Retrd.	1995	12.00	12
1993	Otter-Water Sport 1200QEC1245	Retrd.	1995	12.00	12
1993	Pig-Pee Wee Porker 750QEC1263	Retrd.	1995	7.50	8
1994	Polar Bear McKinley 1800QEC1226	Retrd.	1995	18.00	18
1993	Reclining Terrier Dreamer 750QEC1265	Retrd.	1995	7.50	8
1993	Seated Rabbit Bashful 1000QEC1253	Retrd.	1995	10.00	10
1993	Shih Tzu-Daddy's Girl 750QEC1293	Retrd.	1995	7.50	8
1994	Sitting Pig Li'l Piggy 1000QEC1224	Retrd.	1995	10.00	10
1993	Spaniel & Beagle 1500QEC1283	Retrd.	1995	12.00	12
1993	Squirrel-Cheeky 750QEC1223	Retrd.	1995	7.50	8
1993	Turtle-Tenderfoot 1200QEC1225	Retrd.	1995	12.00	12
1993	White Seal Sea Baby 1000QEC1235	Retrd.	1995	10.00	10

Lou Rankin's Creations - L. Rankin

YEAR ISSUE		EDITION LIMIT	YEAR RETD.	ISSUE PRICE	QUOTE U.S.$
1993	Backyard Bandit Raccoon 3000QHG9920	19,500	1995	30.00	30
1992	Basset Hound -Faithful Friend 3800QHG9908	19,500	1995	38.00	38
1994	Bulldog 3800QHG9926	19,500	1995	38.00	38
1992	Bulldog and Beagle -Best Buddies 4800QHG9906	9,500	1995	48.00	48
1994	Cocker Spaniel Pal 3500QHG9924	19,500	1995	35.00	35
1993	Fairbanks Polar Bear 7000QHG9916	19,500	1995	70.00	70
1994	Frog Pucker Up Baby 3500QHG9923	19,500	1995	35.00	35
1992	Happy Frog -Feelin' Fine 3500QHG9918	19,500	1995	35.00	35
1993	Mini Paws Happy-Looking Cat 2500QHG9922	19,500	1995	25.00	25
1992	Orangutan -The Thinker 3800QHG9915	19,500	1995	38.00	38
1992	Pair of Pigs -Pork & Beans 3800QHG9902	19,500	1995	38.00	38
1992	Pig with Head Raised - Fair Lady 3500QHG9903	19,500	1995	35.00	35
1992	Reclining Bear 3500QHG9901	19,500	1995	35.00	35
1992	Reclining Cat -Birdwatcher 3000QHG9912	19,500	1995	30.00	30
1993	Seal Winsome 3200QHG9921	19,500	1995	32.00	32
1992	Seated Bear 3000QHG9905	19,500	1995	30.00	30
1992	Seated Rabbit 3000QHG9911	19,500	1995	30.00	30
1992	Shih Tzu -The Sophisticate 3000QHG9907	19,500	1995	30.00	30
1993	Slowpoke Turtle 3000QHG9917	19,500	1995	30.00	30
1992	Squirrel I -Satisfied 2500QHG9909	19,500	1995	25.00	25
1992	Squirrel II -Sassy 2500QHG9910	19,500	1995	25.00	25
1992	Two Otters -Two's Company 4500QHG9914	9,500	1995	45.00	45
1994	Two Pigs 4500QHG9925	19,500	1995	45.00	45

Majestic Wilderness - M. Newman

YEAR ISSUE		EDITION LIMIT	YEAR RETD.	ISSUE PRICE	QUOTE U.S.$
1992	American Bald Eagle 1QHG2009	1,200	1993	195.00	195
1993	American Wilderness Mini Environment Set 1QHG2029	2,500	1995	225.00	225
1992	American Wilderness Mini Environment With Dome 8000QHG2019	Retrd.	1995	80.00	80
1994	Arctic Wolves 13000QHG2031	4,500	1995	130.00	130
1992	Bighorn Sheep 1QHG2005	4,500	1995	125.00	125
1992	Bison 1QHG2016	4,500	1995	120.00	120
1994	Elk in Water 12000QHG2032	4,500	1995	120.00	120
1992	Grizzly Mother with Cub 1QHG2004	2,500	1995	135.00	135
1992	Large Base 3500QHG2028	Retrd.	1995	3.50	4
1992	The Launch 1QHG2025	2,500	1995	165.00	165
1992	Lidded Box/Deer 4000QHG2010	9,500	1995	40.00	40
1992	Lidded Box/Wolves 4000QHG2011	9,500	1995	40.00	40
1992	Male Grizzly 1QHG2001	2,500	1995	145.00	145
1992	Mini Black Bear 2800QHG2020	14,500	1995	28.00	28
1992	Mini Cottontail Rabbits 2000QHG2021	14,500	1995	20.00	20
1994	Mini Deer 2500QHG2036	14,500	1995	25.00	25
1992	Mini Eagle 2800QHG2026	14,500	1995	28.00	28
1992	Mini Mule Deer 2800QHG2024	14,500	1995	28.00	28
1992	Mini Raccoons 2000QHG2022	14,500	1995	20.00	20
1992	Mini Red Fox 2000QHG2023	14,500	1995	20.00	20
1994	Mini Snow Owl 1800QHG2034	14,500	1995	18.00	18
1994	Mini Snowshoe Rabbits 2000QHG2037	14,500	1995	20.00	20
1994	Mini White Tailed Buck 2500QHG2035	14,500	1995	25.00	25
1992	Mountain Lion 7500QHG2006	4,500	1995	75.00	75
1992	Red Fox 7500QHG2017	4,500	1995	75.00	75
1992	Small Base 2500QHG2027	Retrd.	1995	2.50	3
1992	Snowshoe Rabbit 7000QHG2007	4,500	1995	70.00	70
1992	Timber Wolves 1QHG2003	2,500	1995	135.00	135
1992	White-tailed Buck 1QHG2008	2,500	1995	135.00	135
1992	White-tailed Doe with Fawn 1QHG2002	2,500	1995	135.00	135
1994	Winter Environment 7000QHG2033	Retrd.	1995	70.00	70
1994	Winter Environment Set 1QHG2038	2,500	1995	160.00	160

Mary Engelbreit Friendship Garden - M. Engelbreit

YEAR ISSUE		EDITION LIMIT	YEAR RETD.	ISSUE PRICE	QUOTE U.S.$
1993	Birdhouse 4500QHG5013	9,500	1995	45.00	45
1993	Blue Teapot 5000QHG5004	9,500	1995	50.00	50
1993	Cherry Teapot 5000QHG5005	9,500	1995	50.00	50
1993	Cookie Jar 5000QHG5009	9,500	1995	50.00	50
1993	Mini Tea Set 4500QHG5007	9,500	1995	45.00	45
1993	Teatime Table and Chairs 7500QHG5014	12,500	1995	75.00	75
1993	Watering Can 3000QHG5008	9,500	1994	30.00	30
1993	Yellow Teapot 5000QHG5006	9,500	1995	50.00	50

Moustershire - D. Rhodus

YEAR ISSUE		EDITION LIMIT	YEAR RETD.	ISSUE PRICE	QUOTE U.S.$
1992	Acorn Inn Customers 2800QHG8020	9,500	1995	28.00	28
1992	Acorn Inn/Timothy Duzmuch 6500QHG8009	9,500	1995	65.00	65
1992	Andrew Allsgood- Honorable Citizen 1000QHG8001	Retrd.	1995	10.00	10
1992	Bakery/Dunne Eaton 5500QHG8010	9,500	1994	55.00	55
1992	Bandstand/Cyrus & Cecilia Sunnyside 5000QHG8011	9,500	1995	50.00	50
1992	Chelsea Goforth- Ingenue 1000QHG8002	Retrd.	1995	10.00	10
1992	Claire Lovencare- Nanny 1800QHG8014	19,500	1995	18.00	18
1992	Colin Tuneman- Musician of Note 1000QHG8004	Retrd.	1995	10.00	10
1992	Hattie Chapeau- Milliner 1500QHG8015	19,500	1995	15.00	15
1992	Henrietta Seaworthy 1500QHG8026	19,500	1995	15.00	15
1992	Hillary Hemstitch- Seamstress 1000QHG8006	Retrd.	1995	10.00	10
1992	Hyacinth House 6500QHG8021	9,500	1995	65.00	65
1992	L.E. Hosten- Innkeeper 1000QHG8007	Retrd.	1995	10.00	10
1992	Malcolm Cramwell- Mouserly Scholar 1000QHG8008	Retrd.	1995	10.00	10
1993	Michael McFogg At Lighthouse 5500QHG8025	9,500	1995	55.00	55
1992	Miles Fielding- Farmer 1000QHG8003	Retrd.	1995	10.00	10
1992	Nigel Puffmore- Talented Tubist 1000QHG8012	19,500	1995	10.00	10
1992	Olivia Puddingsby- Baker 1000QHG8005	Retrd.	1994	10.00	10
1992	The Park Gate 6000QHG8019	9,500	1995	60.00	60
1992	Peter Philpott- Gardener 1200QHG8022	19,500	1995	12.00	12
1992	The Picnic/Tree 5000QHG8017	9,500	1995	50.00	50
1992	Robin Ripengood- Grocer 2800QHG8013	19,500	1995	28.00	28
1992	Tess Tellingtale/Well 2800QHG8024	19,500	1995	28.00	28
1992	Trio 2300QHG8016	19,500	1995	23.00	23
1992	Village/Bay Crossroads Sign 1000QHG8023	19,500	1995	10.00	10

Tender Touches - E. Seale

YEAR ISSUE		EDITION LIMIT	YEAR RETD.	ISSUE PRICE	QUOTE U.S.$
1990	Baby Bear in Backpack 1600QEC9863	Retrd.	1991	16.00	26
1988	Baby Raccoon 2000QHG7031	Retrd.	1992	20.00	40
1991	Baby's 1st Riding Rocking Bear 1600QEC9349	Retrd.	1991	16.00	16
1989	Bear Decorating Tree 1800QHG7050	Retrd.	1995	18.00	40
1992	Bear Family Christmas 4500QHG7002	9,500	1995	45.00	45
1990	Bear Graduate 1500QHG7043	Retrd.	1995	15.00	15
1988	Bear w/ Umbrella 1600QHG7029	Retrd.	1994	16.00	35
1990	Bear's Easter Parade 2300QHG7040	Retrd.	1995	23.00	23
1990	Bears Playing Baseball 2000QHG7039	Retrd.	1994	20.00	20
1990	Bears w/ Gift 1800QEC9461	Retrd.	1991	18.00	50-65
1992	Beaver Growth Chart 2000QHG7007	19,500	1995	20.00	20
1992	Beaver w/ Double Bass 1800QHG7058	Retrd.	1995	18.00	18
1990	Beavers w/Tree 2300QHG7052	Retrd.	1994	23.00	23
1989	Birthday Mouse 1600QHG7010	Retrd.	1993	16.00	45
1992	Breakfast in Bed 1800QHG7059	Retrd.	1995	18.00	18
1989	Bride & Groom 2000QHG7009	Retrd.	1994	20.00	40
1992	Building a Pumpkin Man 1800QHG7061	Retrd.	1995	18.00	18
1990	Bunnies Eating Ice Cream 2000QHG7038	Retrd.	1995	20.00	20
1990	Bunnies w/ Slide 2000QHG7016	Retrd.	1994	20.00	20
1990	Bunny Cheerleader 1600QHG7018	Retrd.	1994	16.00	45
1992	Bunny Clarinet 1600QHG7063	Retrd.	1994	16.00	16
1990	Bunny Hiding Valentine 1600QHG7035	Retrd.	1995	16.00	16
1990	Bunny in Boat 1800QHG7021	Retrd.	1994	18.00	30
1989	Bunny in Flowers 1600QHG7012	Retrd.	1992	16.00	26
1991	Bunny in High Chair 1600QHG7054	Retrd.	1995	16.00	16
1990	Bunny Pulling Wagon 2300QHG7008	Retrd.	1994	23.00	23
1990	Bunny w/ Ice Cream 1500QHG7020	Retrd.	1993	15.00	15
1992	Bunny w/ Kite 1900QHG7006	19,500	1995	19.00	19
1991	Bunny w/ Large Eggs 1600QHG7056	Retrd.	1995	16.00	16
1990	Bunny w/ Stocking 1500QEC9416	Retrd.	1990	15.00	25
1992	Chatting Mice 2300QHG7003	19,500	1995	23.00	23
1989	Chipmunk Praying 1800QEC9431	Retrd.	1991	18.00	75
1989	Chipmunk w/Roses 1600QHG7023	Retrd.	1992	16.00	26
1992	Chipmunks w/Album 2300QHG7057	Retrd.	1995	23.00	23
1991	Christmas Bunny Skiing 1800QHG7046	Retrd.	1995	18.00	18
1990	Dad and Son Bears 2300QHG7015	Retrd.	1992	23.00	33
1992	Delightful Fright 2300QHG7067	19,500	1995	23.00	23
1993	Downhill Dash 2300QHG7080	Retrd.	1995	23.00	23
1990	Easter Egg Hunt 1800QEC9866	Retrd.	1991	18.00	28
1993	Easter Stroll 2100QHG7084	Retrd.	1995	21.00	21
1993	Ensemble Chipmunk Kettledrum 1800QHG7087	Retrd.	1994	18.00	18
1991	Father Bear Barbequing 2300QHG7041	Retrd.	1995	23.00	23
1994	Fireman 2300QHG7090	Retrd.	1995	23.00	23
1991	First Christmas Mice @ Piano 2300QEC9357	Retrd.	1991	23.00	23
1992	Fitting Gift 2300QHG7065	Retrd.	1995	23.00	23
1991	Foxes in Rowboat 2300QHG7053	Retrd.	1995	23.00	23
1992	From Your Valentine 2000QHG7071	Retrd.	1995	20.00	20
1993	Garden Capers 2000QHG7078	Retrd.	1995	20.00	20
1994	Golfing 2300QHG7091	Retrd.	1995	23.00	23
1994	Halloween 2300QHG7093	Retrd.	1995	23.00	23
1989	Halloween Trio 1800QEC9714	Retrd.	1990	18.00	150
1993	Handling a Big Thirst 2100QHG7076	Retrd.	1995	21.00	21
1994	Happy Campers 2500QHG7092	Retrd.	1995	25.00	25
1994	Jesus, Mary, Joseph 2300QHG7094	Retrd.	1995	23.00	23
1993	Love at First Sight 2300QHG7085	Retrd.	1995	23.00	23
1991	Love-American Gothic-Farmer Raccoons 2000QHG7047	Retrd.	1995	20.00	20
1993	Making A Splash 2000QHG7088	Retrd.	1995	20.00	20
1988	Mice at Tea Party 2300QHG7028	Retrd.	1993	23.00	23
1991	Mice Couple Slow Waltzing 2000QEC9437	Retrd.	1991	20.00	20
1990	Mice in Red Car 2100QEC9886	Retrd.	1991	20.00	30
1988	Mice in Rocking Chair 1800QHG7030	Retrd.	1994	18.00	18
1990	Mice w/Mistletoe 2000QEC9423	Retrd.	1990	20.00	30
1990	Mice w/Quilt 2000QHG7017	Retrd.	1994	20.00	45
1992	Mom's Easter Bonnet 1800QHG7072	Retrd.	1995	18.00	18
1991	Mother Raccoon Reading Bible Stories 2000QHG7042	Retrd.	1994	20.00	20
1989	Mouse at Desk 1800QEC9434	Retrd.	1990	18.00	50
1991	Mouse Couple Sharing Soda 2300QHG7055	Retrd.	1995	23.00	23
1990	Mouse in Pumpkin 1800QEC9473	Retrd.	1991	18.00	28
1992	Mouse Matinee 2200QHG7073	Retrd.	1995	22.00	22

YEAR ISSUE		EDITION LIMIT	YEAR RETD.	ISSUE PRICE	QUOTE U.S.$
1990	Mouse Nurse 1500QHG7037	Retrd.	1995	15.00	15
1988	Mouse w/Heart 1800QHG7024	Retrd.	1993	18.00	18
1989	Mouse w/Violin 1600QHG7049	Retrd.	1992	16.00	50
1993	Mr. Repair Bear 1800QHG7075	Retrd.	1995	18.00	18
1992	New World, Ahoy! 2500QHG7068	Retrd.	1995	25.00	25
1992	Newsboy Bear 1600QHG7060	Retrd.	1995	16.00	16
1993	The Old Swimming Hole 6000QHG7086	9,500	1995	45.00	60
1990	Pilgrim Bear Praying 1800QEC9466	Retrd.	1991	18.00	65
1989	Pilgrim Mouse 1600QEC9721	Retrd.	1990	16.00	95
1993	Playground Go-Round 2300QHG7089	Retrd.	1995	23.00	23
1989	Rabbit Painting Egg 1800QHG7022	Retrd.	1994	18.00	18
1988	Rabbit w/Ribbon 1500QHG7027	Retrd.	1994	15.00	15
1988	Rabbits at Juice Stand 2300QHG7033	Retrd.	1994	23.00	23
1989	Rabbits Ice Skating 1800QEC9391	Retrd.	1991	18.00	28
1988	Rabbits w/Cake 2000QHG7025	Retrd.	1992	20.00	40
1992	Raccoon in Bath 1800QHG7069	Retrd.	1993	18.00	18
1990	Raccoon Mail Carrier 1600QHG7013	Retrd.	1995	16.00	16
1988	Raccoon w/Cake 1800QEC9724	Retrd.	1991	18.00	45
1990	Raccoon Watering Roses 2000QHG7036	Retrd.	1994	20.00	20
1991	Raccoon Witch 1600QHG7045	Retrd.	1994	16.00	16
1988	Raccoons Fishing 1800QHG7034	Retrd.	1994	18.00	18
1992	Raccoons on Bridge 2500QHG7004	19,500	1995	25.00	25
1988	Raccoons Playing Ball 1800QEC9771	Retrd.	1991	18.00	40
1990	Raccoons w/Flag 2300QHG7044	Retrd.	1994	23.00	23
1990	Raccoons w/Wagon 2300QHG7014	Retrd.	1993	23.00	23
1990	Romeo & Juliet Mice 2500QEC9903	Retrd.	1991	25.00	35
1990	Santa in Chimney 1800QHG7051	Retrd.	1994	18.00	18
1989	Santa Mouse in Chair 2000QEC9394	Retrd.	1990	20.00	135
1993	Sculpting Santa 2000QHG7083	Retrd.	1995	20.00	20
1992	Soapbox Racer 2300QHG7005	19,500	1995	23.00	23
1988	Squirrels w/Bandage 1800QHG7032	Retrd.	1993	18.00	18
1992	Stealing a Kiss 2300QHG7066	19,500	1995	23.00	23
1992	Sweet Sharing 2000QHG7062	Retrd.	1995	20.00	20
1992	Swingtime Love 2100QHG7070	Retrd.	1993	21.00	21
1990	Teacher & Student Chipmunks 2000QHG7019	Retrd.	1992	20.00	30
1988	Teacher w/Student 1800QHG7026	Retrd.	1995	18.00	18
1993	Teeter For Two 2300QHG7077	Retrd.	1995	23.00	23
1992	Tender Touches Tree House 5500QHG7001	9,500	1995	55.00	55
1992	Thanksgiving Family Around Table 2500QHG7048	Retrd.	1995	25.00	25
1990	Tucking Baby in Bed 1800QHG7011	Retrd.	1993	18.00	18
1992	Waiting for Santa 2000QHG7064	Retrd.	1995	20.00	20
1993	Woodland Americana-Liberty Mouse 2100QHG7081	Retrd.	1995	21.00	21
1993	Woodland Americana-Patriot George 2500QHG7082	Retrd.	1995	25.00	25
1993	Woodland Americana-Stitching the Stars and Stripes 2100QHG7079	Retrd.	1995	21.00	21
1992	Younger Than Springtime 3500QHG7074	19,500	1995	35.00	35

Times to Cherish - Various

YEAR ISSUE		EDITION LIMIT	YEAR RETD.	ISSUE PRICE	QUOTE U.S.$
1992	Beautiful Dreamer 6500QHG6010 - T. Andrews	4,500	1994	65.00	65
1992	A Child's Prayer 3500QHG6006 - T. Andrews	4,500	1994	35.00	35
1992	Daily Devotion 4000QHG6005 - T. Andrews	4,500	1994	40.00	40
1992	Dancer's Dream 5000QHG6009 - T. Andrews	4,500	1994	50.00	50
1992	The Embrace 6000QHG6002 - T. Andrews	4,500	1994	60.00	60
1992	The Joys of Fatherhood 6000QHG6001 - T. Andrews	4,500	1994	60.00	60
1992	Mother's Blessing 6500QHG6008 - T. Andrews	4,500	1994	65.00	65
1992	A Mother's Touch 6000QHG6007 - T. Andrews	4,500	1994	60.00	60
1993	Showing The Way 4500QHG6011 - P. Andrews	4,500	1994	45.00	45
1992	Sister Time 5500QHG6003 - T. Andrews	4,500	1994	55.00	55
1993	Spring Tulip Lidded Box 2500QHG6012 - P. Andrews	4,500	1994	25.00	25

Tobin Fraley Carousels - T. Fraley

YEAR ISSUE		EDITION LIMIT	YEAR RETD.	ISSUE PRICE	QUOTE U.S.$
1994	Armour 6000QHG25	4,500	1995	60.00	60
1992	C.W. Parker/1922 3000QHG5	4,500	1995	30.00	30
1992	C.W. Parker/1922/musical 4000QHG13	4,500	1995	40.00	40
1992	Charles Carmel, circa 1914/musical 4000QHG16	4,500	1995	40.00	40
1992	Charles Carmel/1914 3000QHG8	4,500	1995	30.00	30
1992	Charles Looff/1915 5000QHG1	4,500	1995	50.00	50
1992	Charles Looff/1915/musical 6000QHG09	2,500	1995	60.00	60
1994	Floral 6000QHG27	4,500	1995	60.00	60
1994	Indian 6000QHG28	4,500	1995	60.00	60
1992	M.C. Illions & Sons/1910 3000QHG6	4,500	1995	30.00	30
1992	M.C. Illions & Sons/1910 5000QHG3	4,500	1995	50.00	50
1992	M.C. Illions & Sons/1910/musical 4000QHG14	4,500	1995	40.00	40
1992	M.C. Illions & Sons/1910/musical 6000QHG11	2,500	1995	60.00	60
1992	Musical Premier Horse 1QHG21	1,200	1995	275.00	275
1994	Patriot 6000QHG26	4,500	1995	60.00	60
1992	Philadelphia Toboggan Co/1910 3000QHG7	4,500	1995	30.00	30
1992	Philadelphia Toboggan Co/1910/musical 4000QHG15	4,500	1995	40.00	40
1992	Philadelphia Toboggan Co/1928 5000QHG2	4,500	1995	50.00	50
1992	Philadelphia Toboggan Co/1928/musical 6000QHG10	2,500	1994	60.00	60
1992	Playland Carousel/musical 1QHG17	1,200	1993	195.00	195
1992	Revolving Brass/Wood Display 4000QHG19	4,500	1995	40.00	40
1992	Stein & Goldstein/1914 5000QHG4	4,500	1995	50.00	50
1992	Stein & Goldstein/1914/musical 6000QHG12	2,500	1995	60.00	60

Victorian Memories - Various

YEAR ISSUE		EDITION LIMIT	YEAR RETD.	ISSUE PRICE	QUOTE U.S.$
1992	Doll Trunk IQHG1015 - J. Greene	7,500	1995	125.00	125
1993	Gloria Summer Figurine 6000QHG1032 - Greene/Lyle	9,500	1994	60.00	60
1993	Hobby Horse 1800QHG1028 - J. Greene	9,500	1994	18.00	18
1992	Lillian-cold cast 5500QHG1001 - J. Lyle	9,500	1994	55.00	55
1993	Mini Snow Globe 1800QHG1031 - J. Greene	9,500	1995	18.00	18
1992	Music Box 5000QHG1025 - J. Greene	9,500	1995	50.00	50
1992	Musical Jack-in-the Box 2000QHG9502 - J. Greene	9,500	1995	20.00	20
1992	Rabbit (on wheels) 6500QHG1022 - J. Greene	4,500	1995	65.00	65
1992	Rebecca-cold cast 6000QHG1024 - J. Lyle	9,500	1994	60.00	60
1992	Sarah-cold cast 6000QHG1003 - J. Lyle	9,500	1994	60.00	60
1993	Shoo-Fly Rocking Horse 1800QHG1036 - J. Greene	9,500	1995	18.00	18
1992	Tea Set 3500QHG1026 - J. Greene	9,500	1995	35.00	35
1993	Toy Cradle 2000QHG1027 - J. Greene	9,500	1995	20.00	20
1993	Victorian Toy Cupboard 7500QHG1038 - J. Greene	7,500	1995	75.00	75
1992	Wicker Rocker 4500QHG9510 - J. Greene	4,500	1994	45.00	45
1992	Wooden Doll Carriage-miniature 2000QHG9506 - J. Greene	9,500	1995	20.00	20
1992	Wooden Horse Pull Toy-miniature 2000QHG9504 - J. Greene	9,500	1995	18.00	18
1992	Wooden Jewelry Box 1800QHG9505 - J. Greene	9,500	1995	18.00	18
1992	Wooden Noah's Ark-miniature 1500QHG9503 - J. Greene	9,500	1995	15.00	15
1992	Wooden Rocking Horse 7500QHG9511 - J. Greene	4,500	1995	75.00	75
1992	Wooden Train-miniature 2200QHG9501 - J. Greene	9,500	1995	15.00	15

Hamilton Collection

American Garden Flowers - D. Fryer

YEAR ISSUE		EDITION LIMIT	YEAR RETD.	ISSUE PRICE	QUOTE U.S.$
1987	Azalea	15,000		75.00	75
1988	Calla Lilly	15,000		75.00	75
1987	Camelia	9,800		55.00	75
1988	Day Lily	15,000		75.00	75
1987	Gardenia	15,000		75.00	75
1989	Pansy	15,000		75.00	75
1988	Petunia	15,000		75.00	75
1987	Rose	15,000		75.00	75

American Wildlife Bronze Collection - H./N. Deaton

YEAR ISSUE		EDITION LIMIT	YEAR RETD.	ISSUE PRICE	QUOTE U.S.$
1980	Beaver	7,500		60.00	65
1979	Bobcat	7,500		60.00	75
1979	Cougar	7,500		60.00	125
1980	Polar Bear	7,500		60.00	65
1980	Sea Otter	7,500		60.00	65
1979	White-Tailed Deer	7,500		60.00	105

A Celebration of Roses - N/A

YEAR ISSUE		EDITION LIMIT	YEAR RETD.	ISSUE PRICE	QUOTE U.S.$
1989	Brandy	Open		55.00	55
1989	Color Magic	Open		55.00	55
1989	Honor	Open		55.00	55
1989	Miss All-American Beauty	Open		55.00	55
1991	Ole'	Open		55.00	55
1990	Oregold	Open		55.00	55
1991	Paradise	Open		55.00	55
1989	Tiffany	Open		55.00	55

Coral Kingdom - N/A

YEAR ISSUE		EDITION LIMIT	YEAR RETD.	ISSUE PRICE	QUOTE U.S.$
1995	Athena	Open		35.00	35

Freshwater Challenge - M. Wald

YEAR ISSUE		EDITION LIMIT	YEAR RETD.	ISSUE PRICE	QUOTE U.S.$
1992	Prized Catch	Open		75.00	75
1991	Rainbow Lure	Open		75.00	75
1991	The Strike	Open		75.00	75
1991	Sun Catcher	Open		75.00	75

Heroes of Baseball-Porcelain Baseball Cards - N/A

YEAR ISSUE		EDITION LIMIT	YEAR RETD.	ISSUE PRICE	QUOTE U.S.$
1990	Brooks Robinson	Open		19.50	20
1991	Casey Stengel	Open		19.50	20
1990	Duke Snider	Open		19.50	20
1991	Ernie Banks	Open		19.50	20
1991	Gil Hodges	Open		19.50	20
1991	Jackie Robinson	Open		19.50	20
1991	Mickey Mantle	Open		19.50	20
1990	Roberto Clemente	Open		19.50	20
1991	Satchel Page	Open		19.50	20
1991	Whitey Ford	Open		19.50	20
1990	Willie Mays	Open		19.50	20
1991	Yogi Berra	Open		19.50	20

International Santa - N/A

YEAR ISSUE		EDITION LIMIT	YEAR RETD.	ISSUE PRICE	QUOTE U.S.$
1995	Alpine Santa	Open		55.00	55
1993	Belsnickel	Open		55.00	55
1995	Dedushka Moroz	Open		55.00	55
1992	Father Christmas	Open		55.00	55
1992	Grandfather Frost	Open		55.00	55
1993	Jolly Old St. Nick	Open		55.00	55
1993	Kris Kringle	Open		55.00	55
1994	Pére Nôel	Open		55.00	55
1992	Santa Claus	Open		55.00	55
1994	Yuletide Santa	Open		55.00	55

Little Friends of the Arctic - N/A

YEAR ISSUE		EDITION LIMIT	YEAR RETD.	ISSUE PRICE	QUOTE U.S.$
1995	The Young Prince	Open		37.50	38

Little Night Owls - D.T. Lyttleton

YEAR ISSUE		EDITION LIMIT	YEAR RETD.	ISSUE PRICE	QUOTE U.S.$
1990	Barn Owl	Open		45.00	45
1991	Barred Owl	Open		45.00	45
1991	Great Grey Owl	Open		45.00	45
1991	Great Horned Owl	Open		45.00	45
1991	Short-Eared Owl	Open		45.00	45
1990	Snowy Owl	Open		45.00	45
1990	Tawny Owl	Open		45.00	45
1991	White-Faced Owl	Open		45.00	45

Masters of the Evening Wilderness - N/A

YEAR ISSUE		EDITION LIMIT	YEAR RETD.	ISSUE PRICE	QUOTE U.S.$
1995	Autumn Barn Owls	Open		37.50	38
1995	Great Grey Owl	Open		37.50	38
1995	Great Horned Owl	Open		37.50	38
1994	The Great Snowy Owl	Open		37.50	38

Mystic Spirits - S. Douglas

YEAR ISSUE		EDITION LIMIT	YEAR RETD.	ISSUE PRICE	QUOTE U.S.$
1995	Spirit of the Wolf	Open		55.00	55

Nature's Majestic Cats - D. Geentz

YEAR ISSUE		EDITION LIMIT	YEAR RETD.	ISSUE PRICE	QUOTE U.S.$
1995	Tigress and Cubs	Open		55.00	55

Nesting Instincts - R. Willis

YEAR ISSUE		EDITION LIMIT	YEAR RETD.	ISSUE PRICE	QUOTE U.S.$
1995	By Mother's Side	Open		19.50	20
1995	Learning to Fly	Open		19.50	20
1995	Like Mother, Like Son	Open		19.50	20
1995	A Mother's Pride	Open		19.50	20
1995	Peaceful Perch	Open		19.50	20
1995	Safe and Sound	Open		19.50	20
1995	Under Mother's Wings	Open		19.50	20
1995	A Watchful Eye	Open		19.50	20

Noble American Indian Women - N/A

YEAR ISSUE		EDITION LIMIT	YEAR RETD.	ISSUE PRICE	QUOTE U.S.$
1994	Falling Star	Open		55.00	55
1995	Lily of the Mohawks	Open		55.00	55
1995	Lozen	Open		55.00	55
1994	Minnehaha	Open		55.00	55
1994	Pine Leaf	Open		55.00	55
1995	Pocahontas	Open		55.00	55
1993	Sacajawea	Open		55.00	55
1993	White Rose	Open		55.00	55

The Noble Swan - G. Granget

YEAR ISSUE		EDITION LIMIT	YEAR RETD.	ISSUE PRICE	QUOTE U.S.$
1985	The Noble Swan	5,000		295.00	295

Noble Warriors - N/A

YEAR ISSUE		EDITION LIMIT	YEAR RETD.	ISSUE PRICE	QUOTE U.S.$
1993	Deliverance	Open		135.00	135
1994	Spirit of the Plains	Open		135.00	135
1995	Top Gun	Open		135.00	135
1995	Windrider	Open		135.00	135

The Nolan Ryan Collectors Edition-Porcelain Baseball Cards - N/A

YEAR ISSUE		EDITION LIMIT	YEAR RETD.	ISSUE PRICE	QUOTE U.S.$
1993	Angels 1972-C #595	Open		19.50	20
1993	Astros 1985-C #7	Open		19.50	20
1993	Mets 1968-C #177	Open		19.50	20
1993	Mets 1969-C #533	Open		19.50	20
1993	Rangers 1990-C #1	Open		19.50	20
1993	Rangers 1992-C #1	Open		19.50	20

Ocean Odyssey - W. Youngstrom

YEAR ISSUE		EDITION LIMIT	YEAR RETD.	ISSUE PRICE	QUOTE U.S.$
1995	Breaching the Waters	Open		55.00	55
1995	Riding the Waves	Open		55.00	55

Princess of the Plains - N/A

YEAR ISSUE		EDITION LIMIT	YEAR RETD.	ISSUE PRICE	QUOTE U.S.$
1995	Nature's Guardian	Open		55.00	55
1994	Noble Guardian	Open		55.00	55
1994	Snow Princess	Open		55.00	55
1994	Wild Flower	Open		55.00	55

YEAR ISSUE		EDITION LIMIT	YEAR RETD.	ISSUE PRICE	QUOTE U.S.$
1995	Winter's Rose	Open		55.00	55

Protect Nature's Innocents - R. Manning

1995	African Elephant	Open		14.95	15

Puppy Playtime Sculpture Collection - J. Lamb

1991	Cabin Fever	Open		29.50	30
1991	Catch of the Day	Open		29.50	30
1990	Double Take	Open		29.50	30
1991	Fun and Games	Open		29.50	30
1991	Getting Acquainted	Open		29.50	30
1991	Hanging Out	Open		29.50	30
1991	A New Leash on Life	Open		29.50	30
1991	Weekend Gardner	Open		29.50	30

Puss in Boots - P. Cooper

1993	All Dressed Up	Open		35.00	35
1992	Caught Napping	Open		35.00	35
1994	Daydreamer	Open		35.00	35
1993	Hide'n Go Seek	Open		35.00	35
1993	Sitting Pretty	Open		35.00	35
1992	Sweet Dreams	Open		35.00	35
1994	Tee Time	Open		35.00	35
1993	Tennis Anyone?	Open		35.00	35

Ringling Bros. Circus Animals - P. Cozzolino

1983	Acrobatic Seal	9,800		49.50	50
1983	Baby Elephant	9,800		49.50	55
1983	Miniature Show Horse	9,800		49.50	68
1983	Mr. Chimpanzee	9,800		49.50	50
1984	Parade Camel	9,800		49.50	50
1983	Performing Poodles	9,800		49.50	50
1984	Roaring Lion	9,800		49.50	50
1983	Skating Bear	9,800		49.50	50

Santa Clothtique - Possible Dreams

1995	Baking Christmas Cheer	Open		95.00	95
1992	Checking His List	Open		95.00	95
1993	Last Minute Details	Open		95.00	95
1994	O Tannenbaum!	Open		95.00	95
1993	Twas the Nap Before Christmas	Open		95.00	95
1994	Upon the Rooftop	Open		95.00	95

Snuggle Babies - Jacqueline B.

1988	Baby Bears	Open		35.00	35
1988	Baby Bunnies	Open		35.00	35
1989	Baby Chipmunks	Open		35.00	35
1989	Baby Fawns	Open		35.00	35
1988	Baby Foxes	Open		35.00	35
1989	Baby Raccoons	Open		35.00	35
1988	Baby Skunks	Open		35.00	35
1989	Baby Squirrels	Open		35.00	35

Spirit of the Eagle - T. Sullivan

1995	Blazing Majestic Skies	Open		55.00	55
1995	Noble and Free	Open		55.00	55
1995	Proud Symbol of Freedom	Open		55.00	55
1994	Spirit of Independence	Open		55.00	55

Tropical Treasures - M. Wald

1990	Beaked Coral Butterfly Fish	Open		37.50	38
1990	Blue Girdled Angel Fish	Open		37.50	38
1989	Flag-tail Surgeonfish	Open		37.50	38
1989	Pennant Butterfly Fish	Open		37.50	38
1989	Sail-finned Surgeonfish	Open		37.50	38
1989	Sea Horse	Open		37.50	38
1990	Spotted Angel Fish	Open		37.50	38
1990	Zebra Turkey Fish	Open		37.50	38

Unbridled Spirits - C. DeHaan

1994	Wild Fury	Open		135.00	135

Visions of Christmas - M. Griffin

1995	Gifts From St. Nick	Open		135.00	135
1994	Mrs. Claus' Kitchen	Open		135.00	135
1993	Santa's Delivery	Open		135.00	135
1993	Toys in Progress	Open		135.00	135

Wild Ducks of North America - C. Burgess

1988	American Widgeon	15,000		95.00	95
1988	Bufflehead	15,000		95.00	95
1987	Common Mallard	15,000		95.00	95
1987	Green Winged Teal	15,000		95.00	95
1987	Hooded Merganser	15,000		95.00	95
1988	Northern Pintail	15,000		95.00	95
1988	Ruddy Duck Drake	15,000		95.00	95
1987	Wood Duck	15,000		95.00	95

Wolves of the Wilderness - D. Geenty

1995	Mother's Watch	Open		55.00	55
1995	A Wolf's Pride	Open		55.00	55

Harbour Lights

Great Lakes Region - Harbour Lights

1992	Buffalo NY 122	5,500		60.00	62
1992	Cana Island WI 119	5,500	1995	60.00	66
1991	Fort Niagara NY 113	5,500	1995	60.00	63
1992	Grosse Point IL 120	5,500		60.00	62
1994	Holland (Big Red) MI 142	5,500	1995	60.00	200
1992	Marblehead OH 121	5,500	1995	50.00	120
1992	Michigan City IN 123	5,500		60.00	62
1992	Old Mackinac Point MI 118	5,500	1995	65.00	135-180
1995	Round Island MI 153	9,500		66.00	85
1991	Sand Island WS 112	5,500		60.00	64
1992	Split Rock MI 124 (misspelled)	Closed	1992	60.00	1450-1650
1992	Split Rock MN 124	Retrd.	1995	60.00	120-200
1995	Tawas Pt. MI 152	5,500		75.00	75
1995	Wind Point WS 154	9,500		78.00	78

Great Lighthouses of the World - Harbour Lights

1994	Cape Hatteras NC 401	Open		50.00	50

Gulf Coast Region - Harbour Lights

1995	Biloxi MS 149	5,500		60.00	60
1995	Bolivar TX 146	5,500		70.00	70
1995	New Canal LA 148	5,500		65.00	65
1995	Pensacola FL 150	9,000		80.00	80
1995	Port Isabel TX 147	5,500		65.00	65

Harbour Lights Collector's Society - Harbour Lights

1995	Point Fermin CA 501 (Charter Member Piece)	4/96		80.00	80

Northeast Region - Harbour Lights

1993	Barnegat NJ 139	5,500	1995	60.00	150
1991	Boston Harbor MA 117	5,500	1995	60.00	120-150
1995	Brant Point MA 162	9,500		N/A	N/A
1994	Cape Neddick (Nubble) ME 141	5,500	1995	66.00	125-200
1991	Castle Hill RI 116	5,500		60.00	60
1991	Gt. Captain's Island CT 114	5,500		60.00	66
1995	Highland MA 161	9,500		N/A	N/A
1992	Minot's Ledge MA 131	5,500		60.00	60
1994	Montauk NY 143	5,500	1995	85.00	180-300
1992	Nauset MA 126	5,500	1995	66.00	135-180
1992	New London Ledge CT 129	5,500	1995	66.00	120-135
1992	Portland Breakwater ME 130	5,500		60.00	60
1992	Portland Head ME 125	5,500	1994	66.00	170-200
1991	Sandy Hook NJ 104	Retrd.	1994	60.00	135-200
1992	Southeast Block Island RI 128	5,500	1994	71.00	175-200
1991	West Quoddy Head ME 103	5,500	1995	60.00	120-150
1992	Whaleback NH 127	5,500		60.00	60

Southeast Region - Harbour Lights

1994	Assateague VA 145-mold one	988	1994	69.00	375-800
1994	Assateague VA 145-mold two	4,562	1995	69.00	75
1991	Cape Hatteras NC 102 (with house)	Retrd.	1991	60.00	1900-3000
1992	Cape Hatteras NC 102R	Retrd.	1993	60.00	450-650
1993	Hilton Head SC 136	5,500	1994	60.00	150
1995	Jupiter FL 151	9,500		77.00	77
1993	Key West FL 134	5,500	1995	60.00	130
1993	Ocracoke NC 135	5,500	1995	60.00	62
1993	Ponce de Leon FL 132	5,500	1994	60.00	135-200
1993	St. Augustine FL 138	5,500	1994	71.00	150
1993	St. Simons GA 137	5,500	1995	66.00	150-175
1993	Tybee GA 133	5,500	1995	60.00	135-150

Special Editions - Harbour Lights

1995	Christmas 1995 - Big Bay Point MI 700	5,000		75.00	75
1995	Legacy Light 601	Open		65.00	65

Stamp Series - Harbour Lights

1995	Marblehead OH 413	Open		50.00	50
1995	Spectacle Reef MI 410	Open		60.00	60
1995	Split Rock MN 412	Open		60.00	60
1995	St. Joseph MI 411	Open		60.00	60
1995	Thirty Mile Point NY 414	Open		62.00	62
1995	Five Piece Matched Numbered Set 400	5,000		275.00	275

Western Region - Harbour Lights

1991	Admiralty Head WA 101(misspelled)	Closed	1994	60.00	110-140
1991	Admiralty Head WA 101	Retrd.	1994	60.00	135-250
1991	Burrows Island OR 108 (misspelled)	Closed	1991	60.00	400-600
1991	Burrows Island WA 108	Retrd.	1994	60.00	140-155
1991	Cape Blanco OR 109	5,500		60.00	60
1991	Coquille River OR 111	1,138	1993	60.00	2300-2600
1994	Diamond Head HI 140	5,500	1995	60.00	120-135
1994	Heceta Head OR 144	5,500		65.00	72
1991	North Head WA 106	5,500		60.00	60
1991	Old Point Loma CA 105	5,500	1995	60.00	120-150
1995	Pt. Arena CA 156	9,500		80.00	80
1991	St. George's Reef CA 115	5,500		60.00	60
1991	Umpqua River OR 107	5,500		60.00	60
1991	Yaquina Head WA 110	5,500		60.00	62

Hawthorne Architectural Register

Beacons of Freedom (Illuminated) - Unkn.

1995	Portland Head Lighthouse	Open		39.90	40
1995	West Quaddy Head	Open		39.90	40

Chestnut Hill Station - K.&H. LeVan

1994	Bicycle Shop	Open		29.90	30
1994	Chestnut Hill Depot	Closed	1994	29.90	30
1993	Parkside Cafe	Open		29.90	30
1993	Wishing Well Cottage	Closed	1994	29.90	30

Concord: The Hometown of American Literature - K.&H. LeVan

1993	Alcott's Orchard House	Closed	1995	34.90	35
1992	Emerson's Old Manse	Closed	1995	34.90	35
1992	Hawthorne's Wayside Retreat	Closed	1995	34.90	35

Currier & Ives: The Art of American Literature - C&I Inspired

1994	American Homestead Winter	Open		29.90	30
1995	Feeding the Chickens	Open		29.90	30
1994	The Snow Storm	Open		29.90	30

England of My Dreams - R. Dowding

1994	Mayfair Hill	Closed	1994	59.90	60

The Fairytale Forest - S. Smith

1994	Goldilocks and the Three Bears	Open		24.90	25
1994	Little Red Riding Hood including figurines	Open		49.80	50

Gone With the Wind (Illuminated) - Unkn.

1994	Atlanta Church	Open		39.90	40
1995	Butler Mansion	Open		39.90	40
1994	Kennedy Store	Open		39.90	40
1994	Red Horse Saloon	Open		39.90	40
1993	Tara	Open		39.90	40
1994	Twelve Oaks	Open		39.90	40

Gone With the Wind Collection - K.&H. LeVan

1993	Against Her Will	Open		42.90	43
1994	Alone	Open		45.90	46
1994	Burning of Atlanta	10,000		79.95	80
1995	Dignity & Respect	Open		45.90	46
1994	Hope for a New Tomorrow	Closed	1995	42.90	43
1995	I Have Done Enough	Open		45.90	46
1994	Kennedy House	Open		45.90	46
1994	Merriweather House	Open		45.90	46
1993	A Message for Captain Butler	Open		42.90	43
1995	Revenge on Shantytown	Open		45.90	46
1993	Rhett Returns	Open		39.90	40
1994	Swept Away	Open		45.90	46
1994	Take Me to Tara	Open		45.90	46
1992	Tara . . .Scarlett's Pride	Closed	1995	39.90	40
1992	Twelve Oaks: The Romance Begins	Closed	1995	39.90	40

Helen Steiner Rice: Windows of Gold - S. Smith

1994	Inspiration Point Lighthouse	Open		34.90	35
1994	Peace of Faith	Open		39.90	40
1994	Winter's Warmth	Open		39.90	40

Hershey, PA: An American Dream Comes True - Unkn.

1995	Birthplace of Milton Hershey	Open		34.90	35

Hometown America - Rockwell Inspired

1993	Evergreen Cottage	Open		34.95	35
1994	Evergreen General Store	Open		39.95	40
1994	Evergreen Valley Church	Open		37.95	38
1993	Evergreen Valley School	Open		34.95	35
1993	The Village Bakery	Closed	1994	37.95	38
1994	Waiting For Santa	Closed	1995	39.95	40
1994	Woodcutter's Rest	Open		37.95	38

Hummel's Bavarian Village - M.I. Hummel Inspired

1994	Angel's Duet	Open		49.90	50
1994	The Bakery	Open		49.90	50
1995	Company's Coming	Open		49.90	50

Inside Gone With the Wind Collection - K.&H. LeVan

1994	Pride and Passion	Open		39.90	40

Kinkade's Candlelight Cottages (Illuminated) - Kinkade-Inspired

1993	Chandler's Cottage	Closed	1994	29.90	30
1993	Olde Porterfield Tea Room	Closed	1994	29.90	30

Kinkade's Candlelight Cottages - Kinkade-Inspired

1994	Candlelit Cottage	Open		29.90	30
1994	Cedar Nooke Cottage	Open		29.90	30
1993	Chandler's Cottage	Open		24.90	25
1994	Merritt's Cottage	Open		27.90	28
1993	Olde Porterfield Tea Room	Open		24.90	25
1994	Seaside Cottage	Open		27.90	28
1993	Swanbrooke Cottage	Open		24.90	25
1994	Sweatheart Cottage	Open		27.90	28

Kinkade's Christmas Memories - Kinkade-Inspired

1995	Home to Grandma's	Open		34.90	35
1995	Olde Porterfield Gift & Shoppe	Open		34.90	35
1995	Silent Night	Open		34.90	35
1995	Warmth of Home	Open		34.90	35

Kinkade's Enchanted Cottages - Kinkade-Inspired

1995	Julianne's Cottage	Open		29.90	30
1995	McKenna's Cottage	Open		29.90	30

Kinkade's St. Nicholas Square (Illuminated) - Kinkade-Inspired

1994	Evergreen Apothecary	Open		39.90	40
1994	The Firehouse	Open		39.90	40
1994	Holly House Inn	Open		39.90	40

Year Issue		Edition Limit	Year Retd.	Issue Price	Quote U.S.$
1994	Kringle Brothers	Open		39.90	40
1994	Mrs. C. Bakery	Open		39.90	40
1994	Noel Chapel (free sign in box)	Open		39.90	40
1994	S.C. Toy Maker	Open		39.90	40
1993	Town Hall	Open		39.90	40

P.O. #1, North Pole Collection (Illuminated) - G. Hoover

Year Issue		Edition Limit	Year Retd.	Issue Price	Quote U.S.$
1995	Santa's Candy Shop	Open		39.90	40
1995	Santa's Gift Wrap Central	Open		39.90	40
1994	Santa's Post Office	Open		39.90	40
1994	Santa's Toy Shoppe with Sign	Open		39.90	40

Peaceable Kingdom - K.& H. LeVan

Year Issue		Edition Limit	Year Retd.	Issue Price	Quote U.S.$
1993	Squire Boone's Homestead	Open		34.90	35
1994	White Horse Inn	Open		34.90	35

Peppercricket Grove - C. Wysocki

Year Issue		Edition Limit	Year Retd.	Issue Price	Quote U.S.$
1995	Peppercricket Farm	Open		44.90	45
1995	Virginia's Nest	Open		44.90	45

Rockwell's Christmas in Stockbridge (Illuminated) - Rockwell-Inspired

Year Issue		Edition Limit	Year Retd.	Issue Price	Quote U.S.$
1993	The Antique Shop	Open		29.90	30
1993	The Bank	Open		29.90	30
1993	The Country Store	Open		29.90	30
1993	The Library	Open		29.90	30
1993	The Red Lion Inn	Open		29.90	30
1993	Rockwell's Studio	Open		29.90	30
1993	The Town Offices	Open		29.90	30

Rockwell's Four Freedoms (Illuminated) - Rockwell-Inspired

Year Issue		Edition Limit	Year Retd.	Issue Price	Quote U.S.$
1994	Freedom from Fear: The Rockwell Homestead	Open		39.90	40
1995	Freedom of Speech: Town Hall	Open		39.90	40
1994	Freedom of Worship: Arlington Church	Open		39.90	40
1995	TBA	Open		N/A	N/A

Rockwell's Heart of Stockbridge (Illuminated) - Rockwell-Inspired

Year Issue		Edition Limit	Year Retd.	Issue Price	Quote U.S.$
1995	Bell Tower	Open		39.90	40
1995	Church on the Green	Open		39.90	40
1995	Firehouse	Open		39.90	40
1995	Rockwell's Home	Open		39.90	40
1995	Rockwell's Studio	Open		39.90	40

Rockwell's Home for the Holidays - Rockwell-Inspired

Year Issue		Edition Limit	Year Retd.	Issue Price	Quote U.S.$
1995	"Ready & Waiting"	Open		41.90	42
1994	Arlington Town Hall	Open		41.90	42
1992	Bringing Home the Christmas Tree	Closed	1994	34.90	35
1992	Carolers In The Church Yard	Open		37.90	38
1992	Christmas Eve at the Studio	Closed	1994	34.90	35
1994	Firestation	Open		41.90	42
1994	A Golden Memory	Open		41.90	42
1994	Howard's Store	Open		39.90	40
1994	Late for the Dance	Open		41.90	42
1993	Letters to Santa	Open		39.90	40
1993	Over the River	Closed	1995	37.90	38
1993	A Room at the Inn	Open		39.90	40
1993	School's Out	Closed	1994	39.90	40
1993	Three-Day Pass	Open		37.90	38
1994	A White Christmas	Closed	1995	41.90	42

Rockwell's Neighborhood Collection - Rockwell-Inspired

Year Issue		Edition Limit	Year Retd.	Issue Price	Quote U.S.$
1994	Fido's New Home	Open		29.90	30
1994	The Lemonade Stand	Open		29.90	30
1994	Sidewalk Speedster	Open		29.90	30

Stonefield Valley - K.& H. LeVan

Year Issue		Edition Limit	Year Retd.	Issue Price	Quote U.S.$
1992	Church in the Glen	Closed	1994	37.90	38
1993	Ferryman's Cottage	Closed	1994	39.90	40
1993	Hillside Country Store	Closed	1994	39.90	40
1992	Meadowbrook School	Closed	1994	34.90	35
1993	Parson's Cottage	Closed	1994	37.90	38
1992	Springbridge Cottage	Closed	1994	34.90	35
1994	Valley View Farm	Closed	1994	39.90	40
1992	Weaver's Cottage	Closed	1994	37.90	38

Strolling Through Colonial America - K.&H. LeVan

Year Issue		Edition Limit	Year Retd.	Issue Price	Quote U.S.$
1992	Captain Lee's Grammar School	Closed	1995	39.90	40
1992	Court House on the Green	Closed	1995	37.90	38
1992	Eastbrook Church	Closed	1995	37.90	38
1993	Everette's Joiner Shop	Closed	1993	39.90	40
1992	Higgins' Grist Mill	Closed	1995	37.90	38
1991	Jefferson's Ordinarie	Closed	1995	34.90	35
1992	Millrace Store	Closed	1995	34.90	35
1992	The Village Smithy	Closed	1993	39.90	40

Tara: The Only Thing Worth Fighting For - K.& H. LeVan

Year Issue		Edition Limit	Year Retd.	Issue Price	Quote U.S.$
1994	Carriage House	Open		29.90	30
1994	A Dream Remembered	Open		29.90	30
1994	Kitchen & Gateway	Open		29.90	30
1994	Spring House & Hideaway	Closed	1995	29.90	30
1994	The Stable	Open		29.90	30
1994	Tara Mill	Open		29.90	30

Thatcher's Crossing - R. Dowding

Year Issue		Edition Limit	Year Retd.	Issue Price	Quote U.S.$
1994	Chapel Crossing	Open		29.90	30

Year Issue		Edition Limit	Year Retd.	Issue Price	Quote U.S.$
1993	Midsummer's Cottage	Open		29.90	30
1993	Rose Arbour Cottage	Closed	1994	29.90	30
1994	Woodcutter's Cottage	Open		29.90	30

Victorian Grove Collection - K.& H. LeVan

Year Issue		Edition Limit	Year Retd.	Issue Price	Quote U.S.$
1993	Cherry Blossom	Closed	1994	34.90	35
1992	Lilac Cottage	Closed	1995	34.90	35
1992	Rose Haven	Closed	1994	34.90	35

Watercolor Cottages - K.& H. LeVan

Year Issue		Edition Limit	Year Retd.	Issue Price	Quote U.S.$
1994	Sunrise Cove	Open		34.90	35

Welcome to Mayberry - Unkn.

Year Issue		Edition Limit	Year Retd.	Issue Price	Quote U.S.$
1994	The Courthouse	Open		39.90	40
1994	Floyd's Barber Shop	Open		39.90	40
1994	Mayberry Methodist Church	Open		39.90	40
1994	Post Office	Open		39.90	40
1994	The Taylor Home	Open		39.90	40
1994	Wally's Gas Station	Open		39.90	40

Welcome to Mayberry Accessories - Unkn.

Year Issue		Edition Limit	Year Retd.	Issue Price	Quote U.S.$
1995	Andy & Barney	Open		21.90	22
1995	Aunt Bee & Opey	Open		21.90	22
1995	Patrol Car & Gas Pumps	Open		21.90	22

Wizard of Oz - Unkn.

Year Issue		Edition Limit	Year Retd.	Issue Price	Quote U.S.$
1995	The Journey Begins	Open		149.50	150

Historical Miniatures

American Heritage: Cape May, N.J. - M. Weisser

Year Issue		Edition Limit	Year Retd.	Issue Price	Quote U.S.$
1994	The Abbey	Open		39.00	39
1994	The Linda Lee	Open		39.80	40

American Heritage: Charleston - M. Weisser

Year Issue		Edition Limit	Year Retd.	Issue Price	Quote U.S.$
1994	Citadel's Summerall Chapel	Open		36.00	36
1994	The City Market	Open		39.00	39
1994	The Pink House	Open		36.00	36
1994	Rainbow Row:Blue #1	Open		36.00	36
1994	Rainbow Row:Green #1	Open		36.00	36
1994	Rainbow Row:Pink #1	Open		36.00	36
1994	Rutledge House	Open		50.00	50

American Heritage: Miami Beach: Deco District - M. Weisser

Year Issue		Edition Limit	Year Retd.	Issue Price	Quote U.S.$
1994	Hotel Carlyle	Open		36.00	36
1994	Hotel Century	Open		31.00	31
1994	Hotel Taft	Open		29.90	30

American Heritage: New Orleans - M. Weisser

Year Issue		Edition Limit	Year Retd.	Issue Price	Quote U.S.$
1994	Chart House	Open		34.00	34
1994	Royal Cafe	Open		39.00	39

Doors & Gates of America: Charleston - M. Weisser

Year Issue		Edition Limit	Year Retd.	Issue Price	Quote U.S.$
1994	Bull Street Door:Blue/Beige	Open		15.00	15
1994	The Charleston College Gate	Open		16.00	16
1994	The Harp Gate	Open		15.00	15
1994	The Pineapple Gate	Open		16.00	16

Doors & Gates of America: Miami Beach: Deco District - M. Weisser

Year Issue		Edition Limit	Year Retd.	Issue Price	Quote U.S.$
1994	The Flamingo Door	Open		15.00	15
1994	Key West Door	Open		15.00	15
1994	The Moon Gate	Open		16.00	16
1994	Residential Door #1	Open		16.00	16
1994	Residential Door #2	Open		15.00	15

Iris Arc Crystal

Collector's Society Edition - C. Hughes

Year Issue		Edition Limit	Year Retd.	Issue Price	Quote U.S.$
1992	Gramophone	Retrd.	N/A	100.00	180
1993	Classic Telephone	Retrd.	N/A	150.00	250
1994	Antique Clock	Retrd.	1995	150.00	150

Limited Editions - Various

Year Issue		Edition Limit	Year Retd.	Issue Price	Quote U.S.$
1989	Angel - M. Goena	Retrd.	N/A	180.00	240
1991	Basket of Flowers - M. Goena	Retrd.	N/A	250.00	300
1993	Basket of Violets - M. Goena	750	1995	190.00	190
1993	Birdbath - M. Goena	Retrd.	N/A	190.00	190
1994	Bluebird Basket - M. Goena	1,000		190.00	190
1987	Carousel - T. Holliman	Retrd.	N/A	600.00	720
1986	Classic Car - T. Holliman	Retrd.	N/A	500.00	600
1993	Country Church - M. Goena	350		590.00	590
1991	Country Cottage - M. Goena	300		1500.00	1500
1987	Eagle - P. Hale	Retrd.	N/A	700.00	840
1983	Elephant - P. Hale	Retrd.	N/A	190.00	228
1994	Garden Cottage - C. Hughes	500		390.00	390
1988	Horse and Foal - M. Goena	Retrd.	N/A	1000.00	1200
1994	Hummingbirds - M. Goena	750		290.00	290
1994	Mystic Star Castle - M. Goena	500		390.00	390
1993	Nob Hill Victorian - C. Hughes	250		1000.00	1000
1983	Peacock - P. Hale	Retrd.	N/A	140.00	168
1992	Rainbow Cathedral - M. Goena	150		2500.00	2500
1990	Rainbow Enchanted Castle - C. Hughes	500	1995	1500.00	1500
1983	Teddy Bear with Heart (Rose) - P. Hale	Retrd.	N/A	170.00	204
1983	Teddy Bear with Heart (Silver) - P. Hale	Retrd.	N/A	170.00	204
1991	Vase of Flowers - P. Hale	750		250.00	250

Year Issue		Edition Limit	Year Retd.	Issue Price	Quote U.S.$
1992	Victorian House - C. Hughes	750		270.00	290
1992	Water Mill - M. Goena	350		900.00	950

John Hine N.A. Ltd.

David Winter Collectors Guild Exclusives - D. Winter

Year Issue		Edition Limit	Year Retd.	Issue Price	Quote U.S.$
1987	The Village Scene	Closed	1988	Gift	225-500
1987	Robin Hood's Hideaway	Closed	1989	54.00	250-325
1987	Queen Elizabeth Slept Here	Closed	1989	183.00	250-350
1988	Black Bess Inn	Closed	1990	60.00	95-115
1988	The Pavillion	Closed	1990	52.00	80-100
1988	Street Scene	Closed	1988	Gift	100-250
1989	Home Guard	Closed	1991	105.00	75-105
1989	Coal Shed	Closed	1991	112.00	120
1990	The Plucked Ducks	Closed	1990	Gift	50
1990	The Cobblers	Closed	1992	40.00	40-90
1990	The Pottery	Closed	1992	40.00	40-90
1990	Cartwright's Cottage	Closed	1990	45.00	55-75
1991	Pershore Mill	Closed	1991	Gift	40-75
1991	Tomfool's Cottage	Closed	1993	100.00	85-100
1991	Will-O' The Wisp	Closed	1993	120.00	100-125
1992	Irish Water Mill	Closed	1992	Gift	50-80
1992	Patrick's Water Mill	Closed	1992	Gift	150-225
1992	Candlemaker's	Closed	1992	65.00	65-85
1992	Beekeeper's	Closed	1992	65.00	65-80
1993	On The River Bank	Closed	1993	Gift	50-75
1993	Thameside	Closed	1993	79.00	75-90
1993	Swan Upping Cottage	Closed	1993	69.00	65-90
1993	Horatio Pernickety's Amorous Intent	9,900	1993	375.00	350-375
1994	15 Lawnside Road	Closed	1994	Gift	50
1994	While Away Cottage	Closed	1994	70.00	70
1994	Ashe Cottage	Closed	1994	62.00	75
1995	Buttercup Cottage	Yr.Iss.		60.00	60
1995	The Flowershop	Yr.Iss.		150.00	150
1995	Gardener's Cottage	Yr.Iss.		Gift	Gift

David Winter Special Event Pieces - D. Winter

Year Issue		Edition Limit	Year Retd.	Issue Price	Quote U.S.$
1992	Birthstone Wishing Well	Closed	1993	40.00	55-75
1993	Birthday Cottage	Closed	1994	55.00	60-75
1994	Wishing Falls Cottage	Closed	1995	65.00	65
1995	Whisper Cottage	12/95		65.00	65

David Winter Tour Special Event Piece - D. Winter

Year Issue		Edition Limit	Year Retd.	Issue Price	Quote U.S.$
1993	Arches Thrice	Closed	1993	150.00	100-200

David Winter Appearance Piece - D. Winter

Year Issue		Edition Limit	Year Retd.	Issue Price	Quote U.S.$
1994	Winter Arch	Closed	1994	N/A	N/A
1995	Grumbleweed's Potting Shed	Yr.Iss.		99.00	99

David Winter At The Centre of the Village Collection - D. Winter

Year Issue		Edition Limit	Year Retd.	Issue Price	Quote U.S.$
1983	The Bakehouse	Open		31.40	60
1984	The Chapel	Closed	1992	48.80	75
1985	The Cooper Cottage	Closed	1993	57.90	65-100
1983	The Green Dragon Inn	Open		31.40	60
1982	Ivy Cottage	Closed	1992	22.00	45
1980	Little Market	Closed	1993	28.90	30-45
1980	Market Street	Open		48.80	90
1984	Parsonage	Open		390.00	560
1980	Rose Cottage	Open		28.90	55
1984	Spinner's Cottage	Closed	1990	28.90	40-95
1982	The Village Shop	Open		22.00	35
1980	The Wine Merchant	Closed	1993	28.90	55

David Winter British Traditions - D. Winter

Year Issue		Edition Limit	Year Retd.	Issue Price	Quote U.S.$
1990	Blossom Cottage	Closed	1995	59.00	45-69
1990	The Boat House	Closed	1995	37.50	65-69
1990	Bull & Bush	Closed	1995	37.50	45-55
1990	Burns' Reading Room	Closed	1995	31.00	56
1990	Grouse Moor Lodge	Closed	1995	48.00	70
1990	Guy Fawkes	Closed	1995	31.00	50
1990	Harvest Barn	Closed	1995	31.00	53
1990	Knight's Castle	Closed	1995	59.00	85
1991	The Printers and The Bookbinders	Closed	1994	120.00	140
1990	Pudding Cottage	Closed	1995	78.00	85-96
1990	St. Anne's Well	Closed	1995	48.00	78
1990	Staffordshire Vicarage	Closed	1995	48.00	70
1990	Stonecutters Cottage	Closed	1995	48.00	45-70

David Winter Cameos - D. Winter

Year Issue		Edition Limit	Year Retd.	Issue Price	Quote U.S.$
1992	Barley Malt Kilns	Open		12.50	15
1992	Brooklet Bridge	Open		12.50	15
1992	Diorama-Bright	Open		50.00	50
1992	Diorama-Light	Closed	1992	30.00	65
1992	Greenwood Wagon	Open		12.50	15
1992	Lych Gate	Open		12.50	15
1992	Market Day	Open		12.50	15
1992	One Man Jail	Open		12.50	15
1992	Penny Wishing Well	Open		12.50	15
1992	The Potting Shed	Open		12.50	15
1992	Poultry Ark	Open		12.50	15
1992	The Privy	Open		12.50	15
1992	Saddle Steps	Open		12.50	15
1992	Welsh Pig Pen	Open		12.50	15

David Winter Castle Collection - D. Winter

Year Issue		Edition Limit	Year Retd.	Issue Price	Quote U.S.$
1995	Bishopsgate	Open		175.00	175
1995	Bishopsgate Premier	3,500		225.00	225

FIGURINES/COTTAGES

David Winter Celebration Cottages - D. Winter

YEAR ISSUE		EDITION LIMIT	YEAR RETD.	ISSUE PRICE	QUOTE U.S.$
1994	Celebration Chapel	Open		75.00	75
1994	Celebration Chapel Premier	3,500		150.00	150
1995	Mother's Cottage	Open		65.00	65
1995	Mother's Cottage Premier	3,500		89.50	90
1994	Spring Hollow	Open		65.00	65
1994	Spring Hollow Premier	3,500		125.00	125
1995	Stork Cottage Boy	Open		65.00	65
1995	Stork Cottage Girl	Open		65.00	65
1994	Sweetheart Haven	Open		60.00	60
1994	Sweetheart Haven Premier	3,500		115.00	115

David Winter Christmas - D. Winter

YEAR ISSUE		EDITION LIMIT	YEAR RETD.	ISSUE PRICE	QUOTE U.S.$
1987	Ebenezer Scrooge's Counting House	Closed	1988	96.90	100-125
1988	Christmas in Scotland & Hogmanay	Closed	1988	100.00	135-195
1989	A Christmas Carol	Closed	1989	135.00	100-250
1990	Mr. Fezziwig's Emporium	Closed	1990	135.00	75-100
1991	Fred's Home: "A Merry Christmas, Uncle Ebenezer saids Scrooge's Nephew Fred, and a Happy New Year.	Closed	1991	145.00	75-100
1992	Scrooge's School	Closed	1992	160.00	125-225
1993	Old Joe's Beetling Shop A Veritable Den of Iniquity!	Closed	1993	175.00	185-195
1994	Scrooge's Family Home	Closed	1994	175.00	190-275
1994	Scrooge's Family Home Premier	Closed	1994	230.00	250
1994	Scrooge's Family Home, Plaque	3,500	1994	125.00	150
1995	Miss Belle's Cottage	Yr.Iss.		185.00	185
1995	Miss Belle's Cottage Premier	2,200		235.00	235
1995	Miss Belle's Christmas Plaque	4,000		120.00	120

David Winter English Village - D. Winter

YEAR ISSUE		EDITION LIMIT	YEAR RETD.	ISSUE PRICE	QUOTE U.S.$
1994	Cat & Pipe	Open		53.00	53
1994	Chandlery	Open		53.00	53
1994	Church & Vestry	Open		57.00	57
1994	Constabulary	Open		60.00	60
1994	Crystal Cottage	Open		53.00	53
1994	Engine House	Open		55.00	55
1994	Glebe Cottage	Open		53.00	53
1994	Guardian Castle	8,490	1994	275.00	350-475
1994	Guardian Castle Premier	1,500	1994	350.00	510-600
1994	The Hall	Open		55.00	55
1994	One Acre Cottage	Open		55.00	55
1994	The Post Office	Open		53.00	53
1994	The Quack's Cottage	Open		57.00	57
1994	The Rectory	Open		55.00	55
1994	The Seminary	Open		57.00	57
1994	The Smithy	Open		50.00	50
1994	The Tannery	Open		50.00	50

David Winter Garden Cottages of England - D. Winter

YEAR ISSUE		EDITION LIMIT	YEAR RETD.	ISSUE PRICE	QUOTE U.S.$
1995	Spencer Hall Gardens	4,300		395.00	395
1995	Spencer Hall Gardens, Premier	2,200		495.00	495
1995	Willow Gardens	4,300		225.00	225
1995	Willow Gardens, Premier	2,200		299.00	299

David Winter Heart of England Series - D. Winter

YEAR ISSUE		EDITION LIMIT	YEAR RETD.	ISSUE PRICE	QUOTE U.S.$
1985	The Apothecary Shop	Open		24.10	50
1985	Blackfriars Grange	Closed	1994	24.10	75
1985	Craftsmen's Cottages	Open		24.10	40
1985	The Hogs Head Tavern	Open		24.10	50
1985	Meadowbank Cottages	Open		24.10	40
1985	The Schoolhouse	Open		24.10	45
1985	Shirehall	Open		24.10	50
1985	St. George's Church	Open		24.10	45
1985	The Vicarage	Open		24.10	45
1985	The Windmill	Open		37.50	50
1985	Yeoman's Farmhouse	Open		24.10	40

David Winter In The Country Collection - D. Winter

YEAR ISSUE		EDITION LIMIT	YEAR RETD.	ISSUE PRICE	QUOTE U.S.$
1983	The Bothy	Open		31.40	60
1982	Brookside Hamlet	Closed	1990	74.80	65-75
1982	Drover's Cottage	Open		22.00	35
1983	Fisherman's Wharf	Open		31.40	60
1994	Guardian Gate	Open		150.00	150
1994	Guardian Gate Premier	3,500	1995	199.00	199
1987	John Benbow's Farmhouse	Closed	1993	78.00	85-100
1983	Pilgrim's Rest	Closed	1993	48.80	65-75
1984	Snow Cottage	Closed	1992	74.80	85-100
1986	There was a Crooked House	Open		96.90	155
1984	Tollkeeper's Cottage	Closed	1992	87.00	110

David Winter Irish Collection - D. Winter

YEAR ISSUE		EDITION LIMIT	YEAR RETD.	ISSUE PRICE	QUOTE U.S.$
1992	Fogartys	Closed	1994	75.00	85
1992	Irish Round Tower	Open		65.00	70
1992	Murphys	Open		100.00	110
1992	O'Donovan's Castle	Open		145.00	170
1992	Only A Span Apart	Closed	1993	80.00	75-85
1992	Secret Shebeen	Closed	1993	70.00	75-100

David Winter Landowners - D. Winter

YEAR ISSUE		EDITION LIMIT	YEAR RETD.	ISSUE PRICE	QUOTE U.S.$
1984	Castle Gate	Closed	1992	155.00	220-325
1982	The Dower House	Closed	1993	22.00	45-55
1988	The Grange	Closed	1989	120.00	750-100
1985	Squire Hall	Closed	1990	92.30	75-95
1981	Tudor Manor House	Closed	1990	48.80	65-75

David Winter Main Collection - D. Winter

YEAR ISSUE		EDITION LIMIT	YEAR RETD.	ISSUE PRICE	QUOTE U.S.$
1983	The Alms Houses	Closed	1987	59.90	250-300
1992	Audrey's Tea Room	Closed	1992	90.00	150-180
1992	Audrey's Tea Shop	Closed	1992	90.00	125-150
1982	Blacksmith's Cottage	Closed	1986	22.00	225-450
1991	Castle in the Air	10,000		675.00	710
1981	Castle Keep	Closed	1982	30.00	900-1200
1981	Chichester Cross	Closed	1981	50.00	3200-3700
1980	The Coaching Inn	Closed	1983	165.00	3200-3800
1981	Cornish Cottage	Closed	1986	30.00	850
1983	Cornish Tin Mine	Closed	1988	22.00	50-85
1983	Cotton Mill	Closed	1988	41.30	300-550
1981	Double Oast	Closed	1982	60.00	3300
1980	Dove Cottage	Closed	1983	60.00	1850
1982	Fairytale Castle	Closed	1989	115.00	240-275
1986	Falstaff's Manor	10,000	1990	242.00	295-300
1980	The Forge	Closed	1983	60.00	1900
1983	The Haybarn	Closed	1987	22.00	275
1985	Hermit's Humble Home	Closed	1988	87.00	200-250
1984	House of the Master Mason	Closed	1988	74.80	250-300
1982	House on Top	Closed	1988	92.30	325
1991	Inglenook Cottage	Open		60.00	75
1988	Jim'll Fixit	Closed	1988	350.00	2850-3250
1994	Kingmaker's Castle	Open		225.00	225
1980	Little Forge	Closed	1983	40.00	1650
1980	Little Mill	Closed	1980	40.00	1200
1980	Little Mill-remodeled	Closed	1983	Unkn.	1600
1992	Mad Baron Fourthrite's Folly	Closed	1992	275.00	175-300
1980	Mill House	Closed	1980	50.00	2500
1980	Mill House-remodeled	Closed	1983	50.00	1900
1983	Miner's Cottage	Closed	1987	22.00	140-185
1991	Moonlight Haven	Open		120.00	155
1982	Moorland Cottage	Closed	1987	22.00	150-250
1995	Newtown Millhouse	4,500		195.00	195
1981	The Old Curiosity Shop	Closed	1983	40.00	1200
1980	Quayside	Closed	1985	60.00	900-1800
1994	Quindene Manor	3,000	1994	695.00	700-800
1994	Quindene Manor Premier	1,500	1994	850.00	900-1000
1982	Sabrina's Cottage	Closed	1982	30.00	2000-2350
1981	St. Paul's Cathedral	Closed	1982	40.00	1800-2000
1985	Suffolk House	Closed	1989	48.80	55-75
1980	Three Duck Inn	Closed	1981	60.00	1450
1981	Tythe Barn	Closed	1986	39.30	1600
1981	The Village	Open		362.00	580
1991	The Weaver's Lodgings	Open		65.00	75
1995	Welcome Home Cottage	12/95		99.00	99
1995	Welcome Home Cottage Military	12/95		99.00	99
1982	William Shakespeare's Birthplace (large)	Closed	1984	60.00	1300
1983	Woodcutter's Cottage	Closed	1988	87.00	275-350

David Winter Midlands Collection - D. Winter

YEAR ISSUE		EDITION LIMIT	YEAR RETD.	ISSUE PRICE	QUOTE U.S.$
1988	Bottle Kilns	Closed	1990	78.00	65-85
1988	Coal Miner's Row	Open		90.00	120
1988	Derbyshire Cotton Mill	Closed	1994	65.00	90-125
1988	The Gunsmiths	Open		78.00	100
1988	Lacemaker's Cottage	Open		120.00	155
1988	Lock-keepers Cottage	Open		65.00	85

David Winter Porridge Pot Alley - D. Winter

YEAR ISSUE		EDITION LIMIT	YEAR RETD.	ISSUE PRICE	QUOTE U.S.$
1995	Cob's Bakery	Open		125.00	125
1995	Cob's Bakery Premier	3,500		165.00	165
1995	Sweet Dreams	Open		79.00	79
1995	Sweet Dreams Premier	3,500		99.00	99
1995	Tartan Teahouse	Open		99.00	99
1995	Tartan Teahouse Premier	3,500		129.00	129

David Winter Regions Collection - D. Winter

YEAR ISSUE		EDITION LIMIT	YEAR RETD.	ISSUE PRICE	QUOTE U.S.$
1982	Cotswold Cottage	Open		22.00	35
1981	Cotswold Village	Closed	1990	59.90	50-75
1983	Hertford Court	Closed	1992	87.00	75-100
1985	Kent Cottage	Open		48.80	110
1981	Single Oast	Closed	1993	22.00	30-50
1981	Stratford House	Open		74.80	130
1982	Sussex Cottage	Open		22.00	50
1981	Triple Oast (old version)	Closed	1994	59.90	150-250

David Winter Scenes - Cameo Guild, unless otherwise noted

YEAR ISSUE		EDITION LIMIT	YEAR RETD.	ISSUE PRICE	QUOTE U.S.$
1992	At Rose cottage Vignette - D. Winter	5,000		39.00	39
1992	Daughter - D. Winter	5,000		30.00	30
1992	Father	5,000		45.00	45
1992	Mother	5,000		50.00	50
1992	Son	5,000		30.00	30
1992	At The Bake House Vignette - D. Winter	5,000		35.00	35
1992	Girl Selling Eggs	5,000		30.00	30
1992	Hot Cross Bun Seller	5,000		60.00	60
1992	Lady Customer	5,000		45.00	45
1992	Small Boy And Dog	5,000		45.00	45
1992	Woman At Pump	5,000		45.00	45
1992	At The Bothy Vignette Base - D. Winter	5,000		39.00	39
1992	Farm Hand And Spade	5,000		40.00	40
1992	Farmer And Plough	5,000		60.00	60
1992	Farmer's Wife	5,000		45.00	45
1992	Goose Girl	5,000		45.00	45
1993	Christmas Snow Vignette - D. Winter	5,000		50.00	50
1993	Bob Cratchit And Tiny Tim	5,000		50.00	50
1993	Ebenezer Scrooge	5,000		45.00	45
1993	Fred	5,000		35.00	35
1993	Miss Belle	5,000		35.00	35
1993	Mrs. Fezziwig	5,000		35.00	35
1993	Tom The Street Shoveler	5,000		60.00	60

David Winter Scottish Collection - D. Winter

YEAR ISSUE		EDITION LIMIT	YEAR RETD.	ISSUE PRICE	QUOTE U.S.$
1988	Crofter's Cottage	Closed	1989	51.00	60-80
1989	Gatekeeper's Cottage	Open		65.00	85
1989	Gillie's Cottage	Open		65.00	85
1989	The House on the Loch	Closed	1994	65.00	75-85
1989	MacBeth's Castle	Open		200.00	260
1982	Old Distillery	Closed	1993	312.00	500
1989	Scottish Crofter's	Open		42.00	65

David Winter Seaside Boardwalk - D. Winter

YEAR ISSUE		EDITION LIMIT	YEAR RETD.	ISSUE PRICE	QUOTE U.S.$
1995	The Barnacle Theatre	4,500		175.00	175
1995	Dock Accessory	Open		Gift	N/A
1995	The Fisherman's Shanty	Open		110.00	110
1995	Harbour Master's Watch-House	Open		125.00	125
1995	Jolly Roger Tavern	Open		199.00	199
1995	Lodgings and Sea Bathing	Open		165.00	165
1995	Waterfront Market	Open		125.00	125

David Winter Sherwood Forest Collection - D. Winter

YEAR ISSUE		EDITION LIMIT	YEAR RETD.	ISSUE PRICE	QUOTE U.S.$
1995	Friar Tuck's Sanctum	Open		45.00	45
1995	King Richard's Bower	Open		45.00	45
1995	Little John's Riverloft	Open		45.00	45
1995	Loxley Castle	Open		150.00	150
1995	Maid Marian's Retreat	Open		49.50	50
1995	Much's Mill	Open		45.00	45
1995	Sherwood Forest Diorama	Open		100.00	100
1995	Will Scarlett's Den	Open		49.50	50

David Winter Shires Collection - D. Winter

YEAR ISSUE		EDITION LIMIT	YEAR RETD.	ISSUE PRICE	QUOTE U.S.$
1993	Berkshire Milking Byre	Closed	1995	38.00	30-40
1993	Buckinghamshire Bull Pen	Open	1994	38.00	30-40
1993	Cheshire Kennels	Closed	1995	36.00	30-40
1993	Derbyshire Dovecote	Closed	1995	36.00	30-40
1993	Gloucestershire Greenhouse	Closed	1995	40.00	30-40
1993	Hampshire Hutches	Closed	1995	34.00	30-40
1993	Lancashire Donkey Shed	Closed	1995	38.00	30-40
1993	Oxfordshire Goat Yard	Open	1994	32.00	30-40
1993	Shropshire Pig Shelter	Closed	1995	32.00	30-40
1993	Staffordshire Stable	Closed	1995	36.00	30-40
1993	Wiltshire Waterwheel	Closed	1995	34.00	30-40
1993	Yorkshire Sheep Fold	Closed	1995	38.00	30-40

David Winter Tiny Series - D. Winter

YEAR ISSUE		EDITION LIMIT	YEAR RETD.	ISSUE PRICE	QUOTE U.S.$
1980	Anne Hathaway's Cottage	Closed	1981	Unkn.	750
1980	Cotswold Farmhouse	Closed	1982	Unkn.	450-700
1980	Crown Inn	Closed	1982	Unkn.	600-700
1980	St. Nicholas' Church	Closed	1982	Unkn.	600-900
1980	Sulgrave Manor	Closed	1982	Unkn.	450-700
1980	William Shakespeare's Birthplace	Closed	1981	Unkn.	750

David Winter Welsh Collection - D. Winter

YEAR ISSUE		EDITION LIMIT	YEAR RETD.	ISSUE PRICE	QUOTE U.S.$
1993	A Bit of Nonsense	Closed	1995	50.00	50
1993	Pen-y-Craig	Open		88.00	90
1993	Tyddyn Siriol	Closed	1994	88.00	60-80
1993	Y' Ddraig Goch	Closed	1994	88.00	60-80

David Winter West Country Collection - D. Winter

YEAR ISSUE		EDITION LIMIT	YEAR RETD.	ISSUE PRICE	QUOTE U.S.$
1988	Cornish Engine House	Open		120.00	155
1988	Cornish Harbour	Open		120.00	155
1986	Devon Combe	Closed	1994	73.00	110
1986	Devon Creamery	Open		62.90	110
1987	Orchard Cottage	Closed	1990	91.30	75-95
1986	Smuggler's Creek	Open		390.00	520
1986	Tamar Cottage	Open		45.30	75

David Winter Winterville Collection - D. Winter

YEAR ISSUE		EDITION LIMIT	YEAR RETD.	ISSUE PRICE	QUOTE U.S.$
1994	The Christmastime Clocktower	Open		165.00	165
1994	The Christmastime Clocktower Premier	3,500	1994	215.00	215
1995	St. Stephen's	5,750		150.00	150
1995	St. Stephen's Premier	1,750		195.00	195
1994	Toymaker	Open		135.00	135
1994	Toymaker Premier	3,500	1994	175.00	175
1995	Ye Merry Gentlemen's Lodgings	5,750		125.00	125
1995	Ye Merry Gentlemen's Lodgings Premier	1,750		170.00	170

Disneyana Convention - John Hine Studio

YEAR ISSUE		EDITION LIMIT	YEAR RETD.	ISSUE PRICE	QUOTE U.S.$
1992	Cinderella Castle	500	1992	250.00	1100
1993	Sleeping Beauty Castle	500	1993	250.00	450-800
1994	Euro Disney Castle	500	1994	250.00	350-450

Father Christmas - J. King

YEAR ISSUE		EDITION LIMIT	YEAR RETD.	ISSUE PRICE	QUOTE U.S.$
1988	Falling	Closed	N/A	70.00	70
1988	Feet	Closed	N/A	70.00	70
1988	Standing	Closed	N/A	70.00	70

Father Time Clocks - J. Herbert

YEAR ISSUE		EDITION LIMIT	YEAR RETD.	ISSUE PRICE	QUOTE U.S.$
1992	Castle	Open		110.00	110
1992	Farmhouse	Open		99.00	99
1992	Little Thatched	Open		78.00	78
1992	The Manor	Open		90.00	90
1993	Marshland Castle	Open		99.00	99
1993	Riverside Haven	Open		99.00	99
1992	Treehouse	Open		99.00	99
1993	Tudor Ruin	Open		94.00	94
1992	Watermill	Open		99.00	99
1992	Windmill	Open		120.00	120

Great British Pubs - M. Cooper

YEAR ISSUE		EDITION LIMIT	YEAR RETD.	ISSUE PRICE	QUOTE U.S.$
1989	The Bell	Closed	N/A	79.50	100-350
1989	Black Swan	Closed	1990	79.50	100-200

YEAR ISSUE		EDITION LIMIT	YEAR RETD.	ISSUE PRICE	QUOTE U.S.$
1989	Blue Bell	Closed	N/A	57.50	58
1989	Coach & Horses	Closed	N/A	79.50	80
1989	The Crown Inn	Closed	N/A	79.50	80
1989	Dickens Inn	Closed	N/A	100.00	100
1989	The Feathers	Closed	N/A	200.00	200
1989	The George	Closed	N/A	57.50	58
1989	George Somerset	Closed	N/A	100.00	100
1989	Hawkeshead	Closed	N/A	Unkn.	900
1989	Jamaica Inn	Closed	N/A	39.50	40
1989	King's Arms	Closed	N/A	28.00	28
1989	The Lion	Closed	N/A	57.50	58
1989	Montague Arms	Closed	N/A	57.50	58
1989	Old Bridge House	Closed	N/A	37.50	38
1989	Old Bull Inn	Closed	N/A	87.50	88
1989	The Plough	Closed	N/A	28.00	95
1989	Sherlock Holmes	Closed	N/A	100.00	200
1989	Smith's Arms	Closed	N/A	28.00	28
1989	White Horse	Closed	N/A	39.50	40
1989	White Tower	Closed	N/A	35.00	35
1989	Ye Grapes	Closed	N/A	87.50	88
1989	Ye Olde Spotted Horse	Closed	N/A	79.50	80

Great British Pubs -Yard of Pubs - M. Cooper

YEAR ISSUE		EDITION LIMIT	YEAR RETD.	ISSUE PRICE	QUOTE U.S.$
1989	Black Friars	Closed	N/A	25.00	25
1989	Dirty Duck	Closed	N/A	25.00	25
1989	The Eagle	Closed	N/A	35.00	35
1989	Falkland Arms	Closed	N/A	25.00	25
1989	The Falstaff	Closed	N/A	35.00	35
1989	George & Pilgrims	Closed	N/A	25.00	25
1989	The Green Man	Closed	N/A	Unkn.	75
1989	Grenadier	Closed	N/A	25.00	25
1989	Lygon Arms	Closed	N/A	35.00	35
1989	Suffolk Bull	Closed	N/A	35.00	35
1989	The Swan	Closed	N/A	35.00	35
1989	Wheatsheaf	Closed	N/A	35.00	35

Heartstrings - S. Kuck

YEAR ISSUE		EDITION LIMIT	YEAR RETD.	ISSUE PRICE	QUOTE U.S.$
1992	Day Dreaming	Closed	N/A	92.50	93
1992	Hush, It's Sleepytime	Closed	N/A	97.50	98
1992	Taking Tea	Closed	N/A	92.50	93
1992	Watch Me Waltz	Closed	N/A	97.50	98

Mushrooms - C. Lawrence

YEAR ISSUE		EDITION LIMIT	YEAR RETD.	ISSUE PRICE	QUOTE U.S.$
1989	The Cobblers	Closed	N/A	265.00	265
1989	The Constables	Closed	N/A	200.00	200
1989	The Elders Mushroom	Closed	N/A	175.00	175
1989	The Gift Shop	Closed	N/A	350.00	420
1989	The Ministry	Closed	N/A	185.00	185
1989	The Mush Hospital for Malingerers	Closed	N/A	250.00	250
1989	The Princess Palace	Closed	N/A	600.00	730
1989	Royal Bank of Mushland	Closed	N/A	235.00	235

Santa's Big Day - J. King

YEAR ISSUE		EDITION LIMIT	YEAR RETD.	ISSUE PRICE	QUOTE U.S.$
1992	Booting Up	Closed	N/A	40.00	40
1992	Feet First	Closed	N/A	55.00	55
1992	Heave Ho!	Closed	N/A	70.00	70
1992	Home Rudolph	Closed	N/A	50.00	50
1992	Ready Boys?	Closed	N/A	80.00	80
1992	Reindeer Breakfast	Closed	N/A	50.00	50
1992	Rest-a-while	Closed	N/A	60.00	60
1992	Santa's Night Ride	Closed	N/A	55.00	55
1992	Tight Fit!	Closed	N/A	55.00	55
1992	Wakey, Wakey!	Closed	N/A	55.00	55
1992	Whoops!	Closed	N/A	60.00	60
1992	Zzzzz...	Closed	N/A	85.00	85

The Shoemaker's Dream - J. Herbert

YEAR ISSUE		EDITION LIMIT	YEAR RETD.	ISSUE PRICE	QUOTE U.S.$
1991	Baby Booty (blue)	Open		45.00	45
1991	Baby Booty (pink)	Open		45.00	45
1991	Castle Boot	Open		55.00	55
1991	The Chapel	Open		55.00	55
1992	Christmas Boot	Open		55.00	55
1991	The Clocktower Boot	Open		60.00	60
1992	Clown Boot	Open		45.00	45
1991	The Crooked Boot	Open		35.00	35
1991	The Gate Lodge	Open		65.00	65
1992	The Golf Shoe	Open		35.00	40
1991	The Jester Boot	Closed	1994	29.00	29
1991	River Shoe Cottage	Closed	1994	55.00	55
1991	Rosie's Cottage	Closed	1994	40.00	40
1993	Shiver me Timbers	Open		45.00	55
1991	Shoemaker's Palace	Open		50.00	50
1992	The Sports Shoe	Open		35.00	40
1991	Tavern Boot	Open		55.00	55
1992	Upside Down Boot	Open		45.00	45
1991	Watermill Boot	Closed	1994	60.00	60
1993	Wedding Bells	Open		45.00	50
1991	Windmill Boot	Open		65.00	65
1992	Wishing Well Shoe	Open		32.00	35
1993	The Woodcutter's Shoe	Open		40.00	40

Wideman - M. Wideman

YEAR ISSUE		EDITION LIMIT	YEAR RETD.	ISSUE PRICE	QUOTE U.S.$
1992	Moe's Clubhouse	Closed	1993	40.00	200-250

Wideman-American Collection - M. Wideman

YEAR ISSUE		EDITION LIMIT	YEAR RETD.	ISSUE PRICE	QUOTE U.S.$
1989	Band Stand	Closed	1993	90.00	72-90
1989	Barber Shop	Closed	1993	40.00	30
1989	The Blockhouse	Closed	1993	25.00	16-55
1989	Cajun Cottage	Closed	1993	50.00	40
1989	California Winery	Closed	1993	180.00	145-180
1989	Cherry Hill School	Closed	1993	45.00	46-96
1991	Church in the Dale	Closed	1993	130.00	90
1989	Colonial Wellhouse	Closed	1993	15.00	14-30
1991	Desert Storm Tent	Closed	1991	75.00	75-120
1989	Dog House	Closed	1993	10.00	10-15
1991	Fire Station	Closed	1993	160.00	125-160
1989	Forty-Niner Cabin	Closed	1993	50.00	40-60
1989	Garconniere	Closed	1993	25.00	20
1989	The Gingerbread House	Closed	1993	60.00	52-65
1992	Grain Elevator	Closed	1993	110.00	110
1989	Hacienda	Closed	1993	51.00	40-80
1989	Haunted House	Closed	1993	100.00	100
1989	Hawaiian Grass Hut	Closed	1992	45.00	45
1991	Joe's Service Station	Closed	1993	90.00	108
1989	King William Tavern	Closed	1993	99.00	80-150
1989	The Kissing Bridge	Closed	1992	50.00	40-50
1989	The Log Cabin	Closed	1993	45.00	40-60
1989	The Maple Sugar Shack	Closed	1993	50.00	40-50
1991	Milk House	Closed	1993	20.00	20
1989	The Mission	Closed	1993	99.00	80-100
1991	Mo At Work	Closed	1991	35.00	35-65
1991	Moe's Diner	Closed	1993	100.00	300-800
1989	The New England Church	Closed	1993	79.00	72-80
1989	New England Lighthouse	Closed	1993	99.00	80-120
1992	News Stand	Closed	1993	30.00	30-72
1989	Octagonal House	Closed	1993	40.00	32-52
1989	The Old Mill	Closed	1993	100.00	80-100
1989	The Opera House	Closed	1992	89.00	72-90
1989	The Out House	Closed	1993	15.00	15-30
1989	Oxbow Saloon	Closed	1993	90.00	65-90
1989	The Pacific Lighthouse	Closed	1993	89.00	80-200
1991	Paul Revere's House	Closed	1992	90.00	72-95
1989	Plantation House	Closed	1993	119.00	90-210
1989	Prairie Forge	Closed	1993	65.00	65-135
1989	Railhead Inn	Closed	1993	250.00	195-250
1989	The River Bell	Closed	1993	99.00	95-120
1989	Seaside Cottage	Closed	1992	225.00	190
1989	Sierra Mine	Closed	1992	120.00	90-120
1989	Sod House	Closed	1992	40.00	25-40
1989	Star Cottage	Closed	1993	30.00	24
1989	Sweetheart Cottage	Closed	1993	45.00	35-45
1992	Telephone Booth	Closed	1993	15.00	30
1989	Tobacconist	Closed	1993	45.00	45
1992	Topper's Drive-In	Closed	1993	120.00	125-145
1989	Town Hall	Closed	1993	129.00	125-150
1989	Tree House	Closed	1993	45.00	40-45
1992	Village Mercantile	Closed	1993	60.00	60
1989	Wisteria	Closed	1993	15.00	20

Wideman-First Nation Collection - M. Wideman

YEAR ISSUE		EDITION LIMIT	YEAR RETD.	ISSUE PRICE	QUOTE U.S.$
1993	Elm Bark Longhouse	Closed	1993	56.00	56
1993	The First Nation Collection, set of 8	Closed	1993	500.00	1000
1993	Igloo	Closed	1993	60.00	90
1993	Mandan Earth Lodge	Closed	1993	56.00	300
1993	Plains Teepee	Closed	1993	68.00	300
1993	Stilt House	Closed	1993	60.00	60-90
1993	Sweat Lodge	Closed	1993	34.00	100
1993	West Coast Longhouse	Closed	1993	100.00	100
1993	Wigwam	Closed	1993	65.00	300

Woodly Wise - T. Slack

YEAR ISSUE		EDITION LIMIT	YEAR RETD.	ISSUE PRICE	QUOTE U.S.$
1995	Arbor Stone 500044	Open		55.00	55
1995	Brambly Perch 500020	Open		49.00	49
1995	Chimney Pot Lodge 500082	Open		79.00	79
1995	Crooked Climb 500051	Open		55.00	55
1995	Roundabout 500013	Open		29.00	29
1995	Snow Chapel 500099	2,950		99.00	99
1995	Timberskeep 500075	Open		79.00	79
1995	Water's End 500037	Open		55.00	55
1995	Wendy House 500068	2,950		99.00	99

June McKenna Collectibles, Inc.

7" Limited Edition - J. McKenna

YEAR ISSUE		EDITION LIMIT	YEAR RETD.	ISSUE PRICE	QUOTE U.S.$
1991	Christmas Bishop	7,500	1993	110.00	150
1993	Christmas Cheer 1st ed.	7,500	1993	120.00	250
1993	Christmas Cheer 2nd. ed.	7,500		120.00	120
1990	Christmas Delight	7,500	1992	100.00	100
1995	Christmas Lullaby	7,500		120.00	120
1988	Christmas Memories	7,500	1991	90.00	150
1992	Christmas Wizard	7,500	1994	110.00	150
1990	Ethnic Santa	7,500	1992	100.00	140
1988	Joyful Christmas	7,500	1991	90.00	150
1994	Mrs. Claus, Dancing to the Tune	7,500		120.00	120
1989	Old Fashioned Santa	7,500	1991	100.00	150
1989	Santa's Bag of Surprises	7,500	1991	100.00	150
1994	Santa's One Man Band	7,500		120.00	120

Black Folk Art - J. McKenna

YEAR ISSUE		EDITION LIMIT	YEAR RETD.	ISSUE PRICE	QUOTE U.S.$
1987	Aunt Bertha - 3D	Closed	1991	36.00	75-100
1983	Black Boy With Watermelon, available in 3 colors	Closed	1988	12.00	100
1986	Black Butler	Closed	1989	13.00	75
1983	Black Girl With Watermelon, available in 3 colors	Closed	1988	12.00	95
1984	Black Man With Pig, available in 3 colors	Closed	1988	13.00	180
1984	Black Woman With Broom, available in 3 colors	Closed	1988	13.00	130
1989	Delia	Closed	1991	16.00	50
1992	Fishing John -3D	1,000		160.00	160
1989	Jake	Closed	1991	16.00	50
1985	Kids in a Tub - 3D	Closed	1990	30.00	85-120
1985	Kissing Cousins - sill sitter	Closed	1990	36.00	75-125
1990	Let's Play Ball -3D	Closed	1993	45.00	50
1987	Lil' Willie -3D	Closed	1991	36.00	75
1984	Mammie Cloth Doll	Closed	1988	90.00	400-500
1985	Mammie With Kids - 3D	Closed	1990	90.00	105-130
1985	Mammie With Spoon	Closed	1989	13.00	200
1988	Netty	Closed	1991	16.00	50
1984	Remus Cloth Doll	Closed	1988	90.00	350-400
1988	Renty	Closed	1991	16.00	50
1990	Sunday's Best -3D	Closed	1993	45.00	50
1987	Sweet Prissy -3D	Closed	1991	36.00	75
1992	Sweet Sister Sue -3D	1,000		160.00	160
1990	Tasha	Closed	1991	17.00	40
1985	Toaster Cover	Closed	1988	50.00	350
1990	Tyree	Closed	1991	17.00	40
1987	Uncle Jacob- 3D	Closed	1991	36.00	55-70
1985	Watermelon Patch Kids	Closed	1990	24.00	100

Carolers - J. McKenna

YEAR ISSUE		EDITION LIMIT	YEAR RETD.	ISSUE PRICE	QUOTE U.S.$
1985	Boy Caroler	Closed	1989	36.00	50
1992	Carolers, Grandparents	Closed	1994	70.00	70
1991	Carolers, Man With Girl	Closed	1994	50.00	50
1991	Carolers, Woman With Boy	Closed	1994	50.00	50
1994	Children Carolers	Open		90.00	90
1985	Girl Caroler	Closed	1989	36.00	70
1985	Man Caroler	Closed	1989	36.00	80
1995	Santa Caroling	Open		90.00	90
1985	Woman Caroler	Closed	1989	36.00	60

June McKenna Figurines - J. McKenna

YEAR ISSUE		EDITION LIMIT	YEAR RETD.	ISSUE PRICE	QUOTE U.S.$
1989	16th Century Santa - 3D, blue	Closed	1991	60.00	175-290
1989	16th Century Santa - 3D, green	Closed	1989	60.00	250-290
1989	17th Century Santa - 3D, red	Closed	1991	70.00	175
1993	Angel Name Plaque	Closed	1994	70.00	70
1983	Boy Rag Doll	Closed	N/A	12.00	300-450
1985	Bride w/o base-3D	Closed	1985	25.00	175-235
1985	Bride-3D	Closed	1987	25.00	200
1993	Children Ice Skaters	Closed	1994	60.00	60
1992	Choir of Angels	Closed	1993	60.00	60
1992	Christmas Santa	Closed	1993	60.00	70
1994	Conductor	Open		70.00	70
1987	Country Rag Boy (sitting)	Closed	1990	40.00	150-160
1987	Country Rag Girl (sitting)	Closed	1990	40.00	150-160
1994	Decorating for Christmas	Open		70.00	70
1985	Father Times - 3D	Closed	1991	40.00	110-185
1995	Finishing Touch	Open		70.00	70
1983	Girl Rag Doll	Closed	N/A	12.00	300-450
1993	A Good Night's Sleep	Open		70.00	70
1985	Groom w/o base-3D	Closed	1985	25.00	175-235
1985	Groom-3D	Closed	1987	25.00	150-200
1989	Jolly Ole Santa - 3D	Closed	1991	44.00	90-150
1992	Let It Snow	Open		60.00	60
1986	Little St. Nick	Closed	1990	50.00	130-160
1986	Male Angel	Closed	1986	44.00	1300-1700
1988	Mr. Santa - 3D	Closed	1991	44.00	125-200
1993	Mr. Snowman	Closed	1994	40.00	50
1988	Mrs. Santa - 3D	Closed	1989	50.00	100-200
1987	Name Plaque	Closed	1992	50.00	120-150
1990	Noel - 3D	Closed	1992	50.00	125
1987	Patriotic Santa	Closed	1989	50.00	225-300
1993	Santa and Friends	Open		70.00	70
1993	Santa Name Plaque	Open		70.00	70
1995	Santa Tree Topper	Open		90.00	90
1993	The Snow Family	Closed	1994	40.00	40
1994	Snowman and Child	Open		70.00	70
1985	Soldier	Closed	1988	40.00	160-225
1994	Star of Bethlehem-Angel	Open		40.00	40
1995	A Surprise For Joey	Open		70.00	70
1992	Taking A Break	Open		60.00	70
1995	Travel Plans	Open		70.00	70
1984	Tree Topper	Closed	1987	70.00	350-425

Limited Edition - J. McKenna

YEAR ISSUE		EDITION LIMIT	YEAR RETD.	ISSUE PRICE	QUOTE U.S.$
1988	Bringing Home Christmas	4,000	1990	170.00	275-475
1987	Christmas Eve	4,000	1989	170.00	350-500
1992	Christmas Gathering	4,000		220.00	300
1991	Coming to Town	4,000	1994	220.00	300
1983	Father Christmas	4,000	1986	90.00	2400-2800
1987	Kris Kringle	4,000	1990	350.00	500-700
1990	Night Before Christmas	1,500	1993	750.00	750
1984	Old Saint Nick	4,000	1986	100.00	700-1100
1993	The Patriot	4,000		250.00	250
1995	Peaceful Journey	4,000		250.00	250
1988	Remembrance of Christmas Past	4,000	1992	400.00	350
1991	Santa's Hot Air Balloon	1,500	1993	800.00	800
1989	Santa's Wardrobe	1,500	1992	750.00	800-1000
1989	Seasons Greetings	4,000	1992	200.00	350
1994	St. Nicholas	4,000		240.00	240
1986	Victorian	4,000	1988	150.00	500-900
1990	Wilderness	4,000	1994	200.00	250-375
1985	Woodland	4,000	1987	140.00	750-1500

Limited Edition Flatback - J. McKenna

YEAR ISSUE		EDITION LIMIT	YEAR RETD.	ISSUE PRICE	QUOTE U.S.$
1991	Bag of Stars	10,000	1993	34.00	40
1993	Bells of Christmas	10,000		40.00	40
1989	Blue Christmas	10,000	1991	32.00	100
1995	Christmas Delivery	10,000		40.00	40
1992	Deck The Halls	10,000	1994	34.00	40
1991	Farewell Santa	10,000	1993	34.00	50

YEAR ISSUE		EDITION LIMIT	YEAR RETD.	ISSUE PRICE	QUOTE U.S.$
1992	Good Tidings	10,000	1994	34.00	40
1995	Light of Christmas	10,000		40.00	40
1990	Medieval Santa	10,000	1992	34.00	60
1988	Mystical Santa	10,000	1991	30.00	75
1994	Not Once But Twice	10,000		40.00	40
1990	Old Time Santa	10,000	1992	34.00	60
1994	Post Marked North Pole	10,000		40.00	40
1993	Santa's Love	10,000		40.00	40
1988	Toys of Joy	10,000	1991	30.00	60-70
1989	Victorian	10,000	1991	32.00	100-120

Nativity Set - J. McKenna

YEAR ISSUE		EDITION LIMIT	YEAR RETD.	ISSUE PRICE	QUOTE U.S.$
1993	Cow	Open		30.00	30
1993	Donkey	Open		30.00	30
1988	Nativity - 6 Pieces	Open		130.00	150
1993	Ram & Ewe	Open		30.00	30
1991	Sheep With Shepherds - 2 Pieces	Open		60.00	60
1989	Three Wise Men	Open		60.00	90

Personal Appearance Figurines - J. McKenna

YEAR ISSUE		EDITION LIMIT	YEAR RETD.	ISSUE PRICE	QUOTE U.S.$
1989	Father Christmas	Closed	1993	30.00	150-200
1990	Old Saint Nick	Closed	1994	30.00	200
1991	Woodland	4-Yr.		35.00	35
1992	Victorian	4-Yr.		35.00	35
1993	Christmas Eve	4-Yr.		35.00	35
1994	Bringing Home Christmas	4-Yr.		35.00	35

Registered Edition - J. McKenna

YEAR ISSUE		EDITION LIMIT	YEAR RETD.	ISSUE PRICE	QUOTE U.S.$
1991	Checking His List	Closed	1994	230.00	275
1986	Colonial	Closed	1990	150.00	250-350
1992	Forty Winks	Closed	1994	250.00	300
1988	Jolly Ole St. Nick	Closed	1990	170.00	300
1995	Mrs. Santa Down on the Farm	Open		250.00	250
1995	Santa Down on the Farm	Open		260.00	260
1994	Say Cheese, Please	Open		250.00	250
1993	Tomorrow's Christmas	Open		250.00	250
1990	Toy Maker	Closed	1993	200.00	400
1989	Traditional	Closed	1991	180.00	300
1987	White Christmas	Closed	1987	170.00	1100-1500

Special Limited Edition - J. McKenna

YEAR ISSUE		EDITION LIMIT	YEAR RETD.	ISSUE PRICE	QUOTE U.S.$
1994	All Aboard-North Pole Express	Open		500.00	500
1995	All Aboard-Toy Car	Yr.Iss.		250.00	250
1993	Baking Cookies	2,000		450.00	450
1991	Bedtime Stories	2,000	1994	500.00	500
1990	Christmas Dreams	4,000	1992	280.00	350
1990	Christmas Dreams (Hassock)	63	1990	280.00	2000
1989	Last Gentle Nudge	4,000	1991	280.00	350-400
1989	Santa & His Magic Sleigh	4,000	1992	280.00	450
1992	Santa's Arrival	2,000	1994	300.00	350
1990	Santa's Reindeer	1,500	1993	400.00	400-450
1995	Show Me The Way	1,000		500.00	500
1990	Up On The Rooftop	4,000	1991	280.00	400
1994	Welcome to the World	2,000		400.00	400

Victorian Limited Edition - J. McKenna

YEAR ISSUE		EDITION LIMIT	YEAR RETD.	ISSUE PRICE	QUOTE U.S.$
1990	Edward - 3D	1,000	1991	180.00	450
1990	Elizabeth - 3D	1,000	1991	180.00	450
1990	Joseph - 3D	Closed	1991	50.00	50-250
1990	Victoria - 3D	Closed	1991	50.00	50-250

Kaiser

Animals - W. Gawantka, unless otherwise noted

YEAR ISSUE		EDITION LIMIT	YEAR RETD.	ISSUE PRICE	QUOTE U.S.$
1979	Bear & Cub-521, color bisque	900		400.00	1072
1979	Bear & Cub-521, white bisque	Closed		125.00	378
1980	Bison-630, color bisque - G. Tagliariol	2,000		620.00	1044
1980	Bison-690, white bisque - G. Tagliariol	2,000		350.00	488
1985	Brook Trout-739, color bisque	Open		250.00	488
1975	Dolphin Group (4)-508, white bisque	Closed		Unkn.	575
1978	Dolphin Group (4)-596/4, white bisque	4,500		75.00	956
1975	Dolphin Group (5)-520/5, white bisque	800		850.00	3002
1975	German Shepherd-528, color bisque	Closed		250.00	652
1975	German Shepherd-528, white bisque	Closed		185.00	420
1976	Irish Setter-535, color bisque	1,000		290.00	652
1976	Irish Setter-535, white/base	1,500		Unkn.	424
1978	Killer Whale-579, color/bisque	2,000		420.00	798
1978	Killer Whale-579, white/bisque	2,000		85.00	404
1978	Killer Whales (2)-594, color	2,000		925.00	2008
1978	Killer Whales (2)-594, white	2,000		425.00	1024
1991	Lion-701201, white bisque	1,500		650.00	650
1991	Lion-701203, color bisque	1,500		1300.00	1300
1985	Pike-737, color bisque	Open		350.00	682
1969	Porpoise Group (3)-478, white bisque	Closed		85.00	375
1985	Rainbow Trout-739, color bisque	Open		250.00	488
1985	Trout-739, color bisque	Open		95.00	488
1982	Two wild Boars-664, color bisque - H. Liederly	1,000		650.00	890

Birds of America Collection - W. Gawantka, unless otherwise noted

YEAR ISSUE		EDITION LIMIT	YEAR RETD.	ISSUE PRICE	QUOTE U.S.$
XX	Baby Titmice-501, color/base	Closed	N/A	400.00	500
19XX	Baby Titmice-501, white/base	1,200		200.00	754
1978	Baby Titmice-601, color/base - G. Tagliariol	2,000		Unkn.	956
1978	Baby Titmice-601, white/base - G. Tagliariol	2,000		Unkn.	562
1969	Bald Eagle I -464, color - U. Netzsch	Closed	N/A	Unkn.	650
1969	Bald Eagle I -464, white - U. Netzsch	Closed	N/A	Unkn.	250
1973	Bald Eagle II -497, color bisque - G. Tagliariol	Closed	N/A	Unkn.	1300
XX	Bald Eagle II-497, Colored - Kaiser	Closed	N/A	Unkn.	1300
1974	Bald Eagle III -513, color bisque	Closed	N/A	Unkn.	850
1974	Bald Eagle III -513,white bisque	Closed	N/A	Unkn.	378
1976	Bald Eagle IV-552, color/base	1,500		450.00	998
1976	Bald Eagle IV-552, white/base	1,500		210.00	572
1984	Bald Eagle IX-714, color/base	3,500		500.00	850
1984	Bald Eagle IX-714, white/base	4,000		190.00	374
1978	Bald Eagle V-600, color/base - G. Tagliariol	1,500		Unkn.	3848
1980	Bald Eagle VI-634, white/base	3,000		Unkn.	672
XX	Bald Eagle VII-637, color/base - G. Tagliariol	200		Unkn.	20694
1982	Bald Eagle VIII-656, color/base - G. Tagliariol	Closed	N/A	800.00	880
1982	Bald Eagle VIII-656, white/base - G. Tagliariol	1,000		400.00	904
1985	Bald Eagle X-746, color/base	1,500		Unkn.	1198
1985	Bald Eagle X-746, white/base	1,500		375.00	672
1985	Bald Eagle XI-751, color/base	1,000		880.00	1422
1985	Bald Eagle XI-751, white/base	1,000		Unkn.	902
1976	Baltimore Oriole-536, color/base - G. Tagliariol	1,000		280.00	746
1972	Blue Bird-496, color/base	2,500		120.00	480
1973	Blue Jay-503, color/base	1,500		475.00	1198
1976	Canadian Geese-550, white/base - G. Tagliariol	1,500		1500.00	3490
1973	Cardinal-504, color/base	1,500		60.00	600
1974	Falcon-507, color/base	1,500		820.00	1928
XX	Fighting Peacocks -337, color glaze - G. Bochman	Closed	N/A	Unkn.	340
1972	Goshawk-491, color/base	1,500		2400.00	4326
1972	Goshawk-491, white/base	1,500		850.00	1992
XX	Horned Owl II- 524, color/base - G. Tagliariol	1,000		650.00	2170
XX	Horned Owl II-524, white/base - G. Tagliariol	1,000		Unkn.	918
1982	Hummingbird Group-660, color/base - G. Tagliariol	3,000		650.00	1232
1981	Kingfisher-639, color/base - G. Tagliariol	Closed	N/A	45.00	60
1969	Owl -476, white bisque	Closed	N/A	Unkn.	180
1977	Owl IV-559, color/base - G. Tagliariol	1,000		Unkn.	1270
1969	Owl-476, color bisque	Closed	N/A	Unkn.	550
1978	Pair of Mallards II-572, color/base - G. Tagliariol	1,500		Unkn.	1156
1978	Pair of Mallards II-572, white/base - G. Tagliariol	1,500		Unkn.	2366
1968	Pair of Mallards-456, color/base - U. Netzsch	Closed	N/A	150.00	500
1968	Pair of Mallards-456, white/base - U. Netzsch	2,000		75.00	518
XX	Paradise Bird-318, white bisque - Kaiser	Closed	N/A	Unkn.	135
1976	Pelican-534, color/base - G. Tagliariol	1,200		925.00	1768
XX	Pelican-534, white/base - G. Tagliariol	Closed	N/A	Unkn.	625
1984	Peregrine Falcon-723, color/base - M. Tandy	1,500		850.00	4946
1976	Pheasant-556, color/base - G. Tagliariol	1,500		3200.00	6020
1984	Pheasant-715, color/base - G. Tagliariol	1,500		1000.00	1962
1968	Pidgeon Group-475, color/base - U. Netzsch	1,500		150.00	812
1968	Pidgeon Group-475, white/base - U. Netzsch	2,000		60.00	412
1985	Pintails-747, color/base - Kaiser	1,500		Unkn.	838
1985	Pintails-747, white/base - Kaiser	1,500		Unkn.	364
1981	Quails-640, color/base - G. Tagliariol	1,500		Unkn.	2366
1972	Roadrunner-492, color bisque	1,000		175.00	199
XX	Roadrunner-492, color/base - Kaiser	Closed	N/A	350.00	900
XX	Robin & Worm, color/base - Kaiser	Closed	N/A	60.00	90
XX	Robin II-537, color/base - Kaiser	1,000		260.00	888
1973	Robin-502, color/base	1,500		340.00	718
1981	Rooster-642, color/base - G. Tagliariol	1,500		860.00	1304
1981	Rooster-642, white/base - G. Tagliariol	1,500		380.00	688
1970	Scarlet Tanager, color/base - Kaiser	Closed	N/A	60.00	90
1976	Screech Owl-532, color bisque	Closed	N/A	Unkn.	175
1976	Screech Owl-532, white/base	Closed	N/A	175.00	199
1973	Seagull-498, color bisque	Closed	N/A	Unkn.	1150
1972	Seagull-498, color/base	Closed	N/A	850.00	1150
1972	Seagull-498, white/base	700		550.00	1586
XX	Snowy Owl -776, color/base - Kaiser	1,500		Unkn.	1146
XX	Snowy Owl -776, white/base - Kaiser	1,500		Unkn.	668
XX	Sparrow Hawk-749, color/base - Kaiser	3,000		575.00	906
1986	Sparrow Hawk-777, colored bisque - M. Tandy	10,000		950.00	1336
1986	Sparrow Hawk-777, white bisque - M. Tandy	1,000		440.00	716
1975	Sparrow-516, color/base - G. Tagliariol	1,500		300.00	596
1979	Swan-602, color/base - G. Tagliariol	2,000		Unkn.	1370
XX	Wild Ducks-456, color bisque - Kaiser	Closed	N/A	Unkn.	500
1968	Wild Ducks-456, white bisque - Kaiser	2,000		Unkn.	175
1975	Wood Ducks-514, color/base - G. Tagliariol	800		Unkn.	2804
1975	Woodpeckers-515, color/base - G. Tagliariol	800		900.00	1762

Horse Sculpture - W. Gawantka

YEAR ISSUE		EDITION LIMIT	YEAR RETD.	ISSUE PRICE	QUOTE U.S.$
1969	Arabian Stallion-Comet, color/bisque	Closed	N/A	Unkn.	850
1990	Argos-633101/wht. bisq./base	1,000		578.00	672
1990	Argos-633103/lt. color/base	1,000		1194.00	1388
1990	Argos-633143/color/base	1,000		1194.00	1388
1978	Capitano/Lipizzaner- 597, color	1,500		625.00	1496
1978	Capitano/Lipizzaner- 597, white	Closed	N/A	275.00	574
1976	Hassan/Arabian-553, color/base	1,500		600.00	1100-1200
1976	Hassan/Arabian-553, white/base	Closed	N/A	250.00	600
1975	Lipizzaner/Maestoso-517/color bisque	Closed	N/A	Unkn.	1150
1975	Lipizzaner/Maestoso-517white bisque	Closed	N/A	Unkn.	750
1975	Mare & Foal II-510, color/base	Closed	N/A	650.00	775
1975	Mare & Foal II-510, white/bisque	Closed	N/A	Unkn.	775
1980	Mare & Foal III-636, color/base	1,500		950.00	1632
1980	Mare & Foal III-636, white/base	1,500		300.00	646
1980	Orion/Arabian-629, color/base	2,000		600.00	1038
1980	Orion/Arabian-629, white/base	2,000		250.00	442
1987	Pacer-792, color/base	1,500		1217.00	1350
1987	Pacer-792, white/base	1,500		574.00	652
1971	Pony Group-488, color bisque	Closed	N/A	Unkn.	350
1971	Pony Group-488, color/base	Closed	N/A	Unkn.	350
1971	Pony Group-488, white/base	2,500		50.00	418
1987	Trotter-780, color/base	1,500		1217.00	1350
1987	Trotter-780, white/base	1,500		574.00	652

Human Figures - W. Gawantka, unless otherwise noted

YEAR ISSUE		EDITION LIMIT	YEAR RETD.	ISSUE PRICE	QUOTE U.S.$
XX	Father & Daughter-752, color - Kaiser	2,500		390.00	710
XX	Father & Daughter-752, white - Kaiser	2,500		175.00	362
1982	Father & Son-659, color/base	2,500		400.00	712
1982	Father & Son-659, white/base	2,500		100.00	384
1982	Ice Princess-667, color	5,000		375.00	732
1982	Ice Princess-667, white	5,000		200.00	416
1960	Mother & Child-398, white bisque - G. Bochmann	Open		Unkn.	312
XX	Mother & Child-757, color - Kaiser	3,500		600.00	864
XX	Mother & Child-757, white - Kaiser	4,000		300.00	430
XX	Mother & Child-775, color - Kaiser	3,500		600.00	864
XX	Mother & Child-775, white - Kaiser	4,000		300.00	430
1983	Mother & Child/bust-696, color	3,500		500.00	1066
1983	Mother & Child/bust-696, white	4,000		225.00	428
1982	Swan Lake Ballet-641, color	2,500		650.00	1276
1982	Swan Lake Ballet-641, white	2,500		200.00	974

Kurt S. Adler, Inc.

Christmas Legends - P.F. Bolinger

YEAR ISSUE		EDITION LIMIT	YEAR RETD.	ISSUE PRICE	QUOTE U.S.$
1994	Aldwyn of the Greenwood J8196	Open		145.00	145
1994	Berwyn the Grand J8198	Open		175.00	175
1995	Bountiful J8234	Open		164.00	164
1994	Caradoc the Kind J8199	Open		70.00	70
1994	Florian of the Berry Bush J8199	Open		70.00	70
1994	Gustave the Gutsy J8199	Open		70.00	70
1995	Luminatus J8241	Open		136.00	136
1994	Silvanus the Cheerful J8197	Open		165.00	165

The Fabriché™ Bear & Friends Series - KSA Design Team

YEAR ISSUE		EDITION LIMIT	YEAR RETD.	ISSUE PRICE	QUOTE U.S.$
1992	Laughing All The Way J1567	Retrd.	1994	83.00	83
1992	Not A Creature Was Stirring W1534	Open		67.00	67
1993	Teddy Bear Parade W1601	Open		73.00	73

Fabriché™ Angel Series - K.S. Adler

YEAR ISSUE		EDITION LIMIT	YEAR RETD.	ISSUE PRICE	QUOTE U.S.$
1992	Heavenly Messenger W1584	Retrd.	1994	41.00	41

Fabriché™ Camelot Figure Series - P. Mauk

YEAR ISSUE		EDITION LIMIT	YEAR RETD.	ISSUE PRICE	QUOTE U.S.$
1994	King Arthur J3372	7,500		110.00	110
1993	Merlin the Magician J7966	7,500		120.00	120
1993	Young Arthur J7967	7,500		120.00	120

Fabriché™ Holiday Figurines - KSA Design Team, unless otherwise noted

YEAR ISSUE		EDITION LIMIT	YEAR RETD.	ISSUE PRICE	QUOTE U.S.$
1995	All Aboard For Christmas W1679	Open		56.00	56
1994	All Star Santa W1652	Open		56.00	56
1993	All That Jazz W1620	Retrd.	1994	67.00	67
1992	An Apron Full of Love W1582 - M. Rothenberg	Open		75.00	75
1995	Armchair Quarterback W1693	Open		90.00	90
1994	Basket of Goodies W1650	Open		60.00	60
1992	Bringin in the Yule Log W1589 - M. Rothenberg	5,000		200.00	200
1993	Bringing the Gifts W1605	Open		60.00	60
1992	Bundles of Joy W1578	Retrd.	1994	78.00	78
1995	Captain Claus W1680	Open		56.00	56
1994	Checking His List W1643	Open		60.00	60
1993	Checking It Twice W1604	Open		56.00	56
1992	Christmas is in the Air W1590	Retrd.	1995	110.00	125

Year Issue		Edition Limit	Year Retd.	Issue Price	Quote U.S.$
1995	Diet Starts Tomorrow W1691	Open		60.00	60
1995	Father Christmas W1687	Open		56.00	56
1994	Firefighting Friends W1654	Open		72.00	72
1993	Forever Green W1607	Retrd.	1994	56.00	56
1994	Friendship W1642	Open		65.00	65
1995	Gift From Heaven W1694	Open		60.00	60
1992	He Did It Again J7944 - T. Rubel	Open		160.00	160
1993	Here Kitty W1618 - M. Rothenberg	Retrd.	1994	90.00	125
1994	Ho, Ho, Ho Santa W1632	Open		56.00	56
1994	Holiday Express W1636	Open		100.00	100
1992	Homeward Bound W1568	Open		61.00	65
1992	Hugs and Kisses W1531	Retrd.	1994	67.00	67
1992	I'm Late, I'm Late J7947 - T. Rubel	Retrd.	1995	100.00	100
1992	It's Time To Go J7943 - T. Rubel	Retrd.	1994	150.00	150
1995	Kris Kringle W1685	Open		55.00	55
1994	Mail Must Go Through W1667 - KSA/WRG	Open		110.00	110
1992	Merry Kissmas W1548 - M. Rothenberg	Retrd.	1993	140.00	140
1995	Merry Memories W1735	Open		56.00	56
1994	Merry St. Nick W1641 - Giordano	Open		100.00	100
1995	Mrs. Santa Caroller W1690 - M. Rothenberg	Open		70.00	70
1995	Night Before Christmas W1692 - Wood River Gallery	Open		60.00	60
1994	Officer Claus W1677	Open		56.00	56
1993	Par For The Claus W1603	Open		60.00	60
1994	Peace Santa W1631	Open		60.00	60
1995	Pere Noel W1686	Open		55.00	55
1993	Playtime For Santa W1619	Retrd.	1994	67.00	67
1994	Santa Calls W1678 - W. Joyce	Open		55.00	55
1995	Santa Caroller W1689 - M. Rothenberg	Open		70.00	70
1991	Santa Fiddler W1549 - M. Rothenberg	Retrd.	1992	100.00	100
1992	Santa Steals A Kiss & A Cookie W1581 - M. Rothenberg	Retrd.	1994	150.00	175
1992	Santa's Cat Nap W1504 - M. Rothenberg	Retrd.	1992	98.00	110
1994	Santa's Fishtales W1640	Open		60.00	60
1992	Santa's Ice Capades W1588 - M. Rothenberg	Retrd.	1995	110.00	110
1994	Schussing Claus W1651	Open		78.00	78
1992	St. Nicholas The Bishop W1532	Open		78.00	78
1994	Star Gazing Santa W1656 - M. Rothenberg	Open		120.00	120
1993	Stocking Stuffer W1622	Retrd.	1994	56.00	56
1995	Strike Up The Band W1681	Open		55.00	55
1995	Tee Time W1734	Open		60.00	60
1993	Top Brass W1630	Retrd.	1995	67.00	67
1993	With All The Trimmings W1616	Open		76.00	76
1995	Woodland Santa W1731 - R. Volpi	Open		67.00	67

Fabriché™ Santa at Home Series - M. Rothenberg

Year Issue		Edition Limit	Year Retd.	Issue Price	Quote U.S.$
1995	Baby Burping Santa W1732	Open		80.00	80
1994	The Christmas Waltz 1635	Open		135.00	135
1995	Family Portrait W1727	Open		140.00	140
1993	Grandpa Santa's Piggyback Ride W1621	7,500		84.00	84
1995	Santa's Horsey Ride W1728	Open		80.00	80
1994	Santa's New Friend W1655	Open		110.00	110

Fabriché™ Santa's Helpers Series - M. Rothenberg

Year Issue		Edition Limit	Year Retd.	Issue Price	Quote U.S.$
1993	Little Olde Clockmaker W1629	5,000		134.00	134
1992	A Stitch in Time W1591	5,000		135.00	135

Fabriché™ Smithsonian Museum Series - KSA/Smithsonian

Year Issue		Edition Limit	Year Retd.	Issue Price	Quote U.S.$
1992	Holiday Drive W1556	Retrd.	1995	155.00	155
1993	Holiday Flight W1617	Retrd.	1995	144.00	144
1992	Peace on Earth Angel Treetop W1583	Retrd.	1995	52.00	52
1992	Peace on Earth Flying Angel W1585	Retrd.	1995	49.00	49
1991	Santa On A Bicycle W1527	Retrd.	1994	150.00	150
1995	Toys For Good Boys and Girls W1696	Open		75.00	75

Fabriché™ Thomas Nast Figurines - KSA Design Team

Year Issue		Edition Limit	Year Retd.	Issue Price	Quote U.S.$
1992	Caught in the Act W1577	Retrd.	1993	133.00	133
1992	Christmas Sing-A-Long W1576	12,000		110.00	110
1993	Dear Santa W1602	Retrd.	1993	110.00	110
1991	Hello! Little One W1552	12,000	1994	90.00	90

Gallery of Angels - KSA Design Team

Year Issue		Edition Limit	Year Retd.	Issue Price	Quote U.S.$
1994	Guardian Angel M1099	2,000		150.00	150
1994	Unspoken Word M1100	2,000		150.00	150

Ho Ho Ho Gang - P.F. Bolinger

Year Issue		Edition Limit	Year Retd.	Issue Price	Quote U.S.$
1994	Christmas Goose J8201	Open		25.00	25
1995	Cookie Claus J8286	Open		40.00	40
1995	Do Not Disturb J8233	Open		56.00	56
1994	Holy Mackerel J8202	Open		25.00	25
1995	No Hair Day J8287	Open		50.00	50
1995	North Pole (large) J8237	Open		60.00	60
1995	North Pole (small) J8238	Open		48.00	48
1994	Santa Cob J8203	Open		28.00	28
1994	Surprise J8201	Open		25.00	25
1994	Will He Make It? J8203	Open		28.00	28
1995	Will Work For Cookies J8235	Open		40.00	40
1995	Wishful Thinking J8239	Open		39.00	39

Jim Henson's Muppet Nutcrackers - KSA/JHP

Year Issue		Edition Limit	Year Retd.	Issue Price	Quote U.S.$
1993	Kermit The Frog H1223	Retrd.	1995	90.00	90

Mickey Unlimited - KSA/Disney

Year Issue		Edition Limit	Year Retd.	Issue Price	Quote U.S.$
1994	Donald Duck Drummer W1671	Open		45.00	45
1993	Donald Duck H1235	Open		90.00	90
1992	Goofy H1216	Open		78.00	78
1994	Mickey Bandleader W1669	Open		45.00	45
1992	Mickey Mouse Soldier H1194	Open		72.00	72
1992	Mickey Mouse Sorcerer H1221	Open		100.00	100
1993	Mickey Mouse With Gift Boxes W1608	Open		78.00	78
1994	Mickey Santa Nutcracker H1237	Open		90.00	90
1994	Minnie Mouse Soldier Nutcrackers H1236	Open		90.00	90
1994	Minnie With Cymbals W1670	Open		45.00	45
1993	Pinnochio H1222	Open		110.00	110

Old World Santa Series - J. Mostrom

Year Issue		Edition Limit	Year Retd.	Issue Price	Quote U.S.$
1992	Chelsea Garden Santa W2721	Retrd.	1994	33.50	34
1993	Good King Wenceslas W2928	3,000		134.00	134
1992	Large Black Forest Santa W2717	Retrd.	1994	110.00	110
1992	Large Father Christmas W2719	Retrd.	1994	106.00	106
1993	Medieval King of Christmas W2881	3,000	1994	390.00	390
1992	Mrs. Claus W2714	5,000		37.00	37
1992	Patriotic Santa W2720	3,000	1994	128.00	128
1992	Pere Noel W2723	Retrd.	1994	33.50	34
1992	Small Black Forest Santa W2712	Retrd.	1994	40.00	40
1992	Small Father Christmas W2712	Retrd.	1994	33.50	34
1992	Small Father Frost W2716	Retrd.	1994	43.00	43
1992	Small Grandfather Frost W2718	Retrd.	1994	106.00	106
1992	St. Nicholas W2713	Retrd.	1994	30.00	30
1992	Workshop Santa W2715	5,000		43.00	43

Sesame Street Series - KSA/JHP

Year Issue		Edition Limit	Year Retd.	Issue Price	Quote U.S.$
1993	Big Bird Fabrich, Figurine J7928	Open		60.00	60
1993	Big Bird Nutcracker H1199	Retrd.	1994	60.00	60

Steinbach Camelot Smoking Figure Series - KSA/Steinbach

Year Issue		Edition Limit	Year Retd.	Issue Price	Quote U.S.$
1993	King Arthur ES832	7,500		175.00	175
1992	Merlin The Magician ES830	7,500		150.00	150

Steinbach Nutcracker Collectors' Club - KSA/Steinbach

Year Issue		Edition Limit	Year Retd.	Issue Price	Quote U.S.$
1995	King Wenceslaus	12/96		225.00	225
1995	The Town Crier	12/96		Gift	N/A

Steinbach Nutcracker American Presidents Series - KSA/Steinbach

Year Issue		Edition Limit	Year Retd.	Issue Price	Quote U.S.$
1992	Abraham Lincoln ES622	12,000		195.00	225
1993	Ben Franklin ES622	12,000		225.00	225
1992	George Washington ES623	12,000	1994	195.00	500
1993	Teddy Roosevelt ES644	10,000		225.00	225

Steinbach Nutcracker Camelot Series - KSA/Steinbach

Year Issue		Edition Limit	Year Retd.	Issue Price	Quote U.S.$
1992	King Arthur ES621	Retrd.	1993	195.00	1500
1991	Merlin The Magician ES610	Retrd.	1991	185.00	1300-1800
1995	Queen Guenevere ES869	10,000		245.00	245
1994	Sir Galahad ES862	12,000		225.00	225
1993	Sir Lancelot ES638	12,000		225.00	225
1994	Sir Lancelot Smoker ES833	7,500		150.00	150

Steinbach Nutcracker Christmas Legends Series - KSA/Steinbach

Year Issue		Edition Limit	Year Retd.	Issue Price	Quote U.S.$
1995	1930s Santa Claus ES891	7,500		245.00	245
1993	Father Christmas ES645	7,500		225.00	225
1994	St. Nicholas, The Bishop ES865	7,500		225.00	225

Steinbach Nutcracker Collection - KSA/Steinbach

Year Issue		Edition Limit	Year Retd.	Issue Price	Quote U.S.$
1991	Columbus ES697	Retrd.	1992	194.00	225
1992	Happy Santa ES601	Open		190.00	220
1984	Oil Sheik	Retrd.	1985	100.00	500

Steinbach Nutcracker Famous Chieftans Series - KSA/Steinbach

Year Issue		Edition Limit	Year Retd.	Issue Price	Quote U.S.$
1995	Black Hawk ES889	7,500		245.00	245
1993	Chief Sitting Bull ES637	8,500		225.00	225
1994	Chief Sitting Bull Smoker ES834	7,500		150.00	150
1994	Red Cloud ES864	8,500		225.00	225

Steinbach Nutcracker Tales of Sherwood Forest - KSA/Steinbach

Year Issue		Edition Limit	Year Retd.	Issue Price	Quote U.S.$
1995	Friar Tuck ES890	7,500		245.00	245
1992	Robin Hood ES863	7,500		225.00	225

Visions Of Santa Series - KSA Design Team

Year Issue		Edition Limit	Year Retd.	Issue Price	Quote U.S.$
1992	Santa Coming Out Of Fireplace J1023	Retrd.	1993	29.00	29
1992	Santa Holding Child J826	Retrd.	1993	24.50	25
1992	Santa Spilling Bag Of Toys J1022	7,500	1994	25.50	26
1992	Santa With Little Girls On Lap J1024	7,500		24.50	25
1992	Santa With Sack Holding Toy J827	7,500	1994	24.50	25
1992	Workshop Santa J825	7,500	1994	27.00	27

Zuber Nutcracker Series - KSA/Zuber

Year Issue		Edition Limit	Year Retd.	Issue Price	Quote U.S.$
1992	The Annapolis Midshipman EK7	5,000	1994	125.00	125
1992	The Bavarian EK16	5,000	1994	130.00	130
1992	Bronco Billy The Cowboy EK1	5,000	1994	125.00	125
1992	The Chimney Sweep EK6	5,000	1993	125.00	125
1992	The Country Singer EK19	5,000	1993	125.00	125
1992	The Fisherman EK17	5,000		125.00	125
1994	The Gardner EK26	2,500		150.00	150
1992	Gepetto, The Toymaker EK9	5,000	1994	125.00	125
1992	The Gold Prospector EK18	5,000	1994	125.00	125
1992	The Golfer EK5	5,000	1994	125.00	125
1993	Herr Drosselmeir Nutcracker EK21	5,000	1995	150.00	300-450
1993	The Ice Cream Vendor EK24	5,000		150.00	150
1992	The Indian EK15	5,000	1994	135.00	135
1994	Jazz Player EK25	2,500		145.00	145
1994	Kurt the Traveling Salesman EK28	2,500	1994	155.00	155
1994	Mouse King EK31	2,500		150.00	150
1993	Napoleon Bonaparte EK23	5,000	1994	150.00	150
1992	The Nor' Easter Sea Captain EK3	5,000		125.00	125
1992	Paul Bunyan The Lumberjack EK2	5,000	1993	125.00	125
1994	Peter Pan EK28	2,500		145.00	145
1992	The Pilgrim EK14	5,000	1994	125.00	125
1993	The Pizzamaker EK22	5,000		150.00	150
1994	Scuba Diver EK27	2,500		150.00	150
1994	Soccer Player EK30	2,500		145.00	145
1992	TheTyrolean EK4	5,000	1994	125.00	125
1992	The West Point Cadet With Canon EK8	5,000	1994	130.00	130

Lalique Society of America

Lalique Society Annual Series - Various

Year Issue		Edition Limit	Year Retd.	Issue Price	Quote U.S.$
1989	Degas Box 10585 - R. Lalique	Yr.Iss.		295.00	725
1990	Hestia Medallion 61051 - M.C. Lalique	Yr.Iss.		295.00	700
1991	Lily of Valley (perfume bottle) 61053 - R. Lalique	Yr.Iss.		275.00	450
1992	La Patineuse (paperweight) 61054 - M.C. Lalique	Yr.Iss.		325.00	375
1993	Enchantment (figurine) 61055 - M.C. Lalique	Yr.Iss.		395.00	395
1994	Eclipse (perfume bottle) - M.C. Lalique	Yr.Iss.		395.00	395

Lance Corporation

Chilmark MetalART™ The Great Chiefs - J. Slockbower

Year Issue		Edition Limit	Year Retd.	Issue Price	Quote U.S.$
1992	Chief Joseph	750	1992	975.00	15-1900
1993	Crazy Horse	750		975.00	975
1992	Geronimo	750	1992	975.00	975
1993	Sitting Bull	750		1075.00	1075

Chilmark MetalART™ Mickey & Co. On the Road - Staff

Year Issue		Edition Limit	Year Retd.	Issue Price	Quote U.S.$
1994	Beach Bound	350	1994	350.00	650-1100
1992	Cruising	350	1992	275.00	1325-2000
1993	Sunday Drive	350	1993	325.00	900-1500
1993	Mixed & Matched Numbrd. set/3	350	1993	950.00	3000-7000

Chilmark MetalART™ The Seekers - A. McGrory

Year Issue		Edition Limit	Year Retd.	Issue Price	Quote U.S.$
1993	Bear Vision	500		1375.00	1375
1992	Buffalo Vision	500	1993	1075.00	1075
1993	Eagle Vision	500		1250.00	1250

Chilmark MetalART™ To The Great Spirit - T. Sullivan

Year Issue		Edition Limit	Year Retd.	Issue Price	Quote U.S.$
1993	Gray Elk	950		775.00	775
1992	Shooting Star	950	1994	775.00	775
1994	Thunder Cloud	950		775.00	775
1993	Two Eagles	950		775.00	775

Chilmark Pewter American West - D. Polland, unless otherwise noted

Year Issue		Edition Limit	Year Retd.	Issue Price	Quote U.S.$
1981	Ambushed	294	1991	2370.00	2700
1985	Bear Meet - S. York	Retrd.	1992	500.00	600-800
1982	Blood Brothers - M. Boyett	717	1991	250.00	610-995
1979	Border Rustlers	500	1989	1295.00	1500
1983	Bounty Hunter	264	1987	250.00	300-600
1976	Buffalo Hunt	2,250	1980	300.00	1625
1982	Buffalo Prayer	2,500	1989	95.00	225-400
1990	Buffalo Spirit	2,500	1993	110.00	185
1979	Cavalry Officer - D. LaRocca	500	1985	125.00	400-650
1974	Cheyenne	2,800	1980	200.00	2700-3000
1976	Cold Saddles, Mean Horses	2,800	1986	200.00	800
1974	Counting Coup	2,800	1980	225.00	1600-2000
1979	Cowboy - D. LaRocca	950	1984	125.00	500-750
1974	Crow Scout	3,000	1983	250.00	1000-1700
1978	Dangerous Encounter - B. Rodden	746	1977	475.00	600-950
1990	Eagle Dancer (deNatura)	614	1993	300.00	300
1981	Enemy Tracks	2,500	1988	225.00	700-725
1984	Flat Out for Red River Station - M. Boyett	2,500	1991	3000.00	45-7200
1979	Getting Acquainted	950	1988	215.00	800-1100
1985	Horse of A Different Color - S. York	Retrd.	1992	500.00	600-800
1979	Indian Warrior - D. LaRocca	1,186	1988	95.00	400
1982	Jemez Eagle Dancer	2,500	1989	95.00	250-450
1991	Kiowa Princess (deNatura)	444	1993	300.00	300
1982	Last Arrow	2,500	1988	95.00	300-400
1983	Line Rider	2,500	1988	195.00	975
1979	Mandan Hunter	5,000	1985	65.00	780-900
1975	Maverick Calf	2,500	1981	250.00	1300-1700

YEAR ISSUE		EDITION LIMIT	YEAR RETD.	ISSUE PRICE	QUOTE U.S.$
1976	Monday Morning Wash	2,500	1986	200.00	1000
1979	Mountain Man - D. LaRocca	764	1988	95.00	500-650
1983	Now or Never	693	1991	265.00	800
1975	The Outlaws	2,500	1989	450.00	900-1180
1976	Painting the Town	2,250	1983	300.00	1500-1700
1990	Pequot Wars	950	1990	395.00	450-800
1981	Plight of the Huntsman - M. Boyett	950	1987	495.00	850
1985	Postal Exchange - S. York	Retrd.	1992	300.00	400-600
1990	Red River Wars	950	1990	425.00	700-850
1976	Rescue	2,500	1980	275.00	1150
1979	Running Battle - B. Rodden	761	1987	400.00	750-900
1990	Running Wolf (deNatura)	720	1993	350.00	350
1982	Sioux War Chief	2,500	1989	95.00	240-480
1990	Tecumseh's Rebellion	950	1990	350.00	700
1983	Too Many Aces	1,717	1993	400.00	495
1981	U.S. Marshal	1,500	1986	95.00	450
1981	War Party	1,066	1991	550.00	975-1150
1981	When War Chiefs Meet	2,500	1988	300.00	800
1983	The Wild Bunch	285	1987	200.00	225-400
1982	Yakima Salmon Fisherman	2,500	1987	200.00	700
1991	Yellow Boy (deNatura)	460	1993	350.00	350

Chilmark Pewter American West Christmas Special - D. Polland

YEAR ISSUE		EDITION LIMIT	YEAR RETD.	ISSUE PRICE	QUOTE U.S.$
1991	Merry Christmas Neighbor	1,240	1991	395.00	600
1992	Merry Christmas My Love	819	1992	350.00	350-450
1993	Almost Home	520	1994	375.00	375
1994	Cowboy Christmas	427	1994	250.00	250

Chilmark Pewter American West Event Specials - D. Polland

YEAR ISSUE		EDITION LIMIT	YEAR RETD.	ISSUE PRICE	QUOTE U.S.$
1991	Uneasy Truce	737	1991	125.00	175-195
1992	Irons In The Fire	612	1992	125.00	125
1994	Bacon 'N' Beans Again?	458	1994	150.00	150
1995	Renegade Apache	Annual		150.00	150

Chilmark Pewter American West Redemption Specials - D. Polland, unless otherwise noted

YEAR ISSUE		EDITION LIMIT	YEAR RETD.	ISSUE PRICE	QUOTE U.S.$
1983	The Chief	2,459	1984	275.00	1400-2000
1984	Unit Colors	1,394	1985	250.00	1200-1700
1985	Oh Great Spirit	3,180	1986	300.00	1000-1300
1986	Eagle Catcher - M. Boyett	1,840	1987	300.00	850-1200
1987	Surprise Encounter - F. Barnum	1,534	1988	250.00	600-800
1988	I Will Fight No More Forever (Chief Joseph)	3,404	1989	350.00	850
1989	Geronimo	1,866	1990	375.00	650-750
1990	Cochise	1,778	1991	400.00	500-600
1991	Crazy Horse	2,067	1992	295.00	600-700
1992	Strong Hearts to the Front	1,252	1993	425.00	600
1993	Sacred Ground Reclaimed	861	1994	495.00	550-650
1994	Horse Breaking	504	1995	395.00	395
1995	The Rainmaker - M. Boyett	Yr.Iss.		350.00	350

Chilmark Pewter Civil War - F. Barnum

YEAR ISSUE		EDITION LIMIT	YEAR RETD.	ISSUE PRICE	QUOTE U.S.$
1993	Abraham Lincoln Bust (Bronze)	50	1993	2000.00	2250
1988	A Father's Farewell	2,500	1994	150.00	275
1988	Johnny Shiloh	2,500	1992	100.00	220
1992	Kennesaw Mountain	350	1992	650.00	1500
1992	Parson's Battery	500	1993	495.00	500-575
1987	Saving The Colors	Retrd.	1992	350.00	600-700

Chilmark Pewter Civil War Christmas Specials - F. Barnum

YEAR ISSUE		EDITION LIMIT	YEAR RETD.	ISSUE PRICE	QUOTE U.S.$
1992	Merry Christmas Yank	810	1992	350.00	500
1993	Silent Night	591	1993	350.00	475
1994	Christmas Truce	Retrd.	1994	295.00	295
1995	Peace on Earth	Annual		350.00	350

Chilmark Pewter Civil War Event Specials - F. Barnum

YEAR ISSUE		EDITION LIMIT	YEAR RETD.	ISSUE PRICE	QUOTE U.S.$
1991	Boots and Saddles	437	1991	95.00	200
1992	140th NY Zouave	389	1992	95.00	150
1993	Johnny Reb	889	1993	95.00	125
1994	Billy Yank	Retrd.	1994	95.00	95
1995	Seaman, CSS Alabama	Retrd.	1995	95.00	95

Chilmark Pewter Civil War Redemption Specials - F. Barnum

YEAR ISSUE		EDITION LIMIT	YEAR RETD.	ISSUE PRICE	QUOTE U.S.$
1989	Lee To The Rear	1,088	1990	300.00	800-900
1990	Lee And Jackson	1,040	1991	375.00	525
1991	Stonewall Jackson	1,169	1992	295.00	500
1992	Zouaves 1st Manassas	640	1993	375.00	500
1993	Letter to Sarah	Retrd.	1994	395.00	395
1994	Angel of Fredericksburg	Retrd.	1995	275.00	275
1995	Rebel Yell	Yr.Iss.		N/A	N/A

Chilmark Pewter Eagles - Various

YEAR ISSUE		EDITION LIMIT	YEAR RETD.	ISSUE PRICE	QUOTE U.S.$
1991	Cry of Freedom - S. Knight	Suspd.	1993	395.00	395
1981	Freedom Eagle - G. deLodzia	2,500	1983	195.00	750-900
1989	High and Mighty - A. McGrory	Suspd.	1993	185.00	200
1987	Winged Victory - J. Mullican	Suspd.	1993	275.00	315
1982	Wings of Liberty - M. Boyett	950	1986	625.00	1200

Chilmark Pewter Horses - Various

YEAR ISSUE		EDITION LIMIT	YEAR RETD.	ISSUE PRICE	QUOTE U.S.$
1980	Affirmed - M. Jovine	145	1987	850.00	1275
1980	Born Free - B. Rodden	950	1988	250.00	675
1977	The Challenge - B. Rodden	1,600	1977	175.00	250-300
1981	Clydesdale Wheel Horse - C. Keim	2,808	1989	120.00	430
1978	Paddock Walk - A. Petitto	1,277	1991	85.00	215
1977	Rise and Shine - B. Rodden	1,500	1977	135.00	200
1976	Running Free - B. Rodden	2,500	1977	75.00	300
1976	Stallion - B. Rodden	2,500	1977	75.00	260
1982	Tender Persuasion - J. Mootry	155	1987	950.00	1250
1985	Wild Stallion - D. Polland	179	1988	145.00	350

Chilmark Pewter Legacy of Courage - M. Boyett

YEAR ISSUE		EDITION LIMIT	YEAR RETD.	ISSUE PRICE	QUOTE U.S.$
1983	Along the Cherokee Trace	624	1991	295.00	720
1981	Apache Signals	765	1987	175.00	550-575
1982	Arapaho Sentinel	678	1991	195.00	500
1981	Blackfoot Snow Hunter	984	1988	175.00	650
1981	Buffalo Stalker	1,034	1991	175.00	560
1983	Circling the Enemy	Retrd.	1992	295.00	395
1981	Comanche	1,553	1991	175.00	530-670
1982	Dance of the Eagles	Retrd.	1992	150.00	215
1983	Forest Watcher	658	1991	215.00	540
1981	Iroquois Warfare	1,477	1991	125.00	600
1982	Kiowa Scout	292	1987	195.00	525
1982	Listening For Hooves	883	1991	150.00	400
1982	Mandan Buffalo Dancer	1,494	1991	195.00	450-600
1983	Moment of Truth	1,145	1991	295.00	550-620
1982	Plains Talk-Pawnee	421	1987	195.00	625
1983	Rite of the Whitetail	Retrd.	1992	295.00	400
1982	Shoshone Eagle Catcher	2,500	1985	225.00	16-2000
1982	The Tracker Nez Perce	686	1988	150.00	575
1981	Unconquered Seminole	1,021	1991	175.00	540
1981	Victor Cheyenne	1,299	1991	175.00	500
1983	A Warrior's Tribute	Retrd.	1992	335.00	635
1983	Winter Hunt	756	1991	295.00	400

Chilmark Pewter Masters of the American West - Various

YEAR ISSUE		EDITION LIMIT	YEAR RETD.	ISSUE PRICE	QUOTE U.S.$
1985	Bronco Buster (Large) - C. Rousell	766	1989	400.00	400
1986	Buffalo Hunt - A. McGrory	172	1989	550.00	800
1984	Cheyenne (Remington) - C. Rousell	285	1988	400.00	600
1988	End of the Trail (Mini) - A. McGrory	2,500	1992	225.00	325

Chilmark Pewter Mickey & Co. - Staff

YEAR ISSUE		EDITION LIMIT	YEAR RETD.	ISSUE PRICE	QUOTE U.S.$
1989	"Gold Edition" Hollywood Mickey	Retrd.	1990	200.00	750
1989	Hollywood Mickey	Suspd.	1991	165.00	200-300
1994	Lights, Camera, Action (Bronze)	50		3250.00	3250
1994	Lights, Camera, Action (Pewter)	500		1500.00	1500
1994	Mickey on Parade (Bronze)	50	1994	950.00	950-1450
1994	Mickey on Parade (MetalART))	350	1994	500.00	500-950
1994	Mickey on Parade (Pewter)	750		375.00	375
1991	Mickey's Carousel Ride	2,500		150.00	160
1992	Minnie's Carousel Ride	2,500		150.00	160
1994	Mouse in a Million (Bronze)	50	1994	1250.00	1400-2000
1994	Mouse in a Million (MetalART))	250	1994	650.00	700-1200
1994	Mouse in a Million (Pewter)	500	1994	500.00	500-900
1994	Puttin' on the Ritz (Bronze)	50	1994	2000.00	2100-2400
1994	Puttin' on the Ritz (MetalART))	250		1000.00	1000
1994	Puttin' on the Ritz (Pewter)	350		750.00	750

Chilmark Pewter Mickey & Co. Annual Christmas Special - Staff

YEAR ISSUE		EDITION LIMIT	YEAR RETD.	ISSUE PRICE	QUOTE U.S.$
1993	Hanging the Stockings	Annual	1993	295.00	330-500
1994	Trimming the Tree	Annual	1994	350.00	350
1995	Holiday Harmony?	Annual		395.00	395

Chilmark Pewter Mickey & Co. Annual Santa - Staff

YEAR ISSUE		EDITION LIMIT	YEAR RETD.	ISSUE PRICE	QUOTE U.S.$
1993	Checking it Twice	Annual	1993	195.00	250-450
1994	Just For You	Annual	1994	265.00	350-450
1995	Surprise, Santa!	Annual		225.00	225

Chilmark Pewter Mickey & Co. Annual Special - Staff

YEAR ISSUE		EDITION LIMIT	YEAR RETD.	ISSUE PRICE	QUOTE U.S.$
1994	Bicycle Built For Two	Retrd.	1994	195.00	200-250
1995	Riding the Rails	Yr.Iss.		295.00	295

Chilmark Pewter Mickey & Co. Comic Capers - Staff

YEAR ISSUE		EDITION LIMIT	YEAR RETD.	ISSUE PRICE	QUOTE U.S.$
1995	Crack the Whip (Bronze)	50		2000.00	2000
1995	Crack the Whip (Pewter)	500		750.00	750
1994	Foursome Follies (Bronze)	50	1994	2000.00	2000
1994	Foursome Follies (Pewter)	500	1994	750.00	800-1500

Chilmark Pewter Mickey & Co. Generations of Mickey - Staff

YEAR ISSUE		EDITION LIMIT	YEAR RETD.	ISSUE PRICE	QUOTE U.S.$
1987	Antique Mickey	2,500	1990	95.00	475-900
1990	The Band Concert	2,500		185.00	195
1990	The Band Concert (Painted)	500	1993	215.00	400
1990	Disneyland Mickey	2,500		150.00	160
1989	Mickey's Gala Premiere	2,500		150.00	160
1991	The Mouse-1935	1,200		185.00	195
1991	Plane Crazy-1928	2,500		175.00	185
1989	Sorcerer's Apprentice	2,500	1993	150.00	250-500
1989	Steamboat Willie	2,500	1993	165.00	200-700

Chilmark Pewter Mickey & Co. Mickey and Friends - Staff

YEAR ISSUE		EDITION LIMIT	YEAR RETD.	ISSUE PRICE	QUOTE U.S.$
1994	Donald (Bronze)	75	1994	325.00	325
1994	Donald (Pewter)	1,500		150.00	150
1994	Goofy (Bronze)	75	1994	375.00	375
1994	Goofy (Pewter)	1,500		175.00	175
1994	Mickey (Bronze)	75	1994	325.00	325
1994	Mickey (Pewter)	1,500		150.00	150
1994	Minnie (Bronze)	75	1994	325.00	325
1994	Minnie (Pewter)	1,500		150.00	150
1994	Pluto (Bronze)	75	1994	325.00	325
1994	Pluto (Pewter)	1,500		150.00	150

Chilmark Pewter Mickey & Co. Sweethearts - Staff

YEAR ISSUE		EDITION LIMIT	YEAR RETD.	ISSUE PRICE	QUOTE U.S.$
1994	Jitterbugging	500	1994	450.00	450
1995	Mice on Ice	500	1995	425.00	425
1994	Rowboat Serenade	500	1994	495.00	500-550

Chilmark Pewter Mickey & Co. The Sorcerer's Apprentice - Staff

YEAR ISSUE		EDITION LIMIT	YEAR RETD.	ISSUE PRICE	QUOTE U.S.$
1990	The Dream	12/95		225.00	240
1990	The Incantation	12/95		150.00	175
1990	The Repentant Apprentice	Retrd.	1994	195.00	215
1990	The Sorcerer's Apprentice	12/95		225.00	240
1990	The Whirlpool	12/95		225.00	260

Chilmark Pewter Mickey & Co. Two Wheeling - Staff

YEAR ISSUE		EDITION LIMIT	YEAR RETD.	ISSUE PRICE	QUOTE U.S.$
1994	Get Your Motor Runnin' (Bronze)	50	1994	1200.00	1300-2000
1994	Get Your Motor Runnin' (MetalART)	950	1994	475.00	550-700
1994	Head Out on the Highway (Bronze)	50		1200.00	1200
1994	Head Out on the Highway (MetalART)	950		475.00	475
1995	Looking For Adventure (Bronze)	50		1200.00	1200
1995	Looking For Adventure (MetalART)	950		475.00	475

Chilmark Pewter OffCanvas™ - A. T. McGrory

YEAR ISSUE		EDITION LIMIT	YEAR RETD.	ISSUE PRICE	QUOTE U.S.$
1991	Blanket Signal	350	1993	750.00	850
1990	Smoke Signal	950	1990	345.00	550-700
1990	Vigil	950	1990	345.00	500-700
1990	Warrior	950	1990	300.00	350-600

Chilmark Pewter Sculptures - Various

YEAR ISSUE		EDITION LIMIT	YEAR RETD.	ISSUE PRICE	QUOTE U.S.$
1981	Budweiser Wagon - Keim/Hazen	890	1989	2000.00	3000
1986	Camelot Chess Set - P. Jackson	Retrd.	1991	2250.00	2250
1979	Carousel - R. Sylvan	950	1983	115.00	115
1980	Charge of the 7th Cavalry - B. Rodden	394	1988	600.00	950
1983	Dragon Slayer - D. LaRocca	290	1988	385.00	500
1979	Moses - B. Rodden	2,500	1989	140.00	235
1979	Pegasus - R. Sylvan	527	1981	95.00	175
1979	Unicorn - R. Sylvan	2,500	1982	115.00	550

Chilmark Pewter The Adversaries - F. Barnum

YEAR ISSUE		EDITION LIMIT	YEAR RETD.	ISSUE PRICE	QUOTE U.S.$
1991	Robert E. Lee	950	1992	350.00	1800
1992	Stonewall Jackson	950	1992	375.00	500
1992	Ulysses S. Grant	950	1992	350.00	600-750
1993	Wm. Tecumseh Sherman	950	1993	375.00	375-750
1993	Set of 4		1993	1450.00	3500

Chilmark Pewter The Cavalry Generals - F. Barnum

YEAR ISSUE		EDITION LIMIT	YEAR RETD.	ISSUE PRICE	QUOTE U.S.$
1993	George Armstrong Custer	950		375.00	375
1992	J.E.B. Stuart	950	1992	375.00	500
1993	Nathan Bedford Forrest	950		375.00	375
1994	Philip Sheridan	950		375.00	375

Chilmark Pewter Turning Points - F. Barnum

YEAR ISSUE		EDITION LIMIT	YEAR RETD.	ISSUE PRICE	QUOTE U.S.$
1994	Clashing Sabers	500		600.00	600
1993	The High Tide	500	1993	600.00	900

Chilmark Pewter Wildlife - Various

YEAR ISSUE		EDITION LIMIT	YEAR RETD.	ISSUE PRICE	QUOTE U.S.$
1978	Buffalo - B. Rodden	950	1986	170.00	375-400
1980	Duel of the Bighorns - M. Boyett	137	1987	650.00	1200
1979	Elephant - D. Polland	750	1987	315.00	450-550
1979	Giraffe - D. Polland	414	1981	145.00	145
1979	Kudu - D. Polland	204	1981	160.00	160
1980	Lead Can't Catch Him - M. Boyett	397	1987	645.00	845
1980	Prairie Sovereign - M. Boyett	247	1987	550.00	800
1979	Rhino - D. Polland	142	1981	135.00	135-550
1980	Ruby-Throated Hummingbird - V. Hayton	500	1983	275.00	350
1980	Voice of Experience - M. Boyett	174	1987	645.00	850

Chilmark Pewter/MetalART™ The Medicine Men - D. Polland

YEAR ISSUE		EDITION LIMIT	YEAR RETD.	ISSUE PRICE	QUOTE U.S.$
1992	False Face (MetalART)	1,000		550.00	550
1992	False Face (pewter)	500	1992	375.00	375

Chilmark Pewter/MetalART™ The Warriors - D. Polland

YEAR ISSUE		EDITION LIMIT	YEAR RETD.	ISSUE PRICE	QUOTE U.S.$
1993	Son of the Morning Star (MetalART)	1,000		495.00	495
1993	Son of the Morning Star (pewter)	500	1993	375.00	460
1992	Spirit of the Wolf (MetalART)	1,000		500.00	500
1992	Spirit of the Wolf (pewter)	500	1993	350.00	850

Chilmark Polland Collectors Society Annual Redemption Special - Various

YEAR ISSUE		EDITION LIMIT	YEAR RETD.	ISSUE PRICE	QUOTE U.S.$
1995	Thunder Pipe	Yr.Iss.		395.00	395

Chilmark Polland Collectors Society Membership Sculptures - D. Polland

YEAR ISSUE		EDITION LIMIT	YEAR RETD.	ISSUE PRICE	QUOTE U.S.$
1995	Mystic Medicine Man	Yr.Iss.		Gift	N/A

See also Polland Studios

cp smithshire™ Annual Santa - C. Smith

YEAR ISSUE		EDITION LIMIT	YEAR RETD.	ISSUE PRICE	QUOTE U.S.$
1993	St. Nicholai	Yr.Iss.	1993	75.00	150
1994	Santa and Nicky	Yr.Iss.	1994	90.00	90
1995	Santa's Endless Journey	12/95		70.00	70

cp smithshire™ Event Figurine - C. Smith

YEAR ISSUE		EDITION LIMIT	YEAR RETD.	ISSUE PRICE	QUOTE U.S.$
1993	Sap	Yr.Iss.	1993	60.00	60

YEAR ISSUE		EDITION LIMIT	YEAR RETD.	ISSUE PRICE	QUOTE U.S.$
1995	Pied Piper	12/95		40.00	40

cp smithshire™ Society Member Only Redemption Specials - C. Smith

1993	Dentzel	Yr.Iss.	1994	90.00	90
1995	Cherni	12/95		70.00	70

cp smithshire™ Society Membership Figurines - C. Smith

1993	Fellowship Inn	Yr.Iss.	1994	Gift	N/A
1995	Corey Place	12/95		Gift	N/A

cp smithshire™-Gone Home to the Forest - C. Smith

1993	Abraham	Closed	1995	85.00	100
1993	Andrea and Theodora	Closed	1995	80.00	100
1993	Benjamin	Closed	1995	85.00	85
1993	Chipper	Closed	1994	70.00	100
1993	Florence and Lila	Closed	1994	80.00	100
1993	Granny Smith	Closed	1995	60.00	100
1993	Have and Have Not (No Mushroom)	Closed	1993	80.00	160
1993	Heather (No Mushroom)	Closed	1993	50.00	100
1993	Hyde N' Seek	Closed	1994	70.00	70
1993	Jack O' Lantern (No Mushroom)	Closed	1993	75.00	150
1994	Pepe	Closed	1995	85.00	85
1993	Rushmore	Closed	1995	85.00	85
1993	Tyrus	Closed	1995	75.00	75

Hudson Pewter Figures - P.W. Baston, unless otherwise noted

1972	Benjamin Franklin	Closed	1974	15.00	75-100
1969	Betsy Ross	Closed	1971	30.00	100-125
1969	Colonial Blacksmith	Closed	1971	30.00	100-125
1975	Declaration Wall Plaque	100	1975	Unkn.	300-500
1975	The Favored Scholar - P.W. Baston	6	1975	Unkn.	600-1000
1972	George Washington	Closed	1974	15.00	75-100
1969	George Washington (Cannon)	Closed	1971	35.00	75-100
1972	James Madison	Closed	1974	15.00	50-75
1972	John Adams	Closed	1974	15.00	75-100
1969	John Hancock	Closed	1971	15.00	100-125
1975	Lee's Ninth General Order	Closed	1975	Unkn.	300-400
1975	Lincoln's Gettysburg Address	Closed	1975	Unkn.	300-400
1975	Neighboring Pews	6	1975	Unkn.	600-1000
1975	Spirit of '76 - P.W. Baston	12	1975	Unkn.	750-1500
1972	Thomas Jefferson - P.W. Baston	Closed	1974	15.00	75-100
1975	Washington's Letter of Acceptance - P.W. Baston	Closed	1975	Unkn.	300-400
1975	Weighing the Baby - P.W. Baston	6	1975	Unkn.	600-1000

Hudson Pewter Mickey & Co. - Staff

1988	Happy Birthday Mickey	Yr.Iss.	1989	60.00	150

Hudson Pewter Mickey & Co. -Registered - Staff

1994	Be My Valentine	Closed	1994	65.00	75-125
1994	Christmas Waltz	Closed	1994	65.00	75-125

Hudson Pewter World of Mickey - Staff

1991	Mouse Waltz	Retrd.	1994	41.00	41
1988	Sweethearts	Retrd.	1993	45.00	45

Pere Noel Collection - C. Smith

1994	Checking His List	3,500		70.00	75
1994	Christ Kindle	3,500		85.00	95
1994	Father Christmas	Closed	1994	150.00	150
1994	Grandfather Frost	3,500		65.00	75
1995	Kriss Kringle	3,500		75.00	75
1994	Pere Noel	3,500		65.00	75
1994	Santa Claus	3,500		75.00	75
1995	Santa McClaus	750		110.00	110
1994	Sinter Klaas	3,500		70.00	75
1995	St. Nikkolo	3,500		65.00	65
1995	Stars & Stripes Santa	3,500		85.00	85

Sebastian Miniatures Collectors Society - P.W. Baston, unless otherwise noted

1980	S.M.C. Society Plaque ('80 Charter)	11,914	1980	Gift	20-35
1981	S.M.C. Society Plaque	4,957	1981	Gift	20-30
1982	S.M.C. Society Plaque	1,530	1982	Gift	20-30
1983	S.M.C. Society Plaque	1,167	1983	Gift	20-30
1984	S.M.C. Society Plaque	505	1984	Gift	20-30
1984	Self Portrait	Retrd.	1994	Gift	45
1995	Grace - P.W. Baston, Jr.	Annual		Gift	N/A

Sebastian Miniatures Holiday Memories-Member Only - P.W. Baston, Jr.

1990	Thanksgiving Helper	Yr.Iss.	1991	39.50	40
1990	Leprechaun	Yr.Iss.	1991	27.50	28
1991	Trick or Treat	Yr.Iss.	1992	25.50	50-75
1993	Father Time	Yr.Iss.	1994	27.50	28
1993	New Year Baby	Yr.Iss.	1994	27.50	28
1994	Look What the Easter Bunny Left Me	Yr.Iss.		27.50	28
1995	On Parade	Yr.Iss.		N/A	N/A

Sebastian Miniatures Member Only - P.W. Baston, Jr.

1989	The Collectors	Yr.Iss.	1990	39.50	40
1992	Christopher Columbus	Yr.Iss.	1993	28.50	29

Sebastian Miniature Figurines - P.W. Baston, Jr.

1991	America Salutes Desert Storm-bronze	Retrd.	1994	26.50	100
1991	America Salutes Desert Storm-painted	350	1991	49.50	200-250
1990	America's Hometown	4,750		34.00	34
1994	Boston Light	3,500		45.00	45
1994	Egg Rock Light	3,500		55.00	55
1992	Firefighter	500	1992	28.00	50
1991	Happy Hood Holidays	2,000	1991	32.50	85
1983	Harry Hood	1,000	1983	Unkn.	200-250
1992	I Know I Left It Here Somewhere	1,000		28.50	29
1985	It's Hoods (Wagon)	3,250	1985	N/A	75-100
1994	A Job Well Done	1,000		27.50	28
1993	The Lamplighter	1,000		28.00	28
1994	Nubble Light	3,500		45.00	45
1993	Pumpkin Island Light	3,500		55.00	55
1993	Soap Box Derby	500		45.00	45
1986	Statue of Liberty (AT & T)	1,000	1986	N/A	175-200
1987	White House (Gold, Oval Base)	250	1987	17.00	35-50

Sebastian Miniatures America Remembers - P.W. Baston

1983	Family Feast	4,147	1983	37.50	50-100
1982	Family Fishing	8,734	1982	34.50	50-100
1980	Family Picnic	16,527	1980	29.50	60-100
1981	Family Reads Aloud	21,027	1981	34.50	50-75
1979	Family Sing	7,358	1979	29.50	50-125

Sebastian Miniatures Children At Play - P.W. Baston

1979	Building Days Boy	10,000	1980	19.50	30-50
1979	Building Days Girl	10,000	1980	19.50	30-50
1981	Sailing Days Boy	10,000	1981	19.50	30-50
1981	Sailing Days Girl	10,000	1981	19.50	30-50
1982	School Days Boy	10,000	1982	19.50	40-60
1982	School Days Girl	10,000	1982	19.50	40-60
1978	Sidewalk Days Boy	10,000	1980	19.50	40-60
1978	Sidewalk Days Girl	10,000	1980	19.50	40-60
1980	Snow Days Boy	10,000	1980	19.50	40-60
1980	Snow Days Girl	10,000	1980	19.50	40-60

Sebastian Miniatures Christmas - P.W. Baston, Jr.

1993	Caroling With Santa	1,000		29.00	29
1993	Harmonizing With Santa	1,000		27.00	27
1994	Victorian Christmas Skaters	1,000		32.50	33
1995	Midnight Snacks	1,000		28.50	29

Sebastian Miniatures Exchange Figurines - P.W. Baston, Jr., unless otherwise noted

1984	First Things First	1,267	1985	30.00	45
1987	It's About Time	576	1988	25.00	40
1986	News Wagon	1,422	1987	35.00	45
1983	Newspaper Boy - P.W. Baston	1,708	1984	28.50	60-95
1985	Newstand	1,454	1986	30.00	45

Sebastian Miniatures Firefighter Collection - P.W. Baston, Jr.

1993	Firefighter No. 1	950		48.00	48
1994	Firefighter No. 2	950		48.00	48
1994	Firefighter No. 3	950		48.00	48
1995	Firefighter No. 4	950		48.00	48

Sebastian Miniatures Jimmy Fund - P.W. Baston, Jr., unless otherwise noted

1993	Boy With Ducks	500	1993	27.50	28
1984	Catcher - P.W. Baston	1,872	1984	24.50	35-75
1987	Football Player	1,270	1988	26.50	27
1995	Girl in Riding Outfit	500		28.00	28
1994	Girl on Bench	500	1994	28.00	28
1985	Hockey Player	1,836	1986	24.50	35-50
1988	Santa	500	1988	32.50	33
1983	Schoolboy - P.W. Baston	3,567	1983	24.50	25-35
1986	Soccer Player	1,166	1987	25.00	25

Sebastian Miniatures Private Label - P.W. Baston Jr.

1993	Adams Academy w/ Steeple (Blossom Shop)	75	N/A	100.00	200-225
1993	Adams Academy w/o Steeple (Blossom Shop)	750	N/A	30.00	30

Sebastian Miniatures Shakespearean-Member Only - P.W. Baston, unless otherwise noted

1984	Anne Boleyn	3,897	1984	17.50	35
1984	Henry VIII	4,578	1984	19.50	35
1985	Falstaff	3,357	1985	19.50	35
1985	Mistress Ford	2,836	1985	17.50	35
1986	Juliet	2,620	1986	17.50	35
1986	Romeo	2,853	1986	19.50	35
1987	Countess Olivia	1,893	1987	19.50	35
1987	Malvolio	2,093	1987	21.50	35
1988	Audrey	1,548	1988	22.50	35
1988	Shakespeare - P.W. Baston, Jr.	Retrd.	1989	23.50	35
1988	Touchstone	1,770	1988	22.50	35
1989	Cleopatra	Retrd.	1989	27.00	35
1989	Mark Antony	Retrd.	1989	27.00	35

Sebastian Miniatures Washington Irving-Member Only - P.W. Baston

1980	Rip Van Winkle	12,005	1983	19.50	35
1981	Ichabod Crane	9,069	1983	19.50	35
1981	Dame Van Winkle	11,217	1983	19.50	35
1982	Brom Bones (Headless Horseman)	6,610	1983	22.50	35
1982	Katrina Van Tassel	7,367	1983	19.50	35
1983	Diedrich Knickerbocker	5,528	1983	22.50	35

Legends

Annual Collectors Edition - C. Pardell

1990	The Night Before	S/O	1991	990.00	1300-1900
1991	Medicine Gift of Manhood	S/O	1992	990.00	1900-2400
1992	Spirit of the Wolf	S/O	1992	950.00	1800-2100
1993	Tomorrow's Warrior	S/O	1993	590.00	1000-1300
1994	Guiding Hand	S/O	1994	590.00	800-850
1995	Gift of the Sacred Calf	500	1995	650.00	650

Collectors Only - Various

1993	Give Us Peace - C. Pardell	1,250	1993	270.00	350-750
1994	First Born - C. Pardell	1,250	1994	350.00	550-700
1994	River Bandits - K. Cantrell	1,250		350.00	350
1995	Sonata - K. Cantrell	1,250		250.00	250
1995	Daydreams of Manhood - C. Pardell	2,500		390.00	390

American Heritage - D. Edwards

1987	Grizz Country (Bronze)	Retrd.	1990	350.00	350
1987	Grizz Country (Pewter)	Retrd.	1990	370.00	370
1987	Winter Provisions (Bronze)	Retrd.	1990	340.00	340
1987	Winter Provisions (Pewter)	Retrd.	1990	370.00	370
1987	Wrangler's Dare (Bronze)	Retrd.	1990	630.00	630
1987	Wrangler's Dare (Pewter)	Retrd.	1990	660.00	660

American Indian Dance Premier Edition - C. Pardell

1993	Drum Song	750	1995	2800.00	2950
1994	Footprints of the Butterfly	750		1800.00	1800
1994	Image of the Eagle	750		1900.00	1990
1995	Spirit of the Mountain	750		1750.00	1750

American West Premier Edition - C. Pardell

1992	American Horse	950	1995	1300.00	1300
1992	Defending the People	950		1350.00	1350
1991	First Coup	950	1993	1150.00	1250
1993	Four Bears' Challenge	950		990.00	990
1994	Season of Victory	950		1500.00	1500
1991	Unexpected Rescuer	950	1991	990.00	1800

Animal Dreamer - M. Boyett

1995	Breaking of the War Horse	950		590.00	590
1995	Buffalo Runner	950		550.00	550
1995	He Hunts with the Eagle Medicine	950		490.00	490
1995	In the Path of the Wolf Spirit	950		490.00	490

Classic Equestrian Collection - C. Pardell

1988	Lippizzaner (Bronze)	Retrd.	N/A	200.00	200

Clear Visions - Various

1993	Salmon Falls - W. Whitten	950		950.00	980
1994	Saving Their Skins - C. Pardell	950		1590.00	1630

Culture Covenant Premier Edition - C. Pardell

1995	Each, to the Other	500		1300.00	1300
1995	Our Kind, with All Others	500		1300.00	1300
1994	Our Past, to Our Future	500		1350.00	1350

The Endangered Wildlife Collection - K. Cantrell

1993	Big Pine Survivor	950		390.00	390
1990	Forest Spirit	950	1991	290.00	1300-1600
1991	Mountain Majesty	950		350.00	370
1991	Old Tusker	950		390.00	390
1992	Plains Monarch	950		350.00	370
1994	Prairie Phantom	950		370.00	370
1990	Savannah Prince	950		290.00	300
1993	Silvertip	950		370.00	390
1992	Songs of Autumn	950		390.00	390
1992	Spirit Song	950	1992	350.00	350-900
1994	Twilight	950		290.00	290
1992	Unchallenged	950		350.00	370

Endangered Wildlife Eagle Series - K. Cantrell

1989	Aquila Libre	2,500	1995	280.00	300
1993	Defiance	2,500		350.00	350
1992	Food Fight	2,500		650.00	690
1989	Outpost	2,500	1995	280.00	300
1989	Sentinel	2,500	1993	280.00	650-850
1993	Spiral Flight	2,500		290.00	290
1992	Sunday Brunch	2,500		550.00	590
1989	Unbounded	2,500	1994	280.00	300

Gallery Editions - Various

1994	Center Fire - W. Whitten	350		2500.00	2500
1994	Mountain Family - D. Lemon	150		7900.00	7900
1993	Over the Rainbow - K. Cantrell	600	1995	2900.00	3050
1992	Resolute - C. Pardell	250	1992	7950.00	800-1400
1993	Visionary - C. Pardell	350		7500.00	7500
1993	The Wanderer - K. Cantrell	350		3500.00	3500

The Great Outdoorsman - C. Pardell

1988	Both Are Hooked (Bronze)	Retrd.	N/A	320.00	320
1988	Both Are Hooked (Pewter)	Retrd.	N/A	320.00	320

Happy Trails Collection - W. Whitten

YEAR ISSUE		EDITION LIMIT	YEAR RETD.	ISSUE PRICE	QUOTE U.S.$
1994	Cowboy Soul	750	1994	450.00	450

Hidden Images Collection - D. Lemon

YEAR ISSUE		EDITION LIMIT	YEAR RETD.	ISSUE PRICE	QUOTE U.S.$
1994	In Search of Bear Rock	350		1300.00	1300
1995	Sensed, But Unseen	350		990.00	990
1995	Spirit	350		990.00	990

Indian Arts Collection - C. Pardell

YEAR ISSUE		EDITION LIMIT	YEAR RETD.	ISSUE PRICE	QUOTE U.S.$
1990	Chief's Blanket	1,500	1992	350.00	500-1000
1990	Indian Maiden	1,500		240.00	240
1990	Indian Potter	1,500		260.00	260
1990	Kachina Carver	1,500	1993	270.00	500-1000
1990	Story Teller	1,500	1993	290.00	500-600

Kachina Dancers Collection - C. Pardell

YEAR ISSUE		EDITION LIMIT	YEAR RETD.	ISSUE PRICE	QUOTE U.S.$
1991	Ahote	2,500		370.00	390
1991	Angakchina	2,500		370.00	390
1994	Deer Kachina	2,500		390.00	390
1994	Eototo	2,500		390.00	390
1991	Hilili	2,500		390.00	390
1993	Koshari	2,500		370.00	390
1991	Koyemsi	2,500		370.00	390
1992	Kwahu	2,500		390.00	390
1993	Mongwa	2,500		390.00	390
1994	Palhik Mana	2,500		390.00	390
1992	Tawa	2,500		390.00	390
1994	Wiharu	2,500		390.00	390

The Legacies Of The West Premier Edition - C. Pardell

YEAR ISSUE		EDITION LIMIT	YEAR RETD.	ISSUE PRICE	QUOTE U.S.$
1991	Defiant Comanche	950	1991	1300.00	1300-1800
1993	Eminent Crow	950	1994	1500.00	1500
1994	Enduring	950		1250.00	1350
1992	Esteemed Warrior	950	1992	1750.00	2000-3000
1990	Mystic Vision	950	1990	990.00	2500-3000
1991	No More, Forever	950	1992	1500.00	1700
1992	Rebellious	950		1500.00	1600
1990	Victorious	950	1990	1275.00	3200-3800

The Legendary West Collection - C. Pardell

YEAR ISSUE		EDITION LIMIT	YEAR RETD.	ISSUE PRICE	QUOTE U.S.$
1992	Beating Bad Odds	2,500		390.00	390
1989	Bustin' A Herd Quitter	2,500		590.00	630
1993	Cliff Hanger	2,500		990.00	990
1992	Crazy Horse	2,500	1992	390.00	750-1200
1989	Eagle Dancer	2,500		370.00	390
1993	Hunter's Brothers	2,500		590.00	630
1989	Johnson's Last Fight	2,500	1991	590.00	1000-1650
1990	Keeper of Eagles	2,500		370.00	390
1987	Pony Express (Bronze)	2,500	N/A	320.00	320-450
1989	Pony Express (Mixed Media)	2,500		390.00	390
1987	Pony Express (Pewter)	2,500	N/A	320.00	320-450
1989	Sacajawea	2,500	N/A	380.00	380
1990	Shhh	2,500		390.00	390
1990	Stand of the Sash Wearer	2,500		390.00	390
1989	Tables Turned	2,500		680.00	720
1990	Unbridled	2,500		290.00	290
1991	Warning	2,500		390.00	390
1989	White Feather's Vision	2,500	1991	390.00	900-1300

The Legendary West Premier Edition - C. Pardell

YEAR ISSUE		EDITION LIMIT	YEAR RETD.	ISSUE PRICE	QUOTE U.S.$
1990	Crow Warrior	750	1990	1225.00	2000-3000
1992	The Final Charge	750	1992	1250.00	1500-2000
1989	Pursued	750	1989	750.00	2000-4000
1988	Red Cloud's Coup	750	1988	480.00	5000-6700
1989	Songs of Glory	750	1989	850.00	3300-3500
1991	Triumphant	750	1991	1150.00	1500-1700

Mystical Quest Collection - D. Medina

YEAR ISSUE		EDITION LIMIT	YEAR RETD.	ISSUE PRICE	QUOTE U.S.$
1993	Hunter's Quest	950		990.00	990
1994	Peace Quest	950		1150.00	1150
1992	Vision Quest	950		990.00	990

Native American Spirits - W. Whitten

YEAR ISSUE		EDITION LIMIT	YEAR RETD.	ISSUE PRICE	QUOTE U.S.$
1994	Buffalo Dreamer	1,250		250.00	250
1995	Calling the Buffalo	1,250		250.00	250
1994	Cheyenne War Shield	1,250		250.00	250
1995	Flying Shield	1,250		250.00	250
1994	Peace Pipe	1,250		250.00	250
1994	War Bonnet	1,250		250.00	250
1995	Wolf Headdress	1,250		290.00	290

The North & South Collection - W. Whitten

YEAR ISSUE		EDITION LIMIT	YEAR RETD.	ISSUE PRICE	QUOTE U.S.$
1993	Brother Against Brother	950		550.00	550
1993	The Noble Heart	950		450.00	450
1994	Stonewall	950		450.00	450
1992	Victory at Hand	950		390.00	390

The North American Collection - K. Cantrell

YEAR ISSUE		EDITION LIMIT	YEAR RETD.	ISSUE PRICE	QUOTE U.S.$
1994	Artful Dodger	2,500		160.00	160
1994	Buffalo Spirit	2,500		150.00	160
1994	Eagles Realm	2,500		150.00	160
1994	Elusive	2,500		150.00	160
1994	Northern Express	2,500		150.00	160
1994	Spirit of the Wolf	2,500		150.00	160
1994	Wild Music	2,500		150.00	160
1994	Wind Blown	2,500		160.00	160

North American Wildlife - D. Edwards

YEAR ISSUE		EDITION LIMIT	YEAR RETD.	ISSUE PRICE	QUOTE U.S.$
1988	Defenders of Freedom (Bronze)	Retrd.	N/A	340.00	340
1988	Defenders of Freedom (Pewter)	Retrd.	N/A	370.00	370
1988	Double Trouble (Bronze)	Retrd.	N/A	300.00	300
1988	Double Trouble (Pewter)	Retrd.	N/A	320.00	320
1988	Downhill Run (Bronze)	Retrd.	N/A	330.00	330
1988	Downhill Run (Pewter)	Retrd.	N/A	340.00	340
1988	Grizzly Solitude (Bronze)	Retrd.	N/A	310.00	310
1988	Grizzly Solitude (Pewter)	Retrd.	N/A	330.00	330
1988	Last Glance (Bronze)	Retrd.	N/A	300.00	300
1988	Last Glance (Pewter)	Retrd.	N/A	320.00	320
1988	The Proud American (Bronze)	Retrd.	N/A	330.00	330
1988	The Proud American (Pewter)	Retrd.	N/A	340.00	340
1988	Ridge Runners (Bronze)	Retrd.	N/A	300.00	300
1988	Ridge Runners (Pewter)	Retrd.	N/A	310.00	310
1988	Sudden Alert (Bronze)	Retrd.	N/A	300.00	300
1988	Sudden Alert (Pewter)	Retrd.	N/A	320.00	320

Oceanic World - D. Medina

YEAR ISSUE		EDITION LIMIT	YEAR RETD.	ISSUE PRICE	QUOTE U.S.$
1989	Freedom's Beauty (Bronze)	Retrd.	N/A	330.00	330
1989	Freedom's Beauty (Pewter)	Retrd.	N/A	130.00	130
1989	Together (Bronze)	Retrd.	N/A	140.00	140
1989	Together (Pewter)	Retrd.	N/A	130.00	130

Relics of the Americas - W. Whitten

YEAR ISSUE		EDITION LIMIT	YEAR RETD.	ISSUE PRICE	QUOTE U.S.$
1993	Dream Medicine	950		1150.00	1210
1994	Flared Glory	950		1350.00	1350
1995	Walks With Wolves	950		1250.00	1250

Special Commissions - Various

YEAR ISSUE		EDITION LIMIT	YEAR RETD.	ISSUE PRICE	QUOTE U.S.$
1988	Alpha Pair (Bronze) - C. Pardell	Retrd.	N/A	330.00	330
1988	Alpha Pair (Mixed Media) - C. Pardell	S/O	N/A	390.00	600-995
1988	Alpha Pair (Pewter) - C. Pardell	Retrd.	N/A	330.00	330
1995	Father-The Power Within - D. Medina	350		1500.00	1500
1990	Lakota Love Song - C. Pardell	Retrd.	1990	380.00	1950
1987	Mama's Joy (Bronze) - D. Edwards	Retrd.	N/A	200.00	200
1987	Mama's Joy (Pewter) - D. Edwards	Retrd.	N/A	250.00	250
1995	Rapture - W. Whitten	350		1750.00	1750
1995	Scent in the Air - K. Cantrell	750		990.00	990
1991	Symbols of Freedom - K. Cantrell	2,500		490.00	520
1987	Wild Freedom (Bronze) - D. Edwards	Retrd.	N/A	320.00	320
1987	Wild Freedom (Pewter) - D. Edwards	Retrd.	N/A	330.00	330
1992	Yellowstone Bound - K. Cantrell	600	1994	2500.00	2500

Warriors of the Sacred Circle - W. Whitten

YEAR ISSUE		EDITION LIMIT	YEAR RETD.	ISSUE PRICE	QUOTE U.S.$
1993	Coup Feather	950		450.00	450
1992	Dog Soldier	950		450.00	450
1992	Peace Offering	950		550.00	550
1994	Traditional Weapons	950		550.00	550
1993	Yellow Boy	950		450.00	450

Way of the Cat Collection - K. Cantrell

YEAR ISSUE		EDITION LIMIT	YEAR RETD.	ISSUE PRICE	QUOTE U.S.$
1995	Encounter	500	1995	750.00	750

Way of the Warrior Collection - C. Pardell

YEAR ISSUE		EDITION LIMIT	YEAR RETD.	ISSUE PRICE	QUOTE U.S.$
1991	Clan Leader	1,600	1994	170.00	200-250
1991	Elder Chief	1,600	1994	170.00	200-295
1991	Medicine Dancer	1,600	1994	170.00	200-250
1991	Rite of Manhood	1,600	1994	170.00	200-250
1991	Seeker of Visions	1,600	1994	170.00	200-250
1991	Tribal Defender	1,600	1994	170.00	200-250

Way of the Wolf Collection - K. Cantrell

YEAR ISSUE		EDITION LIMIT	YEAR RETD.	ISSUE PRICE	QUOTE U.S.$
1993	Courtship	500	1993	590.00	700-1000
1994	Missed by a Hare	500	1994	700.00	700
1994	Renewal	500	1994	700.00	900-1000
1995	Stink Bomb	500	1995	750.00	750

Western Memories Premier Edition - D. Lemon

YEAR ISSUE		EDITION LIMIT	YEAR RETD.	ISSUE PRICE	QUOTE U.S.$
1995	Ole Mossy Horn	500		1450.00	1450
1994	Vacant Thunder	500		1900.00	1900
1995	Winds of Memory	500		1750.00	1750

Wild Realm Collection - C. Pardell

YEAR ISSUE		EDITION LIMIT	YEAR RETD.	ISSUE PRICE	QUOTE U.S.$
1988	Fly Fisher (Bronze)	Retrd.	N/A	330.00	330
1988	Fly Fisher (Pewter)	Retrd.	N/A	330.00	330

Wild Realm Premier Edition - C. Pardell

YEAR ISSUE		EDITION LIMIT	YEAR RETD.	ISSUE PRICE	QUOTE U.S.$
1989	High Spirit	1,600		870.00	920
1991	Speed Incarnate	1,600	N/A	790.00	790

Lenox Collections

American Fashion - Unknown

YEAR ISSUE		EDITION LIMIT	YEAR RETD.	ISSUE PRICE	QUOTE U.S.$
1986	Belle of the Ball	Open		95.00	95
1987	Centennial Bride	Open		95.00	95
1984	First Waltz	Open		95.00	95
1987	Gala at the Whitehouse	Open		95.00	95
1985	Governor's Garden Party	Open		95.00	95
1986	Grand Tour	Open		95.00	95
1992	Royal Reception	Open		95.00	95
1983	Springtime Promenade	Open		95.00	95
1984	Tea at the Ritz	Open		95.00	95

Baby Bears - Unknown

YEAR ISSUE		EDITION LIMIT	YEAR RETD.	ISSUE PRICE	QUOTE U.S.$
1991	Polar Bear	Open		45.00	45

Baby Bird Pairs - Unknown

YEAR ISSUE		EDITION LIMIT	YEAR RETD.	ISSUE PRICE	QUOTE U.S.$
1992	Chickadee	Open		64.00	64
1992	Orioles	Open		64.00	64
1991	Robins	Open		64.00	64

Breed Puppies - Unknown

YEAR ISSUE		EDITION LIMIT	YEAR RETD.	ISSUE PRICE	QUOTE U.S.$
1995	Dachshund	Open		75.00	75

Carousel Animals - Unknown

YEAR ISSUE		EDITION LIMIT	YEAR RETD.	ISSUE PRICE	QUOTE U.S.$
1992	Camelot Horse	Open		152.00	152
1990	Carousel Charger	Open		136.00	152
1989	Carousel Circus Horse	Open		136.00	152
1990	Carousel Elephant	Open		136.00	152
1987	Carousel Horse	Open		136.00	152
1990	Carousel Lion	Open		136.00	152
1991	Carousel Polar Bear	Open		152.00	152
1989	Carousel Reindeer	Open		136.00	152
1988	Carousel Unicorn	Open		136.00	152
1992	Christmas Horse 1992	Yr.Iss.	1992	156.00	156
1993	Christmas Horse 1993	Yr.Iss.	1993	156.00	156
1994	Christmas Horse 1994	Yr.Iss.	1994	156.00	156
1994	Midnight Charger	9,500		156.00	156
1993	Nautical Horse	Open		156.00	156
1991	Pride of America	Closed	1991	152.00	152
1993	Rose Prancer	9,500		156.00	156
1993	Statement Horse #1 Victorian Romance	2,500		395.00	395
1994	Statement Horse #2 Ribbons & Roses	2,500		395.00	395
1992	Statement Piece	Open		395.00	395
1992	Tropical Horse	Open		156.00	156
1992	Victorian Romance Horse	Open		156.00	156
1991	Western Horse	Open		152.00	152

Carousels - Unknown

YEAR ISSUE		EDITION LIMIT	YEAR RETD.	ISSUE PRICE	QUOTE U.S.$
1995	Carousel Courtship (Spec. Ed.)	5,500		195.00	195
1995	Jeweled Prancer Carousel	Open		154.00	154

Classical Goddesses - Unknown

YEAR ISSUE		EDITION LIMIT	YEAR RETD.	ISSUE PRICE	QUOTE U.S.$
1992	Aphrodite	Open		95.00	95
1992	Aphrodite, Painted	Open		136.00	136

Crystal Animal Pairs - Unknown

YEAR ISSUE		EDITION LIMIT	YEAR RETD.	ISSUE PRICE	QUOTE U.S.$
1994	Lord & Lady, Wolves	Open		76.00	76
1994	Preen & Serene, Cats	Open		76.00	76
1993	Prim & Proper, Cats	Open		76.00	76
1993	Silk & Satin, Rabbits	Open		76.00	76

Crystal Eagles - Unknown

YEAR ISSUE		EDITION LIMIT	YEAR RETD.	ISSUE PRICE	QUOTE U.S.$
1994	Soaring Majesty	Open		195.00	195
1995	Wings of the Sun	Open		195.00	195

Doves & Roses - Unknown

YEAR ISSUE		EDITION LIMIT	YEAR RETD.	ISSUE PRICE	QUOTE U.S.$
1992	Doves of Honor	Open		119.00	119
1993	Doves of Love	Open		119.00	119
1991	Doves of Peace	Open		95.00	95
1991	Love's Promise	Open		95.00	95

Endangered Baby Animals - Unknown

YEAR ISSUE		EDITION LIMIT	YEAR RETD.	ISSUE PRICE	QUOTE U.S.$
1991	Baby Florida Panther	Open		57.00	57
1991	Baby Grey Wolf	Open		57.00	57
1994	Baby Orangatan	Open		58.00	58
1992	Baby Rhinocerous	Open		57.00	57
1994	Bridled Nail-Tailed Wallaby Joey	Open		58.00	58
1994	Burmese Deer	Open		58.50	59
1991	Elephant	Open		57.00	57
1993	Indian Elephant Calf	Open		57.00	57
1990	Panda	Open		39.00	39
1994	Pigmy Hippo	Open		58.00	58
1994	Sumatra Tiger Cub	Open		58.00	58

Exotic Birds - Unknown

YEAR ISSUE		EDITION LIMIT	YEAR RETD.	ISSUE PRICE	QUOTE U.S.$
1993	"Plum Headed" Parakeet	Open		49.50	50
1991	Cockatoo	Open		45.00	45

Floral Sculptures - Unknown

YEAR ISSUE		EDITION LIMIT	YEAR RETD.	ISSUE PRICE	QUOTE U.S.$
1987	Iris	Open		119.00	136
1988	Magnolia	Open		119.00	136
1988	Peace Rose	Open		119.00	136
1986	Rubrum Lily	Open		119.00	136

Garden Birds - Unknown

YEAR ISSUE		EDITION LIMIT	YEAR RETD.	ISSUE PRICE	QUOTE U.S.$
1987	American Goldfinch	Open		39.00	45
1990	Baltimore Oriole	Open		45.00	45
1993	Barn Swallow	Open		45.00	45
1986	Blue Jay	Open		39.00	45
1991	Broadbilled Hummingbird	Open		45.00	45
1987	Cardinal	Open		39.00	45
1988	Cedar Waxwing	Open		39.00	45
1985	Chickadee	Open		39.00	45
1990	Chipping Sparrow	Open		45.00	45
1993	Chipping Sparrow	Open		45.00	45
1994	Christmas Dove	Yr.Iss.		45.00	45
1991	Dark Eyed Junco	Open		45.00	45
1989	Downy Woodpecker	Open		39.00	45
1986	Eastern Bluebird	Open		39.00	45
1994	Female BlueJay	Open		45.00	45
1993	Female Cardinal	Open		45.00	45
1994	Female Chickadee	Open		45.00	45
1993	Female Kinglet	Open		45.00	45
1991	Golden Crowned Kinglet	Open		45.00	45
1988	Hummingbird	Open		39.00	45
1993	Indigo Bunting	Open		45.00	45
1992	Magnificent Hummingbird	Open		45.00	45
1990	Marsh Wren	Open		45.00	45
1993	Mockingbird	Open		45.00	45
1993	Mountain Bluebird	Open		45.00	45

YEAR ISSUE		EDITION LIMIT	YEAR RETD.	ISSUE PRICE	QUOTE U.S.$
1991	Purple Finch	Open		45.00	45
1994	Purple Martin	Open		45.00	45
1993	Red Winged Blackbird	Open		45.00	45
1987	Red-Breasted Nuthatch	Open		39.00	45
1989	Robin	Open		39.00	45
1991	Rose Grosbeak	Open		45.00	45
1989	Saw Whet Owl	Open		45.00	45
1992	Scarlet Tanger	Open		45.00	45
1993	Statement Piece	Open		45.00	45
1986	Tufted Titmouse	Open		39.00	45
1987	Turtle Dove	Open		39.00	45
1994	Vermillion Flycatcher	Open		45.00	45
1992	Western Meadowlark	Open		45.00	45
1994	Western Tanager	Open		45.00	45
1990	Wood Duck	Open		45.00	45
1993	Yellow Warbler	Open		45.00	45

Garden Flowers - Unknown

1991	Calla Lily	Open		45.00	45
1991	Camelia	Open		45.00	45
1990	Carnation	Open		45.00	45
1988	Cattleya Orchid	Open		39.00	45
1995	Crocus	Open		39.00	39
1990	Daffodil	Open		45.00	45
1990	Day Lily	Open		45.00	45
1995	Gardenia	Open		39.00	39
1995	Gladiolus	Open		39.00	39
1989	Iris	Open		45.00	45
1995	Keepsake Rose (Statement)	Open		95.00	95
1991	Magnolia	Open		45.00	45
1991	Morning Glory	Open		45.00	45
1988	Parrot Tulip	Open		39.00	39
1991	Poinsettia	Open		39.00	39
1993	Red Rose	Open		45.00	45
1988	Tea Rose	Open		39.00	45

Gentle Majesty - Unknown

1990	Bear Hug Polar Bear	Open		76.00	76
1991	Keeping Warm (Foxes)	Open		76.00	76
1990	Penguins	Open		76.00	76

Hunters of the Sky - Unknown

1993	Challenge of the Eagles, Double Eagles	Open		275.00	275
1994	Challenge of the Red Tailed Hawks	Open		295.00	295
1994	Golden Conquerors	Open		295.00	295
1994	Masters of the Wind, Peregian Falcons	Open		295.00	295

International Brides - Unknown

1992	Japanese Bride, Kiyoshi	Open		136.00	136
1990	Russian Bride	Open		136.00	136

International Horse Sculptures - Unknown

1990	Appaloosa	Open		136.00	136
1988	Arabian Knight	Open		136.00	136
1990	Lippizan	Open		136.00	136
1989	Thoroughbred	Open		136.00	136

International Songbirds - Unknown

1992	American Goldfinch	Open		152.00	152
1992	European Goldfinch	Open		152.00	152

Jessie Willcox Smith - J.W.Smith

1991	Feeding Kitty	Open		60.00	60
1991	Rosebuds	Open		60.00	60

Kings of the Sky - Unknown

1991	Defender of Freedom, American Bald Eagle	Closed		234.00	234
1991	Eagle of Glory, Golden Eagle	Open		234.00	234
1994	Eagle of Splendor, American Bald Eagle	Open		252.00	252
1993	Foundation of Freedom	Open		252.00	252
1989	Lord of Skies, American Bald Eagle	Open		195.00	195
1992	Wings of Majesty, American Bald Eagle	Open		252.00	252
1993	Wings of Power, Golden Eagle	Open		252.00	252
1994	Wings of Pride, Golden Eagle	Open		252.00	252

Legendary Princesses - Unknown

1988	Cinderella	Open		136.00	136
1990	Cleopatra	Open		136.00	136
1994	Fairy Godmother	9,500		156.00	156
1992	Firebird	Open		156.00	156
1994	Frog Princess	Open		156.00	156
1990	Guinevere	Open		136.00	136
1990	Juliet	Open		136.00	136
1993	Little Mermaid, Princess of the Sea	Open		156.00	156
1994	Maid Marion	Open		156.00	156
1991	Peacock Maiden	Open		136.00	136
1991	Pocohontas	9,500	1992	136.00	165
1993	Princes Beauty	Open		156.00	156
1993	Princess and the Pea	Open		156.00	156
1985	Rapunzel	Open		119.00	136
1992	Sheherezade	Open		156.00	156
1986	Sleeping Beauty	Open		119.00	136
1987	Snow Queen	Open		119.00	136
1989	Snow White	Open		136.00	136
1989	Swan Princess	Open		136.00	136

Lenox Baby Book - Unknown

1991	Baby's First Christmas	Open		57.00	57
1992	Baby's First Portrait	Open		57.00	57
1990	Baby's First Shoes	Open		57.00	57
1991	Baby's First Steps	Open		57.00	57

Lenox Puppy Collection - Unknown

1990	Beagle	Open		76.00	76
1991	Cocker Spaniel	Open		76.00	76
1994	German Shepherd	Open		75.00	75
1992	Poodle	Open		76.00	76

Lenox Sea Animals - Unknown

1994	Adventure of Fur Seals	Open		136.00	136
1991	Dance of the Dolphins	Open		119.00	119
1993	Flight of the Dolphins	Open		119.00	119
1993	Journey of the Whales	Open		136.00	136
1993	Otter Escapade	Open		136.00	136
1994	Penguins at Play	Open		136.00	136
1992	Song of the Whales	Open		136.00	136
1994	Voyage of the Sea Turtles	Open		136.00	136

Life of Christ - Unknown

1992	A Child's Comfort	Open		95.00	95
1992	A Child's Prayer	Open		95.00	95
1993	Children's Adoration	Open		95.00	95
1990	The Children's Blessing	Open		95.00	95
1992	Childrens's Devotion (Painted)	Open		195.00	195
1990	The Good Shepherd	Open		95.00	95
1993	Jesus, The Carpenter	Open		95.00	95
1991	Jesus, The Teacher	9,500		95.00	95
1990	Madonna And Child	Open		95.00	95
1992	Mary & Christ Child (Painted)	Open		195.00	195
1991	The Savior	Open		95.00	95

Miniature Santas Around the World-8" - Unknown

1993	Americana Santa	Open		19.50	20
1993	Bavarian Santa	Open		19.50	20
1994	Befona	Open		19.50	20
1994	Christkindle	Open		19.50	20
1993	Father Christmas	Open		19.50	20
1993	Grandfather Frost	Open		19.50	20
1993	Kris Kringle	Open		19.50	20
1994	Patriotic Santa	Open		19.50	20
1993	Pere Noel	Open		19.50	20
1994	Sanct Herr Nikolaus	Open		19.50	20
1994	Santa Lucia	Open		19.50	20
1994	Sinterklaus	Open		19.50	20
1994	St. Mikulase	Open		19.50	20
1993	St. Nick	Open		19.50	20
1994	Victorian Santa	Open		19.50	20

Mother & Child - Unknown

1991	Afternoon Stroll	7,500		136.00	136
1990	Bedtime Prayers	Open		119.00	119
1986	Cherished Moment	Open		119.00	119
1989	Christening	Open		119.00	119
1991	Evening Lullaby	7,500		136.00	136
1992	Morning Playtime	Open		136.00	136
1988	The Present	Open		119.00	119
1987	Storytime	Open		119.00	119
1986	Sunday in the Park	Open		119.00	119

Nativity - Unknown

1989	Angels of Adoration	Open		136.00	152
1988	Animals of the Nativity	Open		119.00	152
1990	Children of Bethlehem	Open		136.00	152
1986	Holy Family	Open		119.00	136
1988	Shepherds	Open		119.00	152
1991	Standing Camel & Driver	9,500		152.00	152
1987	Three Kings	Open		119.00	152
1991	Townspeople of Bethlehem	Open		136.00	152

Nature's Beautiful Butterflies - Unknown

1991	Adonis	Open		45.00	45
1993	American Painted Lady	Open		45.00	45
1993	Black Swallowtail	Open		45.00	45
1989	Blue Temora	Open		39.00	45
1993	Great Orange Wingtip	Open		45.00	45
1991	Malachite	Open		45.00	45
1990	Monarch	Open		39.00	45
1990	Purple Emperor	Open		45.00	45
1994	Rainforest Dazzler	Open		45.00	45
1990	Yellow Swallowtail	Open		39.00	45

North American Bird Pairs - Unknown

1991	Blue Jay Pairs	Open		119.00	119
1992	Cardinal	Open		119.00	119
1991	Chickadees	Open		119.00	119
1990	Hummingbirds	Open		119.00	119

North American Wildlife - Unknown

1991	White Tailed Deer	Open		195.00	195

Owls of America - Unknown

1989	Barn Owl	Open		136.00	136
1991	Great Horned Owl	9,500		136.00	136
1990	Screech Owl	Open		136.00	136
1988	Snowy Owl	Open		136.00	136

Parent & Child Bird Pairs - Unknown

1992	Blue Jay Pairs	Open		119.00	119

Porcelain Duck Collection - Unknown

1992	Blue Winged Teal Duck	Open		45.00	45
1991	Mallard Duck	Open		45.00	45
1993	Pintail Duck	Open		45.00	45
1991	Wood Duck	Open		45.00	45

Religious Sculptures - Unknown

1994	Footsteps in the Sand	Open		152.00	152
1993	Last Supper	Open		152.00	152
1992	Moses	Open		95.00	95
1994	Pieta	Open		152.00	152
1995	Praying Hands	Open		95.00	95

Renaissance Nativity - Unknown

1991	Angels	Open		195.00	195
1995	Angels of Harmony	Open		195.00	195
1991	Animals of the Nativity	Open		195.00	195
1993	Camel & Driver	9,500		195.00	195
1994	Children of Bethlehem	9,500		195.00	195
1991	Holy Family	Open		195.00	195
1991	Shepherds of Bethlehem	Open		195.00	195
1991	Three Kings	Open		195.00	195

Santa Claus Collection - Unknown

1991	Americana Santa	Open		136.00	136
1994	Bavarian Santa	Open		136.00	136
1990	Father Christmas	Open		136.00	136
1992	Grandfather Frost	Open		136.00	136
1991	Kris Kringle	Open		136.00	136
1992	Pere Noel	Open		136.00	136
1993	St. Nick	Open		136.00	136
1994	Victorian Santa	Open		136.00	136

Street Crier Collection - Unknown

1991	Belgian Lace Maker	Open		136.00	136
1990	French Flower Maiden	Open		136.00	136

Unicorns - Unknown

1995	Celestial Unicorn (Statement #2)	4,500		295.00	295
1993	Eternal Enchantment (Statement #1)	Open		245.00	245
1994	Golden Grace	Open		149.00	149
1995	Love's Celebration (Anniversary/Spec. Ed.)	9,500		136.00	136
1994	Love's Magic	Open		119.00	119
1994	Love's Messenger (Valentine)	Open		119.00	119
1993	Love's Paradise	Open		119.00	119
1993	Love's Pride	Open		119.00	119
1995	Mid-Summer's Night Unicorn (Spec. Ed.)	9,500		149.00	149
1994	Platinum Purity	Open		149.00	149
1994	Royal Court Unicorn	Open		136.00	136
1994	Unicorn of Summer	Open		119.00	119
1992	Yuletide Blessing (Christmas)	Yr.Iss.	1992	119.00	119
1993	Yuletide Magic (Christmas)	Yr.Iss.	1993	119.00	119
1994	Yuletide Splendor (Christmas)	Yr.Iss.	1994	119.00	119

Wildlife of the Seven Continents - Unknown

1988	African Lion	Open		136.00	136
1987	Antarctic Seals	Open		136.00	136
1985	Asian Elephant	Open		120.00	120
1985	Australian Koala	Open		120.00	120
1987	European Red Deer	Open		136.00	136
1984	North American Bighorn Sheep	Open		120.00	120
1986	South American Puma	Open		120.00	120

Woodland Animals - Unknown

1991	Autumn Adventure (Chipmunk)	Open		39.00	39
1993	Autumn Splendor (Fawn)	Open		45.00	45
1992	Daybreak Discovery (Rabbit)	Open		39.00	39
1994	Early Morning Surprise (Fox)	Open		45.00	45
1995	Forest Friends (Statement)	Open		97.00	97
1994	Nature's Reward (Mouse)	Open		45.00	45
1994	Playful Pursuit (Black Bear)	Open		45.00	45
1993	Scent of Spring (Skunk)	Open		45.00	45
1995	Spring Shadow (Ground Hog)	Open		45.00	45
1990	Springtime Skamper (Red Squirrel)	Open		39.00	39
1994	Summer Delight (Chipmunk)	Open		45.00	45
1990	Twilight Mischief (Raccoon)	Open		39.00	39
1994	Woodland Worker (Beaver)	Open		45.00	45

Lilliput Lane Ltd.

Collectors Club Specials - Various

1986	Packhorse Bridge - D. Tate	Retrd.	1987	Gift	700
1986	Packhorse Bridge (dealer) - D. Tate	Retrd.	1987	Gift	450-750
1986	Crendon Manor - D. Tate	Retrd.	1989	285.00	850
1986	Gulliver - Unknown	Retrd.	1986	65.00	300
1987	Little Lost Dog - D. Tate	Retrd.	1988	Gift	375
1987	Yew Tree Farm - D. Tate	Retrd.	1988	160.00	230
1988	Wishing Well - D. Tate	Retrd.	1989	Gift	105
1989	Dovecot - D. Tate	Retrd.	1990	Gift	95
1989	Wenlock Rise - D. Tate	Retrd.	1989	175.00	150-200
1990	Cosy Corner - D. Tate	Retrd.	1991	Gift	75-100
1990	Lavender Cottage - D. Tate	Retrd.	1991	50.00	75
1990	Bridle Way - D. Tate	Retrd.	1991	100.00	150-225

YEAR ISSUE		EDITION LIMIT	YEAR RETD.	ISSUE PRICE	QUOTE U.S.$
1991	Puddlebrook - D. Tate	Retrd.	1992	Gift	60-100
1991	Gardeners Cottage - D. Tate	Retrd.	1992	120.00	175-225
1991	Wren Cottage - D. Tate	Retrd.	1993	13.95	60-100
1992	Pussy Willow - D. Tate	Retrd.	1993	Gift	36-60
1992	Forget-Me-Not - D. Tate	Retrd.	1993	130.00	150
1993	The Spinney - Lilliput Lane	Retrd.	1994	Gift	100
1993	Heaven Lea Cottage - Lilliput Lane	Retrd.	1994	150.00	250
1993	Curlew Cottage - Lilliput Lane	Retrd.	1995	18.95	19
1994	Petticoat Cottage - Lilliput Lane	Retrd.	1995	Gift	50-95
1994	Woodman's Retreat - Lilliput Lane	Retrd.	1995	135.00	135-195
1995	Thimble Cottage - Lilliput Lane	4/96		Gift	N/A
1995	Porlock Down - Lilliput Lane	4/96		135.00	135

Anniversary Special - Lilliput Lane

YEAR ISSUE		EDITION LIMIT	YEAR RETD.	ISSUE PRICE	QUOTE U.S.$
1992	Honeysuckle Cottage	Yr.Iss.	1992	195.00	300-450
1993	Cotman Cottage	Yr.Iss.	1993	220.00	265-350
1994	Watermeadows	Yr.Iss.	1994	189.00	189
1995	Gertrude's Garden	Yr.Iss.		192.00	192

Special Event Collection - Various

YEAR ISSUE		EDITION LIMIT	YEAR RETD.	ISSUE PRICE	QUOTE U.S.$
1989	1989 South Bend-Commemorative Medallion - D. Tate	Retrd.	1989	N/A	130-200
1990	1990 South Bend-Rowan Lodge D. Tate	Retrd.	1990	N/A	200-400
1991	1991 South Bend-Gamekeepers Cottage - D. Tate	Retrd.	1991	N/A	200
1992	1992 South Bend-Ashberry Cottage - D. Tate	Retrd.	1992	N/A	255-400
1993	1993 South Bend-Magnifying Glass - Lilliput Lane	Retrd.	1993	N/A	N/A

American Collection - D. Tate

YEAR ISSUE		EDITION LIMIT	YEAR RETD.	ISSUE PRICE	QUOTE U.S.$
1984	Adobe Church	Retrd.	1985	22.50	600-900
1984	Adobe Village	Retrd.	1985	60.00	800-1500
1984	Cape Cod	Retrd.	1985	22.50	570-910
1984	Country Church	Retrd.	1985	22.50	500-800
1984	Covered Bridge	Retrd.	1985	22.50	1000-2000
1984	Forge Barn	Retrd.	1985	22.50	550-660
1984	General Store	Retrd.	1985	22.50	600-1000
1984	Grist Mill	Retrd.	1985	22.50	500-785
1984	Light House	Retrd.	1985	22.50	650-900
1984	Log Cabin	Retrd.	1985	22.50	625-1000
1984	Midwest Barn	Retrd.	1985	22.50	250
1984	San Francisco House	Retrd.	1985	22.50	840
1984	Wallace Station	Retrd.	1985	22.50	400

American Landmark Series - R. Day

YEAR ISSUE		EDITION LIMIT	YEAR RETD.	ISSUE PRICE	QUOTE U.S.$
1992	16.9 Cents Per Gallon	Open		150.00	160
1994	Birdsong	Open		120.00	120
1990	Country Church	Retrd.	1992	82.50	110-175
1989	Countryside Barn	Retrd.	1992	75.00	120-200
1990	Covered Memories	Retrd.	1993	110.00	200
1989	Falls Mill	Retrd.	1992	130.00	225-300
1991	Fire House 1	Open		87.50	110
1994	Fresh Bread	Open		150.00	150
1992	Gold Miners' Claim	Open		110.00	120
1990	Great Point Light	Open		39.50	55
1994	Harvest Mill	3,500		395.00	395
1994	Holy Night	Open		225.00	225
1992	Home Sweet Home	Open		120.00	130
1990	Hometown Depot	Retrd.	1993	68.00	100-125
1989	Mail Pouch Barn	Retrd.	1993	75.00	130
1990	Pepsi Cola Barn	Retrd.	1991	87.00	225
1990	Pioneer Barn	Retrd.	1991	30.00	75
1991	Rambling Rose	Retrd.	1995	60.00	85
1990	Riverside Chapel	Retrd.	1993	82.50	130-150
1990	Roadside Coolers	Retrd.	1994	75.00	110-190
1991	School Days	Open		60.00	80
1993	See Rock City	N/A		60.00	60
1993	Shave and A Haircut	N/A		160.00	160
1990	Sign Of The Times	Open		27.50	35
1993	Simply Amish	Open		160.00	160
1992	Small Town Library	Retrd.	1995	130.00	140
1994	Spring Victorian	Open		250.00	250
1991	Victoriana	Retrd.	1992	295.00	350-650
1992	Winnie's Place	Retrd.	1993	395.00	550-850

Blaise Hamlet Classics - Lilliput Lane

YEAR ISSUE		EDITION LIMIT	YEAR RETD.	ISSUE PRICE	QUOTE U.S.$
1993	Circular Cottage	Retrd.	1995	95.00	95
1993	Dial Cottage	Retrd.	1995	95.00	95
1993	Diamond Cottage	Retrd.	1995	95.00	95
1993	Double Cottage	Retrd.	1995	95.00	95
1993	Jasmine Cottage	Retrd.	1995	95.00	95
1993	Oak Cottage	Retrd.	1995	95.00	95
1993	Rose Cottage	Retrd.	1995	95.00	145
1993	Sweet Briar Cottage	Retrd.	1995	95.00	95
1993	Vine Cottage	Retrd.	1995	95.00	135

Blaise Hamlet Collection - D. Tate

YEAR ISSUE		EDITION LIMIT	YEAR RETD.	ISSUE PRICE	QUOTE U.S.$
1989	Circular Cottage	Retrd.	1993	110.00	100-150
1990	Dial Cottage	Retrd.	1995	110.00	100-150
1989	Diamond Cottage	Retrd.	1993	110.00	100-150
1991	Double Cottage	Open		200.00	100-150
1991	Jasmine Cottage	Open		140.00	100-150
1989	Oak Cottage	Retrd.	1993	110.00	100-150
1991	Rose Cottage	Open		140.00	150
1990	Sweetbriar Cottage	Retrd.	1995	110.00	100-150
1990	Vine Cottage	Retrd.	1995	110.00	100-150

Christmas Collection - Various

YEAR ISSUE		EDITION LIMIT	YEAR RETD.	ISSUE PRICE	QUOTE U.S.$
1992	Chestnut Cottage	Open		46.50	50
1992	Cranberry Cottage	Open		46.50	50
1988	Deer Park Hall - D. Tate	Retrd.	1989	120.00	200-350
1993	The Gingerbread Shop	Open		50.00	50
1992	Hollytree House	Open		46.50	50
1991	The Old Vicarage at Christmas D. Tate	Retrd.	1992	180.00	175-350
1993	Partridge Cottage	Open		50.00	50
1994	Ring O' Bells	Open		50.00	50
1993	St. Joseph's Church	Open		70.00	70
1994	St. Joseph's School	Open		50.00	50
1989	St. Nicholas Church - D. Tate	Retrd.	1990	130.00	150-250
1994	The Vicarage	Open		50.00	200-350
1990	Yuletide Inn - D. Tate	Retrd.	1991	145.00	120-150

Christmas Lodge Collection - Lilliput Lane

YEAR ISSUE		EDITION LIMIT	YEAR RETD.	ISSUE PRICE	QUOTE U.S.$
1993	Eamont Lodge	Retrd.	1993	185.00	300
1992	Highland Lodge	Retrd.	1992	180.00	120-300
1995	Kerry Lodge	Yr.Iss.		160.00	160
1994	Snowdon Lodge	Retrd.	1994	175.00	175

Countryside Scene Plaques - D. Simpson

YEAR ISSUE		EDITION LIMIT	YEAR RETD.	ISSUE PRICE	QUOTE U.S.$
1989	Bottle Kiln	Retrd.	1991	49.50	50
1989	Cornish Tin Mine	Retrd.	1991	49.50	50
1989	Country Inn	Retrd.	1991	49.50	50
1989	Cumbrian Farmhouse	Retrd.	1991	49.50	50
1989	Lighthouse	Retrd.	1991	49.50	50
1989	Norfolk Windmill	Retrd.	1991	49.50	50
1989	Oasthouse	Retrd.	1991	49.50	50
1989	Old Smithy	Retrd.	1991	49.50	50
1989	Parish Church	Retrd.	1991	49.50	50
1989	Post Office	Retrd.	1991	49.50	50
1989	Village School	Retrd.	1991	49.50	50
1989	Watermill	Retrd.	1991	49.50	50

Dutch Collection - D. Tate

YEAR ISSUE		EDITION LIMIT	YEAR RETD.	ISSUE PRICE	QUOTE U.S.$
1991	Aan de Amstel	Open		79.00	85
1991	Begijnhof	Open		55.00	60
1991	Bloemenmarkt	Open		79.00	85
1991	De Branderij	Open		72.50	80
1991	De Diamantair	Open		79.00	85
1991	De Pepermolen	Open		55.00	60
1991	De Wolhandelaar	Open		72.50	80
1991	De Zijdewever	Open		79.00	85
1991	Rembrant van Rijn	Open		120.00	130
1991	Rozengracht	Open		72.50	80

English Cottages - D. Tate, unless otherwise noted

YEAR ISSUE		EDITION LIMIT	YEAR RETD.	ISSUE PRICE	QUOTE U.S.$
1982	Acorn Cottage-Mold 1	Retrd.	1983	30.00	250-350
1983	Acorn Cottage-Mold 2	Retrd.	1987	30.00	65
1982	Anne Hathaway's-Mold 1	Retrd.	1983	40.00	2500
1983	Anne Hathaway's-Mold 2	Retrd.	1984	40.00	400-600
1984	Anne Hathaway's-Mold 3	Retrd.	1988	40.00	375
1989	Anne Hathaway's-Mold 4	Open		130.00	150
1991	Anne of Cleves	Open		360.00	395
1994	Applejack Cottage - Lilliput Lane	Open		45.00	45
1982	April Cottage-Mold 1	Retrd.	1984	Unkn.	300
1982	April Cottage-Mold 2	Retrd.	1989	Unkn.	125
1991	Armada House	Open		175.00	185
1989	Ash Nook	Retrd.	1995	47.50	60
1986	Bay View	Retrd.	1988	39.50	90-125
1987	Beacon Heights - Lilliput Lane	Retrd.	1992	125.00	150
1989	Beehive Cottage	Retrd.	1995	72.50	95
1993	Birdlip Bottom - Lilliput Lane	Open		80.00	80
1992	Bow Cottage	Open		128.00	135
1990	Bramble Cottage	Retrd.	1995	55.00	70
1988	Bredon House	Retrd.	1990	145.00	150-275
1989	The Briary	Retrd.	1995	47.50	60
1982	Bridge House-Mold 1	Retrd.	N/A	15.95	450
1982	Bridge House-Mold 2	Retrd.	1990	15.95	175
1991	Bridge House-Mold 3	Open		25.00	30
1988	Brockbank	Retrd.	1993	58.00	80
1985	Bronte Parsonage	Retrd.	1987	72.00	80
1982	Burnside	Retrd.	1985	30.00	550
1990	Buttercup Cottage	Retrd.	1992	40.00	65
1989	Butterwick	Open		52.50	70
1995	Button Down - Lilliput Lane	Open		37.50	38
1994	Camomile Lawn - Lilliput Lane	Open		125.00	125
1982	Castle Street	Retrd.	1986	130.00	240-350
1993	Cat's Coombe Cottage - Lilliput Lane	Retrd.	1995	95.00	95
1991	Chatsworth View	Open		250.00	275
1995	Cherry Blossom Cottage - Lilliput Lane	Open		128.00	128
1990	Cherry Cottage	Retrd.	1995	33.50	45
1989	Chiltern Mill	Retrd.	1995	87.50	110
1989	Chine Cot-Mold 1	Retrd.	1989	36.00	N/A
1989	Chine Cot-Mold 2	Open		36.00	50
1995	Chipping Combe - Lilliput Lane	3,000		525.00	525
1992	The Chocolate House - Lilliput Lane	Open		130.00	140
1985	Clare Cottage	Retrd.	1993	30.00	63
1993	Cley-next-the-sea - Lilliput Lane	2,500		725.00	725
1987	Clover Cottage	Retrd.	1994	27.50	58
1982	Coach House	Retrd.	1985	100.00	11-1895
1986	Cobblers Cottage - D. Hall	Retrd.	1994	42.00	65
1990	Convent in The Woods	Open		175.00	220
1983	Coopers	Retrd.	1986	15.00	440-825
1994	Creel Cottage - Lilliput Lane	Open		40.00	40
1988	Crown Inn	Retrd.	1992	120.00	120-215
1991	Daisy Cottage	Open		37.50	40
1982	Dale Farm-Mold 1	Retrd.	1986	30.00	1300
1982	Dale Farm-Mold 2	Retrd.	1986	30.00	875
1986	Dale Head	Retrd.	1988	75.00	85-200
1982	Dale House	Retrd.	1986	25.00	840
1992	Derwent-le-Dale - Lilliput Lane	Open		75.00	80
1983	Dove Cottage-Mold 1	Retrd.	1984	35.00	725-1800
1984	Dove Cottage-Mold 2	Retrd.	1988	35.00	55-85
1991	Dovetails	Open		90.00	95
1982	Drapers-Mold 1	Retrd.	1983	15.95	5000
1982	Drapers-Mold 2	Retrd.	1983	15.95	4025
1995	Duckdown Cottage - Lilliput Lane	Open		95.00	95
1994	Elm Cottage - Lilliput Lane	Open		65.00	65
1985	Farriers	Retrd.	1990	40.00	40
1991	Farthing Lodge	Open		37.50	40
1992	Finchingfields - Lilliput Lane	Retrd.	1995	82.50	95
1985	Fisherman's Cottage	Retrd.	1989	30.00	70
1989	Fiveways	Retrd.	1995	42.50	55
1991	The Flower Sellers	Open		110.00	120
1987	Four Seasons - M. Adkinson	Retrd.	1991	70.00	100-140
1993	Foxglove Fields - Lilliput Lane	Open		130.00	130
1987	The Gables - Lilliput Lane	Retrd.	1992	145.00	165
1992	Granny Smiths	Open		60.00	65
1992	Grantchester Meadows - Lilliput Lane	Open		275.00	275
1989	Greensted Church	Retrd.	1995	72.50	95
1994	Gulliver's Gate - Lilliput Lane	Open		45.00	45
1989	Helmere Cottage	Retrd.	1995	65.00	80-125
1992	High Ghyll Farm - Lilliput Lane	Open		360.00	395
1982	Holly Cottage	Retrd.	1988	42.50	85
1987	Holme Dyke	Retrd.	1990	50.00	65
1982	Honeysuckle	Retrd.	1987	45.00	130-200
1991	Hopcroft Cottage	Retrd.	1995	120.00	130
1987	Inglewood	Retrd.	1994	27.50	40
1987	Izaak Waltons Cottage	Retrd.	1989	75.00	80-200
1991	John Barleycorn Cottage	Open		130.00	140
1993	Junk and Disorderly - Lilliput Lane	Open		150.00	150
1987	Keepers Lodge	Retrd.	1988	75.00	85-125
1985	Kentish Oast	Retrd.	1990	55.00	150
1990	The King's Arms	Retrd.	1995	450.00	550
1991	Lace Lane	Open		90.00	95
1995	Ladybird Cottage - Lilliput Lane	Open		40.00	40
1982	Lakeside House-Mold 1	Retrd.	1983	40.00	1500
1982	Lakeside House-Mold 2	Retrd.	1986	40.00	810-940
1991	Lapworth Lock	Retrd.	1993	82.50	85
1995	Larkrise - Lilliput Lane	Open		50.00	50
1995	Lazy Days - Lilliput Lane	Open		60.00	60
1994	Lenora's Secret - Lilliput Lane	Retrd.	1994	350.00	450
1995	Little Hay - Lilliput Lane	Open		55.00	55
1995	Little Smithy - Lilliput Lane	Open		65.00	65
1987	Magpie Cottage	Retrd.	1990	70.00	85-250
1993	Marigold Meadow - Lilliput Lane	Open		120.00	120
1991	Micklegate Antiques	Open		90.00	95
1995	Milestone Cottage - Lilliput Lane	Open		40.00	40
1983	Millers	Retrd.	1986	15.00	120-200
1983	Miners-Mold 1	Retrd.	1985	15.00	590
1983	Miners-Mold 2	Retrd.	1985	15.00	375-455
1991	Moonlight Cove	Open		82.50	85
1985	Moreton Manor	Retrd.	1989	55.00	70
1990	Mrs. Pinkerton's Post Office	Open		72.50	85
1992	The Nutshell - Lilliput Lane	Retrd.	1995	75.00	80
1982	Oak Lodge	Retrd.	1987	40.00	100
1992	Oakwood Smithy	Open		450.00	475
1985	Old Curiosity Shop	Retrd.	1989	62.50	100
1982	Old Mine	Retrd.	1983	15.95	6500
1993	Old Mother Hubbard's - Lilliput Lane	Open		185.00	185
1982	The Old Post Office	Retrd.	1986	35.00	500
1984	Old School House	Retrd.	1985	25.00	1000-1400
1991	Old Shop at Bignor	Open		215.00	220
1989	Olde York Toll	Retrd.	1991	82.50	83-110
1994	Orchard Farm Cottage - Lilliput Lane	Open		145.00	145
1985	Ostlers Keep	Retrd.	1991	55.00	150-200
1990	Otter Reach	Open		33.50	45
1991	Paradise Lodge	Open		130.00	140
1988	Pargetters Retreat	Retrd.	1990	75.00	100-150
1991	Pear Tree House	Retrd.	1995	82.50	85
1995	Penny's Post - Lilliput Lane	Open		55.00	55
1990	Periwinkle Cottage	Open		165.00	220
1995	Pipit Toll - Lilliput Lane	Open		64.00	64
1992	Pixie House	Retrd.	1995	55.00	60
1991	The Priest's House	Open		180.00	195
1991	Primrose Hill	Open		46.50	50
1992	Puffin Row	Open		128.00	135
1993	Purbeck Stores - Lilliput Lane	Open		55.00	55
1983	Red Lion Inn	Retrd.	1987	125.00	360
1988	Rising Sun	Retrd.	1992	58.00	84-105
1987	Riverview	Retrd.	1994	27.50	40
1990	Robin's Gate	Open		33.50	45
1988	Royal Oak	Retrd.	1991	145.00	150-300
1990	Runswick House	Open		62.50	80
1992	Rustic Root House	Open		110.00	120
1995	The Rustlings - Lilliput Lane	Open		128.00	128
1987	Rydal View	Retrd.	1989	220.00	200
1987	Saddlers Inn - M. Adkinson	Retrd.	1989	50.00	50-70
1994	Saffron House - Lilliput Lane	Open		220.00	220
1985	Sawrey Gill	Retrd.	1992	30.00	175-230
1991	Saxham St. Edmunds	Retrd.	1994	1550.00	1850
1988	Saxon Cottage	Retrd.	1989	245.00	200
1986	Scroll on the Wall	Retrd.	1987	55.00	170
1987	Secret Garden - M. Adkinson	Retrd.	1994	145.00	220
1988	Ship Inn - Lilliput Lane	Retrd.	1992	210.00	228-325
1988	Smallest Inn	Retrd.	1991	42.50	65
1986	Spring Bank	Retrd.	1991	42.00	50-70
1994	Spring Gate Cottage - Lilliput Lane	Open		130.00	130

YEAR ISSUE		EDITION LIMIT	YEAR RETD.	ISSUE PRICE	QUOTE U.S.$
1989	St. Lawrence Church	Open		110.00	140
1988	St. Marks	Retrd.	1991	75.00	150-225
1985	St. Mary's Church	Retrd.	1988	40.00	75-125
1989	St. Peter's Cove	Retrd.	1991	1375.00	1500-2500
1993	Stocklebeck Mill - Lilliput Lane	Open		325.00	325
1982	Stone Cottage-Mold 1	Retrd.	1983	40.00	1500
1982	Stone Cottage-Mold 2	Retrd.	1986	40.00	170
1986	Stone Cottage-Mold 3	Retrd.	1986	40.00	200
1987	Stoneybeck	Retrd.	1992	45.00	60-75
1993	Stradling Priory - Lilliput Lane	Open		130.00	130
1990	Strawberry Cottage	Open		36.00	45
1987	Street Scene No. 1 - Unknown	Retrd.	1987	40.00	120
1987	Street Scene No. 2 - Unknown	Retrd.	1987	45.00	120
1987	Street Scene No. 3 - Unknown	Retrd.	1987	45.00	120
1987	Street Scene No. 4 - Unknown	Retrd.	1987	45.00	120
1987	Street Scene No. 5 - Unknown	Retrd.	1987	40.00	120
1987	Street Scene No. 6 - Unknown	Retrd.	1987	40.00	120
1987	Street Scene No. 7 - Unknown	Retrd.	1987	40.00	120
1987	Street Scene No. 8 - Unknown	Retrd.	1987	40.00	120
1987	Street Scene No. 9 - Unknown	Retrd.	1987	45.00	120
1987	Street Scene No. 99 - Unknown	Retrd.	1987	45.00	120
1987	Street Scene Set - Unknown	Retrd.	1987	425.00	800-1000
1990	Sulgrave Manor	Retrd.	1992	120.00	130-280
1987	Summer Haze	Retrd.	1993	90.00	130
1994	Sunnyside - Lilliput Lane	Open		40.00	40
1982	Sussex Mill	Retrd.	1986	25.00	325-500
1988	Swan Inn	Retrd.	1992	120.00	170-225
1994	Sweet Pea Cottage - Lilliput Lane	Open		40.00	40
1988	Swift Hollow	Retrd.	1990	75.00	75-175
1989	Tanglewood Lodge	Retrd.	1992	97.00	150-200
1987	Tanners Cottage	Retrd.	1992	27.50	45
1994	Teacaddy Cottage - Lilliput Lane	Open		79.00	79
1983	Thatcher's Rest	Retrd.	1988	185.00	250
1986	Three Feathers	Retrd.	1989	115.00	200-250
1991	Tillers Green	Retrd.	1995	60.00	65
1984	Tintagel	Retrd.	1988	39.50	175
1994	Tired Timbers - Lilliput Lane	Open		80.00	80
1989	Titmouse Cottage	Retrd.	1995	92.50	120
1993	Titwillow Cottage - Lilliput Lane	Open		70.00	70
1983	Toll House	Retrd.	1987	15.00	150
1983	Troutbeck Farm	Retrd.	1987	125.00	250
1983	Tuck Shop	Retrd.	1986	35.00	650
1986	Tudor Court - Lilliput Lane	Retrd.	1992	260.00	275
1994	Two Hoots - Lilliput Lane	Open		75.00	75
1989	Victoria Cottage	Retrd.	1993	52.50	65
1991	Village School	Open		120.00	130
1983	Warwick Hall-Mold 1	Retrd.	1983	185.00	3000-4000
1983	Warwick Hall-Mold 2	Retrd.	1985	185.00	1300-1800
1985	Watermill	Retrd.	1993	40.00	68
1994	Waterside Mill - Lilliput Lane	Open		65.00	65
1987	Wealden House	Retrd.	1990	125.00	140
1992	Wedding Bells - Lilliput Lane	Open		75.00	80
1991	Wellington Lodge	Retrd.	1995	55.00	60
1992	Wheyside Cottage - Lilliput Lane	Open		46.50	50
1989	Wight Cottage	Retrd.	1994	52.50	65
1982	William Shakespeare-Mold 1	Retrd.	1983	55.00	1500-3000
1983	William Shakespeare-Mold 2	Retrd.	1986	55.00	240
1986	William Shakespeare-Mold 3	Retrd.	1989	55.00	215
1989	William Shakespeare-Mold 4	Retrd.	1992	130.00	150
1991	Witham Delph	Retrd.	1994	110.00	120
1983	Woodcutters	Retrd.	1987	15.00	190

English Tea Room Collection - Lilliput Lane

1995	Bargate Cottage Tea Room	Open		160.00	160
1995	Bo-Peep Tea Rooms	Open		120.00	120
1995	Grandma Batty's Tea Room	Open		120.00	120
1995	Kendal Tea House	Open		120.00	120
1995	New Forest Teas	Open		160.00	160

Framed English Plaques - D. Tate

1990	Ashdown Hall	Retrd.	1991	59.50	70
1990	Battleview	Retrd.	1991	59.50	70
1990	Cat Slide Cottage	Retrd.	1991	59.50	70
1990	Coombe Cot	Retrd.	1991	59.50	70
1990	Fell View	Retrd.	1991	59.50	70
1990	Flint Fields	Retrd.	1991	59.50	70
1990	Huntingdon House	Retrd.	1991	59.50	70
1990	Jubilee Lodge	Retrd.	1991	59.50	70
1990	Stowside	Retrd.	1991	59.50	70
1990	Trevan Cove	Retrd.	1991	59.50	70

Framed Irish Plaques - D. Tate

1990	Ballyteag House	Retrd.	1991	59.50	70
1990	Crockuna Croft	Retrd.	1991	59.50	70
1990	Pearses Cottages	Retrd.	1991	59.50	70
1990	Shannons Bank	Retrd.	1991	59.50	70

Framed Scottish Plaques - D. Tate

1990	Barra Black House	Retrd.	1991	59.50	70
1990	Fife Ness	Retrd.	1991	59.50	70
1990	Kyle Point	Retrd.	1991	59.50	70
1990	Preston Oat Mill	Retrd.	1991	59.50	70

French Collection - D. Tate

1991	L' Auberge d'Armorique	Open		220.00	250
1991	La Bergerie du Perigord	Open		230.00	250
1991	La Cabane du Gardian	Open		55.00	60
1991	La Chaumiere du Verger	Open		120.00	130
1991	La Maselle de Nadaillac	Open		130.00	140
1991	La Porte Schoenenberg	Open		75.00	85
1991	Le Manoir de Champfleuri	Open		265.00	295
1991	Le Mas du Vigneron	Open		120.00	130
1991	Le Petite Montmartre	Open		130.00	140
1991	Locmaria	Open		65.00	80

German Collection - D. Tate

1992	Alte Schmiede	Open		175.00	185
1987	Das Gebirgskirchlein	Open		120.00	140
1988	Das Rathaus	Open		140.00	160
1992	Der Bücherwurm	Open		140.00	160
1988	Der Familienschrein	Retrd.	1991	52.50	110
1988	Die Kleine Backerei	Retrd.	1994	68.00	80
1987	Haus Im Rheinland	Open		220.00	250
1987	Jaghutte	Open		82.50	95
1987	Meersburger Weinstube	Open		82.50	95
1987	Moselhaus	Open		140.00	160
1987	Nurnberger Burgerhaus	Open		140.00	160
1992	Rosengartenhaus	Open		120.00	130
1987	Schwarzwaldhaus	Open		140.00	160
1992	Strandvogthaus	Open		120.00	130

Historic Castles of England - Lilliput Lane

1994	Bodiam Castle	Open		129.00	129
1994	Castell Coch	Open		149.00	149
1995	Penkhill Castles	Open		130.00	130
1994	Stokesay Castle	Open		99.00	99

Irish Cottages - D. Tate

1989	Ballykerne Croft	Open		75.00	95
1987	Donegal Cottage	Retrd.	1992	29.00	60
1989	Hegarty's Home	Retrd.	1992	68.00	75
1989	Kennedy Homestead	Open		33.50	45
1989	Kilmore Quay	Retrd.	1992	68.00	100
1989	Limerick House	Retrd.	1992	110.00	160-170
1989	Magilligans	Open		33.50	45
1989	O'Lacey's Store	Open		68.00	85
1989	Pat Cohan's Bar	Open		110.00	140
1989	Quiet Cottage	Retrd.	1992	72.50	120
1989	St. Columba's School	Open		47.50	60
1989	St. Kevin's Church	Open		55.00	70
1989	St. Patrick's Church	Retrd.	1993	185.00	185
1989	Thoor Ballylee	Retrd.	1992	105.00	160-170

Lakeland Bridge Plaques - D. Simpson

1989	Aira Force	Retrd.	1991	35.00	35
1989	Ashness Bridge	Retrd.	1991	35.00	35
1989	Birks Bridge	Retrd.	1991	35.00	35
1989	Bridge House	Retrd.	1991	35.00	105-120
1989	Hartsop Packhorse	Retrd.	1991	35.00	35
1989	Stockley Bridge	Retrd.	1991	35.00	35

Lakeland Christmas - Lilliput Lane

1995	Langdale Cottage	Open		48.00	48
1995	Patterdale Cottage	Open		48.00	48
1995	Rydal Cottage	Open		44.75	45

London Plaques - D. Simpson

1989	Big Ben	Retrd.	1991	39.50	40
1989	Buckingham Palace	Retrd.	1991	39.50	40
1989	Piccadilly Circus	Retrd.	1991	39.50	40
1989	Tower Bridge	Retrd.	1991	39.50	40
1989	Tower of London	Retrd.	1991	39.50	40
1989	Trafalgar Square	Retrd.	1991	39.50	40

Scottish Collection - D. Tate, unless otherwise noted

1985	7 St. Andrews Square - A. Yarrington	Retrd.	1986	15.95	110-225
1995	Amisfield Tower - Lilliput Lane	Open		55.00	55
1989	Blair Atholl	Retrd.	1992	275.00	375
1985	Burns Cottage	Retrd.	1988	35.00	95
1989	Carrick House	Open		47.50	60
1990	Cawdor Castle	Retrd.	1992	295.00	400-500
1989	Claypotts Castle	Open		72.50	95
1989	Craigievar Castle	Retrd.	1991	185.00	300-525
1984	The Croft (renovated)	Retrd.	1991	36.00	75-200
1982	The Croft (without sheep)	Retrd.	1984	29.00	800-1250
1989	Culloden Cottage	Open		36.00	45
1992	Culross House	Open		90.00	95
1992	Duart Castle	3,000		450.00	475
1987	East Neuk	Retrd.	1991	29.00	60-75
1993	Edzell Summer House - Lilliput Lane	Open		110.00	110
1990	Eilean Donan	Open		145.00	185
1992	Eriskay Croft	Open		50.00	55
1990	Fishermans Bothy	Open		36.00	45
1990	Glenlochie Lodge	Retrd.	1993	110.00	120
1990	Hebridean Hame	Retrd.	1992	55.00	65-120
1989	Inverlochie Hame	Open		47.50	60
1989	John Knox House	Retrd.	1992	68.00	250
1989	Kenmore Cottage	Retrd.	1993	87.00	110
1990	Kinlochness	Retrd.	1993	79.00	85-125
1990	Kirkbrae Cottage	Retrd.	1993	55.00	70-95
1994	Ladybank Lodge - Lilliput Lane	Open		80.00	80
1992	Mair Haven	Open		46.50	50
1985	Preston Mill-Mold 1	Retrd.	1986	45.00	175-200
1986	Preston Mill-Mold 2	Retrd.	1992	62.50	78
1989	Stockwell Tenement	Open		62.50	80

Specials - Various

1993	Aberford Gate - Lilliput Lane	Retrd.	1993	95.00	95
1985	Bermuda Cottage (3 Colors) - D. Tate	Retrd.	1991	29.00	40-50
1985	Bermuda Cottage (3 Colors)-set - D. Tate	Retrd.	1991	87.00	175-345
1983	Bridge House Dealer Sign - D. Tate	Retrd.	1984	N/A	120-170
1988	Chantry Chapel - D. Tate	Retrd.	1991	N/A	220-265
1983	Cliburn School - D. Tate	Retrd.	1984	Gift	6000-7000
1987	Clockmaker's Cottage - D. Tate	Retrd.	1990	40.00	200-235
1993	Counting House Corner	3,093	1993	N/A	N/A
1993	Counting House Corner(mounted)	3,093	1993	N/A	N/A
1991	Gamekeeper's Cottage	Retrd.	1992	75.00	200
1987	Guildhall - D. Tate	Retrd.	1989	N/A	145
1994	Leagrave Cottage	Open		75.00	75
1989	Mayflower House - D. Tate	Retrd.	1990	79.50	120-175
1992	Ploughman's Cottage	Retrd.	1993	75.00	75
1991	Rose Cottage Skirsgill-Mold 1	200	1991	N/A	700
1991	Rose Cottage Skirsgill-Mold 2	Retrd.	1991	N/A	250-300
1994	Rose Cottage Skirsgill-Mold 3	Open		N/A	N/A
1990	Rowan Lodge - D. Tate	Retrd.	1991	50.00	120
1986	Seven Dwarf's Cottage - D. Tate	Retrd.	1986	146.80	500-900
1994	Wycombe Toll House	Retrd.	1994	33.00	240-330

Studley Royal Collection - Lilliput Lane

1994	Banqueting House	5,000		65.00	65
1995	Fountains Abbey	3,500		395.00	395
1994	Octagon Tower	5,000		85.00	85
1994	St. Mary's Church	5,000		115.00	115
1994	Temple of Piety	5,000		95.00	95

Unframed Plaques - D. Tate

1989	Large Lower Brockhampton	Retrd.	1991	120.00	120
1989	Large Somerset Springtime	Retrd.	1991	130.00	130
1989	Medium Cobble Combe Cottage	Retrd.	1991	68.00	68
1989	Medium Wishing Well	Retrd.	1991	75.00	75
1989	Small Stoney Wall Lea	Retrd.	1991	47.50	48
1989	Small Woodside Farm	Retrd.	1991	47.50	48

Village Shop Collection - Various

1995	The Baker's Shop	Open		120.00	120
1995	The Chine Shop	Open		120.00	120
1992	The Greengrocers - D. Tate	Open		120.00	130
1993	Jones The Butcher	Open		120.00	120
1992	Penny Sweets	Open		130.00	130
1993	Toy Shop	Open		120.00	120

Welsh Collection - Various

1986	Brecon Bach - D. Tate	Retrd.	1993	42.00	65
1991	Bro Dawel - D. Tate	Open		37.50	40
1985	Hermitage - D. Tate	Retrd.	1986	30.00	250
1987	Hermitage Renovated - D. Tate	Retrd.	1990	42.50	100
1992	St. Govan's Chapel	Open		75.00	80
1991	Tudor Merchant - D. Tate	Open		90.00	95
1991	Ugly House - D. Tate	Open		55.00	60

A Year In An English Garden - Lilliput Lane

1994	Autumn Hues	Open		120.00	120
1995	Spring Glory	Open		120.00	120
1995	Summer Impressions	Open		120.00	120
1994	Winter's Wonder	Open		120.00	120

Lladro

Lladro Collectors Society - Lladro

1985	Little Pals S7600	Closed	1985	95.00	2000-3400
1985	LCS Plague w/blue writing S7601	Closed	N/A	35.00	75-125
1986	Little Traveler S7602	Closed	1986	95.00	1000-1700
1987	Spring Bouquets S7603	Closed	1987	125.00	700-1100
1988	School Days S7604	Closed	1988	125.00	500-800
1988	Flower Song S7607	Closed	1988	175.00	500-800
1989	My Buddy S7609	Closed	1989	145.00	250-600
1990	Can I Play? S7610	Closed	1990	150.00	300-600
1991	Summer Stroll S7611	Closed	1992	195.00	250-550
1991	Picture Perfect S7612	Closed	1991	350.00	350-650
1992	All Aboard S7619	Closed	1993	165.00	250-450
1993	Best Friend S7620	Closed	1993	195.00	250-400
1994	Basket of Love S7622	Closed	1994	225.00	300
1995	10 Year Society Anniversary - Ten and Growing S7635	Yr.Iss.		395.00	395
1995	Afternoon Promenade S7636	Yr.Iss.		240.00	240
1995	Now and Forever (10 year membership piece) S7642	N/A		395.00	395

Lladro Event Figurines - Lladro

1991	Garden Classic L7617G	Closed	1991	295.00	400-750
1992	Garden Song L7618G	Closed	1992	295.00	500-600
1993	Pick of the Litter L7621G	Closed	1993	350.00	350-500
1994	Little Riders L7623P	Closed	1994	250.00	250-350
1995	For A Perfect Performance L7641	Closed	1995	310.00	450

Capricho - Lladro

1988	Bust w/ Black Veil & base C1538	Open		650.00	975
1988	Small Bust w/ Veil & base C1539	Open		225.00	455
1987	Orchid Arrangement C1541	Closed	1990	500.00	1700-2100
1987	Iris Arrangement C1542	Closed	1990	800.00	1000-1500
1987	Fan C1546	Closed	1987	650.00	900-1600
1987	Fan C1546.3	Closed	1987	650.00	900-1600
1987	Iris with Vase C1551	Closed	1991	110.00	375
1987	Flowers Chest C1572	Open		550.00	900
1987	Flat Basket with Flowers C1575	Closed	1991	450.00	850
1989	White Rosary C1647	Closed	1991	290.00	340

FIGURINES/COTTAGES

YEAR ISSUE		EDITION LIMIT	YEAR RETD.	ISSUE PRICE	QUOTE U.S.$
1989	Romantic Lady / Black Veil w/base C1666	Closed	1993	420.00	520
1969	Frosted Angel w/Guitar C4507	Closed	1985	55.00	425
XX	White Bust w/ Veil & base C5927	Open		550.00	865
XX	Special Museum Flower Basket C7606	Closed	1991	N/A	300

Limited Edition - Lladro

YEAR ISSUE		EDITION LIMIT	YEAR RETD.	ISSUE PRICE	QUOTE U.S.$
1971	Hamlet LL1144	750	1973	125.00	3000-4000
1971	Othello and Desdemona LL1145	750	1973	275.00	2250
1971	Antique Auto LL1146	750	1975	1000.00	5500-7000
1971	Floral LL1184	200	1978	400.00	2200
1971	Floral LL1185	200	1974	475.00	1800
1971	Floral LL1186	200	1976	575.00	2200
1972	Eagles LL1189	750	1978	450.00	3200
1972	Sea Birds with Nest LL1194	500	1975	300.00	2750
1972	Turkey Group LL1196	350	1982	325.00	1800
1972	Peace LL1202	150	1973	550.00	7500
1972	Eagle Owl LL1223	750	1983	225.00	1050
1972	Hansom Carriage LL1225	750	1975	1450.00	1100-1400
1973	Hunting Scene LL1238	800	1976	400.00	2000
1973	Turtle Doves LL1240	850	1976	250.00	2300-2500
1973	The Forest LL1243	500	1976	625.00	3300
1974	Soccer Players LL1266	500	1983	1000.00	7500
1974	Man From LaMancha LL1269	1,500	1977	700.00	3700
1974	Queen Elizabeth II LL1275	250	1985	3650.00	5000
1974	Judge LL1281	1,200	1978	325.00	1200-1400
1974	The Hunt LL1308	750	1984	4750.00	6900
1974	Ducks at Pond LL1317	1,200	1984	4250.00	5700
1976	Impossible Dream LL1318	1,000	1983	1200.00	4400
1976	Comforting Baby LL1329	750	1978	350.00	1050
1976	Mountain Country Lady LL1330	750	1983	900.00	1700
1976	My Baby LL1331	1,000	1981	275.00	900
1978	Flight of Gazelles LL1352	1,500	1984	1225.00	3100
1978	Car in Trouble LL1375	1,500	1987	3000.00	5250
1978	Fearful Flight LL1377	750		7000.00	14500
1978	Henry VIII LL 1384	1,200	1993	650.00	850
1981	Venus and Cupid LL1392	750	1993	1100.00	1600-2100
1982	First Date w/base LL1393	1,500		3800.00	5900
1982	Columbus LL1432G	1,200	1988	535.00	1200
1983	Venetian Serenade LL1433	750	1989	2600.00	3750
1985	Festival in Valencia w/base LL1457	3,000	1994	1400.00	2350
1985	Camelot LL1458	3,000	1994	950.00	1650
1985	Napoleon Planning Battle w/base LL1459	12/95		825.00	1450
1985	Youthful Beauty w/base LL1461	5,000		750.00	1200
1985	Flock of Birds w/base LL1462	1,500		1060.00	1750
1985	Classic Spring LL1465	12/95		620.00	975
1985	Classic Fall LL1466	12/95		620.00	975
1985	Valencian Couple on Horse LL1472	3,000		885.00	1550
1985	Coach XVIII Century w/base LL1485	500		14000.00	26000
1986	The New World w/base LL1486	4,000		700.00	1350
1986	Fantasia w/base LL1487	5,000		1500.00	2700
1986	Floral Offering w/base LL1490	3,000		2500.00	4450
1986	Oriental Music w/base LL1491	5,000		1350.00	2445
1986	Three Sisters w/base LL1492	3,000		1850.00	3250
1986	At the Stroke of Twelve w/base LL1493	1,500	N/A	4250.00	6300-7500
1986	Hawaiian Festival w/base LL1496	4,000		1850.00	3200
1987	A Sunday Drive w/base LL1510	1,000		3400.00	4000
1987	Listen to Don Quixote w/base LL1520	750		1800.00	2900
1987	A Happy Encounter LL1523	1,500		2900.00	4900
1988	Japanese Vase LL1536	750	1989	2600.00	3250
1988	Garden Party w/base LL1578	500		5500.00	7250
1988	Blessed Lady w/base LL1579	1,000	1991	1150.00	3000
1988	Return to La Mancha w/base LL1580	500		6400.00	8350
1989	Southern Tea LL1597	12/95		1775.00	2300
1989	Kitakami Cruise w/base LL1605	500		5800.00	7500-9000
1989	Mounted Warriors w/base LL1608	500		2850.00	3450
1989	Circus Parade w/base LL1609	1,000		5200.00	6550
1989	"Jesus the Rock" w/base LL1615	1,000		1175.00	1550
1989	Hopeful Group LL1723	1,000	1993	1825.00	1825
1991	Valencian Cruise LL1731	1,000		2700.00	2950
1991	Venice Vows LL1732	1,500		3755.00	4100
1991	Liberty Eagle LL1738	1,500		1000.00	1100
1991	Heavenly Swing LL1739	1,000		1900.00	2050
1991	Columbus, Two Routes LL1740	12/95		1500.00	1650
1991	Columbus Reflecting LL1741	1,000	1994	1850.00	1995
1991	Onward! LL1742	1,000	1993	2500.00	2850
1991	The Prophet LL1743	300		800.00	875
1991	My Only Friend LL1744	200	1993	1400.00	2000-2550
1991	Dawn LL1745	N/A	1993	1200.00	2500
1991	Champion LL1746	300	1994	1800.00	1950
1991	Nesting Doves LL1747	300	1994	800.00	875
1991	Comforting News LL1748	300		1200.00	1325
1991	Baggy Pants LL1749	300	1994	1500.00	1650
1991	Circus Show LL1750	300	1994	1400.00	1525
1991	Maggie LL1751	300	1994	900.00	990
1991	Apple Seller LL1752	300	1994	900.00	1000-1150
1991	The Student LL1753	300		1300.00	1425
1991	Tree Climbers LL1754	300	1994	1500.00	1650
1991	The Princess And The Unicorn LL1755	1,500	1994	1750.00	1950-2250
1991	Outing In Seville LL1756	500		23000.00	24500
1992	Hawaiian Ceremony LL1757	1,000		9800.00	10250
1992	Circus Time LL1758	2,500		9200.00	9650
1992	Tea In The Garden LL1759	2,000		9500.00	9750
1993	Paella Valenciano w/base LL1762	500		10000.00	10000
1993	Trusting Friends w/base LL1763	350		1200.00	1200
1993	He's My Brother w/base LL1764	350		1500.00	1500
1993	The Course of Adventure LL1765	250		1625.00	1625
1993	Ties That Bind LL1766	250		1700.00	1700
1993	Motherly Love LL1767	250		1330.00	1330
1993	Travellers' Respite w/base LL1768	250		1825.00	1825
1993	Fruitful Harvest LL1769	350		1300.00	1300
1993	Gypsy Dancers LL1770	250		2250.00	2400
1993	Country Doctor w/base LL1771	250		1475.00	1475
1993	Back To Back LL1772	350		1450.00	1450
1993	Mischevous Musician LL1773	350		975.00	1045
1993	A Treasured Moment w/base LL1774	350		950.00	950
1993	Oriental Garden w/base LL1775	750		22500.00	22500
1994	Conquered by Love w/base LL1776	2,500		2850.00	2890
1994	Farewell Of The Samurai w/base LL1777	2,500		3950.00	3950
1994	Pegasus w/base LL1778	1,500		1950.00	1950
1994	High Speed w/base LL1779	1,500		3830.00	3830
1994	Indian Princess w/base LL1780	3,000		1630.00	1630
1994	Allegory of Time LL1781	5,000		1290.00	1290
1994	Circus Fanfare w/base LL1783	1,500		14240.00	14240
1994	Flower Wagon w/base LL1784	3,000		3290.00	3290
1994	Cinderella's Arrival w/base LL1785	1,500		25950.00	25950
1994	Floral Figure w/base LL1788	300		2198.00	2198
1994	Natural Beauty LL1795	500		650.00	650
1994	Floral Enchantment w/base LL1796	300		2990.00	2990
1995	Enchanted Outing w/base LL1797	3,000		3950.00	3950
1995	Far Away Thoughts LL1798	1,500		3600.00	3600
1995	Immaculate Virgin w/base LL1799	2,000		2250.00	2250
1995	To the Rim w/base LL1800	1,500		2475.00	2475
1995	Vision of Peace w/base LL1803	1,500		1895.00	1895
1995	Portrait of a Family w/base LL1805	2,500		1750.00	1750
1995	A Family of Love w/base LL1806	2,500		1750.00	1750
1995	A Dream of Peace w/base LL1807	2,000		1160.00	1160
1970	Girl with Guitar LL2016	750	1982	325.00	1800
1970	Madonna with Child LL2018	300	1974	450.00	1750
1971	Oriental Man LL2021	500	1983	500.00	1850
1971	Three Girls LL2028	500	1976	950.00	3500
1971	Eve at Tree LL2029	600	1976	450.00	3000
1971	Oriental Horse LL2030	350	1983	1100.00	35-5000
1971	Lyric Muse LL2031	400	1982	750.00	2100
1971	Madonna and Child LL2043	300	1974	400.00	1500
1973	Peasant Woman LL2049	750	1977	200.00	1300
1973	Passionate Dance LL2051	500	1975	375.00	4500
1977	St. Theresa LL2061	1,200	1987	387.50	1600
1977	Concerto LL2063	1,200	1988	500.00	1235
1977	Flying Partridges LL2064	1,200	1987	1750.00	4300
1987	Christopher Columbus w/base LL2176	1,000	1994	1000.00	1350
1990	Invincible w/base LL2188	300		1100.00	1250
1993	Flight of Fancy w/base LL2243	300		1400.00	1400
1993	The Awakening w/base LL2244	300		1200.00	1200
1993	Inspired Voyage w/base LL2245	1,000		4800.00	4800
1993	Days of Yore w/base LL2248	1,000		1950.00	2050
1993	Holiday Glow w/base LL2249	1,500		750.00	750
1993	Autumn Glow w/base LL2250	1,500		750.00	750
1993	Humble Grace w/base LL2255	2,000		2150.00	2150
1983	Dawn w/base LL3000	300		325.00	550
1983	Monks w/base LL3001	300	1993	1675.00	2550
1983	Waiting w/base LL3002	125	1991	1550.00	1900
1983	Indolence LL3003	150		1465.00	2100
1983	Venus in the Bath LL3005	N/A	1991	1175.00	1450
1987	Classic Beauty w/base LL3012	500		1300.00	1750
1987	Youthful Innocence w/base LL3013	500		1300.00	1750
1987	The Nymph w/base LL3014	250		1000.00	1450
1987	Dignity w/base LL3015	150		1400.00	1900
1988	Passion w/base LL3016	750		865.00	1200
1988	Muse w/base LL3017	300	1993	650.00	875
1988	Cellist w/base LL3018	300	1993	650.00	875
1988	True Affection w/base LL3019	300		750.00	1025
1989	Demureness w/base LL3020	300	1994	400.00	700
1990	Daydreaming w/base LL3022	500		550.00	775
1990	After The Bath w/base LL3023	300	1991	350.00	800-1300
1990	Discoveries w/Base LL3024	100		1500.00	1750
1991	Resting Nude LL3025	200	1992	650.00	1000
1991	Unadorned Beauty LL3026	200		1700.00	1850
1994	Ebony w/base LL3027	300		1295.00	1295
1994	Modesty w/base LL3028	300		1295.00	1295
1994	Danae LL3029	300		2880.00	2880
1995	Nude Kneeling LL3030	300		975.00	975
1982	Elk LL3501	500	1987	950.00	1200
1978	Nude with Dove LL3503	1,500	1981	250.00	700-1100
1981	The Rescue LL3504	1,500	1987	2900.00	5000
1978	St. Michael w/base LL3515	1,500		2200.00	4690
1980	Turtle Dove Nest w/base LL3519	1,200	1994	3600.00	6050
1980	Turtle Dove Group w/base LL3520	750		6800.00	11900
1981	Philippine Folklore LL3522	12/95		1450.00	2400
1981	Nest of Eagles w/base LL3523	300	1994	6900.00	11500
1981	Drum Beats/Watusi Queen w/base LL3524	1,500	1994	1875.00	3050
1982	Togetherness LL3527	75	1987	375.00	900
1982	Wrestling LL3528	50	1987	950.00	1125
1983	Companionship w/base LL3529	65		1000.00	1790
1983	Anxiety w/base LL3530	125	1993	1075.00	1875
1983	Victory LL3531	90	1988	1500.00	1800
1983	Plentitude LL3532	50	1988	1000.00	1375
1983	The Observer w/base LL3533	115	1993	900.00	1650
1983	In the Distance LL3534	75	1988	525.00	1275
1983	Slave LL3535	50	1988	950.00	1150
1983	Relaxation LL3536	100	1988	525.00	1000
1983	Dreaming w/base LL3537	250	1994	475.00	1475
1983	Youth LL3538	250	1988	525.00	1120
1983	Dantiness LL3539	100	1988	1000.00	1400
1983	Pose LL3540	100	1988	1250.00	1450
1983	Tranquility LL3541	75	1988	1000.00	1400
1983	Yoga LL3542	125	1991	650.00	900
1983	Demure LL3543	100	1988	1250.00	1700
1983	Reflections w/base LL3544	75		650.00	1050
1983	Adoration LL3545	150	1990	1050.00	1600
1983	African Woman LL3546	50	1988	1300.00	2000
1983	Reclining Nude LL3547	75	1988	650.00	875
1983	Serenity w/base LL3548	300	1993	925.00	1550
1983	Reposing LL3549	80	1988	425.00	575
1983	Boxer w/base LL3550	300	1993	850.00	1450
1983	Bather LL3551	300	1988	975.00	1300
1982	Blue God LL3552	1,500	1994	900.00	1575
1982	Fire Bird LL3553	1,500	1994	800.00	1350
1982	Desert People w/base LL3555	750		1680.00	3100
1982	Road to Mandalay LL3556	750	1989	1390.00	2500
1982	Jesus in Tiberias w/base LL3557	1,200		2600.00	4910
1992	The Reader LL3560	200		2650.00	2815
1993	Trail Boss LL3561M	1,500		2450.00	2595
1993	Indian Brave LL3562M	1,500		2250.00	2250
1994	Saint James The Apostle w/base LL3563	1,000		950.00	950
1994	Gentle Moment w/base LL3564	1,000		1795.00	1835
1994	At Peace w/base LL3565	1,000		1650.00	170
1994	Indian Chief w/base LL3566	3,000		1095.00	1095
1994	Trapper w/base LL3567	3,000		950.00	950
1994	American Cowboy w/base LL3568	3,000		950.00	950
1994	A Moment's Pause w/base LL3569	3,500		1495.00	1635
1994	Ethereal Music w/base LL3570	1,000		2450.00	2500
1994	At The Helm w/base LL3571	3,500		1495.00	1495
1995	Proud Warrior w/base LL3572	3,000		995.00	995
1995	Golgotha w/base LL3573	1, 000		1650.00	1650
1980	Successful Hunt LL5098	Closed	1993	5200.00	5200
1985	Napoleon Bonaparte LL 5338	5,000	1994	275.00	495
1985	Beethoven w/base LL 5339	3,000	1993	760.00	1300
1985	Thoroughbred Horse w/base LL5340	1,000	1993	625.00	1050
1985	I Have Found Thee, Dulcinea LL5341	750	1990	1460.00	2000-3000
1985	Pack of Hunting Dogs w/base LL5342	3,000	1994	925.00	1650
1985	Love Boat w/base LL5343	3,000		825.00	1350
1986	Fox Hunt w/base LL5362	1,000		5200.00	8750
1986	Rey De Copas w/base LL5366	2,000	1993	325.00	600
1986	Rey De Oros w/base LL5367	2,000	1993	325.00	600
1986	Rey De Espadas w/base LL5368	2,000	1993	325.00	600
1986	Rey De Bastos w/base LL5369	2,000	1993	325.00	600
1986	Pastoral Scene w/base LL5386	12/95		1100.00	2290
1987	Inspiration LL5413	500	1993	1200.00	2100
1987	Carnival Time w/base LL5423	1,000	1993	2400.00	3900
1989	"Pious" LL5541	N/A	1991	1075.00	1550
1989	Freedom LL5602	1,500	1989	875.00	950
1990	A Ride In The Park LL5718	N/A	1991	3200.00	3500
1991	Youth LL5800	500	1993	650.00	725
1991	Charm LL5801	500	1994	650.00	725
1991	New World Medallion LL5808	5,000	1994	200.00	215
1992	The Voyage of Columbus LL5847	7,500	1994	1450.00	1450-1950
1992	Sorrowful Mother LL5849	1,500		1750.00	1850
1992	Justice Eagle LL5863	1,500		1700.00	1840
1992	Maternal Joy LL5864	1,500		1600.00	1700
1992	Motoring In Style LL5884	1,500		3700.00	3850
1992	The Way Of The Cross LL5890	2,000		975.00	1050
1992	Presenting Credentials LL5911	1,500		19500.00	20500
1992	Young Mozart LL5915	2,500	1994	500.00	1000-1250
1993	Jester's Serenade w/base LL5932	3,000		1995.00	1995
1993	The Blessing w/base LL5942	2,000		1345.00	1345
1993	Our Lady of Rocio w/base LL5951	2,000		3500.00	3500
1993	Where to Sir w/base LL5952	1,500		5250.00	5250
1993	Discovery Mug LL5967	1,992	1994	90.00	90
1993	Graceful Moment w/base LL6033	3,000		1475.00	1475
1993	The Hand of Justice w/base LL6033	1,000		1250.00	1250
1992	Tinkerbell LL7518	1,000		350.00	2200-2700
1993	Peter Pan LL7529	3,000		400.00	1000-1500
1994	Cinderella and Fairy Godmother LL7553G	2,500	1994	875.00	850-1250
1995	Abraham Lincoln w/base LL7554	2,500		2190.00	2190
1994	Snow Beauty Dance	1,000	1995	1280.00	1500-2500

Lladro - Lladro

YEAR ISSUE		EDITION LIMIT	YEAR RETD.	ISSUE PRICE	QUOTE U.S.$
1963	Hunting Dog 308.13	Closed	N/A	N/A	2000
1966	Poodle 325.13	Closed	N/A	N/A	2300
1970	Girl with Pigtails L357.13G	Closed	N/A	N/A	1100
1969	Shepherdess with Goats L1001G	Closed	1987	80.00	675
1969	Shepherdess with Goats L1001M	Closed	1987	80.00	450
1969	Girl's Head L1003G	Closed	1985	150.00	675
1969	Girl's Head L1003M	Closed	1985	150.00	700-900
1969	Pan with Cymbals L1006	Closed	1975	45.00	575
1969	Girl With Lamb L1010G	Closed	1993	26.00	200-375
1969	Girl With Pig L1011G	Open		13.00	90
1969	Centaur Girl L1012M	Closed	1989	45.00	400-450
1969	Centaur Boy L1013M	Closed	1989	425.00	400

FIGURINES/COTTAGES

YEAR ISSUE		EDITION LIMIT	YEAR RETD.	ISSUE PRICE	QUOTE U.S.$
1969	Dove L1015 G	Closed	1994	21.00	105
1969	Dove L1016 G	12/95		36.00	190
1969	Idyl L1017G	Closed	1991	115.00	650
1969	Idyl L1017M	Closed	1991	115.00	550-615
1969	King Gaspar L1018M	Open		345.00	1895
1969	King Melchior L1019M	Open		345.00	1850
1969	King Baltasar L1020M	Open		345.00	1850
1969	Horse Group L1021G	Closed	1975	950.00	1600
1969	Horse Group/All White L1022M	Open		465.00	2100
1969	Flute Player L1025G	Closed	1978	73.00	700
1969	Clown with Concertina L1027G	Closed	1993	95.00	795
1969	Don Quixote w/Stand L1030G	Open		225.00	1450
1969	Sancho Panza L1031G	Closed	1989	65.00	550
1969	Old Folks L1033G	Closed	1985	140.00	1400
1969	Old Folks L1033M	Closed	1985	140.00	1400
1969	Shepherdess with Dog L1034	Closed	1991	30.00	275
1969	Girl with Geese L1035G	12/95		37.50	180
1969	Girl With Geese L1035M	Closed	1992	37.50	165
1969	Horseman L1037G	Closed	1970	170.00	2500
1969	Girl with Turkeys L1038G	Closed	1978	95.00	650
1969	Violinist and Girl L1039G	Closed	1991	120.00	1000-1200
1969	Violinist and Girl L1039M	Closed	1991	120.00	825
1969	Hunters L1048	Closed	1986	115.00	1400
1969	Del Monte (Boy) L1050	Closed	1978	65.00	N/A
1969	Girl with Duck L1052G	Open		30.00	205
1969	Girl with Duck L1052M	Closed	1992	30.00	190
1969	Bird L1053G	Closed	1985	13.00	100
1969	Bird L1054G	Closed	1985	14.00	125
1969	Duck L1056G	Closed	1978	19.00	275
1969	Girl with Pheasant L1055G	Closed	1978	105.00	N/A
1969	Panchito L1059	Closed	1980	28.00	N/A
1969	Deer L1064	Closed	1986	27.50	275
1969	Fox and Cub L1065G	Closed	1985	17.50	350
1969	Basset L1066G	Closed	1981	23.50	500
1969	Old dog L1067G	Closed	1978	40.00	500
1969	Afghan (sitting) L1069G	Closed	1985	36.00	500
1969	Beagle Puppy L1070G	Closed	1991	16.50	180-225
1969	Beagle Puppy L1071G	Closed	1992	16.50	225
1969	Beagle Puppy L1071M	Closed	1992	16.50	225
1969	Beagle Puppy L1072G	Closed	1991	16.50	225
1969	Dutch Girl L1077G	Closed	1981	57.50	250-450
1969	Herald L1078G	Closed	1970	110.00	1100
1969	Girl With Brush L1081G	Closed	1985	14.50	300
1969	Girl Manicuring L1082G	Closed	1985	14.50	300
1969	Girl With Doll L1083G	Closed	1985	14.50	300
1969	Girl with Mother's Shoe L1084G	Closed	1985	14.50	300
1969	Girl Seated with Flowers L1088G	Closed	1989	45.00	700
1971	Lawyer (Face) L1089G	Closed	1973	35.00	950
1971	Girl and Gazelle L1091G	Closed	1975	225.00	1200
1971	Satyr with Snail L1092G	Closed	1975	30.00	300
1969	Beggar L1094G	Closed	1981	65.00	650
1971	Pelusa Clown L1125G	Closed	1978	70.00	875-1150
1971	Clown with Violin L1126G	Closed	1978	71.00	1400
1971	Puppy Love L1127G	Open		50.00	310
1971	Dog in the Basket L1128G	Closed	1985	17.50	450
1971	Faun L1131G	Closed	1972	155.00	1200
1971	Horse L1133G	Closed	1972	115.00	900
1971	Bull L1134G	Closed	1972	130.00	1500
1971	Dog and Snail L1139G	Closed	1981	40.00	270
1971	Girl with Bonnet L1147G	Closed	1985	20.00	275
1971	Dog's Head L1149G	Closed	1981	27.50	350
1971	Elephants (3) L1150G	Open		100.00	795
1971	Elephants (2) L1151G	Open		45.00	420
1971	Dog Playing Guitar L1152G	Closed	1978	32.50	600
1971	Dog Playing Guitar L1153G	Closed	1978	32.50	525
1971	Dog Playing Bass Fiddle L1154G	Closed	1978	36.50	425
1971	Dog w/Microphone L1155G	Closed	1978	35.00	400
1971	Dog Playing Bongos L1156	Closed	1978	32.50	600
1971	Seated Torero L1162G	Closed	1973	35.00	700
1971	Kissing Doves L1169G	Open		32.00	145
1971	Kissing Doves L1169M	Closed	N/A	32.00	150
1971	Kissing Doves L1170G	Closed	1988	25.00	250
1971	Girl With Flowers L1172G	Closed	1993	27.00	295
1971	Girl With Domino L1175G	Closed	1981	34.00	350
1971	Girl With Dice L1176G	Closed	1981	25.00	350
1971	Girl With Ball L1177G	Closed	1981	27.50	425
1971	Girl With Accordian L1178G	Closed	1981	34.00	425
1971	Clown on Domino L1179G	Closed	1981	34.00	300
1971	Platero and Marcelino L1181G	Closed	1981	50.00	400
1972	Little Girl with Cat L1187G	Closed	1989	37.00	375
1972	Boy Meets Girl L1188G	Closed	1989	310.00	350
1972	Eskimo L1195G	Open		30.00	135
1972	Horse Resting L1203G	Closed	1981	40.00	375
1972	Attentive Bear, brown L1204G	Closed	1989	16.00	100-125
1972	Good Bear, brown L1205G	Closed	1989	16.00	100-125
1972	Bear Seated, brown L1206G	Closed	1989	16.00	100-125
1972	Attentive Polar Bear, white L1207G	Open		16.00	75
1972	Bear, white L1208G	Open		16.00	75
1972	Bear, white L1209G	Open		16.00	75
1972	Round Fish L1210G	Closed	1981	35.00	450
1972	Girl With Doll L1211G	Closed	1993	72.00	440
1972	Woman Carrying Water L1212G	Closed	1983	100.00	475
1972	Little Jug Magno L1222.3G	Closed	1979	35.00	300
1972	Young Harlequin L1229G	Open		70.00	520
1972	Friendship L1230G	Closed	1991	68.00	475
1972	Friendship L1230M	Closed	1991	68.00	325
1972	Angel with Lute L1231G	Closed	1988	60.00	450
1972	Angel with Clarinet L1232G	Closed	1988	60.00	450
1972	Angel with Flute L1233G	Closed	1988	60.00	350
1972	Little Jesus of Prag L1234G	Closed	1978	70.00	725
1973	Christmas Carols L1239G	Closed	1981	125.00	800-900
1973	Girl with Wheelbarrow L1245G	Closed	1981	75.00	500-600
1972	Caress and Rest L1246G	Closed	1990	50.00	300
1974	Happy Harlequin L1247M	Closed	1983	220.00	1150
1974	Honey Lickers L1248G	Closed	1990	100.00	475
1974	The Race L1249G	Closed	1988	450.00	1800-2250
1974	Lovers from Verona L 1250G	Closed	1990	330.00	1200
1974	Pony Ride L1251G	Closed	1979	220.00	1200
1974	Shepherd L1252G	Closed	1981	100.00	N/A
1974	Sad Chimney Sweep L1253G	Closed	1983	180.00	1200
1974	Hamlet and Yorick L1254G	Closed	1983	325.00	1100-1200
1974	Seesaw L1255G	Closed	1993	110.00	550
1974	Mother with Pups L1257G	Closed	1981	50.00	700
1974	Playing Poodles L1258G	Closed	1981	47.50	650-850
1974	Poodle L1259G	Closed	1985	27.50	300-400
1974	Flying Duck L1263G	Open		20.00	90
1974	Flying Duck L1264G	Open		20.00	90
1974	Flying Duck L1265G	Open		20.00	90
1974	Girl with Ducks L1267G	Closed	1993	55.00	375
1974	Reminiscing L1270G	Closed	1988	975.00	1375
1974	Thoughts L1272G	Open		87.50	3490
1974	Lovers in the Park L1274G	Closed	1993	450.00	1365
1974	Christmas Seller L1276G	Closed	1981	120.00	750
1974	Feeding Time L1277G	Closed	1993	120.00	350
1974	Feeding Time L1277M	Closed	N/A	120.00	415
1974	Devotion L1278G	Closed	1990	140.00	475
1974	The Wind L1279M	Open		250.00	830
1974	Playtime L1280G	Closed	1983	160.00	650
1974	Afghan Standing L1282G	Closed	1985	45.00	400-475
1974	Little Gardener L1283G	Open		250.00	785
1974	"My Flowers" L1284G	Open		200.00	550
1974	"My Goodness" L1285G	12/95		190.00	415
1974	Flower Harvest L1286G	Open		200.00	495
1974	Picking Flowers L1287G	Open		170.00	440
1974	Aggressive Duck L1288G	12/95		170.00	475
1974	Good Puppy L1289G	Closed	1985	16.60	100-200
1974	Victorian Girl on Swing L1297G	Closed	1990	520.00	1750
1974	Valencian Lady with Flowers L1304G	Open		200.00	625
1974	"On the Farm" L1306G	Closed	1990	130.00	240
1974	Ducklings L1307G	Open		47.50	150
1974	Girl with Cats L1309G	Open		120.00	310
1974	Girl with Puppies in Basket L1311G	Open		120.00	345
1974	Schoolgirl L1313G	Closed	1990	201.00	600
1976	Collie L1316G	Closed	1981	45.00	400
1976	IBIS L1319G	Open		1550.00	2625
1977	Angel with Tamborine L1320G	Closed	1985	125.00	350-450
1977	Angel with Lyre L1321G	Closed	1985	125.00	450-500
1977	Angel with Song L1322G	Closed	1985	125.00	475
1977	Angel with Accordian L1323G	Closed	1985	125.00	400
1977	Angel with Mandolin L1324G	Closed	1985	125.00	400
1976	The Helmsman L1325M	Closed	1988	600.00	900-1200
1976	Playing Cards L1327 M, numbered series	Open		3800.00	6600
1977	Dove Group L1335G	Closed	1990	950.00	1700
1977	Blooming Roses L1339G	Closed	1988	325.00	425
1977	Male Jockey L1341G	Closed	1979	120.00	450
1977	Wrath of Don Quixote L1343G	Closed	1990	250.00	900-1000
1977	Derby L1344G	Closed	1985	1125.00	2500
1978	Sacristan L1345G	Closed	1979	385.00	2300
1978	Under the Willow L1346G	Closed	1990	1600.00	2150
1978	Mermaid on Wave L1347G	Closed	1983	425.00	1800
1978	Nautical Vision L1349G	Closed	1983	Unkn.	3000
1978	In the Gondola L1350G, numbered series	Open		1850.00	3250
1978	Lady with Girl L1353G	Closed	1985	175.00	600
1978	Growing Roses L1354G	Closed	1988	485.00	635
1978	Phyllis L1356G	Closed	1993	75.00	225
1978	Shelley L1357G	Closed	1993	75.00	175-225
1978	Beth L1358G	Closed	1993	75.00	225
1978	Heather L1359G	Closed	1993	75.00	225
1978	Laura L1360G	Closed	1993	75.00	225
1978	Julia L1361G	Closed	1993	75.00	175-225
1978	Swinging L1366G	Closed	1988	825.00	1375
1978	Playful Dogs L1367	Closed	1982	160.00	700
1978	Spring Birds L1368G	Closed	1990	1600.00	2500
1978	Anniversary Waltz L1372G	Open		260.00	570
1978	Chestnut Seller L1373G	Closed	1981	800.00	750-900
1978	Waiting in the Park L1374G	Closed	1993	235.00	450
1978	Watering Flowers L1376G	Closed	1990	400.00	1150
1978	Suzy and Her Doll L1378G	Closed	1985	215.00	600-800
1978	Debbie and Her Doll L1379G	Closed	1985	215.00	600-825
1978	Cathy and Her Doll L1380G	Closed	1985	215.00	570-950
1978	Medieval Girl L1381G	Closed	1985	11.80	400-600
1978	Medieval Boy L1382G	Closed	1985	235.00	650-700
1978	A Rickshaw Ride L1383G	Open		1500.00	2150
1978	The Brave Knight L1385G	Closed	1988	350.00	750
1981	St. Joseph L1386G	Open		250.00	385
1981	Mary L1387G	Open		240.00	385
1981	Baby Jesus L1388G	Open		85.00	140
1981	Donkey L1389G	Open		95.00	190
1981	Cow L1390G	Open		95.00	190
1982	Holy Mary L1394G, numbered series	Open		1000.00	1475
1982	Full of Mischief L1395G	Open		420.00	825
1982	Appreciation L1396G	Open		420.00	825
1982	Second Thoughts L1397G	Open		420.00	820
1982	Reverie L1398G	Open		490.00	970
1982	Dutch Woman with Tulips L1399G	Closed	1988	750.00	750
1982	Valencian Boy L1400G	Closed	1988	298.00	400
1982	Sleeping Nymph L1401G	Closed	1988	210.00	600-875
1982	Daydreaming Nymph L1402G	Closed	1988	210.00	500-550
1982	Pondering Nymph L1403G	Closed	1988	210.00	525-625
1982	Matrimony L1404G	Open		320.00	585
1982	Illusion L1413G	Open		115.00	260
1982	Fantasy L1414G	Open		115.00	260
1982	Mirage L1415G	Open		115.00	260
1982	From My Garden L1416G	Open		140.00	295
1982	Nature's Bounty L1417G	12/95		160.00	340
1982	Flower Harmony L1418G	12/95		130.00	270
1982	A Barrow of Blossoms L1419G	Open		390.00	675
1982	Born Free w/base L1420G	Open		1520.00	3140
1982	Mariko w/base L1421G	12/95		860.00	1575
1982	Miss Valencia L1422G	Open		175.00	395
1982	King Melchior L1423G	Open		225.00	440
1982	King Gaspar L1424G	Open		265.00	475
1982	King Balthasar L1425G	Open		315.00	585
1982	Male Tennis Player L1426M	Closed	1988	200.00	350
1982	Female Tennis Player L1427M	Closed	1988	200.00	350
1982	Afternoon Tea L1428G	Open		115.00	275
1982	Afternoon Tea L1428M	Open		115.00	275
1982	Winter Wonderland w/base L1429G	Open		1025.00	2125
1982	High Society L1430G	Closed	1993	305.00	645
1982	The Debutante L1431G	Open		115.00	275
1982	The Debutante L1431M	Open		115.00	275
1983	Vows L1434G	Closed	1991	600.00	900
1983	Blue Moon L1435G	Closed	1988	98.00	550
1983	Moon Glow L1436G	Closed	1988	98.00	450
1983	Moon Light L1437G	Closed	1988	98.00	450
1983	Full Moon L1438G	Closed	1988	115.00	675
1983	"How Do You Do!" L1439G	Open		185.00	295
1983	Pleasantries L1440G	Closed	1991	960.00	1900
1983	A Litter of Love L1441G	Open		385.00	645
1983	Kitty Confrontation L1442G	Open		155.00	285
1983	Bearly Love L1443G	Open		55.00	120
1983	Purr-Fect L1444G	Open		350.00	615
1983	Springtime in Japan L1445G	Open		965.00	1800
1983	"Here Comes the Bride" L1446G	Open		518.00	995
1983	Michiko L1447G	Open		235.00	460
1983	Yuki L1448G	Open		285.00	550
1983	Mayumi L1449G	Open		235.00	495
1983	Kiyoko L1450G	Open		235.00	495
1983	Teruko L1451G	Open		235.00	495
1983	On the Town L1452G	Closed	1993	220.00	450
1983	Golfing Couple L1453G	Open		248.00	530
1983	Flowers of the Season L1454G	Open		1460.00	2550
1983	Reflections of Hamlet L1455G	Closed	1988	1000.00	1400
1983	Cranes w/base L1456G	Open		1000.00	1950
1985	A Boy and His Pony L1460G	Closed	1988	285.00	800
1985	Carefree Angel with Flute L1463G	Closed	1988	220.00	500
1985	Carefree Angel with Lyre L1464G	Closed	1988	220.00	575-650
1985	Girl on Carousel Horse L1469G	Open		470.00	935
1985	Boy on Carousel Horse L1470G	Open		470.00	935
1985	Wishing On A Star L1475G	Closed	1988	130.00	600
1985	Star Light Star Bright L1476G	Closed	1988	130.00	350
1985	Star Gazing L1477G	Closed	1988	130.00	375
1985	Hawaiian Dancer/Aloha! L1478G	Open		230.00	440
1985	In a Tropical Garden L1479G	12/95		230.00	440
1985	Aroma of the Islands L1480G	Open		260.00	480
1985	Sunning L1481G	Closed	1988	145.00	650
1985	Eve L1482	Closed	1988	145.00	700
1985	Free As a Butterfly L1483G	Closed	1988	145.00	550
1986	Lady of the East w/base L1488G	Closed	1993	625.00	1100
1986	Valencian Children L1489G	Open		700.00	1225
1986	My Wedding Day L1494G	Open		800.00	1495
1986	A Lady of Taste L1495G	Open		575.00	1025
1986	Don Quixote & The Windmill L1497G	Open		1100.00	2050
1986	Tahitian Dancing Girls L1498G	12/95		750.00	1325
1986	Blessed Family L1499G	Open		200.00	395
1986	Ragamuffin L1500G	Closed	1991	125.00	350
1986	Ragamuffin L1500M	Closed	1991	125.00	300
1986	Rag Doll L1501G	Closed	1991	125.00	350
1986	Rag Doll L1501M	Closed	1991	125.00	300
1986	Forgotten L1502G	Closed	1991	125.00	350
1986	Forgotten L1502M	Closed	1991	125.00	300
1986	Neglected L1503G	Closed	1991	125.00	350
1986	Neglected L1503M	Closed	1991	125.00	300
1986	The Reception L1504G	Closed	1990	625.00	1050
1986	Nature Boy L1505G	Closed	1991	100.00	250-375
1986	Nature Boy L1505M	Closed	1991	100.00	N/A
1986	A New Friend L1506G	Closed	1991	110.00	250
1986	A New Friend L1506M	Closed	1991	110.00	285
1986	Boy & His Bunny L1507G	Closed	1991	90.00	250
1986	Boy & His Bunny L1507M	Closed	1991	90.00	N/A
1986	In the Meadow L1508G	Closed	1991	100.00	175-250
1986	In the Meadow L1508M	Closed	1991	100.00	N/A
1986	Spring Flowers L1509G	Closed	1991	100.00	250
1986	Spring Flowers L1509M	Closed	1991	100.00	N/A
1987	Cafe De Paris L1511G	12/95		1900.00	2950
1987	Hawaiian Beauty L1512G	Closed	1990	575.00	1000
1987	A Flower for My Lady L1513G	Closed	1990	1150.00	1500
1987	Gaspar 's Page L1514G	Closed	1990	275.00	300-500
1987	Melchior's Page L1515G	Closed	1990	290.00	650
1987	Balthasar's Page L1516G	Closed	1990	275.00	900-950
1987	Circus Train L1517G	Closed	1994	2900.00	4350
1987	Valencian Garden L1518G	Closed	1991	1100.00	1795
1987	Stroll in the Park L1519G	Open		1600.00	2600
1987	The Landau Carriage L1521G	Open		2500.00	3850
1987	I am Don Quixote! L1522G	Open		2600.00	3950
1987	Valencian Bouquet L1524G	Closed	1991	250.00	400
1987	Valencian Dreams L1525G	Closed	1991	240.00	450

YEAR ISSUE		EDITION LIMIT	YEAR RETD.	ISSUE PRICE	QUOTE U.S.$
1987	Valencian Flowers L1526G	Closed	1991	375.00	550
1987	Tenderness L1527G	Open		260.00	430
1987	I Love You Truly L1528G	Open		375.00	595
1987	Momi L1529G	Closed	1990	275.00	500
1987	Leilani L1530G	Closed	1990	275.00	500
1987	Malia L1531G	Closed	1990	275.00	500
1987	Lehua L1532G	Closed	1990	275.00	575
1987	Not So Fast! L1533G	Open		175.00	265
1988	Little Sister L1534G	Open		180.00	240
1988	Sweet Dreams L1535G	Open		150.00	220
1988	Stepping Out L1537G	Open		230.00	325
1988	Pink Ballet Slippers L1540	Closed	1991	275.00	400
1987	Wild Stallions w/base L1566G	Closed	1993	1100.00	1465
1987	Running Free w/base L1567G	Open		1500.00	1600
1987	Grand Dame L1568G	Open		290.00	425
1989	Fluttering Crane L1598G	Open		115.00	145
1989	Nesting Crane L1599G	Open		95.00	115
1989	Landing Crane L1600G	Open		115.00	145
1989	Rock Nymph L1601G	12/95		665.00	795
1989	Spring Nymph L1602G	12/95		665.00	825
1989	Latest Addition L1606G	Open		385.00	480
1989	Flight Into Egypt w/base L1610G	Open		885.00	1150
1989	Courting Cranes L1611G	Open		565.00	695
1989	Preening Crane L1612G	Open		385.00	485
1989	Bowing Crane L1613G	Open		385.00	485
1989	Dancing Crane L1614G	Open		385.00	485
1988	Cellist L1700M	Closed	1993	1200.00	1750
1988	Saxophone Player L1701M	Closed	1993	835.00	1840
1988	Boy at the Fair (Decorated) L1708M	Closed	1993	650.00	650
1988	Exodus L1709M	Closed	1993	875.00	875
1988	School Boy L1710M	Closed	1993	750.00	750
1988	School Girl L1711M	Closed	1993	950.00	950
1988	On Our Way Home (decorated) L1715M	Closed	1993	2000.00	2000
1988	Nanny L1714M	Closed	1993	700.00	700
1988	Harlequin with Puppy L1716M	Closed	1993	825.00	1000
1988	Harlequin with Dove L1717M	Closed	1993	900.00	1000
1988	Dress Rehearsal L1718M	Closed	1993	1150.00	1150
1989	Back From the Fair L1719M	Closed	1993	1825.00	1825
1990	Sprite w/base L1720G, numbered series	Open		1200.00	1400
1990	Leprechaun w/base L1721G, numrd series	Open		1200.00	1395
1989	Group Discussion L1722M	Closed	1993	1500.00	1500
1989	Hopeful Group L1723M	Closed	1993	1825.00	1825
1989	Belle Epoque L1724M	Closed	1993	700.00	700
1989	Young Lady with Parasol L1725M	Closed	1993	950.00	950
1989	Young Lady with Fan L1726M	Closed	1993	750.00	750
1989	Pose L1727M	Closed	1993	725.00	725
1991	Nativity L1730M	Open		725.00	725
1970	Gothic King L2002G	Closed	1975	25.00	450
1970	Gothic Queen L2003G	Closed	1975	25.00	450
1970	Shepherdess with Lamb L2005M	Closed	1981	100.00	710
1970	Water Carrier Girl Lamp L2006M	Closed	1975	30.00	600
1971	Girl with Dog L2013M	Closed	1975	300.00	N/A
1971	Little Eagle Owl L2020M	Closed	1985	15.00	425
1971	Boy/Girl Eskimo L2038.3M	Closed	N/A	100.00	275-455
1974	Setter's Head L2045M	Closed	1981	42.50	550
1974	Magistrates L2052M	Closed	1981	135.00	950
1974	Oriental L2056M	Open		35.00	105
1974	Oriental L2057M	Open		30.00	100
1974	Thailandia L2058M	Open		650.00	1885
1974	Muskateer L2059M	Closed	1981	900.00	2000-3
1977	Monk L2060M	Open		60.00	145
1977	Dogs-Bust L2067M	Closed	1979	280.00	800
1977	Thai Dancers L2069M	Open		300.00	745
1977	A New Hairdo L2070M	Closed	1991	1060.00	1430
1977	Graceful Duo L2073M	Closed	1994	775.00	1650
1977	Nuns L2075M	Open		90.00	250
1978	Lonely L2076M	Open		72.50	185
1978	Rain in Spain L2077M	Closed	1990	190.00	475-550
1978	Woman L2080M	Closed	1985	625.00	625
1978	Don Quixote Dreaming L2084M	Closed	1985	550.00	2050
1978	The Little Kiss L2086M	Closed	1985	180.00	475
1978	Girl in Rocking Chair L2089	Closed	1981	235.00	600
1978	Saint Francis L2090	Closed	1981	565.00	N/A
1978	Holy Virgin L2092M	Closed	1981	200.00	N/A
1978	Girl Waiting L2093M	12/95		90.00	185
1978	Tenderness L2094M	Open		100.00	205
1978	Duck Pulling Pigtail L2095M	Open		110.00	275
1978	Nosy Puppy L2096M	Closed	1993	190.00	410
1978	Laundress L2109M	Closed	1983	325.00	325-650
1980	Marujita with Two Ducks L2113M	Closed	1993	240.00	295
1980	Kissing Father L2114M	Closed	1981	575.00	575
1980	Mother's Kiss L2115M	Closed	1981	575.00	700
1980	The Whaler L2121M	Closed	1988	820.00	1050
1981	Lost in Thought L2125M	Closed	1990	210.00	250
1983	Indian Chief L2127M	Closed	1988	525.00	750
1983	Venus L2128M	Closed	N/A	650.00	1150
1983	Waiting for Santa L2129M	Closed	1985	325.00	600
1983	Egyptian Cat L2130M	Closed	1985	75.00	500
1983	Mother & Son L2131M, numbered series	Open		850.00	1550
1983	Spring Sheperdess L2132M	Closed	1985	450.00	N/A
1983	Autumn Sheperdess L2133M	Closed	1985	285.00	N/A
1984	Nautical Watch L2134M	Closed	1988	450.00	750
1984	Mystical Joseph L2135M	Closed	1988	428.00	700
1984	The King L2136M	Closed	1988	510.00	710
1984	Fairy Ballerina L2137M	Closed	1988	500.00	1250
1984	Friar Juniper L2138M	Closed	1993	160.00	400
1984	Aztec Indian L2139M	Closed	1988	553.00	600
1984	Pepita wth Sombrero L2140M	Open		97.50	200
1984	Pedro with Jug L2141M	Open		100.00	205
1984	Sea Harvest L2142M	Closed	1990	535.00	700
1984	Aztec Dancer L2143M	Closed	1988	463.00	650
1984	Leticia L2144M	12/95		100.00	190
1984	Gabriela L2145M	Closed	1994	100.00	170
1984	Desiree L2146M	12/95		100.00	190
1984	Alida L2147M	Closed	1994	100.00	170
1984	Head of Congolese Woman L2148M	Closed	1988	55.00	500-700
1985	Young Madonna L2149M	Closed	1988	400.00	675
1985	A Tribute to Peace w/base L2150M	Open		470.00	930
1985	A Bird on Hand L2151M	Open		118.00	255
1985	Chinese Girl L2152M	Closed	1990	90.00	200-250
1985	Chinese Boy L2153	Closed	1990	90.00	200-250
1985	Hawaiian Flower Vendor L2154M	Open		245.00	460
1985	Arctic inter L2156M	Open		75.00	145
1985	Eskimo Girl with Cold Feet L2157M	Open		140.00	285
1985	Pensive Eskimo Girl L2158M	Open		100.00	210
1985	Pensive Eskimo Boy L2159M	Open		100.00	210
1985	Flower Vendor L2160M	12/95		110.00	215
1985	Fruit Vendor L2161M	Closed	1994	120.00	230
1985	Fish Vendor L2162M	Closed	1994	110.00	205
1987	Mountain Shepherd L2163M	Open		120.00	210
1987	My Lost Lamb L2164M	Open		100.00	175
1987	Chiquita L2165M	Closed	1993	100.00	170
1987	Paco L2166M	Closed	1993	100.00	170
1987	Fernando L2167M	Closed	1993	100.00	170
1987	Julio L2168M	Closed	1993	100.00	170
1987	Repose L2169M	Open		120.00	195
1987	Spanish Dancer L2170M	Open		190.00	345
1987	Ahoy Tere L2173M	Open		190.00	325
1987	Andean Flute Player L2174M	Closed	1990	250.00	350
1988	Harvest Helpers L2178M	Open		190.00	265
1988	Sharing the Harvest L2179M	Open		190.00	265
1988	Dreams of Peace w/base L2180M	Open		880.00	1125
1988	Bathing Nymph w/base L2181M	Open		560.00	795
1988	Daydreamer w/base L2182M	Open		560.00	795
1989	Wakeup Kitty L2183M	Closed	1993	225.00	325
1989	Angel and Friend L2184M	Closed	1994	150.00	185
1989	Devoted Reader L2185M	Closed	1994	125.00	160
1989	The Greatest Love L2186M	Open		235.00	320
1989	Jealous Friend L2187M	12/95		275.00	365
1990	Mother's Pride L2189M	Open		300.00	375
1990	To The Well L2190M	Open		250.00	295
1990	Forest Born L2191M	Closed	1991	230.00	450
1990	King Of The Forest L2192M	Closed	N/A	290.00	310
1990	Heavenly Strings L2194M	Closed	1993	170.00	215
1990	Heavenly Sounds L2195M	Closed	1993	170.00	215
1990	Heavenly Solo L2196M	Closed	1993	170.00	215
1990	Heavenly Song L2197M	Closed	1993	175.00	185
1990	A King is Born w/base L2198M	Open		750.00	895
1990	Devoted Friends w/base L2199M	12/95		700.00	895
1990	A Big Hug! L2200M	Open		250.00	310
1990	Our Daily Bread L2201M	Closed	1994	150.00	185
1990	A Helping Hand L2202M	Closed	1993	150.00	185
1990	Afternoon Chores L2203M	Closed	1994	150.00	185
1990	Farmyard Grace L2204M	Closed	1993	180.00	210
1990	Prayerful Stitch L2205M	Closed	1994	160.00	190
1990	Sisterly Love L2206M	Open		300.00	375
1990	What A Day! L2207M	Open		550.00	640
1990	Let's Rest L2208M	Open		550.00	665
1991	Long Dy L2209M	Open		295.00	340
1991	Lazy Day L2210M	Open		240.00	260
1991	Patrol Leader L2212M	Closed	1993	390.00	420
1991	Nature's Friend L2213M	Closed	1993	390.00	420
1991	Seaside Angel L2214M	Open		150.00	165
1991	Friends in Flight L2215M	Open		165.00	180
1991	Laundry Day L2216M	Open		350.00	400
1991	Gentle Play L2217M	Closed	1993	380.00	415
1991	Costumed Couple L2218M	Closed	1993	680.00	750
1992	Underfoot L2219M	Open		360.00	410
1992	Free Spirit L2220M	Closed	1994	235.00	245
1992	Spring Beauty L2221M	Closed	1994	285.00	295
1992	Tender Moment L2222M	Open		400.00	450
1992	New Lamb L2223M	Open		365.00	385
1992	Cherish L2224M	Open		1750.00	1850
1992	FriendlySparrow L2225M	Open		295.00	325
1992	Boy's Best Friend L2226M	Open		390.00	410
1992	Artic Allies L2227M	Open		585.00	615
1992	Snowy Sunday L2228M	Open		550.00	625
1992	Seasonal Gifts L2229M	Open		450.00	475
1992	Mary's Child L2230M	Closed	1994	525.00	550
1992	Afternoon Verse L2231M	Open		580.00	595
1992	Poor Little Bear L2232M	Open		250.00	265
1992	Guess What I Have L2233M	Open		340.00	375
1992	Playful Push L2234M	Open		850.00	875
1993	Adoring Mother L2235M	Open		405.00	440
1993	Frosty Outing L2236M	Open		375.00	410
1993	The Old Fishing Hole L2237M	Open		625.00	640
1993	Learning Together L2238M	Open		500.00	500
1993	Valencian Courtship L2239M	Open		880.00	895
1993	WingedLove L2240M	12/95		285.00	310
1993	Winged Harmony L2241M	12/95		285.00	310
1993	Away to School L2242M	Open		465.00	465
1993	Lion Tamer L2246M	12/95		375.00	375
1993	Just Us L2247M	12/95		650.00	650
1993	Noella L2251M	Open		405.00	420
1993	Waiting For Father L2252M	Open		660.00	660
1993	Noisy Friend L2253M	Open		280.00	280
1993	Step Aside L2254M	Open		280.00	280
1994	Solitude L2256M	Open		398.00	435
1994	Constant Companions L2257M	Open		575.00	625
1994	Family Love L2258M	Open		450.00	485
1994	Little Fisherman L2259M	Open		298.00	330
1994	Artic Friends L2260M	Open		345.00	380
1995	Jesus and Joseph L2294M	Open		550.00	550
1995	Peaceful Rest L2295M	Open		390.00	390
1995	Life's Small Wonders L2296M	Open		370.00	370
1995	Elephants L2297M	Open		875.00	875
1995	Hindu Children L2298M	Open		450.00	450
1995	Poetic Moment L2299M	Open		465.00	465
1995	Emperor L2300M	Open		765.00	765
1995	Empress L2301M	Open		795.00	795
1995	Twilight Years L2302M	Open		385.00	385
1995	Not So Fast L2303M	Open		350.00	350
1995	Love in Bloom L2304M	Open		420.00	420
1995	Fragrant Bouquet L2305M	Open		330.00	330
1995	Hurray Now L2306M	Open		310.00	310
1995	Happy Birthday L2307M	Open		150.00	150
1995	Let's Make Up L2308M	Open		265.00	265
1995	Windblown Girl L2309M	Open		320.00	320
1995	Chit-Chat L2310M	Open		270.00	270
1995	Good Night L2311M	Open		280.00	280
1995	Goose Trying to Eat L2312M	Open		325.00	325
1995	Who's the Fairest L2313M	Open		230.00	230
1995	Breezy Afternoon L2314M	Open		220.00	220
1995	On the Green L2315M	Open		575.00	575
1995	Closing Scene L2316M	Open		560.00	560
1995	Talk to Me L2317M	Open		175.00	175
1995	Taking Time L2318M	Open		175.00	175
1995	A Lesson Shared L2319M	Open		215.00	215
1995	Cat Nap L2320M	Open		265.00	265
1995	All Tuckered Out L2321M	Open		275.00	275
1995	Naptime L2322M	Open		275.00	275
1995	Water Girl L2323M	Open		245.00	245
1995	A Basket of Fun L2324M	Open		320.00	320
1995	Spring Splendor L2325M	Open		440.00	440
1995	Physician L2326M	Open		350.00	350
1995	Sad Sax L2327M	Open		225.00	225
1995	Circus Sam L2328M	Open		225.00	225
1995	Daily Chores L2329M	Open		345.00	345
1978	Native L3502M	Open		700.00	2450
1978	Letters to Dulcinea L3509M, numbered series	Open		875.00	2175
1978	Horse Heads L3511M	Closed	1990	260.00	700
1978	Girl With Pails L3512M	Open		140.00	285
1978	A Wintry Day L3513M	Closed	1988	525.00	750
1978	Pensive w/ base L3514M	Open		500.00	1050
1978	Jesus Christ L3516M	Closed	1988	1050.00	1450
1978	Nude with Rose w/ base L3517M	Open		225.00	780
1980	Lady Macbeth L3518M	Closed	1981	385.00	425-1000
1980	Mother's Love L3521M	Closed	1990	1000.00	1100
1981	Weary w/ base L3525M	Open		360.00	685
1982	Contemplation w/ base L3526M	Open		265.00	590
1982	Stormy Sea w/base L3554M	Open		675.00	1445
1984	Innocence w/base/green L3558M	Closed	1991	960.00	1650
1984	Innocence w/base/red L3558.3M	Closed	1987	960.00	1200
1985	Peace Offering w/base L3559M	Open		397.00	665
1969	Marketing Day L4502G	Closed	1985	40.00	300
1969	Girl with Lamb L4505G	Open		20.00	125
1969	Boy with Kid L4506M	Closed	1985	22.50	425
1969	Boy with Lambs L4509G	Closed	1981	37.50	275
1969	Girl with Parasol and Geese L4510G	Closed	1993	40.00	245
1969	Nude L4511M	Closed	1985	45.00	750
1969	Man on Horse L4515G	Closed	1985	180.00	1000
1969	Female Equestrian L4516G	Open		170.00	745
1969	Flamenco Dancers L4519G	Closed	1993	150.00	1200
1970	Boy With Dog L4522M	Closed	N/A	25.00	155
1969	Girl With Slippers L4523G	Closed	1993	17.00	100
1969	Girl With Slippers L4523M	Closed	1993	17.00	100
1969	Donkey in Love L4524G	Closed	1985	15.00	350
1969	Donkey in Love L4524M	Closed	1985	15.00	350
1969	Violinist L4527G	Closed	1985	75.00	500
1969	Ballet Lamp L4528G	Closed	1985	120.00	850
1969	Joseph L4533G	Open		60.00	110
1969	Joseph L4533M	Open		60.00	110
1969	Mary L4534G	Open		60.00	85
1969	Mary L4534M	Open		60.00	85
1971	Baby Jesus L4535.3G	Open		60.00	70
1969	Baby Jesus L4535.3M	Open		60.00	70
1969	Angel, Chinese L4536G	Open		45.00	90
1969	Angel, Chinese L4536M	Open		45.00	90
1969	Angel, Black L4537G	Open		13.00	90
1969	Angel, Black L4537M	Open		13.00	90
1969	Angel, Praying L4538G	Open		13.00	90
1969	Angel, Praying L4538M	Open		13.00	90
1969	Angel, Thinking L4539G	Open		13.00	90
1969	Angel, Thinking L4539M	Open		13.00	90
1969	Angel with Horn L4540G	Open		13.00	90
1969	Angel with Horn L4540M	Open		13.00	90
1969	Angel Reclining L4541G	Open		13.00	90
1969	Angel Reclining L4541M	Open		13.00	90
1969	Group of Angels L4542G	Open		31.00	195
1969	Group of Angels L4542M	Open		31.00	195
1969	Geese Group L4549G	Open		28.50	230
1969	Geese Group L4549M	Closed	1992	28.50	230
1969	Flying Dove L4550G	Open		47.50	265
1969	Flying Dove L4550M	Closed	1992	47.50	165
1969	Ducks, set of 3 asst. L4551-3G	Open		18.00	140
1969	Shepherd L4554	Closed	1972	69.00	N/A
1969	Sad Harlequin L4558G	Closed	1993	110.00	575
1969	Waiting Backstage L4559G	Closed	1993	110.00	440

YEAR ISSUE		EDITION LIMIT	YEAR RETD.	ISSUE PRICE	QUOTE U.S.$
1969	Couple with Parasol L4563G	Closed	1985	180.00	625
1969	Girl with Geese L4568G	Closed	1993	45.00	220
1969	Girl With Turkey L4569G	Closed	1981	28.50	375
1969	Shepherd Resting L4571G	Closed	1981	60.00	475
1969	Girl with Piglets L4572G	Closed	1985	70.00	400
1969	Girl with Piglets L4572M	Closed	1985	70.00	400
1969	Mother & Child L4575G	Open		50.00	265
1969	New Shepherdess L4576G	Closed	1985	37.50	315
1969	Girl with Sheep L4584G	Closed	1993	27.00	170
1969	Holy Family L4585G	Closed		18.00	135
1969	Holy Family L4585M	Closed		18.00	135
1969	Madonna L4586G	Closed	1979	32.50	350
1969	White Cockeral L4588G	Closed	1979	17.50	300
1969	Girl with Pitcher L4590G	Closed	1981	47.50	425
1969	Shepherdess with Basket L4591G	Closed	1993	20.00	275
1969	Lady with Greyhound L4594G	Closed	1981	60.00	800
1969	Fairy L4595G	Closed	1994	27.50	140
1969	Playfull Horses L4597	Closed	1990	240.00	925-1000
1969	Doctor L4602.3G	Open		33.00	198
1969	Nurse-L4603.3G	Open		35.00	200
1969	Clown with Girl L4605	Closed	1985	160.00	900-1000
1969	Accordian Player L4606	Closed	1978	60.00	550
1969	Cupid L4607G	Closed	1980	15.00	150
1969	Cook in Trouble L4608	Closed	1985	27.50	650-775
1969	Nuns L4611G	Open		37.50	155
1969	Nuns L4611M	Open		37.50	155
1969	Girl Singer L4612G	Closed	1979	14.00	450
1969	Boy With Cymbals L4613G	Closed	1979	14.00	400
1969	Boy With Guitar L4614G	Closed	1979	19.50	400
1969	Boy with Double Bass L4615G	Closed	1979	22.50	400
1969	Boy With Drum L4616G	Closed	1979	16.50	350
1969	Group of Musicians L4617G	Closed	1979	33.00	500
1969	Clown L4618G	Open		70.00	415
1969	Sea Captain L4621G	Closed	1993	45.00	325
1969	Sea Captain L4621M	Closed	N/A	42.50	255
1969	Old Man with Violin L4622G	Closed	1982	45.00	700
1969	Angel with Child L4635G	Open		15.00	110
1969	Honey Peddler L4638G	Closed	1978	60.00	575
1969	Cow With Pig L4640	Closed	1981	42.50	700
1969	Pekinese L4641G	Closed	1985	20.00	400-550
1969	Dog L4642	Closed	1981	22.50	500
1969	Skye Terrier L4643G	Closed	1985	15.00	450-600
1969	Andalucians Group L4647G	Closed	1990	412.00	1400
1969	Valencian Couple on Horseback L4648	Closed	1990	900.00	950
1969	Madonna Head L4649G	Open		25.00	155
1969	Madonna Head L4649M	Open		25.00	155
1969	Girl with Calla Lillies L4650G	Open		18.00	145
1969	Cellist L4651G	Closed	1978	70.00	650
1969	Happy Travelers L4652	Closed	1978	115.00	650
1969	Orchestra Conductor L4653G	Closed	1979	95.00	850
1969	Horses L4655G	Open		110.00	760
1969	Shepherdess L4660G	Closed	1993	21.00	175
1969	Girl with Basket L4665G	Closed	1979	50.00	450
1969	Birds L4667G	Closed	1985	25.00	200
1969	Maja Head L4668G	Closed	1985	50.00	650
1969	Baby Jesus L4670BG	Open		18.00	55
1969	Mary L4671G	Open		33.00	75
1969	St. Joseph L4672G	Open		33.00	90
1969	King Melchior L4673G	Open		35.00	95
1969	King Gaspar L4674G	Open		35.00	95
1969	King Balthasar L4675G	Open		35.00	95
1969	Shepherd with Lamb L4676G	Open		14.00	110
1969	Girl with Rooster L4677G	Open		14.00	90
1969	Shepherdess with Basket L4678G	Open		13.00	90
1969	Donkey L4679G	Open		36.50	100
1969	Cow L4680G	Open		36.50	90
1970	Girl with Milkpail L4682G	Closed	1991	28.00	325
1970	Hebrew Student L4684G	Closed	1985	33.00	500-625
1970	Gothic Queen L4689	Closed	1975	20.00	695
1970	Troubadour in Love L4699	Closed	1975	60.00	1000
1970	Dressmaker L4700G	Closed	1993	45.00	500
1970	Mother & Child L4701G	Open		45.00	295
1970	Bird Watcher L4730	Closed	1985	35.00	400-600
1971	Small dog L4749	Closed	1985	5.50	125-200
1971	Romeo and Juliet L4750G	Open		150.00	1250
1971	Doncel With Roses L4757G	Closed	1979	35.00	500
1974	Lady with Dog L4761G	Closed	1993	60.00	300
1971	Dentist L4762	Closed	1978	36.00	500-600
1971	Dentist (Reduced) L4762. 3G	Closed	1985	30.00	450
1971	Obstetrician L4763G	Closed	1973	47.50	450
1971	Obstetrician L4763.3G	Open		40.00	255
1971	Rabbit L4772G	Open		17.50	135
1971	Rabbit L4773G	Open		17.50	130
1971	Dormouse L4774	Closed	1983	30.00	375
1972	Girl Tennis Player L4778	Closed	1975	50.00	400
1971	Children, Praying L4779G	Open		36.00	195
1971	Children, Praying L4779M	Closed	1992	36.00	153
1971	Boy with Goat L4780	Closed	1978	80.00	600
1972	Gypsy with Brother L4800G	Closed	1979	36.00	400
1972	The Teacher L4801G	Closed	1978	45.00	500
1972	Girl with Dog L4806G	Closed	1981	80.00	550
1972	Geisha L4807G	Closed	1993	190.00	475
1972	Wedding L4808G	Open		50.00	190
1972	Wedding L4808M	Open		50.00	190
1972	Going Fishing L4809G	Open		33.00	160
1972	Young Sailor L4810G	Open		33.00	175
1972	Boy with Pails L4811	Closed	1988	30.00	350
1972	Getting Her Goat L4812G	Closed	1988	55.00	500
1972	Girl with Geese L4815G	Closed	1991	72.00	400
1972	Girl with Geese L4815M	Closed	1991	72.00	295
1972	Little Shepherd with Goat L4817M	Closed	1981	50.00	475
1972	Burro L4821G	Closed	1979	24.00	450
1974	Peruvian Girl with Baby L4822	Closed	1981	65.00	775
1974	Legionary L4823	Closed	1978	55.00	400-500
1972	Male Golfer L4824G	Open		66.00	295
1972	Veterinarian L4825	Closed	1985	48.00	500
1972	Girl Feeding Rabbit L4826G	Closed	1993	40.00	225
1972	Caressing Calf L4827G	Closed	1981	55.00	475
1972	Cinderella L4828G	Open		47.00	245
1975	Swan L4829G	Closed	1983	16.00	275-500
1972	Shepherdess L4835G	Closed	1991	42.00	350
1973	Clean Up Time L4838G	Closed	1993	36.00	250-300
1973	Clean Up Time L4838M	Closed	1992	36.00	250
1972	Oriental Flower Arranger/Girl L4840G	Open		90.00	415
1972	Oriental Flower Arranger/Girl L4840M	Open		90.00	515
1974	Girl from Valencia L4841G	Open		35.00	225
1973	Donkey Ride L4843	Closed	1981	86.00	700
1973	Pharmacist L4844G	Closed	1985	70.00	1500-2500
1973	Classic Dance L4847G	Closed	1985	80.00	600
1973	Feeding The Ducks L4849G	12/95		60.00	270
1973	Feeding The Ducks L4849M	Closed	1992	60.00	250
1973	Aesthetic Pose L4850G	Closed	1985	110.00	650
1973	Lady Golfer L4851M	Closed	1992	70.00	250
1973	Gardner in Trouble L4852	Closed	1981	65.00	500
1974	Cobbler L4853G	Closed	1985	100.00	750
1973	Don Quixote L4854G	Open		40.00	205
1973	Ballerina L4855G	Open		45.00	330
1983	Ballerina, white L4855.3	Closed	1987	110.00	250
1974	Waltz Time L4856G	Closed	1985	65.00	550
1974	Dog L4857G	Closed	1979	40.00	450
1974	Peddler L4859G	Closed	1985	180.00	900
1974	Dutch Girl L4860G	Closed	1985	45.00	250
1974	Horse L4861	Closed	1978	55.00	425
1974	Horse L4862	Closed	1978	55.00	425
1974	Horse L4863	Closed	1978	55.00	400
1974	Embroiderer L4865G	Closed	1994	115.00	700
1974	Girl with Swan and Dog L4866G	Closed	1993	26.00	205
1974	Seesaw L4867G	Open		55.00	350
1974	Girl with Candle L4868G	Open		13.00	90
1974	Girl with Candle L4868M	Closed	1992	13.00	80
1974	Boy Kissing L4869G	Open		13.00	90
1974	Boy Kissing L4869M	Closed	1992	13.00	150-175
1974	Boy Yawning L4870G	Open		13.00	90
1974	Boy Yawning L4870M	Closed	1992	13.00	175
1974	Girl with Guitar L4871G	Open		13.00	90
1974	Girl with Guitar L4871M	Closed	1992	13.00	80
1974	Girl Stretching L4872G	Open		13.00	90
1974	Girl Stretching L4872M	Closed	1992	13.00	80
1974	Girl Kissing L4873G	Open		13.00	90
1974	Girl Kissing L4873M	Closed	1992	13.00	80
1974	Boy & Girl L4874G	Open		25.00	150
1974	Boy & Girl L4874M	Closed	1992	25.00	135
1974	Girl with Jugs L4875G	Closed	1985	40.00	300
1974	Boy Thinking L4876G	Closed	1993	20.00	135
1974	Boy Thinking L4876M	Closed	1992	20.00	120
1974	Lady with Parasol L4879G	Open		48.00	325
1974	Carnival Couple L4882G	12/95		60.00	300
1974	Seraph's Head No.1 L4884	Closed	1985	10.00	100
1974	Seraph's Head No.2 L4885	Closed	1985	10.00	100
1974	Seraph's Head No.3 L4886	Closed	1985	10.00	100
1974	The Kiss L4888G	Closed	1983	150.00	700
1979	Spanish Policeman L4889G	Closed	1991	55.00	400
1976	"My Dog" L4893G	Open		85.00	230
1974	Tennis Player Boy L4894	Closed	1980	75.00	450
1974	Ducks L4895G	Open		45.00	95
1974	Ducks L4895M	Closed	1992	45.00	85
1974	Boy with Snails L4896G	Closed	1979	50.00	400
1974	Boy From Madrid L4898G	Open		55.00	150
1974	Boy From Madrid L4898M	Closed	1992	55.00	130
1974	Boy with Smoking Jacket L4900	Closed	1983	45.00	200
1974	Barrister L4908G	Closed	1985	100.00	585
1974	Girl With Dove L4909G	Closed	1982	70.00	450
1974	Young Lady in Trouble L4912G	Closed	1985	110.00	500-600
1975	Lady with Shawl L4914G	Open		220.00	730
1975	Girl with Pigeons L4915	Closed	1990	110.00	225-250
1976	Chinese Noblewoman L4916G	Closed	1978	300.00	2000
1976	Gypsy Woman L4919G	Closed	1981	165.00	1100
1974	A Girl at the Pond L4918G	Closed	1985	85.00	350
1974	Country Lass with Dog L4920G	12/95		185.00	495
1974	Country Lass with Dog L4920M	Closed	1992	185.00	450
1974	Windblown Girl L4922G	Open		150.00	375
1974	Lanquid Clown L4924G	Closed	1983	200.00	1500
1974	Sisters L4930	Closed	1981	250.00	625
1974	Children with Fruits L4931G	Closed	1981	210.00	500
1974	Dainty Lady L4934G	Closed	1985	60.00	400
1974	"Closing Scene" L4935G	Open		180.00	520
1983	"Closing Scene"/white L4935.3M	Closed	1987	213.00	265
1974	Spring Breeze L4936G	Open		145.00	410
1976	Baby's Outing L4938G	Open		250.00	725
1977	Missy L4951M	Closed	1985	300.00	600-850
1977	Meditation L4952M	Closed	1979	200.00	N/A
1977	Tavern Drinkers L4956G	Closed	1985	1125.00	3500
1977	Attentive Dogs L4957G	Closed	1981	350.00	1500-2200
1977	Cherub, Puzzled L4959G	Open		40.00	110
1977	Cherub, Smiling L4960G	Open		40.00	110
1977	Cherub, Dreaming L4961G	Open		40.00	110
1977	Cherub, Wondering L4962G	Open		40.00	110
1977	Cherub, Wondering L4962M	Closed	1992	40.00	100
1977	Infantile Candour L4963G	Closed	1979	285.00	800
1977	Little Red Riding Hood L4965G	Closed	1983	210.00	550
1977	Tennis Player Puppet L4966G	Closed	1985	60.00	250
1977	Soccer Puppet L4967G	Closed	1985	65.00	425
1977	Oympic Puppet L4968	Closed	1983	65.00	800
1977	Cowboy & Sheriff Puppet L4969G	Closed	1985	85.00	650
1977	Skier Puppet L4970G	Closed	1983	85.00	500-900
1977	Hunter Puppet L4971G	Closed	1985	95.00	750
1977	Girl with Calla Lillies sitting L4972G	Open		65.00	180
1977	Choir Lesson L4973G	Closed	1981	350.00	1450
1977	Augustina of Aragon L4976G	Closed	1979	475.00	1500-1800
1977	Harlequin Serenade L4977	Closed	1979	185.00	675
1977	Milkmaid with Wheelbarrow L4979G	Closed	1981	220.00	950
1977	Ironing Time L4981G	Closed	1985	80.00	350
1978	Naughty Dog L4982G	12/95		130.00	250
1978	Gossip L4984G	Closed	1985	260.00	875
1978	Oriental Spring L4988G	Open		125.00	325
1978	Sayonara L4989G	Open		125.00	300
1978	Chrysanthemum L4990G	Open		125.00	310
1978	Butterfly L4991G	Open		125.00	295
1978	Dancers Resting L4992G	Closed	1983	350.00	850
1978	Gypsy Venders L4993G	Closed	1985	165.00	475
1978	Ready to Go L4996G	Closed	1981	425.00	1400
1978	Don Quixote & Sancho L4998G	Closed	1983	875.00	3300
1978	Reading L5000G	Open		150.00	275
1978	Elk Family L5001G	Closed	1981	550.00	700
1978	Sunny Day L5003G	Closed	1993	193.00	360
1978	Naughty L5006G	Open		55.00	150
1978	Bashful L5007G	Open		55.00	150
1978	Static-Girl w/Straw Hat L5008G	Open		55.00	150
1978	Curious-Girl w/Straw Hat L5009G	Open		55.00	150
1978	Coiffure-Girl w/Straw Hat L5010G	Open		55.00	150
1978	Trying on a Straw Hat L5011G	Open		55.00	150
1978	Daughters L5013G	Closed	1991	425.00	900
1978	Painful Monkey L5018	Closed	1981	135.00	750
1978	Painful Giraffe L5019	Closed	1981	115.00	750
1978	Woman With Scarf L5024G	Closed	1985	141.00	450
1980	A Clean Sweep L5025G	Open	1985	100.00	275
1980	Planning the Day L5026G	Open	1985	90.00	275
1979	Flower Curtsy L5027G	Open		230.00	470
1980	Boy with Tricycle & Flowers L5029G	Closed	1985	675.00	12-1350
1980	Wildflower L5030G	Closed	1994	360.00	695
1979	Little Friskies L5032G	Open		108.00	220
1979	Avoiding the Goose L5033G	Closed	1993	160.00	350
1979	Goose Trying To Eat L5034G	Open		135.00	310
1980	Act II w/base L5035G	Open		700.00	1425
1979	Jockey with Lass L5036G	Open		950.00	2240
1980	Sleighride w/base L5037G	Open		585.00	1140
1980	Candid L5039G	Closed	1981	145.00	475
1979	Girl Walking L5040G	Closed	1981	150.00	420-450
1980	Girl Kneeling and Tulips L5041G	Closed	1981	160.00	650
1980	Ladies Talking L5042G	Closed	1983	385.00	575-1000
1980	Hind and Baby Deer L5043G	Closed	1981	650.00	3600
1980	Girl with Toy Wagon L5044G	Open		115.00	245
1980	Belinda with Doll L5045G	12/95		115.00	215
1980	Organ Grinder L5046G	Closed	1981	328.00	1600
1980	Teacher Woman L5048G	Closed	1981	115.00	585-675
1979	Dancer L5050G	Open		85.00	205
1980	Samson and Delilah L5051G	Closed	1981	350.00	1600
1980	Clown and Girl/ At the Circus L5052G	Closed	1985	525.00	1250
1980	Festival Time L5053G	Closed	1985	250.00	450
1980	Little Senorita L5054G	Closed	1985	235.00	600
1980	Ship-Boy with Baskets L5055G	Closed	1985	140.00	400
1980	Boy Clown with Clock L5056G	Closed	1985	290.00	825
1980	Boy Clown with Violin and Top Hat L5057G	Closed	1985	270.00	750-900
1980	Boy Clown with Concertina L5058G	Closed	1985	290.00	500-600
1980	Boy Clown with Saxaphone L5059G	Closed	1985	320.00	600
1980	Girl Clown with Trumpet L5060G	Closed	1985	290.00	550
1980	Girl Bending/March Wind L5061G	Closed	1983	370.00	650
1980	Kristina L5062G	Closed	1985	225.00	400
1980	Dutch Girl With Braids L5063G	Closed	1985	265.00	425-450
1980	Dutch Girl, Hands Akimbo L5064G	Closed	1990	255.00	500
1980	Ingrid L5065G	Closed	1990	370.00	800
1980	Ilsa L5066G	Closed	1990	275.00	600
1981	Snow White with Apple L5067G	Closed	1983	450.00	1250
1980	Fairy Godmother L5068G	Closed	1983	625.00	950-1150
1980	Choir Boy L5070G	Closed	1983	240.00	850
1980	Nostalgia L5071G	Closed	1993	185.00	350
1980	Courtship L5072	Closed	1990	327.00	750
1980	Country Flowers L5073	Closed	1985	315.00	1500
1980	My Hungry Brood L5074G	Open		295.00	415
1980	Little Harlequin "A" L5075G	Closed	1985	217.50	410
1980	Little Harlequin "B" L5076G	Closed	1985	185.00	375
1980	Little Harlequin "C" L5077G	Closed	1985	185.00	500
1980	Teasing the Dog L5078G	Closed	1985	300.00	750
1980	Woman Painting Vase L5079G	Closed	1985	300.00	600-750
1980	Boy Pottery Seller L5080G	Closed	1985	320.00	650-700
1980	Girl Pottery Seller L5081G	Closed	1985	300.00	725
1980	Flower Vendor L5082G	Closed	1985	750.00	1850
1980	A Good Book L5084G	Closed	1985	175.00	350-525
1980	Mother Amabilis L5086G	Closed	1983	275.00	400
1980	Roses for My Mom L5088G	Closed	1988	645.00	1150

FIGURINES/COTTAGES

YEAR ISSUE		EDITION LIMIT	YEAR RETD.	ISSUE PRICE	QUOTE U.S.$
1980	Scare-Dy Cat/Playful Cat L5091G	Open		65.00	95
1980	After the Dance L5092G	Closed	1983	165.00	350
1980	A Dancing Partner L5093G	Closed	1983	165.00	500
1980	Ballet First Step L5094G	Closed	1983	165.00	400
1980	Ballet Bowing L5095G	Closed	1983	165.00	300
1989	Her Ladyship, L5097G	Closed	1991	5900.00	6700
1982	Playful Tot L5099G	Closed	1985	58.00	N/A
1982	Cry Baby L5100G	Closed	1985	58.00	275-300
1982	Learning to Crawl L5101G	Closed	1985	58.00	275-300
1982	Teething L5102G	Closed	1985	58.00	300
1982	Time for a Nap L5103G	Closed	1985	58.00	275
1982	Natalia L5106G	Closed	1985	85.00	350
1982	Little Ballet Girl L5108G	Closed	1985	85.00	400
1982	Little Ballet Girl L5109G	Closed	1985	85.00	400
1982	Dog Sniffing L5110G	Closed	1985	50.00	450-700
1982	Timid Dog L5111G	Closed	1985	44.00	400-500
1982	Play with Me L5112G	Open		40.00	80
1982	Feed Me L5113G	Open		40.00	80
1982	Pet Me L5114G	Open		40.00	80
1982	Little Boy Bullfighter L5115G	Closed	1985	123.00	400
1982	A Victory L5116G	Closed	1985	123.00	400-500
1982	Proud Matador L5117G	Closed	1985	123.00	500
1982	Girl in Green Dress L5118G	Closed	1985	170.00	600
1982	Girl in Bluish Dress L5119G	Closed	1985	170.00	600
1982	Girl in Pink Dress L5120G	Closed	1985	170.00	600
1982	August Moon L5122G	Closed	1993	185.00	325
1982	My Precious Bundle L5123G	Open		150.00	235
1982	Dutch Couple with Tulips L5124G	Closed	1985	310.00	900
1982	Amparo L5125G	Closed	1990	130.00	330-350
1982	Sewing A Trousseau L5126G	Closed	1990	185.00	425
1982	Marcelina L5127G	Closed	1985	255.00	255
1982	Lost Love L5128G	Closed	1988	400.00	650-750
1982	Jester w/base L5129G	Open		220.00	445
1982	Pensive Clown w/base L5130G	Open		250.00	445
1982	Cervantes L5132G	Closed	1988	925.00	1175
1982	Trophy with Base L5133G	Closed	1983	250.00	650
1982	Girl Soccer Player L5134G	Closed	1983	140.00	500
1982	Billy Football Player L5135G	Closed	1983	140.00	600-775
1982	Billy Skier L5136G	Closed	1983	140.00	700
1982	Billy Baseball Player L5137G	Closed	1983	140.00	650
1982	A New Doll House L5139G	Closed	1983	185.00	750
1982	Feed Her Son L5140G	Closed	1991	170.00	375
1982	Balloons for Sale L5141G	Open		145.00	250
1982	Comforting Daughter L5142G	Closed	1991	195.00	350
1982	Scooting L5143G	Closed	1988	575.00	850-1000
1982	Amy L5145G	Closed	1985	110.00	1500
1982	Ellen L5146G	Closed	1985	110.00	1150
1982	Ivez L5147G	Closed	1985	100.00	600
1982	Olivia L5148G	Closed	1985	100.00	250-425
1982	Ursula L5149G	Closed	1985	100.00	450
1982	Girl's Head L5151G	Closed	1983	380.00	575
1982	Girl's Head L5153G	Closed	1983	475.00	575
1982	First Prize L5154G	Closed	1985	90.00	N/A
1982	Monks at Prayer L5155M	Open		130.00	275
1982	Susan and the Doves L5156G	Closed	1991	203.00	325-360
1982	Bongo Beat L5157G	Open		135.00	230
1982	A Step In Time L5158G	Open		90.00	195
1982	Harmony L5159G	Open		270.00	495
1982	Rhumba L5160G	Open		113.00	185
1982	Cycling To A Picnic L5161G	Closed	1985	2000.00	2800
1982	Mouse Girl/Mindy L5162G	Closed	1985	125.00	425-450
1982	Bunny Girl/Bunny L5163G	Closed	1985	125.00	425-450
1982	Cat Girl/Kitty L5164G	Closed	1985	125.00	450
1982	A Toast by Sancho L5165	Closed	1990	100.00	400
1982	Sea Fever L5166M	Closed	1993	130.00	235
1982	Sea Fever L5166G	Closed	1993	130.00	375
1982	Jesus L5167G	Open		130.00	265
1982	King Solomon L5168G	Closed	1985	205.00	750
1982	Abraham L5169G	Closed	1985	155.00	650
1982	Moses L5170G	Open		175.00	395
1982	Madonna with Flowers L5171G	Open		173.00	310
1982	Fish A'Plenty L5172G	Closed	1994	190.00	385
1982	Pondering L5173G	Closed	1993	300.00	495
1982	Roaring 20's L5174G	Closed	1993	173.00	295
1982	Flapper L5175G	12/95		185.00	365
1982	Rhapsody in Blue L5176G	Closed	1985	325.00	1375
1982	Dante L5177G	Closed	1983	263.00	600
1982	Stubborn Mule L5178G	Closed	1993	250.00	500
1983	Three Pink Roses w/base L5179M	Closed	1990	70.00	110
1983	Dahlia L5180M	Closed	1990	65.00	140
1983	Japanese Camelia w/base L5181M	Closed	1990	60.00	90
1983	White Peony L5182M	Closed	1990	85.00	125
1983	Two Yellow Roses L5183M	Closed	1990	57.50	100
1983	White Carnation L5184M	Closed	1990	65.00	100
1983	Lactiflora Peony L5185M	Closed	1990	65.00	100
1983	Begonia L5186M	Closed	1990	67.50	100
1983	Rhododendrom L5187M	Closed	1990	67.50	100
1983	Miniature Begonia L5188M	Closed	1990	80.00	120
1983	Chrysanthemum L5189M	Closed	1990	100.00	150
1983	California Poppy L5190M	Closed	1990	97.50	180
1983	Predicting the Future L5191G	Closed	1985	135.00	400
1984	Lolita L5192G	Open		80.00	165
1984	Juanita L5193G	Open		80.00	165
1984	Roving Photographer L5194G	Closed	1985	145.00	1200
1983	Say "Cheese!" L5195G	Closed	1990	170.00	525
1983	"Maestro, Music Please!" L5196G	Closed	1988	135.00	500
1983	Female Physician L5197	Open		120.00	260
1984	Boy Graduate L5198G	Open		160.00	290
1984	Girl Graduate L5199G	Open		160.00	285
1984	Male Soccer Player L5200G	Closed	1988	155.00	475
1984	Special Male Soccer Player L5200.3G	Closed	1988	150.00	450
1983	Josefa Feeding Duck L5201G	Closed	1991	125.00	250-300
1983	Aracely with Ducks L5202G	Closed	1991	125.00	250-300
1984	Little Jester L5203G	Closed	1993	75.00	200-250
1984	Little Jester L5203M	Closed	1992	75.00	200-250
1983	Sharpening the Cutlery L5204	Closed	1988	210.00	750
1983	Lamplighter L5205G	Open		170.00	395
1983	Yachtsman L5206G	Closed	1994	110.00	210
1983	A Tall Yarn L5207G	Open		260.00	545
1983	Professor L5208G	Closed	1990	205.00	550-750
1983	School Marm L5209G	Closed	1990	205.00	700
1984	Jolie L5210G	Open		105.00	220
1984	Angela L5211G	Open		105.00	220
1984	Evita L5212G	Open		105.00	195
1983	Lawyer L5213G	Open		250.00	570
1983	Architect L5214G	Closed	1990	140.00	400
1983	Fishing with Gramps w/base L5215G	Open		410.00	850
1983	On the Lake L5216G	Closed	1988	660.00	900
1983	Spring L5217G	Open		90.00	185
1983	Spring L5217M	Open		90.00	185
1983	Autumn L5218G	Open		90.00	185
1983	Autumn L5218M	Open		90.00	185
1983	Summer L5219G	Open		90.00	185
1983	Summer L5219M	Open		90.00	185
1983	Winter L5220G	Open		90.00	185
1983	Winter L5220M	Open		90.00	185
1983	Sweet Scent L5221G	Open		80.00	145
1983	Sweet Scent L5221M	Open		80.00	145
1983	Pretty Pickings L5222G	Open		80.00	145
1983	Pretty Pickings L5222M	Open		80.00	145
1983	Spring is Here L5223G	Open		80.00	145
1983	Spring is Here L5223M	Open		80.00	145
1984	The Quest L5224G	Open		125.00	295
1984	Male Candleholder L5226	Closed	1985	660.00	1200
1984	Playful Piglets L5228G	Open		80.00	150
1983	Storytime L5229G	Closed	1990	245.00	800
1984	Graceful Swan L5230G	Open		35.00	90
1984	Swan with Wings Spread L5231G	Open		50.00	125
1983	Playful Kittens L5232G	Open		130.00	280
1983	Charlie the Tramp L5233G	Closed	1991	150.00	625-750
1984	Artistic Endeavor L5234G	Closed	1988	225.00	400-750
1984	Ballet Trio L5235G	Open		785.00	1650
1984	Cat and Mouse L5236G	Open		55.00	98
1984	Cat and Mouse L5236M	Closed	1992	55.00	95
1984	School Chums L5237G	Open		225.00	485
1984	Eskimo Boy with Pet L5238G	Open		55.00	115
1984	Eskimo Boy with Pet L5238M	Closed	1992	55.00	95
1984	Wine Taster L5239G	Open		190.00	395
1984	Lady from Majorca L5240G	Closed	1990	120.00	350
1984	Best Wishes L5244G	Closed	1986	185.00	275
1984	A Thought for Today L5245	Closed	1986	180.00	300
1984	St. Christopher L5246	Closed	1988	265.00	600
1984	Penguin L5247G	Closed	1988	70.00	200
1984	Penguin L5248G	Closed	1988	70.00	200
1984	Penguin L5249G	Closed	1988	70.00	175
1984	Exam Day L5250G	Closed	1994	115.00	210
1984	Torch Bearer L5251G	Closed	1988	100.00	300
1984	Dancing the Polka L5252G	Closed	1994	205.00	425
1984	Cadet L5253G	Closed	1984	150.00	750
1984	Making Paella L5254G	Closed	1993	215.00	490
1984	Spanish Soldier L5255G	Closed	1988	185.00	650
1984	Folk Dancing L5256G	Closed	1990	205.00	400-600
1984	Vase L5257.30	Closed	1988	55.00	200
1985	Bust of Lady from Elche L5269M	Closed	1988	432.00	750
1985	Racing Motor Cyclist L5270G	Closed	1988	360.00	675
1985	Gazelle L5271G	Closed	1988	205.00	425-550
1985	Biking in the Country L5272G	Closed	1990	295.00	775
1985	Civil Guard at Attention L5273G	Closed	1988	170.00	450
1985	Wedding Day L5274G	Open		240.00	435
1985	Weary Ballerina L5275G	12/95		175.00	310
1985	Weary Ballerina L5275M	Closed	1992	175.00	310
1985	Sailor Serenades His Girl L5276G	Closed	1988	315.00	950
1985	Pierrot with Puppy L5277G	Open		95.00	160
1985	Pierrot with Puppy and Ball L5278G	Open		95.00	160
1985	Pierrot with Concertina L5279G	Open		95.00	160
1985	Hiker L5280G	Closed	1988	195.00	425
1985	Nativity Scene "Haute Relief" L5281M	Closed	1988	210.00	450
1985	Over the Threshold L5282G	Open		150.00	290
1985	Socialite of the Twenties L5283G	Open		175.00	340
1985	Glorious Spring L5284G	Open		355.00	710
1985	Summer on the Farm L5285G	Open		235.00	455
1985	Fall Clean-up L5286G	Open		295.00	565
1985	Winter Frost L5287G	Open		270.00	520
1985	Mallard Duck L5288G	Closed	1994	310.00	520
1985	Little Leaguer Exercising L5289	Closed	1990	150.00	400
1985	Little Leaguer, Catcher L5290	Closed	1990	150.00	500
1985	Little Leaguer on Bench L5291	Closed	1990	150.00	500
1985	Love in Bloom L5292G	Open		225.00	425
1985	Mother and Child and Lamb L5299G	Closed	1988	180.00	750
1985	Medieval Courtship L5300G	Closed	1990	735.00	800
1985	Waiting to Tee Off L5301G	Open		145.00	295
1985	Antelope Drinking L5302	Closed	1988	215.00	650
1985	Playing with Ducks at the Pond L5303G	Closed	1990	425.00	875
1985	Children at Play L5304	Closed	1990	220.00	450-550
1985	A Visit with Granny L5305G	Closed	1993	275.00	625
1985	Young Street Musicians L5306G	Closed	1988	300.00	1500
1985	Mini Kitten L5307G	Closed	1993	35.00	100
1985	Mini Cat L5308G	Closed	1993	35.00	65-100
1985	Mini Cocker Spaniel Pup L5309G	Closed	1993	35.00	75-110
1985	Mini Cocker Spaniel L5310G	Closed	1993	35.00	85-110
1985	Mini Puppies L5311G	Closed	1990	65.00	200
1985	Mini Bison Resting L5312G	Closed	1990	50.00	163
1985	Mini Bison Attacking L5313G	Closed	1990	57.50	163
1985	Mini Deer L5314G	Closed	1990	40.00	70-140
1985	Mini Seal Family L5318G	Closed	1990	77.50	275
1985	Wistful Centaur Girl L5319G	Closed	1990	157.00	450
1985	Demure Centaur Girl L5320	Closed	1990	157.00	425
1985	Parisian Lady L5321G	12/95		193.00	325
1985	Viennese Lady L5322G	Closed	1994	160.00	295
1985	Milanese Lady L5323G	Closed	1994	180.00	400
1985	English Lady L5324G	Closed	1994	225.00	475
1985	Ice Cream Vendor L5325G	12/95		380.00	650
1985	The Tailor L5326G	Closed	1988	335.00	900-1300
1985	Nippon Lady L5327G	Open		325.00	575
1985	Lady Equestrian L5328G	Closed	1988	160.00	400-425
1985	Gentleman Equestrian L5329G	Closed	1988	160.00	525
1985	Concert Violinist L5330G	Closed	1988	220.00	425-500
1985	Gymnast with Ring L5331	Closed	1988	95.00	295
1985	Gymnast Balancing Ball L5332	Closed	1988	95.00	350
1985	Gymnast Exercising with Ball L5333G	Closed	1988	95.00	250
1985	Aerobics Push-Up L5334G	Closed	1988	110.00	295
1985	Aerobics Floor Exercies L5335G	Closed	1988	110.00	300
1985	"La Giaconda" L5337G	Closed	1988	110.00	400
1986	A Stitch in Time L5344G	Open		425.00	795
1986	A New Hat L5345G	Closed	1990	200.00	375
1986	Nature Girl L5346G	Closed	1988	450.00	950
1986	Bedtime L5347G	Open		300.00	545
1986	On The Scent L5348G	Closed	1990	47.50	175
1986	Relaxing L5349G	Closed	1990	47.50	150
1986	On Guard L5350G	Closed	1990	50.00	200
1986	Woe is Me L5351G	Closed	1990	45.00	200
1986	Hindu Children L5352G	Open		250.00	445
1986	Eskimo Riders L5353G	Open		150.00	250
1986	Eskimo Riders L5353M	Open		150.00	250
1986	A Ride in the Country L5354G	Closed	1993	225.00	415
1986	Consideration L5355M	Closed	1988	100.00	225
1986	Wolf Hound L5356G	Closed	1990	45.00	200-300
1986	Oration L5357G	Open		170.00	295
1986	Little Sculptor L5358G	Closed	1990	160.00	325-400
1986	El Greco L5359G	Closed	1990	300.00	550
1986	Sewing Circle L5360G	Closed	1990	600.00	1250
1986	Try This One L5361G	Open		225.00	385
1986	Still Life L5363G	Open		180.00	395
1986	Litter of Fun L5364G	Open		275.00	465
1986	Sunday in the Park L5365G	Open		375.00	625
1986	Can Can L5370G	Closed	1990	700.00	1100-1400
1986	Family Roots L5371G	Open		575.00	935
1986	Lolita L5372G	Closed	1993	120.00	200
1986	Carmencita L5373G	Closed	1993	120.00	200
1986	Pepita L5374G	Closed	1993	120.00	350
1986	Teresita L5375G	Closed	1993	120.00	350
1986	This One's Mine L5376G	12/95		300.00	520
1986	A Touch of Class L5377G	Open		475.00	795
1986	Time for Reflection L5378G	Open		425.00	745
1986	Children's Games L5379G	Closed	1991	325.00	650
1986	Sweet Harvest L5380G	Closed	1990	450.00	915
1986	Serenade L5381	Closed	1990	450.00	625
1986	Lovers Serenade L5382G	Closed	1990	350.00	850
1986	Petite Maiden L5383	Closed	1990	110.00	350
1986	Petite Pair L5384	Closed	1990	225.00	400
1986	Scarecrow & the Lady L5385G	Open		350.00	680
1986	St. Vincent L5387	Closed	1990	190.00	350
1986	Sidewalk Serenade L5388G	Closed	1988	750.00	11-1300
1986	Deep in Thought L5389G	Closed	1990	170.00	400
1986	Spanish Dancer L5390G	Closed	1990	170.00	400
1986	A Time to Rest L5391G	Closed	1990	170.00	400
1986	Balancing Act L5392G	Closed	1990	35.00	200
1986	Curiosity L5393G	Closed	1990	25.00	150
1986	Poor Puppy L5394G	Closed	1990	25.00	150-175
1986	Valencian Boy L5395G	Closed	1991	200.00	400
1986	The Puppet Painter L5396G	Open		500.00	850
1986	The Poet L5397G	Closed	1988	425.00	900
1986	At the Ball L5398G	Closed	1991	375.00	700
1987	Time To Rest L5399G	Closed	1993	175.00	295
1987	The Wanderer L5400G	Open		150.00	245
1987	My Best Friend L5401G	Closed		150.00	240
1987	Desert Tour L5402G	Closed	1990	950.00	1050
1987	The Drummer Boy L5403G	Closed	1990	225.00	400
1987	Cadet Captain L5404G	Closed	1990	175.00	360
1987	The Flag Bearer L5405G	Closed	1990	200.00	450
1987	The Bugler L5406G	Closed	1990	175.00	375
1987	At Attention L5407G	Closed	1990	175.00	325
1987	Sunday Stroll L5408G	Closed	1990	250.00	600
1987	Courting Time L5409	Closed	1990	425.00	550
1987	Pilar L5410G	Closed	1990	200.00	400
1987	Teresa L5411G	Closed	1990	225.00	430
1987	Isabel L5412G	Closed	1990	225.00	450
1987	Mexican Dancers L5415G	Open		800.00	1195
1987	In the Garden L5416G	Open		200.00	325
1987	Artist's Model L5417	Closed	1990	425.00	475
1987	Short Eared Owl L5418G	Closed	1990	200.00	360
1987	Great Gray Owl L5419G	Closed	1990	190.00	195-225
1987	Horned Owl L5420G	Closed	1990	150.00	300
1987	Barn Owl L5421G	Closed	1990	120.00	175
1987	Hawk Owl L5422G	Closed	1990	120.00	195-225
1987	Intermezzo L5424	Closed	1990	325.00	550

FIGURINES/COTTAGES

YEAR ISSUE		EDITION LIMIT	YEAR RETD.	ISSUE PRICE	QUOTE U.S.$
1987	Studying in the Park L5425G	Closed	1991	675.00	950
1987	Studying in the Park L5425M	Closed	1989	675.00	950
1987	One, Two, Three L5426G	12/95		240.00	390
1987	Saint Nicholas L5427G	Closed	1991	425.00	600-700
1987	Feeding the Pigeons L5428	Closed	1990	490.00	700
1987	Happy Birthday L5429G	Open		100.00	155
1987	Music Time L5430G	Closed	1990	500.00	700
1987	Midwife L5431	Closed	1990	175.00	575
1987	Monkey L5432G	Closed	1990	60.00	150
1987	Kangaroo L5433G	Closed	1990	65.00	150-175
1987	Miniature Polar Bear L5434G	Open		65.00	110
1987	Cougar L5435G	Closed	1990	65.00	300
1987	Lion L5436G	Closed	1990	50.00	150-300
1987	Rhino L5437G	Closed	1990	50.00	175
1987	Elephant L5438G	Closed	1990	50.00	175
1987	The Bride L5439G	12/95		250.00	425
1987	Poetry of Love L5442G	Open		500.00	865
1987	Sleepy Trio L5443G	Open		190.00	305
1987	Will You Marry Me? L5447G	Closed	1994	750.00	1250
1987	Naptime L5448G	Open		135.00	250
1987	Naptime L5448M	Open		135.00	250
1987	Goodnight L5449	Open		225.00	375
1987	I Hope She Does L5450G	Open		190.00	345
1988	Study Buddies L5451G	Open		225.00	295
1988	Masquerade Ball L5452G	Closed	1993	220.00	375
1988	Masquerade Ball L5452M	Closed	1992	220.00	265
1988	For You L5453G	Open		450.00	640
1988	For Me? L5454G	Open		290.00	395
1988	Bashful Bather L5455G	Open		150.00	190
1988	Bashful Bather L5455M	Closed	1992	150.00	180
1988	New Playmates L5456G	Open		160.00	230
1988	New Playmates L5456M	Closed	1992	160.00	190
1988	Bedtime Story L5457G	Open		275.00	355
1988	Bedtime Story L5457M	Closed	1992	275.00	330
1988	A Barrow of Fun L5460G	Open		370.00	525
1988	A Barrow of Fun L5460M	Closed	1992	370.00	450
1988	Koala Love L5461G	Closed	1993	115.00	150-225
1988	Practice Makes Perfect L5462G	Open		375.00	545
1988	Look At Me! L5465G	Open		375.00	495
1988	Look At Me! L5465M	Closed	1992	375.00	435
1988	"Chit-Chat" L5466G	Open		150.00	198
1988	"Chit-Chat" L5466M	Closed	1992	150.00	180
1988	May Flowers L5467G	Open		160.00	215
1988	May Flowers L5467M	Closed	1992	160.00	190
1988	"Who's The Fairest?" L5468G	Open		150.00	200
1988	"Who's The Fairest?" L5468M	Closed	1992	150.00	180
1988	Lambkins L5469G	Closed	1993	150.00	210
1988	Lambkins L5469M	Closed	1989	150.00	195
1988	Tea Time L5470G	Open		280.00	385
1988	Sad Sax L5471G	Open		175.00	205
1988	Circus Sam L5472G	Open		175.00	205
1988	How You've Grown! L5474G	Open		180.00	250
1988	How You've Grown! L5474M	Closed	1992	180.00	215
1988	A Lesson Shared L5475G	Open		150.00	190
1988	A Lesson Shared L5475M	Closed	1992	150.00	170
1988	St. Joseph L5476G	Open		210.00	270
1988	Mary L5477G	Open		130.00	165
1988	Baby Jesus L5478G	Open		55.00	75
1988	King Melchior L5479G	Open		210.00	265
1988	King Gaspar L5480G	Open		210.00	265
1988	King Balthasar L5481G	Open		210.00	265
1988	Ox L5482G	Open		125.00	175
1988	Donkey L5483G	Open		125.00	175
1988	Lost Lamb L5484G	Open		100.00	140
1988	Shepherd Boy L5485G	Open		140.00	190
1988	Debutantes L5486G	Open		490.00	695
1988	Debutantes L5486M	Closed	1992	490.00	635
1988	Ingenue L5487G	Open		110.00	145
1988	Ingenue L5487M	Closed	1992	110.00	130
1988	Sandcastles L5488G	Closed	1993	160.00	220
1988	Sandcastles L5488M	Closed	1992	160.00	200
1988	Justice L5489G	Closed	1993	675.00	825
1988	Flor Maria L5490G	Open		500.00	635
1988	Heavenly Strings L5491G	Closed	1993	140.00	160
1988	Heavenly Cellist L5492G	Closed	1993	240.00	240
1988	Angel with Lute L5493G	Closed	1993	140.00	160
1988	Angel with Clarinet L5494G	Closed	1993	140.00	160
1988	Angelic Choir L5495G	Closed	1993	300.00	295-475
1988	Recital L5496G	Open		190.00	285
1988	Dress Rehearsal L5497G	Open		290.00	420
1988	Opening Night L5498G	Open		190.00	285
1988	Pretty Ballerina L5499G	Open		190.00	285
1988	Prayerful Moment (blue) L5500G	Open		90.00	110
1988	Time to Sew (blue) L5501G	Open		90.00	110
1988	Meditation (blue) L5502G	Open		90.00	110
1988	Hurry Now L5503G	Open		180.00	250
1988	Hurry Now L5503M	Closed	1992	180.00	240
1989	Flowers for Sale L5537G	Open		1200.00	1550
1989	Puppy Dog Tails L5539G	Open		1200.00	1595
1989	An Evening Out L5540G	Closed	1991	350.00	425
1989	Melancholy w/base L5542G	Open		375.00	455
1989	"Hello, Flowers" L5543G	Closed	1993	385.00	545
1989	Reaching the Goal L5546G	Open		215.00	275
1989	Only the Beginning L5547G	Open		215.00	275
1989	Pretty Posies L5548G	Closed	1994	425.00	530
1989	My New Pet L5549G	Open		150.00	185
1989	Serene Moment (blue) L5550G	Closed	1993	115.00	195
1989	Serene Moment (white) L5550.3G	Closed	1991	115.00	135
1989	Serene Moment (white) L5550.3M	Closed	1991	115.00	135
1989	Call to Prayer (blue) L5551G	Closed	1993	100.00	195
1989	Call to Prayer (white) L5551.3G	Closed	1991	100.00	120
1989	Call to Prayer (white) L5551.3M	Closed	1991	100.00	120
1989	Morning Chores (blue) L5552G	Closed	1993	115.00	195
1989	Wild Goose Chase L5553G	Open		175.00	230
1989	Pretty and Prim L5554G	Open		215.00	270
1989	"Let's Make Up" L5555G	Open		215.00	265
1989	Green Clover Vase L5561G	Closed	1991	130.00	225
1989	Sad Parting L5583G	Closed	1991	375.00	525
1989	Daddy's Girl/Father's Day L5584G	Open		315.00	395
1989	Fine Melody w/base L5585G	Closed	1993	225.00	295
1989	Sad Note w/base L5586G	Closed	1993	185.00	295
1989	Wedding Cake L5587G	Open		595.00	750
1989	Blustery Day L5588G	Closed	1993	185.00	230
1989	Pretty Pose L5589G	Closed	1993	185.00	230
1989	Spring Breeze L5590G	Closed	1993	185.00	230
1989	Garden Treasures L5591G	Closed	1993	185.00	230
1989	Male Siamese Dancer L5592G	Closed	1993	345.00	420
1989	Siamese Dancer L5593G	Closed	1993	345.00	420
1989	Playful Romp L5594G	Open		215.00	270
1989	Joy in a Basket L5595G	Open		215.00	270
1989	A Gift of Love L5596G	Open		400.00	495
1989	Summer Soiree L5597G	Open		150.00	180
1989	Bridesmaid L5598G	Open		150.00	180
1989	Coquette L5599G	Open		150.00	180
1989	The Blues w/base L5600G	Closed	1993	265.00	375
1989	"Ole" L5601G	Open		365.00	460
1989	Close To My Heart L5603G	Open		125.00	165
1989	Spring Token L5604G	Open		175.00	230
1989	Floral Treasures L5605G	Open		195.00	250
1989	Quiet Evening L5606G	Closed	1993	125.00	165
1989	Calling A Friend L5607G	Open		125.00	165
1989	Baby Doll L5608G	Open		150.00	180
1989	Playful Friends L5609G	12/95		135.00	170
1989	Star Struck w/base L5610G	Open		335.00	420
1989	Sad Clown w/base L5611G	Open		335.00	420
1989	Reflecting w/base L5612G	Closed	1994	335.00	420
1989	Startled L5614G	Closed	1991	265.00	425
1989	Bathing Beauty L5615G	Closed	1991	265.00	330-400
1989	Candleholder L5626	Closed	1990	90.00	125
1989	Lladro Vase L5631G	Closed	1990	150.00	195-275
1990	Water Dreamer Vase L5633G	Closed	1990	150.00	195
1990	Cat Nap L5640G	Open		125.00	145
1990	The King's Guard w/base L5642G	Closed	1993	950.00	1100
1990	Cathy L5643G	Open		200.00	235
1990	Susan L5644G	Open		190.00	215
1990	Elizabeth L5645G	Open		190.00	215
1990	Cindy L5646G	Open		190.00	215
1990	Sara L5647G	Open		200.00	230
1990	Courtney L5648G	Open		200.00	230
1990	Nothing To Do L5649G	Open		190.00	220
1990	Anticipation L5650G	Closed	1993	300.00	350
1990	Musical Muse L5651G	Open		375.00	440
1989	Marbella Clock L5652	Closed	1994	125.00	215
1990	Venetian Carnival L5658G	Closed	1993	500.00	575
1990	Barnyard Scene L5659G	Open		200.00	245
1990	Sunning In Ipanema L5660G	Closed	1993	370.00	475
1990	Traveling Artist L5661G	Closed	1994	250.00	290
1990	May Dance L5662G	Open		170.00	210
1990	Spring Dance L5663G	Open		170.00	210
1990	Giddy Up L5664G	Closed	1994	190.00	230
1990	Hang On! L5665G	12/95		225.00	285
1990	Trino At The Beach L5666G	12/95		390.00	460
1990	Valencian Harvest L5668G	Closed	1993	175.00	205
1990	Valencian FLowers L5669G	Closed	1993	370.00	420
1990	Valencian Beauty L5670G	Closed	1993	175.00	205
1990	Little Dutch Gardener L5671G	Closed	1993	400.00	475
1990	Hi There! L5672G	Open		450.00	520
1990	A Quiet Moment L5673G	Open		450.00	520
1990	A Faun And A Friend L5674G	Open		450.00	520
1990	Tee Time L5675G	Closed	1993	280.00	315
1990	Wandering Minstrel L5676G	Closed	1993	270.00	310
1990	Twilight Years L5677G	Open		370.00	420
1990	I Feel Pretty L5678G	Open		190.00	230
1990	In No Hurry L5679G	Closed	1994	550.00	640
1990	Traveling In Style L5680G	Closed	1994	425.00	495
1990	On The Road L5681G	Closed	1991	320.00	500
1990	Breezy Afternoon L5682G	Open		180.00	195
1990	Breezy Afternoon L5682M	Open		180.00	195
1990	Beautiful Burro L5683G	Closed	1993	280.00	345
1990	Barnyard Reflections L5684G	Closed	1993	460.00	525
1990	Promenade L5685G	Closed	1994	275.00	325
1990	On The Avenue L5686G	Closed	1994	275.00	325
1990	Afternoon Stroll L5687G	Closed	1994	275.00	325
1990	Dog's Best Friend L5688G	Open		250.00	295
1990	Can I Help? L5689G	Open		250.00	325
1990	Marshland Mates w/base L5691G	Open		950.00	1200
1990	Street Harmonies w/base L5692G	Closed	1993	3200.00	3750
1990	Circus Serenade L5694G	Closed	1994	300.00	360
1990	Concertina L5695G	Closed	1994	300.00	360
1990	Mandolin Serenade L5696G	Closed	1994	300.00	360
1990	Over The Clouds L5697G	Open		275.00	310
1990	Don't Look Down L5698G	Open		330.00	395
1990	Sitting Pretty L5699G	Open		300.00	340
1990	Southern Charm L5700G	Open		675.00	1025
1990	Just A Little Kiss L5701G	Open		320.00	375
1990	Back To School L5702G	Closed	1993	350.00	300-445
1990	Behave! L5703G	Closed	1994	230.00	265
1990	Swan Song L5704G	12/95		350.00	410
1990	The Swan And The Princess L5705G	Closed	1994	350.00	415
1990	We Can't Play L5706G	Open		200.00	235
1990	After School L5707G	Closed	1993	280.00	315
1990	My First Class L5708G	Closed	1993	280.00	315
1990	Between Classes L5709G	Closed	1993	280.00	315
1990	Fantasy Friend L5710G	Closed	1993	420.00	495
1990	A Christmas Wish L5711G	Open		350.00	410
1990	Sleepy Kitten L5712G	Open		110.00	130
1990	The Snow Man L5713G	Open		300.00	350
1990	First Ballet L5714G	Open		370.00	420
1990	Mommy, it's Cold! L5715G	Closed	1994	360.00	415
1990	Land of The Giants L5716G	Closed	1994	275.00	315
1990	Rock A Bye Baby L5717G	Open		300.00	365
1990	Sharing Secrets L5720G	Open		290.00	335
1990	Once Upon A Time L5721G	Open		550.00	650
1990	Follow Me L5722G	Open		140.00	160
1990	Heavenly Chimes L5723G	Open		100.00	120
1990	Angelic Voice L5724G	Open		125.00	145
1990	Making A Wish L5725G	Open		125.00	145
1990	Sweep Away The Clouds L5726G	Open		125.00	145
1990	Angel Care L5727G	Open		190.00	210
1990	Heavenly Dreamer L5728G	Open		100.00	120
1991	Carousel Charm L5731G	Closed	1994	1700.00	1850
1991	Carousel Canter L5732G	Closed	1994	1700.00	1850
1991	Horticulturist L5733G	Closed	1993	450.00	495
1991	Pilgrim Couple L5734G	Closed	1993	490.00	525
1991	Big Sister L5735G	Open		650.00	685
1991	Puppet Show L5736G	Open		280.00	295
1991	Little Prince L5737G	Closed	1993	295.00	315
1991	Best Foot Forward L5738G	Closed	1994	280.00	305
1991	Lap Full Of Love L5739G	12/95		275.00	295
1991	Alice In Wonderland L5740G	Open		440.00	485
1991	Dancing Class L5741G	Open		340.00	365
1991	Bridal Portrait L5742G	12/95		480.00	560
1991	Don't Forget Me L5743G	Open		150.00	160
1991	Bull & Donkey L5744G	Open		250.00	275
1991	Baby Jesus L5745G	Open		170.00	185
1991	St. Joseph L5746G	Open		350.00	375
1991	Mary L5747G	Open		275.00	295
1991	Shepherd Girl L5748G	Open		150.00	165
1991	Shepherd Boy L5749G	Open		225.00	245
1991	Little Lamb L5750G	Open		40.00	42
1991	Walk With Father L5751G	Closed	1994	375.00	410
1991	Little Virgin L5752G	Closed	1994	295.00	325
1991	Hold Her Still L5753G	Closed	1993	650.00	695
1991	Singapore Dancers L5754G	Closed	1993	950.00	1125
1991	Claudette L5755G	Closed	1993	265.00	300-350
1991	Ashley L5756G	Closed	1993	265.00	300
1991	Beautiful Tresses L5757G	Closed	1993	725.00	825
1991	Sunday Best L5758G	Open		725.00	785
1991	Presto! L5759G	Closed	1993	275.00	325
1991	Interrupted Nap L5760G	12/95		325.00	350
1991	Out For A Romp L5761G	12/95		375.00	410
1991	Checking The Time L5762G	12/95		560.00	595
1991	Musical Partners L5763G	12/95		625.00	675
1991	Seeds Of Laughter L5764G	12/95		525.00	575
1991	Hats Off To Fun L5765G	12/95		475.00	510
1991	Charming Duet L5766G	Open		575.00	625
1991	First Sampler L5767G	12/95		625.00	680
1991	Academy Days L5768G	Closed	1993	280.00	310
1991	Faithful Steed L5769G	Closed	1994	370.00	395
1991	Out For A Spin L5770G	Closed	1994	390.00	420
1991	The Magic Of Laughter L5771G	Open		950.00	1050
1991	Little Dreamers L5772G	Open		230.00	240
1991	Little Dreamers L5772M	Open		230.00	240
1991	Graceful Offering L5773G	12/95		850.00	895
1991	Nature's Gifts L5774G	Closed	1994	900.00	975
1991	Gift Of Beauty L5775G	12/95		850.00	895
1991	Lover's Paradise L5779G	Open		2250.00	2450
1991	Walking The Fields L5780G	Closed	1993	725.00	795
1991	Not Too Close L5781G	Closed	1994	365.00	450
1991	My Chores L5782G	12/95		325.00	355
1991	Special Delivery L5783G	Closed	1994	525.00	550
1991	A Cradle Of Kittens L5784G	Open		360.00	385
1991	Ocean Beauty L5785G	Open		625.00	665
1991	Story Hour L5786G	Open		550.00	625
1991	Sophisticate L5787G	Open		185.00	195
1991	Talk Of The Town L5788G	Open		185.00	195
1991	The Flirt L5789G	Open		185.00	195
1991	Carefree L5790G	Open		300.00	325
1991	Fairy Godmother L5791G	Closed	1994	375.00	410
1991	Reverent Moment L5792G	Closed	1994	295.00	320
1991	Precocious Ballerina L5793G	12/95		575.00	625
1991	Precious Cargo L5794G	Closed	1994	460.00	495
1991	Floral Getaway L5795G	Closed	1993	625.00	745
1991	Holy Night L5796G	Closed	1994	330.00	360
1991	Come Out And Play L5797G	Closed	1994	275.00	295
1991	Milkmaid L5798G	Closed	1993	450.00	495
1991	Shall We Dance? L5799G	Closed	1993	600.00	695
1991	Elegant Promenade L5802G	Open		775.00	825
1991	Playing Tag L5804G	Closed	1993	170.00	190
1991	Tumbling L5805G	Closed	1993	130.00	140
1991	Tumbling L5805M	Closed	1992	130.00	140
1991	Tickling L5806G	Closed	1993	130.00	145
1991	Tickling L5806M	Closed	1992	130.00	145
1991	My Puppies L5807G	Closed	1993	325.00	360
1991	Musically Inclined L5810G	Closed	1993	235.00	250
1991	Littlest Clown L5811G	Open		225.00	240
1991	Tired Friend L5812G	Open		225.00	245
1991	Having A Ball L5813G	Open		225.00	240

FIGURINES/COTTAGES

YEAR ISSUE		EDITION LIMIT	YEAR RETD.	ISSUE PRICE	QUOTE U.S.$
1991	Curtain Call L5814G	Closed	1994	490.00	520
1991	Curtain Call L5814M	Closed	1994	490.00	520
1991	In Full Relave L5815G	Closed	1994	490.00	520
1991	In Full Relave L5815M	Closed	1994	490.00	520
1991	Prima Ballerina L5816G	Closed	1994	490.00	520
1991	Prima Ballerina L5816M	Closed	1994	490.00	520
1991	Backstage Preparation L5817G	Closed	1994	490.00	520
1991	Backstage Preparation L5817M	Closed	1994	490.00	520
1991	On Her Toes L5818G	Closed	1994	490.00	520
1991	On Her Toes L5818M	Closed	1994	490.00	520
1991	Allegory Of Liberty L5819G	Open		1950.00	2100
1991	Dance Of Love L5820G	Closed	1993	575.00	625
1991	Minstrel's Love L5821G	Closed	1993	525.00	575
1991	Little Unicorn L5826G	Open		275.00	295
1991	Little Unicorn L5826M	Open		275.00	295
1991	I've Got It L5827G	12/95		170.00	180
1991	Next At Bat L5828G	Open		170.00	180
1991	Heavenly Harpist L5830	Yr.Iss.	1991	135.00	140-175
1991	Jazz Horn L5832G	Open		295.00	310
1991	Jazz Sax L5833G	Open		295.00	315
1991	Jazz Bass L5834G	Open		395.00	425
1991	I Do L5835G	Open		165.00	190
1991	Sharing Sweets L5836G	Open		220.00	245
1991	Sing With Me L5837G	Open		240.00	250
1991	On The Move L5838G	Open		340.00	395
1992	A Quiet Afternoon L5843G	12/95		1050.00	1125
1992	Flirtatious Jester L5844G	Open		890.00	925
1992	Dressing The Baby L5845G	Open		295.00	295
1992	All Tuckered Out L5846G	Open		220.00	255
1992	All Tuckered Out L5846M	Open		220.00	255
1992	The Loving Family L5848G	Closed	1994	950.00	985
1992	Inspiring Muse L5850G	Closed	1994	1200.00	1250
1992	Feathered Fantasy L5851G	Open		1200.00	1250
1992	Easter Bonnets L5852G	Closed	1993	265.00	325
1992	Floral Admiration L5853G	Closed	1994	690.00	725
1992	Floral Fantasy L5854G	12/95		690.00	710
1992	Afternoon Jaunt L5855G	Closed	1993	420.00	440
1992	Circus Concert L5856G	Open		570.00	585
1992	Grand Entrance L5857G	Closed	1994	265.00	275
1992	Waiting to Dance L5858G	12/95		295.00	335
1992	At The Ball L5859G	Open		295.00	330
1992	Fairy Garland L5860G	12/95		630.00	650
1992	Fairy Flowers L5861G	12/95		630.00	655
1992	Fragrant Bouquet L5862G	Open		350.00	360
1992	Dressing For The Ballet L5865G	12/95		395.00	415
1992	Final Touches L5866G	12/95		395.00	415
1992	Serene Valenciana L5867G	Closed	1994	365.00	385
1992	Loving Valenciana L5868G	12/95		365.00	385
1992	Fallas Queen L5869G	12/95		420.00	440
1992	Olympic Torch w/Fantasy Logo L5870G	Closed	1994	165.00	145
1992	Olympic Champion w/Fantasy Logo L5871G	Closed	1994	165.00	145
1992	Olympic Pride w/Fantasy Logo L5872G	Closed	1994	165.00	495
1992	Modern Mother L5873G	Open		325.00	335
1992	Off We Go L5874G	Closed	1994	365.00	385
1992	Angelic Cymbalist L5876	Yr.Iss.	1992	140.00	140-175
1992	Guest Of Honor L5877G	Open		195.00	200
1992	Sister's Pride L5878G	Open		595.00	615
1992	Shot On Goal L5879G	Open		1100.00	1150
1992	Playful Unicorn L5880G	Open		295.00	320
1992	Playful Unicorn L5880M	Open		295.00	320
1992	Mischievous Mouse L5881G	Open		285.00	295
1992	Restful Mouse L5882G	Open		285.00	295
1992	Loving Mouse L5883G	Open		285.00	295
1992	From This Day Forward L5885G	Open		265.00	285
1992	Hippity Hop L5886G	12/95		95.00	95
1992	Washing Up L5887G	12/95		95.00	95
1992	That Tickles! L5888G	12/95		95.00	105
1992	Snack Time L5889G	12/95		95.00	105
1992	The Aviator L5891G	Open		375.00	415
1992	Circus Magic L5892G	Open		470.00	495
1992	Friendship In Bloom L5893G	12/95		650.00	685
1992	Precious Petals L5894G	Open		395.00	415
1992	Bouquet of Blossoms L5895G	Open		295.00	295
1992	The Loaves & Fishes L5896G	Open		695.00	760
1992	Trimming The Tree L5897G	Open		900.00	925
1992	Spring Splendor L5898G	Open		440.00	450
1992	Just One More L5899G	Open		450.00	495
1992	Sleep Tight L5900G	Open		450.00	495
1992	Surprise L5901G	Open		325.00	335
1992	Easter Bunnies L5902G	Open		240.00	250
1992	Down The Aisle L5903G	Open		295.00	295
1992	Sleeping Bunny L5904G	Open		75.00	75
1992	Attentive Bunny L5905G	Open		75.00	75
1992	Preening Bunny L5906G	Open		75.00	80
1992	Sitting Bunny L5907G	Open		75.00	80
1992	Just A Little More L5908G	Open		370.00	380
1992	All Dressed Up L5909G	Open		440.00	450
1992	Making A Wish L5910G	Open		790.00	825
1992	Swans Take Flight L5912G	Open		2850.00	2950
1992	Rose Ballet L5919G	Open		210.00	215
1992	Swan Ballet L5920G	Open		210.00	215
1992	Take Your Medicine L5921G	Open		360.00	370
1990	Floral Clock L5924	Closed		N/A	155
1992	Jazz Clarinet L5928G	Open		295.00	295
1992	Jazz Drums L5929G	Open		595.00	610
1992	Jazz Duo L5930G	Open		795.00	885
1993	The Ten Commandments w/Base L5933G	Open		930.00	930
1993	The Holy Teacher L5934G	Open		375.00	375
1993	Nutcracker Suite L5935G	Open		620.00	620
1993	Little Skipper L5936G	Open		320.00	320
1993	Riding The Waves L5941G	Open		405.00	405
1993	World of Fantasy L5943G	12/95		295.00	295
1993	The Great Adventure L5944G	Closed	1994	325.00	325
1993	A Mother's Way L5946G	Open		1350.00	1350
1993	General Practitioner L5947G	Open		360.00	360
1993	Physician L5948G	Open		360.00	360
1993	Angel Candleholder w/Lyre L5949G	Open		295.00	315
1993	Angel Candleholder w/Tambourine L5950G	Open		295.00	315
1993	Sounds of Summer L5953G	Open		125.00	142
1993	Sounds of Winter L5954G	Open		125.00	142
1993	Sounds of Fall L5955G	Open		125.00	142
1993	Sounds of Spring L5956G	Open		125.00	142
1993	The Glass Slipper L5957G	Open		475.00	475
1993	Country Ride w/base L5958G	Open		2850.00	2875
1993	It's Your Turn L5959G	Open		365.00	365
1993	On Patrol L5960G	Open		395.00	445
1993	The Great Teacher w/base L5961G	Open		850.00	850
1993	Angelic Melody L5963	Yr.Iss.	1993	145.00	145
1993	The Great Voyage L5964G	Closed	1994	50.00	50
1993	The Clipper Ship w/base L5965M	Open		240.00	250
1993	Flowers Forever w/base L5966G	Open		4150.00	4150
1993	Honeymoon Ride w/base L5968G	12/95		2750.00	2750
1993	A Special Toy L5971G	Open		815.00	815
1993	Before the Dance w/base L5972G	Open		3550.00	3550
1993	Before the Dance w/base L5972M	Open		3550.00	3550
1993	Family Outing w/base L5974G	Open		4275.00	4275
1993	Up and Away w/base L5975G	Open		2850.00	2850
1993	The Fireman L5976G	Open		395.00	445
1993	Revelation w/base (white) L5977G	12/95		310.00	310
1993	Revelation w/base (black) L5978M	12/95		310.00	310
1993	Revelation w/base (sand) L5979M	12/95		310.00	310
1993	The Past w/base (white) L5980G	12/95		310.00	310
1993	The Past w/base (black) L5981M	12/95		310.00	310
1993	The Past w/base (sand) L5982M	12/95		310.00	310
1993	Beauty w/base (white) L5983G	12/95		310.00	310
1993	Beauty w/base (black) L5984M	12/95		310.00	310
1993	Beauty w/base (sand) L5985M	12/95		310.00	310
1993	Sunday Sermon L5986G	Open		425.00	425
1993	Talk to Me L5987G	Open		145.00	165
1993	Taking Time L5988G	Open		145.00	165
1993	A Mother's Touch L5989G	Open		470.00	470
1993	Thoughtful Caress L5990G	Open		225.00	225
1993	Love Story L5991G	Open		2800.00	2800
1993	Unicorn and Friend L5993G	Open		355.00	355
1993	Unicorn and Friend L5993M	Open		355.00	355
1993	Meet My Friend L5994G	Open		695.00	695
1993	Soft Meow L5995G	Open		480.00	515
1993	Bless the Child L5996G	Closed	1994	465.00	465
1993	One More Try L5997G	Open		715.00	715
1993	My Dad L6001G	12/95		550.00	550
1993	Down You Go L6002G	Open		815.00	815
1993	Ready To Learn L6003G	Open		650.00	650
1993	Bar Mitzvah Day L6004G	Open		395.00	430
1993	Christening Day w/base L6005G	12/95		1425.00	1425
1993	Oriental Colonade w/base L6006G	12/95		1875.00	1875
1993	The Goddess & Unicorn w/base L6007G	Open		1675.00	1675
1993	Joyful Event L6008G	Open		825.00	825
1993	Monday's Child (Boy) L6011G	Open		245.00	270
1993	Monday's Child (Girl) L6012G	Open		260.00	290
1993	Tuesday's Child (Boy) L6013G	Open		225.00	250
1993	Tuesday's Child (Girl) L6014G	Open		245.00	270
1993	Wednesday's Child (Boy) L6015G	Open		245.00	270
1993	Wednesday's Child (Girl) L6016G	Open		245.00	270
1993	Thursday's Child (Boy) L6017G	Open		225.00	250
1993	Thursday's Child (Girl) L6018G	Open		245.00	270
1993	Friday's Child (Boy) L6019G	Open		225.00	250
1993	Friday's Child (Girl) L6020G	Open		225.00	250
1993	Saturday's Child (Boy) L6021G	Open		245.00	270
1993	Saturday's Child (Girl) L6022G	Open		245.00	270
1993	Angelic Melody-L5963G	Yr.Iss.	1993	145.00	145-175
1993	Sunday's Child (Boy) L6023G	Open		225.00	250
1993	Sunday's Child (Girl) L6024G	Open		225.00	250
1993	Barnyard See Saw L6025G	Open		500.00	500
1993	My Turn L6026G	Open		515.00	515
1993	Hanukah Lights L6027G	Open		345.00	395
1993	Mazel Tov! L6028G	Open		380.00	395
1993	Hebrew Scholar L6029G	Open		225.00	245
1993	On The Go L6031G	12/95		475.00	485
1993	On The Green L6032G	Open		645.00	645
1993	Monkey Business L6034G	Closed	1994	745.00	745
1993	Young Princess L6036G	Open		240.00	240
1994	Saint James L6084G	Open		310.00	310
1994	Angelic Harmony L6085G	Open		495.00	550
1994	Allow Me L6086G	Open		1625.00	1625
1994	Loving Care L6087G	Open		250.00	270
1994	Communion Prayer (Boy) L6088G	Open		194.00	200
1994	Communion Prayer (Girl) L6089G	Open		198.00	210
1994	Baseball Player L6090G	Open		295.00	310
1994	Basketball Player L6091G	Open		295.00	310
1994	The Prince L6092G	Open		325.00	325
1994	Songbird L6093G	Open		395.00	395
1994	The Sportsman L6096G	Open		495.00	540
1994	Sleeping Bunny With Flowers L6097G	Open		110.00	110
1994	Attentive Bunny With Flowers L6098G	Open		140.00	140
1994	Preening Bunny With Flowers L6099G	Open		140.00	140
1994	Sitting Bunny With Flowers L6100G	Open		110.00	110
1994	Follow Us L6101G	Open		198.00	215
1994	Mother's Little Helper L6102G	Open		275.00	285
1994	Beautiful Ballerina L6103G	Open		250.00	270
1994	Finishing Touches L6104	Open		240.00	250
1994	Spring Joy L6106G	Open		795.00	795
1994	Football Player L6107	Open		295.00	310
1994	Hockey Player L6108G	Open		295.00	310
1994	Meal Time L6109G	Open		495.00	515
1994	Medieval Maiden L6110G	Open		150.00	165
1994	Medieval Soldier L6111G	Open		225.00	245
1994	Medieval Lord L6112G	Open		285.00	300
1994	Medieval Lady L6113G	Open		225.00	225
1994	Medieval Princess L6114G	Open		245.00	245
1994	Medieval Prince L6115G	Open		295.00	315
1994	Medieval Majesty L6116G	Open		315.00	325
1994	Constance L6117G	Open		195.00	205
1994	Musketeer Portos L6118G	Open		220.00	230
1994	Musketeer Aramis L6119G	Open		275.00	295
1994	Musketeer Dartagnan L6120G	Open		245.00	270
1994	Musketeer Athos L6121G	Open		245.00	270
1994	A Great Adventure L6122	Open		198.00	215
1994	Out For a Stroll L6123G	Open		198.00	215
1994	Travelers Rest L6124G	Open		275.00	295
1994	Angelic Violinist L6126G	Yr.Iss.	1994	150.00	150-175
1994	Sweet Dreamers L6127G	Open		280.00	290
1994	Christmas Melodies L6128G	Open		375.00	385
1994	Little Friends L6129G	Open		225.00	235
1994	Angel of Peace L6131G	Open		345.00	370
1994	Angel with Garland L6133G	Open		345.00	370
1994	Birthday Party L6134G	Open		395.00	425
1994	Football Star L6135	Open		295.00	295
1994	Basketball Star L6136G	Open		295.00	295
1994	Baseball Star L6137G	Open		295.00	295
1994	Globe Paperweight L6138M	Open		95.00	95
1994	Springtime Friends L6140G	Open		485.00	485
1994	Kitty Cart L6141G	Open		750.00	795
1994	Indian Pose L6142G	Open		475.00	475
1994	Indian Dancer L6143G	Open		475.00	475
1995	Caribbean Kiss L6144G	Open		340.00	340
1994	Heavenly Prayer L6145	Open		675.00	695
1994	Spring Angel L6146G	Open		250.00	265
1994	Fall Angel L6147G	Open		250.00	265
1994	Summer Angel L6148G	Open		220.00	220
1994	Winter Angel L6149G	Open		250.00	265
1994	Playing The Flute L6150G	Open		175.00	190
1994	Bearing Flowers L6151G	Open		175.00	190
1994	Flower Gazer L6152G	Open		175.00	190
1994	American Love L6153G	Open		225.00	225
1994	African Love L6154G	Open		225.00	225
1994	European Love L6155G	Open		225.00	225
1994	Asian Love L6156G	Open		225.00	225
1994	Polynesian Love L6157G	Open		225.00	225
1995	Fiesta Dancer L6163G	Open		285.00	285
1994	Wedding Bells L6164G	Open		175.00	185
1995	Pretty Cargo L6165G	Open		500.00	500
1995	Dear Santa L6166G	Open		250.00	250
1995	Delicate Bundle L6167G	Open		275.00	275
1994	The Apollo Landing L6168G	Closed	1995	450.00	450
1995	Seesaw Friends L6169G	Open		795.00	795
1995	Under My Spell L6170G	Open		195.00	195
1995	Magical Moment L6171G	Open		180.00	180
1995	Coming of Age L6172G	Open		345.00	345
1995	A Moment's Rest L6173G	Open		130.00	130
1995	Graceful Pose L6174G	Open		195.00	195
1995	Graceful Pose L6174M	Open		195.00	195
1995	White Swan L6175G	Open		90.00	90
1995	Communion Bell L6176G	Open		85.00	85
1995	Asian Scholar L6177G	Open		315.00	315
1995	Little Matador L6178G	Open		245.00	245
1995	Peaceful Moment L6179G	Open		385.00	385
1995	Sharia L6180G	Open		235.00	235
1995	Velisa L6181G	Open		180.00	180
1995	Preparing For The Sabbath L6183G	Open		385.00	385
1995	For a Better World L6186G	Open		575.00	575
1995	European Boy L6187G	Open		185.00	185
1995	Asian Boy L6188G	Open		225.00	225
1995	African Boy L6189G	Open		195.00	195
1995	Polynesian Boy L6190G	Open		250.00	250
1995	All American L6191G	Open		225.00	225
1995	American Indian Boy L6192G	Open		225.00	225
1995	Summer Serenade L6193G	Open		375.00	375
1995	Summer Serenade L6193M	Open		375.00	375
1995	Carnival Companions L6195G	Open		650.00	650
1995	Seaside Companions L6196G	Open		230.00	230
1995	Seaside Serenade L6197G	Open		275.00	275
1995	Soccer Practice L6198G	Open		195.00	195
1995	In The Procession L6199G	Open		250.00	250
1995	In The Procession L6199M	Open		250.00	250
1995	Bridal Bell L6200G	Open		125.00	125
1995	Cuddly Kitten L6201G	Open		270.00	270
1995	Daddy's Little Sweetheart L6202G	Open		595.00	595

YEAR ISSUE		EDITION LIMIT	YEAR RETD.	ISSUE PRICE	QUOTE U.S.$
1995	Grace and Beauty L6204G	Open		325.00	325
1995	Grace and Beauty L6204M	Open		325.00	325
1995	Graceful Dance L6205G	Open		340.00	340
1995	Reading the Torah L6208G	Open		535.00	535
1995	The Rabbi L6209G	Open		250.00	250
1995	Gentle Surprise L6210G	Open		125.00	125
1995	New Friend L6211G	Open		120.00	120
1995	Little Hunter L6212G	Open		115.00	115
1995	Lady Of Nice L6213G	Open		198.00	198
1995	Lady Of Nice L6213M	Open		198.00	198
1995	Leo L6214G	Open		198.00	198
1995	Virgo L6215G	Open		198.00	198
1995	Aquarius L6216G	Open		198.00	198
1995	Sagittarius L6217G	Open		198.00	198
1995	Taurus L6218G	Open		198.00	198
1995	Gemini L6219G	Open		198.00	198
1995	Libra L6220G	Open		198.00	198
1995	Aries L6221G	Open		198.00	198
1995	Capricorn L6222G	Open		196.00	198
1995	Pisces L6223G	Open		198.00	198
1995	Cancer L6224G	Open		198.00	198
1995	Scorpio L6225G	Open		198.00	198
1995	Snuggle Up L6226G	Open		170.00	170
1995	Trick or Treat L6227G	Open		250.00	250
1995	Special Gift L6228G	Open		265.00	265
1995	Contented Companion L6229G	Open		195.00	195
1995	Oriental Dance L6230G	Open		198.00	198
1995	Oriental Lantern L6231G	Open		198.00	198
1995	Oriental Beauty L6232G	Open		198.00	198
1995	Chef's Apprentice L6233G	Open		260.00	260
1995	Chef's Apprentice L6233M	Open		260.00	260
1995	The Great Chef L6234G	Open		195.00	195
1995	The Great Chef L6234M	Open		195.00	195
1995	Dinner is Served L6235G	Open		185.00	185
1995	Dinner is Served L6235M	Open		185.00	185
1995	Lady of Monaco L6236G	Open		250.00	250
1995	Lady of Monaco L6236M	Open		250.00	250
1995	The Young Jester-Mandolin L6237G	Open		235.00	235
1995	The Young Jester-Mandolin L6237M	Open		235.00	235
1995	The Young Jester-Trumpet L6238G	Open		235.00	235
1995	The Young Jester-Trumpet L6238M	Open		235.00	235
1995	The Young Jester-Singer L6239G	Open		235.00	235
1995	The Young Jester-Singer L6239M	Open		235.00	235
1995	Graceful Ballet L6240G	Open		795.00	795
1995	Graceful Ballet L6240M	Open		795.00	795
1995	Allegory of Spring L6241G	Open		735.00	735
1995	Allegory of Spring L6241M	Open		735.00	735
1995	Challenge L6247M	Yr.Iss.		350.00	350
1995	Regatta L6248G	Yr.Iss.		695.00	695
1985	Lladro Plaque L7116	Open		17.50	18
1985	Lladro Plaque L7118	Closed	N/A	17.00	18
1992	Special Torch L7513G	Open		165.00	165
1992	Special Champion L7514G	Open		165.00	165
1992	Special Pride L7515G	Open		165.00	165
1993	Courage L7522G	Open		195.00	200
1994	Dr. Martin Luther King, Jr. L7528G	Open		345.00	345
1994	Spike L7543G	Open		95.00	105
1994	Brutus L7544G	Open		125.00	140
1994	Rocky L7545G	Open		110.00	120
1994	Stretch L7546G	Open		125.00	140
1994	Rex L7547G	Open		125.00	140
1994	Snow White L7555G (Disney Theme Park issue-back stamp)	Closed	N/A	295.00	660-880
1995	16th Century Globe Paperweight	Open		105.00	105
1989	Starting Forward/Lolo L7605G	Closed	1989	125.00	350

Lladro Limited Edition Egg Series - Lladro

YEAR ISSUE		EDITION LIMIT	YEAR RETD.	ISSUE PRICE	QUOTE U.S.$
1993	1993 Limited Edition Egg L6083M	Closed	1993	145.00	145-250
1994	1994 Limited Edition Egg L7532M	Closed	1994	150.00	150
1995	1995 Limited Edition Egg L7548M	12/95		150.00	195

Maruri USA

African Safari Animals - W. Gaither

YEAR ISSUE		EDITION LIMIT	YEAR RETD.	ISSUE PRICE	QUOTE U.S.$
1983	African Elephant	Closed	N/A	3500.00	3500
1983	Black Maned Lion	Closed	N/A	1450.00	1450
1983	Cape Buffalo	Closed	N/A	2200.00	2200
1983	Grant's Zebras, pair	500		1200.00	1200
1981	Nyala	300		1450.00	1450
1983	Sable	Closed	N/A	1200.00	1200
1983	Southern Greater Kudu	Closed	N/A	1800.00	1800
1983	Southern Impala	Closed	N/A	1200.00	1200
1983	Southern Leopard	Closed	1994	1450.00	1450
1983	Southern White Rhino	150		3200.00	3200

American Eagle Gallery - Maruri Studios

YEAR ISSUE		EDITION LIMIT	YEAR RETD.	ISSUE PRICE	QUOTE U.S.$
1985	E-8501	Closed	1989	45.00	75
1985	E-8502	Open		55.00	65
1985	E-8503	Open		60.00	65
1985	E-8504	Open		65.00	75
1985	E-8505	Closed	1989	65.00	150
1985	E-8506	Open		75.00	90
1985	E-8507	Open		75.00	90
1985	E-8508	Closed	1989	75.00	85
1985	E-8509	Closed	1989	85.00	125
1985	E-8510	Open		85.00	95
1985	E-8511	Closed	1989	85.00	125
1985	E-8512	Open		295.00	325
1987	E-8721	Open		40.00	50
1987	E-8722	Open		45.00	55
1987	E-8723	Closed	1989	55.00	60
1987	E-8724	Open		175.00	195
1989	E-8931	Open		55.00	60
1989	E-8932	Open		75.00	80
1989	E-8933	Open		95.00	95
1989	E-8934	Open		135.00	140
1989	E-8935	Open		175.00	185
1989	E-8936	Open		185.00	195
1991	E-9141 Eagle Landing	Open		60.00	60
1991	E-9142 Eagle w/ Totem Pole	Open		75.00	75
1991	E-9143 Pair in Flight	Open		95.00	95
1991	E-9144 Eagle w/Salmon	Open		110.00	110
1991	E-9145 Eagle w/Snow	Open		135.00	135
1991	E-9146 Eagle w/Babies	Open		145.00	145
1995	E-9551 Eagle	Open		60.00	60
1995	E-9552 Eagle	Open		65.00	65
1995	E-9553 Eagle	Open		75.00	75
1995	E-9554 Eagle	Open		80.00	80
1995	E-9555 Eagle	Open		90.00	90
1995	E-9556 Eagle	Open		110.00	110

Americana - W. Gaither

YEAR ISSUE		EDITION LIMIT	YEAR RETD.	ISSUE PRICE	QUOTE U.S.$
1981	Grizzley Bear and Indian	Closed	N/A	650.00	650
1982	Sioux Brave and Bison	Closed	N/A	985.00	985

Baby Animals - W. Gaither

YEAR ISSUE		EDITION LIMIT	YEAR RETD.	ISSUE PRICE	QUOTE U.S.$
1981	African Lion Cubs	1,500		195.00	195
1981	Black Bear Cubs	Closed	N/A	195.00	195
1981	Wolf Cubs	Closed	N/A	195.00	195

Birds of Prey - W. Gaither

YEAR ISSUE		EDITION LIMIT	YEAR RETD.	ISSUE PRICE	QUOTE U.S.$
1981	Screech Owl	300		960.00	960
1981	American Bald Eagle I	Closed	N/A	165.00	1750
1982	American Bald Eagle II	Closed	N/A	245.00	2750
1983	American Bald Eagle III	Closed	N/A	445.00	1750
1984	American Bald Eagle IV	Closed	N/A	360.00	1750
1986	American Bald Eagle V	Closed	N/A	325.00	1250

Eyes Of The Night - Maruri Studios

YEAR ISSUE		EDITION LIMIT	YEAR RETD.	ISSUE PRICE	QUOTE U.S.$
1988	Double Barn Owl O-8807	Closed	1993	125.00	130
1988	Double Snowy Owl O-8809	Closed	1993	245.00	250
1988	Single Great Horned Owl O-8803	Closed	1993	60.00	65
1988	Single Great Horned Owl O-8808	Closed	1993	145.00	150
1988	Single Screech Owl O-8801	Closed	1993	50.00	55
1988	Single Screech Owl O-8806	Closed	1993	90.00	95
1988	Single Snowy Owl O-8802	Closed	1993	50.00	55
1988	Single Snowy Owl O-8805	Closed	1993	80.00	85
1988	Single Tawny Owl O-8804	Closed	1993	60.00	65

Gentle Giants - Maruri Studios

YEAR ISSUE		EDITION LIMIT	YEAR RETD.	ISSUE PRICE	QUOTE U.S.$
1992	Baby Elephant Sitting GG-9252	Open		65.00	65
1992	Baby Elephant Standing GG-9251	Open		50.00	50
1992	Elephant Pair GG-9255	Open		220.00	220
1992	Elephant Pair Playing GG-9253	Open		80.00	80
1992	Mother & Baby Elephant GG-9254	Open		160.00	160

Graceful Reflections - Maruri Studios

YEAR ISSUE		EDITION LIMIT	YEAR RETD.	ISSUE PRICE	QUOTE U.S.$
1991	Mute Swan w/Baby SW-9152	Closed	1993	95.00	95
1991	Pair-Mute Swan SW-9153	Closed	1993	145.00	145
1991	Pair-Mute Swan SW-9154	Closed	1993	195.00	195
1991	Single Mute Swan SW-9151	Closed	1993	85.00	85

Horses Of The World - Maruri Studios

YEAR ISSUE		EDITION LIMIT	YEAR RETD.	ISSUE PRICE	QUOTE U.S.$
1993	Arabian HW-9356	Open		175.00	175
1993	Camargue HW-9354	Open		150.00	150
1993	Clydesdale HW-9351	Open		145.00	145
1993	Paint Horse HW-9355	Open		160.00	160
1993	Quarter Horse HW-9353	Open		145.00	145
1993	Thoroughbred HW-9352	Open		145.00	145

Hummingbirds - Maruri Studios

YEAR ISSUE		EDITION LIMIT	YEAR RETD.	ISSUE PRICE	QUOTE U.S.$
1995	Allen's & Babies w/Rose H-9523	Open		120.00	120
1995	Allen's w/Easter Lily H-9522	Open		95.00	95
1989	Allew's w/Hibiscus H-8906	Open		195.00	195
1989	Anna's w/Lily H-8905	Open		160.00	160
1995	Anna's w/Trumpet Creeper H-9524	Open		130.00	130
1995	Broad-Billed w/Amaryllis H-9526	Open		150.00	150
1989	Calliope w/Azalea H-8904	Open		120.00	120
1989	Ruby-Throated w/Azalea H-8911	Open		75.00	75
1989	Ruby-Throated w/Orchid H-8914	Open		150.00	150
1989	Rufous w/Trumpet Creeper H-8901	Open		70.00	75
1989	Violet-crowned w/Gentian H-8903	Open		90.00	90
1989	Violet-Crowned w/Gentian H-8913	Open		75.00	75
1995	Violet-Crowned w/Iris H-9521	Open		95.00	95
1989	White-eared w/Morning Glory H-8902	Open		85.00	85
1989	White-Eared w/Morning Glory H-8912	Open		75.00	75
1995	White-Eared w/Tulip H-9525	Open		145.00	145

Legendary Flowers of the Orient - Ito

YEAR ISSUE		EDITION LIMIT	YEAR RETD.	ISSUE PRICE	QUOTE U.S.$
1985	Cherry Blossom	15,000		45.00	55
1985	Chinese Peony	15,000		45.00	55
1985	Chrysanthemum	15,000		45.00	55
1985	Iris	15,000		45.00	55
1985	Lily	15,000		45.00	55
1985	Lotus	15,000		45.00	45
1985	Orchid	15,000		45.00	55
1985	Wisteria	15,000		45.00	55

Majestic Owls of the Night - D. Littleton

YEAR ISSUE		EDITION LIMIT	YEAR RETD.	ISSUE PRICE	QUOTE U.S.$
1988	Barred Owl	15,000		55.00	55
1987	Burrowing Owl	15,000		55.00	55
1988	Elf Owl	15,000		55.00	55

National Parks - Maruri Studios

YEAR ISSUE		EDITION LIMIT	YEAR RETD.	ISSUE PRICE	QUOTE U.S.$
1993	Baby Bear NP-9301	Open		60.00	60
1993	Bear Family NP-9304	Open		160.00	160
1993	Buffalo NP-9306	Open		170.00	170
1993	Cougar Cubs NP-9302	Open		70.00	70
1993	Deer Family NP-9303	Open		120.00	120
1993	Eagle NP-9307	Open		180.00	180
1993	Falcon NP-9308	Open		195.00	195
1993	Howling Wolves NP-9305	Open		165.00	165

North American Game Animals - W. Gaither

YEAR ISSUE		EDITION LIMIT	YEAR RETD.	ISSUE PRICE	QUOTE U.S.$
1984	White Tail Deer	950		285.00	285

North American Game Birds - W. Gaither

YEAR ISSUE		EDITION LIMIT	YEAR RETD.	ISSUE PRICE	QUOTE U.S.$
1983	Bobtail Quail, female	Closed	N/A	375.00	375
1983	Bobtail Quail, male	Closed	N/A	375.00	375
1981	Canadian Geese, pair	Closed	N/A	2000.00	2000
1981	Eastern Wild Turkey	Closed	N/A	300.00	300
1982	Ruffed Grouse	Closed	N/A	1745.00	1745
1983	Wild Turkey Hen with Chicks	Closed	N/A	300.00	300

North American Songbirds - W. Gaither

YEAR ISSUE		EDITION LIMIT	YEAR RETD.	ISSUE PRICE	QUOTE U.S.$
1982	Bluebird	Closed	N/A	95.00	95
1983	Cardinal, female	Closed	N/A	95.00	95
1982	Cardinal, male	Closed	N/A	95.00	95
1982	Carolina Wren	Closed	N/A	95.00	95
1982	Chickadee	Closed	N/A	95.00	95
1982	Mockingbird	Closed	N/A	95.00	95
1983	Robin	Closed	N/A	95.00	95

North American Waterfowl I - W. Gaither

YEAR ISSUE		EDITION LIMIT	YEAR RETD.	ISSUE PRICE	QUOTE U.S.$
1981	Blue Winged Teal	200		980.00	980
1981	Canvasback Ducks	Closed	1994	780.00	780
1981	Flying Wood Ducks	Closed	N/A	880.00	880
1981	Mallard Drake	Closed	N/A	2380.00	2380
1981	Wood Duck, decoy	950		480.00	480

North American Waterfowl II - W. Gaither

YEAR ISSUE		EDITION LIMIT	YEAR RETD.	ISSUE PRICE	QUOTE U.S.$
1982	Bufflehead Ducks Pair	1,500		225.00	225
1982	Goldeneye Ducks Pair	Closed	N/A	225.00	225
1983	Loon	Closed	1989	245.00	245
1981	Mallard Ducks Pair	1,500		225.00	225
1982	Pintail Ducks Pair	Closed	1994	225.00	225
1982	Widgeon, female	Closed	N/A	225.00	225
1982	Widgeon, male	Closed	N/A	225.00	225

Polar Expedition - Maruri Studios

YEAR ISSUE		EDITION LIMIT	YEAR RETD.	ISSUE PRICE	QUOTE U.S.$
1992	Arctic Fox Cubs Playing-P-9223	Open		65.00	65
1990	Baby Arctic Fox-P-9002	Open		50.00	55
1990	Baby Emperor Penguin-P-9001	Open		45.00	50
1992	Baby Harp Seal-P-9221	Open		55.00	55
1990	Baby Harp Seals-P-9005	Open		65.00	70
1992	Emperor Penguins-P-9222	Open		60.00	60
1990	Mother & Baby Emperor Penguins-P-9006	Open		80.00	85
1990	Mother & Baby Harp Seals -P-9007	Open		90.00	95
1990	Mother & Baby Polar Bears -P-9008	Open		125.00	130
1990	Polar Bear Cub Sliding-P-9003	Open		50.00	55
1990	Polar Bear Cubs Playing-P-9004	Open		60.00	65
1992	Polar Bear Family-P-9224	Open		90.00	90
1990	Polar Expedition Sign-PES-001	Open		18.00	18

Precious Panda - Maruri Studios

YEAR ISSUE		EDITION LIMIT	YEAR RETD.	ISSUE PRICE	QUOTE U.S.$
1992	Lazy Lunch PP-9202	Open		60.00	60
1992	Mother's Cuddle-PP-9204	Open		120.00	120
1992	Snack Time PP-9201	Open		60.00	60
1992	Tug Of War PP-9203	Open		70.00	70

Shore Birds - W. Gaither

YEAR ISSUE		EDITION LIMIT	YEAR RETD.	ISSUE PRICE	QUOTE U.S.$
1984	Pelican	Closed	N/A	260.00	260
1984	Sand Piper	Closed	N/A	285.00	285

Signature Collection - W. Gaither

YEAR ISSUE		EDITION LIMIT	YEAR RETD.	ISSUE PRICE	QUOTE U.S.$
1985	American Bald Eagle	Closed	N/A	60.00	60
1985	Canada Goose	Closed	N/A	60.00	60
1985	Hawk	Closed	N/A	60.00	60
1985	Pintail Duck	Closed	N/A	60.00	60
1985	Snow Goose	Closed	N/A	60.00	60
1985	Swallow	Closed	N/A	60.00	60

Songbirds Of Beauty - Maruri Studios

YEAR ISSUE		EDITION LIMIT	YEAR RETD.	ISSUE PRICE	QUOTE U.S.$
1991	Bluebird w/ Apple Blossom SB-9105	Closed	1994	85.00	85

YEAR ISSUE		EDITION LIMIT	YEAR RETD.	ISSUE PRICE	QUOTE U.S.$
1991	Cardinal w/ Cherry Blossom SB-9103	Closed	1994	85.00	85
1991	Chickadee w/ Roses SB-9101	Closed	1994	85.00	85
1991	Dbl. Bluebird w/ Peach Blossom SB-9107	Closed	1994	145.00	145
1991	Dbl. Cardinal w/ Dogwood SB-9108	Closed	1994	145.00	145
1991	Goldfinch w/ Hawthorne SB-9102	Closed	1994	85.00	85
1991	Robin & Baby w/ Azalea SB-9106	Closed	1994	115.00	115
1991	Robin w/ Lilies SB-9104	Closed	1994	85.00	85

Special Commissions - W. Gaither

YEAR ISSUE		EDITION LIMIT	YEAR RETD.	ISSUE PRICE	QUOTE U.S.$
1982	Cheetah	Closed	N/A	995.00	995
1983	Orange Bengal Tiger	240		340.00	340
1981	White Bengal Tiger	240		340.00	340

Studio Collection - Maruri Studios

YEAR ISSUE		EDITION LIMIT	YEAR RETD.	ISSUE PRICE	QUOTE U.S.$
1990	Majestic Eagles-MS-100	Closed	N/A	350.00	800
1991	Delicate Motion-MS-200	3,500		325.00	325
1992	Imperial Panda-MS-300	3,500		350.00	350
1993	Wild Wings-MS-400	3,500		395.00	450
1994	Waltz of the Dolphins-MS-500	3,500		300.00	300
1995	"Independent Spirit" MS-600	3,500		395.00	395

Stump Animals - W. Gaither

YEAR ISSUE		EDITION LIMIT	YEAR RETD.	ISSUE PRICE	QUOTE U.S.$
1984	Bobcat	Closed	N/A	175.00	175
1984	Chipmunk	Closed	N/A	175.00	175
1984	Gray Squirrel	1,200		175.00	175
1983	Owl	Closed	N/A	175.00	175
1983	Raccoon	Closed	1989	175.00	175
1982	Red Fox	Closed	N/A	175.00	175

Upland Birds - W. Gaither

YEAR ISSUE		EDITION LIMIT	YEAR RETD.	ISSUE PRICE	QUOTE U.S.$
1981	Mourning Doves	Closed	N/A	780.00	780

Wings of Love Doves - Maruri Studios

YEAR ISSUE		EDITION LIMIT	YEAR RETD.	ISSUE PRICE	QUOTE U.S.$
1987	D-8701 Single Dove w/ Forget-Me-Not	Closed	1994	45.00	55
1987	D-8702 Double Dove w/ Primrose	Open		55.00	65
1987	D-8703 Single Dove w/Buttercup	Closed	1994	65.00	70
1987	D-8704 Double Dove w/Daisy	Open		75.00	85
1987	D-8705 Single Dove w/Blue Flax	Closed	1994	95.00	95
1987	D-8706 Double Dove w/Cherry Blossom	Open		175.00	195
1990	D-9021 Double Dove w/Gentian	Open		50.00	55
1990	D-9022 Double Dove w/Azalea	Open		75.00	75
1990	D-9023 Double Dove w/Apple Blossom	Open		115.00	120
1990	D-9024 Double Dove w/Morning Glory	Open		150.00	160

Wonders of the Sea - Maruri Studios

YEAR ISSUE		EDITION LIMIT	YEAR RETD.	ISSUE PRICE	QUOTE U.S.$
1994	Dolphin WS-9401	Open		70.00	70
1994	Great White Shark WS-9406	Open		90.00	90
1994	Green Sea Turtle WS-9405	Open		85.00	85
1994	Humpback Mother & Baby WS-9409	Open		150.00	150
1994	Manatee & Baby WS-9403	Open		75.00	75
1994	Manta Ray WS-9404	Open		80.00	80
1994	Orca Mother & Baby WS-9410	Open		150.00	150
1994	Sea Otter & Baby WS-9402	Open		75.00	75
1994	Three Dolphins WS-9408	Open		135.00	135
1994	Two Dolphins WS-9407	Open		120.00	120

Michael's Limited

Collectors' Corner - B. Baker

YEAR ISSUE		EDITION LIMIT	YEAR RETD.	ISSUE PRICE	QUOTE U.S.$
1993	City Cottage (Membership House)-rose/grn.1682	Retrd.	1994	35.00	50-95
1993	Brian's First House (Redemption House)-red1496	Retrd.	1994	71.00	135-150
1994	Gothic Cottage (Membership Sculpture) 1571	Retrd.	1995	35.00	50-75
1994	Duke of Gloucester Street (Redemption House) 1459	Retrd.	1995	69.00	100-125
1995	Marie's Cottage-grey (Membership Sculpture) 1942	12/95		35.00	35
1995	Welcome Home-brick (Redemption House) 1599	Retrd.	1995	65.00	65
1996	Queen Ann Cottage-rose/blue (Membership Sculpture) 1676	Yr. Iss.		39.00	39
1996	Oak Street-brick/brown (Redemption House) 1685	Yr. Iss.		65.00	65

Brian Baker's Déjà Vu Collection - B. Baker

YEAR ISSUE		EDITION LIMIT	YEAR RETD.	ISSUE PRICE	QUOTE U.S.$
1988	Adam Colonial Cottage-blue/white 1515	Retrd.	1993	53.00	53
1993	Admiralty Head Lighthouse-wh. 1532	Retrd.	1995	62.00	62
1992	Alpine Ski Lodge-br./wh. 1012	Retrd.	1994	62.00	92
1988	Andulusian Village-white 1060	Retrd.	1993	53.00	63
1992	Angel of the Sea-blue/white 1587	Open		67.00	67
1992	Angel of the Sea-mauve/wh 1586	Open		67.00	67
1989	Antebellum Mansion-bl./rose 1505	Retrd.	1994	53.00	73
1988	Antebellum Mansion-bl./wh. 1519	Retrd.	1989	49.00	49
1989	Antebellum Mansion-peach 1506	Retrd.	1992	49.00	56
1988	Antebellum Mansion-peach 1517	Retrd.	1989	49.00	49
1988	Antebellum Mansion-wh./gr 1518	Retrd.	1988	49.00	49
1994	Barber Shop 1164	Open		53.00	53
1987	Bavarian Church-white 1021	Retrd.	1989	38.00	38
1987	Bavarian Church-yellow 1020	Retrd.	1988	38.00	38
1987	The Bernese Guesthouse -golden brown 1010	Retrd.	1991	49.00	49
1989	Blumen Shop-white/brown 1023	Retrd.	1994	53.00	73
1996	Brick & Brackets-brick 1933	Open		65.00	65
1994	Cabbagetown 1704	Open		65.00	65
1996	Cape Cottage-grey/white 1442	Open		N/A	N/A
1988	Casa Chiquita-natural 1400	Retrd.	1993	53.00	60
1994	Castle in the Clouds 1090	Retrd.	1995	75.00	75
1993	Charleston Single House-blue/white 1583	Open		60.00	60
1993	Charleston Single House-peach/white 1584	Open		60.00	60
1996	Chateau in the Woods 1683	Yr. Iss.		79.00	79
1994	Christmas at Church 1223	Open		63.00	63
1988	Christmas House-blue 1225	Retrd.	1993	51.00	51
1990	Classic Victorian-blue/white 1555	Retrd.	1994	60.00	80
1990	Classic Victorian-peach 1557	Retrd.	1994	60.00	80
1990	Classic Victorian-rose/blue 1556	Retrd.	1994	60.00	80
1991	Colonial Color-brown 1508	Retrd.	1994	62.00	82
1991	Colonial Cottage-white/bue 1509	Retrd.	1994	59.00	80
1987	Colonial House-blue 1510	Retrd.	1989	49.00	70
1987	Colonial House-wine 1511	Retrd.	1987	40.00	60
1987	Colonial Store-brick 1512	Retrd.	1994	53.00	73
1993	Corner Grocery-brick 1141	Open		67.00	67
1987	The Cottage House-blue 1531	Retrd.	1988	42.00	42
1987	The Cottage House-white 1530	Retrd.	1994	47.00	67
1989	Country Barn-blue 1528	Retrd.	1992	49.00	70
1989	Country Barn-red 1527	Retrd.	1994	53.00	73
1996	Country Christmas-red 1219	Open		68.00	68
1988	Country Church-white/blue 1522	Retrd.	1994	49.00	50-70
1992	Country Station-blue/rust 1156	Open		64.00	64
1994	Country Store 1435	Open		61.00	61
1994	Covered Bridge 1513	Open		69.00	69
1994	Craftsman Cottage-cream 1478	Open		56.00	56
1994	Craftsman Cottage-grey 1477	Open		56.00	56
1989	Deja Vu Sign-ivory/brown 1600	Retrd.	1991	21.00	24-29
1992	Deja Vu Sign-ivory/brown 1999	Open		21.00	21
1993	Dinard Mansion-beige/brick 1005	Open		67.00	67
1996	Dixie Landing-white 1740	Open		68.00	68
1994	Ellis Island 1250	Open		62.00	62
1993	Enchanted Cottage-natural 1205	Retrd.	1995	63.00	63
1988	Fairy Tale Cottage-white/brown 1200	Retrd.	1993	46.00	46
1987	The Farm House-beige/bl. 1525	Retrd.	1992	49.00	49
1987	The Farm House-spiced tan 1526	Retrd.	1991	49.00	49
1992	Firehouse-brick 1140	Open		60.00	60
1992	Flower Store-tan/green 1145	Open		67.00	67
1988	French Colonial Cottage-beige 1516	Retrd.	1991	42.00	65
1988	Georgian Colonial House-white/blue 1514	Retrd.	1993	53.00	53
1990	Gothic Victorian-blue/mauve 1534	Retrd.	1991	47.00	52-54
1988	Gothic Victorian-peach 1536	Retrd.	1993	51.00	60
1988	Gothic Victorian-sea green 1537	Retrd.	1991	47.00	47
1993	Grandpa's Barn-brown 1498	Open		63.00	63
1988	Hampshire House-brick 1040	Retrd.	1989	49.00	60
1989	Hampshire House-brick 1041	Retrd.	1991	49.00	56
1996	Harbor Sentry-white 1590	Open		N/A	N/A
1989	Henry VIII Pub-white/brown 1043	Retrd.	1994	56.00	76
1993	Homestead Christmas-red 1224	Retrd.	1995	57.00	57
1987	Hotel Couronne (original)wh./br. 1000	Retrd.	1989	49.00	49
1989	Hotel Couronne-white/brown 1003	Retrd.	1993	55.00	55
1987	Italianate Victorian-brown 1543	Retrd.	1991	51.00	51
1987	Italianate Victorian-lavendar 1550	Retrd.	1988	45.00	45
1987	Italianate Victorian-mauve/bl. 1545	Retrd.	1992	49.00	49
1989	Italianate Victorian-peach/teal 1552	Retrd.	1992	51.00	62
1989	Italianate Victorian-rose/bl. 1551	Retrd.	1992	51.00	55-58
1987	Italianate Victorian-rust/bl. 1544	Retrd.	1989	49.00	49
1987	Japanese House-wh./br. 1100	Retrd.	1989	47.00	47
1996	Japanese Tea House-br./wh. 1101	Open		61.00	61
1987	The Lighthouse-white 1535	Retrd.	1993	53.00	60
1991	Log Cabin-brown 1501	Retrd.	1994	55.00	75
1992	Looks Like Nantucket-grey 1451	Open		62.00	62
1995	Main Street Cafe-blue 1142	Open		61.00	61
1993	Mansard Lady-blue/rose 1606	Open		64.00	64
1993	Mansard Lady-tan/green 1607	Open		64.00	64
1995	Maple Lane-blue/white 1904	Open		72.00	72
1995	Maple Lane-desert/white 1905	Open		72.00	72
1991	Mayor's Mansion-bl./peach 1585	Retrd.	1994	57.00	77
1996	Meditternaean Ave-cream/tile 1741	Open		N/A	N/A
1995	Mesa Manor 1733	Open		75.00	75
1994	Mission Dolores (no umbrella) 1435	Retrd.	N/A	47.00	75
1994	Mission Dolores 1435	Open		47.00	47
1993	Monday's Wash-cream/bl. 1450	Open		62.00	62
1993	Monday's Wash-white/blue 1449	Open		62.00	62
1995	Mountain Homestead-br. 1401	Open		78.00	78
1994	Mukilteo Lighthouse 1569	Open		55.00	55
1989	Norwegian House-brown 1051	Retrd.	1991	51.00	58
1990	Old Country Cottage-blue 1502	Retrd.	1993	51.00	58
1990	Old Country Cottage-peach 1504	Retrd.	1992	47.00	65
1990	Old Country Cottage-red 1503	Retrd.	1993	51.00	65
1996	Old Glory-brick 1567	Open		N/A	N/A
1994	The Old School House 1439	Open		61.00	61
1987	Old West General Store-wh./gr. 1520	Retrd.	1992	50.00	68
1987	Old West General Store-yellow 1521	Retrd.	1988	50.00	50
1993	Old West Hotel-cream 1120	Open		62.00	62
1995	Old West Sheriff-red 1125	Open		56.00	56
1995	Old White Church-white 1424	Open		65.00	65
1988	One Room School House-red 1524	Retrd.	1994	53.00	73
1994	Orleans Cottage-white/blue 1447	Open		63.00	63
1994	Orleans Cottage-white/red 1448	Open		63.00	63
1990	Palm Villa-desert/green 1421	Retrd.	1995	54.00	61
1990	Palm Villa-white/blue 1420	Retrd.	1995	54.00	61
1994	Paris by the Bay 1004	Open		55.00	55
1989	Parisian Apartment-beige/bl 1002	Retrd.	1994	53.00	73
1987	Parisian Apartment-golden brown 1001	Retrd.	1994	53.00	73
1995	Peggy's Cove Light-white 1533	Open		56.00	56
1996	Pennridge-white/stone 1429	Open		70.00	70
1994	Police Station 1147	Open		55.00	55
1993	Post Office-light green 1146	Open		60.00	60
1987	Queen Ann Victorian-peach/green 1540	Retrd.	1994	53.00	73
1987	Queen Ann Victorian-rose 1541	Retrd.	1994	53.00	73
1987	Queen Ann Victorian-rust/green 1542	Retrd.	1988	49.00	49
1995	Quiet Afternoon-cream/gr. 1623	Open		71.00	71
1995	Quiet Afternoon-rose/blue 1622	Open		71.00	71
1995	River Belle-white 1092	Open		70.00	70
1994	Riverside Mill 1507	Open		65.00	65
1988	Roeder Gate, Rothenburg-brown 1022	Retrd.	1991	49.00	49
1992	Rose Cottage-grey 1443	Open		59.00	59
1996	Ruby's Watch-blue/white 1630	Open		56.00	56
1996	Ruby's Watch-cream/white 1631	Open		56.00	56
1994	San Francisco Stick-brick/teal 1625	Open		61.00	61
1994	San Francisco Stick-cream/blue 1624	Open		61.00	61
1995	Scenic Route 100-red/green 1426	Open		71.00	71
1995	Scenic Route 100-red/yell. 1425	Open		71.00	71
1996	Seaside Cottage 1691	Open		N/A	N/A
1996	Seaside Cottage-rose/white 1690	Open		N/A	N/A
1988	Second Empire House-sea grn./desert 1539	Retrd.	1992	50.00	50
1988	Second Empire House-white/blue 1538	Retrd.	1994	54.00	74
1993	Smuggler's Cove-grey/br. 1529	Open		72.00	72
1987	Snow Cabin-brown/white 1500	Retrd.	1994	51.00	70
1995	Southern Exposure-cream/rose 1582	Open		62.00	62
1995	Southern Exposure-tan/gr. 1581	Open		62.00	62
1995	Southern Mansion-brick 1744	Yr.Iss.	1995	79.00	79
1995	St. Nicholas Church-white/bl. 1409	Open		56.00	56
1993	Steiner Street-peach/green 1674	Open		63.00	63
1993	Steiner Street-rose/blue 1675	Open		63.00	63
1993	The Stone House-stone/bl. 1453	Open		63.00	63
1988	Stone Victorians-browns 1554	Retrd.	1994	56.00	76
1993	Sunday Afternoon-brick 1523	Retrd.	1995	62.00	62
1989	Swedish House-Swed.red 1050	Retrd.	1991	51.00	58
1991	Teddy's Place-teal/rose 1570	Open		61.00	61
1994	Towered Lady-blue/rose 1688	Open		65.00	65
1994	Towered Lady-rose 1689	Open		65.00	65
1992	Tropical Fantasy-blue/coral 1410	Open		67.00	67
1992	Tropical Fantasy-rose/blue 1411	Open		67.00	67
1992	Tropical Fantasy-yell./teal 1412	Open		67.00	67
1996	Tropical Paradise-white/br. 1115	Open		65.00	65
1995	Tudor Christmas-red brick 1221	Open		67.00	67
1995	Tudor Home-tan brick 1222	Open		67.00	67
1987	Turreted Victorian-beige/bl. 1546	Retrd.	1993	55.00	55
1987	Turreted Victorian-peach 1547	Retrd.	1993	55.00	57
1987	Ultimate Victorian-lt. bl/rose 1549	Retrd.	1994	60.00	80
1987	Ultimate Victorian-maroon/slate 1548	Retrd.	1994	60.00	80
1989	Ultimate Victorian-peach/gr 1553	Retrd.	1994	60.00	65
1992	Victorian Bay View-cream/teal 1564	Open		63.00	63
1992	Victorian Bay View-rose/bl. 1563	Open		63.00	63
1992	Victorian Charm-cream 1588	Open		61.00	61
1992	Victorian Charm-mauve 1589	Open		61.00	61
1990	Victorian Country Estate-desert/brown 1560	Retrd.	1994	62.00	82
1990	Victorian Country Estate -peach/bl 1562	Retrd.	1994	62.00	82
1990	Victorian Country Estate -rose/blue 1561	Retrd.	1994	62.00	82
1991	Victorian Farmhouse -goldenbrown 1565	Retrd.	1994	59.00	90
1995	Victorian Living-clay/white 1927	Open		70.00	70
1995	Victorian Living-teal/tan 1926	Open		70.00	70
1992	Victorian Tower House -blue/maroon 1558	Open		63.00	63
1992	Victorian Tower House -peach/blue 1559	Open		63.00	63
1996	Village Pharmacy-brick 1157	Open		65.00	65
1996	Willow Road-brick 1713	Open		68.00	68
1991	Wind and Roses-brick 1470	Open		63.00	63
1989	Windmill on the Dike -beige/grey 1034	Retrd.	1994	60.00	90

Limited Editions From Brian Baker - B. Baker

YEAR ISSUE		EDITION LIMIT	YEAR RETD.	ISSUE PRICE	QUOTE U.S.$
1993	American Classic-rose, Numbrd.1566	Retrd.	1993	99.00	550-595
1987	Amsterdam Canal-brown, S/N 1030	Retrd.	1993	79.00	200
1994	Hill Top Mansion 1598	Retrd.	1994	97.00	97
1993	James River Plantation-brick, Numbrd.1454	Retrd.	1993	108.00	300-500
1996	London 1045	1,000		119.00	119
1994	Painted Ladies 1190	Retrd.	1994	125.00	125
1995	Philadelphia-brick 1441	1,500	1995	110.00	110
1994	White Point 1596	Retrd.	1994	100.00	150

Midwest of Cannon Falls

Belenes Puig Nativity Collection - J.P. Llobera

YEAR ISSUE		EDITION LIMIT	YEAR RETD.	ISSUE PRICE	QUOTE U.S.$
1989	Angel 02087-6	Open		50.00	55
1989	Baby Jesus 02085-2	S/O	N/A	62.00	62
1989	Donkey 02082-1	S/O	N/A	26.00	26
1989	Joseph 02086-9	Open		62.00	62
1989	Mother Mary 02084-5	Open		62.00	62
1985	Nativity, set/6: Holy Family, Angel,Animals 6 3/4" 00205-6	S/O	N/A	250.00	250
1989	Ox 02083-8	S/O	N/A	26.00	26
1990	Resting Camel 04025-6	Open		115.00	115
1986	Sheep, set/3 00475-3	Open		28.00	28
1987	Shepherd & Angel Scene, set/7 06084-1	S/O	N/A	305.00	305
1989	Shepherd Carrying Lamb 02092-0	Open		56.00	56
1989	Shepherd with Staff 02091-3	Open		56.00	56
1985	Shepherd, set/2 00458-6	Open		110.00	110
1988	Standing Camel 08792-3	Open		115.00	115
1989	Wise Man with Frankincense 02088-3	Open		66.00	66
1989	Wise Man with Frankincense on Camel 02077-7	Open		155.00	156
1989	Wise Man with Gold 02089-0	Open		66.00	66
1989	Wise Man with Gold on Camel 02075-3	Open		155.00	156
1989	Wise Man with Myrrh 02090-6	Open		66.00	66
1989	Wise Man with Myrrh on Camel 02076-0	Open		155.00	156
1985	Wise Men, set/3 00459-3	Open		185.00	185

Cannon Valley Figurines and Accessories - Midwest

YEAR ISSUE		EDITION LIMIT	YEAR RETD.	ISSUE PRICE	QUOTE U.S.$
1994	Apple Tree 2 asst. 11484-1	Open		10.00	10
1995	Apple Tree, set/3 12677-6	Open		7.00	7
1994	Cannon Valley Sign 11297-7	Open		5.50	6
1994	Chicken, 3 asst. 11299-1	Open		2.00	2
1995	Chickens, 3 asst. 12657-8	Open		3.00	3
1994	Children, 2 asst. 11461-2	Open		5.50	6
1995	Cow with Calf, 2 asst. 12673-8	Open		6.50	7
1994	Cow, 3 asst. 11309-7	Open		5.50	6
1995	Dog by Doghouse 12658-5	Open		5.00	5
1995	Farm Cat 12808-4	Open		5.00	5
1995	Farm Children, 4 asst. 12671-4	Open		7.50	8
1994	Farm Couple, 2 asst. 11458-2	Open		5.50	6
1994	Farm Town Windmill 11306-6	Open		9.50	10
1994	Farm Tractor 11305-9	Open		9.50	10
1995	Farmer with Feed Bag 12672-1	Open		7.50	8
1995	Farmyard Light 12683-7	Open		5.00	5
1995	Fire Hydrant 12685-1	Open		3.00	3
1994	Flagpole 11300-4	Retrd.	1994	5.30	6
1995	Grandparents, 2 asst. 12661-5	Open		6.00	6
1995	Gravel Road 12682-0	Open		9.00	9
1994	Hay Wagon and Horse Set 11303-5	Open		19.00	19
1994	Horse, 2 asst. 11485-8	Open		10.00	10
1994	Mailbox and Water Pump, 2 asst. 11301-1	Open		4.00	4
1995	Mechanic 12660-8	Open		6.00	6
1995	Minister 12674-5	Open		6.00	6
1995	Outhouse 12668-4	Open		11.00	11
1995	Parking Meter 12686-8	Open		3.00	3
1995	Picket Fence 13260-9	Open		6.00	6
1994	Pickup Truck 11304-2	Open		12.00	12
1994	Pig and Piglets 11302-8	Open		5.30	6
1995	Pine Tree, set/2 12680-6	Open		7.50	8
1995	Silo 12667-7	Open		16.00	16
1995	Split Rail Fence 12676-9	Open		2.00	2
1994	Storekeeper 11459-9	Open		5.50	6
1995	Sunday Best Couple with Children, 2 asst. 12670-7	Open		7.50	8
1994	Teacher and Children, 3 asst. 11460-5	Open		5.50	6
1995	Telephone Pole 12684-4	Open		5.00	5
1995	Turkey, 2 asst. 12659-2	Open		5.00	5
1995	Water Tower 13116-9	Open		13.00	13
1995	Woody Car 12669-1	Open		12.00	12

Cannon Valley Houses - Midwest

YEAR ISSUE		EDITION LIMIT	YEAR RETD.	ISSUE PRICE	QUOTE U.S.$
1995	Ace's Garage (lighted) 12665-3	Open		45.00	45
1995	Church (lighted) 12664-6	Open		45.00	45
1995	Dairy Barn (lighted) 12666-0	5,000		49.00	4900
1994	Family Farmhouse (lighted) 11292-2	Open		43.00	45
1995	Four Square Farmhouse (lighted) 12662-2	Open		49.00	49
1994	General Store (lighted) 11295-3	Open		43.00	45
1995	Grain Elevator (lighted) 12663-9	Open		45.00	45
1994	Hen House (lighted) 11294-6	Open		33.00	33
1994	Little Red Schoolhouse (lighted) 11293-9	Open		43.00	45
1994	Red Barn (lighted) 11296-0	Open		43.00	45

Christian Ulbricht "A Christmas Carol" Nutcrackers - C. Ulbricht

YEAR ISSUE		EDITION LIMIT	YEAR RETD.	ISSUE PRICE	QUOTE U.S.$
1993	Bob Cratchit &Tiny Tim 09577-5	6,000		240.00	250
1994	Ghost of Christmas Present 12041-5	5,000		190.00	200
1993	Scrooge 09584-3	6,000		210.00	240

Christian Ulbricht "American Folk Hero" Nutcracker Collection - C. Ulbricht

YEAR ISSUE		EDITION LIMIT	YEAR RETD.	ISSUE PRICE	QUOTE U.S.$
1994	Davy Crockett 12960-9	2,500		190.00	200
1994	Johnny Appleseed 12959-3	2,500		196.00	200
1995	Paul Bunyan 12800-8	2,500		220.00	220

Christian Ulbricht "Nutcracker Fantasy" Nutcrackers - C. Ulbricht

YEAR ISSUE		EDITION LIMIT	YEAR RETD.	ISSUE PRICE	QUOTE U.S.$
1991	Clara , 11 1/2" 03657-0	Open		125.00	153
1991	Herr Drosselmeyer , 16 1/4" 03656-3	Open		170.00	200
1991	Mouse King Nutcracker, 13 1/2" 04510-7	Open		170.00	200
1991	Prince, 17" 03665-5	Open		160.00	190
1991	Toy Soldier, 14" 03666-2	Open		160.00	190

Christian Ulbricht "Traditional Santa Series" Nutcracker - C. Ulbricht

YEAR ISSUE		EDITION LIMIT	YEAR RETD.	ISSUE PRICE	QUOTE U.S.$
1992	Father Christmas Nutcracker 07094-9	2,500	1992	190.00	500
1995	King of Christmas Nutcracker 13665-2	2,500		250.00	250
1993	Toymaker Nutcracker 09531-7	2,500		220.00	250
1994	Victorian Santa Nutcracker 12961-1	2,500		220.00	250

Christian Ulbricht Nutcracker Collection - C. Ulbricht

YEAR ISSUE		EDITION LIMIT	YEAR RETD.	ISSUE PRICE	QUOTE U.S.$
1995	Biker Nutcracker 13187-9	S/O	N/A	220.00	220
1995	Clown Nutcracker 13188-6	Open		200.00	200
1995	Drummer Nutcracker 12792-6	S/O	N/A	220.00	220
1995	Father Time Nutcracker 12794-0	Open		220.00	220
1995	Female Health Care Professional Nutcracker 13189-3	Open		200.00	200
1995	Female Volleyball Player Nutcracker 13986-8	Open		200.00	200
1995	Huck Finn Nutcracker 12788-9	S/O	N/A	220.00	220
1995	King Nutcracker 13190-9	Open		200.00	200
1993	Leprechaun Nutcracker 09110-4	Open		170.00	190
1995	Moses Nutcracker 13186-2	S/O	N/A	220.00	220
1995	Mother Goose Nutcracker 13182-4	Open		220.00	220
1993	Mr. Claus Nutcracker 09588-1	5,000		180.00	200
1993	Mrs. Claus Nutcracker 09587-4	5,000		180.00	200
1995	Nature Santa with Birdhouse Nutcracker 12790-2	S/O	N/A	220.00	220
1986	Pilgrim, 16 1/2" 00393-0	Open		145.00	170
1995	Pinocchio Nutcracker 13184-8	Open		200.00	200
1994	Prince on Rocking Horse Nutcracker 12964-7	Open		160.00	190
1995	Santa Cookie Baker Nutcracker 13191-6	S/O	N/A	220.00	220
1995	Santa Riding Rocking Reindeer Nutcracker 12786-5	Retrd.	1995	200.00	200
1995	Santa with Tree Nutcracker 12791-9	S/O	N/A	200.00	200
1995	Witch Nutcracker 13183-1	Open		220.00	220

Cottontail Lane Figurines and Accessories - Midwest

YEAR ISSUE		EDITION LIMIT	YEAR RETD.	ISSUE PRICE	QUOTE U.S.$
1994	Arbor w/ Fence Set 02188-0	Open		14.00	15
1994	Birdbath, Bench & Mailbox, 02184-2	Retrd.	1993	4.00	4
1994	Birdhouse, Sundial & Fountain, 3 asst. 00371-8	Open		4.50	5
1994	Bridge & Gazebo, 2 asst. 02182-9	Open		11.50	12
1995	Bunny Chef, 2 asst. 12433-8	Open		5.00	5
1994	Bunny Child Collecting Eggs, 2 asst. 02880-3	Retrd.	1993	4.20	5
1995	Bunny Couple at Cafe Table 12444-4	Open		7.00	7
1994	Bunny Couple on Bicycle 02978-7	Retrd.	1994	5.30	6
1995	Bunny Kids at Carrot Juice Stand 12437-6	Open		5.30	6
1994	Bunny Marching Band, 6 asst. 00355-8	Open		4.20	5
1995	Bunny Minister, Soloist, 2 asst. 12434-8	Open		5.00	5
1995	Bunny Playing Piano 12439-0	Open		5.30	6
1995	Bunny Playing, 2 asst. 12442-0	Open		6.50	7
1995	Bunny Popcorn, Balloon Vendor, 2 asst. 12443-7	Open		6.70	7
1994	Bunny Preparing for Easter, 3 asst. 02971-8	Open		4.20	5
1994	Bunny Shopping Couple, 2 asst. 10362-3	Open		4.20	5
1994	Cobblestone Road 10072-1	Open		9.00	9
1994	Cone-Shaped Tree Set 10369-2	Open		7.50	8
1994	Cottontail Lane Sign 10063-9	Open		5.00	5
1994	Easter Bunny Figure, 2 asst. 00356-5	Open		4.20	5
1994	Egg Stand & Flower Cart, 2 asst. 10354-8	Open		6.00	6
1995	Electric Street Lamppost, set/4 12461-1	Open		25.00	25
1994	Lamppost, Birdhouse & Mailbox, 3 asst. 02187-3	Retrd.	1994	4.50	5
1995	Mayor Bunny and Bunny with Flag Pole, 2 asst. 12441-3	Open		5.50	6
1995	Outdoor Bunny, 3 asst. 12435-2	Open		5.00	5
1994	Policeman, Conductor Bunny, 2 asst.00367-1	Open		4.20	5
1995	Professional Bunny, 3 asst. 12438-3	Open		5.00	5
1995	Street Sign, 3 asst. 12433-8	Open		4.50	5
1994	Strolling Bunny, 2 asst. 02976-3	Retrd.	1994	4.20	5
1995	Strolling Bunny, 2 asst. 12440-6	Open		5.50	6
1994	Sweeper & Flower Peddler Bunny Couple, 2 asst. 00359-6	Open		4.20	5
1994	Topiary Trees, 3 asst. 00346-6	Retrd.	1994	2.50	3
1994	Train Station Couple, 2 asst. 00357-2	Open		4.20	5
1994	Tree & Shrub, 2 asst. 00382-4	Open		5.00	5
1994	Trees, 3 asst. 02194-1	Retrd.	1994	6.20	7
1994	Wedding Bunny Couple, 2 asst. 00347-3	Open		4.20	5

Cottontail Lane Houses - Midwest

YEAR ISSUE		EDITION LIMIT	YEAR RETD.	ISSUE PRICE	QUOTE U.S.$
1993	Bakery (lighted) 01396-0	Open		43.00	45
1993	Bed & Breakfast House (lighted) 00337-4	Open		43.00	45
1995	Boutique and Beauty Shop (lighted) 12301-0	Open		45.00	45
1995	Cafe (lighted) 12303-4	Open		45.00	45
1995	Cathedral (lighted) 12302-7	Open		47.00	47
1993	Chapel (lighted) 00331-2	Retrd.	1993	43.00	45
1993	Church (lighted) 01385-4	Retrd.	1993	42.00	140
1993	Confectionary Shop (lighted) 06335-5	Retrd.	1994	43.00	85
1993	Cottontail Inn (lighted) 01394-6	Open		43.00	45
1993	Flower Shop (lighted) 06333-9	Retrd.	1994	43.00	85
1993	General Store (lighted) 00340-4	Open		43.00	45
1993	Painting Studio (lighted) 01395-5	Retrd.	1994	43.00	45
1993	Rose Cottage (lighted) 01386-1	Retrd.	1994	43.00	45
1995	Rosebud Manor (lighted) 12304-1	3,500	1994	45.00	45
1993	Schoolhouse (lighted) 01378-6	Open		43.00	45
1993	Springtime Cottage (lighted) 06329-8	Retrd.	1994	43.00	85
1995	Town Hall (lighted) 12300-3	Open		45.00	45
1993	Train Station (lighted) 00330-5	Open		43.00	45
1993	Victorian House (lighted) 06332-1	Open		43.00	45

Creepy Hollow Figurines and Accessories - Midwest

YEAR ISSUE		EDITION LIMIT	YEAR RETD.	ISSUE PRICE	QUOTE U.S.$
1994	Black Picket Fence 10685-3	Open		13.50	14
1995	Cemetery Gate 13366-8	Open		16.00	16
1994	Creepy Hollow Sign 10647-1	Open		5.50	6
1995	Flying Witch, Ghost, 2 asst. 13362-0	Open		11.00	11
1994	Ghost, 3 asst. 10652-5	Open		6.00	6
1995	Ghoul Usher 13515-0	Open		6.50	7
1995	Ghoulish Organist Playing Organ 13363-7	Open		13.00	13
1995	Grave Digger, 2 asst. 13360-6	Open		10.00	10
1993	Halloween Sign, 2 asst. 06709-3	Open		6.00	7
1993	Haunted Tree, 2 asst. 05892-3	Open		7.00	7
1995	Hearse with Monsters 13364-4	Open		15.00	15
1993	Hinged Dracula's Coffin 08545-5	Open		11.00	11
1995	Hinged Tomb 13516-7	Open		15.00	15
1995	Hunchback 13359-0	Open		9.00	9
1994	Mad Scientist 10646-4	Open		6.00	7
1994	Outhouse 10648-8	Open		7.00	7
1994	Phantom of the Opera 10645-7	Open		6.00	7
1993	Pumpkin Head Ghost 06661-4	Retrd.	1994	5.50	6
1993	Pumpkin Patch Sign, 2 asst. 05898-5	Retrd.	1995	6.50	7
1995	Pumpkin Street Lamp, set/4 13365-1	Open		25.00	25
1993	Resin Skeleton 06651-5	Retrd.	1994	5.50	6
1995	Road of Bones 13371-2	Open		9.00	9
1994	Street Sign, 2 asst. 10644-0	Open		5.70	6
1995	Street Sign, 3 asst. 13357-6	Open		5.50	6
1995	Theatre Goer, set/2 13358-3	Open		9.00	15
1995	Ticket Seller 13361-3	Open		10.00	10
1994	Tombstone Sign, 3 asst. 10642-6	Open		3.50	4
1993	Trick or Treater, 3 asst. 08591-2	Retrd.	1995	5.50	6
1994	Werewolf 10643-4	Open		6.00	7
1993	Witch 06706-2	Open		6.00	6

Creepy Hollow Houses - Midwest

YEAR ISSUE		EDITION LIMIT	YEAR RETD.	ISSUE PRICE	QUOTE U.S.$
1995	Bewitching Belfry (lighted) 13355-2	Open		50.00	50
1993	Blood Bank (lighted) 08548-6	Open		40.00	43
1994	Cauldron Cafe (lighted) 10649-5	Open		40.00	43
1993	Dr. Frankenstein's House (lighted) 01621-3	Retrd.	1995	40.00	43
1993	Dracula's Castle (lighted) 01627-5	Retrd.	1995	40.00	43
1995	Funeral Parlor (lighted) 13356-9	Open		50.00	50
1993	Haunted Hotel (lighted) 08549-3	Open		40.00	43
1994	Medical Ghoul School (lighted) 10651-8	Open		40.00	43
1993	Mummy's Mortuary (lighted) 01641-1	Open		40.00	43
1994	Phantom's Opera (lighted) 10650-1	Open		40.00	43
1993	Shoppe of Horrors (lighted) 08550-9	Open		40.00	43
1995	Skeleton Cinema (lighted) 13354-5	5,000		50.00	50
1993	Witches Cove (lighted) 01665-7	Open		40.00	43

Folk Art Gallery Collection - Various

YEAR ISSUE		EDITION LIMIT	YEAR RETD.	ISSUE PRICE	QUOTE U.S.$
1995	"Fresh Garden Seeds" Rabbit Scene 15744-2 - P. Schifferl	Open		70.00	70
1995	"May Golden Rays Fill Your Days" Plaque 16124-1 L. Schifferl	Open		60.00	60
1995	Angel Triptych 13785-7 L. Schifferl	Open		65.00	70
1995	Bearing Gifts 13878-6 L. Schifferl	Open		140.00	145
1995	The Bird Watcher 15889-0 R. Tate	Open		60.00	60
1995	Birdhouse Clock 15743-5 P. Schifferl	Open		50.00	50
1995	Casey at Bat 15739-8 - R. Tate	Open		85.00	85
1995	Caught in the Act 13503-7 R. Tate	Open		19.00	19

YEAR ISSUE		EDITION LIMIT	YEAR RETD.	ISSUE PRICE	QUOTE U.S.$
1995	Christmas Peace Dove Weather-vane 13877-9 - L. Schifferl	Retrd.	1995	60.00	60
1995	Circus Bear 13508-2 - P. Herrick	Open		90.00	90
1995	Dancing Around the Maypole 13784-0 - P. Herrick	Open		150.00	150
1995	Don't Cry Over Spilled Milk Cow 15738-1 - R. Tate	Open		80.00	80
1995	Door Arch with Verse 13644-7 - Origin by Sticks	Retrd.	1995	120.00	120
1995	Dream Box 15947-7 - P. Herrick	Open		100.00	100
1995	Fisherman's Dilemma Wall Piece 13505-1 - R. Tate	Open		45.00	45
1995	Fishing Cat 15742-8 - P. Schifferl	Open		45.00	45
1995	Flower Garden Peg Rack Shelf 15894-4 - R. Tate	Open		90.00	90
1995	Folk Santa Broom 13504-4 R. Tate	Retrd.	1995	35.00	35
1995	For All Good Children Reversible Block set/5 13786-4 - P. Schifferl	Open		97.00	97
1995	Frog and Turtle Buddy Bookends 13782-6 - P. Herrick	Open		90.00	90
1995	Frog Prince Butler 13615-7 - P. Herrick	Open		73.00	73
1995	Gardener 15741-1 - R. Tate	Open		50.00	50
1995	Gardener Bunny 15891-3 R. Jones	Open		40.00	40
1995	Gardening Angel 15893-7 P. Schifferl	Open		70.00	70
1995	Gopher Golfer 16119-7 P. Herrick	Open		67.00	67
1995	Happy Faces Rack 13510-5 P. Herrick	Open		112.00	112
1995	Hummingbirds and Flowers 15895-1 - R. Tate	Open		60.00	60
1995	Hunt Scene Rock 16092-3 R. Tate	Open		55.00	55
1995	Jointed Gardening Bluebird 15892-0 - R. Jones	Open		20.00	20
1995	Life's Gifts Wall Plaque 13634-8 Origin by Sticks	Open		65.00	65
1995	Mr. Scared-A-Crows 13496-2 - R. Jones	Open		60.00	60
1995	Nature's Friend Hunter 13506-8 R. Tate	Open		89.00	89
1995	O Starry Night Mantle Piece 13783-3 - P. Herrick	Open		90.00	90
1995	Party Animal Shelf Sitter (3 asst.) 15897-5 - P. Herrick	Open		70.00	70
1995	Pumpkin Man 13509-9 - P. Herrick	Open		90.00	93
1995	Ride a Blue Moon 13507-3 - P. Herrick	Open		50.00	50
1995	Round 'em Up Cowboy with Hay Bale, set/2 15948-4 - R. Jones	Open		60.00	60
1995	Santa Branches, set/3 13635-5 - Origin by Sticks	Open		65.00	65
1995	Santa's Bluebird 13501-3 P. Herrick	Open		37.00	37
1995	St. Francis 15740-4 - R. Tate	Open		97.00	97
1995	Star Gazing Snowman 13495-5 R. Jones	Open		60.00	60
1995	Time for a Nap Wall Hanging 13492-4 - R. Jones	Open		20.00	20
1995	Tortoise and Hare 15888-3 P. Herrick	Open		100.00	100
1995	Turtle and Frog Doll Size Chair 15896-8 - P. Herrick	Open		120.00	120

Heritage Santa Collection - Midwest

1994	American Santa 11622-7	Retrd.	1994	20.00	20
1991	Father Christmas 01798-2	Retrd.	1994	26.50	28
1990	Herr Kristmas 00537-8	Retrd.	1993	26.50	28
1990	MacNicholas 00538-5	Retrd.	1994	26.50	28
1990	Papa Frost 00539-2	Retrd.	1994	26.50	28
1992	Pere Noel 06771-0	Retrd.	1993	26.50	27
1993	Santa España 07368-1	Retrd.	1994	25.00	27
1991	Santa Niccolo 01797-5	Retrd.	1994	26.50	28
1992	Santa Nykolai 06772-7	Retrd.	1993	26.50	27
1993	Santa O'Nicholas 07370-4	Retrd.	1994	25.00	27
1990	Scanda Klaus 00536-1	Retrd.	1994	26.50	28

Heritage Santa Collection Fabric Mache - Midwest

1994	American Santa Fabric Mache set 11944-0	Retrd.	1994	180.00	180
1991	Father Christmas Fabric Mache set 01800-2	Retrd.	1994	160.00	180
1990	Herr Kristmas Fabric Mache set 00515-6	Retrd.	1992	160.00	170
1990	MacNicholas Fabric Mache set 00516-3	Retrd.	1994	160.00	180
1990	Papa Frost Fabric Mache set 00517-0	Retrd.	1993	160.00	170
1992	Pere Noel Fabric Mache set 06766-6	Retrd.	1994	160.00	180
1993	Santa España Fabric Mache set 07357-5	Retrd.	1994	170.00	180
1991	Santa Niccolo Fabric Mache set 01799-9	Retrd.	1994	160.00	180
1992	Santa Nykolai Fabric Mache set 06767-3	Retrd.	1994	160.00	180
1993	Santa O'Nicholas Fabric Mache set 07365-0	Retrd.	1994	170.00	180
1990	Scanda Klaus Fabric Mache set 00514-9	Retrd.	1992	160.00	170

Heritage Santa Collection Music Boxes - Midwest

1994	American Santa Music Box 11618-0	Retrd.	1994	59.00	59
1991	Father Christmas Music Box 01802-6	Retrd.	1993	53.00	59
1990	Herr Kristmas Music Box 00533-1	Retrd.	1992	53.00	56
1990	MacNicholas Music Box 00534-7	Retrd.	1993	53.00	59
1990	Papa Frost Music Box 00535-4	Retrd.	1994	53.00	59
1992	Pere Noel Music Box 06789-5	Retrd.	1993	53.00	59
1993	Santa España Music Box 07366-7	Retrd.	1994	56.00	59
1991	Santa Niccolo Music Box 01801-9	Retrd.	1993	53.00	56
1992	Santa Nykolai Music Box 06790-1	Retrd.	1993	53.00	59
1993	Santa O'Nicholas Music Box 07367-4	Retrd.	1994	56.00	59
1990	Scanda Klaus Music Box 00532-3	Retrd.	1994	53.00	59

Heritage Santa Collection Snowglobes - Midwest

1994	American Santa Snowglobe 11623-4	Retrd.	1994	45.00	45
1991	Father Christmas Snowglobe 01794-4	Retrd.	1994	40.00	45
1990	Herr Kristmas Snowglobe 00525-5	Retrd.	1992	40.00	43
1990	MacNicholas Snowglobe 00526-2	Retrd.	1994	40.00	45
1990	Papa Frost Snowglobe 00527-9	Retrd.	1992	40.00	43
1992	Pere Noel Snowglobe 06778-9	Retrd.	1994	40.00	45
1993	Santa España Snowglobe 07371-1	Retrd.	1994	43.00	45
1991	Santa Niccolo Snowglobe 01793-7	Retrd.	1993	40.00	43
1992	Santa Nykolai Snowglobe 06783-3	Retrd.	1993	40.00	43
1993	Santa O'Nicholas Snowglobe 07372-8	Retrd.	1994	43.00	45
1990	Scanda Klaus Snowglobe 00524-8	Retrd.	1993	40.00	45

Heritage Santa Roly-Polys - Midwest

1994	American Santa Roly-Poly 11620-3	Retrd.	1994	17.00	17
1991	Father Christmas Roly-Poly 01796-8	Retrd.	1994	24.00	25
1990	Herr Kristmas Roly-Poly 00529-3	Retrd.	1993	24.00	25
1990	MacNicholas Roly-Poly 00530-9	Retrd.	1994	24.00	25
1990	Papa Frost Roly-Poly 00531-6	Retrd.	1994	24.00	25
1992	Pere Noel Roly-Poly 06768-0	Retrd.	1993	24.00	24
1993	Santa España Roly-Poly 07373-5	Retrd.	1994	20.00	24
1991	Santa Niccolo Roly-Poly 01795-1	Retrd.	1993	24.00	25
1992	Santa Nykolai Roly-Poly 06769-7	Retrd.	1994	24.00	24
1993	Santa O'Nicholas Roly-Poly 07375-9	Retrd.	1994	20.00	24
1990	Scanda Klaus Roly-Poly 00528-6	Retrd.	1993	24.00	25

Leo R. Smith III Collection - L. R. Smith

1995	"Circle of Nature" Wreath 16120-3	1,000		200.00	200
1995	Angel with Lion and Lamb 13990-5	1,500		125.00	125
1991	Cossack Santa 01092-1	1,700	1993	103.00	130
1993	Dancing Santa 09042-8	5,000	1995	170.00	170
1992	Dreams of Night Buffalo 07999-7	5,000		250.00	270
1991	Fisherman Santa 03311-1	5,000	1995	270.00	290
1993	Folk Angel 05444-4	2,095		145.00	150
1995	Gardening Angel 16118-0	2,500		130.00	130
1994	Gift Giver Santa 12056-9	1,500		180.00	180
1993	Gnome Santa on Deer 05206-8	1,463		270.00	270
1992	Great Plains Santa 08049-8	5,000	1994	270.00	293
1995	Hare Leaping Over the Garden 16121-0	1,000		100.00	100
1992	Leo Smith Name Plaque 07881-5	5,000		12.00	12
1995	Maize Maiden Angel 13992-9	2,500		45.00	45
1991	Milkmaker 03541-2	5,000	1994	170.00	184
1992	Ms. Liberty 07866-2	5,000	1994	190.00	210
1994	Old-World Santa 12053-8	1,500	1994	75.00	250
1995	Orchard Santa 13989-9	1,500		125.00	125
1995	Otter Wall Hanging 16122-7	2,000		150.00	150
1995	Owl Lady 13988-2	1,000		100.00	105
1991	Pilgrim Man 03313-5	5,000	1994	84.00	150
1991	Pilgrim Riding Turkey 03312-8	5,000	1994	230.00	250
1991	Pilgrim Woman 03315-9	5,000	1995	84.00	150
1993	Santa Fisherman 08979-8	1,748		250.00	300
1995	Santa in Sleigh 13987-5	1,500		125.00	125
1992	Santa of Peace 07328-5	5,000	1994	250.00	270
1994	Santa Skier 12054-5	1,500		190.00	190
1994	Star of the Roundup Cowboy 11966-1	1,500		100.00	100
1991	Stars and Stripes Santa 01743-2	5,000	1994	190.00	200
1995	Sunbringer Santa 13991-2	1,500		125.00	125
1991	Tis a Witching Time 03544-3	609	1991	140.00	1200
1991	Toymaker 03540-5	5,000	1994	120.00	130
1993	Voyageur 09043-5	788		170.00	170
1994	Weatherwise Angel 12055-2	1,500		150.00	150
1995	Wee Willie Santa 13993-6	2,500	1995	50.00	50
1992	Woodland Brave 07867-9	1,500	1993	87.00	250
1991	Woodsman Santa 03310-4	5,000	1995	230.00	250

Ore Mountain "A Christmas Carol" Nutcrackers - Midwest

1993	Bob Cratchit, 09421-1	5,000		120.00	130
1994	Ghost of Christmas Future, 10449-1	4,000		116.00	125
1994	Ghost of Christmas Past, 10447-7	4,000		116.00	125
1993	Ghost of Christmas Present 12041-5	5,000		116.00	200
1994	Marley's Ghost, 10448-4	4,000		116.00	125
1993	Scrooge, 05522-9	5,000		104.00	125

Ore Mountain "Nutcracker Fantasy" Nutcrackers - Midwest

1995	Clara, 12801-5	5,000		125.00	125
1991	Clara, 8" 01254-3	Open		77.00	100
1994	Herr Drosselmeyer, 10456-9	5,000		110.00	125
1988	Herr Drosselmeyer, 14 1/2" 07506-7	Open		75.00	115
1993	The Mouse King, 05350-8	5,000		100.00	125
1988	The Mouse King, 10" 07509-8	Open		60.00	85
1994	Nutcracker Prince, 11001-0	5,000		104.00	125
1988	The Prince, 12 3/4" 07507-4	Open		75.00	105
1988	The Toy Soldier, 11" 07508-1	Open		70.00	95
1995	Toy Soldier, 12804-6	5,000		125.00	125

Ore Mountain Easter Nutcrackers - Midwest

1992	Bunny Painter, 06480-1	Retrd.	1993	77.00	80
1991	Bunny with Egg, 00145-5	Retrd.	1993	77.00	80
1984	March Hare, 00312-1	Retrd.	1993	77.00	80

Ore Mountain Nutcracker Collection - Midwest

1995	American Country Santa, 13195-4	Open		165.00	165
1994	Annie Oakley, 10464-4	Retrd.	1995	128.00	130
1995	August the Strong, 13185-5	Open		190.00	190
1995	Barbeque Dad, 13193-0	Open		176.00	176
1994	Baseball Player, 10459-0	Retrd.	1995	111.00	120
1995	Basketball Player, 12784-1	Open		135.00	135
1995	Beefeater, 12797-1	Open		175.00	175
1994	Black Santa, 10460-6	Retrd.	1995	74.00	74
1993	Cat Witch, 09426-6	Retrd.	1995	93.00	93
1994	Cavalier, 12952-4	Open		80.00	95
1994	Cavalier, 12953-1	Open		65.00	77
1994	Cavalier, 12958-6	Open		57.00	65
1995	Chimney Sweep, 00326-8	Open		70.00	70
1992	Christopher Columbus, 00152-3	Retrd.	1992	80.00	80
1991	Clown, 03561-0	Retrd.	1994	115.00	118
1994	Confederate Soldier, 12837-4	Open		93.00	105
1989	Country Santa, 09326-9	Open		95.00	150
1992	Cowboy, 00298-8	Retrd.	1995	97.00	150
1995	Downhill Santa Skier, 13197-8	Open		145.00	145
1990	Elf, 04154-3	Retrd.	1993	70.00	73
1994	Engineer, 10454-5	Retrd.	1995	108.00	108
1992	Farmer, 01109-6	Retrd.	1994	65.00	77
1993	Fireman with Dog, 06592-1	Open		134.00	140
1989	Fisherman, 09327-6	Retrd.	1995	90.00	100
1994	Gardening Lady, 10450-7	Open		104.00	112
1993	Gepetto Santa, 09417-4	Retrd.	1995	115.00	115
1989	Golfer, 09325-2	Retrd.	1994	85.00	90
1995	Handyman, 12806-0	Open		136.00	137
1995	Hockey Player, 12783-4	Open		155.00	155
1995	Hunter Nutcracker 12785-8	Open		136.00	136
1992	Indian, 00195-0	Retrd.	1994	96.00	100
1995	Jack Frost, 12803-9	Open		150.00	150
1995	Jolly St. Nick with Toys, 13709-3	Open		135.00	135
1995	King Richard the Lionhearted, 12798-8	Open		165.00	165
1995	Law Scholar, 12789-6	Open		127.00	127
1990	Merlin the Magician, 04207-6	Open		67.00	75
1994	Miner, 10493-4	Retrd.	1995	110.00	120
1994	Nature Lover, 10446-0	Retrd.	1995	112.00	112
1988	Nordic Santa, 08872-2	Retrd.	1995	84.00	110
1991	Nutcracker-Maker, 03601-3	Retrd.	1993	62.00	65
1995	Peddler, 12805-3	Open		140.00	140
1995	Pierre Le Chef, 12802-2	Open		147.00	147
1992	Pilgrim, 00188-2	Retrd.	1994	96.00	100
1994	Pinecone Santa, 10461-3	Retrd.	1994	92.00	92
1984	Pinocchio, 00160-8	Open		60.00	68
1995	Pizza Baker, 13194-7	Open		170.00	170
1994	Prince Charming, 10457-6	Retrd.	1994	125.00	130
1994	Pumpkin Head Scarecrow, 10451-1	Open		127.00	140
1994	Regal Prince, 10452-1	Open		140.00	152
1992	Ringmaster, 00196-7	Retrd.	1993	135.00	137
1995	Riverboat Gambler, 12787-2	Open		137.00	137
1995	Royal Lion, 13985-1	Open		130.00	130
1995	Santa at Workbench, 13335-4	Open		130.00	130
1994	Santa in Nightshirt, 10462-0	Retrd.	1995	108.00	120
1988	Santa w/Tree & Toys, 07666-8	Retrd.	1993	76.00	87
1993	Santa with Animals, 09424-2	Retrd.	1994	117.00	117
1994	Santa with Basket, 10472-9	Open		80.00	100
1992	Santa with Skis, 01305-2	Retrd.	1994	100.00	110
1990	Sea Captain, 04157-4	Retrd.	1994	86.00	95
1994	Snow King, 10470-5	Retrd.	1995	108.00	120
1994	Soccer Player, 10494-1	Open		97.00	107
1994	Sorcerer, 10471-2	Retrd.	1995	100.00	100
1994	Sultan King, 10455-2	Retrd.	1995	130.00	145
1995	Teacher, 13196-1	Open		165.00	165
1994	Toy Vendor, 11987-7	Open		124.00	135
1990	Uncle Sam, 04206-9	Retrd.	1993	50.00	62
1994	Union Soldier, 12836-7	Open		93.00	105
1992	Victorian Santa, 00187-5	Retrd.	1994	130.00	140
1993	White Santa, 09533-1	Retrd.	1995	100.00	100
1990	Windsor Club, 04160-4	Retrd.	1994	85.00	87
1990	Witch, 04159-8	Retrd.	1995	75.00	76
1990	Woodland Santa, 04191-8	Retrd.	1995	105.00	150

Wendt and Kuhn Collection - Wendt/Kuhn

1989	Angel at Piano 09403-7	Open		31.00	37
1983	Angel Brass Musicians, set/6 00470-8	Open		92.00	110
1983	Angel Conductor on Stand 00469-2	Open		21.00	24

YEAR ISSUE		EDITION LIMIT	YEAR RETD.	ISSUE PRICE	QUOTE U.S.$
1990	Angel Duet in Celestial Stars 04158-1	S/O	N/A	60.00	63
1983	Angel Percussion Musicians set/6 00443-2	Open		110.00	130
1979	Angel Playing Violin 00403-6	S/O	N/A	34.00	35
1980	Angel Pulling Wagon 00553-8	S/O	N/A	43.00	50
1983	Angel String & Woodwind Musicians, set/6 00465-4	Open		108.00	120
1983	Angel String Musicians, set/6 00455-5	Open		105.00	120
1979	Angel Trio, set/3 00471-5	Open		140.00	170
1981	Angel w/Tree & Basket 01190-8	S/O	N/A	24.00	25
1976	Angel with Sled 02940-4	S/O	N/A	36.50	38
1981	Angels at Cradle, set/4 01193-5	Open		73.00	80
1984	Angels Bearing Toys, set/6 00451-7	Open		97.00	110
1979	Bavarian Moving Van 02854-4	Open		134.00	150
1991	Birdhouse 01209-3	S/O	N/A	22.50	23
1991	Boy on Rocking Horse, 2 asst. 01202-4	S/O	N/A	35.00	36
1994	Busy Elf, 3 asst. 12856-5	Open		22.00	24
1987	Child on Skis, 2 asst. 06083-4	S/O	N/A	28.00	29
1987	Child on Sled 06085-8	S/O	N/A	25.50	27
1994	Child with Flowers Set 12947-0	Open		45.00	50
1988	Children Carrying Lanterns Procession, set/6 01213-0	Open		117.00	150
1991	Display Base for Wendt und Kuhn Figures, 12 1/2 x 2" 01214-7	Open		32.00	39
1991	Flower Children, set/6 01213-0	Open		130.00	150
1979	Girl w/Cradle, set/2 01203-1	S/O	N/A	37.50	40
1979	Girl w/Porridge Bowl 01198-0	Open		29.00	32
1979	Girl w/Scissors 01197-3	Open		25.00	32
1983	Girl w/Wagon 01196-6	S/O	N/A	27.00	29
1991	Girl with Doll 01200-0	Open		31.50	35
1980	Little People Napkin Rings 6 asst. 03504-7	Open		21.00	25
1988	Lucia Parade Figures, set/3 07667-5	S/O	N/A	75.00	80
1978	Madonna w/Child 01207-9	Open		120.00	135
1979	Magarita Angels, set/6 02938-1	Open		94.00	110
1983	Margarita Birthday Angels, set/3 00480-7	S/O	N/A	44.00	53
1979	Pied Piper and Children, set/7 02843-8	S/O	N/A	120.00	130
1981	Santa w/Angel in Sleigh 01192-8	S/O	N/A	52.00	60
1976	Santa with Angel 00473-9	Open		50.00	55
1994	Santa with Tree 12942-5	Open		29.00	32
1994	Sun, Moon, Star Set 12943-2	Open		69.00	75
1992	Wendt und Kuhn Display Sign w/ Sitting Angel 07535-7	Open		20.00	23
1991	White Angel with Violin 01205-5	S/O	N/A	25.50	27

Wendt and Kuhn Collection Music Boxes - Wendt/Kuhn

YEAR ISSUE		EDITION LIMIT	YEAR RETD.	ISSUE PRICE	QUOTE U.S.$
1978	Angel at Pipe Organ 01929-0	Open		176.00	200
1994	Angel Under Stars Crank Music Box 12974-6	300		150.00	190
1991	Angels & Santa Around Tree 01211-6	Open		300.00	330
1976	Girl Rocking Cradle 09215-6	S/O	N/A	180.00	190
1978	Rotating Angels 'Round Cradle 01911-5	Open		270.00	300

Wendt and Kuhn Figurines Candleholders - Wendt/Kuhn

YEAR ISSUE		EDITION LIMIT	YEAR RETD.	ISSUE PRICE	QUOTE U.S.$
1976	Angel Candleholder Pair 00472-2	Open		70.00	85
1991	Angel with Friend Candleholder 01191-1	S/O	N/A	33.30	34
1994	Angel with Wagon Candleholder 12860-2	Open		35.00	38
1980	Large Angel Candleholder Pair 01201-7	S/O	N/A	270.00	277
1986	Pair of Angels Candleholder 01204-8	S/O	N/A	30.00	32
1987	Santa Candleholder 06082-7	S/O	N/A	53.00	54
1991	Small Angel Candleholder Pair 01195-9	S/O	N/A	60.00	63
1991	White Angel Candleholder 01206-2	S/O	N/A	28.00	29

Museum Collections, Inc.

American Family I - N. Rockwell

YEAR ISSUE		EDITION LIMIT	YEAR RETD.	ISSUE PRICE	QUOTE U.S.$
1979	Baby's First Step	22,500		90.00	175-200
1980	Birthday Party	22,500		110.00	140
1981	Bride and Groom	22,500		110.00	120
1980	First Haircut	22,500		90.00	150
1980	First Prom	22,500		90.00	95
1980	Happy Birthday, Dear Mother	22,500		90.00	135
1980	Little Mother	22,500		110.00	125
1981	Mother's Little Helpers	22,500		110.00	125
1980	The Student	22,500		110.00	140
1980	Sweet Sixteen	22,500		90.00	125
1980	Washing Our Dog	22,500		110.00	125
1980	Wrapping Christmas Presents	22,500		90.00	125

Christmas - N. Rockwell

YEAR ISSUE		EDITION LIMIT	YEAR RETD.	ISSUE PRICE	QUOTE U.S.$
1980	Checking His List	Yr.Iss.		65.00	110
1983	High Hopes	Yr.Iss.		95.00	175
1981	Ringing in Good Cheer	Yr.Iss.		95.00	100
1984	Space Age Santa	Yr.Iss.		65.00	100
1982	Waiting for Santa	Yr.Iss.		95.00	110

Classic - N. Rockwell

YEAR ISSUE		EDITION LIMIT	YEAR RETD.	ISSUE PRICE	QUOTE U.S.$
1984	All Wrapped Up	Closed		65.00	90-95
1980	Bedtime	Closed		65.00	90-95
1984	The Big Race	Closed		65.00	90-95
1983	Bored of Education	Closed		65.00	90-95
1983	Braving the Storm	Closed		65.00	90-95
1980	The Cobbler	Closed		65.00	95
1982	The Country Doctor	Closed		65.00	90-95
1981	A Dollhouse for Sis	Closed		65.00	90-95
1982	Dreams in the Antique Shop	Closed		65.00	90-95
1983	A Final Touch	Closed		65.00	90-95
1980	For A Good Boy	Closed		65.00	90-95
1984	Goin' Fishin'	Closed		65.00	90-95
1983	High Stepping	Closed		65.00	90-95
1982	The Kite Maker	Closed		65.00	100
1980	Lighthouse Keeper's Daughter	Closed		65.00	95-100
1980	Memories	Closed		65.00	90-95
1981	The Music Lesson	Closed		65.00	90-95
1981	Music Master	Closed		65.00	90-95
1981	Off to School	Closed		65.00	90-95
1981	Puppy Love	Closed		65.00	90-95
1984	Saturday's Hero	Closed		65.00	90-95
1983	A Special Treat	Closed		65.00	90-95
1982	Spring Fever	Closed		65.00	90-95
1980	The Toymaker	Closed		65.00	90-95
1981	While The Audience Waits	Closed		65.00	85
1983	Winter Fun	Closed		65.00	90-95
1982	Words of Wisdom	Closed		65.00	90-95

Commemorative - N. Rockwell

YEAR ISSUE		EDITION LIMIT	YEAR RETD.	ISSUE PRICE	QUOTE U.S.$
1985	Another Masterpiece by Norman Rockwell	5,000		125.00	200-250
1981	Norman Rockwell Display	5,000		125.00	200-250
1983	Norman Rockwell, America's Artist	5,000		125.00	200-250
1984	Outward Bound	5,000		125.00	200-250
1986	The Painter and the Pups	5,000		125.00	250
1982	Spirit of America	5,000		125.00	200-250

My Friends and Me

My Chautauqua Friends - My Friends And Me

YEAR ISSUE		EDITION LIMIT	YEAR RETD.	ISSUE PRICE	QUOTE U.S.$
1994	Athenaeum Hotel 0612	Open		25.95	26
1994	The Brown's Bunglow 0614	Open		22.95	23
1994	Janes Gingerbread Cottage 0616	Open		22.95	23
1994	Miller Bell Tower 0613	Open		25.95	26
1994	Morris Cottage 0617	Open		22.95	23
1994	Smith Cottage 0615	Open		25.95	26
1994	Welcome Sign 0611	Open		22.95	23

My Church Friends I - My Friends And Me

YEAR ISSUE		EDITION LIMIT	YEAR RETD.	ISSUE PRICE	QUOTE U.S.$
1994	Western Reserve Chapel 0504	Open		25.95	26

My Cleveland Friends - My Friends And Me

YEAR ISSUE		EDITION LIMIT	YEAR RETD.	ISSUE PRICE	QUOTE U.S.$
1995	The Arcade CLE003	Open		24.95	25
1995	The Old Stone Church CLE002	Open		24.95	25
1995	Terminal Tower CLE001	Open		24.95	25
1995	West Side Market CLE004	Open		24.95	25

My Country Friends I - My Friends And Me

YEAR ISSUE		EDITION LIMIT	YEAR RETD.	ISSUE PRICE	QUOTE U.S.$
1995	Covered Bridge 0418	Open		22.95	23
1994	Post Office 0416	Open		22.95	23
1994	Thompson Bank Barn 0417	Open		25.95	26
1994	Turner's Mill 0415	Open		22.95	23

My East Coast Lighthouse Friends - My Friends And Me

YEAR ISSUE		EDITION LIMIT	YEAR RETD.	ISSUE PRICE	QUOTE U.S.$
1995	Harbour Town Lighthouse LH0002	Open		23.95	24
1995	Tybee Island Lighthouse LH0001	Open		23.95	24

My Main Street Friends I - My Friends And Me

YEAR ISSUE		EDITION LIMIT	YEAR RETD.	ISSUE PRICE	QUOTE U.S.$
1994	Baker Hardware and Campbell Harness Shop 0321	Open		22.95	23
1994	John's Boots and Shoes 0322	Open		22.95	23
1994	Robert's Frame Shop 0323	Open		22.95	23
1994	Wright Store 0324	Open		22.95	23

My Public Square Friends I - My Friends And Me

YEAR ISSUE		EDITION LIMIT	YEAR RETD.	ISSUE PRICE	QUOTE U.S.$
1994	Bandstand 0721	Open		25.95	26
1994	Clock Tower 0719	Open		25.95	26
1994	Engine House 0722	Open		25.95	26
1994	National Bank 0720	Open		22.95	23

My Rainbow Row Friends - My Friends And Me

YEAR ISSUE		EDITION LIMIT	YEAR RETD.	ISSUE PRICE	QUOTE U.S.$
1995	89 East Bay Street RR89	Open		25.95	26
1995	91 East Bay Street RR91	Open		25.95	26
1995	93 East Bay Street RR93	Open		25.95	26
1995	95 East Bay Street RR95	Open		25.95	26
1995	97 East Bay Street RR97	Open		25.95	26
1995	99-101 East Bay Street RR99-101	Open		25.95	26

My Savannah Friends - My Friends And Me

YEAR ISSUE		EDITION LIMIT	YEAR RETD.	ISSUE PRICE	QUOTE U.S.$
1995	Andrew Low House SAV31404	Open		25.95	26
1995	Cathedral of St. John the Baptist SAV31403	Open		25.95	26
1995	The Herb House SAV31406	Open		25.95	26
1995	Isaiah Davenport House SAV31402	Open		25.95	26
1995	Owens Thomas House SAV31401	Open		25.95	26
1995	The Pink House SAV31405	Open		25.95	26

My South Carolina Friends - My Friends And Me

YEAR ISSUE		EDITION LIMIT	YEAR RETD.	ISSUE PRICE	QUOTE U.S.$
1995	Boyleston House SC2923	Open		24.95	25
1995	Governor's Mansion SC2922	Open		24.95	25
1995	Lace House SC2925	Open		24.95	25
1995	Longstreet Theatre SC2924	Open		24.95	25
1995	State Capital SC2921	Open		25.95	26

My Village Friends I - My Friends And Me

YEAR ISSUE		EDITION LIMIT	YEAR RETD.	ISSUE PRICE	QUOTE U.S.$
1994	Buss House, Storekeeper 0914	Open		25.95	26
1994	Davis House, Landowner 0915	Open		22.95	23
1994	Miller House, Merchant 0916	Open		22.95	23
1994	Osborn House, Railroad Conductor 0913	Open		22.95	23

My Village Friends II - My Friends And Me

YEAR ISSUE		EDITION LIMIT	YEAR RETD.	ISSUE PRICE	QUOTE U.S.$
1994	King House, Dry Goods Store Owner 0917	Open		22.95	23
1994	Pettingell House, Carpenter 0919	Open		22.95	23
1994	Taylor House, Clergyman 0918	Open		22.95	23

New Release - My Friends And Me

YEAR ISSUE		EDITION LIMIT	YEAR RETD.	ISSUE PRICE	QUOTE U.S.$
1995	Quaker Sqaure AKR443-01	Open		23.95	24

Old World Christmas

Candleholders - E.M. Merck

YEAR ISSUE		EDITION LIMIT	YEAR RETD.	ISSUE PRICE	QUOTE U.S.$
1989	Angel 9015	Retrd.	1994	7.50	8
1989	Hummingbird 9013	Retrd.	1994	7.50	8
1989	Nutcracker 9016	Retrd.	1994	7.50	8
1989	Rocking Horse 9011	Retrd.	1994	7.50	8
1989	Santa 9012	Retrd.	1992	7.55	10
1989	Teddy Bear 9014	Retrd.	1994	7.50	8

Collectibles - O.W.C.

YEAR ISSUE		EDITION LIMIT	YEAR RETD.	ISSUE PRICE	QUOTE U.S.$
1992	Candle Arch with Church 862	Retrd.	1993	28.50	40
1992	Large Seiffener Candle Arch 8616	Retrd.	1994	450.00	450
1991	Noah's Ark 861	Open		250.00	250
1992	Weather House 86109	Retrd.	1994	31.50	32

Halloween - E.M. Merck

YEAR ISSUE		EDITION LIMIT	YEAR RETD.	ISSUE PRICE	QUOTE U.S.$
1988	Black Cat on Wire 9208	Retrd.	1992	8.35	10
1989	Black Cat/Witch with Cart (A) 9251	Retrd.	1994	10.00	10
1989	Cast Iron Scarecrow 9218	Retrd.	1994	32.50	33
1987	Ghost Light 9205	Retrd.	1992	37.00	65
1989	Ghost Votive 9211	Retrd.	1994	8.50	9
1988	Haunted House Waterglobe 9206	Retrd.	1989	22.50	27
1987	Haunted House with Lights 9203	Retrd.	1994	99.50	100
1988	Large Pumpkin Bowl 9273	Retrd.	1994	18.50	19
1987	Lighted Ghost Dish 9204	Retrd.	1994	45.00	45
1988	Pumpkin Head on Wire 9207	Retrd.	1992	7.35	10
1987	Pumpkin Light with Ghosts 9201	Retrd.	1994	39.50	40
1987	Pumpkin Light with Scarecrow 9202	Retrd.	1991	37.00	37
1988	Pumpkin Taper Holder 9272	Retrd.	1992	5.65	7
1988	Pumpkin Votive 9271	Retrd.	1991	8.90	10
1989	Witch on Moon Night Light 9212	Retrd.	1994	37.50	38
1988	Witch Taper Holder 9282	Retrd.	1993	11.00	15
1988	Witch Votive Holder 9281	Retrd.	1994	29.50	30

Night Lights - E.M. Merck

YEAR ISSUE		EDITION LIMIT	YEAR RETD.	ISSUE PRICE	QUOTE U.S.$
1986	ABC Block 529713	Retrd.	1994	37.00	43
1986	Angel 529703	Retrd.	1992	18.00	85
1990	Father Christmas 529721	Retrd.	1992	45.00	110
1985	Santa 529701	Retrd.	1987	37.00	300-450
1988	Santa Hugging Tree 529717	Retrd.	1990	42.00	175
1986	Santa in Chimney 529707	Retrd.	1988	37.00	225
1995	Santa in Sleigh 529729	Open		49.50	50
1989	Santa on Locomotive 529719	Retrd.	1991	42.00	165
1995	Santa Toymaker 529731	Open		59.00	59
1992	Santa with Nutcracker 529725	Retrd.	1992	45.00	195
1991	Santa with Stocking 529723	Retrd.	1993	45.00	175
1987	Santa with Tree 529715	Retrd.	1989	39.50	225
1986	Snowman 529709	Retrd.	1988	37.00	110
1986	Teddy Bear 529711	Retrd.	1991	37.00	110

Nutcrackers - E.M. Merck, unless otherwise noted

YEAR ISSUE		EDITION LIMIT	YEAR RETD.	ISSUE PRICE	QUOTE U.S.$
1993	Altenburger Grandma, 7266	Open		135.00	135
1993	Altenburger Grandpa, 7267	Open		135.00	135
1987	Austrian General, 72043 - K.W.O.	Open		57.50	58
1992	Austrian Hussar, 72058 - K.W.O.	Open		62.50	63
1987	Austrian Musketeer, 72048 - K.W.O.	Retrd.	1995	57.50	58
1993	Berchtesgaden Doctor, 7273	Open		110.00	110
1993	Berliner Baker, 7253	Open		110.00	110
1994	Black Cat, 7298	Open		140.00	140
1993	Bohemian Beekeeper, 7264	Open		110.00	110
1993	Brandenburger Guard, 7250	Retrd.	1994	110.00	110
1993	Bremer Sea Captain, 7269	Open		110.00	110
1987	British General, 72042 - K.W.O.	Open		55.00	55
1987	British Guard, 72041 - K.W.O.	Retrd.	1995	60.00	60
1989	British Major, 72050 - K.W.O.	Open		65.00	65
1992	Carved Hunter, 72213 - O.W.C.	Retrd.	1992	150.00	150
1993	Chemnitzer Clown 7255	Open		110.00	110
1987	Chimney Sweep, 72014 - K.W.O.	Open		48.50	49
1993	Coburger Chimney Sweep, 7265	Open		110.00	110
1987	Dutch Guard, 72040 - K.W.O.	Open		55.00	55
1994	Easter Bunny, 7297	Open		140.00	140
1993	Exceptional Guard, 7231 - K.W.O.	50		995.00	995
1992	Exceptional King, 7230	50	1994	950.00	950
1993	Falkensteiner Wizard 7261	Open		110.00	110

FIGURINES/COTTAGES

YEAR ISSUE		EDITION LIMIT	YEAR RETD.	ISSUE PRICE	QUOTE U.S.$
1992	Farmer, 72064 - K.W.O.	Open		62.50	63
1993	Freitaler Fisherman, 7260	Open		110.00	110
1992	French Officer, 72053 - K.W.O.	Open		67.50	68
1993	Fuessen Father Christmas, 7274	Open		135.00	135
1994	Garmish Groom, 7280	Open		110.00	110
1994	Giessener Gardener, 7278	Open		110.00	110
1987	Guard, 72015 - K.W.O.	Open		52.50	53
1995	Harzburg King of Hearts Nutcraker 7288	Open		65.00	65
1992	Hungarian Hussar, 72059 - K.W.O.	Open		62.50	63
1993	Hunter, 72070 - K.W.O.	Open		59.50	60
1991	Inlaid Natural King, 7214 - O.W.C.	Retrd.	1992	150.00	150
1991	Inlaid Natural Muskateer 7225 - O.W.C.	Retrd.	1992	150.00	150
1987	King, 72031 - K.W.O.	Open		50.00	50
1995	Konigsee 7285	Open		125.00	125
1993	Kulmbacher Beer Drinker, 7270	Open		110.00	110
1992	Large Austrian King, 72243 - K.W.O.	Open		130.00	130
1992	Large Austrian Musketeer, 72148 - K.W.O.	Open		87.50	88
1992	Large Bavarian Duke, 72242 K.W.O.	Retrd.	1995	130.00	130
1992	Large British Guard 72141 K.W.O.	Retrd.	1994	90.00	90
1991	Large Carved Hunter, 721 K.W.O.	Open		175.00	175
1992	Large Carved Santa, 7223 K.W.O.	Retrd.	1994	175.00	175
1992	Large Dutch Guard, 72140 K.W.O.	Retrd.	1994	90.00	90
1995	Large Father Christmas, 72403	Open		130.00	130
1992	Large Fireman, 72240 - K.W.O.	Open		99.50	100
1995	Large Guard, 72419	Open		110.00	110
1991	Large Hunter, 7228 - K.W.O.	Retrd.	1994	97.50	98
1993	Large King, 72033 - K.W.O.	Retrd.	1994	79.95	80
1992	Large Prussian Hussar, 72144 K.W.O.	Open		90.00	90
1992	Large Prussian King, 72244 K.W.O.	Retrd.	1994	130.00	130
1992	Large Prussian Sargeant 72145 K.W.O.	Retrd.	1995	90.00	90
1992	Large Saxon Duke, 72241 K.W.O.	Open		130.00	130
1992	Large Snow Prince, 7277	Retrd.	1992	100.00	100
1992	Large Traditional Red King, 7237 - K.W.O.	Open		115.00	115
1992	Natural Guard, 72915 - K.W.O.	Retrd.	1994	52.50	53
1994	Neuschwanstein Knight 7281	Open		110.00	110
1993	Neustadter Nurse, 7272	Open		135.00	135
1994	Nuremberger Nightwatchman 7282	Open		110.00	110
1995	Olbernhau Toy Maker Nutcraker 7285	Open		67.50	68
1994	Partinkirchen Bride 7279	Open		140.00	140
1992	Portuguese Guard, 72055 K.W.O.	Open		65.00	65
1987	Prussian Hussar, 72044 - K.W.O.	Open		60.00	60
1993	Prussian King, 7251	Open		110.00	110
1992	Prussian Officer, 72052 - K.W.O.	Open		65.00	65
1987	Prussian Sergeant, 72045 K.W.O.	Retrd.	1995	60.00	60
1993	Rostocker Pirate, 7252	Open		110.00	110
1993	Saalfelder Shepherd, 7263	Open		110.00	110
1994	Salzburger St. Nicholas, 7275	Open		140.00	140
1987	Saxon Guard, 72049 - K.W.O.	Open		65.00	65
1992	Saxonian Officer, 72051 - K.W.O.	Open		65.00	65
1993	Schneeberger Skier, 7271	Open		135.00	135
1993	Seiffener Santa, 7257	Retrd.	1994	110.00	110
1992	Skier, 7294	Retrd.	1992	82.50	83
1995	Small Beer Drinker, 72018	Open		45.00	45
1994	Small Chimney Sweep, 72025	Open		42.00	42
1994	Small Cook, 72020	Open		42.00	42
1995	Small Father Christmas, 72003	Open		55.00	55
1995	Small Garden Gnome, 72016	Open		45.00	45
1994	Small Gardener, 72023	Open		44.00	44
1995	Small Guard, 72019	Open		45.00	45
1995	Small Hunter, 72017	Open		45.00	45
1995	Small King, 72004	Open		55.00	55
1987	Small King, 72030 - K.W.O.	Open		40.00	40
1995	Small Nightwatchman Elf, 72013	Open		45.00	45
1995	Small Santa's Elf, 72012	Open		45.00	45
1994	Small Santa, 72024	Open		42.00	42
1994	Small Skier, 72021	Open		44.00	44
1995	Small Sugar Plum Fairy, 72002	Open		55.00	55
1994	Small Toy Peddler, 72022	Open		44.00	44
1995	Small Wizard, 72005	Open		55.00	55
1993	Snowman, 7295	Open		110.00	110
1993	Sonnenberger Toy Peddler, 7256	Open		110.00	110
1987	Spanish Guard, 72046 - K.W.O.	Open		65.00	65
1993	Stained King with Crown, 72034 - K.W.O.	Open		65.00	65
1992	Swedish Officer, 72056 - K.W.O.	Open		67.50	68
1993	Teddy Bear, 7296	Retrd.	1994	135.00	135
1993	Tegernsee Golfer, 7259	Open		135.00	135
1993	Traditional Erzgebirge, 72067 - K.W.O.	Open		62.50	63
1993	Waldheimer Hunter, 7254	Open		110.00	110
1994	Waldkirchen Father Christmas 7276	Open		140.00	140
1993	Wittlicher Witch, 7268	Open		135.00	135
1994	Wyker Viking, 7283	Open		110.00	110

Paper Maché - E.M. Merck

YEAR ISSUE		EDITION LIMIT	YEAR RETD.	ISSUE PRICE	QUOTE U.S.$
1988	52 cm. Father Christmas 9652	Retrd.	1990	175.00	175
1988	Assorted Father Christmas 9615	Retrd.	1989	44.00	44
1989	Assorted Santas 9691	Retrd.	1991	35.00	35
1988	Blue Father Christmas 9602	Retrd.	1988	19.50	20
1988	Father Christmas (A) 9600	Retrd.	1988	19.50	20
1989	Father Christmas 9612	Retrd.	1989	38.50	39
1988	Father Christmas with Gifts 9610	Retrd.	1988	32.50	33
1989	Father Christmas with Pack 9638	Retrd.	1989	40.00	40
1988	Red Father Christmas 9601	Retrd.	1988	19.50	20
1989	Santa in Sleigh 9672	Retrd.	1989	39.50	40
1988	Small Traditional Belznickel 9662	Retrd.	1994	35.00	35
1988	Traditional Belznickel 9661	Retrd.	1994	40.00	40
1988	White Father Christmas 9603	Retrd.	1988	19.50	20
1988	White Father Christmas 9616	Retrd.	1989	50.00	50

Porcelain Christmas - E.M. Merck

YEAR ISSUE		EDITION LIMIT	YEAR RETD.	ISSUE PRICE	QUOTE U.S.$
1987	Angels, set of 3 9421	Retrd.	1987	15.50	16
1988	Bear on Skates Music Box 9492	Retrd.	1988	44.00	44
1988	Bunny on Skies Music Box 9491	Retrd.	1988	44.00	44
1987	Cast Iron Santa 9419	Retrd.	1993	35.00	40
1987	Cast Iron Santa on Horse 9418	Retrd.	1993	37.50	43
1995	Father Christmas 9710	Open		9.50	10
1987	Four Castles of Germany 9450	Retrd.	1988	31.00	40
1995	Frosty Friends 9706	Open		10.50	11
1995	Gifts for You 9709	Open		9.95	10
1995	Mr. C's Roadster 9708	Retrd.	1994	9.95	10
1995	Northern Light 9703	Open		9.95	10
1988	Penguin with Gifts Music Box 9493	Retrd.	1988	44.00	44
1995	Polar Express 9701	Open		8.95	9
1995	A Polar Visit 9704	Open		10.50	11
1987	Roly-Poly Santa 9440	Retrd.	1987	27.00	27
1987	Santa Head Night Light 9412	Retrd.	1989	19.00	26
1987	Santa Head Stocking Holder 9414	Retrd.	1987	18.00	22
1987	Santa Head Votive 9411	Retrd.	1988	10.00	15
1987	Santa in Chimney Music Box 9413	Retrd.	1987	44.00	44
1988	Santa in Swing 9473	Retrd.	1988	6.25	7
1988	Santa on Polar Bear 9471	Retrd.	1988	6.25	7
1988	Santa on Teeter-Totter 9475	Retrd.	1988	6.25	7
1988	Santa Visiting Igloo 9476	Retrd.	1988	6.25	7
1988	Santa Visiting Lighthouse 9472	Retrd.	1988	6.25	7
1988	Santa with Angel 9474	Retrd.	1988	6.25	7
1995	Santa's Express 9707	Open		10.50	11
1995	Swinging into the Season 9705	Retrd.	1994	10.50	11
1995	A Touch of Heaven 9702	Open		8.95	9

Pyramids - O.W.C., unless otherwise noted

YEAR ISSUE		EDITION LIMIT	YEAR RETD.	ISSUE PRICE	QUOTE U.S.$
1992	3-Tier Forest 882	Retrd.	1995	225.00	225
1992	3-Tier Nativity 883	Open		250.00	250
1991	3-Tier Painted Nativity 8818	Retrd.	1993	225.00	225
1992	4-Tier White with Music 8837 - K.W.O.	Open		550.00	550
1992	5ft Hand-Carved 884007	Retrd.	1992	1295.00	1295
1992	6ft Hand-Carved 884006	Retrd.	1992	4000.00	4000
1986	Angel Musicians 88001 - K.W.O.	Open		58.50	59
1991	Camel Caravan 8812	Retrd.	1995	92.50	93
1991	Deer in Forest 8810	Open		97.50	98
1992	Detailed Nativity 8851	Retrd.	1993	175.00	175
1992	Fairytale 888	Open		175.00	175
1992	Mini Natural Angel 8819	Open		42.50	43
1992	Mini Painted Angel 8823	Open		47.50	48
1992	Mini-Pyramid, Santa 8820	Retrd.	1994	32.50	33
1992	Miniature Choir 885	Retrd.	1995	35.00	35
1992	Miniature Forest 884	Retrd.	1994	35.00	35
1992	Miniature Music Band 886	Retrd.	1993	30.00	30
1991	Musical 4-Tier 8815	Retrd.	1991	775.00	775
1992	Natural with Deer 8821	Open		65.00	65
1992	Santa with Angels 887	Retrd.	1993	175.00	175
1991	Santa with Train 8817	Retrd.	1991	62.50	63
1992	Small Choir 8879	Retrd.	1993	68.50	69
1992	Small Nativity 8822	Open		110.00	110
1992	Small Nativity 889	Retrd.	1993	82.00	82
1992	Traditional 3-Tier 8826 - K.W.O.	Open		175.00	175
1992	Traditional 4-Tier 8836 - K.W.O.	Open		225.00	225
1991	White 3-Tier 8816	Retrd.	1992	225.00	225
1992	White with Angels 8824	Retrd.	1993	55.00	55

Smoking Men - O.W.C., unless otherwise noted

YEAR ISSUE		EDITION LIMIT	YEAR RETD.	ISSUE PRICE	QUOTE U.S.$
1992	Alpenhorn Player 7058	Open		70.00	70
1992	Angler with Crate 7062	Open		150.00	150
1988	Antique Style Coachman 70053 - K.W.O.	Retrd.	1988	28.00	28
1988	Antique Style Cook 70052 K.W.O.	Retrd.	1989	27.50	28
1988	Artist 70047 - K.W.O.	Open		50.00	50
1986	Artist 7020 - E.M. Merck	Retrd.	1993	55.00	55
1991	Baker 7044	Retrd.	1992	49.50	50
1993	Basket Peddler 70069 - K.W.O.	Open		58.50	59
1992	Basket Peddler 7040	Retrd.	1993	130.00	130
1991	Bavarian Hunter 7032	Retrd.	1994	79.50	80
1991	Beer Drinker 7033	Retrd.	1994	67.50	68
1988	Bird Seller 70046 - K.W.O.	Open		56.00	56
1991	Bird Seller 7014	Retrd.	1992	50.00	50
1987	Blacksmith 70041 - K.W.O.	Open		50.00	50
1991	Butcher 7043	Retrd.	1992	49.50	50
1992	Captain 7052	Open		80.00	80
1986	Carved Hunter 70100	Retrd.	1991	90.00	90
1992	Carved Hunter 7054	Retrd.	1993	200.00	200
1992	Carved King 7072	Open		68.50	69
1992	Carved Santa 7035	Open		67.50	68
1992	Carved Shepherd 7053	Retrd.	1993	150.00	150
1992	Carved Woodsman 7015	Retrd.	1994	67.50	68
1991	Champion Archer 7041	Open		67.50	68
1985	Chimney Sweep 70024 - K.W.O.	Open		47.50	48
1989	Chimney Sweep 7017 - E.M. Merck	Retrd.	1993	55.00	55
1992	Christmas Tree Vendor 709	Open		150.00	150
1992	Clock Salesman 7039	Retrd.	1992	275.00	275
1992	Coachman 70062 - K.W.O.	Open		50.00	50
1991	Coachman 7057	Retrd.	1992	60.00	60
1991	Cook 70061 - K.W.O.	Open		49.00	49
1991	Cook 7025	Retrd.	1993	55.00	55
1992	Farmer 7026	Retrd.	1993	55.00	55
1992	Farmer with Crate 7023	Retrd.	1994	150.00	150
1992	Father Christmas 70113-1	Retrd.	1989	45.00	45
1994	Father Christmas 70150 - K.W.O.	Open		110.00	110
1986	Father Christmas 702	Retrd.	1994	60.00	60
1991	Father Christmas 7051	Open		80.00	80
1993	Father Christmas 7063	Retrd.	1993	45.00	45
1986	Father Christmas with Toys 7010	Retrd.	1992	60.00	60
1987	Fisherman 70042 - K.W.O.	Open		49.50	50
1991	Fisherman 7029	Retrd.	1993	55.00	55
1991	Frosty Snowman 703	Retrd.	1993	22.50	23
1985	Gardener 70040 - K.W.O.	Open		57.00	57
1991	Gardener 7045	Retrd.	1992	49.50	50
1991	Gardner 7016 - E.M. Merck	Retrd.	1993	55.00	55
1994	Grandma 70077 - K.W.O.	Open		59.50	60
1992	Grandma 702622	Retrd.	1993	42.50	43
1985	Grandpa 702615	Retrd.	1993	42.50	43
1994	Grandpa at Oven 70073 - K.W.O.	Open		72.00	72
1994	Grandpa with Accordion 70076 - K.W.O.	Open		59.50	60
1993	Highwayman 70070 - K.W.O.	Open		50.00	50
1985	Hunter 70023 - K.W.O.	Open		49.50	50
1986	Hunter 701	Retrd.	1992	30.00	30
1991	Hunter 7018 - E.M. Merck	Retrd.	1993	55.00	55
1992	Hunter with Crate 7021	Retrd.	1994	150.00	150
1991	Ice Skater 7038 - E.M. Merck	Retrd.	1992	60.00	60
1992	Innkeeper 70268	Retrd.	1993	54.00	54
1991	Innkeeper 7037	Open		60.00	60
1992	King 70229 - E.M. Merck	Retrd.	1993	95.00	95
1993	Large Clock Peddler 70101 K.W.O.	Open		120.00	120
1993	Large Flower Peddler 70103 K.W.O.	Open		120.00	120
1985	Large Hunter 70021-9 - K.W.O.	Open		250.00	250
1986	Large Old World Santa 70203	Retrd.	1988	77.50	78
1993	Large Peddler 70066-9 - K.W.O.	Open		295.00	295
1993	Large Pottery Peddler 70104 K.W.O.	Open		120.00	120
1994	Large Red Santa 70064-9 K.W.O.	Open		270.00	270
1985	Large Toy Peddler Smoker 70020-9 - K.W.O.	Open		280.00	280
1995	Leprechaun Smoker 70110 E.M. Merck	Open		115.00	115
1992	Minstrel 7061	Retrd.	1994	85.00	85
1991	Mountain Climber 7036	Open		67.50	68
1994	Mushroom Collector 70071 K.W.O.	Open		50.00	50
1991	Natural Father Christmas 7012	Retrd.	1992	60.00	60
1991	Natural Santa 706	Retrd.	1992	40.00	40
1991	Nightwatchman 7027	Retrd.	1993	55.00	55
1985	Nightwatchman 7034	Retrd.	1993	32.50	33
1985	Nightwatchman Smoker 70022 K.W.O.	Open		48.50	49
1986	Old World Santa 70204	Retrd.	1988	42.50	43
1992	Peddler 70066 - K.W.O.	Open		59.50	60
1993	Poacher 70068 - K.W.O.	Open		47.50	48
1988	Postman 70048 - K.W.O.	Open		48.50	49
1991	Postman 7028	Retrd.	1993	55.00	55
1991	Prussian Soldier 7056	Retrd.	1993	60.00	60
1992	Red Santa 70064 - K.W.O.	Open		60.00	60
1992	Robber with Crate 7022	Open		150.00	150
1989	Santa 7086	Retrd.	1992	55.00	55
1991	Santa Claus 705	Retrd.	1993	45.00	45
1992	Santa in Crate 707	Retrd.	1994	165.00	165
1986	Santa Smoker/Candleholder 704	Retrd.	1994	55.00	55
1991	Santa with Toys 70060 - K.W.O.	Open		57.00	57
1987	Shepherd 70045 - K.W.O.	Open		49.00	49
1994	Sitting Hunter 70082 - K.W.O.	Open		60.00	60
1986	Skier 702616	Retrd.	1992	54.00	54
1992	Skier 7059	Open		59.50	60
1986	Small Old World Santa 70202	Retrd.	1988	37.50	38
1992	Small Santa 7011	Open		37.50	38
1985	Snowman 702621	Retrd.	1991	30.00	30
1991	Snowman on Skis 7092	Retrd.	1992	30.00	30
1988	Snowman with Bird 708	Open	1993	26.00	26
1992	St. Peter 70228	Retrd.	1993	95.00	95
1987	Tailor 70044 - K.W.O.	Open		50.00	50
1992	Teal Santa 70065 - K.W.O.	Open		60.00	60
1991	Toy Peddler 7030	Retrd.	1993	60.00	60
1991	Toy Peddler 7055	Retrd.	1993	60.00	60
1992	Toy Peddler 7060	Retrd.	1994	110.00	110
1985	Toy Peddler Smoker 70020 K.W.O.	Open		55.00	55
1992	Tyrolian 702613	Retrd.	1993	45.00	45
1992	White Santa 70063 - K.W.O.	Open		60.00	60
1992	Witch 70543 - E.M. Merck	Retrd.	1993	49.50	50
1991	Wood Worker 7031	Retrd.	1994	79.50	80
1987	Woodcarver 70043 - K.W.O.	Retrd.	1990	40.00	40
1991	Woodsman 7013	Retrd.	1993	60.00	60
1991	Woodsman 7019 - E.M. Merck	Retrd.	1993	55.00	55
1985	Woodsman Smoker 70021 - K.W.O.	Open		50.00	50
1994	Zither Player 70083 - K.W.O.	Open		63.00	63

FIGURINES/COTTAGES

Olszewski Studios

Olszewski Studios - R. Olszewski

YEAR ISSUE		EDITION LIMIT	YEAR RETD.	ISSUE PRICE	QUOTE U.S.$
1994	The Grand Entrance SM1	1,500	1994	225.00	280
1994	Tinker's Treasure Chest SM2	Closed	1994	235.00	475
1994	To Be (included w/Treasure Chest) SM3	Closed	1994	Set	Set
1994	The Little Tinker SM4	750	1995	235.00	250
1995	Special Treat SM5	800	1995	220.00	225
1995	Mockingbird	800	1995	230.00	230
1995	Lady With An Urn	1,000	1995	235.00	235

Pacific Rim Import Corp.

Bristol Township - Various

YEAR ISSUE		EDITION LIMIT	YEAR RETD.	ISSUE PRICE	QUOTE U.S.$
1990	Bedford Manor - P. Sebern	Open		30.00	30
1990	Black Swan Millinery - P. Sebern	Open		30.00	30
1991	Bridgestone Church - P. Sebern	Retrd.	1993	30.00	30
1990	Bristol Books - P. Sebern	Open		35.00	35
1995	Bristol Channel Lighthouse P. Sebern	Open		30.00	30
1990	Bristol Township Sign P. Sebern	Open		10.00	10
1993	Chesterfield House - P. Sebern	Open		30.00	30
1990	Coventry House - P. Sebern	Retrd.	1995	30.00	30
1991	Elmstone House - P. Sebern	Retrd.	1993	30.00	45
1991	Flower Shop - P. Sebern	Open		30.00	30
1993	Foxdown Manor - P. Sebern	Open		30.00	30
1990	Geo. Straith Grocer R. S. Benson	Open		25.00	25
1991	Hardwicke House - P. Sebern	Retrd.	1993	30.00	45
1990	High Gate Mill - P. Sebern	Open		40.00	40
1990	Iron Horse Livery - P. Sebern	Retrd.	1993	30.00	30
1991	Kilby Cottage - P. Sebern	Retrd.	1993	30.00	45
1995	King's Gate School - P. Sebern	Open		30.00	30
1990	Maps & Charts - P. Sebern	Open		25.00	25
1991	Pegglesworth Inn - P. Sebern	Retrd.	1995	40.00	40
1990	Queen's Road Church P. Sebern	Open		40.00	40
1994	Shotwick Inn/Surgery - P. Sebern	Open		35.00	35
1990	Silversmith - P. Sebern	Open		30.00	30
1990	Southwick Church - P. Sebern	Open		30.00	30
1994	Surrey Road Church - P. Sebern	Open		40.00	40
1990	Trinity Church - P. Sebern	Retrd.	1993	30.00	30
1990	Violin Shop - P. Sebern	Open		30.00	30
1990	Wexford Manor - P. Sebern	Open		25.00	25

Bristol Waterfront - P. Sebern

YEAR ISSUE		EDITION LIMIT	YEAR RETD.	ISSUE PRICE	QUOTE U.S.$
1992	Admiralty Shipping - P. Sebern	Open		30.00	30
1992	Avon Fish Co.	Open		30.00	30
1993	Bristol Point Lighthouse	Open		45.00	45
1994	Bristol Tattler	Open		40.00	40
1992	Chandler	Open		30.00	30
1992	Customs House	Open		40.00	40
1992	Hawke Exports	Open		40.00	40
1993	Lower Quay Chapel	Open		40.00	40
1994	Portshead Lighthouse	Open		30.00	30
1992	Quarter Deck Inn	Open		40.00	40
1992	Regent Warehouse	Open		40.00	40
1993	Rusty Knight Inn	Open		35.00	35

Bunny Toes - Various

YEAR ISSUE		EDITION LIMIT	YEAR RETD.	ISSUE PRICE	QUOTE U.S.$
1995	Annie With Strawberries P. Sebern	Open		15.00	15
1995	Bunny Gazebo - Pacific Rim Team	Open		50.00	50
1995	Bunny Toes Sign - P. Sebern	Open		20.00	20
1995	Garden Trellis - Pacific Rim Team	Open		30.00	30
1995	Hannah Strolls With Carriage Pacific Rim Team	Open		15.00	15
1995	Hannah With Maximillian Pacific Rim Team	Open		13.00	13
1994	Mazie at Play - Pacific Rim Team	Open		13.00	13
1994	Phoebe Goes Ballooning Pacific Rim Team	Open		7.00	7
1995	Rustic Garden Accessory Group (6 pcs) - P. Sebern	Open		40.00	40
1994	Sophie Pops Out - Pacific Rim Team	Open		7.00	7
1995	Spring Garden Accessory Group (6 pcs) - P. Sebern	Open		40.00	40
1994	Sweethearts (lighted) - Pacific Rim Team	Open		50.00	50
1994	Tillie Making a Wreath - Pacific Rim Team	Open		13.00	13
1995	Tillie With Her Bike - Pacific Rim Team	Open		15.00	15
1995	Timothy With Eggs - Pacific Rim Team	Open		13.00	13
1994	Timothy With Flower Cart Pacific Rim Team	Open		17.00	17
1994	Timothy With Tulips - Pacific Rim Team	Open		13.00	13
1995	Tommy's Joy Ride - P. Sebern	Open		15.00	15
1994	Wendell at the Mail Box - Pacific Rim Team	Open		17.00	17
1995	Wendell Play The Cello - Pacific Rim Team	Open		13.00	13
1994	Wendell With Eggs in Hat Pacific Rim Team	Open		13.00	13
1995	Wendell With Flowers - Pacific Rim Team	Open		13.00	13
1994	Willis & Skeeter - Pacific Rim Team	Open		17.00	17
1995	Willis & Skeeter Gardening Pacific Rim Team	Open		15.00	15
1995	Winifred Paints Eggs - Pacific Rim Team	Open		15.00	15
1994	Winifred With Blooms - Pacific Rim Team	Open		13.00	13

Bunny Toes Birthday Bunnies - P. Sebern

YEAR ISSUE		EDITION LIMIT	YEAR RETD.	ISSUE PRICE	QUOTE U.S.$
1995	Anabell Gliding Along	Open		20.00	20
1995	Beth Back to School	Open		20.00	20
1995	Callie Bundle Up	Open		20.00	20
1995	Carly Striking a Pose	Open		20.00	20
1995	Charlotte Best of the Bunch	Open		20.00	20
1995	Chester Sharing With Friends	Open		20.00	20
1995	Christopher & Cory The Best Shot	Open		20.00	20
1995	Dinah Irresistible	Open		20.00	20
1995	Douglas Frosty Friends	Open		20.00	20
1995	Goldie Taking Turns	Open		20.00	20
1995	Harvey Giddy-Up and Go	Open		20.00	20
1995	Jeremy Clear Sailing	Open		20.00	20
1995	Joey Autumn Chores	Open		20.00	20
1995	Maggie Joy of Giving	Open		20.00	20
1995	Molly Sweet Wishes	Open		20.00	20
1995	Nicholas Between Tides	Open		20.00	20
1995	Penelope Wishful Thinking	Open		20.00	20
1995	Phoebe First Outing	Open		20.00	20
1995	Pieter Higher Education	Open		20.00	20
1995	Russel & Robby Sharing the Harvest	Open		20.00	20
1995	Violet Thank You Notes	Open		20.00	20
1995	Wilbur Lazy Daze	Open		20.00	20
1995	Wiley Winter Games	Open		20.00	20
1995	Zachary Waitin' on the Wind	Open		20.00	20

Pemberton & Oakes

Zolan's Children - D. Zolan

YEAR ISSUE		EDITION LIMIT	YEAR RETD.	ISSUE PRICE	QUOTE U.S.$
1982	Erik and the Dandelion	17,000		48.00	90
1983	Sabina in the Grass	6,800		48.00	115
1985	Tender Moment	10,000		29.00	80
1984	Winter Angel	8,000		28.00	150

PenDelfin

PenDelfin Family Circle Collectors' Club - J. Heap

YEAR ISSUE		EDITION LIMIT	YEAR RETD.	ISSUE PRICE	QUOTE U.S.$
1993	Herald	Closed	1993	Gift	50
1993	Bosun	Closed	1993	50.00	100
1994	Buttons	Closed	1994	Gift	30
1994	Puffer	Yr.Iss.		85.00	85
1995	Bellman	Yr.Iss.		Gift	N/A
1995	Georgie and the Dragon	Yr.Iss.		125.00	125

40th Anniversary Piece - PenDelfin

YEAR ISSUE		EDITION LIMIT	YEAR RETD.	ISSUE PRICE	QUOTE U.S.$
1994	Aunt Ruby	10,000		275.00	275

Band Series - Various

YEAR ISSUE		EDITION LIMIT	YEAR RETD.	ISSUE PRICE	QUOTE U.S.$
XX	Bandstand - J. Heap	Open		70.00	85
XX	Casanova - J. Heap	Open		35.00	42
XX	Clanger - J. Heap	Open		35.00	42
1994	Mike - D. Roberts	Open		55.00	55
XX	Piano - D. Roberts	Open		25.00	30
XX	Rocky - J. Heap	Open		32.00	37
XX	Rolly - J. Heap	Open		17.50	22
XX	Rosa - J. Heap	Open		40.00	48
XX	Thumper - J. Heap	Open		25.00	32

Bed Series - Various

YEAR ISSUE		EDITION LIMIT	YEAR RETD.	ISSUE PRICE	QUOTE U.S.$
XX	Dodger - J. Heap	Open		24.00	28
1993	Forty Winks - D. Roberts	Open		57.00	57
XX	Parsley - D. Roberts	Open		25.00	30
XX	Peeps - J. Heap	Open		21.00	25
XX	Poppet - D. Roberts	Open		23.00	28
XX	Snuggles - J. Heap	Open		20.00	25
XX	Snuggles Awake - J. Heap	Open		60.00	63
1992	Sunny - D. Roberts	Open		40.00	43
1995	Teddy - D. Roberts	Open		45.00	45
XX	Twins - J. Heap	Open		25.00	30
XX	Victoria - J. Heap	Open		47.50	58
XX	Wakey - J. Heap	Open		24.00	28

Event Piece - J. Heap

YEAR ISSUE		EDITION LIMIT	YEAR RETD.	ISSUE PRICE	QUOTE U.S.$
1994	Event Piece	2-Yr.		75.00	75

Fisherman Series - Various

YEAR ISSUE		EDITION LIMIT	YEAR RETD.	ISSUE PRICE	QUOTE U.S.$
XX	The Jetty - J. Heap	Open		180.00	200
XX	The Raft - J. Heap	Open		70.00	80
XX	Whopper - D. Roberts	Open		35.00	43

Nursery Rhymes - Various

YEAR ISSUE		EDITION LIMIT	YEAR RETD.	ISSUE PRICE	QUOTE U.S.$
1956	Little Bo Peep - J. Heap	Retrd.	1959	2.00	N/A
1956	Little Jack Horner - J. Heap	Retrd.	1959	2.00	N/A
1956	Mary Mary Quite Contrary - J. Heap	Retrd.	1959	2.00	N/A
1956	Miss Muffet - J. Heap	Retrd.	1959	2.00	N/A
1956	Tom Tom the Piper's Son - J. Heap	Retrd.	1959	2.00	N/A
1956	Wee Willie Winkie - J. Heap	Retrd.	1959	2.00	N/A

Picnic Series - Various

YEAR ISSUE		EDITION LIMIT	YEAR RETD.	ISSUE PRICE	QUOTE U.S.$
XX	Barrow Boy - J. Heap	Open		35.00	45
XX	Oliver - D. Roberts	Open		25.00	30
XX	Picnic Island - J. Heap	Open		85.00	110
XX	Picnic Midge - J. Heap	Open		25.00	30
1994	Pipkin - J. Heap	Open		50.00	50
XX	Scrumpy - J. Heap	Open		35.00	42
1993	Vanilla - D. Roberts	Open		41.00	43

Retired Figurines - Various

YEAR ISSUE		EDITION LIMIT	YEAR RETD.	ISSUE PRICE	QUOTE U.S.$
1985	Apple Barrel - J. Heap	Retrd.	1992	N/A	15-25
1963	Aunt Agatha - J. Heap	Retrd.	1965	N/A	1500-2000
1955	Balloon Woman - J. Heap	Retrd.	1956	1.00	N/A
1967	The Bath Tub - J. Heap	Retrd.	1972	4.50	70-100
1955	Bell Man - J. Heap	Retrd.	1956	1.00	N/A
1984	Blossom - D. Roberts	Retrd.	1989	35.00	60-75
1955	Bobbin Woman - J. Heap	Retrd.	1956	N/A	N/A
1964	Bongo - D. Roberts	Retrd.	1987	31.00	75-150
1966	Cakestand - J. Heap	Retrd.	1972	2.00	250-500
1953	Cauldron Witch - J. Heap	Retrd.	1959	3.50	N/A
1959	Cha Cha - J. Heap	Retrd.	1961	N/A	1000-1200
1990	Charlotte - D. Roberts	Retrd.	1992	25.00	75-90
1989	Chirpy - D. Roberts	Retrd.	1992	31.50	60-100
1985	Christmas Set - D. Roberts	2,000	1989	N/A	450-550
1962	Cornish Prayer (Corny) - J. Heap	Retrd.	1965	N/A	500-900
1980	Crocker - D. Roberts	Retrd.	1989	20.00	60-75
1963	Cyril Squirrel - J. Heap	Retrd.	1965	N/A	750-1300
1955	Daisy Duck - J. Heap	Retrd.	1958	N/A	N/A
1956	Desmond Duck - J. Heap	Retrd.	1958	2.50	N/A
1955	Elf - J. Heap	Retrd.	1956	1.00	N/A
1954	Fairy Jardiniere - N/A	Retrd.	1958	N/A	N/A
1953	The Fairy Shop - J. Heap	Retrd.	1958	N/A	N/A
1961	Father Mouse (grey) - J. Heap	Retrd.	1966	N/A	500-750
1955	Flying Witch - J. Heap	Retrd.	1956	1.00	N/A
1969	The Gallery Series: Wakey, Pieface, Poppet, Robert, Dodger J. Heap	Retrd.	1971	N/A	200-400
1961	Grand Stand (mold 1) - J. Heap	Retrd.	1969	35.00	400-775
1960	Gussie - J. Heap	Retrd.	1968	N/A	400
1989	Honey - D. Roberts	Retrd.	1994	40.00	60
XX	Humphrey Go-Kart - J. Heap	Retrd.	1995	70.00	100
1986	Jim-Lad - D. Roberts	Retrd.	1992	22.50	45-75
1985	Jingle - D. Roberts	Retrd.	1992	11.25	25-45
XX	Little Mo - D. Roberts	Retrd.	1995	35.00	43
1961	Lollipop (grey) (Mouse) - J. Heap	Retrd.	1966	N/A	500-700
1960	Lucy Pocket - J. Heap	Retrd.	1967	4.20	300-400
1956	Manx Kitten - J. Heap	Retrd.	1958	2.00	N/A
1955	Margot - J. Heap	Retrd.	1961	2.00	350-550
1967	Maud - J. Heap	Retrd.	1970	N/A	300-550
1961	Megan - J. Heap	Retrd.	1967	3.00	400-500
1956	Midge (Replaced by Picnic Midge) - J. Heap	Retrd.	1965	2.00	300-600
1966	Milk Jug Stand - J. Heap	Retrd.	1972	2.00	250-500
1960	Model Stand - J. Heap	Retrd.	1964	4.00	400-750
1961	Mother Mouse (grey) - J. Heap	Retrd.	1966	N/A	450-800
1965	Mouse House (bronze) - J. Heap	Retrd.	1969	N/A	300-400
1965	Mouse House (stoneware) J. Heap	Retrd.	N/A	N/A	500-700
1965	Muncher - D. Roberts	Retrd.	1983	26.00	60-100
1981	Nipper - D. Roberts	Retrd.	1989	20.50	75
1955	Old Adam - J. Heap	Retrd.	1956	4.00	N/A
1955	Old Father (remodeled)- J. Heap	Retrd.	1970	50.	700-1000
1957	Old Mother - J. Heap	Retrd.	1978	6.25	550-800
1955	Original Father - J. Heap	Retrd.	1960	50.00	1000-1500
1956	Original Robert - J. Heap	Retrd.	1967	2.50	200-400
1953	Pendle Witch (stoneware) J. Heap	Retrd.	1957	4.00	800-1200
1967	Phumf - J. Heap	Retrd.	1985	24.00	75
1955	Phynnodderee (Commissioned-Exclusive) - J. Heap	Retrd.	N/A	1.00	N/A
1966	Picnic Basket - J. Heap	Retrd.	1968	2.00	350-600
1965	Picnic Stand - J. Heap	Retrd.	1985	62.50	150-175
1967	Picnic Table - J. Heap	Retrd.	1972	N/A	250-600
1966	Pieface - D. Roberts	Retrd.	1987	31.00	60-75
1965	Pixie Bods - J. Heap	Retrd.	1967	N/A	N/A
1953	Pixie House - J. Heap	Retrd.	1958	N/A	N/A
1962	Pooch - D. Roberts	Retrd.	1987	24.50	60-75
1958	Rabbit Book Ends - J. Heap	Retrd.	1965	10.00	1500-2000
1954	Rhinegold Lamp - J. Heap	Retrd.	1956	21.00	N/A
1967	Robert w/lollipop - D. Roberts	Retrd.	1979	12.00	100-250
1957	Romeo & Juliet - J. Heap	Retrd.	1959	11.00	N/A
1960	Shiner w/black eye - J. Heap	Retrd.	1967	2.50	300-500
XX	Shrimp Stand - D. Roberts	Retrd.	1995	70.00	80
1985	Solo - D. Roberts	Retrd.	1994	40.00	50-75
1960	Squeezy - J. Heap	Retrd.	1970	2.50	300-550
1957	Tammy - D. Roberts	Retrd.	1987	24.50	75
XX	Tennyson - D. Roberts	Retrd.	1995	35.00	42
1956	Timber Stand - J. Heap	Retrd.	1982	35.00	150-200
1953	Tipsy Witch - J. Heap	Retrd.	1959	3.50	N/A
1955	Toper - J. Heap	Retrd.	1956	1.00	N/A
1971	Totty - J. Heap	Retrd.	1981	21.00	150-250
1959	Uncle Soames - J. Heap	Retrd.	1985	105.00	300-400
1991	Wordsworth - D. Roberts	Retrd.	1994	60.00	75

School Series - Various

YEAR ISSUE		EDITION LIMIT	YEAR RETD.	ISSUE PRICE	QUOTE U.S.$
XX	Angelo - J. Heap	Open		90.00	95
XX	Boswell - J. Heap	Open		37.50	47
XX	Digit - D. Roberts	Open		35.00	38
XX	Duffy - J. Heap	Open		50.00	55
XX	Euclid - J. Heap	Open		35.00	38
XX	New Boy - D. Roberts	Open		50.00	55
XX	Old School House - J. Heap	Open		250.00	250

Sport Series - Various

YEAR ISSUE		EDITION LIMIT	YEAR RETD.	ISSUE PRICE	QUOTE U.S.$
XX	Birdie - J. Heap	Open		47.50	53
1993	Campfire - D. Roberts	Open		30.00	30
1995	Dobbin - J. Heap	Open		70.00	70

YEAR ISSUE		EDITION LIMIT	YEAR RETD.	ISSUE PRICE	QUOTE U.S.$
XX	Rambler - D. Roberts	Open		65.00	68
XX	Scout - D. Roberts	Open		100.00	100

Toy Shop Series - Various

XX	Jacky - D. Roberts	Open		45.00	48
XX	The Toy Shop - D. Roberts	Open		325.00	325

Various - Various

XX	Barney - J. Heap	Open		18.00	23
XX	Butterfingers - D. Roberts	Open		55.00	55
1993	Cousin Beau - D. Roberts	Open		55.00	55
XX	Dandy - D. Roberts	Open		50.00	60
XX	Mother with baby - J. Heap	Open		150.00	160
XX	Scoffer - D. Roberts	Open		55.00	55

Village Series - Various

XX	Balcony Scene - D. Roberts	Open		175.00	175
XX	Caravan - D. Roberts	Open		350.00	350
XX	Castle Tavern - D. Roberts	Open		120.00	130
XX	Cobble Cottage - D. Roberts	Open		80.00	90
XX	Curiosity Shop - J. Heap	Open		350.00	350
XX	Fruit Shop - J. Heap	Open		125.00	150
1992	Grand Stand (mold 2)- J. Heap	Open		150.00	150
XX	Large House - J. Heap	Open		275.00	300
1995	Robin's Cave (display piece) - J. Heap	Open		285.00	285

Polland Studios

Collector Society - D. Polland

1987	I Come In Peace	Closed	1987	35.00	400-600
1987	Silent Trail	Closed	1987	300.00	1300
1987	I Come In Peace, Silent Trail Matched Numbered Set	Closed	1987	335.00	15-1895
1988	The Hunter	Closed	1988	35.00	545
1988	Disputed Trail	Closed	1988	300.00	700-1045
1988	The Hunter, Disputed Trail Matched Numbered Set	Closed	1988	335.00	11-1450
1989	Crazy Horse	Closed	1989	35.00	300-470
1989	Apache Birdman	Closed	1989	300.00	700-970
1989	Crazy Horse, Apache Birdman Matched Numbered Set	Closed	1989	335.00	13-1700
1990	Chief Pontiac	Closed	1990	35.00	420
1990	Buffalo Pony	Closed	1990	300.00	600-800
1990	Chief Pontiac, Buffalo Pony Matched Numbered Set	Closed	1990	335.00	900-1350
1991	War Drummer	Closed	1991	35.00	330
1991	The Signal	Closed	1991	350.00	730
1991	War Drummer, The Signal Matched Numbered Set	Closed	1991	385.00	900-1150
1992	Cabinet Sign	Closed	1992	35.00	125
1992	Warrior's Farewell	Closed	1992	350.00	400
1992	Cabinet Sign, Warrior's Farewell Matched Numbered Set	Closed	1992	385.00	465
1993	Mountain Man	Closed	1993	35.00	125
1993	Blue Bonnets & Yellow Ribbon	Closed	1993	350.00	350-400
1993	Mountain Man, Blue Bonnets & Yellow Ribbon Matched Numbered Set	Closed	1993	385.00	385
1994	The Wedding Robe	Closed	1995	45.00	45
1994	The Courtship Race	Closed	1995	375.00	375
1994	The Wedding Robe, The Courtside Race Matched Numbered Set	Closed	1995	385.00	420

See also Lance Corporation Chilmark Pewter Polland Collector Society

Possible Dreams

Santa Claus Network® Collectors Club - Unknown

1992	The Gift Giver-805001	Closed	1993	Gift	40
1993	Santa's Special Friend-805050	Closed	1993	59.00	59
1993	Special Delivery-805002	Closed	1994	Gift	N/A
1994	On a Winter's Eve-805051	Closed	1994	65.00	65
1994	Jolly St. Nick-805003	Closed	1995	Gift	N/A
1995	Marionette Santa-805052	Yr.Iss.		50.00	50

The Citizens of Londonshire® - Unknown

1990	Admiral Waldo-713407	Open		65.00	68
1992	Albert-713426	Closed	1994	65.00	68
1991	Bernie-713414	Open		68.00	71
1992	Beth-713417	Open		35.00	37
1992	Christopher-713418	Open		35.00	37
1992	Countess of Hamlett-713419	Open		65.00	68
1992	David-713423	Open		37.50	39
1992	Debbie-713422	Open		37.50	39
1990	Dianne-713413	Open		33.00	35
1990	Dr. Isaac-713409	Closed	1995	65.00	68
1989	Earl of Hamlett-713400	Closed	1994	65.00	68
1992	Jean Claude-713421	Open		35.00	37
1989	Lady Ashley-713405	Open		65.00	68
1989	Lord Nicholas-713402	Open		72.00	76
1989	Lord Winston of Riverside-713403	Closed	1994	65.00	68
1994	Maggie-713428	Closed	1994	57.00	57
1990	Margaret of Foxcroft-713408	Open		65.00	68
1992	Nicole-713420	Open		35.00	37
1993	Nigel As Santa-713427	Open		53.50	56
1990	Officer Kevin-713406	Closed	1994	65.00	68
1990	Phillip-713412	Open		33.00	35
1992	Rebecca-713424	Open		35.00	37
1992	Richard-713425	Open		35.00	37
1989	Rodney-713404	Open		65.00	68
1991	Sir Red-713415	Closed	1994	72.00	76
1989	Sir Robert-713401	Open		65.00	68
1992	Tiffany Sorbet-713416	Open		65.00	68
1990	Walter-713410	Closed	1994	33.00	35
1990	Wendy-713411	Closed	1994	33.00	35

Clothtique® American Artist Collection™ - Various

1991	Alpine Christmas-15003 - J. Brett	Closed	1994	129.00	135
1992	An Angel's Kiss-15008 J. Griffith	Closed	1995	85.00	89
1993	A Beacon of Light-15022 J. Vaillancourt	Open		60.00	63
1993	A Brighter Day-15024 J. St. Denis	Open		67.50	70
1994	Captain Claus-15030 M. Monteiro	Open		77.00	77
1995	Christmas Caller-15035 J. Vaillancourt	Open		57.50	58
1992	Christmas Company-15011 T. Browning	Closed	1995	77.00	125
1994	Christmas Surprise-15033 M. Alvin	Open		88.00	88
1995	Country Sounds-15042 M. Monteiro	Open		74.00	74
1993	Easy Putt-15018 - T. Browning	Open		110.00	115
1991	Father Christmas-15007 J. Vaillancourt	Closed	1995	59.50	63
1993	Father Earth-15017 - M. Monteiro	Open		77.00	80
1991	A Friendly Visit-15005 T. Browning	Closed	1994	99.50	105
1994	The Gentle Craftsman-15031 J. Griffith	Open		81.00	81
1994	Gifts from the Garden-15032 J. Griffith	Open		77.00	77
1995	Giving Thanks-15045 - M. Alvin	Open		45.50	46
1995	A Good Round-15041 T. Browning	Open		73.00	73
1992	Heralding the Way-15014 J. Griffith	Closed	1995	72.00	75
1993	Ice Capers-15025 - T. Browning	Open		99.50	105
1993	Just Scooting Along-15023 J. Vaillancourt	Open		79.50	83
1992	Lighting the Way-15012 L. Bywaters	Open		85.00	89
1991	The Magic of Christmas-15001 L. Bywaters	Closed	1994	132.00	139
1992	Music Makers-15010 T. Browning	Closed	1995	135.00	165
1993	Nature's Love-15016 - M. Alvin	Open		75.00	79
1992	Out of the Forest-15013 J. Vaillancourt	Closed	1995	60.00	68
1995	Patchwork Santa-15039 J. Cleveland	Open		67.50	68
1992	Peace on Earth-15009 - M. Alvin	Closed	1995	87.50	92
1991	A Peaceful Eve-15002 L. Bywaters	Closed	1994	99.50	105
1995	Riding High-15040 - L. Nillson	Open		115.00	115
1994	Santa and Feathered Friend-15026 - D. Wenzel	Open		84.00	84
1995	Santa and the Ark-15038 J. Griffith	Open		71.50	72
1992	Santa in Rocking Chair-713090 M. Monteiro	Closed	1995	85.00	100
1991	Santa's Cuisine-15006 T. Browning	Closed	1994	138.00	148
1995	Southwest Santa-15043 V. Wiseman	Open		65.00	65
1994	Spirit of Christmas Past-15036 - J. Vaillancourt	Open		79.00	79
1994	Spirit of Santa-15028 T. Browning	Open		68.00	68
1995	The Storyteller-15029 T. Browning	Open		76.00	76
1993	Strumming the Lute-15015 M. Alvin	Open		79.00	83
1995	Sunflower Santa-15044 J. Griffith	Open		75.00	75
1994	Tea Time-15034 - M. Alvin	Open		90.00	90
1994	Teddy Love-15037 - J. Griffith	Open		89.00	89
1994	A Touch of Magic-15027 T. Browning	Open		95.00	95
1991	Traditions-15004 - T. Blackshear	Closed	1994	50.00	65
1993	The Tree Planter-15020 J. Griffith	Open		79.50	84
1993	The Workshop-15019 T. Browning	Closed	1995	140.00	150

Clothtique® Limited Edition Santas - Unknown

1988	Father Christmas-3001	10,000	1993	240.00	240
1988	Kris Kringle-3002	10,000	1992	240.00	240
1988	Patriotic Santa-3000	10,000	1994	240.00	240
1989	Traditional Santa 40's-3003	10,000	1994	240.00	252

Clothtique® Pepsi® Santa Collection - Various

1994	Holiday Host-3605 - Unknown	Open		62.00	62
1995	Jolly Traveler-3606 - B. Prata	Open		90.00	90
1990	Pepsi Cola Santa 1940's-3601 Unknown	Open		68.00	74
1992	Pepsi Santa Sitting-3603 Unknown	Closed	1994	84.00	95
1991	Rockwell Pepsi Santa 1952-3602 - N. Rockwell	Closed	1994	75.00	82

Clothtique® Santas Collection - Unknown

1992	1940's Traditional Santa-713049	Closed	1994	44.00	65
1992	African American Santa-713056	Closed	1995	65.00	68
1993	African-American Santa w/ Doll-713102	Open		40.00	42
1989	Baby's First Christmas-713042	Closed	1992	42.00	46
1995	Baby's First Noel-713120	Open		62.00	62
1988	Carpenter Santa-713033	Closed	1992	38.00	44
1994	Christmas Cheer-713109	Open		58.00	58
1994	A Christmas Guest-713112	Open		79.00	79
1994	Christmas is for Children-713115	Open		62.00	62
1986	Christmas Man-713027	Closed	1989	34.50	35
1987	Colonial Santa-713032	Closed	1990	38.00	40
1995	Down Hill Santa-713123	Open		66.50	67
1992	Engineer Santa-713057	Closed	1995	130.00	137
1993	European Santa-713095	Open		53.00	55
1989	Exhausted Santa-713043	Closed	1992	60.00	65
1991	Father Christmas-713087	Closed	1993	43.00	47
1995	Finishing Touch-713121	Open		54.70	55
1993	Fireman & Child-713106	Open		55.00	58
1992	Fireman Santa-713053	Open		60.00	63
1995	Frisky Friend-713130	Open		45.50	46
1988	Frontier Santa-713034	Closed	1991	40.00	42
1994	Good Tidings-713107	Open		51.00	51
1990	Harlem Santa-713046	Closed	1994	46.00	55
1993	His Favorite Color-713098	Open		48.00	50
1994	Holiday Friend-713110	Open		104.00	104
1995	Home Spun Holidays-713128	Open		49.50	50
1995	Hook Line and Santa-713129	Open		49.70	50
1991	Kris Kringle-713088	Closed	1993	43.00	46
1993	A Long Trip-713105	Open		95.00	100
1993	May Your Wishes Come True-713096	Open		59.00	62
1993	The Modern Shopper-713103	Open		40.00	42
1994	A Most Welcome Visitor-713113	Open		63.00	63
1991	Mrs. Claus in Coat -713078	Closed	1995	47.00	56-65
1989	Mrs. Claus w/doll-713041	Closed	1992	42.00	43
1994	Mrs. Claus-713118	Open		58.00	58
1992	Nicholas-713052	Closed	1994	57.50	60
1994	Our Hero-713116	Open		62.00	62
1989	Pelze Nichol-713039	Closed	1993	40.00	47
1994	Playmates-713111	Open		104.00	104
1994	Puppy Love-713117	Open		62.00	62
1988	Russian St. Nicholas-713036	Open		40.00	43
1990	Santa "Please Stop Here"-713045	Closed	1992	63.00	66
1991	Santa Decorating Christmas Tree-713079	Closed	1992	60.00	60
1991	Santa in Bed-713076	Closed	1994	76.00	83
1992	Santa on Motorbike-713054	Closed	1994	115.00	130
1992	Santa on Reindeer-713058	Closed	1995	75.00	83
1992	Santa on Sled-713050	Closed	1994	75.00	79
1992	Santa on Sleigh-713091	Closed	1995	79.00	83
1991	Santa Shelf Sitter-713089	Closed	1995	55.50	60
1990	Santa w/Blue Robe-713048	Closed	1992	46.00	50
1989	Santa w/Embroidered Coat-713040	Closed	1991	43.00	43
1993	Santa w/Groceries-713099	Open		47.50	50
1986	Santa w/Pack-713026	Closed	1989	34.50	35
1991	Siberian Santa-713077	Closed	1993	49.00	52
1990	Skiing Santa -713047	Closed	1993	62.00	65
1995	Sounds of Christmas-713127	Open		57.50	58
1995	A Special Treat-713122	Open		50.50	51
1988	St. Nicholas-713035	Closed	1991	40.00	42
1995	The Stockings Were Hung-713126	Open		N/A	N/A
1987	Traditional Deluxe Santa-713030	Closed	1990	38.00	38
1986	Traditional Santa-713028	Closed	1989	34.50	125
1989	Traditional Santa-713038	Closed	1992	42.00	43
1991	The True Spirit of Christmas-713075	Closed	1992	97.00	97
1987	Ukko-713031	Closed	1990	38.00	38
1995	Victorian Evergreen-713125	Open		49.00	49
1995	Victorian Puppeteer-713124	Open		51.50	52
1993	Victorian Santa-713097	Open		55.50	58
1988	Weihnachtsman-713037	Closed	1991	40.00	43
1994	A Welcome Visit-713114	Open		62.00	62
1990	Workbench Santa-713044	Closed	1993	72.00	76
1994	Yuletide Journey-713108	Open		58.00	58

Clothtique® Saturday Evening Post J. C. Leyendecker - J. Leyendecker

1991	Hugging Santa-3599	Closed	1994	129.00	150
1992	Santa on Ladder-3598	Closed	1995	135.00	142
1991	Traditional Santa-3600	Closed	1992	100.00	125

Clothtique® Saturday Evening Post Norman Rockwell - N. Rockwell

1992	Balancing the Budget-3064	Open		120.00	126
1989	Christmas "Dear Santa"-3050	Closed	1992	160.00	180
1989	Christmas "Santa with Globe"-3051	Closed	1992	154.00	175
1991	Doctor and Doll-3055	Closed	1995	196.00	206
1991	The Gift-3057	Open		160.00	168
1991	Gone Fishing-3054	Closed	1995	250.00	263
1991	Gramps at the Reins-3058	Open		290.00	305
1990	Hobo-3052	Open		159.00	167
1990	Love Letters-3053	Open		172.00	180
1991	Man with Geese-3059	Open		120.00	126
1992	Marriage License-3062	Open		195.00	205
1991	Santa Plotting His Course-3060	Open		160.00	168
1992	Santa's Helpers-3063	Closed	1994	170.00	179
1991	Springtime-3056	Open		130.00	137
1992	Triple Self Portrait-3061	Closed	1995	230.00	250

Clothtique® Signature Series® - Stanley/Chang

1995	Department Store Santa, USA/Circa 1940s-721001	Open		108.00	108
1995	Father Christmas, England/Circa 1890s-721002	Open		90.00	90

The Thickets at Sweetbriar® - B. Ross

1995	Angel Dear-350123	Open		32.00	32

Year	Issue	Edition Limit	Year Retd.	Issue Price	Quote U.S.$
1993	The Bride-Emily Feathers-350112	Open		30.00	30
1995	Buttercup-350121	Open		32.00	32
1995	Cecily Pickwick-350125	Open		32.00	32
1995	Clem Jingles-350130	Open		37.00	37
1993	Clovis Buttons-350101	Open		24.15	25
1993	The Groom-Oliver Doone-350111	Open		30.00	30
1993	Jewel Blossom-350106	Open		36.75	37
1995	Katy Hollyberry-350124	Open		35.00	35
1995	Kris Krinkle-350414	Open		12.50	13
1994	Lady Slipper-350116	Open		20.00	20
1993	Lily Blossom-350105	Open		36.75	37
1993	Maude Tweedy-350100	Closed	1994	26.25	27
1994	Morning Dew-350113	Open		30.00	30
1993	Morning Glory-350104	Open		30.45	31
1993	Mr. Claws-350109	Open		34.00	34
1993	Mrs. Claws-350110	Open		34.00	34
1993	Orchid Beasley-350103	Open		26.25	27
1995	Parsley Divine-350129	Open		37.00	37
1993	Peablossom Thorndike-350102	Closed	1994	26.25	27
1995	Penny Pringle-350128	Open		32.00	32
1995	Pittypat-350122	Open		32.00	32
1994	Precious Petals-350115	Open		34.00	34
1993	Raindrop-350108	Open		47.25	48
1995	Riley Pickens-350127	Open		32.00	32
1993	Rose Blossom-350107	Open		36.75	37
1994	Sunshine-350118	Open		33.00	33
1994	Sweetie Flowers-350114	Open		33.00	33
1995	Tillie Lilly-350120	Open		32.00	32
1995	Timmy Evergreen-350126	Open		29.00	29
1995	Violet Wiggles-350119	Open		32.00	32

Precious Art/Panton

Krystonia Collector's Club - Panton

Year	Issue	Edition Limit	Year Retd.	Issue Price	Quote U.S.$
1989	Pultzr	Retrd.	1990	55.00	500
1989	Key	Retrd.	1990	Gift	100-130
1991	Dragons Play	Retrd.	1992	65.00	200-400
1991	Kephrens Chest	Retrd.	1992	Gift	130
1992	Vaaston	Retrd.	1993	65.00	120-220
1992	Lantern	Retrd.	1993	Gift	80-100
1993	Sneaking A Peak	Retrd.	1994	Gift	N/A
1993	Spreading His Wings	Retrd.	1994	60.00	100-105
1994	All Tuckered Out	Retrd.	1995	65.00	65
1994	Filler-Up	Retrd.	1995	Gift	N/A
1995	Twingnuk	Yr.Iss.		55.00	55
1995	Kappah Krystal	Yr.Iss.		Gift	N/A

World of Krystonia - Panton

Year	Issue	Edition Limit	Year Retd.	Issue Price	Quote U.S.$
1992	Azael -3811	Retrd.	1995	85.00	85
1989	Babul -1402	Retrd.	1995	25.00	25
1994	Boll-3912	Retrd.	1994	52.00	52
1989	Caught At Last! -1107	Retrd.	1992	150.00	225
1992	Dubious Alliance -1109	Retrd.	1995	195.00	195
1991	Flayla w/Sumbly -1105	Retrd.	1995	104.00	104
1980	Gateway to Kystonia-3301	Retrd.	1994	35.00	45
1987	Grackene -1051	Retrd.	1995	50.00	50
1989	Graffyn on Grunch (waterglobe) -9006	Retrd.	1992	42.00	150
1987	Groc -1044	Retrd.	1995	50.00	50
1987	Grumblypeg Grunch -1081	Retrd.	1992	52.00	110
1989	Kephren -2702	Retrd.	1994	56.00	65
1989	Krystonia Sign -701	Retrd.	1993	N/A	25
1987	Large Graffyn on Grumblypeg Grunch -1011	Retrd.	1992	52.00	110
1991	Large Grunch's Toothache -1082	Retrd.	1994	76.00	80
1987	Large Haapf -1901	Retrd.	1991	38.00	85-125
1987	Large Krak N'Borg -3001	Retrd.	1990	240.00	250-500
1987	Large Moplos -1021	Retrd.	1991	90.00	205-400
1987	Large Myzer -1201	Retrd.	1991	50.00	90-130
1987	Large N' Chakk -2101	Retrd.	1995	140.00	140
1987	Large N'Borg -1092	Retrd.	1994	98.00	140
1988	Large N'Grall -2201	Retrd.	1990	108.00	250
1987	Large Rueggan -1701	Retrd.	1989	55.00	175-300
1987	Large Turfen -1601	Retrd.	1991	50.00	75-100
1987	Large Wodema -1301	Retrd.	1990	50.00	120
1991	Maj-Dron Migration -1108	Retrd.	1994	145.00	155
1988	Medium N'Grall -2202	Retrd.	1994	70.00	80
1988	Medium Rueggan -1702	Retrd.	1993	48.00	70
1987	Medium Stoope -1101	Retrd.	1990	52.00	225
1987	Medium Wodema -1302	Retrd.	1993	44.00	70
1992	Mini N' Grall -611	Retrd.	1995	27.00	27
1992	N' Leila-3801	Retrd.	1994	60.00	65
1991	N'Borg-Mini -609	Retrd.	1994	29.00	29
1990	N'Chakk-Mini -607	Retrd.	1994	29.00	29
1990	Owhey (waterglobe) -9004	Retrd.	1995	42.00	100
1987	Owhey -1071	Retrd.	1990	32.00	100
1990	Shadra -3401	Retrd.	1994	30.00	35
1987	Small Graffyn/Grunch -1012	Retrd.	1989	45.00	155-255
1987	Small Groc -1042B	Retrd.	1987	24.00	4600
1987	Small Krak N' Borg -3003	Retrd.	1993	60.00	175
1987	Small N' Borg -1091	Retrd.	1989	50.00	225
1987	Small N' Tormet -2602	Retrd.	1993	44.00	65
1988	Small Rueggau -1703	Retrd.	1995	42.00	42
1987	Small Shepf -1152	Retrd.	1990	40.00	100
1987	Small Stoope -1102	Retrd.	1995	46.00	46
1988	Small Tulan Captain -2502	Retrd.	1991	44.00	80
1987	Spyke -1061	Retrd.	1993	50.00	80
1989	Stoope (waterglobe) -9003	Retrd.	1991	40.00	156
1988	Tarnhold-Med. -3202	Retrd.	1992	120.00	175
1987	Tarnhold-Small -3203	Retrd.	1995	60.00	60
1988	Tokkel -2401	Retrd.	1995	42.00	42
1992	Zanzibar -3431	Retrd.	1994	45.00	50

Princeton Gallery

Baby bird Trios - Unknown

Year	Issue	Edition Limit	Year Retd.	Issue Price	Quote U.S.$
1991	Cardinals	Open		45.00	45
1991	Woodland Symphony (Bluebirds)	Open		45.00	45

Enchanted Nursery - Unknown

Year	Issue	Edition Limit	Year Retd.	Issue Price	Quote U.S.$
1992	Caprice	Open		57.00	57
1993	Pegasus	Open		57.00	57

Garden Capers - Unknown

Year	Issue	Edition Limit	Year Retd.	Issue Price	Quote U.S.$
1990	Any Mail?	Open		29.50	30
1991	Blue Jays	Open		29.50	30
1992	Bluebird, Spring Planting	Open		29.50	30
1992	Goldfinch, Home Sweet Home	Open		29.50	30
1991	Robin	Open		29.50	30

Lady And The Unicorn - Unknown

Year	Issue	Edition Limit	Year Retd.	Issue Price	Quote U.S.$
1992	Love's Innocence	Open		119.00	119

Pegasus - Unknown

Year	Issue	Edition Limit	Year Retd.	Issue Price	Quote U.S.$
1992	Wings of Magic	Open		95.00	95

Playful Pups - Unknown

Year	Issue	Edition Limit	Year Retd.	Issue Price	Quote U.S.$
1990	Beagle	Open		19.50	20
1990	Dalmation-Where's The Fire	Open		19.50	20
1991	Labrador Retriever	Open		19.50	20
1991	St. Bernard	Open		19.50	20
1991	Wrinkles (Shar Pei)	Open		19.50	20

Unicorn Collection - Unknown

Year	Issue	Edition Limit	Year Retd.	Issue Price	Quote U.S.$
1991	Christmas Unicorn	Yr.Iss.		85.00	85
1993	Love's Courtship	Open		95.00	95
1990	Love's Delight	Open		75.00	75
1991	Love's Devotion	Open		119.00	119
1992	Love's Fancy	Open		95.00	95
1991	Love's Majesty	Open		95.00	95
1991	Love's Purity	Open		95.00	95
1990	Love's Sweetness	Open		75.00	75

R.R. Creations, Inc.

Collectors' Club - D. Ross

Year	Issue	Edition Limit	Year Retd.	Issue Price	Quote U.S.$
1994	Cape Cod 9400	Retrd.	1994	9.95	10
1995	Grist Mill 9500	12/95		11.95	12

Accessories - D. Ross

Year	Issue	Edition Limit	Year Retd.	Issue Price	Quote U.S.$
1989	4" Brick Fence 8913	Retrd.	1991	3.75	4
1987	4" Corral Fence 8726	Retrd.	1992	3.60	4
1989	4" Fence 8917	Retrd.	1992	3.25	4
1991	4" Fence w/ Tree 9124	Open		7.20	8
1989	8" Brick Fence 8912	Retrd.	1991	3.75	4
1990	Cactus Set/2 9014	Retrd.	1992	2.80	3
1993	Honey Pine Shelf 9333	Open		9.95	12
1990	Large Flag Pole 9017	Open		2.95	4
1989	Large Lamp Post 8911	Open		2.75	5
1990	Mainstreet Sign 9018	Open		2.75	4
1990	Natural Windmill 9019	Retrd.	1992	3.60	4
1991	Oak Tree 9123	Open		3.50	5
1992	Pine Tree 9250	Open		3.50	5
1989	Pine Tree w/Bow other side 8915	Retrd.	1991	3.75	4
1989	Shade Tree 8914	Retrd.	1991	3.75	4
1992	Sisters Sled 9252	Open		5.95	7
1992	Small Flag Pole 9251	Retrd.	1994	2.95	3
1992	Small Lamp Post 9254	Retrd.	1994	2.95	3
1990	Sunflower 9016	Open		2.80	4
1989	Trees 8914	Retrd.	1991	3.25	4
1992	Trolley 9255	Retrd.	1994	5.95	6
1987	Welcome Mat 8717	Retrd.	1994	1.80	2
1993	Welcome R.R. Sign 9332	Retrd.	1994	4.50	5
1990	Wheat 9015	Open		2.80	4
1987	Windmill 8725	Open		3.60	4

Amish Accessories - D. Ross

Year	Issue	Edition Limit	Year Retd.	Issue Price	Quote U.S.$
1990	Amish Buggy 9013	Open		4.40	7
1991	Amish Family 9120	Open		4.40	7
1993	Amish Garden 9330	Open		5.95	7
1991	Amish Outhouse 9104	Open		4.25	5
1994	Buggies in a Row 9432	Open		6.50	7
1992	Clothesline 9253	Open		2.95	7
1994	Cows 9434	Open		6.50	7
1994	Milk Cans 9433	Open		6.50	7
1994	No Sunday Sales 9431	Open		3.60	4
1991	Slow Moving Vehicle 9121	Open		2.95	4

Amish Collection Series I - D. Ross

Year	Issue	Edition Limit	Year Retd.	Issue Price	Quote U.S.$
1991	Amish Barn 9102	Retrd.	1994	8.95	11
1991	Amish House 9101	Retrd.	1994	8.95	11
1991	Amish School 9103	Retrd.	1994	8.95	11
1992	Barn Raising 9220	Retrd.	1994	8.95	11
1992	Quilt Shop 9204	Retrd.	1994	8.95	11

Amish Collection Series II - D. Ross

Year	Issue	Edition Limit	Year Retd.	Issue Price	Quote U.S.$
1993	Blacksmith 9329	12/95		8.95	11
1993	Harness & Buggy 9331	12/95		8.95	11
1993	Troyer Bakery 9328	12/95		8.95	11

Author Collection Series I - D. Ross

Year	Issue	Edition Limit	Year Retd.	Issue Price	Quote U.S.$
1994	Edgar Allan Poe 9403	2,500		11.00	11
1994	Harriet Beecher Stowe 9404	2,500		11.00	11
1994	Mark Twain 9401	2,500		11.00	11

Christmas Memories Series I - D. Ross

Year	Issue	Edition Limit	Year Retd.	Issue Price	Quote U.S.$
1992	Christmas Chapel 9216	Retrd.	1994	8.95	11
1992	Christmas F Douglass 9218	Retrd.	1994	8.95	11
1992	Daniel Boone 9219	Retrd.	1994	8.95	11

Christmas Memories Series II - D. Ross

Year	Issue	Edition Limit	Year Retd.	Issue Price	Quote U.S.$
1993	Boscobel 9320	12/95		8.95	11
1993	Christmas Church 9318	12/95		8.95	11
1993	Dell House 9321	12/95		8.95	11
1992	Sister Sled 9252	Open		5.95	7

Christmas Memories Series III - D. Ross

Year	Issue	Edition Limit	Year Retd.	Issue Price	Quote U.S.$
1995	Apothecary 9513	2,500		11.00	11
1995	Butcher 9515	2,500		11.00	11
1995	Cobbler 9514	2,500		11.00	11

Colonial Collection Series I - D. Ross

Year	Issue	Edition Limit	Year Retd.	Issue Price	Quote U.S.$
1989	Boot & Shoemaker 8910	Retrd.	1993	8.95	9
1989	Colonial Inn 8903	Retrd.	1993	8.95	9
1989	Easton House 8918	Retrd.	1993	8.95	9
1989	Silversmith 8909	Retrd.	1993	8.95	9
1989	Tavern 8908	Retrd.	1993	8.95	9

Colonial Collection Series II - D. Ross

Year	Issue	Edition Limit	Year Retd.	Issue Price	Quote U.S.$
1989	C.L. Edwards 8901	Retrd.	1994	8.95	11
1989	Dry Good 8904	Retrd.	1994	8.95	11
1989	G. Dressmaker 8920	Retrd.	1994	8.95	11
1989	Kiistner 8902	Retrd.	1994	8.95	11
1989	Town Hall 8906	Retrd.	1994	8.95	11

Court House Collection - D. Ross

Year	Issue	Edition Limit	Year Retd.	Issue Price	Quote U.S.$
1989	Chase Country 8924	Retrd.	1993	8.95	9
1990	Franklin County 9011	Retrd.	1993	8.95	9
1990	Mount Holly 9010	Retrd.	1993	8.95	9

Grandpa's Farm Coll. Series I (No Open Window/Printed Both Sides) - D. Ross

Year	Issue	Edition Limit	Year Retd.	Issue Price	Quote U.S.$
1987	Barn 8721	Retrd.	1992	8.95	9
1987	Chicken Coop 8722	Retrd.	1992	6.50	7
1987	Farm House 8720	Retrd.	1992	8.95	9
1987	Outhouse 8724	Retrd.	1992	4.25	5
1987	Wash House 8723	Retrd.	1992	6.00	6

Grandpa's Farm Collection Series II - D. Ross

Year	Issue	Edition Limit	Year Retd.	Issue Price	Quote U.S.$
1993	Chicken Coop 9326	12/95		6.50	11
1993	Hofacre House 9323	12/95		8.95	11
1993	New Barn 9324	12/95		8.95	11
1992	Outhouse 9327	Open		4.25	5
1993	Wash House 9325	12/95		6.50	11

Historical Collection Series I - D. Ross

Year	Issue	Edition Limit	Year Retd.	Issue Price	Quote U.S.$
1992	Canfield 9205	Retrd.	1994	8.95	11
1992	Hexagon 9208	Retrd.	1994	8.95	11
1992	Lincoln 9217	Retrd.	1994	8.95	11
1992	Smith-Bly 9201	Retrd.	1994	8.95	11
1992	Susan B. Anthony 9222	Retrd.	1994	8.95	11

Historical Collection Series II - D. Ross

Year	Issue	Edition Limit	Year Retd.	Issue Price	Quote U.S.$
1993	Betsy Ross 9305	12/95		8.95	11
1993	Kennedy Home 9308	12/95		8.95	11
1993	Stone House 9319	12/95		8.95	11

In The Country Series I - D. Ross

Year	Issue	Edition Limit	Year Retd.	Issue Price	Quote U.S.$
1989	Church 8905	Retrd.	1993	8.95	9
1990	Grist Mill 9001	Retrd.	1993	8.95	9
1989	School 8907	Retrd.	1993	8.95	9

In The Country Series II - D. Ross

Year	Issue	Edition Limit	Year Retd.	Issue Price	Quote U.S.$
1993	Country Church 9322	12/95		8.95	11
1993	Country Livin' Shop 9307	12/95		8.95	11
1993	Toll House 9301	12/95		8.95	11

In The Country Series III - D. Ross

Year	Issue	Edition Limit	Year Retd.	Issue Price	Quote U.S.$
1995	Depot 9512	2,500		11.00	11
1995	Grist Mill 9510	2,500		11.00	11
1995	School House 9511	2,500		11.00	11

Inn Collection Series I - D. Ross

Year	Issue	Edition Limit	Year Retd.	Issue Price	Quote U.S.$
1994	Black Horse Inn 9411	2,500		11.00	11
1994	Herlong Mansion 9412	2,500		11.00	11
1994	Nathaniel Porter Inn 9410	2,500		11.00	11

Landmark Collection Series I - D. Ross

Year	Issue	Edition Limit	Year Retd.	Issue Price	Quote U.S.$
1994	Locust Grove 9405	2,500		11.00	11
1994	Longfellow 9408	2,500		11.00	11
1994	Melrose 9409	2,500		11.00	11

Lighthouse Collection Series I - D. Ross

Year	Issue	Edition Limit	Year Retd.	Issue Price	Quote U.S.$
1994	Mystic Sea Port 9406	2,500		11.00	11
1994	Old Point Betsie 9402	2,500		11.00	11
1994	Quoddy Head 9407	2,500		11.00	11

Lighthouse Collection Series II - D. Ross

Year	Issue	Edition Limit	Year Retd.	Issue Price	Quote U.S.$
1995	Block Island S.E. 9506	2,500		11.00	11
1995	Drum Point Lighthouse 9504	2,500		11.00	11

YEAR ISSUE		EDITION LIMIT	YEAR RETD.	ISSUE PRICE	QUOTE U.S.$
1995	Old Port Boca 9505	2,500		11.00	11

Main Street Collection Series I - D. Ross

YEAR ISSUE		EDITION LIMIT	YEAR RETD.	ISSUE PRICE	QUOTE U.S.$
1989	Barron Theatre 8922	Retrd.	1993	8.95	9
1989	Gas Station 8923	Retrd.	1993	8.95	9
1989	Kingman Firehouse 8919	Retrd.	1993	8.95	9
1990	Library 9007	Retrd.	1993	8.95	9
1989	Myerstown Depot 8921	Retrd.	1993	8.95	9
1990	Santa Fe Depot 9006	Retrd.	1993	8.95	9
1991	Telephone Company 9107	Retrd.	1993	8.95	9

Main Street Collection Series II - D. Ross

YEAR ISSUE		EDITION LIMIT	YEAR RETD.	ISSUE PRICE	QUOTE U.S.$
1992	Bakery 9212	Retrd.	1994	8.95	11
1992	Bank 9211	Retrd.	1994	8.95	11
1992	Beauty Shop 9209	Retrd.	1994	8.95	11
1991	Chautaqua Hills Jelly 9105	Retrd.	1994	8.95	11
1989	Harrold's Hardware 8925	Retrd.	1994	8.95	11
1992	Oak Brook Fire Co. 9207	Retrd.	1994	8.95	11

Nostalgia Collection Series I - D. Ross

YEAR ISSUE		EDITION LIMIT	YEAR RETD.	ISSUE PRICE	QUOTE U.S.$
1995	Drive In 9507	2,500		11.00	11
1995	Mae's Diner 9508	2,500		11.00	11
1995	Soda Shop 9509	2,500		11.00	11

On the Square I (No Open Window/Printed Both Sides) - D. Ross

YEAR ISSUE		EDITION LIMIT	YEAR RETD.	ISSUE PRICE	QUOTE U.S.$
1987	Antique Shop 8708	Retrd.	1992	8.95	9
1987	Bakery 8710	Retrd.	1992	8.95	9
1987	Book Store 8709	Retrd.	1992	8.95	9
1987	Candle Shop 8712	Retrd.	1992	8.95	9
1987	Craft Shop 8711	Retrd.	1992	8.95	9
1988	Flower Shop 8807	Retrd.	1992	8.95	9
1988	Ice Cream Parlor 8806	Retrd.	1992	8.95	9

On the Square II - D. Ross

YEAR ISSUE		EDITION LIMIT	YEAR RETD.	ISSUE PRICE	QUOTE U.S.$
1993	Antique Shop 9314	12/95		8.95	11
1993	Book Store 9309	12/95		8.95	11
1993	Candle Shop 9312	12/95		8.95	11
1993	Craft Shop 9313	12/95		8.95	11
1993	Flower Shop 9311	12/95		9.95	11
1993	Ice Cream Shop 9310	12/95		9.95	11

Pre-Open Window Series - D. Ross

YEAR ISSUE		EDITION LIMIT	YEAR RETD.	ISSUE PRICE	QUOTE U.S.$
1990	Adobe House 9005	Retrd.	1992	8.50	9
1991	Faulkner House 9108	Retrd.	1992	8.50	9
1990	Fox Theater 9009	Retrd.	1992	8.50	9
1988	Hardesty House 8808	Retrd.	1992	8.95	9
1991	John Hayes House 9109	Retrd.	1992	11.95	12
1991	Memphis Mansion 9110	Retrd.	1992	8.50	9
1990	Mission 9004	Retrd.	1992	8.50	9
1990	Stone Barn 9003	Retrd.	1992	8.50	9
1990	Stone House 9002	Retrd.	1991	8.50	9
1990	Strater Hotel 9008	Retrd.	1992	8.50	9

Victorian Collection Series I - D. Ross

YEAR ISSUE		EDITION LIMIT	YEAR RETD.	ISSUE PRICE	QUOTE U.S.$
1992	Chapline 9206	Retrd.	1994	8.95	11
1992	Queen Anne 9203	Retrd.	1994	8.95	11
1991	Victorian Michigan 9106	Retrd.	1994	8.95	11

Williamsburg Collection Series I - D. Ross

YEAR ISSUE		EDITION LIMIT	YEAR RETD.	ISSUE PRICE	QUOTE U.S.$
1992	Davidson Shop 9213	Retrd.	1994	8.95	11
1992	Orrell House 9214	Retrd.	1994	8.95	11
1992	Tarpley's Shop 9215	Retrd.	1994	8.95	11

Williamsburg Collection Series II - D. Ross

YEAR ISSUE		EDITION LIMIT	YEAR RETD.	ISSUE PRICE	QUOTE U.S.$
1993	Capitol 9303	12/95		8.95	11
1993	Court House 9302	12/95		8.95	11
1993	Governors Palace 9304	12/95		8.95	11

Rawcliffe Corporation

Angel Fairies™ of the Seasons - J. deStefano

YEAR ISSUE		EDITION LIMIT	YEAR RETD.	ISSUE PRICE	QUOTE U.S.$
1994	Angel Fairy of the Fall	4,500		95.00	95
1994	Angel Fairy of the Spring	4,500		95.00	95
1994	Angel Fairy of the Summer	4,500		95.00	95
1994	Angel Fairy of the Winter	4,500		95.00	95

Baby Bubble Fairies™ - J. deStefano

YEAR ISSUE		EDITION LIMIT	YEAR RETD.	ISSUE PRICE	QUOTE U.S.$
1992	Turquoise-January	6,700		70.00	70
1992	Magenta-February	6,700		70.00	70
1992	Blush-March	6,700		70.00	70
1992	Chartreuse-April	6,700		70.00	70
1992	Violet-May	6,700		70.00	70
1992	Coral-June	6,700		70.00	70
1992	Saffron-July	6,700		70.00	70
1992	Azure-August	6,700		70.00	70
1992	Lavender-September	6,700		70.00	70
1992	Amber-October	6,700		70.00	70
1992	Vermilion-November	6,700		70.00	70
1992	Emerald-December	6,700		70.00	70

Classic Collection - Rawcliffe

YEAR ISSUE		EDITION LIMIT	YEAR RETD.	ISSUE PRICE	QUOTE U.S.$
1995	1956 T-bird Hardtop	Open		72.00	72
1995	1958 T-bird Convertible	Open		70.00	70
1995	928 Porsche	Open		72.00	72
1995	B-17 Bomber	Open		40.00	40
1995	B-52 Bomber	Open		80.00	80
1995	DC-3	Open		72.00	72
1995	F4U-1 Corsair	Open		72.00	72
1995	P-51 Mustang	Open		72.00	72
1995	VW Beetle	Open		72.00	72
1995	World War II Fleet Tugboat	Open		130.00	130
1995	World War II Submarine	Open		72.00	72

Four Seasons Fairies™ - J. deStefano

YEAR ISSUE		EDITION LIMIT	YEAR RETD.	ISSUE PRICE	QUOTE U.S.$
1991	Snow-Winter	9,500		95.00	95
1991	Petal-Spring	9,500		95.00	95
1991	Aria-Summer	9,500		95.00	95
1991	Harvest-Fall	9,500		95.00	95

Garden Fairies™ - J. deStefano

YEAR ISSUE		EDITION LIMIT	YEAR RETD.	ISSUE PRICE	QUOTE U.S.$
1993	The Dew Fairy	4,500		115.00	115
1993	The Dream Fairy	4,500		115.00	115
1993	The Fairy Slipper	4,500		115.00	115
1993	The Illusive Fairy	4,500		115.00	115

Original Bubble Fairy™ Collection - J. deStefano

YEAR ISSUE		EDITION LIMIT	YEAR RETD.	ISSUE PRICE	QUOTE U.S.$
1988	Bliss	Open		85.00	85
1988	Breeze	Retrd.	1993	85.00	85
1988	Echo	Open		85.00	85
1988	Luna	Open		145.00	145
1988	Meadow	Retrd.	1993	145.00	145
1988	Mist	Retrd.	1993	145.00	145
1988	Nimbus	Retrd.	1993	85.00	85
1988	Sky	Open		145.00	145
1988	Sunbeam	Retrd.	1993	85.00	85
1988	Twilight	Open		85.00	85
1988	Whisper	Open		85.00	85
1988	Wishes	Retrd.	1993	85.00	85

Star Trek™ Starships - M. Schwabe

YEAR ISSUE		EDITION LIMIT	YEAR RETD.	ISSUE PRICE	QUOTE U.S.$
1993	USS Enterprise (The Next Generation)	15,000		100.00	100

Star Wars™ Starships - M. Schwabe

YEAR ISSUE		EDITION LIMIT	YEAR RETD.	ISSUE PRICE	QUOTE U.S.$
1993	Darth Vader Tie Fighter Ship	15,000		135.00	135
1993	Millenium Falcon	15,000		115.00	115
1993	X-Wing Fighter	15,000		95.00	95

Wish Fairy™ Collection - J. deStefano

YEAR ISSUE		EDITION LIMIT	YEAR RETD.	ISSUE PRICE	QUOTE U.S.$
1994	Dreams	Open		30.00	30
1994	Friendship	Open		30.00	30
1994	Fun	Open		30.00	30
1994	Good Fortune	Open		30.00	30
1994	Good Luck	Open		30.00	30
1994	Happiness	Open		30.00	30
1994	Health	Open		30.00	30
1994	Laughter	Open		30.00	30
1994	Love	Open		30.00	30
1994	Rainbows	Open		30.00	30
1994	Success	Open		30.00	30
1994	Sunshine	Open		30.00	30

Reco International

Clown Figurines by John McClelland - J. McClelland

YEAR ISSUE		EDITION LIMIT	YEAR RETD.	ISSUE PRICE	QUOTE U.S.$
1988	Mr. Cool	9,500		35.00	35
1987	Mr. Cure-All	9,500		35.00	35
1988	Mr. Heart-Throb	9,500		35.00	35
1987	Mr. Lovable	9,500		35.00	35
1988	Mr. Magic	9,500		35.00	35
1987	Mr. One-Note	9,500		35.00	35
1987	Mr. Tip	9,500		35.00	35

Faces of Love - J. McClelland

YEAR ISSUE		EDITION LIMIT	YEAR RETD.	ISSUE PRICE	QUOTE U.S.$
1988	Cuddles	Open		29.50	33
1988	Sunshine	Open		29.50	33

Granget Crystal Sculpture - G. Granget

YEAR ISSUE		EDITION LIMIT	YEAR RETD.	ISSUE PRICE	QUOTE U.S.$
1973	Long Earred Owl, Asio Otus	Retrd.	1974	2250.00	2250
XX	Ruffed Grouse	Retrd.	1976	1000.00	1000

Laughables - J. Bergsma

YEAR ISSUE		EDITION LIMIT	YEAR RETD.	ISSUE PRICE	QUOTE U.S.$
1995	Annie, Geoge & Harry	Open		17.50	18
1995	Cody & Spot	Open		15.00	15
1995	Daffodil & Prince	Open		13.50	14
1995	Daisy & Jeremiah	Open		15.00	15
1995	Joey & Jumper	Open		15.00	15
1995	Merlin & Gemini	Open		15.00	15
1995	Millie & Mittens	Open		15.00	15
1995	Patches and Pokey	Open		15.00	15
1995	Patty & Petunia	Open		16.50	17
1995	Sunny	Open		13.50	14
1995	Whiskers & Willie	Open		13.50	14

Porcelains in Miniature by John McClelland - J. McClelland

YEAR ISSUE		EDITION LIMIT	YEAR RETD.	ISSUE PRICE	QUOTE U.S.$
XX	Alice	10,000		34.50	35
XX	Autumn Dreams	Open		29.50	30
XX	The Baker	Open		29.50	30
XX	Batter Up	Retrd.	1993	29.50	30
XX	Center Ice	Open		29.50	30
XX	Cheerleader	Open		29.50	30
XX	Chimney Sweep	10,000		34.50	35
XX	The Clown	Open		29.50	30
XX	Club Pro	Open		29.50	30
XX	Country Lass	Open		29.50	30
XX	Cowboy	Open		29.50	30
XX	Cowgirl	Open		29.50	30
XX	Doc	Open		29.50	30
XX	Dressing Up	10,000		34.50	35
XX	The Farmer	Open		29.50	30
XX	Farmer's Wife	Open		29.50	30
XX	The Fireman	Open		29.50	30
XX	First Outing	Open		29.50	30
XX	First Solo	Open		29.50	30
XX	Highland Fling	7,500		34.50	35
XX	John	10,000		34.50	35
XX	Lawyer	Open		29.50	30
XX	Love 40	Open		29.50	30
XX	The Nurse	Open		29.50	30
XX	The Painter	Open		29.50	30
XX	The Policeman	Open		29.50	30
XX	Quiet Moments	Open		29.50	30
XX	Smooth Smailing	Open		29.50	30
XX	Special Delivery	Open		29.50	30
XX	Sudsie Suzie	Open		29.50	30
XX	Tuck-Me-In	Open		29.50	30
XX	Winter Fun	Open		29.50	30

The Reco Angel Collection - J. McClelland

YEAR ISSUE		EDITION LIMIT	YEAR RETD.	ISSUE PRICE	QUOTE U.S.$
1986	Adoration	Open		24.00	24
1986	Devotion	Open		15.00	15
1986	Faith	Retrd.	1995	24.00	24
1986	Gloria	Open		12.00	12
1986	Harmony	Retrd.	1994	12.00	12
1986	Hope	Open		24.00	24
1986	Innocence	Open		12.00	12
1986	Joy	Retrd.	1994	15.00	15
1986	Love	Open		12.00	12
1988	Minstral	Retrd.	1995	12.00	12
1986	Peace	Open		24.00	24
1986	Praise	Open		20.00	20
1988	Reverence	Retrd.	1995	12.00	12
1986	Serenity	Open		24.00	24

The Reco Clown Collection - J. McClelland

YEAR ISSUE		EDITION LIMIT	YEAR RETD.	ISSUE PRICE	QUOTE U.S.$
1985	Arabesque	Open		12.00	13
1985	Bow Jangles	Open		12.00	13
1985	Curly	Open		12.00	13
1987	Disco Dan	Open		12.00	13
1987	Domino	Open		12.00	13
1987	Happy George	Open		12.00	13
1985	Hobo	Open		12.00	13
1987	The Joker	Open		12.00	13
1987	Jolly Joe	Open		12.00	13
1987	Love	Open		12.00	13
1987	Mr. Big	Open		12.00	13
1985	The Professor	Open		12.00	13
1985	Ruffles	Open		12.00	13
1985	Sad Eyes	Open		12.00	13
1985	Scamp	Open		12.00	13
1987	Smiley	Open		12.00	13
1985	Sparkles	Open		12.00	13
1985	Top Hat	Open		12.00	13
1987	Tramp	Open		12.00	13
1987	Twinkle	Open		12.00	13
1985	Whoopie	Open		12.00	13
1985	Winkie	Retrd.	1994	12.00	13
1987	Wistful	Open		12.00	13
1987	Zany Jack	Open		12.00	13

Reco Creche Collection - J. McClelland

YEAR ISSUE		EDITION LIMIT	YEAR RETD.	ISSUE PRICE	QUOTE U.S.$
1988	Cow	Open		15.00	15
1988	Donkey	Open		16.50	17
1987	Holy Family (3 Pieces)	Open		49.00	49
1988	King/Frankincense	Open		22.50	23
1988	King/Gold	Open		22.50	23
1988	King/Myrrh	Open		22.50	23
1987	Lamb	Open		9.50	10
1987	Shepherd-Kneeling	Open		22.50	23
1987	Shepherd-Standing	Open		22.50	23

Rhodes Studio

Rockwell's Age of Wonder - Rockwell-Inspired

YEAR ISSUE		EDITION LIMIT	YEAR RETD.	ISSUE PRICE	QUOTE U.S.$
1992	The Birthday Party	Closed	N/A	39.95	40
1991	Hush-A-Bye	Closed	N/A	34.95	35
1991	School Days	Closed	N/A	36.95	37
1991	Splish Splash	Closed	N/A	34.95	35
1991	Stand by Me	Closed	N/A	36.95	37
1991	Summertime	Closed	N/A	39.95	40

Rockwell's Beautiful Dreamers - Rockwell-Inspired

YEAR ISSUE		EDITION LIMIT	YEAR RETD.	ISSUE PRICE	QUOTE U.S.$
1991	Dear Diary	Closed	N/A	37.95	38
1992	Debutante's Dance	Closed	N/A	42.95	43
1991	Secret Sonnets	Closed	N/A	39.95	40
1991	Sitting Pretty	Closed	N/A	37.95	38
1991	Springtime Serenade	Closed	N/A	39.95	40
1992	Walk in the Park	Closed	N/A	42.95	43

Rockwell's Gems of Wisdom - Rockwell-Inspired

YEAR ISSUE		EDITION LIMIT	YEAR RETD.	ISSUE PRICE	QUOTE U.S.$
1991	Love Cures All	Closed	N/A	39.95	40
1991	Practice Makes Perfect	Closed	N/A	39.95	40
1991	A Stitch In Time	Closed	N/A	42.95	43

Rockwell's Heirloom Santa Collection - Rockwell-Inspired

YEAR ISSUE		EDITION LIMIT	YEAR RETD.	ISSUE PRICE	QUOTE U.S.$
1991	Christmas Dream	150-day		49.95	50
1992	Making His List	Closed	N/A	49.95	50
1990	Santa's Workshop	150-day		49.95	50

Rockwell's Hometown - Rockwell Inspired, unless otherwise noted

YEAR ISSUE		EDITION LIMIT	YEAR RETD.	ISSUE PRICE	QUOTE U.S.$
1991	Bell Tower	Closed	N/A	36.95	37
1992	The Berkshire Playhouse	Closed	N/A	42.95	43
1991	Church On The Green	Closed	N/A	39.95	40
1992	Citizen's Hall	Closed	N/A	42.95	43
1991	Firehouse	Closed	N/A	36.95	37
1991	Greystone Church - Rhodes	Closed	N/A	34.95	35
1992	Mission House	Closed	N/A	42.95	43
1992	Old Corner House	Closed	1994	42.95	43
1991	Rockwell's Residence - Rhodes	Closed	N/A	34.95	35
1992	Town Hall	Closed	N/A	39.95	40

Rockwell's Main Street - Rockwell-Inspired

YEAR ISSUE		EDITION LIMIT	YEAR RETD.	ISSUE PRICE	QUOTE U.S.$
1990	The Antique Shop	150-day		28.00	150
1991	The Bank	150-day		36.00	36
1990	The Country Store	150-day		32.00	36
1991	The Library	150-day		36.00	36
1991	Red Lion Inn	150-day		39.00	39
1990	Rockwell's Studio	150-day		28.00	85
1990	The Town Offices	150-day		32.00	36

Rick Cain Studios

Collectors Guild - R. Cain

YEAR ISSUE		EDITION LIMIT	YEAR RETD.	ISSUE PRICE	QUOTE U.S.$
1992	High Point	S/O	1992	82.00	82
1992	Visor	Retrd.	1992	Gift	75
1993	Strider	S/O	1993	82.00	82
1993	Star Shadow	Retrd.	1993	Gift	75
1994	Midnight Son	1,225	1994	297.00	350-400
1994	Arctic Moon II	Retrd.	1994	Gift	55-60
1995	Family Tree	Yr.Iss.		260.00	260
1995	Bonsai	Yr.Iss.		Gift	N/A

African Fragments - R. Cain

YEAR ISSUE		EDITION LIMIT	YEAR RETD.	ISSUE PRICE	QUOTE U.S.$
1995	Ancient Passage 1810	3,000		110.00	110
1995	Plains Master 1811	3,000		110.00	110

Birds of Prey (Miniatures) - R. Cain

YEAR ISSUE		EDITION LIMIT	YEAR RETD.	ISSUE PRICE	QUOTE U.S.$
1992	Bald Eagle 1800	3,000		49.50	50
1992	Golden Eagle 1801	3,000		49.50	50
1992	Kestrel Hawk 1802	3,000		49.50	50
1992	Night Owl 1803	3,000		49.50	50
1992	Peregrine Falcon 1804	3,000		49.50	50
1992	Red Tail Hawk 1805	3,000		49.50	50

Eco-Sculpture - R. Cain

YEAR ISSUE		EDITION LIMIT	YEAR RETD.	ISSUE PRICE	QUOTE U.S.$
1991	Highland Voyager 1605	2,000		132.00	132
1991	Orchestration 1708	2,000		132.00	132
1992	Polar Eclipse 1910	2,000		110.00	110

Fragments - R. Cain

YEAR ISSUE		EDITION LIMIT	YEAR RETD.	ISSUE PRICE	QUOTE U.S.$
1995	Who	3,000		50.00	50

Gallery I - R. Cain

YEAR ISSUE		EDITION LIMIT	YEAR RETD.	ISSUE PRICE	QUOTE U.S.$
1992	American Dream 2	500		3300.00	3300
1995	American Universe 5	900		1800.00	1800
1995	Perimeters 4	900		2000.00	2000
1993	Raven Shadow 3	900		2200.00	2200
1992	Wind Spirit 1	1,500		1650.00	1650

Master Series - R. Cain

YEAR ISSUE		EDITION LIMIT	YEAR RETD.	ISSUE PRICE	QUOTE U.S.$
1986	Aerial Hunter 1114	5,000	1990	70.40	85
1991	Aerial Victor 1707	2,000	1995	115.00	120-150
1986	African Youth 1109	5,000		137.00	137
1991	Alpha Sprout 1601	2,000		99.00	99
1990	Aquarian 1504	2,000		203.00	203
1995	Arctic Heir 1951	2,500		240.00	240
1993	Arctic Moon 1917	2,000	1993	231.00	500-1100
1993	Arctic Son 1927	2,000	1993	275.00	510-750
1988	The Balance 1302	5,000	1992	374.00	400-515
1992	Bathing Hole 1901	2,000	1994	102.00	155
1994	Bear Rising 1934	2,000		180.00	200
1988	Blackberry Summer 1201	300	1994	165.00	190
1991	Blossom 1705	2,000		99.00	99
1985	Box Turtle 1101	5,000		66.00	66
1993	Buffalo's Son 1924	2,000		143.00	143
1991	Cain Sign 1600	2,000		55.00	55
1991	Cameo 1700	2,000		154.00	154
1995	Canopy 1959	2,000		250.00	250
1985	Catchmaster 1104	5,000	1990	184.80	325-500
1991	Cheetah 1603	2,000		105.00	105
1990	Dark Feather 1501	2,000	1994	86.00	155
1993	Dark Shadow 1918	900		1650.00	1650
1994	Den Meditation 1943	2,000		375.00	375
1989	Domain 1205	5,000	1992	187.00	260
1986	Dragon Sprout 1112	5,000	1990	92.50	300
1987	Dragon Sprout II 1122	5,000		159.00	159
1994	Dragon's Dream 1940	1,500		240.00	300
1987	Dragonflies Dance 1123	5,000	1992	55.00	85
1990	Dual Motion 1503	2,000		185.00	185
1986	Elder 1113	2,500	1993	550.00	750
1989	Encompass 1202	5,000		104.00	104
1988	Fair Atlantis 1130	5,000	1993	319.00	375
1990	Falcon Lore 1406	5,000	1992	86.00	155-200
1985	Featherview 1103	5,000	1993	151.80	180-300
1995	Feet of Clay 1946	2,000		150.00	150
1995	Fire and Ice 1950	2,000		690.00	690
1994	Flight Feathers 1937	1,500		180.00	200
1994	Forest Nimble 1931	2,000		218.00	218
1993	Fountain of Youth 1915	2,000		132.00	132
1994	Four Bears 1933	2,000		1100.00	1100
1988	Guardian 1301	5,000	1995	325.00	370
1987	Habitat 1116	5,000		93.00	93
1989	Hatchling 1205	1,250	1994	85.00	100
1988	Heron Pass 1128	5,000		231.00	231
1991	Highland Voyager 1805	2,000	1995	120.00	120
1987	Innerview 1203	1,500	1994	84.00	100
1994	Ivory Hunter 1939	2,500		160.00	160
1991	Jungle Graces 1706	2,000		110.00	110
1991	La Kimono 1701	2,000		176.00	176
1988	Lady Reflecting 1129	5,000	1995	93.00	93
1992	Leading Wolf 1904	2,000	1992	143.00	450
1987	Liquid Universe 1117	5,000	1995	540.00	615
1993	Little Bears 1921	2,000		220.00	220
1990	Majestic Cradle 1505	900	1995	440.00	500
1986	Marshkeeper 1110	5,000		231.00	231
1993	Medicine Bowl 1920	2,000		220.00	220
1992	Medicine Hawk 1905	2,000		187.00	187
1995	Mergence 1948	2,000		240.00	240
1994	Moon Walk 1930	2,000	1994	198.00	300
1994	Mountain Pass 1938	2,000		180.00	200
1995	Mountain Sketch 1955	2,500		70.00	70
1985	Nightmaster 1105	5,000	1990	184.80	350
1988	Old Man of the Forest 1126	5,000	1992	132.00	185
1988	Orbist 1127	5,000	1992	108.00	150-200
1992	The Pack 1902	2,000	1992	105.50	400
1988	Paradise Found 1124	575	1994	308.00	425
1990	Pathfinder 1403	2,000	1991	101.00	155-200
1994	Pathways 1942	2,500		125.00	125
1990	Pondering 1407	2,000		108.00	108
1992	Power of One 1909	2,000	1995	77.00	100
1992	Prairie Thunder 1903	2,000	1994	110.00	170
1991	Pride 1602	2,000		105.00	105
1992	Radiance 1911	2,000		132.00	132
1994	Rebirth 1928	2,000		180.00	180
1990	Rising Shadow 1408	2,000		187.00	187
1993	Rites of Passage 1916	2,000		165.00	165
1986	Sandmaster 1115	5,000	1995	93.00	105-110
1990	Scarlett Wing 1404	365	1994	101.00	185
1985	Sea View 1107	5,000	1993	70.40	115
1990	Searchers 1502	2,000	1994	174.00	200-250
1987	Sentinel Crest 1119	5,000	1994	121.00	140-170
1992	Seven Bears 1908	2,000	1993	231.00	350-650
1995	Snow Pause 1952	2,000		140.00	140
1991	Soft Wave 1604	2,000		121.00	121
1995	Son and Daughters of the Wind 1947	2,000		165.00	165
1993	Speaks to Strangers 1923	2,000		132.00	132
1991	Spirit Dog 1702	2,000	1992	198.00	450-550
1992	Spirit Eagle 1908	2,000	1993	121.00	200
1994	Spirit of the Mountain 1941	2,000		350.00	440
1993	Spirit Totem 1922	2,000	1993	286.00	435
1993	Steppin' Wolf 1925	2,000	1993	210.00	320
1995	Taking the Lead 1957	2,500		250.00	250
1987	Teller 1120	5,000	1992	308.00	425
1992	Three Bears 1907	2,000		187.00	187
1991	Thunderbowl 1703	2,000		242.00	242
1985	Tidemaster 1108	2,500	1994	242.00	275
1990	Tropic Array 1405	2,000		100.00	100
1986	Tropical Flame 1111	5,000	1992	209.00	290
1989	Universes 1204	5,000	1995	115.00	130-150
1994	Vision Bear 1935	2,000		250.00	250
1994	Waiting Wolf 1929	2,000	1994	198.00	270
1995	Water Dance 1956	2,000		90.00	90
1988	Watercourse Way 1125	5,000		99.00	99
1995	Wedgestone Dragon 1954	2,000		190.00	190
1993	Where Bear 1926	2,000		253.00	253
1986	Wind Horse 1108	5,000	1992	70.00	100
1987	Winged Fortress 1118	5,000	1994	363.00	415
1995	Winged Victor 1953	2,500		170.00	170
1993	Wolf Crossing 1914	2,000		715.00	715
1994	Wolf Prince 1932	2,000		325.00	325
1993	Wolf Trail 1919	2,000	1993	121.00	200-300
1990	Wood Flight 1401	2,000	1992	105.50	145
1993	Wood Song 1912	2,000	1993	143.00	225-425
1985	Woodland Spirit 1102	5,000		165.00	165
1987	Yore Castle 1121	5,000	1992	165.00	230

Path of the Sacred Journey - R. Cain

YEAR ISSUE		EDITION LIMIT	YEAR RETD.	ISSUE PRICE	QUOTE U.S.$
1995	Story Teller 1958	2,500		250.00	250
1994	Tales of Old 1936	2,500		315.00	315

Transcendental Wolves - R. Cain

YEAR ISSUE		EDITION LIMIT	YEAR RETD.	ISSUE PRICE	QUOTE U.S.$
1995	Transcendental Grey Wolf 1949	2,500		315.00	315
1994	Transcendental White Wolf 1944	2,500		315.00	315

Vision Quest - R. Cain

YEAR ISSUE		EDITION LIMIT	YEAR RETD.	ISSUE PRICE	QUOTE U.S.$
1992	Alphascape 1900	2,000	1993	210.00	350-400
1991	Silver Shadow 1606	2,000		176.00	176
1994	Vision Bear 1935	2,000		315.00	315
1995	Vision Ride 1960	2,000		250.00	250
1993	White Vision 1913	2,000		242.00	242

Water's Edge - R. Cain

YEAR ISSUE		EDITION LIMIT	YEAR RETD.	ISSUE PRICE	QUOTE U.S.$
1994	Winged Pass 1945	2,000		115.00	115

Wolf Fragments - R. Cain

YEAR ISSUE		EDITION LIMIT	YEAR RETD.	ISSUE PRICE	QUOTE U.S.$
1994	Devining Wolf 1806	3,000		110.00	110
1994	Pinnacle 1807	3,000		110.00	110

River Shore

Rockwell Single Issues - N. Rockwell

YEAR ISSUE		EDITION LIMIT	YEAR RETD.	ISSUE PRICE	QUOTE U.S.$
1982	Grandpa's Guardian	9,500	N/A	125.00	195
1981	Looking Out To Sea	9,500	N/A	85.00	200

Roman, Inc.

Bill Jauquet Americana "Molly's World" Collection - B. Jauquet

YEAR ISSUE		EDITION LIMIT	YEAR RETD.	ISSUE PRICE	QUOTE U.S.$
1995	Dicky & Dancy Duck Dancing	Open		75.00	75
1995	Ducky Doodle Dee Pulling Wagon	Open		59.50	60
1995	Ducky Doodle Dee Pushing Cart	Open		59.50	60
1995	Father Rabbit	Open		24.50	25
1995	George Duck	Open		19.50	20
1995	Junior Rabbit	Open		17.50	18
1995	Molly Duck	Open		19.50	20
1995	Mother Rabbit	Open		19.50	20
1995	Rabbits Playing Checkers	Open		65.00	65

Bill Jauquet Americana Collection - B. Jauquet

YEAR ISSUE		EDITION LIMIT	YEAR RETD.	ISSUE PRICE	QUOTE U.S.$
1995	Carefree Days	Open		125.00	125
1995	Faithful Voyage	Open		650.00	650
1995	Heading for Home	Open		135.00	135
1995	Heading to Town	Open		150.00	150
1993	Last Train Out	Open		125.00	125
1995	Noah and Friends	Open		350.00	350
1995	Standing Proud	Open		160.00	160
1993	Sunday Driver	Open		395.00	395
1993	Sunrise Ride	Open		175.00	175
1995	Sunrise River	Open		175.00	175

Bristol Falls Carolers Society - E. Simonetti

YEAR ISSUE		EDITION LIMIT	YEAR RETD.	ISSUE PRICE	QUOTE U.S.$
1994	Albert Sinclair	Open		23.50	25
1993	Amos Eleazor Whipple	Open		23.50	25
1994	Caroline Williams	Open		23.50	30
1993	Catherine Lucy Lancaster	Open		23.50	25
1995	Charity and Charles	Open		29.50	30
1993	Chester Adams	Open		23.50	25
1993	Elizabeth Anne Abbot & Stephen	Open		23.50	25
1995	Emily Adams	Open		24.50	25
1994	Jack O'Halloran	Open		23.50	25
1993	James Fisk Cushing	Open		27.50	30
1994	Margaret Louise Winslow Smith	Open		23.50	25
1994	Mary Beth Lancaster	Open		23.50	25
1994	Mayor Jeremiah Bradshaw Smith	Open		23.50	25
1993	Timothy Palmer	Open		27.50	30

Catnippers - I. Spencer

YEAR ISSUE		EDITION LIMIT	YEAR RETD.	ISSUE PRICE	QUOTE U.S.$
1985	A Baffling Yarn	15,000		45.00	45
1985	Can't We Be Friends	15,000		45.00	45
1985	A Christmas Mourning	15,000		45.00	50
1985	Flora and Felina	15,000		45.00	50
1985	Flying Tiger-Retired	15,000		45.00	45
1985	The Paw that Refreshes	15,000		45.00	45
1985	Sandy Claws	15,000		45.00	45
1985	A Tail of Two Kitties	15,000		45.00	45

Ceramica Excelsis - Unknown

YEAR ISSUE		EDITION LIMIT	YEAR RETD.	ISSUE PRICE	QUOTE U.S.$
1978	Assumption Madonna	5,000		56.00	56
1978	Christ Entering Jerusalem	5,000		96.00	96
1978	Christ in the Garden of Gethsemane	5,000		40.00	60
1977	Christ Knocking at the Door	5,000		60.00	60
1980	Daniel in the Lion's Den	5,000		80.00	80
1980	David	5,000		77.00	77
1978	Flight into Egypt	5,000		59.00	90
1983	Good Shepherd	5,000		49.00	49
1978	Guardian Angel with Boy	5,000		69.00	69
1978	Guardian Angel with Girl	5,000		69.00	69
1983	Holy Family	5,000		72.00	72
1978	Holy Family at Work	5,000		96.00	96
1978	Infant of Prague	5,000		37.50	60
1981	Innocence	5,000		95.00	95
1979	Jesus Speaks in Parables	5,000		90.00	90
1983	Jesus with Children	5,000		74.00	74
1981	Journey to Bethlehem	5,000		89.00	89
1983	Kneeling Santa	5,000		95.00	95
1977	Madonna and Child with Angels	5,000		60.00	60
1977	Madonna with Child	5,000		65.00	65
1979	Moses	5,000		77.00	77
1979	Noah	5,000		77.00	77
1981	Sermon on the Mount	5,000		56.00	56
1983	St. Anne	5,000		49.00	49
1983	St. Francis	5,000		59.50	60
1977	St. Francis	5,000		60.00	60
1981	Way of the Cross	5,000		59.00	59
1980	Way to Emmaus	5,000		155.00	155
1977	What Happened to Your Hand?	5,000		60.00	60

A Child's World 1st Edition - F. Hook

YEAR ISSUE		EDITION LIMIT	YEAR RETD.	ISSUE PRICE	QUOTE U.S.$
1980	Beach Buddies, signed	15,000		29.00	600
1980	Beach Buddies, unsigned	15,000		29.00	450
1980	Helping Hands	Closed	N/A	45.00	85
1980	Kiss Me Good Night	15,000		29.00	40
1980	My Big Brother	Closed	N/A	39.00	200
1980	Nighttime Thoughts	Closed	N/A	25.00	65
1980	Sounds of the Sea	15,000	N/A	45.00	150

A Child's World 2nd Edition - F. Hook

YEAR ISSUE		EDITION LIMIT	YEAR RETD.	ISSUE PRICE	QUOTE U.S.$
1981	All Dressed Up	15,000		36.00	70
1981	Cat Nap	15,000	N/A	42.00	125
1981	I'll Be Good	15,000	N/A	36.00	80
1981	Making Friends	15,000		42.00	46
1981	The Sea and Me	15,000	N/A	39.00	80
1981	Sunday School	15,000		39.00	70

A Child's World 3rd Edition - F. Hook

YEAR ISSUE		EDITION LIMIT	YEAR RETD.	ISSUE PRICE	QUOTE U.S.$
1981	Bear Hug	15,000		42.00	45
1981	Pathway to Dreams	15,000		47.00	50
1981	Road to Adventure	15,000		47.00	50
1981	Sisters	15,000	N/A	64.00	75
1981	Spring Breeze	15,000	N/A	37.50	50
1981	Youth	15,000		37.50	40

A Child's World 4th Edition - F. Hook

YEAR ISSUE		EDITION LIMIT	YEAR RETD.	ISSUE PRICE	QUOTE U.S.$
1982	All Bundled Up	15,000		37.50	40
1982	Bedtime	15,000		35.00	38
1982	Birdie	15,000		37.50	40
1982	Flower Girl	15,000		42.00	45
1982	My Dolly!	15,000		39.00	40
1982	Ring Bearer	15,000		39.00	40

A Child's World 5th Edition - F. Hook

YEAR ISSUE		EDITION LIMIT	YEAR RETD.	ISSUE PRICE	QUOTE U.S.$
1983	Brothers	15,000		64.00	70
1983	Finish Line	15,000		39.00	42
1983	Handful of Happiness	15,000		36.00	40
1983	He Loves Me...	15,000		49.00	55
1983	Puppy's Pal	15,000		39.00	42
1983	Ring Around the Rosie	15,000		99.00	105

A Child's World 6th Edition - F. Hook

YEAR ISSUE		EDITION LIMIT	YEAR RETD.	ISSUE PRICE	QUOTE U.S.$
1984	Can I Help?	15,000		37.50	40
1984	Future Artist	15,000		42.00	45
1984	Good Doggie	15,000		47.00	50
1984	Let's Play Catch	15,000		33.00	35
1984	Nature's Wonders	15,000		29.00	31
1984	Sand Castles	15,000		37.50	40

A Child's World 7th Edition - F. Hook

YEAR ISSUE		EDITION LIMIT	YEAR RETD.	ISSUE PRICE	QUOTE U.S.$
1985	Art Class	15,000		99.00	105
1985	Don't Tell Anyone	15,000		49.00	50
1985	Look at Me!	15,000		42.00	45
1985	Mother's Helper	15,000		45.00	50
1985	Please Hear Me	15,000		29.00	30
1985	Yummm!	15,000		36.00	39

A Child's World 8th Edition - F. Hook

YEAR ISSUE		EDITION LIMIT	YEAR RETD.	ISSUE PRICE	QUOTE U.S.$
1985	Chance of Showers	15,000		33.00	35
1985	Dress Rehearsal	15,000		33.00	35
1985	Engine	15,000		36.00	40
1985	Just Stopped By	15,000		36.00	40
1985	Private Ocean	15,000		29.00	31
1985	Puzzling	15,000		36.00	40

A Child's World 9th Edition - F. Hook

YEAR ISSUE		EDITION LIMIT	YEAR RETD.	ISSUE PRICE	QUOTE U.S.$
1987	Hopscotch	15,000		67.50	70
1987	Li'l Brother	15,000		60.00	65

Classic Brides of the Century - E. Williams

YEAR ISSUE		EDITION LIMIT	YEAR RETD.	ISSUE PRICE	QUOTE U.S.$
1989	1900-Flora	5,000		175.00	175
1989	1910-Elizabeth Grace	5,000		175.00	175
1989	1920-Mary Claire	5,000		175.00	175
1989	1930-Kathleen	5,000		175.00	175
1989	1940-Margaret	5,000		175.00	175
1989	1950-Barbara Ann	5,000		175.00	175
1989	1960-Dianne	5,000		175.00	175
1989	1970-Heather	5,000		175.00	175
1989	1980-Jennifer	5,000		175.00	175
1992	1990-Stephanie Helen	5,000		175.00	175

Divine Servant - M. Greiner Jr.

YEAR ISSUE		EDITION LIMIT	YEAR RETD.	ISSUE PRICE	QUOTE U.S.$
1993	Divine Servant, pewter sculpture	Open		200.00	200
1993	Divine Servant, porcelain sculpture	Open		59.50	60
1993	Divine Servant, resin sculpture	Open		250.00	250

Dolfi Original-10" Stoneart - L. Martin

YEAR ISSUE		EDITION LIMIT	YEAR RETD.	ISSUE PRICE	QUOTE U.S.$
1989	Barefoot In Spring	Open		400.00	400
1989	Big Chief Sitting Dog	Open		325.00	325
1989	Birdland Cafe	Open		300.00	300
1989	Dress Rehearsal	Open		495.00	495
1989	Flower Child	Open		300.00	300
1989	Friends & Flowers	Open		400.00	400
1989	Garden Secrets	Open		300.00	300
1989	Have I Been That Good	Open		495.00	495
1989	Holiday Herald	Open		300.00	300
1989	Little Santa	Open		325.00	325
1989	Mary & Joey	Open		495.00	495
1989	Merry Little Light	Open		325.00	325
1989	Mother Hen	Open		300.00	300
1989	Mud Puddles	Open		300.00	300
1989	My Favorite Things	Open		400.00	400
1989	My First Cake	Open		300.00	300
1989	My First Kitten	Open		300.00	300
1989	Pampered Puppies	Open		300.00	300
1989	Puppy Express	Open		300.00	300
1989	A Shoulder to Lean On	Open		400.00	400
1989	Sing a Song of Joy	Open		400.00	400
1989	Sleepyhead	Open		300.00	300
1989	Study Break	Open		325.00	325
1989	Wrapped in Love	Open		300.00	300

Dolfi Original-10" Wood - L. Martin

YEAR ISSUE		EDITION LIMIT	YEAR RETD.	ISSUE PRICE	QUOTE U.S.$
1989	Barefoot In Spring	2,000		1000.00	1000
1989	Big Chief Sitting Dog	2,000		825.00	825
1989	Birdland Cafe	2,000		750.00	750
1989	Dress Rehearsal	2,000		1250.00	1250
1989	Flower Child	2,000		750.00	750
1989	Friends & Flowers	2,000		1000.00	1000
1989	Garden Secrets	2,000		750.00	750
1989	Have I Been That Good	2,000		1250.00	1250
1989	Holiday Herald	2,000		750.00	750
1989	Little Santa	2,000		825.00	825
1989	Mary & Joey	2,000		1250.00	1250
1989	Merry Little Light	2,000		825.00	825
1989	Mother Hen	2,000		750.00	750
1989	Mud Puddles	2,000		750.00	750
1989	My Favorite Things	2,000		1000.00	1000
1989	My First Cake	2,000		750.00	750
1989	My First Kitten	2,000		750.00	750
1989	Pampered Puppies	2,000		750.00	750
1989	Puppy Express	2,000		750.00	750
1989	A Shoulder to Lean On	2,000		1000.00	1000
1989	Sing a Song of Joy	2,000		1000.00	1000
1989	Sleepyhead	2,000		750.00	750
1989	Study Break	2,000		825.00	825
1989	Wrapped in Love	2,000		750.00	750

Dolfi Original-5" Wood - L. Martin

YEAR ISSUE		EDITION LIMIT	YEAR RETD.	ISSUE PRICE	QUOTE U.S.$
1989	Barefoot In Spring	5,000		300.00	300
1989	Big Chief Sitting Dog	5,000		250.00	250
1989	Birdland Cafe	5,000		230.00	230
1989	Dress Rehearsal	5,000		375.00	375
1989	Flower Child	5,000		230.00	230
1989	Friends & Flowers	5,000		300.00	300
1989	Garden Secrets	5,000		230.00	230
1989	Have I Been That Good	5,000		375.00	375
1989	Holiday Herald	5,000		230.00	230
1989	Little Santa	5,000		250.00	250
1989	Mary & Joey	5,000		375.00	375
1989	Merry Little Light	5,000		250.00	250
1989	Mother Hen	5,000		230.00	230
1989	Mud Puddles	5,000		230.00	230
1989	My Favorite Things	5,000		300.00	300
1989	My First Cake	5,000		230.00	230
1989	My First Kitten	5,000		230.00	230
1989	Pampered Puppies	5,000		230.00	230
1989	Puppy Express	5,000		230.00	230
1989	A Shoulder to Lean On	5,000		300.00	300
1989	Sing a Song of Joy	5,000		300.00	300
1989	Sleepyhead	5,000		230.00	230
1989	Study Break	5,000		250.00	250
1989	Wrapped In Love	5,000		230.00	230

Dolfi Original-7" Stoneart - L. Martin

YEAR ISSUE		EDITION LIMIT	YEAR RETD.	ISSUE PRICE	QUOTE U.S.$
1989	Barefoot In Spring	Open		150.00	150
1989	Big Chief Sitting Dog	Open		120.00	120
1989	Birdland Cafe	Open		110.00	110
1989	Dress Rehearsal	Open		185.00	185
1989	Flower Child	Open		110.00	110
1989	Friends & Flowers	Open		150.00	150
1989	Garden Secrets	Open		110.00	110
1989	Have I Been That Good	Open		185.00	185
1989	Holiday Herald	Open		110.00	110
1989	Little Santa	Open		120.00	120
1989	Mary & Joey	Open		185.00	185
1989	Merry Little Light	Open		120.00	120
1989	Mother Hen	Open		110.00	110
1989	Mud Puddles	Open		110.00	110
1989	My Favorite Things	Open		150.00	150
1989	My First Cake	Open		110.00	110
1989	My First Kitten	Open		110.00	110
1989	Pampered Puppies	Open		110.00	110
1989	Puppy Express	Open		110.00	110
1989	A Shoulder to Lean On	Open		150.00	150
1989	Sleepyhead	Open		110.00	110
1989	Sing a Song of Joy	Open		150.00	150
1989	Study Break	Open		120.00	120
1989	Wrapped In Love	Open		110.00	110

Fontanini Collectors' Club Member's Only - E. Simonetti

YEAR ISSUE		EDITION LIMIT	YEAR RETD.	ISSUE PRICE	QUOTE U.S.$
1991	The Pilgrimage	Yr.Iss.		24.95	25
1992	She Rescued Me	Yr.Iss.		23.50	24
1993	Christmas Symphony	Yr.Iss.		13.50	14
1994	Sweet Harmony	Yr.Iss.		13.50	14
1995	Faith: The Fifth Angel	Yr.Iss.		22.50	23

Fontanini Collector Club Renewal Gift - E. Simonetti

YEAR ISSUE		EDITION LIMIT	YEAR RETD.	ISSUE PRICE	QUOTE U.S.$
1993	He Comforts Me	Yr.Iss.		12.50	13
1994	I'm Heaven Bound	Yr.Iss.		12.50	13
1995	Gift of Joy	Yr.Iss.		12.50	13

Fontanini Collectors' Club Special Event Piece - E. Simonetti

YEAR ISSUE		EDITION LIMIT	YEAR RETD.	ISSUE PRICE	QUOTE U.S.$
1990	Gideon	Open		15.00	15

Fontanini Collectors' Club First Year Welcome Gift - E. Simonetti

YEAR ISSUE		EDITION LIMIT	YEAR RETD.	ISSUE PRICE	QUOTE U.S.$
1990	I Found Him	Open		Gift	N/A

Fontanini 5" Collection - E. Simonetti

YEAR ISSUE		EDITION LIMIT	YEAR RETD.	ISSUE PRICE	QUOTE U.S.$
1994	Aaron (Resculptured)	Open		11.50	12
1994	Jeremiah	Open		11.50	12
1994	Josiah (Resculptured)	Open		11.50	12
1995	Kneeling Angel (Resculptured)	Open		11.50	12
1994	Len (Resculptured)	Open		11.50	12
1994	Miriam (Resculptured)	Open		11.50	12
1994	Rachel (Resculptured)	Open		11.50	12
1995	Standing Angel (Resculptured)	Open		11.50	12

Fontanini 7.5" Collection - E. Simonetti

YEAR ISSUE		EDITION LIMIT	YEAR RETD.	ISSUE PRICE	QUOTE U.S.$
1994	Deborah	Open		24.50	25
1994	Eli	Open		24.50	25
1994	Gariel (Resculptured)	Open		24.50	25
1994	Jesus (Resculptured)	Open		24.50	25
1994	Joseph (Resculptured)	Open		24.50	25
1995	King Balthazar (Resculptured)	Open		24.50	25
1995	King Gaspar (Resculptured)	Open		24.50	25
1995	King Melchior (Resculptured)	Open		24.50	25
1994	Mary (Resculptured)	Open		24.50	25
1994	Michael	Open		24.50	25
1994	Miriam	Open		24.50	25
1994	Rachel	Open		24.50	25

Fontanini Heirloom Nativity - E. Simonetti

YEAR ISSUE		EDITION LIMIT	YEAR RETD.	ISSUE PRICE	QUOTE U.S.$
1979	Balthazar (5")	Retrd.	1993	11.50	12
1979	Gabriel (5")	Retrd.	1993	11.50	12
1979	Gaspar (5")	Retrd.	1993	11.50	12
1974	Jesus (5")	Closed	1991	2.50	10
1974	Joseph (5")	Closed	1991	2.50	10
1974	Mary (5")	Closed	1991	2.50	10
1979	Melchior (5")	Retrd.	1993	11.50	12
1993	New Balthazar (5")	Open		11.50	12
1993	New Gabriel (5")	Open		11.50	12
1993	New Gaspar (5")	Open		11.50	12
1991	New Jesus (5")	Open		11.50	12
1991	New Joseph (5")	Open		11.50	12
1991	New Mary (5")	Open		11.50	12
1993	New Melchior (5")	Open		11.50	12

Fontanini Heirloom Nativity Limited Edition Figurines - E. Simonetti

YEAR ISSUE		EDITION LIMIT	YEAR RETD.	ISSUE PRICE	QUOTE U.S.$
1994	Abigail & Peter	25,000		29.50	30
1992	Ariel	Yr.Iss.		29.50	30
1995	Gabriela	25,000		18.00	18
1993	Jeshua & Adin	Yr.Iss.		29.50	30

Fontanini, The Collectible Creche - E. Simonetti

YEAR ISSUE		EDITION LIMIT	YEAR RETD.	ISSUE PRICE	QUOTE U.S.$
1973	10cm., (15 piece Set)	Closed	1992	63.60	89
1973	12cm., (15 piece Set)	Closed	1992	76.50	102
1979	16cm., (15 piece Set)	Closed	1992	178.50	285
1982	17cm., (15 piece Set)	Closed	1992	189.00	305
1973	19cm., (15 piece Set)	Closed	1992	175.50	280
1980	30cm., (15 piece Set)	Closed	1992	670.00	759

Frances Hook's Four Seasons - F. Hook

YEAR ISSUE		EDITION LIMIT	YEAR RETD.	ISSUE PRICE	QUOTE U.S.$
1984	Winter	12,500		95.00	100
1985	Spring	12,500		95.00	100
1985	Summer	12,500		95.00	100
1985	Fall	12,500		95.00	100

Heartbeats - I. Spencer

YEAR ISSUE		EDITION LIMIT	YEAR RETD.	ISSUE PRICE	QUOTE U.S.$
1986	Miracle	5,000		145.00	145
1987	Storytime	5,000		145.00	145

Hook - F. Hook

YEAR ISSUE		EDITION LIMIT	YEAR RETD.	ISSUE PRICE	QUOTE U.S.$
1986	Carpenter Bust	Yr.Iss.		95.00	95
1986	Carpenter Bust-Heirloom Edition	Yr.Iss.		95.00	95
1987	Little Children, Come to Me	15,000		45.00	45
1987	Madonna and Child	15,000		39.50	40
1982	Sailor Mates	2,000		290.00	315
1982	Sun Shy	2,000		290.00	315

Jam Session - E. Rohn

YEAR ISSUE		EDITION LIMIT	YEAR RETD.	ISSUE PRICE	QUOTE U.S.$
1985	Banjo Player	7,500		145.00	145
1985	Bass Player	7,500		145.00	145
1985	Clarinet Player	7,500		145.00	145
1985	Coronet Player	7,500		145.00	145
1985	Drummer	7,500		145.00	145
1985	Trombone Player	7,500		145.00	145

The Masterpiece Collection - Various

YEAR ISSUE		EDITION LIMIT	YEAR RETD.	ISSUE PRICE	QUOTE U.S.$
1979	Adoration - F. Lippe	5,000		73.00	73
1981	The Holy Family - G. delle Notti	5,000		98.00	98
1982	Madonna of the Streets - R. Ferruzzi	5,000		65.00	65
1980	Madonna with Grapes - P. Mignard	5,000		85.00	85

The Museum Collection by Angela Tripi - A. Tripi

YEAR ISSUE		EDITION LIMIT	YEAR RETD.	ISSUE PRICE	QUOTE U.S.$
1995	The Batter	1,000		95.00	95
1993	Be a Clown	1,000		95.00	95
1994	Blackfoot Woman with Baby	1,000		95.00	95
1991	The Caddie	1,000		135.00	135
1992	Checking It Twice	2,500		95.00	95
1991	Christopher Columbus	1,000		250.00	250
1994	Crow Warrior	1,000		195.00	195
1991	The Fiddler	1,000		175.00	176
1992	Flying Ace	1,000		95.00	95
1993	For My Next Trick	1,000		95.00	95
1992	Fore!	1,000		175.00	175
1992	The Fur Trapper	1,000		175.00	175

YEAR ISSUE		EDITION LIMIT	YEAR RETD.	ISSUE PRICE	QUOTE U.S.$
1991	A Gentleman's Game	1,000	1994	175.00	175
1992	The Gift Giver	2,500		95.00	95
1994	Iroquois Warrior	1,000		95.00	95
1995	Jesus in Gethsemane	1,000		95.00	95
1993	Jesus, The Good Shepherd	1,000		95.00	95
1992	Justice for All	1,000		95.00	95
1992	Ladies' Day	1,000		175.00	175
1992	Ladies' Tee	1,000		250.00	250
1990	The Mentor	1,000		290.00	291
1994	Native American Chief	1,000		95.00	95
1994	Native American Woman-Cherokee Maiden	1,000		95.00	95
1992	Nativity Set-8 pc.	2,500		425.00	425
1995	Nurse	1,000		95.00	95
1993	One Man Band Clown	1,000		95.00	95
1992	Our Family Doctor	1,000		95.00	95
1995	The Pitcher	1,000		95.00	95
1993	Preacher of Peace	1,000		175.00	175
1992	Prince of the Plains	1,000		175.00	175
1993	Public Protector	1,000		95.00	95
1994	Rhapsody	1,000		95.00	95
1993	Right on Schedule	1,000		95.00	95
1993	Road Show	1,000		95.00	95
1995	The Runner	1,000		95.00	95
1994	Serenade	1,000		95.00	95
1994	Sonata	1,000		95.00	95
1991	St. Francis of Assisi	1,000		175.00	175
1992	The Tannenbaum Santa	2,500		95.00	95
1992	The Tap In	1,000		175.00	175
1995	Teacher	1,000		95.00	95
1991	Tee Time at St. Andrew's	1,000	1993	175.00	175
1992	This Way, Santa	2,500		95.00	95
1992	To Serve and Protect	1,000		95.00	95
1993	Tripi Crucifix-Large	Open		59.00	59
1993	Tripi Crucifix-Medium	Open		35.00	35
1993	Tripi Crucifix-Small	Open		27.50	28

The Richard Judson Zolan Collection - R.J. Zolan

YEAR ISSUE		EDITION LIMIT	YEAR RETD.	ISSUE PRICE	QUOTE U.S.$
1992	Summer at the Seashore	1,200		125.00	125
1994	Terrace Dancing	1,200		175.00	175

Rohn's Clowns - E. Rohn

YEAR ISSUE		EDITION LIMIT	YEAR RETD.	ISSUE PRICE	QUOTE U.S.$
1984	Auguste	7,500		95.00	95
1984	Hobo	7,500		95.00	95
1984	White Face	7,500		95.00	95

Seraphim Classics - Seraphim Studios

YEAR ISSUE		EDITION LIMIT	YEAR RETD.	ISSUE PRICE	QUOTE U.S.$
1995	Alyssa - Nature's Angel	Yr.Iss.		145.00	145

Spencer - I. Spencer

YEAR ISSUE		EDITION LIMIT	YEAR RETD.	ISSUE PRICE	QUOTE U.S.$
1985	Flower Princess	5,000		195.00	195
1985	Moon Goddess	5,000		195.00	195

Tender Expressions - B. Sargent

YEAR ISSUE		EDITION LIMIT	YEAR RETD.	ISSUE PRICE	QUOTE U.S.$
1994	Each Day is Special...And So Are You	Open		29.50	30
1992	The Greatest Love Shines From A Mother's Face	Open		27.50	28
1994	Home Is In Mother's Heart	Open		32.50	33
1992	I Count My Blessings...And There You Are!	Open		27.50	28
1992	I Even Love the Rain When You Share My Umbrella	Open		27.50	28
1994	I Saved A Place For You In My Heart	Open		29.50	30
1992	I Tell Everyone How Special You Are	Open		27.50	28
1994	I'm On Top of the World When I'm With You	Open		29.50	30
1994	Know What's Special About You?...Everything	Open		29.50	30
1994	Life Gives Us Precious Moments To Fill Our Hearts With Joy	Open		39.50	40
1994	Magic Happens When You Smile	Open		29.50	30
1994	Safely Rest, By Angels Blessed	Open		32.50	33
1994	Tender Moments Last Forever	Open		29.50	30
1992	Thoughts Of You Are In My Heart	Open		27.50	28
1994	The Tiniest Flower Blossoms With Love	Open		29.50	30
1992	You Are Always in the Thoughts That Fill My Day	Open		27.50	28
1994	You Fill My Days With Tiny Blessings	Open		39.50	40
1994	You're In Every Little Prayer (Boy)	Open		29.50	30
1994	You're In Every Little Prayer (Girl)	Open		29.50	30

Ron Lee's World of Clowns

The Ron Lee Collector's Club Gifts - R. Lee

YEAR ISSUE		EDITION LIMIT	YEAR RETD.	ISSUE PRICE	QUOTE U.S.$
1987	Hooping It Up CCG1	Closed	N/A	Gift	N/A
1988	Pudge CCG2	Closed	N/A	Gift	N/A
1989	Pals CCG3	Closed	N/A	Gift	N/A
1990	Potsie CCG4	Closed	N/A	Gift	N/A
1991	Hi! Ya! CCG5	Closed	N/A	Gift	N/A
1992	Bashful Beau CCG6	Closed	N/A	Gift	N/A
1993	Lit'l Mate CCG7	Closed	N/A	Gift	N/A
1994	Chip Off the Old Block CCG8	Closed	N/A	Gift	N/A
1995	Rock-A-Billy	Yr.Iss.	N/A	Gift	N/A

The Ron Lee Collector's Club Renewal Sculptures - R. Lee

YEAR ISSUE		EDITION LIMIT	YEAR RETD.	ISSUE PRICE	QUOTE U.S.$
1987	Doggin' Along CC1	Yr.Iss.	N/A	75.00	115
1988	Midsummer's Dream CC2	Yr.Iss.	N/A	97.00	140
1989	Peek-A-Boo Charlie CC3	Yr.Iss.	N/A	65.00	100
1990	Get The Message CC4	Yr.Iss.	N/A	65.00	65
1991	I'm So Pretty CC5	Yr.Iss.	N/A	65.00	65
1992	It's For You CC6	Yr.Iss.	N/A	65.00	65
1993	My Son Keven CC7	Yr.Iss.	N/A	70.00	70

Around the World With Hobo Joe - R. Lee

YEAR ISSUE		EDITION LIMIT	YEAR RETD.	ISSUE PRICE	QUOTE U.S.$
1994	Hobo Joe in Caribbean L412	750	1995	110.00	110
1994	Hobo Joe in Egypt L415	750	1995	110.00	110
1994	Hobo Joe in England L411	750	1995	110.00	110
1994	Hobo Joe in France L407	750	1995	110.00	110
1994	Hobo Joe in Italy L406	750	1995	110.00	110
1994	Hobo Joe in Japan L408	750	1995	110.00	110
1994	Hobo Joe in Norway L413	750	1995	110.00	110
1994	Hobo Joe in Spain L414	750	1995	110.00	110
1994	Hobo Joe in Tahiti L410	750	1995	110.00	110
1994	Hobo Joe in the U.S.A L409	750	1995	110.00	110

The Betty Boop Collection - R. Lee

YEAR ISSUE		EDITION LIMIT	YEAR RETD.	ISSUE PRICE	QUOTE U.S.$
1992	Bamboo Isle BB715	1,500		240.00	240
1992	Boop Oop A Doop BB705	1,500		97.00	97
1992	Harvest Moon BB700	1,500		93.00	93
1992	Max's Cafe BB720	1,500		99.00	99
1992	Spicy Dish BB710	1,500		215.00	215

Center Ring - R. Lee

YEAR ISSUE		EDITION LIMIT	YEAR RETD.	ISSUE PRICE	QUOTE U.S.$
1994	According To L-431SE	750	1995	125.00	125
1994	Aristocrat L-424SE	750	1995	125.00	125
1994	Barella L-423SE	750	1995	125.00	135
1994	Belt-a-Loon L-427SE	750	1995	125.00	125
1994	Boo-Boo L-430SE	750	1995	125.00	125
1994	Bubbles L-422SE	750	1995	125.00	125
1994	Carpetbagger L-421SE	750	1995	125.00	125
1994	Daisy L-417SE	750	1995	125.00	125
1994	Forget-Me-Not L-428SE	750	1995	125.00	125
1994	Glamour Boy L-433SE	750	1995	125.00	125
1994	Hoop-De-Doo L-434SE	750	1995	125.00	125
1994	Hot Dog L-418SE	750	1995	125.00	125
1994	Kandy L-419SE	750	1995	125.00	125
1994	Maid in the USA L-432SE	750	1995	125.00	125
1994	Mal-Lett L-426SE	750	1995	125.00	125
1994	Poodles L-420SE	750	1995	125.00	125
1994	Puddles L-416SE	750	1995	125.00	125
1994	Rabbit's Foot L-429SE	750	1995	125.00	125
1994	Ruffles L-435SE	750	1995	125.00	125
1994	Snacks L-425SE	750	1995	125.00	125

The Classics - R. Lee

YEAR ISSUE		EDITION LIMIT	YEAR RETD.	ISSUE PRICE	QUOTE U.S.$
1991	Huckleberry Hound HB815	2,750	1995	90.00	90
1991	Quick Draw McGraw HB805	2,750	1995	90.00	90
1991	Scooby Doo & Shaggy HB810	2,750	1995	114.00	114
1991	Yogi Bear & Boo Boo HB800	2,750	1995	95.00	95

The Commemorative Collection - R. Lee

YEAR ISSUE		EDITION LIMIT	YEAR RETD.	ISSUE PRICE	QUOTE U.S.$
1995	April 12th L455	2,500		180.00	180
1995	Between Shows L456	2,500		250.00	250
1995	Filet of Sole L460	2,500		180.00	180
1995	The Highwayman L457	2,500		165.00	165
1995	Just Plain Tired L459	2,500		195.00	195
1995	Practice Swing...Not!! L458	2,500		180.00	180

The E.T. Collection - R. Lee

YEAR ISSUE		EDITION LIMIT	YEAR RETD.	ISSUE PRICE	QUOTE U.S.$
1992	E.T. ET100	1,500	1995	94.00	94
1993	Flight ET115	1,500	1995	325.00	325
1993	Friends ET110	1,500	1995	125.00	125
1992	It's Mee...E.T. ET105	1,500	1995	94.00	94

The Flintstones - R. Lee

YEAR ISSUE		EDITION LIMIT	YEAR RETD.	ISSUE PRICE	QUOTE U.S.$
1991	Bedrock Serenade HB130	2,750		250.00	250
1991	Bogey Buddies HB150	2,750		143.00	143
1991	Buffalo Brothers HB170	2,750		134.00	134
1991	The Flinstones HB100	2,750		410.00	410
1991	Joyride-A-Saurus HB140	2,750		107.00	107
1991	Saturday Blues HB120	2,750		105.00	105
1991	Vac-A-Saurus HB160	2,750		105.00	110
1991	Yabba-Dabba-Doo HB110	2,750		230.00	230

History of Golf - R. Lee

YEAR ISSUE		EDITION LIMIT	YEAR RETD.	ISSUE PRICE	QUOTE U.S.$
1994	20th Century GTA700	10,000		150.00	150
1994	Age of Chivalry GTA400	10,000		150.00	150
1994	Caesar GTA300	10,000		150.00	150
1994	Dawn of Man GTA100	10,000		150.00	150
1994	New Frontiers GTA800	10,000		150.00	150
1994	Old West GTA600	10,000		150.00	150
1994	The Pharaoh GTA200	10,000		150.00	150
1994	Plymouth GTA500	10,000		150.00	150

Holiday Special - R. Lee

YEAR ISSUE		EDITION LIMIT	YEAR RETD.	ISSUE PRICE	QUOTE U.S.$
1995	Santa's Other Sleigh L461	750		195.00	195

The Jetsons - R. Lee

YEAR ISSUE		EDITION LIMIT	YEAR RETD.	ISSUE PRICE	QUOTE U.S.$
1991	4 O'Clock Tea HB550	2,750	1995	203.00	203
1991	Astro: Cosmic Canine HB520	2,750	1995	275.00	275
1991	The Cosmic Couple HB510	2,750	1995	105.00	105
1991	I Rove Roo HB530	2,750	1995	105.00	105
1991	The Jetsons HB500	2,750	1995	500.00	500
1991	Scare-D-Dog HB540	2,750	1995	160.00	160

Musical Clowns in Harmony - R. Lee

YEAR ISSUE		EDITION LIMIT	YEAR RETD.	ISSUE PRICE	QUOTE U.S.$
1994	Aristocrat L-424	750	1995	175.00	175
1994	Barella L-423	750	1995	175.00	175
1994	Bubbles L-422	750	1995	175.00	175
1994	Carpet Bagger L-421	750	1995	175.00	175
1994	Daisy L-417	750	1995	175.00	175
1994	Hot Dog L-418	750	1995	175.00	175
1994	Kandy L-419	750	1995	175.00	175
1994	Poodles L-420	750	1995	175.00	175
1994	Puddles L-416	750	1995	175.00	175
1994	Snacks L-425	750	1995	175.00	175

The Original Ron Lee Collection-1976 - R. Lee

YEAR ISSUE		EDITION LIMIT	YEAR RETD.	ISSUE PRICE	QUOTE U.S.$
1976	Alligator Bowling 504	Closed	N/A	15.00	35-78
1976	Bear Fishing 511	Closed	N/A	15.00	35-78
1976	Clown and Dog Act 101	Closed	N/A	48.00	78-140
1976	Clown and Elephant Act 107	Closed	N/A	56.00	85-140
1976	Clown Tightrope Walker 104	Closed	N/A	50.00	82-155
1976	Dog Fishing 512	Closed	N/A	15.00	35-78
1976	Frog Surfing 502	Closed	N/A	15.00	35-78
1976	Hippo on Scooter 505	Closed	N/A	15.00	35-78
1976	Hobo Joe Hitchiking 116	Closed	N/A	55.00	65
1976	Hobo Joe with Balloons 120	Closed	N/A	63.00	90
1976	Hobo Joe with Pal 115	Closed	N/A	63.00	85-170
1976	Hobo Joe with Umbrella 117	Closed	N/A	58.00	65-160
1976	Kangaroos Boxing 508	Closed	N/A	15.00	35-78
1976	Owl With Guitar 500	Closed	N/A	15.00	35-78
1976	Penguin on Snowskis 503	Closed	N/A	15.00	35-78
1976	Pig Playing Violin 510	Closed	N/A	15.00	35-78
1976	Pinky Lying Down 112	Closed	N/A	25.00	125
1976	Pinky Sitting 119	Closed	N/A	25.00	150
1976	Pinky Standing 118	Closed	N/A	25.00	45-130
1976	Pinky Upside Down 111	Closed	N/A	25.00	125
1976	Rabbit Playing Tennis 507	Closed	N/A	15.00	35-78
1976	Turtle On Skateboard 501	Closed	N/A	15.00	35-78

The Original Ron Lee Collection-1977 - R. Lee

YEAR ISSUE		EDITION LIMIT	YEAR RETD.	ISSUE PRICE	QUOTE U.S.$
1977	Bear On Rock 523	Closed	N/A	18.00	30-80
1977	Koala Bear In Tree 514	Closed	N/A	15.00	35-78
1977	Koala Bear On Log 516	Closed	N/A	15.00	35-78
1977	Koala Bear With Baby 515	Closed	N/A	15.00	35-78
1977	Monkey With Banana 521	Closed	N/A	18.00	30-80
1977	Mouse and Cheese 520	Closed	N/A	18.00	30-80
1977	Mr. Penguin 518	Closed	N/A	18.00	39-85
1977	Owl Graduate 519	Closed	N/A	22.00	44-90
1977	Pelican and Python 522	Closed	N/A	18.00	30-80

The Original Ron Lee Collection-1978 - R. Lee

YEAR ISSUE		EDITION LIMIT	YEAR RETD.	ISSUE PRICE	QUOTE U.S.$
1978	Bobbi on Unicyle 204	Closed	N/A	45.00	65-98
1978	Bow Tie 222	Closed	N/A	67.50	93-215
1978	Butterfly and Flower 529	Closed	N/A	22.00	40-85
1978	Clancy, the Cop 210	Closed	N/A	55.00	72-130
1978	Clara-Bow 205	Closed	N/A	52.00	70-120
1978	Coco-Hands on Hips 218	Closed	N/A	70.00	85-250
1978	Corky, the Drummer Boy 202	Closed	N/A	53.00	85-130
1978	Cuddles 208	Closed	N/A	37.00	55-110
1978	Dolphins 525	Closed	N/A	22.00	40-85
1978	Driver the Golfer 211	Closed	N/A	55.00	200-225
1978	Elephant on Ball 214	Closed	N/A	26.00	42-80
1978	Elephant on Stand 213	Closed	N/A	26.00	42-80
1978	Elephant Sitting 215	Closed	N/A	26.00	42-80
1978	Fancy Pants 224	Closed	N/A	55.00	90-120
1978	Fireman with Hose 216	Closed	N/A	62.00	85-170
1978	Hey Rube 220	Closed	N/A	35.00	53-92
1978	Hummingbird 528	Closed	N/A	22.00	40-85
1978	Jeri In a Barrel 219	Closed	N/A	75.00	110-180
1978	Jocko with Lollipop 221	Closed	N/A	67.50	93-215
1978	Oscar On Stilts 223	Closed	N/A	55.00	90-120
1978	Pierrot Painting 207	Closed	N/A	50.00	80-170
1978	Polly, the Parrot & Crackers 201	Closed	N/A	63.00	100-170
1978	Poppy with Puppet 209	Closed	N/A	60.00	75-140
1978	Prince Frog 526	Closed	N/A	22.00	40-85
1978	Sad Sack 212	Closed	N/A	48.00	62-210
1978	Sailfish 524	Closed	N/A	18.00	40-95
1978	Sea Otter on Back 531	Closed	N/A	22.00	40-85
1978	Sea Otter on Rock 532	Closed	N/A	22.00	40-85
1978	Seagull 527	Closed	N/A	22.00	40-85
1978	Skippy Swinging 239	Closed	N/A	52.00	65-85
1978	Sparky Skating 206	Closed	N/A	55.00	72-260
1978	Tinker Bowing 203	Closed	N/A	37.00	55-110
1978	Tobi-Hands Outstretched 217	Closed	N/A	70.00	98-260
1978	Turtle on Rock 530	Closed	N/A	22.00	40-85

The Original Ron Lee Collection-1979 - R. Lee

YEAR ISSUE		EDITION LIMIT	YEAR RETD.	ISSUE PRICE	QUOTE U.S.$
1979	Buttons Bicycling 229	Closed	N/A	75.00	110-150
1979	Carousel Horse 232	Closed	N/A	119.00	130-195
1979	Darby Tipping Hat 238	Closed	N/A	35.00	60-140
1979	Darby with Flower 235	Closed	N/A	35.00	60-140
1979	Darby with Umbrella 236	Closed	N/A	35.00	60-140
1979	Darby With Violin 237	Closed	N/A	35.00	60-140
1979	Doctor Sawbones 228	Closed	N/A	75.00	110-150
1979	Fearless Fred in Cannon 234	Closed	N/A	80.00	105-300
1979	Harry and the Hare 233	Closed	N/A	69.00	102-180
1979	Kelly at the Piano 241	Closed	N/A	185.00	285-510
1979	Kelly in Kar 230	Closed	N/A	164.00	210-380
1979	Kelly's Kar 231	Closed	N/A	75.00	90-280
1979	Lilli 227	Closed	N/A	75.00	105-145
1979	Timmy Tooting 225	Closed	N/A	35.00	52-85
1979	Tubby Tuba 226	Closed	N/A	35.00	55-90

The Original Ron Lee Collection-1980 - R. Lee

YEAR ISSUE		EDITION LIMIT	YEAR RETD.	ISSUE PRICE	QUOTE U.S.$
1980	Alexander's One Man Band 261	Closed	N/A	N/A	N/A
1980	Banjo Willie 258	Closed	N/A	68.00	85-195

YEAR ISSUE		EDITION LIMIT	YEAR RETD.	ISSUE PRICE	QUOTE U.S.$
1980	Carousel Horse 248	Closed	N/A	88.00	115-285
1980	Carousel Horse 249	Closed	N/A	88.00	115-285
1980	Chuckles Juggling 244	Closed	N/A	98.00	105-150
1980	Cubby Holding Balloon 240	Closed	N/A	50.00	65-70
1980	Dennis Playing Tennis 252	Closed	N/A	74.00	95-185
1980	Doctor Jawbones 260	Closed	N/A	85.00	110-305
1980	Donkey What 243	Closed	N/A	60.00	92-250
1980	Emile 257	Closed	N/A	43.00	82-190
1980	Happy Waving 255	Closed	N/A	43.00	82-190
1980	Hobo Joe in Tub 259	Closed	N/A	96.00	105-125
1980	Horse Drawn Chariot 263	Closed	N/A	N/A	N/A
1980	Jaque Downhill Racer 253	Closed	N/A	74.00	90-210
1980	Jingles Telling Time 242	Closed	N/A	75.00	90-190
1980	Jo-Jo at Make-up Mirror 250	Closed	N/A	86.00	125-185
1980	The Menagerie 262	Closed	N/A	N/A	N/A
1980	Monkey 251	Closed	N/A	60.00	85-210
1980	P. T. Dinghy 245	Closed	N/A	65.00	80-190
1980	Peanuts Playing Concertina 247	Closed	N/A	65.00	150-285
1980	Roni Riding Horse 246	Closed	N/A	115.00	180-290
1980	Ruford 254	Closed	N/A	43.00	80-190
1980	Zach 256	Closed	N/A	43.00	82-190

The Original Ron Lee Collection-1981 - R. Lee

YEAR ISSUE		EDITION LIMIT	YEAR RETD.	ISSUE PRICE	QUOTE U.S.$
1981	Al at the Bass 284	Closed	N/A	48.00	52-112
1981	Barbella 273	Closed	N/A	N/A	N/A
1981	Bojangles 276	Closed	N/A	N/A	N/A
1981	Bosom Buddies 299	Closed	N/A	135.00	90-280
1981	Bozo On Unicycle 279	Closed	N/A	28.00	99-185
1981	Bozo Playing Cymbols 277	Closed	N/A	28.00	99-185
1981	Bozo Riding Car 278	Closed	N/A	28.00	99-185
1981	Carney and Seal Act 300	Closed	N/A	63.00	75-290
1981	Carousel Horse 280	Closed	N/A	88.00	125-290
1981	Carousel Horse 281	Closed	N/A	88.00	125-290
1981	Cashew On One Knee 275	Closed	N/A	N/A	N/A
1981	Elephant Reading 271	Closed	N/A	N/A	N/A
1981	Executive Hitchiking 267	Closed	N/A	23.00	45-110
1981	Executive Reading 264	Closed	N/A	23.00	45-110
1981	Executive Resting 266	Closed	N/A	23.00	45-110
1981	Executive with Umbrella 265	Closed	N/A	23.00	45-110
1981	Harpo 296	Closed	N/A	120.00	190-350
1981	Hobo Joe Praying 298	Closed	N/A	57.00	65-85
1981	Kevin at the Drums 283	Closed	N/A	50.00	92-150
1981	Larry and His Hotdogs 274	Closed	N/A	76.00	90-200
1981	Louie Hitching A Ride 269	Closed	N/A	47.00	58-135
1981	Louie on Park Bench 268	Closed	N/A	56.00	85-160
1981	Louie On Railroad Car 270	Closed	N/A	77.00	95-180
1981	Mickey With Umbrella 291	Closed	N/A	50.00	75-140
1981	Mickey Tightrope Walker 292	Closed	N/A	50.00	75-140
1981	Mickey Upside Down 293	Closed	N/A	50.00	75-140
1981	My Son Darren 295	Closed	N/A	57.00	72-140
1981	Nicky Sitting on Ball 289	Closed	N/A	39.00	48-92
1981	Nicky Standing on Ball 290	Closed	N/A	39.00	48-92
1981	Perry Sitting With Balloon 287	Closed	N/A	37.00	50-95
1981	Perry Standing With Balloon 288	Closed	N/A	37.00	50-95
1981	Pickles and Pooch 297	Closed	N/A	90.00	200-240
1981	Pistol Pete 272	Closed	N/A	76.00	85-180
1981	Rocketman 294	Closed	N/A	77.00	92-150
1981	Ron at the Piano 285	Closed	N/A	46.00	55-110
1981	Ron Lee Trio 282	Closed	N/A	144.00	280-435
1981	Timothy In Big Shoes 286	Closed	N/A	37.00	50-95

The Original Ron Lee Collection-1982 - R. Lee

YEAR ISSUE		EDITION LIMIT	YEAR RETD.	ISSUE PRICE	QUOTE U.S.$
1982	Ali on His Magic Carpet 335	Closed	N/A	105.00	150-210
1982	Barnum Feeding Bacon 315	Closed	N/A	120.00	160-270
1982	Beaver Playing Accordian 807	Closed	N/A	23.00	35-92
1982	Benny Pulling Car 310	Closed	N/A	190.00	235-360
1982	Burrito Bandito 334	Closed	N/A	150.00	190-260
1982	Buster in Barrel 308	Closed	N/A	85.00	90-120
1982	Camel 818	Closed	N/A	57.00	75-150
1982	Captain Cranberry 320	Closed	N/A	115.00	145-180
1982	Captain Mis-Adventure 703	Closed	N/A	250.00	300-550
1982	Carney and Dog Act 301	Closed	N/A	63.00	75-149
1982	Charlie Chaplain 701	Closed	N/A	230.00	285-650
1982	Charlie in the Rain 321	Closed	N/A	80.00	90-160
1982	Chico Playing Guitar 336	Closed	N/A	70.00	95-180
1982	Clancy, the Cop and Dog 333	Closed	N/A	115.00	140-250
1982	Clarence - The Lawyer 331	Closed	N/A	100.00	140-230
1982	Denny Eating Ice Cream 305	Closed	N/A	39.00	50-170
1982	Denny Holding Gift Box 306	Closed	N/A	39.00	50-170
1982	Denny Juggling Ball 307	Closed	N/A	39.00	50-170
1982	Dog Playing Guitar 805	Closed	N/A	23.00	35-92
1982	Dr. Painless and Patient 311	Closed	N/A	195.00	240-385
1982	Fireman Watering House 303	Closed	N/A	99.00	99-180
1982	Fish With Shoe 803	Closed	N/A	23.00	35-92
1982	Fox In An Airplane 806	Closed	N/A	23.00	35-92
1982	Georgie Going Anywhere 302	Closed	N/A	95.00	125-256
1982	Giraffe 816	Closed	N/A	57.00	75-150
1982	Herbie Balancing Hat 327	Closed	N/A	26.00	40-110
1982	Herbie Dancing 325	Closed	N/A	26.00	40-110
1982	Herbie Hands Outstretched 326	Closed	N/A	26.00	40-110
1982	Herbie Legs in Air 329	Closed	N/A	26.00	40-110
1982	Herbie Lying Down 328	Closed	N/A	26.00	40-110
1982	Herbie Touching Ground 330	Closed	N/A	26.00	40-110
1982	Hobo Joe on Cycle 322	Closed	N/A	125.00	170-280
1982	Horse 819	Closed	N/A	57.00	75-150
1982	Kukla and Friend 316	Closed	N/A	100.00	140-210
1982	Laurel & Hardy 700	Closed	N/A	225.00	290-500
1982	Limousine Service 705	Closed	N/A	330.00	375-750
1982	Lion 817	Closed	N/A	57.00	75-150
1982	Marion With Marrionette 317	Closed	N/A	105.00	135-225
1982	Murphy On Unicycle 337	Closed	N/A	115.00	160-288
1982	Nappy Snoozing 346	Closed	N/A	110.00	125-210
1982	Norman Painting Dumbo 314	Closed	N/A	126.00	150-210
1982	Ostrich 813	Closed	N/A	57.00	75-150
1982	Parrot Rollerskating 809	Closed	N/A	23.00	35-92
1982	Pig Brick Layer 800	Closed	N/A	23.00	35-92
1982	Pinball Pal 332	Closed	N/A	150.00	195-287
1982	Quincy Lying Down 304	Closed	N/A	80.00	92-210
1982	Rabbit With Egg 801	Closed	N/A	23.00	35-92
1982	Reindeer 812	Closed	N/A	57.00	75-150
1982	Robin Resting 338	Closed	N/A	110.00	125-210
1982	Ron Lee Carousel	Closed	N/A	1000.00	12500
1982	Rooster 815	Closed	N/A	57.00	75-150
1982	Rooster With Barbell 808	Closed	N/A	23.00	35-92
1982	Sammy Riding Elephant 309	Closed	N/A	90.00	125-250
1982	Seal Blowing His Horns 804	Closed	N/A	23.00	35-92
1982	Self Portrait 702	Closed	N/A	355.00	2500
1982	Slim Charging Bull 313	Closed	N/A	195.00	265-410
1982	Smokey, the Bear 802	Closed	N/A	23.00	35-92
1982	Steppin' Out 704	Closed	N/A	325.00	390-700
1982	Three Man Valentinos 319	Closed	N/A	55.00	70-120
1982	Tiger 814	Closed	N/A	57.00	75-150
1982	Too Loose-L'Artiste 312	Closed	N/A	150.00	180-290
1982	Tou Tou 323	Closed	N/A	70.00	90-190
1982	Toy Soldier 324	Closed	N/A	95.00	140-270
1982	Turtle With Gun 811	Closed	N/A	57.00	75-150
1982	Two Man Valentinos 318	Closed	N/A	45.00	60-130
1982	Walrus With Umbrella 810	Closed	N/A	23.00	35-92

The Original Ron Lee Collection-1983 - R. Lee

YEAR ISSUE		EDITION LIMIT	YEAR RETD.	ISSUE PRICE	QUOTE U.S.$
1983	The Bandwagon 707	Closed	N/A	900.00	2000
1983	Beethoven's Fourth Paws 358	Closed	N/A	59.00	110-165
1983	Black Carousel Horse 1001	Closed	N/A	450.00	450-600
1983	Bumbles Selling Balloons 353	Closed	N/A	80.00	170-240
1983	Buster and His Balloons 363	Closed	N/A	47.00	90-125
1983	Captain Freddy 375	Closed	N/A	85.00	200-425
1983	Casey Cruising 351	Closed	N/A	57.00	95-170
1983	Catch the Brass Ring 708	Closed	N/A	510.00	900-1350
1983	Cecil and Sausage 354	Closed	N/A	90.00	200-270
1983	Chef's Cuisine 361	Closed	N/A	57.00	100-110
1983	Chestnut Carousel Horse 1002	Closed	N/A	450.00	700-1100
1983	Cimba the Elephant 706	Closed	N/A	225.00	300-550
1983	Clyde Juggling 339	Closed	N/A	39.00	100-115
1983	Clyde Upside Down 340	Closed	N/A	39.00	100-115
1983	Coco and His Compact 369	Closed	N/A	55.00	145-175
1983	Cotton Candy 377	Closed	N/A	150.00	200-400
1983	Daring Dudley 367	Closed	N/A	65.00	100-200
1983	Door to Door Dabney 373	Closed	N/A	100.00	200-285
1983	Engineer Billie 356	Closed	N/A	190.00	275-550
1983	Flipper Diving 345	Closed	N/A	115.00	200-350
1983	Gazebo 1004	Closed	N/A	750.00	13-1750
1983	Gilbert Tee'd Off 376	Closed	N/A	60.00	100-200
1983	Hobi in His Hammock 344	Closed	N/A	85.00	175
1983	I Love You From My Heart 360	Closed	N/A	35.00	95-105
1983	The Jogger 372	Closed	N/A	75.00	120-220
1983	Josephine 370	Closed	N/A	55.00	145-175
1983	Knickers Balancing Feather 366	Closed	N/A	47.00	120-135
1983	The Last Scoop 379	Closed	N/A	175.00	300-475
1983	The Last Scoop 900	Closed	N/A	325.00	300-725
1983	Little Horse - Head Down 342	Closed	N/A	29.00	72
1983	Little Horse - Head Up 341	Closed	N/A	29.00	72
1983	Little Saturday Night 348	Closed	N/A	53.00	200
1983	Lou Proposing 365	Closed	N/A	57.00	120-170
1983	Matinee Jitters 378	Closed	N/A	175.00	200-450
1983	Matinee Jitters 901	Closed	N/A	325.00	355
1983	My Daughter Deborah 357	Closed	N/A	63.00	125-185
1983	No Camping or Fishing 902	Closed	N/A	325.00	350-600
1983	On The Road Again 355	Closed	N/A	220.00	300-650
1983	Riches to Rags 374	Closed	N/A	55.00	200-265
1983	Ride 'em Roni 347	Closed	N/A	125.00	200-375
1983	Rufus and His Refuse 343	Closed	N/A	65.00	160
1983	Say It With Flowers 359	Closed	N/A	35.00	95-110
1983	Singin' In The Rain 362	Closed	N/A	105.00	350
1983	Tatters and Balloons 352	Closed	N/A	65.00	125-200
1983	Teeter Tottie Scottie 350	Closed	N/A	55.00	105-165
1983	Tottie Scottie 349	Closed	N/A	39.00	75-115
1983	Up, Up and Away 364	Closed	N/A	50.00	100-150
1983	White Carousel Horse 1003	Closed	N/A	450.00	700-1100
1983	Wilt the Stilt 368	Closed	N/A	49.00	100-155

The Original Ron Lee Collection-1984 - R. Lee

YEAR ISSUE		EDITION LIMIT	YEAR RETD.	ISSUE PRICE	QUOTE U.S.$
1984	Baggy Pants 387	Closed	N/A	98.00	250-300
1984	Black Circus Horse 711A	Closed	N/A	305.00	350-520
1984	A Bozo Lunch 390	Closed	N/A	148.00	250-400
1984	Bozo's Seal of Approval 389	Closed	N/A	138.00	200-350
1984	Chestnut Circus Horse 710A	Closed	N/A	305.00	350-520
1984	Give a Dog a Bone 383	Closed	N/A	95.00	95-182
1984	Just For You 386	Closed	N/A	110.00	150-250
1984	Look at the Birdy 388	Closed	N/A	138.00	200-300
1984	Mortimer Fishing 382	Closed	N/A	N/A	N/A
1984	My Fellow Americans 391	Closed	N/A	138.00	250-425
1984	No Camping or Fishing 380	Closed	N/A	175.00	275-450
1984	No Loitering 392	Closed	N/A	113.00	150-250
1984	The Peppermints 384	Closed	N/A	150.00	180-250
1984	Rudy Holding Balloons 713	Closed	N/A	230.00	300-550
1984	Saturday Night 714	Closed	N/A	250.00	600-825
1984	T.K. and OH!! 385	Closed	N/A	85.00	200-325
1984	Tisket and Tasket 393	Closed	N/A	93.00	150-250
1984	Wheeler Sheila 381	Closed	N/A	75.00	175-225
1984	White Circus Horse 709	Closed	N/A	305.00	350-520

The Original Ron Lee Collection-1985 - R. Lee

YEAR ISSUE		EDITION LIMIT	YEAR RETD.	ISSUE PRICE	QUOTE U.S.$
1985	Bull-Can-Rear-You 422	Closed	N/A	120.00	206
1985	Cannonball 466	Closed	N/A	43.00	83
1985	Catch of the Day 441	Closed	N/A	170.00	305
1985	Clowns of the Caribbean PS101	Closed	N/A	1250.00	2-2800
1985	Dr. Sigmund Fraud 457	Closed	N/A	98.00	190
1985	Dr. Timothy DeCay 459	Closed	N/A	98.00	185
1985	Duster Buster 461	Closed	N/A	43.00	90
1985	The Finishing Touch 409	Closed	N/A	178.00	305
1985	Fred Figures 903	Closed	N/A	175.00	595
1985	From Riches to Rags 374	Closed	N/A	108.00	250
1985	Get the Picture 456	Closed	N/A	70.00	140
1985	Gilbert TeeOd OFF 376	Closed	N/A	63.00	55-63
1985	Giraffe Getting a Bath 428	Closed	N/A	160.00	350-450
1985	Ham Track 451	Closed	N/A	240.00	430
1985	Hi Ho Blinky 462	Closed	N/A	53.00	105
1985	One Wheel Winky 464	Closed	N/A	43.00	83
1985	Pee Wee With Balloons 435	Closed	N/A	50.00	100
1985	Pee Wee With Umbrella 434	Closed	N/A	50.00	100
1985	Policy Paul 904	Closed	N/A	175.00	190
1985	Rosebuds 433	Closed	N/A	155.00	315
1985	Twas the Night Before 408	Closed	N/A	235.00	405
1985	Whiskers Bathing 749	Closed	N/A	305.00	500-800
1985	Whiskers Hitchhiking 745	Closed	N/A	240.00	800
1985	Whiskers Holding Balloons 746	Closed	N/A	265.00	500-800
1985	Whiskers Holding Umbrella 747	Closed	N/A	265.00	500-800
1985	Whiskers On The Bench 750	Closed	N/A	230.00	600-700
1985	Whiskers Sweeping 744	Closed	N/A	240.00	850
1985	Yo Yo Stravinsky-Attoney at Law 458	Closed	N/A	98.00	185

The Original Ron Lee Collection-1986 - R. Lee

YEAR ISSUE		EDITION LIMIT	YEAR RETD.	ISSUE PRICE	QUOTE U.S.$
1986	Bathing Buddies 450	Closed	N/A	145.00	250-375
1986	Bums Day at the Beach L105	Closed	N/A	97.00	N/A
1986	Captain Cranberry 469	Closed	N/A	140.00	175-335
1986	Christmas Morning Magic L107	Closed	N/A	99.00	N/A
1986	Getting Even 485	Closed	N/A	85.00	125-225
1986	Hari and Hare 454	Closed	N/A	57.00	85-135
1986	High Above the Big Top L112	Closed	N/A	162.00	N/A
1986	The Last Stop L106	Closed	N/A	99.00	N/A
1986	Most Requested Toy L108	Closed	N/A	264.00	N/A
1986	Puppy Love's Portrait L113	Closed	N/A	168.00	250
1986	Ride 'Em Peanuts 463	Closed	N/A	55.00	70-135
1986	Wet Paint 436	Closed	N/A	80.00	100-200

The Original Ron Lee Collection-1987 - R. Lee

YEAR ISSUE		EDITION LIMIT	YEAR RETD.	ISSUE PRICE	QUOTE U.S.$
1987	First & Main L110	Closed	N/A	368.00	500-775
1987	Happines Is L116	Closed	N/A	155.00	N/A
1987	Heartbroken Harry L101	Closed	N/A	63.00	125-225
1987	Lovable Luke L102	Closed	N/A	70.00	150
1987	Puppy Love L103	Closed	N/A	71.00	150
1987	Show of Shows L115	Closed	N/A	175.00	N/A
1987	Sugarland Express L109	Closed	N/A	342.00	400-600
1987	Would You Like To Ride? L104	Closed	N/A	246.00	300-475

The Original Ron Lee Collection-1988 - R. Lee

YEAR ISSUE		EDITION LIMIT	YEAR RETD.	ISSUE PRICE	QUOTE U.S.$
1988	Anchors-A-Way L120	Closed	N/A	195.00	N/A
1988	Boulder Bay L124	Closed	N/A	700.00	N/A
1988	Bozorina L118	Closed	N/A	95.00	120
1988	Cactus Pete L125	Closed	N/A	495.00	N/A
1988	Dinner for Two L119	Closed	N/A	140.00	N/A
1988	The Fifth Wheel L117	Closed	N/A	250.00	375
1988	Fore! L122	Closed	N/A	135.00	150
1988	New Ron Lee Carousel	Closed	N/A	7000.00	9500
1988	Pumpkuns Galore L121	Closed	N/A	135.00	N/A
1988	To The Rescue L127	Closed	N/A	130.00	160-550
1988	Together Again L126	Closed	N/A	130.00	195
1988	Tunnel of Love L123	Closed	N/A	490.00	600-800
1988	When You're Hot, You're Hot! L128	Closed	N/A	221.00	220

The Original Ron Lee Collection-1989 - R. Lee

YEAR ISSUE		EDITION LIMIT	YEAR RETD.	ISSUE PRICE	QUOTE U.S.$
1989	The Accountant L173	Closed	N/A	68.00	150-200
1989	The Baseball Player L189	Closed	N/A	72.00	150-200
1989	The Basketball Player L187	Closed	N/A	68.00	150-200
1989	Be Happy L198	Closed	N/A	160.00	N/A
1989	Be It Ever So Humble L111	Closed	N/A	900.00	950-1250
1989	The Beautician L183	Closed	N/A	68.00	150-200
1989	Beauty Is In The Eye Of L140	Closed	N/A	190.00	N/A
1989	Birdbrain L206	Closed	N/A	110.00	250
1989	The Bowler L191	Closed	N/A	68.00	150-200
1989	Butt-R-Fly L151	Closed	N/A	47.00	75
1989	Butterflies Are Free L204	Closed	N/A	225.00	N/A
1989	Candy Apple L155	Closed	N/A	47.00	75
1989	Candy Man L217	Closed	N/A	350.00	350
1989	Catch A Falling Star L148	Closed	N/A	57.00	75
1989	The Chef L178	Closed	N/A	65.00	150-200
1989	The Chiropractor L180	Closed	N/A	68.00	150-200
1989	Circus Little L143	Closed	N/A	990.00	1250
1989	Craps L212	Closed	N/A	530.00	N/A
1989	Dang It L200	Closed	N/A	47.00	N/A
1989	The Dentist L175	Closed	N/A	65.00	150-200
1989	The Doctor L170	Closed	N/A	65.00	150-200
1989	Eye Love You L136	Closed	N/A	68.00	N/A
1989	The Fireman L169	Closed	N/A	68.00	150-200
1989	The Fisherman L194	Closed	N/A	72.00	150-200
1989	The Football Player L186	Closed	N/A	65.00	150-200
1989	Get Well L131	Closed	N/A	79.00	N/A
1989	The Golfer L188	Closed	N/A	72.00	150-200
1989	The Greatest Little Shoe On Earth L210	Closed	N/A	165.00	200-300
1989	Happy Chanakah L162	Closed	N/A	106.00	N/A
1989	Hot Diggity Dog L201	Closed	N/A	47.00	50
1989	The Housewife L181	Closed	N/A	75.00	150-200
1989	Hughie Mungus L144	Closed	N/A	250.00	300-825
1989	I Ain't Got No Money L195	Closed	N/A	325.00	N/A

FIGURINES/COTTAGES

YEAR ISSUE		EDITION LIMIT	YEAR RETD.	ISSUE PRICE	QUOTE U.S.$
1989	I Just Called! L153	Closed	N/A	47.00	75
1989	I Pledge Allegiance L134	Closed	N/A	131.00	150-250
1989	I Should've When I Could've L196	Closed	N/A	325.00	340
1989	I-D-D-D-Do! L215	Closed	N/A	180.00	N/A
1989	If I Were A Rich Man L133	Closed	N/A	315.00	400-600
1989	If That's Your Drive How's Your Putts L164	Closed	N/A	260.00	N/A
1989	In Over My Head L135	Closed	N/A	95.00	250
1989	Jingles Hitchhiking L209	Closed	N/A	90.00	175
1989	Jingles Holding Balloon L208	Closed	N/A	90.00	200
1989	Jingles With Umbrella L207	Closed	N/A	90.00	175
1989	Just Carried Away L138	Closed	N/A	135.00	230
1989	Just Go! L156	Closed	N/A	47.00	75
1989	The Lawyer 171	Closed	N/A	68.00	150-200
1989	Maestro L132	Closed	N/A	173.00	N/A
1989	Marcelle L150	Closed	N/A	47.00	N/A
1989	The Mechanic L184	Closed	N/A	68.00	150-200
1989	Memories L197	Closed	N/A	325.00	N/A
1989	Merry Xmas L159	Closed	N/A	94.00	N/A
1989	My Affections L157	Closed	N/A	47.00	75
1989	My First Tree L161	Closed	N/A	92.00	125
1989	My Heart Beats For You L137	Closed	N/A	74.00	95
1989	My Last Chip L213	Closed	N/A	550.00	N/A
1989	My Money's OnThe Bull L142	Closed	N/A	187.00	160-187
1989	The New Self Portrait L218	Closed	N/A	800.00	950
1989	No Fishing L130	Closed	N/A	247.00	N/A
1989	Not A Ghost Of A Chance L145	Closed	N/A	195.00	250
1989	The Nurse L168	Closed	N/A	65.00	N/A
1989	O' Solo Mia L139	Closed	N/A	85.00	90-150
1989	The Optometrist L174	Closed	N/A	65.00	150-200
1989	Over 21 L214	Closed	N/A	550.00	N/A
1989	The Pharmacist L166	Closed	N/A	65.00	N/A
1989	The Photographer L172	Closed	N/A	68.00	150-200
1989	The Plumber L176	Closed	N/A	65.00	150-200
1989	The Policeman L165	Closed	N/A	68.00	100-200
1989	Rain Bugs Me L203	Closed	N/A	225.00	N/A
1989	The Real Estate Lady L185	Closed	N/A	70.00	150-200
1989	The Real Estate Man L177	Closed	N/A	65.00	150-200
1989	Rest Stop L149	Closed	N/A	47.00	75
1989	The Salesman L167	Closed	N/A	68.00	N/A
1989	Santa's Dilemma L160	Closed	N/A	97.00	250
1989	The Secretary L179	Closed	N/A	65.00	150-200
1989	The Serenade L202	Closed	N/A	47.00	N/A
1989	Sh-h-h-h! L146	Closed	N/A	210.00	450
1989	She Loves Me Not L205	Closed	N/A	225.00	N/A
1989	The Skier L193	Closed	N/A	75.00	150-200
1989	Slots Of Luck L211	Closed	N/A	90.00	175
1989	Snowdrifter L163	Closed	N/A	230.00	240
1989	Stormy Weathers L152	Closed	N/A	47.00	N/A
1989	Sunflower L154	Closed	N/A	47.00	N/A
1989	The Surfer L192	Closed	N/A	72.00	150-200
1989	Tee for Two L141	Closed	N/A	125.00	N/A
1989	The Tennis Player L190	Closed	N/A	72.00	150-200
1989	Today's Catch L147	Closed	N/A	230.00	350
1989	Two a.m. Blues L199	Closed	N/A	125.00	150
1989	The Veterinarian L182	Closed	N/A	72.00	150-200
1989	Wintertime Pals L158	Closed	N/A	90.00	N/A
1989	Wishful Thinking L114	Closed	N/A	230.00	250-500
1989	You Must Be Kidding L216	Closed	N/A	N/A	800

The Original Ron Lee Collection-1990 - R. Lee

YEAR ISSUE		EDITION LIMIT	YEAR RETD.	ISSUE PRICE	QUOTE U.S.$
1990	All Show No Go L238	1,500		285.00	285
1990	The Big Wheel L236	Closed	N/A	240.00	245
1990	Carousel Horse L219	Closed	N/A	150.00	N/A
1990	Carousel Horse L220	Closed	N/A	150.00	N/A
1990	Carousel Horse L221	Closed	N/A	150.00	N/A
1990	Carousel Horse L222	Closed	N/A	150.00	N/A
1990	Fill'er Up L248	Closed	N/A	280.00	300
1990	Flapper Riding Carousel L223	Closed	N/A	190.00	N/A
1990	Heart of My Heart L246	5,500	1995	55.00	55
1990	Heartbroken Hobo L233	Closed	N/A	116.00	160
1990	Henry 8-3/4 L260	Closed	N/A	37.00	50
1990	Horsin' Around L262	Closed	N/A	37.00	37-50
1990	I Love You L242	5,500	1995	55.00	55
1990	I.Q. Two L253	2,750	1995	33.00	33
1990	Jo-Jo Riding Carousel L226	Closed	N/A	190.00	N/A
1990	Kiss! Kiss! L251	Closed	N/A	37.00	37
1990	L-O-V-E L245	5,500	1995	55.00	55
1990	Loving You L244	5,500		55.00	55
1990	Me Too!! L231	Closed	1995	70.00	70-80
1990	My Heart's on for You L240	5,500	1995	55.00	55
1990	Na! Na! L252	Closed	N/A	33.00	33
1990	New Pinky Lying Down L228	8,500		42.00	42
1990	New Pinky Sitting L230	8,500		42.00	42
1990	New Pinky Standing L229	8,500		42.00	42
1990	New Pinky Upside Down L227	8,500		42.00	42
1990	Paddle L259	2,750	1995	33.00	33
1990	Par Three L232	2,750	1995	144.00	144
1990	Peaches Riding Carousel L224	Closed	N/A	190.00	N/A
1990	Pitch L261	2,750	1995	35.00	35
1990	Push and Pull L249	Closed	N/A	260.00	280
1990	Q.T. Pie L257	2,750	1995	37.00	50
1990	Rascal Riding Carousel L225	Closed	N/A	190.00	N/A
1990	Same To "U" L255	2,750	1995	37.00	37
1990	Scooter L234	Closed	1995	240.00	275
1990	Skiing My Way L239	2,500	1995	400.00	695
1990	Snowdrifter II L250	Closed	N/A	340.00	280
1990	Squirt L258	2,750	1995	37.00	37
1990	Stuck on Me L243	5,500	1995	55.00	55
1990	Swinging on a Star L241	5,500	1995	55.00	55
1990	Tandem Mania L235	Closed	N/A	360.00	360
1990	Uni-Cycle L237	Closed	N/A	240.00	240
1990	Watch Your Step L247	2,500		78.00	78
1990	Yo Mama L256	2,750	1995	35.00	35
1990	Your Heaviness L254	2,750	1995	37.00	37

The Original Ron Lee Collection-1991 - R. Lee

YEAR ISSUE		EDITION LIMIT	YEAR RETD.	ISSUE PRICE	QUOTE U.S.$
1991	Ain't No Havana L315	500	1995	230.00	230
1991	Anywhere? L269	Closed	N/A	125.00	155
1991	Banjo Willie L293	1,750		90.00	90
1991	Business is Business L266	Closed	1995	110.00	125
1991	Clarence Clarinet L289	1,750	1995	42.00	42
1991	Cruising L265	Closed	N/A	170.00	170-175
1991	Droopy Drummer L290	1,750	1995	42.00	42
1991	Eight Ball-Corner Pocket L311	1,750		224.00	225
1991	Fall L282	1,500		120.00	120-125
1991	Geronimo L304	1,750		127.00	127
1991	Gilbert's Dilemma L270	Closed	N/A	90.00	125
1991	Give Me Liberty L313	Closed	N/A	155.00	155-165
1991	Happy Birthday Puppy Love L278	Closed	N/A	73.00	85
1991	Harley Horn L291	1,750	1995	42.00	42
1991	Hobi Daydreaming L299	1,750		112.00	112
1991	Hook, Line and Sinker L303	1,750		100.00	60-100
1991	Hot Dawg! L316	500	1995	255.00	255
1991	I'm Singin' In The Rain L268	Closed	N/A	135.00	150
1991	IRS or Bust L285	1,500	1995	122.00	122
1991	Lit'l Snowdrifter L298	1,750		70.00	85
1991	Makin Tracks L283	1,500	1995	142.00	142
1991	Marcelle I L271	2,250	1995	50.00	50
1991	Marcelle II L272	2,250	1995	50.00	50
1991	Marcelle III L273	2,250	1995	50.00	50
1991	Marcelle IV L274	2,250	1995	50.00	50
1991	New Darby Tipping Hat L310	1,250	1995	57.00	57
1991	New Darby with Flower L307	1,250	1995	57.00	57
1991	New Darby with Umbrella L308	1,250	1995	57.00	57
1991	New Darby with Violin L309	1,250	1995	57.00	57
1991	New Harpo L305	1,250	1995	130.00	130
1991	New Toy Soldier L306	1,250	1995	115.00	115
1991	Our Nation's Pride L312	Closed	N/A	150.00	150
1991	Puppy Love Scootin' L275	Closed	N/A	73.00	73-80
1991	Puppy Love's Free Ride L276	Closed	N/A	73.00	100
1991	Puppy Love's Treat L277	Closed	N/A	73.00	73-80
1991	Refugee L267	1,750	1995	88.00	88
1991	Sand Trap L301	1,750		100.00	100
1991	Soap Suds Serenade L284	1,750		85.00	85
1991	Spring L280	1,500		95.00	95-110
1991	Strike!!! L302	1,750		76.00	76
1991	Summer L281	1,500	N/A	95.00	125
1991	Surf's Up L300	1,750		80.00	80
1991	TA DA L294	Closed	N/A	220.00	200-295
1991	Tender-Lee L264	1,750	1995	96.00	96
1991	This Won't Hurt L296	1,750	1995	110.00	110
1991	Tootie Tuba L286	1,750	1995	42.00	42
1991	Trash Can Sam L295	1,750	1995	118.00	118
1991	Truly Trumpet L287	1,750	1995	42.00	42
1991	Trusty Trombone L288	1,750	1995	42.00	42
1991	Two For Fore L297	1,750		120.00	120
1991	United We Stand L314	Closed	N/A	150.00	165
1991	The Visit L263	1,750	1995	100.00	100
1991	Winter L279	1,500		115.00	115-125

The Original Ron Lee Collection-1992 - R. Lee

YEAR ISSUE		EDITION LIMIT	YEAR RETD.	ISSUE PRICE	QUOTE U.S.$
1992	Baloony L350	2,500		26.00	27
1992	Beats Nothin' L357	1,500		145.00	145
1992	Beau Regards L342	2,500		26.00	27
1992	Big Wheel Kop RLC1005	1,750	1995	65.00	65
1992	Birdy The Hard Way L352	1,750		85.00	85
1992	Bo-Bo Balancing RLC1003	1,750	1995	75.00	75
1992	Break Point L335	2,500		26.00	27
1992	Brokenhearted Huey RLC1006	1,750	1995	65.00	65
1992	Buster Too PC100	1,500	1995	65.00	65
1992	Cannonball RLC1009	1,750	1995	95.00	95
1992	Clar-A-Bow L336	2,500		26.00	27
1992	Cyclin' Around L322	2,500		26.00	27
1992	Dreams L332	2,500		26.00	27
1992	Dudley's Dog Act RLC1010	1,750	1995	75.00	75
1992	Dunkin' L328	2,500		26.00	27
1992	Fish in Pail L358	1,500		130.00	130
1992	Flyin' High L340	2,500		26.00	27
1992	Forget Me Not L341	2,500		26.00	27
1992	Gassing Up RLC1004	1,750	1995	70.00	70
1992	Go Man Go L344	2,500		26.00	27
1992	Handy Standy L321	2,500		26.00	27
1992	Heel's Up L329	2,500		26.00	27
1992	Hi-Five L339	2,500		26.00	27
1992	Hippolong Cassidy L320	Closed	N/A	166.00	140
1992	Howdy L325	2,500		26.00	27
1992	Jo-Jo Juggling RLC1002	1,750	1995	70.00	70
1992	Juggles L347	2,500		26.00	27
1992	Little Pard L349	2,500		26.00	27
1992	Lolly L326	2,500		26.00	27
1992	Love Ya' Baby L355	1,250		190.00	190
1992	Miles PC105	1,500	1995	65.00	65
1992	My Pal L334	2,500		26.00	27
1992	My Portrait L354	Closed	N/A	315.00	315
1992	Myak Kyak L337	2,500		26.00	27
1992	On My Way L348	2,500		26.00	27
1992	Penny Saver L333	2,500		26.00	27
1992	Popcorn & Cotton Candy RLC1001	1,750	1995	70.00	70
1992	Scrub-A- Dub-Dub L319	Closed	N/A	185.00	195
1992	Seven's Up L356	1,250		165.00	165
1992	Shake Jake L324	2,500		26.00	27
1992	Ship Ahoy L345	2,500		26.00	27
1992	Shufflin' L343	2,500		26.00	27
1992	Snowdrifter Blowin' In Wind L317	1,750		77.50	78
1992	Snowdrifter's Special Delivery L318	1,750		136.00	136
1992	Steamer L338	2,500		26.00	27
1992	Stop Cop L331	2,500		26.00	27
1992	Strike Out L323	2,500		26.00	27
1992	Struttin' L346	2,500		26.00	27
1992	Sure-Footed Freddie RLC1007	1,750	1995	80.00	80
1992	To-Tee L327	2,500		26.00	27
1992	Topper PC110	1,500	1995	65.00	65
1992	Twirp Chirp L330	2,500		26.00	27
1992	Vincent Van Clown L353	Closed	N/A	160.00	160
1992	Walking A Fine Line RMB7000	1,750	1995	65.00	65
1992	Webb-ster PC115	1,500	1995	65.00	65
1992	Wrong Hole Clown L351	1,750		125.00	125

The Original Ron Lee Collection-1993 - R. Lee

YEAR ISSUE		EDITION LIMIT	YEAR RETD.	ISSUE PRICE	QUOTE U.S.$
1993	Andy Jackson L364	950	1995	87.00	87
1993	Anywhere Warm L398	950		90.00	90
1993	Bellboy L390	950	1995	80.00	80
1993	Blinky Lying Down L384	1,200		45.00	45
1993	Blinky Sitting L383	1,200		45.00	45
1993	Blinky Standing L382	1,200		45.00	45
1993	Blinky Upside Down L385	1,200		45.00	45
1993	Bo-Bo L365	950	1995	95.00	95
1993	Britches L377	750		205.00	205
1993	Bumper Fun L403	750		330.00	330
1993	Buster L368	950	1995	87.00	87
1993	Charkles L381	750	1995	220.00	220
1993	Chattanooga Choo-Choo L374	750		420.00	420
1993	Dave Bomber L360	950	1995	90.00	90
1993	Happy Trails L369	950	1995	90.00	90
1993	Honk Honk L370	950	1995	90.00	90
1993	Hot Buns L376	750		175.00	175
1993	Lollipop L363	950	1995	87.00	87
1993	Merry Go Clown L405	750		375.00	375
1993	Moto Kris L380	750		255.00	255
1993	North Pole L396	950	1995	75.00	75
1993	Piggy Backin' L379	750		205.00	205
1993	Pretzels L372	750		195.00	195
1993	Sailin' L366	950	1995	95.00	95
1993	Scrubs L361	950	1995	87.00	87
1993	Sho-Sho L373	750		115.00	115
1993	Shriner Cop L404	750		175.00	175
1993	Skittles L367	950	1995	95.00	95
1993	Snoozin' L399	950		90.00	90
1993	Soft Shoe L400	750		275.00	275
1993	Sole-Full L375	750		250.00	250
1993	Special Occasion L402	750		280.00	280
1993	Taxi L378	750		470.00	470
1993	Tinker And Toy L359	950	1995	95.00	95
1993	Wagone Hes L371	750		210.00	210
1993	Wanderer L401	750		255.00	255
1993	Yo-Yo L362	950	1995	87.00	87

The Popeye Collection - R. Lee

YEAR ISSUE		EDITION LIMIT	YEAR RETD.	ISSUE PRICE	QUOTE U.S.$
1992	Liberty P001	1,750	1995	184.00	184
1992	Men!!! P002	1,750	1995	230.00	230
1992	Oh Popeye P005	1,750	1995	230.00	230
1992	Par Excellence P006	1,750	1995	220.00	220
1992	Strong to The Finish P003	1,750	1995	95.00	95
1992	That's My Boy P004	1,750	1995	145.00	145

Premier Dealer Collection - R. Lee

YEAR ISSUE		EDITION LIMIT	YEAR RETD.	ISSUE PRICE	QUOTE U.S.$
1992	Dream On PD002	Closed	N/A	125.00	125
1992	Framed Again PD001	Closed	N/A	110.00	110
1993	Jake-A-Juggling Balls PD008	500		85.00	85
1993	Jake-A-Juggling Clubs PD007	500		85.00	85
1993	Jake-A-Juggling Cylinder PD006	500		85.00	85
1994	Joe's Feline Friend PD009	500		105.00	105
1994	Just Big Enough PD010	500		115.00	115
1992	Moonlighting PD004	Closed	N/A	125.00	125
1992	Nest to Nothing PD003	Closed	N/A	110.00	115
1994	Off The Toe PD011	500		105.00	105
1993	Pockets PD005	500		175.00	175
1994	Storm Warning PD012	500		115.00	115
1994	Trading Places PD013	500		190.00	190

Rocky & Bullwinkle And Friends Collection - R. Lee

YEAR ISSUE		EDITION LIMIT	YEAR RETD.	ISSUE PRICE	QUOTE U.S.$
1992	Dudley Do-Right RB610	1,750	1995	175.00	175
1992	KA-BOOM! RB620	1,750	1995	175.00	175
1992	My Hero RB615	1,750	1995	275.00	275
1992	Rocky & Bullwinkle RB600	1,750	1995	120.00	120
1992	The Swami RB605	1,750	1995	175.00	175

The Ron Lee Disney Collection Exclusives - R. Lee

YEAR ISSUE		EDITION LIMIT	YEAR RETD.	ISSUE PRICE	QUOTE U.S.$
1993	Aladdin MM560	500		550.00	550
1995	Autopia MM770	750		220.00	220
1992	Bambi MM330	2,750		195.00	195
1990	The Bandleader MM100	Closed	N/A	75.00	75
1992	Beauty & The Beast (shadow box) DIS100	500		1650.00	1650
1994	Beauty & The Beast MM610	800		170.00	170
1992	Big Thunder Mountain MM460	250	1995	1650.00	2000-3000
1992	Captain Hook MM320	2,750		175.00	175
1995	The Carousel MM730	750		125.00	125
1992	Christmas '92 MM420	1,500		145.00	145
1993	Cinderella's Slipper MM510	1,750	1995	115.00	115
1993	Darkwing Duck MM470	1,750		105.00	105

YEAR ISSUE		EDITION LIMIT	YEAR RETD.	ISSUE PRICE	QUOTE U.S.$
1991	Decorating Donald MM210	2,750		60.00	60
1992	The Dinosaurs MM370	2,750		195.00	195
1991	Dopey MM120	2,750	1995	80.00	80
1990	Dumbo MM600	2,750		110.00	110
1995	Ear Force One MM790	500	1995	600.00	600
1995	Engine No. One	500		650.00	650
1994	Engine Number One MM690	500	1995	650.00	650
1995	Fantasyland MM780	750		285.00	285
1992	Finishing Touch MM440	1,500		85.00	85
1993	Flying With Dumbo MM530	1,000		330.00	330
1995	Frontierland MM740	750		160.00	160
1992	Genie MM450	2,750		110.00	110
1991	Goofy MM110	2,750		115.00	115
1991	Goofy's Gift MM230	2,750		70.00	70
1994	Grumpy Playing Organ MM590	800	1995	150.00	150
1991	Jiminy's List MM250	2,750		60.00	60
1991	Lady and the Tramp MM280	1,500	1995	295.00	295
1993	Letters to Santa MM550	1,500		170.00	170
1991	Lion Around MM270	2,750		140.00	140
1994	The Lion King MM640	1,750		170.00	170
1992	Litt'l Sorcerer MM340	2,750		57.00	57
1992	Little Mermaid MM310	2,750		230.00	230
1992	Lumiere & Cogsworth MM350	2,750		145.00	145
1995	Main Street MM710	750		120.00	120
1995	The Matterhorn MM750	750		240.00	240
1991	Mickey & Minnie at the Piano MM180	2,750		195.00	195
1991	Mickey's Adventure MM150	2,750		195.00	195
1990	Mickey's Christmas MM400	2,750		95.00	95
1991	Mickey's Delivery MM220	2,750		70.00	70
1993	Mickey's Dream MM520	250	1995	400.00	850
1994	Mickey's Limousine MM650	500	1995	450.00	450
1994	Mickey, Brave Little Tailor MM570	1,750	1995	72.00	72
1991	Minnie Mouse MM170	2,750		80.00	80
1994	Minnie, Brave Little Tailor MM580	1,750	1995	72.00	72
1994	MM/MM/Goofy, Limo	500		500	600
1992	Mrs. Potts & Chip MM360	2,750		125.00	125
1991	Mt. Mickey MM900	2,750		175.00	175
1994	New Tinkerbell MM680	300	1995	99.00	99
1994	Official Conscience MM620	300	1995	65.00	65
1995	The People Mover MM760	750		190.00	190
1990	Pinocchio MM500	2,750	1995	85.00	85
1991	Pluto's Treat MM240	2,750		60.00	60
1994	Pongo & Pups MM670	800	1995	124.00	124
1993	Santa's Workshop MM540	1,500		170.00	170
1994	Snow White & Doc MM630	800		135.00	135
1990	Snow White & Grumpy MM800	2,750		140.00	140
1993	Snow White & The Seven Dwarfs (shadow box) DIS200	250		1800.00	1800
1990	The Sorcerer MM200	Closed	N/A	85.00	120
1992	Sorcerer's Apprentice MM290	2,750		125.00	125
1990	Steamboat Willie MM300	2,750	1995	95.00	95
1992	Stocking Stuffer MM410	1,500		63.00	63
1991	The Tea Cup Ride (Disneyland Exclusive) MM260	1,250		225.00	225
1994	Tigger on Rabbit MM660	800	1995	110.00	110
1993	Tinker Bell MM490	1,750	1995	85.00	85
1995	The Topiary MM720	750		145.00	145
1991	Tugboat Mickey MM160	2,750		180.00	180
1991	Two Gun Mickey MM140	2,750		115.00	115
1990	Uncle Scrooge MM700	2,750		110.00	110
1993	Winnie The Pooh MM480	1,750		125.00	125
1992	Winnie The Pooh & Tigger MM390	2,750	1995	105.00	105
1992	Wish Upon A Star MM430	1,500		80.00	80
1991	The Witch MM130	2,750		115.00	115
1992	Workin' Out MM380	2,750		95.00	95
1992	Workin' Out MM380	2,750		95.00	95

The Ron Lee Emmett Kelly, Sr. Collection - R. Lee

YEAR ISSUE		EDITION LIMIT	YEAR RETD.	ISSUE PRICE	QUOTE U.S.$
1991	Emmett Kelly, Sr. Sign E208	Closed	N/A	110.00	110
1991	God Bless America EK206	Closed	N/A	130.00	250
1991	Help Yourself EK202	Closed	N/A	145.00	350
1991	Love at First Sight EK204	Closed	N/A	197.00	197
1991	My Protege EK207	Closed	N/A	160.00	165
1991	Spike's Uninvited Guest EK203	Closed	N/A	165.00	295
1991	That-A-Way EK201	Closed	N/A	125.00	135
1991	Time for a Change EK205	Closed	N/A	190.00	305

The Ron Lee Looney Tunes Collection - R. Lee

YEAR ISSUE		EDITION LIMIT	YEAR RETD.	ISSUE PRICE	QUOTE U.S.$
1991	1940 Bugs Bunny LT165	Closed	N/A	85.00	85
1991	Bugs Bunny LT150	Closed	N/A	123.00	125
1991	Daffy Duck LT140	Closed	N/A	80.00	80-85
1991	Elmer Fudd LT125	Closed	N/A	87.00	87-90
1991	Foghorn Leghorn & Henry Hawk LT160	Closed	N/A	115.00	115
1991	Marvin the Martian LT170	Closed	N/A	75.00	75
1991	Michigan J. Frog LT110	Closed	N/A	115.00	115
1991	Mt. Yosemite LT180	850		160.00	160-300
1991	Pepe LePew & Penelope LT145	Closed	N/A	115.00	115
1991	Porky Pig LT115	Closed	N/A	97.00	97-100
1991	Sylvester & Tweety LT135	Closed	N/A	110.00	110-115
1991	Tasmanian Devil LT120	Closed	N/A	105.00	105
1991	Tweety LT155	Closed	N/A	110.00	110-115
1991	Western Daffy Duck LT105	Closed	N/A	87.00	87-90
1991	Wile E. Coyote & Roadrunner LT175	Closed	N/A	165.00	175
1991	Yosemite Sam LT130	Closed	N/A	110.00	110

The Ron Lee Looney Tunes II Collection - R. Lee

YEAR ISSUE		EDITION LIMIT	YEAR RETD.	ISSUE PRICE	QUOTE U.S.$
1992	Beep Beep LT220	1,500		115.00	115
1992	Ditty Up LT200	2,750		110.00	110
1992	For Better or Worse LT190	1,500		285.00	285
1992	Leopold & Giovanni LT205	1,500		225.00	225
1992	No Pain No Gain LT210	950		270.00	270
1992	Rackin' Frackin' Varmint LT225	950		260.00	260
1992	Speedy Gonzales LT185	2,750		73.00	73
1992	Van Duck LT230	950		335.00	335
1992	The Virtuosos LT235	950		350.00	350
1992	What The ...? LT195	1,500		240.00	240
1992	What's up Doc? LT215	950		270.00	270

The Ron Lee Looney Tunes III Collection - R. Lee

YEAR ISSUE		EDITION LIMIT	YEAR RETD.	ISSUE PRICE	QUOTE U.S.$
1992	Bugs Bunny w/ Horse LT245	1,500		105.00	105
1992	Cowboy Bugs LT290	1,500		70.00	70
1992	Daffy Duck w/ Horse LT275	1,500		105.00	105
1992	Elmer Fudd w/ Horse LT270	1,500		105.00	105
1992	Pepe Le Pew w/ Horse LT285	1,500		105.00	105
1992	Porky Pig w/ Horse LT260	1,500		105.00	105
1992	Sylvester w/ Horse LT250	1,500		105.00	105
1992	Tasmanian Devil w/ Horse LT255	1,500		105.00	105
1992	Wile E. Coyote w/ Horse LT280	1,500		105.00	105
1992	Yosemite Sam w/ Horse LT265	1,500		105.00	105

The Ron Lee Looney Tunes IV Collection - R. Lee

YEAR ISSUE		EDITION LIMIT	YEAR RETD.	ISSUE PRICE	QUOTE U.S.$
1993	Bugs LT330	1,200		79.00	79
1993	A Christmas Carrot LT320	1,200		175.00	175
1993	The Essence of Love LT310	1,200		145.00	145
1993	Martian's Best Friend LT305	1,200		140.00	140
1993	Me Deliver LT295	1,200		110.00	110
1993	Puttin' on the Glitz LT325	1,200		79.00	79
1993	The Rookie LT315	1,200		75.00	75
1993	Yo-Ho-Ho- LT300	1,200		105.00	105

The Ron Lee Looney Tunes V Collection - R. Lee

YEAR ISSUE		EDITION LIMIT	YEAR RETD.	ISSUE PRICE	QUOTE U.S.$
1994	Bugs LT330	1,200		79.00	79
1994	A Carrot a Day LT350	1,200		85.00	85
1994	Guilty LT345	1,200		80.00	80
1994	Ma Cherie LT340	1,200		185.00	185
1994	No H20 LT355	1,200		160.00	160
1994	Puttin' on the Glitz LT325	1,200		79.00	79
1994	Smashing LT335	1,200		80.00	80
1994	Taz On Ice LT360	1,200		115.00	115

The Ron Lee Looney Tunes VI Collection - R. Lee

YEAR ISSUE		EDITION LIMIT	YEAR RETD.	ISSUE PRICE	QUOTE U.S.$
1994	Bugs Pharoah LT370	500		130.00	130
1994	Cleopatra's Barge LT400	500		550.00	550
1994	Cruising Down the Nile LT385	500		295.00	295
1994	King Bugs and Friends LT395	500		480.00	480
1994	Ramases & Son LT380	500		230.00	230
1994	Tweety Pharoah LT365	500		110.00	110
1994	Warrior Taz LT375	500		140.00	140
1994	Yosemite's Chariot LT390	500		310.00	310

The Ron Lee Looney Tunes Western Collection - R. Lee

YEAR ISSUE		EDITION LIMIT	YEAR RETD.	ISSUE PRICE	QUOTE U.S.$
1995	Acme Junction LT435	500		290.00	290
1995	Bwanding Iron LT420	500		210.00	210
1995	Heap Big Chief LT415	500		230.00	230
1995	Lit'l Trooper LT405	500		157.00	157
1995	Roadrunner Express LT425	500		240.00	240
1995	Saturday Serenade LT430	500		255.00	255
1995	Whoa!! LT410	500		215.00	215

The Ron Lee Warner Bros. Collection - R. Lee

YEAR ISSUE		EDITION LIMIT	YEAR RETD.	ISSUE PRICE	QUOTE U.S.$
1993	Courtly Gent WB003	1,000		102.00	102
1992	Dickens' Christmas WB400	850		198.00	198
1993	Duck Dodgers WB005	1,000		300.00	300
1993	Gridiron Glory WB002	1,000		102.00	102
1993	Hair-Raising Hare WB006	1,000		300.00	300
1993	Hare Under Par WB001	1,000		102.00	102
1993	Home Plate Heroes WB004	1,000		102.00	102
1991	The Maltese Falcon WB100	Closed	N/A	175.00	175
1991	Robin Hood Bugs WB200	1,000		190.00	190
1992	Yankee Doodle Bugs WB300	850		195.00	195

Shriner Clowns - R. Lee

YEAR ISSUE		EDITION LIMIT	YEAR RETD.	ISSUE PRICE	QUOTE U.S.$
1994	Bubbles L437	1,750		120.00	120
1994	Helping Hand L436	1,750		145.00	145

Sports & Professionals - R. Lee

YEAR ISSUE		EDITION LIMIT	YEAR RETD.	ISSUE PRICE	QUOTE U.S.$
1994	The Baseball Player L448	2,500		77.00	77
1994	The Basketball Player L450	2,500		74.00	74
1994	The Chef L441	2,500		74.00	74
1994	The Dentist L446	2,500		70.00	70
1994	The Doctor L439	2,500		70.00	70
1994	The Fireman L444	2,500		90.00	90
1994	The Fisherman L452	2,500		77.00	77
1994	The Football Player L449	2,500		74.00	74
1994	The Golfer L447	2,500		77.00	77
1994	The Hockey Player L454	2,500		80.00	80
1994	The Lawyer L445	2,500		70.00	70
1994	The Nurse L443	2,500		74.00	74
1994	The Pilot L440	2,500		74.00	74
1994	The Policeman L442	2,500		77.00	77
1994	The Skier L453	2,500		77.00	77
1994	The Teacher L438	2,500		70.00	70
1994	The Tennis Player L451	2,500		74.00	74

Superman I - R. Lee

YEAR ISSUE		EDITION LIMIT	YEAR RETD.	ISSUE PRICE	QUOTE U.S.$
1993	Help Is On The Way SP100	750	1995	280.00	280
1993	Meteor Moment SP115	750	1995	314.00	314
1993	Metropolis SP110	750	1995	320.00	320
1993	Proudly We Wave SP105	750	1995	185.00	185

Superman II - R. Lee

YEAR ISSUE		EDITION LIMIT	YEAR RETD.	ISSUE PRICE	QUOTE U.S.$
1994	Good and Evil SP135	750	1995	190.00	190
1994	More Powerful SP130	750	1995	420.00	420
1994	Quick Change SP120	750	1995	125.00	125
1994	To The Rescue SP125	750	1995	195.00	195

The Wizard of Oz Collection - R. Lee

YEAR ISSUE		EDITION LIMIT	YEAR RETD.	ISSUE PRICE	QUOTE U.S.$
1992	The Cowardly Lion WZ425	750		620.00	620
1992	Kansas WZ400	750		550.00	550
1992	The Munchkins WZ405	750		620.00	620
1992	The Ruby Slippers WZ410	750		620.00	620
1992	The Scarecrow WZ415	750		510.00	510
1992	The Tin Man WZ420	750		530.00	530

Wizard of Oz II - R. Lee

YEAR ISSUE		EDITION LIMIT	YEAR RETD.	ISSUE PRICE	QUOTE U.S.$
1994	The Cowardly Lion WZ445	500		130.00	130
1994	Dorothy WZ430	500		150.00	150
1994	Glinda WZ455	500		225.00	225
1994	The Scarecrow WZ435	500		130.00	130
1994	The Tinman WZ440	500		110.00	110
1994	The Wicked Witch WZ450	500		125.00	125

The Woody Woodpecker & Friends Collection - R. Lee

YEAR ISSUE		EDITION LIMIT	YEAR RETD.	ISSUE PRICE	QUOTE U.S.$
1992	1940 Woody Woodpecker WL020	1,750		73.00	73
1992	Andy and Miranda Panda WL025	1,750		140.00	140
1992	Birdy for Woody WL005	1,750		117.00	117
1992	Pals WL030	1,750		179.00	179
1992	Peck of My Heart WL010	1,750		370.00	395
1992	Woody Woodpecker WL015	1,750		73.00	73

Royal Doulton

Royal Doulton Collectors' Club - N/A

YEAR ISSUE		EDITION LIMIT	YEAR RETD.	ISSUE PRICE	QUOTE U.S.$
1980	John Doulton Jug (8 O'Clock) D6656	Yr.Iss.		70.00	125
1981	Sleepy Darling Figure HN2953	Yr.Iss.		100.00	195
1982	Dog of Fo-Flambe	Yr.Iss.		50.00	150
1982	Prized Possessions Figure HN2942	Yr.Iss.		125.00	450
1983	Loving Cup	Yr.Iss.		75.00	150
1983	Springtime HN3033	Yr.Iss.		125.00	325
1984	Sir Henry Doulton Jug D6703	Yr.Iss.		50.00	115
1984	Pride & Joy Figure HN2945	Yr.Iss.		125.00	275
1985	Top of the Hill Plate HN2126	Yr.Iss.		35.00	100
1985	Wintertime Figure HN3060	Yr.Iss.		125.00	225
1986	Albert Sagger Toby Jug	Yr.Iss.		35.00	85
1986	Auctioneer Figure HN2988	Yr.Iss.		150.00	150
1987	Collector Bunnykins	Yr.Iss.		40.00	400-650
1987	Summertime Figurine HN3137	Yr.Iss.		140.00	150
1988	Top of the Hill Miniature Figurine HN2126	Yr.Iss.		95.00	125
1988	Beefeater Tiny Jug	Yr.Iss.		25.00	125
1988	Old Salt Tea Pot	Yr.Iss.		135.00	250
1989	Geisha Flambe Figure HN3229	Yr.Iss.		195.00	195
1989	Flower Sellers Children Plate	Yr.Iss.		65.00	70-100
1990	Autumntime Figure HN3231	Yr.Iss.		190.00	195
1990	Jester Mini Figure HN3196	Yr.Iss.		115.00	115
1990	Old King Cole Tiny Jug	Yr.Iss.		35.00	35
1991	Bunny's Bedtime Figure HN3370	Yr.Iss.		195.00	195
1991	Charles Dickens Jug D6901	Yr.Iss.		100.00	100
1991	L'Ambiteuse Figure (Tissot Lady)	Yr.Iss.		295.00	295
1991	Christopher Columbus Jug D6911	Yr.Iss.		95.00	95
1992	Discovery Figure HN3428	Yr.Iss.		160.00	100
1992	King Edward Jug D6923	Yr.Iss.		250.00	250
1992	Master Potter Bunnykins DB131	Yr.Iss.		50.00	50-95
1992	Eliza Farren Prestige Figure HN3442	Yr.Iss.		335.00	200
1993	Barbara Figure	Yr.Iss.		285.00	285
1993	Lord Mountbatten L/S Jug	N/A		225.00	225
1993	Punch & Judy Double Sided Jug	2,500		400.00	400
1993	Flambe Dragon HN3552	N/A		260.00	260
1994	Diane HN3604	N/A		250.00	250

Age of Innocence - N. Pedley

YEAR ISSUE		EDITION LIMIT	YEAR RETD.	ISSUE PRICE	QUOTE U.S.$
1991	Feeding Time HN3373	9,500	1994	245.00	290
1992	First Outing HN3377	9,500	1994	275.00	310
1991	Making Friends HN3372	9,500	1994	270.00	310
1991	Puppy Love HN3371	9,500	1994	270.00	310

Beatrix Potter Figures - Various

YEAR ISSUE		EDITION LIMIT	YEAR RETD.	ISSUE PRICE	QUOTE U.S.$
1992	And This Pig Had None P3319 - M. Alcock	Open		29.95	30
1971	Appley Dapply P2333 - A. Hallam	Open		29.95	30
1970	Aunt Pettitoes P2276 - A. Hallam	Retrd.	1993	29.95	45-75
1989	Babbity Bumble P2971 - W. Platt	Retrd.	1993	29.95	75
1992	Benjamin Ate a Lettuce Leaf P3317 - M. Alcock	Open		29.95	30
1948	Benjamin Bunny P1105 A. Gredington	Open		29.95	30
1983	Benjamin Bunny Sat on a Bank P2803 - D. Lyttleton	Open		29.95	30
1975	Benjamin Bunny with Peter Rabbit P2509 - A. Musiankowski	Open		39.95	50
1995	Benjamin Bunny-large size P3403 - M. Alcock	Open		65.00	65
1991	Benjamin Wakes Up P3234 A. Hughes-Lubeck	Open		29.95	30
1965	Cecily Parsley P1941 A. Gredington	Retrd.	1993	29.95	45-85
1979	Chippy Hackee P2627 D. Lyttleton	Retrd.	1993	29.95	49-55

YEAR ISSUE		EDITION LIMIT	YEAR RETD.	ISSUE PRICE	QUOTE U.S.$
1991	Christmas Stocking P3257 M. Alcock	Retrd.	1994	65.00	65
1985	Cottontail at Lunchtime P2878 - D. Lyttleton	Open		29.95	30
1970	Cousin Ribby P2284 - A. Hallam	Retrd.	1993	29.95	45-65
1982	Diggory Diggory Delvet P2713 - D. Lyttleton	Open		29.95	30
1995	F.W. Gent-large size P3450 M. Alcock	Open		65.00	65
1977	Fierce Bad Rabbit P2586 D. Lyttleton	Open		29.95	30
1954	Flopsy Mopsy and Cottontail P1274 - A. Gredington	Open		29.95	30
1990	Foxy Reading Country News P3219 - A. Hughes-Lubeck	Open		49.95	55
1954	Foxy Whiskered Gentleman P1277 - A. Gredington	Open		29.95	30
1990	Gentleman Mouse Made a Bow P3200 - T. Chawner	Open		29.95	30
1986	Goody and Timmy Tiptoes P2957 - D. Lyttleton	Open		49.95	55
1961	Goody Tiptoes P1675 A. Gredington	Open		29.95	30
1951	Hunca Munca P1198 A. Gredington	Open		29.95	30
1992	Hunca Munca Spills the Beads P3288 - M. Alcock	Open		29.95	30
1977	Hunca Munca Sweeping P2584 D. Lyttleton	Open		29.95	30
1990	Jemema Puddleduck-Foxy Whiskered Gentleman P3193 - T. Chawner	Open		49.95	80
1983	Jemima Puddleduck Made a Feather Nest-P2823 D. Lyttleton	Open		29.95	30
1948	Jemima Puddleduck P1092 A. Gredington	Open		29.95	30
1993	Jemima Puddleduck-Large size P3373 - M. Alcock	Open		49.95	65
1988	Jeremy Fisher Digging P3090 T. Chawner	Retrd.	1994	50.00	75
1950	Jeremy Fisher P1157 A. Gredington	Open		29.95	30
1995	Jeremy Fisher-large size P3372 M. Alcock	Open		65.00	65
1990	John Joiner P2965 - G. Tongue	Open		29.95	30
1954	Johnny Townmouse P1276 A. Gredington	Retrd.	1993	29.95	45-55
1988	Johnny Townmouse with Bag P3094 - T. Chawner	Retrd.	1994	50.00	75
1990	Lady Mouse Made a Curtsy P3220 - A. Hughes-Lubeck	Open		29.95	30
1950	Lady Mouse P1183 A. Gredington	Open		29.95	30
1977	Little Black Rabbit P2585 D. Lyttleton	Open		29.95	30
1987	Little Pig Robinson Spying P3031 - T. Chawner	Retrd.	1993	29.95	95
1991	Miss Dormouse P3251 M. Alcock	Open		65.00	65
1990	Mittens & Moppet P3197 T. Chawner	Retrd.	1994	50.00	50
1989	Mother Ladybird P2966 - W. Platt	Open		29.95	30
1973	Mr. Alderman Ptolemy P2424 G. Tongue	Open		29.95	30
1965	Mr. Benjamin Bunny P1940 A. Gredington	Open		29.95	30
1979	Mr. Drake Puddleduck P2628 D. Lyttleton	Open		29.95	30
1974	Mr. Jackson P2453 - A. Hallam	Open		29.95	30
1988	Mr. Tod P3091 - T. Chawner	Retrd.	1993	29.95	95
1965	Mrs. Flopsy Bunny P1942 A. Gredington	Open		29.95	30
1992	Mrs. Rabbit Cooking P3278 M. Alcock	Open		29.95	30
1951	Mrs. Rabbit P1200 A. Gredington	Open		29.95	30
1976	Mrs. Rabbit with Bunnies P2543 D. Lyttleton	Open		29.95	30
1995	Mrs. Rabbit-large size P3398 M. Alcock	Open		65.00	65
1951	Mrs. Ribby P1199 A. Gredington	Open		29.95	30
1948	Mrs. Tittlemouse P1103 A. Gredington	Retrd.	1993	29.95	45-55
1992	No More Twist P3325 - M. Alcock	Open		29.95	30
1986	Old Mr. Bouncer P2956 D. Lyttleton	Open		29.95	30
1963	Old Mr. Brown P1796 - A. Hallam	Open		29.95	30
1983	Old Mr. Pricklepin P2767 - N/A	Retrd.	1982	29.95	115-125
1959	Old Woman Who Lived in a Shoe P1545 - C. Melbourne	Open		29.95	30
1983	Old Woman Who Lived in a Shoe, Knitting P2804 D. Lyttleton	Open		29.95	30
1991	Peter & The Red Handkerchief P3242 - M. Alcock	Open		39.95	45
1995	Peter in Bed P3473 - M. Alcock	Open		39.95	40
1989	Peter Rabbit in the Gooseberry Net P3157 - D. Lyttleton	Open		39.95	50
1948	Peter Rabbit P1098 A. Gredington	Open		29.95	30
1993	Peter Rabbit-large size P3356 - M. Alcock	Open		65.00	65
1971	Pickles P2334 - N/A	Retrd.	1982	29.95	375-675
1948	Pig Robinson P1104 A. Gredington	Open		29.95	30
1955	Pigling Bland P1365 - G. Orwell	Open		29.95	30
1991	Pigling Eats Porridge P3252 M. Alcock	Retrd.	1994	50.00	50
1976	Poorly Peter Rabbit P2560 D. Lyttleton	Open		29.95	30
1981	Rebeccah Puddleduck P2647 D. Lyttleton	Open		29.95	30
1992	Ribby and the Patty Pan P3280 M. Alcock	Open		29.95	30
1974	Sally Henry Penney P2452 A. Hallam	Retrd.	1993	29.95	65-75
1948	Samuel Whiskers P1106 A. Gredington	Open		29.95	30
1948	Squirrel Nutkin P1102 A. Gredington	Open		29.95	30
1961	Tabitha Twitchitt P1676 A. Gredington	Open		29.95	30
1976	Tabitha Twitchitt with Miss Moppett P2544 - D. Lyttleton	Retrd.	1993	29.95	75-95
1949	Tailor of Gloucester P1108 A. Gredington	Open		29.95	30
1995	Tailor of Gloucester-large size P3449 - M. Alcock	Open		65.00	65
1948	Tiggy Winkle P1107 A. Gredington	Open		29.95	30
1985	Tiggy Winkle Takes Tea P2877 D. Lyttleton	Open		29.95	30
1948	Timmy Tiptoes P1101 A. Gredington	Open		29.95	30
1949	Timmy Willie P1109 A. Gredington	Retrd.	1993	29.95	45-195
1986	Timmy Willie Sleeping P2996 G. Tongue	Open		29.95	30
1948	Tom Kitten P1100 A. Gredington	Open		29.95	30
1995	Tom Kitten-large size P3405 M. Alcock	Open		65.00	65
1987	Tom Kittten and Butterfly P3030 T. Chawner	Retrd.	1994	50.00	50
1987	Tom Thumb P2989 - W. Platt	Open		29.95	30
1955	Tommy Brock P1348 - G. Orwell	Open		29.95	30

British Sporting Heritage - V. Annand

YEAR ISSUE		EDITION LIMIT	YEAR RETD.	ISSUE PRICE	QUOTE U.S.$
1994	Ascot HN3471	5,000		475.00	475
1993	Henley HN3367	5,000		475.00	475
1995	Wimbledon HN3366	5,000		475.00	475

Bunnykins - Various

YEAR ISSUE		EDITION LIMIT	YEAR RETD.	ISSUE PRICE	QUOTE U.S.$
1995	Bathtime DB148 - M. Alcock	Open		40.00	40
1987	Be Prepared DB56 - D. Lyttleton	Open		40.00	40
1987	Bed Time DB55 - D. Lyttleton	Open		40.00	40
1991	Bride DB101 - A. Hughes	Open		40.00	40
1987	Brownie DB61 - W. Platt	Retrd.	1993	39.00	65
1990	Cook DB85- W. Platt	Retrd.	1994	35.00	40-65
1995	Easter Greetings - M. Alcock	Open		50.00	50
1988	Father, Mother, Victoria DB68 M. Alcock	Open		40.00	40
1989	Fireman DB75 - M. Alcock	Open		40.00	40
1990	Fisherman DB84- W. Platt	Retrd.	1993	39.00	75-95
1991	Groom DB102 - M. Alcock	Open		40.00	40
XX	Halloween Bunnykin DB132 N/A	Open		50.00	50
1983	Happy Birthday DB21 G. Tongue	Open		40.00	40
1988	Harry DB73 - M. Alcock	Retrd.	1993	34.00	60
1972	Helping Mother DB2 - A Hallam	Retrd.	1993	34.00	55-75
1986	Home Run DB43 - D. Lyttleton	Retrd.	1993	39.00	55-85
1990	Ice Cream DB82 - W. Platt	Retrd.	1993	39.00	60-75
1982	Mr. Bunnykin Easter Parade DB18 - G. Tongue	Retrd.	1993	39.00	65-75
1982	Mrs. Bunnykin Easter Parade DB19 - D. Lyttleton	Open		40.00	40
1989	Nurse DB74 - M. Alcock	Open		35.00	40
1989	Paper Boy DB77 - M. Alcock	Retrd.	1993	39.00	65
1972	Playtime DB8 - A Hallam	Retrd.	1993	34.00	60
1988	Policeman DB69 - M. Alcock	Open		40.00	40
1988	Polly DB71 - M. Alcock	Retrd.	1993	34.00	40-65
1995	Rainy Day DB147 - M. Alcock	Open		40.00	40
1981	Santa Bunnykins DB17 D. Lyttleton	Open		40.00	40
1987	School Days DB57 - D. Lyttleton	Retrd.	1994	40.00	55
1982	School Master DB60 - W. Platt	Open		40.00	40
1974	Sleepytime DB15 A. Musiankowski	Retrd.	1993	39.00	65
1972	Sleigh Ride DB4 - A Hallam	Open		40.00	40
1972	Story Time DB9 - A Hallam	Open		35.00	40
1988	Susan DB70 - M. Alcock	Retrd.	1993	34.00	40-60
XX	Sweetheart Bunnykin DB130 N/A	Open		40.00	40
1988	Tom DB72 - M. Alcock	Retrd.	1993	34.00	45-65
1986	Uncle Sam DB50 - D. Lyttleton	Open		40.00	40
1988	William DB69 - M. Alcock	Retrd.	1993	34.00	40-65

Character Jug of the Year - Various

YEAR ISSUE		EDITION LIMIT	YEAR RETD.	ISSUE PRICE	QUOTE U.S.$
1991	Fortune Teller D6824 - S. Taylor	Closed	1991	130.00	160-250
1992	Winston Churchill D6907 S. Taylor	Closed	1992	195.00	195
1993	Vice-Admiral Lord Nelson D6932 S. Taylor	Closed	1993	225.00	225
1994	Captain Hook - M. Alcock	Closed	1994	235.00	235
1995	Captain Bligh D6967 - S. Taylor	Yr.Iss.	1994	200.00	200

Character Jugs - Various

YEAR ISSUE		EDITION LIMIT	YEAR RETD.	ISSUE PRICE	QUOTE U.S.$
1993	Abraham Lincoln - M. Alcock	2,500	1994	190.00	190
1991	Airman, sm. - W. Harper	Open		82.50	83
1995	Alfred Hitchcock D6987 D. Biggs	Open		200.00	200
1990	Angler, sm. - S. Taylor	Open		82.50	83
1947	Beefeater, lg. - Unknown	Open		150.00	150
1947	Beefeater, sm. - Unknown	Open		82.50	83
1995	Charles Dickens D6939 W. Harper	2,500		500.00	500
1989	Clown, lg.- S. Taylor	Open		205.00	205
1991	Columbus, lg.- S. Taylor	Open		160.00	160
1983	D'Artagnan, lg.- S. Taylor	Open		150.00	150
1983	D'Artagnan, sm.- S. Taylor	Open		82.50	83
1991	Equestrian, sm.- S. Taylor	Open		82.50	83
1995	George Washington - M. Alcock	2,500		200.00	200
XX	George Washington, lg. Unknown	Retrd.	1994	150.00	150
1994	Glenn Miller - M. Alcock	Open		270.00	270
1971	Golfer, lg. - D. Biggs	Open		150.00	150
1993	Graduate-Male, sm.- S. Taylor	Open		85.00	85
1986	Guardsman, lg.- S. Taylor	Open		150.00	150
1986	Gurardsman, sm.- S. Taylor	Open		82.50	83
1990	Guy Fawkes, lg. - W. Harper	Open		150.00	150
1975	Henry VIII, lg. - E. Griffiths	Open		150.00	150
1975	Henry VIII, sm. - E. Griffiths	Open		82.50	83
1991	Jockey, sm.- S. Taylor	Open		82.50	83
1995	Judge and Thief Toby D6988 S. Taylor	Open		185.00	185
1959	Lawyer, lg. - M. Henk	Open		150.00	150
1959	Lawyer, sm. - M. Henk	Open		82.50	83
1990	Leprechaun, lg. - W. Harper	Open		205.00	205
1990	Leprechaun, sm. - W. Harper	Open		85.00	85
1986	London Bobby, lg.- S. Taylor	Open		150.00	150
1986	London Bobby, sm.- S. Taylor	Open		82.50	83
1952	Long John Silver, lg. - M. Henk	Open		150.00	150
1952	Long John Silver, sm. - M. Henk	Open		82.50	83
1960	Merlin, lg. - G. Sharpe	Open		150.00	150
1960	Merlin, sm. - G. Sharpe	Open		82.50	83
1990	Modern Golfer, sm.- S. Taylor	Open		82.50	83
1955	Rip Van Winkle, lg. - M. Henk	Open		150.00	150
1955	Rip Van Winkle, sm. - M. Henk	Open		82.50	83
1991	Sailor, sm. - W. Harper	Open		82.50	83
1984	Santa Claus, lg. - M. Abberley	Open		150.00	150
1984	Santa Claus, sm. - M. Abberley	Open		82.50	83
1993	Shakespeare, sm. - W. Harper	Open		99.00	99
1973	The Sleuth, lg.- A. Moore	Open		150.00	150
1973	The Sleuth, sm. - A. Moore	Open		82.50	83
1991	Snooker Player, sm.- S. Taylor	Open		82.50	83
1991	Soldier, sm. - W. Harper	Open		82.50	83
1994	Thomas Jefferson - M. Alcock	2,500		200.00	200
XX	Town Crier, lg. - Unknown	Retrd.	1994	170.00	170
1993	Winston Churchill, sm.- S. Taylor	Open		99.00	99
1990	Wizard, lg.- S. Taylor- S. Taylor	Open		175.00	175
1990	Wizard, sm.- S. Taylor	Open		85.00	85
1991	Yeoman of the Guard, lg. S. Taylor	Open		150.00	150

Character Sculptures - Various

YEAR ISSUE		EDITION LIMIT	YEAR RETD.	ISSUE PRICE	QUOTE U.S.$
1993	Captain Hook - R. Tabbenor	Open		250.00	250
1994	D' Artagnan - R. Tabbenor	Open		260.00	260
1993	Dick Turpin - R. Tabbenor	Open		250.00	250
1995	Gulliver - D. Biggs	Open		285.00	285
1993	Long John Silver A. Maslankowski	Open		250.00	250
1994	Pied Piper - A. Maslankowski	Open		260.00	260
1993	Robin Hood - A. Maslankowski	Open		250.00	250

Diamond Anniversary Tinies - N/A

YEAR ISSUE		EDITION LIMIT	YEAR RETD.	ISSUE PRICE	QUOTE U.S.$
1994	John Barleycorn	2,500	94	350.00	350
1994	The Cellarer	2,500	94	set	Set
1994	Dick Turpin	2,500	94	set	Set
1994	Granny	2,500	94	set	Set
1994	Jester	2,500	94	set	Set
1994	Parson Brown	2,500	94	set	Set

Femmes Fatales - P. Davies

YEAR ISSUE		EDITION LIMIT	YEAR RETD.	ISSUE PRICE	QUOTE U.S.$
1979	Cleopatra HN2868	750		750.00	1350
1984	Eve HN2466	750		1250.00	1250
1981	Helen of Troy HN2387	750	1993	1250.00	1350
1985	Lucrezia Borgia HN2342	750	1993	1250.00	1250
1982	Queen of Sheba HN2328	750		1250.00	1300-1400
1983	Tz'u-Hsi HN2391	750		1250.00	1250

Figure of the Year - Various

YEAR ISSUE		EDITION LIMIT	YEAR RETD.	ISSUE PRICE	QUOTE U.S.$
1991	Amy HN3316 - P. Gee	Closed	1991	195.00	500
1992	Mary HN3375 - P. Gee	Closed	1992	225.00	400
1993	Patricia HN3365 - V. Annand	Closed	1993	250.00	250
1994	Jennifer HN3447 - P. Gee	Closed	1994	250.00	250
1995	Deborah - HN3644 - N. Pedley	Yr.Iss.		225.00	225

The Four Seasons - V. Annand

YEAR ISSUE		EDITION LIMIT	YEAR RETD.	ISSUE PRICE	QUOTE U.S.$
1993	Springtime HN3477	Open		325.00	325
1994	Summertime HN3478	Open		325.00	325
1993	Autumntime HN3621	Open		325.00	325
1993	Wintertime HN3622	Open		325.00	650

Gainsborough Ladies - P. Gee

YEAR ISSUE		EDITION LIMIT	YEAR RETD.	ISSUE PRICE	QUOTE U.S.$
1991	Countess of Sefton HN3010	5,000	1994	650.00	650
1991	Hon Frances Duncombe HN3009	5,000	1994	650.00	650-700
1991	Lady Sheffield HN3008	5,000	1994	650.00	650-700
1990	Mary, Countess Howe HN3007	5,000	1994	650.00	650

Great Lovers - R. Jefferson

YEAR ISSUE		EDITION LIMIT	YEAR RETD.	ISSUE PRICE	QUOTE U.S.$
1994	Robin Hood and Maid Marian HN3111	150		5250.00	5250
1993	Romeo and Juliet HN3113	150		5250.00	5250

Images - Various

YEAR ISSUE		EDITION LIMIT	YEAR RETD.	ISSUE PRICE	QUOTE U.S.$
1991	Bride & Groom HN3281 R. Tabbenor	Open		85.00	85
1991	Bridesmaid HN3280 R. Tabbenor	Open		85.00	85
1993	Brother & Sister HN3460 A. Hughes	Retrd.	N/A	52.50	99
1991	Brothers HN3191 - E. Griffiths	Open		90.00	99

YEAR ISSUE		EDITION LIMIT	YEAR RETD.	ISSUE PRICE	QUOTE U.S.$
1981	Family HN2720 - E. Griffiths	Open		187.50	188
1988	First Love HN2747 - D. Tootle	Open		170.00	188
1991	First Steps HN3282 R. Tabbenor	Open		142.00	188
1993	Gift of Freedom HN3443 - N/A	Retrd.	N/A	90.00	215
1989	Happy Anniversary HN3254 D. Tootle	Open		187.50	188
1981	Lovers HN2762 - D. Tootle	Retrd.	N/A	187.50	188
1980	Mother & Daughter HN2841 E. Griffiths	Open		187.50	188
1993	Our First Christmas HN3452 N/A	Open		185.00	188
1989	Over the Threshold HN3274 R. Tabbenor	Open		187.50	188
1983	Sisters HN3018 - P. Parson	Open		90.00	99
1987	Wedding Day HN2748 D. Tootle	Open		187.50	188

Limited Edition Character Jugs - Various

YEAR ISSUE		EDITION LIMIT	YEAR RETD.	ISSUE PRICE	QUOTE U.S.$
1992	Abraham Lincoln D6936 S. Taylor	2,500	1994	190.00	190
1994	Aladdin's Genie D6971 D. Biggs	1,500	1994	335.00	350
1993	Clown Toby - N/A	3,000		175.00	175
1993	Elf Miniature D6942 - N/A	2,500	1994	55.00	55
XX	Father Christmas Toby - N/A	3,500		125.00	125
1990	Henry VIII - N/A	Open		150.00	150
1991	Henry VIII - W. Harper	1,991		395.00	950
1991	Jester - S. Taylor	2,500		125.00	150
1994	King & Queen of Diamonds D6969 - J. Taylor	2,500	1994	260.00	260
1992	King Charles I D6917 W. Harper	2,500		450.00	450
1994	Leprechaun Toby - N/A	2,500		150.00	150
1992	Mrs. Claus Miniature D6922 N/A	2,500		50.00	55
1993	Napoleon (Large size) D6941 S. Taylor	2,000	1994	225.00	225
1994	Oliver Cromwell D6968 W. Harper	2,500	1994	475.00	475
1991	Santa Claus Miniature D6900 N/A	5,000		50.00	55
1988	Sir Francis Drake D6805 P .Gee	Closed	N/A	N/A	100
XX	Snake Charmer - N/A	2,500		210.00	210
1994	Thomas Jefferson - N/A	2,500		200.00	200
1992	Town Crier D6895 - S. Taylor	2,500		175.00	175
1992	William Shakespeare D6933 W. Harper	2,500	1994	625.00	635

Limited Editions - Various

YEAR ISSUE		EDITION LIMIT	YEAR RETD.	ISSUE PRICE	QUOTE U.S.$
1992	Christopher Columbus HN3392 A. Maslankowski	1,492		1950.00	1950
1993	Duke of Wellington HN3432 A. Maslankowski	1,500		1750.00	1750
1994	Field Marshal Montgomery HN3405 - N/A	1,944		1100.00	1100
1993	General Robert E. Lee HN3404 R. Tabbenor	5,000		1175.00	1175
1993	Lt. General Ulysses S. Grant HN3403 - R. Tabbenor	5,000		1175.00	1175
1992	Napoleon at Waterloo HN3429 A. Maslankowski	1,500		1900.00	1900
1993	Vice Admiral Lord Nelson HN3489 - A. Maslankowski	950		1750.00	1750
1993	Winston S. Churchill HN3433 - A. Maslankowski	5,000		595.00	595

Myths & Maidens - R. Jefferson

YEAR ISSUE		EDITION LIMIT	YEAR RETD.	ISSUE PRICE	QUOTE U.S.$
1986	Diana The Huntress HN2829	300		2950.00	3000
1985	Europa & Bull HN2828	300		2950.00	3000
1984	Juno & Peacock HN2827	300		2950.00	3000
1982	Lady & Unicorn HN2825	S/O		2500.00	2500
1983	Leda & Swan HN2826	300		2950.00	3000

Prestige Figures - Various

YEAR ISSUE		EDITION LIMIT	YEAR RETD.	ISSUE PRICE	QUOTE U.S.$
1982	Columbine HN2738 - D. Tootle	N/A		1250.00	1350
1982	Harlequin HN2737 - D. Tootle	N/A		1250.00	1350
1964	Indian Brave HN2376 - M. Davis	500	N/A	2500.00	5500
1952	Jack Point HN2080 - C.J. Noke	N/A		2900.00	3100
1950	King Charles HN2084 C.J. Noke	N/A		2500.00	2500
1964	Matador and Bull HN2324 M. Davis	N/A		21500.00	23000
1952	The Moor HN2082 - C.J. Noke	N/A		2500.00	2700
1964	The Palio HN2428 - M. Davis	500	N/A	2500.00	6500
1952	Princess Badoura HN2081 - N/A	N/A		28000.00	30000
1978	St George and Dragon HN2856 W.K. Harper	N/A		13600.00	14500

Queens of Realm - P. Parsons

YEAR ISSUE		EDITION LIMIT	YEAR RETD.	ISSUE PRICE	QUOTE U.S.$
1989	Mary, Queen of Scots HN3142	S/O	N/A	550.00	850
1988	Queen Anne HN3141	Retrd.	N/A	525.00	600
1986	Queen Elizabeth I HN3099	S/O	N/A	495.00	495-650
1987	Queen Victoria HN3125	S/O	N/A	495.00	950
1987	Set of 4	S/O	N/A	2065.00	3000

Reynolds Collection - P. Gee

YEAR ISSUE		EDITION LIMIT	YEAR RETD.	ISSUE PRICE	QUOTE U.S.$
1992	Countess Harrington HN3317	5,000		550.00	595
1993	Countess Spencer HN3320	5,000		595.00	595
1991	Lady Worsley HN3318	5,000		550.00	595
1992	Mrs. Hugh Bonfoy HN3319	5,000		550.00	595

Royal Doulton Figurines - Various

YEAR ISSUE		EDITION LIMIT	YEAR RETD.	ISSUE PRICE	QUOTE U.S.$
1933	Beethoven - R. Garbe	25	N/A	N/A	6500
1987	Life Boatman HN2764 W. Harper	Closed	N/A	N/A	225
1975	The Milkmaid HN2057A L. Harradine	Closed	N/A	N/A	225
1924	Tony Weller HN684 - C. Noke	Closed	N/A	N/A	1800

Royalty - Various

YEAR ISSUE		EDITION LIMIT	YEAR RETD.	ISSUE PRICE	QUOTE U.S.$
1986	Duchess Of York HN3086 E. Griffiths	1,500		495.00	750
1981	Duke Of Edinburgh HN2386 P. Davis	750		395.00	450
1982	Lady Diana Spencer HN2885 E. Griffiths	1,500		395.00	600
1981	Prince Of Wales HN2883 E. Griffiths	1,500		395.00	750
1981	Prince Of Wales HN2884 E. Griffiths	1,500		750.00	1000
1982	Princess Of Wales HN2887 E. Griffiths	1,500		750.00	1200
1973	Queen Elizabeth II HN2502 P. Davis	750		N/A	1800
1982	Queen Elizabeth II HN2878 E. Griffiths	2,500		N/A	450
1992	Queen Elizabeth II, 2nd. Version HN3440 - P. Gee	3,500		460.00	460
1989	Queen Elizabeth, the Queen Mother as the Duchess of York HN3230 - P. Parsons	9,500		N/A	450
1990	Queen Elizabeth, the Queen Mother HN3189 - E. Griffiths	2,500		N/A	450
1980	Queen Mother HN2882 P. Davis	1,500		650.00	1250

Royal Worcester

Bicentennial Limited Edition Commemoratives - P.W. Baston

YEAR ISSUE		EDITION LIMIT	YEAR RETD.	ISSUE PRICE	QUOTE U.S.$
1973	Blacksmith	500		Unkn.	500
1973	Cabinetmaker	500		Unkn.	300-400
1975	Clockmaker	Unkn.		Unkn.	500
1973	Potter	500		Unkn.	300-400

Dorothy Doughty Porcelains - D. Doughty

YEAR ISSUE		EDITION LIMIT	YEAR RETD.	ISSUE PRICE	QUOTE U.S.$
1935	American Redstarts and Hemlock	66		Unkn.	5500
1941	Apple Blossoms	250		400.00	1400-3750
1963	Audubon Warblers	500		1350.00	2100-4200
1938	Baltimore Orioles	250		350.00	Unkn.
1956	Bewick's Wrens & Yellow Jasmine	500		600.00	2100-3800
1964	Blue Tits & Pussy Willow	500		250.00	3000
1936	Bluebirds	350		500.00	8500-9000
1940	Bobwhite Quail	22		275.00	11000
1959	Cactus Wrens	500		1250.00	1700-4500
1960	Canyon Wrens	500		750.00	2000-4000
1937	Cardinals	500		500.00	2000-9000
1968	Carolina Paroquet, Color	350		1200.00	1900-2200
1968	Carolina Paroquet, White	75		600.00	Unkn.
1965	Cerulean Warblers & Red Maple	500		1350.00	1400-3000
1938	Chickadees & Larch	300		350.00	85-8900
1965	Chuffchaff	500		1500.00	1300-2900
1942	Crabapple Blossom Sprays And A Butterfly	250		Unkn.	800
1940	Crabapples	250		400.00	3700-4250
1967	Downy Woodpecker & Pecan, Color	400		1500.00	1000-2400
1967	Downy Woodpecker & Pecan, White	75		1000.00	1900
1959	Elf Owl	500		875.00	Unkn.
1955	Gnatcatchers	500		600.00	2700-4900
1972	Goldcrests, Pair	500		4200.00	Unkn.
1936	Goldfinches & Thistle	250		350.00	4300
1968	Gray Wagtail	500		600.00	Unkn.
1961	Hooded Warblers	500		950.00	4300
1950	Hummingbirds And Fuchsia	500		Unkn.	2800
1942	Indigo Bunting And Plum Twig	5,000		Unkn.	Unkn.
1942	Indigo Buntings, Blackberry Sprays	500		375.00	1700-3500
1965	Kingfisher Cock & Autumn Beech	500		1250.00	1900-2300
1952	Kinglets & Noble Pine	500		450.00	1300-4800
1966	Lark Sparrow	500		750.00	Unkn.
1962	Lazuli Bunting & Chokecherries, Color	500		1350.00	3000-4500
1962	Lazuli Bunting & Chokecherries, White	100		1350.00	2600-3000
1964	Lesser Whitethroats	500		350.00	1200-4000
1950	Magnolia Warbler	150		1100.00	1900-3600
1977	Meadow Pipit	500		1800.00	1800
1950	Mexican Feijoa	250		600.00	2600-4900
1940	Mockingbirds	500		450.00	7200-7750
1942	Mockingbirds and Peach Blossom	500		Unkn.	Unkn.
1964	Moorhen Chick	500		1000.00	Unkn.
1964	Mountain Bluebirds	500		950.00	1700-2300
1955	Myrtle Warblers	500		550.00	1300-4000
1971	Nightingale & Honeysuckle	500		2500.00	2500-2750
1947	Orange Blossoms & Butterfly	250		500.00	4200-4500
1957	Ovenbirds	250		650.00	4500
1957	Parula Warblers	500		600.00	1700-3600
1958	Phoebes On Flame Vine	500		750.00	2200-3500
1952	Red-Eyed Vireos	500		450.00	2000
1968	Redstarts & Gorse	500		1900.00	2300
1964	Robin	500		750.00	Unkn.
1956	Scarlet Tanagers	500		675.00	3000-4200
1962	Scissor-Tailed Flycatcher, Color	250		950.00	Unkn.
1962	Scissor-Tailed Flycatcher, White	75		950.00	1300-1600
1963	Vermillion Flycatchers	500		250.00	1100-3400
1964	Wrens & Burnet Rose	500		650.00	1000
1952	Yellow-Headed Blackbirds	350		650.00	2000-2400
1958	Yellowthroats on Water Hyacinth	350		750.00	1700-4000

Equestrians - D. Linder

YEAR ISSUE		EDITION LIMIT	YEAR RETD.	ISSUE PRICE	QUOTE U.S.$
1973	American Saddle Horse	Closed	N/A	1525.00	1525
1969	Appaloosa	Closed	N/A	1350.00	1350
1936	At The Meet	Closed	N/A	944.00	944
1936	Cantering to the Post	Closed	N/A	944.00	944
1977	Clydesdale	Closed	N/A	2300.00	2300
1968	Duke of Edinburgh	Closed	N/A	2400.00	2400
1960	Foxhunter	Closed	N/A	1200.00	1200
1974	Galloping in Winter	Closed	N/A	8500.00	8500
1974	Galloping Ponies (colored)	Closed	N/A	4600.00	4600
1974	Galloping Ponies (white)	Closed	N/A	2900.00	2900
1977	Grundy	Closed	N/A	3400.00	3400
1976	Hackney Pony	Closed	N/A	2000.00	2000
1936	Hog Hunting	Closed	N/A	1277.00	1277
1936	Huntsman and Hounds	Closed	N/A	1110.00	1110
1965	Hyperion	Closed	N/A	1000.00	1000
1972	M Coakes Mould on Stroller	Closed	N/A	1600.00	1600
1975	Meade on Laurieston	Closed	N/A	3600.00	3600
1963	Merand	Closed	N/A	1550.00	1550
1975	Mill Reef	Closed	N/A	2300.00	2300
1976	New Born (colored)	Closed	N/A	2700.00	2700
1976	New Born (white)	Closed	N/A	1600.00	1600
1972	Nijinsky	Closed	N/A	2300.00	2300
1961	Officer Royal Horse Guards	Closed	N/A	1400.00	1400
1936	Over the Sticks	Closed	N/A	944.00	944
1971	Palomino	Closed	N/A	1350.00	1350
1966	Percheron	Closed	N/A	1450.00	1450
1936	Polo Player	Closed	N/A	1055.00	1055
1971	Prince's Grace & Foal (colored)	Closed	N/A	2700.00	2700
1971	Prince's Grace & Foal (white)	Closed	N/A	2600.00	2600
1973	Princess Anne on Doublet	Closed	N/A	8000.00	8000
1962	Quarter Horse	Closed	N/A	900.00	900
1976	Red Rum	Closed	N/A	2000.00	2000
1966	Royal Canadian Policeman	Closed	N/A	1700.00	1700
1964	Shire Stallion	Closed	N/A	1500.00	1500
1969	Suffolk Punch	Closed	N/A	1350.00	1350
1936	Three Circus Horses Rearing	Closed	N/A	4440.00	4440
1950	Two Galloping Horses	Closed	N/A	2553.00	2553
XX	Winner Brown/Bay	Closed	N/A	1721.00	1721
XX	Winner Grey/Bay	Closed	N/A	1721.00	1721

Ronald Van Ruyckevelt Porcelains - R. Van Ruyckevelt

YEAR ISSUE		EDITION LIMIT	YEAR RETD.	ISSUE PRICE	QUOTE U.S.$
XX	Alice	500		1875.00	1875
1970	American Pintail, Pair	500		Unkn.	3000
1969	Argenteuil A-108	338		Unkn.	Unkn.
1968	Blue Angel Fish	500		375.00	900
1965	Blue Marlin	500		500.00	1000
1967	Bluefin Tuna	500		500.00	Unkn.
1969	Bobwhite Quail, Pair	500		Unkn.	2000
1967	Butterfly Fish	500		375.00	1600
1969	Castelneau Pink	429		Unkn.	825-875
1969	Castelneau Yellow	163		Unkn.	825-875
XX	Cecilia	500		1875.00	1875
1968	Dolphin	500		500.00	900
1971	Elaine	750		600.00	600-650
1962	Flying Fish	300		400.00	450
1971	Green-Winged Teal	500		1450.00	1450
1962	Hibiscus	500		300.00	350
1956	Hogfish & Sergeant Major	500		375.00	650
1968	Honfleur A-105	290		Unkn.	600
1968	Honfleur A-106	290		Unkn.	600
1971	Languedoc	216		Unkn.	1150
1968	Mallards	500		Unkn.	2000
1968	Mennecy A-101	338		Unkn.	675-725
1968	Mennecy A-102	334		Unkn.	675-725
1961	Passionflower	500		300.00	400
1976	Picnic	250		2850.00	2850
1976	Queen Elizabeth I	250		3850.00	3850
1977	Queen Elizabeth II	250		Unkn.	Unkn.
1976	Queen Mary I	250		4850.00	4850
1968	Rainbow Parrot Fish	500		1500.00	1500
1958	Red Hind	500		375.00	900
1968	Ring-Necked Pheasants	500		Unkn.	32-3400
1964	Rock Beauty	500		425.00	850
1962	Sailfish	500		400.00	550
1969	Saint Denis A-109	500		Unkn.	925-950
1961	Squirrelfish	500		400.00	9000
1966	Swordfish	500		575.00	650
1964	Tarpon	500		500.00	975
1972	White Doves	25		3600.00	27850

Ruth Van Ruyckevelt Porcelains - R. Van Ruyckevelt

YEAR ISSUE		EDITION LIMIT	YEAR RETD.	ISSUE PRICE	QUOTE U.S.$
1960	Beatrice	500		125.00	Unkn.
1969	Bridget	500		300.00	600-700
1960	Caroline	500		125.00	Unkn.
1968	Charlotte and Jane	500		1000.00	15-1650
1967	Elizabeth	750		300.00	750-800
1969	Emily	500		300.00	600
1978	Esther	500		Unkn.	Unkn.
1971	Felicity	750		600.00	600
1959	Lisette	500		100.00	Unkn.
1962	Louisa	500		400.00	975
1968	Madeline	500		300.00	750-800
1968	Marion	500		275.00	575-625
1964	Melanie	500		150.00	Unkn.
1959	Penelope	500		100.00	Unkn.
1964	Rosalind	500		150.00	Unkn.
1963	Sister of London Hospital	500		Unkn.	475-500
1963	Sister of St. Thomas Hospital	500		Unkn.	475-500
1970	Sister of the Red Cross	750		Unkn.	525-1500
1966	Sister of University College Hospital	500		Unkn.	475-500

YEAR ISSUE		EDITION LIMIT	YEAR RETD.	ISSUE PRICE	QUOTE U.S.$
1964	Tea Party	250		400.00	7000

Salvino Inc.

Collector Club Figurines - Salvino

YEAR ISSUE		EDITION LIMIT	YEAR RETD.	ISSUE PRICE	QUOTE U.S.$
1993	6" Mario Lemieux-Painted Away Uniform (Unsigned)	Closed	N/A	70.00	90
1993	Joe Montana-"KC" Away Uniform (Hand Signed)	Closed	N/A	275.00	275

Boston Celtic Greats - Salvino

YEAR ISSUE		EDITION LIMIT	YEAR RETD.	ISSUE PRICE	QUOTE U.S.$
1991	Larry Bird	S/O	N/A	285.00	350
1993	Larry Bird (Special Edition)	S/O	N/A	375.00	400-450

Boxing Greats - Salvino

YEAR ISSUE		EDITION LIMIT	YEAR RETD.	ISSUE PRICE	QUOTE U.S.$
1990	Muhammed Ali	S/O	N/A	250.00	300-400
1990	Muhammed Ali (Special Edition)	S/O	N/A	375.00	350-700

Brooklyn Dodger - Salvino

YEAR ISSUE		EDITION LIMIT	YEAR RETD.	ISSUE PRICE	QUOTE U.S.$
1989	Don Drysdale	S/O	N/A	185.00	200-300
1989	Don Drysdale AP	300		200.00	400
1993	Duke Snider	1,000		275.00	275
1990	Roy Campanella	2,000		395.00	350-500
1990	Roy Campanella (Special Edition)	S/O	N/A	550.00	600-900
1989	Sandy Koufax	S/O	N/A	195.00	225-300
1989	Sandy Koufax AP	500		250.00	400

Chicago Bears Greats - Salvino

YEAR ISSUE		EDITION LIMIT	YEAR RETD.	ISSUE PRICE	QUOTE U.S.$
1992	Gale Sayers	1,000		275.00	275

Collegiate Series - Salvino

YEAR ISSUE		EDITION LIMIT	YEAR RETD.	ISSUE PRICE	QUOTE U.S.$
1992	Joe Montana	S/O	N/A	275.00	325
1992	OJ Simpson	1,000		275.00	350

Dealer Special Series - Salvino

YEAR ISSUE		EDITION LIMIT	YEAR RETD.	ISSUE PRICE	QUOTE U.S.$
1992	Joe Namath	S/O	N/A	700.00	700
1992	Mickey Mantle #6	S/O	N/A	700.00	1100
1992	Mickey Mantle #7	S/O	N/A	700.00	700
1993	Willie Mays	S/O	N/A	700.00	700

Green Bay Packer Legends - Salvino

YEAR ISSUE		EDITION LIMIT	YEAR RETD.	ISSUE PRICE	QUOTE U.S.$
1992	Bart Starr	500		250.00	250
1992	Jim Taylor	500		250.00	250
1992	Paul Hornung	500		250.00	250

Heroes of the Diamond - Salvino

YEAR ISSUE		EDITION LIMIT	YEAR RETD.	ISSUE PRICE	QUOTE U.S.$
1993	Brooks Robinson	1,000		275.00	275
1992	Mickey Mantle Batting	S/O	N/A	395.00	700
1992	Mickey Mantle Fielding	S/O	N/A	395.00	450-700
1991	Rickey Henderson (Away)	600		275.00	275
1991	Rickey Henderson (Home)	S/O	N/A	275.00	275
1991	Rickey Henderson (Special Edition)	550		375.00	375
1992	Willie Mays New York	750		395.00	395
1992	Willie Mays San Francisco	750		395.00	395

Hockey Greats - Salvino

YEAR ISSUE		EDITION LIMIT	YEAR RETD.	ISSUE PRICE	QUOTE U.S.$
1991	Mario Lemieux	S/O	N/A	275.00	300-600
1992	Mario Lemieux (Special Editon)	S/O	N/A	285.00	400
1994	Wayne Gretzky	S/O	N/A	395.00	395

NBA Laker Legends - Salvino

YEAR ISSUE		EDITION LIMIT	YEAR RETD.	ISSUE PRICE	QUOTE U.S.$
1991	Elgin Baylor	700		250.00	250
1991	Elgin Baylor (Special Edition)	300		350.00	350
1991	Jerry West	700		250.00	250
1991	Jerry West (Special Edition)	300		350.00	350

NFL Superstar - Salvino

YEAR ISSUE		EDITION LIMIT	YEAR RETD.	ISSUE PRICE	QUOTE U.S.$
1990	Jim Brown	S/O	N/A	275.00	275-325
1990	Jim Brown (Special Edition)	S/O	N/A	525.00	450-550
1990	Joe Montana	S/O	N/A	275.00	275-325
1990	Joe Montana (Special Edition)	S/O	N/A	395.00	395
1993	Joe Montana 49'er	1,000		275.00	275
1993	Joe Montana Chiefs	450		275.00	400
1990	Joe Namath	2,500		275.00	275
1990	Joe Namath (Special Edition)	500		375.00	375-475
1990	OJ Simpson	1,000		250.00	300-400

Pittsburgh Stealer Greats - Salvino

YEAR ISSUE		EDITION LIMIT	YEAR RETD.	ISSUE PRICE	QUOTE U.S.$
1992	Terry Bradshaw	S/O	N/A	275.00	275

Racing Legends - Salvino

YEAR ISSUE		EDITION LIMIT	YEAR RETD.	ISSUE PRICE	QUOTE U.S.$
1991	AJ Foyt	S/O	N/A	250.00	250
1991	Darrell Waltrip	S/O	N/A	250.00	250
1991	Richard Petty	S/O	N/A	250.00	250
1991	Richard Petty (Special Edition)	S/O	N/A	279.00	350-400
1993	Richard Petty Farewell Tour	2,500		275.00	275

Tennis Greats - Salvino

YEAR ISSUE		EDITION LIMIT	YEAR RETD.	ISSUE PRICE	QUOTE U.S.$
1993	Bjorn Borg	500		275.00	275

Unsigned Collection - Salvino

YEAR ISSUE		EDITION LIMIT	YEAR RETD.	ISSUE PRICE	QUOTE U.S.$
1993	Mario Lemieux 6" cold-cast pewter	S/O	N/A	43.95	44
1993	Mario Lemieux 6" hand-painted	S/O	N/A	69.95	70
1993	Mario Lemieux 8" cold-cast pewter	S/O	N/A	99.95	100
1993	Mario Lemieux cold-cast pewter plaque	S/O	N/A	24.95	25
1993	Richard Petty 6" cold-cast pewter	5,000		43.95	44
1993	Richard Petty 6" hand-painted	2,500		69.95	70
1993	Richard Petty 8" cold-cast pewter	2,500		99.95	100
1993	Richard Petty cold-cast pewter plaque	5,000		24.95	25
1994	Roberto Clemente	1,750		125.00	125

Sarah's Attic, Inc.

Collector's Club Promotion - Sarah's Attic

YEAR ISSUE		EDITION LIMIT	YEAR RETD.	ISSUE PRICE	QUOTE U.S.$
1991	Diamond 3497	Closed	1992	36.00	100
1991	Ruby 3498	Closed	1992	42.00	100
1992	Christmas Love Santa 3522	Closed	1992	45.00	45
1992	Forever Frolicking Friends 3523	Closed	1992	Gift	75
1992	Love One Another 3561	Closed	1992	60.00	60
1992	Sharing Dreams 3562	Closed	1993	75.00	100
1992	Life Time Friends 3563	Closed	1993	75.00	125
1992	Love Starts With Children 3607	Closed	1993	Gift	75
1993	First Forever Friend Celebration 3903	Closed	1993	50.00	50
1993	Pledge of Allegiance 3749	Closed	1993	45.00	90
1993	Love Starts With Children II 3837	Closed	1994	Gift	65
1993	Gem White Girl w/Basket 3842	Closed	1994	33.00	65
1993	Rocky Black Boy w/Marbles 3843	Closed	1994	25.00	65
1994	America Boy 4191	Closed	1994	25.00	25
1994	America Girl 4192	Closed	1994	25.00	25
1994	Saturday Night Round Up 4232	Closed	1995	Gift	25
1994	Billy Bob 4233	Closed	1995	38.00	38
1994	Jimmy Dean 4234	Closed	1995	38.00	38
1994	Sally/Jack 4235	Closed	1995	55.00	55
1994	Ellie/T.J. 4236	Closed	1995	55.00	55
1995	Flags in Heaven	12/95		45.00	45
1995	Friends Forever 4444	5/96		60.00	60
1995	Playtime Pals 4446	7/96		65.00	65
1995	Horsin' around 4445	7/96		65.00	65

Angels In The Attic - Sarah's Attic

YEAR ISSUE		EDITION LIMIT	YEAR RETD.	ISSUE PRICE	QUOTE U.S.$
1989	Abbee-Angel-2336	Closed	1991	10.00	20
1990	Adora Girl Angel Standing 3276	4,000	1990	35.00	100-165
1994	Adora w/Harp 4137	4,000		26.00	26
1989	Alex-Angel 2335	Closed	1991	10.00	14
1989	Amelia-Angel 2334	Closed	1991	10.00	14
1991	Angel Adora With Bunny 3390	Closed	1993	50.00	65
1990	Angel Bear in Basket 3294	Closed	1990	23.00	23
1994	Angel Bear with Horse 4243	2,050		26.00	26
1994	Angel Bunny with Cage 4241	2,050		20.00	20
1991	Angel Enos With Frog 3391	10,000	1993	50.00	65
1994	Angel Kitty with Basket 4240	2,050		20.00	20
1992	Angel Pup 3519	Closed	1993	14.00	20
1994	Angel Pup with Victrola 4242	2,050		20.00	20
1990	Angel Rabbit in Basket 3293	Closed	1990	25.00	25
1989	Angelica Angel 3201	6,000	1992	25.00	25
1989	Ashbee-Angel 2337	Closed	1991	10.00	20
1989	Ashlee Angel 2354	Closed	1990	14.00	28
1991	Bert Angel 3416	1,000	1992	60.00	120
1989	Bevie-Angel 2361	Closed	1990	10.00	10
1990	Billi-Angel 3295	Closed	1991	18.00	22
1994	Black Boy-Wings of Love 4203	1,000	1995	36.00	36
1994	Black Girl-Wings of Love 4202	1,000	1995	36.00	36
1993	Blessed is He 3952	1,994	1994	48.00	110-200
1994	Blessed is He II 4189	2,500		66.00	66
1995	Blessed is He III 4387	4,000		60.00	60
1989	Bonnie-Angel 2328	Closed	1991	17.00	20
1990	Buster-Angel 3302	Closed	1991	15.00	15
1994	Casey Angel 4245	2,050		32.00	32
1995	Christine 4420	5,000		26.00	26
1990	Cindi-Angel 3296	Closed	1991	18.00	22
1989	Clyde-Angel 2329	Closed	1991	17.00	20
1992	Contentment 3500	500	1992	100.00	200
1989	Daisy Angel 2352	Closed	1990	14.00	14
1995	Dignity 4330	Open		55.00	55
1991	Donald Angel 3415	1,000	1992	50.00	50
1989	Dusty Angel 2358	Closed	1990	12.00	95
1989	Eddie-Angel 2331	Closed	1990	10.00	10
1989	Emmy Lou Angel 2359	Closed	1990	12.00	12
1992	Enos & Adora-Small 3671	5,000	1993	35.00	45
1990	Enos Boy Angel Sitting 3275	4,000	1990	33.00	100
1994	Enos w/Horn 4138	4,000		26.00	26
1993	Faith-Black Angel 3953	1,994		40.00	40
1989	Floppy-Angel 2330	Closed	1990	10.00	20
1990	Flossy-Angel 3301	Closed	1991	15.00	24
1993	Grace-White Angel 3954	1,994		40.00	40
1989	Gramps Angel 2357	Closed	1990	17.00	95
1989	Grams Angel 2356	Closed	1990	17.00	95
1992	Harmony Angel 3710	3,500	1994	26.00	26
1992	Heavenly Caring 3661	2,500	1993	70.00	90
1992	Heavenly Giving 3663	Closed	1993	70.00	90
1989	Heavenly Guardian 3213	6,000	1990	40.00	40
1992	Heavenly Loving 3664	2,500	1993	70.00	90
1993	Heavenly Peace 3833	2,500	1994	47.00	47
1993	Heavenly Protecting 3795	2,500	1994	40.00	40
1992	Heavenly Sharing 3662	2,500	1993	70.00	90
1993	Heavenly Uniting 3794	2,500	1994	45.00	45
1992	Hope Angel 3659	Closed	1994	40.00	40
1989	Jeffrey-Angel 2333	Closed	1990	14.00	14
1989	Jessica-Angel 2332	Closed	1990	14.00	14
1994	Jonathon Angel 4253	2,050		32.00	32
1994	Jovae Angel 4252	2,050		32.00	32
1992	Joy Angel 3711	3,500	1994	26.00	26
1995	Labor of Love - Baby Black Girl 4288	Open		25.00	25
1995	Labor of Love - Beach White Boy 4302	Closed	1995	29.00	29
1995	Labor of Love - Birthday White Girl 4299	Open		29.00	29
1995	Labor of Love - Birthday Black Boy 4301	Open		29.00	29
1995	Labor of Love - Birthday Black Girl 4290	Open		29.00	29
1995	Labor of Love - Birthday White Boy 4303	Open		29.00	29
1995	Labor of Love - Blk Boy Stocking 4436	Open		18.00	18
1995	Labor of Love - Blk Boy Trumpet 4432	Open		18.00	18
1995	Labor of Love - Blk Girl Wreath 4435	Open		18.00	18
1995	Labor of Love - Bottle White Girl 4306	Closed	1995	29.00	29
1995	Labor of Love - Campfire White Girl 4293	Closed	1995	29.00	29
1995	Labor of Love - Canning White Girl 4297	Closed	1995	29.00	29
1995	Labor of Love - Computer Black Boy 4304	Open		29.00	29
1995	Labor of Love - Fishing Black Boy 4300	Open		29.00	29
1995	Labor of Love - Golfing Black Boy 4308	Open		29.00	29
1995	Labor of Love - Growing Black Girl 4305	Open		29.00	29
1995	Labor of Love - Happiness White Girl 4291	Open		29.00	29
1995	Labor of Love - Heals Black Girl 4292	Open		29.00	29
1995	Labor of Love - Ironing White Girl 4289	Open		29.00	29
1995	Labor of Love - Mechanic White Boy 4298	Closed	1995	29.00	29
1995	Labor of Love - Mowing Black Boy 4296	Closed	1995	29.00	29
1995	Labor of Love - Planting White Girl 4287	Open		29.00	29
1995	Labor of Love - Roller Blading White Boy 4309	Open		29.00	29
1995	Labor of Love - Sending Smiles Black Girl 4307	Open		29.00	29
1995	Labor of Love - Sewing Black Girl 4295	Open		29.00	29
1995	Labor of Love - Studying Black Boy 4294	Open		25.00	25
1995	Labor of Love - Tools White Boy 4310	Closed	1995	29.00	29
1995	Labor of Love - Wht Boy Wreath 4434	Open		18.00	18
1995	Labor of Love - Wht Girl Praying 4431	Open		18.00	18
1995	Labor of Love - Wht Girl Stocking 4433	Open		18.00	18
1995	Labor of Love Mini- Black Boy, blue 4383	Open		12.00	12
1995	Labor of Love Mini- Black Boy, gold 4382	Open		12.00	12
1995	Labor of Love Mini- Black Girl, gold 4378	Open		12.00	12
1995	Labor of Love Mini- Black Girl, pink 4379	Open		12.00	12
1995	Labor of Love Mini- White Boy, blue 4385	Open		12.00	12
1995	Labor of Love Mini- White Boy, gold 4384	Open		12.00	12
1995	Labor of Love Mini- White Girl, gold 4380	Open		12.00	12
1995	Labor of Love Mini- White Girl, pink 4381	Open		12.00	12
1994	Lacy Angel 4244	2,050		32.00	32
1990	Lena-Angel 3297	Closed	1991	36.00	40
1995	Louise Angel 4472	2,500		34.00	34
1990	Louise-Angel 3300	Closed	1991	17.00	24
1992	Love 3501	500	1992	80.00	200
1995	Love 4328	Open		40.00	40
1993	Mr. Ward-Happy Me 3971	500	1994	40.00	40
1992	Noble Angel 3712	3,500	1994	24.00	24
1989	Patsy Angel 2353	Closed	1990	13.00	13
1995	Prayer of Love 4437	500	1995	85.00	170
1992	Priscilla-Angel 3511	5,000	1993	46.00	46
1989	Rayburn-Angel 2338	Closed	1990	12.00	19
1989	Reba-Angel 2340	Closed	1990	12.00	12
1989	Reggie-Angel 2339	Closed	1990	12.00	15
1989	Regina 3208	Closed	1989	24.00	24
1995	Respect 4329	Open		32.00	32
1993	Risen Christ 3931	1,994		48.00	48
1989	Ruthie-Angel 2341	Closed	1990	12.00	12
1989	Saint Willie Bill 2360	Closed	1991	30.00	40
1989	Shooter Angel 2355	Closed	1991	12.00	24
1992	Sincerity Angel 3713	3,500	1994	24.00	24
1988	Small Angel Resin Candle 3071	Closed	1989	9.00	9
1989	St. Anne 2323	Closed	1991	29.00	32
1989	St. Gabbe 2322	Closed	1991	30.00	33
1989	St. George 3211	Closed	1991	60.00	65
1990	Trapper-Angel 3299	Closed	1991	17.00	24
1990	Trudy-Angel 3298	Closed	1991	36.00	36
1989	Wendall-Angel 2324	Closed	1991	10.00	20
1989	Wendy-Angel 2326	Closed	1991	10.00	20
1989	Wilbur-Angel 2327	Closed	1991	10.00	20
1995	Willie Bill Angel 4471	2,500		34.00	34
1989	Winnie-Angel 2325	Closed	1991	10.00	20

Beary Adorables Collection - Sarah's Attic

YEAR ISSUE		EDITION LIMIT	YEAR RETD.	ISSUE PRICE	QUOTE U.S.$
1987	Abbee Bear 2005	Closed	1989	6.00	12
1987	Alex Bear 2003	Closed	1989	10.00	12
1987	Amelia Bear 2004	Closed	1989	8.00	12
1988	Americana Bear 3047	Closed	1990	50.00	115

YEAR ISSUE		EDITION LIMIT	YEAR RETD.	ISSUE PRICE	QUOTE U.S.$
1988	Americana Bear w/Bow 2072	Closed	1990	10.00	10
1988	Americana Bear w/Jacket 2073	Closed	1990	10.00	10
1988	Americana Collectible Bear 2074	Closed	1989	18.00	18
1992	Andy-Father Bear 3727	3,500	1994	20.00	20
1989	Angel Bear 3105	Closed	1990	24.00	25
1988	Arti Boy Bear 6319	Closed	1990	7.00	15
1987	Ashbee Bear 2006	Closed	1989	6.00	12
1992	Aunt Eunice Bathtime 3924	Open		40.00	40
1992	Aunt Eunice Bear 3917	Open		24.00	24
1990	Bailey 50's Papa Bear 3250	4,000	1991	30.00	30
1995	Bay City Beauty 4334	Closed	1995	26.00	26
1995	Bay City Beauty w/Trunk 4335	Open		40.00	40
1988	Bear Clown 6276	Closed	1990	12.00	13
1988	Bear in Basket 4022	Closed	1989	48.00	48
1987	Bear on Cart 5148	Closed	1989	6.00	6
1987	Bear on Heart 5154	Closed	1989	6.00	6
1987	Bear on Trunk 5126	Closed	1989	16.00	20
1986	Bear Resin Candle 2022	Closed	1987	12.00	12
1987	Bear with Bow 5130	Closed	1990	8.00	8
1993	Beary Happy Halloween 3830	Closed	1994	18.00	18
1993	Beary Huggable Bear 3760	Closed	1994	18.00	18
1993	Beary Merry Christmas 3831	Closed	1994	20.00	20
1994	Beary Special Birthday Bear 3962	Closed	1994	20.00	20
1993	Beary Special Brother Bear 3873	Closed	1994	18.00	18
1993	Beary Special Father Bear 3875	Closed	1994	22.00	22
1994	Beary Special Friend Bear 3961	Closed	1994	20.00	20
1993	Beary Special Mother Bear 3874	Closed	1994	18.00	18
1993	Beary Special Sister Bear 3872	Closed	1994	18.00	18
1990	Belinda 50's Girl Bear 3253	4,000	1991	25.00	25
1992	Bellhop & Second-Hand Rose 3920	Open		40.00	40
1992	Bellhop Bear 3914	Open		24.00	24
1988	Benni Bear 6267	Closed	1990	7.00	7
1989	Betsy Bear w/Flag 3097	Closed	1990	22.00	28
1990	Beulah 50's Mama Bear 3251	4,000	1991	30.00	30
1990	Birkey 50's Boy Bear Teddy 3252	4,000	1991	25.00	25
1988	Boy Bear Resin Candle 3070	Closed	1989	12.00	12
1992	Brandy-Baby Bear 3728	3,500	1994	14.00	14
1986	Collectible Bear 2035	Closed	1989	14.00	14
1989	Colonial Bear w/Hat 3098	Closed	1990	22.00	25
1989	Daisy Bear 3101	Closed	1990	48.00	55
1987	Double Bear on Swing 5114	Closed	1987	20.00	20
1987	Double Bears w/Wood Heart 5400	Closed	1989	10.00	10
1992	Dowager Twins Bear 3910	Open		24.00	24
1993	Dowager Twins on Couch 3927	Closed	1994	60.00	60
1991	Dudley Bear 3355	2,500	1990	32.00	32
1993	Eddie Bear 3915	Closed	1994	24.00	24
1992	Eddie w/Trunk 3918	Open		40.00	40
1988	Einstein Bear 6266	Closed	1990	8.00	9
1991	Franny Bear 3358	2,500	1991	32.00	32
1994	Get Well Soon Bear 3992	Closed	1994	20.00	20
1988	Ghost Bear 3028	Closed	1989	9.00	20
1988	Girl Bear Resin Candle 3027	Closed	1989	11.00	11
1989	Griswald Bear 3102	Closed	1990	48.00	55
1988	Honey Ma Bear 6316	Closed	1990	16.00	20
1993	I Love You Bears 3812	Closed	1994	22.00	22
1993	I'm Beary Sorry Bear 3763	Closed	1994	18.00	18
1992	Irish Bear 3908	Open		24.00	24
1992	Irish Bear at Pub 3928	Open		40.00	40
1991	Joey Bear 3357	2,500	1990	32.00	32
1992	Just Ted Bear 3909	Open		24.00	24
1992	Just Ted w/Mirror 3923	Open		40.00	40
1988	Lefty Bear in Stocking 3049	Closed	1990	70.00	70
1993	Librarian Bear 3916	Closed	1994	24.00	24
1992	Librarian w/Desk 3919	Open		40.00	40
1995	Love Heals All 4438	Open		28.00	28
1992	Mandy-Mother Bear 3726	3,500	1994	20.00	20
1991	Margie Bear 3356	2,500	1991	32.00	32
1988	Marti Girl Bear 6318	Closed	1990	12.00	20
1992	Me and My Shadow Bear 3911	Open		26.00	26
1993	Me and My Shadow w/Chair 3926	Closed	1994	45.00	45
1992	Michaud Bear Sign 3929	Open		35.00	35
1989	Mikey Bear 3104	Closed	1990	26.00	30
1989	Mini Boy Bear 2316	Closed	1990	5.00	5
1989	Mini Girl Bear 2315	Closed	1990	5.00	5
1989	Mini Sleeping Bear 2317	Closed	1990	5.00	5
1989	Mini Teddy Bear 3110	Closed	1990	5.00	5
1991	Miss Love Bear 3354	2,500	1992	42.00	42
1993	Miss You Beary Much Bear 3761	Closed	1994	18.00	18
1989	Missy Bear 3103	Closed	1990	26.00	30
1991	Oliver Bear 3359	2,500	1990	32.00	32
1993	Professor Bear 3906	Open		24.00	24
1992	Professor w/Board 3925	Open		40.00	40
1995	Proxy Bear 4332	Closed	1995	20.00	20
1995	Proxy w/Jewelry Box 4333	Closed	1995	33.00	33
1988	Rufus Pa Bear 6317	Closed	1990	15.00	20
1989	Sammy Boy Bear 3111	Closed	1990	12.00	15
1989	Sarah's Bear 3096	Closed	1989	7.25	8
1992	Second Hand-Rose Bear 3912	Open		24.00	24
1989	Sid Papa Bear 3092	Closed	1990	18.00	25
1989	Sophie Mama Bear 3093	Closed	1990	18.00	25
1989	Spice Bear Crawling 3109	Closed	1990	12.00	15
1989	Sugar Bear Sitting 3112	Closed	1990	12.00	12
1992	Tommy w/Dog 3922	Open		40.00	40
1992	Tommy's Bear 3907	Open		24.00	24
1993	Witchie Bear 3913	Closed	1994	24.00	24
1993	Witchie w/Pot 3921	Closed	1994	40.00	40
1993	You're Beary Special Bear 3762	Closed	1994	18.00	18

Black Heritage Collection - Sarah's Attic

YEAR ISSUE		EDITION LIMIT	YEAR RETD.	ISSUE PRICE	QUOTE U.S.$
1995	Alicia/Yvette on Pew 4410	5,000		50.00	50
1995	Bessie Coleman 4313	2,500		50.00	50
1993	Bessie Gospel Singer 3754	2,500		40.00	40
1995	Bill Pickett 4281	2,500		56.00	56
1991	Black Baby Tansy 3388	Closed	1993	40.00	50
1995	Blessed is She 4312	5,000		50.00	50
1995	Book of Wisdom 4315	4,000		52.00	52
1992	Booker T. Washington 3648	3,000	1993	80.00	175
1992	Boys Night Out 3660	2,000	1994	350.00	450-695
1993	Brewster Clapping Singer 3758	2,500	1995	27.00	27
1990	Brotherly Love 3336	5,000	1991	80.00	175
1992	Buffalo Soldier 3524	5,000	1993	80.00	125
1995	Buffalo Soldier 4285	5,000		65.00	65
1991	Caleb w/ Football 3485	6,000	1993	40.00	40
1991	Caleb w/Vegetables 3375	4,000	1991	50.00	50
1990	Caleb-Lying Down 3232	Closed	1994	23.00	35
1995	Calvin 4319	4,000		28.00	28
1992	Calvin Prayer Time 3510	5,000	1993	46.00	46
1993	Carter Woodson 3845	3,000		45.00	45
1995	Charity 4318	4,000		28.00	28
1993	Claudia w/Tamborine Singer 3757	2,500	1995	27.00	27
1994	Coretta Scott King 4178	12/96		60.00	60
1991	Corporal Pervis 3366	8,000	1993	60.00	125
1995	Elroy Praying w/Bible 4411	5,000		25.00	25
1992	Esther w/Butter Churn 3536	Closed	1994	70.00	70
1995	Frederick Douglass 4402	2,500		55.00	55
1993	George Washington Carver 3848	3,000		45.00	45
1987	Gramps 5104	Closed	1988	16.00	100
1987	Grams 5105	Closed	1988	16.00	100
1992	Granny Wynne & Olivia 3535	5,000	1994	85.00	85
1990	Harpster w/Banjo 3257	4,000	1990	60.00	175-275
1991	Harpster w/Harmonica II 3384	8,000	1993	60.00	125
1992	Harriet Tubman 3687	3,000	1993	60.00	125
1994	Harriet Tubman II 4110	2,500		50.00	50
1991	Hattie Quilting 3483	6,000	1993	60.00	125
1990	Hattie-Knitting 3233	4,000	1990	40.00	75-100
1995	Henry O. Flipper 4403	2,500		55.00	55
1995	Hugs 4185	Open		36.00	36
1992	Ida B. Wells & Frederick Douglass 3642	3,000	1993	160.00	200-300
1995	Ida B. Wells and Son 4400	2,500		65.00	65
1993	Jesse Gospel Singer 3755	2,500		40.00	40
1992	Jomo-African Boy 3652	4,000	1994	27.00	27
1992	Kaminda-African Woman 3679	4,000	1994	50.00	50
1995	Kisses 4186	Open		30.00	30
1994	Kitty w/Microphone 4141	2,000		50.00	50
1995	Libby w/Candle 4396	4,000		26.00	26
1994	Libby w/Jacks 4139	4,000		26.00	26
1990	Libby w/Overalls 3259	4,000	1990	36.00	150
1991	Libby w/Puppy 3386	10,000	1993	50.00	70
1995	Lift Your Hearts 4413	5,000		50.00	50
1995	Love 4187	Open		50.00	50
1995	Loving Touch 4314	4,000		66.00	66
1995	Lucas w/Bear 4397	4,000		26.00	26
1991	Lucas w/Dog 3387	10,000	1993	50.00	70
1990	Lucas w/Overalls 3260	4,000	1990	36.00	150
1994	Lucas w/Papers 4140	4,000		26.00	26
1993	Madame CJ Walker 3849	3,000		45.00	45
1995	Martin Luther King Birmingham Jail 4407	12/96		65.00	65
1995	Martin Luther King Wedding 4406	12/96		85.00	85
1994	Martin Luther King, Jr. 4179	12/96		65.00	65
1994	Mary Church Terrell 4122	2,500		50.00	50
1993	Mary McLeod Bethune 3847	3,000		45.00	45
1993	Miles Boy Angel 3752	2,500	1995	27.00	40
1992	Miss Lettie-Teacher 3513	6,000	1993	50.00	50
1993	Moriah Girl Angel 3759	2,500	1994	27.00	45
1992	Muffy-Prayer Time 3509	5,000	1993	46.00	55
1992	Music Masters 3533	1,000	1992	300.00	350
1992	Music Masters II 3621	1,000	1994	250.00	300
1994	Music Masters III 4142	2,000		80.00	80
1993	Nat Love Cowboy (Isom Dart) 3792	2,500	1993	45.00	225-350
1994	Nat Love w/Saddle 4121	2,500		60.00	60
1991	Nighttime Pearl 3362	Closed	1993	50.00	65
1991	Nighttime Percy 3363	Closed	1993	50.00	65
1992	Nurturing with Love-3686	2,000	1993	60.00	60
1995	Old Time Tunes 4317	4,000		54.00	54
1995	Olivia A. D. Washington 4404	2,500		51.00	51
1993	Otis Redding 3793	Closed	1994	70.00	300
1991	Pappy Jake & Susie Mae 3482	6,000	1993	60.00	60
1989	Pappy Jake 3100	Closed	1990	40.00	100
1994	Peaches-Clown 4135	4,000		29.00	29
1990	Pearl-Black Girl Dancing 3291	5,000	1992	45.00	75
1990	Percy-Black Boy Dancing 3292	5,000	1993	45.00	75
1993	Phillis Wheatley 3846	3,000		45.00	45
1992	Porter 3525	5,000	1993	80.00	125
1991	Portia Quilting 3484	6,000	1993	40.00	40
1990	Portia Reading Book 3256	Closed	1991	30.00	45-65
1991	Portia-Victorian Dress 3373	7,000	1992	35.00	35
1990	Praise the Lord I (Preacher I) 3277	4,000	1991	55.00	135-150
1991	Praise the Lord II w/Kids 3376	5,000	1994	100.00	100
1993	Praise the Lord III 3753	2,500	1994	44.00	55
1995	Praise the Lord IV 4369	5,000		55.00	55
1994	Pug-Clown 4136	4,000		29.00	29
1989	Quilting Ladies 3099	Closed	1991	90.00	300
1992	Rhythm & Blues 3620	5,000	1994	80.00	80
1995	Rosa Parks 4401	6/97		65.00	65
1991	Sadie & Osie Mae 3365	8,000	1993	70.00	70
1992	Shamba-African Man 3680	4,000	1994	50.00	50
1992	Sojourner Truth 3629	3,000	1993	80.00	150
1995	Stitch of Love 4316	4,000		60.00	60
1990	Susie Mae 3231	Closed	1994	22.00	22
1995	Tuskegee Airman W.W. II 4405	2,500		60.00	60
1991	Uncle Reuben 3389	8,000	1993	70.00	125
1993	Vanessa Gospel Singer 3756	2,500		40.00	100
1994	W.E.B. DuBois 4123	2,500		60.00	60
1991	Webster-Victorian Suit 3374	7,000	1992	35.00	35
1990	Whoopie & Wooster 3255	4,000	1990	50.00	300
1991	Whoopie & Wooster II 3385	8,000	1993	70.00	125

Classroom Memories - Sarah's Attic

YEAR ISSUE		EDITION LIMIT	YEAR RETD.	ISSUE PRICE	QUOTE U.S.$
1991	Achieving Our Goals 3417	10,000	1994	80.00	80
1988	Miss Pritchet 6505	Closed	1993	28.00	35

Cookie Kids & Friends - Sarah's Attic

YEAR ISSUE		EDITION LIMIT	YEAR RETD.	ISSUE PRICE	QUOTE U.S.$
1995	Chip - Wh Boy w/Dog C004	Open		29.50	30
1995	Cookie Kids Displayer C000	Open		20.00	20
1995	Cookie Kids Sign C001	Open		39.00	39
1995	Honey - Bl School Girl C007	Open		29.50	30
1995	Oatie - Bl Boy w/Bike C002	Open		29.50	30
1995	Peanut - Wh Girl w/Dome C005	Open		29.50	30
1995	Sprinkles - Bl Clown Boy C006	Open		29.50	30
1995	Sugar - Bl Girl Baking C003	Open		29.50	30

Cotton Tale Collection - Sarah's Attic

YEAR ISSUE		EDITION LIMIT	YEAR RETD.	ISSUE PRICE	QUOTE U.S.$
1988	Americana Bunny 3048	Closed	1990	58.00	190
1988	Amos Hare 3040	Closed	1990	11.00	11
1992	Annabelle Mom Rabbit 3704	2,500	1994	40.00	40
1988	Billi Rabbit 6283	Closed	1990	27.00	35
1987	Bonnie 5727	Closed	1989	30.00	125
1988	Boy Rabbit Resin Candle 3026	Closed	1989	9.00	9
1988	Bunny in Basket 4021	4,000	1989	48.00	55
1993	Bunny Love Rabbit 3799	Closed	1994	18.00	18
1991	Chuckles Rabbit 3350	Closed	1993	53.00	53
1988	Cindi Rabbit 6282	Closed	1990	27.00	35
1987	Clyde 5728	Closed	1989	30.00	125
1989	Cookie Rabbit 3078	Closed	1990	29.00	125
1991	Cookie Rabbit 3351	Closed	1993	47.00	47
1994	Cookie-Rabbit Quilting 4196	6/96		40.00	40
1994	Corkey-Rabbit Chair 4197	6/96		30.00	30
1989	Crumb Rabbit 3077	Closed	1990	29.00	35-43
1991	Crumb Rabbit 3352	Closed	1993	53.00	53
1994	Crumb-Rabbit w/Book 4195	6/96		40.00	40
1992	Dustin Boy Rabbit 3700	2,500	1993	32.00	32
1987	Floppy 5729	Closed	1989	19.00	19
1992	Flower Girl Rabbit 3699	2,500	1993	32.00	32
1994	Fluff-Angel Bunny 4199	6/96		19.00	19
1995	Giddy-up 4280	Closed	1995	38.00	38
1988	Girl Rabbit Resin candle 3025	Closed	1989	9.00	9
1995	Glimmer 4362	1,000		50.00	50
1995	Glitz 4363	1,000		50.00	50
1990	Hannah Mom Rabbit 3264	Closed	1992	32.00	32
1993	Hannah w/Muff 3733	Closed	1993	30.00	30
1990	Henry Dad Rabbit w/Pipe 3263	Closed	1992	32.00	32
1993	Henry w/Wreath 3734	Closed	1993	30.00	30
1990	Herbie Boy Rabbit 3265	Closed	1992	22.00	22
1993	Herbie Sitting 3736	Closed	1993	25.00	25
1990	Hether Girl Rabbit 3266	Closed	1992	22.00	22
1993	Hether in Sled 3735	Closed	1993	30.00	30
1992	Higgins Dad Rabbit 3703	2,500	1994	40.00	40
1988	Izzy Hare 3038	Closed	1990	8.00	8
1988	Lizzy Hare 3037	Closed	1990	8.00	8
1988	Maddy Hare 3039	Closed	1990	11.00	11
1990	Molly Rabbit w/Vest 3240	Closed	1991	75.00	75
1989	Nana Rabbit 3080	Closed	1990	50.00	60-75
1991	Nana Rabbit w/Washboard 3349	Closed	1993	100.00	100
1994	Nana-Rabbit w/Book 4193	6/96		55.00	55
1990	Ollie Rabbit w/Vest 3239	Closed	1991	75.00	96
1989	Papa Rabbit 3079	Closed	1990	50.00	60-75
1991	Papa Rabbit w/Hat 3348	Closed	1993	80.00	80
1994	Papa-Rabbit w/Paper 4194	6/96		55.00	55
1992	Petals Girl Rabbit 3701	2,500	1994	30.00	30
1992	Pockets Boy Rabbit 3702	2,500	1994	30.00	30
1989	Sleepy Rabbit 3088	Closed	1990	16.00	25
1991	Sleepy Rabbit 3353	Closed	1993	35.00	35
1994	Sleepy-Bunny 4198	6/96		23.00	23
1990	Snowball Rabbit 3329	Closed	1993	8.00	8
1992	Tabitha Christmas 3688	2,500	1993	24.00	24
1993	Tabitha Cowgirl 3738	2,500	1994	30.00	30
1991	Tabitha Victorian Rabbit 3371	Closed	1993	30.00	45
1994	Tabitha-Valentine 4117	Closed	1994	24.00	24
1989	Tessy Rabbit 3086	Closed	1990	15.00	20
1991	Tessy Victorian Rabbit 3370	Closed	1993	20.00	35
1993	Tessy-Easter 3950	1,994		24.00	24
1989	Thelma Rabbit 3084	Closed	1990	33.00	40
1991	Thelma Victorian Rabbit 3368	Closed	1993	60.00	60
1993	Thelma-Easter 3948	1,994		26.00	26
1989	Thomas Rabbit 3085	Closed	1990	33.00	40
1991	Thomas Victorian Rabbit 3367	Closed	1993	60.00	60
1993	Thomas-Easter 3949	1,994		26.00	26
1989	Toby Rabbit 3087	Closed	1990	17.00	20
1991	Toby Victorian Rabbit 3369	Closed	1993	40.00	55
1992	Toby w/Hobby Horse 3689	2,500	1993	32.00	32
1992	Toby w/Train-Small 3673	5,000	1992	35.00	35
1993	Toby with Book/Christmas 3737	2,500	1994	20.00	20
1993	Toby-Easter 3951	1,994		24.00	24
1994	Toby-Valentine 4118	Closed	1994	24.00	24
1991	Tucker Victorian Rabbit 3372	Closed	1993	37.00	37
1988	Wendall Mini Rabbit 6268	Closed	1990	8.00	12
1987	Wendall Rabbit 5285	Closed	1989	14.00	25

YEAR ISSUE		EDITION LIMIT	YEAR RETD.	ISSUE PRICE	QUOTE U.S.$
1988	Wendy Mini Rabbit 6270	Closed	1990	8.00	12
1987	Wendy Rabbit 5286	Closed	1989	15.00	25
1988	Wilbur Mini Rabbit 6269	Closed	1990	8.00	12
1987	Wilbur Rabbit 5287	Closed	1989	13.00	25
1988	Winnie Mini Rabbit 6271	Closed	1990	8.00	8
1986	Winnie Rabbit 2036	Closed	1989	14.00	14
1990	Zeb Pa Rabbit w/Carrots 3217	500	1990	18.00	32
1990	Zeb Sailor Dad 3319	Closed	1992	28.00	28
1990	Zeke Boy Rabbit w/Carrots 3219	500	1990	17.00	32
1990	Zeke Sailor Boy 3321	Closed	1992	26.00	26
1990	Zelda Ma Rabbit w/Carrots 3218	500	1990	18.00	32
1990	Zelda Sailor Mom 3320	Closed	1992	28.00	28
1987	Zoe Girl Rabbit w/Carrots 3220	500	1990	17.00	32
1990	Zoe Sailor Girl 3322	Closed	1992	26.00	26

Daisy Collection - Sarah's Attic

YEAR ISSUE		EDITION LIMIT	YEAR RETD.	ISSUE PRICE	QUOTE U.S.$
1990	Bomber-Tom 3309	Closed	1993	52.00	57
1990	Jack Boy Ball & Glove 3249	Closed	1993	40.00	44
1993	Jack Boy w/Broken Arm 3970	2,000	1994	30.00	60
1990	Jewel-Julie 3310	Closed	1993	62.00	68
1989	Sally Booba 2344	Closed	1993	40.00	60
1990	Sparky-Mark 3307	Closed	1993	55.00	60
1990	Spike-Tim 3308	Closed	1993	46.00	51
1990	Stretch-Mike 3311	Closed	1993	52.00	57

Dreams of Tomorrow - Sarah's Attic

YEAR ISSUE		EDITION LIMIT	YEAR RETD.	ISSUE PRICE	QUOTE U.S.$
1994	Annie-Nurse 4128	3,000		33.00	33
1992	Annie-Teacher 3507	6,000	1993	55.00	55
1991	Benjamin w/Drums 3487	10,000	1993	46.00	58
1994	Bernie-Teacher 4132	3,000		38.00	38
1992	Blossom 3502	5,000	1993	50.00	50
1994	Boyd-Basketball 4279	2,000		36.00	36
1994	Boyd-Teacher 4130	3,000		34.00	34
1992	Bubba-Doctor 3506	6,000	1993	60.00	66
1994	Bubba-Fireman 4229	2,000		37.00	37
1994	Bubba-Football 4272	2,000		36.00	36
1992	Bubba-Policeman 3685	3,000	1993	46.00	51
1992	Bud-Fireman 3668	6,000	1993	50.00	55
1994	Bud-Police (blue) 4260	2,000		45.00	45
1994	Bud-Police (brown) 4261	2,000		45.00	45
1994	Calvin-Black Golfer 4161	3,000		35.00	35
1994	Calvin-Soccer 4275	2,000		36.00	36
1994	Champ-Soccer 4277	2,000		36.00	36
1993	Champ-White Boy Baseball 3776	Open		32.00	32
1991	Charity Sewing Flags 3486	10,000	1993	46.00	51
1992	Chips-Graduate 3532	6,000	1993	46.00	46
1993	Cody-Cowboy 3886	2,000		30.00	30
1994	Cody-Hockey 4271	2,000		38.00	38
1992	Cricket-Graduate 3531	6,000	1993	46.00	46
1992	Cupcake-Ballerina 3683	3,000	1993	46.00	46
1994	Cupcake-Dentist 4116	3,000		33.00	33
1992	Cupcake-Nurse 3514	6,000	1993	46.00	46
1994	Cupcake-Soccer 4276	2,000		36.00	36
1993	Dana-White Waitress 3779	2,000	1994	34.00	34
1994	Dedication-White Doctor 4111	3,000		38.00	38
1994	Devotion-Black Doctor 4112	3,000		33.00	33
1994	Hewett-Police (blue) 4258	2,000		45.00	45
1994	Hewett-Police (brown) 4259	2,000		45.00	45
1994	Jack Boy-Graduate 3984	3,000		30.00	30
1993	Jack-Boy White Pharmacist 3781	2,000		34.00	34
1994	Joe-Farmer w/Basket 4120	3,000		33.00	33
1994	John-Farmer w/Tractor 4119	3,000		36.00	36
1993	Jojo-White Girl Basketball 3777	Open		32.00	32
1994	Josh-Hockey 4270	2,000		38.00	38
1993	Josh-Jogger 3887	2,000		25.00	25
1994	Judy-Teacher 4131	3,000		38.00	38
1994	Juliana-Teacher 4129	3,000		34.00	34
1992	Katie-Executive 3665	6,000	1993	46.00	46
1994	Katie-Nurse 3987	3,000		33.00	33
1993	Katie-Pharmacist 3898	2,000		32.00	32
1993	Logan-White Boy Graduate 3740	2,000	1993	35.00	35
1993	Lottie-White Girl Graduate 3739	2,000	1993	35.00	35
1992	Madge-Farmer 3503	2,500	1993	50.00	50
1992	Marty-Farmer 3504	2,500	1993	50.00	50
1994	Moose-Football 4273	2,000		36.00	36
1993	Noah-Black Pharmacist 3780	2,000		34.00	34
1992	Noah-Executive 3508	6,000	1993	46.00	46
1992	Pansy-Ballerina 3682	3,000	1993	46.00	46
1993	Pansy-Black Waitress 3778	2,000	1994	40.00	40
1992	Pansy-Nurse 3505	6,000	1993	46.00	51
1993	Pansy-Pharmacist 3899	2,000		32.00	32
1994	Peaches-Dentist 4113	3,000		33.00	33
1994	Pug-Dentist 4114	3,000		33.00	33
1994	R. C. Mounted Police 4228	2,000		32.00	32
1993	Rachel-Photographer 3871	2,000		27.00	32
1994	Sally Booba-Graduate 3983	3,000		30.00	30
1992	Shelby-Executive 3666	6,000	1993	46.00	50
1994	Shelby-Nurse 4127	3,000		33.00	33
1991	Skip Building Houses 3489	10,000	1993	50.00	50
1994	Spike-Basketball 4278	2,000		36.00	36
1994	Spike-White Golfer 4162	3,000		35.00	35
1991	Susie Painting Train 3488	10,000	1993	46.00	46
1993	Tillie-Girl Basketball 3774	Open		32.00	32
1994	Tillie-Graduate 3985	3,000		30.00	30
1994	Tillie-Nurse 3989	3,000		33.00	33
1993	Tillie-Photographer 3870	2,000		27.00	32
1994	Tillie-Soccer 4274	2,000		36.00	36
1992	Tillie-Teacher 3520	6,000	1993	50.00	50
1992	Twinkie-Doctor 3515	6,000	1993	50.00	50
1993	Twinkie-Pilot 3869	2,000		27.00	35
1992	Twinkie-Policeman 3684	3,000	1993	46.00	46
1994	Twinkie-White Dentist 4115	3,000		33.00	33
1994	Whimpy-Doctor 3988	3,000		33.00	33
1992	Whimpy-Executive 3521	6,000	1993	46.00	46
1994	Whimpy-Fireman 4230	2,000		37.00	37
1993	Willie-Boy Baseball 3775	Open		32.00	32
1994	Willie-Doctor 3990	3,000		33.00	33
1992	Willie-Fireman 3667	6,000	1993	46.00	46
1994	Willie-Graduate 3986	3,000		30.00	30
1993	Willie-Pilot 3868	2,000		27.00	27
1994	Willie-Police (blue) 4256	2,000		32.00	32
1994	Willie-Police (brown) 4257	2,000		32.00	32

Happy Collection - Sarah's Attic

YEAR ISSUE		EDITION LIMIT	YEAR RETD.	ISSUE PRICE	QUOTE U.S.$
1988	Americana Clown 4025	4,000	1990	80.00	80
1988	Christmas Clown 4026	4,000	1990	88.00	88

Matt & Maggie - Sarah's Attic

YEAR ISSUE		EDITION LIMIT	YEAR RETD.	ISSUE PRICE	QUOTE U.S.$
1988	Large Matt 3029	4,000	1989	48.00	58
1986	Maggie 2029	4,000	1989	14.00	28
1989	Maggie Bench Sitter 3083	Closed	1990	32.00	42
1986	Maggie Candle Holder 2026	Closed	1987	12.00	12
1987	Maggie on Heart 5145	Closed	1989	9.00	15
1987	Matt & Maggie w/ Bear 5730	100	1987	100.00	150
1986	Matt 2030	Closed	1989	14.00	28
1989	Matt Bench Sitter 3082	Closed	1990	32.00	42
1986	Matt Candle Holder 2025	Closed	1987	12.00	12
1987	Matt on Heart 5144	Closed	1989	9.00	15
1989	Mini Maggie 2314	Closed	1989	6.00	12
1989	Mini Matt 2313	Closed	1989	6.00	12
1988	Small Sitting Maggie 5284	Closed	1989	11.50	35
1988	Small Sitting Matt 5283	Closed	1989	11.50	35
1987	Standing Maggie 2014	Closed	1989	11.00	15
1987	Standing Matt 2013	Closed	1989	11.00	15

Santas Of The Month-Series A - Sarah's Attic

YEAR ISSUE		EDITION LIMIT	YEAR RETD.	ISSUE PRICE	QUOTE U.S.$
1988	January White Santa	Closed	1990	50.00	135-150
1988	January Black Santa	Closed	1990	50.00	200-300
1988	February White Santa	Closed	1990	50.00	135-150
1988	February Black Santa	Closed	1990	50.00	200-300
1988	March White Santa	Closed	1990	50.00	135-150
1988	March Black Santa	Closed	1990	50.00	200-300
1988	April White Santa	Closed	1990	50.00	135-150
1988	April Black Santa	Closed	1990	50.00	200-300
1988	May White Santa	Closed	1990	50.00	135-150
1988	May Black Santa	Closed	1990	50.00	200-300
1988	June White Santa	Closed	1990	50.00	135-150
1988	June Black Santa	Closed	1990	50.00	200-300
1988	July White Santa	Closed	1990	50.00	175
1988	July Black Santa	Closed	1990	50.00	200-300
1988	August White Santa	Closed	1990	50.00	135-150
1988	August Black Santa	Closed	1990	50.00	200-300
1988	September White Santa	Closed	1990	50.00	135-150
1988	September Black Santa	Closed	1990	50.00	200-300
1988	October White Santa	Closed	1990	50.00	135-150
1988	October Black Santa	Closed	1990	50.00	200-300
1988	November White Santa	Closed	1990	50.00	135-150
1988	November Black Santa	Closed	1990	50.00	200-300
1988	December White Santa	Closed	1990	50.00	135-150
1988	December Black Santa	Closed	1990	50.00	225-375
1988	Mini January White Santa	Closed	1990	14.00	33-35
1988	Mini January Black Santa	Closed	1990	14.00	35
1988	Mini February White Santa	Closed	1990	14.00	33-35
1988	Mini February Black Santa	Closed	1990	14.00	35
1988	Mini March White Santa	Closed	1990	14.00	33-35
1988	Mini March Black Santa	Closed	1990	14.00	35
1988	Mini April White Santa	Closed	1990	14.00	33-35
1988	Mini April Black Santa	Closed	1990	14.00	35
1988	Mini May White Santa	Closed	1990	14.00	33-35
1988	Mini May Black Santa	Closed	1990	14.00	35
1988	Mini June White Santa	Closed	1990	14.00	33-35
1988	Mini June Black Santa	Closed	1990	14.00	35
1988	Mini July White Santa	Closed	1990	14.00	40
1988	Mini July Black Santa	Closed	1990	14.00	50
1988	Mini August White Santa	Closed	1990	14.00	33-35
1988	Mini August Black Santa	Closed	1990	14.00	35
1988	Mini September White Santa	Closed	1990	14.00	33-35
1988	Mini September Black Santa	Closed	1990	14.00	35
1988	Mini October White Santa	Closed	1990	14.00	33-35
1988	Mini October Black Santa	Closed	1990	14.00	35
1988	Mini November White Santa	Closed	1990	14.00	33-35
1988	Mini November Black Santa	Closed	1990	14.00	35
1988	Mini December White Santa	Closed	1990	14.00	33-35
1988	Mini December Black Santa	Closed	1990	14.00	35

Santas Of The Month-Series B - Sarah's Attic

YEAR ISSUE		EDITION LIMIT	YEAR RETD.	ISSUE PRICE	QUOTE U.S.$
1990	Jan. Santa Winter Fun 7135	Closed	1991	80.00	100
1990	Feb. Santa Cupids Help 7136	Closed	1991	120.00	120
1990	Mar. Santa Irish Delight 7137	Closed	1991	120.00	150
1990	Apr. Santa Spring/Joy 7138	Closed	1991	150.00	150
1990	May Santa Par For Course 7139	Closed	1991	100.00	125
1990	June Santa Graduation 7140	Closed	1991	70.00	70
1990	July Santa God Bless 7141	Closed	1991	100.00	125
1990	Aug. Santa Summers Tranquility 7142	Closed	1991	110.00	130
1990	Sep. Santa Touchdown 7143	Closed	1991	90.00	90
1990	Oct. Santa Seasons Plenty 7144	Closed	1991	120.00	120
1990	Nov. Santa Give Thanks 7145	Closed	1991	100.00	125
1990	Dec. Santa Peace 7146	Closed	1991	120.00	125
1990	January Mrs. Winter Fun 7147	Closed	1991	80.00	100
1990	February Mrs. Cupid's Helper 7148	Closed	1991	110.00	110
1990	March Mrs. Irish Delight7149	Closed	1991	80.00	100
1990	April Mrs. Spring Joy 7150	Closed	1991	110.00	110
1990	May Mrs. Par for the Course 7151	Closed	1991	80.00	100
1990	June Mrs. Graduate 7152	Closed	1991	70.00	100
1990	July Mrs. God Bless America 7153	Closed	1991	100.00	125
1990	August Mrs. Summer Tranquility 7154	Closed	1991	90.00	112
1990	September Mrs. Touchdown 7155	Closed	1991	90.00	100
1990	October Mrs. Seasons of Plenty 7156	Closed	1991	90.00	112
1990	November Mrs. Give Thanks 7157	Closed	1991	90.00	112
1990	December Mrs. Peace 7158	Closed	1991	110.00	137

Santas Of The Month-Series C - Sarah's Attic

YEAR ISSUE		EDITION LIMIT	YEAR RETD.	ISSUE PRICE	QUOTE U.S.$
1990	Jan. Fruits of Love 3400	Closed	1993	90.00	90
1990	Feb. From The Heart 3401	Closed	1993	90.00	90
1990	Mar. Irish Love 3402	Closed	1993	100.00	100
1990	Apr. Spring Time 3403	Closed	1993	90.00	90
1990	May Caddy Chatter 3404	Closed	1993	100.00	100
1990	June Homerun 3405	Closed	1993	90.00	100
1990	July Celebrate America 3406	Closed	1993	90.00	90
1990	Aug. Fun In The Sun 3407	Closed	1993	90.00	90
1990	Sept. Lessons In Love 3408	Closed	1993	90.00	90
1990	Oct. Masquerade 3409	Closed	1993	120.00	120
1990	Nov. Harvest Of Love 3410	Closed	1993	120.00	120
1990	Dec. A Gift Of Peace 3411	Closed	1993	90.00	90

Santas Of The Month-Series D - Sarah's Attic

YEAR ISSUE		EDITION LIMIT	YEAR RETD.	ISSUE PRICE	QUOTE U.S.$
1993	January White Wintertime Santa 3881	Closed	1994	35.00	35
1993	February White Valentine Santa 3882	Closed	1994	35.00	35
1993	March White St. Patrick's Santa 3885	Closed	1994	35.00	40
1993	April White Easter Santa 3741	Closed	1994	35.00	35
1993	May White Springtime Santa 3742	Closed	1994	35.00	35
1993	June White Summertime Santa 3743	Closed	1994	35.00	35
1993	July White Americana Santa 3815	Closed	1994	35.00	35
1993	August White Beachtime Santa 3816	Closed	1994	35.00	35
1993	September White Classroom Santa 3817	Closed	1994	35.00	35
1992	Oct. White Halloween Santa 3696	Closed	1994	35.00	35
1992	Nov. White Harvest Santa 3697	Closed	1994	35.00	35
1992	Dec. White Father X-Mas Santa 3698	Closed	1994	35.00	35

Santas Of The Month-Series E - Sarah's Attic

YEAR ISSUE		EDITION LIMIT	YEAR RETD.	ISSUE PRICE	QUOTE U.S.$
1993	January Black Wintertime Santa 3880	Closed	1994	35.00	35
1993	February Black Valentine Santa 3883	Closed	1994	35.00	35
1993	March Black St. Patrick's Santa 3884	Closed	1994	35.00	35
1993	April Black Easter Santa 3746	Closed	1994	35.00	35
1993	May Black Springtime Santa 3747	Closed	1994	35.00	35
1993	June Black Summertime Santa 3748	Closed	1994	35.00	35
1993	July Black Americana Santa 3818	Closed	1994	35.00	35
1993	August Black Beachtime Santa 3819	Closed	1994	35.00	35
1993	September Black Classroom Santa 3820	Closed	1994	35.00	35
1992	Oct. Black Halloween Santa 3729	Closed	1994	35.00	35
1992	Nov. Black Harvest Santa 3730	Closed	1994	35.00	35
1992	Dec. Black Father X-Mas Santa 3731	Closed	1994	35.00	35

Sarah's Gang Collection - Sarah's Attic

YEAR ISSUE		EDITION LIMIT	YEAR RETD.	ISSUE PRICE	QUOTE U.S.$
1989	Baby Rachel 2306	Closed	1994	20.00	20
1990	Baby Rachel-Beachtime 3248	Closed	1992	35.00	53
1988	Cupcake 4027	Closed	1994	20.00	20
1995	Cupcake 4346	Open		28.00	28
1989	Cupcake Clown 3144	Closed	1989	21.00	35
1993	Cupcake on Bench 3766	Closed	1994	28.00	28
1987	Cupcake on Heart 5140	Closed	1989	9.00	20
1987	Cupcake w/Rope 5119	Closed	1988	16.00	16
1993	Cupcake w/Snowman 3822	2,500	1994	35.00	35
1989	Cupcake-Americana 2304	Closed	1993	21.00	25
1990	Cupcake-Beachtime 3244	Closed	1992	35.00	53
1990	Cupcake-Devil 3314	Closed	1992	40.00	40
1986	Cupcake-Original 2034	Closed	1988	14.00	20-75
1989	Cupcake-Small School 2309	Closed	1990	11.00	20
1993	Cupcake-Spring 3937	1,994		30.00	30
1993	Katie & Rachel in Chair 3764	Closed	1994	60.00	60
1990	Katie & Whimpy-Beachtime 3243	Closed	1992	60.00	60-75
1988	Katie 4029	Closed	1994	20.00	20
1995	Katie 4344	Open		28.00	28
1987	Katie On Heart 5141	Closed	1989	9.00	20
1992	Katie On Sled 3707	2,500	1994	35.00	35
1987	Katie Sitting 2002	Closed	1987	14.00	20
1989	Katie-Americana 2302	Closed	1993	21.00	25
1991	Katie-Bride 3431	Closed	1994	47.00	52
1986	Katie-Original 2032	Closed	1988	14.00	20
1989	Katie-Small Sailor 2307	Closed	1990	14.00	20
1993	Katie-Spring 3935	1,994		28.00	28
1991	Katie-Thanksgiving 3468	10,000	1993	32.00	32

FIGURINES/COTTAGES

YEAR ISSUE		EDITION LIMIT	YEAR RETD.	ISSUE PRICE	QUOTE U.S.$
1990	Katie-Witch 3312	Closed	1992	40.00	50
1991	Peaches-Flower Girl 3438	Closed	1994	40.00	40
1991	Percy-Minister 3440	Closed	1994	50.00	55
1991	Pug-Ringbearer 3439	Closed	1994	40.00	44
1995	Rachel 4348	Open		28.00	28
1993	Rachel in Snowsuit 3823	2,500	1994	25.00	25
1991	Rachel-Americana 3364	Closed	1993	30.00	30
1991	Rachel-Flower Girl 3432	Closed	1994	40.00	40
1990	Rachel-Pumpkin 3318	Closed	1992	40.00	50
1993	Rachel-Spring 3940	1,994		30.00	30
1991	Rachel-Thanksgiving 3474	10,000	1993	32.00	35
1988	Tillie 4032	Closed	1994	20.00	30
1995	Tillie 4342	Open		28.00	28
1991	Tillie Masquerade 3412	Closed	1993	45.00	50
1987	Tillie On Heart 5150	Closed	1989	9.00	20
1992	Tillie On Log 3705	2,500	1994	35.00	35
1986	Tillie Resin Candle 2024	Closed	1987	12.00	12
1993	Tillie w/Bear 3769	Closed	1994	28.00	28
1989	Tillie-Americana 2301	Closed	1993	21.00	25
1990	Tillie-Beachtime 3247	Closed	1992	35.00	53
1991	Tillie-Bride 3436	Closed	1994	47.00	47
1990	Tillie-Clown 3316	Closed	1992	40.00	50
1986	Tillie-Original 2027	Closed	1988	14.00	20
1989	Tillie-Small Country 2312	Closed	1992	16.00	26
1993	Tillie-Spring 3938	1,994		30.00	30
1991	Tillie-Thanksgiving 3472	10,000	1993	32.00	32
1988	Twinkie 4028	Closed	1994	20.00	20
1995	Twinkie 4347	Open		28.00	28
1989	Twinkie Clown 3145	Closed	1989	19.00	35
1987	Twinkie On Heart 5143	Closed	1989	9.00	20
1993	Twinkie w/Football 3765	Closed	1994	28.00	28
1987	Twinkie w/Pole 5107	Closed	1988	20.00	20
1993	Twinkie w/Snowballs 3821	2,500	1994	35.00	35
1989	Twinkie-Americana 2305	Closed	1993	21.00	25
1990	Twinkie-Beachtime 3245	Closed	1992	35.00	53
1990	Twinkie-Devil 3315	Closed	1992	40.00	50
1991	Twinkie-Minister 3435	Closed	1994	50.00	50
1986	Twinkie-Original 2033	Closed	1988	14.00	20
1989	Twinkie-Small School 2310	Closed	1990	11.00	20
1993	Twinkie-Spring 3936	1,994		28.00	28
1991	Tyler-Ring Bearer 3433	Closed	1994	40.00	44
1988	Whimpy 4030	Closed	1994	20.00	20
1995	Whimpy 4345	Open		28.00	28
1987	Whimpy on Heart 5142	Closed	1989	9.00	20
1987	Whimpy Sitting 2001	Closed	1987	14.00	20
1992	Whimpy w/Book 3708	2,500	1994	35.00	35
1993	Whimpy w/Train 3767	Closed	1994	28.00	28
1989	Whimpy-Americana 2303	Closed	1993	21.00	25
1991	Whimpy-Groom 3430	Closed	1994	47.00	52
1986	Whimpy-Original 2031	Closed	1988	14.00	20
1990	Whimpy-Scarecrow 3313	Closed	1992	40.00	40
1989	Whimpy-Small Sailor 2308	Closed	1990	14.00	20
1993	Whimpy-Spring 3934	1,994		28.00	28
1991	Whimpy-Thanksgiving 3469	10,000	1993	32.00	32
1988	Willie 4031	Closed	1994	20.00	30
1995	Willie 4343	Open		28.00	28
1993	Willie Lying w/Pillow 3768	Closed	1994	28.00	28
1987	Willie On Heart 5151	Closed	1989	9.00	20
1986	Willie Resin Candle 2023	Closed	1987	12.00	12
1992	Willie w/Skates 3706	2,500	1994	35.00	35
1989	Willie-Americana 2300	Closed	1993	21.00	25
1990	Willie-Beachtime 3246	Closed	1992	35.00	53
1990	Willie-Clown 3317	Closed	1992	40.00	50
1991	Willie-Groom 3437	Closed	1994	47.00	47
1986	Willie-Original 2028	Closed	1988	14.00	20-75
1989	Willie-Small Country 2311	Closed	1992	18.00	26
1993	Willie-Spring 3939	1,994		28.00	28
1991	Willie-Thanksgiving 3473	10,000	1993	32.00	32

Sarah's Neighborhood Friends - Sarah's Attic

YEAR ISSUE		EDITION LIMIT	YEAR RETD.	ISSUE PRICE	QUOTE U.S.$
1987	Amber-Small Girl standing 5797	Closed	1989	14.00	14
1988	Americana Beau 2076	Closed	1988	25.00	25
1988	Americana Buttons 2077	Closed	1988	25.00	25
1991	Annie Nativity (Mary) 3419	Closed	1994	30.00	30
1991	Annie w/Flower Basket 3380	Closed	1992	56.00	56
1990	Annie w/Violin 3272	Closed	1992	40.00	40
1987	Archie-Small Boy standing 5798	Closed	1989	14.00	14
1987	Ashlee 5726	Closed	1989	44.00	44
1991	Babes-Nativity Jesus 3427	Closed	1994	20.00	20
1989	Baby Doll-mini 2318	Closed	1990	5.00	5
1991	Baby Tansy-white 2402	10,000	1993	40.00	40
1987	Bare Bottom Baby 5799	Closed	1988	8.00	8
1987	Beau-Cupie Boy 5861	Closed	1988	20.00	20
1987	Bevie 5103	Closed	1989	14.00	14
1987	Blondie-Girl doll sitting 5796	Closed	1989	14.00	14
1990	Bubba w/Lantern 3268	Closed	1992	40.00	40
1991	Bubba w/Lemonade Stand 3382	Closed	1992	54.00	108
1991	Bubba-Nativity King 3422	Closed	1994	40.00	40
1991	Bud Nativity (Joseph) 3420	Closed	1994	34.00	34
1990	Bud w/Book 3270	Closed	1992	40.00	40
1991	Bud w/Newspaper 3378	Closed	1992	40.00	40
1987	Butch-Boy Book sitting 5795	Closed	1989	14.00	14
1987	Buttons-Cupie Girl 5862	Closed	1988	20.00	20
1995	Chilly & Jingles - Lge 4417	100	1995	80.00	80
1995	Chilly - Snowman 4418	1,000		44.00	44
1987	Clementine-Girl Sailor Suit 5794	Closed	1989	12.00	12
1990	Cody-Victorian Boy 3229	4,000	1990	46.00	46
1987	Corky-Boy Sailor Suit 5793	Closed	1989	12.00	12
1987	Daisy 3002	Closed	1989	24.00	24
1991	Dolly Nativity (Jesus) 3418	Closed	1994	20.00	20
1987	Dusty 5106	Closed	1988	19.00	19
1987	Eddie 5337	Closed	1989	14.00	14
1993	Ellie-Girl w/Book 3784	Closed	1993	28.00	28
1993	Emily & Gideon-Small 3670	Closed	1993	40.00	40
1987	Emmy Lou 5112	Closed	1988	14.00	14
1993	Evan-Boy w/Bowl 3785	Closed	1993	28.00	28
1995	Flurry & Boo 4414	1,000		30.00	30
1987	Gramps-white 5104	Closed	1988	16.00	98
1993	Grams w/Rolling Pin 3782	Closed	1993	50.00	50
1987	Grams-white 5105	Closed	1988	16.00	98
1991	Hewett w/Apples 3377	Closed	1992	40.00	40
1990	Hewett w/Drum 3273	Closed	1992	40.00	40
1991	Hewitt-Nativity King 3424	Closed	1994	40.00	40
1988	Jeffrey Boy w/Clown 6151	Closed	1989	26.00	26
1989	Jennifer & Max 2319	4,000	1990	57.00	65
1988	Jessica 4033	Closed	1989	30.00	30
1988	Lena-w/Doll 3043	Closed	1990	40.00	40
1992	Misty 3616	4,000	1993	60.00	60
1989	Moose Boy Sitting 3215	Closed	1993	20.00	20
1991	Noah-Nativity Jesus 3428	Closed	1994	36.00	36
1991	Pansy Pushing Carriage 3381	Closed	1992	50.00	50
1990	Pansy w/Sled 3269	Closed	1992	35.00	35
1991	Pansy-Nativity Angel 3425	Closed	1994	30.00	30
1987	Patsy-Cheerleader 5120	Closed	1988	19.00	19
1993	Rosie on Crate 3783	Closed	1993	50.00	50
1991	Shelby-Nativity Mary 3429	Closed	1994	30.00	30
1987	Shooter 5110	Closed	1988	20.00	20
1995	Snowy 4416	1,000		30.00	30
1989	Sweet Rose 3214	6,000	1990	50.00	50
1990	Tiffany Victorian Girl 3328	Closed	1992	40.00	60
1988	Trudy-w/Teacup 3042	Closed	1990	34.00	34
1990	Tyler Victorian Boy 3327	Closed	1992	40.00	60
1990	Weasel w/Cap 3271	Closed	1992	40.00	40
1991	Weasel w/Newspaper 3383	Closed	1992	40.00	40
1991	Weasel-Nativity King 3423	Closed	1994	40.00	40
1987	Willie Bill 5108	Closed	1988	20.00	20

Snowflake Collection - Sarah's Attic

YEAR ISSUE		EDITION LIMIT	YEAR RETD.	ISSUE PRICE	QUOTE U.S.$
1993	Blizzard Snowman News 3866	4,000		20.00	20
1989	Boo Mini Snowman 3200	Closed	1993	6.00	12
1993	Bottles Snowman Milkman 3867	4,000		20.00	20
1992	Christmas Love-Small 3674	5,000	1992	30.00	33
1993	Cruiser Snowwman on Bike 3865	4,000		23.00	23
1992	Crystal Mother Snowman 3721	3,500		20.00	20
1989	Flurry 2342	Closed	1993	12.00	20
1990	Old Glory Snowman 3225	4,000	1992	24.00	26
1993	Sparkles & Topper on Log 3840	4,000		28.00	28
1992	Sparkles Baby Snowman 3723	3,500		14.00	14
1992	Topper Father Snowman 3722	3,500		20.00	20
1989	Winter Frolic 3209	Closed	1992	60.00	70

Spirit of America - Sarah's Attic

YEAR ISSUE		EDITION LIMIT	YEAR RETD.	ISSUE PRICE	QUOTE U.S.$
1993	Abraham Lincoln 3876	1,863	1994	60.00	60
1994	Asthon-Mother Indian 3977	1,000	1994	40.00	40
1994	Benjamin Franklin 4124	1,776	1994	70.00	70
1988	Betsy Ross 3024	Closed	1992	34.00	40
1991	Bright Sky Mother Indian 3345	Closed	1992	70.00	90-140
1995	Buffalo Bill 4311	2,500	1995	60.00	60
1995	Chief Joseph 4282	2,500		56.00	56
1994	Daniel Boone 4109	1,769	1994	60.00	60
1993	Democrat Donkey 3955	1,840	1994	40.00	40
1991	Forever in Our Hearts 3413	10,000	1994	90.00	90
1993	George Washington 3878	1,789	1994	60.00	60
1993	George Washington's Birth House 3879	Closed	1994	45.00	45
1992	Gray Wolf Father Indian 3692	2,000	1994	46.00	46
1994	Hogan-Indian House 3981	1,000	1994	40.00	40
1994	Hosteen-Father Indian 3978	1,000	1994	40.00	40
1988	Indian Brave 4007	Closed	1990	10.00	10
1988	Indian Girl 4008	Closed	1990	10.00	10
1991	Iron Hawk Father Indian 3344	Closed	1992	70.00	90-140
1993	Lincoln's Birth House 3877	Closed	1994	34.00	34
1991	Little Dove Girl Indian 3346	Closed	1992	40.00	60-85
1992	Moon Dance Girl Indian 3695	2,000	1994	30.00	30
1992	Morning Flower Indian 3693	2,000	1994	46.00	46
1988	Pilgrim Boy 4009	Closed	1990	12.00	20
1988	Pilgrim Girl 4010	Closed	1990	12.00	24
1992	Red Feather Boy Indian 3694	2,000	1994	30.00	30
1993	Republican Elephant 3956	1,854	1994	40.00	60
1994	Shine-Boy Indian 3980	1,000	1994	25.00	50
1994	Siyah-Girl Indian 3979	1,000	1994	25.00	50
1991	Spotted Eagle Boy Indian 3347	Closed	1992	30.00	45-85
1993	Tallman House 3900	1,856	1994	50.00	50

Spirit of Christmas Collection - Sarah's Attic

YEAR ISSUE		EDITION LIMIT	YEAR RETD.	ISSUE PRICE	QUOTE U.S.$
1995	Ahmad - Nativity 4453	7,500		23.00	23
1995	America Santa 4467	1,776		100.00	100
1995	Angelika - Nativity 4456	7,500		25.00	25
1988	Baby Jesus-Natural 2082	Closed	1988	7.00	7
1993	Been Good Santa/Boy 3813	2,500	1994	60.00	60
1990	Bells of Christmas 3326	5,000	1994	35.00	35
1989	Blessed Christmas 2350	7,500	1993	100.00	100
1992	Blessed Christmas-Small 3669	5,000	1993	40.00	40
1995	Blessed Family Nativity 4364	5,000		70.00	70
1989	Blinkey Elf Ball 3187	Closed	1990	16.00	16
1995	Care Basket 4424	5,000		26.00	26
1995	Caring - Boy w/Globe 4423	5,000		29.00	29
1995	Cherish the Children 4466	1,000		70.00	70
1994	Christine-Christmas 4149	Closed	1994	24.00	24
1993	Christmas Bear 3853	Closed	1993	23.00	23
1994	Christmas Bear 4157	Closed	1994	23.00	23
1993	Christmas Christine 3855	Closed	1993	30.00	30
1995	Christmas Dreams 4463	1,000		64.00	64
1993	Christmas Holly Santa 3859	Closed	1993	50.00	50
1993	Christmas Jaleesa 3856	Closed	1993	25.00	25
1993	Christmas Jeb 3854	Closed	1993	25.00	25
1993	Christmas Jessica 3858	Closed	1993	25.00	25
1989	Christmas Joy 3177	6,000	1990	32.00	32
1995	Christmas Joy 4331	2,000		60.00	60
1993	Christmas Justin 3857	Closed	1993	25.00	25
1990	Christmas Music 3305	5,000	1991	60.00	60
1993	Christmas Proclaim. Love Santa 3860	Closed	1993	50.00	50
1993	Christmas Rabbit 3852	Closed	1993	23.00	23
1994	Christmas Rabbit 4158	Closed	1994	23.00	23
1990	Christmas Wishes 3325	5,000	1994	50.00	50
1990	Christmas Wonder Santa 3278	3,000	1991	50.00	50
1987	Colonel Santa 3007	Closed	1989	30.00	30
1989	Colonel Santa II 3179	6,000	1990	35.00	35
1989	Colonel Santa-Mini 3188	Closed	1990	14.00	14
1994	Deck the Halls-Black Santa 4159	3,000		30.00	30
1988	Elf Grabbing Hat 3041	Closed	1989	8.00	8
1988	Elf w/Gift 6239	Closed	1989	8.00	14
1987	Father Snow 2049	Closed	1990	42.00	42
1989	Father Snow II 2351	6,000	1992	32.00	36
1989	Father Snow-Mini 3191	Closed	1990	16.00	16
1994	Gift of Christmas-White Santa 4146	2,000		60.00	60
1994	Gift of Love-Black Santa 4145	2,000		60.00	60
1992	Gifts of Christmas Santa 3677	Closed	1993	90.00	90
1992	Gifts of Love Santa 3678	Closed	1993	90.00	90
1994	Golden Memories Santa 4254	1,000		70.00	70
1995	Happiness 4426	5,000		34.00	34
1995	Helpfulness 4425	5,000		37.00	37
1988	Ho Ho Santa w/Elf 3053	Closed	1990	84.00	84
1995	Ishamael - Nativity 4454	7,500		23.00	23
1995	Jabari - Nativity 4455	7,500		23.00	23
1994	Jalessa-Christmas 4154	Closed	1994	28.00	28
1995	Jarrell - Nativity 4452	7,500		23.00	23
1994	Jeb-Christmas 4155	Closed	1994	28.00	28
1994	Jessica-Christmas 4147	Closed	1994	28.00	28
1987	Jesus 5136	Closed	1987	11.00	11
1988	Jesus 6309	Closed	1990	11.00	11
1987	Jingle Bells 2050	Closed	1989	20.00	20
1989	Jingle Bells II 3178	6,000	1990	26.00	26
1989	Jingle Bells-Mini 3190	Closed	1990	16.00	16
1995	Joah - Nativity 4451	7,500		23.00	23
1989	Jolly II 2347	6,000	1993	17.00	17
1989	Jolly-Mini 3193	Closed	1990	10.00	10
1987	Joseph 5135	Closed	1987	12.00	12
1988	Joseph 6308	Closed	1990	19.00	19
1988	Joseph-Natural 2081	Closed	1988	11.00	11
1995	Joy to the World 4462	1,000		64.00	64
1995	Joyfulness 4428	5,000		28.00	28
1994	Justin-Christmas 4148	Closed	1994	30.00	30
1995	Kindness 4427	5,000		30.00	30
1987	Kris Kringle-Black 5860	Closed	1990	100.00	100
1987	Kris Kringle-White 5860	Closed	1990	100.00	100
1994	Labor of Love-Christmas 4151	Closed	1994	30.00	35
1995	Lakeisha - Nativity 4450	7,500		25.00	25
1988	Large Mrs. Claus Resin Candle 3069	Closed	1989	11.00	11
1988	Large Santa Resin Candle 3068	Closed	1989	11.00	11
1987	Large Santa w/Cane 5124	Closed	1989	27.00	27
1993	Let The Be Peace Santa 3797	2,000	1994	70.00	70
1993	Let There Be Love Santa 3796	2,000	1994	70.00	70
1987	Long Journey 2051	Closed	1989	19.00	35
1989	Long Journey II 3184	6,000	1992	35.00	40
1989	Long Journey-Mini 3192	Closed	1990	11.00	11
1990	Love the Children 3324	5,000	1994	75.00	75
1992	Love the Children-Small 3672	5,000	1993	35.00	35
1989	Mama Santa sitting 3181	Closed	1990	30.00	40
1989	Mama Santa Stocking 3183	Closed	1990	50.00	50
1987	Mary 5134	Closed	1987	12.00	12
1988	Mary 6307	Closed	1990	19.00	19
1988	Mary-Mini 3034	Closed	1989	6.00	6
1988	Mary-Natural 2080	Closed	1988	11.00	11
1988	Mini Jesus 3036	Closed	1989	4.00	4
1988	Mini Joseph-Natural 2088	Closed	1988	5.00	5
1988	Mini Joseph-Natural 3035	Closed	1989	6.00	6
1988	Mini Mary-Natural 2087	Closed	1988	5.00	5
1988	Mini Santa Resin Candle 3074	Closed	1989	7.00	7
1987	Mini Santa w/Cane 5123	Closed	1990	8.00	8
1988	Mini-Jesus 2089	Closed	1988	4.00	4
1987	Mrs. Claus 5289	Closed	1989	26.00	26
1988	Mrs. Claus Small 6272	Closed	1989	11.00	11
1995	Mrs. Santa 4430	5,000		42.00	42
1987	Naughty or Nice 2048	Closed	1989	100.00	100
1989	Naughty or Nice-Mini 3210	Closed	1990	20.00	20
1993	Oh My! Santa/Girl 3814	2,500		55.00	55
1989	Papa Santa Sitting 3180	Closed	1990	30.00	40
1989	Papa Santa Stocking 3182	Closed	1990	50.00	60
1995	Peace on Earth 4464	1,000		80.00	80
1994	Rejoice-White Santa 4160	3,000		34.00	34
1987	Santa /wBasket 3020	Closed	1989	9.00	9
1995	Santa 4429	5,000		45.00	45
1990	Santa Claus Express 3304	4,000	1993	150.00	150
1987	Santa Head-3/4 3018	Closed	1989	8.00	8
1987	Santa Head-Full 3019	Closed	1988	8.00	8
1988	Santa in Chimney 4020	4,000	1990	110.00	150
1988	Santa Kneeling 4011	Closed	1989	22.00	22
1987	Santa Sitting 5122	Closed	1988	18.00	18
1991	Santa Tex 3392	500	1990	30.00	75
1995	Santa's Love 4465	1,000		98.00	98
1987	Santa's Workshop 3006	Closed	1990	50.00	100
1987	Santa-Necklace 5408	Closed	1988	10.00	10
1994	Sarah Elizabeth Christmas 4150	Closed	1994	27.00	27
1991	Sharing Love Santa 3491	3,000	1993	120.00	140

YEAR ISSUE		EDITION LIMIT	YEAR RETD.	ISSUE PRICE	QUOTE U.S.$
1989	Silent Night 2343	6,000	1991	33.00	50
1988	Sitting Elf 6238	Closed	1989	7.00	14
1988	Small Mrs. Claus Resin Candle 3073	Closed	1989	10.00	10
1988	Small Santa Resin Candle 3072	Closed	1989	10.00	10
1987	Small Santa w/Tree 5125	Closed	1989	14.00	14
1988	Small sitting Santa 6258	Closed	1989	11.00	11
1989	Spirit of Christmas Santa 2320	4,000	1993	80.00	80
1987	St. Nick 3005	Closed	1989	28.00	28
1989	St. Nick II 2349	6,000	1990	43.00	43
1989	St. Nick-Mini 3189	Closed	1990	14.00	14
1989	Stinky Elf sitting 3185	Closed	1990	16.00	20
1994	Teapot-Christmas 4156	Closed	1994	4.00	4
1995	Tillie - Caroling 4461	5,000		26.00	26
1991	Treasures of Love Santa 3490	3,000	1993	140.00	140
1995	Willie - Caroling 4460	5,000		26.00	26
1989	Winky Elf Letter 3186	Closed	1990	16.00	20
1989	Woodland Santa 2345	7,500	1990	100.00	150
1989	Yule Tiding II 2348	6,000	1991	23.00	30

Tender Moments - Sarah's Attic

YEAR ISSUE		EDITION LIMIT	YEAR RETD.	ISSUE PRICE	QUOTE U.S.$
1995	All Done 4395	3,000		29.00	29
1993	Always & Forever Black Wedding 3834	4,000		60.00	60
1992	Black Baby Boy 1-2 3518	Closed	1993	50.00	50
1992	Black Baby Boy Birth 3516	Closed	1993	50.00	55
1992	Black Baby Girl 1-2 3517	Closed	1993	50.00	55
1992	Black Baby Girl Birth 3526	Closed	1993	50.00	50
1993	Black Boy 3-4/In Wagon 3745	Open		40.00	40
1994	Black Boy w/Hobby Horse 4-5 3958	Open		33.00	33
1993	Black Girl 3-4/Tricycle 3744	Open		40.00	60
1994	Black Girl on Horse 4-5 3957	Open		37.00	37
1993	Bless This Child- White Couple 3838	2,500	1994	60.00	60
1995	Bundle of Joy 4392	3,000		20.00	20
1995	Bundle of Love 4393	3,000		29.00	29
1993	Catch of Love White Men Fishing 3827	4,000		50.00	50
1993	Days to Remember Black Men Fishing 3828	4,000		50.00	50
1995	Family is Love 4320	4,000	1995	60.00	60
1992	Generations of Love	Closed	1994	293.00	425
1993	Gentle Touch Black Girls 3825	2,500		40.00	40
1994	Get Well Soon-Sign 4220	Open		16.00	16
1995	Having Fun 4322	4,000		44.00	44
1993	Joy of Motherhood Black Pregnant Woman 3791	1,000	1994	55.00	70
1993	Little Blessing Black Couple 3839	2,500	1994	75.00	90
1995	Little Engineer 4389	3,000		25.00	25
1995	Love & Hugs Girl 4255	Open		38.00	38
1993	Love of Life-Black Couple 3788	1,000	1993	70.00	100-200
1995	Lullaby 4390	3,000		29.00	29
1995	Me Big Girl 4394	3,000		29.00	29
1992	Misty 3616	Closed	1993	60.00	60
1993	New Beginning White Pregnant Woman 3790	1,000	1994	55.00	55
1995	Precious Dreams 4391	3,000		28.00	28
1993	Promise of Love White Wedding 3835	4,000		60.00	60
1995	Remembrance 4470	2,000		100.00	100
1992	Small Black Boy 2-3 3676	Closed	1993	50.00	55
1992	Small Black Girl 2-3 3675	Closed	1993	50.00	50
1993	Special Black Boy in Wheelchair 3969	Open		38.00	38
1994	Special Black Girl 4126	Open		38.00	38
1993	Special Times White Girls 3826	2,500		40.00	40
1994	Special White Boy 4125	Open		38.00	38
1993	Special White Girl in Wheelchair 3968	Open		38.00	38
1995	Study Time 4325	4,000	1995	32.00	32
1995	Sweet Dreams 4388	3,000		29.00	29
1994	Timeless Knowledge 4323	4,000		47.00	47
1995	Treasured Moments 4321	4,000	1995	70.00	70
1993	True Love-White Couple 3789	1,000	1994	70.00	80
1992	White Baby Boy 1 3527	Closed	1993	60.00	66
1992	White Baby Girl 1 3528	Closed	1993	60.00	65
1992	White Boy 1-2 3530	Closed	1993	60.00	60
1992	White Boy 2-3 3624	Closed	1993	60.00	60
1992	White Boy 3-4 3691	Closed	1993	50.00	50
1994	White Boy w/Fire Truck 4-5 3960	Open		40.00	40
1992	White Girl 1-2 3529	Closed	1993	60.00	60
1992	White Girl 2-3 3623	Closed	1993	60.00	66
1992	White Girl 3-4 3690	Closed	1993	50.00	50
1994	White Girl w/Trunk 4-5 3959	Open		40.00	40
1995	Wow! 4324	4,000	1995	36.00	36

United Hearts Collection - Sarah's Attic

YEAR ISSUE		EDITION LIMIT	YEAR RETD.	ISSUE PRICE	QUOTE U.S.$
1992	Adora Angel-May 3632	Closed	1993	50.00	50
1991	Adora Christmas-December 3479	Closed	1992	36.00	45
1991	Annie & Waldo Beach-August 3460	Closed	1992	40.00	40
1991	Barney the Great-October 3466	Closed	1992	40.00	48
1991	Bibi & Biff Clowns-October 3467	Closed	1992	35.00	42
1991	Bibi-Miss Liberty Bear-July 3457	Closed	1992	30.00	36
1991	Bubba Beach-August 3461	Closed	1992	34.00	41
1992	Carrotman-January 3619	Closed	1993	30.00	40
1991	Chilly Snowman-January 3443	Closed	1992	33.00	40
1991	Chuckles-September 3464	Closed	1992	26.00	26
1991	Cookie w/Kitten-September 3462	Closed	1992	28.00	28
1992	Cookie-July 3638	Closed	1993	34.00	34
1991	Crumb on Stool-September 3463	Closed	1992	32.00	39
1992	Crumb-July 3639	Closed	1993	34.00	34
1992	Cupcake-November 3649	Closed	1993	35.00	35
1991	Cupcake-Thanksgiving 3470	Closed	1993	36.00	36
1992	December Tree 3655	Closed	1993	40.00	40
1991	Emily-Springtime May 3452	Closed	1992	53.00	60
1992	Enos Angel-May 3633	Closed	1993	50.00	50
1991	Enos Christmas-December 3480	Closed	1992	36.00	36
1992	Ethan Angel-August 3641	Closed	1993	46.00	46
1992	Fluffy Bear-February 3625	Closed	1993	35.00	35
1991	Gideon-Springtime May 3453	Closed	1992	40.00	43
1992	Herbie-January 3618	Closed	1993	26.00	26
1992	Hether-January 3617	Closed	1993	26.00	26
1991	Hewett w/Leprechaun-March 3448	Closed	1992	56.00	67
1991	Jack Boy Graduation-June 3455	Closed	1992	40.00	40
1992	Jewels-April 3630	Closed	1993	60.00	60
1992	Katie-September 3643	Closed	1993	35.00	35
1992	Kyu Lee-March 3628	Closed	1993	40.00	40
1992	Mrs. Claus December 3653	Closed	1993	45.00	45
1991	Noah w/Pot of Gold-March 3447	Closed	1992	36.00	43
1991	Pansy Beach-August 3459	Closed	1992	34.00	41
1991	Papa Barney & Biff-July 3458	Closed	1992	64.00	76
1992	Peaches-October 3647	Closed	1993	30.00	30
1991	Peanut-February 3445	Closed	1992	32.00	32
1991	Prissy w/Shaggy-February 3444	Closed	1992	36.00	36
1992	Puffy Bear-Febuary 3626	Closed	1993	35.00	35
1992	Pug-October 3646	Closed	1993	47.00	47
1991	Sally Booba Graduation-June 3454	Closed	1992	45.00	50
1992	Santa-December 3654	Closed	1993	45.00	45
1991	Shelby w/Shamrock-March 3446	Closed	1992	36.00	43
1991	Sparky Dog Graduation-June 3456	Closed	1992	16.00	16
1992	Stretch-April 3631	Closed	1993	50.00	50
1991	Tabitha April 3449	Closed	1992	32.00	32
1992	Tabitha w/Glove-June 3636	Closed	1993	34.00	34
1992	Tessie w/Ball-June 3637	Closed	1993	34.00	34
1991	Tillie-January 3441	Closed	1992	32.00	40
1991	Toby & Tessie-April 3450	Closed	1992	44.00	44
1992	Toby w/Bat-June 3635	Closed	1993	34.00	34
1992	Twinkie-November 3650	Closed	1993	35.00	35
1991	Twinkie-Thanksgiving 3471	Closed	1993	32.00	32
1991	Willie-January 3442	Closed	1992	32.00	40
1992	Willie-September 3644	Closed	1993	35.00	35
1992	Young Kim-March 3627	Closed	1993	40.00	40
1992	Zena Angel-August 3640	Closed	1993	46.00	46

Schmid

Lowell Davis Farm Club - L. Davis

YEAR ISSUE		EDITION LIMIT	YEAR RETD.	ISSUE PRICE	QUOTE U.S.$
1986	The Bride 221001 / 20993	Closed	1987	45.00	400-450
1987	The Party's Over 221002 / 20994	Closed	1988	50.00	100-190
1988	Chow Time 221003 / 20995	Closed	1989	55.00	85-100
1989	Can't Wait 221004 / 20996	Closed	1990	75.00	125
1990	Pit Stop 221005 / 20997	Closed	1991	75.00	125-150
1991	Arrival Of Stanley 221006 / 20998	Yr.Iss.	1992	100.00	85-100
1991	Don't Pick The Flowers 221007 / 21007	Yr.Iss.	1992	100.00	143
1992	Hog Wild	Yr.Iss.	1993	100.00	100
1992	Check's in the Mail	Yr.Iss.	1993	100.00	100
1993	The Survivor 25371	Yr.Iss.	1994	70.00	70
1993	Summer Days	Yr.Iss.		100.00	100
1994	Dutch Treat	Yr.Iss.		100.00	100
1995	Free Kittens	Yr.Iss.		40.00	40

Lowell Davis Farm Club - L. Davis

YEAR ISSUE		EDITION LIMIT	YEAR RETD.	ISSUE PRICE	QUOTE U.S.$
1994	Feathering Her Nest	Yr.Iss.		Gift	N/A
1995	After the Rain	Yr.Iss.		Gift	N/A

Lowell Davis Farm Club Renewal Figurine - L. Davis

YEAR ISSUE		EDITION LIMIT	YEAR RETD.	ISSUE PRICE	QUOTE U.S.$
1986	Thirsty? 892050 / 92050	Yr.Iss.		Gift	40
1987	Cackle Berries 892051 / 92051	Yr.Iss.	1989	Gift	N/A
1988	Ice Cream Churn 892052 / 92052	Yr.Iss.	1990	Gift	50
1990	Not A Sharing Soul 892053 / 92053	Yr.Iss.	1991	Gift	40
1991	New Arrival 892054 / 92054	Yr.Iss.	1992	Gift	40
1992	Garden Toad 92055	Yr.Iss.	1993	Gift	N/A
1993	Luke 12:6 25372	Yr.Iss.	1994	Gift	N/A

Davis Cat Tales Figurines - L. Davis

YEAR ISSUE		EDITION LIMIT	YEAR RETD.	ISSUE PRICE	QUOTE U.S.$
1982	Company's Coming 25205	Closed	N/A	60.00	225-275
1982	Flew the Coop 25207	Closed	N/A	60.00	300-365
1982	On the Move 25206	Closed	N/A	70.00	550-650
1982	Right Church, Wrong Pew 25204	Closed	N/A	70.00	288-350

Davis Country Christmas Figurines - L. Davis

YEAR ISSUE		EDITION LIMIT	YEAR RETD.	ISSUE PRICE	QUOTE U.S.$
1995	Bah Humbug	2,500		200.00	200
1987	Blossom's Gift 23554	Closed	N/A	150.00	350
1992	Born on a Starry Night 23559	2,500		225.00	225
1985	Christmas at Fox Fire Farm 23552	Closed	N/A	80.00	275
1986	Christmas at Red Oak 23553	Closed	N/A	80.00	200
1991	Christmas At Red Oak II 23558	Closed	N/A	250.00	250
1984	Country Christmas 23551	Closed	N/A	80.00	450
1988	Cutting the Family Christmas Tree 23555	Closed	N/A	80.00	350
1983	Hooker at Mailbox with Presents 23550	Closed	N/A	80.00	750
1989	Peter and the Wren 23556	Closed	N/A	165.00	300-450
1994	Visions of Sugar Plums	2,500		250.00	250
1993	Waiting For Mr. Lowell 23606	2,500		250.00	250
1990	Wintering Deer 23557	Closed	N/A	165.00	280

Davis Country Pride - L. Davis

YEAR ISSUE		EDITION LIMIT	YEAR RETD.	ISSUE PRICE	QUOTE U.S.$
1981	Bustin' with Pride 25202	Closed	N/A	100.00	225-250
1981	Duke's Mixture 25203	Closed	N/A	100.00	160-300
1981	Plum Tuckered Out 25201	Closed	N/A	100.00	950
1981	Surprise in the Cellar 25200	Closed	N/A	100.00	930-1000

Davis Dealer Counter Signs - L. Davis

YEAR ISSUE		EDITION LIMIT	YEAR RETD.	ISSUE PRICE	QUOTE U.S.$
1985	Fox Fire Farm 888907	Closed	N/A	30.00	250
1992	Little Critters 25515	Open		50.00	50
1990	Mr. Lowell's Farm 25302	Open		50.00	55-70
1980	RFD America 888902	Closed	N/A	40.00	200
1981	Uncle Remus 888904	Closed	N/A	30.00	300

Davis Farm Set - L. Davis

YEAR ISSUE		EDITION LIMIT	YEAR RETD.	ISSUE PRICE	QUOTE U.S.$
1985	Barn 25352	Closed	N/A	47.50	425
1985	Chicken House 25358	Closed	N/A	19.00	50
1985	Corn Crib and Sheep Pen 25354	Closed	N/A	25.00	65-80
1985	Garden and Wood Shed 25359	Closed	N/A	25.00	65
1985	Goat Yard and Studio 25353	Closed	N/A	32.50	85
1985	Hen House 25356	Closed	N/A	32.50	80
1985	Hog House 25355	Closed	N/A	27.50	85
1985	Main House 25351	Closed	N/A	42.50	100
1985	Privy 25348	Closed	N/A	12.50	35
1985	Remus' Cabin 25350	Closed	N/A	42.50	95
1985	Smoke House 25357	Closed	N/A	12.50	65
1985	Windmill 25349	Closed	N/A	25.00	40

Davis Friends of Mine - L. Davis

YEAR ISSUE		EDITION LIMIT	YEAR RETD.	ISSUE PRICE	QUOTE U.S.$
1992	Cat and Jenny Wren 23633	5,000		170.00	175
1992	Cat and Jenny Wren Mini Figurine 23634	Open		35.00	35
1989	Sun Worshippers 23620	5,000	1993	120.00	134
1989	Sun Worshippers Mini Figurine 23621	5,000	1993	32.50	33
1990	Sunday Afternoon Treat 23625	5,000	1993	120.00	170
1990	Sunday Afternoon Treat Mini Figurine 23626	Closed	1993	32.50	38
1991	Warm Milk 23629	Closed	1993	120.00	200
1991	Warm Milk Mini Figurine 23630	5,000	1993	32.50	38

Davis Little Critters - L. Davis

YEAR ISSUE		EDITION LIMIT	YEAR RETD.	ISSUE PRICE	QUOTE U.S.$
1992	Charivari 25707	950		250.00	250
1991	Christopher Critter 25514	1,192	1993	150.00	150
1992	Double Yolker 25516	Yr.Iss.		70.00	70
1989	Gittin' a Nibble 25294	Closed	N/A	50.00	57
1991	Great American Chicken Race 25500	2,500		225.00	275
1991	Hittin' The Sack 25510	Closed	N/A	70.00	70
1990	Home Squeezins 25504	Closed	1993	90.00	90
1991	Itiskit, Itasket 25511	Open		45.00	45
1991	Milk Mouse 25503	2,500		175.00	228
1992	Miss Private Time 25517	Yr.Iss.		35.00	35
1990	Outing With Grandpa 25502	2,500	1993	200.00	250
1990	Private Time 25506	Closed	1993	18.00	40
1990	Punkin' Pig 25505	2,500	1993	250.00	350
1991	Punkin' Wine 25501	Closed		100.00	150
1991	Toad Strangler 25509	Closed	N/A	57.00	57
1991	When Coffee Never Tasted So Good 25507	1,250		800.00	800
1992	A Wolf in Sheep's Clothing 25518	Yr.Iss.		110.00	110

Davis Pen Pals - L. Davis

YEAR ISSUE		EDITION LIMIT	YEAR RETD.	ISSUE PRICE	QUOTE U.S.$
1993	The Old Home Place 25802	1,200		200.00	200
1993	The Old Home Place Mini Figurine 25801	Open		30.00	30

Davis Promotional Figurine - L. Davis

YEAR ISSUE		EDITION LIMIT	YEAR RETD.	ISSUE PRICE	QUOTE U.S.$
1994	Don't Forget Me 227130	N/A	1994	70.00	70
1992	Hen Scratch Prom 225968	N/A	1992	90.00	95
1993	Leapin' Lizard 225969	N/A	1993	80.00	80
1991	Leavin' The Rat Race 225512	N/A	1991	80.00	200
1995	Nasty Stuff 95103	N/A		40.00	40

Davis RFD America - L. Davis

YEAR ISSUE		EDITION LIMIT	YEAR RETD.	ISSUE PRICE	QUOTE U.S.$
1984	Anybody Home 25239	Closed	N/A	35.00	100
1994	Attic Antics	Open		100.00	100
1982	Baby Blossom 25227	Closed	N/A	40.00	325
1982	Baby Bobs 25222	Closed	N/A	47.50	200-250
1985	Barn Cats 25257	Open		39.50	80
1993	Be My Valentine 27561	Open		35.00	35
1986	Bit Off More Than He Could Chew 25279	Open		15.00	60
1979	Blossom 25032	Closed	N/A	180.00	1800
1982	Blossom and Calf 25326	Closed	N/A	250.00	700-1000
1995	Blossom's Best	750		300.00	300
1987	Bottoms Up 25270	Open	1992	80.00	105
1989	Boy's Night Out 25339	1,500		190.00	225
1982	Brand New Day 25226	Closed	N/A	23.50	150-175
1979	Broken Dreams 25035	Closed	N/A	165.00	1000-1300
1988	Brothers 25286	Closed	1990	55.00	75-100
1984	Catnapping Too? 25247	Closed	1991	70.00	150
1987	Chicken Thief 25338	Closed	N/A	200.00	300
1983	City Slicker 25329	Closed	N/A	150.00	270
1991	Cock Of The Walk 25347	2,500		300.00	300
1986	Comfy? 25273	Open		40.00	80
1994	Companion pc. And Down the Hatch	6 mo.	1994	135.00	135
1994	Companion pc. Open The Lid	6 mo.	1994	135.00	135
1989	Coon Capers 25291	Open		67.50	90
1990	Corn Crib Mouse 25295	Closed	1993	35.00	45

YEAR ISSUE		EDITION LIMIT	YEAR RETD.	ISSUE PRICE	QUOTE U.S.$
1983	Counting the Days 25233	Closed	1992	40.00	60
1981	Country Boy 25213	Closed	N/A	37.50	250-375
1985	Country Cousins 25266	Open		42.50	80
1982	Country Crook 25280	Closed	N/A	37.50	350
1985	Country Crooner 25256	Open		25.00	50
1984	Country Kitty 25246	Closed	N/A	52.00	115-125
1979	Country Road 25030	Closed	N/A	100.00	900
1984	Courtin' 25220	Closed	N/A	45.00	125
1980	Creek Bank Bandit 25038	Closed	N/A	37.50	400
1995	Cussin' Up a Storm	Open		45.00	45
1993	Don't Open Till Christmas 27562	Open		35.00	35
1992	Don't Play With Fire 25319	Open		120.00	120
1985	Don't Play with Your Food 25258	Closed	1992	28.50	100
1981	Double Trouble 25211	Closed	N/A	35.00	475
1981	Dry as a Bone 25216	Closed	N/A	45.00	275-325
1993	Dry Hole 25374	Open		30.00	30
1987	Easy Pickins 25269	Closed	1990	45.00	85
1983	Fair Weather Friend 25236	Closed	N/A	25.00	85
1983	False Alarm 25237	Closed	N/A	65.00	150-185
1989	Family Outing 25289	Open		45.00	60
1985	Feelin' His Oats 25275	1,500		150.00	260
1990	Finder's Keepers 25299	Open		39.50	45
1991	First Offense 25304	Closed	1993	70.00	75
1994	First Outing	Open		65.00	65
1988	Fleas 25272	Open		20.00	24
1980	Forbidden Fruit 25022	Closed	N/A	25.00	150
1990	Foreplay 25300	Closed	1993	59.50	80
1979	Fowl Play 25033	Closed	N/A	100.00	275-325
1992	Free Lunch 25321	Open		85.00	85
1993	The Freeloaders 95042	1,250		230.00	230
1985	Furs Gonna Fly 25335	1,500		145.00	240-450
1987	Glutton for Punishment 25268	Closed	1991	95.00	160
1988	Goldie and Her Peeps 25283	Open		25.00	37
1984	Gonna Pay for His Sins 25243	Open		27.50	55
1980	Good, Clean Fun 25020	Closed	1989	40.00	100
1984	Gossips 25248	Closed	N/A	110.00	200
1992	The Grass is Always Greener 25367	Open		195.00	195
1991	Gun Shy 25305	Closed	1993	70.00	70
1990	Hanky Panky 25298	Closed	1993	65.00	95
1993	Happy Birthday My Sweet 27560	Open		35.00	35
1988	Happy Hour 25287	Open		57.50	75-100
1983	Happy Hunting Ground 25330	Closed	N/A	160.00	235
1984	Headed Home 25240	Closed	1991	25.00	50
1992	Headed South 25327	Open		45.00	45
1991	Heading For The Persimmon Grove 25306	Closed	1993	80.00	80
1994	Helpin Himself	Open		65.00	65
1983	Hi Girls, The Name's Big Jack 25328	Closed	N/A	200.00	385
1981	Hightailing It 25214	Closed	N/A	50.00	375-500
1983	His Eyes Are Bigger Than His Stomach 25332	Closed	N/A	235.00	350
1984	His Master's Dog 25244	Closed	N/A	45.00	150
1994	Hittin The Trail	1,250		250.00	250
1985	Hog Heaven 25336	1,500		165.00	260-450
1992	The Honeymoon's Over 25370	1,950		300.00	300
1984	Huh? 25242	Closed	1989	40.00	90-160
1993	I'm Thankful For You 27563	Open		35.00	35
1982	Idle Hours 25230	Closed	N/A	37.50	225-300
1993	If You Can't Beat Em Join Em 25379	1,750		250.00	250
1979	Ignorance is Bliss 25031	Closed	N/A	165.00	1300
1988	In a Pickle 25284	Open		40.00	50
1980	Itching Post 25037	Closed	N/A	30.00	75-115
1993	King of The Mountain 25380	750		500.00	500
1991	Kissin' Cousins 25307	Closed	1993	80.00	80
1990	The Last Straw 25301	Open		125.00	180
1989	Left Overs 25290	Open		90.00	100
1983	Licking Good 25234	Closed	N/A	35.00	200-250
1990	Little Black Lamb (Baba) 25297	Closed	1993	30.00	38
1990	Long Days, Cold Nights 25344	2,500	1993	175.00	190
1991	Long, Hot Summer 25343	1,950		250.00	250
1985	Love at First Sight 25267	Closed	1992	70.00	115
1984	Mad As A Wet Hen 25334	Closed	N/A	185.00	700-800
1987	Mail Order Bride 25263	Closed	1991	150.00	185-260
1983	Makin' Tracks 25238	Closed	1989	70.00	125
1988	Making a Bee Line 25274	Closed	1990	75.00	125
1994	Mama Can Willie Stay For Supper	1,250		200.00	200
1983	Mama's Prize Leghorn 25235	Closed	N/A	55.00	125
1986	Mama? 25277	Closed	1991	15.00	45
1989	Meeting of Sheldon 25293	Closed	1992	120.00	150
1980	Milking Time 25023	Closed	N/A	20.00	240
1988	Missouri Spring 25278	Closed	1992	115.00	175
1982	Moon Raider 25325	Closed	N/A	190.00	325
1989	Mother Hen 25292	Open		37.50	50
1982	Moving Day 25225	Closed	N/A	43.50	325
1992	My Favorite Chores 25362	1,500		750.00	750
1980	New Day 25025	Closed	N/A	20.00	165
1989	New Friend 25288	Open		45.00	60
1993	No Hunting 25375	1,000		95.00	95
1988	No Private Time 25316	Closed	N/A	200.00	300-355
1994	Not a Happy Camper	Open		75.00	75
1994	Oh Mother What is it?	1,000		250.00	250
1992	OH Sheeeit . . . 25363	Open		120.00	120
1993	Oh Where is He Now 95041	1,250		250.00	250
1984	One for the Road 25241	Open		37.50	60-70
1987	The Orphans 25271	Open		50.00	85
1985	Out-of-Step 25259	Open		45.00	90
1985	Ozark Belle 25264	Closed	1990	35.00	70
1992	Ozark's Vittles 25318	Open		60.00	60
1984	Pasture Pals 25245	Closed	1990	52.00	130
1994	Pecking Order	Open		200.00	200
1993	Peep Show 25376	Open		35.00	35
1988	Perfect Ten 25282	Closed	1990	95.00	180
1990	Piggin' Out 25345	Closed	N/A	190.00	250
1984	Prairie Chorus 25333	Closed	N/A	135.00	1000-1500
1981	Punkin' Seeds 25219	Closed	N/A	225.00	1200-1750
1994	Qu'est - Ceque C'est?	Open		200.00	200
1985	Renoir 25261	Closed	1991	45.00	85
1981	Rooted Out 25217	Closed	1989	45.00	85-115
1992	Safe Haven 25320	Open		95.00	95
1988	Sawin' Logs 25260	Open		85.00	105
1981	Scallawags 25221	Closed	N/A	65.00	150
1992	School Yard Dogs 25369	Open		100.00	100
1990	Seein' Red (Gus w/shoes) 25296	Closed	1993	35.00	47
1992	She Lay Low 25364	Open		120.00	120
1993	Sheep Sheerin Time 25388	1,200		500.00	500
1982	A Shoe to Fill 25229	Closed	N/A	37.50	150-175
1979	Slim Pickins 25034	Closed	N/A	165.00	525-700
1992	Snake Doctor 25365	Open		70.00	70
1991	Sooieee 25360	1,500		350.00	350
1981	Split Decision 25210	Closed	N/A	45.00	175-325
1995	Sticks and Stones	Open		30.00	30
1983	Stirring Up Trouble 25331	Closed	N/A	160.00	260
1980	Strawberry Patch 25021	Closed	1989	25.00	95
1982	Stray Dog 25223	Closed	N/A	35.00	75
1981	Studio Mouse 25215	Closed	N/A	60.00	360
1980	Sunday Afternoon 25024	Closed	N/A	22.50	225-250
1993	Sweet Tooth 25373	Open		60.00	60
1982	Thinking Big 25231	Closed	N/A	35.00	70-90
1985	Too Good to Waste on Kids 25262	Open		70.00	130
1982	Treed 25327	Closed	N/A	155.00	320
1989	A Tribute to Hooker 25340	Closed	N/A	180.00	215-300
1993	Trick or Treat 27565	Open		35.00	35
1990	Tricks Of The Trade 25346	Closed	N/A	300.00	300-375
1987	Two in the Bush 25337	Closed	N/A	150.00	320
1994	Two Timer	Open		95.00	95
1982	Two's Company 25224	Closed	N/A	43.50	200
1981	Under the Weather 25212	Closed	1991	25.00	85
1995	Uninvited Caller	Open		35.00	35
1981	Up To No Good 25218	Closed	N/A	200.00	850-950
1982	Waiting for His Master 25281	Closed	N/A	50.00	300
1994	Warmin'	1,250		270.00	270
1991	Washed Ashore 25308	Closed	1993	70.00	75
1982	When Mama Gets Mad 25228	Closed	N/A	37.50	300-375
1987	When the Cat's Away 25276	Open		40.00	60
1988	When Three Foot's a Mile 25315	Closed	N/A	230.00	300
1980	Wilbur 25029	Closed	N/A	100.00	585
1985	Will You Still Respect Me in the Morning 25265	Open		35.00	75
1988	Wintering Lamb 25317	Closed	N/A	200.00	250
1988	Wishful Thinking 25285	Open		55.00	70
1983	Woman's Work 25232	Closed	1989	35.00	75-100

Davis Route 66 - L. Davis

YEAR ISSUE		EDITION LIMIT	YEAR RETD.	ISSUE PRICE	QUOTE U.S.$
1992	Fresh Squeezed? (w/ wooden base) 25609	350		600.00	600
1992	Fresh Squeezed? 25608	2,500		450.00	450
1992	Going To Grandma's 25619	Open		80.00	80
1993	Home For Christmas 25621	Open		80.00	80
1991	Just Check The Air 25600	350	1995	700.00	1500
1991	Just Check The Air 25603	2,500		550.00	550
1993	Kickin' Himself 25622	Open		80.00	80
1991	Little Bit Of Shade 25602	Open		100.00	100
1991	Nel's Diner 25601	350	1995	700.00	1700
1991	Nel's Diner 25604	2,500		550.00	550
1992	Quiet Day at Maple Grove 25618	Open		130.00	130
1992	Relief 25605	Open		80.00	80
1993	Summer Days 25607	Yr.Iss.		100.00	100
1992	Welcome Mat (w/ wooden base) 25606	1,500		400.00	400-500
1992	What Are Pals For? 25620	Open		100.00	100

Davis Special Edition Figurines - L. Davis

YEAR ISSUE		EDITION LIMIT	YEAR RETD.	ISSUE PRICE	QUOTE U.S.$
1983	The Critics 23600	Closed	N/A	400.00	900-1300
1989	From A Friend To A Friend 23602	1,200		750.00	1700
1985	Home from Market 23601	Closed	N/A	400.00	1500
1992	Last Laff 23604	1,200		900.00	1000
1990	What Rat Race? 23603	1,200		800.00	1025

Davis Uncle Remus - L. Davis

YEAR ISSUE		EDITION LIMIT	YEAR RETD.	ISSUE PRICE	QUOTE U.S.$
1981	Brer Bear 25251	Closed	N/A	80.00	900-1200
1981	Brer Coyote 25255	Closed	N/A	80.00	500
1981	Brer Fox 25250	Closed	N/A	70.00	900-950
1981	Brer Rabbit 25252	Closed	N/A	85.00	2000
1981	Brer Weasel 25254	Closed	N/A	80.00	700
1981	Brer Wolf 25253	Closed	N/A	85.00	500

Don Polland Figurines I - D. Polland

YEAR ISSUE		EDITION LIMIT	YEAR RETD.	ISSUE PRICE	QUOTE U.S.$
1983	Challenge	2,000	1989	275.00	600
1983	Dangerous Moment	2,000	1989	250.00	350
1986	Down From The High Country	2,250	1989	225.00	295
1983	Downed	2,500	1989	250.00	600
1986	Eagle Dancer	2,500	1989	170.00	295
1983	Escape	2,500	1989	175.00	650
1983	Fighting Bulls	2,500	1989	200.00	600
1983	The Great Hunt	350	1989	3750.00	3750
1983	Hot Pursuit	2,500	1989	225.00	550
1983	The Hunter	2,500	1989	225.00	500
1986	Plains Warrior	1,250	1989	350.00	550
1986	Running Wolf-War Chief	2,500	1989	170.00	295
1986	Second Chance	2,000	1989	125.00	650
1983	A Second Chance	2,000	1989	350.00	650
1986	Shooting the Rapids	2,500	1989	195.00	495
1986	War Trophy	2,250	1989	225.00	500
1983	Young Bull	2,750	1989	125.00	250

Kitty Cucumber Musical Figurine - M. Lillemoe

YEAR ISSUE		EDITION LIMIT	YEAR RETD.	ISSUE PRICE	QUOTE U.S.$
1992	Butterfly 30221	5,000		50.00	50
1992	Dance 'Round the Maypole 30215	5,000		55.00	55

RFD America - L. Davis

YEAR ISSUE		EDITION LIMIT	YEAR RETD.	ISSUE PRICE	QUOTE U.S.$
1989	Woodscolt 25342	Closed	N/A	300.00	380
1993	You're a Basket Full of Fun 27564	Open		35.00	35

Sebastian Studios

Large Ceramastone Figures - P.W. Baston

YEAR ISSUE		EDITION LIMIT	YEAR RETD.	ISSUE PRICE	QUOTE U.S.$
1963	Abraham Lincoln Toby Jug	Closed	N/A	Unkn.	600-1000
1963	Anne Boleyn	Closed	N/A	Unkn.	600-1000
1940	Basket	Closed	N/A	Unkn.	300-400
1973	Blacksmith	Closed	N/A	Unkn.	300-400
1940	Breton Man	Closed	N/A	Unkn.	1000-1500
1940	Breton Woman	Closed	N/A	Unkn.	1000-1500
1973	Cabinetmaker	Closed	N/A	Unkn.	300-400
1940	Candle Holder	Closed	N/A	Unkn.	300-400
1940	Caroler	Closed	N/A	Unkn.	300-400
1973	Clockmaker	Closed	N/A	Unkn.	600-1000
1964	Colonial Boy	Closed	N/A	Unkn.	600-1000
1964	Colonial Girl	Closed	N/A	Unkn.	600-1000
1964	Colonial Man	Closed	N/A	Unkn.	600-1000
1964	Colonial Woman	Closed	N/A	Unkn.	600-1000
1963	David Copperfield	Closed	N/A	Unkn.	600-1000
1965	The Dentist	Closed	N/A	Unkn.	600-1000
1963	Dora	Closed	N/A	Unkn.	600-1000
1963	George Washington Toby Jug	Closed	N/A	Unkn.	600-1000
1966	Guitarist	Closed	N/A	Unkn.	600-1000
1963	Henry VIII	Closed	N/A	Unkn.	600-1000
1940	Horn of Plenty	Closed	N/A	Unkn.	300-400
1964	IBM Father	Closed	N/A	Unkn.	600-1000
1964	IBM Mother	Closed	N/A	Unkn.	600-1000
1964	IBM Photographer	Closed	N/A	Unkn.	600-1000
1964	IBM Son	Closed	N/A	Unkn.	600-1000
1964	IBM Woman	Closed	N/A	Unkn.	600-1000
1967	Infant of Prague	Closed	N/A	Unkn.	600-1000
1956	Jell-O Cow Milk Pitcher	Closed	N/A	Unkn.	175-225
1940	Jesus	Closed	N/A	Unkn.	300-400
1963	John F. Kennedy Toby Jug	Closed	N/A	Unkn.	600-1000
1940	Lamb	Closed	N/A	Unkn.	300-400
1947	Large Victorian Couple	Closed	N/A	Unkn.	600-1000
1940	Mary	Closed	N/A	Unkn.	600-1000
1963	Mending Time	Closed	N/A	Unkn.	600-1000
1975	Minuteman	Closed	N/A	Unkn.	600-1000
1978	Mt. Rushmore	Closed	N/A	Unkn.	400-500
1965	N.E. Home For Little Wanderers	Closed	N/A	Unkn.	600-1000
1939	Paul Revere Plaque	Closed	N/A	Unkn.	400-500
1973	Potter	Closed	N/A	Unkn.	300-400
XX	Santa Fe...All The Way	Closed	N/A	Unkn.	600-1000
XX	St. Francis (Plaque)	Closed	N/A	Unkn.	600-1000
1965	Stanley Music Box	Closed	N/A	Unkn.	300-500
1958	Swift Instrument Girl	Closed	N/A	Unkn.	500-750
1963	Tom Sawyer	Closed	N/A	Unkn.	600-1000
1959	Wasp Plaque	Closed	N/A	Unkn.	500-750
1948	Woody at Three	Closed	N/A	Unkn.	600-1000

Sebastian Miniatures - P.W. Baston

YEAR ISSUE		EDITION LIMIT	YEAR RETD.	ISSUE PRICE	QUOTE U.S.$
1956	77th Bengal Lancer (Jell-O)	Closed	N/A	Unkn.	600-1000
1942	Accordion	Closed	N/A	Unkn.	325-375
1952	Aerial Tramway	Closed	N/A	Unkn.	300-600
1959	Alcoa Wrap PS	Closed	N/A	Unkn.	350-400
1959	Alexander Smith Weaver	Closed	N/A	Unkn.	350-425
1956	Alike, But Oh So Different	Closed	N/A	Unkn.	300-350
1957	Along the Albany Road PS	Closed	N/A	Unkn.	600-1000
1940	Ann Styyvesant	Closed	N/A	Unkn.	75-100
1940	Annie Oakley	Closed	N/A	Unkn.	75-100
1956	Arthritic Hands (J & J)	Closed	N/A	Unkn.	600-1000
XX	Babe Ruth	Closed	N/A	Unkn.	600-1000
1952	Baby (Jell-O)	Closed	N/A	Unkn.	525-600
1939	Benjamin Franklin	Closed	N/A	Unkn.	75-100
1962	Big Brother Bob Emery	Closed	N/A	Unkn.	600-1000
1953	Blessed Julie Billart	Closed	N/A	Unkn.	400-500
1962	Blue Belle Highlander	Closed	N/A	Unkn.	200-250
1954	Bluebird Girl	Closed	N/A	Unkn.	400-450
XX	Bob Hope	Closed	N/A	Unkn.	600-1000
1957	Borden's Centennial (Elsie the Cow)	Closed	N/A	Unkn.	600-1000
1971	Boston Gas Tank	Closed	N/A	Unkn.	300-500
1953	Boy Jesus in the Temple	Closed	N/A	Unkn.	350-400
1949	Boy Scout Plaque	Closed	N/A	Unkn.	300-350
1940	Buffalo Bill	Closed	N/A	Unkn.	75-100
1961	Bunky Knudsen	Closed	N/A	Unkn.	600-1000
1954	Campfire Girl	Closed	N/A	Unkn.	400-450
1955	Captain Doliber	Closed	N/A	Unkn.	300-350
1968	Captain John Parker	Closed	N/A	Unkn.	300-350
1951	Carl Moore (WEEI)	Closed	N/A	Unkn.	200-300
1951	Caroline Cabot (WEEI)	Closed	N/A	Unkn.	200-350
1940	Catherine LaFitte	Closed	N/A	Unkn.	75-100
1958	CBS Miss Columbia PS	Closed	N/A	Unkn.	600-1000
1951	Charles Ashley (WEEI)	Closed	N/A	Unkn.	200-350
1951	Chief Pontiac	Closed	N/A	Unkn.	400-700
1951	Chiquita Banana	Closed	N/A	Unkn.	350-400
1951	Christopher Columbus	Closed	N/A	Unkn.	250-300
1958	Cliquot Club Eskimo PS	Closed	N/A	Unkn.	10-2300

YEAR ISSUE		EDITION LIMIT	YEAR RETD.	ISSUE PRICE	QUOTE U.S.$
1957	Colonial Fund Doorway PS	Closed	N/A	Unkn.	600-1000
1958	Commodore Stephen Decatur	Closed	N/A	Unkn.	125-175
1958	Connecticut Bank & Trust	Closed	N/A	Unkn.	225-275
1939	Coronado	Closed	N/A	Unkn.	75-100
1939	Coronado's Senora	Closed	N/A	Unkn.	75-100
XX	Coronation Crown	Closed	N/A	Unkn.	600-1000
1942	Cymbals	Closed	N/A	Unkn.	325-375
1954	Dachshund (Audiovox)	Closed	N/A	Unkn.	300-350
1947	Dahl's Fisherman	Closed	N/A	Unkn.	150-175
1940	Dan'l Boone	Closed	N/A	Unkn.	75-100
1953	Darned Well He Can	Closed	N/A	Unkn.	300-350
1955	Davy Crockett	Closed	N/A	Unkn.	225-275
1939	Deborah Franklin	Closed	N/A	Unkn.	75-100
1948	Democratic Victory	Closed	N/A	Unkn.	350-500
1963	Dia-Mel Fat Man	Closed	N/A	Unkn.	375-400
1947	Dilemma	Closed	N/A	Unkn.	275-300
1967	Doc Berry of Berwick (yellow shirt)	Closed	N/A	Unkn.	300-350
1941	Doves	Closed	N/A	Unkn.	600-1000
1947	Down East	Closed	N/A	Unkn.	125-150
1942	Drum	Closed	N/A	Unkn.	325-375
1941	Ducklings	Closed	N/A	Unkn.	600-1000
1949	Dutchman's Pipe	Closed	N/A	Unkn.	175-225
1951	E. B. Rideout (WEEI)	Closed	N/A	Unkn.	200-350
XX	Eagle Plaque	Closed	N/A	Unkn.	1000-1500
1956	Eastern Paper Plaque	Closed	N/A	Unkn.	350-400
1940	Elizabeth Monroe	Closed	N/A	Unkn.	150-175
1956	Elsie the Cow Billboard	Closed	N/A	Unkn.	600-1000
1949	Emmett Kelly	Closed	N/A	Unkn.	200-300
1949	Eustace Tilly	Closed	N/A	Unkn.	750-1500
1939	Evangeline	Closed	N/A	Unkn.	100-125
1952	The Fat Man (Jell-O)	Closed	N/A	Unkn.	525-600
1952	The Favored Scholar	Closed	N/A	Unkn.	200-300
1959	Fiorello LaGuardia	Closed	N/A	Unkn.	125-175
1947	First Cookbook Author	Closed	N/A	Unkn.	125-150
1952	The First House, Plimoth Plantation	Closed	N/A	Unkn.	150-195
1947	Fisher Pair PS	Closed	N/A	Unkn.	400-1000
1959	Fleischmann's Margarine PS	Closed	N/A	Unkn.	225-325
1939	Gabriel	Closed	N/A	Unkn.	100-125
1966	Gardener Man	Closed	N/A	Unkn.	250-300
1966	Gardener Women	Closed	N/A	Unkn.	250-300
1966	Gardeners (Thermometer)	Closed	N/A	Unkn.	300-400
1949	Gathering Tulips	Closed	N/A	Unkn.	225-250
1972	George & Hatchet	Closed	N/A	Unkn.	400-450
1939	George Washington	Closed	N/A	Unkn.	35-75
1949	Giant Royal Bengal Tiger	Closed	N/A	Unkn.	1000-1500
1959	Giovanni Verrazzano	Closed	N/A	Unkn.	125-175
1955	Giraffe (Jell-O)	Closed	N/A	Unkn.	350-375
1956	Girl on Diving Board	Closed	N/A	Unkn.	400-450
1951	Great Stone Face	Closed	N/A	Unkn.	600-1000
1956	The Green Giant	Closed	N/A	Unkn.	400-500
1959	H.P. Hood Co. Cigar Store Indian	Closed	N/A	Unkn.	600-1000
1958	Hannah Duston PS	Closed	N/A	Unkn.	250-325
1940	Hannah Penn	Closed	N/A	Unkn.	100-150
1959	Harvard Trust Co. Town Crier	Closed	N/A	Unkn.	350-400
1958	Harvard Trust Colonial Man	Closed	N/A	Unkn.	275-325
1948	A Harvey Girl	Closed	N/A	Unkn.	250-300
1959	Henry Hudson	Closed	N/A	Unkn.	125-175
1965	Henry Wadsworth Longfellow	Closed	N/A	Unkn.	275-325
1953	Holgrave the Daguerrotypist	Closed	N/A	Unkn.	200-250
1954	Horizon Girl	Closed	N/A	Unkn.	400-450
1942	Horn	Closed	N/A	Unkn.	325-375
1955	Horse Head PS	Closed	N/A	Unkn.	350-375
1947	Howard Johnson Pieman	Closed	N/A	Unkn.	300-450
1957	IBM 305 Ramac	Closed	N/A	Unkn.	400-450
1939	Indian Maiden	Closed	N/A	Unkn.	100-125
1939	Indian Warrior	Closed	N/A	Unkn.	100-125
1960	The Infantryman	Closed	N/A	Unkn.	600-1000
1951	The Iron Master's House	Closed	N/A	Unkn.	350-500
1958	Jackie Gleason	Closed	N/A	Unkn.	600-1000
1963	Jackie Kennedy Toby Jug	Closed	N/A	Unkn.	600-1000
1940	James Monroe	Closed	N/A	Unkn.	150-175
1957	Jamestown Church	Closed	N/A	Unkn.	400-450
1957	Jamestown Ships	Closed	N/A	Unkn.	350-475
1940	Jean LaFitte	Closed	N/A	Unkn.	75-100
1951	Jesse Buffman (WEEI)	Closed	N/A	Unkn.	200-350
1939	John Alden	Closed	N/A	Unkn.	35-50
1963	John F. Kennedy Toby Jug	Closed	N/A	Unkn.	600-1000
1940	John Harvard	Closed	N/A	Unkn.	125-150
1940	John Smith	Closed	N/A	Unkn.	75-150
1958	Jordan Marsh Observer	Closed	N/A	Unkn.	175-275
1948	Jordan Marsh Observer	Closed	N/A	Unkn.	150-175
1951	Jordon Marsh Observer Rides the A.W. Horse	Closed	N/A	Unkn.	300-325
1951	Judge Pyncheon	Closed	N/A	Unkn.	175-225
1954	Kernel-Fresh Ashtray	Closed	N/A	Unkn.	400-450
XX	The King	Closed	N/A	Unkn.	600-1000
1941	Kitten (Sitting)	Closed	N/A	Unkn.	600-1000
1941	Kitten (Sleeping)	Closed	N/A	Unkn.	600-1000
1953	Lion (Jell-O)	Closed	N/A	Unkn.	350-375
1966	Little George	Closed	N/A	Unkn.	350-450
1952	Lost in the Kitchen (Jell-O)	Closed	N/A	Unkn.	350-375
1942	Majorette	Closed	N/A	Unkn.	325-375
1952	Marblehead High School Plaque	Closed	N/A	Unkn.	200-300
1939	Margaret Houston	Closed	N/A	Unkn.	75-100
1960	Marine Memorial	Closed	N/A	Unkn.	300-400
1949	The Mark Twain Home in Hannibal, MO	Closed	N/A	Unkn.	600-1000
1972	Martha & the Cherry Pie	Closed	N/A	Unkn.	350-400
1939	Martha Washington	Closed	N/A	Unkn.	35-75
1948	Mary Lyon	Closed	N/A	Unkn.	250-300
1960	Masonic Bible	Closed	N/A	Unkn.	300-400
1966	Massachusetts SPCA	Closed	N/A	Unkn.	250-350
1957	Mayflower PS	Closed	N/A	Unkn.	300-325
1949	Menotomy Indian	Closed	N/A	Unkn.	175-250
1961	Merchant's Warren Sea Capt.	Closed	N/A	Unkn.	200-250
1960	Metropolitan Life Tower PS	Closed	N/A	Unkn.	350-400
1956	Michigan Millers PS	Closed	N/A	Unkn.	200-275
1951	Mit Seal	Closed	N/A	Unkn.	350-425
1954	Moose (Jell-O)	Closed	N/A	Unkn.	350-375
1951	Mother Parker (WEEI)	Closed	N/A	Unkn.	200-350
1947	Mr. Beacon Hill	Closed	N/A	Unkn.	50-75
1950	Mr. Obocell	Closed	N/A	Unkn.	75-125
1948	Mr. Rittenhouse Square	Closed	N/A	Unkn.	150-175
1948	Mr. Sheraton	Closed	N/A	Unkn.	400-500
1947	Mrs. Beacon Hill	Closed	N/A	Unkn.	50-75
1940	Mrs. Dan'l Boone	Closed	N/A	Unkn.	75-100
1940	Mrs. Harvard	Closed	N/A	Unkn.	125-150
1956	Mrs. Obocell	Closed	N/A	Unkn.	400-450
1948	Mrs. Rittenhouse Square	Closed	N/A	Unkn.	150-175
1959	Mrs. S.O.S.	Closed	N/A	Unkn.	300-350
1958	Mt. Vernon	Closed	N/A	Unkn.	400-500
1957	Nabisco Buffalo Bee	Closed	N/A	Unkn.	600-1000
1957	Nabisco Spoonmen	Closed	N/A	Unkn.	600-1000
1948	Nathaniel Hawthorne	Closed	N/A	Unkn.	175-200
1950	National Diaper Service	Closed	N/A	Unkn.	250-300
1963	Naumkeag Indian	Closed	N/A	Unkn.	225-275
1952	Neighboring Pews	Closed	N/A	Unkn.	200-300
1956	NYU Grad School of Bus. Admin. Bldg.	Closed	N/A	Unkn.	300-350
1951	The Observer & Dame New England.	Closed	N/A	Unkn.	325-375
1952	Old Powder House	Closed	N/A	Unkn.	250-300
1953	Old Put Enjoys a Licking	Closed	N/A	Unkn.	300-350
1955	Old Woman in the Shoe (Jell-O)	Closed	N/A	Unkn.	500-600
1957	Olde James Fort	Closed	N/A	Unkn.	250-300
XX	Ortho Gynecic	Closed	N/A	Unkn.	600-1000
1967	Ortho-Novum	Closed	N/A	Unkn.	600-1000
1952	Our Lady of Good Voyage	Closed	N/A	Unkn.	200-250
1954	Our Lady of Laleche	Closed	N/A	Unkn.	300-350
1965	Panti-Legs Girl PS	Closed	N/A	Unkn.	250-300
1949	Patrick Henry	Closed	N/A	Unkn.	100-125
1949	Paul Bunyan	Closed	N/A	Unkn.	150-250
1966	Paul Revere Plaque (W.T. Grant)	Closed	N/A	Unkn.	300-350
1941	Peacock	Closed	N/A	Unkn.	600-1000
1956	Permacel Tower of Tape Ashtray	Closed	N/A	Unkn.	600-1000
1960	Peter Stvyvesant	Closed	N/A	Unkn.	125-175
1940	Peter Stvyvesant	Closed	N/A	Unkn.	75-100
1941	Pheasant	Closed	N/A	Unkn.	600-1000
1950	Phoebe, House of 7 Gables	Closed	N/A	Unkn.	150-175
1940	Pocohontas	Closed	N/A	Unkn.	75-150
1961	Pope John 23rd	Closed	N/A	Unkn.	400-450
1965	Pope Paul VI	Closed	N/A	Unkn.	400-500
1956	Praying Hands	Closed	N/A	Unkn.	250-300
1947	Prince Philip	Closed	N/A	Unkn.	200-300
1947	Princess Elizabeth	Closed	N/A	Unkn.	200-300
1939	Priscilla	Closed	N/A	Unkn.	35-50
1951	Priscilla Fortesue (WEEI)	Closed	N/A	Unkn.	200-350
1946	Puritan Spinner	Closed	N/A	Unkn.	500-1000
1953	R.H. Stearns Chestnut Hill Mall	Closed	N/A	Unkn.	225-275
1954	Rabbit (Jell-O)	Closed	N/A	Unkn.	350-375
1956	Rarical Blacksmith	Closed	N/A	Unkn.	300-500
1948	Republican Victory	Closed	N/A	Unkn.	600-1000
1954	Resolute Ins. Co. Clipper PS	Closed	N/A	Unkn.	300-325
1956	Robin Hood & Friar Tuck	Closed	N/A	Unkn.	400-500
1956	Robin Hood & Little John	Closed	N/A	Unkn.	400-500
1958	Romeo & Juliet	Closed	N/A	Unkn.	400-500
1941	Rooster	Closed	N/A	Unkn.	600-1000
1958	Salem Savings Bank	Closed	N/A	Unkn.	250-300
1939	Sam Houston	Closed	N/A	Unkn.	75-100
1955	Santa (Jell-O)	Closed	N/A	Unkn.	500-600
1949	Sarah Henry	Closed	N/A	Unkn.	100-125
1946	Satchel-Eye Dyer	Closed	N/A	Unkn.	125-150
1953	The Schoolboy of 1850	Closed	N/A	Unkn.	350-400
1952	Scottish Girl (Jell-O)	Closed	N/A	Unkn.	350-375
1954	Scuba Diver	Closed	N/A	Unkn.	400-450
1962	Seaman's Bank for Savings	Closed	N/A	Unkn.	300-350
1961	Seb. Dealer Plaque (Marblehead)	Closed	N/A	Unkn.	300-350
1955	Second Bank-State St. Trust PS	Closed	N/A	Unkn.	300-325
1941	Secrets	Closed	N/A	Unkn.	600-1000
1938	Shaker Lady	Closed	N/A	Unkn.	50-100
1938	Shaker Man	Closed	N/A	Unkn.	50-100
1959	Siesta Coffee PS	Closed	N/A	Unkn.	600-1000
1951	Sir Frances Drake	Closed	N/A	Unkn.	250-300
1948	Sitzmark	Closed	N/A	Unkn.	175-200
1948	Slalom	Closed	N/A	Unkn.	175-200
1960	Son of the Desert	Closed	N/A	Unkn.	200-275
1957	Speedy Alka Seltzer	Closed	N/A	Unkn.	600-1000
1952	St. Joan d'Arc	Closed	N/A	Unkn.	300-350
1961	St. Jude Thaddeus	Closed	N/A	Unkn.	400-500
1954	St. Pius X	Closed	N/A	Unkn.	400-475
1952	St. Sebastian	Closed	N/A	Unkn.	300-350
1953	St. Teresa of Lisieux	Closed	N/A	Unkn.	225-275
1965	State Street Bank Globe	Closed	N/A	Unkn.	250-300
1954	Stimalose (Men)	Closed	N/A	Unkn.	600-1000
1954	Stimalose (Woman)	Closed	N/A	Unkn.	175-200
1952	Stork (Jell-O)	Closed	N/A	Unkn.	425-525
1960	Supp-Hose Lady	Closed	N/A	Unkn.	300-500
1941	Swan	Closed	N/A	Unkn.	600-1000
1954	Swan Boat Brooch-Empty Seats	Closed	N/A	Unkn.	600-1000
1954	Swan Boat Brooch-Full Seats	Closed	N/A	Unkn.	600-1000
1948	Swedish Boy	Closed	N/A	Unkn.	250-500
1948	Swedish Girl	Closed	N/A	Unkn.	250-500
XX	Sylvania Electric-Bulb Display	Closed	N/A	Unkn.	600-1000
1952	Tabasco Sauce	Closed	N/A	Unkn.	400-500
1956	Texcel Tape Boy	Closed	N/A	Unkn.	350-425
1949	The Thinker	Closed	N/A	Unkn.	175-250
1956	Three Little Kittens (Jell-O)	Closed	N/A	Unkn.	375-400
1947	Tollhouse Town Crier	Closed	N/A	Unkn.	125-175
1961	Tony Piet	Closed	N/A	Unkn.	600-1000
1966	Town Lyne Indian	Closed	N/A	Unkn.	600-1000
1971	Town Meeting Plaque	Closed	N/A	Unkn.	350-400
1942	Tuba	Closed	N/A	Unkn.	325-375
1949	Uncle Mistletoe	Closed	N/A	Unkn.	250-300
1970	Uncle Sam in Orbit	Closed	N/A	Unkn.	350-400
1968	Watermill Candy Plaque	Closed	N/A	Unkn.	600-1000
1952	Weighing the Baby	Closed	N/A	Unkn.	200-300
1954	Whale (Jell-O)	Closed	N/A	Unkn.	350-375
1940	William Penn	Closed	N/A	Unkn.	100-150
1954	William Penn	Closed	N/A	Unkn.	175-225
1939	Williamsburg Governor	Closed	N/A	Unkn.	75-100
1939	Williamsburg Lady	Closed	N/A	Unkn.	75-100
1962	Yankee Clipper Sulfide	Closed	N/A	Unkn.	600-1000

Seymour Mann, Inc.

Bunny Musical Figurines - Kenji

YEAR ISSUE		EDITION LIMIT	YEAR RETD.	ISSUE PRICE	QUOTE U.S.$
1991	Bunny In Teacup MH-781	Open		25.00	25
1991	Bunny In Teapot MH-780	Open		25.00	25

Cat Musical Figurines - Kenji

YEAR ISSUE		EDITION LIMIT	YEAR RETD.	ISSUE PRICE	QUOTE U.S.$
1990	Bride/Groom Cat MH-738	Closed	1995	37.50	38
1991	Brown Cat in Bag	Closed	1995	30.00	30
1987	Brown Cat in Bag MH-617B/6	Closed	1995	30.00	30
1991	Brown Cat in Hat	Closed	1995	35.00	35
1988	Brown Cat in Hat MH-634B/6	Closed	1995	35.00	35
1991	Brown Cat in Teacup	Closed	1995	30.00	30
1987	Brown Cat in Teacup MH-600VGB16	Closed	1995	30.00	30
1987	Cat in Garbage Can MH-490	Closed	1995	35.00	35
1987	Cat in Rose Teacup MH-600VG	Closed	1995	30.00	30
1990	Cat Asleep MH-735	Closed	1995	17.50	18
1990	Cat Calico in Easy Chair MH-743VG	Closed	1995	27.50	28
1991	Cat in Bag	Closed	1995	30.00	30
1991	Cat in Bag	Closed	1995	30.00	30
1987	Cat in Bag MH-614	Closed	1995	30.00	30
1987	Cat in Bag MH-617	Closed	1995	30.00	30
1989	Cat in Basinet MH-714	Closed	1995	35.00	35
1989	Cat in Basket MH-713B	Closed	1995	35.00	35
1991	Cat in Basket MH-768	Closed	1995	35.00	35
1991	Cat in Bootie	Closed	1995	35.00	35
1990	Cat in Bootie MH-728	Closed	1995	35.00	35
1990	Cat in Dress MH-751VG	Closed	1995	37.50	38
1989	Cat in Flower MH-709	Closed	1995	35.00	35
1991	Cat in Garbage Can	Closed	1995	35.00	35
1989	Cat in Gift Box Musical MH-732	Closed	1995	40.00	40
1991	Cat in Hat	Closed	1995	35.00	35
1991	Cat in Hat Box	Closed	1995	35.00	35
1988	Cat in Hat Box MH-634	Closed	1995	35.00	35
1988	Cat in Hat MH-634B	Closed	1995	35.00	35
1991	Cat in Rose Teacup	Closed	1995	30.00	30
1989	Cat in Shoe MH-718	Closed	1995	30.00	30
1991	Cat in Teacup	Closed	1995	30.00	30
1987	Cat in Teacup MH-600VGG	Closed	1995	30.00	30
1991	Cat in Teapot Brown	Closed	1995	30.00	30
1987	Cat in Teapot Brown MH-600VGB	Closed	1995	30.00	30
1989	Cat in Water Can Musical MH-712	Closed	1995	35.00	35
1991	Cat Momma MH-758	Closed	1995	35.00	35
1989	Cat on Basket MH-713	Closed	1995	35.00	35
1990	Cat on Gift Box Music MH-740	Closed	1995	40.00	40
1990	Cat on Pillow MH-731	Closed	1995	17.50	18
1991	Cat on Tipped Garbage Can	Closed	1995	35.00	35
1987	Cat on Tipped Garbage Can MH-498	Closed	1995	35.00	35
1990	Cat Sailor in Rocking Boat MH-734	Closed	1995	45.00	45
1990	Cat w/Bow on Pink Pillow MH-741P	Closed	1995	33.50	34
1989	Cat w/Coffee Cup Musical MH-706	Closed	1995	35.00	35
1990	Cat w/Parrot Musical MH-730	Closed	1995	37.50	38
1989	Cat w/Swing Musical MH-710	Closed	1995	35.00	35
1991	Cat Watching Butterfly MH-784	Closed	1995	17.50	18
1991	Cat Watching Canary MH-783	Closed	1995	25.00	25
1991	Cat With Bow on Pink Pillow MH-741P	Closed	1995	33.50	34
1991	Cats Ball Shape	Closed	1995	25.00	25
1985	Cats Ball Shape MH-303A/G	Closed	1995	25.00	25
1990	Cats Graduation MH-745	Closed	1995	27.50	28
1989	Cats in Basket XMAS-664	Closed	1995	7.50	8
1991	Cats w/Ribbon	Closed	1995	30.00	30
1986	Cats w/Ribbon MH-481A/C	Closed	1995	30.00	30
1991	Family Cat MH-770	Closed	1995	35.00	35
1991	Grey Cat in Bootie	Closed	1995	35.00	35
1990	Grey Cat in Bootie MH-728G/6	Closed	1995	35.00	35
1991	Kitten Picking Tulips MH-756	Closed	1995	40.00	40
1990	Kitten Trio in Carriage MH-742	Closed	1995	37.50	38
1991	Kittens w/Balls of Yarn	Closed	1995	30.00	30
1987	Kittens w/Balls of Yarn MH-612	Closed	1995	30.00	30
1991	Musical Bear	Closed	1995	27.50	28
1987	Musical Bear MH-602	Closed	1995	27.50	28

YEAR ISSUE		EDITION LIMIT	YEAR RETD.	ISSUE PRICE	QUOTE U.S.$
1991	Revolving Cat with Butterfly MH-759	Closed	1995	40.00	40
1991	Teapot Cat	Closed	1995	30.00	30
1987	Teapot Cat MH-631	Closed	1995	30.00	30
1987	Valentine Cat in Bag Musical MH-600	Closed	1995	33.50	34
1987	Valentine Cat in Teacup MH-600VLT	Closed	1995	33.50	34

Christmas Collection - Various

YEAR ISSUE		EDITION LIMIT	YEAR RETD.	ISSUE PRICE	QUOTE U.S.$
1991	2 Tone Stone Church MER-360B - J. White	Closed	1993	35.00	35
1986	Antique Santa Musical XMAS-364 - J. White	Closed	1987	20.00	20
1990	Antique Shop Lite Up House MER-376 - J. White	Closed	1993	27.50	28
1991	Apothecary Lite Up CJ-128 Jaimy	Closed	1993	33.50	34
1990	Bakery Lite Up House MER-373 J. White	Closed	1993	27.50	28
1991	Beige Church Lite Up House MER-360A - Jaimy	Closed	1993	35.00	35
1990	Bethlehem Lite Up Set 3 CP-59893 - J. White	Closed	1993	120.00	120
1991	Boy and Girl on Bell CJ-132 Jaimy	Closed	1993	13.50	14
1991	Boy on Horse CJ-457 - Jaimy	Closed	1993	6.00	6
1990	Brick Church Lite Up House MER-360C - J. White	Closed	1993	35.00	35
1991	Carolers Under Lamppost CJ-114A - Jaimy	Closed	1993	7.50	8
1989	Cat in Teacup Musical XMAS-600 - J. White	Closed	1992	30.00	30
1990	Cathedral Lite Up House MER-362 - J. White	Closed	1993	37.50	38
1991	Church Lite Up MER-410 J. White	Closed	1993	17.50	18
1990	Church Lite Up House MER-310 - J. White	Closed	1993	27.50	28
1991	Church w/Blue Roof Lite Up House MER-360E - J. White	Closed	1993	35.00	35
1991	Covered Bridge CJ-101 - Jaimy	Closed	1993	27.50	28
1990	Deep Gold Church Lite Up House MER-360D - J. White	Closed	1993	35.00	35
1990	Double Store Lite Up House MER-311 - J. White	Closed	1993	27.50	28
1991	Elf w/Doll House CB-14 E. Mann	Closed	1993	30.00	30
1991	Elf w/Hammer CB-11 - E. Mann	Closed	1993	30.00	30
1991	Elf w/Reindeer CJ-422 - Jaimy	Closed	1993	9.00	9
1991	Elf w/Rocking Horse CB-10 E. Mann	Closed	1993	30.00	30
1991	Elf w/Teddy Bear CB-12 E. Mann	Closed	1993	30.00	30
1991	Emily's Toys CJ-127 - Jaimy	Closed	1993	35.00	35
1991	Father and Mother w/Daughter CJ-133 - Jaimy	Closed	1993	13.50	14
1991	Father Christmas CJ-233	Closed	1993	33.50	34
1991	Father Christmas w/Holly CJ-239 - Jaimy	Closed	1993	35.00	35
1991	Fire Station CJ-129 - Jaimy	Closed	1993	50.00	50
1990	Fire Station Lite Up House XMS-1550C - E.Mann	Closed	1993	25.00	25
1991	Four Men Talking CJ-138 - Jaimy	Closed	1993	27.50	28
1991	Gift Shop Lite Up CJ-125 - Jaimy	Closed	1993	33.50	34
1991	Girls w/Instruments CJ-131 Jaimy	Closed	1993	13.50	14
1990	Grist Mill Lite Up House MER-372 - J. White	Closed	1993	27.50	28
1991	Horse and Coach CJ-207 - Jaimy	Closed	1993	25.00	25
1990	Inn Lite Up House MER-316 J. White	Closed	1993	27.50	28
1986	Jumbo Santa/Toys XMAS-38 J. White	Closed	1987	45.00	45
1991	Kids Building Igloo CJ-137 Jaimy	Closed	1993	13.50	14
1991	Lady w/Dogs CJ-208 - Jaimy	Closed	1993	13.50	14
1990	Leatherworks Lite Up House MER-371 - J. White	Closed	1993	27.50	28
1990	Library Lite Up House MER-317 J. White	Closed	1993	27.50	28
1990	Light House Lite Up House MER-370 - J. White	Closed	1993	27.50	28
1991	Man w/Wheelbarrow CJ-134 Jaimy	Closed	1993	13.50	14
1990	Mansion Lite Up House MER-319 - J. White	Closed	1993	27.50	28
1990	Mr/Mrs Santa Musical CJ-281 Jaimy	Closed	1993	37.50	38
1990	New England Church Lite Up House MER-375 - J. White	Closed	1993	27.50	28
1990	New England General Store Lite Up House MER-377 - J. White	Closed	1993	27.50	28
1991	Newsboy Under Lamppost CJ-144B - Jaimy	Closed	1993	15.00	15
1991	Old Curiosity Lite Up CJ-201 Jaimy	Closed	1993	37.50	38
1991	Playhouse Lite Up CJ-122 Jaimy	Closed	1993	50.00	50
1991	Public Library Lite Up CJ-121 Jaimy	Closed	1993	45.00	45
1990	Railroad Station Lite Up House MER-374 - J. White	Closed	1993	27.50	28
1991	Reindeer Barn Lite Up House CJ-421 - Jaimy	Closed	1993	55.00	55
1991	Restaurant Lite Up House MER-354 - J. White	Closed	1993	27.50	28
1990	Roly Poly Santa 3 Asst. CJ-253/4/7 - Jaimy	Closed	1993	17.50	18
1991	Santa Cat Roly Poly CJ-252 Jaimy	Closed	1993	17.50	18
1991	Santa Fixing Sled CJ-237 - Jaimy	Closed	1993	35.00	35
1991	Santa In Barrel Waterball CJ-243 - Jaimy	Closed	1993	33.50	34
1989	Santa in Sled w/Reindeer CJ-3 Jaimy	Closed	1992	25.00	25
1991	Santa In Toy Shop CJ-441 Jaimy	Closed	1993	33.50	34
1989	Santa Musicals CJ-1/4 - Jaimy	Closed	1992	27.50	28
1990	Santa on Chimney Musical CJ-212 - Jaimy	Closed	1993	33.50	34
1989	Santa on Horse CJ-33A - Jaimy	Closed	1992	33.50	34
1990	Santa on See Saw TR-14 E. Mann	Closed	1993	30.00	30
1991	Santa On Train CJ-458 - Jaimy	Closed	1993	6.00	6
1991	Santa On White Horse CJ-338 E. Mann	Closed	1993	33.50	34
1991	Santa Packing Bag CJ-210 Jaimy	Closed	1993	33.50	34
1990	Santa Packing Bag CJ-210 Jaimy	Closed	1993	33.50	34
1991	Santa Packing Bag CJ-236 Jaimy	Closed	1993	35.00	35
1991	Santa Sleeping Musical CJ-214 Jaimy	Closed	1993	30.00	30
1991	Santa w/Bag and List CJ-431 Jaimy	Closed	1993	33.50	34
1991	Santa w/Deer Musical CJ-21R Jaimy	Closed	1993	33.50	34
1991	Santa w/Girl Waterball CJ-241 Jaimy	Closed	1993	33.50	34
1991	Santa w/Lantern Musical CJ-211 Jaimy	Closed	1993	33.50	34
1990	Santa w/List CJ-23 - Jaimy	Closed	1993	27.50	28
1989	Santa w/List CJ-23 - Jaimy	Closed	1992	27.50	28
1991	Santa w/List CJ-23R - Jaimy	Closed	1993	27.50	28
1990	School Lite Up House MER-320 J. White	Closed	1993	27.50	28
1991	The Skaters CJ-205 - Jaimy	Closed	1993	25.00	25
1991	Snowball Fight CJ-124B - Jaimy	Closed	1993	25.00	25
1991	Soup Seller Waterball CJ-209 - Jaimy	Closed	1993	25.00	25
1991	Stone Cottage Lite Up CJ-100 - Jaimy	Closed	1993	37.50	38
1991	Stone House Lite Up CJ-102 - Jaimy	Closed	1993	45.00	45
1991	The Story Teller CJ-204 - Jaimy	Closed	1993	20.00	20
1991	Teddy Bear On Wheels CB-42 - E. Mann	Closed	1993	25.00	25
1991	Three Ladies w/Food CJ-136 - Jaimy	Closed	1993	13.50	14
1990	Town Hall Lite Up House MER-315 - J. White	Closed	1993	27.50	28
1991	The Toy Seller CJ-206 - Jaimy	Closed	1993	13.50	14
1991	Toy Store Lite Up House MER-355 - J. White	Closed	1993	27.50	28
1991	Trader Santa Musical CJ-442 - Jaimy	Closed	1993	30.00	30
1991	Train Set MER-378 - J. White	Closed	1993	25.00	25
1985	Trumpeting Angel w/Jesus XMAS-527 - J. White	Closed	1987	40.00	40
1991	Two Old Men Talking CJ-107 - Jaimy	Closed	1993	13.50	14
1991	Village Mill Lite Up CJ-104 - Jaimy	Closed	1993	30.00	30
1991	Village People CJ-116A - Jaimy	Closed	1993	60.00	60
1985	Virgin w/Christ Musical XMAS-528 - J. White	Closed	1987	33.50	34
1991	Woman w/Cow CJ-135 - Jaimy	Closed	1993	15.00	15
1991	Ye Olde Town Tavern CJ-130 - Jaimy	Closed	1993	45.00	45

Christmas In America - Various

YEAR ISSUE		EDITION LIMIT	YEAR RETD.	ISSUE PRICE	QUOTE U.S.$
1990	Cart With People - E. Mann	Closed	1992	25.00	35
1988	Doctor's Office Lite Up - E. Mann	Closed	1990	27.50	28
1991	New England Church Lite Up House MER-375 - J. White	Closed	1992	27.50	28
1991	New England General Store Lite Up House MER-377 - J. White	Closed	1992	27.50	28
1989	Santa in Sleigh - E. Mann	Closed	1990	25.00	45
1988	Set Of 3, Capitol, White House, Mt. Vernon - E. Mann	Closed	1990	75.00	150

Christmas Village - L. Sciola

YEAR ISSUE		EDITION LIMIT	YEAR RETD.	ISSUE PRICE	QUOTE U.S.$
1991	Away, Away	Closed	1993	30.00	30
1991	Counsil House	Closed	1993	60.00	60
1991	Curiosity Shop	Closed	1993	45.00	45
1991	Emily's Toys	Closed	1993	45.00	45
1991	The Fire Station	Closed	1993	60.00	60
1991	On Thin Ice	Closed	1993	30.00	30
1991	The Playhouse	Closed	1993	60.00	60
1991	Public Library	Closed	1993	50.00	50
1991	Scrooge/Marley's Counting House	Closed	1993	45.00	45
1991	Story Teller	Closed	1993	20.00	20
1991	Ye Old Gift Shoppe	Closed	1993	50.00	50

Dickens Collection - Various

YEAR ISSUE		EDITION LIMIT	YEAR RETD.	ISSUE PRICE	QUOTE U.S.$
1990	Black Swan Inn Lite Up XMS-7000E - J. White	Closed	1993	30.00	30
1990	Cratchit Family MER-121 - J. White	Closed	1993	37.50	38
1991	Cratchit's Lite Up House CJ-200 Jaimy	Closed	1993	37.50	38
1991	Cratchit/Tiny Tim Musical CJ-117 - Jaimy	Closed	1993	33.50	34
1990	Cratchit/Tiny Tim Musical MER-105 - J. White	Closed	1993	33.50	34
1989	Cratchits Lite Up XMS-7000A - J. White	Closed	1991	30.00	30
1989	Fezziwigs Lite Up XMS-7000C - J. White	Closed	1991	30.00	30
1989	Gift Shoppe Lite Up XMS-7000D - J. White	Closed	1991	30.00	30
1990	Hen Poultry Lite Up XMS-7000H J. White	Closed	1993	30.00	30
1991	Scrooge Musical CJ-118 - Jaimy	Closed	1993	30.00	30
1991	Scrooge/Marley Counting House CJ-202 - Jaimy	Closed	1993	37.50	38
1989	Scrooge/Marley Lite Up XMS-7000B - J. White	Closed	1991	30.00	30
1990	Tea and Spice Lite Up XMS-7000F - J. White	Closed	1993	30.00	30
1990	Waite Fish Store Lite Up XMS-7000G - J. White	Closed	1993	30.00	30

Gingerbread Christmas Collection - J. Sauerbrey

YEAR ISSUE		EDITION LIMIT	YEAR RETD.	ISSUE PRICE	QUOTE U.S.$
1991	Gingerbread Angel CJ-411	Closed	1993	7.50	8
1991	Gingerbread Church Lite Up House CJ-403	Closed	1993	65.00	65
1991	Gingerbread House CJ-416	Closed	1993	7.50	8
1991	Gingerbread House Lite Up CJ-404	Closed	1993	65.00	65
1991	Gingerbread Man CJ-415	Closed	1993	7.50	8
1991	Gingerbread Mansion Lite Up CJ-405	Closed	1993	70.00	70
1991	Gingerbread Mouse/Boot CJ-409	Closed	1993	7.50	8
1991	Gingerbread Mrs. Claus CJ-414	Closed	1993	7.50	8
1991	Gingerbread Reindeer CJ-410	Closed	1993	7.50	8
1991	Gingerbread Rocking Horse Music CJ-460	Closed	1993	33.50	34
1991	Gingerbread Santa CJ-408	Closed	1993	7.50	8
1991	Gingerbread Sleigh CJ-406	Closed	1993	7.50	8
1991	Gingerbread Snowman CJ-412	Closed	1993	7.50	8
1991	Gingerbread Swan Musical CJ-462	Closed	1993	33.50	34
1991	Gingerbread Sweet Shop Lite Up House	Closed	1993	60.00	60
1991	Gingerbread Teddy Bear Music CJ-461	Closed	1993	33.50	34
1991	Gingerbread Toy Shop Lite Up House CJ-402	Closed	1993	60.00	60
1991	Gingerbread Tree CJ-407	Closed	1993	7.50	8
1991	Gingerbread Village Lite Up House CJ-400	Closed	1993	60.00	60

Victorian Christmas Collection - Various

YEAR ISSUE		EDITION LIMIT	YEAR RETD.	ISSUE PRICE	QUOTE U.S.$
1991	Antique Shop Lite Up House MER-353 - J. White	Closed	1993	27.50	28
1991	Beige Church Lite Up House MER-351 - J. White	Closed	1993	35.00	35
1991	Book Store Lite Up House MER-351 - J. White	Closed	1993	27.50	28
1991	Church Lite Up House MER-350 - J. White	Closed	1993	37.50	38
1991	Country Store Lite Up House MER-356 - J. White	Closed	1993	27.50	28
1993	Couple Against Wind CJ-420 - Jaimy	Closed	1994	15.00	15
1991	Inn Lite Up House MER-352 - J. White	Closed	1993	27.50	28
1991	Little Match Girl CJ-419 - Jaimy	Closed	1993	9.00	9
1990	Toy/Doll House Lite Up MER-314 - J. White	Closed	1993	27.50	28
1990	Two Boys w/Snowman CJ-106 - Jaimy	Closed	1993	12.00	12
1990	Victorian House Lite Up House MER-312 - J. White	Closed	1993	27.50	28
1990	Yarn Shop Lite Up House MER-313 - J. White	Closed	1993	27.50	28

Wizard Of Oz - 40th Anniversary - E. Mann

YEAR ISSUE		EDITION LIMIT	YEAR RETD.	ISSUE PRICE	QUOTE U.S.$
1979	Dorothy, Scarecrow, Lion, Tinman	Closed	1981	7.50	45
1979	Dorothy, Scarecrow, Lion, Tinman, Musical	Closed	1981	12.50	75

Shelia's Collectibles

Shelia's Collectors' Society - S. Thompson

YEAR ISSUE		EDITION LIMIT	YEAR RETD.	ISSUE PRICE	QUOTE U.S.$
1993	Susan B. Anthony CGA93	Retrd.	1994	Gift	65
1993	Anne Peacock House SOC01	Retrd.	1994	16.00	55-75
1994	Helen Keller's Birthplace-Ivy Green CGA94	Retrd.	1995	Gift	55
1994	Seaview Cottage SOC02	Retrd.	1995	17.00	50
1995	Red Cross CGA95	4/96		Gift	N/A
1995	Pink Lady SOC03	5/96		20.00	20

Accessories - S. Thompson

YEAR ISSUE		EDITION LIMIT	YEAR RETD.	ISSUE PRICE	QUOTE U.S.$
1994	Amish Quilt Line COL12	Retrd.	1994	18.00	25-45
1993	Apple Tree COL09	Open		12.00	12
1993	Dogwood Tree COL08	Open		12.00	12
1992	Fence 5" COL04	Retrd.	1993	9.00	17
1992	Fence 7" COL05	Retrd.	1995	10.00	18
1995	Flower Garden ACC02	Open		13.00	13
1994	Formal Garden COL13	Retrd.	1994	18.00	35
1992	Gazebo With Victorian Lady COL02	Retrd.	1995	11.00	12-25
1992	Lake With Swan COL06	Retrd.	1993	11.00	15-25
1992	Oak Bower COL03	Retrd.	1993	11.00	20-50
1995	Real Estate Sign ACC03	Open		12.00	12
1994	Sunrise At 80 Meeting COL10	Retrd.	1994	18.00	30-35
1992	Tree With Bush COL07	Open		10.00	10
1994	Victorian Arbor COL11	Retrd.	1994	18.00	24-30
1995	Wisteria Arbor ACC01	Open		12.00	12
1992	Wrought Iron Gate With Magnolias COL01	Retrd.	1993	11.00	15-45

American Barns - S. Thompson

YEAR ISSUE		EDITION LIMIT	YEAR RETD.	ISSUE PRICE	QUOTE U.S.$
1995	Casey Barn BAR04	Open		18.00	18
1995	Mail Pouch Barn BAR03	Open		18.00	18
1995	Pennsylvania Dutch Barn AP BAR02	Retrd.	1995	20.00	20-40
1995	Pennsylvania Dutch Barn BAR02	Open		18.00	18
1994	Rock City Barn AP BAR01	Retrd.	1994	20.00	20-40

Year	Issue	Edition Limit	Year Retd.	Issue Price	Quote U.S.$
1994	Rock City Barn BAR01	Open		18.00	18

Amish Village - S. Thompson

Year	Issue	Edition Limit	Year Retd.	Issue Price	Quote U.S.$
1994	Amish Barn (renovated) AMS04II	Open		17.00	17
1993	Amish Barn AMS04	Open		17.00	17
1993	Amish Barn, AP AMS04	Retrd.	1993	20.00	20-30
1994	Amish Buggy (renovated) AMS05II	Open		12.00	12
1993	Amish Buggy AMS05	Open		12.00	12
1993	Amish Buggy, AP AMS05	Retrd.	1993	16.00	25-35
1994	Amish Home (renovated) AMS01II	Open		17.00	17
1993	Amish Home AMS01	Open		17.00	17
1993	Amish Home, AP AMS01	Retrd.	1993	20.00	25-35
1994	Amish School (renovated) AMS02II	Open		15.00	15
1993	Amish School AMS02	Open		15.00	15
1993	Amish School, AP AMS02	Retrd.	1993	20.00	25-35
1994	Covered Bridge (renovated) AMS03II	Open		16.00	16
1993	Covered Bridge AMS03	Open		16.00	16
1993	Covered Bridge, AP AMS03	Retrd.	1993	20.00	25-35
1995	Roadside Stand AMS06	Open		17.00	17
1995	Roadside Stand, AP AMS06	Retrd.	1995	24.00	30-40

Atlanta - S. Thompson

Year	Issue	Edition Limit	Year Retd.	Issue Price	Quote U.S.$
1995	Fox Theatre ATL06	Open		19.00	19
1995	Hammond's House ATL05	Open		18.00	18
1995	Swan House ATL03	Open		18.00	18
1995	Tallie Smith House ATL01	Open		17.00	17
1995	Victorian Playhouse ATL02	Open		17.00	17
1995	Wren's Nest ATL04	Open		19.00	19

Charleston - S. Thompson

Year	Issue	Edition Limit	Year Retd.	Issue Price	Quote U.S.$
1994	#2 Meeting Street (renovated) CHS06II	Open		16.00	16
1991	#2 Meeting Street CHS06	Open		15.00	15
1990	90 Church St. CHS17	Retrd.	1993	12.00	25-50
1994	Ashe House (renovated) CHS51II	Open		16.00	16
1993	Ashe House CHS51	Open		16.00	16
1991	Beth Elohim Temple CHS20	Retrd.	1993	15.00	20-30
1994	The Citadel (renovated) CHS22II	Open		16.00	16
1993	The Citadel CHS22	Open		16.00	16
1993	City Hall CHS21	Retrd.	1993	15.00	60-100
1991	City Market (closed gates) CHS07	Retrd.	1991	15.00	45-65
1991	City Market (open gates) CHS07	Open		15.00	15
1994	City Market (renovated) CHS07II	Open		15.00	15
1994	College of Charleston (renovated) CHS40II	Open		16.00	16
1993	College of Charleston CHS40	Open		16.00	16
1993	College of Charleston, AP CHS40	Retrd.	1993	20.00	36
1992	Dock Street Theater (chimney) CHS08	Retrd.	1993	15.00	23-50
1991	Dock Street Theater (no chimney) CHS08	Retrd.	1992	15.00	65
1994	Edmonston-Alston (renovated) CHS04II	Retrd.	1995	16.00	25
1991	Edmonston-Alston CHS04	Retrd.	1995	15.00	30
1990	Exchange Building CHS15	Retrd.	1994	15.00	25-30
1990	Heyward-Washington House CHS02	Retrd.	1993	15.00	25-35
1994	John Rutledge House Inn (renovated) CHS50II	Open		16.00	16
1993	John Rutledge House Inn CHS50	Open		16.00	16
1991	Magnolia Plantation House (beige curtains) CHS03	Open		16.00	16
1994	Magnolia Plantation House (renovated) CHS03II	Open		16.00	16
1991	Magnolia Plantation House (white curtains) CHS03	Open		16.00	16
1990	Manigault House CHS01	Retrd.	1993	15.00	23-35
1990	Middleton Plantation CHS19	Retrd.	1991	9.00	150
1990	Pink House CHS18	Retrd.	1993	12.00	16-30
1990	Powder Magazine CHS16	Retrd.	1991	9.00	100-200
1994	Single Side Porch (renovated) CHS30II	Open		16.00	16
1993	Single Side Porch CHS30	Open		16.00	16
1993	Single Side Porch, AP CHS30	Retrd.	1993	20.00	36
1990	St. Michael's Church CHS14	Retrd.	1994	15.00	30-40
1994	St. Philip's Church (renovated) CHS05II	Open		15.00	15
1991	St. Philip's Church CHS05	Open		15.00	15
1991	St. Phillip's Church (misspelling Phillips) CHS05	Open		15.00	15

Charleston Gold Seal - S. Thompson

Year	Issue	Edition Limit	Year Retd.	Issue Price	Quote U.S.$
1988	90 Church St. CHS17	Retrd.	1990	9.00	40
1988	CHS31 Rainbow Row-rust	Retrd.	1990	9.00	N/A
1988	CHS32 Rainbow Row-tan	Retrd.	1990	9.00	N/A
1988	CHS33 Rainbow Row-cream	Retrd.	1990	9.00	N/A
1988	CHS34 Rainbow Row-green	Retrd.	1990	9.00	N/A
1988	CHS35 Rainbow Row-lavender	Retrd.	1990	9.00	N/A
1988	CHS36 Rainbow Row-pink	Retrd.	1990	9.00	N/A
1988	CHS37 Rainbow Row-blue	Retrd.	1990	9.00	N/A
1988	CHS38 Rainbow Row-lt. yellow	Retrd.	1990	9.00	N/A
1988	CHS39 Rainbow Row-lt. pink	Retrd.	1990	9.00	N/A
1988	Exchange Building CHS15	Retrd.	1990	9.00	N/A
1988	Middleton Plantation CHS19	Retrd.	1990	9.00	100
1988	Pink House CHS18	Retrd.	1990	9.00	N/A
1988	Powder Magazine CHS16	Retrd.	1990	9.00	200-250
1988	St. Michael's Church CHS14	Retrd.	1990	9.00	N/A

Charleston II - S. Thompson

Year	Issue	Edition Limit	Year Retd.	Issue Price	Quote U.S.$
1995	Boone Hall Plantation CHS56	Open		18.00	18
1995	Boone Hall Plantation, AP CHS56	Retrd.	1995	24.00	30-40
1994	Drayton House CHS52	Open		18.00	18
1994	Drayton House, AP CHS52	Retrd.	1994	24.00	30-75
1995	O'Donnell's Folly CHS55	Open		18.00	18
1995	O'Donnell's Folly, AP CHS55	Retrd.	1995	24.00	30-40

Charleston Rainbow Row - S. Thompson

Year	Issue	Edition Limit	Year Retd.	Issue Price	Quote U.S.$
1990	CHS31 Rainbow Row-rust	Retrd.	1993	9.00	25-40
1990	CHS32 Rainbow Row-cream	Retrd.	1993	9.00	25-40
1990	CHS33 Rainbow Row-tan	Retrd.	1993	9.00	25-40
1990	CHS34 Rainbow Row-green	Retrd.	1993	9.00	25-40
1990	CHS35 Rainbow Row-lavender	Retrd.	1993	9.00	25-40
1990	CHS36 Rainbow Row-pink	Retrd.	1993	9.00	25-40
1990	CHS37 Rainbow Row-blue	Retrd.	1993	9.00	25-40
1990	CHS38 Rainbow Row-lt. yellow	Retrd.	1993	9.00	25-40
1990	CHS39 Rainbow Row-lt. pink	Retrd.	1993	9.00	25-40
1993	CHS41 Rainbow Row-aurora	Open		13.00	13
1994	CHS41II Rainbow Row-aurora (renovated)	Open		13.00	13
1993	CHS42 Rainbow Row-off-white	Open		13.00	13
1994	CHS42II Rainbow Row-off-white (renovated)	Open		13.00	13
1993	CHS43 Rainbow Row-cream	Open		13.00	13
1994	CHS43II Rainbow Row-cream (renovated)	Open		13.00	13
1993	CHS44 Rainbow Row-green	Open		13.00	13
1994	CHS44II Rainbow Row-green (renovated)	Open		13.00	13
1993	CHS45 Rainbow Row-lavender	Open		13.00	13
1994	CHS45II Rainbow Row-lavender (renovated)	Open		13.00	13
1993	CHS46 Rainbow Row-pink	Open		13.00	13
1994	CHS46II Rainbow Row-pink (renovated)	Open		13.00	13
1993	CHS47 Rainbow Row-blue	Open		13.00	13
1994	CHS47II Rainbow Row-blue (renovated)	Open		13.00	13
1993	CHS48 Rainbow Row-yellow	Open		13.00	13
1994	CHS48 Rainbow Row-yellow (renovated)	Open		13.00	13
1993	CHS49 Rainbow Row-gray	Open		13.00	13
1994	CHS49II Rainbow Row-gray (renovated)	Open		13.00	13
1993	Rainbow Row Sign	Retrd.	N/A	12.50	20

Dicken's Village - S. Thompson

Year	Issue	Edition Limit	Year Retd.	Issue Price	Quote U.S.$
1991	Butcher Shop XMS03	Retrd.	1993	15.00	25-35
1991	Evergreen Tree XMS08	Retrd.	1993	11.00	20-35
1991	Gazebo & Carolers XMS06	Retrd.	1993	12.00	30-40
1991	Scrooge & Marley's Shop XMS01	Retrd.	1993	15.00	35-45
1991	Scrooge's Home XMS05	Retrd.	1993	15.00	33
1991	Toy Shoppe XMS04	Retrd.	1993	15.00	25-35
1991	Victorian Apartment Building XMS02	Retrd.	1993	15.00	33
1992	Victorian Church XMS09	Retrd.	1993	15.00	25-55
1991	Victorian Skaters XMS07	Retrd.	1993	12.00	37
1992	Set	Retrd.	1993	125.00	200-300

Galveston - S. Thompson

Year	Issue	Edition Limit	Year Retd.	Issue Price	Quote U.S.$
1995	Beissner House GLV04	Open		18.00	18
1995	Dancing Pavillion GLV03	Open		18.00	18
1995	Frenkel House GLV01	Open		18.00	18
1995	Reymershoffer House GLV02	Open		18.00	18

Ghost House Series - S. Thompson

Year	Issue	Edition Limit	Year Retd.	Issue Price	Quote U.S.$
1995	Gaffos House GHO04	Open		19.00	19
1994	Inside-Outside House GHO01	Open		18.00	18
1994	Inside-Outside House, AP GHO01	Retrd.	1994	20.00	30-40
1994	Pirates' House GHO02	Open		18.00	18
1994	Pirates' House, AP GHO02	Retrd.	1994	20.00	25-40
1995	Red Castle GHO03	Open		19.00	19

Gone with the Wind - S. Thompson

Year	Issue	Edition Limit	Year Retd.	Issue Price	Quote U.S.$
1995	Aunt Pittypat's GWW03	Open		24.00	24
1995	Aunt Pittypat's, AP GWW03	Retrd.	1995	30.00	35
1995	General Store GWW04	Open		24.00	24
1995	General Store, AP GWW04	Retrd.	1995	30.00	35
1995	Loew's Grand GWW05	Open		24.00	24
1995	Loew's Grand, AP GWW05	Retrd.	1995	30.00	35
1995	Tara GWW01	Open		24.00	24
1995	Tara, AP GWW01	Retrd.	1995	30.00	35
1995	Twelve Oaks GWW02	Open		24.00	24
1995	Twelve Oaks, AP GWW02	Retrd.	1995	30.00	35
1995	Set of 5, AP	Retrd.	1995	150.00	250

Inventor Series - S. Thompson

Year	Issue	Edition Limit	Year Retd.	Issue Price	Quote U.S.$
1993	Ford Motor Company (green) INV01	Retrd.	1993	17.00	35-45
1993	Ford Motor Company (grey) INV01	Retrd.	1994	17.00	20
1993	Ford Motor Company, AP INV01	Retrd.	1993	20.00	40
1993	Menlo Park Laboratory (cream) INV02	Retrd.	1993	16.00	45
1993	Menlo Park Laboratory (grey) INV02	Retrd.	1994	16.00	20
1993	Menlo Park Laboratory, AP INV02	Retrd.	1993	20.00	24
1993	Noah Webster House INV03	Retrd.	1994	15.00	20
1993	Noah Webster House, AP INV03	Retrd.	1993	20.00	24-35
1993	Wright Cycle Shop INV04	Retrd.	1994	17.00	25
1993	Wright Cycle Shop, AP INV04	Retrd.	1993	20.00	24-35

Jazzy New Orleans Series - S. Thompson

Year	Issue	Edition Limit	Year Retd.	Issue Price	Quote U.S.$
1994	Beauregard-Keys House JNO04	Open		18.00	18
1994	Beauregard-Keys House, AP JNO04	Retrd.	1994	20.00	30-40
1994	Gallier House JNO02	Open		18.00	18
1994	Gallier House, AP JNO02	Retrd.	1994	20.00	30-40
1994	La Branche Building JNO01	Open		18.00	18
1994	La Branche Building, AP JNO01	Retrd.	1994	20.00	30-40
1994	LePretre House JNO03	Open		18.00	18
1994	LePretre House, AP JNO03	Retrd.	1994	20.00	30-40

Key West - S. Thompson

Year	Issue	Edition Limit	Year Retd.	Issue Price	Quote U.S.$
1995	Artist House KEY06	Open		19.00	19
1995	Artist House, AP KEY06	Retrd.	1995	24.00	30-40
1995	Eyebrow House KEY01	Open		18.00	18
1995	Eyebrow House, AP KEY01	Retrd.	1995	24.00	30-40
1995	Hemingway House KEY07	Open		19.00	19
1995	Hemingway House, AP KEY07	Retrd.	1995	24.00	30-40
1995	Illingsworth Gingerbread House KEY05	Open		19.00	19
1995	Illingsworth Gingerbread House, AP KEY05	Retrd.	1995	24.00	30-40
1995	Shotgun House KEY03	Open		17.00	17
1995	Shotgun House, AP KEY03	Retrd.	1995	24.00	30-40
1995	Shotgun Sister KEY04	Open		17.00	17
1995	Shotgun Sister, AP KEY04	Retrd.	1995	24.00	30-40
1995	Southernmost House KEY02	Open		19.00	19
1995	Southernmost House, AP KEY02	Retrd.	1995	24.00	30-40

Lighthouse Series - S. Thompson

Year	Issue	Edition Limit	Year Retd.	Issue Price	Quote U.S.$
1991	Anastasia Lighthouse (burgundy) FL103	Retrd.	1991	15.00	25
1991	Anastasia Lighthouse (red) FL103	Retrd.	1994	15.00	25
1993	Assateague Island Light LTS07	Open		17.00	17
1994	Assateague Island Light, AP LTS07	Retrd.	1994	20.00	30-40
1995	Cape Hatteras Light LTS09	Open		17.00	17
1995	Cape Hatteras Light, AP LTS09	Retrd.	1995	24.00	30-40
1991	Cape Hatteras Lighthouse NC103	Retrd.	1994	15.00	25
1994	Charleston Light (renovated) LTS01	Retrd.	1995	15.00	25
1993	Charleston Light LTS01	Retrd.	1995	15.00	25
1993	New London Ledge Light LTS08	Open		17.00	17
1994	New London Ledge Light, AP LTS08	Retrd.	1994	20.00	30-40
1993	Round Island Light LTS06	Open		17.00	17
1994	Round Island Light, AP LTS06	Retrd.	1994	20.00	30-40
1990	Stage Harbor Lighthouse NEW06	Retrd.	1993	15.00	45-90
1993	Thomas Point Light LTS05	Open		17.00	17
1994	Thomas Point Light, AP LTS05	Retrd.	1994	20.00	30-40
1990	Tybee Lighthouse SAV07	Retrd.	1994	15.00	25-35

Limited Edition American Gothic - S. Thompson

Year	Issue	Edition Limit	Year Retd.	Issue Price	Quote U.S.$
1993	Gothic Revival Cottage ACL01	Retrd.	1993	20.00	40
1993	Mele House ACL04	Retrd.	1993	20.00	40
1993	Perkins House ACL02	Retrd.	1993	20.00	40
1993	Rose Arbor ACL05	Retrd.	1993	14.00	40
1993	Roseland Cottage ACL03	Retrd.	1993	20.00	30
1993	Set of 5	Retrd.	1993	94.00	150

Limited Edition Mail-Order Victorians (Barber Houses) - S. Thompson

Year	Issue	Edition Limit	Year Retd.	Issue Price	Quote U.S.$
1994	Brehaut House ACL09	3,300	1994	24.00	25-40

Limited Edition Mail-Order Victorians - S. Thompson

Year	Issue	Edition Limit	Year Retd.	Issue Price	Quote U.S.$
1994	Goeller House ACL08	3,300	1994	24.00	25-45
1994	Henderson House ACL07	3,300	1994	24.00	25-50
1994	Titman House ACL06	3,300	1994	24.00	25-40
1994	Set of 4	3,300	1994	96.00	125

Limited Pieces

Year	Issue	Edition Limit	Year Retd.	Issue Price	Quote U.S.$
1991	Bridgetown Library NJ102	Retrd.	N/A	16.00	25
1993	Comly-Rich House XXX01	Retrd.	N/A	12.00	25-75
1991	Delphos City Hall OH101	Retrd.	N/A	15.00	100-200
1991	Historic Burlington County Clubhouse NJ101	Retrd.	N/A	16.00	N/A
1991	Mark Twain Boyhood Home MO101	Retrd.	N/A	15.00	N/A
1990	Newton County Court House GA101	Retrd.	N/A	16.00	N/A

Martha's Vineyard - S. Thompson

Year	Issue	Edition Limit	Year Retd.	Issue Price	Quote U.S.$
1994	Alice's Wonderland (renovated) MAR08II	Open		16.00	16
1993	Alice's Wonderland MAR08	Open		16.00	16
1993	Alice's Wonderland, AP MAR08	Retrd.	1993	20.00	30
1995	Blue Cottage MAR13	Open		17.00	17
1995	Blue Cottage, AP MAR13	Retrd.	1995	24.00	30-40
1994	Campground Cottage (renovated) MAR07II	Retrd.	1995	16.00	16
1993	Campground Cottage MAR07	Retrd.	1995	16.00	20
1993	Campground Cottage, AP MAR07	Retrd.	1993	20.00	30
1994	Gingerbread Cottage-grey (renovated) MAR09II	Open		16.00	16
1993	Gingerbread Cottage-grey AP MAR09	Retrd.	1993	20.00	30
1993	Gingerbread Cottage-grey MAR09	Open		16.00	16
1995	Trails End MAR11	Open		17.00	17
1995	Trails End, AP MAR11	Retrd.	1995	24.00	30-40
1995	White Cottage MAR12	Open		17.00	17
1995	White Cottage, AP MAR12	Retrd.	1995	24.00	30-40

FIGURINES/COTTAGES

YEAR ISSUE		EDITION LIMIT	YEAR RETD.	ISSUE PRICE	QUOTE U.S.$
1994	Wood Valentine (renovated) MAR10II	Open		16.00	16
1993	Wood Valentine MAR10	Open		16.00	16
1993	Wood Valentine, AP MAR10	Retrd.	1993	20.00	30-40

New England - S. Thompson

YEAR ISSUE		EDITION LIMIT	YEAR RETD.	ISSUE PRICE	QUOTE U.S.$
1991	Faneuil Hall NEW09	Retrd.	1993	15.00	25-80
1990	Longfellow's House NEW01	Retrd.	1993	15.00	25-50
1990	Malden Mass. Victorian Inn NEW05	Retrd.	1992	10.00	60-100
1990	Martha's Vineyard Cottage-blue/mauve MAR06	Retrd.	1993	15.00	25-75
1990	Martha's Vineyard Cottage-blue/orange MAR05	Retrd.	1993	15.00	20-50
1990	Motif #1 Boathouse NEW02	Retrd.	1993	15.00	25-70
1990	Old North Church NEW04	Retrd.	1993	15.00	30-90
1990	Paul Revere's Home NEW03	Retrd.	1993	15.00	30-90
1991	President Bush's Home NEW07	Retrd.	1993	15.00	30-95
1991	Wedding Cake House NEW08	Retrd.	1993	15.00	30-70

North Carolina - S. Thompson

YEAR ISSUE		EDITION LIMIT	YEAR RETD.	ISSUE PRICE	QUOTE U.S.$
1990	Josephus Hall House NC101	Retrd.	1993	15.00	30
1990	Presbyterian Bell Tower NC102	Retrd.	1993	15.00	50
1991	The Tryon Palace NC104	Retrd.	1993	15.00	30-75

Old-Fashioned Christmas - S. Thompson

YEAR ISSUE		EDITION LIMIT	YEAR RETD.	ISSUE PRICE	QUOTE U.S.$
1994	Conway Scenic Railroad Station OFC04	Open		18.00	18
1994	Conway Scenic Railroad Station, AP OFC04	Retrd.	1994	20.00	30-50
1994	Dwight House OFC02	Open		18.00	18
1994	Dwight House, AP OFC02	Retrd.	1994	20.00	30-50
1994	General Merchandise OFC03	Open		18.00	18
1994	General Merchandise, AP OFC03	Retrd.	1994	20.00	30-50
1994	Old First Church OFC01	Open		18.00	18
1994	Old First Church, AP OFC01	Retrd.	1994	20.00	30-50
1994	Set of 4 1994 AP	Retrd.	1994	80.00	199
1995	Christmas Inn OFC05	Open		18.00	18
1995	Town Square Tree OFC06	Open		18.00	18

Painted Ladies I - S. Thompson

YEAR ISSUE		EDITION LIMIT	YEAR RETD.	ISSUE PRICE	QUOTE U.S.$
1990	The Abbey LAD08	Retrd.	1992	10.00	85-175
1990	Atlanta Queen Anne LAD07	Retrd.	1992	10.00	100-200
1990	Cincinnati Gothic LAD05	Retrd.	1992	10.00	75-125
1990	Colorado Queen Anne LAD04	Retrd.	1992	10.00	75-125
1990	Illinois Queen Anne LAD06	Retrd.	1991	10.00	385-450
1990	San Francisco Italianate-yellow LAD03	Retrd.	1992	10.00	115-150
1990	San Francisco Stick House-blue LAD02	Retrd.	1991	10.00	60-80
1990	San Francisco Stick House-yellow LAD01	Retrd.	1991	10.00	70-125
1990	Painted Ladies I Sign	Retrd.	N/A	12.50	20

Painted Ladies II - S. Thompson

YEAR ISSUE		EDITION LIMIT	YEAR RETD.	ISSUE PRICE	QUOTE U.S.$
1994	Cape May Gothic (renovated) LAD13II	Retrd.	1995	16.00	20
1992	Cape May Gothic LAD13	Retrd.	1995	15.00	20
1994	Cape May Victorian Pink House (renovated) LAD16II	Open		16.00	16
1992	Cape May Victorian Pink House LAD16	Open		15.00	15
1994	The Gingerbread Mansion (renovated) LAD09II	Retrd.	1994	16.00	25
1992	The Gingerbread Mansion LAD09	Retrd.	1993	15.00	20-35
1994	Morningstar Inn (renovated) LAD15II	Retrd.	1994	16.00	25
1992	Morningstar Inn LAD15	Retrd.	1994	15.00	23
1994	Pitkin House (renovated) LAD10II	Open		16.00	16
1992	Pitkin House LAD10	Open		15.00	15
1994	Queen Anne Townhouse (renovated) LAD12II	Retrd.	1994	16.00	25
1992	Queen Anne Townhouse LAD12	Retrd.	1994	15.00	23
1994	The Victorian Blue Rose (renovated) LAD14II	Open		16.00	16
1992	The Victorian Blue Rose LAD14	Open		15.00	15
1994	The Young-Larson House (renovated) LAD11II	Open		16.00	16
1992	The Young-Larson House LAD11	Open		15.00	15

Painted Ladies III - S. Thompson

YEAR ISSUE		EDITION LIMIT	YEAR RETD.	ISSUE PRICE	QUOTE U.S.$
1994	Cape May Green Stockton Row (renovated) LAD20II	Retrd.	1995	16.00	20
1993	Cape May Green Stockton Row LAD20	Retrd.	1995	16.00	20
1994	Cape May Linda Lee (renovated) LAD17II	Open		16.00	16
1993	Cape May Linda Lee LAD17	Open		16.00	16
1994	Cape May Pink Stockton Row (renovated)LAD19II	Open		16.00	16
1993	Cape May Pink Stockton Row LAD19	Open		16.00	16
1994	Cape May Tan Stockton Row (renovated)LAD18II	Open		16.00	16
1993	Cape May Tan Stockton Row LAD18	Open		16.00	16
1995	Steiner Cottage LAD21	Open		17.00	17
1995	Steiner Cottage, AP LAD21	Retrd.	1995	24.00	25-40

Philadelphia - S. Thompson

YEAR ISSUE		EDITION LIMIT	YEAR RETD.	ISSUE PRICE	QUOTE U.S.$
1990	"Besty" Ross House (misspelling) PHI03	Retrd.	1990	15.00	20-45
1990	Betsy Ross House PHI03	Retrd.	1993	15.00	30-75
1990	Carpenter's Hall PHI01	Retrd.	1993	15.00	25-35
1990	Elphreth's Alley PHI05	Retrd.	1993	15.00	30-65
1990	Graff House PHI07	Retrd.	1993	15.00	35-75
1990	Independence Hall PHI04	Retrd.	1993	15.00	30-75
1990	Market St. Post Office PHI02	Retrd.	1993	15.00	33
1990	Old City Hall PHI08	Retrd.	1993	15.00	25-40
1990	Old Tavern PHI06	Retrd.	1993	15.00	25-35

Plantations - S. Thompson

YEAR ISSUE		EDITION LIMIT	YEAR RETD.	ISSUE PRICE	QUOTE U.S.$
1995	Farley PLA04	Open		18.00	18
1995	Farley, AP PLA04	Retrd.	1995	24.00	30-40
1995	Longwood PLA02	Open		19.00	19
1995	Longwood, AP PLA02	Retrd.	1995	24.00	30-40
1995	Merry Sherwood PLA03	Open		18.00	18
1995	Merry Sherwood, AP PLA03	Retrd.	1995	24.00	30-40
1995	San Francisco PLA01	Open		19.00	19
1995	San Francisco, AP PLA01	Retrd.	1995	24.00	30-40

San Francisco - S. Thompson

YEAR ISSUE		EDITION LIMIT	YEAR RETD.	ISSUE PRICE	QUOTE U.S.$
1995	Brandywine SF101	Open		18.00	18
1995	Brandywine, AP SF101	Retrd.	1995	24.00	30-40
1995	Eclectic Blue SF103	Open		19.00	19
1995	Eclectic Blue, AP SF103	Retrd.	1995	24.00	30-40
1995	Edwardian Green SF104	Open		18.00	18
1995	Edwardian Green, AP SF104	Retrd.	1995	24.00	30-40
1995	Queen Rose SF102	Open		19.00	19
1995	Queen Rose, AP SF102	Retrd.	1995	24.00	30-40

Savannah - S. Thompson

YEAR ISSUE		EDITION LIMIT	YEAR RETD.	ISSUE PRICE	QUOTE U.S.$
1990	Andrew Low Mansion SAV02	Retrd.	1994	15.00	20-45
1994	Catherdral of St. John (renovated) SAV09II	Retrd.	1995	16.00	30
1992	Catherdral of St. John SAV09	Retrd.	1995	16.00	20-40
1994	Chestnut House SAV11	Open		18.00	18
1994	Chestnut House, AP SAV11	Retrd.	1994	24.00	75
1990	Davenport House SAV03	Retrd.	1994	15.00	20-50
1990	Herb House SAV05	Retrd.	1993	15.00	25-75
1994	Juliette Low House (renovated) SAV04II	Open		15.00	15
1990	Juliette Low House (w/logo) SAV04	Open		15.00	15
1990	Juliette Low House (w/o logo) SAV04	Open		15.00	15
1995	Mercer House SAV12	Open		18.00	18
1995	Mercer House, AP SAV12	Retrd.	1995	24.00	75
1990	Mikve Israel Temple SAV06	Retrd.	1994	15.00	25-75
1994	Olde Pink House (renovated) SAV01II	Open		15.00	15
1990	Olde Pink House SAV01	Open		15.00	15
1994	Owens Thomas House (renovated) SAV10II	Open		16.00	16
1993	Owens Thomas House AP SAV10	Retrd.	1993	20.00	75
1993	Owens Thomas House SAV10	Open		16.00	16
1990	Savannah Gingerbread House I SAV08	Retrd.	1990	15.00	200-325
1990	Savannah Gingerbread House II SAV08	Retrd.	1992	15.00	200-325

Signing Only Pieces - S. Thompson

YEAR ISSUE		EDITION LIMIT	YEAR RETD.	ISSUE PRICE	QUOTE U.S.$
1994	Star Barn SOP01	Retrd.	1994	24.00	25-45
1995	Shelia's Real Estate Office SOP02	12/95		20.00	20

South Carolina - S. Thompson

YEAR ISSUE		EDITION LIMIT	YEAR RETD.	ISSUE PRICE	QUOTE U.S.$
1991	All Saints' Church SC105	Retrd.	1993	15.00	30-55
1990	The Governor's Mansion (misspelling) SC102	Retrd.	1990	15.00	15
1994	The Governor's Mansion (renovated) SC102II	Retrd.	1995	15.00	35
1990	The Governor's Mansion SC102	Retrd.	1995	15.00	25-30
1994	The Hermitage (renovated) SC101II	Retrd.	1995	15.00	20
1990	The Hermitage SC101	Retrd.	1995	15.00	25
1994	The Lace House (renovated) SC103II	Retrd.	1995	15.00	15
1990	The Lace House SC103	Retrd.	1995	15.00	50
1994	The State Capitol (renovated) SC104II	Retrd.	1994	15.00	40
1991	The State Capitol SC104	Retrd.	1994	15.00	35

St. Augustine - S. Thompson

YEAR ISSUE		EDITION LIMIT	YEAR RETD.	ISSUE PRICE	QUOTE U.S.$
1991	Anastasia Lighthousekeeper's House FL104	Retrd.	1993	15.00	25-40
1991	Mission Nombre deDios FL105	Retrd.	1993	15.00	30-50
1991	Old City Gates FL102	Retrd.	1993	15.00	25-30
1991	The "Oldest House" FL101	Retrd.	1993	15.00	30-50

Texas - S. Thompson

YEAR ISSUE		EDITION LIMIT	YEAR RETD.	ISSUE PRICE	QUOTE U.S.$
1990	The Alamo TEX01	Retrd.	1993	15.00	150-200
1990	Mission Concepcion TEX04	Retrd.	1993	15.00	50-75
1990	Mission San Francisco TEX03	Retrd.	1993	15.00	30-75
1990	Mission San Jose' TEX02	Retrd.	1993	15.00	30-75
1990	Texas Sign	Retrd.	N/A	12.50	20

Victorian Springtime - S. Thompson

YEAR ISSUE		EDITION LIMIT	YEAR RETD.	ISSUE PRICE	QUOTE U.S.$
1993	Heffron House VST03	Open		17.00	17
1993	Heffron House, AP VST03	Retrd.	1993	20.00	30-45
1993	Jacobsen House VST04	Open		17.00	17
1993	Jacobsen House, AP VST04	Retrd.	1993	20.00	30-45
1993	Ralston House VST01	Open		17.00	17
1993	Ralston House, AP VST01	Retrd.	1993	20.00	30-45
1993	Sessions House VST02	Open		17.00	17
1993	Sessions House, AP VST02	Retrd.	1993	20.00	30-45
1993	Set of 4, AP	Closed		100.00	180

Victorian Springtime II - S. Thompson

YEAR ISSUE		EDITION LIMIT	YEAR RETD.	ISSUE PRICE	QUOTE U.S.$
1995	Dragon House VST07	Open		18.00	18
1995	Dragon House, AP VST07	Retrd.	1995	24.00	30-40
1995	E.B. Hall House VST08	Open		19.00	19
1995	E.B. Hall House, AP VST08	Retrd.	1995	24.00	30-40
1995	Gibney Home VST09	Open		18.00	18
1995	Gibney Home, AP VST09	Retrd.	1995	24.00	30-40
1995	Ray Home VST05	Open		18.00	18
1995	Ray Home, AP VST05	Retrd.	1995	24.00	30-40
1995	Victoria VST06	Open		18.00	18
1995	Victoria, AP VST06	Retrd.	1995	24.00	30-40

Washington D.C. - S. Thompson

YEAR ISSUE		EDITION LIMIT	YEAR RETD.	ISSUE PRICE	QUOTE U.S.$
1992	Cherry Trees DC005	Retrd.	1993	12.00	30-50
1992	Library of Congress DC002	Retrd.	1993	16.00	20-50
1991	National Archives DC001	Retrd.	1993	16.00	30-50
1991	Washington Monument DC004	Retrd.	1993	16.00	20-50
1992	White House DC003	Retrd.	1993	16.00	70-145
1992	Set of 5	Retrd.	1993	76.00	350

West Coast Lighthouse Series - S. Thompson

YEAR ISSUE		EDITION LIMIT	YEAR RETD.	ISSUE PRICE	QUOTE U.S.$
1995	East Brother Light WCL01	Open		19.00	19
1995	East Brother Light, AP WCL01	Retrd.	1995	24.00	30-40
1995	Mukilteo Light WCL02	Open		18.00	18
1995	Mukilteo Light, AP WCL02	Retrd.	1995	24.00	30-40
1995	Point Fermin Light WCL04	Open		18.00	18
1995	Point Fermin Light, AP WCL04	Retrd.	1995	24.00	30-40
1995	Yaquina Bay Light WCL03	Open		18.00	18
1995	Yaquina Bay Light, AP WCL03	Retrd.	1995	24.00	30-40

Williamsburg - S. Thompson

YEAR ISSUE		EDITION LIMIT	YEAR RETD.	ISSUE PRICE	QUOTE U.S.$
1990	Apothecary WIL09	Retrd.	1994	12.00	20-30
1994	Bruton Parish Church (renovated) WIL13II	Open		15.00	15
1992	Bruton Parish Church WIL13	Open		15.00	15
1995	Capitol WIL15	Open		18.00	18
1995	Capitol, AP WIL15	Retrd.	1995	24.00	30-40
1994	Courthouse (renovated) WIL11II	Retrd.	1995	15.00	20
1990	Courthouse WIL11	Retrd.	1995	15.00	20
1990	The Golden Ball Jeweler WIL07	Retrd.	1994	12.00	20-30
1994	Governor's Palace (renovated) WIL04II	Open		15.00	15
1990	Governor's Palace WIL04	Open		15.00	15
1994	Homesite (renovated) WIL12II	Open		15.00	15
1990	Homesite WIL12	Open		15.00	15
1994	King's Arm Tavern (renovated) WIL10II	Retrd.	1995	15.00	25-35
1990	King's Arm Tavern WIL10	Retrd.	1995	15.00	15
1990	Milliner WIL06	Retrd.	1994	12.00	20-45
1990	Nicolson Shop WIL08	Retrd.	1994	12.00	20-35
1990	The Printing Offices WIL05	Retrd.	1993	12.00	20-30
1995	Raleigh Tavern WIL14	Open		18.00	18
1995	Raleigh Tavern, AP WIL14	Retrd.	1995	24.00	30-40

Sports Impressions/Enesco

Collectors' Club Members Only - Various

YEAR ISSUE		EDITION LIMIT	YEAR RETD.	ISSUE PRICE	QUOTE U.S.$
1990	The Mick-Mickey Mantle 5000-1	Yr.Iss.	N/A	75.00	85
1991	Rickey Henderson-Born to Run 5001-11	Yr.Iss.	N/A	49.95	50
1991	Nolan Ryan-300 Wins 5002-01	Yr.Iss.	N/A	125.00	125
1991	Willie, Mickey & Duke plate 5003-04	Yr.Iss.	N/A	39.95	40
1992	Babe Ruth 5006-11	Yr.Iss.	N/A	40.00	40
1992	Walter Payton 5015-01	Yr.Iss.	N/A	50.00	50
1993	The 1927 Yankees plate - R.Tanenbaum	Yr.Iss.	N/A	60.00	75

Collectors' Club Symbol of Membership - Sports Impressions

YEAR ISSUE		EDITION LIMIT	YEAR RETD.	ISSUE PRICE	QUOTE U.S.$
1991	Mick/7 plate 5001-02	Yr.Iss.	N/A	Gift	20
1992	USA Basketball team plate 5008-30	Yr.Iss.	N/A	Gift	N/A
1993	Nolan Ryan porcelain card	Yr.Iss.	N/A	Gift	25

Baseball Superstar Figurines - Sports Impressions

YEAR ISSUE		EDITION LIMIT	YEAR RETD.	ISSUE PRICE	QUOTE U.S.$
1988	Al Kaline	2,500	N/A	90.00	125
1988	Andre Dawson	2,500	N/A	90.00	125-200
1988	Bob Feller	2,500	N/A	90.00	125-200
1992	Cubs Ryne Sandberg Home 1118-23	975	1993	150.00	195
1987	Don Mattingly	Closed	N/A	90.00	250
1987	Don Mattingly (Franklin glove variation)	Closed	N/A	90.00	750
1989	Duke Snider	2,500	N/A	90.00	125
1994	Giants Barry Bonds (signed) 1160-46	975	1995	150.00	150
1992	Johnny Bench (hand signed) 1126-23	975	1994	150.00	150
1988	Jose Canseco	Closed	N/A	90.00	125-200
1987	Keith Hernandez	2,500	N/A	90.00	125-200
1989	Kirk Gibson	Closed	N/A	90.00	125-200
1987	Mickey Mantle	Closed	N/A	90.00	175-295
1996	Mickey Mantle "The Greatest Switch Hitter" (hand signed) 1228-46 - T. Treadway	975		395.00	395
1990	Nolan Ryan	Closed	N/A	50.00	50
1992	Nolan Ryan Figurine/plate/stand 1134-31	500	1994	260.00	260
1990	Nolan Ryan Kings of K	Closed	N/A	125.00	125
1990	Nolan Ryan Mini	Closed	N/A	50.00	50
1990	Nolan Ryan Supersize	Closed	N/A	250.00	250
1993	Oakland A's Reggie Jackson (signed) 1048-46	975	1994	150.00	150
1993	Rangers Nolan Ryan (signed) 1127-46	975	1994	175.00	175
1994	Rangers Nolan Ryan (signed) Farewell 1161-49	975	1994	150.00	150

YEAR	ISSUE	EDITION LIMIT	YEAR RETD.	ISSUE PRICE	QUOTE U.S.$
1990	Ted Williams	Closed	N/A	90.00	200-375
1987	Wade Boggs	Closed	N/A	90.00	150-225
1989	Will Clark	Closed	N/A	90.00	125-250
1993	Yankees Mickey Mantle (signed) 1038-46	975	1993	195.00	195

Basketball Superstar Figurines - Sports Impressions

YEAR	ISSUE	EDITION LIMIT	YEAR RETD.	ISSUE PRICE	QUOTE U.S.$
1993	Julius Erving 76ers (hand signed) 4102-46	975	1994	150.00	150
1993	Julius Erving 76ers (hand signed) 4102-61	76	1994	295.00	295

Football Superstar Figurines - Sports Impressions

YEAR	ISSUE	EDITION LIMIT	YEAR RETD.	ISSUE PRICE	QUOTE U.S.$
1993	Gale Sayers Bears (hand signed) 3029-23	975	1994	150.00	150
1992	John Unitas Colts (hand signed) 3016-23	975	1994	150.00	150
1993	Kenny Stabler Raiders (hand signed) 3026-23	975	1994	150.00	150
1993	Walter Payton Bears (hand signed) 3028-23	975	1994	150.00	150

NASCAR

YEAR	ISSUE	EDITION LIMIT	YEAR RETD.	ISSUE PRICE	QUOTE U.S.$
1995	Bill Elliott (hand signed) 8100-46	975		150.00	150

Plaques - Various

YEAR	ISSUE	EDITION LIMIT	YEAR RETD.	ISSUE PRICE	QUOTE U.S.$
1995	Life of a Legend Mickey Mantle 1228-71 - T. Fogarty	Open		40.00	40
1995	Profiles in Courage Mickey Mantle 1231-62 - M. Petronella	Open		40.00	40

Swarovski America Ltd.

Collectors Society Editions - Various

YEAR	ISSUE	EDITION LIMIT	YEAR RETD.	ISSUE PRICE	QUOTE U.S.$
1987	Togetherness-The Lovebirds Schreck/Stocker	Yr.Iss.	1987	150.00	3200-4000
1988	Sharing-The Woodpeckers A. Stocker	Yr.Iss.	1988	165.00	1150-1900
1988	Mini Cactus	Yr.Iss.	1988	Gift	200-225
1989	Amour-The Turtledoves A. Stocker	Yr.Iss.	1989	195.00	750-1100
1989	SCS Key Chain	Yr.Iss.	1989	Gift	50-75
1990	Lead Me-The Dolphins M. Stamey	Yr.Iss.	1990	225.00	900-1700
1990	Mini Chaton	Yr.Iss.	1990	Gift	60-85
1991	Save Me-The Seals - M. Stamey	Yr.Iss.	1991	225.00	450-700
1991	Dolphin Brooch	Yr.Iss.	1991	75.00	125-150
1991	SCS Pin	Yr.Iss.	1991	Gift	45
1992	Care For Me - The Whales M. Stamey	Yr.Iss.	1992	265.00	375-700
1992	SCS Pen	Yr.Iss.	1992	Gift	25-75
1992	5th Anniversary Edition-The Birthday Cake - G. Stamey	Yr.Iss.	1992	85.00	125-225
1993	Inspiration Africa-The Elephant M. Zendron	Yr.Iss.	1993	325.00	750-1100
1993	Elephant Brooch	Yr.Iss.	1993	85.00	100-150
1993	Leather Luggage Tag	Yr.Iss.	1993	Gift	15-25
1994	Inspiration Africa-The Kudu M. Stamey	Yr.Iss.	1994	295.00	375-600
1994	Leather Double Picture Frame	Yr.Iss.	1994	Gift	20
1995	Inspiration Africa-The Lion A. Stocker	12/95		325.00	325
1995	Centenary Swan Brooch	12/95		125.00	125
1995	Miniature Crystal Swan	12/95		Gift	N/A

African Wildlife - Various

YEAR	ISSUE	EDITION LIMIT	YEAR RETD.	ISSUE PRICE	QUOTE U.S.$
1995	Baby Elephant - M. Zendron	Open		155.00	155
1994	Cheetah - M. Stamey	Open		275.00	275
1989	Elephant-Small - A. Stocker	Open		50.00	65

Among Flowers And Foliage - C. Schneiderbauer

YEAR	ISSUE	EDITION LIMIT	YEAR RETD.	ISSUE PRICE	QUOTE U.S.$
1992	Bumblebee	Open		85.00	85
1994	Butterfly on Leaf	Open		75.00	85
1995	Dragonfly	Open		85.00	85
1992	Hummingbird	Open		195.00	210

Barnyard Friends - Various

YEAR	ISSUE	EDITION LIMIT	YEAR RETD.	ISSUE PRICE	QUOTE U.S.$
1993	Dick Gosling - A. Stocker	Open		37.50	38
1993	Harry Gosling - A. Stocker	Open		37.50	38
1984	Medium Pig - M. Schreck	Open		35.00	55
1988	Mini Chicks (Set of 3) G. Stamey	Open		35.00	45
1987	Mini Hen - G. Stamey	Open		35.00	45
1982	Mini Pig - M. Schreck	Open		16.00	30
1987	Mini Rooster - G. Stamey	Open		35.00	55
1993	Mother Goose - A. Stocker	Open		75.00	75
1993	Tom Gosling - A. Stocker	Open		37.50	38

Beauties of the Lake - Various

YEAR	ISSUE	EDITION LIMIT	YEAR RETD.	ISSUE PRICE	QUOTE U.S.$
1983	Drake-Mini - M. Schreck	Open		20.00	45
1994	Frog - G. Stamey	Open		49.50	50
1989	Mallard-Giant - M. Stamey	Open		2000.00	4500
1986	Standing Duck-Mini - A. Stocker	Open		22.00	38
1977	Swan-Large - M. Schreck	Open		55.00	95
1995	Swan-Maxi - A. Hirzinger	Open		4500.00	4500
1977	Swan-Medium - M. Schreck	Open		44.00	85
1989	Swan-Small - M. Schreck	Open		35.00	50
1986	Swimming Duck-Mini A. Stocker	Open		16.00	38

Centenary Edition - A. Hirzinger

YEAR	ISSUE	EDITION LIMIT	YEAR RETD.	ISSUE PRICE	QUOTE U.S.$
1995	Centenary Swan	12/95		150.00	150

Commemorative Single Issues - Team

YEAR	ISSUE	EDITION LIMIT	YEAR RETD.	ISSUE PRICE	QUOTE U.S.$
1990	Elephant,(Introduced by Swarovski America as a commemorative item during Design Celebration/January '90 in Walt Disney World)	Closed	N/A	125.00	850-1200
1993	Elephant,(Introduced by Swarovski America as a commemorative item during Design Celebration/January '93 in Walt Disney World)	Open		150.00	150

Crystal Melodies - M. Zendron

YEAR	ISSUE	EDITION LIMIT	YEAR RETD.	ISSUE PRICE	QUOTE U.S.$
1993	Grand Piano	Open		250.00	260
1992	Harp	Open		175.00	210
1992	Lute	Open		125.00	140

Decorative Items For The Desk (Paperweights) - M. Schreck

YEAR	ISSUE	EDITION LIMIT	YEAR RETD.	ISSUE PRICE	QUOTE U.S.$
1990	Chaton-Giant 7433NR180000	Open		4500.00	4500
1987	Chaton-Large 7433NR80	Open		190.00	260
1987	Chaton-Small 7433NR50	Open		50.00	65
1987	Pyramid-Small Crystal Cal. 7450NR40095	Open		100.00	125
1987	Pyramid-Small Vitrail Med. 7450NR40087	Open		100.00	125

Endangered Species - Various

YEAR	ISSUE	EDITION LIMIT	YEAR RETD.	ISSUE PRICE	QUOTE U.S.$
1993	Baby Panda - A. Stocker	Open		24.50	25
1991	Kiwi - M. Stamey	Open		37.50	45
1987	Koala - A. Stocker	Open		50.00	65
1989	Mini Koala - A. Stocker	Open		35.00	45
1992	Mother Beaver - A. Stocker	Open		110.00	125
1993	Mother Kangaroo with Baby G. Stamey	Open		95.00	95
1993	Mother Panda - A. Stocker	Open		120.00	125
1992	Sitting Baby Beaver - A. Stocker	Open		47.50	50
1981	Turtle-Giant - M. Schreck	Open		2500.00	4500
1977	Turtle-Large - M. Schreck	Open		48.00	75
1977	Turtle-Small - M. Schreck	Open		35.00	50

Exquisite Accents - Various

YEAR	ISSUE	EDITION LIMIT	YEAR RETD.	ISSUE PRICE	QUOTE U.S.$
1995	Angel - A. Stocker	Open		210.00	210
1980	Birdbath - M. Schreck	Open		150.00	210
1987	Birds' Nest	Open		90.00	125
1987	Dinner Bell-Medium M. Schreck	Open		80.00	95
1987	Dinner Bell-Small - M. Schreck	Open		60.00	65
1992	The Rose - M. Stamey	Open		150.00	155

Feathered Friends - A. Hirzinger

YEAR	ISSUE	EDITION LIMIT	YEAR RETD.	ISSUE PRICE	QUOTE U.S.$
1993	Pelican	Open		37.50	38

Game of Kings - M. Schreck

YEAR	ISSUE	EDITION LIMIT	YEAR RETD.	ISSUE PRICE	QUOTE U.S.$
1984	Chess Set	Open		950.00	1375

Horses on Parade - M. Zendron

YEAR	ISSUE	EDITION LIMIT	YEAR RETD.	ISSUE PRICE	QUOTE U.S.$
1993	White Stallion	Open		250.00	260

In A Summer Meadow - Various

YEAR	ISSUE	EDITION LIMIT	YEAR RETD.	ISSUE PRICE	QUOTE U.S.$
1982	Butterfly	Open		44.00	85
1994	Field Mice (set of 3) - A. Stocker	Open		42.50	45
1991	Field Mouse - A. Stocker	Open		47.50	50
1985	Hedgehog-Large - M. Schreck	Open		120.00	140
1985	Hedgehog-Medium - M. Schreck	Open		70.00	85
1987	Hedgehog-Small - M. Schreck	Open		50.00	55
1995	Ladybug - E. Mair	Open		29.50	30
1986	Mini Butterfly	Open		16.00	45
1988	Mini Sitting Rabbit - A. Stocker	Open		35.00	45
1988	Mother Rabbit - A. Stocker	Open		60.00	75
1992	Sparrow - C. Schneiderbauer	Open		29.50	30

Kingdom Of Ice And Snow - Various

YEAR	ISSUE	EDITION LIMIT	YEAR RETD.	ISSUE PRICE	QUOTE U.S.$
1986	Large Polar Bear - A. Stocker	Open		140.00	210
1986	Mini Baby Seal - A. Stocker	Open		30.00	45
1984	Mini Penguin - M. Schreck	Open		16.00	38

Our Candleholders - Various

YEAR	ISSUE	EDITION LIMIT	YEAR RETD.	ISSUE PRICE	QUOTE U.S.$
1987	Star-Large 7600NR143	Open		250.00	375
1989	Star-Medium 7600NR143001	Open		200.00	260
1985	Water Lily-Large 7600NR125 - M. Schreck	Open		200.00	375
1983	Water Lily-Medium 7600NR123 M. Schreck	Open		150.00	260
1985	Water Lily-Small 7600NR124 M. Schreck	Open		100.00	175

Our Woodland Friends - Various

YEAR	ISSUE	EDITION LIMIT	YEAR RETD.	ISSUE PRICE	QUOTE U.S.$
1981	Bear-Large - M. Schreck	Open		75.00	95
1985	Bear-Mini - M. Schreck	Open		16.00	55
1987	Fox - A. Stocker	Open		50.00	75
1988	Mini Running Fox - A. Stocker	Open		35.00	45
1988	Mini Sitting Fox - A. Stocker	Open		35.00	45
1989	Mushrooms - A. Stocker	Open		35.00	45
1983	Owl-Giant - M. Schreck	Open		1200.00	2000
1979	Owl-Large - M. Schreck	Open		90.00	125
1979	Owl-Mini - M. Schreck	Open		16.00	30
1995	Owlet - A. Hirzinger	Open		45.00	45
1994	Roe Deer Fawn - E. Mair	Open		75.00	75
1985	Squirrel - M. Schreck	Open		35.00	55

Pets' Corner - Various

YEAR	ISSUE	EDITION LIMIT	YEAR RETD.	ISSUE PRICE	QUOTE U.S.$
1993	Beagle Playing - A. Stocker	Open		49.50	50
1990	Beagle Puppy - A. Stocker	Open		40.00	50
1992	Poodle - A. Stocker	Open		125.00	140
1990	Scotch Terrier - A. Stocker	Open		60.00	75
1991	Sitting Cat - M. Stamey	Open		75.00	85
1993	Sitting Poodle - A. Stocker	Open		85.00	85

Retired - Various

YEAR	ISSUE	EDITION LIMIT	YEAR RETD.	ISSUE PRICE	QUOTE U.S.$
1992	Angel 6475NR000009	Retrd.	1994	65.00	75-100
XX	Apple Photo Stand-Kg Sz (Gold) 7504NR060G	Retrd.	1989	120.00	350-600
XX	Apple Photo Stand-Kg Sz (Rhodium) 7504NR060R M. Schreck	Retrd.	1989	120.00	500
XX	Apple Photo Stand-Lg (Gold) 7504NR050G	Retrd.	1991	80.00	235-300
XX	Apple Photo Stand-Lg. 7504NR050R	Retrd.	1987	80.00	200-400
XX	Apple Photo Stand-Sm. (Gold) 7504NR030G	Retrd.	1991	40.00	125-200
XX	Apple Photo Stand-Sm. 7504NR030R	Retrd.	1987	40.00	125-200
XX	Ashtray 7461NR100	Retrd.	1991	45.00	250
XX	Ashtray 7501NR061	Retrd.	1981	45.50	1000-1200
XX	Bear-Giant Size 7637NR112 - M. Schreck	Retrd.	1988	125.00	1200-1700
XX	Bear-Kg Sz 7637NR92 M. Schreck	Retrd.	1987	95.00	1000-1700
1984	Bear-Mini 7670NR32 M. Schreck	Retrd.	1989	16.00	120-180
1982	Bear-Sm 7637NR054000 M. Schreck	Retrd.	1995	44.00	85
1992	Beaver-Baby Lying 7616NR000003 - A. Stocker	Retrd.	1995	47.50	50
1985	Bee (Gold) 7553NR100	Retrd.	1989	200.00	950-1200
1985	Bee (Rhodium) 7553NR200	Retrd.	1987	200.00	1200-1600
XX	Beetle Bottle Opener (Gold) 7505NR76	Retrd.	1984	80.00	850-1500
XX	Beetle Bottle Opener (Rhodium) 7505NR76	Retrd.	1984	80.00	600-1200
1984	Blowfish-Lg 7644NR41	Retrd.	1992	40.00	90-150
1985	Butterfly (Gold) 7551NR100	Retrd.	1989	200.00	700-1100
1985	Butterfly (Rhodium) 7551NR200	Retrd.	1987	200.00	1300-1700
XX	Butterfly-Mini 7671NR30	Retrd.	1989	16.00	75-120
XX	Cardholders-Lg. , Set/4 7403NR30095	Retrd.	1990	45.00	250-400
XX	Cardholders-Small , Set/4-7403NR20095	Retrd.	1990	25.00	185
1977	Cat-Lg 7634NR70 - M. Schreck	Retrd.	1992	44.00	90-125
19XX	Cat-Medium 7634NR52	Retrd.	1987	38.00	275-400
1982	Cat-Mini 7659NR31 - M. Schreck	Retrd.	1992	16.00	40-85
1981	Chess Set/Wooden Board 7550NR432032	Retrd.	1987	950.00	1200-1700
XX	Chicken-Mini 7651NR20	Retrd.	1989	16.00	40-100
XX	Cigarette Box 7503NR050	Retrd.	1982	136.00	2500
XX	Cigarette Holder 7463NR062	Retrd.	1991	85.00	200-300
1991	City Gates 7474NR000023 G. Stamey	Retrd.	1995	95.00	110-125
1991	City Tower 7474NR000022 G. Stamey	Retrd.	1995	37.50	45-75
1984	Dachshund-Lg 7641NR75 M. Schreck	Retrd.	1992	48.00	80-125
XX	Dachshund-Mini 7672NR42 A. Stocker	Retrd.	1989	20.00	85-125
1987	Dachshund-Mini 7672NR042000 A. Stocker	Retrd.	1995	20.00	50
1981	Dinner Bell-Lg. 7467NR071000 M. Schreck	Retrd.	1992	80.00	145-175
XX	Dog (standing) 7635NR70	Retrd.	1991	44.00	75-115
XX	Duck-Lg 7653NR75	Retrd.	1987	44.00	225-265
XX	Duck-Medium 7653NR55	Retrd.	1988	38.00	75-125
XX	Duck-Mini 7653NR45	Retrd.	1989	16.00	50-100
XX	Elephant 7640NR55	Retrd.	1990	90.00	150-250
1988	Elephant-Lg 7640NR060000 A. Stocker	Retrd.	1995	70.00	175-200
1984	Falcon Head-Lg 7645NR100 M. Schreck	Retrd.	1992	600.00	800-1200
1986	Falcon Head-Sm 7645NR45 M. Schreck	Retrd.	1992	60.00	125
1984	Frog (black eyes) 7642NR48 M. Schreck	Retrd.	1992	30.00	75-90
1984	Frog (clear eyes) 7642NR48 M. Schreck	Retrd.	1992	30.00	125-225
XX	Grapes-Large 7550NR30015	Retrd.	1989	250.00	800-1100
1985	Grapes-Medium 7550NR20029	Retrd.	1995	300.00	375
1985	Grapes-Small 7550NR20015	Retrd.	1995	200.00	260
XX	Hedgehog-Kg. Sz. 7630NR60 M. Schreck	Retrd.	1987	98.00	350-450
XX	Hedgehog-Lg 7630NR50 M. Schreck	Retrd.	1987	65.00	220-250
XX	Hedgehog-Med 7630NR40 M. Schreck	Retrd.	1987	44.00	100-150
XX	Hedgehog-Sm 7630NR30 M. Schreck	Retrd.	1987	38.00	350-500
1988	Hippopotamus 7626NR65 A. Stocker	Retrd.	1993	70.00	125-150
1989	Hippopotamus-Sm. 7626NR055000 - A. Stocker	Retrd.	1995	70.00	75-85
1991	Holy Family w/Arch 7475NR001	Retrd.	1994	250.00	275-350
1985	Hummingbird (Gold) 7552NR100	Retrd.	1989	200.00	850-1200
1985	Hummingbird (Rhodium) 7552NR200	Retrd.	1987	200.00	1800
1990	Kingfisher 7621NR000001 M. Stamey	Retrd.	1993	75.00	100-150
1991	Kitten 7634NR028000 M. Stamey	Retrd.	1995	47.50	50-60
XX	Lighter 7462NR062	Retrd.	1991	160.00	250
XX	Lighter 7500NR050	Retrd.	1982	160.00	2300
1986	Mallard 7647NR80 - M. Schreck	Retrd.	1995	80.00	125-150
XX	Mouse-Kg. Sz. 7631NR60 M. Schreck	Retrd.	1987	95.00	550-650

YEAR ISSUE		EDITION LIMIT	YEAR RETD.	ISSUE PRICE	QUOTE U.S.$
XX	Mouse-Lg. 7631NR50 M. Schreck	Retrd.	1987	69.00	150-275
1976	Mouse-Med 7631NR040000 M. Schreck	Retrd.	1995	48.00	90
XX	Mouse-Mini 7655NR23	Retrd.	1989	16.00	50-125
XX	Mouse-Sm. 7631NR30 M. Schreck	Retrd.	1992	35.00	50-75
1989	Old Timer Automobile 7473NR000001 - G. Stamey	Retrd.	1995	130.00	155
1989	Owl 7621NR000003 - M. Stamey	Retrd.	1993	70.00	120-170
1979	Owl-Sm 7636NR046000 M. Schreck	Retrd.	1995	59.00	85-120
1989	Parrot 7621NR000004 M. Stamey	Retrd.	1993	70.00	125-150
1987	Partridge 7625NR50 - A. Stocker	Retrd.	1991	85.00	135-200
1984	Penguin-Lg 7643NR085000 M. Schreck	Retrd.	1995	44.00	95
XX	Picture Frame/Oval 7505NR75G	Retrd.	1990	90.00	225-300
XX	Picture Frame/Square 7506NR60G	Retrd.	1990	100.00	250
XX	Pig-Lg 7638NR65 - M. Schreck	Retrd.	1987	50.00	200-250
1985	Pineapple/Rhodium-Giant 7507NR26002 - M. Schreck	Retrd.	1987	1750.00	3500
1982	Pineapple/Rhodium-Lg 7507NR105002 - M. Schreck	Retrd.	1987	150.00	275-400
1987	Pineapple/Rhodium-Sm 7507NR060002 - M. Schreck	Retrd.	1987	55.00	100-175
XX	Pprwgt-Atomic-Crystal Cal 7454NR60095	Retrd.	1985	80.00	500-800
XX	Pprwgt-Atomic-Vitrl Med 7454NR60087	Retrd.	1985	80.00	550-800
XX	Pprwgt-Barrel-Crystal Cal 7453NR60095	Retrd.	1989	80.00	200-300
XX	Pprwgt-Barrel-Vitrl Med 7453NR60087	Retrd.	1989	80.00	175
XX	Pprwgt-Carousel-Crystal Cal 7451NR60095	Retrd.	1985	80.00	650-1000
XX	Pprwgt-Carousel-Vitrl Med 7451NR60087	Retrd.	1985	80.00	700-1000
1982	Pprwgt-Cone Crystal Cal 7452NR60095 - M. Schreck	Retrd.	1993	80.00	180-225
1982	Pprwgt-Cone Vitrl Med 7452NR60087 - M. Schreck	Retrd.	1993	80.00	150-250
1981	Pprwgt-Egg 7458NR63069 M. Schreck	Retrd.	1993	60.00	100-135
XX	Pprwgt-Geometric 7432NR57002N	Retrd.	1991	75.00	100-175
XX	Pprwgt-Octron-Crystal Cal 7456NR41	Retrd.	1992	75.00	120-160
XX	Pprwgt-Octron-Vitrl Med 7456NR41087	Retrd.	1992	75.00	120-175
XX	Pprwgt-One Ton 7495NR65	Retrd.	1991	75.00	100-175
XX	Pprwgt-Rd.-Berm Blue 7404NR30MM	Retrd.	N/A	15.00	200-400
XX	Pprwgt-Rd.-Berm Blue 7404NR40MM	Retrd.	N/A	20.00	200-400
XX	Pprwgt-Rd.-Berm Blue 7404NR50MM	Retrd.	N/A	40.00	300-500
XX	Pprwgt-Rd.-Crystal Cal 7404NR30095/30MM	Retrd.	1989	15.00	75
XX	Pprwgt-Rd.-Crystal Cal 7404NR40095/40MM	Retrd.	1989	20.00	50-95
XX	Pprwgt-Rd.-Crystal Cal 7404NR50095/50MM	Retrd.	1989	40.00	200
XX	Pprwgt-Rd.-Crystal Cal 7404NR60095/60MM	Retrd.	1989	50.00	250
XX	Pprwgt-Rd.-Green 7404NR30	Retrd.	N/A	15.00	200-400
XX	Pprwgt-Rd.-Green 7404NR40	Retrd.	N/A	20.00	200-400
XX	Pprwgt-Rd.-Green 7404NR50	Retrd.	N/A	40.00	300-500
XX	Pprwgt-Rd.-Sahara 7404NR30	Retrd.	1983	15.00	200-400
XX	Pprwgt-Rd.-Sahara 7404NR40	Retrd.	1982	20.00	200-400
XX	Pprwgt-Rd.-Sahara 7404NR50	Retrd.	1983	40.00	300-500
XX	Pprwgt-Rd.-Vitrl Med 7404NR30087/30MM	Retrd.	1989	15.00	75
XX	Pprwgt-Rd.-Vitrl Med 7404NR40087/40MM	Retrd.	1989	20.00	95
XX	Pprwgt-Rd.-Vitrl Med 7404NR50087/50MM	Retrd.	1989	40.00	200
XX	Pprwgt-Rd.-Vitrl Med 7404NR60087/60MM	Retrd.	1989	50.00	175-250
1987	Pyramid-Lg.-Crystal Cal 7450NR50095 - M. Schreck	Retrd.	1994	90.00	175-250
1987	Pyramid-Lg.-Vitrl Med 7450NR50087 - M. Schreck	Retrd.	1994	90.00	200-250
XX	Rabbit-Lg 7652NR45	Retrd.	1988	38.00	150-210
XX	Rabbit-Mini 7652NR20	Retrd.	1989	16.00	55-100
1988	Rabbit-Mini Lying 7678NR030000 - A. Stocker	Retrd.	1995	35.00	50
1988	Rhinoceros 7622NR70 A. Stocker	Retrd.	1993	70.00	100-125
1990	Rhinoceros-Sm 7622NR060000 A. Stocker	Retrd.	1995	70.00	75-90
XX	Salt and Pepper Shakers 7508NR068034	Retrd.	1989	80.00	200-350
XX	Schnapps Glasses, Set/6-7468NR039000	Retrd.	1991	150.00	225-300
1985	Seal-Large 7646NR085000 M. Schreck	Retrd.	1995	44.00	85-95
1992	Shepherd 7475NR000007	Retrd.	1994	65.00	75-125
1990	Silver Crystal City-Cathedral 7474NR000021 - G. Stamey	Retrd.	1995	95.00	120-130
1990	Silver Crystal City-Houses I& II (Set/2) 7474NR100000 G. Stamey	Retrd.	1995	75.00	75-100
1990	Silver Crystal City-Houses III & IV (Set/2) 7474NR200000 G. Stamey	Retrd.	1995	75.00	85-115
1990	Silver Crystal City-Poplars (Set/3) 7474NR020003 G. Stamey	Retrd.	1995	40.00	50-75
1986	Snail 7648NR030000 M. Stamey	Retrd.	1995	35.00	55
1991	South Sea Shell 7624NR72000 - M. Stamey	Retrd.	1995	110.00	120-135
XX	Sparrow-Lg 7650NR32	Retrd.	1988	38.00	120-150
1979	Sparrow-Mini 7650NR20 M. Schreck	Retrd.	1992	16.00	45-60
XX	Swan-Mini 7658NR27 M. Schreck	Retrd.	1989	16.00	100-130
XX	Table Magnifyer (no chain) 7510NR01G	Retrd.	1984	70.00	600-1100
XX	Table Magnifyer (no chain) 7510NR01R	Retrd.	1984	80.00	600-1100
1989	Toucan 7621NR000002 M. Stamey	Retrd.	1993	70.00	100-135
1993	Town Hall 7474NR000027 G. Stamey	Retrd.	1995	135.00	135-175
XX	Treasure Box (Heart/Butterfly)7465NR52/100	Retrd.	1991	80.00	175-200
XX	Treasure Box (Heart/Flower)7465NR52	Retrd.	1989	80.00	200-250
XX	Treasure Box (Oval/Butterfly)7466NR063100	Retrd.	1989	80.00	200-300
XX	Treasure Box (Oval/Flower) 7466NR063000	Retrd.	1991	80.00	150-250
XX	Treasure Box (Round/Butterfly) 7464NR50/100	Retrd.	1989	80.00	175-250
XX	Treasure Box (Round/Flower) 7464NR50	Retrd.	1991	80.00	150-250
XX	Turtle-King Size 7632NR75 M. Schreck	Retrd.	1988	58.00	200-240
XX	Vase 7511NR70	Retrd.	1991	50.00	175-225
1989	Walrus 7620NR100000 M. Stamey	Retrd.	1994	120.00	125-175
1988	Whale 7628NR80 - M. Stamey	Retrd.	1992	70.00	125-150
1992	Wise Men (Set/3) 7475NR200000	Retrd.	1994	175.00	185-250

Retired Candleholders - Various

YEAR ISSUE		EDITION LIMIT	YEAR RETD.	ISSUE PRICE	QUOTE U.S.$
XX	Candleholder 7600NR101	Retrd.	1982	23.00	100-200
XX	Candleholder 7600NR102	Retrd.	1987	35.00	100-125
XX	Candleholder 7600NR103	Retrd.	1988	40.00	110-175
XX	Candleholder 7600NR104	Retrd.	1988	95.00	200-300
XX	Candleholder 7600NR106	Retrd.	1986	85.00	265-400
XX	Candleholder 7600NR107	Retrd.	1986	100.00	270-400
XX	Candleholder 7600NR109	Retrd.	1986	37.00	110-200
XX	Candleholder 7600NR110	Retrd.	1987	40.00	120-160
XX	Candleholder 7600NR111	Retrd.	1986	100.00	275-400
XX	Candleholder 7600NR112	Retrd.	1986	75.00	300
XX	Candleholder 7600NR114	Retrd.	1986	37.00	150-225
XX	Candleholder 7600NR115	Retrd.	1987	185.00	400-450
XX	Candleholder 7600NR116	Retrd.	1986	350.00	1000-1200
XX	Candleholder 7600NR119	Retrd.	1989	N/A	500
XX	Candleholder 7600NR122	Retrd.	1988	85.00	180
XX	Candleholder 7600NR127	Retrd.	1987	65.00	270
XX	Candleholder 7600NR128	Retrd.	1987	100.00	200
XX	Candleholder 7600NR129	Retrd.	1987	120.00	265-300
XX	Candleholder 7600NR130	Retrd.	1986	275.00	850-1050
XX	Candleholder 7600NR131 (Set/6)	Retrd.	N/A	43.00	605-900
XX	Candleholder 7600NR138	Retrd.	1987	160.00	480-500
XX	Candleholder 7600NR139	Retrd.	1987	140.00	245-500
XX	Candleholder 7600NR140	Retrd.	1987	120.00	500-650
XX	Candleholder-Baroque 7600NR121	Retrd.	1987	150.00	350
XX	Candleholder-European Style 7600NR103	Retrd.	1991	N/A	750
XX	Candleholder-European Style 7600NR108	Retrd.	1990	N/A	400-500
XX	Candleholder-European Style 7600NR141	Retrd.	1991	N/A	750
XX	Candleholder-European Style 7600NR142	Retrd.	1990	N/A	550
XX	Candleholder-Global-Kg. Sz. 7600NR135	Retrd.	1989	50.00	200
XX	Candleholder-Global-Lg. 600NR134	Retrd.	1991	40.00	75-80
XX	Candleholder-Global-Med. (2) 7600NR133	Retrd.	1991	40.00	75-100
XX	Candleholder-Global-Sm. (4) 7600NR132	Retrd.	1990	60.00	115-250
1990	Candleholder-Neo-Classic-Lg. 7600NR144090 - A. Stocker	Retrd.	1993	220.00	400-550
1990	Candleholder-Neo-Classic-Med. 600NR144080 - A. Stocker	Retrd.	1993	190.00	350
1990	Candleholder-Neo-Classic-Sm. 7600NR144070 - A. Stocker	Retrd.	1993	170.00	300
XX	Candleholder-Pineapple 7600NR136G	Retrd.	1987	150.00	250-450
XX	Candleholder-Pineapple 7600NR136R	Retrd.	1987	150.00	300-600
XX	Candleholder-w/Flowers-Lg. 7600NR137	Retrd.	1991	150.00	400
XX	Candleholder-w/Flowers Sm. 7600NR120	Retrd.	1987	60.00	330
XX	Candleholder-w/Leaves-Sm. 7600NR126	Retrd.	1987	100.00	200-330

South Sea - Various

YEAR ISSUE		EDITION LIMIT	YEAR RETD.	ISSUE PRICE	QUOTE U.S.$
1987	Blowfish-Mini	Open		22.00	30
1986	Blowfish-Small	Open		35.00	55
1991	Butterfly Fish - M. Stamey	Open		150.00	175
1995	Conch - M. Stamey	Open		29.50	30
1995	Dolphin - M. Stamey	Open		210.00	210
1995	Maritime Trio (Shell, Starfish, Conch) - M. Stamey	Open		104.00	104
1988	Open Shell w/Pearl - M. Stamey	Open		120.00	175
1993	Sea Horse - M. Stamey	Open		85.00	85
1995	Shell - M. Stamey	Open		45.00	45
1995	Starfish - M. Stamey	Open		29.50	30
1993	Three South Sea Fish - M. Stamey	Open		135.00	140

Sparkling Fruit - Various

YEAR ISSUE		EDITION LIMIT	YEAR RETD.	ISSUE PRICE	QUOTE U.S.$
1991	Apple - M. Stamey	Open		175.00	185
1991	Pear - M. Stamey	Open		175.00	185
1981	Pineapple-Giant /Gold M. Schreck	Open		1750.00	3250
1981	Pineapple-Large /Gold M. Schreck	Open		150.00	260
1986	Pineapple-Small /Gold M. Schreck	Open		55.00	85

Swarovski Silver Crystal Worldwide Limited Editions - A. Stocker

YEAR ISSUE		EDITION LIMIT	YEAR RETD.	ISSUE PRICE	QUOTE U.S.$
1995	Eagle	10,000	1995	1750.00	4500-6000

When We Were Young - Various

YEAR ISSUE		EDITION LIMIT	YEAR RETD.	ISSUE PRICE	QUOTE U.S.$
1990	Airplane - A. Stocker	Open		135.00	155
1993	Kris Bear - M. Zendron	Open		75.00	75
1988	Locomotive - G. Stamey	Open		150.00	155
1990	Petrol Wagon - G. Stamey	Open		75.00	95
1994	Replica Cat	Open		37.50	38
1994	Replica Hedgehog	Open		37.50	38
1994	Replica Mouse	Open		37.50	38
1994	Sailboat - G. Stamey	Open		195.00	210
1991	Santa Maria - G. Stamey	Open		375.00	375
1994	Starter Set	Open		112.50	113
1988	Tender - G. Stamey	Open		55.00	55
1993	Tipping Wagon - G. Stamey	Open		95.00	95
1995	Train-Mini - G. Stamey	Open		125.00	125
1988	Wagon - G. Stamey	Open		85.00	95

Todays' Creations Inc.

Times to Remember - A. Gordon

YEAR ISSUE		EDITION LIMIT	YEAR RETD.	ISSUE PRICE	QUOTE U.S.$
1995	Bride with Bouquet	5,000		85.00	85
1995	Bride with Bouquet-white	5,000		70.00	70
1995	Daddy's Little Girl	5,000		95.00	95
1995	Daddy's Little Girl-musical	5,000		125.00	125
1995	Daddy's Little Girl-white	5,000		75.00	75
1995	Daddy's Little Girl-white-musical	5,000		115.00	115
1995	First Dance	5,000		95.00	95
1995	First Dance-musical	5,000		125.00	125
1995	First Dance-white	5,000		75.00	75
1995	First Dance-white-musical	5,000		115.00	115
1995	Mother and Bride	5,000		95.00	95
1995	Mother and Bride-white	5,000		75.00	75
1995	Slice of Life	5,000		100.00	100
1995	Slice of Life-white	5,000		80.00	80
1995	With This Ring	5,000		95.00	95
1995	With This Ring-white	5,000		75.00	75

The Tudor Mint Inc.

Arthurian Legend - M. Locker, unless otherwise noted

YEAR ISSUE		EDITION LIMIT	YEAR RETD.	ISSUE PRICE	QUOTE U.S.$
1990	3200 Merlin	Open		18.60	34
1990	3201 Into Merlin's Care Mold 1	Closed	N/A	25.40	250
1990	3201 Into Merlin's Care Mold 2	Closed	1993	25.40	95
1990	3202 Excaliber - M.L./R.G.	Open		18.60	34
1990	3203 Camelot	Open		25.40	42
1990	3204 King Arthur - M.L./R.G.	Open		18.60	34
1990	3205 Queen Guinevere	Open		18.60	34
1990	3206 Sir Percival & the Grail	Closed	1993	18.60	225
1990	3207 Morgan Le Fey	Open		25.40	42
1990	3208 Sir Lancelot	Open		25.40	42
1992	3209 Vigil of Sir Galahad A. Slocombe	Open		31.45	42
1992	3210 Sir Mordred - R. Gibbons	Open		23.70	34
1992	3211 Return of Excalibur	Open		23.70	34
1993	3212 Sir Gawain - A. Slocombe	Open		25.40	34
1993	3213 King Arthur/Sir Bedevere	Open		33.90	42

Dark Secrets - Various

YEAR ISSUE		EDITION LIMIT	YEAR RETD.	ISSUE PRICE	QUOTE U.S.$
1994	6201 Dark Secrets - A. Slocombe	Open		84.90	112
1994	6202 Guardian of the Skulls R. Gibbons	Open		30.18	40
1994	6203 The Skull Gateway M. Locker	Open		33.90	44
1994	6204 The Tortured Skull M. Locker	Open		33.90	44
1994	6205 The Serpent of the Skulls - S. Darnley	Open		33.90	44
1994	6206 The Altar of the Skulls M. Locker	Open		25.40	36
1994	6207 The Skull Master R. Gibbons	Open		33.90	44
1994	6208 The Vampire of the Skulls A. Slocombe	Open		25.40	36
1994	6209 The Chamber of the Skulls - A. Slocombe	Open		101.90	142
1994	6210 The Guardian of the Demons - M. Locker	Open		30.18	40
1994	6211 The Ice Demon S. Darnley	Open		25.40	36
1994	6212 The Demon of the Pit S. Darnley	Open		25.40	36
1994	6213 The Demon of the Night - M. Locker	Open		25.40	36
1994	6214 The Demon of the Catacombs - R. Gibbons	Open		25.40	36
1994	6215 The Demon Slayer M. Locker	Open		25.40	36
1994	6216 The Demon Jailer S. Darnley	Open		25.40	36
1994	6217 The Chamber of the Demons - A. Slocombe	Open		101.90	142
1994	6218 The Guardian of Skeletons - R. Gibbons	Open		30.51	42
1994	6219 The Vigil of the Skeleton R. Gibbons	Open		25.40	36

YEAR ISSUE		EDITION LIMIT	YEAR RETD.	ISSUE PRICE	QUOTE U.S.$
1994	6220 The Forgotten Skeleton R. Gibbons	Open		30.51	42
1994	6221 The Prisoners of the Sword - A. Slocombe	Open		30.51	42
1994	6222 The Executioner M. Locker	Open		30.51	42
1994	6223 The Finder of the Treasure - A. Slocombe	Open		25.40	36
1994	6224 The Skeleton Warrior S. Darnley	Open		30.51	42
1994	6225 The Chamber of Skeletons - A. Slocombe	Open		101.90	142

Dinosaur Collection - Various

YEAR ISSUE		EDITION LIMIT	YEAR RETD.	ISSUE PRICE	QUOTE U.S.$
1993	6001 Pteranodon - M. Locker	Closed	1994	25.40	70
1993	6002 Triceratops - A. Slocombe	Closed	1994	25.40	70
1993	6003 Stegosaurus A. Slocombe	Closed	1994	25.40	70
1993	6004 Brontosaurus - M. Locker	Closed	1994	25.40	70
1993	6005 Tyrannosaurus Rex A. Slocombe	Closed	1994	25.40	70
1993	6006 Spinosaurus - R. Gibbons	Closed	1994	25.40	70

Hobbit Collection - A. Slocombe, unless otherwise noted

YEAR ISSUE		EDITION LIMIT	YEAR RETD.	ISSUE PRICE	QUOTE U.S.$
1991	5001 Bilbo Baggins - R. Gibbons	Open		23.70	38
1991	5002 Gandalf	Open		42.41	64
1991	5003 Thorn Oakenshield R. Gibbons	Closed	1992	23.70	87
1991	5004 The Great Goblin R. Gibbons	Closed	1993	23.70	55
1991	5005 Gollum	Open		29.75	46
1991	5006 Beorn	Closed	1992	42.41	85
1991	5007 The Elven King	Closed	1992	29.75	85
1991	5008 Smaug the Dragon	Closed	1993	93.41	135
1991	5009 Bard - M. Locker	Closed	1992	23.70	87
1991	5010 'Good Morn.' at Bag End - R. Gibbons	Closed	1993	67.90	125
1991	5011 Moon Letters	Closed	1992	93.41	140-240
1991	5012 Finding the 'Precious' R. Gibbons	Closed	1992	67.90	165
1991	5013 The Capture of Bilbo	Closed	1992	67.90	150-200
1991	5014 'Riddles in the Dark'	Closed	1992	56.01	125-150
1991	5015 Escape From the Wargs - R. Gibbons	Closed	1992	67.90	150-200
1991	5016 Barrels Out of Bond M. Locker	Closed	1992	67.90	150-200
1991	5017 The 'Courage of the Bilbo'	Closed	1992	56.01	125-150
1991	5018 Prisoner of Elven King	Closed	1992	67.90	125-150
1991	5019 The Enchanted Door M. Locker	Closed	1992	93.41	260
1991	5020 The Wrath of Beorn - M. Locker	Closed	1992	67.90	185
1991	5021 Journey's End R. Gibbons	Closed	1993	67.90	150
1991	5022 The Troll's Clearing R. Gibbons	Closed	1992	251.51	600
1991	5023 Burglar Steals Smaug's	Closed	1993	254.91	400
1991	5024 Farewell, King Under Mt. - M. Locker	Closed	1992	254.91	500-600

Lord of the Rings - Various

YEAR ISSUE		EDITION LIMIT	YEAR RETD.	ISSUE PRICE	QUOTE U.S.$
1992	5025 Frodo Baggins R. Gibbons	Open		25.40	38
1992	5026 Bilbo's Tale - M. Locker	Open		25.40	38
1992	5027 Gimli the Dwarf M. Locker	Open		25.40	38
1992	5028 Sam Gamgee - R. Gibbons	Open		25.40	38
1992	5029 Aragorn (Strider) A. Slocombe	Open		25.40	38
1992	5030 An Orc - R. Gibbons	Closed	1994	30.51	55
1992	5031 Legolas the Elf A. Slocombe	Open		30.51	46
1992	5032 The Mirror of Galadriel R. Gibbons	Open		30.51	46
1992	5033 Saruman - A. Slocombe	Closed	1994	43.78	75
1992	5034 The Balrog - R. Gibbons	Open		67.90	100
1992	5035 Gandalf & Shadowfax M. Locker	Open		67.90	100
1992	5036 A Black Rider A. Slocombe	Open		67.90	100
1992	5037 Pippin - A. Slocombe	Closed	1994	25.40	48
1992	5038 Merry - A. Slocombe	Closed	1994	25.40	48
1992	5039 Boromir - R. Gibbons	Closed	1994	25.40	48
1992	5040 Treebeard (Fangorn) R. Gibbons	Closed	1994	43.78	70

Myth & Magic Club - Various

YEAR ISSUE		EDITION LIMIT	YEAR RETD.	ISSUE PRICE	QUOTE U.S.$
1990	9001 The Quest For the Truth R.G./M.L.	Closed	1991	84.90	600
1991	9002 The Game of Strax R. Gibbons	Closed	1991	25.40	550
1991	9003 The Well of Aspirations A. Slocombe	Closed	1992	84.90	500
1992	9004 Playmates - R. Gibbons	Closed	1992	28.80	260
1992	9005 Friends - A. Slocombe	Closed	1993	32.20	175
1992	9006 The Enchanted Pool R. Gibbons	Closed	1993	84.90	260
1993	9007 The Mystical Encounter A. Slocombe	Closed	1994	33.58	87
1994	9008 Keeper of the Dragons R. Gibbons	Closed	1994	84.90	125
1994	9009 The Crystal Shield M. Locker	Closed	1995	44.00	60
1994	9010 Battle for the Crystal A. Slocombe	Closed	1995	108.00	108
1995	9011 Starstruck - S. Darnley	Open		44.00	44
1990	CC01 The Protector R. Gibbons	Closed	1991	Gift	425
1991	CC02 The Jovial Wizard M. Locker	Closed	1992	Gift	270
1992	CC03 Dragon of Destiny R. Gibbons	Closed	1993	Gift	150-200
1993	CC04 Dragon of Methtintdour A. Slocombe	Closed	1994	Gift	80-140
1994	CC05 The Dreamy Dragon M. Locker	Closed	1995	Gift	N/A
1995	CC06 The Regal Dragon A. Slocombe	Open		Gift	N/A

Myth & Magic Extravaganza Study - Various

YEAR ISSUE		EDITION LIMIT	YEAR RETD.	ISSUE PRICE	QUOTE U.S.$
1992	3600 Sauria - A. Slocombe	Closed	1992	33.90	34
1993	3602 Deinos - R. Gibbons	Closed	1993	33.90	34
1994	3604 Lithia - M. Locker	Closed	1994	31.92	32
1995	3608 Imperia - S. Darnley	Closed	1995	41.25	42

Myth & Magic Large - Various

YEAR ISSUE		EDITION LIMIT	YEAR RETD.	ISSUE PRICE	QUOTE U.S.$
1990	3300 The Dragon Master R. Gibbons	7,500		297.50	404
1990	3301 The Magical Encounter R. Gibbons	Open		30.50	42
1990	3302 The Keeper of the Magic R. Gibbons	Closed	1995	59.40	108
1990	3303 Summoning the Elements R. Gibbons	Closed	1993	59.40	295
1990	3304 Sorceror's Apprentice R. Gibbons	Closed	1991	59.40	350
1990	3305 The Nest of Dragons M. Locker	Closed	1993	59.40	225
1990	3306 Meeting of the Unicorns M. Locker	Open		59.40	86
1990	3307 Sentinels at the Portal R. Gibbons	Closed	1991	59.40	350
1990	3308 The VII Seekers of Knowledge - M. Locker	7,500		297.50	404
1990	3309 Le Morte D'Arthur A. Slocombe	Open		84.90	122
1990	3310 The Magical Vision A. Slocombe	Closed	1995	84.90	153
1990	3311 The Dance of the Dolphins - R. Gibbons	1,537	1993	297.50	550
1991	3312 Altar of Enlightenment M. Locker	Open		84.90	122
1991	3313 Power of the Crystal A. Slocombe	3,500		595.00	595
1992	3314 The Awakening J. Pickering	Closed	1995	64.50	108
1992	3315 The Crystal Dragon A. Slocombe	Open		101.90	122
1992	3318 The Gathering of the Unicorns - A.S./R.G.	5,000		314.50	404
1993	3319 The Invocation - M. Locker	Closed	1995	84.90	153
1993	3320 The Fighting Dragons A. Slocombe	Open		67.90	86
1993	3321 The Playful Dolphins M. Locker	Open		56.95	68
1993	3322 The Dragon of Darkness A. Slocombe	Open		67.90	90
1994	3323 The Destroyer of the Crystal - S. Darnley	Open		84.90	114
1994	3324 A Tranquil Moment M. Locker	Open		84.90	114
1994	3325 Great Earth Dragon R. Gibbons	Open		101.90	136
1995	3326 The Great Sun Dragon - A. Slocombe	Open		136.00	136
1995	3327 The Great Moon Dragon R. Gibbons	Open		136.00	136
1995	3328 The Great Sea Dragon M. Locker	Open		136.00	136

Myth & Magic Miniatures - R. Gibbons, unless otherwise noted

YEAR ISSUE		EDITION LIMIT	YEAR RETD.	ISSUE PRICE	QUOTE U.S.$
1989	3500 The Incantation	Closed	1991	8.42	100
1989	3501 The Book of Spells R.G./M.L.	Closed	1995	8.42	19
1989	3502 The Enchanted Castle	Closed	1993	8.42	28
1989	3503 The Cauldron of Light M.L./R.G	Open		8.42	12
1989	3504 The Winged Serpent	Closed	1995	8.42	19
1989	3505 The White Witch R.G./M.L.	Closed	1991	8.42	83
1989	3506 The Master Wizard	Closed	1995	8.42	19
1989	3507 The Guardian Dragon	Open		8.42	12
1989	3508 The Unicorn	Open		8.42	12
1989	3509 Pegasus	Open		8.42	12
1989	3510 The Castle of Dreams	Closed	1993	8.42	38
1989	3511 The Light of Knowledge R.G./M.L.	Closed	1991	8.42	25-80
1990	3512 The Siren	Closed	1991	8.42	160
1990	3513 The Crystal Queen	Closed	1992	8.76	28-50
1990	3514 The Astronomer R.G./M.L.	Closed	1991	8.76	50-100
1990	3515 The Alchemist - R.G./M.L.	Closed	1991	8.76	50-100
1990	3516 The Minotaur	Closed	1991	8.76	150
1990	3517 The Grim Reaper R.G./M.L.	Closed	1995	8.76	19
1990	3518 The Castle of Souls	Closed	1993	8.76	41
1990	3519 The Dragon Gateway	Closed	1995	8.76	19
1990	3520 The Dragon Rider R.G./M.L.	Closed	1991	8.76	150
1990	3521 The Dragon's Kiss	Closed	1992	8.76	55
1990	3522 The Witch & Familiar	Closed	1991	8.76	240
1990	3523 The Oriental Dragon R.G./M.L.	Closed	1993	8.76	30
1990	3524 The Reborn Dragon	Open		8.76	12
1990	3525 The Fire Dragon R.G./M.L.	Closed	1994	8.76	28
1990	3526 The Giant Sorceror R.G./M.L.	Closed	1991	8.76	120
1990	3527 The Wizard of Light	Closed	1994	8.76	28
1990	3528 Keeper of the Treasure	Closed	1992	8.76	82
1990	3529 The Old Hag	Closed	1991	8.76	240
1991	3530 Mother Nature	Closed	1994	9.44	25
1991	3531 The Earth Wizard R.G./M.L.	Closed	1992	9.44	74
1991	3532 The Fire Wizard	Closed	1994	9.44	27
1991	3533 The Water Wizard	Closed	1992	9.44	14
1991	3534 The Air Wizard	Closed	1992	9.44	70
1991	3535 The Dragon of the Lake	Closed	1994	9.44	35
1991	3536 The Dragon's Spell R.G./M.L.	Closed	1991	9.44	14
1991	3537 Merlin - M. Locker	Open		9.44	12
1991	3538 Excalibur - M.L./R.G.	Closed	1993	9.44	25
1991	3539 Camelot - M. Locker	Open		9.44	12
1991	3540 King Arthur - M.L./R.G.	Open		9.44	12
1991	3541 Queen Guinevere M. Locker	Closed	1993	9.44	30
1992	3542 Dragon of the Forest	Closed	1995	10.11	18
1992	3543 Dragon of the Moon	Closed	1995	10.11	18
1992	3544 Wizard of Winter	Closed	1995	10.11	18
1992	3545 Dragon of Wisdom	Closed	1995	10.11	18
1992	3546 Dragon of the Sun - M. Locker	Closed	1995	10.11	18
1992	3547 Dragon of the Clouds M. Locker	Closed	1995	10.11	18
1993	3548 Moon Wizard A. Slocombe	Open		10.62	12
1993	3549 Unicorn of Light - A. Slocombe	Open		10.62	12
1993	3550 Return of Excalibur M. Locker	Closed	1994	10.62	25
1993	3551 Magical Encounter	Open		10.62	12
1993	3552 Ice Dragon - A. Slocombe	Closed	1995	10.62	18
1993	3553 Sleepy Dragon - M. Locker	Open		10.62	12
1994	3554 Keeper of the Skulls	Open		10.80	12
1994	3555 The Dark Dragon A. Slocombe	Open		10.80	12
1994	3556 Protector of the Young M.L./R.G.	Open		10.80	12
1994	3557 Dragon of Light - R.G./A.S.	Open		10.80	12
1994	3558 Unicorns of Freedom	Open		10.80	12
1994	3559 Defender of the Crystal	Open		10.80	12
1995	3560 The Loving Dragons - N/A	Open		12.00	12
1995	3561 The Wizard of the Lake N/A	Open		12.00	12
1995	3562 The Hatch Wings - N/A	Open		12.00	12
1995	3563 The Dragon of the Treasure - N/A	Open		12.00	12
1995	3564 The Armoured Dragon N/A	Open		12.00	12
1995	3565 The Sword Master - N/A	Open		12.00	12

Myth & Magic One Year Only Piece - Various

YEAR ISSUE		EDITION LIMIT	YEAR RETD.	ISSUE PRICE	QUOTE U.S.$
1993	OY93 The Flying Dragon A. Slocombe	Closed	1993	67.90	315
1994	OY94 Dragon of Underworld R. Gibbons	Closed	1994	70.55	250
1995	OY95 Guardian of the Crystal A. Slocombe	Closed	1995	84.90	135

Myth & Magic Promotion - Various

YEAR ISSUE		EDITION LIMIT	YEAR RETD.	ISSUE PRICE	QUOTE U.S.$
1993	3601 Dactrius - R.G./M.L./A.S.	Closed	1993	67.90	225-350
1994	3603 Vexius - A. Slocombe	Closed	1994	70.55	122
1995	3606 Viamphe - M. Locker	Closed	1995	73.42	45
1995	3607 Quargon - A. Slocombe	Closed	1995	26.32	27

Myth & Magic Standard - R. Gibbons, unless otherwise noted

YEAR ISSUE		EDITION LIMIT	YEAR RETD.	ISSUE PRICE	QUOTE U.S.$
1989	3001 The Incantation	Open		16.90	34
1989	3002 The Siren	Closed	1995	16.90	48
1989	3003 The Evil of Greed	Closed	1989	16.90	250
1989	3004 The Book of Spells M. Locker	Open		16.90	34
1989	3005 The Enchanted Castle	Closed	1991	16.90	75-125
1989	3006 The Cauldron of Light M.L./R.G.	Open		16.90	34
1989	3007 The Winged Serpent	Closed	1991	16.90	75-125
1989	3008 The White Witch M. Locker	Closed	1991	16.90	75-100
1989	3009 The Master Wizard	Closed	1993	16.90	50-75
1989	3010 The Infernal Demon	Closed	1989	16.90	220
1989	3011 The Warrior Knight Mold 1	Closed	N/A	16.90	500
1989	3011 The Warrior Knight Mold 2	Closed	1990	16.90	300
1989	3012 The Deadly Combat	Closed	1989	16.90	300
1989	3013 The Old Hag Mold 1	Closed	N/A	16.90	700
1989	3013 The Old Hag Mold 2	Closed	1990	16.90	350
1989	3014 The Crystal Queen	Closed	1993	16.90	75
1989	3015 The Astronomer M. Locker	Closed	1990	16.90	135
1989	3016 The Pipes of Pan	Closed	1990	16.90	175
1989	3017 Mischievous Goblin	Closed	1990	16.90	70-130
1989	3018 The Gorgon Medusa R.G./M.L.	Closed	1990	16.90	150
1989	3019 The Alchemist - M. Locker	Closed	1990	16.90	125
1989	3020 The Merman - M. Locker	Closed	1990	16.90	120
1989	3021 The Guardian Dragon	Closed	1995	16.90	34
1989	3022 The Minotaur	Closed	1991	16.90	175
1989	3023 The Grim Reaper	Open		16.90	34
1989	3024 The Unicorn	Open		16.90	34
1989	3027 The Castle of Souls	Closed	1995	22.00	55
1989	3028 The Dragon Gateway	Closed	1995	22.00	55
1989	3029 The Dragon Rider M. Locker	Closed	1995	16.90	48
1989	3030 The Dragon's Kiss Mold 1 M. Locker	Closed	N/A	16.90	160

YEAR ISSUE		EDITION LIMIT	YEAR RETD.	ISSUE PRICE	QUOTE U.S.$
1989	3030 The Dragon's Kiss Mold 2 M. Locker	Closed	1993	16.90	82
1989	3031 The Witch and Familiar	Closed	1990	16.90	240
1989	3032 The Oriental Dragon Mold 1 - M. Locker	Closed	N/A	16.90	600
1989	3032 The Oriental Dragon Mold 2 - M. Locker	Closed	N/A	16.90	480
1989	3032 The Oriental Dragon Mold 3 - M. Locker	Closed	1993	16.90	295
1989	3033 The Reborn Dragon	Open		16.90	34
1989	3034 The Fire Dragon M. Locker	Closed	1993	16.90	82
1989	3035 The Giant Sorceror	Closed	1993	16.90	82
1989	3036 The Wizard of Light	Open		16.90	34
1989	3037 The Light of Knowledge M. Locker	Closed	1991	16.90	165
1989	3038 Pegasus	Open		16.90	34
1990	3039 The Earth Wizard	Closed	1991	18.60	70-150
1990	3040 The Fire Wizard	Closed	1994	18.60	80
1990	3041 The Water Wizard	Closed	1991	18.60	70-150
1990	3042 The Air Wizard	Closed	1991	18.60	100-150
1990	3043 Mother Nature	Open		18.60	34
1990	3044 The Dragon of the Lake	Closed	1993	26.10	195
1990	3045 The Dragon's Spell	Closed	1992	18.60	100
1990	3046 The Keeper of the Treasure	Closed	1995	18.60	45
1990	3047 George & the Dragon	Closed	1990	18.60	525
1990	3048 Dragon of the Sea	Closed	1993	18.60	80
1990	3049 Dragon of the Forest	Closed	1994	18.65	70
1990	3050 Dragon of Wisdom	Open		18.60	34
1990	3051 Spirits of the Forest	Closed	1995	18.60	45
1990	3052 Virgin and Unicorn	Closed	1993	26.10	85
1991	3053 The Wizard of Autumn	Open		22.00	34
1991	3054 The Wizard of Winter	Open		22.00	34
1991	3055 The Wizard of Spring A. Slocombe	Closed	1995	22.00	45
1991	3056 The Wizard of Summer	Open		22.00	34
1991	3057 The Dragon of the Moon	Open		22.00	34
1991	3058 The Sun Dragon M. Locker	Open		22.00	34
1991	3059 Dragon of the Clouds M. Locker	Open		22.00	34
1991	3060 The Spirited Pegasus	Closed	1994	22.00	75
1991	3061 The Castle of Spires A. Slocombe	Closed	1993	29.75	75-125
1991	3062 The Castle in the Clouds A. Slocombe	Closed	1992	22.00	75
1991	3063 The Moon Wizard A. Slocombe	Open		22.00	34
1991	3064 Dragon of the Stars M. Locker	Closed	1995	29.75	45
1991	3065 The Sorceress of Light M. Locker	Closed	1994	22.00	40
1991	3066 The Jewelled Dragon A. Slocombe	Open		22.00	34
1991	3067 Old Father Time M. Locker	Closed	1993	29.75	110
1991	3068 Runelore	Open		29.75	42
1992	3069 The Fairy Queen A. Slocombe	Closed	1993	23.70	70
1992	3070 The Dragon Queen A. Slocombe	Open		32.20	42
1992	3071 The Ice Dragon A. Slocombe	Open		23.70	34
1992	3072 The Sleepy Dragon M. Locker	Open		23.70	34
1992	3073 Unicorn of Light A. Slocombe	Open		23.70	34
1992	3074 Starspell - M. Locker	Open		23.70	34
1992	3075 The Visionary	Open		32.20	42
1992	3076 The Crystal Spell M. Locker	Closed	1995	23.70	45
1992	3077 Unicorn Rider A. Slocombe	Open		23.70	34
1992	3078 The Loremaker A. Slocombe	Open		23.70	34
1992	3079 Dragon's Enchantress A. Slocombe	Closed	1994	32.20	45
1992	3080 The Leaf Spirit	Closed	1994	23.70	70
1992	3081 The Wizard of the Future	Open		23.70	34
1992	3082 The Swamp Dragon A. Slocombe	Open		23.70	34
1992	3083 The Dragon of the Skulls	Open		23.70	34
1992	3084 The Dark Dragon A. Slocombe	Open		23.70	34
1992	3085 The Dragon of Light R.G./A.S.	Open		23.70	34
1993	3092 The Fountain of Light A. Slocombe	Closed	1995	25.00	45
1993	3093 The Dawn of the Dragon- R. Gibbons	Open		25.00	34
1993	3094 The Dragon of Prehistory	Closed	1995	25.00	45
1993	3095 Defender of the Crystal A. Slocombe	Open		25.00	34
1993	3096 Rising of the Phoenix M. Locker	Closed	1995	25.00	48
1993	3097 The Protector of Young M. Locker	Open		25.00	34
1993	3098 The Unicorns of Freedom A. Slocombe	Open		25.00	34
1993	3099 The Keeper of the Skulls	Open		33.60	42
1993	3100 The Wizard of the Serpents - M. Locker	Open		25.00	34
1993	3101 The Loving Dragons M. Locker	Open		25.00	34
1993	3102 The Sword Master A. Slocombe	Open		25.00	34
1993	3103 Dragon of Mystery M. Locker	Open		25.00	34
1994	3104 The Wizard of the Skies M. Locker	Open		25.40	36
1994	3105 The Dragon of the Treasure - A. Slocombe	Open		25.40	36
1994	3106 The Wizard of the Lake	Open		25.40	36
1994	3107 Banishing the Dragon S. Darnley	Open		25.40	36
1994	3108 The Dragon's Castle	Open		25.40	44
1994	3109 The Mystical Traveller M. Locker	Open		25.40	36
1994	3110 The Armoured Dragon S. Darnley	Open		25.40	36
1994	3111 The Hatchlings S. Darnley	Open		25.40	36
1994	3112 Dragon of Ice Crystals A. Slocombe	Open		30.50	42
1994	3113 Mischievous Dragon S. Darnley	Open		25.40	36
1994	3114 The Crystal Unicorn S. Darnley	Open		30.50	42
1994	3115 Summoner of Light M. Locker	Open		30.50	42
1994	3116 The Majestic Dragon A. Slocombe	Open		30.50	42
1994	3117 The Proud Pegasus	Open		25.40	36
1995	3118 The Dragon Warrior S. Darnley	Open		40.00	42
1995	3119 The Crystal Serpent M. Locker	Open		54.00	54
1995	3120 The Dragon of the Deep M. Locker	Open		34.00	34
1995	3121 The Celtic Dragon A. Slocombe	Open		42.00	42
1995	3122 The Unicorn of Justice A. Slocombe	Open		34.00	34
1995	3123 The Dragon King M. Locker	Open		64.00	64
1995	3124 The Castle of Light	Open		34.00	34
1995	3125 The Dragon's Nest A. Slocombe	Open		42.00	42
1995	3126 The Mischievous Dragonets	Open		42.00	42
1995	3127 The Guardian of Light	Open		54.00	54
1995	3128 The Dragon Thief	Open		42.00	42
1995	3129 The Earth Dragon	Open		54.00	54
1995	3130 The Studious Dragon A. Slocombe	Open		42.00	42
1995	3131 Finding the Dragonets M. Locker	Open		34.00	34
1995	3132 Learning to Fly	Open		34.00	34
1995	3133 The Wizard's Best Friend	Open		34.00	34
1995	3134 Reflections - M. Locker	Open		42.00	42
1995	3135 The Lord of the Wizards A. Slocombe	Open		42.00	42
1995	3136 The Solar Dragon S. Darnley	Open		54.00	54
1995	3137 The Lunar Dragon	Open		54.00	54
1995	3138 Wizard Mountain	Open		28.00	28
1995	3139 The Crystal Chalice	Open		32.00	32
1995	3140 The Wizard's Scroll A. Slocombe	Open		28.00	28
1995	3141 The Magic Glade S. Darnley	Open		32.00	32
1995	3142 The Magic Staff M. Locker	Open		28.00	28
1995	3143 The Wrong Spell M. Locker	Open		32.00	32

United Design Corp.

Angels Collection - D. Newburn, unless otherwise noted

YEAR ISSUE		EDITION LIMIT	YEAR RETD.	ISSUE PRICE	QUOTE U.S.$
1993	Angel of Flight AA-032 K. Memoli	10,000		100.00	100
1993	Angel w/ Birds AA-034	10,000	1995	75.00	75
1994	Angel w/ Book AA-058	10,000		84.00	84
1994	Angel w/ Christ Child AA-061 K. Memoli	10,000		84.00	84
1993	Angel w/ Lillies, Crimson AA-040	10,000		80.00	80
1993	Angel w/ Lillies-033	10,000		80.00	80
1992	Angel, Lamb & Critters AA-021 S. Bradford	10,000		90.00	95
1992	Angel, Lion & Lamb AA-020 K. Memoli	10,000	1994	135.00	225-325
1994	Angel, Roses and Bluebirds AA-054	10,000		65.00	65
1993	Autumn Angel AA-035	10,000		70.00	70
1993	Autumn Angel, Emerald AA-041	10,000		70.00	70
1995	Celestial Guardian Angel AA-069 - S. Bradford	10,000		120.00	120
1991	Christmas Angel AA-003 S. Bradford	10,000	1994	125.00	125
1991	Classical Angel AA-005 S. Bradford	10,000		79.00	79
1994	Dreaming of Angels AA-060 K. Memoli	10,000		120.00	120
1994	Earth Angel AA-059 - S. Bradford	10,000		84.00	84
1992	The Gift '92 AA-018 S. Bradford	3,500	1992	140.00	275-400
1993	The Gift '93 AA-037 - S. Bradford	3,500	1993	120.00	200-350
1994	The Gift '94 AA-057	5,000	1994	140.00	175
1995	The Gift '95 AA-067	5,000		140.00	140
1991	The Gift AA-009 - S. Bradford	2,500	1991	135.00	490-600
1995	Guardian Angel, Lion & Lamb AA-083 - S. Bradford	10,000		165.00	165
1995	Guardian Angel, Lion & Lamb, lt. AA-068 - S. Bradford	10,000		165.00	165
1994	Harvest Angel AA-063 S. Bradford	10,000		84.00	84
1991	Heavenly Shepherdess AA-008 S. Bradford	10,000		99.00	99
1992	Joy To The World AA-016	10,000		90.00	95
1995	A Little Closer to Heaven AA-081 - K. Memoli	10,000		230.00	230
1995	A Little Closer to Heaven, lt. AA-085 - K. Memoli	10,000		230.00	230
1993	Madonna AA-031 - K. Memoli	10,000		100.00	100
1991	Messenger of Peace AA-006 S. Bradford	10,000		75.00	79
1992	Peaceful Encounter AA-017	10,000		100.00	100
1995	Starlight Starbright AA-066	10,000		70.00	70
1991	Trumpeter Angel AA-004 S. Bradford	10,000		99.00	99
1992	Winter Angel AA-019	10,000		75.00	75
1991	Winter Rose Angel AA-007 S. Bradford	10,000	1994	65.00	65

Backyard Birds - Various

YEAR ISSUE		EDITION LIMIT	YEAR RETD.	ISSUE PRICE	QUOTE U.S.$
1994	Allen's on Pink Flowers BB-044 P.J. Jonas	Open		22.00	22
1994	Allen's on Purple Morning Glory BB-051 - P.J. Jonas	Open		22.00	22
1989	Baltimore Oriole BB-024 S. Bradford	Open		19.50	22
1989	Blue Jay BB-026 - S. Bradford	Open		19.50	22
1989	Blue Jay, Baby BB-027 S. Bradford	Open		15.00	15
1990	Bluebird (Upright) BB-031 S. Bradford	Open		20.00	20
1988	Bluebird BB-009 - S. Bradford	Open		15.00	21
1988	Bluebird Hanging BB-017 S. Bradford	Retrd.	1990	11.00	17
1988	Bluebird, Small BB-001 S. Bradford	Open		10.00	11
1994	Broadbill on Blue Morning Glory BB-053 - P.J. Jonas	Open		22.00	22
1994	Broadbill on Trumpet Vine BB-043 - P.J. Jonas	Open		22.00	22
1994	Broadbill on Yellow Fuscia BB-055 - P.J. Jonas	Open		22.00	22
1994	Broadbill Pair on Yellow Flowers BB-048 - P.J. Jonas	Open		30.00	30
1988	Cardinal Hanging BB-018 S. Bradford	Retrd.	1990	11.00	11
1988	Cardinal, Female BB-011 S. Bradford	Open		15.00	17
1988	Cardinal, Male BB-013 S. Bradford	Open		15.00	18
1988	Cardinal, Small BB-002 S. Bradford	Open		10.00	11
1990	Cedar Waxwing Babies BB-033 S. Bradford	Open		22.00	22
1990	Cedar Waxwing BB-032 S. Bradford	Open		20.00	20
1988	Chickadee BB-010 - S. Bradford	Open		15.00	18
1988	Chickadee Hanging BB-019 S. Bradford	Retrd.	1990	11.00	11
1988	Chickadee, Small BB-003 S. Bradford	Open		10.00	11
1990	Evening Grosbeak BB-034 S. Bradford	Open		22.00	22
1989	Goldfinch BB-028 - S. Bradford	Open		16.50	20
1989	Hoot Owl BB-025 - S. Bradford	Open		15.00	20
1988	Humingbird BB-012 - S. Bradford	Open		15.00	18
1988	Hummingbird Female, Small BB-005 - S. Bradford	Retrd.	1991	10.00	10
1988	Hummingbird Flying, Small BB-004 - S. Bradford	Open		10.00	11
1988	Hummingbird Sm., Hanging BB-022 - S. Bradford	Retrd.	1990	11.00	11
1988	Hummingbird, Lg., Hanging BB-023 - S. Bradford	Retrd.	1990	15.00	15
1990	Indigo Bunting BB-036 S. Bradford	Open		20.00	20
1990	Indigo Bunting, Female BB-039 S. Bradford	Open		20.00	20
1994	Magnificent Pair on Trumpet VIne BB-046 - P.J. Jonas	Open		30.00	30
1990	Nuthatch, White-throated BB-037 - S. Bradford	Open		20.00	20
1990	Painted Bunting BB-040 S. Bradford	Open		20.00	20
1990	Painted Bunting, Female BB-041 S. Bradford	Open		20.00	20
1990	Purple Finch BB-038 S. Bradford	Open		20.00	20
1988	Red-winged Blackbird BB-014 S. Bradford	Retrd.	1991	15.00	17
1988	Robin Babies BB-008 S. Bradford	Open		15.00	19
1988	Robin Baby, Small BB-006 S. Bradford	Open		10.00	11
1988	Robin BB-015 - S. Bradford	Open		15.00	21
1988	Robin Hanging BB-020 S. Bradford	Retrd.	1990	11.00	11
1990	Rose Breasted Grosbeak BB-042 - S. Bradford	Open		20.00	20
1994	Rubythroat on Pink Fuscia BB-054 - P.J. Jonas	Open		22.00	22
1994	Rubythroat on Red Morning Glory BB-052 - P.J. Jonas	Open		22.00	22
1994	Rubythroat on Thistle BB-049 - P.J. Jonas	Open		16.50	17
1994	Rubythroat on Yellow Flowers BB-045 - P.J. Jonas	Open		22.00	22
1994	Rubythroat Pair on Pink Flowers BB-047 - P.J. Jonas	Open		30.00	30
1989	Saw-Whet Owl BB-029 S. Bradford	Open		15.00	18
1988	Sparrow BB-016 - S. Bradford	Open		15.00	17
1988	Sparrow Hanging BB-021 S. Bradford	Retrd.	1990	11.00	11
1988	Sparrow, Small BB-007 S. Bradford	Open		10.00	11
1989	Woodpecker BB-030 S. Bradford	Open		16.50	20

Easter Bunny Family - D. Kennicutt

YEAR ISSUE		EDITION LIMIT	YEAR RETD.	ISSUE PRICE	QUOTE U.S.$
1994	All Hidden SEC-045	Open		24.50	25
1989	Auntie Bunny SEC-008	Retrd.	1992	20.00	23
1992	Auntie Bunny w/Cake SEC-033R	Retrd.	1994	20.00	22
1991	Baby in Buggy, Boy SEC-027R	Retrd.	1994	20.00	22
1991	Baby in Buggy, Girl SEC-029R	Retrd.	1994	20.00	22
1994	Babysitter SEC-049	Open		24.50	25
1994	Bath Time SEC-044	Open		24.50	25
1995	Bed Time SEC-057	Open		24.00	24
1992	Boy Bunny w/Large Egg SEC-034R	Retrd.	1994	20.00	22
1991	Bubba In Wheelbarrow SEC-021	Retrd.	1993	20.00	20
1990	Bubba w/Wagon SEC-016	Retrd.	1993	16.50	18
1988	Bunnies, Basket Of SEC-001	Retrd.	1991	13.00	18
1991	Bunny Boy w/Basket SEC-025	Retrd.	1993	20.00	20
1988	Bunny Boy w/Duck SEC-002	Retrd.	1991	13.00	18
1988	Bunny Girl w/Hen SEC-004	Retrd.	1991	13.00	18
1989	Bunny w/Prize Egg SEC-010	Retrd.	1993	19.50	20
1988	Bunny, Easter SEC-003	Retrd.	1991	15.00	18
1993	Christening Day SEC-040	Retrd.	1995	20.00	22
1989	Ducky w/Bonnet, Blue SEC-015	Retrd.	1992	10.00	12
1989	Ducky w/Bonnet, Pink SEC-014	Retrd.	1992	10.00	12
1992	Easter Bunny w/Back Pack SEC-030	Open		20.00	22
1990	Easter Bunny w/Crystal SEC-017	Retrd.	1995	23.00	25
1993	Easter Bunny, Chocolate Egg SEC-041	Open		23.00	25
1995	Easter Cookies SEC-052	Open		24.00	24
1989	Easter Egg Hunt SEC-012	Retrd.	1995	16.50	22
1993	Egg Roll SEC-036	Open		23.00	25
1991	Fancy Find SEC-028	Retrd.	1995	20.00	22
1995	First Outing SEC-054	Open		19.00	19
1994	First Steps SEC-048	Open		24.50	25
1994	Gift Carrot SEC-046	Open		22.00	22
1993	Girl Bunny w/Basket SEC-039	Open		20.00	22
1992	Girl Bunny w/Large Egg SEC-035R	Retrd.	1994	20.00	22
1993	Grandma & Quilt SEC-037	Open		23.00	25
1992	Grandma w/ Bible SEC-031	Open		20.00	22
1992	Grandpa w/Carrots SEC-032R	Retrd.	1994	20.00	22
1990	Hen w/Chick SEC-018	Retrd.	1992	23.00	23
1994	Large Prize Egg SEC-047	Open		22.00	22
1989	Little Sis w/Lolly SEC-009	Retrd.	1992	14.50	18
1993	Lop Ear Dying Eggs SEC-042	Open		23.00	25
1991	Lop-Ear w/Crystal SEC-022	Open		23.00	25
1993	Mom Storytime SEC-043	Open		20.00	22
1990	Momma Making Basket SEC-019	Retrd.	1992	23.00	23
1990	Mother Goose SEC-020	Retrd.	1992	16.50	20
1991	Nest of Bunny Eggs SEC-023	Open		17.50	22
1995	Printing Lessons SEC-053	Open		19.00	19
1995	Quality Inspection SEC-055	Open		19.00	19
1988	Rabbit, Grandma SEC-005	Retrd.	1991	15.00	20
1988	Rabbit, Grandpa SEC-006	Retrd.	1991	15.00	20
1988	Rabbit, Momma w/Bonnet SEC-007	Retrd.	1991	15.00	20
1989	Rock-A-Bye Bunny SEC-013	Retrd.	1995	20.00	25
1993	Rocking Horse SEC-038	Open		20.00	22
1989	Sis & Bubba Sharing SEC-011	Open		22.50	25
1995	Spring Flying SEC-058	Open		19.00	19
1995	Team Work SEC-051	Open		24.00	24
1995	Two in a Basket SEC-056	Open		24.00	24
1991	Victorian Auntie Bunny SEC-026	Retrd.	1993	20.00	20
1991	Victorian Momma SEC-024	Retrd.	1993	20.00	20
1994	Wheelbarrow SEC-050	Open		24.50	25

Easter Bunny Family Babies - D. Kennicutt

YEAR ISSUE		EDITION LIMIT	YEAR RETD.	ISSUE PRICE	QUOTE U.S.$
1995	Baby in Basket SEC-815	Open		8.00	8
1994	Baby on Blanket, Naptime SEC-807	Open		6.50	7
1995	Basket of Carrots SEC-812	Open		8.00	8
1994	Boy Baby with Blocks SEC-805	Open		6.50	7
1995	Boy w/Butterfly SEC-814	Open		8.00	8
1994	Boy with Baseball Bat SEC-801	Open		6.50	7
1994	Boy with Basket and Egg SEC-802	Open		6.50	7
1994	Boy with Stick Horse SEC-803	Open		6.50	7
1995	Gift Egg SEC-808	Open		8.00	8
1994	Girl with Big Egg SEC-806	Open		6.50	7
1994	Girl with Blanket SEC-800	Open		6.50	7
1994	Girl with Toy Rabbit SEC-804	Open		6.50	7
1995	Hostess SEC-810	Open		8.00	8
1995	Lop Ear & Flower Pot SEC-809	Open		8.00	8
1995	Spring Flowers SEC-813	Open		8.00	8
1995	Tea Party SEC-811	Open		8.00	8

Easter Bunny Family Miniatures - Various

YEAR ISSUE		EDITION LIMIT	YEAR RETD.	ISSUE PRICE	QUOTE U.S.$
1994	Auntie Bunny mini SEC-525 D. Newburn	Open		8.50	9
1993	Baby Boy with Pail SEC-512 D. Newburn	Open		8.50	9
1993	Baby Girl with Bunny SEC-513 D. Newburn	Open		7.50	8
1993	Baby in Cradle SEC-515 P.J. Jonas	Open		7.50	8
1993	Basket of Bunnies mini SEC-504 P.J. Jonas	Open		7.50	8
1993	Boy Bunny with Blocks SEC-506 P.J. Jonas	Open		8.50	9
1993	Bubba with Goose mini SEC-505 - D. Newburn	Open		7.50	8
1994	Bunny and Goose Reading SEC-516 - P.J. Jonas	Open		8.50	9
1993	Bunny under Bonnet SEC-500 P.J. Jonas	Open		7.50	8
1994	Bunny with Toy Cow SEC-527 P.J. Jonas	Open		7.50	8
1994	Easter Bonnet (Lop Ear) SEC-523 - D. Newburn	Open		7.50	8
1993	Easter Bunny mini SEC-510 D. Newburn	Open		8.50	9
1993	Girl Bunny with Carrots SEC-501 - P.J. Jonas	Open		8.50	9
1993	Girl Bunny with Hen mini SEC-502 - P.J. Jonas	Open		7.50	8
1993	Grandma Rabbit mini SEC-507 P.J. Jonas	Open		8.50	9
1993	Grandpa Rabbit mini SEC-508 P.J. Jonas	Open		8.50	9
1993	Lilly mini SEC-514 - D. Newburn	Open		7.50	8
1994	Little Lop Artist SEC-520 D. Newburn	Open		8.50	9
1994	Little Sis with Lolly mini SEC-519 - D. Newburn	Open		8.50	9
1993	Lop Ear and Paint Bucket SEC-503 - D. Newburn	Open		8.50	9
1994	Lop Ear Boy with Wagon SEC-526 - D. Newburn	Open		7.50	8
1993	Lop Ear Girl with Egg SEC-509 D. Newburn	Open		7.50	8
1994	Mini Momma with Basket SEC-517 - P.J. Jonas	Open		8.50	9
1994	Mini Prize Egg SEC-524 P.J. Jonas	Open		7.50	8
1993	Momma Rabbit mini SEC-511 D. Newburn	Open		8.50	9
1994	Spring Showers SEC-522 P.J. Jonas	Open		8.50	9
1994	Victorian Auntie Bunny mini SEC-521 - P.J. Jonas	Open		7.50	8
1994	Victorian Momma Bunny mini SEC-518 - D. Newburn	Open		8.50	9

Legend of Santa Claus - L. Miller, unless otherwise noted

YEAR ISSUE		EDITION LIMIT	YEAR RETD.	ISSUE PRICE	QUOTE U.S.$
1992	Arctic Santa CF-035 S. Bradford	7,500		90.00	100-140
1988	Assembly Required CF-017	7,500	1994	79.00	119
1991	Blessed Flight CF-032 K. Memoli	7,500	1994	159.00	225-525
1987	Checking His List CF-009	15,000	1994	75.00	120
1989	Christmas Harmony CF-020 S. Bradford	7,500	1992	85.00	130
1992	The Christmas Tree CF-038	7,500	1995	90.00	90
1993	Dear Santa CF-046 - K. Memoli	7,500		170.00	170
1995	Dear Santa, Vict. CF-063	10,000		170.00	170
1987	Dreaming Of Santa CF-008 S. Bradford	15,000	1988	65.00	325
1992	Earth Home Santa CF-040 S. Bradford	7,500		135.00	140
1986	Elf Pair CF-005	10,000	1992	60.00	130
1988	Father Christmas CF-018 S. Bradford	7,500	1993	75.00	110
1991	For Santa CF-029	7,500		99.00	135
1990	Forest Friends CF-025	7,500	1993	90.00	110
1995	Getting Santa Ready CF-056	10,000		170.00	170
1989	Hitching Up CF-021	7,500	1993	90.00	100
1995	Into the Wind CF-061	10,000		140.00	140
1995	Into the Wind, Vict. CF-062	10,000		140.00	140
1993	Jolly St. Nick CF-045 - K. Memoli	7,500		130.00	130
1993	Jolly St. Nick, Victorian CF-050 K. Memoli	7,500		120.00	120
1986	Kris Kringle CF-002	10,000	1991	60.00	175
1992	Letters to Santa CF-036	7,500	1995	125.00	130
1988	Load 'Em Up CF-016 S. Bradford	7,500	1990	79.00	350
1987	Loading Santa's Sleigh CF-010	15,000	1993	100.00	110
1992	Loads of Happiness CF-041 K. Memoli	7,500		100.00	110
1994	Long Stocking Dilemma, Victorian CF-055 - K. Memoli	7,500		170.00	170
1994	Longstocking Dilemma CF-052 K. Memoli	7,500		170.00	170
1987	Mrs. Santa CF-006 - S. Bradford	15,000	1991	60.00	195
1993	The Night Before Christmas CF-043	7,500		100.00	100
1993	Northwoods Santa CF-047 S. Bradford	7,500		100.00	100
1987	On Santa's Knee-CF007 S. Bradford	15,000	1994	65.00	110
1990	Puppy Love CF-024	7,500	1994	100.00	130
1989	A Purrr-Fect Christmas CF-019 S. Bradford	7,500	1994	95.00	130
1991	Reindeer Walk CF-031 K. Memoli	7,500		150.00	165
1995	The Ride CF-057	10,000		130.00	130
1986	Rooftop Santa CF-004 S. Bradford	10,000	1991	65.00	170
1990	Safe Arrival CF-027 Memoli/Jonas	7,500		150.00	175
1992	Santa and Comet CF-037	7,500	1995	110.00	110
1992	Santa and Mrs. Claus CF-039 K. Memoli	7,500		150.00	150
1992	Santa and Mrs. Claus, Victorian CF-042 - K. Memoli	7,500		135.00	140
1986	Santa At Rest CF-001	10,000	1988	70.00	600
1991	Santa At Work CF-030	7,500	1995	99.00	110
1987	Santa On Horseback CF-011 S. Bradford	15,000	1990	75.00	295
1994	Santa Riding Dove CF-053	7,500		120.00	120
1986	Santa With Pups CF-003 S. Bradford	10,000	1988	65.00	570
1993	Santa's Friends CF-044	7,500		100.00	100
1995	Santa, Dusk & Dawn CF-060	10,000		150.00	150
1988	St. Nicholas CF-015	7,500	1992	75.00	135
1994	Star Santa w/ Polar Bear CF-054 - S. Bradford	7,500		130.00	130
1995	Starlight Express CF-059	10,000		170.00	170
1994	The Story of Christmas CF-051 K. Memoli	10,000		180.00	180
1993	Victorian Lion & Lamb Santa CF-048 - S. Bradford	7,500		100.00	100
1990	Victorian Santa CF-028 S. Bradford	7,500	1992	125.00	250-450
1991	Victorian Santa w/ Teddy CF-033 - S. Bradford	7,500		150.00	160
1990	Waiting For Santa CF-026 S. Bradford	7,500	1995	100.00	130

Legend Of The Little People - L. Miller

YEAR ISSUE		EDITION LIMIT	YEAR RETD.	ISSUE PRICE	QUOTE U.S.$
1989	Adventure Bound LL-002	Retrd.	1993	35.00	50
1989	Caddy's Helper LL-007	Retrd.	1993	35.00	50
1991	The Easter Bunny's Cart LL-020	Retrd.	1994	45.00	50
1991	Fire it Up LL-023	Retrd.	1994	50.00	55
1990	Fishin' Hole LL-012	Retrd.	1994	35.00	50
1989	A Friendly Toast LL-003	Retrd.	1993	35.00	50
1990	Gathering Acorns LL-014	Retrd.	1994	100.00	100
1991	Got It LL-021	Retrd.	1994	45.00	50
1990	Hedgehog In Harness LL-010	Retrd.	1994	45.00	50
1990	Husking Acorns LL-008	Retrd.	1994	60.00	65
1991	It's About Time LL-022	Retrd.	1994	55.00	60
1990	A Little Jig LL-018	Retrd.	1994	45.00	50
1990	A Look Through The Spyglass LL-015	Retrd.	1994	40.00	50
1989	Magical Discovery LL-005	Retrd.	1993	45.00	50
1990	Ministral Magic LL-017	Retrd.	1994	45.00	50
1990	A Proclamation LL-013	Retrd.	1994	45.00	55
1989	Spring Water Scrub LL-006	Retrd.	1993	35.00	50
1990	Traveling Fast LL-009	Retrd.	1994	45.00	50
1989	Treasure Hunt LL-004	Retrd.	1993	45.00	50
1991	Viking LL-019	Retrd.	1994	45.00	50
1989	Woodland Cache LL-001	Retrd.	1993	35.00	50
1990	Woodland Scout LL-011	Retrd.	1994	40.00	50
1990	Writing The Legend LL-016	Retrd.	1994	35.00	65

Lil' Dolls - Various

YEAR ISSUE		EDITION LIMIT	YEAR RETD.	ISSUE PRICE	QUOTE U.S.$
1992	Clara & The Nutcracker LD-017 D. Newburn	Retrd.	1994	35.00	35
1991	The Nutcracker LD-006 P.J. Jonas	Retrd.	1994	35.00	35

Music Makers - Various

YEAR ISSUE		EDITION LIMIT	YEAR RETD.	ISSUE PRICE	QUOTE U.S.$
1991	A Christmas Gift MM-015 D. Kennicutt	Retrd.	1993	59.00	59
1991	Crystal Angel MM-017 D. Kennicutt	Retrd.	1993	59.00	59
1991	Dashing Through The Snow MM-013 - D. Kennicutt	Retrd.	1993	59.00	59
1989	Evening Carolers MM-005 D. Kennicutt	Retrd.	1993	69.00	69
1989	Herald Angel MM-011 S. Bradford	Retrd.	1993	79.00	79
1991	Nutcracker MM-024 - P.J. Jonas	Retrd.	1994	69.00	69
1991	Peace Descending MM-025 P.J. Jonas	Retrd.	1993	69.00	69
1991	Renaissance Angel MM-028 P.J. Jonas	Retrd.	1994	69.00	69
1989	Santa's Sleigh MM-004 - L. Miller	Retrd.	1993	69.00	69
1991	Teddy Bear Band #2 MM-023 D. Kennicutt	Retrd.	1994	90.00	90
1989	Teddy Bear Band MM-012 S. Bradford	Retrd.	1993	99.00	100
1989	Teddy Drummers MM-009 D. Kennicutt	Retrd.	1993	69.00	69
1991	Teddy Soldiers MM-018 D. Kennicutt	Retrd.	1994	69.00	84
1991	Victorian Santa MM-026 L. Miller	Retrd.	1993	69.00	69

Party Animals™ - L. Miller, unless otherwise noted

YEAR ISSUE		EDITION LIMIT	YEAR RETD.	ISSUE PRICE	QUOTE U.S.$
1992	Democratic Donkey ('92) K. Memoli	Retrd.	1994	20.00	20
1984	Democratic Donkey ('84) D. Kennicutt	Retrd.	1986	14.50	16
1986	Democratic Donkey ('86)	Retrd.	1988	14.50	15
1988	Democratic Donkey ('88)	Retrd.	1990	14.50	16
1990	Democratic Donkey ('90) D. Kennicutt	Retrd.	1992	16.00	16
1984	GOP Elephant ('84)	Retrd.	1986	14.50	16
1986	GOP Elephant ('86)	Retrd.	1988	14.50	15
1988	GOP Elephant ('88)	Retrd.	1990	14.50	16
1990	GOP Elephant ('90) - D. Kennicutt	Retrd.	1992	16.00	16
1992	GOP Elephant ('92) - K. Memoli	Retrd.	1994	20.00	20

PenniBears™ - P.J. Jonas

YEAR ISSUE		EDITION LIMIT	YEAR RETD.	ISSUE PRICE	QUOTE U.S.$
1992	After Every Meal PB-058	Retrd.	1994	22.00	22
1992	Apple For Teacher PB-069	Retrd.	1994	24.00	24
1989	Attic Fun PB-019	Retrd.	1992	20.00	40
1989	Baby Hugs PB-007	Retrd.	1992	20.00	35
1991	Baking Goodies PB-043	Retrd.	1993	26.00	30
1989	Bathtime Buddies PB-023	Retrd.	1992	20.00	25
1992	Batter Up PB-066	Retrd.	1994	22.00	22
1991	Bear Footin' it PB-037	Retrd.	1993	24.00	24
1992	Bear-Capade PB-073	Retrd.	1994	22.00	22
1991	Bearly Awake PB-033	Retrd.	1993	22.00	25
1989	Beautiful Bride PB-004	Retrd.	1992	20.00	35
1993	Big Chief Little Bear PB-088	12/95		28.00	28
1989	Birthday Bear PB-018	Retrd.	1992	20.00	40
1991	Boo Hoo Bear PB-050	Retrd.	1994	22.00	22
1990	Boooo Bear PB-025	Retrd.	1993	20.00	22
1991	Bountiful Harvest PB-045	Retrd.	1994	24.00	24

YEAR ISSUE		EDITION LIMIT	YEAR RETD.	ISSUE PRICE	QUOTE U.S.$
1989	Bouquet Boy PB-003	Retrd.	1992	20.00	45
1989	Bouquet Girl PB-001	Retrd.	1992	20.00	45
1991	Bump-bear-Crop PB-035	Retrd.	1993	26.00	30
1991	Bunny Buddies PB-042	Retrd.	1993	22.00	25
1989	Butterfly Bear PB-005	Retrd.	1992	20.00	45-50
1990	Buttons & Bows PB-012	Retrd.	1992	20.00	45
1992	Christmas Cookies PB-075	Retrd.	1994	22.00	22
1991	Christmas Reinbear PB-046	Retrd.	1994	28.00	28
1992	Cinderella PB-056	Retrd.	1994	22.00	22
1992	Clowning Around PB-065	Retrd.	1994	22.00	22
1989	Cookie Bandit PB-006	Retrd.	1992	20.00	30
1990	Count Bearacula PB-027	Retrd.	1993	22.00	24
1991	Country Lullabye PB-036	Retrd.	1993	24.00	25
1990	Country Quilter PB-030	Retrd.	1993	22.00	30
1990	Country Spring PB-013	Retrd.	1992	20.00	45
1991	Curtain Call PB-049	Retrd.	1994	24.00	24
1992	Decorating The Wreath PB-076	Retrd.	1994	22.00	22
1989	Doctor Bear PB-008	Retrd.	1992	20.00	30
1992	Downhill Thrills PB-070	Retrd.	1994	24.00	24
1990	Dress Up Fun PB-028	Retrd.	1993	22.00	30
1992	Dust Bunny Roundup PB-062	Retrd.	1994	22.00	22
1992	First Prom PB-064	Retrd.	1994	22.00	22
1990	Garden Path PB-014	Retrd.	1992	20.00	45-50
1993	Getting 'Round On My Own PB-085	12/95		26.00	26
1990	Giddiap Teddy PB-011	Retrd.	1992	20.00	35
1991	Goodnight Little Prince PB-041	Retrd.	1993	26.00	30
1991	Goodnight Sweet Princess PB-040	Retrd.	1993	26.00	30
1993	Gotta Try Again PB-082	12/95		24.00	24
1989	Handsome Groom PB-015	Retrd.	1992	20.00	40
1993	Happy Birthday PB-084	12/95		26.00	26
1993	A Happy Camper PB-077	12/95		28.00	28
1991	Happy Hobo PB-051	Retrd.	1994	26.00	26
1989	Honey Bear PB-002	Retrd.	1992	20.00	45
1992	I Made It Boy PB-061	Retrd.	1994	22.00	22
1992	I Made It Girl PB-060	Retrd.	1994	22.00	22
1989	Lazy Days PB-009	Retrd.	1992	20.00	25
1992	Lil' Devil PB-071	Retrd.	1994	24.00	24
1991	Lil' Mer-teddy PB-034	Retrd.	1993	24.00	24
1992	Lil' Sis Makes Up PB-074	Retrd.	1994	22.00	22
1993	Little Bear Peep PB-083	12/95		24.00	24
1993	Making It Better PB-087	12/95		24.00	24
1993	May Joy Be Yours PB-080	12/95		24.00	24
1993	My Forever Love PB-078	12/95		28.00	28
1989	Nap Time PB-016	Retrd.	1992	20.00	22
1989	Nurse Bear PB-017	Retrd.	1992	20.00	35
1992	On Your Toes PB-068	Retrd.	1994	24.00	24
1989	Petite Mademoiselle PB-010	Retrd.	1992	20.00	40
1991	Pilgrim Provider PB-047	Retrd.	1994	32.00	32
1992	Pot O' Gold PB-059	Retrd.	1994	22.00	22
1992	Puddle Jumper PB-057	Retrd.	1994	24.00	24
1989	Puppy Bath PB-020	Retrd.	1992	20.00	25
1989	Puppy Love PB-021	Retrd.	1992	20.00	25
1993	Rest Stop PB-079	12/95		24.00	24
1992	Sandbox Fun PB-063	Retrd.	1994	22.00	22
1990	Santa Bear-ing Gifts PB-031	Retrd.	1993	24.00	30
1993	Santa's Helper PB-081	12/95		28.00	28
1990	Scarecrow Teddy PB-029	Retrd.	1993	24.00	25
1992	Smokey's Nephew PB-055	Retrd.	1994	22.00	22
1990	Sneaky Snowball PB-026	Retrd.	1993	20.00	25
1989	Southern Belle PB-024	Retrd.	1992	20.00	35
1992	Spanish Rose PB-053	Retrd.	1994	24.00	24
1990	Stocking Surprise PB-032	Retrd.	1993	22.00	26
1993	Summer Belle PB-086	12/95		24.00	24
1991	Summer Sailing PB-039	Retrd.	1993	26.00	30
1991	Sweet Lil 'Sis PB-048	Retrd.	1994	22.00	22
1991	Sweetheart Bears PB-044	Retrd.	1993	28.00	30
1992	Tally Ho! PB-054	Retrd.	1994	22.00	22
1992	Touchdown PB-072	Retrd.	1994	22.00	22
1989	Tubby Teddy PB-022	Retrd.	1992	20.00	22
1991	A Wild Ride PB-052	Retrd.	1994	26.00	26
1992	Will You Be Mine? PB-067	Retrd.	1994	22.00	22
1991	Windy Day PB-038	Retrd.	1993	24.00	24

PenniBears™ Collector's Club Members Only Editions - P.J. Jonas

1990	1990 First Collection PB-C90	Retrd.	1990	26.00	125
1991	1991 Collecting Makes Cents PB-C91	Retrd.	1991	26.00	75
1992	1992 Today's Pleasures, Tomorrow's Treasures PB-C92	Retrd.	1992	26.00	100
1993	1993 Chalkin Up Another Year PB-C93	Retrd.	1993	26.00	35
1994	1994 Artist's Touch-Collector's Treasure PB-C94	Retrd.	1994	26.00	26

Storytime Rhymes & Tales - H. Henriksen

1991	Humpty Dumpty SL-008	Retrd.	1993	64.00	64
1991	Little Jack Horner SL-007	Retrd.	1993	50.00	50
1991	Little Miss Muffet SL-006	Retrd.	1993	64.00	64
1991	Mistress Mary SL-002	Retrd.	1993	64.00	64
1991	Mother Goose SL-001	Retrd.	1993	64.00	64
1991	Owl & Pussy Cat SL-004	Retrd.	1993	100.00	100
1991	Simple Simon SL-003	Retrd.	1993	90.00	90
1991	Three Little Pigs SL-005	Retrd.	1993	100.00	100

VickiLane

Collector Club Series - V. Anderson

1993	Sweet Secrets	Retrd.	1994	30.00	30
1994	Take Me Home-Little Miss April	Retrd.	1995	28.00	28
1995	Hopping Forward	Yr.Iss.		28.00	28

Mice Memories - V. Anderson

1990	Happiness Together	1,000		65.00	73
1990	Mouse on the Beach	Retrd.	1993	28.00	28

Sweet Thumpins - V. Anderson

1995	"Fore You" Boy Golfer Bunny	Open		22.00	22
1995	"I Gotch Ya" Cowboy Bunny	Open		24.00	24
1995	"Sneaking Up on You" Indian Bunny	Open		24.00	24
1995	"What a Hit" Girl Golfer Bunny	Open		22.00	22
1995	Bride and Groom Bunny	Open		20.00	20
1986	Bunnies in Frilly Dress with Pillows	Retrd.	1994	22.00	22
1987	Bunny Sleeping in a Basket	Retrd.	1993	18.00	18
1993	Bunny Throwing Snowball	Retrd.	1994	31.00	31
1988	Bunny with Christmas Wreath	Retrd.	1994	19.00	19
1992	Cookie Peddler	750		90.00	90
1988	Farmer Bunny with Carrots	Retrd.	1993	18.00	18
1995	Flower Girl Bunny	Open		16.00	16
1988	Girl Bunny with a Hat and Doll	Retrd.	1993	18.00	18
1990	Just For You, Girl Bunny with Carrot	Retrd.	1994	29.00	29
1990	Making Memories	1,000		70.00	73
1995	Minister Bunny	Open		16.00	16
1995	Ring Bearer Bunny	Open		16.00	16
1995	Summer Daze	500		85.00	85
1990	Tea Time	1,000		79.00	82
1990	Venture into Sweet Thumpins	Retrd.	1993	60.00	73
1995	Wedding Family on Pew	Open		24.00	24

Time For Teddy - V. Anderson

1983	Bear Holding His Foot	Retrd.	1993	14.00	14
1989	Boy Teddy Building Sandcastles	Retrd.	1993	17.00	17
1989	Girl Teddy Sunbathing	Retrd.	1993	18.00	18
1984	Sailor Bear	Retrd.	1994	17.00	17
1986	Sailor Bear with Duck	Retrd.	1994	16.00	16
1985	Teddy Bear with a Bow	Retrd.	1993	14.00	14
1984	Teddy Bear with Bow & Heart	Retrd.	1993	13.50	14
1986	Teddy Riding Goose	Retrd.	1994	20.50	21
1990	Teddy with Antique Radio	Retrd.	1994	18.00	18
1986	Wedding Pair Bears	Retrd.	1994	19.00	19

WACO Products Corp.

From a Child's Heart - P. Willingham

1995	Against the Odds	Open		20.00	20
1995	Our Spirit Is Unshakable	Open		20.00	20
1995	We Can Weather Any Storm	Open		20.00	20
1995	Will This Help?	Open		20.00	20

The Herman Collection - J. Unger

1990	Birthday Cake	Retrd.	1995	20.00	20
1990	Bowling/Wife	Retrd.	1995	20.00	20
1990	Doctor/Fat Man	Retrd.	1993	20.00	20
1990	Doctor/High Cost	Retrd.	1995	20.00	20
1990	Fry Pan/Fisherman	Retrd.	1993	20.00	20
1990	Golf/Camel	Retrd.	1993	20.00	20
1990	Husband/Check	Open		20.00	20
1990	Husband/Newspaper	Retrd.	1993	20.00	20
1990	Lawyer/Cabinet	Retrd.	1993	20.00	20
1990	Stop Smoking	Open		20.00	20
1990	Tennis/Wife	Open		20.00	20
1990	Wedding Ring	Retrd.	1993	20.00	20

Melody In Motion/Collector's Society - S. Nakane

1992	Amazing Willie the One-Man Band	Retrd.	1994	130.00	250-300
1992	Willie The Conductor	Retrd.	1994	Gift	35
1993	Charmed Bunnies	Retrd.	1993	Gift	45
1994	Willie The Collector	Yr. Iss.		200.00	200
1994	Springtime	Retrd.	1994	Gift	45
1995	Best Friends	Yr. Iss.		Gift	45

Melody In Motion/Madame - S. Nakane

1988	Madame Cello Player	Retrd.	1991	130.00	130
1988	Madame Cello Player (glazed)	Retrd.	1993	170.00	170
1988	Madame Flute Player	Retrd.	1992	130.00	130
1988	Madame Flute Player (glazed)	Retrd.	1993	170.00	170
1988	Madame Harp Player	Open		130.00	180
1988	Madame Harp Player (glazed)	Retrd.	1993	190.00	190
1988	Madame Harpsichord Player	Retrd.	1991	130.00	130
1988	Madame Harpsichord Player (glazed)	Retrd.	1993	170.00	170
1988	Madame Lyre Player	Retrd.	1994	130.00	130
1988	Madame Mandolin Player	Retrd.	1994	130.00	130
1988	Madame Violin Player	Retrd.	1991	130.00	130

Melody In Motion/Santa - S. Nakane

1986	1986-Santa Claus	Retrd.	1986	100.00	2500
1987	1987-Santa Claus	Retrd.	1987	130.00	700-2000
1988	1988-Santa Claus	Retrd.	1988	130.00	1000
1989	1989-Willie The Santa	Retrd.	1989	130.00	N/A
1990	1990-Santa Claus	Retrd.	1990	150.00	200-225
1991	1991-Santa Claus	Retrd.	1991	150.00	160
1992	1992-Santa Claus	Open		160.00	160
1993	1993-Coca-Cola Santa Claus	Retrd.	1993	180.00	225
1994	1994-Coca-Cola Santa Claus	Retrd.	1994	190.00	225
1995	1995 Santa Claus	6,000		190.00	190

Melody In Motion/Spotlight Clown - S. Nakane

1989	Spotlight Clown Banjo	Retrd.	1992	85.00	200
1989	Spotlight Clown Cornet	Retrd.	1992	85.00	125-200
1989	Spotlight Clown Trombone	Retrd.	1992	85.00	200
1989	Spotlight Clown Tuba	Retrd.	1992	85.00	200
1989	Spotlight Clown w/Bingo The Dog	Open		85.00	85
1989	Spotlight Clown w/Upright Bass	Retrd.	1994	85.00	85

Melody In Motion/Timepiece - S. Nakane

1989	Clockpost Willie	Open		150.00	200
1992	Golden Mountain Clock	Open		250.00	280
1990	Grandfather's Clock	Retrd.	1994	200.00	295
1991	Hunter Timepiece	Retrd.	1994	250.00	320
1989	Lull'aby Willie	Retrd.	1992	170.00	170
1992	Wall Street Willie	Open		180.00	240

Melody In Motion/Various - Various

1990	Accordion Boy - S. Nakane	Retrd.	1992	120.00	200
1987	Accordion Clown - S. Nakane	Retrd.	1991	110.00	250
1987	Balloon Clown - S. Nakane	Open		110.00	145
1990	Blacksmith - S. Nakane	Retrd.	1993	110.00	200
1994	Blue Danube Carousel S. Nakane	Open		280.00	280
1994	Campfire Cowboy - S. Nakane	Open		180.00	180
1987	The Carousel (1st Edition) S. Nakane	Retrd.	1993	240.00	260
1991	The Carousel (2nd Edition) S. Nakane	Retrd.	1995	240.00	350
1986	The Cellist - S. Nakane	Open		130.00	160
1994	Christmas Caroler Boy S. Nakane	10,000		172.00	172
1994	Christmas Caroler Girl S. Nakane	10,000		172.00	172
1987	Clarinet Clown - S. Nakane	Retrd.	1991	110.00	300
1995	Coca-Cola Norman Rockwell "Gone Fishing" - S. Nakane	Open		194.00	194
1994	Day's End - S. Nakane	Open		240.00	240
1986	The Fiddler - S. Nakane	Retrd.	1995	130.00	160
1989	The Grand Carousel - S. Nakane	Open		3000.00	3000
1986	The Guitarist - S. Nakane	Retrd.	1994	130.00	200
1990	Hunter - S. Nakane	Retrd.	1994	110.00	150
1992	King of Clowns Carousel S. Nakane	Open		740.00	850
1991	Little John - C. Johnson	Retrd.	1992	180.00	300
1994	Low Pressure Job - S. Nakane	Open		240.00	240
1991	Robin Hood - C. Johnson	Retrd.	1991	180.00	350
1985	Salty 'N' Pepper - S. Nakane	Retrd.	1992	176.00	400
1987	Saxophone Clown - S. Nakane	Retrd.	1991	110.00	250
1990	Shoemaker - S. Nakane	Retrd.	1993	110.00	200
1993	South of the Border - S. Nakane	Open		180.00	180
1991	Victoria Park Carousel S. Nakane	Open		300.00	340
1987	Violin Clown - S. Nakane	Retrd.	1992	110.00	200
1994	When I Grow Up - S. Nakane	Open		200.00	200
1990	Woodchopper - S. Nakane	Retrd.	1993	110.00	200

Melody In Motion/Vendor - S. Nakane

1989	Ice Cream Vendor	Retrd.	1994	140.00	200
1987	Organ Grinder	Retrd.	1994	130.00	200
1989	Peanut Vendor	Retrd.	1994	140.00	200

Melody In Motion/Willie - S. Nakane

1993	The Artist	Open		240.00	240
1994	Chattanooga Choo Choo	Open		180.00	180
1992	Dockside Willie	Open		160.00	190
1993	Heartbreak Willie	Open		180.00	180
1994	Jackpot Willie	Open		180.00	180
1993	Lamp Light Willie	Open		220.00	220
1987	Lamppost Willie	Open		110.00	140
1994	Longest Drive	Open		150.00	150
1994	Smooth Sailing	Open		200.00	200
1992	Wild West Willie	Open		175.00	200
1995	Willie the Conductor (10th Anniversary)	Open		220.00	220
1991	Willie The Fisherman	Open		150.00	190
1994	Willie the Golfer - Hour on the Hour Clock	Open		240.00	240
1993	Willie The Golfer - Quartz Alarm Clock	Open		240.00	240
1985	Willie The Hobo	Open		130.00	160
1985	Willie The Trumpeter	Open		130.00	160
1985	Willie The Whistler	Open		130.00	160
1995	Willie the Yodeler	Open		158.00	158

Whimsicals- Sri Lanka/Thailand - S. Nakane

1995	Cheers	Open		38.00	38
1995	The Entertainer	Open		38.00	38
1995	Happy Endings	Open		38.00	38
1995	Just For You	Open		38.00	38
1995	Pals	Open		38.00	38
1995	Pampered Pets	Open		38.00	38

Whimsicals-Japan - S. Nakane

1992	Apple Pickin' Time	Retrd.	1994	60.00	60
1992	Bon Voyage	Retrd.	1994	60.00	60
1992	Cheers	Retrd.	1995	60.00	60
1992	The Entertainer	Retrd.	1995	60.00	60
1992	Happy Endings	Retrd.	1995	60.00	60
1992	Just For You	Retrd.	1995	60.00	60
1992	The Merrymakers	Retrd.	1994	60.00	60
1992	Pals	Retrd.	1995	60.00	60
1992	Pampered Pets	Retrd.	1995	60.00	60
1992	Showtime	Retrd.	1994	60.00	60
1992	Special Delivery	Retrd.	1994	60.00	60
1992	Storytime	Retrd.	1994	60.00	60
1992	Tea Time	Retrd.	1994	60.00	60

Walt Disney

Walt Disney Collectors Society - Disney Studios

Year	Issue	Edition Limit	Year Retd.	Issue Price	Quote U.S.$
1993	Jiminy Cricket Kit	Closed	1993	Gift	220
1993	Jiminy Cricket 4" /wheel	Closed	1993	Gift	150-225
1993	Jiminy Cricket/clef	Closed	1993	Gift	120-175
1993	Brave Little Tailor 7 1/4"	Closed	1994	160.00	250-325
1994	Cheshire Cat 4 3/4"/clef	Closed	1994	Gift	95-135
1994	Cheshire Cat 4 3/4"/flower	Closed	1994	Gift	85-110
1994	Pecos Bill 9 1/2"	Closed	1994	650.00	650-775
1994	Admiral Duck 6 1/4"	Closed	1995	165.00	200-225
1995	Dumbo	12/95		Gift	N/A
1995	Cruella De Vil 10 1/4"	12/95		250.00	250
1995	Dumbo Ornament	12/95		20.00	20

Classics Collection-Special Event - Disney Studios

Year	Issue	Edition Limit	Year Retd.	Issue Price	Quote U.S.$
1993	Flight of Fancy 3" 41051	Closed	1994	35.00	40-55
1994	Mr. Smee 5" 41062	Closed	1995	90.00	90-115
1994	Mr. Smee 5" 41062 (teal stamp)	Closed	1995	90.00	110-140
1995	Lucky 41080	Closed	1995	40.00	40
1995	Wicked Witch 41084	3/96		130.00	130

Classics Collection-3 Caballeros - Disney Studios

Year	Issue	Edition Limit	Year Retd.	Issue Price	Quote U.S.$
1995	Amigo Donald 7" 41076	Open		180.00	180
1995	Amigo Jose 7" 41077	Open		180.00	180
1995	Amigo Panchito 7" 41078	Open		180.00	180

Classics Collection-Bambi - Disney Studios

Year	Issue	Edition Limit	Year Retd.	Issue Price	Quote U.S.$
1992	Bambi 6" 41033	Open		195.00	195
1992	Bambi 6" 41033/wheel	Closed	1992	195.00	235-250
1992	Bambi & Flower 6" 41010	10,000	1993	298.00	450-550
1992	Field Mouse-not touching 5 3/5" 41012	7,500	1993	195.00	1300-1800
1992	Field Mouse-touching 5 3/5" 41012	7,500	1993	195.00	1250-1400
1992	Flower 3"41034	Open		78.00	78
1992	Flower 3"41034/wheel	Closed	1992	78.00	140-155
1992	Friend Owl 8 3/5" 41011	Open		195.00	195
1992	Friend Owl 8 3/5" 41011/wheel	Closed	1992	195.00	195-225
1992	Thumper 3" 41013	Open		55.00	55
1992	Thumper 3" 41013/wheel	Closed	1992	55.00	60-80
1992	Thumper's Sisters 3 3/5" 41014	Open		69.00	69
1992	Thumper's Sisters 3 3/5" 41014/wheel	Closed	1992	69.00	75-90
1992	Bambi-Opening Title 41015	Open		29.00	29
1992	Bambi-Opening Title 41015/wheel	Closed	1992	29.00	35-50

Classics Collection-Cinderella - Disney Studios

Year	Issue	Edition Limit	Year Retd.	Issue Price	Quote U.S.$
1993	A Dress For Cinderelly 41030/wheel & clef	5,000	1993	800.00	2000-2375
1992	Birds With Sash 6 2/5" 41005	Closed	1994	149.00	155-170
1992	Chalk Mouse 3 2/5" 41006	Closed	1994	65.00	75-100
1992	Cinderella 6" 41000/clef	Closed	1993	195.00	300-345
1992	Cinderella 6" 41000/wheel	Closed	1992	195.00	325-365
1995	Cinderella & The Prince 41079	Open		275.00	275
1992	Cinderella, Lucifer, Bruno, set of 3/wheel & clef	Closed	1993	333.00	475-550
1992	Gus 3 2/5" 41007	Closed	1994	65.00	75-100
1992	Bruno 4 2/5" 41002/wheel & clef	Closed	1993	69.00	90-125
1992	Jaq 4 1/5" 41008	Closed	1994	65.00	65-100
1992	Lucifer 2 3/5" 41001/wheel & clef	Closed	1993	69.00	90-125
1992	Needle Mouse 5 4/5" 41004	Closed	1994	69.00	75-90
1992	Sewing Book 41003	Closed	1994	69.00	75
1992	Sewing Book 41003/no mark	Closed	1994	69.00	95-110
1992	Cinderella-Opening Title 41009	Open		29.00	29
1992	Cinderella-Opening Title-Technicolor 41009	Closed	1993	29.00	40-55
1992	Cinderella-Opening Title-Technicolor 41009/wheel	Closed	1993	29.00	45

Classics Collection-Fantasia - Disney Studios

Year	Issue	Edition Limit	Year Retd.	Issue Price	Quote U.S.$
1993	Blue Centaurette-Beauty in Bloom 7 1/2" 41041	Retrd.	1995	195.00	200-250
1992	Broom, 5 4/5" 41017	Retrd.	1995	75.00	85-100
1992	Broom, w/water spots 5 4/5" 41017/wheel	Closed	1992	75.00	135-175
1994	Hop Low 2 3/4" 41067	Open		35.00	35
1993	Love's Little Helpers 8" 41042	Retrd.	1995	290.00	300-350
1994	Mushroom Dancer-Medium 4 1/4" 41068	Open		50.00	50
1994	Mushroom Dancer-Medium 4 1/4" 41068/teal stamp	Closed	1994	50.00	60-95
1994	Mushroom Dancer-Large 4 3/4" 41058	Open		60.00	60
1994	Mushroom Dancer-Large 4 3/4" 41058/teal stamp	Closed	1994	60.00	65-100
1993	Pink Centaurette-Romantic Reflections 7 1/2" 41040	Retrd.	1995	175.00	200-250
1992	Sorcerer Mickey 5 1/8" 41016	Retrd.	1995	195.00	225-240
1992	Fantasia-Opening Title 41018	Open		29.00	29
1992	Fantasia-Opening Title-blank 41018	Closed	1994	29.00	30-50
1992	Fantasia-Opening Title-Technicolor 41018	Closed	1993	29.00	40-55

Classics Collection-Holiday Series - Disney Studios

Year	Issue	Edition Limit	Year Retd.	Issue Price	Quote U.S.$
1995	Presents for My Pals 41086	12/95		150.00	150

Classics Collection-Mr. Duck - Disney Studios

Year	Issue	Edition Limit	Year Retd.	Issue Price	Quote U.S.$
1993	Donald & Daisy 6 3/5" 41024/clef	5,000	1993	298.00	550-675
1993	Donald & Daisy 6 3/5" 41024/wheel	5,000	1993	298.00	650-850
1993	Mr. Duck Steps Out-Opening Title 41023	Open		29.00	29
1993	Mr. Duck Steps Out-Opening Title 41023/clef	Closed	1993	29.00	35-45
1993	Nephew Duck-Dewey 4" 41025	Open		65.00	65
1993	Nephew Duck-Dewey 4" 41025/wheel	Closed	1993	65.00	80-90
1993	Nephew Duck-Huey 4" 41049	Open		65.00	65
1993	Nephew Duck-Huey 4" 41049/clef	Closed	1993	65.00	65-85
1993	Nephew Duck-Louie 4" 41050	Open		65.00	65
1993	Nephew Duck-Louie 4" 41050/clef	Closed	1993	65.00	65-85
1994	With Love From Daisy 6 1/4" 41060	Open		180.00	180

Classics Collection-Peter Pan - Disney Studios

Year	Issue	Edition Limit	Year Retd.	Issue Price	Quote U.S.$
1993	Captain Hook 8" 41044	Open		275.00	275
1993	Captain Hook 8" 41044/clef	Closed	1994	275.00	875-950
1993	The Crocodile 6 1/4" 41054	Open		315.00	315
1993	Peter Pan 7 1/2" 41043	Open		165.00	165
1993	Peter Pan 7 1/2"41043/clef	Closed	1994	165.00	200-225
1993	Tinkerbell 5" 41045/clef	12,500	1994	215.00	500-700
1993	Tinkerbell 5" 41045/flower	12,500	1994	215.00	350-425
1993	Peter Pan-Opening Title 41047	Open		29.00	29
1993	Peter Pan-Opening Title 41047/clef	Closed	1994	29.00	35-50

Classics Collection-Snow White - Disney Studios

Year	Issue	Edition Limit	Year Retd.	Issue Price	Quote U.S.$
1994	Snow White 8 1/4" 41063/flower	Closed	1994	165.00	185-250
1994	Snow White 8 1/4" 41063	Open		165.00	165
1995	Bashful 5" 91069	Open		95.00	95
1995	Doc 5 1/4" 41071	Open		95.00	95
1995	Dopey 5" 41074	Open		95.00	95
1995	Grumpy 7 3/4" 41065	Open		180.00	180
1995	Happy 5 1/2" 41064	Open		125.00	125
1995	Sleepy 3 1/4" 41066	Open		95.00	95
1995	Sneezy 4 1/2" 41073	Open		90.00	90
1995	Snow White-Opening Title 41083	Open		29.00	29

Classics Collection-Symphony Hour - Disney Studios

Year	Issue	Edition Limit	Year Retd.	Issue Price	Quote U.S.$
1993	Clarabelle 6 4/5" 41027/wheel	Closed	1993	198.00	250-275
1993	Clarabelle 6 4/5"41027	Open		198.00	198
1994	Clara Cluck	Open		185.00	185
1993	Goofy 6 4/5" 41026/wheel	Closed	1993	198.00	1400-1650
1993	Goofy 6 4/5" 41026	Open		198.00	198
1993	Horace 6 4/5" 41028	Open		198.00	198
1993	Horace 6 4/5" 41028/wheel	Closed	1993	198.00	210-250
1993	Mickey Conductor 7 3/8" 41029	Open		185.00	185
1993	Mickey Conductor 7 3/8" 41029/wheel	Closed	1993	185.00	225-250
1993	Symphony Hour-Opening Title 41031	Open		29.00	29
1993	Symphony Hour-Opening Title 41031/clef	Closed	1993	29.00	35-50

Classics Collection-The Delivery Boy - Disney Studios

Year	Issue	Edition Limit	Year Retd.	Issue Price	Quote U.S.$
1992	Delivery Boy-Opening Title 41019	Open		29.00	29
1992	Delivery Boy-Opening Title 41019/clef	Closed	1993	29.00	35-50
1992	Mickey 6" 41020	Open		125.00	135
1992	Mickey 6" 41020/wheel	Closed	1992	125.00	195-225
1992	Minnie 6" 41021	Open		125.00	135
1992	Minnie 6" 41021/wheel	Closed	1992	125.00	195-225
1992	Pluto (raised letters) 3 3/5" 41022/wheel	Closed	1992	125.00	280-350
1992	Pluto 3 3/5" 41022	Open		125.00	125
1992	Pluto 3 3/5" 41022/wheel	Closed	1992	125.00	175-200

Classics Collection-Three Little Pigs - Disney Studios

Year	Issue	Edition Limit	Year Retd.	Issue Price	Quote U.S.$
1993	Big Bad Wolf (short tooth) 41039 1st version	S/O	1994	295.00	900-1100
1993	Big Bad Wolf 41039	7,500	1994	295.00	700-800
1993	Fiddler Pig 4 1/2" 41038	Open		75.00	75
1993	Fiddler Pig 4 1/2" 41038/clef	Closed	1993	75.00	75-115
1993	Fifer Pig 4 1/2" 41037	Open		75.00	75
1993	Fifer Pig 4 1/2" 41037/clef	Closed	1993	75.00	75-115
1993	Practical Pig 4 1/2" 41036	Open		75.00	75
1993	Practical Pig 4 1/2" 41036/clef	Closed	1993	75.00	75-115
1993	Three Little Pigs-Opening Title 41046	Open		29.00	30-40
1993	Three Little Pigs-Opening Title 41046/clef	Closed	1993	29.00	35

Classics Collection-Tribute Series - Disney Studios

Year	Issue	Edition Limit	Year Retd.	Issue Price	Quote U.S.$
1995	Pals Forever 41085	Closed	1995	175.00	175
1995	Slue Foot Sue 41075	Closed	1995	695.00	695

Disney's Enchanted Places - Disney Studios

Year	Issue	Edition Limit	Year Retd.	Issue Price	Quote U.S.$
1995	Dwarf's Cottage	Open		180.00	180
1995	White Rabbit's Cottage	Open		175.00	175
1995	Woodcutter's Cottage	Open		170.00	170

Wee Forest Folk

Animals - A. Petersen, unless otherwise noted

Year	Issue	Edition Limit	Year Retd.	Issue Price	Quote U.S.$
1974	Baby Hippo H-2	Closed	1977	7.00	N/A
1978	Beaver Wood Cutter BV-1 W. Petersen	Closed	1980	8.00	250-475
1974	Miss and Baby Hippo H-3	Closed	1977	15.00	800-1000
1973	Miss Ducky D-1	Closed	1977	6.00	N/A
1974	Miss Hippo H-1	Closed	1977	8.00	N/A
1977	Nutsy Squirrel SQ-1 W. Petersen	Closed	1977	3.00	400-500
1979	Turtle Jogger TS-1	Closed	1980	4.00	300-400

Bears - A. Petersen

Year	Issue	Edition Limit	Year Retd.	Issue Price	Quote U.S.$
1978	Big Lady Bear BR-4	Closed	1980	7.50	N/A
1977	Blueberry Bears BR-1	Closed	1982	8.75	550
1977	Boy Blueberry Bear BR-3	Closed	1982	4.50	250-700
1995	Don't Be Shy BB-1	Open		76.00	76
1995	Father's Night BB-5	Open		159.00	159
1977	Girl Blueberry Bear BR-2	Closed	1982	4.25	400-550
1995	Good Pickin's BB-4	Open		64.00	64
1995	Just a Peek BB-6	Open		159.00	159
1995	Lunch on a Log BB-3	Open		89.00	89
1978	Traveling Bear BR-5	Closed	1980	8.00	250-375
1995	Welcome Home BB-2	Open		108.00	108

Book / Figurine - W. Petersen

Year	Issue	Edition Limit	Year Retd.	Issue Price	Quote U.S.$
1988	Tom & Eon BK-1	Suspd.	1991	45.00	225

Bunnies - A. Petersen, unless otherwise noted

Year	Issue	Edition Limit	Year Retd.	Issue Price	Quote U.S.$
1977	Batter Bunny B-9	Closed	1982	4.50	350-400
1973	Broom Bunny B-6	Closed	1978	9.50	N/A
1972	Double Bunnies B-1	Closed	1980	4.25	400
1972	Housekeeping Bunny B-2	Closed	1980	4.50	400
1973	Market Bunny B-8	Closed	1977	9.00	N/A
1973	Muff Bunny B-7	Closed	1977	9.00	N/A
1973	The Professor B-4	Closed	1980	4.75	350-400
1980	Professor Rabbit B-11 W. Petersen	Closed	1981	14.00	400-500
1973	Sir Rabbit B-3 - W. Petersen	Closed	1980	4.50	300-400
1973	Sunday Bunny B-5	Closed	1978	4.75	N/A
1977	Tennis Bunny BS-1	Closed	1980	3.75	250-350
1985	Tiny Easter Bunny B-12 D. Petersen	Closed	1992	25.00	90
1978	Wedding Bunnies B-10 W. Petersen	Closed	1981	12.50	500
1992	Windy Day! B-13 - D. Petersen	Open		37.00	42

Christmas Carol Series - A. Petersen

Year	Issue	Edition Limit	Year Retd.	Issue Price	Quote U.S.$
1987	Bob Cratchit and Tiny Tim CC-2	Open		36.00	45
1988	The Fezziwigs CC-7	Open		65.00	82
1987	Ghost of Christmas Past CC-4	Open		24.00	31
1987	Ghost of Christmas Present CC-5	Open		54.00	61
1987	Ghost of Christmas Yet to Come CC-6	Open		24.00	30
1987	Marley's Ghost CC-3	Open		24.00	31
1987	Scrooge CC-1	Open		23.00	30

Cinderella Series - A. Petersen

Year	Issue	Edition Limit	Year Retd.	Issue Price	Quote U.S.$
1988	Cinderella's Slipper (with Prince) C-1	Closed	1989	62.00	175
1989	Cinderella's Slipper C-1a	Closed	1994	32.00	90-105
1988	Cinderella's Wedding C-5	Closed	1994	62.00	153
1989	The Fairy Godmother C-7	Closed	1994	69.00	175
1988	Flower Girl C-6	Closed	1994	22.00	72-85
1988	The Flower Girls C-4	Closed	1994	42.00	95-115
1988	The Mean Stepmother C-3	Closed	1994	32.00	90-140
1988	The Ugly Stepsisters C-2	Closed	1994	62.00	148

Fairy Tale Series - A. Petersen

Year	Issue	Edition Limit	Year Retd.	Issue Price	Quote U.S.$
1980	Red Riding Hood & Wolf FT-1	Closed	1982	29.00	1200
1980	Red Riding Hood FT-2	Closed	1982	13.00	550

Forest Scene - A. Petersen, unless otherwise noted

Year	Issue	Edition Limit	Year Retd.	Issue Price	Quote U.S.$
1989	Hearts and Flowers FS-2 W. Petersen	Open		110.00	124
1992	Love Letter FS-5 - W. Petersen	Open		98.00	110
1991	Mountain Stream FS-4 W. Petersen	Open		128.00	144
1990	Mousie Comes A-Calling FS-3 W. Petersen	Open		128.00	146
1993	Picnic on the Riverbank FS-6	Open		150.00	180
1994	Wayside Chat FS-7	Open		170.00	170
1988	Woodland Serenade FS-1 W. Petersen	Closed	1994	125.00	345

Foxes - A. Petersen

Year	Issue	Edition Limit	Year Retd.	Issue Price	Quote U.S.$
1978	Barrister Fox FX-3	Closed	1980	7.50	695
1977	Dandy Fox FX-2	Closed	1979	6.00	500
1977	Fancy Fox FX-1	Closed	1979	4.75	500

Frogs - A. Petersen, unless otherwise noted

Year	Issue	Edition Limit	Year Retd.	Issue Price	Quote U.S.$
1977	Frog Friends F-3 - W. Petersen	Closed	1981	5.75	350-450
1974	Frog on Rock F-2	Closed	1977	6.00	N/A
1977	Grampa Frog F-5 - W. Petersen	Closed	1981	6.00	500
1974	Prince Charming F-1 W. Petersen	Closed	1977	7.50	400-500
1978	Singing Frog F-6	Closed	1979	5.50	250-300
1977	Spring Peepers F-4	Closed	1979	3.50	N/A

Limited Edition - A. Petersen, unless otherwise noted

Year	Issue	Edition Limit	Year Retd.	Issue Price	Quote U.S.$
1981	Beauty and the Beast BB-1 W. Petersen	Closed	1981	89.00	1500-2000
1985	Helping Hand LTD-2	Closed	1985	62.00	700-750
1984	Postmouster LTD-1 W. Petersen	Closed	1984	46.00	700-750
1987	Statue in the Park LTD-3 W. Petersen	Closed	1987	93.00	850-950
1988	Uncle Sammy LTD-4	Closed	1988	85.00	295

Mice - A. Petersen, unless otherwise noted

Year	Issue	Edition Limit	Year Retd.	Issue Price	Quote U.S.$
1992	Adam's Apples M-187	Open		148.00	158
1988	Aloha! M-158	Closed	1994	32.00	75-95
1991	April Showers M-180	Open		27.00	37

FIGURINES/COTTAGES

YEAR ISSUE		EDITION LIMIT	YEAR RETD.	ISSUE PRICE	QUOTE U.S.$
1982	Arty Mouse M-71	Closed	1991	19.00	85-150
1985	Attic Treasure M-126	Closed	1994	42.00	145
1977	Baby Sitter M-19	Closed	1981	5.75	395
1982	Baby Sitter M-66	Closed	1993	23.50	95
1981	Barrister Mouse M-57	Closed	1982	16.00	495
1987	Bat Mouse M-154	Closed	1994	25.00	65-95
1982	Beach Mousey M-76	Closed	1993	19.00	95-110
1982	Beddy-bye Mousey M-69	Open		29.00	54
1983	Birthday Girl M-99	Open		18.50	34
1981	Blue Devil M-61	Closed	N/A	12.50	125
1982	Boy Sweetheart M-81	Closed	1982	13.50	500
1975	Bride Mouse M-9	Closed	1978	4.00	550
1978	Bridge Club Mouse M-20	Closed	1979	6.00	300
1978	Bridge Club Mouse Partner M-21	Closed	1979	6.00	300
1995	Broom Service M-205 D. Petersen	Open		62.00	62
1984	Campfire Mouse M-109 W. Petersen	Closed	1986	26.00	350-395
1981	The Carolers M-63	Closed	1981	29.00	400-600
1980	Carpenter Mouse M-49	Closed	1981	15.00	400
1995	Caught in the Act M-209 W. Petersen	Open		49.00	49
1983	Chief Geronimouse M-107a	Closed	1994	21.00	95
1994	Chief Mouse-asoit M-197	Open		90.00	90
1978	Chief Nip-a-Way Mouse M-26	Closed	1981	7.00	300-600
1987	Choir Mouse M-147 - W. Petersen	Closed	1990	23.00	75-140
1979	Chris-Miss M-32	Closed	1982	9.00	395
1979	Chris-Mouse M-33	Closed	1982	9.00	115-250
1984	Chris-Mouse Pageant M-117	Open		38.00	59
1990	Chris-Mouse Slipper M-166	Open		35.00	42
1985	Chris-Mouse Tree M-124	Open		28.00	48
1986	Christ-Mouse Stocking M-142	Open		34.00	42
1993	Christmas Eve M-191	Open		145.00	158
1983	Christmas Morning M-92	Closed	1987	35.00	200-350
1995	Christmas Wish M-203	Open		156.00	156
1995	Clementine M-204 - D. Petersen	Open		86.00	86
1983	Clown Mouse M-98	Closed	1984	22.00	350-450
1990	Colleen O'Green M-167	Open		40.00	49
1986	Come & Get It! M-141	Closed	1988	34.00	125
1985	Come Play! M-131	Closed	1991	18.00	85
1989	Commencement Day M-161 W. Petersen	Open		28.00	36
1980	Commo-Dormouse M-42 W. Petersen	Closed	1981	14.00	500-900
1978	Cowboy Mouse M-25	Closed	1981	6.00	300-600
1983	Cupid Mouse M-94 - W. Petersen	Open		22.00	43
1981	Doc Mouse & Patient M-55 W. Petersen	Closed	1981	14.00	400-475
1987	Don't Cry! M-149	Closed	1990	33.00	95-120
1986	Down the Chimney M-143	Closed	1988	48.00	225-295
1987	Drummer M-153b - W. Petersen	Closed	1989	29.00	65
1982	Easter Bunny Mouse M-82	Open		18.00	38
1989	Elf Tales M-163	Closed	1994	48.00	55-120
1985	Family Portrait M-127	Closed	1987	54.00	250-350
1976	Fan Mouse M-10	Closed	1979	5.75	450-500
1974	Farmer Mouse M-5	Closed	1979	3.75	350-450
1989	Father Chris-Mouse M-164	Open		34.00	41
1985	Field Mouse M-133 W. Petersen	Open		46.00	94
1983	First Christmas M-93	Closed	1986	16.00	300-350
1986	First Date M-134 - W. Petersen	Open		60.00	68
1984	First Day of School M-112	Closed	1985	27.00	165-192
1986	First Haircut M-137 W. Petersen	Closed	1992	58.00	225
1993	First Kiss! M-192	Open		65.00	65
1980	Fishermouse M-41	Closed	1981	16.00	500-700
1981	Flower Girl M-53	Closed	1983	15.00	350
1988	Forty Winks M-159 - W. Petersen	Open		36.00	46
1986	Fun Float M-138 - W. Petersen	Open		34.00	39
1979	Gardener Mouse M-37	Closed	1981	12.00	400
1983	Get Well Soon! M-96	Closed	1983	15.00	390
1982	Girl Sweetheart M-80	Open		13.50	24
1974	Good Knight Mouse M-4 W. Petersen	Closed	1977	7.50	350-500
1981	Graduate Mouse M-58	Closed	1988	15.00	115
1991	Grammy-Phone M-176	Open		75.00	88
1992	Greta M-169b	Closed	1993	35.00	95
1992	Hans M-169a	Closed	1993	35.00	93
1990	Hans & Greta M-169	Closed	1992	64.00	150-180
1982	Happy Birthday! M-83	Open		17.50	35
1983	Harvest Mouse M-104 W. Petersen	Closed	1984	23.00	375-475
1989	Haunted Mouse House M-165 D. Petersen	Open		125.00	184
1995	Heavenly Slumber M-210	Open		49.00	49
1995	High Flyer M-207 - W. Petersen	Open		88.00	88
1992	High on the Hog M-186	Closed	1994	52.00	135
1982	Holly Mouse M-87	Open		13.50	32
1995	Jack in the Sandbox M-206 D. Petersen	Open		108.00	108
1976	June Belle M-13	Closed	1979	4.25	350-400
1986	Just Checking M-140	Open		34.00	42
1977	King "Tut" Mouse TM-1	Closed	1979	4.50	N/A
1982	Lamplight Carolers M-86	Closed	1987	35.00	250-350
1981	Little Devil M-61	Open		12.50	32
1982	Little Fire Chief M-77 W. Petersen	Closed	1984	29.00	575
1981	Little Ghost M-62	Open		8.50	22
1993	Little Mice Who Lived in a Shoe M-189 - D. Petersen	Open		395.00	425
1982	Little Sledders M-85	Closed	1985	24.00	250-400
1991	Little Squirt M-181 - W. Petersen	Open		49.00	57
1982	Littlest Angel M-88	Closed	1986	15.00	75
1987	Littlest Witch and Skeleton M-155	Open		49.00	64

YEAR ISSUE		EDITION LIMIT	YEAR RETD.	ISSUE PRICE	QUOTE U.S.$
1987	Littlest Witch M-156	Closed	1993	24.00	75-100
1981	Lone Caroler M-64	Closed	1981	15.50	375-575
1993	Lord & Lady Mousebatten M-195	Open		85.00	92
1976	Mama Mouse with Baby M-18	Closed	1979	6.00	350-450
1987	Market Mouse M-150 W. Petersen	Closed	1993	49.00	120-150
1972	Market Mouse M-1a	Closed	1978	4.25	175-350
1976	May Belle M-12	Closed	1980	4.25	225-375
1982	Me and Raggedy Ann M-70	Open		18.50	37
1983	Merry Chris-Miss M-90	Closed	1985	17.00	350-395
1983	Merry Chris-Mouse M-91	Closed	1985	16.00	350-395
1994	Midnight Snack M-201	Open		230.00	230
1980	Miss Bobbin M-40	Open		22.00	64
1992	Miss Daisy M-182	Open		42.00	48
1972	Miss Mouse M-1	Closed	1978	4.25	300-350
1972	Miss Mousey M-2	Closed	1978	4.00	250-350
1972	Miss Mousey w/ Bow Hat M-2b	Closed	1979	4.25	250-350
1972	Miss Mousey w/ Straw Hat M-2a	Closed	1980	4.25	250-350
1987	Miss Noel M-146	Open		32.00	42
1973	Miss Nursey Mouse M-3	Closed	1980	4.00	450-650
1980	Miss Polly Mouse M-46	Closed	1984	23.00	375
1982	Miss Teach & Pupil M-73	Closed	1984	29.50	450
1980	Miss Teach M-45	Closed	1980	18.00	400-500
1984	Mom & Ginger Baker M-115 W. Petersen	Open		38.00	66
1981	Mom and Squeaky Clean M-60	Open		27.00	59
1982	Moon Mouse M-78	Closed	1984	15.50	500-800
1981	Mother's Helper M-52	Closed	1983	11.00	300-600
1979	Mouse Artiste M-39	Closed	1981	12.50	400-600
1979	Mouse Ballerina M-38	Closed	1979	12.50	400-450
1983	Mouse Call M-97 - W. Petersen	Closed	1983	24.00	700-800
1979	Mouse Duet M-29	Closed	1982	25.00	550-700
1986	Mouse on Campus M-139 W. Petersen	Closed	1988	25.00	125
1979	Mouse Pianist M-30	Closed	1984	17.00	500-600
1985	Mouse Talk M-130	Closed	1993	44.00	115-135
1979	Mouse Violinist M-31	Closed	1984	9.00	300
1976	Mouse with Muff M-16	Closed	1977	9.00	N/A
1979	Mousey Baby, heart book M-34	Closed	1982	9.50	250-450
1981	Mousey Express M-65	Closed	1993	22.00	95-150
1983	Mousey Nurse M-95	Open		15.00	31
1983	Mousey's Cone M-100	Closed	1994	22.00	60-85
1983	Mousey's Dollhouse M-102	Closed	1985	30.00	475
1988	Mousey's Easter Basket M-160	Closed	N/A	32.00	115-125
1982	Mousey's Teddy M-75	Closed	1985	29.00	375-475
1983	Mousey's Tricycle M-101	Open		24.00	49
1991	Mousie's Egg Factory M-175	Open		73.00	94
1976	Mrs. Mousey M-15	Closed	1978	4.00	N/A
1976	Mrs. Mousey w/ Hat M-15a	Closed	1979	4.25	N/A
1992	Mrs. Mousey's Studio M-184 W. Petersen	Open		150.00	165
1980	Mrs. Tidy M-51	Closed	1981	19.50	350-500
1980	Mrs. Tidy and Helper M-50	Closed	1981	24.00	550
1993	The Mummy M-194	Open		34.00	38
1991	Night Prayer M-178	Open		52.00	63
1976	Nightie Mouse M-14	Closed	1979	4.75	350-500
1981	Nurse Mousey M-54	Closed	1982	14.00	410
1991	The Nutcracker M-174 D. Petersen	Open		49.00	62
1982	Office Mousey M-68	Closed	1984	23.00	430-650
1992	The Old Black Stove M-185 D. Petersen	Open		130.00	145
1993	One-Mouse Band M-196	Open		95.00	104
1983	Pack Mouse M-106 W. Petersen	Closed	1984	19.00	350
1987	Pageant Angel M-145	Open		19.00	26
1985	Pageant Shepherds M-122	Closed	1985	35.00	275
1987	Pageant Stable M-144	Open		56.00	74
1985	Pageant Wiseman M-121	Closed	1985	58.00	200-300
1981	Pearl Knit Mouse M-59	Closed	1985	20.00	235
1992	Peekaboo! M-183 - D. Petersen	Open		52.00	56
1984	Pen Pal Mousey M-114	Closed	1985	26.00	375
1993	Peter Pumpkin Eater M-190	Closed	1994	98.00	110-175
1984	Peter's Pumpkin M-118	Closed	1992	19.00	85-125
1980	Photographer Mouse M-48 W. Petersen	Closed	1981	23.00	400-700
1978	Picnic Mice M-23 - W. Petersen	Closed	1979	7.25	375-500
1985	Piggy-Back Mousey M-129 W. Petersen	Closed	1986	28.00	400-450
1994	Pilgrim's Welcome M-198	Open		55.00	55
1978	Pirate Mouse M-27	Closed	1979	6.50	400
1980	Pirate Mouse M-47 - W. Petersen	Closed	1981	16.00	1500
1990	Polly's Parasol M-170	Closed	1993	39.00	85-145
1982	Poorest Angel M-89	Closed	1986	15.00	130
1989	Prima Ballerina M-162	Open		35.00	44
1984	Prudence Pie Maker M-119	Closed	1992	18.50	85-125
1977	Queen "Tut" Mouse TM-2	Closed	1979	4.50	N/A
1985	Quilting Bee M-125 W. Petersen	Open		30.00	44
1979	Raggedy and Mouse M-36	Closed	1981	12.00	350-410
1991	Red Riding Hood at Grand-mother's House - D. Petersen	Open		295.00	295
1987	The Red Wagon M-151 W. Petersen	Closed	1991	54.00	150-250
1979	Rock-a-bye Baby Mouse M-35	Closed	1981	17.00	350-450
1983	Rocking Tot M-103	Closed	1990	19.00	60-90
1983	Rope 'em Mousey M-108	Closed	1984	19.00	350-435
1983	Running Doe/Little Deer M-107b	Open		35.00	44
1980	Santa Mouse M-43	Closed	1985	12.00	275-350
1984	Santa's Trainee M-116 W. Petersen	Closed	1984	36.50	550
1982	Say "Cheese" M-72 W. Petersen	Closed	1983	15.50	500
1981	School Marm Mouse M-56	Closed	1981	19.50	500
1987	Scooter Mouse M-152 W. Petersen	Open		34.00	43

YEAR ISSUE		EDITION LIMIT	YEAR RETD.	ISSUE PRICE	QUOTE U.S.$
1991	Sea Sounds M-179	Open		34.00	41
1978	Secretary, Miss Spell/Miss Pell M-22	Closed	1981	4.50	375-500
1976	Shawl Mouse M-17	Closed	1977	9.00	N/A
1985	Shepherd Kneeling M-122a	Open		20.00	29
1985	Shepherd Standing M-122b	Open		20.00	29
1991	Silent Night M-173	Open		64.00	76
1987	Skeleton Mousey M-157	Closed	1993	27.00	93
1992	Snow Buddies M-188 D. Petersen	Open		58.00	64
1982	Snowmouse & Friend M-84	Closed	1985	23.50	400
1984	Spring Gardener M-111	Open		26.00	42
1990	Stars & Stripes M-168	Open		34.00	40
1985	Strolling with Baby M-128	Open		42.00	61
1995	Struggling Artist M-208 W. Petersen	Open		49.00	49
1985	Sunday Drivers M-132 W. Petersen	Closed	1994	58.00	275
1986	Sweet Dreams M-136	Closed	1992	58.00	150-200
1982	Sweethearts M-79	Closed	1982	26.00	375-500
1991	Tea For Three M-177 D. Petersen	Open		135.00	162
1982	Tea for Two M-74	Closed	1984	26.00	300-410
1976	Tea Mouse M-11	Closed	1979	5.75	450-500
1984	Tidy Mouse M-113	Closed	1985	38.00	350-450
1987	Tooth Fairy M-148	Open		32.00	40
1978	Town Crier Mouse M-28	Closed	1979	10.50	500
1984	Traveling Mouse M-110	Closed	1987	28.00	290
1987	Trumpeter M-153a - W. Petersen	Closed	1989	29.00	65
1987	Tuba Player M-153c W. Petersen	Closed	1989	29.00	65
1992	Tuckered Out! M-136a	Closed	1993	46.00	165
1975	Two Mice with Candle M-7	Closed	1979	4.50	350-450
1975	Two Tiny Mice M-8	Closed	1979	4.50	350-500
1985	Under the Chris-Mouse Tree M-123	Open		48.00	84
1986	Waltzing Matilda M-135 W. Petersen	Closed	1993	48.00	120-195
1995	Wanderlust M-211	Open		68.00	68
1983	Wash Day M-105	Closed	1984	23.00	400-650
1994	We Gather Together M-199	Open		90.00	90
1978	Wedding Mice M-24 W. Petersen	Closed	1981	7.50	375-750
1982	Wedding Mice M-67 W. Petersen	Closed	1993	29.50	140
1994	The Wedding Pair M-200	Open		98.00	98
1993	Welcome Chick! M-193	Open		64.00	70
1985	Wise Man in Robe M-121b	Open		26.00	37
1985	Wise Man Kneeling M-121c	Open		29.00	39
1985	Wise Man with Turban M-121a	Open		28.00	39
1980	Witch Mouse M-44	Closed	1983	12.00	175-275
1984	Witchy Boo! M-120	Open		21.00	38
1974	Wood Sprite M-6a	Closed	1978	4.00	350-500
1974	Wood Sprite M-6b	Closed	1978	4.00	350-500
1974	Wood Sprite M-6c	Closed	1978	4.00	350-500
1994	The Yard Sale M-202	Open		325.00	325
1990	Zelda M-171	Open		37.00	47

Minutemice - A. Petersen, unless otherwise noted

1979	Concord Minute Mouse MM-10 - W. Petersen	Open		14.00	14
1974	Concordian On Drum with Glasses MM-4	Closed	1977	9.00	N/A
1974	Concordian Wood Base w/Hat MM-4b	Closed	1977	8.00	N/A
1974	Concordian Wood Base w/Tan Coat MM-4a	Closed	1977	7.50	N/A
1974	Little Fifer on Drum MM-5b	Closed	1977	8.00	N/A
1974	Little Fifer on Drum with Fife MM-5	Closed	1977	8.00	N/A
1974	Little Fifer on Wood Base MM-5a	Closed	1977	8.00	N/A
1979	Minute Mouse and Red Coat MM-9 - W. Petersen	Open		28.00	28
1974	Mouse Carrying Large Drum MM-3	Closed	1977	8.00	N/A
1974	Mouse on Drum with Black Hat MM-2	Closed	1977	9.00	N/A
1974	Mouse on Drum with Fife MM-1	Closed	1977	9.00	N/A
1974	Mouse on Drum with Fife Wood Base MM-1a	Closed	1977	9.00	N/A
1979	Red Coat Mouse MM-11 W. Petersen	Open	1977	14.00	14

Moles - A. Petersen

1994	Bell Ringer Mole MO-2	Open		44.00	44
1978	Mole Scout MO-1	Closed	1980	4.25	225-400
1995	Mole's Red Sled MO-3	Open		59.00	59

Mouse Sports - A. Petersen, unless otherwise noted

1975	Bobsled Three MS-1	Closed	1977	12.00	400-500
1994	Camping Out MS-16	Open		75.00	75
1985	Fishin' Chip MS-14 - W. Petersen	Closed	1992	46.00	225
1981	Golfer Mouse MS-10	Closed	1984	15.50	465-550
1977	Golfer Mouse MS-7	Closed	1980	5.25	300
1989	Joe Di'Mousio MS-15	Open		39.00	48
1984	Land Ho! MS-12	Closed	1987	36.50	245
1976	Mouse Skier MS-3	Closed	1979	4.25	300-400
1975	Skater Mouse MS-2	Closed	1980	4.50	300-400
1980	Skater Mouse MS-8	Closed	1983	16.50	400
1977	Skating Star Mouse MS-6	Closed	1979	3.75	250-400
1980	Skier Mouse (Red/Yellow, Red/Green) MS-9	N/A	1983	13.00	225-400
1980	Skier Mouse MS-9	Open		13.00	41
1984	Tennis Anyone? MS-13	Closed	1988	18.00	115-145
1976	Tennis Star MS-4	Closed	1978	3.75	150-300
1976	Tennis Star MS-5	Closed	1981	3.75	150-300
1982	Two in a Canoe MS-11 W. Petersen	Open		29.00	62

Owls - A. Petersen, unless otherwise noted

YEAR	ISSUE	EDITION LIMIT	YEAR RETD.	ISSUE PRICE	QUOTE U.S.$
1975	Colonial Owls O-4	Closed	1977	11.50	350-500
1979	Grad Owl O-5 - W. Petersen	Closed	1979	4.25	350-550
1980	Graduate Owl (On Books) O-6 W. Petersen	Closed	1980	12.00	330-500
1974	Mr. and Mrs. Owl O-1	Closed	1981	6.00	500
1974	Mr. Owl O-3	Closed	1981	3.25	150-300
1974	Mrs. Owl O-2	Closed	1981	3.00	150-300

Piggies - A. Petersen

YEAR	ISSUE	EDITION LIMIT	YEAR RETD.	ISSUE PRICE	QUOTE U.S.$
1978	Boy Piglet/ Picnic Piggy P-6	Closed	1981	4.00	700
1978	Girl Piglet/Picnic Piggy P-5	Closed	1981	4.00	700
1981	Holly Hog P-11	Closed	1981	25.00	350-425
1978	Jolly Tar Piggy P-3	Closed	1979	4.50	200-250
1978	Miss Piggy School Marm P-1	Closed	1979	4.50	225-325
1980	Nurse Piggy P-10	Closed	1981	15.50	200-225
1978	Picnic Piggies P-4	Closed	1981	7.75	200-300
1980	Pig O' My Heart P-9	Closed	1981	12.00	200-275
1978	Piggy Baker P-2	Closed	1981	4.50	225-425
1980	Piggy Ballerina P-7	Closed	1981	15.50	200-275
1978	Piggy Jogger PS-1	Closed	1981	4.50	125-200
1980	Piggy Policeman P-8	Closed	1981	17.50	200-350

Raccoons - A. Petersen

YEAR	ISSUE	EDITION LIMIT	YEAR RETD.	ISSUE PRICE	QUOTE U.S.$
1978	Bird Watcher Raccoon RC-3	Closed	1981	6.50	600
1977	Hiker Raccoon RC-2	Closed	1980	4.50	700
1977	Mother Raccoon RC-1	Closed	1980	4.50	300-475
1978	Raccoon Skater RCS-1	Closed	1980	4.75	250-400
1978	Raccoon Skier RCS-2	Closed	1980	6.00	350-450

Rats - A. Petersen, unless otherwise noted

YEAR	ISSUE	EDITION LIMIT	YEAR RETD.	ISSUE PRICE	QUOTE U.S.$
1975	Doc Rat R-2 - W. Petersen	Closed	1980	5.25	200-400
1975	Seedy Rat R-1	Closed	1977	5.25	1200

Robin Hood Series - A. Petersen

YEAR	ISSUE	EDITION LIMIT	YEAR RETD.	ISSUE PRICE	QUOTE U.S.$
1990	Friar Tuck RH-3	Closed	1994	32.00	90
1990	Maid Marion RH-2	Closed	1994	32.00	90
1990	Robin Hood RH-1	Closed	1994	37.00	90

Single Issues - A. Petersen, unless otherwise noted

YEAR	ISSUE	EDITION LIMIT	YEAR RETD.	ISSUE PRICE	QUOTE U.S.$
1980	Cave Mouse - W. Petersen	Closed	N/A	N/A	500-600
1980	Cave Mouse with Baby W. Petersen	Closed	N/A	26.00	N/A
1979	Ezra Ripley	Open		40.00	40-95
1972	Party Mouse in Plain Dress	Closed	N/A	N/A	N/A
1972	Party Mouse in Polka-Dot Dress	Closed	N/A	N/A	N/A
1972	Party Mouse in Sailor Suit	Closed	N/A	N/A	N/A
1972	Party Mouse with Bow Tie	Closed	N/A	N/A	N/A
1979	Sarah Ripley	Open		48.00	48-110
1980	Screech Owl - W. Petersen	Closed	1982	N/A	N/A
1983	Wee Forest Folk Display Piece	Open		70.00	70

Tiny Teddies - D. Petersen

YEAR	ISSUE	EDITION LIMIT	YEAR RETD.	ISSUE PRICE	QUOTE U.S.$
1984	Boo Bear T-3	Suspd.		20.00	75
1987	Christmas Teddy T-10	Suspd.		26.00	75
1984	Drummer Bear T-4	Suspd.		22.00	70
1988	Hansel & Gretel Bears @ Witch's House T-11	Suspd.		175.00	245
1986	Huggy Bear T-8	Suspd.		26.00	85
1984	Little Teddy T-1	Closed	1986	20.00	125
1989	Momma Bear T-12	Suspd.		27.00	125-150
1985	Ride 'em Teddy! T-6	Suspd.		32.00	95
1984	Sailor Teddy T-2	Suspd.		20.00	75
1984	Santa Bear T-5	Suspd.		27.00	115
1985	Seaside Teddy T-7	Suspd.		28.00	95
1983	Tiny Teddy TT-1	Closed	1983	16.00	150-175
1987	Wedding Bears T-9	Suspd.		54.00	135

Wind in the Willows - A. Petersen, unless otherwise noted

YEAR	ISSUE	EDITION LIMIT	YEAR RETD.	ISSUE PRICE	QUOTE U.S.$
1982	Badger WW-2	Closed	1983	18.00	495
1982	Mole WW-1	Closed	1983	18.00	595
1982	Ratty WW-4	Closed	1983	18.00	495
1982	Toad WW-3 - W. Petersen	Closed	1983	18.00	495

GRAPHICS

American Artists

Fred Stone - F. Stone

YEAR	ISSUE	EDITION LIMIT	YEAR RETD.	ISSUE PRICE	QUOTE U.S.$
1979	Affirmed, Steve Cauthen Up	750	N/A	100.00	600
1988	Alysheba	950	N/A	195.00	650
1992	The American Triple Crown I, 1948-1978	1,500		325.00	325
1993	The American Triple Crown II, 1937-1946	1,500		325.00	325
1993	The American Triple Crown III, 1919-1935	1,500		225.00	225
1983	Andalusian, The	750	N/A	150.00	350
1981	Arabians, The	750	N/A	115.00	525
1989	Battle For The Triple Crown	950	N/A	225.00	650
1980	The Belmont-Bold Forbes	500	N/A	100.00	375
1991	Black Stallion	1,500		225.00	250
1988	Cam-Fella	950	N/A	175.00	350
1981	Contentment	750	N/A	115.00	525
1992	Dance Smartly-Pat Day Up	950	N/A	225.00	325
1995	Dancers, canvas litho	350		375.00	375
1995	Dancers, print	Open		60.00	60
1983	The Duel	750	N/A	150.00	400
1985	Eternal Legacy	950	N/A	175.00	950
1980	Exceller-Bill Shoemaker	500	N/A	90.00	800
1990	Final Tribute- Secretariat	1,150	N/A	265.00	1300
1987	The First Day	950	N/A	175.00	225
1991	Forego	1,150		225.00	250
1986	Forever Friends	950	N/A	175.00	725
1985	Fred Stone Paints the Sport of Kings (Book)	750	N/A	265.00	750
1980	Genuine Risk	500	N/A	100.00	700
1991	Go For Wand-A Candle in the Wind	1,150		225.00	225
1986	Great Match Race-Ruffian & Foolish Pleasure	950	N/A	175.00	375
1995	Holy Bull, canvas litho	350		375.00	375
1995	Holy Bull, litho	1,150		225.00	225
1981	John Henry-Bill Shoemaker Up	595	N/A	160.00	1500
1985	John Henry-McCarron Up	750	N/A	175.00	500-750
1995	Julie Krone - Colonial Affair	1,150		225.00	225
1985	Kelso	950	N/A	175.00	750
1980	The Kentucky Derby	750	N/A	100.00	650
1980	Kidnapped Mare-Franfreluche	750	N/A	115.00	575
1987	Lady's Secret	950	N/A	175.00	425
1982	Man O'War "Final Thunder"	750	N/A	175.00	2500-3100
1979	Mare and Foal	500	N/A	90.00	500
1979	The Moment After	500	N/A	90.00	350
1986	Nijinski II	950	N/A	175.00	275
1984	Northern Dancer	950	N/A	175.00	625
1982	Off and Running	750	N/A	125.00	250-350
1990	Old Warriors Shoemaker-John Henry	1,950	N/A	265.00	595
1979	One, Two, Three	500	N/A	100.00	1000
1980	The Pasture Pest	500	N/A	100.00	875
1979	Patience	1,000	N/A	90.00	1200
1989	Phar Lap	950	N/A	195.00	275
1982	The Power Horses	750	N/A	125.00	250
1987	The Rivalry-Alysheba and Bet Twice	950	N/A	195.00	550
1979	The Rivals-Affirmed & Alydar	500	N/A	90.00	500
1983	Ruffian-For Only a Moment	750	N/A	175.00	1100
1983	Secretariat	950	N/A	175.00	995-1200
1989	Shoe Bald Eagle	950	N/A	195.00	675
1981	The Shoe-8,000 Wins	395	N/A	200.00	7000
1980	Spectacular Bid	500	N/A	65.00	350-400
1995	Summer Days, canvas litho	350		375.00	375
1995	Summer Days, litho	1,150		225.00	225
XX	Sunday Silence	950	N/A	195.00	425
1981	The Thoroughbreds	750	N/A	115.00	425
1983	Tranquility	750	N/A	150.00	525
1984	Turning For Home	750	N/A	150.00	425
1982	The Water Trough	750	N/A	125.00	575

Anheuser-Busch, Inc.

Anheuser-Busch - H. Droog

YEAR	ISSUE	EDITION LIMIT	YEAR RETD.	ISSUE PRICE	QUOTE U.S.$
1994	Gray Wolf Mirror N4570	2,500		135.00	150

Armani

Wall Art - G. Armani

YEAR	ISSUE	EDITION LIMIT	YEAR RETD.	ISSUE PRICE	QUOTE U.S.$
1994	Abiding Love 105A	675		475.00	475
1994	Abiding Love A/P 111A	25	1995	675.00	675
1994	The Embrace 103A	675		475.00	475
1994	The Embrace A/P 109A	25	1995	675.00	675
1994	La Pieta 102A	675		475.00	475
1994	La Pieta A/P 108A	25	1995	675.00	675
1994	Lady w/Mirror 101A	675		475.00	475
1994	Lady w/Mirror A/P 107A	25	1995	675.00	675
1994	Lady w/Peacock 100A	675		475.00	475
1994	Lady w/Peacock A/P 106A	25	1995	675.00	675
1994	Wind Song 104A	675		475.00	475
1994	Wind Song A/P 110A	25	1995	675.00	675

Artaffects

Perillo - G. Perillo

YEAR	ISSUE	EDITION LIMIT	YEAR RETD.	ISSUE PRICE	QUOTE U.S.$
1980	Babysitter, S/N	3,000		45.00	125-350
1988	By the Stream, S/N	950		100.00	125
1985	Chief Crazy Horse, S/N	950		125.00	450
1982	Chief Pontiac, S/N	950		75.00	100
1985	Chief Sitting Bull, S/N	500		125.00	350
1982	Hoofbeats, S/N	950		100.00	150
1982	Indian Style, S/N	950		75.00	100
1986	Learning His Ways, S/N	325		150.00	250
1982	Lonesome Cowboy, S/N	950		75.00	150
1978	Madonna of the Plains, S/N	500		125.00	200-600
1977	Madre, S/N	500		125.00	350
1988	Magnificent Seven, S/N	950		125.00	125
1982	Maria, S/N	550		150.00	350
1985	Marigold, S/N	500		125.00	150-450
1983	The Moment Poster, S/N	495		20.00	60
1984	Navajo Love, S/N	300		125.00	700
1984	Out of the Forest, S/N	Unkn.		Unkn.	450
1990	The Pack, S/N	950		150.00	200
1982	Papoose, S/N	950		125.00	125
1981	Peaceable Kingdom, S/N	950		100.00	375-800
1986	The Pout, S/N	325		150.00	200-450
1980	Puppies, S/N	3,000		45.00	200
1986	The Rescue, S/N	325		150.00	200-550
1985	Secretariat, S/N	950		125.00	150
1979	Sioux Scout and Buffalo Hunt, matched set	500		150.00	250-850
1978	Snow Pals, S/N	500		125.00	150-550
1982	Tender Love, S/N	950		75.00	125-450
1982	Tinker, S/N	3,000		45.00	100-350
1986	War Pony, S/N	325		150.00	150
1985	Whirlaway, S/N	950		125.00	150

Circle Fine Art

Rockwell - N. Rockwell

YEAR	ISSUE	EDITION LIMIT	YEAR RETD.	ISSUE PRICE	QUOTE U.S.$
XX	American Family Folio	200		Unkn.	17500
XX	The Artist at Work	130		Unkn.	3500
XX	At the Barber	200		Unkn.	4900
XX	Autumn	200		Unkn.	3500
XX	Autumn/Japon	25		Unkn.	3600
XX	Aviary	200		Unkn.	4200
XX	Barbershop Quartet	200		Unkn.	4200
XX	Baseball	200		Unkn.	3600
XX	Ben Franklin's Philadelphia	200		Unkn.	3600
XX	Ben's Belles	200		Unkn.	3500
XX	The Big Day	200		Unkn.	3400
XX	The Big Top	148		Unkn.	2800
XX	Blacksmith Shop	200		Unkn.	6300
XX	Bookseller	200		Unkn.	2700
XX	Bookseller/Japon	25		Unkn.	2750
XX	The Bridge	200		Unkn.	3100
XX	Cat	200		Unkn.	3400
XX	Cat/Collotype	200		Unkn.	4000
XX	Cheering	200		Unkn.	3600
XX	Children at Window	200		Unkn.	3600
XX	Church	200		Unkn.	3400
XX	Church/Collotype	200		Unkn.	4000
XX	Circus	200		Unkn.	2650
XX	County Agricultural Agent	200		Unkn.	3900
XX	The Critic	200		Unkn.	4650
XX	Day in the Life of a Boy	200		Unkn.	6200
XX	Day in the Life of a Boy/Japon	25		Unkn.	6500
XX	Debut	200		Unkn.	3600
XX	Discovery	200		Unkn.	5900
XX	Doctor and Boy	200		Unkn.	9400
XX	Doctor and Doll-Signed	200		Unkn.	11900
XX	Dressing Up/Ink	60		Unkn.	4400
XX	Dressing Up/Pencil	200		Unkn.	3700
XX	The Drunkard	200		Unkn.	3600
XX	The Expected and Unexpected	200		Unkn.	3700
XX	Family Tree	200		Unkn.	5900
XX	Fido's House	200		Unkn.	3600
XX	Football Mascot	200		Unkn.	3700
XX	Four Seasons Folio	200		Unkn.	13500
XX	Four Seasons Folio/Japon	25		Unkn.	14000
XX	Freedom from Fear-Signed	200		Unkn.	6400
XX	Freedom from Want-Signed	200		Unkn.	6400
XX	Freedom of Religion-Signed	200		Unkn.	6400
XX	Freedom of Speech-Signed	200		Unkn.	6400
XX	Gaiety Dance Team	200		Unkn.	4300
XX	Girl at Mirror-Signed	200		Unkn.	8400
XX	The Golden Age	200		Unkn.	3500
XX	Golden Rule-Signed	200		Unkn.	4400
XX	Golf	200		Unkn.	3600
XX	Gossips	200		Unkn.	5000
XX	Gossips/Japon	25		Unkn.	5100
XX	Grotto	200		Unkn.	3400
XX	Grotto/Collotype	200		Unkn.	4000
XX	High Dive	200		Unkn.	3400
XX	The Homecoming	200		Unkn.	3700
XX	The House	200		Unkn.	3700
XX	Huck Finn Folio	200		Unkn.	35000
XX	Ichabod Crane	200		Unkn.	6700
XX	The Inventor	200		Unkn.	4100
XX	Jerry	200		Unkn.	4700
XX	Jim Got Down on His Knees	200		Unkn.	4500
XX	Lincoln	200		Unkn.	11400
XX	Lobsterman	200		Unkn.	5500
XX	Lobsterman/Japon	25		Unkn.	5750
XX	Marriage License	200		Unkn.	6900
XX	Medicine	200		Unkn.	3400
XX	Medicine/Color Litho	200		Unkn.	4000
XX	Miss Mary Jane	200		Unkn.	4500
XX	Moving Day	200		Unkn.	3900
XX	Music Hath Charms	200		Unkn.	4200
XX	My Hand Shook	200		Unkn.	4500
XX	Out the Window	200		Unkn.	3400
XX	Out the Window/ Collotype	200		Unkn.	4000
XX	Outward Bound-Signed	200		Unkn.	7900
XX	Poor Richard's Almanac	200		Unkn.	24000
XX	Prescription	200		Unkn.	4900
XX	Prescription/Japon	25		Unkn.	5000
XX	The Problem We All Live With	200		Unkn.	4500
XX	Puppies	200		Unkn.	3700
XX	Raliegh the Dog	200		Unkn.	3900
XX	Rocket Ship	200		Unkn.	3650
XX	The Royal Crown	200		Unkn.	3500
XX	Runaway	200		Unkn.	3800
XX	Runaway/Japon	200		Unkn.	5700
XX	Safe and Sound	200		Unkn.	3800
XX	Saturday People	200		Unkn.	3300
XX	Save Me	200		Unkn.	3600
XX	Saying Grace-Signed	200		Unkn.	7400
XX	School Days Folio	200		Unkn.	14000
XX	Schoolhouse	200		Unkn.	4500
XX	Schoolhouse/Japon	25		Unkn.	4650
XX	See America First	200		Unkn.	5650
XX	See America First/Japon	25		Unkn.	6100
XX	Settling In	200		Unkn.	3600
XX	Shuffelton's Barbershop	200		Unkn.	7400

GRAPHICS

YEAR ISSUE		EDITION LIMIT	YEAR RETD.	ISSUE PRICE	QUOTE U.S.$
XX	Smoking	200		Unkn.	3400
XX	Smoking/Collotype	200		Unkn.	4000
XX	Spanking	200		Unkn.	3400
XX	Spanking/ Collotype	200		Unkn.	4000
XX	Spelling Bee	200		Unkn.	6500
XX	Spring	200		Unkn.	3500
XX	Spring Flowers	200		Unkn.	5200
XX	Spring/Japon	25		Unkn.	3600
XX	Study for the Doctor's Office	200		Unkn.	6000
XX	Studying	200		Unkn.	3600
XX	Summer	200		Unkn.	3500
XX	Summer Stock	200		Unkn.	4900
XX	Summer Stock/Japon	25		Unkn.	5000
XX	Summer/Japon	25		Unkn.	3600
XX	The Teacher	200		Unkn.	3400
XX	Teacher's Pet	200		Unkn.	3600
XX	The Teacher/Japon	25		Unkn.	3500
XX	The Texan	200		Unkn.	3700
XX	Then For Three Minutes	200		Unkn.	4500
XX	Then Miss Watson	200		Unkn.	4500
XX	There Warn't No Harm	200		Unkn.	4500
XX	Three Farmers	200		Unkn.	3600
XX	Ticketseller	200		Unkn.	4200
XX	Ticketseller/Japon	25		Unkn.	4400
XX	Tom Sawyer Color Suite	200		Unkn.	30000
XX	Tom Sawyer Folio	200		Unkn.	26500
XX	Top of the World	200		Unkn.	4200
XX	Trumpeter	200		Unkn.	3900
XX	Trumpeter/Japon	25		Unkn.	4100
XX	Two O'Clock Feeding	200		Unkn.	3600
XX	The Village Smithy	200		Unkn.	3500
XX	Welcome	200		Unkn.	3500
XX	Wet Paint	200		Unkn.	3800
XX	When I Lit My Candle	200		Unkn.	4500
XX	White Washing	200		Unkn.	3400
XX	Whitewashing the Fence/Collotype	200		Unkn.	4000
XX	Window Washer	200		Unkn.	4800
XX	Winter	200		Unkn.	3500
XX	Winter/Japon	25		Unkn.	3600
XX	Ye Old Print Shoppe	200		Unkn.	3500
XX	Your Eyes is Lookin'	200		Unkn.	4500

Cross Gallery, Inc.

Bandits & Bounty Hunters - P.A. Cross

YEAR ISSUE		EDITION LIMIT	YEAR RETD.	ISSUE PRICE	QUOTE U.S.$
1995	Bandits	865		225.00	225
1994	Bounty Hunters	865	1995	225.00	225

The Gift - P.A. Cross

YEAR ISSUE		EDITION LIMIT	YEAR RETD.	ISSUE PRICE	QUOTE U.S.$
1989	B' Achua Dlubh-bia Bii Noskiiyahi The Gift, Part II	S/O	1989	225.00	650
1993	The Gift, Part III	S/O	1993	225.00	350-1000

Half Breed Series - P.A. Cross

YEAR ISSUE		EDITION LIMIT	YEAR RETD.	ISSUE PRICE	QUOTE U.S.$
1989	Ach-hua Dlubh: (Body Two), Half Breed	S/O	1989	190.00	1450
1989	Ach-hua Dlubh: (Body Two), Half Breed II	S/O	1989	225.00	800-1100
1990	Ach-hua Dlubh: (Body Two), Half Breed III	S/O	1990	225.00	850
1995	Ach-hua Dlubh: (Body Two), Half Breed IV	S/O	1995	225.00	225

Limited Edition Original Graphics - P.A. Cross

YEAR ISSUE		EDITION LIMIT	YEAR RETD.	ISSUE PRICE	QUOTE U.S.$
1991	Bia-A-Hoosh (A Very Special Woman), Stone Lithograph	S/O	1991	500.00	500
1987	Caroline, Stone Lithograph	S/O	1987	300.00	600
1988	Maidenhood Hopi, Stone Lithograph	S/O	1988	950.00	1150
1990	Nighteyes, I, Serigraph	S/O	1990	225.00	425
1989	The Red Capote, Serigraph	S/O	1989	750.00	1150
1989	Rosapina, Etching	74		1200.00	1200
1991	Wooltalkers, Serigraph	275		750.00	750

Limited Edition Prints - P.A. Cross

YEAR ISSUE		EDITION LIMIT	YEAR RETD.	ISSUE PRICE	QUOTE U.S.$
1991	Ashpahdua Hagay Ashae-Gyoke (My Home & Heart Is Crow)	S/O	1991	225.00	225-350
1983	Ayla-Sah-Xuh-Xah (Pretty Colours, Many Designs)	S/O	1983	150.00	450
1990	Baape Ochia (Night Wind, Turquoise)	S/O	1990	185.00	370
1990	Biaachee-itah Bah-achbeh (Medicine Woman Scout)	S/O	1990	225.00	525
1984	Blue Beaded Hair Ties	S/O	1984	85.00	330
1991	The Blue Shawl	S/O	1991	185.00	275
1987	Caroline	S/O	1987	45.00	145
1989	Chey-ayjeh: Prey	S/O	1989	190.00	325-600
1988	Dance Apache	S/O	1988	190.00	360
1987	Dii-tah-shteh Ee-wihza-ahook (A Coat of much Value)	S/O	1987	90.00	740
1989	The Dreamer	S/O	1989	190.00	600
1987	The Elkskin Robe	S/O	1987	190.00	640
1990	Eshte	S/O	1990	185.00	200
1986	Grand Entry	S/O	1986	85.00	85
1983	Isbaaloo Eetshiileehcheek (Sorting Her Beads)	S/O	1983	150.00	1750
1990	Ishia-Kahda #1 (Quiet One)	S/O	1990	185.00	400
1988	Ma-a-luppis-she-La-dus (She is above everything, nothing can touch her)	S/O	1988	190.00	525
1984	Profile of Caroline	S/O	1984	85.00	185
1986	The Red Capote	S/O	1986	150.00	850
1987	The Red Necklace	S/O	1987	90.00	210
1989	Teesa Waits To Dance	S/O	1989	135.00	180
1984	Thick Lodge Clan Boy: Crow Indian	475		85.00	85
1987	Tina	S/O	1987	45.00	110
1985	The Water Vision	S/O	1985	150.00	325
1984	Whistling Water Clan Girl: Crow Indian	S/O	1984	85.00	85
1993	Winter Girl Bride	1,730		225.00	225
1986	Winter Morning	S/O	1986	185.00	1450
1986	The Winter Shawl	S/O	1986	150.00	1600

Miniature Line - P.A. Cross

YEAR ISSUE		EDITION LIMIT	YEAR RETD.	ISSUE PRICE	QUOTE U.S.$
1991	BJ	S/O	1995	80.00	80
1993	Braids	447		80.00	80
1993	Daybreak	447		80.00	80
1991	The Floral Shawl	S/O	1995	80.00	80
1991	Kendra	S/O	1995	80.00	80
1993	Ponytails	447		80.00	80
1993	Sundown	447		80.00	80
1991	Watercolour Study #2 For Half Breed	S/O	1995	80.00	80

The Painted Ladies' Suite - P.A. Cross

YEAR ISSUE		EDITION LIMIT	YEAR RETD.	ISSUE PRICE	QUOTE U.S.$
1992	Acoria (Crow; Seat of Honor)	S/O	1995	185.00	185
1992	Avisola	S/O	1995	185.00	185
1992	Dah-say (Crow; Heart)	S/O	1995	185.00	185
1992	Itza-chu (Apache; The Eagle)	S/O	1995	185.00	185
1992	Kel'hoya (Hopi; Little Sparrow Hawk)	S/O	1995	185.00	185
1992	The Painted Ladies	S/O	1992	225.00	1200
1995	Sus(h)gah-daydus(h) (Crow; Quick)	447		185.00	185
1995	Tze-go-juni (Chiricahua Apache)	447		185.00	185

Star Quilt Series - P.A. Cross

YEAR ISSUE		EDITION LIMIT	YEAR RETD.	ISSUE PRICE	QUOTE U.S.$
1988	The Quilt Makers	S/O	1988	190.00	1200
1986	Reflections	S/O	1986	185.00	865
1985	Winter Warmth	S/O	1985	150.00	900-1215

Wolf Series - P.A. Cross

YEAR ISSUE		EDITION LIMIT	YEAR RETD.	ISSUE PRICE	QUOTE U.S.$
1990	Agninaug Amaguut;Inupiag (Women With Her Wolves)	S/O	1993	325.00	350-750
1993	Ahmah-ghut, Tuhtu-loo; Eelahn-nuht Kah-auhk (Wolves and Caribou; My Furs and My Friends)	1,050		255.00	255
1989	Biagoht Eecuebeh Hehsheesh-Checah: (Red Ridinghood and Her Wolves), Gift I	S/O	1989	225.00	1500-2500
1985	Dii-tah-shteh Bii-wik; Chedah-bah liidah (My Very Own Protective Covering; Walks w/the Wolf Woman)	S/O	1985	185.00	3275
1987	The Morning Star Gives Long Otter His Hoop Medicine Power	S/O	1987	190.00	1800-2500

Flambro Imports

Emmett Kelly Jr. Lithographs - B. Leighton-Jones

YEAR ISSUE		EDITION LIMIT	YEAR RETD.	ISSUE PRICE	QUOTE U.S.$
1995	All Star Circus	2 Yr.		150.00	150
1994	EKJ 70th Birthday Commemorative	1,994		150.00	150
1994	I Love You	2 Yr.		90.00	90
1994	Joyful Noise	2 Yr.		90.00	90
1994	Picture Worth 1,000 Words	2 Yr.		90.00	90

Gartlan USA

Lithograph - Various

YEAR ISSUE		EDITION LIMIT	YEAR RETD.	ISSUE PRICE	QUOTE U.S.$
1986	George Brett-"The Swing" - J. Martin	2,000		85.00	200
1991	Joe Montana - M. Taylor	500	1994	495.00	600-700
1989	Kareem Abdul Jabbar-The Record Setter - M. Taylor	1,989	1993	85.00	300-350
1991	Negro League 1st World Series (print) - Unknown	1,924	1993	109.00	125
1987	Roger Staubach - C. Soileau	1,979	1992	85.00	200-300

Greenwich Workshop

Bama - J. Bama

YEAR ISSUE		EDITION LIMIT	YEAR RETD.	ISSUE PRICE	QUOTE U.S.$
1993	Art of James Bama Book with Chester Medicine Crow Fathers Flag Print	2,500	N/A	345.00	345
1981	At a Mountain Man Wedding	1,500	N/A	145.00	275
1981	At Burial Gallager and Blind Bill	1,650	N/A	135.00	150
1988	Bittin' Up-Rimrock Ranch	1,250	N/A	195.00	1000
1992	Blackfeet War Robe	1,000		195.00	195
1987	Buck Norris-Crossed Sabres Ranch	1,000	N/A	195.00	850
1990	Buffalo Bill	1,250	N/A	210.00	210
1993	The Buffalo Dance	1,000		195.00	195
1991	Ceremonial Lance	1,250		225.00	225
1994	Cheyenne Dog Soldier	1,000		225.00	225
1991	Chuck Wagon	1,000		225.00	225
1975	Chuck Wagon in the Snow	1,000	N/A	50.00	50
1992	Coming' Round the Bend	1,000		195.00	195
1978	Contemporary Sioux Indian	1,000	N/A	75.00	400
1992	Crow Cavalry Scout	1,000		195.00	195
1977	A Crow Indian	1,000	N/A	65.00	125
1982	Crow Indian Dancer	1,250		150.00	150
1988	Crow Indian From Lodge Grass	1,250		225.00	225
1988	Dan-Mountain Man	1,250	N/A	195.00	195
1983	The Davilla Brothers-Bronc Riders	1,250		145.00	145
1983	Don Walker-Bareback Rider	1,250	N/A	85.00	85
1991	The Drift on Skull Creek Pass	1,500		225.00	225
1979	Heritage	1,500	N/A	75.00	100
1978	Indian at Crow Fair	1,500	N/A	75.00	75
1988	Indian Wearing War Medicine Bonnet	1,000	N/A	225.00	225
1980	Ken Blackbird	1,500	N/A	95.00	95
1974	Ken Hunder, Working Cowboy	1,000	N/A	55.00	55
1989	Little Fawn-Cree Indian Girl	1,250	N/A	195.00	195
1979	Little Star	1,500	N/A	80.00	1000
1993	Magua-"The Last of the Mohicans"	1,000		225.00	225
1993	Making Horse Medicine	1,000		225.00	225
1978	Mountain Man	1,000	N/A	75.00	430
1980	Mountain Man 1820-1840 Period	1,500	N/A	115.00	150
1979	Mountain Man and His Fox	1,500	N/A	90.00	350
1982	Mountain Man with Rifle	1,250	N/A	135.00	135
1978	A Mountain Ute	1,000	N/A	75.00	75
1992	Northern Cheyene Wolf Scout	1,000		195.00	195
1981	Old Arapaho Story-Teller	1,500	N/A	135.00	135
1980	Old Saddle in the Snow	1,500	N/A	75.00	150
1980	Old Sod House	1,500	N/A	80.00	350
1981	Oldest Living Crow Indian	1,500	N/A	135.00	135
1993	On the North Fork of the Shoshoni	1,000		195.00	195
1990	Paul Newman as Butch Cassidy & Video	2,000		250.00	250
1981	Portrait of a Sioux	1,500	N/A	135.00	135
1979	Pre-Columbian Indian with Atlatl	1,500	N/A	75.00	75
1991	Ready to Rendezvous	1,000		225.00	225
1995	Ready to Ride	1,000		185.00	185
1990	Ridin' the Rims	1,250	N/A	210.00	210
1991	Riding the High Country	1,250		225.00	225
1978	Rookie Bronc Rider	1,000	N/A	75.00	100
1976	Sage Grinder	1,000	N/A	65.00	1800
1980	Sheep Skull in Drift	1,500	N/A	75.00	75
1974	Shoshone Chief	1,000	N/A	65.00	65
1982	Sioux Indian with Eagle Feather	1,250	N/A	150.00	150
1992	Sioux Subchief	1,000		195.00	195
1994	Slim Warren, The Old Cowboy	1,000		125.00	125
1983	Southwest Indian Father & Son	1,250		145.00	145
1977	Timber Jack Joe	1,000	N/A	65.00	450
1988	The Volunteer	1,500		225.00	225
1987	Winter on Trout Creek	1,000	N/A	150.00	525
1981	Winter Trapping	1,500	N/A	150.00	300
1980	Young Plains Indian	1,500	N/A	125.00	1300
1990	Young Sheepherder	1,500		225.00	225

Bean - A. Bean

YEAR ISSUE		EDITION LIMIT	YEAR RETD.	ISSUE PRICE	QUOTE U.S.$
1993	Conrad Gordon and Bean:The Fantasy	1,000		385.00	385
1987	Helping Hands	850		150.00	150
1988	How It Felt to Walk on the Moon	850	N/A	150.00	150
1992	In Flight	850		385.00	385
1994	In The Beginning Apollo 25 C/S	1,000	N/A	450.00	900

Blackshear - T. Blackshear

YEAR ISSUE		EDITION LIMIT	YEAR RETD.	ISSUE PRICE	QUOTE U.S.$
1994	Beauty and the Beast	1,000		225.00	225
1993	Hero Frederick Douglass	746		20.00	20
1993	Hero Harriet Tubman	753		20.00	20
1993	Hero Martin Luther King, Jr.	762		20.00	20
1993	Heroes of Our Heritage Portfolio	5,000		35.00	35
1995	Intimacy	550		850.00	850
1995	Night in Day	850		195.00	195
1994	Swansong	1,000		175.00	175

Blake - B. Blake

YEAR ISSUE		EDITION LIMIT	YEAR RETD.	ISSUE PRICE	QUOTE U.S.$
1995	The Old Double Diamond	850		175.00	175
1994	West of the Moon	650		195.00	195

Blossom - C. Blossom

YEAR ISSUE		EDITION LIMIT	YEAR RETD.	ISSUE PRICE	QUOTE U.S.$
1990	Ebb Tide	950		175.00	175
1989	Harbor Light	950		165.00	165
1988	Heading Home	950	N/A	150.00	250
1992	Port of Call	850		175.00	175
1992	Silhouette	850		175.00	175
1994	Traveling in Company	850		175.00	175
1994	Traveling in Company, Remarque	100		415.00	415
1992	Windward	950		175.00	175

Bralds - B. Bralds

YEAR ISSUE		EDITION LIMIT	YEAR RETD.	ISSUE PRICE	QUOTE U.S.$
1995	Bag Ladies	2,500		150.00	150

Bullas - W. Bullas

YEAR ISSUE		EDITION LIMIT	YEAR RETD.	ISSUE PRICE	QUOTE U.S.$
1995	The Big Game	1,500		95.00	95
1993	Billy the Pig	850		95.00	172
1995	The Chimp Shot	1,000		95.00	95
1994	Clucks Unlimited	850		95.00	95
1994	Court of Appeals	850		95.00	95
1995	Dog Byte	1,000		95.00	95
1994	Ductor	850		95.00	95
1995	fowl ball...	1,500		95.00	95
1994	Fridays After Five	850		95.00	95
1993	Mr. Harry Buns	850	N/A	95.00	95
1993	Our Ladies of the Front Lawn	850		95.00	95
1993	The Pale Prince	850		110.00	110
1993	Sand Trap Pro	850		95.00	95
1993	Some Set of Buns	850		95.00	95
1995	tennis, anyone?	1,000		95.00	95
1993	Wine-Oceros	850		95.00	95
1993	You Rang, Madam?	850		95.00	114

Christensen - J. Christensen

YEAR ISSUE		EDITION LIMIT	YEAR RETD.	ISSUE PRICE	QUOTE U.S.$
1989	The Annunciation	850	N/A	175.00	175
1995	Balancing Act	3,500		185.00	185
1994	Bird Hunters (Bronze)	50	N/A	4500.00	4500
1990	The Burden of the Responsible Man	850	N/A	145.00	800-1200
1991	The Candleman	850	N/A	160.00	260
1990	The Candleman, AP (Bronze)	100	N/A	737.00	4500
1993	College of Magical Knowledge	4,500	N/A	185.00	220-325
1993	College of Magical Knowledge, remarque	500	N/A	252.50	325
1991	Diggery Diggery Dar- Etching	75	N/A	210.00	465
1994	Evening Angels	4,000		195.00	195
1989	The Fish Walker (Bronze)	100	N/A	711.00	4500
1994	Framed Evening Angels	200	N/A	800.00	800
1993	Getting it Right	4,000		185.00	185
1985	The Gift For Mrs. Claus	3,500	N/A	80.00	415
1991	Jack Be Nimble-Etching	75	N/A	210.00	425
1986	Jonah	850	N/A	95.00	200
1991	Lawrence and a Bear	850		145.00	250
1987	Low Tech	2,000	N/A	35.00	35
1991	Man in the Moon-Etching	75	N/A	210.00	450-600
1988	The Man Who Minds the Moon	850	N/A	145.00	650
1991	Mother Goose-Etching	75	N/A	210.00	450
1987	Old Man with a Lot on His Mind	850	N/A	85.00	380-560
1986	Olde World Santa	3,500	N/A	80.00	425
1992	The Oldest Angel	850	N/A	125.00	485
1991	Once Upon a Time	1,500	N/A	175.00	1075
1991	Once Upon a Time, remarque	500	N/A	220.00	1150
1991	Pelican King	850	N/A	115.00	245
1991	Peter Peter Pumpkin Eater-Etching	75	N/A	210.00	450-600
1995	Piscatorial Percussionist	3,000		125.00	125
1992	The Reponsible Woman	2,500	N/A	175.00	190
1990	Rhymes & Reasons w/Booklet	3,000	N/A	150.00	240
1990	Rhymes & Reasons w/Booklet, remarque	500	N/A	208.00	330
1993	The Royal Music Barque	2,750	N/A	375.00	375
1992	The Royal Processional	1,500	N/A	185.00	340
1992	The Royal Processional, remarque	500	N/A	252.50	650
1993	The Scholar	3,250	N/A	125.00	400
1995	Serenade For an Orange Cat	3,000		125.00	125
1995	Sisters of the Sea	2,000		195.00	195
1994	Six Bird Hunters-Full Camouflage 3	4,662	N/A	165.00	165
1994	Sometimes the Spirit Touches w/book	3,600	N/A	195.00	300
1991	Three Blind Mice-Etching	75	N/A	210.00	450
1991	Three Wise Men of Gotham-Etching	75	N/A	210.00	450
1991	Tweedle Dee & Tweedle Dum-Etching	75	N/A	210.00	400
1994	Two Angels Discussing Botticelli	2,950		145.00	145
1990	Two Sisters	650	N/A	325.00	325
1987	Voyage of the Basset w/Journal	850	N/A	225.00	1200
1993	Waiting for the Tide	2,250	N/A	150.00	150
1988	The Widows Mite	850	N/A	145.00	2500
1986	Your Plaice, or Mine?	850	N/A	125.00	125

Combes - S. Combes

YEAR ISSUE		EDITION LIMIT	YEAR RETD.	ISSUE PRICE	QUOTE U.S.$
1992	African Oasis	650	N/A	375.00	500
1981	Alert	1,000	N/A	95.00	95
1987	The Angry One	850		95.00	95
1988	Bushwhacker	850	N/A	145.00	145
1983	Chui	275	N/A	250.00	250
1988	Confrontation	850		145.00	145
1988	The Crossing	1,250	N/A	245.00	245
1994	Disdain	850		110.00	110
1980	Facing the Wind	1,500	N/A	75.00	75
1993	Fearful Symmetry	850	N/A	110.00	110
1995	Golden Silhouette	950		175.00	175
1990	The Guardian (Silverback)	1,000		185.00	185
1992	The Hypnotist	1,250		145.00	145
1994	Indian Summer	950		175.00	175
1980	Interlude	1,500	N/A	85.00	85
1995	Jungle Phantom	950		175.00	175
1991	Kilimanjaro Morning	850		185.00	185
1981	Leopard Cubs	1,000	N/A	95.00	95
1992	Lookout	1,250		95.00	95
1980	Manyara Afternoon	1,500	N/A	75.00	250
1989	Masai-Longonot, Kenya	850		145.00	145
1992	Midday Sun (Lioness & Cubs)	850		125.00	125
1989	Mountain Gorillas	550	N/A	135.00	135
1995	Pride	950		175.00	175
1980	Serengeti Monarch	1,500	N/A	85.00	85
1995	Serious Intent	950		175.00	175
1995	Siberian Winter	950		175.00	175
1988	Simba	850		125.00	125
1980	Solitary Hunter	1,500	N/A	75.00	75
1990	Standoff	850	N/A	375.00	375
1991	Study in Concentration	850	N/A	185.00	225
1987	Tall Shadows	850	N/A	150.00	425
1985	Tension at Dawn	825	N/A	145.00	1000
1985	Tension at Dawn, remarque	25	N/A	275.00	1200
1989	The Watering Hole	850		225.00	225
1986	The Wildebeest Migration	450	N/A	350.00	1900

Crowley - D. Crowley

YEAR ISSUE		EDITION LIMIT	YEAR RETD.	ISSUE PRICE	QUOTE U.S.$
1981	Afterglow	1,500	N/A	110.00	110
1992	Anna Thorne	650		160.00	160
1980	Apache in White	1,500	N/A	85.00	85
1979	Arizona Mountain Man	1,500	N/A	85.00	85
1980	Beauty and the Beast	1,500	N/A	85.00	85
1992	Colors of the Sunset	650		175.00	175
1979	Desert Sunset	1,500	N/A	75.00	75
1978	Dorena	1,000	N/A	75.00	75
1994	The Dreamer	650		150.00	150
1981	Eagle Feathers	1,500	N/A	95.00	95
1988	Ermine and Beads	550	N/A	85.00	85
1989	The Gunfighters	3,000	N/A	35.00	35
1981	The Heirloom	1,000	N/A	125.00	125
1982	Hopi Butterfly	275	N/A	350.00	350
1978	Hudson's Bay Blanket	1,000	N/A	75.00	75
1980	The Littlest Apache	275	N/A	325.00	850
1994	Plumes and Ribbons	650		160.00	160
1979	Security Blanket	1,500	N/A	65.00	65
1981	Shannandoah	275	N/A	325.00	325
1978	The Starquilt	1,000	N/A	65.00	300-450
1986	The Trapper	550		75.00	75

Dawson - J. Dawson

YEAR ISSUE		EDITION LIMIT	YEAR RETD.	ISSUE PRICE	QUOTE U.S.$
1992	The Attack (Cougars)	850		175.00	175
1993	Berry Contented	850		150.00	150
1993	Berry Contented (Remarque)	100		235.00	235
1994	The Face Off (Right & Left Panel)	850		150.00	150
1993	Looking Back	850		110.00	110
1993	Otter Wise	850		150.00	150
1993	Taking a Break	850	N/A	150.00	150

Doolittle - B. Doolittle

YEAR ISSUE		EDITION LIMIT	YEAR RETD.	ISSUE PRICE	QUOTE U.S.$
1983	Art of Camouflage, signed	2,000	1983	55.00	300
1980	Bugged Bear	1,000	1980	85.00	3500-4000
1987	Calling the Buffalo	8,500	1987	245.00	1025
1983	Christmas Day, Give or Take a Week	4,581	1983	80.00	1500
1988	Doubled Back	15,000	1988	245.00	1200
1992	Eagle Heart	48,000	1992	285.00	285
1982	Eagle's Flight	1,500	1982	185.00	3000-4000
1983	Escape by a Hare	1,500	1983	80.00	630
1984	Forest Has Eyes, The	8,544	1984	175.00	5200
1980	Good Omen, The	1,000	1980	85.00	4500-5200
1987	Guardian Spirits	13,238	1987	295.00	1200
1990	Hide and Seek (Composite & Video)	25,000	1990	300.00	300
1990	Hide and Seek Suite	25,000	1990	900.00	1200
1984	Let My Spirit Soar	1,500	1984	195.00	4000-4500
1979	Pintos	1,000	1979	65.00	8000-9500
1993	Prayer for the Wild Things	65,000	1993	325.00	375
1983	Runs With Thunder	1,500	1983	150.00	1330
1983	Rushing War Eagle	1,500	1983	150.00	1150
1991	Sacred Circle (Print & Video)	40,192	1991	325.00	425
1989	Sacred Ground	69,996	1989	265.00	950
1987	Season of the Eagle	36,548	1987	245.00	975
1991	The Sentinel	35,000	1991	275.00	750
1981	Spirit of the Grizzly	1,500	1981	150.00	3400-4000
1995	Spirit Takes Flight	48,000		225.00	225
1986	Two Bears of the Blackfeet	2,650	1986	225.00	1130
1985	Two Indian Horses	12,253	1985	225.00	4000-4500
1995	Two More Indian Horses	48,000		225.00	225
1981	Unknown Presence	1,500	1981	135.00	2700-3000
1992	Walk Softly (Chapbook)	40,192	1992	225.00	225
1994	When The Wind Had Wings	57,500	1994	325.00	325
1986	Where Silence Speaks, Doolittle The Art of Bev Doolittle	3,500	1986	650.00	2700
1980	Whoo !?	1,000	1980	75.00	1300
1993	Wilderness? Wilderness!	50,000	1993	65.00	65
1985	Wolves of the Crow	2,650	1985	225.00	1700
1981	Woodland Encounter	1,500	1981	145.00	8100-9000

Ferris - K. Ferris

YEAR ISSUE		EDITION LIMIT	YEAR RETD.	ISSUE PRICE	QUOTE U.S.$
1990	The Circus Outbound	1,000		225.00	225
1991	Farmer's Nightmare	850		185.00	185
1991	Linebacker in the Buff	1,000		225.00	225
1983	Little Willie Coming Home	1,000	N/A	145.00	1900-2100
1994	Real Trouble	1,000		195.00	195
1982	Sunrise Encounter	1,000	N/A	145.00	145
1993	A Test of Courage	850		185.00	185
1991	Too Little, Too Late w/Video	1,000		245.00	245

Frederick - R. Frederick

YEAR ISSUE		EDITION LIMIT	YEAR RETD.	ISSUE PRICE	QUOTE U.S.$
1990	Autumn Leaves	1,250	N/A	175.00	175
1989	Barely Spring	1,500		165.00	165
1994	Beeline (C)	1,000		195.00	195
1987	Before the Storm (Diptych)	550	N/A	350.00	950
1991	Breaking the Ice	2,750	N/A	235.00	235
1989	Colors of Home	1,500	N/A	165.00	225
1995	Drifters	850		175.00	175
1985	Early Evening Gathering	475	N/A	325.00	355
1990	An Early Light Breakfast	1,750	N/A	235.00	235
1990	Echoes of Sunset	1,750	N/A	235.00	500
1987	Evening Shadows (White-Tail Deer)	1,500	N/A	125.00	125
1992	Fast Break	2,250		235.00	235
1992	Fire and Ice (Suite of 2)	1,750		175.00	175
1984	First Moments of Gold	825	N/A	145.00	170
1984	First Moments of Gold, remarque	25	N/A	172.50	185
1984	From Timber's Edge	850	N/A	125.00	140-165
1989	Gifts of the Land #2	500	N/A	150.00	150
1988	Gifts of the Land w/Wine & Wine Label	500	N/A	150.00	150
1988	Glimmer of Solitude	1,500		145.00	145
1993	Glory Days	1,750		115.00	115
1986	Great Horned Owl	1,250	N/A	115.00	135
1995	High Country Harem	1,000		185.00	185
1985	High Society	950	N/A	115.00	200-400
1991	The Long Run	1,750	N/A	235.00	300-400
1991	The Long Run, AP	200	N/A	167.50	300
1985	Los Colores De Chiapas	950	N/A	85.00	85
1994	The Lost World	1,000		175.00	175
1985	Misty Morning Lookout	950	N/A	145.00	145
1984	Misty Morning Sentinel	850	N/A	125.00	145
1989	Monarch of the North	2,000		150.00	150
1990	Morning Surprise	1,750	N/A	165.00	165
1991	Morning Thunder	1,750	N/A	185.00	250
1988	The Nesting Call	2,500		150.00	150
1988	The Nesting Call, remarque	1,000	N/A	165.00	165
1993	New Heights	1,950		195.00	195
1987	Northern Light	1,500	N/A	165.00	165
1986	Out on a Limb	1,250	N/A	145.00	350
1993	Point of View	1,000		235.00	235
1992	Rain Forest Rendezvous	1,500	N/A	225.00	225
1988	Rim Walk	1,500	N/A	90.00	100
1988	Shadows of Dusk	1,500	N/A	165.00	165
1990	Silent Watch (High Desert Museum)	2,000	N/A	35.00	35
1994	Snow Pack	1,000		175.00	175
1992	Snowstorm	1,750		195.00	195
1990	Snowy Reflections (Snowy Egret)	1,500		150.00	150
1986	Sounds of Twilight	1,500	N/A	135.00	200
1991	Summer's Song (Triptych)	2,500		225.00	225
1993	Temple of the Jaguar	1,500		225.00	225
1988	Timber Ghost w/Mini Wine Label	3,000	N/A	150.00	175
1994	Tropic Moon	850		165.00	165
1987	Tundra Watch (Snowy Owl)	1,500	N/A	145.00	145
1994	Way of the Caribou	1,235		235.00	235
1987	Winter's Brilliance (Cardinal)	1,500	N/A	135.00	140
1986	Winter's Call	1,250	N/A	165.00	450-600
1986	Winter's Call Raptor, AP	100	N/A	165.00	600
1987	Woodland Crossing (Caribou)	1,500	N/A	145.00	145
1988	World of White	2,500	N/A	150.00	150

Gurney - J. Gurney

YEAR ISSUE		EDITION LIMIT	YEAR RETD.	ISSUE PRICE	QUOTE U.S.$
1992	Birthday Pageant	2,500	N/A	60.00	60
1992	Birthday Pageant, remarque	300	N/A	275.00	340
1995	Cottage Reflections	3,000		195.00	195
1991	Dinosaur Boulevard	2,000	N/A	125.00	125
1991	Dinosaur Boulevard, remarque	250	N/A	196.00	1500
1990	Dinosaur Parade	1,995	1995	125.00	125
1990	Dinosaur Parade, remarque	150		130.00	1500-2000
1992	Dream Canyon	N/A	N/A	125.00	125
1992	Dream Canyon, remarque	150	N/A	196.00	300
1993	The Excursion	3,500		175.00	175
1993	Garden of Hope	3,500		175.00	175
1990	Morning in Treetown	1,500	N/A	175.00	260
1993	Palace in the Clouds	3,500	N/A	175.00	175
1993	Ring Riders	2,500	N/A	175.00	175
1995	Rumble & Mist	2,500		175.00	175
1990	Seaside Romp	1,000	N/A	175.00	290
1992	Skyback Print w/Dinotopia Book	3,500	N/A	295.00	295
1994	Small Wonder	3,299	N/A	75.00	75
1994	Steep Street	3,500		95.00	95
1991	Waterfall City	3,000	N/A	125.00	125
1991	Waterfall City, remarque	250	N/A	186.00	425
1995	The World Beneath Collectors' Book w/ print	3,000		195.00	195

Gustafson - S. Gustafson

YEAR ISSUE		EDITION LIMIT	YEAR RETD.	ISSUE PRICE	QUOTE U.S.$
1995	The Alice in Wonderland Suite	4,000		195.00	195
1994	Frog Prince	3,500	1994	125.00	125
1993	Goldilocks and the Three Bears	3,500	1993	125.00	250-400
1995	Hansel & Gretel	3,000		125.00	125
1993	Humpty Dumpty	3,500	1993	125.00	125
1995	Jack in the Beanstalk	3,500		125.00	125
1993	Little Red Riding Hood	3,500	1993	125.00	165
1994	Pat-A-Cake	4,000	1994	125.00	125
1993	Snow White and the Seven Dwarfs	3,500	1993	165.00	250-350
1995	Touched by Magic	4,000		185.00	185

Hartough - L. Hartough

YEAR ISSUE		EDITION LIMIT	YEAR RETD.	ISSUE PRICE	QUOTE U.S.$
1995	7th Hole Pebble Beach Golf Links	850		225.00	225

Johnson - J. Johnson

YEAR ISSUE		EDITION LIMIT	YEAR RETD.	ISSUE PRICE	QUOTE U.S.$
1994	Moose River	650		175.00	175
1994	Sea Treasures	650		125.00	125
1994	Winter Thaw	650		150.00	150
1993	Wolf Creek	550	N/A	165.00	200

Kennedy - S. Kennedy

YEAR ISSUE		EDITION LIMIT	YEAR RETD.	ISSUE PRICE	QUOTE U.S.$
1988	After Dinner Music	2,500	N/A	175.00	300
1995	Alaskan Malamute	1,000		125.00	125
1992	Aurora	2,250	N/A	195.00	195
1991	A Breed Apart	2,750	N/A	225.00	225
1992	Cabin Fever	2,250		175.00	175
1988	Distant Relations	950	N/A	200.00	500
1988	Eager to Run	950	N/A	200.00	1700
1990	Fish Tales	5,500	N/A	225.00	225
1991	In Training	3,350	N/A	165.00	165
1991	In Training, remarque	150	N/A	215.50	216
1995	The Lesson	1,000		125.00	125
1993	Midnight Eyes	1,750		125.00	125
1993	Never Alone	2,250		225.00	225
1993	Never Alone, remarque	250	N/A	272.50	273
1990	On the Edge	4,000		225.00	225
1995	On the Heights	850		175.00	175

YEAR ISSUE		EDITION LIMIT	YEAR RETD.	ISSUE PRICE	QUOTE U.S.$
1994	Quiet Time Companions-Samoyed	1,000		125.00	125
1994	Quiet Time Companions-Siberian Husky	1,000	N/A	125.00	125
1994	Silent Observers	1,250	N/A	165.00	265
1989	Snowshoes	4,000	N/A	185.00	185
1994	Spruce and Fur	1,500		165.00	165
1993	The Touch	1,500		115.00	115
1989	Up a Creek	2,500	N/A	185.00	285

Kodera - C. Kodera

YEAR ISSUE		EDITION LIMIT	YEAR RETD.	ISSUE PRICE	QUOTE U.S.$
1986	The A Team (K10)	850		145.00	145
1995	A.M. Sortie	1,000		225.00	225
1991	Darkness Visible (Stealth)	2,671	N/A	40.00	40
1987	Fifty Years a Lady	550	N/A	150.00	325
1988	The Great Greenwich Balloon Race	1,000		145.00	145
1990	Green Light-Jump!	650	N/A	145.00	200
1992	Halsey's Surprise	850		95.00	95
1994	Last to Fight	1,000		225.00	225
1992	Looking For Nagumo	1,000		225.00	225
1992	Memphis Belle/Dauntless Dotty	1,250		245.00	245
1990	A Moment's Peace	1,250		150.00	150
1988	Moonlight Intruders	1,000		125.00	125
1989	Springtime Flying in the Rockies	550	N/A	95.00	95
1992	Thirty Seconds Over Tokyo	1,000	N/A	275.00	275
1991	This is No Drill w/Video	1,000		225.00	225
1994	This is No Time to Lose an Engine	850		150.00	150
1994	Tiger's Bite	850		150.00	150
1987	Voyager: The Skies Yield	1,500		225.00	225

Landry - P. Landry

YEAR ISSUE		EDITION LIMIT	YEAR RETD.	ISSUE PRICE	QUOTE U.S.$
1993	The Antique Shop	1,250	N/A	125.00	125
1992	Apple Orchard	1,250		150.00	150
1992	Aunt Martha's Country Farm	1,500	N/A	185.00	185
1987	Bluenose Country	550	N/A	115.00	175
1992	Boardwalk Promenade	1,250		175.00	175
1989	A Canadian Christmas	1,250		125.00	125
1989	Cape Cod Welcome Cameo	850	N/A	75.00	400
1990	The Captain's Garden	1,000	N/A	165.00	250
1993	Christmas at Mystic Seaport	2,000		125.00	125
1992	Christmas at the Flower Market	2,500		125.00	125
1994	Christmas Carousel Pony	2,000		125.00	125
1990	Christmas Treasures	2,500		165.00	165
1992	Cottage Garden	1,250	N/A	160.00	160
1995	Cottage Reflections	850		135.00	135
1994	An English Cottage	850		150.00	150
1994	Flower Barn	1,000		175.00	175
1988	Flower Boxes	550	N/A	75.00	225
1991	Flower Market	1,500	N/A	185.00	700
1990	Flower Wagon	1,500	N/A	165.00	175
1994	Flowers For Mary Hope	1,250		165.00	165
1995	Harbor Garden	1,000		160.00	160
1993	Hometown Parade	1,250		165.00	165
1990	Morning Papers	1,250	N/A	135.00	200
1994	Morning Walk	850		135.00	135
1991	Nantucket Colors	1,500		150.00	150
1993	Paper Boy	1,500		150.00	150
1993	A Place in the Park	1,500		185.00	185
1984	Regatta	500	N/A	75.00	135
1984	Regatta, remarque	50	N/A	97.50	145
1990	Seaside Carousel	1,500	N/A	165.00	200
1988	Seaside Cottage	550	N/A	125.00	125
1986	Seaside Mist	450	N/A	85.00	300
1985	The Skaters	500		75.00	75
1985	The Skaters, remarque	50	N/A	97.50	98
1995	Spring Song	2,500		145.00	145
1991	Summer Concert	1,500		195.00	195
1989	Summer Garden	850	N/A	125.00	400
1995	Summer Mist (Fine Art Original Lithograph)	550		750.00	750
1992	Sunflowers	1,250	N/A	125.00	125
1991	The Toymaker	1,500	N/A	165.00	165
1991	Victorian Memories	1,500	N/A	150.00	150

Lyman - S. Lyman

YEAR ISSUE		EDITION LIMIT	YEAR RETD.	ISSUE PRICE	QUOTE U.S.$
1990	Among The Wild Brambles	1,750	1990	185.00	185
1985	Autumn Gathering	850	N/A	115.00	115
1985	Bear & Blossoms (C)	850	N/A	75.00	450
1987	Canadian Autumn	1,500	1987	165.00	175
1995	Cathedral Snow	4,000		245.00	245
1989	Color In The Snow (Pheasant)	1,500	N/A	165.00	200-375
1991	Dance of Cloud and Cliff	1,500	1991	225.00	225
1991	Dance of Water and Light	3,000	1991	225.00	225
1983	Early Winter In The Mountains	850	N/A	95.00	300
1987	An Elegant Couple (Wood Ducks)	1,000	N/A	125.00	125
1991	Embers at Dawn	3,500	1991	225.00	975
1983	End Of The Ridge	850	N/A	95.00	450
1990	Evening Light	2,500	1990	225.00	1300
1995	Evening Star w/collector's edition book	9,500		195.00	195
1993	Fire Dance	8,500	1993	235.00	300
1984	Free Flight	850		70.00	70
1987	High Creek Crossing	1,000	N/A	165.00	600-800
1989	High Light	1,250	1989	165.00	255
1986	High Trail At Sunset	1,000	N/A	125.00	420
1988	The Intruder	1,500	N/A	150.00	150
1993	Lake of the Shining Rocks	2,250	1993	235.00	250
1992	Lantern Light Print w Firelight Chapbook	10,000	1993	195.00	195
1989	Last Light of Winter	1,500	1989	175.00	875
1995	Midnight Fire	8,500		245.00	245
1994	Moon Fire	7,500	1994	245.00	525
1987	Moon Shadows	1,500	N/A	135.00	135
1994	Moonlit Flight on Christmas Night	2,750	1994	165.00	245
1986	Morning Solitude	850	N/A	115.00	600
1990	A Mountain Campfire	1,500	1990	195.00	2050
1994	New Kid on the Rock	2,250		185.00	185
1987	New Territory (Grizzly & Cubs)	1,000	N/A	135.00	135
1984	Noisy Neighbors	675	N/A	95.00	600
1984	Noisy Neighbors, remarque	25	N/A	127.50	900
1994	North Country Shores	3,000	1994	225.00	225
1983	The Pass	850	N/A	95.00	600-850
1989	Quiet Rain	1,500	N/A	165.00	400-800
1988	The Raptor's Watch	1,500	N/A	150.00	475
1988	Return Of The Falcon	1,500	N/A	150.00	200
1993	Riparian Riches	2,500	1993	235.00	250
1992	River of Light (Geese)	2,950	N/A	225.00	225
1991	Secret Watch (Lynx)	2,250		150.00	150
1990	Silent Snows	1,750	N/A	210.00	210
1988	Snow Hunter	1,500	N/A	135.00	135
1986	Snowy Throne (C)	850	N/A	85.00	300
1993	The Spirit of Christmas	2,750	1993	165.00	200
1995	Thunderbolt	7,000		235.00	235
1987	Twilight Snow (C)	950	N/A	85.00	150
1988	Uzumati: Great Bear of Yosemite	1,750		150.00	500
1992	Warmed by the View	8,500	1992	235.00	300
1992	Wilderness Welcome	8,500	N/A	235.00	425
1992	Wildflower Suite (Hummingbird)	2,250		175.00	175
1992	Woodland Haven	2,500	N/A	195.00	255

Marris - B. Marris

YEAR ISSUE		EDITION LIMIT	YEAR RETD.	ISSUE PRICE	QUOTE U.S.$
1987	Above the Glacier	850	N/A	145.00	145
1986	Best Friends	850	N/A	85.00	300
1994	Big Gray's Barn and Bistro	1,000		125.00	125
1989	Bittersweet	1,000	N/A	135.00	135
1990	Bugles and Trumpets!	1,000	N/A	175.00	175
1992	The Comeback	1,250		175.00	175
1991	Cops & Robbers	1,000	N/A	165.00	165
1988	Courtship	850	N/A	145.00	145
1995	Dairy Queens	1,000		125.00	125
1995	The Dartmoor Ponies	1,000		165.00	165
1987	Desperados	850	N/A	135.00	135
1991	End of the Season	1,000		165.00	165
1985	The Fishing Lesson	1,000		145.00	145
1995	The Gift	1,000		125.00	125
1987	Honey Creek Whitetales	850	N/A	145.00	145
1985	Kenai Dusk	1,000	N/A	145.00	300
1994	Lady Marmalade's Bed & Breakfast	1,000		125.00	125
1990	Mom's Shadow	1,000		165.00	165
1994	Moonshine	1,000		95.00	95
1989	New Beginnings	1,000	N/A	175.00	300
1990	Of Myth and Magic	1,500	N/A	175.00	175
1986	Other Footsteps	950		75.00	75
1989	The Playgroud Showoff	850	N/A	165.00	165
1992	Security Blanket	1,250		175.00	175
1993	Spring Fever	1,000		165.00	165
1991	The Stillness (Grizzly & Cubs)	1,000	N/A	165.00	165
1992	Sun Bath	1,000		95.00	95
1992	To Stand and Endure	1,000	N/A	195.00	195
1991	Under the Morning Star	1,500		175.00	175
1988	Waiting For the Freeze	1,000	N/A	125.00	125

McCarthy, Frank - F. McCarthy

YEAR ISSUE		EDITION LIMIT	YEAR RETD.	ISSUE PRICE	QUOTE U.S.$
1984	After the Dust Storm	1,000	N/A	145.00	145
1982	Alert	1,000	N/A	135.00	135
1984	Along the West Fork	1,000	N/A	175.00	200
1978	Ambush, The	1,000	N/A	125.00	300
1982	Apache Scout	1,000	N/A	165.00	165
1988	Apache Trackers (C)	1,000	N/A	95.00	95
1992	The Art of Frank McCarthy	10,418	N/A	60.00	60
1982	Attack on the Wagon Train	1,400	N/A	150.00	150
1977	The Beaver Men	1,000	N/A	75.00	400
1980	Before the Charge	1,000	N/A	115.00	200
1978	Before the Norther	1,000	N/A	90.00	325
1990	Below The Breaking Dawn	1,250	N/A	225.00	225
1994	Beneath the Cliff (Petraglyphs)	1,500		295.00	295
1989	Big Medicine	1,000	N/A	225.00	370
1983	Blackfeet Raiders	1,000	N/A	90.00	300
1992	Breaking the Moonlit Silence	650	N/A	375.00	300-375
1986	The Buffalo Runners	1,000	N/A	195.00	170
1980	Burning the Way Station	1,000	N/A	125.00	250
1993	By the Ancient Trails They Passed	1,000	N/A	245.00	245
1989	Canyon Lands	1,250	N/A	225.00	225
1982	The Challenge	1,000	N/A	175.00	300
1985	Charging the Challenger	1,000	N/A	150.00	550
1991	The Chase	1,000		225.00	225
1986	Children of the Raven	1,000	N/A	185.00	550
1987	Chiricahua Raiders	1,000	N/A	165.00	200
1977	Comanche Moon	1,000	N/A	75.00	250
1992	Comanche Raider-Bronze	100		812.50	813
1986	Comanche War Trail	1,000	N/A	165.00	170
1989	The Coming Of The Iron Horse	1,500	N/A	225.00	225
1989	The Coming Of The Iron Horse (Print/Pewter Train Special Publ. Ed.)	100	N/A	1500.00	1600-2150
1981	The Coup	1,000	N/A	125.00	250
1981	Crossing the Divide (The Old West)	1,500	N/A	850.00	700
1984	The Decoys	450	N/A	325.00	500
1977	Distant Thunder	1,500	N/A	75.00	300
1989	Down From The Mountains	1,500	N/A	245.00	245
1986	The Drive (C)	1,000	N/A	95.00	95-175
1977	Dust Stained Posse	1,000	N/A	75.00	450
1985	The Fireboat	1,000	N/A	175.00	200
1994	Flashes of Lighting-Thunder of Hooves	550		435.00	435
1987	Following the Herds	1,000	N/A	195.00	250
1980	Forbidden Land	1,000	N/A	125.00	125
1978	The Fording	1,000	N/A	75.00	200
1987	From the Rim	1,000	N/A	225.00	225
1981	Headed North	1,000	N/A	150.00	225
1992	Heading Back	1,000		225.00	200-225
1990	Hoka Hey: Sioux War Cry	1,250		225.00	225
1987	The Hostile Land	1,000	N/A	225.00	235
1976	The Hostiles	1,000	N/A	75.00	400
1984	Hostiles, signed	1,000	N/A	55.00	55
1974	The Hunt	1,000	N/A	75.00	620-930
1988	In Pursuit of the White Buffalo	1,500	N/A	225.00	900
1992	In the Land of the Ancient Ones	1,250	N/A	245.00	245
1983	In The Land Of The Sparrow Hawk People	1,000	N/A	165.00	180
1987	In The Land Of The Winter Hawk	1,000	N/A	225.00	225
1978	In The Pass	1,500	N/A	90.00	125
1985	The Last Crossing	550	N/A	350.00	450-500
1989	The Last Stand: Little Big Horn	1,500	N/A	225.00	225
1984	Leading the Charge, signed	1,000	N/A	55.00	55
1974	Lone Sentinel	1,000	N/A	55.00	1400-1800
1979	The Loner	1,000	N/A	75.00	275
1974	Long Column	1,000	N/A	75.00	400
1985	The Long Knives	1,000	N/A	175.00	400
1989	Los Diablos	1,250	N/A	225.00	225
1983	Moonlit Trail	1,000	N/A	90.00	100
1992	Navajo Ponies Comanchie Warriors	1,000		225.00	225
1978	Night Crossing	1,000	N/A	75.00	200
1974	The Night They Needed a Good Ribbon Man	1,000	N/A	65.00	300
1977	An Old Time Mountain Man	1,000	N/A	65.00	200
1990	On The Old North Trail (Triptych)	650	N/A	550.00	750
1979	On the Warpath	1,000	N/A	75.00	150
1983	Out Of The Mist They Came	1,000	N/A	165.00	175
1990	Out Of The Windswept Ramparts	1,250		225.00	225
1976	Packing In	1,000	N/A	65.00	400
1991	Pony Express	1,000		225.00	225
1991	Pony Express-Bronze	10		934.00	934
1979	The Prayer	1,500	N/A	90.00	550-600
1991	The Pursuit	650	N/A	550.00	550
1981	Race with the Hostiles	1,000	N/A	135.00	135
1987	Red Bull's War Party	1,000	N/A	165.00	165
1979	Retreat to Higher Ground	2,000	N/A	90.00	200
1975	Returning Raiders	1,000	N/A	75.00	300
1980	Roar of the Norther	1,000	N/A	90.00	200
1977	Robe Signal	850	N/A	60.00	400
1988	Saber Charge	2,250		225.00	225-250
1984	The Savage Taunt	1,000	N/A	225.00	225
1985	Scouting The Long Knives	1,400	N/A	195.00	250-300
1993	Shadows of Warriors (3 Print Suite)	1,000		225.00	225
1994	Show of Defiance	1,000		195.00	195
1993	Sighting the Intruders	1,000		225.00	225
1978	Single File	1,000	N/A	75.00	300
1976	Sioux Warriors	650	N/A	55.00	250
1975	Smoke Was Their Ally	1,000	N/A	75.00	425-550
1980	Snow Moon	1,000	N/A	115.00	250
1986	Spooked	1,400	N/A	195.00	200
1981	Surrounded	1,000	N/A	150.00	195-275
1975	The Survivor	1,000	N/A	65.00	250
1980	A Time Of Decision	1,150	N/A	125.00	175
1978	To Battle	1,000	N/A	75.00	370
1985	The Traders	1,000	N/A	195.00	195
1980	The Trooper	1,000	N/A	90.00	125
1988	Turning The Leaders	1,500	N/A	225.00	225
1983	Under Attack	5,676	N/A	125.00	500
1981	Under Hostile Fire	1,000	N/A	150.00	200
1975	Waiting for the Escort	1,000	N/A	75.00	125
1976	The Warrior	650	N/A	55.00	200
1982	The Warriors	1,000	N/A	150.00	150
1984	Watching the Wagons	1,400	N/A	175.00	440
1994	The Way of the Ancient Migrations	1,250		245.00	245
1987	When Omens Turn Bad	1,000	N/A	165.00	325
1992	When the Land Was Theirs	1,000		225.00	225
1992	Where Ancient Ones Had Hunted	1,000	N/A	245.00	245
1992	Where Others Had Passed	1,000	N/A	245.00	245
1986	Where Tracks Will Be Lost	550	N/A	350.00	350
1982	Whirling He Raced to Meet the Challenge	1,000	N/A	175.00	450
1991	The Wild Ones	1,000	N/A	225.00	225
1990	Winter Trail	1,500	N/A	235.00	235
1993	With Pistols Drawn	1,000		195.00	195

McCarthy, Kevin - K. McCarthy

YEAR ISSUE		EDITION LIMIT	YEAR RETD.	ISSUE PRICE	QUOTE U.S.$
1991	Comanche Rider-Bronze	100	N/A	812.50	813
1991	Pony Express-Bronze	10	N/A	934.00	934
1994	Thunder of Hooves-Bronze	10	N/A	875.00	875

Mitchell - D. Mitchell

YEAR ISSUE		EDITION LIMIT	YEAR RETD.	ISSUE PRICE	QUOTE U.S.$
1994	Bonding Years	550		175.00	175
1993	Country Church	550		175.00	175
1995	Innocence	1,000		150.00	150
1995	Let Us Pray	850		175.00	175
1993	Psalms 4:1	550	N/A	195.00	195
1992	Rowena	550	N/A	195.00	300

Mo Da-Feng - M. Da-Feng

YEAR ISSUE		EDITION LIMIT	YEAR RETD.	ISSUE PRICE	QUOTE U.S.$
1994	Ocean Mist	850		150.00	150

Parker, E. - E. Parker

Year Issue		Edition Limit	Year Retd.	Issue Price	Quote U.S.$
1995	The Glorious 4th	850		150.00	150

Parker, R. - R. Parker

Year Issue		Edition Limit	Year Retd.	Issue Price	Quote U.S.$
1995	The Breakfast Club	850		125.00	125
1995	Coastal Morning	850		195.00	195
1995	Evening Solitude	850		195.00	195
1994	Forest Flight	850		195.00	195
1994	Grizzlies at the Falls	850		225.00	225
1994	Morning Flight	4,000		20.00	20

Phillips - W. Phillips

Year Issue		Edition Limit	Year Retd.	Issue Price	Quote U.S.$
1982	Advantage Eagle	1,000	N/A	135.00	250
1992	Alone No More	850		195.00	195
1988	America on the Move	1,500	N/A	185.00	210
1994	Among the Columns of Thor	1,000		295.00	295
1993	And Now the Trap	850		175.00	175
1986	Changing of the Guard	500		100.00	100
1993	Chasing the Daylight	850		185.00	185
1994	Christmas Leave When Dreams Come True	1,500	N/A	185.00	230
1986	Confrontation at Beachy Head	1,000		150.00	150
1991	Dauntless Against a Rising Sun	850	N/A	195.00	195
1991	Fifty Miles Out	1,000		175.00	175
1983	The Giant Begins to Stir	1,250	N/A	185.00	1800
1990	Going in Hot w/Book	1,500		250.00	250
1985	Heading For Trouble	1,000	N/A	125.00	250
1984	Hellfire Corner	1,225	N/A	185.00	650
1984	Hellfire Corner, remarque	25	N/A	225.80	675
1990	Hunter Becomes the Hunted w/video	1,500		265.00	265
1992	I Could Never Be So Lucky Again	850	N/A	295.00	750
1993	If Only in My Dreams	1,000	N/A	175.00	365
1984	Into the Teeth of the Tiger	975	N/A	135.00	900
1984	Into the Teeth of the Tiger, remarque	25	N/A	167.50	2000
1994	Into the Throne Room of God w/book "The Glory of Flight"	750	N/A	195.00	400
1991	Intruder Outbound	1,000		225.00	225
1991	Last Chance	1,000	N/A	165.00	165
1985	Lest We Forget	1,250	N/A	195.00	195
1994	Lethal Encounter	1,000		225.00	225
1988	The Long Green Line	3,500		185.00	185
1992	The Long Ride Home (P-51D)	850	N/A	195.00	195
1991	Low Pass For the Home Folks, BP	1,000	N/A	175.00	175
1986	Next Time Get 'Em All	1,500	N/A	225.00	300
1989	No Empty Bunks Tonight	1,500	N/A	165.00	165
1989	No Flying Today	1,500		185.00	185
1989	Over the Top	1,000		165.00	165
1985	The Phantoms and the Wizard	850	N/A	145.00	625
1992	Ploesti: Into the Fire and Fury	850		195.00	195
1987	Range Wars	1,000		160.00	160
1987	Shore Birds at Point Lobos	1,250	N/A	175.00	175
1989	Sierra Hotel	1,250	N/A	175.00	175
1987	Sunward We Climb	1,000		175.00	175
1983	Those Clouds Won't Help You Now	625	N/A	135.00	300
1983	Those Clouds Won't Help You Now, remarque	25	N/A	275.00	325
1987	Those Last Critical Moments	1,250	N/A	185.00	300
1993	Threading the Eye of the Needle	1,000		195.00	195
1986	Thunder in the Canyon	1,000	N/A	165.00	650
1990	A Time of Eagles	1,250		245.00	245
1989	Time to Head Home	1,500		165.00	165
1986	Top Cover for the Straggler	1,000	N/A	145.00	210
1983	Two Down, One to Go	3,000	N/A	15.00	15
1982	Welcome Home Yank	1,000	N/A	135.00	850
1993	When Prayers are Answered	850		245.00	245
1991	When You See Zeros, Fight Em'	1,000		N/A	N/A

Reynolds - J. Reynolds

Year Issue		Edition Limit	Year Retd.	Issue Price	Quote U.S.$
1994	Arizona Cowboys	850	N/A	195.00	225
1994	Cold Country, Hot Coffee	1,000		185.00	185
1994	The Henry	850	N/A	195.00	195
1994	Quiet Place	1,000	N/A	185.00	185
1994	Spring Showers	1,000		225.00	225

Simpkins - J. Simpkins

Year Issue		Edition Limit	Year Retd.	Issue Price	Quote U.S.$
1994	All My Love	850		125.00	125
1993	Angels	850		225.00	225
1994	Gold Falls	1,750		195.00	195
1995	Mrs. Tenderhart	1,000		175.00	175
1995	Pavane in Gold	2,500		175.00	175
1994	Reverence For Life w/border & card	750	N/A	175.00	335
1994	Reverence For Life w/frame	100	N/A	600.00	600

Smith - T. Smith

Year Issue		Edition Limit	Year Retd.	Issue Price	Quote U.S.$
1992	The Challenger	1,300		185.00	185
1995	The Refuge	1,000		245.00	245

Terpning - H. Terpning

Year Issue		Edition Limit	Year Retd.	Issue Price	Quote U.S.$
1992	Against the Coldmaker	1,000	N/A	195.00	195
1993	The Apache Fire Makers	1,000	N/A	235.00	235
1993	Army Regulations	1,000		235.00	235
1987	Blackfeet Among the Aspen	1,000	N/A	225.00	225
1985	Blackfeet Spectators	475	N/A	350.00	1600
1988	Blood Man	1,250	N/A	95.00	365
1982	CA Set Pony Soldiers/Warriors	1,000	N/A	200.00	200
1985	The Cache	1,000		175.00	175
1992	Capture of the Horse Bundle	1,250		235.00	235
1982	Chief Joseph Rides to Surrender	1,000	N/A	150.00	2550
1986	Comanche Spoilers	1,000		195.00	195
1990	Cree Finery	1,000		225.00	225
1983	Crossing Medicine Lodge Creek	1,000	N/A	150.00	700
1994	Crow Camp, 1864	1,000	N/A	235.00	235
1984	Crow Pipe Holder	1,000		150.00	150
1991	Digging in at Sappa Creek MW	650	N/A	375.00	375
1994	The Feast	1,850	N/A	245.00	245
1992	Four Sacred Drummers	1,000	N/A	225.00	225
1988	Hope Springs Eternal-Ghost Dance	2,250	N/A	225.00	225
1994	Isdzan-Apache Woman	1,000	N/A	175.00	175
1991	The Last Buffalo	1,000		225.00	225
1991	Leader of Men	1,250	N/A	235.00	235
1984	The Long Shot, signed	1,000	N/A	55.00	55
1984	Medicine Man of the Cheyene	450	N/A	350.00	3350
1993	Medicine Pipe	1,000	N/A	150.00	175
1985	One Man's Castle	1,000		150.00	150
1983	Paints	1,000	N/A	140.00	250
1992	Passing Into Womanhood	650	N/A	375.00	435
1987	The Ploy	1,000	N/A	195.00	1250
1992	Prairie Knights	1,000	N/A	225.00	225
1987	Preparing for the Sun Dance	1,000	N/A	175.00	270
1988	Pride of the Cheyene	1,250		195.00	195
1993	Profile of Wisdom	1,000		175.00	175
1989	Scout's Report	1,250		225.00	225
1985	The Scouts of General Crook	1,000	N/A	175.00	175
1988	Search For the Pass	1,000	N/A	225.00	270
1982	Search For the Renegades	1,000	N/A	150.00	150
1989	Shepherd of the Plains Cameo	1,250		125.00	125
1982	Shield of Her Husband	1,000	N/A	150.00	1200
1983	Shoshonis	1,250	N/A	85.00	225
1985	The Signal	1,250	N/A	90.00	650
1981	Sioux Flag Carrier	1,000	N/A	125.00	125
1981	Small Comfort	1,000	N/A	135.00	475
1993	Soldier Hat	1,000		235.00	235
1981	The Spectators	1,000	N/A	135.00	250
1994	Spirit of the Rainmaker	1,500	N/A	235.00	235
1983	Staff Carrier	1,250	N/A	90.00	700
1986	Status Symbols	1,000	N/A	185.00	1450
1981	Stones that Speak	1,000	N/A	150.00	1350
1989	The Storyteller w/Video & Book	1,500	N/A	950.00	950
1992	The Strength of Eagles	1,250		235.00	235
1988	Sunday Best	1,250		195.00	195
1990	Telling of the Legends	1,250	N/A	225.00	765
1986	Thunderpipe and the Holy Man	550	N/A	350.00	500
1995	Trading Post at Chadron Creek	1,000	N/A	225.00	225
1991	Transferring the Medicine Shield	850	N/A	375.00	1300
1981	The Victors	1,000	N/A	150.00	545
1985	The Warning	1,650	N/A	175.00	500
1986	Watching the Column	1,250	N/A	90.00	90
1990	When Careless Spelled Disaster	1,000	N/A	225.00	255
1987	Winter Coat	1,250	N/A	95.00	95
1984	Woman of the Sioux	1,000	N/A	165.00	825

Townsend - B. Townsend

Year Issue		Edition Limit	Year Retd.	Issue Price	Quote U.S.$
1994	Autumn Hillside	1,000		175.00	175
1993	Dusk	1,250		195.00	195
1995	Gathering of the Herd	1,000		195.00	195
1993	Hailstorm Creek	1,250		195.00	195
1994	Mountain Light	1,000		195.00	195
1992	Open Ridge	1,500	N/A	225.00	225
1993	Out of the Shadows	1,500		195.00	195
1992	Riverbend	1,000	N/A	185.00	335

Weiss - J. Weiss

Year Issue		Edition Limit	Year Retd.	Issue Price	Quote U.S.$
1984	Basset Hound Puppies	1,000	N/A	65.00	65
1988	Black Labrador Head Study Cameo	1,000		90.00	90
1984	Cocker Spaniel Puppies	1,000	N/A	75.00	265
1992	Cuddle Time	850		95.00	95
1993	A Feeling of Warmth	1,000	N/A	165.00	300
1994	Forever Friends	1,000	1994	95.00	200
1983	Golden Retriever Puppies	1,000	N/A	65.00	600
1988	Goldens at the Shore	850	N/A	145.00	500
1995	I Didn't Do It	1,250		125.00	125
1982	Lab Puppies	1,000	N/A	65.00	65
1992	No Swimming Lessons Today	1,000		140.00	140
1984	Old English Sheepdog Puppies	1,000	N/A	65.00	240
1993	Old Friends	1,000	1993	95.00	95
1986	One Morning in October	850	N/A	125.00	340
1985	Persian Kitten	1,000	N/A	65.00	65
1982	Rebel & Soda	1,000	N/A	45.00	90
1991	Wake Up Call	850		165.00	165
1988	Yellow Labrador Head Study Cameo	1,000		90.00	90

Williams - B.D. Williams

Year Issue		Edition Limit	Year Retd.	Issue Price	Quote U.S.$
1993	Avant Garde S&N	500	N/A	60.00	60
1993	Avant Garde unsigned	2,603	N/A	30.00	30

Wootton - F. Wootton

Year Issue		Edition Limit	Year Retd.	Issue Price	Quote U.S.$
1990	Adlertag, 15 August 1940 & Video	1,500	N/A	245.00	245
1993	April Morning:France, 1918	850		245.00	245
1983	The Battle of Britain	850	N/A	150.00	225
1988	Encounter with the Red Baron	850	N/A	165.00	165
1985	Huntsmen and Hounds	650		115.00	115
1982	Knights of the Sky	850	N/A	165.00	300
1993	Last Combat of the Red Baron	850		185.00	185
1992	The Last of the First F. Wooten	850		235.00	235
1994	Peenemunde	850		245.00	245
1986	The Spitfire Legend	850	N/A	195.00	195

Wysocki - C. Wysocki

Year Issue		Edition Limit	Year Retd.	Issue Price	Quote U.S.$
1987	'Twas the Twilight Before Christmas	7,500	N/A	95.00	150
1988	The Americana Bowl	3,500		295.00	295
1983	Amish Neighbors	1,000	N/A	150.00	500
1989	Another Year At Sea	2,500	N/A	175.00	250-410
1983	Applebutter Makers	1,000	N/A	135.00	500
1987	Bach's Magnificat in D Minor	2,250	N/A	150.00	500
1991	Beauty And The Beast	2,000	N/A	125.00	125
1990	Belly Warmers	2,500		150.00	195-200
1984	Bird House Cameo	1,000	N/A	85.00	450
1985	Birds of a Feather	1,250	N/A	145.00	400
1989	Bostonians And Beans (PC)	6,711	N/A	225.00	565-600
1979	Butternut Farms	1,000	N/A	75.00	1000
1980	Caleb's Buggy Barn	1,000	N/A	80.00	300
1984	Cape Cod Cold Fish Party	1,000	N/A	150.00	150
1986	Carnival Capers	620		200.00	200
1981	Carver Coggins	1,000	N/A	145.00	900
1989	Christmas Greeting	11,000	N/A	125.00	100
1982	Christmas Print, 1982	2,000	N/A	80.00	700
1984	Chumbuddies, signed	1,000		55.00	55
1985	Clammers at Hodge's Horn	1,000	N/A	150.00	1500
1983	Commemorative Print, 1983	2,000	N/A	55.00	55
1983	Commemorative Print, 1984	2,000		55.00	55
1984	Commemorative Print, 1985	2,000		55.00	55
1985	Commemorative Print, 1986	2,000		55.00	55
1984	Cotton Country	1,000	N/A	150.00	200
1983	Country Race	1,000	N/A	150.00	400
1986	Daddy's Coming Home	1,250	N/A	150.00	1100
1987	Dahalia Dinalhaven Makes a Dory Deal	2,250	N/A	150.00	250
1986	Dancing Pheasant Farms	1,750	N/A	165.00	350
1980	Derby Square	1,000	N/A	90.00	1100
1986	Devilbelly Bay	1,000	N/A	145.00	300
1986	Devilstone Harbor/An American Celebration (Print & Book)	3,500	N/A	195.00	400
1989	Dreamers	3,000		175.00	350
1992	Ethel the Gourmet	10,179	N/A	150.00	350
1979	Fairhaven by the Sea	1,000	N/A	75.00	700
1988	Feathered Critics	2,500		150.00	150
1979	Fox Run	1,000	N/A	75.00	1700
1984	The Foxy Fox Outfoxes the Fox Hunters	1,500	N/A	150.00	600
1992	Frederick the Literate	6,500	N/A	150.00	2000
1989	Fun Lovin' Silly Folks	3,000	N/A	185.00	300-400
1984	The Gang's All Here	Open		65.00	65
1984	The Gang's All Here, remarque	250		90.00	90
1992	Gay Head Light	2,500		165.00	165
1986	Hickory Haven Canal	1,500	N/A	165.00	800
1988	Home Is My Sailor	2,500	N/A	150.00	150
1985	I Love America	2,000		20.00	20
1990	Jingle Bell Teddy and Friends	5,000		125.00	125
1980	Jolly Hill Farms	1,000	N/A	75.00	850
1986	Lady Liberty's Independence Day Enterprising Immigrants	1,500	N/A	140.00	200-300
1992	Love Letter From Laramie	1,500		150.00	150
1989	The Memory Maker	2,500		165.00	165
1985	Merrymakers Serenade	1,250	N/A	135.00	135
1986	Mr. Swallobark	2,000	N/A	145.00	1500
1982	The Nantucket	1,000	N/A	145.00	400
1981	Olde America	1,500	N/A	125.00	700
1981	Page's Bake Shoppe	1,000	N/A	115.00	500
1983	Plum Island Sound, signed	1,000	N/A	55.00	55
1983	Plum Island Sound, unsigned	Open	N/A	40.00	40
1981	Prairie Wind Flowers	1,000	N/A	125.00	1800
1992	Proud Little Angler	2,750	N/A	150.00	150
1994	Remington w/Book-Heartland	15,000		195.00	195
1990	Robin Hood	2,000		165.00	165
1991	Rockland Breakwater Light	2,500		165.00	280
1985	Salty Witch Bay	475	N/A	350.00	2400
1991	Sea Captain's Wife Abiding	1,500	N/A	150.00	150
1979	Shall We?	1,000	N/A	75.00	500
1982	Sleepy Town West	1,500	N/A	150.00	500
1984	Storin' Up	450	N/A	325.00	1000
1982	Sunset Hills, Texas Wildcatters	1,000	N/A	125.00	150
1984	Sweetheart Chessmate	1,000	N/A	95.00	350
1983	Tea by the Sea	1,000	N/A	145.00	1500
1993	The Three Sisters of Nauset, 1880	2,500	N/A	165.00	200
1984	A Warm Christmas Love	3,951	N/A	80.00	350
1990	Wednesday Night Checkers	2,500		175.00	175
1991	West Quoddy Head Light, Maine	2,500		165.00	165
1990	Where The Bouys Are	2,750	N/A	175.00	200
1991	Whistle Stop Christmas	5,000		125.00	125
1980	Yankee Wink Hollow	1,000	N/A	95.00	1300
1987	Yearning For My Captain	2,000	N/A	150.00	285-300
1987	You've Been So Long at Sea, Horatio	2,500	N/A	150.00	200

Guildhall, Inc.

DeHaan - C. DeHaan

Year Issue		Edition Limit	Year Retd.	Issue Price	Quote U.S.$
1992	73o In Amarillo...Yesterday	925		140.00	140
1993	Appeasing The Water People	925		150.00	150
1993	As The Buffalo Leave	925		150.00	150
1983	Crossin' Horse Creek	650		100.00	625
1992	Crossing At The Big Trees	925		140.00	200
1990	Crow Autumn	925		135.00	250
1987	Crow Ceremonial Dress	750		100.00	175
1989	Crows	800		135.00	525
1991	The Encounter	925		140.00	300

GRAPHICS

YEAR ISSUE		EDITION LIMIT	YEAR RETD.	ISSUE PRICE	QUOTE U.S.$
1990	Escape	925		135.00	200
1979	Foggy Mornin' Wait	650		75.00	2525
1981	Forgin' The Keechi	650		85.00	725
1993	Goosed	925		150.00	150
1990	High Plains Drifters	925		140.00	200
1985	Horsemen of the West (Suite of 3)	650		145.00	975
1984	Jake	650		100.00	600
1985	Keechi Country	750		100.00	375
1983	Keep A Movin' Dan	750		85.00	125
1989	Kentucky Blue	750		125.00	575
1986	The Loner (with matching buckle)	750		145.00	425
1981	MacTavish	650		75.00	1000
1986	Moon Dancers	750		100.00	165
1988	Mornin' Gather	750		100.00	350
1987	Murphy's Law	750		100.00	225
1986	The Mustangers	750		100.00	400
1982	O' That Strawberry Roan	750		85.00	125
1985	Oklahoma Paints	750		100.00	425
1990	The Pipe Carrier	925		140.00	175
1991	The Prideful Ones (Set of 2)	925		150.00	200
1989	The Quarter Horse	800		125.00	325
1993	The Return	925		150.00	150
1983	Ridin' Ol' Paint	750		85.00	625
1986	The Searchers	650		100.00	375
1992	Silent Trail Talk	925		140.00	175
1987	Snow Birds	750		100.00	350
1984	Spooked	650		95.00	1825
1988	Stage To Deadwood	750		100.00	275
1991	Sundance	925		140.00	175
1987	Supremacy	750		100.00	175
1981	Surprise Encounter	750		85.00	475
1980	Texas Panhandle	650		75.00	1525
1985	Up the Chisholm	750		85.00	125
1989	Village Markers	750		125.00	525
1990	War Cry	925		135.00	275
1988	Water Breakin'	750		125.00	600

Hadley House

Capser - M. Capser

YEAR ISSUE		EDITION LIMIT	YEAR RETD.	ISSUE PRICE	QUOTE U.S.$
1993	Briar and Brambles	999		100.00	100
1992	Comes the Dawn	600		100.00	100
1994	Dashing Through the Snow	999		100.00	100
1994	Down the Lane	Open		30.00	30
1995	Enchanted Waters	999		100.00	100
1995	Grapevine Estates	999		100.00	100
1994	The Lifting Fog	Open		30.00	30
1995	Mariner's Point	999		100.00	100
1994	Nappin'	999		100.00	100
1994	A Night's Quiet	999		100.00	100
1995	On Gentle Wings	999		100.00	100
1993	Pickets & Vines	999	1994	100.00	100
1992	Reflections	600	1993	100.00	100
1993	Rock Creek Spring	999		80.00	80
1994	September Blush	999		100.00	100
1992	Silence Unbroken	600		100.00	100
1993	Skyline Serenade	600	1993	100.00	100
1995	Spring Creek Fever	999		100.00	100
1993	A Summer's Glow	999		60.00	60
1994	A Time For Us	999		125.00	125
1994	To Search Again	Open		30.00	30
1992	The Watch	600	1993	100.00	150
1994	The Way Home	Open		30.00	30
1993	Whispering Wings	1,500	1994	100.00	100

Franca - O. Franca

YEAR ISSUE		EDITION LIMIT	YEAR RETD.	ISSUE PRICE	QUOTE U.S.$
1988	The Apache	950	1990	70.00	175
1990	Blue Navajo	1,500	1991	125.00	125
1990	Blue Tranquility	999	1990	100.00	100
1988	Cacique	950	1990	70.00	175
1990	Cecy	1,500	1992	125.00	225
1990	Destiny	999	1990	100.00	100
1991	Early Morning	3,600		125.00	225
1993	Evening In Taos	4,000		80.00	80
1988	Feathered Hair Ties	600	1988	80.00	300
1990	Feathered Hair Ties II	999	1990	100.00	300
1991	The Lovers	2,400	1991	125.00	900
1991	The Model	1,500	1991	125.00	400
1992	Navajo Daydream	3,600	1993	175.00	360
1989	Navajo Fantasy	999	1989	80.00	150
1992	Navajo Meditating	4,000		80.00	125
1992	Navajo Reflection	4,000	1992	80.00	225
1990	Navajo Summer	999	1988	100.00	240
1991	Olympia	1,500	1991	125.00	250
1989	Pink Navajo	999	1989	80.00	250
1988	The Red Shawl	600	1990	80.00	300
1991	Red Wolf	1,500	1991	125.00	225
1990	Santa Fe	1,500	1991	125.00	300
1988	Sitting Bull	950	1990	70.00	250
1988	Slow Bull	950	1990	70.00	250
1990	Turqoise Necklace	999	1990	100.00	450
1990	Wind Song	999	1990	100.00	425
1992	Wind Song II	4,000	1992	80.00	150
1989	Winter	999	1989	80.00	220
1989	Young Warrior	999	1989	80.00	425

Hanks - S. Hanks

YEAR ISSUE		EDITION LIMIT	YEAR RETD.	ISSUE PRICE	QUOTE U.S.$
1994	All Gone Awry	2,000		150.00	150
1994	All In a Row	2,000	1994	150.00	150
1995	A Captive Audience	1,500		150.00	150
1995	Cat's Lair	1,500		150.00	150
1993	Catching The Sun	999	1993	150.00	450
1992	Conferring With the Sea	999	1993	125.00	500
1990	Contemplation	999		100.00	150
1995	Country Comfort	999		100.00	100
1995	Drip Castles	4,000		30.00	30
1991	Duet	999	1993	150.00	600-750
1990	Emotional Appeal	999		150.00	225
1993	Gathering Thoughts	1,500	1995	150.00	150
1992	An Innocent View	999	1992	150.00	500-600
1994	The Journey Is The Goal	1,500	1995	150.00	150
1995	Kali	Open		25.00	25
1993	Little Black Crow	1,500		150.00	150
1994	Michaela and Friends/Book	2,500		200.00	200
1993	The New Arrival	1,500		150.00	200
1995	Pacific Sanctuary	1,500		150.00	150
1993	Peeking Out	Open		40.00	40
1993	Places I Remember	1,500		150.00	150
1990	Quiet Rapport	999		150.00	300
1993	A Sense of Belonging	1,500		150.00	150
1995	Small Miracle	1,500		125.00	125
1992	Sometimes It's the Little Things	999		125.00	225
1994	Southwestern Bedroom	999		150.00	180-225
1992	Stepping Stones	999	1993	150.00	170-200
1991	Sunday Afternoon	Open		40.00	40
1992	Things Worth Keeping	999	1991	125.00	1800
1993	The Thinkers	1,500		150.00	150
1994	Water Lilies In Bloom	750		295.00	295
1993	When Her Blue Eyes Close	999		100.00	100
1994	Where The Light Shines Brightest	1,500		150.00	150
1991	A World For Our Children	999	1992	125.00	1500

Hulings - C. Hulings

YEAR ISSUE		EDITION LIMIT	YEAR RETD.	ISSUE PRICE	QUOTE U.S.$
1990	Ancient French Farmhouse	999		150.00	240
1989	Chechaquene-Morocco Market Square	999	1993	150.00	225
1992	Cuernavaca Flower Market	580		225.00	225
1988	Ile de la Cite-Paris	580	1990	150.00	225
1990	The Lonely Man	999	1993	150.00	150
1988	Onteniente	580	1989	150.00	425
1991	Place des Ternes	580	1991	195.00	700
1989	Portuguese Vegetable Woman	999	1993	85.00	85
1994	The Red Raincoat	580		225.00	225
1990	Spanish Shawl	999	1994	125.00	125
1993	Spring Flowers	580		225.00	225
1992	Sunday Afternoon	580		195.00	300
1988	Three Cats on a Grapevine	580	1989	65.00	225
1993	Washday In Provence	580		225.00	225

Redlin - T. Redlin

YEAR ISSUE		EDITION LIMIT	YEAR RETD.	ISSUE PRICE	QUOTE U.S.$
1981	1981 MN Duck Stamp Print	7,800	1981	125.00	150
1982	1982 MN Trout Stamp Print	960	1982	125.00	600
1983	1983 ND Duck Stamp Print	3,438	1983	135.00	150
1984	1984 Quail Conservation	1,500	1984	135.00	135
1985	1985 MN Duck Stamp	4,385	1985	135.00	135
1985	Afternoon Glow	960	1985	150.00	1600
1979	Ageing Shoreline	960	1979	40.00	375
1981	All Clear	960	1981	150.00	300
1994	America, America	29,500		250.00	250
1994	And Crown Thy Good w/Brotherhood	29,500		250.00	250
1977	Apple River Mallards	Retrd.	1977	10.00	100
1981	April Snow	960	1981	100.00	450
1989	Aroma of Fall	6,800	1989	200.00	1450
1987	Autumn Afternoon	4,800	1987	100.00	725
1993	Autumn Evening	29,500		250.00	250
1980	Autumn Run	960	1980	60.00	400
1983	Autumn Shoreline	Retrd.	1983	50.00	200
1978	Back from the Fields	720	1978	40.00	250-400
1985	Back to the Sanctuary	960	1986	150.00	400
1978	Backwater Mallards	720	1978	40.00	1000
1983	Backwoods Cabin	960	1983	150.00	900
1990	Best Friends (AP Only)	570	1993	1000.00	1500
1982	The Birch Line	960	1982	100.00	500
1984	Bluebill Point (AP)	240	1984	300.00	650
1988	Boulder Ridge	4,800		150.00	150
1980	Breaking Away	960	1980	60.00	430
1985	Breaking Cover	960	1985	150.00	500
1981	Broken Covey	960	1981	100.00	525
1985	Brousing	960	1985	150.00	800
1994	Campfire Tales	29,500		250.00	250
1988	Catching the Scent	2,400		200.00	200
1986	Changing Seasons-Autumn	960	1986	150.00	500
1987	Changing Seasons-Spring	960	1987	200.00	475
1984	Changing Seasons-Summer	960	1984	150.00	1400
1986	Changing Seasons-Winter	960	1986	200.00	600
1985	Clear View	1,500	1985	300.00	500
1980	Clearing the Rail	960	1980	60.00	650-850
1984	Closed for the Season	960	1984	150.00	300
1979	Colorful Trio	960	1979	40.00	550
1991	Comforts of Home	22,900		175.00	450
1986	Coming Home	2,400	1986	100.00	1400
1992	The Conservationists	29,500		175.00	175
1988	Country Neighbors	4,800	1988	150.00	425-550
1980	Country Road	960	1980	60.00	650-745
1987	Deer Crossing	2,400	1987	200.00	950
1985	Delayed Departure	1,500	1985	150.00	500-1000
1980	Drifting	960	1980	60.00	400
1987	Evening Chores (print & book)	2,400	1988	400.00	775-1000
1985	Evening Company	960	1985	150.00	500
1983	Evening Glow	960	1983	150.00	1600-1800
1987	Evening Harvest	960	1987	200.00	1300
1982	Evening Retreat (AP)	300	1982	400.00	2800
1990	Evening Solitude	9,500	1990	200.00	775
1983	Evening Surprise	960	1983	150.00	1100-2000
1990	Evening With Friends	19,500	1991	225.00	850-1200
1990	Family Traditions	Retrd.	1993	80.00	100
1979	Fighting a Headwind	960	1979	30.00	350
1991	Flying Free	14,500		200.00	200
1993	For Amber Waves of Grain	29,500		250.00	250
1993	For Purple Mountains Majesty	29,500		250.00	250
1995	From Sea to Shining Sea	29,500		250.00	250
1994	God Shed His Grace on Thee	29,500		250.00	250
1987	Golden Retreat (AP)	500	1986	800.00	2000
1995	Harvest Moon Ball	9,500	1995	275.00	500
1986	Hazy Afternoon	2,560	1986	200.00	850
1990	Heading Home	Retrd.	1993	80.00	200
1983	Hidden Point	960	1983	150.00	525
1981	High Country	960	1981	100.00	600
1981	Hightailing	960	1981	75.00	300
1980	The Homestead	960	1980	60.00	640
1989	Homeward Bound	Retrd.	1994	80.00	250
1988	Homeward Bound	Retrd.	1993	70.00	150
1988	House Call	6,800	1990	175.00	500-900
1991	Hunter's Haven (A/P)	1,000	N/A	175.00	900-1200
1989	Indian Summer	4,800	1989	200.00	600-725
1980	Intruders	960	1980	60.00	310
1982	The Landing	Retrd.	1982	30.00	80
1981	The Landmark	960	1981	100.00	400
1984	Leaving the Sanctuary	960	1984	150.00	475
1994	Lifetime Companions	29,500		250.00	250
1988	Lights of Home	9,500	1988	125.00	700
1979	The Loner	960	1979	40.00	300
1990	Master of the Valley	6,800		200.00	200
1988	The Master's Domain	2,400	1988	225.00	800
1988	Moonlight Retreat (A/P)	530		1000.00	1400
1979	Morning Chores	960	1979	40.00	1350
1984	Morning Glow	960	1984	150.00	1200
1981	Morning Retreat (AP)	240		400.00	2800
1989	Morning Rounds	6,800	1992	175.00	475
1991	Morning Solitude	12,107	1991	250.00	460
1984	Night Harvest	960	1984	150.00	850
1985	Night Light	1,500	1985	300.00	600
1986	Night Mapling	960	1986	200.00	550
1995	A Night on the Town	29,500		150.00	150
1980	Night Watch	2,400	1980	60.00	800
1984	Nightflight (AP)	360	1984	600.00	2200
1982	October Evening	960	1982	100.00	750
1989	Office Hours	6,800	1991	175.00	500-900
1992	Oh Beautiful for Spacious Skies	29,500		250.00	250
1978	Old Loggers Trail	720	1978	40.00	950-1200
1983	On the Alert	960	1983	125.00	400
1977	Over the Blowdown	Retrd.	1977	20.00	100
1978	Over the Rushes	720	1978	40.00	450
1981	Passing Through	960	1981	100.00	225
1983	Peaceful Evening	960	1983	100.00	350
1991	Pleasures of Winter	24,500	1992	150.00	275-400
1986	Prairie Monuments	960	1986	200.00	650
1988	Prairie Morning	4,800	1988	150.00	500
1984	Prairie Skyline	960	1984	150.00	550
1983	Prairie Springs	960	1983	150.00	325
1987	Prepared for the Season	Retrd.	1994	70.00	100
1990	Pure Contentment	9,500	1989	150.00	500
1978	Quiet Afternoon	720	1978	40.00	575
1988	Quiet of the Evening	4,800	1988	150.00	700
1982	Reflections	960	1982	100.00	500
1985	Riverside Pond	960	1985	150.00	525
1984	Rural Route	960	1984	150.00	350
1983	Rushing Rapids	960	1983	125.00	400
1980	Rusty Refuge I	960	1980	60.00	520
1981	Rusty Refuge II	960	1980	100.00	550-650
1984	Rusty Refuge III	960	1984	150.00	500
1985	Rusty Refuge IV	960	1985	150.00	500
1980	Secluded Pond	960	1980	60.00	290
1982	Seed Hunters	960	1982	100.00	575
1985	Sharing Season I	Retrd.	1993	60.00	150
1986	Sharing Season II	Retrd.	1993	60.00	150
1981	Sharing the Bounty	960	1981	100.00	1500
1994	Sharing the Evening	29,500		175.00	175
1987	Sharing the Solitude	2,400	1987	125.00	800
1986	Silent Flight	960	1986	150.00	335
1980	Silent Sunset	960	1980	60.00	780
1984	Silent Wings Suite (set of 4)	960	1984	200.00	750
1981	Soft Shadows	960	1984	100.00	325
1989	Special Memories (AP)	570		1000.00	1000
1982	Spring Mapling	960	1982	100.00	800
1981	Spring Run-Off	1,700	1981	125.00	450
1980	Spring Thaw	960	1980	60.00	460
1980	Squall Line	960	1980	60.00	300
1978	Startled	720	1978	30.00	750
1986	Stormy Weather	1,500	1986	200.00	550
1992	Summertime	24,900		225.00	225
1984	Sundown	960	1984	300.00	575
1986	Sunlit Trail	960	1986	150.00	350
1984	Sunny Afternoon	960	1984	150.00	700
1987	That Special Time	2,400	1987	125.00	650-1200
1987	Together for the Season	Open		70.00	100
1995	Total Comfort	9,500	1995	275.00	275
1986	Twilight Glow	960	1986	200.00	700
1988	Wednesday Afternoon	6,800	1989	175.00	500-800
1990	Welcome to Paradise	14,500	1990	150.00	450-650
1985	Whistle Stop	960	1985	150.00	550
1979	Whitecaps	960	1979	40.00	520
1982	Whitewater	960	1982	100.00	400
1982	Winter Haven	500	1982	85.00	800
1977	Winter Snows	Retrd.	1977	20.00	100

YEAR ISSUE		EDITION LIMIT	YEAR RETD.	ISSUE PRICE	QUOTE U.S.$
1984	Winter Windbreak	960	1984	150.00	750
1992	Winter Wonderland	29,500	1993	150.00	275

Hallmark Galleries

Innocent Wonders - T. Blackshear

YEAR ISSUE		EDITION LIMIT	YEAR RETD.	ISSUE PRICE	QUOTE U.S.$
1992	Pinkie Poo 7500QHG4016	9,500	1995	75.00	75

Majestic Wilderness - M. Newman

YEAR ISSUE		EDITION LIMIT	YEAR RETD.	ISSUE PRICE	QUOTE U.S.$
1992	Timber Wolves 7500QHG2013	9,500	1995	75.00	75
1992	White-tailed Deer 7500QHG2014	9,500	1995	75.00	75

Tobin Fraley Carousel Collection - Fraley/ Taylor Bruce

YEAR ISSUE		EDITION LIMIT	YEAR RETD.	ISSUE PRICE	QUOTE U.S.$
1993	Magical Ride 8000QHG22	9,500	1995	80.00	80

John Hine N.A. Ltd.

Rambles - A. Wyatt

YEAR ISSUE		EDITION LIMIT	YEAR RETD.	ISSUE PRICE	QUOTE U.S.$
1989	Blue Tit	Closed	N/A	33.00	33
1989	Bluebell Cottage	Closed	N/A	50.00	50
1989	Castle Street	Closed	N/A	42.00	42
1989	Frog	Closed	N/A	33.00	33
1989	Garden Gate	Closed	N/A	59.90	60
1989	Hedgerow	Closed	N/A	59.90	60
1989	Kingfisher	Closed	N/A	33.00	33
1989	Lobster Pot	Closed	N/A	50.00	50
1989	Otter's Holt	Closed	N/A	50.00	50
1989	Puffin Rock	Closed	N/A	50.00	50
1989	Riverbank	Closed	N/A	59.90	60
1989	Shirelarm	Closed	N/A	42.00	42
1989	St. Mary's Church	Closed	N/A	42.00	42
1989	Summer Harvest	Closed	N/A	59.90	60
1989	The Swan	Closed	N/A	42.00	42
1989	Two for Joy	Closed	N/A	59.90	60
1989	Waters Edge	Closed	N/A	59.90	60
1989	Wren	Closed	N/A	33.00	33

Lightpost Publishing

Kinkade Member's Only Collectors' Society - T. Kinkade

YEAR ISSUE		EDITION LIMIT	YEAR RETD.	ISSUE PRICE	QUOTE U.S.$
1992	Skater's Pond	Closed	N/A	295.00	400-515
1992	Morning Lane	Closed	N/A	Gift	100
1994	Collector's Cottage I	Closed	1995	315.00	350-400
1994	Painter of Light Book	Closed	1995	Gift	50-75
1995	Lochavan Cottage	Yr.Iss.		295.00	295
1995	Gardens Beyond Autumn Gate	3/96		Gift	90

Kinkade-Archival Paper/Canvas-Combined Edition-Framed - T. Kinkade

YEAR ISSUE		EDITION LIMIT	YEAR RETD.	ISSUE PRICE	QUOTE U.S.$
1990	Blue Cottage (Paper)	Retrd.	1993	125.00	350
1990	Blue Cottage (Canvas)	Retrd.	1993	495.00	1500
1990	Moonlit Village (Paper)	Closed	N/A	225.00	1100-1200
1990	Moonlit Village (Canvas)	Closed	N/A	595.00	3000-3500
1989	New York, 1932 (Paper)	Closed	N/A	225.00	1250-1750
1989	New York, 1932 (Canvas)	Closed	N/A	595.00	3000-3800
1989	Skating in the Park (Paper)	Closed	1994	225.00	1200-1500
1989	Skating in the Park (Canvas)	Closed	1994	595.00	1400-2000

Kinkade-Canvas Editions-Framed - T. Kinkade

YEAR ISSUE		EDITION LIMIT	YEAR RETD.	ISSUE PRICE	QUOTE U.S.$
1991	Afternoon Light, Dogwood A/P	98	1991	595.00	1800-2400
1991	Afternoon Light, Dogwood S/N	980	N/A	495.00	1700-2300
1992	Amber Afternoon A/P	200	1992	715.00	1200
1992	Amber Afternoon S/N	980	N/A	615.00	1000-1200
1994	Autumn at Ashley's Cottage A/P	395		590.00	615
1994	Autumn at Ashley's Cottage S/N	3,950		440.00	465
1991	The Autumn Gate A/P	200	N/A	695.00	3200-3700
1991	The Autumn Gate R/P	Retrd.	1992	695.00	3200-3700
1991	The Autumn Gate S/N	980	N/A	595.00	3000-3500
1995	Autumn Lane A/P	295		840.00	840
1995	Autumn Lane G/P	1,240		790.00	790
1995	Autumn Lane S/N	2,950		690.00	690
1994	Beacon of Hope A/P	275	1994	765.00	865-995
1994	Beacon of Hope S/N	2,750	1994	615.00	800-1000
1993	Beside Still Waters A/P	400	N/A	745.00	1300-1800
1993	Beside Still Waters G/P	490	N/A	745.00	1200-1450
1993	Beside Still Waters S/N	1,280	N/A	595.00	1100-1600
1993	Beyond Autumn Gate A/P	600	1993	915.00	3600
1993	Beyond Autumn Gate G/P	500	N/A	915.00	3300
1993	Beyond Autumn Gate S/N	1,750	N/A	815.00	3000-3500
1993	The Blessings of Autumn A/P	200	1994	715.00	900
1993	The Blessings of Autumn G/P	250	1994	715.00	900
1993	The Blessings of Autumn S/N	1,250	1994	615.00	815-1000
1994	The Blessings of Spring A/P	275	1994	665.00	825
1994	The Blessings of Spring G/P	685	1994	665.00	825
1994	The Blessings of Spring S/N	2,750	1994	515.00	615-700
1995	Blessings of Summer A/P	495		1015.00	1070
1995	Blessings of Summer G/P	1,240		965.00	965
1995	Blessings of Summer S/N	4,950		865.00	920
1995	Blossom Bridge A/P	295		730.00	730
1995	Blossom Bridge G/P	740		685.00	680
1995	Blossom Bridge S/N	2,950		580.00	580
1992	Blossom Hill Church A/P	200	1994	695.00	800-1400
1992	Blossom Hill Church R/P	Retrd.	1993	695.00	695
1992	Blossom Hill Church S/N	980	1994	595.00	800-1100
1991	Boston A/P	50	N/A	595.00	2000-2500
1991	Boston S/N	550	N/A	495.00	1600-2200
1992	Broadwater Bridge A/P	200	N/A	595.00	1950
1992	Broadwater Bridge G/P	200	N/A	645.00	2000
1992	Broadwater Bridge S/N	980	N/A	495.00	1700-1900
1995	Brookside Hideaway A/P	395	1995	695.00	695
1995	Brookside Hideaway G/P	990	1995	695.00	695
1995	Brookside Hideaway S/N	3,950		545.00	580
1991	Carmel, Delores Street and the Tuck Box Tea Room A/P	200	1992	745.00	3000-3300
1991	Carmel, Delores Street and the Tuck Box Tea Room R/P	Retrd.	1992	745.00	745
1991	Carmel, Delores Street and the Tuck Box Tea Room S/N	980	1992	645.00	2900
1989	Carmel, Ocean Avenue A/P	Closed	N/A	795.00	6500-7000
1989	Carmel, Ocean Avenue S/N	Closed	N/A	645.00	4000-6000
1991	Cedar Nook Cottage R/P	200	1991	295.00	695
1991	Cedar Nook Cottage S/N	1,960	1991	195.00	400-500
1990	Chandler's Cottage S/N	Closed	N/A	495.00	2000-3000
1992	Christmas At the Ahwahnee A/P	200		615.00	730
1992	Christmas At the Ahwahnee S/N	980		515.00	580
1990	Christmas Cottage 1990 A/P	Closed	1990	295.00	2300-2600
1990	Christmas Cottage 1990 S/N	Closed	N/A	295.00	1600-2000
1991	Christmas Eve A/P	200	1991	495.00	1000-1600
1991	Christmas Eve R/P	Retrd.	1991	495.00	1500-1800
1991	Christmas Eve S/N	980	N/A	395.00	800-1400
1994	Christmas Memories A/P	345	N/A	695.00	895
1994	Christmas Memories G/P	863		695.00	895
1994	Christmas Memories S/N	3,450	N/A	545.00	545-895
1994	Christmas Tree Cottage A/P	395		590.00	615
1994	Christmas Tree Cottage G/P	988		590.00	615
1994	Christmas Tree Cottage S/N	3,950		440.00	465
1992	Cottage-By-The-Sea A/P	200	1992	695.00	2000
1992	Cottage-By-The-Sea G/P	200	N/A	745.00	1600-2200
1992	Cottage-By-The-Sea S/N	980	N/A	595.00	1400-1900
1992	Country Memories A/P	200	1992	495.00	800-1000
1992	Country Memories G/P	200		495.00	665
1992	Country Memories S/N	980	N/A	395.00	600-900
1994	Creekside Trail A/P	198	1994	840.00	840
1994	Creekside Trail G/P	496		840.00	840
1994	Creekside Trail S/N	1,984		670.00	690
1994	Days of Peace A/P	198		840.00	840
1994	Days of Peace G/P	496		840.00	840
1994	Days of Peace S/N	1,984		690.00	690
1994	Dusk in the Valley A/P	198		840.00	840
1994	Dusk in the Valley G/P	496		840.00	840
1994	Dusk in the Valley S/N	1,984		690.00	690
1994	Emerald Isle Cottage A/P	275	1994	665.00	665
1994	Emerald Isle Cottage G/P	685		665.00	665
1994	Emerald Isle Cottage S/N	2,750		515.00	580
1993	End of a Perfect Day I A/P	400	N/A	615.00	1900-2200
1993	End of a Perfect Day I G/P	300	N/A	665.00	2100
1993	End of a Perfect Day I S/N	1,250	N/A	515.00	1500-1900
1994	End of a Perfect Day II A/P	275	1994	965.00	2100-2400
1994	End of a Perfect Day II G/P	685	1994	965.00	1400-2200
1994	End of a Perfect Day II S/N	2,750	1995	815.00	1400-2000
1995	End of a Perfect Day III A/P	495	1995	1145.00	1145-1500
1995	End of a Perfect Day III G/P	1,240		1145.00	1245
1995	End of a Perfect Day III S/N	4,950		995.00	1055
1989	Entrance to Manor House A/P	Closed	N/A	595.00	2000-2500
1989	Entrance to Manor House S/N	Closed	N/A	495.00	1700-2000
1989	Evening at Merritt's Cottage A/P	Closed	N/A	595.00	2700-3000
1989	Evening at Merritt's Cottage S/N	Closed	N/A	495.00	2500-3000
1992	Evening at Swanbrooke Cottage Thomashire A/P	Closed	N/A	595.00	2000-2800
1992	Evening at Swanbrooke Cottage Thomashire G/P	Closed	N/A	645.00	2000-2800
1992	Evening at Swanbrooke Cottage Thomashire S/N	Closed	N/A	495.00	2000-2800
1992	Evening Carolers A/P	200		415.00	505
1992	Evening Carolers G/P	200		415.00	505
1992	Evening Carolers S/N	1,960		315.00	355
1995	Evening in the Forest A/P	495		695.00	730
1995	Evening in the Forest G/P	1,250		645.00	680
1995	Evening in the Forest S/N	4,950		545.00	580
1993	Fisherman's Wharf; San Francisco A/P	275	1993	1065.00	1200-1400
1993	Fisherman's Wharf; San Francisco G/P	550	N/A	1065.00	1200-1400
1993	Fisherman's Wharf; San Francisco S/N	2,750	N/A	965.00	1100-1200
1991	Flags Over The Capitol A/P	200		695.00	840
1991	Flags Over The Capitol R/P	Closed	N/A	695.00	795-1000
1991	Flags Over The Capitol S/N	980		595.00	690
1993	The Garden of Promise A/P	300		715.00	1000-1300
1993	The Garden of Promise G/P	400	N/A	715.00	1300-1500
1993	The Garden of Promise S/N	1,250	1994	615.00	1200-1400
1992	The Garden Party A/P	200		595.00	650
1992	The Garden Party G/P	200		595.00	
1992	The Garden Party S/N	980		495.00	580
1994	Gardens Beyond Autumn Gate S/N	3/96		1025.00	1025
1993	Glory of Evening A/P	400	1993	365.00	415-500
1993	Glory of Evening G/P	400		365.00	
1993	Glory of Evening S/N	1,980	1994	315.00	315-475
1993	Glory of Morning A/P	400	1993	365.00	415
1993	Glory of Morning G/P	400	1993	365.00	415
1993	Glory of Morning S/N	1,980	1994	315.00	400-600
1993	Glory of Winter A/P	300		715.00	715-765
1993	Glory of Winter G/P	250		715.00	840
1993	Glory of Winter S/N	1,250		615.00	690
1994	Guardian Castle A/P	475		1015.00	1070
1994	Guardian Castle G/P	1,190		1015.00	1070
1994	Guardian Castle S/N	4,750		865.00	920
1993	Heather's Hutch A/P	400	1993	515.00	645-695
1993	Heather's Hutch G/P	300		515.00	565-695
1993	Heather's Hutch S/N	1,250	N/A	415.00	500-800
1994	Hidden Arbor A/P	375		665.00	730
1994	Hidden Arbor G/P	685		665.00	730
1994	Hidden Arbor S/N	3,750		515.00	580
1990	Hidden Cottage I A/P	Closed	N/A	595.00	2000-4000
1990	Hidden Cottage I S/N	Closed	N/A	495.00	2300-3100
1993	Hidden Cottage II A/P	400	1993	615.00	700-765
1993	Hidden Cottage II G/P	600	1995	665.00	765-815
1993	Hidden Cottage II S/N	1,480	1994	515.00	665-900
1994	Hidden Gazebo A/P	240	1994	665.00	765-945
1994	Hidden Gazebo G/P	600	1994	665.00	765-975
1994	Hidden Gazebo S/N	2,400	1994	515.00	600-900
1991	Home For The Evening A/P	200	1994	295.00	800-1000
1991	Home For The Evening S/N	980	N/A	195.00	400-700
1991	Home For The Holidays A/P	200	1991	695.00	3000
1991	Home For The Holidays R/P	Closed	1991	695.00	3000
1991	Home For The Holidays S/N	980	N/A	595.00	1600-2300
1992	Home is Where the Heart Is A/P	200	N/A	695.00	1900
1992	Home is Where the Heart Is G/P	200	N/A	695.00	1900
1992	Home is Where the Heart Is S/N	980	N/A	595.00	1650-2000
1993	Homestead House A/P	300		715.00	715
1993	Homestead House G/P	250		715.00	840
1993	Homestead House S/N	1,250		615.00	690
1995	Hometown Chapel A/P	495		1045.00	1100
1995	Hometown Chapel G/P	1,240		995.00	1050
1995	Hometown Chapel S/N	4,950		895.00	950
1995	Hometown Memories I A/P	495		1015.00	1070
1995	Hometown Memories I G/P	1,240		1015.00	1020
1995	Hometown Memories I S/N	4,950		865.00	920
1992	Julianne's Cottage A/P	200	N/A	495.00	1700-2000
1992	Julianne's Cottage G/P	200	N/A	565.00	1700-1900
1992	Julianne's Cottage S/N	980	N/A	395.00	1500-1800
1993	Lamplight Brooke A/P	400	1994	715.00	1900-2100
1993	Lamplight Brooke G/P	330	1994	715.00	1900-2300
1993	Lamplight Brooke S/N	1,650	1994	615.00	1700-1900
1994	Lamplight Inn A/P	275	1994	765.00	875-900
1994	Lamplight Inn G/P	685	1994	765.00	875
1994	Lamplight Inn S/N	2,750	1994	615.00	725
1993	Lamplight Lane A/P	Closed	N/A	695.00	3000-3500
1993	Lamplight Lane G/P	200	1994	695.00	3600
1993	Lamplight Lane S/N	Closed	N/A	595.00	3000-3400
1995	Lamplight Village A/P	495	1995	800.00	900
1995	Lamplight Village G/P	1,240		800.00	900
1995	Lamplight Village S/N	4,950	1995	650.00	650-750
1995	A Light in the Storm A/P	395		840.00	840
1995	A Light in the Storm G/P	1,240		840.00	840
1995	A Light in the Storm S/N	3,950		690.00	690
1991	The Lit Path A/P	200	1991	395.00	395
1991	The Lit Path R/P	Retrd.	1991	395.00	395-495
1991	The Lit Path S/N	1,960	1994	195.00	315-415
1995	Main Street Celebration A/P	125	1995	800.00	800
1995	Main Street Celebration S/N	1,250		650.00	690
1995	Main Street Courthouse A/P	125	1995	800.00	800
1995	Main Street Courthouse S/N	1,250		650.00	690
1995	Main Street Matinee A/P	125	1995	800.00	800
1995	Main Street Matinee S/N	1,250		650.00	690
1995	Main Street Trolley A/P	125	1995	800.00	800
1995	Main Street Trolley S/N	1,250		650.00	690
1991	McKenna's Cottage A/P	200		595.00	730
1991	McKenna's Cottage G/P	200		615.00	
1991	McKenna's Cottage S/N	980	1995	495.00	615
1992	Miller's Cottage, Thomashire A/P	200	N/A	595.00	1000-1300
1992	Miller's Cottage, Thomashire G/P	200	N/A	595.00	1000-1300
1992	Miller's Cottage, Thomashire S/N	980	1994	495.00	1000-1400
1994	Moonlight Lane I A/P	240	1995	665.00	665
1994	Moonlight Lane I G/P	600		665.00	665
1994	Moonlight Lane I S/N	2,400		515.00	580
1992	Moonlit Sleigh Ride A/P	200		395.00	505
1992	Moonlit Sleigh Ride S/N	1,960	1994	295.00	315-365
1995	Morning Dogwood A/P	495		645.00	675
1995	Morning Dogwood G/P	1,240		595.00	625
1995	Morning Dogwood S/N	4,950		495.00	525
1995	Morning Glory Cottage A/P	495		695.00	730
1995	Morning Glory Cottage G/P	1,240		645.00	680
1995	Morning Glory Cottage S/N	4,950		545.00	580
1990	Morning Light A/P	Closed	N/A	695.00	2000-2300
1992	Olde Porterfield Gift Shoppe A/P	200	1995	595.00	615-765
1992	Olde Porterfield Gift Shoppe G/P	200		595.00	
1992	Olde Porterfield Gift Shoppe S/N	980	1994	495.00	515-615
1991	Olde Porterfield Tea Room A/P	200	N/A	595.00	900-1600
1991	Olde Porterfield Tea Room R/P	Closed	1991	595.00	900-1700
1991	Olde Porterfield Tea Room S/N	980	N/A	495.00	1000-1500
1991	Open Gate, Sussex A/P	200	1994	295.00	415
1991	Open Gate, Sussex R/P	Closed	1992	295.00	500-600
1991	Open Gate, Sussex S/N	980	1994	195.00	315-415
1993	Paris, City of Lights A/P	600	1994	765.00	1600-1900
1993	Paris, City of Lights G/P	600	N/A	815.00	1900-2000
1993	Paris, City of Lights S/N	1,980	N/A	695.00	1600-2200
1994	Paris, Eiffel Tower A/P	275	1994	945.00	1400-1500
1994	Paris, Eiffel Tower G/P	685	1995	945.00	1400-1500
1994	Paris, Eiffel Tower S/N	2,750	1994	795.00	900-1200
1995	Petals of Hope A/P	395		730.00	730
1995	Petals of Hope G/P	990		680.00	680
1995	Petals of Hope S/N	3,950		580.00	580
1994	The Power & The Majesty A/P	275		765.00	840
1994	The Power & The Majesty G/P	685		765.00	840
1994	The Power & The Majesty S/N	2,750		615.00	690
1991	Pye Corner Cottage A/P	200		295.00	395
1991	Pye Corner Cottage R/P	200		295.00	395
1991	Pye Corner Cottage S/N	1,960		195.00	245
1990	Rose Arbor A/P	Closed	N/A	595.00	1900-2400
1990	Rose Arbor S/N	Closed	N/A	495.00	1500-2000

GRAPHICS

YEAR ISSUE		EDITION LIMIT	YEAR RETD.	ISSUE PRICE	QUOTE U.S.$
1994	San Francisco Market Street A/P	750	1994	945.00	945-1045
1994	San Francisco Market Street G/P	1,875		945.00	945
1994	San Francisco Market Street S/N	7,500		795.00	845
1992	San Francisco, Nob Hill (California St.) A/P	Closed	N/A	715.00	4000-5000
1992	San Francisco, Nob Hill (California St.) P/P	Closed	N/A	815.00	5000
1992	San Francisco, Nob Hill (California St.) S/N	Closed	N/A	645.00	4000-4500
1989	San Francisco, Union Square A/P	Closed	N/A	795.00	5000-6000
1989	San Francisco, Union Square S/N	Closed	N/A	595.00	5500-6000
1992	Silent Night A/P	200	N/A	495.00	1025
1992	Silent Night G/P	200	N/A	495.00	1000
1992	Silent Night S/N	980	N/A	395.00	800-1000
1995	Simpler Times I A/P	345		840.00	840
1995	Simpler Times I G/P	870		790.00	790
1995	Simpler Times I S/N	3,450		690.00	690
1990	Spring At Stonegate A/P	50	N/A	395.00	600-800
1990	Spring At Stonegate S/N	550	1995	295.00	515-600
1994	Spring in the Alps A/P	198		725.00	730
1994	Spring in the Alps G/P	500		725.00	730
1994	Spring in the Alps S/N	1,984		575.00	580
1993	St. Nicholas Circle A/P	420	1995	715.00	715-915
1993	St. Nicholas Circle G/P	350	1995	715.00	900
1993	St. Nicholas Circle S/N	1,750	1994	615.00	615-815
1993	Stonehearth Hutch A/P	400	N/A	515.00	695-845
1993	Stonehearth Hutch G/P	300	1994	515.00	695-895
1993	Stonehearth Hutch S/N	1,650	N/A	415.00	600-800
1993	Studio in the Garden A/P	400		515.00	615
1993	Studio in the Garden G/P	600		515.00	600
1993	Studio in the Garden S/N	1,480		415.00	465
1992	Sunday at Apple Hill A/P	200	1993	595.00	1195
1992	Sunday at Apple Hill G/P	200	N/A	595.00	1195
1992	Sunday at Apple Hill S/N	980	1993	495.00	1000-1500
1993	Sunday Outing A/P	200	N/A	595.00	1150
1993	Sunday Outing G/P	200	N/A	595.00	1100-1200
1993	Sunday Outing S/N	980	N/A	495.00	900-1400
1992	Sweetheart Cottage I A/P	200	1992	595.00	1200-1300
1992	Sweetheart Cottage I G/P	200	N/A	595.00	1200-1300
1992	Sweetheart Cottage I S/N	980	N/A	495.00	1000-1200
1993	Sweetheart Cottage II A/P	400	1993	695.00	1450-1700
1993	Sweetheart Cottage II G/P	490	N/A	745.00	1400-1700
1993	Sweetheart Cottage II S/N	980	N/A	595.00	1300-1700
1994	Sweetheart Cottage III A/P	165	1994	765.00	865-1200
1994	Sweetheart Cottage III G/P	410	1994	765.00	865-1200
1994	Sweetheart Cottage III S/N	1,650	1994	615.00	715-1000
1992	Victorian Christmas I A/P	200	1992	695.00	1800-2200
1992	Victorian Christmas I G/P	200	1992	695.00	1800-2400
1992	Victorian Christmas I S/N	980	1992	595.00	2000-2200
1993	Victorian Christmas II A/P	400	1994	715.00	1500-1700
1993	Victorian Christmas II G/P	300	1994	715.00	1350-1800
1993	Victorian Christmas II S/N	1,650	1994	615.00	1000-1500
1994	Victorian Christmas III A/P	395	1994	800.00	800
1994	Victorian Christmas III G/P	990		800.00	800
1994	Victorian Christmas III S/N	3,950		650.00	690
1995	Victorian Christmas IV S/N	Yr.Iss.	1995	650.00	650
1991	Victorian Evening	Closed	1993	495.00	1300-1500
1992	Victorian Garden A/P	200	1993	895.00	2200-2600
1992	Victorian Garden G/P	200	1993	895.00	2000-2400
1992	Victorian Garden S/N	980	1993	795.00	2500-2900
1993	Village Inn A/P	400		615.00	730
1993	Village Inn G/P	400		615.00	730
1993	Village Inn S/N	1,200	1994	515.00	515-750
1994	The Warmth of Home A/P	345		590.00	615
1994	The Warmth of Home G/P	860		590.00	615
1994	The Warmth of Home S/N	3,450		440.00	465
1992	Weathervane Hutch A/P	200	1995	395.00	415-615
1992	Weathervane Hutch G/P	200		395.00	415
1992	Weathervane Hutch S/N	1,960	1992	295.00	315-515
1993	Winter's End A/P	400		715.00	840
1993	Winter's End G/P	490		715.00	840
1993	Winter's End S/N	1,450		615.00	690
1991	Woodman's Thatch A/P	200	1995	295.00	315-495
1991	Woodman's Thatch R/P	200	N/A	295.00	315-495
1991	Woodman's Thatch S/N	1,960	1994	195.00	315
1992	Yosemite A/P	200		695.00	840
1992	Yosemite G/P	200		695.00	840
1992	Yosemite S/N	980		595.00	690

Kinkade-Premium Paper-Unframed - T. Kinkade

YEAR ISSUE		EDITION LIMIT	YEAR RETD.	ISSUE PRICE	QUOTE U.S.$
1991	Afternoon Light, Dogwood A/P	98	N/A	295.00	1225
1991	Afternoon Light, Dogwood S/N	980	N/A	185.00	825
1992	Amber Afternoon S/N	980		225.00	265
1994	Autumn at Ashley's Cottage A/P	245		335.00	395
1994	Autumn at Ashley's Cottage S/N	2,450		185.00	195
1991	The Autumn Gate S/N	980	1994	225.00	500-950
1995	Autumn Lane A/P	285		400.00	400
1995	Autumn Lane S/N	2,850		250.00	250
1994	Beacon of Hope S/N	2,750		235.00	265
1993	Beside Still Waters S/N	1,280	1994	185.00	525-600
1993	Beyond Autumn Gate S/N	1,750	1994	285.00	500-900
1985	Birth of a City	Closed	N/A	150.00	900-1300
1993	The Blessings of Autumn S/N	1,250		235.00	265
1994	The Blessings of Spring A/P	275		345.00	370
1994	The Blessings of Spring S/N	2,750		195.00	220
1995	Blessings of Summer A/P	485		450.00	450
1995	Blessings of Summer S/N	4,850		300.00	300
1995	Blossom Bridge S/N	2,850		205.00	205
1992	Blossom Hill Church S/N	980		225.00	265
1991	Boston S/N	550	1994	175.00	350-750
1992	Broadwater Bridge S/N	980	1994	225.00	400-700
1995	Brookside Hideaway A/P	385		355.00	355

YEAR ISSUE		EDITION LIMIT	YEAR RETD.	ISSUE PRICE	QUOTE U.S.$
1995	Brookside Hideaway S/N	3,850		205.00	220
1991	Carmel, Delores Street and the Tuck Box Tea Room S/N	980	1994	275.00	800-1000
1989	Carmel, Ocean Avenue S/N	Closed	N/A	225.00	2200-2500
1990	Chandler's Cottage S/N	Closed	N/A	125.00	1000-1500
1992	Christmas At the Ahwahnee S/N	980		175.00	220
1990	Christmas Cottage 1990 S/N	Closed	N/A	95.00	350-700
1991	Christmas Eve S/N	980		125.00	195
1994	Christmas Tree Cottage A/P	295		335.00	395
1994	Christmas Tree Cottage S/N	2,950		185.00	195
1992	Cottage-By-The-Sea S/N	980	N/A	235.00	500-800
1992	Country Memories S/N	980		185.00	195
1994	Creekside Trail A/P	198		400.00	425
1994	Creekside Trail S/N	1,984		250.00	275
1984	Dawson	Closed	N/A	150.00	1200-1600
1994	Days of Peace A/P	198		400.00	415
1994	Days of Peace S/N	1,984		250.00	275
1994	Dusk in the Valley A/P	198		400.00	425
1994	Dusk in the Valley S/N	1,984		250.00	275
1994	Emerald Isle Cottage A/P	275		345.00	355
1994	Emerald Isle Cottage S/N	2,750		195.00	220
1993	End of a Perfect Day I S/N	1,250	1994	195.00	625-800
1994	End of a Perfect Day II A/P	275		435.00	435
1994	End of a Perfect Day II S/N	2,750		285.00	300
1995	End of a Perfect Day III A/P	485		475.00	475
1995	End of a Perfect Day III S/N	4,850		325.00	345
1989	Entrance to the Manor House	Closed	N/A	125.00	800-1000
1989	Evening at Merritt's Cottage	Closed	N/A	125.00	1000-1400
1992	Evening at Swanbrooke Cottage, S/N	980	1994	250.00	600-1000
1995	Evening in the Forest A/P	485		355.00	355
1995	Evening in the Forest S/N	4,850		205.00	205
1985	Evening Service	Closed	N/A	90.00	600-900
1991	Flags Over The Capitol S/N	1,991		195.00	265
1993	The Garden of Promise S/N	1,250	1994	235.00	500
1992	The Garden Party S/N	980		175.00	220
1994	Gardens Beyond Autumn Gate S/N	3/96		325.00	325
1993	Glory of Winter S/N	1,250		235.00	265
1994	Guardian Castle A/P	275		450.00	450
1994	Guardian Castle G/P	685		450.00	450
1994	Guardian Castle S/N	2,750		300.00	320
1993	Heather's Hutch S/N	1,250		175.00	195
1994	Hidden Arbor S/N	2,750	N/A	195.00	195
1990	Hidden Cottage	Closed	N/A	125.00	1000
1993	Hidden Cottage II S/N	1,480		195.00	195
1994	Hidden Gazebo A/P	275		345.00	355
1994	Hidden Gazebo, S/N	2,400	1995	195.00	205
1991	Home For The Evening S/N	Closed	N/A	100.00	200-300
1991	Home For The Holidays S/N	980	1994	225.00	500-700
1992	Home is Where the Heart Is, S/N	980	1994	225.00	450-700
1993	Homestead House S/N	1,250		235.00	265
1995	Hometown Memories I A/P	485		450.00	470
1995	Hometown Memories I S/N	4,850		300.00	320
1992	Julianne's Cottage S/N	Closed	N/A	185.00	550-750
1993	Lamplight Brook S/N	1,650		235.00	235
1994	Lamplight Inn A/P	275		385.00	415
1994	Lamplight Inn S/N	2,750		235.00	265
1993	Lamplight Lane S/N	Closed	N/A	225.00	500-1000
1995	Lamplight Village A/P	485		400.00	415
1995	Lamplight Village S/N	4,850		250.00	265
1995	A Light in the Storm A/P	385		415.00	415
1995	A Light in the Storm S/N	3,850		265.00	265
1995	Main Street Celebration A/P	195		400.00	400
1995	Main Street Celebration S/N	1,950		250.00	250
1995	Main Street Courthouse A/P	195		400.00	400
1995	Main Street Courthouse S/N	1,950		250.00	250
1995	Main Street Matinee A/P	195		400.00	400
1995	Main Street Matinee S/N	1,950		250.00	250
1995	Main Street Trolley A/P	195		400.00	400
1995	Main Street Trolley S/N	1,950		250.00	250
1991	McKenna's Cottage S/N	980		150.00	220
1992	Miller's Cottage S/N	980	1995	175.00	195-350
1994	Moonlight Lane I A/P	240		345.00	345
1994	Moonlight Lane I S/N	2,400		195.00	195
1985	Moonlight on the Riverfront	Closed	N/A	150.00	1800
1995	Morning Dogwood A/P	485		345.00	345
1995	Morning Dogwood S/N	4,850		195.00	205
1995	Morning Glory Cottage A/P	485		355.00	355
1995	Morning Glory Cottage S/N	4,850		205.00	205
1986	New York, 6th Avenue	Closed	N/A	150.00	1700-2000
1992	Olde Porterfield Gift Shoppe S/N	980		175.00	195
1991	Olde Porterfield Tea Room	980	N/A	150.00	195-395
1991	Open Gate, Sussex S/N	980		100.00	115
1993	Paris, City of Lights S/N	1,980		285.00	285
1994	Paris, Eiffel Tower A/P	275		445.00	445
1994	Paris, Eiffel Tower S/N	2,750		295.00	310
1995	Petals of Hope A/P	385		355.00	355
1995	Petals of Hope S/N	3,850		205.00	205
1984	Placerville, 1916 S/N	Closed	N/A	90.00	1800-2800
1994	The Power & The Majesty A/P	275		385.00	385
1994	The Power & The Majesty S/N	2,750		235.00	265
1988	Room with a View S/N	Closed	N/A	150.00	800-1000
1990	Rose Arbor S/N	Closed	1994	125.00	350-700
1994	San Francisco Market Street A/P	750		525.00	550
1994	San Francisco Market Street S/N	7,500		375.00	400
1986	San Francisco, 1909 S/N	Closed	N/A	150.00	1800-2300
1993	San Francisco, Fisherman's Wharf S/N	2,750		305.00	305
1992	San Francisco, Nob Hill (California St.) S/N	Closed	N/A	275.00	1500-1800
1989	San Francisco, Union Square S/N	Closed	N/A	225.00	2000-2700
1992	Silent Night S/N	980	1994	175.00	185-275

YEAR ISSUE		EDITION LIMIT	YEAR RETD.	ISSUE PRICE	QUOTE U.S.$
1995	Simpler Time I A/P	335		400.00	400
1995	Simpler Time I S/N	3,350		250.00	250
1990	Spring At Stonegate S/N	550	N/A	95.00	185-250
1994	Spring in the Alps A/P	198		375.00	375
1994	Spring in the Alps S/N	1,984		225.00	225
1993	St. Nicholas Circle S/N	1,750		235.00	265
1993	Stonehearth Hutch S/N	1,650		175.00	195
1993	Studio in the Garden S/N	980	1995	175.00	175
1992	Sunday At Apple Hill, S/N	980	1994	175.00	275-425
1993	Sunday Outing S/N	980		175.00	205
1992	Sweetheart Cottage I S/N	980	1995	150.00	200-400
1993	Sweetheart Cottage II S/N	980	1994	150.00	400-600
1993	Sweetheart Cottage III A/P	165		385.00	400
1993	Sweetheart Cottage III S/N	1,650		235.00	265
1992	Victorian Christmas I S/N	980	N/A	235.00	400-700
1993	Victorian Christmas II S/N	1,650		235.00	250
1994	Victorian Christmas III S/N	2,950		250.00	250
1995	Victorian Christmas IV S/N	Retrd.	1995	250.00	250
1991	Victorian Evening, S/N	Retrd.	1993	150.00	200-400
1992	Victorian Garden, S/N	980	1994	275.00	500-900
1993	Village Inn S/N	1,200		195.00	220
1994	The Warmth of Home A/P	245		335.00	345
1994	The Warmth of Home S/N	2,450		185.00	195
1993	Winter's End S/N	875		235.00	265
1992	Yosemite S/N	980		225.00	265

Lightpost Publishing/ Recollections

American Heroes Collection-Framed - Recollections

YEAR ISSUE		EDITION LIMIT	YEAR RETD.	ISSUE PRICE	QUOTE U.S.$
1992	Abraham Lincoln	7,500		150.00	150
1993	Babe Ruth	2,250		95.00	95
1993	Ben Franklin	1,000		95.00	95
1994	Dwight D. Eisenhower	Open		30.00	30
1994	Eternal Love (Civil War)	1,861		195.00	195
1994	Franklin D. Roosevelt	Open		30.00	30
1992	George Washington	7,500		150.00	150
1994	George Washington	Open		30.00	30
1992	John F. Kennedy	7,500		150.00	150
1994	John F. Kennedy	Open		30.00	30
1992	Mark Twain	7,500		150.00	150
1994	A Nation Divided	1,000		150.00	150
1993	A Nation United	1,000		150.00	150

Cinema Classics Collection-Framed - Recollections

YEAR ISSUE		EDITION LIMIT	YEAR RETD.	ISSUE PRICE	QUOTE U.S.$
1993	As God As My Witness	Open		40.00	40
1994	Attempted Deception	Open		30.00	30
1994	A Chance Meeting	Open		30.00	30
1993	A Dream Remembered	Open		40.00	40
1993	The Emerald City	Open		40.00	40
1993	Follow the Yellow Brick Road	Open		40.00	40
1993	Frankly My Dear	Open		40.00	40
1994	The Gift	Open		30.00	30
1993	Gone With the Wind-Movie Ticket	2,000		40.00	40
1994	If I Only Had a Brain	Open		30.00	30
1994	If I Only Had a Heart	Open		30.00	30
1994	If I Only Had the Nerve	Open		30.00	30
1993	The Kiss	Open		40.00	40
1993	Not A Marrying Man	12,500		150.00	150
1993	Over The Rainbow	7,500		150.00	150
1994	The Proposal	Open		30.00	30
1993	The Ruby Slippers	Open		40.00	40
1993	Scarlett & Her Beaux	12,500		150.00	150
1994	There's No Place Like Home	Open		30.00	30
1993	We're Off to See the Wizard	Open		40.00	40
1993	You Do Waltz Divinely	12,500		195.00	195
1993	You Need Kissing	12,500		195.00	195

The Elvis Collection - Recollections

YEAR ISSUE		EDITION LIMIT	YEAR RETD.	ISSUE PRICE	QUOTE U.S.$
1994	Celebrity Soldier/Regular G.I.	Open		30.00	30
1994	Dreams Remembered/Dreams Realized	Open		30.00	30
1994	Elvis the King	2,750		195.00	195
1994	Elvis the Pelvis	2,750		195.00	195
1994	The King/The Servant	Open		30.00	30
1994	Lavish Spender/Generous Giver	Open		30.00	30
1994	Professional Artist/Practical Joker	Open		30.00	30
1994	Public Image/Private Man	Open		30.00	30
1994	Sex Symbol/Boy Next Door	Open		30.00	30
1994	To Elvis with Love	2,750		195.00	195
1994	Vulgar Showman/Serious Musician	Open		30.00	30

Gone With the Wind - Recollections

YEAR ISSUE		EDITION LIMIT	YEAR RETD.	ISSUE PRICE	QUOTE U.S.$
1995	Final Parting Classic Clip	Open		30.00	30
1995	A Parting Kiss Classic Clip	Open		30.00	30
1995	The Red Dress Classic Clip	Open		30.00	30
1995	Sweet Revenge Classic Clip	Open		30.00	30

The Wizard of Oz - Recollections

YEAR ISSUE		EDITION LIMIT	YEAR RETD.	ISSUE PRICE	QUOTE U.S.$
1995	Glinda the Good Witch	Open		30.00	30
1995	Toto	Open		30.00	30
1995	The Wicked Witch	Open		30.00	30
1995	The Wizard	Open		30.00	30

Marty Bell

Members Only Collectors Club - M. Bell

YEAR ISSUE		EDITION LIMIT	YEAR RETD.	ISSUE PRICE	QUOTE U.S.$
1991	Little Thatch Twilight	Closed	1992	288.00	575
1991	Charter Rose, The	Closed	1992	Gift	N/A
1992	Candle At Eventide	Closed	1993	Gift	N/A
1992	Blossom Lane	Closed	1993	288.00	288

YEAR ISSUE		EDITION LIMIT	YEAR RETD.	ISSUE PRICE	QUOTE U.S.$
1993	Laverstoke Lodge	Closed	1994	328.00	328
1993	Chideock Gate	Closed	1994	Gift	N/A
1994	Hummingbird Hill	Closed	1995	320.00	495
1994	The Hummingbird	Closed	1995	Gift	N/A
1995	The Bluebird Victorian	Yr.Iss.		320.00	340
1995	The Bluebird	Yr.Iss.		Gift	N/A

America the Beautiful - M. Bell

YEAR ISSUE		EDITION LIMIT	YEAR RETD.	ISSUE PRICE	QUOTE U.S.$
1993	The Abbey	750		400.00	424
1994	Bayside Morning	750		400.00	424
1993	Idaho Hideaway	750		400.00	424
1993	Jones Victorian	750	1994	400.00	1050
1994	Love Tide	750		400.00	424
1995	Majesty	500		700.00	742
1994	Mendocino Twilight	750		400.00	424
1994	My Garden	750		430.00	456
1994	Summerland	750		400.00	424
1995	Telegraph Hill	750		150.00	150
1995	The Tuck Box Tea Room, Carmel	500	1995	456.00	1200
1993	Turlock Spring	500		700.00	742
1994	Woodland Garden	750		460.00	488

Christmas - M. Bell

YEAR ISSUE		EDITION LIMIT	YEAR RETD.	ISSUE PRICE	QUOTE U.S.$
1989	Fireside Christmas	500	1989	136.00	750
1990	Ready For Christmas	700	1990	148.00	495
1991	Christmas in Rochester	900	1991	148.00	275-350
1992	McCoy's Toy Shoppe	900	1992	148.00	350
1993	Christmas Treasures	900		200.00	200
1994	Rocky Mountain Christmas	750		400.00	424

England - M. Bell

YEAR ISSUE		EDITION LIMIT	YEAR RETD.	ISSUE PRICE	QUOTE U.S.$
1987	Alderton Village	500	1988	235.00	750-899
1988	Allington Castle, Kent	1,800		540.00	572
1992	Antiques of Rye	1,100		220.00	234
1990	Arbor Cottage	900	1990	130.00	150-250
1993	Arundel Row	750		130.00	138
1991	Bay Tree Cottage, Rye	1,100	1992	230.00	230-520
1981	Bibury Cottage	500	1988	280.00	800-1000
1981	Big Daddy's Shoe	700	1989	64.00	150-300
1988	The Bishop's Roses	900	1989	220.00	695
1989	Blush of Spring	1,200	1990	96.00	120-160
1995	Blyton Cottage	750		100.00	100
1988	Bodiam Twilight	900	1991	520.00	900-1100
1988	Brendon Hills Lane	900		304.00	318
1992	Briarwood	217	1993	220.00	220
1993	Broadway Cottage	750		330.00	350
1987	Broughton Village	900	1988	128.00	400-500
1984	Brown Eyes	312	1993	296.00	296
1990	Bryants Puddle Thatch	900	1990	130.00	150-295
1986	Burford Village Store	500	1988	106.00	500-1500
1995	Burton Cottage	750		100.00	100
1993	Byfleet	900		180.00	200
1994	Canterbury Roses	750		180.00	190
1981	Castle Combe Cottage	500	1988	230.00	895
1993	The Castle Tearoom	900	1993	88.00	88
1987	The Chaplains Garden	500	1987	235.00	1000-2000
1992	Chelsea Roses	750		298.00	318
1989	Cherry Tree Thatch	2,400		88.00	96
1991	Childswickham Morning	305	1993	396.00	396
1987	Chippenham Farm	500	1988	120.00	300-900
1988	Clove Cottage	900	1988	128.00	500
1988	Clover Lane Cottage	1,800	1988	272.00	750-1400
1991	Cobblestone	1,200		374.00	404
1993	Coln St. Aldwyn's	1,000	1995	730.00	1200
1986	Cotswold Parish Church	500	1988	98.00	1500-2000
1988	Cotswold Twilight	900	1988	128.00	200-495
1993	Cottontail Lodge	700		375.00	398
1991	Cozy Cottage	900	1991	130.00	130
1993	Craigton Cottage	500		130.00	138
1982	Crossroads Cottage	S/O	1987	38.00	200
1992	Devon Cottage	900		374.00	404
1991	Devon Roses	1,200	1991	78.00	195-500
1991	Dorset Roses	1,200	1991	96.00	195
1987	Dove Cottage Garden	900	1990	260.00	304-495
1987	Driftstone Manor	500	1988	440.00	1500
1987	Ducksbridge Cottage	500	1988	400.00	2000-2400
1987	Eashing Cottage	900	1988	120.00	200-400
1992	East Sussex Roses (Archival)	1,200	1993	184.00	184
1989	Elegance of Spring	1,800		396.00	456
1989	Fernbank Cottage	2,400		96.00	106
1985	Fiddleford Cottage	500	1986	78.00	1950
1993	Flower Box, The	900		300.00	318
1988	Friday Street Lane	1,800	1992	280.00	600
1989	The Game Keeper's Cottage	900	1989	560.00	1800-2000
1992	Garlands Flower Shop	900	1992	220.00	220
1988	Ginger Cottage	1,800	1988	320.00	550-800
1989	Glory Cottage	911	1993	96.00	96
1989	Goater's Cottage	900	1991	368.00	400-560
1990	Gomshall Flower Shop	900	1990	396.00	2900
1993	Graffam House	900		180.00	200
1987	Halfway Cottage	900	1988	260.00	300-500
1992	Happy Heart Cottage	1,200		368.00	398
1989	Hideaway Cottage	2,400		88.00	96
1992	Hollybush	1,200	1994	560.00	560
1991	Horsham Farmhouse	1,200		180.00	200
1986	Housewives Choice	500	1987	98.00	750-1000
1988	Icomb Village Garden	900	1988	620.00	1300-1500
1988	Jasmine Thatch	900	1991	272.00	495
1989	Larkspur Cottage	900	1989	220.00	495
1985	Little Boxford	500	1987	78.00	300-900
1991	Little Bromley Lodge	1,200		456.00	488
1991	Little Timbers	900	1992	130.00	130
1987	Little Tulip Thatch	500	1988	120.00	400-700
1990	Little Well Thatch	950	1990	130.00	150-250
1990	Longparish Cottage	900	1991	368.00	300-550
1990	Longstock Lane	900	1990	130.00	200
1986	Lorna Doone Cottage	500	1987	380.00	8000-9000
1990	Lower Brockhampton Manor	900	1990	640.00	1800
1988	Lullabye Cottage	900	1988	220.00	300-400
1990	Martin's Market, Rye	1,100		304.00	318
1987	May Cottage	900	1988	120.00	200-699
1988	Meadow School	816	1993	220.00	350
1985	Meadowlark Cottage	500	1987	78.00	450-699
1990	Mermaid Inn, Rye, The	1,100		560.00	594
1987	Millpond, Stockbridge, The	500	1987	120.00	1100
1992	Miss Hathaway's Garden	1,800		694.00	742
1987	Morning Glory Cottage	500	1988	120.00	450-599
1988	Morning's Glow	1,800	1989	280.00	320-650
1994	Mother Hubbard's Garden	2-Yr.		230.00	244
1988	Murrle Cottage	1,800	1988	320.00	450-650
1983	Nestlewood	500	1987	300.00	2500
1989	Northcote Lane	1,160	1993	88.00	88
1989	Old Beams Cottage	900	1990	368.00	650
1988	Old Bridge, Grasmere	453	1993	640.00	640
1990	Old Hertfordshire Thatch	900	1990	396.00	2000
1993	Old Mother Hubbard's Cottage	2-Yr.	1995	230.00	244
1989	Overbrook	827	1993	220.00	350
1992	Pangbourne on Thames	900	1994	304.00	400-650
1984	Penshurst Tea Rooms (Archival)	1,000	1988	335.00	950
1984	Penshurst Tea Rooms (Canvas)	500	1987	335.00	15-3600
1989	Periwinkle Tea Rooms, The	2,400		694.00	742
1989	Pride of Spring	1,200	1990	96.00	200-400
1989	Primrose Cottage	2,400		88.00	96
1988	Rodway Cottage	900	1989	694.00	700-1500
1989	Rose Bedroom, The	515	1993	388.00	388
1995	Rose Bower Cottage (Triple)	500		520.00	520
1990	Sanctuary	900	1992	220.00	450
1982	Sandhills Cottage	S/O	1987	38.00	38
1988	Sandy Lane Thatch	375	1993	380.00	500
1982	School Lane Cottage	S/O	1987	38.00	38
1993	Selborne Cottage	750		300.00	318
1992	Sheffield Roses	750		298.00	318
1988	Shere Village Antiques	900	1988	272.00	304-699
1993	Simon the Pieman, Rye	1,100		240.00	255
1995	Sissinghurst Garden	750		488.00	488
1991	Somerset Inn	1,200		180.00	200
1993	Speldhurst Farm	1,200		248.00	265
1981	Spring in the Santa Ynez	500	1991	400.00	1100
1991	Springtime at Scotney	1,200	1992	730.00	950-1200
1989	St. Martin's Ashurst	243	1993	344.00	344
1992	Strand Quay, Rye, The	1,100		248.00	265
1990	Summer's Garden	900	1991	78.00	400-800
1994	Summer's Song, Scotney	1,200		730.00	774
1985	Summers Glow	500	1987	98.00	600-1000
1987	Sunrise Thatch	900	1988	120.00	200-300
1985	Surrey Garden House	500	1986	98.00	850-1499
1991	Swan Cottage Tea Room, Rye	1,100		176.00	200
1989	Sweet Blue	1,800		396.00	456
1985	Sweet Pine Cottage	500	1987	78.00	350-1499
1988	Sweet Twilight	900	1988	220.00	350-600
1990	Sweetheart Thatch	900	1993	220.00	220
1991	Tea Time	900	1991	130.00	300
1982	Thatchcolm Cottage	S/O	1987	38.00	38
1989	Thimble Pub, The	641	1993	344.00	344
1993	Tithe Barn Cottage	900		368.00	398
1993	Umbrella Cottage	900		176.00	200
1991	Upper Chute	900	1991	496.00	850-1500
1992	Valentine Cottage	900		304.00	318
1987	The Vicar's Gate	500	1988	110.00	600
1987	Wakehurst Place	900	1988	480.00	1750
1987	Well Cottage, Sandy Lane	500	1988	440.00	650-1500
1991	Wepham Cottage	1,200	1991	396.00	1200
1984	West Kington Dell	500	1988	215.00	650
1992	West Sussex Roses (Archival)	1,200	1993	184.00	184
1994	Westminster Roses	750		180.00	190
1990	Weston Manor	900	1995	694.00	742
1987	White Lilac Thatch	900	1988	260.00	400-700
1992	Wild Rose Cottage	155	1993	248.00	248
1985	Windsong Cottage	500	1987	156.00	350-799
1991	Windward Cottage, Rye	1,100	1991	228.00	550-635
1991	Ye Olde Bell, Rye	1,100		196.00	212
1986	York Garden Shop	500	1988	98.00	250-999

HuggaBells - M. Bell

YEAR ISSUE		EDITION LIMIT	YEAR RETD.	ISSUE PRICE	QUOTE U.S.$
1995	The Luv Boat	350		110.00	116
1995	Motherlove	350		116.00	116
1995	Storytime	350		110.00	116
1995	Tea with Miss Teddy	350	1995	128.00	185
1995	Wedded Bliss	350		116.00	116

Mill Pond Press

Bateman - R. Bateman

YEAR ISSUE		EDITION LIMIT	YEAR RETD.	ISSUE PRICE	QUOTE U.S.$
1982	Above the River-Trumpeter Swans	950	1984	200.00	1000
1984	Across the Sky-Snow Geese	950	1985	220.00	800
1980	African Amber-Lioness Pair	950	1980	175.00	575
1979	Afternoon Glow-Snowy Owl	950	1979	125.00	600
1990	Air, The Forest and The Watch	42,558	N/A	325.00	350
1984	Along the Ridge-Grizzly Bears	950	1984	200.00	1200
1984	American Goldfinch-Winter Dress	950	1984	75.00	200
1979	Among the Leaves-Cottontail Rabbit	950	1980	75.00	1200
1980	Antarctic Elements	950	1980	125.00	150
1991	Arctic Cliff-White Wolves	13,000	1991	325.00	525
1982	Arctic Evening-White Wolf	950	1982	185.00	1400
1980	Arctic Family-Polar Bears	950	1980	150.00	1700
1992	Arctic Landscape-Polar Bear	5,000	N/A	345.00	700
1992	Arctic Landscape-Polar Bear-Premier Ed.	450		800.00	800
1982	Arctic Portrait-White Gyrfalcon	950	1982	175.00	280
1985	Arctic Tern Pair	950	1985	175.00	200
1981	Artist and His Dog	950	1983	150.00	300
1980	Asleep on the Hemlock-Screech Owl	950	1980	125.00	375
1991	At the Cliff-Bobcat	12,500	1991	325.00	325
1992	At the Feeder-Cardinal	950	1992	125.00	125
1987	At the Nest-Secretary Birds	950	1987	290.00	290
1982	At the Roadside-Red-Tailed Hawk	950	1984	185.00	650
1980	Autumn Overture-Moose	950	1980	245.00	1800
1980	Awesome Land-American Elk	950	1980	245.00	1500
1989	Backlight-Mute Swan	950	1989	275.00	500
1983	Bald Eagle Portrait	950	1983	185.00	280
1982	Baobab Tree and Impala	950	1986	245.00	300
1980	Barn Owl in the Churchyard	950	1981	125.00	850
1989	Barn Swallow and Horse Collar	950	N/A	225.00	225
1982	Barn Swallows in August	950	N/A	245.00	425
1992	Beach Grass and Tree Frog	1,250		345.00	350
1985	Beaver Pond Reflections	950	1985	185.00	225
1984	Big Country, Pronghorn Antelope	950	1985	185.00	200
1986	Black Eagle	950	1986	200.00	250
1993	Black Jaguar-Premier Edition	450		850.00	1200
1986	Black-Tailed Deer in the Olympics	950	1986	245.00	245
1986	Blacksmith Plover	950	1986	185.00	185
1991	Bluebird and Blossoms	4,500		235.00	235
1991	Bluebird and Blossoms-Prestige Edition	450		625.00	625
1980	Bluffing Bull-African Elephant	950	1981	135.00	1125
1981	Bright Day-Atlantic Puffins	950	1985	175.00	875
1989	Broad-Tailed Hummingbird Pair	950	1989	225.00	225
1980	Brown Pelican and Pilings	950	1980	165.00	950
1979	Bull Moose	950	1979	125.00	1275
1978	By the Tracks-Killdeer	950	1980	75.00	1200
1983	Call of the Wild-Bald Eagle	950	1983	200.00	250
1985	Canada Geese Family(stone lithograph)	260	1985	350.00	1000
1985	Canada Geese Over the Escarpment	950	1985	135.00	175
1986	Canada Geese With Young	950	1986	195.00	325
1981	Canada Geese-Nesting	950	1981	295.00	2950
1993	Cardinal and Sumac	2,510	N/A	235.00	235
1988	Cardinal and Wild Apples	12,183	1988	235.00	235
1989	Catching The Light-Barn Owl	2,000	1990	295.00	295
1988	Cattails, Fireweed and Yellowthroat	950	1988	235.00	275
1989	Centennial Farm	950	1989	295.00	450
1988	The Challenge-Bull Moose	10,671		325.00	325
1980	Chapel Doors	950	1985	135.00	375
1986	Charging Rhino	950	1986	325.00	500
1982	Cheetah Profile	950	1985	245.00	500
1978	Cheetah With Cubs	950	1980	95.00	450
1988	Cherrywood with Juncos	950	1988	245.00	245-345
1990	Chinstrap Penguin	810	1991	150.00	150
1992	Clan of the Raven	950	1992	235.00	600
1981	Clear Night-Wolves	950	1981	245.00	6500-8100
1988	Colonial Garden	950	1988	245.00	245
1987	Continuing Generations-Spotted Owls	950	1987	525.00	1150
1991	Cottage Lane-Red Fox	950	1991	285.00	285
1984	Cougar Portrait	950	1984	95.00	200
1979	Country Lane-Pheasants	950	1981	85.00	300
1981	Courting Pair-Whistling Swans	950	1981	245.00	550
1981	Courtship Display-Wild Turkey	950	1981	175.00	175
1980	Coyote in Winter Sage	950	1980	245.00	3600
1992	Cries of Courtship-Red Crowned Cranes	950	1992	350.00	350
1980	Curious Glance-Red Fox	950	1980	135.00	1200
1986	Dark Gyrfalcon	950	1986	225.00	325
1993	Day Lilies and Dragonflies	1,250		345.00	345
1982	Dipper By the Waterfall	950	1985	165.00	225
1989	Dispute Over Prey	950		325.00	325
1989	Distant Danger-Raccoon	1,600	1989	225.00	225
1984	Down for a Drink-Morning Dove	950	1985	135.00	200
1978	Downy Woodpecker on Goldenrod Gall	950	1979	50.00	1425
1988	Dozing Lynx	950	1988	335.00	1900
1986	Driftwood Perch-Striped Swallows	950	1986	195.00	250
1983	Early Snowfall-Ruffed Grouse	950	1985	195.00	225
1983	Early Spring-Bluebird	950	1984	185.00	450
1981	Edge of the Ice-Ermine	950	1981	175.00	475
1982	Edge of the Woods-Whitetail Deer, w/Book	950	1983	745.00	1400
1991	Elephant Cow and Calf	950	1991	300.00	300
1986	Elephant Herd and Sandgrouse	950	1986	235.00	235
1991	Encounter in the Bush-African Lions	950	1991	295.00	325
1987	End of Season-Grizzly	950	1987	325.00	500
1991	Endangered Spaces-Grizzly	4,008	1991	325.00	425
1985	Entering the Water-Common Gulls	950	1986	195.00	200
1986	European Robin and Hydrangeas	950	1986	130.00	225
1989	Evening Call-Common Loon	950	1989	235.00	525
1980	Evening Grosbeak	950	1980	125.00	1175

YEAR ISSUE		EDITION LIMIT	YEAR RETD.	ISSUE PRICE	QUOTE U.S.$
1983	Evening Idyll-Mute Swans	950	1984	245.00	450-525
1981	Evening Light-White Gyrfalcon	950	1981	245.00	1100
1979	Evening Snowfall-American Elk	950	1980	150.00	1900
1987	Everglades	950	1987	360.00	360
1980	Fallen Willow-Snowy Owl	950	1980	200.00	950
1987	Farm Lane and Blue Jays	950	1987	225.00	450
1986	Fence Post and Burdock	950	1987	130.00	130
1991	Fluid Power-Orca	290		2500.00	2500
1980	Flying High-Golden Eagle	950	1980	150.00	975
1982	Fox at the Granary	950	1985	165.00	225
1982	Frosty Morning-Blue Jay	950	1982	185.00	1000
1982	Gallinule Family	950		135.00	135
1981	Galloping Herd-Giraffes	950	1981	175.00	1200
1985	Gambel's Quail Pair	950	1985	95.00	350
1982	Gentoo Penguins and Whale Bones	950	1986	205.00	300
1983	Ghost of the North-Great Gray Owl	950	1983	200.00	2675
1982	Golden Crowned Kinglet and Rhododendron	950	1982	150.00	2575
1979	Golden Eagle	950	1981	150.00	250
1985	Golden Eagle Portrait	950	1987	115.00	175
1989	Goldfinch In the Meadow	1,600	1989	150.00	200
1983	Goshawk and Ruffed Grouse	950	1984	185.00	400-700
1988	Grassy Bank-Great Blue Heron	950	1988	285.00	285
1981	Gray Squirrel	950	1981	180.00	1250
1979	Great Blue Heron	950	1980	125.00	1300
1987	Great Blue Heron in Flight	950	1987	295.00	550
1988	Great Crested Grebe	950	1988	135.00	135
1987	Great Egret Preening	950	1987	315.00	500
1983	Great Horned Owl in the White Pine	950	1983	225.00	575
1987	Greater Kudu Bull	950	1987	145.00	145
1993	Grizzly and Cubs	2,250		335.00	400
1991	Gulls on Pilings	1,950		265.00	265
1988	Hardwood Forest-White-Tailed Buck	630	1988	300.00	2100
1988	Harlequin Duck-Bull Kelp-Executive Ed.	623	1988	550.00	550
1988	Harlequin Duck-Bull Kelp-Gold Plated	950	1988	300.00	300
1980	Heron on the Rocks	950	1980	75.00	300
1981	High Camp at Dusk	950	1985	245.00	300
1979	High Country-Stone Sheep	950	1982	125.00	325
1987	High Kingdom-Snow Leopard	950	1987	325.00	675-850
1990	Homage to Ahmed	290		3300.00	3300
1984	Hooded Mergansers in Winter	950	1984	210.00	650-700
1984	House Finch and Yucca	950	1984	95.00	175
1986	House Sparrow	950	1986	125.00	350
1987	House Sparrows and Bittersweet	950	1987	220.00	400
1986	Hummingbird Pair Diptych	950	1986	330.00	475
1987	Hurricane Lake-Wood Ducks	950		135.00	200
1981	In for the Evening	950	1981	150.00	1500
1994	In His Prime-Mallard	950	N/A	195.00	295-350
1984	In the Brier Patch-Cottontail	950	1985	165.00	350
1986	In the Grass-Lioness	950	1986	245.00	245
1985	In the Highlands-Golden Eagle	950	1985	235.00	425
1985	In the Mountains-Osprey	950	1987	95.00	125
1992	Intrusion-Mountain Gorilla	2,250		325.00	325
1990	Ireland House	950	1990	265.00	318
1985	Irish Cottage and Wagtail	950	1990	175.00	175
1992	Junco in Winter	1,250	1992	185.00	185
1990	Keeper of the Land	290		3300.00	3300
1993	Kestrel and Grasshopper	1,250		335.00	335
1979	King of the Realm	950	1979	125.00	675
1987	King Penguins	950	1987	130.00	135
1981	Kingfisher and Aspen	950	1981	225.00	600
1980	Kingfisher in Winter	950	1981	175.00	825
1980	Kittiwake Greeting	950	1980	75.00	550
1981	Last Look-Bighorn Sheep	950	1986	195.00	225
1987	Late Winter-Black Squirrel	950	1987	165.00	165
1981	Laughing Gull and Horseshoe Crab	950	1981	125.00	125
1982	Leopard Ambush	950	1986	245.00	600
1988	Leopard and Thomson Gazelle Kill	950	1988	275.00	275
1985	Leopard at Seronera	950	1985	175.00	280
1980	Leopard in a Sausage Tree	950	1980	150.00	1250
1984	Lily Pads and Loon	950	1984	200.00	1875
1987	Lion and Wildebeest	950	1987	265.00	265
1980	Lion at Tsavo	950	1983	150.00	275
1978	Lion Cubs	950	1981	125.00	800
1987	Lioness at Serengeti	950	1987	325.00	325
1985	Lions in the Grass	950	1985	265.00	1250
1981	Little Blue Heron	950	1981	95.00	275
1982	Lively Pair-Chickadees	950	1982	160.00	450
1983	Loon Family	950	1983	200.00	750
1990	Lunging Heron	1,250	1990	225.00	225
1978	Majesty on the Wing-Bald Eagle	950	1979	150.00	2650
1988	Mallard Family at Sunset	950	1988	235.00	235
1986	Mallard Family-Misty Marsh	950	1986	130.00	175
1986	Mallard Pair-Early Winter	41,740	1986	135.00	200
1985	Mallard Pair-Early Winter 24K Gold	950	1986	1650.00	2000
1986	Mallard Pair-Early Winter Gold Plated	7,691	1986	250.00	375
1989	Mangrove Morning-Roseate Spoonbills	2,000	1989	325.00	325
1991	Mangrove Shadow-Common Egret	1,250		285.00	285
1993	Marbled Murrelet	55	1993	1200.00	1200
1986	Marginal Meadow	950	1986	220.00	350
1979	Master of the Herd-African Buffalo	950	1980	150.00	2250
1984	May Maple-Scarlet Tanager	950	1984	175.00	825
1982	Meadow's Edge-Mallard	950	1982	175.00	900
1982	Merganser Family in Hiding	950	1982	200.00	525
1994	Meru Dusk-Lesser Kudu	950		135.00	135
1989	Midnight-Black Wolf	25,352	1989	325.00	2300
1980	Mischief on the Prowl-Raccoon	950	1980	85.00	350
1980	Misty Coast-Gulls	950	1980	135.00	600
1984	Misty Lake-Osprey	950	1985	95.00	300
1981	Misty Morning-Loons	950	1981	150.00	3000
1986	Moose at Water's Edge	950	1986	130.00	225
1990	Morning Cove-Common Loon	950	1990	165.00	165
1985	Morning Dew-Roe Deer	950	1985	175.00	175
1983	Morning on the Flats-Bison	950	1983	200.00	300
1984	Morning on the River-Trumpeter Swans	950	1984	185.00	300
1990	Mossy Branches-Spotted Owl	4,500	1990	300.00	525
1990	Mowed Meadow	950	1990	190.00	190
1986	Mule Deer in Aspen	950	1986	175.00	175
1983	Mule Deer in Winter	950	1983	200.00	275-350
1988	Muskoka Lake-Common Loons	2,500	1988	265.00	450
1989	Near Glenburnie	950		265.00	265
1983	New Season-American Robin	950	1983	200.00	450
1986	Northern Reflections-Loon Family	8,631	1986	255.00	2100
1985	Old Whaling Base and Fur Seals	950	1985	195.00	550
1987	Old Willow and Mallards	950	1987	325.00	390
1980	On the Alert-Chipmunk	950	1980	60.00	500
1993	On the Brink-River Otters	1,250		345.00	345
1985	On the Garden Wall	950	1985	115.00	300
1985	Orca Procession	950	1985	245.00	2525
1981	Osprey Family	950	1981	245.00	325
1983	Osprey in the Rain	950	1983	110.00	650
1987	Otter Study	950	1987	235.00	375
1981	Pair of Skimmers	950	1981	150.00	150
1988	Panda's At Play (stone lithograph)	160	1988	400.00	1650
1994	Path of the Panther	1,950		295.00	295
1984	Peregrine and Ruddy Turnstones	950	1985	200.00	350
1985	Peregrine Falcon and White-Throated Swifts	950	1985	245.00	550
1987	Peregrine Falcon on the Cliff-Stone Litho	525	1988	350.00	625
1983	Pheasant in Cornfield	950	1983	200.00	375
1988	Pheasants at Dusk	950	1988	325.00	525
1982	Pileated Woodpecker on Beech Tree	950	1982	175.00	525
1990	Pintails in Spring	9,651	1989	135.00	135
1982	Pioneer Memories-Magpie Pair	950	1982	175.00	250
1987	Plowed Field-Snowy Owl	950	1987	145.00	400
1990	Polar Bear	290	1990	3300.00	3300
1982	Polar Bear Profile	950	1982	210.00	2350
1982	Polar Bears at Bafin Island	950	1982	245.00	875
1990	Power Play-Rhinoceros	950	1990	320.00	320
1980	Prairie Evening-Short-Eared Owl	950	1983	150.00	200
1994	Predator Portfolio/Black Bear	950		475.00	475
1992	Predator Portfolio/Cougar	950		465.00	465
1993	Predator Portfolio/Grizzly	950		475.00	475
1993	Predator Portfolio/Polar Bear	950		485.00	485
1993	Predator Portfolio/Wolf	950	N/A	475.00	475
1988	Preening Pair-Canada Geese	950	1988	235.00	300
1987	Pride of Autumn-Canada Goose	15,294	1987	135.00	245
1986	Proud Swimmer-Snow Goose	950	1986	185.00	185
1989	Pumpkin Time	950		195.00	195
1982	Queen Anne's Lace and American Goldfinch	950	1982	150.00	1000
1984	Ready for Flight-Peregrine Falcon	950	1984	185.00	500
1982	Ready for the Hunt-Snowy Owl	950	1982	245.00	550
1993	Reclining Snow Leopard	1,250		335.00	335
1988	Red Crossbills	950	1988	125.00	125
1984	Red Fox on the Prowl	950	1984	245.00	1500
1982	Red Squirrel	950	1982	175.00	700
1986	Red Wolf	950	1986	250.00	525
1981	Red-Tailed Hawk by the Cliff	950	1981	245.00	550
1981	Red-Winged Blackbird and Rail Fence	950	1981	195.00	225
1984	Reeds	950	1984	185.00	575
1986	A Resting Place-Cape Buffalo	950	1986	265.00	265
1986	Resting Pair-Cape Buffalo	950		265.00	265
1987	Rhino at Ngoro Ngoro	950	1988	325.00	325
1993	River Otter-North American Wilderness	350		325.00	500
1993	River Otters	290		1500.00	1500
1986	Robins at the Nest	950	1986	185.00	225
1987	Rocky Point-October	950	1987	195.00	275
1980	Rocky Wilderness-Cougar	950	1980	175.00	1425
1990	Rolling Waves-Lesser Scaup	3,330		125.00	125
1993	Rose-breasted Grosbeak	290		450.00	450
1981	Rough-Legged Hawk in the Elm	950	1991	175.00	250
1981	Royal Family-Mute Swans	950	1981	245.00	1100
1983	Ruby Throat and Columbine	950	1983	150.00	2200
1987	Ruddy Turnstones	950	1987	175.00	175
1994	Salt Spring Sheep	1,250		235.00	235
1981	Sarah E. with Gulls	950	1981	245.00	2625
1993	Saw Whet Owl and Wild Grapes	950		185.00	185
1991	The Scolding-Chickadees & Screech Owl	12,500		235.00	235
1991	Sea Otter Study	950	1991	150.00	150
1993	Shadow of the Rain Forest	9,000	1993	345.00	500
1981	Sheer Drop-Mountain Goats	950	1981	245.00	2800
1988	Shelter	950	1988	325.00	1000
1992	Siberian Tiger	4,500		325.00	325
1984	Smallwood	950	1985	200.00	500
1990	Snow Leopard	290	1990	2500.00	3500
1985	Snowy Hemlock-Barred Owl	950	1985	245.00	400
1994	Snowy Nap-Tiger	950	1994	185.00	185
1994	Snowy Owl	150	N/A	265.00	1000
1987	Snowy Owl and Milkweed	950	1987	235.00	950
1983	Snowy Owl on Driftwood	950	1983	245.00	1450
1983	Spirits of the Forest	950	1984	170.00	1750
1986	Split Rails-Snow Buntings	950	1986	220.00	220
1980	Spring Cardinal	950	1980	125.00	600
1982	Spring Marsh-Pintail Pair	950	1982	200.00	275
1980	Spring Thaw-Killdeer	950	1980	85.00	150
1982	Still Morning-Herring Gulls	950	1982	200.00	250
1987	Stone Sheep Ram	950	1987	175.00	175
1985	Stream Bank June	950	1986	160.00	175
1984	Stretching-Canada Goose	950	1984	225.00	3600-3900
1985	Strutting-Ring-Necked Pheasant	950	1985	225.00	325
1985	Sudden Blizzard-Red-Tailed Hawk	950	1985	245.00	600
1990	Summer Morning Pasture	950	1990	175.00	175
1984	Summer Morning-Loon	950	1984	185.00	1250
1986	Summertime-Polar Bears	950	1986	225.00	475
1979	Surf and Sanderlings	950	1980	65.00	450
1981	Swift Fox	950	1981	175.00	350
1986	Swift Fox Study	950	1986	115.00	150
1987	Sylvan Stream-Mute Swans	950	1987	125.00	125
1984	Tadpole Time	950	1985	135.00	475
1988	Tawny Owl In Beech	950		325.00	600
1992	Tembo (African Elephant)	1,550		350.00	350
1984	Tiger at Dawn	950	1984	225.00	2500
1983	Tiger Portrait	950	1983	130.00	400
1988	Tree Swallow over Pond	950	1988	290.00	290
1991	Trumpeter Swan Family	290		2500.00	2500
1985	Trumpeter Swans and Aspen	950	1985	245.00	550
1979	Up in the Pine-Great Horned Owl	950	1981	150.00	550
1980	Vantage Point	950	1980	245.00	1300
1993	Vigilance	9,500		330.00	330
1989	Vulture And Wildebeest	550		295.00	295
1981	Watchful Repose-Black Bear	950	1981	245.00	700
1985	Weathered Branch-Bald Eagle	950	1985	115.00	300
1991	Whistling Swan-Lake Erie	1,950		325.00	325
1980	White Encounter-Polar Bear	950	1980	245.00	4200-4800
1990	White on White-Snowshoe Hare	950	1990	195.00	590
1982	White World-Dall Sheep	950	1982	200.00	450
1985	White-Breasted Nuthatch on a Beech Tree	950	1985	175.00	300
1980	White-Footed Mouse in Wintergreen	950	1980	60.00	650
1982	White-Footed Mouse on Aspen	950	1983	90.00	180
1992	White-Tailed Deer Through the Birches	10,000		335.00	335
1984	White-Throated Sparrow and Pussy Willow	950	1984	150.00	580
1991	Wide Horizon-Tundra Swans	2,862		325.00	350-450
1991	Wide Horizon-Tundra Swans Companion	2,862		325.00	325
1986	Wildbeest	950		185.00	185
1982	Willet on the Shore	950	N/A	125.00	225
1979	Wily and Wary-Red Fox	950	1979	125.00	1500
1984	Window into Ontario	950	1984	265.00	1500
1983	Winter Barn	950	1984	170.00	400
1979	Winter Cardinal	950	1979	75.00	3550
1992	Winter Coat	1,250		245.00	245
1985	Winter Companion	950	1985	175.00	500
1980	Winter Elm-American Kestrel	950	1980	135.00	600
1986	Winter in the Mountains-Raven	950	1987	200.00	200
1981	Winter Mist-Great Horned Owl	950	1981	245.00	900
1980	Winter Song-Chickadees	950	1980	95.00	900
1984	Winter Sunset-Moose	950	1984	245.00	2700
1992	Winter Trackers	4,500	1992	335.00	375
1981	Winter Wren	950	1981	135.00	250
1983	Winter-Lady Cardinal	950	1983	200.00	1500
1979	Winter-Snowshoe Hare	950	1980	95.00	1200
1987	Wise One, The	950	1987	325.00	800
1979	Wolf Pack in Moonlight	950	1979	95.00	3000
1994	Wolf Pair in the Snow	290		795.00	795
1994	Wolverine Porfolio	950		275.00	275
1983	Wolves on the Trail	950	1983	225.00	700
1985	Wood Bison Portrait	950	1985	165.00	200
1983	Woodland Drummer-Ruffed Grouse	950	1984	185.00	250
1981	Wrangler's Campsite-Gray Jay	950	1981	195.00	550
1979	Yellow-Rumped Warbler	950	1980	50.00	575
1978	Young Barn Swallow	950	1979	75.00	700
1983	Young Elf Owl-Old Saguaro	950	1983	95.00	250
1991	Young Giraffe	290		850.00	850
1989	Young Kittiwake	950		195.00	195
1988	Young Sandhill-Cranes	950	1988	325.00	325
1989	Young Snowy Owl	950	1990	195.00	195

Brenders - C. Brenders

YEAR ISSUE		EDITION LIMIT	YEAR RETD.	ISSUE PRICE	QUOTE U.S.$
1986	The Acrobat's Meal-Red Squirrel	950	1989	65.00	275
1988	Apple Harvest	950	1989	115.00	350
1989	The Apple Lover	1,500	1990	125.00	275
1987	Autumn Lady	950	1989	150.00	375
1991	The Balance of Nature	1,950		225.00	225
1993	Black Sphinx	950		235.00	235
1986	Black-Capped Chickadees	950	1989	40.00	450
1990	Blond Beauty	1,950	1990	185.00	185
1986	Bluebirds	950	1989	40.00	200-300
1988	California Quail	950	1989	95.00	350-400
1991	Calm Before the Challenge-Moose	1,950	1991	225.00	225
1987	Close to Mom	950	1988	150.00	1500
1993	Collectors Group (Butterfly Collections)	290		375.00	375
1986	Colorful Playground-Cottontails	950	1989	75.00	475
1989	The Companions	18,036	1989	200.00	900-1250
1994	Dall Sheep Portrait	950		115.00	115
1992	Den Mother-Pencil Sketch	2,500	1992	135.00	135

YEAR ISSUE		EDITION LIMIT	YEAR RETD.	ISSUE PRICE	QUOTE U.S.$
1992	Den Mother-Wolf Family	25,000	1992	250.00	400
1986	Disturbed Daydreams	950	1989	95.00	425
1987	Double Trouble-Raccoons	950	1988	120.00	500-750
1993	European Group (Butterfly Collections)	290		375.00	375
1993	Exotic Group (Butterfly Collections)	290		375.00	375
1989	Forager's Reward-Red Squirrel	1,250	1989	135.00	135
1988	Forest Sentinel-Bobcat	950	1988	135.00	500
1990	Full House-Fox Family	20,106	1990	235.00	400
1990	Ghostly Quiet-Spanish Lynx	1,950	1990	200.00	200
1986	Golden Season-Gray Squirrel	950	1987	85.00	450-525
1986	Harvest Time-Chipmunk	950	1989	65.00	150-250
1988	Hidden In the Pines-Immature Great Hor	950	1988	175.00	1500
1988	High Adventure-Black Bear Cubs	950	1989	105.00	375
1988	A Hunter's Dream	950	1988	165.00	850
1993	In Northern Hunting Grounds	1,750		375.00	375
1992	Island Shores-Snowy Egret	2,500		250.00	250
1987	Ivory-Billed Woodpecker	950	1989	95.00	500
1988	Long Distance Hunters	950	1988	175.00	2250
1989	Lord of the Marshes	1,250	1989	135.00	175
1986	Meadowlark	950	1989	40.00	150
1989	Merlins at the Nest	1,250	1989	165.00	300-375
1985	Mighty Intruder	950	1989	95.00	275
1987	Migration Fever-Barn Swallows	950	1989	150.00	295
1990	The Monarch is Alive	4,071	1990	265.00	400
1993	Mother of Pearls	5,000		275.00	275
1990	Mountain Baby-Bighorn Sheep	1,950		165.00	165
1987	Mysterious Visitor-Barn Owl	950	1989	150.00	250
1993	Narrow Escape-Chipmunk	1,750		150.00	150
1991	The Nesting Season-House Sparrow	1,950	1991	195.00	200-250
1989	Northern Cousins-Black Squirrels	950	1989	150.00	250
1984	On the Alert-Red Fox	950	1986	95.00	475
1990	On the Old Farm Door	1,500	1990	225.00	450
1991	One to One-Gray Wolf	10,000	1991	245.00	450
1992	Pathfinder-Red Fox	5,000	1992	245.00	375
1984	Playful Pair-Chipmunks	950	1987	60.00	400
1994	Power and Grace	2,500	1994	265.00	265
1989	The Predator's Walk	1,250	1989	150.00	375
1992	Red Fox Study	1,250	1992	125.00	125
1994	Riverbank Kestrel	2,500		225.00	225
1988	Roaming the Plains-Pronghorns	950	1989	150.00	150
1986	Robins	950	1989	40.00	125
1993	Rocky Camp-Cougar Family	5,000		275.00	275
1993	Rocky Camp-Cubs	950		225.00	225
1992	Rocky Kingdom-Bighorn Sheep	1,750		255.00	255
1991	Shadows in the Grass-Young Cougars	1,950	1991	235.00	235
1990	Shoreline Quartet-White Ibis	1,950		265.00	265
1984	Silent Hunter-Great Horned Owl	950	1987	95.00	450
1984	Silent Passage	950	1988	150.00	495
1990	Small Talk	1,500	1990	125.00	150-250
1992	Snow Leopard Portrait	1,750	1993	150.00	150
1990	Spring Fawn	1,500	1990	125.00	300
1990	Squirrel's Dish	1,950		110.00	110
1989	Steller's Jay	1,250	1989	135.00	175
1991	Study for One to One	1,950		120.00	200
1993	Summer Roses-Winter Wren	1,500	1993	250.00	350
1989	The Survivors-Canada Geese	1,500	1989	225.00	850-950
1994	Take Five-Canadian Lynx	1,500		245.00	245
1988	Talk on the Old Fence	950	1988	165.00	550
1990	A Threatened Symbol	1,950	1990	145.00	300
1994	Tundra Summit-Arctic Wolves	6,061	1994	265.00	325
1984	Waterside Encounter	950	1987	95.00	1000
1987	White Elegance-Trumpeter Swans	950	1989	115.00	390
1993	White Wolves-North American Wilderness Portfolio	350		325.00	475
1988	Witness of a Past-Bison	950	1990	110.00	110
1992	Wolf Scout #1	2,500	1992	105.00	105
1992	Wolf Scout #2	2,500	1992	105.00	105
1991	Wolf Study	950	1991	125.00	125
1987	Yellow-Bellied Marmot	950	1989	95.00	425
1989	A Young Generation	1,250	1989	165.00	375-425

Calle - P. Calle

YEAR ISSUE		EDITION LIMIT	YEAR RETD.	ISSUE PRICE	QUOTE U.S.$
1981	Almost Home	950	1981	150.00	150
1991	Almost There	950	1991	165.00	165
1989	And A Good Book For Company	950	1990	135.00	190
1993	And A Grizzly Claw Necklace	750		150.00	150
1981	And Still Miles to Go	950	1981	245.00	300
1981	Andrew At The Falls	950	1981	150.00	175
1989	The Beaver Men	950		125.00	125
1984	A Brace for the Spit	950	1985	110.00	275
1980	Caring for the Herd	950	1981	110.00	110
1985	The Carrying Place	950	1990	195.00	195
1984	Chance Encounter	950	1986	225.00	300
1981	Chief High Pipe (Color)	950	1981	265.00	275
1980	Chief High Pipe (Pencil)	950	1980	75.00	165
1980	Chief Joseph-Man of Peace	950	1980	135.00	150
1990	Children of Walpi	350		160.00	160
1990	The Doll Maker	950		95.00	95
1982	Emerging from the Woods	950	1987	110.00	110-160
1981	End of a Long Day	950	1981	150.00	150-190
1984	Fate of the Late Migrant	950	1985	110.00	300
1983	Free Spirits	950	1985	195.00	325
1983	Free Trapper Study	550	1985	75.00	125-300
1981	Fresh Tracks	950	1981	150.00	165
1991	Friend of Foe	950		125.00	125
1981	Friends	950	1987	150.00	150
1985	The Frontier Blacksmith	950		245.00	245
1989	The Fur Trapper	550		75.00	175
1982	Generations in the Valley	950	1987	245.00	245
1985	The Grandmother	950	1987	400.00	400
1989	The Great Moment	950		350.00	350
1992	Hunter of Geese	950		125.00	125
1993	I Call Him Friend	950		235.00	235
1983	In Search of Beaver	950	1983	225.00	600
1991	In the Beginning . . . Friends	1,250	1993	250.00	250
1987	In the Land of the Giants	950	1988	245.00	780
1990	Interrupted Journey	1,750	1991	265.00	265
1990	Interrupted Journey-Prestige Ed.	290	1991	465.00	465
1987	Into the Great Alone	950	1988	245.00	600
1981	Just Over the Ridge	950	1982	245.00	325
1980	Landmark Tree	950	1980	125.00	225
1991	Man of the Fur Trade	550		110.00	110
1984	Mountain Man	550	1988	95.00	250-550
1993	Mountain Man-North American Wilderness Portfolio	350		325.00	N/A
1989	The Mountain Men	300	1989	400.00	400
1989	Navajo Madonna	650		95.00	95
1988	A New Day	950		150.00	150
1981	One With The Land	950	1981	245.00	325
1992	Out of the Silence	2,500		265.00	265
1992	Out of the Silence-Prestige	290		465.00	465
1981	Pause at the Lower Falls	950	1981	110.00	125
1980	Prayer to the Great Mystery	950	1980	245.00	400
1982	Return to Camp	950	1982	245.00	400
1991	The Silenced Honkers	1,250		250.00	250
1980	Sioux Chief	950	1980	85.00	85-140
1986	Snow Hunter	950	1988	150.00	250-410
1980	Something for the Pot	950	1980	175.00	1000
1990	Son of Sitting Bull	950		95.00	95
1985	Storyteller of the Mountains	950	1985	225.00	575
1983	Strays From the Flyway	950	1983	195.00	250-340
1981	Teton Friends	950	1981	150.00	200
1991	They Call Me Matthew	950		125.00	125
1992	Through the Tall Grass	950		175.00	175
1988	Trapper at Rest	550		95.00	95
1982	Two from the Flock	950	1982	245.00	400
1980	View from the Heights	950	1980	245.00	350
1988	Voyageurs and Waterfowl...Constant	950	1988	265.00	265
1980	When Snow Came Early	950	1980	85.00	250-340
1984	When Trails Cross	950	1984	245.00	750
1991	When Trails Grow Cold	2,500		265.00	265
1991	When Trails Grow Cold-Prestige Edition	290	1991	465.00	465-600
1994	When Trappers Meet	750		165.00	165
1989	Where Eagles Fly	1,250	1990	265.00	265
1989	A Winter Feast	1,250	1989	265.00	265
1989	A Winter Feast-Prestige Ed.	290	1989	465.00	465
1981	Winter Hunter (Color)	950	1981	245.00	725
1980	Winter Hunter (Pencil)	950	1980	65.00	450
1983	A Winter Surprise	950	1984	195.00	800

Cross - T. Cross

YEAR ISSUE		EDITION LIMIT	YEAR RETD.	ISSUE PRICE	QUOTE U.S.$
1994	April	750		55.00	55
1994	August	750		55.00	55
1993	Ever Green	750		135.00	135
1993	Flame Catcher	750	1993	185.00	185
1993	Flicker, Flash and Twirl	525		165.00	165
1994	July	750		55.00	55
1994	June	750		55.00	55
1994	March	750		55.00	55
1994	May	750		55.00	55
1992	Shell Caster	750	1993	150.00	150
1993	Sheperds of Magic	750		135.00	135
1993	Spellbound	750		85.00	85
1994	Spring Forth	750		145.00	145
1992	Star Weaver	750	1993	150.00	150
1994	Summer Musings	750		145.00	145
1993	The Summons...And Then They Are One	750	1993	195.00	195
1994	When Water Takes to Air	750		135.00	135
1993	Wind Sifter	750	1993	150.00	150

Daly - J. Daly

YEAR ISSUE		EDITION LIMIT	YEAR RETD.	ISSUE PRICE	QUOTE U.S.$
1990	The Big Moment	1,500		125.00	125
1991	Cat's Cradle-Prestige Edition	950		450.00	450
1994	Catch of My Dreams	4,500		45.00	45
1994	Childhood Friends	950		110.00	110
1990	Confrontation	1,500	1992	85.00	85
1990	Contentment	1,500	1990	95.00	300
1992	Dominoes	1,500		155.00	155
1992	Favorite Gift	2,500	1992	175.00	175
1987	Favorite Reader	950	1990	85.00	85
1986	Flying High	950	1988	50.00	350
1992	The Flying Horse	950		325.00	325
1993	Good Company	1,500		155.00	155
1992	Her Secret Place	1,500	1992	135.00	250
1991	Home Team: Zero	1,500		150.00	150
1991	Homemade	1,500	1992	125.00	125
1990	Honor and Allegiance	1,500	1993	110.00	110
1990	The Ice Man	1,500	1992	125.00	125
1992	The Immigrant Spirit	5,000		125.00	125
1992	The Immigrant Spirit-Prestige Edition	950		125.00	125
1989	In the Doghouse	1,500	1990	75.00	300
1990	It's That Time Again	1,500		120.00	120
1992	Left Out	1,500		110.00	110
1989	Let's Play Ball	1,500	1991	75.00	150
1990	Make Believe	1,500	1990	75.00	125
1994	Mud Mates	950		150.00	150
1994	My Best Friends	950		85.00	85
1991	A New Beginning	5,000		125.00	125
1993	The New Citizen	5,000		125.00	125
1993	The New Citizen-Prestige Edition	950		125.00	125
1987	Odd Man Out	950	1988	85.00	85
1988	On Thin Ice	950	1993	95.00	95
1991	Pillars of a Nation-Charter Edition	20,000		175.00	200
1992	Playmates	1,500	1992	155.00	350
1990	Radio Daze	1,500		150.00	150
1983	Saturday Night	950	1985	85.00	1125
1990	The Scholar	1,500	N/A	110.00	110
1993	Secret Admirer	1,500		150.00	150
1994	Slugger	950		75.00	75
1982	Spring Fever	950	1988	85.00	750
1993	Sunday Afternoon	1,500		150.00	150
1988	Territorial Rights	950	1990	85.00	85
1989	The Thief	1,500	1990	95.00	175
1989	The Thorn	1,500	1990	125.00	125
1988	Tie Breaker	950	1990	95.00	95
1991	Time-Out	1,500	1993	125.00	125
1993	To All a Good Night	1,500		160.00	160
1992	Walking the Rails	1,500		175.00	175
1993	When I Grow Up	1,500		175.00	175
1994	Wind-Up, The	950		75.00	75
1988	Wiped Out	1,250	1990	125.00	125

Morrissey - D. Morrissey

YEAR ISSUE		EDITION LIMIT	YEAR RETD.	ISSUE PRICE	QUOTE U.S.$
1994	The Amazing Time Elevator	950		195.00	195
1993	Charting the Skies	1,250	1993	195.00	195
1993	Charting the Skies-Caprice Edition	550	1993	375.00	375
1993	Draft of a Dream	175	1993	250.00	250
1993	Draft of Dream	175		250.00	250
1994	The Dreamer's Trunk	1,500		195.00	195
1993	Drifting Closer	1,250		175.00	175
1993	The Mystic Mariner	750	1993	150.00	250
1993	The Redd Rocket	1,250		175.00	375
1994	The Redd Rocket-Pre-Flight	950	1993	110.00	110
1992	The Sandman's Ship of Dreams	750	1993	150.00	150
1994	Sighting off the Stern	950		135.00	135
1993	Sleeper Flight	1,250	1993	195.00	195
1993	The Telescope of Time	5,000		195.00	195

Olsen - G. Olsen

YEAR ISSUE		EDITION LIMIT	YEAR RETD.	ISSUE PRICE	QUOTE U.S.$
1993	Airship Adventures	750		150.00	150
1993	Angels of Christmas	750	1993	135.00	135
1993	Dress Rehearseal	750	1993	165.00	620
1993	The Fraternity Tree	750		195.00	195
1994	Little Girls Will Mothers Be	750	N/A	135.00	135
1994	Mother's Love	750	1994	165.00	165
1994	Summerhouse	750		165.00	165

Seerey-Lester - J. Seerey-Lester

YEAR ISSUE		EDITION LIMIT	YEAR RETD.	ISSUE PRICE	QUOTE U.S.$
1994	Abandoned	950		175.00	175
1986	Above the Treeline-Cougar	950	1986	130.00	175
1986	After the Fire-Grizzly	950	1990	95.00	95
1986	Along the Ice Floe-Polar Bears	950		200.00	200
1987	Alpenglow-Artic Wolf	950	1987	200.00	275
1987	Amboseli Child-African Elephant	950		160.00	160
1984	Among the Cattails-Canada Geese	950	1985	130.00	425
1984	Artic Procession-Willow Ptarmigan	950	1988	220.00	600
1990	Artic Wolf Pups	290		500.00	500
1987	Autumn Mist-Barred Owl	950	1987	160.00	225
1987	Autumn Thunder-Muskoxen	950		150.00	150
1985	Awakening Meadow-Cottontail	950		50.00	50
1992	Banyan Ambush- Black Panther	950	1992	235.00	400
1984	Basking-Brown Pelicans	950	1988	115.00	125
1988	Bathing-Blue Jay	950		95.00	95
1987	Bathing-Mute Swan	950	1992	175.00	175
1989	Before The Freeze-Beaver	950		165.00	165
1990	Bittersweet Winter-Cardinal	1,250	1990	150.00	275
1992	Black Jade	1,950	1992	275.00	275
1992	Black Magic-Panther	750	1992	195.00	195
1993	Black Wolf-North American Wilderness	350		325.00	N/A
1984	Breaking Cover-Black Bear	950	N/A	130.00	130
1987	Canyon Creek-Cougar	950	1987	195.00	450
1992	The Chase-Snow Leopard	950		200.00	200
1994	Child of the Outback	950		175.00	175
1985	Children of the Forest-Red Fox Kits	950	1985	110.00	150
1985	Children of the Tundra-Artic Wolf Pup	950	1985	110.00	225
1988	Cliff Hanger-Bobcat	950		200.00	200
1984	Close Encounter-Bobcat	950	1989	130.00	190
1988	Coastal Clique-Harbor Seals	950		160.00	160
1986	Conflict at Dawn-Heron and Osprey	950	1989	130.00	130
1983	Cool Retreat-Lynx	950	1988	85.00	100
1986	Cottonwood Gold-Baltimore Oriole	950		85.00	85
1985	Cougar Head Study	950		60.00	60
1989	Cougar Run	950	1989	185.00	350-450
1994	The Courtship	950		175.00	175
1993	Dark Encounter	3,500	N/A	200.00	200
1990	Dawn Majesty	1,250	1991	185.00	185
1987	Dawn on the Marsh-Coyote	950		200.00	200
1985	Daybreak-Moose	950		135.00	135
1991	Denali Family-Grizzly Bear	950	1991	195.00	195
1986	Early Arrivals-Snow Buntings	950		75.00	75
1983	Early Windfall-Gray Squirrels	950		85.00	85

YEAR ISSUE		EDITION LIMIT	YEAR RETD.	ISSUE PRICE	QUOTE U.S.$
1988	Edge of the Forest-Timber Wolves	950	1988	500.00	700
1989	Evening Duet-Snowy Egrets	1,250		185.00	185
1991	Evening Encounter-Grizzly & Wolf	1,250		185.00	185
1988	Evening Meadow-American Goldfinch	950		150.00	150
1991	Face to Face	1,250		200.00	200
1985	Fallen Birch-Chipmunk	950	1985	60.00	250
1985	First Light-Gray Jays	950	1985	130.00	200
1983	First Snow-Grizzly Bears	950	1984	95.00	250
1987	First Tracks-Cougar	950		150.00	150
1989	Fluke Sighting-Humback Whales	950	1989	185.00	185
1993	Freedom I	350		500.00	500
1993	Frozen Moonlight	2,500	1993	225.00	225
1985	Gathering-Gray Wolves, The	950	1987	165.00	350
1989	Gorilla	290	1989	400.00	600
1993	Grizzly Impact	950		225.00	225
1990	Grizzly Litho	290	1990	400.00	600
1989	Heavy Going-Grizzly	950	1989	175.00	300
1986	Hidden Admirer-Moose	950	1986	165.00	275
1988	Hiding Place-Saw-Whet Owl	950		95.00	95
1989	High and Mighty-Gorilla	950	1989	185.00	375
1986	High Country Champion-Grizzly	950	1986	175.00	275
1984	High Ground-Wolves	950	1984	130.00	325
1987	High Refuge-Red Squirrel	950		120.00	120
1984	Icy Outcrop-White Gyrfalcon	950	1986	115.00	200
1987	In Deep-Black Bear Cub	950		135.00	135
1990	In Their Presence	1,250		200.00	200
1985	Island Sanctuary-Mallards	950	1987	95.00	175
1986	Kenyan Family-Cheetahs	950		130.00	130
1986	Lakeside Family-Canada Geese	950		75.00	75
1988	Last Sanctuary-Florida Panther	950	1993	175.00	175
1983	Lone Fisherman-Great Blue Heron	950	1985	85.00	300
1993	Loonlight	1,500		225.00	225
1986	Low Tide-Bald Eagles	950		130.00	130
1987	Lying in Wait-Arctic Fox	950		175.00	175
1984	Lying Low-Cougar	950	1986	85.00	450
1991	Monsoon-White Tiger	950	1994	195.00	195
1991	Moonlight Chase-Cougar	1,250		195.00	195-220
1988	Moonlight Fishermen-Raccoons	950	1990	175.00	175
1988	Moose Hair	950		165.00	165
1988	Morning Display-Common Loons	3,395	1988	135.00	300
1986	Morning Forage-Ground Squirrel	950	1988	75.00	75
1993	Morning Glory-Bald Eagle	1,250	N/A	225.00	225
1984	Morning Mist-Snowy Owl	950	1988	95.00	95-180
1990	Mountain Cradle	1,250		200.00	300
1988	Night Moves-African Elephants	950		150.00	150
1990	Night Run-Artic Wolves	1,250	1990	200.00	250
1993	Night Specter	1,250		195.00	195
1986	Northwoods Family-Moose	950		75.00	75
1987	Out of the Blizzard-Timber Wolves	950	1987	215.00	350
1992	Out of the Darkness	290		200.00	200
1987	Out of the Mist-Grizzly	950	1990	200.00	200
1991	Out on a Limb-Young Barred Owl	950		185.00	185
1991	Panda Trilogy	950		375.00	375
1993	Phantoms of the Tundra	950		235.00	235
1984	Plains Hunter-Prairie Falcon	950		95.00	95
1990	The Plunge-Northern Sea Lions	1,250		200.00	200
1986	Racing the Storm-Artic Wolves	950	1986	200.00	350
1987	Rain Watch-Belted Kingfisher	950		125.00	125
1993	The Rains-Tiger	950		225.00	225
1992	Ranthambhore Rush	950		225.00	225
1983	The Refuge-Raccoon	950	1983	85.00	300
1992	Regal Majesty	290		200.00	200
1985	Return to Winter-Pintails	950	1990	135.00	135
1983	River Watch-Peregrine Falcon	950		85.00	85
1988	Savana Siesta-African Lions	950		165.00	165
1990	Seasonal Greeting-Cardinal	1,250		150.00	150
1993	Seeking Attention	950		200.00	200
1991	Sisters-Artic Wolves	1,250		185.00	185
1989	Sneak Peak	950		185.00	185
1986	Snowy Excursion-Red Squirrel	950		75.00	75
1988	Snowy Watch-Great Gray Owl	950		175.00	175
1989	Softly, Softly-White Tiger	950	1989	220.00	490
1991	Something Stirred (Bengal Tiger)	950		195.00	195
1988	Spanish Mist-Young Barred-Owl	950		175.00	175
1984	Spirit of the North-White Wolf	950	1986	130.00	185
1990	Spout	290		500.00	500
1989	Spring Flurry-Adelie Penguins	950		185.00	185
1986	Spring Mist-Chickadees	950	1986	105.00	150
1990	Suitors-Wood Ducks	3,313	1989	135.00	135
1990	Summer Rain-Common Loons	4,500	1990	200.00	200
1990	Summer Rain-Common Loons (Prestige)	450		425.00	425
1987	Sundown Alert-Bobcat	950		150.00	150
1985	Sundown Reflections-Wood Ducks	950		85.00	85
1990	Their First Season	1,250	1990	200.00	200
1990	Togetherness	1,250		125.00	185
1986	Treading Thin Ice-Chipmunk	950		75.00	75
1988	Tundra Family-Arctic Wolves	950		200.00	200
1985	Under the Pines-Bobcat	950	1986	95.00	275
1989	Water Sport-Bobcat	950	1989	185.00	185
1990	Whitetail Spring	1,250	1990	185.00	185
1988	Winter Grazing-Bison	950		185.00	185
1986	Winter Hiding-Cottontail	950		75.00	75
1983	Winter Lookout-Cougar	950	1985	85.00	500
1986	Winter Perch-Cardinal	950	1986	85.00	175
1985	Winter Rendezvous-Coyotes	950	1985	140.00	225
1988	Winter Spirit-Gray Wolf	950		200.00	200
1987	Winter Vigil-Great Horned Owl	950	1990	175.00	175
1993	Wolong Whiteout	950		225.00	225
1986	The Young Explorer-Red Fox Kit	950		75.00	75

Smith - D. Smith

YEAR ISSUE		EDITION LIMIT	YEAR RETD.	ISSUE PRICE	QUOTE U.S.$
1993	African Ebony-Black Leopard	1,250		195.00	195
1992	Armada	950		195.00	195
1993	Catching the Scent-Polar Bear	950		175.00	175
1994	Curious Presence-Whitetail Deer	950		195.00	195
1991	Dawn's Early Light-Bald Eagles	950		185.00	185
1993	Echo Bay-Loon Family	1,150		185.00	250
1992	Eyes of the North	2,500		225.00	225
1993	Guardians of the Den	1,500		195.00	350
1991	Icy Reflections-Pintails	500		250.00	250
1992	Night Moves-Cougar	950		185.00	185
1994	Parting Reflections	950		185.00	185
1993	Shrouded Forest-Bald Eagle	950		150.00	950
1991	Twilight's Calling-Common Loons	950	1991	175.00	300
1993	What's Bruin	1,750		185.00	275

New Masters Publishing

Bannister - P. Bannister

YEAR ISSUE		EDITION LIMIT	YEAR RETD.	ISSUE PRICE	QUOTE U.S.$
1982	Amaryllis	500	N/A	285.00	1900
1988	Apples and Oranges	485	N/A	265.00	600
1982	April	300	N/A	200.00	1100
1984	April Light	950	N/A	150.00	600
1978	Bandstand	250	N/A	75.00	450
1991	Celebration	662	N/A	350.00	700
1989	Chapter One	485	N/A	265.00	1300
1991	Crossroads	485	N/A	295.00	590
1993	Crowning Glory	485	N/A	265.00	265
1992	Crystal Bowl	485	N/A	265.00	265
1989	Daydreams	485	N/A	265.00	530
1993	Deja Vu	663	N/A	265.00	265
1983	The Duchess	500	N/A	250.00	1800
1980	Dust of Autumn	200	N/A	200.00	1225
1981	Easter	300	N/A	260.00	950
1982	Emily	500	N/A	285.00	800
1980	Faded Glory	200	N/A	200.00	1225
1984	The Fan Window	950	N/A	195.00	450
1987	First Prize	950	N/A	115.00	175
1988	Floribunda	485	N/A	265.00	550
1994	From Russia With Love	950	N/A	165.00	165
1980	Gift of Happiness	200	N/A	200.00	2000
1980	Girl on the Beach	200	N/A	200.00	1200
1990	Good Friends	485	N/A	265.00	750
1988	Guinevere	485	N/A	265.00	1000
1993	Into The Woods	485	N/A	265.00	265
1982	Ivy	500	N/A	285.00	700
1982	Jasmine	500	N/A	285.00	650
1981	Juliet	300	N/A	260.00	5000
1990	Lavender Hill	485	N/A	265.00	625
1992	Love Letters	485	N/A	265.00	265
1988	Love Seat	485	N/A	230.00	500
1989	Low Tide	485	N/A	265.00	550
1982	Mail Order Brides	500	N/A	325.00	2300
1984	Make Believe	950	N/A	150.00	600
1989	March Winds	485	N/A	265.00	530
1983	Mementos	950	N/A	150.00	1400
1982	Memories	500	N/A	235.00	500
1992	Morning Mist	485	N/A	265.00	265
1981	My Special Place	300	N/A	260.00	1850
1982	Nuance	500	N/A	235.00	470
1994	Once Upon A Time	950	N/A	265.00	265
1983	Ophelia	950	N/A	150.00	675
1989	Peace	485	N/A	265.00	1100
1981	Porcelain Rose	300	N/A	260.00	2000
1982	The Present	500	N/A	260.00	800
1986	Pride & Joy	950	N/A	150.00	300
1991	Pudding & Pies	485	N/A	265.00	265
1987	Quiet Corner	950	N/A	115.00	300
1989	The Quilt	485	N/A	265.00	900
1993	Rambling Rose	485	N/A	265.00	265
1981	Rehearsal	300	N/A	260.00	1850
1990	Rendezvous	485	N/A	265.00	650
1984	Scarlet Ribbons	950	N/A	150.00	325
1980	Sea Haven	300	N/A	260.00	1100
1990	Seascapes	485	N/A	265.00	550
1987	September Harvest	950	N/A	150.00	300
1980	The Silver Bell	200	N/A	200.00	2000
1990	Sisters	485	N/A	265.00	950
1990	Songbird	485	N/A	265.00	550
1991	String of Pearls	485	N/A	265.00	850
1988	Summer Choices	300	N/A	250.00	800
1991	Teatime	485	N/A	295.00	600
1980	Titania	350	N/A	260.00	900
1991	Wildflowers	485	N/A	295.00	590
1983	Window Seat	950	N/A	150.00	600

Past Impressions

Maley - A. Maley

YEAR ISSUE		EDITION LIMIT	YEAR RETD.	ISSUE PRICE	QUOTE U.S.$
1989	Alexandria	750	1994	125.00	125
1989	Beth	750	1994	125.00	125
1991	Between Friends	750		275.00	275
1988	The Boardwalk	Closed	N/A	250.00	340
1990	Cafe Royale	750		275.00	275
1989	Catherine	750	1994	125.00	125
1992	Circle of Love	500		250.00	250
1988	Day Dreams	Closed	N/A	200.00	350-450
1992	An Elegant Affair	500		260.00	260
1989	English Rose	Closed	N/A	250.00	285
1990	Evening Performance	750		150.00	150
1990	Festive Occasion	Closed	N/A	250.00	250
1984	Glorious Summer	Closed	N/A	150.00	725
1990	Gracious Era	750		275.00	275
1995	Grand Entrance	500		250.00	250
1989	In Harmony	750	1995	250.00	250
1992	Intimate Moment	750		250.00	250
1988	Joys of Childhood	Closed	N/A	250.00	250
1995	The Letter	500		250.00	250
1967	Love Letter	Closed	N/A	200.00	300-550
1995	The New Carriage	500		100.00	100
1994	New Years Eve	500		250.00	250
1988	Opening Night	Closed	N/A	250.00	2000
1994	Parisian Beauties	500		275.00	275
1985	Passing Elegance	Closed	N/A	150.00	750
1987	The Promise	Closed	N/A	200.00	315
1993	Rags and Riches	500		250.00	250
1994	The Recital	500		275.00	275
1990	Romantic Engagement	750		275.00	275
1984	Secluded Garden	Closed	N/A	150.00	970
1985	Secret Thoughts	Closed	N/A	150.00	850
1993	Sleigh Bells	500		260.00	260
1991	Summer Carousel	750		200.00	200
1994	Summer Elegance	500		275.00	275
1990	Summer Pastime	Closed	N/A	250.00	250
1995	Summer Romance	500		250.00	250
1991	Sunday Afternoon	750		275.00	275
1986	Tell Me	Closed	N/A	150.00	850
1988	Tranquil Moment	Closed	N/A	250.00	315
1989	Victoria	750	1994	125.00	125
1988	Victorian Trio	Closed	N/A	250.00	340
1994	Visiting The Nursery	500		250.00	250
1992	A Walk in the Park	500		260.00	260
1991	Winter Carousel	750		200.00	200
1989	Winter Impressions	750		250.00	315
1986	Winter Romance	Closed	N/A	150.00	650

Pemberton & Oakes

Canvas Replicas - D. Zolan

YEAR ISSUE		EDITION LIMIT	YEAR RETD.	ISSUE PRICE	QUOTE U.S.$
1992	Quiet Time	Retrd.	N/A	18.80	50
1992	September Girl	Retrd.	N/A	18.80	40
1992	Summer Garden	Retrd.	N/A	18.80	45

Canvas Transfer - D. Zolan

YEAR ISSUE		EDITION LIMIT	YEAR RETD.	ISSUE PRICE	QUOTE U.S.$
1992	Daisy Days	Retrd.	N/A	24.20	45
1993	It's Grandma & Grandpa	Retrd.	N/A	24.20	45
1993	Spring Duet	Retrd.	N/A	24.40	45

Grandparents Day-Miniature Lithographs - D. Zolan

YEAR ISSUE		EDITION LIMIT	YEAR RETD.	ISSUE PRICE	QUOTE U.S.$
1992	Letter to Grandma	Retrd.	N/A	35.00	41

Membership-Miniature Lithographs - D. Zolan

YEAR ISSUE		EDITION LIMIT	YEAR RETD.	ISSUE PRICE	QUOTE U.S.$
1992	Brotherly Love	Retrd.	N/A	18.00	68
1993	New Shoes	Retrd.	N/A	18.00	42
1993	Country Walk	Retrd.	N/A	22.00	40
1994	Enchanted Forest	Retrd.	N/A	22.00	40

Miniature Replicas of Oils - D. Zolan

YEAR ISSUE		EDITION LIMIT	YEAR RETD.	ISSUE PRICE	QUOTE U.S.$
1990	Brotherly Love	Retrd.	N/A	24.40	77
1991	Crystal's Creek	Retrd.	N/A	24.40	45
1990	Daddy's Home	Retrd.	N/A	24.40	71
1992	It's Grandma & Grandpa	Retrd.	N/A	24.40	41
1992	Mother's Angels	Retrd.	N/A	24.40	40
1992	Touching the Sky	Retrd.	N/A	24.40	37

Quiet Moments-Miniature Lithographs - D. Zolan

YEAR ISSUE		EDITION LIMIT	YEAR RETD.	ISSUE PRICE	QUOTE U.S.$
1993	Birthday Greetings	Retrd.	N/A	22.00	42
1993	Country Kitten	Retrd.	N/A	22.00	42
1993	Crystal's Creek	Retrd.	N/A	22.00	43
1992	One Summer Day	Retrd.	N/A	22.00	40

Single Issues-Miniature Lithographs - D. Zolan

YEAR ISSUE		EDITION LIMIT	YEAR RETD.	ISSUE PRICE	QUOTE U.S.$
1993	A Christmas Prayer 1993	Retrd.	N/A	35.00	42
1993	Daddy's Home	Retrd.	N/A	22.00	50
1993	First Kiss	Retrd.	N/A	22.00	45-80
1994	A Gift for Laurie	Retrd.	N/A	22.00	40
1993	Letter To Grandma	Retrd.	N/A	22.00	42
1994	Rodeo Girl	Retrd.	N/A	35.00	42
1991	Tender Moment	Retrd.	N/A	35.00	75

Zolan's Children-Lithographs - D. Zolan

YEAR ISSUE		EDITION LIMIT	YEAR RETD.	ISSUE PRICE	QUOTE U.S.$
1989	Almost Home	Retrd.	N/A	98.00	255
1991	Autumn Leaves	Retrd.	N/A	98.00	120
1993	The Big Catch	Retrd.	N/A	98.00	130
1989	Brotherly Love	Retrd.	N/A	98.00	295
1982	By Myself	Retrd.	N/A	98.00	230
1989	Christmas Prayer	Retrd.	N/A	98.00	175-225
1990	Colors of Spring	Retrd.	N/A	98.00	175-240
1990	Crystal's Creek	Retrd.	N/A	98.00	175
1989	Daddy's Home	Retrd.	N/A	98.00	310
1988	Day Dreamer	Retrd.	N/A	35.00	130
1992	Enchanted Forest	Retrd.	N/A	98.00	110-135
1982	Erik and the Dandelion	Retrd.	N/A	98.00	400
1990	First Kiss	Retrd.	N/A	98.00	240
1991	Flowers for Mother	Retrd.	N/A	98.00	160
1993	Grandma's Garden	Retrd.	N/A	98.00	135
1989	Grandma's Mirror	Retrd.	N/A	98.00	140-195
1990	Laurie and the Creche	Retrd.	N/A	98.00	115-165
1989	Mother's Angels	Retrd.	N/A	98.00	175-240
1992	New Shoes	Retrd.	N/A	98.00	150

YEAR ISSUE		EDITION LIMIT	YEAR RETD.	ISSUE PRICE	QUOTE U.S.$
1989	Rodeo Girl	Retrd.	N/A	98.00	160
1984	Sabina in the Grass	Retrd.	N/A	98.00	625
1988	Small Wonder	Retrd.	N/A	98.00	250
1989	Snowy Adventure	Retrd.	N/A	98.00	205
1991	Summer Suds	Retrd.	N/A	98.00	140-175
1989	Summer's Child	Retrd.	N/A	98.00	225
1986	Tender Moment	Retrd.	N/A	98.00	275
1988	Tiny Treasures	Retrd.	N/A	150.00	215
1987	Touching the Sky	Retrd.	N/A	98.00	175-225
1988	Waiting to Play	Retrd.	N/A	35.00	135
1988	Winter Angel	Retrd.	N/A	98.00	230

Zolan's Children-Miniature Lithographs - D. Zolan

YEAR ISSUE		EDITION LIMIT	YEAR RETD.	ISSUE PRICE	QUOTE U.S.$
1992	Colors of Spring	Retrd.	N/A	35.00	40
1992	Forest & Fairytales	Retrd.	N/A	22.00	42
1992	The Little Fisherman	Retrd.	N/A	35.00	43
1991	Morning Discovery	Retrd.	N/A	35.00	55

Reco International

Fine Art Canvas Reproduction - J. McClelland

YEAR ISSUE		EDITION LIMIT	YEAR RETD.	ISSUE PRICE	QUOTE U.S.$
1990	Beach Play	350		80.00	80
1991	Flower Swing	350		100.00	100
1991	Summer Conversation	350		80.00	80

Limited Edition Print - S. Kuck

YEAR ISSUE		EDITION LIMIT	YEAR RETD.	ISSUE PRICE	QUOTE U.S.$
1986	Ashley	500		85.00	150
1985	Heather	Retrd.	1987	75.00	150
1984	Jessica	Retrd.	1986	60.00	400

McClelland - J. McClelland

YEAR ISSUE		EDITION LIMIT	YEAR RETD.	ISSUE PRICE	QUOTE U.S.$
XX	I Love Tammy	500		75.00	100
XX	Just for You	300		155.00	155
XX	Olivia	300		175.00	175
XX	Reverie	300		110.00	110
XX	Sweet Dreams	300		145.00	145

Roman, Inc.

Abble Williams - A. Williams

YEAR ISSUE		EDITION LIMIT	YEAR RETD.	ISSUE PRICE	QUOTE U.S.$
1988	Mary, Mother of the Carpenter	Closed	N/A	100.00	100

The Discovery of America Miniature Art Print - I. Spencer

YEAR ISSUE		EDITION LIMIT	YEAR RETD.	ISSUE PRICE	QUOTE U.S.$
1991	The Discovery of America	Open		2.00	2

Divine Servant - M. Greiner Jr.

YEAR ISSUE		EDITION LIMIT	YEAR RETD.	ISSUE PRICE	QUOTE U.S.$
1993	Divine Servant, print of drawing	Open		35.00	35
1994	Divine Servant, print of painting	Yr.Iss.		75.00	75
1994	Divine Servant, print of painting	Yr.Iss.		150.00	150
1994	Divine Servant, print of painting w/remarque	Yr.Iss.		75.00	75
1994	Divine Servant, print of painting w/remarque	Yr.Iss.		150.00	150

Fishers of Men - M. Greiner, Jr.

YEAR ISSUE		EDITION LIMIT	YEAR RETD.	ISSUE PRICE	QUOTE U.S.$
1994	Fishers of Men 8x10	Open		10.00	10
1994	Fishers of Men 11x14	Open		20.00	20
1994	Fishers of Men 16x20	Open		35.00	35

Hook - F. Hook

YEAR ISSUE		EDITION LIMIT	YEAR RETD.	ISSUE PRICE	QUOTE U.S.$
1982	Bouquet	1,200		70.00	350
1981	The Carpenter	Yr.Iss		100.00	1000
1981	The Carpenter (remarque)	Yr.Iss		100.00	3000
1982	Frolicking	1,200		60.00	350
1982	Gathering	1,200		60.00	350-450
1982	Little Children, Come to Me	1,950		50.00	500
1982	Little Children, Come to Me, remarque	50		100.00	500
1982	Posing	1,200		70.00	350
1982	Poulets	1,200		60.00	350
1982	Surprise	1,200		50.00	350

Portraits of Love - F. Hook

YEAR ISSUE		EDITION LIMIT	YEAR RETD.	ISSUE PRICE	QUOTE U.S.$
1988	Expectation	2,500		25.00	25
1988	In Mother's Arms	2,500		25.00	25
1988	My Kitty	2,500		25.00	25
1988	Remember When...	2,500		25.00	25
1988	Sharing	2,500		25.00	25
1988	Sunkissed Afternoon	2,500		25.00	25

Schmid

Ferrandiz Lithographs - J. Ferrandiz

YEAR ISSUE		EDITION LIMIT	YEAR RETD.	ISSUE PRICE	QUOTE U.S.$
1983	Friendship	460	1983	165.00	450
1983	Friendship, remarque	15	1983	1200.00	2300
1982	He Seems to Sleep	450	1982	150.00	700
1982	He Seems to Sleep, remarque	25	1982	300.00	3200
1981	Heart of Seven Colors	600	1981	100.00	395
1981	Heart of Seven Colors, remarque	75	1981	175.00	1300
1982	Mirror of the Soul	225	1982	150.00	425
1982	Mirror of the Soul, remarque	35	1982	250.00	2400
1980	Most Precious Gift	425	1980	125.00	1200
1980	Most Precious Gift, remarque	50	1980	225.00	2800
1980	My Star	675	1980	100.00	650
1980	My Star, remarque	75	1980	175.00	1800
1982	Oh Small Child	450	1982	125.00	495
1982	Oh Small Child, remarque	50	1982	225.00	1450
1982	On the Threshold of Life	425	1982	150.00	450
1982	On the Threshold of Life, remarque	50	1982	275.00	1350
1982	Riding Through the Rain	900	1982	165.00	350
1982	Riding Through the Rain, remarque	100	1982	300.00	950
1982	Spreading the Word	675	1982	125.00	190-250
1982	Spreading the Word, remarque	75	1982	225.00	1075
1984	Star in the Teapot	410	1984	165.00	165
1984	Star in the Teapot, remarque	15	1984	1200.00	2100

V.F. Fine Arts

Angels of Joy-Series I - S. Kuck

YEAR ISSUE		EDITION LIMIT	YEAR RETD.	ISSUE PRICE	QUOTE U.S.$
1994	Charity	750		195.00	195
1994	Grace	750		195.00	195
1994	Gratitude	750		195.00	195
1994	Mischief	750		195.00	195

Kuck - S. Kuck

YEAR ISSUE		EDITION LIMIT	YEAR RETD.	ISSUE PRICE	QUOTE U.S.$
1993	Best Friend, proof	250	N/A	175.00	175
1993	Best Friends, Canvas Transfer	250	N/A	500.00	500
1993	Best Friends, S/N	2,500	N/A	145.00	150
1994	Best of Days, S/N	750	1994	160.00	175
1989	Bundle of Joy, S/N	1,000	1989	125.00	250
1993	Buttons & Bows, proof	95	N/A	125.00	135
1993	Buttons & Bows, S/N	950	N/A	95.00	110
1990	Chopsticks, proof	150	1991	120.00	125
1990	Chopsticks, remarque	25	1991	160.00	195
1990	Chopsticks, S/N	1,500	1990	80.00	95
1987	The Daisy, proof	90	1988	40.00	175
1987	The Daisy, S/N	900	1988	30.00	100
1989	Day Dreaming, proof	90	1989	225.00	250
1989	Day Dreaming, remarque	50	1989	300.00	350
1989	Day Dreaming, S/N	900	1989	150.00	200
1994	Dear Santa, S/N	950	1994	95.00	95
1992	Duet, Canvas Framed	500	1994	255.00	275
1992	Duet, proof	95	N/A	175.00	200
1992	Duet, S/N	950	N/A	125.00	135
1988	First Recital, proof	25	1988	250.00	750
1988	First Recital, remarque	25	1988	400.00	1200
1988	First Recital, S/N	150	1988	200.00	550
1990	First Snow, proof	50	1990	150.00	275
1990	First Snow, remarque	25	1990	200.00	350
1990	First Snow, S/N	500	1990	95.00	175
1987	The Flower Girl, proof	90	1987	50.00	95
1987	The Flower Girl, S/N	900	1987	40.00	65
1994	Garden Memories, Canvas Transfer	250	N/A	500.00	500
1994	Garden Memories, S/N	2,500	N/A	145.00	165
1991	God's Gift, proof	150	N/A	150.00	175
1991	God's Gift, S/N	1,500	1993	95.00	110
1993	Good Morning, Canvas	250	1993	500.00	500
1993	Good Morning, proof	50	N/A	175.00	195
1993	Good Morning, S/N	2,500	N/A	145.00	165
1989	Innocence, proof	90	1989	225.00	255
1989	Innocence, remarque	50	1989	300.00	350
1989	Innocence, S/N	900	1989	150.00	220
1992	Joyous Day, Canvas Transfer	250	N/A	250.00	275
1992	Joyous Day, proof	120	N/A	175.00	200
1992	Joyous Day, S/N	1,200	1993	125.00	135
1988	The Kitten, proof	50	1988	150.00	1400
1988	The Kitten, remarque	25	1988	250.00	950
1988	The Kitten, S/N	350	1988	120.00	1200
1990	Le Beau, proof	150	1990	120.00	225
1990	Le Beau, remarque	25	1990	160.00	275
1990	Le Beau, S/N	1,500	1990	80.00	175
1987	Le Papillion, proof	35	1990	110.00	175
1987	Le Papillion, remarque	7	1990	150.00	250
1987	Le Papillion, S/N	350	1990	90.00	150
1990	Lilly Pond, color remarque	125	1990	500.00	500
1990	Lilly Pond, proof	75	1990	200.00	200
1990	Lilly Pond, S/N	750	1990	150.00	150
1988	Little Ballerina, proof	25	1988	150.00	350
1988	Little Ballerina, remarque	25	1988	225.00	450
1988	Little Ballerina, S/N	150	1988	110.00	275
1987	The Loveseat, proof	90	1987	40.00	150
1987	The Loveseat, S/N	900	1987	30.00	95
1991	Memories, S/N	5,000	1991	195.00	225
1987	Mother's Love, proof	12	1987	225.00	1400
1987	Mother's Love, S/N	150	1987	195.00	750
1988	My Dearest, proof	50	1988	200.00	1000
1988	My Dearest, remarque	25	1988	325.00	1200
1988	My Dearest, S/N	350	1988	160.00	750
1995	Playful Kitten	950	1995	95.00	95
1989	Puppy, proof	50	1989	180.00	650
1989	Puppy, remarque	50	1989	240.00	850
1989	Puppy, S/N	500	1989	120.00	600
1987	A Quiet Time, proof	90	1987	50.00	90
1987	A Quiet Time, S/N	900	1987	40.00	60
1987	The Reading Lesson, proof	90	1987	70.00	200
1987	The Reading Lesson, S/N	900	1987	60.00	150
1995	Rhapsody & Lace	1,150		95.00	95
1989	Rose Garden, proof	50	1989	150.00	450
1989	Rose Garden, remarque	50	1989	200.00	600
1989	Rose Garden, S/N	500	1989	95.00	390
1986	Silhouette, proof	25	1987	90.00	250
1986	Silhouette, S/N	250	1987	80.00	200
1989	Sisters, proof	90	1989	150.00	450
1989	Sisters, remarque	50	1989	200.00	500
1989	Sisters, S/N	900	1988	95.00	225
1989	Sonatina, proof	90	1989	225.00	500
1989	Sonatina, remarque	50	1989	300.00	650
1989	Sonatina, S/N	900	1989	150.00	375
1986	Summer Reflections, proof	90	1987	70.00	300
1986	Summer Reflections, S/N	900	1987	60.00	250
1986	Tender Moments, proof	50	1986	80.00	295
1986	Tender Moments, S/N	500	1986	70.00	200
1993	Thinking of You, Canvas Transfer	250	1993	500.00	500
1993	Thinking of You, S/N	2,500	N/A	145.00	175
1988	Wild Flowers, proof	50	1988	175.00	300
1988	Wild Flowers, remarque	25	1988	250.00	400
1988	Wild Flowers, S/N	350	1988	160.00	250
1992	Yesterday, Canvas Framed	550	N/A	195.00	200
1992	Yesterday, proof	95	N/A	150.00	150
1992	Yesterday, S/N	950	N/A	95.00	95

PLATES

American Artists

The Best of Fred Stone-Mares & Foals Series (6 1/2 ") - F. Stone

YEAR ISSUE		EDITION LIMIT	YEAR RETD.	ISSUE PRICE	QUOTE U.S.$
1991	Patience	19,500		25.00	25-30
1992	Water Trough	19,500		25.00	25
1992	Pasture Pest	19,500		25.00	25
1992	Kidnapped Mare	19,500		25.00	25
1993	Contentment	19,500		25.00	25
1993	Arabian Mare & Foal	19,500		25.00	25
1994	Diamond in the Rough	19,500		25.00	25
1995	The First Day	19,500		25.00	25

Famous Fillies Series - F. Stone

YEAR ISSUE		EDITION LIMIT	YEAR RETD.	ISSUE PRICE	QUOTE U.S.$
1987	Lady's Secret	9,500		65.00	90
1988	Ruffian	9,500		65.00	85
1988	Genuine Risk	9,500		65.00	90
1992	Go For The Wand	9,500		65.00	80-90

Fred Stone Classic Series - F. Stone

YEAR ISSUE		EDITION LIMIT	YEAR RETD.	ISSUE PRICE	QUOTE U.S.$
1986	The Shoe-8,000 Wins	9,500		75.00	95-100
1986	The Eternal Legacy	9,500		75.00	100
1988	Forever Friends	9,500		75.00	95
1989	Alysheba	9,500		75.00	75-95

Gold Signature Series - F. Stone

YEAR ISSUE		EDITION LIMIT	YEAR RETD.	ISSUE PRICE	QUOTE U.S.$
1990	Secretariat Final Tribute, signed	4,500		150.00	375
1990	Secretariat Final Tribute, unsigned	7,500		75.00	75
1991	Old Warriors, signed	4,500		150.00	425
1991	Old Warriors, unsigned	7,500		75.00	75

Gold Signature Series II - F. Stone

YEAR ISSUE		EDITION LIMIT	YEAR RETD.	ISSUE PRICE	QUOTE U.S.$
1991	Northern Dancer, double signature	1,500		175.00	250
1991	Northern Dancer, single signature	3,000		150.00	150
1991	Northern Dancer, unsigned	7,500		75.00	75
1991	Kelso, double signature	1,500		175.00	175
1991	Kelso, single signature	3,000		150.00	150
1991	Kelso, unsigned	7,500		75.00	75

Gold Signature Series III - F. Stone

YEAR ISSUE		EDITION LIMIT	YEAR RETD.	ISSUE PRICE	QUOTE U.S.$
1992	Dance Smartly-Pat Day, Up, double signature	1,500		175.00	175
1992	Dance Smartly-Pat Day, Up, single signature	3,000		150.00	150
1992	Dance Smartly-Pat Day, Up, unsigned	7,500		75.00	75
1993	American Triple Crown-1937-1946, signed	2,500		195.00	195
1993	American Triple Crown-1937-1946, unsigned	7,500		75.00	75
1993	American Triple Crown-1948-1978, signed	2,500		195.00	195
1993	American Triple Crown-1948-1978, unsigned	7,500		75.00	175
1994	American Triple Crown-1919-1935, signed	2,500		95.00	95
1994	American Triple Crown-1919-1935, unsigned	7,500		75.00	75

Gold Signature Series IV - F. Stone

YEAR ISSUE		EDITION LIMIT	YEAR RETD.	ISSUE PRICE	QUOTE U.S.$
1995	Julie Krone - Colonial Affair	7,500		75.00	75
1995	Julie Krone - Colonial Affair, signed	2,500		150.00	150

The Horses of Fred Stone - F. Stone

YEAR ISSUE		EDITION LIMIT	YEAR RETD.	ISSUE PRICE	QUOTE U.S.$
1982	Patience	9,500		55.00	200
1982	Arabian Mare and Foal	9,500		55.00	175
1982	Safe and Sound	9,500		55.00	125
1983	Contentment	9,500		55.00	125

Mare and Foal Series - F. Stone

YEAR ISSUE		EDITION LIMIT	YEAR RETD.	ISSUE PRICE	QUOTE U.S.$
1986	Water Trough	12,500		49.50	175
1986	Tranquility	12,500		49.50	75
1986	Pasture Pest	12,500		49.50	110
1987	The Arabians	12,500		49.50	55

Mare and Foal Series II - F. Stone

YEAR ISSUE		EDITION LIMIT	YEAR RETD.	ISSUE PRICE	QUOTE U.S.$
1989	The First Day	Open		35.00	35
1989	Diamond in the Rough	Retrd.		35.00	35

Racing Legends - F. Stone

YEAR ISSUE		EDITION LIMIT	YEAR RETD.	ISSUE PRICE	QUOTE U.S.$
1989	Phar Lap	9,500		75.00	75
1989	Sunday Silence	9,500		75.00	75
1990	John Henry-Shoemaker	9,500		75.00	75

PLATES

Sport of Kings Series - F. Stone

YEAR ISSUE		EDITION LIMIT	YEAR RETD.	ISSUE PRICE	QUOTE U.S.$
1984	Man O'War	9,500		65.00	125
1984	Secretariat	9,500		65.00	295
1985	John Henry	9,500		65.00	100
1986	Seattle Slew	9,500		65.00	75

The Stallion Series - F. Stone

YEAR ISSUE		EDITION LIMIT	YEAR RETD.	ISSUE PRICE	QUOTE U.S.$
1983	Black Stallion	19,500		49.50	150
1983	Andalusian	19,500		49.50	150

Anheuser-Busch, Inc.

1992 Olympic Team Series - A-Busch, Inc.

YEAR ISSUE		EDITION LIMIT	YEAR RETD.	ISSUE PRICE	QUOTE U.S.$
1991	1992 Olympic Team Winter Plate N3180	Retrd.	1994	35.00	35
1992	1992 Olympic Team Summer Plate N3122	Retrd.	1994	35.00	35

Archives Plate Series - D. Langeneckert

YEAR ISSUE		EDITION LIMIT	YEAR RETD.	ISSUE PRICE	QUOTE U.S.$
1992	1893 Columbian Exposition N3477	25-day		27.50	28
1992	Ganymede N4004	25-day		27.50	28
1995	Budweiser's Greatest Triumph Plate N5195	25-day		27.50	28
1995	Mirror of Truth Plate N5196	25-day		27.50	28

Civil War Series - D. Langeneckert

YEAR ISSUE		EDITION LIMIT	YEAR RETD.	ISSUE PRICE	QUOTE U.S.$
1992	General Grant N3478	Retrd.	1994	45.00	45
1993	General Robert E. Lee N3590	Retrd.	1994	45.00	45
1993	President Abraham Lincoln N3591	Retrd.	1994	45.00	45

Collector Edition Series - M. Urdahl

YEAR ISSUE		EDITION LIMIT	YEAR RETD.	ISSUE PRICE	QUOTE U.S.$
1995	"This Bud's For You" N4945	25-day		27.50	28

Holiday Plate Series - Various

YEAR ISSUE		EDITION LIMIT	YEAR RETD.	ISSUE PRICE	QUOTE U.S.$
1989	Winters Day N2295 - B. Kemper	Retrd.	N/A	30.00	65-80
1990	An American Tradition N2767 - S. Sampson	Retrd.	N/A	30.00	35-45
1991	The Season's Best N3034 - S. Sampson	25-day		30.00	30
1992	A Perfect Christmas N3440 - S. Sampson	25-day		27.50	28
1993	Special Delivery N4002 - N. Koerber	Retrd.		27.50	28
1994	Hometown Holiday N4572 - B. Kemper	25-day		27.50	28
1995	Lighting the Way Home N5215 - T. Jester	25-day		27.50	28

Man's Best Friend Series - M. Urdahl

YEAR ISSUE		EDITION LIMIT	YEAR RETD.	ISSUE PRICE	QUOTE U.S.$
1990	Buddies N2615	Retrd.	N/A	30.00	50-80
1990	Six Pack N3005	Retrd.	N/A	30.00	35-45
1992	Something's Brewing N3147	Retrd.	1994	30.00	30
1993	Outstanding in Their Field N4003	25-day		27.50	28

Anna-Perenna Porcelain

American Silhouettes Family Series - P. Buckley Moss

YEAR ISSUE		EDITION LIMIT	YEAR RETD.	ISSUE PRICE	QUOTE U.S.$
1982	Family Outing	5,000		75.00	95
1982	John and Mary	5,000		75.00	95
1984	Homemakers Quilting	5,000		75.00	85-195
1983	Leisure Time	5,000		75.00	85

American Silhouettes Valley Series - P. Buckley Moss

YEAR ISSUE		EDITION LIMIT	YEAR RETD.	ISSUE PRICE	QUOTE U.S.$
1982	Frosty Frolic	5,000		75.00	85-95
1984	Hay Ride	5,000		75.00	85
1983	Sunday Ride	5,000		75.00	85-100
1983	Market Day	5,000		75.00	120

American Silhouettes-Childrens Series - P. Buckley Moss

YEAR ISSUE		EDITION LIMIT	YEAR RETD.	ISSUE PRICE	QUOTE U.S.$
1981	Fiddlers Two	5,000		75.00	95
1982	Mary With The Lambs	5,000		75.00	85
1983	Ring-Around-the-Rosie	5,000		75.00	200
1983	Waiting For Tom	5,000		75.00	175

Annual Christmas Plate - P. Buckley Moss

YEAR ISSUE		EDITION LIMIT	YEAR RETD.	ISSUE PRICE	QUOTE U.S.$
1984	Noel, Noel	5,000		67.50	325
1985	Helping Hands	5,000		67.50	225
1986	Night Before Christmas	5,000		67.50	150
1987	Christmas Sleigh	5,000		75.00	95
1988	Christmas Joy	7,500		75.00	75
1989	Christmas Carol	7,500		80.00	95
1990	Christmas Eve	7,500		80.00	80
1991	The Snowman	7,500		80.00	80
1992	Christmas Warmth	7,500		85.00	85
1993	Joy to the World	7,500		85.00	85

The Celebration Series - P. Buckley Moss

YEAR ISSUE		EDITION LIMIT	YEAR RETD.	ISSUE PRICE	QUOTE U.S.$
1986	Wedding Joy	5,000		100.00	200-350
1987	The Christening	5,000		100.00	175
1988	The Anniversary	5,000		100.00	120-190
1990	Family Reunion	5,000		100.00	150

Uncle Tad's Cats - T. Krumeich

YEAR ISSUE		EDITION LIMIT	YEAR RETD.	ISSUE PRICE	QUOTE U.S.$
1979	Oliver's Birthday	5,000		75.00	200
1980	Peaches & Cream	5,000		75.00	100
1981	Princess Aurora	5,000		80.00	100
1981	Walter's Window	5,000		80.00	120

ANRI

ANRI Father's Day - Unknown

YEAR ISSUE		EDITION LIMIT	YEAR RETD.	ISSUE PRICE	QUOTE U.S.$
1972	Alpine Father & Children	Closed	1972	35.00	100
1973	Alpine Father & Children	Closed	1973	40.00	95
1974	Cliff Gazing	Closed	1974	50.00	100
1975	Sailing	Closed	1975	60.00	90

ANRI Mother's Day - Unknown

YEAR ISSUE		EDITION LIMIT	YEAR RETD.	ISSUE PRICE	QUOTE U.S.$
1972	Alpine Mother & Children	Closed	1972	35.00	50
1973	Alpine Mother & Children	Closed	1973	40.00	50
1974	Alpine Mother & Children	Closed	1974	50.00	55
1975	Alpine Stroll	Closed	1975	60.00	65
1976	Knitting	Closed	1976	60.00	65

Christmas - J. Malfertheiner, unless otherwise noted

YEAR ISSUE		EDITION LIMIT	YEAR RETD.	ISSUE PRICE	QUOTE U.S.$
1971	St. Jakob in Groden	6,000	1971	37.50	65
1972	Pipers at Alberobello	6,000	1972	45.00	75
1973	Alpine Horn	6,000	1973	45.00	390
1974	Young Man and Girl	6,000	1974	50.00	95
1975	Christmas in Ireland	6,000	1975	60.00	60
1976	Alpine Christmas	6,000	1976	65.00	190
1977	Legend of Heligenblut	6,000	1977	65.00	91
1978	Klockler Singers	6,000	1978	80.00	80
1979	Moss Gatherers - Unknown	6,000	1979	135.00	177
1980	Wintry Churchgoing - Unknown	6,000	1980	165.00	165
1981	Santa Claus in Tyrol - Unknown	6,000	1981	165.00	200
1982	The Star Singers - Unknown	6,000	1982	165.00	165
1983	Unto Us a Child is Born - Unknown	6,000	1983	165.00	310
1984	Yuletide in the Valley - Unknown	6,000	1984	165.00	170
1985	Good Morning, Good Cheer	6,000	1985	165.00	165
1986	A Groden Christmas	6,000	1986	165.00	200
1987	Down From the Alps	6,000	1987	195.00	250
1988	Christkindl Markt	6,000	1988	220.00	230
1989	Flight Into Egypt	6,000	1989	275.00	275
1990	Holy Night	6,000	1990	300.00	300

Disney Four Star Collection - Disney Studios

YEAR ISSUE		EDITION LIMIT	YEAR RETD.	ISSUE PRICE	QUOTE U.S.$
1989	Mickey Mini Plate	5,000	1989	40.00	55
1990	Minnie Mini Plate	5,000	1990	40.00	55
1991	Donald Mini Plate	5,000	1991	50.00	55

Ferrandiz Christmas - J. Ferrandiz

YEAR ISSUE		EDITION LIMIT	YEAR RETD.	ISSUE PRICE	QUOTE U.S.$
1972	Christ In The Manger	4,000	1972	35.00	230
1973	Christmas	4,000	1973	40.00	225
1974	Holy Night	4,000	1974	50.00	100
1975	Flight into Egypt	4,000	1975	60.00	95
1976	Tree of Life	4,000	1976	60.00	85
1977	Girl with Flowers	4,000	1977	65.00	185
1978	Leading the Way	4,000	1978	77.50	180
1979	The Drummer	4,000	1979	120.00	175
1980	Rejoice	4,000	1980	150.00	160
1981	Spreading the Word	4,000	1981	150.00	150
1982	The Shepherd Family	4,000	1982	150.00	150
1983	Peace Attend Thee	4,000	1983	150.00	150

Ferrandiz Mother's Day Series - J. Ferrandiz

YEAR ISSUE		EDITION LIMIT	YEAR RETD.	ISSUE PRICE	QUOTE U.S.$
1972	Mother Sewing	3,000	1972	35.00	200
1973	Alpine Mother & Child	3,000	1973	40.00	150
1974	Mother Holding Child	3,000	1974	50.00	150
1975	Dove Girl	3,000	1975	60.00	150
1976	Mother Knitting	3,000	1976	60.00	200
1977	Alpine Stroll	3,000	1977	65.00	125
1978	The Beginning	3,000	1978	75.00	150
1979	All Hearts	3,000	1979	120.00	170
1980	Spring Arrivals	3,000	1980	150.00	165
1981	Harmony	3,000	1981	150.00	150
1982	With Love	3,000	1982	150.00	150

Ferrandiz Wooden Birthday Plates - J. Ferrandiz

YEAR ISSUE		EDITION LIMIT	YEAR RETD.	ISSUE PRICE	QUOTE U.S.$
1972	Boy	Unkn.		15.00	150
1972	Girl	Unkn.		15.00	160
1973	Boy	Unkn.		20.00	200
1973	Girl	Unkn.		20.00	150
1974	Boy	Unkn.		22.00	160
1974	Girl	Unkn.		22.00	160

Ferrandiz Wooden Wedding Plates - J. Ferrandiz

YEAR ISSUE		EDITION LIMIT	YEAR RETD.	ISSUE PRICE	QUOTE U.S.$
1972	Boy and Girl Embracing	Closed	1972	40.00	150
1973	Wedding Scene	Closed	1973	40.00	150
1974	Wedding	Closed	1974	48.00	150
1975	Wedding	Closed	1975	60.00	150
1976	Wedding	Closed	1976	60.00	90-150

Armstrong's

Classic Memory Collection - R. Skelton

YEAR ISSUE		EDITION LIMIT	YEAR RETD.	ISSUE PRICE	QUOTE U.S.$
1995	The Donut Dunker (signed)	1,000		375.00	375

Commemorative Issues - R. Skelton

YEAR ISSUE		EDITION LIMIT	YEAR RETD.	ISSUE PRICE	QUOTE U.S.$
1983	70 Years Young (10 1/2")	15,000		85.00	85-125
1984	Freddie the Torchbearer (8 1/2")	15,000		62.50	63
1994	Red & His Friend	160		700.00	950

Freedom Collection of Red Skelton - R. Skelton

YEAR ISSUE		EDITION LIMIT	YEAR RETD.	ISSUE PRICE	QUOTE U.S.$
1990	The All American, (signed)	1,000		195.00	300
1990	The All American	9,000		62.50	63
1991	Independence Day? (signed)	1,000		195.00	200
1991	Independence Day?	9,000		62.50	63
1992	Let Freedom Ring, (signed)	1,000		195.00	195
1992	Let Freedom Ring	9,000		62.50	63
1993	Freddie's Gift of Life, (signed)	1,000		195.00	195
1993	Freddie's Gift of Life	9,000		62.50	63

Happy Art Series - W. Lantz

YEAR ISSUE		EDITION LIMIT	YEAR RETD.	ISSUE PRICE	QUOTE U.S.$
1981	Woody's Triple Self-Portrait, Signed	1,000		100.00	150
1981	Woody's Triple Self-Portrait	9,000		39.50	40
1983	Gothic Woody, Signed	1,000		100.00	150
1983	Gothic Woody	9,000		39.50	40
1984	Blue Boy Woody, Signed	1,000		100.00	150
1984	Blue Boy Woody	9,000		39.50	40

The Signature Collection - R. Skelton

YEAR ISSUE		EDITION LIMIT	YEAR RETD.	ISSUE PRICE	QUOTE U.S.$
1986	Anyone for Tennis?	9,000		62.50	63
1986	Anyone for Tennis? (signed)	1,000		125.00	350
1987	Ironing the Waves	9,000		62.50	63
1987	Ironing the Waves (signed)	1,000		125.00	300
1988	The Cliffhanger	9,000		62.50	63
1988	The Cliffhanger (signed)	1,000		150.00	250
1988	Hooked on Freddie	9,000		62.50	63
1988	Hooked on Freddie (signed)	1,000		175.00	200

Sports - Schenken

YEAR ISSUE		EDITION LIMIT	YEAR RETD.	ISSUE PRICE	QUOTE U.S.$
1985	Pete Rose h/s (10 1/4")	1,000		100.00	400
1985	Pete Rose u/s (10 1/4")	10,000		45.00	100

Armstrong's/Crown Parlan

Freddie The Freeloader - R. Skelton

YEAR ISSUE		EDITION LIMIT	YEAR RETD.	ISSUE PRICE	QUOTE U.S.$
1979	Freddie in the Bathtub	10,000		60.00	200
1980	Freddie's Shack	10,000		60.00	100
1981	Freddie on the Green	10,000		60.00	60
1982	Love that Freddie	10,000		60.00	60

Freddie's Adventures - R. Skelton

YEAR ISSUE		EDITION LIMIT	YEAR RETD.	ISSUE PRICE	QUOTE U.S.$
1982	Captain Freddie	15,000		60.00	100-125
1982	Bronco Freddie	15,000		60.00	40-75
1983	Sir Freddie	15,000		62.50	55-100
1984	Gertrude and Heathcliffe	15,000		62.50	65

Artaffects

Club Member Limited Edition Redemption Offerings - G. Perillo

YEAR ISSUE		EDITION LIMIT	YEAR RETD.	ISSUE PRICE	QUOTE U.S.$
1992	The Pencil	Yr. Iss.		35.00	75
1992	Studies in Black and White (Set of 4)	Yr. Iss.		75.00	100
1993	Watcher of the Wilderness	Yr. Iss.		60.00	60

America's Indian Heritage - G. Perillo

YEAR ISSUE		EDITION LIMIT	YEAR RETD.	ISSUE PRICE	QUOTE U.S.$
1987	Cheyenne Nation	10-day		24.50	45
1988	Arapaho Nation	10-day		24.50	45
1988	Kiowa Nation	10-day		24.50	45
1988	Sioux Nation	10-day		24.50	45
1988	Chippewa Nation	10-day		24.50	45
1988	Crow Nation	10-day		24.50	45
1988	Nez Perce Nation	10-day		24.50	45
1988	Blackfoot Nation	10-day		24.50	45

Arctic Friends - G. Perillo

YEAR ISSUE		EDITION LIMIT	YEAR RETD.	ISSUE PRICE	QUOTE U.S.$
1982	Siberian Love	7,500		100.00	100
1982	Snow Pals	7,500		set	Set

Chieftains I - G. Perillo

YEAR ISSUE		EDITION LIMIT	YEAR RETD.	ISSUE PRICE	QUOTE U.S.$
1979	Chief Sitting Bull	7,500		65.00	350
1979	Chief Joseph	7,500		65.00	110
1980	Chief Red Cloud	7,500		65.00	120
1980	Chief Geronimo	7,500		65.00	85
1981	Chief Crazy Horse	7,500		65.00	150

Chieftains II - G. Perillo

YEAR ISSUE		EDITION LIMIT	YEAR RETD.	ISSUE PRICE	QUOTE U.S.$
1983	Chief Pontiac	7,500		70.00	110
1983	Chief Victorio	7,500		70.00	85
1984	Chief Tecumseh	7,500		70.00	85
1984	Chief Cochise	7,500		70.00	85
1984	Chief Black Kettle	7,500		70.00	110

Child's Life - G. Perillo

YEAR ISSUE		EDITION LIMIT	YEAR RETD.	ISSUE PRICE	QUOTE U.S.$
1983	Siesta	10,000		45.00	50
1984	Sweet Dreams	10,000		45.00	50

Council of Nations - G. Perillo

YEAR ISSUE		EDITION LIMIT	YEAR RETD.	ISSUE PRICE	QUOTE U.S.$
1992	Strength of the Sioux	14-day		29.50	45
1992	Pride of the Cheyenne	14-day		29.50	35
1992	Dignity of the Nez Perce	14-day		29.50	35
1992	Courage of the Arapaho	14-day		29.50	35
1992	Power of the Blackfoot	14-day		29.50	35
1992	Nobility of the Algonquin	14-day		29.50	35
1992	Wisdom of the Cherokee	14-day		29.50	35
1992	Boldness of the Seneca	14-day		29.50	35

Indian Bridal - G. Perillo

YEAR ISSUE		EDITION LIMIT	YEAR RETD.	ISSUE PRICE	QUOTE U.S.$
1990	Yellow Bird (6 1/2")	14-day		25.00	25
1990	Autumn Blossom (6 1/2")	14-day		25.00	25
1990	Misty Waters (6 1/2")	14-day		25.00	25
1990	Sunny Skies (6 1/2")	14-day		25.00	25

Indian Nations - G. Perillo

YEAR ISSUE		EDITION LIMIT	YEAR RETD.	ISSUE PRICE	QUOTE U.S.$
1983	Blackfoot	7,500		140.00	350
1983	Cheyenne	7,500		set	Set

YEAR ISSUE		EDITION LIMIT	YEAR RETD.	ISSUE PRICE	QUOTE U.S.$
1983	Apache	7,500		set	Set
1983	Sioux	7,500		set	Set

Legends of the West - G. Perillo

1982	Daniel Boone	10,000		65.00	65
1983	Davy Crockett	10,000		65.00	65
1983	Kit Carson	10,000		65.00	65
1983	Buffalo Bill	10,000		65.00	65

March of Dimes: Our Children - G. Perillo

1989	A Time to Be Born	150-day		29.00	40

Masterpieces of Rockwell - N. Rockwell

1980	After the Prom	17,500		42.50	43
1980	The Challenger	17,500		50.00	50
1982	Girl at the Mirror	17,500		50.00	50
1982	Missing Tooth	17,500		50.00	50

Mother's Love - G. Perillo

1988	Feelings	Yr.Iss.		35.00	90
1989	Moonlight	Yr.Iss.		35.00	65
1990	Pride & Joy	Yr.Iss.		39.50	50
1991	Little Shadow	Yr.Iss.		39.50	45

Motherhood Series - G. Perillo

1983	Madre	10,000		50.00	75
1984	Madonna of the Plains	3,500		50.00	75
1985	Abuela	3,500		50.00	75
1986	Nap Time	3,500		50.00	75

Native American Christmas - G. Perillo

1993	The Little Shepherd	Annual		35.00	55
1994	Joy to the World	Annual		45.00	45

Nature's Harmony - G. Perillo

1982	The Peaceable Kingdom	12,500		100.00	125-200
1982	Zebra	12,500		50.00	50
1982	Bengal Tiger	12,500		50.00	60
1983	Black Panther	12,500		50.00	70
1983	Elephant	12,500		50.00	80

North American Wildlife - G. Perillo

1989	Mustang	14-day		29.50	35-55
1989	White-Tailed Deer	14-day		29.50	35
1989	Mountain Lion	14-day		29.50	35
1990	American Bald Eagle	14-day		29.50	35
1990	Timber Wolf	14-day		29.50	35
1990	Polar Bear	14-day		29.50	35
1990	Buffalo	14-day		29.50	35-55
1990	Bighorn Sheep	14-day		29.50	35

Perillo Christmas - G. Perillo

1987	Shining Star	Yr.Iss.		29.50	75-100
1988	Silent Light	Yr.Iss.		35.00	100
1989	Snow Flake	Yr.Iss.		35.00	50
1990	Bundle Up	Yr.Iss.		39.50	75
1991	Christmas Journey	Yr.Iss.		39.50	50

Perillo's Four Seasons - G. Perillo

1991	Summer (6 1/2")	14-day		25.00	25
1991	Autumn (6 1/2")	14-day		25.00	25
1991	Winter (6 1/2")	14-day		25.00	25
1991	Spring (6 1/2")	14-day		25.00	25

Portraits of American Brides - R. Sauber

1986	Caroline	10-day		29.50	50-85
1986	Jacqueline	10-day		29.50	45
1987	Elizabeth	10-day		29.50	45
1987	Emily	10-day		29.50	45
1987	Meredith	10-day		29.50	50
1987	Laura	10-day		29.50	45
1987	Sarah	10-day		29.50	45
1987	Rebecca	10-day		29.50	65

Pride of America's Indians - G. Perillo

1986	Brave and Free	10-day		24.50	50
1986	Dark-Eyed Friends	10-day		24.50	45
1986	Noble Companions	10-day		24.50	35
1987	Kindred Spirits	10-day		24.50	35
1987	Loyal Alliance	10-day		24.50	75
1987	Small and Wise	10-day		24.50	35
1987	Winter Scouts	10-day		24.50	25-40
1987	Peaceful Comrades	10-day		24.50	37-50

The Princesses - G. Perillo

1982	Lily of the Mohawks	7,500		50.00	85-175
1982	Pocahontas	7,500		50.00	75-100
1982	Minnehaha	7,500		50.00	50-100
1982	Sacajawea	7,500		50.00	50-100

Proud Young Spirits - G. Perillo

1990	Protector of the Plains	14-day		29.50	45
1990	Watchful Eyes	14-day		29.50	55
1990	Freedom's Watch	14-day		29.50	35-45
1990	Woodland Scouts	14-day		29.50	35-45
1990	Fast Friends	14-day		29.50	35-45
1990	Birds of a Feather	14-day		29.50	50
1990	Prairie Pals	14-day		29.50	35-45
1990	Loyal Guardian	14-day		29.50	35

Special Issue - G. Perillo

1981	Apache Boy	5,000		95.00	175
1983	Papoose	3,000		100.00	125
1983	Indian Style	17,500		50.00	50
1984	The Lovers	Closed	N/A	50.00	100
1984	Navajo Girl	3,500		95.00	175
1986	Navajo Boy	3,500		95.00	175

Studies in Black and White-Collector's Club Only (Miniatures) - G. Perillo

1992	Dignity	Yr. Iss.		75.00	100
1992	Determination	Yr. Iss.		set	Set
1992	Diligence	Yr. Iss.		set	Set
1992	Devotion	Yr. Iss.		set	Set

The Thoroughbreds - G. Perillo

1984	Whirlaway	9,500		50.00	125
1984	Secretariat	9,500		50.00	65
1984	Man o' War	9,500		50.00	65
1984	Seabiscuit	9,500		50.00	65

War Ponies of the Plains - G. Perillo

1992	Nightshadow	75-day		27.00	27
1992	Windcatcher	75-day		27.00	27
1992	Prairie Prancer	75-day		27.00	27
1992	Thunderfoot	75-day		27.00	27
1992	Proud Companion	75-day		27.00	27
1992	Sun Dancer	75-day		27.00	27
1992	Free Spirit	75-day		27.00	27
1992	Gentle Warrior	75-day		27.00	27

The Young Chieftains - G. Perillo

1985	Young Sitting Bull	5,000		50.00	75-100
1985	Young Joseph	5,000		50.00	75-100
1986	Young Red Cloud	5,000		50.00	75-100
1986	Young Geronimo	5,000		50.00	75-100
1986	Young Crazy Horse	5,000		50.00	75-100

Artists of the World

Celebration Series - T. DeGrazia

1993	The Lord's Candle	5,000		39.50	45
1993	Pinata Party	5,000		39.50	45
1993	Holiday lullaby	5,000		39.50	45
1993	Caroling	5,000		39.50	45

Children (Signed) - T. DeGrazia

1978	Los Ninos, signed	500		100.00	900
1978	White Dove, signed	500		100.00	450
1978	Flower Girl, signed	500		100.00	450
1979	Flower Boy, signed	500		100.00	450
1980	Little Cocopah Girl, signed	500		100.00	320
1981	Beautiful Burden, signed	500		100.00	320
1981	Merry Little Indian, signed	500		100.00	450

Children - T. DeGrazia

1976	Los Ninos	5,000		35.00	900
1977	White Dove	5,000		40.00	100
1978	Flower Girl	9,500		45.00	105
1979	Flower Boy	9,500		45.00	105
1980	Little Cocopah	9,500		50.00	65
1981	Beautiful Burden	9,500		50.00	120
1982	Merry Little Indian	9,500		55.00	120
1983	Wondering	10,000		60.00	130
1984	Pink Papoose	10,000		65.00	140
1985	Sunflower Boy	10,000		65.00	50-65

Children at Play - T. DeGrazia

1985	My First Horse	15,000		65.00	65-100
1986	Girl With Sewing Machine	15,000		65.00	65-100
1987	Love Me	15,000		65.00	65-100
1988	Merrily, Merrily, Merrily	15,000		65.00	65-100
1989	My First Arrow	15,000		65.00	65-100
1990	Away With My Kite	15,000		65.00	65-100

Children Mini-Plates - T. DeGrazia

1980	Los Ninos	5,000		15.00	300
1981	White Dove	5,000		15.00	100
1982	Flower Girl	5,000		15.00	100
1982	Flower Boy	5,000		15.00	100
1983	Little Cocopah Indian Girl	5,000		15.00	100
1983	Beautiful Burden	5,000		20.00	100
1984	Merry Little Indian	5,000		20.00	100
1984	Wondering	5,000		20.00	100
1985	Pink Papoose	5,000		20.00	100
1985	Sunflower Boy	5,000		20.00	100

Children of the Sun - T. DeGrazia

1987	Spring Blossoms	150-day		34.50	50
1987	My Little Pink Bird	150-day		34.50	50
1987	Bright Flowers of the Desert	150-day		37.90	50
1988	Gifts from the Sun	150-day		37.90	50
1988	Growing Glory	150-day		37.90	50
1988	The Gentle White Dove	150-day		37.90	50
1988	Sunflower Maiden	150-day		39.90	50
1989	Sun Showers	150-day		39.90	50

Fiesta of the Children - T. DeGrazia

1990	Welcome to the Fiesta	150-day		34.50	40
1990	Castanets in Bloom	150-day		34.50	40
1991	Fiesta Flowers	150-day		34.50	45
1991	Fiesta Angels	150-day		34.50	35

Floral Fiesta - T. DeGrazia

1994	Little Flower Vendor	5,000		39.50	40
1994	Flowers For Mother	5,000		39.50	40
1995	Floral Innocence	5,000		39.50	40
1995	Floral Bouquet	5,000		39.50	40

Holiday (Signed) - T. DeGrazia

1976	Festival of Lights, signed	500		100.00	350
1977	Bell of Hope, signed	500		100.00	200
1978	Little Madonna, signed	500		100.00	350
1979	The Nativity, signed	500		100.00	200
1980	Little Pima Drummer, signed	500		100.00	200
1981	A Little Prayer, signed	500		100.00	200
1982	Blue Boy, signed	96		100.00	200

Holiday - T. DeGrazia

1976	Festival of Lights	9,500		45.00	125
1977	Bell of Hope	9,500		45.00	50-100
1978	Little Madonna	9,500		45.00	50
1979	The Nativity	9,500		50.00	65-100
1980	Little Pima Drummer	9,500		50.00	55
1981	A Little Prayer	9,500		55.00	65
1982	Blue Boy	10,000		60.00	65
1983	Heavenly Blessings	10,000		65.00	65
1984	Navajo Madonna	10,000		65.00	65
1985	Saguaro Dance	10,000		65.00	65

Holiday Mini-Plates - T. DeGrazia

1980	Festival of Lights	5,000		15.00	250
1981	Bell of Hope	5,000		15.00	95
1982	Little Madonna	5,000		15.00	95
1982	The Nativity	5,000		15.00	95
1983	Little Pima Drummer	5,000		15.00	25
1983	Little Prayer	5,000		20.00	25
1984	Blue Boy	5,000		20.00	25
1984	Heavenly Blessings	5,000		20.00	25
1985	Navajo Madonna	5,000		20.00	25
1985	Saguaro Dance	5,000		20.00	25

Western - T. DeGrazia

1986	Morning Ride	5,000		65.00	90
1987	Bronco	5,000		65.00	90
1988	Apache Scout	5,000		65.00	90
1989	Alone	5,000		65.00	90

Bareuther

Christmas - H. Mueller, unless otherwise noted

1967	Stiftskirche	10,000		12.00	85
1968	Kapplkirche	10,000		12.00	25
1969	Christkindlesmarkt	10,000		12.00	18
1970	Chapel in Oberndorf	10,000		12.50	22
1971	Toys for Sale - From Drawing By L. Richter	10,000		12.75	27
1972	Christmas in Munich	10,000		14.50	25
1973	Sleigh Ride	10,000		15.00	35
1974	Black Forest Church	10,000		19.00	19
1975	Snowman	10,000		21.50	30
1976	Chapel in the Hills	10,000		23.50	26
1977	Story Time	10,000		24.50	40
1978	Mittenwald	10,000		27.50	31
1979	Winter Day	10,000		35.00	35
1980	Mittenberg	10,000		37.50	39
1981	Walk in the Forest	10,000		39.50	40
1982	Bad Wimpfen	10,000		39.50	43
1983	The Night before Christmas	10,000		39.50	40
1984	Zeil on the River Main	10,000		42.50	45
1985	Winter Wonderland	10,000		42.50	57
1986	Christmas in Forchheim	10,000		42.50	70
1987	Decorating the Tree	10,000		42.50	85
1988	St. Coloman Church	10,000		52.50	65
1989	Sleigh Ride	10,000		52.50	80-90
1990	The Old Forge in Rothenburg	10,000		52.50	53
1991	Christmas Joy	10,000		56.50	57
1992	Market Place in Heppenheim	10,000		59.50	60
1993	Winter Fun	10,000		59.50	60
1994	Coming Home For Christmas	10,000		59.50	60

Belleek

Christmas - Unknown

1970	Castle Caldwell	7,500	1970	25.00	70-85
1971	Celtic Cross	7,500	1971	25.00	60
1972	Flight of the Earls	7,500	1972	30.00	35
1973	Tribute To Yeats	7,500	1973	38.50	40
1974	Devenish Island	7,500	1974	45.00	190
1975	The Celtic Cross	7,500	1975	48.00	80
1976	Dove of Peace	7,500	1976	55.00	55
1977	Wren	7,500	1977	55.00	55

Holiday Scenes in Ireland - Unknown

1991	Traveling Home	7,500		75.00	75
1992	Bearing Gifts	7,500		75.00	75
1994	The Ice Skaters	7,500		75.00	75

Berlin Design

Christmas - Unknown

YEAR ISSUE		EDITION LIMIT	YEAR RETD.	ISSUE PRICE	QUOTE U.S.$
1970	Christmas in Bernkastel	4,000		14.50	125
1971	Christmas in Rothenburg	20,000		14.50	45
1972	Christmas in Michelstadt	20,000		15.00	55
1973	Christmas in Wendlestein	20,000		20.00	55
1974	Christmas in Bremen	20,000		25.00	53
1975	Christmas in Dortland	20,000		30.00	35
1976	Christmas in Augsburg	20,000		32.00	75
1977	Christmas in Hamburg	20,000		32.00	32
1978	Christmas in Berlin	20,000		36.00	85
1979	Christmas in Greetsiel	20,000		47.50	60
1980	Christmas in Mittenberg	20,000		50.00	55
1981	Christmas Eve In Hahnenklee	20,000		55.00	55
1982	Christmas Eve In Wasserberg	20,000		55.00	50
1983	Christmas in Oberndorf	20,000		55.00	65
1984	Christmas in Ramsau	20,000		55.00	55
1985	Christmas in Bad Wimpfen	20,000		55.00	59
1986	Christmas Eve in Gelnhaus	20,000		65.00	65
1987	Christmas Eve in Goslar	20,000		65.00	65
1988	Christmas Eve in Ruhpolding	20,000		65.00	90
1989	Christmas Eve in Friedechsdadt	20,000		80.00	80
1990	Christmas Eve in Partenkirchen	20,000		80.00	80
1991	Christmas Eve in Allendorf	20,000		80.00	80

Bing & Grondahl

American Christmas Heritage Collection - C. Magadini

YEAR ISSUE		EDITION LIMIT	YEAR RETD.	ISSUE PRICE	QUOTE U.S.$
1996	The Statue of Liberty	Yr.Iss.		47.50	48

Centennial Anniversary Commemoratives - Various

YEAR ISSUE		EDITION LIMIT	YEAR RETD.	ISSUE PRICE	QUOTE U.S.$
1995	Centennial Plaquettes: Series of 10 5" plates featuring B&G motifs: 1895, 1905, 1919, 1927, 1932, 1945, 1954, 1967, 1974, 1982	Yr.Iss.	1995	250.00	250
1995	Centennial Plate: Behind the Frozen Window - F.A. Hallin	10,000	1995	39.50	40
1995	Centennial Platter: Towers of Copenhagen - J. Nielsen	7,500	1995	195.00	195

Centennial Collection - Various

YEAR ISSUE		EDITION LIMIT	YEAR RETD.	ISSUE PRICE	QUOTE U.S.$
1991	Crows Enjoying Christmas D. Jensen	Annual	1991	59.50	60
1992	Copenhagen Christmas H. Vlugenring	Annual	1992	59.50	60
1993	Christmas Elf - H. Thelander	Annual	1993	59.50	60
1994	Christmas in Church H. Thelander	Annual	1994	59.50	60
1995	Behind The Frozen Window A. Hallin	Annual	1995	59.50	60

Children's Day Plate Series - Various

YEAR ISSUE		EDITION LIMIT	YEAR RETD.	ISSUE PRICE	QUOTE U.S.$
1985	The Magical Tea Party - C. Roller	Annual	1985	24.50	25
1986	A Joyful Flight - C. Roller	Annual	1986	26.50	55
1987	The Little Gardeners - C. Roller	Annual	1987	29.50	75
1988	Wash Day - C. Roller	Annual	1988	34.50	45
1989	Bedtime - C. Roller	Annual	1989	37.00	60
1990	My Favorite Dress S. Vestergaard	Annual	1990	37.00	75
1991	Fun on the Beach S. Vestergaard	Annual	1991	45.00	60
1992	A Summer Day in the Meadow S. Vestergaard	Annual	1992	45.00	60-75
1993	The Carousel - S. Vestergaard	Annual	1993	45.00	55-60
1994	The Little Fisherman S. Vestergaard	Annual	1994	45.00	46
1995	My First Book - S. Vestergaard	Annual	1995	45.00	45
1996	The Little Racers S. Vestergaard	Annual		45.00	45

Christmas - Various

YEAR ISSUE		EDITION LIMIT	YEAR RETD.	ISSUE PRICE	QUOTE U.S.$
1895	Behind The Frozen Window F.A. Hallin	Annual	1895	.50	5000
1896	New Moon - F.A. Hallin	Annual	1896	.50	2200-2500
1897	Sparrows - F.A. Hallin	Annual	1897	.75	1425-1600
1898	Roses and Star - F. Garde	Annual	1898	.75	800-900
1899	Crows - F. Garde	Annual	1899	.75	1200-1800
1900	Church Bells - F. Garde	Annual	1900	.75	1200-1350
1901	Three Wise Men - S. Sabra	Annual	1901	1.00	450-540
1902	Gothic Church Interior D. Jensen	Annual	1902	1.00	310-450
1903	Expectant Children - M. Hyldahl	Annual	1903	1.00	250-450
1904	Fredericksberg Hill - C. Olsen	Annual	1904	1.00	125-225
1905	Christmas Night - D. Jensen	Annual	1905	1.00	150-215
1906	Sleighing to Church - D. Jensen	Annual	1906	1.00	115-130
1907	Little Match Girl - E. Plockross	Annual	1907	1.00	150
1908	St. Petri Church - P. Jorgensen	Annual	1908	1.00	80-105
1909	Yule Tree - Aarestrup	Annual	1909	1.50	100-135
1910	The Old Organist - C. Ersgaard	Annual	1910	1.50	95-113
1911	Angels and Shepherds H. Moltke	Annual	1911	1.50	75-90
1912	Going to Church - E. Hansen	Annual	1912	1.50	80-95
1913	Bringing Home the Tree T. Larsen	Annual	1913	1.50	90-105
1914	Amalienborg Castle - T. Larsen	Annual	1914	1.50	85-95
1915	Dog Outside Window - D. Jensen	Annual	1915	1.50	100-135
1916	Sparrows at Christmas P. Jorgensen	Annual	1916	1.50	70-85
1917	Christmas Boat - A. Friis	Annual	1917	1.50	83
1918	Fishing Boat - A. Friis	Annual	1918	1.50	90
1919	Outside Lighted Window - A. Friis	Annual	1919	2.00	75-90
1920	Hare in the Snow - A. Friis	Annual	1920	2.00	75-95
1921	Pigeons - A. Friis	Annual	1921	2.00	60-75
1922	Star of Bethlehem - A. Friis	Annual	1922	2.00	60-90
1923	The Ermitage - A. Friis	Annual	1923	2.00	93
1924	Lighthouse - A. Friis	Annual	1924	2.50	89
1925	Child's Christmas - A. Friis	Annual	1925	2.50	60-90
1926	Churchgoers - A. Friis	Annual	1926	2.50	80-90
1927	Skating Couple - A. Friis	Annual	1927	2.50	90-100
1928	Eskimos - A. Friis	Annual	1928	2.50	60-85
1929	Fox Outside Farm - A. Friis	Annual	1929	2.50	90-103
1930	Town Hall Square H. Flugenring	Annual	1930	2.50	95-115
1931	Christmas Train - A. Friis	Annual	1931	2.50	95
1932	Life Boat - H. Flugenring	Annual	1932	2.50	60-83
1933	Korsor-Nyborg Ferry H. Flugenring	Annual	1933	3.00	90-100
1934	Church Bell in Tower - H. Flugenring	Annual	1934	3.00	65-90
1935	Lillebelt Bridge - O. Larson	Annual	1935	3.00	75-90
1936	Royal Guard - O. Larson	Annual	1936	3.00	77
1937	Arrival of Christmas Guests O. Larson	Annual	1937	3.00	93
1938	Lighting the Candles - I. Tjerne	Annual	1938	3.00	200-400
1939	Old Lock-Eye, The Sandman I. Tjerne	Annual	1939	3.00	180-250
1940	Christmas Letters - O. Larson	Annual	1940	4.00	180-205
1941	Horses Enjoying Meal O. Larson	Annual	1941	4.00	175-300
1942	Danish Farm - O. Larson	Annual	1942	4.00	125-210
1943	Ribe Cathedral - O. Larson	Annual	1943	5.00	210-288
1944	Sorgenfri Castle - O. Larson	Annual	1944	5.00	80-105
1945	The Old Water Mill - O. Larson	Annual	1945	5.00	170-180
1946	Commemoration Cross M. Hyldahl	Annual	1946	5.00	80-105
1947	Dybbol Mill - M. Hyldahl	Annual	1947	5.00	135-190
1948	Watchman - M. Hyldahl	Annual	1948	5.50	95-105
1949	Landsoldaten - M. Hyldahl	Annual	1949	5.50	90-105
1950	Kronborg Castle - M. Hyldahl	Annual	1950	5.50	150-190
1951	Jens Bang - M. Hyldahl	Annual	1951	6.00	120-195
1952	Thorsvaldsen Museum B. Pramvig	Annual	1952	6.00	90-120
1953	Snowman - B. Pramvig	Annual	1953	7.50	95
1954	Royal Boat - K. Bonfils	Annual	1954	7.00	115-195
1955	Kaulundorg Church - K. Bonfils	Annual	1955	8.00	115-150
1956	Christmas in Copenhagen K. Bonfils	Annual	1956	8.50	145-285
1957	Christmas Candles - K. Bonfils	Annual	1957	9.00	90-165
1958	Santa Claus - K. Bonfils	Annual	1958	9.50	80-110
1959	Christmas Eve - K. Bonfils	Annual	1959	10.00	110-165
1960	Village Church - K. Bonfils	Annual	1960	10.00	170-200
1961	Winter Harmony - K. Bonfils	Annual	1961	10.50	50-95
1962	Winter Night - K. Bonfils	Annual	1962	11.00	55-90
1963	The Christmas Elf - H. Thelander	Annual	1963	11.00	70-120
1964	The Fir Tree and Hare H. Thelander	Annual	1964	11.50	50
1965	Bringing Home the Tree H. Thelander	Annual	1965	12.00	50-70
1966	Home for Christmas H. Thelander	Annual	1966	12.00	45-60
1967	Sharing the Joy - H. Thelander	Annual	1967	13.00	35-50
1968	Christmas in Church H. Thelander	Annual	1968	14.00	30-60
1969	Arrival of Guests - H. Thelander	Annual	1969	14.00	27
1970	Pheasants in Snow H. Thelander	Annual	1970	14.50	15-25
1971	Christmas at Home H. Thelander	Annual	1971	15.00	15
1972	Christmas in Greenland H. Thelander	Annual	1972	16.50	20
1973	Country Christmas H. Thelander	Annual	1973	19.50	25
1974	Christmas in the Village H. Thelander	Annual	1974	22.00	25
1975	Old Water Mill - H. Thelander	Annual	1975	27.50	28
1976	Christmas Welcome H. Thelander	Annual	1976	27.50	28
1977	Copenhagen Christmas H. Thelander	Annual	1977	29.50	30
1978	Christmas Tale - H. Thelander	Annual	1978	32.00	32
1979	White Christmas - H. Thelander	Annual	1979	36.50	38
1980	Christmas in Woods H. Thelander	Annual	1980	42.50	70
1981	Christmas Peace - H. Thelander	Annual	1981	49.50	50
1982	Christmas Tree - H. Thelander	Annual	1982	54.50	55
1983	Christmas in Old Town H. Thelander	Annual	1983	54.50	55
1984	The Christmas Letter - E. Jensen	Annual	1984	54.50	55
1985	Christmas Eve at the Farmhouse - E. Jensen	Annual	1985	54.50	55
1986	Silent Night, Holy Night E. Jensen	Annual	1986	54.50	55
1987	The Snowman's Christmas Eve E. Jensen	Annual	1987	59.50	75
1988	In the Kings Garden - E. Jensen	Annual	1988	64.50	65
1989	Christmas Anchorage E. Jensen	Annual	1989	59.50	70
1990	Changing of the Guards E. Jensen	Annual	1990	64.50	68
1991	Copenhagen Stock Exchange E. Jensen	Annual	1991	69.50	75
1992	Christmas At the Rectory J. Steensen	Annual	1992	69.50	85
1993	Father Christmas in Copenhagen - J. Nielsen	Annual	1993	69.50	95
1994	A Day At The Deer Park J. Nielsen	Annual	1994	72.50	80
1995	The Towers of Copenhagen J. Nielsen	Annual	1995	72.50	80
1996	Winter at the Old Mill - J. Nielsen	Yr.Iss.		74.50	75

Christmas In America - J. Woodson

YEAR ISSUE		EDITION LIMIT	YEAR RETD.	ISSUE PRICE	QUOTE U.S.$
1986	Christmas Eve in Williamsburg	Annual	1986	29.50	165
1987	Christmas Eve at the White House	Annual	1987	34.50	35
1988	Christmas Eve at Rockefeller Center	Annual	1988	34.50	60
1989	Christmas In New England	Annual	1989	37.00	55
1990	Christmas Eve at the Capitol	Annual	1990	39.50	55
1991	Christmas Eve at Independence Hall	Annual	1991	45.00	60
1992	Christmas in San Francisco	Annual	1992	47.50	60
1993	Coming Home For Christmas	Annual	1993	47.50	48
1994	Christmas Eve In Alaska	Annual	1994	47.50	48
1995	Christmas Eve in Mississippi	Annual	1995	47.50	48

Christmas in America Anniversary Plate - J. Woodson

YEAR ISSUE		EDITION LIMIT	YEAR RETD.	ISSUE PRICE	QUOTE U.S.$
1991	Christmas Eve in Williamsburg	Annual	1991	69.50	70
1995	The Capitol - J. Woodson	Annual		74.50	75

Jubilee-5 Year Cycle - Various

YEAR ISSUE		EDITION LIMIT	YEAR RETD.	ISSUE PRICE	QUOTE U.S.$
1915	Frozen Window - F.A. Hallin	Annual	1915	Unkn.	190-225
1920	Church Bells - F. Garde	Annual	1920	Unkn.	60-75
1925	Dog Outside Window - D. Jensen	Annual	1925	Unkn.	160-300
1930	The Old Organist - C. Ersgaard	Annual	1930	Unkn.	210
1935	Little Match Girl - E. Plockross	Annual	1935	Unkn.	450-760
1940	Three Wise Men - S. Sabra	Annual	1940	Unkn.	1800
1945	Amalienborg Castle - T. Larsen	Annual	1945	Unkn.	100-200
1950	Eskimos - A. Friis	Annual	1950	Unkn.	100-220
1955	Dybbol Mill - M. Hyldahl	Annual	1955	Unkn.	215
1960	Kronborg Castle - M. Hyldahl	Annual	1960	25.00	100-160
1965	Chruchgoers - A. Friis	Annual	1965	25.00	105
1970	Amalienborg Castle - T. Larsen	Annual	1970	30.00	30
1975	Horses Enjoying Meal O. Larson	Annual	1975	40.00	60
1980	Yule Tree - Aarestrup	Annual	1980	60.00	60
1985	Lifeboat at Work - H. Flugenring	Annual	1985	65.00	80
1990	The Royal Yacht Dannebrog J. Bonfils	Annual	1990	95.00	80-95
1995	Centennial Platter - J. Nielsen	7,500	1995	195.00	195

Mother's Day - Various

YEAR ISSUE		EDITION LIMIT	YEAR RETD.	ISSUE PRICE	QUOTE U.S.$
1969	Dogs and Puppies - H. Thelander	Annual	1969	9.75	400-500
1970	Bird and Chicks - H. Thelander	Annual	1970	10.00	25-45
1971	Cat and Kitten - H. Thelander	Annual	1971	11.00	12
1972	Mare and Foal - H. Thelander	Annual	1972	12.00	20
1973	Duck and Ducklings H. Thelander	Annual	1973	13.00	25
1974	Bear and Cubs - H. Thelander	Annual	1974	16.50	20
1975	Doe and Fawns - H. Thelander	Annual	1975	19.50	20
1976	Swan Family - H. Thelander	Annual	1976	22.50	23
1977	Squirrel and Young H. Thelander	Annual	1977	23.50	27
1978	Heron and Young - H. Thelander	Annual	1978	24.50	30
1979	Fox and Cubs - H. Thelander	Annual	1979	27.50	33
1980	Woodpecker and Young H. Thelander	Annual	1980	29.50	35
1981	Hare and Young - H. Thelander	Annual	1981	36.50	38
1982	Lioness and Cubs - H. Thelander	Annual	1982	39.50	40
1983	Raccoon and Young H. Thelander	Annual	1983	39.50	45
1984	Stork and Nestlings H. Thelander	Annual	1984	39.50	50
1985	Bear and Cubs - H. Thelander	Annual	1985	39.50	45
1986	Elephant with Calf - H. Thelander	Annual	1986	39.50	40-55
1987	Sheep with Lambs H. Thelander	Annual	1987	42.50	75-85
1988	Crested Plover and Young H. Thelander	Annual	1988	47.50	60
1988	Lapwing Mother with Chicks H. Thelander	Annual	1988	49.50	90
1989	Cow With Calf - H. Thelander	Annual	1989	49.50	55
1990	Hen with Chicks - L. Jensen	Annual	1990	52.50	65-90
1991	The Nanny Goat and her Two Frisky Kids - L. Jensen	Annual	1991	54.50	55-75
1992	Panda With Cubs - L. Jensen	Annual	1992	59.50	65-90
1993	St. Bernard Dog and Puppies A. Therkelsen	Annual	1993	59.50	88
1994	Cat with Kittens - A. Therkelsen	Annual	1994	59.50	88
1995	Hedgehog with Young A. Therkelsen	Annual		59.50	60
1996	Koala with Young - A. Therkelsen	Annual		59.50	60

Mother's Day Jubilee-5 Year Cycle - Thelander

YEAR ISSUE		EDITION LIMIT	YEAR RETD.	ISSUE PRICE	QUOTE U.S.$
1979	Dog & Puppies	Yr.Iss.	1979	55.00	55
1984	Swan Family	Yr.Iss.	1984	65.00	65
1989	Mare & Colt	Yr.Iss.	1989	95.00	110
1994	Woodpecker & Young	Yr.Iss.	1994	95.00	95

Olympic - Unknown

YEAR ISSUE		EDITION LIMIT	YEAR RETD.	ISSUE PRICE	QUOTE U.S.$
1972	Munich, Germany	Closed	1972	20.00	15-25
1976	Montreal, Canada	Closed	1976	29.50	60
1980	Moscow, Russia	Closed	1980	43.00	89
1984	Los Angeles, USA	Closed	1984	45.00	259
1988	Seoul, Korea	Closed	1988	60.00	65
1992	Barcelona, Spain	Closed	1992	74.50	75

Santa Around the World - H. Hansen

YEAR ISSUE		EDITION LIMIT	YEAR RETD.	ISSUE PRICE	QUOTE U.S.$
1995	Santa in Greenland	Yr.Iss.	1995	74.50	75

Statue of Liberty - Unknown

YEAR ISSUE		EDITION LIMIT	YEAR RETD.	ISSUE PRICE	QUOTE U.S.$
1985	Statue of Liberty	10,000	1985	60.00	80

Boehm Studios

Panda - Boehm

YEAR ISSUE		EDITION LIMIT	YEAR RETD.	ISSUE PRICE	QUOTE U.S.$
1982	Panda, Harmony	5,000		65.00	65
1982	Panda, Peace	5,000		65.00	65

The Bradford Exchange/Russia

The Nutcracker - N. Zaitseva

Year	Issue	Edition Limit	Year Retd.	Issue Price	Quote U.S.$
1993	Marie's Magical Gift	95-day		39.87	40
1993	Dance of Sugar Plum Fairy	95-day		39.87	40
1993	Waltz of the Flowers	95-day		39.87	40
1993	Battle With the Mice King	95-day		39.87	40

The Bradford Exchange/United States

101 Dalmatians - Al White Studios

Year	Issue	Edition Limit	Year Retd.	Issue Price	Quote U.S.$
1993	Watch Dogs	95-day		29.90	30
1994	A Happy Reunion	95-day		29.90	30
1994	Hello Darlings	95-day		32.90	33
1994	Sergeant Tibs Saves the Day	95-day		32.90	33
1994	Halfway Home	95-day		32.90	33
1994	True Love	95-day		32.90	33
1995	Bedtime	95-day		34.90	35
1995	A Messy Good Time	95-day		34.90	35

Aladdin - Disney Studio Artists

Year	Issue	Edition Limit	Year Retd.	Issue Price	Quote U.S.$
1993	Magic Carpet Ride	95-day		29.90	30
1993	A Friend Like Me	95-day		29.90	30
1994	Aladdin in Love	95-day		29.90	30
1994	Traveling Companions	95-day		29.90	30
1994	Make Way for Prince Ali	95-day		29.90	30
1994	Aladdin's Wish	95-day		29.90	30
1995	Bee Yourself	95-day		29.90	30
1995	Group Hug	95-day		29.90	30

Alice in Wonderland - S. Gustafson

Year	Issue	Edition Limit	Year Retd.	Issue Price	Quote U.S.$
1993	The Mad Tea Party	95-day		29.90	95
1993	The Cheshire Cat	95-day		29.90	30
1994	Croquet with the Queen	95-day		29.90	30
1994	Advice from a Caterpillar	95-day		29.90	30

America's Favorite Classic Cars - D. Everhart

Year	Issue	Edition Limit	Year Retd.	Issue Price	Quote U.S.$
1993	1957 Corvette	Closed	1995	54.00	75
1993	1956 Thunderbird	Closed	1995	54.00	125
1994	1957 Bel Air	Closed	1995	54.00	54
1994	1965 Mustang	Closed	1995	54.00	54

America's Triumph in Space - R. Schaar

Year	Issue	Edition Limit	Year Retd.	Issue Price	Quote U.S.$
1993	The Eagle Has Landed	95-day		29.90	30
1993	The March Toward Destiny	95-day		29.90	30
1994	Flight of Glory	95-day		32.90	33
1994	Beyond the Bounds of Earth	95-day		32.90	33
1994	Conquering the New Frontier	95-day		32.90	33
1994	Rendezvous With Victory	95-day		34.90	35
1994	The New Explorers	95-day		34.90	35
1994	Triumphant Finale	95-day		34.90	35

American Frontier - C. Wysocki

Year	Issue	Edition Limit	Year Retd.	Issue Price	Quote U.S.$
1993	Timberline Jack's Trading Post	95-day		29.90	30
1994	Dr. Livingwell's Medicine Show	95-day		29.90	30
1994	Bustling Boomtown	95-day		29.90	30
1994	Kirbyville	95-day		29.90	30
1994	Hearty Homesteaders	95-day		29.90	30
1994	Oklahoma or Bust	95-day		29.90	30

Ancient Seasons - M. Silversmith

Year	Issue	Edition Limit	Year Retd.	Issue Price	Quote U.S.$
1995	Edge of Night	95-day		29.90	30

Autumn Encounters - C. Fisher

Year	Issue	Edition Limit	Year Retd.	Issue Price	Quote U.S.$
1995	Woodland Innocents	95-day		29.90	30

Babe Ruth Centennial - P. Heffernan

Year	Issue	Edition Limit	Year Retd.	Issue Price	Quote U.S.$
1995	The 60th Homer	95-day		34.90	35

Baskets of Love - A. Isakov

Year	Issue	Edition Limit	Year Retd.	Issue Price	Quote U.S.$
1993	Andrew and Abbey	95-day		29.90	30
1993	Cody and Courtney	95-day		29.90	30
1993	Emily and Elliott	95-day		32.90	33
1993	Heather and Hannah	95-day		32.90	33
1993	Justin and Jessica	95-day		32.90	33
1993	Katie and Kelly	95-day		34.90	35
1994	Louie and Libby	95-day		34.90	35
1994	Sammy and Sarah	95-day		34.90	35

Battles of/American Civil War - J. Griffin

Year	Issue	Edition Limit	Year Retd.	Issue Price	Quote U.S.$
1994	Gettysburg	95-day		29.90	30
1995	Vicksburg	95-day		29.90	30

Beneath the Waves - D. Terbush

Year	Issue	Edition Limit	Year Retd.	Issue Price	Quote U.S.$
1995	Sea of Light	95-day		29.90	30
1995	All God's Children	95-day		29.90	30
1995	Humpback Whales	95-day		29.90	30

The Bunny Workshop - J. Maday

Year	Issue	Edition Limit	Year Retd.	Issue Price	Quote U.S.$
1995	Make Today Eggstra Special	95-day		19.95	20

By Gone Days - L. Dubin

Year	Issue	Edition Limit	Year Retd.	Issue Price	Quote U.S.$
1994	Soda Fountain	95-day		29.90	30
1995	Sam's Grocery Store	95-day		29.90	30
1995	Saturday Matinee	95-day		29.90	30
1995	The Corner News Stand	95-day		29.90	30
1995	Main Street Splendor	95-day		29.90	30
1995	The Barber Shop	95-day		29.90	30

Cabins of Comfort River - F. Buchwitz

Year	Issue	Edition Limit	Year Retd.	Issue Price	Quote U.S.$
1995	Comfort by Camplights Fire	95-day		29.90	30

Carousel Daydreams - Tseng

Year	Issue	Edition Limit	Year Retd.	Issue Price	Quote U.S.$
1995	Swept Away	4/96		39.90	40

Charles Wysocki's Peppercricket Grove - C. Wysocki

Year	Issue	Edition Limit	Year Retd.	Issue Price	Quote U.S.$
1993	Peppercricket Farms	95-day		24.90	25
1993	Gingernut Valley Inn	95-day		24.90	25
1993	Budzen's Fruits and Vegetables	95-day		24.90	25
1993	Virginia's Market	95-day		24.90	25
1993	Pumpkin Hollow Emporium	95-day		24.90	25
1993	Liberty Star Farms	95-day		24.90	25
1993	Overflow Antique Market	95-day		24.90	25
1993	Black Crow Antique Shoppe	95-day		24.90	25

Cherished Traditions - M. Lesher

Year	Issue	Edition Limit	Year Retd.	Issue Price	Quote U.S.$
1995	The Wedding Ring	95-day		29.90	30

Cherubs of Innocence - W. Bouguereau

Year	Issue	Edition Limit	Year Retd.	Issue Price	Quote U.S.$
1994	The First Kiss	95-day		29.90	30
1995	Love at Rest	95-day		29.90	30
1995	Thoughts of Love	95-day		32.90	33

Chosen Messengers - G. Running Wolf

Year	Issue	Edition Limit	Year Retd.	Issue Price	Quote U.S.$
1994	The Pathfinders	95-day		29.90	30
1994	The Overseers	95-day		29.90	30
1994	The Providers	95-day		32.90	33
1994	The Surveyors	95-day		32.90	33

A Christmas Carol - L. Garrison

Year	Issue	Edition Limit	Year Retd.	Issue Price	Quote U.S.$
1993	God Bless Us Everyone	95-day		29.90	65
1993	Ghost of Christmas Present	95-day		29.90	30
1994	A Merry Christmas to All	95-day		29.90	30
1994	A Visit From Marley's Ghost	95-day		29.90	30
1994	Remembereing Christmas Past	95-day		29.90	30
1994	A Spirit's Warning	95-day		29.90	30
1994	The True Spirit of Christmas	95-day		29.90	30
1994	Merry Christmas, Bob	95-day		29.90	30

Christmas Memories - J. Tanton

Year	Issue	Edition Limit	Year Retd.	Issue Price	Quote U.S.$
1993	A Winter's Tale	95-day		29.90	30
1993	Finishing Touches	95-day		29.90	48
1993	Welcome to Our Home	95-day		29.90	30
1993	Christmas Celebration	95-day		29.90	30

Classic Melodies from the "Sound of Music" - M. Hampshire

Year	Issue	Edition Limit	Year Retd.	Issue Price	Quote U.S.$
1995	Sing Along with Maria	95-day		29.90	30

The Costuming of A Legend: Dressing Gone With The Wind - D. Klauba

Year	Issue	Edition Limit	Year Retd.	Issue Price	Quote U.S.$
1993	The Red Dress	95-day		29.90	30
1993	The Green Drapery Dress	95-day		29.90	30
1994	The Green Sprigged Dress	95-day		29.90	30
1994	Black & White Bengaline Dress	95-day		29.90	30
1994	Widow's Weeds	95-day		29.90	30
1994	The Country Walking Dress	95-day		29.90	30
1994	Plaid Business Attire	95-day		29.90	30
1994	Orchid Percale Dress	95-day		29.90	30
1994	The Mourning Gown	95-day		29.90	30
1994	The Green Muslin Dress	95-day		29.90	30

A Country Wonderland - W. Goebel

Year	Issue	Edition Limit	Year Retd.	Issue Price	Quote U.S.$
1995	The Quiet Hour	95-day		29.90	30

Deer Friends at Christmas - J. Thornbrugh

Year	Issue	Edition Limit	Year Retd.	Issue Price	Quote U.S.$
1994	All a Glow	95-day		29.90	30
1994	A Glistening Season	95-day		29.90	30
1994	Holiday Sparkle	95-day		29.90	30
1995	Woodland Splendor	95-day		29.90	30

Desert Rhythms - M. Cowdery

Year	Issue	Edition Limit	Year Retd.	Issue Price	Quote U.S.$
1994	Partner With A Breeze	95-day		29.90	30
1994	Wind Dancer	95-day		29.90	30
1994	Riding On Air	95-day		29.90	30

Dog Days - J. Gadamus

Year	Issue	Edition Limit	Year Retd.	Issue Price	Quote U.S.$
1993	Sweet Dreams	95-day		29.90	30
1993	Pier Group	95-day		29.90	30
1993	Wagon Train	95-day		32.90	33
1993	First Flush	95-day		32.90	33
1993	Little Rascals	95-day		32.90	33
1993	Where'd He Go	95-day		32.90	33

Elvis: Young & Wild - B. Emmett

Year	Issue	Edition Limit	Year Retd.	Issue Price	Quote U.S.$
1993	The King of Creole	95-day		29.90	30
1993	King of the Road	95-day		29.90	30
1994	Tough But Tender	95-day		32.90	33
1994	With Love, Elvis	95-day		32.90	33
1994	The Picture of Cool	95-day		32.90	33
1994	Kissing Elvis	95-day		34.90	35
1994	The Perfect Take	95-day		34.90	35
1994	The Rockin' Rebel	95-day		34.90	35

Faces of the Wild - D. Parker

Year	Issue	Edition Limit	Year Retd.	Issue Price	Quote U.S.$
1995	The Wolf	95-day		39.90	40

Fairyland - M. Jobe

Year	Issue	Edition Limit	Year Retd.	Issue Price	Quote U.S.$
1994	Trails of Starlight	95-day		29.90	30

Year	Issue	Edition Limit	Year Retd.	Issue Price	Quote U.S.$
1994	Twilight Trio	95-day		29.90	30
1994	Forest Enchantment	95-day		32.90	33
1995	Silvery Splasher	95-day		32.90	33
1995	Magical Mischief	95-day		32.90	33
1995	Farewell to the Night	95-day		34.90	35

Family Circles - R. Rust

Year	Issue	Edition Limit	Year Retd.	Issue Price	Quote U.S.$
1993	Great Gray Owl Family	95-day		29.90	30
1994	Great Horned Owl Family	95-day		29.90	30
1994	Barred Owl Family	95-day		29.90	30
1994	Spotted Owl Family	95-day		29.90	30

Field Pup Follies - L. Kaatz

Year	Issue	Edition Limit	Year Retd.	Issue Price	Quote U.S.$
1994	Sleeping on the Job	Closed	1995	29.90	30
1994	Hat Check	Closed	1995	29.90	30
1994	Fowl Play	Closed	1995	29.90	30
1994	Tackling Lunch	1/96		29.90	30

Fleeting Encounters - M. Budden

Year	Issue	Edition Limit	Year Retd.	Issue Price	Quote U.S.$
1995	Autumn Retreat	95-day		29.90	30

Floral Frolics - G. Kurz

Year	Issue	Edition Limit	Year Retd.	Issue Price	Quote U.S.$
1994	Spring Surprises	95-day		29.90	30
1994	Bee Careful	95-day		29.90	30
1995	Fuzzy Fun	95-day		32.90	33
1995	Sunny Hideout	95-day		32.90	33

Floral Greetings - L. Liu

Year	Issue	Edition Limit	Year Retd.	Issue Price	Quote U.S.$
1994	Circle of Love	95-day		29.90	30
1994	Circle of Elegance	95-day		29.90	30
1994	Circle of Harmony	95-day		32.90	33
1994	Circle of Joy	95-day		32.90	33
1994	Circle of Romance	95-day		34.90	35
1995	Circle of Inspiration	95-day		34.90	35

Footsteps of the Brave - H. Schaare

Year	Issue	Edition Limit	Year Retd.	Issue Price	Quote U.S.$
1993	Noble Quest	95-day		24.90	25
1993	At Storm's Passage	95-day		24.90	25
1993	With Boundless Vision	95-day		27.90	28
1993	Horizons of Destiny	95-day		27.90	28
1993	Path of His Forefathers	95-day		27.90	28
1993	Soulful Reflection	95-day		29.90	30
1993	The Reverent Trail	95-day		29.90	30
1994	At Journey's End	95-day		34.90	35

Forever Glamorous Barbie - C. Falberg

Year	Issue	Edition Limit	Year Retd.	Issue Price	Quote U.S.$
1995	Enchanted Evening	6/96		49.90	50

Fracé's Kingdom of the Great Cats: Signature Collection - C. Fracé

Year	Issue	Edition Limit	Year Retd.	Issue Price	Quote U.S.$
1994	Mystic Realm	95-day		39.90	40
1994	Snow Leopard	95-day		39.90	40
1994	Emperor of Siberia	95-day		39.90	40
1994	His Domain	95-day		39.90	40
1994	American Monarch	95-day		39.90	40

Freshwater Game Fish of North America - E. Totten

Year	Issue	Edition Limit	Year Retd.	Issue Price	Quote U.S.$
1994	Rainbow Trout	95-day		29.90	30
1995	Largemouth Bass	95-day		29.90	30
1995	Blue Gills	95-day		29.90	30
1995	Northern Pike	95-day		29.90	30
1995	Brown Trout	95-day		29.90	30

Friendship in Bloom - L. Chang

Year	Issue	Edition Limit	Year Retd.	Issue Price	Quote U.S.$
1994	Paws in the Posies	95-day		34.90	35
1995	Cozy Petunia Patch	95-day		34.90	35
1995	Patience & Impatience	95-day		34.90	35

Gallant Men of Civil War - J. Strain

Year	Issue	Edition Limit	Year Retd.	Issue Price	Quote U.S.$
1994	Robert E. Lee	95-day		29.90	30
1995	Stonewall Jackson	95-day		29.90	30
1995	Nathan Bedford Forest	95-day		29.90	30
1995	Joshua Chamberlain	95-day		29.90	30
1995	John Hunt Morgan	95-day		29.90	30

Gardens of Innocence - D. Richardson

Year	Issue	Edition Limit	Year Retd.	Issue Price	Quote U.S.$
1994	Hope	95-day		29.90	30
1994	Charity	95-day		29.90	30
1994	Joy	95-day		32.90	33
1994	Faith	95-day		32.90	33
1994	Grace	95-day		32.90	33
1995	Serenity	95-day		34.90	35
1995	Peace	95-day		34.90	35
1995	Patience	95-day		34.90	35

Getting Away From It All - D. Rust

Year	Issue	Edition Limit	Year Retd.	Issue Price	Quote U.S.$
1995	Mountain Hideaway	95-day		29.90	30

Gone With The Wind - M. Phalen

Year	Issue	Edition Limit	Year Retd.	Issue Price	Quote U.S.$
1995	Scarlett Radiance	95-day		39.90	40
1995	Rhett's Bright Promise	95-day		39.90	40

Gone With The Wind: Musical Treasures - A. Jenks

Year	Issue	Edition Limit	Year Retd.	Issue Price	Quote U.S.$
1994	Tara: Scarlett's True Love	95-day		29.90	30
1994	Scarlett: Belle of/12 Oaks BBQ	95-day		29.90	30
1995	Charity Bazaar	95-day		32.90	33
1995	The Proposal	95-day		32.90	33

Great Moments in Baseball - S. Gardner

Year	Issue	Edition Limit	Year Retd.	Issue Price	Quote U.S.$
1993	Joe DiMaggio: The Streak	95-day		29.90	30

YEAR ISSUE		EDITION LIMIT	YEAR RETD.	ISSUE PRICE	QUOTE U.S.$
1993	Stan Musial: 5 Homer Double Header	95-day		29.90	30
1994	Bobby Thomson: Shot Heard Round the World	95-day		32.90	33
1994	Bill Mazeroski: Winning Home Run	95-day		32.90	33
1994	Don Larsen: Perfect Series Game	95-day		32.90	33
1994	J. Robinson: Saved Pennant	95-day		34.90	35
1994	Satchel Paige: Greatest Games	95-day		34.90	35
1994	Billy Martin: The Rescue Catch	95-day		34.90	35
1994	Dizzy Dean: The World Series Shutout	95-day		34.90	35
1995	Carl Hubbell: The 1934 All State	95-day		36.90	37

Great Superbowl Quarterbacks - R. Brown

1995	Joe Montana: King of Comeback	95-day		29.90	30

Guidance From Above - B. Jaxon

1994	Prayer to the Storm	95-day		29.90	30
1995	Appeal to Thunder	95-day		29.90	30
1995	Blessing the Future	95-day		29.90	30

Happy Hearts - J. Daly

1995	Contentment	95-day		29.90	30
1995	Playmates	95-day		29.90	30
1995	Childhood Friends	95-day		32.90	33
1995	Favorite Gift	95-day		32.90	33

Heart of Heart - Raphael

1995	Thinking of You	95-day		29.90	30

Heaven on Earth - T. Kinkade

1994	I Am the Light of/World	95-day		29.90	30
1995	I Am the Way	95-day		29.90	30
1995	Thy Word is a Lamp	95-day		29.90	30
1995	For Thou Art My Lamp	95-day		29.90	30
1995	In Him Was Life	95-day		29.90	30
1995	But The Path of Just	95-day		29.90	30

Heaven Sent - L. Bogle

1994	Sweet Dreams	95-day		29.90	30
1994	Puppy Dog Tails	95-day		29.90	30
1994	Timeless Treasure	95-day		32.90	33
1995	Precious Gift	95-day		32.90	33

Heirloom Memories - A. Pech

1994	Porcelain Treasure	95-day		29.90	40
1994	Rhythms in Lace	95-day		29.90	40
1994	Pink Lemonade Roses	95-day		29.90	30
1994	Victorian Romance	95-day		29.90	30
1994	Teatime Tulips	95-day		29.90	30
1994	Touch of the Irish	95-day		29.90	30

A Hidden World - R. Rust

1993	Two by Night, Two by Light	95-day		29.90	30
1993	Two by Steam, Two in Dream	95-day		29.90	30
1993	Two on Sly, Two Watch Nearby	95-day		32.90	33
1993	Hunter Growls, Spirits Prowl	95-day		32.90	33
1993	In Moonglow One Drinks	95-day		32.90	33
1993	Sings at the Moon, Spirits Sing in Tune	95-day		34.90	35
1994	Two Cubs Play As Spirits Show the Way	95-day		34.90	35
1994	Young Ones Hold on Tight As Spirits Stay in Sight	95-day		34.90	35

Hideaway Lake - R. Rust

1993	Rusty's Retreat	95-day		34.90	35
1993	Fishing For Dreams	95-day		34.90	35
1993	Sunset Cabin	95-day		34.90	35
1993	Echoes of Morning	95-day		34.90	35

Hometown Memories - C. Wysocki

1994	Small Talk at Birdie's Perch	95-day		29.90	30
1995	Tranquil Days/Ravenswhip Cove	95-day		29.90	30
1995	Summer Delights	95-day		29.90	30
1995	Capturing the Moment	95-day		29.90	30
1995	A Farewell Kiss	95-day		29.90	30
1995	Jason Sparklin the Lighthouse	95-day		29.90	30

Hunters of the Spirit - R. Docken

1995	Provider	95-day		29.90	30

Illusions of Nature - M. Bierlinski

1995	A Trio of Wolves	95-day		29.90	30

Immortals of the Diamond - C. Jackson

1994	The Sultan of Swat	95-day		39.90	40
1995	Pride of the Yankees	95-day		39.90	40

In A Hidden Garden - T. Clausnitzer

1993	Curious Kittens	95-day		29.90	30
1994	Through Eyes of Blue	95-day		29.90	30
1994	Amber Gaze	95-day		29.90	30
1994	Fascinating Find	95-day		29.90	30

Keepsakes of the Heart - C. Layton

1993	Forever Friends	95-day		29.90	30
1993	Afternoon Tea	95-day		29.90	30
1993	Riding Companions	95-day		29.90	30
1993	Sentimental Sweethearts	95-day		29.90	30

Kindred Thoughts - C. Puolin

1995	Sisters	95-day		29.90	30

Kingdom of the Unicorn - M. Ferraro

1993	The Magic Begins	95-day		29.90	40
1993	In Crystal Waters	95-day		29.90	50
1993	Chasing a Dream	95-day		29.90	45
1993	The Fountain of Youth	95-day		29.90	30

Kinkade's Illuminated Cottages - T. Kinkade

1994	The Flagstone Path	1/96		34.90	35
1995	The Garden Walk	3/96		34.90	35
1995	Cherry Blossom Hideaway	5/96		34.90	35

Lamplight Village - T. Kinkade

1995	Lamplight Brooke	95-day		29.90	30
1995	Lamplight Lane	95-day		29.90	30
1995	Lamplight Inn	95-day		29.90	30

Land of Oz: New Dimension - D. Cherry

1995	Step into the Emerald City	95-day		34.90	35

Legend of the White Buffalo - D. Stanley

1995	Mystic Spirit	95-day		29.90	30

Lena Liu's Beautiful Gardens - Inspired by L. Liu

1994	Iris Garden	12/95		34.00	34
1994	Peony Garden	2/96		34.00	34
1994	The Rose Garden	4/96		39.00	39
1995	Lily Garden	95-day		39.00	39

The Life of Christ - R. Barrett

1994	The Passion in the Garden	95-day		29.90	30
1994	Jesus Enters Jerusalem	95-day		29.90	30
1994	Jesus Calms the Waters	95-day		32.90	33
1994	Sermon on the Mount	95-day		32.90	33
1994	The Last Supper	95-day		32.90	33
1994	The Ascension	95-day		34.90	35
1994	The Resurrection	95-day		34.90	35
1995	The Crucifixion	95-day		34.90	35

The Light of the World - C. Nick

1995	The Last Supper	95-day		29.90	30

Lincoln's Portraits of Valor - B. Maguire

1993	The Gettysburg Address	95-day		29.90	30
1993	Emancipation Proclamation	95-day		29.90	30
1993	The Lincoln-Douglas Debates	95-day		29.90	30
1993	The Second Inaugural Address	95-day		29.90	30

The Lion King - Disney Studios

1994	The Circle of Life	95-day		29.90	30
1995	Like Father, Like Son	95-day		29.90	30
1995	A Crunchy Feast	95-day		32.90	33

Little Bandits - C. Jagodits

1993	Handle With Care	95-day		29.90	70
1993	All Tied Up	95-day		29.90	35
1993	Everything's Coming Up Daisies	95-day		32.90	48
1993	Out of Hand	95-day		32.90	33
1993	Pupsicles	95-day		32.90	33
1993	Unexpected Guests	95-day		32.90	33

Lord of Forest & Canyon - G. Beecham

1994	Mountain Majesty	95-day		29.90	30
1995	Proud Legacy	95-day		29.90	30
1995	Golden Monarch	95-day		29.90	30
1995	Forest Emperor	95-day		29.90	30

Majestic Patriots - G. Dieckhoner

1995	My Country Tis of Thee	95-day		29.90	30

Mickey and Minnie's Through the Years - Disney Studios

1995	Mickey's Birthday Party 1942	95-day		29.90	30
1995	Brave Little Tailor	95-day		29.90	30

Moments at Home - S. Kuck

1995	Moments of Caring	95-day		29.90	30

A Mother's Love - J. Anderson

1995	Remembrance	95 days		29.90	30

Musical Tribute to Elvis the King - B. Emmett

1994	Rockin' Blue Suede Shoes	95-day		29.90	30
1994	Hound Dog Bop	95-day		29.90	30
1995	Red, White & Gl Blues	95-day		32.90	33
1995	American Dream	95-day		32.90	33

Mysterious Case of Fowl Play - B.H. Bond

1994	Inspector Clawseau	95-day		29.90	30
1994	Glamourpuss	95-day		29.90	30
1994	Sophisicat	95-day		29.90	30
1994	Kool Cat	95-day		29.90	30
1994	Sneakers & High-Top	95-day		29.90	30
1995	Tuxedo	95-day		29.90	30

Mystic Guardians - S. Hill

1993	Soul Mates	95-day		29.90	30
1993	Majestic Messenger	95-day		29.90	30
1993	Companion Spirits	95-day		32.90	33
1994	Faithful Fellowship	95-day		32.90	33
1994	Spiritual Harmony	95-day		32.90	33
1994	Royal Unity	95-day		32.90	33

Mystic Spirits - V. Crandell

1995	Moon Shadows	95-day		29.90	30
1995	Midnight Snow	95-day		29.90	30
1995	Arctic Nights	95-day		32.90	33

Native American Legends: Chiefs of Destiny - C. Jackson

1994	Sitting Bull	2/96		39.90	40
1994	Chief Joseph	4/96		39.90	40
1995	Red Cloud	6/96		44.90	45

Native Beauty - L. Bogle

1994	The Promise	95-day		29.90	30
1994	Afterglow	95-day		29.90	30
1994	White Feather	95-day		29.90	30
1995	First glance	95-day		29.90	30
1995	Morning Star	95-day		29.90	30
1995	Quiet Time	95-day		29.90	30
1995	Warm Thoughts	95-day		29.90	30

Native Visions - J. Cole

1995	Bringers of the Storm	95-day		29.90	30
1995	Water Vision	95-day		29.90	30

Nature's Little Treasures - L. Martin

1994	Garden Whispers	95-day		29.90	30
1994	Wings of Grace	95-day		29.90	30
1994	Delicate Splendor	95-day		32.90	33
1994	Perfect Jewels	95-day		32.90	33
1994	Miniature Glory	95-day		32.90	33
1994	Precious Beauties	95-day		34.90	35
1994	Minute Enchantment	95-day		34.90	35
1994	Rare Perfection	95-day		34.90	35
1995	Misty Morning	95-day		36.90	37

New Horizons - R. Copple

1993	Building For a New Generation	95-day		29.90	45
1993	The Power of Gold	95-day		29.90	30
1994	Wings of Snowy Grandeur	95-day		32.90	33
1994	Master of the Chase	95-day		32.90	33
1995	Coastal Domain	95-day		32.90	33

Night Fairies - M. Jobe

1994	Trails of Starlight	95-day		29.90	30

Nightsong: The Loon - J. Hansel

1994	Moonlight Echoes	95-day		29.90	30
1994	Evening Mist	95-day		29.90	30
1994	Nocturnal Glow	95-day		32.90	33
1994	Tranquil Reflections	95-day		32.90	33
1994	Peaceful Waters	95-day		32.90	33
1994	Silently Nestled	95-day		34.90	35
1994	Night Light	95-day		34.90	35
1995	Peaceful Homestead	95-day		34.90	35
1995	Loons by the Lily Pad	95-day		34.90	35

Nightwatch: The Wolf - D. Ningewance

1994	Moonlight Serenade	95-day		29.90	30
1994	Midnight Guard	95-day		29.90	30
1994	Snowy Lookout	95-day		29.90	30
1994	Silent Sentries	95-day		29.90	30
1994	Song to the Night	95-day		29.90	30
1994	Winter Passage	95-day		29.90	30

Northern Companions - K. Weisberg

1995	Midnight Harmony	95-day		29.90	30

Northwoods Spirit - D. Wenzel

1994	Timeless Watch	95-day		29.90	30
1994	Woodland Retreat	95-day		29.90	30
1995	Forest Echo	95-day		29.90	30
1995	Timberland Gaze	95-day		29.90	30
1995	Evening Respite	95-day		29.90	30

Nosy Neighbors - P. Weirs

1994	Cat Nap	95-day		29.90	30
1994	Special Delivery	95-day		29.90	30
1995	House Sitting	95-day		29.90	30
1995	Observation Deck	95-day		32.90	33
1995	Surprise Visit	95-day		32.90	33

Notorious Disney Villains - Disney Studios

1993	The Wicked Queen	95-day		29.90	30
1994	Maleficent	95-day		29.90	30
1994	Ursella	95-day		29.90	30
1994	Cruella De Vil	95-day		29.90	30

Old Fashioned Christmas with Thomas Kinkade - T. Kinkade

1993	All Friends Are Welcome	95-day		29.90	35
1993	Winters Memories	95-day		29.90	30
1993	A Holiday Gathering	95-day		32.90	33
1994	Christmas Tree Cottage	95-day		32.90	33
1995	The Best Tradition	95-day		32.90	33

Panda Bear Hugs - W. Nelson

1994	Loving Advice	Closed	1995	39.00	39

YEAR ISSUE	EDITION LIMIT	YEAR RETD.	ISSUE PRICE	QUOTE U.S.$
1994 A Playful Interlude	Closed	1995	39.00	39
1994 A Taste of Life	Closed	1995	39.00	39

Pathways of the Heart - J. Barnes

YEAR ISSUE	EDITION LIMIT	YEAR RETD.	ISSUE PRICE	QUOTE U.S.$
1993 October Radiance	95-day		29.90	30
1993 Daybreak	95-day		29.90	30
1994 Harmony with Nature	95-day		29.90	30
1994 Distant Lights	95-day		29.90	30
1994 A Night to Remember	95-day		29.90	30
1994 Peaceful Evening	95-day		29.90	30

Peace on Earth - D. Geisness

YEAR ISSUE	EDITION LIMIT	YEAR RETD.	ISSUE PRICE	QUOTE U.S.$
1993 Winter Lullaby	95-day		29.90	30
1994 Heavenly Slumber	95-day		29.90	30
1994 Sweet Embrace	95-day		32.90	33
1994 Woodland Dreams	95-day		32.90	33
1994 Snowy Silence	95-day		32.90	33
1994 Dreamy Whispers	95-day		32.90	33

Picked from an English Garden - W. Von Schwarzbek

YEAR ISSUE	EDITION LIMIT	YEAR RETD.	ISSUE PRICE	QUOTE U.S.$
1994 Inspired by Romance	95-day		29.90	30
1995 Lasting Treasures	95-day		29.90	30
1995 Nature's Wonders	95-day		29.90	30

Pinegrove's Winter Cardinals - S. Timm

YEAR ISSUE	EDITION LIMIT	YEAR RETD.	ISSUE PRICE	QUOTE U.S.$
1994 Evening in Pinegrove	95-day		29.90	30
1994 Pinegrove's Sunset	95-day		29.90	30
1994 Pinegrove's Twilight	95-day		29.90	30
1994 Daybreak in Pinegrove	95-day		29.90	30
1994 Pinegrove's Morning	95-day		29.90	30
1994 Afternoon in Pinegrove	95-day		29.90	30
1994 Midnight in Pinegrove	95-day		29.90	30
1994 At Home in Pinegrove	95-day		29.90	30

Portraits of Majesty - D. Braud

YEAR ISSUE	EDITION LIMIT	YEAR RETD.	ISSUE PRICE	QUOTE U.S.$
1994 Snowy Monarch	95-day		29.90	30
1995 Reflections of Kings	95-day		29.90	30
1995 Emperor of His Realm	95-day		29.90	30
1995 Solemn Sovereign	95-day		29.90	30

Postcards from Thomas Kinkade - T. Kinkade

YEAR ISSUE	EDITION LIMIT	YEAR RETD.	ISSUE PRICE	QUOTE U.S.$
1995 San Francisco	95-day		34.90	35
1995 Paris	95-day		34.90	35
1995 New York City	95-day		34.90	35

Practice Makes Perfect - L. Kaatz

YEAR ISSUE	EDITION LIMIT	YEAR RETD.	ISSUE PRICE	QUOTE U.S.$
1994 What's a Mother to Do?	95-day		29.90	30
1994 The Ones That Got Away	95-day		29.90	30
1994 Pointed in the Wrong Direction	95-day		32.90	33
1994 Fishing for Compliments	95-day		32.90	33
1994 Dandy Distraction	95-day		32.90	33
1995 On The Right Track	95-day		34.90	35
1995 More Than a Mouthful	95-day		34.90	35

Precious Angels - S. Kuck

YEAR ISSUE	EDITION LIMIT	YEAR RETD.	ISSUE PRICE	QUOTE U.S.$
1994 Angel of Sharing	95-day		29.90	30
1995 Angel of Sunshine	95-day		29.90	30
1995 Angel of Laughter	95-day		29.90	30
1995 Angel of Hope	95-day		29.90	30
1995 Angel of Grace	95-day		29.90	30

Precious Visions - J. Grande

YEAR ISSUE	EDITION LIMIT	YEAR RETD.	ISSUE PRICE	QUOTE U.S.$
1994 Brilliant Moment	95-day		29.90	30
1995 Brief Interlude	95-day		29.90	30
1995 Timeless Radiance	95-day		29.90	30
1995 Enduring Elegance	95-day		32.90	33

Pride of America - J. Spurlock

YEAR ISSUE	EDITION LIMIT	YEAR RETD.	ISSUE PRICE	QUOTE U.S.$
1995 Wings of Glory	95-day		29.90	30

Promise of a Savior - Various

YEAR ISSUE	EDITION LIMIT	YEAR RETD.	ISSUE PRICE	QUOTE U.S.$
1993 An Angel's Message	95-day		29.90	30
1993 Gifts to Jesus	95-day		29.90	30
1993 The Heavenly King	95-day		29.90	30
1993 Angels Were Watching	95-day		29.90	30
1993 Holy Mother and Child	95-day		29.90	30
1994 A Child is Born	95-day		29.90	30

Proud Heritage - M. Amerman

YEAR ISSUE	EDITION LIMIT	YEAR RETD.	ISSUE PRICE	QUOTE U.S.$
1994 Mystic Warrior: Medicine Crow	95-day		34.90	35
1994 Great Chief: Sitting Bull	95-day		34.90	35
1994 Brave Leader: Geronimo	95-day		34.90	35
1995 Peaceful Defender	95-day		34.90	35

Quiet Moments - K. Daniel

YEAR ISSUE	EDITION LIMIT	YEAR RETD.	ISSUE PRICE	QUOTE U.S.$
1994 Time for Tea	95-day		29.90	30
1995 A Loving Hand	95-day		29.90	30
1995 Kept with Care	95-day		29.90	30
1995 Puppy Love	95-day		29.90	30

Radiant Messengers - L. Martin

YEAR ISSUE	EDITION LIMIT	YEAR RETD.	ISSUE PRICE	QUOTE U.S.$
1994 Peace	95-day		29.90	30
1994 Hope	95-day		29.90	30
1994 Beauty	95-day		29.90	30
1994 Inspiration	95-day		29.90	30

Reflections of Marilyn - C. Notarile

YEAR ISSUE	EDITION LIMIT	YEAR RETD.	ISSUE PRICE	QUOTE U.S.$
1994 All That Glitters	95-day		29.90	30
1994 Shimmering Heat	95-day		29.90	30
1994 Million Dollar Star	95-day		29.90	30
1995 A Twinkle in Her Eye	95-day		29.90	30

Remembering Elvis - N. Giorgio

YEAR ISSUE	EDITION LIMIT	YEAR RETD.	ISSUE PRICE	QUOTE U.S.$
1994 The King	95-day		29.90	30
1995 The Legend	95-day		29.90	30

Rockwell Commemorative Stamps - N. Rockwell

YEAR ISSUE	EDITION LIMIT	YEAR RETD.	ISSUE PRICE	QUOTE U.S.$
1994 Triple Self Portrait	95-day		29.90	30
1994 Freedom From Want	95-day		29.90	30
1994 Freedom From Fear	95-day		29.90	30
1995 Freedom of Speech	95-day		29.90	30
1995 Freedom of Worship	95-day		29.90	30

Royal Enchantments - J. Penchoff

YEAR ISSUE	EDITION LIMIT	YEAR RETD.	ISSUE PRICE	QUOTE U.S.$
1995 The Gift	6/96		39.90	40
1995 The Courtship	8/96		39.90	40

Sacred Circle - K. Randle

YEAR ISSUE	EDITION LIMIT	YEAR RETD.	ISSUE PRICE	QUOTE U.S.$
1993 Before the Hunt	95-day		29.90	30
1993 Spiritual Guardian	95-day		29.90	30
1993 Ghost Dance	95-day		32.90	33
1994 Deer Dance	95-day		32.90	33
1994 The Wolf Dance	95-day		32.90	33
1994 The Painted Hourse	95-day		34.90	35
1994 Transformation Dance	95-day		34.90	35
1994 Elk Dance	95-day		34.90	35

Sandra Kuck's Mother's Day Collection - S. Kuck

YEAR ISSUE	EDITION LIMIT	YEAR RETD.	ISSUE PRICE	QUOTE U.S.$
1995 Home is Where/Heart Is	95-day		35.00	35

Santa's Little Helpers - B. Higgins Bond

YEAR ISSUE	EDITION LIMIT	YEAR RETD.	ISSUE PRICE	QUOTE U.S.$
1994 Stocking Stuffers	95-day		24.90	25
1994 Wrapping Up the Holidays	95-day		24.90	25
1994 Not a Creature Was Stirring	95-day		24.90	25
1994 Santa's Little Helper	95-day		24.90	25
1995 Cozy Kittens	95-day		24.90	25
1995 Holiday Mischief	95-day		24.90	25

Santa's On His Way - S. Gustafson

YEAR ISSUE	EDITION LIMIT	YEAR RETD.	ISSUE PRICE	QUOTE U.S.$
1994 Checking It Twice	95-day		29.90	30
1994 Up, Up & Away	95-day		29.90	30
1995 Santa's First Stop	95-day		29.90	30
1995 Gifts for One and All	95-day		29.90	30

Signs of Spring - J. Thornbrugh

YEAR ISSUE	EDITION LIMIT	YEAR RETD.	ISSUE PRICE	QUOTE U.S.$
1994 A Family Feast	95-day		29.90	30
1995 How Fast They Grow	95-day		29.90	30
1995 Our First Home	95-day		29.90	30
1995 Awaiting New Arrivals	95-day		29.90	30

Silent Journey - D. Casey

YEAR ISSUE	EDITION LIMIT	YEAR RETD.	ISSUE PRICE	QUOTE U.S.$
1994 Where Paths Cross	95-day		29.90	30
1994 On Eagle's Wings	95-day		29.90	30
1994 Seeing the Unseen	95-day		29.90	30
1995 Where the Buffalo Roam	95-day		29.90	30
1995 Unbridled Majesty	95-day		29.90	30
1995 Wisdom Seeker	95-day		29.90	30
1995 Journey of the Wild	95-day		29.90	30

Soft Elegance - R. Iverson

YEAR ISSUE	EDITION LIMIT	YEAR RETD.	ISSUE PRICE	QUOTE U.S.$
1994 Priscilla in Pearls	95-day		29.90	30
1995 Tabitha on Taffeta	95-day		29.90	30
1995 Emily in Emeralds	95-day		29.90	30
1995 Alexandra in Amethysts	95-day		29.90	30

Some Beary Nice Places - J. Tanton

YEAR ISSUE	EDITION LIMIT	YEAR RETD.	ISSUE PRICE	QUOTE U.S.$
1994 Welcome to the Library	95-day		29.90	30
1994 Welcome to Our Country Kitchen	95-day		29.90	30
1995 Bearennial Garden	95-day		32.90	33
1995 Welcome to Our Music	95-day		32.90	33

Soul Mates - L. Bogle

YEAR ISSUE	EDITION LIMIT	YEAR RETD.	ISSUE PRICE	QUOTE U.S.$
1995 The Lovers	95-day		29.90	30
1995 The Awakening	95-day		29.90	30

Sovereigns of the Sky - G. Dieckhoner

YEAR ISSUE	EDITION LIMIT	YEAR RETD.	ISSUE PRICE	QUOTE U.S.$
1994 Spirit of Freedom	Closed	1995	39.00	39
1994 Spirit of Pride	Closed	1995	39.00	39
1994 Spirit of Valor	12/95		44.00	44
1994 Spirit of Majesty	2/96		44.00	44
1995 Spirit of Glory	95-day		44.00	44

Sovereigns of the Wild - D. Grant

YEAR ISSUE	EDITION LIMIT	YEAR RETD.	ISSUE PRICE	QUOTE U.S.$
1993 The Snow Queen	95-day		29.90	30
1994 Let Us Survive	95-day		29.90	30
1994 Cool Cats	95-day		29.90	30
1994 Siberian Snow Tigers	95-day		29.90	30
1994 African Evening	95-day		29.90	30
1994 First Outing	95-day		29.90	30

Superstars of Baseball - T. Sizemore

YEAR ISSUE	EDITION LIMIT	YEAR RETD.	ISSUE PRICE	QUOTE U.S.$
1994 Willie "Say Hey" Mays	95-day		29.90	30
1995 Carl "Yaz" Yastrzemski	95-day		29.90	30
1995 Frank "Robby" Robinson	95-day		32.90	33
1995 Bob Gibson	95-day		32.90	33

Superstars of Country Music - N. Giorgio

YEAR ISSUE	EDITION LIMIT	YEAR RETD.	ISSUE PRICE	QUOTE U.S.$
1993 Dolly Parton: I Will Always Love You	95-day		29.90	30
1993 Kenny Rogers: Sweet Music Man	95-day		29.90	30
1994 Barbara Mandrell	95-day		32.90	33
1994 Glen Campbell: Rhinestone Cowboy	95-day		32.90	33

Tale of Peter Rabbit & Benjamin Bunny - R. Akers

YEAR ISSUE	EDITION LIMIT	YEAR RETD.	ISSUE PRICE	QUOTE U.S.$
1994 A Pocket Full of Onions	3/96		39.00	39
1994 Beside His Cousin	95-day		39.00	39
1995 Round that Corner	95-day		39.00	39
1995 Safely Home	95-day		44.00	44

That's What Friends Are For - A. Isakov

YEAR ISSUE	EDITION LIMIT	YEAR RETD.	ISSUE PRICE	QUOTE U.S.$
1994 Friends Are Forever	95-day		29.90	30
1994 Friends Are Comfort	95-day		29.90	30
1994 Friends Are Loving	95-day		29.90	30
1995 Friends Are Fun	95-day		29.90	30

Through a Child's Eyes - K. Noles

YEAR ISSUE	EDITION LIMIT	YEAR RETD.	ISSUE PRICE	QUOTE U.S.$
1994 Little Butterfly	95-day		29.90	30
1995 Woodland Rose	95-day		29.90	30
1995 Treetop Wonder	95-day		29.90	30
1995 Little Red Squirrel	95-day		32.90	33
1995 Water Lily	95-day		32.90	33
1995 Prairie Song	95-day		32.90	33

Thundering Waters - F. Miller

YEAR ISSUE	EDITION LIMIT	YEAR RETD.	ISSUE PRICE	QUOTE U.S.$
1994 Niagara Falls	95-day		34.90	35
1994 Lower Falls, Yellowstone	95-day		34.90	35
1994 Bridal Veil Falls	95-day		34.90	35
1995 Havasu Falls	95-day		29.90	30

Tidings of Joy - S. Kuck

YEAR ISSUE	EDITION LIMIT	YEAR RETD.	ISSUE PRICE	QUOTE U.S.$
1994 Noel	75-day		38.00	38

Trains of the Great West - K. Randle

YEAR ISSUE	EDITION LIMIT	YEAR RETD.	ISSUE PRICE	QUOTE U.S.$
1993 Moonlit Journey	95-day		29.90	45
1993 Mountain Hideaway	95-day		29.90	44
1993 Early Morning Arrival	95-day		29.90	30
1994 The Snowy Pass	95-day		29.90	30

Triumph in the Air - H. Krebs

YEAR ISSUE	EDITION LIMIT	YEAR RETD.	ISSUE PRICE	QUOTE U.S.$
1994 Checkmate!	95-day		34.90	35
1994 One Heck of a Deflection Shot	95-day		34.90	35
1994 Hunting Fever	95-day		34.90	35
1995 Struck by Thunder	95-day		34.90	35

Twilight Memories - J. Barnes

YEAR ISSUE	EDITION LIMIT	YEAR RETD.	ISSUE PRICE	QUOTE U.S.$
1995 Winter's Twilight	95-day		29.90	30

Two's Company - S. Eide

YEAR ISSUE	EDITION LIMIT	YEAR RETD.	ISSUE PRICE	QUOTE U.S.$
1994 Golden Harvest	95-day		29.90	30
1995 Brotherly Love	95-day		29.90	30
1995 Seeing Double	95-day		29.90	30
1995 Spring Spaniels	95-day		29.90	30

Under A Snowy Veil - C. Sams

YEAR ISSUE	EDITION LIMIT	YEAR RETD.	ISSUE PRICE	QUOTE U.S.$
1995 Winter's Warmth	95-day		29.90	30
1995 Snow Mates	95-day		29.90	30
1995 Winter's Dawn	95-day		29.90	30
1995 First Snow	95-day		29.90	30

Untamed Spirits - P. Weirs

YEAR ISSUE	EDITION LIMIT	YEAR RETD.	ISSUE PRICE	QUOTE U.S.$
1993 Wild Hearts	95-day		29.90	50
1994 Breakaway	95-day		29.90	45
1994 Forever Free	95-day		29.90	30
1994 Distant Thunder	95-day		29.90	30

Untamed Wilderness - P. Weirs

YEAR ISSUE	EDITION LIMIT	YEAR RETD.	ISSUE PRICE	QUOTE U.S.$
1995 Unexpected Encounter	95-day		29.90	30

Vanishing Paradises - G. Dieckhoner

YEAR ISSUE	EDITION LIMIT	YEAR RETD.	ISSUE PRICE	QUOTE U.S.$
1993 The Rainforest	95-day		29.90	30
1993 The Panda's World	95-day		29.90	30
1993 Splendors of India	95-day		29.90	30
1993 An African Safari	95-day		29.90	30

Visions from Eagle Ridge - D. Casey

YEAR ISSUE	EDITION LIMIT	YEAR RETD.	ISSUE PRICE	QUOTE U.S.$
1995 Assembly of Pride	95-day		29.90	30

Visions of Glory - D. Cook

YEAR ISSUE	EDITION LIMIT	YEAR RETD.	ISSUE PRICE	QUOTE U.S.$
1995 Iwo Jima	95-day		29.90	30

Visions of Our Lady - H. Garrido

YEAR ISSUE	EDITION LIMIT	YEAR RETD.	ISSUE PRICE	QUOTE U.S.$
1994 Our Lady of Lourdes	95-day		29.90	30
1994 Our Lady of Medjugorje	95-day		29.90	30
1994 Our Lady of Fatima	95-day		29.90	30
1994 Our Lady of Guadeloupe	95-day		29.90	30
1994 Our Lady of Grace	95-day		29.90	30
1994 Our Lady of Mt. Carmel	95-day		29.90	30

Visions of the Sacred - D. Stanley

YEAR ISSUE	EDITION LIMIT	YEAR RETD.	ISSUE PRICE	QUOTE U.S.$
1994 Snow Rider	95-day		29.90	30
1994 Spring's Messenger	95-day		29.90	30
1994 The Cheyenne Prophet	95-day		32.90	33
1995 Buffalo Caller	95-day		32.90	33
1995 Journey of Harmony	95-day		32.90	33

A Visit from St. Nick - C. Jackson

YEAR ISSUE	EDITION LIMIT	YEAR RETD.	ISSUE PRICE	QUOTE U.S.$
1995 Twas the Night Before Christmas	5/96		49.00	49
1995 Up to the Housetop	9/96		49.00	49

A Visit to Brambly Hedge - J. Barklem

YEAR ISSUE	EDITION LIMIT	YEAR RETD.	ISSUE PRICE	QUOTE U.S.$
1994 Summer Story	Closed	1995	39.90	40
1994 Spring Story	Closed	1995	39.90	40
1994 Autumn Story	Closed	1995	39.90	40

YEAR ISSUE		EDITION LIMIT	YEAR RETD.	ISSUE PRICE	QUOTE U.S.$
1994	Winter Story	12/95		39.90	40

Warm Country Moments - M.A. Lasher

YEAR ISSUE		EDITION LIMIT	YEAR RETD.	ISSUE PRICE	QUOTE U.S.$
1994	Mabel's Sunny Retreat	95-day		29.90	30
1994	Annebelle's Simple Pleasures	95-day		29.90	30
1994	Harriet's Loving Touch	95-day		29.90	30
1994	Emily and Alice in a Jam	95-day		29.90	30
1995	Hanna's Secret Garden	95-day		29.90	30

Welcome to the Neighborhood - B. Mock

YEAR ISSUE		EDITION LIMIT	YEAR RETD.	ISSUE PRICE	QUOTE U.S.$
1994	Ivy Lane	95-day		29.90	30
1994	Daffodil Drive	95-day		29.90	30
1995	Lilac Lane	95-day		34.90	35
1995	Tulip Terrace	95-day		34.90	35

When All Hearts Come Home - J. Barnes

YEAR ISSUE		EDITION LIMIT	YEAR RETD.	ISSUE PRICE	QUOTE U.S.$
1993	Oh Christmas Tree	95-day		29.90	30
1993	Night Before Christmas	95-day		29.90	30
1993	Comfort and Joy	95-day		29.90	30
1993	Grandpa's Farm	95-day		29.90	30
1993	Peace on Earth	95-day		29.90	30
1993	Night Departure	95-day		29.90	30
1993	Supper and Small Talk	95-day		29.90	30
1993	Christmas Wish	95-day		29.90	30

When Dreams Blossom - R. McGinnis

YEAR ISSUE		EDITION LIMIT	YEAR RETD.	ISSUE PRICE	QUOTE U.S.$
1994	Dreams to Gather	95-day		29.90	30
1994	Where Friends Dream	95-day		29.90	30
1994	The Sweetest of Dreams	95-day		32.90	33
1994	Dreams of Poetry	95-day		32.90	33
1995	A Place to Dream	95-day		32.90	33
1995	Dreaming of You	95-day		32.90	33

Where Eagles Soar - F. Mittelstadt

YEAR ISSUE		EDITION LIMIT	YEAR RETD.	ISSUE PRICE	QUOTE U.S.$
1994	On Freedom's Wing	95-day		29.90	30
1994	Allegiance with the Wind	95-day		29.90	30
1995	Lakeside Eagles	95-day		29.90	30
1995	Lighthouse Eagles	95-day		29.90	30
1995	Noble Legacy	95-day		29.90	30

Windows on a World of Song - K. Daniel

YEAR ISSUE		EDITION LIMIT	YEAR RETD.	ISSUE PRICE	QUOTE U.S.$
1993	The Library: Cardinals	95-day		34.90	35
1993	The Den: Black-Capped Chickadees	95-day		34.90	35
1993	The Bedroom: Bluebirds	95-day		34.90	35
1994	The Kitchen: Goldfinches	95-day		34.90	35

Winnie the Pooh: 3D - C. Jackson

YEAR ISSUE		EDITION LIMIT	YEAR RETD.	ISSUE PRICE	QUOTE U.S.$
1994	Time For a Little Something	2/96		39.90	40
1995	Bouncing Tiggers Do Best	4/96		39.90	40

Winter Shadows - N. Glazier

YEAR ISSUE		EDITION LIMIT	YEAR RETD.	ISSUE PRICE	QUOTE U.S.$
1995	Canyon Moon	95-day		29.90	30
1995	Shadows of Gray	95-day		29.90	30

Wish You Were Here - T. Kinkade

YEAR ISSUE		EDITION LIMIT	YEAR RETD.	ISSUE PRICE	QUOTE U.S.$
1994	End of a Perfect Day	95-day		29.90	30
1994	A Quiet Evening/Riverlodge	95-day		29.90	30
1994	Soft Morning Light	95-day		29.90	30

Woodland Tranquility - G. Alexander

YEAR ISSUE		EDITION LIMIT	YEAR RETD.	ISSUE PRICE	QUOTE U.S.$
1994	Winter's Calm	95-day		29.90	30
1995	Frosty Morn	95-day		29.90	30
1995	Crossing Boundaries	95-day		29.90	30

Woodland Wings - J. Hansel

YEAR ISSUE		EDITION LIMIT	YEAR RETD.	ISSUE PRICE	QUOTE U.S.$
1994	Twilight Flight	95-day		34.90	35
1994	Gliding on Gilded Skies	95-day		34.90	35
1994	Sunset Voyage	95-day		34.90	35
1995	Peaceful Journey	95-day		34.90	35

The World of the Eagle - J. Hansel

YEAR ISSUE		EDITION LIMIT	YEAR RETD.	ISSUE PRICE	QUOTE U.S.$
1994	Sentinel of the Night	95-day		29.90	50
1994	Silent Guard	95-day		29.90	55
1994	Night Flyer	95-day		32.90	33
1995	Midnight Duty	95-day		32.90	55

A World of Wildlife: Celebrating Earth Day - T. Clausnitzer

YEAR ISSUE		EDITION LIMIT	YEAR RETD.	ISSUE PRICE	QUOTE U.S.$
1995	A Delicate Balance	95-day		29.90	30

WWII: A Remembrance - J. Griffin

YEAR ISSUE		EDITION LIMIT	YEAR RETD.	ISSUE PRICE	QUOTE U.S.$
1994	D-Day	95-day		29.90	30
1994	The Battle of Midway	95-day		29.90	30
1994	The Battle of The Bulge	95-day		32.90	33
1995	Battle of the Philippines	95-day		32.90	33
1995	Doolittle's Raid Over Tokyo	95-day		32.90	33

Cavanagh Group Intl.

Coca-Cola Brand Heritage Collection - Various

YEAR ISSUE		EDITION LIMIT	YEAR RETD.	ISSUE PRICE	QUOTE U.S.$
1995	Boy Fishing - N. Rockwell	5,000		60.00	60
1995	Hilda Clark with Roses - CGI	5,000		60.00	60
1994	Santa at His Desk - Sundblom	5,000		60.00	60

Dave Grossman Creations

Emmett Kelly Plates - B. Leighton-Jones

YEAR ISSUE		EDITION LIMIT	YEAR RETD.	ISSUE PRICE	QUOTE U.S.$
1986	Christmas Carol	Yr.Iss.		20.00	400
1987	Christmas Wreath	Yr.Iss.		20.00	225
1988	Christmas Dinner	Yr.Iss.		20.00	49
1989	Christmas Feast	Yr.Iss.		20.00	39
1990	Just What I Needed	Yr.Iss.		24.00	39
1991	Emmett The Snowman	Yr.Iss.		25.00	45
1992	Christmas Tunes	Yr.Iss.		25.00	35
1993	Downhill-Christmas Plate	Yr.Iss.		30.00	30
1994	Holiday Skater EKP-94	Yr.Iss.		30.00	30

Saturday Evening Post Collection - Rockwell-Inspired

YEAR ISSUE		EDITION LIMIT	YEAR RETD.	ISSUE PRICE	QUOTE U.S.$
1991	Downhill Daring BRP-91	Yr.Iss.		25.00	25
1991	Missed BRP-101	Yr.Iss.		25.00	25
1992	Choosin Up BRP-102	Yr.Iss.		25.00	25

Dave Grossman Designs

Norman Rockwell Collection - Rockwell-Inspired

YEAR ISSUE		EDITION LIMIT	YEAR RETD.	ISSUE PRICE	QUOTE U.S.$
1979	Leapfrog NRP-79	Retrd.		50.00	50
1980	Lovers NRP-80	Retrd.		60.00	60
1981	Dreams of Long Ago NRP-81	Retrd.		60.00	60
1982	Doctor and Doll NRP-82	Retrd.		65.00	95
1983	Circus NRP-83	Retrd.		65.00	65
1984	Visit With Rockwell NRP-84	Retrd.		65.00	65
1980	Christmas Trio RXP-80	Retrd.		75.00	75
1981	Santa's Good Boys RXP-81	Retrd.		75.00	75
1982	Faces of Christmas RXP-82	Retrd.		75.00	75
1983	Christmas Chores RXP-83	Retrd.		75.00	75
1984	Tiny Tim RXP-84	Retrd.		75.00	75
1980	Back To School RMP-80	Retrd.		24.00	24
1981	No Swimming RMP-81	Retrd.		25.00	25
1982	Love Letter RMP-82	Retrd.		27.00	30
1983	Doctor and Doll RMP-83	Retrd.		27.00	27
1984	Big Moment RMP-84	Retrd.		27.00	27
1979	Butterboy RP-01	Retrd.		40.00	40
1982	American Mother RGP-42	Retrd.		45.00	45
1983	Dreamboat RGP-83	Retrd.		24.00	30
1978	Young Doctor RDP-26	Retrd.		50.00	65

Norman Rockwell Collection-Boy Scout Plates - Rockwell-Inspired

YEAR ISSUE		EDITION LIMIT	YEAR RETD.	ISSUE PRICE	QUOTE U.S.$
1981	Can't Wait BSP-01	Retrd.		30.00	45
1982	Guiding Hand BSP-02	Retrd.		30.00	35
1983	Tomorrow's Leader BSP-03	Retrd.		30.00	45

Norman Rockwell Collection-Huck Finn Plates - Rockwell-Inspired

YEAR ISSUE		EDITION LIMIT	YEAR RETD.	ISSUE PRICE	QUOTE U.S.$
1979	Secret HFP-01	Retrd.		40.00	40
1980	ListeningHFP-02	Retrd.		40.00	40
1980	No Kings HFP-03	Retrd.		40.00	40
1981	Snake Escapes HFP-04	Retrd.		40.00	40

Norman Rockwell Collection-Tom Sawyer Plates - Rockwell-Inspired

YEAR ISSUE		EDITION LIMIT	YEAR RETD.	ISSUE PRICE	QUOTE U.S.$
1975	Whitewashing the Fence TSP-01	Retrd.		26.00	35
1976	First Smoke TSP-02	Retrd.		26.00	35
1977	Take Your Medicine TSP-03	Retrd.		26.00	40
1978	Lost in Cave TSP-04	Retrd.		26.00	40

Delphi

The Beatles '67-'70 - D. Sivavec

YEAR ISSUE		EDITION LIMIT	YEAR RETD.	ISSUE PRICE	QUOTE U.S.$
1992	Sgt. Pepper the 25th Anniversary	150-day		27.75	28
1992	All You Need is Love	150-day		27.75	28
1993	Magical Mystery Tour	150-day		30.75	31
1993	Hey Jude	150-day		30.75	31
1993	Abbey Road	150-day		30.75	31
1993	Let It Be	150-day		30.75	31

The Beatles Collection - N. Giorgio

YEAR ISSUE		EDITION LIMIT	YEAR RETD.	ISSUE PRICE	QUOTE U.S.$
1991	The Beatles, Live In Concert	150-day		24.75	40-50
1991	Hello America	150-day		24.75	50-60
1991	A Hard Day's Night	150-day		27.75	50-60
1992	Beatles '65	150-day		27.75	45
1992	Help	150-day		27.75	45
1992	The Beatles at Shea Stadium	150-day		29.75	30
1992	Rubber Soul	150-day		29.75	30
1992	Yesterday and Today	150-day		29.75	30

Commemorating The King - M. Stutzman

YEAR ISSUE		EDITION LIMIT	YEAR RETD.	ISSUE PRICE	QUOTE U.S.$
1993	The Rock and Roll Legend	95-day		29.75	35-55
1993	Las Vegas, Live	95-day		29.75	50-60
1993	Blues and Black Leather	95-day		29.75	30
1993	Private Presley	95-day		29.75	30
1993	Golden Boy	95-day		29.75	30
1993	Screen Idol	95-day		29.75	30
1993	Outstanding Young Man	95-day		29.75	30
1993	The Tiger: Faith, Spirit & Discipline	95-day		29.75	30

Dream Machines - P. Palma

YEAR ISSUE		EDITION LIMIT	YEAR RETD.	ISSUE PRICE	QUOTE U.S.$
1988	'56 T-Bird	150-day		24.75	25
1988	'57 'Vette	150-day		24.75	25
1989	'58 Biarritz	150-day		27.75	28
1989	'56 Continental	150-day		27.75	28
1989	'57 Bel Air	150-day		27.75	50
1989	'57 Chrysler 300C	150-day		27.75	30

Elvis on the Big Screen - B. Emmett

YEAR ISSUE		EDITION LIMIT	YEAR RETD.	ISSUE PRICE	QUOTE U.S.$
1992	Elvis in Loving You	150-day		29.75	45
1992	Elvis in G.I. Blues	150-day		29.75	55
1992	Viva Las Vegas	150-day		32.75	70
1993	Elvis in Blue Hawaii	150-day		32.75	40
1993	Elvis in Jailhouse Rock	150-day		32.75	45
1993	Elvis in Spinout	150-day		34.75	43
1993	Elvis in Speedway	150-day		34.75	35
1993	Elvis in Harum Scarum	150-day		34.75	35

The Elvis Presley Hit Parade - N. Giorgio

YEAR ISSUE		EDITION LIMIT	YEAR RETD.	ISSUE PRICE	QUOTE U.S.$
1992	Heartbreak Hotel	150-day		29.75	30
1992	Blue Suede Shoes	150-day		29.75	30
1992	Hound Dog	150-day		32.75	33
1992	Blue Christmas	150-day		32.75	33
1992	Return to Sender	150-day		32.75	33
1993	Teddy Bear	150-day		34.75	35
1993	Always on My Mind	150-day		34.75	35
1993	Mystery Train	150-day		34.75	35
1993	Blue Moon of Kentucky	150-day		34.75	35
1993	Wear My Ring Around Your Neck	150-day		36.75	37
1993	Suspicious Minds	150-day		36.75	37
1993	Peace in the Valley	150-day		36.75	37

Elvis Presley: In Performance - B. Emmett

YEAR ISSUE		EDITION LIMIT	YEAR RETD.	ISSUE PRICE	QUOTE U.S.$
1990	'68 Comeback Special	150-day		24.75	52-60
1991	King of Las Vegas	150-day		24.75	70
1991	Aloha From Hawaii	150-day		27.75	65
1991	Back in Tupelo, 1956	150-day		27.75	70
1991	If I Can Dream	150-day		27.75	50-60
1991	Benefit for the USS Arizona	150-day		29.75	50-60
1991	Madison Square Garden, 1972	150-day		29.75	60-70
1991	Tampa, 1955	150-day		29.75	50-60
1991	Concert in Baton Rouge, 1974	150-day		29.75	50-60
1992	On Stage in Wichita, 1974	150-day		31.75	50
1992	In the Spotlight: Hawaii, '72	150-day		31.75	48
1992	Tour Finale: Indianapolis 1977	150-day		31.75	43

Elvis Presley: Looking At A Legend - B. Emmett

YEAR ISSUE		EDITION LIMIT	YEAR RETD.	ISSUE PRICE	QUOTE U.S.$
1988	Elvis at/Gates of Graceland	150-day		24.75	90
1989	Jailhouse Rock	150-day		24.75	85
1989	The Memphis Flash	150-day		27.75	45-60
1989	Homecoming	150-day		27.75	45-60
1990	Elvis and Gladys	150-day		27.75	60
1990	A Studio Session	150-day		27.75	35-45
1990	Elvis in Hollywood	150-day		29.75	60
1990	Elvis on His Harley	150-day		29.75	70
1990	Stage Door Autographs	150-day		29.75	50
1991	Christmas at Graceland	150-day		32.75	80
1991	Entering Sun Studio	150-day		32.75	55
1991	Going for the Black Belt	150-day		32.75	50
1991	His Hand in Mine	150-day		32.75	35-45
1991	Letters From Fans	150-day		32.75	40
1991	Closing the Deal	150-day		34.75	40
1992	Elvis Returns to the Stage	150-day		34.75	45

Fabulous Cars of the '50's - G. Angelini

YEAR ISSUE		EDITION LIMIT	YEAR RETD.	ISSUE PRICE	QUOTE U.S.$
1993	'57 Red Corvette	95-day		24.75	40-50
1993	'57 White T-Bird	95-day		24.75	85
1993	'57 Blue Belair	95-day		27.75	60
1993	'59 Cadillac	95-day		27.75	45
1993	'56 Lincoln Premier	95-day		27.75	45
1994	'59 Red Ford Fairlane	95-day		27.75	45

In the Footsteps of the King - D. Sivavec

YEAR ISSUE		EDITION LIMIT	YEAR RETD.	ISSUE PRICE	QUOTE U.S.$
1993	Graceland: Memphis, Tenn.	95-day		27.75	40
1994	Elvis' Birthplace: Tupelo, Miss	95-day		29.75	30
1994	Day Job: Memphis, Tenn.	95-day		32.75	33
1994	Flying Circle G. Ranch: Walls, Miss.	95-day		32.75	33
1994	The Lauderdale Courts	95-day		32.75	33
1995	Patriotic Soldier	95-day		34.75	35

Indiana Jones - V. Gadino

YEAR ISSUE		EDITION LIMIT	YEAR RETD.	ISSUE PRICE	QUOTE U.S.$
1989	Indiana Jones	150-day		24.75	25-35
1989	Indiana Jones and His Dad	150-day		24.75	45
1990	Indiana Jones/Dr. Schneider	150-day		27.75	35
1990	A Family Discussion	150-day		27.75	50
1990	Young Indiana Jones	150-day		27.75	50
1991	Indiana Jones/The Holy Grail	150-day		27.75	60

Legends of Baseball - Various

YEAR ISSUE		EDITION LIMIT	YEAR RETD.	ISSUE PRICE	QUOTE U.S.$
1992	Babe Ruth: The Called Shot B. Benger	150-day		24.95	30
1992	Lou Gehrig: The Luckiest Man - J. Barson	150-day		24.75	25
1993	Ty Cobb: The Georgia Peach J. Barson	150-day		27.95	28
1993	Cy Young: The Perfect Game J. Barson	150-day		27.75	28
1993	Roger Hornsby: .424 Season J. Barson	150-day		27.75	28
1993	Honus Wagner: Flying Dutchman - J. Barson	150-day		29.75	30
1993	Jimmie Fox: The Beast J. Barson	150-day		29.75	30
1993	Walter Johnson: The Shutout J. Barson	150-day		29.75	30
1993	Tris Speaker: The Gray Eagle - J. Barson	150-day		29.75	30
1994	Christy Matthewson: 1905 W. Series - J. Barson	150-day		31.75	32
1994	Mel Ott: Master Melvin J. Barson	150-day		31.75	32
1994	Lefty Grove: His Greatest Season - J. Barson	150-day		31.75	32
1994	Shoeless Joe Jackson: Where Triples Go to Die - J. Barson	150-day		31.75	32
1995	Pie Traynor: Pittsburgh Champ J. Barson	150-day		33.75	32
1995	Mickey Cochrane: Black Mike J. Barson	150-day		33.75	32

YEAR ISSUE		EDITION LIMIT	YEAR RETD.	ISSUE PRICE	QUOTE U.S.$
1995	Grover Alexander - J. Barson	150-day		33.75	32

The Magic of Marilyn - C. Notarile

YEAR ISSUE		EDITION LIMIT	YEAR RETD.	ISSUE PRICE	QUOTE U.S.$
1992	For Our Boys in Korea, 1954	150-day		24.75	30
1992	Opening Night	150-day		24.75	40
1993	Rising Star	150-day		27.75	55
1992	Stopping Traffic	150-day		27.75	28
1992	Strasberg's Student	150-day		27.75	28
1993	Photo Opportunity	150-day		29.75	30
1993	Shining Star	150-day		29.75	30
1993	Curtain Call	150-day		29.75	30

The Marilyn Monroe Collection - C. Notarile

YEAR ISSUE		EDITION LIMIT	YEAR RETD.	ISSUE PRICE	QUOTE U.S.$
1989	Marilyn Monroe/7 Year Itch	150-day		24.75	60-80
1990	Diamonds/Girls Best Friend	150-day		24.75	85-90
1991	Marilyn Monroe/River of No Return	150-day		27.75	100
1992	How to Marry a Millionaire	150-day		27.75	95
1992	There's No Business/Show Business	150-day		27.75	65-75
1992	Marilyn Monroe in Niagra	150-day		29.75	80
1992	My Heart Belongs to Daddy	150-day		29.75	50-60
1992	Marilyn Monroe as Cherie in Bus Stop	150-day		29.75	75
1992	Marilyn Monroe in All About Eve	150-day		29.75	50-60
1992	Marilyn Monroe in Monkey Business	150-day		31.75	50-60
1992	Marilyn Monroe in Don't Bother to Knock	150-day		31.75	75
1992	Marilyn Monroe in We're Not Married	150-day		31.75	65

Portraits of the King - D. Zwierz

YEAR ISSUE		EDITION LIMIT	YEAR RETD.	ISSUE PRICE	QUOTE U.S.$
1991	Love Me Tender	150-day		27.75	45
1991	Are You Lonesome Tonight?	150-day		27.75	35
1991	I'm Yours	150-day		30.75	31
1991	Treat Me Nice	150-day		30.75	35
1992	The Wonder of You	150-day		30.75	31
1992	You're a Heartbreaker	150-day		32.75	33
1992	Just Because	150-day		32.75	33
1992	Follow That Dream	150-day		32.75	33

Take Me Out To The Ballgame - D. Henderson

YEAR ISSUE		EDITION LIMIT	YEAR RETD.	ISSUE PRICE	QUOTE U.S.$
1993	Wrigley Field: The Friendly Confines	95-day		29.75	30
1993	Yankee Stadium: House that Ruth Built	95-day		29.75	30
1993	Fenway Park: Home of the Green Monster	95-day		32.75	33
1993	Briggs Stadium: Home of the Tigers	95-day		32.75	33
1993	Comiskey Park: Home of the White Sox	95-day		32.75	33
1994	Cleveland Stadium: Home of the Indians	95-day		34.75	35
1994	Memorial Stadium: Home of the Orioles	95-day		34.75	35
1994	County Stadium: Home of the 1957 Champions	95-day		34.75	35
1994	Ebbets Field: Home of the Dodgers	95-day		34.75	35

Take Me Out to the Ballgame - D. Henderson

YEAR ISSUE		EDITION LIMIT	YEAR RETD.	ISSUE PRICE	QUOTE U.S.$
1995	Shibe Park	95-day		36.75	37

Department 56

A Christmas Carol - R. Innocenti

YEAR ISSUE		EDITION LIMIT	YEAR RETD.	ISSUE PRICE	QUOTE U.S.$
1991	The Cratchit's Christmas Pudding, 5706-1	18,000	1991	60.00	60-80
1992	Marley's Ghost Appears To Scrooge, 5721-5	18,000	1992	60.00	65
1993	The Spirit of Christmas Present, 5722-3	18,000	1993	60.00	60
1994	Visions of Christmas Past 5723-1	18,000	1994	60.00	60

Dickens' Village - Department 56

YEAR ISSUE		EDITION LIMIT	YEAR RETD.	ISSUE PRICE	QUOTE U.S.$
1987	Dickens' Village Porcelain Plates, 5917-0 Set of 4	Closed	1990	140.00	220

Duncan Royale

History of Santa Claus I - S. Morton

YEAR ISSUE		EDITION LIMIT	YEAR RETD.	ISSUE PRICE	QUOTE U.S.$
1985	Medieval	Retrd.	N/A	40.00	75
1985	Kris Kringle	Retrd.	N/A	40.00	75
1985	Pioneer	10,000	N/A	40.00	40
1986	Russian	Retrd.	N/A	40.00	65
1986	Soda Pop	Retrd.	N/A	40.00	75
1986	Civil War	10,000	N/A	40.00	40
1986	Nast	Retrd.	N/A	40.00	75
1987	St. Nicholas	Retrd.	N/A	40.00	75
1987	Dedt Moroz	10,000	N/A	40.00	45
1987	Black Peter	10,000	N/A	40.00	60
1987	Victorian	Retrd.	N/A	40.00	45
1987	Wassail	Retrd.	N/A	40.00	45
XX	Collection of 12 Plates	Retrd.	N/A	480.00	480

Edna Hibel Studios

Allegro - E. Hibel

YEAR ISSUE		EDITION LIMIT	YEAR RETD.	ISSUE PRICE	QUOTE U.S.$
1978	Plate & Book	7,500		120.00	150

Arte Ovale - E. Hibel

YEAR ISSUE		EDITION LIMIT	YEAR RETD.	ISSUE PRICE	QUOTE U.S.$
1980	Takara, gold	300		1000.00	4200
1980	Takara, blanco	700		450.00	1200
1980	Takara, cobalt blue	1,000		595.00	2350
1984	Taro-kun, gold	300		1000.00	2700
1984	Taro-kun, blanco	700		450.00	825
1984	Taro-kun, cobalt blue	1,000		995.00	1050

Christmas Annual - E. Hibel

YEAR ISSUE		EDITION LIMIT	YEAR RETD.	ISSUE PRICE	QUOTE U.S.$
1985	The Angels' Message	Yr.Iss.		45.00	225
1986	Gift of the Magi	Yr.Iss.		45.00	275
1987	Flight Into Egypt	Yr.Iss.		49.00	250
1988	Adoration of the Shepherds	Yr.Iss.		49.00	175
1989	Peaceful Kingdom	Yr.Iss.		49.00	165
1990	The Nativity	Yr.Iss.		49.00	125-150

David Series - E. Hibel

YEAR ISSUE		EDITION LIMIT	YEAR RETD.	ISSUE PRICE	QUOTE U.S.$
1979	Wedding of David & Bathsheba	5,000		250.00	650
1980	David, Bathsheba & Solomon	5,000		275.00	425
1982	David the King	5,000		275.00	295
1982	David the King, cobalt A/P	25		275.00	1200
1984	Bathsheba	5,000		275.00	295
1984	Bathsheba, cobalt A/P	100		275.00	1200

Edna Hibel Holiday - E. Hibel

YEAR ISSUE		EDITION LIMIT	YEAR RETD.	ISSUE PRICE	QUOTE U.S.$
1991	The First Holiday	Yr.Iss.		49.00	85
1991	The First Holiday, gold	1,000		99.00	150
1992	The Christmas Rose	Yr.Iss.		49.00	70
1992	The Christmas Rose, gold	1,000		99.00	100-125

Eroica - E. Hibel

YEAR ISSUE		EDITION LIMIT	YEAR RETD.	ISSUE PRICE	QUOTE U.S.$
1990	Compassion	10,000		49.50	65
1992	Darya	10,000		49.50	50

Famous Women & Children - E. Hibel

YEAR ISSUE		EDITION LIMIT	YEAR RETD.	ISSUE PRICE	QUOTE U.S.$
1980	Pharaoh's Daughter & Moses, gold	2,500		350.00	625
1980	Pharaoh's Daughter & Moses, cobalt blue	500		350.00	1350
1982	Cornelia & Her Jewels, gold	2,500		350.00	495
1982	Cornelia & Her Jewels, cobalt blue	500		350.00	350
1982	Anna & The Children of the King of Siam, gold	2,500		350.00	495
1982	Anna & The Children of the King of Siam, colbalt blue	500		350.00	1350
1984	Mozart & The Empress Marie Theresa, gold	2,500		350.00	395
1984	Mozart & The Empress Marie Theresa, cobalt blue	500		350.00	975

Flower Girl Annual - E. Hibel

YEAR ISSUE		EDITION LIMIT	YEAR RETD.	ISSUE PRICE	QUOTE U.S.$
1985	Lily	15,000		79.00	300
1986	Iris	15,000		79.00	225
1987	Rose	15,000		79.00	175
1988	Camellia	15,000		79.00	165
1989	Peony	15,000		79.00	100-125
1992	Wisteria	15,000		79.00	90

International Mother Love French - E. Hibel

YEAR ISSUE		EDITION LIMIT	YEAR RETD.	ISSUE PRICE	QUOTE U.S.$
1985	Yvette Avec Ses Enfants	5,000		125.00	225
1991	Liberte, Egalite, Fraternite	5,000		95.00	95

International Mother Love German - E. Hibel

YEAR ISSUE		EDITION LIMIT	YEAR RETD.	ISSUE PRICE	QUOTE U.S.$
1982	Gesa Und Kinder	5,000		195.00	195
1983	Alexandra Und Kinder	5,000		195.00	195

March of Dimes: Our Children Our Future - E. Hibel

YEAR ISSUE		EDITION LIMIT	YEAR RETD.	ISSUE PRICE	QUOTE U.S.$
1990	A Time To Embrace	150-day		29.00	29

Mother and Child - E. Hibel

YEAR ISSUE		EDITION LIMIT	YEAR RETD.	ISSUE PRICE	QUOTE U.S.$
1973	Colette & Child	15,000		40.00	725
1974	Sayuri & Child	15,000		40.00	425
1975	Kristina & Child	15,000		50.00	400
1976	Marilyn & Child	15,000		55.00	400
1977	Lucia & Child	15,000		60.00	350
1981	Kathleen & Child	15,000		85.00	275

Mother's Day - E. Hibel

YEAR ISSUE		EDITION LIMIT	YEAR RETD.	ISSUE PRICE	QUOTE U.S.$
1992	Molly & Annie	Yr.Iss.		39.00	70-100
1992	Molly & Annie, gold	2,500		95.00	150
1992	Molly & Annie, platinum	500		275.00	275

Mother's Day Annual - E. Hibel

YEAR ISSUE		EDITION LIMIT	YEAR RETD.	ISSUE PRICE	QUOTE U.S.$
1984	Abby & Lisa	Yr.Iss.		29.50	400
1985	Erica & Jamie	Yr.Iss.		29.50	250
1986	Emily & Jennifer	Yr.Iss.		29.50	150-300
1987	Catherine & Heather	Yr.Iss.		34.50	200
1988	Sarah & Tess	Yr.Iss.		34.90	175
1989	Jessica & Kate	Yr.Iss.		34.90	100
1990	Elizabeth, Jorday & Janie	Yr.Iss.		36.90	95
1991	Michele & Anna	Yr.Iss.		36.90	65
1992	Olivia & Hildy	Yr.Iss.		39.90	80

Museum Commemorative - E. Hibel

YEAR ISSUE		EDITION LIMIT	YEAR RETD.	ISSUE PRICE	QUOTE U.S.$
1977	Flower Girl of Provence	12,750		175.00	425
1980	Diana	3,000		350.00	395

Nobility Of Children - E. Hibel

YEAR ISSUE		EDITION LIMIT	YEAR RETD.	ISSUE PRICE	QUOTE U.S.$
1976	La Contessa Isabella	12,750		120.00	425
1977	Le Marquis Maurice Pierre	12,750		120.00	225
1978	Baronesse Johanna-Maryke Van Vollendam Tot Marken	12,750		130.00	175
1979	Chief Red Feather	12,750		140.00	200

Nordic Families - E. Hibel

YEAR ISSUE		EDITION LIMIT	YEAR RETD.	ISSUE PRICE	QUOTE U.S.$
1987	A Tender Moment	7,500		79.00	95

Oriental Gold - E. Hibel

YEAR ISSUE		EDITION LIMIT	YEAR RETD.	ISSUE PRICE	QUOTE U.S.$
1975	Yasuko	2,000		275.00	3000
1976	Mr. Obata	2,000		275.00	2100
1978	Sakura	2,000		295.00	1800
1979	Michio	2,000		325.00	1500

Scandinavian Mother & Child - E. Hibel

YEAR ISSUE		EDITION LIMIT	YEAR RETD.	ISSUE PRICE	QUOTE U.S.$
1987	Pearl & Flowers	7,500		55.00	225
1989	Anemone & Violet	7,500		75.00	95
1990	Holly & Talia	7,500		75.00	85

To Life Annual - E. Hibel

YEAR ISSUE		EDITION LIMIT	YEAR RETD.	ISSUE PRICE	QUOTE U.S.$
1986	Golden's Child	5,000		99.00	275
1987	Triumph! Everyone A Winner	19,500		55.00	60
1988	The Whole Earth Bloomed as a Sacred Place	15,000		85.00	60
1989	Lovers of the Summer Palace	5,000		65.00	75
1992	People of the Fields	5,000		49.00	49

Tribute To All Children - E. Hibel

YEAR ISSUE		EDITION LIMIT	YEAR RETD.	ISSUE PRICE	QUOTE U.S.$
1984	Giselle	19,500		55.00	95
1984	Gerard	19,500		55.00	95
1985	Wendy	19,500		55.00	125
1986	Todd	19,500		55.00	125

The World I Love - E. Hibel

YEAR ISSUE		EDITION LIMIT	YEAR RETD.	ISSUE PRICE	QUOTE U.S.$
1981	Leah's Family	17,500		85.00	225
1982	Kaylin	17,500		85.00	375
1983	Edna's Music	17,500		85.00	195
1983	O' Hana	17,500		85.00	195

Edwin M. Knowles

Aesop's Fables - M. Hampshire

YEAR ISSUE		EDITION LIMIT	YEAR RETD.	ISSUE PRICE	QUOTE U.S.$
1988	The Goose That Laid the Golden Egg	150-day		27.90	28
1988	The Hare and the Tortoise	150-day		27.90	28
1988	The Fox and the Grapes	150-day		30.90	31
1989	The Lion And The Mouse	150-day		30.90	35
1989	The Milk Maid And Her Pail	150-day		30.90	32
1989	The Jay And The Peacock	150-day		30.90	31

American Innocents - Marsten/Mandrajji

YEAR ISSUE		EDITION LIMIT	YEAR RETD.	ISSUE PRICE	QUOTE U.S.$
1986	Abigail in the Rose Garden	100-day		19.50	20
1986	Ann by the Terrace	100-day		19.50	20
1986	Ellen and John in the Parlor	100-day		19.50	20
1986	William on the Rocking Horse	100-day		19.50	46

The American Journey - M. Kunstler

YEAR ISSUE		EDITION LIMIT	YEAR RETD.	ISSUE PRICE	QUOTE U.S.$
1987	Westward Ho	150-day		29.90	30
1988	Kitchen With a View	150-day		29.90	30
1988	Crossing the River	150-day		29.90	30
1988	Christmas at the New Cabin	150-day		29.90	30

Americana Holidays - D. Spaulding

YEAR ISSUE		EDITION LIMIT	YEAR RETD.	ISSUE PRICE	QUOTE U.S.$
1978	Fourth of July	Yr.Iss.		26.00	26
1979	Thanksgiving	Yr.Iss.		26.00	26
1980	Easter	Yr.Iss.		26.00	26
1981	Valentine's Day	Yr.Iss.		26.00	26
1982	Father's Day	Yr.Iss.		26.00	26
1983	Christmas	Yr.Iss.		26.00	26
1984	Mother's Day	Yr.Iss.		26.00	27

Amy Brackenbury's Cat Tales - A. Brackenbury

YEAR ISSUE		EDITION LIMIT	YEAR RETD.	ISSUE PRICE	QUOTE U.S.$
1987	A Chance Meeting: White American Shorthairs	150-day		21.50	30
1987	Gone Fishing: Maine Coons	150-day		21.50	40
1988	Strawberries and Cream: Cream Persians	150-day		24.90	40
1988	Flower Bed: British Shorthairs	150-day		24.90	25
1988	Kittens and Mittens: Silver Tabbies	150-day		24.90	25
1988	All Wrapped Up: Himalayans	150-day		24.90	45

Annie - W. Chambers

YEAR ISSUE		EDITION LIMIT	YEAR RETD.	ISSUE PRICE	QUOTE U.S.$
1983	Annie and Sandy	100-day		19.00	19
1983	Daddy Warbucks	100-day		19.00	19
1983	Annie and Grace	100-day		19.00	19
1984	Annie and the Orphans	100-day		21.00	21
1985	Tomorrow	100-day		21.00	21
1986	Annie and Miss Hannigan	100-day		21.00	21
1986	Annie, Lily and Rooster	100-day		24.00	30
1986	Grand Finale	100-day		24.00	25

Baby Owls of North America - J. Thornbrugh

YEAR ISSUE		EDITION LIMIT	YEAR RETD.	ISSUE PRICE	QUOTE U.S.$
1991	Peek-A-Whoo:Screech Owls	150-day		27.90	37
1991	Forty Winks: Saw-Whet Owls	150-day		29.90	40
1991	The Tree House: Northern Pygmy Owls	150-day		30.90	45
1991	Three of a Kind: Great Horned Owls	150-day		30.90	45
1991	Out on a Limb: Great Gray Owls	150-day		30.90	50
1991	Beginning to Explore: Boreal Owls	150-day		32.90	50
1992	Three's Company: Long Eared Owls	150-day		32.90	45
1992	Whoo's There: Barred Owl	150-day		32.90	50

PLATES

Backyard Harmony - J. Thornbrugh

YEAR ISSUE		EDITION LIMIT	YEAR RETD.	ISSUE PRICE	QUOTE U.S.$
1991	The Singing Lesson	150-day		27.90	38
1991	Welcoming a New Day	150-day		27.90	40
1991	Announcing Spring	150-day		30.90	60
1992	The Morning Harvest	150-day		30.90	45
1992	Spring Time Pride	150-day		30.90	50
1992	Treetop Serenade	150-day		32.90	60
1992	At The Peep Of Day	150-day		32.90	40
1992	Today's Discoveries	150-day		32.90	45

Bambi - Disney Studios

YEAR ISSUE		EDITION LIMIT	YEAR RETD.	ISSUE PRICE	QUOTE U.S.$
1992	Bashful Bambi	150-day		34.90	40
1992	Bambi's New Friends	150-day		34.90	60
1992	Hello Little Prince	150-day		37.90	65
1992	Bambi's Morning Greetings	150-day		37.90	60
1992	Bambi's Skating Lesson	150-day		37.90	38
1993	What's Up Possums?	150-day		37.90	38

Beauty and the Beast - Disney Studios

YEAR ISSUE		EDITION LIMIT	YEAR RETD.	ISSUE PRICE	QUOTE U.S.$
1993	Love's First Dance	150-day		29.90	30
1993	A Blossoming Romance	150-day		29.90	30
1993	Warming Up	150-day		32.90	33
1993	Learning to Love	150-day		32.90	33
1993	Papa's Workshop	150-day		32.90	33
1993	Be Our Guest	150-day		34.90	35
1993	Belle's Favorite Story	150-day		34.90	35
1993	A Mismatch	150-day		34.90	35
1994	A Spot of Tea	150-day		34.90	35
1994	Enchanté, Cherie	150-day		34.90	35
1994	A Gift for Belle	150-day		34.90	35
1994	The Spell is Broken	150-day		34.90	35

Biblical Mothers - E. Licea

YEAR ISSUE		EDITION LIMIT	YEAR RETD.	ISSUE PRICE	QUOTE U.S.$
1983	Bathsheba and Solomon	Yr.Iss.		39.50	40
1984	Judgment of Solomon	Yr.Iss.		39.50	40
1984	Pharaoh's Daughter and Moses	Yr.Iss.		39.50	40
1985	Mary and Jesus	Yr.Iss.		39.50	40
1985	Sarah and Isaac	Yr.Iss.		44.50	45
1986	Rebekah, Jacob and Esau	Yr.Iss.		44.50	45

Birds of the Seasons - S. Timm

YEAR ISSUE		EDITION LIMIT	YEAR RETD.	ISSUE PRICE	QUOTE U.S.$
1990	Cardinals In Winter	150-day		24.90	40
1990	Bluebirds In Spring	150-day		24.90	30
1991	Nuthatches In Fall	150-day		27.90	28
1991	Baltimore Orioles In Summer	150-day		27.90	30
1991	Blue Jays In Early Fall	150-day		27.90	45
1991	Robins In Early Spring	150-day		27.90	30
1991	Cedar Waxwings in Fall	150-day		29.90	65
1991	Chickadees in Winter	150-day		29.90	55

Call of the Wilderness - K. Daniel

YEAR ISSUE		EDITION LIMIT	YEAR RETD.	ISSUE PRICE	QUOTE U.S.$
1991	First Outing	150-day		29.90	50
1991	Howling Lesson	150-day		29.90	90
1991	Silent Watch	150-day		32.90	50
1991	Winter Travelers	150-day		32.90	50
1992	Ahead of the Pack	150-day		32.90	65
1992	Northern Spirits	150-day		34.90	50
1992	Twilight Friends	150-day		34.90	35
1992	A New Future	150-day		34.90	35
1992	Morning Mist	150-day		36.90	37
1992	The Silent One	150-day		36.90	37

Carousel - D. Brown

YEAR ISSUE		EDITION LIMIT	YEAR RETD.	ISSUE PRICE	QUOTE U.S.$
1987	If I Loved You	150-day		24.90	25
1988	Mr. Snow	150-day		24.90	25
1988	The Carousel Waltz	150-day		24.90	25
1988	You'll Never Walk Alone	150-day		24.90	25

Casablanca - J. Griffin

YEAR ISSUE		EDITION LIMIT	YEAR RETD.	ISSUE PRICE	QUOTE U.S.$
1990	Here's Looking At You, Kid	150-day		34.90	38
1990	We'll Always Have Paris	150-day		34.90	40
1991	We Loved Each Other Once	150-day		37.90	38
1991	Rick's Cafe Americain	150-day		37.90	40
1991	A Franc For Your Thoughts	150-day		37.90	55
1991	Play it Sam	150-day		37.90	60

China's Natural Treasures - T.C. Chiu

YEAR ISSUE		EDITION LIMIT	YEAR RETD.	ISSUE PRICE	QUOTE U.S.$
1992	The Siberian Tiger	150-day		29.90	43
1992	The Snow Leopard	150-day		29.90	35
1992	The Giant Panda	150-day		32.90	35
1992	The Tibetan Brown Bear	150-day		32.90	40
1992	The Asian Elephant	150-day		32.90	50
1992	The Golden Monkey	150-day		34.90	45

Christmas in the City - A. Leimanis

YEAR ISSUE		EDITION LIMIT	YEAR RETD.	ISSUE PRICE	QUOTE U.S.$
1992	A Christmas Snowfall	150-day		34.90	35
1992	Yuletide Celebration	150-day		34.90	55
1993	Holiday Cheer	150-day		34.90	60
1993	The Magic of Christmas	150-day		34.90	65

Cinderella - Disney Studios

YEAR ISSUE		EDITION LIMIT	YEAR RETD.	ISSUE PRICE	QUOTE U.S.$
1988	Bibbidi, Bobbidi, Boo	150-day		29.90	65-95
1988	A Dream Is A Wish Your Heart Makes	150-day		29.90	60
1989	Oh Sing Sweet Nightingale	150-day		32.90	50-70
1989	A Dress For Cinderelly	150-day		32.90	90
1989	So This Is Love	150-day		32.90	70
1990	At The Stroke Of Midnight	150-day		32.90	60
1990	If The Shoe Fits	150-day		34.90	65-75
1990	Happily Ever After	150-day		34.90	35

Classic Fairy Tales - S. Gustafson

YEAR ISSUE		EDITION LIMIT	YEAR RETD.	ISSUE PRICE	QUOTE U.S.$
1991	Goldilocks and the Three Bears	150-day		29.90	55
1991	Little Red Riding Hood	150-day		29.90	60
1991	The Three Little Pigs	150-day		32.90	55
1991	The Frog Prince	150-day		32.90	63
1992	Jack and the Beanstalk	150-day		32.90	60
1992	Hansel and Gretel	150-day		34.90	60
1992	Puss in Boots	150-day		34.90	43
1992	Tom Thumb	150-day		34.90	45

Classic Mother Goose - S. Gustafson

YEAR ISSUE		EDITION LIMIT	YEAR RETD.	ISSUE PRICE	QUOTE U.S.$
1992	Little Miss Muffet	150-day		29.90	35
1992	Mary had a Little Lamb	150-day		29.90	50
1992	Mary, Mary, Quite Contrary	150-day		29.90	55
1992	Little Bo Peep	150-day		29.90	50

The Comforts of Home - H. Hollister Ingmire

YEAR ISSUE		EDITION LIMIT	YEAR RETD.	ISSUE PRICE	QUOTE U.S.$
1992	Sleepyheads	150-day		24.90	25
1992	Curious Pair	150-day		24.90	25
1993	Mother's Retreat	150-day		27.90	28
1993	Welcome Friends	150-day		27.90	28
1993	Playtime	150-day		27.90	28
1993	Feline Frolic	150-day		29.90	30
1993	Washday Helpers	150-day		29.90	30
1993	A Cozy Fireside	150-day		29.90	30

Cozy Country Corners - H. H. Ingmire

YEAR ISSUE		EDITION LIMIT	YEAR RETD.	ISSUE PRICE	QUOTE U.S.$
1990	Lazy Morning	150-day		24.90	40-50
1990	Warm Retreat	150-day		24.90	35-40
1991	A Sunny Spot	150-day		27.90	40
1991	Attic Afternoon	150-day		27.90	45
1991	Mirror Mischief	150-day		27.90	60
1991	Hide and Seek	150-day		29.90	45
1991	Apple Antics	150-day		29.90	75
1991	Table Trouble	150-day		29.90	68

Csatari Grandparent - J. Csatari

YEAR ISSUE		EDITION LIMIT	YEAR RETD.	ISSUE PRICE	QUOTE U.S.$
1980	Bedtime Story	100-day		18.00	18
1981	The Skating Lesson	100-day		20.00	25
1982	The Cookie Tasting	100-day		20.00	25
1983	The Swinger	100-day		20.00	25
1984	The Skating Queen	100-day		22.00	22
1985	The Patriot's Parade	100-day		22.00	22
1986	The Home Run	100-day		22.00	22
1987	The Sneak Preview	100-day		22.00	22

The Disney Treasured Moments Collection - Disney Studios

YEAR ISSUE		EDITION LIMIT	YEAR RETD.	ISSUE PRICE	QUOTE U.S.$
1992	Cinderella	150-day		29.90	30
1992	Snow White and the Seven Dwarves	150-day		29.90	30
1993	Alice in Wonderland	150-day		32.90	33
1993	Sleeping Beauty	150-day		32.90	33
1993	Peter Pan	150-day		32.90	33
1993	Pinocchio	150-day		34.90	35
1993	The Jungle Book	150-day		34.90	35
1994	Beauty & The Beast	150-day		34.90	35

Ency. Brit. Birds of Your Garden - K. Daniel

YEAR ISSUE		EDITION LIMIT	YEAR RETD.	ISSUE PRICE	QUOTE U.S.$
1985	Cardinal	100-day		19.50	30
1985	Blue Jay	100-day		19.50	30
1985	Oriole	100-day		22.50	30
1986	Chickadees	100-day		22.50	30
1986	Bluebird	100-day		22.50	30
1986	Robin	100-day		22.50	30
1986	Hummingbird	100-day		24.50	30
1987	Goldfinch	100-day		24.50	30
1987	Downy Woodpecker	100-day		24.50	35
1987	Cedar Waxwing	100-day		24.90	35

Fantasia: (The Sorcerer's Apprentice) Golden Anniversary - Disney Studios

YEAR ISSUE		EDITION LIMIT	YEAR RETD.	ISSUE PRICE	QUOTE U.S.$
1990	The Apprentice's Dream	150-day		29.90	60
1990	Mischievous Apprentice	150-day		29.90	65
1991	Dreams of Power	150-day		32.90	55
1991	Mickey's Magical Whirlpool	150-day		32.90	50
1991	Wizardry Gone Wild	150-day		32.90	45
1991	Mickey Makes Magic	150-day		34.90	63
1991	The Penitent Apprentice	150-day		34.90	47
1992	An Apprentice Again	150-day		34.90	50

Father's Love - B. Bradley

YEAR ISSUE		EDITION LIMIT	YEAR RETD.	ISSUE PRICE	QUOTE U.S.$
1984	Open Wide	100-day		19.50	20
1984	Batter Up	100-day		19.50	20
1985	Little Shaver	100-day		19.50	20
1985	Swing Time	100-day		22.50	23

Field Puppies - L. Kaatz

YEAR ISSUE		EDITION LIMIT	YEAR RETD.	ISSUE PRICE	QUOTE U.S.$
1987	Dog Tired-The Springer Spaniel	150-day		24.90	45
1987	Caught in the Act-The Golden Retriever	150-day		24.90	40
1988	Missing/Point/Irish Setter	150-day		27.90	28
1988	A Perfect Set-Labrador	150-day		27.90	40
1988	Fritz's Folly-German Shorthaired Pointer	150-day		27.90	40
1988	Shirt Tales: Cocker Spaniel	150-day		27.90	45
1989	Fine Feathered Friends-English Setter	150-day		29.90	30
1989	Command Performance/ Wiemaraner	150-day		29.90	35

Field Trips - L. Kaatz

YEAR ISSUE		EDITION LIMIT	YEAR RETD.	ISSUE PRICE	QUOTE U.S.$
1990	Gone Fishing	150-day		24.90	25
1991	Ducking Duty	150-day		24.90	25
1991	Boxed In	150-day		27.90	28
1991	Pups 'N Boots	150-day		27.90	30
1991	Puppy Tales	150-day		27.90	28
1991	Pail Pals	150-day		29.90	35
1991	Chesapeake Bay Retrievers	150-day		29.90	32
1991	Hat Trick	150-day		29.90	30

First Impressions - J. Giordano

YEAR ISSUE		EDITION LIMIT	YEAR RETD.	ISSUE PRICE	QUOTE U.S.$
1991	Taking a Gander	150-day		29.90	40
1991	Two's Company	150-day		29.90	35
1991	Fine Feathered Friends	150-day		32.90	45
1991	What's Up?	150-day		32.90	40
1991	All Ears	150-day		32.90	65
1992	Between Friends	150-day		32.90	45

The Four Ancient Elements - G. Lambert

YEAR ISSUE		EDITION LIMIT	YEAR RETD.	ISSUE PRICE	QUOTE U.S.$
1984	Earth	75-day		27.50	28
1984	Water	75-day		27.50	28
1985	Air	75-day		29.50	30
1985	Fire	75-day		29.50	40

Frances Hook Legacy - F. Hook

YEAR ISSUE		EDITION LIMIT	YEAR RETD.	ISSUE PRICE	QUOTE U.S.$
1985	Fascination	100-day		19.50	20
1985	Daydreaming	100-day		19.50	20
1986	Discovery	100-day		22.50	23
1986	Disappointment	100-day		22.50	23
1986	Wonderment	100-day		22.50	23
1987	Expectation	100-day		22.50	23

Free as the Wind - M. Budden

YEAR ISSUE		EDITION LIMIT	YEAR RETD.	ISSUE PRICE	QUOTE U.S.$
1992	Skyward	150-day		29.90	56
1992	Aloft	150-day		29.90	60
1992	Airborne	150-day		32.90	45
1993	Flight	150-day		32.90	33
1993	Ascent	150-day		32.90	33
1993	Heavenward	150-day		32.90	33

Friends I Remember - J. Down

YEAR ISSUE		EDITION LIMIT	YEAR RETD.	ISSUE PRICE	QUOTE U.S.$
1983	Fish Story	97-day		17.50	18
1984	Office Hours	97-day		17.50	18
1985	A Coat of Paint	97-day		17.50	18
1985	Here Comes the Bride	97-day		19.50	20
1985	Fringe Benefits	97-day		19.50	20
1986	High Society	97-day		19.50	20
1986	Flower Arrangement	97-day		21.50	22
1986	Taste Test	97-day		21.50	22

Friends of the Forest - K. Daniel

YEAR ISSUE		EDITION LIMIT	YEAR RETD.	ISSUE PRICE	QUOTE U.S.$
1987	The Rabbit	150-day		24.50	26
1987	The Raccoon	150-day		24.50	35
1987	The Squirrel	150-day		27.90	28
1988	The Chipmunk	150-day		27.90	28
1988	The Fox	150-day		27.90	28
1988	The Otter	150-day		27.90	28

Garden Secrets - B. Higgins Bond

YEAR ISSUE		EDITION LIMIT	YEAR RETD.	ISSUE PRICE	QUOTE U.S.$
1993	Nine Lives	150-day		24.90	50
1993	Floral Purr-fume	150-day		24.90	80
1993	Bloomin' Kitties	150-day		24.90	60
1993	Kitty Corner	150-day		24.90	50
1993	Flower Fanciers	150-day		24.90	25
1993	Meadow Mischief	150-day		24.90	25
1993	Pussycat Potpourri	150-day		24.90	25
1993	Frisky Business	150-day		24.90	25

Gone with the Wind - R. Kursar

YEAR ISSUE		EDITION LIMIT	YEAR RETD.	ISSUE PRICE	QUOTE U.S.$
1978	Scarlett	100-day		21.50	150-185
1979	Ashley	100-day		21.50	75-100
1980	Melanie	100-day		21.50	40-70
1981	Rhett	100-day		23.50	35-60
1982	Mammy Lacing Scarlett	100-day		23.50	50-70
1983	Melanie Gives Birth	100-day		23.50	55-65
1984	Scarlet's Green Dress	100-day		25.50	35-55
1985	Rhett and Bonnie	100-day		25.50	65
1985	Scarlett and Rhett: The Finale	100-day		29.50	45-70

Great Cats Of The Americas - L. Cable

YEAR ISSUE		EDITION LIMIT	YEAR RETD.	ISSUE PRICE	QUOTE U.S.$
1989	The Jaguar	150-day		29.90	40-50
1989	The Cougar	150-day		29.90	35-45
1989	The Lynx	150-day		32.90	33
1990	The Ocelot	150-day		32.90	33
1990	The Bobcat	150-day		32.90	33
1990	The Jaguarundi	150-day		32.90	35
1990	The Margay	150-day		34.90	35
1991	The Pampas Cat	150-day		34.90	35

Heirlooms And Lace - C. Layton

YEAR ISSUE		EDITION LIMIT	YEAR RETD.	ISSUE PRICE	QUOTE U.S.$
1989	Anna	150-day		34.90	40-50
1989	Victoria	150-day		34.90	65
1990	Tess	150-day		37.90	70-80
1990	Olivia	150-day		37.90	110
1991	Bridget	150-day		37.90	110
1991	Rebecca	150-day		37.90	90

Hibel Christmas - E. Hibel

YEAR ISSUE		EDITION LIMIT	YEAR RETD.	ISSUE PRICE	QUOTE U.S.$
1985	The Angel's Message	Yr.Iss.		45.00	45
1986	The Gifts of the Magi	Yr.Iss.		45.00	45
1987	The Flight Into Egypt	Yr.Iss.		49.00	49

Year Issue		Edition Limit	Year Retd.	Issue Price	Quote U.S.$
1988	Adoration of the Shepherd	Yr.Iss.		49.00	50-60
1989	Peaceful Kingdom	Yr.Iss.		49.00	49
1990	Nativity	Yr.Iss.		49.00	75

Home Sweet Home - R. McGinnis

Year Issue		Edition Limit	Year Retd.	Issue Price	Quote U.S.$
1989	The Victorian	150-day		39.90	40
1989	The Greek Revival	150-day		39.90	40
1989	The Georgian	150-day		39.90	40
1990	The Mission	150-day		39.90	40

It's a Dog's Life - L. Kaatz

Year Issue		Edition Limit	Year Retd.	Issue Price	Quote U.S.$
1992	We've Been Spotted	150-day		29.90	30
1992	Literary Labs	150-day		29.90	30
1993	Retrieving Our Dignity	150-day		32.90	33
1993	Lodging a Complaint	150-day		32.90	33
1993	Barreling Along	150-day		32.90	33
1993	Play Ball	150-day		34.90	35
1993	Dogs and Suds	150-day		34.90	35
1993	Paws for a Picnic	150-day		34.90	35

J. W. Smith Childhood Holidays - J. W. Smith

Year Issue		Edition Limit	Year Retd.	Issue Price	Quote U.S.$
1986	Easter	97-day		19.50	21
1986	Thanksgiving	97-day		19.50	20
1986	Christmas	97-day		19.50	20
1986	Valentine's Day	97-day		22.50	23
1987	Mother's Day	97-day		22.50	23
1987	Fourth of July	97-day		22.50	23

Jerner's Less Travelled Road - B. Jerner

Year Issue		Edition Limit	Year Retd.	Issue Price	Quote U.S.$
1988	The Weathered Barn	150-day		29.90	30
1988	The Murmuring Stream	150-day		29.90	30
1988	The Covered Bridge	150-day		32.90	33
1989	Winter's Peace	150-day		32.90	33
1989	The Flowering Meadow	150-day		32.90	33
1989	The Hidden Waterfall	150-day		32.90	33

Jewels of the Flowers - T.C. Chiu

Year Issue		Edition Limit	Year Retd.	Issue Price	Quote U.S.$
1991	Sapphire Wings	150-day		29.90	30
1991	Topaz Beauties	150-day		29.90	41
1991	Amethyst Flight	150-day		32.90	35
1991	Ruby Elegance	150-day		32.90	45
1991	Emerald Pair	150-day		32.90	52
1991	Opal Splendor	150-day		34.90	35-45
1992	Pearl Luster	150-day		34.90	60
1992	Aquamarine Glimmer	150-day		34.90	35

Keepsake Rhymes - S. Gustafson

Year Issue		Edition Limit	Year Retd.	Issue Price	Quote U.S.$
1992	Humpty Dumpty	150-day		29.90	30-45
1993	Peter Pumpkin Eater	150-day		29.90	85
1993	Pat-a-Cake	150-day		29.90	90
1993	Old King Cole	150-day		29.90	50

The King and I - W. Chambers

Year Issue		Edition Limit	Year Retd.	Issue Price	Quote U.S.$
1984	A Puzzlement	150-day		19.50	20
1985	Shall We Dance?	150-day		19.50	20
1985	Getting to Know You	150-day		19.50	20
1985	We Kiss in a Shadow	150-day		19.50	20

Lady and the Tramp - Disney Studios

Year Issue		Edition Limit	Year Retd.	Issue Price	Quote U.S.$
1992	First Date	150-day		34.90	56
1992	Puppy Love	150-day		34.90	70
1992	Dog Pound Blues	150-day		37.90	38
1992	Merry Christmas To All	150-day		37.90	38
1993	Double Siamese Trouble	150-day		37.90	38
1993	Ruff House	150-day		39.90	40
1993	Telling Tails	150-day		39.90	40
1993	Moonlight Romance	150-day		39.90	40

Lincoln Man of America - M. Kunstler

Year Issue		Edition Limit	Year Retd.	Issue Price	Quote U.S.$
1986	The Gettysburg Address	150-day		24.50	25-30
1987	The Inauguration	150-day		24.50	25
1987	The Lincoln-Douglas Debates	150-day		27.50	28
1987	Beginnings in New Salem	150-day		27.90	28
1988	The Family Man	150-day		27.90	28
1988	Emancipation Proclamation	150-day		27.90	28

The Little Mermaid - Disney Studio Artists

Year Issue		Edition Limit	Year Retd.	Issue Price	Quote U.S.$
1993	A Song From the Sea	95-day		29.90	30
1993	A Visit to the Surface	95-day		29.90	30
1993	Daddy's Girl	95-day		32.90	33
1993	Underwater Buddies	95-day		32.90	33
1993	Ariel's Treasured Collection	95-day		32.90	33
1993	Kiss the Girl	95-day		32.90	33
1994	Fireworks at First Sight	95-day		34.90	35
1994	Forever Love	95-day		34.90	35

Living with Nature-Jerner's Ducks - B. Jerner

Year Issue		Edition Limit	Year Retd.	Issue Price	Quote U.S.$
1986	The Pintail	150-day		19.50	30
1986	The Mallard	150-day		19.50	40
1987	The Wood Duck	150-day		22.50	35
1987	The Green-Winged Teal	150-day		22.50	40
1987	The Northern Shoveler	150-day		22.90	30
1987	The American Widgeon	150-day		22.90	35
1987	The Gadwall	150-day		24.90	35
1988	The Blue-Winged Teal	150-day		24.90	30

Majestic Birds of North America - D. Smith

Year Issue		Edition Limit	Year Retd.	Issue Price	Quote U.S.$
1988	The Bald Eagle	150-day		29.90	30-40
1988	Peregrine Falcon	150-day		29.90	30
1988	The Great Horned Owl	150-day		32.90	33
1989	The Red-Tailed Hawk	150-day		32.90	33
1989	The White Gyrfalcon	150-day		32.90	33
1989	The American Kestral	150-day		32.90	33
1990	The Osprey	150-day		34.90	35
1990	The Golden Eagle	150-day		34.90	35

Mary Poppins - M. Hampshire

Year Issue		Edition Limit	Year Retd.	Issue Price	Quote U.S.$
1989	Mary Poppins	150-day		29.90	50
1989	A Spoonful of Sugar	150-day		29.90	40
1990	A Jolly Holiday With Mary	150-day		32.90	37
1990	We Love To Laugh	150-day		32.90	45
1991	Chim Chim Cher-ee	150-day		32.90	39
1991	Tuppence a Bag	150-day		32.90	50

Mickey's Christmas Carol - Disney Studios

Year Issue		Edition Limit	Year Retd.	Issue Price	Quote U.S.$
1992	Bah Humbug	150-day		29.90	40
1992	What's So Merry About Christmas?	150-day		29.90	50
1993	God Bless Us Every One	150-day		32.90	63
1993	A Christmas Surprise	150-day		32.90	33
1993	Yuletide Greetings	150-day		32.90	33
1993	Marley's Warning	150-day		34.90	35
1993	A Cozy Christmas	150-day		34.90	35
1993	A Christmas Feast	150-day		34.90	35

Musical Moments From the Wizard of Oz - K. Milnazik

Year Issue		Edition Limit	Year Retd.	Issue Price	Quote U.S.$
1993	Over the Rainbow	95-day		29.90	30
1993	We're Off to See the Wizard	95-day		29.90	30
1993	Munchkin Land	95-day		29.90	30
1993	If I Only Had a Brain	95-day		29.90	30
1993	Ding Dong The Witch is Dead	95-day		29.90	30
1993	The Lullabye League	95-day		29.90	30
1994	If I Were King of the Forest	95-day		29.90	30
1994	Merry Old Land of Oz	95-day		29.90	30

My Fair Lady - W. Chambers

Year Issue		Edition Limit	Year Retd.	Issue Price	Quote U.S.$
1989	Opening Day at Ascot	150-day		24.90	25
1989	I Could Have Danced All Night	150-day		24.90	25
1989	The Rain in Spain	150-day		27.90	28
1989	Show Me	150-day		27.90	28
1990	Get Me To/Church On Time	150-day		27.90	28
1990	I've Grown Accustomed/Face	150-day		27.90	40

Nature's Child - M. Jobe

Year Issue		Edition Limit	Year Retd.	Issue Price	Quote U.S.$
1990	Sharing	150-day		29.90	31
1990	The Lost Lamb	150-day		29.90	30
1990	Seems Like Yesterday	150-day		32.90	35
1990	Faithful Friends	150-day		32.90	33
1990	Trusted Companion	150-day		32.90	50
1991	Hand in Hand	150-day		32.90	45

Nature's Garden - C. Decker

Year Issue		Edition Limit	Year Retd.	Issue Price	Quote U.S.$
1994	Peaceful Harmony	95-day		34.90	35
1993	Springtime Friends	95-day		29.90	30
1993	A Morning Splash	95-day		29.90	30
1993	Flury of Activity	95-day		32.90	33
1993	Hanging Around	95-day		32.90	33
1993	Tiny Twirling Treasures	95-day		32.90	33
1994	Peaceful Harmony	95-day		29.90	30

Nature's Nursery - J. Thornbrugh

Year Issue		Edition Limit	Year Retd.	Issue Price	Quote U.S.$
1992	Testing the Waters	150-day		29.90	50
1993	Taking the Plunge	150-day		29.90	45
1993	Race Ya Mom	150-day		29.90	46
1993	Time to Wake Up	150-day		29.90	40
1993	Hide and Seek	150-day		29.90	30
1993	Piggyback Ride	150-day		29.90	30

Not So Long Ago - J. W. Smith

Year Issue		Edition Limit	Year Retd.	Issue Price	Quote U.S.$
1988	Story Time	150-day		24.90	25
1988	Wash Day for Dolly	150-day		24.90	25
1988	Suppertime for Kitty	150-day		24.90	30
1988	Mother's Little Helper	150-day		24.90	30

Oklahoma! - M. Kunstler

Year Issue		Edition Limit	Year Retd.	Issue Price	Quote U.S.$
1985	Oh, What a Beautiful Mornin'	150-day		19.50	20
1986	Surrey with the Fringe on Top'	150-day		19.50	20
1986	I Cain't Say No	150-day		19.50	20
1986	Oklahoma	150-day		19.50	20

The Old Mill Stream - C. Tennant

Year Issue		Edition Limit	Year Retd.	Issue Price	Quote U.S.$
1990	New London Grist Mill	150-day		39.90	40
1991	Wayside Inn Grist Mill	150-day		39.90	42
1991	Old Red Mill	150-day		39.90	40
1991	Glade Creek Grist Mill	150-day		39.90	40

Old-Fashioned Favorites - M. Weber

Year Issue		Edition Limit	Year Retd.	Issue Price	Quote U.S.$
1991	Apple Crisp	150-day		29.90	75
1991	Blueberry Muffins	150-day		29.90	65
1991	Peach Cobbler	150-day		29.90	98
1991	Chocolate Chip Oatmeal Cookies	150-day		29.90	205

Once Upon a Time - K. Pritchett

Year Issue		Edition Limit	Year Retd.	Issue Price	Quote U.S.$
1988	Little Red Riding Hood	150-day		24.90	25
1988	Rapunzel	150-day		24.90	25
1988	Three Little Pigs	150-day		27.90	30
1989	The Princess and the Pea	150-day		27.90	30
1989	Goldilocks and the Three Bears	150-day		27.90	35
1989	Beauty and the Beast	150-day		27.90	50

Pinocchio - Disney Studios

Year Issue		Edition Limit	Year Retd.	Issue Price	Quote U.S.$
1989	Gepetto Creates Pinocchio	150-day		29.90	75
1990	Pinocchio And The Blue Fairy	150-day		29.90	85
1990	It's an Actor's Life For Me	150-day		32.90	60
1990	I've Got No Strings On Me	150-day		32.90	50
1991	Pleasure Island	150-day		32.90	50
1991	A Real Boy	150-day		32.90	55

Portraits of Motherhood - W. Chambers

Year Issue		Edition Limit	Year Retd.	Issue Price	Quote U.S.$
1987	Mother's Here	150-day		29.50	30
1988	First Touch	150-day		29.50	30

Precious Little Ones - M. T. Fangel

Year Issue		Edition Limit	Year Retd.	Issue Price	Quote U.S.$
1988	Little Red Robins	150-day		29.90	30
1988	Little Fledglings	150-day		29.90	30
1988	Saturday Night Bath	150-day		29.90	33
1988	Peek-A-Boo	150-day		29.90	32

Proud Sentinels of the American West - N. Glazier

Year Issue		Edition Limit	Year Retd.	Issue Price	Quote U.S.$
1993	Youngblood	150-day		29.90	55
1993	Cat Nap	150-day		29.90	70
1993	Desert Bighorn-Mormon Ridge	150-day		32.90	50
1993	Crown Prince	150-day		32.90	65

Purrfect Point of View - J. Giordano

Year Issue		Edition Limit	Year Retd.	Issue Price	Quote U.S.$
1992	Unexpected Visitors	150-day		29.90	30
1992	Wistful Morning	150-day		29.90	50
1992	Afternoon Catnap	150-day		29.90	32
1992	Cozy Company	150-day		29.90	40

Pussyfooting Around - C. Wilson

Year Issue		Edition Limit	Year Retd.	Issue Price	Quote U.S.$
1991	Fish Tales	150-day		24.90	25
1991	Teatime Tabbies	150-day		24.90	25
1991	Yarn Spinners	150-day		24.90	30
1991	Two Maestros	150-day		24.90	32

Romantic Age of Steam - R.B. Pierce

Year Issue		Edition Limit	Year Retd.	Issue Price	Quote U.S.$
1992	The Empire Builder	150-day		29.90	45
1992	The Broadway Limited	150-day		29.90	75
1992	Twentieth Century Limited	150-day		32.90	33
1992	The Chief	150-day		32.90	33
1992	The Crescent Limited	150-day		32.90	33
1993	The Overland Limited	150-day		34.90	35
1993	The Jupiter	150-day		34.90	35
1993	The Daylight	150-day		34.90	35

Santa's Christmas - T. Browning

Year Issue		Edition Limit	Year Retd.	Issue Price	Quote U.S.$
1991	Santa's Love	150-day		29.90	45
1991	Santa's Cheer	150-day		29.90	40-50
1991	Santa's Promise	150-day		32.90	65
1991	Santa's Gift	150-day		32.90	70
1992	Santa's Surprise	150-day		32.90	50-60
1992	Santa's Magic	150-day		32.90	45-65

Season For Song - M. Jobe

Year Issue		Edition Limit	Year Retd.	Issue Price	Quote U.S.$
1991	Winter Concert	150-day		34.90	43
1991	Snowy Symphony	150-day		34.90	60
1991	Frosty Chorus	150-day		34.90	65
1991	Silver Serenade	150-day		34.90	50

Seasons of Splendor - K. Randle

Year Issue		Edition Limit	Year Retd.	Issue Price	Quote U.S.$
1992	Autumn's Grandeur	150-day		29.90	45
1992	School Days	150-day		29.90	40
1992	Woodland Mill Stream	150-day		32.90	65
1992	Harvest Memories	150-day		32.90	55
1992	A Country Weekend	150-day		32.90	60
1993	Indian Summer	150-day		32.90	60

Shadows and Light: Winter's Wildlife - N. Glazier

Year Issue		Edition Limit	Year Retd.	Issue Price	Quote U.S.$
1993	Winter's Children	150-day		29.90	50
1993	Cub Scouts	150-day		29.90	65
1993	Little Snowman	150-day		29.90	50
1993	The Snow Cave	150-day		29.90	50

Singin' In The Rain - M. Skolsky

Year Issue		Edition Limit	Year Retd.	Issue Price	Quote U.S.$
1990	Singin' In The Rain	150-day		32.90	35
1990	Good Morning	150-day		32.90	34
1991	Broadway Melody	150-day		32.90	45
1991	We're Happy Again	150-day		32.90	50

Sleeping Beauty - Disney Studios

Year Issue		Edition Limit	Year Retd.	Issue Price	Quote U.S.$
1991	Once Upon A Dream	150-day		39.90	50
1991	Awakened by a Kiss	150-day		39.90	100
1991	Happy Birthday Briar Rose	150-day		42.90	55
1992	Together At Last	150-day		42.90	55

Small Blessings - C. Layton

Year Issue		Edition Limit	Year Retd.	Issue Price	Quote U.S.$
1992	Now I Lay Me Down to Sleep	150-day		29.90	40-50
1992	Bless Us O Lord For These, Thy Gifts	150-day		29.90	45-55
1992	Jesus Loves Me, This I Know	150-day		32.90	48
1992	This Little Light of Mine	150-day		32.90	33
1992	Blessed Are The Pure In Heart	150-day		32.90	33
1993	Bless Our Home	150-day		32.90	33

Snow White and the Seven Dwarfs - Disney Studios

Year Issue		Edition Limit	Year Retd.	Issue Price	Quote U.S.$
1991	The Dance of Snow White/Seven Dwarfs	150-day		29.90	60-80
1991	With a Smile and a Song	150-day		29.90	80
1991	A Special Treat	150-day		32.90	50-60
1992	A Kiss for Dopey	150-day		32.90	50-60
1992	The Poison Apple	150-day		32.90	65-70
1992	Fireside Love Story	150-day		34.90	65

YEAR ISSUE		EDITION LIMIT	YEAR RETD.	ISSUE PRICE	QUOTE U.S.$
1992	Stubborn Grumpy	150-day		34.90	50
1992	A Wish Come True	150-day		34.90	64
1992	Time To Tidy Up	150-day		34.50	35
1993	May I Have This Dance?	150-day		36.90	37
1993	A Surprise in the Clearing	150-day		36.50	37
1993	Happy Ending	150-day		36.90	37

Songs of the American Spirit - H. Bond

1991	The Star Spangled Banner	150-day		29.90	30
1991	Battle Hymn of the Republic	150-day		29.90	55
1991	America the Beautiful	150-day		29.90	45
1991	My Country 'Tis of Thee	150-day		29.90	45

Sound of Music - T. Crnkovich

1986	Sound of Music	150-day		19.50	20
1986	Do-Re-Mi	150-day		19.50	20
1986	My Favorite Things	150-day		22.50	23
1986	Laendler Waltz	150-day		22.50	26
1987	Edelweiss	150-day		22.50	23
1987	I Have Confidence	150-day		22.50	23
1987	Maria	150-day		24.90	25
1987	Climb Ev'ry Mountain	150-day		24.90	30

South Pacific - E. Gignilliat

1987	Some Enchanted Evening	150-day		24.50	25
1987	Happy Talk	150-day		24.50	25
1987	Dites Moi	150-day		24.90	25
1988	Honey Bun	150-day		24.90	25

Stately Owls - J. Beaudoin

1989	The Snowy Owl	150-day		29.90	55
1989	The Great Horned Owl	150-day		29.90	45
1990	The Barn Owl	150-day		32.90	35
1990	The Screech Owl	150-day		32.90	35
1990	The Short-Eared Owl	150-day		32.90	33
1990	The Barred Owl	150-day		32.90	35
1990	The Great Grey Owl	150-day		34.90	35
1991	The Saw-Whet Owl	150-day		34.90	35

The Story of Christmas by Eve Licea - E. Licea

1987	The Annunciation	Yr.Iss.		44.90	50
1988	The Nativity	Yr.Iss.		44.90	50
1989	Adoration Of The Shepherds	Yr.Iss.		49.90	53
1990	Journey Of The Magi	Yr.Iss.		49.90	50
1991	Gifts Of The Magi	Yr.Iss.		49.90	50-60
1992	Rest on the Flight into Egypt	Yr.Iss.		49.90	50-65

Sundblom Santas - H. Sundblom

1989	Santa By The Fire	Closed		27.90	30
1990	Christmas Vigil	Closed		27.90	45
1991	To All A Good Night	Closed		32.90	70
1992	Santa's on His Way	Closed		32.90	75

A Swan is Born - L. Roberts

1987	Hopes and Dreams	150-day		24.50	25
1987	At the Barre	150-day		24.50	25
1987	In Position	150-day		24.50	25
1988	Just For Size	150-day		24.50	40

Sweetness and Grace - J. Welty

1992	God Bless Teddy	150-day		34.90	40
1992	Sunshine and Smiles	150-day		34.90	60
1992	Favorite Buddy	150-day		34.90	35-45
1992	Sweet Dreams	150-day		34.90	35-45

Thomas Kinkade's Enchanted Cottages - T. Kinkade

1993	Fallbrooke Cottage	95-day		29.90	30
1993	Julianne's Cottage	95-day		29.90	30
1993	Seaside Cottage	95-day		29.90	30
1993	Sweetheart Cottage	95-day		29.90	30
1993	Weathervane Cottage	95-day		29.90	30
1993	Rose Garden Cottage	95-day		29.90	30

Thomas Kinkade's Garden Cottages of England - T. Kinkade

1991	Chandler's Cottage	150-day		27.90	60-90
1991	Cedar Nook Cottage	150-day		27.90	50-60
1991	Candlelit Cottage	150-day		30.90	60
1991	Open Gate Cottage	150-day		30.90	40-60
1991	McKenna's Cottage	150-day		30.90	45-60
1991	Woodsman's Thatch Cottage	150-day		32.90	45-60
1992	Merritt's Cottage	150-day		32.90	55-80
1992	Stonegate Cottage	150-day		32.90	70-80

Thomas Kinkade's Home for the Holidays - T. Kinkade

1991	Sleigh Ride Home	150-day		29.90	40-50
1991	Home to Grandma's	150-day		29.90	45
1991	Home Before Christmas	150-day		32.90	45-55
1991	The Warmth of Home	150-day		32.90	60
1992	Homespun Holiday	150-day		32.90	45
1992	Hometime Yuletide	150-day		34.90	50-60
1992	Home Away From Home	150-day		34.90	55
1992	The Journey Home	150-day		34.90	35

Thomas Kinkade's Home is Where the Heart Is - T. Kinkade

1992	Home Sweet Home	150-day		29.90	65
1992	A Warm Welcome Home	150-day		29.90	55
1992	A Carriage Ride Home	150-day		32.90	65
1993	Amber Afternoon	150-day		32.90	33
1993	Country Memories	150-day		32.90	33

YEAR ISSUE		EDITION LIMIT	YEAR RETD.	ISSUE PRICE	QUOTE U.S.$
1993	The Twilight Cafe	150-day		34.90	35
1993	Our Summer Home	150-day		34.90	35
1993	Hometown Hospitality	150-day		34.90	35

Thomas Kinkade's Thomashire - T. Kinkade

1992	Olde Porterfield Tea Room	150-day		29.90	50-60
1992	Olde Thomashire Mill	150-day		29.90	65-80
1992	Swanbrook Cottage	150-day		32.90	75-100
1992	Pye Corner Cottage	150-day		32.90	50-70
1993	Blossom Hill Church	150-day		32.90	33
1993	Olde Garden Cottage	150-day		32.90	33

Thomas Kinkade's Yuletide Memories - T. Kinkade

1992	The Magic of Christmas	150-day		29.90	75-90
1992	A Beacon of Faith	150-day		29.90	50-60
1993	Moonlit Sleighride	150-day		29.90	40-80
1993	Silent Night	150-day		29.90	40-70
1993	Olde Porterfield Gift Shoppe	150-day		29.90	30
1993	The Wonder of the Season	150-day		29.90	30
1993	A Winter's Walk	150-day		29.90	30
1993	Skater's Delight	150-day		32.90	33

Tom Sawyer - W. Chambers

1987	Whitewashing the Fence	150-day		27.50	28
1987	Tom and Becky	150-day		27.90	28
1987	Tom Sawyer the Pirate	150-day		27.90	28
1988	First Pipes	150-day		27.90	28

Under Mother's Wing - J. Beaudoin

1992	Arctic Spring: Snowy Owls	150-day		29.90	45
1992	Forest's Edge: Great Gray Owls	150-day		29.90	40
1992	Treetop Trio: Long-Eared Owls	150-day		32.90	45
1992	Woodland Watch: Spotted Owls	150-day		32.90	60
1992	Vast View: Saw Whet Owls	150-day		32.90	50
1992	Lofty-Limb: Great Horned Owl	150-day		34.90	50
1993	Perfect Perch: Barred Owls	150-day		34.90	45
1993	Happy Home: Short-Eared Owl	150-day		34.90	45

Upland Birds of North America - W. Anderson

1986	The Pheasant	150-day		24.50	25
1986	The Grouse	150-day		24.50	25
1987	The Quail	150-day		27.50	28
1987	The Wild Turkey	150-day		27.50	28
1987	The Gray Partridge	150-day		27.50	28
1987	The Woodcock	150-day		27.90	28

Windows of Glory - J. Welty

1993	King of Kings	95-day		29.90	30
1993	Prince of Peace	95-day		29.90	30
1993	The Messiah	95-day		32.90	33
1993	The Good Shepherd	95-day		32.90	33
1993	The Light of the World	95-day		32.90	33
1993	The Everlasting Father	95-day		32.90	33

Wizard of Oz - J. Auckland

1977	Over the Rainbow	100-day		19.00	45-55
1978	If I Only Had a Brain	100-day		19.00	40
1978	If I Only Had a Heart	100-day		19.00	35-45
1978	If I Were King of the Forest	100-day		19.00	45-50
1979	Wicked Witch of the West	100-day		19.00	55-65
1979	Follow the Yellow Brick Road	100-day		19.00	50
1979	Wonderful Wizard of Oz	100-day		19.00	60
1980	The Grand Finale	100-day		24.00	55

Wizard of Oz: A National Treasure - R. Laslo

1991	Yellow Brick Road	150-day		29.90	50
1992	I Haven't Got a Brain	150-day		29.90	50
1992	I'm a Little Rusty Yet	150-day		32.90	50
1992	I Even Scare Myself	150-day		32.90	60
1992	We're Off To See the Wizard	150-day		32.90	50
1992	I'll Never Get Home	150-day		34.90	35
1992	I'm Melting	150-day		34.90	35
1992	There's No Place Like Home	150-day		34.90	35

Yesterday's Innocents - J. Wilcox Smith

1992	My First Book	150-day		29.90	30
1992	Time to Smell the Roses	150-day		29.90	50
1993	Hush, Baby's Sleeping	150-day		32.90	40
1993	Ready and Waiting	150-day		32.90	60

Enchantica

Retired Enchantica Collection - Various

1992	Winter Dragon-Grawlfang-2200 - J. Woodward	Retrd.	1993	50.00	75
1992	Spring Dragon-Gorgoyle-2201 - J. Woodward	Retrd.	1993	50.00	75
1993	Summer Dragon-Arangast-2202 - J. Woodward	Retrd.	1993	50.00	75
1993	Autumn Dragon-Snarlgard-2203 - J. Woodward	Retrd.	1993	50.00	75
1992	Cave Dragon-2065 - A. Bill	Retrd.	1994	200.00	225
1991	Snappa Caught Napping-2039 - A. Hull	Retrd.	1994	39.50	60

Enesco Corporation

Barbie-Bob Mackie JC Penney Exclusive - Enesco

1995	Queen of Hearts Barbie-11276	7,500	1995	30.00	30

Barbie-FAO Schwarz Exclusive - Enesco

1994	Silver Screen Barbie-128805	3,600	1995	30.00	30

YEAR ISSUE		EDITION LIMIT	YEAR RETD.	ISSUE PRICE	QUOTE U.S.$
1995	Circus Star Barbie-150339	3,600	1995	30.00	30

Barbie-Glamour - Enesco

1996	Here Comes The Bride, 1966-170984	Open		30.00	30

Barbie-Great Eras - Enesco

1996	Gibson Girl Barbie-171468	5,000		30.00	30
1996	1920's Flapper Barbie-174777	5,000		30.00	30

Barbie-Happy Holiday - Enesco

1994	Happy Holidays Barbie, 1994-115088	5,000	1994	30.00	100-150
1995	Happy Holidays Barbie, 1995-143154	Yr.Iss.		30.00	30
1995	Happy Holidays Barbie, 1988-154180	Yr.Iss.		30.00	30

Barbie-Hollywood Legends - Enesco

1996	Barbie As Scarlett O'Hara in Green Velvet-171085	5,000		30.00	30
1996	Barbie As Scarlett O'Hara in Green Velvet Bas Relief-174742	Yr.Iss.		30.00	30

Barbie-Nostalgic - Enesco

1993	35th Anniversary Barbie-655112	5,000	1994	30.00	30
1994	Barbie Solo In The Spotlight, 1959-114383	5,000	1995	30.00	45
1996	Barbie Enchanted Evening, 1960-175587	5,000		30.00	30

Cherished Teddies - P. Hillman

1995	Jack/Jill Nursery Rhyme - 114901	Open		35.00	35
1995	Mary/Lamb Nursery Rhyme - 128902	Open		35.00	35
1995	Old King Cole Nursery Rhyme - 135437	Open		35.00	35
1995	Girl in Green Dress Dtd 95 - 141550	Yr.Iss.		35.00	35

Memories of Yesterday Dated Plate Series - Various

1993	Look Out-Something Good Is Coming Your Way!-530298 - S. Butcher	Yr.Iss.		50.00	50
1994	Pleasant Dreams and Sweet Repose-528102 - M. Atwell	Yr.Iss.		50.00	50
1995	Join Me For a Little Song-134880 - M. Atwell	Yr.Iss.		50.00	50

Precious Moments Beauty of Christmas Collection - S. Butcher

1994	You're as Pretty as a Christmas Tree - 530409	Yr.Iss.		50.00	50
1995	He Covers the Earth With His Beauty - 142670	Yr.Iss.		50.00	50

Precious Moments Christmas Blessings - S. Butcher

1990	Wishing You A Yummy Christmas-523801	Yr.Iss.		50.00	50
1991	Blessings From Me To Thee-523860	Yr.Iss.		50.00	55
1992	But The Greatest of These Is Love-527742	Yr.Iss.		50.00	50
1993	Wishing You the Sweetest Christmas-530204	Yr.Iss.		50.00	50

Precious Moments Christmas Collection - S. Butcher

1981	Come Let Us Adore Him-E-5646	15,000		40.00	48-60
1982	Let Heaven and Nature Sing-E-2347	15,000		40.00	40
1983	Wee Three Kings-E-0538	15,000		40.00	40
1984	Unto Us a Child Is Born-E-5395	15,000		40.00	40

Precious Moments Christmas Love Series - S. Butcher

1986	I'm Sending You a White Christmas-101834	Yr.Iss.		45.00	55
1987	My Peace I Give Unto Thee-102954	Yr.Iss.		45.00	90
1988	Merry Christmas Deer-520284	Yr.Iss.		50.00	55
1989	May Your Christmas Be A Happy Home-523003	Yr.Iss.		50.00	55

Precious Moments Inspired Thoughts Series - S. Butcher

1985	Love One Another-E-5215	15,000		40.00	66
1982	Make a Joyful Noise-E-7174	15,000		40.00	40
1983	I Believe In Miracles-E-9257	15,000		40.00	40
1984	Love is Kind-E-2847	15,000		40.00	40

Precious Moments Joy of Christmas Series - S. Butcher

1982	I'll Play My Drum For Him-E-2357	Yr.Iss.		40.00	90-93
1983	Christmastime is for Sharing-E-0505	Yr.Iss.		40.00	60-75
1984	The Wonder of Christmas-E-5396	Yr.Iss.		40.00	45
1985	Tell Me the Story of Jesus-15237	Yr.Iss.		40.00	90-115

Precious Moments Mother's Day Series - S. Butcher

1993	Thinking of You is What I Really Like to Do-531766	Yr.Iss.		50.00	50
1995	He Hath Made Everything Beautiful In His Time-129151	Yr.Iss.		50.00	50

Precious Moments Mother's Love Series - S. Butcher

1981	Mother Sew Dear-E-5217	15,000		40.00	50
1982	The Purr-fect Grandma-E-7173	15,000		40.00	40

YEAR ISSUE		EDITION LIMIT	YEAR RETD.	ISSUE PRICE	QUOTE U.S.$
1983	The Hand that Rocks the Future-E-9256	15,000		40.00	40
1984	Loving Thy Neighbor-E-2848	15,000		40.00	40

Precious Moments Open Editions - S. Butcher

YEAR ISSUE		EDITION LIMIT	YEAR RETD.	ISSUE PRICE	QUOTE U.S.$
1982	Our First Christmas Together-E-2378	Suspd.		30.00	45-55
1981	The Lord Bless You and Keep You-E-5216	Suspd.		30.00	40-45
1982	Rejoicing with You-E-7172	Suspd.		30.00	40
1983	Jesus Loves Me-E-9275	Suspd.		30.00	45-48
1983	Jesus Loves Me-E-9276	Suspd.		30.00	45-48
1994	Bring The Little Ones To Jesus-531359	Yr.Iss.		50.00	50

Precious Moments The Four Seasons Series - S. Butcher

YEAR ISSUE		EDITION LIMIT	YEAR RETD.	ISSUE PRICE	QUOTE U.S.$
1985	The Voice of Spring-12106	Yr.Iss.		40.00	110-120
1985	Summer's Joy-12114	Yr.Iss.		40.00	85-110
1986	Autumn's Praise-12122	Yr.Iss.		40.00	53
1986	Winter's Song-12130	Yr.Iss.		40.00	58

Ernst Enterprises/Porter & Price, Inc.

A Beautiful World - S. Morton

YEAR ISSUE		EDITION LIMIT	YEAR RETD.	ISSUE PRICE	QUOTE U.S.$
1981	Tahitian Dreamer	Retrd.	1987	27.50	30
1982	Flirtation	Retrd.	1987	27.50	30
1984	Elke of Oslo	Retrd.	1987	27.50	30

Classy Cars - S. Kuhnly

YEAR ISSUE		EDITION LIMIT	YEAR RETD.	ISSUE PRICE	QUOTE U.S.$
1982	The 26T	Retrd.	1990	24.50	25
1982	The 31A	Retrd.	1990	24.50	25
1983	The Pickup	Retrd.	1990	24.50	25
1984	Panel Van	Retrd.	1990	24.50	25

Commemoratives - S. Morton

YEAR ISSUE		EDITION LIMIT	YEAR RETD.	ISSUE PRICE	QUOTE U.S.$
1981	John Lennon	Retrd.	1988	39.50	100-150
1982	Elvis Presley	Retrd.	1988	39.50	75-125
1982	Marilyn Monroe	Retrd.	1988	39.50	100
1983	Judy Garland	Retrd.	1988	39.50	70
1984	John Wayne	Retrd.	1988	39.50	95

Elvira - S. Morton

YEAR ISSUE		EDITION LIMIT	YEAR RETD.	ISSUE PRICE	QUOTE U.S.$
1988	Night Rose	90-day		29.50	45
1988	Red Velvet	90-day		29.50	35
1988	Mistress of the Dark	90-day		29.50	35

Elvis Presley - S. Morton

YEAR ISSUE		EDITION LIMIT	YEAR RETD.	ISSUE PRICE	QUOTE U.S.$
1987	The King	Retrd.	1991	39.50	90
1987	Loving You	Retrd.	1991	39.50	90
1987	Early Years	Retrd.	1991	39.50	90
1987	Tenderly	Retrd.	1991	39.50	90
1988	Forever Yours	Retrd.	1991	39.50	90
1988	Rockin in the Moonlight	Retrd.	1991	39.50	90
1988	Moody Blues	Retrd.	1991	39.50	60-85
1988	Elvis Presley	Retrd.	1991	39.50	75
1989	Elvis Presley-Special Request	Retrd.	1991	150.00	250-300

Hollywood Greats - S. Morton

YEAR ISSUE		EDITION LIMIT	YEAR RETD.	ISSUE PRICE	QUOTE U.S.$
1981	John Wayne	Retrd.	1988	29.95	100
1981	Gary Cooper	Retrd.	1988	29.95	30
1982	Clark Gable	Retrd.	1988	29.95	65
1984	Alan Ladd	Retrd.	1988	29.95	40-60

Hollywood Walk of Fame - S. Morton

YEAR ISSUE		EDITION LIMIT	YEAR RETD.	ISSUE PRICE	QUOTE U.S.$
1989	Jimmy Stewart	Retrd.	1992	39.50	45
1989	Elizabeth Taylor	Retrd.	1992	39.50	45
1989	Tom Selleck	Retrd.	1992	39.50	45
1989	Joan Collins	Retrd.	1992	39.50	45
1990	Burt Reynolds	Retrd.	1992	39.50	50
1990	Sylvester Stallone	Retrd.	1992	39.50	45

The Republic Pictures Library - S. Morton

YEAR ISSUE		EDITION LIMIT	YEAR RETD.	ISSUE PRICE	QUOTE U.S.$
1991	Showdown With Laredo	28-day		37.50	38
1991	The Ride Home	28-day		37.50	38
1991	Attack at Tarawa	28-day		37.50	38
1991	Thoughts of Angelique	28-day		37.50	38
1992	War of the Wildcats	28-day		37.50	38
1992	The Fighting Seabees	28-day		37.50	38
1992	The Quiet Man	28-day		37.50	38
1992	Angel and the Badman	28-day		37.50	38
1993	Sands of Iwo Jima	28-day		37.50	38
1993	Flying Tigers	28-day		37.50	38
1993	The Tribute (12")	28-day		97.50	98
1994	The Tribute (8 1/4")	9,500		29.50	30

Seems Like Yesterday - R. Money

YEAR ISSUE		EDITION LIMIT	YEAR RETD.	ISSUE PRICE	QUOTE U.S.$
1981	Stop & Smell the Roses	Retrd.	1988	24.50	30
1982	Home by Lunch	Retrd.	1988	24.50	35
1982	Lisa's Creek	Retrd.	1988	24.50	25
1983	It's Got My Name on It	Retrd.	1988	24.50	30
1983	My Magic Hat	Retrd.	1988	24.50	25
1984	Little Prince	Retrd.	1988	24.50	25

Star Trek - S. Morton

YEAR ISSUE		EDITION LIMIT	YEAR RETD.	ISSUE PRICE	QUOTE U.S.$
1984	Mr. Spock	Retrd.	1989	29.50	100-200
1985	Dr. McCoy	Retrd.	1989	29.50	75-125
1985	Sulu	Retrd.	1989	29.50	60-100
1985	Scotty	Retrd.	1989	29.50	60-100
1985	Uhura	Retrd.	1989	29.50	60-100
1985	Chekov	Retrd.	1989	29.50	60-100
1985	Captain Kirk	Retrd.	1989	29.50	100-125
1985	Beam Us Down Scotty	Retrd.	1989	29.50	75
1985	The Enterprise	Retrd.	1989	39.50	80-135

Star Trek: Commemorative Collection - S. Morton

YEAR ISSUE		EDITION LIMIT	YEAR RETD.	ISSUE PRICE	QUOTE U.S.$
1987	The Trouble With Tribbles	Retrd.	1989	29.50	100-175
1987	Mirror, Mirror	Retrd.	1989	29.50	170
1987	A Piece of the Action	Retrd.	1989	29.50	75-175
1987	The Devil in the Dark	Retrd.	1989	29.50	90-165
1987	Amok Time	Retrd.	1989	29.50	75-175
1987	The City on the Edge of Forever	Retrd.	1989	29.50	100-150
1987	Journey to Babel	Retrd.	1989	29.50	115-150
1987	The Menagerie	Retrd.	1989	29.50	100-200

Turn of The Century - R. Money

YEAR ISSUE		EDITION LIMIT	YEAR RETD.	ISSUE PRICE	QUOTE U.S.$
1981	Riverboat Honeymoon	Retrd.	1987	35.00	40
1982	Children's Carousel	Retrd.	1987	35.00	40
1984	Flower Market	Retrd.	1987	35.00	35
1985	Balloon Race	Retrd.	1987	35.00	35

Women of the West - D. Putnam

YEAR ISSUE		EDITION LIMIT	YEAR RETD.	ISSUE PRICE	QUOTE U.S.$
1979	Expectations	Retrd.	1986	39.50	40
1981	Silver Dollar Sal	Retrd.	1986	39.50	40
1982	School Marm	Retrd.	1986	39.50	40
1983	Dolly	Retrd.	1986	39.50	40

Fairmont

Famous Clowns - R. Skelton

YEAR ISSUE		EDITION LIMIT	YEAR RETD.	ISSUE PRICE	QUOTE U.S.$
1976	Freddie the Freeloader	10,000		55.00	400
1977	W. C. Fields	10,000		55.00	100
1978	Happy	10,000		55.00	100
1979	The Pledge	10,000		55.00	100

Spencer Special - I. Spencer

YEAR ISSUE		EDITION LIMIT	YEAR RETD.	ISSUE PRICE	QUOTE U.S.$
1978	Hug Me	10,000		55.00	150
1978	Sleep Little Baby	10,000		65.00	125

Fenton Art Glass Company

American Classic Series - M. Dickinson

YEAR ISSUE		EDITION LIMIT	YEAR RETD.	ISSUE PRICE	QUOTE U.S.$
1986	Jupiter Train on Opal Satin	5,000	1986	75.00	75
1986	Studebaker-Garford Car on Opal Satin	5,000	1986	75.00	75

American Craftsman Carnival - Fenton

YEAR ISSUE		EDITION LIMIT	YEAR RETD.	ISSUE PRICE	QUOTE U.S.$
1970	Glassmaker	Closed	1970	10.00	25-50
1971	Printer	Closed	1971	10.00	25-50
1972	Blacksmith	Closed	1972	10.00	25-50
1973	Shoemaker	Closed	1973	10.00	25-50
1974	Pioneer Cooper	Closed	1974	11.00	25-50
1975	Paul Revere (Patriot & Silversmith)	Closed	1975	12.50	25-50
1976	Gunsmith	Closed	1976	13.50	25-50
1977	Potter	Closed	1977	15.00	25-50
1978	Wheelwright	Closed	1978	15.00	25-50
1979	Cabinetmaker	Closed	1979	15.00	25-50
1980	Tanner	Closed	1980	16.50	25-50
1981	Housewright	Closed	1981	17.50	25-50

Artist Series - Various

YEAR ISSUE		EDITION LIMIT	YEAR RETD.	ISSUE PRICE	QUOTE U.S.$
1982	After The Snow (3 1/4") D. Johnson	15,000	1982	14.50	15
1983	Winter Chapel (3 1/4") D. Johnson	15,000	1984	15.00	15
1985	Flying Geese (3 1/4") D. Johnson	15,000	1985	15.00	15
1986	The Hummingbird (3 1/4") D. Johnson	15,000	1986	15.00	15
1987	Out in the Country (3 1/4") L. Everson	15,000	1987	15.00	15
1988	Serenity (3 1/4") - F. Burton	5,000	1988	16.50	17
1989	Househunting (3 1/4") D. Barbour	5,000	1989	16.50	17

Childhood Treasurers Series - Various

YEAR ISSUE		EDITION LIMIT	YEAR RETD.	ISSUE PRICE	QUOTE U.S.$
1983	Teddy Bear (3 1/4") - D. Johnson	15,000	1983	15.00	15
1984	Hobby Horse (3 1/4") L. Everson	15,000	1984	15.00	15
1985	Clown (3 1/4") - L. Everson	15,000	1985	17.50	18
1986	Playful Kitten (3 1/4") L. Everson	15,000	1986	15.00	16
1987	Frisky Pup (3 1/4") - D. Barbour	15,000	1987	15.00	15
1988	Castles in the Air (3 1/4") D. Barbour	5,000	1988	16.50	17
1989	A Child's Cuddly Friend (3 1/4") D. Johnson	5,000	1989	16.50	17

Christmas - Various

YEAR ISSUE		EDITION LIMIT	YEAR RETD.	ISSUE PRICE	QUOTE U.S.$
1979	Nature's Christmas K. Cunningham	Yr.Iss.	1979	35.00	35
1980	Going Home - D. Johnson	Yr.Iss.	1980	38.50	39
1981	All Is Calm - D. Johnson	Yr.Iss.	1981	42.50	43
1982	Country Christmas - R. Spindler	Yr.Iss.	1982	42.50	43
1983	Anticipation - D. Johnson	7,500	1983	45.00	45
1984	Expectation - D. Johnson	7,500	1984	50.00	50
1985	Heart's Desire - D. Johnson	7,500	1986	50.00	50
1987	Sharing The Spirit - L. Everson	Yr.Iss.	1987	50.00	50
1987	Cardinal in the Churchyard D. Johnson	4,500	1987	39.50	40
1988	A Chickadee Ballet - D. Johnson	4,500	1988	39.50	40
1989	Downy Pecker - Chisled Song D. Johnson	4,500	1989	39.50	40
1990	A Blue Bird in Snowfall D. Johnson	4,500	1990	39.50	40
1990	Sleigh Ride - F. Burton	3,500	1990	45.00	45
1991	Christmas Eve - F. Burton	3,500	1991	45.00	45
1992	Family Tradition - F. Burton	3,500	1992	49.00	49
1993	Family Holiday - F. Burton	3,500	1993	49.00	49
1994	Silent Night - F. Burton	1,500	1994	65.00	65
1995	Our Home Is Blessed - F. Burton	1,500		65.00	65

Christmas In America - Fenton

YEAR ISSUE		EDITION LIMIT	YEAR RETD.	ISSUE PRICE	QUOTE U.S.$
1970	Little Brown Church in the Vale, Bradford, IA, Blue Satin	Closed	1970	12.50	15
1970	Little Brown Church in the Vale, Bradford, IA, Carnival	Closed	1970	12.50	15
1970	Little Brown Church in the Vale, Bradford, IA, White Satin	Closed	1970	12.50	15
1971	The Old Brick Church, Isle of Wight County, VA, Blue Satin	Closed	1971	12.50	15
1971	The Old Brick Church, Isle of Wight County, VA, Carnival	Closed	1971	12.50	15
1971	The Old Brick Church, Isle of Wight County, VA, White Satin	Closed	1971	12.50	15
1972	The Two Horned Church, Marietta, OH, Blue Satin	Closed	1972	12.50	15
1972	The Two Horned Church, Marietta, OH, Carnival	Closed	1972	12.50	15
1972	The Two Horned Church, Marietta, OH, White Satin	Closed	1972	12.50	15
1973	St. Mary's in the Mountain, Virginia City, NV, Blue Satin	Closed	1973	12.50	15
1973	St. Mary's in the Mountain, Virginia City, NV, Carnival	Closed	1973	12.50	15
1973	St. Mary's in the Mountain, Virginia City, NV, White Satin	Closed	1973	12.50	15
1974	The Nation's Church, Philadelphia, PA, Blue Satin	Closed	1974	13.50	15
1974	The Nation's Church, Philadelphia, PA, Carnival	Closed	1974	13.50	15
1974	The Nation's Church, Philadelphia, PA, White Satin	Closed	1974	13.50	15
1975	Birthplace of Liberty, Richmond, VA, Blue Satin	Closed	1975	13.50	15
1975	Birthplace of Liberty, Richmond, VA, Carnival	Closed	1975	13.50	15
1975	Birthplace of Liberty, Richmond, VA, White Satin	Closed	1975	13.50	15
1976	The Old North Church, Boston, MA, Blue Satin	Closed	1976	15.00	15
1976	The Old North Church, Boston, MA, Carnival	Closed	1976	15.00	15
1976	The Old North Church, Boston, MA, White Satin	Closed	1976	15.00	15
1977	San Carlos Borromeo de Carmelo, Carmel, CA, Blue Satin	Closed	1977	15.00	15
1977	San Carlos Borromeo de Carmelo, Carmel, CA, Carnival	Closed	1977	15.00	15
1977	San Carlos Borromeo de Carmelo, Carmel, CA, White Satin	Closed	1977	15.00	15
1978	The Church of Holy Trinity, Philadelphia, PA, Blue Satin	Closed	1978	15.00	15
1978	The Church of Holy Trinity, Philadelphia, PA, Carnival	Closed	1978	15.00	15
1978	The Church of Holy Trinity, Philadelphia, PA, White Satin	Closed	1978	15.00	15
1979	San Jose Y Miguel de Aguayo, San Antonio, TX, Blue Satin	Closed	1979	15.00	15
1979	San Jose Y Miguel de Aguayo, San Antonio, TX, Carnival	Closed	1979	15.00	15
1979	San Jose Y Miguel de Aguayo, San Antonio, TX, White Satin	Closed	1979	15.00	15
1980	Christ Church, Alexandria, VA, Blue Satin	Closed	1980	16.50	17
1980	Christ Church, Alexandria, VA, Carnival	Closed	1980	16.50	17
1980	Christ Church, Alexandria, VA, White Satin	Closed	1980	16.50	17
1981	San Xavier Del Bac, Tucson, AZ, Blue Satin	Closed	1981	18.50	19
1981	San Xavier Del Bac, Tucson, AZ, Carnival	Closed	1981	18.50	19
1981	San Xavier Del Bac, Tucson, AZ, White Satin	Closed	1981	18.50	19
1981	San Xavier Del Bac, Tucson, AZ, Florentine	Closed	1981	25.00	25

Designer Series - Various

YEAR ISSUE		EDITION LIMIT	YEAR RETD.	ISSUE PRICE	QUOTE U.S.$
1983	Lighthouse Point - M. Dickinson	1,000	1983	65.00	65
1983	Down Home - G. Finn	1,000	1983	65.00	65
1984	Smoke 'N Cinders - M. Dickinson	1,250	1984	65.00	65
1984	Majestic Flight - B. Cumberledge	1,250	1984	65.00	65
1985	In Season - M. Dickinson	1,250	1985	65.00	65
1985	Nature's Grace - B. Cumberland	1,250	1985	65.00	65
1985	Statue of Liberty - S. Bryan	1,250	1985	65.00	65
1986	Statue of Liberty - S. Bryan	1,250	1986	65.00	65

Easter Series - M. Reynolds

YEAR ISSUE		EDITION LIMIT	YEAR RETD.	ISSUE PRICE	QUOTE U.S.$
1995	Covered Hen & Egg	950	1995	95.00	95

Mary Gregory - M. Reynolds

YEAR ISSUE		EDITION LIMIT	YEAR RETD.	ISSUE PRICE	QUOTE U.S.$
1994	Plate w/stand, 9"	Closed	1994	65.00	65
1995	Plate w/stand, 9"	Closed	1995	65.00	65

Mother's Day Series - Fenton, unless otherwise noted

YEAR ISSUE		EDITION LIMIT	YEAR RETD.	ISSUE PRICE	QUOTE U.S.$
1971	Madonna w/Sleeping Child, Carnival	Closed	1971	10.75	15
1971	Madonna w/Sleeping Child, Blue Satin	Closed	1971	10.75	15
1972	Madonna of the Goldfinch, Carnival	Closed	1972	12.50	15

YEAR ISSUE		EDITION LIMIT	YEAR RETD.	ISSUE PRICE	QUOTE U.S.$
1972	Madonna of the Goldfinch, Blue Satin	Closed	1972	12.50	15
1972	Madonna of the Goldfinch, White Satin	Closed	1972	12.50	15
1973	The Small Cowper Madonna, Carnival	Closed	1973	12.50	15
1973	The Small Cowper Madonna, Blue Satin	Closed	1973	12.50	15
1973	The Small Cowper Madonna, White Satin	Closed	1973	12.50	15
1974	Madonna of the Grotto, Carnival	Closed	1974	13.50	15
1974	Madonna of the Grotto, Blue Satin	Closed	1974	13.50	15
1974	Madonna of the Grotto, White Satin	Closed	1974	13.50	15
1975	Taddei Madonna, Blue Satin	Closed	1975	13.50	15
1975	Taddei Madonna, Carnival	Closed	1975	13.50	15
1975	Taddei Madonna, White Satin	Closed	1975	13.50	15
1976	The Holly Night, Cardinal	Closed	1976	13.50	15
1976	The Holly Night, Blue Satin	Closed	1976	13.50	15
1976	The Holly Night, White Satin	Closed	1976	13.50	15
1977	Madonna & Child w/Pomegrantate, Carnival	Closed	1977	15.00	15
1977	Madonna & Child w/Pomegrantate, Blue Satin	Closed	1977	15.00	15
1977	Madonna & Child w/Pomegrantate, White Satin	Closed	1977	15.00	15
1978	The Madonnina, Cardinal	Closed	1978	15.00	15
1978	The Madonnina, Blue Satin	Closed	1978	15.00	15
1978	The Madonnina, White Satin	Closed	1978	15.00	15
1979	Madonna of the Rose Hedge, Carnival	Closed	1979	15.00	15
1979	Madonna of the Rose Hedge, Blue Satin	Closed	1979	15.00	15
1979	Madonna of the Rose Hedge, White Satin	Closed	1979	15.00	15
1979	Madonna of the Rose Hedge, Ruby Carnival	Closed	1979	35.00	35
1980	New Born - L. Everson	Closed	1980	28.50	29
1981	Gentle Fawn - L. Everson	Closed	1981	32.50	33
1982	Nature's Awakening - L. Everson	Closed	1982	35.00	35
1983	Where's Mom - L. Everson	Closed	1983	35.00	35
1984	Precious Panda - L. Everson	Closed	1984	35.00	35
1985	Mother's Little Lamb - L. Everson	Closed	1985	35.00	35
1990	Mother Swan - L. Everson	Closed	1990	45.00	50
1991	Mother's Watchful Eye - M. Reynolds	Closed	1991	45.00	50
1992	Let's Play With Mom - M. Reynolds	Closed	1992	49.50	50
1993	Mother Deer - M. Reynolds	Closed	1993	49.50	50
1994	Loving Puppy - M. Reynolds	Closed	1994	49.50	50

Flambro Imports

Emmett Kelly Jr. Plates - Various

YEAR ISSUE		EDITION LIMIT	YEAR RETD.	ISSUE PRICE	QUOTE U.S.$
1983	Why Me? Plate I - C. Kelly	10,000		40.00	450
1984	Balloons For Sale Plate II C. Kelly	10,000		40.00	350
1985	Big Business Plate III - C. Kelly	10,000		40.00	350
1986	And God Bless America IV C. Kelly	10,000		40.00	325
1988	Tis the Season - D. Rust	10,000		50.00	80-125
1989	Looking Back- 65th Birthday D. Rust	6,500		50.00	125
1991	Winter - D. Rust	10,000		30.00	30
1992	Spring - D. Rust	10,000		30.00	30
1992	Summer - D. Rust	10,000		30.00	30
1992	Autumn - D. Rust	10,000		30.00	30
1993	Santa's Stowaway - D. Rust	10,000		30.00	30
1994	70th Birthday Commemorative D. Rust	5,000		30.00	30
1995	All Wrapped Up in Christmas Undis.	5,000		30.00	30

Fountainhead

As Free As The Wind - M. Fernandez

YEAR ISSUE		EDITION LIMIT	YEAR RETD.	ISSUE PRICE	QUOTE U.S.$
1989	As Free As The Wind	Unkn.		295.00	300-600

The Wings of Freedom - M. Fernandez

YEAR ISSUE		EDITION LIMIT	YEAR RETD.	ISSUE PRICE	QUOTE U.S.$
1985	Courtship Flight	2,500		250.00	1300-2000
1986	Wings of Freedom	2,500		250.00	1000-1300

Gartlan USA

Carlton Fisk - M. Taylor

YEAR ISSUE		EDITION LIMIT	YEAR RETD.	ISSUE PRICE	QUOTE U.S.$
1992	Signed Plate (10 1/4")	950	1993	70-150.	175
1992	Signed Plate (10 1/4") A/P	300		175.00	175
1992	Plate (8 1/2")	10,000		30.00	30
1992	Plate (3 1/4")	Open		15.00	15

George Brett Gold Crown Collection - J. Martin

YEAR ISSUE		EDITION LIMIT	YEAR RETD.	ISSUE PRICE	QUOTE U.S.$
1986	George Brett "Baseball's All Star" (3 1/4")	Open		12.95	15-20
1986	George Brett "Baseball's All Star" (10 1/4") signed	2,000		100.00	200

Joe Montana - M. Taylor

YEAR ISSUE		EDITION LIMIT	YEAR RETD.	ISSUE PRICE	QUOTE U.S.$
1991	Signed Plate (10 1/4")	2,250		125.00	150-300
1991	Signed Plate (10 1/4") A/P	250		195.00	195
1991	Plate (8 1/2")	10,000		30.00	30
1991	Plate (3 1/4")	Open		15.00	15

Johnny Bench - M. Taylor

YEAR ISSUE		EDITION LIMIT	YEAR RETD.	ISSUE PRICE	QUOTE U.S.$
1989	Collector Plate (10 1/4") signed	1,989		100.00	200
1989	Collector Plate (3 1/4")	Open		15.00	15

Kareem Abdul-Jabbar Sky-Hook Collection - M. Taylor

YEAR ISSUE		EDITION LIMIT	YEAR RETD.	ISSUE PRICE	QUOTE U.S.$
1989	Kareem Abdul-Jabbar "Path of Glory" (10 1/4"), signed	1,989		100.00	175-295
1989	Collector plate (3 1/4")	Closed		16.00	30

Magic Johnson Gold Rim Collection - R. Winslow

YEAR ISSUE		EDITION LIMIT	YEAR RETD.	ISSUE PRICE	QUOTE U.S.$
1987	Magic Johnson "The Magic Show" (10 1/4"), signed	1,987		100.00	450-550
1987	Magic Johnson "The Magic Show" (3 1/4")	Closed		14.50	25-35

Mike Schmidt "500th" Home Run Edition - C. Paluso

YEAR ISSUE		EDITION LIMIT	YEAR RETD.	ISSUE PRICE	QUOTE U.S.$
1987	Mike Schmidt "Power at the Plate" (10 1/4"), signed	1,987		100.00	395-495
1987	Mike Schmidt "Power at the Plate" (3 1/4")	Open		14.50	19
1987	Mike Schmidt A/P	56		150.00	150
1987	Mike Schmidt (signed & dated)	50		100.00	595

Pete Rose Diamond Collection - Forbes

YEAR ISSUE		EDITION LIMIT	YEAR RETD.	ISSUE PRICE	QUOTE U.S.$
1988	Pete Rose "The Reigning Legend" (10 1/4"), signed	950		195.00	250-300
1988	Pete Rose "The Reigning Legend" (10 1/4"), signed A/P	50		300.00	395
1988	Pete Rose "The Reigning Legend"(3 1/4")	Open		14.50	15

Pete Rose Platinum Edition - T. Sizemore

YEAR ISSUE		EDITION LIMIT	YEAR RETD.	ISSUE PRICE	QUOTE U.S.$
1985	Pete Rose "The Best of Baseball"(3 1/4")	Open		12.95	15-20
1985	Pete Rose "The Best of Baseball"(10 1/4")	4,192		100.00	385
1985	Pete Rose "The Best of Baseball"(10 1/4"), (signed & dated)	50		100.00	675

Roger Staubach Sterling Collection - C. Soileau

YEAR ISSUE		EDITION LIMIT	YEAR RETD.	ISSUE PRICE	QUOTE U.S.$
1987	Roger Staubach (3 1/4" diameter)	Open		12.95	15-20
1987	Roger Staubach (10 1/4" diameter) signed	1,979		100.00	125-195

Wayne Gretzky - M. Taylor

YEAR ISSUE		EDITION LIMIT	YEAR RETD.	ISSUE PRICE	QUOTE U.S.$
1989	Collector Plate (10 1/4"), signed by Gretzky and Howe	1,851		225.00	225-350
1989	Collector Plate (10 1/4") A/P, signed by Gretzky and Howe	300		300.00	450-575
1989	Collector Plate (8 1/2")	10,000		45.00	45-50
1989	Collector Plate (3 1/4")	Open		15.00	15

Georgetown Collection, Inc.

Children of the Great Spirit - C. Theroux

YEAR ISSUE		EDITION LIMIT	YEAR RETD.	ISSUE PRICE	QUOTE U.S.$
1993	Buffalo Child	35-day		29.95	30
1993	Winter Baby	35-day		29.95	30

Goebel/M.I. Hummel

M.I. Hummel Club Exclusive-Celebration - M.I. Hummel

YEAR ISSUE		EDITION LIMIT	YEAR RETD.	ISSUE PRICE	QUOTE U.S.$
1986	Valentine Gift (Hum 738)	Closed		90.00	90-120
1987	Valentine Joy (Hum 737)	Closed		98.00	90-120
1988	Daisies Don't Tell (Hum 736)	Closed		115.00	115-130
1989	It's Cold (Hum 735)	Closed		120.00	120-150

M.I. Hummel Collectibles Anniversary Plates - M.I. Hummel

YEAR ISSUE		EDITION LIMIT	YEAR RETD.	ISSUE PRICE	QUOTE U.S.$
1975	Stormy Weather 280	Closed		100.00	75-120
1980	Spring Dance 281	Closed		225.00	50-100
1985	Auf Wiedersehen 282	Closed		225.00	100-250

M.I. Hummel Collectibles-Annual Plates - M.I. Hummel

YEAR ISSUE		EDITION LIMIT	YEAR RETD.	ISSUE PRICE	QUOTE U.S.$
1971	Heavenly Angel 264	Closed		25.00	550-625
1972	Hear Ye, Hear Ye 265	Closed		30.00	40-60
1973	Glober Trotter 266	Closed		32.50	75-120
1974	Goose Girl 267	Closed		40.00	45-75
1975	Ride into Christmas 268	Closed		50.00	60
1976	Apple Tree Girl 269	Closed		50.00	50-60
1977	Apple Tree Boy 270	Closed		52.50	80-110
1978	Happy Pastime 271	Closed		65.00	50-85
1979	Singing Lesson 272	Closed		90.00	65-90
1980	School Girl 273	Closed		100.00	90
1981	Umbrella Boy 274	Closed		100.00	60-100
1982	Umbrella Girl 275	Closed		100.00	125-150
1983	The Postman 276	Closed		108.00	175-195
1984	Little Helper 277	Closed		108.00	75-105
1985	Chick Girl 278	Closed		110.00	90-110
1986	Playmates 279	Closed		125.00	125-170
1987	Feeding Time 283	Closed		135.00	250-350
1988	Little Goat Herder 284	Closed		145.00	100-120
1989	Farm Boy 285	Closed		160.00	130-150
1990	Shepherd's Boy 286	Closed		170.00	170-250
1991	Just Resting 287	Closed		196.00	125-170
1992	Wayside Harmony 288	Closed		210.00	210-230
1993	Doll Bath 289	Closed		210.00	210-225
1994	Doctor 290	Closed		225.00	225-250
1995	Come Back Soon 291	Yr.Iss.		250.00	250

M.I. Hummel-Friends Forever - M.I. Hummel

YEAR ISSUE		EDITION LIMIT	YEAR RETD.	ISSUE PRICE	QUOTE U.S.$
1992	Meditation 292	Open		180.00	195
1993	For Father 293	Open		195.00	195
1994	Sweet Greetings 294	Open		205.00	205
1995	Surprise 295	Open		210.00	210

M.I. Hummel-Little Music Makers - M.I. Hummel

YEAR ISSUE		EDITION LIMIT	YEAR RETD.	ISSUE PRICE	QUOTE U.S.$
1984	Little Fiddler 744	Closed		30.00	30-70
1985	Serenade 741	Closed		30.00	30-70
1986	Soloist 743	Closed		35.00	35-70
1987	Band Leader 742	Closed		40.00	40-70

M.I. Hummel-The Little Homemakers - M.I. Hummel

YEAR ISSUE		EDITION LIMIT	YEAR RETD.	ISSUE PRICE	QUOTE U.S.$
1988	Little Sweeper (Hum 745)	Closed		45.00	45
1989	Wash Day (Hum 746)	Closed		50.00	50
1990	A Stitch in Time (Hum 747)	Closed		50.00	50
1991	Chicken Licken (Hum 748)	Closed		70.00	70

Gorham

(Four Seasons) A Boy and His Dog Plates - N. Rockwell

YEAR ISSUE		EDITION LIMIT	YEAR RETD.	ISSUE PRICE	QUOTE U.S.$
1971	Boy Meets His Dog	Annual	1971	50.00	225
1971	Adventures Between Adventures	Annual	1971	Set	Set
1971	The Mysterious Malady	Annual	1971	Set	Set
1971	Pride of Parenthood	Annual	1971	Set	Set

(Four Seasons) A Helping Hand Plates - N. Rockwell

YEAR ISSUE		EDITION LIMIT	YEAR RETD.	ISSUE PRICE	QUOTE U.S.$
1979	Year End Court	Annual	1979	100.00	100-125
1979	Closed for Business	Annual	1979	Set	Set
1979	Swatter's Rights	Annual	1979	Set	Set
1979	Coal Season's Coming	Annual	1979	Set	Set

(Four Seasons) Dad's Boys Plates - N. Rockwell

YEAR ISSUE		EDITION LIMIT	YEAR RETD.	ISSUE PRICE	QUOTE U.S.$
1980	Ski Skills	Annual	1980	135.00	90-135
1980	In His Spirits	Annual	1980	Set	Set
1980	Trout Dinner	Annual	1980	Set	Set
1980	Careful Aim	Annual	1980	Set	Set

(Four Seasons) Four Ages of Love - N. Rockwell

YEAR ISSUE		EDITION LIMIT	YEAR RETD.	ISSUE PRICE	QUOTE U.S.$
1973	Gaily Sharing Vintage Time	Annual	1973	60.00	165
1973	Flowers in Tender Bloom	Annual	1973	Set	Set
1973	Sweet Song So Young	Annual	1973	Set	Set
1973	Fondly We Do Remember	Annual	1973	Set	Set

(Four Seasons) Going on Sixteen Plates - N. Rockwell

YEAR ISSUE		EDITION LIMIT	YEAR RETD.	ISSUE PRICE	QUOTE U.S.$
1977	Chilling Chore	Annual	1977	75.00	95
1977	Sweet Serenade	Annual	1977	Set	Set
1977	Shear Agony	Annual	1977	Set	Set
1977	Pilgrimage	Annual	1977	Set	Set

(Four Seasons) Grand Pals Four Plates - N. Rockwell

YEAR ISSUE		EDITION LIMIT	YEAR RETD.	ISSUE PRICE	QUOTE U.S.$
1976	Snow Sculpturing	Annual	1976	70.00	120
1976	Soaring Spirits	Annual	1976	Set	Set
1976	Fish Finders	Annual	1976	Set	Set
1976	Ghostly Gourds	Annual	1976	Set	Set

(Four Seasons) Grandpa and Me Plates - N. Rockwell

YEAR ISSUE		EDITION LIMIT	YEAR RETD.	ISSUE PRICE	QUOTE U.S.$
1974	Gay Blades	Annual	1974	60.00	90
1974	Day Dreamers	Annual	1974	Set	Set
1974	Goin' Fishing	Annual	1974	Set	Set
1974	Pensive Pals	Annual	1974	Set	Set

(Four Seasons) Landscapes - N. Rockwell

YEAR ISSUE		EDITION LIMIT	YEAR RETD.	ISSUE PRICE	QUOTE U.S.$
1980	Summer Respite	Annual	1980	45.00	80
1981	Autumn Reflection	Annual	1981	45.00	65
1982	Winter Delight	Annual	1982	50.00	63
1983	Spring Recess	Annual	1983	60.00	60

(Four Seasons) Life with Father Plates - N. Rockwell

YEAR ISSUE		EDITION LIMIT	YEAR RETD.	ISSUE PRICE	QUOTE U.S.$
1982	Big Decision	Annual	1982	100.00	100
1982	Blasting Out	Annual	1982	Set	Set
1982	Cheering the Champs	Annual	1982	Set	Set
1982	A Tough One	Annual	1982	Set	Set

(Four Seasons) Me and My Pals Plates - N. Rockwell

YEAR ISSUE		EDITION LIMIT	YEAR RETD.	ISSUE PRICE	QUOTE U.S.$
1975	A Lickin' Good Bath	Annual	1975	70.00	115
1975	Young Man's Fancy	Annual	1975	Set	Set
1975	Fisherman's Paradise	Annual	1975	Set	Set
1975	Disastrous Daring	Annual	1975	Set	Set

(Four Seasons) Old Buddies Plates - N. Rockwell

YEAR ISSUE		EDITION LIMIT	YEAR RETD.	ISSUE PRICE	QUOTE U.S.$
1983	Shared Success	Annual	1983	115.00	115
1983	Endless Debate	Annual	1983	Set	Set
1983	Hasty Retreat	Annual	1983	Set	Set
1983	Final Speech	Annual	1983	Set	Set

(Four Seasons) Old Timers Plates - N. Rockwell

YEAR ISSUE		EDITION LIMIT	YEAR RETD.	ISSUE PRICE	QUOTE U.S.$
1981	Canine Solo	Annual	1981	100.00	100
1981	Sweet Surprise	Annual	1981	Set	Set
1981	Lazy Days	Annual	1981	Set	Set
1981	Fancy Footwork	Annual	1981	Set	Set

(Four Seasons) Tender Years Plates - N. Rockwell

YEAR ISSUE		EDITION LIMIT	YEAR RETD.	ISSUE PRICE	QUOTE U.S.$
1978	New Year Look	Annual	1978	100.00	100-125
1978	Spring Tonic	Annual	1978	Set	Set
1978	Cool Aid	Annual	1978	Set	Set
1978	Chilly Reception	Annual	1978	Set	Set

(Four Seasons) Young Love Plates - N. Rockwell

YEAR ISSUE		EDITION LIMIT	YEAR RETD.	ISSUE PRICE	QUOTE U.S.$
1972	Downhill Daring	Annual	1972	60.00	100-180
1972	Beguiling Buttercup	Annual	1972	Set	Set
1972	Flying High	Annual	1972	Set	Set
1972	A Scholarly Pace	Annual	1972	Set	Set

American Artist - R. Donnelly

YEAR ISSUE		EDITION LIMIT	YEAR RETD.	ISSUE PRICE	QUOTE U.S.$
1976	Apache Mother & Child	9,800	1980	25.00	56

Barrymore - Barrymore

YEAR ISSUE		EDITION LIMIT	YEAR RETD.	ISSUE PRICE	QUOTE U.S.$
1971	Quiet Waters	15,000	1980	25.00	25
1972	San Pedro Harbor	15,000	1980	25.00	25
1972	Nantucket, Sterling	1,000	1972	100.00	100
1972	Little Boatyard, Sterling	1,000	1972	100.00	145

Bas Relief - N. Rockwell

YEAR ISSUE		EDITION LIMIT	YEAR RETD.	ISSUE PRICE	QUOTE U.S.$
1981	Sweet Song So Young	Undis.	1984	100.00	100
1981	Beguiling Buttercup	Undis.	1984	62.50	70
1982	Flowers in Tender Bloom	Undis.	1984	100.00	100
1982	Flying High	Undis.	1984	62.50	65

Boy Scout Plates - N. Rockwell

YEAR ISSUE		EDITION LIMIT	YEAR RETD.	ISSUE PRICE	QUOTE U.S.$
1975	Our Heritage	18,500	1980	19.50	40
1976	A Scout is Loyal	18,500	1990	19.50	55
1977	The Scoutmaster	18,500	1990	19.50	60
1977	A Good Sign	18,500	1990	19.50	50
1978	Pointing the Way	18,500	1990	19.50	50
1978	Campfire Story	18,500	1990	19.50	25
1980	Beyond the Easel	18,500	1990	45.00	45

Charles Russell - C. Russell

YEAR ISSUE		EDITION LIMIT	YEAR RETD.	ISSUE PRICE	QUOTE U.S.$
1980	In Without Knocking	9,800	1990	38.00	75
1981	Bronc to Breakfast	9,800	1990	38.00	50-75
1982	When Ignorance is Bliss	9,800	1990	45.00	75-115
1983	Cowboy Life	9,800	1990	45.00	100

China Bicentennial - Gorham

YEAR ISSUE		EDITION LIMIT	YEAR RETD.	ISSUE PRICE	QUOTE U.S.$
1972	1776 Plate	18,500	1980	17.50	35
1976	1776 Bicentennial	8,000	1980	17.50	35

Christmas - N. Rockwell

YEAR ISSUE		EDITION LIMIT	YEAR RETD.	ISSUE PRICE	QUOTE U.S.$
1974	Tiny Tim	Annual	1974	12.50	30-40
1975	Good Deeds	Annual	1975	17.50	20-30
1976	Christmas Trio	Annual	1976	19.50	30
1977	Yuletide Reckoning	Annual	1977	19.50	45
1978	Planning Christmas Visit	Annual	1978	24.50	30
1979	Santa's Helpers	Annual	1979	24.50	25
1980	Letter to Santa	Annual	1980	27.50	32
1981	Santa Plans His Visit	Annual	1981	29.50	30
1982	Jolly Coachman	Annual	1982	29.50	30
1983	Christmas Dancers	Annual	1983	29.50	35
1984	Christmas Medley	17,500	1984	29.95	30
1985	Home For The Holidays	17,500	1985	29.95	30
1986	Merry Christmas Grandma	17,500	1986	29.95	65
1987	The Homecoming	17,500	1987	35.00	45
1988	Discovery	17,500	1988	37.50	45

Christmas/Children's Television Workshop - Unknown

YEAR ISSUE		EDITION LIMIT	YEAR RETD.	ISSUE PRICE	QUOTE U.S.$
1981	Sesame Street Christmas	Annual	1981	17.50	18
1982	Sesame Street Christmas	Annual	1982	17.50	18
1983	Sesame Street Christmas	Annual	1983	19.50	20

Encounters, Survival and Celebrations - J. Clymer

YEAR ISSUE		EDITION LIMIT	YEAR RETD.	ISSUE PRICE	QUOTE U.S.$
1982	A Fine Welcome	7,500	1983	50.00	75
1983	Winter Trail	7,500	1984	50.00	125
1983	Alouette	7,500	1984	62.50	63
1983	The Trader	7,500	1984	62.50	63
1983	Winter Camp	7,500	1984	62.50	75
1983	The Trapper Takes a Wife	7,500	1984	62.50	63

Gallery of Masters - Various

YEAR ISSUE		EDITION LIMIT	YEAR RETD.	ISSUE PRICE	QUOTE U.S.$
1971	Man with a Gilt Helmet - Rembrandt	10,000	1975	50.00	50
1972	Self Portrait with Saskia - Rembrandt	10,000	1975	50.00	50
1973	The Honorable Mrs. Graham - Gainsborough	7,500	1975	50.00	50

Gorham Museum Doll Plates - Gorham

YEAR ISSUE		EDITION LIMIT	YEAR RETD.	ISSUE PRICE	QUOTE U.S.$
1984	Lydia	5,000	1984	29.00	125
1984	Belton Bebe	5,000	1984	29.00	55
1984	Christmas Lady	7,500	1984	32.50	33
1985	Lucille	5,000	1985	29.00	35
1985	Jumeau	5,000	1985	29.00	35

Julian Ritter - J. Ritter

YEAR ISSUE		EDITION LIMIT	YEAR RETD.	ISSUE PRICE	QUOTE U.S.$
1977	Christmas Visit	9,800	1977	24.50	29
1978	Valentine, Fluttering Heart	7,500	1978	45.00	45

Julian Ritter, Fall In Love - J. Ritter

YEAR ISSUE		EDITION LIMIT	YEAR RETD.	ISSUE PRICE	QUOTE U.S.$
1977	Enchantment	5,000	1977	100.00	100
1977	Frolic	5,000	1977	set	Set
1977	Gutsy Gal	5,000	1977	set	Set
1977	Lonely Chill	5,000	1977	set	Set

Julian Ritter, To Love a Clown - J. Ritter

YEAR ISSUE		EDITION LIMIT	YEAR RETD.	ISSUE PRICE	QUOTE U.S.$
1978	Awaited Reunion	5,000	1978	120.00	120
1978	Twosome Time	5,000	1978	120.00	120
1978	Showtime Beckons	5,000	1978	120.00	120
1978	Together in Memories	5,000	1978	120.00	120

Leyendecker Annual Christmas Plates - J. C. Leyendecker

YEAR ISSUE		EDITION LIMIT	YEAR RETD.	ISSUE PRICE	QUOTE U.S.$
1988	Christmas Hug	10,000	1988	37.50	50

Moppet Plates-Anniversary - Unknown

YEAR ISSUE		EDITION LIMIT	YEAR RETD.	ISSUE PRICE	QUOTE U.S.$
1976	Anniversary	20,000	1977	13.00	13

Moppet Plates-Christmas - Unknown

YEAR ISSUE		EDITION LIMIT	YEAR RETD.	ISSUE PRICE	QUOTE U.S.$
1973	Christmas	Annual	1973	10.00	35
1974	Christmas	Annual	1974	12.00	12
1975	Christmas	Annual	1975	13.00	13
1976	Christmas	Annual	1976	13.00	15
1977	Christmas	Annual	1977	13.00	14
1978	Christmas	Annual	1978	10.00	10
1979	Christmas	Annual	1979	12.00	12
1980	Christmas	Annual	1980	12.00	12
1981	Christmas	Annual	1981	12.00	12
1982	Christmas	Annual	1982	12.00	12
1983	Christmas	Annual	1983	12.00	12

Moppet Plates-Mother's Day - Unknown

YEAR ISSUE		EDITION LIMIT	YEAR RETD.	ISSUE PRICE	QUOTE U.S.$
1973	Mother's Day	Annual	1973	10.00	30
1974	Mother's Day	Annual	1974	12.00	20
1975	Mother's Day	Annual	1975	13.00	15
1976	Mother's Day	Annual	1976	13.00	15
1977	Mother's Day	Annual	1977	13.00	15
1978	Mother's Day	Annual	1978	10.00	10

Pastoral Symphony - B. Felder

YEAR ISSUE		EDITION LIMIT	YEAR RETD.	ISSUE PRICE	QUOTE U.S.$
1982	When I Was a Child	7,500	1983	42.50	50
1982	Gather the Children	7,500	1983	42.50	50
1984	Sugar and Spice	7,500	1985	42.50	50
XX	He Loves Me	7,500	1985	42.50	50

Pewter Bicentennial - R. Pailthorpe

YEAR ISSUE		EDITION LIMIT	YEAR RETD.	ISSUE PRICE	QUOTE U.S.$
1971	Burning of the Gaspee	5,000	1971	35.00	35
1972	Boston Tea Party	5,000	1972	35.00	35

Presidential - N. Rockwell

YEAR ISSUE		EDITION LIMIT	YEAR RETD.	ISSUE PRICE	QUOTE U.S.$
1976	John F. Kennedy	9,800	1976	30.00	65
1976	Dwight D. Eisenhower	9,800	1976	30.00	35

Remington Western - F. Remington

YEAR ISSUE		EDITION LIMIT	YEAR RETD.	ISSUE PRICE	QUOTE U.S.$
1973	A New Year on the Cimarron	Annual	1973	25.00	35-50
1973	Aiding a Comrade	Annual	1973	25.00	30-125
1973	The Flight	Annual	1973	25.00	30-95
1973	The Fight for the Water Hole	Annual	1973	25.00	30-125
1975	Old Ramond	Annual	1975	20.00	35-60
1975	A Breed	Annual	1975	20.00	35-65
1976	Cavalry Officer	5,000	1976	37.50	60-75
1976	A Trapper	5,000	1976	37.50	60-75

Silver Bicentennial - Various

YEAR ISSUE		EDITION LIMIT	YEAR RETD.	ISSUE PRICE	QUOTE U.S.$
1972	1776 Plate - Gorham	500	1972	500.00	500
1972	Burning of the Gaspee - R. Pailthorpe	750	1972	500.00	500
1973	Boston Tea Party - R. Pailthorpe	750	1973	550.00	575

Single Release - N. Rockwell

YEAR ISSUE		EDITION LIMIT	YEAR RETD.	ISSUE PRICE	QUOTE U.S.$
1974	The Golden Rule	Annual	1974	12.50	30
1975	Ben Franklin	Annual	1975	19.50	35

Single Release - F. Quagon

YEAR ISSUE		EDITION LIMIT	YEAR RETD.	ISSUE PRICE	QUOTE U.S.$
1976	The Black Regiment 1778	7,500	1978	25.00	58

Single Release - N. Rockwell

YEAR ISSUE		EDITION LIMIT	YEAR RETD.	ISSUE PRICE	QUOTE U.S.$
1974	Weighing In	Annual	1974	12.50	80-99
1976	The Marriage License	Numbrd	1985	37.50	52-75
1978	Triple Self Portrait Memorial	Annual	1978	37.50	75
1980	The Annual Visit	Annual	1980	32.50	70
1981	Day in Life of Boy	Annual	1981	50.00	80
1981	Day in Life of Girl	Annual	1981	50.00	80-108

Time Machine Teddies Plates - B. Port

YEAR ISSUE		EDITION LIMIT	YEAR RETD.	ISSUE PRICE	QUOTE U.S.$
1986	Miss Emily, Bearing Up	5,000	1986	32.50	50
1987	Big Bear, The Toy Collector	5,000	1987	32.50	45
1988	Hunny Munny	5,000	1988	37.50	40

Vermeil Bicentennial - Gorham

YEAR ISSUE		EDITION LIMIT	YEAR RETD.	ISSUE PRICE	QUOTE U.S.$
1972	1776 Plate	250	1972	750.00	800

Hackett American

Sports - Various

YEAR ISSUE		EDITION LIMIT	YEAR RETD.	ISSUE PRICE	QUOTE U.S.$
1981	Reggie Jackson h/s - Paluso	Retrd.	N/A	100.00	1065
1983	Steve Garvey h/s - Paluso	Retrd.	N/A	100.00	150-250
1983	Nolan Ryan h/s - Paluso	Retrd.	N/A	100.00	825
1983	Tom Seaver h/s - Paluso	3,272	N/A	100.00	350
1984	Steve Carlton h/s - Paluso	Retrd.	N/A	100.00	275
1985	Willie Mays h/s - Paluso	Retrd.	N/A	125.00	350-445
1985	Whitey Ford h/s - Paluso	Retrd.	N/A	125.00	295
1985	Hank Aaron h/s - Paluso	Retrd.	N/A	125.00	350-445
1985	Sandy Koufax h/s - Paluso	1,000	N/A	125.00	300-500
1985	H. Killebrew d/s - Paluso	Retrd.	N/A	125.00	200-360
1985	E. Mathews d/s - Paluso	Retrd.	N/A	125.00	225-300
1986	T. Seaver 300 d/s - Paluso	1,200	N/A	125.00	250
1986	Roger Clemens d/s - Paluso	Retrd.	N/A	125.00	600-900
1986	Reggie Jackson d/s - Paluso	Retrd.	N/A	125.00	395
1986	Wally Joyner d/s - Paluso	Retrd.	N/A	125.00	295
1986	Don Sutton d/s (great events)-Paluso	300	N/A	125.00	250
XX	Gary Carter d/s - Simon	Retrd.	N/A	125.00	175
1985	Dwight Gooden u/s - Simon	Retrd.	N/A	55.00	85
XX	Arnold Palmer h/s - Alexander	Retrd.	N/A	125.00	225
XX	Gary Player h/s - Alexander	Retrd.	N/A	125.00	350
1983	Reggie Jackson h/s - Alexander	Retrd.	N/A	125.00	695
1983	Reggie Jackson, proof - Alexander	Retrd.	N/A	250.00	1695
1986	Joe Montana d/s - Alexander	Retrd.	N/A	125.00	595

Hadley House

American Memories Series - T. Redlin

YEAR ISSUE		EDITION LIMIT	YEAR RETD.	ISSUE PRICE	QUOTE U.S.$
1987	Coming Home	9,500		85.00	85
1988	Lights of Home	9,500	1994	85.00	150
1989	Homeward Bound	9,500		85.00	85
1991	Family Traditions	9,500		85.00	85

Annual Christmas Series - T. Redlin

YEAR ISSUE		EDITION LIMIT	YEAR RETD.	ISSUE PRICE	QUOTE U.S.$
1991	Heading Home	9,500	1994	65.00	125
1992	Pleasures Of Winter	19,500		65.00	125
1993	Winter Wonderland	19,500		65.00	125
1994	Almost Home	19,500		65.00	125
1995	Sharing the Evening	45-day		29.95	30

Country Doctor Collection - T. Redlin

YEAR ISSUE		EDITION LIMIT	YEAR RETD.	ISSUE PRICE	QUOTE U.S.$
1995	Wednesday Afternoon	45-day		29.95	30
1995	Office Hours	45-day		29.95	30
1995	House Calls	45-day		29.95	30
1995	Morning Rounds	45-day		29.95	30

Glow Series - T. Redlin

YEAR ISSUE		EDITION LIMIT	YEAR RETD.	ISSUE PRICE	QUOTE U.S.$
1985	Evening Glow	5,000	1986	55.00	400
1985	Morning Glow	5,000	1986	55.00	200
1985	Twilight Glow	5,000	1988	55.00	100
1988	Afternoon Glow	5,000	1989	55.00	55

Lovers Collection - O. Franca

YEAR ISSUE		EDITION LIMIT	YEAR RETD.	ISSUE PRICE	QUOTE U.S.$
1992	Lovers	9,500		50.00	50

Navajo Visions Suite - O. Franca

YEAR ISSUE		EDITION LIMIT	YEAR RETD.	ISSUE PRICE	QUOTE U.S.$
1993	Navajo Fantasy	9,500		50.00	50
1993	Young Warrior	9,500		50.00	50

Navajo Woman Series - O. Franca

YEAR ISSUE		EDITION LIMIT	YEAR RETD.	ISSUE PRICE	QUOTE U.S.$
1990	Feathered Hair Ties	5,000	1994	50.00	50
1991	Navajo Summer	5,000		50.00	50
1992	Turquoise Necklace	5,000		50.00	50
1993	Pink Navajo	5,000		50.00	50

Retreat Series - T. Redlin

YEAR ISSUE		EDITION LIMIT	YEAR RETD.	ISSUE PRICE	QUOTE U.S.$
1987	Morning Retreat	9,500	1988	65.00	100
1987	Evening Retreat	9,500	1989	65.00	100
1988	Golden Retreat	9,500	1989	65.00	100
1989	Moonlight Retreat	9,500	1993	65.00	65

Seasons - T. Redlin

YEAR ISSUE		EDITION LIMIT	YEAR RETD.	ISSUE PRICE	QUOTE U.S.$
1994	Autumn Evening	45-day		29.95	30
1995	Spring Fever	45-day		29.95	30
1995	Summertime	45-day		29.95	30
1995	Wintertime	45-day		29.95	30

That Special Time - T. Redlin

YEAR ISSUE		EDITION LIMIT	YEAR RETD.	ISSUE PRICE	QUOTE U.S.$
1991	Evening Solitude	9,500	1994	65.00	65
1991	That Special Time	9,500	1993	65.00	65
1992	Aroma of Fall	9,500	1994	65.00	65
1993	Welcome To Paradise	9,500		65.00	65

Tranquility - O. Franca

YEAR ISSUE		EDITION LIMIT	YEAR RETD.	ISSUE PRICE	QUOTE U.S.$
1994	Blue Navajo	9,500		50.00	50
1994	Blue Tranquility	9,500		50.00	50
1994	Navajo Meditating	9,500		50.00	50
1995	Navajo Reflection	9,500		50.00	50

Wildlife Memories - T. Redlin

YEAR ISSUE		EDITION LIMIT	YEAR RETD.	ISSUE PRICE	QUOTE U.S.$
1994	Best Friends	19,500		65.00	65
1994	Comforts of Home	19,500		65.00	65
1994	Pure Contentment	19,500		65.00	65
1994	Sharing in the Solitude	19,500		65.00	65

Windows to the Wild - T. Redlin

YEAR ISSUE		EDITION LIMIT	YEAR RETD.	ISSUE PRICE	QUOTE U.S.$
1990	Master's Domain	9,500		65.00	65
1991	Winter Windbreak	9,500		65.00	65
1992	Evening Company	9,500		65.00	65
1994	Night Mapling	9,500		65.00	65

Hallmark Galleries

Days to Remember-The Art of Norman Rockwell - Rockwell-Inspired

YEAR ISSUE		EDITION LIMIT	YEAR RETD.	ISSUE PRICE	QUOTE U.S.$
1992	A Boy Meets His Dog (pewter medallion) 4500QHG9715	9,500	1994	45.00	45
1992	Sweet Song So Young (pewter medallion) 4500QHG9716	9,500	1994	45.00	45
1992	Fisherman's Paradise (pewter medallion) 4500QHG9717	9,500	1994	45.00	45
1992	Sleeping Children (pewter medallion) 4500QHG9718	9,500	1994	45.00	45
1993	Breaking Home Ties 3500QHG9723	9,500	1995	35.00	35
1994	Growing Years 3500QHG9724	9,500	1995	35.00	35

Easter Plate - L. Votruba

YEAR ISSUE		EDITION LIMIT	YEAR RETD.	ISSUE PRICE	QUOTE U.S.$
1994	Collector's Plate-(1st Ed.) 775QEO8233	Yr.Iss.	1995	7.75	25

Enchanted Garden - E. Richardson

YEAR ISSUE		EDITION LIMIT	YEAR RETD.	ISSUE PRICE	QUOTE U.S.$
1992	Neighborhood Dreamer 4500QHG3001	9,500	1994	45.00	45
1992	Swan Lake (tile) 3500QHG3010	9,500	1994	35.00	35

PLATES

YEAR ISSUE		EDITION LIMIT	YEAR RETD.	ISSUE PRICE	QUOTE U.S.$
1992	Fairy Bunny Tale: The Beginning (tile) 2500QHG3011	14,500	1994	25.00	25
1992	Fairy Bunny Tale: Beginning II (tile) 3500QHG3015	14,500	1994	35.00	35

Innocent Wonders - T. Blackshear

YEAR ISSUE		EDITION LIMIT	YEAR RETD.	ISSUE PRICE	QUOTE U.S.$
1992	Pinkie Poo 3500QHG4017	9,500	1995	35.00	35
1992	Dinky Toot 3500QHG4019	9,500	1995	35.00	35
1993	Pockets 3500QHG4022	9,500	1995	35.00	35
1994	Twinky Wink 3500QHG4023	9,500	1995	35.00	35

Majestic Wilderness - M. Englebreit

YEAR ISSUE		EDITION LIMIT	YEAR RETD.	ISSUE PRICE	QUOTE U.S.$
1994	Golden Rule (tile) 3000QHG5010	14,500	1995	30.00	30
1994	Recipe for Happiness (tile) 3000QHG5011	14,500	1995	30.00	30

Majestic Wilderness - M. Newman

YEAR ISSUE		EDITION LIMIT	YEAR RETD.	ISSUE PRICE	QUOTE U.S.$
1992	Timber Wolves (porcelain) 3500QHG2012	9,500	1995	35.00	35
1992	Vixen & Kits 3500QHG2018	9,500	1995	35.00	35
1994	White Tail Buck 3500QHG2030	9,500	1995	35.00	35

Tobin Fraley Carousels - T. Fraley

YEAR ISSUE		EDITION LIMIT	YEAR RETD.	ISSUE PRICE	QUOTE U.S.$
1992	Philadelphia Toboggan Co/1920 (pewter medallion) 4500QHG20	9,500	1994	45.00	45
1993	Magical Ride 3500QHG30	9,500	1995	35.00	35
1994	Riding to Adventure 3500QHG23	9,500	1995	35.00	35

Hamilton Collection

All in a Day's Work - J. Lamb

YEAR ISSUE		EDITION LIMIT	YEAR RETD.	ISSUE PRICE	QUOTE U.S.$
1994	Where's the Fire?	28-day		29.50	30
1994	Lunch Break	28-day		29.50	30
1994	Puppy Patrol	28-day		29.50	30
1994	Decoy Delivery	28-day		29.50	30
1994	Budding Artist	28-day		29.50	30
1994	Garden Guards	28-day		29.50	30
1994	Saddling Up	28-day		29.50	30
1995	Taking the Lead	28-day		29.50	30

America's Greatest Sailing Ships - T. Freeman

YEAR ISSUE		EDITION LIMIT	YEAR RETD.	ISSUE PRICE	QUOTE U.S.$
1988	USS Constitution	14-day		29.50	40
1988	Great Republic	14-day		29.50	40
1988	America	14-day		29.50	45
1988	Charles W. Morgan	14-day		29.50	40
1988	Eagle	14-day		29.50	48
1988	Bonhomme Richard	14-day		29.50	40
1988	Gertrude L. Thebaud	14-day		29.50	45
1988	Enterprise	14-day		29.50	36

The American Civil War - D. Prechtel

YEAR ISSUE		EDITION LIMIT	YEAR RETD.	ISSUE PRICE	QUOTE U.S.$
1990	General Robert E. Lee	14-day		37.50	55-75
1990	Generals Grant and Lee At Appomattox	14-day		37.50	50-55
1990	General Thomas "Stonewall" Jackson	14-day		37.50	55
1990	Abraham Lincoln	14-day		37.50	50-60
1991	General J.E.B. Stuart	14-day		37.50	45-54
1991	General Philip Sheridan	14-day		37.50	60
1991	A Letter from Home	14-day		37.50	60
1991	Going Home	14-day		37.50	45
1992	Assembling The Troop	14-day		37.50	75
1992	Standing Watch	14-day		37.50	75

The American Wilderness - M. Richter

YEAR ISSUE		EDITION LIMIT	YEAR RETD.	ISSUE PRICE	QUOTE U.S.$
1995	Gray Wolf	28-day		29.95	30

Andy Griffith - R. Tanenbaum

YEAR ISSUE		EDITION LIMIT	YEAR RETD.	ISSUE PRICE	QUOTE U.S.$
1992	Sheriff Andy Taylor	28-day		29.50	45
1992	A Startling Conclusion	28-day		29.50	40
1993	Mayberry Sing-a-long	28-day		29.50	30
1993	Aunt Bee's Kitchen	28-day		29.50	30
1993	Surprise! Surprise!	28-day		29.50	30
1993	An Explosive Situation	28-day		29.50	30
1993	Meeting Aunt Bee	28-day		29.50	30
1993	Opie's Big Catch	28-day		29.50	30

The Angler's Prize - M. Susinno

YEAR ISSUE		EDITION LIMIT	YEAR RETD.	ISSUE PRICE	QUOTE U.S.$
1991	Trophy Bass	14-day		29.50	36
1991	Blue Ribbon Trout	14-day		29.50	33
1991	Sun Dancers	14-day		29.50	30
1991	Freshwater Barracuda	14-day		29.50	36
1991	Bronzeback Fighter	14-day		29.50	36
1991	Autumn Beauty	14-day		29.50	36
1992	Old Mooneyes	14-day		29.50	36
1992	Silver King	14-day		29.50	33

Beauty Of Winter - N/A

YEAR ISSUE		EDITION LIMIT	YEAR RETD.	ISSUE PRICE	QUOTE U.S.$
1992	Silent Night	28-day		29.50	30
1993	Moonlight Sleighride	28-day		29.50	30

The Best Of Baseball - R. Tanenbaum

YEAR ISSUE		EDITION LIMIT	YEAR RETD.	ISSUE PRICE	QUOTE U.S.$
1993	The Legendary Mickey Mantle	28-day		29.50	30
1993	The Immortal Babe Ruth	28-day		29.50	30
1993	The Great Willie Mays	28-day		29.50	30
1993	The Unbeatable Duke Snider	28-day		29.50	30
1993	The Extraordinary Lou Gehrig	28-day		29.50	30
1993	The Phenomenal Roberto Clemente	28-day		29.50	30
1993	The Remarkable Johnny Bench	28-day		29.50	30
1993	The Incredible Nolan Ryan	28-day		29.50	30
1993	The Exceptional Brooks Robinson	28-day		29.50	30
1993	The Unforgettable Phil Rizzuto	28-day		29.50	30
1995	The Incomparable Reggie Jackson	28-day		29.50	30

Bialoskyr & Friends - P./A.Bialosky

YEAR ISSUE		EDITION LIMIT	YEAR RETD.	ISSUE PRICE	QUOTE U.S.$
1992	Family Addition	28-day		29.50	30
1993	Sweetheart	28-day		29.50	30
1993	Let's Go Fishing	28-day		29.50	30
1993	U.S. Mail	28-day		29.50	30
1993	Sleigh Ride	28-day		29.50	30
1993	Honey For Sale	28-day		29.50	30
1993	Breakfast In Bed	28-day		29.50	36
1993	My First Two-Wheeler	28-day		29.50	30

Big Cats of the World - D. Manning

YEAR ISSUE		EDITION LIMIT	YEAR RETD.	ISSUE PRICE	QUOTE U.S.$
1989	African Shade	14-day		29.50	30
1989	View from Above	14-day		29.50	30
1990	On The Prowl	14-day		29.50	30
1990	Deep In The Jungle	14-day		29.50	30
1990	Spirit Of The Mountain	14-day		29.50	30
1990	Spotted Sentinel	14-day		29.50	30
1990	Above the Treetops	14-day		29.50	30
1990	Mountain Dweller	14-day		29.50	30
1992	Jungle Habitat	14-day		29.50	30
1992	Solitary Sentry	14-day		29.50	30

Bundles of Joy - B. P. Gutmann

YEAR ISSUE		EDITION LIMIT	YEAR RETD.	ISSUE PRICE	QUOTE U.S.$
1988	Awakening	14-day		24.50	75
1988	Happy Dreams	14-day		24.50	60-99
1988	Tasting	14-day		24.50	36-59
1988	Sweet Innocence	14-day		24.50	30
1988	Tommy	14-day		24.50	30
1988	A Little Bit of Heaven	14-day		24.50	75
1988	Billy	14-day		24.50	30-35
1988	Sun Kissed	14-day		24.50	30-35

Butterfly Garden - P. Sweany

YEAR ISSUE		EDITION LIMIT	YEAR RETD.	ISSUE PRICE	QUOTE U.S.$
1987	Spicebush Swallowtail	14-day		29.50	45
1987	Common Blue	14-day		29.50	38
1987	Orange Sulphur	14-day		29.50	35-50
1987	Monarch	14-day		29.50	38
1987	Tiger Swallowtail	14-day		29.50	35
1987	Crimson Patched Longwing	14-day		29.50	38
1988	Morning Cloak	14-day		29.50	35
1988	Red Admiral	14-day		29.50	38

The Call of the North - J. Tift

YEAR ISSUE		EDITION LIMIT	YEAR RETD.	ISSUE PRICE	QUOTE U.S.$
1993	Winter's Dawn	28-day		29.50	30
1994	Evening Silence	28-day		29.50	30
1994	Moonlit Wilderness	28-day		29.50	30
1994	Silent Snowfall	28-day		29.50	30
1994	Snowy Watch	28-day		29.50	30
1994	Sentinels of the Summit	28-day		29.50	30
1994	Arctic Seclusion	28-day		29.50	30
1994	Forest Twilight	28-day		29.50	30
1994	Mountain Explorer	28-day		29.50	30
1994	The Cry of Winter	28-day		29.50	30

Call to Adventure - R. Cross

YEAR ISSUE		EDITION LIMIT	YEAR RETD.	ISSUE PRICE	QUOTE U.S.$
1993	USS Constitution	28-day		29.50	30
1993	The Bounty	28-day		29.50	30
1994	Bonhomme Richard	28-day		29.50	30
1994	Old Nantucket	28-day		29.50	30
1994	Golden West	28-day		29.50	30
1994	Boston	28-day		29.50	30
1994	Hannah	28-day		29.50	30
1994	Improvement	28-day		29.50	30
1995	Anglo-American	28-day		29.50	30
1995	Challenge	28-day		29.50	30

Cameo Kittens - Q. Lemonds

YEAR ISSUE		EDITION LIMIT	YEAR RETD.	ISSUE PRICE	QUOTE U.S.$
1993	Ginger Snap	28-day		29.50	30
1993	Cat Tails	28-day		29.50	30
1993	Lady Blue	28-day		29.50	30
1993	Tiny Heart Stealer	28-day		29.50	30
1993	Blossom	28-day		29.50	30
1994	Whisker Antics	28-day		29.50	30
1994	Tiger's Temptation	28-day		29.50	30
1994	Scout	28-day		29.50	30
1995	Timid Tabby	28-day		29.50	30

A Child's Best Friend - B. P. Gutmann

YEAR ISSUE		EDITION LIMIT	YEAR RETD.	ISSUE PRICE	QUOTE U.S.$
1985	In Disgrace	14-day		24.50	90-175
1985	The Reward	14-day		24.50	60-140
1985	Who's Sleepy	14-day		24.50	90-100
1985	Good Morning	14-day		24.50	73
1985	Sympathy	14-day		24.50	55
1985	On the Up and Up	14-day		24.50	75-100
1985	Mine	14-day		24.50	90
1985	Going to Town	14-day		24.50	60-95

A Child's Christmas - J. Ferrandiz

YEAR ISSUE		EDITION LIMIT	YEAR RETD.	ISSUE PRICE	QUOTE U.S.$
1995	Asleep in the Hay	28-day		29.95	30
1995	Merry Little Friends	28-day		29.95	30
1995	Love is Warm All Over	28-day		29.95	30
1995	Little Shepard Family	28-day		29.95	30

Childhood Reflections - B.P. Gutmann

YEAR ISSUE		EDITION LIMIT	YEAR RETD.	ISSUE PRICE	QUOTE U.S.$
1991	Harmony	14-day		29.50	100
1991	Kitty's Breakfast	14-day		29.50	30
1991	Friendly Enemies	14-day		29.50	60
1991	Smile, Smile, Smile	14-day		29.50	30
1991	Lullaby	14-day		29.50	30
1991	Oh! Oh! A Bunny	14-day		29.50	65
1991	Little Mother	14-day		29.50	30
1991	Thank You, God	14-day		29.50	36

Children of the American Frontier - D. Crook

YEAR ISSUE		EDITION LIMIT	YEAR RETD.	ISSUE PRICE	QUOTE U.S.$
1986	In Trouble Again	10-day		24.50	35
1986	Tubs and Suds	10-day		24.50	27
1986	A Lady Needs a Little Privacy	10-day		24.50	38
1986	The Desperadoes	10-day		24.50	27
1986	Riders Wanted	10-day		24.50	30
1987	A Cowboy's Downfall	10-day		24.50	25
1987	Runaway Blues	10-day		24.50	25
1987	A Special Patient	10-day		24.50	38

Civil War Generals - M. Gnatek

YEAR ISSUE		EDITION LIMIT	YEAR RETD.	ISSUE PRICE	QUOTE U.S.$
1994	Robert E. Lee	28-day		29.50	30
1994	J.E.B. Stewart	28-day		29.50	30
1994	Joshua L. Chamberlain	28-day		29.50	30
1994	George Armstrong Custer	28-day		29.50	30
1994	Nathan Bedford Forrest	28-day		29.50	30
1994	James Longstreet	28-day		29.50	30
1995	Thomas "Stonewall" Jackson	28-day		29.50	30

Classic American Santas - G. Hinke

YEAR ISSUE		EDITION LIMIT	YEAR RETD.	ISSUE PRICE	QUOTE U.S.$
1993	A Christmas Eve Visitor	28-day		29.50	30
1994	Up on the Rooftop	28-day		29.50	30
1994	Santa's Candy Kitchen	28-day		29.50	30
1994	A Christmas Chorus	28-day		29.50	30
1994	An Exciting Christmas Eve	28-day		29.50	30
1994	Rest Ye Merry Gentlemen	28-day		29.50	30
1994	Preparing the Sleigh	28-day		29.50	30
1994	The Reindeer's Stable	28-day		29.50	30
1994	He's Checking His List	28-day		29.50	30

Classic Corvettes - M. Lacourciere

YEAR ISSUE		EDITION LIMIT	YEAR RETD.	ISSUE PRICE	QUOTE U.S.$
1994	1957 Corvette	28-day		29.50	30
1994	1963 Corvette	28-day		29.50	30
1994	1968 Corvette	28-day		29.50	30
1994	1986 Corvette	28-day		29.50	30
1995	1967 Corvette	28-day		29.50	30
1995	1953 Corvette	28-day		29.50	30
1995	1962 Corvette	28-day		29.50	30
1995	1990 Corvette	28-day		29.50	30

Classic Sporting Dogs - B. Christie

YEAR ISSUE		EDITION LIMIT	YEAR RETD.	ISSUE PRICE	QUOTE U.S.$
1989	Golden Retrievers	14-day		24.50	55-70
1989	Labrador Retrievers	14-day		24.50	60
1989	Beagles	14-day		24.50	36
1989	Pointers	14-day		24.50	30
1989	Springer Spaniels	14-day		24.50	40
1990	German Short-Haired Pointers	14-day		24.50	55
1990	Irish Setters	14-day		24.50	40
1990	Brittany Spaniels	14-day		24.50	48

Classic TV Westerns - K. Milnazik

YEAR ISSUE		EDITION LIMIT	YEAR RETD.	ISSUE PRICE	QUOTE U.S.$
1990	The Lone Ranger and Tonto	14-day		29.50	55-75
1990	Bonanza ™	14-day		29.50	60
1990	Roy Rogers and Dale Evans	14-day		29.50	60
1991	Rawhide	14-day		29.50	60
1991	Wild Wild West	14-day		29.50	60
1991	Have Gun, Will Travel	14-day		29.50	60
1991	The Virginian	14-day		29.50	50
1991	Hopalong Cassidy	14-day		29.50	60

Cloak of Visions - A. Farley

YEAR ISSUE		EDITION LIMIT	YEAR RETD.	ISSUE PRICE	QUOTE U.S.$
1994	Visions in a Full Moon	28-day		29.50	30
1994	Protector of the Child	28-day		29.50	30
1995	Spirits of the Canyon	28-day		29.50	30
1995	Freedom Soars	28-day		29.50	30
1995	Mystic Reflections	28-day		29.50	30
1995	Staff of Life	28-day		29.50	30
1995	Springtime Hunters	28-day		29.50	30

Coral Paradise - H. Bond

YEAR ISSUE		EDITION LIMIT	YEAR RETD.	ISSUE PRICE	QUOTE U.S.$
1989	The Living Oasis	14-day		29.50	30
1990	Riches of the Coral Sea	14-day		29.50	30
1990	Tropical Pageantry	14-day		29.50	36
1990	Caribbean Spectacle	14-day		29.50	33
1990	Undersea Village	14-day		29.50	36
1990	Shimmering Reef Dwellers	14-day		29.50	36
1990	Mysteries of the Galapagos	14-day		29.50	33
1990	Forest Beneath the Sea	14-day		29.50	30

Cottage Puppies - K. George

YEAR ISSUE		EDITION LIMIT	YEAR RETD.	ISSUE PRICE	QUOTE U.S.$
1993	Little Gardeners	28-day		29.50	30
1993	Springtime Fancy	28-day		29.50	30
1993	Endearing Innocence	28-day		29.50	30
1994	Picnic Playtime	28-day		29.50	30
1994	Lazy Afternoon	28-day		29.50	30
1994	Summertime Pals	28-day		29.50	30
1994	A Gardening Trio	28-day		29.50	30
1994	Taking a Break	28-day		29.50	30

Council Of Nations - G. Perillo

YEAR ISSUE		EDITION LIMIT	YEAR RETD.	ISSUE PRICE	QUOTE U.S.$
1991	Strength of the Sioux	28-day		29.50	30
1992	Pride of the Cheyenne	28-day		29.50	30
1992	Dignity of the Nez Parce	28-day		29.50	30
1992	Courage of the Arapaho	28-day		29.50	30
1992	Power of the Blackfoot	28-day		29.50	30
1992	Nobility of the Algonqui	28-day		29.50	30
1992	Wisdom of the Cherokee	28-day		29.50	30

YEAR	ISSUE	EDITION LIMIT	YEAR RETD.	ISSUE PRICE	QUOTE U.S.$
1992	Boldness of the Seneca	28-day		29.50	30

Country Garden Cottages - E. Dertner

YEAR	ISSUE	EDITION LIMIT	YEAR RETD.	ISSUE PRICE	QUOTE U.S.$
1992	Riverbank Cottage	28-day		29.50	36
1992	Sunday Outing	28-day		29.50	30
1992	Shepherd's Cottage	28-day		29.50	30
1993	Daydream Cottage	28-day		29.50	30
1993	Garden Glorious	28-day		29.50	30
1993	This Side of Heaven	28-day		29.50	30
1993	Summer Symphony	28-day		29.50	30
1993	April Cottage	28-day		29.50	30

Country Kitties - G. Gerardi

YEAR	ISSUE	EDITION LIMIT	YEAR RETD.	ISSUE PRICE	QUOTE U.S.$
1989	Mischief Makers	14-day		24.50	45
1989	Table Manners	14-day		24.50	36
1989	Attic Attack	14-day		24.50	45
1989	Rock and Rollers	14-day		24.50	55
1989	Just For the Fern of It	14-day		24.50	50
1989	All Washed Up	14-day		24.50	50
1989	Stroller Derby	14-day		24.50	39
1989	Captive Audience	14-day		24.50	50

A Country Season of Horses - J.M. Vass

YEAR	ISSUE	EDITION LIMIT	YEAR RETD.	ISSUE PRICE	QUOTE U.S.$
1990	First Day of Spring	14-day		29.50	36
1990	Summer Splendor	14-day		29.50	33
1990	A Winter's Walk	14-day		29.50	33
1990	Autumn Grandeur	14-day		29.50	30
1990	Cliffside Beauty	14-day		29.50	30
1990	Frosty Morning	14-day		29.50	30
1990	Crisp Country Morning	14-day		29.50	30
1990	River Retreat	14-day		29.50	30

A Country Summer - N. Noel

YEAR	ISSUE	EDITION LIMIT	YEAR RETD.	ISSUE PRICE	QUOTE U.S.$
1985	Butterfly Beauty	10-day		29.50	36
1985	The Golden Puppy	10-day		29.50	30
1986	The Rocking Chair	10-day		29.50	36
1986	My Bunny	10-day		29.50	33
1988	The Piglet	10-day		29.50	30
1988	Teammates	10-day		29.50	30

Curious Kittens - B. Harrison

YEAR	ISSUE	EDITION LIMIT	YEAR RETD.	ISSUE PRICE	QUOTE U.S.$
1990	Rainy Day Friends	14-day		29.50	36
1990	Keeping in Step	14-day		29.50	36
1991	Delightful Discovery	14-day		29.50	36
1991	Chance Meeting	14-day		29.50	36
1991	All Wound Up	14-day		29.50	36
1991	Making Tracks	14-day		29.50	36
1991	Playing Cat and Mouse	14-day		29.50	36
1991	A Paw's in the Action	14-day		29.50	36
1992	Little Scholar	14-day		29.50	36
1992	Cat Burglar	14-day		29.50	36

Daughters Of The Sun - K. Thayer

YEAR	ISSUE	EDITION LIMIT	YEAR RETD.	ISSUE PRICE	QUOTE U.S.$
1993	Sun Dancer	28-day		29.50	30
1993	Shining Feather	28-day		29.50	30
1993	Delighted Dancer	28-day		29.50	30
1993	Evening Dancer	28-day		29.50	30
1993	A Secret Glance	28-day		29.50	30
1993	Chippewa Charmer	28-day		29.50	30
1994	Pride of the Yakima	28-day		29.50	30
1994	Radiant Beauty	28-day		29.50	30

Dear to My Heart - J. Hagara

YEAR	ISSUE	EDITION LIMIT	YEAR RETD.	ISSUE PRICE	QUOTE U.S.$
1990	Cathy	14-day		29.50	30-60
1990	Addie	14-day		29.50	30
1990	Jimmy	14-day		29.50	30
1990	Dacy	14-day		29.50	30
1990	Paul	14-day		29.50	30
1991	Shelly	14-day		29.50	30
1991	Jenny	14-day		29.50	30
1991	Joy	14-day		29.50	30

Dolphin Discovery - D. Queen

YEAR	ISSUE	EDITION LIMIT	YEAR RETD.	ISSUE PRICE	QUOTE U.S.$
1995	Sunrise Reverie	28-day		29.50	30
1995	Coral Garden	28-day		29.95	30
1995	Coral Cove	28-day		29.95	30

Dreamsicles - K. Haynes

YEAR	ISSUE	EDITION LIMIT	YEAR RETD.	ISSUE PRICE	QUOTE U.S.$
1994	The Flying Lesson	28-day		19.50	20
1995	By the Light of the Moon	28-day		19.50	20

Dreamsicles Special Friends - K. Haynes

YEAR	ISSUE	EDITION LIMIT	YEAR RETD.	ISSUE PRICE	QUOTE U.S.$
1995	A Hug From the Heart	28-day		29.95	30
1995	Heaven's Little Helper	28-day		29.95	30
1995	Bless Us All	28-day		29.95	30

Drivers of Victory Lane - R. Tanenbaum

YEAR	ISSUE	EDITION LIMIT	YEAR RETD.	ISSUE PRICE	QUOTE U.S.$
1994	Bill Elliott	28-day		29.50	30
1994	Jeff Gordon	28-day		29.50	30
1994	Rusty Wallace	28-day		29.50	30
1995	Geoff Bodine	28-day		29.50	30
1995	Dale Earnhardt	28-day		29.50	30

Easyriders - M. Lacourciere

YEAR	ISSUE	EDITION LIMIT	YEAR RETD.	ISSUE PRICE	QUOTE U.S.$
1995	American Classic	28-day		29.95	30
1995	Symbols of Freedom	28-day		29.95	30

Elvis Remembered - S. Morton

YEAR	ISSUE	EDITION LIMIT	YEAR RETD.	ISSUE PRICE	QUOTE U.S.$
1989	Loving You	90-day		37.50	95-125
1989	Early Years	90-day		37.50	50-100
1989	Tenderly	90-day		37.50	95-125
1989	The King	90-day		37.50	130
1989	Forever Yours	90-day		37.50	100
1989	Rockin in the Moonlight	90-day		37.50	100-125
1989	Moody Blues	90-day		37.50	100-110
1989	Elvis Presley	90-day		37.50	130-150

Enchanted Seascapes - J. Enright

YEAR	ISSUE	EDITION LIMIT	YEAR RETD.	ISSUE PRICE	QUOTE U.S.$
1993	Sanctuary of the Dolphin	28-day		29.50	30
1994	Rhapsody of Hope	28-day		29.50	30
1994	Oasis of the Gods	28-day		29.50	30
1994	Sphere of Life	28-day		29.50	30
1994	Edge of Time	28-day		29.50	30
1994	Sea of Light	28-day		29.50	30
1994	Lost Beneath the Blue	28-day		29.50	30
1994	Blue Paradise	28-day		29.50	30
1995	Morning Odyssey	28-day		29.50	30
1995	Paradise Cove	28-day		29.50	30

English Country Cottages - M. Bell

YEAR	ISSUE	EDITION LIMIT	YEAR RETD.	ISSUE PRICE	QUOTE U.S.$
1990	Periwinkle Tea Room	14-day		29.50	45
1991	Gamekeeper's Cottage	14-day		29.50	75
1991	Ginger Cottage	14-day		29.50	60
1991	Larkspur Cottage	14-day		29.50	45
1991	The Chaplain's Garden	14-day		29.50	33
1991	Lorna Doone Cottage	14-day		29.50	45
1991	Murrle Cottage	14-day		29.50	36
1991	Lullabye Cottage	14-day		29.50	30

Eternal Wishes of Good Fortune - Shuho

YEAR	ISSUE	EDITION LIMIT	YEAR RETD.	ISSUE PRICE	QUOTE U.S.$
1983	Friendship	10-day		34.95	35
1983	Purity and Perfection	10-day		34.95	35
1983	Illustrious Offspring	10-day		34.95	35
1983	Longevity	10-day		34.95	35
1983	Youth	10-day		34.95	35
1983	Immortality	10-day		34.95	35
1983	Marital Bliss	10-day		34.95	35
1983	Love	10-day		34.95	35
1983	Peace	10-day		34.95	35
1983	Beauty	10-day		34.95	35
1983	Fertility	10-day		34.95	35
1983	Fortitude	10-day		34.95	35

Exotic Tigers of Asia - K. Ottinger

YEAR	ISSUE	EDITION LIMIT	YEAR RETD.	ISSUE PRICE	QUOTE U.S.$
1995	Lord of the Rainforest	28-day		29.50	30
1995	Snow King	28-day		29.50	30
1995	Ruler of the Wetlands	28-day		29.50	30
1995	Majestic Vigil	28-day		29.50	30

Farmyard Friends - J. Lamb

YEAR	ISSUE	EDITION LIMIT	YEAR RETD.	ISSUE PRICE	QUOTE U.S.$
1992	Mistaken Identity	28-day		29.50	30
1992	Little Cowhands	28-day		29.50	30
1993	Shreading the Evidence	28-day		29.50	30
1993	Partners in Crime	28-day		29.50	30
1993	Fowl Play	28-day		29.50	30
1993	Follow The Leader	28-day		29.50	30
1993	Pony Tales	28-day		29.50	30
1993	An Apple A Day	28-day		29.50	30

Favorite American Songbirds - D. O'Driscoll

YEAR	ISSUE	EDITION LIMIT	YEAR RETD.	ISSUE PRICE	QUOTE U.S.$
1989	Blue Jays of Spring	14-day		29.50	36
1989	Red Cardinals of Winter	14-day		29.50	36
1989	Robins & Apple Blossoms	14-day		29.50	36
1989	Goldfinches of Summer	14-day		29.50	36
1990	Autumn Chickadees	14-day		29.50	36
1990	Bluebirds and Morning Glories	14-day		29.50	36
1990	Tufted Titmouse and Holly	14-day		29.50	30
1991	Carolina Wrens of Spring	14-day		29.50	30

Favorite Old Testament Stories - S. Butcher

YEAR	ISSUE	EDITION LIMIT	YEAR RETD.	ISSUE PRICE	QUOTE U.S.$
1994	Jacob's Dream	28-day		35.00	35
1995	The Baby Moses	28-day		35.00	35
1995	Esther's Gift To Her People	28-day		35.00	35
1995	A Prayer For Victory	28-day		35.00	35
1995	Where You Go, I Will Go	28-day		35.00	35
1995	A Prayer Answered, A Promise Kept	28-day		35.00	35

The Fierce And The Free - F. McCarthy

YEAR	ISSUE	EDITION LIMIT	YEAR RETD.	ISSUE PRICE	QUOTE U.S.$
1992	Big Medicine	28-day		29.50	30
1993	Land of the Winter Hawk	28-day		29.50	30
1993	Warrior of Savage Splendor	28-day		29.50	30
1994	War Party	28-day		29.50	30
1994	The Challenge	28-day		29.50	30
1994	Out of the Rising Mist	28-day		29.50	30
1994	The Ambush	28-day		29.50	30
1994	Dangerous Crossing	28-day		29.50	30

Forging New Frontiers - J. Deneen

YEAR	ISSUE	EDITION LIMIT	YEAR RETD.	ISSUE PRICE	QUOTE U.S.$
1994	The Race is On	28-day		29.50	30
1994	Big Boy	28-day		29.50	30
1994	Cresting the Summit	28-day		29.50	30
1994	Spring Roundup	28-day		29.50	30
1994	Winter in the Rockies	28-day		29.50	30
1994	High Country Logging	28-day		29.50	30
1994	Confrontation	28-day		29.50	30
1994	A Welcome Sight	28-day		29.50	30

A Garden Song - M. Hanson

YEAR	ISSUE	EDITION LIMIT	YEAR RETD.	ISSUE PRICE	QUOTE U.S.$
1994	Winter's Splendor	28-day		29.50	30
1994	In Full Bloom	28-day		29.50	30
1994	Golden Glories	28-day		29.50	30
1995	Autumn's Elegance	28-day		29.50	30
1995	First Snowfall	28-day		29.50	30
1995	Robins in Spring	28-day		29.50	30

Glory of Christ - C. Micarelli

YEAR	ISSUE	EDITION LIMIT	YEAR RETD.	ISSUE PRICE	QUOTE U.S.$
1992	The Ascension	48-day		29.50	30
1992	Jesus Teaching	48-day		29.50	30
1993	Last Supper	48-day		29.50	30
1993	The Nativity	48-day		29.50	30
1993	The Baptism of Christ	48-day		29.50	30
1993	Jesus Heals the Sick	48-day		29.50	30
1994	Jesus Walks on Water	48-day		29.50	30
1994	Descent From the Cross	48-day		29.50	30

Glory of the Game - T. Fogarty

YEAR	ISSUE	EDITION LIMIT	YEAR RETD.	ISSUE PRICE	QUOTE U.S.$
1994	"Hank Aaron's Record-Breaking Home Run"	28-day		29.50	30
1994	"Bobby Thomson's Shot Heard 'Round the World"	28-day		29.50	30
1994	1969 Miracle Mets	28-day		29.50	30
1995	Reggie Jackson: Mr. October	28-day		29.50	30
1995	Don Larsen's Perfect World	28-day		29.50	30
1995	Babe Ruth's Called Shot	28-day		29.50	30
1995	Wille Mays: Greatest Catch	28-day		29.50	30
1995	Bill Mazeroski's Series	28-day		29.50	30

The Golden Age of American Railroads - T. Xaras

YEAR	ISSUE	EDITION LIMIT	YEAR RETD.	ISSUE PRICE	QUOTE U.S.$
1991	The Blue Comet	14-day		29.50	45
1991	The Morning Local	14-day		29.50	60
1991	The Pennsylvania K-4	14-day		29.50	90
1991	Above the Canyon	14-day		29.50	90
1991	Portrait in Steam	14-day		29.50	75
1991	The Santa Fe Super Chief	14-day		29.50	105
1991	The Big Boy	14-day		29.50	60
1991	The Empire Builder	14-day		29.50	60
1992	An American Classic	14-day		29.50	33
1992	Final Destination	14-day		29.50	36

Golden Discoveries - L. Budge

YEAR	ISSUE	EDITION LIMIT	YEAR RETD.	ISSUE PRICE	QUOTE U.S.$
1995	Boot Bandits	28-day		29.95	30
1995	Hiding the Evidence	28-day		29.95	30
1995	Decoy Dilemma	28-day		29.95	30

Golden Puppy Portraits - P. Braun

YEAR	ISSUE	EDITION LIMIT	YEAR RETD.	ISSUE PRICE	QUOTE U.S.$
1994	Do Not Disturb!	28-day		29.50	30
1995	Teething Time	28-day		29.50	30
1995	Table Manners	28-day		29.50	30
1995	A Golden Bouquet	28-day		29.50	30

Good Sports - J. Lamb

YEAR	ISSUE	EDITION LIMIT	YEAR RETD.	ISSUE PRICE	QUOTE U.S.$
1990	Wide Retriever	14-day		29.50	45
1990	Double Play	14-day		29.50	36
1990	Hole in One	14-day		29.50	45
1990	The Bass Masters	14-day		29.50	36
1990	Spotted on the Sideline	14-day		29.50	36
1990	Slap Shot	14-day		29.50	45
1991	Net Play	14-day		29.50	50
1991	Bassetball	14-day		29.50	36
1992	Boxer Rebellion	14-day		29.50	33
1992	Great Try	14-day		29.50	39

Great Fighter Planes Of World War II - R. Waddey

YEAR	ISSUE	EDITION LIMIT	YEAR RETD.	ISSUE PRICE	QUOTE U.S.$
1992	Old Crow	14-day		29.50	30
1992	Big Hog	14-day		29.50	30
1992	P-47 Thunderbolt	14-day		29.50	30
1992	P-40 Flying Tiger	14-day		29.50	30
1992	F4F Wildcat	14-day		29.50	30
1992	P-38F Lightning	14-day		29.50	30
1993	F6F Hellcat	14-day		29.50	30
1993	P-39M Airacobra	14-day		29.50	30
1995	Memphis Belle	14-day		29.50	30
1995	The Dragon and His Tail	14-day		29.50	30

Great Mammals of the Sea - Wyland

YEAR	ISSUE	EDITION LIMIT	YEAR RETD.	ISSUE PRICE	QUOTE U.S.$
1991	Orca Trio	14-day		35.00	45
1991	Hawaii Dolphins	14-day		35.00	38
1991	Orca Journey	14-day		35.00	43
1991	Dolphin Paradise	14-day		35.00	45
1991	Children of the Sea	14-day		35.00	60
1991	Kissing Dolphins	14-day		35.00	39
1991	Islands	14-day		35.00	60
1991	Orcas	14-day		35.00	45

The Greatest Show on Earth - F. Moody

YEAR	ISSUE	EDITION LIMIT	YEAR RETD.	ISSUE PRICE	QUOTE U.S.$
1981	Clowns	10-day		30.00	30-45
1981	Elephants	10-day		30.00	30
1981	Aerialists	10-day		30.00	30
1981	Great Parade	10-day		30.00	30
1981	Midway	10-day		30.00	30
1981	Equestrians	10-day		30.00	30
1982	Lion Tamer	10-day		30.00	30
1982	Grande Finale	10-day		30.00	30

Growing Up Together - P. Brooks

YEAR	ISSUE	EDITION LIMIT	YEAR RETD.	ISSUE PRICE	QUOTE U.S.$
1990	My Very Best Friends	14-day		29.50	36
1990	Tea for Two	14-day		29.50	30
1990	Tender Loving Care	14-day		29.50	30
1990	Picnic Pals	14-day		29.50	30
1991	Newfound Friends	14-day		29.50	30
1991	Kitten Caboodle	14-day		29.50	30
1991	Fishing Buddies	14-day		29.50	30

YEAR ISSUE		EDITION LIMIT	YEAR RETD.	ISSUE PRICE	QUOTE U.S.$
1991	Bedtime Blessings	14-day		29.50	30

Historic Rails - T. Xaras

1995	Harper's Ferry	28-day		29.95	30

The I Love Lucy Plate Collection - J. Kritz

1989	California, Here We Come	14-day		29.50	100-175
1989	It's Just Like Candy	14-day		29.50	100-155
1990	The Big Squeeze	14-day		29.50	100-155
1990	Eating the Evidence	14-day		29.50	175-300
1990	Two of a Kind	14-day		29.50	125-150
1991	Queen of the Gypsies	14-day		29.50	90-120
1992	Night at the Copa	14-day		29.50	75-100
1992	A Rising Problem	14-day		29.50	100-150

Japanese Floral Calendar - Shuho/Kage

1981	New Year's Day	10-day		32.50	33
1982	Early Spring	10-day		32.50	33
1982	Spring	10-day		32.50	33
1982	Girl's Doll Day Festival	10-day		32.50	33
1982	Buddha's Birthday	10-day		32.50	33
1982	Early Summer	10-day		32.50	33
1982	Boy's Doll Day Festival	10-day		32.50	33
1982	Summer	10-day		32.50	33
1982	Autumn	10-day		32.50	33
1983	Festival of the Full Moon	10-day		32.50	33
1983	Late Autumn	10-day		32.50	33
1983	Winter	10-day		32.50	33

The Jeweled Hummingbirds - J. Landenberger

1989	Ruby-throated Hummingbirds	14-day		37.50	38
1989	Great Sapphire Wing Hummingbirds	14-day		37.50	38
1989	Ruby-Topaz Hummingbirds	14-day		37.50	38
1989	Andean Emerald Hummingbirds	14-day		37.50	38
1989	Garnet-throated Hummingbirds	14-day		37.50	38
1989	Blue-Headed Sapphire Hummingbirds	14-day		37.50	38
1989	Pearl Coronet Hummingbirds	14-day		37.50	38
1989	Amethyst-throated Sunangels	14-day		37.50	38

Kitten Classics - P. Cooper

1985	Cat Nap	14-day		29.50	36
1985	Purrfect Treasure	14-day		29.50	30
1985	Wild Flower	14-day		29.50	30
1985	Birdwatcher	14-day		29.50	30
1985	Tiger's Fancy	14-day		29.50	33
1985	Country Kitty	14-day		29.50	33
1985	Little Rascal	14-day		29.50	30
1985	First Prize	14-day		29.50	30

The Last Warriors - C. Ren

1993	Winter of '41	28-day		29.50	30
1993	Morning of Reckoning	28-day		29.50	30
1993	Twilights Last Gleaming	28-day		29.50	30
1993	Lone Winter Journey	28-day		29.50	30
1994	Victory's Reward	28-day		29.50	30
1994	Solitary Hunter	28-day		29.50	30
1994	Solemn Reflection	28-day		29.50	30
1994	Confronting Danger	28-day		29.50	30
1995	Moment of Contemplation	28-day		29.50	30
1995	The Last Sunset	28-day		29.50	30

The Legend of Father Christmas - V. Dezerin

1994	The Return of Father Christmas	28-day		29.50	30
1994	Gifts From Father Christmas	28-day		29.50	30
1994	The Feast of the Holiday	28-day		29.50	30
1995	Christmas Day Visitors	28-day		29.50	30
1995	Decorating the Tree	28-day		29.50	30
1995	The Snow Sculpture	28-day		29.50	30
1995	Skating on the Pond	28-day		29.50	30
1995	Holy Night	28-day		29.50	30

Legendary Warriors - M. Gentry

1995	White Quiver and Scout	28-day		29.95	30
1995	Lakota Rendezvous	28-day		29.95	30
1995	Crazy Horse	28-day		29.95	30
1995	Sitting Bull's Vision	28-day		29.95	30

A Lisi Martin Christmas - L. Martin

1992	Santa's Littlest Reindeer	28-day		29.50	30
1993	Not A Creature Was Stirring	28-day		29.50	30
1993	Christmas Dreams	28-day		29.50	30
1993	The Christmas Story	28-day		29.50	30
1993	Trimming The Tree	28-day		29.50	30
1993	A Taste Of The Holidays	28-day		29.50	30
1993	The Night Before Christmas	28-day		29.50	30
1993	Christmas Watch	28-day		29.50	30
1995	Christmas Presence	28-day		29.50	30
1995	Nose to Nose	28-day		29.50	30

Little Fawns of the Forest - R. Manning

1995	In the Morning Light	28-day		29.95	30
1995	Cool Reflections	28-day		29.95	30

Little Ladies - M.H. Bogart

1989	Playing Bridesmaid	14-day		29.50	75
1990	The Seamstress	14-day		29.50	60
1990	Little Captive	14-day		29.50	45
1990	Playing Mama	14-day		29.50	60
1990	Susanna	14-day		29.50	35
1990	Kitty's Bath	14-day		29.50	55

YEAR ISSUE		EDITION LIMIT	YEAR RETD.	ISSUE PRICE	QUOTE U.S.$
1990	A Day in the Country	14-day		29.50	45
1991	Sarah	14-day		29.50	45
1991	First Party	14-day		29.50	30
1991	The Magic Kitten	14-day		29.50	30

The Little Rascals - Unknown

1985	Three for the Show	10-day		24.50	35
1985	My Gal	10-day		24.50	45
1985	Skeleton Crew	10-day		24.50	25
1985	Roughin' It	10-day		24.50	45
1985	Spanky's Pranks	10-day		24.50	25
1985	Butch's Challenge	10-day		24.50	25
1985	Darla's Debut	10-day		24.50	25
1985	Pete's Pal	10-day		24.50	25

Little Shopkeepers - G. Gerardi

1990	Sew Tired	14-day		29.50	30
1991	Break Time	14-day		29.50	30
1991	Purrfect Fit	14-day		29.50	30
1991	Toying Around	14-day		29.50	36
1991	Chain Reaction	14-day		29.50	45
1991	Inferior Decorators	14-day		29.50	36
1991	Tulip Tag	14-day		29.50	36
1991	Candy Capers	14-day		29.50	36

Lore Of The West - L. Danielle

1993	A Mile In His Mocassins	28-day		29.50	30
1993	Path of Honor	28-day		29.50	30
1993	A Chief's Pride	28-day		29.50	30
1994	Pathways of the Pueblo	28-day		29.50	30
1994	In Her Seps	28-day		29.50	30
1994	Growing Up Brave	28-day		29.50	30
1994	Nomads of the Southwest	28-day		29.50	30
1994	Sacred Spirit of the Plains	28-day		29.50	30
1994	We'll Fight No More	28-day		29.50	30
1994	The End of the Trail	28-day		29.50	30

Love's Messengers - J. Grossman

1995	To My Love	28-day		29.50	30
1995	Cupid's Arrow	28-day		29.50	30
1995	Love's Melody	28-day		29.50	30
1995	A Token of Love	28-day		29.50	30
1995	Harmony of Love	28-day		29.50	30

The Lucille Ball (Official) Commemorative Plate - Morgan

1993	Lucy	28-day		37.50	125

Madonna And Child - Various

1992	Madonna Della Sedia R. Sanzio	28-day		37.50	38
1992	Virgin of the Rocks - L. DaVinci	28-day		37.50	38
1993	Madonna of Rosary B. E. Murillo	28-day		37.50	38
1993	Sistine Madonna - R. Sanzio	28-day		37.50	38
1993	Virgin Adoring Christ Child A. Correggio	28-day		37.50	38
1993	Virgin of the Grape - P. Mignard	28-day		37.50	38
1993	Madonna del Magnificat S. Botticelli	28-day		37.50	38
1993	Madonna col Bambino S. Botticelli	28-day		37.50	38

The Magical World of Legends & Myths - J. Shalatain

1993	A Mother's Love	28-day		35.00	35
1993	Dreams of Pegasus	28-day		35.00	35
1994	Flight of the Pegasus	28-day		35.00	35
1994	The Awakening	28-day		35.00	35
1994	Once Upon a Dream	28-day		35.00	35
1994	The Dawn of Romance	28-day		35.00	35
1994	The Astral Unicorn	28-day		35.00	35
1994	Flight into Paradise	28-day		35.00	35
1995	Pegasus in the Stars	28-day		35.00	35
1995	Unicorn of the Sea	28-day		35.00	35

Majestic Birds of Prey - C.F. Riley

1983	Golden Eagle	12,500		55.00	55
1983	Cooper's Hawk	12,500		55.00	55
1983	Great Horned Owl	12,500		55.00	55
1983	Bald Eagle	12,500		55.00	55
1983	Barred Owl	12,500		55.00	55
1983	Sparrow Owl	12,500		55.00	55
1983	Peregrine Falcon	12,500		55.00	55
1983	Osprey	12,500		55.00	55

Majesty of Flight - T. Hirata

1989	The Eagle Soars	14-day		37.50	48
1989	Realm of the Red-Tail	14-day		37.50	39
1989	Coastal Journey	14-day		37.50	45
1989	Sentry of the North	14-day		37.50	48
1989	Commanding the Marsh	14-day		37.50	38
1990	The Vantage Point	14-day		29.50	45
1990	Silent Watch	14-day		29.50	48
1990	Fierce and Free	14-day		29.50	45

Man's Best Friend - L. Picken

1992	Special Delivery	28-day		29.50	30
1992	Making Waves	28-day		29.50	30
1992	Good Catch	28-day		29.50	30
1993	Time For a Walk	28-day		29.50	45
1993	Faithful Friend	28-day		29.50	30
1993	Let's Play Ball	28-day		29.50	30
1993	Sitting Pretty	28-day		29.50	30

YEAR ISSUE		EDITION LIMIT	YEAR RETD.	ISSUE PRICE	QUOTE U.S.$
1993	Bedtime Story	28-day		29.50	30
1993	Trusted Companion	28-day		29.50	30

Mike Schmidt - R. Tanenbaum

1994	The Ultimate Competitor: Mike Schmidt	28-day		29.50	30
1995	A Homerun King	28-day		29.50	30
1995	An All Time, All Star	28-day		29.50	30
1995	A Career Retrospective	28-day		29.50	30

Milestones in Space - D. Dixon

1994	Moon Landing	28-day		29.50	30
1995	Space Lab	28-day		29.50	30
1995	Maiden Flight of Columbia	28-day		29.50	30
1995	Free Walk in Space	28-day		29.50	30
1995	Lunar Rover	28-day		29.50	30
1995	Handshake in Space	28-day		29.50	30

Mixed Company - P. Cooper

1990	Two Against One	14-day		29.50	36
1990	A Sticky Situation	14-day		29.50	36
1990	What's Up	14-day		29.50	30
1990	All Wrapped Up	14-day		29.50	36
1990	Picture Perfect	14-day		29.50	30
1991	A Moment to Unwind	14-day		29.50	33
1991	Ole	14-day		29.50	33
1991	Picnic Prowlers	14-day		29.50	30

Murals From The Precious Moments Chapel - S. Butcher

1995	The Pearl of Great Price	28-day		35.00	35
1995	The Good Samaritan	28-day		35.00	35

Mystic Warriors - C. Ren

1992	Deliverance	28-day		29.50	30
1992	Mystic Warrior	28-day		29.50	35
1992	Sun Seeker	28-day		29.50	30
1992	Top Gun	28-day		29.50	30
1992	Man Who Walks Alone	28-day		29.50	30
1992	Windrider	28-day		29.50	30
1992	Spirit of the Plains	28-day		29.50	30
1993	Blue Thunder	28-day		29.50	30
1993	Sun Glow	28-day		29.50	30
1993	Peace Maker	28-day		29.50	30

Nature's Majestic Cats - M. Richter

1993	Siberian Tiger	28-day		29.50	30
1993	Himalayan Snow Leopard	28-day		29.50	30
1993	African Lion	28-day		29.50	30
1994	Asian Clouded Leopard	28-day		29.50	30
1994	American Cougar	28-day		29.50	30
1994	East African Leopard	28-day		29.50	30
1994	African Cheetah	28-day		29.50	30
1994	Canadian Lynx	28-day		29.50	30

Nature's Nighttime Realm - G. Murray

1992	Bobcat	28-day		29.50	30
1992	Cougar	28-day		29.50	30
1993	Jaguar	28-day		29.50	30
1993	White Tiger	28-day		29.50	30
1993	Lynx	28-day		29.50	30
1993	Lion	28-day		29.50	30
1993	Snow Leopard	28-day		29.50	30
1993	Cheetah	28-day		29.50	30

Nature's Quiet Moments - R. Parker

1988	A Curious Pair	14-day		37.50	38
1988	Northern Morning	14-day		37.50	38
1988	Just Resting	14-day		37.50	38
1989	Waiting Out the Storm	14-day		37.50	38
1989	Creekside	14-day		37.50	38
1989	Autumn Foraging	14-day		37.50	38
1989	Old Man of the Mountain	14-day		37.50	38
1989	Mountain Blooms	14-day		37.50	38

Noble American Indian Women - D. Wright

1989	Sacajawea	14-day		29.50	35-50
1990	Pocahontas	14-day		29.50	45
1990	Minnehaha	14-day		29.50	40
1990	Pine Leaf	14-day		29.50	45
1990	Lily of the Mohawk	14-day		29.50	36
1990	White Rose	14-day		29.50	35-45
1991	Lozen	14-day		29.50	33
1991	Falling Star	14-day		29.50	35-45

Noble Owls of America - J. Seerey-Lester

1986	Morning Mist	15,000		55.00	55
1987	Prairie Sundown	15,000		55.00	55
1987	Winter Vigil	15,000		55.00	55
1987	Autumn Mist	15,000		75.00	75
1987	Dawn in the Willows	15,000		55.00	55
1987	Snowy Watch	15,000		60.00	60
1988	Hiding Place	15,000		55.00	55
1988	Waiting for Dusk	15,000		55.00	55

Nolan Ryan - R. Tanenbaum

1994	The Strikeout Express	28-day		29.50	30
1994	Birth of a Legend	28-day		29.50	30
1994	Mr. Fastball	28-day		29.50	30
1994	Million-Dollar Player	28-day		29.50	30
1994	27 Seasons	28-day		29.50	30
1994	Farewell	28-day		29.50	30

YEAR ISSUE	EDITION LIMIT	YEAR RETD.	ISSUE PRICE	QUOTE U.S.$
1994 The Ryan Express	28-day		29.50	30

Norman Rockwell's Saturday Evening Post Baseball - N. Rockwell

YEAR ISSUE	EDITION LIMIT	YEAR RETD.	ISSUE PRICE	QUOTE U.S.$
1992 100th Year of Baseball	Open		19.50	20
1993 The Rookie	Open		19.50	20
1993 The Dugout	Open		19.50	20
1993 Bottom of the Sixth	Open		19.50	20

North American Ducks - R. Lawrence

YEAR ISSUE	EDITION LIMIT	YEAR RETD.	ISSUE PRICE	QUOTE U.S.$
1991 Autumn Flight	14-day		29.50	36
1991 The Resting Place	14-day		29.50	30
1991 Twin Flight	14-day		29.50	30
1992 Misty Morning	14-day		29.50	30
1992 Springtime Thaw	14-day		29.50	30
1992 Summer Retreat	14-day		29.50	30
1992 Overcast	14-day		29.50	30
1992 Perfect Pintails	14-day		29.50	30

North American Gamebirds - J. Killen

YEAR ISSUE	EDITION LIMIT	YEAR RETD.	ISSUE PRICE	QUOTE U.S.$
1990 Ring-necked Pheasant	14-day		37.50	38
1990 Bobwhite Quail	14-day		37.50	45
1990 Ruffed Grouse	14-day		37.50	38
1990 Gambel Quail	14-day		37.50	42
1990 Mourning Dove	14-day		37.50	45
1990 Woodcock	14-day		37.50	45
1991 Chukar Partridge	14-day		37.50	45
1991 Wild Turkey	14-day		37.50	45

North American Waterbirds - R. Lawrence

YEAR ISSUE	EDITION LIMIT	YEAR RETD.	ISSUE PRICE	QUOTE U.S.$
1988 Wood Ducks	14-day		37.50	54
1988 Hooded Mergansers	14-day		37.50	54
1988 Pintails	14-day		37.50	45
1988 Canada Geese	14-day		37.50	45
1989 American Widgeons	14-day		37.50	54
1989 Canvasbacks	14-day		37.50	55
1989 Mallard Pair	14-day		37.50	60
1989 Snow Geese	14-day		37.50	45

The Nutcracker Ballet - S. Fisher

YEAR ISSUE	EDITION LIMIT	YEAR RETD.	ISSUE PRICE	QUOTE U.S.$
1978 Clara	28-day		19.50	36
1979 Godfather	28-day		19.50	20
1979 Sugar Plum Fairy	28-day		19.50	45
1979 Snow Queen and King	28-day		19.50	40
1980 Waltz of the Flowers	28-day		19.50	20
1980 Clara and the Prince	28-day		19.50	45

Official Honeymooner's Commemorative Plate - D. Bobnick

YEAR ISSUE	EDITION LIMIT	YEAR RETD.	ISSUE PRICE	QUOTE U.S.$
1993 The Official Honeymooner's Commemorative Plate	28-day		37.50	100

The Official Honeymooners Plate Collection - D. Kilmer

YEAR ISSUE	EDITION LIMIT	YEAR RETD.	ISSUE PRICE	QUOTE U.S.$
1987 The Honeymooners	14-day		24.50	100-200
1987 The Hucklebuck	14-day		24.50	100-175
1987 Baby, You're the Greatest	14-day		24.50	100-200
1988 The Golfer	14-day		24.50	100-200
1988 The TV Chefs	14-day		24.50	100-120
1988 Bang! Zoom!	14-day		24.50	95-110
1988 The Only Way to Travel	14-day		24.50	100-120
1988 The Honeymoon Express	14-day		24.50	125-150

On Wings of Eagles - J. Pitcher

YEAR ISSUE	EDITION LIMIT	YEAR RETD.	ISSUE PRICE	QUOTE U.S.$
1994 "By Dawn's Early Light"	28-day		29.50	30
1994 Winter's Majestic Flight	28-day		29.50	30
1994 Over the Land of the Free	28-day		29.50	30
1995 Free Flight	28-day		29.50	30
1995 Morning Majesty	28-day		29.50	30

Our Cherished Seas - S. Barlowe

YEAR ISSUE	EDITION LIMIT	YEAR RETD.	ISSUE PRICE	QUOTE U.S.$
1992 Whale Song	48-day		37.50	38
1992 Lions of the Sea	48-day		37.50	38
1992 Flight of the Dolphins	48-day		37.50	38
1992 Palace of the Seals	48-day		37.50	38
1993 Orca Ballet	48-day		37.50	38
1993 Emporers of the Ice	48-day		37.50	38
1993 Sea Turtles	48-day		37.50	38
1993 Splendor of the Sea	48-day		37.50	38

Petals and Purrs - B. Harrison

YEAR ISSUE	EDITION LIMIT	YEAR RETD.	ISSUE PRICE	QUOTE U.S.$
1988 Blushing Beauties	14-day		24.50	55
1988 Spring Fever	14-day		24.50	38
1988 Morning Glories	14-day		24.50	45
1988 Forget-Me-Not	14-day		24.50	36
1989 Golden Fancy	14-day		24.50	30
1989 Pink Lillies	14-day		24.50	30
1989 Summer Sunshine	14-day		24.50	55
1989 Siamese Summer	14-day		24.50	55

Portraits of Jesus - W. Sallman

YEAR ISSUE	EDITION LIMIT	YEAR RETD.	ISSUE PRICE	QUOTE U.S.$
1994 Jesus, The Good Shepherd	28-day		29.50	30
1994 Jesus in the Garden	28-day		29.50	30
1994 Jesus, Children's Friend	28-day		29.50	30
1994 The Lord's Supper	28-day		29.50	30
1994 Christ at Dawn	28-day		29.50	30
1994 Christ at Heart's Door	28-day		29.50	30
1994 Portrait of Christ	28-day		29.50	30
1994 Madonna and Christ Child	28-day		29.50	30

Portraits of the Bald Eagle - J. Pitcher

YEAR ISSUE	EDITION LIMIT	YEAR RETD.	ISSUE PRICE	QUOTE U.S.$
1993 Ruler of the Sky	28-day		37.50	38
1993 In Bold Defiance	28-day		37.50	38
1993 Master Of The Summer Skies	28-day		37.50	38
1993 Spring's Sentinel	28-day		37.50	38

Portraits of the Wild - J. Meger

YEAR ISSUE	EDITION LIMIT	YEAR RETD.	ISSUE PRICE	QUOTE U.S.$
1994 Interlude	28-day		29.50	30
1994 Winter Solitude	28-day		29.50	30
1994 Devoted Protector	28-day		29.50	30
1994 Call of Autumn	28-day		29.50	30
1994 Watchful Eyes	28-day		29.50	30
1994 Babies of Spring	28-day		29.50	30
1994 Rocky Mountain Grandeur	28-day		29.50	30
1995 Unbridled Power	28-day		29.50	30
1995 Moonlight Vigil	28-day		29.50	30

Precious Moments Bible Story - S. Butcher

YEAR ISSUE	EDITION LIMIT	YEAR RETD.	ISSUE PRICE	QUOTE U.S.$
1990 Come Let Us Adore Him	28-day		29.50	30
1992 They Followed The Star	28-day		29.50	30
1992 The Flight Into Egypt	28-day		29.50	30
1992 The Carpenter Shop	28-day		29.50	30
1992 Jesus In The Temple	28-day		29.50	30
1992 The Crucifixion	28-day		29.50	30
1993 He Is Not Here	28-day		29.50	30

Precious Moments Classics - S. Butcher

YEAR ISSUE	EDITION LIMIT	YEAR RETD.	ISSUE PRICE	QUOTE U.S.$
1993 God Loveth A Cheerful Giver	28-day		35.00	35
1993 Make A Joyful Noise	28-day		35.00	35
1994 Love One Another	28-day		35.00	35
1994 You Have Touched So Many Hearts	28-day		35.00	35
1994 Praise the Lord Anyhow	28-day		35.00	35
1994 I Believe in Miracles	28-day		35.00	35
1994 Good Friends Are Forever	28-day		35.00	35
1994 Jesus Loves Me	28-day		35.00	35
1995 Friendship Hits the Spot	28-day		35.00	35
1995 To My Deer Friend	28-day		35.00	35

Precious Moments Plates - T. Utz

YEAR ISSUE	EDITION LIMIT	YEAR RETD.	ISSUE PRICE	QUOTE U.S.$
1979 Friend in the Sky	28-day		21.50	50
1980 Sand in her Shoe	28-day		21.50	27
1980 Snow Bunny	28-day		21.50	18
1980 Seashells	28-day		21.50	38
1981 Dawn	28-day		21.50	27
1982 My Kitty	28-day		21.50	36

Precious Portraits - B. P. Gutmann

YEAR ISSUE	EDITION LIMIT	YEAR RETD.	ISSUE PRICE	QUOTE U.S.$
1987 Sunbeam	14-day		24.50	36
1987 Mischief	14-day		24.50	30
1987 Peach Blossom	14-day		24.50	36
1987 Goldilocks	14-day		24.50	30
1987 Fairy Gold	14-day		24.50	36
1987 Bunny	14-day		24.50	30

The Prideful Ones - C. DeHaan

YEAR ISSUE	EDITION LIMIT	YEAR RETD.	ISSUE PRICE	QUOTE U.S.$
1994 Village Markers	28-day		29.50	30
1994 His Pride	28-day		29.50	30
1994 Appeasing the Water People	28-day		29.50	30
1994 Tribal Guardian	28-day		29.50	30
1994 Autumn Passage	28-day		29.50	30
1994 Winter Hunter	28-day		29.50	30
1994 Silent Trail Break	28-day		29.50	30
1994 Water Breaking	28-day		29.50	30
1994 Crossing at the Big Trees	28-day		29.50	30
1995 Winter Songsinger	28-day		29.50	30

Princesses of the Plains - D. Wright

YEAR ISSUE	EDITION LIMIT	YEAR RETD.	ISSUE PRICE	QUOTE U.S.$
1993 Prairie Flower	28-day		29.50	30
1993 Snow Princess	28-day		29.50	30
1993 Wild Flower	28-day		29.50	30
1993 Noble Beauty	28-day		29.50	30
1993 Winter's Rose	28-day		29.50	30
1993 Gentle Beauty	28-day		29.50	30
1994 Nature's Guardian	28-day		29.50	30
1994 Mountain Princess	28-day		29.50	30
1995 Proud Dreamer	28-day		29.50	30
1995 Spring Maiden	28-day		29.50	30

Proud Indian Families - K. Freeman

YEAR ISSUE	EDITION LIMIT	YEAR RETD.	ISSUE PRICE	QUOTE U.S.$
1991 The Storyteller	14-day		29.50	30
1991 The Power of the Basket	14-day		29.50	30
1991 The Naming Ceremony	14-day		29.50	30
1992 Playing With Tradition	14-day		29.50	30
1992 Preparing the Berry Harvest	14-day		29.50	30
1992 Ceremonial Dress	14-day		29.50	30
1992 Sounds of the Forest	14-day		29.50	30
1992 The Marriage Ceremony	14-day		29.50	30
1993 The Jewelry Maker	14-day		29.50	30
1993 Beautiful Creations	14-day		29.50	30

Proud Innocence - J. Schmidt

YEAR ISSUE	EDITION LIMIT	YEAR RETD.	ISSUE PRICE	QUOTE U.S.$
1994 Desert Bloom	28-day		29.50	30
1994 Little Drummer	28-day		29.50	30
1995 Young Archer	28-day		29.50	30
1995 Morning Child	28-day		29.50	30
1995 Wise One	28-day		29.50	30
1995 Sun Blossom	28-day		29.50	30
1995 Laughing Heart	28-day		29.50	30
1995 Gentle Flower	28-day		29.50	30

The Proud Nation - R. Swanson

YEAR ISSUE	EDITION LIMIT	YEAR RETD.	ISSUE PRICE	QUOTE U.S.$
1989 Navajo Little One	14-day		24.50	50
1989 In a Big Land	14-day		24.50	25
1989 Out with Mama's Flock	14-day		24.50	25
1989 Newest Little Sheepherder	14-day		24.50	30
1989 Dressed Up for the Powwow	14-day		24.50	30
1989 Just a Few Days Old	14-day		24.50	30
1989 Autumn Treat	14-day		24.50	30
1989 Up in the Red Rocks	14-day		24.50	25

Puppy Playtime - J. Lamb

YEAR ISSUE	EDITION LIMIT	YEAR RETD.	ISSUE PRICE	QUOTE U.S.$
1987 Double Take-Cocker Spaniels	14-day		24.50	75
1987 Catch of the Day-Golden Retrievers	14-day		24.50	45
1987 Cabin Fever-Black Labradors	14-day		24.50	45
1987 Weekend Gardener-Lhasa Apsos	14-day		24.50	36
1987 Getting Acquainted-Beagles	14-day		24.50	36
1987 Hanging Out-German Shepherd	14-day		24.50	45
1987 New Leash on Life-Mini Schnauzer	14-day		24.50	45
1987 Fun and Games-Poodle	14-day		24.50	36

Quiet Moments Of Childhood - D. Green

YEAR ISSUE	EDITION LIMIT	YEAR RETD.	ISSUE PRICE	QUOTE U.S.$
1991 Elizabeth's Afternoon Tea	14-day		29.50	45
1991 Christina's Secret Garden	14-day		29.50	36
1991 Eric & Erin's Storytime	14-day		29.50	30
1992 Jessica's Tea Party	14-day		29.50	33
1992 Megan & Monique's Bakery	14-day		29.50	36
1992 Children's Day By The Sea	14-day		29.50	30
1992 Jordan's Playful Pups	14-day		29.50	33
1992 Daniel's Morning Playtime	14-day		29.50	30

The Quilted Countryside: A Signature Collection by Mel Steele - M. Steele

YEAR ISSUE	EDITION LIMIT	YEAR RETD.	ISSUE PRICE	QUOTE U.S.$
1991 The Old Country Store	14-day		29.50	36
1991 Winter's End	14-day		29.50	36
1991 The Quilter's Cabin	14-day		29.50	45
1991 Spring Cleaning	14-day		29.50	36
1991 Summer Harvest	14-day		29.50	30
1991 The Country Merchant	14-day		29.50	36
1992 Wash Day	14-day		29.50	30
1992 The Antiques Store	14-day		29.50	33

Remembering Norma Jeane - F. Accornero

YEAR ISSUE	EDITION LIMIT	YEAR RETD.	ISSUE PRICE	QUOTE U.S.$
1994 The Girl Next Door	28-day		29.50	30
1994 Her Day in the Sun	28-day		29.50	30
1994 A Star is Born	28-day		29.50	30
1994 Beauty Secrets	28-day		29.50	30
1995 In the Spotlight	28-day		29.50	30
1995 Bathing Beauty	28-day		29.50	30
1995 Young & Carefree	28-day		29.50	30
1995 Free Spirit	28-day		29.50	30
1995 A Country Girl at Heart	28-day		29.50	30

The Renaissance Angels - L. Bywaters

YEAR ISSUE	EDITION LIMIT	YEAR RETD.	ISSUE PRICE	QUOTE U.S.$
1994 Doves of Peace	28-day		29.50	30
1994 Angelic Innocence	28-day		29.50	30
1994 Joy to the World	28-day		29.50	30
1995 Angel of Faith	28-day		29.50	30
1995 The Christmas Star	28-day		29.50	30
1995 Trumpeter's Call	28-day		29.50	30
1995 Harmonious Heavens	28-day		29.50	30
1995 The Angels Sing	28-day		29.50	30

Rockwell Home of the Brave - N. Rockwell

YEAR ISSUE	EDITION LIMIT	YEAR RETD.	ISSUE PRICE	QUOTE U.S.$
1981 Reminiscing	18,000		35.00	53
1981 Hero's Welcome	18,000		35.00	53
1981 Back to his Old Job	18,000		35.00	53
1981 War Hero	18,000		35.00	35
1982 Willie Gillis in Church	18,000		35.00	53
1982 War Bond	18,000		35.00	35
1982 Uncle Sam Takes Wings	18,000		35.00	75
1982 Taking Mother over the Top	18,000		35.00	35

Romance of the Rails - D. Tutwiler

YEAR ISSUE	EDITION LIMIT	YEAR RETD.	ISSUE PRICE	QUOTE U.S.$
1994 Starlight Limited	28-day		29.50	30
1994 Portland Rose	28-day		29.50	30
1994 Orange Blossom Special	28-day		29.50	30
1994 Morning Star	28-day		29.50	30
1994 Crescent Limited	28-day		29.50	30
1994 Sunset Limited	28-day		29.50	30
1994 Western Star	28-day		29.50	30
1994 Sunrise Limited	28-day		29.50	30
1995 The Blue Bonnett	28-day		29.50	30
1995 The Pine Tree Limited	28-day		29.50	30

Romantic Castles of Europe - D. Sweet

YEAR ISSUE	EDITION LIMIT	YEAR RETD.	ISSUE PRICE	QUOTE U.S.$
1990 Ludwig's Castle	19,500		55.00	55
1991 Palace of the Moors	19,500		55.00	55
1991 Swiss Isle Fortress	19,500		55.00	55
1991 The Legendary Castle of Leeds	19,500		55.00	55
1991 Davinci's Chambord	19,500		55.00	55
1991 Eilean Donan	19,500		55.00	55
1992 Eltz Castle	19,500		55.00	55
1992 Kylemore Abbey	19,500		55.00	55

Romantic Flights of Fancy - Q. Lemonds

YEAR ISSUE	EDITION LIMIT	YEAR RETD.	ISSUE PRICE	QUOTE U.S.$
1994 Sunlit Waltz	28-day		29.50	30
1994 Morning Minuet	28-day		29.50	30
1994 Evening Solo	28-day		29.50	30
1994 Summer Sonata	28-day		29.50	30
1995 Twilight Tango	28-day		29.50	30
1995 Sunset Ballet	28-day		29.50	30

PLATES

Romantic Victorian Keepsake - J. Grossman

Year Issue		Edition Limit	Year Retd.	Issue Price	Quote U.S.$
1992	Dearest Kiss	28-day		35.00	35
1992	First Love	28-day		35.00	35
1992	As Fair as a Rose	28-day		35.00	35
1992	Springtime Beauty	28-day		35.00	35
1992	Summertime Fancy	28-day		35.00	35
1992	Bonnie Blue Eyes	28-day		35.00	35
1992	Precious Friends	28-day		35.00	35
1994	Bonnets and Bouquets	28-day		35.00	35
1994	My Beloved Teddy	28-day		35.00	35
1994	A Sweet Romance	28-day		35.00	35

The Saturday Evening Post - N. Rockwell

Year Issue		Edition Limit	Year Retd.	Issue Price	Quote U.S.$
1989	The Wonders of Radio	14-day		35.00	35
1989	Easter Morning	14-day		35.00	60
1989	The Facts of Life	14-day		35.00	35
1990	The Window Washer	14-day		35.00	45
1990	First Flight	14-day		35.00	54
1990	Traveling Companion	14-day		35.00	35
1990	Jury Room	14-day		35.00	35
1990	Furlough	14-day		35.00	35

Scenes of An American Christmas - B. Perry

Year Issue		Edition Limit	Year Retd.	Issue Price	Quote U.S.$
1994	I'll Be Home for Christmas	28-day		29.50	30
1994	Christmas Eve Worship	28-day		29.50	30
1994	A Holiday Happening	28-day		29.50	30
1994	A Long Winter's Night	28-day		29.50	30
1994	The Sounds of Christmas	28-day		29.50	30
1994	Dear Santa	28-day		29.50	30
1995	An Afternoon Outing	28-day		29.50	30
1995	Winter Worship	28-day		29.50	30

Seasons of the Bald Eagle - J. Pitcher

Year Issue		Edition Limit	Year Retd.	Issue Price	Quote U.S.$
1991	Autumn in the Mountains	14-day		37.50	45
1991	Winter in the Valley	14-day		37.50	38
1991	Spring on the River	14-day		37.50	38
1991	Summer on the Seacoast	14-day		37.50	38

Sharing Life's Most Precious Memories - S. Butcher

Year Issue		Edition Limit	Year Retd.	Issue Price	Quote U.S.$
1995	Thee I Love	28-day		35.00	35
1995	The Joy of the Lord Is My Strength	28-day		35.00	35
1995	May Your Every Wish Come True	28-day		35.00	35

Sharing the Moments - S. Butcher

Year Issue		Edition Limit	Year Retd.	Issue Price	Quote U.S.$
1995	You Have Touched So Many Hearts	28-day		35.00	35

Single Issues - T. Utz

Year Issue		Edition Limit	Year Retd.	Issue Price	Quote U.S.$
1983	Princess Grace	21-day		39.50	60

Small Wonders of the Wild - C. Frace

Year Issue		Edition Limit	Year Retd.	Issue Price	Quote U.S.$
1989	Hideaway	14-day		29.50	45
1990	Young Explorers	14-day		29.50	36
1990	Three of a Kind	14-day		29.50	75
1990	Quiet Morning	14-day		29.50	36
1990	Eyes of Wonder	14-day		29.50	30
1990	Ready for Adventure	14-day		29.50	30
1990	Uno	14-day		29.50	45
1990	Exploring a New World	14-day		29.50	30

Spirit of the Mustang - C. DeHaan

Year Issue		Edition Limit	Year Retd.	Issue Price	Quote U.S.$
1995	Winter's Thunder	28-day		29.95	30

Sporting Generation - J. Lamb

Year Issue		Edition Limit	Year Retd.	Issue Price	Quote U.S.$
1991	Like Father, Like Son	14-day		29.50	36-45
1991	Golden Moments	14-day		29.50	35
1991	The Lookout	14-day		29.50	35
1992	Picking Up The Scent	14-day		29.50	30
1992	First Time Out	14-day		29.50	30
1992	Who's Tracking Who	14-day		29.50	30
1992	Springing Into Action	14-day		29.50	30
1992	Point of Interest	14-day		29.50	30

STAR TREK® : 25th Anniversary Commemorative - T. Blackshear

Year Issue		Edition Limit	Year Retd.	Issue Price	Quote U.S.$
1991	STAR TREK 25th Anniversary Commemorative Plate	14-day		37.50	120-175
1991	SPOCK	14-day		35.00	100-150
1991	Kirk	14-day		35.00	75-140
1992	McCoy	14-day		35.00	45
1992	Uhura	14-day		35.00	45
1992	Scotty	14-day		35.00	45
1993	Sulu	14-day		35.00	45
1993	Chekov	14-day		35.00	45
1994	U.S.S. Enterprise NCC-1701	14-day		35.00	49

STAR TREK® : Captain James T. Kirk Autographed Wall Plaque - N/A

Year Issue		Edition Limit	Year Retd.	Issue Price	Quote U.S.$
1995	Captain James T. Kirk	5,000		195.00	195

STAR TREK® : Captain Jean-Luc Picard Autographed Wall Plaque - N/A

Year Issue		Edition Limit	Year Retd.	Issue Price	Quote U.S.$
1994	Captain Jean-Luc Picard	5,000		195.00	100-200

STAR TREK® : Deep Space 9 - M. Weistling

Year Issue		Edition Limit	Year Retd.	Issue Price	Quote U.S.$
1994	Commander Benjamin Sisko	28-day		35.00	35
1994	Security Chief Odo	28-day		35.00	35
1994	Major Kira Nerys	28-day		35.00	35
1994	Space Station	28-day		35.00	35
1994	Proprietor Quark	28-day		35.00	35
1995	Doctor Julian Bashir	28-day		35.00	35
1995	Lieutenant Jadzia Dax	28-day		35.00	35
1995	Chief Miles O'Brien	28-day		35.00	35

STAR TREK® : First Officer Spock® Autographed Wall Plaque - N/A

Year Issue		Edition Limit	Year Retd.	Issue Price	Quote U.S.$
1994	First Officer Spock®	2,500		195.00	195

STAR TREK® : The Movies - M. Weistling

Year Issue		Edition Limit	Year Retd.	Issue Price	Quote U.S.$
1994	STAR TREK IV: The Voyage Home	28-day		35.00	35
1994	STAR TREK II: The Wrath of Khan	28-day		35.00	35
1994	STAR TREK VI: The Undiscovered Country	28-day		35.00	35
1995	STAR TREK III: The Search For Spock	28-day		35.00	35
1995	STAR TREK V: The Final Frontier	28-day		35.00	35

STAR TREK® : The Next Generation - T. Blackshear

Year Issue		Edition Limit	Year Retd.	Issue Price	Quote U.S.$
1993	Captain Jean-Luc Picard	28-day		35.00	35
1993	Commander William T. Riker	28-day		35.00	35
1994	Lieutenant Commander Data	28-day		35.00	35
1994	Lieutenant Worf	28-day		35.00	35
1994	Counselor Deanna Troi	28-day		35.00	35
1995	Dr. Beverly Crusher	28-day		35.00	35

STAR TREK® : The Next Generation The Episodes - K. Birdsong

Year Issue		Edition Limit	Year Retd.	Issue Price	Quote U.S.$
1994	The Best of Both Worlds	28-day		35.00	35
1994	Encounter at Far Point	28-day		35.00	35
1995	Unification	28-day		35.00	35
1995	Yesterday's Enterprise	28-day		35.00	35
1995	All Good Things	28-day		35.00	35
1995	Descent	28-day		35.00	35

STAR TREK® : The Spock® Commemorative Wall Plaque - N/A

Year Issue		Edition Limit	Year Retd.	Issue Price	Quote U.S.$
1993	Spock®/STAR TREK VI The Undiscovered Country	2,500		195.00	195

STAR TREK® : The Voyagers - K. Birdsong

Year Issue		Edition Limit	Year Retd.	Issue Price	Quote U.S.$
1994	U.S.S. Enterprise NCC-1701	28-day		35.00	35
1994	U.S.S. Enterprise NCC-1701-D	28-day		35.00	35
1994	Klingon Battlecruiser	28-day		35.00	35
1994	Romulan Warbird	28-day		35.00	35
1994	U.S.S. Enterprise NCC-1701-A	28-day		35.00	35
1995	Ferengi Marauder	28-day		35.00	35
1995	Klingon Bird of Prey	28-day		35.00	35
1995	Triple Nacelled U.S.S. Enterprise	28-day		35.00	35
1995	Cardassian Galor Warship	28-day		35.00	35

Star Wars 10th Anniversary Commemorative - T. Blackshear

Year Issue		Edition Limit	Year Retd.	Issue Price	Quote U.S.$
1990	Star Wars 10th Anniversary Commemorative Plates	14-day		39.50	100-145

Star Wars Plate Collection - T. Blackshear

Year Issue		Edition Limit	Year Retd.	Issue Price	Quote U.S.$
1987	Hans Solo	14-day		29.50	75-125
1987	R2-D2 and Wicket	14-day		29.50	75-125
1987	Luke Skywalker and Darth Vader	14-day		29.50	75-125
1987	Princess Leia	14-day		29.50	100-125
1987	The Imperial Walkers	14-day		29.50	100-125
1987	Luke and Yoda	14-day		29.50	100
1988	Space Battle	14-day		29.50	300-345
1988	Crew in Cockpit	14-day		29.50	230

Star Wars Space Vehicles - S. Hillios

Year Issue		Edition Limit	Year Retd.	Issue Price	Quote U.S.$
1995	Millenium Falcon	28-day		35.00	35
1995	TIE Fighters	28-day		35.00	35
1995	Red Five X-Wing Fighters	28-day		35.00	35
1995	Imperial Shuttle	28-day		35.00	35

Star Wars Trilogy - M. Weistling

Year Issue		Edition Limit	Year Retd.	Issue Price	Quote U.S.$
1993	Star Wars	28-day		37.50	38
1993	The Empire Strikes Back	28-day		37.50	38
1993	Return Of The Jedi	28-day		37.50	38

Symphony of the Sea - R. Koni

Year Issue		Edition Limit	Year Retd.	Issue Price	Quote U.S.$
1995	Fluid Grace	28-day		29.95	30
1995	Dolphin's Dance	28-day		29.95	30
1995	Orca Ballet	28-day		29.95	30
1995	Moonlit Minuet	28-day		29.95	30
1995	Sailfish Serenade	28-day		29.95	30
1995	Starlit Waltz	28-day		29.95	30
1995	Sunset Splendor	28-day		29.95	30

Those Delightful Dalmations - N/A

Year Issue		Edition Limit	Year Retd.	Issue Price	Quote U.S.$
1995	You Missed a Spot	28-day		29.95	30
1995	Here's a Good Spot	28-day		29.95	30

Timeless Expressions of the Orient - M. Tsang

Year Issue		Edition Limit	Year Retd.	Issue Price	Quote U.S.$
1990	Fidelity	15,000		75.00	95
1991	Femininity	15,000		75.00	75
1991	Longevity	15,000		75.00	75
1991	Beauty	15,000		55.00	55
1992	Courage	15,000		55.00	55

Treasured Days - H. Bond

Year Issue		Edition Limit	Year Retd.	Issue Price	Quote U.S.$
1987	Ashley	14-day		29.50	60
1987	Christopher	14-day		24.50	45
1987	Sara	14-day		24.50	30
1987	Jeremy	14-day		24.50	45
1987	Amanda	14-day		24.50	45
1988	Nicholas	14-day		24.50	45
1988	Lindsay	14-day		24.50	45
1988	Justin	14-day		24.50	45

A Treasury of Cherished Teddies - P. Hillman

Year Issue		Edition Limit	Year Retd.	Issue Price	Quote U.S.$
1994	Happy Holidays, Friend	28-day		29.50	30
1995	A New Year with Old Friends	28-day		29.50	30
1995	Valentines For You	28-day		29.50	30

Unbridled Spirit - C. DeHaan

Year Issue		Edition Limit	Year Retd.	Issue Price	Quote U.S.$
1992	Surf Dancer	28-day		29.50	30
1992	Winter Renegade	28-day		29.50	30
1992	Desert Shadows	28-day		29.50	30
1993	Painted Sunrise	28-day		29.50	30
1993	Desert Duel	28-day		29.50	30
1993	Midnight Run	28-day		29.50	30
1993	Moonlight Majesty	28-day		29.50	30
1993	Autumn Reverie	28-day		29.50	30
1993	Blizzard's Peril	28-day		29.50	30
1993	Sunrise Surprise	28-day		29.50	30

Under the Sea - C. Bragg

Year Issue		Edition Limit	Year Retd.	Issue Price	Quote U.S.$
1993	Tales of Tavarua	28-day		29.50	30
1993	Water's Edge	28-day		29.50	30
1994	Beauty of the Reef	28-day		29.50	30
1994	Rainbow Reef	28-day		29.50	30
1994	Orca Odyssey	28-day		29.50	30
1994	Rescue the Reef	28-day		29.50	30
1994	Underwater Dance	28-day		29.50	30
1994	Gentle Giants	28-day		29.50	30
1995	Undersea Enchantment	28-day		29.50	30
1995	Penguin Paradise	28-day		29.50	30

Undersea Visions - J. Enright

Year Issue		Edition Limit	Year Retd.	Issue Price	Quote U.S.$
1995	Secret Sanctuary	28-day		29.95	30
1995	Temple of Treasures	28-day		29.95	30

Utz Mother's Day - T. Utz

Year Issue		Edition Limit	Year Retd.	Issue Price	Quote U.S.$
1983	A Gift of Love	N/A		27.50	38
1983	Mother's Helping Hand	N/A		27.50	28
1983	Mother's Angel	N/A		27.50	28

Vanishing Rural America - J. Harrison

Year Issue		Edition Limit	Year Retd.	Issue Price	Quote U.S.$
1991	Quiet Reflections	14-day		29.50	45
1991	Autumn's Passage	14-day		29.50	45
1991	Storefront Memories	14-day		29.50	30
1991	Country Path	14-day		29.50	36
1991	When the Circus Came To Town	14-day		29.50	36
1991	Covered in Fall	14-day		29.50	45
1991	America's Heartland	14-day		29.50	33
1991	Rural Delivery	14-day		29.50	33

Victorian Christmas Memories - J. Grossman

Year Issue		Edition Limit	Year Retd.	Issue Price	Quote U.S.$
1992	A Visit from St. Nicholas	28-day		29.50	30
1993	Christmas Delivery	28-day		29.50	30
1993	Christmas Angels	28-day		29.50	30
1992	With Visions of Sugar Plums	28-day		29.50	30
1993	Merry Olde Kris Kringle	28-day		29.50	30
1993	Grandfather Frost	28-day		29.50	30
1993	Joyous Noel	28-day		29.50	30
1993	Christmas Innocence	28-day		29.50	30
1993	Dreaming of Santa	28-day		29.50	30
1993	Mistletoe & Holly	28-day		29.50	30

Victorian Playtime - M. H. Bogart

Year Issue		Edition Limit	Year Retd.	Issue Price	Quote U.S.$
1991	A Busy Day	14-day		29.50	30
1992	Little Masterpiece	14-day		29.50	30
1992	Playing Bride	14-day		29.50	36
1992	Waiting for a Nibble	14-day		29.50	30
1992	Tea and Gossip	14-day		29.50	30
1992	Cleaning House	14-day		29.50	30
1992	A Little Persuasion	14-day		29.50	30
1992	Peek-a-Boo	14-day		29.50	30

Warrior's Pride - C. DeHaan

Year Issue		Edition Limit	Year Retd.	Issue Price	Quote U.S.$
1994	Crow War Pony	28-day		29.50	30
1994	Running Free	28-day		29.50	30
1994	Blackfoot War Pony	28-day		29.50	30
1994	Southern Cheyenne	28-day		29.50	30
1995	Shoshoni War Ponies	28-day		29.50	30
1995	A Champion's Revelry	28-day		29.50	30
1995	Battle Colors	28-day		29.50	30
1995	Call of the Drums	28-day		29.50	30

The West of Frank McCarthy - F. McCarthy

Year Issue		Edition Limit	Year Retd.	Issue Price	Quote U.S.$
1991	Attacking the Iron Horse	14-day		37.50	60
1991	Attempt on the Stage	14-day		37.50	45
1991	The Prayer	14-day		37.50	54
1991	On the Old North Trail	14-day		37.50	48
1991	The Hostile Threat	14-day		37.50	45
1991	Bringing Out the Furs	14-day		37.50	45
1991	Kiowa Raider	14-day		37.50	45
1991	Headed North	14-day		37.50	38

Wilderness Spirits - P. Koni

Year Issue		Edition Limit	Year Retd.	Issue Price	Quote U.S.$
1994	Eyes of the Night	28-day		29.95	30
1995	Midnight Call	28-day		29.95	30
1995	Breaking the Silence	28-day		29.95	30
1995	Moonlight Run	28-day		29.95	30

YEAR ISSUE		EDITION LIMIT	YEAR RETD.	ISSUE PRICE	QUOTE U.S.$
1995	Sunset Vigil	28-day		29.95	30
1995	Sunrise Spirit	28-day		29.95	30

Winged Reflections - R. Parker

YEAR ISSUE		EDITION LIMIT	YEAR RETD.	ISSUE PRICE	QUOTE U.S.$
1989	Following Mama	14-day		37.50	38
1989	Above the Breakers	14-day		37.50	38
1989	Among the Reeds	14-day		37.50	38
1989	Freeze Up	14-day		37.50	38
1989	Wings Above the Water	14-day		37.50	38
1990	Summer Loon	14-day		29.50	30
1990	Early Spring	14-day		29.50	30
1990	At The Water's Edge	14-day		29.50	30

Winter Rails - T. Xaras

YEAR ISSUE		EDITION LIMIT	YEAR RETD.	ISSUE PRICE	QUOTE U.S.$
1992	Winter Crossing	28-day		29.50	30
1993	Coal Country	28-day		29.50	30
1993	Daylight Run	28-day		29.50	30
1993	By Sea or Rail	28-day		29.50	30
1993	Country Crossroads	28-day		29.50	30
1993	Timber Line	28-day		29.50	30
1993	The Long Haul	28-day		29.50	30
1993	Darby Crossing	28-day		29.50	30
1995	East Broad Top	28-day		29.50	30
1995	Landsdowne Station	28-day		29.50	30

Winter Wildlife - J. Seerey-Lester

YEAR ISSUE		EDITION LIMIT	YEAR RETD.	ISSUE PRICE	QUOTE U.S.$
1989	Close Encounters	15,000		55.00	55
1989	Among the Cattails	15,000		55.00	55
1989	The Refuge	15,000		55.00	55
1989	Out of the Blizzard	15,000		55.00	55
1989	First Snow	15,000		55.00	55
1989	Lying In Wait	15,000		55.00	55
1989	Winter Hiding	15,000		55.00	55
1989	Early Snow	15,000		55.00	55

Wizard of Oz Commemorative - T. Blackshear

YEAR ISSUE		EDITION LIMIT	YEAR RETD.	ISSUE PRICE	QUOTE U.S.$
1988	We're Off to See the Wizard	14-day		24.50	110-200
1988	Dorothy Meets the Scarecrow	14-day		24.50	75-125
1989	The Tin Man Speaks	14-day		24.50	105-160
1989	A Glimpse of the Munchkins	14-day		24.50	115-150
1989	The Witch Casts A Spell	14-day		24.50	100-160
1989	If I Were King Of The Forest	14-day		24.50	125-160
1989	The Great and Powerful Oz	14-day		24.50	125-160
1989	There's No Place Like Home	14-day		24.50	125-160

Wizard of Oz-Fifty Years of Oz - T. Blackshear

YEAR ISSUE		EDITION LIMIT	YEAR RETD.	ISSUE PRICE	QUOTE U.S.$
1989	Fifty Years of Oz	14-day		37.50	100-200

Wizard of Oz-Portraits From Oz - T. Blackshear

YEAR ISSUE		EDITION LIMIT	YEAR RETD.	ISSUE PRICE	QUOTE U.S.$
1989	Dorothy	14-day		29.50	120-175
1989	Scarecrow	14-day		29.50	100-140
1989	Tin Man	14-day		29.50	110-150
1990	Cowardly Lion	14-day		29.50	120-150
1990	Glinda	14-day		29.50	75-140
1990	Wizard	14-day		29.50	125-140
1990	Wicked Witch	14-day		29.50	100-200
1990	Toto	14-day		29.50	150-200

The Wonder Of Christmas - J. McClelland

YEAR ISSUE		EDITION LIMIT	YEAR RETD.	ISSUE PRICE	QUOTE U.S.$
1991	Santa's Secret	28-day		29.50	30
1991	My Favorite Ornament	28-day		29.50	30
1991	Waiting For Santa	28-day		29.50	30
1993	The Caroler	28-day		29.50	30

Woodland Babies - P. Manning

YEAR ISSUE		EDITION LIMIT	YEAR RETD.	ISSUE PRICE	QUOTE U.S.$
1995	Hollow Hideaway	28-day		29.95	30

Woodland Encounters - G. Giordano

YEAR ISSUE		EDITION LIMIT	YEAR RETD.	ISSUE PRICE	QUOTE U.S.$
1991	Want to Play?	14-day		29.50	30
1991	Peek-a-boo!	14-day		29.50	30
1991	Lunchtime Visitor	14-day		29.50	33
1991	Anyone for a Swim?	14-day		29.50	36
1991	Nature Scouts	14-day		29.50	36
1991	Meadow Meeting	14-day		29.50	33
1991	Hi Neighbor	14-day		29.50	30
1992	Field Day	14-day		29.50	36

The World Of Zolan - D. Zolan

YEAR ISSUE		EDITION LIMIT	YEAR RETD.	ISSUE PRICE	QUOTE U.S.$
1992	First Kiss	28-day		29.50	30
1992	Morning Discovery	28-day		29.50	30
1993	The Little Fisherman	28-day		29.50	30
1993	Letter to Grandma	28-day		29.50	30
1993	Twilight Prayer	28-day		29.50	30
1993	Flowers for Mother	28-day		29.50	30

Year Of The Wolf - A. Agnew

YEAR ISSUE		EDITION LIMIT	YEAR RETD.	ISSUE PRICE	QUOTE U.S.$
1993	Broken Silence	28-day		29.50	30
1993	Leader of the Pack	28-day		29.50	30
1993	Solitude	28-day		29.50	30
1994	Tundra Light	28-day		29.50	30
1994	Guardians of the High Country	28-day		29.50	30
1994	A Second Glance	28-day		29.50	30
1994	Free as the Wind	28-day		29.50	30
1994	Song of the Wolf	28-day		29.50	30
1995	Lords of the Tundra	28-day		29.50	30
1995	Wilderness Companions	28-day		29.50	30

Young Lords of The Wild - M. Richter

YEAR ISSUE		EDITION LIMIT	YEAR RETD.	ISSUE PRICE	QUOTE U.S.$
1994	Siberian Tiger Club	28-day		29.95	30
1995	Snow Leopard Cub	28-day		29.95	30
1995	Lion Cub	28-day		29.95	30
1995	Clouded Leopard Cub	28-day		29.95	30

Hamilton/Boehm

Award Winning Roses - Boehm

YEAR ISSUE		EDITION LIMIT	YEAR RETD.	ISSUE PRICE	QUOTE U.S.$
1979	Peace Rose	15,000		45.00	63
1979	White Masterpiece Rose	15,000		45.00	63
1979	Tropicana Rose	15,000		45.00	63
1979	Elegance Rose	15,000		45.00	63
1979	Queen Elizabeth Rose	15,000		45.00	63
1979	Royal Highness Rose	15,000		45.00	63
1979	Angel Face Rose	15,000		45.00	63
1979	Mr. Lincoln Rose	15,000		45.00	63

Gamebirds of North America - Boehm

YEAR ISSUE		EDITION LIMIT	YEAR RETD.	ISSUE PRICE	QUOTE U.S.$
1984	Ring-Necked Pheasant	15,000		62.50	63
1984	Bob White Quail	15,000		62.50	63
1984	American Woodcock	15,000		62.50	63
1984	California Quail	15,000		62.50	63
1984	Ruffed Grouse	15,000		62.50	63
1984	Wild Turkey	15,000		62.50	63
1984	Willow Partridge	15,000		62.50	63
1984	Prairie Grouse	15,000		62.50	63

Hummingbird Collection - Boehm

YEAR ISSUE		EDITION LIMIT	YEAR RETD.	ISSUE PRICE	QUOTE U.S.$
1980	Calliope	15,000		62.50	80
1980	Broadbilled	15,000		62.50	63
1980	Rufous Flame Bearer	15,000		62.50	80
1980	Broadtail	15,000		62.50	63
1980	Streamertail	15,000		62.50	80
1980	Blue Throated	15,000		62.50	80
1980	Crimson Topaz	15,000		62.50	63
1980	Brazilian Ruby	15,000		62.50	80

Owl Collection - Boehm

YEAR ISSUE		EDITION LIMIT	YEAR RETD.	ISSUE PRICE	QUOTE U.S.$
1980	Boreal Owl	15,000		45.00	75
1980	Snowy Owl	15,000		45.00	63
1980	Barn Owl	15,000		45.00	63
1980	Saw Whet Owl	15,000		45.00	63
1980	Great Horned Owl	15,000		45.00	63
1980	Screech Owl	15,000		45.00	63
1980	Short Eared Owl	15,000		45.00	63
1980	Barred Owl	15,000		45.00	63

Water Birds - Boehm

YEAR ISSUE		EDITION LIMIT	YEAR RETD.	ISSUE PRICE	QUOTE U.S.$
1981	Canada Geese	15,000		62.50	75
1981	Wood Ducks	15,000		62.50	63
1981	Hooded Merganser	15,000		62.50	87
1981	Ross's Geese	15,000		62.50	63
1981	Common Mallard	15,000		62.50	63
1981	Canvas Back	15,000		62.50	63
1981	Green Winged Teal	15,000		62.50	63
1981	American Pintail	15,000		62.50	63

Haviland

Twelve Days of Christmas - R. Hetreau

YEAR ISSUE		EDITION LIMIT	YEAR RETD.	ISSUE PRICE	QUOTE U.S.$
1970	Partridge	30,000		25.00	54
1971	Two Turtle Doves	30,000		25.00	25
1972	Three French Hens	30,000		27.50	28
1973	Four Calling Birds	30,000		28.50	30
1974	Five Golden Rings	30,000		30.00	30
1975	Six Geese a'laying	30,000		32.50	33
1976	Seven Swans	30,000		38.00	38
1977	Eight Maids	30,000		40.00	40
1978	Nine Ladies Dancing	30,000		45.00	67
1979	Ten Lord's a'leaping	30,000		50.00	50
1980	Eleven Pipers Piping	30,000		55.00	65
1981	Twelve Drummers	30,000		60.00	60

Haviland & Parlon

Christmas Madonnas - Various

YEAR ISSUE		EDITION LIMIT	YEAR RETD.	ISSUE PRICE	QUOTE U.S.$
1972	By Raphael - Raphael	5,000		35.00	42
1973	By Feruzzi - Feruzzi	5,000		40.00	78
1974	By Raphael - Raphael	5,000		42.50	43
1975	By Murillo - Murillo	7,500		42.50	43
1976	By Botticelli - Botticelli	7,500		45.00	45
1977	By Bellini - Bellini	7,500		48.00	48
1978	By Lippi - Lippi	7,500		48.00	53
1979	Madonna of The Eucharist - Botticelli	7,500		49.50	112

Hutschenreuther

The Glory of Christmas - W./C. Hallett

YEAR ISSUE		EDITION LIMIT	YEAR RETD.	ISSUE PRICE	QUOTE U.S.$
1982	The Nativity	25,000		80.00	125
1983	The Annunciation	25,000		80.00	115
1984	The Shepherds	25,000		80.00	100
1985	The Wiseman	25,000		80.00	100

Gunther Granget - G. Granget

YEAR ISSUE		EDITION LIMIT	YEAR RETD.	ISSUE PRICE	QUOTE U.S.$
1972	American Sparrows	5,000		50.00	150
1972	European Sparrows	5,000		30.00	65
1973	American Kildeer	2,250		75.00	90
1973	American Squirrel	2,500		75.00	75
1973	European Squirrel	2,500		35.00	50
1974	American Partridge	2,500		75.00	90
1975	American Rabbits	2,500		90.00	90
1976	Freedom in Flight	5,000		100.00	100
1976	Wrens	2,500		100.00	110
1976	Freedom in Flight, Gold	200		200.00	200
1977	Bears	2,500		100.00	100
1978	Foxes' Spring Journey	1,000		125.00	200

Imperial Ching-te Chen

Beauties of the Red Mansion - Z. HuiMin

YEAR ISSUE		EDITION LIMIT	YEAR RETD.	ISSUE PRICE	QUOTE U.S.$
1986	Pao-chai	115-day		27.92	40
1986	Yuan-chun	115-day		27.92	45-60
1987	Hsi-feng	115-day		30.92	31
1987	Hsi-chun	115-day		30.92	31-35
1988	Miao-yu	115-day		30.92	31
1988	Ying-chun	115-day		30.92	35
1988	Tai-yu	115-day		32.92	35
1988	Li-wan	115-day		32.92	50
1988	Ko-Ching	115-day		32.92	35
1988	Hsiang-yun	115-day		34.92	35
1989	Tan-Chun	115-day		34.92	40
1989	Chiao-chieh	115-day		34.92	35

Blessings From a Chinese Garden - Z. Song Mao

YEAR ISSUE		EDITION LIMIT	YEAR RETD.	ISSUE PRICE	QUOTE U.S.$
1988	The Gift of Purity	175-day		39.92	42
1989	The Gift of Grace	175-day		39.92	40
1989	The Gift of Beauty	175-day		42.92	43
1989	The Gift of Happiness	175-day		42.92	43
1990	The Gift of Truth	175-day		42.92	43
1990	The Gift of Joy	175-day		42.92	43

Flower Goddesses of China - Z. HuiMin

YEAR ISSUE		EDITION LIMIT	YEAR RETD.	ISSUE PRICE	QUOTE U.S.$
1991	The Lotus Goddess	175-day		34.92	35
1991	The Chrysanthemum Goddess	175-day		34.92	35
1991	The Plum Blossom Goddess	175-day		37.92	40
1991	The Peony Goddess	175-day		37.92	55
1991	The Narcissus Goddess	175-day		37.92	60
1991	The Camellia Goddess	175-day		37.92	50

The Forbidden City - S. Fu

YEAR ISSUE		EDITION LIMIT	YEAR RETD.	ISSUE PRICE	QUOTE U.S.$
1990	Pavilion of 10,000 Springs	150-day		39.92	40
1990	Flying Kites/Spring Day	150-day		39.92	40
1990	Pavilion/Floating Jade Green	150-day		42.92	44
1991	The Lantern Festival	150-day		42.92	46
1991	Nine Dragon Screen	150-day		42.92	55
1991	The Hall of the Cultivating Mind	150-day		42.92	43
1991	Dressing the Empress	150-day		45.92	46
1991	Pavilion of Floating Cups	150-day		45.92	50

Garden of Satin Wings - J. Xue-Bing

YEAR ISSUE		EDITION LIMIT	YEAR RETD.	ISSUE PRICE	QUOTE U.S.$
1992	A Morning Dream	115-day		29.92	30
1993	An Evening Mist	115-day		29.92	30
1993	A Garden Whisper	115-day		29.92	40
1993	An Enchanting Interlude	115-day		29.92	30

Legends of West Lake - J. Xue-Bing

YEAR ISSUE		EDITION LIMIT	YEAR RETD.	ISSUE PRICE	QUOTE U.S.$
1989	Lady White	175-day		29.92	40
1990	Lady Silkworm	175-day		29.92	40
1990	Laurel Peak	175-day		29.92	45
1990	Rising Sun Terrace	175-day		32.92	45
1990	The Apricot Fairy	175-day		32.92	33
1990	Bright Pearl	175-day		32.92	33
1990	Thread of Sky	175-day		34.92	35
1991	Phoenix Mountain	175-day		34.92	35-40
1991	Ancestors of Tea	175-day		34.92	45
1991	Three Pools Mirroring/Moon	175-day		36.92	45
1991	Fly-In Peak	175-day		36.92	40
1991	The Case of the Folding Fans	175-day		36.92	40

Maidens of the Folding Sky - J. Xue-Bing

YEAR ISSUE		EDITION LIMIT	YEAR RETD.	ISSUE PRICE	QUOTE U.S.$
1992	Lady Lu	175-day		29.92	35
1992	Mistress Yang	175-day		29.92	45
1992	Bride Yen Chun	175-day		32.92	80
1993	Parrot Maiden	175-day		32.92	80

Scenes from the Summer Palace - Z. Song Mao

YEAR ISSUE		EDITION LIMIT	YEAR RETD.	ISSUE PRICE	QUOTE U.S.$
1988	The Marble Boat	175-day		29.92	32
1988	Jade Belt Bridge	175-day		29.92	32
1989	Hall that Dispels the Clouds	175-day		32.92	38
1989	The Long Promenade	175-day		32.92	35
1989	Garden/Harmonious Pleasure	175-day		32.92	35
1989	The Great Stage	175-day		32.92	33
1989	Seventeen Arch Bridge	175-day		34.92	35
1989	Boaters on Kumming Lake	175-day		34.92	35

International Silver

Bicentennial - M. Deoliveira

YEAR ISSUE		EDITION LIMIT	YEAR RETD.	ISSUE PRICE	QUOTE U.S.$
1972	Signing Declaration	7,500		40.00	310
1973	Paul Revere	7,500		40.00	160
1974	Concord Bridge	7,500		40.00	115
1975	Crossing Delaware	7,500		50.00	80
1976	Valley Forge	7,500		50.00	65
1977	Surrender at Yorktown	7,500		50.00	60

John Hine N.A. Ltd.

David Winter Plate Collection - M. Fisher

YEAR ISSUE		EDITION LIMIT	YEAR RETD.	ISSUE PRICE	QUOTE U.S.$
1991	A Christmas Carol	10,000	1993	30.00	35-60
1991	Cotswold Village Plate	10,000	1993	30.00	35-60

PLATES

YEAR ISSUE		EDITION LIMIT	YEAR RETD.	ISSUE PRICE	QUOTE U.S.$
1992	Chichester Cross Plate	10,000	1993	30.00	35-60
1992	Little Mill Plate	10,000	1993	30.00	35-60
1992	Old Curiosity Shop	10,000	1993	30.00	35-60
1992	Scrooge's Counting House	10,000	1993	30.00	35-60
1993	Dove Cottage	10,000		30.00	35
1993	Little Forge	10,000		30.00	35

Kaiser

Bicentennial Plate - J. Trumball

1976	Signing Declaration	Closed		75.00	150

Christmas Plates - Various

1970	Waiting for Santa Claus - T. Schoener	Closed		12.50	25
1971	Silent Night - K. Bauer	Closed		13.50	23
1972	Welcome Home - K. Bauer	Closed		16.50	43
1973	Holy Night - T. Schoener	Closed		18.00	44
1974	Christmas Carolers - K. Bauer	Closed		25.00	30
1975	Bringing Home the Tree - J. Northcott	Closed		25.00	30
1976	Christ/Saviour Born - C. Maratti	Closed		25.00	35
1977	The Three Kings - T. Schoener	Closed		25.00	25
1978	Shepherds in The Field - T. Schoener	Closed		30.00	30
1979	Christmas Eve - H. Blum	Closed		32.00	45
1980	Joys of Winter - H. Blum	Closed		40.00	43
1981	Adoration by Three Kings - K. Bauer	Closed		40.00	41
1982	Bringing Home the Tree - K. Bauer	Closed		40.00	45

Egyptian - Unknown

1980	Nefertiti	10,000		275.00	458
1980	Tutankhamen	10,000		275.00	458

King Tut - Unknown

1978	King Tut	Closed		65.00	100

Mother's Day - Various

1971	Mare and Foal - T. Schoener	Closed		13.00	25
1972	Flowers for Mother - T. Schoener	Closed		16.50	20
1973	Cats - T. Schoener	Closed		17.00	40
1974	Fox - T. Schoener	Closed		20.00	40
1975	German Shepherd - T. Schoener	Closed		25.00	100
1976	Swan and Cygnets - T. Schoener	Closed		25.00	28
1977	Mother Rabbit and Young T. Schoener	Closed		25.00	30
1978	Hen and Chicks - T. Schoener	Closed		30.00	50
1979	A Mother's Devotion - N. Peterner	Closed		32.00	40
1980	Raccoon Family - J. Northcott	Closed		40.00	45
1981	Safe Near Mother - H. Blum	Closed		40.00	40
1982	Pheasant Family - K. Bauer	Closed		40.00	44
1983	Tender Care - K. Bauer	Closed		40.00	65

KPM-Royal Berlin

Christmas - Unknown

1969	Christmas Star	5,000		28.00	380
1970	Three Kings	5,000		28.00	300
1971	Christmas Tree	5,000		28.00	290
1972	Christmas Angel	5,000		31.00	300
1973	Christ Child on Sled	5,000		33.00	280
1974	Angel and Horn	5,000		35.00	180
1975	Shepherds	5,000		40.00	165
1976	Star of Bethlehem	5,000		43.00	140
1977	Mary at Crib	5,000		46.00	100
1978	Three Wise Men	5,000		49.00	54
1979	The Manger	5,000		55.00	55
1980	Shepherds in Fields	5,000		55.00	55

Lalique Society of America

Annual - M. Lalique

1965	Deux Oiseaux (Two Birds)	2,000		25.00	1300
1966	Rose de Songerie (Dream Rose)	5,000		25.00	115
1967	Ballet de Poisson (Fish Ballet)	5,000		25.00	100
1968	Gazelle Fantaisie (Gazelle Fantasy)	5,000		25.00	75
1969	Papillon (Butterfly)	5,000		30.00	50
1970	Paon (Peacock)	5,000		30.00	60
1971	Hibou (Owl)	5,000		35.00	70
1972	Coquillage (Shell)	5,000		40.00	75
1973	Petit Geai (Jayling)	5,000		42.50	100
1974	Sous d'Argent (Silver Pennies)	5,000		47.50	100
1975	Duo de Poisson (Fish Duet)	5,000		50.00	140
1976	Aigle (Eagle)	5,000		60.00	90

Lance Corporation

American Expansion (Hudson Pewter) - P.W. Baston

1975	Spirit of '76 (6" Plate)	4,812	1975	27.50	100-120
1975	American Independence	18,462	N/A	Unkn.	100-125
1975	American Expansion	2,250	N/A	Unkn.	50-75
1975	The American War Between the States	825	N/A	Unkn.	150-200

Sebastian Plates - P.W. Baston

1978	Motif No. 1	4,878	1985	75.00	50-75
1979	Grand Canyon	2,492	1985	75.00	50-75
1980	Lone Cypress	718	1985	75.00	150-175
1980	In The Candy Store	9,098	1985	39.50	40
1981	The Doctor	7,547	1985	39.50	40
1983	Little Mother	2,710	1985	39.50	40
1984	Switching The Freight	706	1985	42.50	80-100

Lenox China

Annual Holiday - Unknown

1991	1991 Holiday Plate-Sleigh	Yr.Iss.	1992	75.00	75
1992	1992 Holiday Plate-Rock Horse	Yr.Iss.	1993	75.00	75
1993	1993 Holiday Plate-Fireplace	Yr.Iss.	1994	75.00	75
1994	1994 Annual Holiday-Santa	Yr.Iss.	1995	75.00	75

Christmas Trees Around the World - Unknown

1991	Germany	Yr.Iss.	1992	75.00	75
1992	France	Yr.Iss.	1993	75.00	75
1993	England	Yr.Iss.	1994	75.00	75
1994	Poland	Yr.Iss.	1995	75.00	75

Colonial Christmas Wreath - Unknown

1981	Colonial Virginia	Yr.Iss.	1982	65.00	76
1982	Massachusetts	Yr.Iss.	1983	70.00	93
1983	Maryland	Yr.Iss.	1984	70.00	79
1984	Rhode Island	Yr.Iss.	1985	70.00	82
1985	Connecticut	Yr.Iss.	1986	70.00	75
1986	New Hampshire	Yr.Iss.	1987	70.00	75
1987	Pennsylvania	Yr.Iss.	1988	70.00	75
1988	Delaware	Yr.Iss.	1989	70.00	70
1989	New York	Yr.Iss.	1990	75.00	82
1990	New Jersey	Yr.Iss.	1991	75.00	78
1991	South Carolina	Yr.Iss.	1992	75.00	75
1992	North Carolina	Yr.Iss.	1993	75.00	75
1993	Georgia	Yr.Iss.	1994	75.00	75

Nativity Vignettes - Unknown

1993	The Holy Family	Yr.Iss.	1994	57.00	57
1994	The Wisemen	Yr.Iss.	1995	59.00	59

Lenox Collections

Adventures of the Deep Plate Collection - Unknown

1994	Let's Play	Open		39.50	40
1994	A New Day	Open		39.50	40
1994	Shining On	Open		39.50	40
1994	Polar Strollers	Open		39.50	40
1994	New Birth	Open		39.50	40
1994	Gratitude	Open		39.50	40
1994	After Hours	Open		39.50	40
1994	Sea of Joy	Open		39.50	40

American Wildlife - N. Adams

1982	Red Foxes	9,500		65.00	65
1982	Ocelots	9,500		65.00	65
1982	Sea Lions	9,500		65.00	65
1982	Raccoons	9,500		65.00	65
1982	Dall Sheep	9,500		65.00	65
1982	Black Bears	9,500		65.00	65
1982	Mountain Lions	9,500		65.00	65
1982	Polar Bears	9,500		65.00	65
1982	Otters	9,500		65.00	65
1982	White Tailed Deer	9,500		65.00	65
1982	Buffalo	9,500		65.00	65
1982	Jack Rabbits	9,500		65.00	65

Amish Life Plates - D. Patterson

1994	Barn Raising	Open		39.50	40
1994	Country Kids	Open		39.50	40

Annual Christmas Plates - Various

1992	Sleigh - Unknown	Yr.Iss.	1992	75.00	75
1993	Midnight Sleighride - L. Bywater	90-day	1993	119.00	119

Arctic Wolves - J. VanZyle

1993	Far Country Crossing	90-day	1994	29.90	30
1993	Cry of the Wild	90-day	1994	29.90	30
1993	Nightwatch	90-day	1994	29.90	30
1993	Midnight Renegade	90-day	1994	29.90	30
1993	On the Edge	90-day	1994	29.90	30
1993	Picking Up the Trail	90-day	1994	29.90	30

Big Cats of the World - Q. Lemonds

1993	Black Panther	Open		39.50	40
1993	Chinese Leopard	Open		39.50	40
1993	Cougar	Open		39.50	40
1993	Bobcat	Open		39.50	40
1993	White Tiger	Open		39.50	40
1993	Tiger	Open		39.50	40
1993	Lion	Open		39.50	40
1993	Snow Leopard	Open		39.50	40

Birds of the Garden - W. Mumm

1992	Spring Glory, Cardinals	Open		39.50	40
1993	Sunbright Songbirds, Goldfinch	Open		39.50	40
1993	Bluebirds Haven, Bluebirds	Open		39.50	40
1993	Blossoming Bough, Chickadees	Open		39.50	40
1993	Jewels of the Garden, Hummingbirds	Open		39.50	40
1993	Indigo Meadow, Indigo Buntings	Open		39.50	40
1993	Scarlet Tanagers	Open		39.50	40

Boehm Birds - E. Boehm

1970	Wood Thrush	Yr.Iss.	1970	35.00	100
1971	Goldfinch	Yr.Iss.	1971	35.00	50
1972	Mountain Bluebird	Yr.Iss.	1972	37.50	45
1973	Meadowlark	Yr.Iss.	1973	50.00	50
1974	Rufous Hummingbird	Yr.Iss.	1974	45.00	50
1975	American Redstart	Yr.Iss.	1975	50.00	50
1976	Cardinals	Yr.Iss.	1976	53.00	53
1977	Robins	Yr.Iss.	1977	55.00	55
1978	Mockingbirds	Yr.Iss.	1978	58.00	58
1979	Golden-Crowned Kinglets	Yr.Iss.	1979	65.00	95
1980	Black-Throated Blue Warblers	Yr.Iss.	1980	80.00	112
1981	Eastern Phoebes	Yr.Iss.	1981	92.50	100

Boehm Woodland Wildlife - E. Boehm

1973	Racoons	Yr.Iss.	1973	50.00	50
1974	Red Foxes	Yr.Iss.	1974	52.50	53
1975	Cottontail Rabbits	Yr.Iss.	1975	58.50	59
1976	Eastern Chipmunks	Yr.Iss.	1976	62.50	63
1977	Beaver	Yr.Iss.	1977	67.50	68
1978	Whitetail Deer	Yr.Iss.	1978	70.00	70
1979	Squirrels	Yr.Iss.	1979	76.00	76
1980	Bobcats	Yr.Iss.	1980	82.50	83
1981	Martens	Yr.Iss.	1981	100.00	150
1982	River Otters	Yr.Iss.	1982	100.00	180

Cat Family Portrait - G. Coheleach

1994	Cougars	Open		39.50	40
1994	Lynx	Open		39.50	40
1994	Tigers	Open		39.50	40
1994	Snow Leopard	Open		39.50	40

Children of the Sun & Moon - D. Crowley

1993	Desert Blossom	Open		39.50	40
1993	Shy One	Open		39.50	40
1993	Feathers & Furs	Open		39.50	40
1994	Little Flower	Open		39.90	40
1994	Daughter of the Sun	Open		39.90	40
1994	Red Feathers	Open		39.90	40
1994	Stars in Her Eyes	Open		39.90	40
1994	Indigo Girl	Open		39.90	40

Crystal Hunter - Unknown

1994	Crystal Tiger	Open		39.50	40
1994	Dreamscape	Open		39.50	40
1994	Crystal Domain	Open		39.50	40
1994	Heart of Crystal	Open		39.50	40

Cubs of the Big Cats - Q. Lemonds

1993	Jaquar Cub	90-day	1994	29.90	30

Darling Dalmations - L. Picken

1993	Three Alarm Fire	90-day	1994	29.90	30
1993	All Fired Up	90-day	1994	29.90	30
1993	Fire Brigade	90-day	1994	29.90	30
1993	Pup in Boots	90-day	1994	29.90	30
1993	Caught in the Act	90-day	1994	29.90	30
1993	Please Don't Pick the Flowers	90-day	1994	29.90	30

Dolphins of the Seven Seas - J. Holderby

1993	Bottlenose Dolphins	Open		39.50	40

Eagle Conservation - R. Kelley

1993	Soaring the Peaks	Open		39.50	40
1993	Solo Flight	Open		39.50	40
1993	Northern Heritage	Open		39.50	40
1993	Lone Sentinel	Open		39.50	40
1993	River Scout	Open		39.50	40
1993	Eagles on Mt. McKinley	Open		39.50	40
1993	Daybreak on River's Edge	Open		39.50	40
1993	Northwood's Legend	Open		39.50	40

Enchanted World of the Unicorn - R. Sanderson

1992	Hidden Glade of Unicorn	90-day	1993	29.90	30
1992	Secret Garden of Unicorn	90-day	1993	29.90	30
1993	Joyful Meadow of Unicorn	90-day	1994	29.90	30
1993	Misty Hills of Unicorn	90-day	1994	29.90	30
1993	Tropical Paradise of Unicorn	90-day	1994	29.90	30
1993	Springtime Pasture of Unicorn	90-day	1994	29.90	30

English Country Cats - A. Mortimer

1994	Pepper & Ginger	Open		39.50	40
1994	Bluebell & Sage	Open		39.50	40
1994	Bib & Tucker	Open		39.50	40
1994	Calico & Cosmos	Open		39.50	40
1994	Peaches & Cream	Open		39.50	40
1994	Buttons & Buster	Open		39.50	40
1994	Sweet Prince & Pansy	Open		39.50	40
1994	Felix & Oscar	Open		39.50	40

Garden Bird Plate Collection - Unknown

1988	Chickadee	Open		48.00	48
1988	Bluejay	Open		48.00	48
1989	Hummingbird	Open		48.00	48
1991	Dove	Open		48.00	48
1991	Cardinal	Open		48.00	48
1992	Goldfinch	Open		48.00	48

Great Castles of the World - Unknown

1994	Neuschwanstein	Open		39.50	40
1994	Alcazar de Segovia	Open		39.50	40

YEAR ISSUE		EDITION LIMIT	YEAR RETD.	ISSUE PRICE	QUOTE U.S.$
1994	Chateau de Chambord	Open		39.50	40
1994	Houses of Parliment	Open		39.50	40
1994	West Minster	Open		39.50	40
1994	Taj Mahal	Open		39.50	40
1994	St. Basil	Open		39.50	40

Great Cats of the World - G. Coheleach

1993	Siberian Tiger	Open		39.50	40
1993	Lion	Open		39.50	40
1993	Lioness	Open		39.50	40
1993	Snow Leopard	Open		39.50	40
1993	White Tiger	Open		39.50	40
1993	Jaquar	Open		39.50	40
1993	Cougar	Open		39.50	40
1993	Chinese Leopard	Open		39.50	40
1994	Puma	Open		39.50	40

Heaven Sent - Lenox

1994	Cherubs in Clouds	Open		39.50	40
1994	Heaven's Messengers	Open		39.50	40
1994	Angel Blues	Open		39.50	40

I Love Labradors - L. Picken

1994	Little Helpers	Open		39.50	40
1994	Rookie of the Year	Open		39.50	40
1994	Catch of the Day	Open		39.50	40
1994	Just Ducky	Open		39.50	40

International Victorian Santas - R. Hoover

1992	Kris Kringle	90-day	1993	39.50	40
1993	Father Christmas	90-day	1994	39.50	40
1994	Grandfather Frost	90-day	1995	39.50	40
1995	American Santa Claus	90-day	1995	39.50	40

Kimble Barnyard - Kimble

1994	Statement Plate 1	Open		39.50	40
1994	Statement Plate 2	Open		39.50	40

Kimble Cats - Kimble

1994	Happy Cat	Open		39.50	40
1994	Welcome Cat	Open		39.50	40
1994	Fat Cat	Open		39.50	40
1994	Taffy Cat	Open		39.50	40
1994	Cool Cat	Open		39.50	40
1994	Proper Cats	Open		39.50	40
1994	Happy Family Cats	Open		39.50	40
1994	Lucky Cat	Open		39.50	40

King of the Plains - S. Combes

1994	Tsava Elephant	Open		39.90	40
1994	Guardian	Open		39.90	40
1994	Rainbow Trail	Open		39.90	40
1994	African Ancients	Open		39.90	40
1994	Protecting the Flanks	Open		39.90	40
1994	The Last Elephant	Open		39.90	40
1994	End of the Line	Open		39.90	40
1994	Sparring Bulls	Open		39.90	40

Land of Buffalo - T. Lovell

1994	Fire in Buffalo Grass	Open		39.50	40
1994	Four Times to the Sun	Open		39.50	40
1994	Listening for the Drums	Open		39.50	40
1994	Finishing Touch	Open		39.50	40
1994	Long Ago Creature	Open		39.50	40
1994	The Wolf Man	Open		39.50	40
1994	War Bonnet Ceremony	Open		39.50	40
1994	The Gift	Open		39.50	40

Larry Chandler Puppy Portraits - L. Chandler

1994	Smoky	Open		39.50	40
1994	Dutch	Open		39.50	40
1994	Custard	Open		39.50	40
1994	Ebony & Ivory	Open		39.50	40

Life of Christ - J. Fuentes DeFalamanca

1994	Holy Family	Open		39.50	40
1994	Baptism	Open		39.50	40
1994	Crucifiction	Open		39.50	40
1994	Last Supper	Open		39.50	40
1994	Jesus the Good Shepherd	Open		39.50	40
1994	Agony in the Garden	Open		39.50	40
1994	Ascension	Open		39.50	40
1994	Resurrection	Open		39.50	40

Loveable Labs - L. Chandler

1994	Photo Labs	Open		39.50	40
1994	Space Labs	Open		39.50	40
1994	Dental Labs	Open		39.50	40
1994	Science Labs	Open		39.50	40

Magic of Christmas - L. Bywaters

1993	Santa of the Northen Forest	Open		39.50	40
1993	Santa's Gift of Peace	Open		39.50	40
1993	Gifts For All	Open		39.50	40
1994	Coming Home	Open		39.50	40
1994	Santa's Sentinels	Open		39.50	40
1994	Wonder of Wonders	Open		39.50	40
1994	A Berry Merry Christmas	Open		39.50	40

Magnificent Dolphins of the 7 Seas - J. Holderby

1994	Bottlenose Dophin	Open		39.50	40
1994	Dolphins in Ruins	Open		39.50	40

Miracles of Christ - M. Weistling

1994	Wedding at Canna	Open		39.50	40
1994	Walking on Water	Open		39.50	40

Moonlight Fantasy - B. Chall

1994	Moonlight Highway	Open		39.50	40
1994	Moonlight Enchantment	Open		39.50	40
1994	Moonlight Voyager	Open		39.50	40
1994	Orca Moon	Open		39.50	40

Mumm-Birds in Snow - W. Mumm

1994	Cardinals in Winter	Open		39.50	40
1994	Chickadees	Open		39.50	40
1994	Juncos	Open		39.50	40

Nature's Collage - C. McClung

1992	Cedar Waxwing, Among The Berries	Open		34.50	35
1992	Gold Finches, Golden Splendor	Open		34.50	35
1993	Bluebirds, Summer Interlude	90-day	1994	39.50	40
1993	Chickadees, Rose Morning	90-day	1994	39.50	40
1993	Bluejays, Winter Song	90-day	1994	39.50	40
1993	Cardinals, Spring Courtship	90-day	1994	39.50	40
1993	Hummingbirds, Jeweled Glory	90-day	1994	39.50	40
1993	Indigo Buntings, Indigo Evening	90-day	1994	39.50	40

Nature's Nestlings - C. McClung

1994	Golden Moments	Open		39.50	40
1994	New Beginnings	Open		39.50	40
1994	Precious Treasures	Open		39.50	40
1994	Morning Song	Open		39.50	40
1994	Goldfinches	Open		39.50	40
1994	Cardinals	Open		39.50	40
1994	Wren Family	Open		39.50	40
1994	Cardinal Family	Open		39.50	40

Owls of North America - L. Laffin

1993	Spirit of the Arctic, Snowy Owl	Open		39.50	40

Pierced Nativity - Unknown

1993	Holy Family	Open		45.00	45
1994	Three Kings	Open		45.00	45
1994	Heralding Angels	Open		45.00	45
1994	Shepherds	Open		45.00	45

Pierced Religious Plates - Unknown

1994	Pierced Pieta	Open		39.50	40

Royal Cats of Guy Coheleach - G. Coheleach

1994	Afternoon Shade	Open		39.50	40
1994	Jungle Jaquar	Open		39.50	40
1994	Rocky Mountain Puma	Open		39.50	40
1994	Rocky Refuge	Open		39.50	40
1994	Siesta	Open		39.50	40
1994	Ambush in the Snow	Open		39.50	40
1994	Lion in Wait	Open		39.50	40
1994	Cat Nap	Open		39.50	40

Spirit of the Navajo - Unknown

1994	Navajo Hug	Open		39.50	40
1994	Six Days Old	Open		39.50	40
1994	Jewel	Open		39.50	40
1994	The Sentinel	Open		39.50	40
1994	Never Alone	Open		39.50	40
1994	Windy but Warm	Open		39.50	40
1994	Ride to the Song	Open		39.50	40
1994	Girl Holding Puppy	Open		39.50	40

Spirits of the Sky - M. Fields

1994	Soul of the Wolf	Open		39.50	40
1994	Spirit Riders	Open		39.50	40
1994	Medicine Woman	Open		39.50	40
1994	Spirit Lovers	Open		39.50	40
1994	Spirit 8	Open		39.50	40

Victorian Santas - D. Morgan

1994	Kris Kringle	Open		39.50	40
1994	Father Christmas	Open		39.50	40
1994	Grandfather Frost	Open		39.50	40
1994	American Santa	Open		39.50	40
1994	Victorian Santa	Open		39.50	40
1994	97 Santa	Open		39.50	40
1994	Belsnickle	Open		39.50	40
1994	The Magic Never Ends	Open		39.50	40
1994	Checking His List	Open		39.50	40
1994	Twas the Night	Open		39.50	40

Whale Conservation - J. Holderby

1993	Orca	Open		39.50	40

Wilderness Solitude - T. Doughty

1994	Snowy Haven	Open		39.50	40
1994	Midnight Lookout	Open		39.50	40
1994	Old Homestead	Open		39.50	40

Wreaths of the Month - Unknown

1994	Winter Greetings-December	Open		39.50	40
1994	Spring Blessings-May	Open		39.50	40

Lightpost Publishing

Kinkade-Thomas Kinkade Signature Collection - T. Kinkade

1991	Chandler's Cottage	2,500		49.95	50
1991	Cedar Nook	2,500		49.95	50
1991	Sleigh Ride Home	2,500		49.95	50
1991	Home To Grandma's	2,500		49.95	50

Lilliput Lane Ltd.

American Landmarks Collection - R. Day

1990	Country Church	5,000		35.00	35
1990	Riverside Chapel	5,000		35.00	35

Lladro

Lladro Plate Collection - Lladro

1993	The Great Voyage L5964G	Open		50.00	50
1993	Looking Out L5998G	Open		38.00	38
1993	Swinging L5999G	Open		38.00	38
1993	Duck Plate L6000G	Open		38.00	38
1994	Friends L6158	Open		32.00	32
1994	Apple Picking L6159M	Open		32.00	32
1994	Turtledove L6160	Open		32.00	32
1994	Flamingo L6161M	Open		32.00	32
1994	Resting L6162M	Open		32.00	32

March of Dimes

Our Children, Our Future - Various

1989	A Time for Peace - D. Zolan	150-day		29.00	32
1989	A Time To Love - S. Kuck	150-day		29.00	45
1989	A Time To Plant - J. McClelland	150-day		29.00	32
1989	A Time To Be Born - G. Perillo	150-day		29.00	35
1990	A Time To Embrace - E. Hibel	150-day		29.00	55
1990	A Time To Laugh - A. Williams	150-day		29.00	32

Marigold

Sport - Carreno

1989	Mickey Mantle handsigned	Retrd.		100.00	700-1000
1989	Mickey Mantle unsigned	Retrd.		60.00	100
1989	Joe DiMaggio handsigned	Retrd.		100.00	1475
1989	Joe DiMaggio f/s (blue sig.)	Retrd.		60.00	195
1990	Joe DiMaggio AP handsigned	Retrd.		N/A	2375

Maruri USA

Eagle Plate Series - W. Gaither

1984	Free Flight	Closed	1993	150.00	150-198

Museum Collections, Inc.

American Family I - N. Rockwell

1979	Baby's First Step	9,900		28.50	48
1979	Happy Birthday Dear Mother	9,900		28.50	45
1979	Sweet Sixteen	9,900		28.50	35
1979	First Haircut	9,900		28.50	60
1979	First Prom	9,900		28.50	35
1979	Wrapping Christmas Presents	9,900		28.50	35
1979	The Student	9,900		28.50	35
1979	Birthday Party	9,900		28.50	35
1979	Little Mother	9,900		28.50	35
1979	Washing Our Dog	9,900		28.50	35
1979	Mother's Little Helpers	9,900		28.50	35
1979	Bride and Groom	9,900		28.50	35

American Family II - N. Rockwell

1980	New Arrival	22,500		35.00	55
1980	Sweet Dreams	22,500		35.00	38
1980	Little Shaver	22,500		35.00	40
1980	We Missed You Daddy	22,500		35.00	38
1980	Home Run Slugger	22,500		35.00	38
1980	Giving Thanks	22,500		35.00	38
1980	Space Pioneers	22,500		35.00	38
1980	Little Salesman	22,500		35.00	38
1980	Almost Grown up	22,500		35.00	38
1980	Courageous Hero	22,500		35.00	38
1981	At the Circus	22,500		35.00	38
1981	Good Food, Good Friends	22,500		35.00	38

Christmas - N. Rockwell

1979	Day After Christmas	Yr.Iss		75.00	75
1980	Checking His List	Yr.Iss		75.00	75
1981	Ringing in Good Cheer	Yr.Iss		75.00	75
1982	Waiting for Santa	Yr.Iss		75.00	75
1983	High Hopes	Yr.Iss		75.00	75
1984	Space Age Santa	Yr.Iss		55.00	55

Norman Rockwell Gallery

Norman Rockwell Centennial - Rockwell Inspired

1993	The Toymaker	Closed		39.90	40
1993	The Cobbler	Closed		39.90	40

Rockwell's Christmas Legacy - Rockwell Inspired

YEAR ISSUE		EDITION LIMIT	YEAR RETD.	ISSUE PRICE	QUOTE U.S.$
1992	Santa's Workshop	Closed		49.90	50
1993	Making a List	Closed		49.90	50
1993	While Santa Slumbers	Closed		54.90	55
1993	Visions of Santa	Closed		54.90	55

Pemberton & Oakes

Adventures of Childhood Collection - D. Zolan

YEAR ISSUE		EDITION LIMIT	YEAR RETD.	ISSUE PRICE	QUOTE U.S.$
1989	Almost Home	Retrd.		19.60	55
1989	Crystal's Creek	Retrd.		19.60	47
1989	Summer Suds	Retrd.		22.00	35-45
1990	Snowy Adventure	Retrd.		22.00	42
1991	Forests & Fairy Tales	Retrd.		24.40	40

The Best of Zolan in Miniature - D. Zolan

YEAR ISSUE		EDITION LIMIT	YEAR RETD.	ISSUE PRICE	QUOTE U.S.$
1985	Sabina	Retrd.		12.50	112
1986	Erik and Dandelion	Retrd.		12.50	100
1986	Tender Moment	Retrd.		12.50	85
1986	Touching the Sky	Retrd.		12.50	83
1987	A Gift for Laurie	Retrd.		12.50	77-85
1987	Small Wonder	Retrd.		12.50	77

Childhood Discoveries (Miniature) - D. Zolan

YEAR ISSUE		EDITION LIMIT	YEAR RETD.	ISSUE PRICE	QUOTE U.S.$
1990	Colors of Spring	Retrd.		14.40	40-50
1990	Autumn Leaves	Retrd.		14.40	43
1991	Enchanted Forest	Retrd.		16.60	35-55
1991	Just Ducky	Retrd.		16.60	42
1991	Rainy Day Pals	Retrd.		16.60	40
1992	Double Trouble	Retrd.		16.60	36-50
1990	First Kiss	Retrd.		14.40	50-63
1993	Peppermint Kiss	Retrd.		16.60	43-70
1995	Tender Hearts	19-day		16.60	33

Childhood Friendship Collection - D. Zolan

YEAR ISSUE		EDITION LIMIT	YEAR RETD.	ISSUE PRICE	QUOTE U.S.$
1986	Beach Break	Retrd.		19.00	54
1987	Little Engineers	Retrd.		19.00	45-66
1988	Tiny Treasures	Retrd.		19.00	51
1988	Sharing Secrets	Retrd.		19.00	60-70
1988	Dozens of Daisies	Retrd.		19.00	42-68
1990	Country Walk	Retrd.		19.00	41-62

Children and Pets - D. Zolan

YEAR ISSUE		EDITION LIMIT	YEAR RETD.	ISSUE PRICE	QUOTE U.S.$
1984	Tender Moment	Retrd.		19.00	35-70
1984	Golden Moment	Retrd.		19.00	45-68
1985	Making Friends	Retrd.		19.00	42-59
1985	Tender Beginning	Retrd.		19.00	45
1986	Backyard Discovery	Retrd.		19.00	40-50
1986	Waiting to Play	Retrd.		19.00	45

Children at Christmas - D. Zolan

YEAR ISSUE		EDITION LIMIT	YEAR RETD.	ISSUE PRICE	QUOTE U.S.$
1981	A Gift for Laurie	Retrd.		48.00	75-95
1982	Christmas Prayer	Retrd.		48.00	90-110
1983	Erik's Delight	Retrd.		48.00	68
1984	Christmas Secret	Retrd.		48.00	67
1985	Christmas Kitten	Retrd.		48.00	60-75
1986	Laurie and the Creche	Retrd.		48.00	60-75

Christmas (Miniature) - D. Zolan

YEAR ISSUE		EDITION LIMIT	YEAR RETD.	ISSUE PRICE	QUOTE U.S.$
1993	Snowy Adventure	Retrd.		16.60	27-37
1994	Candlelight Magic	19-day		16.60	25-35

Christmas - D. Zolan

YEAR ISSUE		EDITION LIMIT	YEAR RETD.	ISSUE PRICE	QUOTE U.S.$
1991	Candlelight Magic	Retrd.		24.80	35-70

Companion to Brotherly Love - D. Zolan

YEAR ISSUE		EDITION LIMIT	YEAR RETD.	ISSUE PRICE	QUOTE U.S.$
1989	Sisterly Love	Retrd.		22.00	45-75

Easter (Miniature) - D. Zolan

YEAR ISSUE		EDITION LIMIT	YEAR RETD.	ISSUE PRICE	QUOTE U.S.$
1991	Easter Morning	Retrd.		16.60	30-40

Father's Day (Miniature) - D. Zolan

YEAR ISSUE		EDITION LIMIT	YEAR RETD.	ISSUE PRICE	QUOTE U.S.$
1994	Two of a Kind	Retrd.		16.60	36

Father's Day - D. Zolan

YEAR ISSUE		EDITION LIMIT	YEAR RETD.	ISSUE PRICE	QUOTE U.S.$
1986	Daddy's Home	Retrd.		19.00	118

Grandparent's Day - D. Zolan

YEAR ISSUE		EDITION LIMIT	YEAR RETD.	ISSUE PRICE	QUOTE U.S.$
1990	It's Grandma & Grandpa	Retrd.		24.40	41
1993	Grandpa's Fence	Retrd.		24.40	40-55

Heirloom Ovals - D. Zolan

YEAR ISSUE		EDITION LIMIT	YEAR RETD.	ISSUE PRICE	QUOTE U.S.$
1992	My Kitty	Retrd.		18.80	47

March of Dimes: Our Children, Our Future - D. Zolan

YEAR ISSUE		EDITION LIMIT	YEAR RETD.	ISSUE PRICE	QUOTE U.S.$
1989	A Time for Peace	Retrd.		29.00	40-50

Members Only Single Issue (Miniature) - D. Zolan

YEAR ISSUE		EDITION LIMIT	YEAR RETD.	ISSUE PRICE	QUOTE U.S.$
1990	By Myself	Retrd.		14.40	62
1993	Summer's Child	Retrd.		16.60	43
1994	Little Slugger	10-day		16.60	37

Membership (Miniature) - D. Zolan

YEAR ISSUE		EDITION LIMIT	YEAR RETD.	ISSUE PRICE	QUOTE U.S.$
1987	For You	Retrd.		12.50	102
1988	Making Friends	Retrd.		12.50	75
1989	Grandma's Garden	Retrd.		12.50	72
1990	A Christmas Prayer	Retrd.		14.40	54
1991	Golden Moment	Retrd.		15.00	47
1992	Brotherly Love	Retrd.		15.00	60-90
1993	New Shoes	Retrd.		17.00	40
1994	My Kitty	19-day		Gift	34

Moments To Remember (Miniature) - D. Zolan

YEAR ISSUE		EDITION LIMIT	YEAR RETD.	ISSUE PRICE	QUOTE U.S.$
1992	Just We Two	Retrd.		16.60	40-50
1992	Almost Home	Retrd.		16.60	35
1993	Tiny Treasures	Retrd.		16.60	35
1993	Forest Friends	Retrd.		16.60	35

Mother's Day (Miniature) - D. Zolan

YEAR ISSUE		EDITION LIMIT	YEAR RETD.	ISSUE PRICE	QUOTE U.S.$
1990	Flowers for Mother	Retrd.		14.40	35-45
1992	Twilight Prayer	Retrd.		16.60	30-40
1993	Jessica's Field	Retrd.		16.60	35-45
1994	One Summer Day	Retrd.		16.60	36

Mother's Day - D. Zolan

YEAR ISSUE		EDITION LIMIT	YEAR RETD.	ISSUE PRICE	QUOTE U.S.$
1988	Mother's Angels	Retrd.		19.00	75

Nutcracker II - Various

YEAR ISSUE		EDITION LIMIT	YEAR RETD.	ISSUE PRICE	QUOTE U.S.$
1981	Grand Finale - S. Fisher	Retrd.		24.40	36
1982	Arabian Dancers - S. Fisher	Retrd.		24.40	68
1983	Dew Drop Fairy - S. Fisher	Retrd.		24.40	40
1984	Clara's Delight - S. Fisher	Retrd.		24.40	45
1985	Bedtime for Nutcracker S. Fisher	Retrd.		24.40	45
1986	The Crowning of Clara S. Fisher	Retrd.		24.40	36
1987	Dance of the Snowflakes D. Zolan	Retrd.		24.40	50-70
1988	The Royal Welcome R. Anderson	Retrd.		24.40	45
1989	The Spanish Dancer - M. Vickers	Retrd.		24.40	45

Plaques - D. Zolan

YEAR ISSUE		EDITION LIMIT	YEAR RETD.	ISSUE PRICE	QUOTE U.S.$
1991	New Shoes	Retrd.		18.80	37-60
1992	Grandma's Garden	Retrd.		18.80	37-50
1992	Small Wonder	Retrd.		18.80	36
1992	Easter Morning	Retrd.		18.80	38

Plaques-Single Issues - D. Zolan

YEAR ISSUE		EDITION LIMIT	YEAR RETD.	ISSUE PRICE	QUOTE U.S.$
1991	Flowers for Mother	Retrd.		16.80	35-45

Single Issue - D. Zolan

YEAR ISSUE		EDITION LIMIT	YEAR RETD.	ISSUE PRICE	QUOTE U.S.$
1993	Winter Friends	Retrd.		18.80	37

Single Issue Bone China (Miniature) - D. Zolan

YEAR ISSUE		EDITION LIMIT	YEAR RETD.	ISSUE PRICE	QUOTE U.S.$
1992	Window of Dreams	Retrd.		18.80	30-40

Single Issue Day to Day Spode - D. Zolan

YEAR ISSUE		EDITION LIMIT	YEAR RETD.	ISSUE PRICE	QUOTE U.S.$
1991	Daisy Days	Retrd.		48.00	55

Single Issues (Miniature) - D. Zolan

YEAR ISSUE		EDITION LIMIT	YEAR RETD.	ISSUE PRICE	QUOTE U.S.$
1986	Backyard Discovery	Retrd.		12.50	107
1986	Daddy's Home	Retrd.		12.50	820
1989	Sunny Surprise	Retrd.		12.50	66
1989	My Pumpkin	Retrd.		14.40	70-80
1991	Backyard Buddies	Retrd.		16.60	40
1991	The Thinker	Retrd.		16.60	50-80
1993	Quiet Time	Retrd.		16.60	45-60
1994	Little Fisherman	19-day		16.60	30-40

Special Moments of Childhood Collection - D. Zolan

YEAR ISSUE		EDITION LIMIT	YEAR RETD.	ISSUE PRICE	QUOTE U.S.$
1988	Brotherly Love	Retrd.		19.00	75-95
1988	Sunny Surprise	Retrd.		19.00	40-55
1989	Summer's Child	Retrd.		22.00	45-55
1990	Meadow Magic	Retrd.		22.00	38
1990	Cone For Two	Retrd.		24.60	38
1990	Rodeo Girl	Retrd.		24.60	35

Tenth Anniversary - D. Zolan

YEAR ISSUE		EDITION LIMIT	YEAR RETD.	ISSUE PRICE	QUOTE U.S.$
1988	Ribbons and Roses	Retrd.		24.40	45-55

Thanksgiving (Miniature) - D. Zolan

YEAR ISSUE		EDITION LIMIT	YEAR RETD.	ISSUE PRICE	QUOTE U.S.$
1993	I'm Thankful Too	Retrd.		16.60	37

Thanksgiving - D. Zolan

YEAR ISSUE		EDITION LIMIT	YEAR RETD.	ISSUE PRICE	QUOTE U.S.$
1981	I'm Thankful Too	Retrd.		19.00	85-100

Times To Treasure Bone China (Miniature) - D. Zolan

YEAR ISSUE		EDITION LIMIT	YEAR RETD.	ISSUE PRICE	QUOTE U.S.$
1993	Little Traveler	Retrd.		16.60	30-40
1993	Garden Swing	Retrd.		16.60	29
1994	Summer Garden	19-day		16.60	30
1994	September Girl	19-day		16.60	30

Wonder of Childhood - D. Zolan

YEAR ISSUE		EDITION LIMIT	YEAR RETD.	ISSUE PRICE	QUOTE U.S.$
1982	Touching the Sky	Retrd.		19.00	40-55
1983	Spring Innocence	Retrd.		19.00	35-45
1984	Winter Angel	Retrd.		22.00	50-60
1985	Small Wonder	Retrd.		22.00	35-50
1986	Grandma's Garden	Retrd.		22.00	45
1987	Day Dreamer	Retrd.		22.00	40-50

Yesterday's Children (Miniature) - D. Zolan

YEAR ISSUE		EDITION LIMIT	YEAR RETD.	ISSUE PRICE	QUOTE U.S.$
1994	Little Friends	19-day		16.60	35-55
1994	Seaside Treasures	19-day		16.60	35

Zolan's Children - D. Zolan

YEAR ISSUE		EDITION LIMIT	YEAR RETD.	ISSUE PRICE	QUOTE U.S.$
1978	Erik and Dandelion	Retrd.		19.00	255
1979	Sabina in the Grass	Retrd.		22.00	195-250
1980	By Myself	Retrd.		24.00	50-60
1981	For You	Retrd.		24.00	30-43

PenDelfin

Plate Series - Various

YEAR ISSUE		EDITION LIMIT	YEAR RETD.	ISSUE PRICE	QUOTE U.S.$
XX	Mother With Baby - J. Heap	10,000	1985	40.00	200
XX	Father - J. Heap	7,500	1986	40.00	40
XX	Whopper - D. Roberts	7,500	1987	50.00	50
XX	Gingerbread Day - J. Heap	7,500	1988	55.00	55
XX	Caravan - D. Roberts	7,500	1989	60.00	60
XX	Old Schoolhouse - J. Heap	7,500	1990	60.00	60

Pickard

Mother's Love - I. Spencer

YEAR ISSUE		EDITION LIMIT	YEAR RETD.	ISSUE PRICE	QUOTE U.S.$
1980	Miracle	7,500		95.00	95
1981	Story Time	7,500		110.00	110
1982	First Edition	7,500		115.00	115
1983	Precious Moment	7,500		120.00	145

Symphony of Roses - I. Spencer

YEAR ISSUE		EDITION LIMIT	YEAR RETD.	ISSUE PRICE	QUOTE U.S.$
1982	Wild Irish Rose	10,000		85.00	95
1983	Yellow Rose of Texas	10,000		90.00	100-110
1984	Honeysuckle Rose	10,000		95.00	135
1985	Rose of Washington Square	10,000		100.00	175

Princeton Gallery

Arctic Wolves - J. Van Zyle

YEAR ISSUE		EDITION LIMIT	YEAR RETD.	ISSUE PRICE	QUOTE U.S.$
1991	Song of the Wilderness	90-day		29.50	30
1992	In The Eye of the Moon	90-day		29.50	30

Circus Friends Collection - R. Sanderson

YEAR ISSUE		EDITION LIMIT	YEAR RETD.	ISSUE PRICE	QUOTE U.S.$
1989	Don't Be Shy	Unkn.		29.50	30
1990	Make Me A Clown	Unkn.		29.50	30
1990	Looks Like Rain	Unkn.		29.50	30
1990	Cheer Up Mr. Clown	Unkn.		29.50	30

Cubs Of The Big Cats - Q. Lemond

YEAR ISSUE		EDITION LIMIT	YEAR RETD.	ISSUE PRICE	QUOTE U.S.$
1990	Cougar Cub	Unkn.		29.50	30
1991	Lion Cub	90-day		29.50	30
1991	Snow Leopard	90-day		29.50	30
1991	Cheetah	90-day		29.50	30
1991	Tiger	90-day		29.50	30
1992	Lynx Cub	90-day		29.50	30
1992	White Tiger Cub	90-day		29.50	30

Darling Dalmations - L. Picken

YEAR ISSUE		EDITION LIMIT	YEAR RETD.	ISSUE PRICE	QUOTE U.S.$
1991	Dalmatian	90-day		29.50	30
1992	Firehouse Frolic	90-day		29.50	30

Enchanted World of the Unicorn - R. Sanderson

YEAR ISSUE		EDITION LIMIT	YEAR RETD.	ISSUE PRICE	QUOTE U.S.$
1991	Rainbow Valley	90-day		29.50	30
1992	Golden Shore	90-day		29.50	30

Reco International

Amish Traditions - B. Farnsworth

YEAR ISSUE		EDITION LIMIT	YEAR RETD.	ISSUE PRICE	QUOTE U.S.$
1994	Golden Harvest	95-day		29.50	30
1994	Family Outing	95-day		29.50	30
1994	The Quilting Bee	95-day		29.50	30
1995	Last Day of School	95-day		29.50	30

Barefoot Children - S. Kuck

YEAR ISSUE		EDITION LIMIT	YEAR RETD.	ISSUE PRICE	QUOTE U.S.$
1987	Night-Time Story	Retrd.	1994	29.50	40
1987	Golden Afternoon	14-day		29.50	40
1988	Little Sweethearts	Retrd.	1995	29.50	40
1988	Carousel Magic	14-day		29.50	49
1988	Under the Apple Tree	Retrd.	1995	29.50	40
1988	The Rehearsal	Retrd.	1995	29.50	40
1988	Pretty as a Picture	Retrd.	1993	29.50	45
1988	Grandma's Trunk	Retrd.	1993	29.50	45

Becky's Day - J. McClelland

YEAR ISSUE		EDITION LIMIT	YEAR RETD.	ISSUE PRICE	QUOTE U.S.$
1985	Awakening	90-day		24.50	29
1985	Getting Dressed	Retrd.	1988	24.50	29
1986	Breakfast	Retrd.	1987	27.50	35
1986	Learning is Fun	Retrd.	1988	27.50	28
1986	Muffin Making	Retrd.	1989	27.50	28
1986	Tub Time	Retrd.	1989	27.50	35
1986	Evening Prayer	Retrd.	1990	27.50	28

Birds of the Hidden Forest - G. Ratnavira

YEAR ISSUE		EDITION LIMIT	YEAR RETD.	ISSUE PRICE	QUOTE U.S.$
1994	Macaw Waterfall	96-day		29.50	30
1994	Paradise Valley	96-day		29.50	30
1995	Toucan Treasure	96-day		29.50	30

Bohemian Annuals - Factory Artist

YEAR ISSUE		EDITION LIMIT	YEAR RETD.	ISSUE PRICE	QUOTE U.S.$
1974	1974	Retrd.	1975	130.00	155
1975	1975	Retrd.	1976	140.00	160
1976	1976	Retrd.	1978	150.00	160

Castles & Dreams - J. Bergsma

YEAR ISSUE		EDITION LIMIT	YEAR RETD.	ISSUE PRICE	QUOTE U.S.$
1992	The Birth of a Dream	48-day		29.50	30
1992	Dreams Come True	48-day		29.50	30
1993	Believe In Your Dreams	48-day		29.50	30
1994	Follow Your Dreams	48-day		29.50	30

A Childhood Almanac - S. Kuck

YEAR ISSUE		EDITION LIMIT	YEAR RETD.	ISSUE PRICE	QUOTE U.S.$
1985	Fireside Dreams-January	Retrd.	1991	29.50	45-49
1985	Be Mine-February	Retrd.	1992	29.50	45
1986	Winds of March-March	Retrd.	1994	29.50	45-49

Year	Issue	Edition Limit	Year Retd.	Issue Price	Quote U.S.$
1985	Easter Morning-April	Retrd.	1992	29.50	55
1985	For Mom-May	Retrd.	1992	29.50	45
1985	Just Dreaming-June	Retrd.	1992	29.50	55
1985	Star Spangled Sky-July	14-day		29.50	45
1985	Summer Secrets-August	Retrd.	1991	29.50	53
1985	School Days-September	Retrd.	1991	29.50	60
1986	Indian Summer-October	Retrd.	1991	29.50	45
1986	Giving Thanks-November	Retrd.	1995	29.50	45-49
1985	Christmas Magic-December	Retrd.	1995	35.00	70

A Children's Christmas Pageant - S. Kuck

Year	Issue	Edition Limit	Year Retd.	Issue Price	Quote U.S.$
1986	Silent Night	Retrd.	1987	32.50	75-90
1987	Hark the Herald Angels Sing	Retrd.	1988	32.50	35
1988	While Shepherds Watched...	Retrd.	1990	32.50	33
1989	We Three Kings	Yr.Iss.		32.50	35

The Children's Garden - J. McClelland

Year	Issue	Edition Limit	Year Retd.	Issue Price	Quote U.S.$
1993	Garden Friends	120-day		29.50	32
1993	Tea for Three	120-day		29.50	30
1993	Puppy Love	120-day		29.50	30

Christening Gift - S. Kuck

Year	Issue	Edition Limit	Year Retd.	Issue Price	Quote U.S.$
1995	God's Gift	Open		29.90	30

The Christmas Series - J. Bergsma

Year	Issue	Edition Limit	Year Retd.	Issue Price	Quote U.S.$
1990	Down The Glistening Lane	14-day		35.00	39
1991	A Child Is Born	14-day		35.00	35
1992	Christmas Day	14-day		35.00	35
1993	I Wish You An Angel	14-day		35.00	35

Christmas Wishes - J. Bergsma

Year	Issue	Edition Limit	Year Retd.	Issue Price	Quote U.S.$
1994	I Wish You Love	75-day		29.50	30
1995	I Wish You Joy	75-day		29.50	30

Days Gone By - S. Kuck

Year	Issue	Edition Limit	Year Retd.	Issue Price	Quote U.S.$
1983	Sunday Best	Retrd.	1984	29.50	40-55
1983	Amy's Magic Horse	Retrd.	1985	29.50	50-70
1984	Little Anglers	Retrd.	1985	29.50	27
1984	Afternoon Recital	Retrd.	1985	29.50	50-75
1984	Little Tutor	Retrd.	1985	29.50	30
1985	Easter at Grandma's	Retrd.	1985	29.50	30
1985	Morning Song	Retrd.	1986	29.50	30
1985	The Surrey Ride	Retrd.	1987	29.50	30

Dresden Christmas - Factory Artist

Year	Issue	Edition Limit	Year Retd.	Issue Price	Quote U.S.$
1971	Shepherd Scene	Retrd.	1978	15.00	50
1972	Niklas Church	Retrd.	1978	15.00	25
1973	Schwanstein Church	Retrd.	1978	18.00	35
1974	Village Scene	Retrd.	1978	20.00	30
1975	Rothenburg Scene	Retrd.	1978	24.00	30
1976	Village Church	Retrd.	1978	26.00	35
1977	Old Mill	Retrd.	1978	28.00	30

Dresden Mother's Day - Factory Artist

Year	Issue	Edition Limit	Year Retd.	Issue Price	Quote U.S.$
1972	Doe and Fawn	Retrd.	1979	15.00	20
1973	Mare and Colt	Retrd.	1979	16.00	25
1974	Tiger and Cub	Retrd.	1979	20.00	23
1975	Dachshunds	Retrd.	1979	24.00	28
1976	Owl and Offspring	Retrd.	1979	26.00	30
1977	Chamois	Retrd.	1979	28.00	30

The Enchanted Norfin Trolls - C. Hopkins

Year	Issue	Edition Limit	Year Retd.	Issue Price	Quote U.S.$
1993	Troll Maiden	75-day		19.50	20
1993	The Wizard Troll	75-day		19.50	20
1993	The Troll and His Dragon	75-day		19.50	20
1994	Troll in Shinning Armor	75-day		19.50	20
1994	Minstrel Troll	75-day		19.50	20
1994	If Trolls Could Fly	75-day		19.50	20
1994	Chef le Troll	75-day		19.50	20
1994	Queen of Trolls	75-day		19.50	20

The Flower Fairies Year Collection - C.M. Barker

Year	Issue	Edition Limit	Year Retd.	Issue Price	Quote U.S.$
1990	The Red Clover Fairy	14-day		29.50	30
1990	The Wild Cherry Blossom Fairy	14-day		29.50	30
1990	The Pine Tree Fairy	14-day		29.50	30
1990	The Rose Hip Fairy	14-day		29.50	30

Four Seasons - J. Poluszynski

Year	Issue	Edition Limit	Year Retd.	Issue Price	Quote U.S.$
1973	Spring	Retrd.	1975	50.00	75
1973	Summer	Retrd.	1975	50.00	75
1973	Fall	Retrd.	1975	50.00	75
1973	Winter	Retrd.	1975	50.00	75

Furstenberg Christmas - Factory Artist

Year	Issue	Edition Limit	Year Retd.	Issue Price	Quote U.S.$
1971	Rabbits	Retrd.	1977	15.00	30
1972	Snowy Village	Retrd.	1977	15.00	20
1973	Christmas Eve	Retrd.	1977	18.00	35
1974	Sparrows	Retrd.	1977	20.00	30
1975	Deer Family	Retrd.	1977	22.00	30
1976	Winter Birds	Retrd.	1977	25.00	25

Furstenberg Deluxe Christmas - E. Grossberg

Year	Issue	Edition Limit	Year Retd.	Issue Price	Quote U.S.$
1971	Wise Men	Retrd.	1974	45.00	45
1972	Holy Family	Retrd.	1974	45.00	45
1973	Christmas Eve	Retrd.	1974	60.00	65

Furstenberg Easter - Factory Artist

Year	Issue	Edition Limit	Year Retd.	Issue Price	Quote U.S.$
1971	Sheep	Retrd.	1973	15.00	150
1972	Chicks	Retrd.	1975	15.00	60
1973	Bunnies	Retrd.	1976	16.00	80
1974	Pussywillow	Retrd.	1976	20.00	33
1975	Easter Window	Retrd.	1977	22.00	30
1976	Flower Collecting	Retrd.	1977	25.00	25

Furstenberg Mother's Day - Factory Artist

Year	Issue	Edition Limit	Year Retd.	Issue Price	Quote U.S.$
1972	Hummingbirds, Fe	Retrd.	1974	15.00	45
1973	Hedgehogs	Retrd.	1974	16.00	40
1974	Doe and Fawn	Retrd.	1974	20.00	30
1975	Swans	Retrd.	1976	22.00	23
1976	Koala Bears	Retrd.	1976	25.00	30

Furstenberg Olympic - J. Poluszynski

Year	Issue	Edition Limit	Year Retd.	Issue Price	Quote U.S.$
1972	Munich	Retrd.	1972	20.00	75
1976	Montreal	Retrd.	1976	37.50	38

Games Children Play - S. Kuck

Year	Issue	Edition Limit	Year Retd.	Issue Price	Quote U.S.$
1979	Me First	Retrd.	1983	45.00	50
1980	Forever Bubbles	Retrd.	1983	45.00	48
1981	Skating Pals	Retrd.	1983	45.00	48
1982	Join Me	10,000		45.00	45

Gardens of Beauty - D. Barlowe

Year	Issue	Edition Limit	Year Retd.	Issue Price	Quote U.S.$
1988	English Country Garden	14-day		29.50	30
1988	Dutch Country Garden	14-day		29.50	30
1988	New England Garden	14-day		29.50	30
1988	Japanese Garden	14-day		29.50	30
1989	Italian Garden	14-day		29.50	30
1989	Hawaiian Garden	14-day		29.50	30
1989	German Country Garden	14-day		29.50	30
1989	Mexican Garden	14-day		29.50	30
1992	Colonial Splendor	48-day	1994	29.50	30

Gift of Love Mother's Day Collection - S. Kuck

Year	Issue	Edition Limit	Year Retd.	Issue Price	Quote U.S.$
1993	Morning Glory	Retrd.	1994	65.00	65
1994	Memories From The Heart	Retrd.	1994	65.00	65

The Glory Of Christ - C. Micarelli

Year	Issue	Edition Limit	Year Retd.	Issue Price	Quote U.S.$
1992	The Ascension	48-day		29.50	30
1993	Jesus Teaching	48-day		29.50	30
1993	The Last Supper	48-day		29.50	30
1993	The Nativity	48-day		29.50	30
1993	The Baptism Of Christ	48-day		29.50	30
1993	Jesus Heals The Sick	48-day		29.50	30
1994	Jesus Walks On Water	48-day		29.50	30
1994	Descent From The Cross	48-day		29.50	30

God's Own Country - I. Drechsler

Year	Issue	Edition Limit	Year Retd.	Issue Price	Quote U.S.$
1990	Daybreak	14-day		30.00	30
1990	Coming Home	14-day		30.00	30
1990	Peaceful Gathering	14-day		30.00	30
1990	Quiet Waters	14-day		30.00	30

The Grandparent Collector's Plates - S. Kuck

Year	Issue	Edition Limit	Year Retd.	Issue Price	Quote U.S.$
1981	Grandma's Cookie Jar	Yr.Iss.		37.50	38
1981	Grandpa and the Dollhouse	Yr.Iss.		37.50	38

Great Stories from the Bible - G. Katz

Year	Issue	Edition Limit	Year Retd.	Issue Price	Quote U.S.$
1987	Moses in the Bulrushes	14-day	1994	29.50	35
1987	King Saul & David	14-day	1994	29.50	35
1987	Moses and the Ten Commandments	14-day	1994	29.50	38
1987	Joseph's Coat of Many Colors	14-day	1994	29.50	35
1988	Rebekah at the Well	14-day	1994	29.50	35
1988	Daniel Reads the Writing on the Wall	14-day	1994	29.50	35
1988	The Story of Ruth	14-day	1994	29.50	35
1988	King Solomon	14-day	1994	29.50	35

Guardians Of The Kingdom - J. Bergsma

Year	Issue	Edition Limit	Year Retd.	Issue Price	Quote U.S.$
1990	Rainbow To Ride On	Retrd.	1993	35.00	37
1990	Special Friends Are Few	17,500		35.00	35
1990	Guardians Of The Innocent Children	17,500		35.00	38
1990	The Miracle Of Love	17,500		35.00	37
1991	The Magic Of Love	17,500		35.00	35
1991	Only With The Heart	17,500		35.00	35
1991	To Fly Without Wings	17,500		35.00	35
1991	In Faith I Am Free	17,500		35.00	35

Haven of the Hunters - H. Roe

Year	Issue	Edition Limit	Year Retd.	Issue Price	Quote U.S.$
1994	Eagle's Castle	96-day		29.50	30
1994	Sanctuary of the Hawk	96-day		29.50	30

Hearts And Flowers - S. Kuck

Year	Issue	Edition Limit	Year Retd.	Issue Price	Quote U.S.$
1991	Patience	120-day		29.50	30-45
1991	Tea Party	120-day		29.50	30-55
1992	Cat's In The Cradle	120-day		32.50	50
1992	Carousel of Dreams	120-day		32.50	55
1992	Storybook Memories	120-day		32.50	33
1993	Delightful Bundle	120-day		34.50	35
1993	Easter Morning Visitor	120-day		34.50	35
1993	Me and My Pony	120-day		34.50	35

In The Eye of The Storm - W. Lowe

Year	Issue	Edition Limit	Year Retd.	Issue Price	Quote U.S.$
1991	First Strike	120-day		29.50	35
1992	Night Force	120-day		29.50	35
1992	Tracks Across The Sand	120-day		29.50	30
1992	The Storm Has Landed	120-day		29.50	30

J. Bergsma Mother's Day Series - J. Bergsma

Year	Issue	Edition Limit	Year Retd.	Issue Price	Quote U.S.$
1990	The Beauty Of Life	14-day		35.00	35
1992	Life's Blessing	14-day		35.00	35
1993	My Greatest Treasures	14-day		35.00	35
1994	Forever In My Heart	14-day		35.00	35

King's Christmas - Merli

Year	Issue	Edition Limit	Year Retd.	Issue Price	Quote U.S.$
1973	Adoration	Retrd.	1974	100.00	265
1974	Madonna	Retrd.	1975	150.00	250
1975	Heavenly Choir	Retrd.	1976	160.00	235
1976	Siblings	Retrd.	1978	200.00	225

King's Flowers - A. Falchi

Year	Issue	Edition Limit	Year Retd.	Issue Price	Quote U.S.$
1973	Carnation	Retrd.	1974	85.00	130
1974	Red Rose	Retrd.	1975	100.00	145
1975	Yellow Dahlia	Retrd.	1976	110.00	162
1976	Bluebells	Retrd.	1977	130.00	165
1977	Anemones	Retrd.	1979	130.00	175

King's Mother's Day - Merli

Year	Issue	Edition Limit	Year Retd.	Issue Price	Quote U.S.$
1973	Dancing Girl	Retrd.	1974	100.00	225
1974	Dancing Boy	Retrd.	1975	115.00	250
1975	Motherly Love	Retrd.	1976	140.00	225
1976	Maiden	Retrd.	1978	180.00	200

Kingdom of the Great Cats - P. Jepson

Year	Issue	Edition Limit	Year Retd.	Issue Price	Quote U.S.$
1995	Out of the Mist	36-day		29.50	30
1995	Summit Sanctuary	36-day		29.50	30

Kittens 'N Hats - S. Somerville

Year	Issue	Edition Limit	Year Retd.	Issue Price	Quote U.S.$
1994	Opening Night	48-day		29.50	30
1994	Sitting Pretty	48-day		29.50	30
1995	Little League	48-day		29.50	30

Little Angel Plate Collection - S. Kuck

Year	Issue	Edition Limit	Year Retd.	Issue Price	Quote U.S.$
1994	Angel of Charity	95-day		29.50	30
1994	Angel of Joy	95-day		29.50	30

Little Professionals - S. Kuck

Year	Issue	Edition Limit	Year Retd.	Issue Price	Quote U.S.$
1982	All is Well	Retrd.	1983	39.50	43-65
1983	Tender Loving Care	Retrd.	1985	39.50	50-75
1984	Lost and Found	10,000		39.50	45
1985	Reading, Writing and...	Retrd.	1989	39.50	45

Magic Companions - J. Bergsma

Year	Issue	Edition Limit	Year Retd.	Issue Price	Quote U.S.$
1994	Believe in Love	48-day		29.50	30
1994	Imagine Peace	48-day		29.50	30
1995	Live in Harmony	48-day		29.50	30
1995	Trust in Magic	48-day		29.50	30

March of Dimes: Our Children, Our Future - Various

Year	Issue	Edition Limit	Year Retd.	Issue Price	Quote U.S.$
1989	A Time to Love (2nd in Series) - S. Kuck	Retrd.	1993	29.00	45
1989	A Time to Plant (3rd in Series) - J. McClelland	150-day	1993	29.00	50

Marmot Christmas - Factory Artist

Year	Issue	Edition Limit	Year Retd.	Issue Price	Quote U.S.$
1970	Polar Bear, Fe	Retrd.	1971	13.00	60
1971	Buffalo Bill	Retrd.	1972	16.00	55
1972	Boy and Grandfather	Retrd.	1973	20.00	50
1971	American Buffalo	Retrd.	1973	14.50	35
1973	Snowman	Retrd.	1974	22.00	45
1974	Dancing	Retrd.	1975	24.00	30
1975	Quail	Retrd.	1976	30.00	40
1976	Windmill	Retrd.	1978	40.00	40

Marmot Father's Day - Factory Artist

Year	Issue	Edition Limit	Year Retd.	Issue Price	Quote U.S.$
1970	Stag	Retrd.	1970	12.00	100
1971	Horse	Retrd.	1972	12.50	40

Marmot Mother's Day - Factory Artist

Year	Issue	Edition Limit	Year Retd.	Issue Price	Quote U.S.$
1972	Seal	Retrd.	1973	16.00	60
1973	Bear with Cub	Retrd.	1974	20.00	140
1974	Penguins	Retrd.	1975	24.00	50
1975	Raccoons	Retrd.	1976	30.00	45
1976	Ducks	Retrd.	1977	40.00	40

The McClelland Children's Circus Collection - J. McClelland

Year	Issue	Edition Limit	Year Retd.	Issue Price	Quote U.S.$
1982	Tommy the Clown	Retrd.	1973	29.50	49
1982	Katie, the Tightrope Walker	Retrd.	1975	29.50	49
1983	Johnny the Strongman	Retrd.	1976	29.50	39
1984	Maggie the Animal Trainer	100-day	1978	29.50	30

Memories Of Yesterday - M. Attwell

Year	Issue	Edition Limit	Year Retd.	Issue Price	Quote U.S.$
1993	Hush	Open		29.50	30
1993	Time For Bed	Open		29.50	30
1993	I'se Been Painting	Open		29.50	30
1993	Just Looking Pretty	Open		29.50	30
1994	Give it Your Best Shot	Open		29.50	30
1994	I Pray The Lord My Soul to Keep	Open		29.50	30
1994	Just Thinking About You	Open		29.50	30
1994	What Will I Grow Up To Be	Open		29.50	30

Moments At Home - S. Kuck

Year	Issue	Edition Limit	Year Retd.	Issue Price	Quote U.S.$
1995	Moments of Caring	95-day		29.90	30
1995	Moments of Tenderness	95-day		29.90	30
1995	Moments of Friendship	95-day		29.90	30
1995	Moments of Sharing	95-day		29.90	30
1995	Moments of Love	95-day		29.90	30

Moser Christmas - Factory Artist

Year	Issue	Edition Limit	Year Retd.	Issue Price	Quote U.S.$
1970	Hradcany Castle	Retrd.	1971	75.00	170
1971	Karlstein Castle	Retrd.	1972	75.00	80

YEAR ISSUE		EDITION LIMIT	YEAR RETD.	ISSUE PRICE	QUOTE U.S.$
1972	Old Town Hall	Retrd.	1973	85.00	85
1973	Karlovy Vary Castle	Retrd.	1974	90.00	100

Moser Mother's Day - Factory Artist

1971	Peacocks	Retrd.	1971	75.00	100
1972	Butterflies	Retrd.	1972	85.00	90
1973	Squirrels	Retrd.	1973	90.00	95

Mother Goose - J. McClelland

1979	Mary, Mary	Retrd.	1979	22.50	75
1980	Little Boy Blue	Retrd.	1980	22.50	30
1981	Little Miss Muffet	Yr.Iss.		24.50	28
1982	Little Jack Horner	Retrd.	1982	24.50	30
1983	Little Bo Peep	Yr.Iss.		24.50	30
1984	Diddle, Diddle Dumpling	Yr.Iss.		24.50	28
1985	Mary Had a Little Lamb	Yr.Iss.		27.50	28
1986	Jack and Jill	Retrd.	1988	27.50	32

Mother's Day Collection - S. Kuck

1985	Once Upon a Time	Retrd.	1987	29.50	65-75
1986	Times Remembered	Yr.Iss.		29.50	50-75
1987	A Cherished Time	Yr.Iss.		29.50	55
1988	A Time Together	Yr.Iss.		29.50	59

Noble and Free - Kelly

1994	Gathering Storm	95-day		29.50	30
1994	Protected Journey	95-day		29.50	30
1994	Moonlight Run	95-day		29.50	30

The Nutcracker Ballet - C. Micarelli

1989	Christmas Eve Party	14-day	1994	35.00	35
1990	Clara And Her Prince	14-day		35.00	37
1990	The Dream Begins	14-day		35.00	35
1991	Dance of the Snow Fairies	14-day	1994	35.00	35
1992	The Land of Sweets	14-day		35.00	35
1992	The Sugar Plum Fairy	14-day		35.00	35

Oscar & Bertie's Edwardian Holiday - P.D. Jackson

1991	Snapshot	48-day		29.50	30
1992	Early Rise	48-day		29.50	30
1992	All Aboard	48-day		29.50	30
1992	Learning To Swim	48-day		29.50	30

Our Cherished Seas - S. Barlowe

1991	Whale Song	48-day		37.50	38
1991	Lions of the Sea	48-day		37.50	38
1991	Flight of the Dolphins	48-day		37.50	38
1992	Palace of the Seals	48-day		37.50	38
1992	Orca Ballet	48-day		37.50	38
1993	Emperors of the Ice	48-day		37.50	38
1993	Turtle Treasure	48-day		37.50	38
1993	Splendor of the Sea	48-day		37.50	38

Plate Of The Month Collection - S. Kuck

1990	January	28-day		25.00	25
1990	February	28-day		25.00	25
1990	March	28-day		25.00	25
1990	April	28-day		25.00	25
1990	May	28-day		25.00	25
1990	June	28-day		25.00	25
1990	July	28-day		25.00	25
1990	August	28-day		25.00	25
1990	September	28-day		25.00	25
1990	October	28-day		25.00	25
1990	November	28-day		25.00	25
1990	December	28-day		25.00	25

Precious Angels - S. Kuck

1995	Angel of Grace	95-day		29.90	30
1995	Angel of Happiness	95-day		29.90	30
1995	Angel of Hope	95-day		29.90	30
1995	Angel of Laughter	95-day		29.90	30
1995	Angel of Love	95-day		29.90	30
1995	Angel of Peace	95-day		29.90	30
1995	Angel of Sharing	95-day		29.90	30
1995	Angel of Sunshine	95-day		29.90	30

The Premier Collection - J. McClelland

1991	Love	7,500		75.00	75

Premier Collection - S. Kuck

1991	Puppy	Retrd.	1993	95.00	125-150
1991	Kitten	Retrd.	1992	95.00	150-200
1992	La Belle	7,500		95.00	95
1992	Le Beau	7,500		95.00	95

Royal Mother's Day - Factory Artist

1970	Swan and Young	Retrd.	1971	12.00	80
1971	Doe and Fawn	Retrd.	1972	13.00	55
1972	Rabbits	Retrd.	1973	16.00	40
1973	Owl Family	Retrd.	1974	18.00	40
1974	Duck and Young	Retrd.	1975	22.00	40
1975	Lynx and Cubs	Retrd.	1976	26.00	40
1976	Woodcock and Young	Retrd.	1978	27.50	33
1977	Koala Bear	Retrd.	1978	30.00	30

Royale - Factory Artist

1969	Apollo Moon Landing	Retrd.	1969	30.00	80

Royale Christmas - Factory Artist

1969	Christmas Fair	Retrd.	1970	12.00	125
1970	Vigil Mass	Retrd.	1971	13.00	110
1971	Christmas Night	Retrd.	1972	16.00	50
1972	Elks	Retrd.	1973	16.00	45
1973	Christmas Down	Retrd.	1974	20.00	38
1974	Village Christmas	Retrd.	1975	22.00	60
1975	Feeding Time	Retrd.	1976	26.00	35
1976	Seaport Christmas	Retrd.	1977	27.50	30
1977	Sledding	Retrd.	1978	30.00	30

Royale Father's Day - Factory Artist

1970	Frigate Constitution	Retrd.	1971	13.00	80
1971	Man Fishing	Retrd.	1972	13.00	35
1972	Mountaineer	Retrd.	1973	16.00	55
1973	Camping	Retrd.	1974	18.00	45
1974	Eagle	Retrd.	1975	22.00	35
1975	Regatta	Retrd.	1976	26.00	35
1976	Hunting	Retrd.	1977	27.50	33
1977	Fishing	Retrd.	1978	30.00	30

Royale Game Plates - Various

1972	Setters - J. Poluszynski	Retrd.	1974	180.00	200
1973	Fox - J. Poluszynski	Retrd.	1975	200.00	250
1974	Osprey - W. Schiener	Retrd.	1976	250.00	250
1975	California Quail - W. Schiener	Retrd.	1976	265.00	265

Royale Germania Christmas Annual - Factory Artist

1970	Orchid	Retrd.	1971	200.00	650
1971	Cyclamen	Retrd.	1972	200.00	325
1972	Silver Thistle	Retrd.	1973	250.00	290
1973	Tulips	Retrd.	1974	275.00	310
1974	Sunflowers	Retrd.	1975	300.00	320
1975	Snowdrops	Retrd.	1976	450.00	500

Royale Germania Crystal Mother's Day - Factory Artist

1971	Roses	Retrd.	1971	135.00	650
1972	Elephant and Youngster	Retrd.	1972	180.00	250
1973	Koala Bear and Cub	Retrd.	1973	200.00	225
1974	Squirrels	Retrd.	1974	240.00	250
1975	Swan and Young	Retrd.	1975	350.00	360

Sandra Kuck Mothers' Day - S. Kuck

1995	Home is Where the Heart Is	48-day		35.00	35
1996	Dear To The Heart	48-day		35.00	35

The Sophisticated Ladies Collection - A. Fazio

1985	Felicia	21-day		29.50	33
1985	Samantha	21-day	1994	29.50	33
1985	Phoebe	21-day	1994	29.50	33
1985	Cleo	21-day		29.50	33
1986	Cerissa	21-day	1994	29.50	33
1986	Natasha	21-day	1994	29.50	33
1986	Bianka	21-day	1994	29.50	33
1986	Chelsea	21-day	1994	29.50	33

Special Occasions by Reco - S. Kuck

1988	The Wedding	Open		35.00	35
1989	Wedding Day (6 1/2")	Open		25.00	25
1990	The Special Day	Open		25.00	25

Special Occasions-Wedding - C. Micarelli

1991	From This Day Forward (9 1/2")	Open		35.00	35
1991	From This Day Forward (6 1/2")	Open		25.00	25
1991	To Have And To Hold (9 1/2")	Open		35.00	35
1991	To Have And To Hold (6 1/2")	Open		25.00	25

Sugar and Spice - S. Kuck

1993	Best Friends	95-day		29.90	30
1993	Sisters	95-day		29.90	30
1994	Little One	95-day		32.90	33
1994	Teddy Bear Tales	95-day		32.90	33
1994	Morning Prayers	95-day		32.90	33
1995	First Snow	95-day		34.90	35
1994	Garden of Sunshine	95-day		34.90	35
1995	A Special Day	95-day		34.90	35

Tidings Of Joy - S. Kuck

1992	Peace on Earth	N/A		35.00	50
1993	Rejoice	N/A		35.00	50
1994	Noel	75-day		35.00	38

Totems of the West - J. Bergsma

1994	The Watchmen	96-day		29.50	30
1995	Peace At Last	96-day		29.50	30
1995	Never Alone	96-day		35.00	35

Town And Country Dogs - S. Barlowe

1990	Fox Hunt	36-day		35.00	35
1991	The Retrieval	36-day		35.00	35
1991	Golden Fields (Golden Retriever)	36-day		35.00	35
1993	Faithful Companions (Cocker Spaniel)	36-day		35.00	35

Trains of the Orient Express - R. Johnson

1993	The Golden Arrow-England	N/A		29.50	30
1994	Austria	N/A		29.50	30
1994	Bavaria	N/A		29.50	30
1994	Rumania	N/A		29.50	30
1994	Greece	N/A		29.50	30
1994	Frankonia	N/A		29.50	30
1994	Turkey	N/A		29.50	30
1994	France	N/A		29.50	30

Treasured Songs of Childhood - J. McClelland

1987	Twinkle, Twinkle, Little Star	Retrd.	1990	29.50	30
1988	A Tisket, A Tasket	150-day	1991	29.50	30
1988	Baa, Baa, Black Sheep	Retrd.	1991	32.90	33
1989	Round The Mulberry Bush	150-day		32.90	35
1989	Rain, Rain Go Away	Retrd.	1993	32.90	33
1989	I'm A Little Teapot	Retrd.	1993	32.90	33
1989	Pat-A-Cake	150-day		34.90	35
1990	Hush Little Baby	150-day		34.90	35

Vanishing Animal Kingdoms - S. Barlowe

1986	Rama the Tiger	21,500		35.00	35
1986	Olepi the Buffalo	21,500		35.00	35
1987	Coolibah the Koala	21,500		35.00	42
1987	Ortwin the Deer	21,500		35.00	39
1987	Yen-Poh the Panda	21,500		35.00	40
1988	Mamakuu the Elephant	21,500		35.00	59

Victorian Christmas - S. Kuck

1995	Dear Santa	72-day		35.00	35

Victorian Mother's Day - S. Kuck

1989	Mother's Sunshine	Retrd.	1990	35.00	45-85
1990	Reflection Of Love	Retrd.	1991	35.00	50-80
1991	A Precious Time	Retrd.	1992	35.00	45-75
1992	Loving Touch	Retrd.	1993	35.00	45-49

Western - E. Berke

1974	Mountain Man	Retrd.		165.00	165

Women of the Plains - C. Corcilius

1994	Pride of a Maiden	36-day		29.50	30
1995	No Boundaries	36-day		29.50	30
1995	Silent Companions	36-day		35.00	35

The Wonder of Christmas - J. McClelland

1991	Santa's Secret	48-day		29.50	50
1992	My Favorite Ornament	48-day		29.50	55
1992	Waiting For Santa	48-day		29.50	55
1993	Candlelight Christmas	48-day		29.50	55

The World of Children - J. McClelland

1977	Rainy Day Fun	10,000	1977	50.00	50
1978	When I Grow Up	15,000	1978	50.00	55
1979	You're Invited	15,000	1979	50.00	55
1980	Kittens for Sale	15,000	1980	50.00	55

River Shore

Baby Animals - R. Brown

1979	Akiku	20,000		50.00	80
1980	Roosevelt	20,000		50.00	90
1981	Clover	20,000		50.00	65
1982	Zuela	20,000		50.00	65

Famous Americans - Rockwell-Brown

1976	Brown's Lincoln	9,500		40.00	40
1977	Rockwell's Triple Self-Portrait	9,500		45.00	45
1978	Peace Corps	9,500		45.00	45
1979	Spirit of Lindbergh	9,500		50.00	50

Little House on the Prairie - E. Christopherson

1985	Founder's Day Picnic	10-day		29.50	50
1985	Women's Harvest	10-day		29.50	45
1985	Medicine Show	10-day		29.50	45
1985	Caroline's Eggs	10-day		29.50	45
1985	Mary's Gift	10-day		29.50	45
1985	A Bell for Walnut Grove	10-day		29.50	45
1985	Ingall's Family	10-day		29.50	45
1985	The Sweetheart Tree	10-day		29.50	45

Norman Rockwell Single Issue - N. Rockwell

1979	Spring Flowers	17,000		75.00	145
1980	Looking Out to Sea	17,000		75.00	195
1982	Grandpa's Guardian	17,000		80.00	80
1982	Grandpa's Treasures	17,000		80.00	80

Puppy Playtime - J. Lamb

1987	Double Take	14-day		24.50	32-35
1988	Catch of the Day	14-day		24.50	25
1988	Cabin Fever	14-day		24.50	25
1988	Weekend Gardener	14-day		24.50	25
1988	Getting Acquainted	14-day		24.50	25
1988	Hanging Out	14-day		24.50	25
1988	A New Leash On Life	14-day		24.50	30
1987	Fun and Games	14-day		24.50	30

Rockwell Four Freedoms - N. Rockwell

1981	Freedom of Speech	17,000		65.00	80-99
1982	Freedom of Worship	17,000		65.00	80
1982	Freedom from Fear	17,000		65.00	65
1982	Freedom from Want	17,000		65.00	65

Rockwell Society

Christmas - N. Rockwell

1974	Scotty Gets His Tree	Yr.Iss.		24.50	60-95
1975	Angel with Black Eye	Yr.Iss.		24.50	40
1976	Golden Christmas	Yr.Iss.		24.50	35
1977	Toy Shop Window	Yr.Iss.		24.50	50-75

YEAR ISSUE		EDITION LIMIT	YEAR RETD.	ISSUE PRICE	QUOTE U.S.$
1978	Christmas Dream	Yr.Iss.		24.50	25
1979	Somebody's Up There	Yr.Iss.		24.50	25
1980	Scotty Plays Santa	Yr.Iss.		24.50	25
1981	Wrapped Up in Christmas	Yr.Iss.		25.50	27
1982	Christmas Courtship	Yr.Iss.		25.50	26
1983	Santa in the Subway	Yr.Iss.		25.50	26-35
1984	Santa in the Workshop	Yr.Iss.		27.50	28
1985	Grandpa Plays Santa	Yr.Iss.		27.90	28
1986	Dear Santy Claus	Yr.Iss.		27.90	28
1987	Santa's Golden Gift	Yr.Iss.		27.90	36
1988	Santa Claus	Yr.Iss.		29.90	30
1989	Jolly Old St. Nick	Yr.Iss.		29.90	35
1990	A Christmas Prayer	Yr.Iss.		29.90	30
1991	Santa's Helpers	Yr.Iss.		32.90	33
1992	The Christmas Surprise	Yr.Iss.		32.90	40
1993	The Tree Brigade	Yr.Iss.		32.90	45
1994	Christmas Marvel	Yr.Iss.		32.90	84
1995	Filling The Stockings	Yr.Iss.		32.90	33

Colonials-The Rarest Rockwells - N. Rockwell

1985	Unexpected Proposal	150-day		27.90	28
1986	Words of Comfort	150-day		27.90	28
1986	Light for the Winter	150-day		30.90	31
1987	Portrait for a Bridegroom	150-day		30.90	31
1987	The Journey Home	150-day		30.90	31
1987	Clinching the Deal	150-day		30.90	31
1988	Sign of the Times	150-day		32.90	33
1988	Ye Glutton	150-day		32.90	33

Coming Of Age - N. Rockwell

1990	Back To School	150-day		29.90	40
1990	Home From Camp	150-day		29.90	35
1990	Her First Formal	150-day		32.90	65
1990	The Muscleman	150-day		32.90	33
1990	A New Look	150-day		32.90	35
1991	A Balcony Seat	150-day		32.90	33
1991	Men About Town	150-day		34.90	35
1991	Paths of Glory	150-day		34.90	35
1991	Doorway to the Past	150-day		34.90	40
1991	School's Out!	150-day		34.90	60

Heritage - N. Rockwell

1977	Toy Maker	Yr.Iss.		14.50	80-100
1978	Cobbler	Yr.Iss.		19.50	40
1979	Lighthouse Keeper's Daughter	Yr.Iss.		19.50	25
1980	Ship Builder	Yr.Iss.		19.50	20
1981	Music maker	Yr.Iss.		19.50	20
1982	Tycoon	Yr.Iss.		19.50	25
1983	Painter	Yr.Iss.		19.50	20
1984	Storyteller	Yr.Iss.		19.50	20
1985	Gourmet	Yr.Iss.		19.50	20
1986	Professor	Yr.Iss.		22.90	23
1987	Shadow Artist	Yr.Iss.		22.90	30
1988	The Veteran	Yr.Iss.		22.90	23
1988	The Banjo Player	Yr.Iss.		22.90	25
1990	The Old Scout	Yr.Iss.		24.90	30
1991	The Young Scholar	Yr.Iss.		24.90	30
1991	The Family Doctor	Yr.Iss.		27.90	45
1992	The Jeweler	Yr.Iss.		27.90	47
1993	Halloween Frolic	Yr.Iss.		27.90	53
1994	The Apprentice	Yr.Iss.		29.90	30

Innocence and Experience - N. Rockwell

1991	The Sea Captain	150-day		29.90	30
1991	The Radio Operator	150-day		29.90	30
1991	The Magician	150-day		32.90	30
1992	The American Heroes	150-day		32.90	35

A Mind of Her Own - N. Rockwell

1986	Sitting Pretty	150-day		24.90	30
1987	Serious Business	150-day		24.90	28
1987	Breaking the Rules	150-day		24.90	40
1987	Good Intentions	150-day		27.90	28
1988	Second Thoughts	150-day		27.90	28
1988	World's Away	150-day		27.90	28
1988	Kiss and Tell	150-day		29.90	30
1988	On My Honor	150-day		29.90	30

Mother's Day - N. Rockwell

1976	A Mother's Love	Yr.Iss.		24.50	75
1977	Faith	Yr.Iss.		24.50	45
1978	Bedtime	Yr.Iss.		24.50	33
1979	Reflections	Yr.Iss.		24.50	25
1980	A Mother's Pride	Yr.Iss.		24.50	25
1981	After the Party	Yr.Iss.		24.50	25
1982	The Cooking Lesson	Yr.Iss.		24.50	30
1983	Add Two Cups and Love	Yr.Iss.		25.50	28
1984	Grandma's Courting Dress	Yr.Iss.		25.50	26
1985	Mending Time	Yr.Iss.		27.50	28
1986	Pantry Raid	Yr.Iss.		27.90	28
1987	Grandma's Surprise	Yr.Iss.		29.90	30
1988	My Mother	Yr.Iss.		29.90	32
1989	Sunday Dinner	Yr.Iss.		29.90	30
1990	Evening Prayers	Yr.Iss.		29.90	30
1991	Building Our Future	Yr.Iss.		32.90	33
1991	Gentle Reassurance	Yr.Iss.		32.90	33
1992	A Special Delivery	Yr.Iss.		32.90	35

Rockwell on Tour - N. Rockwell

1983	Walking Through Merrie Englande	150-day		16.00	16
1983	Promenade a Paris	150-day		16.00	16
1983	When in Rome	150-day		16.00	16
1984	Die Walk am Rhein	150-day		16.00	16

Rockwell's American Dream - N. Rockwell

1985	A Young Girl's Dream	150-day		19.90	20
1985	A Couple's Commitment	150-day		19.90	27
1985	A Family's Full Measure	150-day		22.90	30
1986	A Mother's Welcome	150-day		22.90	25
1986	A Young Man's Dream	150-day		22.90	30
1986	The Musician's Magic	150-day		22.90	25
1987	An Orphan's Hope	150-day		24.90	26
1987	Love's Reward	150-day		24.90	30

Rockwell's Golden Moments - N. Rockwell

1987	Grandpa's Gift	150-day		19.90	30
1987	Grandma's Love	150-day		19.90	35
1988	End of day	150-day		22.90	40
1988	Best Friends	150-day		22.90	23
1989	Love Letters	150-day		22.90	23
1989	Newfound Worlds	150-day		22.90	23
1989	Keeping Company	150-day		24.90	25
1989	Evening's Repose	150-day		24.90	25

Rockwell's Light Campaign - N. Rockwell

1983	This is the Room that Light Made	150-day		19.50	20
1984	Grandpa's Treasure Chest	150-day		19.50	20
1984	Father's Help	150-day		19.50	20
1984	Evening's Ease	150-day		19.50	20
1984	Close Harmony	150-day		21.50	22
1984	The Birthday Wish	150-day		21.50	22

Rockwell's Rediscovered Women - N. Rockwell

1984	Dreaming in the Attic	100-day		19.50	20
1984	Waiting on the Shore	100-day		22.50	23
1984	Pondering on the Porch	100-day		22.50	23
1984	Making Believe at the Mirror	100-day		22.50	23-30
1984	Waiting at the Dance	100-day		22.50	27
1984	Gossiping in the Alcove	100-day		22.50	23
1984	Standing in the Doorway	100-day		22.50	20-35
1984	Flirting in the Parlor	100-day		22.50	23-35
1984	Working in the Kitchen	100-day		22.50	33
1984	Meeting on the Path	100-day		22.50	23
1984	Confiding in the Den	100-day		22.50	23
1984	Reminiscing in the Quiet	100-day		22.50	33
XX	Complete Collection	100-day		267.00	267

Rockwell's The Ones We Love - N. Rockwell

1988	Tender Loving Care	150-day		19.90	30
1989	A Time to Keep	150-day		19.90	30
1989	The Inventor And The Judge	150-day		22.90	35
1989	Ready For The World	150-day		22.90	30
1989	Growing Strong	150-day		22.90	25
1990	The Story Hour	150-day		22.90	35
1990	The Country Doctor	150-day		24.90	25
1990	Our Love of Country	150-day		24.90	25
1990	The Homecoming	150-day		24.90	25
1991	A Helping Hand	150-day		24.90	25

Rockwell's Treasured Memories - N. Rockwell

1991	Quiet Reflections	150-day		29.90	30
1991	Romantic Reverie	150-day		29.90	35
1991	Tender Romance	150-day		32.90	33
1991	Evening Passage	150-day		32.90	33
1991	Heavenly Dreams	150-day		32.90	34
1991	Sentimental Shores	150-day		32.90	34

Roman, Inc.

Abbie Williams Collection - A. Williams

1991	Legacy of Love	Open		29.50	30
1991	Bless This Child	Open		29.50	30

Catnippers - I. Spencer

1986	Christmas Mourning	9,500		34.50	35
1992	Happy Holidaze	9,500		34.50	35

A Child's Play - F. Hook

1982	Breezy Day	30-day		29.95	39
1982	Kite Flying	30-day		29.95	39
1984	Bathtub Sailor	30-day		29.95	35
1984	The First Snow	30-day		29.95	35

A Child's World - F. Hook

1980	Little Children, Come to Me	15,000		45.00	49

Fontanini Annual Christmas Plate - E. Simonetti

1986	A King Is Born	Yr.Iss.		60.00	60
1987	O Come, Let Us Adore Him	Yr.Iss.		60.00	65
1988	Adoration of the Magi	Yr.Iss.		70.00	75
1989	Flight Into Egypt	Yr.Iss.		75.00	85

Frances Hook Collection-Set I - F. Hook

1982	I Wish, I Wish	15,000		24.95	35-39
1982	Baby Blossoms	15,000		24.95	35-39
1982	Daisy Dreamer	15,000		24.95	35-39
1982	Trees So Tall	15,000		24.95	35-39

Frances Hook Collection-Set II - F. Hook

1983	Caught It Myself	15,000		24.95	25
1983	Winter Wrappings	15,000		24.95	25
1983	So Cuddly	15,000		24.95	25
1983	Can I Keep Him?	15,000		24.95	25

Frances Hook Legacy - F. Hook

1985	Fascination	100-day		19.50	35-39
1985	Daydreaming	100-day		19.50	35-39
1985	Discovery	100-day		22.50	35-39
1985	Disappointment	100-day		22.50	35-39
1985	Wonderment	100-day		22.50	35-39
1985	Expectation	100-day		22.50	35-39

God Bless You Little One - A. Williams

1991	Baby's First Birthday (Girl)	Open		29.50	30
1991	Baby's First Birthday (Boy)	Open		29.50	30
1991	Baby's First Smile	Open		19.50	20
1991	Baby's First Word	Open		19.50	20
1991	Baby's First Step	Open		19.50	20
1991	Baby's First Tooth	Open		19.50	20

The Ice Capades Clown - G. Petty

1983	Presenting Freddie Trenkler	30-day		24.50	25

The Lord's Prayer - A. Williams

1986	Our Father	10-day		24.50	25
1986	Thy Kingdom Come	10-day		24.50	25
1986	Give Us This Day	10-day		24.50	25
1986	Forgive Our Trespasses	10-day		24.50	34
1986	As We Forgive	10-day		24.50	25
1986	Lead Us Not	10-day		24.50	25
1986	Deliver Us From Evil	10-day		24.50	25
1986	Thine Is The Kingdom	10-day		24.50	25

The Love's Prayer - A. Williams

1988	Love Is Patient and Kind	14-day		29.50	30
1988	Love Is Never Jealous or Boastful	14-day		29.50	30
1988	Love Is Never Arrogant or Rude	14-day		29.50	30
1988	Love Does Not Insist on Its Own Way	14-day		29.50	30
1988	Love Is Never Irritable or Resentful	14-day		29.50	30
1988	Love Rejoices In the Right	14-day		29.50	30
1988	Love Believes All Things	14-day		29.50	30
1988	Love Never Ends	14-day		29.50	30

The Magic of Childhood - A. Williams

1985	Special Friends	10-day		24.50	35
1985	Feeding Time	10-day		24.50	35
1985	Best Buddies	10-day		24.50	35
1985	Getting Acquainted	10-day		24.50	35
1986	Last One In	10-day		24.50	35
1986	A Handful Of Love	10-day		24.50	35
1986	Look Alikes	10-day		24.50	35
1986	No Fair Peeking	10-day		24.50	35

March of Dimes: Our Children, Our Future - A. Williams

1990	A Time To Laugh	150-day		29.00	39-49

The Masterpiece Collection - Various

1979	Adoration - F. Lippe	5,000		65.00	65
1980	Madonna with Grapes - P. Mignard	5,000		87.50	88
1981	The Holy Family - G. Delle Notti	5,000		95.00	95
1982	Madonna of the Streets - R. Ferruzzi	5,000		85.00	85

Millenium Series - Various

1992	Silent Night - Morcaldo/Lucchesi	Closed	1992	49.50	50
1993	The Annunciation - Morcaldo/Lucchesi	5,000	1993	49.50	50
1994	Peace On Earth - Morcaldo/Lucchesi	5,000	1994	49.50	50
1995	Cause of Our Joy - M. Lucchesi	7,500		49.50	50

Precious Children - A. Williams

1993	Bless Baby Brother	N/A		29.50	30
1993	Blowing Bubbles	N/A		29.50	30
1993	Don't Worry, Mother Duck	N/A		29.50	30
1993	Treetop Discovery	N/A		29.50	30
1993	The Tea Party	N/A		29.50	30
1993	Mother's Little Angel	N/A		29.50	30
1993	Picking Daisies	N/A		29.50	30
1993	Let's Say Grace	N/A		29.50	30

Pretty Girls of the Ice Capades - G. Petty

1983	Ice Princess	30-day		24.50	25

Promise of a Savior - Unknown

1993	An Angel's Message	95-day		29.90	30
1993	Gifts to Jesus	95-day		29.90	30
1993	The Heavenly King	95-day		29.90	30
1993	Angels Were Watching	95-day		29.90	30
1993	Holy Mother & Child	95-day		29.90	30
1993	A Child is Born	95-day		29.90	30

The Richard Judson Zolan Collection - R.J. Zolan

1992	The Butterfly Net	100-day		29.50	30
1994	The Ring	100-day		29.50	30
1994	Terrace Dancing	100-day		29.50	30

Roman Cats - Unknown

YEAR ISSUE		EDITION LIMIT	YEAR RETD.	ISSUE PRICE	QUOTE U.S.$
1984	Grizabella	30-day		29.50	30
1984	Mr. Mistoffelees	30-day		29.50	30
1984	Rum Rum Tugger	30-day		29.50	30

Roman Memorial - F. Hook

YEAR ISSUE		EDITION LIMIT	YEAR RETD.	ISSUE PRICE	QUOTE U.S.$
1984	The Carpenter	Yr.Iss.		100.00	135

Sepaphim Collection by Faro - Faro

YEAR ISSUE		EDITION LIMIT	YEAR RETD.	ISSUE PRICE	QUOTE U.S.$
1994	Rarest of Heaven	7,200	1995	65.00	65
1995	Heaven's Herald	7,200		65.00	65

Single Releases - A. Williams

YEAR ISSUE		EDITION LIMIT	YEAR RETD.	ISSUE PRICE	QUOTE U.S.$
1987	The Christening	Open		29.50	30
1990	The Dedication	Open		29.50	30
1990	The Baptism	Open		29.50	30

The Sweetest Songs - I. Spencer

YEAR ISSUE		EDITION LIMIT	YEAR RETD.	ISSUE PRICE	QUOTE U.S.$
1986	A Baby's Prayer	30-day		39.50	45
1986	This Little Piggie	30-day		39.50	40
1988	Long, Long Ago	30-day		39.50	40
1989	Rockabye	30-day		39.50	40

Tender Expressions - B. Sargent

YEAR ISSUE		EDITION LIMIT	YEAR RETD.	ISSUE PRICE	QUOTE U.S.$
1992	Thoughts of You Are In My Heart	100-day		29.50	30

Rorstrand

Christmas - G. Nylund

YEAR ISSUE		EDITION LIMIT	YEAR RETD.	ISSUE PRICE	QUOTE U.S.$
1968	Bringing Home the Tree	Annual	N/A	12.00	300-400
1969	Fisherman Sailing Home	Annual	N/A	13.50	45
1970	Nils with His Geese	Annual	N/A	13.50	30
1971	Nils in Lapland	Annual	N/A	15.00	30
1972	Dalecarlian Fiddler	Annual	N/A	15.00	20-22
1973	Farm in Smaland	Annual	N/A	16.00	60
1974	Vadslena	Annual	N/A	19.00	43
1975	Nils in Vastmanland	Annual	N/A	20.00	35
1976	Nils in Uapland	Annual	N/A	20.00	43-49
1977	Nils in Varmland	Annual	N/A	29.50	30
1978	Nils in Fjallbacka	Annual	N/A	32.50	49
1979	Nils in Vaestergoetland	Annual	N/A	38.50	39
1980	Nils in Halland	Annual	N/A	55.00	60
1981	Nils in Gotland	Annual	N/A	55.00	45
1982	Nils at Skansen	Annual	N/A	47.50	40
1983	Nils in Oland	Annual	N/A	42.50	55
1984	Angerman land	Annual	N/A	42.50	35
1985	Nils in Jamtland	Annual	N/A	42.50	70
1986	Nils in Karlskr	Annual	N/A	42.50	50
1987	Dalsland, Forget-Me-Not	Annual	N/A	47.50	150
1988	Nils in Halsingland	Annual	N/A	55.00	60
1989	Nils Visits Gothenborg	Annual		60.00	61
1990	Nils in Kvikkjokk	Annual	N/A	75.00	75
1991	Nils in Medelpad	Annual	N/A	85.00	85
1992	Gastrikland, Lily of the Valley	Annual	N/A	92.50	93
1993	Orebro Castle in Narkes	Annual		92.50	93
1994	Gripsholm Castle Sodermanland	Annual		92.50	93
1995	Nils in Härjedalen	Annual		92.50	93

Rosenthal

Christmas - Unknown

YEAR ISSUE		EDITION LIMIT	YEAR RETD.	ISSUE PRICE	QUOTE U.S.$
1910	Winter Peace	Annual		Unkn.	550
1911	Three Wise Men	Annual		Unkn.	325
1912	Stardust	Annual		Unkn.	255
1913	Christmas Lights	Annual		Unkn.	235
1914	Christmas Song	Annual		Unkn.	350
1915	Walking to Church	Annual		Unkn.	180
1916	Christmas During War	Annual		Unkn.	240
1917	Angel of Peace	Annual		Unkn.	200
1918	Peace on Earth	Annual		Unkn.	200
1919	St. Christopher with Christ Child	Annual		Unkn.	225
1920	Manger in Bethlehem	Annual		Unkn.	325
1921	Christmas in Mountains	Annual		Unkn.	200
1922	Advent Branch	Annual		Unkn.	200
1923	Children in Winter Woods	Annual		Unkn.	200
1924	Deer in the Woods	Annual		Unkn.	200
1925	Three Wise Men	Annual		Unkn.	200
1926	Christmas in Mountains	Annual		Unkn.	195
1927	Station on the Way	Annual		Unkn.	200
1928	Chalet Christmas	Annual		Unkn.	185
1929	Christmas in Alps	Annual		Unkn.	225
1930	Group of Deer Under Pines	Annual		Unkn.	225
1931	Path of the Magi	Annual		Unkn.	225
1932	Christ Child	Annual		Unkn.	185
1933	Thru the Night to Light	Annual		Unkn.	190
1934	Christmas Peace	Annual		Unkn.	190
1935	Christmas by the Sea	Annual		Unkn.	190
1936	Nurnberg Angel	Annual		Unkn.	195
1937	Berchtesgaden	Annual		Unkn.	195
1938	Christmas in the Alps	Annual		Unkn.	195
1939	Schneekoppe Mountain	Annual		Unkn.	195
1940	Marien Chrch in Danzig	Annual		Unkn.	250
1941	Strassburg Cathedral	Annual		Unkn.	250
1942	Marianburg Castle	Annual		Unkn.	300
1943	Winter Idyll	Annual		Unkn.	300
1944	Wood Scape	Annual		Unkn.	300
1945	Christmas Peace	Annual		Unkn.	400
1946	Christmas in an Alpine Valley	Annual		Unkn.	240
1947	Dillingen Madonna	Annual		Unkn.	985
1948	Message to the Shepherds	Annual		Unkn.	875
1949	The Holy Family	Annual		Unkn.	185
1950	Christmas in the Forest	Annual		Unkn.	185
1951	Star of Bethlehem	Annual		Unkn.	450
1952	Christmas in the Alps	Annual		Unkn.	195
1953	The Holy Light	Annual		Unkn.	195
1954	Christmas Eve	Annual		Unkn.	195
1955	Christmas in a Village	Annual		Unkn.	195
1956	Christmas in the Alps	Annual		Unkn.	195
1957	Christmas by the Sea	Annual		Unkn.	195
1958	Christmas Eve	Annual		Unkn.	195
1959	Midnight Mass	Annual		Unkn.	195
1960	Christmas in a Small Village	Annual		Unkn.	195
1961	Solitary Christmas	Annual		Unkn.	225
1962	Christmas Eve	Annual		Unkn.	195
1963	Silent Night	Annual		Unkn.	195
1964	Christmas Market in Nurnberg	Annual		Unkn.	225
1965	Christmas Munich	Annual		Unkn.	185
1966	Christmas in Ulm	Annual		Unkn.	275
1967	Christmas in Reginburg	Annual		Unkn.	185
1968	Christmas in Bremen	Annual		Unkn.	195
1969	Christmas in Rothenburg	Annual		Unkn.	220
1970	Christmas in Cologne	Annual		Unkn.	175
1971	Christmas in Garmisch	Annual		42.00	100
1972	Christmas in Franconia	Annual		50.00	95
1973	Lubeck-Holstein	Annual		77.00	105
1974	Christmas in Wurzburg	Annual		85.00	100

Nobility of Children - E. Hibel

YEAR ISSUE		EDITION LIMIT	YEAR RETD.	ISSUE PRICE	QUOTE U.S.$
1976	La Contessa Isabella	12,750		120.00	120
1977	La Marquis Maurice-Pierre	12,750		120.00	120
1978	Baronesse Johanna	12,750		130.00	140
1979	Chief Red Feather	12,750		140.00	180

Oriental Gold - E. Hibel

YEAR ISSUE		EDITION LIMIT	YEAR RETD.	ISSUE PRICE	QUOTE U.S.$
1976	Yasuko	2,000		275.00	650
1977	Mr. Obata	2,000		275.00	500
1978	Sakura	2,000		295.00	400
1979	Michio	2,000		325.00	375

Wiinblad Christmas - B. Wiinblad

YEAR ISSUE		EDITION LIMIT	YEAR RETD.	ISSUE PRICE	QUOTE U.S.$
1971	Maria & Child	Undis.		100.00	700
1972	Caspar	Undis.		100.00	290
1973	Melchior	Undis.		125.00	335
1974	Balthazar	Undis.		125.00	300
1975	The Annunciation	Undis.		195.00	195
1976	Angel with Trumpet	Undis.		195.00	195
1977	Adoration of Shepherds	Undis.		225.00	225
1978	Angel with Harp	Undis.		275.00	295
1979	Exodus from Egypt	Undis.		310.00	310
1980	Angel with Glockenspiel	Undis.		360.00	360
1981	Christ Child Visits Temple	Undis.		375.00	375
1982	Christening of Christ	Undis.		375.00	375

Royal Copenhagen

Christmas - Various

YEAR ISSUE		EDITION LIMIT	YEAR RETD.	ISSUE PRICE	QUOTE U.S.$
1908	Madonna and Child - C. Thomsen	Annual	1908	1.00	3000-4000
1909	Danish Landscape - S. Ussing	Annual	1909	1.00	150-225
1910	The Magi - C. Thomsen	Annual	1910	1.00	100-150
1911	Danish Landscape - O. Jensen	Annual	1911	1.00	125-165
1912	Christmas Tree - C. Thomsen	Annual	1912	1.00	140-165
1913	Frederik Church Spire A. Boesen	Annual	1913	1.50	147-165
1914	Holy Spirit Church - A. Boesen	Annual	1914	1.50	100-225
1915	Danish Landscape - A. Krog	Annual	1915	1.50	125-175
1916	Shepherd at Christmas R. Bocher	Annual	1916	1.50	115-135
1917	Our Savior Church - O. Jensen	Annual	1917	2.00	115-168
1918	Sheep and Shepherds O. Jensen	Annual	1918	2.00	105-180
1919	In the Park - O. Jensen	Annual	1919	2.00	120-135
1920	Mary and Child Jesus - G. Rode	Annual	1920	2.00	120-175
1921	Aabenraa Marketplace O. Jensen	Annual	1921	2.00	75-175
1922	Three Singing Angels E. Selschau	Annual	1922	2.00	75-90
1923	Danish Landscape - O. Jensen	Annual	1923	2.00	92
1924	Sailing Ship - B. Olsen	Annual	1924	2.00	135-165
1925	Christianshavn - O. Jensen	Annual	1925	2.00	115-140
1926	Christianshavn Canal - R. Bocher	Annual	1926	2.00	115-175
1927	Ship's Boy at Tiller - B. Olsen	Annual	1927	2.00	145-180
1928	Vicar's Family - G. Rode	Annual	1928	2.00	105-135
1929	Grundtvig Church - O. Jensen	Annual	1929	2.00	105-140
1930	Fishing Boats - B. Olsen	Annual	1930	2.50	135-140
1931	Mother and Child - G. Rode	Annual	1931	2.50	135-175
1932	Frederiksberg Gardens O. Jensen	Annual	1932	2.50	118
1933	Ferry and the Great Belt B. Olsen	Annual	1933	2.50	165-225
1934	The Hermitage Castle O. Jensen	Annual	1934	2.50	175-275
1935	Kronborg Castle - B. Olsen	Annual	1935	2.50	225
1936	Roskilde Cathedral - R. Bocher	Annual	1936	2.50	200-300
1937	Main Street Copenhagen N. Thorsson	Annual	1937	2.50	230
1938	Round Church in Osterlars H. Nielsen	Annual	1938	3.00	300-460
1939	Greenland Pack-Ice - S. Nielsen	Annual	1939	3.00	325-430
1940	The Good Shepherd - K. Lange	Annual	1940	3.00	450-685
1941	Danish Village Church T. Kjolner	Annual	1941	3.00	465-510
1942	Bell Tower - N. Thorsson	Annual	1942	4.00	450-600
1943	Flight into Egypt - N. Thorsson	Annual	1943	4.00	650-750
1944	Danish Village Scene - V. Olson	Annual	1944	4.00	250-370
1945	A Peaceful Motif - R. Bocher	Annual	1945	4.00	375-450
1946	Zealand Village Church N. Thorsson	Annual	1946	4.00	255
1947	The Good Shepherd - K. Lange	Annual	1947	4.50	285-550
1948	Nodebo Church - T. Kjolner	Annual	1948	4.50	260-300
1949	Our Lady's Cathedral H. Hansen	Annual	1949	5.00	125-175
1950	Boeslunde Church - V. Olson	Annual	1950	5.00	225-300
1951	Christmas Angel - R. Bocher	Annual	1951	5.00	250-350
1952	Christmas in the Forest K. Lange	Annual	1952	5.00	175
1953	Frederiksberg Castle - T. Kjolner	Annual	1953	6.00	200-265
1954	Amalienborg Palace - K. Lange	Annual	1954	6.00	100-150
1955	Fano Girl - K. Lange	Annual	1955	7.00	150-300
1956	Rosenborg Castle - K. Lange	Annual	1956	7.00	270
1957	The Good Shepherd - H. Hansen	Annual	1957	8.00	130
1958	Sunshine over Greenland H. Hansen	Annual	1958	9.00	130-200
1959	Christmas Night - H. Hansen	Annual	1959	9.00	180
1960	The Stag - H. Hansen	Annual	1960	10.00	150-185
1961	Training Ship - K. Lange	Annual	1961	10.00	150-225
1962	The Little Mermaid - Unknown	Annual	1962	11.00	250-315
1963	Hojsager Mill - K. Lange	Annual	1963	11.00	60
1964	Fetching the Tree - K. Lange	Annual	1964	11.00	60-90
1965	Little Skaters - K. Lange	Annual	1965	12.00	60
1966	Blackbird - K. Lange	Annual	1966	12.00	33-50
1967	The Royal Oak - K. Lange	Annual	1967	13.00	30-75
1968	The Last Umiak - K. Lange	Annual	1968	13.00	30
1969	The Old Farmyard - K. Lange	Annual	1969	14.00	30
1970	Christmas Rose and Cat K. Lange	Annual	1970	14.00	40-55
1971	Hare In Winter - K. Lange	Annual	1971	15.00	21
1972	In the Desert - K. Lange	Annual	1972	16.00	21
1973	Train Homeward Bound K. Lange	Annual	1973	22.00	25
1974	Winter Twilight - K. Lange	Annual	1974	22.00	30
1975	Queen's Palace - K. Lange	Annual	1975	27.50	25
1976	Danish Watermill S. Vestergaard	Annual	1976	27.50	40
1977	Immervad Bridge - K. Lange	Annual	1977	32.00	40
1978	Greenland Scenery - K. Lange	Annual	1978	35.00	30
1979	Choosing Christmas Tree K. Lange	Annual	1979	42.50	65
1980	Bringing Home the Tree K. Lange	Annual	1980	49.50	50
1981	Admiring Christmas Tree K. Lange	Annual	1981	52.50	53
1982	Waiting for Christmas - K. Lange	Annual	1982	54.50	65
1983	Merry Christmas - K. Lange	Annual	1983	54.50	64
1984	Jingle Bells - K. Lange	Annual	1984	54.50	60
1985	Snowman - K. Lange	Annual	1985	54.50	80-90
1986	Christmas Vacation - K. Lange	Annual	1986	54.50	85
1987	Winter Birds - S. Vestergaard	Annual	1987	59.50	70
1988	Christmas Eve in Copenhagen S. Vestergaard	Annual	1988	59.50	60-70
1989	The Old Skating Pond S. Vestergaard	Annual	1989	59.50	80-90
1990	Christmas at Tivoli S. Vestergaard	Annual	1990	64.50	125
1991	The Festival of Santa Lucia S. Vestergaard	Annual	1991	69.50	70-90
1992	The Queen's Carriage S. Vestergaard	Annual	1992	69.50	77
1993	Christmas Guests S. Vestergaard	Annual	1993	69.50	75-90
1994	Christmas Shopping S. Vestergaard	Annual	1994	72.50	75
1995	Christmas at the Manor House S. Vestergaard	Annual	1995	72.50	75
1996	Lighting the Street Lamps S. Vestergaard	Annual		74.50	75

Royal Devon

Rockwell Christmas - N. Rockwell

YEAR ISSUE		EDITION LIMIT	YEAR RETD.	ISSUE PRICE	QUOTE U.S.$
1975	Downhill Daring	Yr.Iss.		24.50	30
1976	The Christmas Gift	Yr.Iss.		24.50	35
1977	The Big Moment	Yr.Iss.		27.50	50
1978	Puppets for Christmas	Yr.Iss.		27.50	28
1979	One Present Too Many	Yr.Iss.		31.50	32
1980	Gramps Meets Gramps	Yr.Iss.		33.00	33

Rockwell Mother's Day - N. Rockwell

YEAR ISSUE		EDITION LIMIT	YEAR RETD.	ISSUE PRICE	QUOTE U.S.$
1975	Doctor and Doll	Yr.Iss.		23.50	50
1976	Puppy Love	Yr.Iss.		24.50	104
1977	The Family	Yr.Iss.		24.50	85
1978	Mother's Day Off	Yr.Iss.		27.00	35
1979	Mother's Evening Out	Yr.Iss.		30.00	32
1980	Mother's Treat	Yr.Iss.		32.50	35

Royal Doulton

Christmas Plates - N/A

YEAR ISSUE		EDITION LIMIT	YEAR RETD.	ISSUE PRICE	QUOTE U.S.$
1993	Royal Doulton-Together For Christmas	N/A		45.00	45
1993	Royal Albert-Sleighride	N/A		45.00	45

Family Christmas Plates - N/A

YEAR ISSUE		EDITION LIMIT	YEAR RETD.	ISSUE PRICE	QUOTE U.S.$
1991	Dad Plays Santa	Yr.Iss.		60.00	60

Royal Worcester

Birth Of A Nation - P.W. Baston

YEAR ISSUE		EDITION LIMIT	YEAR RETD.	ISSUE PRICE	QUOTE U.S.$
1972	Boston Tea Party	10,000		45.00	140-275
1973	Paul Revere	10,000		45.00	140-250
1974	Concord Bridge	10,000		50.00	140

YEAR ISSUE		EDITION LIMIT	YEAR RETD.	ISSUE PRICE	QUOTE U.S.$
1975	Signing Declaration	10,000		65.00	140
1976	Crossing Delaware	10,000		65.00	140
1977	Washington's Inauguration	1,250		65.00	140

Currier and Ives Plates - P.W. Baston

1974	Road in Winter	5,570		59.50	55-100
1975	Old Grist Mill	3,200		59.50	55-100
1976	Winter Pastime	1,500		59.50	55-125
1977	Home to Thanksgiving	546		59.50	200-250

Kitten Classics - P. Cooper

1985	Cat Nap	14-day		29.50	36
1985	Purrfect Treasure	14-day		29.50	30
1985	Wild Flower	14-day		29.50	30
1985	Birdwatcher	14-day		29.50	30
1985	Tiger's Fancy	14-day		29.50	33
1985	Country Kitty	14-day		29.50	33
1985	Little Rascal	14-day		29.50	30
1986	First Prize	14-day		29.50	30

Kitten Encounters - P. Cooper

1987	Fishful Thinking	14-day		29.50	30-54
1987	Puppy Pal	14-day		29.50	36
1987	Just Ducky	14-day		29.50	36
1987	Bunny Chase	14-day		29.50	30
1987	Flutter By	14-day		29.50	30
1987	Bedtime Buddies	14-day		29.50	30
1988	Cat and Mouse	14-day		29.50	33
1988	Stablemates	14-day		29.50	48

Sarah's Attic, Inc.

Classroom Memories - Sarah's Attic

1991	Classroom Memories 3495	6,000	1993	80.00	80

Schmid

Christmas - B. Hummel

1971	Angel	Annual		15.00	20
1972	Angel With Flute	Annual		15.00	15
1973	The Nativity	Annual		15.00	60
1974	The Guardian Angel	Annual		18.50	19
1975	Christmas Child	Annual		25.00	25
1976	Sacred Journey	Annual		27.50	28
1977	Herald Angel	Annual		27.50	28
1978	Heavenly Trio	Annual		32.50	33
1979	Starlight Angel	Annual		38.00	38
1980	Parade Into Toyland	Annual		45.00	45
1981	A Time To Remember	Annual		45.00	45
1982	Angelic Procession	Annual		45.00	49
1983	Angelic Messenger	Annual		45.00	45
1984	A Gift from Heaven	Annual		45.00	48
1985	Heavenly Light	Annual		45.00	45
1986	Tell The Heavens	Annual		45.00	45
1987	Angelic Gifts	Annual		47.50	48
1988	Cheerful Cherubs	Annual		53.00	60
1989	Angelic Musician	Annual		53.00	53
1990	Angel's Light	Annual		53.00	53
1991	Message From Above	Annual		60.00	60
1992	Sweet Blessings	Annual		65.00	65

Davis Cat Tales Plates. - L. Davis

1982	Right Church, Wrong Pew	12,500		37.50	200
1982	Company's Coming	12,500		37.50	180
1982	On the Move	12,500		37.50	145
1982	Flew the Coop	12,500		37.50	90

Davis Christmas Plates - L. Davis

1983	Hooker at Mailbox With Present	7,500		45.00	130
1984	Country Christmas	7,500		45.00	75-100
1985	Christmas at Foxfire Farm	7,500		45.00	150
1986	Christmas at Red Oak	7,500		45.00	50-75
1987	Blossom's Gift	7,500		47.50	100
1988	Cutting the Family Christmas Tree	7,500		47.50	50-100
1989	Peter and the Wren	7,500		47.50	75
1990	Wintering Deer	7,500		47.50	48
1991	Christmas at Red Oak II	7,500		55.00	75
1992	Born On A Starry Night	7,500		55.00	55
1993	Waiting For Mr. Lowell	5,000		55.00	55
1994	Visions of Sugarplums	5,000		55.00	55
1995	Bah Humbug	5,000		55.00	55

Davis Country Pride Plates - L. Davis

1981	Surprise in the Cellar	7,500		35.00	175-225
1981	Plum Tuckered Out	7,500		35.00	70-125
1981	Duke's Mixture	7,500		35.00	190
1982	Bustin' with Pride	7,500		35.00	75

Davis Red Oak Sampler - L. Davis

1986	General Store	5,000		45.00	175
1987	Country Wedding	5,000		45.00	125
1989	Country School	5,000		45.00	75
1990	Blacksmith Shop	5,000		52.50	53

Davis Special Edition Plates - L. Davis

1983	The Critics	12,500		45.00	60-145
1984	Good Ole Days Privy Set 2	5,000		60.00	80-125
1986	Home From Market	7,500		55.00	145

Disney Annual - Disney Studios

1983	Sneak Preview	20,000		22.50	23
1984	Command Performance	20,000		22.50	23
1985	Snow Biz	20,000		22.50	23
1986	Tree For Two	20,000		22.50	23
1987	Merry Mouse Medley	20,000		25.00	25
1988	Warm Winter Ride	20,000		25.00	25
1989	Merry Mickey Claus	20,000		32.50	60
1990	Holly Jolly Christmas	20,000		32.50	33
1991	Mickey and Minnie's Rockin' Christmas	20,000		37.00	37

Disney Christmas - Disney Studios

1973	Sleigh Ride	Annual		10.00	250-300
1974	Decorating The Tree	Annual		10.00	70-80
1975	Caroling	Annual		12.50	14
1976	Building A Snowman	Annual		13.00	15
1977	Down The Chimney	Annual		13.00	17
1978	Night Before Christmas	Annual		15.00	25
1979	Santa's Suprise	15,000		17.50	27
1980	Sleigh Ride	15,000		17.50	33
1981	Happy Holidays	15,000		17.50	25
1982	Winter Games	15,000		18.50	25

Disney Mother's Day - Disney Studios

1974	Flowers For Mother	Annual		10.00	45
1975	Snow White & Dwarfs	Annual		12.50	50
1976	Minnie Mouse	Annual		13.00	25
1977	Pluto's Pals	Annual		13.00	18
1978	Flowers For Bambi	Annual		15.00	40
1979	Happy Feet	10,000		17.50	20
1980	Minnie's Surprise	10,000		17.50	30
1981	Playmates	10,000		17.50	35
1982	A Dream Come True	10,000		18.50	40

Disney Special Edition Plates - Disney Studios

1978	Mickey Mouse At Fifty	15,000		25.00	65-100
1980	Happy Birthday Pinocchio	7,500		17.50	25-60
1981	Alice in Wonderland	7,500		17.50	18
1982	Happy Birthday Pluto	7,500		17.50	39
1982	Goofy's Golden Jubilee	7,500		18.50	29
1987	Snow White Golden Anniversary	5,000		47.50	90
1988	Mickey Mouse & Minnie Mouse 60th	10,000		50.00	95-125
1989	Sleeping Beauty 30th Anniversary	5,000		80.00	95
1990	Fantasia-Sorcerer's Apprentice	5,000		59.00	59-99
1990	Pinocchio's Friend	Annual		25.00	25
1990	Fantasia Relief Plate	20,000		25.00	39

Ferrandiz Beautiful Bounty Porcelain Plates - J. Ferrandiz

1982	Summer's Golden Harvest	10,000		40.00	40
1982	Autumn's Blessing	10,000		40.00	40
1982	A Mid-Winter's Dream	10,000		40.00	43
1982	Spring Blossoms	10,000		40.00	40

Ferrandiz Music Makers Porcelain Plates - J. Ferrandiz

1981	The Flutist	10,000		25.00	29
1981	The Entertainer	10,000		25.00	29
1982	Magical Medley	10,000		25.00	29
1982	Sweet Serenade	10,000		25.00	32

Ferrandiz Porcelain Christmas Plates - J. Ferrandiz

1972	Christ in the Manger	Unkn.		30.00	179
1973	Christmas	Unkn.		30.00	229

The Littlest Night - B. Hummel

1993	The Littlest Night	Annual		25.00	25

Mother's Day - B. Hummel

1972	Playing Hooky	Annual		15.00	15
1973	Little Fisherman	Annual		15.00	33
1974	Bumblebee	Annual		18.50	20
1975	Message of Love	Annual		25.00	29
1976	Devotion For Mother	Annual		27.50	30
1977	Moonlight Return	Annual		27.50	29
1978	Afternoon Stroll	Annual		32.50	33
1979	Cherub's Gift	Annual		38.00	38
1980	Mother's Little Helpers	Annual		45.00	52
1981	Playtime	Annual		45.00	52
1982	The Flower Basket	Annual		45.00	48
1983	Spring Bouquet	Annual		45.00	54
1984	A Joy to Share	Annual		45.00	45
1985	A Mother's Journey	Annual		45.00	45
1986	Home From School	Annual		45.00	55
1988	Young Reader	Annual		52.50	81
1989	Pretty as a Picture	Annual		53.00	75
1990	Mother's Little Athlete	Annual		53.00	53
1991	Soft & Gentle	Annual		55.00	55

Peanuts Christmas - C. Schulz

1972	Snoopy Guides the Sleigh	Annual		10.00	45
1973	Christmas Eve at Doghouse	Annual		10.00	100
1974	Christmas At Fireplace	Annual		10.00	48
1975	Woodstock and Santa Claus	Annual		12.50	19
1976	Woodstock's Christmas	Annual		13.00	20
1977	Deck The Doghouse	Annual		13.00	19
1978	Filling the Stocking	Annual		15.00	35
1979	Christmas at Hand	15,000		17.50	45
1980	Waiting for Santa	15,000		17.50	50
1981	A Christmas Wish	15,000		17.50	28
1982	Perfect Performance	15,000		18.50	45

Peanuts Special Edition Plate - C. Schulz

1976	Bi-Centennial	Unkn.		13.00	30

Peanuts Valentine's Day Plates - C. Schulz

1977	Home Is Where the Heart is	Unkn.		13.00	33
1978	Heavenly Bliss	Unkn.		13.00	30
1979	Love Match	Unkn.		17.50	28
1980	From Snoopy, With Love	Unkn.		17.50	25
1981	Hearts-A-Flutter	Unkn.		17.50	20
1982	Love Patch	Unkn.		17.50	18

Peanuts World's Greatest Athlete - C. Schulz

1982	Go Deep	10,000		17.50	25
1982	The Puck Stops Here	10,000		17.50	23
1982	The Way You Play The Game	10,000		17.50	20
1982	The Crowd Went Wild	10,000		17.50	18

Raggedy Ann Annual Plates - Unknown

1980	The Sunshine Wagon	10,000		17.50	80-100
1981	The Raggedy Shuffle	10,000		17.50	28-75
1982	Flying High	10,000		18.50	19
1983	Winning Streak	10,000		22.50	23
1984	Rocking Rodeo	10,000		22.50	23

Raggedy Ann Bicentennial Plate - Unknown

1976	Bicentennial Plate	Unkn.		13.00	30-60

Raggedy Ann Christmas Plates - Unknown

1975	Gifts of Love	Unkn.		12.50	45
1976	Merry Blades	Unkn.		13.00	38
1977	Christmas Morning	Unkn.		13.00	23
1978	Checking the List	Unkn.		15.00	20
1979	Little Helper	Unkn.		17.50	20

Raggedy Ann Valentine's Day Plates - Unknown

1978	As Time Goes By	Unkn.		13.00	25
1979	Daisies Do Tell	Unkn.		17.50	20

Seymour Mann, Inc.

Connoisseur Collection - M. Bernini

1995	Bluebird CLT-13	25,000		50.00	50
1995	Canary CLT-10	25,000		50.00	50
1995	Cardinal CLT-7	25,000		50.00	50
1995	Dove Duo CLT-1	25,000		50.00	50
1995	Hummingbird Duo CLT-4	25,000		50.00	50
1995	Pink Rose CLT-70	25,000		50.00	50
1995	Robin CLT-16	25,000		50.00	50
1995	Swan Duo CLT-50	25,000		50.00	50

Sports Impressions/Enesco

Gold Edition Plates - Various

XX	A's Jose Canseco Gold (10 1/4") 1028-04 - J. Canseco	2,500	N/A	125.00	125
1990	Andre Dawson - R. Lewis	Closed		150.00	150
1988	Brooks Robinson - R. Simon	Closed		125.00	225
1987	Carl Yastrzemski - R. Simon	Closed		125.00	175
1992	Chicago Bulls '92 World Champions - C. Hayes	Closed		150.00	150
1993	Chicago Bulls 1993 World Championship Gold (10 1/4") 4062-04 - B. Vann	1,993	1994	150.00	150
1987	Darryl Strawberry #1 - R. Simon	Closed		125.00	125
1989	Darryl Strawberry #2 - T. Fogerty	Closed		125.00	125
1986	Don Mattingly - B. Johnson	Closed		125.00	125
1991	Dream Team (1st Ten Chosen) L. Salk	Closed		150.00	300
1992	Dream Team - R.Tanenbaum	Closed		150.00	175
1992	Dream Team 1992 (8 1/2") 5507-03 - C. Hayes	7,500	1994	60.00	60
1992	Dream Team 1992 Gold (10 1/4") 5509-04 - R. Tanenbaum	1,992	1994	150.00	150
1991	Hawks Dominique Wilkins J. Catalano	Closed		150.00	195
1990	Joe Montana 49ers - J. Catalano	Closed		150.00	195
1990	Joe Montana 49ers Gold (10 1/4") 3000-04 - J. Catalano	1,990	1991	150.00	150
1986	Keith Hernandez - R. Simon	Closed		125.00	175
1991	Lakers Magic Johnson W.C. Mundy	Closed		150.00	225
1991	Larry Bird - J. Catalano	Closed		150.00	195
1986	Larry Bird - R. Simon	Closed		125.00	200
1988	Larry Bird - R. Simon	Closed		125.00	275
1990	Living Triple Crown - R. Lewis	Closed		150.00	150-225
1993	Magic Johnson (4042-04) R.Tanenbaum	Closed		150.00	150
1988	Magic Johnson - R. Simon	Closed		125.00	225
1993	Magic Johnson - T. Fogerty	Closed		150.00	175
1991	Magic Johnson Lakers Gold (10 1/4") 4007-04 - C.W. Mundy	1,991	1991	150.00	175
1992	Magic Johnson Lakers Gold (10 1/4") 4042-04 - R. Tanenbaum	1,992	1994	150.00	150
1991	Magic Johnson Lakers Platinum (8 1/2") 4007-03 - M. Petronella	5,000	1992	60.00	60
1989	Mantle Switch Hitter - J. Catalano	Closed		150.00	295-325
1990	Michael Jordan - J. Catalano	Closed		150.00	275-325
1991	Michael Jordan - J. Catalano	Closed		150.00	195
1992	Michael Jordan - R.Tanenbaum	Closed		150.00	175
1993	Michael Jordan - T. Fogerty	Closed		150.00	200

YEAR ISSUE		EDITION LIMIT	YEAR RETD.	ISSUE PRICE	QUOTE U.S.$
1992	Michael Jordan Bulls (10 1/4") 4032-04 - R. Tanenbaum	1,991	1992	150.00	275-325
1993	Michael Jordan Bulls Gold (10 1/4") 4046-04 - T. Fogarty	2,500	1993	150.00	150
1991	Michael Jordan Gold (10 1/4") 4002-04 - J. Catalano	1,991	1992	150.00	150
1991	Michael Jordan Platinum (8 1/2") 4002-03 - M. Petronella	1,991	1993	60.00	95
1995	Mickey Mantle "My Greatest Year 1956" 1229-04 - B. Vann	1,956		100.00	100
1991	Mickey Mantle 7 - B. Simon	Closed		150.00	195
1986	Mickey Mantle At Night - R. Simon	Closed		125.00	250
1995	Mickey Mantle double plate set 176923 - T. Treadway	2,401		75.00	75
1987	Mickey, Willie, & Duke - R. Simon	Closed		150.00	500
1992	NBA 1st Ten Chosen Gold (10 1/4") 5501-04 - L. Salk	1,992	1992	150.00	175-300
1992	NBA 1st Ten Chosen Platinum (8 1/2") (blue) 5502-03 - J. Catalano	7,500	1993	60.00	95
1992	NBA 1st Ten Chosen Platinum (8 1/2") (red) 5503-03 - C.W. Mundy	7,500	1993	60.00	95
1990	Nolan Ryan 300 - J. Catalano	Closed		150.00	175
1990	Nolan Ryan 300 Gold 1091-04 - T. Fogarty	1,990	1992	150.00	150
1995	Profiles in Courage Mickey Mantle 1231-03 - M. Petronella	Open		30.00	30
1990	Rickey Henderson - R. Lewis	Closed		150.00	150
XX	Roberto Clemente 1090-03 - R. Lewis	10,000	N/A	75.00	75
1993	Shaquille O'Neal Gold (10 1/4") 4047-04 - T. Fogarty	2,500	1994	150.00	150
1987	Ted Williams (signed) - R. Simon	Closed		125.00	450-550
1990	Tom Seaver - R. Lewis	Closed		150.00	150
1986	Wade Boggs - B. Johnson	Closed		125.00	150
1989	Will Clark - J. Catalano	Closed		125.00	150
1988	Yankee Tradition - J. Catalano	Closed		150.00	175-225

The Tudor Mint Inc.

Collector Plates - J. Mulholland

YEAR ISSUE		EDITION LIMIT	YEAR RETD.	ISSUE PRICE	QUOTE U.S.$
1992	4401 Meeting of Unicorns	Closed	1993	27.10	35
1992	4402 Cauldron of Light	Closed	1993	27.10	35
1992	4403 The Guardian Dragon	Closed	1993	27.10	35
1992	4404 The Dragon's Nest	Closed	1993	27.10	35

V-Palekh Art Studios

Russian Legends - Various

YEAR ISSUE		EDITION LIMIT	YEAR RETD.	ISSUE PRICE	QUOTE U.S.$
1988	Ruslan and Ludmilla - G. Lubimov	195-day		29.87	30-45
1988	The Princess/Seven Bogatyrs - A. Kovalev	195-day		29.87	35-45
1988	The Golden Cockerel - V. Vleshko	195-day		32.87	35
1988	Lukomorya - R. Belousov	195-day		32.87	35
1989	Fisherman and the Magic Fish - N. Lopatin	195-day		32.87	35
1989	Tsar Saltan - G. Zhiryakova	195-day		32.87	35
1989	The Priest and His Servant - O. An	195-day		34.87	35
1990	Stone Flower - V. Bolshakova	195-day		34.87	40
1990	Sadko - E. Populor	195-day		34.87	45
1990	The Twelve Months - N. Lopatin	195-day		36.87	80
1990	Silver Hoof - S. Adeyanor	195-day		36.87	65
1990	Morozko - N. Lopatin	195-day		36.87	60

Villeroy & Boch

Flower Fairy - C. Barker

YEAR ISSUE		EDITION LIMIT	YEAR RETD.	ISSUE PRICE	QUOTE U.S.$
1979	Lavender	21-day		35.00	125
1980	Sweet Pea	21-day		35.00	125
1980	Candytuft	21-day		35.00	89
1981	Heliotrope	21-day		35.00	75
1981	Blackthorn	21-day		35.00	75
1981	Appleblossom	21-day		35.00	95

Russian Fairytales Maria Morevna - B. Zvorykin

YEAR ISSUE		EDITION LIMIT	YEAR RETD.	ISSUE PRICE	QUOTE U.S.$
1982	Maria Morevna and Tsarevich Ivan	27,500		70.00	85
1982	Koshchey Carries Off Maria Morevna	27,500		70.00	70
1982	Tsarevich Ivan and the Beautiful Castle	27,500		70.00	90

Russian Fairytales The Firebird - B. Zvorykin

YEAR ISSUE		EDITION LIMIT	YEAR RETD.	ISSUE PRICE	QUOTE U.S.$
1981	In Search of the Firebird	27,500		70.00	75-95
1981	Ivan and Tsarevna on the Grey Wolf	27,500		70.00	70
1981	The Wedding of Tsarevna Elena the Fair	27,500		70.00	90

Russian Fairytales The Red Knight - B. Zvorykin

YEAR ISSUE		EDITION LIMIT	YEAR RETD.	ISSUE PRICE	QUOTE U.S.$
1981	The Red Knight	27,500		70.00	40-70
1981	Vassilissa and Her Stepsisters	27,500		70.00	45-77
1981	Vassilissa is Presented to the Tsar	27,500		70.00	56-75

Villeroy & Boch - B. Zvorykin

YEAR ISSUE		EDITION LIMIT	YEAR RETD.	ISSUE PRICE	QUOTE U.S.$
1980	The Snow Maiden	27,500		70.00	110
1981	Snegurochka at the Court of Tsar Berendei	27,500		70.00	45-70
1981	Snegurochka and Lei, the Shepherd Boy	27,500		70.00	44-70

W.S. George

Alaska: The Last Frontier - H. Lambson

YEAR ISSUE		EDITION LIMIT	YEAR RETD.	ISSUE PRICE	QUOTE U.S.$
1991	Icy Majesty	150-day		34.50	34
1991	Autumn Grandeur	150-day		34.50	35
1992	Mountain Monarch	150-day		37.50	45
1992	Down the Trail	150-day		37.50	38
1992	Moonlight Lookout	150-day		37.50	60
1992	Graceful Passage	150-day		39.50	56
1992	Arctic Journey	150-day		39.50	70
1992	Summit Domain	150-day		39.50	50

Along an English Lane - M. Harvey

YEAR ISSUE		EDITION LIMIT	YEAR RETD.	ISSUE PRICE	QUOTE U.S.$
1993	Summer's Bright Welcome	95-day		29.50	32
1993	Greeting the Day	95-day		29.50	55
1993	Friends and Flowers	95-day		29.50	60
1993	Cottage Around the Bend	95-day		29.50	30

America the Beautiful - H. Johnson

YEAR ISSUE		EDITION LIMIT	YEAR RETD.	ISSUE PRICE	QUOTE U.S.$
1988	Yosemite Falls	150-day		34.50	35
1989	The Grand Canyon	150-day		34.50	30
1989	Yellowstone River	150-day		37.50	38
1989	The Great Smokey Mountains	150-day		37.50	38
1990	The Everglades	150-day		37.50	38
1990	Acadia	150-day		37.50	40
1990	The Grand Tetons	150-day		39.50	45
1990	Crater Lake	150-day		39.50	40

America's Pride - R. Richert

YEAR ISSUE		EDITION LIMIT	YEAR RETD.	ISSUE PRICE	QUOTE U.S.$
1992	Misty Fjords	150-day		29.50	60
1992	Rugged Shores	150-day		29.50	45
1992	Mighty Summit	150-day		32.50	45
1993	Lofty Reflections	150-day		32.50	60
1993	Tranquil Waters	150-day		32.50	55
1993	Mountain Majesty	150-day		34.50	65
1993	Canyon Climb	150-day		34.50	45
1993	Golden Vista	150-day		34.50	35

Art Deco - M. McDonald

YEAR ISSUE		EDITION LIMIT	YEAR RETD.	ISSUE PRICE	QUOTE U.S.$
1989	A Flapper With Greyhounds	150-day		39.50	50
1990	Tango Dancers	150-day		39.50	55-75
1990	Arriving in Style	150-day		39.50	55
1990	On the Town	150-day		39.50	75

Bear Tracks - J. Seerey-Lester

YEAR ISSUE		EDITION LIMIT	YEAR RETD.	ISSUE PRICE	QUOTE U.S.$
1992	Denali Family	150-day		29.50	40
1993	Their First Season	150-day		29.50	45
1993	High Country Champion	150-day		29.50	30
1993	Heavy Going	150-day		29.50	30
1993	Breaking Cover	150-day		29.50	30
1993	Along the Ice Flow	150-day		29.50	30

Beloved Hymns of Childhood - C. Barker

YEAR ISSUE		EDITION LIMIT	YEAR RETD.	ISSUE PRICE	QUOTE U.S.$
1988	The Lord's My Shepherd	150-day		29.50	50
1988	Away In a Manger	150-day		29.50	40
1989	Now Thank We All Our God	150-day		32.50	33
1989	Love Divine	150-day		32.50	33
1989	I Love to Hear the Story	150-day		32.50	35
1989	All Glory, Laud and Honour	150-day		32.50	40
1990	All People on Earth Do Dwell	150-day		34.50	35
1990	Loving Shepherd of Thy Sheep	150-day		34.50	35

A Black Tie Affair: The Penguin - C. Jagodits

YEAR ISSUE		EDITION LIMIT	YEAR RETD.	ISSUE PRICE	QUOTE U.S.$
1992	Little Explorer	150-day		29.50	50
1992	Penguin Parade	150-day		29.50	50
1992	Baby-Sitters	150-day		29.50	45
1993	Belly Flopping	150-day		29.50	48

Blessed Are The Children - W. Rane

YEAR ISSUE		EDITION LIMIT	YEAR RETD.	ISSUE PRICE	QUOTE U.S.$
1990	Let the/Children Come To Me	150-day		29.50	45
1990	I Am the Good Shepherd	150-day		29.50	50
1991	Whoever Welcomes/Child	150-day		32.50	45
1991	Hosanna in the Highest	150-day		32.50	40
1991	Jesus Had Compassion on Them	150-day		32.50	45
1991	Blessed are the Peacemakers	150-day		34.50	55
1991	I am the Vine, You are the Branches	150-day		34.50	55
1991	Seek and You Will Find	150-day		34.50	45

Bonds of Love - B. Burke

YEAR ISSUE		EDITION LIMIT	YEAR RETD.	ISSUE PRICE	QUOTE U.S.$
1989	Precious Embrace	150-day		29.50	30
1990	Cherished Moment	150-day		29.50	35
1991	Tender Caress	150-day		32.50	35
1992	Loving Touch	150-day		32.50	35
1992	Treasured Kisses	150-day		32.50	40
1994	Endearing Whispers	150-day		32.50	65

The Christmas Story - H. Garrido

YEAR ISSUE		EDITION LIMIT	YEAR RETD.	ISSUE PRICE	QUOTE U.S.$
1992	Gifts of the Magi	150-day		29.50	30
1993	Rest on the Flight into Egypt	150-day		29.50	30
1993	Journey of the Magi	150-day		29.50	30
1993	The Nativity	150-day		29.50	30
1993	The Annunciation	150-day		29.50	30
1993	Adoration of the Shepherds	150-day		29.50	30

Classic Waterfowl: The Ducks Unlimited - L. Kaatz

YEAR ISSUE		EDITION LIMIT	YEAR RETD.	ISSUE PRICE	QUOTE U.S.$
1988	Mallards at Sunrise	150-day		36.50	40
1988	Geese in the Autumn Fields	150-day		36.50	37
1989	Green Wings/Morning Marsh	150-day		39.50	40
1989	Canvasbacks, Breaking Away	150-day		39.50	40
1989	Pintails in Indian Summer	150-day		39.50	40
1990	Wood Ducks Taking Flight	150-day		39.50	40
1990	Snow Geese Against November Skies	150-day		41.50	42
1990	Bluebills Coming In	150-day		41.50	42

Columbus Discovers America: The 500th Anniversary - J. Penalva

YEAR ISSUE		EDITION LIMIT	YEAR RETD.	ISSUE PRICE	QUOTE U.S.$
1992	Under Full Sail	150-day		29.50	30
1992	Ashore at Dawn	150-day		29.50	35
1992	Columbus Raises the Flag	150-day		32.50	35
1992	Bringing Together Two Cultures	150-day		32.50	47
1992	The Queen's Approval	150-day		32.50	45
1992	Treasures From The New World	150-day		32.50	90

Country Bouquets - G. Kurz

YEAR ISSUE		EDITION LIMIT	YEAR RETD.	ISSUE PRICE	QUOTE U.S.$
1991	Morning Sunshine	150-day		29.50	45
1991	Summer Perfume	150-day		29.50	50
1991	Warm Welcome	150-day		32.50	50
1991	Garden's Bounty	150-day		32.50	65

Country Nostalgia - M. Harvey

YEAR ISSUE		EDITION LIMIT	YEAR RETD.	ISSUE PRICE	QUOTE U.S.$
1989	The Spring Buggy	150-day		29.50	30
1989	The Apple Cider Press	150-day		29.50	40
1989	The Vintage Seed Planter	150-day		29.50	40
1989	The Old Hand Pump	150-day		32.50	50
1990	The Wooden Butter Churn	150-day		32.50	45
1990	The Dairy Cans	150-day		32.50	33
1990	The Forgotten Plow	150-day		34.50	40
1990	The Antique Spinning Wheel	150-day		34.50	40

Critic's Choice: Gone With The Wind - P. Jennis

YEAR ISSUE		EDITION LIMIT	YEAR RETD.	ISSUE PRICE	QUOTE U.S.$
1991	Marry Me, Scarlett	150-day		27.50	50
1991	Waiting for Rhett	150-day		27.50	55
1991	A Declaration of Love	150-day		30.50	50
1991	The Paris Hat	150-day		30.50	50-60
1991	Scarlett Asks a Favor	150-day		30.50	50-65
1992	Scarlett Gets Her Way	150-day		32.50	50
1992	The Smitten Suitor	150-day		32.50	45
1992	Scarlett's Shopping Spree	150-day		32.50	40
1992	The Buggy Ride	150-day		32.50	50
1992	Scarlett Gets Down to Business	150-day		34.50	50
1993	Scarlett's Heart is with Tara	150-day		34.50	45
1993	At Cross Purposes	150-day		34.50	35

A Delicate Balance: Vanishing Wildlife - G. Beecham

YEAR ISSUE		EDITION LIMIT	YEAR RETD.	ISSUE PRICE	QUOTE U.S.$
1992	Tomorrow's Hope	95-day		29.50	30
1993	Today's Future	95-day		29.50	30
1993	Present Dreams	95-day		32.50	33
1993	Eyes on the New Day	95-day		32.50	33

Dr. Zhivago - G. Bush

YEAR ISSUE		EDITION LIMIT	YEAR RETD.	ISSUE PRICE	QUOTE U.S.$
1990	Zhivago and Lara	150-day		39.50	40
1991	Love Poems For Lara	150-day		39.50	40
1991	Zhivago Says Farewell	150-day		39.50	45
1991	Lara's Love	150-day		39.50	55

The Elegant Birds - J. Faulkner

YEAR ISSUE		EDITION LIMIT	YEAR RETD.	ISSUE PRICE	QUOTE U.S.$
1988	The Swan	150-day		32.50	33
1988	Great Blue Heron	150-day		32.50	33
1989	Snowy Egret	150-day		32.50	36
1989	The Anhinga	150-day		35.50	36
1989	The Flamingo	150-day		35.50	36
1990	Sandhill and Whooping Crane	150-day		35.50	36

Enchanted Garden - E. Antonaccio

YEAR ISSUE		EDITION LIMIT	YEAR RETD.	ISSUE PRICE	QUOTE U.S.$
1993	A Peaceful Retreat	95-day		24.50	25
1993	Pleasant Pathways	95-day		24.50	25
1993	A Place to Dream	95-day		24.50	25
1993	Tranquil Hideaway	95-day		24.50	25

Eyes of the Wild - D. Pierce

YEAR ISSUE		EDITION LIMIT	YEAR RETD.	ISSUE PRICE	QUOTE U.S.$
1993	Eyes in the Mist	95-day		29.50	60
1993	Eyes in the Pines	95-day		29.50	45
1993	Eyes on the Sly	95-day		29.50	30
1993	Eyes of Gold	95-day		29.50	30
1993	Eyes of Silence	95-day		29.50	30
1993	Eyes in the Snow	95-day		29.50	30
1993	Eyes of Wonder	95-day		29.50	30
1994	Eyes of Strength	95-day		29.50	30

The Faces of Nature - J. Kramer Cole

YEAR ISSUE		EDITION LIMIT	YEAR RETD.	ISSUE PRICE	QUOTE U.S.$
1992	Canyon of the Cat	150-day		29.50	55
1992	Wolf Ridge	150-day		29.50	70
1993	Trail of the Talisman	150-day		29.50	30
1993	Wolfpack of the Ancients	150-day		29.50	30
1993	Two Bears Camp	150-day		29.50	30
1993	Wintering With the Wapiti	150-day		29.50	30
1993	Within Sunrise	150-day		29.50	30
1993	Wambli Okiye	150-day		29.50	30

The Federal Duck Stamp Plate Collection - N. Anderson

YEAR ISSUE		EDITION LIMIT	YEAR RETD.	ISSUE PRICE	QUOTE U.S.$
1990	The Lesser Scaup	150-day		27.50	40
1990	Mallard	150-day		27.50	50
1990	The Ruddy Ducks	150-day		30.50	31
1990	Canvasbacks	150-day		30.50	42
1991	Pintails	150-day		30.50	35
1991	Wigeons	150-day		30.50	35
1991	Cinnamon Teal	150-day		32.50	33
1991	Fulvous Wistling Duck	150-day		32.50	55
1991	The Redheads	150-day		32.50	50
1991	Snow Goose	150-day		32.50	35

PLATES

Feline Fancy - H. Ronner

YEAR ISSUE		EDITION LIMIT	YEAR RETD.	ISSUE PRICE	QUOTE U.S.$
1993	Globetrotters	95-day		34.50	40
1993	Little Athletes	95-day		34.50	50
1993	Young Adventurers	95-day		34.50	36
1993	The Geographers	95-day		34.50	50

Field Birds of North America - D. Bush

YEAR ISSUE		EDITION LIMIT	YEAR RETD.	ISSUE PRICE	QUOTE U.S.$
1991	Winter Colors: Ring-Necked Pheasant	150-day		39.50	50
1991	In Display: Ruffed Goose	150-day		39.50	45
1991	Morning Light: Bobwhite Quail	150-day		42.50	60
1991	Misty Clearing: Wild Turkey	150-day		42.50	85
1992	Autumn Moment: American Woodcock	150-day		42.50	50
1992	Season's End: Willow Ptarmigan	150-day		42.50	60

Floral Fancies - C. Callog

YEAR ISSUE		EDITION LIMIT	YEAR RETD.	ISSUE PRICE	QUOTE U.S.$
1993	Sitting Softly	95-day		34.50	35
1993	Sitting Pretty	95-day		34.50	35
1993	Sitting Sunny	95-day		34.50	35
1993	Sitting Pink	95-day		34.50	35

Flowers From Grandma's Garden - G. Kurz

YEAR ISSUE		EDITION LIMIT	YEAR RETD.	ISSUE PRICE	QUOTE U.S.$
1990	Country Cuttings	150-day		24.50	45
1990	The Morning Bouquet	150-day		24.50	40
1991	Homespun Beauty	150-day		27.50	40
1991	Harvest in the Meadow	150-day		27.50	40
1991	Gardener's Delight	150-day		27.50	55
1991	Nature's Bounty	150-day		27.50	60
1991	A Country Welcome	150-day		29.50	55
1991	The Springtime Arrangement	150-day		29.50	55

Flowers of Your Garden - V. Morley

YEAR ISSUE		EDITION LIMIT	YEAR RETD.	ISSUE PRICE	QUOTE U.S.$
1988	Roses	150-day		24.50	35
1988	Lilacs	150-day		24.50	50
1988	Daisies	150-day		27.50	35
1988	Peonies	150-day		27.50	28
1988	Chrysanthemums	150-day		27.50	28
1989	Daffodils	150-day		27.50	28
1989	Tulips	150-day		29.50	30
1989	Irises	150-day		29.50	30

Garden of the Lord - C. Gillies

YEAR ISSUE		EDITION LIMIT	YEAR RETD.	ISSUE PRICE	QUOTE U.S.$
1992	Love One Another	150-day		29.50	30
1992	Perfect Peace	150-day		29.50	30
1992	Trust In the Lord	150-day		32.50	33
1992	The Lord's Love	150-day		32.50	33
1992	The Lord Bless You	150-day		32.50	33
1992	Ask In Prayer	150-day		34.50	35
1993	Peace Be With You	150-day		34.50	35
1993	Give Thanks To The Lord	150-day		34.50	35

Gardens of Paradise - L. Chang

YEAR ISSUE		EDITION LIMIT	YEAR RETD.	ISSUE PRICE	QUOTE U.S.$
1992	Tranquility	150-day		29.50	50
1992	Serenity	150-day		29.50	55
1993	Splendor	150-day		32.50	33
1993	Harmony	150-day		32.50	33
1993	Beauty	150-day		32.50	33
1993	Elegance	150-day		32.50	33
1993	Grandeur	150-day		32.50	33
1993	Majesty	150-day		32.50	33

Gentle Beginnings - W. Nelson

YEAR ISSUE		EDITION LIMIT	YEAR RETD.	ISSUE PRICE	QUOTE U.S.$
1991	Tender Loving Care	150-day		34.50	45
1991	A Touch of Love	150-day		34.50	50
1991	Under Watchful Eyes	150-day		37.50	50
1991	Lap of Love	150-day		37.50	55
1992	Happy Together	150-day		37.50	85
1992	First Steps	150-day		37.50	70

Glorious Songbirds - R. Cobane

YEAR ISSUE		EDITION LIMIT	YEAR RETD.	ISSUE PRICE	QUOTE U.S.$
1991	Cardinals on a Snowy Branch	150-day		29.50	35
1991	Indigo Buntings and/Blossoms	150-day		29.50	30
1991	Chickadees Among The Lilacs	150-day		32.50	33
1991	Goldfinches in/Thistle	150-day		32.50	33
1991	Cedar Waxwing/Winter Berries	150-day		32.50	34
1991	Bluebirds in a Blueberry Bush	150-day		34.50	35
1991	Baltimore Orioles/Autumn Leaves	150-day		34.50	45
1991	Robins with Dogwood in Bloom	150-day		34.50	50

The Golden Age of the Clipper Ships - C. Vickery

YEAR ISSUE		EDITION LIMIT	YEAR RETD.	ISSUE PRICE	QUOTE U.S.$
1989	The Twilight Under Full Sail	150-day		29.50	30
1989	The Blue Jacket at Sunset	150-day		29.50	30
1989	Young America, Homeward	150-day		32.50	33
1990	Flying Cloud	150-day		32.50	33
1990	Davy Crocket at Daybreak	150-day		32.50	35
1990	Golden Eagle Conquers Wind	150-day		32.50	35
1990	The Lightning in Lifting Fog	150-day		34.50	35
1990	Sea Witch, Mistress/Oceans	150-day		34.50	35

Gone With the Wind: Golden Anniversary - H. Rogers

YEAR ISSUE		EDITION LIMIT	YEAR RETD.	ISSUE PRICE	QUOTE U.S.$
1988	Scarlett and Her Suitors	150-day		24.50	55-90
1988	The Burning of Atlanta	150-day		24.50	55
1988	Scarlett and Ashley After the War	150-day		27.50	50-60
1988	The Proposal	150-day		27.50	80
1989	Home to Tara	150-day		27.50	50
1989	Strolling in Atlanta	150-day		27.50	50
1989	A Question of Honor	150-day		29.50	45
1989	Scarlett's Resolve	150-day		29.50	45
1989	Frankly My Dear	150-day		29.50	55-65
1989	Melane and Ashley	150-day		32.50	40
1990	A Toast to Bonnie Blue	150-day		32.50	45-55
1990	Scarlett and Rhett's Honeymoon	150-day		32.50	45

Gone With the Wind: The Passions of Scarlett O'Hara - P. Jennis

YEAR ISSUE		EDITION LIMIT	YEAR RETD.	ISSUE PRICE	QUOTE U.S.$
1992	Fiery Embrace	150-day		29.50	65
1992	Pride and Passion	150-day		29.50	75
1992	Dreams of Ashley	150-day		32.50	75
1992	The Fond Farewell	150-day		32.50	45-55
1992	The Waltz	150-day		32.50	75
1992	As God Is My Witness	150-day		34.50	40
1993	Brave Scarlett	150-day		34.50	55
1993	Nightmare	150-day		34.50	35
1993	Evening Prayers	150-day		34.50	35
1993	Naptime	150-day		36.50	37
1993	Dangerous Attraction	150-day		36.50	37
1994	The End of An Era	150-day		36.50	37

Grand Safari: Images of Africa - C. Fracé

YEAR ISSUE		EDITION LIMIT	YEAR RETD.	ISSUE PRICE	QUOTE U.S.$
1992	A Moment's Rest	150-day		34.50	45
1992	Elephant's of Kilimanjaro	150-day		34.50	50
1992	Undivided Attention	150-day		37.50	38
1993	Quiet Time in Samburu	150-day		37.50	38
1993	Lone Hunter	150-day		37.50	38
1993	The Greater Kudo	150-day		37.50	38

Heart of the Wild - G. Beecham

YEAR ISSUE		EDITION LIMIT	YEAR RETD.	ISSUE PRICE	QUOTE U.S.$
1991	A Gentle Touch	150-day		29.50	50
1992	Mother's Pride	150-day		29.50	50-60
1992	An Afternoon Together	150-day		32.50	55
1992	Quiet Time?	150-day		32.50	60

Hollywood's Glamour Girls - E. Dzenis

YEAR ISSUE		EDITION LIMIT	YEAR RETD.	ISSUE PRICE	QUOTE U.S.$
1989	Jean Harlow-Dinner at Eight	150-day		24.50	35
1990	Lana Turner-Postman Ring Twice	150-day		29.50	30
1990	Carol Lombard-The Gay Bride	150-day		29.50	30
1990	Greta Garbo-In Grand Hotel	150-day		29.50	30

Hometown Memories - H.T. Becker

YEAR ISSUE		EDITION LIMIT	YEAR RETD.	ISSUE PRICE	QUOTE U.S.$
1993	Moonlight Skaters	150-day		29.50	30
1993	Mountain Sleigh Ride	150-day		29.50	30
1993	Heading Home	150-day		29.50	30
1993	A Winter Ride	150-day		29.50	30

Last of Their Kind: The Endangered Species - W. Nelson

YEAR ISSUE		EDITION LIMIT	YEAR RETD.	ISSUE PRICE	QUOTE U.S.$
1988	The Panda	150-day		27.50	55
1989	The Snow Leopard	150-day		27.50	45
1989	The Red Wolf	150-day		30.50	31
1989	The Asian Elephant	150-day		30.50	31
1990	The Slender-Horned Gazelle	150-day		30.50	31
1990	The Bridled Wallaby	150-day		30.50	31
1990	The Black-Footed Ferret	150-day		33.50	34
1990	The Siberian Tiger	150-day		33.50	35
1991	The Vicuna	150-day		33.50	34
1991	Przewalski's Horse	150-day		33.50	34

Lena Liu's Basket Bouquets - L. Liu

YEAR ISSUE		EDITION LIMIT	YEAR RETD.	ISSUE PRICE	QUOTE U.S.$
1992	Roses	150-day		29.50	45
1992	Pansies	150-day		29.50	50
1992	Tulips and Lilacs	150-day		32.50	33
1992	Irises	150-day		32.50	50
1992	Lilies	150-day		32.50	60
1992	Parrot Tulips	150-day		32.50	45
1992	Peonies	150-day		32.50	45
1993	Begonias	150-day		32.50	33
1993	Magnolias	150-day		32.50	33
1993	Calla Lilies	150-day		32.50	33
1993	Orchids	150-day		32.50	33
1993	Hydrangeas	150-day		32.50	33

Lena Liu's Flower Fairies - L. Liu

YEAR ISSUE		EDITION LIMIT	YEAR RETD.	ISSUE PRICE	QUOTE U.S.$
1993	Magic Makers	95-day		29.50	30
1993	Petal Playmates	95-day		29.50	30
1993	Delicate Dancers	95-day		32.50	33
1993	Mischief Masters	95-day		32.50	33
1993	Amorous Angels	95-day		32.50	33
1993	Winged Wonders	95-day		34.50	35
1993	Miniature Mermaids	95-day		34.50	35
1993	Fanciful Fairies	95-day		34.50	35

Lena Liu's Hummingbird Treasury - L. Liu

YEAR ISSUE		EDITION LIMIT	YEAR RETD.	ISSUE PRICE	QUOTE U.S.$
1992	The Ruby-Throated Hummingbird	150-day		29.50	30
1992	Anna's Hummingbird	150-day		29.50	30
1992	Violet-Crowned Hummingbird	150-day		32.50	33
1992	The Rufous Hummingbird	150-day		32.50	33
1993	White-Eared Hummingbird	150-day		32.50	33
1993	Broad-Billed Hummingbird	150-day		34.50	35
1993	Calliope Hummingbird	150-day		34.50	35
1993	The Allen's Hummingbird	150-day		34.50	35

Little Angels - B. Burke

YEAR ISSUE		EDITION LIMIT	YEAR RETD.	ISSUE PRICE	QUOTE U.S.$
1992	Angels We Have Heard on High	150-day		29.50	45
1992	O Tannenbaum	150-day		29.50	60
1993	Joy to the World	150-day		32.50	100
1993	Hark the Herald Angels Sing	150-day		32.50	45
1993	It Came Upon a Midnight Clear	150-day		32.50	50
1993	The First Noel	150-day		32.50	33

A Loving Look: Duck Families - B. Langton

YEAR ISSUE		EDITION LIMIT	YEAR RETD.	ISSUE PRICE	QUOTE U.S.$
1990	Family Outing	150-day		34.50	35
1991	Sleepy Start	150-day		34.50	35
1991	Quiet Moment	150-day		37.50	40
1991	Safe and Sound	150-day		37.50	40
1991	Spring Arrivals	150-day		37.50	40
1991	The Family Tree	150-day		37.50	50

The Majestic Horse - P. Wildermuth

YEAR ISSUE		EDITION LIMIT	YEAR RETD.	ISSUE PRICE	QUOTE U.S.$
1992	Classic Beauty: Thoroughbred	150-day		34.50	55
1992	American Gold: The Quarterhorse	150-day		34.50	65
1992	Regal Spirit: The Arabian	150-day		34.50	50
1992	Western Favorite: American Paint Horse	150-day		34.50	75

Melodies in the Mist - A. Sakhavarz

YEAR ISSUE		EDITION LIMIT	YEAR RETD.	ISSUE PRICE	QUOTE U.S.$
1993	Early Morning Rain	95-day		34.50	35
1993	Among the Dewdrops	95-day		34.50	35
1993	Feeding Time	95-day		37.50	38
1993	The Garden Party	95-day		37.50	38
1993	Unpleasant Surprise	95-day		37.50	38
1993	Spring Rain	95-day		37.50	38

Memories of a Victorian Childhood - Unknown

YEAR ISSUE		EDITION LIMIT	YEAR RETD.	ISSUE PRICE	QUOTE U.S.$
1992	You'd Better Not Pout	150-day		29.50	30
1992	Sweet Slumber	150-day		29.50	55
1992	Through Thick and Thin	150-day		32.50	50
1992	An Armful of Treasures	150-day		32.50	60
1993	A Trio of Bookworms	150-day		32.50	55
1993	Pugnacious Playmate	150-day		32.50	60

Nature's Legacy - J. Sias

YEAR ISSUE		EDITION LIMIT	YEAR RETD.	ISSUE PRICE	QUOTE U.S.$
1990	Blue Snow at Half Dome	150-day		24.50	30
1991	Misty Morning/Mt. McKinley	150-day		24.50	30
1991	Mount Ranier	150-day		27.50	30
1991	Havasu Canyon	150-day		27.50	28
1991	Autumn Splendor in the Smoky Mts.	150-day		27.50	35
1991	Winter Peace in Yellowstone Park	150-day		29.50	30
1991	Golden Majesty/Rocky Mountains	150-day		29.50	35
1991	Radiant Sunset Over the Everglades	150-day		29.50	30

Nature's Lovables - C. Fracé

YEAR ISSUE		EDITION LIMIT	YEAR RETD.	ISSUE PRICE	QUOTE U.S.$
1990	The Koala	150-day		27.50	35
1991	New Arrival	150-day		27.50	40
1991	Chinese Treasure	150-day		27.50	28
1991	Baby Harp Seal	150-day		30.50	45
1991	Bobcat: Nature's Dawn	150-day		30.50	35
1991	Clouded Leopard	150-day		32.50	35
1991	Zebra Foal	150-day		32.50	45
1991	Bandit	150-day		32.50	45

Nature's Playmates - C. Fracé

YEAR ISSUE		EDITION LIMIT	YEAR RETD.	ISSUE PRICE	QUOTE U.S.$
1991	Partners	150-day		29.50	40
1991	Secret Heights	150-day		29.50	45
1991	Recess	150-day		32.50	45
1991	Double Trouble	150-day		32.50	40
1991	Pals	150-day		32.50	40
1992	Curious Trio	150-day		34.50	50
1992	Playmates	150-day		34.50	50
1992	Surprise	150-day		34.50	50-70
1992	Peace On Ice	150-day		36.50	75
1992	Ambassadors	150-day		36.50	70

Nature's Poetry - L. Liu

YEAR ISSUE		EDITION LIMIT	YEAR RETD.	ISSUE PRICE	QUOTE U.S.$
1989	Morning Serenade	150-day		24.50	45
1989	Song of Promise	150-day		24.50	45
1990	Tender Lullaby	150-day		27.50	28
1990	Nature's Harmony	150-day		27.50	40
1990	Gentle Refrain	150-day		27.50	30
1990	Morning Chorus	150-day		27.50	35
1990	Melody at Daybreak	150-day		29.50	30
1991	Delicate Accord	150-day		29.50	30
1991	Lyrical Beginnings	150-day		29.50	30
1991	Song of Spring	150-day		32.50	40
1991	Mother's Melody	150-day		32.50	40
1991	Cherub Chorale	150-day		32.50	50

On Golden Wings - W. Goebel

YEAR ISSUE		EDITION LIMIT	YEAR RETD.	ISSUE PRICE	QUOTE U.S.$
1993	Morning Light	95-day		29.50	30
1993	Early Risers	95-day		29.50	30
1993	As Day Breaks	95-day		32.50	33
1993	Daylight Flight	95-day		32.50	33
1993	Winter Dawn	95-day		32.50	33
1994	First Light	95-day		34.50	35

On Gossamer Wings - L. Liu

YEAR ISSUE		EDITION LIMIT	YEAR RETD.	ISSUE PRICE	QUOTE U.S.$
1988	Monarch Butterflies	150-day		24.50	35
1988	Western Tiger Swallowtails	150-day		24.50	40
1988	Red-Spotted Purple	150-day		27.50	50
1988	Malachites	150-day		27.50	28
1988	White Peacocks	150-day		27.50	40
1989	Eastern Tailed Blues	150-day		27.50	28
1989	Zebra Swallowtails	150-day		29.50	30
1989	Red Admirals	150-day		29.50	30

On the Wing - T. Humphrey

YEAR ISSUE		EDITION LIMIT	YEAR RETD.	ISSUE PRICE	QUOTE U.S.$
1992	Winged Splendor	150-day		29.50	30

YEAR ISSUE		EDITION LIMIT	YEAR RETD.	ISSUE PRICE	QUOTE U.S.$
1992	Rising Mallard	150-day		29.50	45
1992	Glorious Ascent	150-day		32.50	50-60
1992	Taking Wing	150-day		32.50	45
1992	Upward Bound	150-day		32.50	40
1993	Wondrous Motion	150-day		34.50	45
1993	Springing Forth	150-day		34.50	35
1993	Graceful Climb	150-day		34.50	35

On Wings of Snow - L. Liu

1991	The Swans	150-day		34.50	40
1991	The Doves	150-day		34.50	60
1991	The Peacocks	150-day		37.50	55
1991	The Egrets	150-day		37.50	55
1991	The Cockatoos	150-day		37.50	50
1992	The Herons	150-day		37.50	50

Our Woodland Friends - C. Brenders

1989	Fascination	150-day		29.00	29
1990	Beneath the Pines	150-day		29.50	32
1990	High Adventure	150-day		32.50	33
1990	Shy Explorers	150-day		32.50	40
1991	Golden Season:Gray Squirrel	150-day		32.50	35
1991	Full House Fox Family	150-day		32.50	55
1991	A Jump Into Life: Spring Fawn	150-day		34.50	35
1991	Forest Sentinel:Bobcat	150-day		34.50	40

Paw Prints: Baby Cats of the Wild - C. Fracé

1992	Morning Mischief	95-day		29.50	45
1993	Togetherness	95-day		29.50	50
1993	The Buddy System	95-day		32.50	33
1993	Nap Time	95-day		32.50	33

Petal Pals - L. Chang

1992	Garden Discovery	150-day		24.50	25
1992	Flowering Fascination	150-day		24.50	25
1993	Alluring Lilies	150-day		24.50	25
1993	Springtime Oasis	150-day		24.50	25
1993	Blossoming Adventure	150-day		24.50	25
1993	Dancing Daffodils	150-day		24.50	25
1993	Summer Surprise	150-day		24.50	25
1993	Morning Melody	150-day		24.50	25

Poetic Cottages - C. Valente

1992	Garden Paths of Oxfordshire	150-day		29.50	50
1992	Twilight at Woodgreen Pond	150-day		29.50	55
1992	Stonewall Brook Blossoms	150-day		32.50	35
1992	Bedfordshire Evening Sky	150-day		32.50	33
1993	Wisteria Summer	150-day		32.50	33
1993	Wiltshire Rose Arbor	150-day		32.50	33
1993	Alderbury Gardens	150-day		32.50	33
1993	Hampshire Spring Splendor	150-day		32.50	33

Portraits of Christ - J. Salamanca

1991	Father, Forgive Them	150-day		29.50	70
1991	Thy Will Be Done	150-day		29.50	50
1991	This is My Beloved Son	150-day		32.50	50
1991	Lo, I Am With You	150-day		32.50	55
1991	Become as Little Children	150-day		32.50	55
1991	Peace I Leave With You	150-day		34.50	55
1992	For God So Loved the World	150-day		34.50	55
1992	I Am the Way, the Truth and the Life	150-day		34.50	65
1992	Weep Not For Me	150-day		34.50	65
1992	Follow Me	150-day		34.50	60

Portraits of Exquisite Birds - C. Brenders

1990	Backyard Treasure/Chickadee	150-day		29.50	30
1990	The Beautiful Bluebird	150-day		29.50	30
1991	Summer Gold: The Robin	150-day		32.50	33
1991	The Meadowlark's Song	150-day		32.50	33
1991	Ivory-Billed Woodpecker	150-day		32.50	33
1991	Red-Winged Blackbird	150-day		32.50	33

Purebred Horses of the Americas - D. Schwartz

1989	The Appalosa	150-day		34.50	35
1989	The Tenessee Walker	150-day		34.50	35
1990	The Quarterhorse	150-day		37.50	38
1990	The Saddlebred	150-day		37.50	45
1990	The Mustang	150-day		37.50	39
1990	The Morgan	150-day		37.50	70

Rare Encounters - J. Seerey-Lester

1993	Softly, Softly	95-day		29.50	50
1993	Black Magic	95-day		29.50	50
1993	Future Song	95-day		32.50	40
1993	High and Mighty	95-day		32.50	33
1993	Last Sanctuary	95-day		32.50	33
1993	Something Stirred	95-day		34.50	35

Romantic Gardens - C. Smith

1989	The Woodland Garden	150-day		29.50	30
1989	The Plantation Garden	150-day		29.50	30
1990	The Cottage Garden	150-day		32.50	33
1990	The Colonial Garden	150-day		32.50	33

Romantic Harbors - C. Vickery

1993	Advent of the Golden Bough	95-day		34.50	40
1993	Christmas Tree Schooner	95-day		34.50	60
1993	Prelude to the Journey	95-day		37.50	50
1993	Shimmering Light of Dusk	95-day		37.50	40

Romantic Roses - V. Morley

1993	Victorian Beauty	95-day		29.50	30
1993	Old-Fashioned Grace	95-day		29.50	30
1993	Country Charm	95-day		32.50	33
1993	Summer Romance	95-day		32.50	33
1993	Pastoral Delight	95-day		32.50	33
1993	Springtime Elegance	95-day		34.50	35
1993	Vintage Splendor	95-day		34.50	35
1994	Heavenly Perfection	95-day		34.50	35

Scenes of Christmas Past - L. Garrison

1987	Holiday Skaters	150-day		27.50	30
1988	Christmas Eve	150-day		27.50	35
1989	The Homecoming	150-day		30.50	31
1990	The Toy Store	150-day		30.50	31
1991	The Carollers	150-day		30.50	31
1992	Family Traditions	150-day		32.50	45
1993	Holiday Past	150-day		32.50	50
1994	A Gathering of Faith	150-day		32.50	55

The Secret World Of The Panda - J. Bridgett

1990	A Mother's Care	150-day		27.50	35
1991	A Frolic in the Snow	150-day		27.50	28
1991	Lazy Afternoon	150-day		30.50	31
1991	A Day of Exploring	150-day		30.50	31
1991	A Gentle Hug	150-day		32.50	35
1991	A Bamboo Feast	150-day		32.50	75

Soaring Majesty - C. Fracé

1991	Freedom	150-day		29.50	35
1991	The Northern Goshhawk	150-day		29.50	40
1991	Peregrine Falcon	150-day		32.50	33
1991	Red-Tailed Hawk	150-day		32.50	33
1991	The Ospray	150-day		32.50	35
1991	The Gyrfalcon	150-day		34.50	45
1991	The Golden Eagle	150-day		34.50	50
1992	Red-Shouldered Hawk	150-day		34.50	35

Sonnets in Flowers - G. Kurz

1992	Sonnet of Beauty	150-day		29.50	40
1992	Sonnet of Happiness	150-day		34.50	45
1992	Sonnet of Love	150-day		34.50	35
1992	Sonnet of Peace	150-day		34.50	55

The Sound of Music: Silver Anniversary - V. Gadino

1991	The Hills are Alive	150-day		29.50	35
1992	Let's Start at the Very Beginning	150-day		29.50	35
1992	Something Good	150-day		32.50	45
1992	Maria's Wedding Day	150-day		32.50	50

Spirit of Christmas - J. Sias

1990	Silent Night	150-day		29.50	37
1991	Jingle Bells	150-day		29.50	30
1991	Deck The Halls	150-day		32.50	40
1991	I'll Be Home For Christmas	150-day		32.50	45
1991	Winter Wonderland	150-day		32.50	40
1991	O Christmas Tree	150-day		32.50	35

Spirits of the Sky - C. Fisher

1992	Twilight Glow	150-day		29.50	40
1992	First Light	150-day		29.50	40
1992	Evening Glimmer	150-day		32.50	75
1992	Golden Dusk	150-day		32.50	40
1993	Sunset Splendor	150-day		32.50	33
1993	Amber Flight	150-day		34.50	35
1993	Winged Radiance	150-day		34.50	35
1993	Day's End	150-day		34.50	35

Symphony of Shimmering Beauties - L. Liu

1991	Iris Quartet	150-day		29.50	54
1991	Tulip Ensemble	150-day		29.50	35
1991	Poppy Pastorale	150-day		32.50	43
1991	Lily Concerto	150-day		32.50	55
1991	Peony Prelude	150-day		32.50	45
1991	Rose Fantasy	150-day		34.50	60
1991	Hibiscus Medley	150-day		34.50	40
1992	Dahlia Melody	150-day		34.50	55
1992	Hollyhock March	150-day		34.50	45
1992	Carnation Serenade	150-day		36.50	45
1992	Gladiolus Romance	150-day		36.50	37
1992	Zinnia Finale	150-day		36.50	37

Tis the Season - J. Sias

1993	A World Dressed in Snow	95-day		29.50	40
1993	A Time for Tradition	95-day		29.50	45
1993	We Shall Come Rejoining	95-day		29.50	30
1993	Our Family Tree	95-day		29.50	30

Tomorrow's Promise - W. Nelson

1992	Curiosity: Asian Elephants	150-day		29.50	45
1992	Playtime Pandas	150-day		29.50	40
1992	Innocence: Rhinos	150-day		32.50	65
1992	Friskiness: Kit Foxes	150-day		32.50	45

Touching the Spirit - J. Kramer Cole

1993	Running With the Wind	95-day		29.50	60
1993	Kindred Spirits	95-day		29.50	40
1993	The Marking Tree	95-day		29.50	30
1993	Wakan Tanka	95-day		29.50	30
1993	He Who Watches	95-day		29.50	30
1993	Twice Traveled Trail	95-day		29.50	30

1993	Keeper of the Secret	95-day		29.50	30
1993	Camp of the Sacred Dogs	95-day		29.50	30

A Treasury of Songbirds - R. Stine

1995	Alluring Daylight	150 days		34.5	
1995	Sapphire Dawn	150days		34.5	
1992	Springtime Splendor	150-day		29.50	48
1992	Morning's Glory	150-day		29.50	50
1992	Golden Daybreak	150-day		32.50	45
1992	Afternoon Calm	150-day		32.50	50
1992	Dawn's Radiance	150-day		32.50	50
1993	Scarlet Sunrise	150-day		34.50	35
1993	Sapphire Dawn	150-day		34.50	35
1993	Alluring Daylight	150-day		34.50	35

The Vanishing Gentle Giants - A. Casay

1991	Jumping For Joy	150-day		32.50	40
1991	Song of the Humpback	150-day		32.50	40
1991	Monarch of the Deep	150-day		35.50	45
1991	Travelers of the Sea	150-day		35.50	65
1991	White Whale of the North	150-day		35.50	65
1991	Unicorn of the Sea	150-day		35.50	50

Victorian Cat - H. Bonner

1990	Mischief With The Hatbox	150-day		24.50	50
1991	String Quartet	150-day		24.50	55
1991	Daydreams	150-day		27.50	40
1991	Frisky Felines	150-day		27.50	50
1991	Kittens at Play	150-day		27.50	45
1991	Playing in the Parlor	150-day		29.50	55
1991	Perfectly Poised	150-day		29.50	65
1992	Midday Repose	150-day		29.50	45

Victorian Cat Capers - Various

1992	Who's the Fairest of Them All? - F. Paton	150-day		24.50	65
1992	Puss in Boots - Unknown	150-day		24.50	60
1992	My Bowl is Empty - W. Hepple	150-day		27.50	35
1992	A Curious Kitty - W. Hepple	150-day		27.50	35
1992	Vanity Fair - W. Hepple	150-day		27.50	30
1992	Forbidden Fruit - W. Hepple	150-day		29.50	50
1993	The Purr-fect Pen Pal - W. Hepple	150-day		29.50	35
1993	The Kitten Express - W. Hepple	150-day		29.50	40

Wild Innocents - C. Fracé

1993	Reflections	95-day		29.50	45
1993	Spiritual Heir	95-day		29.50	45
1993	Lion Cub	95-day		29.50	50
1993	Sunny Spot	95-day		29.50	30

Wild Spirits - T. Hirata

1992	Solitary Watch	150-day		29.50	40
1992	Timber Ghost	150-day		29.50	50
1992	Mountain Magic	150-day		32.50	33
1993	Silent Guard	150-day		32.50	33
1993	Sly Eyes	150-day		32.50	33
1993	Mighty Presence	150-day		34.50	35
1993	Quiet Vigil	150-day		34.50	35
1993	Lone Vanguard	150-day		34.50	35

Wings of Winter - D. Rust

1992	Moonlight Retreat	150-day		29.50	30
1993	Twilight Serenade	150-day		29.50	30
1993	Silent Sunset	150-day		29.50	30
1993	Night Lights	150-day		29.50	30
1993	Winter Haven	150-day		29.50	30
1993	Full Moon Companions	150-day		29.50	30
1993	White Night	150-day		29.50	30
1993	Winter Reflections	150-day		29.50	30

Winter's Majesty - C. Fracé

1992	The Quest	150-day		34.50	40
1992	The Chase	150-day		34.50	40
1993	Alaskan Friend	150-day		34.50	55
1993	American Cougar	150-day		34.50	35
1993	On Watch	150-day		34.50	35
1993	Solitude	150-day		34.50	35

Wonders Of The Sea - R. Harm

1991	Stand By Me	150-day		34.50	35
1991	Heart to Heart	150-day		34.50	35
1991	Warm Embrace	150-day		34.50	45
1991	A Family Affair	150-day		34.50	35

The World's Most Magnificent Cats - C. Fracé

1991	Fleeting Encounter	150-day		24.50	40
1991	Cougar	150-day		24.50	55
1991	Royal Bengal	150-day		27.50	40
1991	Powerful Presence	150-day		27.50	50
1991	Jaguar	150-day		27.50	50
1991	The Clouded Leopard	150-day		29.50	55
1991	The African Leopard	150-day		29.50	50
1991	Mighty Warrior	150-day		29.50	60
1992	The Cheetah	150-day		31.50	60
1992	Siberian Tiger	150-day		31.50	70

Waterford Wedgwood USA

Bicentennial - Unknown

1972	Boston Tea Party	Annual		40.00	40
1973	Paul Revere's Ride	Annual		40.00	115

YEAR ISSUE		EDITION LIMIT	YEAR RETD.	ISSUE PRICE	QUOTE U.S.$
1974	Battle of Concord	Annual		40.00	55
1975	Across the Delaware	Annual		40.00	105
1975	Victory at Yorktown	Annual		45.00	53
1976	Declaration Signed	Annual		45.00	45

Wedgwood Christmas - Various

YEAR ISSUE		EDITION LIMIT	YEAR RETD.	ISSUE PRICE	QUOTE U.S.$
1969	Windsor Castle - T. Harper	Annual		25.00	200
1970	Trafalgar Square - T. Harper	Annual		30.00	60
1971	Picadilly Circus - T. Harper	Annual		30.00	50
1972	St. Paul's Cathedral - T. Harper	Annual		35.00	50
1973	Tower of London - T. Harper	Annual		40.00	90
1974	Houses of Parliament - T. Harper	Annual		40.00	40
1975	Tower Bridge - T. Harper	Annual		45.00	45
1976	Hampton Court - T. Harper	Annual		50.00	50
1977	Westminister Abbey - T. Harper	Annual		55.00	60
1978	Horse Guards - T. Harper	Annual		60.00	60
1979	Buckingham Palace - Unknown	Annual		65.00	65
1980	St. James Palace - Unknown	Annual		70.00	70
1981	Marble Arch - Unknown	Annual		75.00	75
1982	Lambeth Palace - Unknown	Annual		80.00	90
1983	All Souls, Langham Palace Unknown	Annual		80.00	80
1984	Constitution Hill - Unknown	Annual		80.00	80
1985	The Tate Gallery - Unknown	Annual		80.00	80
1986	The Albert Memorial - Unknown	Annual		80.00	150
1987	Guildhall - Unknown	Annual		80.00	85
1988	The Observatory/Greenwich Unknown	Annual		80.00	90
1989	Winchester Cathedral - Unknown	Annual		88.00	88

STEINS

Anheuser-Busch, Inc.

A & Eagle Historical Trademark Series-Giftware Edition - Various

YEAR ISSUE		EDITION LIMIT	YEAR RETD.	ISSUE PRICE	QUOTE U.S.$
1993	The 1872 Edition CS191, boxed D. Langeneckert	Retrd.	N/A	22.00	30-45
1993	The 1872 Edition CS201, tin D. Langeneckert	Retrd.	N/A	31.00	40-55
1993	The 1890 Edition CS218, tin A-Busch, Inc.	Retrd.	N/A	24.00	30-50
1994	The 1890 Edition CS219, boxed A-Busch, Inc.	Retrd.	N/A	24.00	30-50
1994	The 1900 Edition CS238, tin A-Busch, Inc.	20,000	1994	28.00	35-45
1994	A & Eagle Trademark III stein CS240, boxed - D. Langeneckert	20,000		25.00	25
1994	A & Eagle Trademark III stein CS238, tin - D. Langeneckert	30,000	1994	28.00	30-45

Anheuser-Busch Collectors Club - Various

YEAR ISSUE		EDITION LIMIT	YEAR RETD.	ISSUE PRICE	QUOTE U.S.$
1995	Budweiser Clydesdales at the Bauernhof - A. Leon	Yr.Iss.		Gift	N/A
1995	The Brew House Clock Tower D. Thompson	4/96		150.00	150

1992 Olympic Team Series-Collector Edition - A-Busch, Inc.

YEAR ISSUE		EDITION LIMIT	YEAR RETD.	ISSUE PRICE	QUOTE U.S.$
1991	1992 Winter Olympic Stein CS162	25,000		85.00	85
1992	1992 Summer Olympic Stein CS163	Retrd.	1994	85.00	85
1992	1992 U.S.Olympic Stein CS168	50,000		16.00	19

Anheuser-Busch Founder Series-Premier Collection - A-Busch, Inc.

YEAR ISSUE		EDITION LIMIT	YEAR RETD.	ISSUE PRICE	QUOTE U.S.$
1993	Adophus Busch CS216	10,000		180.00	180
1994	August A. Busch, Sr. CS229	10,000		220.00	220
1995	Adolphus Busch III CS265	10,000		220.00	220

Archives Series-Collector Edition - Various

YEAR ISSUE		EDITION LIMIT	YEAR RETD.	ISSUE PRICE	QUOTE U.S.$
1992	1893 Columbian Exposition CS169 - A-Busch, Inc.	75,000	1995	35.00	35
1992	Ganymede CS190 D. Langeneckert	Retrd.	1995	35.00	45-60
1994	Budweiser's Greatest Triumph CS222 - D. Langeneckert	75,000		35.00	35
1995	Mirror of Truth Stein CS252 D. Langeneckert	75,000		35.00	35

Birds of Prey Series-Premier Edition - P. Ford

YEAR ISSUE		EDITION LIMIT	YEAR RETD.	ISSUE PRICE	QUOTE U.S.$
1991	American Bald Eagle CS164	25,000	1995	125.00	125
1992	Peregrine Falcon CS183	25,000		125.00	125
1994	Osprey CS212	Retrd.	1994	135.00	250-350
1995	Great Horned Owl CS264	25,000		137.00	137

Bud Label Series-Giftware Edition - A-Busch, Inc.

YEAR ISSUE		EDITION LIMIT	YEAR RETD.	ISSUE PRICE	QUOTE U.S.$
1989	Budweiser Label CS101	Retrd.	1995	14.00	15-25
1990	Antique Label II CS127	Retrd.	N/A	14.00	16-25
1990	Bottled Beer III CS136	Retrd.	1995	15.00	15-30

Budweiser Military Series-Giftware Edition - M. Watts

YEAR ISSUE		EDITION LIMIT	YEAR RETD.	ISSUE PRICE	QUOTE U.S.$
1994	Army CS224	Open		19.00	19
1994	Air Force CS228	Open		19.00	19
1995	Budweiser Salutes the Navy CS243	Open		19.50	20
1995	Marines stein CS256	Open		22.00	22

Budweiser Racing Series-Giftware Edition - Various

YEAR ISSUE		EDITION LIMIT	YEAR RETD.	ISSUE PRICE	QUOTE U.S.$
1992	Budweiser Racing Elliot/Johnson N3553 - M. Watts	Retrd.	1995	19.00	25-45
1993	Budweiser RacingTeam CS194 H. Droog	Retrd.	1995	19.00	19

Civil War Series-Premier Edition - D. Langeneckert

YEAR ISSUE		EDITION LIMIT	YEAR RETD.	ISSUE PRICE	QUOTE U.S.$
1992	General Grant CS181	25,000	1995	150.00	150
1993	General Robert E. Lee CS188	25,000	1995	150.00	150
1993	President Abraham Lincoln CS189	25,000	1995	150.00	150

Classic Series - A-Busch, Inc.

YEAR ISSUE		EDITION LIMIT	YEAR RETD.	ISSUE PRICE	QUOTE U.S.$
1988	1st Edition CS93	Retrd.	N/A	34.95	145-175
1989	2nd Edition CS104	Retrd.	N/A	54.95	100-150
1990	3rd Edition CS113	Retrd.	N/A	65.00	45-85
1991	4th Edition CS130	Retrd.	N/A	75.00	40-90

Clydesdales Holiday Series - A-Busch, Inc.

YEAR ISSUE		EDITION LIMIT	YEAR RETD.	ISSUE PRICE	QUOTE U.S.$
1980	1st Holiday CS19	Retrd.	N/A	9.95	100-150
1976	Budweiser Champion Clydesdales CS19A	Retrd.	N/A	N/A	185-250
1981	2nd Holiday CS50	Retrd.	N/A	9.95	225-275
1982	3rd Holiday CS57 50th Anniversary	Retrd.	N/A	9.95	85-100
1983	4th Holiday CS58	Retrd.	N/A	9.95	30-45
1984	5th Holiday CS62	Retrd.	N/A	9.95	15-25
1985	6th Holiday CS63	Retrd.	N/A	9.95	15-30
1986	7th Holiday CS66	Retrd.	N/A	9.95	30-40
1987	8th Holiday CS70	Retrd.	N/A	9.95	12-25
1988	9th Holiday CS88	Retrd.	N/A	9.95	12-20
1989	10th Holiday CS89	Retrd.	N/A	12.95	12-20

Clydesdales Series-Giftware Edition - A-Busch, Inc.

YEAR ISSUE		EDITION LIMIT	YEAR RETD.	ISSUE PRICE	QUOTE U.S.$
1987	Eight Horse Hitch CS74	Retrd.	N/A	9.95	20-40
1988	Mare & Foal CS90	Retrd.	N/A	11.50	25
1989	Parade Dress CS99	Retrd.	N/A	11.50	40-65
1991	Training Hitch CS131	Retrd.	N/A	13.00	20-25
1992	Clydesdales on Parade CS161	Retrd.	N/A	16.00	16-30
1994	Proud and Free CS223	Open		17.00	17

Collector Edition - J. Tull

YEAR ISSUE		EDITION LIMIT	YEAR RETD.	ISSUE PRICE	QUOTE U.S.$
1994	Budweiser World Cup Stein CS230	25,000	1994	40.00	40-50

Discover America Series-Collector Edition - A-Busch, Inc.

YEAR ISSUE		EDITION LIMIT	YEAR RETD.	ISSUE PRICE	QUOTE U.S.$
1990	Nina CS107	100,000	1995	40.00	40
1991	Pinta CS129	100,000	1995	40.00	40
1992	Santa Maria CS138	100,000	1995	40.00	40

Endangered Species Series-Collector Edition - B. Kemper

YEAR ISSUE		EDITION LIMIT	YEAR RETD.	ISSUE PRICE	QUOTE U.S.$
1989	Bald Eagle CS106 (First)	Retrd.	N/A	24.95	280-400
1990	Asian Tiger CS126 (Second)	Retrd.	N/A	27.50	65-75
1991	African Elephant CS135 (Third)	100,000	1995	29.00	30
1992	Giant Panda CS173 (Fourth)	100,000		29.00	29
1993	Grizzly CS199 (Fifth)	100,000		29.50	30
1994	Gray Wolf Stein CS226 (Sixth)	100,000		29.50	30
1995	Cougar Stein CS253 (Seventh)	100,000		32.00	32

Giftware Edition - A-Busch, Inc.

YEAR ISSUE		EDITION LIMIT	YEAR RETD.	ISSUE PRICE	QUOTE U.S.$
1992	1992 Rodeo CS184	Retrd.	N/A	18.00	18-25
1993	Bud Man Character Stein CS213	Open		45.00	45
1994	"Fore!" Budweiser Golf Bag Stein CS225	Open		16.00	16
1994	"Walking Tall" Budweiser Cowboy Boot Stein CS251	Open		17.50	18
1995	"Play Ball" Baseball Mitt stein CS244	Open		18.00	18

Historical Landmark Series - A-Busch, Inc.

YEAR ISSUE		EDITION LIMIT	YEAR RETD.	ISSUE PRICE	QUOTE U.S.$
1986	Brew House CS67 (First)	Retrd.	N/A	19.95	35
1987	Stables CS73 (Second)	Retrd.	N/A	19.95	25-35
1988	Grant Cabin CS83 (Third)	Retrd.	N/A	19.95	45
1988	Old School House CS84 (Fourth)	Retrd.	N/A	19.95	25-35

Horseshoe Series - A-Busch, Inc.

YEAR ISSUE		EDITION LIMIT	YEAR RETD.	ISSUE PRICE	QUOTE U.S.$
1986	Horseshoe CS68	Retrd.	N/A	14.95	35-45
1987	Horsehead CS76	Retrd.	N/A	16.00	30-40
1986	Horseshoe CS77	Retrd.	N/A	16.00	40-75
1987	Horsehead CS78	Retrd.	N/A	14.95	45-75
1988	Harness CS94	Retrd.	N/A	16.00	45-75

Hunter's Companion Series-Collector Edition - Various

YEAR ISSUE		EDITION LIMIT	YEAR RETD.	ISSUE PRICE	QUOTE U.S.$
1993	Labrador Retriever CS195 L. Freeman	50,000		32.50	33
1994	The Setter Stein CS205 S. Ryan	50,000		32.50	33
1995	The Golden Retreiver Stein CS248 - S. Ryan	50,000		34.00	34

Limited Edition Series - A-Busch, Inc.

YEAR ISSUE		EDITION LIMIT	YEAR RETD.	ISSUE PRICE	QUOTE U.S.$
1985	Ltd. Ed. I Brewing & Fermenting CS64	Retrd.	N/A	29.95	175-200
1986	Ltd. Ed. II Aging & Cooperage CS65	Retrd.	N/A	29.95	50-75
1987	Ltd. Ed. III Transportation CS71	Retrd.	N/A	29.95	30-50
1988	Ltd. Ed. IV Taverns & Public Houses CS75	Retrd.	N/A	29.95	30-50
1989	Ltd. Ed.V Festival Scene CS98	Retrd.	N/A	34.95	30-50

Logo Series Steins-Giftware Edition - A-Busch, Inc.

YEAR ISSUE		EDITION LIMIT	YEAR RETD.	ISSUE PRICE	QUOTE U.S.$
1991	Budweiser CS143	Retrd.	N/A	16.00	16
1991	Bud Light CS144	Retrd.	N/A	16.00	16
1991	Michelob CS145	Retrd.	N/A	16.00	16
1991	Michelob Dry CS146	Retrd.	N/A	16.00	16
1991	Busch CS147	Retrd.	N/A	16.00	16
1991	A&Eagle CS148	Retrd.	N/A	16.00	16
1991	Bud Dry Draft CS156	Open		16.00	16

Marine Conservation Series-Collector Edition - B. Kemper

YEAR ISSUE		EDITION LIMIT	YEAR RETD.	ISSUE PRICE	QUOTE U.S.$
1994	Manatee Stein CS203	25,000		33.50	34
1995	Great White Shark Stein CS247	25,000		39.50	40

Octoberfest Series-Giftware Edition - A-Busch, Inc.

YEAR ISSUE		EDITION LIMIT	YEAR RETD.	ISSUE PRICE	QUOTE U.S.$
1991	1991 Octoberfest N3286	25,000	N/A	19.00	20-30
1992	1992 Octoberfest CS185	35,000		16.00	16
1993	1993 Octoberfest CS202	35,000	N/A	18.00	18

Olympic Centennial Collection - A-Busch, Inc.

YEAR ISSUE		EDITION LIMIT	YEAR RETD.	ISSUE PRICE	QUOTE U.S.$
1995	1996 U.S. Olympic Team "Gymnastics" Stein CS262	10,000		85.00	85
1995	1996 U.S. Olympic Team "Track & Field" Stein CS246	10,000		85.00	85
1995	Centennial Olympic Games Giftware Stein CS266	Open		25.00	25
1995	Collector's Edition Official Centennial Olympics Games Stein CS259	12/96		50.00	50

Porcelain Heritage Series-Premier Edition - Various

YEAR ISSUE		EDITION LIMIT	YEAR RETD.	ISSUE PRICE	QUOTE U.S.$
1990	Berninghaus CS105 Berninghaus	Retrd.	1994	75.00	75
1991	After The Hunt CS155 A-Busch, Inc.	Retrd.	1994	100.00	100
1992	Cherub CS182 - D. Langeneckert	25,000		100.00	100

Premier Collection - H. Droog

YEAR ISSUE		EDITION LIMIT	YEAR RETD.	ISSUE PRICE	QUOTE U.S.$
1993	Bill Elliott CS196	25,000	1995	150.00	150
1993	Bill Elliott, Signature Edition, CS196SE	1,500	1995	295.00	295

Sea World Series-Collector Edition - A-Busch, Inc.

YEAR ISSUE		EDITION LIMIT	YEAR RETD.	ISSUE PRICE	QUOTE U.S.$
1992	Killer Whale CS186	25,000		100.00	100
1992	Dolphin CS187	22,500		90.00	90

Specialty Steins - A-Busch, Inc.

YEAR ISSUE		EDITION LIMIT	YEAR RETD.	ISSUE PRICE	QUOTE U.S.$
1975	Bud Man CS1	Retrd.	N/A	N/A	350-425
1975	A&Eagle CS2	Retrd.	N/A	N/A	175-275
1975	A&Eagle Lidded CSL2 (Reference CS28)	Retrd.	N/A	N/A	200-325
1975	Katakombe CS3	Retrd.	N/A	N/A	225-300
1975	Katakombe Lidded CSL3	Retrd.	N/A	N/A	350-400
1975	German Olympia CS4	Retrd.	N/A	N/A	60-150
1975	Senior Grande Lidded CSL4	Retrd.	N/A	N/A	625-650
1975	German Pilique CS5	Retrd.	N/A	N/A	400-500
1975	German Pilique Lidded CSL5	Retrd.	N/A	N/A	500-550
1975	Senior Grande CS6	Retrd.	N/A	N/A	600-700
1975	German Olympia Lidded CSL6	Retrd.	N/A	N/A	250-275
1975	Miniature Bavarian CS7	Retrd.	N/A	N/A	300
1976	Budweiser Centennial Lidded CSL7	Retrd.	N/A	N/A	400-500
1976	U.S. Bicentennial Lidded CSL8	Retrd.	N/A	N/A	400-500
1976	Natural Light CS9	Retrd.	N/A	N/A	175-225
1976	Clydesdales Hofbrau Lidded CSL9	Retrd.	N/A	N/A	200-300
1976	Blue Delft CS11	Retrd.	N/A	N/A	1800-2400
1976	Clydesdales CS12	Retrd.	N/A	N/A	200-275
1976	Budweiser Centennial CS13	Retrd.	N/A	N/A	300-450
1976	U.S. Bicentennial CS14	Retrd.	N/A	N/A	300-450
1976	Clydesdales Grants Farm CS15	Retrd.	N/A	N/A	175-275
1976	German Cities (6 assorted) CS16	Retrd.	N/A	N/A	1800-2000
1976	Americana CS17	Retrd.	N/A	N/A	350-550
1976	Budweiser Label CS18	Retrd.	N/A	N/A	350
1980	Budweiser Ladies (4 assorted) CS20	Retrd.	N/A	N/A	2000-2500
1977	Budweiser Girl CS21	Retrd.	N/A	N/A	400
1976	Budweiser Centennial CS22	Retrd.	N/A	N/A	400-450
1977	A&Eagle CS24	Retrd.	N/A	N/A	350
1976	A&Eagle Barrel CS26	Retrd.	N/A	N/A	125-175
1976	Michelob CS27	Retrd.	N/A	N/A	150-225
1976	A&Eagle Lidded CS28 (Reference CSL2)	Retrd.	N/A	N/A	200-300
1976	Clydesdales Lidded CS29	Retrd.	N/A	N/A	225-350
1976	Coracao Decanter Set (7 piece) CS31	Retrd.	N/A	N/A	500
1976	German Wine Set (7 piece) CS32	Retrd.	N/A	N/A	500
1976	Clydesdales Decanter CS33	Retrd.	N/A	N/A	1100-1200
1976	Holanda Brown Decanter Set (7 piece) CS34	Retrd.	N/A	N/A	350
1976	Holanda Blue Decanter Set (7 piece) CS35	Retrd.	N/A	N/A	500
1976	Canteen Decanter Set (7 piece) CS36	Retrd.	N/A	N/A	N/A
1976	St. Louis Decanter CS37	Retrd.	N/A	N/A	400
1976	St. Louis Decanter Set (7 piece) CS38	Retrd.	N/A	N/A	1200
1980	Wurzburger Hofbrau CS39	Retrd.	N/A	N/A	300-450
1980	Budweiser Chicago Skyline CS40	Retrd.	N/A	N/A	125-150
1978	Busch Gardens CS41	Retrd.	N/A	N/A	225-350
1980	Oktoberfest— "The Old Country" CS42	Retrd.	N/A	N/A	225-350
1980	Natural Light Label CS43	Retrd.	N/A	N/A	175
1980	Busch Label CS44	Retrd.	N/A	N/A	175
1980	Michelob Label CS45	Retrd.	N/A	N/A	75-125
1980	Budweiser Label CS46	Retrd.	N/A	N/A	75-125
1981	Budweiser Chicagoland CS51	Retrd.	N/A	N/A	40-50
1981	Budweiser Texas CS52	Retrd.	N/A	N/A	55
1981	Budweiser California CS56	Retrd.	N/A	N/A	50
1983	Budweiser San Francisco CS59	Retrd.	N/A	N/A	175
1984	Budweiser Olympic Games CS60	Retrd.	N/A	N/A	20-50

YEAR ISSUE		EDITION LIMIT	YEAR RETD.	ISSUE PRICE	QUOTE U.S.$
1983	Bud Light Baron CS61	Retrd.	N/A	N/A	35-60
1987	Santa Claus CS79	Retrd.	N/A	N/A	65-75
1987	King Cobra CS80	Retrd.	N/A	N/A	250
1987	Winter Olympic Games, Lidded CS81	Retrd.	N/A	49.95	65-75
1988	Budweiser Winter Olympic Games CS85	Retrd.	N/A	24.95	25
1988	Summer Olympic Games, Lidded CS91	Retrd.	N/A	54.95	50
1988	Budweiser Summer Olympic Games CS92	Retrd.	N/A	54.95	25
1988	Budweiser/ Field&Stream Set (4 piece) CS95	Retrd.	N/A	69.95	250-350
1989	Bud Man CS100	Retrd.	N/A	29.95	40-50
1990	Baseball Cardinal Stein CS125	Retrd.	N/A	30.00	30
1991	Bevo Fox Stein CS160	Retrd.	1994	250.00	200-250

Sports History Series-Giftware Edition - A-Busch, Inc.

1990	Baseball, America's Favorite Pastime CS124	Retrd.	N/A	20.00	25
1990	Football, Gridiron Legacy CS128	Retrd.	N/A	20.00	23
1991	Auto Racing, Chasing The Checkered Flag CS132	100,000	1995	22.00	23
1991	Basketball, Heroes of the Hardwood CS134	100,000		22.00	22
1992	Golf, Par For The Course CS165	100,000	1995	22.00	23
1993	Hockey, Center Ice CS209	100,000		22.00	22

Sports Legend Series-Collector Edition - Various

1991	Babe Ruth CS142 - A-Busch	50,000	1995	85.00	85
1992	Jim Thorpe CS171 - M. Caito	50,000	1995	85.00	85
1993	Joe Louis CS206 - M. Caito	Retrd.	1994	85.00	85-100

St. Patrick's Day Series-Giftware Edition - A-Busch, Inc.

1991	1991 St. Patrick's Day CS109	Retrd.	N/A	15.00	45-60
1992	1992 St. Patrick's Day CS166	100,000	N/A	15.00	15-20
1993	1993 St. Patrick's Day CS193	Retrd.	N/A	15.30	25-30
1994	Luck O' The Irish CS210	Open		18.00	18
1995	1995 St. Patrick's Day Stein CS242	Open		19.00	19

Wholesaler Holiday Series - Various

1990	An American Tradition, CS112, 1990 - S. Sampson	Retrd.	N/A	13.50	14
1990	An American Tradition, CS112-SE, 1990 - S. Sampson	Retrd.	N/A	50.00	65-80
1991	The Season's Best, CS133, 1991 - S. Sampson	Retrd.	N/A	14.50	15
1991	The Season's Best, CS133-SE Signature Edition, 1991 S. Sampson	Retrd.	N/A	50.00	40-50
1992	The Perfect Christmas, CS167, 1992 - S. Sampson	Retrd.	N/A	14.50	15
1992	The Perfect Christmas, CS167-SE Signature Edition, 1992 - S. Sampson	Open		50.00	25
1993	Special Delivery, CS192, 1993 N. Koerber	Retrd.	N/A	15.00	20-40
1993	Special Delivery, CS192-SE Signature Edition, 1993 - N. Koerber	Retrd.	N/A	60.00	125
1994	Hometown Holiday, CS211, 1994 - B. Kemper	Retrd.	1994	14.00	15
1994	Hometown Holiday, CS211-SE Signature Edition, 1994 B. Kemper	Retrd.	N/A	65.00	100-120
1995	Lighting the Way Home, CS263 T. Jester	Open		17.00	17
1995	Lighting the Way Home, CS263-SE Signature Edition T. Jester	10,000		75.00	75

Anheuser-Busch, Inc./Gerz Meisterwerke

American Heritage Collection - Gerz

1993	John F. Kennedy Stein-GM-4	10,000		220.00	220

Gerz Collectorwerke - Various

1993	The Dugout-GL1 - A-Busch, Inc.	10,000		110.00	110
1994	Winchester Stein-GL2 A-Busch, Inc.	10,000		120.00	120
1995	"Saturday Evening Post" Christmas Stein GL5 J.C. Leyendecker	5,000		105.00	105

Gerz Meisterwerke Collection - A-Busch, Inc.

1994	Norman Rockwell-Triple Self Portrait GM6	5,000		250.00	250
1994	Mallard Stein GM7	5,000		220.00	220
1994	Winchester "Model 94" Centennial Stein GM10	5,000		150.00	150
1995	Giant Panda Stein GM-8	3,500		210.00	210
1995	Rosie the Riveter Stein GM-9	5,000		165.00	165

Gerz Meisterwerke First Hunt Series - P. Ford

1992	Golden Retriever GM-2	10,000		150.00	150
1994	Springer Spaniel GM-5	10,000		170.00	170
1995	Pointer Stein GM-16	10,000		190.00	190

Gerz Saturday Evening Post Collection - J.C. Leyendecker

1993	Santa's Mailbag GM-1	Retrd.		195.00	250
1993	Santa's Helper GM-3	7,500		200.00	200
1994	"All I Want For Christmas" GM-13	5,000		220.00	220

Artaffects

Perillo Steins - G. Perillo

YEAR ISSUE		EDITION LIMIT	YEAR RETD.	ISSUE PRICE	QUOTE U.S.$
1989	Buffalo Hunt	5,000		125.00	125
1991	Hoofbeats	5,000		125.00	125

CUI/Carolina Collection/Dram Tree

Classic Car Series - Various

1992	1957 Chevy - G. Geivette	Retrd.		100.00	100
1993	Classic T-Birds - K. Eberts	6,950		100.00	100

Ducks Unlimited - Various

1987	Wood Duck Edition I - K. Bloom	Retrd.		80.00	200
1988	Mallard Edition II - M. Bradford	Retrd.		80.00	125
1989	Canvasbacks Edition III L. Barnicle	Retrd.		80.00	100
1990	Pintails Edition IV R. Plasschaert	Retrd.		80.00	90
1991	Canada Geese Edition V J. Meger	20,000		80.00	80

Ducks Unlimited Classic Decoy Series - D. Boncela

1992	1930's Bert Graves Mallard Decoys Edition I	Retrd.		100.00	100

Elvis Presley Deluxe Series - Unknown

1993	Comeback Special-25th Anniversary	1,968		130.00	130
1994	Life of Elvis Deluxe	1,977		130.00	130
1994	Elvis:Aloha from Hawaii Deluxe	1,973		130.00	130

Federal Duck Stamp - Various

1990	Lesser Scaup Edition I N. Anderson	6,950		80.00	80
1991	Black Bellied Whistling Duck Edition II - J. Hautman	6,950		80.00	80
1992	King Eiders Edition III - N. Howe	Retrd.		80.00	80
1993	Spectacled Eiders - J. Hautman	6,950		80.00	80
1993	50th Anniversary Commemorative - W.C. Morris	6,950		85.00	85
1994	Canvasbacks - B. Miller	6,950		80.00	80

Great American Achievements - CUI

1986	First Successful Flight Edition I	Retrd.		10.95	75-95
1987	The Model T Edition II	Retrd.		12.95	30-55
1988	First Transcontinental Railway Edition III	Retrd.		15.95	28-55
1989	The First River Steamer Edition IV	Retrd.		25.00	25
1990	Man's First Walk on the Moon Edition V	Retrd.		25.00	25

The History of Billiards - Various

1993	1694 Louis XIV - Trouvian	Retrd.		39.50	40
1993	1745 Ich Mache Nur Colle Unknown	Retrd.		39.50	40
1993	1823 Indifference - D. Egerton	Retrd.		39.50	40
1993	1859 First Major Stake Match Unknown	Retrd.		39.50	40
1993	1875 Grand Union Hotel, Saratoga NY - Unknown	Retrd.		39.50	40
1993	1905 Untitled Print - M. Neuman	Retrd.		39.50	40

North American Fishing Club - V. Beck

1992	Jumpin' Hog	6,950		90.00	90

Quarterback Legends - CUI

1992	Hall of Fame - John Unitas Edition I	4,950		175.00	175
1992	Hall of Fame - Y.A. Tittle Edition II	4,950		175.00	175
1992	Hall of Fame - Bart Starr	4,950		175.00	175
1992	Hall of Fame - Otto Graham	Retrd.		175.00	175

Still the King - Various

1992	Elvis Presley Postage Stamp - Unknown	Retrd.		60.00	60
1993	'68 Comeback Special - CUI	45-day		60.00	60
1994	Gates of Graceland - Unknown	45-day		60.00	60
1994	Elvis in the Army - Unknown	45-day		65.00	65
1994	Elvis: Aloha from Hawaii Unknown	45-day		65.00	65
1994	Elvis in Las Vegas - Unknown	45-day		65.00	65

Stroh Bavaria Collection - CUI

1990	Dancers Edition I - Bavaria I	Retrd.		45.00	45
1990	Dancers Pewter Figure Edition I Bavaria I	Retrd.		70.00	70
1991	Barrel Pusher Edition II Bavaria II	Retrd.		45.00	45
1991	Barrel Pusher Pewter Edition II Bavaria II	Retrd.		70.00	70
1992	The Aging Cellar-Edition III	Retrd.		45.00	45
1992	The Aging Cellar-Pewter Edition III	Retrd.		70.00	70
1993	Bandwagon Street Party-Pewter Edition II	Retrd.		70.00	70
1993	Bandwagon Street Party Edition IV	Retrd.		45.00	45

Stroh Heritage Collection - CUI

1984	Horsedrawn Wagon - Heritage I	Retrd.		11.95	15-25
1985	Kirn Inn Germany - Heritage II	Retrd.		12.95	15-22
1986	Lion Brewing Company - Heritage III	Retrd.		13.95	25-35
1987	Bohemian Beer - Heritage IV	Retrd.		14.95	19-22
1988	Delivery Vehicles - Heritage V	Retrd.		25.00	25
151989	Fire Brewed - Heritage V I	Retrd.		16.95	19

Hadley House

Annual Christmas Series - T. Redlin

YEAR ISSUE		EDITION LIMIT	YEAR RETD.	ISSUE PRICE	QUOTE U.S.$
1994	Almost Home	45-day		39.95	40
1995	Winter Wonderland	45-day		39.95	40

Hamilton Collection

The STAR TREK® Tankard Collection - T. Blackshear

1994	SPOCK	Open		49.50	50
1995	Kirk	Open		49.50	50
1995	McCoy	Open		49.50	50
1995	Uhura	Open		49.50	50
1995	Scotty	Open		49.50	50
1995	Sulu	Open		49.50	50
1995	Chekov	Open		49.50	50
1995	U.S.S. Enterprise NCC-1701	Open		49.50	50

Warriors of the Plains Tankards - G. Stewart

1992	Thundering Hooves	Open		125.00	125
1995	Warrior's Choice	Open		125.00	125
1995	Healing Spirits	Open		125.00	125
1995	Battle Grounds	Open		125.00	125

Sports Impressions/Enesco

Baseball Steins - Various

1990	Nolan Ryan Rangers - R. Lewis	Closed	N/A	30.00	30
1990	Life Of A Legend Mickey Mantle T. Fogarty	Closed	N/A	30.00	30
1990	Kings of K - J. Catalano	Closed	N/A	30.00	30
1990	Rangers Nolan Ryan 300th Win J. Catalano	Closed	N/A	30.00	30
1995	Life of a Legend Mickey Mantle (17 oz.) 1228-72 - T. Fogarty	Open		15.00	15

Football Steins - J. Catalano

1990	Dan Marino	2,500	N/A	30.00	30
1991	Jim Kelly	2,500	N/A	30.00	30
1990	Joe Montana 49ers 3000-06	2,500	1992	30.00	30
1991	Troy Aikman Cowboys 3008-06	2,500	1993	30.00	30

INDEX

4 Q. *WHAT'S THE LATEST NEWS IN THE WORLD OF COLLECTIBLES?*

A. THE CIB REPORT & SHOWCASE

Read all about the latest news on the everchanging world of collectibles with the CIB REPORT & SHOWCASE. This quarterly newsletter keeps you in touch with the fast-paced world of limited edition collectibles. Each issue brings you the information you need to help make collecting even more fun and exciting.

You'll enjoy page after page of news about...

- **New Product Introductions, some complete with color photography**
- **Collector Club Activities**
- **Artist Signings and Open Houses**
- **Convention News**
- **Feature columns on the world of collecting**

5 Q. *HOW DO I FIND RECENT ISSUES THAT ARE NOT AVAILABLE TO ME LOCALLY?*

A. DIRECTORY TO LIMITED EDITION COLLECTIBLE STORES.

This directory features over 1,000 collectible stores from coast to coast and in Canada. It's a must for collectors who wish to purchase collectibles by phone, mail or in person. Retailers are listed by state for easy reference, making it an ideal travel companion for collectors. A comprehensive, easy-to-use index lets you find the information you need about individual collectible lines instantly.

COLLECTORS' INFORMATION BUREAU Publications are filled with information about...

KURT S. ADLER, INC. • ANHEUSER-BUSCH, INC. • ANNALEE MOBILITEE DOLLS, INC. • ARMANI/MILLER IMPORT • ANRI WOODSCULPTURES • THE ASHTON-DRAKE GALLERIES • ATTIC BABIES • BAND CREATIONS • THE BRADFORD EXCHANGE • BRANDYWINE COLLECTIBLES • THE BOYDS COLLECTION LTD. • BYERS' CHOICE LTD. • RICK CAIN STUDIOS • CALABAR CREATIONS • CAST ART INDUSTRIES, INC. • CAVANAGH GROUP INTERNATIONAL • CHRISTOPHER RADKO • CLASSIC COLLECTABLES BY UNIQUELY YOURS • CREART • DEPARTMENT 56, INC. • THE WALT DISNEY COMPANY • *eggspressions! inc.* • ENESCO CORP. • THE FENTON ART GLASS CO. • F.J. DESIGNS/THE CAT'S MEOW • FLAMBRO IMPORTS • FORMA VITRUM • THE FRANKLIN MINT • FRASER INTERNATIONAL • MARGARET FURLONG DESIGNS • GANZ • GEORGETOWN COLLECTION • GOEBEL OF NORTH AMERICA • THE GREAT AMERICAN TAYLOR COLLECTIBLES CORP. • THE GREENWICH WORKSHOP • HALLMARK KEEPSAKE ORNAMENTS COLLECTORS' CLUB • THE HAMILTON COLLECTION • HAND & HAMMER SILVERSMITHS • HARBOUR LIGHTS • HAWTHORNE ARCHITECTURAL REGISTER • M.I. HUMMEL CLUB • LADIE AND FRIENDS, INC. • THE LANCE CORPORATION • THE LAWTON DOLL COMPANY • RON LEE'S WORLD OF CLOWNS • GEORGE Z. LEFTON CO. • LEGENDS • LENOX COLLECTIONS • LILLIPUT LANE • LLADRO SOCIETY • SEYMOUR MANN, INC. • MARURI U.S.A. • JUNE MCKENNA COLLECTIBLES, INC. • MEDIA ARTS GROUP • MICHAEL'S LIMITED • MIDWEST OF CANNON FALLS • MISS MARTHA ORIGINALS, INC. • MY FRIENDS & ME • OLD WORLD CHRISTMAS • PACIFIC RIM IMPORT CORP. • PENDELFIN STUDIOS • POSSIBLE DREAMS • PRECIOUS ART/PANTON • R.R. CREATIONS • RAWCLIFFE CORP. • RECO INTERNATIONAL CORP. • ROMAN, INC. • ROYAL COPENHAGEN/BING & GRONDAHL • ROYAL DOULTON • SARAH'S ATTIC • SCHMID • SHELIA'S, INC. • SWAROVSKI AMERICA LIMITED • TODAY'S CREATIONS • THE TUDOR MINT • UNITED DESIGN CORP. • VICKILANE • WACO PRODUCTS CORP. •

▼▼▼

USE THIS FORM FOR EASY ORDERING!

YES! Please send me the books I've indicated below.

Description	Quantity	Price Each	Total
Market Guide & Price Index		$22.95	
Collectibles Price Guide		$12.95	
Directory to Secondary Market Retailers		$11.95	
CIB Report & Showcase 1-year Subscription		$15.00	
Directory to Limited Edition Collectible Stores		$14.95	
	Shipping (see chart at left)		
	Handling charge (per order)		$1.00
	Illinois residents add 7.75% sales tax Michigan residents add 6% sales tax		
	GRAND TOTAL		

Shipping Charges

Up to $14.95	$2.00
$15.00 - $22.95	$3.00
$23.00 - $61.00	$5.00
$62.00 and up	10% of total order

All orders must be prepaid.
Please allow 2 weeks for delivery.

Prices subject to change without notice.

Send To:

Name ______________________________
Please print clearly.

Address ______________________________

City ______________________ State ________ Zip ________

❑ My check or money order, payable to the Collectors' Information Bureau, is enclosed.

❑ Please charge my credit card. ❑ VISA ❑ MasterCard

Account Number ______________________________

Expiration Date ______________________________

Signature ______________________________

Telephone number (   ) ______________________________

Please write us for our Canadian price list. MG-13

Detach at perforation and mail to: **Order Dept., Collectors' Information Bureau, 5065 Shoreline Road, Suite 200, Barrington, IL 60010.**

NOTES